australia & new zealand
on a shoestring

Paul Smitz, Sandra Bao, Pete Cruttenden, George Dunford, Simone Egger, Susannah Farfor, Justin Flynn, Sarina Singh, Justine Vaisutis, Sarah Wintle

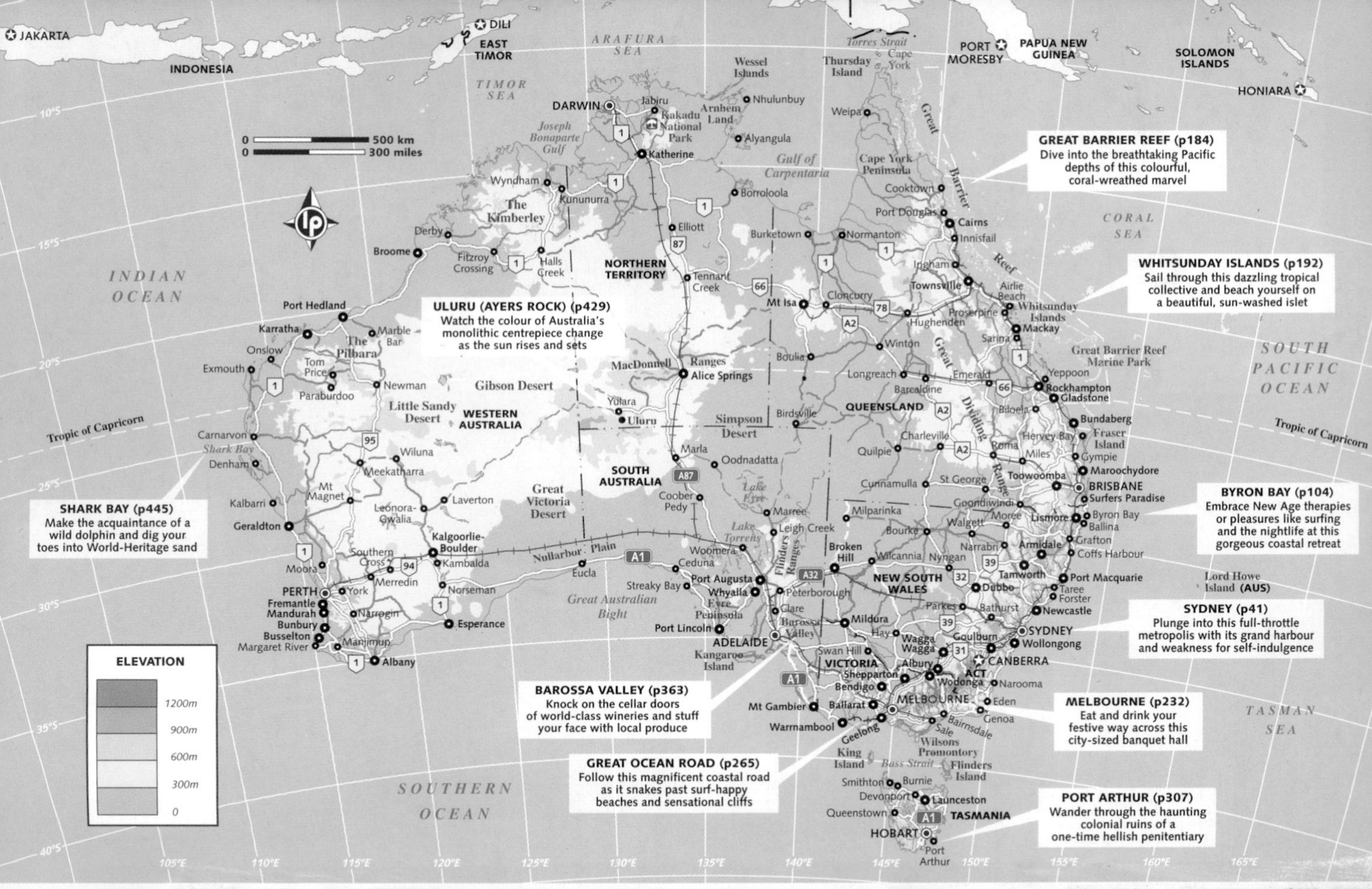
GREAT BARRIER REEF (p184)
Dive into the breathtaking Pacific depths of this colourful, coral-wreathed marvel
WHITSUNDAY ISLANDS (p192)
Sail through this dazzling tropical collective and beach yourself on a beautiful, sun-washed islet
BYRON BAY (p104)
Embrace New Age therapies or pleasures like surfing and the nightlife at this gorgeous coastal retreat
SYDNEY (p41)
Plunge into this full-throttle metropolis with its grand harbour and weakness for self-indulgence
MELBOURNE (p232)
Eat and drink your festive way across this city-sized banquet hall
PORT ARTHUR (p307)
Wander through the haunting colonial ruins of a one-time hellish penitentiary
GREAT OCEAN ROAD (p265)
Follow this magnificent coastal road as it snakes past surf-happy beaches and sensational cliffs
BAROSSA VALLEY (p363)
Knock on the cellar doors of world-class wineries and stuff your face with local produce
ULURU (AYERS ROCK) (p429)
Watch the colour of Australia's monolithic centrepiece change as the sun rises and sets
SHARK BAY (p445)
Make the acquaintance of a wild dolphin and dig your toes into World-Heritage sand
ELEVATION
1200m
900m
600m
300m
0
0 500 km
0 300 miles
INDIAN OCEAN
SOUTHERN OCEAN
SOUTH PACIFIC OCEAN
CORAL SEA
TASMAN SEA
ARAFURA SEA
TIMOR SEA
WESTERN AUSTRALIA
NORTHERN TERRITORY
SOUTH AUSTRALIA
QUEENSLAND
NEW SOUTH WALES
VICTORIA
TASMANIA
ACT
INDONESIA
EAST TIMOR
PAPUA NEW GUINEA
SOLOMON ISLANDS
Tropic of Capricorn

Responsible Travel

As travellers, we all like the places we visit to have a positive effect on us, so it's only fitting that we repay the favour. In Australia and New Zealand, this is particularly important when it comes to the local wildlife that you've travelled so far to see.

When you visit the Great Barrier Reef, you'll want to be inspired by the vivid colours of the living coral reef, not see coral that's died from being manhandled or been broken off so someone can stuff it in their pocket. When you hike down the Milford Track, you'll want to breathe in pristine rainforest, not see discarded cigarettes and plastic bags, or trailside plants crushed by careless boots. And the close-up experiences of penguins, dolphins and koalas that you've been so looking forward to will be denied to you if the animals have been scared off or their habitats damaged.

Your impact on the locals doesn't stop there. You will be paying your respects to Aborigines and Maoris when you buy products they make themselves rather than imitation souvenirs manufactured elsewhere. And (in Australia) by conserving water, you'll be helping everyone out – domesticated humans and wild animals alike – when things get a bit dry.

The self-awareness that grows with each new day on the road is one of your greatest strengths as a traveller. Feel free to put this quality to good use throughout your explorations.

For tips on social etiquette, see the Getting Started chapter.

HOW YOU CAN HELP

- **Conserve water** Keep showers short and don't leave the tap running while washing dishes or brushing teeth, as Australia is afflicted by drought-induced water shortages.
- **Shop originally and legally** Buy authentic indigenous goods directly from artists where possible (they're usually better anyway), and stay away from products made from endangered or protected species.
- **Stick up for the wildlife** Refrain from interfering with wildlife, and take issue with anyone who does.
- **Support conscientious tours** If your guide has a 'Who cares?' attitude to the environment, take your business elsewhere and warn other travellers.

WEB RESOURCES

- **www.acfonline.org.au** Australia's biggest nongovernment conservation organisation
- **www.doc.govt.nz** New Zealand's Department of Conservation
- **www.coralreefalliance.org** Everything about coral reefs
- **www.ecotourism.org.au** Lists 'eco'-certified tour operators

Contents

Lonely Planet books provide independent advice. Lonely Planet does not accept advertising in guidebooks, nor do we accept payment in exchange for listing or endorsing any place or business. Lonely Planet writers do not accept discounts or payments in exchange for positive coverage of any sort.

The Authors

PAUL SMITZ — Coordinating Author

Working on a guidebook is one of the few times when being inbred can be positive, as Paul's discovered though many years of exploring and writing about his home country, Australia. It's a cliché (he's full of them – read the rest of the book), but no matter how many parts of this ridiculously large continent he visits or revisits, he remains infatuated with its strangeness, beauty, unpredictability and self-deprecating humour. Paul's also travelled around New Zealand for Lonely Planet, and finds its melodramatic scenery, isolation, hyperactivity and innate friendliness just as beguiling.

Paul compiled the front and end chapters of this book, including the Directory and Transport chapters. He also updated New Zealand's North and South Island chapters.

SANDRA BAO — Sydney

Sandra was born and lived in Buenos Aires, Argentina until she was nine. She then emigrated to the USA, became an American citizen, and decided to spend much of the next 25 years of her life travelling, covering more than 50 countries. In between travels she earned a psychology degree at University of California Santa Cruz (doing little to help her future career as a Lonely Planet author) and got hitched to a fellow Lonely Planet author (and editor) Ben Greensfelder.

Sydney reigns supreme among her favourite cities and Lonely Planet gigs, and during her research for this book Sandra has learned to appreciate echidnas, the Aussie accent and munching on fish and chips at the beach.

PETE CRUTTENDEN — Outback Australia (the Red Centre)

West Australian–born, East-Coast raised, and Melburnian by preference, Pete's always headed inland to Australia's mountains, forests, rivers and deserts to clean the stink of the city off his skin. Lonely Planet has helped him flee in recent years, sending him up the Queensland coast for the first edition of *East Coast Australia,* into Western Australia's northern tropical reaches for *Australia* (12th edition) and into the remote and spectacular central deserts for *Outback Australia*. This latest trip allowed him to reacquaint himself with Australia's iconic Red Centre – a place that definitely bears repeat visits.

GEORGE DUNFORD — New South Wales (including the Australian Capital Territory)

Hailing from the Snowy Mountains originally, George jumped at the chance to head back to his old haunts. It bought back memories of waitering in Canberra's Laos embassy while he studied for his honours in history, family holidays on golden Byron beaches and long 'are-we-there-yet' car journeys out west. George is a freelance writer in Melbourne, where it's colder, but he likes to think the culture keeps him warm.

SIMONE EGGER — Melbourne & Victoria

Simone Egger lives in Melbourne and works as a freelance photojournalist. Simone had a stint with Lonely Planet as an editor before crossing over to authoring. Travel has always been in her biography. The novelty of being a traveller in her home state and a tourist in her home town will never wear off.

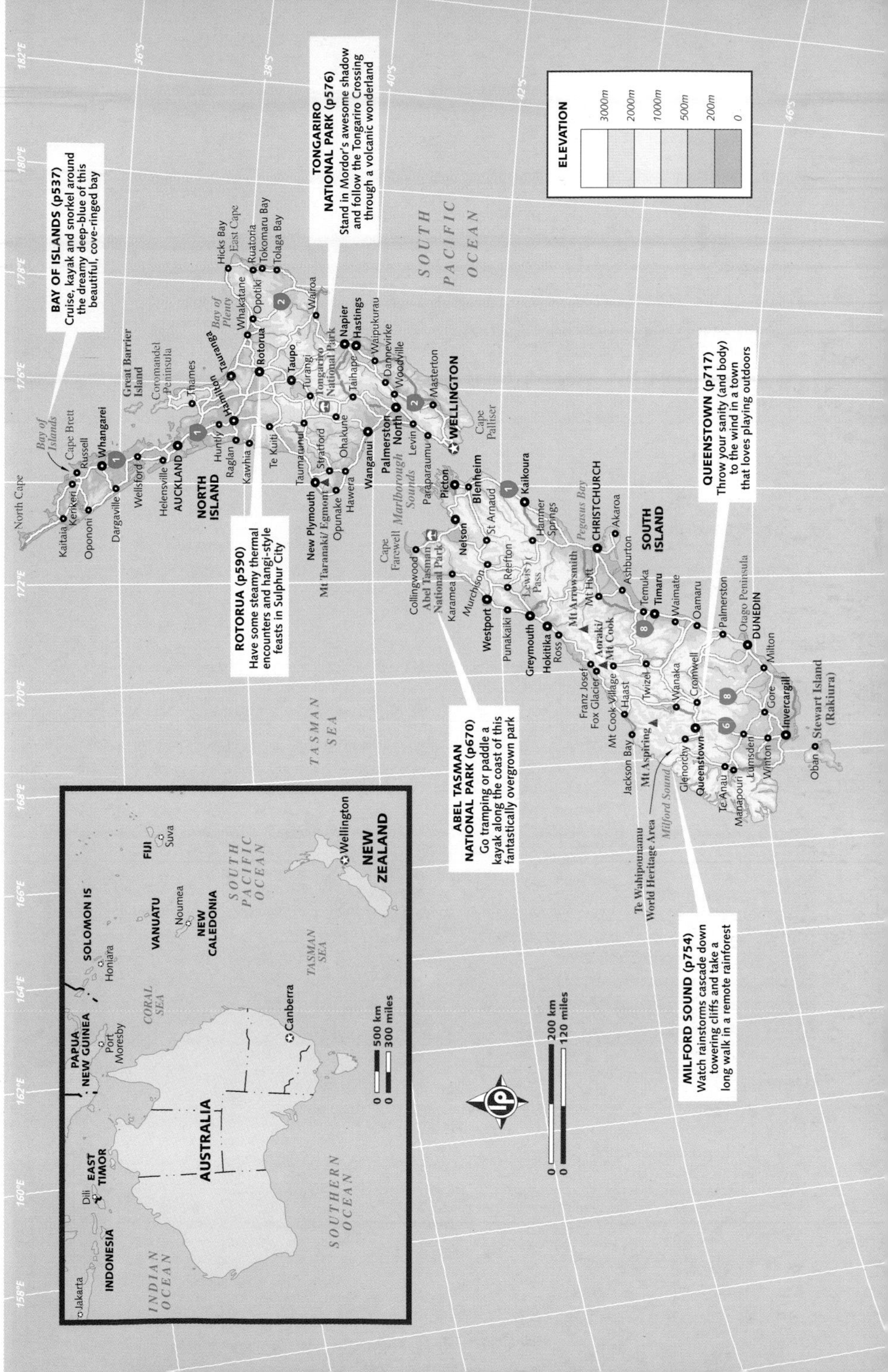

BAY OF ISLANDS (p537) Cruise, kayak and snorkel around the dreamy deep-blue of this beautiful, cove-ringed bay

TONGARIRO NATIONAL PARK (p576) Stand in Mordor's awesome shadow and follow the Tongariro Crossing through a volcanic wonderland

ROTORUA (p590) Have some steamy thermal encounters and hangi-style feasts in Sulphur City

ABEL TASMAN NATIONAL PARK (p670) Go tramping or paddle a kayak along the coast of this fantastically overgrown park

QUEENSTOWN (p717) Throw your sanity (and body) to the wind in a town that loves playing outdoors

MILFORD SOUND (p754) Watch rainstorms cascade down towering cliffs and take a long walk in a remote rainforest

SUSANNAH FARFOR

Adelaide & Around, Outback Australia (Coober Pedy)

Susannah's a Melbourne-based writer and editor, whose work often covers adventure-related travel, and food publications. For this title she cruised, snorkelled and surfed the coasts, hiked the hills, explored caves and put an oenology course to good use by quaffing South Australia's wines, along with its array of gourmet produce. Fascinated by the more remote regions of Australia, she has travelled in every state and also wrote Lonely Planet's *Northern Territory* guidebook.

JUSTIN FLYNN

Perth & Around, Outback Australia (Up the West Coast)

Justin professes a love of all things West Australian, from the Eagles and the Dockers (when they're thrashed by his beloved Richmond Tigers) to a robust Margaret River red and a spectacular sunset over Cottesloe Beach. He started out as a sports journalist before doing a stint as a TV reporter with WIN TV in Mildura. He then set off on the obligatory backpacking trip around the UK and Europe, and has been travelling ever since. He now divides his time between the office at Lonely Planet where he's an editor and his home in gorgeous Barwon Heads. This was Justin's first authoring assignment for Lonely Planet and he vows it won't be his last.

SARINA SINGH

Tasmania

Sarina lived in SA's Adelaide and Mt Gambier before moving to Melbourne, aged 10. She finished a business degree in Melbourne and pursued a corporate traineeship with the Sheraton in India but later ditched hotels for newspapers, working as a freelance journalist and foreign correspondent. After four years in south Asia she returned to Australia, got postgraduate journalism qualifications and wrote/directed a documentary film. Sarina has worked on more than 15 Lonely Planet books including *Aboriginal Australia & the Torres Strait Islands*. She has also contributed to various international publications such as the *Sunday Times* and *National Geographic Traveler*.

JUSTINE VAISUTIS

Queensland

Justine became addicted to the nomadic lifestyle living in South Africa and South Korea as a little tacker. Mostly, she grew up in Canberra, exploiting the Australian way of life every summer on the NSW coast. As a teenager she experienced her first Queensland winter and confused it with Utopia. For this title she thoroughly enjoyed reliving the fabrication in the aquatic playground of the Queensland coast. Having carted a backpack around South America and Africa on previous budget exploits, Queensland was a veritable shoestring Shangri La, but discovering a taste for the local brew, local sights and well…locals was just as rewarding.

SARAH WINTLE

Darwin & Around, Outback Australia (Broome & the Kimberley)

Sarah jumped at the chance to trade in her regular marketing role at Lonely Planet to explore her homeland's remote reaches in the Kimberley and the Top End. Maybe it's symptomatic of going to the same holiday spot as a kid, but this yoga devotee's had travel wanderlust for years. Sarah's travelled from New York to Nepal, and extensively in Australia, Asia and Europe. She thrives in cities but also loves the wilderness. Just don't ask her to name her favourite destination – she's loved everywhere. Yet she's still fond of going back to her family holiday haunt to relax and hit the waves.

CONTRIBUTING AUTHORS

Susie Ashworth wrote most of the Snapshot Australia chapter. Susie is a Melbourne-based freelance writer and enthusiastic traveller. On her longest Australian trip, she and a trusty Holden spent six months exploring the country's Outback, coast and country towns.

Professor Tim Flannery wrote the Environment section of Snapshot Australia. Tim's a naturalist and explorer and the author of a number of award-winning books, including *The Future Eaters, Throwim Way Leg* (an account of his adventures as a biologist working in New Guinea) and the landmark ecological history of North America, *The Eternal Frontier*. His latest book, written about Australia, is *Country*. Tim lives in Adelaide where he is director of the South Australian Museum and a professor at the University of Adelaide.

Josh Kronfeld wrote the Surfing in NZ boxed text in the New Zealand Directory chapter. Josh is an ex–All Black flanker, whose passion for surfing NZ's beaches is legendary.

Dr David Millar wrote the Health chapter. David Millar is a travel medicine specialist, diving doctor and lecturer in wilderness medicine who graduated in Hobart, Tasmania. He has worked in all states of Australia (except the Northern Territory) and as an expedition doctor with the Maritime Museum of Western Australia, accompanying a variety of expeditions around Australia. Dr Millar is currently a medical director with the Travel Doctor in Auckland.

Nina Rousseau wrote most of the Snapshot New Zealand chapter. Nina worked for Lonely Planet as an editor before jumping the fence to explore the world (and motel rooms) as a Lonely Planet author, including several trips around Australia and NZ. She currently works as a freelance writer and editor.

Nandor Tanczos MP wrote the Environmental Issues in Aotearoa New Zealand boxed text in the Snapshot New Zealand chapter. New Zealand's first Rastafarian member of Parliament, he's the Greens' spokesperson on Treaty of Waitangi issues and a high-profile campaigner on genetic engineering and cannabis law reform.

Vaughan Yarwood wrote the Environment section of Snapshot New Zealand. Vaughan is an Auckland-based writer whose most recent book, *The History Makers: Adventures in New Zealand Biography,* is published by Random House. Earlier work includes *The Best of New Zealand,* a collection of essays on NZ life and culture by prominent Kiwis, which he edited, and the regional history *Between Coasts: from Kaipara to Kawau.*

Vaughan has written widely for NZ and international publications and is the former associate editor of *New Zealand Geographic,* for which he continues to write International assignments have taken him to many countries in Europe, Asia and the Pacific. Most recently he travelled to Antarctica to research a book on polar exploration.

Thanks also to **Steve Irwin** (Crikey – Quarantine Matters! boxed text in the Australia Directory chapter) and **Sir Ian McKellen** (Sandflies boxed text in the New Zealand Directory chapter) for their contributions.

Destination Australia & New Zealand

GRANT DIXON

Beach south of Eddystone Point, northeast coast (p316), Tasmania, Australia

Your flight to the bottom end of the Pacific has taken you far from home, and you tumble off the plane feeling a mixture of excitement, anxiety and the prickle of long-haul weariness. You've heard about the amazing landscapes of Australia and New Zealand, and that the locals are a friendly bunch with an infectious enthusiasm. So you've travelled here with high expectations of spectacular sights, mind-blowing activities and all-round fun, unaware that those expectations are about to be completely overwhelmed.

You sit in a raucous pub sipping a freshly poured beer, thinking 'Nice people, strange accents'. Then you're suddenly being dumped onto a sun-cooked beach by an energetic wave. Now you sit on your bum in the outback watching the biggest rock you've ever seen glow red in the twilight. You try to outstare psychedelic little fish beneath the overhang of a massive coral reef, sit in a bus weaving past sea-sculpted limestone cliffs, and listen to a Tasmanian devil ransack your camping supplies as you sleep under a wilderness sky.

You're struck by déjà vu as you sit in another raucous pub across the Tasman Sea, thinking 'Nice people, strange accents'. You step along a cliff top above a rainforest-choked valley, moved to silence by the prehistoric calm. You watch a dolphin swim past in surreal, underwater slow motion. Then you're sliding your fingers along the depthless blue ice of a glacier cave, scrambling up the side of a volcano, jumping into space with a rubber cord unfurling behind you, and yelling yourself hoarse just for the hell of it at a rugby match.

Surprisingly (or perhaps not), going home now seems like the furthest thing from your mind.

CHRISTOPHER GROENHOUT

Opera House and Harbour Bridge in Sydney Harbour (p43), Sydney, Australia

HIGHLIGHTS

BEST URBAN EXPERIENCES

Sydney (Australia) ■ hedonistic harbourside city where the single-minded pursuit of pleasure is both a social requirement and a spectator sport (p41)

Auckland (NZ) ■ New Zealand's entertainment capital, where diverse inner-city venues happily co-exist with an energetic outdoor culture (p508)

Melbourne (Australia) ■ sports-crazed habitat, famous for the international flavour of its eating scene, and its laneway bars and earthy pubs (p232)

Rotorua (NZ) ■ backpackers steam up their senses, gawk at geysers and soak their cares away in thermal baths at this hot Kiwi destination (p590)

BEST OUTDOOR ACTIVITIES

Walking (Australia & NZ) ■ walk the walks: the Milford, Routeburn, Kepler and Tongariro tracks in NZ (p777); or Tasmania's Overland Track (p321)

Snorkelling & diving (Australia) ■ dive into the Coral Sea to float beside the world's biggest population of polyps, the Great Barrier Reef (p184)

Bungy mania (NZ) ■ take leave of your senses by throwing yourself into thin air off a ledge, a bridge or a gondola in Queenstown (p719)

Swimming with dolphins & watching whales (NZ) ■ take to the low seas with a dusky dolphin, a fur seal or a whale as a chaperone, in Kaikoura (p657)

ANDERS BLOMQVIST

Bungy jumping over Waikato River (p570), New Zealand

DAVID WALL

Yachts docked in Opua, Bay of Islands (p537), New Zealand

BEST ISLANDS & BEACHES

Whitsunday Islands (Australia) ■ paradisal mini-archipelago with coral-fringed beaches, perfect for cruising and snoozing (p192)

Bay of Islands (NZ) ■ island-speckled ocean refuge brimming with boats, water-sports options, and pods of local dolphins (p537)

Bondi Beach (Australia) ■ iconic swimming spot in the suntanned hurly burly of Sydney: it has an appealing mixture of tattiness and glam (p56)

Stewart Island (NZ) ■ wilderness getaway off the South Island, blanketed by a pristine national park (p763)

BEST OFF-THE-BEATEN-TRACK PLACES

The Catlins (NZ) ■ disconcertingly beautiful coastal sanctuary yielding forests, swathes of sand dunes and wind-blasted promontories (p769)

Kangaroo Island (Australia) ■ superb natural environment that has little-explored coves and forests, and is overrun with native wildlife (p371)

East Cape (NZ) ■ an unspoilt frontierland that treats visitors to driftwood-decorated beaches, friendly Maori settlements and magical seclusion (p623)

The Kimberley (Australia) ■ rugged chunk of the outback encompassing chasms, craters and the striped, stony towers of Purnululu (p432)

ROSS BARNETT

The Remarkable Rocks (p373), Flinders Chase National Park, Kangaroo Island, South Australia

ITINERARIES

THE KITCHEN SINK

How long?
2-8 months
When to go?
Sep-May
Budget?
A$45-60 per day;
NZ$50-70 per day

To circumnavigate both Australia and NZ means to experience independent travel at its most fulfilling.

After exploring east coast Australia, head due west from **Townsville** (p195) to leave a vigorous trail of footprints around the Red Centre destinations of **Alice Springs** (p419) and **Uluru** (p429) before dog-legging it to **Darwin** (p326).

Cross into Western Australia for a pit stop at pretty **Kununurra** (p444) and let the Great Northern Hwy transport you to the getaway town of **Broome** (p433). Take a peninsular sidetrack to the marine brilliance of **Ningaloo Reef** (p449) and the snorkel-friendly **Cape Range National Park** (p450), followed by a date with a bottle-nosed dolphin at **Monkey Mia** (p447). Continue south to the 'life is a beach' city of **Perth** (p380) and the latte-sipping enclave of **Freo** (p391), then wine away the hours at **Margaret River** (p404) until you're ready to tackle the flat, empty immensity of the Nullarbor Plain.

In South Australia, bushwalkers trudge towards the challenging **Flinders Ranges** (p375) while tipplers charge their palates in the **Barossa Valley** (p363). Beyond **Adelaide** (p352) it's a shortish trek into Victoria to check out surfboard-strewn **Torquay** (p265) and food-loving **Melbourne** (p232), from where there's a ferry to the unmissable island highlights in **Tasmania** (p293). Then enjoy the secluded wilderness of **Wilsons Promontory National Park** (p276) in Victoria, cruise around **Narooma** (p114) and bask in idyllic

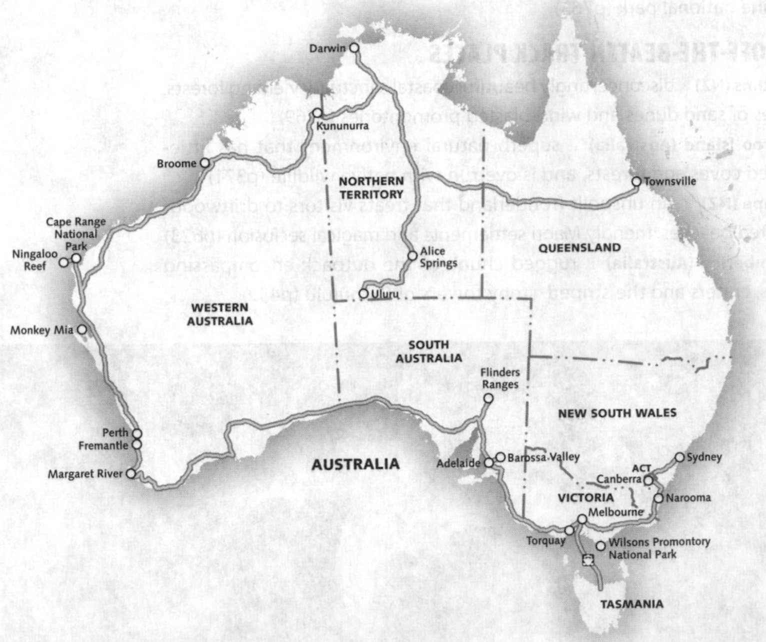

Jervis Bay (p113), both in New South Wales. After you've detoured to the national capital, **Canberra** (p115), return to lively **Sydney** (p41).

In NZ, leave **Auckland** (p508) for a snorkel off **Goat Island Beach** (p537), then continue to the iconic **Bay of Islands** (p537) to see where a landmark treaty was signed at **Waitangi** (p540). Swing north to the desolate dunes of **Ninety Mile Beach** (p551) and loop through the ancient **Waipoua Kauri Forest** (p552) back to Auckland. Head east to the splendidly forested **Coromandel Peninsula** (p563), then make for sulphurous **Rotorua** (p590). Explore the karst glory of **Waitomo** (p558), gaze at the massive dormant cone of **Mt Taranaki/Egmont** (p587), then go north via the still-smoking volcanoes of **Tongariro National Park** (p576) to sparkling **Lake Taupo** (p568). See **Napier** (p609) decked out in its roaring thirties Art Deco wardrobe, then finish your North Island jaunt in windy, cosmopolitan **Wellington** (p624).

Beyond Cook Strait, travel south to the deepwater wildlife of **Kaikoura** (p657) then double back to the grape-wreathed vineyards around **Blenheim** (p654). Arc around the coast to the stunning bays of **Abel Tasman National Park** (p670) before travelling west to the strikingly layered rocks of **Punakaiki** (p709), jade-polishing **Hokitika** (p706) and the magnificent seracs of **Franz Josef Glacier** (p711) and **Fox Glacier** (p714). Over Haast Pass are the perpetually active towns of **Wanaka** (p732) and **Queenstown** (p717). Detour from **Te Anau** (p750) north to divine **Milford Sound** (p754) and south to **Manapouri** (p758) to access the fantastically remote **Doubtful Sound** (p758). From low-rise **Invercargill** (p760), a secondary road skirts the grand ecology of **The Catlins** (p769). Forge north to Scottish-bred **Dunedin** (p738) before ducking inland to **Aoraki/Mt Cook** (p702). Continue beyond the turquoise brilliance of **Lake Tekapo** (p700) to cathedral-centred **Christchurch** (p673).

Experiencing the furthest reaches of the Aussie and Kiwi land masses means over 19,700km of main roads, not counting side trips to beaches, forests, mountains, reefs, towns… Where you start and finish is up to your imagination, but ideally allow for around eight months of discovery.

GOING TO EXTREMES

Journey to the ends of NZ and Australian terra firma and experience places far removed from ordinary life on this all-points-of-the-compass tour. Our suggested starting and stopping points are fairly arbitrary – you can begin or end this trip pretty much anywhere you like.

How long?
1½-6½ months
When to go?
Sep-May
Budget?
A$45-60 per day; NZ$50-70 per day

From the bright lights of **Sydney** (p41), venture down to the heel of the state of Victoria to explore the faunal riches and captivating walking tracks of **Wilsons Promontory** (p276). Freshen up in **Melbourne** (p232) before catching a ferry over to the island-state of Tasmania, where you'll find the touchingly sombre **Port Arthur** (p307) and the postcard-perfect, dreamy **Freycinet Peninsula** (p310). On the other side of the continent are the beachy city of **Perth** (p380) and, just offshore, the sparkling sands of **Rottnest Island** (p396). From here you can trek northwards to the dolphin-harbouring waters of **Shark Bay** (p445) and the amazing **Ningaloo Marine Park** (p449). Further north is the awesomely peaceful **Kimberley** (p432) and the ecological splendour of its Top End neighbour, **Kakadu National Park** (p340). Finally, to the east across the Gulf of Carpentaria and Cape York Peninsula are the extraordinary rainforests of **Cape Tribulation** (p223).

Once on NZ soil, head north from **Auckland** (p508) up along the dunes of Aupouri Peninsula to the tip of **Cape Reinga** (p551), which is wrapped in eerie solitude and Maori legend. Head back down through Auckland and skirt the Bay of Plenty to the wilderness-choked ranges of **East Cape** (p623). From **Wellington** (p624), hop over to the South Island and lose yourself in the myriad wonderful waterways of **Marlborough Sounds** (p650). Take the less-travelled trail to the West Coast to visit the icy brilliance of **Fox Glacier** (p714) and **Franz Josef Glacier** (p711) before continuing south

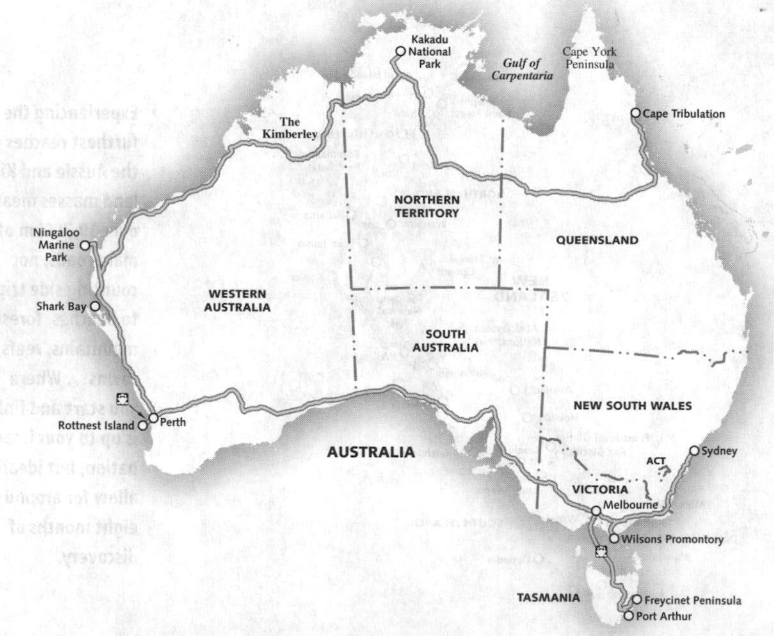

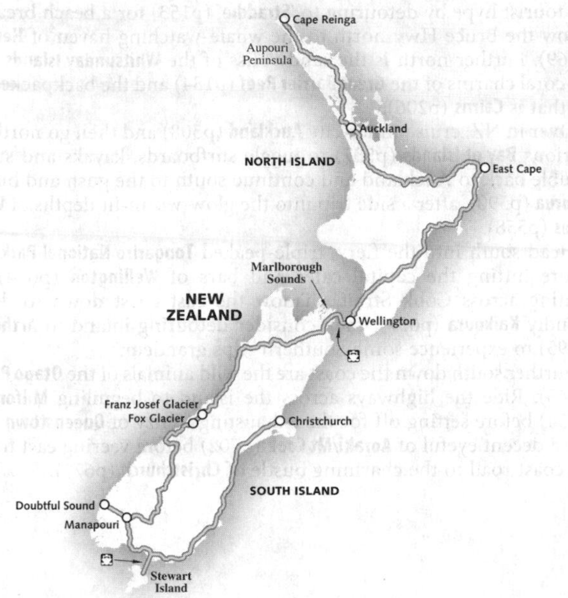

If you travel from one far-flung corner of Australia to another, and from NZ's northernmost fingernail to its detached southern toe, you'll tally around 16,900km of unforgettably diverse experiences. You could spend a mere two months on the road, but why would you if you had seven months up your sleeve?

to **Manapouri** (p758), from where you can travel through the magnificent wilds of Fiordland to utterly isolated **Doubtful Sound** (p758). Now ferry yourself out to **Stewart Island** (p763) to commune with nature before journeying on to **Christchurch** (p673).

BACKPACKER CLASSIC

How long?
3 weeks-3 months
When to go?
Sep-May
Budget?
A$45-60 per day; NZ$50-70 per day

The routes that initiate most backpackers to the joys of travel in this part of the South Pacific are the sea-hugging, sun-seeking run up the beach-sprinkled east coast of mainland Australia, and the dizzying loop around both islands of NZ that starts in Auckland and ends in Christchurch.

We start this itinerary in Australia, but many travellers familiarise themselves with Kiwi territory first before jetting across the Tasman. Similarly, for the Australian leg, most travellers fly into Sydney and then head north, but there's no reason why you can't tackle the route from the other end; ditto the NZ leg, which can be started in either Auckland or Christchurch.

In Australia, once you've tasted the big-city trappings of **Sydney** (p41) and the cliff-top magnificence of the **Blue Mountains** (p84), let the Pacific Hwy transport you north along some idyllic stretches of coastline to the sheltered serenity of **Port Stephens** (p96), the extreme sportiness of **Port Macquarie** (p97) and the marine wildlife of **Coffs Harbour** (p101). After seeing the lifestyles of the feral and famous in bemusing **Byron Bay** (p104) and the trippy hippiness of **Nimbin** (p109), head over the state border into Queensland and follow the smell of tanning oil to the overwhelming

Combine the Australian east coast with NZ's main attractions and you have a 6570km odyssey. You can tackle this well-travelled trail in as little as three weeks, but give yourself three months to really savour its pleasures.

kitsch and night-time glitz of **Surfers Paradise** (p155), and then into the relaxed streets of **Brisbane** (p138). Take time out from the crowds and the tourist hype by detouring to **'Straddie'** (p153) for a beach break, then follow the Bruce Hwy north to the whale-watching haven of **Hervey Bay** (p169). Further north is the sandy bliss of the **Whitsunday Islands** (p192), the coral charms of the **Great Barrier Reef** (p184) and the backpacker carnival that is **Cairns** (p206).

Over in NZ, cruise inner-city **Auckland** (p508) and then go north to the glorious **Bay of Islands** (p537) to juggle surfboards, kayaks and snorkels. Double back to Auckland and continue south to the gush and bubble of **Rotorua** (p590), after a side trip into the glow-worm-lit depths of **Waitomo Caves** (p558).

Head south into the fiery, triple-peaked **Tongariro National Park** (p576) before hitting the capital cafés and bars of **Wellington** (p624). After floating across Cook Strait, shadow the east coast down to dolphin-friendly **Kaikoura** (p657), then consider detouring inland to **Arthur's Pass** (p695) to experience some Southern Alps grandeur.

Further south down the coast are the wild animals of the **Otago Peninsula** (p745). Ride the highways across the island to beguiling **Milford Sound** (p754) before setting off for the exhausting frenzy of **Queenstown** (p717). Get a decent eyeful of **Aoraki/Mt Cook** (p702) before veering east to regain the coast road to the charming bustle of **Christchurch** (p673).

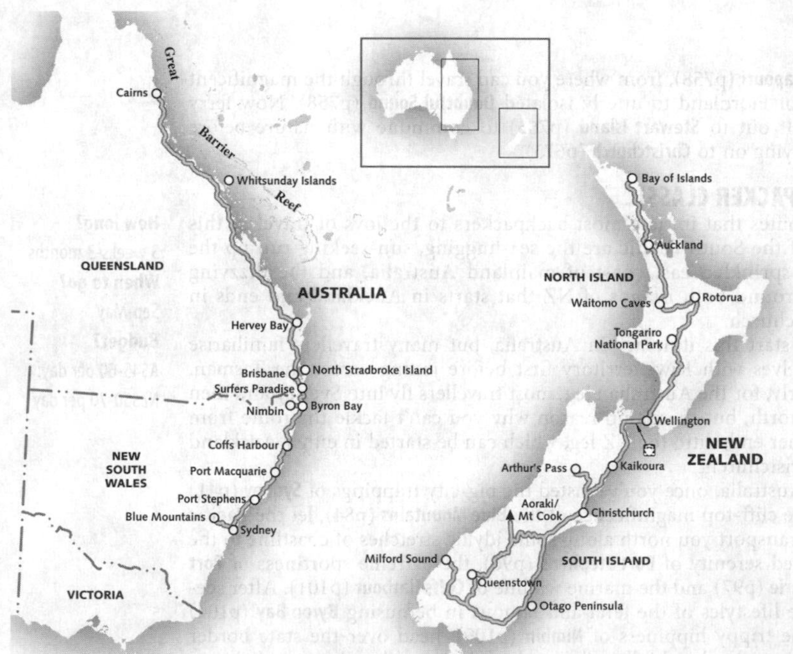

Getting Started

Travelling on a shoestring doesn't mean threadbare experiences. Nor do you need years of on-the-road experience to use common sense when assessing accommodation and transport options, particularly in Australia and NZ where tourism is a big, well-organised business. To help you on your way, see the Australia Directory (p458) and New Zealand Directory (p773) chapters for everything from business hours to visas. Also see Responsible Travel (p4) for some empowering advice.

WHEN TO GO

Any time is a good time to be *somewhere* in Australia. When it's cold down south, it's magnificent in the north and the Centre; when it's too hot up north, the southern states are at their finest. The Australian high season, when traveller numbers are highest, is over the three months of summer. In NZ, the warmer months between November and April form the extended high season, with the cooler, less trafficked months of October/November and April/May arguably the best times to visit; note it's usually a few degrees cooler on the South Island than on the North Island.

See under Climate in the Australia Directory (p463) and New Zealand Directory (p779) chapters for more information, including climate charts.

The NZ and Australian seasons are the antithesis of those in Europe and North America. It's summer from December to February, when the weather and longer daylight hours prompt outdoor escapades. June through August is winter, with temperatures dropping the further south you travel. Winter is officially the tourism low season in Australia, but it's also when travellers head north where the humidity of the wet season has subsided and the temperature is agreeable. Meanwhile, across the Tasman, snow is thick on the ground and Kiwi ski resorts are in full swing. Autumn (March to May) and spring (September to November) generally enjoy a lack of climatic extremes.

Unless you like competing with hordes of grimly determined locals for seats on buses, better-standard budget rooms, camp sites and premium vantage points at major attractions, avoid prime destinations during

WHAT TO TAKE

- **Camping gear** It's usually easy to rent or buy outdoor equipment in Australia and NZ, but if you're in for serious camping or walking/tramping it'll be more convenient and cheaper to carry your own stuff.
- **Clothes** Both countries have diverse climates, so pack all-weather clothes; NZ's weather can change very quickly, which anyone tramping at high altitudes should keep in mind.
- **Humour** Bring your sense of humour, for all those inevitable, minor backpacking mishaps, so you can begin to appreciate (perhaps even understand) the antipodean love of irony.
- **Insect repellent** And make it extra-strength repellent or it won't measure up against the formidable (and numerous) mosquitoes, flies and sandflies.
- **Insurance** If you plan to do any of the high-risk activities that these countries are famous for (eg bungy jumping or rock climbing), make sure you're fully covered by your travel insurance policy.
- **Photocopies** Make copies of important documents such as your passport, plane ticket, travellers cheque serial numbers, credit and debit cards, and pack them separately from the originals; also leave some copies at home.
- **Sunglasses** The sunlight can be pretty intense, so bring your sunnies along.

school holidays (particularly mid-December to mid-January and over Easter) and public holidays.

Festival-loving backpackers will find Kiwis hold numerous summer-time food and wine festivals, concerts and sports events, with other big occasions scattered throughout the year. Australians seize any excuse for a celebration and make public spectacles of themselves year-round.

HOW MUCH?

Bottle of beer A$2.50-3.80; NZ$3-5

Bottled water A$2-3; NZ$2-3

Coffee A$2.50-3; NZ$3-4

Hostel bunk A$15-25; NZ$18-25

Internet access A$2.50-6 per hr; NZ$3-10 per hr

Meal A$8-15; NZ$7-15

Movie ticket A$9-14; NZ$9-13

Petrol average A$0.90-1.10 per litre; NZ$1.05 per litre

COSTS & MONEY

Travellers who camp, or sleep in hostels, eat in cheap cafés or cook their own meals, tackle attractions independently (forgoing tours), restrict their socialising and travel by bus, or in a cheap, locally bought vehicle, can explore Australia for as little as A$45 per day, and NZ for as little as NZ$50 per day. But if you want to enjoy the occasional restaurant-cooked meal and entertaining over-indulgence (like a hard night of partying), then A$60 per day in Australia and NZ$70 per day in NZ is far more realistic.

Access to money via ATMs or credit card is hardly ever a problem, except in remote destinations. A true budgeting unknown when it comes to your trip, however, is the cost of activities. This could figure prominently in your expenses and it helps to decide in advance what you'd prefer to spend on. Travellers who intend on being very active should consider staying in the cheapest accommodation to help finance their exertions, while more-sedentary types who prefer sitting on a beach or a bar stool to dangling at the end of a bungy cord should limit their organised activities.

For more information, including exchange rates, see under Money in the Australia Directory (p470) and New Zealand Directory (p784) chapters.

LIFE ON THE ROAD

You pile out of the bus to collect your dust-smeared backpack, ears ringing with the chatter of the insecure fellow traveller you've sat next to for four hours. You check into your oddly familiar, historic yet refurbished hostel, claiming the top bunk in your dorm and hoping the bed below won't be occupied by a snorer with the lung capacity of an asthmatic bear. You test the bunk and are reassured to find it doesn't sag, then inspect

10 TIPS TO STAY ON A BUDGET

- Ask other travellers for their opinions of the best deals and worst rip-offs.
- Bring your own (BYO) camping gear rather than renting equipment for overnight walks.
- Don't shop in tourist districts.
- Compare prices of tours held several times a day – tours departing around lunchtime (eg Milford Sound cruises) are usually the most expensive.
- Eat frequently at food courts, markets and decent bakeries, and try to cook for yourself a few times a week.
- Figure out what you can afford to spend each day, and keep a diary of what you actually spend.
- Join or form groups to cut the cost of transport hire and sightseeing tours.
- Pack light so that using foot power to get around town is doable if necessary.
- 'Shouting' (buying your companions a drink) is an Australian custom, but it can be a real wallet-emptier depending on the size of the group and what they're drinking – it's OK to decline someone's offer of a shout and just buy your own.
- Use inner-city public transport (including late-night services) rather than taxis.

WHOOPS! *Paul Smitz*

Feeling weary during a recent NZ research trip, I took an upstairs pub room and settled in for a sound sleep. Unfortunately, I forgot to first check if there was any live music in the pub bar that night. The first violent drum beats and distorted guitars started underneath my mattress around 9pm, and the encores and loud drunken applause didn't finish until 3am. Not happy.

the modern kitchen and well-scrubbed bathroom, all the while nodding vigorously to complete strangers until your neck gets sore.

After getting the lowdown from the hostel's staff, who helpfully book you on a tour the following day, you wander into town with other new arrivals to explore your surroundings, comparing opinions of museums, beaches, quality of takeaway food and the attractiveness of the locals (and how weird their accents are) as you go. Later, you decide to find a good pub where you can take the first step towards tomorrow's hangover, though first you have to lose the guy who hasn't stopped complaining about how this place is so 'boring' compared to the primeval African jungle he recently hacked through with a blunt pair of scissors. Later still, you're at a table in your fourth bar of the evening, enthusiastically describing your upcoming three-day rainforest walk and first-ever skydive to several glassy-eyed people whose names you can't remember. The next morning, you get up (late) and leave your brain in bed while the rest of you finds a funky café for breakfast, where you can re-energise yourself for another unpredictable day.

CONDUCT

Generally, Australians and New Zealanders have metaphorically thick skins and friendly, nonjudgemental dispositions. It's usually only extreme behaviour that will incite extreme displeasure.

One thing that denizens of both countries take seriously is their attachment to the town or city where they live. Where it's deeply entrenched, this parochialism fuels defensiveness and intolerance of criticism from so-called outsiders, so think twice before you stand in the middle of a pub and openly condemn the place you're in as a 'shithole'. Adamantly comparing a place unfavourably to your own home city or country will also probably not win you friends, mostly because the locals will find it downright rude, but sometimes because such complaints tap into an old vein of xenophobia.

Aussies and Kiwis also take drinking seriously. Visitors may find themselves judged socially by how much alcohol they can hold, but the dangers of trying to live up to such expectations (particularly when they're established by seasoned drinkers) are obvious. The great Australian shout (buying a round of drinks) is a fine tradition, but don't let someone else shout you a drink if you've no intention of (or no money for) reciprocating.

DO'S & DON'TS

- Always acknowledge a greeting, even if it's from a stranger.
- Ask before taking photographs of indigenous Australians or Maoris.
- Don't light up a cigarette in someone's home without asking if it's OK.
- Home-town pride can be strong, so be discreet with criticisms.
- Ignore local regulations at your peril; they're usually there for a reason.
- Play by local pool table rules, which can change from town to town (sometimes from pub to pub).

TOP TENS

MUST-SEE MOVIES

One of the best places to do your essential trip preparation (ie daydreaming) is in a comfy lounge room with a bowl of popcorn in one hand, a remote control in the other and your eyeballs glued to a small screen.

- *Mad Max* (Australia, 1979) Director: George Miller
- *Lord of the Rings: The Fellowship of the Ring* (NZ, 2001) Director: Peter Jackson
- *Lantana* (Australia, 2001) Director: Ray Lawrence
- *Whale Rider* (NZ, 2003) Director: Niki Caro
- *Once Were Warriors* (NZ, 1994) Director: Lee Tamahori
- *Picnic at Hanging Rock* (Australia, 1975) Director: Peter Weir
- *Rabbit-Proof Fence* (Australia, 2002) Director: Phillip Noyce
- *The Piano* (NZ, 1993) Director: Jane Campion
- *An Angel at My Table* (NZ, 1990) Director: Jane Campion
- *Japanese Story* (Australia, 2003) Director: Sue Brooks

ESSENTIAL READS

Be it through escapist plots, multilayered fiction or character-driven social commentary, Australian and Kiwi literature tell you much about each country's unsettled history, growing cultural awareness and the physical power of the landscape.

- *The Vintner's Luck* (NZ, 2000) Elizabeth Knox
- *True History of the Kelly Gang* (Australia, 2000) Peter Carey
- *Dirt Music* (Australia, 2003) Tim Winton
- *Dreams Lost Never Walked* (NZ, 2003) Raumoa Ormsby
- *A Child's Book of True Crime* (Australia, 2002) Chloe Hooper
- *In a Fishbone Church* (NZ, 1998) Catherine Chidgey
- *The Carpathians* (NZ, 1988) Janet Frame
- *Gould's Book of Fish* (Australia, 2003) Richard Flanagan
- *The Hunter* (Australia, 1999) Julia Leigh
- *The Bone People* (NZ, 1988) Keri Hulme

OUR FAVOURITE FESTIVALS & EVENTS

These are our top 10 reasons to get into the festive spirit during your travels.

- World Buskers Festival, January, Christchurch, South Island, NZ (p682)
- Auckland Anniversary Day Regatta, January, North Island, NZ (p518)
- Summer City Festival, January and February, Wellington, North Island, NZ (p634)
- Sydney Gay & Lesbian Mardi Gras, February, NSW, Australia (p61)
- Harvest Hawke's Bay, February, North Island, NZ (p616)
- Adelaide Fringe, March, SA, Australia (p357)
- Beer Can Regatta, July/August, Darwin, NT, Australia (p331)
- Montana World of Wearable Art Show, NZ (p664)
- AFL Grand Final, September, Melbourne, Victoria, Australia (p247)
- Stompen Ground Festival, September/October, WA, Australia (p437)

Australia

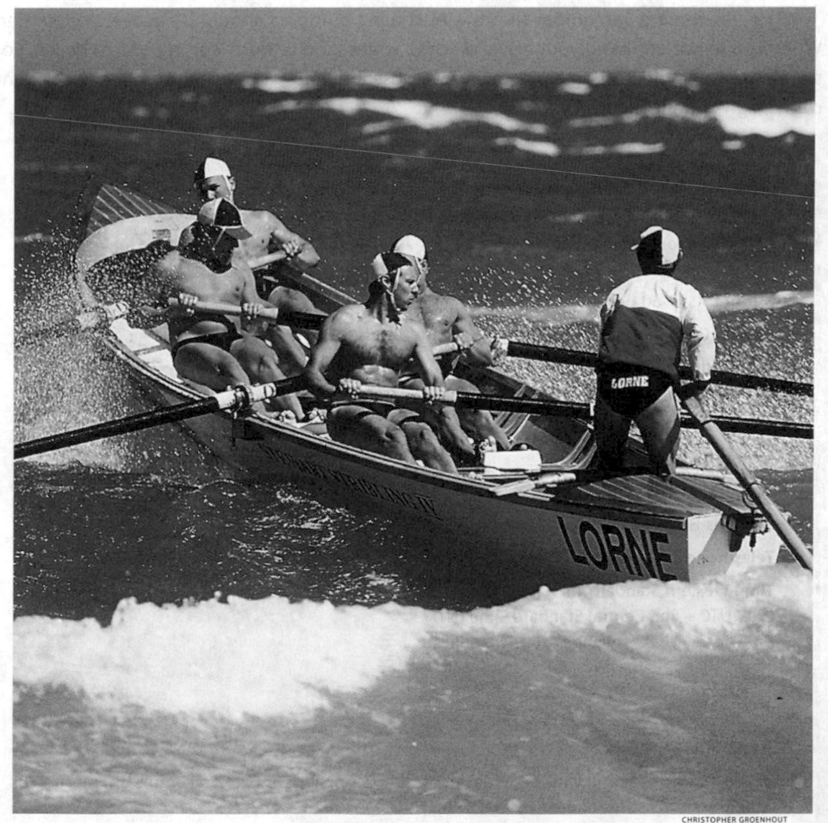

CHRISTOPHER GROENHOUT

Australia

Australia is like a huge backpacker beacon, pulling travellers by their tens of thousands across the Pacific and Indian Oceans to gawk at one of the world's most diverse landscapes. The sheer immensity of the continent makes it feel like an unexplored land – no matter how many other travellers tell you what to expect, when you first lay eyes on the ochre tinge of Uluru, the enormous rainforests of southwestern Tasmania, the fleshy majesty of a humpback whale in Hervey Bay, or the bewitching twists and turns of the Great Ocean Rd, you'll feel as if you're the first person who's ever seen them.

The idiosyncratic locals are an experience in themselves: they'll say 'g'day' to complete strangers but use words sparingly with friends; they're self-effacing, yet sometimes fiercely parochial; energetic yet laidback; outwardly playful, inwardly serious. The fascinating indigenous culture shows its true spirit through a powerful kinship with the land and Dreaming art.

While you're here, remember that the Australian outdoors should be actively celebrated. When you're not unfurling your towel on crisp white sand or body-surfing onto a beach, you should be striding across an alpine meadow, abseiling into narrow chasms or snowboarding down high-country slopes.

FAST FACTS

- **Area** 7,686,850 sq km
- **ATMs** In all tourist areas and many small towns
- **Budget** A$45-60 per day
- **Capital** Canberra
- **Costs** Dorm bed A$15-25; beer A$2.50-3.80; takeaway snack A$2-3
- **Electricity** 220-240V AC, 50Hz
- **Money** US$1 = A$0.69
- **Population** 19,826,000
- **Seasons** High Dec-Feb; low Jun-Aug
- **Telephone** Country code ☎ 61
- **Time** Western Standard Time (WA) = GMT/UTC + 8hr; Central Standard Time (NT & SA) = GMT/UTC + 9½hr; Eastern Standard Time (Queensland, NSW, ACT, Victoria and Tasmania) = GMT/UTC + 10hr

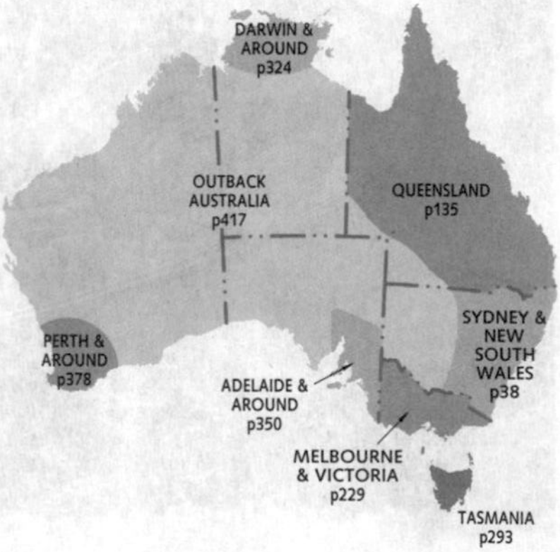

DARWIN & AROUND p324
OUTBACK AUSTRALIA p417
QUEENSLAND p135
PERTH & AROUND p378
SYDNEY & NEW SOUTH WALES p38
ADELAIDE & AROUND p350
MELBOURNE & VICTORIA p229
TASMANIA p293

TRAVEL HINT

Travellers roaming far and wide should check out hop-on, hop-off backpacker bus options (p478) and the discount passes offered by major bus lines (p479).

Snapshot Australia

CURRENT EVENTS

Despite its faraway location in the Pacific Ocean, Australia has not escaped the terrible events of the international scene, with Iraq, war and terrorism in the headlines and a constant source of discussion and argument in pubs and workplaces around the land. In October 2002, the Bali bombings killed over 190 people (including 89 Australians) and brought terrorism frighteningly close to home, prompting an outpouring of grief and soul-searching over Australia's foreign policy.

The government has thrown itself behind its traditional allies, the United States and Britain, echoing their antiterrorism messages, joining the 'coalition of the willing' and sending troops to Iraq. But throughout the conflict, Australians were divided over their country's military presence in the Gulf. Some looked longingly and approvingly at their nearby neighbour, New Zealand, who decided early to stay well out of it. A high-profile governmental slanging match arose over whether Australia had made itself a greater target for terrorists by joining George Dubya's Iraq campaign. During the election campaign of 2004, the Australian Labor Party (ALP) leader Mark Latham controversially promised to bring Aussie troops home from Iraq by Christmas. Prime Minister John Howard insisted they remain in Iraq 'until the job was done'. Ultimately (and surprisingly), the Iraq conflict took a backseat to domestic issues during the campaign.

Stuart Macintyre's *A Concise History of Australia* is a highly readable account of the national past. A very direct sense of connection between the past and today prevades the text and has given it a name as the best single-volume history of Australia available.

On 9 October 2004, after a drawn-out election campaign and more than eight years in power, conservative Liberal Party leader John Howard won his fourth term of office as prime minister of Australia. His main opponent was working-class-boy-made-good Mark Latham, who as the Labor leader and potential PM, promised to restore much-needed money to public health and education services and assist lower-income workers improve their lot in life. Other issues on Latham's agenda were saving Tasmania's old-growth forests and reducing public funding to elite private schools. Ultimately, scepticism over Latham's ability to manage the economy, and fear over rising interest rates led the majority of Aussies to vote for the devil they knew.

Up to the election, John Howard had presided over a relatively stable economic period, with continued annual growth and consistently low interest rates (a winning formula for the huge number of Australian home owners). In 2003, the economy boasted a 4% growth rate and the Aussie dollar gained about 30% against the US dollar – great for Aussie travellers heading overseas, but not so great for exporters.

During his long haul as PM, Howard has exchanged his 'Honest John' nickname for 'the Man of Steel', winning fans from Australians who support his hard-line stance over asylum seekers trying to enter Australia through 'nonofficial' channels. Those people arriving on Aussie shores in leaky boats find themselves promptly thrown into detention centres, often in remote, inhospitable regions around the country. Once again, this issue is a highly divisive one, with strong opposition from left-leaning locals who abhor the treatment of asylum seekers.

At the time of writing, Prime Minister John Howard was still ebullient over his election win, particularly as it became apparent that the coalition would also gain full control of the Senate, opening the floodgates for legislation that had been held back by Labor and the minor parties for eight years. Likely changes include the full sale of Telstra (fully privatising the half public-owned telecommunications company) and changes to cross-media ownership laws, which could dramatically alter the media landscape of the country.

In *The Explorers* (1998), Tim Flannery brings together an interesting collection of first-hand accounts by explorers, from James Cook and Joseph Banks to John Batman and Ludwig Leichhardt.

Ironically, barely a week after the federal election, the government began to make predictions about a slowing economy and rising interest rates. It seemed that the public's greatest fear was on the cards anyway. At the same time, media commentators continued to speculate about whether sexagenarian John Howard was going to stick around or hand over to his loyal treasurer Peter Costello, who has been waiting for the top job for several years.

Environmentally, Australia is a continent of extremes, and each year brings its fair share of drought, oppressive heat, bushfires, floods and cyclones. Recently, the country has suffered from a long-term drought, enduring significant water shortages and agricultural losses. Water restrictions have become an annual summer burden for city slickers, but a daily struggle for country folk who have even less access to water supplies.

But when life gets too serious, Australians love to turn their focus on the things that really matter – sport, and their latest Hollywood hopeful doing Australia proud. Following the fortunes of our Nic, Cate, Naomi, Heath and even Russ (don't say he's a Kiwi) is a national pastime, and the country rejoices with every award and international accolade.

HISTORY

Australia was the last great landmass to be discovered by Europeans. Long before the British claimed it, European explorers and traders dreamt of the riches to be found in the unknown southern land *(terra australis)*. The continent they eventually found had already been inhabited for tens of thousands of years.

If you want to know more about Captain James Cook, his ships, travels, journals and tragic end, see www.captaincooksociety.com.

Australian Aboriginal society has a continuous cultural history going back at least 50,000 years. It's almost certain that the first humans crossed the sea from Southeast Asia, but when is the subject of hot debate. The favoured options are between 35,000 and 60,000 years ago.

Australia's Aboriginal people lived in extended family groups or clans. Rituals, traditions and laws linked the people of each clan to the land they occupied. Clan members came together to perform rituals to honour their ancestral spirits and the creators of the Dreaming. These beliefs were the basis of the Aboriginal people's ties to the land they lived on.

European Discovery & Exploration

It's thought that Portuguese navigators probably sighted the Australian coast in the first half of the 16th century, and were followed by Dutch sailors in the early 1600s. In 1642 the Dutch East India Company set out for an exploration of the southern land, with Abel Tasman making two voyages in the 1640s, discovering the region he called Van Diemen's Land (renamed Tasmania 200 years later).

TIMELINE

8000 BC: Tasmania's Aborigines are separated from the mainland when sea levels rise

60000 BC — 8000 BC — 1640

60,000 – 35,000 BC: The date is debatable, but Aborigines settle in Australia sometime during this period

1642 AD: Abel Tasman discovers Tasmania and names it Van Diemen's Land after a Dutch governor

The prize for being Australia's first English visitor goes to the enterprising pirate William Dampier, who made the first investigations ashore about 40 years after Tasman. Dampier gave the continent a bad rap, and Europeans began to see it as a primitive and godless place. In 1768, Captain James Cook set out from Britain to begin a search for the Great South Land. On 19 April 1770, the extreme southeastern tip of the continent was sighted and named Point Hicks. Cook and his ships then hung a right, followed the coast north, and nine days later found sheltered anchorage in a harbour they named Botany Bay. After navigating the Great Barrier Reef and rounding Cape York, Cook put ashore to raise the Union Jack, rename the continent New South Wales, and claimed it for the British in the name of King George III.

Convicts & Settlement

Cook's botanist companion, Joseph Banks, suggested New South Wales would be a fine site for a colony of thieves. That the continent was already inhabited was not considered significant. In January 1788, the First Fleet sailed into Botany Bay under the command of Captain Arthur Phillip, who was to be the colony's first governor. For the newly arrived convicts, New South Wales was a harsh and horrible place; their sentences, of at least seven years with hard labour, were as good as life sentences as there was little hope of returning home.

Robert Hughes' bestseller *The Fatal Shore* (1987) offers a colourful and exhaustive historical account of convict transportation from Britain to Australia.

During the 1830s and 1840s the number of free settlers to the colonies of New South Wales, Western Australia, Van Diemen's Land (present-day Tasmania) and Port Phillip (Victoria) increased, but it was the discovery of gold in the 1850s that dramatically changed the young country.

By the time convict transportation was abolished (1852 in the eastern colonies and 1868 in the west), more than 168,000 convicts had been shipped to Australia.

Colonial Exploration & Expansion

By 1800 there were only two small settlements in Australia – at Sydney Cove and on Norfolk Island. While unknown areas on world maps were dwindling, most of Australia was still a mystery. The next 40 years were a great period of discovery, with thrill-seeking explorers trudging across the vast land, and settlements established at Hobart, Brisbane, Perth, Adelaide and Melbourne.

For a harrowing insight into the realities of life in a penal colony, grab a copy of the Australian 19th-century classic *For the Term of His Natural Life* (1874), by Marcus Clarke.

Notable early explorers were Matthew Flinders who sailed right around Australia in 1802; Blaxland, Wentworth and Lawson, who were the first to forge a trail through the Blue Mountains (west of Sydney); Hume and Hovell, who made the first overland journey southwards in 1824: from present-day Canberra to the western shores of Port Phillip Bay; and Robert Burke and William Wills who crossed the continent from south to north, then starved to death on the return trip.

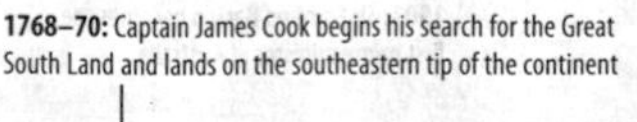

1768–70: Captain James Cook begins his search for the Great South Land and lands on the southeastern tip of the continent

1802: Matthew Flinders circumnavigates Australia with his faithful companion, Trim the cat

1760 1780 1800 1820

1788: The First Fleet arrives at Sydney Harbour with its cargo of convicts

1824: Hume and Hovell make the first overland trip from Sydney to Port Phillip Bay

Devastation of the Aborigines

It is believed that when Sydney Cove was first settled by the British there were about 300,000 Aboriginal people in Australia with around 250 different languages. Despite the presence of the Aboriginal people, the newly arrived Europeans considered the new continent to be *terra nullius* – a land belonging to no one.

Continent of Hunter-Gatherers: New Perspectives in Australian Prehistory by H Lourandos is an interesting survey of significant pre-European Aboriginal sites, set within the range of environmental zones across the continent.

Many Aborigines were driven from their land by force, and many more succumbed to introduced diseases such as smallpox and tuberculosis. As the European invaders encroached on Aboriginal lands, they introduced feral and domestic animals that destroyed water holes and ruined the habitats that had sustained mammals, reptiles and vegetable foods for tens of thousands of years. Starving Aborigines took colonists' livestock and then suffered reprisal raids that often left many dead. For the first 100 years of 'settlement' very few Europeans were prosecuted for killing Aboriginal people, although the practice was widespread.

Full-blood Aboriginal people in Tasmania were wiped out, and Aboriginal society elsewhere in Australia suffered terribly. By the 1880s only relatively small groups deep in the outback were still unscathed by the European invasion.

Gold!

The discovery of gold in the 1850s changed the social and economic face of Australia, particularly in Victoria where most of the gold was found.

The discovery of large reserves near Bathurst in 1851 caused a rush of miners from Sydney. The same year, one of the largest gold finds in history was made in central Victoria at Ballarat, followed by others at Bendigo and Mt Alexander (Castlemaine), starting a gold rush of unprecedented size.

The finds were big news around the world, and the image of Australia as a penal colony made way for that of a new El Dorado. While the first diggers at the goldfields came from the other Australian colonies, it wasn't long before thousands of Irish, Scots, English, other Europeans, Americans and Chinese began to arrive, all in search of the precious ore.

'Such is life' – Ned Kelly's last words before being hanged at Old Melbourne Gaol.

Although few people made their fortunes on the goldfields, many stayed on, as workers, shopkeepers and farmers. In Victoria, many tried to scratch a living from a small scrap of land granted by the government. Tough times and clashes with oppressive police created a climate of dissent. Ned Kelly (1855–80), a bushranger whose gang killed three policemen, came from such a setting. Despite his gruesome crimes and execution by hanging, Ned Kelly continues to be one of Australia's most persistent folk heroes.

Federation & WWI

With Federation on 1 January 1901, Australia became a nation, but its loyalty and many of its legal and cultural ties to Britain remained. The mother country still expected military support and, many times during the 20th century, Australia willingly followed its Western soul-mates to war.

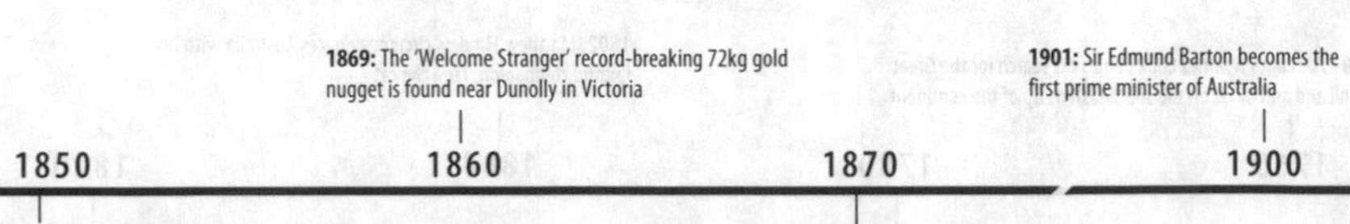
1869: The 'Welcome Stranger' record-breaking 72kg gold nugget is found near Dunolly in Victoria
1901: Sir Edmund Barton becomes the first prime minister of Australia
1850
1860
1870
1900
1851: The rush begins when gold is discovered near Bathurst, west of the Blue Mountains
1878: Ned Kelly and his gang of bushrangers shoot dead three police officers at Stringybark Creek

The extent to which Australia regarded itself as a European outpost was highlighted by the passage of the Immigration Restriction Bill of 1901. The discriminatory bill, known as the White Australia policy, was designed to prevent the immigration of Asians and Pacific Islanders.

When war broke out in Europe in 1914, Australian troops were sent to fight far from home. To Australians, the most infamous of the WWI battles was that at Gallipoli. Due to British military errors, Australian and New Zealander troops landed at the Turkish beach only to be slaughtered by well-equipped and strategically positioned Turkish soldiers. The sacrifices made by Australian soldiers are commemorated on Anzac Day, 25 April, the anniversary of the Gallipoli landing.

To learn more about the tragic Gallipoli campaign, see www.anzacsite.gov.au.

'Protection & Assimilation' of Aboriginal People

By the early 1900s, legislation designed to segregate and 'protect' Aboriginal people had been passed in all states. It imposed restrictions on their rights to own property and seek employment, and the Aboriginals Ordinance of 1918 allowed the state to remove children from their Aboriginal mother if it was suspected that the father was not an Aborigine – the children were placed in foster homes or child-care institutions. This practice continued until the 1960s. Today, those removed in this way are collectively known as the 'stolen generation'.

After WWII, government policy was the 'assimilation' of Aboriginal people into white society. Inevitably, the rights of Aboriginal people were eroded further. In the 1960s many white Australians condemned the assimilationist policy, and in 1967 non-Aboriginal Australians voted to give Aborigines and Torres Strait Islanders the status of citizens. Assimilationist policy was dumped by the newly elected Whitlam government in 1972. It was replaced by a policy of 'self-determination', which for the first time enabled Aboriginal people to participate in decision-making processes, by granting them rights to their land.

DID YOU KNOW?

On 26 May 1998, Australia celebrated its first National Sorry Day, with hundreds of thousands of Aussies signing Sorry Books and taking part in ceremonies in the spirit of reconciliation with the Aboriginal community.

WWII & Postwar Australia

When war broke out in 1939 Australian troops fought alongside the British in Europe and the Middle East, but after the Japanese bombed Pearl Harbor, Australia started to feel threatened. Singapore fell, the northern Australian towns of Darwin and Broome and the New Guinean town of Port Moresby were bombed, and the Japanese advanced southward. When Britain called for more Australian troops, Prime Minister John Curtin refused; Australian soldiers were needed closer to home.

Ultimately it was the USA that helped protect Australia from the Japanese, defeating them in the Battle of the Coral Sea. This event was to mark the beginning of a profound shift in Australia's allegiance away from Britain and towards the USA.

Needing labour and a larger population, 'populate or perish' became the catch phrase in postwar Australia; more than 800,000 non-British

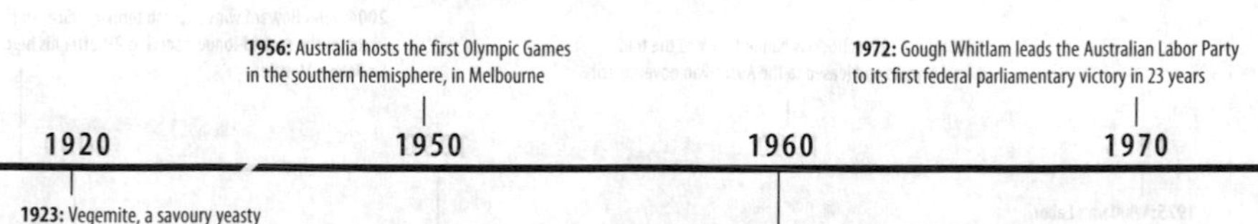

1956: Australia hosts the first Olympic Games in the southern hemisphere, in Melbourne
1972: Gough Whitlam leads the Australian Labor Party to its first federal parliamentary victory in 23 years
1920
1950
1960
1970
1923: Vegemite, a savoury yeasty breakfast spread, is invented in Melbourne
1967: Aborigines are finally given the status of citizens

European migrants were encouraged to move 'down under' between the years of 1947 and 1968.

Swept up in the anticommunist fever of the 1950s and led by the conservative government of Robert Menzies, Australia followed the USA into the Korean War.

In 1965 Australia once again committed troops to help the USA – this time in Vietnam. But the reasons for war and the conscription of thousands of young Aussie men troubled many in Australia. The marches, protests and civil unrest that followed contributed to the 1972 election of the Australian Labor Party, under the leadership of Gough Whitlam. The Whitlam government withdrew troops from Vietnam, abolished national service and higher-education fees, instituted a system of free and universally available health care, and supported land rights for Aboriginal people.

On 11 November 1975, the governor-general took the unprecedented step of dismissing parliament

But the Whitlam government was hampered by a hostile Senate and accusations of mismanagement. On 11 November 1975, the governor-general (the British monarch's representative in Australia) took the unprecedented step of dismissing parliament and installing a caretaker government led by the leader of the opposition Liberal Party, Malcolm Fraser. Fraser's conservative coalition won the ensuing election. A Labor government was not returned until 1983, when a former trade union leader, Bob Hawke, became prime minister.

Today

After a period of recession and high unemployment in the early 1990s, the electorate eventually lost faith in the Labor government and, in early 1996, Labor leader Paul Keating was defeated by the Liberal/National Party coalition led by John Howard.

In the late 1990s, republicanism was the hot issue, and many lobbied to replace Britain's queen with an Australian president as head of state. But no one could agree on how the new system would work and the 1999 referendum was a victory for the status quo.

The next big issue was the dilemma of asylum seekers landing on Australian shores.

In 2001, several hundred asylum seekers aboard a sinking boat were rescued just offshore by the *Tampa*, a Norwegian vessel, and then denied sanctuary in Australia. In the midst of the national hysteria that followed (an overwhelming majority of Australians supported the government's action), the asylum seekers were accused by the government of trying to throw their children overboard. This accusation was eventually proved false, but not before the government won a huge majority at the November 2001 federal election.

At the time of writing, John Howard was on cloud nine after winning his fourth election in a row, on 9 October 2004.

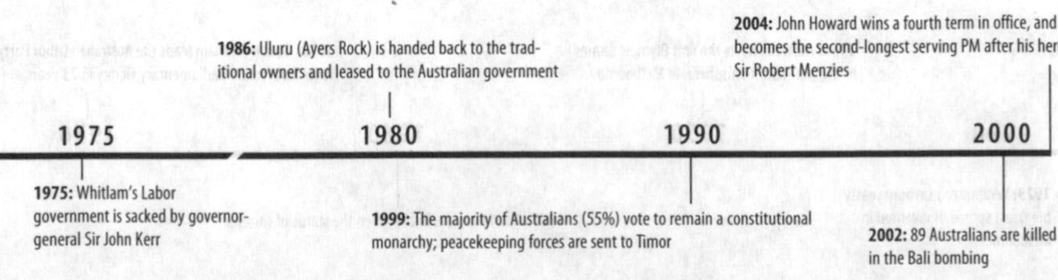
1986: Uluru (Ayers Rock) is handed back to the traditional owners and leased to the Australian government
2004: John Howard wins a fourth term in office, and becomes the second-longest serving PM after his hero Sir Robert Menzies
1975
1980
1990
2000
1975: Whitlam's Labor government is sacked by governor-general Sir John Kerr
1999: The majority of Australians (55%) vote to remain a constitutional monarchy; peacekeeping forces are sent to Timor
2002: 89 Australians are killed in the Bali bombing

THE CULTURE

The National Psyche

Despite the stereotype of tanned, outback-dwelling, muscle-bound, croc-wrestlers, most Australians are urban and urbane, more comfortable wrangling a bruschetta-and-macchiato brunch than wrestling an oversized reptile.

Despite its sophisticated lifestyles, the Australian landscape has shaped a national character that is used to hardship. Living with adversity has also helped mould an anti-authoritarian, rebellious nature rooted in a down-trodden (and for some, convict) past. Most Aussies prefer to support the underdog over someone who has become too successful, too popular or 'too big for their boots'. Australians also tend to be modest and not crow about success. Boasting is an unforgivable sin in a society where egalitarian values are held in high regard.

Australians often use humour as a social levelling tool. For those not familiar with its unique character, a first encounter with Aussie humour can be a confusing experience. Aussie kids are infused with the essential characteristics of the local humour – self-deprecation, black humour, sarcasm, irony and the occasional obscenity. One of the worst social faux pas in Australia is to take yourself too seriously, and youngsters must learn how 'to take a joke' along with how to walk and talk.

Social interaction, particularly at the pub, is often a mix of jokes, amusing anecdotes and personal teasing. Visitors can be shocked to hear best mates trading insults ('taking the piss') or labelling each other a '!%! bastard', until they realise it's meant in the nicest possible way. Swear words are often used as terms of affection, and if you're being teased it usually means that you are liked and are being accepted in the group.

Make sure you're always in on the joke with Lonely Planet's *Australian Phrasebook*, which has 250 pages of rhyming slang, Aussie expressions, national songs, Aboriginal languages and other cultural titbits.

Along with its indigenous population, a steady stream of immigrants continues to make its imprint on Australian culture, with large populations of Brits, Irish, New Zealanders, continental Europeans and Asians bringing their own unique histories, stories, food and cultures to the melting pot. To many migrants, Australia is a land of opportunity, a perfect place to start a new life. So while on your travels in Australia you may still hear 'g'day' from an Akubra-wearing, laconic, sixth-generation bush larrikin, but his voice will be just one among many.

Lifestyle

The Australian landscape's riches forged the nickname 'the lucky country', and for most Australians this rings true. Most Aussies are city-dwellers, living a modern, comfortable life near the coast where they enjoy warm weather, a high standard of living, pristine beaches and a laidback atmosphere that can be found even in the busiest cities. Most locals you'll meet will be relaxed and friendly. They're blessed with the good life and know it.

Life's still a beach for many Aussies, who strip off the business suit at the end of the day and head for the closest stretch of coastline they can find – for more than 85% of Australians their nearest beach is within 50km of home. The beach holiday is still very much the annual summer pilgrimage for most families, who flock to beaches (many dragging caravans) in search of long, lazy sun-kissed days on the sand and in the surf. (On your travels, beware of the most popular beach resorts during school holidays: it's a crush that can get pretty ugly.)

The Australian Dream has long been to own a house on a quarter-acre block, and the majority of folks still rate home ownership highly on their 'to do' list. Inside the average middle-class suburban home, you'll probably find a married heterosexual couple, though it is becoming increasingly likely they will be de facto, or in their second marriage.

Our 'mum and dad' couple will have an average of 1.4 children, probably called Jessica and Jack, Australia's names of the moment. But the birth rate has been falling over the last few years as more couples put off having children, preferring to focus on higher education, travel and financial security before parenthood. Politicians from both the major parties have been scrambling to come up with ideas to encourage more breeding, from family-friendly work policies to 'baby bonuses'. Despite their efforts, at the time of writing, a quarter of Aussie women of child-bearing age were expected to remain childless.

People

Australia has been strongly influenced by immigration, and its multicultural mix is among the most diverse in the world. At the last census (2001), 23% of the population were foreign-born, compared with an estimated 11.5% in the USA. Many foreign-born Australians came from Italy and Greece after WWII, but recent immigrants have mostly come from NZ and the UK, and from China, Vietnam, Africa and India. Some 2.2% of the population identify themselves as being of Aboriginal origin; most of them living in the Northern Territory, which has, not coincidently, the lowest life expectancy rates in the country. Australia's other indigenous people, Torres Strait Islanders, are primarily Melanesian, living in north Queensland and on the islands of the Torres Strait between Cape York and Papua New Guinea.

There are 19,826,000 people in Australia, with a whopping 64% living in cities. Population density is the lowest in the world, with an average of 2.5 people per square kilometre. Most people live along the eastern seaboard, between Melbourne and Brisbane, with a smaller concentration on the coastal region in and around Perth. Most of the outback is empty.

Arts

Check out Message Stick for indigenous arts and music information: www.abc.net.au/message.

Australians are known for having a love affair with sport and little more than a fleeting attraction to the arts, but statistics prove otherwise. The most popular pastime is cinema, with 67% of the population lining up for flicks and popcorn each year. Book-lovers in Australia fork out about A$1 billion on books each year, around 25% of Australians attend a music concert annually, and some 21% of Australians gallery-hop.

LITERATURE

The *Oxford Companion to Australian Literature* (1994), edited by William H Wilde, Joy Hooton & Barry Andrews, is a comprehensive guide to Australian authors and writing from European settlement to the 1990s.

Through story and ballads, early literature mythologised the hardships of European pioneers and unjust governments. Nationalism was a driving force, especially in the late 1800s with the celebration of the country's centenary (1888) and Federation in 1901. AB 'Banjo' Paterson was *the* bush poet of the time, famous for his poems *The Man from Snowy River*, *Clancy of the Overflow* and *Waltzing Matilda*, the country's on-again-off-again national anthem. Henry Lawson, a contemporary of Paterson, wrote short stories evoking the era; one of his best, *The Drover's Wife*, is a moving tale of one woman's lot in the pioneering life.

In the postwar era, Australian writers began to re-evaluate their colonial past. Patrick White, arguably Australia's finest novelist and the country's only Nobel Prize winner for Literature to date, helped turn the tables on the earlier writers' fascination with romanticism with *Voss* (1957) and his despair-inducing *The Tree of Man* (1955). Later novelists, such as the Booker-prize winner Thomas Keneally, keenly felt the devastation and

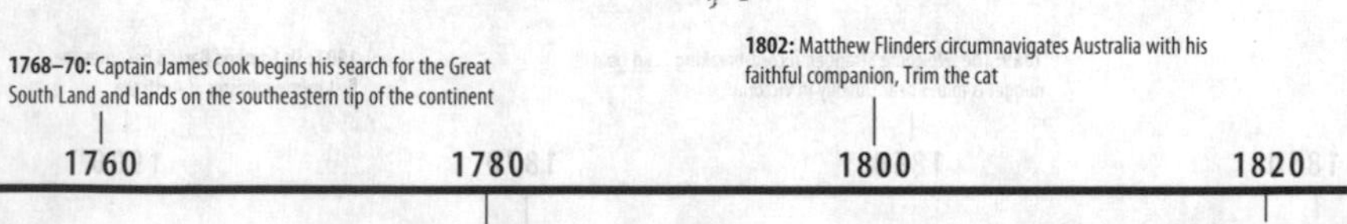

Devastation of the Aborigines

It is believed that when Sydney Cove was first settled by the British there were about 300,000 Aboriginal people in Australia with around 250 different languages. Despite the presence of the Aboriginal people, the newly arrived Europeans considered the new continent to be *terra nullius* – a land belonging to no one.

Many Aborigines were driven from their land by force, and many more succumbed to introduced diseases such as smallpox and tuberculosis. As the European invaders encroached on Aboriginal lands, they introduced feral and domestic animals that destroyed water holes and ruined the habitats that had sustained mammals, reptiles and vegetable foods for tens of thousands of years. Starving Aborigines took colonists' livestock and then suffered reprisal raids that often left many dead. For the first 100 years of 'settlement' very few Europeans were prosecuted for killing Aboriginal people, although the practice was widespread.

Continent of Hunter-Gatherers: New Perspectives in Australian Prehistory by H Lourandos is an interesting survey of significant pre-European Aboriginal sites, set within the range of environmental zones across the continent.

Full-blood Aboriginal people in Tasmania were wiped out, and Aboriginal society elsewhere in Australia suffered terribly. By the 1880s only relatively small groups deep in the outback were still unscathed by the European invasion.

Gold!

The discovery of gold in the 1850s changed the social and economic face of Australia, particularly in Victoria where most of the gold was found.

The discovery of large reserves near Bathurst in 1851 caused a rush of miners from Sydney. The same year, one of the largest gold finds in history was made in central Victoria at Ballarat, followed by others at Bendigo and Mt Alexander (Castlemaine), starting a gold rush of unprecedented size.

The finds were big news around the world, and the image of Australia as a penal colony made way for that of a new El Dorado. While the first diggers at the goldfields came from the other Australian colonies, it wasn't long before thousands of Irish, Scots, English, other Europeans, Americans and Chinese began to arrive, all in search of the precious ore.

'Such is life' – Ned Kelly's last words before being hanged at Old Melbourne Gaol.

Although few people made their fortunes on the goldfields, many stayed on, as workers, shopkeepers and farmers. In Victoria, many tried to scratch a living from a small scrap of land granted by the government. Tough times and clashes with oppressive police created a climate of dissent. Ned Kelly (1855–80), a bushranger whose gang killed three policemen, came from such a setting. Despite his gruesome crimes and execution by hanging, Ned Kelly continues to be one of Australia's most persistent folk heroes.

Federation & WWI

With Federation on 1 January 1901, Australia became a nation, but its loyalty and many of its legal and cultural ties to Britain remained. The mother country still expected military support and, many times during the 20th century, Australia willingly followed its Western soul-mates to war.

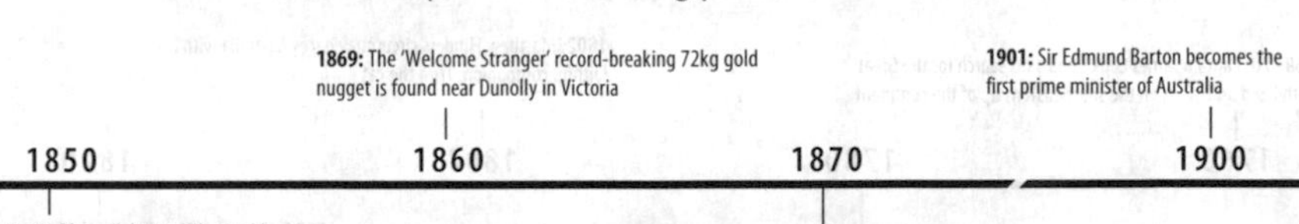
1869: The 'Welcome Stranger' record-breaking 72kg gold nugget is found near Dunolly in Victoria
1901: Sir Edmund Barton becomes the first prime minister of Australia
1850
1860
1870
1900
1851: The rush begins when gold is discovered near Bathurst, west of the Blue Mountains
1878: Ned Kelly and his gang of bushrangers shoot dead three police officers at Stringybark Creek

The extent to which Australia regarded itself as a European outpost was highlighted by the passage of the Immigration Restriction Bill of 1901. The discriminatory bill, known as the White Australia policy, was designed to prevent the immigration of Asians and Pacific Islanders.

When war broke out in Europe in 1914, Australian troops were sent to fight far from home. To Australians, the most infamous of the WWI battles was that at Gallipoli. Due to British military errors, Australian and New Zealander troops landed at the Turkish beach only to be slaughtered by well-equipped and strategically positioned Turkish soldiers. The sacrifices made by Australian soldiers are commemorated on Anzac Day, 25 April, the anniversary of the Gallipoli landing.

To learn more about the tragic Gallipoli campaign, see www.anzacsite.gov.au.

'Protection & Assimilation' of Aboriginal People

By the early 1900s, legislation designed to segregate and 'protect' Aboriginal people had been passed in all states. It imposed restrictions on their rights to own property and seek employment, and the Aboriginals Ordinance of 1918 allowed the state to remove children from their Aboriginal mother if it was suspected that the father was not an Aborigine – the children were placed in foster homes or child-care institutions. This practice continued until the 1960s. Today, those removed in this way are collectively known as the 'stolen generation'.

After WWII, government policy was the 'assimilation' of Aboriginal people into white society. Inevitably, the rights of Aboriginal people were eroded further. In the 1960s many white Australians condemned the assimilationist policy, and in 1967 non-Aboriginal Australians voted to give Aborigines and Torres Strait Islanders the status of citizens. Assimilationist policy was dumped by the newly elected Whitlam government in 1972. It was replaced by a policy of 'self-determination', which for the first time enabled Aboriginal people to participate in decision-making processes, by granting them rights to their land.

DID YOU KNOW?

On 26 May 1998, Australia celebrated its first National Sorry Day, with hundreds of thousands of Aussies signing Sorry Books and taking part in ceremonies in the spirit of reconciliation with the Aboriginal community.

WWII & Postwar Australia

When war broke out in 1939 Australian troops fought alongside the British in Europe and the Middle East, but after the Japanese bombed Pearl Harbor, Australia started to feel threatened. Singapore fell, the northern Australian towns of Darwin and Broome and the New Guinean town of Port Moresby were bombed, and the Japanese advanced southward. When Britain called for more Australian troops, Prime Minister John Curtin refused; Australian soldiers were needed closer to home.

Ultimately it was the USA that helped protect Australia from the Japanese, defeating them in the Battle of the Coral Sea. This event was to mark the beginning of a profound shift in Australia's allegiance away from Britain and towards the USA.

Needing labour and a larger population, 'populate or perish' became the catch phrase in postwar Australia; more than 800,000 non-British

1920 **1950** **1960** **1970**

1923: Vegemite, a savoury yeasty breakfast spread, is invented in Melbourne

1956: Australia hosts the first Olympic Games in the southern hemisphere, in Melbourne

1967: Aborigines are finally given the status of citizens

1972: Gough Whitlam leads the Australian Labor Party to its first federal parliamentary victory in 23 years

European migrants were encouraged to move 'down under' between the years of 1947 and 1968.

Swept up in the anticommunist fever of the 1950s and led by the conservative government of Robert Menzies, Australia followed the USA into the Korean War.

In 1965 Australia once again committed troops to help the USA – this time in Vietnam. But the reasons for war and the conscription of thousands of young Aussie men troubled many in Australia. The marches, protests and civil unrest that followed contributed to the 1972 election of the Australian Labor Party, under the leadership of Gough Whitlam. The Whitlam government withdrew troops from Vietnam, abolished national service and higher-education fees, instituted a system of free and universally available health care, and supported land rights for Aboriginal people.

On 11 November 1975, the governor-general took the unprecedented step of dismissing parliament

But the Whitlam government was hampered by a hostile Senate and accusations of mismanagement. On 11 November 1975, the governor-general (the British monarch's representative in Australia) took the unprecedented step of dismissing parliament and installing a caretaker government led by the leader of the opposition Liberal Party, Malcolm Fraser. Fraser's conservative coalition won the ensuing election. A Labor government was not returned until 1983, when a former trade union leader, Bob Hawke, became prime minister.

Today

After a period of recession and high unemployment in the early 1990s, the electorate eventually lost faith in the Labor government and, in early 1996, Labor leader Paul Keating was defeated by the Liberal/National Party coalition led by John Howard.

In the late 1990s, republicanism was the hot issue, and many lobbied to replace Britain's queen with an Australian president as head of state. But no one could agree on how the new system would work and the 1999 referendum was a victory for the status quo.

The next big issue was the dilemma of asylum seekers landing on Australian shores.

In 2001, several hundred asylum seekers aboard a sinking boat were rescued just offshore by the *Tampa*, a Norwegian vessel, and then denied sanctuary in Australia. In the midst of the national hysteria that followed (an overwhelming majority of Australians supported the government's action), the asylum seekers were accused by the government of trying to throw their children overboard. This accusation was eventually proved false, but not before the government won a huge majority at the November 2001 federal election.

At the time of writing, John Howard was on cloud nine after winning his fourth election in a row, on 9 October 2004.

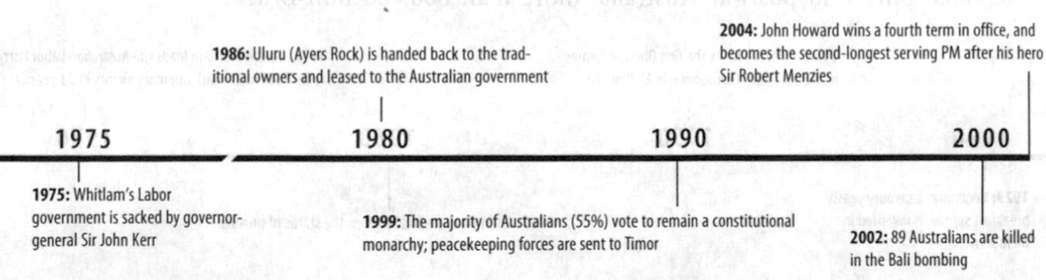

2004: John Howard wins a fourth term in office, and becomes the second-longest serving PM after his hero Sir Robert Menzies
1986: Uluru (Ayers Rock) is handed back to the traditional owners and leased to the Australian government
1975
1980
1990
2000
1975: Whitlam's Labor government is sacked by governor-general Sir John Kerr
1999: The majority of Australians (55%) vote to remain a constitutional monarchy; peacekeeping forces are sent to Timor
2002: 89 Australians are killed in the Bali bombing

TOP READS

- *Eucalyptus* (Murray Bail) A spellbinding contemporary fairy tale about a man's strange search for the perfect suitor for his daughter. Wonderful evocative prose for lovers of trees and nature.
- *True History of the Kelly Gang* (Peter Carey) The tale of infamous Aussie bushranger Ned Kelly, told in the evocative, ungrammatical voice of Kelly's Jerilderie letter.
- *Cloudstreet* (Tim Winton) An epic family saga based in postwar Perth and full of Winton's distinctive poetic narrative.
- *My Place* (Sally Morgan) Moving autobiography of the author's discovery of her Aboriginal heritage.
- *Voss* (Patrick White) Described as White's most challenging but most impressive work, this superbly written novel explores the colonial exploration era in Australia.

rage of the Aborigines, as depicted in his excellent novel *The Chant of Jimmy Blacksmith* (1972), also made into a film.

Australia's literary scene has evolved in the last few decades to better reflect the country's multicultural makeup. Sally Morgan's successful autobiography *My Place* (1987) charts the author's aboriginality (only discovered in her teens) and her search for her true identity. Kim Scott's excellent *Benang* (1999), which won the Miles Franklin award in 2000, is a confronting but rewarding read about the assimilation policies of the 20th century and the devastating effect they had on Aboriginal Australia.

Australia's best-known novelist and twice winner of the prestigious Booker Prize, Peter Carey, writes knock-out books; his most popular are *Oscar & Lucinda* (1988) and *True History of the Kelly Gang* (2000).

Another of Australia's celebrated contemporary writers is Tim Winton. His books celebrate the beauty of the landscape, particularly his nostalgic *Land's Edge* (1993), where he affectionately reminisces about childhood summers on the coast. His award-winning *Cloudstreet* (1991), an epic family saga, has also received rave reviews from local and international audiences – and the unofficial title of 'Australia's most popular novel'.

CINEMA

Australia loved moving pictures from the start, having created the world's first full-length feature film in 1905, *The Story of the Kelly Gang* (directed by the Tait brothers). Other early silent classics include *The Sentimental Bloke* (1919), based on a humorous poem by CJ Dennis; and *For the Term of His Natural Life* (1926), about a beleaguered convict.

DID YOU KNOW?

All the *Star Wars* prequels were largely shot at Fox Studios Sydney.

By the time the 1960s rolled around, Aussies were glued to their TV screens and the film industry suffered a prolonged drought. But in the 1970s there was a revival, with the government funding the new Australian Film, TV & Radio School and the Australian Film Commission. Big names from this period include directors Peter Weir, Fred Schepisi and Bruce Beresford, and actors Judy Davis and Mel Gibson. Seventies' films worth a look are *Walkabout* (1971), a fascinating insight into indigenous culture and the harsh conditions of the outback; and *Picnic at Hanging Rock* (1975), a haunting tale of some school girls who mysteriously disappear into the bush. Two powerful movies with an antiwar message are *Breaker Morant* (1980) and *Gallipoli* (1981), which featured Mel Gibson before his meteoric rise. *Mad Max* (1979) and *Mad Max II* (1981) were genre-busters and box-office hits that did well overseas – to everyone's surprise. And then there was *Crocodile Dundee* (1986), a huge international

TOP FLICKS

- *Muriel's Wedding* (PJ Hogan) Timeless celebration of kitsch, following loveable ABBA devotee Muriel on her journey of self-discovery.
- *Shine* (Scott Hicks) True life tale of emotionally disturbed musical genius David Helfgott.
- *Breaker Morant* (Bruce Beresford) Aussie classic about war crimes and justice during the late stages of the Boer War.
- *Picnic at Hanging Rock* (Peter Weir) Haunting flick about the mysterious disappearance of school girls at Hanging Rock.
- *Lantana* (Ray Lawrence) Mesmerising contemporary story of love, trust and betrayal in relationships.

success, but a movie that did nothing to counter stereotypes of stubbled Aussie blokes.

In the late '80s and '90s the spotlight turned homeward to the suburban quarter-acre block where the larrikin Aussie battler fought for a 'fair go' in satirical celebrations of Australian myths and stereotypes. The best of these were *Muriel's Wedding* (1994) and *The Castle* (1997).

The building of Fox Studios Australia (Sydney) and Warner Roadshow Studios on the Gold Coast (Queensland) in the past few years has attracted big-budget US productions like *Mission Impossible II*, *The Matrix* trilogy and *Moulin Rouge* to the country.

In the last few years most films made for an Australian audience have abandoned stereotypes and started to explore the country's diversity. Indigenous stories have found a mainstream voice on the big screen, with films such as *The Tracker* (2002) and *Rabbit Proof Fence* (2002), illustrations of a nation starting to come to terms with its racist past and present. By staying relevant to contemporary Australians, the industry continues to survive and thrive.

MUSIC

For a 100% dose of Aussie music, tune into the national radio station Triple J for 'Home and Hosed', 9pm to 11pm weeknights www.triplej.net.au/listen.

Australian popular music really kicked off in the '70s, fed by a thriving pub-rock scene and the huge success of *Countdown*, a music TV show that exposed local bands.

F-off rock legends AC/DC started out in the early '70s; their 1980 album *Back in Black* blitzed some 10 million sales in the USA alone. Cold Chisel also started out around that time, their stubbled Aussie blokedom and earnest rock an instant success; *Cold Chisel* and *East* are their best albums. Paul Kelly's first forays in the music scene were in the '70s, too, though his solo album *Post* (1985) put his passionate folk ballad blend on the map. Midnight Oil's politico-pop reached a head at the time of *Diesel and Dust* (1987); while the Divinyls, with lead siren Chrissy Amphlett, are best remembered for the raunchy single 'I Touch Myself'. Nick Cave is one of a number of indie performers who came to prominence in the late '70s and left for overseas in a diaspora of Aussie talent in the '80s.

By the late '80s, notably around the time *Countdown* was wound down (1987), Australian rock music began to be dominated by the lucrative ditty-pop market. Enter Kylie Minogue, one-time fluffy-haired nymphet from *Neighbours*, whose bum first hit the stage with *Locomotion* in 1987, and the rest, as they say, is history.

Feeding on the pub-rock legacy of the '70s, live music continues to find an audience, with local bands like Powderfinger, The Avalanches, Grinspoon, The Whitlams, Gerling and Spiderbait working hard on the local scene, but not competing internationally with the big-name Oz exports Kylie, Natalie Imbruglia, Silverchair, Jet and The Vines.

Contemporary indigenous music is thriving, and the annual Deadlys awards are a good place to find out who's setting the pace (www.vibe.com.au). Jimmy Little, the country-folk stalwart, began his career in the '50s, but it was in the '90s that indigenous music hit mainstream, thanks largely to the immense popularity of Yothu Yindi and the single 'Treaty', lifted from their excellent album, *Tribal Voice* (1991).

Grab a copy of *Great Southern Land* (2003, Festival Mushroom Records). This best-of album selects 19 Oz classics from Cold Chisel's 'Khe Sanh', The Angels' 'Am I Ever Gonna See Your Face Again?' (response: no way, get fucked, fuck off!) to Men at Work's 'Down Under'.

Sport

Sport is a national obsession, and there's no sport that arouses more passion and pride than football, whether it be the brawny battlers of the National Rugby League (NRL) or the tight-shorted titans of the Australian Football League (AFL, or Aussie Rules).

The national **AFL** (http://afl.com.au) competition developed from the league in Victoria, a state that is sports mad and fiercely parochial about its beloved game. If you're travelling in autumn or winter and get the chance, head to Melbourne to hear the roar of the crowd at a game in the MCG. These days, much to the chagrin of many Victorians, the AFL includes successful teams from other states, including Queensland, Western Australia, NSW and South Australia.

In Sydney and Brisbane, the rough and tough game of rugby league is the dominant code. The majority of teams that play in the **NRL** (www.nrl.com.au) come from NSW, plus others from Queensland, Victoria and even NZ.

The sibling code of rugby union is also played in NSW, the ACT and Queensland, with teams competing in a Southern Hemisphere Super-12 competition that includes teams from NZ and South Africa.

In summer, sports fans' focus quickly shifts and the hordes head for the cricket grounds to catch the drama of one-day and test match cricket (the five-day international version of the game). There are regular four-day interstate matches for the national championship (formerly known as the Sheffield Shield but now named after a brand of cow juice). The one-day game is easier for newbies to appreciate than the full five-day version, which some nonfans consider as exciting as watching paint dry. If you're keen, go to a test match and ask someone to explain it to you – but be prepared to be confused and possibly bored.

In the international arena, Australians take their sport just as seriously, churning out champion swimmers and athletes at their taxpayer-funded Australian Institute of Sport in preparation for each Olympic Games. But they don't compete for just personal satisfaction: winning gold for Australia can set up a young athlete for a lifetime of lucrative public speaking engagements and appearances in women's magazines.

ENVIRONMENT Tim Flannery

Australia's plants and animals are just about the closest things to alien life you are likely to encounter on earth. That's because Australia has been isolated from the other continents for a very long time – at least 45 million years. Its birds, mammals, reptiles and plants have taken their own separate and very different evolutionary journey, and the result is the world's most distinct – and one of its most diverse – natural realms.

Tim Flannery is a naturalist, explorer and writer. His latest book, about Australia, is *Country*. Tim Flannery lives in Adelaide where he is director of the South Australian Museum and a professor at the University of Adelaide.

The first naturalists to investigate Australia were astonished by what they found. Here the swans were black – to Europeans this was a metaphor for the impossible – while mammals such as the platypus and echidna were discovered to lay eggs. It really was an upside-down world, where many of the larger animals hopped, where each year the trees shed their bark rather than their leaves, and where the 'pears' were made of wood (the woody pear is a relative of the waratah).

The Land

There are two big factors that go a long way towards explaining nature in Australia: its soils and its climate. Both are unique. Australian soils are the more subtle and difficult to notice of the two, but they have been fundamental in shaping life here. On the other continents, in recent geological times processes such as volcanism, mountain building and glacial activity have been busy creating new soil. Just think of the glacial-derived soils of North America, north Asia and Europe. They feed the world today, and were made by glaciers grinding up rock of differing chemical composition over the last two million years. The rich soils of India and parts of South America were made by rivers eroding mountains, while Java in Indonesia owes its extraordinary richness to volcanoes.

Tim Flannery's *The Future Eaters* is a 'big picture' overview of evolution in Australasia, covering the last 120 million years of history, with thoughts on how the environment has shaped Australasia's human cultures.

All of these soil-forming processes have been almost absent from Australia in more recent times. Only volcanoes have made a contribution, and they cover less than 2% of the continent's land area. In fact, for the last 90 million years, beginning deep in the age of dinosaurs, Australia has been geologically comatose. It was too flat, warm and dry to attract glaciers, its crust too ancient and thick to be punctured by volcanoes or folded into mountains. Look at Uluru and Kata Tjuta (the Olgas). They are the stumps of mountains that 350 million years ago were the height of the Andes. Yet for hundreds of millions of years they've been nothing but nubbins.

DID YOU KNOW?

Australia is the world's sixth-largest country and covers around 5% of the world's land surface. It's about 4000km from east to west and 3200km from north to south, with a coastline 36,735km long.

Under such conditions no new soil is created and the old soil is leached of all its goodness, and is blown and washed away. The leaching is done by rain. Even if just 30cm of it falls each year, that adds up to a column of water 30 million kilometres high passing through the soil over 100 million years, and that can do a great deal of leaching! Almost all of Australia's mountain ranges are more than 90 million years old, so you will see a lot of sand here, and a lot of country where the rocky 'bones' of the land are sticking up through the soil. It is an old, infertile landscape, and life in Australia has been adapting to these conditions for aeons.

Australia's misfortune in respect to soils is echoed in its climate. In most parts of the world outside the wet tropics, life responds to the rhythm of the seasons – summer to winter, or wet to dry. Most of Australia experiences seasons – sometimes very severe ones – yet life does not respond solely to them. This can clearly be seen by the fact that even though there's plenty of snow and cold country in Australia, there are almost no trees that shed their leaves in winter, nor do any Australian animals hibernate. Instead there is a far more potent climatic force that Australian life must obey: El Niño.

The cycle of flood and drought that El Niño brings to Australia is profound. The rivers – even the mighty Murray River, the nation's largest, which runs through the southeast – can be miles wide one year, while you can literally step over its flow the next. This is the power of El Niño, and its effect, when combined with Australia's poor soils, manifests itself compellingly. As you might expect from this, relatively few of Australia's birds are seasonal breeders, and few migrate. Instead, they breed when the rain comes, and a large percentage are nomads, following the rain across the breadth of the continent.

Wildlife

Australia is, of course, famous as being the home of the kangaroo and other marsupials. Unless you visit a wildlife park, such creatures are not easy to see as most are nocturnal. Their lifestyles, however, are exquisitely attuned to Australia's harsh conditions. Have you ever wondered why kangaroos, alone among the world's larger mammals, hop? It turns out that hopping is the most efficient way of getting about at medium speeds. This is because the energy of the bounce is stored in the tendons of the legs – much like in a pogo-stick – while the intestines bounce up and down like a piston, emptying and filling the lungs without needing to activate the chest muscles. When you travel long distances to find meagre feed, such efficiency is a must.

Marsupials are so efficient that they need to eat a fifth less food than equivalent-sized placental mammals (everything from bats to rats, whales and ourselves). But some marsupials have taken energy efficiency much further. If you get to visit a wildlife park or zoo you might notice that far-away look in a koala's eyes. It seems as if nobody is home – and this in fact is near the truth. Several years ago biologists announced that koalas are the only living creatures that have brains that don't fit their skulls. Instead they have a shrivelled walnut of a brain that rattles around in a fluid-filled cranium. Other researchers have contested this finding, however, pointing out that the brains of the koalas examined for the study may have shrunk because these organs are so soft. Whether soft-brained or empty-headed, there is no doubt that the koala is not the Einstein of the animal world, and we now believe that it has sacrificed its brain to energy efficiency. Brains cost a lot to run – our brains typically weigh 2% of our bodyweight, but use 20% of the energy we consume. Koalas eat gum leaves, which are so toxic that they use 20% of their energy just detoxifying this food. This leaves little energy for the brain, and living in the treetops where there are so few predators means that they can get by with very few wits.

Pizzey and Knight's *Field Guide to Birds of Australia* is an indispensable guide for bird-watchers and anyone else even peripherally interested in Australia's feathered tribes. Knight's illustrations are both beautiful and helpful in identification.

One of the more common marsupials you might catch a glimpse of in the national parks around Australia's major cities are the species of antechinus. These nocturnal, rat-sized creatures lead an extraordinary life. The males live for just 11 months, the first 10 of which consist of a concentrated burst of eating and growing. And like teenage males, the day comes when their minds turn to sex, and in the antechinus this becomes an obsession. As they embark on their quest for females they forget to eat and sleep. Instead they gather in logs and woo passing females by serenading them with squeaks. By the end of August – just two weeks after they reach 'puberty' – every single male is dead, exhausted by sex and burdened with carrying around swollen testes. This extraordinary life history may also have evolved in response to Australia's trying environmental conditions. It seems likely that if the males survived mating, they would compete with the females as they tried to find enough food to feed their growing young. Basically, antechinus dads are disposable. They do better for antechinus posterity if they go down in a testosterone-fuelled blaze of glory.

B Beale and P Fray's *The Vanishing Continent* gives an excellent overview of soil erosion across Australia. Fine colour photographs make the issue more graphic.

Australia's plants can be irresistibly fascinating. If you happen to be in the Perth area in spring, it's well worth taking a wildflower tour. The best flowers grow on the arid and monotonous sand plains, and the blaze of colour produced by the kangaroo paws, banksias and similar native plants can be dizzying. The sheer variety of flowers is amazing, with 4000 species crowded into the southwestern corner of the continent.

This diversity of prolific flowering plants has long puzzled botanists. Again, Australia's poor soils seem to be the cause. The sand plain is about the poorest soil in Australia – almost pure quartz. This prevents any one fast-growing species from dominating. Instead, thousands of specialist plant species have learned to find a narrow niche, and so co-exist. Some live at the foot of the metre-high sand dunes, some on top, some on an east-facing slope, some on the west and so on. Their flowers need to be striking in order to attract pollinators, for nutrients are so lacking in this sandy world that even insects such as bees are rare.

If you are very lucky, you might see a honey possum. This tiny marsupial is an enigma. Somehow it gets all of its dietary requirements from nectar and pollen, and in the southwest there are always enough flowers around for it to survive. No one, though, knows why the males need sperm larger even than those of the blue whale, or why their testes are so massive. Were humans as well endowed, men would be walking around with the equivalent of a 4kg bag of potatoes between their legs!

National & State Parks

Australia has more than 500 national parks – nonurban protected wilderness areas of environmental or natural importance. Each state defines and runs its own national parks, but the principle is the same throughout Australia. National parks include rainforests, vast tracts of empty outback, strips of coastal dune land and rugged mountain ranges.

Several of Australia's most beautiful national parks are included on the World Heritage Register. For more information about these sites see http://whc.unesco.org/heritage.htm.

Public access is encouraged as long as safety and conservation regulations are observed. In all parks you're asked to do nothing to damage or alter the natural environment. Camping grounds (often with toilets and showers), walking tracks and information centres are often provided for visitors. In most national parks there are restrictions on bringing in pets.

State parks and state forests are other forms of nature reserves, owned by state governments and with fewer regulations than national parks. Although state forests can be logged, they are often recreational areas with camping grounds, walking tracks and signposted forest drives. Some permit horses and dogs. For a list of useful web links to national and state park authorities, see the Department of Environment & Heritage website: www.deh.gov.au/parks/links/index.html.

Environmental Challenges

The European colonisation of Australia, commencing in 1788, heralded a period of catastrophic environmental upheaval, with the result that Australians today are struggling with some of the most severe environmental problems to be found anywhere. It may seem strange that a population of just 20 million, living in a continent the size of the USA minus Alaska, could inflict such damage on its environment, but Australia's long isolation, its fragile soils and difficult climate have made it particularly vulnerable to human-induced change.

Damage to Australia's environment has been inflicted several ways, the most important being the introduction of pest species, destruction of forests, overstocking rangelands, inappropriate agriculture and interference with water flows. Beginning with the escape of domestic cats into the Australian bush shortly after 1788, a plethora of vermin, from foxes to wild camels and cane toads, have run wild in Australia, causing extinctions in the native fauna. One out of every 10 native mammals living in Australia prior to European colonisation is now extinct, and many more are highly endangered. Extinctions have also affected native plants, birds and amphibians.

The destruction of forests has also had a profound effect. Most of Australia's rainforests have suffered clearing, while conservationists fight with loggers over the fate of the last unprotected stands of 'old growth'. Many Australian rangelands have been chronically overstocked for more than a century, the result being extreme vulnerability of both soils and rural economies to Australia's drought and flood cycle, as well as extinction of many native species. The development of agriculture has involved land clearance and the provision of irrigation, and here again the effect has been profound. Clearing of the diverse and spectacular plant communities of the Western Australian wheatbelt began just a century ago, yet today up to one-third of that country is degraded by salination of the soils. Between 70kg and 120kg of salt lies below every square metre of the region, and clearing of native vegetation has allowed water to penetrate deep into the soil, dissolving the salt crystals and carrying brine towards the surface.

For more on the biggest environmental issues of the moment, see the website of the largest nongovernmental organisation involved in conservation, the Australian Conservation Foundation www.acfonline.org.au.

In terms of financial value, just 1.5% of Australia's land surface provides over 95% of agricultural yield, and much of this land lies in the irrigated regions of the Murray-Darling Basin. This is Australia's agricultural heartland, yet it too is under severe threat from salting of soils and rivers. Irrigation water penetrates into the sediments laid down in an ancient sea, carrying salt into the catchments and fields. If nothing is done, the lower Murray River will become too salty to drink in a decade or two, threatening the water supply of Adelaide, a city of more than a million people.

Despite the enormity of the biological crisis engulfing Australia, governments and the community have been slow to respond. It was in the 1980s that coordinated action began to take place, but not until the '90s that major steps were taken. The establishment of **Landcare** (www.landcareaustralia.com.au), an organisation enabling people to effectively address local environmental issues, and the expenditure of A$2.5 billion through the National Heritage Trust Fund have been important national initiatives. Yet so difficult are some of the issues the nation faces that, as yet, little has been achieved in terms of halting the destructive processes.

Individuals are also banding together to help. Groups such as the **Australian Bush Heritage Fund** (www.bushheritage.asn.au) and the **Australian Wildlife Conservancy** (AWC; www.australianwildlife.org) allow people to donate funds and time to the conservation of native species. Some such groups have been spectacularly successful; the AWC, for example, already manages many endangered species over its 1.3 million acre holdings.

So severe are Australia's problems that it will take a revolution before they can be overcome, for sustainable practices need to be implemented in every arena of life – from farms to suburbs and city centres. Renewable energy, sustainable agriculture and water use lie at the heart of these changes, and Australians are only now developing the road-map to sustainability that they so desperately need if they are to have a long-term future on the continent.

Sydney & New South Wales

CONTENTS

HIGHLIGHTS

- **Sydney Harbour** Get to know the sparkling harbour – whether you're on it, in it, above it or beside it (p43)
- **Bondi Beach** Bum around this beach with the bold and the beautiful while everyone else is at work (p56)
- **Royal National Park** Strap on the hiking boots and get amongst this park's chasms and creeks (p82)
- **South Coast** Chill on the unspoilt beaches and endearing fishing villages along this length of coast (p110)
- **Blue Mountains** Hang out with the Three Sisters and enjoy the crazy haze here (p84)
- **Kosciuszko National Park** Delve into caves, hike through bushland and slice the slopes through the ski resorts (p129)
- **Byron Bay** Grow your dreads, buy a rainbow T-shirt and mellow out, man (p104)

- **Cheer for:** South Sydney Rabittohs – the original underdogs in the NRL (rugby league)
- **Eat:** fish & chips on the beach at Manly (p59)
- **Drink:** a schooner (425mL) of Tooheys
- **Listen to:** silverchair's *Frogstomp* (p92), Spiderbait's *Tonight Alright*
- **Watch:** animated kid-flick *Nemo* or crime comedy *Two Hands*
- **Party at:** Coogee (p57) in Sydney or Byron Bay (p104)
- **Swim at:** Newcastle (p90) or Sydney's beaches (p58)
- **Avoid:** funnel-web spiders, real-estate agents called Gordon who can do you a deal on a nice little bridge with harbour views
- **Locals' nickname:** Cockroaches

TELEPHONE CODE: 02	WEBSITE: www.visitnsw.com.au

When Captain James Cook first set foot on this stunning coastline in 1770, the most praiseworthy place he could compare it to was Wales: hence the name. The UK then shipped its convicts to the sunnier clime and golden beaches, but was surprised that this punishment didn't deter crime. Most modern visitors – far from heading here for punishment – arrive in Australia via Sydney and are wowed by the natural beauty of the city's harbour. Travellers who explore further find a fascinatingly diverse state and are privy to why New South Wales (NSW) is Australia's most populous state.

The rest of NSW is more than just Sydney's backyard – it has several cosmopolitan cities, alpine ski extremes, artsy outback oases, cool rainforests and gorgeous white-sanded beaches. Despite a bitter struggle with Victoria, NSW even wangles the nation's capital within its borders, although technically the Australian Capital Territory (ACT) remains an independent state. Most travellers follow the coast north and south of Sydney, with detours inland to destinations like Canberra (the bush capital) or out to stark Broken Hill (p452). From the transport hub of Sydney, planes, trains, buses and roads all head out to explore the state – so grab yourself a ticket or park yourself behind the wheel for one helluva ride.

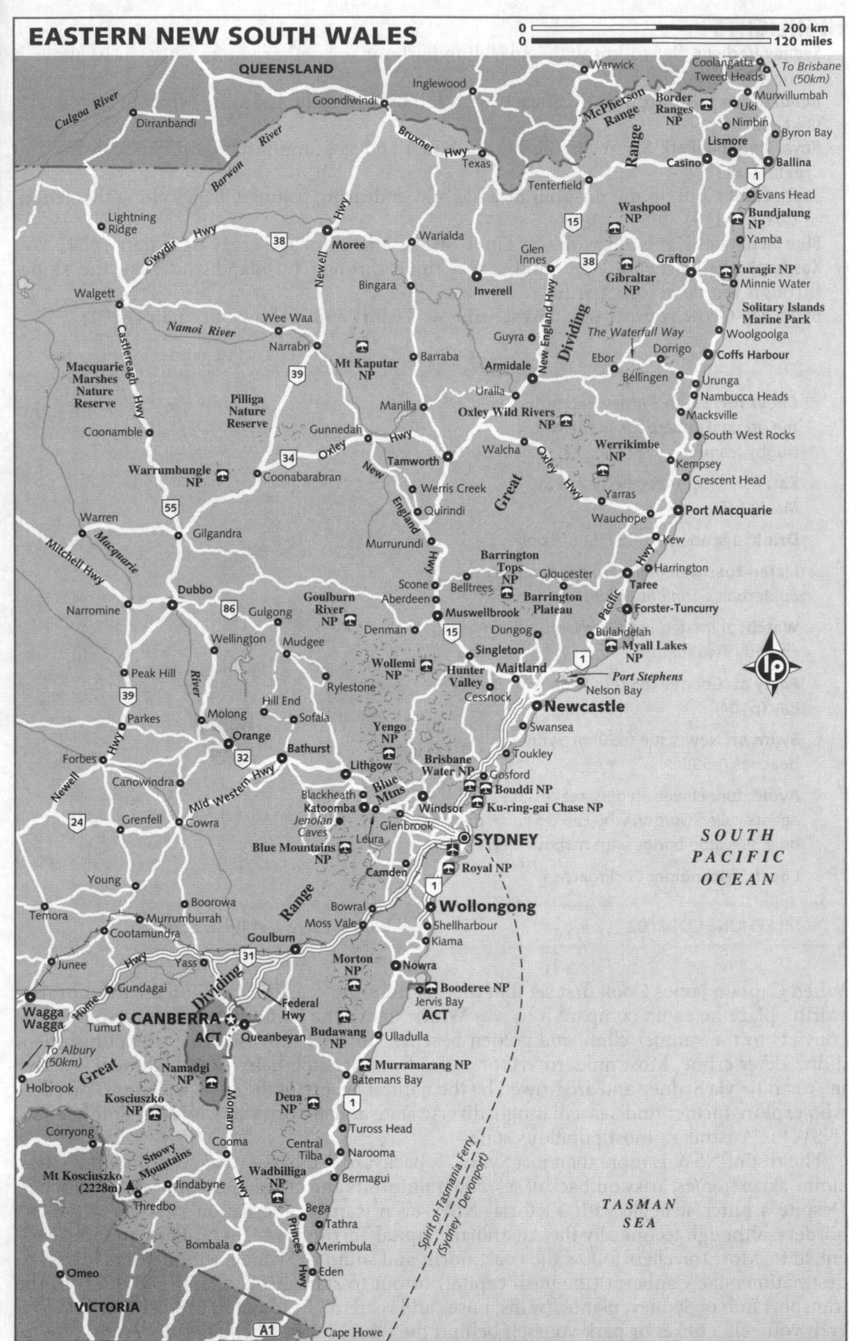
EASTERN NEW SOUTH WALES
0 200 km
0 120 miles
QUEENSLAND
Culgoa River
Dirranbandi
Goondiwindi
Inglewood
Warwick
Coolangatta
Tweed Heads
To Brisbane (50km)
Murwillumbah
McPherson Range
Border Ranges NP
Uki
Nimbin
Byron Bay
Lismore
Casino
Ballina
Barwon River
Bruxner Hwy
Texas
Range
Tenterfield
Evans Head
Bundjalung NP
Yamba
Washpool NP
Lightning Ridge
Gwydir Hwy
Newell Hwy
Moree
Warialda
Glen Innes
Grafton
Yuragir NP
Minnie Water
Gibraltar NP
Solitary Islands Marine Park
Walgett
Bingara
Inverell
New England Hwy
Dividing
The Waterfall Way
Woolgoolga
Namoi River
Wee Waa
Guyra
Dorrigo
Coffs Harbour
Castlereagh Hwy
Narrabri
Mt Kaputar NP
Barraba
Armidale
Ebor
Bellingen
Urunga
Macquarie Marshes Nature Reserve
Pilliga Nature Reserve
Uralla
Nambucca Heads
Manilla
Oxley Wild Rivers NP
Macksville
Coonamble
Gunnedah
Oxley Hwy
South West Rocks
Walcha
Werrikimbe NP
Tamworth
Kempsey
Warrumbungle NP
Coonabarabran
New England Hwy
Great
Crescent Head
Werris Creek
Yarras
Quirindi
Port Macquarie
Wauchope
Warren
Gilgandra
Kew
Macquarie
Murrurundi
Mitchell Hwy
Barrington Tops NP
Gloucester
Harrington
Pacific Hwy
Dubbo
Scone
Belltrees
Taree
Goulburn River NP
Aberdeen
Barrington Plateau
Narromine
Gulgong
Muswellbrook
Forster-Tuncurry
Denman
Dungog
Wellington
Mudgee
Singleton
Bulahdelah
Myall Lakes NP
Wollemi NP
Hunter Valley
Maitland
Peak Hill
River
Rylestone
Port Stephens
Nelson Bay
Cessnock
Hill End
Newcastle
Parkes
Molong
Sofala
Swansea
Orange
Yengo NP
Bathurst
Toukley
Forbes
Lithgow
Brisbane Water NP
Gosford
Canowindra
Mid Western Hwy
Bouddi NP
Blackheath
Blue Mtns
Ku-ring-gai Chase NP
Katoomba
Windsor
Jenolan Caves
Grenfell
Cowra
Glenbrook
Leura
SYDNEY
SOUTH PACIFIC OCEAN
Blue Mountains NP
Royal NP
Camden
Young
Boorowa
Range
Bowral
Wollongong
Temora
Murrumburrah
Moss Vale
Shellharbour
Cootamundra
Goulburn
Kiama
Junee
Yass
Hume Hwy
Dividing
Morton NP
Nowra
Gundagai
Federal Hwy
Booderee NP
Wagga Wagga
CANBERRA
Tumut
ACT
Queanbeyan
Jervis Bay
ACT
Budawang NP
Ulladulla
To Albury (50km)
Great
Namadgi NP
Murramarang NP
Holbrook
Batemans Bay
Kosciuszko NP
Monaro Hwy
Deua NP
Corryong
Snowy Mountains
Cooma
Tuross Head
Central Tilba
Narooma
Mt Kosciuszko (2228m)
Jindabyne
Wadbilliga NP
Bermagui
Thredbo
Spirit of Tasmania Ferry (Sydney - Devonport)
TASMAN SEA
Bega
Tathra
Bombala
Princes Hwy
Merimbula
Omeo
Eden
VICTORIA
A1
Cape Howe
1
15
38
39
34
55
86
32
24
31

SYDNEY

☎ 02 / pop 4 million

Australia's oldest and largest European settlement is a vibrant city built around a simply spectacular harbour. Instantly recognisable thanks to its opera house, harbour and bridge, Sydney also boasts lesser-known attractions like the historic Rocks, Victorian-era Paddington, heavenly beaches such as Bondi and Manly, and two superb coastal national parks on the city fringe. An array of ethnic groups contribute to the city's social life – in particular, the dynamism of the Chinese community has played an important role in altering the city's Anglo-Mediterranean fabric, and in preparing it to become a key player in Asia. The success of the 2000 Olympic Games only served to bolster Sydneysiders' pride in their waterside playground. It's a place that combines relaxed hedonism, brash industriousness and look-at-me antics.

Don't Miss: The Opera House (like you would!); strolling across the Harbour Bridge and into the North Shore; checking out that hot spot, The Rocks; relaxing in the Botanic Gardens; hangin' out in Bondi, Coogee or Manly; eating on the cheap (but well) in Chinatown and Surry Hills; partying hard in Kings Cross and strutting down Paddington's fashionable Oxford St.

HISTORY

It was at Sydney Cove, where the ferries run from Circular Quay today, that the first European settlement was established in 1788, so it's not surprising that Sydney has a strong sense of history. But that doesn't stop the city from being far brasher and livelier than many of its younger Australian counterparts.

The city is built on land once occupied by the Eora tribe, whose presence lingers in the place names of some suburbs and whose artistic legacy can be seen at many Aboriginal rock-engraving sites around the city.

Many ascribe Sydney's raffish spirit to the fact that essentially the military were in charge in the late 18th century and early 19th century. Paying for labour and local products in rum (hence the name Rum Corps), the soldiers upset, defied and outmanoeuvred three of the colony's early governors, including one William Bligh, of *Bounty* mutiny fame.

ORIENTATION

The harbour divides Sydney into northern and southern halves, with the Sydney Harbour Bridge and the Harbour Tunnel joining the two shores. The city centre is roughly from Circular Quay to Central Station. To the west is Darling Harbour, and further west of the centre are the gentrified suburbs of Pyrmont, Glebe and Balmain. Newtown and Leichhardt are slightly beyond these.

East of the centre lies Darlinghurst, Kings Cross and Paddington. To the southeast, along the coast, are the ocean-beach suburbs of Bondi and Coogee.

The suburbs north of the bridge, including McMahon's Point, Lavender Bay, Cremorne Point, Mosman and Balmoral, are known collectively as the North Shore.

Maps

Just about every brochure you pick up includes a map of the city centre, but Lonely Planet's *Sydney City Map* is an exceptional choice. The *Sydney* UBD street directory (A$30) is invaluable for drivers.

For a great selection of travel maps (and guidebooks) check out **Map World** (Map pp48-50; ☎ 9261 3601; www.mapworld.net.au; 280 Pitt St, City; 🕒 8.30pm-5.30pm Mon-Wed & Fri, to 6.30pm Thu, 10am-3.30pm Sat). For aerial, topographic and many other maps, visit the **Department of Land and Water Conservation** (DLWC; Map pp48-50; ☎ 9228 6111; 23-33 Bridge St, City; 🕒 8.30am-4.30pm Mon-Fri).

INFORMATION

Bookshops

Desire Books (Map p59; ☎ 9977 0888; 3/3 Whistler St, Manly; 🕒 10am-6pm Fri-Wed, to 11pm Thu) Chess on Thursday nights, book-club meetings, sofas out the back – oh yeah, it also sells new and used books.

Dymocks Books (Map pp48-50; ☎ 9235 0155; 424 George St, City; 🕒 9am-6.30pm Mon-Wed & Fri, to 9pm Thu, to 6pm Sat, 10am-5.30pm Sun) In excess of 250,000 titles spread over three floors; includes a Lonely Planet aisle!

Elizabeth's Bookshops (Map pp48-50; ☎ 9332 1444; 126 Oxford St, Darlinghurst; 🕒 9.30am-10.30pm Mon-Sat, to 10pm Sun) Buy, sell or exchange your books, DVDs and CDs.

Gleebooks (Map pp44-5; ☎ 9660 2333; 49 Glebe Point Rd, Glebe; 🕒 9am-9pm) Frequent winner of 'bookshop of the year' awards. Also has used-books shop at 191 Glebe Point Rd.

Travel Bookshop (Map pp48-50; ☎ 9261 8200; 175 Liverpool St, City; 🕒 9am-6pm Mon-Sat, 10am-5pm Sun) Crammed with – you guessed it – travel books. Also has used books (trade 'em in).

GETTING INTO TOWN

Sydney's **Kingsford Smith Airport** (☎ 9667 9111; www.sydneyairport.com.au) is 10km south of the city centre; the international and domestic terminals are a 4km bus trip apart on either side of the runway. One of the easiest ways to get from the airport into the centre is with a shuttle company. These take you straight to your hostel/hotel and cost about A$9 to A$12. All go into the city centre; some reach surrounding suburbs and beach destinations. Companies include **Kingsford Smith Transport** (KST; ☎ 9666 9988; www.kst.com.au), **Super Shuttle** (☎ 0500 881 113, 9311 3789; www.supershuttle.com.au) and **Shuttle Bus Services** (SBS; ☎ 0500 503 220; www.shuttlebusservices.com).

The cheapest way to Bondi is by taking bus No 400 or 400 express (A$4) to Bondi Junction, then the L82, 380, 381 or 382 to Bondi. from the airport.

Airport Link (☎ 13 15 00; www.airportlink.com.au) is a train line that runs to and from city stations to the airport terminals (domestic and international) every 10 to 15 minutes. Trains run from approximately 5am to midnight (A$11).

Taxi fares from the airport are A$25 to Circular Quay, A$35 to North Sydney and Bondi, and A$50 to Manly.

Emergency

Lifeline (☎ 13 11 14) Has 24-hour phone counselling services, including suicide prevention.
NRMA (Map pp48-50; ☎ 13 21 32; 388 George St, City) For car insurance and roadside service.
Police Station City (Map pp48-50; 570 George St); The Rocks (Map pp48-50; 132 George St) Dial 000 for emergency police assistance.
Rape Crisis Centre (☎ 1800 424 017, 9819 6565)
Wayside Chapel (Map p55; ☎ 9358 6577; 29 Hughes St, Potts Point) Crisis centre (🕑 7am to 10pm) in the heart of Kings Cross.

Internet Access

Internet cafés are found throughout Sydney, especially around Kings Cross, Bondi and Glebe. Some stay open 24 hours. Rates are around A$3 an hour. Plenty of hostels and hotels offer Internet access for their guests, as do public libraries (you'll need to book for the latter, though).
Global Gossip (Map p55; ☎ 9326 9777; 111 Darlinghurst Rd, Kings Cross; 🕑 8am-midnight) Also in Bondi, near Central Station and in the city.
Travellers Contact Point (Map pp48-50; ☎ 9221 8744; Level 7, 428 George St, City; 🕑 9am-6pm Mon-Fri, 10am-4pm Sat) Free email for the first 30 minutes.

Internet Resources

For more information on Sydney, check out these websites:
www.cityofsydney.nsw.gov.au City news and politics.
www.sydney.citysearch.com.au What's happening in Sydney.
www.viewsydney.com.au Features live images from around the city.
www.visitnsw.com.au Info on Sydney and NSW, including weather.
www.whitepages.com.au Find a business or service anywhere in Australia.

Left Luggage

Any hotel or hostel should store luggage for you if you've stayed there.
McCafferty's office (Map pp48-50; ☎ 9212 3433; Central Station; 🕑 6am-10pm) Has luggage lockers for A$7 to A$12 per day.
Travellers Contact Point (Map pp48-50; ☎ 9221 8744; Level 7, 428 George St, City) Stores luggage for A$20 per piece per month.

Media

The Metro lift-out in Friday's *Sydney Morning Herald* provides a comprehensive weekly listing of what's on in the city. The Wednesday SLM inset in *The Daily Telegraph* does the same. Free music and entertainment papers include *Drum Media*, *Revolver*, *3D World* and *Sydney Star Observer* (www.ssonet.com.au) – the latter is gay-focused.

There are plenty of guidebooks that cover Sydney. Lonely Planet's *Sydney*, *New South Wales* and *East Coast Australia* are general guides and there's also the handy-sized *Best of Sydney* guide.

Medical Services

Kings Cross Travellers Clinic (Map p55; ☎ 9358 3066; 13 Springfield Ave, Kings Cross; 🕑 9am-1pm & 2-6pm Mon-Fri, 10am-noon Sat) Bookings advised for morning-after pill scripts and dive medicals.
Sydney Hospital (Map pp48-50; ☎ 9382 7111; 8 Macquarie St, City) Has a 24-hour emergency ward.

Travellers Medical & Vaccination Centre (Map pp48-50; ☎ 9221 7133; Level 7, 428 George St, City; 8am-5.30pm Mon-Wed & Fri, to 7.30pm Thu, 9am-1pm Sat) The best place to get your vaccinations and medical advice related to travel.

Money

There are banks and ATMs throughout Sydney. Exchange bureaus open seven days a week include two at Central Station (open 8am to 5pm Monday to Friday and 9am to 6pm Saturday and Sunday), another opposite Wharf 6 at Circular Quay (open 8am to 8.30pm) and one near Roslyn St and Darlinghurst Rd, Kings Cross (open 9am to 8pm Monday to Friday and 9.30am to 6.30pm Saturday and Sunday). The airport's exchange bureaus open until the last flight comes in.

American Express (Map pp48-50; ☎ 1300 139 060; 105 Pitt St, City; 9am-5pm Mon-Fri, 10am-1pm Sat) Helps with travel arrangements; has other branches throughout town, including an exchange booth inside the Travel Bookshop (p41).

Travelex (Map pp48-50; ☎ 9231 2523; 175 Pitt St, City; 9am-5.30pm Mon-Fri, 10am-2pm Sat) Plus other branches throughout Sydney and in HSBC banks.

Post

There are many post office branches throughout the city centre. See the map on pp48–50 for locations.

General Post Office (GPO; Map pp48-50; 1 Martin Place, City; 8.15am-5.30pm Mon-Fri, 10am-2pm Sat)

Poste-restante service (Map pp48-50; 310 George St, City; 8.15am-5.30pm Mon-Fri) In the Hunter Connection building. You'll need identification.

Telephone

Public phones can be found all over the city. Most take magnetic phonecards that you can buy from corner stores.

Global Gossip (Map p55; ☎ 9326 9777; 111 Darlinghurst Rd, Kings Cross; 8am-midnight) Offers discount long-distance and international calls.

Telstra phone centre (Map pp48-50; ☎ 9201 9320; 231 Elizabeth St, City; 7am-11pm Mon-Fri, to 7pm Sat & Sun)

Tourist Information

All hours below vary with the seasons; summer hours (listed below) are longer.

City Host Information Kiosks (9am-6pm) Circular Quay (Map pp48-50; cnr Pitt & Alfred Sts); Martin Place (Map pp48-50; btwn Elizabeth & Castlereagh Sts); Town Hall (Map pp48-50; cnr George & Bathurst Sts)

Darling Harbour visitors centre (Map pp48-50; ☎ 9240 8788; Darling Harbour; 10am-6pm) Under the highway and behind the IMAX Theatre.

Sydney visitors centre (☎ 9667 6053; www.visitnsw.com.au; Sydney International Airport; 6am-11pm) Book discounted hotel rooms and onward travel here.

Sydney visitors centre (Map pp48-50; ☎ 9240 8788; www.sydneyvisitorscentre.com; 106 George St, The Rocks; 9am-6pm) Very helpful and stuffed full of brochures.

Travel Agencies

Backpackers World (Map p55; ☎ 9380 2700; www.backpackersworld.com.au; 212 Victoria St, Kings Cross; 9am-7pm Mon-Fri, 10am-6pm Sat, 11am-5pm Sun) Five Sydney locations.

STA Travel (Map pp48-50; ☎ 9252 8022; www.statravel.com.au; Shop 1, 2 Bridge St, City; 9.30-5.30 Mon-Sat) Has 20 Sydney branches.

Travellers Contact Point (Map pp48-50; ☎ 9221 8744; www.travellers.com.au; Level 7, 428 George St, City; 9am-6pm Mon-Fri, 10am-4pm Sat) Full-blown backpacker agency. Also holds mail and has a good bulletin board.

YHA Membership & Travel Centre (Map pp48-50; ☎ 9261 1111; www.yha.com.au/yhainfo/membership_travel.cfm; 422 Kent St, City; 9am-5pm Mon-Wed & Fri, to 6pm Thu, to 2pm Sat) YHA bookings worldwide – also try the travel agent in the Sydney Central YHA (p63).

Traveller Services

Travellers Aid Society (Map pp48-50; ☎ 9211 2469; Platform 1, Central Station; 8am-2.30pm Mon-Sat) Provides general information, travel assistance, phone recharging and hot showers.

SIGHTS

Sydney's chock-full of things to see and do. Much of it doesn't cost a cent, but some of it does. If you plan on seeing an exceptional number of museums, attractions and tours, check out the **Smartvisit card** (☎ 1300 661 711; www.seesydneycard.com), available from the guided tours desk at Sydney Opera House (p47).

Practically all sights and museums in Sydney have good disabled access.

Sydney Harbour

Sydney's stunning harbour (Port Jackson; Map pp44–5) is both a major port and the city's playground. It stretches some 20km inland to join the mouth of the Parramatta River. The headlands at the entrance are known as North Head and South Head. The most scenic part of the harbour is between the Heads and the Harbour Bridge, 8km inland. Middle Harbour is a large inlet that

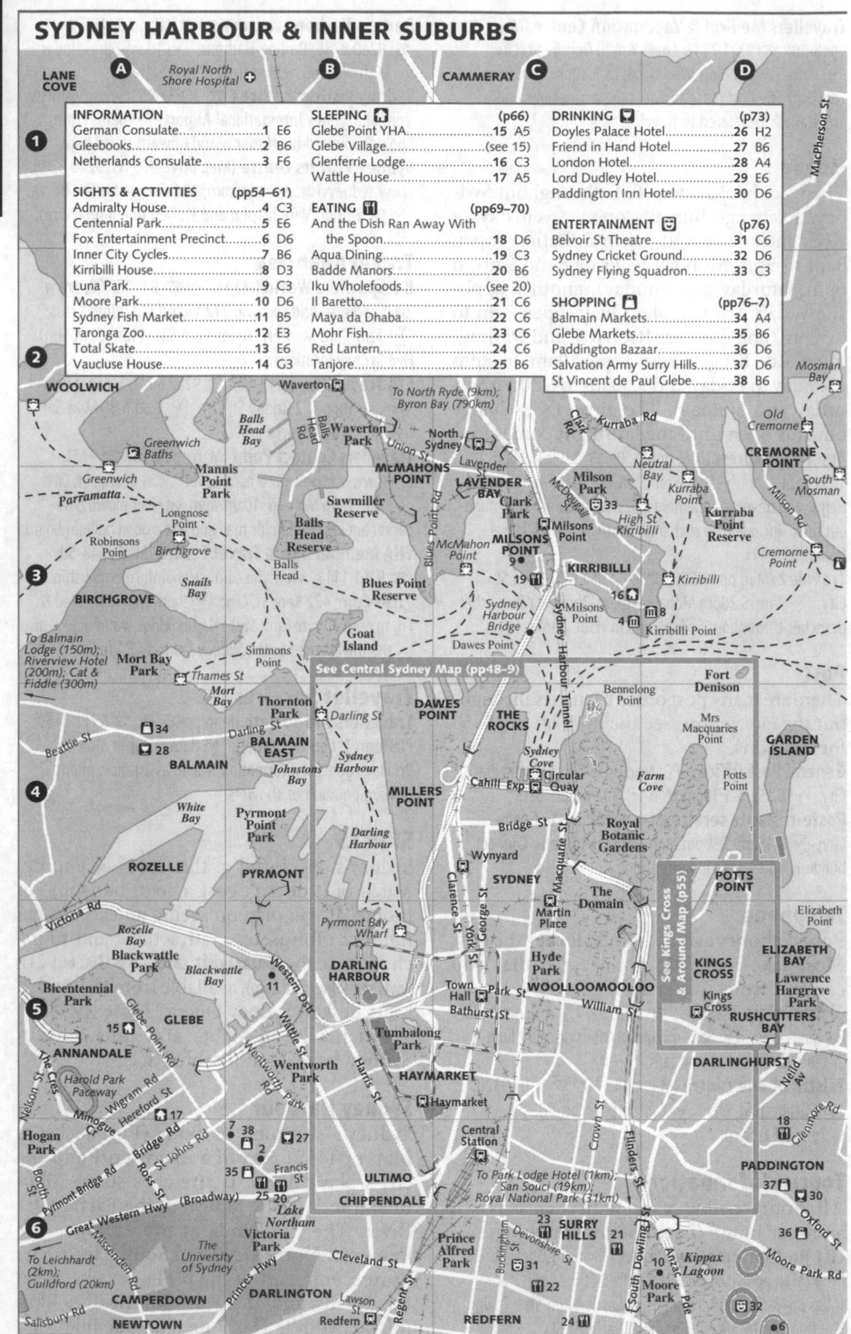
SYDNEY HARBOUR & INNER SUBURBS
INFORMATION
German Consulate 1 E6
Gleebooks 2 B6
Netherlands Consulate 3 F6
SIGHTS & ACTIVITIES (pp54–61)
Admiralty House 4 C3
Centennial Park 5 E6
Fox Entertainment Precinct 6 D6
Inner City Cycles 7 B6
Kirribilli House 8 D3
Luna Park 9 C3
Moore Park 10 D6
Sydney Fish Market 11 B5
Taronga Zoo 12 E3
Total Skate 13 E6
Vaucluse House 14 G3
SLEEPING (p66)
Glebe Point YHA 15 A5
Glebe Village (see 15)
Glenferrie Lodge 16 C3
Wattle House 17 A5
EATING (pp69–70)
And the Dish Ran Away With the Spoon 18 D6
Aqua Dining 19 C3
Badde Manors 20 B6
Iku Wholefoods (see 20)
Il Baretto 21 C6
Maya da Dhaba 22 C6
Mohr Fish 23 C6
Red Lantern 24 C6
Tanjore 25 B6
DRINKING (p73)
Doyles Palace Hotel 26 H2
Friend in Hand Hotel 27 B6
London Hotel 28 A4
Lord Dudley Hotel 29 E6
Paddington Inn Hotel 30 D6
ENTERTAINMENT (p76)
Belvoir St Theatre 31 C6
Sydney Cricket Ground 32 D6
Sydney Flying Squadron 33 C3
SHOPPING (pp76–7)
Balmain Markets 34 A4
Glebe Markets 35 B6
Paddington Bazaar 36 D6
Salvation Army Surry Hills 37 D6
St Vincent de Paul Glebe 38 B6
LANE COVE
Royal North Shore Hospital
CAMMERAY
MacPherson St
WOOLWICH
Waverton
To North Ryde (9km); Byron Bay (790km)
Mosman Bay
Old Cremorne
CREMORNE POINT
South Mosman
Greenwich Baths
Greenwich
Parramatta
Mannis Point Park
Balls Head Bay
Balls Head Rd
Waverton Park
Union St
North Sydney
Lavender St
McMAHONS POINT
LAVENDER BAY
Clark Rd
Kurraba Rd
Neutral Bay
Milson Park
Kurraba Point
Kurraba Point Reserve
Milson Rd
Longnose Point
Robinsons Point
Birchgrove
Sawmiller Reserve
Balls Head Reserve
Blues Point Rd
McMahon Point
Clark Park
McDougall St
Milsons Point
MILSONS POINT
High St
Kirribilli
Cremorne Point
Balls Head
Snails Bay
BIRCHGROVE
Blues Point Reserve
KIRRIBILLI
Sydney Harbour Bridge
Milsons Point
Kirribilli Point
To Balmain Lodge (150m); Riverview Hotel (200m); Cat & Fiddle (300m)
Mort Bay Park
Simmons Point
Goat Island
Dawes Point
Sydney Harbour Tunnel
Thames St
Mort Bay
Thornton Park
See Central Sydney Map (pp48–9)
Darling St
DAWES POINT
THE ROCKS
Fort Denison
Bennelong Point
Mrs Macquaries Point
GARDEN ISLAND
Beattie St
BALMAIN
BALMAIN EAST
Johnstons Bay
Sydney Harbour
Sydney Cove
Circular Quay
Cahill Exp
Farm Cove
Potts Point
MILLERS POINT
White Bay
Pyrmont Point Park
Darling Harbour
Bridge St
Macquarie St
Royal Botanic Gardens
ROZELLE
PYRMONT
Wynyard
SYDNEY
Clarence St
George St
York St
Martin Place
The Domain
See Kings Cross & Around Map (p55)
POTTS POINT
Elizabeth Point
Victoria Rd
Rozelle Bay
Blackwattle Park
Blackwattle Bay
Pyrmont Bay Wharf
DARLING HARBOUR
Hyde Park
KINGS CROSS
Kings Cross
ELIZABETH BAY
Western Dstr
Town Hall
Park St
Bathurst St
WOOLLOOMOOLOO
William St
Lawrence Hargrave Park
RUSHCUTTERS BAY
Bicentennial Park
GLEBE
Glebe Point Rd
Wattle St
Tumbalong Park
ANNANDALE
The Cres
Harold Park Paceway
Wentworth Park
Wentworth Park Rd
Harris St
HAYMARKET
Haymarket
DARLINGHURST
Neild Av
Nelson St
Wigram Rd
Hereford St
Minogue Cr
Crown St
Glenmore Rd
Hogan Park
Bridge Rd
St Johns Rd
Central Station
Flinders St
Booth St
Ross St
Pyrmont Bridge Rd
Francis St
ULTIMO
To Park Lodge Hotel (1km); San Souci (19km); Royal National Park (31km)
PADDINGTON
CHIPPENDALE
Great Western Hwy
(Broadway)
Lake Northam
Victoria Park
Prince Alfred Park
Devonshire St
Buckingham St
SURRY HILLS
South Dowling St
Anzac Pde
Oxford St
To Leichhardt (2km); Guildford (20km)
Missenden Rd
The University of Sydney
Princes Hwy
Cleveland St
Kippax Lagoon
Moore Park
Moore Park Rd
CAMPERDOWN
DARLINGTON
Lawson St
Regent St
Salisbury Rd
NEWTOWN
Redfern
REDFERN

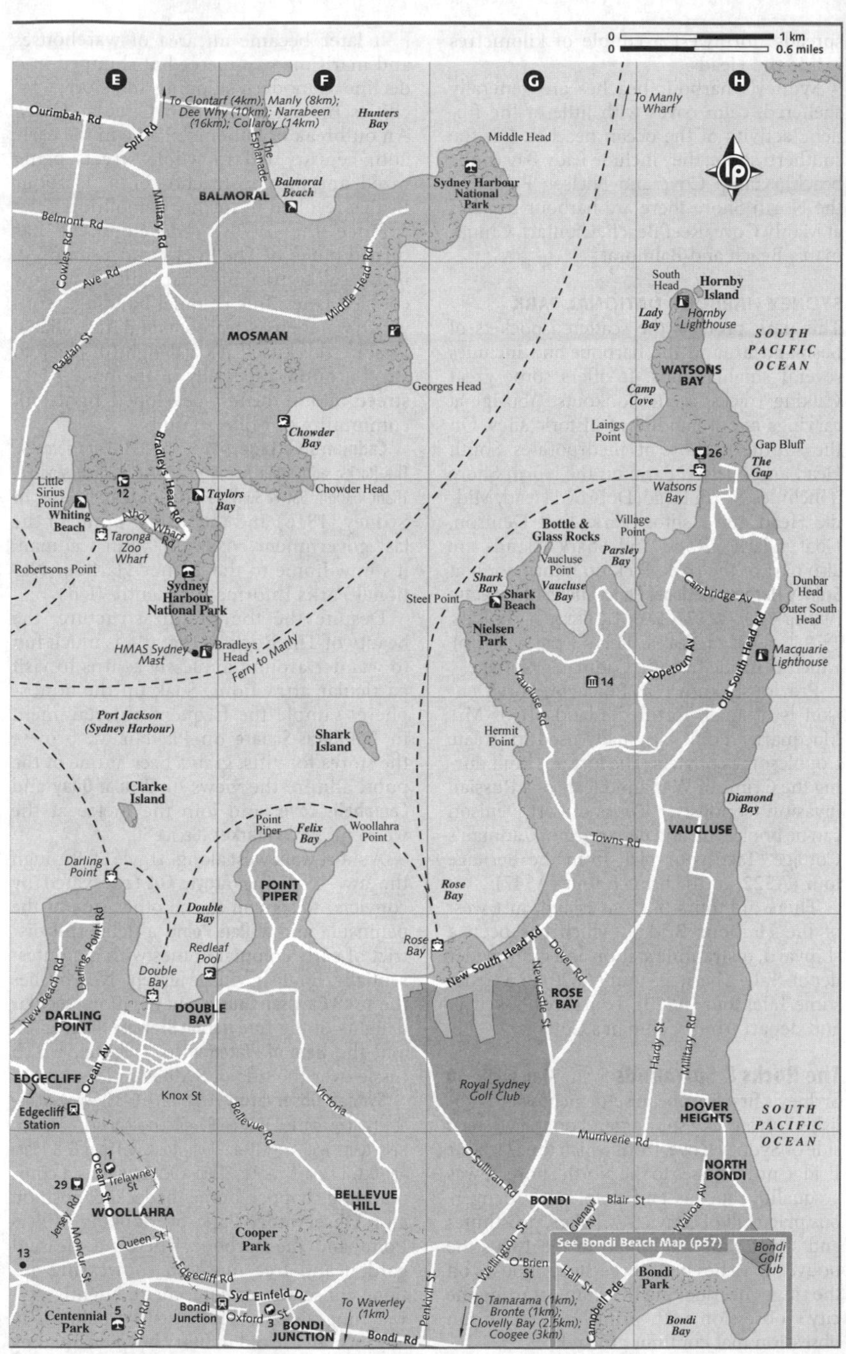

0 1 km
0 0.6 miles
E
F
G
H
To Clontarf (4km); Manly (8km); Dee Why (10km); Narrabeen (16km); Collaroy (14km)
To Manly Wharf
Ourimbah Rd
Spit Rd
Hunters Bay
The Esplanade
Middle Head
Balmoral Beach
BALMORAL
Military Rd
Sydney Harbour National Park
Belmont Rd
Cowles Rd
Ave Rd
Middle Head Rd
South Head
Hornby Island
Hornby Lighthouse
Lady Bay
MOSMAN
Raglan St
SOUTH PACIFIC OCEAN
WATSONS BAY
Georges Head
Camp Cove
Chowder Bay
Laings Point
Bradleys Head Rd
Gap Bluff
26
The Gap
Little Sirius Point
12
Taylors Bay
Chowder Head
Watsons Bay
Whiting Beach
Athol Wharf Rd
Taronga Zoo Wharf
Bottle & Glass Rocks
Village Point
Robertsons Point
Vaucluse Point
Parsley Bay
Shark Bay
Vaucluse Bay
Sydney Harbour National Park
Steel Point
Shark Beach
Cambridge Av
Dunbar Head
Outer South Head
Nielsen Park
HMAS Sydney Mast
Bradleys Head
Ferry to Manly
Macquarie Lighthouse
Old South Head Rd
Vaucluse Rd
14
Hopetoun Av
Port Jackson (Sydney Harbour)
Shark Island
Hermit Point
Clarke Island
Diamond Bay
VAUCLUSE
Point Piper
Felix Bay
Woollahra Point
Towns Rd
Darling Point
POINT PIPER
Rose Bay
Double Bay
Darling Point Rd
Redleaf Pool
Rose Bay
New South Head Rd
Dover Rd
Newcastle St
New Beach Rd
Double Bay
ROSE BAY
DARLING POINT
DOUBLE BAY
Hardy St
Military Rd
EDGECLIFF
Ocean Av
Knox St
Royal Sydney Golf Club
Victoria
Edgecliff Station
Bellevue Rd
DOVER HEIGHTS
SOUTH PACIFIC OCEAN
Murriverie Rd
1
Ocean St
Trelawney St
O'Sullivan Rd
NORTH BONDI
29
BELLEVUE HILL
BONDI
Blair St
Jersey Rd
WOOLLAHRA
Glenayr Av
Wairoa Av
Cooper Park
Wellington St
See Bondi Beach Map (p57)
Bondi Golf Club
13
Queen St
Moncur St
O'Brien St
Hall St
Bondi Park
Edgecliff Rd
Syd Einfeld Dr
To Waverley (1km)
Penkivil St
To Tamarama (1km); Bronte (1km); Clovelly Bay (2.5km); Coogee (3km)
Campbell Pde
Centennial Park
5
Bondi Junction
Oxford St
3
BONDI JUNCTION
Bondi Rd
York Rd
Bondi Bay

spreads northwest a couple of kilometres inside the Heads.

Sydney's harbour beaches are generally sheltered, calm coves with little of the frenetic activity of the ocean beaches. On the southern shore, they include Lady Bay (nude beach), Camp Cove and Nielsen Park. On the North Shore there are harbour beaches at Manly Cove, Reef Beach, Clontarf, Chinaman's Beach and Balmoral.

SYDNEY HARBOUR NATIONAL PARK

This park protects the scattered pockets of bushland around the harbour and includes several small islands. It offers some great walking tracks, scenic lookouts, Aboriginal carvings and a handful of historic sites. On the southern shore it incorporates South Head and Nielsen Park; on the North Shore it includes North Head, Dobroyd Head, Middle Head and Ashton Park. Fort Denison, Goat, Clarke, Rodd and Shark Islands are also part of the park. Pick up information at **Sydney Harbour National Parks Information Centre** (Map pp48-50; ☎ 9247 5033; 110 George St, The Rocks; 🕑 9.30am-4.30pm Mon-Fri, 10am-4.30pm Sat & Sun), which is inside historic Cadman's Cottage.

Previously known as Pinchgut, Fort Denison is a small, fortified island off of Mrs Macquaries Point, originally used to isolate troublesome convicts. The fort was built during the Crimean War amid fears of a Russian invasion (seriously!). Tours of Fort Denison can be booked at, and depart from, Cadman's Cottage. Take your pick from the heritage tour (A$22) or the brunch tour (A$47).

There are tours of Goat Island, just west of the Harbour Bridge, which has been a shipyard, quarantine station and gunpowder depot. Take a heritage tour (A$20) or a Gruesome Tales tour (A$25). Tours are booked at, and depart from, Cadman's Cottage.

The Rocks & Surrounds Map pp48–50

Sydney's first European settlement was established on a rocky spur of land on the western side of Sydney Cove, from which the Harbour Bridge now crosses to the North Shore. It was a squalid, raucous and notoriously dangerous place full of convicts, whalers, prostitutes and street gangs, although in the 1820s the nouveaux riches built three-storey houses on the ridges overlooking the slums, starting the city's obsession with prime real estate (an obsession that continues today).

It later became an area of warehouses and maritime commerce but slumped into decline as modern shipping and storage facilities moved away from Circular Quay. An outbreak of bubonic plague in the early 20th century led to whole streets being razed, and the construction of the Harbour Bridge resulted in further demolition.

Since the 1970s, redevelopment has turned much of The Rocks into a sanitised, historical tourist precinct, full of narrow cobbled lanes, fine colonial buildings, converted warehouses, tearooms and Australiana. Despite the kitsch it's a delightful place to stroll around, especially in the poky backstreets and in the less-developed, tight-knit community of Millers Point.

Cadman's Cottage (☎ 9247 5033; 110 George St, The Rocks; admission free; 🕑 9.30am-4.30pm Mon-Fri, 10am-4.30pm Sat & Sun) is the oldest house in Sydney (1816) and the former home of the last government coxswain, John Cadman; it's now home to the Sydney Harbour National Parks Information Centre (left).

Despite the tourist infrastructure, the beauty of The Rocks is that it's as much fun to wander around aimlessly as it is to visit particular attractions. Soak up the atmosphere, sample the frequent entertainment in **The Rocks Square** on Playfair St, browse the stores for gifts, grab a beer at one of the pubs, admire the views of **Circular Quay** and **Campbells Cove**, and join the melee at the weekend **Rocks Market** (George St).

A short walk west along Argyle St, through the awe-inspiring **Argyle Cut** (excavated by convicts) takes you to the other side of the peninsula and **Millers Point**, a delightful district of early colonial homes with a quintessentially English village green. Nearby lies the 1848 **Garrison Church** and the more-secular delights of the **Lord Nelson Brewery Hotel** (p72) and the **Hero of Waterloo** (p72) hotel, which tussle over the title of Sydney's oldest pub.

Sydney Observatory (☎ 9217 0485; www.sydneyobservatory.com.au; Watson Rd, Observatory Hill; admission free, tours A$6; 🕑 10am-5pm, tours 6.15pm & 8.15pm Apr-Oct, 8.15pm Nov-Mar, 8.30pm Dec & Jan) has a commanding, copper dome–bedecked position atop Observatory Park, overlooking Millers Point and the harbour. There's a pleasant garden and free museum showcasing antique conservatory equipment. Nightly sky-watching visits (A$15) must be paid for in advance. In the old military hospital building close by (within the National Trust centre), the **SH Ervin Gallery** (☎ 9258 0123; Watson Rd, Observatory Hill; adult/concession A$6/4; 11am-5pm Tue-Fri, noon-5pm Sat & Sun) has temporary exhibitions of Australian art. It's also the home of the annual Salon des Refuses show, for rejected Archibald Prize (see p53) contenders. The café here serves good food.

At **Dawes Point**, on Walsh Bay, just west of the Harbour Bridge, are several renovated wharves. Pier One now houses a luxury hotel; Pier Four is the home of the prestigious Sydney Theatre, Bangarra Dance Theatre, Sydney Dance Company and Australian Theatre for Young People (ATYP). Other wharves appear to be getting the 'luxury waterfront apartments' treatment.

Sydney Harbour Bridge

The beloved 'old coat hanger' crosses the harbour at one of the harbour's narrowest points, linking the southern and northern shores and joining central Sydney with the satellite business district in North Sydney. The bridge (Map pp44–5) was completed in 1932 at a cost of A$20 million and has always been a favourite icon. This is partly because of its sheer size, partly because of its function in uniting the city and partly because it boosted employment during the Depression.

You can climb up almost 200 stairs inside the southeastern stone pylon, which houses a small (free) museum and the **Pylon Lookout** (Map pp48-50; ☎ 9240 1100; www.pylonlookout.com.au; admission A$8.50; 10am-5pm), or you can spend quite a bit more to join a climbing group and scale the bridge itself. **BridgeClimb** (Map pp48-50; ☎ 8274 7777; www.bridgeclimb.com.au; 5 Cumberland St, The Rocks; climbs A$155-225), a brilliantly executed tourist attraction, offers the adventurous traveller an unforgettable climb up and over the bridge. While it's certainly not cheap, this unique 3½-hour tour includes thorough safety checks, your own climbing suit and an enthusiastic guide. Twilight trips cost more, as do the photographs taken of you and the Opera House way down below (one group photo is included in the price). No dangling objects (including cameras) are allowed while on the climb, and everyone's given a breathalyser test beforehand – drunks aren't allowed, either.

Cars, trains, cyclists, joggers and pedestrians use the bridge. The bike path is on the western side and the pedestrian walkway on the eastern; stair access is from Cumberland St in The Rocks and near Milsons Point Station on the North Shore.

The best way to experience the bridge is undoubtedly on foot; don't expect much of a view crossing by car or train. Driving south (only) there's a A$3 toll.

Sydney Opera House

The postcard-perfect **Sydney Opera House** (Map pp48–50) is dramatically situated on the eastern headland of Circular Quay. Its soaring shell-like (there are 1,056,006 Swedish tiles on the roof) exterior is one of *the* must-see sights in the world – don't visit Sydney without clapping eyes on it. Its construction was an operatic blend of personal vision, long delays, bitter feuding, budget blowouts and pusillanimous politicking. Construction began in 1959 after Danish architect Jorn Utzon won an international design competition with his plans for a A$7 million building. After political interference, Utzon quit in disgust in 1966, leaving a consortium of Australian architects to design a compromised interior, at a cost of A$102 million (Uzton hasn't personally seen the Opera House since, but is involved, as a consultant, in a refurbishment that will improve its acoustics and access). Finally completed in 1973, it was lumbered with an impractical (for staging operas) internal design. The first public performance here was, tellingly, Sergei Prokofiev's *War and Peace* opera. Today some 3000 events are staged here annually.

A worthwhile, hour-long **tour** (☎ 9250 7250; www.sydneyoperahouse.com; adult/concession A$20/14; 9am-5pm) of the Opera House buildings is almost compulsory and very informative. Not every tour can visit all theatres because of rehearsals, but you're more likely to see everything if you take an early tour. Tours run every half-hour and include a free drink. Phone or email beforehand if you need wheelchair access.

Circular Quay **pp48–50**

Built around Sydney Cove, **Circular Quay** is one of the city's major focal points. The first European settlement grew around the Tank Stream, which now runs underground into the harbour near Wharf 6. For many years this was the shipping centre of Sydney, but it's now both a commuting hub and a recreational space. It combines ferry quays,

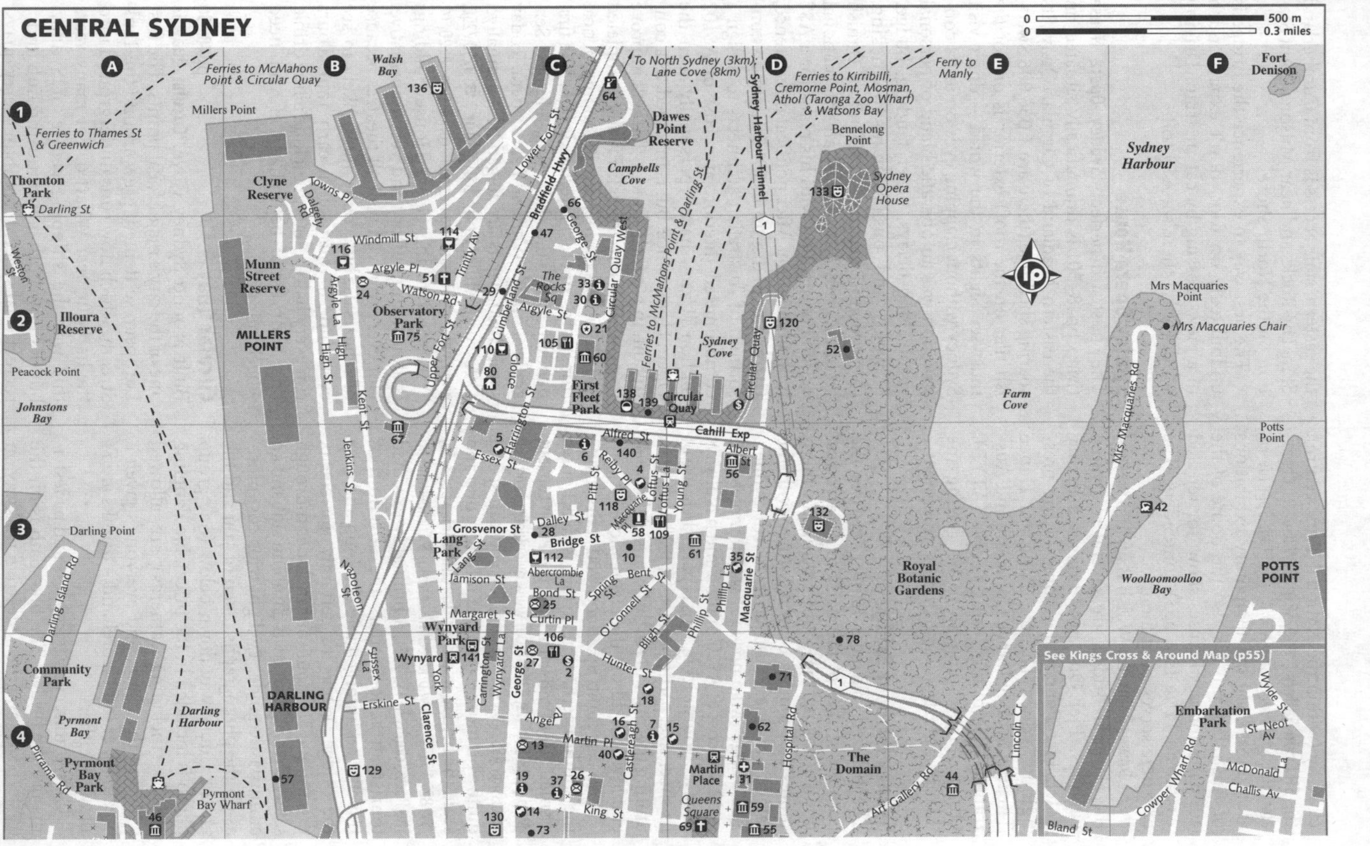
CENTRAL SYDNEY
0
500 m
0
0.3 miles
A
B
C
D
E
F
1
2
3
4
Ferries to McMahons Point & Circular Quay
Walsh Bay
To North Sydney (3km); Lane Cove (8km)
Ferries to Kirribilli, Cremorne Point, Mosman, Athol (Taronga Zoo Wharf) & Watsons Bay
Ferry to Manly
Fort Denison
Millers Point
Ferries to Thames St & Greenwich
Thornton Park
Darling St
Weston St
Illoura Reserve
Peacock Point
Johnstons Bay
Darling Point
Darling Island Rd
Community Park
Pyrmont Bay
Pyrmont Bay Park
Pirrama Rd
Pyrmont Bay Wharf
Darling Harbour
DARLING HARBOUR
MILLERS POINT
Munn Street Reserve
Clyne Reserve
Towns Pl
Dalgety Rd
Windmill St
Argyle Pl
Watson Rd
Argyle La
High La
High St
Trinity Av
Observatory Park
Upper Fort St
Kent St
Jenkins St
Napoleon St
Sussex La
Erskine St
Clarence St
York
Wynyard
Wynyard Park
Carrington St
Wynyard La
George St
Lower Fort St
Bradfield Hwy
Cumberland St
Glouce
Harrington St
Essex St
The Rocks Sq
Argyle St
George St
Circular Quay West
First Fleet Park
Dawes Point Reserve
Campbells Cove
Ferries to McMahons Point & Darling St
Sydney Harbour Tunnel
Sydney Cove
Circular Quay
Cahill Exp
Alfred St
Albert St
Reiby Pl
Pitt St
Loftus St
Loftus La
Young St
Macquarie Pl
Grosvenor St
Dalley St
Bridge St
Lang Park
Lang St
Jamison St
Abercrombie La
Bond St
Margaret St
Curtin Pl
Spring St
Bent St
O'Connell St
Bligh St
Phillip St
Phillip La
Macquarie St
Hunter St
Castlereagh St
Angel Pl
Martin Pl
Martin Place
Queens Square
King St
Hospital Rd
The Domain
Art Gallery Rd
Lincoln Cr
Royal Botanic Gardens
Bennelong Point
Sydney Opera House
Farm Cove
Sydney Harbour
Mrs Macquaries Point
Mrs Macquaries Chair
Mrs Macquaries Rd
Potts Point
Woolloomooloo Bay
POTTS POINT
See Kings Cross & Around Map (p55)
Embarkation Park
Wylde St
St Neot Av
McDonald La
Challis Av
Cowper Wharf Rd
Bland St

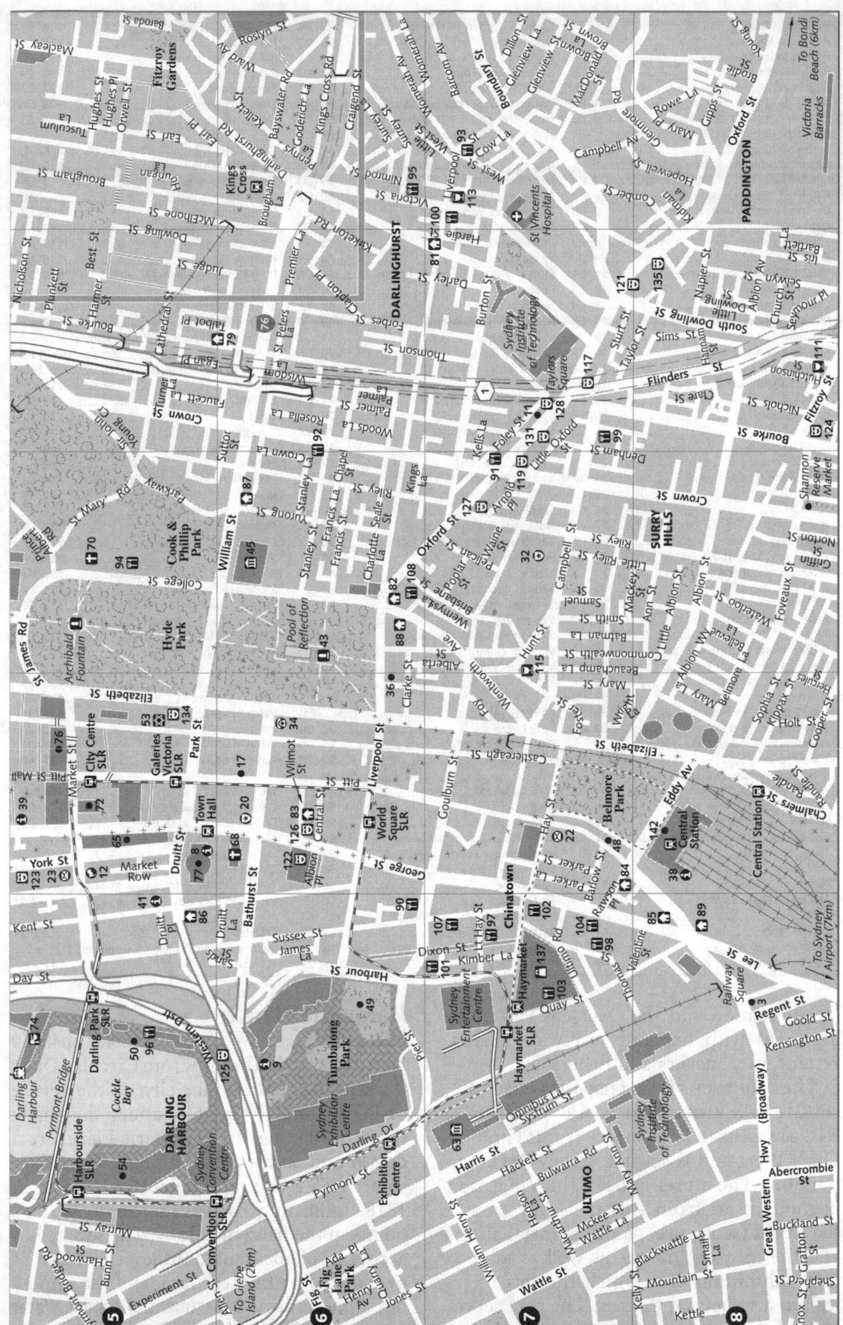
DARLING HARBOUR
Darling Harbour
Cockle Bay
Pyrmont Bridge
Harbourside SLR
Darling Park SLR
Convention SLR
Sydney Convention Centre
Sydney Exhibition Centre
Exhibition Centre
Tumbalong Park
Sydney Entertainment Centre
Haymarket SLR
Haymarket
Chinatown
ULTIMO
Sydney Institute of Technology
Fig Lane Park
To Glebe Island (2km)
Western Dstr
Market Row
Town Hall
Galeries Victoria SLR
City Centre SLR
World Square SLR
Central Station
Railway Square
Belmore Park
To Sydney Airport (7km)
Hyde Park
Archibald Fountain
Pool of Reflection
Cook & Phillip Park
SURRY HILLS
Shannon Reserve Market
DARLINGHURST
Kings Cross
Fitzroy Gardens
Sydney Institute of Technology
Taylors Square
St Vincents Hospital
PADDINGTON
Victoria Barracks
To Bondi Beach (6km)
Pyrmont Bridge Rd
Harwood St
Bunn St
Murray St
Experiment St
Allen St
Pyrmont St
Jones St
Harris St
Wattle St
William Henry St
Macarthur St
Mary Ann St
Kelly St
Blackwattle La
Mountain St
Kettle St
Knox St
Shepherd St
Grafton St
Buckland St
Abercrombie St
Great Western Hwy (Broadway)
Kensington St
Goold St
Regent St
Lee St
Quay St
Ultimo Rd
Thomas St
Harbour St
Darling Dr
Pier St
Day St
Kent St
Sussex St
Dixon St
Druitt St
Bathurst St
Liverpool St
York St
George St
Pitt St
Pitt St Mall
Market St
Park St
Castlereagh St
Elizabeth St
Goulburn St
Hay St
Campbell St
Wentworth Ave
Oxford St
College St
William St
St James Rd
Prince Albert Rd
St Mary's Rd
Crown St
Bourke St
Riley St
Foveaux St
Albion St
Cooper St
Chalmers St
Eddy Av
Flinders St
South Dowling St
Darlinghurst Rd
Victoria St
Liverpool St
Burton St
Forbes St
Kings Cross Rd
Bayswater Rd
Roslyn St
Craigend St
Boundary St
Glenmore Rd
Oxford St
Nicholson St
Macleay St
Dowling St
McElhone St
Brougham St
Cathedral St
Judge St

INFORMATION
American Express 1 D2
American Express 2 C4
Backpacker's World (see 123)
Bicycle NSW 3 B8
British Consulate General 4 C3
Canadian High Commission 5 C3
City Host Information Kiosk (Circular Quay) 6 C3
City Host Information Kiosk (Martin Place) 7 C4
City Host Information Kiosk (Town Hall) 8 C5
Darling Harbour Visitors Centre 9 B6
Department of Land & Water Conservation 10 C3
Dymocks Books (see 39)
Elizabeth's Bookshops 11 E7
French Consulate 12 C5
General Post Office 13 C4
Irish Consulate 14 C4
Japanese Consulate 15 D4
Korean Consulate 16 C4
Map World 17 C6
New Zealand High Commission 18 C4
NRMA 19 C4
Police Station 20 C6
Police Station 21 C2
Post Office 22 C7
Post Office 23 C5
Post Office 24 B2
Post Office 25 C3
Post Office 26 C4
Poste Restante Service Office 27 C4
STA Travel 28 C3
Stair access to Harbour Bridge 29 C2
Sydney Harbour National Parks Information Centre 30 C2
Sydney Hospital 31 D4
Sydney Police Centre 32 D7
Sydney Visitors Centre 33 C2
Telstra Phone Centre 34 C6
Thai Consulate 35 D3
Travel Bookshop 36 C6
Travelex 37 C4
Travellers Aid Society 38 C8
Travellers Contact Point 39 C5
Travellers Medical & Vaccination Centre (see 39)
US Consulate General 40 C4
YHA Membership & Travel Centre 41 B5

SIGHTS & ACTIVITIES (pp43–60)
Andrew 'Boy' Charlton Pool 42 F3
Anzac Memorial 43 D6
Art Gallery of NSW 44 E4
Australian Museum 45 D6
Australian National Maritime Museum 46 A4
BridgeClimb 47 C2
Cadmans Cottage (see 30)
Cheeky Monkey 48 C7
Chinese Garden of Friendship 49 B6
Cockle Bay Wharf 50 B5
Garrison Church 51 B2
Government House 52 D2
Great Synagogue 53 C5
Harbourside Shopping Centre 54 A5
Hyde Park Barracks Museum 55 D4
Justice & Police Museum 56 D3
King St Wharf 57 B4
Macquarie Place Obelisk 58 C3
Mint Building 59 D4
Museum of Contemporary Art 60 C2
Museum of Sydney 61 D3
Parliament House 62 D4
Powerhouse Museum 63 A7
Pylon Lookout 64 C1
Queen Victoria Building (QVB) 65 C5
Rocks Market 66 C1
SH Ervin Gallery 67 B3
St Andrew's Cathedral 68 C6
St James Church 69 D4
St Mary's Cathedral 70 D5
State Library of NSW 71 D4
State Theatre 72 C5
Strand Arcade 73 C4
Sydney Aquarium 74 B5
Sydney Observatory 75 B2
Sydney Tower 76 C5
Sydney Town Hall 77 C5
Sydney Tropical Centre 78 D4

SLEEPING (pp63–7)
Australian Backpackers 79 E6
Bed & Breakfast Sydney Harbour 80 C2
Royal Sovereign Hotel 81 E7
Stellar Suites 82 D6
Sydney Backpackers 83 C6
Sydney Central YHA 84 C7
Wake Up! 85 B8
Wanderers on Kent 86 B5
Woodduck Inn 87 D6
Y on the Park 88 D6
YHA Railway Square Hostel 89 B8

EATING (pp67–71)
BBQ King 90 B6
Betty's Soup Kitchen 91 D7
Bill & Toni's 92 E6
Bills 93 F7
Blackbird Café (see 96)
Bodhi 94 D5
Burgerman 95 F6
Chinta Ria...Temple of Love 96 B5
Dixon House Food Court 97 B7
Emperor's Garden BBQ & Noodles 98 B7
Foodgame 99 E7
Fu Manchu 100 F7
Harbour Plaza Eating World 101 B7
Marigold Citymark 102 B7
Market City Shopping Centre 103 B7
Mint Café (see 59)
Pho Pasteur 104 B7
Rockpool 105 C2
Sailor's Thai (see 33)
Salad Works 106 C4
Sussex Centre 107 B7
Uchi Lounge 108 D6
Wagamama 109 C3

DRINKING (pp72–4)
Australian Hotel 110 C2
Cricketers Arms 111 E8
Darlo Bar (see 81)
Establishment 112 C3
Green Park Hotel 113 F7
Hero of Waterloo 114 C2
Hollywood Hotel 115 D7
Lord Nelson Brewery Hotel 116 B2

ENTERTAINMENT (pp74–6)
ARQ 117 E7
Australian Theatre for Young People (ATYP) (see 136)
Bangarra Dance Theatre (see 136)
Basement 118 C3
Colombian 119 D7
Dendy 120 D2
Goodbar 121 E7
Greater Union Hoyts Cinemas 122 C6
Halftix 123 C5
Hopetoun Hotel 124 E8
IMAX 125 B6
Metro Theatre 126 C6
Midnight Shift 127 D7
Oxford Hotel 128 E7
Slip Inn 129 B4
Soup Plus 130 C4
Stonewall 131 E7
Sydney Conservatorium of Music 132 D3
Sydney Dance Company (see 136)
Sydney Opera House 133 D1
Sydney Philharmonic Choirs (see 136)
Sydney Theatre (see 136)
Ticketek 134 C5
Verona Cinema 135 E8
Wharf Theatre 136 B1

SHOPPING (pp76–7)
Paddy's Market 137 B7

TRANSPORT (pp77–80)
CountryLink Travel Centre 138 C2
Ferry Information Office 139 C2
McCafferty's Office (Left Luggage) (see 142)
Transit Shop 140 C3
Transportation Information Booth (see 138)
Wynyard Park Bus Exchange 141 C4

OTHER
Sydney Coach Terminal & Travellers Information Service 142 C8

a train station and the Overseas Passenger Terminal with harbour walkways, parks, restaurants, buskers and fisherfolk.

The **Museum of Contemporary Art** (MCA; ☎ 9241 5892; www.mca.com.au; 140 George St, The Rocks; admission free; 10am-5pm) fronts Circular Quay West and is set in a stately Art Deco building. The museum has a fine collection of modern art from Australia and around the world (sculpture, painting, installations and the moving image), as well as temporary exhibitions (for which the price varies) on a variety of themes. The café serves classy food in a classy atmosphere.

Macquarie Place & Surrounds

Map pp48–50

Narrow lanes lead south from Circular Quay towards the centre of the city. At the corner of Loftus and Bridge Sts, under the shady Moreton Bay figs in Macquarie Place, are a **cannon** and **anchor** from the First Fleet flagship, HMS *Sirius*, and an **obelisk**, erected in 1818, indicating road distances to various points in the nascent colony. The square has a couple of pleasant outdoor cafés and is overlooked by the rear façade of the imposing 19th-century **Department of Land & Water Conservation Building** on Bridge St.

Sydney buffs will enjoy the excellent **Museum of Sydney** (☎ 9251 5988; www.hht.net.au; 37 Phillip St, City; adult/concession A$7/3; 9.30am-5pm), two blocks east of Macquarie Place and on the site of the first and infamously fetid government house, built in 1788. Sydney's early history (including pre-1788) comes to life here in whisper, argument, gossip and artefacts. There's also a worthy café on the premises and a damn fine gift shop.

The 1856 **Justice & Police Museum** (☎ 9252 1144; www.hht.net.au; 8 Phillip St, City; adult/concession A$7/3; 10am-5pm Sat & Sun), in the old water-police court and station on the corner of Phillip and Albert Sts, has fascinating exhibitions on crime and policing, with a Sydney focus. The drug and addiction exhibition (with its creative bongs) is especially interesting. Wheelchair access is to the ground floor only, but Braille and audio guides are available. Open daily in January.

City Centre

Map pp48–50

Central Sydney stretches from **Circular Quay** in the north to Central Station in the south. The business hub is towards the northern end, but most redevelopment is occurring at the southern end and this is gradually shifting the focus of the city.

Sydney lacks a true civic centre, but Martin Place lays claim to the honour, if only by default. This grand, revamped pedestrian mall extends from Macquarie St to George St and is impressively lined by the monumental buildings of financial institutions and the colonnaded Victorian post office at No 1. There's plenty of public seating, a cenotaph commemorating Australia's war dead and an amphitheatre where lunch-time entertainment is sometimes staged.

The **Sydney Town Hall**, a few blocks south of here on the corner of George and Druitt Sts, was built in 1874. The elaborate chamber room and concert hall inside matches its outrageously ornate exterior. Next door, the Anglican **St Andrew's Cathedral**, built around the same time, is the oldest cathedral in Australia.

The city's most sumptuous shopping complex, the Byzantine-style **Queen Victoria Building** (QVB), is next to the town hall and takes up an entire city block bordered by George, Druitt, York and Market Sts. Another lovingly restored shopping centre is the **Strand Arcade**, between Pitt St Mall and George St.

There are 45-minute tours (A$12) of the splendidly over-the-top **State Theatre** (☎ 9373 6652; 49 Market St; 11.30am-3pm Mon-Fri), which was built in 1929.

To the southwest of here are the **Spanish Quarter** and **Chinatown** – dynamic areas spreading and breathing life into the city's lacklustre southeastern zone. Central Station lies isolated on the southern periphery.

Darling Harbour

Map pp48–50

This huge waterfront leisure park on the city centre's western edge, once a thriving dockland area, was reinvigorated in the 1980s by a combination of vision, politicking and big money. The supposed centrepiece is the Harbourside complex (which has shops and restaurants) – a development that's struggled to shrug off its 'white elephant' tag, despite extensive refurbishment in the last few years. The real attractions of Darling Harbour are the aquarium, excellent museums and Chinese Garden.

Until recently, the emphasis here was on tacky tourist 'entertainment', but the snazzy new wining and dining precincts of **Cockle Bay Wharf** (built opposite Harbourside) and **King St Wharf** have lent the area a bit more kudos with Sydneysiders and visitors alike. The Monorail and Metro Light Rail link Darling Harbour to the city centre.

Ferries leave from Circular Quay's Wharf 5 and stop at Darling Harbour's Aquarium Pier and Pyrmont Bay wharf (A$4.50).

The main pedestrian approaches to Darling Harbour are across footbridges from Market and Liverpool Sts. The one from Market St leads to Pyrmont Bridge, now a pedestrian-and-monorail-only route, but once famous as the world's first electrically operated swingspan bridge.

The **Darling Harbour visitors centre** (☎ 9240 8788; 10am-6pm) is under the highway and behind the IMAX theatre.

SYDNEY AQUARIUM

Near the eastern end of Pyrmont Bridge, this good **aquarium** (☎ 9262 2300; www.sydneyaquarium.com.au; Aquarium Pier, Darling Harbour; adult/concession A$24/16; 9am-10pm) displays the richness of Australian marine life. Three 'oceanariums' are moored in the harbour with sharks, rays and big fish in one, and Sydney Harbour marine life and seals in the others. There are also informative and well-presented exhibits of freshwater fish and coral gardens. The transparent underwater tunnels are mesmerising.

AUSTRALIAN NATIONAL MARITIME MUSEUM

This wonderful thematic **museum** (☎ 9298 3777; www.anmm.gov.au; 2 Murray St, City; admission free; 9.30am-5pm) tells the story of Australia's relationship with the sea, from Aboriginal canoes and the First Fleet to surf culture and the America's Cup. Even the building, with its sail-like roof and wave-like lines, harkens to the sea. Admission to the ship and submarine cost extra (adult/concession A$10/6).

POWERHOUSE MUSEUM

Covering the decorative arts, social history and science and technology, this is Sydney's hippest **museum** (☎ 9217 0100; www.powerhousemuseum.com; 500 Harris St, Ultimo; adult/concession A$10/5; 10am-5pm). It has eclectic exhibitions ranging from costume jewellery and musical instruments to steam locomotives and space capsules. The collections are well displayed and the emphasis is on hands-on interaction. Find it behind the Sydney Exhibition Centre – it's in a former power station that once ran Sydney's now-defunct trams.

CHINESE GARDEN OF FRIENDSHIP

In the southeastern corner of Darling Harbour, the tranquil **Chinese Garden** (☎ 9281 6863; adult/concession A$6/3; 9.30am-5.30pm) was designed by landscape architects from Guangdong, and is an oasis of lush serenity. Enter through the Courtyard of Welcoming Fragrance, circle the Lake of Brightness and finish with tea and cake in the **Chinese teahouse** (10am-4.30pm), or by having your photo taken in a Chinese opera costume (A$10).

Macquarie Street Map pp48–50

Sydney's greatest concentration of early public buildings grace Macquarie St, which runs along the eastern edge of the city from Hyde Park to the Opera House. Many of the buildings were commissioned by Lachlan Macquarie, the first governor to have a vision of the city beyond it being a convict colony. He enlisted convict forger Francis Greenway as an architect to realise his plans.

Two Greenway gems on Queens Sq, at the northern end of Hyde Park, are **St James Church** (1819–24) and the 1819 Georgian-style **Hyde Park Barracks Museum** (☎ 9223 8922; www.hht.net.au; Queens Sq; Macquarie St, City; adult/concession A$7/3; 9.30am-5pm). The barracks were first convict quarters, then became an immigration depot, and later a court. The museum details the building's history and provides an interesting perspective on Sydney's social history, with the best use of rats you'll ever see in a display. Next door is the lovely **Mint Building** (☎ 9217 0311; 10 Macquarie St, City), which was originally the

BEST VIEWS IN TOWN...

Sydney is an ostentatious city that offers visitors a dramatic spectacle. You can see the complete panorama by whooshing to the top of **Sydney Tower** (AMP tower; Map pp48-50; ☎ 9223 0933; www.sydneyskytour.com.au; cnr Market & Castlereagh Sts; adult/concession A$22/16; 9am-10.30pm Sun-Fri, to 11.30pm Sat), a needle-like column with an observation deck and revolving restaurants set 250m above the ground. The views extend west to the Blue Mountains and east to the ocean, as well as to the streets of inner Sydney below. Skytour is a half-hour virtual reality ride through Australia's history and landscape, and is included in the admission price. To get to the tower, enter Centrepoint from Market St and take the lift to the podium level where you buy your ticket.

The **Harbour Bridge** is another obvious vantage point: try the **Pylon Lookout** or, if you've got the bucks, a **Bridgeclimb** tour (see p47).

There are impressive ground-level views of the city and harbour from **Mrs Macquaries Point** (Map pp48–50) and from **Observatory Hill** (Map pp48–50) in Millers Point. **Blues Point Reserve** (Map pp44–5) and **Bradleys Head** (Map pp44–5) are the best vantage points on the North Shore.

The most enjoyable and atmospheric way to view Sydney is by boat. If you can't persuade someone to take you sailing (or you don't want to pay for a cruise), jump aboard a ferry at Circular Quay. The Manly ferry offers the obligatory cruise down the length of the harbour east of the bridge for a mere A$5.80.

If you're in the vicinity of Kings Cross, the northern end of Victoria St in Potts Point is an excellent vantage point from which to take in the cityscape and its best-known icons, especially at night.

southern wing of the infamous Rum Hospital. The hospital was built by two Sydney merchants in 1816 in return for a monopoly on the rum trade. It became a branch of the Royal Mint in 1854. There's a fancy café on the premises (see Mint Café, p67), but nothing else is open to the public.

The Mint's twin is **Parliament House** (☎ 9230 2047; Macquarie St, City; admission free; 🕑 9.30am-4pm Mon-Fri), which was originally the northern wing of the Rum Hospital. This simple, proud building has been home to the NSW Parliament since 1829. The public gallery is open on days when parliament is sitting.

Next to Parliament House is the **State Library of NSW** (☎ 9273 1414; www.sl.nsw.gov.au; Macquarie St, City; 🕑 9am-5pm Mon-Fri, 11am-5pm Sat & Sun), which is more of a cultural centre than a traditional library. It holds over five million tomes (the smallest being a tablet-sized Lord's Prayer) and hosts innovative, free, temporary exhibitions in its **galleries** (🕑 9am-5pm Mon-Fri, 10am-5pm Sat & Sun). The library's modern wing also has a great bookshop filled with Australian titles. Free one-hour tours are given Tuesday at 11am and Thursday at 2pm.

The **Sydney Conservatorium of Music** (☎ 9351 1222; www.usyd.edu.au/su/conmusic; Macquarie St, City) was built by Greenway as the stables and servants' quarters of Macquarie's planned government house. Macquarie was replaced as governor before the house could be finished, partly because of the project's extravagance. See p75 for more information about the music recitals held here.

Built between 1837 and 1845, **Government House** (☎ 9931 5222; www.hht.net.au; Macquarie St, City; admission free; 🕑 grounds 10am-4pm daily, house 10am-3pm Fri-Sun) dominates the western headland of Farm Cove and, until early 1996, was the official residence of the governor of NSW. It's a marvellous example of the Gothic Revival style. Tours of the house depart every half-hour from 10.30am (unless a special event means tours are cancelled).

Art Gallery of New South Wales

Located at The Domain, east of Macquarie St, the **art gallery** (AGNSW; Map pp48-50; ☎ 9225 1744; www.artgallery.nsw.gov.au; Art Gallery Rd, City; admission free; 🕑 10am-5pm) has excellent permanent displays of 19th- and 20th-century Australian art, Aboriginal and Torres Strait Islander art and 15th- to 19th-century European and Asian art. It also has some inspired temporary exhibits, and a free Aboriginal dance performance at noon Tuesday to Saturday. The frequently controversial Archibald Prize exhibition is held here annually, with portraits of the famous and not-so-famous bringing out the art critic in almost every Sydneysider. There's usually a charge for temporary exhibitions; free tours are held at 1pm.

Australian Museum

On the eastern flank of Hyde Park, on the corner of College and William Sts, this natural history **museum** (Map pp48-50; ☎ 9320 6000; www.amonline.net.au; 6 College St, City; adult/concession A$8/4; 🕑 9.30am-5pm) has an excellent Australian wildlife collection (including skeletons). It also has a gallery tracing Aboriginal history and the Dreamtime, and there's an indigenous performance at noon and 2pm every Sunday.

Royal Botanic Gardens — Map pp48–50

The city's favourite picnic spot, jogging route and place to stroll is the enchanting **Royal Botanic Gardens** (☎ 9231 8111; www.rbgsyd.gov.au; Mrs Macquaries Rd, City; admission free; 🕑 gardens 7am-sunset, visitors centre 10am-4pm), which borders Farm Cove, southeast of the Opera House. The gardens were established in 1816 and feature plant life from the South Pacific. They include the site of the colony's first paltry vegetable patch, which has been preserved as the First Farm exhibit.

There's a fabulous, leech-free **Sydney Tropical Centre** (adult A$2.20; 🕑 10am-4pm) in the interconnecting Arc and Pyramid glasshouses. The multistorey Arc has a collection of rampant climbers and trailers from the world's rainforests, while the Pyramid houses the Australian collection, including monsoonal, woodland and tropical rainforest plants. Other attractions in the gardens include the Fernery, the Succulent Garden and the Rose Garden.

Free tours depart at 10.30am daily except public holidays (and at 1pm Monday to Friday except public holidays and December to February) from the information booth at the Gardens Shop. As far as wildlife goes, you can't fail to notice the gardens' resident colony of grey-headed flying foxes (*Pteropus poliocephalus* – fruit bats), who spend their days chittering loudly and hanging around upside down until it's time to commute south across the city at dusk. Cockatoos, small reptiles and large orb spiders can also be seen. The park's paths are, for the most part, wheelchair accessible, although there are some flights of stairs scattered about.

Other Parks & Gardens

The Domain (Map pp48–50) is a pleasant grassy area east of Macquarie St that was set aside by Governor Phillip for public recreation. Today it's used by city workers as a place to escape the hubbub, and on Sunday afternoon it's the gathering place for soapbox speakers who do their best to engage or enrage their listeners.

On the eastern edge of the city centre is the formal **Hyde Park** (Map pp48–50), once the colony's first racetrack and cricket pitch. It has a grand avenue of trees, delightful fountains and a giant public chessboard. It contains the dignified **Anzac Memorial** (Map pp48-50; 9am-5pm), which has a free exhibition on the ground floor that covers the 10 overseas conflicts in which Australians have fought. **St Mary's Cathedral** (Map pp48-50; ☎ 9220 0400; cnr College St & St Mary's Rd, City; 6.30am-6.30pm), with its new copper spires, overlooks the park from the east, while the 1878 **Great Synagogue** (Map pp48-50; ☎ 9267 2477; 187a Elizabeth St) stands on the west. Tours of the synagogue take place at noon Tuesday and Thursday (A$5; entry at 166 Castlereagh St).

Sydney's biggest park is **Centennial Park** (Map pp44–5), which has running, cycling, skating and horse-riding tracks, duck ponds, barbecue sites and sports pitches. It's 5km from the centre, just southeast of Paddington.

Moore Park (Map pp44–5) abuts the western flank of Centennial Park and contains sports pitches, a golf course, an equestrian centre, the Fox Entertainment Precinct, the Aussie Stadium and the Sydney Cricket Ground (SCG).

Kings Cross & Around — Map p55

The Cross is a bizarre cocktail of strip joints, prostitution, crime and drugs shaken and stirred. Add a handful of great restaurants, smart cafés, upmarket hotels and backpacker hostels and you'll get the idea. It attracts an odd mix of highlife, lowlife, sailors, tourists and suburbanites looking for a big night out.

The Cross has always been lovably roguish, from its early days as a centre of bohemianism to the Vietnam War era, when it became the vice centre of Australia. It appeals to the larrikin spirit, which always enjoys a bit of devil-may-care and 24-hour drinking. Many budget travellers begin and end their Australian adventures in the Cross (many of Sydney's hostels are here) – it's a good place to swap information, meet up with friends, find work, browse notice boards and buy or sell a car. **Darlinghurst Rd** is the trashy main drag, though new construction is beautifying the area. This doglegs into Macleay St, which continues into more upmarket Potts Point. Most hostels are on Victoria St, which diverges from Darlinghurst Rd just north of William St, near the iconic Coca Cola sign. There's a market every Sunday near the thistle-like **El Alamein Fountain** in the Fitzroy Gardens.

In the dip between the Cross and the city is Woolloomooloo, one of Sydney's oldest areas, and an interesting place to stroll around. The Finger Wharf houses apartments, restaurants and a hotel. **Harry's Café de Wheels**, next to the wharf, must be one of the few pie carts in the world to be a tourist attraction. It opened in 1945, stays open 18 hours a day (till way after midnight on weekends) and offers the cheapest water-view meals in town (you'll be sitting on a bench, though).

Inner East

The backbone of Darlinghurst, Surry Hills and Paddington, **Oxford St** (Map pp48–50) is one of the more happening places for late-night action. It's a strip of shops, cafés, bars and nightclubs whose flamboyance and spirit can be largely attributed to the vibrant and vocal gay community. The route of the **Sydney Gay & Lesbian Mardi Gras** (p61) parade passes this way.

The main drag of Oxford St runs from the southeastern corner of Hyde Park to the northwestern corner of Centennial Park, although it continues in name to Bondi Junction. Taylor Sq is the main hub. (An orientation warning: Oxford St's street numbers restart on the Darlinghurst-Paddington border, west of the junction with South Dowling and Victoria Sts.) Bus Nos 380 and 382 from Circular Quay, and No 378 from Railway Sq, run the length of the street.

DARLINGHURST — Map pp48–50

This is a vital area of urban cool, full of bright young things. There's no better way to soak

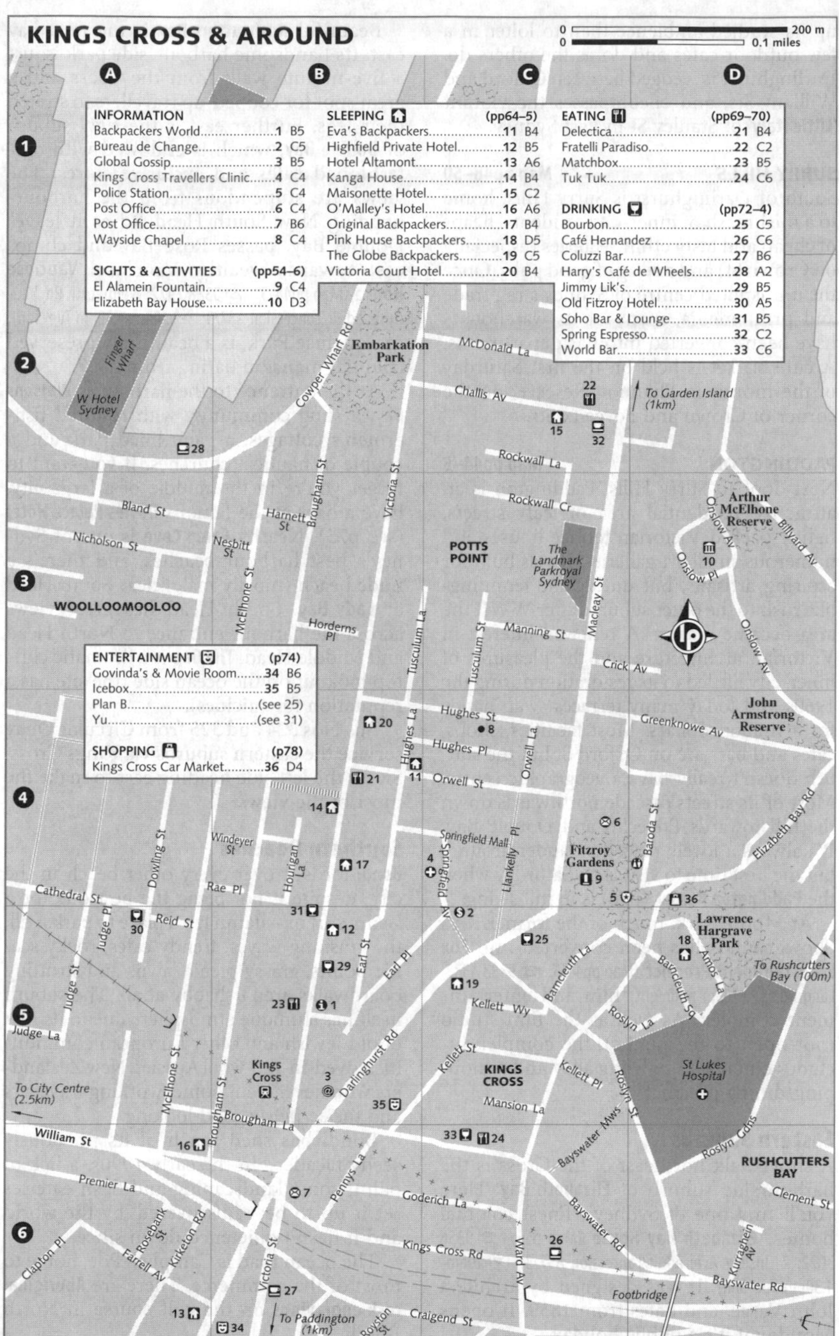
KINGS CROSS & AROUND
0 200 m
0 0.1 miles
A
B
C
D
1
2
3
4
5
6
INFORMATION
Backpackers World....1 B5
Bureau de Change....2 C5
Global Gossip....3 B5
Kings Cross Travellers Clinic....4 C4
Police Station....5 C4
Post Office....6 C4
Post Office....7 B6
Wayside Chapel....8 C4
SIGHTS & ACTIVITIES (pp54–6)
El Alamein Fountain....9 C4
Elizabeth Bay House....10 D3
SLEEPING (pp64–5)
Eva's Backpackers....11 B4
Highfield Private Hotel....12 B5
Hotel Altamont....13 A6
Kanga House....14 B4
Maisonette Hotel....15 C2
O'Malley's Hotel....16 A6
Original Backpackers....17 B4
Pink House Backpackers....18 D5
The Globe Backpackers....19 C5
Victoria Court Hotel....20 B4
EATING (pp69–70)
Delectica....21 B4
Fratelli Paradiso....22 C2
Matchbox....23 B5
Tuk Tuk....24 C6
DRINKING (pp72–4)
Bourbon....25 C5
Café Hernandez....26 C6
Coluzzi Bar....27 B6
Harry's Café de Wheels....28 A2
Jimmy Lik's....29 B5
Old Fitzroy Hotel....30 A5
Soho Bar & Lounge....31 B5
Spring Espresso....32 C2
World Bar....33 C6
ENTERTAINMENT (p74)
Govinda's & Movie Room....34 B6
Icebox....35 B5
Plan B....(see 25)
Yu....(see 31)
SHOPPING (p78)
Kings Cross Car Market....36 D4
Finger Wharf
W Hotel Sydney
Cowper Wharf Rd
Embarkation Park
McDonald La
Challis Av
To Garden Island (1km)
Rockwall La
Rockwall Cr
Bland St
Harnett St
Brougham St
Victoria St
Nicholson St
Nesbitt St
POTTS POINT
The Landmark Parkroyal Sydney
Arthur McElhone Reserve
Onslow Av
Billyard Av
Onslow Pl
WOOLLOOMOOLOO
McElhone St
Horderns Pl
Tusculum La
Tusculum St
Manning St
Macleay St
Crick Av
John Armstrong Reserve
Greenknowe Av
Hughes St
Hughes Pl
Hughes La
Orwell La
Orwell St
Elizabeth Bay Rd
Windeyer St
Dowling St
Hourigan La
Springfield Mall
Springfield Av
Llankelly Pl
Fitzroy Gardens
Baroda St
Cathedral St
Rae Pl
Reid St
Judge Pl
Judge St
Judge La
Earl St
Earl Pl
Barncleuth La
Barncleuth Sq
Lawrence Hargrave Park
Ameos La
To Rushcutters Bay (100m)
Kellett Wy
Roslyn La
Darlinghurst Rd
Kellett St
KINGS CROSS
Kellett Pl
Kings Cross
St Lukes Hospital
To City Centre (2.5km)
Mansion La
Roslyn St
Brougham La
William St
Bayswater Mws
Roslyn Gdns
RUSHCUTTERS BAY
Clement St
Premier La
Pennys La
Goderich La
Bayswater Rd
Rosebank St
Kirketon Rd
Ward Av
Clapton Pl
Farrell Av
Kings Cross Rd
Kurraheen Av
Victoria St
Footbridge
To Paddington (1km)
Royston St
Craigend St

up its studied ambience than to loiter in a few outdoor cafés and do as the others do. Darlinghurst is wedged between Oxford and William Sts, and encompasses the vibrant **'Little Italy'** of Stanley St in East Sydney.

SURRY HILLS — Map pp48–50

South of Darlinghurst is Surry Hills, home to a mishmash of inner-city residents, heaps of cheap and tasty ethnic eateries (especially on Crown St) and a swag of good pubs. Once the undisputed centre of Sydney's rag trade and print media, many of its warehouses have been converted into flash apartments. A cute **market** is held on the first Saturday of the month in Shannon Reserve, on the corner of Crown and Foveaux Sts.

PADDINGTON — Map pp44–5

Next door to Surry Hills, Paddington is an attractive residential area of leafy streets, tightly packed Victorian terrace houses and numerous small art galleries. It was built for aspiring artisans, but during the lemming-like rush to the outer suburbs after WWII the area became a slum. A renewed interest in Victorian architecture and the pleasures of inner-city life led to its restoration during the 1960s and today many terraces swap hands for a million dollars. Most facilities, shops, cafés and bars are on Oxford St but the suburb doesn't really have a geographic centre. Most of its streets cascade northwards down the hill towards Edgecliff and Double Bay. It's always a lovely place to wander around, but the best time to visit is on Saturday when the **Paddington Bazaar** (p76) is in full swing.

At Moore Park, much of the former RAS Showgrounds has been converted into **Fox Entertainment Precinct** (Map pp44-5; ☎ 9383 4333; Lang Rd; 🕑 10am-midnight) film and entertainment complex. As well as the film studio (not open to the public), the complex includes cinemas, a bowling alley and a shopping/dining precinct.

Eastern Suburbs

A short walk northeast of the Cross is the harbourside suburb of **Elizabeth Bay.** Here you'll find one of Sydney's finest colonial homes, **Elizabeth Bay House** (Map p55; ☎ 9356 3022; 7 Onslow Ave; adult/concession A$7/3; 🕑 10am-4.30pm Tue-Sun). It was designed by architect John Verge, and dates from 1839. It opens Monday if it's a public holiday.

Beautiful **Rushcutters Bay** is the next bay east. Its handsome harbour-side park is just a five-minute walk from the Cross and a great spot for cooped-up travellers to stretch their legs. Further east is the ritzy suburb of **Double Bay**, which is endowed with old-fashioned cafés and exclusive stores. The views are stupendous from the harbour-hugging New South Head Rd as it leaves Double Bay, passes Rose Bay and climbs east towards wealthy Vaucluse. **Vaucluse House** (Map pp44-5; ☎ 9388 7922; Wentworth Rd, Vaucluse; adult/concession A$7/3; 🕑 10am-4.30pm Tue-Sun), in Vaucluse Park, is a beautifully preserved colonial mansion dating from 1827.

At the entrance to the harbour is **Watsons Bay**, a snug community with restored fishermen's cottages, a palm-lined park and a couple of nautical churches. If you want to forget you're in the middle of a large city, have a beer at the famous **Doyles Palace Hotel** (see p73). Nearby **Camp Cove** is one of Sydney's best harbour beaches, and there's a nude beach (mostly male) near South Head at **Lady Bay**. South Head has great views across the harbour entrance to North Head and Middle Head. **The Gap** is a dramatic cliff-top lookout on the ocean side (the site has a reputation for suicides).

Bus Nos 324 and 325 from Circular Quay service the eastern suburbs via Kings Cross. Sit on the left side heading east to make the most of the views.

Southern Beaches

Bondi lords it over every other beach in the city, despite it not being the best one for a swim, surf or – damn it – a place to park. Still, the crashing waves, trendy cafés, rocky scenic points, grassy picnic lawns and strutting boardwalks aren't shabby at all. The suburb itself has a unique atmosphere due to its mix of old Jewish and other European communities, dyed-in-the-wool Aussies, New Zealanders who never went home, working travellers and the *seriously* good-looking.

Bondi has shed much of its previously seedy façade – in the early 1990s, a lick of paint, some landscaping and flash eateries set it up to be 'rediscovered' by the world and it hasn't quietened down since.

The ocean road is Campbell Pde, home to most of the commerce. There are **Aboriginal rock engravings** on the golf course in North Bondi.

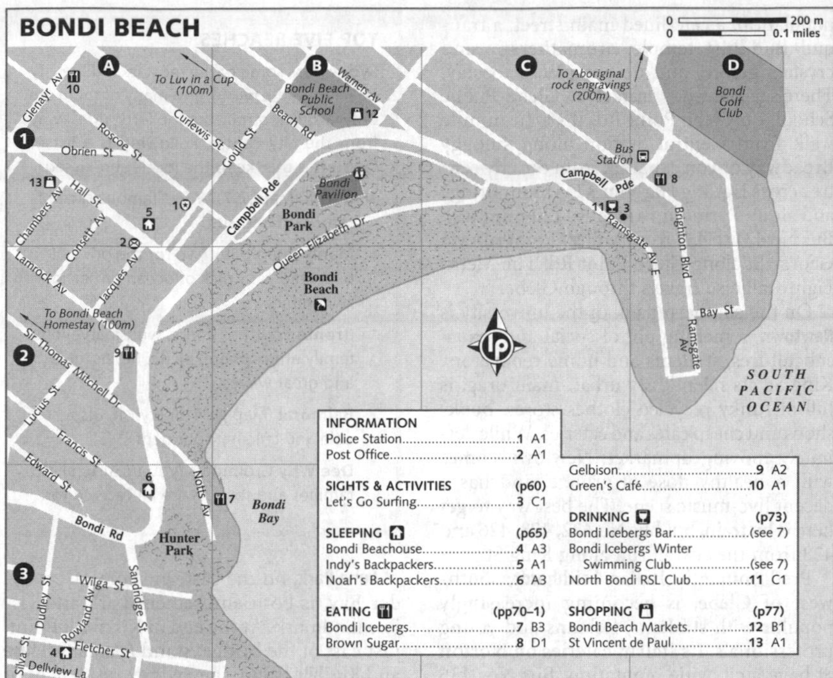

Catch bus No 380, 382, L82 or 389 from the city to get to the beach or, if you're in a hurry, catch a train to Bondi Junction and pick up one of these buses as they pass through the Bondi Junction bus station.

Just south of Bondi is **Tamarama**, a lovely cove with strong rips. Get off the bus as it kinks off Bondi Rd onto Fletcher St, just before it reaches Bondi Beach. Tamarama is a five-minute walk down the hill.

There is a nice beach hemmed in by a bowl-shaped park and sandstone headlands at **Bronte**, south of Tamarama. The cafés with outdoor tables on the edge of the park make it a great chill-out destination. Catch bus No 378 from Railway Sq, or you can catch a train to Bondi Junction and pick up the bus there; sit on the left side for a breathtaking view as the bus descends Macpherson St.

You can walk to Bronte along the wonderful cliff-top footpath from Bondi Beach or from Coogee via Gordon's Bay, Clovelly and the sun-bleached Waverley Cemetery.

Clovelly Bay is a narrow scooped-out beach to the south. There's little surf and it's good for swimming. As well as the saltwater baths here, there's a wheelchair-accessible boardwalk so that the chairbound can take a sea dip. Something of a poor cousin to Bondi, **Coogee** has spruced itself up in recent years. It has a relaxed air, a good sweep of sand and a couple of established hostels and hotels. You can reach Coogee by catching bus No 372 from Railway Sq or No 373 from Circular Quay. Or take a train to Bondi Junction and pick up bus No 314 or 315 from there.

Inner West Map pp44–5

West of the centre is the higgledy-piggledy peninsula suburb of **Balmain**. It was once a notoriously rough neighbourhood of dockyard workers but has been transformed into an artsy, middle-class area of restored Victoriana flush with pubs, cafés and trendy shops. It's a great place for a stroll, and cars will actually stop when you cross the street. Catch a ferry from Circular Quay (A$4.50) or bus No 442 from the QVB building.

Bohemian *and* yuppie **Glebe** is southwest of the centre, on the northern edge of the University of Sydney. It has a large student population, a café-lined main street, a tranquil Buddhist temple, aromatherapy and crystals galore, and decent places to stay. There's a Saturday **market** at Glebe Public School, on Glebe Point Rd. It's a 10-minute walk from Central Station along smoggy Broadway or you can walk from the city centre across Darling Harbour's Pyrmont Bridge and along Pyrmont Bridge Rd (20 minutes). Bus No 431 to 434 from Millers Point run via George St along Glebe Point Rd. The Metro Light Rail also travels through Glebe.

On the southern flank of the university is **Newtown**, a melting pot of social and sexual subcultures, students and home renovators. King St, its relentlessly urban main drag, is full of funky recycled-clothes stores, bookshops and cheap cafés and eateries. While definitely moving upmarket, Newtown comes with a healthy dose of grunge, and has a decent live-music scene. The best way to get here is by train, but bus No 422, 423, 426 and 428 from the city all run along King St.

Predominantly Italian **Leichhardt**, southwest of Glebe, is becoming increasingly popular with students, lesbians and young professionals. Its Italian eateries on Norton St have a citywide reputation. Bus Nos 436 to 440 run from the city to Leichhardt.

SYDNEY FISH MARKET

With over 15 million kg of seafood sold here annually, this large fish **market** (Map pp44-5; ☎ 9004 1100; www.sydneyfishmarket.com.au; cnr Pyrmont Bridge Rd & Bank St, Pyrmont; 🕑 7am-4pm) is the place to get on first-name terms with a bewildering array of scaly critters. You can see fish auctions (early mornings), eat sushi or fish and chips, buy super-fresh seafood and attend seafood cooking classes (call for details). It's west of Darling Harbour, on Blackwattle Bay. The Metro Light Rail is the best way to get here (the stop's called Fish Market).

North Shore Map pp44–5

On the northern side of the Harbour Bridge is **North Sydney**, a high-rise office centre with little to tempt the traveller. **McMahons Point** is a lovely, forgotten suburb wedged between the two business districts, on the western side of the bridge. There's a line of pleasant alfresco cafés on Blues Point Rd, which runs down to Blues Point Reserve on the western headland of Lavender Bay. The reserve has fine city views.

TOP FIVE BEACHES

Sydney has some of the most incredible city beaches in the world, and many of them are only a quick stroll, bus or ferry ride away from the city centre. Following is a list of favourites that keep the locals sun-kissed.

- **Bondi** (Map p57) World-famous slice of sand, surf and sun.
- **Manly** (Map p59) Two for the price of one: take your pick of ocean or harbour swimming.
- **Bronte** South of Bondi, with marvellous family atmosphere, picnic tables, grass and great waves.
- **Balmoral** (Map pp44–5) Stylish, respectable and chic harbour gem.
- **Dee Why** Grommets (young surfers), families and tourists are all catered for.

Luna Park, on the eastern shore of Lavender Bay, is both amusement park and visible landmark. At the end of Kirribilli Point, just east of the bridge, stand **Admiralty House** and **Kirribilli House**, the Sydney residences of the governor general and the prime minister respectively (Admiralty House is the one nearer the bridge; both are closed to the public). East of here are the upmarket suburbs of **Neutral Bay**, **Cremorne** and **Mosman**, all with pleasant coves and harbour-side parks perfect for picnics. Ferries go to all of these suburbs from Circular Quay.

On the northern side of Mosman is the pretty beach suburb of Balmoral, which faces Manly across Middle Harbour. There are picnic areas, a promenade and three beaches.

TARONGA ZOO

In a superb harbourside setting, **Taronga Zoo** (Map pp44-5; ☎ 9969 2777; www.zoo.nsw.gov.au; Bradleys Head Rd, Mosman; adult/concession A$25/19; 🕑 9am-5pm) has some 3000 critters (from seals to tigers, koalas to giraffes and echidnas to platypuses), all in decent habitats and well cared for. Ferries to the zoo depart from Circular Quay's Wharf 2 half-hourly from 7.15am Monday to Friday and 8.45am Saturday and Sunday. Bus No 247 gets you here from the QVB building (A$3.50). A ZooPass (A$31.70), sold at Circular Quay and elsewhere, includes return ferry rides and zoo admission. Bring a picnic if you want to avoid expensive zoo food.

Manly

Map p59

The jewel of the North Shore, Manly is on a narrow peninsula that ends at the dramatic cliffs of North Head. It boasts harbour and ocean beaches, a ferry wharf, all the trappings of a touristy beach destination and a great sense of community. It's a sun-soaked place not afraid to show a bit of tack and brashness to attract visitors, and makes a refreshing change from the prim upper-middle-class harbour enclaves nearby.

The **Manly visitors centre** (☎ 9977 1088; Manly Wharf; 9am-5pm Mon-Fri, 10am-4pm Sat & Sun), just outside the ferry wharf, has free pamphlets on the 10km **Manly Scenic Walkway** and bus information. Ferries and JetCat catamarans operate between Circular Quay and Manly. JetCats seem to traverse the harbour before you get a chance to blink (well, about 15 minutes), while the ferries do the trip in a cool 30 minutes and offer fantastic views.

The ferry wharf is on the Manly Cove foreshore. A short walk along Manly's pedestrian mall, **The Corso**, brings you to the **ocean beach** lined with towering Norfolk pines. The road running along the foreshore changes name from North Steyne to South Steyne. A footpath follows the shoreline from South Steyne around the small headland to tiny **Fairy Bower Beach** and the picturesque cove of **Shelly Beach**.

On the Manly Cove foreshore, the small **Manly Art Gallery & Museum** (☎ 9949 1776; West Esplanade Reserve; adult/concession A$3.50/1.10; 10am-5pm Tue-Sun), focuses on the suburb's special relationship with the beach.

Oceanworld (☎ 9949 2644; West Esplanade; adult/concession A$16.50/12; 10am-5.30pm) is next door. The big attractions are the sharks and stingrays – try to view divers feeding the sharks. An underwater tunnel offers dramatic (but dry) close encounters with the fish. After 3.30pm the admission price drops by 15%.

Behind the Manly Art Gallery is the wonderful 10km-long **Manly Scenic Walkway**, which has a 2km-long wheelchair accessible path. Bring water as there are no shops along the way.

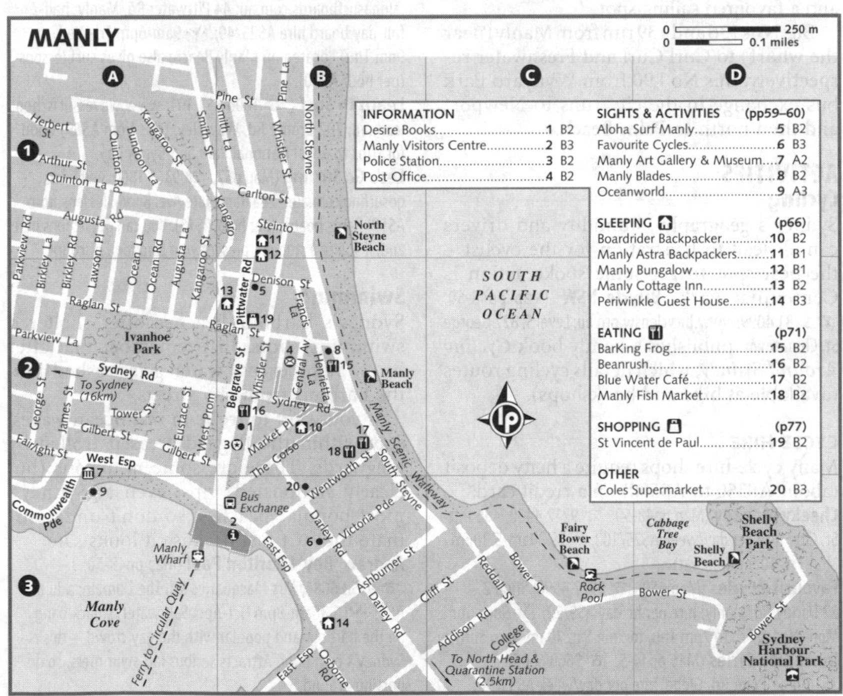

North Head, at the entrance to Sydney Harbour, is about 3km south of Manly. Most of the dramatic headland is in Sydney Harbour National Park. The **Quarantine Station** represents an interesting slice of Sydney's social history; it housed suspected disease carriers from 1832 right up until 1984. To visit the station, book a guided **tour** (☎ 9247 5033; adult A$11; ⌚ tours 1.15pm Tue & Thu, 1.15pm & 3.30pm Sat & Sun). The station is reputedly haunted and there are spooky three-hour ghost tours at night (A$22 Wednesday, A$28 Friday to Sunday).

Northern Beaches

A string of ocean-front suburbs sweeps 30km north along the coast from Manly, ending at beautiful, well-heeled Palm Beach and the spectacular Barrenjoey Heads at the entrance to Broken Bay. Beaches along the way include Freshwater, Curl Curl, Dee Why, Collaroy and Narrabeen. The most spectacular are Whale Beach and Bilgola (near Palm Beach), both with dramatic, steep headlands. Several of the northernmost beach suburbs also back onto Pittwater, a lovely inlet off Broken Bay and a favoured sailing spot.

Bus Nos 136 and 139 run from Manly (near the wharf) to Curl Curl and Freshwater respectively. Bus No L90 from Wynyard Park bus exchange in the city runs to Newport and then north to Palm Beach.

ACTIVITIES

Cycling

Sydney's geography, humidity and drivers can all lead to frustration for the cyclist – the best spot to get some spoke action is Centennial Park. **Bicycle NSW** (Map pp48-50; ☎ 9281 4099; www.bicyclensw.org.au; Level 5, 822 George St, Chinatown) publishes a handy book *Cycling Around Sydney*, which details cycling routes (available at bike and bookshops).

CYCLE HIRE

Many cycle-hire shops require a hefty deposit (about A$350 to A$500) on a credit card.

Cheeky Monkey (Map pp48-50; ☎ 9212 4460; 456 Pitt St, City; hire per day/week A$25/100; ⌚ 8.30am-5.30pm Mon-Fri, 10am-4pm Sat)

Favourite Cycles (Map p59; ☎ 9977 4590; Shop 2, 22 Darley Rd, Manly; hire per hr/day A$9/22; ⌚ 9am-6pm Mon-Wed & Fri, to 7pm Thu, to 5pm Sat, 10am-4pm Sun)

Inner City Cycles (Map pp44-5; ☎ 9660 6605; 151 Glebe Point Rd, Glebe; hire per day/week A$33/90; ⌚ 9.30am-6pm Mon-Wed & Fri, to 8pm Thu, to 4pm Sat, 11am-3pm Sun)

In-line Skating

The beach promenades at Bondi and Manly and the paths of Centennial Park are the most favoured spots for skating.

Manly Blades (Map p59; ☎ 9976 3833; 49 North Steyne, Manly; ⌚ 9am-6pm) Rents in-line skates (from A$12), scooters (from A$7) and baby joggers (from A$12).

Total Skate (Map pp44-5; ☎ 9380 6356; 36 Oxford St, Woollahra; hire 1st/subsequent hour A$10/5) Near Centennial Park; fee includes safety equipment.

Surfing

South of the Heads, the best spots are Bondi, Tamarama, Bronte and Maroubra. Cronulla, south of Botany Bay, is also a serious surfing spot. On the North Shore, there are a dozen surf beaches between Manly and Palm Beach; the best are Manly, Curl Curl, Dee Why, North Narrabeen, Mona Vale, Newport Reef, North Avalon and Palm Beach itself. For current wave activity check www.wavecam.com.au.

Aloha Surf Manly (Map p59; ☎ 9977 3777; www.alohasurfboards.com.au; 44 Pittwater Rd, Manly; half-/full-day board hire A$25/40; ⌚ 9am-6pm Fri-Wed, to 9pm Thu) Located on Manly Beach; also gives surf lessons (per hour A$50).

Learn to Surf (☎ 1800 851 101; www.wavessurfschool.com.au; 192 Bronte Rd, Waverley; trips from A$69) Good for trips to Royal National Park and Byron Bay.

Let's Go Surfing (Map p57; ☎ 9365 1800; www.letsgosurfing.com.au; 128a Ramsgate Ave, Bondi; lessons from A$59) Rents boards (per hour A$15). You can get lessons here and, if you're a student, present your card for a discount.

Swimming

Sydney's harbour beaches offer sheltered swimming spots. Just remember that after heavy rains excess water gets washed into the harbour from city streets.

If you want to frolic in real ocean waves, stay within the flagged areas patrolled by lifeguards. There are some notorious (but clearly signposted) rips, even at Sydney's most popular beaches, so don't underestimate the surf just because it looks safe.

Andrew 'Boy' Charlton Pool (Map pp48-50; ☎ 9358 6686; Mrs Macquaries Rd, The Domain; adult A$5; ⌚ 6.30am-8pm Oct-Apr) Salt water, smack bang on the harbour and popular with the gay crowd – this is Sydney's best pool. Attracts serious lap-swimmers, so no horsing around.

Wylie's Baths (☎ 9665 2838; Neptune St, Coogee; admission A$3; 7am-6pm) The waves wash in, but the sharks don't. It's like swimming in the ocean, but you're in a salt-water pool. Pretty cool.

TOURS

Sydney offers many kinds of tours, from harbour cruises to walks to flights over the water. The more affordable ones are listed below.

Walking Tours

Maureen Fry (☎ 9660 7157; www.ozemail.com.au/~mpfry; 15 Arcadia Rd, Glebe) Maureen caters mainly for groups, but may be able to take individuals. Two-hour guided walks around Sydney cost A$16 per person (minimum 10 people).

Sydney Architecture Walks (☎ 8239-2211; www.sydneyarchitecture.org; adult/concession A$20/15) Open your eyes to Sydney's architecture, both old and new. Strolls last two hours.

The Rocks Walking Tours (☎ 9247-6678; Shop K4, Kendall Lane, The Rocks) Guides are wonderfully enthusiastic, pointing out things you'd never have noticed. There are 90-minute tours thrice weekdays, twice on weekends; in January twice a day every day of week. Costs A$17.50

Harbour Cruises

There's a wide range of cruises on the harbour, from paddle-steamers to sailing yachts. Smart penny-pinchers just take the A$5.80 ferry to Manly and call it a night.

Excellent **Harboursights Cruises** (☎ 13 15 00; cruises adult from A$15), run by STA Travel, let you to take in the sights, sounds and smells of the harbour. Choose from the morning (one hour), afternoon (2½ hours) or evening (1½ hours) cruises. Tickets can be bought at ferry ticket offices in Circular Quay.

Also recommended (these run hourly and include a drink):

Magistic Cruises (☎ 8296 7222; www.magisticcruises.com.au; King St Wharf 5, Darling Harbour or Wharf 6, Circular Quay; cruises A$22)

Matilda Rocket Express (☎ 9264 7377; www.matilda.com.au; Aquarium Pier, Pier 26, Darling Harbour; cruises A$22)

FESTIVALS & EVENTS

Sydney has plenty of festivals and special goings-on year-round. Ask at the visitor centres to find out what's on when you're in town.

January

Sydney Festival This massive event floods the city with art in January, including free outdoor concerts in The Domain.

Australia Day (26 January) Australia's birthday is celebrated with barbecues, picnics and fireworks on the harbour.

February

Chinese New Year Celebrated in Chinatown with fireworks in late January or early February.

Tropfest This home-grown, short-film festival ensures its flicks are fresh with the inclusion of compulsory props (announced just before the competition so no one gets too much of a headstart). Big-name stars are often the judges (eg Keanu Reeves, Nicole Kidman, Russell Crowe).

Sydney Gay & Lesbian Mardi Gras (www.mardigras.org.au) The highlight of this world-famous festival, held in late February (sometimes early March) is the colourful, sequined parade along Oxford St. The parade culminates in a bacchanalian party at the Fox Entertainment Precinct in Moore Park.

March/April

Royal Easter Show This 12-day event is an agricultural show and funfair held at Homebush Bay (you can even pet the baby animals).

May

Sydney Writers' Festival Celebrates the literary in Sydney, with guest authors, talks and forums.

June

Sydney Film Festival (www.sydneyfilmfestival.org) A 14-day orgy of cinema held at the State Theatre and other cinemas.

Sydney Biennale An international art festival held in even-numbered years at the Art Gallery of NSW, the Powerhouse Museum and other venues.

August

City to Surf Run This 14km-long fun run takes place on the second Sunday in August and attracts a mighty 40,000 entrants who run from Hyde Park to Bondi Beach.

September

Carnivale There's plenty of colour at this multicultural arts festival held in early spring.

Royal Botanic Gardens Spring Festival Spring into spring, with concerts, colourful flower displays and plenty of pollen.

October

Rugby League Grand Final The two best teams left standing in the National Rugby League (NRL) meet to decide who's best.

Manly Jazz Festival Held over the Labour Day long weekend in early October and featuring lots of jazz performances (mostly free).

Kings Cross Carnival Taking place in late October or early November, this street fair includes a bed race.

GAY & LESBIAN SYDNEY

In Sydney, one could be forgiven for thinking that gay is the new straight. Gay and lesbian culture forms a vocal, dynamic, well-organised and colourful part of Sydney's social fabric. In 2002 Sydney played host to the best-dressed Olympics ever – the **Gay Games**.

February's colourful **Sydney Gay & Lesbian Mardi Gras** (see p61) is Australia's biggest annual tourist event, and the joyful-hedonism-meets-political-protest Oxford St parade is watched by over half-a-million people. The **Sleaze Ball** (a Mardi Gras fundraiser) takes place in October, with leather taking the place of Lycra. The parties for both events are held in Moore Park. Tickets are restricted to Mardi Gras members. Gay and lesbian international visitors wishing to attend the parties should contact the **Mardi Gras** (☎ 9568 8600; www.mardigras.org.au) office well in advance – tickets sell fast.

The **Taylor Sq** region of Oxford St is the hub of gay life in Sydney, although there are 'pockets' in suburbs such as **Paddington**, **Newtown**, **Alexandria** and **Leichhardt**. Gay beach life is focused on **Lady Bay** (nude) and **Tamarama** (also known as Glamarama). You may also want to check out **Redleaf Pool**, on New South Head Rd just past Double Bay, or **Andrew 'Boy' Charlton pool** (p60).

However, there's still a homophobic side to some 'true blue' Aussies, and violence against homosexuals isn't unheard of, particularly during school holidays. For the record, in New South Wales (NSW) the age of consent for homosexual sex is 16 for both men and women.

The free gay press includes the **Sydney Star Observer** and **Lesbians on the Loose** (www.lotl.com). These can be found in shops and cafés in the inner east and west. They all have excellent listings of gay and lesbian organisations, services and events. **Gay & Lesbian Tourism Australia** (GALTA; www.galta.com.au) can provide a wealth of information about gay and lesbian travel in Oz.

If you're keen to take part in Sydney's gay nightlife scene you can find plenty of listings in the local gay press. The following represent a mix of old favourites and newer club nights that cover both low-key and 'out there' bases.

Admission prices for nightclubs usually run from A$10, but bars let you in for free.

ARQ (Map pp48-50; ☎ 9380 8700; 16 Flinders St, Darlinghurst) This excellent, large club has a 24-hour licence and flattering lighting. Good DJs are often heard here, and it's a popular place to 'recover' on Sundays. Opens at 10pm on weekends.

Colombian (Map pp48-50; ☎ 9360 2151; cnr Oxford & Crown Sts, Darlinghurst; 🕑 10am-4am Sun-Thu, 9am-6am Fri & Sat) It's a good mix of spiffy décor, handlebar moustaches, good music, buff bods, plenty of space and quite a few women.

Midnight Shift (Map pp48-50; ☎ 9360 4319; 85 Oxford St, Darlinghurst; 🕑 noon-3am Mon-Thu, 1pm-6am Fri-Sun) The ground floor is quite pubby despite the disco balls, but upstairs it's a licence to booze and cruise with less conversation. We like the fact that you can find a range of men here.

Newtown Hotel (☎ 9517 1728; 174 King St, Newtown; 🕑 10am-midnight Mon-Sat, to 10pm Sun) In Sydney's other gay enclave, the Newtown does a roaring trade with gay folk who just want to go to the local and have a good time. The drag acts are pretty good and the staff sport interesting haircuts.

Oxford Hotel (Map pp48-50; ☎ 9331 3467; 134 Oxford St, Darlinghurst; 🕑 downstairs 24hr; upstairs 5pm-1am Mon-Wed, to 9am Thu-Sun) With an industrial hard-core theme going on at the ground-level bar and a more upmarket 'mixed' atmosphere in the cocktail bar upstairs, this place covers the bases on Taylor Sq.

Stonewall (Map pp48-50; ☎ 9360 1963; 175 Oxford St, Darlinghurst; 🕑 10.30am-4am Mon-Thu, 10.30am-7am Fri & Sat) The nightly shows and good vibes make this friendly spot a popular one, and the nice airy location also helps. The ceiling collapsed here, causing one DJ to proclaim 'I finally brought the house down!'

Looking for a gay-friendly hotel? Try **Park Lodge Hotel** (Map pp44-5; ☎ 1800 818 239, 9318 2393; www.parklodgehotel.com; 747 South Dowling St, Moore Park; d A$85-200;) where 20 comfortable rooms await at this intimate three-star Victorian hotel. The service is personal, the furnishings antique-ish and there's kitchen access. Disadvantages are that it's on a busy thoroughfare (although quiet inside) and a bit far from the centre. The cheapest rooms have unattached bathrooms; the most expensive come with kitchenette. Negotiate on price in slow seasons.

November

Sculpture by the Sea (www.sculpturebythesea.com) Held in mid-November, the Bondi-to-Bronte walk is transformed into an outdoor sculpture gallery.

December

Christmas Day (25 December) Thousands of backpackers descend on Bondi Beach on Christmas Day, much to the consternation of the civil authorities and the overworked lifesavers.

Boxing Day (26 December) Sydney Harbour is a sight to behold as hundreds of boats crowd its waters to farewell the yachts competing in the gruelling Sydney to Hobart Yacht Race.

New Year's Eve (31 December) The Rocks, Kings Cross and Bondi Beach are traditional gathering places for alcohol-sodden celebrations on New Year's Eve, although alcohol-free zones and a massive police presence are aimed at quelling the rowdier elements.

SLEEPING

Sydney has a huge variety of accommodation. You can grab some shut-eye at a cosy B&B, seedy motel, authentic Aussie pub or five-star luxury behemoth with harbour views. However, most budget travellers choose to stay in hostels, and – luckily – Sydney has its share of the heap.

The largest concentration of hostels is in Kings Cross, but many have also popped up at the beach magnets of Manly, Bondi and Coogee. Or, if you're looking for something more serene and away from the action, check out the pleasant suburbs of Kirribilli, Glebe or Newtown (all served by public transport).

Most hostels offer discounts if you have Youth Hostelling Australia (YHA) or VIP cards, the International Student Identity Card (ISIC), or if you're staying longer, such as a week or more. Prices are highest during the peak of summer (December and January), and often drop for the slow winter months (prices in this section reflect mostly summer tariffs). Some places have 'shoulder-season' prices (covering the period in between the low and high seasons).

For long-stay accommodation, peruse the 'flats to let' and 'share accommodation' ads in the *Sydney Morning Herald* on Wednesday and Saturday. Hostel notice boards are also good sources of information. Or try these websites: www.gumtree.com.au, www.domain.com.au, www.sleepingwiththeenemy.com and www.flatmates.com.au.

Keep in mind that some long-term lodgings require deposits (or bonds) and don't come furnished.

Hostels & Hotels

CITY CENTRE **Map pp48–50**

Sydney Central YHA (☎ 9281 9111; www.yha.com.au; 11 Rawson Pl; dm A$27-33, d A$85-95; Ⓟ ⊠ 💻 ♿) The Cadillac of Sydney hostels, this huge heritage-listed building offers 500-plus beds, artfully decorated spaces, a games room, nightly movies, all the services you'd expect (including a full-on travel agency) and even an ATM in the foyer. And don't forget the rooftop swimming pool! It's within spitting distance of Central Station, and is popular, so reserve in advance (although a sister hostel has recently been built close by at Railway Sq – the YHA Railway Square Hostel). Wheelchair accessible.

Wake Up! (☎ 9288 7888; www.wakeup.com.au; 509 Pitt St; dm A$28, d A$90-100, ⊠ 💻) Trendy backpackers flock to this large, modern and artsy hostel right near Central Station. Spiffy spaces await them (the seven floors each have a theme and colour), as do all the services they could ask for. There's a

SPLURGE!

Stellar Suites on Wentworth (Map pp48-50; ☎ 1800 025 575, 9264 9754; www.stellarsuites.com.au; 4 Wentworth Ave; r A$110-350; Ⓟ ⊠ 💻) Gorgeous, luxurious rooms heal well-travelled bones at this hip boutique hotel, nicely located right near Hyde Park. All 38 modern rooms have kitchenette, telephone, safe and Internet connection, and a three-bedroom apartment is available. Parking and breakfast cost extra.

Bed & Breakfast Sydney Harbour (Map pp48-50; ☎ 9247 1130; www.bedandbreakfastsydney.com; 140-142 Cumberland St, The Rocks; s A$140-220, d A$155-260; ⊠) When you're halfway through your trip and sorely missing home, shell out a few bucks and treat yourself to some homey comfort. Each of the nine rooms in these twin heritage buildings is charmingly unique, and all come with soft sheets, a full hot breakfast and relaxing moments in the leafy courtyard. The Rocks location is great, and there's a pleasant kitchen. Note that a few rooms share bathrooms.

sunny café on the main floor and gloomy restaurant-bar downstairs.

Wanderers on Kent (☎ 1800 424 444, 9267 7718; 477 Kent St; dm A$24-33; d A$85;) This popular hostel is in a great central location between the Sydney Town Hall and Darling Harbour. Facilities and services are good, and there's a solarium, for that sun-damaged look. Wheelchair accessible.

Y on the Park (☎ 9264 2451; www.ywca-sydney.com.au; 5-11 Wentworth Ave; s A$75-115, d & tw A$100-135;) This YWCA hotel (men welcome) is ideally located right near Hyde Park, with the city centre and Oxford St a short walk away. Rooms are clean and modern, with deluxe versions sporting safes. Four-bed dorms (no bunks!) cost A$33 per person. Breakfast included.

Sydney Backpackers (☎ 1800 887 766, 9267 7772; www.sydneybackpackers.com; 7 Wilmot St; dm A$30, d A$85;) The best thing about this hostel is its location – right in the city centre. Every dorm has its own bathroom, doubles come with fridge and TV and there's a nice rooftop terrace for everyone. Good security.

KINGS CROSS

Highfield Private Hotel (Map p55; ☎ 9326 9539; www.highfieldhotel.com; 166 Victoria St; s/d A$55/70) A clean and welcoming hotel owned by a Swedish family (therefore a magnet for Swedish travellers), this well-run place offers good security, simple rooms (shared bathrooms), 24-hour access and a spot-on location. Small dorms cost A$25 per head.

Original Backpackers (Map p55; ☎ 1800 807 130, 9356 3232; www.originalbackpackers.com.au; 160-162 Victoria St; dm/s/d A$23/50/65;) Smack dab in the centre of Kings Cross and set in a wonderful historic mansion, this long-running hostel has 176 beds, friendly staff and great outdoor spaces. It's open 24 hours, all rooms have fridges and there's free pick-up from the airport.

Pink House Backpackers (Map p55; ☎ 1800 806 385, 9358 1689; www.pinkhouse.com.au; 6-8 Barncleuth Sq; dm A$22-26, d A$55-65,) Yes, it's pink, but it's also a beautiful historic mansion with charming personality and some fine patios. There's a great atmosphere and the location is pretty darn good, which makes this a popular place.

Eva's Backpackers (Map p55; ☎ 9358 2185; www.evasbackpackers.com.au; 6-8 Orwell St; dm A$24, d & tw A$60;) A perennial favourite with many travellers, this well-managed hostel has colourful halls, good small dorms and a pretty rooftop with great views. Doubles share bathrooms; breakfast is included. It's a popular place, so book ahead.

Maisonette Hotel (Map p55; ☎ 9357 3878; maisonettehotel@bigpond.com; 31 Challis Ave; s/d A$60/95) Not a bad deal for this clean, friendly hotel, and the price drops a bit if you stay longer than a night. The small, bright rooms come with kitchenette and TV, although the cheapest singles share bathrooms.

O'Malley's Hotel (Map p55; ☎ 9357 2211; www.omalleyshotel.com.au; 228 William St; s & d A$70, t A$90;) This friendly Irish pub comes attached to traditionally decorated, well-furnished rooms with fridge and TV. It's a great deal, and surprisingly quiet given its location, although there is a lot of Irish music played here (take heed, if you're allergic to jigs). A larger apartment is also available (A$99).

Globe Backpackers (Map p55; ☎ 1800 806 384; www.globebackpackers.com; 40 Darlinghurst Rd; dm A$20-22, d A$60;) In the heart of Kings Cross is this slightly funky hostel with good chill-out spaces and a small veranda. It's not the spiffiest but does have interesting murals. Call ahead, as reception is open limited hours. Free breakfast and airport pick-up.

Kanga House (Map p55; ☎ 1800 452 642, 9357 7897; www.kangahouse.com.au; 141 Victoria St; dm A$18-23, d A$55;) If you stay here, be sure to get a room out the back with views of the Opera House and Harbour Bridge. Otherwise, it's your average hostel with decent facilities and services. All rooms share baths; breakfast is included.

SPLURGE!

Victoria Court Hotel (Map p55; ☎ 9357 3200; www.victoriacourt.com.au; 122 Victoria St; d A$135-165; P) Looking for a quiet, comfortable room with a lovely Victorian air? How about some old-fashioned service to go along? The search is over at this quaint boutique hotel, where plush flowery-decorated beds comfort you at night, while in the morning a breakfast buffet is served in the indoor glass-covered patio. Sweet, but still too dear for your wallet? Try for the one room with an unattached but private bathroom (A$95).

DARLINGHURST AREA

Royal Sovereign Hotel (Map pp48-50; ☎ 9331 3672; royalsov@solotel.com.au; cnr Liverpool St & Darlinghurst Rd; d from A$80-90, ❄) Perched above one of Sydney's favourite drinking dens, these small but sharply decorated rooms all come with TV and clean shared bathrooms. Upper rooms are quieter but more expensive, and come with fridge and coffeepot.

Hotel Altamont (Map p55; ☎ 1800 991 110, 9360 6000; www.altamont.com.au; 207 Darlinghurst Rd; d A$115-130; ❄) Flashy in a rustic sort of way, this modern boutique hotel offers immaculate rooms and a smart, intimate foyer strewn with leather chairs. There's a great terrace, and even dorm rooms are available! Continental breakfast is included (dorms pay A$2 extra). A great deal, considering the surroundings, services and location (near Kings Cross). Reception is open 8am to 8pm.

Woodduck Inn (Map p55; ☎ 1800 110 025; www.woodduckinn.com.au; 49 William St; dm A$20-22, d A$60) The location's great and the rooftop views are awesome (watch the fruit bats commute at dusk). Dorms are small and there are only two doubles, but you get a free beer at check-in. Breakfast included, airport pick-up and beach shuttle.

Australian Backpackers (Map pp48-50; ☎ 1800 350 211; www.australianbackpackers.com.au; 132 Bourke St; dm A$20, d A$60) It ain't eye candy and the facilities are nothing to write to mum about, but that's not why you're here – you come here if you want work. Nick, the manager, pretty much guarantees you some kind of job. And the only rules are no stealing or fighting, so you get the casual picture. Free breakfast, airport pick-up and surf lessons.

BALMAIN

Balmain Lodge (Map pp44-5; ☎ 9810 3700; www.balmainlodge.com.au; 415 Darling St; s/d A$65/80; P) Located on Balmain's backbone, Darling St, this place offers capable management and clean, no-frills rooms with kitchenettes and patios. Every two rooms share a bathroom. It's popular with long-term tenants, so call ahead (reception is open 8am to 6pm Monday to Friday). Wheelchair access.

BONDI

Map p57

Bondi Beachouse YHA (☎ 9365 2088; www.bondibeachouse.com.au; 63 Fletcher St; dm A$27, s/d from A$60/70; ❄ 💻) Bondi's best hostel, offering clean rooms (some boasting water views) and an unsurpassable rooftop terrace with spa. Cheap meals, free sporting-equipment use and nightly activities also on tap. Catch bus No 380 from the city or Bondi Junction and alight at the Fletcher St stop.

Bondi Beach Homestay (☎ 9300 0800; www.bondibeachhomestay.com.au; 10 Forest Knoll Ave; s/d A$80/135; P 💻) In a charmingly decorated home with friendly owners, this is one of Bondi's hidden gems. Immaculate bathrooms are shared among the four homey rooms, and comfortable common areas include a lounge and sunny veranda. Breakfast included; kitchen access.

Indy's Backpackers (☎ 8300 8802; www.indysbackpackers.com.au; 35a Hall St; dm A$28; 💻) With a relaxed, easy-going vibe and definite surfing slant, this hostel is a socially gregarious option. Facilities are well used (with a downright grungy edge), but a table-tennis table spices things up in patio area. Free sporting-equipment use, nightly activities.

Noah's Backpackers (☎ 1800 226 662; www.noahsbondibeach.com; 2 Campbell Pde; dm A$22-25, d A$55-60; 💻) It's large, basic and somewhat impersonal, and the kitchen's not too clean. The huge rooftop terrace, however, has great beach views – and there's a pool table in the lounge. Doubles sport fridges and TVs.

COOGEE

Coogee Beachside Accommodation (☎ 9315 8511; www.sydneybeachside.com.au; 178 Coogee Bay Rd; d A$55-95) A good option for budget travellers seeking simple but clean rooms with fridge, TV and shared bathrooms. In a converted house with kitchen facilities.

Wizard of Oz Backpackers (☎ 9315 7876; www.wizardofoz.com.au; 172 Coogee Bay Rd; dm A$27) Just a few blocks from the hot beach sands, this laid-back place is run by the same people as Coogee Beachside Accommodation (free airport pick-up available for both, and office hours are also similar – about 8am to noon and from 5pm to 8pm).

Grand Pacific Private Hotel (☎ 9665 6301; 136a Beach St; s/d A$35/45) Curt management rules at this very *un*-grand, gritty and somewhat smelly joint. Yet that scruffy charm and those dirt-cheap prices keep the hordes coming, so reserve ahead – and try to get a room with a balcony! All rooms share bathrooms and come with TV and fridge. Kitchen available.

NORTH SHORE

Glenferrie Lodge (Map pp44-5; ☎ 9955 1685; www.glenferrielodge.com; 12a Carabella St, Kirribilli; s A$50-55, d & tw A$85-95; 💻) In a large, beautiful old house with a can't-miss sculpture out the front, this place's best feature is the wonderfully grassy back garden. Rooms come with fridge, and shared bathrooms are clean (dorm beds are also available at A$35). Accessible from Milsons Point train station or Kirribilli wharf by ferry.

Sydney Beachhouse YHA (☎ 9981 1177; www.sydneybeachouse.com.au; 4 Collaroy St, Collaroy; dm A$20-26, d & tw A$65) This clean, airy hostel comes with great outdoor spaces, including a pool! It's also wheelchair friendly and lies close to some of Sydney's best beaches. To get here, catch bus No L90 or L88 from Railway Sq, Town Hall or Wynyard train stations. From Manly, take bus Nos 155 or 156.

MANLY — Map p59

Manly Bungalow (☎ 9977 5494; www.manlybungalow.com; 64 Pittwater Rd; d A$75, tr A$90) Just a handful of rooms are available for those who seek quiet, secure and pleasant rooms with a small, serene garden nearby. All share bathrooms and come with kitchenette and TV. Book ahead; office hours are limited.

Manly Cottage Inn (☎ 9976 0297; www.hostelworld.com; 25 Pittwater Rd; dm A$25; Ⓟ) Located well inland on busy Pittwater Rd, this small hostel is nonetheless fairly intimate and relatively pleasant, with a small patio out the front. One double is available (A$75).

Boardrider Backpacker (☎ 9977 6077; www.boardrider.com.au; Rear 63, The Corso; dm A$28, d A$75-85; 💻) Right in the middle of The Corso, Manly's happenin' pedestrian mall, this hostel caters to the young and surfing. It has a large TV room and rents water-sport equipment. The rooftop patio's pretty cool, and there's a balcony from where you can check out the waves.

> **SPLURGE!**
>
> **Periwinkle Guest House** (Map p59; ☎ 9977 4668; www.periwinkle.citysearch.com.au; 18-19 East Esplanade, Manly; s A$100-135, d A$130-185; Ⓟ) This beautifully restored Victorian house has 18 pleasant and well-appointed rooms, all with fridges and TVs (and some with stunning water views). There's a family atmosphere and a relaxing shady courtyard. Cook up dinner in the nifty kitchen, but remember that a light breakfast is on the house.

Manly Astra Backpackers (☎/fax 9977 2092; 68 Pittwater Rd; d A$60) On offer here are 12 good, no-nonsense rooms with shared bathrooms and kitchen access. There's a decent communal feel and free use of body boards. Call ahead, as reception is only open 9am to noon and 6pm to 7pm.

GLEBE — Map pp44–5

Wattle House (☎ 9552 4997; www.wattlehouse.com.au; 44 Hereford St; dm A$27, d A$85; ⊠) Here's the homiest, most intimate hostel you could hope for – all wrapped up in a lovely Victorian house accommodating just 26 people. It's also tidy, friendly, efficient and comes with a sweet little garden. Not your party place, so expect some quiet – and be sure to call ahead.

Glebe Point YHA (☎ 9692 8418; www.yha.com.au; 262-264 Glebe Point Rd; dm A$24-28, d A$70; 💻) Well run and pleasant, this large, friendly hostel offers good facilities and simple but clean rooms with sinks. There's a covered rooftop area with picnic tables and a barbecue.

Glebe Village (☎ 1800 801 983; www.bakpakgroup.com/glebevillage; 256 Glebe Point Rd; dm A$26-28, d A$75; 💻) Looking for a party hostel? This is probably the place to come. Hang out in the leafy front patio with good music playing, and try not to stress the laid-back staff. Rooms are quirky, breakfast is included and reception's open from 7.30am to 8.30pm.

NEWTOWN

Billabong Gardens (☎ 1800 806 419, 9550 3236; www.billabonggardens.com.au; 5-11 Egan St; dm A$20-23, s A$50, d A$70-90; 💻) This long-standing, brick-and-tile motel/hostel is clean and quiet and has some pleasant common spaces. There's a kitchen, cosy TV room and tiny pool, and it's close to hoppin' King St. From Railway Sq catch bus No 422, 423, 426 or 428 up King St and get off at Missenden Rd. By train, go to Newtown Station and turn right; Egan St is four blocks up on the left.

TEMPE (NEAR AIRPORT)

Old Rectory (☎ 8504 2615; http://oldrectory.idx.com.au; 2 Samuel St; s A$50-65, d A$60-80; ⊠ 💻) Great if you need to be within a 10-minute drive of the airport. A helpful couple manages nine basic, comfortable rooms (most with shared bathrooms) in this modest yet historic Tempe house. There's a communal kitchen and grassy lawn. It's on a very busy street, so traffic (both ground vehicles and airplanes) is noisy at times. Breakfast and pick-up from the airport included.

Camping

Sydney's caravan parks, most of which also have sites for tents, are a fair way out of town. The following are up to 26km from the city centre. Note that the peak seasons (like Christmas) see rates rise.

Lane Cove River Tourist Park (☎ 9888 9133; www.lanecoverivertouristpark.com.au; Plassey Rd, North Ryde; camp sites per 2 people A$26, caravan sites A$26-28, cabins A$100-150) This cheery place lies 14km north of the city and has good facilities (including over 150 caravan sites). You can chill out in the pool when temperatures swelter.

Sydney Lakeside Holiday Park (☎ 9913 7845; www.sydneylakeside.com.au; Lake Park Rd, Narrabeen; camp & caravan sites per 2 people A$28-33, cabins & villas A$130-185) Located 26km north of Sydney, this nifty place occupies prime real estate around the northern beaches. If roughing it doesn't appeal, there are good cabins and lakeside 'villas'.

Grand Pines Tourist Park (☎ 9529 7329; www.thegrandpines.com.au; 289 The Grand Pde, Sans Souci; camp & caravan sites per 2 people A$39-45, cabins A$70-154) This friendly, good-quality caravan park is 17km south of Sydney on beautiful Botany Bay. Take your pick from sites, vans and cabins. High standards are maintained, and feedback is positive.

EATING

With great local produce, innovative chefs and BYO (bring your own alcohol) licensing laws, it's no surprise that eating out is one of the great delights of a visit to Sydney.

City Centre — Map pp48–50

There's no shortage of places for a snack or meal in the city, especially on weekdays (when most restaurants cater to the business crowds).

Wagamama (☎ 9252 9593; cnr Bridge & Loftus Sts, City; mains A$11-18.50; ⏲ lunch & dinner) Long, no-nonsense picnic tables and minimalist décor help you concentrate on slurping the delicious ramen and udon. There are also curry and rice dishes. This popular branch restaurant lets you do it all in Japanese fast-food style.

SPLURGE!

Rockpool (Map pp48-50; ☎ 9252 1888; 107 George St, The Rocks; mains A$54-60; ⏲ dinner Tue-Sat) It's one of the best eateries in Sydney, with good reason. Chef Neil Perry churns out beautiful (in all senses) dishes, and the seafood especially shines. Go for the southern rock lobster tagine with roast apricots and couscous for two, while enjoying the shiny, modern atmosphere – you'll thank us later.

Bodhi (☎ 9360 2523; College St, Phillip Park, City; yum cha A$4-9; ⏲ lunch Mon, lunch & dinner Tue-Sun) Vegans need look no further than this flashy spot, located underneath the plaza in front of the cathedral. Lunch means tasty yum cha, although the outdoor seating can be windy. There's another (smaller) branch at Central Station.

Mint Café (☎ 9233 3337; 10 Macquarie St, City; mains A$4.50-16; ⏲ breakfast & lunch) It's located in Sydney's old mint, but your wallet won't feel it. Plop down on the pleasant balcony and enjoy the leek and pumpkin frittata (A$12) or tandoori lamb (A$13). Makes a good break if you're sightseeing around here.

Salad Works (☎ 9223 0677; 17 Hunter St, City; salads from A$8; ⏲ breakfast & lunch Mon-Fri) This one's for you, salad-lovers – choose from Greek, chicken or Caesar, or make your own. But don't expect tables at this mostly takeaway joint, although there are seven stools against the wall. Breakfast pastries are also available.

Sailor's Thai (☎ 9251 2466; 106 George St, The Rocks; mains A$17-26; ⏲ lunch & dinner Mon-Sat) Sit at the long, communal stainless steel table and feast on some of the best Thai food this side of Bangkok. A power crowd of arts bureaucrats and politicians mingles with the young and lively, all to good effect. Look for it right next to the tourist office.

Uchi Lounge (☎ 9261 3524; 15 Brisbane St, Surry Hills; mains A$14-17; ⏲ dinner) Dress up creatively – your server certainly will, and might be sporting a colourful hairstyle to boot. While the décor looks like a final-year art school exhibition, the blissful Japanese food takes centre stage. And the groovy ground-floor bar is the perfect place to wait for your no-reservations table.

Chinatown Map pp48–50

Some of Sydney's cheapest (and tastiest) food can be found in bustling Chinatown.

Pho Pasteur (☎ 9212 5622; 709 George St; mains A$7.50-9; ⏰ lunch & dinner) Super-spartan, super-quick and super-crowded at lunch time. And some of the best *pho* (Vietnamese beef noodle soup) around.

BBQ King (☎ 9267 2586; 18-20 Goulburn St; mains A$12-24; ⏰ lunch & dinner) Vegetarians should give this place a wide berth, 'cause roast duck and barbecued pork are the main attractions. It's an old-school Chinese eatery, with bustling service, generous pots of tea and a lack of fancy décor. Open till 2am.

Marigold Citymark (☎ 9281 3388; Levels 4 & 5, 683-689 George St, Haymarket; yum cha A$8; ⏰ lunch & dinner) The mostly Asian clientele is always a good sign at this cavernous yum cha place. There's also an extensive menu of other dishes, including vegetarian.

Emperor's Garden BBQ & Noodles (☎ 9281 9899; 213-215 Thomas St; mains A$6-12; ⏰ lunch & dinner) Busy eatery specialising in meat and poultry dishes. The little takeaway section out the front has many goodies, including some crimson-hued offerings hanging in the window.

FILLING UP AT A FOOD COURT

One quick, easy and cheap way to stop your tummy rumbling as you pound the pavements of Darling Harbour and Chinatown is the ubiquitous food court. Packed with small kitchens offering a variety of Asian dishes, they're worth dipping your chopsticks into – *if* you can find a table during lunch time! Meals cost around A$7 to A$8, and the stalls are open until about 9pm daily.

Harbour Plaza Eating World (Map pp48-50; cnr Dixon & Goulburn Sts, Chinatown) Being renovated at the time of research, so will be spiffy-new when you get here.

Market City Shopping Centre (Map pp48-50; ☎ 9212 1388; 9-13 Hay St, Chinatown) Way up on the top floor, with Paddy's Market and outlet stores underneath.

Sussex Centre (Map pp48-50; 401 Sussex St, Chinatown) On the top floor, but not as big as Market City.

Dixon House Food Court (Map pp48-50; cnr Little Hay & Dixon Sts, Chinatown) Down in the basement, and a bit claustrophobic.

Darling Harbour Map pp48–50

The areas around Darling Harbour have dining options as far as the eye can see – some hit, many miss. Most have nice views, although they don't usually come cheap.

Blackbird Café (☎ 9283 7385; Level 2, Sussex St, Cockle Bay Wharf; mains A$6-17; ⏰ breakfast, lunch & dinner) A good budget option in this area, with typical café fare (such as pizza, pasta and salad) on tap. The shady outdoor balcony is pleasant, as are the harbour views. Open late.

Chinta Ria...Temple of Love (☎ 9264 3211; Level 2, Cockle Bay Wharf, 201 Sussex St; mains A$15-26; ⏰ lunch & dinner) It ain't particularly cheap Malaysian food but it sure is fun. The enormous Buddha greets you as you enter, while the spicy chicken laksa (A$15) is worth getting excited about. Jazzy music, colourful décor, clanging dishes and efficient service abound.

Darlinghurst & Paddington

Victoria St sports the most eateries in Darlinghurst. There's a second cluster of (mostly Italian) restaurants on Stanley St, just south of William St between Crown and Riley Sts.

Fu Manchu (Map pp48-50; ☎ 9360 9424; 249 Victoria St, Darlinghurst; mains A$9-20; ⏰ dinner Tue-Sun) The original Fu, with some of the best Asian eating in Darlinghurst. The vibe is 21st-century Hong Kong slick chic, with chopsticks and elbows getting a thorough workout (it's a narrow space). Grab some steamed barbecue pork or vegetarian buns (A$6).

Bill & Toni's (Map pp48-50; ☎ 9360 4702; 74 Stanley St, Darlinghurst; mains A$13) Folks come here because it's a tradition for basic Italian cuisine, a stalwart of the cheap and cheerful and, in our opinion, a national treasure. The service is lightning-fast, you get your orange cordial for free and everyone leaves with a smile. The café downstairs has good coffee.

Burgerman (Map pp48-50; ☎ 9361 0268; 116 Surrey St, Darlinghurst; mains A$7-11; ⏰ lunch & dinner) Does a lamb fillet with eggplant, garlic and basil mayo sound good? How about a beetroot and horseradish mayo burger? These and other tasty treats are cooked up in a small, open space with simple yet smart décor. Grab a pavement table and enjoy.

Betty's Soup Kitchen (Map pp48-50; ☎ 9360 9698; 84 Oxford St, Darlinghurst; mains A$7-12; ⏰ lunch & dinner) Basic comfort food, quick and easy. Soups, salad bar, pasta, bangers and mash, and lamb stew – no surprises, no disappointments. All cheap.

Foodgame (Map pp48-50; ☎ 9380 8585; 185 Campbell St, Darlinghurst; mains A$7-15; ⌚ lunch & dinner) The steel deli counters work well with the plush lounge area, communal table and pavement seating. Wherever you sit, you'll enjoy the salads (Thai to Caesar), burgers (satay to steak) and pasta (ravioli to fettuccini). And don't even think about leaving without dessert (lemon tart, sticky date pudding, lime-infused coconut pannacotta…).

And the Dish Ran Away With the Spoon (Map pp44-5; ☎ 9361 6131; 226 Glenmore Rd, Paddington; mains A$5-10; ⌚ breakfast, lunch & dinner) Local yuppies cram this charming little Paddington deli to lunch on great pasta and burgers, and it's a primo spot to pick up picnic fixings or takeaway lunches and dinners. Try the low-fat 'skinny burger' (A$7.20) – it tastes too good to be true.

Bill's (Map pp48-50; ☎ 9360 9631; 433 Liverpool St, Darlinghurst; mains A$17-23; ⌚ breakfast & lunch) Beautifully presented food. Gleaming open kitchen. Fresh flowers and fashion 'zines. Large communal table for conversations about your sweet corn frittata with bacon (A$18.50) and his seared Atlantic salmon (A$22.50). Unbearable weekend brunch crowds. No sign outside. Bill Granger.

Surry Hills — Map pp44–5

Crown St is the main thoroughfare through Surry Hills, but it's a long street and the restaurants appear in fits and starts. It's worth a wander along, though, as it also has worthwhile shops.

Il Baretto (☎ 9361 6163; 496 Bourke St; mains A$10-18; ⌚ breakfast, lunch & dinner Tue-Sat, breakfast & lunch Sun) Packed to the rafters and dishing up some of the most heavenly pasta in Sydney. It's tiny and chaotic, but once you've put your name down for a table, wait patiently at the pub across the road – staff will come to get you. Try the *spaghetti alle vongole* (spaghetti with clams; A$18).

Red Lantern (☎ 9698 4355; 545 Crown St; mains A$12-20; ⌚ lunch Tue-Sun, dinner daily) Before anything else, call to make reservations – and ask for a front patio table. This hot new Vietnamese joint serves up some great rice-paper shrimp rolls (A$9) and pork cutlets (A$16), all the while softly glowing in atmospheric lighting.

Mohr Fish (☎ 9318 1326; 202 Devonshire St; mains A$7-18; ⌚ lunch & dinner) Don't expect a fancy eatery – this place takes up a space the size of your living room. It's very casual and has only a short, simple menu of fried seafood – can you say 'fish and chips' (A$7.50)? Expect the locals to join you at the crowded counter.

> **SPLURGE!**
>
> **Aqua Dining** (Map pp44-5; ☎ 9964 9998; cnr Paul & Northcliff Sts, Milsons Point; lunch A$33-36, dinner A$41-42; ⌚ lunch Sun-Fri, dinner daily) The fit-out here was accomplished by Soma design, with muted mushroom tones and clean lines. However, the design never really competes with the view of the Opera House and Harbour Bridge, let alone the Olympic swimming pool with bathers underneath. Expect sterling service and supreme food (the hickory-smoked Yamba prawns are especially good) – all worth the hike out to the North Shore. Reservations are a good idea.

There are half-a-dozen nondescript but good-value Lebanese eateries around the corner of Cleveland and Elizabeth Sts, at the southern end of Surry Hills, where most dishes cost between A$5 and A$10. Also, many cheap Indian and Turkish places spice up Cleveland St between Crown and Bourke Sts.

Maya da Dhaba (☎ 8399 3785; 431 Cleveland St; mains A$8-15; ⌚ dinner) Better-than-average Indian fare is served in natty surroundings at this popular restaurant. The *andrakhi* lamb chops (grilled lamb chops; A$14.50) arrive sizzling and juicy, while the chicken *makhani* (butter chicken; A$13) is also quite tasty, but there are plenty of vegetarian choices as well.

Kings Cross & Around — Map p55

The Cross has a good mixture of tiny cafés, swanky eateries and fast-food joints serving greasy fare designed mainly to soak up beer.

Fratelli Paradiso (☎ 9357 1744; 12 Challis Ave, Potts Point; mains A$12-28; ⌚ breakfast, lunch & dinner Mon-Fri, breakfast & lunch Sat & Sun) It's worth getting out of bed in the morning for the breakfast here. The eggs are magnificent, the rice pudding superb, the coffee out of this world. Service is friendly, sometimes cheeky, and always brisk – just like in Italy.

Delectica (☎ 9380 1390; 130 Victoria St, Potts Point; mains A$8-14; ⌚ breakfast & lunch) This pleasant café is modern, airy and comes with charming service. You might be amid backpacker chaos, but you won't really care – the food's that tasty.

Tuk Tuk (☎ 9380 4500; 28 Bayswater Rd; mains A$12-18; lunch Mon-Fri, dinner daily) After meeting that backpacker of your dreams, bring 'em here for a romantic wooing session. It's a beautifully airy and classy atmosphere at reasonable prices, and the Thai food's not bad. Other branches around the city.

Matchbox (☎ 9326 9860; 197 Victoria St; mains A$10-12; breakfast & lunch) Tiny as a matchbox indeed – there are just four small pavement tables and a wrap-around counter. And this trendy breakfast place (where brekky is served all day) gets packed on weekends, so come early.

Glebe

Map pp44–5

Glebe Point Rd was Sydney's original 'eat street', but what it lacks in cutting-edge dining experiences it has in laid-back, unpretentious atmosphere and good-value food.

Tanjore (☎ 9660 6332; 34 Glebe Point Rd; mains A$8-16; dinner Sat-Wed) A pioneer of South Indian food in Australia, Tanjore attracts a range of locals, Indian-food lovers and celebrities. Everything is cooked to order and the tandoori dishes are so good you'll need to make reservations.

Iku Wholefoods (☎ 9692 8720; 25a Glebe Point Rd; mains A$3-9; lunch & dinner) Here's one of the best vegan places in town, offering cheap and healthy takeaway (mostly organic) treats. Point, order, pay – and go picnic at nearby Victoria Park. Closes relatively early on weekends (11am to 8pm Saturday, noon to 7.30pm Sunday).

Badde Manors (☎ 9660 3797; 37 Glebe Point Rd; mains A$7-13; breakfast, lunch & dinner) This long-established corner haunt is especially popular on market day. It can be pretty hectic here, so just remember it's called Badde Manors for a reason. The cakes and tarts are excellent and best enjoyed at a pavement table.

Newtown

A swag of funky cafés and restaurants line King St offering an interesting introduction to the suburb's community life. Many places cater to university students.

Green Gourmet (☎ 9519 5330; 115 King St; mains A$13-15; lunch & dinner) Spotlessly clean and kind to animals, Green Gourmet offers great Chinese-Malaysian vegetarian grub. On weekends, grab a few morsels of yum cha and wash it all down with one of the excellent teas on offer. There's a buffet lunch on weekdays.

Bacigalupo (☎ 9565 5238; 284 King St; mains A$9-15; breakfast, lunch & dinner) If traipsing along King St has caused your tummy to rumble, Bacigalupo's mammoth blackboard full of hearty breakfast, pasta and salad dishes will ease the pain. It's a cheery, high-ceilinged place, with egg-yolk yellow walls and lots of loud conversation.

Old Fish Shop Café (☎ 9519 4295; 239a King St; mains A$9-10; breakfast, lunch & dinner) Yep, it used to be a fish shop. Now it's a tiny corner café with garlic hanging from above, paint peeling off the walls, open windows to catch King St's fumes and simple, tasty sandwiches and pizzas. Closes at 7pm.

Thai Pothong (☎ 9550 6277; 294 King St; mains A$7-20; lunch Tue-Sun, dinner daily) Voted 'Best Thai' more than once by those who should know, this popular restaurant serves up an interesting and affordable range of veggie dishes, seafood, curries and salads. What more can you ask for?

Leichhardt

You can still get a cheap spaghetti in Norton St, but the classic bistros are now rubbing shoulders with flashy restaurants, plus a few Greek, Chinese and Thai interlopers.

Bar Italia (☎ 9560 9981; 169-171 Norton St; mains A$10-17; breakfast, lunch & dinner) This enormously popular restaurant, café and gelataria offers pasta, salads, focaccia and – for those who can take it – plenty of veal. The pavement tables, good honest food and famous gelato (a must-have accessory for any Norton St stroll) attracts couples and families alike.

Grind (☎ 9568 5535; 151 Norton St; mains A$9-15; breakfast & lunch) Try the delicious pasta dishes or go for the focaccia sandwiches (how does roast beef, caramelised onions, arugula and tomato chutney sound?). Either way you'll be golden, and you can even smoke afterwards if you're on the balcony above.

Bondi

Map p57

The tourist-trap greasy spoons are still in plentiful supply along Campbell Pde between Hall St and Beach Rd, but on other streets they're being squeezed out by fancy bistros and a slew of serious foodie joints. You'll generally have to forego a table with sea view

SPLURGE!

Bondi Icebergs (Map p57; ☎ 9365 9000; www.idrb.com; 1 Notts Ave; mains A$32-44; 🕑 lunch Tue-Sun, dinner Tue-Sat) So damn hot we get scorch marks just walking past this place, this supremely upmarket restaurant (and bar – see p73) epitomises the flash of Sydney's best restaurants. Not only are the food and wine fantastic (check out the changing menus on its website), but the views over Bondi come unmatched. Reservations, needless to say, are crucial (as is decent dress).

if you're seriously pinching pennies, but a bag of takeaway and a patch of sand can work just as well.

Brown Sugar (☎ 9365 6262; 100 Brighton Blvd; mains A$8-14; 🕑 breakfast & lunch) This cramped space churns out brekky to the smooth set on weekends – and one bite of its blackstone eggs (A$13) will tell you why. Weekdays are much less frantic, but the lunch dishes and salads taste just as good.

Green's Café (☎ 9130 6181; 140 Glenayr Ave; mains A$8-14; 🕑 breakfast & lunch Wed-Mon) A green-hued, homey, laid-back experience awaits those seeking tasty and healthy salads, sandwiches and scrambles. The teas are special, too. (It's not vegetarian only, despite the name.)

Luv in a Cup (106 Glenayr Ave; mains A$8-13; 🕑 breakfast & lunch) As cute and cramped as a bug's ear, this mostly breakfast joint cooks up some fantastic 'love eggs' (A$12) and 'love waffles' (A$7.50). The lunch menu is limited, but breakfast is served until 4pm.

Gelbison (☎ 9130 4042; 10 Lamrock Ave; mains A$10-19; 🕑 dinner) An old favourite with many beach bums, film-industry types (including Mel Gibson) and assorted gluttons looking for great Italian staples. It never seems to change, and in Bondi that's a rare thing.

House of Soy (☎ 9300 0033; 294b Campbell Pde; mains A$5-14; 🕑 lunch & dinner Wed-Mon; closes 6pm Sat) Five words: soy-based organic vegan pies.

Coogee

There is a number of cheap takeaways on Coogee Bay Rd – but you're better off on the side-street cafés, which have healthier food, sunnier interiors and outdoor tables.

A Fish Called Coogee (☎ 9664 7700; 229 Coogee Bay Rd; mains A$4.50-8; 🕑 lunch & dinner) This busy little fishmonger sells fresh seafood cooked many different ways. Grab some great takeaway fish and chips (A$8) and sit on the beach, 'cause you may not snag one of those gleaming pavement tables.

Rice (☎ 1300 887 423; 100 Beach St; mains A$11-17; 🕑 dinner) Stunning in its dark colour scheme, this fancy noodle joint serves up the goods to your specifications. Curries, salads, stir-fries and meat dishes are also available. It's up the hill from the beach, which puts it nicely away from the beach crowds.

Erciyes 2 (☎ 9664 1913; 240 Coogee Bay Rd; mains A$8-13; 🕑 café lunch & dinner, restaurant dinner) The café up the front serves quick pizza, pies and kebabs, while the restaurant out the back serves similar fare but with belly dancing on top (Friday and Saturday only).

Manly

Map p59

The ocean end of The Corso (Manly's pedestrian mall) is jam-packed with takeaway places and outside tables. Manly Wharf and South Steyne have plenty of airy eateries that catch the sea breeze and bustle on sunny weekends.

Manly Fish Market (☎ 9976 3777; Shop 1, Wentworth St; mains A$8-12; 🕑 breakfast, lunch & dinner) A small fish shop with just two tables, although with the beach so near most folks grab the delicious fish and chips bag and head to the water.

Blue Water Café (☎ 9976 2051; 28 South Steyne; mains A$14-25; 🕑 breakfast, lunch & dinner) The huge portions are a major attraction at this bustling, popular beach café. The whopping lemon chicken burger (A$14) will really satisfy a post-surf hunger, although all the boards on the wall will remind you to get back into the foam.

BarKing Frog (☎ 9977 6307; 48 North Steyne; lunch A$12-18, dinner A$21-28; 🕑 breakfast, lunch & dinner) This is an attractive place, great for watching the beach world go by. The healthy menu does good lunch-time fare (think pasta and burgers), while in the evenings a more Mod Oz list takes over. Sunday night is popular.

Beanrush (☎ 9977 2236; 7 Whistler St; mains A$2.20-9.50; 🕑 breakfast & lunch Mon-Sat) A small hole-in-the-wall café with truly great coffee and sweet staff. Definitely worth a visit if your engine needs revving. The snacks are mighty fine, too. Closes at 5.30pm.

DRINKING

Bars & Pubs

There are *plenty* of drinking holes everywhere in Sydney. Generally, big nights on the turps take place in The Rocks and around Kings Cross – where you'll hear and smell the action pretty quickly. Attractive, more low-key places can be found in inner-city suburbs such as Surry Hills and Darlinghurst, and big breezy barns make for great drinking sessions by the ocean beaches.

Some of the cheapest drinks can be found at RSL (Returned & Services League) club bars or other special member clubs all over Sydney. These places serve cheap food and beer but they don't usually have that 'young traveller' atmosphere, so it may be best to go with a local friend or turn up in a group. You will have to produce ID that proves you live at least 5km away from the establishment, although temporary memberships are inexpensive. Avoid the poker machines (pokies) here.

You must be at least 18 years old to legally drink alcohol in Australia.

CITY CENTRE

Establishment (Map pp48-50; ☎ 9240 3000; 252 George St, City) Cashed-up and convinced it's still the '80s, the smartly suited crowd here appreciates the fine art of a flashy cocktail after a hard day's stockbroking. It's like the marble foyer of an elegant hotel, but with noise levels approaching a dull roar.

THE ROCKS Map pp48–50

Lord Nelson Brewery Hotel (☎ 9251 4044; 19 Kent St, The Rocks) This atmospheric old (1842) pub claims to be the 'oldest pub' in town (although others do, too!) and brews its own beers (Quayle Ale, Trafalgar Pale Ale, Victory Bitter, Three Sheets, Old Admiral and Nelsons Blood). Go ahead and try them all.

Hero of Waterloo (☎ 9252 4553; 81 Lower Fort St, Millers Point) This venue has a wonderful stone interior and nightly music (see p76). Downstairs is an original dungeon, where drinkers would sleep off a heavy night before a stint on the high seas.

Australian Hotel (☎ 9247 2229; 100 Cumberland St, The Rocks) Grab a pleasant pavement table at this laid-back, friendly hotel and watch the traffic go by. There are renowned local brews on tap along with popular gourmet pizzas (try the crocodile, emu and 'roo toppings).

KINGS CROSS, WOOLLOOMOOLOO & DARLINGHURST

Jimmy Lik's (Map p55; ☎ 8354 1400; 188 Victoria St, Kings Cross) Long benches and a long cocktail list suit the highfalutin atmosphere. Folks wait here for a table at Jimmy Lik's restaurant, which serves excellent Southeast Asian food (try the smoked eel in betel leaf; A$3).

Soho Bar & Lounge (Map p55; ☎ 9358 6511; 171 Victoria St, Kings Cross) In an old Art Deco pub, this revamped ground-floor bar forms the centre of many Sydneysiders' social lives. It's a dark, relaxed drinking lounge, but you'll want to wear your sleekest.

Old Fitzroy Hotel (Map p55; ☎ 9356 3848; 129 Dowling St, Woolloomooloo) Is it a pub? A theatre? A bistro? Actually, it's all three. Grab a bowl of laksa, see the acting stars of tomorrow and wash it all down with a beer (about A$30). The little balcony is unbeatable on a hot night, and there are also pavement tables.

Bourbon (Map p55; ☎ 9358 1144; 24 Darlinghurst Rd, Kings Cross) Flash to the max and attracting young, hip and upper-crust crowds that come to lounge in booths, sit back on sofas or overlook the park and bustling pavement. Hip music, mod lighting and great service are included. Open until 6am.

World Bar (Map p55; ☎ 9357 7700; 24 Bayswater Rd, Kings Cross) Three floors of cool spaces attract the backpacking crowd, and two-for-one cocktails such as 'cocksucking cowboy' or 'horny monkey' keep them happy (grab a discount flyer from your hostel). There's a patio out front, free pool until 6pm and DJs nightly. On Sunday the barbecue costs only A$0.50 with a beer purchase.

Green Park Hotel (Map pp48-50; ☎ 9380 5311; 360 Victoria St, Darlinghurst) The good old Green Park has tiled walls and a bar; it's a popular local watering hole and a cool hang-out for pool-shooters. The last dose of renovations provided much-needed drinking space and better toilets, and the high chairs, low sofas and pavement tables are cool, too.

Darlo Bar (Map pp48-50; ☎ 9331 3672; 306 Liverpool St, Darlinghurst) The service is friendly, the furniture retro mix 'n' match, and there's a boisterous (and crowded) scene on weekends. Comfortable atmosphere and interesting neighbourhood.

SURRY HILLS Map pp48–50

Cricketers Arms (☎ 9331 3301; 106 Fitzroy St) A cosy vibe fills this friendly pub with arty locals (many gathered at the wrap-around bar). Those appreciative of good DJ skills turn up Thursday to Sunday. There are also open fireplaces.

Hollywood Hotel (☎ 9281 2765; 2 Foster St) This Art Deco pub looks nondescript from the outside, but the inside reveals one of Sydney's most appealing Friday night drinking dens. A mixed (dare we say, bohemian) crowd crams in and gets down to the business of starting the weekend with gusto.

PADDINGTON **Map pp44–5**

Paddington Inn Hotel (☎ 9380 5913; 338 Oxford St) This is a popular, sociable pub, but it's pretty large so there's room for everyone. The interior is surprisingly swanky, so grab a window seat and listen to the music (described as 'funky shit' by one staff member).

Lord Dudley Hotel (☎ 9327 5399; 236 Jersey Rd, Woollahra) The Lord Dudley is as close as Sydney really gets to an English pub atmosphere, with dark walls and wood, and good beer in pint glasses. It gets packed with rugby union fans, and there's good food served downstairs.

BALMAIN & GLEBE **Map pp44–5**

London Hotel (☎ 9555 1377; 234 Darling St, Balmain) At this beautiful historical building, be sure to snag an outside counter stool that overlooks the street. It's a good place for a cleansing ale, especially after a trawl through the nearby Saturday markets. Sundays are good locals' days.

Riverview Hotel (☎ 9810 1151; 29 Birchgrove Rd, Balmain) This avowedly local pub was once owned by Australian swimming legend Dawn Fraser (a Balmain icon if ever there was one), who occasionally makes an appearance. It's low-key, a bit of a treasure and great for chatting up the locals.

Friend in Hand Hotel (☎ 9660 2326; 58 Cowper St, Glebe) It's hardly yuppie and not very relaxing (what with all that betting going on), but you can enjoy the poetry slams on Tuesday, hermit crab races on Wednesday or comedy gigs on Thursday. Or just grab an eyeful of the bric-a-brac around you.

BONDI **Map p57**

North Bondi RSL Club (☎ 9130 8770; 118-120 Ramsgate) The views are wonderful for the price (cheap), though it has no-nonsense décor (and avoid the pokies). There's trivia on Tuesdays, live music Wednesdays and a DJ on Sundays. Bring ID, because if you're not a member you need to prove you live at least 5km away.

Bondi Icebergs Bar (☎ 9365 9000; 1 Notts Ave) This is one of Sydney's best-located drinking spots. The hanging rattan chairs and colourful sofa loungers make for a relaxing yet classy setting, and the stunning water views don't hurt. If you're willing to dish out the cash, head into the dining room for a top-notch meal (p71), providing there's a table waiting for you.

Bondi Icebergs Winter Swimming Club (☎ 9130 3120; 1 Notts Ave) Located just below the Bondi Icebergs Bar, this is a more affordable and laid-back bar, but with practically the same views. It serves popular café food (pizza and burgers) and A$3.50 beers. Bring ID, because if you're not a member you need to prove you live at least 5km away.

COOGEE

Coogee Bay Hotel (☎ 9315 6019; cnr Arden St & Coogee Bay Rd) Four bars live on the premises here, so think about whether you want a water view, patio, balcony or sport on TV. Whatever you choose, you'll be drinking with the popular crowd in the heart of Coogee.

WATSONS BAY

Doyles Palace Hotel (Map pp44-5; ☎ 9337 5444; 10 Marine Pde) Surrounded by pricey seafood restaurants and home to a lovely boutique hotel, you'll be pleased to know that you can have the Doyles experience simply by buying a jug of beer, sitting down in the beer garden and enjoying the superlative view of Sydney Harbour. A time-honoured tradition, but avoid weekends, when it's packed to the gills.

Cafés

Coluzzi Bar (Map p55; ☎ 9380 5420; 322 Victoria St, Darlinghurst; snacks A$5-8; 🕒 5am-7pm) You come here for traditional Italian coffee (it's got a nice bite), so grab a pavement table and relax. They've achieved legendary status by making coffee for over 50 years, and claim to have started the coffee craze.

Spring Espresso (Map p55; ☎ 9331 0190; 65 Macleay St, Potts Point; mains A$8-12; 🕒 6.30am-6.30pm) For good coffee and good snacks, try this diminutive and bustling café; entry is via Challis Ave. You may have a bit of a wait on your hands during the morning rush, when it seems that half of Potts Point needs a heart-starter.

Café Hernandez (Map p55; ☎ 9331 2343; 60 Kings Cross Rd, Kings Cross; snacks A$5-9; 24hr) With a delightful old-world atmosphere and some of the best coffee in Sydney, Hernandez has been attracting everyone from taxi drivers to arty students for years. At times you'll think you're in Madrid, especially when it's 3am and this joint's jumping.

CLUBBING

Sydney's dance-club scene is alive and kicking, with local and international DJs revving up thousands of people every weekend. Some places have strict door policies and a lot of attitude; others are great places to catch up with all sorts of people. Cover charges, ranging from A$10 to A$20, are quoted below. For information on gay- and lesbian-friendly clubs, see p62.

Slip Inn (Map pp48-50; ☎ 9299 4777; 111 Sussex St, City; admission A$15-20) Warren-like and sporting three different rooms (and themes), this place is full of cool kids and those who love a bit of turntablist-inspired dancing – with funky house and hip-hop breaks on the menu.

Yu (Map p55; ☎ 9358 6511; 171 Victoria St, Kings Cross; admission A$10-20) Yu wants you to get down to the best of house and funk, played by some of Sydney's most venerable DJs. We love After Ours, which solves the dilemma of what to do on a Sunday night. The club itself is slick-looking and attached to a fancy ground-floor bar.

Icebox (Map p55; ☎ 9331 0058; 2 Kellett St, Kings Cross; admission A$10-15) If you're hankering for those 'summer of love' sounds of the late '80s and early '90s, Icebox has Stun on Wednesday night. Progressive and hard house can be heard Thursday to Sunday, for those who like to party hard until the wee hours.

GoodBar (Map pp48-50; ☎ 9360 6759; 11a Oxford St, Paddington; admission A$10) This hanky-sized club is still attracting gorgeous young fly-girls and B-boys who manage to get past the face control at the door. The bar's Thursday night groove-fest – Step Forward – is easily its best night, with reggae, funk and hip-hop.

Plan B (Map p55; ☎ 9358 1144; 24 Darlinghurst Rd, Kings Cross; admission A$15-20) This classy disco sports a glowing pink bar, lounge area for wallflowers and, of course, the hoppin' dance floor. Wear your best and head on upstairs.

ENTERTAINMENT

The *Sydney Morning Herald* Metro lift-out (published on Friday) and *The Daily Telegraph* SLM lift-out (published on Wednesday) list events in town for the coming week. Free newspapers, such as *Drum Media*, *Revolver* and *3D World* also have useful listings and are available from bookshops, bars, cafés and music stores.

Ticketek (Map pp48-50; ☎ 9266 4800; www.ticketek.com.au; 195 Elizabeth St, City; 9am-7pm Mon-Fri, to 4pm Sat) The city's main booking agency for theatre, concerts, sport and other events. Phone and Internet bookings are available and it also has agencies around town.

Halftix (Map pp48-50; ☎ 8235 7093; www.halftix.com.au; 91 York St, City; 9am-6pm Tue-Fri) Sells half-price seats for shows. Tickets are mainly available for shows that night, and they can't tell you where you'll be sitting. Phone and Internet bookings are available.

Cinemas

Generally, cinema tickets cost between A$12 and A$15 for adults (less for concessions). Tuesday is often discount day, with tickets going for about A$10. Movie listings can be found in Sydney's daily newspapers.

Greater Union Hoyts Cinemas (Map pp48-50; www.greaterunion.com.au; ☎ 9273 7431; 505 George St, City) This monster-sized movie palace has 17 screens – the biggest in NSW – in an orgy of popcorn-fuelled mainstream entertainment.

Dendy (Map pp48-50; ☎ 9247 3800; www.dendy.com.au; Shop 9, 2 Circular Quay East; general/concession A$10.50/14) Found right near the Opera House, this is a lavish cinema with well-chosen first-run movies and a great bar (for ticket-holders only). On Monday movies cost A$9 for everyone.

Verona Cinema (Map pp48-50; ☎ 9360 6099; Level 1, 17 Oxford St, Paddington; admission A$14) This cinema also has a café and bar, so you can discuss the good (invariably nonmainstream) flick you've just seen.

IMAX (Map pp48-50; ☎ 9281 3300; www.imax.com.au; Southern Promenade, Cockle Bay; admission A$17; 10am-10pm) If you're into being wowed by massive images, some in 3-D, then the IMAX is for you. Movies shown tend to be either thrill-fests or nature docos.

Govinda's & Movie Room (Map p55; ☎ 9380 5155; www.govindas.com.au; 112 Darlinghurst Rd, Darlinghurst; dinner & movie A$20; 6-10.30pm) The Hare-Krishna Govinda's is an all-you-can-gobble vegetarian smorgasbord, which also gives you admission to the cinema upstairs (where you can lie back on the floor cushioning), which shows mainstream and indie films.

Live Music

Sydney doesn't have as dynamic a music scene as Melbourne, but you can still find live music most nights of the week. For listings of venues and acts, see the papers mentioned under Entertainment (opposite).

CLASSICAL

Sydney Opera House (Map pp48-50; ☎ 9250 7777; www.sydneyoperahouse.com; Bennelong Point, Circular Quay East) This is the classical performance centre in Australia, with the Concert Hall and Opera Hall holding about 2600 and 1500 people respectively. Everything is performed here – theatre, comedy, music, dance, ballet and opera – but it's the latter art form that really shines. The box office opens from 9am to 8.30pm Monday to Saturday and two hours before a Sunday performance. And don't be late for your performance or you'll be shut out 'till intermission!

Sydney Conservatorium of Music (Map pp48-50; ☎ 9351 1222; www.usyd.edu.au/su/conmusic; Macquarie St, City) This historic music venue showcases the talents of its students and teachers. Choral, jazz, operatic and chamber concerts are held here from March to July, along with free lunch-time recitals on Wednesday and Friday at 1.10pm (March to November).

JAZZ & BLUES

Sydney has a healthy and innovative jazz and blues circuit, with quite a few venues worth a swing. Cover charges range from A$5 to A$50.

Basement (Map pp48-50; ☎ 9251 2797; 29 Reiby Pl, Circular Quay; admission A$12-50) This place has decent food, good music (plus the odd spoken word and comedy gig) and some big international names occasionally dropping by (making the cover charge skyrocket).

Empire Hotel (☎ 9557 1701; www.sydneyblues.com; 103a Parramatta Rd, Annandale; admission Fri & Sat A$5-15) Blues (along with ska and rockabilly) buffs should look no further than the well-run Empire for live acts (aided by a very good sound system) Tuesday to Sunday nights.

Soup Plus (Map pp48-50; ☎ 9299 7728; 383 George St, City; admission after 9pm A$10) This casual basement venue offers live jazz and cheap food for lunch and dinner. It's the mainstream end of jazz (for the most part), so don't expect any radical tonal experimentation.

ROCK & POP

Sometimes there's no charge to see young local bands, while between A$5 and A$20 is charged for well-known local acts, with up to A$60 for international performers.

Annandale Hotel (☎ 9550 1078; 17 Parramatta Rd, Annandale; tickets A$8-20) This venue plays host to a sometimes eclectic assortment of local and international alternative music acts. Loud rock, heavy metal, dance and acoustic gigs jam nightly from Tuesday to Sunday, while cult movies play Monday nights. Say what?

Cat & Fiddle (☎ 9810 7931; 456 Darling St, Balmain) Nightly live music plays at 7.30pm, with local bands providing the energy at this smoky venue. Tall stools and tables seat the crowd, happy hour runs from 8am to 6pm (!) and

FREE SOUNDS

On summer weekends there are free music performances in many parks, especially in **The Domain** (Map pp48–50) during the Sydney Festival in January, when you can catch 'Opera in the Domain' and 'Symphony in the Park' (bring a picnic!). At **St Andrew's Cathedral** (Map pp48–50) you can catch free 'Young Music' concerts at noon on Thursdays and organ recitals at 1.10pm Friday. Every Wednesday at 1.15pm from March to December, there's a free organ recital at **St James' Church** (Map pp48–50) at the end of King St. Over the Labour Day long weekend (early October), there are free outdoor jazz concerts as part of the **Manly International Jazz Festival** (p61). You can be entertained by buskers around the Opera House and Circular Quay, in The Rocks and Kings Cross, and along The Corso in Manly. Alternatively, you can listen to the mad and the erudite venting their obsessions at Speakers' Corner in **The Domain** on Sunday afternoon. Sometimes there are free concerts at the **Art Gallery of NSW** (p53), performed by students of the Australian Institute of Music. Concerts take place between 12.30pm and 1.30pm Sunday. The **Sydney Conservatorium of Music** (above) offers concerts at 1.10pm on Wednesday and Friday from March to November.

there's even a small theatre on the premises (about 30 seats).

Metro Theatre (Map pp48-50; ☎ 9287 2000; 624 George St, City; tickets A$10-75) This is easily the best place to see well-chosen local and alternative international acts (plus the odd DJ) in well-ventilated comfort.

Hopetoun Hotel (Map pp48-50; ☎ 9361 5257; 416 Bourke St, Surry Hills; admission A$6-12) This great little venue offers flexibility for artists and patrons alike and features an array of modern musical styles – from folk to rap to DJs to local bands getting their first taste of life on the road. Occasional international groups also visit.

Sandringham Hotel (☎ 9557 1254; 387 King St, Newtown) You can still pay a minimal amount of money (A$5 to A$15) and get your earwax blasted out almost nightly while munching on tapas (A$6). There are pool competitions on Wednesday afternoon.

TRADITIONAL

Hero of Waterloo (Map pp48-50; ☎ 9252 4553; 81 Lower Fort St, Millers Point) This pub (p72) has traditional piano Monday to Thursday, folk on Friday and Saturday and Irish tunes on Sunday (a popular night).

Sport

Sydney's sunshine, parks, beaches and love of showing off all conspire to make this a delightful city for staying fit or watching sport. If you like to watch, have a credit card handy and book tickets to a variety of sporting events, big and small. If you're the one being sporty, it can be as simple as putting your feet in some jogging shoes or putting in some laps at a beach-side pool.

The **Sydney Cricket Ground** (SCG), at Moore Park, is the venue for sparsely attended state cricket matches, well-attended five-day Test matches and sell-out one-day World Series cricket matches.

Sydney is one of rugby league's world capitals. **National Rugby League** (NRL; www.nrl.com.au) games are played from March to October at a variety of venues, including Aussie Stadium in Moore Park and Telstra Stadium in Homebush Bay.

The (sometimes) high-flying footy team Sydney Swans, NSW's contribution to the **Australian Football League** (AFL; www.afl.com.au), plays matches between March and September. Its home ground is the SCG.

Sydney's oldest and largest 18-footer yacht club is the **Sydney Flying Squadron** (Map pp44-5; ☎ 9955 8350; www.sydneyflyingsquadron.com.au; 76 McDougall St, Milsons Point). Catch its ferry at Milsons Point to watch skiff racing from 2pm to 4.30pm on Saturday between September and April (A$15).

Theatre & Comedy

Wharf Theatre (Map pp48-50; ☎ 9250 1700; www.sydneytheatre.com.au; Pier 4, Hickson Rd, Walsh Bay) Also home to the **Australian Theatre for Young People** (ATYP; 9251 3900), **Bangarra Dance Theatre** (☎ 9251 5333), **Sydney Philharmonia Choirs** (☎ 9251 2024) and the **Sydney Dance Company** (☎ 9221 4811).

Belvoir St Theatre (Map pp44-5; ☎ 9699 3444; www.belvoir.com.au; 25 Belvoir St, Surry Hills; tickets adult A$27-45, concession A$21-30) Something of a home for original and often experimental Australian theatre, its excellent resident production company is known as Company B, which gets actors like Geoffrey Rush to say 'no' to Hollywood in return for a meaty stage role.

Sydney Theatre (Map pp48-50; ☎ 9250 1999; www.sydneytheatre.org.au; 22 Hickson Rd, Walsh Bay) Managed by the Sydney Theatre Company, this 850-seat, state-of-the-art theatre (which opened in January 2004) offers drama and dance productions of national and international stature. Past plays have included direction by William S Burroughs, Tom Waits and Robert Wilson.

SHOPPING

The hub of city shopping is Pitt St Mall (Map pp48–50), with department stores, shopping centres and numerous shops all within arm's reach. However, it's much more relaxing to shop for fashion on popular inner-city strips such as Oxford St in Paddington. For furnishings and antiques head for Queen St, Woollahra; for CDs try around Crown St, Surry Hills; and for outdoor gear visit the corner of Kent and Bathurst Sts in town. Or test out Sydney's popular markets. The Rocks is where you'll generally find what's known as 'Australiana' (ie souvenirs), although it won't be cheap here. Try Paddy's Markets instead.

Markets

Markets are generally open from 9am-4pm, though some may open an hour earlier or close an hour later.

Paddington Bazaar (Map pp44-5; ☎ 9331 2923; St John's Church, 395 Oxford St, Paddington; 🕑 Sat) Very

THRIFT STORES

Need some new duds? Lost your towel at the beach? Looking for a good book to read? You don't have to pay retail prices if you're OK with second-hand stuff. The St Vincent de Paul Society (better known as St Vinnies) and the Salvation Army (the Salvos) have quite a few stores spread over the city. Here are a few:

St Vincent de Paul Paddington (☎ 9360 4151; 292 Oxford; 🕑 9.30am-5.30pm Mon-Wed & Fri, to 7.30 Thu, 10am-5pm Sat)

St Vincent de Paul Bondi (Map p57; ☎ 9300 0585; 60 Hall St; 🕑 9.30am-5.30pm Mon-Fri, 9am-4pm Sat)

St Vincent de Paul Newtown (☎ 9557 1996; 189 King St; 9am-5pm Mon-Fri, 10am-4pm Sat)

St Vincent de Paul Glebe (Map pp44-5; ☎ 9552 6031; 179 Glebe Point Rd; 🕑 9am-4.30pm Mon-Fri, 10am-4pm Sat)

St Vincent de Paul Manly (Map p59; ☎ 9977 1574; 2-20 Pittwater Rd; 🕑 9am-5pm Mon-Fri, to noon Sat)

Salvation Army Glebe (☎ 9552 2589; 654 Glebe Point Rd; 🕑 10am-5.45pm Mon-Sat)

Salvation Army Surry Hills (☎ 9360 1710; 339 Crown St; 🕑 9.30am-2.30pm Mon-Fri)

popular, upmarket and pricey, with vintage clothing, creative crafts, beautiful jewellery, tasty food and holistic treatments.

Paddy's Markets (Map pp48-50; ☎ 1300 361 589; www.paddysmarkets.com.au; cnr Hay & Thomas Sts, Haymarket; 🕑 9am-5pm Thu-Sun) In the heart of Chinatown, this Sydney institution is a great place to find cheap souvenirs, clothing, cosmetics and other usual market items. Be prepared for crowds.

Rocks Market (Map pp48-50; ☎ 9240 8717; George St, The Rocks; 🕑 Sat & Sun) Held at the top end of George St, this market is a little touristy but worth a look for the jewellery, souvenirs (how about some 'roo balls?) and wonderful crafts made of metal, ceramics, stone, leather and glass.

Balmain Markets (Map pp44-5; ☎ 0418 765 736; St Andrew's Church, 223 Darling St, Balmain; 🕑 Sat) This small but good local market offers crafty stuff like handmade candles and soaps, jewellery, exotic textiles, artwork, and used clothing and books. Buy a snack in the church hall.

Rozelle Second-Hand Markets (☎ 9818 5373; Rozelle Public School, Darling St, Rozelle; 🕑 9am-4pm Sat & Sun) Used clothes, shoes, books, knick-knacks and junk in general; a 30-minute walk southwest of Balmain.

Glebe Markets (Map pp44-5; Glebe Public School, cnr Glebe Point Rd & Derby Pl, Glebe; 🕑 Sat) A large and very popular market with the usual books, vintage clothing, leather goods, hippy crafts and curios.

Bondi Beach Markets (Map p57; ☎ 9315 8988; Bondi Beach Public School, cnr Campbell Pde & Warners Ave; 🕑 Sun) At the northern end of Campbell Pde, this market is good for hippy clothing, swimwear, jewellery, knick-knacks and people-watching.

GETTING THERE & AWAY

Air

Sydney's Kingsford Smith Airport is Australia's busiest, so don't be surprised if there are delays. It's only 10km south of the city centre, making access easy, but this also means that flights cease between 11pm and 5am due to noise regulations.

You can fly into Sydney from all the usual international points and from all over Australia. Jetstar, Qantas and Virgin run frequent flights to other capital cities. Low-end one-way fares at the time of writing started at: Melbourne A$70, Brisbane A$80, Cairns A$170, Adelaide A$110, Perth A$200 and Alice Springs A$190. (One-off specials can be cheaper than these prices.) Smaller airlines, linked to Qantas, fly within NSW.

Air Link (☎ 13 17 13; www.airlinkairlines.com.au) Services regional NSW.

Alliance Airlines (☎ 1300 130 092; www.allianceairlines.com.au) Services regional NSW.

Jetstar (☎ 13 15 38, www.jetstar.com.au)

Qantas (☎ 13 13 13; www.qantas.com.au)

Regional Express (Rex; ☎ 13 17 13; www.regionalexpress.com.au) Services regional NSW and Victoria.

Virgin Blue (☎ 13 67 89, www.virginblue.com.au)

Bus & Train

The long-distance train and bus services, including those leaving from Central Station, are competitive and efficient. Book these tickets in advance. The government's **CountryLink** (Map pp48-50; ☎ 13 22 32, after hours ☎ 9379 1600; www.countrylink.info; Platform 1 Central Station; 🕑 6.45am-8.45pm) network of trains and buses offers good fares (there's also a branch at Circular Quay). Sample destinations include Brisbane (A$132), Canberra (A$50) and Melbourne (A$132), but with two weeks' notice you can cut these fares by 50%. Whichever transport you take, remember that showing a student, youth or even hostel card often gets you a discount.

Major bus operators include **McCafferty's/ Greyhound** (☎ 9212 3433; www.mccaffertys.com.au) and **Premier Motor Service** (☎ 13 34 10; www.premierms.com.au). Sample destinations include Brisbane (A$90), Canberra (A$35) and Melbourne (A$65).

A ferry operates between Sydney and Devonport (Tasmania). **TT-Line** (☎ 1800 634 906; www.spiritoftasmania.com.au) runs the *Spirit of Tasmania III* (from A$230 per person, 20 hours) departing from Sydney at 4pm on Friday and 5pm Sunday, arriving around 1pm and 2pm, respectively, the next day. During periods of high demand (over Christmas and New Year), there is also a Tuesday sailing at 6pm.

GETTING AROUND

For information on buses, ferries and trains, contact the **Transport Infoline** (☎ 13 15 00; www.131500.com.au). Call between 6am and 10pm daily; the operators can tell you exactly how to get from one point to another. For information on getting into the city from the airport, see p42.

Bus

Sydney's bus network extends to most suburbs. Fares depend on the number of 'sections' you pass through. As a rough guide, short jaunts cost A$1.60 and most other fares in the inner suburbs are A$2.70. If you plan on taking many buses it's cheaper to buy passes (see opposite). Regular buses run between 5am and midnight, when Nightrider buses take over.

The major starting points for bus routes are Circular Quay, Argyle St in Millers Point, Wynyard Park, the Queen Victoria Building (York St) and Railway Sq. Most buses head out of the city on George or Castlereagh Sts and take George or Elizabeth Sts coming in. Pay the driver as you enter, or dunk your prepaid ticket in the green ticket machines by the door.

At Circular Quay there's a **Transit Shop** (Map pp48-50; 🕑 7am-7pm Mon-Fri, 8am-5.30pm Sat & Sun) that sells bus passes and dispenses bus route information. Look for this kiosk right in front of the McDonald's at Alfred and Loftus Sts. Other bus Transit Shops also sell passes. For more bus information you can call ☎ 9244 1991 or ☎ 13 15 00, or check www.sydneybuses.nsw.gov.au.

Car & Motorcycle

BUYING/SELLING A CAR

Sydney is the capital of car sales for most travellers. Parramatta Rd is lined with used-car lots. The **Kings Cross Car Market** (Map p55; ☎ 1800 808 188, 9358 5000; www.carmarket.com.au; cnr Ward Ave & Elizabeth Bay Rd, Kings Cross; 🕑 9am-5pm) gets mixed reports, but it seems popular with travellers. Always read the fine print on anything you sign with regard to buying or selling a car. Several dealers will sell you a car with an undertaking to buy it back at an agreed price. However, do not accept any verbal guarantees – get them in writing.

The *Trading Post*, a weekly rag available from all newsagents and online (www.tradingpost.com.au), is also a good place to look for second-hand vehicles. Another resource is the *Sydney Morning Herald's* classified section (www.smh.com.au). Car prices will probably be a bit cheaper if you buy from a private party.

Yet another option is going to a car auction. One place is **Auto Auctions** (☎ 9724 9111; www.auto-auctions.com.au; 682 Woodville Rd, Guildford).

Before you buy any vehicle, regardless of the seller, we strongly recommend that you have it thoroughly checked by a competent mechanic. For this service, the **NRMA** (Map pp48-50; ☎ 13 21 32, 13 11 22; www.nrma.com.au; 74 King St, City; 🕑 9am-5pm Mon-Fri) charges A$240 for nonmembers (A$200 for members). We've heard some real horror stories from readers who've failed to get their vehicles checked.

The **Register of Encumbered Vehicles** (REVS; ☎ 9633 6333; www.revs.nsw.gov.au) is a government organisation that can check to ensure the car you're buying is fully paid-up and owned by the seller. Other helpful websites, especially if you have problems with your vehicle, are www.fairtrading.nsw.gov.au and www.accc.gov.au.

CAR RENTAL

Avis (☎ 13 63 33), **Budget** (☎ 13 27 27), Delta **Europcar** (☎ 1300 131 390), **Hertz** (☎ 13 30 39) and **Thrifty** (☎ 1300 367 227) all have desks at the airport. Their rates sometimes include insurance and unlimited kilometres. Some companies require you to be over 25 years old. Avis and

Hertz also provide hand-controlled cars for disabled travellers. The *Yellow Pages* (www.yellowpages.com.au) lists many other car-hire companies, some specialising in renting near-wrecks at rock-bottom prices – always read the fine print on your rental agreement carefully if you decide on this option.

TOLL ROADS

The Harbour Tunnel shoulders some of the Harbour Bridge's workload. It begins about half a kilometre south of the Opera House, crosses under the harbour just to the east of the bridge, and rejoins the highway on the northern side. There's a southbound (only) toll of A$3 for both the tunnel and the bridge. If you're heading from the North Shore to the eastern suburbs, it's much easier to use the harbour tunnel. The Eastern Distributor imposes a northbound toll (A$4).

The new Cross City Tunnel is presently being built, with the hope that it will ease traffic congestion and improve east–west travel across the city. It will link the Western Distributor to New South Head and connect the Eastern Distributor to Domain Tunnel. It's due to be completed in 2005 and tolls will range from A$1.10 to A$2.50 for cars.

Fare Deals

The SydneyPass offers three, five or seven days unlimited travel over a seven-day period on all STA buses and ferries, as well as the red TravelPass zone (inner suburbs) of the rail network. The passes cover the Airport Express, Explorers, JetCats, RiverCats and three STA-operated harbour cruises. The passes cost A$90 for three days, A$120 for five days and A$140 for seven days.

TravelPasses are designed for commuters and offer cheap weekly travel. There are various colour-coded grades offering combinations of distance and service. A Red TravelPass (train, bus and ferry) costs A$32.

If you're just catching buses, get a TravelTen ticket, which gives a big discount on 10 bus trips. There are various colour codes for distances, so check which is the most appropriate for you. A red TravelTen costs A$25 and can be used to reach most places mentioned in the Sydney section of this guide.

All the passes above are sold at train stations, bus Transit Shops and major newsagents.

Ferry Ten tickets are similar and cost from A$29 for 10 inner-harbour (ie short) ferry trips, or A$45 including the Manly ferry. They can be purchased at the Circular Quay ferry ticket office.

Several transport-plus-entry tickets are available, which work out cheaper than catching a ferry and paying entry separately. They include the ZooPass (A$32) and the AquariumPass (A$30), which can be purchased at the ferry terminals.

Ferry

Sydney Ferries (☎ 9207 3196; www.sydneyferries.info) provides the most enjoyable way to get around. Many people use ferries to commute so there are frequent connecting bus services. Some ferries operate between 6am and midnight, although ferries servicing tourist attractions operate much shorter hours. Popular places accessible by ferry include Darling Harbour, Balmain, Hunters Hill and Parramatta to the west; McMahons Point, Kirribilli, Neutral Bay, Cremorne, Mosman, Taronga Zoo and Manly on the North Shore; and Double Bay, Rose Bay and Watsons Bay in the eastern suburbs.

There are three kinds of ferry: regular STA ferries, fast JetCats that go to Manly (A$7.50) and RiverCats that traverse the Parramatta River to Parramatta (A$7). All ferries depart from Circular Quay. At Wharf 4 you'll find the **ferry information office** (Map pp48-50; ☎ 9207 3170; 7am-5.45pm Mon-Sat, 8am-5.45pm Sun) near the ticket booths. Most regular harbour ferries cost A$4.50, although the longer trip to Manly costs A$5.80.

Metro Light Rail & Monorail

The **Metro Light Rail** (MLR; ☎ 9285 5600, www.metrolightrail.com.au) and the **Metro Monorail** (☎ 9285 5600; www.metromonorail.com.au) are of limited use for Sydney residents but are a little more useful for tourists. The MLR operates 24 hours a day between Central Station and Pyrmont via Darling Harbour and Chinatown. The service runs to Lilyfield via the Fish Market, Wentworth Park, Glebe, Jubilee Park and Rozelle Bay from 6am to 11pm Sunday to Thursday (to midnight Friday and Saturday). Tickets cost A$2.80 to A$5.20 per adult, and A$1.40 to A$3.70 per concession fare. Tickets can be purchased on board.

The Monorail circles Darling Harbour and links it to the city centre. There's a monorail every three to five minutes, and the full loop takes about 14 minutes. A single trip costs A$4, but with the day pass (A$8) you can ride as often as you like for a full day. The monorail operates from 7am to 10pm Monday to Thursday, to midnight on Friday and Saturday and from 8am to 10pm Sunday.

Taxi

There are heaps of taxis in Sydney. Flag fall is A$2.65, and the metered fair is A$1.53 per kilometre and A$0.67 per minute waiting time. There are extra charges for fares between 10pm and 6am, for heavy luggage, and for harbour-bridge and tunnel tolls. There's also a radio booking fee. The four big taxi companies offer a reliable service:

Legion (☎ 13 14 51)
Premier Cabs (☎ 13 10 17)
RSL Cabs (☎ 13 22 11)
Taxis Combined (☎ 8332 8888)

Train

Sydney has a vast suburban rail network and frequent services, making trains much quicker than buses. The underground City Circle comprises seven city-centre stations. Lines radiate from the City Circle, but do not extend to the northern and southern beaches, Balmain or Glebe. All city-bound suburban trains stop at Central Station, and usually one or more of the other City Circle stations as well (a ticket to the city will take you to any station on the City Circle). Trains run from around 5am to midnight.

After 9am on weekdays and at any time on weekends, you can buy an off-peak return ticket for not much more than a standard one-way fare.

Staffed ticket booths are supplemented by automatic ticket machines at stations. If you have to change trains, it's cheaper to buy a ticket to your ultimate destination – but don't depart from an another station en route to your destination or your ticket will be invalid.

All stations have train information. Central Station has a good **information kiosk** (🕑 6am-10pm) near platforms 4 and 5. The **transportation information booth** (Map pp48-50; 🕑 9am-5pm) at Circular Quay also hands out advice; it's right next to Countrylink. You can also check www.cityrail.info.

AROUND SYDNEY

Although it's a sprawling metropolis, Sydney has its fair share of national parks, with loads of opportunities to bushwalk, rock climb or just laze on a secluded beach. The Blue Mountains National Park is the pick of the bunch with the majestic Three Sisters rock formations, pleasant towns and thick scrub to explore. Ku-ring-gai Chase National Park is an impressive mix of sandstone and bushland, while Royal National Park has the advantage of stunning coastal cliffs. Then there's historic Botany Bay, where Captain Cook first raised the flag and controversially claimed the country for mother England.

The greatest advantage of Sydney's bushland is that it's all easy to get to – a train line runs to the Blue Mountains and most of the other parks are all accessible by public transport. Day trips are easy, but on weekends you might find half of Sydney keeping you company.

BOTANY BAY

Most people assume that Sydney was built around Botany Bay, probably due to the bad folk songs about it (such as 'Bound for Botany Bay'). Botany Bay is actually 10km to 15km south of the city's fringe. Today it's a major industrial centre so its unspoilt landscapes are long gone. The bay retains a few pretty stretches and holds a special place in Australian history. During a landfall here, Captain Cook first encountered Aboriginal people, and the area was named by Joseph Banks (the expedition's naturalist) for the botanical bonanza he found in the environs.

The **Botany Bay National Park** (www.nationalparks.nsw.gov.au; admission per car A$7; 🕑 7am-7.30pm) encompasses both headlands of the bay. At Kurnell, on the southern headland, Cook's landing place is marked by a series of monuments. The 436-hectare park has bushland and coastal walking tracks, picnic areas and an 8km bike track. The park's **Discovery Centre** (☎ 02-9668 9111; 🕑 10am-3pm) documents the shocking impact of European arrival, and has information on the surrounding wetlands. Pedestrians are not charged the park's admission fee, so you can park outside and walk in (the monuments and most walking tracks are close to the entrance). From Cronulla train station (10km away), you can catch the

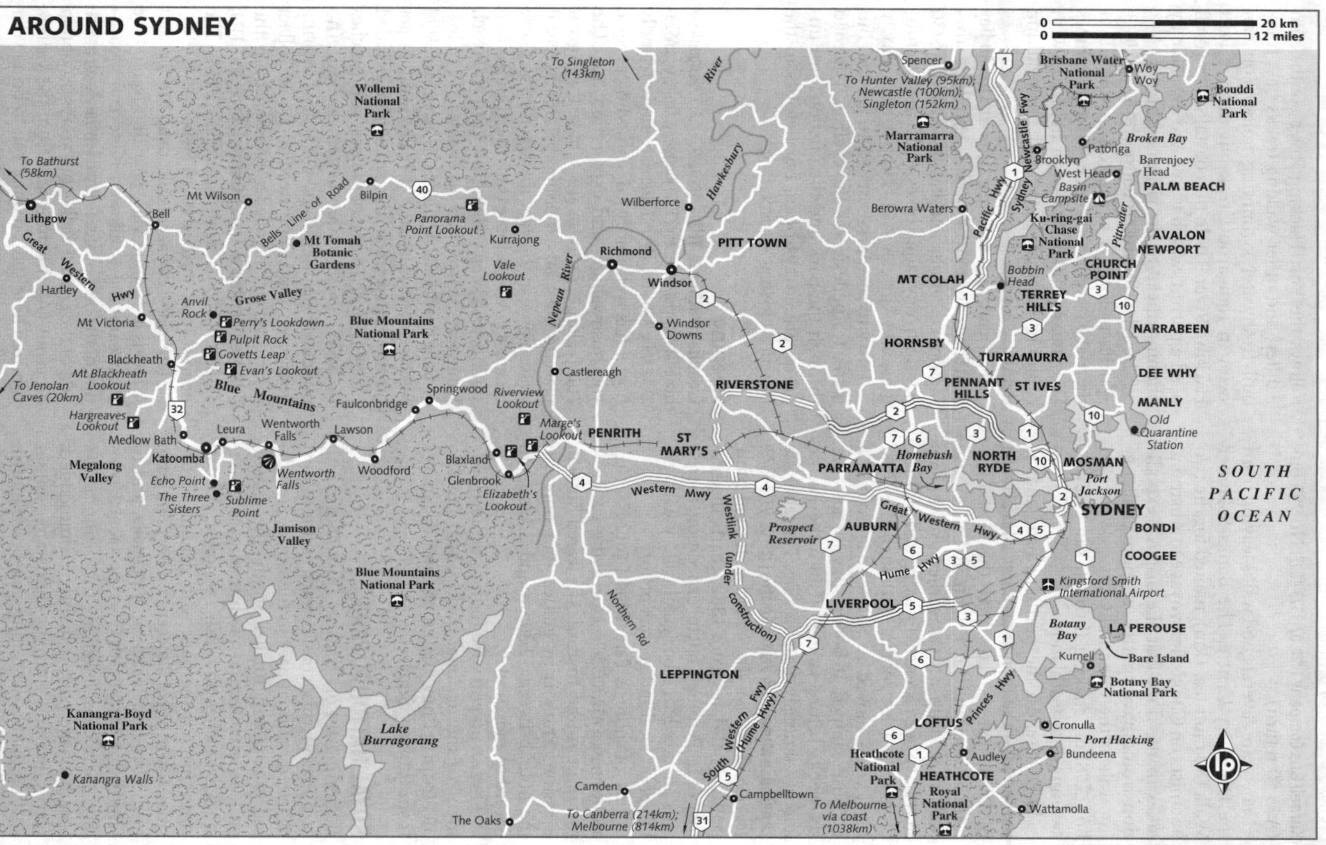
AROUND SYDNEY
0 20 km
0 12 miles
SOUTH PACIFIC OCEAN
To Bathurst (58km)
Lithgow
Great Western Hwy
Hartley
To Jenolan Caves (20km)
Bell
Mt Victoria
Blackheath
Mt Blackheath Lookout
Hargreaves Lookout
Medlow Bath
Megalong Valley
Katoomba
Echo Point
The Three Sisters
Leura
Sublime Point
Wentworth Falls
Jamison Valley
Mt Wilson
Anvil Rock
Perry's Lookdown
Pulpit Rock
Govetts Leap
Evan's Lookout
Blue Mountains
Grose Valley
Bells Line of Road
Mt Tomah Botanic Gardens
Bilpin
Wollemi National Park
Blue Mountains National Park
Kanangra-Boyd National Park
Kanangra Walls
Lake Burragorang
Lawson
Woodford
Faulconbridge
Springwood
Blaxland
Glenbrook
Elizabeth's Lookout
Riverview Lookout
Marge's Lookout
Vale Lookout
Panorama Point Lookout
Kurrajong
Castlereagh
Nepean River
Richmond
Windsor
Windsor Downs
Wilberforce
To Singleton (143km)
Hawkesbury River
PITT TOWN
RIVERSTONE
PENRITH
ST MARY'S
Western Mwy
Westlink (under construction)
Northern Rd
LEPPINGTON
Camden
The Oaks
To Canberra (214km); Melbourne (814km)
Campbelltown
South Western Fwy (Hume Hwy)
Prospect Reservoir
PARRAMATTA
Homebush Bay
Great Western Hwy
Hume Hwy
AUBURN
LIVERPOOL
To Melbourne via coast (1038km)
Heathcote National Park
HEATHCOTE
Royal National Park
LOFTUS
Audley
Princes Hwy
Wattamolla
Bundeena
Port Hacking
Cronulla
Kurnell
Botany Bay National Park
Botany Bay
Bare Island
LA PEROUSE
Kingsford Smith International Airport
COOGEE
BONDI
SYDNEY
Port Jackson
MOSMAN
NORTH RYDE
PENNANT HILLS
ST IVES
TURRAMURRA
HORNSBY
MT COLAH
Berowra Waters
Marramarra National Park
Spencer
To Hunter Valley (95km); Newcastle (100km); Singleton (152km)
Pacific Hwy
Sydney Newcastle Fwy
Brooklyn
Ku-ring-gai Chase National Park
Bobbin Head
TERREY HILLS
CHURCH POINT
West Head
Basin Campsite
Pittwater
Patonga
Brisbane Water National Park
Woy Woy
Broken Bay
Barrenjoey Head
PALM BEACH
Bouddi National Park
AVALON
NEWPORT
NARRABEEN
DEE WHY
MANLY
Old Quarantine Station

Kurnell Bus Company (☎ 02-9523 4047) No 987 bus (A$5.50 return).

There are several good walks leaving from the Discovery Centre. The Banks-Solander Walk (30 minutes, 1km), named for the two botanists on Cook's first voyage to Australia, takes in the flora that the original expedition would have spotted. A more challenging walk is the Cape Baily Coast Walk (2½ hours, 8km) snaking through sand dunes, swamps and heathlands.

La Perouse, on the northern headland, is named after the French explorer who arrived in 1788, just six days after the First Fleet claimed the land for Britain. If La Perouse had showed up a week earlier, Australians may have been French-speaking and scoffing croissants a lot sooner. Although the First Fleet soon moved to Sydney Harbour, La Perouse camped at Botany Bay for another six weeks before sailing off into the Pacific and mysteriously disappearing. The fabulous **Laperouse Museum & Visitor Centre** (☎ 02-9311 3379; adult A$5.50; 10am-4pm Wed-Sun), in the old cable station that dates from 1882, charts the history of La Perouse's fateful expedition; there's also an excellent Aboriginal gallery with exhibits on local indigenous history.

Just offshore is **Bare Island** (☎ 02-9247 5033; adult/concession A$7.70/5.50), a decaying concrete fort built in 1885 to ward off a feared Russian invasion. Entry is by guided tour only, on the hour between 12.30pm and 3.30pm on Saturday and Sunday.

There's no entry fee to the northern segment of the national park. Catch bus No 394 from Sydney's Circular Quay or No 393 from Railway Square.

ROYAL NATIONAL PARK

Beginning at Port Hacking (just 30km south of Sydney) this coastal park is the oldest gazetted national park in the world. Stretching over 20km further south, the coastal park is a collection of dramatic cliffs, secluded beaches and lush rainforest. A road runs through the park with detours to the small township of **Bundeena** on Port Hacking, to the beautiful beach at **Wattamolla**, and to windswept **Garie Beach**. The spectacular two-day, 26km coastal walking track running the length of the park is highly recommended. Garie, Era and Burning Palms are popular surfing spots; swimming can be delightful at Wattamolla. A walking and cycling track follows the Port Hacking River south from Audley, and other walking tracks pass tranquil freshwater swimming holes. You can swim in Kangaroo Creek but not the Port Hacking River. To do the coastal walks you'll need a permit, which is free and available by phoning ahead to the visitors centre.

The friendly **visitors centre** (☎ 02-9542 0648; 8.30am-4.30pm) is at the top of the hill at the park's main entrance, off the Princes Hwy near Audley. Staff can help you with camping permits, maps and bushwalking details.

You can hire exercise gear at the **Audley Boat Shed** (☎ 02-9545 4967; Farnell Rd), where rowing boats, canoes and kayaks cost A$16/30 per hour/day, aqua bikes A$12 per 30 minutes, and bicycles A$14/30 per hour/day.

Entry to the park costs A$10 per car, but is free for pedestrians and cyclists. The road through the park and the offshoot to Bundeena are always open, but detours to the beaches close at sunset.

Sleeping

Cronulla Beachouse YHA (☎ 02-9527 7772; enquiries@cronullabeachyha.com; Level 1, 40 Kingsway, Cronulla; s A$25-27, d & tw A$60-66; P) This extremely friendly hostel has well-informed staff who can give you bushwalking and exploration tips. The comfy, large common areas make this a great place to meet others doing the 26km coastal walk. You can also get the key for the Garie Beach YHA. Catch the train to Cronulla train station, and keep walking left until you reach Kingsway. Wheelchair accessible.

Garie Beach YHA (☎ 02-9261 1111; Garie Beach, Royal National Park; dm A$10) If you really want to get off the beaten track, this small and secluded hostel is close to one of the best surf beaches in NSW. Facilities are extremely basic (no phones or electricity) and you'll need to bring your own food. You need to book, collect a key and get detailed directions from the **YHA Membership & Travel Centre** (☎ 02-9261 1111; 422 Kent St, City) or from Cronulla's YHA. The nearest food store is 10km away.

The only car-accessible **camp site** (per adult A$7.50) is at Bonnie Vale, near Bundeena. Free bush camping is allowed in several areas – one of the best places is **Providential Head**, at the end of the coastal walk – but you must obtain a permit (A$3) beforehand from the visitors centre. These spots require you to bring your own drinking water and fires are forbidden.

Getting There & Away

You can get to the national park from either Wollongong or Sydney. From Sydney, take the Princes Hwy and turn off south of Loftus to reach the northern end of the park. From Wollongong the coast road north offers spectacular views of the Illawarra escarpment and the coast from Bald Hill Lookout (just north of Stanwell Park, on the southern boundary of the park). Enter the park at Otford. There's another entrance at Waterfall, just off the Princes Hwy.

Four kilometres from the park's entrance and a further 2km from the visitors centre, Loftus is the closest station on the Sydney–Wollongong train line. The distance seems shorter if you bring a bike on the train, especially as there is a refreshing 10km ride through the bush on a vehicle-free track, just half an hour's ride from Sutherland station. Engadine, Heathcote, Waterfall and Otford are on the park's boundary and have walking tracks leading into the park.

A scenic route to the park is to take a train from Sydney to Cronulla (changing at Sutherland on the way; A$4.40), then a **Cronulla National Park Ferries** (☎ 02-9523 2990) boat to Bundeena in the northeastern corner of the park (adult A$3.30). Ferries depart from Cronulla Wharf, just below the train station. Cronulla National Park Ferries also offers daily Hacking River cruises in summer (adult A$15), with a reduced timetable in winter.

KU-RING-GAI CHASE NATIONAL PARK

Attracting more than two million visitors a year, Ku-ring-gai is known for the dizzying drop-offs and spectacular valleys that riddle the 15,000-hectare national park. Just 24km north of the city centre, the park borders the southern edge of Broken Bay and the western shore of Pittwater. It has that classic Sydney mixture of sandstone, native scrub and water surrounds, plus walking tracks, horse-riding trails, picnic areas, Aboriginal rock engravings and spectacular views of Broken Bay, particularly from West Head at

CITY-SIDE SANCTUARIES

Blessed with bush on its fringes, Sydney has several spots just outside the city where you can cuddle a koala or eyeball an emu.

Koala Park Sanctuary

Set in 4.5 hectares of rainforest, **Koala Park Sanctuary** (☎ 02-9484 3141; www.koalaparksanctuary.com.au; 84 Castle Hill Rd, West Pennant Hills; adult A$18; 9am-5pm) is as much a sanctuary for visitors as it is for the little grey tourist-pullers. Feeding takes place at 10.20am, 11.45am, 2pm and 3pm, which is the best time to hug and hold these adorable creatures. The park is also home to kangaroos, wombats, echidnas, dingoes and a host of native birds. To get here by public transport, take a train to Pennant Hills station and then catch the Glenorie bus (ask the driver where to get off).

Featherdale Wildlife Park

One of the largest private collections of Australian animals inhabits **Featherdale Wildlife Park** (☎ 02-9622 1644; www.featherdale.com.au; 217-229 Kildare Rd, Doonside; adult A$18; 9am-5pm), and most of the creatures wander free. Cuddling a koala is old hat when you can also feed a joey, pat a wallaby or walk with wombats. There's also a diversity of native birds and an impressive crocodile exhibit. To get here via public transport, take a train to Blacktown, then bus No 725.

Calga Springs Sanctuary

There's a terrific array of animals north of Sydney at **Calga Springs Sanctuary** (☎ 02-4375 1100; www.calgasanctuary.com; Peats Ridge Rd, Leichhardt; adult A$15; 10am-5pm) – wallabies that wander into the café for patting, echidnas, kookaburras and gangly emus. The sanctuary aims to protect native animals from introduced species. There are even a few Aboriginal rock engravings and stencils that staff point out during guided tours at 10.30am, 1pm and 2.30pm. You'll need your own wheels to get here, but the exit is well-signposted off the F3 freeway (roughly 45 minutes from Sydney Harbour Bridge).

the park's northeastern tip. There are several roads through the park and four entrances. Admission is A$10 per car.

The **Kalkari visitors centre** (☎ 02-9457 9853; 9am-5pm) is about 2.5km into the park from the Mt Colah entrance on Ku-ring-gai Chase Rd. Centre staff are cheerful volunteers who are clued up on local walking tracks. The short wheelchair-accessible Discovery Walk (30 minutes) around the visitors centre takes in lookouts, a kangaroo grazing area, and a tree believed to have been here since Captain Cook landed.

The road descends from the visitors centre to the picnic area at **Bobbin Head** on Cowan Creek. **Halvorsen** (☎ 02-9457 9011; Bobbin Head) rents rowing boats for A$25/60 per hour/day and eight-seater motorboats for A$60/130. There's another **visitors centre** (☎ 02-9472 8949; Bobbin Head wharf; 10am-4pm) doling out similar information to Kalkari, and with a coffee shop. The **Bobbin Head Inn** (sandwiches A$3-5.50; breakfast & lunch) provides a good bite. For a walk that begins just past Bobbin Head, you can take the Sphinx and Warrimoo track (3½ hours, 9.6km). There's also a mangrove boardwalk at Bobbin Head.

The Basin Trail (three hours, 7km) is a more-difficult leg-stretcher that takes in **Aboriginal engravings** and a detour to the nearby river before concluding at the camping ground (see below). The more-demanding Resolute Track (three hours, 7km) passes more engravings and a cave that was once an Aboriginal home. Also worth checking out is the **Red Hands Cave**, not far from Resolute picnic area.

Sharks make swimming at Broken Bay impossible, but there are netted swimming areas at Illawong Bay and the Basin.

Sleeping

Basin camp sites (☎ 02-9974 1011; camp sites per person A$9) Camping at the Basin on the western side of Pittwater is a popular getaway for many Sydneysiders, so be sure to book ahead by phoning the message service. You can either walk from West Head Rd (about 2½ hours), or catch a ferry or water taxi from Palm Beach (see right).

Pittwater YHA (☎ 02-9999 5748; pittwater@hansw.org.au; Ku-ring-gai Chase National Park, via Church Point; dm A$22, d & tw A$60) With spectacular views across to Pittwater, this beautifully situated hostel (just a couple of kilometres south of the Basin) is known for its friendly wildlife and helpful staff. You'll need to book ahead and stock up on food. To get here, take bus No 156 from Manly Wharf to Church Point, then the ferry from Church Point to Halls Wharf. After all that, make a 10-minute uphill walk – but it's definitely worth the effort.

Getting There & Away

There are four roads from Sydney to the park: Mt Colah (turning off the Pacific Hwy onto Ku-ring-gai Chase Rd); Turramurra, in the southwest; and Terrey Hills and Church Point, in the southeast. **Shorelink Buses** (☎ 02-9457 8888) runs bus No 577 every 30 minutes from Turramurra station to the park entrance (A$3.10) on weekdays; one bus goes as far as Bobbin Head. The schedule changes on weekends with fewer buses going to the entrance but more to Bobbin Head.

The **Palm Beach Ferry Service** (☎ 02-9918 2747) runs to the Basin hourly from 9am to 5pm Monday to Thursday, 9am to 8pm Friday and 9am to 6pm Saturday, Sunday and public holidays (adult/concession A$8/4). You can also use **Church Point Water Taxis** (☎ 0428-238 190) for the trip between Church Point and Palm Beach (A$38.50 for up to six people).

BLUE MOUNTAINS

Artsy counterculture, New Age hideaway, wilderness getaway or bushwalker's mecca – the Blue Mountains is Sydney's alter ego. For the past century Sydneysiders have been escaping for weekends or dropping out entirely to appreciate the high altitude, eucalyptus haze and magnificent scenery – all of which have a restorative effect. The rugged crags, sheer cliffs and staggering chasms may have impeded the progress of early explorers, but for nature nuts they represent a peerless escape ideal for bushwalking, rock climbing or abseiling. Recent tourism has seen mountaineering operators and the café culture boom, so if you want to pamper yourself or rough it, there are plenty of options.

Activities

Whether you're into abseiling or bushwalking, there's plenty of outdoor action to be had in the Blue Mountains. The Jamison Valley is the best place for bushwalking

CLIMATIC CHANGE

If the weather is fine in Sydney, don't assume it'll be sunny in the Blue Mountains. There's considerable climatic difference between coastal Sydney and the high altitudes of Katoomba. It's even been known to snow during winter, so bring cold-/wet-weather gear, particularly if you're bushwalking.

with spectacular cliffs and dense bush all around. Further out Grose Valley has more great walks that are usually less busy than Jamison Valley.

The best base for rock climbing and mountaineering is definitely Katoomba, where there are heaps of great outfits with rental gear and professionals to give you tips.

Further out Jenolan Caves has good spelunking and can be a cool relief from bushwalking during hotter summer months.

Orientation

The Great Western Hwy (becoming the Western Motorway) takes you out of Sydney's urban sprawl and follows a scenic ridge running east–west through the Blue Mountains. Here, quaint towns merge into each other – Glenbrook, Springwood, Woodford, Lawson, Wentworth Falls, Leura, Katoomba, Medlow Bath, Blackheath, Mt Victoria and Hartley.

Getting There & Away

Katoomba is 109km from Sydney's city centre, but it's almost a satellite suburb with half-hourly trains from Central Station. The trip to Katoomba takes two hours (A$11.40), but because there are regular trains you can hop off at smaller townships along the way. For an affordable day trip, **CityRail** (☎ 13 15 00; www.cityrail.info) has the Blue Mountains ExplorerLink ticket (A$38.90), which includes same-day trains to and from Katoomba, a day's travel on the Blue Mountains Explorer Bus and admission to several attractions.

By car, leave the city via Parramatta Rd and detour onto the Western Motorway toll road (M4; A$2.20) at Strathfield. For an alternative scenic route, try the Bells Line of Rd (p89) by heading out on Parramatta Rd and from Parramatta drive northwest on the Windsor Rd to Windsor.

GLENBROOK TO LEURA

Sights & Activities

South of Glenbrook, the Blue Mountains National Park hosts the ancient **Red Hand Cave**, an Aboriginal shelter with an axe-grinding site and hand stencils on the walls. It's an easy four-hour return walk, southwest of the National Parks & Wildlife Service (NPWS) visitors centre.

The famous artist and author Norman Lindsay (1879–1969) lived in Faulconbridge from 1912 until his death. His home is now the **Norman Lindsay Gallery & Museum** (☎ 02-4751 1067; www.hermes.net.au/nlg; 14 Norman Lindsay Cres, Faulconbridge; adult A$8; 🕑 10am-4pm). It houses his cartoons, sculptures and risqué paintings, as well as puppets from *The Magic Pudding*.

Just south of Wentworth Falls are great views of the Jamison Valley. You can see the spectacular 300m **Wentworth Falls** from Falls Reserve, a small park in Wentworth Falls, which is the starting point for a network of half-day walking tracks. These include a walk to **Rocket Point** (one hour, 2km), offering closer views of the falls.

South of Leura, **Sublime Point** is an exquisite cliff lookout. You can have a picnic at nearby **Gordon Falls Reserve** and from here follow the cliff-top path or Cliff Dr 4km west to Katoomba's Echo Point.

Tours

For a unique and indigenous perspective of the Blue Mountains, join **Blue Mountains Walkabout** (☎ 0408-443 822; www.bluemountainswalkabout.com; adult A$95), which includes bushwalking with an Aboriginal guide. Don't forget your swimmers!

Sleeping & Eating

Hawkesbury Heights YHA (☎ 4754 5621; 836 Hawkesbury Rd, Hawkesbury Heights; dm A$19) Set in bush 8km from Springwood, this hostel takes its ecofriendly credentials seriously with solar power, a green toilet and a wood stove. Trees even sneak into the architecture with trunks used as beams. You'll need to book ahead and having your own transport to get there is a must.

Alexandra Hotel (☎ 4782 4422; 62 Great Western Hwy, Leura; s A$56-60, d & tw A$70-80) Has good pub rooms with cosy electric blankets and all-day Continental breakfasts, although light sleepers should be aware of the Thursday night disco. Meals (A$10 to A$12) are solid

THE ARTISTS' HIDEAWAY

Because of it's proximity to Sydney, many artists, writers and culture vultures have hidden out in the Blue Mountains. The most prominent is Norman Lindsay – cartoonist, painter, writer and all-round ratbag, depending on who you believe. His most famous (and harmless) drawings were of the Magic Pudding – an inexhaustible pudding bowl that could change into any type of dessert you desired. It was recently made into a film, with John Cleese voicing the loudmouthed pudding. Lindsay's other works included scandalous nudes (pretty tame by modern standards) and political cartoons that depicted Australia's wartime paranoias and racism. Many of Lindsay's works are on display in his former home in Faulconbridge (see p85).

Other writers have holed up here to write the Great Australian Novel, including Kit Denton (author of *Breaker Morant*) and novelist Eleanor Dark, whose picturesque Katoomba home – *Varuna* – still offers retreat fellowships to writers. More recently, the Blue Mountains produced the Down Under Beats Crew – a hip-hop outfit that won Triple J radio's prestigious 'Unearthed' award for best new band.

pub fare – steak, veggie lasagne and pies, all served with chips.

There are NPWS camping areas accessible by road at Euroka Clearing near Glenbrook, Murphys Glen near Woodford, and Ingar near Wentworth Falls. You can camp at Euroka Clearing by getting a permit (A$5) from the **Richmond NPWS** (☎ 02-4588 5247; Bowmans Cottage, 370 George St, Richmond); bring your own drinking water.

For authentic Japanese food, **Hana** (☎ 02-4784 1345; 121 The Mall, Leura; set menus A$12-15; 🕑 lunch Tue-Sat, dinner daily) dishes up excellent set-menu options, bento lunchboxes and great sushi and sashimi for dinner. For a bullish appetite, **Stockmarket** (☎ 02-4784 3121; 179 The Mall, Leura; pastries A$2.50-5, mains A$7.50-13.50; 🕑 breakfast & lunch) has lunch salads trading well and danishes booming at this economical bakery with a loungey feel.

KATOOMBA

☎ 02 / pop 17,900

Spooky thick mists, Art Deco guesthouses and cafés, the grand Three Sisters within strolling distance and the odd snowfall make this town a real curiosity. Katoomba (meaning 'shining tumbling water') has been the big tourist attraction of the Blue Mountains since the 1920s when development peaked, leaving several magnificent examples of architecture. It's the easiest base from which to explore the Blue Mountains – the really lazy need only walk down the street to ogle Echo Point. The more intrepid can plan their adventures further afield from this well-connected hub town. There's a definite hippy vibe (think incense burning in cafés, and beards with pony-tails), but this town is cosmopolitan enough to include all sorts.

Orientation

Steep Katoomba St is the main drag that eventually leads to **Echo Point**. The train station is conveniently at the head of (you guessed it) Katoomba St.

Information

Echo Point visitors centre (☎ 1300 653 408; www.bluemountainstourism.org.au; Echo Point; 🕑 9am-5pm)

Katoomba Book Exchange (☎ 4782 9997; 34 Katoomba St; per hr A$8; 🕑 10am-6pm Tue-Sat, noon-6pm Sun & Mon) Internet access.

Sights

The awe-inspiring **Echo Point** is easily the most popular and most photographed spot in the mountains. To the east are spectacular views of the **Three Sisters** rock formations – even more stunning when floodlit at night. Below are ant-like bushwalkers inching their way along various tracks through the **Jamison Valley**.

To the west of Echo Point, at the junction of Cliff Dr and Violet St, is **Scenic World** (☎ 4782 2699; www.scenicworld.com.au; 🕑 9am-5pm), a theme-parkish complex with rides that hurtle into the views. The **Scenic Railway** runs to the bottom of the Jamison Valley (A$14). The hair-raising 45-degree incline means this is one of the steepest train rides in the world, and is well worth screaming about. The popular six-hour walk to the **Ruined Castle** rock formation begins at the bottom of the valley. The **Scenic Skyway** (A$14) is a cable car half crossing Katoomba Falls gorge, conveniently pausing for photo opportunities. The **Scenisender** is an enclosed cable car (A$14) that also drops off in the Jamison Valley. By the time you're reading this, the Scenic empire will have expanded to include a new skyway that may go all the way across to Echo Point.

Activities

Before going out in the Blue Mountains wilderness, it's a good idea to check conditions at a NPWS office or visitors centre, as areas can be off-limits due to bushfires, landslides or other changes in conditions. Checking the weather is also a necessity as conditions are very changeable in the mountains.

ABSEILING, CANYONING & ROCK CLIMBING

A plethora of Katoomba operators offer excellent services for exploring the cliffs and crags of the region. Most offer discounts for YHA/VIP members and students.

At the **Australian School of Mountaineering** (☎ 4782 2014; www.asmguides.com; 166b Katoomba St; courses A$125-295) there are day-long rock climbing (A$165), abseiling (A$125) and bushcraft courses (A$295). It also arranges guided climbs (A$150).

Katoomba Adventure Centre (☎ 1800 624 226; www.kacadventures.com; 1 Katoomba St; trips A$85-140) organises half-/full-day abseiling (A$85/140), canyoning (A$100/140) and full-day rock climbing (A$140). It also leads mountain-biking trips through gorges and caverns (A$95 to A$160). As a bonus, staff do a CD photo album of your adventure (A$5).

Specialising in rock climbing, **High 'n' Wild Mountain Adventures** (☎ 4782 6224; www.high-n-wild.com.au; Shop 3, 5 Katoomba St; 9am-5pm; trip A$85-990) offers full-day abseiling (A$85 to A$150), half-/full-day climbing (A$110/160) and full-day canyoning (A$155). Mountain-biking trips (half-/full-day A$110/160) are also possible. It does a sideline in snow and ice climbing in the Mt Kosciuszko National Park with a four-day skills-focused trip (A$990).

Another good local outfit is **Blue Mountains Adventure Company** (☎ 4782 1271; bmac.com.au; 84a Bathurst Rd; trips A$85-155), arranging abseiling (from A$120), canyoning (from A$145), rock climbing (from A$155), bushwalking (from A$85) and mountain biking (from A$95) for a day or longer.

BUSHWALKING

The best way to really experience the Blue Mountains is on foot with walks ranging from 30 minutes to a few days. The two most popular walking areas are Jamison Valley (south of Katoomba) and Grose Valley (east of Blackheath).

Visit an NPWS visitors centre for walking suggestions or ask at one of the tourist information centres. It's very rugged country and walkers sometimes get lost, so it's highly advisable to: get reliable information; tell someone where you're going; and not go alone. Many Blue Mountains watercourses are polluted, so you have to sterilise water or take your own. Also, be prepared for sudden weather changes.

For a good basic walk, the Prince Henry Cliff Walk (two hours, 9km) starts at Echo Point and takes in the Katoomba Cascades and Jamison Valley. To get down into the valley, many walkers descend the Giant Stairway, 841 steps that leave even the fittest puffing on the return trip. The walk to the Ruined Castle is a difficult, longer walk (eight hours) that starts at the Katoomba Falls Kiosk.

Tours

Wonderbus (☎ 9555 9800, 0403-327 143; www.wonderbus.com) is a backpacker-friendly outfit with day tours of the Blue Mountains (A$70 to A$100) and overnight trips (A$215) that include the Jenolan Caves, dorm accommodation at the Blue Mountains YHA Hostel (you don't have to be a YHA member) and a bushwalk. Book in person at Sydney's **YHA Membership & Travel Centre** (Map pp48-50; ☎ 9261 1111; www.yha.com.au/yhainfo/membership_travel.cfm; 422 Kent St) or at any YHA hostel in Sydney.

An environmentally conscious outfit, **Tread Lightly Eco Tours** (☎ 4788 1229; www.treadlightly.com.au; 100 Great Western Hwy, Medlow Bath) does tours as easy as a two-hour bushwalk (A$30) or as tough as a full-day rainforest trek (A$165).

Festivals & Events

Yulefest is a Christmas in July celebration throughout the Blue Mountains, with parades and traditional dinners. Because it's held in winter, there's always the possibility that it will be a 'white Christmas'.

Sleeping

Blue Mountains YHA (☎ 4782 1416; www.yha.com.au; 207 Katoomba St; dm A$22-28, d & tw A$70-80, A$3.50

surcharge for YHA nonmembers;) This large Art Deco property has been renovated to highlight the large verandas and huge dining room. There's a barbecue, videos and bicycles, plus very helpful staff with details on discounts and local walks.

Blue Mountains Backpackers (1800 624 226; 190 Bathurst St; dm A$20; d & tw A$60;) This small, laid-back hostel has large common areas and a big backyard (including hammocks) in which to laze. For rainy days there's a good video collection, although the helpful owners can get you outside when it's sunny. (The place operates Katoomba Adventure Centre – see Activities, p87).

No 14 (4782 7104; www.bluemts.com.au/no14; 14 Lovell St; dm A$22, s A$45-50, d & tw A$60-65) Across the road from a meditation centre, this place has absorbed neighbouring karma to create a chilled and comfortable bungalow. Rooms are bright and clean, although it can get a bit crowded and is a little way from the centre of town.

Katoomba Mountain Lodge (4782 3933; kmtlodge@pnc.com.au; 31 Lurline St; dm A$18-20, s A$40-50, d & tw A$60) This backstreet bargain has an emphasis on price, not style, with simple rooms and meals extra. Tea and coffee are always available gratis and upper-level rooms have window-seat views of the valley.

Cecil Guesthouse (47821411; 108 Katoomba St; s A$55-65, d A$85-95) This cosy little spot is showing its age a little, but excellent views and huge common rooms and a tennis court are excellent bonuses.

Clarendon Guesthouse (4782 1322; www.clarendonguesthouse.com.au; 68 Lurline St; d A$90;) On the corner of Lurline and Waratah Sts, this guesthouse has both old-fashioned and motel-style rooms, with log fires, a cocktail bar and a swimming pool. It's also a popular venue for live music and cabaret acts. Breakfast is included.

Katoomba Falls Caravan Park (4782 1835; Katoomba Falls Rd; caravan sites from A$16, cabins A$80-95) About 2km south of the highway, this well-managed caravan park also has good cabins. Set in lush bush surrounds, some of the camp sites are a little worn down, making for uncomfortable nights.

SPLURGE!

Carrington Hotel (4782 1111; www.thecarrington.com.au; 15-47 Katoomba St; d A$120-450) Check in to the Carrington for lavish luxury. Elegantly refurbished to highlight the Art Deco charm, this hotel is Katoomba's masterpiece. Rooms range from basic traditional rooms (really plush pub rooms) to elaborate suites. The buffet breakfasts (included with room rates) are ridiculously generous – typical luxury from a hotel named after 'Champagne Charlie' Carrington, a governor infamous for enjoying a glass or two of bubbly to start the day.

Eating & Drinking

The best eating is found by simply strolling down Katoomba St. To stock up on groceries, head for **Coles** (4782 6133; cnr Waratah & Parke Sts). The cheapest bakery in town is **Katoomba French Hot Bread** (4782 4820; 135 Katoomba St; pastries A$1.50-2.50; 9am-6pm) with bargain fresh pastries and pies.

Paragon Café (4782 2928; 65 Katoomba St; mains A$15-22; breakfast, lunch & dinner) This is Katoomba's unmissable Art Deco highlight. Some come for the indulgent chocolate counter, others for the huge tea range, but the fancy cocktail bar out the back is perfect for meeting Al Capone over a Manhattan. The menu is a little unimaginative, but the surroundings more than make up for it.

Solitary (4782 1164; 90 Cliff Dr, Leura Falls; mains A$24-32; lunch & dinner) This is *the* hot-date restaurant in town. Impress with the selection of tagines and stylish food, washed down with a bottle from the sophisticated wine list. Finish off with a downright sexy dessert. Reservations essential on weekends.

Parakeet Café (4782 2347; 195b Katoomba St; mains A$6.50-13; breakfast, lunch & dinner) This bohemian hang-out is just the spot to pose with poets (poetry readings every second Monday) and installation artists who sculpt napkins and salt shakers. It's bright and breezy with great breakfasts.

Flapping Curtain Café (4782 1622; 10 Katoomba St; mains A$3.50-10.50, breakfast, lunch & dinner) A quirky eatery that dishes up burgers and sandwiches (even an authentic chip butty) with bubbly service.

Katoomba's pubs are a bit average, but they all serve beer. **Gearins Hotel** (4782 4395; 273 Great Western Hwy) is Katoomba's best watering hole, with matey locals and a delicious 'chocolate draught'.

Entertainment

Clarendon (☎ 4782 1322; www.clarendonguesthouse.com.au; 68 Lurline St) is known for its outrageous cabaret acts and quality live music.

Trieseles (☎ 4782 4026; 287 Bathurst Rd) For DJs and live music, this place belts out the beats Thursday to Saturday nights.

Edge Cinema (☎ 4782 8900; www.edgecinema.com.au; 225 Great Western Hwy; adult/concession A$12/11) Film buffs should check out this cinema showing current releases, as well as a 40-minute Blue Mountains documentary called *The Edge* (adult/concession A$13.50/11.50), on a giant screen.

Getting Around

BICYCLE

You can hire bicycles from **Cycle Tech** (☎ 4782 2800; 182 Katoomba St; hire half-/full day A$28/50), where prices include a spares kit and helmet.

BUS

Blue Mountains Bus Company (☎ 4782 4213; Highland St, Leura) Runs between Katoomba train station, Echo Point, and Scenic World. Buses are roughly every 45 minutes.

Blue Mountains Explorer Bus (☎ 4782 4807; www.explorerbus.com.au; tickets A$25) Does a hop-on/hop-off hourly circuit (from 9.30am to 5.30pm) of attractions around Katoomba and Leura. Package passes include entry into Scenic World and Jenolan Caves tours.

Trolley Bus (☎ 1800 801 577; www.trolleytours.com.au; 285 Main St) Drives around the main sights of Leura and Katoomba.

Mountainlink (☎ 4751 1077; www.mountainlink.com.au) Runs a service between Echo Point and Gordon Falls via Katoomba St and Leura Mall (Monday to Saturday).

BLACKHEATH AREA

Many visitors use quaint Blackheath as a base for visiting the Grose and Megalong Valleys. You can easily wander to the awesome lookouts a few kilometres east of town, such as **Govetts Leap** and **Evan's Lookout**. To the northeast, via Hat Hill Rd, are **Pulpit Rock**, **Perry's Lookdown** and **Anvil Rock**.

A cliff-top track leads from Govetts Leap to Pulpit Rock, and there are several walks from Govetts Leap down into the Grose Valley. Get details on the walks from the **NPWS visitors centre** (☎ 02-4787 8877; Govetts Leap Rd, Blackheath; 🕓 9am-4.30pm). Perry's Lookdown is the beginning of the shortest route to the beautiful **Blue Gum Forest** (four hours, 5km) in the base of the valley. Another good information source is the **Blue Mountains Heritage Centre** (☎ 02-4787 8877; Govetts Leap Rd, Blackheath; 🕓 9am-4.30pm), about 3km off the Great Western Hwy.

Sleeping

There's bushwalker camping at Acacia Flat, in the Grose Valley near the Blue Gum Forest. It's a steep descent from Govetts Leap or Perry's Lookdown. You can also camp at Perry's Lookdown, which has a car park acting as a convenient base for walks into the Grose Valley. However, you'll need to bring your own water.

Gardners Inn (☎ 4787 8347; 255 Great Western Hwy; s/d A$45/80) This cosy and friendly pub is the oldest hotel (1832) in the Blue Mountains. Some rooms are showing (and smelling) their age, but they do come with a hearty breakfast.

Blackheath Caravan Park (☎ 4787 8101; Prince Edward St; camp/caravan sites per person A$10/14; on-site caravans per 2 people A$45) This friendly caravan park is off Govetts Leap Rd, just 600m from the highway. Caravans are basic (there's no linen), but serviceable.

JENOLAN CAVES

Australia's best-known limestone caves have been spooking kids since 1867, when **Jenolan Caves** (☎ 6359 3311; www.jenolancaves.org.au) were first opened to the public. Parts of the system remain unexplored, but you can visit nine caves by guided tour. There are roughly 11 tours a day (10am and 4.30pm weekdays, 9.30am and 5pm weekends). Cave passes are priced individually, starting with **Lucas Cave** (adult/concession A$15/10) to the awesome **Temple of Baal** (adult/concession A$22/15). There is a variety of themed tours that usually run on weekends, such as the eerie Ghost Tour (A$28). For climbers, there's a series of adventure caves (A$55 to A$190) that involve varying levels of scrambling. During school holidays, you should arrive early as the best caves can sell out by 10am.

BELLS LINE OF ROAD

If you've got your own transport, this back road between Richmond and Lithgow is the most scenic route across the Blue Mountains. There are fine views towards the coast from Kurrajong Heights on the eastern slopes of the range, there are orchards around Bilpin, and there are sandstone cliffs and bush scenery all the way to Lithgow.

NORTH COAST

Stretching from Sydney to the Queensland border, the golden sands, sunny days and crashing waves of NSW's northerly coast are the dream stuff of Australian holidays. Whether you're looking to surf, stretch out in the glorious sun or take a moody coastal walk, this uninterrupted run of beaches won't let you down. Bustling Byron Bay has become a second home for many Sydneysiders, and overdeveloped patches dot the coastline, but there are still a few undiscovered places on which to unfurl your towel.

Most surprising is the range of experiences on offer along the coast. Where else could you start your day getting photographed with a giant concrete banana, then do a spot of dolphin-watching, de-stress at a yoga class before heading out for a night of word-class live music, and then go clubbing till dawn? Just remember that if you visit during the school holidays you'll be sharing the attractions with loads of holidaying families who make the regular pilgrimage to the coast. Then there's the last week of November, marked on calendars as Schoolies Week – a post-exam blowout that attracts around 50,000 high-schoolers from across Australia to book up places all the way to the Gold Coast and beyond.

Activities

The weather's good and there are hundreds of operators keen to get you exploring the great outdoors. Water lovers can catch the curl at Newcastle's Nobby's Beach, a great surf beach for beginners or the more advanced, or snorkel among grey nurse sharks and blossoming coral in Solitary Islands Marine Parks. For an awesome natural high, challenge the sky and the waves (and probably the beach) by kitesurfing in Byron Bay.

Hike through rainforest to the top of the ex-volcano Mt Warning, or take a bumpy camel ride across Port Macquarie's Lighthouse Beach.

NEWCASTLE

☎ 02 / pop 133,690

A short hop from Sydney and close enough to hear corks popping in the Hunter Valley, Newcastle definitely has a lot to offer. Lazing on golden beaches or searching out the next big thing in Oz rock at a local pub, make it worth the pilgrimage. Out-of-touch Australians might still remember Newcastle as a city of heavy industry, but the metropolis has been re-inventing itself. Since the 1987 closure of the steel plant, Newcastle has undergone an urban renaissance, making it one of Australia's most liveable cities.

Orientation

The central business district (CBD) sits on a peninsula bordered by the Hunter River and the sea, tapering down to the long sand spit out to Nobby's Head. The train station is at the CBD's northeastern edge – the East End. The shopping centre is Hunter St, a pedestrian mall between Newcomen and Perkins Sts. The lively suburb of Hamilton is adjacent to Newcastle West; Cooks Hill (including Darby St, the famous dining precinct) is south of Hunter St. Stockton is north across the river. If you get disoriented, Queens Wharf Tower is always visible to the north.

Newcastle has two airports (Belmont and Williamtown), both about 40km from the city. **Port Stephens Coaches** (☎ 4982 2940; http://pscoaches.com.au; 17a Port Stephens Dr, Anna Bay) travels to Williamtown airport frequently (A$5.10, 35 minutes) en route to Nelson Bay. Local bus Nos 310, 311, 322 and 363 go to Belmont from Newcastle train station (A$2.50, 1½ hours). A **taxi** (☎ 4979 3000) costs A$42 to either airport.

Information

You can log on at most hostels (Nomads Backpackers By the Beach is the cheapest – see p93).

Royal Newcastle Hospital (☎ 4923 6000; Pacific St) Right by the YHA. However the Royal has no emergency department.

Visitors centre (☎ 1800 654 558, 4974 2999; www.newcastletourism.com; 363 Hunter St; 9am-5pm Mon-Fri, 10am-3.30pm Sat & Sun;) The always-helpful Newcastle books accommodation and tours, and has extensive Hunter Valley information.

Sights & Activities

SWIMMING & SURFING

The whole town heads for an after-work swim at **Newcastle Beach** (just east of the CBD), especially at the 1922 **ocean baths**. Surfers should check out **Nobby's Beach**, just north of the baths. For newbie grommets, **Avago Sports**

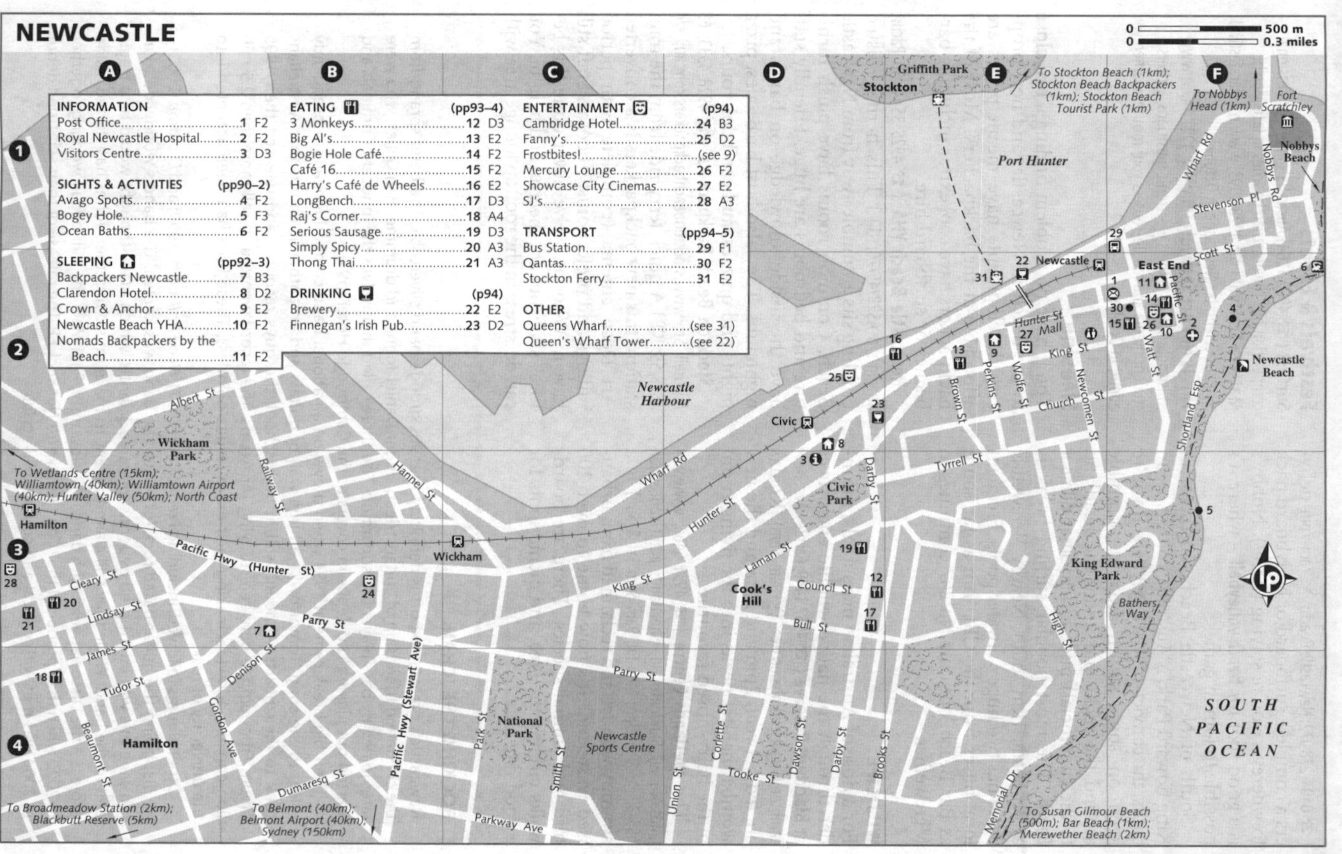
NEWCASTLE
0 500 m
0 0.3 miles
INFORMATION
Post Office 1 F2
Royal Newcastle Hospital 2 F2
Visitors Centre 3 D3
SIGHTS & ACTIVITIES (pp90–2)
Avago Sports 4 F2
Bogey Hole 5 F3
Ocean Baths 6 F2
SLEEPING (pp92–3)
Backpackers Newcastle 7 B3
Clarendon Hotel 8 D2
Crown & Anchor 9 E2
Newcastle Beach YHA 10 F2
Nomads Backpackers by the Beach 11 F2
EATING (pp93–4)
3 Monkeys 12 D3
Big Al's 13 E2
Bogie Hole Café 14 F2
Café 16 15 F2
Harry's Café de Wheels 16 E2
LongBench 17 D3
Raj's Corner 18 A4
Serious Sausage 19 D3
Simply Spicy 20 A3
Thong Thai 21 A3
DRINKING (p94)
Brewery 22 E2
Finnegan's Irish Pub 23 D2
ENTERTAINMENT (p94)
Cambridge Hotel 24 B3
Fanny's 25 D2
Frostbites! (see 9)
Mercury Lounge 26 F2
Showcase City Cinemas 27 E2
SJ's 28 A3
TRANSPORT (pp94–5)
Bus Station 29 F1
Qantas 30 F2
Stockton Ferry 31 E2
OTHER
Queens Wharf (see 31)
Queen's Wharf Tower (see 22)
Griffith Park
Stockton
To Stockton Beach (1km); Stockton Beach Backpackers (1km); Stockton Beach Tourist Park (1km)
To Nobbys Head (1km)
Fort Scratchley
Nobbys Beach
Port Hunter
Newcastle Harbour
East End
Newcastle Beach
Civic Park
Cook's Hill
King Edward Park
Bathers Way
SOUTH PACIFIC OCEAN
Wickham Park
Wickham
Hamilton
National Park
Newcastle Sports Centre
To Wetlands Centre (15km); Williamtown (40km); Williamtown Airport (40km); Hunter Valley (50km); North Coast
To Broadmeadow Station (2km); Blackbutt Reserve (5km)
To Belmont (40km); Belmont Airport (40km); Sydney (150km)
To Susan Gilmour Beach (500m); Bar Beach (1km); Merewether Beach (2km)

(☎ 0404-278 072; Newcastle Beach; ⏲ 7am-7pm) delivers a complete surfboard or bodyboard pack to wherever you're staying (A$39). Nobby's is a good spot for **beach volleyball** – where it's possible to join in games.

South of Newcastle Beach, northeast of King Edward Park, is Australia's oldest ocean baths, the convict-carved **Bogey Hole**. If you're keen on some skinny-dipping, scramble around the rocks and under the headland to the (unofficial) nude beach, **Susan Gilmour Beach**. The most popular surfing break is at **Bar Beach**, 1km south. Nearby **Merewether Beach** has two huge saltwater pools. Frequent local buses from the CBD run as far south as Bar Beach, but only No 207 continues to Merewether.

WILDLIFE

For a dose of Australian marsupials, meander through the native wildlife enclosures at **Blackbutt Reserve** (☎ 4952 1449; Carnley Ave, New Lambton Heights; admission free; ⏲ 9am-5pm). Koalas are fed between 2pm and 3pm and the new wombat habitat peeks into the living room of the hairy-nosed favourite.

The **Wetlands Centre** (☎ 4951 6466; www.wetlands.org.au; Sandgate Rd, Shortland; adult/concession A$5/3; ⏲ 9am-3pm Mon-Fri, 9am-5pm Sat & Sun) is a swampy wonderland reclaimed from urbanised wasteland. It's now home to over 200 bird and animal species. There are boardwalks circling the area, and picnic spots for a good day out.

Festivals & Events

Surfest (☎ 4982 1264) Australia's oldest professional competition hits Novocastrian beaches in late March.
Mattara Festival (☎ 4928 4093; www.mattarafestival.org.au) Celebrates Newcastle in October.
This Is Not Art Festival (TINA; ☎ 4927 1475; www.thisisnotart.org) Gathers electronic musicians, writers, student media and rabble-rousers your mother warned you about; in October.

Sleeping

You'll have no problem finding a bed close to the beach in Newcastle, and new property developments have meant prices are affordable at the backpackers. Most of the backpackers have cool extras including barbecues or surfboard hire.

Newcastle Beach YHA (☎ 4925 3544; 30 Pacific St; dm/s/d A$28/45/70; 💻) This heritage-listed building sits a stumble away from Newcastle Beach. Common rooms have plush furniture and bedrooms are huge. Friendly staff have the inside knowledge on bands and nightclubs. They also host barbecues, pizza nights and quizzes, and can book tours.

Stockton Beach Backpackers (☎ 4928 4333; 68 Mitchell St; www.stocktonbeachbackpackers.com.au; s/d A$28/55; 💻) A quick ferry ride from the train station, this new backpackers is a converted Art Deco cinema (complete with period railings and projectionist's booth). Staff still have a 'Whoops, we've never done this before!' style, but are cheerful and helpful. You can de-stress in the rooftop lounge area with

ROCKING THE 'CHAIR

Newcastle's greatest export is definitely the '90s grunge band silverchair. The band sprang from the childhood friendship of guitarist/lead singer Daniel Johns and drummer Ben Gillies, who were later joined by bass player Chris Joannou. The three called themselves the Innocent Criminals and started out playing Led Zeppelin covers at the Cambridge Hotel (p94).

Their big break came in 1994 when they won a national band competition, and subsequently released the song 'Tomorrow' – a huge wall of guitars and an anthemic chorus that Australians took to their hearts. Although still in high school, the guys recorded and released their 1995 album *Frogstomp* in between studying for exams. The record went on to sell more than 2.5 million copies worldwide, making their exam results pointless. These boys had been accepted into the university of rock.

Other albums followed, including *Freak Show* (1997), *Neon Ballroom* (1999) and *Diorama* (2002) – all displaying the guitar-based rock for which the band was known. The band's worldwide touring schedule was interrupted by Johns' reactive arthritis, which many thought would be a tragic end to the band. While they still claim to want to make music together, Johns has started a side project – the Dissociatives – with dance-music auteur, Paul Mac. The pair began working together in 2000 when they produced the *I Can't Believe It's Not Rock* EP. The release of their self-titled debut in 2004 was met with critical and commercial acclaim.

SPLURGE!

Clarendon Hotel (☎ 4927 0966; www.clarendonhotel.com.au; 347 Hunter St; d A$121-132, ste A$143-154;) Boutique to its britches, the Clarendon has seen a 'hip replacement'. It's an old pub styled uber-fashionably with expansive beds and funked-up couches. Walls are vividly painted, so every room has its own colour scheme (from lipstick red to bold blues). There are cheaper rates midweek, and good packages including champagne, dinner and breakfast can be found on its website.

excellent city views, or unwind with a spa and sauna (A$5).

Nomads Backpackers by the Beach (☎ 4926 3472; www.backpackersbythebeach.com.au; 34 Hunter St; dm/d A$20/50;) Fresh, clean and damn close to the beach, this multistorey hostel (expect some stair climbing) is relaxed. Occasionally it teams up with other hostels for full-on backpacker barbecues. Buried in the basement is the most affordable Internet in town.

Backpackers Newcastle (☎ 4969 3436; www.newcastlebackpackers.com; 42-44 Denison St, Hamilton; dm A$20, d from A$50;) With a pool table, table tennis and solar-heated pool, there's plenty to bring you out to Hamilton. Staff are mad-keen surfers offering tips, gear and lifts to the best breaks. They'll also pick up and drop off at any Newcastle train station.

Crown & Anchor (☎ 4929 1027; 189 Hunter St; dm A$20) This hotel has clean, new rooms with basic facilities (there are no kitchens or common rooms). The club downstairs is raucous Wednesday to Saturday nights, making it a good central spot if you're out all night.

Stockton Beach Tourist Park (☎ 4928 1393; Pitt St, Stockton; camp sites per 2 people from A$16, cabins A$50-90) This time-worn caravan park is handy to the CBD via the Stockton–Newcastle ferry.

Eating

In the battle of the eat streets, Darby St is kicking Beaumont's arse for choice and style. The East End also has a few options, although they're pricier.

EAST END

Bogie Hole Café (☎ 4926 1790; cnr Hunter & Pacific Sts; mains A$10-20; breakfast, lunch & dinner) Always packed, this eatery has generous serves and is handy to the beach. Pavement dining in this quieter part of town makes for a great breakfast or dinner – usually including menu mainstays such as pastas, salads, burgers, steaks and chicken.

Big Al's (☎ 4929 2717; cnr King & Brown Sts; burgers A$3.20-5, rolls A$3.10-5.10; lunch & dinner) This gangster-themed (more Al Capone than Ice-T) burger joint is a quirky Newcastle institution. Burgers are generous, each with a kooky name – The Godfather is a beef burger with enough eggs and bacon to make Marlon Brando worry about his cholesterol.

Cafe 16 (☎ 4927 5622; 16 Watt St; mains A$12-14; breakfast & lunch Mon-Sat) For a munch of the Middle East right in the CBD, this place has a great menu. There's Moroccan sausages and eggs for breakfast or tiger prawns with chermoula for a terrific lunch. Wash it all down with a cup of fresh mint tea.

Harry's Café de Wheels (☎ 4926 2165; on the waterfront; pies A$3; open lunch & dinner, late) Set in an old tram car, this is the spot for late-night hot dogs and surprisingly good pies. You can take on the Tiger – a pie heaped with mashed potato and peas.

BEAUMONT STREET

Raj's Corner (☎ 4962 1827; cnr Beaumont & James Sts; plates A$7.90-12 lunch & dinner Mon-Sat) This Indian lunch option has familiar dishes – tikka, korma, butter chicken – all piled on to a plate. Vegetarians have a fair choice here, too.

Simply Spice (☎ 4965 4688; Shop 5-6, 79 Beaumont St; mains A$8-13; lunch & dinner Mon-Sat) Heaped serves of traditional Singaporean food and a simple décor make this another good, quick bite. You should definitely try its Asian drinks, including chai and iced *bandung* (a milky drink made from rose syrup and condensed milk). Weekday lunches are a bargain at A$6.

Thong Thai (☎ 4969 5655; 74 Beaumont St; mains A$10-15; dinner Wed-Mon) Delicious and spicy, this laminated-table eatery serves up all the classics to Novocastrian families wanting a quick, cheap feed.

DARBY STREET

LongBench (☎ 4927 8888; 161 Darby St; breakfast A$8-14; lunch & dinner A$11-18; breakfast, lunch & dinner) Funky interiors and zippy staff make this a great dinner spot. It serves mammoth burgers, pastas and fish – the Mod Oz works. Out the back is a roomy courtyard in which to luxuriate. Coffee bowls are a must for the morning after – a perfect hangover antidote.

Serious Sausage (☎ 4929 2278; 76 Darby St; burgers A$9.50; ⏰ breakfast, lunch & dinner Mon-Fri, breakfast & lunch Sat & Sun) There's no fooling with these guys when it comes to snags. All its produce is organic, with burgers using local beef (there are also gluten-free options for burgers). Spicy kransky dogs and chicken or veggie burgers make great quick bites.

3 Monkeys (☎ 4926 3779; 131 Darby St; light meals A$11-18, mains A$20-25; ⏰ breakfast, lunch & dinner) Tempura vegies and mind-blowing smoothies (try the A$5.50 Cookie Monster – blended choc-chip cookies in malt and ice cream) make this a good spot for a casual meal. The chilled-out courtyard is ideal to drink the night away.

Drinking

Brewery (☎ 4929 6333; www.qwb.com.au; 150 Wharf Rd) Has unmissable schooners of mind-numbing alcoholic ginger beer, with a mixed crowd of suits and uni students.

Finnegan's Irish Pub (☎ 4926 4777; 21-23 Darby St) A cut above most wannabe Irish boozers, and you'll find a jolly Novocastrian crowd rolling out of this comfy establishment.

Clubbing

Most places in town don't warm up until 11pm.

Mercury Lounge (☎ 4926 1119; 23 Watt St; ⏰ 8pm-4.30am) Hosts visiting DJs in a moodily lit bar and serves cocktails.

Fanny's (☎ 4929 2025; www.fannys.com.au; 311 Wharf Rd; ⏰ Wed-Sun 8pm-3am; admission A$5-20) Has hard breakbeats, electronica and a pick-up joint reputation.

Frostbites! (☎ 4929 1027; 1st fl, Crown & Anchor; 189 Hunter St; ⏰ 6pm-late Tue-Sun) Has top 40 dancing, but everyone comes here to sample a brain-tingling alcoholic snow cone.

Entertainment

CINEMAS

Showcase City Cinemas (☎ 4929 5019; 31 Wolfe St; admission A$10) Alternates Hollywood new releases with foreign and independent movies.

LIVE MUSIC

Newcastle's brightest musical star was silverchair (see p92), the grunge powerhouse that conquered the world after cutting its teeth in local backrooms. Newcastle's live scene remains strong, but is changeable, so check with hostel staff or Thursday's *Newcastle Herald*. The biweekly street press magazine *U Turn* (www.uturn.net.au) also has an extensive gig guide. Most pubs only have gigs Wednesday to Sunday.

Cambridge Hotel (☎ 4962 2459; 789 Hunter St) Has been launching live music in Newcastle for years, so it's a good bet for bands – usually locals and the odd national act.

SJ's (☎ 4961 2537; cnr Beaumont & Hudson Sts) Sleekly refitted, SJ's has a huge band room and purple pool table.

Newcastle Entertainment Centre (☎ 4921 2121; www.nentcent.com.au; Brown Rd, Broadmeadow). Big international acts periodically pack out this centre.

Getting There & Away

AIR

At the time of writing, low-end fares to Sydney started at A$100, Brisbane A$80 and Melbourne A$70.

Brindabella Airlines (☎ 1300 668 824, 02-6248 8711; www.brindabella-airlines.com.au) Flies from Williamtown to Canberra (A$290).

Jetstar (☎ 13 15 38; www.jetstar.com.au)

Qantas (☎ 13 13 13; www.qantas.com.au; 79 Hunter St)

Virgin Blue (☎ 13 67 89; www.virginblue.com.au)

BUS

Nearly all long-distance buses stop behind Newcastle station.

McCafferty's (☎ 13 14 99; www.mccaffertys.com.au) goes daily to Sydney (A$35, 2½ hours) and all stops to Brisbane (A$80, 14 hours), while **Port Stephens Coaches** (☎ 4982 2940; http://pscoaches.com.au; 17a Port Stephens Dr, Anna Bay) also runs daily to Sydney (A$38, two hours). **Sid Fogg's Coaches** (☎ 4928 1088; www.sidfoggs.com.au; RMB 2324 Main Rd, Fullerton Cove) travels to Sydney's Liverpool Station (A$27, three hours, once daily) and Canberra (A$52, 7½ hours, once daily).

TRAIN

CityRail (☎ 13 15 00; www.cityrail.nsw.gov.au) trains travel frequently to Sydney (A$17, three hours).

Getting Around

BOAT

From Queens Wharf, the Stockton ferry (A$1.80) runs half-hourly from 5.15am to 11pm Monday to Thursday (to midnight Friday and Saturday, to 10pm Sunday).

BUS

Most **local buses** (☎ 13 15 00; www.newcastle.sta.nsw.gov.au) operate every half-hour on weekdays, less frequently on weekends. Fares are time-based: one-/four-hourly A$2.50/4.90 or all day for A$7.60.

HUNTER VALLEY

The Hunter Valley's a name you might groggily recall from wine bottles. Some of Australia's best wines are grown right here – it's celebrated for big reds, but there are some whites that are well worth looking for. Most of the wineries are clustered around the New England Hwy and to the south along Wollombi/Maitland Rd. Cessnock is the nearest town. Get started with a copy of the *Hunter Valley Wine Country Visitors Guide* (available at most NSW visitors centres) with vineyard summaries and an excellent map. Another great source of information: **Vintage Hunter Wine & Visitors Centre** (☎ 02-4990 4477; www.winecountry.com.au; 455 Wine Country Dr, Pokolbin; 9am-5pm Mon-Sat, to 4pm Sun).

Wineries

Most wineries have free 'cellar door' tastings from 10am to 5pm – buying isn't compulsory, but if you find a wine you like many wineries have good outdoor areas in which to enjoy a picnic.

The huge new development is **Hunter Valley Gardens** (☎ 02-4998 7600; www.hvg.com.au; Broke Rd, Pokolbin). It's a combination of cellar door, restaurant, orchard, speciality shops and decorative garden. This is the place to sample Roche wines, although the gardens are really only for botanical buffs.

Affordable and laid-back, **McGuigan Cellars** (☎ 02-4998 7402; www.mcguiganwines.com.au; McDonalds Rd; tours A$2; tours 11am, noon & 2pm Sat & Sun) is Australia's third-largest winery, with an excellent cheese factory. A smaller vineyard with a big reputation is **Brokenwood Wines** (☎ 02-4998 7559; www.brokenwood.com.au; McDonalds Rd) with a reliable semillon and a gutsy shiraz.

For a quick sampler, the **Small Winemakers Centre** (☎ 02-4998 7668; www.smallwinemakerscentre.com.au; McDonalds Rd) serves as an ambassador for 10 winemakers that don't have their own cellar doors. It's a good place to discover an unknown bottle. The Australian Regional Food Centre & Café is attached with a variety of jams, chutneys and cordials that make good souvenirs. If you're getting peckish, **Pokolbin Estate Vineyard** (☎ 02-4998 7524; www.pokolbinestate.com.au; McDonalds Rd) is a boutique winery (most of its wines aren't exported) that also offers delicious olive tastings.

If you're over wine, make a beeline for **Bluetongue Brewery** (☎ 4998 7777; www.bluetonguebrewery.com.au; Hunter Resort Country Estate, Hermitage Rd),

TOP FIVE WINE-TASTING TIPS

Despite the dramatic sloshing-around-the-mouth rituals and the complicated language ('Yes, definitely woody hints of cinnamon in this one'), wine tasting is a fairly simple business. Everyone has different tastes, though, so it's a good idea to sample several varietals. Getting into the grapes and then driving is just stupid, so here's a few tips that'll let you enjoy a good drop and still come home with your driver's licence.

- Designate a driver: roads in the area are dodgy, with curvy stretches and several unpaved (dirt) roads. A driver needs to be sober enough to deal with unfamiliar roads. Being the designated driver is a tough job, so buy him or her a bottle to enjoy when they get home.
- Monitor your drinks: if you are driving keep an eye on how many drinks you're having. Tastes are usually in 20mL doses. Five an hour puts a woman close to being over the limit, while a big guy could possibly have twice as much.
- Take a tour: this way you can drink as much as you want, safe in the knowledge that someone else has the car keys (see p96).
- Use spittoons: they may look like props from an old cowboy movie, but they mean you can taste without swallowing. Professional wine tasters opt for the spittoon so they can sample a lot of wine without losing the plot.
- Start with whites, finish with reds: to enjoy the subtler flavours, drink whites in the morning and take on the heavier reds and dessert wines in the afternoon.

BEHIND THE SCENES: WINERY TOURS

If simply tasting isn't enough, then joining a winery tour can be an education, showing you how wine is made as well as providing a few inside tips on the best vintages. Here are a few winning wineries that offer free daily tours:

Drayton's Family Wines (☎ 02-4998 7513; www.draytonswines.com.au; Oakley Creek Rd; tours 11am)

The Rothbury Estate (☎ 02-4998 7363; Broke Rd; tours 10.30am)

Tyrrell's Vineyard (☎ 02-4993 7000; www.tyrrells.com.au; Broke Rd; tours 1.30pm Mon-Sat)

Wyndham Estate (☎ 02-4938 3444; www.wyndhamestate.com; 700 Dalwood Rd; tours 11am)

If you're prepared to pay a few bucks, **Hunter Valley Wine School** (☎ 4998 7777; Hermitage Rd, Hunter Resort; 2hr hard-hat tour A$25, winery tour A$5) has an in-depth tour and discussion of appreciation and wine styles.

which has concocted a very good ginger beer and some other excellent varieties that are ripe for the tasting.

TOURS

Visitors centres and various accommodation places in both Sydney and Newcastle often book tours to the Hunter Valley. For tours of individual wineries, see above.

Grapemobile (☎ 0500 804 039; www.grapemobile.com.au; cnr McDonalds Rd & Palmers Lane; bike hire per day A$30) Organises bike hire and tours through the vineyards, including a support bus and meals.

Grape-X-pectations (☎ 4991 1578; www.grape-x-pectations.com.au; 1-day tours A$70) Specialises in discovering boutique wineries, and can do transfers from Newcastle.

Hunter Valley Day Tours (☎ 4938 5031; www.huntertourism.com/daytours; ⌚ 8am-9pm; 1-day tours A$95) Takes you on a wine- and cheese-tasting outing. It can pick you up from Newcastle.

Wine Rover (☎ 1800 801 012, 0427 001 100; www.rovercoaches.com.au; 1-day tours A$35-40) Offers a hop-on/hop-off bus that goes to most of the big wineries, departing from the Wine Country Tourism Office.

Barrington Tops National Park

This **World Heritage wilderness** lies on the rugged Barrington Plateau with one of Australia's most diverse ecosystems. There are walking tracks and lookouts near Gloucester Tops, Careys Peak, Williams River (wheelchair accessible) and Jerusalem Creek. Always check conditions with Gloucester **NPWS office** (☎ 02-6538 5300) before heading out, as weather is very unpredictable. Gloucester NPWS also books camping at **Devil's Hole** (camp sites free), **Junction Pools** (camp sites for 2 people A$3) and **Gloucester River** (camp sites for 2 people A$5).

Day tours to Barrington Tops can be organised through Nelson Bay **visitors centre** (☎ 1800 808 900, 02-4981 1579; www.portstephens.org.au; Victoria Pde; ⌚ 9am-5pm). **Barrington Canoe Adventures** (☎ 02-6558 4316; www.canoebarrington.com.au; 774 Barrington East Rd, Barrington; 1-day rental A$55) runs white-water trips out of its riverside lodge, 14km from Gloucester. Weekend packages including accommodation and guide cost A$304.

Myall Lakes National Park

This park is a patchwork of coastal lakes, islands, forest and beaches. It has bushwalks through coastal rainforest and past dunes at **Mungo Brush**. The best surf beaches are in the north around **Seal Rocks**. Book ahead for **Seal Rocks Camping Reserve** (☎ 1800 112 234, 4977 6164; Kinka Rd, Seal Rocks; camp sites per 2 people A$13, cabins A$50). Bulahdelah **visitors centre** (☎ 4997 4981; cnr Crawford St & Pacific Hwy; ⌚ 9am-5pm) has guides for bushwalkers and information about camping grounds. Canoes, sailboards and runabouts can be hired here.

To get to the national park, drive north from Newcastle along the Pacific Hwy, turning off at Bulahdelah. **Great Lakes Coaches** (☎ 1800 043 263) services this route, charging A$47 from Sydney or A$30 from Newcastle.

NEWCASTLE TO PORT MACQUARIE

As you drive north from Newcastle, the suburban landscape soon peters out to the secluded holiday area of **Port Stephens**, where Novocastrian families come to get away from it all. It's easy to see why, as it's just an hour's drive from Newcastle and has over 32km of beach. The self-professed 'dolphin capital of Australia', **Nelson Bay** (population 7000) is the biggest town in the area and makes a good base from which to explore the region.

Port Stephens

☎ 02

Staff at **Nelson Bay visitors centre** (☎ 1800 808 900, 4981 1579; www.portstephens.org.au; Victoria Pde;

(9am-5pm) can help plan your Port Stephens activities.

SIGHTS & ACTIVITIES

At the mouth of the Myall River, opposite Nelson Bay, are the small towns of **Tea Gardens**, on the river, and **Hawks Nest**, on the beach. **Jimmy's Beach** at Hawks Nest fronts a glass-like stretch of water, while **Bennett's Beach** has great views of Broughton Island.

On the southern side of the Tomaree Peninsula, **One Mile Beach** is usually deserted except for surfers. Further south you can hang out in the surf-side village of **Anna Bay**, backed by the incredible **Stockton Bight**, the longest barrier sand dune in Australia, which stretches 35km to Newcastle. At the far western end of the beach the wreck of the *Sygna* founders in the water.

To get out among the dolphins take a tour with **Moonshadow** (☎ 4984 9388; Shop 3, 35 Stockton St, Nelson Bay; 1½hr tours A$18), a long-running outfit with three modern vessels.

Get even deeper with dive gear from **Hawks Nest Dive Centre** (☎ 4997 0442; www.hawksnestdive.com.au; 87a Marine Dr, Tea Gardens; dive courses A$90-500), which runs dive courses from beginners (A$90) to comprehensive Open Water certification (A$500). A cheaper option is to take one of its snorkelling tours (A$40).

Even if you've never been on a horse before, **Horse Paradise** (☎ 4965 1877; www.users.bigpond.com/horseparadise; Nelson Bay Rd, Williamtown; tours from A$35) will take you on an expedition through the dunes or through Port Stephens bushland.

Try sand-boarding with one of the tour operators.

TOURS

Port Stephens 4WD Eco-Tours (☎ 4982 7277; tours from A$20) Drive around Stockton sand dunes, visit the *Sygna* and go sand-boarding (you'll be cleaning out the crannies for days afterwards).

Sand Safaris (☎ 4965 0215; www.sandsafaris.com.au; 173 Nelson Bay Rd, Williamtown; tours A$110) Sand Safaris gives you your very own quad bike (a super-stable motorcycle that looks embarrassingly like a lawnmower) and takes you out on the dunes for some full-on – yet ecologically sensitive – hooning around.

SLEEPING & EATING

In Nelson Bay, Government St is lined with motels and hotels. Shoal Bay – virtually a suburb of Nelson Bay – mixes accommodation with stores and restaurants. Anna Bay is the closest hamlet to One Mile Beach. Prices rise and availability tightens with school holidays, when crowds come to the region.

Shoal Bay Holiday Park (☎ 1800 600 200, 4981 1427; www.beachsideholidays.com.au; Shoal Bay Rd, Shoal Bay; powered camp sites per 2 people from A$30, bungalows from A$45;) The best value at this first-rate caravan park are the budget-style 'Safari Bungalows' with generous verandas on which to laze. There are regular activities, including karaoke.

Port Stephens YHA Samurai Beach Bungalows (☎ 4982 1921; www.portstephens.org.au/samurai; cnr Frost Rd & Robert Connell Close, Anna Bay; dm A$26; d A$95) Set amid verdant bush, these cabins are a perfect getaway. There's an outdoor camp kitchen, surfboards and bikes.

Nelson Bay marina has several places at which to eat, suitable for most budgets and tastes.

Rob's on the Boardwalk (☎ 4984 4444; D'Albora Marina, Nelson Bay; mains A$12-27) A highlight of the many seafood restaurants along the waterfront, with great oysters, a good wine list and relaxed outdoor dining.

Incredible Edibles (☎ 4981 4511; cnr Donaldson & Stockton Sts, Nelson Bay; sandwiches from A$5) For a budget bite try, try this great little deli that makes for gourmet picnic fodder.

Lazy Dayz Café & Tea Shoppe (☎ 4997 1889; 71 Marine Dr, Tea Gardens; mains A$5-18) A good takeaway with a country-café feel; serves fresh fish, burgers, salads and steaks.

GETTING THERE & AROUND

To drive from Nelson Bay to Tea Gardens, you have to backtrack to Raymond Terrace.

Port Stephens Coaches (☎ 4982 2940; http://pscoaches.com.au; 17a Port Stephens Dr, Anna Bay) goes from Nelson Bay via Anna Bay to Newcastle (A$10.40, 1¼ hours, 11 times daily). The 9am bus from Nelson Bay continues to Sydney (A$31, 3½ hours).

Port Stephens Ferry Service (☎ 4981 3798; Nelson Bay Public Jetty) chugs from Nelson Bay to Tea Gardens and back three times a day (A$15 return, one hour).

PORT MACQUARIE

☎ 02 / pop 33,700

At the mouth of the Hastings River, Port Macquarie was once a penal settlement for hardened convicts for whom Sydney was considered too cushy, but it's a lot more salubrious these days. Port (as locals call it) has embraced the koala as a mascot and has a challenging range of extreme sports, often cheaper than at other coastal towns. If you're heading north from Sydney it's a good spot to find a less crowded beach and to bask in a sunny laid-back town.

Information

NPWS office (☎ 6586 8300; 152 Horton St; ⌚ 9am-4.30pm Mon-Fri)

Port Surf Hub (☎ 6584 4744; 57 Clarence St; per hr A$6; ⌚ 10am-7pm) Internet access.

Visitors centre (☎ 6581 8000, 1300 303 155; www.portmacquarieinfo.com.au; Clarence St; ⌚ 8.30am-5pm Mon-Fri, 9am-4pm Sat & Sun)

Sights & Activities

The **Koala Hospital** (☎ 6584 1522; www.midcoast.com.au/users/koalahos/; Lord St; admission by donation; ⌚ 9am-5pm) cares for koalas injured around Port Macquarie – check the cute names on the patients' board. It's Australia's oldest koala hospital, and you can wander through the outdoor enclosures or watch feeding (3pm). To get your hands on a koala, visit **Billabong Koala Park** (☎ 6585 1060; 61 Billabong Dr, adult A$9.50; ⌚ 9am-5pm), which breeds marsupials for zoos. Come for the pattings at 10.30am, 1.30pm and 3.30pm.

About 3km south of town, **Sea Acres Rainforest Centre** (☎ 6582 3355; Pacific Dr; adult A$10; ⌚ 9am-4.30pm) protects a 72-hectare pocket of coastal rainforest, where you can spot brush turkeys and lace monitors (goannas). There are access points to **Kooloonbung Creek Nature Reserve**, which has boardwalks and bushwalking tracks, around the town centre.

There's great swimming and surfing at several beaches, starting at **Town Beach** and running south. Walk the **breakwall** and read the entertaining graffiti of previous visitors, including hundreds of multilingual versions of 'I was 'ere'.

Cruise operators line the waterfront near Town Wharf. For a guided canoe trip up the Hastings River, **Port Macquarie Sea Kayak** (☎ 6584 1039; Sea Rescue Shed; 2hr-trip A$30) is just the ticket.

To get under the surface, **Rick's Dive School** (☎ 0422-063 528; intro course A$60, PADI course A$170) is an excellent deal, particularly if you want to complete a PADI course. Most of the diving is shore diving, but trips to **Delicate Nobby** can be arranged with a few days' notice.

For a better view of the dramatic landscapes and sandy beaches, strap into a hang-glider with **High Adventure** (☎ 1800 063 648; www.highadventure.com.au; tandem paragliding/hang-gliding A$155/250), who gets you airborne and adrenalised.

A shoreline camel ride is a must with **Port Macquarie Camel Safaris** (☎ 1800 501 879, 6583 7650; www.nnsw.worldtourism.com.au/pmcamelsafaris; Lighthouse Beach, Matthew Flinders Dr; 30min/1hr ride A$20/A$35), which can be a quick 30-minute gallop along Lighthouse Beach. It can also do barbecue packages for larger groups.

Practise your rock climbing at **Centre of Gravity** (☎ 6581 3899; 52 Jindalee Rd; climbing admission & equipment hire A$30, laserzone game A$8; ⌚ noon-5pm Wed, Fri & Sat, to 9pm Tue & Thu), which boasts the biggest climbing gym between Sydney and Queensland. It also has indoor laserzone, where you compete in mock battles as a great way to sort out problems with travel companions ('Eat laser-death, toothpaste-thief!').

Tours

Port Macquarie Cruise Adventures (☎ 1300 555 890; www.cruiseadventures.com.au; Town Wharf, Clarence St; 1-day cruises A$20-50) Has five different cruises that explore inland waterways, with dolphin-spotting in glass-sided boats.

Winery Tours (☎ 6584 8887, 0414-664 694; 1-day tours A$29) Offers tours of the region's up-and-coming wineries (including Cassegrain and Innes Lake) in an air-con bus that collects from all accommodation places.

Sleeping

Gordon St has several cheap motels, although they can be a long walk to the beach. Hostels offer loads of extras to woo travellers.

Ozzie Pozzie Backpackers (☎ 6583 8133; ozziepozzie@bigpond.com; 36 Waugh Street; dm/d A$26/60; 💻) This suburban hostel is a good spot to chill out. Friendly staff offer free pick-ups, bikes (A$5), fishing gear, bodyboards and barbecue nights. Some lucky guests are greeted with lollypops on arrival.

Lindel Port Macquarie Backpackers (☎ 1800 688 882, 6583 1791; Hastings River Dr; dm/s/d from A$25/40/60; 💻 🏊) This building – one of Port's oldest houses – retains its period pressed-tin walls, although it's a bit dim inside. The palm-surrounded pool, rental bikes and fishing gear all make for a good stay. At the time of writing, it was up for sale, so we can only hope this institution continues.

Port Macquarie YHA (☎ 6583 5512; portmacqyha@hotmail.com; 40 Church St; dm/d A$20/50) Brightly

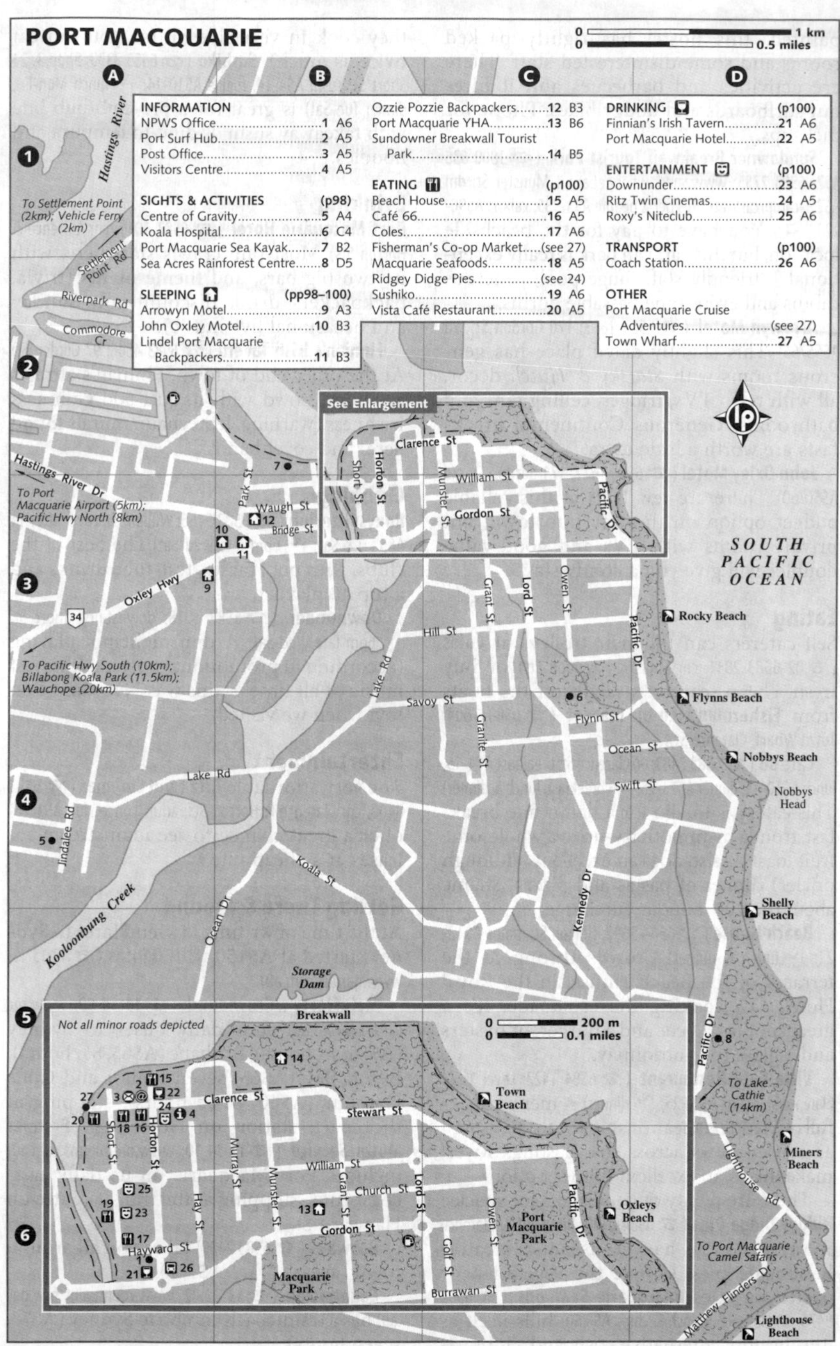
PORT MACQUARIE
0 1 km
0 0.5 miles
A
B
C
D
1
2
3
4
5
6
INFORMATION
NPWS Office 1 A6
Port Surf Hub 2 A5
Post Office 3 A5
Visitors Centre 4 A5
SIGHTS & ACTIVITIES (p98)
Centre of Gravity 5 A4
Koala Hospital 6 C4
Port Macquarie Sea Kayak 7 B2
Sea Acres Rainforest Centre 8 D5
SLEEPING (pp98–100)
Arrowyn Motel 9 A3
John Oxley Motel 10 B3
Lindel Port Macquarie Backpackers 11 B3
Ozzie Pozzie Backpackers 12 B3
Port Macquarie YHA 13 B6
Sundowner Breakwall Tourist Park 14 B5
EATING (p100)
Beach House 15 A5
Café 66 16 A5
Coles 17 A6
Fisherman's Co-op Market (see 27)
Macquarie Seafoods 18 A5
Ridgey Didge Pies (see 24)
Sushiko 19 A6
Vista Café Restaurant 20 A5
DRINKING (p100)
Finnian's Irish Tavern 21 A6
Port Macquarie Hotel 22 A5
ENTERTAINMENT (p100)
Downunder 23 A6
Ritz Twin Cinemas 24 A5
Roxy's Niteclub 25 A6
TRANSPORT (p100)
Coach Station 26 A6
OTHER
Port Macquarie Cruise Adventures (see 27)
Town Wharf 27 A5
Hastings River
To Settlement Point (2km); Vehicle Ferry (2km)
Settlement Point Rd
Riverpark Rd
Commodore Cr
Hastings River Dr
To Port Macquarie Airport (5km); Pacific Hwy North (8km)
Park St
Waugh St
Bridge St
Oxley Hwy
34
To Pacific Hwy South (10km); Billabong Koala Park (11.5km); Wauchope (20km)
See Enlargement
Clarence St
Short St
Horton St
Munster St
William St
Gordon St
Pacific Dr
SOUTH PACIFIC OCEAN
Grant St
Lord St
Owen St
Hill St
Lake Rd
Savoy St
Granite St
Flynn St
Ocean St
Swift St
Rocky Beach
Flynns Beach
Nobbys Beach
Nobbys Head
Jindalee Rd
Koala St
Kooloonbung Creek
Ocean Dr
Kennedy Dr
Storage Dam
Shelly Beach
To Lake Cathie (14km)
Miners Beach
Lighthouse Rd
To Port Macquarie Camel Safaris
Matthew Flinders Dr
Lighthouse Beach
Not all minor roads depicted
Breakwall
0 200 m
0 0.1 miles
Town Beach
Stewart St
Murray St
Hay St
Church St
Hayward St
Golf St
Burrawan St
Macquarie Park
Port Macquarie Park
Oxleys Beach

painted, this hostel has tightly packed rooms and some disinterested staff. There are activities and barbecues and it hires out surfboards and dodgy bikes. Phone for pick-ups.

Sundowner Breakwall Tourist Park (☎ 1800 636 452, 6583 2755; www.sundowner.net.au; 1 Munster St; dm A$22, camp/caravan sites per 2 people A$32/35, cabins A$90-220; 💻) You have to pay for the beachside location, but this caravan park is really exceptional – friendly staff, huge pool, generous cabins and even some passable dorms.

Arrowyn Motel (☎ 6583 1633; 170 Gordon St; s/d A$55/65) This slightly dated place has generous rooms with *Starsky & Hutch* décor, all with retro TVs, fridges, ceiling fans and bathrooms. Generous Continental breakfasts are worth a little extra.

John Oxley Motel (☎ 6583 1677; 171 Gordon St; s/d A$50/60) There are few frills at this reliable budget option on the way into town, but private rooms with TVs and good-value doubles will give you a comfy stay.

Eating

Self-caterers can fill their trolleys at **Coles** (☎ 02-6583 2831; cnr Short & Haywood Sts) or buy fresh, cheap seafood straight off the boats from **Fisherman's Co-op market** (☎ 6583 1604; Town Wharf, Clarence St).

Café 66 (☎ 6583 2483; 66 Clarence St; breakfast A$4-15, lunch A$10-15, dinner A$13-25; 🕒 breakfast, lunch & dinner) This eatery is the go for a damn fine breakfast, from a mammoth fry-up to a wholesome fruit toast. It also does an excellent (although pricier) dinner of pastas and pizzas. Shame about the 10% Sunday surcharge.

Beach House (☎ 6584 5692; Horton St; mains A$12-22; 🕒 lunch & dinner) Crowds throng to the terraces of the Beach House, in the Royal Hotel. Overlooking the esplanade, it's a great spot for a beer and a burger, or oysters and a glass of chardonnay.

Vista Café Restaurant (☎ 6584 1422; Level 1, 74 Clarence St; mains A$20-25; 🕒 dinner) A menu chock-full of Mediterranean-inspired cuisine, as well as sunset views across the Hastings River, make this is an excellent dinner option.

There are plenty of good spots for snacks: **Ridgey Didge Pies** (☎ 6584 0720; Ritz Centre, Clarence St; pies A$2.50-3.50) has grouse and creative handmade pies; sample the vegetarian or oyster varieties. **Macquarie Seafoods** (☎ 6583 8476; 68 Clarence St; fish & chips A$6.50) bills itself as 'the healthy alternative' fish and chips, as they cook in vegetable oil (so you can eat twice as much). **Sushiko** (☎ 6583 3333; Shop 3, 21 Short St; sushi A$4-14, mains A$10-14; 🕒 lunch Mon-Fri, dinner Tue-Sat) is great for a pre-club/pub bite with takeaway sushi or dine-in tempura and noodles.

Drinking

Port Macquarie Hotel (☎ 6583 1011, cnr Clarence & Horton Sts) Most pub crawls start here, with its two big bars, and theme nights (trivia, backpackers drink discounts on Sunday and occasional live music).

Finnian's Irish Tavern (☎ 6583 4646; 97 Gordon St) At the other end of town, Finnian's attracts an older crowd with its just-add-Guinness Irishness (warning: leprechaun murals found here) and cover bands.

Clubbing

Roxys Niteclub (☎ 6583 5466; William St; cover after 11 A$5 Fri & Sat; 🕒 6pm-late Wed-Sat) The best of the clubs, with pool tables, test-tube drinks and a top 40 playlist.

Downunder (☎ 6583 4018; downstairs, Short St; 🕒 6pm-late Wed-Sat) A dim nightspot playing (according to promotional posters) 'the best music of all time' – this was Nelly and Bon Jovi when we visited.

Entertainment

The very affordable **Ritz Twin Cinemas** (☎ 6583 8400; cnr Clarence & Horton Sts; adult/concession A$10/8) offer a great chance to see mainstream releases at a cheap rate.

Getting There & Around

At the time of writing, low-end fares to Sydney started at A$150 with **Qantas** (☎ 13 13 13; www.qantas.com.au).

McCafferty's/Greyhound (☎ 13 14 99; www.mccaffertys.com.au) runs daily buses to Sydney (A$60, six hours), Brisbane (A$65, 8½ hours), Byron Bay (A$65, seven hours) and Coffs Harbour (A$40, three hours), stopping at the coach station on Horton St. **Premier Motor Service** (☎ 13 34 10; www.premierms.com.au) includes Port Macquarie on its daily east-coast runs, stopping at the transit centre on Hayward St.

Busways (☎ 6583 2499) takes you all around town (average fare A$1.20).

CountryLink (☎ 13 22 32; www.countrylink.nsw.gov.au) has a train/coach combo to Sydney (A$75, seven hours).

COFFS HARBOUR

☎ 02 / pop 60,000

Better known as Coffs, this welcoming town has been on a banana bender since the first yellow fruit was grown here in the 1880s. But these days there's more to Coffs – apart from a gorgeous beach, there's excellent white-water rafting and diving to be had. The Great Dividing Range nuzzles the sea at Coffs, creating an intriguing environment and fauna (see Wild Coffs, below). For a town this size, there's also an impressive dining culture with particularly fine dining around the Jetty. The combination of action and sophistication is probably why Russell Crowe has a ranch not far from Coffs.

Orientation

The junction of Grafton and High Sts marks the city centre. After the pedestrian mall, High St becomes the main road to the Jetty a few kilometres east (although locals call this stretch Harbour Dr).

Information

Coffs Coast visitors centre (☎ 1300 369 070, 6652 1522; www.coffscoast.com.au; cnr Pacific Hwy & Mclean St; 🕑 9am-5pm)
Internet Room (☎ 6651 9155; Shop 21, Jetty Village Centre, High St; per hr A$5.50)
Jetty Dive Centre (☎ 6651 1611; www.jettydive.com.au; 398 Harbour Dr; per hr A$5) Internet access; see p102 for dive-trip information.
Main post office (Ground fl, Palms Centre shopping centre, High St pedestrian mall)

Sights & Activities

Kitschy and cultish, the **Big Banana** (☎ 6652 4355; www.bigbanana.com; Pacific Hwy; 🕑 8am-5pm) is Coff's best-known sight. Sure, the kiddie rides are lame, but the choc-dipped bananas are worth the trip. Weirdly, there are winter sports – ice-skating (A$12) and fake-slope skiing (A$15) – plus banana viewing on the 'skywalk' (A$5) or train/plantation tours (A$12). The souvenir shop has more banana-inspired gear – banana fridge magnets, soap and even harmonicas – than you're ever likely to see again.

In the same kitschy league, the **Clog Barn** (☎ 6652 4633; www.clogbiz.com; 215 Pacific Hwy; adult A$4.50; 🕑 11am-4pm) is a miniature Dutch village populated by tiny Dutch people and lizards – making it an optimum location to shoot your own budget remake of *Godzilla*. The clog-crazy manager hosts free clog-making demonstrations at 11am and 4pm.

For beach bums, the main beach is **Park Beach**, but beware of vicious rips. **Jetty Beach** is sheltered and locals swear by the Jetty-jump around high tide. **Diggers Beach**, off the highway near the Big Banana, bares all with a nude section. Surfers head for Diggers and **Macauleys Headland**.

The massive **North Coast Botanic Gardens** (☎ 6648 4188; Hardacre St; admission by donation; 🕑 9am-5pm) harbours endangered species and examples of the region's rainforest types. Take the 6km **Coffs Creek Habitat Walk**, starting opposite the council chambers on Coff St.

The harbour's northern breakwall runs out to **Muttonbird Island**, named for the more than

WILD COFFS

Creating Solitary Islands Marine Park in 1998 was a recognition by Coffs of the area's unique environment and marine life. Humpback whales regularly pass through on their migrations, although divers are keener to spot endangered grey nurse sharks and colourful blooms of coral. What makes the water so special is the blending of warm and cool currents, creating a mix of species where fish swim through temperate seaweeds and corals. It all combines into a marine life cocktail that makes it worth strapping on a snorkel.

You don't have to get wet to see Coffs' wildlife. Muttonbird Island hosts thousands of the cute birds, who travel more than 10,000km to breed. They come in May and June, enjoying elaborate mating rituals before nesting in the same burrows year after year.

Year-round residents include the town's colonies of bats, seen scattering into the sky in a magnificent nightly show. Far from being blood-sucking menaces, environmentalists theorise that bats beneficially spread seeds and eat pesky insects.

And then there's the less pleasant local fauna – the cockroach. The proximity of banana plantations gives these odious critters warm, moist, breeding grounds, so you'll see a few of them no matter where you stay. We've encountered them scurrying out of bins in the main street.

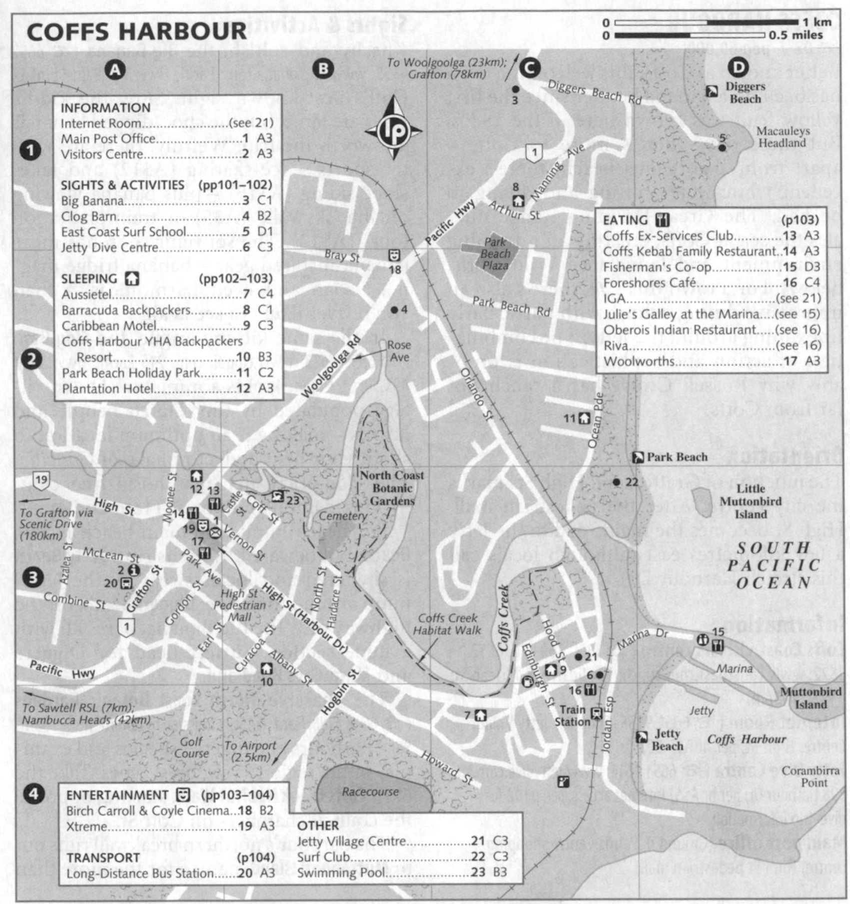

12,000 pairs of birds who migrate here annually. The hill-top observation deck affords great views of the city, seasonally snogging mutton birds and passing whales.

Muttonbird Island marks the start of **Solitary Islands Marine Park**, where tropical and temperate currents meet, attracting unusual fish life (see Wild Coffs, p101). The easiest way to enjoy surrounding marine life is by snorkelling with **Jetty Dive Centre** (☎ 6651 1611; www.jettydive.com.au; 398 High St (Harbour Dr); snorkelling A$90, dive trip A$90; 🕑 8.30am-5pm). It also offers snorkelling and diving tours (A$45) and cheap dive certification courses (A$200).

Liquid Assets (☎ 6658 0850; www.surfrafting.com; half-/full-day trips A$80/125) specialises in white-water rafting trips to the Nymboida River, with surf-rafting (A$40) also available. Get harnessed into a kite with **Leading Edge Kite Company** (☎ 6658 5585, 0407-057 405; www.lekite.com.au; 1hr intro course A$150), with whom you can cut the waves with kiteboard courses or bash the sand on kitebuggies. Specialising in women's classes, staff at **East Coast Surf School** (☎ 6651 5515; www.eastcoastsurfschool.com.au; Diggers Beach; 1-day lesson A$40) reckon they can get anyone standing on a board in just a few hours.

Sleeping

Motels are affordable and most hostels work extra hard in Coffs.

Aussietel (☎ 6651 1871; fun@aussietel.com; 312 High St; dm/d A$26/65; 💻) Near Jetty restaurants and the beach, Aussietel is friendly, roomy and clean. Staff are generous with advice on what to do around town and there are loads of organised activities. Good hire bikes are available (A$5 per day).

Caribbean Motel (☎ 6652 1500; www.stayincoffs.com.au; 353 High St; d A$70-185;) Clean and colourful, this motel is handily placed across from the Jetty restaurants, and well-appointed rooms often have ocean views. Extras include balconies, breakfasts and spas.

Barracuda Backpackers (☎ 6651 3514; www.backpackers.coffs.tv; 19 Arthur St; dm/d A$22/55;) Not too far from the beach, but closer to the Big Banana, this sometimes-grubby hostel packs in the bunks, but does have a pool and barbecue. Readers rave about the helpfulness of staff, who can help find fruit-picking work in season (or you can check its job board for opportunities).

Coffs Harbour YHA Backpackers Resort (☎ 6652 6462; coffsyha@key.net.au; 110 Albany St; dm/d A$22/55;) This time-worn hostel offers loads of activities, including bikes, boards and golf clubs available for hire (A$10). Friendly staff do pick-ups.

Plantation Hotel (☎ 6652 3855; www.plantationhotel.com.au; 88 Grafton St; dm A$19-22, d A$55, tr A$70) This place provides affordable beds in converted hotel rooms, although cramped kitchens, small common areas and band noise from downstairs point to an identity crisis – is it a pub, live-music venue or hostel?

Park Beach Holiday Park (☎ 6648 4888; Ocean Pde; camp sites per 2 people A$21, cabins A$52;) On the beach, this massive park includes a cool pool with waterslides, and seahorse fountains to swim through. It's well set up for families, but takes all comers.

Eating & Drinking

JETTY

The Jetty is the main restaurant strip, but self-caterers can stock up at **IGA supermarket** (☎ 6650 0014; 25 Jetty Shopping Village Centre; 8am-9pm) or **Woolworths** (☎ 6652 6866; 7 Park Ave; 7am-midnight Mon-Fri, to 10pm Sat, 8am-9pm Sun).

Foreshores Café (☎ 6652 3127; 394 Harbour Dr; mains A$6-18; breakfast & lunch) Quick and friendly service, huge breakfasts (including good veggie options) and ocean breezes on the terrace make this a great spot to start the day.

Riva (☎ 6650 0195; 384A Harbour Dr; tapas A$6.50-12.50, mains A$22-24; dinner) Packed with paella posers and tapas tossers, this is where Coffs' smart set enjoys a glass of wine or shares a pizza (we loved the tandoori chicken with cashews and yogurt). Funky décor and a glossary explaining the menu complete the too-cool-for-school image.

Oberois Indian Restaurant (☎ 6651 9699; 376 Harbour Dr; mains A$8.50-14.50; dinner) For no-worries curries grab yourself a table in this gaudy curry house. All the old favourites are here – tikka, korma and biryani – but the chef's specials all innovatively use seafood. Spice junkies should opt for the very hot setting to really cleanse the sinuses.

MARINA

This spot is becoming quite touristy, although you can still find well-priced food.

Fisherman's Co-op (☎ 6652 2811; 69 Marina Dr; 9am-6pm) Specialising in 'strollable food', the Co-op is where you can grab fish and chips (A$6.50), super-fresh sushi lunchboxes (A$7) or gelati as you explore the marina.

Julie's Galley at the Marina (☎ 6650 0188; Marina Dr; burgers A$4-7; 8am-6.30pm) Blokes off the fishing boats swear by the chicken satay burgers here, but you can also grab a breakfast egg-and-bacon roll or go for a veggie option.

CBD

The city centre is good for takeaway lunch or coffee, but most places are closed in the evening.

Coffs Kebab Family Restaurant (☎ 6651 8889; 93 Grafton St; kebabs A$5.50-7.50; lunch & dinner daily, to 1am Fri & Sat) Serving up a flavoursome, end-of-the-night kebab is this place's speciality. The tabouleh is fresh and there are a few other takeaway options.

Coffs Ex-Services Club (☎ 6652 3888; www.cex.com.au; cnr Pacific Hwy & Vernon St; mains A$8-17; lunch & dinner) Cheap drinks mean most pub crawls start here. Some reckon the chilly air-con is cryogenically preserving the old codgers in the front bar, but the back room gets a younger crowd with cocktails and the danceable end of top 40. Meals here are basic – think meat and two veg.

Entertainment

Locals hang out in pubs, and Thursday's edition of the *Coffs Harbour Advocate* lists gigs.

Xtreme (☎ 6652 6426; 15 High St mall; admission A$5-10; 7pm-5am Thu-Sat) Coff's only club is a dance/pick-up venue that hots up after 11pm. Before then you can kill time on the pool tables, but relax because it's open until 5am.

Plantation Hotel (☎ 6652 3855; www.plantationhotel.com.au; 88 Grafton St) The hot new pub that attracts a diverse crowd with live bands and young crowds. See also the review under Sleeping, p103.

Sawtell RSL Club (☎ 6653 1577; 1st Ave, Sawtell) Big-name touring bands usually play here, about 5km south of town.

Birch Carroll & Coyle cinema (☎ 6651 5568; Bray St; adult A$11-12.50, concession A$9.50; 🕑 10.30am-11pm) The place to catch mainstream movies.

Getting There & Away

AIR

At the time of writing, low-end fares to Sydney started at A$100.

Qantas (☎ 13 13 13; www.qantas.com.au)
Virgin Blue (☎ 13 67 89, www.virginblue.com.au)

BUS

The long-distance bus station is beside the visitors centre.

McCafferty's/Greyhound (☎ 13 14 99; www.mccaffertys.com.au) runs twice-daily buses to Sydney (A$60, seven hours), Brisbane (A$55, seven hours), Byron Bay (A$45, four hours) and Port Macquarie (A$40, three hours).
Premier Motor Service (☎ 133 410; www.premierms.com.au) heads up and down the coast, stopping at Byron Bay (A$45, four hours), Sydney (A$57, 7½ hours) and Brisbane (A$51, eight hours).

TRAIN

CountryLink (☎ 13 22 32; www.countrylink.nsw.gov.au) runs to Sydney (A$80, eight hours), Byron Bay (A$45, 4½ hours) and Brisbane (A$75, 5½ hours).

Getting Around

Kings Bros (☎ 6652 2877; www.kingsbrosbus.com.au) runs the useful No 365 bus, looping along High St and Ocean Pde to Park Beach Plaza.

BYRON BAY

☎ 02 / pop 5400

In a past life, Byron (as just about everyone knows this town) may have been a sleepy beach town, but you'd have to put it through a lot of regression therapy and float tanks to find its inner self today. With jaw-dropping beaches, a hippy vibe, an exhausting array of activities and a booty-shaking nightlife, you won't be the first to discover Byron's charms. So many people make the pilgrimage from Sydney that Byron has been dubbed North Bondi, but that could also be for the awesome surfing. During the festivals (see Festivals & Events, p107) alterna-gods including Michael Franti and Ben Harper have been known to play a few gigs and then hit the surf or join a local yoga class.

Orientation

The main drag is Jonson St, which has the bus terminal at its southern end and curves onto the beachside Bay Rd. To get from Ballina airport jump aboard Byron Bay Airbus (see Getting There & Away, p108)

The closest airport is at Ballina but most people use the larger Coolangatta airport (see p155).

Information

INTERNET ACCESS

Internet Outpost (☎ 6680 7986; Soundwaves, 58 Jonson St; www.internet-outpost.com; per hr A$4)
Global Gossip (☎ 6680 9140; Byron Bus & Backpacker Centre, 84 Jonson St; per hr A$4.50; 🕑 9am-midnight summer, to 10pm winter)

MONEY

Most banks are represented along the Jonson St strip.

Byron Foreign Exchange (☎ 6685 7787; 4 Central Arcade, Byron St; 🕑 9am-8pm Mon-Sat, 10am-4pm Sun) Provides foreign exchange, cash and transfers.

TRAVEL AGENCIES

Byron Bus & Backpacker Centre (☎ 6685 5517; 84 Jonson St; 🕑 7am-7pm) Handles transport, accommodation and activity bookings and has a Global Gossip Internet outlet.

TOURIST INFORMATION

Visitors centre (☎ 6680 9271; www.visitbyronbay.com; Stationmaster's Cottage, 80 Jonson St; 🕑 9am-5pm) Has copies of the local paper, *Echo* (www.echo.net.au), the bible for news and entertainment; and *Body & Soul* (a guide to natural therapists).

Sights

CAPE BYRON

Named by Captain Cook, this stunning stretch of ocean is full of dolphins. There are also cameos from humpback whales who pass during their northern (June and July) and southern (September to November)

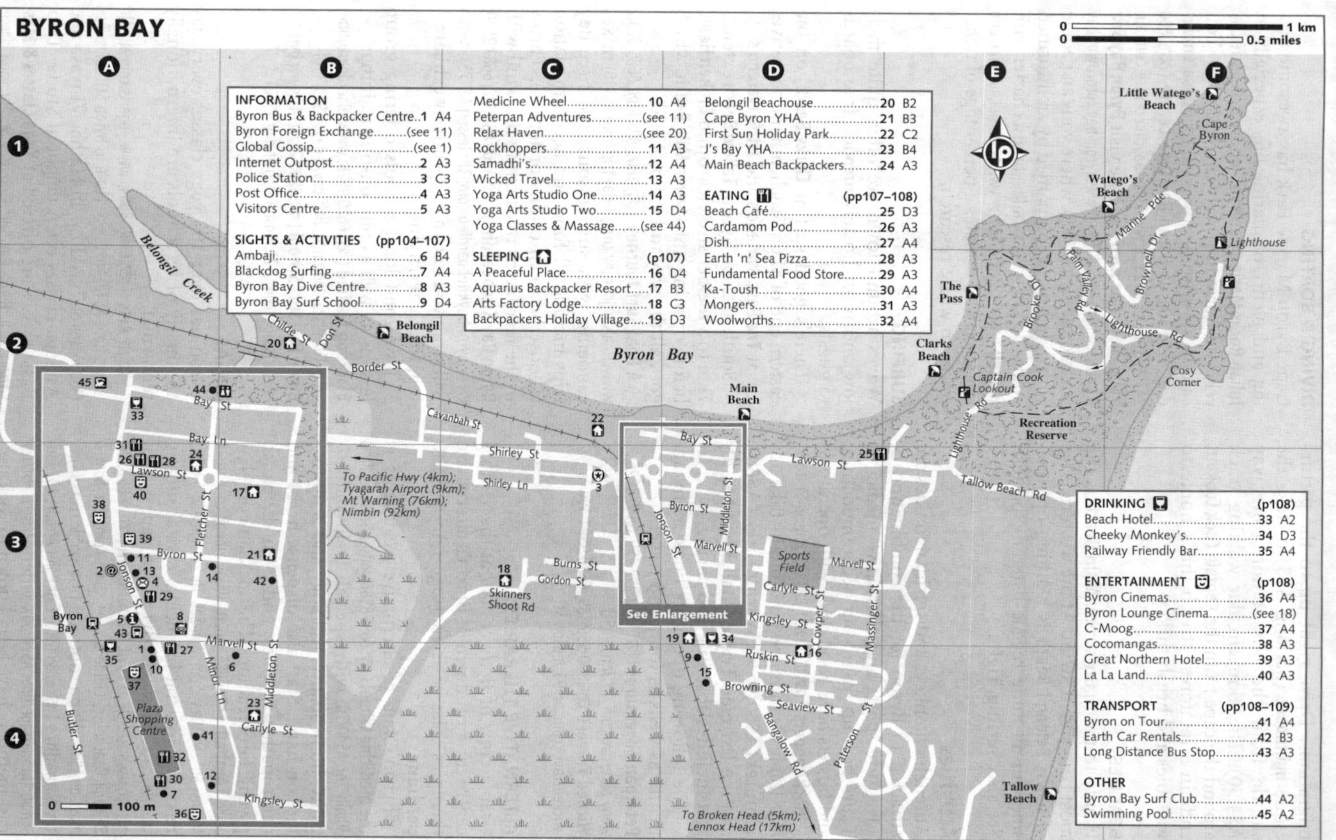
BYRON BAY
0 1 km
0 0.5 miles
INFORMATION
Byron Bus & Backpacker Centre..1 A4
Byron Foreign Exchange.........(see 11)
Global Gossip..........................(see 1)
Internet Outpost.......................2 A3
Police Station...........................3 C3
Post Office...............................4 A3
Visitors Centre..........................5 A3
SIGHTS & ACTIVITIES (pp104–107)
Ambaji.......................................6 B4
Blackdog Surfing.......................7 A4
Byron Bay Dive Centre..............8 A3
Byron Bay Surf School...............9 D4
Medicine Wheel.......................10 A4
Peterpan Adventures.............(see 11)
Relax Haven..........................(see 20)
Rockhoppers...........................11 A3
Samadhi's...............................12 A4
Wicked Travel.........................13 A3
Yoga Arts Studio One.............14 A3
Yoga Arts Studio Two.............15 D4
Yoga Classes & Massage.......(see 44)
SLEEPING (p107)
A Peaceful Place.....................16 D4
Aquarius Backpacker Resort.....17 B3
Arts Factory Lodge..................18 C3
Backpackers Holiday Village.....19 D3
Belongil Beachouse.................20 B2
Cape Byron YHA.....................21 B3
First Sun Holiday Park.............22 C2
J's Bay YHA............................23 B4
Main Beach Backpackers.........24 A3
EATING (pp107–108)
Beach Café.............................25 D3
Cardamom Pod........................26 A3
Dish..27 A4
Earth 'n' Sea Pizza..................28 A3
Fundamental Food Store.........29 A3
Ka-Toush................................30 A4
Mongers..................................31 A3
Woolworths.............................32 A4
DRINKING (p108)
Beach Hotel............................33 A2
Cheeky Monkey's....................34 D3
Railway Friendly Bar................35 A4
ENTERTAINMENT (p108)
Byron Cinemas........................36 A4
Byron Lounge Cinema...........(see 18)
C-Moog...................................37 A4
Cocomangas...........................38 A3
Great Northern Hotel..............39 A3
La La Land.............................40 A3
TRANSPORT (pp108–109)
Byron on Tour.........................41 A4
Earth Car Rentals....................42 B3
Long Distance Bus Stop...........43 A3
OTHER
Byron Bay Surf Club................44 A2
Swimming Pool.......................45 A2
Byron Bay
Belongil Creek
Belongil Beach
Main Beach
Clarks Beach
The Pass
Wategos Beach
Little Watego's Beach
Cape Byron
Lighthouse
Cosy Corner
Captain Cook Lookout
Recreation Reserve
Tallow Beach
Sports Field
Plaza Shopping Centre
See Enlargement
To Pacific Hwy (4km); Tyagarah Airport (9km); Mt Warning (76km); Nimbin (92km)
To Broken Head (5km); Lennox Head (17km)
0 100 m
Childe St
Don St
Border St
Cavanbah St
Shirley St
Shirley Ln
Bay St
Bay Ln
Lawson St
Jonson St
Byron St
Fletcher St
Middleton St
Marvell St
Minor Ln
Carlyle St
Kingsley St
Butler St
Burns St
Gordon St
Skinners Shoot Rd
Ruskin St
Browning St
Seaview St
Bangalow Rd
Paterson St
Cowper St
Massinger St
Tallow Beach Rd
Lighthouse Rd
Brooke Dr
Palm Valley Rd
Brownell Dr
Marine Pde

migrations. Drive right up to the picturesque **lighthouse** (parking A$5) or take the shuttle from the bus station (one way A$4.50). The 4km circular walking track around the cape from the **Captain Cook Lookout** ends in a rainforest stretch that's home to wallabies and brush turkeys.

BEACHES

Handy to the main street, **Main Beach** is the most convenient swim. At the western edge of town **Belongil Beach** is clothing-optional since an all-nude reggae-listening protest. See also Surfing, right.

Activities

Adrenalin monkeys and spiritual junkies are attracted to Byron for the combination of adventure sports and alternative medicine. Tours pick up from your accommodation, and hostels have good deals with operators.

Rockhoppers (☎ 0500 881 881; 87 Jonson St; tours A$59-120) leads rainforest mountain-bike adventures (A$80), a Mt Warning trek (A$60), and the Extreme Triple Challenge (A$120) that includes abseiling and caving.

The following operators book many activities as wells as tours and travel:

Peterpan Adventures (☎ 1800 252 459, 6880 8926; www.peterpan.com; 87 Jonson St)

Wicked Travel (☎ 1800 555 339, 6680 9594; www.wickedtravel.com.au; 91 Jonson St)

ALTERNATIVE THERAPIES

Grab a copy of *Body & Soul* at the visitors centre for a rundown of Byron's alternative therapies. The basic massage rate is A$40 per hour.

Byron's hub of alternative treatments is the **Medicine Wheel** (☎ 6685 8366; Jonson St; all sessions 30min/1hr A$40/70) with specialists in naturopathy, homeopathy, iridology and acupuncture on hand. Staff also dispense herbs and naturopathic supplies, and even dabble in psychic tarot readings. The unashamedly New Age **Ambaji** (☎ 6685 6620; www.ambaji.com.au; 6 Marvell St; 🕐 10am-5pm Mon-Sat; 1hr session A$60) offers reiki, craniosacral balancing, crystal singing bowls and massage. Byron's cheapest float and massage deal is at **Relax Haven** (☎ 6685 8304; Belongil Beachouse, Childe St; 🕐 10am-8pm; 1hr float & massage A$40). For a soothing hot-rock massage, try **Samadhi's** (☎ 6685 6905; East Point Arcade, 107 Jonson St; 1hr massage/float A$70/50), where *Big Brother* cast members have been known to rock up.

DIVING & BOATING

Cape Byron Marine Park has awesome diving and plenty of marine life, especially at **Julian Rocks Marine Reserve**, where cold southerly and warm northerly currents meet. You can do an introductory scuba course (half-day A$130) at **Byron Bay Dive Centre** (☎ 1800 243 483, 6685 8333; www.byronbaydivecentre.com.au; 9 Marvell St). For more sea life visit **Byron Bay Sea Kayaks** (☎ 6685 4161; www.byron-bay.com/byronbayseakayaks; half-day tour A$60), where you can paddle with dolphins, accompanied by an informed guide. To sail with whales, take a charter with **Baysail** (☎ 0418-656 160; www.baysail.net.au; 3hr cruise from A$70), who donates a percentage of ticket prices to whale research.

SURFING

Waves around town are often quite mellow and most hostels provide free boards to guests.

There's good surf at **Clarks Beach**, on the eastern end of Main Beach, but the best waves are at **The Pass**, **Watego's** and **Little Watego's**.

South of Cape Byron, **Tallow Beach** extends 7km to a rockier stretch around **Broken Head**, before opening onto **Seven Mile Beach**, which goes all the way to Lennox Head.

A Real Surf Journey (☎ 1800 828 888, 6685 3738; www.arealsurfjourney.com; 3-day trip from A$110) mixes canoeing with surf lessons. Its three-day trips include all food and accommodation (choose between cabins or tepees). Throw in the fear factor of catching the wind with **Byron Bay Kiteboarding** (☎ 1300 888 938, 6687 2570; www.byronbaykiteboarding.com; 3hr lesson A$175), who will strap you onto a kite – utterly exhilarating, totally terrifying.

Two good local schools offering group lessons as well as one-on-one training:

Blackdog Surfing (☎ 6680 9828; www.blackdogsurfing.com; The Plaza, Jonson St; half-day/3 days A$45/110)

Byron Bay Surf School (☎ 1800 707 274; www.byronbaysurfschool.com; 127 Jonson St; half-day A$60)

YOGA

Byron has over 100 yoga classes every day and many of its schools are internationally renowned.

Yoga Arts (☎ 6680 8684; www.yogarts.com.au; 1hr classes from A$12) Studio One (1st fl, 6 Byron St); Studio Two (130 Jonson St) has drop-in Hatha, Vinyasa and Astanga classes often taught at Studio Two. Basic classes are offered at **Yoga Classes & Massage** (1st fl, Byron Bay Surf Club, Bay St; 1hr yoga classes

A$10; ⌚ classes 9am & 10am), a casual (just sign up on the board downstairs) Hatha introduction with a great beach location. For an Iyengar/Hatha fusion, go for a come-to-you private lesson at **Yoga With Flo** (☎ 6685 9910; www.intouchyogabyronbay.com; 2hr private lessons A$100).

Festivals & Events

East Coast Blues and Roots Festival (☎ 9266 4800; www.bluesfest.com.au; tickets from A$50) This Easter festival brings in R & B–based music.

Splendour in the Grass (www.splendourinthegrass.com) Hot new bands in a camp-out environment in July.

Byron Bay Writers Festival (☎ 6685 5115; www.byronbaywritersfestival.com.au) Attracts international and local wordsmiths in August.

Sleeping

There's a lot of competition for the backpacker dollar in Byron so standards are often high. Book well in advance for festival accommodation.

Arts Factory Lodge (☎ 6685 7709; www.artsfactory.com.au; Skinners Shoot Rd; camp sites per person A$11, dm A$22-33, d 50-80; 💻 🏊) Set in reclaimed swampland, this place is like a 1960s commune gone right. Choose from dorms, tepees or even the love shack. There's plenty of entertainment: didgeridoo-making lessons, fire-twirling classes and the Byron Lounge Cinema (see p108).

A Peaceful Place (☎ 6685 6560; www.byron-bay.com/apeacefulplace; 41 Ruskin St; s/d A$45/78) The almost-invisible signage makes this a secluded B&B, as friendly owners (Stan and Zetta) encourage healing here – note the huge crystal in the foyer. Rooms are bright and spacious, and breakfasts, including fresh orange juice, are a real bonus. Stan's glass studio out the front sometimes hosts classes for guests.

Main Beach Backpackers (☎ 1800 150 233, 6685 8695; 19-23 Lawson St; dm A$25, d A$60-100; ❄ 🏊) This established hostel has a courtyard pool, huge kitchen, regular free barbecues and a choice of indoor or outdoor pool tables – what more could you want? The noticeboard is a good place to find rides or used cars. Four-bed dorms represent the best value for money.

Cape Byron YHA (☎ 1800 652 627, 6685 8788; www.capebyronhostel.com.au; cnr Middleton & Byron Sts; dm A$22-28, d with bathroom A$70-110, without bathroom A$30-40; 🏊) This complex – including a travel agency and dive shop – is close to the town centre and has a generous pool in the courtyard. Plus there's a pool table, pinball and TV-VCR in the common room and a quieter reading room.

Aquarius Backpacker Resort (☎ 1800 028 909, 6685 7663; www.byron-bay.com/aquarius; 16 Lawson St; dm from A$28, d A$75-160; 💻 🏊) Formerly a resort, Aquarius still has some resort trappings – such as dorms with fridges, TVs or private bathrooms. Recent renovations have included a great on-site café and solar-heated pool. Only a short hop to the beach.

Other recommendations:

Backpackers Holiday Village (☎ 1800 350 388, 6685 8888; 116 Jonson St; dm A$25-28, d A$60-75; 💻) Lively common areas, clean dorms and a travel desk. The doubles are self-contained two-bedroom apartments.

Belongil Beachouse (☎ 6685 7868; www.belongilbeachouse.com; Childe St; dm A$25-28, d A$65-70, apt A$80-120, cottages A$140-195; 💻) Secluded and great value, although some dorms are crowded. Polished floorboards and stained glass add to the atmosphere. Relax Haven spa (see opposite) is on the premises.

J's Bay YHA (☎ 1800 678 195, 6685 8853; www.byron-bay.com/jsbay; 7 Carlyle St; dm A$25-27, d A$60-100; 💻 🏊) Clean and friendly, with plenty of activities. Give Ziggy the dog a pat by the pool.

First Sun Holiday Park (☎ 6685 6544; www.bshp.com.au/first; Lawson St; camp/caravan sites per 2 people A$24/26, cabins A$70-90) Right in the town centre and just a stroll to Main Beach, this council-run caravan park is the pick of the bunch.

Eating

Byron has plenty of affordable dining options. For basic groceries there's **Woolworths** (☎ 6685 7202; Plaza Shopping Centre, Jonson St; ⌚ 8am-9pm Mon-Fri, 8am-8pm Sat, 10am-6pm Sun).

Fundamental Food Store (☎ 6685 6424; 61 Jonson St; salads A$6.50, burgers A$9; ⌚ lunch & dinner) This vegetarian institution has a great supermarket catering to vegan and gluten-free diets, but don't miss the excellent salad bar with delightfully dippy staff.

Ka-Tousch (☎ 6680 7718; Plaza Shopping Centre, Jonson St, pita pockets A$5-9.50, snacks A$6.50-10.50, mains A$14-16; ⌚ breakfast, lunch & dinner) Going beyond basic kebabs, this café excels in Middle Eastern cuisine, including vibrant salads and Moroccan pastries served with zesty dips. Rock your kasbah in the evenings lounging on cushions and enjoying occasional belly dancing.

Cardamom Pod (☎ 6680 7383; 8 Pier Arcade, Lawson St; mains A$6-11.50; ⌚ lunch & dinner) This simple Hare Krishna eatery does flavoursome Indian and charges by the serve – so you can eat as

SPLURGE!

Dish (☎ 6685 7320; cnr Jonson & Marvell Sts; mains A$27-30; ⌚ dinner Tue-Sun) For a stylish hot date, grab a bite at this Modern Australian restaurant. It's set in a rainforest garden with a hefty wine list and superb seafood. Afterwards, hit the adjoining Dish Raw Bar – with swanky black-and-white leather furnishings – for a cocktail and rich, gooey dessert.

much or as little as you like. Friday night is an all-you-can-eat feast (A$12.50).

Mongers (☎ 6680 8080; 1 Bay Lane; fish & chips A$9-13; ⌚ lunch & dinner) This gourmet fish and chip shop wows locals with hand-cut chips, succulent calamari and tempura prawns. Grab the mammoth family box for a beach picnic.

Earth 'n' Sea Pizza (☎ 6685 6029; 11 Lawson St; pizzas A$14-30; ⌚ lunch & dinner) Some swear by the pizza, but there's good gelati for afters. Vegetarians go for the Mullumbimby Madness pizza, while hotheads love the lava-ly spicy Krakatoa.

Beach Café (☎ 6685 7598; Lawson St; breakfast A$9-15, ⌚ breakfast & lunch) Overlooking Clarks Beach, go for breakfast (although there are yummy lunches).

Drinking

Beach Hotel (☎ 6685 6402; cnr Jonson & Bay Sts) With a beachfront beer garden where everyone drinks after a swim. Look out for *Crocodile Dundee* props in the barn-like interior.

Cheeky Monkey's (☎ 6685 5886; 115 Jonson St; ⌚ 7pm to 3am Thu-Sat) Love it or leave it, this backpacker haunt has loud music, frequent theme nights and traveller discounts. Expect dancing on the tables, and solid drinking.

Railway Friendly Bar (☎ 6685 7662; Jonson St) The carriage-shaped bar is the local hangout, where many start the night's drinking or finish it by jumping on a train.

Entertainment

Byron Bay's nightlife is the tripped-out star of the north coast, with plenty of live music and clubbing.

CINEMAS

Byron Lounge Cinema (☎ 6685 7709; Skinners Shoot Rd; admission A$11) Plays art-house at the Arts Factory Lodge, offering 'dinner and movie' deals nightly. Faux-fur seats and lie-down front rows make this the best way to catch a flick.

Byron Cinemas (☎ 6680 8555; www.byroncinemas.com; 108 Jonson St; adult/concession A$12.50/10) Screen Hollywood blockbusters, with cheap Monday deals.

CLUBBING

Cocomangas (☎ 6685 8493; 32 Jonson St; ⌚ 8pm-3am Mon-Sat) A mainstreet mainstay with loads of theme nights spinning retro and funk to a pop-loving crowd.

C-Moog (☎ 6680 7022; www.c-moog.com.au; The Plaza, Jonson St; admission A$5-20; ⌚ 7pm-3am Tue-Sat) This late-nighter breaks out beats, funk and hip-hop with visiting DJs.

La La Land (☎ 6680 7070; www.lalaland.com.au; 6 Lawson St; ⌚ 7pm-3am) Hidden upstairs, La La Land is a Melbourne chain club with a cool crowd that appreciates the moodily dark setting, Sunday sessions and eclectic music (techno to '80s retro).

LIVE MUSIC

Great Northern Hotel (☎ 6685 6454; Jonson St) The back room of this hotel is synonymous with big-name Australian bands and stellar international tourists.

Railway Friendly Bar (☎ 6685 7662; Jonson St) This bar (left), called the Rails by locals, has guitar-based music most nights, but better bands rock out on weekends.

Getting There & Away

AIR

At the time of writing, low-end air fares from Ballina to Sydney started at A$100 and Melbourne at A$150.

Qantas (☎ 13 13 13; www.qantas.com.au)
Virgin Blue (☎ 136 789, www.virginblue.com.au)

BUS

Long-distance buses stop on Jonson St.

McCafferty's/Greyhound (☎ 13 14 19; www.mccaffertys.com.au) travels twice daily to Brisbane (A$31, three hours), Sydney (A$85, 12 to 14 hours) and Coffs Harbour (A$45, four hours).

Premier Motor Service (☎ 133 410; www.premierms.com.au) has three buses a day to most east coast destinations including Sydney (A$81, 12 to 14 hours), Coffs Harbour (A$45, four hours) and Brisbane (A$30, three hours).

Brisbane Express Bus (☎ 1800 626 222, 07-3342 3564; www.brisbane2byron.com) goes daily to Brisbane (A$28, two hours), while **Byron Bay**

Airbus (☎ 6684 3232; www.byron-bay.com/airbus) operates three times a day to airports at Coolangatta (A$35, one hour) and Ballina (A$30, 30 minutes).

TRAIN

The daily XPT runs to Sydney (A$104, 12 hours) via Coffs Harbour (A$45, 4½ hours), with bookings through **CountryLink** (☎ 13 22 32; www.countrylink.nsw.gov.au).

Getting Around

Byron on Tour (☎ 6680 7006; Shop 3, 95 Jonson St; hire per day A$25) will have you zipping around town in a scootacar – a go-anywhere four-wheel buggy. **Earth Car Rentals** (☎ 6685 7472, 6680 9708; www.byron-bay.com/earthcar; Shop 6, 14 Middleton St) has the best car deals in town from A$38 a day. Most hostels rent bikes.

NIMBIN

From Byron many make the journey west to Nimbin, the alternative centre synonymous with hippies and marijuana. It may feel a little like a bush Amsterdam, but since the 1973 Aquarius Festival Nimbin has been a hippy time capsule. You'll get offered pot in the streets and eventually those persistent dealers become annoying, but Nimbin makes an interesting day trip – just don't inhale.

The **Hemp Embassy** (☎ 6689 1842; www.hempembassy.net; 51 Cullen St; 'whenever') raises consciousness about marijuana legalisation, as well as providing all the implements you'll need to get high. Smokers are welcome at its coffee shop next door. Across the road, **Nimbin Museum** (☎ 6689 1123; 62 Cullen St; admission by donation; 9am-5pm) is a rambling work of art rather than history.

IS IT LEGAL?

Under Australian law, it's illegal for anyone to possess or use cannabis. Busts still happen in Nimbin and penalties can be hefty (see Legal Matters, p469). Yet the town has visible dealing – from kids in tracksuits to mums on mobiles. There's an ongoing struggle to establish legal cannabis cafés, but New South Wales police aren't coming to the party.

Each May the Hemp Embassy (see above) organises 'Mardi Grass' to protest against drug laws, with a whacked-out parade through town. There are a lot of grey goatees and joint smoking, but there are also some interesting opinions on the drug's medicinal/industrial uses. These arguments could come in handy next time you get caught smoking.

Sleeping & Eating

Nimbin Rox Hostel (☎ 6689 0022; home.iprimus.com.au/nimbinrox/; 74 Thorburn St; camp sites per person/dm/d A$10/22/48;) A cool clean hostel with hammocks, permaculture gardens, craft workshops and Thai massage.

Rainbow Café (☎ 6689 1997; 64a Cullen St; mains A$3-7; breakfast, lunch & dinner) This place is good for grabbing a bite, serving cakes and veggie breakfasts, with a big backyard hosting occasional musicians and poets.

Getting There & Around

The **Nimbin Shuttle** (☎ 6680 9189) operates to Byron Bay (one way A$12, Monday to Saturday). **Jim's Alternative Tours** (☎ 6685 7720; www.byron-bay.com/jimstours) is a dependable operator running daily trips from Byron (A$30).

MT WARNING NATIONAL PARK

Named Mt Warning (1157m) by Captain Cook to prevent him from blundering into the coast, this is a spectacular post-volcanic peak. Off the Murwillumbah–Uki road, a 6km access road runs to the car park. There's a 4.5km **summit walk** (five hours return) through lush rainforest, and the track is well marked. However, you'll need a torch for predawn climbing, which rewards with spectacular sunrise views.

BORDER RANGES NATIONAL PARK

This enormous **World Heritage wilderness area** (31,500 hectares) covers the NSW side of the McPherson Range along the Queensland border. More than a quarter of Australia's native bird species can be found within the park.

The eastern section, with escarpments of the massive Mt Warning caldera, is the most easily accessible. The Tweed Range Scenic Dr (gravel but usable in all weather) loops for 100km through the park from Lillian Rock, midway between Uki and Kyogle, to Wiangaree, north of Kyogle on the Woodenbong road. It has some breathtaking lookouts over the Tweed Valley to Mt Warning and the coast. There are rainforest walks from the picnic area at Brindle Creek.

There are a couple of basic **camping grounds** (A$3) on the Tweed Range Scenic Dr, at Forest Tops and Sheep Station Creek. You'll need to bring water. For bookings, call the Kyogle **NPWS** (☎ 02-6632 1473; kyogle@npws.nsw.gov.au).

TWEED HEADS

☎ 07 / pop 55,860

Straddling the NSW–Queensland border, Tweed is where glitzy Coolangatta goes to retire. With a laid-back lifestyle and beautiful beaches, it's easy to see why. There are good budget options around, but when it comes to nightlife the town pulses to the slow beat of grey power. **Tweed Heads visitor centre** (☎ 1800 674 414; www.tweed-coolangatta.com; Tweed Mall, cnr Wharf & Bay Sts; 9am-5pm) is helpful.

The **Captain Cook Memorial**, which straddles the border and is marked by a laser lighthouse, is at Point Danger (named by rock-paranoid Captain Cook). Nearby **Kirra Beach** is a stunning spot for a paddle.

Sleeping & Eating

Accommodation spills over into Coolangatta and up along the Gold Coast (p158), where there's more choice. An excellent caravan park is **Tweed Billabong** (☎ 1800 650 405; www.tweedbillabong.com.au; Holden St; caravan sites per 2 people A$28-45; cabins A$65-170;), with an impressive swimming billabong and palm-fringed pool. The best snacks and breakfasts are at **Seachange Café** (☎ 5599 2031; 275 Boundary Rd; meals A$6-12; breakfast & lunch), with great seascape views.

Getting There & Away

McCafferty's/Greyhound (☎ 13 14 19; www.mccaffertys.com.au) travels daily to Sydney (A$91, 14 hours) or Brisbane (A$15, one hour). **Premier Motor Service** (☎ 13 34 10; www.premierms.com.au) has three buses a day to Sydney (A$85, 13 hours) and three to Brisbane (A$15, one hour).

SOUTH COAST

Expanses of unspoilt coast, humble fishing towns, remote national parks, rich Aboriginal history and superb forests all line the south coast. Sure, it's not as densely populated or as heavily visited as the north coast, but if you don't mind cooler waters there's every chance you'll discover a beach of your own on the 450km of coast between Sydney and the Victorian border. The profusion of national parks makes it easier to clap eyes on wildlife outside of enclosures, and the waters are teeming with tuna, crayfish and even oysters (which are farmed along the coast).

There may not be a party town the likes of Byron Bay, but the south coast is more of a family destination – quieter but worth investigating. Popular beaches are thick with families during the school holidays, but if you come outside these times you'll have space and serenity. If you're looking for outdoor adventures there's bushwalking, scuba diving, fishing, caving, whale-watching and island-exploring, mostly within minutes of the main towns.

Activities

Most of the fun of the south coast is in finding a deserted beach to lie on.

As well, there are great chances to explore Booderee National Park on foot or by camping out. Muramurrang and Mimosa National Parks also offer good bushwalking and some beach camping. There are a few dive places in Jervis Bay, and Wollongong's beaches are a cheaper spot to get a surf lesson.

Getting There & Away

The Princes Hwy runs along the coast from Sydney to the Victorian border – a longer, slower, but more picturesque route to Melbourne than the Hume Hwy.

BUS

Murrays (☎ 13 22 51) has daily buses from Canberra to Batemans Bay (A$24, 2½ hours) and south along the coast to Narooma (A$36, 4½ hours from Canberra; A$16 from Batemans Bay). **Premier Motor Service** (☎ 13 34 10; www.premierms.com.au) runs daily from Canberra to Sydney (A$50, 7½ hours) and Melbourne (A$55, 10 hours), with stops along the way including Narooma (from Melbourne).

Priors (☎ 1800 816 234) runs weekdays between Parramatta and Narooma (A$45, seven hours) and between Sydney and Batemans Bay (A$33, five hours) on Sunday, stopping at most coastal destinations. **Sapphire Coast Express** (☎ 1800 812 135, 03-9763 4473) has buses between Ulladulla/Batemans Bay and Melbourne (A$85, 12 hours) twice a week.

WOLLONGONG

☎ 02 / pop 228,800

Just 80km south of Sydney, Wollongong is the state's third-largest city, but is often forgotten as a suburb of its bigger, showier neighbour. With over 15 surf beaches in the immediate area, it is a waxhead's paradise and much of the action revolves around the beaches.

The city centre and beaches are pleasantly low-rise and low-key, with a large resident student population keeping the town lively. Away from the waves the city can be less attractive – sprawling and industrial with Australia's biggest steelworks at nearby Port Kembla. The area is mistakenly referred to as Illawarra, although this name applies more to the hills (the Illawarra Escarpment) that serve as the city's scenic backdrop.

Orientation

Crown St is the main street, with a pedestrian mall between Keira and Kembla Sts. Keira St is part of the Princes Hwy.

Information

Network Café (☎ 4228 8686; www.networkcafé.com.au; Shop 4-5, 157 Crown St; per hr A$6) Has speedy Internet connections, but can be crowded with LAN gamers.

Tourism Wollongong visitors centre (☎ 1800 240 737, 4227 5545; www.tourismwollongong.com; cnr Crown & Kembla Sts; 9am-5pm Mon-Fri, to 4pm Sat, 10am-4pm Sun)

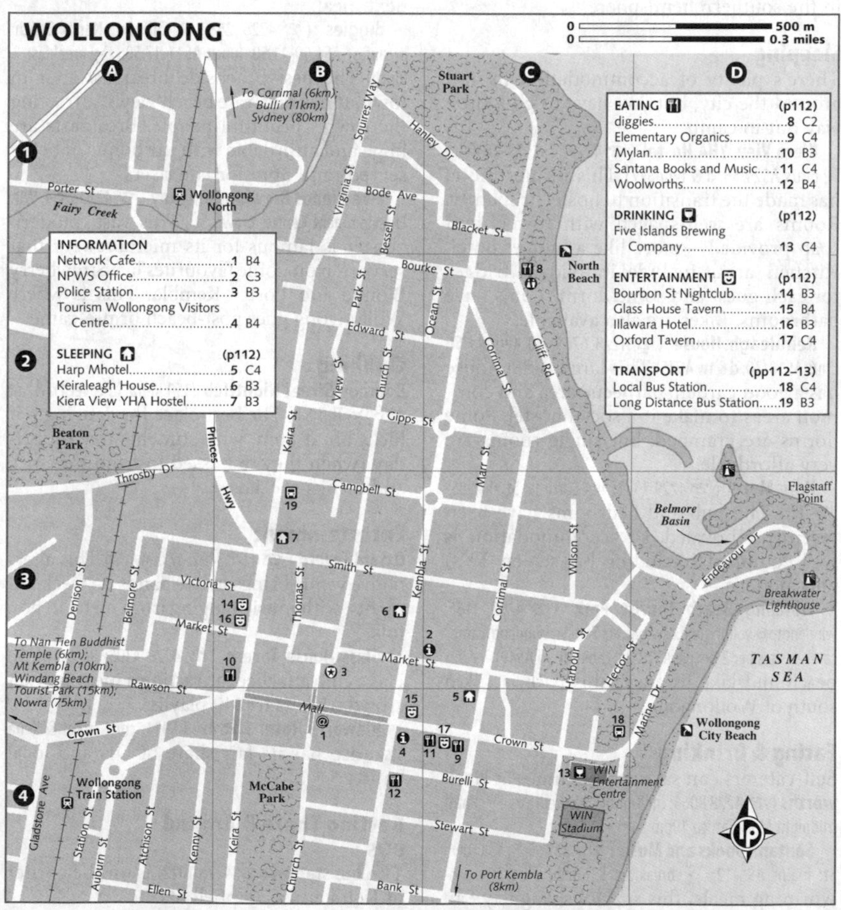

Sights & Activities

Your best bet is to explore the pleasant harbour and the shore for empty expanses of sand. The fishing fleet is based in the southern part of the harbour, **Belmore Basin**, dominated by two late-19th-century lighthouses on the foreshore. Gorgeous **North Beach** generally has better surf than **Wollongong City Beach**. You can take a lesson with **Taupu Surf School** (☎ 4268 0088; www.taupusurfschool.com; 2hr intro course A$49), which gives daily lessons on North Beach and has a special surf-safety course that helps you pick the perfect conditions.

A few kilometres south of the city, the **Nan Tien Buddhist Temple** (☎ 4272 0600; Berkeley Rd, Berkeley; 9am-5pm Tue-Sun) is a peaceful sanctuary that's the biggest Buddhist temple in the southern hemisphere.

Sleeping

There's plenty of accommodation in and around the city, but you have to go a little way out to camp.

Kiera View YHA Hostel (☎ 4229 1132; 73-75 Keira St; dm/s A$24/55, d & tw A$77) This former motel has made the transition to hostel brilliantly. Rooms are well-spaced with towels and soap provided – more like a budget hotel. Kitchen areas include individual fridges for each guest and some dorm rooms have bathrooms. Bikes are also available.

Keiraleagh House (☎ 4228 6765; 60 Kembla St; dm/s A$18/30, d & tw A$45) This large, older house has a good garden, barbecue area and common areas to make it a social hostel. Some dorms are cramped, but single rooms are very affordable.

Harp Motel (☎ 4229 1333; 124 Corrimal St; d A$85-95;) The pub and bedrooms have been recently renovated, so accommodation is well equipped (including big screen TVs) and modern.

Windang Beach Tourist Park (☎ 4297 3166; windangtp@wollongong.nsw.gov.au; Fern St, Windang; camp/caravan sites per 2 people A$19/24, cabins from A$49) With beach and lake frontage, this park is 15km south of Wollongong.

Eating & Drinking

Self-caterers can save their pennies at **Woolworths** (☎ 4228 8066; cnr Kembla & Burelli Sts; 7am-midnight Mon-Sat, to 10pm Sun).

Santana Books and Music (☎ 4227 6603; 53 Crown St; mains A$6-12; breakfast & lunch) For bookworming meals, this spacious, vaguely San Francisco–themed café (sandwiches are named The Haight or other Bay city landmarks) is the place. Flip through magazines (or a volume of Funk & Wagnalls) while enjoying a sandwich, salad or coffee.

Elementary Organics (☎ 4226 6300; 47 Crown St; mains A$7-14; breakfast & lunch) Bristling with health and wheatgrass shots, this little place does fresh juices and neat home-made organic and veggie breakfasts and lunches.

Mylan (☎ 4228 1588; 198 Keira St; mains A$7.50-9; lunch & dinner Mon-Sat) Vietnamese-inspired cuisine in funky minimalist surrounds gives you the feeling this place will be expensive, but it's a surprising bargain. Grab a belly-filling bowl of *pho* (beef noodle soup) or wonton soup and you won't need your next meal.

diggies (☎ 4226 2688; 1 Cliff Rd, North Beach; breakfast A$4.50-11.50, lunch A$11-17.50; breakfast & lunch) The best beachside breakfast spot in town. It has first-rate beach views, attracting the town's beautiful people. Breakfasts are huge and affordable with the bonus of being served until 3pm for late risers.

Five Islands Brewing Company (☎ 4220 2854; WIN Entertainment Centre, Crown St) This vast, modern boozer is famous for its microbrewery that serves flavoursome favourites like Strawberry Blonde and Porter Kembla. This is where Wollongong goes post-beach or pre-game.

Clubbing

Bourbon Street Nightclub (150 Keira St; cover Fri & Sat A$5; Thu-Sat) The best place for dancing – it kicks off at 8pm, with students free on Friday (when they're bussed in from the uni), and drinks specials.

Entertainment

Oxford Tavern (☎ 4228 3892; 47 Crown St) This alternative venue brings in live bands on weekend nights, with music ranging from metal to pop folk.

Glass House Tavern (☎ 4226 4305; 90 Crown St) Has a club attached, attracting a meat-market crowd with its top 40 playlist.

Illawarra Hotel (☎ 4229 5411; cnr Market & Keira Sts) Also has its fair share of DJs and local bands.

Getting There & Around

BUS

The **bus station** (☎ 4226 1022) is on the corner of Keira and Campbell Sts.

Premier Motor Services (☎ 13 34 10; www.premierms.com.au) runs several daily services to Sydney (A$13, two hours) and regular services to Batemans Bay (A$33, three to four hours, two or three daily), Narooma (A$45, 4½ to five hours, two or three daily) and Melbourne (A$70, 15 hours, one daily). **Murrays** (☎ 13 22 51; www.murrays.com.au) goes daily to Canberra (A$31, 3½ hours).

Local bus companies serve the city from the local bus station on Marine Dr. Companies include **Dions** (☎ 4228 9855), **Premier** (☎ 4271 1322) and **Greens** (☎ 4267 3884).

CityRail (☎ 13 15 00) runs several daily trains to Sydney (A$8.80, 1½ hours).

AROUND WOLLONGONG

Wollongong's dramatic backdrop, the **Illawarra Escarpment**, is a place to enjoy woodland walks and grand coastal views. There are walking tracks on Mt Kembla and Mt Keira, less than 10km from the city centre, but you'll need your own transport to get to the tracks. Enjoy spectacular views over the town and coast from the **Bulli Scenic Lookout** (pronounced bull-eye), north off the Princes Hwy. The visitors centre or the local **NPWS office** (☎ 02-4225 1455; Shop 4, 55 Market St, Wollongong; 🕑 8.30am-4.30pm Mon-Fri) should have copies of the useful, free NPWS leaflet guide to the escarpment.

Heading further south, you'll strike **Nowra** (pop 25,000), an agreeable town that has some attractive beaches serving as playgrounds for Australian families. If you've got your own vehicle it can be a good spot to stop on your way to Jervis Bay. Accommodation can be a little pricey, but one option if you're travelling in a group of four or more is **M&Ms Guesthouse** (☎ 4422 8006; www.mmguesthouse.com; 1a Scenic Dr; dm A$25, s/d A$55/75), a rustic little place in a good riverside location. You can grab a bite at the **Tea Club** (46 Berry St; mains around A$10; 🕑 lunch daily, dinner Tue-Sat), a comfortable little café where Nowra's bohemian set hangs out.

JERVIS BAY

Despite extensive development, this sheltered bay area retains its white beaches and crystal-clear water. Dolphins are regularly seen, and whales swing by on their annual migrations (June to November). The small town of **Huskisson** is a good base from which to explore the wilderness of Jervis Bay, but

> **GUARDIAN BIRD**
>
> The Aboriginal people of the Wreck Bay area on the southern peninsula hold one animal as their guardian – the white-bellied eagle. This huge bird grows to a height of 75cm and is easily recognisable by its sheer white under-body. During their breeding session from May to October, you may be lucky enough to spot one of their nests – large stick constructions hidden 30m high in trees.

Booderee National Park is the real highlight. **Vincentia** is another sleepy beach town that almost merges with Huskisson.

A fair chunk of the area belongs to the navy (off-limits to civilians) and is technically part of the ACT, so that Canberra has a strategic sea port during times of war.

The bay's northern shore is harder to reach because of the large size of the bay, which means you have to drive back onto the highway and head south. This probably explains why the northern shore is comparatively underdeveloped.

Beecroft Peninsula forms the northeastern side of Jervis Bay. Currarong, near Beecroft Head, is a small town with camping at **Currarong Tourist Park** (☎ 02-4448 3027; camp/caravan sites per 2 people A$16/20, cabins from A$70).

Jointly administered by the local Aboriginal community, the Booderee National Park occupies Jervis Bay's southeastern spit. Much of it is heathland, with some short walks and gorgeous secluded beaches. The **visitors centre** (☎ 02-4443 0977; www.deh.gov.au/parks/booderee) at the park entrance has walking-track maps and camping information. Inside the park is the **Booderee Botanic Gardens** (🕑 8.30am-5pm), with a number of short walks – none longer than three hours – along stunning beaches. Entry to the park is by the car-load (per car A$10) and is valid for one week. NPWS passes aren't valid in this park.

Activities

To see dolphins and even passing whales, join **Dolphin Watch Cruises** (☎ 1800 246 010; www.dolphinwatch.com.au; Owen St; adult/concession A$25/18), which has several dolphin- and whale-watching trips (June to November is prime whale time). It offers a free trip if dolphins are not spotted.

If you want to get closer to the marine life, two Huskisson outfits offer diving and courses: **Pro Dive** (☎ 02-4441 5255; 64 Owen St; 1-day intro dive/4-day PADI course A$140/420) and **Sea Sports** (☎ 02-4441 5012; 47 Owen St; 1-day intro dive/3-day PADI course A$180/320).

Sleeping & Eating

Jervis Bay Backpackers (☎ 02-4441 6880; www.beachnbush.com.au; 17 Elizabeth St, Vincentia; dm A$25, d & tw A$60) Cheap bunks are available at this homey little place that delivers a free breakfast.

Husky Pub (☎ 02-4441 5001; www.thehuskypub.com.au; Owen St, Huskisson; s/d 40/60) Has reasonable pub rooms, some with bay views (although rooms 1 and 2 have the irritating 'bling bling' of the downstairs gaming lounge).

There are several caravan parks in the area, but **Huskisson Beach Tourist Resort** (☎ 02-4441 5142; Beach St, Huskisson-Vincentia Rd; camp/caravan sites per 2 people A$24/26, cabins A$68;) has a beachside location just a little way out of Huskisson on the road to Vincentia.

In Booderee National Park, there are several camping areas at Green Patch (A$14 to A$17) and Bristol Point, and a rudimentary camping area at Caves Beach (A$9 to A$11). Book sites at the **visitors centre** (☎ 02-4443 0977) at the park entrance. Also in the park, **Bay of Plenty Lodges** (☎ 02-4441 2018; www.bayofplentylodges.com.au; dm A$15-20, cabins A$100-160) is an environmentally friendly outfit set in the bush (kangaroos are the other amiable residents).

Affordable dining options:

Taj Indian Restaurant (☎ 02-4441 7775; Shop 2, 47 Owen St, Huskisson; meals A$8.50-19; dinner) Great curries.

Hawng Khrua Thai Restaurant (☎ 02-4441 7029; Shop 1, The Promenade, Huskisson; meals A$13-15; dinner) Offers lip-smacking Thai dishes.

Getting There & Away

Nowra Coaches (☎ 02-4423 5244) goes to Huskisson (A$10, 30 minutes; two to four daily) and Jervis Bay Village (A$9, 1¼ hours, twice weekly) in Booderee National Park.

MURRAMARANG NATIONAL PARK

Starting about 20km south of Ulladulla and running most of the way south to Batemans Bay, this coastal park has stunning beaches that bring surfers and campers alike.

The best surf beaches are **Merry**, **Pebbly** and **Depot Beaches**. Pebbly Beach is particularly famous for its 'tame' kangaroos, known to wander down to the water and come close enough to pat. There are numerous walking tracks snaking off from the beaches and a steep but enjoyable walk up **Durras Mountain** (283m). Overnight camping means paying the park entry fee of A$6 per car plus any camping fees (around A$5 per person).

BATEMANS BAY

☎ **02 / pop 10,200**

Only 152km away from the nation's capital, Batemans Bay is known as Canberra's beach (public servants are recognisable by tan lines around their forgotten ID tags). It's a busy seaside town that's a popular base for families who day-trip to better beaches further north. The Batemans Bay **visitors centre** (☎ 1800 802 528, 4472 6900; Princes Hwy; 9am-5pm) is near the town centre.

Corrigans Beach is the closest beach to the town centre, with smaller beaches amid rocky shores. Wave-riders head for **Surf Beach**, **Malua Bay** and **Broulee**. Beginners can get a lesson from **Broulee Surf School** (☎ 4471 7370; www.brouleesurfschool.com.au; 1½hr lesson A$42).

Batemans Bay has good budget accommodation as travellers tend to use it as a base to explore the rest of the region. A budget-conscious option is **Shady Willows Holiday Park & YHA** (☎ 4472 4972; www.yha.com.au; Old Princes Hwy; camp sites per person A$12, dm A$21-31, s A$35-38, d A$50-60;), with converted caravans and dorms. Facilities include bike hire and laundry.

NAROOMA & AROUND

The lovely coastal town of **Narooma** boasts serene, forest-edged inlets and lakes, and some rugged coastline. The **visitors centre** (☎ 02-4476 2881; www.naturecoast-tourism.com.au; Princes Hwy; 9am-5pm) is close to the town centre. The **NPWS office** (☎ 02-4476 2888; cnr Field St & Princes Hwy; 9am-5pm Mon-Fri) stocks brochures for all nearby parks.

About 10km off the coast is **Montague Island**, a nature reserve with resident seals and nesting fairy penguins. It's accessible only by boat with an NPWS-accredited guide. The four-hour **NPWS tours** (☎ 0407-909 111; Narooma Town Wharf; adult A$80) depart morning and evening.

A good-value place to stay is **Holiday Lodge Motor Inn** (☎ 02-4476 2282; 141 Wagonga St/Princess Hwy, Narooma; s/d A$70/80;), with dated décor, but good rooms including kitchenettes, verandas and almost sea views (pesky palm trees!). **Lynch's Hotel** (☎ 02-4476 2001; 135 Wagonga St, Narooma; s/d/tw A$40/50/65) deceives with the pub downstairs populated by old men, but upstairs has recently renovated rooms – some with impressive ocean views.

Eating options revolve around seafood. The best is **Quarterdeck Marina** (☎ 02-4476 2763; Riverside Dr; mains A$14-18; lunch & dinner) with creative fish and chips (anyone for Cajun Dory?) and sea birds prospecting the nearby estuary. Don't miss the oysters farmed right in front of the restaurant.

Just 15km south of Narooma is the twee town of **Central Tilba**. Heritage-listed, it's a craft centre that your mum would find 'just darling'. From nearby **Tilba Tilba** you can walk (five hours return) up Mt Dromedary (806m) – a camel-shaped landmass also called Gulaga by local Koori people. After that climb, you've probably earned a tipple at **Tilba Valley Wines** (☎ 02-4473 7308; www.tilbavalleywines.com; 947 Old Princes Hwy; lunches A$9; tastings 10am-5pm) or a sample of award-winning *fromages* from **ABC Cheese Factory** (☎ 4473 7387; Bate St, Central Tilba; 9am-5pm).

Further south, **Umbarra Aboriginal and Cultural Centre** (☎ 02-4473 7232; www.umbarra.com.au; Wallaga Lake; cruises A$30, 4WD tours A$40-65) gives a fascinating insight into indigenous culture, including traditional dwellings. Excellent tours include an off-road excursion and a boat tour spotting the black duck – a totem of the local Yuin people.

South of the beautiful bird-filled **Wallaga Lake** and off the Princes Hwy, **Bermagui** (population 2000) is a pretty fishing port. There are great walks nearby and it's a handy base for visits to both Gulaga/Wallaga Lake and Mimosa Rocks National Parks. Bermagui's **visitors centre** (☎ 02-6493 3054; Lamont St; 10am-4pm) is just beyond the marina.

Stay at Bermagui's **Blue Pacific** (☎ 1800 244 921, 02-6493 4921; 73 Murrah St; dm/s A$25/50), a motel-style place with small but comfortable and well-equipped rooms that are ideal for self-catering. Eat at **Saltwater** (☎ 02-6493 4328; mains A$20; lunch Wed-Sun, dinner Thu-Sat), a bright, modern place on the harbour.

MIMOSA ROCKS NATIONAL PARK

Running along 17km of beautiful coastline, Mimosa Rocks (5624 hectares) is a wonderful coastal park with dense and varied bush and great beaches. There are basic **camp sites** (per person A$5) at Aragunnu Beach, Picnic Point and Middle Beach, and a camping area with no facilities at Gillards Beach. These camping areas and the picnic areas are accessible from the road running between Bermagui and Tathra. Contact the **NPWS office** (☎ 6476 2888) in Narooma for camping bookings.

SOUTH INLAND

There's plenty to tempt you away from the coast with the nation's capital and the state's largest national park both inland. The Australian Capital Territory (ACT) sprawls over 2366 sq km, with the meticulously designed metropolis of Canberra at its heart. Crammed with national monuments and set in idyllic bush, Canberra has plenty to set your camera's flash popping. Further south, the rugged Snowy Mountains are Australia's premier venue for skiing and snow sports. In summer the mountains blossom with wild flowers, making it the perfect time to bushwalk to the summit of Mt Kosciuszko, Australia's highest mountain. Even further south, the town of Albury Wodonga straddles the border with Victoria, and picturesque Wagga Wagga has small town charm with a big city population.

Activities

With the outdoorsy capital Canberra at its centre, the south is abuzz with recreation. If you're adventurous, there are great slopes to carve up on skis or a snowboard: check out Thredbo and Perisher for the best slopes. Better yet, you can combine business and pleasure by working in the snowfields (see Positions Vacant: Snow Fiends, p129).

Canberra itself is crisscrossed by networks of cycle paths, and the central lake makes for loads of water sports, while national parks like Namadgi and Kosciuszko are packed with walking and wildlife-watching options.

CANBERRA & THE AUSTRALIAN CAPITAL TERRITORY

☎ 02 / pop 309,800

Founded by an act of Parliament and the centre of Australian politics ever since, Canberra is an outdoorsy city set amid lakeside parks and rugged bushland. Weekends find Canberrans biking and in-line skating around Lake Burley Griffin or tramping through the surrounding wilderness of

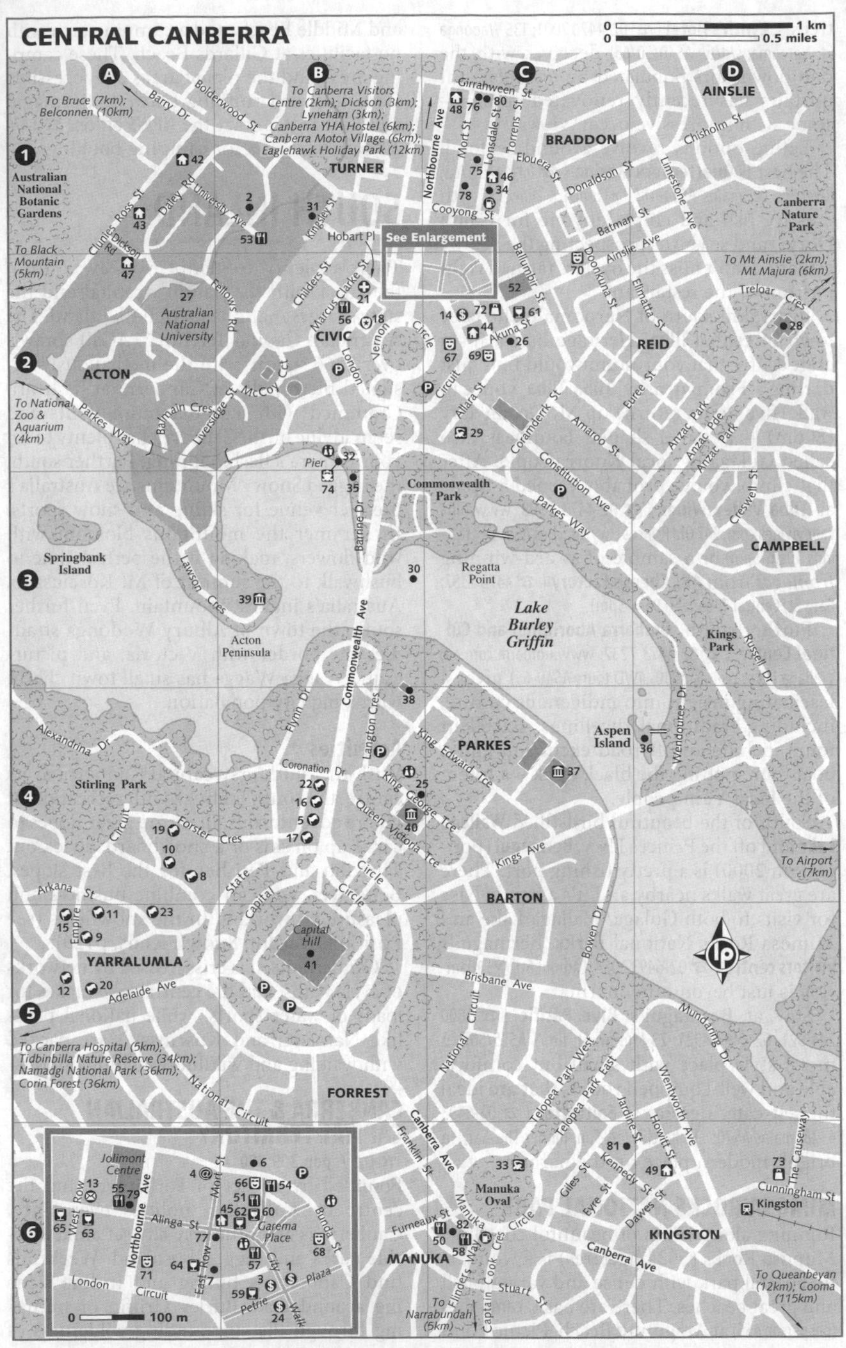
CENTRAL CANBERRA
0 1 km
0 0.5 miles
A
B
C
D
1
2
3
4
5
6
To Bruce (7km); Belconnen (10km)
To Canberra Visitors Centre (2km); Dickson (3km); Lyneham (3km); Canberra YHA Hostel (6km); Canberra Motor Village (6km); Eaglehawk Holiday Park (12km)
AINSLIE
BRADDON
TURNER
Australian National Botanic Gardens
To Black Mountain (5km)
Canberra Nature Park
To Mt Ainslie (2km); Mt Majura (6km)
See Enlargement
Australian National University
ACTON
CIVIC
REID
To National Zoo & Aquarium (4km)
Pier
Commonwealth Park
Regatta Point
CAMPBELL
Springbank Island
Lake Burley Griffin
Acton Peninsula
Kings Park
Aspen Island
PARKES
Stirling Park
BARTON
To Airport (7km)
Capital Hill
YARRALUMLA
To Canberra Hospital (5km); Tidbinbilla Nature Reserve (34km); Namadgi National Park (36km); Corin Forest (36km)
FORREST
Manuka Oval
MANUKA
KINGSTON
Kingston
To Narrabundah (5km)
To Queanbeyan (12km); Cooma (115km)
Jolimont Centre
Garema Place
0 100 m
Barry Dr
Bolderwood St
Girrahween St
Northbourne Ave
Mort St
Lonsdale St
Torrens St
Chisholm St
Elouera St
Donaldson St
Limestone Ave
Cooyong St
Batman St
Ainslie Ave
Daley Rd
University Ave
Kingsley St
Clunies Ross St
Dickson Rd
Hobart Pl
Childers St
Marcus Clarke St
Ballumbir St
Doonkuna St
Elimatta St
Treloar Cres
Fellows Rd
London Circuit
Vernon Circle
Akuna St
Allara St
McCoy Cct
Liversidge St
Balmain Cres
Parkes Way
Coranderrk St
Amaroo St
Euree St
Anzac Park
Anzac Pde
Constitution Ave
Creswell St
Barrine Dr
Commonwealth Ave
Lawson Cres
Flynn Dr
Langton Cres
Wendouree Dr
Russell Dr
Alexandrina Dr
Coronation Dr
King Edward Tce
King George Tce
Queen Victoria Tce
Forster Cres
Kings Ave
Arkana St
Empire Circuit
State Circle
Capital Circle
Bowen Dr
Brisbane Ave
Adelaide Ave
National Circuit
Mundaring Dr
Telopea Park West
Telopea Park East
Canberra Ave
Franklin St
Jardine St
Howitt St
Wentworth Ave
Kennedy St
Giles St
Eyre St
Dawes St
The Causeway
Cunningham St
Furneaux St
Manuka Circle
Flinders Way
Captain Cook Cres
Stuart St
West Row
East Row
Alinga St
Bunda St
City Walk
Petrie Plaza

INFORMATION
American Express 1 B6
ANU Union Building 2 B1
ANZ Bank 3 B6
Café Cactus 4 A6
Canadian High Commission 5 B4
Citizens Advice Bureau ACT 6 B6
Civic Library 7 A6
French Embassy 8 A4
German Embassy 9 A5
Indonesian Embassy 10 A4
Irish Embassy 11 A5
Japanese Embassy 12 A5
Main Post Office 13 A6
National Australia Bank 14 C2
Netherlands Embassy 15 A5
NZ High Commission 16 B4
Papua New Guinea High Commission 17 B4
Police Station 18 B2
Singapore High Commission 19 A4
Thai Embassy 20 A5
Thomas Cook (see 72)
Travellers' Medical & Vaccination Centre 21 B2
UK High Commission 22 B4
US Embassy 23 A5
Westpac Bank 24 B6

SIGHTS & ACTIVITIES (pp118–122)
Aboriginal Tent Embassy 25 B4
Adrenalin Sports 26 C2
Australian National University 27 A2
Australian War Memorial 28 D2
Canberra Olympic Pool 29 C2
Captain Cook Memorial Water Jet 30 B3
Civic YMCA (see 29)
Drill Hall Gallery 31 B1
Lake Burley Griffin Boat Hire 32 B2
Manuka Swimming Pool 33 C6
Mountain Designs 34 C1
Mr Spokes Bike Hire 35 B3
National Carillon 36 D4
National Gallery of Australia 37 C4
National Library of Australia 38 B4
National Museum of Australia 39 B3
National Portrait Gallery (see 40)
Old Parliament House 40 B4
Parliament House 41 B5

SLEEPING (pp122–3)
Bruce Hall 42 A1
Burton & Garran Hall 43 A1
Canberra City Accommodation 44 C2
City Walk Hotel 45 A6
Civic Pub Backpackers 46 C1
John XXIII College 47 A2
Kythera Motel 48 C1
Ursula College (see 47)
Victor Lodge 49 D6

EATING (pp123–4)
Abell's Kopi Tiam 50 C6
Asian Bistro (see 2)
Caffe della Piazza 51 B6
City Market 52 C2
Food Hall (see 72)
Gods Café & Bar 53 B1
Gus' Café 54 B6
Little Saigon 55 A6
Milk & Honey (see 66)
Sage (see 70)
Santa Lucia (see 81)
Shalimar 56 B2
Silo (see 81)
Sizzle Bento 57 B6
Verve 58 C6

DRINKING (pp124–5)
Church Bar (see 44)
Cube 59 B6
Filthy McFadden's (see 81)
Hippo 60 B6
Holy Grail 61 C2
King O'Malley's 62 B6
P.J. O'Reilly's 63 A6
Phoenix 64 A6
Toast (see 69)
Wig & Pen 65 A6

ENTERTAINMENT (pp125–6)
Academy 66 B6
ANU Union Bar (see 2)
Canberra Theatre Centre 67 C2
Club Mombasa 68 B6
Electric Shadows Cinema 69 C2
Gorman House Arts Centre 70 C2
icbm & Insomnia 71 A6

SHOPPING (p126)
Canberra Centre 72 C2
Gorman House Markets (see 70)
Old Bus Depot Markets 73 D6

TRANSPORT (pp126–7)
Action Information Kiosk (see 77)
Acton Park Ferry Terminal 74 B3
Avis 75 C1
Budget 76 C1
Civic Bus Interchange 77 A6
Hertz 78 C1
Qantas 79 A6
Thrifty 80 C1

OTHER
Kingston Shopping Centre 81 C6
Manuka Shopping Centre 82 C6

Namadgi National Park. The city itself delivers plenty of tourist-worthy sites: an array of national monuments, quality cafés and restaurants fit for visiting dignitaries (that's you!) and a thriving pub/club scene that shakes off the grey public-servant image.

The relative serenity and orderliness of the Australian capital (especially of the rambling, homogeneous suburbs) isn't everybody's idea of a good time. But the capital is big enough to reward most visitors with different types of experiences. Club culture is peeking between the gaps in Canberra's (predominantly faux-Irish) pub scene and a flourishing arts scene packs out theatres and galleries. There's some intriguing modern architecture, an active collective of essay-procrastinating university students from around the world, a political enclave from Capital Hill, and a buzzing bar-fly culture. So pack an open mind and investigate the possibilities.

History

When Australia's separate colonies underwent federation in 1901, a decision to build a national capital was written into the constitution. After heated debate between Sydney and Melbourne, a site was selected in 1908 and the Commonwealth government bought land for the ACT in 1911. American architect Walter Burley Griffin won an international competition to design the city and had a lake named after him for his efforts. On 12 March 1913, when the foundations of the new capital were being laid, the city was officially baptised 'Canberra', believed to be an Aboriginal term for 'meeting place'.

Canberra took over from Melbourne as the seat of national government in 1927, but the city's expansion only got under way after WWII. In 1960 the ACT's population was 50,000 and by 1967 had topped 100,000; today it's almost 310,000. In 1988 Canberra was granted self-government, able to control its own purse strings. More recently, Canberra has overcome bushfires in 2003, which damaged large chunks of Namadgi National Park and devastated over 500 homes.

Orientation

Artificial Lake Burley Griffin (called the 'ornamental water' in Walter Burley Griffin's original plans) is the centrepiece of the city. From the north side the main arterial road, Northbourne Ave, runs to Canberra city (aka the suburb of Civic). The pedestrian

THE STATE IT'S IN

The Australian Capital Territory (ACT) is technically an independent city-state and is not part of NSW. When the colonies decided to join together to become a nation in 1901, bickering between Sydney and Melbourne meant that a new capital had to be built between the rival metropolises. The newly created state was administered by the federal government but, in 1988, it shrugged off responsibility and made the ACT self-governing. Most Australians still equate Canberra with the federal government, using it as a curse when 'those bastards in Canberra' increase taxes or make other unpopular moves.

For geographical purposes only, we've included the ACT in this NSW chapter.

malls to the east comprise Canberra's main shopping areas.

To the north of Civic, Dickson and Lyneham are two predominantly residential suburbs with interesting town centres.

South of Civic, Northbourne Ave becomes Commonwealth Ave and crosses Lake Burley Griffin to Capital Circle, which is crowned by Parliament House. Following this road south will take you to Manuka and, further on, the turn-off to Kingston, where you'll find the train station.

The rest of the city is made up of suburban clusters, each with their own 'town centres'.

Canberra's airport is 7km southeast of the city. Taxi fares to the city average A$18. **Deane's Buslines** (☎ 6299 3722) operates the AirLiner bus (A$5, 20 minutes, 11 times daily between 5.30am and 7pm Monday to Friday), which runs between the airport and the city interchange (bay 6).

Information

INTERNET ACCESS

Public libraries (including Civic Library), several hostels and the Jolimont Centre have public Internet access.

Café Cactus (☎ 6248 0449; Shop 1, 7 Mort St, Civic; 🕑 8am-7pm Mon-Fri, 9.30am-9pm Sat, 10.30am-6pm Sun; per hr A$12) An upbeat, friendly Internet café.

MEDICAL SERVICES

Canberra Hospital (☎ 6244 2222, emergency dept 6244 2611; Yamba Dr, Garran)

Travellers Medical & Vaccination Centre (☎ 6257 7156; 5th fl, 8-10 Hobart Pl, Civic; 🕑 8.30am-4.30pm Mon, Wed & Fri, to 7pm Thu) Appointments essential.

MONEY

American Express (☎ 6247 2333; 1st fl, Centrepoint, City Walk, Civic)

Thomas Cook (☎ 6247 9984; Canberra Centre, Bunda St, Civic)

POST

Main post office (☎ 6209 1681; 53-73 Alinga St, Civic) You can pick up poste restante here – have your mail addressed to: Poste Restante Canberra GPO, Canberra City, ACT 2601.

TOURIST INFORMATION

Canberra visitors centre (☎ 1300 554 114, 6205 0044; www.canberratourism.com.au; 330 Northbourne Ave, Dickson; 🕑 9am-5.30pm Mon-Fri, 9am-4pm Sat & Sun) Dispenses detailed visitor information and books accommodation.

Citizens Advice Bureau ACT (☎ 6248 7988; www.citizensadvice.org.au; Griffin Centre, 19 Bunda St, Civic; 🕑 10am-4pm Mon-Fri, to 1pm Wed) Acts as a more central branch of the visitors centre, but is not as thorough.

Sights

You'll notice a lot of sights with the word 'national' in their names – some of them are worth seeing and some can be yawned through. Canberra's many significant buildings, museums and galleries gather around Lake Burley Griffin, while the most appealing natural features lie in the territory's west and southwest. Wheelchair-bound visitors will find most sights are fully accessible.

Bus No 34 from the city interchange is handy for many of the following sights. For more information on bus services see p127.

LOOKOUTS

Black Mountain (812m) is topped by the 195m-high **Telstra Tower** (☎ 1800 806 718; Black Mountain Dr; adult A$3.30; 🕑 9am-10pm), which has been likened to a giant syringe, but the view from the top is truly ecstatic. **Mt Ainslie**, northeast of the city, stands 843m and has fine views day and night; walking tracks to the mountain start behind the War Memorial and end at the 888m **Mt Majura**.

LAKE BURLEY GRIFFIN

Named after Canberra's architect, Lake Burley Griffin was filled by damming the

Molonglo River in 1963. Around its 35km shore are many places of interest.

Built in 1970 for the bicentenary of Cook's landfall, the **Captain Cook Memorial Water Jet** (10am-noon & 2-4pm, also 7-9pm during daylight saving) flings a geyser-like column of water up to 147m into the air. The skeleton globe at nearby **Regatta Point** traces Cook's three great voyages of discovery.

Not content just to send a card, Britain gave the 50m-high **National Carillon** (6257 1068; recitals 12.45-1.35pm Tue & Thu, 2.45-3.35pm Sat & Sun) to Canberra as a 50th anniversary present. The carillon tower is on Aspen Island, and its 53 bronze bells weigh from 7kg to six tonnes and periodically toll to play strange compositions. Bookings are required for Carillon **tours** (adult A$8; 12.45pm Mon, Wed & Fri).

PARLIAMENT HOUSE

Worth a few hours' exploration is Canberra's striking **Parliament House** (6277 5399; www.aph.gov.au; admission free; 9am-5pm). See Designs on Power, below for details on the building's design.

There are free 45-minute **guided tours** on nonsitting days (the days when parliament is not in session) and 20-minute tours on sitting days (every half-hour from 9am to 4pm daily), but you're welcome to self-navigate and watch parliamentary squabblings from the public galleries. Tickets for question time (2pm sitting days) in the **House of Representatives** are free but must be booked in advance through the Sergeant at Arms (6277 4889); tickets aren't required for the **Senate Chamber**.

OLD PARLIAMENT HOUSE

Get a feel for the old-time parliamentary action at **Old Parliament House** (6270 8222; www.oph.gov.au; King George Tce, Parkes; adult/concession A$2/1; 9am-5pm), seat of government from 1927 to 1988. You can wander through the prime minister's suite or try your hand at addressing the House of Representatives. There's a free **guided tour** (40min; 9.30am, 10.15am, 11am, 11.45am, 12.45pm, 1.30pm, 2.30pm & 3.15pm). The building incorporates the **National Portrait Gallery** (6270 8236; www.portrait.gov.au), which exhibits painting, photography and new-media portraiture.

Opposite the main entrance is the culturally significant **Aboriginal Tent Embassy**, established in 1972 to protest against the government's refusal to recognise land rights.

DESIGNS ON POWER

Opened in 1988, Parliament House cost a whopping A$1.1 billion and took eight years to build. It replaced Old Parliament House, which was originally designed as temporary accommodation, but it served for 61 years.

The new Parliament House was built into a hillside and covered by grass to preserve the site's original landscape. Its splendid interior incorporates different combinations of Australian timbers in each main section, and more than 3000 original artworks.

The main axis of Parliament House runs northeast–southwest so that it aligns with Old Parliament House, the Australian War Memorial and Mt Ainslie. Two high, granite-faced walls curve out from the axis to the corners of the building; the House of Representatives (east of the walls) and the Senate (to the west) are linked to the centre by covered walkways.

Enter the building across the 90,000-piece **forecourt mosaic** by Michael Nelson Tjakamarra, the theme of which is 'a meeting place' and that represents possum and wallaby Dreaming. Then go through the white marble **Great Veranda** at the northeastern end of the main axis. In the **foyer**, the grey-green marble columns symbolise a forest, and marquetry wall panels are inlaid with designs of Australian flora.

The 1st floor overlooks the **Great Hall** and its 20m-long **tapestry**, created by the Victorian Tapestry Workshop and inspired by the original Arthur Boyd eucalypt forest painting hanging outside the hall. In the public gallery above the Great Hall is the 16m-long **embroidery**, created by more than 500 members of the embroiderers' guilds of Australia.

The Great Hall is the centre of the building, with passages to chambers on each side. One of only four known copies of the 1297 **Magna Carta** is displayed here.

On the building's grassy rooftop are 360-degree views and an 81m-high flagpole carrying a flag the size of a double-decker bus.

For many Australians, it was the first place they saw the Aboriginal flag.

NATIONAL GALLERY OF AUSTRALIA

With artworks ranging from traditional Aboriginal art to 20th-century works by prominent artists such as Arthur Boyd, the **National Gallery** (☎ 6240 6502; www.nga.gov.au; Parkes Pl, Parkes; permanent collection free; ⏲ 10am-5pm) is essential if you're seeking Australian culture. Sharing gallery space with paintings are sculptures (visit the Sculpture Garden), photographs, furniture, ceramics, fashion and silverware. In addition to regular all-inclusive **guided tours** (⏲ 11am & 2pm), there's also a **tour** (⏲ 11am Thu & Sun) focusing on Aboriginal and Torres Strait Islander art.

NATIONAL MUSEUM OF AUSTRALIA

Everything is on a huge scale at this **museum** (☎ 1800 026 132, 6208 5000; www.nma.gov.au; Lawson Cres, Acton Peninsula; admission free; ⏲ 9am-5pm), which seems to be more abstract Australian storybook than museum. Using humour, creativity, controversy and self-contradiction, the museum puts national identity in a blender, challenging visitors' ideas of Australian-ness. There are giant buses, 'Gardens of Australian Dreams' and a huge red ribbon – making it more rollercoaster ride than fusty traditional museum. If you don't believe us, try the dizzying introductory C show. Bus No 34 runs here. There's also a free bus on weekends and public holidays, departing regularly from 10.30am from platform 7 at the city bus interchange.

AUSTRALIAN NATIONAL BOTANIC GARDENS

On the lower slopes of Black Mountain, 90 hectares of beautiful **gardens** (☎ 6250 9450; www.anbg.gov.au/anbg; Clunies Ross St, Acton; admission free; ⏲ 9am-5pm, to 8pm summer) celebrate Australian floral diversity. The **Aboriginal Plant Use Walk** (45 minutes, 1km) passes through the cool **Rainforest Gully** and has signs explaining how Aborigines related to indigenous plants. The **Eucalypt Lawn** is peppered with 600 species of this ubiquitous tree.

The **visitors centre** (⏲ 9.30am-4.30pm) is the departure point for free **guided walks** (⏲ 11am & 2pm, also 10am summer).

NATIONAL ZOO & AQUARIUM

This engaging **zoo** and **aquarium** (☎ 6287 8400; www.zooquarium.com.au; Lady Denman Dr, Yarralumla; adult/concession A$19/16; ⏲ 9am-5pm) has a roll-call of fascinating animals, including capuchins, diminutive sun (Malay) bears, alpine dingoes and a tigon (the unnatural result of breeding tiger-lion crosses in captivity).

AUSTRALIAN WAR MEMORIAL

Old war movies come to life at the **war memorial** (☎ 6243 4211; www.awm.gov.au; Treloar Cres, Campbell; admission free; ⏲ 10am-5pm), which houses pictures, dioramas, relics and exhibitions detailing Australia's various conflicts. There's an impressive collection of aircraft and machinery in **Anzac Hall** (resting place of the Lancaster bomber called *G for George*) and in the **Aircraft Hall**. Entombed among the Hall of Memory's mosaics is the **Unknown Australian Soldier**, whose remains were returned from a WWI battlefield in 1993 and who symbolises all Australian war casualties.

There are free **guided tours** (90min; 10am, 10.30am, 11am, 1pm, 1.30pm & 2pm) and a *Self-guided Tour* leaflet (A$3).

Along **Anzac Pde**, Canberra's broad commemorative way, are 11 memorials to various campaigns.

NATIONAL LIBRARY OF AUSTRALIA

Drawing on classical architecture, the impressive **library** (☎ 6262 1111; www.nla.gov.au; Parkes Pl, Parkes; admission free; ⏲ main reading room 9am-9pm Mon-Thu, to 5pm Fri & Sat, 1.30-5pm Sun) has accumulated over six million items, most of which can be accessed in one of eight reading rooms. Rarer items including musical recordings, paintings and, of course, books are displayed at the **exhibition gallery** (admission free; ⏲ 9am-5pm). Bookings are required for the free one-hour **guided tour** (☎ 6262 1271).

AUSTRALIAN NATIONAL UNIVERSITY (ANU)

Founded in 1946, the park-like grounds of the **ANU** (☎ 6125 5111; www.anu.edu.au) lay between Civic and Black Mountain and make for a pleasant walk. Drop into the **Drill Hall Gallery** (☎ 6125 5832; Kingsley St; admission free; ⏲ noon-5pm Wed-Sun) to see special exhibitions and paintings from the university's art collection; a permanent fixture is the dazzling hue of Sidney Nolan's *Riverbend*. Collect the ANU *Sculpture Walk* brochure to get a fine-arts appreciation of the university grounds.

AUSTRALIAN INSTITUTE OF SPORT (AIS)

Australia's elite and aspiring-elite athletes train at the **AIS** (☎ 6214 1444; www.ausport.com.au; Leverrier Cres, Bruce), a facility that matches sporting talent with science. Institute **tours** (adult/concession A$12/9) are led by resident sportspeople at 10am, 11.30am, 1pm and 2.30pm. The tours include information on training routines and diets, displays on Australian champions and the Sydney Olympics, and interactive exhibits where you can try your hand at basketball, rowing and skiing.

Activities

The 'bush capital' revels in its outdoors, with swimming in river-fed waterholes, cycling and skating around the lake, and bushwalking in the pleasant surrounds.

ABSEILING & ROCK CLIMBING

The environs of Namadgi National Park offer plenty of places to get out and scramble up some rocks. **Real Fun** (☎ 1800 637 486; www.realfun.com.au; half-day abseiling A$110) can take you out to abseil around Ginninderra Falls (below). To hone your skills indoors, check out the beginners walls at **Civic YMCA** (☎ 6249 8733; Allara St, Civic; climbing A$6, equipment hire A$3).

BOATING

Lake Burley Griffin Boat Hire (☎ 6249 6861; Acton Jetty, Civic; per hr A$12) has canoe, kayak, surf-ski and paddle-boat hire; swimming in the lake, however, isn't recommended.

BUSHWALKING

Not far from the capital, **Namadgi National Park** has eight peaks higher than 1700m, and offers bushwalking – it's on one end of the difficult, 655km-long Australian Alps Walking Track. There's also **camping** (camp sites per person A$2.60-3.40). For information, visit the Namadgi **visitors centre** (☎ 6207 2900; Naas Rd; 🕑 9am-4pm Mon-Fri, 9am-4.30pm Sat & Sun), 2km south of Tharwa.

Tidbinbilla Nature Reserve (☎ 6205 1233; off Paddy's River Rd), 45km southwest of the city, is threaded with bushwalking tracks, many of which are back in action after the bushfires. There are several easy walks, including the Hanging Rock Trail and Church Rock Heritage Loop. Across the NSW border in the northwest is **Ginninderra Falls** (☎ 6278 4222; Parkwood Rd; adult A$4.50; 🕑 10am-6pm summer, to 4pm winter). Swim under the cascade in the fantastic Upper Gorge Pool or follow the pretty walking tracks through the area.

Local bushwalking maps are available at **Mountain Designs** (☎ 6247 7488; 6 Lonsdale St, Braddon). The *Namadgi National Park* map (A$4.40), available from the Canberra and Namadgi visitors centres, details 23 walks.

CYCLING

An intricate bike-path network loops around Canberra, although the most popular track circles the lake. Other paths follow the Murrumbidgee River. The visitors centre sells the *Canberra Cycleways* map (A$6.50) and *Cycle Canberra* (A$15), the latter published by **Pedal Power ACT** (www.pedalpower.org.au).

If you're up for the 27km cycle around the lake, **Mr Spokes Bike Hire** (☎ 6257 1188; Barrine Dr, Civic;; half-/full-day hire A$30/40; 🕑 9am-5pm daily school holidays, 9am-5pm Wed-Sun rest of year) is conveniently located near the Acton Park ferry terminal.

For more bike rental:

Canberra YHA Hostel (p122)
Canberra City Accommodation (p122)
Victor Lodge (p122)

IN-LINE SKATING

Mr Spokes Bike Hire (☎ 6257 1188; Barrine Dr, Civic) has skating for A$11 for the first hour, then A$5.50 for each subsequent hour. It also rents skates, as does **Adrenalin Sports** (☎ 6257 7233; Shop 7, 38 Akuna St, Civic), which charges A$17 for two hours.

SWIMMING

Canberra's swimming pools include the **Canberra Olympic Pool** (☎ 6248 0132; Allara St, Civic) and the heritage-listed **Manuka Swimming Pool** (☎ 6295 1349; Manuka Circle, Manuka; 🕑 6.30am-7pm Mon-Fri, 8am-7pm Sat & Sun).

If you've got your own transport, good swimming spots lie along the **Murrumbidgee** and **Cotter Rivers**. Other popular riverside areas include **Uriarra Crossing, Casuarina Sands, Kambah Pool Reserve**, **Cotter Dam** and **Pine Island**.

SNOW PLAY

There's tonnes of fun to be had at **Corin Forest** (☎ 6235 7333; www.corin.com.au; Corin Rd; 🕑 10am-4pm Mon-Fri, to 5pm Sat & Sun), which has recently got its rides back up after the bushfires. You can hurtle down the silver tube of the bobsled (A$6 per ride), dangle from the flying fox (A$5.50 per ride) or play on the artificial snow (A$6). There are plans to get a full ski slope here, so you might not have to trawl all the way to the Snowies for your snow thrills.

Tours

Canberra Tours (☎ 6298 3344; canberradaytours@bigpond.com; half-/full-day tours A$35/50) whizzes around capital sites and includes the cost of entry.

City Sightseeing (☎ 6257 3423; adult A$30) is a hop-on, hop-off double-decker bus service (departs 9am to 4pm, hourly Monday to Friday, every 40 minutes Saturday and Sunday) with tickets valid for 24 hours and including access to 14 of the most popular attractions. It leaves from Civic Bus Terminal.

SS Maid Marion (☎ 0418-828 357; 1hr cruise adult A$10) cruises to/from lakeside locales such as Acton Park ferry terminal and the National Library, with up to five cruises daily.

The reputable **Go Bush Tours** (☎ 6231 3023; www.gobushtours.com.au; tours adult/concession from A$33/28) does tailored excursions around Canberra, including a circuit of city lookouts. It has a wheelchair-accessible vehicle. To go further out bush, sign up with **Wild Things Tours** (☎ 6254 6304; 1-day tour A$80), which heads out to Namadgi National Park and guarantees kangaroo sightings.

Festivals & Events

Summernats Car Festival (www.summernats.com.au) Revs up in January at Exhibition Park.

National Multicultural Festival (www.multiculturalfestival.com.au) Celebrated over 10 days in February.

Royal Canberra Show End of February.

Celebrate Canberra (www.celebratecanberra.com) The city's extended birthday party in mid-March.

National Folk Festival (www.folkfestival.asn.au) One of the country's largest, held every March/April.

Indy Fest (www.indyfest.com) Independent bands rawk out in March/April.

Floriade festival (www.floriadeaustralia.com) Held in September/October and dedicated to Canberra's spectacular spring flowers.

Metal for the Brain (www.metalforthebrain.com) Headbanging heaven in December.

Sleeping

There is only a handful of accommodation choices in the centre of Canberra. Most hotels and motels are either strung out along Northbourne Ave or hidden in northern suburbs like Ainslie, O'Connor and Downer. The other main accommodation area lies south around Capital Hill, particularly in Kingston and Barton.

HALLS OF RESIDENCE

Conveniently located on Daley Rd, many of ANU's halls of residence rent rooms during university holidays (from late November to late February). Most offer single rooms, some with self-catering, while others provide some meals. Room prices start from around A$50 (up to A$15 more for B&B).

Bruce Hall (☎ 6267 4000) and **Burton & Garran Hall** (☎ 6267 4333) are at the northern end of Daley Rd. The affiliated **Ursula College** (☎ 6279 4303) and **John XXIII College** (☎ 6279 4905) lie to the south, opposite Sullivans Creek.

HOSTELS

Canberra City Accommodation (☎ 6257 3999; www.canberrabackpackers.net.au; 7 Akuna St, Civic; dm A$24-26, s/d A$55/70; P 💻) This bright, well-managed hostel is packed with facilities, including a pool, gym, bicycle hire (A$16 per day) and huge kitchen area. Some readers have found it a little grubby, but the Church Bar (p125) downstairs is a good party venue.

Canberra YHA Hostel (☎ 6248 9155; canberra@yhansw.org.au; 191 Dryandra St, O'Connor; dm/d from A$20/60; P 💻) Set in bushland, this hostel lets you wake up to bird songs and laze under gum trees. Extensive kitchens have great views of the city, plus there's a basketball court and pool table. It's 6km northwest of the centre, so hire a bike or jump on the No 35 bus.

Civic Pub Backpackers (☎ 6248 6488; 8 Lonsdale St, Braddon; dm A$20; 💻) Rooms upstairs in this watering hole are basic, clean and roomy with many just two-bed dorms. The pub downstairs is relatively quiet.

Victor Lodge (☎ 6295 7777; www.victorlodge.com.au; 29 Dawes St, Kingston; dm/s/d A$25/55/70; P 💻) On the south side of the lake, this budget option has slightly squashy rooms, although the dorms represent good value. Breakfast is thrown in and there's also a commercial kitchen and barbecue area. It does pick-ups from train and bus stations; otherwise catch bus No 38, 39 or 80. Take advantage of its bicycle hire (A$15) to scoot around the lake.

MOTELS

Canberra's motels line Northbourne Ave, although many are expensive options.

City Walk Hotel (☎ 1800 600 124, 6257 0124; www.citywalkhotel.com.au; 2 Mort St, Civic; dm A$22-24, s A$45-70, d A$60-80) This centrally located budget hotel is just upstairs from King O'Malley's (p125) for an easy stagger home after a big drinking session. Rooms are compact and common areas are basic, while self-catering kitchens are tightly spaced.

Kythera Motel (☎ 6248 7611; 100 Northbourne Ave; d A$65-95; P) Close to the city, this motel is a simple place with serviceable rooms that have small showers and balconies. There's the bonus of two restaurants downstairs.

CAMPING & CARAVAN PARKS

Canberra Motor Village (☎ 6247 5466; canmotor village@ozemail.com.au; Kunzea St, O'Connor; camp sites per 2 people A$15-21, caravan sites A$28, d A$60-125; P) Dozing in a peaceful bush setting 6km northwest of Civic, this place has an abundance of amenities, motel rooms and self-contained cabins in various sizes, and a laid-back feel.

Eaglehawk Holiday Park (☎ 6241 6411; www.eagle hawk.contact.com.au; Federal Hwy, Sutton; camp/caravan sites per 2 people A$17/22, s & d A$70-125; P) This friendly highway-side complex is 12km north of the centre, just over the NSW border. It has plenty of sheltered accommodation (campers get the edge of a field) and meals are available at the sometimes noisy pub next door.

Eating

Canberra's diverse range of eateries benefit from an affluent diplomatic and political community who has brought a taste for several international cuisines to Canberra. Civic's Garema Pl has many excellent options, although the upmarket selections in Kingston and Manuka are well known for courting big spenders. There's also a fantastic Asian/international strip in Dickson. Self-caterers can fill their trolleys at **City Market** (Bunda St), a collection of fresh fruit and vegetable shops, and a supermarket.

CIVIC

Once a nocturnal skateboarding bowl and drug-dealing centre, Garema Pl has become an outdoor dining mecca. Heading over towards the uni will flush out some cheaper dining options.

Fast food is on the menu at the Canberra Centre's **food hall** (Bunda St; meals A$5-12), including sushi, kebabs, burgers, laksa, gourmet rolls and smoothies.

Milk & Honey (☎ 6247 7722; 29 Garema Pl; mains A$12-22; breakfast, lunch & dinner) Bright staff serve up zesty meals (such as fried haloumi on corn fritters; A$14.50) in this funky, orange-interiored café. People-watchers can take advantage of couches and enjoy great coffee.

Sizzle Bento (☎ 6262 60223; Garema Pl; plates A$2-5; lunch & dinner) All aboard the wasabi express! A revolving train brings around bargain plates of sushi and tempura, and this bargain food is so good you'll want to divert the tracks directly to your taste buds.

Caffe della Piazza (☎ 6248 9711; 19 Garema Pl; mains A$14-20) It's stretching credibility to compare Garema Pl to an authentic piazza, but it's no exaggeration to say that this decade-old restaurant offers excellent, hearty Italian fare and a heady wine list.

Shalimar (☎ 6249 6784; 9 Tasman House, Marcus Clarke St; mains A$13-16; lunch & dinner) Full of flavoursome smells, this family-run curry house has been a long-time local secret. The menu is authentic Indian with large serves that make it perfect for after the pub.

WHAT'S ALL THE GUS ABOUT?

If you're wandering around Civic you'll spot a bronze plaque of a cheeky Austrian fellow smiling up at you. Gus Petersilka (1913–1994) was a popular local character who first campaigned for outdoor dining in Garema Pl. He took on local councils who frequently confiscated his street-side chairs, and legend has it that Gus once locked himself in his café to protest.

Born in Austria, Gus escaped the Nazis and eventually moved to Canberra in the 1960s. The young capital was ready for some new thinking and Gus opened a series of popular European-style eateries that featured seating outside. But the local council had other ideas, opposing the Austrian restaurateur at every turn. Eventually public opinion saw Garema Pl opened up to outdoor dining. For his troublemaking, he was voted Canberran of the Year in 1978 and even unsuccessfully ran for the Legislative Assembly (Canberra's governing body) in 1988. He's fondly remembered by a street named after him (Petersilka St in Gungahlin) and a plaque out the front of **Gus' Café** (☎ 6248 8118; 8 Garema Arcade, Bunda St, Civic; mains A$12-16; breakfast, lunch & dinner), the Canberran institution he opened in 1969 that continues to serve coffee, cake and satisfying meals on the alfresco.

Sage (☎ 6249 6050; Gorman House Arts Centre; Ainslie Ave; mains A$10-22; ⏲ lunch & dinner Tue-Fri, brunch, lunch & dinner Sat) Not just the spot for a quick market bite, Sage has become a restaurant in its own right with a subdued atmosphere and dishes such as pumpkin and roasted garlic gnocchi. The outdoor area is ideal for a sunny lunch.

Gods Café & Bar (☎ 6248 5538; Arts Centre, University Ave, Acton; mains A$8-15) This café in the university district of Acton makes a refreshing pit stop after wandering the university campus. Offerings range from toasted focaccias to grilled veal kidney. Eat in the main low-lit den or in the light-filled side hall.

Asian Bistro (☎ 6125 2446; 1st fl, ANU Union Bldg, University Ave; plates A$6.70-10.20; ⏲ lunch & dinner Mon-Fri) Attracting starving students and the odd pre-soundcheck band from the ANU Union bar (see opposite), this is an all-you-can-eat institution. Stack your plate high with simple curries, stir-fries and other Asian delights, and challenge the random pricing policy, which charges extra for 'excessive plates'.

Little Saigon (☎ 6230 5003; Alinga St; mains A$9-15) There are plenty of dishes to clamp your teeth on in this simple Vietnamese eatery. Early afternoon sees a roaring trade in 'lunch boxes': takeaway chicken, beef, pork or vegetarian dishes (A$5) accompanied by rice or noodles.

MANUKA & KINGSTON

Close to Parliament House, this is the dining area where you can bump into diplomats or give politicians a serve. With such a plush clientele, it's no wonder Manuka has earned a reputation as the posh nosh precinct, although affordable places can be found. Kingston is the new Manuka, outclassing its sophisticated neighbour with its own increasingly stylish restaurant quarter.

Verve (☎ 6239 4666; cnr Franklin St & Flinders Way, Manuka; mains A$15-23; ⏲ lunch & dinner Mon-Sat) A great location for people-watching, this corner café-bar is a fresh flavour in Manuka, serving up innovative pastas, generous risottos and some unmissable duck rolls. Grab a frappé and watch the passing parade.

Abell's Kopi Tiam (☎ 6239 4199; 7 Furneaux St, Manuka; mains A$13-17; ⏲ lunch & dinner Tue-Sat) This excellent Indonesian and Malaysian eatery has loads of vegetarian options and some home-style treats including the zesty My Mum's Laksa. Finish off with *goreng pisang* (Malaysian banana fritter).

Silo (☎ 6260 6060; 36 Giles St, Kingston; lunches A$10-13; ⏲ breakfast & lunch Mon-Sat) This designer bakery packs them in for breakfast (you'll need to get in early or be prepared to wait) and justifiably for the likes of potato, anchovy and chilli jam pizzas.

Santa Lucia (☎ 6295 1813; 21 Kennedy St, Kingston; mains A$12-20; ⏲ lunch & dinner) Canberra's first Italian restaurant is everything you'd expect from clichéd red-and-white-checked tablecloths to hearty serves of pasta. Pizzas are particularly scrumptious.

DICKSON

The consumer precinct here is a UN of the palate, boasting Chinese, Thai, Laotian, Vietnamese, Korean, Japanese, Turkish and Malaysian restaurants. Dickson is about 3km north of Civic.

Âu Lac (☎ 6262 8922; 39 Woolley St; mains A$8-10; ⏲ lunch & dinner) This simple Vietnamese vegetarian restaurant employs the soya bean as a culinary chameleon, making it pretend to be a beef curry, fried fish or honey-roast chicken. The meals are tasty and the service quick.

Kingsland Vegetarian Restaurant (☎ 6262 9350; Shop 5, Dickson Plaza, 28 Challis St, Dickson; mains A$7.50-13; ⏲ lunch & dinner) Vegetarians shouldn't miss the chance to sample the impressive mock meats, including fish and chicken, at this quaint little eatery.

Food Court Family Restaurant (☎ 6247 2477; 28 Woolley St, Dickson; lunch A$10.80, dinner A$16-18; ⏲ lunch Wed-Sun, dinner daily) If you see all-you-can-eat as a challenge, then this upstairs smorgasbord will definitely burst your buttons. Food is pan-Asian with a salad bar and desserts (don't forget to save room).

Drinking

Unlike many other Australian cities where pubs are architectural masterpieces, many of Canberra's pubs are crammed into office buildings (particularly in Civic). To get out from under this shadow, many have developed distinct identities and attract diverse crowds. Irish pubs have become a plague on the Canberra drinking scene.

Phoenix (☎ 6247 1606; 21 East Row, Civic) The ever-cosy Phoenix could be mistaken for just another Irish pub, but its alternative crowd and snug booths make it a homey favourite. It's a good place for a chat with younger locals and to even enjoy a Guinness or 20.

Toast (☎ 6230 0003; City Walk, Civic) Upstairs behind the Electric Shadows cinema, this grungy little bar attracts a diverse crowd – some come for the pool tables, others for the antique computer games, but the place is packed with a young crowd when gigs kick off (see p126).

Church Bar (☎ 6257 3062; 7 Akuna St, Civic; 🕑 11am-late Mon-Sat) Downstairs in Canberra City Accommodation (see p122) this is definitely a boisterous backpacker bar with DJs Thursday to Saturday and a sozzling amount of drink specials.

Hippo (☎ 6257 9090; 17 Garema Pl, Civic) The ultimate chill-out bar, Hippo coolly relishes its chandeliers and designer couch ambience with the casual swilling of cocktails (Frisky Sour and Soho Loves You are just two dreamy concoctions) and hosts lounge-tinged DJs.

Holy Grail (☎ 62579717; cnr Akuna & Bunda Sts) This barn-like bar is a good spot for a drink, with a crowd ranging from students to public servants (they're the ones with ID tags dangling in their drinks).

Wig & Pen (☎ 6248 0171; cnr Alinga St & West Row, Civic) For a British-inspired knees-up, grab a pint of beer (mostly brewed right on the premises). Drinkers are a relaxed group, many from the nearby uni.

King O'Malley's (☎ 6257 0111; 131 City Walk, Civic) The biggest of Canberra's faux-Irish boozers, this tie-loosening Friday night favourite is loud and lively. Ironically, its name takes the piss out of the teetotalling bureaucrat who kept Canberra 'dry' until 1928.

For more of the same, head across Northbourne Ave to **PJ O'Reilly's** (☎ 6230 4752; cnr Alinga St & West Row, Civic), locally referred to as Plastic McPaddy's.

Further afield, **Filthy McFadden's** (☎ 6239 5303; 62 Jardine St, Kingston) is another of Canberra's whisky-drenched Irish dens, but it's worth the trip for the down-to-earth crowd.

Clubbing

The capital's clubs boast variety with plenty of places to get out and shake your rump. Thursday, Friday and Saturday nights are the biggest nights, particularly during uni semesters.

Academy (☎ 6257 3355; www.academyclub.com.au; Bunda St; admission A$5-20; 🕑 4pm-5am Thu-Sat) Canberra's first super-club (capes not included), this funkily converted cinema has a huge dance floor and visiting international DJs. The elevated Candy Bar is a good place from which to watch the action, and they've kept the silver screen for video and effects. Thursday nights are cheapest, with retro.

icbm & Insomnia (☎ 6248 0102; 50 Northbourne Ave, Civic; Insomnia A$5 on Sat; 🕑 icbm 7pm-late daily, Insomnia 9pm-late Wed-Sat) This notorious meat market joint is chock-full of a young crowd. Downstairs, icbm is a bar with top 40 music, while upstairs, Insomnia is a electronic-fuelled club that hosts comedy on weeknights.

Club Mombasa (☎ 0419-609 106; www.clubmombasa.com.au; 128 Bunda St, Civic; events A$5-7; 🕑 8pm-late Wed-Sun) With its pulses of African, reggae and Latin rhythms, you come here for serious dancing.

Cube (☎ 6257 1110; 33 Petrie Pl, Civic; admission A$5-10; 🕑 5pm-late Fri & Sat) This gay- and lesbian-friendly venue has a tight dance floor that's a good place to shake your thang into the early hours of the morning.

Entertainment

The student population keeps Civic pumping with late-night clubs, and bands plug in amps at several reliable spots. For entertainment listings, see the 'Times Out' section of Thursday's *Canberra Times* and the free monthly street mag *bma* (www.bmamag.com).

CINEMAS

Multiplex cinemas can be found on Mort St, Civic, and in various suburban shopping malls.

Electric Shadows Cinema (☎ 6247 5060; City Walk, Civic; adult/concession A$14/8.50) An exile from the mainstream over on City Walk, Electric Shadows plays all the art-house and independent films. It offers matinee and Wednesday discounts.

LIVE MUSIC

Many pubs have free live music, but it's often of the simple 'some bloke who owns a guitar' variety.

ANU Union Bar (Uni Bar; ☎ 6125 2446; www.anuunion.com.au; Union Court, Acton; admission A$5-15; 🕑 gigs usually 8pm) This bar is an institution in Canberra's live music scene, with bands from Wednesday to Saturday during semesters. Big touring acts love the grungy Refectory, and there's a pokier band area for small bands.

Holy Grail (☎ 62579717; cnr Akuna & Bunda Sts) This bar (see left) gets in big-name local bands and a few notable international touring acts.

Tilley's Devine Café Gallery (☎ 6249 1543; cnr Wattle & Brigalow Sts, Lyneham; events usually A$30) Named for the famous madam and gangster, Tilley's is artsy, from its deep dark booths to its poetry nights. Folk-y and rock musicians appear here with occasional comedians. Its bumper hot breakfasts are the accompaniment to a morning paper.

Toast (☎ 6230 0003; City Walk, Civic; admission A$2-5; gigs Fri & Sat) Hosting everything from hip hop to solo acoustic gigs, this bar (see Drinking, p125) is a local scene wildcard. Local bands launch their CDs here and visiting DJs have been known to tweak the decks.

Rock Ape (Northside Fitness Centre, 20 Dickson Pl, Dickson) If you're not wearing a black T-shirt with a tortured demon on it, you'll stand out at this metal bar that hosts visiting guitar gods and hard-core heroes.

Hippo (☎ 6257 9090; 17 Garema Pl, Civic) This ultracool bar (see p125) has Wednesday night jazz (A$5).

PERFORMING ARTS

Canberra Theatre Centre (☎ box office 1800 802 025, 6275 2700; www.canberratheatre.org.au; London Circuit, Civic Sq, Civic; box office 9am-5.30pm Mon-Sat) There are many dramatic goings-on within this highly cultured centre, from Shakespeare to David Williamson plays and indigenous dance troupes. Information and tickets are supplied by Canberra Ticketing, in the adjacent North Building (Eftpos is not available).

Gorman House Arts Centre (☎ 6249 7377; Ainslie Ave, Braddon) Hosts various theatre and dance companies that stage their own productions. On Saturday it's home to the Gorman House Markets (see right).

Shopping

The Australian capital is a crafty place, good for picking up creative gifts and souvenirs from galleries, museum shops or markets.

Canberra Centre (☎ 6247 5611; Bunda St, Civic) The city's best shopping mall houses dozens of speciality stores, including fashion boutiques, food emporiums and jewellery shops.

Old Bus Depot Markets (☎ 6292 8391; cnr Cunningham St & The Causeway, Kingston; 10am-4pm Sun) This popular indoor market specialises in hand-crafted goods and regional edibles, including the output of the Canberra district's 20-plus wineries.

Gorman House Markets (☎ 6249 7377; Ainslie Ave, Braddon; 10am-5pm Sat) This modern bazaar has vintage clothing, second-hand books, food, artworks and even the odd belly-dancing performance.

Getting There & Away

AIR

Canberra airport (☎ 6275 2236) is serviced by Qantas, Virgin Blue and Regional Express. At the time of writing, low-end flights to Sydney started at A$90, Brisbane A$110 and Melbourne A$80.

Brindabella Airlines (☎ 6248 8711, 1300 668 824; www.brindabella-airlines.com.au) Also flies to Albury Wodonga (A$213, one hour) and Newcastle (A$280, one hour).

Qantas (☎ 13 13 13; www.qantas.com.au)

Rex (☎ 13 17 13; www.regionalexpress.com.au)

Virgin Blue (☎ 136 789; www.virginblue.com.au)

BUS

The interstate bus terminal is at the **Jolimont Centre** (Northbourne Ave, Civic), which has left-luggage lockers and free phone lines to the visitors centre and some budget accommodation. Inside the Jolimont Centre, the **Travellers Booking Centre** (☎ 1300 733 323, 6249 6006; 6am-11.45pm) and **CountryLink travel centre** (☎ 13 22 32, 6257 1576; 7.15am-5pm Mon-Fri) book seats on most services.

McCafferty's/Greyhound (☎ 13 14 99; www.mccaffertys.com.au) has frequent services to Sydney (adult A$35, four to five hours), Adelaide (A$130, 20 hours) and Melbourne (A$60, nine hours). There are also regular services to Cooma (A$37, 1½ hours) and Thredbo (adult A$54, three hours) in winter.

Murrays (☎ 13 22 51; www.murrays.com.au; counter 7am-7pm) has daily express services to Sydney (A$35, 3¼ hours) and also runs to Batemans Bay (A$24, 2½ hours), Narooma (A$36, 4½ hours) and Wollongong (A$31, 3½ hours).

Transborder Express (☎ 6241 0033) runs daily to Yass (A$13, 50 minutes), while **Summit Coaches** (☎ 6297 2588) runs to Thredbo (A$51, three hours) via Jindabyne on Monday, Wednesday, Friday and Saturday.

CAR & MOTORCYCLE

The Hume Hwy connects Sydney and Melbourne, passing about 50km north of Canberra. The Federal Hwy runs north to connect with the Hume near Goulburn, and the Barton Hwy meets the Hume near

Yass. To the south, the Monaro Hwy connects Canberra with Cooma and the Snowy Mountains.

Rental car prices start at around A$45 a day. Major companies with Canberra city offices (and desks at the airport):

Avis (☎ 13 63 33, 6249 6088; 17 Lonsdale St, Braddon)
Budget (☎ 1300 362 848, 6257 2200; cnr Mort & Girrahween Sts, Braddon)
Hertz (☎ 13 30 39, 6257 4877; 32 Mort St, Braddon)
Thrifty (☎ 13 61 39, 6247 7422; 29 Lonsdale St, Braddon)

TRAIN

Kingston train station (Wentworth Ave) is the city's rail terminus. You can book trains and connecting buses inside the station at the **CountryLink travel centre** (☎ 13 22 32, 6295 1198; 6.15am-5.30pm Mon-Sat, 10.30am-5.30pm Sun).

Trains run three times a day to Sydney (A$50, four hours). There are no direct trains to Melbourne, but you can catch the daily Countrylink coach to Cootamundra that links with a train to Melbourne (A$90, nine hours). A daily V/Line Canberra Link service involves a train between Melbourne and Albury Wodonga, then a connecting bus to Canberra (A$60, 8½ hours, one daily). A longer but more scenic bus-and-train service to Melbourne is the V/Line Capital Link (A$58, 10½ hours) running every Tuesday and Friday via Cooma and the East Gippsland forests to Sale, where you board the Melbourne-bound train.

Getting Around

BUS

Canberra's public transport provider is the **ACT Internal Omnibus Network** (Action; ☎ 13 17 10, 6207 7611; www.action.act.gov.au). The main city interchange is along Alinga St, East Row and Mort St in Civic. Visit the **Action information kiosk** (East Row, Civic; 7.15am-4pm Mon-Fri) in the interchange for free route maps and timetables, or buy the all-routes *Canberra Bus Map* (A$2) from newsagents.

You can purchase single-trip tickets (adult/concession A$2.40/1.30), but a better bet for most visitors is a daily ticket (adult/concession A$6/3). Tickets are available from bus drivers. You can also prepurchase tickets from Action agents (including the visitors centre and some newsagents), including the good-value 10-trip ticket (adult/concession A$21/10.50).

For details about the hop-on, hop-off double-decker bus service operated by **City Sightseeing** (☎ 6257 3423; adult A$30), see p122.

CAR & MOTORCYCLE

While most cities are laid out on a square grid, Canberra maddeningly uses a circle as its base. To compensate, roads are generally wide and relatively uncluttered. This makes driving easy, even during so-called 'peak hour' times. At night, look out for kangaroos on Tuggeranong Parkway and outer suburban roads.

There's plenty of well-signposted parking in Civic. The visitors centre has a *Motorbike Parking in Canberra* pamphlet.

TAXI

Call **Canberra Cabs** (☎ 13 22 27) if you need a taxi.

SNOWY MOUNTAINS

Affectionately called the Snowies, this section of the Great Dividing Range crosses the NSW–Victoria border. Their peak is Mt Kosciuszko (pronounced 'ko-zee-osko'), Australia's highest summit (2228m). Most of the Snowies are contained within Kosciuszko National Park, an area of year-round interest, with skiing in winter (see p130). Kosciuszko National Park adjoins the Alpine National Park in Victoria.

The upper waters of the Murray River form both the state and national-park boundaries in the southwest. The Snowy River, made famous by Banjo Paterson's poem *The Man from Snowy River* (see The Man Behind the Man, p128), rises just below the summit of Mt Kosciuszko. The Murrumbidgee River also rises in the national park.

GETTING THERE & AWAY

Canberra is the jumping-off point for the park. From there **CountryLink** (☎ 13 22 32) and **V/Line buses** (☎ 13 61 96) travel to Cooma (A$38, 1½ hours).

Summit Coaches (☎ 1800 608 008, 6297 2588) runs to Thredbo from Canberra via Jindabyne and Cooma four times a week. Jindabyne to Thredbo costs A$24 and takes an hour. Shuttles will take you from Cooma or Jindabyne to the ski resorts in winter.

In winter you can normally drive as far as Perisher Valley, but snow chains must be carried (even if there's no snow) and fitted

THE MAN BEHIND THE MAN

Like the Anzac legend, the *Man from Snowy River* has become part of Australia's national dreaming. When AB 'Banjo' Paterson (1864–1941) penned the work he didn't expect that it would spawn two films, a TV series, a musical and lend itself to several place names around the region. But Paterson was a modest bloke, who sold the rights to the unofficial national anthem 'Waltzing Matilda' for just £5 and allowed it be used as a radio jingle for Billy Tea.

Debate still rages about the character who inspired the poem. The poem's simple narrative tells of a bushman who surprises established riders with his skill to round up an unruly horse, the colt from Old Regret. Some reckon the Man from Snowy River was Jack Riley, a local from Corryong who was famous for his horsemanship. It's reason enough for Corryong to host the annual **Man From Snowy River Bush Festival** (www.manfromsnowyriverbushfestival.com.au), a week-long celebration of bush life held every April. Others speculate that 'the man' may have been Charlie McKeahnie, another legendary horseman who was the subject of the poem *On the Range*, by Barcroft Boake. Whoever 'the man' was, it's too late for him to get a share in the million-dollar industry that Banjo Paterson created when he published his humble poem in the *Bulletin*.

to your wheels when directed – there are heavy penalties if you don't have them.

The simple and safe way to get to Perisher/Smiggins from Jindabyne is to take the **Skitube** (☎ 6456 2010; same-day return A$27), a tunnel railway up to Perisher Valley and Mt Blue Cow from below the snow line at Bullocks Flat, on the Alpine Way. The Skitube is all but closed in summer.

Qantas (☎ 13 13 13) flies to Sydney (A$155, one hour) from Cooma airport, about 15km south of Cooma.

Cooma

☎ 02 / pop 6900

Cooma was the construction centre for the Snowy Mountains hydroelectric scheme, built by workers from all over the world. The **Snowy Mountains Scheme Information & Education Centre** (☎ 1800 623 776, 6453 2004; www.snowyhydro.com.au; Princes Hwy; admission free; 🕑 8am-5pm Mon-Fri, to 1pm Sat & Sun) has high-tech interactive exhibits and videos of this amazing project, which took 25 years to complete. The Cooma **visitors centre** (☎ 1800 636 525, 6450 1742; www.visitcooma.com.au; 119 Sharp St; 🕑 9am-5pm; 💻) is a good place to check snow conditions.

SLEEPING & EATING

Prices are lower here than in Jindabyne or the ski resorts, but in winter it's wise to book well ahead.

The most affordable option is the **Bunkhouse Motel** (☎ 6452 2983; www.bunkhousemotel.com.au; 28 Soho St; dm/s/d from A$30/40/55), with generously sized rooms (many with their own facilities).

Decent eateries line Sharp St, including **Organic Vibes** (☎ 6452 6566; 82a Sharp St; lunch A$9-12, dinner A$14-18; 🕑 lunch & dinner) for fresh juices and healthy meals; **Sharp Food** (☎ 6452 7333; 122 Sharp St; lunch A$10; 🕑 breakfast & lunch) has pleasant courtyard lounging; and cosy **Lott** (☎ 6452 1414; 178-180 Sharp St; mains A$7-11; 🕑 breakfast & lunch; 💻) for hearty meals and good coffee.

Jindabyne

☎ 02 / pop 4400

An excellent base for year-round outdoor activities, Jindabyne is a modern town on the shore of the artificial Lake Jindabyne. Winter brings the skiing crowds, while the rest of the year there's horse riding, mountain biking, swimming, sailing and kitesurfing. The NPWS-operated Snowy Region **visitors centre** (☎ 6450 5600; 🕑 8.30am-5pm) is in the heart of town on Kosciuszko Rd.

Paddy Pallin (☎ 6456 2922; Kosciuszko Rd) organises guided walks and adventure activities all year. It also sells and rents outdoor equipment of all sorts. For snow and ice climbing, the Blue Mountains outfit **High 'n' Wild Mountain Adventures** (☎ 4782 6224; www.high-n-wild.com.au; 4-day course A$975) holds a four-day, skills-focused course in Mt Kosciuszko National Park for budding mountaineers.

SLEEPING

Winter sees a huge influx of visitors; prices soar, many places are booked out months ahead and overnight accommodation disappears with minimum bookings of two nights. Prices also rise on Friday and Saturday nights throughout the year.

Snowy Mountains Backpackers (☎ 1800 333 468, 6456 1500; www.snowybackpackers.com.au; 7 Gippsland St; dm/d A$35/80; 🖳) This place has clean, bright rooms, full wheelchair access and a laundry. It's also a good spot to hustle up work in the mountains, plus it offers massage and a book-swap library.

Mad Mooses (☎ 6456 1108; moose@snowy.net.au; 21 Munyang St; B&B dm A$35) This comfortable budget lodge has some kooky moose features, along with breakfast and use of the handmade barbecue.

Banjo Patterson Inn (☎ 1800 046 275, 6456 2372; 1 Kosciuszko Rd; s A$60-75, d from A$70) This large, modern place has lake-view balconies and good facilities, with the bonus of a bar downstairs.

Snowline Caravan Park (☎ 1800 248 148, 6456 2099; camp sites per 2 people/dm/cabins from A$23/30/160) Rates jump higher than the altitude in winter at this convenient lakeside place (in the low season, cabins are available for only A$47, as opposed to the high season rate of A$160), where there is a variety of cabins available.

EATING

Dining options are slightly cheaper than at the resorts (although only slightly).

Il Lago (☎ 6456 1171; 19 Nugget's Crossing; mains A$18; 🕑 dinner Tue-Sat year-round, lunch Tue-Sat high season only) Has a good-value Italian menu that includes local trout dishes and gourmet pizzas.

Bits & Pizzas (☎ 6456 2439; Shopping Centre, off Kosciusko Rd; pizzas A$7.80-22; 🕑 dinner) This simple spot devotes itself to the cheapest mountain meals, including the odd – but enjoyable – Vegemite pizza.

Sundance Bakehouse & Tearooms (☎ 6456 2951; Shop 13, Nugget's Crossing; pies from A$3; 🕑 breakfast, lunch & dinner) This quaint bakery does all the pastry basics brilliantly, throwing in experimental innovations such as pumpkin and pine-nut rolls or the intriguing prawn pie.

Kosciuszko National Park

The state's largest national park (6900 sq km) includes caves, lakes, forest, ski resorts and Mt Kosciuszko. Winter is busiest, but it's also popular in summer when there are excellent bushwalks and sweet alpine wild flowers. There are NPWS offices in Khancoban (p131) and the main visitors centre is in Jindabyne (opposite).

Mt Kosciuszko and the main ski resorts are in the south of the park. There's an 18km round-trip walking track to Australia's highest summit that can be accessed from a lift at Thredbo.

From Jindabyne, Kosciuszko Rd leads through Sawpit Creek (15km) to Perisher Valley (33km) and on to Charlotte Pass (40km). The spectacular Alpine Way runs from Jindabyne to Thredbo (33km) and around to Khancoban (116km) on the southwestern side of the mountains. Accessibility on all roads is subject to snow conditions.

Entry to the national park, including the ski resorts, costs A$15 per car, per day. If you're here for a while, the A$80 annual pass is a worthwhile investment.

Take adequate clothing and be prepared for all conditions; even in summer there is sometimes snow on the ground. At the resorts, the summer (low season) runs from

POSITIONS VACANT: SNOW FIENDS

Keen to ski, but can't afford the mountains of cash? Working in the mountains is just the ticket (or lift pass). If you want to maximise your time on the slopes, try out for a skiing instructor job or, perhaps more realistically, a job as a liftie (a person who works on the lifts). There are plenty of jobs out of the cold including bar staff, housekeepers and equipment-hire staff. They're also after chefs, childcare workers and maintenance staff.

Most jobs mean signing on for the season (at least three months) and the working week is an exhausting 30 to 40 hours, but you can ski on your days off and most resorts throw in free lift passes and equipment hire for staff. Recruitment starts in April, so if you get organised you can be skiing by June.

Here are a few places to try:

Perisher Blue (www.perisherblue.com.au) The resort employs staff early in the year.

Snowy Mountains Backpackers The noticeboard in this hostel often posts jobs for travellers (see left).

Snowy Staff (www.snowystaff.com.au) This employment agency recruits staff for all the big resorts.

Thredbo (www.thredbo.com.au) From December the website has details of positions available, with interviews in Sydney.

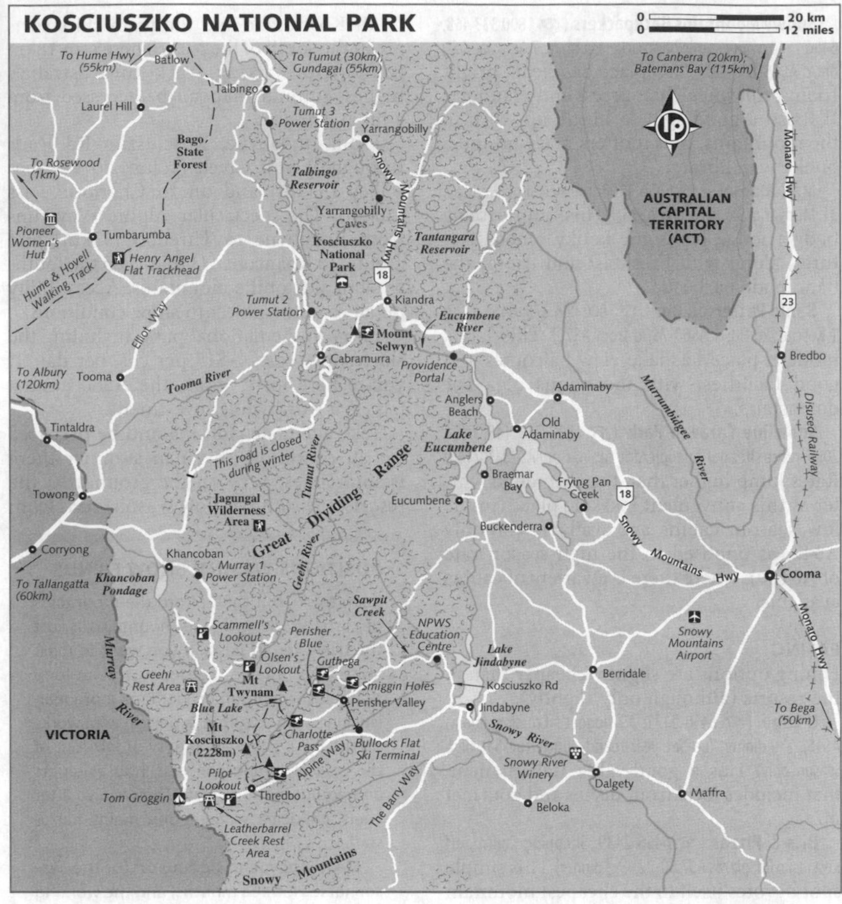

the long weekend in early October to the mid-June long weekend; winter (high season) – and higher prices – starts after that.

Skiing & Ski Resorts

Where else could you snowboard through gum trees or try cross-country or downhill skiing in June? This winter playground has skiing from June to early October, although snow is guaranteed in July, August and September when resorts often crank up their snow-making equipment. The Australian Alps are a ski-tourer's paradise and cross-country skiing is very popular. There's cross-country racing (classic or skating) in Perisher Valley. On the steep slopes of the Main Range near Twynam and Carruthers, cross-country downhill (XCD) fanatics get their adrenaline rushes. In winter, the cliffs near Blue Lake become a practice ground for alpine climbers. Snowboard hire and lessons are widely available, and the major resorts have developed purpose-built runs and bowls.

One of the most affordable ways to get out on the slopes is to get a group of friends and rent a lodge or apartment. Bring food and drink, as supplies at the resorts are expensive. Jindabyne and Cooma, both some distance below the snow line, offer cheaper accommodation (buses shuttle between towns and slopes).

Lift passes and lesson costs vary from resort to resort. Equipment hire costs from A$50 a day at the resorts, less off-mountain.

The route to the snow is lined with garages and hire stores that rent ski equipment and snow chains. **Ski Kaos** (☎ 9976 5555; www.skikaos.com) runs coach-based packages from Sydney from around A$300, and full-week packages from A$600.

THREDBO

☎ 02 / pop 2900 / elevation 1365m

Thredbo has the longest run of all the resorts – 3km through 670m of vertical drop – and some of Australia's best skiing. As well as the long runs, the absence of T-bar lifts makes Thredbo popular with snowboarders. New lifts and turbo snow-making machines should ensure that there is more snow and you can get in more runs. There's a variety of passes available: adult lift-only one-/five-day tickets cost A$80/340; two-day beginner/experienced lift and lesson packages cost A$213/160. Friday Flat is a purpose-built beginners' area with its own slow-speed quad chairlift (A$43).

The chairlift to the top of Mt Crackenback runs through summer (A$22 return). From the top of the chairlift it's a 2km walk to a lookout point with good views of Mt Kosciuszko, or 7km to the top of the mountain itself. In summer mad-keen mountain bikers carry their bikes up on the chairlift to ride helter-skelter down the dirt tracks.

Thredbo attracts a fair crowd in summer, with scenic bushwalking, mountain biking, bobsledding and golfing. **Thredbo Resort Centre** (☎ 1800 020 589, 6459 4294; www.thredbo.com.au; Friday Dr) is well-stocked with visitor information. The free *Summer Walks Map & Activities Guide* is worth picking up.

If the budget's tight, you're better off staying in towns outside of the national park. Prices drop in summer, but there are no spectacular bargains. In the high season, **Thredbo YHA Lodge** (☎ 6457 6376; thredbo@yhansw.org.au; 8 Jack Adams Pathway; dm/tw A$66/132) has members-only accommodation, with a ballot for winter places (during July and August). The YHA website (www.yha.org.au) is the best place to log on to the ballot, which closes in April. Prices in the low season drop dramatically (dorm bed/twin A$21/26).

PERISHER BLUE

☎ 02 / elevation 1680m

Perisher Blue (☎ 6459 4495, 1300 655 811; www.perisherblue.com.au) has 50 lifts accessible with one ticket. There is a variety of alpine and cross-country runs, valley and bowl skiing, snowboarding areas and night-boarding sessions.

An adult one-/five-day lift ticket costs A$80/340; other passes are also available. A combined lesson-and-lift pass costs A$80/295 (for beginners) and A$108/433 (for the experienced).

Accommodation in Perisher Valley and Smiggin Holes is generally very expensive, so your best bet is to live-in and work on the snowfields (see Positions Vacant: Snow Fiends, p129). Perisher Blue is dead in the off-season and most facilities close.

CHARLOTTE PASS

☎ 02 / elevation 1760m

Set at the base of Mt Kosciuszko, **Charlotte Pass** (☎ 6457 5458; www.charlottepass.com.au) is the highest and one of the oldest and most isolated resorts in Australia. In winter you have to take a snowcat the last 8km from Perisher Valley (A$30 each way, book ahead). Five lifts serve rather short but uncrowded runs and this is good ski-touring country. Daily lift passes cost A$85.

Transport pick-up is from the Charlotte Pass Village information desk at the Perisher Skitube terminal.

MT SELWYN

☎ 02 / elevation 1492m

Halfway between Tumut and Cooma, **Mt Selwyn** (☎ 1800 641 064, 6454 9488; www.selwynsnow.com.au), is the bargain resort. With 12 lifts, it's ideal for beginners, but is day-use only; adult lift tickets cost A$58/29 and lift-and-lesson packages A$80.

Adaminaby Bus Service (☎ 6454 2318) runs between Jindabyne and Mt Selwyn in winter; bookings are essential.

THE ALPINE WAY

From Jindabyne this spectacular route runs through bushfire-damaged forest at the southern end of Kosciuszko National Park to **Khancoban**. Two of the best mountain views are from **Olsen's Lookout**, 10km off the road on the Geehi Dam dirt road, and **Scammell's Lookout**, just off the Alpine Way at a good picnic spot. There's an **NPWS office** (☎ 02-6076 9373; Scott St; 🕑 8.30am-noon & 1-4pm) in Khancoban, where you can pick up the self-drive *Alpine Way Guide* and buy park passes.

If you have your own car and road conditions allow passage through to the ski fields, accommodation in Khancoban can be very affordable. **Khancoban Backpackers & Fisherman's Lodge** (☎ 02-6076 9471; www.alpineinn.com.au; Alpine Way; s A$19) is a very basic place (you'll need to supply your own bedding and cooking utensils), but rooms are clean and roomy enough. Booking and check-in is at the nearby **Khancoban Alpine Inn** (☎ 02-6076 9471; www.alpineinn.com.au; Alpine Way; small s/d A$55/65, good-sized A$80/90;), which has motel rooms and a pleasant garden. Also on-site is the **Pickled Parrot bistro** (mains A$7.50), serving home-cooked meals.

Yarrangobilly Caves (per vehicle A$3), 77km after Tumut and 109km from Cooma, are a subterranean secret. Guided tours (adult A$11; 11am, 1pm and 3pm) or self-guided tours (adult A$8.80; 9.30am to 4.30pm) are both excellent explorations. You can fish and bushwalk in this lovely place, and there's a thermal pool – at a balmy 27°C. There is an **NPWS office** (☎ 02-6454 9579; 9.30am to 4.30pm) at the caves.

ALBURY WODONGA

☎ 02 / pop 42,100

Cut in two by the Murray River just below the Hume Weir, the towns of Albury (in NSW) and Wodonga (in Victoria) were once conjoined twins. The Albury side got the more attractive parts of the city with decent restaurants, some lively bars (generally well supported by the local student population) and a few places of interest. The tempestuous upper Murray River relaxes just below Albury so it can be a good spot for low-adrenaline water sports. For most visitors, the twin towns are a break in the journey between Sydney and Melbourne.

Information & Orientation

The main drag is Dean St with most of the eating options and pubs clustered around it. The train station is at the eastern end of Smollet St (parallel to Dean St). The large Albury Wodonga **visitors centre** (☎ 1300 796 222; gateway@alburywodongatourism.biz; Hume Hwy; 9am-5pm), offering information on both NSW and Victoria, is just over the bridge on the Wodonga side.

There's Internet access at **PC Magic** (☎ 6041 3835; www.pcmagic.net.au; 461 Olive St; per hr A$5; 9am-5pm Mon-Fri, to noon Sat).

Sights & Activities

In summer you can swim in the Murray River in **Noreuil Park**. From September to April (water levels permitting) you can take a leisurely **river cruise** (☎ 6041 5558, 0408-200 531) on the paddle-steamer *Cumberoona*. Cruises start at A$13 and schedules change, so ring ahead to check departure times.

The **Botanic Gardens** are at the end of Dean St. A worthwhile walk from the gardens, particularly at dawn or dusk, takes you up the small hill where the white tower of the war memorial commands some agreeable views over the area.

In town, the **Albury Regional Art Gallery** (☎ 6023 8187; 546 Dean St; admission free; 10.30am-5pm Mon-Fri, to 4pm Sat & Sun) has a small, permanent collection that includes contemporary Australian photography and works by Russell Drysdale and Fred Williams.

In November, the annual **Ngangirra Festival**, which features Aboriginal art, music, dance and language, is held at Mungabareena Reserve.

Albury Backpackers (see below) runs half-day to seven-day canoeing trips on the Murray and you don't have to stay at the hostel to join one. It's also worth asking about bike hire here, as there are good bike tracks around town and the visitors centre has a bike-track brochure.

Oz E Wildlife (☎ 6040 3677; Ettamogah; adult/concession A$10/8; 9am-5pm), 10km north of town on the Hume Hwy, is a sanctuary with a fair collection of Aussie animals that originally came here as sickly visitors. The menagerie includes peacocks, koalas, cuter-than-a-button penguins and an other-worldly albino kangaroo. Penguin feeding is at 11am, 1pm and 3pm.

A few kilometres further north of Albury, the massive **Ettamogah Pub** (☎ 6026 2366; Burma Rd; 10am-late) is full of Australiana (cockatoos, beer, blue singlets and, er, dodgem cars) based on the famous Aussie cartoon pub. Still, it does brew its own beer and there's a winery.

Sleeping

Albury Backpackers (☎ 6041 1822, 0417-691 339; 452 David St; dm/d A$17/40;) It's easy to spot this ramshackle hostel with its purple roof and bus wrecks down the side yard. Rooms are bright and there's a selection of videos and DVDs for guests. The friendly staff organise canoeing trips down the Murray and ski trips in winter, but are equally helpful in finding fruit-picking work. Hire-bikes are well maintained.

New Albury (☎ 6021 3599; 491 Kiewa St; s/d A$48/60; ❄) This solid hotel offers basic but good-value rooms that are fresh and clean after a recent renovation.

Eating

Dean St has an array of decent restaurants that have sprung up to suit the cosmopolitan city.

Electra Café (cnr Dean & Macauley Sts; mains A$19; 🕑 breakfast, lunch & dinner) The nomadic menu of European, Middle Eastern and Asian dishes makes this a good hang-out – particularly when there's live music in the cavernous (but relaxed) back room.

Grind Feedstore (☎ 6041 2108; 467 Olive St; mains A$10.50-14; 🕑 breakfast & lunch Mon-Fri, dinner Fri & Sat) With comfy couches, and tapas that's perfect for snacking on with a bottle of wine, this is Albury's most relaxed eatery. A cheeky painting of a can opener on the wall completes the picture.

Gypsy's Food Bar (☎ 6021 4775; 582 Dean St; breakfasts A$6-11, mains A$6-12; 🕑 breakfast, lunch & dinner) This is the spot for a cheap cooked breakfast, but only big appetites need apply for the Gypsy's Famous Breakfast – a delicious orgy of grease. Don't miss the hot cakes.

Entertainment

Hotel Termo (🕑 6041 3544; 417 Dean St) Pub crawls start here, with its laid-back vibe, youngish crowd and a showcase of surprisingly decent live music and local DJing.

Liquid (491 Dean St; admission A$5; 🕑 9pm-'late' Wed-Sat) is Albury's biggest nightclub – there's a young crowd, a decent dance floor and mainstream dance music. It's free entry before 10pm and cheap drinks is Wednesday night.

Getting There & Away

AIR

At the time of writing, low-end fares to Sydney started at A$85 and Melbourne at A$55.

Brindabella Airlines (☎ 6248 8711, 1300 668 824; www.brindabella-airlines.com.au) Flies to Canberra (A$213, one hour).
Qantas (☎ 13 13 13; www.qantas.com.au)
Rex (☎ 13 17 13; www.regionalexpress.com.au)

BUS

McCafferty's/Greyhound (☎ 13 14 99; www.mccaffertys.com.au), running between Sydney (A$60, eight hours) and Melbourne (A$39, three to four hours), stops at Viennaworld (a service station/diner) on the highway across from Noreuil Park, and will stop at the Caltex service station on the northern highway on request. Book at the train station.

TRAIN

CountryLink (☎ 13 22 32, 6041 9555) at the train station books bus and train tickets. The twice-daily **XPT** (☎ 6041 9555) train service between Sydney and Melbourne stops in Albury on its overnight and day service. If you're travelling between the two capital cities it's much cheaper to stop over in Albury on a through ticket than to buy two separate tickets. **V/Line** (☎ 13 61 96) runs to Melbourne (A$70, 3½ hours) and Canberra (A$60, five hours).

WAGGA WAGGA

☎ 02 / pop 44,500

The famous 'town so nice they named it twice' is the state's largest inland city. Despite its size, it feels more like a country town than a city. The name means 'place of many crows' in the local Wiradjuri (one of NSW's largest Aboriginal tribal groups) language and is usually abbreviated to one word, pronounced 'wogga'.

Orientation & Information

The long main street, Baylis St, runs north from the train station and becomes Fitzmaurice St at the northern end. The Wagga Wagga **visitors centre** (☎ 6926 9621; www.tourismwaggawagga.com.au; Tarcutta St; 🕑 9am-5pm) is close to the river.

There's Internet access at **Civic Video** (☎ 6921 8866; 21 Forsyth St; first 15min A$2.20, per subsequent hr A$4; 🕑 10am-10pm). Alternatively, try the cheaper service at the public **library** (Morrow St).

Sights & Activities

There are two wineries nearby: **Wagga Wagga Winery** (☎ 6922 1221; Oura Rd; 🕑 11am-late) and the **Charles Sturt University Winery and Cheese Factory** (☎ 6933 2435; Coolamon Rd; 🕑 11am-5pm Mon-Fri, to 4pm Sat & Sun), which is part of the wine science school at the university.

The **Wiradjuri Walking Track** loops 30km from the visitors centre (pick up a map here) and includes some good lookouts. There's a shorter 10km return walk past Wollundry Lagoon. From the **beach** near the Wagga Wagga Caravan Park you can go swimming and fishing. **River cruises** operate Wednesday to Monday, weather and river levels permitting; ask at the visitors centre. One good operator is **Murrumbidgee River Boats** (☎ 6925 8700; 175 Eunony Bridge Rd; cruises adult A$12) which runs a one-hour cruise at 2pm Thursday to Monday. Bring your own picnic lunch and enjoy a relaxed afternoon on the river.

Sleeping

There's plenty of accommodation, mostly motel style (on Tarcutta St). The pubs are often cheaper options.

Manor (☎ 6921 5962; www.themanor.com.au; 38 Morrow St; B&B s/d A$70/100;) This small, well-restored guesthouse has some comfortable old-fashioned rooms (with shared bathroom) and a fine-dining restaurant.

Victoria Hotel (☎ 6921 5233; www.vichotel.net; Baylis St; s/d A$22/33) This is a convenient, central budget option.

Eating

Baylis/Fitzmaurice St has a surprisingly diverse range of places at which to eat, including several Italian restaurants, good coffee shops and bakeries. **Woolworths** (☎ 6921 4533; cnr Berry & Forsyth Sts) is the place to stock up on groceries.

Vietnamese **Saigon Restaurant** (☎ 6921 2212; 89 Morgan St; dishes A$10; lunch & dinner) is popular for takeaways and good-value restaurant meals. If you crave curry, consider the **Indian Tavern Tandoori** (☎ 6921 3121; 14-16 Pall Mall; mains A$10-20; dinner).

Getting There & Away

At the time of writing, low-end flights to Sydney started at A$75, and to Melbourne at A$75.

Qantas (☎ 13 13 13; www.qantas.com.au)
Rex (☎ 13 17 13; www.regionalexpress.com.au)

McCafferty's/Greyhound (☎ 13 14 99; www.mccaffertys.com.au) and **Fearnes** (☎ 6921 2316) run daily to Sydney (A$55, seven hours).

CountryLink (☎ 13 22 32, 6939 5488) buses leave from the train station (you can make bookings here).

Wagga is on the train line between Sydney (6¼ hours) and Melbourne (4¼ hours); the one-way fare to both cities is A$75 and there are daily services.

Queensland

CONTENTS

HIGHLIGHTS

- **Great Barrier Reef** Get nose to nose with multihued marine life (p184)
- **Whitsundays** Set sail languidly through these islands (p192)
- **Fraser Island** Embark on a reconnoitre of the world's biggest sand island (p173)
- **Great Keppel** Find your own patch of island isolation (p183)
- **Hervey Bay** Watch magnificent whales (p172)
- **Surfers Paradise** Show the locals a party trick or 10 (p160)
- **Noosa** Bronze up on the beach (p164)

- **Cheer for:** Queensland Bulls in the Pura Cup (cricket)
- **Eat:** fresh fruit and fresh seafood, barbecued on the beachfront beside your tent
- **Drink:** pot (285mL) of XXXX
- **Listen to:** Powderfinger's *Internationalist*, Regurgitator's (the Gurge) *Band in a Bubble* (recorded live over 21 days in a glass bubble in Melbourne's Fed Square)
- **Watch:** *The Crocodile Hunter* (really! It's surprisingly funny!) or crime flick *Getting Square*
- **Party at:** Cairns (p212), Surfers (p160) or Brisbane's 'Valley' (p149)
- **Swim at:** North Stradbroke Island (p153) or Coolum or Peregian Beach (p164)
- **Avoid:** box jellyfish, redneck politicians, Surfers Paradise during Schoolies Week
- **Locals' nickname:** Canetoads, Banana Benders

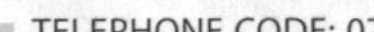

- TELEPHONE CODE: 07
- WEBSITE: www.queenslandholidays.com.au

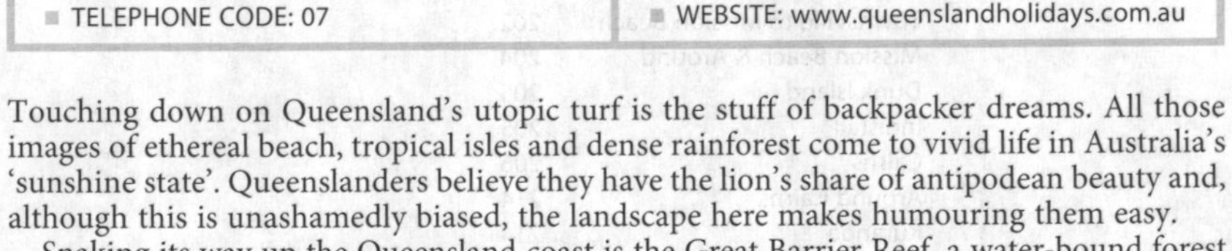

Touching down on Queensland's utopic turf is the stuff of backpacker dreams. All those images of ethereal beach, tropical isles and dense rainforest come to vivid life in Australia's 'sunshine state'. Queenslanders believe they have the lion's share of antipodean beauty and, although this is unashamedly biased, the landscape here makes humouring them easy.

Snaking its way up the Queensland coast is the Great Barrier Reef, a water-bound forest of iridescent coral, fish and thousands of other marine species. One of the seven wonders of the natural world, the reef provides ample and spectacular diving and snorkelling opportunities. You can also explore the reef from above the water while charting a course through the dazzling Whitsunday Islands. Further south is enigmatic Fraser Island; the world's largest sand island, speckled with mineral lakes, rainforests and seemingly infinite beaches. Onshore, Queensland is blessed with a sun-drenched coast and some spectacular national parks scattered over the ranges.

Two well-touristed cities grace either end of the state. Brisbane, the state capital and a lively cosmopolitan city, is in the south. At the northern, tropical end sits Cairns. Just 30km from the Great Barrier Reef, this graceful city lures travellers of all ilk. Inhabiting the two and everywhere in between is the genuine, affable Queensland population.

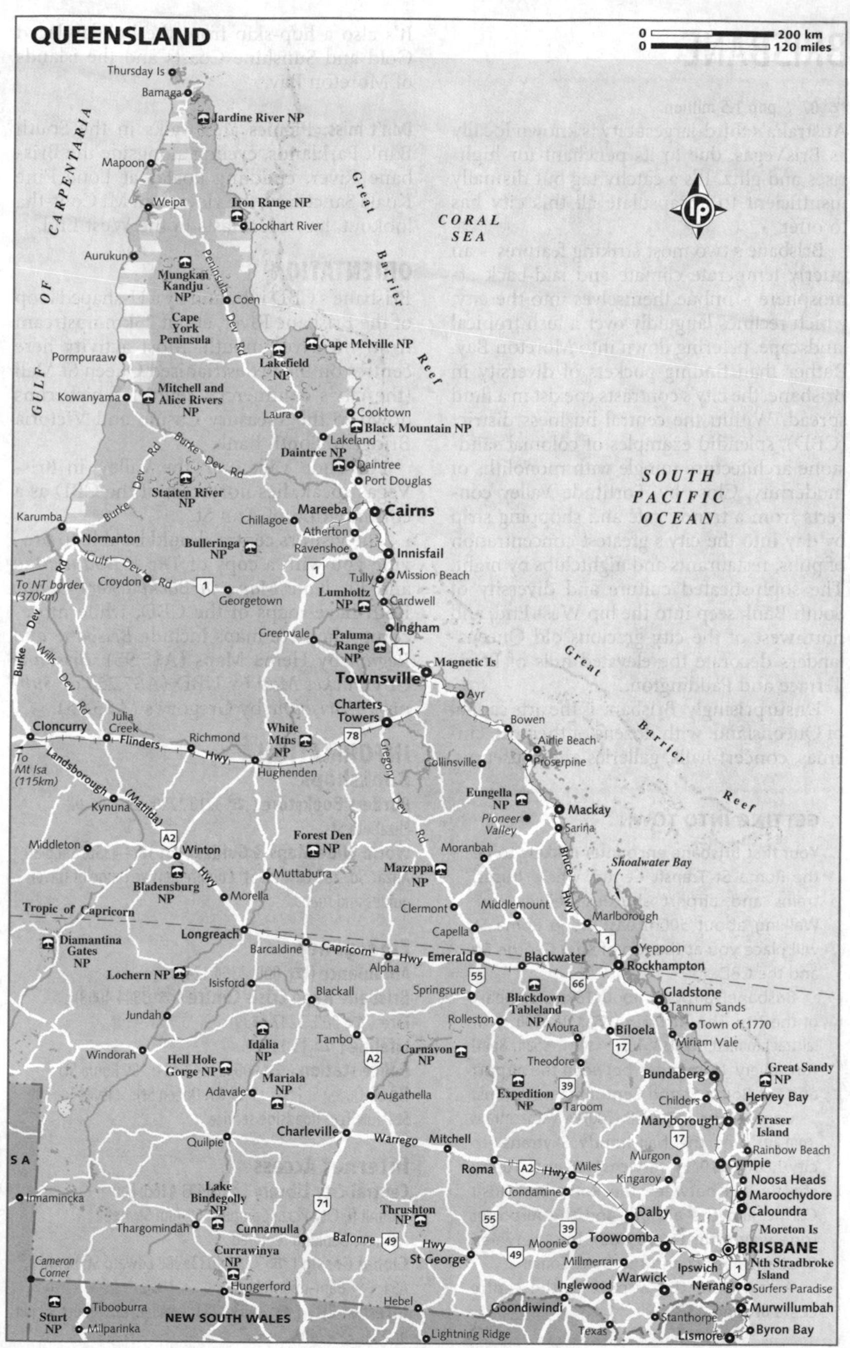
QUEENSLAND
0 200 km
0 120 miles
Thursday Is
Bamaga
Jardine River NP
Mapoon
Weipa
Iron Range NP
Lockhart River
Aurukun
Mungkan Kandju NP
Coen
Cape York Peninsula
Pompuraaw
Lakefield NP
Cape Melville NP
Mitchell and Alice Rivers NP
Kowanyama
Laura
Cooktown
Black Mountain NP
Lakeland
Daintree NP
Daintree
Port Douglas
Staaten River NP
Karumba
Normanton
Mareeba
Cairns
Chillagoe
Atherton
Bulleringa NP
Ravenshoe
Innisfail
Tully
Mission Beach
Croydon
Georgetown
To NT border (370km)
Lumholtz NP
Cardwell
Ingham
Greenvale
Paluma Range NP
Magnetic Is
Townsville
Ayr
Charters Towers
Bowen
Airlie Beach
Proserpine
Cloncurry
Julia Creek
Richmond
White Mtns NP
Hughenden
Collinsville
To Mt Isa (115km)
Kynuna
Eungella NP
Pioneer Valley
Mackay
Sarina
Middleton
Winton
Forest Den NP
Moranbah
Shoalwater Bay
Bladensburg NP
Muttaburra
Mazeppa NP
Morella
Clermont
Middlemount
Marlborough
Tropic of Capricorn
Longreach
Capella
Diamantina Gates NP
Barcaldine
Emerald
Blackwater
Yeppoon
Rockhampton
Alpha
Lochern NP
Isisford
Blackall
Springsure
Blackdown Tableland NP
Gladstone
Tannum Sands
Jundah
Rolleston
Moura
Biloela
Town of 1770
Idalia NP
Tambo
Miriam Vale
Windorah
Hell Hole Gorge NP
Carnarvon NP
Theodore
Great Sandy NP
Bundaberg
Mariala NP
Adavale
Augathella
Expedition NP
Childers
Hervey Bay
Taroom
Maryborough
Fraser Island
Charleville
Quilpie
Warrego
Mitchell
Rainbow Beach
Murgon
Gympie
SA
Roma
Hwy
Miles
Kingaroy
Noosa Heads
Innamincka
Lake Bindegolly NP
Condamine
Maroochydore
Caloundra
Thrushton NP
Dalby
Thargomindah
Cunnamulla
Balonne
Hwy
Moreton Is
Toowoomba
Currawinya NP
Moonie
BRISBANE
Cameron Corner
St George
Millmerran
Ipswich
Nth Stradbroke Island
Hungerford
Warwick
Nerang
Surfers Paradise
Inglewood
Sturt NP
Tibooburra
Hebel
Goondiwindi
Murwillumbah
Milparinka
NEW SOUTH WALES
Stanthorpe
Texas
Lightning Ridge
Lismore
Byron Bay
GULF OF CARPENTARIA
CORAL SEA
Great Barrier Reef
SOUTH PACIFIC OCEAN
Peninsula Dev Rd
Burke Dev Rd
'Gulf' Dev Rd
Burke Dev Wills Dev Rd
Flinders Hwy
Landsborough (Matilda) Hwy
Gregory Dev Rd
Bruce Hwy
Capricorn Hwy

BRISBANE

☎ 07 / pop 1.5 million

Australia's third-largest city is known locally as BrisVegas, due to its penchant for high-rises and glitz. It's a catchy tag but dismally insufficient to encapsulate all this city has to offer.

Brisbane's two most striking features – an utterly temperate climate and laid-back atmosphere – imbue themselves into the city, which reclines languidly over a lush tropical landscape, petering down into Moreton Bay. Rather than finding pockets of diversity in Brisbane, the city's contrasts coexist in a fluid spread. Within the central business district (CBD), splendid examples of colonial sandstone architecture mingle with monoliths of modernity. Close by, Fortitude Valley converts from a trendy café and shopping strip by day into the city's greatest concentration of pubs, restaurants and nightclubs by night. The sophisticated culture and diversity of South Bank seep into the hip West End, and northwest of the city gracious old Queenslanders decorate the elevated hills of Petrie Terrace and Paddington.

Unsurprisingly, Brisbane is the arts capital of Queensland, with dozens of theatres, cinemas, concert halls, galleries and museums.

GETTING INTO TOWN

Your first Brisbane encounter is likely to be the Roma St Transit Centre, where buses, trains and airport shuttles deliver you. Walking about 500m east along Roma St will place you at the top of King George Sq and the CBD.

Brisbane's airport is about 15km northeast of the city. The **Airtrain** (☎ 3215 5000; www.airtrain.com.au; tickets A$10; 🕑 services 5am-8pm) runs every 15 minutes between the airport and the Roma St and Central train stations.

Coachtrans (☎ 3238 4700; www.coachtrans.com.au) runs the half-hourly Skytrans (to city/hostel A$9/11, services 5.45am to 10pm) shuttle bus between the Roma St Transit Centre and the airport, and the Airporter (one-way/return A$35/65) bus between Brisbane airport and the Gold Coast.

A taxi from the airport to the centre costs around A$30.

It's also a hop-skip from the holiday-laced Gold and Sunshine Coasts and the islands of Moreton Bay.

Don't miss: Picnics and walks in the South Bank Parklands, cycling alongside the Brisbane River, cuddling koalas at Lone Pine Koala Sanctuary, the view from Mt Coot-tha lookout, lazy breakfasts in the West End.

ORIENTATION

Brisbane's CBD is bound by a U-shaped loop of the Brisbane River, about 25km upstream from the river mouth. Most activity here centres on the pedestrianised Queen St Mall (the city's commercial centre), which runs down to the Treasury Casino and Victoria Bridge to South Bank.

Fortitude Valley, or 'the Valley' in BrisVegas speak, lies northeast of the CBD as a continuation of Ann St.

The visitors centre should be able to provide you with a copy of *The Brisbane Map* and *Brisbane Map – a Backpackers Guide*. Both have maps of the CBD, while more-comprehensive maps include *Brisbane and Region* by Hema Maps (A$5.95), *Brisbane City Pocket Map* by UBD (A$7.25) or *Suburban Brisbane* by Gregory's (A$5.95).

INFORMATION

Bookshops

Borders Bookstore (☎ 3210 1220; cnr Albert & Elizabeth Sts)

World Wide Maps & Guides (☎ 3221 4330; Shop 30, Anzac Sq, 267 Edward St) Comprehensive range of travel guides and maps.

Emergency

Ambulance (☎ 000, 3364 1246)

Brisbane Rape Crisis Centre (☎ 3844 4008)

Fire (☎ 000, 3247 5539)

Lifeline (☎ 13 11 14)

Police station (☎ 000, 3364 6464; 100 Roma St)

RACQ Queen St (☎ 13 19 05; Queen St); St Pauls Tce 300 St Pauls Tce) Roadside service.

Internet Access

Central City Library (☎ 3403 4166; Lower ground fl, City Plaza Complex, 69 Ann St; free) Advance booking required.

Global Gossip (☎ 3229 4033; 288 Edward St; per hr A$4; 🕑 8am-midnight)

Internet City (☎ 3003 1221; Level 4, 132 Albert St; per hr A$4; 🕑 24hr)

State Library of Queensland (☎ 3840 7666; South Bank; free) Advance booking required.

Internet Resources

www.backpackbrisbane.com Good backpacker-specific source.
www.ourbrisbane.com.au Everything on the where, what, how and why of Brisbane.
www.queenslandholidays.com.au Informative website covering the whole state.
www.tq.webcentral.com.au/accessqld Excellent website for disabled travellers.

Left Luggage

Central station (☎ 3235 2222; Ann St; per 24hr A$4)
Roma St Transit Centre (☎ 3235 2222; Roma St; per 24hr A$6)

Media

This Week in Brisbane & South-East Queensland Available from the Brisbane Visitor Information Centre. Good for cultural events.
Time Off (www.timeoff.com.au) Free weekly mag listing Brisbane's gigs and events.
Rave (www.ravemag.com.au) Gig guide and entertainment section of Brisbane's *Courier Mail* newspaper.

Medical Services

24hr pharmacy (☎ 3221 4585; 141 Queen St)
Brisbane Sexual Health Clinic (☎ 3227 8666; 270 Roma St)
Royal Brisbane Hospital (☎ 3253 8111; Hertson Rd, Hertson; 🕒 24hr casualty ward)
Travellers Medical Service (☎ 1300 369 359, 3211 3611; 1st fl, 245 Albert St; 🕒 7.30am-7pm Mon-Fri, 8.30am-5pm Sat, 9.30am-5pm Sun)
Travellers Medical & Vaccination Centre (TMVC; ☎ 3221 9066; 5th fl, 247 Adelaide St; 🕒 closed Thu, Sat afternoon & Sun) Vaccinations and medical advice for travellers.

Money

There are exchange bureaus at Brisbane airport. Most banks also have exchange facilities, as well as ATMs.
American Express (☎ 1300 139 060; 131 Elizabeth St)
Interforex Brisbane (☎ 3221 3562; Shop Q255, Wintergarden, 171-209 Queen St Mall)
Travelex Edward St (☎ 3221 9422; 276 Edward St); Queen St Mall (☎ 3210 6325; Street level, Myer Centre, Queen St Mall)

Post

Main post office (☎ 13 13 18; 261 Queen St; 🕒 7am-6pm Mon-Fri) Has a poste restante counter.

Tourist Information

Brisbane Visitor Information Centre (☎ 3006 6200; cnr Albert & Queen Sts; 🕒 9am-5.30pm Mon-Thu, 9am-8pm Fri, 9am-5pm Sat, 9.30am-4.30pm Sun) Masses of information on accommodation, eating, sights and activities. It can book almost anything for you.

Travel Agencies

Adventure Travel Bugs (☎ 1800 666 720, 3236 0234; www.oztravelbugs.com; 158 Roma St) A large specialist in budget trips.
Backpackers Travel Centre (☎ 3221 2255; www.backpackerstravel.net.au; 138 Albert St) Cheap Australian tour packages.
STA Travel (☎ 3221 3722; 111 Adelaide St)
Trailfinders (☎ 3229 0887; 91 Elizabeth St)
YHA Membership & Travel Office (☎ 3236 1680; 154 Roma St) Tours, Youth Hostels Association (YHA) membership and hostel bookings.

SIGHTS

Most of Brisbane's major sights can be found in the CBD or inner-city suburbs. A walk through the city will reveal Brisbane's colonial history and architecture, and a ferry ride across the river lands you in the glut of attractions and activities of South Bank. Chinatown and Brunswick St, both in Fortitude Valley, provide a healthy injection of culture, shopping and food to keep you busy and well fed.

Further afield is Mt Coot-tha Reserve, where spectacular views from the lookout are easily accessed by bus.

South Bank Parklands

This beautiful smear of green skirting the western side of the Brisbane River is home to cultural attractions, fine eateries, small rainforests, hidden lawns and gorgeous flora. The **parklands** (admission free; 🕒 dawn-dusk) have a scenic esplanade that offers spectacular views of the city and the whole area is laden with atmosphere and character.

You can easily spend an afternoon meandering here, and there are plenty of pockets in which to enjoy a picnic lunch. The two standout attractions are **Stanley St Plaza** – a renovated section of historic Stanley St lined with cafés, shops and restaurants – and **South Bank Beach**. On hot days, people converge on this beach, which is an artificial swimming hole that wraps around trees, bridges and rockeries before opening up to resemble a tropical lagoon.

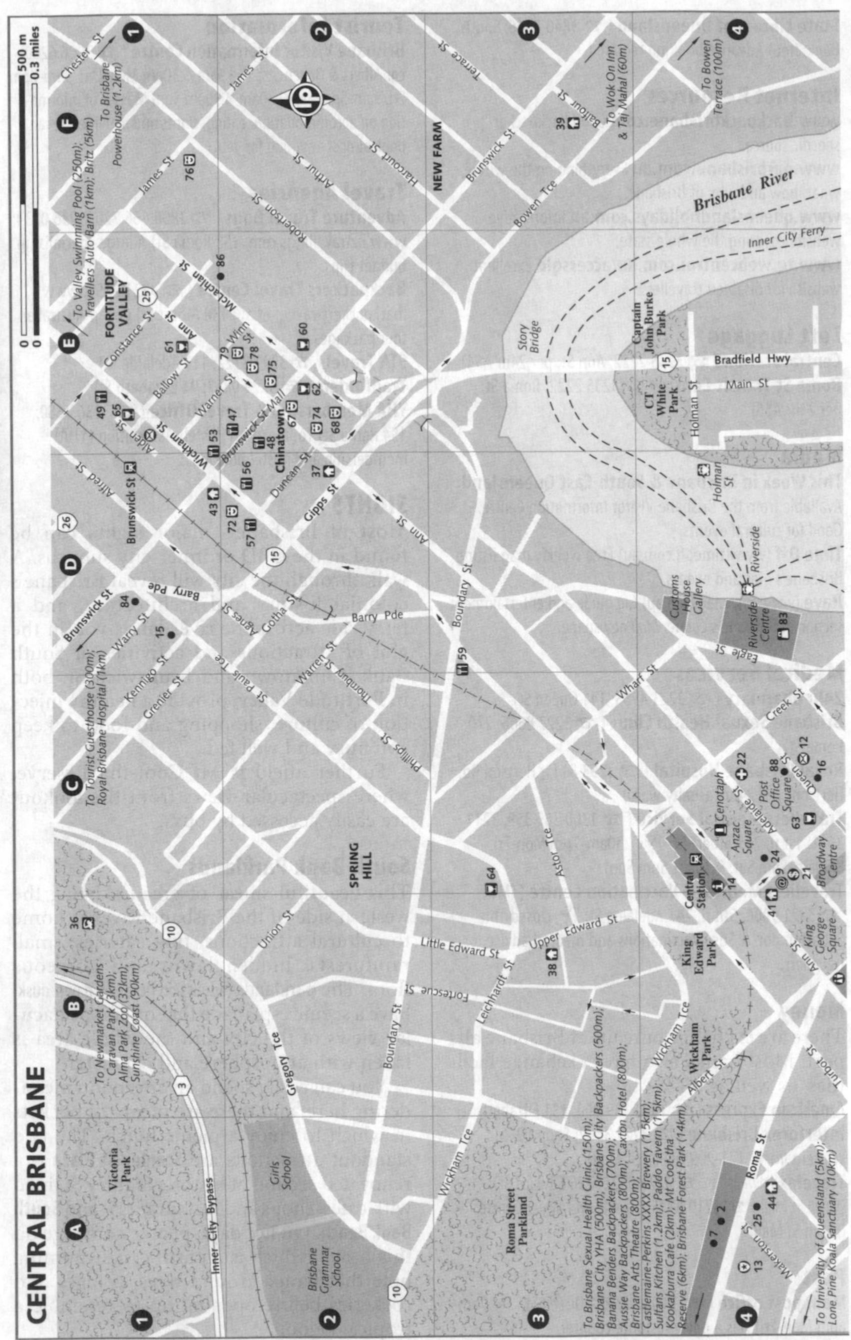
CENTRAL BRISBANE
500 m
0.3 miles
To Newmarket Gardens Caravan Park (3km); Alma Park Zoo (32km); Sunshine Coast (90km)
To Tourist Guesthouse (300m); Royal Brisbane Hospital (1km)
To Valley Swimming Pool (250m); Travellers Auto Barn (1km); Britz (5km)
To Brisbane Powerhouse (1.2km)
To Wok On Inn & Taj Mahal (60m)
To Bowen Terrace (100m)
To Brisbane Sexual Health Clinic (150m); Brisbane City YHA (500m); Brisbane City Backpackers (500m); Banana Benders Backpackers (700m); Caxton Hotel (800m); Aussie Way Backpackers (800m); Brisbane Arts Theatre (800m); Castlemaine-Perkins XXXX Brewery (1.5km); Sultans Kitchen (1.2km); Paddo Tavern (1.5km); Kookaburra Cafe (2km); Mt Coot-tha Reserve (6km); Brisbane Forest Park (14km)
To University of Queensland (5km); Lone Pine Koala Sanctuary (10km)
Victoria Park
Inner City Bypass
Brisbane Grammar School
Girls School
Roma Street Parkland
SPRING HILL
FORTITUDE VALLEY
NEW FARM
Chinatown
Brunswick St Mall
Story Bridge
Brisbane River
Inner City Ferry
Captain John Burke Park
CT White Park
Customs House Gallery
Riverside Centre
Riverside
King Edward Park
Wickham Park
Central Station
Anzac Square
Cenotaph
Post Office Square
King George Square
Broadway Centre
Gregory Tce
Boundary St
Wickham Tce
Leichhardt St
Little Edward St
Upper Edward St
Fortescue St
Astor Tce
Union St
St Pauls Tce
Warren St
Thornbury St
Phillips St
Gotha St
Agnes St
Barry Pde
Brunswick St
Wickham St
Ann St
Gipps St
Duncan St
Warner St
Ballow St
Constance St
Alden St
Alfred St
McLachlan St
Winn St
Robertson St
Arthur St
Harcourt St
James St
Chester St
Terrace St
Brunswick St
Bowen Tce
Balfour St
Bradfield Hwy
Main St
Holman St
Eagle St
Wharf St
Creek St
Adelaide St
Queen St
Albert St
Turbot St
Roma St
Makerston St
Kennigo St
Grenier St
Warry St

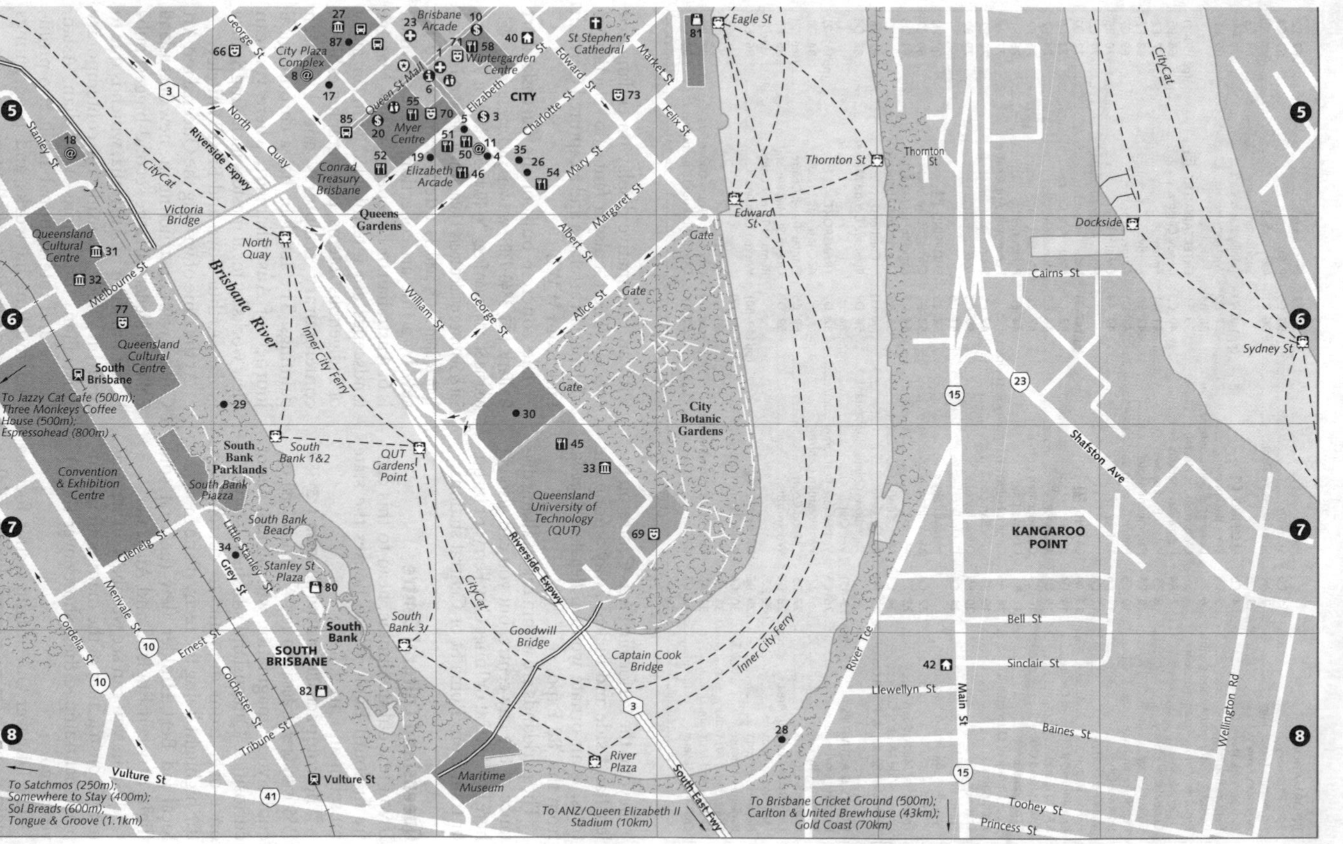
George St
City Plaza Complex
Brisbane Arcade
Wintergarden Centre
Queen St Mall
Elizabeth St
CITY
Myer Centre
Elizabeth Arcade
Conrad Treasury Brisbane
Queens Gardens
Charlotte St
Mary St
Margaret St
Albert St
Edward St
St Stephen's Cathedral
Market St
Felix St
Eagle St
Thornton St
Edward St
Dockside
CityCat
Cairns St
Sydney St
Shafston Ave
KANGAROO POINT
Bell St
Sinclair St
Llewellyn St
Baines St
Main St
Wellington Rd
Toohey St
Princess St
River Tce
Stanley St
North Quay
Riverside Expwy
Victoria Bridge
Queensland Cultural Centre
Melbourne St
Brisbane River
Inner City Ferry
William St
Alice St
Gate
City Botanic Gardens
Queensland University of Technology (QUT)
South Brisbane
To Jazzy Cat Cafe (500m); Three Monkeys Coffee House (500m); Espressohead (800m)
South Bank Parklands
South Bank 1&2
QUT Gardens Point
Convention & Exhibition Centre
South Bank Piazza
South Bank Beach
Little Stanley St
Stanley St Plaza
Grey St
Glenelg St
Merivale St
Cordelia St
Ernest St
South Bank
SOUTH BRISBANE
South Bank 3
Goodwill Bridge
Captain Cook Bridge
Colchester St
Tribune St
Vulture St
River Plaza
Maritime Museum
South East Fwy
To Satchmos (250m); Somewhere to Stay (400m); Sol Breads (600m); Tongue & Groove (1.1km)
To ANZ/Queen Elizabeth II Stadium (10km)
To Brisbane Cricket Ground (500m); Carlton & United Brewhouse (43km); Gold Coast (70km)

QUEENSLAND

INFORMATION

24hr Pharmacy	1	C5
Adventure Travel Bugs	2	A4
American Express	3	C5
Backpackers Travel Centre	4	C5
Borders Bookstore	5	C5
Brisbane Visitor Information Centre	6	B5
Brisbane Visitors Accommodation Service	7	A4
Central City Library	8	B5
Global Gossip	9	C4
Interforex Brisbane	10	C5
Internet City	11	C5
Main Post Office	12	C4
Police Station	13	A4
Queensland Rail Travel Centre	14	C4
RACQ Branch	15	D1
RACQ Head Office	16	C4
STA Travel	17	B5
State Library of Queensland	18	A5
Trailfinders	19	B5
Travelex	20	B5
Travelex	21	C4
Travellers' Medical & Vaccination Centre	22	C4
Travellers' Medical Service	23	B5
World Wide Maps & Guides	24	C4
YHA Membership & Travel Office	25	A4

SIGHTS & ACTIVITIES (pp139–45)

Brisbane Bicycle Sales	26	C5
Brisbane City Gallery	(see 27)	
Brisbane City Hall	27	B5
Cliffs Rock-Climbing Area	28	D8
Museum of Brisbane	(see 27)	
Nepalese Pagoda	29	B6
Parliament House	30	C6
Queensland Art Gallery	31	A6
Queensland Museum	32	A6
QUT Art Museum	33	C7
Riders	34	B7
Skatebiz	35	C5
Splash Leisure Pool	36	B1

SLEEPING (pp146–7)

Bunk Backpackers	37	D2
Dorchester Self-Contained Units	38	B3
Globetrekkers Hostel	39	F3
Palace Backpackers Embassy	40	C5
Palace Backpackers	41	B4
Paramount Motel	42	E8
Prince Consort Backpackers	43	D1
Tinbilly	44	A4

EATING (pp147–9)

Artisans on the Yard	45	C7
Asian Fast-Food Shops	46	C5
Cosmopolitan Coffee	47	E2
Fatboys Cafe	48	E2
Garuva Hidden Tranquility Restaurant & Bar	49	E1
Gilhooley's	50	C5
Govinda's	51	C5
Irish Murphy's	52	B5
McWhirters Marketplace	53	E1
Metro Cafe	54	C5
Myer Centre Food Court	55	B5
Palace Cafe	(see 41)	
Superbowl Chinese Restaurant	56	D2
Veg Out	(see 53)	
Vietnamese Restaurant	57	D2
Wintergarden Centre Food Court	58	C5
Woolworths	59	D3

DRINKING (pp149–50)

Birdee Num Num	(see 37)	
Dooley's	60	E2
Elephant & Wheelbarrow	(see 43)	
GPO	61	E1
Press Club	62	E2
R-Bar	63	C4
Ric's Cafe Bar	(see 48)	
Sportsman's Hotel	64	C3
Tinbilly Bar & Cafe	(see 44)	
Wickham Hotel	65	E1

ENTERTAINMENT (pp150–1)

Dendy Cinema	66	B5
Empire	67	E2
Family	68	E2
Gardens Theatre	69	C7
Greater Union	70	B5
Hoyts Regent Theatre	71	C5
Indie Temple	72	D2
Metro Arts Centre	73	C5
Monastery	74	E2
Mustang Bar	75	E2
Palace Centro	76	F1
Performing Arts Centre	77	A6
Source	78	E2
Zoo	79	E2

SHOPPING (p151)

Crafts Village Market	80	B7
Eagle St Pier Market	81	D5
Queensland Aboriginal Creations	82	B8
Riverside Centre Market	83	D4

TRANSPORT (pp151–2)

ABC Integra	84	D1
Qantas Travel Centre	(see 22)	
Queen St Mall Bus Station	85	B5
Roma St Transit Centre	(see 7)	
Wicked Campers	86	E2

OTHER

City Night Tours Departures	87	B5
City Sights Tour Departures	88	C4

Beyond the Performing Arts Centre, on the left-hand side and tucked away among the trees, is an ornate wooden **Nepalese Pagoda**, from the '88 Expo.

The parklands are within easy walking distance of the city centre, but you can also get here by CityCat or Inner City Ferry, or by bus or train from Roma St or Central stations.

Queensland Cultural Centre

If you're a culture junkie, head to this centre in South Bank, which houses the state museum and art gallery.

The compact **Queensland Museum** (☎ 3840 7555; entry Grey St; admission free; 9.30am-5pm) occupies your imagination with all manner of curiosities. Queensland's history is given a once-over from dinosaur to current day, the highlight being the teeny plane in which local lad Bert Hinkler flew the first solo flight between England and Australia.

Upstairs you can see wombats on steroids in a reconstruction of the mammoth marsupials that tramped these shores over 100,000 years ago.

The Discover Queensland section focuses mainly on the state's current diverse wildlife with an informative display on endangered species. There's also a fantastic selection of Melanesian artefacts and a captured German tank from WWI.

The concrete bulk of the **Queensland Art Gallery** (☎ 3840 7303; www.qag.qld.gov.au; entry Melbourne St; admission free; 10am-5pm Mon-Fri, 9am-5pm Sat & Sun, free guided tours 11am, 1pm & 2pm Mon-Fri, 11am, 1pm & 3pm Sat & Sun) is utterly transformed inside by a fine-art collection, most of which is of Australian or European origins. Massive landscapes are intermingled with an array of indigenous totems, photographic exhibits, contemporary sculptures and European paintings. The 1st floor has a chronological journey of Australian art, where you can view works by local masters including Sidney Nolan, Arthur Boyd and Brett Whiteley.

At the time of writing the Queensland Art Gallery was constructing the new **Queensland Gallery of Modern Art**, the second-biggest public art museum in Australia, which is due to open in 2006. Focusing on contemporary Australian, indigenous Australian, Asian, Pacific and international art, it also promised multimedia works and programmes for art enthusiasts of all ages.

Chinatown

Alongside the funky restaurants and bars of Fortitude Valley is Brisbane's very own Chinatown. Although it only occupies one street (Duncan St), the Chinatown Mall has the same flamboyance and flavour of its counterparts in Sydney and Melbourne.

The Ann St end is guarded by an exquisite Tang dynasty archway and Oriental lions. The mall itself is populated by Chinese restaurants, herbalists, massage therapists and acupuncture businesses. Chinese landscaping includes pagodas and a waterfall.

Brisbane City Hall

This gracious sandstone edifice (☎ 3403 4048; btwn Ann & Adelaide Sts; admission free, viewing tower adult A$2; lift & viewing tower 10am-3pm Mon-Fri, 10am-2pm Sat) overlooks the sculptures and fountains of King George Sq. It's surrounded by modern skyscrapers, but the observation platform up in the bell tower still provides one of the best views across the city.

On the ground floor the **Museum of Brisbane** (☎ 3403 4048; admission free; 10am-5pm) follows Brisbane's physical and cultural progress. The use of audio transcripts and a huge wall dedicated to baby Brisbanites born in the 1980s mingles well with some beautifully antique B&W photographs. The museum also incorporates the **Brisbane City Gallery** (admission free), which features a mixture of local and international artists.

QUT Art Museum

On the Queensland University of Technology (QUT) campus, this small **museum** (☎ 3864 2797; 2 George St; admission free; 10am-4pm Tue-Fri, noon-4pm Sat & Sun) provides an excellent insight into the state's contemporary art, in all its mediums. Best of all are the frequent displays of work by students at the university, demonstrating possible future directions of art in Australia.

Parliament House

Perched imposingly at the edge of the CBD, **Parliament House** (☎ 3406 7111; cnr Alice & George Sts; admission free; 9am-5pm Mon-Fri) dates from 1868, with a roof clad in Mt Isa copper. If you're really keen, on sitting days you can gawk at the law-makers in action from the public balcony. Free tours leave on demand each weekday (only two tours daily when parliament is sitting).

City Botanic Gardens

A deserved drawcard, these **gardens** (☎ 3403 0666; Albert St; 24hr, free guided tours 11am & 1pm Mon-Sat) are a mass of green lawns, towering Moreton Bay figs and tropical flora descending gently from the QUT campus. Crisscrossing paths through the interior and perimeter enable strollers, joggers, picnickers, cyclists and in-line skaters to enjoy the views. The gardens are partly lit up at night and you stand a good chance of seeing possums. There's a pleasant café inside the former curator's cottage at the southern end.

Roma St Parkland

Looking like a mini version of the Botanic Gardens, this **park** (☎ 3006 4545; Albert St; admission free; dawn-dusk, free guided tours 10am & 2pm Thu-Sun Sep-May, 11am & 2pm Thu-Sun Jun-Aug) is home to subtropical gardens (the world's largest in a city centre) and a small outdoor theatre. There are public barbecues here so you can do the very Australian picnic thing.

Mt Coot-tha Reserve

About 7km west of the city centre, **Mt Coot-tha Reserve** is a 220-hectare bushland reserve, teeming with wildlife (mostly of the possum variety). Aside from the chunk of wilderness, the big attractions here are a massive planetarium and the spectacular lookout. The latter affords panoramic daytime views of Brisbane and a few bits beyond, and at night a sea of twinkling lights blanketing the terrain for miles. The lookout has wheelchair access.

Just north of the road to the lookout, on Sir Samuel Griffith Dr, is the turn-off to **JC Slaughter Falls**, reached by a short walking track. Also here is a 1.8km **Aboriginal Art Trail**, which takes you past eight sites with works by local Aboriginal artists.

At the base of Mt Coot-tha, the **Brisbane Botanic Gardens** (☎ 3403 8888; admission free; 8.30am-5.30pm, free guided walks 11am & 1pm Mon-Sat) contains more than 5000 plant species, including Australian varieties.

The **Sir Thomas Brisbane Planetarium** (☎ 3403 2578; adult A$10.50), found within the Brisbane Botanic Gardens, is Australia's largest planetarium with a series of mind-boggling astronomical displays. Highly recommended are the shows at the Cosmic Skydome, which will make you feel like you've stepped on board the *Enterprise*.

To get to Mt Coot-tha and the Brisbane Botanic Gardens take bus No 471 from Adelaide St, opposite King George Sq (A$2.60, 30 minutes, hourly Monday to Friday, six Saturday and Sunday).

Brisbane Forest Park

If the Botanics aren't enough bush for you then join the many Brisbanites who satisfy their wilderness cravings at this 28,500-hectare park in the D'Aguilar Range, about 30 minutes northwest of the city. At the park entrance, the **visitors centre** (☎ 3300 4855; 60 Mt Nebo Rd; 🕑 8.30am-4.30pm Mon-Fri, 9am-4.30pm Sat & Sun) has information about bush **camping** (camp sites per person A$4) in the park, and maps of walking tracks. The birdlife is a big lure here and it's a beautiful spot for a barbecue. There are also walks ranging from a few hundred metres to 8km. To really enjoy the park it's best to organise your own transport, as buses only go as far as the park headquarters. Picnic areas and walking tracks are beyond the headquarters.

Beside the visitors centre is **Walk-About Creek** (adult A$3.50; 🕑 9am-4.30pm), a freshwater study centre where you can see a resident platypus up close, as well as fish, lizards, pythons and turtles.

Lone Pine Koala Sanctuary

Just 11km west of Brisbane's CBD, **Lone Pine Koala Sanctuary** (☎ 3378 1366; Jesmond Rd, Fig Tree Pocket; adult A$15, VIP & YHA cardholder A$12; 🕑 8.30am-5pm) is the world's largest koala sanctuary. With over 130 of the cute and cuddly marsupials you won't lack photo opportunities. A cuddle costs an extra A$15. Keeping the koalas company are wombats, kangaroos, possums, dingoes, Tasmanian devils and other native animals. There are regular talks during the day, and barbecue facilities.

To get here catch the No 430 express bus (A$3.40, 35 minutes, frequently) from the Queen St Mall bus station (under the Myer Centre).

Alternatively, **Mirimar Cruises** (☎ 0412-749 426; return ticket A$28) cruises to the sanctuary from North Quay (next to Victoria Bridge), along the Brisbane River. It departs daily at 10am, returning from Lone Pine at 1.30pm.

Alma Park Zoo

You can also bond with a more multicultural mix of furred and feathered brethren at **Alma Park Zoo** (☎ 3204 6566; Alma Rd, Dakabin; adult/student A$22/20; 🕑 9am-5pm, last entry 4pm), over 35km north of the city centre. Unbearably cute exotics such as tamarin and squirrel monkeys, sun bears and leopards lounge about and you can touch and feed some of them between 11am and 2.30pm.

To get here catch the Zoo Train from Roma St Transit Centre to Dakabin Station (A$3.80, 50 minutes, every 30 minutes) where the complimentary Zoo Bus takes you the rest of the way.

ACTIVITIES

Brisbane's climate and geography are perfect for outdoor activities, and the city's relatively flat topography and numerous parks and gardens enable you to scale walls, walk, cycle, skate and swim to your heart's content.

Cycling

Brisbane has some 500km of bike tracks, all of which are detailed in the *Brisbane Bicycle Experience Guide* booklet, available from visitors centres.

Scenic tracks along the Brisbane River range from 5km to 20km. A good starter takes you from the City Botanic Gardens, across the Goodwill Bridge and out to the University of Queensland. It's about 7km one way and you can stop for a beer at the Regatta pub in Toowong.

Bicycles are allowed on Citytrains, except on weekdays during peak hours. You can also take bikes on CityCats and ferries for free but cycling in malls is a no-go.

Brisbane Bicycle Sales (☎ 3229 2433; www.brizbike.com; 87 Albert St; per hr/day A$12/20; 🕑 8.30am-5.30pm Mon-Fri, to 4pm Sat, 10am-4pm Sun)

Riders (☎ 3846 6200; Shop 9, Little Stanley St, South Bank; per hr/day A$12/30; 🕑 8am-5pm Mon-Sat, 10am-4pm Sun)

Valet Cycle Hire (☎ 0408-003 198; www.valetcyclehire.com; per half-/full day A$30/40) First-class bikes and service plus a daily afternoon guided tour (A$38) with small numbers. Delivery and collection to and from your hotel door.

In-line Skating

You can also traverse all those bike tracks on two legs of course. **Skatebiz** (☎ 3220 0157; 101 Albert St; per 2/24hr A$13/20; 🕑 9am-5.30pm Mon-Thu, to 4pm Sat, 10am-4pm Sun) rents in-line skates. **Planet Inline** (☎ 3255 0033; www.planetinline.com; tours A$15) offers Sunday skate tours that differ each week and last about three hours. **Blade Sensations** (☎ 3844 0606) runs a justifiably popular Full Moon skating tour; no raving or bare bums, just a big bunch of folk floating through the city on wheels.

Swimming

There are several good swimming pools in Brisbane, generally open from 6am or 7am until 7pm and costing around A$5.

South Bank Beach (South Bank Parklands) Free, sceney and scenic.

Splash Leisure Pool (☎ 3831 7665; 400 Gregory Tce, Spring Hill) One of the biggest pools in Brisbane.

Valley Swimming Pool (☎ 3852 1231; 432 Wickham St, Fortitude Valley)

Climbing

If scaling walls is your thing, you can do the Spiderman dance in spectacular fashion at the **cliffs rock-climbing area**, on the southern banks of the Brisbane River at Kangaroo Point. These pink volcanic cliffs are allegedly 200 million years old and regardless of your level of expertise, joining the other scrambling climbers is good (and exhilarating!) fun. Several operators offer climbing and abseiling instruction here:

Jane Clarkson's Outdoor Adventures (☎ 3870 3223; climbing A$15) Join the rock-climbing club any Wednesday night at 5.45pm; just make your way to the base of the cliffs.

Worth Wild Rock Climbing (☎ 3395 6450; www.worthwild.com.au; group instruction per person A$75)

Other Activities

Brisbane's Chinatown offers travel-weary bones, muscles and minds blissful respite in the form of free **tai chi** classes every Sunday morning at 11am in the Chinatown Mall (Duncan St).

One of the best ways to see Brisbane is to fling yourself out of a plane skydiving. It will set you back about A$250.

Brisbane Skydiving Centre (☎ 1800 061 555; www.brisbaneskydive.com.au)

Ripcord Skydivers (☎ 3399 3552; www.ripcord-skydivers.com.au)

TOURS

If you're a fan of the amber fluid you'll enjoy touring the **Castlemaine-Perkins XXXX Brewery** (☎ 3361 7597; www.xxxx.com.au; cnr Black & Paton Sts, Milton; adult A$18; ⏲ tours hourly 10am-4pm Mon-Fri, plus 6pm Wed). Most hostels organise tours or you can call and book yourself. The brewery is about 1.5km west of Roma St Transit Centre; the closest train station is Milton.

You can also tour the **Carlton & United Brewhouse** (☎ 3826 5858; cnr Mulles Rd & Pacific Hwy, Yatala; admission with/without bus A$30/15; ⏲ tours 10am, noon & 2pm Mon-Fri), halfway between Brisbane and the Gold Coast. Apparently this is one of the most technologically advanced breweries in the world, pumping out three million bottles of the good stuff each day. Just to see this much liquid gold in one spot is awesome – Homer, eat your heart out.

The **City Sights bus tour** (day tickets A$20) is a hop-on-hop-off shuttle taking in 19 of Brisbane's major landmarks. Tours depart every 45 minutes between 9am and 3.45pm from Post Office Sq on Queen St. The same ticket covers you for unlimited use of conventional city bus and ferry services. Its **City Nights tour** (A$20; ⏲ 6pm Mar-Oct, 6.30pm Nov-Feb), departing from City Hall, goes a little further afield and includes Mt Coot-tha Lookout and a CityCat cruise.

Brisbane Day Tours (☎ 3236 1240; tours A$100) Whale-watching trips to Moreton Bay between June and November.

Brisbackpacker Tours (☎ 3342 7813; www.brisbackpacker.com; day tours incl lunch A$60) City tours with a local flavour.

River City Cruises (☎ 0428-278 472; www.rivercitycruises.com; 1½hr cruise A$20) Swans up and down the Brisbane River, taking in the sights.

For tours from Brisbane of the Gold Coast hinterland and Glass House Mountains, see p157 and p162.

FESTIVALS & EVENTS

Information on festivals and events in Brisbane can be found at visitors centres or at www.ourbrisbane.com/whatson/festivals. Major happenings:

Cockroach Races A bizarre ritual that takes place at the Story Bridge Hotel on Australia Day (26 January).

Chinese New Year Always a popular event in Fortitude Valley in February.

Tropfest Nationwide short film festival telecast live at South Bank.

International Film Festival 10 days of quality films in July, shown at various locations.

Valley Fiesta Food and music festival held in Chinatown and Brunswick St Mall in mid-July.

'Ekka' Royal National Agricultural Show The country comes to town in early August.

Livid Annual one-day alternative rock festival in October.

Woodford Folk Festival Six days and nights between Christmas and New Year, 78km north of Brisbane in Woodford.

GAY & LESBIAN BRISBANE

While Brisbane can't compete with the prolific gay and lesbian scenes of Sydney and Melbourne, what you'll find here is quality rather than quantity.

Most action, centred in Fortitude Valley, is covered by the fortnightly *Q News* (www.qnews.com.au). *Queensland Pride*, another gay publication, takes in the whole of the state. *Dykes on Mykes* (www.queerradio.org), a radio show on Wednesday from 9pm to 11pm on FM102.1, is another source of information. Major events on the year's calendar include the **Queer Film Festival** held in late March (showcasing gay, lesbian, bisexual and transgender films and videos) and the **Brisbane Pride Festival** in June. Pride attracts up to 25,000 people every year and peaks during the parade held mid-festival. For more information on the Pride Festival, call ☎ 0418-152 801.

Brisbane's most popular gay and lesbian venue is the **Wickham Hotel** (☎ 3852 1301; Wickham St, Fortitude Valley), a classic old Victorian pub with good dance music, drag shows and dancers. The Wickham celebrates the Sydney Mardi Gras and the Pride Festival in style and grandeur.

Other good options:

Sportsman's Hotel (☎ 3831 2892; 130 Leichhardt St, Spring Hill) Another fantastically popular gay venue, with a different theme or show for each night of the week.

GPO (☎ 3252 1322; 740 Ann St, Fortitude Valley) Funky bar filled with young trendies.

Family Brisbane's best nightclub (p150).

QUEENSLAND

SLEEPING

Brisbane's hostels are generally of a high standard and will almost always have laundry facilities, a TV lounge, Internet access and plenty of information.

Apart from their proximity to the CBD, city centre hostels are close to the Roma St Transit Centre and consequently handy when arriving or leaving.

Staying in the alternative neighbourhood of Fortitude Valley and nearby New Farm puts you next door to Chinatown, Brunswick St's café strip and the city's most concentrated nightlife scene. West End, south of the river, has a decidedly chilled-out atmosphere and some great cafés and restaurants.

The **Brisbane Visitors Accommodation Service** (☎ 3236 2020; 3rd fl, Roma St Transit Centre) has a free booking service, and brochures and information on hostels and other budget options in Brisbane and up and down the coast.

CITY CENTRE

Tinbilly (☎ 1800 446 646, 3238 5888; www.tinbilly.com; 462 George St; 13-/7-/4-bed dm A$20/23/26, d & tw A$75; [air-con] [internet]) Ultramodern Tinbilly flaunts its youth with a sleek, modern interior, excellent facilities and clinical cleanliness. Each room has a bathroom and individual lockers, and is wheelchair accessible. Downstairs, a happy, helpful buzz swims around the job centre, travel agency and very popular bar.

Palace Backpackers (☎ 1800 676 340, 3211 2433; www.palacebackpackers.com.au; cnr Ann & Edward Sts; dm/s/d A$23/36/60; [internet]) This colossal backpacker institution caters to everybody: loners, partygoers and just about everyone in between in an ageing, multistorey labyrinth. The rooms are a little cramped, but there are comfy TV rooms, a huge kitchen, a job club, a tour-information desk and a great rooftop sundeck.

Other options:

Palace Backpackers Embassy (☎ 1800 676 340, 3002 5777; cnr Elizabeth & Edward Sts; dm/s/d A$23/36/60; [internet]) Smaller offshoot of Palace Backpackers.

Dorchester Self-Contained Units (☎ 3831 2967; dorchesterinn@bigpond.com; 484 Upper Edward St; s/d/tr A$70/80/90; [parking] [air-con]) Spacious, self-contained units. Great-value doubles.

PETRIE TERRACE

Brisbane City YHA (☎ 3236 1004; brisbanecity@yhaqld.org; 392 Upper Roma St; dm A$23, d & tw A$55-70; [parking] [air-con] [internet]) You can't miss this place, with its Legoland exterior, but inside it's classy, spacious and comfortable. There's a great café as well as a tour desk and provisions for the disabled. It's very popular, attracting all ages and groups.

Banana Benders Backpackers (☎ 1800 241 157, 3367 1157; www.bananabenders.com; 118 Petrie Tce; dm A$21-23, d & tw A$50; [internet]) Sporting one of Queensland's fruity mascots, this yellow-and-blue number is small, relaxed and personal. The owners can help you find work and, if you're hanging around, the one-bedroom apartments (A$130 per week) are lovely.

Also here:

Aussie Way Backpackers (☎ 3369 0711; 34 Cricket St; dm/d A$22/50) Like a homey B&B without the second B.

Brisbane City Backpackers (☎ 1800 062 572, 3211 3221; www.citybackpackers.com; 380 Upper Roma St; dm A$16-23, s/d A$45/65; P) Average dorms but heavy partying. Wheelchair accessible.

FORTITUDE VALLEY & NEW FARM

Bunk Backpackers (☎ 1800 682 865; www.bunkbrisbane.com.au; cnr Ann & Gipps Sts, Fortitude Valley; dm A$23-26, d & tw A$60; P) The pick of the bunch. Bunk is more like a snazzy hotel, with generous dorms (with bathroom), luscious mattresses, gleaming kitchens and bathrooms, and funky décor. It's extremely secure and the faaaabulous bar and swimming pool belong on a CD cover. It's also wheelchair friendly.

Tourist Guesthouse (☎ 1800 800 589, 3252 4171; www.touristguesthouse.com.au; 555 Gregory Tce, New Farm; dm/s/d/tr A$17/55/70/75; P) A short walk from Brunswick St, this hotel/hostel is scrubbed-up rustic; plenty of faded pine but mod cons too. All rooms have TVs and fridges and the doubles are excellent value.

Prince Consort Backpackers (☎ 1800 225 005, 3257 2252; www.nomadsworld.com; 230 Wickham St, Fortitude Valley; dm A$16-20, d & tw A$48-52) Conveniently perched above the Elephant & Wheelbarrow (p149), this character-laden hostel has high ceilings, big arched windows, appealing dorms and good facilities. They're super-professional here but beware the noise from downstairs.

Other recommendations:

Bowen Terrace (☎ 3254 1575; fax 3358 1488; 365 Bowen Tce, New Farm; s A$35, d with/without bathroom A$55/50) Tranquil, friendly, old guesthouse.

Globetrekkers Hostel (☎ 3358 1251; www.globetrekkers.net; 35 Balfour St, New Farm; dm/s A$19/$35, d & tw with/without bathroom A$48/44) Small and super-relaxed. Campervan friendly.

> **SPLURGE!**
>
> **Paramount Motel** (☎ 3393 1444; www.paramountmotel.com.au; 649 Main St, Kangaroo Point; s/d/tw A$70/75/80, 4-bed units from A$100; P) This modern motel is impeccably clean and has bright and spacious rooms with terrifically cheerful décor. Indulgent mod cons and extras include TVs, fully equipped kitchens and hairdryers. There's also a barbecue by the pool and the staff is friendly and helpful.

WEST END

Somewhere to Stay (☎ 1800 812 398, 3846 2858; www.somewheretostay.com.au; 45 Brighton Rd; dm A$16-25, s from A$32, d A$45-60; P) In a mammoth Queenslander, Somewhere to Stay houses a good variety of rooms, from simple, six-bed dorms to indulgent doubles with TV, bathroom and fridge. The relaxed atmosphere is fashioned by breezy balconies and spectacular city views.

CAMPING

Newmarket Gardens Caravan Park (☎ 3356 1458; stay@newmarketgardens.com.au; 199 Ashgrove Ave, Ashgrove; camp/caravan sites per 2 people from A$19/36, cabins from A$65) About 4km north of the CBD, this park has sparse tree cover but good facilities and plenty of barbecues. The cabins and vans are decent value but warm in summer. It's connected to town by bus Nos 366 and 377.

Alternatively, Globetrekkers Hostel (left) will allow travellers to camp in the backyard, in their own vehicles.

EATING

Many of Brisbane's restaurants and cafés are in neighbourhoods close to the city centre. Most cafés in the CBD close on weekends.

In the Valley you'll find inexpensive cafés and a smorgasbord of Asian flavours on offer, thanks to Chinatown. The West End is a distinctly cosmopolitan corner, with trendy cafés and eclectic cuisine. Around Paddington and Petrie Tce, Caxton St and its western extension, Given Tce, are the best hunting grounds.

City Centre

SELF-CATERING

There's a Woolworths on the corner of Edward and Elizabeth Sts. Small convenience stores and 7-Elevens are scattered throughout the CBD.

CAFÉS

Metro Cafe (☎ 3221 3181; cnr Albert & Mary Sts; breakfast around A$8, sandwiches A$4-6; breakfast & lunch Mon-Fri) Petite Metro is deservedly popular with the suit brigade, dishing up mountainous breakfasts, sizzling burgers and kebabs and dozens of fresh and tasty sandwiches.

Devoid of the lunch-hour deadline you can munch slowly at the great window seating.

Palace Café (☎ 3211 2433; cnr Ann & Edward Sts; meals A$4-9; breakfast & lunch) Attached to Palace Backpackers (p146), this café is big on quantity rather than haute cuisine. It's kind to your budget, though, and fries a mean bacon and eggs, as well as offering predictable but filling focaccias and burgers.

QUICK EATS

For cheap eats and variety you're best off heading to the food courts in the shopping centres on Queen St Mall. At the Wintergarden and Myer Centres you can dig into sushi, noodles, kebabs, focaccias, curries or roasts for A$5 to A$8. The Charlotte St end of the Elizabeth Arcade also has some excellent fast-food specialising in Asian cuisine.

RESTAURANTS

Govinda's (☎ 3210 0255; 1st fl, 99 Elizabeth St; all you can eat A$8.50, Sun feast A$5; lunch Mon-Sat, dinner Fri, Sun feast from 5pm;) Hare Krishna–run Govinda's is perfect if you like a little enlightenment with your lentils. However, you can still enjoy the vegetarian curries, snacks, salads and stews without a serving of philosophy, and the divine smells and tranquil interior is inviting to all.

Down Under Bar & Grill (☎ 3211 9277; cnr Ann & Edward Sts; mains A$8.50-11; lunch Mon-Fri, dinner daily) Beneath Palace Backpackers, standard-issue T-bones, fish and chips, grilled chicken and veggie patties are all served in sizable quantities here. Nightly specials include the odd adventure like satay or curry. You'll want to eat early before the tables turn to platforms of drunken revelry (see opposite).

Two Irish theme pubs with good fare:

Gilhooley's (☎ 3229 0672; 124 Albert St; mains A$8-16; lunch & dinner)

Irish Murphy's (☎ 3221 4377; cnr George & Elizabeth Sts; mains A$9-16; lunch & dinner)

Further south down George St, is **Artisans on the Yard** (George St, QUT campus; meals A$6-10; lunch Mon-Fri), a chilled student hang-out serving good café fare.

Fortitude Valley & New Farm

SELF-CATERING

McWhirters Marketplace (cnr Brunswick & Wickham Sts, Fortitude Valley) There's a great produce market with fresh fruit and vegies.

CAFÉS

Fatboys Cafe (☎ 3252 3789; 323 Brunswick St, Fortitude Valley; dishes around A$15; breakfast, lunch & dinner Mon-Wed, 24hr Thu-Sun) This trendy café fills its crevices with coffee-sipping 20-somethings without being overly sceney. The menu boasts fairly standard café fare – pastas, paninis and salads – but it's the ambience that most come to ingest.

Cosmopolitan Coffee (☎ 3252 4179; 322 Brunswick St, Fortitude Valley; mains around A$15; breakfast, lunch & dinner) Pizzas, pastas and calzones are the specialities at this elongated café and they're good, particularly in the wee hours. Copious choices suit all palates and it also serves fresh salads and designer breads… oh, and coffee.

Veg Out (☎ 3852 2668; McWhirters Arcade, cnr Brunswick & Wickham Sts, Fortitude Valley; dishes A$8-14; breakfast & lunch) This teeny canteen-style café cooks up super-healthy organic and vegetarian nosh, mostly with Asian overtones.

QUICK EATS

Wok on Inn (☎ 3254 2546; 728 Brunswick St; dishes around A$8; lunch & dinner) A popular noodle bar cooking up hot and tasty noodle mains and soups, with a regular A$6.50 lunch special.

Chinatown hosts several hole-in-the-wall cheap and quick eating options, usually serving predictable but tasty Chinese dishes. Expect to pay around A$8 for a good feed.

RESTAURANTS

Vietnamese Restaurant (☎ 3252 4112; 194 Wickham St, Fortitude Valley; mains A$10-13; lunch & dinner;) Perennially popular and a local favourite. Excellent Vietnamese food in every carnivorous version imaginable (including scallops and squid) is served along with a chunky selection of vegetarian dishes. The shrimp-and-pork roll starters are divine, as is any dish containing the word 'sizzling'.

Garuva Hidden Tranquility Restaurant & Bar (☎ 3216 0124; 324 Wickham St, Fortitude Valley; mains around A$20; dinner;) Dining here is quite an experience. Garuva's rainforested foyer leads to tables with cushioned seating, concealed by walls of fluttering white silk. Choices like Turkish shark and Chinese roast beef, along with dim lighting, smooth soundtracks and lulled voices create a debaucherous air. Fantastic!

Superbowl Chinese Restaurant (☎ 3257 2188; 185 Wickham Tce, Fortitude Valley; mains A$10-15; lunch &

dinner; ☒) Not a football in sight but the exhaustive menu boasts more authentic Chinese cuisine than most. Chef specialities include *congee* (rice porridge), Peking chicken, tom yum clay pots and spicy salt-and-pepper flounder. The hot pots here are fantastic.

Taj Mahal (☎ 3254 2388; 722 Brunswick St, New Farm; mains A$12-15; ⏲ dinner; ☒) Head here for a curry fix.

West End

CAFÉS

Jazzy Cat Cafe (☎ 3864 2544; 56 Mollison St; mains A$15-20; ⏲ breakfast, lunch & dinner) Set in a beautifully restored Queenslander, Jazzy Cat is a wee warren of dining nooks, bohemian vibes and friendly staff. The menu is imaginative and amid the risottos, Asian salads and pastas are tofu steaks, as well as those of the cow variety.

Satchmos (☎ 3846 7746; 185 Boundary St; meals A$5-12; ⏲ breakfast, lunch & dinner) True to its namesake, Satchmos oozes blues and jazz and dining here is always like a long, lazy Sunday breakfast. There's a good all-day A$5.90 big breakfast on the contemporary menu, and live music from Thursday to Sunday.

Three Monkeys Coffee House (☎ 3844 6045; 58 Mollison St; dishes A$10-18; ⏲ breakfast, lunch & dinner; ☒) You can soak up the pseudo-Moroccan décor and ambience here as you munch away on focaccias, paninis, pizzas, salads, nachos…actually, it's a long menu so the list goes on. Delectable coffee and cakes.

Other recommendations:

Espressohead (☎ 3844 8324; 69 Boundary St; meals A$7-10; ⏲ breakfast & lunch) Chilled cube of a café, great coffee.

Sol Breads (☎ 3255 1225; 27 Vulture St; snacks A$2-4; ⏲ breakfast & lunch) Organic breads, cakes and snacks.

SPLURGE!

Sultans Kitchen (☎ 3368 2194; 163 Given Tce, Paddington; dishes A$15-20; ⏲ dinner) If Indian food is your weakness then you must splurge at this award winner. The service is impeccable and flavours from all corners of the subcontinent are represented on the menu. The nine types of naan are a meal unto themselves and you can grab your vino from Paddo Tavern's bottleshop down the road.

Paddington

Inexpensive dining options are more limited in this part of town but **Kookaburra Café** (☎ 3369 2400; 280 Given Tce; meals A$10-25; ⏲ lunch & dinner) serves good grills with a distinctly Aussie twist. Its pizzas have won awards so bring an empty tum. Alternatively, **Paddo Tavern** (☎ 3369 0044; 186 Given Tce; dishes A$8-15; ⏲ lunch & dinner; ☒) has a good bistro, and an inviting patio out front; see also review under Drinking, below.

DRINKING

Brisbane's watering holes are generally situated around the CBD, the Valley, and Petrie Tce. The CBD, however, is often dead on weekends, when most punters head for the more lively inner suburbs.

Down Under Bar & Grill (☎ 3211 9277; cnr Ann & Edward Sts, City) This travellers' haunt is not just a place for a good feed. It also heaves on a nightly basis – things usually start with a few quiet pints before dissolving into a loud and beery mash, by which stage you may feel inclined to add your mark to the graffiti-covered walls.

Elephant & Wheelbarrow (☎ 1800 225 005, 3257 2252; 230 Wickham St, Fortitude Valley; ☒) This cavernous English theme pub may not mirror a Putney local but the ales are good and the atmosphere positively festive. There are plenty of snugs and tables, which fill to bursting on weekends.

Paddo Tavern (☎ 3369 0044; 186 Given Tce, Paddington; ☒) The clientele is local but the décor in this huge pub is kitschy, Wild West saloon bar. An odd marriage, sure, but the punters lap it up along with icy beers, footy telecasts and pool tables. Great beer balcony and Sunday sessions.

Dooley's (☎ 3252 4344; 394 Brunswick St, Fortitude Valley; ☒) Thick with Irish charm, this theme pub is unpretentious and inviting. There's a good combination of local and Irish liquids and a yawning pool hall.

Press Club (☎ 3852 4000; 339 Brunswick St, Fortitude Valley; ☒) This classy bar throbs with heavenly beats in an underworld setting, with minimal lighting, stylish goth décor and plenty of private loungey corners. The soundtrack is courtesy of live DJs and the atmosphere is more chilled-out drinking than beer vacuuming.

Ric's Café Bar (☎ 3854 1772; 321 Brunswick St, Fortitude Valley) Found in the Brunswick St Mall,

Ric's has live bands downstairs, DJs in the lounge bar upstairs, and even space for a bit of quiet conversation at the tables on the street.

Other options:

Caxton Hotel (☎ 3369 5544; 38 Caxton St, Petrie Terrace) Hot on weekends with dance anthems and flashy young things looking to pick up.

Tinbilly Bar & Café (www.tinbilly.com; 462 George St) The ground floor of Tinbilly hostel is all modern chrome and TV screens; see Tinbilly, p146.

Birdee Num Num (☎ 3257 3644; cnr Ann & Gipps Sts) Bunk Backpackers' (see p147) swanky bar appeals to travellers and students.

CLUBBING

Brisbane is proud of its nightclub scene and offers more than a couple of venues at which to dance. Most are open Thursday to Sunday nights, are vigilant about ID and charge between A$5 and A$10 for entry.

Family (☎ 3852 5000; 8 McLachlan St, Fortitude Valley) Voted Australia's best nightclub two years in a row, Family exhilarates dance junkies every weekend with four levels of the latest sounds. Elite DJs from home and away frequently grace the decks, including the likes of Fergie, Don Diablo and Carl Kennedy.

Empire (☎ 3852 1216; 339 Brunswick St, Fortitude Valley) Things get going at this funky club after 9pm on weekends, when DJs upstairs in the Moon Bar serve drum and base, and swanky lithe things mingle in the sceney Corner Bar downstairs.

Monastery (☎ 3257 7081; 621 Ann St, Fortitude Valley) Expect house, techno and break beat in this converted church in the Valley. Friday night is generally heaving.

More club action:

Source (697 Ann St, Fortitude Valley) R & B, live DJs, rap and open mike on Sunday.

R-Bar (☎ 3220 1477; 235 Edward St, Fortitude Valley) Dance tunes from Wednesday to Sunday.

For information on gay-friendly clubs, see p146.

ENTERTAINMENT

Brisbane pulls all the international bands heading to Oz and its clubs are nationally renowned. There's also plenty of theatre. Pick up the free entertainment papers *Time Off* (www.timeoff.com.au), *Rave* (www.ravemag.com.au) and *Scene* (www.sceneonline.com.au) from any café in the Valley. Another good source of information is the website www.brisbane247.com.

Cinemas

Greater Union (☎ 3027 9999; Level A, Myer Centre, Queen St Mall; P) Mainstream blockbusters.

Hoyts Regent Theatre (☎ 3027 9999; 107 Queen St Mall; P) Gorgeous old cinema.

Dendy Cinema (☎ 3211 3244; 346 George St) Art-house and indie flicks.

Palace Centro (☎ 3852 4488; 39 James St) Art-house films.

Live Music

Brisbane's love affair with live music began long before three lanky local lads sang harmonic ditties and called themselves the Bee Gees. In recent years successful acts including, Regurgitator, Powderfinger, Pete Murray (by Queensland default) and the soulful George, embody Brisbane's musical evolution. Get in early to see history in the making. Cover charges start at around A$6.

Zoo (☎ 3854 1381; 711 Ann St, Fortitude Valley) The long queues here start early for a good reason and whether you're into hard rock or electronic soundscapes, Zoo has a gig for you. Musos rate this as an excellent venue and it is one of your best chances to hear some raw, local talent.

Indie Temple (☎ 3852 2851; 210 Wickham St, Fortitude Valley) The emphasis is on alternative music and rock at this student stomping ground. Live music alternates with theme nights. It's also becoming the fashionable small venue for big international acts, so keep an eye out.

Tongue & Groove (☎ 3846 0334; 63 Hardgrave Rd, West End;) This funky little venue hosts everything from reggae and blues to dance beats from Tuesday to Sunday.

Jazz & Blues Bar (☎ 3238 2222; ground fl, Holiday Inn, Roma St;) It's an older crowd here but if you're a sucker for jazz and blues, this is Brisbane's major venue for local and international acts in this genre. Maestros take to the stage Wednesday to Saturday.

Mustang Bar (☎ 3257 4493; 633 Ann St, Fortitude Valley) Live music Wednesday to Sunday for the 'fiscally challenged backpacker and student'.

Sport

You can see interstate cricket matches and international test cricket at the **Brisbane Cricket Ground** (Gabba; ☎ 3008 6166; www.thegabba.org.au; P) in Woolloongabba, just south of

Kangaroo Point. The cricket season runs from October to March.

During the other half of the year, rugby league is the big spectator sport. The Brisbane Broncos play their home games at the **ANZ/Queen Elizabeth II Stadium** in Nathan.

Once dominated by Victorian teams, the Australian Football League (AFL) has been mastered by the Brisbane Lions, after they won the flag in 2001, 2002 and 2003. You can watch them kick the ball and some southern butt at a home game at the **Gabba** between March and September.

Theatre

Performing Arts Centre (☎ 3840 7444; www.qpac.com.au; Queensland Cultural Centre, Stanley St, South Bank; P ♿) The centre features concerts, plays, dance performances and film screenings in its three venues on this one site.

Brisbane Powerhouse (☎ 3358 8600; 119 Lamington St; P ♿) Housed in a stylish, modernised brick building, this progressive little theatre puts on an ambitious programme of plays, music and dance.

Other theatre options:

Metro Arts Centre (☎ 3221 1527; 109 Edward St; P ♿)
Gardens Theatre (☎ 3864 4455; QUT, George St)
Brisbane Arts Theatre (☎ 3369 2344; 210 Petrie Tce; P ♿)

SHOPPING

Several outdoor megastores are in a row along Wickham St in Fortitude Valley, south of Gipps St. It's possible to hire camping gear from a couple of them.

Aboriginal art can be found at **Queensland Aboriginal Creations** (☎ 3224 5730; Little Stanley St).

On weekends the funky Valley Market, with a diverse collection of crafts, clothes and junk, is held in the Brunswick St Mall. The **Crafts Village Market** (Stanley St Plaza) at South Bank has a great range of clothing, arts and crafts from Friday to Sunday.

Every Sunday (8am to 4pm), the carnival-style Riverside Centre Market and Eagle St Pier Market host over 150 craft stalls (glassware, weaving, leatherwork etc).

GETTING THERE & AWAY

Air

You can fly into Brisbane from several international destinations and from all over Australia. Low-end one-way fares at the time of writing started at: Sydney A$80, Melbourne A$120, Cairns A$110, Adelaide A$160, Perth A$280, Alice Springs A$260. (One-off specials can be cheaper than these prices.) Alliance Airlines and Macair fly within Queensland.

Alliance Airlines (☎ 1300 130 092; www.allianceairlines.com.au)
Jetstar (☎ 13 15 38; www.jetstar.com.au)
Macair (☎ 13 13 13; www.macair.com.au)
Qantas (☎ 13 13 13; www.qantas.com.au; 247 Adelaide St)
Virgin Blue (☎ 13 67 89; www.virginblue.com.au)

Bus

Brisbane's **Roma St Transit Centre** (Roma St), about 500m west of the city centre, is the main terminus and booking office for all long-distance buses and trains.

The bus companies have booking desks on the 3rd level of the centre. **McCafferty's/Greyhound** (☎ 13 20 30, 13 14 99; www.mccaffertys.com.au) operates buses between Brisbane and Sydney (A$100, 16 hours, five daily) and Melbourne (A$175, 24 hours, four daily). Services north to Cairns (A$200, 28½ hours, five daily) stop at Noosa Heads (A$19, three hours), Hervey Bay (A$50, five hours), Rockhampton (A$65, 11 hours), Mackay (A$130, 16 hours) and Townsville (A$170, 23 hours). **Premier Motor Service** (☎ 13 34 10; www.premierms.com.au) has all the same services as McCafferty's/Greyhound, but generally for a few dollars less.

McCafferty's/Greyhound also connects Brisbane with Darwin (A$430, 47 hours, two daily).

Car

Car parks in the CBD charge anything from A$7 to A$25 a day and the parking inspectors are merciless about the two-hour limits.

Car-rental agencies in the city:

ABC Integra (☎ 1800 067 414; 3620 3200; www.abcintegra.com.au; 398 St Pauls Tce, Fortitude Valley)
Britz (☎ 1800 331 454; www.britz.com; 647 Kingsford Smith Dr, Eagle Farm)
Travellers Auto Barn (☎ 1800 674 374; www.travellersautobarn.com.au; 2 Maud St, Newstead) Good spot to sell or buy a car.
Wicked Campers (☎ 1800 246 869, 3257 2170; www.wickedcampers.com.au; 79 McLachlan St, Fortitude Valley) Cheap campervan rental.

Train

New South Wales' **CountryLink** (☎ 13 22 32; www.countrylink.nsw.gov.au) has a daily XPT (express

QUEENSLAND

passenger train) service between Brisbane and Sydney (A$120, 14 hours, daily).

Queensland Rail (☎ 1300 131 722; www.traveltrain.qr.com.au) operates numerous services throughout the state. Concessions are available to students with a valid International Student Identity Card (ISIC) card.

Main train routes in the state:

Brisbane to Rockhampton On the *Tilt Train* (economy A$95, seven hours, three weekly).
Brisbane to Townsville On the *Sunlander* (economy adult/student A$165/85, 24 hours, four weekly).
Brisbane to Cairns On the *Sunlander* (economy adult/student A$190/95, 32 hours, four weekly).

GETTING AROUND

Boat

Brisbane's nippy blue CityCat catamarans run from the University of Queensland in the west to Bretts Wharf in the east, and back. They leave every 20 to 30 minutes between 5.50am and 10.30pm. Many of the stops are wheelchair accessible.

Inner City Ferries operate ferries that zigzag across the river between North Quay (near Victoria Bridge) and Mowbray Park. Services run till about 9pm Sunday to Thursday and until about 11.30pm on Friday and Saturday. There are also several cross-river ferries; most useful is the Eagle St Pier to Kangaroo Point (Thornton St) service, as it's the quickest way to access Kangaroo Point from the CBD. Cross-river/entire route fares cost A$1.80/3.80.

Bus

The Loop – a free bus that circles the city area – stopping at QUT, Queen St Mall, City Hall, Central Station and Riverside – runs every 10 minutes on weekdays between 7am and 6pm.

The underground bus station in Queen St Mall's Myer Centre is the main stop for local buses. You can also catch buses from the colour-coded stops along Adelaide St, between George and Edward Sts.

Routes are priced by the sector. Most of the inner suburbs fall into Zone 1 (A$1.80) and Zone 2 (A$2.60).

Buses run every 10 to 20 minutes Monday to Friday, from 5am till about 6pm, and with the same frequency on Saturday morning (starting at 6am). Services are less frequent at other times, and cease at 7pm Sunday and midnight on other days.

Public Transport

For all city bus, train and ferry information, ring the **TransInfo Service** (☎ 13 12 30; www.transinfo.qld.gov.au; 🕒 6am-9pm). Bus and ferry information is also available at the Brisbane Visitor Information Centre and the **Queensland Rail Travel Centre** (Central station, Ann St; 🕒 7am-5pm Mon-Fri, 9am-12.30pm Sat).

The following tickets can save you quite a bit of money:

Day Rover ticket (A$8.40) Unlimited travel on buses, ferries and CityCats.
Off-Peak Saver (A$4.60) Valid on buses, ferries and CityCats between 9am and 3.30pm and after 7pm Monday to Friday, and on buses only all weekend.
Ten-Trip Saver (Zone 1 A$14)
South East Explorer ticket (A$8.60) Valid on buses, ferries, CityCats and Citytrain services.

Taxi

You can usually hail a taxi with ease in most parts of central Brisbane and its neighbouring districts. Two of the main operators in Brisbane are **Black & White** (☎ 13 10 08) and **Yellow Cab Co** (☎ 13 19 24).

Train

The fast Citytrain network has seven lines, which run as far as Gympie North (for the Sunshine Coast) and Nerang and Robina (for the Gold Coast). Trains go through Roma St, Central and Brunswick St stations. A journey in the central area, which includes Central station, Roma St Transit Centre, South Brisbane and Vulture St, costs A$2.

AROUND BRISBANE

The belt of holiday destinations around Brisbane offers travellers everything from bungy jumping to dolphin feeding. If you're after fruit-picking work, try heading southwest of Brisbane to the town of Stanthorpe. But if you'd rather inhale fresh sea air than engage in hard yakka (and who wouldn't), Moreton Bay, at the mouth of the Brisbane River, is reckoned to have about 365 islands, and a couple of these prove to be excellent day trips – or longer – from the city.

Activities

Surfing and 4WDing are the big activities on North Stradbroke Island, while nearby Moreton Island offers some of the best hiking and diving opportunities south of the reef. The Gold Coast also has some fine surfing beaches, but the big activities in Surfers Paradise take bungy jumping to new and creative levels.

STANTHORPE & THE GRANITE BELT

☎ 07

South of Warwick is the Granite Belt, an elevated plateau of the Great Dividing Range.

This 'high country' is renowned for its boutique wineries, but for backpackers the real allure is the abundance of fruit- and vegetable-picking work around Stanthorpe from October to mid-June (provided there has been plenty of rainfall during the year).

Information

Stanthorpe visitors centre (☎ 1800 060 877, 4681 2057; Leslie St; 8.30am-5pm)

Sights

About 26km south of Stanthorpe, a sealed road turns off the highway, leading 9km east to the **Girraween National Park** (visitors centre ☎ 4684 5157), which features towering granite boulders surrounded by eucalypt forests. Wildlife abounds, and the park adjoins Bald Rock National Park over the border in New South Wales. There are two good **camping grounds** (camp sites per person A$4) in Girraween, plus numerous walking tracks.

Sleeping

Backpackers of Queensland (☎ 0429-810 998; www.backpackersofqueensland.com.au; 80 High St, Stanthorpe; dm per night/week A$25/125;) Modern, comfortable stone cabins with good facilities. During fruit-picking season it caters only to working backpackers who stay by the week.

Other recommendations:

Stanthorpe Backpackers, Top of the Town & Caravan Village (☎ 4681 4888; www.stanthorpe-backpackers.com; dm A$20)

Country Style Tourist Park (☎ 4683 4358; New England Hwy, Glen Aplin; camp sites per 2 people with camp kitchen A$16, caravan sites per 2 people A$14, cabins A$65)

Getting There & Away

McCafferty's/Greyhound (☎ 13 20 30) has services between Brisbane and Stanthorpe (A$70, five hours, twice daily).

NORTH STRADBROKE ISLAND

☎ 07

Popularly known as Straddie, this lovely sand island is one of the largest of its kind in the world and is just a 30-minute ferry ride from Cleveland, 30km south of Brisbane. The surf beaches here are excellent and there are some great walking tracks.

Orientation

There are three small settlements on the island: Dunwich, Amity Point and Point Lookout, all grouped around the northern end.

Hugging the eastern side, **Eighteen Mile Beach** is open to 4WD vehicles and campers, and the island's north is littered with walking tracks and old 4WD roads.

Except for the beach, the southern part of the island is closed to visitors because of sand mining.

Information

Stradbroke Island visitors centre (☎ 3409 9555; www.stradbroketourism.com; 8.30am-5pm Mon-Fri, to 3pm Sat & Sun) About 200m from the ferry terminal in Dunwich.

Sights & Activities

Straddie's most obvious appeal is a string of beautiful beaches. At **Point Lookout**, there's a series of points and bays along the headland, and endless stretches of white sand. **Cylinder Beach** and **Amity Point** generally provide calm swimming opportunities, while **Main Beach** churns some good swells and breaks for surfing. You can hire surfboards and bodyboards from several places; kayak hire is around A$20/50 per hour/day, surfboards A$15/40 and bodyboards A$10/30.

Straddie Adventures (☎ 3409 8414; Point Lookout) offers sea-kayaking trips (including snorkelling stops for A$35) around Straddie, and sand-boarding (A$25), which is like snowboarding, except on sand.

Stradbroke Island Scuba Centre (☎ 3409 8888; www.stradbrokeislandscuba.com.au; 1 East Coast Rd, Point Lookout) offers snorkelling trips (two-hour/Open Water Certificate course for A$60/350).

Awesome Wicked Wild (☎ 3409 8045) operates tours of Amity Point and the lakes in 6m glass-bottomed canoes (half-/full day A$35/50).

You can traverse the island by 4WD, or better yet on foot, using the 20km of bitumen road and dirt-track loops. Along the way you'll encounter some of Straddie's

QUEENSLAND

idyllic swimming holes, including the beautiful freshwater **Blue Lake**, reached by a sandy 4WD track off the road to Dunwich, or by a pleasant 2.7km walking track through the forest.

Alternatively you can dip into the glassy waters of **Brown Lake**, about 3km along the Blue Lake road from Dunwich.

Sleeping & Eating

Stradbroke Island Guesthouse (☎ 3409 8888; www.stradbrokeislandscuba.com.au; 1 East Coast Rd; dm A$22, d & tw A$50) By the beach in Point Lookout, this large, clean hostel has excellent facilities including bike hire for A$10/15 for a half-/full day.

Straddie Hostel (☎ 3409 8979; 76 Mooloomba Rd; dm/d A$17/40) Found about halfway between Main and Cylinder Beach, this hostel is very relaxed and hires surfboards.

There are six **camping grounds** (camp sites per person from A$6, foreshore camping per person A$3.80) on Straddie. The scenic Adder Rock and Thankful Rest Camping Areas overlook lovely Home Beach, and Cylinder Beach Camping Area sits right on popular Cylinder Beach. Book in advance through the visitors centre.

Point Lookout has a couple of general stores selling groceries but it's worth bringing supplies. Note that few places to eat are open later than 8pm.

For a cheap chicken parmigiana, duck into the **Point Lookout Bowls Club** (☎ 3409 8182; East Coast Rd, Point Lookout; meals A$5-15). Alternatively, **Stonefish Café** (☎ 3409 8549; cnr Mooloomba Rd & Mintee St; mains A$15-20; breakfast & lunch) dishes up fancier fare and there's a small deli next door.

Getting There & Around

Citytrain (☎ 13 12 30; www.transinfo.qld.gov.au) services travel from Brisbane's Central or Roma St stations to Cleveland station (A$3.80, one hour, every 30 minutes), which is the gateway to the island. Buses meet the trains at the station (A$0.90). From here **Stradbroke Ferries** (☎ 3286 2666; www.stradbrokeferries.com.au) runs a water taxi to Dunwich (A$13 return, 45 minutes, roughly hourly 6am to 6pm) and a less frequent vehicle ferry (vehicle including passengers A$90, 5.30am to 6.30pm)

The **Stradbroke Flyer** (☎ 3826 1964; www.flyer.com.au) operates a catamaran (return A$13, 45 minutes, roughly hourly) to One Mile Jetty, 1.5km north of central Dunwich.

Local buses (☎ 3409 7151) meet the ferries at Dunwich and One Mile Jetty, and run across to Point Lookout (A$9). The last bus to Dunwich leaves Point Lookout at about 6pm. If you miss it, there's the **Stradbroke Cab Service** (☎ 3409 9800).

MORETON ISLAND

North of Stradbroke, Moreton Island comes a close second to Fraser Island for excellent sand-driving and wilderness, yet sees far fewer visitors. It's a harder slog to get here and around, but the prolific birdlife, isolation and spectacular diving opportunities are worthy magnets.

Orientation & Information

Apart from a few rocky headlands, Moreton Island is all sand. There are no paved roads, but 4WD vehicles can travel along beaches and a few cross-island tracks – seek local advice about tides and creek crossings. You can get **EPA** (Environmental Protection Authority; www.epa.qld.gov.au) maps from the vehicle-ferry offices or the **rangers** (☎ 3408 2710). Vehicle permits for the island cost A$30 and are available through the ferry operators or from EPA offices.

Tangalooma, halfway down the western side of the island, is a popular tourist resort sited at an old whaling station. The only other settlements, all on the west coast, are **Bulwer** near the northwestern tip, **Cowan Cowan** between Bulwer and Tangalooma, and **Kooringal** near the southern tip.

Sights & Activities

You can spend several days exploring the island by foot via the good network of tracks and decommissioned 4WD roads. Towering at 280m, **Mt Tempest** is the world's highest coastal sand hill and it's worth making the strenuous trek to the summit, about 3km inland from Eagers Creek.

Off the west coast the deliberately sunk **Tangalooma Wrecks** provide stunning snorkelling and diving.

One of Moreton Island's biggest attractions is the **wild-dolphin feeding**, which takes place at the Tangalooma resort each evening at around sunset.

Several tour companies make it all easy for you, with packages including accommodation, 4WD touring, sand-boarding, kayaking and snorkelling.

Moreton Bay Escapes (☎ 1300 559 355, 3893 1671; www.moretonbayescapes.com.au) Three-day, two-night tours including meals A$320.
Gibren Expeditions (☎ 1300 559 355; www.gibrenexpeditions.com.au) Two-/three-day tours from A$210/250.

Sleeping

There are nine EPA **camping grounds** (camp sites per person A$4) on the island (including four on the beach), all with water, toilets and cold showers. For information and camping permits, contact the **EPA** (☎ 3227 8185; 160 Ann St, Brisbane) or the **ranger** (☎ 3408 2710) at False Patch Wrecks, near Tangalooma.

Getting There & Around

A number of ferries run from the mainland:
Combie Trader (☎ 3203 6399; www.moreton-island.com; vehicle plus 4 passengers/pedestrian A$150/35; departs 8am, 1pm & 5.30pm Sun, 8am & 1pm Mon, 8am Wed-Thu, 8am, 1pm & 7pm Fri, 6am & 11am Sat) Sails between Scarborough and Bulwer.
Moreton Venture (☎ 3895 1000; www.moretonventure.com.au; return vehicle plus 2 passengers/pedestrians A$130/30; departs 8.30am daily, plus 6.30pm Fri & 2.30pm Sun) Travels from the Port of Brisbane to Tangalooma.
Tangalooma Flyer (☎ 3268 6333; www.tangalooma.com/tangalooma/transport; day/overnight trip A$38/64; departs 10am) A bus (A$5) departs from Roma St Transit Centre (9am) to meet this catamaran. Book in advance.

You can hire 4WDs to explore the island from **Moreton Island 4WD Hire** (☎ 3410 1338; www.moretonisland.com.au) in Bulwer, from A$125 per day.

GOLD COAST

☎ 07 / pop 376,500

Like a big, tacky, wild ride, the Gold Coast welcomes you with a blinding and unapologetic smack of tourist development oozing from its theme parks, shopping malls, condominium clusters and other artificial attractions. It turns into party central for thousands of school leavers between mid-November and mid-December for an event locally known as Schoolies Week. Although it's generally a lot of fun for those celebrating, it can be hell for everyone else. Right, now that the introductions are out of the way you'll know to leave your culture hats behind and be prepared for pure hedonism.

The party's epicentre is Surfers Paradise (known locally as Surfers), where the candy-coloured neon is rivalled only by the hue of the cocktails and liquor waiting on every corner. The bonanza of shopping malls, eateries, drinking holes and dizzying fun sucks you into its relentless spin and spits you back out exhausted, but with more than a couple of entries for your diary.

The Gold Coast also offers some excellent surfing breaks and a little-visited but beautiful hinterland, less than 30km from the beach. Two of the national parks in this area – Lamington and Springbrook – are among Queensland's best.

Orientation

Southport is a quiet residential spread and the Gold Coast's entry point from Brisbane. Just south, the Gold Coast Hwy pummels

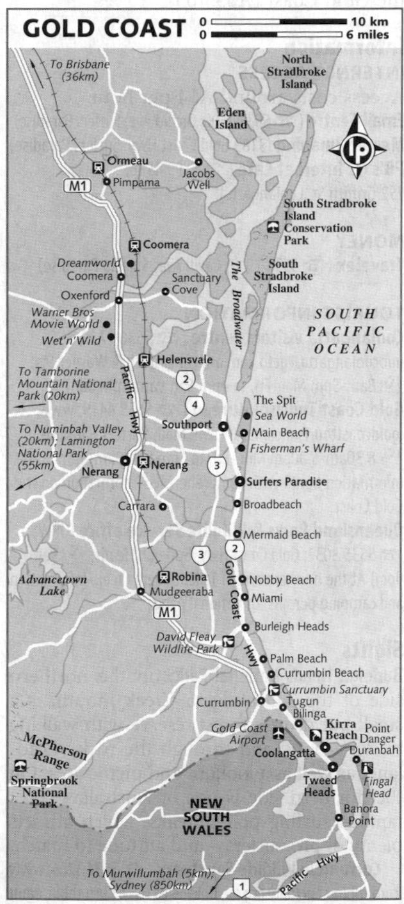

through the heart of Surfers, an area within easy reach of the Gold Coast's theme parks.

Further south the construction diminishes in size and grandeur and there are some excellent surfing breaks at Burleigh Heads and Kirra Beach. The twin towns of Coolangatta (where the airport is located) and Tweed Heads on the NSW border mark the southern end of the Gold Coast.

Gold Coast Tourist Shuttle (☎ 1300 655 655; 5574 5111) provides transfers (one way/return A$14/24) from the Gold Coast airport to points up and down the coast. Otherwise, hop on bus No 1 or 1A for central Surfers (A$4.50/9).

Coachtrans (☎ 3238 4700) operates the Airporter bus between Brisbane airport and the Gold Coast (A$35/65).

Information

INTERNET ACCESS

Access costs around A$4 per hour.

Email Centre (☎ 5538 7500; Orchid Ave, Surfers Paradise)
Mercari Imaging (3189 Gold Coast Hwy, Surfers Paradise)
PB's OZ Internet Cafe (☎ 5599 4536; 152 Griffith St, Coolangatta)

MONEY

Travelex (☎ 5531 7917; Cavill Ave, Surfers Paradise)

TOURIST INFORMATION

Coolangatta visitors centre (☎ 5536 7765; infocoolangatta@gctb.com.au; cnr Griffith & Warner Sts; 🕑 8am-5pm Mon-Fri, to 4pm Sat, 9am-1pm Sun)

Gold Coast Tourism Bureau (☎ 5538 4419; www.goldcoasttourism.com.au; Cavill Mall, Surfers Paradise; 🕑 8.30am-5.30pm Mon-Fri, to 5pm Sat, 9am-4pm Sun) Information booth with comprehensive information on the Gold Coast.

Queensland Parks & Wildlife Service office (QPWS; ☎ 5535 3032; Gold Coast Hwy, Burleigh Heads; 🕑 9am-4pm) At the northern end of Tallebudgera Creek. Information and camping permits for national parks.

Sights

Burleigh Heads National Park, on the northern side of the Tallebudgera Creek mouth, is a small but diverse forest reserve with walking tracks around and through the rocky headland, as well as a lookout and picnic area. On the northern side is one of Australia's most famous surfing point breaks, which attracts plenty of pro-surfers – and attitude to match.

Currumbin Wildlife Sanctuary (☎ 5534 1266; www.currumbin-sanctuary.org.au; Gold Coast Hwy, Currumbin; adult A$22; 🕑 8am-5pm) provides one of your best opportunities (outside of going walkabout) to see Australian native animals in bush and rainforest habitats. Tree kangaroos, koalas, emus, wombats and other cute and fuzzies are joined daily by flocks of brilliantly coloured rainbow lorikeets, which take great delight in eating out of your hand during the daily 8am feeding frenzy. To get here catch Surfside bus No 1 or 1A from Surfers.

David Fleay Wildlife Park (☎ 5576 2411; West Burleigh Rd; adult A$13; 🕑 9am-5pm) is also home to a wide collection of Australian fauna, with an emphasis on rare and endangered species. QPWS rangers give informative talks throughout the day. To get here, take the Surfside bus No 1 or 1A.

Among the highlights of the Gold Coast hinterland is the 600m-high plateau of **Tamborine Mountain**, on a northern spur of the McPherson Range. Patches of the area's original forests remain in nine small national parks. There are gorges, spectacular cascades like **Witches Falls**, **Cameron Falls** and **Cedar Creek Falls** near North Tamborine, and walking tracks to various lookouts with great views over the coast.

In the hinterland's southwest, **Springbrook National Park** is perched atop a 900m-high plateau, which, like the rest of the McPherson Range, is a remnant of the huge volcano that once centred on Mt Warning in NSW. The village of Springbrook is balanced right on the edge of the plateau, with numerous waterfalls (when there's enough rain) that tumble down more than 100m to the coastal plain below. There are several

BREAKFAST AGAIN, ANYONE?

Almost a rite of passage in Surfers is betting your life on the strength of a giant rubber band at **Banzai Bungey** (☎ 07-5526 7611; Cypress Ave; jumps from A$99). But wait! At the same location there are new and inventive ways to revisit your breakfast. The **Flycoaster** (☎ 07-5539 0474; per person A$39) swings you like a pendulum after you've been released from a hoist 20m up. **Sling Shot** (☎ 07-5570 2700; per person A$30) catapults you into the air at around 160km and **Vomatron** (per person A$30) warns you from the get go and whisks you around in a giant arc at about 120km an hour.

GOLD COAST THEME PARKS

If it weren't for the bush you could be forgiven for thinking you'd landed in Los Angeles. Just northwest of Surfers, four American-style theme parks summon you with thrilling rides and entertaining shows. Discount tickets are available at most hostels and tourist offices on the Gold Coast and the 3-Park Super Pass (A$155) covers entry to Sea World, Movie World and Wet'n'Wild.

Dreamworld (☎ 07-5588 1111; www.dreamworld.com.au; Pacific Hwy, Coomera; adult A$60; 9.30am-5pm) This is thrill-ride central, with options like the Giant Drop – a terminal-velocity machine where you free fall from 38 storeys. There are also wildlife shows and the interactive tiger show, one of only two in the world.

Sea World (☎ 07-5588 2222; www.seaworld.com.au; Sea World Dr, Main Beach; adult A$60; 10am-5pm) Not surprisingly, this park's theme is aquatic and apart from the rollercoasters and waterslides, there are numerous dolphin, sea-lion and other marine animal shows throughout the day. Two polar bears are the resident celebrities here.

Warner Bros Movie World (☎ 07-5573 8485; www.movieworld.com.au; Pacific Hwy, Oxenford; adult A$60; 9.30am-5pm) Mingle with your favourite Loony Tunes characters here or take the movie-ride of the moment. Other attractions include stunt shows and movie-themed whizzing rides.

Wet'n'Wild (☎ 07-5573 2255; www.wetnwild.com.au; Pacific Hwy, Oxenford; adult A$35; 10am-9pm summer, to 5pm winter) If the beach is too sedate, this colossal water-sports park offers plenty of creative ways to get wet. You can slippery-slide down inventive waterslides, dip into gigantic pools or zoom down white-water rapids on a giant rubber ring at 70km/h.

places where you can get the giddy thrill of leaning right out over the edge, including **Purling Brook Falls**, near the Gwongorella Picnic Area on Springbrook Rd, and **Best of All Lookout**, which is reached via Lyrebird Ridge Rd.

West of Springbrook, the 200-sq-km **Lamington National Park** covers much of the McPherson Range and adjoins the Border Ranges National Park in NSW. The park includes most of the spectacular Lamington Plateau, which reaches 1100m in places, as well as densely forested valleys below. There are beautiful gorges, caves and waterfalls and lots of wildlife.

Companies offering tours here from Brisbane include **Brisbackpacker Tours** (☎ 07-3342 7813; www.brisbackpacker.com), **Rob's Rainforest Explorer** (☎ 0409-496 607; http://homepage.powerup.com.au/~frogbus7) and **Bushwacker Ecotours** (☎ 07-5520 7238; www.bushwacker-ecotours.com.au). All charge around A$60 to A$80 for a day tour including lunch. See right for tours from the Gold Coast.

Activities

The Gold Coast is an ideal area to learn the craft of surfing, and the modest waves around Surfers Paradise provide the perfect starting point. Two beaches regularly used for both national and international competitions because of their top-notch waves are **Kirra** and **Duranbah**; both are suited to experienced surfers.

Surf schools charge between A$40 and A$50 for a two-hour lesson. The following are recommended:

Cheyne Horan School of Surf (☎ 1800 227 873, 0403-080 484; www.cheynehoran.com.au)

Surfers Beach Hut Beach Hire (☎ 1800 787 337, 5526 7077; Cavill Ave Mall, Surfers Paradise; 8am-5pm) Also hires short boards for A$15/40 per hour/day.

Nancy Emerson School of Surf (☎ 0413-380 933; www.surfclinics.com)

To get even closer to marine life, **Queensland Scuba Diving Company** (☎ 5526 7722; Mariners Cove Marina, Main Beach) organises single dives (including fish feeding) for beginners for A$100.

Tours

If you haven't the patience for surfing, **Splash Safaris** (☎ 0407-741 748; www.seakayakingtours.com; tours A$65) offers day kayaking tours that include snorkelling, dolphin searching, bushwalking and lunch.

Without wheels, the best way to explore the Gold Coast hinterland's Springbrook, Tambourine and Lamington National Parks is on a tour.

Australian Day Tours (☎ 1300 363 436; tours A$65)

O'Reilly's (☎ 5524 4249; tours A$45)

Scenic Hinterland Tours (☎ 5538 2899; www.hinterlandtours.com.au; tours A$40)

Southern Cross 4WD Tours (☎ 1800 067 367, 5547 7120; www.sc4wd.com.au; tours from A$110) Small ecotours off the beaten track.

Two companies operate tours in and out of Surfers' harbour in amphibious vehicles. The **Aquabus** (☎ 5539 0222; www.aquabus.com.au; A$29) makes a 75-minute trip from Orchid Ave up to Main Beach and the Spit, and then sails back on the Broadwater. **Aqua Duck** (☎ 5538 3825; www.aquaduck.com.au; return trip A$29) does exactly the same.

Festivals & Events

In mid-March the **Quiksilver Pro-Surfing Competition** enables you to catch some of the world's best surfers weaving their magic on the waves.

Sleeping

Surfers is littered with hostels and most have pools, bars and Internet access. If you want a quieter experience, head to Southport. However, if you're just looking for good surf and fellow travellers, then bypass the glitz altogether and get straight down to Coolangatta. Most hostels have free pick up from the **Surfers Paradise Transit Centre** (cnr Beach & Cambridge Rds), and put on free shuttle buses to clubs and beaches. The helpful **In Transit** (☎ 5592 2911) tour desk at the Transit Centre makes accommodation bookings for free.

Trekkers (☎ 1800 100 004, 5591 5616; www.trekkersbackpackers.com.au; 22 White St, Southport; dm A$23, d & tw A$60;) You could bottle the charm and friendly vibes of this beautiful Queenslander and make a mint. On a leafy street in Southport, the whole place has been renovated and all the rooms are spotless, homey and comfy. Its character extends into a lovely garden and it organises frequent club treks.

Cheers Backpackers (☎ 1800 636 539, 5531 6539; 8 Pine Ave, Surfers Paradise; dm/d A$23/60; P) Amid the friendly blur of theme nights, karaoke, pool comps, pub crawls, happy hours and barbecues found here, you'll also stumble across adequate rooms and good facilities. Cheers is undeniably a party hostel and the fun frequently trickles out to the nearby action of Surfers.

Sleeping Inn Surfers (☎ 1800 817 832, 5592 4455; www.sleepinginn.com.au; 26 Peninsular Dr; dm A$21, d with/without bath A$65/55;) A bit flashier than your average hostel, this converted motel has modern facilities and a wide choice of rooms, from basic dorms to classier doubles with TV. It's also large enough to cater to party punters as well as those in dire need of a quiet sleep.

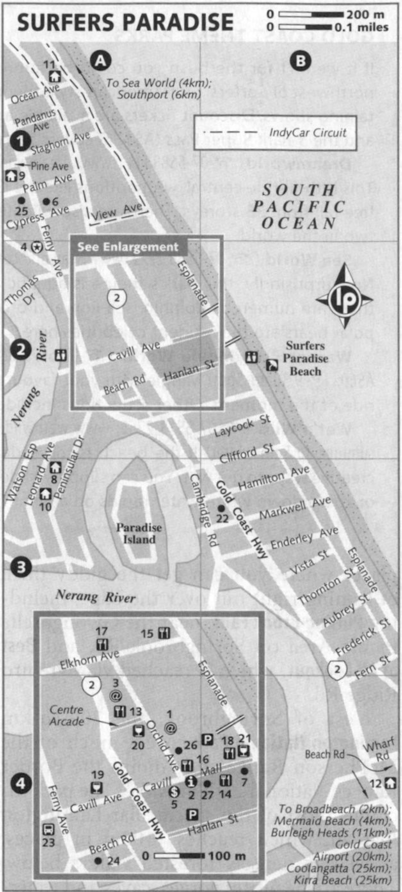

Surf 'n' Sun Backpackers (☎ 1800 678 194, 5592 2363; www.surfnsun-goldcoast.com; 3323 Gold Coast Hwy, Surfers Paradise; dm/d A$23/60;) Rivalling Cheers as party central, this hostel is the best option for Surfers' beach and bars. Staff are chipper, and there are surfboards for hire, pool tables and the constant hum of music, and if the hop-skip to the beach is too strenuous then the pool is a nice, lazy alternative.

Coolangatta YHA (☎ 5536 7644; booking@coolangattayha.com; 230 Coolangatta Rd, Bilinga; dm incl breakfast A$20-23, s/d incl breakfast A$34/50; P) A looong haul from the bustle, this well-equipped YHA is favoured by surf junkies

INFORMATION	
Email Centre	1 A4
Gold Coast Tourism Bureau	2 A4
Mercari Imaging	3 A4
Police Station	4 A2
Post Office	(see 27)
Travelex	5 A4
SIGHTS & ACTIVITIES	**(pp156–7)**
Banzai Bungey	6 A1
Flycoaster	(see 6)
Sling Shot	(see 6)
Surfers Beach Hut Beach Hire	7 B4
Vomatron	(see 6)
SLEEPING	**(pp158–9)**
Backpackers in Paradise	8 A3
Cheers Backpackers	9 A1
In Transit	(see 24)
Sleeping Inn Surfers	10 A3
Surf 'n' Sun Backpackers	11 A1
Surfers Paradise Backpackers Resort	12 B4
EATING	**(p159)**
Arirang	13 A4
Charlies	14 B4
Chateau Beachside	15 A3
La Porchetta	16 A4
La Porchetta	17 A3
Raptis Plaza Food Court	18 B4
Supermarket	(see 27)
DRINKING	**(p160)**
Cocktails & Dreams	(see 1)
Fever	19 A4
Gilhooley's	20 A4
O'Malleys	21 B4
Party	(see 1)
Shooters	(see 1)
TRANSPORT	**(p160)**
All Age Car Rentals	22 B3
Bus Stop for Southport	23 A4
Red Back Rentals	(see 24)
Red Rocket Rent-A-Car	(see 1)
Surfers Paradise Transit Centre	24 A4
Yahoo	25 A1
OTHER	
Aqua Duck	26 A4
Aquabus	(see 26)
Paradise Centre	27 B4

of all vintage who overdose on the excellent breaks across the road. You can also hire boards and bikes. There are courtesy transfers from Coolangatta and Surfers.

Other recommendations:

Surfers Paradise Backpackers Resort (☎ 1800 282 800, 5592 4677; www.surfersparadisebackpackers.com.au; Gold Coast Hwy, Surfers Paradise; dm/d/tr A$22/55/80;) Motel-style hostel with sauna, tennis court, pool room and bar.

Backpackers in Paradise (☎ 5538 4344; fax 5538 2222; 40 Peninsular Dr; dm A$15-20, d A$55;) Walking distance to everything.

Mermaid Beach Motel (☎ 5575 5688; www.mermaidbeachmotel.com.au; 2395 Gold Coast Hwy, Mermaid Beach; r A$55-65;) Small motel with clean, self-contained rooms.

Kirra Beach Tourist Park (☎ 5581 7744; www.gctp.com.au/kirra; Charlotte St, Kirra; camp/caravan sites per 2 people A$24/22, d/cabins A$45/75;) This large park is spread out and has plenty of grassy sites, modern self-contained cabins and good-value doubles. Facilities include a TV room and barbecues, and there is wheelchair access.

Eating

The Gold Coast has a multicultural palate. Most eateries are centralised in Surfers, where Japanese, Korean and Malaysian food is particularly abundant. Outside of Surfers cheap eats are generally limited to pubs and cafés.

Chateau Beachside (☎ 5526 9994; cnr The Esplanade & Elkhorn Ave, Surfers Paradise; meals A$5-10; breakfast & lunch;) Inside this seafront hotel you can vacuum enough carbs to get through the day at the fantastic all-you-can-gobble A$10 buffet breakfast. If you've still got room at lunch its burgers, salads, seafood and pastas are also great value.

La Porchetta (meals A$10-15; breakfast, lunch & dinner;) Orchid Ave (☎ 5527 5273; 3 Orchid Ave, Surfers Paradise); Elkhorn Ave (☎ 5504 5236; Elkhorn Ave, Surfers Paradise) Red-checked tablecloths and high standards reign at this chain of Italian eateries. Tasty pizzas and pastas in copious versions and sizable portions are the mainstay, with gourmet options and meat dishes at the pricier end of the menu.

Arirang (☎ 5539 8008; Shop 8, Centre Arcade, Surfers Paradise; mains A$8-16) Among the bizillion Korean noodle bars, this one shines with unpretentious, no-nonsense décor and authentic Korean cuisine. Lunch-time noodle dishes are a tasty A$8 bargain.

Charlies (☎ 5538 5285; Cavill Mall, Surfers Paradise; meals A$10-20; 24hr) With décor devoted to Charlie Chaplin, who undoubtedly never ate here, this sprawling café has a hint of American diner about it and serves hearty burgers, pizzas, pastas, sandwiches and breakfasts. The outdoor seating is pleasant.

Teeny sushi bars and Asian eateries fill every corner of Surfers, and takeaway sets you back about A$7. Choices in **Raptis Plaza food court** (off Cavill Ave Mall, Surfers Paradise) include Italian, burgers, kebabs, Thai, Japanese and an all-you-can-eat for A$10 Asian buffet.

Shopping centres with supermarkets:

Australia Fair (Marine Pde, Southport)
Paradise Centre (Cavill Ave, Surfers Paradise)
Tweed Mall (Wharf St, Coolangatta)

QUEENSLAND

You can tuck into decent pub grub at O'Malleys (see below), with meals from A$8 to A$10, and Gilhooley's (see below), meals from A$7 to A$11.

Drinking

Surfers takes its drinking more seriously than oxygen. Clubs here offer vouchers for backpackers and Wednesday and Saturday are generally the big party nights. Cover charges are usually between A$5 and A$10.

O'Malleys (☎ 5570 4075; Level 1, 1 Cavill Ave, Surfers Paradise;) By day this is a quaint respite from the hectic heat of Cavill Ave, and the A$8 jugs are pure medicine. The network of booths and stools overlooking the ocean fills up at night when the atmosphere is happy and rowdy. Good pub grub.

Gilhooley's (☎ 5538 9122; 39 Cavill Ave;) Another pseudo-Irish pub nestled into a convenient spot on the main drag, Gilhooley's hosts live Irish music and DJs (not at the same time) and big-screen TV sports…or you can people-watch from the terrace.

Cocktails & Dreams (☎ 5592 1955; Level 1, The Mark, Orchid Ave, Surfers Paradise) This club is a Surfers institution and backpacker favourite. Drink deals, dancing and general debauchery pulls the crowds in and spits them out again in the wee hours after an exhausting good time. Linked by a stairway, the **Party** (☎ 5538 2848; Orchid Ave) offers more of the same with A$2 drink deals from Thursday to Sunday nights, theme nights and bubbly prizes.

Shooters (☎ 5592 1144; 15 Orchid Ave) Apparently food is served here but who could tell with all the alcohol. Another backpacker haunt, Shooters is packed to almost bursting on weekends.

Liquid (☎ 5538 0111; Shop 1, 18 Orchid Ave) Spilling out onto the sidewalk, Liquid swims in glossy blue neon and water-featured walls. Trendy patrons sip cocktails early on but eventually it all ends up naughty and noisy. This is the perfect place to wear that impractical top you brought from home.

Entertainment

It wouldn't be an Irish pub without live music, now would it? Gilhooley's (above) is one that accommodates regularly.

Gold Coast cinemas:

Pacific Square 12 Cinemas (☎ 5572 2666; Pacific Fair shopping centre, cnr Hooker Blvd & Gold Coast Hwy, Broadbeach; P)

Coolangatta 6 Cinema Centre (☎ 5536 8900; Level 2, Showcase on the Beach Centre, Griffith St; P)

Getting There & Away

AIR

Jetstar (☎ 13 15 38; www.jetstar.com.au)

Qantas (☎ 13 13 13; www.qantas.com.au)

Virgin Blue (☎ 13 67 89; www.virginblue.com.au)

BUS

If you're coming by bus, you'll arrive at the **Surfers Paradise Transit Centre** (cnr Beach & Cambridge Rds). Inside are various bus company booking desks, a cafeteria and left-luggage lockers (A$4 per 12 hours).

From Sydney, you can catch **McCafferty's/Greyhound** (☎ 13 20 30) buses to Surfers (A$95, 16 hours, two daily), via Byron Bay (A$25, two hours). These buses continue to Brisbane (A$15, 1½ hours). **Premier Motor Service** (☎ 13 34 10) does the same routes but costs slightly less, and both companies will usually allow you a free stopover on the Gold Coast if you have a through ticket to or from Brisbane. The buses also stop at the stations in Southport, Surfers Paradise and Coolangatta.

CAR & BICYCLE

There are dozens of firms that rent cars, mopeds and bicycles, particularly in Surfers. A few of the cheaper ones:

All Age Car Rentals (☎ 1800 671 361; 3024 Gold Coast Hwy, Surfers Paradise; www.goldcoastcarhire.com) Mopeds and cars.

Freedom Wheels (☎ 5596 7979; info@freedomwheelsrentals.com) Can provide specially designed vehicles for the disabled.

Red Rocket Rent-A-Car (☎ 1800 673 682; 5538 9074; Shop 9, The Mark, Orchid Ave, Surfers Paradise) Bicycles, scooters and cars.

Yahoo (☎ 5592 0227; cnr Palm & Ferny Aves) Used cars from A$15 per day.

TRAIN

From Brisbane, **Citytrain** (☎ 13 12 30; www.transinfo.qld.gov.au) operates a half-hourly service to/from Nerang (A$18.50, 1½ hours) and Robina (A$19, 1¾ hours). Neither of these stations are particularly close to any of the main Gold Coast centres, but you can catch a ride with **Surfside Buslines** (☎ 13 12 30, 5571 6555), which runs shuttles from Nerang and Robina to Surfers (A$3.40, 40 minutes, frequent).

Getting Around

Surfside Buslines (☎ 13 12 30, 5571 6555) provides a frequent service up and down the Gold Coast Hwy from Southport to Tweed Heads and beyond (bus No 1 and 1A), 24 hours a day. You can buy individual fares or get an Ezy Pass for a day's unlimited travel (A$10), or a weekly pass (A$43).

SUNSHINE COAST TO THE WHITSUNDAYS

This stretch of Queensland is possibly the most enigmatic, encompassing brilliant tracts of coastline, the world's largest sand island and islands so exquisite it seems the whole world wants to court their shores.

This is also a great region to indulge in some genuine Queensland hospitality. Tourist trappings are virtually unknown here and the locals redefine the meaning of laid-back. This appealing package enables travellers to immerse themselves in the landscape and culture without feeling like the ubiquitous tourist.

Activities

This section covers a huge stretch of the Queensland coast, where a diversity of activities are on offer. The Sunshine Coast offers great surfing opportunities, particularly around Noosa, where several companies teach the fine art. Just north of Noosa, kayaking and canoeing are popular pursuits in the Everglades section of the Great Sandy National Park. On the Fraser Coast, you can test your mettle by 4WDing up Fraser Island's beach 'highway' or, for something more sedate but no less spectacular, explore the whale-watching opportunities in Hervey Bay between July and October.

More water-based activities abound further north with diving near Bundaberg and sailing around the Whitsunday Islands. If you're a landlubber at heart, Great Keppel Island has some excellent bushwalks.

SUNSHINE COAST

In stark contrast to the sensory overload of the Gold Coast, Queensland's Sunshine Coast is laid-back and offers sufficient services, recreation and the odd giant fruit to keep stimulus-needy folk happy.

The coastline itself is also stunning and the area is a popular weekend getaway from Brisbane.

Suburbia sprouts its concrete limbs between Caloundra and Maroochydore and this string of towns blends into a mishmash of beach and buildings. Apart from good lazing and surfing, here you'll find mostly low-rise shopping malls, cafés, restaurants, pubs and all other things civilised. As the coast travels north the urban density diminishes, particularly around the picturesque towns of Coolum and Peregian Beach.

Further north again plenty of travellers find their nirvana in the Sunshine Coast's jewel – Noosa; a staunchly low-rise and leafy resort that sometimes feels like an antipodean answer to France's Nice.

Glass House Mountains

☎ 07 / pop 660

The Glass House Mountains, about 20km north of the small dairy township of Caboolture, consist of 13 ethereally shaped volcanic crags sticking up from the coastal plain. Standing up to 300m high and, with sheer rocky sides, the Aborigines believed these peaks to be a family of mountain spirits, the

BUCKS IN THE BANK

Harvesting a smorgasbord of fruit, vegetables and fish all year makes Queensland an attractive state for financially challenged backpackers tired of waiting tables and answering phones. The busiest period anywhere in the state is generally between March and November.

The main hotspots are Bundaberg, Childers, Stanthorpe and Bowen, where everything from avocados to zucchini is harvested almost year-round and hostels specialise in finding travellers work. You should also be able to pick up work around Maroochydore and, during January and December, in the Atherton Tablelands and around Tully and Cardwell.

The **National Harvest Labour Information Service** (☎ 1800 062 332; www.jobsearch.gov.au/harvesttrail) is an excellent resource for putting you in contact with employers. Alternatively, check out wwoof.com.au for WWOOFing (Willing Workers on Organic Farms) opportunities.

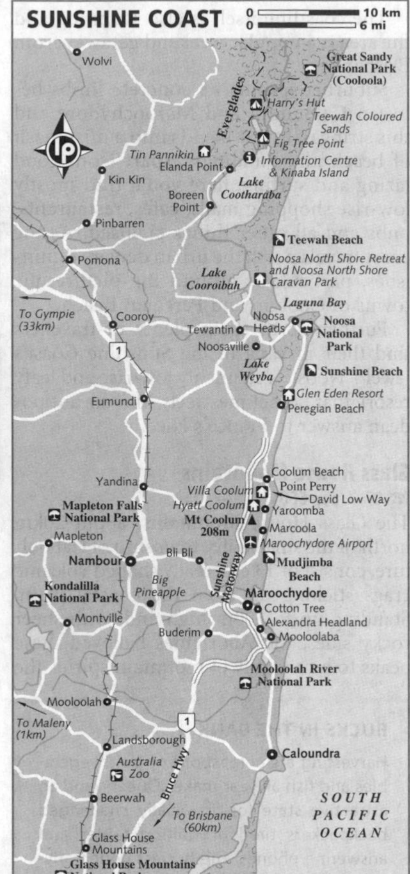

most distinctive of which is the father, Tibrogargan. Small national parks surround Mts Tibrogargan, Beerwah, Coonowrin, Ngungun, Miketeeburnulgrai and Elimbah, with picnic grounds, walking tracks and lookouts. The peaks are reached by a series of sealed and unsealed roads known collectively as Forest Dr, which heads inland from Glass House Mountains Rd.

There are walking tracks (really low-grade mountain climbs) on Tibrogargan, Beerwah and Ngungun. The **District Forest Office** (☎ 5496 0166; Beerburrum) has more information.

Rainforest Rob's Explorer (☎ 0409-496 607; http://homepage.powerup.com.au/~frogbus7; day tours incl lunch A$80) organises small tours here from Brisbane.

Nearby is – crikey! – **Australia Zoo** (☎ 5494 1134; www.crocodilehunter.com; Glasshouse Mountains Rd, Beerwah; adult/student A$27/22; 9am-4.30pm). From a tiny reptile park in the 1980s, this has become huge, as owner Steve 'Crocodile Hunter' Irwin has proved to possess a mesmerising hold over crocs and international TV viewers alike. You won't catch the man himself here often. However, with such a reputation to uphold, this animal Disneyworld doesn't disappoint. There are regular crocodile, snake, otter etc shows. Phone about free transfers from Noosa or Beerwah train stations.

Caloundra to Maroochy

☎ 07

At the southern end of the Sunshine Coast, Caloundra (population 50,150) is a quiet town dominated by low-rise suburbia and a string of lovely beaches. The scenery becomes increasingly commercial as you head north until you hit Maroochy (population 44,100), with its vistas of high-rise apartments dressed in colours not from mother nature's palate. Maroochy is made up of Mooloolaba – the most developed suburb here – Alexandra Headlands, Cotton Tree and Maroochydore, which are catching up fast.

In summer the whole area is flooded with Queensland families indulging in good fishing and surf beaches and Maroochy gets particularly busy. However, it quickly reverts back to the tranquil epitome of coastal Oz for the remainder of the year.

INFORMATION

Caloundra visitors centre (☎ 5491 0202; www.caloundratourism.com.au; 7 Caloundra Rd; 8.30am-5pm Mon-Fri, 9am-5pm Sat & Sun) About 2km west of the town centre.

Information booths Maroochydore airport (☎ 5448 9088; Friendship Dr, Marcoola; 8.45am-4.30pm, depending on flight arrivals); Mooloolaba (☎ 5478 2233; cnr First Ave & Brisbane Rd; 9am-5pm)

Maroochy visitors centre (☎ 1800 882 032, 5479 1566; www.maroochytourism.com; cnr Sixth Ave & Melrose St, Maroochydore; 9am-5pm Mon-Fri, to 4pm Sat & Sun)

SIGHTS & ACTIVITIES

Well worth a visit, **Underwater World** (☎ 5444 8488; www.underwaterworld.com.au; The Wharf, Parkyn Pde, Mooloolaba; adult A$23; 9am-6pm) gives you a glimpse of good and colourful fishy things to come, with an invaluable insight into the diversity of marine life inhabiting nearby waters. It's the southern hemisphere's largest oceanarium, a statistic made vividly obvious in the impressive shark tunnel, which is also home to some 20,000 fish. There are also seal shows.

Scuba World (☎ 5444 8595; The Wharf, Parkyn Pde, Mooloolaba) can get you up close and personal with one of Underwater World's grey nurse sharks (certified/uncertified divers A$95/125). The company also takes certified divers on coral dives off the coast (A$55).

Brothers Neilsen (☎ 5444 3545; cnr The Esplanade & Venning St, Mooloolaba) has surfboards for hire for A$40 a day and bodyboards for A$20 a day (rates drop in winter).

SLEEPING

Cotton Tree Beachouse Backpackers (☎ 5443 1755; www.cottontreebackpackers.com; 15 The Esplanade, Cotton Tree; YHA members dm/d A$19/41, nonmembers A$21/46; 💻) Virtually on the beach, this place is strong on charm, from the leafy front garden to its timber frame. It's homey but the spa and good facilities add a touch of class. Best of all, use of the surfboards, bodyboards and kayaks is free.

Suncoast Backpackers Lodge (☎ 5443 7544; vip_suncoast@hotmail.com; 50 Parker St, Maroochydore; dm/d A$19/40; P 💻) This small and friendly hostel has motel-style rooms and an aversion to the cram-'em-in philosophy – no bunks! Staff bend over backwards to help you out with free pick-ups, loads of tour and activities info and a kicking A$5 barbecue on Wednesday night.

Caloundra City Backpackers (☎ 5499 7655; www.caloundracitybackpackers.com.au; 84 Omrah Ave, Caloundra; dm/tw/d A$17/40/45) Built in 2001, this much-lauded motel-style hostel is spotless and friendly, even if the rooms are not huge. Disabled access is OK.

Cotton Tree Caravan Park (☎ 1800 461 253, 5443 1253; www.maroochypark.qld.gov.au; Cotton Tree Pde, Cotton Tree; camp/caravan sites per 2 people A$20/25) Once upon a time there were two caravan parks that joined forces and became a super caravan park. In summer this right-on-the-beach park is a virtual suburb but most of the time it's a spacious, grassy spot with great facilities. It caters well to disabled travellers.

Other recommendations:

Maroochydore YHA Backpackers (☎ 5443 3151; mail@yhabackpackers.com; 24 Schirmann Dr, Maroochydore; dm/d A$20/45; 💻 🏊) Pleasant collection of older brick buildings, away from the centre.

Hibiscus Holiday Park (☎ 1800 550 138, 5491 1564; fax 5492 6938; cnr Bowman & Landsborough Park Rds, Caloundra; camp/caravan sites per 2 people A$25/30, dm/vans/cabins A$20/55/60; units A$75-85; 👪) Next to Bulcock Beach with small, spotless dorms and spacious units.

EATING

Self-caterers will find supermarkets inside **Sunland Shopping Centre** (Bowman Rd, Caloundra) and **Sunshine Plaza** (Horton Pde, Maroochydore). The latter also has a food court, with meals from A$5 to A$8.

Raw Energy (☎ 5444 2111; Shop 3, The Esplanade, Mooloolaba; dishes A$9-13; 🕐 breakfast & lunch Mon-Sat) Fire yourself up with healthy fuel like paninis, pastas, juices and the inevitable wheatgrass. All dished up in a colourful juice bar.

Krishna's (2/7 First Ave, Maroochydore; lunch A$7, dinner A$8; 🕐 lunch Mon-Fri, dinner Fri & Sun) Krishna's may not have extended its ambience budget too far but the Indian veggie buffet is excellent value and the food is hot and healthy.

Augello's (☎ 5478 3199; cnr The Esplanade & Brisbane Rd, Mooloolaba; dishes A$11-20; 🕐 lunch & dinner; 👪) Concoctions like Moroccan chicken pizza with sun-dried tomatoes and lime-yoghurt dressing have helped make this one of Australia's top spots for pizza, but if all you crave is a margarita, that's fine, too.

The **Caloundra RSL** (☎ 5491 1544; 19 West Tce; A$6.50-20; 🕐 lunch & dinner; 👪) has won several minor dining awards, but its interior is pure Las Vegas.

For somewhere less gaudy, head for the **Blue Orchid** (☎ 5491 9433; 22 Bulcock St, Caloundra; mains A$12-20; 🕐 dinner; 👪) Thai restaurant.

GETTING THERE & AWAY

The Sunshine Coast's airport is at Maroochydore. Flights from Sydney/Melbourne start at around A$120/180.

Jetstar (☎ 13 15 38; www.jetstar.com.au)
Qantas (☎ 13 13 13; www.qantas.com.au)
Virgin Blue (☎ 13 67 89; www.virginblue.com.au)

Long-distance buses stop at the **Suncoast Pacific bus terminal** (☎ 5443 1011; First Ave, Maroochydore), just off Aerodrome Rd. **McCafferty's/Greyhound** (☎ 13 20 30) and **Premier Motor Service** (☎ 13 34 10) have services from Brisbane (A$19, 1½ hours, two daily), as does Suncoast Pacific (adult/student A$24.50/20, 1½ hours, six or seven daily). The latter offers a stand-by fare of A$15 and there are often seats.

Sunshine Coast Hinterland

The hinterland's main tourist attraction, 6km southeast of the commercial town of Nambour, is the **Big Pineapple** (☎ 07-5442 1333; Nambour Connection Rd; admission free; ⏲ 9am-5pm). One of Australia's numerous kitsch 'big things', this 15m-high fibreglass fruit sits beside a pineapple plantation, a macadamia orchard and an extensive souvenir shop. A small train chugs through the plantation.

North of Nambour, locals and visitors flock to the **Eumundi markets** (⏲ 8am-1.30pm Wed, 6am-2pm Sat), where hundreds of stalls sell local produce and lots of alternative, New Age stuff. The local bus between Noosa Heads and Nambour stops here, or there are direct bus transfers for A$15 return.

Inland from Nambour, the Blackall Range creates a scenic hinterland with appealing national parks and rather chintzy rustic villages. The scenic Mapleton to Maleny road runs along the ridge of the range, past rainforests at **Mapleton Falls National Park**, 4km west of Mapleton, and **Kondalilla National Park**, 3km north of Montville. Both Mapleton and Kondalilla **waterfalls** plunge more than 80m, and their lookouts offer wonderful forest views.

The **Woodford Folk Festival**, held annually during the five days leading up to New Year's Eve, is the closest Australia has to Woodstock. Woodford is near Maleny.

Maroochy to Noosa

☎ 07

If you really came to the Sunshine Coast to soak up the sunshine and the coast then head north of Maroochy to the much less-crowded towns of **Coolum Beach** and **Peregian Beach**. The easiest way to get here is by car but Sunbus buses pass through regularly. The area is good for surfing, but also offers wonderful coastal views from **Point Perry** or the chance to climb **Mt Coolum**. Beside the surf lifesaving club, the **tourist information booth** (David Low Way, Coolum Beach; ⏲ 9am-5pm) has brochures on accommodation.

Villa Coolum (☎ 5446 1286; www.villacoolum.com; 102 Coolum Tce, Coolum Beach; r A$50-80; 🅿) has simple self-contained units with leafy verandas.

Noosa

☎ 07 / pop 36,400

The combination of tropical vegetation, crystalline beaches and towering gum trees seems to peak in spectacular fashion in Noosa. In the 1960s this was another of those undeveloped surfing havens, but beauty like this is hard to contain and within 30 years it carried an exclusive label catering to media stars, glammed-up fashionistas and well-moneyed daahlings. They brought with them a glut of inoffensive condominiums and exquisite cuisine, but the beach and bush are still free so the well-heeled simply share the beat with thongs and boardshorts.

Noosa consists of three areas: Noosa Junction, Noosaville and Noosa Heads. The latter is the fanciest sibling, in which trendy Hastings St is dominated by bars, boutiques and bronzed bikini bodies baring their bits. This all culminates in Noosa National Park, thick with stunning views, birdlife and native flora.

Noosaville, to the west, and Sunshine Beach, south, retain a laid-back ambience, while the Sunshine Coast hinterland and the wilderness of the Cooloola coast (Great Sandy National Park) are within easy reach.

INFORMATION

Adventure Travel Bugs (☎ 1800 666 720, 5474 8530; 9 Sunshine Beach Rd, Noosa Junction) Internet access available for A$4 per hour.

Noosa visitors centre (☎ 1800 448 833, 5447 4988; www.tourismnoosa.com.au; Hastings St roundabout, Noosa Heads; ⏲ 9am-5pm)

Peterpan Adventure Travel (☎ 1800 777 115; www.peterpans.com; 3/75 Noosa Dr, Noosa Junction) Internet access available for A$4 per hour.

SIGHTS

The small but lovely **Noosa National Park** extends for about 2km southwest from the headland that marks the end of the Sunshine Coast. It has fine walks, great coastal scenery and a string of popular bays for surfing on the northern side. **Alexandria Bay** on the eastern side has the best sands and is also an informal nudist beach.

The most scenic way to access the national park is to follow the boardwalk along the coast from town. This continues all the way to the park's main entrance at the end of Park Rd (the eastern continuation of Hastings St). Here you'll find a car park, picnic areas and the **EPA centre** (☎ 5447 3243; ⏲ 9am-3pm), from where you can obtain a walking track map.

For a panoramic view, you can walk or drive up Viewland Dr to the **Laguna Lookout** in Noosa Junction.

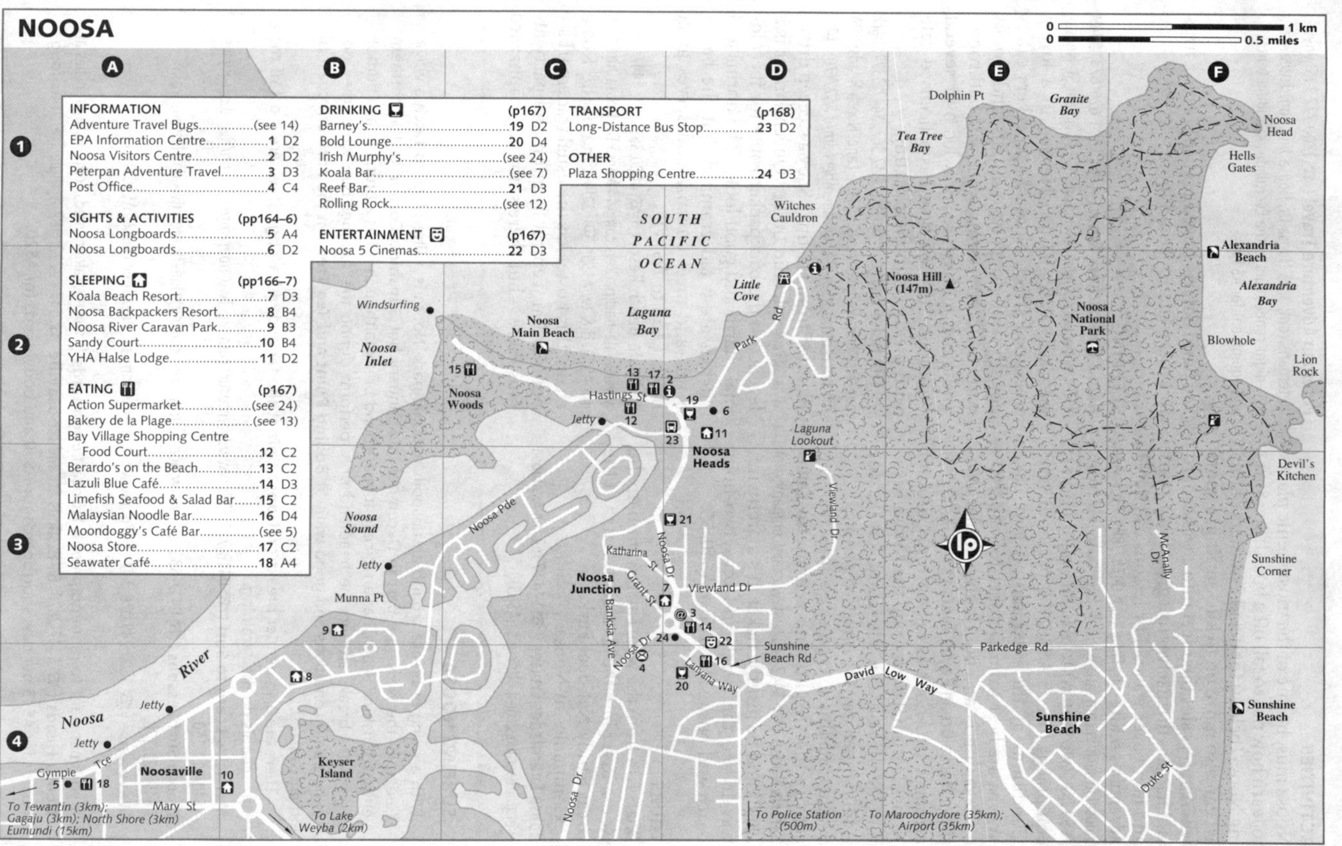
NOOSA
0 1 km
0 0.5 miles
INFORMATION
Adventure Travel Bugs.........(see 14)
EPA Information Centre.........1 D2
Noosa Visitors Centre.........2 D2
Peterpan Adventure Travel.........3 D3
Post Office.........4 C4
SIGHTS & ACTIVITIES (pp164–6)
Noosa Longboards.........5 A4
Noosa Longboards.........6 D2
SLEEPING (pp166–7)
Koala Beach Resort.........7 D3
Noosa Backpackers Resort.........8 B4
Noosa River Caravan Park.........9 B3
Sandy Court.........10 B4
YHA Halse Lodge.........11 D2
EATING (p167)
Action Supermarket.........(see 24)
Bakery de la Plage.........(see 13)
Bay Village Shopping Centre Food Court.........12 C2
Berardo's on the Beach.........13 C2
Lazuli Blue Café.........14 D3
Limefish Seafood & Salad Bar.........15 C2
Malaysian Noodle Bar.........16 D4
Moondoggy's Café Bar.........(see 5)
Noosa Store.........17 C2
Seawater Café.........18 A4
DRINKING (p167)
Barney's.........19 D2
Bold Lounge.........20 D4
Irish Murphy's.........(see 24)
Koala Bar.........(see 7)
Reef Bar.........21 D3
Rolling Rock.........(see 12)
ENTERTAINMENT (p167)
Noosa 5 Cinemas.........22 D3
TRANSPORT (p168)
Long-Distance Bus Stop.........23 D2
OTHER
Plaza Shopping Centre.........24 D3
Dolphin Pt
Granite Bay
Tea Tree Bay
Noosa Head
Hells Gates
Witches Cauldron
SOUTH PACIFIC OCEAN
Alexandria Beach
Alexandria Bay
Little Cove
Noosa Hill (147m)
Noosa National Park
Laguna Bay
Noosa Main Beach
Windsurfing
Noosa Inlet
Blowhole
Lion Rock
Park Rd
Hastings St
Noosa Woods
Jetty
Noosa Heads
Laguna Lookout
Devil's Kitchen
Viewland Dr
Noosa Pde
Noosa Sound
Katharina St
Noosa Dr
McAnally Dr
Sunshine Corner
Noosa Junction
Grant St
Munna Pt
Banksia Ave
Sunshine Beach Rd
Parkedge Rd
Lanyana Way
David Low Way
River
Noosa
Sunshine Beach
Gympie Tce
Noosaville
Keyser Island
Duke St
Mary St
To Tewantin (3km); Gagaju (3km); North Shore (3km) Eumundi (15km)
To Lake Weyba (2km)
To Police Station (500m)
To Maroochydore (35km); Airport (35km)
QUEENSLAND

ACTIVITIES

Noosa must be one of the most scenic places to learn how not to fall off a board. See Surfing Noosa (below) for details. Masters of this art can also move on to kite-surfing, a sport where riders slot their feet into a wakeboard and harness themselves to a giant kite to surf and jump over waves. For lessons call **Noosa Adventures & Kite-Surfing** (☎ 0438-788 573; www.noosakitesurfing.com.au), which has courses from A$120 (two hours) to A$380 (eight hours); equipment hire is A$30/100 per hour/day. Conditions at the river mouth and Lake Weyba are best from October to January.

Kayaking is an enduringly popular pastime. **Noosa Ocean Kayak Tours** (☎ 0418-787 577) arranges two-hour kayaking tours around Noosa National Park or up the Noosa River for A$50. You can also hire kayaks for A$40/50 per day for one/two people.

After all this exercise you may need an activity that requires no activity, so **Camel Safaris Noosa** (☎ 5442 4402; www.camelcompany.com.au) should be just the ticket. It's a pretty fun way to see the beach and one-/two-hour beach and bush safaris cost A$40/55.

TOURS

Boats run from the wharf at Tewantin up the Noosa River into the 'Everglades' area of the Great Sandy National Park.

Companies in Noosa:

Noosa Everglades Cruises (☎ 5449 7362; www.noosaevergladescruises.com; 6hr cruise A$65)

Peterpan Adventure Travel (☎ 1800 777 115; www.peterpans.com; 3/75 Noosa Dr, Noosa Junction) Three-day, two-night canoe tours to the Everglades including tents and equipment for A$110.

See Sand Safaris boxed text (p174) for trips to Fraser Island from Noosa.

SLEEPING

Noosa Backpackers Resort (☎ 1800 626 673, 5449 8151; www.noosabackpackers.com; 9-13 William St, Noosaville; dm/d A$22/55; 🖳 🖳) Nestled in a lovely tree-lined street, Noosa Backpackers caters equally well to party animals and bookworms. Roomy dorms, some with bathroom, and quiet doubles are sprawled over several buildings. Also on-board is a licensed café with plenty of outdoor seating.

YHA Halse Lodge (☎ 1800 242 567, 5447 3377; backpackers@halselodge.com.au; 2 Halse Lane, Noosa Heads; YHA members dm/d A$24/64, non-members dm/d A$27/70; 🖳) Elevated from Hastings St by a steeeep driveway, this splendid timber Queenslander is a legend on the backpacker route for its colonial charm and good looks. The dorms and kitchen are a tad cramped, but the bar is a mix-and-meet bonanza and serves great meals (A$6 to A$11).

Koala Beach Resort (☎ 1800 357 457, 5447 3355; www.koala-backpackers.com; 44 Noosa Dr, Noosa Junction; dm A$22, d & tw A$55; 🖳 🖳) One of the Koala chain, this hostel has the usual trademarks – popular bar, central location and party atmosphere – but there's nothing haphazard

SURFING NOOSA

With a string of breaks around an unspoilt national park, Noosa is a fine place to catch a wave. Generally the waves are best in December and January but **Sunshine Corner**, at the northern end of Sunshine Beach, has an excellent year-round break (although it has a brutal beach dump). The point breaks around the headland only perform during the summer but, when they do, expect wild conditions and good walls at **Boiling Point** and **Tea Tree**, on the northern coast of the headland.

There are also gentler breaks on **Noosa Spit** at the far end of Hastings St, where most of the surf schools do their training.

Merrick's Learn to Surf (☎ 0418-787 577; www.learntosurf.com.au) Two-hour/three-lesson/five-day courses A$40/110/150.

Noosa Surf Lessons (☎ 0412-330 850; www.noosasurflessons.com.au) One-/three-/five-day lessons from A$45/120/170.

Wavesense (☎ 1800 249 076, 5474 9076; www.wavesense.com.au) One/three classes A$50/135.

If you just want to rent equipment, **Noosa Longboards** (www.noosalongboards.com), with branches at **Noosa Heads** (☎ 5447 2828; 64 Hastings St) and **Noosaville** ☎ 5474 2722; 187 Gympie Tce), has longboards for A$45 per day, shortboards for A$30 and bodyboards for A$20.

about this setup. Your buck also buys huge dorms, good facilities, professional staff and plenty of bench seating and grassy patches outside to rest surf-weary bones.

Gagaju (☎ 5474 3522; www.travoholic.com/gagaju; 118 Johns Dr, Tewantin; camp sites per 2 people/dm A$11/17; 💻) This ecocamp, far removed from the bustle of Noosa, offers a completely different experience. A series of rustic lodgings sit on the banks of Lake Coroibah, but be warned: it's utterly basic and modern comforts are a world away, but then that's the point.

Other recommendations:

Sandy Court (☎ 5449 7225; fax 5473 0397; 30 James St, Noosaville; r A$55;) Small budget motel.

Noosa River Caravan Park (☎ 5449 7050; fax 5474 3024; Russel St; camp/caravan sites per 2 people A$25/30) Popular riverside park; book ahead.

EATING

Budget options on Hastings St are extremely limited but Noosaville and Noosa Junction cater to all wallets. However, you can eat well for around A$8 at the **Bay Village Shopping Centre food court** (Hastings St, Noosa Heads). Self-caterers may find the **Noosa Store** (33 Hastings St, Noosa Heads) or **Action** (Plaza Shopping Centre, Sunshine Beach Rd, Noosa Junction) supermarket useful.

Lazuli Blue Café (☎ 5448 0055; 9 Sunshine Beach Rd, Noosa Junction; meals A$7-12; breakfast & lunch) Slow and lazy eating is mandatory at this ultrafriendly and relaxed café, where colossal fresh juices and smoothies are the specialities. The breakfasts, Turkish toasties, salads and meatier dishes like Cajun chicken are pretty special, too.

Seawater Café (☎ 5449 7215; 197 Gympie Tce, Noosaville; meals A$8-20; breakfast, lunch & dinner) This kitsch and colourful restaurant serves excellent seafood. Mermaids, portholes and sea paraphernalia adorn the walls, and calamari, prawns and plenty of fish adorn the menu. If you prefer something nonfishy, the nightly roast and daily sandwiches are also good.

Limefish Seafood & Salad Bar (☎ 5447 4650; Shop 2, 2 Hastings St, Noosa Heads; dishes A$6-12; lunch & dinner) This eat-in or takeaway spot provides the cheapest way to dig into fresh seafood on Hastings Street. There's no silver service, but they sizzle your choice of fish on the spot and the salads are fab.

Berardo's on the Beach (☎ 5448 0888; 49 Hastings St, Noosa Heads; dishes A$10-26; lunch & dinner;) For a superlative splurge and stunning beachside views, this Noosa institution is a winner. The Mod Oz cuisine is an infusion of Asian, Italian and Middle Eastern flavours and not a cent is spared on the ingredients. The seafood here is spectacular.

Other options:

Moondoggy's Café Bar (☎ 5449 9659; 187 Gympie Tce, Noosaville; meals A$5-12; breakfast & lunch) Café fare with a gourmet twist.

Bakery de la Plage (49 Hastings St; snacks A$2-4; breakfast & lunch Mon-Sat) Fabulous French pies and pastries.

Malaysian Noodle Bar (☎ 5448 0311; 36 Sunrise Beach Rd, Noosa Junction; dishes A$8-13; lunch & dinner)

DRINKING

Koala Bar (☎ 1800 357 457, 5447 3355; www.koala-backpackers.com; 44 Noosa Dr, Noosa Junction) Noosa's nightly revelry generally starts at this popular resort (see opposite). The backpacker backdrop flexes its influence with a buzzing vibe, and the beer jugs and thumping soundtrack lay the foundations for new acquaintances and a happy alcoholic glaze.

Reef Bar (☎ 5447 4477; 9 Noosa Dr, Noosa Junction) Once the beer goggles are firmly fastened and the Koala Bar closes its doors, the obvious step is to seek more of the same across the road. There's a strong local feel here, and although you can grasp the secrets of Australian football while listening to Australian rock, you can also dance to doof doof.

Barney's (☎ 5447 4800; Noosa Dr, Noosa Heads) An all-day drinking bonanza, this outdoor bar plays a relentless soundtrack of loud music to an appreciative crowd of 20-somethings. Threads shift from boardshorts to strappy heels and shirts as the sun goes down.

Irish Murphy's (☎ 5455 3344; cnr Sunshine Beach Rd & Noosa Dr;) This member of the Irish theme-bar chain presents no surprises, just good ales and a good pub atmosphere.

Noosa's not exactly a clubbing haven, but if you're looking to dance head to **Rolling Rock** (☎ 5447 2255; Bay Village, off Hastings St, Noosa Heads; admission A$6-7), a long-standing club pumping out techno, funk, progressive house and top 40 tunes nightly. Alternatively, **Bold Lounge** (☎ 5447 3433; Noosa Bowls Club, Lanyana Way, Noosa Junction; admission A$10) hosts a dance party on the first Saturday of each month,

ENTERTAINMENT

Catch the latest blockbuster flicks here at **Noosa 5 Cinemas** (☎ 1300 366 339; 29 Sunshine Beach Rd, Noosa Junction).

GETTING THERE & AROUND

Long-distance buses stop on the corner of Noosa Dr and Noosa Pde, just back from Hastings St. Services from Brisbane take about three hours.

McCafferty's/Greyhound (☎ 13 20 30) serves this route (A$19, three daily), as does **Premier Motor Service** (☎ 13 34 10) for A$18 (two daily), and **Suncoast Pacific** (☎ 5443 1011), which has six to eight buses daily (adult/student/stand-by A$28/23/15).

Several companies have shuttles from Brisbane airport, generally costing A$35 to A$40:

Col's Airport Shuttle (☎ 5473 9966; www.airshuttle.com.au)
Henry's Airport Buses (☎ 5474 0199)
Suncoast Airlink (☎ 5474 1566; sairlink@tpg.com.au)

Riverlight Ferry (☎ 5449 8442) operates ferries between Noosa Heads and Tewantin (one-way/all-day pass A$9.50/14, 30 minutes, six to 10 daily). Tickets include onboard commentary so it's a tour as well as a people-mover.

Sunbus (☎ 5450 7888) services the entire Sunshine Coast, linking the Noosa villages along the way. Fares include Noosa Heads to Maroochydore (A$7.40, one hour, frequent) and Noosa Heads to Nambour train station (A$7.50, one hour, frequent Monday to Saturday, five on Sunday).

Koala Bike Hire (☎ 5474 2733) delivers mountain bikes to your door for A$17 to A$24 per day. Alternatively, most hostels hire bikes for around A$20 per day.

Lake Cooroibah

☎ 07

About 2km north of Tewantin the Noosa River widens out into Lake Cooroibah. You really need wheels to get around and you can catch the **Noosa River Ferry** (☎ 5447 1321; cars A$4.50; 🕒 6am-10.30pm, to 12.30am Fri & Sat) from the end of Moorindil St in Tewantin; each crossing takes about five minutes. You can drive in a conventional vehicle to the lake's eastern shore or the beaches of Laguna Bay.

Those keen to see wildlife, go canoeing or revel in relaxed bush living should stay at **Noosa North Shore** (☎ 5447 1225; www.noosaretreat.com.au; dm/d A$20/50). It's difficult to get from the resort into late-night Noosa without your own transport, but there's a restaurant and pub on-site.

Noosa North Shore Caravan Park (☎ 5447 1706; camp/caravan sites per 2 people from A$14/20) is nearby.

Lake Cootharaba

☎ 07

Lake Cootharaba is reached by driving northwest of Tewantin. **Boreen Point**, on Cootharaba's western shore, is the starting point for kayaking trips into the Cooloola section of the Great Sandy National Park.

From Boreen Point, a partially unsealed road leads up to **Elanda Point**, where there's a **ranger's station** (☎ 5449 7364). Here also is **Elanda Point Canoe Company** (☎ 5485 3165; www.elanda.com.au), which charges A$35 per day for canoes and kayaks; a river taxi to the national park **camping ground** (camp sites per person A$4) costs A$10 each way.

Great Sandy National Park (Cooloola)

East and north of the lakes is the Great Sandy National Park. This 54,000-hectare varied wilderness of mangroves, forest and heathland is traversed by the Noosa River. Kayaking from Boreen Point is a beautiful way to see it and an organised cruise (see p166) will accommodate this. There's an **EPA visitors centre** (☎ 07-5449 7364) at Kinaba Island.

The park has about 10 **camping grounds** (camp sites per person A$4), including Fig Tree Point, at Lake Cootharaba's northern edge; Harry's Hut, 4km further up the river; and Freshwater, about 6km south of Double Island Point on the beach. Contact the rangers at Elanda Point or Kinaba for bookings.

FRASER COAST

As the Bruce Hwy makes its way north through the Fraser Coast, the Queensland landscape leaves the touristed urban spread behind. This area's trump card is Fraser Island; the world's largest sand island, which was created over millennia by longshore drift, and sand washing off Australia's east coast.

By the time you reach Bundaberg further north, you've entered a region of sugar cane, rum and coral. Visitors get a taste of Queensland's uniqueness, and a taste of hard work – this is one of the best spots in Oz to pick up fruit-picking jobs.

Rainbow Beach

☎ 07 / pop 1050

This smidgeon of a town has colourful locals and even more-colourful cliffs. The latter arc their red-hued way around Wide Bay and offer a sweeping panorama from the lighthouse at Double Island Point in the south to Fraser Island in the north.

Rainbow Beach is also inexpensive and utterly devoid of any tourist trappings. These virtues make it the most idyllic kick-off point for Fraser Island, which is a mere 15 minutes by ferry from Inskip Point, 13km north of Rainbow Beach.

INFORMATION

Cooloola Home Video (☎ 5486 3135; Shop 5, 8 Rainbow Beach Rd; per hr A$4) Internet access.

EPA office (☎ 5486 3160; www.epa.qld.gov.au; Rainbow Beach Rd; 7am-4pm) On the way into town.

Rainbow Beach visitors centre (☎ 5486 3227; 8 Rainbow Beach Rd; 7am-6pm)

SIGHTS & ACTIVITIES

The beach here is immense and empty and the view from the Carlo Sandblow, a 120m-high dune on the hill overlooking the town, is breathtaking. **Surf & Sand Safaris** (☎ 5486 3131) runs four-hour trips (A$55) south along the beach, taking in the coloured sands that rise steeply above the beach and the lighthouse. Trips then continue beyond the point to the wreck of the **Cherry Venture** – a freighter that ran aground here in 1973.

The myriad visitors to Rainbow Beach include a pod of dolphins that drops into nearby Tin Can Bay regularly. **Rainbow Beach Dolphin View Sea Kayaking** (☎ 0408-738 192; half-day tour A$65) and **Carlo Canoes** (☎ 5486 3610; day tour A$60) operate dolphin safaris in kayaks and canoes respectively.

Surfing is popular, as is scuba diving at Wolf Rock off Double Island Point, where you'll find gropers, turtles, manta rays and harmless grey nurse sharks. Contact **Wolf Rock Dive Centre** (☎ 5486 8004; wolfrockdive@bigpond.com).

SLEEPING & EATING

Frasers on Rainbow YHA (☎ 1800 100 170, 5486 8885; rainbowbeachyha@bigpond.com; 18 Spectrum St; dm/d A$20/55;) In a nicely converted motel, Frasers has roomy dorms with bathrooms and fabulously comfy beds. Locals join guests for a tipple at the sprawling outdoor bar and there are enough nooks and crannies for a quiet night. Its A$5 dinner deals are great value but order early!

Dingoes on the Beachfront (☎ 1800 111 126, 5486 3711; 3 Spectrum Ave; dm/d A$20/50;) Actually, it's not on the beachfront, and the dorms and facilities are accommodating without being spectacular. Nevertheless, this hostel resembles a swarming menagerie when the 4WD tours get in and hordes of travellers bunker down in the capacious bar for drinks and Fraser Island anecdotes.

Other recommendations:

Rainbow Beach Backpackers Resort (www.rainbowbeachbackpackersresort.com.au; dm A$18, d with/without bath A$55/39; P) Spartan converted motel, close to the beach.

Rainbow Beach Holiday Village & Caravan Park (☎ 5486 3222; www.beach-village.com; Rainbow Beach Rd; camp/caravan sites per 2 people from A$20/22, beachfront caravan site A$23;) Neat as a pin, right by the beach.

For self-caterers there's a supermarket and bakery on Rainbow Beach Rd.

Archie's (☎ 5486 3277; 12 Rainbow Beach Rd; mains A$5.50-15) a popular café, perfectly encapsulates Rainbow's laid-back surfer chic, serving delicious smoothies, veggie burgers, nachos and more.

GETTING THERE & AROUND

McCafferty's/Greyhound (☎ 13 20 30) and **Premier Motor Service** (☎ 13 34 10) have services to Rainbow Beach from Brisbane (A$35, 5½ hours, daily) via Noosa (A$20, 2½ hours), which continue to Hervey Bay (A$19, 1½ hours).

With a 4WD it's possible to drive south along the beach and through the Cooloola section of the Great Sandy National Park to Noosa, as well as head for Fraser Island. Ask the **Rainbow Beach EPA** (☎ 5486 3160; www.epa.qld.gov.au) for a permit if you wish to camp.

Aussie Adventure (☎ 5486 3599; 4/54 Rainbow Beach Rd) and **Safari 4x4** (☎ 1800 689 819, 4124 4244; 27 Goondi St) offer 4WD vehicle hire for A$110 to A$150 per day.

For ferry details, see p176.

Hervey Bay

☎ **07 / pop 36,100**

Hervey Bay is coastal Queensland in a nutshell. Its aesthetic charm, headlined by miles of flawless beach and suburbia, diminishes steadily towards the outskirts where it becomes an industrial jungle. The resulting infrastructure makes Hervey Bay the most popular launching pad to Fraser Island, and its proximity to this marvel is intrinsic to the town's culture. Fortunately, the genuine affability of the locals here prevents Hervey

Bay from becoming a tacky string of souvenir shops and overpriced motels.

Hervey Bay is also a popular stomping ground for whales and this spectacular sight, coupled with sublime swimming and fishing, attracts Queensland families by the truckload in summer. It seems many have been coming for so long that they've not bothered to leave and the town has a healthy percentage of retirees among its permanent population.

INFORMATION

Adventure Travel Centre (☎ 1800 554 400, 4125 9288; 410 The Esplanade; 🕑 7am-10pm) Internet access (per hour A$4) and information.

Hervey Bay Tourism & Development Bureau (☎ 1800 811 728, 4124 2912; cnr Urraween & Maryborough Rds; 🕑 8.30am-5pm Mon-Fri, 10am-4pm Sat & Sun) On the town's outskirts.

Whale Watch Tourist Centre (☎ 1800 358 595; Urangan Marina; 🕑 9am-5pm) Privately run but has good information.

SIGHTS & ACTIVITIES

Hervey Bay's spread of beach is best viewed via the 15km **Esplanade Track**. Amid the views you'll also encounter the 1.5km **Urangan Pier** and more than a couple of warm 'g'days' from passing locals.

At the eastern end of town, **Reef World** (☎ 4128 9828; Pulgul St, Urangan; adult A$14; 🕑 9.30am-5pm) is a small aquarium exquisitely stocked with some of the Great Barrier Reef's most colourful characters. You can get nose to nose through glass with the fish, resident turtles and coral. You can also take a dip with nonpredatory sharks (A$50).

Aboriginal bush-tucker excursions offered by **Tom's Tours** (☎ 4128 1005, after hours 4128 7968; adult A$25) are excellent, even though they include a visit to the rather faded **Hervey Bay Natureworld** (☎ 4124 1733; Fairway Dr). Tom gives you the chance, for a small surcharge, to paint your own boomerang. **Scrub Hill Community Farm** (☎ 4124 6908; adult A$16.50) also has bush-tucker tours.

Between mid-July and late October, whale-watching tours operate out of Hervey Bay daily (weather permitting). Sightings are guaranteed from 1 August to 1 November, when you get a free subsequent trip if the whales don't show. Some inquisitive animals

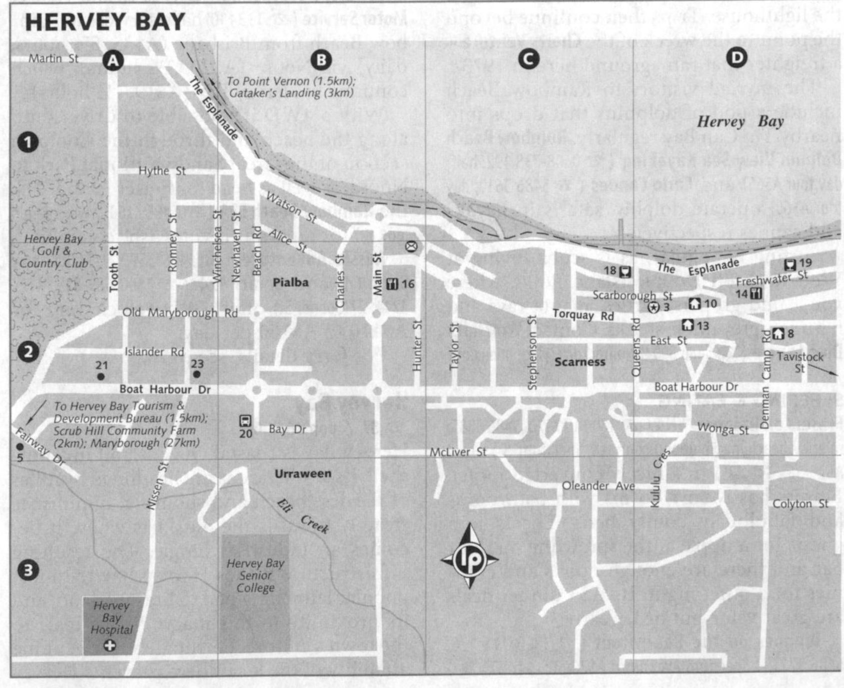

come right up to the boats, surfacing only metres away. At other times of the year, many boats offer dolphin-spotting tours.

Most boats provide underwater viewing, and prices for half-day tours are about A$65. Full-day tours cost only marginally more.

Princess II (4124 0400) Full-day tours with a good track record.

Quick Cat II (1800 671 977, 4128 9611; www.herveybaywhalewatch.com.au) A small vehicle run by an award-winning company.

Whalesong (1800 689 610, 4125 6222; www.whalesong.com.au)

SLEEPING

Hostels are big business in Hervey Bay and you're spoilt for choice. Most arrange pick-ups from the main bus stop, and organise trips to Fraser Island.

A1 Fraser Roving (1800 989 811, 4125 6386; www.fraserroving.com.au; 412 The Esplanade; dm A$18-21, d & tw A$50;) Possibly the friendliest hostel in all of Queensland, Fraser Roving's genuine owners and atmospheric bar guarantee new mates. If you're desperate for a quiet night, however, there's plenty of space to buffer the noise. The rooms are spartan but spacious and there are spotless bathrooms and a decent kitchen. Good wheelchair facilities.

Colonial Log Cabins (1800 818 280, 4125 1844; www.coloniallogcabins.com; 820 Boat Harbour Dr; dm A$22, d & tw from A$55, cabins from A$80;) Dorms, cabins and villas at this excellent YHA are scattered throughout a tranquil pocket of bush in the 'burbs. Possums and parrots entertain regularly and the facilities are excellent. Only some rooms have air-con so be sure to request one of these if the weather's warm.

Happy Wanderer Village (4125 1103; hwanderer@hervey.com.au; 105 Truro St, Torquay; camp/caravan sites per 2 people A$23/27, cabins from A$50;) The delicately manicured lawns and profuse gum cover at this large park make for great tent pitches, but the cabins, studios and two-bedroom units are all excellent for a splurge. The spotless facilities include a spa, laundry and free barbecues, and it's wheelchair accessible.

Koala Beach Resort (1800 354 535; 4125 3601; www.koala-backpackers.com; 408 The Esplanade; dm A$18, d & tw with/without bath A$55/45;) Like its siblings around Queensland, this hostel carries

QUEENSLAND

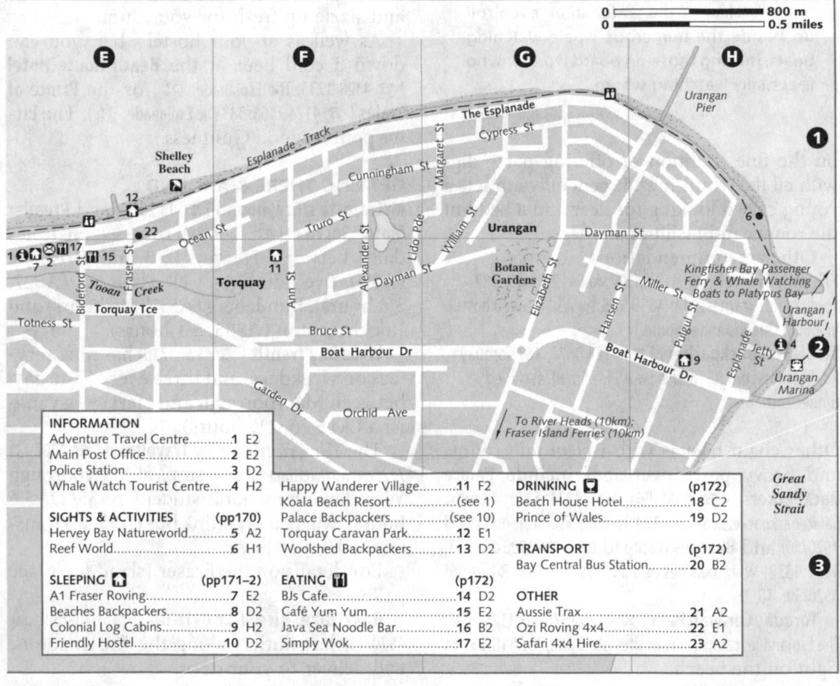

A WHALE OF A TIME

Seeing humpback whales in the flesh certainly surpasses watching a nature documentary. Up to 15m in length and 40 tonnes in weight, they're majestic and awe-inspiring – and seen regularly around the waters of Hervey Bay.

Up to 3000 humpbacks *(Megaptera novaeangliae)* enter the bay between the last week of July and the end of October, on the return leg of their annual migration between Antarctica and the warmer waters off northeastern Australia. Having mated and given birth in the north, they arrive in Hervey Bay in groups of about a dozen (known as pulses), before splitting into smaller groups of two or three (pods).

No-one is quite sure why the whales divert en route back to Antarctica. The prevailing theory is that it offers the adults a chance to enjoy a bit of R&R and gives the new calves more time to develop the layers of blubber necessary for survival in icy southern waters. Whatever the reason, the whales have come to feel increasingly at home in Hervey Bay over the years. With one eye clear of the water some even roll up beside the numerous whale-watching boats, making those on board wonder who is actually watching whom.

on the fine tradition of offering party digs with all the trimmings. It generally attracts a young crowd looking for beer and a bed but the rooms and facilities are decent.

Other recommendations:

Friendly Hostel (☎ 4124 4107; fax 4124 4619; 182 Torquay Rd, Scarness; dm A$19, d & tw A$44) Small hostel in an old Queenslander home.

Woolshed Backpackers (☎ 4124 0677; 181 Torquay Rd, Scarness; dm A$18, d & tw A$44) Small, secluded timber cottages.

Other chain hostels with welcoming rooms and heavy party overtones include **Palace Backpackers** (☎ 1800 063 168, 4124 5331; island@palacebackpackers.com.au; 184 Torquay Rd, Scarness; dm/d A$20/50) and **Beaches Backpackers** (☎ 1800 655 501, 4124 1322; www.beaches.com.au; 195 Torquay Rd; dm/d A$20/50; 💻).

Torquay Caravan Park (☎ 4125 1578; fax 4125 6706; The Esplanade; camp/caravan sites per 2 people A$18/23) is right on the beach.

EATING & DRINKING

The Esplanade around Torquay has plenty of takeaways, but **BJs Cafe** (21 Denman Camp Rd; meals A$4-8; 🕑 lunch & dinner) is a cut above. The Esplanade also has a couple of supermarkets.

Café Yum Yum (☎ 4125 4107; cnr Bideford & Truro Sts; dishes A$5-10; 🕑 breakfast & lunch Mon-Sat) The décor here may be slightly faded but the international menu boasts Thai curries, moussaka, lamb kofta and lavash. The pitta-bread pockets are fantastic and they cook a hearty, healthy breakfast.

Simply Wok (☎ 4125 2077; 417 The Esplanade; meals A$7-15; 🕑 breakfast, lunch & dinner; ⌘) Actually, there's nothing simple about the variety here, which includes gourmet sandwiches, divine salads, seafood and inventive Asian cuisine. The food is positively grown-up but you get to be 10 again with the markers and paper at every table – honestly, it's hard to resist.

Java Sea Noodle Bar (☎ 4123 7267; Shop 1/10 Main St, Pialba; meals around A$8; 🕑 lunch & dinner Mon-Sat) It's a bit out of the way but this noodle bar is ideal if you've had one too many burgers. The choose-your-own-adventure menu allows you to pick your own sauces, noodles and ingredients, which staff throw together and sizzle up fresh for you. Yum.

As well as at your hostel's bar, you can down a cold beer at the **Beach House Hotel** (☎ 4128 1233; The Esplanade; ⌘) or the **Prince of Wales** (☎ 4124 2466; 383 The Esplanade; ⌘). The latter pours a good Guinness.

GETTING THERE & AROUND

McCafferty's/Greyhound (☎ 13 20 30) and **Premier Motor Service** (☎ 13 34 10) run several times daily between Hervey Bay and Brisbane (A$50, five hours) as well as Noosa (A$27, 3½ hours), Bundaberg (A$17, 1½ hours) and Rockhampton (A$55, 5½ hours).

Wide Bay Transit (☎ 4121 3719) has nine services on weekdays, and three every Saturday, between Maryborough and Hervey Bay marina (A$5.25, 1½ hours).

The *Tilt Train*, run by **Traveltrain** (☎ 1300 131 722; www.traveltrain.com.au), stops at Maryborough West (economy adult/student A$55/27, 3½ hours), where a Trainlink bus (A$5.50) transfers to Hervey Bay.

For details on the Fraser Island ferry, see p176.

Rayz Bike Hire (☎ 0417-644 814; half-/full day A$20/15) has outlets along the Esplanade or will deliver to your door.

Fraser Island

☎ 07

Seen from the coast, Fraser Island appears too lush and green to be the world's biggest sand island, but its ecology is one of its many wonders. The fringe of pounding surf belies an interior of rainforests, gorges, mineral streams and some 200 vivid freshwater lakes. All of these dot a landscape that, considering its 120km by 15km surface area and enormous depth, contains more sand than the Sahara desert – reputedly.

Dunes, known locally as 'sandblows', stand up to 220m tall before you, while your 4WD moves slowly along the soft tracks. It's an amazing environment, but as 350,000 people arrive annually to delight in its beauty, Fraser can also feel like a giant sandpit with its own peak hour and congested beach highway.

Coming here, there are certain essentials to know: 4WDs are necessary (see the boxed text Sand Safaris, p174). The lakes are lovely to swim in, but the sea's lethal: undertows and man-eating sharks make it a definite no-go. And feeding the island's dingoes has made them increasingly aggressive in recent years (see p176).

Yet none of this detracts from the enjoyment of a location that's unlike any other on earth. If the dunes, forests, lakes, birds and mammals aren't enough, gaze up at the night sky. With little light behind you, the Milky Way blazes bright.

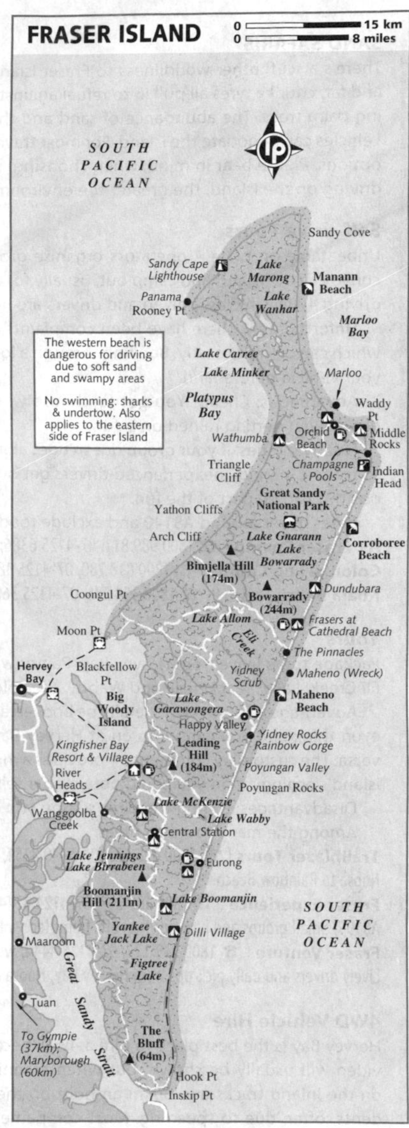

INFORMATION

If travelling independently, you'll need a permit to take a vehicle onto the island and to camp. Pick one up at **QPWS kiosk** (☎ 4125 8473) at the River Heads ferry terminal. Vehicle permits cost A$30, and camping ones A$4. If you forget to buy a vehicle permit on the mainland, it costs A$41 (cash only) on the island, but you could also face a A$50 fine. Permits are also available online at www.epa.qld.gov.au or from EPA offices.

You can pick up supplies and fuel at the island's Cathedral Beach, Eurong, Kingfisher Bay, Happy Valley and Orchid Beach, but you're far better off stocking up on the mainland because island prices are high.

Ranger stations offer information leaflets, tide times, free firewood (one armful per camp) and drinking water. Eurong is the main station; others close outside the high season (usually school holidays, Christmas and Easter).

Ranger stations:

Central Station (☎ 4127 9191; 🕒 10am-noon)
Dundubara (☎ 4127 9138; 🕒 8-9am & 3-4pm)
Eurong (☎ 4127 9128; 🕒 10.30am-4pm Mon, 7am-4pm Tue-Thu, 7am-3pm Fri, 2-4pm Sat & Sun)
Waddy Point (☎ 4127 9190; 🕒 7-8am & 4-4.30pm)

SAND SAFARIS

There's a sci-fi other-worldliness to Fraser Island, as 4WDs and buses with towering wheel bases and fat, chunky tyres all pull in to refuel against an idyllic beach backdrop of white sand and waving palm trees. The abundance of sand and the lack of paved roads mean that only these 4WD vehicles can negotiate the island. For most travellers transport comes down to the following three options. Please bear in mind, when choosing, that the greater the number of individual vehicles driving on the island, the greater the environmental damage.

Self-drive Tours

Unbeatable on price – operators organise groups of about nine per vehicle to drive their own convoy to the island and camp out, usually for two nights and three days. Some instruction about driving 4WD vehicles is given and drivers are nominated.

Unfortunately, there have been complaints about dodgy vehicle damage claims upon return, which can be quite costly. Booking through a local hostel reduces the risk of this. Either way, check your vehicle beforehand.

Advantages: Cheap! You get to choose when and how you see everything. If your group is good, even getting rained on is fun.

Disadvantages: If your group doesn't get along it's a looooong three days. If the weather's rough so is the camping. Inexperienced drivers get bogged in sand all the time, although if it's not serious this can be part of the fun.

Rates hover around A$140 and exclude food and fuel (usually A$30 to A$40). Recommended:

A1 Fraser Roving (☎ 1800 989 811, 07-4125 6386; www.fraserroving.com.au)
Colonial Log Cabins (☎ 1800 818 280, 07-4125 1844; www.coloniallogcabins.com)
Koala Beach Resort (☎ 1800 354 535, 07-4125 3601; www.koala-backpackers.com)

Tours

Package tours leave from Hervey Bay, Rainbow Beach and Noosa, and typically cover rainforests, Eli Creek, Lakes Mackenzie and Wabby, the coloured Pinnacles and the *Maheno* shipwreck.

Advantages: Tours can generally be booked at the last minute, you don't have to cook, drive…or even think and you can jump on at Hervey Bay and return to Rainbow Beach or Noosa, or vice versa. The customary commentary provides a much greater understanding and appreciation of the island's ecology than you could obtain on a self-drive tour.

Disadvantages: During the peak season you could share the experience with 40 others.

Among the many tours on offer:

Trailblazer Tours (☎ 1800 626 673, 07-5449 8151; Noosaville; 3-day safari A$275) Small groups. Pick-ups from Noosa to Rainbow Beach.
Fraser Experience (☎ 1800 689 819, 07-4124 4244; www.safari4wdhire.com.au; Hervey Bay; 2-day tours A$195) Small groups and pick-up/drop offs from Hervey Bay and Rainbow Beach.
Fraser Venture (☎ 1800 249 122, 07-4125 4444, www.fraser-is.com; 1/2/3 days A$100/210/340 twin share) Lively drivers and daily pick-ups from Hervey Bay, Noosa and Rainbow Beach.

4WD Vehicle Hire

Hervey Bay is the best place to hire a 4WD, because there's plenty of choice. A driving instruction video will usually be shown, but when planning your trip, reckon on covering 20km an hour on the inland tracks and 50km an hour on the eastern beach. Fraser has had some nasty accidents, often due to speeding. Most companies will help arrange ferries, and permits, and hire camping gear.

Advantages: Complete freedom to roam the island, and escape the crowds. Disadvantages: It's not cheap and you may have to tackle conditions where even experienced 4WDers have difficulties. Daily rates for multiple-day rentals are about A$120 for a Suzuki Sierra to A$180 for a Toyota Landcruiser. Recommended:

Aussie Trax (☎ 1800 062 275, 07-4124 4433; 56 Boat Harbour Dr, Hervey Bay)
Ozi Roving 4X4 (☎ 07-4125 6355; 10 Fraser St, Torquay)
Safari 4X4 Hire (☎ 1800 689 819, 07-4124 4244; 102 Boat Harbour Dr, Hervey Bay)

SIGHTS & ACTIVITIES

From the island's southern tip, vehicles should use the old mining track between Hook Point and Dilli Village, rather than the beach. From here on, the eastern beach is the main thoroughfare. A short drive north of Dilli will take you to the resort at **Eurong**, the start of the inland track across to Central Station and Wanggoolba Creek (for the ferry to River Heads).

In the middle of the island is **Central Station**, the starting point for numerous walking tracks. From signposted tracks head to the beautiful **Lakes McKenzie**, **Jennings**, **Birrabeen** and **Boomanjin**. Like many of Fraser's lakes, these are 'perched', formed by water accumulating on top of a thin impermeable layer of decaying twigs and leaves. They also join Iceland's famous Blue Lagoon as open-air beauty salons, where you can exfoliate your skin with the mineral sand and soften your hair in the clear water. Lake McKenzie is possibly the most spectacular, but Lake Birrabeen is also amazing, and usually less crowded.

About 4km north of Eurong along the beach is a signposted walking track to **Lake Wabby**. An easier route is from the lookout on the inland track. Wabby is surrounded on three sides by eucalypt forest, while the fourth side is a massive sandblow, which is encroaching on the lake at a rate of about 3m a year. The lake is deceptively shallow and diving is dangerous – in recent years, several people have been paralysed by doing so. You can often find turtles and huge catfish in the eastern corner of the lake under the trees.

Driving north along the beach you will pass **Happy Valley** and **Eli Creek**, a fast-moving, crystal-clear waterway that will carry you effortlessly downstream. It's enough fun to convert even the baddest dude into a 10-year-old wanting another go…and another…and another. About 2km from Eli Creek is the wreck of the *Maheno*, a passenger liner that was blown ashore by a cyclone in 1935 while being towed to a Japanese scrapyard.

Roughly 5km north of the *Maheno* you'll find the **Pinnacles** – a section of coloured sand cliffs – and about 10km beyond, **Dundubara**. Then there's a 20km stretch of beach before you come to the rock outcrop of **Indian Head**, the best vantage point on the island. Sharks, manta rays, dolphins and (during the migration season) whales can often be spotted from the top of the headland.

From Indian Head the track branches inland, passing the **Champagne Pools** (the only safe spot on the island for saltwater swimming). This inland road leads to **Waddy Point** and **Orchid Beach**, the last settlement on the island. Many tracks north of this are closed for environmental protection. The 30km of beach up to **Sandy Cape**, the northern tip, with its lighthouse, is off limits to hire vehicles. The beach from Sandy Cape to Rooney Point is closed to all vehicles, as is the road from Orchid Beach to Platypus Bay.

SLEEPING & EATING

Self-caterers should come well equipped, as supplies on the island are limited and pricey.

The QPWS runs **camping grounds** (camp sites per person A$4) with coin-operated hot showers, toilets and barbecues at Central Station, Dundubara and Waddy Point. Its camping grounds at Lake McKenzie, Lake Boomanjin and Wathumba have cold showers; there are none at the Lake Allom grounds. You can also camp on designated stretches of the eastern beach. To camp in any of these public areas you need a permit. At the time of research Dilli Village camping ground was being refurbished by the University of the Sunshine Coast, which will subsequently manage it. It should be open for business by the time you read this.

Prices for all other accommodation drop considerably outside of school holidays, Christmas and Easter.

WORLD HERITAGE ASHTRAY?

Because Fraser Island is World Heritage–listed nothing should be taken from the island and only tracks should be left behind. This includes even the teeniest bit of litter, and so it is both surprising and sad that many travellers flick their cigarette butts without thinking. A cigarette butt may seem innocuous, but fish and birds assume it's food. Moreover, in peak season the island's most touristed areas begin to resemble an ashtray.

Enjoy Fraser Island – 'butt' don't forget your rubbish.

DEADLY DINGOES

In 2001 the fatal mauling of a nine-year-old Brisbane boy on Fraser Island was the tragic culmination of several dingo attacks in preceding years. Soon after, 30 of the island's estimated 160 dingoes were culled – much to the disgust of Aboriginal and environmental groups. The saddest fact is that this event and the growing aggressiveness of the animals was surely brought about by tourists hand feeding or harassing the dingoes over the years.

Consequently, there's now a minimum A$225 fine for feeding dingoes or leaving food where it may attract them to camping grounds. In its Fraser Island information pack, the Queensland Parks & Wildlife Service (QPWS) provides a leaflet on being 'Dingo Smart'.

Frasers at Cathedral Beach (☎ 4127 9177; www.fraserislandco.com.au; Cathedral Beach; camp sites per 2 people A$18, cabins from A$110) This privately run, family-orientated, park, about 34km north of Eurong, has a comfortable tent village. The cabins are excellent value for a group of four or more.

Eurong Beach Resort (☎ 4127 9122; www.fraser-is.com; Eurong; dm A$17-28, units from A$140;) Bright and cheerful Eurong is the main resort on the east coast and the most accessible for all budgets. Cheaper dorms are spartan and often booked by tour groups, but the comfortable self-contained versions are good value. The resort also has a cavernous restaurant and a number of splurge options. A hard day's sightseeing can be rewarded by a dip in the lagoon-style pool or with a bevvy at the Beach Bar.

Kingfisher Bay Resort (☎ 1800 072 555, 4120 3333; www.kingfisherbay.com; Kingfisher Bay; hotel r from A$270, 2-bedroom villas (3-night min) from A$820;) If you're thinking of blowing the budget (you are in paradise, after all) this elegant ecoresort is the way to go. Sophisticated timber villas are raised from the ground to limit the environmental impact and the interiors are laced with little indulgences. There are also restaurants, bars and shops.

GETTING THERE & AWAY

The most commonly used ferries to Fraser Island are the vehicle ferries from River Heads, about 10km south of Hervey Bay, which land on the island's west coast either at Wanggoolba Creek or Kingfisher Bay. However there's a fast catamaran service for pedestrians from Hervey Bay's Urangan marina to Kingfisher Bay, while yet more vehicle ferries operate from Inskip Point (near Rainbow Beach) to Hook Point in the island's south.

Fraser Venture (☎ 4125 4444; return fare vehicle & driver A$110, additional passenger A$6) makes the 30-minute crossing from River Heads to Wanggoolba Creek. It departs daily from River Heads at 7.15am, 9am, 10.15am, 11am, 2.30pm and 3.30pm, returning from the island at 8.30am, 9.30am, 1pm, 2.30pm, 3.30pm, and 4pm. On Saturday there is also a 7am service from River Heads, returning at 7.30am from the island.

The **Kingfisher Bay Resort** (☎ 1800 072 555, 4120 3333; www.kingfisherbay.com; Kingfisher Bay; return fare vehicle & four passengers A$110, additional passenger A$6) operates two boats. Its vehicle ferry does the 45-minute crossing from River Heads to Kingfisher Bay daily. Departures from River Heads are at 7.15am, 11am and 2.30pm, and from the island at 8.30am, 1.30pm and 4pm. Its fast catamaran passenger ferry (return fare A$44) crosses between the Urangan marina and Kingfisher Bay every few hours from 8.45am to 8pm (later on Friday and Saturday).

The **Rainbow Venture Ferry** (☎ 1800 227 437, 5486 3154; return fare vehicle & occupants A$65) has regular ferries making the 15-minute trip from Inskip Point to Hook Point, from 7am to 5.30pm daily (sometimes later in peak season).

Childers

☎ 07 / pop 1500

This pretty heritage town attracts budget travellers with its year-round fruit-picking opportunities. This is despite an increasing realisation of just how back-breaking this work can be, and despite the Palace Hostel fire in 2000 that killed 15 backpackers. There is a moving **Childers Backpackers Memorial** upstairs in the renovated Palace building. The **visitors centre** (☎ 4126 3886; 9am-4pm Mon-Fri, 9am-3pm Sat & Sun) is downstairs.

Not yet open at the time of research, the brand new **Palace Backpackers** (☎ 4126 2244; fax 4126 1699; 72 Churchill St; dm A$20;) promises excellent facilities and support for working backpackers. It's also a reflection of how much this town embraces working travellers and the life they inject into the community.

Other recommendations:

Sugarbowl Caravan Park (☎ 4126 1521; Churchill St; camp sites per 2 people per night/week from A$18/105) Good amenities.

Childers Tourist Park & Camp (☎ 4126 1371; 111 Stockyard Rd; camp sites per 2 people per night/week from A$16/100) Quiet, convivial site, about 7km from town.

Federal Hotel (☎ 4126 1438; fax 4126 2407; 71 Churchill St; dm per night/week A$19/90) Old but friendly and central pub.

Long-distance buses stop just north of town at the Shell service station. One-way fares to/from Hervey Bay are A$15, Maryborough A$22 and Bundaberg A$15.

Bundaberg

☎ 07 / pop 44,550

From 'the hummock' – the only hill in this flat landscape – the eye sees fields of waving sugar cane from Bundaberg to the coral-fringed coast. That's the source of the famous Bundy rum and of income for some, but not all, local 'cockies' (farmers).

Bundaberg may have seen the odd aesthetic alteration over the years but essentially not much has changed in this typical Australian country town. The main strip, embellished with wide streets and waving palms, is positively gracious. For travellers, Bundaberg offers plenty of fruit-picking work, scuba diving and the chance to see unbearably cute turtles make their first stumble down the beach at nearby Mon Repos.

INFORMATION

Bundaberg visitors centre 186 Bourbong St (☎ 4153 9289; 🕑 8.30am-4.45pm Mon-Fri, 10am-1pm Sat & Sun); 271 Bourbong St (☎ 1800 308 888, 4153 8888; 🕑 9am-5pm)

Cosy Corner Internet Cafe (Barolin St; per hr A$4)

SIGHTS & ACTIVITIES

This small town has bred an Australian icon, and visiting the vats of the **Bundaberg Rum Distillery** (☎ 4131 2900; www.bundabergrum.com.au; Ave St; adult/concession A$9.90/7.70; 🕑 tours 10am-3pm Mon-Fri, 10am-2pm Sat & Sun) is a cultural experience. Well, that's waxing lyrical but the distillery is intrinsically Bundaberg, the tours are good fun and you get a tot of the good stuff at the end.

The best museums in the attractive **Botanic Gardens** (Gin Gin Rd) are the **Fairymead House Sugar Museum** (☎ 4153 6786; admission A$4; 🕑 10am-4pm), with everything from explanatory videos to artefacts by Polynesian 'Kanaka' sugar workers and a colourful collection of 1950s anodised-aluminium sugar containers; and the **Hinkler House Museum** (☎ 4152 0222; admission A$4; 🕑 10am-4pm), one-time home to Bert Hinkler, who in 1928 was the first solo flier between England and Australia. The gardens are 2km north of town across the Burnett River.

The **Bundy Belle** (☎ 0427-099 009) is an old-fashioned ferry that chugs down the Burnett River twice a day for 2½-hour trips (A$15).

The small **Alexandra Park & Zoo** (☎ Quay St; admission free; 🕑 6.30am-3.30pm) is tucked into a green corner on the banks of the Burnett River. A handful of animals including the ubiquitous kangaroo and some vivid and vocal parrots reside here. It's a pretty spot and the adjoining large, grassy park begs for a picnic.

About 16km east of Bundaberg, the small beach hamlet of **Bagara** entices divers and snorkellers with a dazzling bank of coral near the shore around **Barolin Rocks** and in

TALKING TURTLE

You almost expect to hear the hushed commentary of wildlife programme-maker David Attenborough during the egg-laying and hatching at Mon Repos, Australia's most accessible turtle rookery. But on this beach 15km northeast of Bundaberg it's no disappointment to be accompanied instead by the knowledgeable staff from the **Environmental Protection Agency (EPA) visitors centre** (☎ 4159 1562; 🕑 7.30am-4pm Mon-Fri). From November to March, when loggerhead and other marine turtles drag themselves up the beach to lay their eggs, and the young then emerge, the office organises nightly **viewings** (adult A$5; 🕑 7pm-6am). It's best to arrive as early as 5.30pm to queue. After 7pm you'll be allocated to a group and led on to the beach in turns. Alternatively you can take a turtle-watching tour with **Footprints Adventures** (☎ 4152 3659; www.footprintsadventures.com.au). Either way, take warm clothing, rain protection and insect repellent.

the **Woongarra Marine Park**. This is one of the cheapest spots in Australia to dive and you can do a PADI Open Water course for about A$170.

Dive companies in Bundaberg:

Salty's (☎ 4151 6422; 208 Bourbong St)

Aqua Scuba (☎ 4153 5761; julian@aquascuba.com.au; Shop 1, 66 Tarago St)

SLEEPING

Bundaberg Backpackers & Travellers Lodge (☎ 41 52 2080; fax 4151 3355; cnr Targo & Crofton Sts; dm per night/week A$20/110;) The Lodge's bland brick exterior and practical interior furnishings belie a warm, cheerful buzz, perpetuated by helpful owners and a constant stream of working travellers. Little extras like dressers in the dorms and oodles of couches create a homely environment.

Grand Backpackers (☎ 4154 1166; 89 Bourbong St; dm per night/week A$21/115) Above a beautiful old corner pub, this hostel promises more character than your average hostel and doesn't disappoint. Behind a wide timber balcony sits a commodious common area and (a few) accommodating dorms. Plus you've got a great local just downstairs.

In the bus station complex two spartan hostels catering to divers are the **Dive Inn** (☎ 4153 5761; diveinn@aquascuba.com.au; dm for divers/nondivers A$17/15;) and **Salty's Rest** (☎ 4151 6422; dm for divers/nondivers A$15/17;).

Also recommended:

Federal Backpackers (☎ 4153 3711; www.federalbackpackers.com.au; 221 Bourbong St; dm per night/week from A$20/120, d A$50;) Big and functional.

City Centre Backpackers (☎ 4151 3501; 216 Bourbong St; dm per night/week A$20/120, d per night/week A$50/300) Not luxurious, but friendly.

EATING

If you're self-catering, head to the supermarket on Woongarra Street.

Talking Point Cafe (☎ 4152 1811; 79 Bourbong St; dishes A$5-10; breakfast & lunch;) The cooking smells swimming about here are mouth-watering and the paninis, focaccias, soups and coffee are just as divine. The cosy couches by the front window can be difficult to climb out of so you'll just have to stay for cake.

Spices Plus (☎ 4154 3320; cnr Quay & Targo Sts; dishes A$8-14; dinner;) Bundaberg's spicy little secret debunks the myth that small towns don't have culinary delights. The authentic Indian food here will have your taste buds sizzling but bookings are advised as it's deservedly popular.

Delight Cafe (☎ Earls Court, Bourbong St; meals A$4-8; breakfast & lunch Mon-Fri) This nook of a café really is a delight, serving everything from veggie burgers and hot rolls to sushi.

GETTING THERE & AWAY

The main bus stop is **Stewart's coach terminal** (☎ 4153 2646; 66 Targo St). One-way bus fares from Bundaberg include Brisbane (A$65, 6½ hours), Childers (A$15, one hour), Hervey Bay (A$17, 1½ hours), Agnes Waters (A$25, two hours) and Rockhampton (A$55, 4½ hours).

Traveltrain's (☎ 1300 131 722; www.traveltrain.com.au) *Tilt Train* also runs between Brisbane and Bundaberg (A$90, 4½ hours, three weekly).

CAPRICORN COAST

Agnes Water & Town of 1770

☎ 07

Just when you thought Queensland had given away all her secrets, the isolated settlements of Agnes Water and Town of 1770 beckon you with dense tumbles of tropical bush, rugged headland and views to the southern fingers of the Great Barrier Reef so vast they muddle the horizon.

To be honest, the secret was out a while ago – surfers have been heading here for years, testing their courage and skill on the hefty breaks by the shore and off the reef. What keeps the area devoid of a development invasion is its perimeter of national park. These days, this region is where travellers head to escape the highways, chill out and overdose on sand and sun.

INFORMATION

Agnes Water library (☎ 4902 1501; Regional Transition Centre, Captain Cook Dr, Agnes Water; per 30min A$2.20) Internet access, but you must book.

Discovery Centre (☎ 4974 7002; Shop 12, Endeavour Plaza, cnr Captain Cook Dr & Round Hill Rd, Agnes Water; 9am-5pm) Tourist information.

SIGHTS & ACTIVITIES

The best way to enjoy this pocket of tranquillity is to soak up the sun and views on any of the beaches accessible from both towns. A low population provides the kind of seclusion celebs might yearn for and the absence of crowds certainly makes you feel pretty special.

This area is the closest access point to the southernmost section of the Great Barrier Reef. Accessing the islands here is an expensive exercise but well worth the bucks for the gorgeous snorkelling and diving.

Several operators offer day tours from the 1770 marina to **Lady Musgrave Island**, a 15-hectare cay surrounded by an aqua-blue lagoon. Prices generally include lunch and snorkelling. Cruises run by **Captain Cook Great Barrier Reef Cruises** (☎ 1300 666 631, 4974 9077; www.1770reefcruises.com; tours A$130) are on *Spirit of 1770*, a high-speed catamaran, and the company sometimes discounts tickets if you're staying at one of the hostels. Another good operator is **Lady Musgrave Barrier Reef Cruises** (☎ 1800 072 110, 4159 4519; www.lmcruises.com.au; tours A$140).

If you really need to get away from it all, try the even less-trafficked and unspoilt **Fitzroy Reef Lagoon**, a coral outcrop visited by **1770 Holidays** (☎ 1800 177 011, 4974 9422; www.1770holidays.com; tours A$125), which zips off in its *Reef Jet*. The same company also runs enjoyable day tours in its LARCs (large amphibious vehicles); these day trips take in Middle Island, Bustard Head and Eurimbula National Park, operate on Monday, Wednesday and Saturday, and cost A$95.

Locally operated **1770 Adventure Tours** offers sea kayaking and canoe tours (A$35) and a very popular sunset tour (A$5). You won't need to seek them out – staff visit the hostels and plan trips based on interest and numbers.

Agnes Waters' main beach is Queensland's northernmost surfing beach.

SLEEPING & EATING

Cool Bananas Backpackers (☎ 1800 227 660, 4974 7660; fax 4974 7661; 2 Springs Rd, Agnes Water; dm A$23; 💻) A stylish timber-and-tin Shangri-La and one big muscle relaxant. An unyielding soundtrack of the Chillout Sessions, frequent campfires, video nights, a sundrenched patio and snags on the barbecue all trap you in a lackadaisical lull. However, if you've the strength grab a bodyboard and head to the beach.

Backpackers 1770 (☎ 1800 121 770; Captain Cook Dr, Agnes Water; dm/d A$20/40; 💻) Slightly less relaxing than Cool Bananas – but only just – this hostel is functional in a comfy way. All the dorms have bathrooms, the kitchen and outdoor dining area are quite fabulous and the owners are professional and knowledgeable.

There's also beachfront camping with a whopping view at **Town of 1770 Camping Ground** (☎ 4974 9286; Captain Cook Dr, camp/caravan sites per 2 people A$20/23).

There's a supermarket, bakery and butcher in **Endeavor Plaza** (cnr Captain Cook Dr & Round Hill Rd, Agnes Water).

1770 Cafe & Bar (Captain Cook Dr, Town of 1770; meals A$8-20; 🕑 lunch & dinner) The most atmospheric watering hole for miles and best enjoyed at sunset – with a beer in your hand and a melting sun over the reef. After several more bevvies it's time to tuck into one of its divine pizzas.

In Agnes Water you can pick up an outstanding kebab at the **Rock Cafe** (Springs Rd; meals A$4-10; 🕑 breakfast & lunch daily, dinner Tue-Sun) or good takeaway food at **Palms Cafe** (Captain Cook Rd; meals A$2-10; 🕑 breakfast, lunch & dinner).

GETTING THERE & AWAY

Agnes Water is serviced by **McCafferty's/Greyhound** (☎ 13 20 30) from Bundaberg (A$25, two hours) and Rockhampton (A$26, 2½ hours). **Premier Motor Service** (☎ 13 34 10) links Agnes Waters with Bundaberg ($9) and Rockhampton ($25).

Rockhampton

☎ 07 / pop 59,500

Larger-than-life figurines of cattle greet the visitor at nearly every turn in the beef capital of Australia, but there's no bull about Rockhampton. Divided by the mighty Fitzroy River, this bastion of the cowboy is a hodgepodge of heritage buildings and tropical Queensland. Regardless of your gender, you'll almost certainly be called pet, darl or mate in 'Rocky', where political correctness is a term relegated to the bookshops.

An administrative and educational centre, Rocky sits astride the tropic of Capricorn, marking the start of the tropical north. It's a great place from which to head for Yeppoon and Great Keppel Island.

Rockhampton's CBD sits on the southern side of the Fitzroy River, which flows through the heart of the city. Suburban sprawl ebbs on the northern side of the river. A taxi from the airport into town costs A$10 to A$15.

INFORMATION

Capricorn visitors centre (☎ 4927 2055; www.capricorntourism.com.au; Gladstone Rd; 🕑 8am-5pm) About 3km south of town.

QUEENSLAND

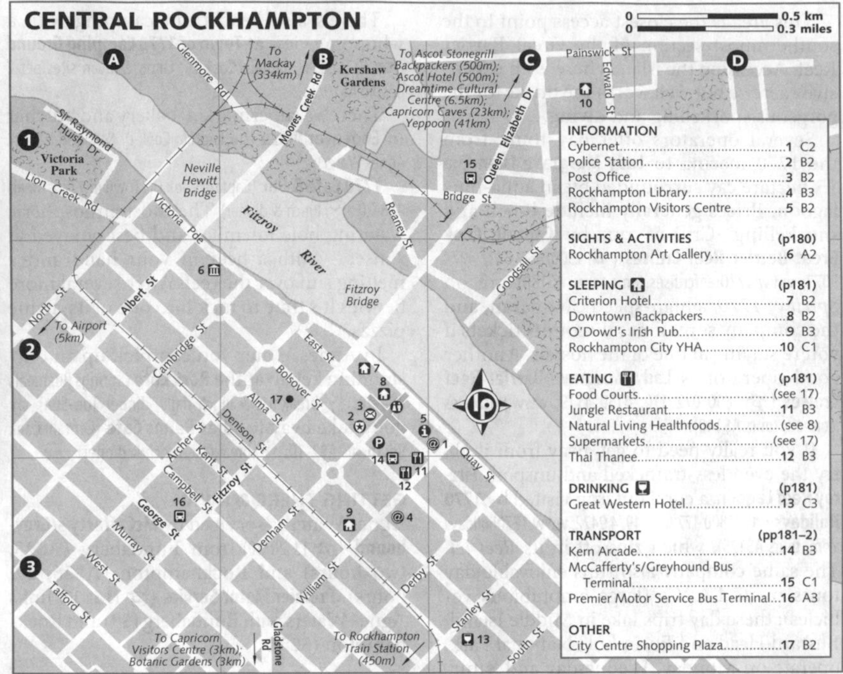

Cybernet (☎ 4927 3633; 12 William St; per hr A$5) Internet access.

Jungle Restaurant (☎ 4921 4900; cnr East & William St; per hr A$5) This restaurant (see opposite) has Internet access.

Rockhampton library (☎ 4936 8265; 69 William St) Free Internet access but you need to book.

Rockhampton visitors centre (☎ 4922 5339; Customs House, 208 Quay St; 8.30am-4.30pm Mon-Fri, 9am-4pm Sat & Sun)

SIGHTS & ACTIVITIES

Rockhampton has some fine old buildings, particularly on Quay St. Leaflets from the visitors centres map out walking routes.

The **Rockhampton Art Gallery** (☎ 4927 7129; 62 Victoria Pde; admission free; 10am-4pm Tue-Fri, 11am-4pm Sat & Sun) is possibly the best regional gallery in Australia. With not a cowboy image in sight, this gallery plays permanent host to Australian masters including Norman Lindsay, Sidney Nolan, Arthur Boyd and Sir Russell Drysdale. Temporary exhibits of mixed mediums including drawings, weavings, pottery and glasswork mostly hail from the Asia-Pacific region, with a strong emphasis on indigenous influences.

Rockhampton's **Botanic Gardens** (☎ 4922 1654; Spencer St; admission free; 6am-6pm), in the city's south, really are memorable, with flaming bougainvilleas, bunya pines, and a small but interesting zoo.

Just across the river from the central district, **Kershaw Gardens** (Moores Creek Rd) is a scenic miscellany of forest, creeks and open grassy areas perfect for some Frisbee action. Walking paths traverse the gardens and avid botanists will appreciate the scientific labels.

Set among 12 hectares of tribal sites and native bush, the **Dreamtime Cultural Centre** (☎ 4936 1655; Bruce Hwy; adult A$13; 10am-3.30pm Mon-Fri) is one of the largest displays of Aboriginal and Torres Strait Islander culture in Australia. It's a genuine opportunity to learn more about Australia's rich and complex indigenous make-up. The tours, at 10.30am and 1pm, are highly recommended.

TOURS

Beef 'n' Reef Adventures (☎ 1800 753 786, 0427-159 655; www.beefnreef.com; half-/full-day tours A$35/75) This tour is a must for anyone hungry to witness a seldom-seen Australia. Owner-operator Dave takes small groups to untouristed corners of the Capricorn Coast, including cattle farms, the Capricorn Caves, Styx River and the Koorana Crocodile Farm. Each tour is tailored to make the most of the weather and other environmental conditions and you'll get no recycled commentary here. Highly recommended.

SLEEPING

All Rocky's hostels arrange pick-ups unless you arrive on the late bus – if this is the case, call and let them know you're coming.

Rockhampton City YHA (☎ 4927 5288; rockhampton@yhaqld.org; 60 MacFarlane St; dm A$23, d & tw A$50;) This well-organised hostel vaguely resembles a school camp – the facilities are more functional than homely but everything is neat, clean and ordered. The kitchen is excellent and although the rooms are cramped, the beds are comfy.

Ascot Stonegrill Backpackers (☎ 1800 224 719, 0427-159 655; www.ascothotel.com.au; 177 Musgrave St; dm A$18, d & tw A$36;) Upstairs from the popular pub and restaurant (right) this hostel is all faded charm and creature comforts. The facilities aren't exceptional but the owners are, and their genuine, affable approach is infectious. It's the kind of place where you come for a day but stay for a week. Reception is open 24 hours.

Downtown Backpackers (☎ 4922 1837; fax 4922 1050; 91 East St; dm/tw A$23/38;) In a very handy location, this hostel has basic, clean accommodation, although the staff can be a bit indifferent.

Two central pubs with gorgeous façades and fair dinkum accommodation:

Criterion Hotel (☎ 4922 1225; www.thecriterion.com.au; 150 Quay St; s/d A$35/45;)

O'Dowd's Irish Pub (☎ 4927 0344; www.odowds.com.au; 100 William St; s/d A$30/45, motel r A$80;)

EATING & DRINKING

If you're self-catering, fill up on the cheap at the supermarkets and small food courts inside **City Centre Shopping Plaza** (cnr Fitzroy and Bolsover Sts).

Rockhampton's culinary delights revolve largely around steak, but there is a modicum of offerings for noncarnivores.

Natural Living Healthfoods (☎ 4927 8235; 4 Denham St; meals A$4-10; breakfast & lunch Mon-Fri) Not strictly Pritikin-esque but by Rocky's standards the quiches, sandwiches, muffins and pies in this popular café are certainly fresh and healthy. Good breakfasts.

Thai Thanee (☎ 4922 1255; cnr William & Bolsover Sts; mains A$10-17; dinner;) The décor may be a tad drab but the cuisine here is positively fragrant. All your favourites adorn the menu and amid the green and red curries are a few lesser knowns.

Jungle Restaurant (☎ 4921 4900; cnr East & William Sts; lunch A$6-10, dinner A$10-20; lunch & dinner;) Polished but unpretentious, this funky restaurant cooks up something for everyone. Sushi, seafood, fajitas, steaks, pasta…you get the picture. Wednesday and Thursday nights are Indian curry nights when you can eat your fill for A$13.

Ascot Hotel (☎ 1800 224 719; 177 Musgrave St; mains A$17-30; lunch & dinner;) Possibly the best of Rocky's steakhouses, the speciality here is a large chunk of beef served on a sizzling stone slab. You can cook it to your taste – sublime! Afterwards, pop into the pub for a bout of karaoke and a beer with the locals.

Great Western Hotel (☎ 4922 1862; 39 Stanley St; admission A$8) This Rocky institution lures urban cowboys for miles, with its saloon-style bar down to its monthly rodeos. If you're brave you can test your skills on a real bull for free on Wednesday nights.

You can also down a cold beer in less energetic surrounds at the memorabilia-clad Criterion Hotel (left) or O'Dowd's Irish Pub (left).

GETTING THERE & AWAY

At the time of writing, low-end flights to Sydney started at A$110, Brisbane A$90 and Melbourne A$180.

Jetstar (☎ 13 15 38; www.jetstar.com.au)
Qantas (☎ 13 13 13; www.qantas.com.au)
Regional Express (Rex; ☎ 13 17 13; www.regionalexpress.com.au)
Virgin Blue (☎ 13 67 89; www.virginblue.com.au)

McCafferty's/Greyhound (☎ 4927 2844; cnr Brown & Linnett Sts) is just north of the Fitzroy Bridge. Destinations include Brisbane (A$65, 11 hours), Mackay (A$50, four hours), Airlie Beach (A$65, 6½ hours) and Townsville (A$65, 11 hours).

Premier Motor Service (☎ 3236 4444; 91 George St) is at the Mobil roadhouse. It services the same routes as McCafferty's, but for several dollars less.

Young's Bus Service (☎ 4922 3813) leaves for Yeppoon from the Kern Arcade (local bus terminal) in Bolsover St 12 times daily from Monday to Friday and six times on Saturday and Sunday ($7.70). **Rothery's Coaches** (☎ 4922 4320) travels twice daily between Rockhampton airport and Rosslyn Bay (A$15) – the marina for Great Keppel Island.

The high-speed *Tilt Train*, run by **Traveltrain** (☎ 1300 131 722; www.traveltrain.com.au), also travels between Brisbane and Rockhampton (economy A$95, seven hours, six weekly).

Around Rockhampton

In the Berserker Range, 23km north of Rockhampton, are the **Capricorn Caves** (☎ 07-4934 2883; www.capricorncaves.com.au; Caves Rd; 9am-4pm). This series of limestone caves and passages is spectacular year-round, but particularly during the summer solstice (1 December to 14 January), when the sun beams vertical light through the roof of the Belfry Cave. A one-hour cathedral tour (A$15), leaving on the hour, and three-hour adventure tour (A$60, bookings required) are offered.

About 120km southwest of Rockhampton and 22km east of Baralaba, **Myella Farm Stay** (☎ 07-4998 1290; www.myella.com; 2-/3-day stay A$170/240) is a 1040-hectare cattle station where travellers can experience life on an Aussie farm; it promises horse riding, campfires, home cooking, kangaroos and red dust. Ring for directions or to arrange a pick-up.

Carnarvon National Park

Sitting 450km southwest of Rockhampton is Carnarvon National Park. Carved out over millions of years by a creek running through sandstone, the highlight here is **Carnarvon Gorge**. This amazing oasis contains river oaks, flooded gums, cabbage palms and moss gardens, plus caves full of Aboriginal art, deep pools and platypuses in the creek. The valley floor sits beneath a sheer 200m rock wall.

From Rockhampton head west to Emerald; the turn-off to the gorge is 60km south of Rolleston. After the turn-off, there's 23km of sealed road, followed by an unsealed 21km. After rain, the dirt sections are impassable.

The road leads to a **visitors centre** (☎ 07-4984 4505; 8am-5pm) and a scenic picnic ground. The main walking track starts from here, following Carnarvon Creek through the gorge, with detours to various points of interest. These include the **Moss Garden** (3.6km from the picnic area), **Ward's Canyon** (4.8km), the **Art Gallery** (5.6km) and **Cathedral Cave** (9.3km) – the last two of which are decorated with Aboriginal stencils and hand paintings. You should allow at least a few days for a visit here, and bring lunch and water because there aren't any shops.

You cannot drive from Carnarvon Gorge to other sections of the park, although you can reach beautiful Mt Moffatt via an unsealed road from Injune (4WD necessary). For further information, contact the **Injune Information Centre** (☎ 07-4626 1053).

There are a couple of camping options within the park, but you need to book well in advance. **Takarakka Bush Resort** (☎ 07-4984 4535; www.takarakka.com.au; Wyseby Rd; camp/caravan sites per 2 people A$18/24, cabins A$70) is a signposted bush oasis with picturesque cabins. Alternatively,

DODGY JELLIES

From around October to April, Queensland's coastal waters from Rockhampton north become a playground for the deadly box jellyfish and the much smaller, but similarly dangerous, Irukandji jellyfish. They may appear harmless enough, but the sting from a box jellyfish has been known to kill in a matter of minutes.

This is all old news for Queenslanders, which is why you'll see plenty of them swimming in superhero suits, minus the cape. All the lusty photography in the world couldn't make these Lycra all-over-the-body numbers sexy, but a 'stinger suit' is your best protection against the deadly floaters. Besides, if everyone else is wearing one then it's not like you stand out. If you're doing any kind of snorkelling, sailing or diving tour most companies provide suits as a matter of course. Many northern beaches also come equipped with stinger nets.

If someone is stung, douse the stings with vinegar (no, vinegar is not the new coconut oil) and call an ambulance because artificial respiration may be required.

Your last alternative is to simply stay out of the sea during the dangerous period, but that's not much fun.

you can rough it at **Big Bend** (☎ 07-4984 4505; fax 4984 4915; camp sites per person A$4), which sits a 10km walk up the gorge. There are toilets but no showers, and fires are forbidden.

There is no public transport to Carnarvon National Park and you'll need your own wheels to get here. The *Spirit of the Outback* train, run by **Traveltrain** (☎ 1300 131 722; www.traveltrain.com.au), goes twice weekly (Tuesdays and Saturdays) from Rockhampton to Emerald (adult/student economy $55/27, five hours) and Longreach (A$110/55, 13½ hours).

Once in Emerald you can rent a car from **Avis** (☎ 4982 2333; www.avis.com.au; Springsure Rd; 7am-6pm Mon-Fri, 7am-11am Sat, 4-6pm Sun). Alternatively, **Sunrover Expeditions** (☎ 1800 353 717, 3880 0719; www.sunrover.com.au; 6-day tours per person A$940) operates fully inclusive tours from Brisbane, which depart on the last Tuesday of every month between March and November.

Yeppoon

☎ 07 / pop 10,780

While it's also the gateway to Great Keppel Island, Yeppoon is an attractive seaside town in its own right. Its pleasant beaches give way in the north to rainforest around Byfield, and the surrounding hills tumble down to a scenic esplanade with palms, pines and a vivid horizon. Just south of Yeppoon, Rosslyn Bay is the departure point for Great Keppel Island.

Capricorn Coast visitors centre (☎ 1800 675 785, 4939 4888; Ross Creek Roundabout; 9am-5pm) at the town entrance is a good source of information, and you can jump online at the **Yellow Door** (☎ 4939 8035; 30 James St; per hr A$4).

Yeppoon Backpackers (☎ 4939 4702; fax 4939 8080; 30 Queen St; dm/d A$20/45;) is a rambling Queenslander with simple dorms and a pool where you can easily waste a day. The owners pick up from Rockhampton once a day. **Beachside Caravan Park** (☎ 4939 3738; Farnborough Rd; camp/caravan sites per 2 people A$14/17) is a small breezy park with good sites.

James St has a supermarket and a healthy dose of good eateries, including **Dreamers** (☎ 4939 5797; 4 James St; dishes A$3-7; breakfast & lunch) and **Food for Thought** (☎ 4939 3335; Shop 6, Normanby St; dishes A$5-12; breakfast & lunch).

Young's Bus Service (☎ 4922 3813) operates a loop service from Rockhampton to Yeppoon, Rosslyn Bay and back (A$7.70, 12 services Monday to Friday, six Saturday and Sunday). **Rothery's Coaches** (☎ 4922 4320) does the same in flashier buses (A$15), twice daily.

Great Keppel Island

☎ 07

Great Keppel's gorgeous landscape is straight off a postcard – expansive beaches with talcy-white sand and motionless, blue water; undulating forests peppered with walking tracks; and intimate coves and coral beaches. These trimmings and a choice of budget-friendly digs make this island a favourite with backpackers, but it's big enough to avoid any peak-hour overtones. Actually, its unblemished surface belies its easy access from the mainland, but bear in mind that this tranquillity comes without artificial entertainment so pack a good book.

SIGHTS & ACTIVITIES

The tips of air-tubes bobbing above the water are testament to the popularity of **snorkelling**. Visitors usually start out at **Shelving Beach**, becoming progressively more adventurous as they hike to **Monkey Point** and **Clam Bay**.

Snorkelling at the more remote beaches involves a bushwalk, but even if you don't fancy a snorkel, the walk itself is worth doing. The longest bush track leads to the lighthouse near **Bald Rock Point** on the island's far side, but it's quite hard going (four to five hours return). The **Mt Wyndham** circuit walk (three hours) takes in the homestead and shearing shed. Whichever trek you choose be aware that the tracks get rough and rocky, and that you should take plenty of water with you.

With 18km of white-sand beaches, you don't need to go far for a swim. **Fisherman's Beach**, where the ferries come in, rarely gets crowded, and it's even quieter just around the corner at **Putney Beach**.

For watersports, **Great Keppel Island Jet Ski** (Putney Beach) and **Contiki Watersports Kiosk** (Fisherman's Beach) both hire sailboards, kayaks and snorkelling gear. **Keppel Reef Scuba Adventures** (☎ 4939 5022; www.keppeldive.com; Putney Beach) offers introductory dives with gear supplied for around A$100, or qualified dives with gear from A$75.

SLEEPING & EATING

Great Keppel YHA Hostel (☎ 4933 6416; yhagreatkeppelisland@bigpond.com.au; dm A$24, s/d tent A$28/56, d & tw cabin A$85) The sizable hostel is spread out on a large patch of Great Keppel greenery and gets a big thumbs up. The bright, immaculate cabins with hospital-corner sheeted beds are

QUEENSLAND

QUEENSLAND

THE GREAT BARRIER REEF (GBR)

Larger than the Great Wall of China and the only living thing visible from space, the Great Barrier Reef is one of the seven wonders of the natural world. The conglomeration of colourful coral that stretches along the Queensland seaboard is the planet's biggest reef system, where 2600 separate reefs form an outer ribbon parallel to the coast.

Scientists lovingly nickname this phenomenon the GBR, while NASA astronauts have eulogised it as a 'white scar on the face of the Pacific Ocean'. One BBC TV programme rated it second only to the Grand Canyon on a list of 50 places to see before you die. Did we mention this reef is pretty ace?

At a Glance

Length 2000km, from north of Bundaberg to Torres Strait
Width 80km at its broadest
Total size Over 345,000 sq km
Distance from shore 300km in the south, 30km in the north
Age Estimated between 600,000 years and 18 million years (contentious)

From Little Polyps, Mighty Reefs Grow

Made up of an industrious family of tiny animals, the coral polyp is responsible for creating the GBR and other reefs. All corals are primitive hollow sacs with tentacles on the top, but it's the hard – as opposed to soft – corals that are the architects and builders. These excrete a small amount of limestone as an outer skeleton to protect and support their soft bodies. As polyps die and new ones grow on top, billions of their skeletons cement together into an ever-growing natural bulwark.

All polyps need sunlight, so few grow deeper than 30m below the surface. The coral's skeletons are white, while the reef's kaleidoscopic colours come from the living polyps.

One of the most spectacular sights on the GBR occurs for a few nights after a full moon in late spring or early summer, when vast numbers of corals spawn. With tiny bundles of sperm and eggs visible to the naked eye, the event looks like a gigantic underwater snowstorm.

So, Then – What Will I See?

Beneath the surface the reef sometimes resembles a peak hour of psychedelically patterned fish, as they teem about each other and the vivid coral. But they aren't alone. Marine environments, including coral reefs, demonstrate the greatest biodiversity of any ecosystems on earth – much more so than rainforests. A simple snorkel is likely to reveal turtles, reef sharks, dolphins and sea cucumbers. If you're lucky, though, you might also spot whales, manta rays, squid and dugongs (sea cows).

OK, Then – Where's the Best Place to See the Reef?

It's said you could dive here every day of your life and still not see the entire reef. Individual areas vary from time to time, depending on the weather or any recent damage, but places to start:

Cairns (p209) The most common choice, so can be overtrafficked.
Port Douglas (p221) Gateway to the Low Isles and the Agincourt Reefs.
Yongala shipwreck (p197) One of Australia's best shipwrecks, off Townsville.
Fitzroy Reef Lagoon (p179) Untouched for years, so tourist numbers are still limited.
Whitsunday Islands (p192)

You can also view fish and coral from a glass-bottomed boat, a semisubmersible boat or an underwater observatory. Tour operators are listed throughout this book. You can also ask the Marine Park Authority for advice, or visit its Reef HQ aquarium (p197) in Townsville to see a living coral reef without leaving dry land.

For more information, see Lonely Planet's *Diving & Snorkeling Australia's Great Barrier Reef* guide.

recommended in summer when a fan is futile against the heat. Otherwise the tents are solid and pleasant.

Great Keppel Island Holiday Village (☎ 1800 180 235, 4939 8655; www.gkiholidayvillage.com.au; dm A$27, d tent A$70, cabins with bath from A$120) Beach shacks and Crusoe-esque surrounds tempt you into hammocks and conversation at this snug hideaway. The barbecue and free snorkelling gear get a good work-out, but maintenance is maybe too relaxed and the bathrooms and dorms could do with a bit of love.

Bringing supplies from the mainland is strongly advised as resources on the island are limited and costly. If you're keen to eat out, the smart and breezy **Keppel Haven Bar Bistro** (☎ 4933 6744; dishes A$7-22; breakfast, lunch & dinner) mixes up its menu with tortillas, fish burgers, stir-fries and steaks. You can chow down on the patio with a sunset.

Elsewhere the cuisine revolves heavily around pizzas and burgers. Two good options in this vein are **Island Pizza** (☎ 4939 4699; lunch A$5.50-28, dinner A$15-28; dinner Tue-Sun, lunch Sat & Sun during school holidays) and Contiki Resort's **Reef Burger Bar** (meals A$10-20; lunch & dinner).

GETTING THERE & AWAY

Two ferry operators leave the mainland from Keppel Bay Marina in Rosslyn Bay, south of Yeppoon. Both hostels pick up from the beach but you'll need to let them know.

Freedom Fast Cats (☎ 1800 336 244, 4933 6244; return ticket A$32) Departs from Rosslyn Bay at 9am, noon and 3pm; leaves Keppel Island at 10am, 2pm and 4pm.

Keppel Tourist Services (☎ 4933 6744; return ticket A$30) Departs from Rosslyn Bay at 7.30am, 9.15am, 11.30am and 3.30pm; leaves Keppel Island at 8.15am, 2pm and 4.30pm.

Rothery's Coaches (☎ 07-922 4320) travels twice daily between Rockhampton airport and Rosslyn Bay (A$15).

WHITSUNDAY COAST

It's time to get wet. Whether you're lazing on a yacht or skimming shallow reefs with mask and snorkel, you'll still wish you had aqualungs and a lifetime to explore the exotic Great Barrier Reef Marine Park beneath these irresistible waters. The Whitsunday Coast is Queensland's water-sports playground, and Airlie Beach its capital.

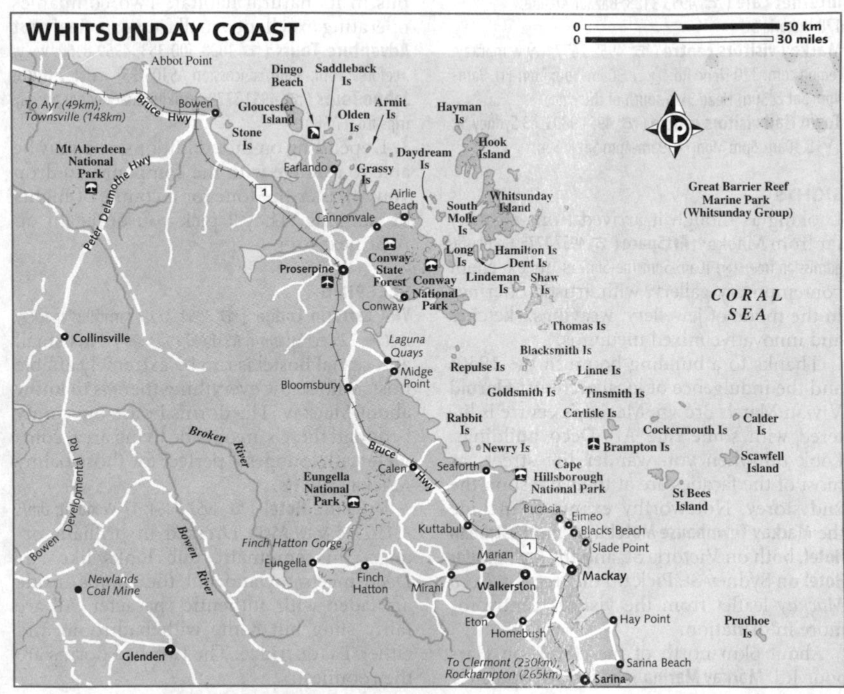

Mackay

☎ 07 / pop 74,000

The largest metropolitan area in the Whitsundays region, Mackay is a melting pot of culture and architecture. The population has evident Aboriginal, Torres Strait Islander and European roots and Mackay's central district is a marriage of Art Deco beauties and functional urbanity. Furnished with lush palms, the streets hum with a vibrant café and bar scene and at sunset squillions of rainbow lorikeets chatter madly in the town's trees. Across the Pioneer River, the constantly transforming marina adds a fancy touch with its glistening boats and swish restaurants.

Mackay is also a great access point for Pioneer Valley and Eungella National Park west of the town, Cape Hillsborough National Park to the north, Brampton and Carlisle Islands, as well as the Great Barrier Reef.

Mackay Taxis (☎ 13 10 08) run from the city centre to the airport, marina or train station for about A$12.

INFORMATION

Easy Internet (☎ 4953 3331; 22 Sydney St)
Internet Cafe (☎ 4953 3188; Bazaar Arcade, 128 Victoria St)
Mackay visitors centre (☎ 4952 2677; www.mackayregion.com; 320 Nebo Rd; 8.30am-5pm Mon-Fri, 9am-4pm Sat & Sun) Head 3km south of the city.
Town Hall visitors centre (☎ 4951 4803; 63 Sydney St; 8.30am-5pm Mon-Fri, 9am-4pm Sat & Sun)

SIGHTS

Looking as though it arrived from a galaxy far from Mackay, **ArtSpace** (☎ 4957 1775; Gordon St; admission free; 10am-5pm Tue-Sun) is an excellent contemporary gallery, with artistic offerings in the mode of jewellery, weavings, sketches and innovative mixed mediums.

Thanks to a building boom in the 1930s and the indulgence of local architect Harold Vivian Marsh Brown, Mackay's centre is littered with some fine Art Deco buildings. Look up when you wander the streets as most of the façades are at their finest on the 2nd storey. Noteworthy examples include the **Mackay Townhouse Motel** and the **Australian Hotel**, both on Victoria St, and the **Ambassador Hotel** on Sydney St. Pick up the free *Art Deco Mackay* leaflet from the visitors centre for more information.

About 6km north of the centre on Harbour Rd, **Mackay Marina** is a dash of opulence with its groovy restaurants and sceney atmosphere. You can picnic here or walk along the breakwater for a surreal view of the sugar-loading terminal. **Harbour Beach**, next to it, is the best swimming close to town, but further north is **Bucasia Beach**, a glorious stretch for swimming and long walks, with a caravan park for holiday-makers.

Illawong Fauna Sanctuary (☎ 4959 1777; illawongsanctuary@bigpond.com; Eungella Rd, Mirani; adult A$13, half-day tour A$60; 9am-6.30pm) is a sanctuary for sick critters and an excellent opportunity to witness native wildlife. Many of the residents are given names and some 'perform' for their carers; check out the barking owl! Feeding times are the best time to visit (crocodiles 2.15pm, koalas 3pm). It's about 43km west of Mackay, but half-day tours include transfers.

TOURS

Beyond Mackay's sugar-cane sea lie the superb rainforest ecologies of Pioneer Valley, Eungella National Park and Finch Hatton Gorge. This area holds one of your best chances of spotting the shy and elusive platypus in its natural habitat. Two companies operating excellent, small tours are **Reeforest Adventure Tours** (☎ 1800 500 353, 4959 8360; www.reeforest.com; adult/concession A$105/95) and **Jungle Johno Tours** (☎ 4951 3728; larrikin@mackay.net.au; day trips from A$80).

Depending on the conditions, you may be able to arrange with the companies to drop you off after the tour for a couple of nights of camping. They'll pick you up again on their next tour.

SLEEPING

YHA Larrikin Lodge (☎ 4951 3728; larrickin@mackay.net.au; 32 Peel St; dm/d A$18/40;) This small and casual hostel is run by extremely affable hosts who know everything there is to know about Mackay. The dorms house big comfy beds and there's an outside living area, complete with lounges – perfect for those balmy Mackay nights.

McGuire's Hotel (☎ 4957 7464; 17 Wood St; dm/s A$15/25, d & tw A$40) Dressed in brilliant orange, this enigmatic pub looks like Art Deco meets toyland but the rooms inside are laden with authentic character. All are fairly snug but come with bathroom and either TV or fridge. The two-bed dorms are the roomiest.

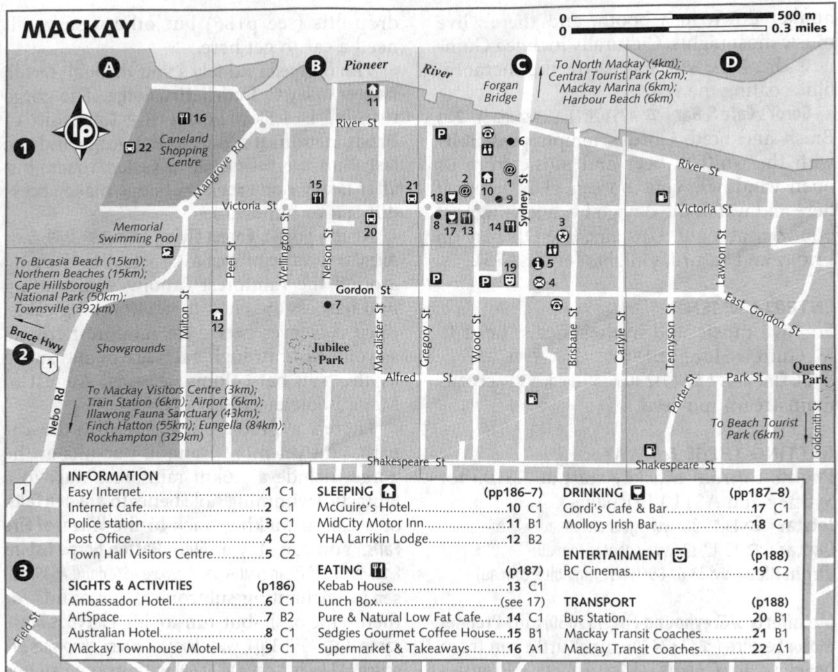

QUEENSLAND

Tucked into a quiet spot by the river on the city's fringe, **MidCity Motor Inn** (☎ 4951 1666; midcitymotel@mackay.net.au; 2 Macalister St; d from A$75;) has slightly dated but accommodating rooms.

Camping options:

Beach Tourist Park (☎ 4957 4021; www.beachtouristpark.com.au; 8 Petrie St, Illawong Beach; camp/caravan sites per 2 people A$18/24;) Catch bus No 1.

Central Tourist Park (☎ 4957 6141; 15 Malcomson St, North Mackay; camp/caravan sites per 2 people A$13/16) Catch bus No 5 or 6.

EATING

Self-caterers should head to **Caneland Shopping Centre** (Mangrove Rd) for takeaways and a supermarket.

Pure & Natural Low Fat Cafe (☎ 4957 6136; Sydney St; dishes A$4-8; breakfast & lunch) Who cares if the food here is healthy – this is some of the best-looking nosh found north of Brisbane. If the choice of delectable chicken and cashew salads, multistorey pasta bakes, tasty tortillas and monster baguettes does it for you, then just wait till you get started on the sweet stuff!

Sedgies Gourmet Coffee House (☎ 4957 4845; cnr Nelson & Victoria Sts; meals A$5-11; breakfast & lunch Mon-Fri;) Brazilian, Black Mountain, Mullimbimby Hinterland…no, these aren't waxing techniques, they're coffee beans and if you've been suffering the instant stuff too long then this café is a tonic. Over 40 teas and coffees are served here and they taste better with a toasted sarni or stuffed spud.

Other recommendations:

Kebab House (☎ 4944 0393; cnr Victoria & Wood Sts; dishes A$5-8; 11am-5am Fri-Sun) Fast and cheap.

Lunch Box (Centrepoint Shopping Centre, Victoria St; meals A$5; breakfast & lunch Mon-Fri) Hot and tasty burgers and rolls.

You can dig into some good pub tucker at Molloys Irish Bar (below), with dishes from A8 to A$15, or Gordi's Café & Bar (p188), dishes from A$10 to A$17.

DRINKING

Molloys Irish Bar (☎ 4957 7737; 148 Victoria St;) Lacking the usual theme-pub kitsch, Molloys is understated and genuine with the usual ales on tap. You can perch on bar stools or hunker down in a booth, and there's live music most nights. Culturally inclined Guinness drinkers will appreciate the memorabilia coating the walls.

Gordi's Café & Bar (☎ 4951 2611; 85 Victoria St;) Brash and bold, Gordi's tempts passers-by with the whiff of beer and music from its open windows. You too can plant yourself here and watch the day go by, but things get bouncier at night. Upstairs, live DJs play on Friday and Saturday nights (entry A$5).

ENTERTAINMENT

For live music and livelier locals, head to McGuire's Hotel (p186).

BC Cinemas (☎ 4942 4066; 30 Gordon St) screens mainstream movies.

GETTING THERE & AWAY

Flights to/from Mackay start at A$100 for Sydney and A$110 Brisbane.

Jetstar (☎ 13 15 38; www.jetstar.com.au)
Qantas (☎ 13 13 13; www.qantas.com.au)
Virgin Blue (☎ 13 67 89; www.virginblue.com.au)

McCafferty's/Greyhound (☎ 13 20 30) and **Premier Motor Service** (☎ 13 34 10) can shuttle you from Mackay to Cairns (McCafferty's/Premier A$110/100, 12 hours), Townsville (A$65/60, 6½ hours), Airlie Beach (A$20/20, two hours) and Brisbane (A$130/120, 16 hours). Both leave from the **bus station** (☎ 4944 2144; cnr Victoria & Macalister Sts; 24hr).

By rail, **Traveltrain's** (☎ 1300 131 722; www.traveltrain.com.au) *Sunlander* runs between Mackay and Brisbane (economy adult/student A$140/70, 29 hours, twice weekly) and between Mackay and Cairns (A$110/55, 12 hours, twice weekly). The train station is at Paget, 5km south of the city centre.

GETTING AROUND

The local bus service is **Mackay Transit Coaches** (☎ 4957 3330). Bus journeys commence from the back of Caneland Shopping Centre or the corner of Victoria and Gregory Sts, outside Centrelink. The visitors centre has timetables.

Around Mackay

☎ 07

You're missing a great country Queensland experience if you don't spend a couple of days enjoying the sights west of Mackay. Some organised tours also do camping drop-offs (see p186) but otherwise you'll need a car to get here.

The Eungella Rd takes you through fertile **Pioneer Valley** to **Finch Hatton Gorge**. The gorge turn-off is 1.5km before the township of Finch Hatton. It's 9km to the gorge and the last 3km are on good, unsealed roads, but after heavy rain creek crossings make access difficult or impossible.

At the gorge, **Forest Flying** (☎ 4958 3359; www.forestflying.com; Finch Hatton; A$45) gets you whizzing around the rainforest canopy while sitting in a harness attached to a 340m-long cable. Keep your eyes peeled for rainforest critters as you brush through palm leaves and swing by the fruit bat colony (seasonal August to May). Book ahead.

There's a pretty picnic area by the car park, and yet more tranquil pursuits at the gorge include a 1.6km rainforest walk to a fantastic swimming hole beneath **Araluen Falls**, or a 2.6km walking track to the **Wheel of Fire Falls**. You can stay at **Finch Hatton Gorge Cabins** (☎ 4958 3281; camp sites per 2 people A$6, dm/d A$19/80), set in enchanting subtropical surrounds, or there's the basic-but-fun-loving **Platypus Bushcamp** (☎ 4958 3204; www.bushcamp.net; camp sites per person A$7.50, huts dm/d A$20/60) with its own swimming hole and platypus viewing.

In the teensy township of Finch Hatton is the **Finch Hatton Caravan Park** (☎ 4958 3222; finchparkau@yahoo.com.au; camp/caravan sites per 2 people A$15/36;).

A further 20km and you reach beautiful **Eungella National Park** (*young*-gulla). Eungella means 'Land of Clouds'. The park has the oldest and longest stretch of subtropical rainforest in Australia and has been cut off from other rainforest areas for roughly 30,000 years. It breeds weird beasties that exist nowhere else, such as the Eungella gastric brooding frog, which incubates its eggs in its stomach and gives birth by spitting out the tadpoles! Charming.

There are excellent rainforest walks signposted on the 5km road between Eungella township and pretty **Broken River**, but it's the shy platypus you'll hope to see (they live at Broken River). You can be fairly sure of seeing platypuses most days from the viewing platform near the bridge. The best times are immediately after dawn and at dusk, but you must be patient, still and silent. Rangers lead night walks that reveal the park's party animals.

If you want to stay in the national park, try the lovely QPWS **Fern Flat Campground** (☎ 4958 4552; Broken River; camp sites per person A$4), run on a first-come, first-served basis, near the **ranger's office** (☎ 4958 4552; 🕑 8am-4pm) and kiosk.

Back at Eungella township, **Hideaway Café** (☎ 4958 4533; dishes around A$10; 🕑 breakfast & lunch) has scrumptious home-made food and the eccentric but utterly enchanting **Suzanne's Magical Garden**. **Eungella General Store** (☎ 4958 4520; snacks around A$8; 🕑 8am-6.30pm) has tasty café meals, groceries and fuel.

Cape Hillsborough National Park

It's all cliffs, dunes, scrub, rainforest and secluded woodland here, so there's little to do but relax and hang out with kangaroos on the beach or spot turtles. This small coastal park, 54km north of Mackay, takes in 300m-high Cape Hillsborough and nearby Andrews Point, which is joined to Wedge Island by a causeway at low tide. There are three short walking tracks and a rangers' office on the foreshore next to a lovely picnic area. Visitors can get information from the Cape Hillsborough Nature Resort.

Cape Hillsborough Nature Resort (☎ 4959 0152; www.capehillsboroughresort.com.au; camp sites per 2 people, A$13, cabins/d A$80/85) is very low-key, with friendly owners, wandering wildlife and a small restaurant.

Bush meets ocean at the grassy QPWS **Smalleys Beach Campground** (☎ 4959 0410; Smalleys Beach; camp sites per person A$4). Register on-site.

Airlie Beach

☎ 07 / pop 3030

Sitting beneath a congregation of dramatic hills and with a plane of turquoise sea tickling the horizon, Airlie is a jumping resort town and gateway to the Whitsunday Islands. Backpackers seem to outnumber everyone else here. Tripping into town by the busload to embark on the mandatory Whitsunday sail, they spend much of their time utilising Airlie's loud and lively nightlife to compensate for three days of blissful lazing.

Shute Harbour Rd is the main drag, along which you'll find cafés, shops, bars and oodles of travel agencies competing for your buck. Most boats to the islands leave from Shute Harbour, 21km east of Airlie Beach, or from the Abel Point Marina, which is 1.5km southwest. Whale-watching boat trips between July and September are another attraction.

INFORMATION

Internet access hovers at around A$1 per hour.

Airlie Beach visitors centre (☎ 1800 819 366, 4946 6665; abtic@whitsunday.net.au; 277 Shute Harbour Rd; 🕑 7.30am-8pm) Privately run tourist information centre.

Airlie Waterfront Travel (☎ 1800 464 000, 4948 1302; 6 The Esplanade) Internet access.

Peterpan Adventure Travel (☎ 1800 213 225, 4948 0866; Shop 1, 398 Shute Harbour Rd) Internet access.

QPWS (☎ 4946 7022; www.epa.qld.gov.au; cnr Shute Harbour & Mandalay Rds; 🕑 9am-5pm Mon-Fri, 9am-1pm Sat) Six kilometres from Airlie towards Shute Harbour.

Tourism Whitsundays visitors centre (☎ 1800 801 252, 4945 3711; www.whitsundaytourism.com; Bruce Hwy, Proserpine 🕑 9am-5pm Mon-Sat, 10am-5pm Sun) The only official tourist centre in the area, this place offers excellent and unbiased information pertaining to the whole Whitsundays area.

SIGHTS & ACTIVITIES

Although Airlie doesn't have any great beaches, a glorious artificial **lagoon**, right on the foreshore, more than makes up for it. It's free, and open 24 hours.

Sailing opportunities are plenty (see p193 for details).

With all that coral and colour just offshore, **diving** is an understandably popular pastime around Airlie Beach. Many of the sailing tours offer diving at an extra cost but you should check whether there's a qualified instructor, how many dives are included and whether they dive on the fringing reefs that surround the Whitsunday Islands or travel further to the Great Barrier Reef. Be wary of extremely cheap dive options; we have had reader reports of unstable diving equipment.

There are a number of scuba-diving schools in town and it's worth talking to the tourist office and other backpackers to get a feel for which companies currently offer the best service. Two reputable companies are **Oceania Dive** (☎ 1800 075 035, 4946 6032; www.whitsundaysonline.com/oceaniadive.php; 257 Shute Harbour Rd) and **Pro Dive** (☎ 4948 1888; www.prodive.com.au; 344 Shute Harbour Rd). Both offer five-day Open Water courses for beginners and three-day courses for certified divers on the Great Barrier Reef for between A$480 and A$540.

The colourful **Airlie Beach Community Markets** (The Esplanade; 7am-1pm Sat) are a combination of live music, fresh produce and kitschy crafts. Perfect Saturday morning stuff.

QUEENSLAND

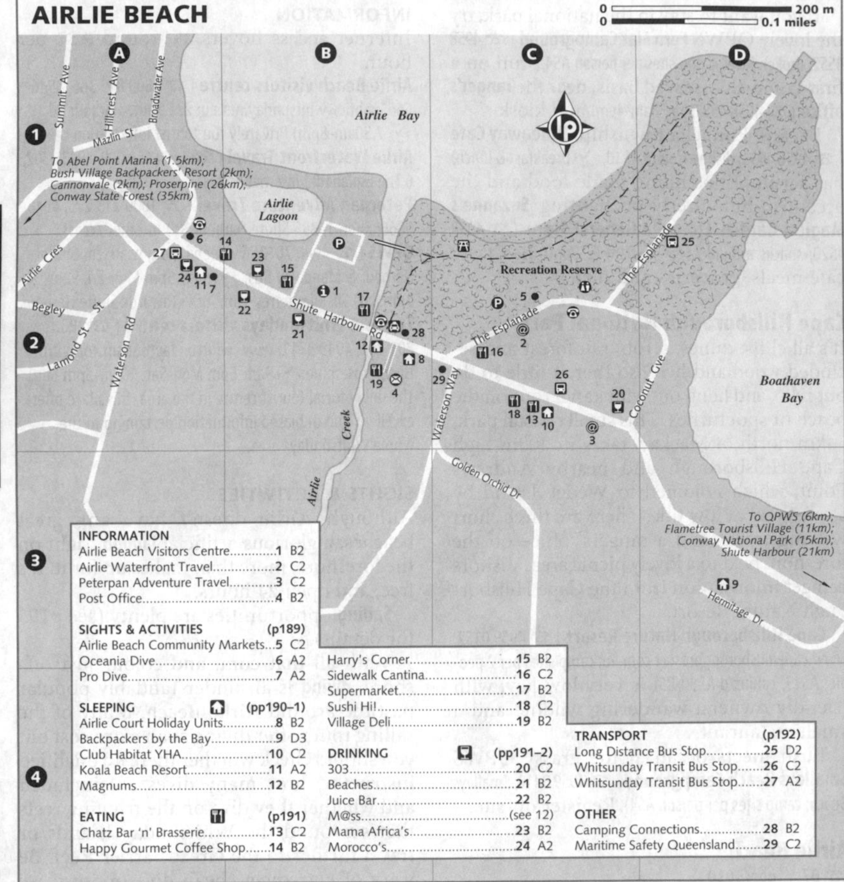

TOURS

Touring the seas in small vessels is a rewarding adventure. Several companies hire kayaks (around A$50 per day), but doing a tour that includes snorkelling, swimming, lunch and commentary is great fun.

Ozone Adventures (☎ 4946 4751; www.ozoneadventures.com; half-/full-day tours A$60/100)

Salty Dog Sea Kayaking (☎ 4946 1388; www.saltydog.com.au; half-/full-day tours A$60/A$95)

Sea Kayaking Whitsundays (☎ 4948 9711; www.seakayakingwhitsundays.com.au; day tours from A$60, full-moon tour A$40)

Fawlty's 4WD Tropical Tours (day tours A$50) is an award-winning outfit operating 4WD eco-tours of the rainforests surrounding Airlie Beach, with lunch thrown in. This is an entertaining way to get an understanding of the area's ecology. Book through the Airlie Beach visitors centre (p189).

Readers rave about **Whitsunday Crocodile Safari** (☎ 4946 5111; www.crocodilesafari.com.au; day tours A$85), an ecotour that takes you on a boat ride through the estuaries of the Proserpine River. The stars of the show are the estuary crocs, but they're joined by a menagerie of wildlife along the way.

SLEEPING

Magnums (☎ 1800 624 634, 4946 6222; www.magnums.com.au; Shute Harbour Rd; camp/caravan sites per 2 people A$15/18, dm A$13-16, d & tw A$44; ⌘ 💻) Disguised as a party behemoth, Magnums offers surprisingly tranquil digs. Dorms and very comfortable doubles are nestled into townhouse-style complexes hidden by a palm tree oasis out the back. Closer to the action, the cheaper dorms are noisy and cramped but who can argue with the price?

Backpackers by the Bay (☎ 1800 646 994, 4946 72 67; www.backpackersbythebay.com; 12 Hermitage Dr; dm/d A$20/48;) Parked on a hill away from the main drag, this snug hostel has compact rooms and a small bar. It manages to escape the party hype without being too far from the action and the sun lounges by the pool have one of the best views in town.

Bush Village Backpackers' Resort (☎ 1800 809 256, 4946 6177; fax 4946 7227; 2 St Martin's Rd, Cannonvale; dm/d from A$22/55;) About 2km west of Airlie, Bush Village has a cosy stretch of top-notch cabins with cooking facilities, fridge, bathroom and TV. There's also a bar and pleasant garden, and rates include breakfast, linen and towels. A courtesy bus runs into town until 11.30pm.

Koala Beach Resort (☎ 1800 800 421, 4946 6001; www.koala-backpackers.com; 336 Shute Harbour Rd; dm A$19, d & tw A$60;) There's plenty of room at this hostel, where a series of bungalows strewn across a sprawling lawn contain dorms with bathrooms, kitchenettes and TVs. The best doubles are numbers 29 to 36. Unfortunately, management dissuades Aussie travellers…something about the noise.

Airlie Court Holiday Units (☎ 4946 6218; www.whitsundayunits.com; 382 Shute Harbour Rd; s/d ste A$80/85;) A step up in price and quality, this small, central motel has self-contained apartments with cushy wicker furnishings. The owners are extremely friendly and helpful.

Other recommendations:

Club Habitat YHA (☎ 1800 247 251, 4946 6312; airliebeach@yhaqld.org; 394 Shute Harbour Rd; dm/d A$23/56;) Clean and comfortable motel-style hostel.

Flametree Tourist Village (☎ 1800 069 388, 4946 9388; www.flametreevillage.com.au; Shute Harbour Rd; camp/caravan sites per 2 people A$17/21, units from A$65) Mini tropical jungle 11km east of Airlie.

EATING

There's a supermarket on Shute Harbour Rd for self-caterers.

Village Deli (☎ 4964 1121; Whitsunday Village Resort, mains A$7-15; breakfast, lunch & dinner;) For fresh gourmet food this deli wins hands down. Here you can hook into pear and couscous salad, bacon and pumpkin pie or delectable sandwiches. The stylish ambience is set by breezy seating and funky tunes.

Happy Gourmet Coffee Shop (☎ 4946 7820; 263 Shute Harbour Rd; meals A$6-13; breakfast & lunch) This wee café has unassuming surrounds and outstanding salads, sandwiches and rolls. The build-your-own burger for A$5 is a steal.

Sidewalk Cantina (☎ 4946 6425; The Esplanade; lunch A$6-12, dinner A$12-20; lunch daily, dinner Thu-Mon;) By day this convivial café offers patrons a fairly standard café menu but the lasagnes, salads and sangers give way to Tex-Mex feasts by night. Then you can treat your taste buds to quesadillas, chimichangas, tortillas and nachos.

Chatz Bar 'n' Brasserie (☎ 4946 7223; 390 Shute Harbour Rd; mains A$13-20; lunch & dinner;) Thai curries, Cajun lamb, towering beef burgers and a whole lot more; this bar cooks up creative and tasty dishes. There's a hint of outdoor seating but most diners opt for the cool, dark interior.

Other recommendations:

Sushi Hi! (☎ 4948 0400; 390 Shute Harbour Rd; mains A$13-20; lunch & dinner) Fresh sushi, soba and tempura.

Harry's Corner (☎ 4946 7459; 273 Shute Harbour Rd; breakfast A$5-7; breakfast & lunch) Lagoon-side, good-value breakfast.

DRINKING

Magnum's (☎ 4946 6266; Shute Harbour Rd) Airlie Beach's most prominent drinking hole, where a sea of wooden tables in a gargantuan outdoor setting fills to capacity most nights. A spirited crowd jostles for cheap jugs of beer at the bar and the god of social things weaves his magic. By night Magnum's M@ss nightclub is one lively crowd-pleaser with top 40 on the speakers, wet T-shirt comps on stage and foam parties regularly.

Mama Africa's (☎ 4948 0438; 263 Shute Harbour Rd;) Cool and sophisticated, this club is all jungle print and tribal motifs. Mama's knows how to rock, though, and this vibe will lift you from the kick-back lounge chairs well enough.

Morocco's (☎ 4946 6001; 336 Shute Harbour Rd) Well entrenched on the backpacker drinking route, Morocco's is an amicable pub with a happy hour that extends from mid-afternoon to 7.30pm. You'll undoubtedly find your beer goggles here along with the mate or beau you met last night.

Juice Bar (☎ 4946 6465; 354 Shute Harbour Rd;) Has a distinctly city edge to its minimalist décor: polished concrete floor, a chill area with frothing, aerated water tanks and a small dance floor to pack the crowd tight. It mixes the music up a little, with R&B, dance and top 40.

Other recommendations:

Beaches (☎ 4946 6244; Shute Harbour Rd) Large outdoor pub with happy hours and happier punters.

303 (☎ 4946 4048; 303 Shute Harbour; gig entry A$5) Darkened windows, live music and indulgent Sunday sessions.

GETTING THERE & AROUND

McCafferty's/Greyhound (☎ 13 20 30) and **Premier Motor Service** (☎ 13 34 10) head into Airlie Beach from Brisbane (McCafferty's/Premier A$150/135, 18 hours), Townsville (A$50/50, four hours), Mackay (A$20/20, two hours) and Cairns (A$110/100, 10 hours). The bus stop is about halfway along The Esplanade. Shute Harbour Rd travel agencies take bookings.

Local bus company **Whitsunday Transit** (☎ 1300 655 449) connects Proserpine, Cannonvale, Abel Point, Airlie Beach and Shute Harbour. Buses operate daily from 6am to 10.30pm and stop outside Mangrove Jack's or just up from Pro Dive. Grab a schedule from any travel agency.

Conway National Park & State Forest

A new walkers' paradise is in the making. By the time you read this, QPWS should have finished its 36km **Whitsundays Great Walk**, traversing the rugged ranges and rainforest valleys, coastal woodlands and mangroves of this area. You'll need to be reasonably fit and have three days to fill. Adventurers seeking altitude should hike the 2.4km up **Mt Rooper Lookout** in the national park for top views of the Whitsunday Passage and islands.

Or there's the beautiful **Cedar Creek Falls** track in the state forest. The turn-off is on your right, 18km from Airlie Beach on the Proserpine–Airlie road. Fawlty's 4WD Tropical Tours (see Tours, p190) runs good-value, full-day rainforest tours to the falls.

Contact **QPWS** (☎ 4946 7022) in Airlie for more park and forest information.

Whitsunday Islands

In 1770 this network of ethereal islands snagged their first tourist when Captain Cook stumbled across their beautiful path. Photographed countless times and believed to epitomise paradise, this smear of marine blue and tropical green is iconic in Queensland's landscape and no trip to the state is complete without an encounter.

The Whitsundays contain over 90 islands, mostly uninhabited and continental (the tips of underwater mountains). The surrounding waterways are a marine park and fall within the Great Barrier Reef World Heritage Area. The reef itself is at least 60km from the mainland but many islands have colourful fringing coral reefs. Regardless of where you swim, remember that we're all responsible for preserving this natural wonderland for future generations to enjoy, so you may kiss the fish if you can catch them, but don't feed them – and please, don't pet the coral.

All but four of the Whitsundays are predominantly or completely national park (the exceptions are Dent Island and the resort islands of Hamilton, Daydream and Hayman). The other main resorts are on South Molle, Lindeman, Long and Hook Islands. People staying in the resorts are generally on cheap package holidays booked in advance, but some resorts offer affordable stand-by rates that may include meals. Ask at Airlie Beach travel agencies.

CAMPING

You can pitch your tent at QPWS camping grounds on 17 of the islands, but you must haul along your own gear, food, drinking water, fuel stoves and nature-loving attitude (leave only footprints). Camping grounds are occasionally closed to alternate traffic between them and minimise the impact on the environment.

To organise your trip, visit the excellent Airlie Beach **QPWS** (☎ 4946 7022; www.epa.qld.gov.au; cnr Shute Harbour & Mandalay Rds), which provides permits (per person A$4) and enthusiastic advice on highlights. You can also purchase permits online at www.epa.qld.gov.au or by calling ☎ 13 13 04.

Camping Connections (☎ 07-4946 5255; Where?-What?How? Travel, Shop 1, 283 Shute Harbour Rd) runs a direct boat service to camping grounds for between A$45 and A$150, return. You need a minimum of four people and camping permits.

Or, relax on a hosted camp. Several companies have been granted permits to run cushy camping tours to most of the islands, and the guides have good local knowledge. Remember to bring your swimming costume.

SAILING THE WHITSUNDAY ISLANDS

A Whitsundays sailing trip is virtually mandatory on every backpackers' itinerary, not least because it's a beautiful and extremely affordable activity.

Dozens of companies operate out of Airlie Beach. Day trips (between A$90 and A$150) generally visit a couple of islands and Whitehaven Beach (on Whitsunday Island) and include lunch and snorkelling. Options range from fast rafts and island-hoppers to a leisurely sail on a ketch or catamaran.

The lure of a high-seas adventure, however, snags most travellers into a three-day, two-night sail. These start at around A$180 and top out at around A$450. Most include snorkelling, boom-netting (reclining on a large net in the water as the boat sails – best not to wear bikini bottoms on one of these) and meals. Like all tours, the price is a good reflection of quality and it's worth asking how many people the boat takes, how long you actually spend at sea (if your boat departs at 4pm it's not *really* three days), how old the boat is and whether the boat shown on the brochure is the same one you will take. Promotional material can be misleading.

At Sea No One Can Hear You Scream

A tempting alternative is to crew on a private boat, but this can be risky. Readers have sent in hair-raising accounts of 'illegal charters' that range from sexual harassment to poor safety and inexperienced crew. Illegal charters are most often advertised on photocopied leaflets that read: 'Crew Wanted: Share an adventurous sailing experience and expenses'. While there are, no doubt, many legitimate private owners who wish to share the beauty of the Whitsundays with you, it's important to research any offer before you sail into the sunset.

Visit the Maritime Safety Officer at **Maritime Safety Queensland** (☎ 07 4946 2200; www.transport.qld.gov.au/maritime; Level 1, 384 Shute Harbour Rd) in Airlie Beach. Officers can tell you the right questions to ask and if the vessel has current commercial registration and is crewed by professionals. You could save yourself from an upsetting – or potentially dangerous – experience. Wise words aside, happy sailing!

Salty Dog Sea Kayaking (☎ 4946 1388; www.saltydog.com.au; 3-day kayaking tours & camping A$390)
Sea Kayaking Whitsundays (☎ 07-4948 9711; www.seakayakingwhitsundays.com.au; 2-day kayaking tours A$275) Seasonal.
Whitsunday Sightseeing (☎ 07-4946 6611; 3-day, 2-night safaris A$280).

GETTING THERE & AROUND

Most of the cruise operators leave from Shute Harbour but include a Whitsunday Transit bus transfer from Airlie Beach.

Fantasea Ferries (☎ 07-4946 5111; www.fantasea.com.au) and **Whitsunday Allover Cruises** (☎ 07-4946 6900, 1300 366 494) are the major operators for transfers to South Molle, Daydream, Long, Lindeman and Hamilton Islands. Both companies operate from Shute Harbour.

Camping Connections (☎ 07-4946 5255; Where?-What?How? Travel, Shop 1, 283 Shute Harbour Rd) does drop-offs to island camping grounds.

LONG ISLAND

There's good rainforest here – it's nearly all national park – with 13km of walking tracks and some fine lookouts. The island is skinny (2km wide) but long enough (9km) to house three resorts and a QPWS **camping ground** (camp sites per person A$4) in seclusion.

SOUTH MOLLE ISLAND

At 4 sq km South Molle is the largest of the Molle group and is virtually joined to Mid Molle and North Molle islands. It has long stretches of beach and is crisscrossed by 15km of wonderful walking tracks. The highest point is **Mt Jeffreys** (198m), but the climb up Spion Kop is also worthwhile. South Molle is comprised mainly of national park, but there's a QPWS **camping ground** (camp sites per person A$4) and a resort in the north, where the boats come in.

HOOK ISLAND

The second-largest of the Whitsundays at 53 sq km, Hook Island is mainly national park and blessed with great beaches and camping grounds. There's impressive snorkelling around the northern camping grounds, and **Crayfish Beach** is an awesome spot.

You can make your own way here with Camping Connections, or with **Adventure Cruises** (☎ 4946 5255; return ticket A$40). Ring the commercial operators for tour/camping options (see p192).

Hook Island Wilderness Resort (☎ 07-4946 9380; camp sites per 2 people A$15, dm A$25, cabins A$80-120;) This backpacker resort has a series of beach shack–style rooms, a very casual bar and a simple kiosk. Activities available include kayaking, fish feeding at the jetty and copious amounts of snorkelling and bushwalking. It's often booked by school groups so check with travel agencies in Airlie Beach before you set out.

WHITSUNDAY ISLAND

This island is food for the soul. The largest of the Whitsundays, it covers 109 sq km and rises to 438m at Whitsunday Peak. On its southeast coast, 6km-long **Whitehaven Beach** is the longest and finest beach in the group (some say in the country), with good snorkelling off its southern end. *Everyone* day-trips to Whitehaven Beach, but it's magic to linger overnight.

Perhaps the most celebrated view of all the Whitsundays comes from here – looking up from Hill Inlet on Tongue Point down towards pristine Whitehaven Beach.

There's plenty of **camping** (per person A$4), but no resort here.

DAYDREAM ISLAND

Tiny Daydream Island, about 1km long and 500m wide, is the nearest island resort to Shute Harbour.

Daydream Island Resort & Spa (☎ 1800 075 040, 07-4948 8488; www.daydream.net.au; 3-night packages from A$470) From the funky, bubbly reception area and friendly staff to fresh, colourfully furnished rooms, Daydream's attitude would improve any mood. It's a mainly couple-oriented resort, but is also family- and wheelchair-friendly, and it has a day spa that rejuvenates sun-battered bodies.

HAMILTON ISLAND

The flashy marina and erupting high-rises of **Hamilton Island** (☎ 1800 075 110, 07-4946 9999; www.hamiltonisland.com.au; d A$305-600;) advertise that here is where you get well and truly into it all rather than away from it all. Skirting the water are 11 restaurants, bars, banks, accommodation for more than 2000 people and even traffic! Getting from A to B on Hamilton is via buggy and these zoom about like it's some crazed golfers' grand prix.

Hamilton, the most developed Whitsunday island, is an appealing day trip from Shute Harbour, and you can use some of the resort's facilities.

LINDEMAN ISLAND

It's a bit of a hike to southerly Lindeman (mostly national park), but the rewards are lots of secluded bays and 20km of impressive walking tracks. Tremendous numbers of grass trees make striking photographs and the view from Mt Oldfield (210m) is grand.

Day-tripping is an option, but it's a *very* long day; call **Whitsunday Allover Cruises** (☎ 07-4946 6900; adult A$120) for details.

There's a QPWS **camping ground** (camp sites per person A$4), or go with a commercial operator (see p192).

Bowen

☎ 07 / pop 13,200

In answer to your question: it's a mango, that huge orange blob outside the visitors centre. It's been placed there to welcome you to Bowen, which is in fact a thriving fruit and vegetable centre in spite of its seemingly wide and empty streets. Most travellers come here for seasonal picking work (April to August) and both **Bowen Backpackers** (☎ 4786 3433; www.users.bigpond.com/bowenbackpackers; beach end Herbert St; dm per night/week A$21/130, d per night/week A$25/155;) and **Barnacles Backpackers** (☎ 4786 4400; barnaclebackpackers@bigpond.com.au; 18 Gordon St; dm/d A$17/19) cater well to them.

There are a couple of modern pubs and cafés in town, but cosy **Horseshoe Bay Café** (☎ 4786 3280; Horseshoe Bay; dishes A$5-12; breakfast & lunch Tue-Sun) produces far from ordinary hot dogs and burgers, and restaurant-style dinners.

The long-distance bus stop is just outside **Bowen Travel** (☎ 4786 2835; William St), from which you can purchase **McCafferty's/Greyhound** (☎ 13 20 30) or **Premier Motor Service** (☎ 13 34 10) bus tickets to a variety of destinations, inlcuding Rockhampton (A$70, eight hours), Airlie Beach (A$18, one hour) and Townsville (A$32, three hours).

TROPICAL NORTH QUEENSLAND

North Queensland is best known for its proximity to the Great Barrier Reef and most visitors to this natural wonder use Townsville, Port Douglas or the ever popular Cairns as a launching pad. In the latter, don't be surprised if your attention is snagged not only by the huge parties on offer every night but also the ancient rainforests of Cape Tribulation, just a smidgeon north.

Surrounding these hot spots are the vast and beautiful Atherton Tablelands and the remote top end of Australia; utopia for those looking to get off the beaten track.

Activities

Understandably, snorkelling, sailing and diving opportunities are abundant in and around Cairns and Port Douglas. Townsville also has some excellent diving, with the *Yongala* shipwreck nearby.

Magnetic Island is a secluded oasis, offering fine bushwalking and plenty of koala-spotting opportunities.

Just south of Cairns, the Tully River thrashes about for most of the year, providing exhilarating white-water rafting.

TOWNSVILLE

☎ 07 / pop 150,000

Townsville is Queensland's second largest city and the 'big smoke' for Queensland's gigantic inland agricultural and mining regions. It's also home to thousands of army boys and girls and university students. This transient population adds significantly to the city's culture, which embraces cosmopolitan dining, a thriving, sceney nightlife and some excellent museums.

Townsville is an attractive spot in which to spend a few days. Behind the compact CBD, verdant hills cast a domineering canvas across low-rise development and suburban sprawl. The Great Barrier Reef lies about two hours east of Townsville and far closer is the popular and gorgeous Magnetic Island.

Orientation

Castle Hill (290m) presides over Townsville. Ross Creek winds through its city centre, which lies on the north side of the creek over the Dean St Bridge or the Victoria Bridge (pedestrians only). The centre is easy to get around on foot.

Flinders Mall, the shopping precinct, stretches southwest from the northern side of Dean St Bridge. To the northeast of the bridge is Flinders St East, lined with many of the town's oldest buildings, plus eateries, nightclubs and the Sunferries terminal for Magnetic Island departures (there's another terminal on Sir Leslie Thiess Dr on the breakwater).

The Townsville Transit Centre, the arrival and departure point for long-distance buses, is on the corner of Palmer and Plume Sts. This is not to be confused with the Transit Mall near Flinders Mall, which is the departure point for local buses and taxis.

Townsville's airport is 5km northwest of the city at Garbutt. A taxi to the centre costs around A$20, or **Airport Transfers** (☎ 4775 5544; one-way/return A$7/11) runs from the Townsville Transit Centre and most accommodation near the city centre.

Information

EMERGENCY

Ambulance (☎ 000)
Police station (☎ 000, 4772 4366; 211 Sturt St)

INTERNET ACCESS

Internet Cafe (Townsville Transit Centre, cnr Palmer & Plume Sts; per hr A$6)
Internet Den (☎ 4721 4500; 265 Flinders Mall; per hr A$6)
Townsville City Library (☎ 4727 9666; Northtown Shopping Centre, Flinders Mall; free)

TOURIST INFORMATION

Flinders Mall visitors centre (☎ 4721 3660; Flinders Mall; 🕑 9am-5pm Mon-Fri, 9am-1pm Sat & Sun)
Great Barrier Reef Marine Park Authority (☎ 4750 0700; www.gbrmpa.gov.au; 2-68 Flinders St East; 🕑 9am-5pm Mon-Fri)
Townsville Enterprise Ltd visitors centre (☎ 4778 3555; www.townsvilleonline.com.au; Bruce Hwy; 🕑 9am-5pm) Well-organised, private tourism organisation, 8km south of the city centre.

TRAVEL AGENCIES

MB Travel (☎ 4721 3444; res@mbtravel.com.au; Townsville Transit Centre, cnr Palmer & Plume Sts) Cheap packages to Magnetic Island.

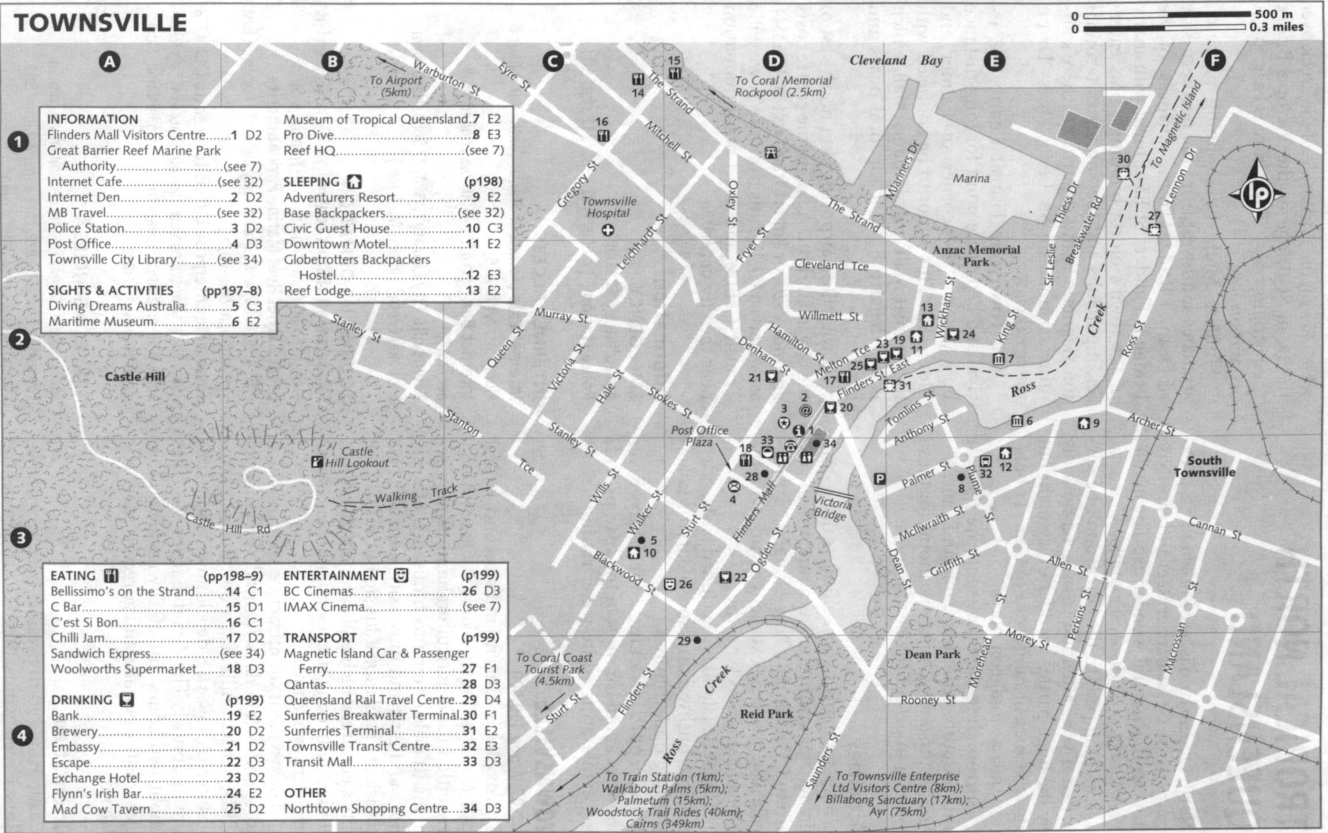
TOWNSVILLE
0 500 m
0 0.3 miles
INFORMATION
Flinders Mall Visitors Centre......1 D2
Great Barrier Reef Marine Park Authority......(see 7)
Internet Cafe......(see 32)
Internet Den......2 D2
MB Travel......(see 32)
Police Station......3 D2
Post Office......4 D3
Townsville City Library......(see 34)
SIGHTS & ACTIVITIES (pp197–8)
Diving Dreams Australia......5 C3
Maritime Museum......6 E2
Museum of Tropical Queensland......7 E2
Pro Dive......8 E3
Reef HQ......(see 7)
SLEEPING (p198)
Adventurers Resort......9 E2
Base Backpackers......(see 32)
Civic Guest House......10 C3
Downtown Motel......11 E2
Globetrotters Backpackers Hostel......12 E3
Reef Lodge......13 E2
EATING (pp198–9)
Bellissimo's on the Strand......14 C1
C Bar......15 D1
C'est Si Bon......16 C1
Chilli Jam......17 D2
Sandwich Express......(see 34)
Woolworths Supermarket......18 D3
DRINKING (p199)
Bank......19 E2
Brewery......20 D2
Embassy......21 D2
Escape......22 D3
Exchange Hotel......23 D2
Flynn's Irish Bar......24 E2
Mad Cow Tavern......25 D2
ENTERTAINMENT (p199)
BC Cinemas......26 D3
IMAX Cinema......(see 7)
TRANSPORT (p199)
Magnetic Island Car & Passenger Ferry......27 F1
Qantas......28 D3
Queensland Rail Travel Centre......29 D4
Sunferries Breakwater Terminal......30 F1
Sunferries Terminal......31 E2
Townsville Transit Centre......32 E3
Transit Mall......33 D3
OTHER
Northtown Shopping Centre......34 D3
Cleveland Bay
To Airport (5km)
To Coral Memorial Rockpool (2.5km)
To Magnetic Island
Marina
Anzac Memorial Park
Townsville Hospital
Castle Hill
Castle Hill Lookout
Walking Track
Castle Hill Rd
Post Office Plaza
Victoria Bridge
South Townsville
Ross Creek
Dean Park
Reid Park
To Coral Coast Tourist Park (4.5km)
To Train Station (1km); Walkabout Palms (5km); Palmetum (15km); Woodstock Trail Rides (40km); Cairns (349km)
To Townsville Enterprise Ltd Visitors Centre (8km); Billabong Sanctuary (17km); Ayr (75km)

Sights

The magical **Reef HQ** (☎ 4750 0800; www.reefhq.org.au; 2-68 Flinders St East; adult A$20; 9am-5pm) is a marine wonderland and miniature version of the Great Barrier Reef. A colossal aquarium dominates the centre, in which gorgeous fishy things in all their brilliant shapes, colours and sizes jostle to and fro in a hurry to nowhere. Here you can learn how sargassum fish and nudibranchs ward off predators, how sunlight affects coral and how all the reef's creatures work in symbiosis to maintain this fragile ecosystem. There are hands-on reef displays and tours scheduled throughout the day.

The **Strand**, northwest of town, is Townsville's vibrant beachfront esplanade and here the city opens up to wide views of the ocean. On board are a marina, cafés, parks and a stinger enclosure. At its top end is the enormous artificial **Coral Memorial Rockpool** on the edge of the ocean, open 24 hours – and it's free.

If you're feeling energetic, the panoramic views from the top of **Castle Hill** are worth the 2km scramble to the summit; the path to the top begins at the end of Victoria St.

Cotter's Market (Flinders Mall; 8.30am-1pm Sun) has about 200 craft and food stalls, as well as live entertainment, and wheelchair access is fine. Alternatively, the **Strand Nightmarkets** (The Strand; 5-9.30pm) are held on the first Friday of every month between May and December.

SANCTUARIES & PARKS

About 17km south of Townsville, **Billabong Sanctuary** (☎ 4778 8344; www.billabongsanctuary.com.au; Bruce Hwy; adult/backpacker A$24/22; 8am-5pm) is a 10-hectare wildlife park where many animals roam free. You can cuddle a koala, wombat or python, and feed a crocodile or eagle at shows that are scheduled throughout the day.

If you fancy a lazy picnic, Townsville is spoiled for pretty parks and gardens. The visitors centre has a complete list. The **Palmetum** (☎ 4727 8330; off University Rd, Douglas; dawn-dusk), about 15km southwest of the city centre, is a lush, 17-hectare botanic garden devoted to native palms that are arranged in natural environments, ranging from desert to rainforest. There's a fine old Queenslander tearoom, in case you forget your picnic.

MUSEUMS

Even if you're not a history buff, you'll love the **Museum of Tropical Queensland** (☎ 4726 0600; www.mtq.qld.gov.au; 70-102 Flinders St East; adult A$9; 9.30am-5pm), which devotes many of its exhibits, talks and demonstrations to the tragic sinking of HMS *Pandora*. The museum also travels down prehistoric, geographic, archaeological and anthropological paths, with a particularly good exhibit on Aboriginal and Torres Strait Islander peoples. You can also gawk at models of enormous and fearsome beasties that filled Queensland's waters at various stages over the last 200 million years.

If you plan to dive to the *Yongala* shipwreck, visit the **Maritime Museum** (☎ 4721 5251; 42-68 Palmer St; adult A$5; 10am-4pm Mon-Fri, 1-4pm Sat & Sun). The *Yongala* was overcome by a cyclone in 1911, and its wreck has since transformed into a coral reef teeming with marine life that seem to guard this underwater cemetery. The museum has relics, historical newspaper articles and a video of the first archaeological survey of the wreck.

Activities

After all that sun, surf and snorkelling it's likely you'll be desperate for some land-based activities, and Townsville has a few cards up its sleeve to accommodate.

Woodstock Trail Rides (☎ 4778 8888; www.woodstocktrailrides.com.au; Flinders Hwy; day tour A$120) runs a terrific outback experience on its cattle station. The price includes transfers, billy tea and damper, cattle mustering, calf branding and whip cracking, as well as a camp-oven lunch and ice-cold beer at day's end. Trail rides and an overnight bush camp are also available.

For adrenalin junkies, **R'n'R White Water Rafting** (☎ 1800 079 977; www.raft.com.au; A$145) has seriously scary rafting on the Tully River, and **Coral Sea Skydivers** (☎ 4772 4889; www.coralseaskydivers.com.au; tandem jump A$290) will dump you from a plane.

But really, this is coastal Queensland, and the sublime snorkelling and diving are big attractions. The beautifully spooky *Yongala* shipwreck is popular – you need to do an Open Water course to see the wreck; these courses generally last five days and cost between A$540 and A$580. It's best to ask other travellers and your hostel for recommendations about courses.

Diving options:

Blue Angel Adventure Diving (☎ 1800 330 191, 4723 0630) Includes three nights with all meals on its boat.

Diving Dreams Australia (☎ 4721 2500; www.divingdreams.com; 252 Walker St; 9am-6pm Mon-Fri, 9am-3pm Sat)

Pro Dive (☎ 1300 131 760, 4721 1760; www.prodivetownsville.com.au; 14 Plume St; 9am-5pm Mon-Fri, 10am-4pm Sat, noon-4pm Sun)

Tours

If superb rainforest, a beautifully restored mining town or Australia's longest waterfall tempt you, **Townsville Tropical Tours** (☎ 4721 6489; www.townsvilletropicaltours.com.au; day trips from A$120) has good-value day trips that take in the Paluma Range National Park, Hidden Valley, Charters Towers or Wallaman Falls. It also tours the Billabong Sanctuary (tours adult/concession A$34/32).

Reef EcoTours (☎ 0419-712 579; www.reefecotours.com; tours from A$50) is a small outfit operated by a marine biologist who complements snorkelling tours with informative commentary.

Sleeping

Globetrotters Backpackers Hostel (☎ 1800 008 533, 4771 3242; www.globetrottersinn.com.au; 45 Palmer St; dm A$22, d & tw A$50-55; P) Staying in this homely Queenslander is like sharing with flatmates…only there's more of them and the kitchen and bathroom are spotless. The rooms here are simple and cosy and there's a friendly communal air.

Base Backpackers (☎ 1800 628 836, 4721 2322; www.basebackpackers.com; cnr Palmer & Plume Sts; dm/d A$17/60;) Right above the transit centre, Base lures weary travellers into exceptionally comfy beds (no foam here!) with its sheer convenience. The dorms are spacious and the bathrooms cater to the masses but the kitchen is sloppy and minuscule. The bar specialises in gargantuan cocktails and a party vibe. Disabled access.

Civic Guest House (☎ 1800 646 619, 4771 5381; www.backpackersinn.com.au; 262 Walker St; dm A$20, s/d from A$40/45, ste A$60; P) The snug rooms in this central hostel are dressed in ageing but charming furniture (which occupies a bit of space but adds flair). The building is dotted with small bathrooms and kitchens and the only (small) drawback is a slight lack of communal space.

Adventurers Resort (☎ 1800 211 522, 4721 1522; www.adventurersresort.com; 79 Palmer St; dm/d A$20/50; P) If it weren't for the friendly staff this large, motel-style hostel could leave you feeling slightly anonymous. The rooms are clinically spartan and an eensy bit cell-like, but everything is immaculate. The attached bistro does a nightly A$5 meal and the resort rents out bicycles.

Two small hostels in the thick of the nightlife strip are **Reef Lodge** (☎ 4721 1112; www.reeflodge.com.au; 4-6 Wickham St; dm A$16-18, d with/without bath A$55/40;) and **Downtown Motel** (☎ 4771 5000; 121 Flinders St; dm A$15-18, d A$60; P). The latter choice has good motel doubles.

Camping options:

Coral Coast Tourist Park (☎ 4774 5295; www.coralcoastpark.com.au; 547 Ingham Rd; camp/caravan sites per 2 people $A18/25;)

Walkabout Palms (☎ 1800 633 562; www.walkaboutpalms.com.au; Bruce Hwy, Wulguru; camp/caravan sites per 2 people A$21/25, tw A$45, cabins A$60;)

Eating

Self-caterers can stock up at Woolworths supermarket in the city centre.

C Bar (☎ 4724 0333; The Strand; mains A$7-16; breakfast, lunch & dinner;) What a classy joint. The C Bar's menu is a fusion of flavours – risotto, ratatouille, lavash rolls and sushi are just a hint. Free with your meal are dazzling views, a chilled ambience and waterfront seating. This place has the best lazy breakfast north of the border.

Bellissimo's on the Strand (☎ 4721 5577; Shop 7, 58 The Strand; meals A$3.50-7; breakfast, lunch & dinner) This industrious little café serves delectable coffee and cake but you can also grab a lunch or dinner of quiche, hot dogs, pies, open grilled sangers and salads. There's a nice splatter of al fresco seating and a well-stocked magazine rack.

Chilli Jam (☎ 4721 5199; 205 Flinders St East; dishes A$7-12; lunch Tue-Fri; dinner Tue-Sun) Inside a clean, chrome interior, this stylish noodle bar serves Singaporean, Thai, Malaysian and Chinese noodles full of fresh and spicy flavour. The heat factor is geared to your taste so chilli freaks can go nuts.

C'est Si Bon (☎ 4772 5828; Shop 2, 48 Gregory St; meals A$6-15; breakfast & lunch daily, dinner Thu-Sat;) From the sleek bench seating to the blunt, earthy hues and soft lighting, this eatery oozes style. The food is a perfect match, with gourmet salads, pastries, pastas and sandwiches with fresh deli ingredients. At night things get a bit funkier and the menu switches to mezes and tapas.

Other recommendations:

Sandwich Express (Northtown Shopping Centre, Flinders Mall; sandwiches A$4-7; lunch Mon-Fri) Speedy sandwiches.

Flynn's Irish Bar (☎ 4721 1655; cnr Wickham & Flinders St East; dishes A$7-13; lunch & dinner Mon-Sat) Beef-and-Guinness pies. See below.

There's also a small cafeteria inside the Transit Centre (on the corner of Palmer and Plume Sts) that serves mountainous focaccias (A$5).

Drinking

Brewery (☎ 4724 9999; 242 Flinders St;) Within a heritage façade of arched columns and yawning windows this boutique brewery hums with a mixed crowd and cool ambience. Joining the usual suspects on tap are six excellent brewery beers, including the aptly named Lager Lout (it's 4.7% alcohol) and its own alcoholic pop called Scuds. DJs hit the decks on weekends.

Mad Cow Tavern (☎ 4771 5727; 129 Flinders St East) In the middle of the party strip, this bar-in-a-cow-suit cooks up spirited mayhem most nights with dim lighting and ferocious socialising. The drinking is no light affair here, either.

Flynn's Irish Bar (☎ 4721 1655; cnr Wickham St & Flinders St East) This warm Irish pub requires no fancy frills to tempt thirsty travellers; it's just a genuine watering hole with the usual Irish ales on tap.

Exchange Hotel (☎ 4771 3335; 151 Flinders St East) Beer, bourbon and live music are the order of the day at this hulking pub. No need to stress too much about your attire, either.

Bank (☎ 4771 6148; 169 Flinders St East; admission A$5;) Definitely the sleekest club in town, Bank is a superbly restored old bank building with a marble bar, padded chill zone and slinky *Basic Instinct* ambience. The bartenders impress with showy bottle tossing. The beat is house and dance. The dress? Whatever's *in*! Admission may not apply after 11pm.

Escape (☎ 4772 4429; 450 Flinders St; admission A$5-12) Catering to a crowd of students looking to dance and party hard, this huge club contains four levels to amuse you. There's live music, pool tables, top 40 tunes and upstairs a den of hard-core techno with DJs. Admission only applies upstairs.

Embassy (☎ 4724 5000; 13 Sturt St;) Sleek and sophisticated, this club also hosts DJs who turn out mostly funk and house.

Entertainment

Head to the **Exchange Hotel** (☎ 4771 3335; 151 Flinders St East) for a spot of live rock or top 40 covers, see left; or for something more sedate, catch a flick at **BC Cinemas** (☎ 4771 4101; cnr Sturt & Blackwood Sts;).

Get up close and personal with the Reef's beauty at **IMAX cinema** (☎ 4721 1481; Reef HQ complex, 2-68 Flinders St East; adult A$12; 10.30am-4.30pm), at its regular showings of the film *The Great Barrier Reef*.

Getting There & Away

AIR

Flights to/from Townsville start at: Sydney (A$160) and Brisbane (A$110).

Alliance Airlines (☎ 1300 130 092; www.allianceairlines.com.au)

Qantas (☎ 13 13 13; www.qantas.com.au; 345 Flinders Mall)

Virgin Blue (☎ 136 789; www.virginblue.com.au)

BUS

McCafferty's/Greyhound (☎ 13 20 30) and **Premier Motor Service** (☎ 13 34 10) have desks at the **Townsville Transit Centre** (☎ 4721 3082; cnr Palmer & Plume Sts). Routes to/from Townsville include Brisbane (McCafferty's/Premier Motor Service A$170/A$160, 23 hours), Rockhampton (A$65/60, 11 hours), Mackay (A$65/60, six hours), Airlie Beach (A$50/50, four hours), Mission Beach (A$45/45, four hours) and Cairns (A$60/55, six hours).

TRAIN

The Brisbane–Cairns *Sunlander* train operates from Brisbane to Townsville (economy adult/student A$165/85, 24 hours, four weekly) and Cairns (A$60/29, 8½ hours). Book at the **Queensland Rail Travel Centre** (☎ 4772 8358; www.traveltrain.qr.com.au; 502 Flinders St; 9am-5pm Mon-Fri, 1-4.30pm Sat, 8.30am-4.15pm Sun, closed for lunch).

Getting Around

Sunbus (☎ 4725 8482; www.sunbus.com.au) runs local bus services around Townsville. Route maps and timetables are available at the visitors centre in Flinders Mall.

Taxis congregate outside the Transit Mall, or call **Townsville Taxis** (☎ 13 10 08, 4778 9555).

MAGNETIC ISLAND

☎ 07 / pop 2500

Magnetic Island greets you with emerald-green water if the sun is shining, but when the clouds roll in over the mountains, it looks more like a pocket of the Rocky Mountains than tropical Queensland.

This is the perfect island getaway. With a little effort you can have a beach all to yourself. With a little more effort you can wend your way through giant granite boulders, hoop pines and eucalypts via a good network of walking tracks. Half the island is national park, and rock wallabies, bats and brushtail possums are prolific.

It's also the largest natural koala sanctuary in Queensland (some say Australia) and, consequently, spotting fuzzy grey bums in the foliage is a mandatory pursuit. The surrounding waters belong to the Great Barrier Reef World Heritage Area.

A visitors centre is planned for Nelly Bay, but until then, pop into Townsville's **Flinders Mall visitors centre** (☎ 4721 3660; Flinders Mall). There's a **QPWS** (☎ 4778 5378; Hurst St; 🕑 7.30am-4pm) at Picnic Bay.

Sights

PICNIC BAY

Perhaps it's the twinkling night views of Townsville that draw travellers to Picnic Bay. The Mall, along the waterfront, has a good handful of eateries and is a favourite hang-out for that elegant, curious bird – the curlew.

To the west of town is **Cockle Bay**, with the wreck of HMS *City of Adelaide*, and secluded **West Point**. Heading east around the coast is **Rocky Bay**, where there's a short, steep walk down to its beautiful beach. The popular **Picnic Bay Golf Course** is open to the public.

NELLY BAY

Nelly Bay is the island's main ferry port. At the time of writing, a three-year waterfront development that includes a marina, accommodation and dining was under way, conspiring to make Nelly Bay the island's happening hub – hopefully a low-key one.

ARCADIA

Arcadia village has the lovely **Alma Bay** cove. There's plenty of shade, picnic tables and a kids' playground here. The main beach, **Geoffrey Bay**, is less appealing but has a reef at its southern end (QPWS discourages reef walking at low tide). It's also the access point for the car ferry, but that may change as Nelly Bay develops.

RADICAL BAY & THE FORTS

Townsville was a supply base for the Pacific during WWII, and the island's **forts** were designed to protect the town from naval attack. The only ammunition they provide now is for your camera – great panoramic views. You can walk to the forts from the Radical and Horseshoe Bay Rds junction, about 2km north of Alma Bay. Or head north to Radical Bay via a rough vehicle track, with walking tracks off it that lead to secluded Arthur and Florence Bays (great for snorkelling), and the old **searchlight station** on the headland between the two.

From Radical Bay you can walk across the headland to beautiful **Balding Bay** (an unofficial nude-bathing beach) and Horseshoe Bay.

HORSESHOE BAY

On the north coast of the island, Horseshoe Bay seems to attract a younger crowd. It has a few shops, accommodation and a long stretch of beach that has water-sports gear for hire. There are walks northeast to Balding and Radical Bays for great swimming.

Activities

The QPWS publishes a leaflet on the island's excellent **bushwalking tracks**. Some walks include: Nelly Bay to Arcadia (5km one way), Picnic Bay to West Point (16km return; no bus access), Horseshoe Bay to Florence Bay (2.5km, one hour). You can catch the bus back at the end of most of these.

There are stinger nets on the beaches around Horseshoe Bay; however, if you're staying in Arcadia locals will tell you their tiny Alma Bay is devoid of stingers and indeed they've not had an incident yet.

If you missed the Whitsundays, you can still indulge in a day's sailing here. **Jazza Sailing Tours** (☎ 0427-373 011, 4758 1887; day trip A$80) runs a day trip on a 13m yacht that includes snorkelling, boom-netting and a seafood lunch. There's also a West Point sunset sail (A$30).

Magnetic Island Sea Kayaks (☎ 4778 5424; www.seakayak.com.au; Horseshoe Bay; half-day tours A$50; 🕑 7am-9pm) has excellent tours of Magnetic

Island's coves and bays, but if you'd rather explore the coastline by horse power, call **Bluey's Horseshoe Ranch** (☎ 4778 5109; Horseshoe Bay; trail rides A$65) about its two-hour beach trails.

Dive companies on Magnetic Island offer plenty of underwater action with certificate courses, and wreck and night dives. Try **Ocean Dive Australia** (☎ 4758 1391; Nelly Bay), based at Coconuts on the Beach, or **Pleasure Divers** (☎ 4778 5788, 1800 797 797; Arcadia), based at Arkies resort.

Sleeping

Magnetic Island is a bit of a cheap package bonanza, but before you pay for anything in Townsville speak to other travellers to confirm the accommodation matches the exuberant description on the brochure.

Geoff's Place (☎ 1800 285 577, 4778 5577; geoffsplace@beyond.net.au; 40 Horseshoe Bay Rd, Horseshoe Bay; camp sites per 2 people A$10, dm A$18, d A$50;) On a sprawling patch of land, this place epitomizes the tropical hideaway with basic A-frame timber cabins and plenty of rich green flora. There's oodles of shady camping spots, a beautiful saltwater pool and enough room left over for a creek!

Arkies (☎ 1800 663 666, 4778 5177; www.arkiesonmagnetic.com; 7 Marine Pde, Arcadia; dm A$15-18, d & tw A$50;) This hefty complex is like a village unto itself: tour desk, pub, pool, bistro, café, beach volleyball and masses of beds. The dorms are uninspiring but roomy enough. Arkies' biggest virtue, however, is its promise of a good party.

Travellers Resort (☎ 1800 000 290, 4778 5166; www.mbtravel.com.au/holiday/ma_travellersresort.asp; The Esplanade, Picnic Bay; dm from A$12, d 50;) The rooms and facilities at this hostel are a little on the tired side but the emphasis is well and truly on the three bars and the shameless pursuit of a good time. There's also a resident crocodile but his partying days seem to be behind him.

Maggies Beach House (☎ 4778 5144; www.maggiesbeachhouse.com.au; Pacific Dr, Horseshoe Bay; dm from A$21, d from A$60;) With the façade of a Mediterranean resort, Maggies' cell-like interior falls short of expectation. Everything is clean enough but the overwhelming grey concrete makes the place feel slightly institutionalised. The lively atmosphere downstairs in the bar compensates though and it *is* right by the beach.

If you want to splurge and get carried away with the whole tropical getaway thing, two good options are **Marshall's B&Bs** (☎ 4778 5112, 3 Endeavour Rd, Arcadia; s/d A$45/65) and **Magnetic Island Tropical Resort** (☎ 1800 691 22, 4778 5955; www.magneticislandresort.com; 56 Yates St, Nelly Bay; d from A$75;).

There are no QPWS camping grounds, but some hostels have camp sites.

Eating

There are small supermarkets in all the villages, and good bakeries in Nelly Bay and Arcadia.

The island's dress code is a shorts and thongs (flip-flops) affair. Opening hours are erratic during quiet periods (late January to March).

Fat Possum Café (☎ 4778 5409; Sooning St, Nelly Bay; dishes A$3.50-10; breakfast & lunch daily, dinner Fri-Tue) This pocket-sized café packs some punch with delicious burgers (go Mexican, veggie or tandoori), freshly baked pies and pastries and authentic noodle dishes for dinner. Great smoothies.

Banister's Seafood (☎ 4778 5585; 22 McCabe Cres, Arcadia; mains A$5-22; lunch & dinner) If you like seafood, pack your appetite. Banister's turns the humble fish-and-chips takeaway into a divine art and the menu only gets fancier from there. All manner of shellfish joins plenty of fish on the menu and you can scoff the lot by candlelight.

Geckos (☎ 4778 5144; Pacific Dr, Horseshoe Bay; meals A$8-20; breakfast, lunch & dinner) A good splash of flavours graces the menu at Geckos, with pizzas, salads, stir-fries, seafood and Thai dishes all getting a spot. The open-air surrounds are pleasant, too, with Horseshoe Bay planted conveniently at your feet. This place is part of Maggie's Beach House (see left).

Wicked Bread Gourmet Fillings (Pacific Dr, Horseshoe Bay; sandwiches A$4-8; breakfast & lunch) The name isn't the only mouthful here. This classy deli-style café offers concoctions like the New York special, protein packer, Bombay chicken and cranberry classic.

Other recommendations:

Feedja Cafe (☎ 4778 5833; Picnic Bay Mall, Picnic Bay; dishes A$4-8; breakfast & lunch) Fresh café fare.

Mermaids (☎ 4778 5433; Picnic Bay Mall, Picnic Bay; meals A$5-10; lunch & dinner) Great fish and chips, and tortilla wraps.

Getting There & Away

Sunferries (☎ 4771 3855; Flinders St East, Townsville; 6.45am-7pm Mon-Fri, 7am-5.30pm Sat & Sun) operates a frequent passenger ferry between Townsville and Magnetic Island (return A$20, 20 minutes). Ferries leave from the terminal on Flinders St East, also stopping at the breakwater terminal on Sir Leslie Thiess Dr.

Magnetic Island Car & Passenger Ferry (☎ 4772 5422; Ross St; ⌚ 6am-5.20pm Mon-Fri, 7.45am-5.20pm Sat & Sun) does the crossing seven times Monday to Thursday, eight times on Friday and six times on each Saturday and Sunday, from the southern side of Ross Creek. Return fares are car A$123, motorcycle A$40, passengers A$17, bicycles free. The car ferry arrives at Arcadia.

Getting Around

Magnetic Island Bus Service (☎ 4778 5130; fares A$2-4.50) plies between Picnic Bay and Horseshoe Bay at least 14 times a day, meeting all ferries and stopping at, or near, all accommodation.

You can rent a scooter (around A$30 per day) or your very own hot-pink little moke (around A$60 per day) to zip around the island. Companies include **Moke Hire** (☎ 4778 5491; Horseshoe Bay), **Roadrunner Scooter Hire** (☎ 4778 5222; Picnic Bay Mall, Picnic Bay) and **Tropical Topless Car Rentals** (☎ 4758 1111; Picnic Bay).

Most hostels rent mountain bikes for A$15 a day.

TOWNSVILLE TO MISSION BEACH

Paluma Range National Park

If you've got wheels, don't miss the beautiful Mt Spec–Big Crystal Creek section of this national park. It straddles the 1000m-plus Paluma Range west of the Bruce Hwy and has Australia's most southerly pocket of tropical rainforest, with wonderful coastal views. It's about 62km north of Townsville.

There are two access routes from the Bruce Hwy. Travelling north from Townsville, take the turn-off left after Rollingstone, then left onto the signposted ring road up to Paluma Range. The uphill road is narrow and spectacular, and winds along the southern edge of the park, passing **Little Crystal Creek** (with a waterfall and good swimming beside a stone bridge) and **McClelland's Lookout** (with three good walking tracks) on the way to the mountain village of Paluma (18km from the ring road).

Travelling south, turn right at Mutarnee to access the ring road, just after the Frosty Mango café. Take the turn-off to **Big Crystal Creek**, which has good swimming, a barbecue area and a self-registration **camping ground** (camp sites per person A$4). To complete the drive, get back onto the ring road and take the right turn-off to Paluma.

The **Jourama Falls** area of the park is 6km along good unsealed road off the highway. The signpost is 91km north of Townsville. **Waterview Creek**, within walking distance of the falls (600m), has good swimming holes with loads of cute turtles, lookouts, a picnic area and a self-registration **camping ground** (camp sites per person A$4) with barbecues. Check availability with the **ranger** (☎ 07-4777 3112) in the peak season.

Townsville Tropical Tours (see p198) runs day trips to the park, or accommodation is available at **Paluma Rainforest Cottages** (☎ 07-4770 8520; d A$90). Make sure you stop at **Frosty Mango** (☎ 07-4770 8184; light meals A$5-10) at Mutarnee. It's a roadside restaurant serving everything mango-ish.

For more information, contact the QPWS or visitors centre (see below), in Ingham. Alternatively, try Townsville's **Flinders Mall visitors centre** (☎ 4721 3660; Flinders Mall; ⌚ 9am-5pm Mon-Fri, 9am-1pm Sat & Sun).

Ingham & Around

☎ **07**

Ingham is a major sugar-producing town and you'll want to stop here for directions to spectacular **Wallaman Falls**, within Lumholtz National Park (50km west of town). These falls have the longest single drop of any in Australia, at 278m. It's a powerful sight in the wet season. There's a self-registration QPWS **camping ground** (camp sites per person A$4) with a swimming hole nearby. Pop into the **Ingham visitors centre** (☎ 4776 5211; cnr Lannercost St & Townsville Rd; ⌚ 9am-5pm Mon-Fri, 9am-2pm Sat & Sun) or the **QPWS** (☎ 4777 2808; 49 Cassidy St) for information.

Buses link Ingham with Townsville ($27, 1½ hours) and Cairns ($43, 3½ hours).

Cardwell

☎ **07 / pop 1420**

Quiet Cardwell is one of north Queensland's earliest towns, yet there's surprisingly little to it. The Port Hinchinbrook marina development, 2km south of town, is the departure point for Hinchinbrook Island and may awaken this beachside stretch in years to come. For travellers with wheels, there are a bunch of great forest drives, picnic spots and walks with swimming holes in the area, including the **Cardwell Forest Dr**, a 26km round trip.

The QPWS **Reef & Rainforest Centre** (☎ 4066 8115; www.epa.qld.gov.au; 8am-4.30pm), beside the main jetty, has a great rainforest interpretative display and information on Hinchinbrook Island and the drives.

On the main strip, the **Hinchinbrook Hop** (☎ 4066 8671; 186 Victoria St; camp sites per 2 people A$12, dm A$14) has small, bright dorms and a good roadside café. The **Kookaburra Holiday Park** (☎ 4066 8648; www.kookaburraholidaypark.com.au; 175 Bruce Hwy; camp sites per 2 people A$11, dm A$18;) includes a YHA hostel. Alternatively, **Cardwell Backpackers Hostel** (☎ 4066 8014; www.backpackers.narod.ru; 178 Bowen St; dm/d A$16/34) is a homely spot.

All buses between Townsville and Cairns stop at Cardwell: Townsville (A$33), Cairns (A$33). Cardwell is also on the Brisbane to Cairns train line. Contact the **Queensland Rails booking service** (☎ 13 22 32; www.traveltrain.qr.com.au; 6am-8.30pm) for more information.

Hinchinbrook Island National Park

☎ 07

Lucky you, if you have time to explore this stunning and unspoiled wilderness. Hinchinbrook's granite mountains rise dramatically from the sea. The mainland side is thick with lush tropical forest, while long, sandy beaches and tangled mangroves curve around its eastern shores. All 399 sq km of the island is national park, and rugged **Mt Bowen** (1121m) is its highest peak. There's plenty of wildlife, especially pretty-faced wallabies and the iridescent-blue Ulysses butterfly. It's definitely worth a day trip.

Hinchinbrook is well known to bushwalkers and naturalists. Walking opportunities here are excellent; however, some tracks may close between November and March due to adverse weather. The highlight is the **Thorsborne Trail** (also known as the East Coast Trail), a 32km track from Ramsay Bay to Zoe Bay (with its stunning waterfall), and on to George Point at the southern tip. It's a three- to five-day walk, although you can walk shorter sections if you don't have that much time. This is the real bush experience – you'll need to draw water from creeks as you go (all water should be chemically purified or boiled before drinking), keep your food out of reach of the native bush rats, and keep an eye out for estuarine crocodiles in the mangroves. Take plenty of insect repellent.

There are six QPWS **camping grounds** (per person A$4) along the Thorsborne Trail, plus others at Macushla and Scraggy Point in the north. There is a limit of 45 people allowed on the main track at any time, so it's necessary to book ahead (up to one year ahead for school-holiday periods). Pick up the informative Thorsborne Trail and Hinchinbrook leaflets from the QPWS **Reef & Rainforest Centre** (☎ 4066 8601) in Cardwell. To purchase camping permits call ☎ 13 13 04 or pay online at www.epa.qld.gov.au.

GETTING THERE & AWAY

From April to October **Hinchinbrook Island Ferries** (☎ 4066 8270; www.hinchinbrookferries.com.au) runs a daily service (three services a week from November to March) from Port Hinchinbrook marina. Services are suspended in February. Day trips and return transfers for campers and walkers all cost A$85. Walkers usually catch a different ferry at the southern end of the island to Lucinda, back on the mainland, with **Hinchinbrook Explorer Fishing and Ecotours** (☎ 4068 9716; one way A$60).

Tully

☎ 07 / pop 2700

The big excitement in tiny Tully is spending five frothy hours white-water rafting its wild river. The town is supposedly the wettest place in Australia with an average annual rainfall of over 4000mm. When you're not surfing the river there's ample work *à la* bananas and sugar cane. Walkers also have good reason to stop, with 150km of new tracks. Even so, nearby Mission Beach has more-appealing creature comforts.

Bilyana National Employer's Employment Services (☎ 4066 5562; Bluff Rd, Bilyana), about 17km south of Tully, can help you find fruit-picking work, and hostels in Tully can do the same.

Day trips with **Raging Thunder Adventures** (☎ 4030 7990; www.ragingthunder.com.au) or **R'n'R White Water Rafting** (☎ 1800 079 039, 4051 7777; www.raft.com.au) cost from A$135 and include barbecue lunch and transfers from Mission Beach, Cairns or Port Douglas.

The new **Misty Mountain** and **Kennedy Trails** cover existing logging roads that wind through the lush Tully Valley and, in part, retrace the steps of explorer Edmund Kennedy. Alternatively, Aboriginal guides share their rainforest survival skills along the old trading route, **Echo Creek Walking Trail**. You can book tours through **El Rancho Del Rey** (☎ 4066 7770; www.elrancho.com.au; Ranch Rd via Davidson Rd, Tully; dm/s A$66/135), which has homestead or bunk accommodation that includes meals. For more information on heritage walking tracks, ask at the **visitors centre** (☎ 4068 2288; 8.30am-4.45pm Mon-Fri, 9am-2.30pm Sat & Sun) on the highway or check Tourism Tropical North Queensland's website at www.tropicalaustralia.com.au.

Tully's limited accommodation is geared towards fruit pickers. There's the loud and high-density **Banana Barracks** (☎ 4068 0455; bananabarracks@comnorth.com.au; 50 Butler St; dm A$18) or the quieter, old-fashioned **Savoy** (☎ 4068 2400; 4 Plumb St; dm A$17).

Buses serve Tully from all coastal points including Townsville ($36, three hours), Ingham ($29, 1½ hours) and Cairns ($26, 2½ hours).

MISSION BEACH & AROUND

☎ 07

A wisp of houses and shops are all that interrupt this long terrain of palm-fringed beach and dense mangrove forest. There's some serious downtime to be had in Mission Beach and its smaller, shouldering neighbours of Bingil Bay and Wongaling Beach, but if you're lonely for action you've got white-water rafting, skydiving and sea-kayaking at your door.

Information

Mission Beach visitors centre (☎ 4068 7099; Porter Promenade; 9am-5pm)

Mission Music (☎ 4068 7955; Shop 9, The Homestead Centre, Mission Beach; per hr A$5) Internet access.

Wet Tropics Centre (Porter Promenade, Mission Beach; 10am-5pm)

Sights & Activities

Mission Beach has all those near-death experiences you've been longing to try. You can **skydive** from here, **raft** the Tully River rapids (see p203), learn to **dive** or go **crocodile spotting** in the mangroves at night.

Sea kayaking is a fantastic way to learn about the Great Barrier Reef Marine Park with guides who really know and love the area. **Coral Sea Kayaking** (☎ 4068 9154; www.coralseakayaking.com) offers half-/full-day trips (A$60/95) around Mission Beach and Dunk Island, and three-, five- and seven-day trips as far as Hinchinbrook Island.

Day trips to pretty Dunk Island (opposite) are popular. **MV Lawrence Kavanagh** (☎ 4068 7211), **Quick Cat Cruises** (☎ 4068 7289) and **Blue Thunder Cruises** (☎ 4088 6007) compete heavily for business at the Clump Point Jetty, offering good-value Great Barrier Reef and Dunk and Bedarra Island trips between them. Day trips cost between A$80 and A$90.

Rainforest walks around Mission Beach can get exciting if you meet a southern cassowary. This large, flightless, blue bird is an endangered species that needs protection, although it can disembowel you with a toenail. Don't feed cassowaries and be careful not to run over them with your car. Mission Beach was their habitat before people built brick nests on their turf.

Sleeping

Sanctuary (☎ 1800 777 012, 4088 6064; www.sanctuaryatmission.com; Holt Rd, Bingil Bay; dm/d A$33/65) A hut with floor-to-ceiling mesh is all that separates you from boisterous rainforest critters at this unique tree-top sanctuary about 11km north of Mission Beach. The gleaming communal treehouse has an excellent café, or you can self-cater. Note – the terrain here is incredibly steep! Transfers are available.

Beach Shack (☎ 1800 333 115, 4068 7783; www.missionbeachshack.com; 86 Porter Promenade, Mission Beach; dm/d A$18/45) This small hostel greets you with a welcome warm enough to make you feel like one of the crew immediately. The open-plan house, frequent barbecues and couch-stocked lounge play their part, too. It also books good-value trips to the Great Barrier Reef.

Treehouse (☎ 4068 7137; treehouse.yha@znet.net.au; Frizzel Rd, Bingil Bay; dm/d A$20/50) Peering over the forest canopy from lofty stilts, this hostel has brilliant views and a vast deck from which to enjoy them. Rooms are fairly rudimentary (it *is* a treehouse) but the facilities aren't. It's a good distance from anywhere, though, so bring a good book.

Other recommendations:

Mission Beach Retreat (☎ 1800 001 056, 4088 6299; 49 Porter Promenade, Mission Beach; dm A$18, d A$40) Neat as a pin and central.

Scotty's Beach House (☎ 1800 665 567, 4068 8676; www.scottysbeachhouse.com.au; 167 Reid Rd, Wongaling

Beach; dm/d A$21/50;) Good café & party bar. Plain dorms in motel-style units.

Hideaway Holiday Village (4068 7104; hideaway@austarnet.com.au; 58-60 Porter Promenade, Mission Beach; camp/caravan sites per 2 people A$24/27, cabins with/without bath A$70/55;) Central and tidy.

Eating & Drinking

If you're self-catering, you'll find Mission Beach Supermarket at the Village Green.

Oceania Bar (4088 6222; 52 Porter Promenade, Mission Beach; meals A$8-20; dinner;) Definitely the coolest joint in town and not just for the bar. The menu is an act of genius with grilled tuna and wasabi burgers, tempeh towers and inventive salads, steaks and pastas. The bar gears into party mode on weekends with live DJs, beach parties and general debauchery.

Piccolo Paradiso (4068 7008; Village Green, Mission Beach; mains A$7-19; breakfast, lunch & dinner Tue-Sun) Impressive pizzas and pastas are the go here but you can also pick up scrumptious lunchtime specials like baguettes, bruschetta, salads and nachos. The atmosphere is relaxed and all that foliage around the outdoor tables makes for very pleasant dining indeed.

Early Birds Coffee Shop (4088 6000; cnr Porter Promenade & Campbell St, Mission Beach; snacks A$4-10; breakfast & lunch) This small café churns out great breakfasts, club sandwiches, hot rolls and burgers. There's a smattering of tables outside or you can just take food away and dine on the beach.

Café Coconutz (4068 7397; Porter Promenade, Mission Beach; mains A$8-20; lunch & dinner) By day this is a cruisy café serving focaccias and salads. By night the atmosphere is decidedly more hip, as is the menu – nasi goreng, rogan josh and a good smattering of steaks for the true carnivore. The attached bar teems with pool-playing drinkers most nights.

Cafe Gecko (4068 7390; Shop 6, Porter Promenade, Mission Beach; snacks A$4-8; breakfast & lunch) sells good coffee, sandwiches and pies.

Getting There & Around

McCafferty's/Greyhound (13 20 30) buses stop at the Port o' Call Cafe in Mission Beach, while **Premier Motor Service** (13 34 10) stops at Wongaling Beach. Both companies take passengers to Cairns (A$15, two hours) and Townsville (A$45, four hours).

Mission Beach Connections (4059 2709; www.missionbeachdunkconnections.com.au) also shuttles folk to and from Cairns (A$15, three daily) in minibuses.

The Mission Beach Bus Service runs regularly from Bingil Bay to South Mission Beach.

DUNK ISLAND

07

Dunk Island is an easy day trip from Mission Beach. It's just 4.5km off the coast and is blessed with nearly 150 species of birdlife and exotic butterflies in season.

Rainforest walks here revive the spirit. From the top of Mt Kootaloo (271m; 5.6km from the base to the top), entrances to the Hinchinbrook Channel fan before you, or there's the rewarding but difficult island circuit (9.2km) that passes by secluded beaches. You can also check out the alternative lifestyle of **Bruce Arthur's Artists Colony** (adult A$4; 10am-1pm Mon & Thu).

The resort on Dunk charges a day pass (A$28), which includes complimentary lunch and a swim in the beachside butterfly pool. You can test your water- or Jet-skiing skills, snorkel, or tube ride at the jetty (for a price, of course), where there's a snack bar serving pizza, pies and light meals (A$5 to A$16).

At the resort's water-sports office the QPWS **camping ground** (4068 8199; camp sites per person A$4) has nine shaded sites with good amenities; call for bookings.

Getting There & Away

A transfer to Dunk Island costs about A$22 per adult, but some operators offer package trips that include lunch and other island stops.

Dunk Island Express Water Taxis (4068 8310)
MV Lawrence Kavanagh (4068 7211)
Quick Cat Cruises (4068 7289)

INNISFAIL

07 / pop 8530

The traffic is always at a standstill around Innisfail's pedestrian-friendly streets, but you won't mind, as it's such a pretty place to stop by. This prosperous sugar city suffered a devastating cyclone in 1918, but its reconstruction came at the height of the sleek 1920s and '30s Art Deco movement. Innisfail's residents are proudly restoring buildings from this glamorous era.

The **visitors centre** (4061 7422; Bruce Hwy; 9am-5pm Mon-Fri, 10am-3pm Sat & Sun), situated

QUEENSLAND

about 3.5km south of town, offers a **town walk** brochure.

Johnstone River Crocodile Farm (☎ 4061 1121; Flying Fish Point Rd; adult/child A$16/8; 8.30am-4.30pm) breeds thousands of crocodiles so that we can enjoy them as handbags and steak. But your skin will crawl at the sight of 300 crocs slam-dancing over a pile of raw chicken heads for dinner (feeding times 11am and 3pm). You can pet a freshwater croc and watch the guides *sit* on one-tonne Gregory, their fattest reptile. Tours run frequently.

Just off the Bruce Hwy about 3.5km south of town, tidy **Mango Tree Van Park** (☎ 4061 1656; mangotreepark@bigpond.com; 6 Couche St; camp sites per 2 people A$15, cabins A$65;) has two great cottage-style cabins.

Hostels cater to the banana plantation workers. The homey atmosphere at **Codge Lodge** (☎ 4061 8055; 63 Rankin St; dm/d A$20/40) makes it the best choice, or there's **Backpackers Paradise** (☎ 4061 2284; 73 Rankin St; dm A$15) and **Walkabout Motel** (☎ 4061 2311; 20-24 McGowan Dr; motelwalkabout@bigpond.com; dm A$15;).

From Innisfail the Palmerston Hwy winds west up to the magical Atherton Tableland, passing through the rainforest of **Palmerston (Wooroonooran National Park)**, which has creeks, waterfalls, scenic walking tracks and a self-registration **camping ground** (camp sites per person A$4) at Henrietta Creek, just off the road.

CAIRNS

☎ 07 / pop 98,981

Sunny Cairns is alive with the carnival atmosphere of travellers year-round and the city is positively booming. There's no denying this gem of the north rides hard on the back of tourism, but Cairns has cultivated a happy marriage of old Queensland character and modest development, with a minimum of tourist traps and tack. In fact, a constantly shifting population of travellers and students injects far more than a boost to the economy, and at times its heart feels like a global village. It has an irrepressible energy and a lush tropical setting.

Apart from limitless accommodation and dining options, markets, culture, shopping and seaside atmosphere, Cairns' big drawcard is its access to the outer tentacles of the Great Barrier Reef. It's also a good base to discover Port Douglas, the Atherton Tableland, Cape Tribulation and beyond. The best news for budget travellers is that you don't have to empty the bank to enjoy it. In the city itself, cosmetic improvements like the glorious swimming lagoon and thick grassy parklands are free. All this is much more fun with a mate and hooking up with fellow travellers here is a highlight of its own.

Orientation

Cairns' CBD is in the area between the Esplanade and McLeod St and Wharf and Aplin Sts. Reef Fleet terminal is the main departure point for reef trips. Trinity Wharf, where long-distance buses arrive and depart, is east of the CBD. Cairns' train station is hidden inside Cairns Central Shopping Centre on McLeod St. Local buses (Sunbus) leave from the Lake St Transit Centre.

The airport is about 5km from central Cairns. **Australia Coach** (☎ 4048 8355; australiacoach@blackandwhitetaxis.com.au; tickets A$8) meets all incoming flights and runs a shuttle bus to the CBD. **Black & White Taxis** (☎ 13 10 08, 4048 8333) charges about A$14 to/from the airport.

Information

BOOKSHOPS

Absells Chart & Map Centre (☎ 4041 2699; Andrejic Arcade, 55-59 Lake St) Sells a broad range of maps and travel guides.

Exchange Bookshop (☎ 4051 1443; 78 Grafton St) New and second-hand books.

EMERGENCY

Ambulance (☎ 000)

Fire (☎ 000)

Police station (☎ 000, 4030 7000; 5 Sheridan St)

INTERNET ACCESS

A cluster of backpacker travel agencies around Shields St offers the cheapest Internet access.

Backpackers World for Travel (☎ 4041 0999; 12 Shields St; per hr A$1)

Global Gossip (☎ 4041 6411; 125 Abbott St; per hr A$4)

Happy Travels (☎ 4041 0666; Shop 9, 7 Shields St; per hr A$2)

Peterpan (☎ 1800 213 225; Level 1, Shop 20-22, Shields St; per hr A$1)

MEDICAL SERVICES

Cairns Base Hospital (☎ 4050 6333; The Esplanade)

Cairns City 24-Hour Medical Centre (☎ 4052 1119; admin@rightroundtheworld.com; cnr Florence & Grafton Sts)

Cairns Travel Clinic (☎ 4041 1699; ctlmed@iig.com.au; 15 Lake St)

MONEY

All of the major banks have branches, with ATMs, throughout central Cairns, and most have foreign-exchange sections. There's also **Travelex** (☎ 4041 0644; 13 Shields St) and **American Express Travel** (☎ 4051 8811; Orchid Plaza, Abbott St).

TOURIST INFORMATION

If you can't find tourist information in Cairns, then you'll never find porn on the Internet either. There are dozens of privately run 'information centres' (basically tour-booking agencies), but official offices are best.

Accommodation Centre (☎ 1800 807 730, 4051 4066; www.accomcentre.com.au; 36 Aplin St) An extremely helpful centre with wheelchair access and tourist information; it's also a contact point for working holidays in Japan.

Cairns visitor centre (☎ 4031 4355; www.cairnsvisitorcentre.com; Shop 2a, Pier Marketplace; 9am-5pm)

QPWS (☎ 4046 6600; www.epa.qld.gov.au; 5b Sheridan St; 8.30am-5pm Mon-Fri) Camping permits and walking-track information.

Tourism Tropical North Queensland (☎ 4031 3588; www.tropicalaustralia.com.au; 51 The Esplanade; 8.30am-6.30pm) Excellent and unbiased.

TRAVEL AGENCIES

On Shields St, a number of agencies specialise in backpacker travel.

Backpackers World for Travel (☎ 4041 0999; 12 Shields St)

Navi Tour (☎ 1300 558 800, 4031 6776; 1st fl, Orchid Plaza, 58 Lake St) Caters for Japanese tourists.

Peterpan (☎ 1800 213 225; www.peterpans.com; Level 1, Shop 20-22, Shields St)

Rendez-Vous Futé (☎ 4031 3533; www.australie-voyages.com, French only; 28 Spence St) French-speaking agency.

STA Travel (☎ 4031 4199; 9 Shields St)

Trailfinders (☎ 1300 651 900; 4041 1100; www.trailfinders.com.au; Hides Cnr, Lake St)

Sights

The undisputed highlight of the **Cairns foreshore promenade** is the 4000-sq-metre saltwater **swimming lagoon**. As though part of a big eye-candy convention, bodies (mostly of the backpacker variety) accumulate here to cool off and bronze up. Fitness enthusiasts inline, cycle and work up a sweat along the **Esplanade Walking Track**, although this is also pleasant for a stroll. Locals and travellers meander lazily up and down **The Esplanade**, popping into restaurants and shops until the wee hours.

One of the best cultural experiences in the state can be found at the Aborigine-owned and operated **Tjapukai Cultural Park** (☎ 4042 9999; www.tjapukai.com.au; Kamerunga Rd, Carevonica; adult A$29, with transfers A$50; 9am-5pm). This complex illustrates the culture of the Tjapukai tribe through galleries and dance performances. It features the Creation legend, told using giant holograms; a corroboree; and boomerang- and spear-throwing demonstrations.

The small **Cairns Regional Gallery** (☎ 4031 6865; www.cairnsregionalgallery.com.au; cnr Abbott & Shields Sts; adult A$4; 10am-5pm Mon-Sat, 1-5pm Sun) is housed within the gorgeous former State Public Office building, built in 1936. The interior of white arches and columns, ornate ceilings, and marble floors is a work of art itself. Gracing the walls of the three galleries are temporary exhibits, diverse in nature and medium. Contentious and contemporary issues are celebrated through the pieces here and it's a far cry from watercolours and pastels.

An excellent way to learn about the reef is at **Reef Teach** (☎ 4031 7794; www.reefteach.com.au; 14 Spence St; adult A$13; 10am-9pm Mon-Sat, lectures 6.15pm & 8.30pm Mon-Sat). The madcap lecturer we encountered here is like an ocean-obsessed Ace Ventura – this guy talks FAST. You'll learn basic fish and coral identification, and how to treat the Reef respectfully. You'll also learn more-obscure facts, such as which creature breathes through its anus.

Flecker Botanic Gardens (☎ 4044 3398; Collins Ave, Edge Hill; 7.30am-5.30pm Mon-Fri, 8.30am-5.30pm Sat & Sun) specialises in cycads, heliconias, gingers and palms, and has a stunning collection of natives and exotics. Informative tours are held at 1pm Monday to Friday (A$5) and there are self-guided walking tracks.

Opposite the gardens a rainforest boardwalk leads to **Saltwater Creek** and **Centenary Lakes**. For more-serious walkers, tracks through **Mt Whitfield Conservation Park** have several lookouts offering spectacular views of Cairns and Trinity Inlet.

Crystal Cascades, 20km south of Cairns, is a series of beautiful swimming holes, but you'll need a car to get here and back. There is a terrific **mangrove boardwalk** on Airport Ave, 200m before the airport.

Cairns Tropical Zoo (☎ 4055 3669; www.cairnstropicalzoo.com; Captain Cook Hwy, Clifton Beach; adult A$25; 8.30am-5pm), 22km north of Cairns, is the area's ultimate wildlife experience. If you haven't cuddled a koala, here's the place. Noncontact critters include kangaroos, wombats and the regional mascot – crocs.

QUEENSLAND

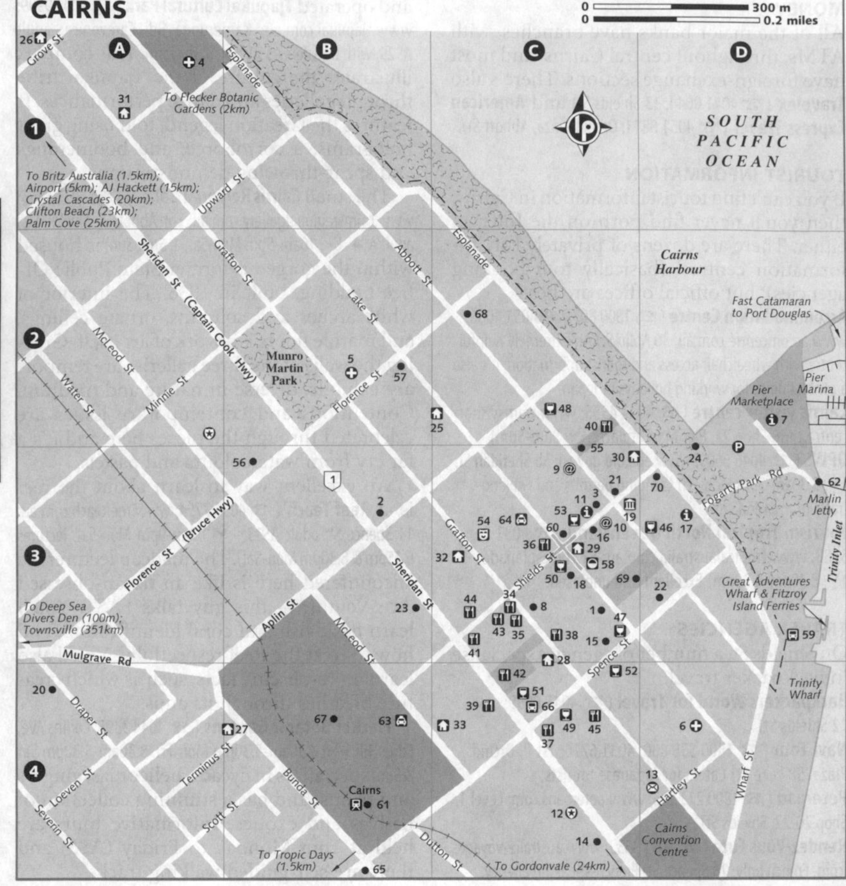

Activities

DIVING & SNORKELLING

Cairns is the scuba capital of the Barrier Reef and a popular place for PADI Open Water courses. There's a plethora of choices, from no-frills, four-day courses with pool training and reef dives (around A$300) to four-day Open Water courses (A$430 to A$580). Five-day courses (A$540 to A$650) include two days of pool theory and three days living on a boat. The live-aboard courses are more rewarding and often have higher safety standards. Find out whether prices include a medical check (around A$45), daily reef tax (A$5) and passport photos (around A$8). Advanced courses are also available for certified divers.

A selection of reputable dive schools in Cairns:

Cairns Reef Dive (☎ 1800 222 252, 4052 1811; www.cairnsreefdive.com.au; Shop 2, 86 Lake St; 🕑 7am-5pm)

Deep Sea Divers Den (☎ 1800 612 223, 4046 7333; www.divers-den.com; 319 Draper St; 🕑 6am-6pm)

Down Under Dive (☎ 1800 079 099; www.downunderdive.com.au; 287 Draper St; 🕑 7am-7pm)

Pro-Dive (☎ 4031 5255; www.prodive-cairns.com.au; cnr Abbott & Shields Sts; 🕑 9am-9pm)

WHITE-WATER RAFTING

There's exciting white-water rafting down the Barron, Tully, Russell and North Johnstone Rivers.

Tours are graded according to difficulty, from armchair rafting (Grade 1) to heart palpitations (Grade 5). Approximate prices for tours (from Cairns) are full-day Tully A$150, half-day Barron A$85, two-/four-day North Johnstone A$650/1500, and full-day Russell A$130; check if wetsuit hire (around A$10) and national park fees (A$6) are included.

Raging Thunder (☎ 4030 7990; www.ragingthunder.com.au) Wide range of adrenalin-inducing tours.

R'n'R White Water Rafting (☎ 4051 4055; www.raft.com.au; 8.30am-5.30pm)

OTHER ACTIVITIES

The range of other activities is enormous and most hostels have an exhaustive list. Some of the more popular sports are skydiving and bungy jumping:

AJ Hackett (☎ 1800 622 888, 4057 7188; www.ajhackett.com.au; end McGregor Rd; bungy A$110-140, s/tw/tr minjin jungle swing per person A$80/59/39, bungy & minjin swing combo A$140; 10am-5pm) Courtesy bus runs 9.15am, noon and 3pm.

Skydive Cairns (☎ 1800 444 568, 4031 5466; www.skydive.net.au; 59 Sheridan St; tandem dives from A$245; 7am-5pm)

Springmount Station (☎ 4093 4493; www.springmountstation.com; half-/full day A$90/110) Horse riding, camp-outs and farmstays.

Tours

DAINTREE RIVER & CAPE TRIBULATION

Cape Tribulation is one of the most popular day-trip destinations from Cairns. Tour operators push the 'safari' angle, but the road is sealed (suitable for a conventional vehicle) until just before the Cape Tribulation Beach House.

Billy Tea Bush Safaris (☎ 4032 0077; www.billytea.com.au; day tours A$130; depart/return 7.10am/6.30pm) Runs ecotours.

Cape Trib Connections (☎ 4053 3833; www.capetribconnections.com; day tours A$110; depart/return 8am/6pm)

Down Under Tours (☎ 4035 5566; res@downundertours.com; day tours A$100)

Jungle Tours (☎ 1800 817 234; www.adventuretours.com.au; day tours A$130; depart/return 7.30am/6.45pm) Recommended by readers.

GREAT BARRIER REEF & ISLANDS

Reef tours usually include lunch, snorkelling gear (with dives an optional extra) and pick-up from your accommodation. Tours start at A$60 and go as high as you want. At the cheaper end:

Compass (☎ 1800 815 811, 4050 0666; www.reeftrip.com; 100 Abbott St; day trips A$60; 8am-5pm) Hastings Reef and Breaking Patches. Maximum 100 people per tour. Boom-netting.

Noah's Ark Cruises (☎ 4041 0036; day trips from A$70) Hastings Reef and Michaelmas Cay. Maximum 32. Lots of snorkelling.

Passions of Paradise (☎ 1800 011 346, 4050 0676; www.passions.com.au; Reef Fleet Terminal; day trips A$75; 9am-5.30pm) Upolu Cay and Paradise Reef. Maximum 65. Catamaran. Party reputation.

PROTECTING THE REEF

The sheer size of the Great Barrier Reef makes it difficult to fathom how this ecosystem could be in danger of destruction, but three main threats – land-based pollutants, overfishing and the big one: global warming – jeopardise the reef's future. Coral polyps need a water temperature of 17.5°C to 28°C to grow and cannot tolerate too much sediment. Global warming and El Niño conditions are occasionally overheating sections of the world's oceans. This rise in temperature is literally bleaching the coral – as the brightly coloured living polyps die, only the white skeleton remains.

Some environmentalists and scientists predict that under the current conditions, coral cover within the reef may be reduced to less than 5% by the year 2050. Because all the living organisms in the reef are symbiotic, the colourful and diverse ecosystem we see today may be gone forever.

Fortunately, it's not all doom and gloom. In July 2004 the Australian government introduced new laws that increased 'no-take' zones, where it is forbidden to remove animal or plant life (eg no fishing), to 33.33% of the reef (it was previously only 4.5%). Although it will be several years before the success of this plan can be measured, it is certainly a huge step towards tackling overfishing and pollution.

Responsible tourism also plays a major role. Take all litter with you, even biodegradable material like apple cores. Admire, but don't touch or harass, marine animals and be aware that if you touch or walk on coral you'll cause damage. (It can also give you some very nasty cuts).

Most cruise operators are conscientious, but if you see staff dumping dodgy substances, question them. Apart from the environmental impact of this type of behaviour, there is a A$4.5 billion tourism industry based on the Great Barrier Reef, and it relies on the reef remaining healthy.

For more information you can contact the **Great Barrier Reef Marine Park Authority** (☎ 4750 0700; www.gbrmpa.gov.au; 2-68 Flinders St East, Townsville; 9am-5pm Mon-Fri).

QUEENSLAND

Tusa Dive (☎ 4031 1028; www.tusadive.com; cnr Esplanade & Shields Sts; day trips A$115; 8am-5pm) Smaller groups and greater coverage of the reef.

OTHER TOURS

For exploring the Atherton Tableland, **Uncle Brian's Tours** (☎ 4050 0615; www.unclebrian.com.au; day tour A$85; depart/return 8am/8.30pm Mon, Wed, Fri & Sat) is recommended, taking in Babinda, Josephine Falls and Lake Eacham.

Sleeping

Gilligan's (☎ 4041 6566; www.gilligansbackpackers.com.au; 57-89 Grafton St; dm/d A$24/60; P) Pure utopia, Gilligan's is essentially a sleek and stylish new hotel modified for backpackers. Each spacious dorm has a bathroom and balcony. Doubles come with TVs and furniture (from this century!) and are the best value in town. Each floor has a kitchen fit for Nigella, and amphitheatre lounge rooms. The only flaw is that it accommodates a small army and can get noisy at night.

Dreamtime Travellers Rest (☎ 4031 6753; www.dreamtimetravel.com.au; 4 Terminus St; dm/d A$20/45;) This small hostel, in a beautiful Queenslander just west of the centre, is outstanding. Behind the big front gates are very comfortable rooms, all with full bedding and towels, smart and spotless bathrooms and very relaxed vibes. The owners are down to earth and helpful.

Tropic Days (☎ 4041 1521; www.tropicdays.com.au; 28 Bunting St; dm/d A$20/45; P) Readers rave about this hostel and deservedly so. More like a casual B&B, the friendly owners have put considerable thought and effort into the tasteful rooms. All the facilities are excellent and tariffs include a free dinner in town. Monday nights here are A$8 'Croc BBQ' affairs – an absolute bargain.

Cairns Girls Hostel (☎ 1800 011 950, 4051 2767; www.cairnsgirlshostel.com.au; 147 Lake St; dm/tw A$16/36;) Sorry guys, this spotless two-storey mansion with three kitchens, two TV rooms and a warren of bathrooms and rooms has a strict oestrogen rule. There's a pervading tranquillity here and Dawn, the incredibly friendly owner, is a guru on all things Cairns. Super-cheap weekly rates.

Global Palace (☎ 1800 819 024, 4031 7921; www.globalpalace.com.au; 86-88 Lake St; dm A$21-23, tw/d A$50/52;) This classy and central hostel has some stylish décor and modern, minimalist rooms. The cheaper dorms are roomy and the more expensive ones bunk-free.

There's also a great wooden balcony overhanging the Shields St pedestrian strip and a TV room large enough to fly in.

International Hostel (☎ 4031 1545; www.internationalhostel.com.au; 67 The Esplanade; dm/d A$15/50;) This central hostel is reminiscent of a colourful university dorm. The simple dorms have adequate space and chunky mattresses while the larger doubles are airy. It's the best of the Esplanade hostels and has pristine views of the lagoon and its bronzing bods.

Calypso Inn (☎ 1800 815 628, 4031 0910; www.calypsobackpackers.com; 5-9 Digger St; dm/s A$21/33, d & tw A$50;) It's not as central as some, but Calypso is a suburban resort. The spacious outdoor area and lagoon-style pool are shaded by towering palms and the bar here is party HQ. Rooms are simple, clean and comfy, and there's a A$7 buffet every night.

Other recommendations:

YHA Cairns Central (☎ 4051 0772; cairnscentral@yhaqld.org; 20-24 McLeod St; dm with/without bath A$23/21, d & tw with/without bath A$60/50; P) Sociable motel-style hostel.

Pete's Backpackers Resort (☎ 1800 122 123; www.petescairns.com.au; 242 Grafton St; dm/s A$18/25, d A$40-45; P) Faded charm and a huge lawn.

Shooting Star Apartments (☎ 4047 7200; www.shootingstarapartments.com.au; 117 Grafton St; apt A$90; P) Stylish apartments for a well-earned splurge.

Eating

Cairns, with its Aussie tucker and hotpot of cuisines, can adapt to any appetite.

Restaurants, cafés and pubs cluster along Shields St (the major eat street) and the Esplanade (for a late-night pit stop and tourist-oriented restaurants). Also, many pubs and clubs serve counter meals.

SELF-CATERING

Cairns has a **Woolworths** (Abbott St), but the wonderful **Rusty's Bazaar** (Sheridan St btwn Shields & Spence Sts; Fri-Sun) is where many locals do their weekly shop. Rusty's sells fresh fruit and vegies, Asian herbs, seafood and honey. Niche self-catering options:

Asian Foods Australia (☎ 4052 1510; 101-105 Grafton St) Asian foodstore. Dry goods.

Neil's Organics (☎ 4051 5688; 21 Sheridan St) Organic produce, including fruit and vegies.

CAFÉS & QUICK EATS

Dotted along the Esplanade are noodle bars and kebab shops where you can gorge for around A$8. Lunch-time food courts can be found upstairs at **Orchid Plaza** (Abbott St) and at the **Night Markets** (The Esplanade), where you can snack on Aussie-Chinese.

Lillipad Café (☎ 4051 9565; 72 Grafton St; meals A$3-8; breakfast & lunch Mon-Sat) Blessed by the god of the spectacular spatula, this bohemian little café pumps out fantastic breakfasts in cheerful surrounds. The toasted Turkish bread or paninis for lunch are also creative, but if you've had bread up to the wazoo then the Mediterranean lasagne and pumpkin and risotto pastries are a delight.

Beethoven Café (☎ 4051 0292; 105 Grafton St; meals A$3.60-7; breakfast & lunch Mon-Sat) This busy bakery-café specialises in tasty and filling sandwiches, using fresh bread baked on the premises. It's also very popular with the locals for breakfast and regardless of what time you're here you should leave room for the gooey sweets and pastries.

City Walk Café (☎ 4051 5075; 95 Lake St; meals A$6-14; breakfast, lunch & dinner;) With commodious booths and perfect views of the pedestrian mall, this café is a great spot to people-watch. To accompany your entertainment you can dig into baguettes, pastas, salads, risotto and burgers. The menu may not be imaginative but the prices easily compensate.

Other recommendations:

Tiny's Juice Bar (☎ 4031 4331; 45 Grafton St; meals A$4-8; breakfast & lunch Mon-Sat) Great veggie option.

Sushi Express (☎ 4041 4388; 1st fl, Orchid Plaza, Abbott St; sushi plates A$2-4; lunch;)

Sushi Zipang (☎ 4051 3328; 39 Shields St; sushi plates A$2-5, meals A$7.50-19; lunch & dinner;)

RESTAURANTS

Gaura Nitai's (☎ 4031 2255; 55 Spence St; meals A$4.50-10; lunch Mon-Fri, dinner Mon-Sat;) This tranquil place is a vegetarian's treasure trove, with heavy subcontinent overtones and an inventive menu. Apart from fragrant and spicy dahls, curries and wontons, you can get cashew loaves and – dare we say it – healthy desserts. Big thumbs up.

Red Ochre Grill (☎ 4051 0100; 43 Shields St; mains A$8-30; lunch & dinner;) Cuisine for cultivated carnivores – Red Ochre pillages the bush and makes wild things yum. How does salt and native pepper crocodile and tiger prawns grab you? Or perhaps quandong-chilli kangaroo sirloin and maybe wattle-seed pavlova to finish? You'll have to ditch the thongs and spend a little but it's definitely worth it.

Rattle 'n' Hum (☎ 4031 3011; 67 The Esplanade; meals A$10-20; ⏰ lunch & dinner) Sedate and sleepy during the day, this bar heaves with meal-munching, cocktail-guzzling, beer-gulping happy campers by night. The wood-fired smells translate into excellent pizza and its salads are a cut above the norm.

Tandoori Oven (☎ 4031 0043; 62b Shields St; meals A$15-22; ⏰ lunch & dinner Mon-Sat) The only thing more authentic than the curries at this North Indian diner is the Indian pop music blaring from the speakers. If you're looking to blow your taste buds you'll get the opportunity here.

Other recommendations:

Gilligan's Bistro (☎ 4041 6566; 57-89 Grafton St; meals A$10-20; ⏰ lunch & dinner) Cosmopolitan fare in very cool surrounds. Part of Gilligan's Backpackers (p210).

Wool Shed (☎ 4031 6304; 24 Shields St; meals A$5-10; ⏰ dinner) Pack-'em-in and fill-'em-up. Oh, and have a drink (below).

Sawaddee (☎ 4031 7993; 62 Shields St; meals A$10-17; ⏰ lunch Thu & Fri, dinner Mon-Sun; ✇) Tasty Thai.

You can pick up a decent counter meal at **Fox & Firkin** (☎ 4031 5305; cnr Lake & Spence Sts; meals A$13-22; ⏰ lunch & dinner) or **Shenannigans** (☎ 4051 2490; 48 Spence St; meals A$8-15; ⏰ lunch & dinner). For full reviews of these places, see right.

Drinking

You won't die of thirst in Cairns – there are pubs on every corner. Street-press magazines *Barfly* and *Cairns Backpacker* cover music gigs, movies, pubs and clubs. Nightclub-goers take note: clubs refuse entry after 3am, and while you can keep drinking if you're in a club already, once you leave you won't be allowed back in. Cairns' bouncers are vigilant, so take your ID.

Gilligan's (☎ 4041 6566; 57-89 Grafton St) Attached to the Backpackers (p210), this enormous bar is fast becoming the most popular joint in town. The chic interior is very Soho, daahling, and the yawning deck outside, littered with tables, is superlative. Most nights it's an absolute drinking, dancing, mingling bonanza, with punters lapping up the stylish yet unpretentious surrounds.

Wool Shed (☎ 4031 6304; 24 Shields St; admission A$5 after 10pm) Things may start quietly at the Wool Shed but before long it's all drunkenness and table dancing. This phenomenally popular get-pissed-quick bar pulls in the crowds with happy hours, theme nights and prize draws. Every Wednesday night you can further your cultural education at the Miss Wet T-Shirt comp.

Sporties (☎ 4041 2533; 33 Spence St; admission A$6) Speaking of cultural education, Sporties' drawcard is Babe Nation every Wednesday night, where girls ditch their tops for body paint and bear nothing but their national flag all night. Tuesday night is one big happy hour and DJs do their thing regularly.

Fox & Firkin (☎ 4031 5305; cnr Lake & Spence Sts; ✇) If all that tomfoolery is a bit complicated, this pub – dressed like an old English local – promises a solid bout of drinking. The cavernous balcony overlooking the pedestrian strip constantly buzzes with folk regaling Reef anecdotes and tucking into large jugs of beer. Its very own Firkin Ale is on tap – yum!

Shenannigans (☎ 4051 2490; 48 Spence St; ✇) The high-backed booths and dark polished wood scream elegance, but the amicable atmosphere in this Irish-style pub does indeed verge on sheer shenanigans as the night draws on. Another of Cairn's great drinking holes, this one comes with good ales, a huge beer garden and outside bistro.

Johno's Nightclub & Bar (☎ 4051 8770; cnr Abbott & Aplin Sts) Johno's is huge: a hang-glider is suspended from the roof. The World-Famous Gong Show is free every Sunday, and chipper bar staff call you 'darlin' and 'bloke'. Packed most nights.

Rattle 'n' Hum (☎ 4031 3011; 67 The Esplanade) This cavernous, dark-wood bar is also a restaurant (left), but in the witching hours – any time after 9pm – the emphasis is well and truly on conversation and consumption. Cocktails and beer are quaffed at a rapid rate and those not talking get into some serious pool.

Other recommendations:

Bar Embassy (☎ 4031 4166; 38 Abbott St) Style bar in the former courthouse.

Nu Trix (☎ 4051 8223; 53 Spence St; admission A$6) Gay and lesbian nightclub open till the wee hours.

PJ O'Briens (☎ 4031 5333; cnr Lake & Shields Sts; ✇)

Entertainment

Johno's Nightclub & Bar (☎ 4051 8770; cnr Abbott & Aplin Sts) Old-school musicians play great blues and rock here every night (free admission before 9pm). See above for more.

Fox & Firkin (☎ 4031 5305; cnr Lake & Spence Sts) Also has live music, see opposite.

Cairns City Cinemas (☎ 4031 1077; 108 Grafton St) and **Central Cinemas** (☎ 4052 1166; Cairns Central, McLeod St) show mainstream, new-release flicks.

Shopping

It seems as though every second shop in Cairns sells 'authentic didgeridoos and boomerangs', although the ratio of quantity to craftsmen just doesn't add up. Ask at your hostel for a good reference or head to Tjapukai Cultural Park (p207), where you can be certain the items are authentic.

Getting There & Away

AIR

Cairns is very well connected to the rest of Australia. Low-end, one-way fares at the time of writing started at: Sydney A$180, Brisbane A$110, Melbourne A$200, Adelaide A$300, Perth A$330, Alice Springs A$290. (Watch for specials though, which can be much cheaper than these prices.)

Alliance Airlines (☎ 1300 130 092; www.allianceairlines.com.au)
Jetstar (☎ 13 15 38; www.jetstar.com.au)
Macair (☎ 13 13 13; www.macair.com.au)
Qantas (☎ 13 13 13, 4050 4033; www.qantas.com.au; cnr Lake & Shields Sts)
Virgin Blue (☎ 13 67 89; www.virginblue.com.au)

BOAT

Quicksilver (☎ 4031 4299; www.quicksilver-cruises.com) has trips from Cairns to Port Douglas, via Palm Cove, for A$25/40 one way/return. It leaves the Pier Marina in Cairns at 8am, and departs from Port Douglas at 5.15pm; the journey takes 1½ hours.

BUS

Companies including **McCafferty's/Greyhound** (☎ 13 20 30), **Premier Motor Service** (☎ 13 34 10) and **Coral Reef Coaches** (☎ 4098 2800; www.coralreefcoaches.com.au) arrive at and depart from the bus station at Trinity Wharf.

McCafferty's/Greyhound operates daily bus services between Cairns and Brisbane (A$200, 28½ hours), Rockhampton (A$130, 17 hours), Mackay (A$110, 12 hours) and Townsville (A$60, six hours), which offer free stopovers, of no more than six nights, along the way. Premier Motor Service does the same routes for slightly less.

Coral Reef Coaches runs regular services between Cairns and Port Douglas, Mossman, Daintree, Cape Tribulation and Cooktown, via either the inland road or the coastal road. It also runs a service to Karumba.

White Car Coaches (☎ 4091 1855; whitecars@top.net.au) travels between Kuranda and Cairns eight times daily (one way/return A$4/8). Services depart from Cairns between 8.30am and 5.30pm Monday to Friday, and 8.30am to 1pm Saturday and Sunday. Buses leave from either the Lake St Transit Centre or 48 Spence St (outside Shenannigans) in Cairns.

The slightly cheaper **John's Bus** (☎ 0418-772 953) runs a similar service to White Car Coaches, with the same frequency between Kuranda and Cairns (A$2), departing from the same spots.

CAR

You can easily get to Cape Tribulation from Cairns with a conventional vehicle. Most companies prohibit you from taking vehicles to Cooktown or Chillagoe as the road is unsealed and rough in parts.

All Day Car Rentals (☎ 4031 3348; www.cairns-car-rentals.com; 60 Abbott St)
Britz Australia (☎ 4032 2611; www.britz.com; 411 Sheridan St) Campervans.
Budget (☎ 1800 020 304, 4051 9222; www.budget.com.au; 153 Lake St)
Travellers Auto Barn (☎ 1800 674 374, 4041 3722; www.travellers-autobarn.com.au; 123 Bunda St) Campervan rental and car yard.

TRAIN

Queensland Rail (☎ 1800 620 324; www.traveltrain.qr.com.au; McLeod St, Cairns Central; 🕐 8am-5pm Mon-Fri, 7am-1pm Sat) can book you tickets for the *Sunlander*, which travels between Brisbane and Cairns (economy adult/student A$190/95, 32 hours, three weekly).

See p216 for information on travelling on the scenic railway to Kuranda.

Getting Around

BICYCLE

If you're here for a while, **Bike Man** (☎ 4041 5566; www.bikeman.com.au; 30 Florence St; weekly rentals from A$13) has excellent weekly rates.

BUS

Running regular services in and around Cairns, **Sunbus** (☎ 4057 7411; www.sunbus.com.au) buses leave from the Lake St Transit Centre at City Place. Schedules for most routes are posted here. Buses run from early morning to late evening. Destinations include Flecker Botanic Gardens (No 7), Clifton Beach (Nos 1 and 1B) and Palm Cove (Nos 1, 1B and 2X). All are served by the (almost) round-the-clock night service (N) on Friday and Saturday. Heading south, bus No 1 goes as far as Gordonvale.

TAXI

Black & White Taxis (☎ 13 10 08, 4048 8333) has a rank on the corner of Lake and Shields Sts and one outside Cairns Central.

AROUND CAIRNS

Cairns' Northern Beaches

☎ 07

You realise where all the locals live when you see Cairns' relaxed northern beaches, a string of coastal communities linked by the Captain Cook Hwy. They offer some pleasant dining and accommodation options if you want to escape the big smoke. Most of these are located around idyllic Palm Cove, the largest of the settlements.

Turn-offs from the highway, to the various beaches, are well signposted if you're travelling by car, and **Sunbus** (☎ 4057 7411; www.sunbus.com.au) runs regular services here.

You can indulge in some beachfront camping at the compact **Yorkeys Knob Beachfront Caravan Park** (☎ 4055 7201; Sims Esplanade, Yorkeys Knob; camp/caravan sites per 2 people A$18/22, cabins A$70) or the less sedate **Palm Cove Cairns City Council Camping Grounds** (☎ 4055 3824; hunter_irene@hotmail.com; camp/caravan sites per 2 people A$12/17). The latter is an incredibly popular spot that's packed during the high season (bookings essential for powered sites). It's next to the jetty, so it's perfect for early-morning fishing.

If you've got a bit of pocket money, **Ellis Beach Oceanfront Bungalows and Leisure Park** (☎ 1800 637 036, 4055 3538; www.ellisbeachbungalows.com.au; Captain Cook Hwy, Ellis Beach; camp/caravan sites per 2 people A$26/32, cabins A$68, bungalows A$129-155; ✇) has lovely cabins with private balconies and well-tended camp sites.

Cocky's at the Cove (☎ 4059 1691; Veivers Rd, Palm Cove; meals A$3.90-9.50; ⏲ breakfast & lunch) is a relaxed eatery serving cheap sandwiches and all-day brekky. For pub grub head to **CSLC** (☎ 4059 1244; Veivers Rd, Palm Cove; meals A$9-20; ⏲ lunch & dinner), a locals' haunt with a fabulous garden bar. CSLC has a strict dress code: 'thongs or shoes must be worn at all times'.

Ellis Beach Bar & Grill (☎ 4055 3534; Captain Cook Hwy, Ellis Beach; meals A$5-22; ⏲ lunch & dinner) pumps out tasty burgers and salad, and has live music every Sunday. **Ellis Beach Surf Life Saving Club** (☎ 4055 3695; Captain Cook Hwy, Ellis Beach) is perfect for a quiet ale.

KURANDA

☎ **07 / pop 1456**

From 10am to 3pm Kuranda is a seething mass of camera-toting tourists with more bum bags than you can poke a didgeridoo at. After 3pm, when the Skyrail and Scenic Rail depart, you can experience the 'real' Kuranda, a mellow mountain town set in stunning rainforest.

The volunteer-run **Kuranda visitors centre** (☎ 4093 9311; www.kuranda.org; Centenary Park; ⏲ 10am-4pm) has maps and a helpful website. **Tower Corner** (☎ /fax 4093 7400; 14 Thongon St; per hr A$$4) has Net access.

Sights & Activities

Kuranda's famous markets, which now heavily target the tourist dollar, are still the village's prime attractions. The markets are split into two sections: **Kuranda Markets** (☎ 4093 8772; 7 Therwine St; ⏲ 9am-3pm Wed-Fri & Sun) is where you'll find food and food products (eg emu oil) and **Kuranda Heritage Markets** (☎ 4093 8060; www.kurandaline.com.au/market; Rob Vievers Dr; ⏲ 9am-3pm) sells tourist-oriented arts and crafts.

Kuranda Arts Co-op (☎ /fax 4093 9026; www.artskuranda.asn.au; Kuranda Settlement Village, 12 Rob Veivers Dr; ⏲ 10am-4pm) is the best place for genuine arts and crafts.

Over the footbridge behind the train station, **Kuranda Riverboat and Rainforest Tours** (☎ 4093 7476; adult A$12; ⏲ cruises hourly 10.30am-2.30pm) runs sedate 45-minute cruises along the Barron River. Check operating times during the wet season (October to March).

There are several signed walks from the markets, and a short walking track through **Jumrum Creek Environmental Park**, off Barron Falls Rd. The park has a big population of fruit bats.

Continuing on, Barron Falls Rd divides: the left fork takes you to a wheelchair-accessible **lookout** over the falls, while further along, the right fork brings you to **Wrights Lookout**, with views down to Barron Gorge National Park.

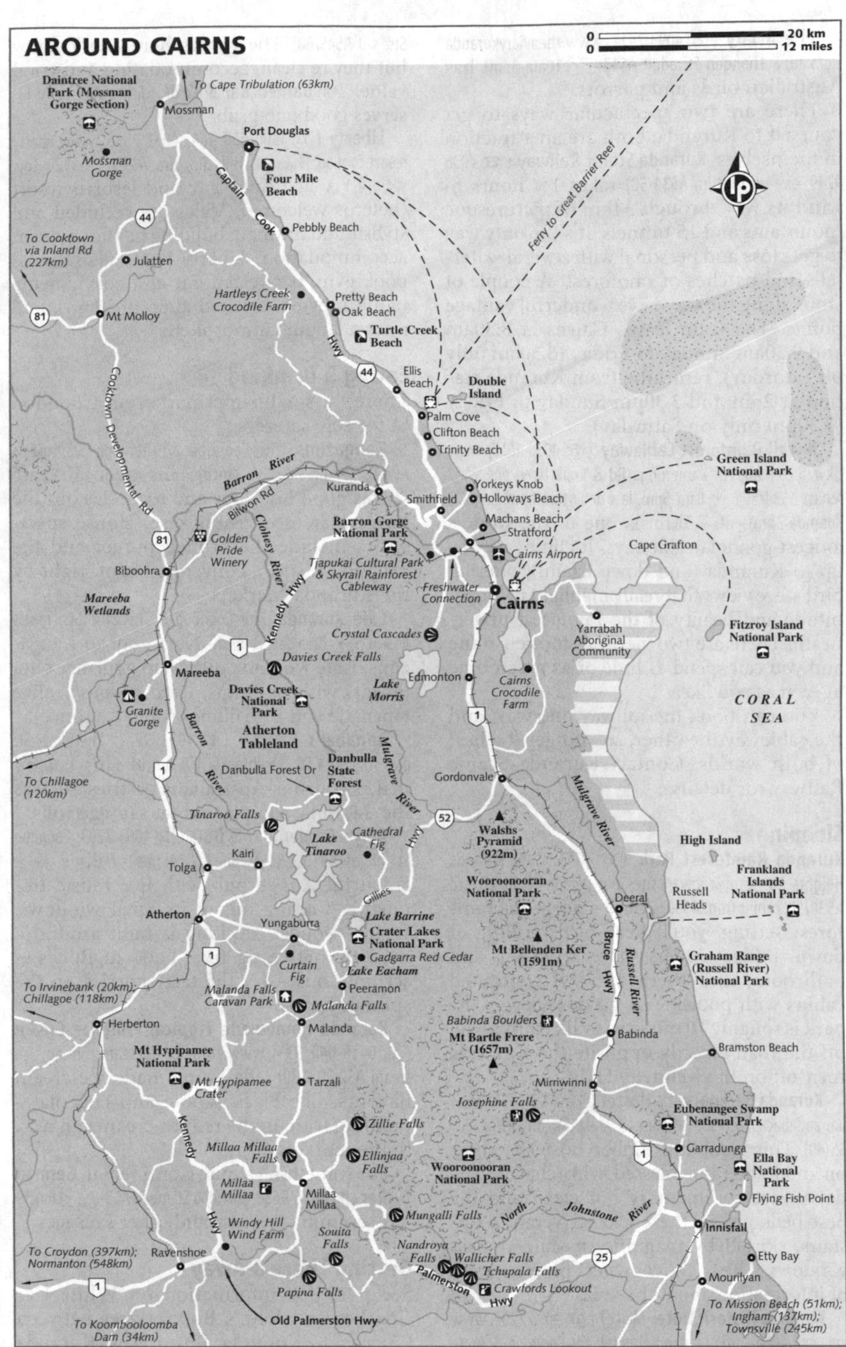
AROUND CAIRNS
0 20 km
0 12 miles
To Cape Tribulation (63km)
Daintree National Park (Mossman Gorge Section)
Mossman
Mossman Gorge
Port Douglas
Four Mile Beach
Ferry to Great Barrier Reef
Captain Cook Hwy
44
Pebbly Beach
To Cooktown via Inland Rd (227km)
Julatten
Hartleys Creek Crocodile Farm
Pretty Beach
Oak Beach
81
Mt Molloy
Turtle Creek Beach
Cooktown Developmental Rd
Ellis Beach
Double Island
Palm Cove
Clifton Beach
Trinity Beach
Green Island National Park
Barron River
Bilwon Rd
Kuranda
Smithfield
Yorkeys Knob
Holloways Beach
Machans Beach
Stratford
Barron Gorge National Park
Golden Pride Winery
Clohesy River
Cairns Airport
Cape Grafton
Biboohra
Tjapukai Cultural Park & Skyrail Rainforest Cableway
Freshwater Connection
Cairns
Mareeba Wetlands
Kennedy Hwy
Yarrabah Aboriginal Community
Fitzroy Island National Park
Crystal Cascades
1
Davies Creek Falls
Mareeba
Edmonton
Granite Gorge
Davies Creek National Park
Lake Morris
Cairns Crocodile Farm
CORAL SEA
Atherton Tableland
Barron River
To Chillagoe (120km)
Danbulla Forest Dr
Danbulla State Forest
Mulgrave River
Gordonvale
Tinaroo Falls
52
Walshs Pyramid (922m)
Mulgrave River
Lake Tinaroo
Cathedral Fig
Hwy
High Island
Tolga
Kairi
Gillies
Wooroonooran National Park
Frankland Islands National Park
Deeral
Russell Heads
Atherton
Yungaburra
Lake Barrine
Crater Lakes National Park
Bruce Hwy
Mt Bellenden Ker (1591m)
Gadgarra Red Cedar
Curtain Fig
Lake Eacham
Russell River
Graham Range (Russell River) National Park
To Irvinebank (20km); Chillagoe (118km)
Malanda Falls Caravan Park
Malanda Falls
Peeramon
Herberton
Malanda
Babinda Boulders
Mt Bartle Frere (1657m)
Babinda
Bramston Beach
Mt Hypipamee National Park
Mt Hypipamee Crater
Tarzali
Mirriwinni
Josephine Falls
Eubenangee Swamp National Park
Kennedy Hwy
Zillie Falls
Millaa Millaa Falls
Ellinjaa Falls
Wooroonooran National Park
Garradunga
Ella Bay National Park
Millaa Millaa
Millaa Millaa
Flying Fish Point
Mungalli Falls
North Johnstone River
Innisfail
Windy Hill Wind Farm
Souita Falls
Nandroya Falls
Wallicher Falls
Tchupala Falls
To Croydon (397km); Normanton (548km)
Ravenshoe
25
Etty Bay
Palmerston Hwy
Crawfords Lookout
Mourilyan
Papina Falls
Old Palmerston Hwy
To Koombooloomba Dam (34km)
To Mission Beach (51km); Ingham (137km); Townsville (245km)

The **Aviary** (4093 7411; www.theaviarykuranda.com.au; 8 Thongon St; adult A$12; 10am-3pm) has Australian birds and parrots.

There are two spectacular ways to get yourself to Kuranda; both are an attraction in themselves. **Kuranda Scenic Railway** (4036 9249; one way/return A$34/50) takes 1¾ hours to wind its way through 34km of picturesque mountains and 15 tunnels. It's the only way to get close and personal with several waterfalls and patches of rainforest. A couple of stops along the way have wonderful vantage points. The train leaves Cairns at 8.30am and 9.30am Sunday to Friday (8.30am only on Saturday), returning from Kuranda station at 2pm and 3.30pm Sunday to Friday (3.30pm only on Saturday).

Skyrail Rainforest Cableway (4038 1555; www.skyrail.com.au; cnr Kamerunga Rd & Cook Hwy; one way/return A$34/50; 8am-5pm, last departure from Cairns & Kuranda 3pm), at 7.5km, is one of the world's longest gondola cableways. It climbs its way up to Kuranda (and down again!), offering bird's-eye views that really highlight the magnitude and beauty of the rainforest underneath. There are two viewing stops en-route and you can spend as little or as much time at each as you like.

You can book the railway one way, and the cableway the other, so you get the best of both worlds. Contact Kuranda Scenic Railway for details.

Sleeping

Kuranda Rainforest Park (4093 7316; Kuranda Heights Rd; camp/caravan sites per person A$10/17, s/d A$30/50, cabins from A$80) Amid a gorgeous rainforest setting, you'll hear birds trilling at dawn. Budget rooms share a kitchen and bathroom, and there are self-contained cabins with poolside or garden views. The park is roughly 10 minutes' walk from town, off the road directly opposite the Kuranda turn-off on the Kennedy Hwy.

Kuranda Backpacker's Hostel (4093 7355; www.kurandabackpackershostel.com; 6 Arara St; dm/s/d A$17/35/40) This rambling timber hostel is short on mod cons but blessed with charm. The dorms are rudimentary but clean and the best beds are in the enclosed veranda upstairs, skirted by magnificent stained-glass windows. The friendly owners have a wealth of information about the area.

Kuranda Historic Hotel-Motel (4093 7206; www.gdaypubs.com.au/kurandahotelmotel; cnr Coondoo & Arara Sts; s/d A$45/60) The rooms here aren't fancy but they're clean, accommodating and good value. Its **Garden Bar & Grill** (dishes A$7 to A$13) serves good pub grub.

Liberty (1300 650 464, 4093 7556; www.libertyresort.com.au; 3 Green Hills Rd; dm A$35, r A$120-260;) A luxurious gay and lesbian resort (heteros welcome). Villas are secluded and stylish, and the main building has fancy dorm accommodation. Liberty has a sensational pool, gym, bar-restaurant and cosy cinema (adult movies screened after 10.30pm), and a sexy, languid atmosphere.

Eating & Drinking

There's a small supermarket on Coondoo St for self-caterers.

Kangazims (cnr Coondoo & Therwine Sts; meals A$4-9; breakfast & lunch) This open-air café serves good hot dogs and focaccias but the burgers are something else. House specialities include the brunch burger and the 'troppo'. It's in a convenient spot, right by the Kuranda Markets.

Café Kuranda (cnr Coondoo & Therwine Sts; meals A$3-10; breakfast & lunch) Next door to Kangazims, Café Kuranda dishes up gourmet pitta breads, with hummus, *baba ganoush*, olive tapenade and Brie fillings (not all at once).

Annabel's Pantry (4093 9271; Therwine St; pies A$3.50-4.50; breakfast & lunch) This bakery makes gourmet Australiana pastries, such as the 'Matilda' roo pie and fat sausage rolls.

Billy's Garden Bar & BBQ (4093 7203; Coondoo St; mains A$10-22; lunch & dinner) Billy's is a colourful Aussie pub with live music frequently wafting out of its open windows. Inside, wooden decking is built around a majestic native fig tree. Food at Billy's is scrumptious – try the tasty curries on the specials board.

Kuranda Homemade Tropical Fruit Ice Cream (0419-644 933; www.kuranda-icecream.com.au; ice cream A$2.80-4.80) sells home-made ice-cream flavours, like black sapote and chocolate-pudding fruit, in the red ice-cream van next to the markets.

For something a mite Continental, **German Tucker** (4057 9688; Coondoo St; meals A$5-8; lunch) has scrummy kransky and other sausages.

Getting There & Away

See p213 for information on White Car Coaches and John's Bus services between Cairns and Kuranda. Buses leave Kuranda from the bus terminal on Therwine St, near the visitors centre.

ATHERTON TABLELAND

Inland from the coast between Innisfail and Cairns, the lush Atherton Tableland is a region of beautiful scenery, with lakes and waterfalls, national parks and state forests, small villages and busy rural centres. The Tableland's altitude is more than 1000m in places.

Nonindigenous Australians and other migrants came to the Tableland in the 1870s searching for gold and (later) tin. Roads and railways were built, and logging and farming became the main industries. The region's traditional owners, the Ngadjonji tribe of the wider Djirbal language group, met the intrusion with violent resistance, but were themselves violently overcome.

The Atherton Tableland is best explored by car but **White Car Coaches** (☎ 07-4091 1855; whitecars@top.net.au) also has regular bus services from Cairns.

Mareeba & Around

☎ 07 / pop 8000

Mareeba, the rough diamond of the Tableland, is where the rainforest meets the outback. It's a great place to pick up seasonal work, and it has a few attractions. If you're around in July, be sure to see the **Mareeba Rodeo**.

First stop is the incredibly helpful **Mareeba Heritage Museum & Tourist Information Centre** (☎ 4092 5674; www.mareebaheritagecentre.com.au; Centenary Park, 345 Byrnes St; 8am-4pm), which has displays and a wide veranda for sitting back with a cool drink.

Mareeba Wetlands (☎ 4093 2514; www.mareebawetlands.com; adult A$8; 10am-4pm Apr-Dec) is a bird-lovers' extravaganza. Two thousand hectares of savannah woodland are home to more than 180 species of birds, and the reserve is a haven for mammals and reptiles. Canoe tours cost A$6/11 for a half-/one-hour trip. To reach the Wetlands, head 7km north from Mareeba and take the Pickford Rd turn-off from Biboohra.

Granite Gorge (admission A$2) offers waterfalls, walking tracks round huge granite formations, rock-wallaby feeding and a camping ground. To reach it, follow Chewco Rd out of Mareeba for 7km; there's a turn-off to your right from there.

Coffee aficionados will love **Coffeeworks** (☎ 1800 355 526; 4092 4101; www.arabicas.com.au; 136 Mason St, Mareeba; coffee A$2.50-3.30, tours adult A$5; 9am-4pm), and you can taste mango wine at **Golden Pride Winery** (☎ 4093 2524; www.goldendrop.com; Bilwon Rd; half-bottle/bottle A$16/25; 8am-5pm). Head north to Biboohra for 11km and turn right at Bilwon Rd. It's another 2km to the winery.

Aviation and military buffs should definitely check out **Beck Museum** (☎ 4092 3979; www.holidaynq.com.au/AthertonTabs/BeckCollection/beck-collection.html; Kennedy Hwy; adult A$13; 10am-4pm).

Without doubt, **Jackaroo Motel** (☎ 4092 2677; www.jackaroomotel.com; 340 Byrnes St; s/d A$66/77;) is the best accommodation in Mareeba. It has clean rooms, wheelchair facilities and a cool saltwater swimming pool.

Arriga Park Farmstay (☎ 4093 2114; www.bnbnq.com.au/arriga; 1720 Dimbula Rd; r A$65) is a working cane farm. Rooms are in a colonial homestead and all produce is organic. Full board is available. Alternatively, **Riverside Caravan Park** (☎ 4092 2309; 13 Egan St, Mareeba; camp/caravan sites per 2 people A$11/14, on-site caravans A$25-35), on the Barron River, has beautiful views.

Natasi's (10 Byrnes St, Mareeba; meals A$3-6.50; lunch;) serves burgers and sandwiches.

Chillagoe

☎ 07 / pop 150

Chillagoe's population is small, unless you count the termites that inhabit the rich ochre mounds dotting its arid landscape. Chillagoe lives up to any romantic notions you may have of the outback. Around town are limestone caves, rock pinnacles, Aboriginal rock art and ruins of early-20th-century smelters. The town is 140km west of Mareeba and close enough to make a day trip from Cairns, but an overnight stay is preferable.

The **Hub** (☎ 4094 7111; jimevans@bigpond.com.au; Queen St; 8am-5pm Mon-Fri, to 3.30pm Sat & Sun) is the visitors centre, and where you book QPWS **cave tours** (A$11-14) of the stunning Donna (9am), Trezkinn (11am) and Royal Arch (1.30pm) limestone caves.

SLEEPING & EATING

Chillagoe Cabins (☎ 4094 7206; www.chillagoe.com; Queen St; s/d A$80/100;) Modelled on old miners' huts, these cabins are comfortable and self-contained. The friendly owners are animal carers and you may be able to pat a convalescing kangaroo. Chillagoe Cabins

QUEENSLAND

also offers package tours, with pick-up from Cairns and Mareeba.

Chillagoe Bush Camp & Eco-Lodge (☎ 4094 7155; bushlodge@bigpond.com; Hospital Ave; s/tw A$28/50, d A$55-70;) Another good option, this property is dripping in foliage and has a range of cabins to suit all budgets. There's also a communal area for meals.

Chillagoe Caves Lodge (☎ 4094 7106; caveslodge chillagoe@bigpond.com; 7 King St; camp sites per person A$7, s A$40-60, d A$45-65;) This pleasant motel has basic rooms with super-clean, spacious bathrooms, and free in-house movies. Budget rooms have shared facilities and there's a restaurant.

Chillagoe Tourist Village (☎ 4094 7177; raewin@ bigpond.com; Queen St; camp/caravan sites per person A$6/8, cabins s/d A$35/45, units s/d A$50/60;) This is a lovely spot if you're camping, although the cabins are also great value. You'll have to share the grounds with the resident guinea fowls.

Post Office Hotel (☎ 4094 7119; 37 Queen St; meals A$10-16; lunch & dinner) Graffiti scrawls cover these walls from skirting board to ceiling, and the solid marble bar is a tangible piece of history. Meals are enormous: a piece of rump covers the plate. The Post Office is the last bastion for punters seeking solace in a quiet beer.

GETTING THERE & AWAY

Take the Cairns to Mareeba **White Car Coach** (☎ 07-4091 1855) to reach Chillagoe. The **Chillagoe Bus Service** (☎ 4094 7155), run by Chillagoe Bush Camp & Eco-Lodge, departs from Chillagoe post office (in the Hub) at 7.30am Monday to Friday and returns from Mareeba train station at 1pm Monday, Tuesday, Thursday and Friday and at 11.30am on Wednesday (A$35/70 one way/return).

If you're travelling by car, be careful when driving from Mareeba to Cairns as there are no fences and the Brahmin cattle certainly don't expect to move out of your way. All but the last 25km of the route is sealed and shouldn't present a problem for conventional vehicles during the dry season.

Atherton

☎ 07 / pop 5889

Atherton is a prosperous town and a handy place to regroup. **Atherton Tableland Information Centre** (☎ 4091 4222; www.athertonsc.qld.gov.au; cnr Robert & Herberton Rds; 9am-5pm) has useful information, and **Washouse Internet café** (☎ 4091 2619; 1 Robert St; per 30min A$3) has Net access.

The best attraction in town is **Crystal Caves** (☎ 4091 2365; www.crystalcaves.com.au; 69 Main St; adult A$11; 8.30am-5pm Mon-Fri, to 4pm Sat, 10am-4pm Sun), a mineralogical museum in an artificial cave that winds for a block underground. You must wear a hard hat, and you need to be there one hour before closing. There is wheelchair access.

As you approach Atherton from Herberton in the southwest, **Hou Wang Temple & Chinatown** (☎ 4091 6945; athchinatn@austarmetro.com.au; 86 Herberton Rd; interpretative museum & tour adult A$7; 10am-4pm) is a 100-year-old Chinese temple on the site of Atherton's original Chinatown (which existed from the late 1800s to the mid-1900s).

Lake Tinaroo

☎ 07

From Atherton or nearby Tolga it's a short drive to this lake created for the Barron River hydroelectric power scheme. A fisherman's haven, Lake Tinaroo is open year-round for barramundi fishing. **Tinaroo Falls**, on the northwestern corner of the lake, is the main settlement.

Lake Tinaroo Holiday Park (☎ 4095 8232; fax 4095 8808; Dam Rd; camp/caravan sites per 2 people A$15/20, cabins A$48-60) is a pleasant camping ground by the lake that also has boat hire (half-/full day A$70/80). BYO (bring your own) linen.

The brightly painted **Pensini's Café & Restaurant** (☎ 4095 8242; Lake Tinaroo Lookout; meals A$7-28) is a modern bar and bistro with a vista of Tinaroo Dam.

From the dam, the unsealed 4WD-only Danbulla Forest Dr winds through the **Danbulla State Forest** beside the lake, finally emerging on the Gillies Hwy 4km northeast of Lake Barrine. The road passes several spectacular self-registration lakeside **camping grounds** (camp sites per person A$4), run by the **QPWS** (☎ 4095 8459) in Lake Tinaroo.

There's a volcanic crater at **Mobo Creek** and, 6km from the Gillies Hwy, a short walk takes you down to the **Cathedral Fig**, a gigantic strangler fig tree.

Yungaburra

☎ 07 / pop 1007

Yungaburra is the archetypal picturesque village: quaint, heritage-listed and full of 19th-century architecture. It's a romantic getaway and the perfect base from which to explore the Atherton Tableland.

Yungaburra Markets (☎ 4095 2111; Gillies Hwy; 🕑 7am-noon) are held on the fourth Saturday of every month when the town is besieged by avid shoppers.

The magnificent **Curtain Fig** tree is a must-see attraction. Spindly aerial roots hang in a feathery curtain and it's like a *Lord of the Rings* prop. There's wheelchair access.

The legendary **On the Wallaby** (☎ 4095 2031; www.onthewallaby.com; 34 Eacham Rd; dm/d A$20/45) is a popular hostel that runs excellent tours (day/overnight/two-night, three-day tours A$80/150/170) of the area, including canoeing and wildlife-spotting. If you can splurge a bit then head to **Lake Eacham Hotel** (☎ 4095 3515; 6 Kehoe Pl; s/d A$55/65), a historic country pub with counter meals and accommodation.

Nick's Swiss-Italian Restaurant (☎ 4095 3330; www.nicksrestaurant.com.au; Gillies Hwy; meals A$9-27; 🕑 lunch Wed-Sun, dinner Tue-Sun) is run by a Yungaburra personality (especially when he gets fired up on the piano accordion) of the same name, and his fun family restaurant serves easy-pleaser pastas, rosti and schnitzels.

Crater Lakes National Park & Around

☎ 07

Part of the Wet Tropics World Heritage Area, the two mirror-like volcanic lakes of Eacham and Barrine, off the Gillies Hwy east of Yungaburra, are beautiful swimming and picnicking spots encircled by **rainforest walking tracks**. Both lakes are national parks, but camping is not allowed.

Accessible from either lake, and 12km from Yungaburra, the native **Gadgarra Red Cedar** is more than 500 years old. On the drive there you may encounter an indignant gaggle of geese.

A secluded lake with whip birds cracking in lush rainforest, Lake Eacham provides the perfect backdrop for a picnic. An excellent information source is the ranger's station, where you may get to hold the native Australian python that lives there.

Lake Eacham Van Park (☎ 4095 3730; www.lakeeachamtouristpark.com; 71 Lakes Dr; camp/caravan sites per 2 people A$13/19, cabins from A$60), less than 2km down the Malanda road from Lake Eacham, has a pretty camping ground.

Spoil yourself with a Devonshire tea at **Lake Barrine Rainforest Cruise & Tea House** (☎ 4095 3847; fax 4095 3260; Gillies Hwy; 🕑 9am-5pm) and spot water dragons and tortoises on the 45-minute cruise (per adult A$10, five daily).

Malanda

☎ 07 / pop 1022

Part of the waterfall circuit, Malanda is about 15km southwest of Lake Eacham. **Malanda Falls Environmental Centre** (☎ 4096 6957; Atherton Rd; 🕑 10am-4pm) has an interpretative display and arranges fascinating 1½-hour **guided rainforest walks** (adult A$5; 🕑 depart 10am & 1pm Thu-Sun) led by a Ngadjonji tribal elder.

On the Atherton road on the outskirts of town are **Malanda Falls**. At the base of these is a natural pool in the midst of lush forest, which doubles as a deservedly popular swimming hole.

Right next to Malanda Falls is the **Malanda Falls Caravan Park** (☎ 4096 5314; 38 Park Ave; camp/caravan sites per 2 people A$15/18, dm A$35, cabins from A$50), surrounded by gorgeous scenery and wildlife.

Next door to the Environmental Centre is the **Tree Kangaroo Café** (☎ 4096 6658; Atherton Rd; meals A$6-10; 🕑 lunch & dinner).

Millaa Millaa & the Waterfall Circuit

☎ 07 / pop 350

The 16km 'waterfall circuit' near this small town, 24km south of Malanda, passes some of the most picturesque falls on the Tableland. You enter the circuit by taking Theresa Creek Rd, 1km east of Millaa Millaa on the Palmerston Hwy. **Millaa Millaa Falls**, the largest of the falls, are a perfect sheet of water dropping over a fern-fringed escarpment. These are the most spectacular and have the best swimming hole. Continuing around the circuit, you reach **Zillie Falls** and then **Ellinjaa Falls**, before returning to the Palmerston Hwy just 2.5km out of Millaa Millaa.

A further 5.5km down the Palmerston Hwy there's a turn-off to **Mungalli Falls**, 5km off the highway.

Mungalli Falls Rainforest Village (☎ 4097 2358; www.mungallifalls.com; Junction Rd; dm A$25, cabins A$50-80), caters mostly to large groups with accommodation for up to 600 people. There's a **kiosk** (meals A$10-A$25), and horse-riding (A$65 for 3½ hours) is available.

Mungalli Creek Dairy (☎ 4097 2232; www.millaa.com/Mungalli/mungalli.htm; 254 Brooks Rd; 🕑 10am-4pm) is a biodynamic dairy farm where you can taste cheese such as kaffir lime quark, and sinfully rich cheesecake.

Set on 2.8 hectares and teeming with wildlife, **Millaa Millaa Tourist Park** (☎ 4097 2290; www.millaapark.com; cnr Malanda Rd & Lodge Ave; camp sites per 2 people A$15, dm A$12, cabins from A$55), 1.5km from Millaa Millaa Falls, has a range of accommodation options, including a four-star villa.

Lunch at the charming **Falls Teahouse** (☎ 4097 2237; Palmerston Hwy; meals A$8-14; ⏰ lunch & dinner), overlooking the rolling Tableland hills, is delicious (scrumptious home-made bread!). Rooms have period furniture, and B&B accommodation is available. It is just out of Millaa Millaa, on the turn-off to Millaa Millaa Falls.

Mt Hypipamee National Park

Between Atherton and Ravenshoe, the Kennedy Hwy passes the eerie Mt Hypipamee crater, which could be a scene from a science-fiction film and is well worth stopping for. It's a scenic 800m (return) walk from the picnic area, past **Dinner Falls**, to this narrow, 138m-deep crater with its moody-looking lake far below.

Herberton

☎ 07 / pop 946

Although a booming tin-mining town in the early 1900s, Herberton, on the banks of Wild River, is now a sleepy – but historic – Tableland town. Many of its buildings are still intact.

As you enter the town from Atherton, you'll pass **Herberton Historical Village** (☎ 4096 2271; 6 Broadway; adult A$10; ⏰ 10am-4pm), with a private collection of 28 original buildings.

Wild River Caravan Park (☎ 4096 2121; 23 Holdcroft Dr; camp/caravan sites per 2 people A$9/17, caravans A$28, units A$39) has self-contained units and a pretty aspect.

Risley's (☎ 4096 2111; 55 Grace St; mains A$22-27; ⏰ lunch Sat & Sun, dinner Wed-Sun) is a high-quality cosmopolitan restaurant in the middle of meat-and-three-veg land. The restaurant incorporates Risley's art collection.

PORT DOUGLAS

☎ 07 / pop 5867

Port Douglas is a beautiful holiday destination – Four Mile Beach, backed by palm trees, stretches languorously along the Coral Sea, and there are stunning views from Flagstaff Hill Lookout. The drive between Cairns and Port Douglas covers some of the most stunning seaside kilometres in the country.

Although Port has wooed the lucrative tourist market with boutique accommodation, stylish eating options and organised tours, the down-to-earth locals have managed to preserve its relaxed village feel.

The town is obsessed with all things nautical. If you hear wolf whistles, don't be surprised to see a magnificent yacht rather than a hot bod. There are some excellent sailing and fishing tours available, and you can make trips to the Low Isles, Great Barrier Reef, Mossman Gorge, Atherton Tableland and Cape Tribulation from here.

Orientation & Information

From the Captain Cook Hwy it's 6km along a low spit of land to Port Douglas. Davidson St, the main entry road, ends at a T-junction with Macrossan St; the shopping strip is to the left, and to the right is the Esplanade and Four Mile Beach.

Port Douglas **visitors centre** (☎ 4099 5599; www.reefandrainforest.com.au; 23 Macrossan St; ⏰ 9am-5.30pm) has maps, and there's Net access at **Dige Images** (☎ 4099 4699; Shop 2, 34 Macrossan St; per hr A$6.50).

Sights & Activities

Like the town it's attached to, **Four Mile Beach** is picturesque and a great spot to get a fix of sun and sea. The more refined clientele of Port Douglas means topless bathing is not a gawk fest but if you want to pursue this passion be considerate of others (and their families!).

'Educational and enjoyable' often conjures up images of tired museums, but the excellent **Rainforest Habitat** (☎ 4099 3235; www.rainforesthabitat.com.au; Port Douglas Rd; adult A$24; ⏰ 8am-5.30pm, last admission 4.30pm) is something special and is well worth the admission fee. It has a series of enclosures containing plant and animal species native to rainforests, wetlands and grasslands. The *Bird & Animal Spotter's Guide* (A$2) is invaluable, and you'll see iridescent parrots, wading birds, fruit bats and prehistoric-looking cassowaries.

Port Douglas Markets (Anzac Park, bottom of Macrossan St; ⏰ 8.30am-1.30pm Sun) make for a leisurely Sunday-morning wander along the grassy banks of Anzac Park. Port's markets were here long before the tourists. Pick up fruit and vegies and local arts and crafts.

St Mary's by the Sea (Anzac Park) is a tiny, nondenominational, white-timber chapel that was built in 1911.

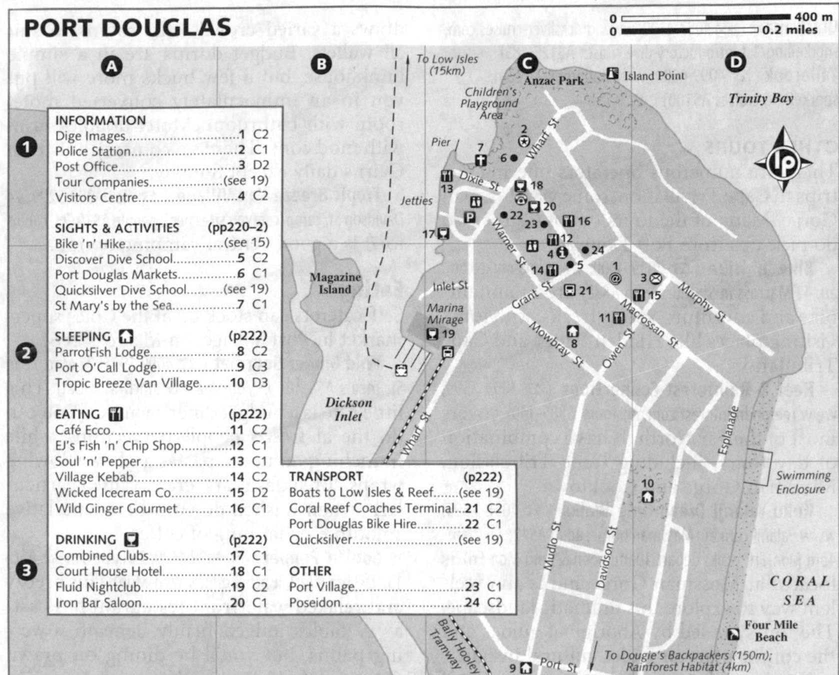

Several companies offer PADI Open Water certification as well as advanced dive certificates. The long-running and well-respected **Discover Dive School** (☎ 4099 5544; www.discoverdiveschool.com; Shop 6, Grant St) runs small classes (a maximum of six people), as does **Quicksilver Dive School** (☎ 4099 5050; www.quicksilverdive.com.au; Marina Mirage, Wharf St). Both have four-day Learn to Dive courses, which include two days' pool and theory in Palm Cove and two days' open water on the Quicksmart boat from Port Douglas.

About 20km north of Port Douglas on the Captain Cook Hwy is Mossman. The Kuku Yalanji people are the traditional owners of the stunning **Mossman Gorge**, east of Mossman. The gorge has some crystal-clear swimming holes, which can be treacherous after heavy rain, and a 2.4km **walking track** that loops through superb lowland forest.

Tours

LOW ISLES TRIPS

There are several cruises to the Low Isles, a small coral cay surrounded by a lagoon and topped by a lighthouse.

Ragamuffin Sail & Snorkel (☎ 4099 5922; ragamuffin@ledanet.com.au; Marina Mirage, Wharf St; adult A$110)

Sailaway (☎ 4099 4772; www.sailawayportdouglas.com; adult A$115)

Zachariah (☎ 4098 5405; adult A$95)

REEF TRIPS

Reef trips from Port Douglas tend to be a bit pricier than those from Cairns, largely due to reduced choice but better quality. All include lunch and snorkelling equipment. Two certified dives cost A$175 to A$195, but many trips offer a free introductory dive in addition to the price of two certified dives. Trips leave daily from the Marina Mirage at around 8.30am.

Aristocat (☎ 4099 4727; www.aristocat.com.au; Shop 18, Marina Mirage, Wharf St; snorkelling cruises A$135)

Calypso (☎ 4099 3377; www.calypsocharters.com.au; snorkelling/1st introductory dive cruises A$140/170)

Haba (☎ 4099 5254; www.habadive.com.au; snorkelling/1st introductory dive cruises A$140/185)

Poseidon (☎ 4099 4134; www.poseidon-cruises.com.au; Shop 2, 32 Macrossan St; snorkelling/1st introductory dive cruises A$140/185)

Quicksmart (☎ 4087 2100; www.quicksilver-cruises.com; snorkelling/1st introductory dive cruises A$125/185)
Tallarook (☎ 4099 6000; www.tallarooksail.com; snorkelling cruises A$100)

OTHER TOURS

There are numerous operators offering day trips to Cape Tribulation, some via Mossman Gorge. Many of the tours out of Cairns also do pick-ups from Port Douglas.

Bike 'n' Hike (☎ 4099 4000; www.bikenhike.com.au; 42 Macrossan St; tours from A$88) are mountain-bike and adventure-sports freaks, with tours visiting places like Hidden Valley and Cape Tribulation.

Reef & Rainforest Connections (☎ 4099 5599; www.reefandrainforest.com.au; tours A$85-140) covers most of the Far North. It has a combination of day tours, including Cape Tribulation, Mossman Gorge and Cooktown.

Kuku-Yalanji Dreamtime Walks (☎ 4098 2595; www.yalanji.com.au; Mossman Gorge; adult A$17; 9am-4pm Mon-Fri, walks depart 10am, noon & 2pm Mon-Fri) is located at Mossman Gorge and is an excellent way to explore this dramatic landscape. The tours are led by Aboriginal guides and the commentary provides cultural insight.

You can also get a bird's-eye view of Port Douglas with **Parasailing** (☎ 4099 3175; xtraactionwater@optusnet.com.au; tandem parasail A$50).

Sleeping

ParrotFish Lodge (☎ 4099 5011; www.parrotfishlodge.com; 37-39 Warner St; dm with/without bath A$26/20;) This modern ecohostel fits Port Douglas' serene surrounds like a glove. Environmental themes dominate, with oceans painted under foot and reef images and Aboriginal art gracing the walls. The generous dorms are spotless and the attached bar has pool tables and plenty of space. What's more, your tariff helps fund conservation of the fragile Daintree Rainforest. Good wheelchair access.

Dougie's Backpackers (☎ 1800 996 200, 4099 6200; www.dougies.com.au; 111 Davidson St; camp sites per person A$10, dm A$21, d & tw A$60, tr A$75;) The shimmering pool and shady palms fronting this friendly hostel beckon like a mini oasis. All the rooms and facilities are neat as a pin and at night languid activity moves to the bar. Courtesy buses run to the town centre.

Port O'Call Lodge (☎ 1800 892 800, 4099 5422; www.portocall.com.au; Port St; dm A$28, budget d A$60-70, motel d A$90-110;) This YHA hostel draws a varied crowd with rooms to suit all wallets. Budget dorms are in a simple bunkhouse, but a few bucks more will put you in an immaculately converted motel room with bathroom. Motel doubles brim with mod cons. There's a courtesy bus from Cairns daily except Sunday.

Tropic Breeze Van Village (☎/fax 4099 5299; 24 Davidson St; camp/caravan sites per 2 people A$19/23, cabins A$72) is a good central camping option.

Eating

Self-caterers can stock up at the Coles supermarket in Port Village, on Macrossan St.

Wild Ginger Gourmet (☎ 4099 5972; 22 Macrossan St; meals A$3-10; breakfast & lunch Mon-Sat) This little café is a budget diner's winner. You can do the al fresco people-perve thing while munching on udon, pastas and overflowing wraps. Breakfasts are great value, particularly when washed down with a superlative smoothie or fat mug of coffee.

Soul 'n' Pepper (☎ 4099 4499; 2 Dixie St; meals A$6-13; breakfast, lunch & dinner Wed-Mon) This breezy and relaxed waterfront restaurant has castaway tables lodged firmly beneath towering palms, but you'll be dining on prawn Caesar salad, goat's cheese and marinated eggplant, and crispy herb-battered fish. The soul end of the tag comes from a cruisy blues soundtrack perpetuating the laid-back vibes.

Café Ecco (☎ 4099 4056; Shop 1, 43 Macrossan St; lunch A$7-16, dinner A$9-20; breakfast & lunch year-round, dinner Easter-Oct) This long, trendy restaurant spills out onto the street, where passers-by salivate over delights from the inventive menu. Thai chicken wraps, fresh spring rolls, tiger prawn salads and veggie lasagnes are all dished up with impeccable service.

EJ's Fish 'n' Chip Shop (☎ 4099 4128; 23 Macrossan St; meals A$3-10; breakfast, lunch & dinner) Sure, you can feast on the regular takeaway staples – burgers, dim sims and toasted sarnis, but this is not your average chippy and the barramundi and steak mains are delectable.

Other recommendations:

Wicked Icecream Co (48 Macrossan St; breakfast & lunch;) To-die-for ice cream, gelati and sorbet.
Village Kebab (Grant St; kebabs A$4-8; lunch & dinner Mon-Fri) Fabulous kebabs.
Port O'Call (☎ 4099 5422; Port St; meals A$10-14; dinner) Asian and seafood mains and huge servings. See also left.

QUEENSLAND

Parrotfish Lodge (☎ 4099 5011; 37/39 Warner St; meals A$10-17; dinner) See also opposite.

Most of Port Douglas' clubs and pubs also serve counter meals, including **Combined Clubs** (☎ 4099 5553; Ashford St; meals A$7.50-14).

Drinking & Entertainment

Iron Bar Saloon (☎ 4099 4776; 5 Macrossan St) Stuffed full of Australiana, this is one of the last of the great outback woolsheds. Cane toads hop to the finish line on Tuesday, Thursday and Sunday. Live music plays Wednesday to Sunday, and the Iron Bar heats up after midnight. Meals are a meat-fest of native beasts (roo etc).

Court House Hotel (☎ 4099 5181; cnr Macrossan & Wharf Sts) Live music, happy hours, oceans of seating and a gorgeous balcony (not to mention the views!). This pub has a distinguished façade but utterly local atmosphere. The garden bistro serves thumping counter meals.

Combined Clubs (☎ 4099 5553; Ashford St) A watering hole popular with locals, this is a comfortable, friendly club with ludicrously cheap pots. The only way to go bankrupt here is on the pokies.

Last stop is **Fluid Nightclub** (☎ 4099 5200; Marina Mirage, Wharf St; 10pm-5am) for the flashing neon and doof-doof beats.

Getting There & Away

Coral Reef Coaches (☎ 4098 2800; www.coralreefcoaches.com.au) runs daily bus services between Port Douglas and Cairns, Mossman, Daintree, Cape Tribulation and Cooktown. All one-way fares are A$20 to A$25. Contact the head office in Mossman (on the number above) to arrange a pick-up.

Quicksilver (☎ 4031 4299; www.quicksilver-cruises.com) travels from Port Douglas to Cairns, via Palm Cove (one way/return A$25/38), leaving Marina Mirage at 5.30pm. The journey takes 1½ hours.

Getting Around

Pedalling around compact Port is a sensible way to go. Hire bikes from **Bike 'n' Hike** (☎ 4099 4000; www.bikenhike.com.au; 42 Macrossan St; half-/full day A$11/16.50; 8.30am-6.30pm Apr-Jan, 9am-5pm Feb & Mar) and **Port Douglas Bike Hire** (☎ 4099 5799; braden@top.net.au; cnr Wharf & Warner Sts; half-day/24hr A$10/14; 9am-5pm).

Port Douglas Taxis (☎ 4099 5345) provides 24-hour service.

DAINTREE

☎ 07

The landscape becomes markedly greener and denser as the Captain Cook Hwy continues from Mossman to Daintree, giving you a taste of the magnificent rainforests that lie across the river in Cape Tribulation. The turn-off to the Daintree River cable ferry is 24km from Mossman.

Daintree Village was originally established as a logging town in the 1870s, and mighty cedars were floated down the Daintree River for further transportation. Now the river is more commonly used for cruises, with frequent crocodile sightings the big selling point. While neither Daintree Village nor the surrounding countryside is part of the Wet Tropics World Heritage Area, there are still pockets of untouched rainforest.

A number of small tour operators offer water safaris here, including **Daintree Rainforest River Trains** (☎ 1800 808 309; www.daintreerivertrain.com; 2½hr cruise A$38) and **Peter Cooper's Mangrove Ecosystem Tours** (☎ 4098 2066; Public Wharf; adult A$20; departs hourly).

If you plan to stay in Daintree Village, **Red Mill House** (☎ 4098 6233; www.redmillhouse.com.au; Stewart St; s/d A$80/105) is an excellent B&B in the centre of town, with comfortable rooms and a lovely spacious garden. It's also wheelchair accessible.

There are a couple of eateries in the village centre, including the casual **Jacanas Restaurant** (meals A$5-18).

Baaru House (☎ 4098 6100; meals A$9-21) is the restaurant attached to the exclusive Daintree Eco Lodge & Spa. It's open to nonguests, though, and is reasonably priced, so make the most of it! The chef uses native produce.

CAPE TRIBULATION AREA

About 11km south of Daintree Village is the turn-off to the Daintree River ferry that takes you into the Cape Tribulation area. After crossing the river it's another 34km by sealed road to Cape Tribulation. The indigenous Kuku Yalanji people called the area Kulki, but the name Cape Tribulation was conferred by Captain Cook after his ship ran aground on Endeavour Reef.

Part of the Wet Tropics World Heritage Area, the region from the Daintree River north to Cape Tribulation is extraordinarily beautiful and famed for its ancient rainforest, sandy beaches and the rugged mountains of

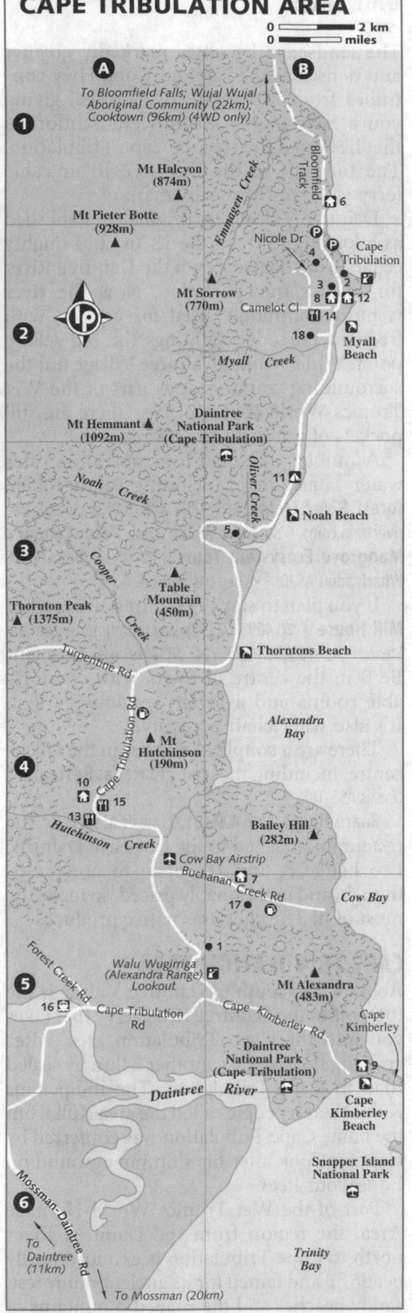

INFORMATION

Daintree Rainforest Environmental Centre	1 B5
Ranger Station	2 B2

SIGHTS & ACTIVITIES (p225)

Bat House	3 B2
Cape Trib Exotic Fruit Farm	4 B2
Jindalba Boardwalk	(see 1)
Marrdja Botanical Walk	5 B3

SLEEPING (pp224–6)

Cape Trib Beach House	6 B1
Crocodylus Village	7 B5
Jungle Lodge	8 B2
Koala Beach Resort Club Daintree	9 B5
Lync Haven Rainforest Retreat	10 A4
Noah Beach Camping Area	11 B3
PK's Jungle Village	12 B2

EATING (pp225–6)

Daintree Ice Cream Company	13 A4
Dragonfly Cafe	14 B2
Fan Palm Boardwalk Café	15 A4

TRANSPORT (pp224–5)

Daintree River Cable Ferry	16 A5

OTHER

Cow Bay Service Station & General Store	17 B5
Mason's Store	18 B2

Thornton Peak (1375m) and **Mt Sorrow** (770m). It's one of the few places in the world where tropical rainforest meets the sea.

Electricity is powered by generators in this section; few places have air-con and not everywhere has 24-hour power. 'Cape Trib' is one of the most popular day trips from Port Douglas and Cairns, and accommodation is booked solid in peak periods.

You can get fuel and supplies at **Cow Bay Service Station & General Store** (☎ 07-4098 9127; Buchanan Creek Rd), and from **Mason's Store** (☎ 07-4098 0070), just past Myall Creek.

Daintree River cable ferry (cars/motorcycles/bicycles & pedestrians one way A$20/10/5; 6am-midnight every 15min) takes two minutes to cross the river.

Coral Reef Coaches (☎ 07-4098 2800; www.coralreefcoaches.com.au) runs daily bus services from Cairns to Cape Tribulation. For information on organised trips to the area, see p209 and p222.

The following sections chart a route from the Daintree River to Cape Tribulation.

Cape Kimberley

☎ 07

Cape Kimberley Rd, 3km beyond the Daintree River crossing, leads to **Cape Kimberley Beach**, a beautiful quiet beach backed with tropical bush that offers some shade.

At the beach is **Koala Beach Resort Club Daintree** (☎ 1800 466 444, 4090 7500; www.koala-backpackers.com; Cape Kimberley Beach; dm A$18-25, d A$85;).

A cut above its cousins further south, this complex spreads out over a remote property with plenty of exquisite flora to add to the atmosphere. Cheaper dorms are in simple four-bed tents and the doubles are motel style. There is, of course, a bar with a goodly supply of alcohol and pub grub (A$7 to A$11). There's a strong emphasis on activities here so you can see the rainforest any which way you choose.

Cow Bay

☎ 07

Cow Bay is simply beautiful. Trees provide beach shade, and you can fish or just lie down and chill out – it doesn't get more relaxing than this.

Before the turn-off to the Jindalba Boardwalk is the **Walu Wugirriga (Alexandra Range) lookout**, with an information board and marvellous views over the **Alexandra Range**.

Daintree Rainforest Environmental Centre (☎ 4098 9171; www.daintree-rec.com.au; adult A$12; 9am-5pm) has a 25m-high tower that starts at the rainforest floor and reaches high into the canopy. Jindalba Boardwalk snakes through the rainforest behind the centre.

Crocodylus Village (☎ 4098 9166; www.crocodyluscapetrib.com; Buchanan Creek Rd; share huts A$23, huts with bathroom A$75;) Definitely one for the quiet traveller, Crocodylus is a picturesque collection of jungle safari tents that look a tad weary but are still accommodating. The doubles, which come with bedding, towels and mosquito nets, are quite lovely. A good network of walking tracks winds its way through the village and for longer trips you can hire a bicycle or take one of its kayak tours.

Lync Haven Rainforest Retreat (☎ 4098 9155; www.lynchaven.com.au; Cape Tribulation Rd; camp/caravan sites per 2 people A$19/22, bungalows A$100) is a hodgepodge of grassy camp sites and small brick bungalows (which are comfortable and self-contained). It's a huge property and also an animal sanctuary. You can visit convalescing wildlife via seven rainforest walking tracks.

You can fill up at **Fan Palm Boardwalk Café** (☎ 4098 9061; 80 Cape Tribulation Rd; meals A$5-12), which makes a tasty toasted sarni and, if you need something heftier, burgers that defy gravity. Staff can also put together a picnic lunch, so if you're interested call in advance with your wish list. **Daintree Ice Cream Company** (☎ 4098 9114; Cape Tribulation Rd; mango juice/ice cream A$3/4; noon-5pm) is pure YUM! Try four delectable flavours in one cup: wattleseed, blueberry, hazelnut and mango.

Noah Beach

☎ 07

The reason to head to **Marrdja Botanical Walk** is the beautiful interpretative boardwalk that follows the creek through the rainforest and mangroves to a lookout over Noah Creek.

Noah Beach Camping Area (☎ 4098 0052; Noah Beach; camp sites per person A$4) is a QPWS self-registration camping ground set 100m back from the beach. Big red-trunked trees provide shade for 16 sites.

Cape Tribulation

☎ 07

The most developed of the area's villages, a small cluster of accommodation options and shops emerge from the forest as you head into 'town'. We're not talking anything fancy – you could blink and miss it and the wilderness is still overwhelming.

Mason's Store (☎ 4098 0070; www.masonstours.com.au; 7am-7pm) is a one-stop supply shop that sells takeaway food and petrol, and runs tours.

At **Bat House** (☎ 4053 4467; www.austrop.org.au/bat_house.html; minimum donation A$2; 10.30am-2.30pm Tue-Fri & Sun) there are environmental displays and a fruit bat called Eggie, whose owner is passionate about bats.

Taste seasonally available tropical fruits at **Cape Trib Exotic Fruit Farm** (☎ 4098 0057; www.capetrib.com.au; tastings A$15; tastings 4-5.45pm, bookings advisable). If you're not a lover of the rather strong-smelling durian, try to miss durian season (November to May) at this pungent fruit farm.

Jungle Adventures (☎ 4099 5651; www.jungleadventurescapetrib.com.au; night walks A$30; depart 7.30pm) runs fun and informative night walks and wildlife-spotting. They'll pick you up from your accommodation so give them a buzz.

SLEEPING & EATING

Cape Trib Beach House (☎ 4098 0030; www.capetribbeach.com.au; Bloomfield Track; dm A$25-32, cabins A$70-125;) This hideaway is sublime. Rooms with flyscreens are set deep in the rainforest, and the complex is right at the beach. There's a friendly open-air bar and small communal kitchen. The Beach House also runs sea-kayaking trips to Myall Beach.

QUEENSLAND

PK's Jungle Village (☎ 1800 232 333, 4098 0082; www.pksjunglevillage.com; Cape Tribulation Rd; camp sites per 2 people A$30, dm A$25, cabins d A$75-100;) PK's is as loud and brash as Cape Tribulation gets. Apart from a vibrant party scene, there is a smorgasbord of activities on offer, including volleyball, kayaking, horse riding and rafting. Rooms are spartan and have no flyscreens, so prepare to be eaten alive unless you have a mosquito net.

Jungle Lodge (☎ 4098 0034; Cape Tribulation Rd; camp sites per person A$11-15, dm A$20-24, d A$70;) Unassuming and barely an interruption in the rainforest, this place has basic but fun safari tents with full linen and towels. Dorm beds are in train-like sleepers and the kitchen and bathrooms are decent. There's a small takeaway attached (snacks A$4 to A$10).

Dragonfly Café (☎ 4098 0121; Camelot Close; meals A$10-15;) A beautiful timber-pole licensed café that showcases local art. It's very chilled out.

CAPE TRIBULATION TO COOKTOWN

North of Cape Tribulation, the spectacular **Bloomfield Track** is unsealed (4WD only) and continues through the forest to the Wujal Wujal Aboriginal Community, on the far side of the Bloomfield River crossing. Some steep sections of the Bloomfield Track may be impassable after heavy rain; check road conditions at **Mason's Store** (☎ 07-4098 0070), just past Myall Creek in Cape Tribulation, before heading off.

A must-see along the way is **Bloomfield Falls** (after crossing the Bloomfield River turn left; the car park is 1km away). North from Wujal Wujal the track heads for 46km through the tiny settlements of **Bloomfield**, **Rossville** and **Helenvale** to meet the sealed Cooktown Developmental Rd, 28km south of Cooktown.

The **Lion's Den Hotel** (☎ 07-4060 3911; fax 07-4060 3958; Helenvale; camp sites per 2 people A$7; meals around A$10) is a colourful 1875 bush pub. With its corrugated, graffiti-covered tin walls and slab-timber bar it attracts a steady stream of travellers and local characters.

COOKTOWN

☎ 07 / pop 1638

Sitting at the mouth of the croc-infested Endeavour River, Cooktown has a reckless, outpost ambience. It's a hard-drinking town and many people seem cast adrift here. The locals go by the relaxed pace of 'Cooktown time' and they *live* to fish. Fishermen will regale you with stories of oversized red emperors and mangrove jacks (none of which ever got away).

Cooktown can claim to be Australia's first nonindigenous settlement, however transient. From June to August 1770, Captain Cook beached his barque *Endeavour* here, during which time the expedition's chief naturalist, Joseph Banks, collected 186 species of Australian plants from the banks of the Endeavour River and wrote the first European description of a kangaroo.

While Cook had amicable contact with the local Aboriginal people, race relations in the area turned sour a century later when Cooktown was founded as the unruly port for the Palmer River gold rush (1873–83). Battle Camp, about 60km inland from Cooktown, was the site of a major battle between Europeans and Aborigines.

In 1874, Cooktown was the second-largest town in Queensland, with 94 pubs and a population over 30,000. As many as half of the inhabitants were Chinese, who were mercilessly persecuted before being driven from the area in the 1880s.

The Peninsula Development Rd, due for completion in 2005, is still unsealed in sections and a 4WD is necessary from Cape Tribulation. The trek to Cooktown is rewarded not only by its welcoming community and frontier atmosphere, but also by some fascinating reminders of the area's past.

Information

Cooktown Library (☎ 4069 5009; Helen St; per hr A$4) Internet access.

Cooktown QPWS (☎ 4069 5777; ian.king@epa.qld.gov.au; Webber Esplanade; 8am-3.30pm Mon-Thu, to 3pm Fri) Permits and information. Ranger often around in the afternoon.

Cooktown Travel Centre (☎ 4069 5446; cooktowntravel@bigpond.com; Charlotte St; 8.30am-5pm Mon-Fri, to noon Sat) Tourist information.

Lure Shop (☎ 4069 5396; Charlotte St; per hr A$4) Internet access.

Sights & Activities

Cooktown hibernates during the wet season (locals call it the dead season), and reduced hours or closure may apply to attractions and tours; call beforehand to check.

Nature's Powerhouse (☎ 4069 6004; www.naturespowerhouse.info; both galleries adult A$2; 9am-5pm) is an environment interpretative centre in Cooktown's **botanic gardens**. The Powerhouse has two excellent galleries: **Charlie Tanner Gallery** (Charlie was Cooktown's 'snake man') has fantastic displays about snakes, termite mounds, crocodiles, 'only on the Cape' wildlife (the bare-backed fruit bat will give you nightmares) and inspirational stories from taipan-bite survivors; and the **Vera Scarth-Johnson Gallery** displays a collection of intricate and beautiful botanical illustrations of the region's native plants. There are **walking tracks** that lead from the gardens to the **beaches** at Cherry Tree and Finch Bays.

Housed in the imposing 1880s St Mary's Convent, the **James Cook Museum** (4069 5386; jcmuseum@tpg.com.au; cnr Furneaux & Helen Sts; adult A$7; 9.30am-4pm) explores Cooktown's intriguing past.

Grassy Hill lookout (162m) has spectacular 360-degree views, and it's a 1½-hour walk to the summit of **Mt Cook** (431m), with even better views. The track starts by the Mt Cook National Park sign on Melaleuca St, beyond the swimming pool.

Charlotte St and Bicentennial Park have a number of interesting **monuments**, including the much-photographed bronze **Captain Cook statue**.

Fishing is a major pastime in Cooktown; to find out about the best fishing spots check out www.cook.qld.gov.au/visitors/FinchBayFish.shtml.

Tours

Tours can be booked directly with the tour companies or at Cooktown Travel Centre. The following are rates for one person, but group bookings are much cheaper.

Cooktown Tours (4069 5125; www.cooktowntours.com; tours A$25-125) runs guided coach and 4WD tours around Cooktown to: Black Mountain and the Lion's Den Hotel; Coloured Sands, Elim Beach and Hopevale Aboriginal Community; and Split Rock galleries and Lakefield National Park.

Bart's Bush Adventures (4069 6229; bartbush@tpg.com.au; 1 Hutchinson St; 8am-5pm) offers a 4WD Miner's Adventure (A$145) and Bloomfield Falls Adventure (A$125) with accredited Savannah Guides (professional tour-guide network).

Wilderness Challenge (4035 4488; www.wilderness-challenge.com.au; 2-day tour A$360; Mon, Wed & Fri) runs all inclusive tours to Cooktown from Brisbane.

Cooktown Cruises (4069 5712; ashtyn@tpg.com.au; adult A$25; 1pm Easter-Dec) runs a sedate two-hour cruise to the head of the Endeavour River.

Sleeping

Pam's Place (4069 5166; www.cooktownhostel.com; cnr Charlotte & Boundary Sts; dm A$20-22, d A$50) A hefty wooden croc acts as the resident welcoming committee at this comfortable YHA hostel and the friendly vibes don't stop at the gate. All the rooms here are quite accommodating and there's a big emphasis on getting you out and about to see the area. Pam's will get you out there on a good array of tours and activities.

Seaview Motel (4069 5377; seaviewm@tpg.com.au; Webber Esplanade; s/d A$65/79) This rambling motel has prime water frontage and spectacular views of Cook's landing site. The rooms are less dramatic than the views, but are clean and comfy.

Alamanda Inn (4069 5203; Hope St; s A$28-56, d A$40-75) This simple hotel is a reasonable option, with pleasant, no-frills rooms.

Other options:

Hillcrest B&B (4069 5305; fax 4069 5893; 130 Hope St; r from A$60) Charming timber B&B.

Tropical Breeze Caravan Park (4069 5417; McIvor Rd; camp sites per 2 people A$16, cabins with fan/air-con A$60/65, units A$55-76) Book ahead for the high season.

Eating & Drinking

Grab supplies from **Martin's IGA supermarket** (4069 5633; cnr Helen & Hogg Sts) and **Cooktown Bakery** (4069 5612; Charlotte St).

Gill'd 'n' Gutt'd (4069 5863; Webber Esplanade; meals A$6-12) Sensational fish-and-chip shop with super-fresh Spanish mackerel and barramundi.

Nonya's Café (4069 5723; Charlotte St; meals A$8-17) A welcome change from the counter-meal circuit, serving fresh salads, tapas, tasty Malay curries with rice and chicken satay, plus the usual takeaway menu.

Seagren's Inn (4069 5357; Charlotte St; mains A$16-30) More upmarket, serving Mod Oz cuisine in a heritage timber building.

Drinking is one of the more popular Cooktown activities, and there are some great old pubs and clubs along Charlotte St that all serve meals.

Cooktown Hotel (☎ 4069 5308; cnr Charlotte & Walker Sts; meals around A$12) Known as the Top Pub, this friendly hotel has heaps of character and is generally *full* of characters.

Bowls Club (☎ 4069 6173; Charlotte St; meals around A$14) Set up in the 1970s by avid bowlers, the Bowls Club is a relaxing place for a beer, and is popular with families. Meals are delicious – it serves excellent, spicy, Thai green chicken curry and grilled reef fish.

RSL Club (☎ 4069 5780; Charlotte St; meals A$8-14) Another top spot for a decent feed and refreshing ale.

Getting There & Around

Coral Reef Coaches (☎ 4098 2800; www.coralreefcoaches.com.au) travels between Cooktown and Cairns.

For a taxi, call ☎ 4069 5387.

CAIRNS TO COOKTOWN – THE INLAND ROAD

The 341km Peninsula Development Rd loops north from Cairns through Kuranda, Mareeba, Mt Molloy, Mt Carbine and Palmer River to Lakeland, where it splits off to Cape York Peninsula. From Lakeland the road to Helenvale is unsealed, but suitable for a conventional vehicle.

Mt Molloy's claim to fame is that the Swedish and Danish version of the TV show *Survivor* was filmed at **Camp Molloy**, the town's camping ground. Five kilometres away is the **National Hotel** (☎ 07-4094 1133; Main St; s/d A$25/50), a country pub serving counter meals (A$6 to A$15).

The Palmer River gold rush (1873–83) occurred about 70km to the west, throwing up boomtowns Palmerville and Maytown; little of either remains today. At the Palmer River crossing, **Palmer River roadhouse** (☎ 07-4060 2020; camp/caravan sites per 2 people A$7/13; 7am-late) is a solitary place with horrendously expensive fuel.

South of Cooktown the road passes through the sinister-looking rock piles of **Black Mountain National Park** – a range of hills formed 260 million years ago and made up of thousands of granite boulders. Aborigines call it Kalcajagga ('place of the spears'), and it's home to unique species of frog, skink and gecko.

Melbourne & Victoria

CONTENTS

HIGHLIGHTS

- **MCG** Be swept up by the roars of 60,000 people during a game of Aussie Rules (p257)
- **Great Ocean Road** Take the passenger seat for a drive with spectacular views and inhale the fresh, salty air (p265)
- **The Grampians** Walk through ancient landscapes (p285)
- **Yarra Valley** Tipple your way through the vineyards (p262)
- **Sovereign Hill** Suspend disbelief at Ballarat's re-creation of an 1860s goldmining township (p279)
- **Wilsons Promontory National Park** Give way to wombats on your way to the beach (p276)
- **Alpine National Park** Feel the sting of winter on your cheeks as you bushwalk or ski (p288)
- **City bars** Stay out late, hopping from one fabulous drinking venue to the next (p254)
- **Bells Beach** Surf Victoria's awesome swells (p266)
- **Echuca** Kick back on a Murray River paddle-steamer (p283)

- **Cheer for:** St Kilda Saints in the AFL (Aussie rules)
- **Eat:** dim sims
- **Drink:** a pot (285mL) of Carlton
- **Listen to:** Jet's *Get Born*, TISM live (in fact, anyone live!)
- **Watch:** *Queen of the Damned* (crummy vampire flick) or *Romper Stomper* (ultra violent Russell Crowe movie, filmed just down the road from the Lonely Planet office)
- **Party at:** St Kilda (p256)
- **Swim at:** Melbourne's Williamstown Beach (p245) or Torquay (p265), along the coast
- **Avoid:** brown snakes, redback spiders, getting your bike wheel stuck in a tram track
- **Locals' nickname:** Mexicans

- TELEPHONE CODE: 03
- WEBSITE: www.visitvictoria.com

Although it's Australia's smallest mainland state, Victoria is crammed with sights and activities. You don't have to travel far before reaching its staggeringly beautiful coast, wilderness and eclectic townships.

Experience the Great Ocean Road's sweeping rugged coastline, the Grampians' ancient wilderness and the glorious Alpine National Park. Wildlife inhabits every corner of the state, from the penguins at Phillip Island to the koalas, kangaroos and lyrebirds that call the numerous protected parks home. A smattering of wineries and a good dose of historic townships add to the state's rich texture. Adventure junkies can surf, cycle, kayak, ski and hang-glide from place to place. Or you can take it down a notch and kick back on seemingly endless beaches.

And then, of course, there's Melbourne. This lush city contains a scandalous array of world-class arts, sporting events, festivals, cuisines, music, bars and shops. Its locals have connections to all parts of the world, which makes for a diverse and creative population. The city sprawls out from the Yarra River, and is almost entirely surrounded by parks and gardens. Melbourne tends to be modest about its treasures, but there's a riot of activity going on behind the city's grid. It's as surprising as its weather and as diverse as its people.

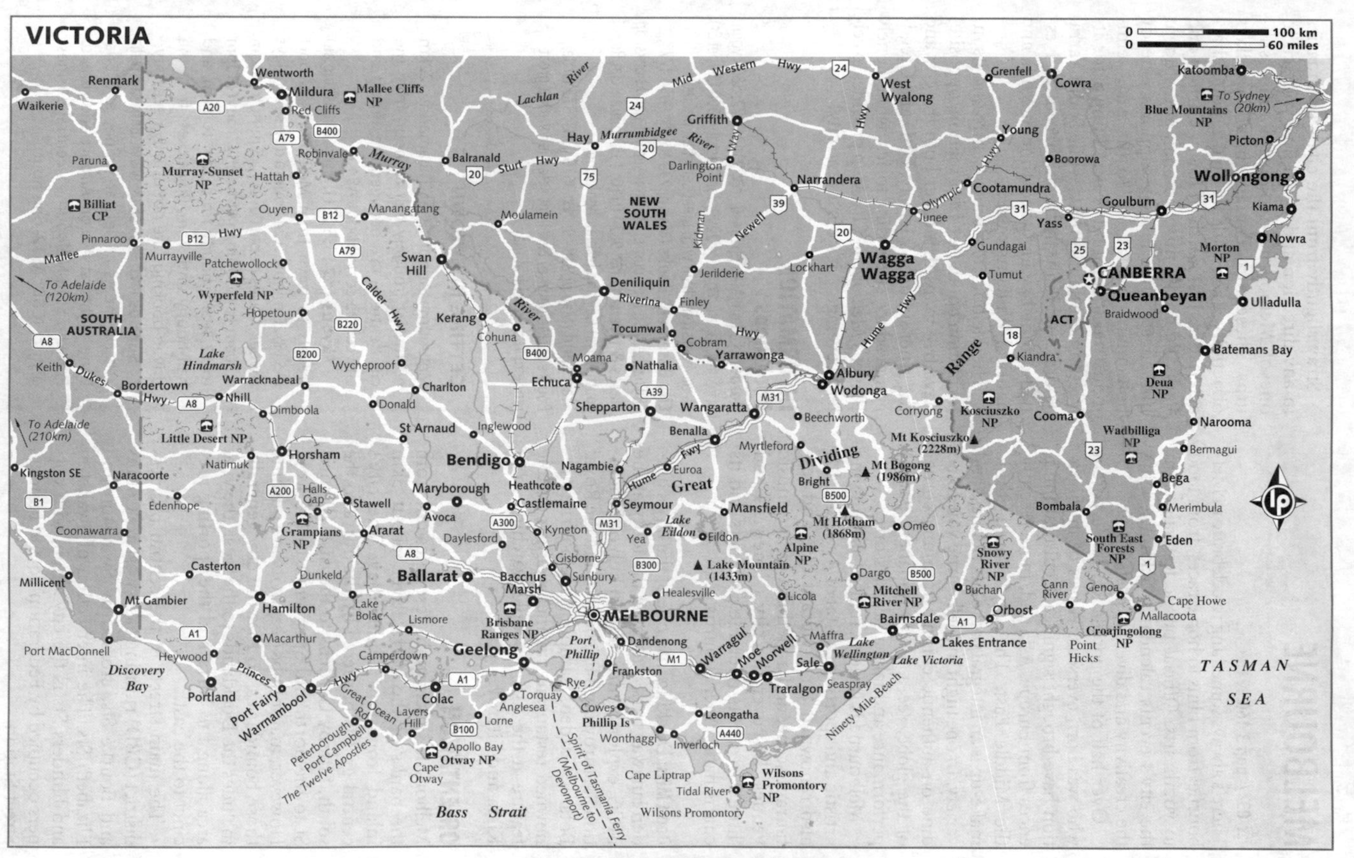
VICTORIA
0 100 km
0 60 miles
Renmark
Waikerie
Wentworth
Mildura
Red Cliffs
Mallee Cliffs NP
Lachlan River
Mid Western Hwy
West Wyalong
Grenfell
Cowra
Katoomba
To Sydney (20km)
Blue Mountains NP
Picton
Wollongong
Kiama
Nowra
Paruna
Murray-Sunset NP
Hattah
Robinvale
Murray
Balranald
Sturt Hwy
Hay
Murrumbidgee River
Griffith
Darlington Point
Narrandera
Young
Boorowa
Cootamundra
Olympic Hwy
Junee
Goulburn
Yass
Billiat CP
Ouyen
Manangatang
Moulamein
NEW SOUTH WALES
Kidman Way
Newell Hwy
Pinnaroo
Murrayville
Mallee
Patchewollock
Swan Hill
Gundagai
Morton NP
To Adelaide (120km)
Wyperfeld NP
Calder Hwy
Deniliquin
Jerilderie
Lockhart
Wagga Wagga
Tumut
CANBERRA
Queanbeyan
Ulladulla
SOUTH AUSTRALIA
Hopetoun
Kerang
River
Riverina
Finley
Braidwood
ACT
Tocumwal
Hwy
Hume Hwy
Cohuna
Cobram
Range
Kiandra
Batemans Bay
Lake Hindmarsh
Wycheproof
Moama
Yarrawonga
Deua NP
Keith
Dukes Hwy
Bordertown
Warracknabeal
Nathalia
Albury
Wodonga
Nhill
Charlton
Echuca
Dimboola
Donald
Shepparton
Wangaratta
Beechworth
Corryong
Kosciuszko NP
Cooma
Narooma
To Adelaide (210km)
St Arnaud
Inglewood
Benalla
Myrtleford
Mt Kosciuszko (2228m)
Wadbilliga NP
Little Desert NP
Horsham
Bermagui
Kingston SE
Natimuk
Bendigo
Nagambie
Euroa
Fwy
Dividing
Mt Bogong (1986m)
Naracoorte
Hume
Great
Bright
Bega
Halls Gap
Stawell
Maryborough
Heathcote
Castlemaine
Seymour
Mansfield
Bombala
Merimbula
Edenhope
Avoca
Mt Hotham (1868m)
Omeo
Grampians NP
Ararat
Lake Eildon
Eildon
Coonawarra
Daylesford
Kyneton
Yea
Alpine NP
Snowy River NP
South East Forests NP
Eden
Gisborne
Casterton
Dunkeld
Ballarat
Bacchus Marsh
Sunbury
Lake Mountain (1433m)
Dargo
Millicent
Healesville
Mitchell River NP
Buchan
Cann River
Genoa
Cape Howe
Mt Gambier
Hamilton
Lake Bolac
Lismore
Brisbane Ranges NP
MELBOURNE
Licola
Bairnsdale
Orbost
Mallacoota
Croajingolong NP
Macarthur
Dandenong
Port Phillip
Warragul
Maffra
Lake Wellington
Lakes Entrance
Lake Victoria
Point Hicks
Port MacDonnell
Heywood
Discovery Bay
Princes Hwy
Camperdown
Geelong
Frankston
Moe
Morwell
Sale
TASMAN SEA
Portland
Port Fairy
Warrnambool
Great Ocean Rd
Colac
Torquay
Rye
Traralgon
Seaspray
Ninety Mile Beach
Anglesea
Cowes
Phillip Is
Leongatha
Lavers Hill
Lorne
Wonthaggi
Inverloch
Peterborough
Port Campbell
The Twelve Apostles
Apollo Bay
Otway NP
Spirit of Tasmania Ferry (Melbourne to Devonport)
Cape Otway
Cape Liptrap
Wilsons Promontory NP
Tidal River
Bass Strait
Wilsons Promontory

MELBOURNE

☎ 03 / pop 3,160,171

There's always something to celebrate in Melbourne: from films to horse races, from food to youth arts. Official public festivals cram the city's events calendar – acknowledging the creativity and diversity of its locals.

Over half of the population has a parent who was born overseas. Waves of immigration have brought significant cultural influences from Europe, Asia and, more recently, the Middle East. The city's multi-ethnic make-up is an integral part of its richness and variety. In one night in Melbourne you could dine on authentic cuisine from any corner of the globe, see a *bhuto* (Japanese dance) performance and take a salsa lesson.

Melbourne is widely credited as being the artistic and sporting capital of Australia. It's also renowned for a vibrant café and restaurant scene, and a plethora of live-music venues. Discover the city's laneways and 'little' streets, its riverside precincts and its charismatic inner suburbs.

Don't Miss: Ducking into one of the city's hidden laneway bars, watching the footy at the MCG, exploring the cultural hub of Federation Sq, throwing a Frisbee around the Royal Botanic Gardens, sampling Melbourne's renowned restaurant cuisine, seeing a double feature at the Astor, people-watching in St Kilda and Fitzroy.

ORIENTATION

Melbourne's metropolis resonates out from the banks of the Yarra River, about 5km inland from Port Phillip Bay. The city's central grid is bordered by the Yarra to the south, Fitzroy Gardens to the east, Victoria St to the north and Spencer St to the west. However, major hubs of activity are pushing those boundaries, so that the city generally includes the Docklands to the west, the vital area along the Yarra and the sporting precinct to the east.

The main streets of the central business district (CBD) running east–west are Collins and Bourke Sts, crossed by Swanston and Elizabeth Sts. The intersection of Swanston and Flinders Sts is the city's hub, with corners occupied by Federation Sq and Flinders Street Station.

Stray slightly from the city's boundaries in any direction and you'll find yourself in one of Melbourne's colourful inner suburbs. These areas contain thriving pockets of activity, each with its own unique characteristics. Just north of town, Carlton and Parkville hold a mix of Italian and student influences, while Fitzroy supports a heady bohemian population. To the east, semi-industrial Richmond is best known for its Vietnamese community, while South Yarra, Toorak and Prahran are chichi central. Nestled on the bay are good-time St Kilda and nautical Williamstown.

The Melbourne Visitor Centre and its information booth (see Information, opposite) have free maps that cover both the city and the inner suburbs. Melway, UBD and Gregory's produce street directories, while Lonely Planet's *Melbourne City Map* provides excellent coverage – it's our home city!

INFORMATION

Bookshops

Borders Carlton (Map pp234-6; ☎ 9348 0222; 380 Lygon St); South Yarra (☎ 9824 2299; Jam Factory, 500 Chapel St) Mega-bookstore chain with great selection of CDs.

City Basement Books (Map pp238-9; ☎ 9654 1773; 28 Elizabeth St, Melbourne) Monster second-hand bookshop.

Hares & Hyenas (☎ 9824 0110; 135 Commercial Rd, South Yarra) Gay and lesbian bookshop.

Map Land (Map pp238–9; ☎ 9670 4383; 372 Little Bourke St, Melbourne) Excellent selection with a great range of topographical maps.

GETTING INTO TOWN

Melbourne Airport is at Tullamarine, 22km northwest (roughly half an hour) from the city centre. A taxi between the airport and city centre costs about A$40.

Skybus (☎ 9335 2811; www.skybus.com.au) travels to town from Melbourne Airport (A$13, 20 minutes) 24 hours a day, seven days a week. Buses depart every 15 minutes from 6.30am to 6.30pm, half-hourly from 6.30pm to 12.30am, hourly from 1am to 5am, and half-hourly until 7am. Buy tickets from the driver; bookings are not usually necessary.

Sunbus (☎ 9689 6888; www.sunbusaustralia.com.au) meets all Jetstar Sydney and Brisbane flights at Avalon Airport and runs to Franklin St in Melbourne's central business district (CBD; A$12, one hour).

McGills (Map pp238–9; ☎ 9602 5566; 187 Elizabeth St, Melbourne) Interstate and foreign newspapers and magazines.
Readings (Map pp234-6; ☎ 9347 6633; 309 Lygon St, Carlton) Melbourne institution offering supreme service.

Emergency
Ambulance (☎ 000)
Fire (☎ 000)
Lifeline (☎ 13 11 14) A 24-hour, seven-day, over-the-phone counselling service in six languages.
Police (☎ 000); Flinders Lane (Map pp238-9; ☎ 9650 7077; 226 Flinders Lane, Melbourne); Flinders St (Map pp234-6; ☎ 9247 6491; 637 Flinders St, Melbourne) Police stations open 24 hours.

Internet Access
Prices are around A$4 per hour.
e:fifty five (Map pp238-9; ☎ 9620 3899; Basement, 55 Elizabeth St, Melbourne) Purchase a drink and get your Internet half-price.
Netcity (Map p244; ☎ 9525 3411; 63 Fitzroy St, St Kilda)
World Wide Wash (Map pp234-6; ☎ 9419 8214; 361 Brunswick St, Fitzroy) Laundrette and Internet café.

Internet Resources
www.backpackvictoria.com The official backpackers' site.
www.melbourne.citysearch.com.au What's-on listings; restaurants, clubs, shopping and accommodation are also listed.

Media
Melbourne has two major daily newspapers: the broadsheet **Age** (www.theage.com.au) and the tabloid **Herald Sun** (www.heraldsun.com.au). The pull-out EG section in Friday's *Age* is excellent for what's-on information.

Free street press is also focused on music and entertainment. Look out for *Beat* and *InPress* in cafés and venues about town.

Art Almanac (A$3) is a comprehensive listing of galleries that's updated monthly, and is available at bookshops and larger art galleries.

Medical Services
Alfred Hospital (☎ 9276 2000; Commercial Rd, Prahran) Has a 24-hour casualty ward.
Chapelgate Pharmacy (☎ 9531 8004; 103 Carlisle St, St Kilda East; 9am-9pm)
Denticare (☎ 9625 1218; www.denticare.com.au) Provides 24-hour emergency service.
Melbourne Sexual Health Centre (Map pp234-6; ☎ 9347 0244; www.mshc.org.au; 580 Swanston St, Carlton) Free check-ups and other medical services; appointments preferred.
St Vincent's Hospital (Map pp238-9; ☎ 9288 2211; 41 Victoria Pde, Fitzroy) Has a 24-hour casualty ward.
Travellers' Medical and Vaccination Centre (TMVC; Map pp238-9; ☎ 9602 5788; Level 2, 393 Little Bourke St, Melbourne) Appointments necessary.

Money
Changing foreign currency or travellers cheques is no problem at most banks, particularly at larger banks such as the **Commonwealth Bank** (Map pp238-9; ☎ 9675 7000; 385 Bourke St, Melbourne). There are foreign-exchange booths (open for all flights) at Melbourne's international airport, and exchange offices such as **Thomas Cook** (Map pp238-9; ☎ 9654 4222; 261 Bourke St, Melbourne; 9am-5pm Mon-Fri, 10am-5pm Sat, 11am-4pm Sun) in the city centre.

Post
Main post office (Map pp238-9; ☎ 13 13 18; 250 Elizabeth St, Melbourne)
Poste restante (Map pp238-9; 380 Bourke St, Melbourne; 6am-6pm Mon-Fri) Mail can be collected from the Private Box Room and is held for a month – bring your passport.

Tourist Information
Backpackers Travel Centre (Map pp238-9; ☎ 9654 8477; Shop 1, 250 Flinders St, Melbourne) Backpacker-oriented travel agency.
Backpackers World (Map pp238-9; ☎ 9639 9686; 450 Elizabeth St, Melbourne) Another backpacker-oriented travel agency.
Information booth (Map pp238–9; Bourke St Mall, Melbourne; 9am-5pm Mon-Fri, 10am-5pm Sat & Sun)
Melbourne Visitor Centre (Map pp238-9; ☎ 9658 9658; www.thatsmelbourne.com.au; Federation Sq, cnr Swanston & Flinders Sts, Melbourne; 9am-6pm) The city's main drop-in visitors centre, offering everything from Internet to accommodation bookings; the place to pick up a public-transport map.
Tourism Victoria (☎ 13 28 42; www.visitvictoria.com) The phone service and website are excellent sources of information to get you up to speed.
YHA Travel (Map pp238–9; ☎ 9670 9611; 83 Hardware Lane, Melbourne) Tour information and bookings.

SIGHTS
Melbourne is relatively compact, and bursting with sights that, although scattered about town, are easy to get to on foot or by tram. Walking allows you to discover its charismatic little streets, laneways and arcades.

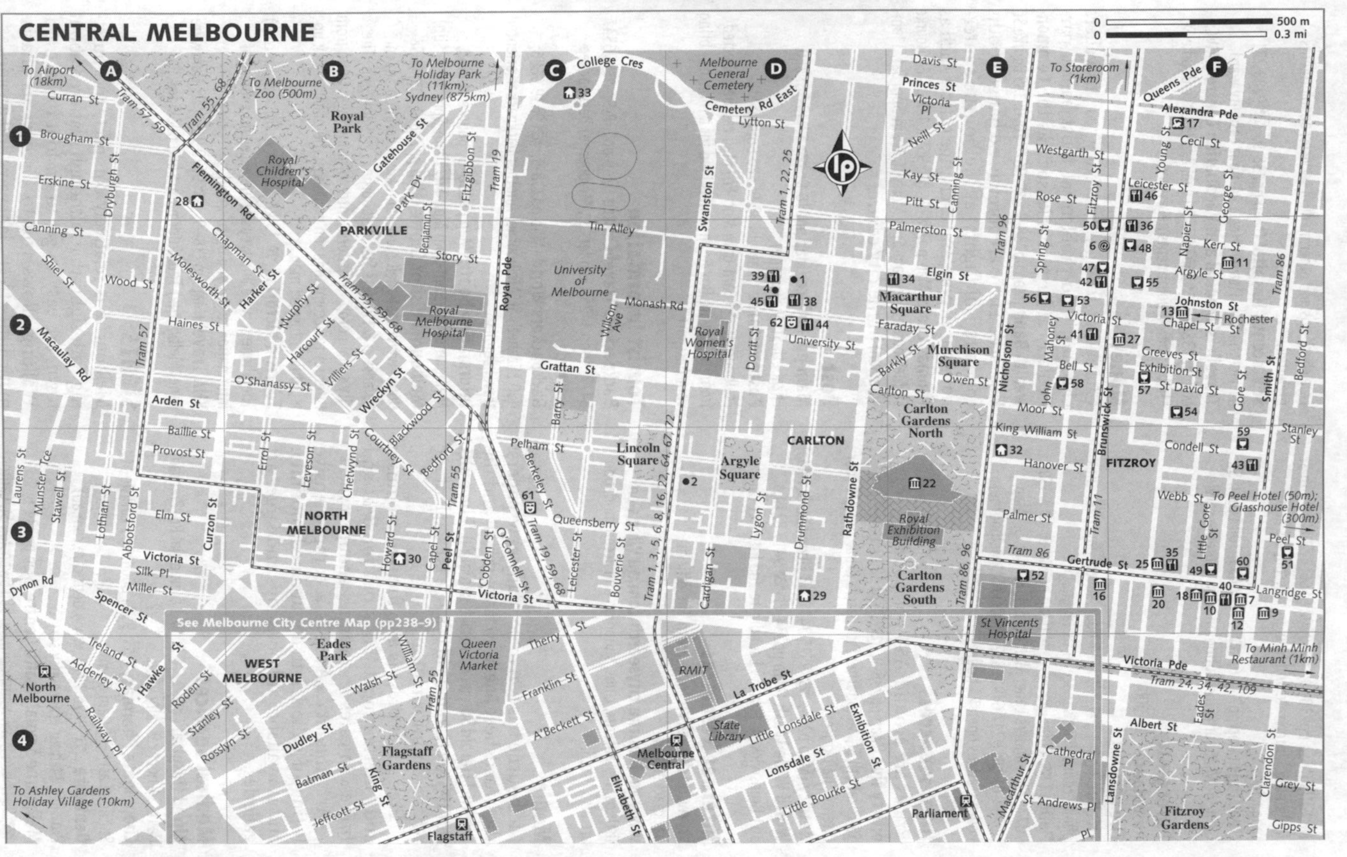
CENTRAL MELBOURNE
0 500 m
0 0.3 mi
To Airport (18km)
To Melbourne Zoo (500m)
To Melbourne Holiday Park (11km); Sydney (875km)
To Storeroom (1km)
To Peel Hotel (50m); Glasshouse Hotel (300m)
To Minh Minh Restaurant (1km)
To Ashley Gardens Holiday Village (10km)
See Melbourne City Centre Map (pp238-9)
Royal Park
Royal Children's Hospital
PARKVILLE
Royal Melbourne Hospital
University of Melbourne
Melbourne General Cemetery
Royal Women's Hospital
NORTH MELBOURNE
WEST MELBOURNE
CARLTON
FITZROY
Carlton Gardens North
Carlton Gardens South
Royal Exhibition Building
Argyle Square
Lincoln Square
Macarthur Square
Murchison Square
Queen Victoria Market
Flagstaff Gardens
Fitzroy Gardens
Eades Park
St Vincents Hospital
State Library
RMIT
Melbourne Central
Parliament
Flagstaff
North Melbourne
Flemington Rd
Royal Pde
Swanston St
Rathdowne St
Nicholson St
Brunswick St
Smith St
Victoria St
Victoria Pde
La Trobe St
Elizabeth St
Exhibition St
Lonsdale St
Spencer St
Peel St
Gertrude St
Johnston St
Grattan St
Alexandra Pde
Queens Pde
Princes St
Elgin St
Macaulay Rd
Arden St
Curzon St
Wreckyn St
Gatehouse St
College Cres
Cemetery Rd East

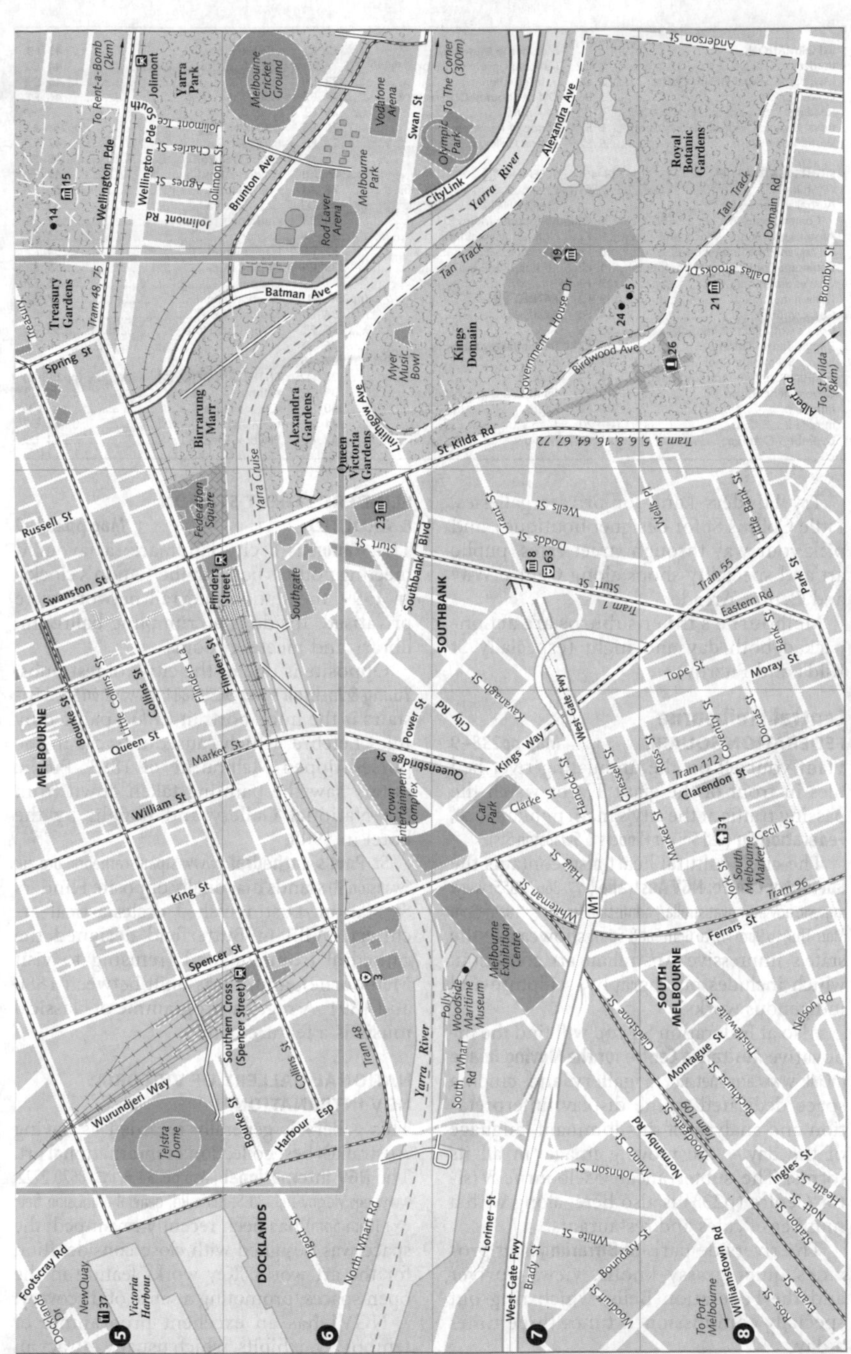
To Rent-a-Bomb (2km)
Jolimont
Yarra Park
Melbourne Cricket Ground
Vodafone Arena
To The Corner (300m)
Anderson St
Swan St
Olympic Park
Melbourne Park
Rod Laver Arena
CityLink
Yarra River
Alexandra Ave
Royal Botanic Gardens
Tan Track
Domain Rd
Bromby St
Dallas Brooks Dr
Government House Dr
Kings Domain
Myer Music Bowl
Birdwood Ave
Linlithgow Ave
Queen Victoria Gardens
Alexandra Gardens
Batman Ave
Brunton Ave
Wellington Pde South
Wellington Pde
Jolimont Tce
Charles St
Agnes St
Jolimont St
Jolimont Rd
Treasury Gardens
Treasury
Tram 48, 75
Spring St
Birrarung Marr
Federation Square
Yarra Cruise
St Kilda Rd
Tram 3, 5, 6, 8, 16, 64, 67, 72
Albert Rd
To St Kilda (8km)
Russell St
Swanston St
Flinders Street
Southgate
Sturt St
Southbank Blvd
Grant St
Dodds St
Wells St
Wells Pl
Little Bank St
Park St
Tram 55
Tram 1
Eastern Rd
SOUTHBANK
Kavanagh St
City Rd
Power St
Queensbridge St
Kings Way
West Gate Fwy
Tope St
Moray St
Bank St
Coventry St
Dorcas St
Tram 112
Clarendon St
Chessell St
Ross St
Hancock St
Clarke St
Car Park
Crown Entertainment Complex
Market St
Cecil St
South Melbourne Market
York St
Tram 96
Haig St
Whiteman St
M1
Ferrars St
MELBOURNE
Bourke St
Little Collins St
Collins St
Flinders La
Flinders St
Queen St
William St
King St
Spencer St
Southern Cross (Spencer Street)
Melbourne Exhibition Centre
Polly Woodside Maritime Museum
South Wharf Rd
Tram 48
Wurundjeri Way
Telstra Dome
Harbour Esp
Collins St
SOUTH MELBOURNE
Gladstone St
Thistlewaite St
Nelson Rd
Montague St
Buckhurst St
Tram 109
Woodgate St
Normanby Rd
Munro St
Johnson St
Ingles St
Heath St
Nott St
Station St
Lorimer St
White St
Boundary St
Williamstown Rd
To Port Melbourne
Woodruff St
Brady St
Ross St
Evans St
North Wharf Rd
Pigott St
DOCKLANDS
Footscray Rd
NewQuay
Docklands Dr
Victoria Harbour
5
6
7
8

INFORMATION		
Borders	1	D2
Melbourne Sexual Health Centre	2	D3
Police Station	3	B6
Readings	4	D2
Royal Botanic Gardens Visitors Centre	5	E7
World Wide Wash	6	E2
SIGHTS & ACTIVITIES	**(pp233–45)**	
69 Smith	7	F3
Australian Centre for Contemporary Art	8	D7
Australian Galleries: Works on Paper	9	F3
Australian Print Workshop	10	F3
Centre for Contemporary Photography	11	F2
Charles Smith	12	F3
Conical Inc	13	F2
Conservatory	14	F5
Cook's Cottage	15	F5
Dianne Tanzer Gallery	16	E3
Fitzroy Swimming Pool	17	F1
Gertrude Contemporary Art Spaces	18	F3
Government House	19	E7
Intrude	20	F3
Intrude 2	(see 20)	
La Trobe's Cottage	21	E8
Melbourne Museum	22	E3
National Gallery of Victoria: NGV International	23	D6
Old Melbourne Observatory	24	E7
Seventh	25	F3
Shrine of Remembrance	26	E8
Sutton Gallery	27	F2
SLEEPING	**(pp247–50)**	
Chapman Gardens YHA Hostel	28	A1
Medley Hall	29	D3
Melbourne Metro YHA	30	B3
Nomads Market Inn	31	C8
Nunnery	32	E3
Ormond College	33	C1
EATING	**(pp250–54)**	
Abla's	34	E2
Arcadia	35	F3
Babka Bakery Cafe	36	F2
Bhoj	37	A5
Brunetti's	38	D2
Jimmy Watson's Wine Bar	39	D2
Ladro	40	F3
Mao's	41	E2
Mario's	42	E2
Old Kingdom	43	F3
Shakahari	44	D2
Tiamo	45	D2
Vegie Bar	46	F1
DRINKING	**(pp254–6)**	
Bar Open	47	E2
Bimbo Deluxe	48	F2
Builders Arms	49	F3
Evelyn Hotel	50	E2
Gay Trade Bar	51	F3
Gertrude's	52	E3
Laundry	53	E2
Napier Hotel	54	F2
Night Cat	55	F2
Old Bar	56	E2
Rainbow Hotel	57	F2
Standard Hotel	58	E2
Union Club Hotel	59	F3
Yelza	60	F3
ENTERTAINMENT	**(pp256–9)**	
Arthouse	61	C3
Cinema Nova	(see 1)	
La Mama	62	D2
Playbox Theatre	63	D7

Try Flinders Lane for private galleries, Little Collins St for designer boutiques, and pick your way through street cafés, public art and speciality shops along Centre Way and Centre Arcade.

Melbourne's inner suburbs are action-packed both day and night (especially St Kilda and Fitzroy).

Central Melbourne

FEDERATION SQUARE — Map pp238–9

Plant yourself on the undulating river-bed tiles in front of the giant TV or watch the passing traffic at the city's main public space, **Federation Sq** (Fed Sq; cnr Flinders & Swanston Sts).

The city's cultural heart also contains the **Ian Potter Centre: NGV Australia** (☎ 8662 1555; www.ngv.vic.gov.au/ngvaustralia/; admission free; 10am-5pm Mon-Thu, to 9pm Fri, to 6pm Sat & Sun), showcasing the state's impressive Australian art collection, which includes photography, sculpture and indigenous works.

Also at Federation Sq you will find the innovative **Australian Centre for the Moving Image** (ACMI; www.acmi.net.au), a gallery and cinema space dedicated to the display, interpretation and analysis of the dominant language of the day – the moving image, in all its forms. The subterranean Melbourne Visitor Centre (p233) is also here, along with a number of cafés and restaurants.

The riverside park of **Birrarung Marr** provides quiet grassy knolls, views upriver and the Federation Bells, which ring out specially commissioned tunes three times a day.

FLINDERS STREET STATION & AROUND — Map pp238–9

The **station** is a city landmark; a favoured meeting point is beneath the station's clocks. In 1999, the station and rail network were privatised. Inside is a crumbling ballroom, library and meeting rooms.

Opposite is one of the city's oldest pubs, **Young & Jackson's** (☎ 9650 3884; 1 Swanston St). Upstairs is the nude portrait *Chloe*, painted by Jules Lefebre, which caused a fracas in the pursed-lipped Melbourne of 1883. Public outcry saw the painting taken down from the National Gallery and bought by the hotel in 1908.

St Paul's Cathedral (www.stpaulscathedral.org.au; Swanston St) stands diagonally opposite Flinders St Station. Distinguished ecclesiastical architect, William Butterfield designed the cathedral from England (refusing to visit Melbourne), and it was built between 1880 and 1891. A regular programme of classical music is a feature here.

NATIONAL GALLERY OF VICTORIA: NGV INTERNATIONAL

This gallery is generally regarded as having Australia's best collection of international art. The **NGV International** (Map pp234-6; ☎ 8620 2222; www.ngv.vic.gov.au; 180 St Kilda Rd; general admission free; 10am-5pm) has been recently revamped; the space was designed with close consideration for the art works. Key works feature in the open spaces, promoting a sense of discovery.

NGVI has an excellent programme of temporary exhibits, which usually attract an admission fee. There's a café, restaurant, shop and sculpture garden within the gallery walls – behind the famous water wall.

The Australian collection is on display at the Ian Potter Centre: NGV Australia (opposite).

RIALTO TOWERS OBSERVATION DECK

The **observation deck** (Map pp238-9; ☎ 9629 8222; www.melbournedeck.com.au; 525 Collins St, Melbourne; adult/concession A$13/9; 10am-10pm) allows for impressive 360-degree views of the city grid and river system. Surveying the city from 253m up is a sensational Melbourne high.

IMMIGRATION MUSEUM

The **museum** (Map pp238-9; ☎ 9927 2700; 400 Flinders St; adult/concession A$6/free; 10am-5pm) in the old Customs House mixes visual displays with audio to convey the migrant experience in Australia. The 2nd-floor galleries host a range of excellent temporary exhibitions exploring multiethnic social and cultural issues, including funeral rituals and cooking traditions.

AUSTRALIAN CENTRE FOR CONTEMPORARY ART

The **Australian Centre for Contemporary Art** (ACCA; Map pp234-6; ☎ 9697 9999; www.accaonline.org.au; 111 Sturt St; admission free; 11am-6pm Tue-Sun) displays contemporary pieces that challenge traditional artistic frameworks. But, it isn't an alienating place: you won't be wondering if the Exit sign is part of the exhibition!

QUEEN VICTORIA MARKET

Chaotic, friendly, odorous – Melbourne's favourite **market** (Map pp234-6; ☎ 9320 5822; www.qvm.com.au; cnr Elizabeth & Victoria Sts; 6am-2pm Tue & Thu, to 6pm Fri, to 3pm Sat, 9am-4pm Sun) should be on your to-do list. Although officially designated as a market in 1878, the land had been put to various uses beforehand, from cattle yards to being part of Melbourne's first cemetery – an estimated 9000 bodies still remain under the car park.

Pick your way through the throng to find everything from gooey Brie to snuggly sheepskin boots. If you're visiting between late November and mid-February, time your visit for the bustling **night market** (5.30-10pm Wed). Throughout the year, eating a bratwurst on Saturday morning while listening to the thigh-slapping musicians outside the deli is a Melbourne must.

The market offers a variety of walks – the popular two-hour **Foodies Dream tour** (☎ 9320 5835; tour A$22; 10am Tue & Thu-Sat) is a great taste-hopping exploration of the market.

CHINATOWN Map pp238–9

Red archways across either end of Little Bourke St's **Chinatown** are your gateways to clattering woks, glowing neon, exotic aromas and shops with floor-to-ceiling chambers of medicinal herbs and tinctures.

The **Museum of Chinese Australian History** (☎ 9662 2888; 22 Cohen Pl; admission A$6.50; 10am-5pm) documents Melbourne's Chinese social history, including two dragons – the retired Dai Loong (Great Dragon), and the Millennium Dragon. If you're here during Chinese New Year (February) or Moomba (March), and fancy being a dragon for a day, the museum is always looking for volunteers to hunker down and help parade the dragon through the streets. The museum also conducts two-hour walking tours (A$15) around Chinatown; bookings are essential.

BOURKE STREET MALL & AROUND Map pp238–9

The section of Bourke St between Elizabeth and Swanston Sts is a pedestrian walkway (shared with trams). The north side of the **mall** is dominated by department stores, including the old main post office which reopened as the **GPO Melbourne** shopping centre in 2004. On the south side, **Royal Arcade**, built in 1869, is Melbourne's oldest arcade; it's lined with an assortment of shops, and shelters the statues of Gog and Magog – mythical giants who've been striking the hour here since 1892.

ROYAL BOTANIC GARDENS & KINGS DOMAIN Map pp234–6

Beside St Kilda Rd, which runs along expansive **Kings Domain**, stands the imposing

TRAM IT

Trams are generally the best way to get to specific sights around town. An extensive network covers every corner of the city, running north–south and east–west along all major roads. Pick up a transport map from the Melbourne Visitor Centre (Map pp238–9) in Federation Sq.

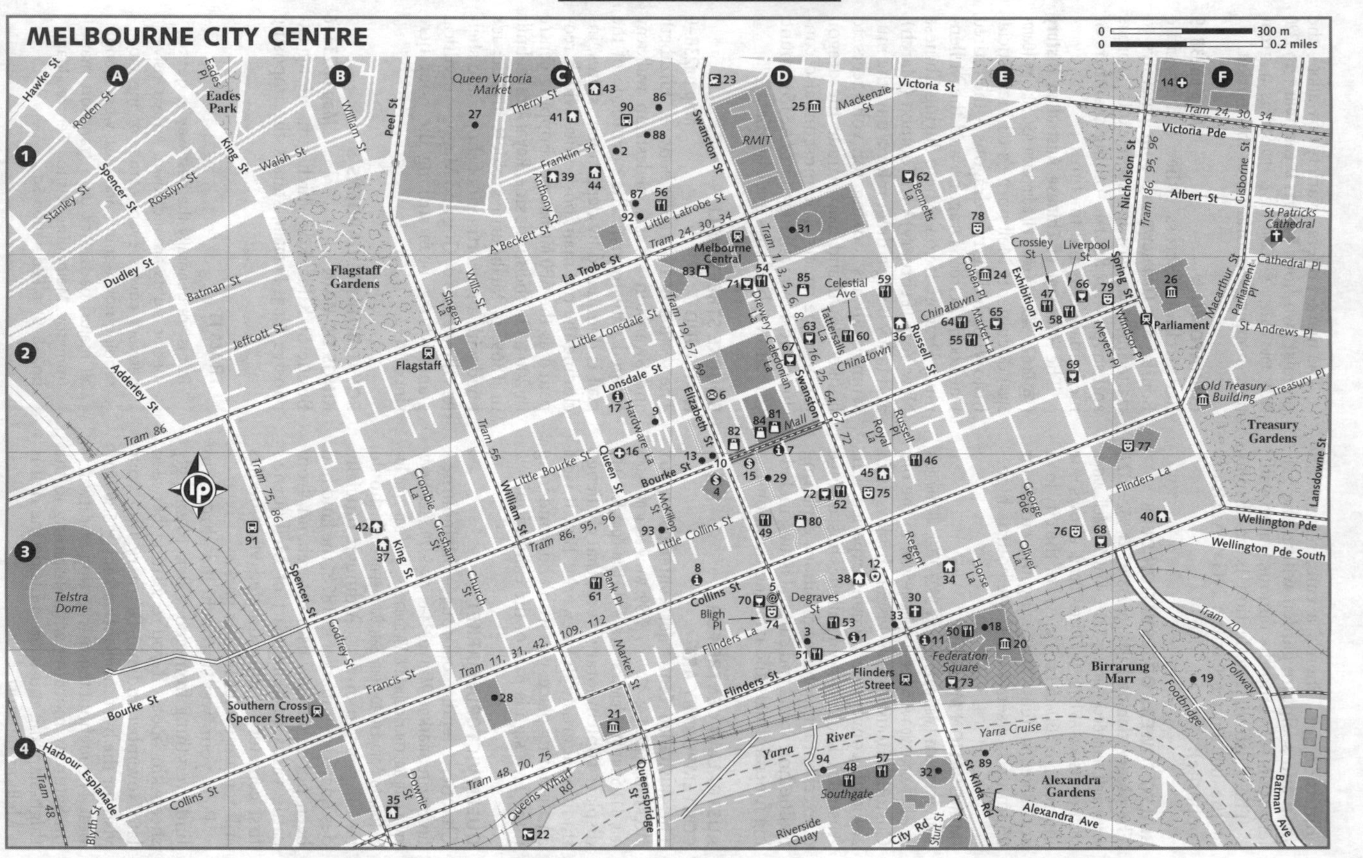
MELBOURNE CITY CENTRE
0 300 m
0 0.2 miles
Queen Victoria Market
Flagstaff Gardens
Flagstaff
Melbourne Central
Parliament
Treasury Gardens
Old Treasury Building
St Patricks Cathedral
Birrarung Marr
Alexandra Gardens
Federation Square
Flinders Street
Southern Cross (Spencer Street)
Telstra Dome
Yarra River
Southgate
Riverside Quay
RMIT
Eades Park
Eades Pl
Chinatown
Footbridge
Tollway
Yarra Cruise
Spencer St
King St
William St
Queen St
Elizabeth St
Swanston St
Swanston Mall
Russell St
Exhibition St
Spring St
Nicholson St
Victoria Pde
Victoria St
Peel St
La Trobe St
Little Lonsdale St
Lonsdale St
Little Bourke St
Bourke St
Little Collins St
Collins St
Flinders La
Flinders St
Wellington Pde
Wellington Pde South
Batman Ave
Alexandra Ave
St Kilda Rd
City Rd
Queensbridge St
Market St
Harbour Esplanade
Adderley St
Dudley St
Batman St
Jeffcott St
Rosslyn St
Hawke St
Roden St
Stanley St
Walsh St
Franklin St
Therry St
A'Beckett St
Little Latrobe St
Albert St
Gisborne St
Macarthur St
Parliament Pl
Cathedral Pl
St Andrews Pl
Treasury Pl
Lansdowne St
Godfrey St
Francis St
Downie St
Church St
Gresham St
Crombie La
McKillop St
Bank Pl
Hardware La
Degraves St
Bligh Pl
Regent Pl
Horse La
Oliver La
George Pde
Royal La
Russell Pl
Bennetts La
Celestial Ave
Tattersalls La
Drewery La
Caledonian La
Cohen Pl
Market La
Crossley St
Liverpool St
Windsor Pl
Meyers Pl
Mackenzie St
Wills St
Singers La
Anthony St
Queens Wharf Rd
Sturt St
Blyth St
Tram 86
Tram 48
Tram 55
Tram 70
Tram 75, 86
Tram 19, 57, 59
Tram 24, 30, 34
Tram 86, 95, 96
Tram 11, 31, 42, 109, 112
Tram 48, 70, 75
Tram 1, 3, 5, 6, 8, 16, 25, 64, 67, 72
A B C D E F
1 2 3 4

INFORMATION

Backpackers Travel Centre ... 1 D3
Backpackers World ... 2 C1
City Basement Books ... 3 D3
Commonwealth Bank ... 4 D3
e:fiftyfive ... 5 D3
General Post Office ... 6 D2
Information Booth ... 7 D2
Information Victoria ... 8 D3
Map Land ... 9 C2
McGills ... 10 D3
Melbourne Visitor Centre ... 11 E3
Police Station ... 12 D3
Poste Restante ... 13 D3
St Vincent's Hospital ... 14 F1
Thomas Cook ... 15 D3
Travellers' Medical & Vaccination Centre ... 16 C2
YHA Travel ... 17 C2

SIGHTS & ACTIVITIES (pp233–41)

AFL Hall of Fame ... (see 85)
Australian Centre for the Moving Image ... 18 E3
Federation Bells ... 19 F4
Ian Potter Centre: NGV Australia ... 20 E3
Immigration Museum ... 21 C4
Melbourne Aquarium ... 22 C4
Melbourne City Baths ... 23 D1
Museum of Chinese Australian History ... 24 E2
Old Melbourne Gaol ... 25 D1
Parliament House ... 26 F2
Queen Victoria Market ... 27 C1
Rialto Towers Observation Deck ... 28 C4
Royal Arcade ... 29 D3
St Paul's Cathedral ... 30 E3
State Library of Victoria ... 31 D1
Victorian Arts Centre ... 32 E4
Young & Jackson's ... 33 E3

SLEEPING (pp247–8)

Adelphi Hotel ... 34 E3
All Nations ... 35 B4
Exford Hotel ... 36 E2
Friendly Backpacker ... 37 B3
Greenhouse Backpackers ... 38 D3
Hotel Bakpak ... 39 C1
Hotel Lindrum ... 40 F3
Hotel Y ... 41 C1
Melbourne Connection Travellers Hostel ... 42 B3
Stork Hotel ... 43 C1
Toad Hall ... 44 C1
Victoria Hotel ... 45 D3

EATING (pp250–1)

Basso ... 46 E3
Becco ... 47 E2
Blue Train Cafe ... 48 D4
Cafe Segovia ... 49 D3
Chocolate Buddha ... 50 E3
Coles Express ... 51 D4
Crossways ... 52 D3
Degraves Espresso Bar ... 53 D3
Don Don Japanese Cafe ... 54 D2
Flower Drum ... 55 E2
Kimchi House ... 56 C1
Mecca ... 57 D4
Pellegrini's ... 58 E2
Stalactites ... 59 D2
Supper Inn ... 60 D2
Syracuse ... 61 C3

DRINKING (pp254–5)

Bennetts Lane Jazz Club ... 62 E1
Cookie ... 63 D2
Croft Institute ... 64 E2
Ding Dong ... 65 E2
Double Happiness ... 66 E2
Hi-Fi Bar & Ballroom ... (see 52)
Lounge ... 67 D2
Phoenix ... 68 E3
Pony ... 69 E2
Robot ... 70 D3
Rue Bebelons ... 71 D2
Tony Starr's Kitten Club ... 72 D3
Transport ... 73 E4

ENTERTAINMENT (pp256–9)

Green Room ... 74 D3
Half-Tix ... 75 D3
Honkytonks ... 76 E3
Kino Dendy ... 77 F2
Lumiere ... 78 E1
Metro Nightclub ... 79 E2

SHOPPING (p259)

Australia on Collins ... 80 D3
David Jones ... 81 D2
GPO Melbourne ... 82 D2
Melbourne Central ... 83 D2
Myer ... 84 D2
QV ... 85 D2

TRANSPORT (pp259–60)

Avis ... 86 C1
Budget ... 87 C1
Hertz ... 88 C1
Hire A Bike ... 89 E4
Melbourne Transit Centre ... 90 C1
Skybus to Airport ... (see 91)
Southern Cross Coach Terminal ... 91 B3
Thrifty ... 92 C1

OTHER

Haunted Melbourne Ghost Tour ... 93 C3
Melbourne River Cruises ... 94 D4

Shrine of Remembrance (10am-5pm), built as a memorial to Victorians killed in WWI. It's worth climbing to the balcony for fine views.

Near the shrine is **La Trobe's Cottage** (☎ 9654 5528; admission A$2.20; 11am-4pm Mon, Wed, Sat & Sun), the original Victorian government house that was sent out from the 'mother country' in prefabricated form in 1839. Its replacement is the imposing **Government House** (☎ 9654 5528; Government House Dr; admission A$11; guided tours Mon & Wed), built to house the governor (Queen's representative). Victoria's current governor, Mr Landy, could be the last if the present push for a republic gains momentum. Admission is by appointment only via one of the guided tours.

The **Royal Botanic Gardens** (www.rbg.vic.gov.au; Birdwood Ave; admission free; 7.30am-8.30pm Nov-Mar, to 5.30pm or 6pm Apr-Oct) form a corner of the Kings Domain. Next to the **Old Melbourne Observatory** is the **visitors centre** (☎ 9252 2429; 9am-5pm Mon-Fri, 10am-5.30pm Sat & Sun), where you can book tours, including Aboriginal heritage walks (A$16).

The beautifully designed gardens feature mini ecosystems set amid vast lawns. Take a book, a picnic or a Frisbee; most importantly, take your time. The gardens sprawl alongside the Yarra and are surrounded by a former horse-exercising track known as the **Tan** (4km), now favoured by joggers.

OLD MELBOURNE GAOL

Displays in the tiny cells of the **gaol and museum** (Map pp238-9; ☎ 9663 7228; Russell St; admission A$13; 9am-5pm) tell stories from the grim old days. Death masks of some of the 100 people hanged here are testimony to the 'science' of the day, which attempted to understand the criminal mind by studying the shape of the head. **Night tours** (tour A$20; 7.30pm & 8.30pm Wed & Fri-Sun), led by the ghost of a gaoler, ham up the facts – book the tours through **Ticketek** (☎ 13 28 49).

PARLIAMENT HOUSE

Australia's first federal parliament sat at this imposing public building from 1901 before moving to Canberra in 1927. Gun slits are visible just below the roof (although they've never been used), and the dungeon is now the cleaners' tearoom. **Parliament House** (Map pp238-9; www.parliament.vic.gov.au; Spring St) is open on weekdays, with regular free **tours** (☎ 9651 8568) when parliament is not in session; ask about the mystery of the stolen ceremonial mace that disappeared from the lower house in 1891 – rumour has it ending up in a brothel. When parliament is in session you can watch proceedings from the public galleries.

VICTORIAN ARTS CENTRE

A major player in Melbourne's cultural life, the **Arts Centre** (Map pp238-9; ☎ 9281 8000; www.vicartscentre.com.au; 100 St Kilda Rd, Southgate) is made up of two buildings: Hamer Hall and the Theatres Building. **Hamer Hall** (🕒 1½hr before performances), the city's official concert hall, is mostly below ground – its décor is inspired by Australia's mineral and gemstone deposits. The **Theatres Building** (🕒 9am-11pm Mon-Sat, 10am-5pm Sun) wears the centre's distinctive spire. It houses a number of theatres, plus two free galleries.

STATE LIBRARY OF VICTORIA

Retreat from the weather into the sedate **state library** (Map pp234-6; ☎ 8664 7000; www.slv.vic.gov.au; 328 Swanston St; 🕒 10am-9pm Mon-Thu, to 6pm Fri-Sun) where you'll find the impressive domed Reading Room, and lose yourself in one of the million books in the library's collection.

MELBOURNE CRICKET GROUND & AROUND — Map pp234–6

The **Melbourne Cricket Ground** (MCG; www.mcg.org.au; Brunton Ave) is one of the world's great sporting venues. It's best visited with about 60,000 other spectators during a footy match (see p257). Understandably, attendance numbers have risen since the first game was played here in 1858. The first Test cricket match between Australia and England was also played here in 1877, and it was the main stadium for the 1956 Olympic Games.

'The G' (as it's also known) underwent a major overhaul in 2004 in preparation for the 2006 Commonwealth Games. You can take a **tour** (☎ 9657 8879; A$10; 🕒 10am-3pm on nonevent days), which is the only way you get to stand on the hallowed turf – unless you're considering a career in football or cricket.

The MCG is the heart of Yarra Park, Melbourne's sporting precinct. Yarra Park encompasses a number of ovals and arenas, including **Melbourne Park (National Tennis Centre)**, **Olympic Park** and **Rod Laver Arena**.

FITZROY GARDENS — Map pp234–6

A few sights are dotted among the elm-lined avenues, expansive lawns and giant trees of **Fitzroy Gardens** (www.fitzroygardens.com; Wellington Pde). **Cook's Cottage** (☎ 9419 4677; admission A$3.70; 🕒 9am-5pm) is believed to be the Yorkshire family home of Captain James Cook, who was credited with 'discovering' Australia. The nearby **Conservatory** (🕒 9am-5pm; admission free) bursts with five floral displays every year.

You'll probably meet some possums in the gardens after dark. As cute as the little darlings are, too many possums in too small an area have caused serious damage to some trees – look out for the sheet-metal collars that prevent the possums from climbing threatened trees. The rangers recommend that you don't feed the possums.

SOUTHGATE

The **Southgate complex** (Map pp238–9), on the south bank of the Yarra, houses three levels of restaurants, cafés and bars, all of which enjoy a fabulous outlook over the river and cityscape. There's an international food hall on the ground floor, as well as retail outlets.

You can take a boat cruise from Berth 1 with **Penguin Waters Cruises** (☎ 9645 0533; 2hr cruise A$55; 🕒 sunset) to see a penguin colony. The cruise includes an on-board barbecue.

CROWN ENTERTAINMENT COMPLEX

Crown Complex (Map pp234-6; ☎ 9292 8888; www.crowncasino.com.au; Southbank) could be labelled with many an adjective, but subtle certainly wouldn't be one of them. The sprawling complex includes the luxury Crown Towers Hotel, a giant cinema complex, nightclubs, restaurants, high-end boutiques, the obligatory Planet Hollywood…oh yes, and a casino, clad in gold leaf and glitz. The casino promises that your ticket to Broadway will pop out of the machine at any moment, if only you'll just keep trying.

MELBOURNE AQUARIUM

On the north side of the river, the **Melbourne Aquarium** (Map pp238-9; ☎ 9620 0999; cnr Queens Wharf Rd & King St; adult/concession A$22/14; 🕒 9.30am-6pm) is the best way to see sharks – with thick glass between you and them. The jellyfish tanks, coral atoll and a simulated billabong with intermittent rain above it are other highlights. Not so impressive are the exorbitant entrance fees, and overall feel of the place, which fails to evoke the beauty and mystery of the deep.

DOCKLANDS **Map pp234–6**

Near the rear of Southern Cross (Spencer St) Station on Spencer St, **Docklands** (☎ 1300 663 008; www.docklands.vic.gov.au) is the city's most recent major development. It comprises residential apartment towers, film studios, shopping complexes and a number of dining options and public spaces. It was the city's main industrial docking area until the mid-1970s, and a Koorie hunting ground for centuries before that. It's intended that development at Docklands will continue into the next decade – much of it will follow the Commonwealth Games in 2006. **NewQuay** is the drinking and dining precinct, and **Telstra Dome** (☎ 8625 7700; www.telstradome.com.au) the venue for sport, with AFL games played here weekly during the season.

Carlton & Parkville **Map pp234–6**

There are two major influences in **Carlton**: the Italian community and the University of Melbourne (established in 1853). Carlton's backbone, Lygon St, was one of Melbourne's original bohemian streets, and some unpretentious restaurants and outlets can still be found at the Elgin St end – away from the touting tourist trattorias nearer town. The **Lygon St Festa** celebrates the area's Italian heritage with a street party every November. Tram No 1 running along Swanston St gets you to Carlton from the city centre, or you can stroll north up Russell St.

Parkville has one of the city's more unusual mixes of residents: exotic animals and world-class athletes. Melbourne's largest parkland, Royal Park, houses its furry and feathered residents in Melbourne Zoo. These critters are set to be joined by around 6000 athletes and officials, with the establishment of the Commonwealth Games Athletes Village in Royal Park.

MELBOURNE MUSEUM

Opened amid controversy due to its location (away from the city's other cultural institutions), design (see for yourself), and aims (theme park–styled interactive displays and sets with gizmos galore) is Melbourne's **museum** (Map pp234-6; ☎ 13 11 02; www.melbourne.museum.vic.gov.au; Carlton Gardens, 11 Nicholson St, Carlton; admission A$6; 🕐 10am-5pm). There's everything here from Bunjilaka (the museum's exceptional Aboriginal centre) to a living forest gallery to the kitchen sink of 26 Ramsay St (from *Neighbours*, if you're not one of the 120 million who watch it daily). The Australian Gallery has a room dedicated to legendary racehorse Phar Lap, which includes his taxidermied hide.

ROYAL PARK

The once-mammoth reservation of **Royal Park** (Map pp234-6; Royal Pde), established in the 1870s, has been eroded over the years by sports ovals, stadiums, a public golf course, Melbourne Zoo and a Commonwealth Games village (the latter due for completion by 2006). In the corner closest to the University of Melbourne is a garden of Australian native plants.

MELBOURNE ZOO

Laying claim to being Australia's oldest zoo (1862), **Melbourne Zoo** (☎ 9285 9300; www.zoo.org.au; Elliott Ave, Parkville; adult/concession A$18/13.50; 🕐 9am-5pm) is a great place to visit. Love or hate zoos, few could deny that Melbourne's has some of the most sympathetic enclosures in the world, and a progressive take on animal welfare. Don't miss 'Bugs & Butterflies', a walk-through tropical enclosure aflutter with native butterflies. It's right by the bug collection, where you can get up close to giant burrowing cockroaches or infamous redback spiders. The collection of better-known Australian animals is also fabulous; the long-flight aviary's a definite plus; and the zoo's elephants have a long-awaited new enclosure. From the city, take tram No 55 from William St (Monday to Saturday), No 68 from Elizabeth St (Sunday), or the Upfield-line train to Royal Park train station.

THE VEGEMITE LEGEND

Open any cupboard in any Melbourne suburb – nay, any Australian suburb – and you'll find a jar of iconic black goo. **Vegemite** (www.vegemite.com.au) was 'discovered' in Melbourne at the Fred Walker Cheese Company in 1922, made from leftover brewer's yeast (used to create beer). This distinctive vegetable-extract spread is no longer Australian owned, but it's no less loved by Australians.

Fitzroy

Map pp234–6

Fitzroy has Melbourne's highest density of cafés, restaurants, bars, galleries and eclectic shops. It contains pockets of the city's highest and lowest income earners, as well as ethnic communities from around the globe. This mix of people interacts with remarkable aplomb. There's a genuine community in Fitzroy, where coffee is the social lubricant and paradoxes abound – the most pronounced being that convention is unconventional.

A 20m slice of **Brunswick St** contains: a pub, five cafés, a perfumery, a bookshop, a hairdresser, a bar and a clothing boutique with a busker camped out the front. It's a frenetic strip of establishments dedicated entirely to dispensable living. Catch tram No 112 from Collins St to get here.

Johnston St is the centre of Melbourne's Latin quarter, with tapas bars, the Spanish club and Hispanic Festival street party in November.

To see what Melbourne artists have to say for themselves, head to **Gertrude St**, with its cluster of contemporary galleries and incumbent bars and cafés.

Glamour-free **Smith St** is the business end of Fitzroy: it's where you'll find the banks and supermarkets. It also has its fair share of drinking dens, Asian and vegetarian stores, cafés, cutting-edge designer boutiques and op shops.

Richmond

This densely packed neighbourhood is one out of the bag. Sandwiched between the city and the Yarra River, it contains pockets of semi-industrial streetscapes, a thriving Vietnamese community and tracts of tranquil bushland.

Victoria St, between Church and Hoddle Sts, is the place to come for the best bowl of *pho* (beef noodle soup) outside of Vietnam. Melburnians cram around tightly spaced tables to fill up on authentic Vietnamese fare for around A$10, every night of the week; tram No 42 or 109 from Collins St gets you here.

Bridge Rd is a mecca for off-the-rack bargain shoppers; a large number of clothing retailers have their factory outlets and seconds' stores between Punt Rd and Church St. Once Bridge Rd crosses Church St, the pace slows a little to accommodate cafés, and new and used furniture stores. Take tram No 48 or 75 from Flinders St to get to Bridge Rd.

Swan St is a hotchpotch of food outlets, retailers and pubs. Its proximity to the MCG (p240) sees thousands trek along here on match days, seeking a post-game ale and a sympathetic ear to dissect the day's play.

FITZROY GALLERY HOP

Entry to the following galleries (all on Map pp234–6) is free; all can be visited on an extended stroll. Opening hours are generally from 11am to 5.30pm Tuesday to Friday and between 1pm and 5pm on Saturday.

Start at **Dianne Tanzer Gallery** (☎ 9416 3956; www.diannetanzergallery.net.au; 108 Gertrude St), which showcases emerging artists. **Intrude** (☎ 9417 6033; www.intrudegallery.com.au; 122 Gertrude St) is next. **Seventh** (☎ 0407-112 482; 155 Gertrude St) is an artist-run space with a new show every two weeks. Cross back to the always-exciting **Gertrude Contemporary Art Spaces** (☎ 9419 3406; www.gertrude.org.au; 200 Gertrude St). **Australian Print Workshop** (☎ 9419 5466; www.australianprintworkshop.com; 210 Gertrude St) is the longest-running public-access print workshop in Victoria, and has a collection of individually editioned prints by Australian artists.

Turn right at Smith St to the artist-run **69 Smith** (☎ 9432 0795; www.vicnet.net.au/~smith69; 69 Smith St), followed by **Charles Smith** (☎ 9419 0880; www.charlessmithgallery.com.au; 65 Smith St) and **Australian Galleries: Works on Paper** (☎ 9417 0800; 50 Smith St), representing established contemporary artists.

Double back down Smith St and turn left into Johnston St for a look-in at the artist-run **Conical Inc** (☎ 9415 6958; www.conical.org.au; 3 Rochester St), and the **Centre for Contemporary Photography** (☎ 9417 1549; www.ccp.org.au; 404 George St; admission by donation) on the opposite side of Johnston St. A left from Johnston St into Brunswick St will take you to **Sutton Gallery** (☎ 9416 0727; www.suttongallery.com.au; 254 Brunswick St) – a quality commercial space. Then it must be about time for a coffee.

The major hub of Richmond train station is on Swan St.

YARRA BEND PARK

Yarra Bend's large areas of bushland are an inner-city oasis, much loved by runners, rowers, cyclists, picnickers and strollers. The park is a short walk along Gipps St from Collingwood train station.

The **Studley Park Boathouse** (☎ 9853 1972; Boathouse Rd, Kew; 🕓 9am-5pm) has a café, and rowing boats and canoes for hire (A$22 per hour for two people); bring photo ID. Kanes footbridge takes you across to the other side of the river, from where it's about a 20-minute walk to **Dights Falls** at the confluence of the Yarra River and Merri Creek. You can also walk to the falls along the southern bank. Bus Nos 200, 201 or 207 from Lonsdale St in the city will drop you a short walk away from the boathouse.

South Yarra, Toorak & Prahran

Welcome to the 'right' side of the river, to the wealthy playgrounds of the bronzed and beautiful. **Toorak** is Melbourne's poshest suburb, where mansions abound and there's an exclusive cluster of shops (known as Toorak Village) along Toorak Rd.

The **South Yarra** end of Toorak Rd is an eclectic mix of shops focused squarely on the grooming industry, from laundries and top-range designer gear (for 40-plus shoppers), to spray-on-tan salons. Tram No 8 from Swanston St in the city takes you along Toorak Rd. Chapel St, between Toorak Rd and Commercial Rd, is where it all happens, darlings. This is where mainstream, style-conscious die-hards flock – it's virtually wall-to-wall clothing boutiques (with a healthy sprinkling of bars, and cafés for latte lovers) – and a great place for people-watching. It's worth taking a wander if you have the time.

The **Prahran** section of Chapel St stretches from Commercial Rd down to Dandenong Rd, becoming grungier with each step away from groomed South Yarra. Prahran has a delightful mix of influences, with a range of ethnic and economic backgrounds all vying for a piece of the action behind charming, if oft-neglected, Art Deco and Victorian shopfronts. Commercial Rd is something of a hub for Melbourne's gay and lesbian community, and has a collection of nightclubs, bars, bookshops and cafés. See Out in Queer Melbourne, (p246) for some of the gay-friendly entertainment options along this strip. You'll also find some of Melbourne's best produce at Prahran Market. Greville St, running off Chapel St beside the Prahran Town Hall, is the area's shopping alternative, with a fabulous assembly of retro, grunge and designer boutiques and bookshops, and some lively bars and cafés.

CAMBERWELL MARKET

A few suburbs east of Toorak is the conservative suburb of Camberwell, where we're sure the overwhelming majority of the population wears twin-sets and pearls. It's also where you'll find the city's best flea market. Serious gleaners fall out of bed before dawn every Sunday to search for treasures by torchlight. It's open from 6am to noon, but six hours is hardly enough time to pick through mounds of Barbie-doll heads, old LPs, '50s clothes, cutlery, tools and photo frames. You'll find the market in the car park off Fairholm Grove, tucked in behind Burke Rd. Take a train from the city to Camberwell station on the Alamein, Belgrave or Lilydale lines.

HERRING ISLAND

Just 3km from the city, **Herring Island** (http://home.vicnet.net.au/~herring) features native gardens that provide a natural habitat for birds and other animals. It's also the site for environmental sculptures created by eminent artists from Australia and abroad. To get here, **Parks Victoria** (☎ 13 19 63; www.parkweb.vic.gov.au; fare A$2) operates a boat on weekends from Como Landing on Alexandra Ave in South Yarra. It runs between noon and 5pm from October to March.

St Kilda

Map p244

St Kilda is Melbourne's celebrity good-time suburb: its lush seaside surrounds are constantly in the limelight, it's home to conspicuous consumption and host to innumerable public parties, and it has a reputation for its seamier side.

The suburb was once a fashionable seaside resort. It entered a gradual decline and by the 1960s was downright seedy. Its cheap rents and faded glory attracted immigrants and refugees, bohemians and down-and-outers.

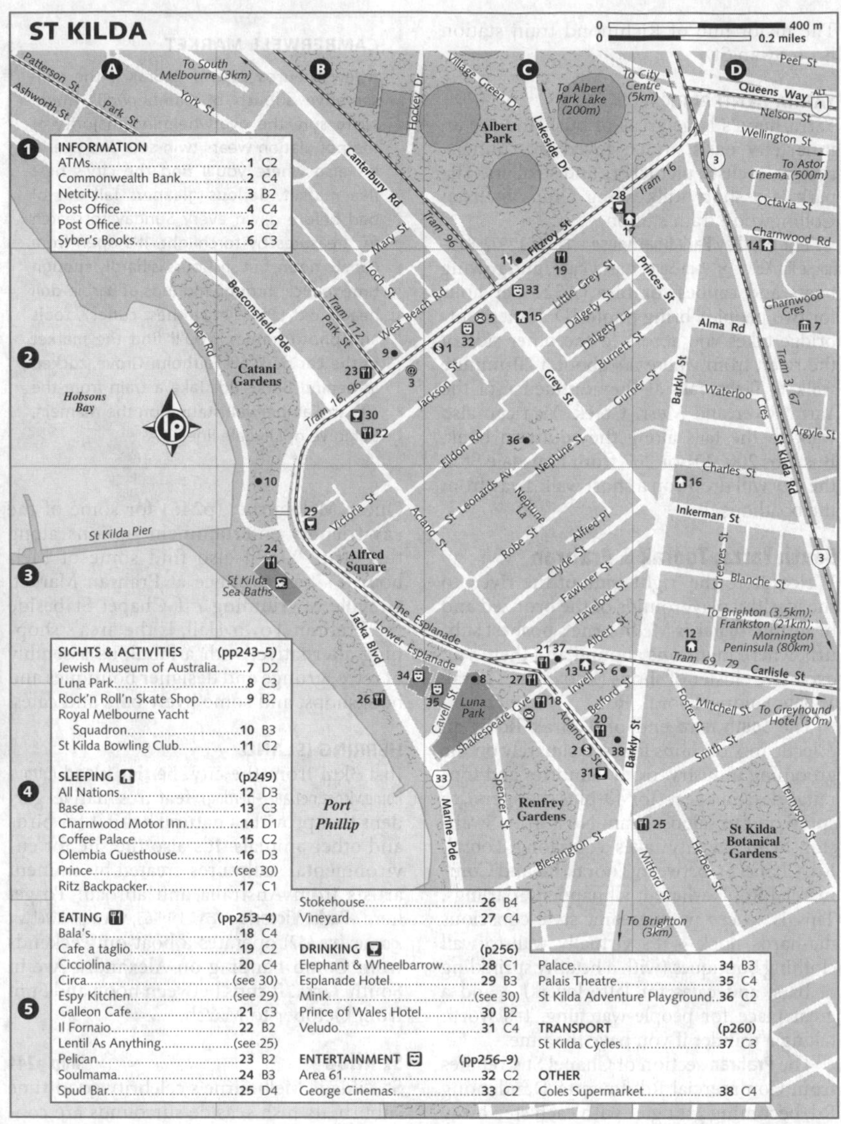

Since the '90s it's undergone an image upgrade, although it's still a place of extremes, with backpacker hostels and fine-dining restaurants, sports cars and street workers.

The idyllic **Albert Park Lake** sprawls just north of one of St Kilda's main streets – **Fitzroy St**. This street is densely packed with bars, clubs and restaurants, and leads down to the postcard-pretty, palm-lined **foreshore**. **St Kilda Pier** is a favoured spot to soak up the city and bay views. **The Esplanade** follows the horizon line to **Acland St** – the strip of the latter street between Carlisle and Barkly Sts is famed for Continental cake shops, delicatessens, and older-style central-European cafés and restaurants. The fun of Acland St starts at the laughing face of **Luna Park** (☎ 1902 240 112; Lower Esplanade; ⏰ 7-11pm Fri, 11am-11pm Sat, to 6pm Sun). A symbol of St Kilda since 1912, Luna Park's old-world charm is best experienced from the heritage-listed roller-coaster ride. Single-ride tickets cost A$7.

If you follow **Carlisle St** across St Kilda Rd and into East St Kilda, you'll stumble onto a hectic shopping strip dominated by European-style delis, kosher food outlets and a number of hip cafés and bars.

Tram No 16 runs down St Kilda Rd to Fitzroy and Acland Sts, as does No 96, from Spencer St. No 67 runs further down St Kilda Rd, intersecting with Carlisle St.

Williamstown & Around

This historic seafaring town is full steam ahead on sunny afternoons, its pavements packed with café-dwellers enjoying stellar views over Hobsons Bay to the city. Williamstown was the bay's main seaport until the Yarra River was deepened and the Port of Melbourne developed in the 1880s. Bypassed and forgotten for years, Williamstown has been rediscovered and is especially popular with day-trippers on weekends.

Arriving by boat at Gem Pier is a fitting way to visit; see p261 for details. **Nelson Pl** follows the foreshore and is lined with historic terraces. The **visitors centre** (☎ 9397 3791; cnr Syme St & Nelson Pl; ⏰ 9am-5pm) sells a great *Heritage Walks* booklet (A$6). **Williamstown Beach**, on the south side of the peninsula, is pleasant for a swim; from Nelson Pl turn into Coles St, go to the end and turn right.

SCIENCEWORKS MUSEUM & MELBOURNE PLANETARIUM

Under the shadow of the Westgate Bridge, the **Scienceworks Museum & Melbourne Planetarium** (☎ 9392 4800; 2 Booker St, Spotswood; admission A$6, incl Planetarium show A$12; ⏰ 10am-4.30pm) offers hands-on gadgets – they're popular with kids, if they can elbow out the dads. The planetarium is a must-see journey through the night sky illustrated on a 15m domed ceiling; shows start at noon, 1pm, 2pm and 3pm. The museum is a 15-minute walk down Hudsons Rd from Spotswood train station, or you can also arrive by ferry (see p261).

ACTIVITIES

Buy yourself a Frisbee or a footy and head to one of the city's parks or gardens. If you're feeling a little more energetic, Melbourne's flat landscape and temperate weather make cycling a perfect way to get out and see the city; see p260. Or you could try one of the following.

In-Line Skating

The best and most popular tracks follow the shoreline from Port Melbourne to Brighton. You can hire from places like **Rock'n Roll'n Skate Shop** (Map p244; ☎ 9525 3434; 22 Fitzroy St, St Kilda) for A$8 for the first hour, less per hour for subsequent hours.

Lawn Bowls

Bowling clubs have opened their doors to nonmembers in the last few years and are gaining a wave of youthful followers. These new proponents of lawn bowls appreciate the social atmosphere, and that you can play in bare feet with a drink in one hand. **St Kilda Bowling Club** (Map p244; ☎ 9537 0370; 66 Fitzroy St, St Kilda; ⏰ noon-sunset Tue-Sun) provides bowls and some friendly instruction for first-timers for between A$5 and A$10.

Sailing

Hobson's Bay Yacht Club (☎ 9397 6393; www.hbyc.asn.au; 268 Nelson Pl, Williamstown) welcomes volunteers Saturday and Sunday. You can join a boat with the **Royal Melbourne Yacht Squadron** (Map p244; ☎ 9534 0227; Pier Rd, St Kilda) from Wednesday to Sunday in summer (A$11).

Swimming

The bay beaches are hotspots during summer, but public pools near the city include the following:

Fitzroy Swimming Pool (Map pp234-6; ☎ 9417 6493; cnr Alexandra Pde & Young St, Fitzroy; ⏰ Nov-Mar) Swim in the 50m outdoor pool for A$3.80.

Melbourne City Baths (Map pp238-9; ☎ 9663 5888; 420 Swanston St, Melbourne) Swim in the 25m indoor pool for A$4; the baths first opened in 1860 to deter Melburnians from bathing in the then seriously polluted Yarra River.

Melbourne Sports and Aquatic Centre (☎ 9926 1555; Aughtie Dr, Albert Park Lake) Swim here for A$5.50; it also has a super wave pool.

Prahran Aquatic Centre (☎ 8290 7140; Essex St, Prahran; ⏰ Oct-Mar) Swim in the 50m outdoor pool with music piped under water for A$3.50.

TOURS

Melbourne has a diverse range of quality tours on hand. The free *Melbourne Events*

OUT IN QUEER MELBOURNE

Melbourne's gay scene enjoys a relaxed, unfussy atmosphere.

To stay up-to-date with what's on, tune in to **JOY FM** (www.joy.org.au; 94.9FM), or pick up one of the local street-press publications: **Melbourne Community Voice** (www.mcv.net.au) and **Bnews** (www.bnews.net.au) are available from cafés and bars around town.

The **ALSO Foundation** (☎ 9827 4999; www.also.org.au) organises some of the hottest dance parties. Its website contains a services directory, which is also available in print at **Hares & Hyenas Bookshop** (☎ 9824 0110; 135 Commercial Rd, South Yarra).

Following are a few venues worth checking out:

Gay Trade Bar (Map pp234–6; ☎ 9417 6700; 9 Peel St, Collingwood; admission free) Relax at this all-week venue, with themed cheap-drinks nights like 'toss the boss', and professional bar dancers.

Glasshouse Hotel (☎ 9419 4748; 51 Gipps St, Collingwood; admission free-A$10) Like some of the girls propped up at the bar, this venue is the mainstay of the fickle lesbian scene. Pick-ups and pool cues are all the rage.

Peel Hotel (☎ 9419 4762; cnr Peel & Wellington Sts, Collingwood; admission Fri & Sat A$10 after 10pm) An infamous institution (where an enormous phallus used to hang over the main bar), the Peel now lets the 'average' guy do his own thing on the dance floor.

Xchange Hotel (☎ 9867 5144; 119 Commercial Rd, South Yarra; admission A$5-8) Boy-band drop-out meets senior sleaze in this popular pub/Internet/video/TV/pole-dancing venue. Something for everyone makes the Xchange worth a visit.

Justine Dalla Riva

guide comes out monthly. It's available from the Melbourne Visitor Centre and has a comprehensive list of tours.

River Cruises

Melbourne River Cruises (Map pp238-9; ☎ 9614 1215; www.melbcruises.com.au; adult/concession from A$17/14) offers a choice of hourly cruises running up or down the Yarra, or a combination of both. A ticket booth is located at Berths 5 and 6 at Southgate. It also ferries to Williamstown (p245), through the city's shipping channels.

Tram Tours

Tour the town for nix on the **City Circle** tram. Every 12 minutes or so between 10am and 6pm, the burgundy-and-gold trams loop anticlockwise along Flinders, Spring and La Trobe Sts to Footscray Rd (near Docklands), and then back along Flinders St.

Walking Tours

The **Capital City Trail** is a 29km self-guided cycling/jogging/walking track encircling the city, linking major parks and providing access to just about everything good in inner Melbourne. The track starts and finishes at Southbank; pick up a brochure from the Melbourne Visitor Centre at Federation Square and follow the identifiable plaques (see p260 for bike hire).

The **Royal Botanic Gardens** (p237) offers various walking tours, including an Aboriginal heritage walk. The **Museum of Chinese Australian History** (p237) offers walks around Chinatown, and the **Queen Victoria Market** (p237) has a cracker Foodies Dream tour, among others.

Hear the call of Melbourne's restless souls on a **Haunted Melbourne Ghost Tour** (Map pp238-9; ☎ 9670 2585; www.haunted.com.au; 15 McKillop St; adult/concession A$20/18) – visiting the buildings and sites that they allegedly haunt. The tour starts at 8pm each Saturday and runs for two hours. Bookings are essential.

If you want to focus on just one food group (the most important one – chocolate), there's a chocolate walking tour. Every Saturday, Suzie Wharton of **Chocoholic Tours** (☎ 9815 1228, 0412-158 017; www.chocoholictours.com.au; 2hr tours A$28) takes groups through Melbourne's historic laneways and arcades and into chocolate havens (with plenty of samples to eat along the way – you'll end up staggering back to your hostel). Bookings are required.

FESTIVALS & EVENTS

Melburnians like any excuse for a knees-up. 'What's-on' lists are available from the Melbourne Visitor Centre and its website (www.thatsmelbourne.com.au). See p257 for ticketing information.

January

Australia Day (26 January) Celebrated with everything from an Aussie barbecue to fireworks at Federation Sq.

Big Day Out (26 January; www.bigdayout.com) Nearly 40,000 revellers go off to over 40 international and Australian alternative rock bands.

February

Midsumma Gay & Lesbian Festival (www.midsumma.org.au) Features the Red Raw rave and Pride March.

Chinese New Year Chinatown becomes a sea of activity.

St Kilda Festival (www.stkildafestival.com.au) Imagine 350,000 people in less than 1 sq km and you've got the biggest free music festival in Australia, a manic one-day riot of music, arts, nosh and beer.

March

Melbourne Moomba Festival (www.melbourne.vic.gov.au) A free four-day family event; water-skiing along the Yarra is a major component. Don't miss the Birdman Rally, where people jump into the Yarra in home-made flying contraptions.

Australian Formula One Grand Prix (www.grandprix.com.au) Held at the Albert Park circuit.

Melbourne Food & Wine Festival (www.melbfoodwinefest.com.au) Enjoy lunch with 999 other diners at one of the festival's highlights, the 'World's Longest Lunch'.

April

Melbourne International Comedy Festival (www.comedyfestival.com.au) Laughs take over the town when local jokesters are joined by a wealth of international acts.

Anzac Day (25 April) Commemorating those who died in war. The day begins with a dawn service at the Shrine of Remembrance, followed by a march along St Kilda Rd to the city.

May

St Kilda Film Festival (www.stkildafilmfestival.com.au) Showcases contemporary Australian short films, with competitors from all genres. There's a healthy cash prize for the best short film.

Next Wave (www.nextwave.org.au) Celebrating unpopular culture from the city's young, emerging artists, Next Wave runs for two weeks at venues across town.

International Jazz Festival (www.mijf.org) This event attracts a wealth of local and overseas performers.

July

Melbourne International Film Festival (www.melbournefilmfestival.com.au) This two-week festival screens the best of local and international film, and includes Q&As with filmmakers.

September

Melbourne Fringe Festival (www.melbournefringe.com.au) Celebrates left-of-centre arts – including those events not likely to make it to October's Melbourne Festival.

AFL Grand Final (www.afl.com.au) The climax of the AFL footy season is played on the last Saturday in September – it's also Melbourne's biggest day for barbecues (see if you can't get yourself invited to one).

October

Melbourne International Festival (www.melbournefestival.com.au) Held at various venues around the city, the festival brings together a programme of visual art, as well as Australian and international performers of theatre, opera, dance and music.

Lygon St Festa This Italian street party in Carlton features community soccer matches, music, food stalls and the famous waiters' race – where a caffe latte is relayed.

November

Melbourne Cup (www.vrc.net.au) This horse race is a public holiday in Victoria. On the first Tuesday of the month Melburnians don silly hats and get plastered, and virtually the whole country grinds to a standstill.

December

Test Match Cricket Beat the post-Christmas slump and head to the MCG on Boxing Day, when tens of thousands turn up for the first day of international cricket.

New Year's Eve Thousands descend on Southgate, Federation Sq and Birrarung Marr for this public party, which includes a massive fireworks display.

SLEEPING

Melbourne has loads of budget options, but during major events and festivals, beds can be scarce. It's best to book ahead, particularly during the Grand Prix in March (expect inflated prices at this time).

If you want to be right in the heart of the action, stay in the city centre. Then you're within stumbling distance of some of Melbourne's best bars and restaurants, and within walking distance of most sights. St Kilda is the perfect choice for sea breezes, pubs and café culture. Fitzroy is another great choice for Melbourne's arty scene, with cafés, restaurants and more very-Melbourne pubs than you can down a pot at.

The Youth Hostels Association (YHA) hostels have the same prices all year, but at the others you can expect to pay a little less in winter than in summer; we quote high-season prices. Most offer cheaper weekly rates.

Colleges can be a good alternative during student holidays. Expect to pay around

A$40 per person. Check the housing website of these places:

RMIT (☎ 9925 2000; www.rmit.edu.au/housing)

Medley Hall (Map pp234-6; ☎ 9663 5847; www.medleyhall.unimelb.edu.au; 48 Drummond St, Carlton) Beautiful, with a top location.

Ormond College (Map pp234-6; ☎ 9348 1688; www.ormond.unimelb.edu.au; College Cres, University of Melbourne)

Hostels & Hotels

CITY CENTRE & AROUND Map pp238–9

Greenhouse Backpackers (☎ 1800 249 207, 9639 6400; www.friendlygroup.com.au; 228 Flinders Lane; dm/s/d A$27/60/78; 💻) A fantastic location in one of the city's bustling one-way streets, the Greenhouse is a colourful, friendly and well-run operation with excellent facilities – plus there's a rooftop garden. Rooms are barren, but spick-and-span. Book ahead.

Friendly Backpacker (☎ 9670 1111; www.friendlygroup.com.au; 197 King St; dm/d A$25/80; ❄ 💻) Friendly by name, friendly by nature. A bed in a small dorm comes with a locker, immaculate shared bathroom, free Internet, hot drinks and breakfast.

Exford Hotel (☎ 9663 2697; www.exfordhotel.com.au; cnr Russell & Little Bourke Sts; dm A$20-25, d A$60; P 💻) Right by buzzing Chinatown, the Exford has a back-slapping bar that parties hard until 7am. You won't have far to crawl to the rooms in the upper section, which are no-frills but OK. Book ahead.

Toad Hall (☎ 9600 9010; www.toadhall-hotel.com.au; 441-451 Elizabeth St; dm/s/d A$25/60/70, d with bathroom A$90; P) Labyrinthine Toad Hall is quiet with clean rooms, if a tad old-fashioned and pokey. There's a pleasant shaded courtyard out the back.

Stork Hotel (☎ 9663 6237; www.storkhotel.com; 504 Elizabeth St; s/d/tr A$45/60/85) Located close to the Queen Victoria Market, this friendly old pub offers basic accommodation upstairs. The rooms are small, simple and brightly coloured, with polished floors. Facilities include a laundry and an adjoining restaurant.

Hotel Bakpak (☎ 1800 645 200, 9329 7525; www.bakpak.com/franklin; 167 Franklin St; dm A$23-26, s/d A$55/65; 💻) This massive hotel has excellent facilities, a basement bar, free brekky, a rooftop 'garden', a zillion activities organised daily and no-frills, ward-like rooms. There's free pick-up from the airport (but ring first to find out times).

All Nations (☎ 9620 1022; www.allnations.com.au; 2 Spencer St; dm A$15-24, d A$60; 💻) This huge place fosters backpacker culture with a great range of facilities, including basic breakfast, free gym use, Internet, and the obligatory heaving bar with drinking games aplenty.

Hotel Y (☎ 9329 5188; www.hotely.com.au; 489 Elizabeth St; r from A$80) The Young Women's Christian Association runs this award-winning hotel. Clearly a good choice for young women, it's also a ripper for other demographics. The 'Y' is fitted with modern facilities, including a budget café and communal kitchen and laundry, and is close to the Queen Victoria Market.

Victoria Hotel (☎ 9653 0441; www.victoriahotel.com.au; 215 Little Collins St; s/d from A$60/80) This old-timer is a city institution, offering a flexible range of comfortable accommodation in the heart of the city's designer-fashion and arts precinct.

Melbourne Connection Travellers Hostel (☎ 9642 4464; www.melbourneconnection.com; 205 King St; dm A$21-25, d A$70) This little charmer follows the small-is-better principle, offering simple, clean and uncluttered budget accommodation in an intimate setting. The hostel has a good kitchen, laundry facilities and a TV room.

SPLURGE!

Take a holiday from your travelling and spend a night in the plush surrounds of one of Melbourne's boutique hotels.

Adelphi Hotel (Map pp238-9; ☎ 9650 7555; www.adelphi.com.au; 187 Flinders Lane, Melbourne; r A$300-540; P) Chic from top to bottom, with an astounding basement restaurant, rooftop bar with city views, and famous glass-bottomed lap pool, which extends over the street.

Prince (Map p244; ☎ 9536 1111; www.theprince.com.au; 2 Acland St, St Kilda; r A$200-520; P) Oh-so-stylish, modern and elegant. Its near-perfect rooms are complemented by the Aurora Spa Retreat and C restaurant, for the ultimate in indulgence.

Hotel Lindrum (Map pp238-9; ☎ 9668 1111; www.hotellindrum.com.au; 26 Flinders St, Melbourne; r A$230-470) All class, Lindrum occupies a stand-out building overlooking Birrarung Marr and the railway line. This former pool hall is an intimate designer hotel with sleek, well-appointed rooms.

SOUTH MELBOURNE

Nomads Market Inn (Map pp234-6; ☎ 9690 2220; www.marketinn.com.au; 115 Cecil St, South Melbourne; dm A$19-23, d A$60; 💻) Within walking distance of Southgate; you may not fully appreciate your 'free beer on arrival' if you arrive early in the day, but you'll love the complimentary breakfast. Book ahead.

NORTH MELBOURNE **Map pp234–6**

Both of Melbourne's YHA hostels are in North Melbourne, 15 minutes' walk northwest of the city centre. Rates listed are for nonmembers.

Melbourne Metro YHA (☎ 9329 8599; www.yha.com.au; 78 Howard St; dm A$27-30, s/d A$65/75, with bathroom A$80/90; P 💻) Formerly known as Queensberry Hill YHA, this huge hostel is the YHA's squeaky-clean showpiece. The facilities are top-notch, with pool table, rooftop gardens and much more, but few would call it homely.

Chapman Gardens YHA Hostel (☎ 9328 3595; www.yha.com.au; 76 Chapman St; dm A$28-30; s/d A$55/65; P 💻) Consisting of mostly twin-share rooms, this option is relatively small and personal, with two communal kitchens and a subdued ambience.

FITZROY

Nunnery (Map pp234-6; ☎ 9419 8637; www.bakpak.com/nunnery; 116 Nicholson St; dm A$23-27, s A$55-65, d A$70-85; 💻) It seems old habits die fast at the Nunnery, with not a hint of lemon-lipped attitude to be seen. This fabulous place oozes atmosphere, with big comfortable lounges and communal areas. Apart from the main building there's also the Nunnery Guesthouse, which has larger rooms in a private setting (singles A$75, doubles A$100 to A$110). Book ahead. From Bourke St, catch tram No 96 to stop 13.

SOUTH YARRA & AROUND

Claremont Accommodation (☎ 9826 8000; www.hotelclaremont.com; 189 Toorak Rd; dm/s/d A$30/70/80; P 💻) Light-filled and large, Claremont offers basic, budget accommodation with shared bathrooms. Rooms are spotless and have polished floorboards. It's a short walk from South Yarra train station and tram No 8 will drop you at the doorstep.

Chapel St Backpackers (☎ 9533 6855; www.csbackpackers.com.au; 22 Chapel St, Prahran; dm A$20-26, d with bathroom A$75; 💻) This tidy place is within walking distance of South Yarra, Prahran and St Kilda. Some dorms have bathrooms, and breakfast is free. Take the Sandringham-line train to Windsor station.

RICHMOND

Richmond Hill Hotel (☎ 9428 6501; www.richmondhillhotel.com.au; 353 Church St; dm A$22, s A$45-75, d A$55-85; P 💻) This grandiose Victorian-era terrace is an excellent option. The mixed bag of rooms range from OK, if drab, dorms to good-value economy rooms; they all have shared bathrooms. In the latter category the best rooms are Nos 53, 54, 56 and 57, which all have private balconies. Book well ahead! To get here, take tram No 75 from Flinders St, and change to tram No 78 or 79, which run along Church St; get off at stop 58.

ST KILDA & AROUND **Map p244**

From Swanston St in the city, tram No 16 takes you down St Kilda Rd to Fitzroy and Acland Sts. There's also the faster light-rail service (No 96 via Spencer and Bourke Sts) to the old St Kilda train station and along Fitzroy and Acland Sts.

Coffee Palace (☎ 1800 654 098, 9534 5283; 24 Grey St; dm A$20-24, d A$60; 💻) This maze-like backpacker is in a big shambolic mansion. If you're here to party, you'll love it – there's always a pub-crawl happening. The rooftop is a bonus, too. Breakfast is included and pick-ups provided.

Ritz Backpacker (☎ 9525 3501; 169 Fitzroy St; dm A$20-23; 💻) If you plan to fall into bed after a day packed with *Neighbours* tours and rowdy drinking sessions at the Elephant & Wheelbarrow pub downstairs, then this is for you. Rooms are basic, and bathrooms are modern and clean.

Base (☎ 9536 6109; www.basebackpackers.com; 17 Carlisle St; dm A$22-28; r A$85; 💻) The most recent addition to the Base chain of accommodation, this sassy, red glass–fronted establishment opened in mid-2004. Sparkling new facilities include a bar, communal kitchen, lounge and dining areas.

Olembia Guesthouse (☎ 9537 1412; www.olembia.com.au; 96 Barkly St; dm/s/d A$24/50/78; reception 🕐 7am-1pm, 5-7pm; P) An excellent and quiet option that's more boutique hotel than hostel – it's a couples' kind of place. The rooms are quite small but well kept and comfy, and there's a good kitchen and plenty of spots to curl up with a book. Book well ahead.

All Nations (☎ 9534 0300; 32 Carlisle St; dm A$18-25; d A$80-120; reception ⏰ noon-5pm;) Cosy, clean rooms belie the ugly '70s exterior. All rooms have bathroom and TV, and there's free use of bikes and the Internet.

Charnwood Motor Inn (☎ 9525 4199; www.charnwoodmotorinn.com; 3 Charnwood Rd; s/d A$85/90; P) Ultra-daggy and a bit tired, but in a quiet, leafy street and with generous-sized rooms.

Camping & Caravan Parks

There are a few caravan and camping parks in the metropolitan area, but the following are the best two options; both are about 10km from the city.

Ashley Gardens Holiday Village (☎ 9318 6866; www.ashleygardens.com.au; 129 Ashley St, Braybrook; camp sites for 2 people A$33, cabins from A$80) A well-kept and well-equipped park with regular bus transport (No 220) to the city.

Melbourne Holiday Park (☎ 9354 3533; www.big4melb.com; 265 Elizabeth St, Coburg East; camp sites for 2 people A$28, cabins from A$67) A good runner-up to Ashley Gardens.

EATING

Melbourne is famous for the quality and the range of its dining options. The city's multiethnic make-up shines in the variety of cuisines and fusion of flavours. There's a dominant café culture, offering some of the world's best coffee. Eating in Melbourne can be as thrifty as an A$8 plate of noodles or as indulgent as a degustation menu, but is generally good value considering the high quality of produce used. Eating out is an essential Melbourne experience: don't miss St Kilda, the city centre and Fitzroy.

Central Melbourne

Melbourne is saturated with good budget eating options. You'll find them in the city's laneways and little streets, such as Centre Way and Chinatown, as well as up near the universities.

TOP FIVE BAR-CAFÉS

Loads of Melbourne's bars also do great food. If you're looking for one venue where you can eat in back-slapping surrounds, check out the following:

- **Cookie** (p255)
- **Rue Bebélons** (p255)
- **Lounge** (p255)
- **Transport** (p255)
- **Orange** (p253)

SELF-CATERING

For fresh produce, you can't go past the Queen Victoria Market (p237). **Coles Express** (Map pp238-9; ☎ 9654 3830; 2-26 Elizabeth St) has all your packaged needs.

CAFÉS

Pellegrini's (Map pp238-9; ☎ 9662 1885; 66 Bourke St; pasta A$11-13; ⏰ lunch & dinner) The clock stopped in 1950 at this fabulous espresso bar. Prop yourself up at the bar, pick from mamma's favourite pasta, pizza and risotto, and enjoy your nosh shoulder-to-shoulder with other Pellegrini's devotees. We love this place; drop in for an espresso any time of day.

Degraves Espresso Bar (Map pp238-9; ☎ 9654 1245; 23 Degraves St; dishes A$7-13; ⏰ breakfast & lunch) The rickety cinema seating and fashionable gloom make Degraves a quintessential Melbourne laneway experience. If you've overindulged in that other Melbourne laneway experience – the hip little bar with no signage – beat your hangover with poached eggs, or French toast with maple syrup, from the all-day breakfast menu.

Blue Train Café (Map pp238-9; ☎ 9696 0440; mid-level, Southgate; dishes A$6-17; ⏰ breakfast, lunch & dinner) Manic Blue Train wrote the winning formula for a popular café: great-looking staff, city views, snappy service and a never-ending menu. Stick to the pasta and wood-fired pizzas here; other meals can go off the rails (sorry) when it's packed on weekends.

Café Segovia (Map pp238-9; ☎ 9650 2373; 33 Block Pl; dishes A$8-15; ⏰ breakfast & lunch daily, dinner Mon-Sat) Segovia barely contains the number of people who stop in for a focaccia, pasta or soup. Punters spill out the door into the laneway, merging with patrons from neighbouring cafés.

QUICK EATS

Basso (Map pp238-9; ☎ 9650 0077; 195 Little Collins St; pizza slice A$4.90-5.50, mains A$15-20; ⏰ lunch & dinner Mon-Fri) Head down to the bunker-like Basso with its clean-cut style, friendly service and up to 20 different slabs of delectable pizza. From the leek and gorgonzola to the mini fuss but maxi taste of the tomato-dolloped pancetta, there's something for everyone. Eat your slice in, or on the run.

SPLURGE!

Uncrumple that one good outfit in your pack and get ready for a dining experience worth writing home about.

Becco (Map pp238-9; ☎ 9663 3000; 11-25 Crossley St; mains A$23-29; ⏲ lunch & dinner Mon-Sat) The city's cool, classic Becco attracts diners with its superb take on traditional Italian favourites, combined with faultless service.

Flower Drum (Map pp238-9; ☎ 9662 3655; 17 Market Lane, Melbourne; mains A$30-50; ⏲ lunch Mon-Sat, dinner daily) It's hard to remember a year when Flower Drum hasn't won the *Age Good Food Guide*'s Best Restaurant award. This mega-plush Melbourne institution offers some of the best Chinese cuisine ever likely to tantalise your tongue. Lunch is a good (and cheaper) option, but book ahead at any time.

Pearl (☎ 9421 4599; 631-33 Church St, Richmond; mains A$28-34; ⏲ breakfast Sat & Sun, lunch & dinner daily) We can't gush enough about this place. The service is impeccable and the adventurous menu sublime; give over to three courses.

C (Map p244; ☎ 9536 1122; 2 Acland St, St Kilda; mains A$30-35; ⏲ breakfast, lunch & dinner) Slick, refined and one of Melbourne's best eateries.

Don Don Japanese Café (Map pp238-9; ☎ 9662 3377; 321 Swanston St; dishes A$4-8; ⏲ lunch Mon-Fri) Students, retailers and city kids swamp this uptown Japanese outlet. The prices are unbelievably cheap, incommensurate with the quality bento boxes, bowls of curry and noodles. Join the throng at this informal eatery to wolf down lunch at an up-tempo pace.

RESTAURANTS

Chocolate Buddha (Map pp238-9; ☎ 9654 5688; Federation Sq, 2 Swanston St; meals A$14-20; ⏲ lunch & dinner) Slurping organic soup noodles, or sharing *gyoza* (dumplings) and the steamed *edamame* (young soya beans) is a relaxed way to enjoy the vibe at Federation Sq. Only the complex rules for ordering here lack Zen calm. Dishes don't come out together and there's no food service at some tables; best you wait to be seated.

Supper Inn (Map pp238-9; ☎ 9663 4759; 15-17 Celestial Ave; dishes A$15-30; ⏲ dinner) So, the word's out: bar-boozers queue behind families who got here just before the groups of students. Open until 2.30am, the Supper Inn is a favourite for late-night noodles, claypots or congee. The décor is nothing flash and the service can be blunt, but the quality dishes are excellent value. Supper Inn is licenced and has BYO (bring your own alcohol).

Mecca (Map pp238-9; ☎ 9682 2999; Mid-level, Southgate; mains A$26-30; ⏲ lunch & dinner) Offering Moroccan, Egyptian and Lebanese influences, the menu offers confident combinations of prime ingredients. Sink your teeth into some harissa-spiced barramundi from the riverside balcony and suddenly the Yarra looks like the Nile. After throwing in the serviette on the nougat parfait, you'll think you're in heaven.

Kimchi House (Map pp238-9; ☎ 9663 5919; 70 Little La Trobe St; mains A$12-14; ⏲ Mon-Sat) This hidden gem looks like a workaday factory from the outside, but inside it's a simple yet intimate and contemporary space. Excellent Korean food is dished up here to those in the know – do it yourself on the charcoal barbecues.

Bhoj (Map pp234-6; ☎ 9600 0884; 54 NewQuay Promenade, Docklands; mains A$8-18) This is the best option at Docklands, lauded by foodies as offering the best Indian in inner Melbourne. We agree, but if you like your curries hot, say so.

Also recommended:

Syracuse (Map pp238-9; ☎ 9670 1777; 23 Bank Pl; tapas A$4-10, mains A$20-25; ⏲ breakfast & lunch Mon-Fri, dinner Mon-Sat) Delicious tapas and chic European ambience.

Stalactites (Map pp238-9; ☎ 9663 3316; cnr Lonsdale & Russell Sts; dishes A$3.50-20; ⏲ 24hr) Greek eats – great souvlakis for lining the stomach.

Crossways (Map pp238-9; ☎ 9650 2939; 123 Swanston St; all-you-can-eat A$5.50; ⏲ lunch Mon-Sat) Vegetarian food – the chanting and literature are free.

Carlton — Map pp234–6

Carlton's Lygon St is still heavily influenced by its Italian heritage. As you head north along Lygon, over Grattan St, the staged smiles and antics from the spruikers outside the many tourist restaurants give way to a more local setting, marked by unfussy bistros.

Brunetti's (☎ 9347 2801; 194-204 Faraday St; café dishes A$3-7, restaurant mains A$12-23; 🕑 breakfast, lunch & dinner) Owner and pastry chef Giorgio Angelé migrated to Australia after entering the country as the pastry chef for the 1956 Italian Olympic team. Brunetti is famous for its exceptional coffee and authentic Roman patisserie. Traditional European cuisine can also be experienced here, but alfresco coffee and biscotti, tiramisu or delicious *graffe* (custard-filled donuts) is the way locals regularly visit.

Tiamo (☎ 9347 5759; 303 Lygon St; dishes A$10.50-16; 🕑 breakfast, lunch & dinner) From 7am, Tiamo's front window has men sitting at the bar, downing espressos and chatting in Italian with waiters. The dark and atmospheric interior has attracted local thespians, artists and Italophiles since the 1960s. Tiamo is licenced and recommended for lunch and dinner. Expect value for money and generous portions of simple and traditional cuisine at this treasured trattoria.

Abla's (☎ 9347 0006; 109 Elgin St; dishes A$16-18; 🕑 lunch Thu & Fri, dinner Mon-Sat) Grab a bottle of your favourite plonk and settle in at homely Abla's. If you're here for the compulsory banquet on Friday and Saturday night, bring a couple of bottles to see you through the 13 courses. Chef/proprietor Abla won't let you leave until you're patting your tummy contentedly; this is hospitality at its best.

FITZROY PUBS

Serving as the neighbourhood's lounge rooms, Fitzroy's pubs (all on Map pp234–6) are more than just beer-swilling hubs. They also dish-up great pub grub to line your stomach, in a social setting.

Builders Arms (☎ 9419 0818; 211 Gertrude St) Old-school grunge; gay night Thursday.

Napier Hotel (☎ 9419 4240; 210 Napier St) Favoured by young locals.

Rainbow Hotel (☎ 9419 4193; 27 St David St) Jumping pub, with regular live music.

Standard Hotel (☎ 9419 4793; 293 Fitzroy St; 🕑 to 11pm) Gorgeous beer garden.

Union Club Hotel (☎ 9417 2926; 164 Gore St) Mixed crowd with loyal following.

Bimbo Deluxe (☎ 9419 8600; 376 Brunswick St) Open till 3am nightly. Cheap pizza weekdays (noon-4pm A$3, 7-11pm A$4).

Jimmy Watson's Wine Bar (☎ 9347 3985; 333 Lygon St; mains A$16-22; 🕑 lunch Mon-Sat, dinner Tue-Sat) Legendary among wine lovers, elegant Jimmy's boasts an extensive wine list complemented by excellent European-style food. The leafy courtyard is a winner; or enjoy a session of pavement people-watching, armed with a glassful of Jimmy's very own chardonnay.

Shakahari (☎ 9347 3848; 201-203 Faraday St; dishes A$14-17; 🕑 lunch Mon-Sat, dinner daily) Established over 20 years ago, Shakahari takes itself seriously, which is mirrored in its at-times earnest atmosphere. If the weather is in your favour, ask to be seated in the palm-fringed courtyard. The curries, tagines and noodle dishes are heroic, whatever the setting.

Fitzroy

Map pp234–6

Fitzroy has more options than you thought possible. It's where Mongolian meets Malaysian, Russian café meets Italian café, and Spanish tapas bar meets vegetarian barn. Most of the action is on Brunswick St, although Gertrude St shouldn't be overlooked.

CAFÉS

Babka Bakery Café (☎ 9416 0091; 358 Brunswick St; dishes A$4-14; 🕑 breakfast & lunch Tue-Sun) The heavenly aroma of cinnamon and freshly baked bread is a good incentive to hang around if waiting for a table. Pastries are sweet, buttery and warm, much like the smiles and service from the waitresses. A Russian influence is present with borsch (a traditional beetroot and potato soup) on the menu.

Mario's (☎ 9417 3343; 303 Brunswick St; dishes A$5-18; 🕑 breakfast, lunch & dinner) Snubbing the easy-come, easy-go wannabe cafés on the strip, this sceney café is one of the originals, and doesn't it know it. Come for the great coffee, gut-buster breakfasts and a selection of good pasta dishes.

Arcadia (☎ 9416 1055; 193 Gertrude St; dishes A$8-14; 🕑 breakfast, lunch & dinner Tue-Sun) Cheerful, colourful, friendly and homely – in a '50s kinda way. It has wholesome and hearty focaccias, soups and pastas.

RESTAURANTS

Mao's (☎ 9419 1919; 263 Brunswick St; mains A$12.50-22; 🕑 lunch & dinner Tue-Sun) Mao's is a favourite for its casual vibe, super-friendly staff, off-beat but stylish fit-out and, most importantly, its modern, delicious twist on classic Chinese food.

Vegie Bar (☎ 9417 6935; 380 Brunswick St; dishes A$3-10; lunch & dinner) A Brunswick St stalwart, the barn-sized, buzzing Vegie Bar is perennially packed with a mixed bag of customers, here for the sometimes-fabulous, sometimes-average all-vegie eats. The burgers are a sure-fire winner any time. Come hungry, as the servings are huge.

Old Kingdom (☎ 9417 2438; 197 Smith St; mains A$8-14; lunch & dinner) We keep coming back for Old Kingdom's speciality, the exquisite Peking duck (one of Melbourne's finest). The expert table-side slicing is a treat in itself, but it wouldn't be so entertaining without the no-fuss charisma of Simon, the head waiter. Order at least a day ahead; one duck (A$40) is enough for three people.

Ladro (☎ 9417 7575; 224a Gertrude St; pizza A$12-20; dinner Wed-Sun) Probably the best pizza you'll ever have, with not one shred of processed ham to be found. Chunks of spicy sausage sit with fennel in melted mozzarella, on traditionally thin bases. Toppings are suited for pizza lovers who possess a more adventurous palate. Communal dining is the culture at Ladro where you book for a seat, not a table; bookings essential.

Richmond

The stretch of Victoria St between Hoddle and Church Sts is wall-to-wall with Asian supermarkets and Vietnamese restaurants: pleasing to the stomach and easy on the pocket. The food is fresh and authentic, and you can have a huge bowl of soup that's a meal in itself for around A$7; main courses generally cost between A$8 and A$15. And there are options on Bridge Rd as well.

Ha Long Bay (☎ 9429 3268; 82 Victoria St; mains A$7-14; breakfast, lunch & dinner) In a long stretch of same-same restaurants, Ha Long is outstanding for its friendly service and cheery surrounds. The extensive menu includes all your Vietnamese favourites: rice and noodles done every way, with a choice of meats and vegetables. Dishes are as sprightly and colourful as the décor.

Minh Minh (☎ 9427 7891; 94 Victoria St; mains A$8-16; lunch & dinner) A smart fit-out and fine Thai, Lao and Vietnamese dishes distinguish Minh Minh. You can't beat the crispy fried calamari with lemongrass and chilli, and the springiest spring rolls on Victoria St. Tables are crammed cheek-by-jowl, with two or more sittings per night.

Richmond Hill Cafe & Larder (☎ 9421 2808; 48-50 Bridge Rd; breakfast A$11-24, dinner A$26-28; breakfast & lunch daily, dinner Tue-Sun) The roomy, understated style of this café is supplemented by the attached produce store – cheese lovers, your search is over.

Tofu Shop International (☎ 9429 6204; 78 Bridge Rd; bowls A$6-13; lunch Mon-Sat, dinner Mon-Fri) Pull up a stool at this popular vegetarian café to enjoy the wholesome range of dishes. Try the hearty 'soy'vlakis or dip into the delights in the *bain-marie*.

South Yarra, Toorak & Prahran

It's perpetually peak hour along Chapel St, with diners and drinkers converging from all corners for a piece of the action. The Prahran end has plenty of budget choices.

Orange (☎ 9529 1644; 126 Chapel St, Prahran; mains A$14-23; breakfast & lunch daily, dinner Wed-Sun) Orange straddles the café-bar label with ease, its well-worn vinyl banquettes cushioning fashionable bums for early breakfasts (from 7am) to late-night beverages (open till 2am Thursday to Sunday). It serves good coffee during the day, and at night Orange slows its grinders and replaces teaspoons with bar coasters.

Windsor Castle (☎ 9525 0239; 89 Albert St, Windsor; mains A$16; lunch Thu-Sun, dinner daily) You know you've arrived when you see the pink elephants walking across the roof. Retro pub favourites are given a modern spin, or dished up plain and simple, like fish fingers with mushy peas. Dine in the chocolate-velour interior or spacious beer garden, especially on a Sunday when the Castle is most popular.

Tusk (☎ 9529 1198; 133 Chapel St; mains A$13-22; breakfast, lunch & dinner) Join the students from the nearby university and circus school, and tuck into a mammoth burger. Grab a window seat or pavement table to watch the passing foot traffic.

St Kilda Map p244

Fitzroy St is one of the city's most famed and popular eating strips; serious dining options mix it with casual choices. Acland St is renowned for its fine European delicatessens and cake shops; an avalanche of cafés, bars and restaurants smother the street.

CAFÉS

Galleon Café (☎ 9534 8934; 9 Carlisle St; dishes A$7.50-11; breakfast & lunch) The beloved Galleon is an enduring hang-out for St Kilda's alternative community. From sardines on toast to porridge or Coco Pops for breakfast, this very welcoming and character-filled spot is proof that food doesn't have to be gourmet or complicated to appeal. Long live the Galleon.

Il Fornaio (☎ 9534 2922; 2 Acland St; dishes A$8-16; ⏲ breakfast/lunch Tue-Sun) This concrete carpark shell retained its edgy industrial feel when it was transformed into this buzzy Italian bakery-café-restaurant. Everything here, from the breads and breakfasts to the lunches and dinners, is excellent. And don't get us started on the cakes.

Café a taglio (☎ 9534 1344; 157 Fitzroy St; pizza slices A$4.50-5.50, mains A$10-18; ⏲ lunch & dinner) Line up at the glass cabinet to select your slice of thin-crust pizza. The hard work done, sip a glass of wine or down a beer while your potato and leek or mushroom and gorgonzola sliver is heated. A range of mains graces the blackboard menu, including a tender barbecued calamari salad.

Lentil As Anything (☎ 9534 5833; 41 Blessington St; ⏲ lunch & dinner) The open kitchen at this hippy café serves up honest, tasty dishes. There are no prices; instead, the customer pays what they feel the meal is worth. Factor on anything upwards of A$10 – unless you want to withdraw from your karma bank.

MELBOURNE & VICTORIA

QUICK EATS

Bala's (☎ 9534 6116; 1e Shakespeare Grove; dishes A$2.50-12; ⏲ lunch & dinner) Always crowded, but with hearty, tasty mains available for under A$12 (and snacks for under A$2), it's not surprising. Eat at one of the few tables in the shop, or grab some takeaway and head down to the beach.

Spud Bar (☎ 9534 8888; 43 Blessington St; potatoes A$6-6.50; ⏲ lunch & dinner) The humble potato takes on a whole new dynamic here, where you can stuff your crispy-skinned spud with as many goodies as you want.

RESTAURANTS

Vineyard (☎ 9534 1942; 71a Acland St; mains A$10-25; ⏲ breakfast, lunch & dinner) It doesn't really get more St Kilda than the Vineyard on a sunny day. Cheek by jowl with Luna Park and so perfectly placed for people-watching, the Vineyard is best enjoyed on a Sunday afternoon over beers and some tasty if fairly unchallenging Mod Oz meals. This relaxed, retro pad is open from 10am to 3am.

Espy Kitchen (☎ 9534 0211; 11 The Esplanade; dishes A$10-16; ⏲ dinner) The Esplanade Hotel's kitchen is always busy, with dishes ranging from burgers to lamb vindaloo. Play a game of pool or catch a band (p256) after you've eaten.

Pelican (☎ 9525 5847; cnr Fitzroy & Park Sts; tapas A$6-10, mains A$18-23; ⏲ breakfast, lunch & dinner) St Kilda's groovy young things love Pelican. Its idiosyncratic design makes the most of the corner position – with a wraparound terrace. Tapas is the hero here, but Pelican's casual ambience sits well with breakfasters, too; especially champagne breakfasters.

Cicciolina (☎ 9525 3333; 130 Acland St; lunch A$7.50-15, dinner A$18-27; ⏲ lunch & dinner) Intimate and dimly lit, this fine Italian eatery is the perfect place to come on a romantic soiree. There's a bar at the back that you can enjoy while you wait for your table, which you invariably will – this gem is popular, but doesn't take bookings.

Soulmama (☎ 9525 3338; St Kilda Baths Complex, Jacka Blvd; bowls A$10-12; ⏲ lunch & dinner) Boasting prime real estate, vegetarian Soulmama resists what the lesser (probably meat-eating) mortals would succumb to: inflated prices. If lining up to choose your food seems like too much work, you can always ask your waiter to make a selection for you. Thanks to the fab location, it's a winning recipe, even if you might have to wait aeons for a table.

Stokehouse (☎ 9525 5555; 30 Jacka Blvd; downstairs mains A$10-20; ⏲ breakfast, lunch & dinner) Great foreshore location with a packed downstairs bar-bistro and outdoor seating (prime for people-watching). There's also good fish and chips and wood-fired pizza, and upstairs is fine-dining.

DRINKING

Melbourne celebrates the sanctioned drug of alcohol with gusto. It's the social lubricant in a highly sociable city. Apart from the city centre, drinking dens abound in the inner suburbs of St Kilda, Fitzroy and Prahran. Bars generally open until 1am weekdays and 3am Friday and Saturday. See www.melbournepubs.com.au for reviews of the city's pubs, bars and clubs.

What's-on information is listed in the Entertainment Guide (EG), published every Friday in the *Age* newspaper and at **CitySearch** (www.melbourne.citysearch.com.au). *Beat* and *Inpress* are free music and entertainment magazines, each with reviews, interviews and a comprehensive gig guide; they're available from pubs, cafés and venues.

Central Melbourne Map pp238–9

Melbourne's bar scene is one of the classiest, dirtiest, most boutique, egalitarian and retro (yet progressive) you'll encounter. Find the bars, and you do have to search to find them, in the city's laneways and alleys: behind unassuming doorways, down in basements and up flights of stairs.

e:fiftyfive (☎ 9620 3899; Basement, 55 Elizabeth St) Atmospheric, seductive lighting, comfy couches – fifty-five's very popular Internet lounge/bar is a great spot to have a beer – or three. It's a travellers' hang-out and is busy most of the time.

Lounge (☎ 9663 2916; 1st fl, 243 Swanston St; Wed-Sat) The Lounge provides the setting for a cracker night that might feature Latin rhythms, soul grooves or hip hop; open till 6am. Lounge also does reasonably priced meals (A$9 to A$16).

Cookie (☎ 9663 7660; 252 Swanston St) What wins a place the *Age Good Food Guide* Bar of the Year award? It could be Cookie's prime locale with balconies overlooking Swanston St, the parquet walls, good-looking staff, perverse collection of music – mostly on vinyl – and 16m marble bar. Fabulous cocktails and 10 beers on tap are further consideration. Still not sold? It does amazing Thai food, too (mains A$15 to A$22).

Ding Dong (☎ 9662 1020; http://dingdonglounge.com.au; 18 Market Lane; Tue-Sun) This rock 'n' roll bar also stages touring and local bands in a space the size of your mum's garage; this is the perfect spot if you wanna let it all hang out.

Transport (☎ 9658 8808; Federation Sq) A modern pub conveniently located across the road from Flinders St Station, with views along the Yarra, of the square and busy St Kilda Rd. Remember to look up and see your beer being transported along transparent beer lines. The building also houses the fine-dining **Taxi Dining Room** (☎ 9654 8808) upstairs.

Robot (☎ 9620 3646; 12 Bligh Pl; Mon-Sat) Set among high-rises, cute little Robot is a favourite for all things Japanese: beers, sake, and nori rolls for munchy-attacks – even Astro Boy makes an appearance in the décor. It has an all-welcome door policy, and animated movies screen free on Tuesday.

Phoenix (☎ 9650 4976; 82 Flinders St; to 1am Sun-Thu, to 4am Fri & Sat) Offering split levels of yellow hues, zebra carpet and dimly lit alcoves, Phoenix is the perfect inner-city nest. Contemporary bar snacks and late closing on weekends ensure its popularity with in-the-know locals. Distinctive food, like crocodile-fillet tapas, make for some pretty snappy bar snacks.

Pony (☎ 9654 5917; 68 Little Collins St; Tue-Sun) Bands thump away upstairs (Wednesday to Saturday) above the low ceilings and smoky din. You can also saddle up for the long haul, as downstairs is open until 7am Friday and Saturday nights.

Croft Institute (☎ 9671 4399; 21-25 Croft Alley; Mon-Sat) Find the cure at this Melbourne Institution. Prescribe yourself a beaker of house-distilled vodka in the laboratory downstairs or jerk like Mr Hyde on the dance-floor-cum-gymnasium-bar upstairs.

Hi-Fi Bar & Ballroom (☎ 9654 7617; www.thehifi.com.au; 125 Swanston St; admission A$5-18; Wed-Sun) This is a popular city venue where more-successful home-grown acts perform, as do irregular international acts. Anything goes at the Hi-Fi, from metal, rock, blues and roots to the occasional tribute night.

Other central Melbourne bars:

Tony Starr's Kitten Club (☎ 9650 2448; 1st fl, 267 Little Collins St; nightly) Prop your gorgeous self at the bar for the signature cocktails.

Double Happiness (☎ 9650 4488; 21 Liverpool St; Mon-Sat) Stylish hole in the wall, with hip doses of Mao propaganda.

Rue Bebélons (☎ 9663 1700; 267 Little Lonsdale St; nightly) An intimate café-bar that's busy by day or night.

Bennetts Lane Jazz Club (☎ 9663 2856; 25 Bennetts Lane; admission A$10-15; Tue-Sun) A great place to toe-tap to contemporary jazz.

Fitzroy Map pp234–6

Bar Open (☎ 9415 9601; 317 Brunswick St) Usually the last stop of the night, this multilevel bar is a haven to all kinds, who are often found lolling or dribbling in the dark corners of this well-worn and very popular spot. Upstairs, bands kick on to all hours.

Evelyn Hotel (☎ 9419 5500; 351 Brunswick St) Perennially popular live-music venue, attracting international and local indie bands and often the first point of call for up-and-coming local acts.

Gertrude's (☎ 9417 6420; 30-32 Gertrude St; Tue-Sat) With a roster of DJs and cosy classic-film nights, Gertrude's is a find. Effortlessly dashing, its amiable interior and deftly prepared drinks are loved by locals. Supplement this with bistro-style food (mains A$15 to A$20) and there's little more you could ask for from a bar.

Night Cat (☎ 9417 0090; 141 Johnston St; admission A$5; ⌚ Thu-Sun) A great atmosphere, innumerable retro suspended lamps, cosy corners, and a dance floor so big you can swing several cats. Expect jazz, soul, blues and funk.

Laundry (☎ 9419 7111; 50 Johnston St; admission free-A$6) Nightly DJs and regular live bands play these two funky floors with everything from electro lounge to karaoke.

Other recommendations:

Yelza (☎ 9416 2689; 245 Gertrude St; ⌚ Wed-Sun) For baroque overload.

Old Bar (☎ 9417 4155; 74 Johnston St) A packed and friendly Gen-X haunt with the Clash et al spinning nightly.

St Kilda Map p244

Elephant & Wheelbarrow (☎ 9534 7888; 169 Fitzroy St; ⌚ nightly) This backpacker hang-out hosts ever-popular *Neighbours* nights on Monday, with visiting cast members (A$38).

Esplanade Hotel (☎ 9534 0211; 11 The Esplanade; ⌚ nightly) Watch your bags, and mind you don't get stuck to the festering carpets. This atmospheric dive ROCKS, and endures a love/hate relationship with the thousands of Melburnians who have staggered through the doors over decades. Bands play nightly, and it has comedy nights and great food (see Espy Kitchen, p254). If you leave Melbourne and haven't been to the Espy, you'll never hear the end of it.

Prince of Wales Hotel (☎ 9536 1111; 29 Fitzroy St; ⌚ nightly) A long-standing institution, this hotel offers a tantalising mix of St Kilda locals, a seedy lowlife, a touch of camp (Monday), and plenty of rough and tumble. A variety of bands and DJs play upstairs.

Other recommendations:

Veludo (☎ 9534 4456; 175 Acland St; ⌚ nightly) A dark and sultry way to lose a few hours. Food runs till late.

Mink (☎ 9536 1199; 2b Acland St; ⌚ nightly) Over 80 different vodkas in slick surrounds.

CLUBBING

Melbourne's club scene could keep you from seeing daylight for days. Generally, clubs get going once the bars close at around 1am; the majority of clubs close between 5am and 7am. When one club closes, another opens for the recovery. Cover charges range from A$10 to A$15.

Prahran has plenty of clubs, and King St in the city has a cluster of big commercial venues.

Metro Nightclub (Map pp238-9; ☎ 9663 4288; 20-30 Bourke St, Melbourne; ⌚ Thu-Sat) This ginormous club has eight bars and two dance floors over three levels, pumped with retro '80s, funky '70s and doofing '90s music. Goo (alternative, supposedly), on Thursday, and Pop (top 40), on Saturday, are the busiest nights.

Revolver Upstairs (☎ 9521 5985; 229 Chapel St, Prahran) Just like an enormous lounge room. There's 54 hours of nonstop music Friday to Sunday, with alternating DJs keeping the shagpile rugs well trodden. The front room is also used for a variety of film screenings and heaps of bands. Out the back there's even a Thai restaurant.

Area 61 (Map p244; ☎ 9537 1999; www.area61.com.au; 61 Fitzroy St, St Kilda; ⌚ Thu-Sun) Everything looks good through the upstairs water wall as you peer down to the dance floor below. Area 61 is a relatively small club catering for about 300 boisterous backpackers. Sunday night, things get a bit dirtier, playing uplifting hard house to those who are still going.

Honkytonks (Map pp238-9; ☎ 9662 4555; Duckboard Pl, Melbourne; ⌚ Wed-Sun) The archetypal lost-up-a-laneway-at-the-top-of-a-dark-staircase bar-club. Down the back, past the grand piano holding the DJ decks, are unhindered panoramic views out over the MCG. The exceptionally well-stocked giant bar is a feature in itself. A number of small separate spaces will keep you comfortable all night. Honkys also hosts some stellar touring acts.

Palace (Map p244; ☎ 9534 0655; Lower Esplanade, St Kilda; ⌚ Wed-Sun) Huge complex with everything from retro sounds to commercial dance beats. Twister on Saturday is the best night by far, and you can party on to greet the birds at 7am.

ENTERTAINMENT

There are so many entertainment options in town, you may wonder whether anyone in Melbourne actually works. See p254 for publications that reveal what's on. The city and Fitzroy have loads of independent galleries showing local artists' work (see Fitzroy Gallery Hop, p242); entry is free. The *Art*

Almanac (A$3; available from bookstores) is a comprehensive listing, updated monthly.

Tickets for major events and some performances are for sale through ticketing agencies. **Ticketmaster** (☎ 13 61 00; www.ticketmaster.com.au) and **Ticketek** (☎ 13 28 49; www.ticketek.com) are the main players.

Half-Tix (Map pp238-9; ☎ 9650 9420; Town Hall, Melbourne; 10am-2pm Mon & Sat, 11am-6pm Tue-Thu, to 6.30pm Fri) sells half-price tickets on the day of the performance; cash payments only.

Live Music

Melbourne is widely considered to be the live-music capital of the country. Big-name international acts stop in town, but there's also a swag of local offerings playing original music in a variety of styles. A number of drinking venues (particularly pubs) double as band venues, which have been the proving ground for many a local success. See Drinking (p254) for venues to potentially hear the next Nick Cave or INXS, as well as for suggested publications with gig listings. Pubs that regularly host live music include the Esplanade Hotel (opposite), Evelyn Hotel (p255), Laundry (opposite) and the Rainbow (p252). Admission prices range from free to A$20, depending on who's playing.

You could also try:

Corner (☎ 9427 7300; 57 Swan St, Richmond) Mid-level alternative acts.

Green Room (Map pp238–9; ☎ 9620 5100; Basement, 33 Elizabeth St, Melbourne; admission up to A$10) Wednesday is karaoke, and bands play Thursday to Saturday.

Duke of Windsor (☎ 9510 1062; 179 Chapel St, Prahran) Any night between Wednesday and Saturday should give you something to look at and rock to.

Arthouse (Map pp234-6; ☎ 9347 3917; cnr Elizabeth & Queensberry Sts, Melbourne) Where to come for death metal, thrash, ska…It features everything from Vaginal Carnage to the Nihilists – you get the picture.

Sport

AUSTRALIAN RULES

The **Australian Football League** (AFL; www.afl.com.au) runs Aussie rules football – otherwise known as 'the footy'. It's incredibly popular, with games at the MCG (p240) regularly pulling crowds of 50,000 to 80,000; the Grand Final on the last Saturday in September fills the ground with more than 90,000 fans. The sheer energy of the barracking at a big game is exhilarating, and despite the fervour, crowd violence is almost unknown.

TRUGO

Melbourne is home to more than footy. In the 1920s, Melbourne rail workers invented Trugo – something like a hybrid of lawn bowls and croquet. Not surprisingly, every aspect of the game relates to trains. Solid rubber rings used as buffers between carriages were knocked about with a sledgehammer, which has since been replaced with a lighter wooden mallet. The pitch's length is that of a train carriage and the goals are the same width apart as an open doorway to a carriage.

A team consists of eight players. Each has six turns at hitting four rings through the goals: a 'true go' according to legend. Men prefer to take a swing backwards through the legs, while the ladies prefer the putt-style swing.

While the Connecticut Extreme Croquet Society showed some interest in the game, it's currently still played exclusively by Melbourne's older generation. The **Victorian Trugo Association** (http://home.vicnet.net.au/~vtrugo) has more on this unique sport.

Being the shrine of Aussie rules, the MCG is the best place to see a match, although the new Telstra Dome has poached its fair share of games. Tickets (between A$14 and A$20) can be bought at the ground for most games. Seats can be booked (this might be necessary for big games) through **Ticketmaster** (☎ 13 61 00) for about A$30.

CRICKET

In summer, international Test matches, one-day internationals, the national cricket competition and local district matches are played at the MCG. General admission to international one-day matches is around A$30; finals cost more. Tickets can usually be bought from the venue on match day, except for potential sell-out matches (like the ever-popular Boxing Day test).

HORSE RACING

Melbourne's horse races are held at Flemington, Caulfield, Moonee Valley and Sandown racecourses.

The **Melbourne Cup** (www.vrc.net.au), one of the world's great horse races, is the feature event of the city's Spring Racing Carnival, which runs through October and climaxes with the Melbourne Cup on the first Tuesday in November. The cup brings the whole country to a standstill. Entry costs A$35, or book in advance for reserved seats through Ticketmaster from A$105. The Thursday after the Cup, Oaks Day, once a 'ladies'-only event, is now almost as popular (with both sexes) as the Cup. Admission costs A$30.

MOTOR SPORTS

Fans of blokes (and the odd 'sheila') driving very fast in circles will be pleased to know that the **Australian Formula One Grand Prix** (www.grandprix.com.au) is held at Albert Park in March. The **Australian Motorcycle Grand Prix** (www.grandprix.com.au/bikes) runs at Phillip Island in October.

RUGBY

Although Melbourne has been slow to catch on, **Rugby Union** has attracted huge crowds to international matches at the MCG and Telstra Dome. **Rugby League**, on the other hand, has made some impact on Melbourne's sport-mad public. **Melbourne Storm** (www.melbournestorm.com.au) is the only Melbourne side in the national league.

April to September is the season for both codes. Melbourne Storm's home matches are played at Olympic Park.

SOCCER

Soccer has a fairly strong following in Melbourne, with two teams competing in the national soccer league's season (October to May). For details on home matches and venues contact the **Victorian Soccer Federation** (☎ 9682 9666; www.soccervictoria.org.au).

PICNICS & FLICKS

During the summer months between December and March, the open-air **Moonlight Cinema** (www.moonlight.com.au; Royal Botanic Gardens, entry via Gate F on Birdwood Ave) screens classic, art-house and cult films. **Open Air Cinema** (Sidney Myer Music Bowl, entry via Gate 1, Kings Domain, Lithgow Ave) has a similar theme. Ticket prices are a little higher than at standard cinemas and are available at the gate or through **Ticketmaster** (☎ 1300 136 166). BYO rug, picnic basket and wine for a night with the stars, under the stars.

TENNIS

For two weeks every January, the Rod Laver Arena at Melbourne Park on Batman Ave hosts the **Australian Open** (www.ausopen.com.au), with top players from around the world competing in the year's first grand-slam tournament. Tickets for the Open range from around A$30 for early rounds to A$100 for finals.

Cinemas

There's a cluster of mainstream cinemas around the intersection of Bourke and Russell Sts in the city, including Hoyts, Greater Union and Village. Tickets cost around A$13.50/10.50 per adult/student. Price for screenings at independent cinemas are practically the same as those at mainstream cinemas. Village also operates the **Coburg Drive-In** (☎ 9354 8630; Newlands Rd, Coburg) and 24-hour cinemas at Crown (p240).

Australian Centre for the Moving Image (Map pp238-9; ACMI; ☎ 8663 2200; Federation Sq, Melbourne) cinemas screen experimental, off-beat films, both genre- and theme-based; see also p236.

The **Astor** (☎ 9510 1414; cnr Chapel St & Dandenong Rd, East St Kilda) is the place for Art Deco nostalgia, cult-classic double bills and brilliant choc-top ice creams.

There are many other independent and art-house cinemas:

Kino Dendy (Map pp238-9; ☎ 9650 2100; Collins Place, 45 Collins St, Melbourne) Monday cheap tickets for A$8.50.

Lumiere (Map pp238-9; ☎ 9639 1055; 108 Lonsdale St, Melbourne) 'Bargain Monday' for A$5 before 5pm, A$7 after 5pm.

Cinema Nova (Map pp234-6; ☎ 9347 5331; 380 Lygon St, Carlton) Monday cheap tickets for A$5 before 4pm, A$7.50 after 4pm.

George Cinemas (Map p244; ☎ 9534 6922; 135 Fitzroy St, St Kilda) Venue for the St Kilda Film Festival (p247).

Cinema Europa (☎ 1300 555 400; Jam Factory, 500 Chapel St, South Yarra) Tuesday cheap tickets for A$9.

Theatre

The city's main theatre company, the **Melbourne Theatre Company** (MTC; ☎ 9684 4500; www.mtc.com.au), performs mainstream works regularly at the Victorian Arts Centre (p240).

Playbox Theatre (Map pp234-6; ☎ 9685 5111; www.playbox.com.au; 113 Sturt St, South Melbourne) Performs edgy Australian works at the atmospheric CUB Malthouse theatre.

For exciting fringe theatre head to the long-standing institution of **La Mama** (Map

MELBOURNE & VICTORIA

pp234-6; ☎ 9347 6142; 205 Faraday St, Carlton), the **Storeroom** (☎ 9486 5651; www.thestoreroom.com.au; 1st fl, rear Parkview Hotel, cnr St Georges Rd & Scotchmer St, Fitzroy North) or **Red Stitch** (☎ 9533 8083; www.redstitch.net; Rear 2 Chapel St, St Kilda).

SHOPPING

Shopping in Melbourne is a highlight for many visitors, with the city and inner suburbs offering a staggering variety of quality goods. Charge up your cards and go.

Central Melbourne Map pp238–9

Major retail centres, with a variety of stores under one roof: **QV** (www.qv.com.au; cnr Lonsdale & Russell Sts), **Melbourne Central** (www.melbournecentral.com.au; La Trobe St), **Australia on Collins** (260 Collins St) and **Southgate** (Southbank), plus the **Myer** and **David Jones** department stores and **GPO Melbourne** shopping centre on Bourke St Mall.

Some of the best stores are tucked away in the city's little streets and laneways. Little Collins St (between Spring and Elizabeth), Flinders Lane, Howey Place Centre Way and Block Arcade have an eclectic array of local designer wares, from jewellery to clothing.

Run out of film? Lost your lens cap? Then try the cluster of camera shops along Elizabeth St between Bourke and Lonsdale Sts.

Quality outdoor gear is found in shops along Little Bourke S between Elizabeth St and Hardware Lane.

The Queen Victoria Market (p237) on a Sunday is a good choice for cheap clothing and knick-knacks.

MARKETS

Arts & crafts market (Victorian Arts Centre, 100 St Kilda Rd, Southgate; 🕐 Sun 10am-5pm) The promenade outside the Victorian Arts Centre displays wares from around 150 stalls, which peddle everything from kaleidoscopes to soaps.

Fitzroy

Brunswick St offers a fabulous range of speciality stores from hip designer, retro and street wear to perfumeries and teashops, as well as its fair share of book and music stores. Gertrude St has an eclectic range of shops and is worthy of a stroll.

Richmond

Bridge Rd, between Punt Rd and Church St, is chock-a-block full of outlets with the latest off-the-rack fashion seconds and samples. Sharpen your elbows and dive in.

South Yarra & Prahran

Chapel St in South Yarra has long had a reputation as Melbourne's premier style strip, and the street continues to be one of the most popular fashion haunts for beautiful people. Expect top labels and top prices.

Once Chapel St crosses Commercial Rd into Prahran things become a little more relaxed, yet edgier. Greville St in Prahran is the place for hip young designer stores, second-hand vintage and retro gear, and a couple of designer outlets.

GETTING THERE & AWAY

Air

International and interstate flights operate out of Melbourne Airport at Tullamarine, with Jetstar's Brisbane and Sydney flights operating from Avalon, near Geelong.

Low-end one-way fares (Jetstar, Qantas and Virgin Blue) at the time of writing started at: Sydney A$70, Brisbane A$120, Cairns A$200, Adelaide A$80, Hobart A$80, Perth A$200 and Alice Springs A$240. Make sure you book these fares early. One-off specials can be significantly cheaper than these prices.

O'Connor, Qantas and Regional Express fly within Victoria.

Jetstar (☎ 13 15 38; www.jetstar.com.au)
O'Connor (☎ 13 13 13, 08-8723 0666; www.oconnor-airlines.com.au)
Qantas (☎ 13 13 13; www.qantas.com.au)
Regional Express (Rex; ☎ 13 17 13; www.regionalexpress.com.au)
Virgin Blue (☎ 13 67 89; www.virginblue.com.au)

Bus

Long-distance bus services for **V/Line** (☎ 13 61 96; www.vlinepassenger.com.au) and **Firefly** (☎ 1300 730 740; www.fireflyexpress.com.au) operate from the Southern Cross coach terminal in Spencer St. **McCafferty's/Greyhound** (☎ 13 20 30; www.mccaffertys.com.au) services operate from the **Melbourne Transit Centre** (Map pp238-9; Franklin St). Basic one-way fares from Melbourne to Sydney cost between A$65 and A$200 (12 hours), Brisbane from A$165 to A$190 (24 hours) and Perth from A$340 to A$490 (3½ days). There are at least six departures per day for these cities.

Ferry

The *Spirit of Tasmania* ferries run by **TT-Line** (☎ 13 20 10; www.spiritoftasmania.com.au) depart from Port Melbourne's Station Pier each night at 9pm, bound for Devonport in Tasmania (10 hours). One-way adult fares range from A$105 to A$260. The cost for vehicles depends on the size of the vehicle and the season. The fare for a standard car (5m or less in length) or a campervan is A$55 in peak season (17 December to 25 January), and is free for the rest of the year.

Train

V/Line (☎ 13 61 96; www.vlinepassenger.com.au) operates long-distance trains around regional Victoria from Southern Cross station (Spencer St station) in Spencer St. It also combines rail and coach interstate services to Adelaide (A$65, 12 hours, four times daily) and Canberra (A$60, eight hours; daily).

Other interstate services are operated by **CountryLink** (☎ 13 22 32; www.countrylink.info) for Sydney and Brisbane, and **Great Southern Railways** (☎ 13 21 47; www.trainways.com.au) for Adelaide, Perth, Darwin and Alice Springs.

GETTING AROUND

See p232 for information on getting to and from Melbourne's airports.

Bicycle

Melbourne is a great city for cycling, with plenty of dedicated bike paths. Some of these are along the foreshore and the Yarra. The Melbourne Visitors Centre (p233) provides information and maps on city paths.

Bicycles can be taken on suburban trains (free) in off-peak times. Tram tracks are a hazard: they're slippery, and it's easy to get your wheel stuck in them, so take care.

Quite a few places have bicycles for hire, with the price including helmet hire (helmets are compulsory) and lock. Try these:

Hire A Bike (Map pp238–9; ☎ 0412-616 633; Princes Bridge, Southbank) Day hire A$35.

St Kilda Cycles (Map p244; ☎ 9534 3074; www.stkildacycles.com.au; 11 Carlisle St, St Kilda) Day hire A$20.

Car & Motorcycle

Treat trams with caution. You can only overtake a tram on the left and must always stop behind a tram when it halts to drop or collect passengers (except where there are central 'islands' for passengers).

Melbourne has a notoriously confusing road rule contrived so as not to delay trams – it's known as the 'hook turn'. To turn right at many major intersections in the city centre, you have to pull to the left, wait until the light of the street you're turning into changes from red to green, then complete the turn. Look for the black-and-white hook-turn sign hanging from overhead cables.

CAR HIRE

These companies have desks at Melbourne airport, and you'll find plenty of other outlets in the city:

Avis (Map pp238-9; ☎ 13 63 33; www.avis.com.au; 20 Franklin St, Melbourne)

Budget (Map pp238-9; ☎ 1300 362 848; www.budget.com.au; 398 Elizabeth St, Melbourne)

Hertz (Map pp238-9; ☎ 13 30 39; www.hertz.com.au; 97 Franklin St, City)

Thrifty (Map pp238-9; ☎ 1300 367 227; www.thrifty.com.au; 390 Elizabeth St, Melbourne)

For disabled travellers, Avis and Hertz provide hand-controlled vehicles. These major companies all offer unlimited-kilometre rates. One-day hire rates for fully licenced drivers over 25 are around A$70 for a small car and A$80 for a big car – obviously, the longer the hire period, the cheaper the daily rate.

The *Yellow Pages* lists car-rental firms, including local operators who rent newer cars but don't have the nationwide network (and overheads) of the big operators. Try **Atlas** (☎ 9663 6233; www.atlasrent.com.au).

Rent-a-wreck operators hire out older vehicles at much lower rates than the larger companies, with rates starting at about A$35 a day. You might try **Rent-a-Bomb** (☎ 9428 0088; www.rentabomb.com.au; 507 Bridge Rd, Richmond).

CITYLINK

Melbourne's **CityLink** (☎ 13 26 29; www.citylink.com.au) tollway system has two main links. The southern link runs from the South Eastern Fwy at Toorak Rd, and branches to the southeastern edge of the city centre at Exhibition St, or to Kings Way. The western link runs from the Calder Fwy intersection with the Tullamarine Fwy to the West Gate Fwy, on the western edge of the city centre.

You can buy a day pass (A$9.90) at any post office, by telephoning CityLink or on the CityLink website – if you go through the toll without a pass, you must ring within 24 hours or you'll cop a fine.

PARKING

If you're lucky enough to find a parking space in the city centre, you'll pay about A$2 an hour. Watch out for clearway zones that operate during peak hours; parking in one means big fines and having your car towed away. Inner residential areas often have 'resident-only' parking zones (with residents requiring a permit), or parking restrictions that run until midnight. This makes parking near nightlife areas in Fitzroy or St Kilda nigh impossible – take a tram or a taxi. Note that a sign telling you you're allowed to park for, say, two hours, reads 2P.

There are more than 70 car parks in the city. Rates vary but you'll pay around A$7 an hour or A$24 a day during the week – less on weekends. You'll pay around an A$8.50 flat rate for parking after 6pm (usually until midnight).

Ferry

Williamstown Ferries (☎ 9682 9555; www.williamstownferries.com.au) operates ferries between the city and Gem Pier in Williamstown, with regular departures from Southgate (Berth 7) between 10.30am and 5pm. The return fare is A$18. You can ask to be dropped at Scienceworks (p245). On weekends there's a ferry between St Kilda Pier and Williamstown, departing from St Kilda hourly between 11.30am and 4.30pm, and departing from Williamstown hourly from 11am to 4pm; the fare is A$6.50.

Melbourne River Cruises (☎ 9629 7233) runs at least three times a day between Federation Sq and Gem Pier, Williamstown for A$14.

Public Transport

Melbourne's comprehensive public transport system covers every nook of the city and surrounds. For timetable and fare information, contact the **Met Information Centre** (☎ 13 16 38; www.victrip.com.au) or drop in to the Melbourne Visitor Centre (p233).

Buying a ticket is as simple as feeding your coins into a machine where you board, or to the bus driver. It's complicated by the limited availability of certain ticket types, however; eg daily tickets aren't available for purchase on trams. Many small businesses, such as newspaper kiosks and milk bars, sell most tickets.

There's an array of tickets and an unpopular automated ticketing system. Once you've bought the ticket, it must be validated for each trip.

The metropolitan area is divided into three zones. Zone 1 covers the city and inner suburbs (including St Kilda), and most visitors won't venture beyond that unless they're going right out of town.

Zone 1 tickets cost A$3 for two hours, A$5.80 for all day and A$25 for a week (longer periods are available). You can break your journey and change between trams, buses and trains with these tickets.

City Saver tickets (A$2.20) allow you to travel two sections on buses or trams in Zone 1, but you can't break your journey.

BUS

Generally, buses continue from where the trains finish, or go to places such as hospitals, universities, suburban shopping centres and the outer suburbs that are not reached by other services.

TRAIN

Suburban trains are faster than trams or buses, but don't go to many inner suburbs. Flinders St train station is the main hub.

During the week, most trains start running at 5am and finish at midnight, and should run every three to eight minutes during peak hour, every 15 to 20 minutes at other times and every 40 minutes after 7pm. On Saturday they run every half-hour from 5am to midnight, while on Sunday it's every 40 minutes from 8am to 11pm.

The city service includes an underground City Loop, which is a quick way to get from one side of town to the other.

TRAM

Tram routes cover the city and inner suburbs. Tram stops are numbered out from the city centre. There are also 'light-rail' services to some suburbs, including St Kilda, running along disused rail lines.

In theory, trams run along most routes every six to eight minutes during peak hour (from around 7.30am to 9.30am & 4.30 to 6.30pm) and every 12 minutes at other times. Services are less frequent on weekends and late at night.

Be extremely careful getting on and off a tram: by law, cars are supposed to stop when a tram stops to pick up and drop off passengers, but they don't always stop.

Taxi

The main taxi ranks in the city are outside the major hotels, outside Flinders St and Southern Cross train stations, on the corner of William and Bourke Sts, and on Lonsdale St outside Myer. Finding an empty taxi in the city on Friday or Saturday night can be *extremely* difficult. Flagfall is A$2.80, and the standard rate is A$1.33 per kilometre. There is a A$1 charge for telephone bookings, and another A$1 is charged for service between midnight and 6am.

There are several taxi companies, but all taxis are painted yellow. Major companies include **Embassy** (☎ 13 17 55) and **Silver Top** (☎ 13 10 08). All companies charge the same fares. Accessible taxis for disabled travellers are plentiful, but you'll need to book ahead (☎ 1300 364 050).

AROUND MELBOURNE

You'll need a full day to explore beyond Melbourne's outlying suburban sprawl. For cool rainforest walks, head to the Dandenongs; tipple your way through the state's premier wine-growing region, the Yarra Valley; or enjoy the pristine coast of the Mornington Peninsula.

Activities

Lace up for some bushwalking in the Dandenong Ranges National Park. Go tobogganing at Lake Mountain during winter. In summer, try board- or bodysurfing along the Mornington Peninsula's rugged back beaches or along the Great Ocean Rd.

THE DANDENONGS

Less than an hour from the city, the Dandenongs are a breath of fresh mountain air, filtered by large stands of tall forests and fern gullies. Over 300km of walking tracks wend through the ranges, providing one of the most accessible bushwalking options close to Melbourne.

There's a **visitors centre** (☎ 03-9758 7522; www.yarrarangestourism.com; 1211 Burwood Hwy, Upper Ferntree Gully; 🕑 9am-5pm) near the Upper Ferntree Gully train station; it has free maps detailing the walking tracks. **Parks Victoria** (☎ 13 19 63; www.parkweb.vic.gov.au) has a downloadable map, and the visitors centre and Parks Victoria both have information on the area's spectacular gardens, such as the National Rhododendron Gardens (best visited in spring and autumn).

The **Dandenong Ranges National Park** supports a range of native wildlife, from the echidna to the lyrebird. The latter is known for its distinctive dance and ability to mimic mechanical sounds, such as camera shutters and cars. Walks through the park range from short strolls to four-hour bushwalks. One of the most accessible areas is Sherbrooke Forest, which has a towering cover of mountain-ash trees. You can reach the start of its eastern loop walk (three hours, 10km) just 1km or so from Belgrave train station, by walking to the end of Old Monbulk Rd past Puffing Billy's station. The walks at Ferntree Gully National Park, home to large numbers of lyrebirds and the infamous Thousand Steps, are 10 minutes' walk from the Upper Ferntree Gully train station.

William Ricketts Sanctuary (☎ 13 19 63; Mt Dandenong Tourist Rd, Mt Dandenong; admission A$6; 🕑 10am-4.30) features Ricketts' sculptures blended beautifully with damp fern gardens – his work was inspired by nature and the years he spent living with Aboriginal people. It's well worth a look. Bus 688 runs here from Croydon train station.

Puffing Billy (☎ 03-9754 6800; www.puffingbilly.com.au; Old Monbulk Rd, Belgrave; Belgrave-Gembrook return A$39) is an extremely popular attraction. The restored steam train puffs its way through the forested hills and fern gullies between Belgrave and Gembrook stations. *Puffing Billy* is at the centre of the Great Train Race, where competitors run for the hills and try to outsteam the train. Billy also graciously steps aside occasionally for *Thomas the Tank Engine* to take the rails.

Puffing Billy operates at least three times a day, departing from the Belgrave Puffing Billy station, a short walk from Belgrave station. At least one train per hour runs from Flinders St train station directly to Belgrave on the Belgrave line.

THE YARRA VALLEY

Neat, furrowed rows of grapevines from over 40 vineyards dominate the Yarra Valley. It's an area famous for its regional produce, as

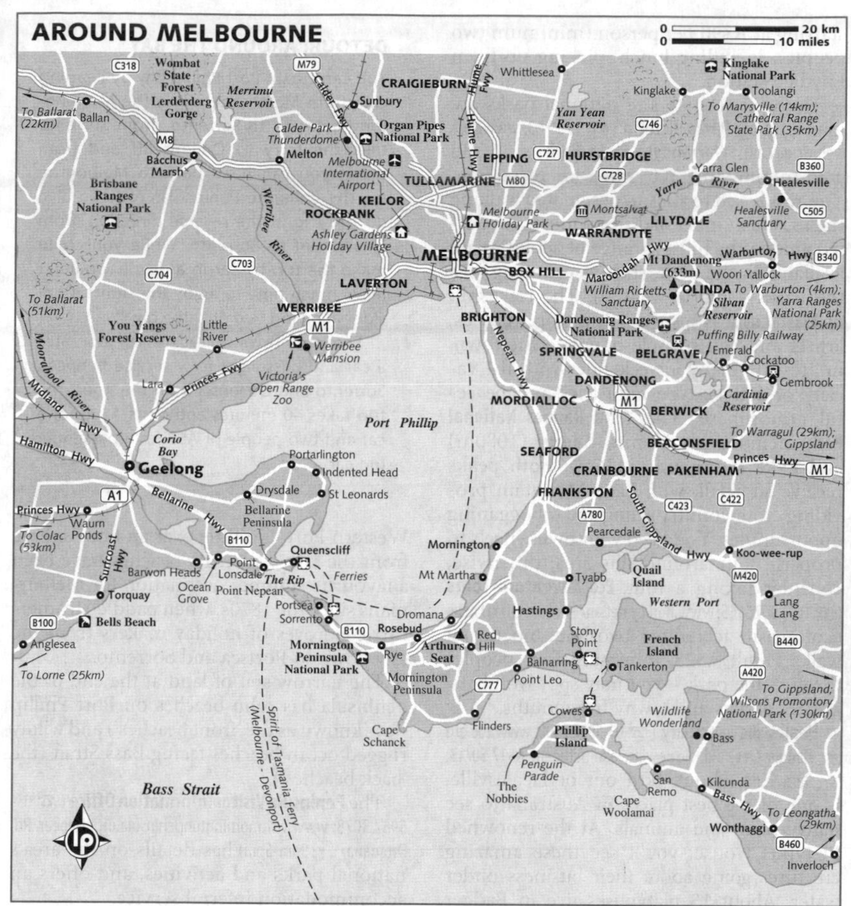

well as substantial tracts of native bushland and the excellent Healesville Sanctuary.

The **visitors centre** (☎ 03-5962 2600; www.yarravalleytourism.asn.au; Harker St, Healesville; 🕑 9am-5pm) is off the highway in Healesville; there's also one in the Upper Yarra Valley, on the highway in Warburton.

Most people visit the Yarra Valley to sample the region's **wines** (www.yarravalleywine.com.au). While buying at the cellar door is no cheaper than buying from large outlets in Melbourne, the experience is a lot more gratifying. Hopping from vineyard to vineyard (to vineyard) often provides the opportunity to meet the personalities behind the labels. Some of the larger wineries also have restaurants that use the fine local produce, and provide much-needed solid sustenance. A superb time to visit the region is during the **Yarra Valley Grape Grazing Festival** (www.grapegrazing.com.au) in February. Over 23 participating wineries provide food, and host loads of live music. Among the more well-known wineries are **De Bortoli** (☎ 5965 2271; www.debortoli.com.au; Pinnacle Lane, Dixons Creek; 🕑 10am-5pm), **Domaine Chandon** (☎ 9739 1110; www.chandon.com.au; Green Point, Maroondah Hwy, Coldstream; 🕑 10.30am-4.30pm) and **Yering Station** (☎ 9730 1107; www.yering.com; 38 Melba Hwy, Yarra Glen; 🕑 10am-5pm Mon-Fri, to 6pm Sat & Sun).

The visitors centre has information and maps for self-drive tours. Suburban trains only goes as far as Lilydale. **Yarra Valley Winery Tours** (☎ 03-5962 3870; www.yarravalleywinerytours.com.au) runs daily bus tours of the wineries starting at A$90 per person (minimum two people), including lunch, picking up from Lilydale station.

The valley's state and national parks are managed by **Parks Victoria** (☎ 13 19 63; www.parkweb.vic.gov.au). **Warrandyte State Park** is an old gold-mining area, reclaimed for recreation. You're advised to stick to designated walking tracks, as a number of disused mines are dotted among the hills. A range of activities are available in the park, such as canoeing (see the Parks Victoria website). The township of **Warrandyte** is also worth a stop: hippies, artists and craftspeople populate the town, impressing many a weekender with the variety of cottage-type industries and peaceful atmosphere. The **Yarra Ranges National Park** includes Mt Donna Buang (1080m) and Lake Mountain (1436m). Both peaks receive snowfall, with Lake Mountain providing cross-country skiing and tobogganing opportunities. You need your own wheels to properly tour around this area; otherwise, consider taking a tour. **Eco Adventure Tours** (☎ 03-5962 5115; www.hotkey.net.au/~ecoadven) offers ecotourism-accredited two-hour nocturnal walks (adult A$23, minimum four people) through the park – you may spot wombats, greater gliders and tawny frogmouths.

Healesville Sanctuary (☎ 03-5957 2800; www.zoo.org.au; Badger Creek Rd, Healesville; adult/student A$17.50/13; 9am-5pm), about 4km out of Healesville, is one of the best places in Australia to see native birds and animals. At the renowned Platypus House, you'll see these amazing creatures going about their business under water. About 15 platypuses live in Badger Creek, which runs through the grounds of the sanctuary itself. The staff give regular demonstrations, such as snake shows, but the best is the amazing Birds of Prey presentation, where raptors swoop above your head. This is held at noon, 2.30pm and 3.30pm (weather permitting). To get here, driving is best, but suburban trains do go as far as Lilydale. **McKenzie's Bus Lines** (☎ 03-5962 5088; www.mckenzies.com.au) has daily services from Lilydale train station to Healesville and on to the Sanctuary. Around one service a day goes from the Southern Cross coach terminal in Spencer St in the city, to Healesville.

DETOUR: AROUND THE BAY

You can circuit Port Phillip Bay by heading east from Melbourne along the Mornington Peninsula to Sorrento. From Sorrento take the ferry to Queenscliff and from there, you can head back to Melbourne via the Bellarine Peninsula. You can also do the trip in the reverse direction, from Queenscliff to Sorrento. While you could make the trip by car in a day, it wouldn't leave much time to enjoy the sights. Consider allowing two or three days.

Searoad (www.searoad.com.au) operates a car and passenger ferry service between Sorrento and Queenscliff on the hour. The trip takes 40 minutes and costs A$46 for a car and two people or A$8 for a passenger (no car).

MORNINGTON PENINSULA

The boot-shaped Mornington Peninsula, which juts out between Port Phillip Bay and Western Port, is a little over an hour's drive from the city centre. Its beaches have been a favourite summer destination for Melburnians since the 1870s, when paddle-steamers carried droves of holiday-makers from the city down to Portsea and Sorrento.

The narrow spit of land at the end of the peninsula has calm beaches on Port Phillip Bay (known as the 'front beaches') and wildly rugged ocean beaches facing Bass Strait (the 'back beaches').

The **Peninsula Visitor Information Office** (☎ 03-5987 3078; www.visitmorningtonpeninsula.org; Nepean Rd, Dromana; 9am-5pm) has details on the area's national parks and activities, and offers an accommodation referral service.

Swimming and surfing top the list of activities, but there are also walking tracks through the **Mornington Peninsula National Park** (www.parkweb.vic.gov.au; admission A$7.20). The coastal strip fronting Bass Strait forms part of the park, and along here you'll find coastal walking tracks and some great surf beaches.

Summer in the historic and fashionable resort town of **Sorrento** is frenetic. In the winter months, sanity returns and Sorrento is once more a sleepy seaside retreat. The town has some fine 19th-century buildings constructed from locally quarried limestone, and it boasts great beaches (the back beach has a great rock pool for swimming in at low tide), and plenty of cafés and restaurants. Sorrento was the site of the first official European settlement in Victoria. The camp only lasted from October 1803 to May 1804, when the group of convicts, marines, civil officers and free settlers moved on to better-watered conditions at Hobart.

From Sorrento you can ferry across Port Phillip bay to Queenscliff on the Bellarine Peninsula (see Detour: Around the Bay, opposite) – keep an eye out for dolphins.

Dolphin-watching cruises on the bay are very popular in season, generally from October to April/May. Local operators, including **Polperro Dolphin Swims** (☎ 03-5988 8437; www.polperro.com.au; 4hr swimming tours A$95, 4hr sightseeing tours A$40) and **Moonraker** (☎ 03-5984 4211; www.moonrakercharters.com.au; 3hr swimming tours A$80, 3hr sightseeing tours A$40) offer a combination of sightseeing cruises of the bay, fishing trips and dolphin-watching cruises.

Multimillion-dollar mansions are ten-a-penny in **Portsea**. The front beach is calm and inviting. If things get too hot, wander up to the Portsea Hotel and enjoy a drink in the grassy (and usually pretty crowded) beer garden that overlooks the pier. The back beach is notoriously wild, and on shore is the impressive natural rock formation **London Bridge**.

From Melbourne take a train to Frankston (Metcard Zone 1, 2 and 3 A$7, one hour). From Frankston train station, bus No 788 leaves for Portsea (A$8.20, 1¾ hour), stopping in Sorrento (A$7.90, 1½ hours), nine times daily (fewer on weekends).

GREAT OCEAN ROAD

Long stretches of ocean beaches, rugged cliffs and shipwrecks on one side contrast with lush forested areas on the other, making the curvy Great Ocean Road (B100) one of the world's most spectacular coastal drives.

The lush Otway Ranges run from Aireys Inlet to Cape Otway, offering great bushwalking. Most of the coastal section of the Otways is part of the Angahook-Lorne State Park. The Great Ocean Road officially starts at Torquay, ending at Allansford where it joins the Princes Hwy and continues along the southeast coast through to South Australia.

Open daily are **visitors centres** (www.greatoceanrd.org.au) in Torquay, Lorne, Apollo Bay, Port Campbell, Warrnambool, Port Fairy and Portland.

Accommodation is scarce during the summer school holidays (middle of December to the end of January) and at Easter, when prices are inflated.

Activities

As you'd expect, most activities focus on the sea. You can take surfing lessons with **Go Ride a Wave** (☎ 1300 132 441; www.graw.com.au) in Torquay, Anglesea and Lorne; the **Westcoast Surf School** (☎ 03-5261 2241) operates in Torquay. A two-hour lesson including a spongy Malibu board and wetsuit will set you back around A$50.

There are plenty of opportunities to ride a horse along the beach and in the bush, as well as chances to hang-glide and sea-kayak.

This is also the setting for spectacular walks in national and state parks, as well as along the shore. The **Surf Coast Walk** follows the coastline from Jan Juc to Moggs Creek, west of Aireys Inlet. While the total distance is around 30km, the walk consists of several shorter, easily accessed sections.

Getting There & Away

V/Line (☎ 13 61 96; www.vlinepassenger.com.au) runs a train from Melbourne to Geelong (A$10.20, one hour); from there a coach runs along the coast to Anglesea (A$5.80, one hour), Lorne (A$14, one hour 35 minutes), and Apollo Bay (A$22, 2½ hours) at least twice daily. On Friday (in December and January) there's a service continuing on from Apollo Bay to Port Campbell and Warrnambool (A$25, 4½ hours). Direct services between Geelong and Warrnambool (along the Princes Hwy) run daily and cost A$45. From Warrnambool coaches continue to Port Fairy (A$5, 30 minutes) and Portland (A$15, 1½ hours).

McHarry's Bus Lines (☎ 03-5223 2111; www.mcharrys.com.au) runs between Geelong train station and Torquay (A$5.30, 40 minutes).

TORQUAY

☎ 03 / pop 8000

Torquay is surf central, with a relatively young population devoted to riding the sea. The town has a range of beaches suited to surfers. Australia's leading surf brands were conceived and developed here, and have commercial centres on the Surfcoast Hwy. A number of outlets hire out gear along here; it's also where you'll find the **visitors centre** (☎ 5261 4219; www.visitsurfcoast.com; Surf City Plaza, Beach Rd; 9am-5pm;).

MELBOURNE & VICTORIA

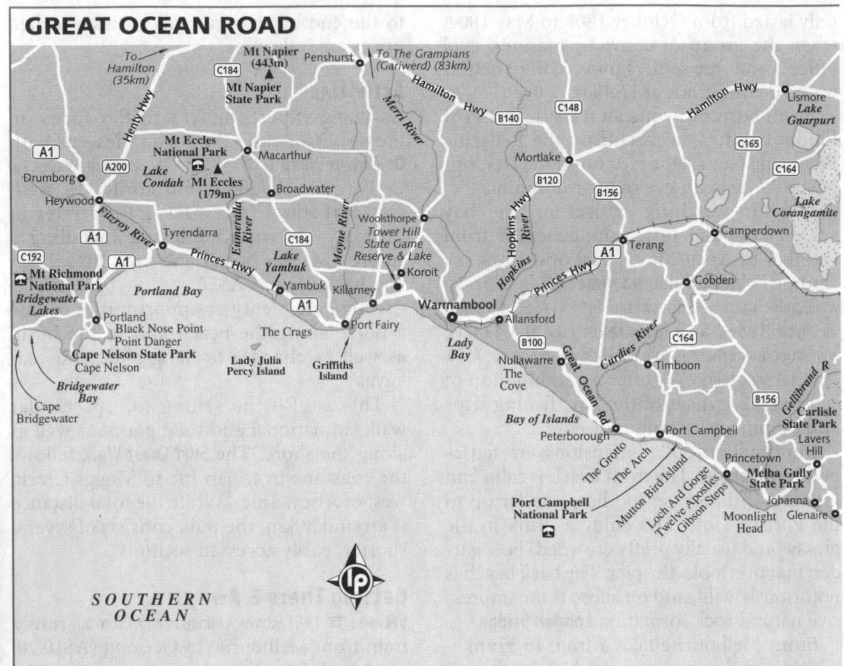

If you're happier on land, you can surf a mechanical 'ball' at **Surfworld Australia Surfing Museum** (☎ 5261 4606; www.surfworld.org.au; Surf City Plaza, Beach Rd; admission A$7.50; 🕒 9am-5pm), which explains the way in which waves are formed.

Nearby beaches with good surfing conditions include **Jan Juc** (about 3km southwest) and the famous **Bells Beach** (7km). The powerful point break at Bells is the site of a world-championship surfing contest every Easter. Every year (since 1964) the event attracts the world's top pro surfers and thousands of spectators. This time of year produces the biggest swells, with waves up to 6m recorded during the contest.

Sleeping & Eating

Bells Beach Lodge (☎ 5261 7070; www.bellsbeachlodge.com.au; 51-53 Surfcoast Hwy; dm/d A$23/60; 💻) A bustling, friendly hostel with lived-in appeal. The owners are able to book tours and they also hire out mountain bikes, cars and surfboards.

Torquay Public Reserve (☎ 5261 7070; www.torquayforeshore.com; Bell St; camp sites A$19-35, on-site caravans A$50-90, cabins A$45-55) This good-sized camping ground is well located just behind the back beach. During the high season it can be fully booked and imposes three-night minimum stays.

Sandbah Café (☎ 5261 6414; 21 Gilbert St; dishes A$6-12; 🕒 breakfast, lunch & dinner Jan & Dec) An easy stroll from the water. Open your mouth wide for Sandbah's big breakfasts and belly-filling lunches, such as burgers and overflowing plates of pasta. There are good vege options, too.

Growlers (☎ 5264 8455; 23 The Esplanade; dishes A$8-21; 🕒 breakfast, lunch & dinner) This funky licenced café-restaurant serves hearty dishes with creative twists on old-time faves, such as toasties and pies filled with ingenious ingredients. The dinner menu is a little more upmarket, commensurate with the prices.

Imperial Rhino (☎ 5261 6780; 3 Bell St; dishes A$6-10; 🕒 breakfast, lunch & dinner) Suitably Zen, with diners sharing a place at the long, wooden tables slurping and twirling loads of noodle offerings such as vermicelli, hokkien and rice noodles.

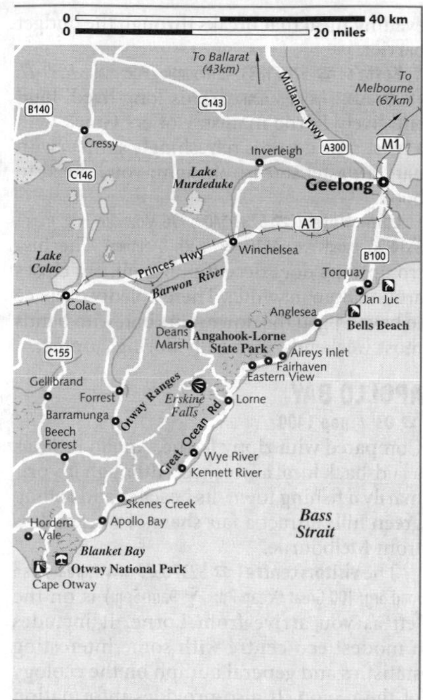

ANGLESEA

☎ 03 / pop 2200

Anglesea is a sedate family-oriented town, with a bustling little shopping strip. You can take to the sea and sand at Anglesea Beach – where the Anglesea River feeds into the sea – or gawk at the hundreds of kangaroos who graze on the fairways of **Anglesea Golf Club** (Noble St).

Anglesea Backpackers (☎ 5263 2664; http://home.iprimus.com.au/angleseabackpacker; 40 Noble St; dm/d A$25/80), just out of town, is a cheery backpackers a short shuffle from the beach, with neat facilities and accommodation. Double rooms have a bathroom; expect cheaper rates in winter.

Of Anglesea's three caravan parks, **Anglesea Family Holiday Park** (☎ 5263 1583; www.angleseafcp.com.au; Cameron Rd; camp sites per 2 people A$22, cabins A$70-120) is the pick of the bunch. It has pole position within earshot of the sea, and tea tree–shaded grounds. Minimum-night stays apply during school holidays, Easter and Christmas.

Surfing Albatross (☎ 5263 1010; 89 Great Ocean Rd; dishes A$10-20; breakfast, lunch & dinner, closed Mon & Wed in winter) is the nexus between café-restaurant and bar. Serving decent café-style fare, it replaces the cutlery with beer coasters at night and hosts a brilliant line-up of live music most Saturday nights.

AIREYS INLET

☎ 03 / pop 1000

If it weren't for the lighthouse, you could easily drive right past Aireys, which consists of a pub, general store and a café or two – and beaches, of course. Beneath the **Split Point Lighthouse** (nicknamed the White Lady), rock pools harbour colourful sea critters, visible at low tide. A walking track follows the clifftop from the lighthouse.

About 2km inland, **Blazing Saddles** (☎ 5289 7322; Bimbadeen Dr) has beachside horse rides (A$75, 2½ hours) and bush rides from A$35 (1¼ hours). **Gorats** (☎ 5289 6841; 63 Pearse Rd; tours per hr from A$45) rents out mountain bikes.

The **Angahook-Lorne State Park** extends between Fairhaven and Kennett River. The northern area of the park around Aireys features heathlands and spring wildflowers. There's a range of walking tracks from 30 minutes' to four hours' duration. The **visitors centres** (www.greatoceanrd.org.au) and the **Parks Victoria** (www.parkweb.vic.gov.au) websites have details.

Aireys Inlet Holiday Park (☎ 5289 6230; www.aicp.com.au; 19-25 Great Ocean Rd; camp/caravan sites A$30/36, cabins from A$100) has excellent facilities, including a campers' kitchen.

LORNE

☎ 03 / pop 1200

Lorne is the most fashionable town on the Great Ocean Rd. Its tidy foreshore curtained by giant pine trees is the setting for some excellent beaches and hip places to eat, drink and hang out. The **visitors centre** (☎ 5289 1152; lornevic@iprimus.com.au; 144 Mountjoy Pde; 9am-5pm) offers an accommodation referral service and posts vacancies in the window after hours.

Some of the best walks in the Angahook-Lorne State Park begin in the hills behind Lorne, with lush fern gullies, waterfalls and wildlife aplenty. If you don't want to bushwalk, at least take a scenic drive. Head up to the magnificent **Teddy Lookout** just at the end of George St (five minutes), follow the Deans Marsh–Lorne road into the Otways or take Erskine Falls Rd inland to **Erskine Falls** (around 15 minutes).

Qdos (☎ 5289 1989; www.qdosarts.com; 35 Allenvale Rd; ⌚ 10am-6pm Thu-Tue) is a mellow, ecofriendly art gallery, sculpture garden and café in a bushland setting that's well worth a visit. There's lots going on, including art classes, regular music gigs and occasional live theatre; the food's pretty good as well.

Perfect your stroke with **Paddle with the Platypus** (☎ 5236 6345; platycat@bigpond.com.au; 4hr trips A$85), which offers half-day canoeing trips to Lake Elizabeth in the Otways, 40km northwest of Lorne, where you're likely to see platypuses. Trips run twice daily, at dawn and at dusk; you'll need your own transport to make the journey to the pick-up point (in the nearby town of Forrest). Bookings are essential.

New Year's Eve in Lorne is spectacularly popular, featuring the **Fall's Festival** (www.fallsfestival.com), a big-time concert out at Erskine Falls. During the first week of January, several thousand swimmers splash their way across Loutit Bay in the **Pier to Pub swim** (www.lornesurfclub.com.au).

Sleeping

Great Ocean Road Backpackers (☎ 5289 1809; lorne@yhavic.org.au; 10 Erskine Ave; dm A$20-23) The best hostel in Lorne, set on a bushy hillside.

Grand Pacific Hotel (☎ 5289 1609; 268 Mountjoy Pde; d A$75) The back part of this luxuriously renovated hotel has a few budget rooms, which retain a bit of the old-style charm.

Erskine River Caravan Park (☎ 5289 1382; 2 Great Ocean Rd; camp sites per 2 people A$20-25, cabins A$80-100) A spiffing site, right by the river.

All five camping grounds in town are managed by the **Lorne Foreshore Committee** (☎ 5289 1382; www.lorneforeshore.asn.au). You'll need to book well in advance for a site at any of the parks during holiday time, when cabins can only be booked by the week.

Eating & Drinking

Mermaids (☎ 5289 2422; 22 Great Ocean Rd; dishes A$6-12; ⌚ breakfast & lunch Thu-Mon) This upstairs hideaway has superb ocean views, making your pancake stack all the more enjoyable. Better-than-average tofu burgers and wraps are the heroes of the lunch-time offerings.

Reif's (☎ 5289 2366; 84 Mountjoy Pde; mains A$12-22; ⌚ breakfast, lunch & dinner) The multitiered decking at Reif's is oh so fine for bumper breakfasts, Modern-Australian lunches or a sassier evening meal that breaks through the budget barrier.

Kosta's (☎ 5289 1883; 48 Mountjoy Pde; mains A$19-27; ⌚ breakfast, lunch & dinner) This long-lived, loud and lively Lorne mainstay offers Greek with a twist. The décor is refreshingly simple, with nary a pastel starfish in sight; you'll need to book.

Lorne Hotel (☎ 5289 1409; 176 Mountjoy Pde; mains A$14-20, bands free-A$10 ⌚ lunch & dinner) The bistro upstairs does decent pub grub, but closes around 8pm in winter. There's plenty of space to have a jig in the downstairs bar, with bands most weekends, especially during summer.

APOLLO BAY

☎ 03 / pop 1400

Compared with zippy Lorne, Apollo Bay has a laid-back local ambience. Although it's primarily a fishing town, its beaches and rolling green hills attract a fair share of weekenders from Melbourne.

The **visitors centre** (☎ 5237 6529; www.greatoceanroad.org; 100 Great Ocean Rd; ⌚ 9am-5pm) is on the left as you arrive from Lorne. It includes a modest eco-centre with some interesting statistics and general bumph on the ecology of the region. It also provides information on local walks and waterfalls.

A 1km drive up Marriners Lookout Rd, followed by a 500m walk, takes you to **Marriner's Lookout**, which has humbling views of the vast coast.

There are plenty of activities, including horse riding at the **Wild Dog Trails** (☎ 5237 6441; 225 Wild Dog Rd; 2hr/all-day horse rides A$55/100) in the bush and along the beaches. If you fancy a little high flying, check out **12 Apostles Aerial Adventures** (☎ 5237 7370; 3 Telford St), which will fly you in a small plane over the Otways (A$55) or the Twelve Apostles (A$140). **Wingsports Flight Academy** (☎ 0419-378 616; www.wingsports.com.au) in Apollo Bay offers tandem powered hang-glides (20 minutes) from A$95.

Apollo Bay Seal Kayaking (☎ 0405-495 909; 2 McMinn Ct, Marengo; 2hr trips A$45) organises kayaking trips among seal colonies, as well as surfing lessons (A$40, 1½ hours) between October and May. **Apollo Bay Fishing & Adventure Tours** (☎ 5237 7888; 16 Seymour Cres) offers half-day fishing trips (A$70, four hours) and scenic wildlife tours (from A$25 per hour), taking in the marine park and seal colony.

The **Apollo Bay Music Festival** (www.apollobaymusicfestival.com) in March will have you bopping about the town's venues to blues, jazz, rock and folk performances.

About 25km west of Apollo Bay is the lush little **Melba Gully State Park**. Its nature track leads through stunning rainforest and, at night, twinkles with the light of glow-worms; guided tours run during holiday seasons (ask at the visitors centre).

Sleeping

Surfside Backpackers (☎ 5237 7263; 7 Gambier St; dm A$20-22, d A$50, self-contained units A$65-80; 💻) Relax in one of the two sitting rooms to the soothing crackle of records, with million-dollar beach views. The retro '50s cabins sleep four to eight people, but book out fast, so get in early. There are facilities for disabled guests.

Pisces Caravan Resort (☎ 5237 6749; www.greatoceanroad.org/pisces; 113 Great Ocean Rd; caravan sites A$20-27, cabins A$60-175) There's something mildly suburban about the carefully manicured landscaping and cheek-by-jowl accommodation, although it's tempered by the gorgeous scenic setting. Facilities include a shared kitchen for campers and a games and TV room. There's also a bathroom equipped for disabled guests.

Lighthouse Keepers Inn (☎ 5237 6278; 175 Great Ocean Rd; d A$105-135; ❄) Some of the bright modern rooms here have stellar views to the beach across the road. This is a genteel guesthouse, with all the modern conveniences.

Eating

Bay Leaf Café (☎ 5237 6470; 131 Great Ocean Rd; mains A$10-20; 🕐 breakfast & lunch year-round, dinner summer) A chummy laid-back place decked with local art and offering beach views. The cuisine is a corking combo of Asian and Australian influences, and there are takeaway treats such as bagels.

Nautigals (☎ 5237 7939; Shop 1, 57 Great Ocean Rd; mains A$5-12; 🕐 dinner; 💻) This restaurant is hot – literally – with chilli-laced dishes, such as *mee goreng* (fried egg noodles) and spicy wedges. Even the squid salad is given the red-hot treatment. Brave curry fans can try the beef vindaloo.

Buffs Bistro (☎ 5237 6403; 51-53 Great Ocean Rd; mains A$9-23; 🕐 lunch & dinner) This friendly restaurant is decorated with famous Fernando Botero prints of a portly lady in the buff. There's a great range of cross-cultural cuisine and some interesting vegetarian options. Keep an ear out for occasional jazz nights.

THE OTWAYS

From Apollo Bay, the road leaves the coast and winds through the Otway National Park, which boasts relatively untouched rainforests, fern gullies and huge forests of mountain ash.

A couple of unsealed roads lead off the highway and run through the park down to the coast. The first, about 6km southwest of Apollo Bay, leads to the **Elliot River picnic area** and **Shelly Beach**. Seventeen kilometres past Apollo Bay is **Maits Rest Rainforest Boardwalk**, a lovely 20-minute walk through a rainforest gully.

About 2km further on, Otway Lighthouse Rd leads 12km down to Cape Otway Light Station. Look out for koalas in the trees (and for other motorists doing the same). The **lighthouse** (☎ 03-5237 9240; Lighthouse Rd; guided tours A$11, self-guided tours A$5; 🕐 9am-5pm, later in summer) is well worth a visit.

Bimbi Park (☎ 03-5237 9246; www.bimbipark.com.au; Manna Gum Dr, Cape Otway; dm A$20-25, camp/caravan sites per 2 people A$15/18, cabins A$60-85) is signposted off Otway Lighthouse Rd about 3km before the lighthouse; facilities are in a remote and dramatic setting deep in the woodland. This is a great base for the Otways. Prices vary according to season. There are trail rides (A$40, 1½ hours) available here.

THE SHIPWRECK COAST

The Victorian coastline between Cape Otway and Port Fairy was a notoriously dangerous stretch of water in the days of sailing ships. Navigation was very difficult due to numerous barely-hidden reefs and frequent heavy fog. More than 80 vessels came to grief on this 120km stretch in just 40 years.

The most famous wreck was that of the iron-hulled clipper *Loch Ard*, which foundered off Mutton Bird Island on the final night of its voyage from England in 1878. Only two of the 55 people on board survived. Eva Carmichael clung to wreckage and was washed into the gorge, where the ship's apprentice officer Tom Pearce rescued her. Eva and Tom were both 18 years old. The press tried to create a romantic story but in reality Eva soon returned to Ireland without seeing Tom again.

There's also accommodation in the lightstation buildings. You'll need to book; phone **Parks Victoria** (☎ 13 19 63; www.parkweb.vic.gov.au). Blanket Bay Rd leads off Otway Lighthouse Rd across to Blanket Bay, where there are walking tracks and bush camping.

PORT CAMPBELL NATIONAL PARK

This is the most photographed stretch of the Great Ocean Road. Dramatic limestone cliffs tower above the ocean. Rock stacks, gorges, arches and blowholes combine to create a stunning organic landscape. The **Gibson Steps** lead down to Gibson Beach, but beware of being stranded by high tides or stormy seas. Beaches along this stretch are dangerous for swimmers.

There's a **visitors centre** and car park here for the **Twelve Apostles**. These are rock stacks in the ocean, only seven of which can be seen from tourist viewing points. These tall rocky stacks have been abandoned to the ocean by the eroding mainland. Constantly pounded by waves, the fate of the seven 'apostles' is tenuous. No-one is sure what happened to the other five – or if there ever were five others. Perhaps a touch of poetic licence was used in the naming.

East of Port Campbell, **Loch Ard Gorge** is named after the wreck of the *Loch Ard*, (see The Shipwreck Coast, p269). The **Arch** and **London Bridge** were once one rock platform linking a stack to the mainland. In 1990 it collapsed, stranding two astonished tourists who were later rescued by helicopter. On moonlit evenings this is a good spot to see penguins.

The **visitors centre** (☎ 1300 137 255, 03-5598 6089; portcampbellvisitor@corangamite.vic.gov.au; 26 Morris St, Port Campbell; 9am-5pm) can book accommodation and trips, and Parks Victoria's information on the area is available here.

Sleeping & Eating

Port Campbell YHA Hostel (☎ 03-5598 6305; portcampbellyha@ansonic.com.au; 18 Tregea St, Port Campbell; camp sites per 2 people A$16, dm A$19, d A$50-65, cabins A$60-70;) This well-oiled operation offers tidy cabins, decent dorms and a spacious communal kitchen and dining area. The managers will book YHA accommodation in advance for you.

Port Of Call (☎ 03-5598 6206; poc@standard.net.au; 37 Lord St, Port Campbell; d A$70-120) This homely place has rustic appeal with a lush garden. There are also more swish units available, as well as a unit with facilities for mobility-impaired guests.

Port Campbell National Park Cabin & Camping Park (☎ 03-5598 6492; campinport@datafast.net.au; Morris St, Port Campbell; camp sites per 2 people A$20, cabins A$75-100) The grassy camp sites here are good value, and there are beach and river frontages. Boat charter can be arranged.

Nico's Pizza & Pasta (☎ 03-5598 6130; 25 Lord St, Port Campbell; mains A$14-18; dinner) This earthy pizza and pasta joint has imaginative choices such as the Persian pizza with walnuts, feta cheese, pears and tomato topped with cumin, coriander, sesame seeds and herbs. Home-made breads here are exceptional, too; try the sun-dried tomato and cheese. YHA discounts are offered and there's wheelchair access.

Cray Pot Bistro (☎ 03-5598 6320; 40 Lord St, Port Campbell; mains A$14-18; lunch & dinner) Out the back of the Port Campbell Hotel, this bistro keeps its menu simple, yet sublime. If you're into 'catch of the day', go for the namesake crayfish.

WARRNAMBOOL

☎ 03 / pop 26,800

Despite being a major commercial and industrial centre, Warrnambool retains a cheery '50s charm. It's also a university town, so it has a number of lively pubs and student hang-outs. A dreary strip of motels and commercial outlets flanks the Princes Hwy approach to town. Head towards the sea for the town's more appealing aspect.

The **visitors centre** (☎ 1800 637 725, 5564 7837; www.warrnamboolinfo.com.au; Flagstaff Hill Maritime Village, Merri St; 9am-5pm) can book accommodation and **Southern IT** (☎ 5561 7280; 200 Timor St; 9am-5pm Mon-Fri;) offers Internet access.

The town was originally established as a whaling and sealing station. Thankfully, the harpoons were replaced with binoculars. **Whale-watching** is now a major attraction between June and early October, when Southern Right whales come to give birth to and nurse their young off Logans Beach. There is a **whale-watching platform** (Logans Beach Rd) with interpretative panels, and the visitors centre has a pamphlet about the biology and migratory patterns of these great creatures.

The main swimming beach is at sheltered **Lady Bay**. **Logans Beach** has the best surf and there are good breaks at **Levy's Beach** and **Second Bay**.

The **Warrnambool Art Gallery** (☎ 5564 7832; 165 Timor St; admission A$4; ⏰ 10am-5pm Mon-Fri, noon-5pm Sat & Sun) has an excellent Australian collection.

The **Mahogany Walking Trail**, starting at the Thunder Point coastal reserve on the western edge of town, is a 22km coastal walk to Port Fairy.

Sleeping

Warrnambool Beach Backpackers (☎ 5562 4874; johnpearson@hotmail.com; 17 Stanley St; dm/d A$20/60; 💻) With more than a few home comforts, such as a giant telly with DVD and surround sound, this is one of Victoria's better backpackers. It's friendly, clean and near the sea to boot. There's free use of bikes and a free pick-up service from the train station or bus stop.

Hotel Warrnambool (☎ 5562 2377; ozone@standard.net.au; cnr Koroit & Kepler Sts; s/d A$40/80) It isn't flash, but it's clean and convenient. Rates include breakfast at the restaurant downstairs, which is often full of happily chomping locals. There's also a great bar here (see Eating & Drinking, below).

Surfside Holiday Park (☎ 5561 2611; alewis@warrnambool.vic.gov.au; Pertobe Rd; camp sites per 2 people A$19-28, cabins A$60-95) Perfectly located near Lake Pertobe, you can spring from your tent to the beach in a jiffy.

Eating & Drinking

Liebig St has a choice selection of eateries.

Fishtales Café (☎ 5561 2957; 63 Liebig St; dishes A$5-20; ⏰ breakfast, lunch & dinner) An extensive menu includes Med, Eastern, veg and fast-food options. The nosh is top-notch, served in cheery surrounds with an outside patio for summer diners and smokers. For something different, try the parsnip or spicy eggplant fritters.

Malaysia (☎ 5562 2051; 69 Liebig St; mains A$13-17; ⏰ dinner) The Southeast Asian cuisine will stop your stomach rumbling, with plenty of noodle and curry choices. Play spot-the-celebrity with the photos adorning the walls.

Seanchai (☎ 5561 7900; 62 Liebig St; ⏰ lunch & dinner) Pronounced 'shanna-kee' (Gaelic for storyteller), this is an Irish pub to be sure, with dimly lit cosy corners and live music on weekends. One of the most popular hang-outs.

Hotel Warrnambool (☎ 5562 2377; ozone@standard.net.au; cnr Koroit & Kepler Sts; ⏰ lunch & dinner) This place is a treasure. A wide range of beers, comfortable seating and absolutely no poker machines allow the gentle art of conversation to flourish. Have a look at the postmodern ceiling. For accommodation details, see Sleeping (left).

Getting There & Away

See p265 for transport information along the Great Ocean Rd. Heading inland, there's a weekday **V/Line** (☎ 13 61 96; www.vline.com.au) service to Ballarat (A$20, three hours).

PORT FAIRY

☎ 03 / pop 2600

The first Europeans to settle this seaside township were whalers and sealers back in 1835. To this day, the bluestone buildings, whitewashed cottages and colourful fishing fleet lend Port Fairy a relaxed, salty feel.

The **visitors centre** (☎ 5568 2682; www.moyne.vic.gov.au; Railway Pl; ⏰ 9am-5pm) has an accommodation referral service. At the **Surfcafé** (☎ 5568 1585; Sackville St; ⏰ 9am-5pm) you can check your emails while surfing your way through a large cappuccino.

The two **history walks** through Port Fairy take in the cottages built by whalers and seamen, as well as grand public buildings and National Trust–classified properties (more than 50 of the town's buildings carry this classification). There is also a **shipwreck walk** along the beach, which incorporates six wreck sites and the **Battery Hill** fortification (established in the 1860s). Brochures are available from the visitors centre.

For bird-watchers, **Griffiths Island**, joined to the mainland by a narrow strip of land, is home to a colony of mutton birds (short-tailed shearwaters).

The **Port Fairy Folk Festival** (www.portfairyfolkfestival.com), one of the country's foremost music festivals, is held over the Labour Day weekend (second Monday in March). Tickets are sold by ballot in October and November but there's plenty of free entertainment. Book accommodation well in advance.

Sleeping

Port Fairy YHA Hostel (☎ 5568 2468; portfairy@yha.vic.org.au; 8 Cox St; dm/s/d A$24/45/60; 💻) Victoria's oldest YHA has had a recent spruce-up. It offers a choice of bunk beds in the main house or more modern units out the back, and is supplemented by a billiards room, as well as a garden with outdoor seating.

Discounts apply for YHA members (less A$3.50 per person) and multinight stays in winter.

Eumeralla Backpackers (☎ 5568 4204; High St, Yambuck; dm A$17) This excellent hostel is in a converted former school building. Run by a local Aboriginal trust, it's off the beaten track, 17km west of Port Fairy on the Princes Hwy. Canoes can be hired (per day A$5) to paddle down the Eumeralla River to Lake Yambuk. The hostel is also handy for bird-watching in the nearby wetlands. There are facilities for the disabled.

Seacombe House & Comfort Inn (☎ 5568 1082; www.seacombehouse.com.au; 22 Sackville St; hotel s/d A$70/90, motel s/d A$125/140, cottages A$180;) The Seacombe's hotel rooms are in the original 1847 inn. For something more swanky try the motel units or National Trust–classified cottages that sleep up to four and have their own kitchen, lounge, spa and open fire.

Gardens Caravan Park (☎ 5568 1060; www.portfairycaravanparks.com/gardensrates.htm; 111 Griffiths St; camp sites per 2 people A$15-19, cabins A$70-85) This park has plenty of grassy space, with sites and cabins surrounding a vast playing field near the river and botanical gardens. There are facilities for the disabled.

Eating

Rebecca's (☎ 5568 2533; 70 Sackville St; dishes A$9-13; breakfast & lunch) This straight-up restaurant serves light lunches such as melts, open sandwiches and salads, as well as heftier fare. The same folk own the home-made ice-creamery next door; round off your meal with a scoop of the yummy mango flavour.

Portofino (☎ 5568 2251; 26 Bank St; mains A$22-27; dinner) Not an extensive menu, but entrées here can double as mains. Meat and fish is served with a fusion of international flavours – you may want to give the pan-fried bull's testicles a miss.

Dublin House Inn (☎ 5568 2022; 57 Bank St; mains A$20-23; dinner) The Dublin specialises in hearty, local dishes and is packed out on weekends. The menu includes game (such as pheasant), plus fillets of kangaroo guaranteed to put a spring in your step.

PORTLAND

☎ 03 / pop 9600

Portland is Victoria's oldest town. From the early 1800s it was a base for whaling and sealing.

These days it's an interesting mix of the historical and the industrial, with old bluestone buildings around the deep-water port and the huge aluminium smelter occupying the narrow headland.

The **visitors centre** (☎ 1800 035 567, 5523 2671; www.portlandnow.net.au; Lee Breakwater Rd; 9am-5pm) operates an accommodation service for call-in visitors. It's at the **Maritime Discovery Centre** (☎ 5521 0000; Lee Breakwater Rd; admission A$8; 9am-5pm), which has displays on exploration, whaling and wildlife. It also houses *Portland Lifeboat*, Australia's oldest intact vessel.

There are some top **surfing** spots at Bridgewater Bay, which is patrolled in summer. Around Point Danger, south of Portland, there are good point breaks at Black Nose Point and nearby Crumpets.

For surfing goods, head to **Portland Surf-In** (☎ 5523 5804; 88 Percy St; 10am-5.30pm Mon-Fri, to noon Sat).

Sleeping & Eating

Portland Backpackers (☎ 0407-854 051; 5523 6390; bpackers@datafast.net.au; 14 Gawler St; dm A$15;) This friendly ramshackle place is in an old bluestone building, with chickens out the back. The owner can impart surfing advice, and hires out bikes, surfboards and snorkelling gear.

Mac's Hotel Bentinck (☎ 5523 2188; www.richmondhenty.com.au/macs/; 41 Bentinck St; s/d A$50/60;) This grandiose 1850s hotel has an imposing corner location and double-storey verandas. The exterior is fancier than the interior, but rooms are perfectly acceptable.

Centenary Caravan Park (☎ 5523 1487; 184 Bentinck St; caravan sites/cabins from A$17/70) Sitting pretty, right on the riverfront, this is also the most central caravan park in town.

Canton Palace (☎ 5523 3677; 9 Julia St; smorgasbord A$15; lunch Tue-Sat, dinner daily) There are no surprises, but the Palace has reliably inexpensive Chinese smorgasbords on Saturday and a cut-price lunch menu the rest of the week.

Fully's Café & Wine Bar (☎ 5523 5355; 55 Bentinck St; mains A$8-15; lunch & dinner) This is a lively waterfront restaurant with a sophisticated East and West menu. What you find here is a choice of vegetarian options such as goat's cheese salad with pine nuts, and stir-fries; the daily specials include homemade soups.

EAST AROUND THE COAST

Containing some of Victoria's favourite locations, the east coast is full of magic. From its fairy penguins, through enchanting French Island, all the way to the splendour of Croajingolong National Park: these are some of Victoria's most special places.

Activities

The east coast of Victoria provides plenty of opportunities to get wet, with equally good swimming and surf beaches. On land, stunning walks through wilderness are an option, including wonderful opportunities for overnight walks. If you prefer to pedal, try cycling around French Island.

PHILLIP ISLAND

☎ 03

Most visitors to Victoria make a beeline to this holiday isle – just 125km southeast of Melbourne by road – for its much-hyped penguin parade. There are other things to see, too, including Seal Rocks and The Nobbies, some lovely walks and the world-renowned surf beaches. The island is connected to the mainland by a bridge at San Remo. The main town is Cowes, on the north coast. The **visitors centre** (☎ 1300 366 422; piinfo@waterfront.net.au; Phillip Island Rd; 9am-5pm) is located 1km beyond the bridge.

Sights & Activities

The island's natural coastline provides a bevvy of attractions. Little penguins (popularly known as fairy penguins) are the smallest penguin species in the world. During the feeding season (November to January) they have to catch a whopping 14 times their weight in food for their offspring. Every evening at Summerland Beach, the penguins emerge from the sea, just after dusk, and toddle up the beach to their nests in what's popularly known as the **Penguin Parade** (☎ 5951 2800; A$16 from 10am). It's a delightful sight, but as this is Victoria's biggest tourist attraction, expect crowds, especially on weekends and holidays. Make sure you bring plenty of warm gear.

Off Point Grant, the extreme southwest tip of the island, a group of rocks called **The Nobbies** rises from the sea, offering spectacular views. Beyond these are **Seal Rocks**, home to Australia's largest colony of fur seals. The rocks are most crowded from October to December.

The **Koala Conservation Centre** (☎ 5951 2800; Phillip Island Tourist Rd; admission A$8.50; 10am-4.30pm) has tree-top boardwalks where you can view koalas up close. The centre is run by the self-funded Phillip Island Nature Park, so part of the revenue from your admission goes into research and conservation.

Get up close with Aussie wildlife at **Wildlife Wonderland** (☎ 5678 2222; Bass Hwy; adult A$11.90; 10am-6pm, last entry 5pm), off the island, on the highway about 10km from San Remo.

The island's birdlife includes colonies of **mutton birds**, found particularly in the sand dunes around Cape Woolamai. These migratory birds arrive for breeding almost on the same day each year – 24 September – and stay on the island until late April before undertaking a journey of a mere 15,000km(!) to the Arctic region. Your best chance of seeing these über-travellers is at the penguin parade, as they fly in at dusk during spring and summer, or at the Forest Caves Reserve near Cape Woolamai.

The island's ocean **beaches** are on the south side; there's a lifesaving club at Woolamai – a beach notorious for its rips and currents, so only swim between the flags. Good beginner surf breaks can be found at Shelly and Smiths beaches; leave Flynn's Reef to the pros. If you're not a good swimmer, head for the bay beaches around Cowes or quieter ocean beaches such as Smiths (which is patrolled during summer holidays). A number of surf shops on the island rent out equipment. **Island Surfboards** (☎ 5952 2578; 147 Thompson Ave, Cowes) offers two-hour surfing lessons, including equipment, for A$40 per person.

Rugged, windswept **Cape Woolamai** has a range of walking tracks, from a two-hour walk to the stunning granite Pinnacles, to a complete loop of the cape (four hours return, 8km). For something more tranquil, take a stroll around the bird-lovers' paradise of **Rhyll Inlet**, where there is a wonderful return walk (30 minutes) to the inlet through mangroves alive with crabs.

Sleeping

There's a bunch of accommodation options, but vacancies can be scarce during school

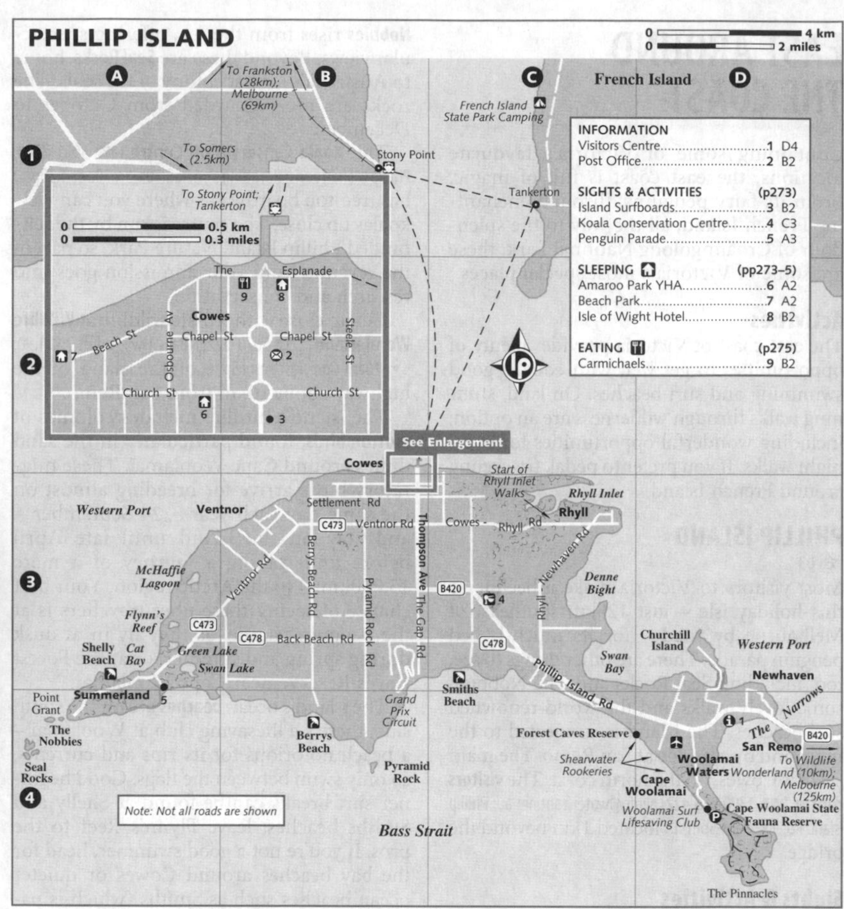

holidays, so book ahead. The visitors centre has an accommodation booking service, and www.phillipisland.net.au is a good place to start. The places listed here are all in Cowes.

Amaroo Park YHA (☎ 5952 2548; phillipisland@yhavic.org.au; 97 Church St; camp site for 2 people A$25, dm/s/d A$23/39/60, cabins with bathroom from A$85;) This well-run hostel is a good base, with leafy grounds, a pool and a charming old homestead. The 10-bed dorms are clean, if a little cramped. V/Line bus drivers drop you about 300m from the door, or ring the hostel about the shuttle service to and from Melbourne (A$20 one way). The hostel also runs Duck Truck tour packages – three nights' dorm accommodation (including three cooked meals), admission to the penguin parade, an island tour, half-day use of a bike and transport to and from Melbourne (A$146). It also takes tours to Wilsons Promontory (p276).

Isle of Wight Hotel (☎ 5952 2301; The Esplanade; s/d A$65/85;) Few would call the poo-brown, motel-like rooms beautiful, but they're clean, right in the swing of things and a stone's throw from the beach. Rates increase in summer. You can also eat and party here – see Eating and Drinking, opposite.

There are a dozen or so caravan parks, most of them in Cowes. Generally, sites range seasonally from A$17 to A$30, and on-site caravans and cabins cost from A$40 to A$90. **Beach Park** (☎ 5952 2113; 2 McKenzie Rd) has a leafy beachside position; book ahead. Note that you aren't allowed to camp or even sleep in your car in any public area on the island.

Eating & Drinking

Several diner-type options pull in the crowds along Cowe's Thompson Ave, but the best eating is along the waterfront on the Esplanade.

Carmichaels (☎ 5952 1300; 17 The Esplanade; mains A$15-32; lunch & dinner) One of the island's best eateries, Carmichaels offers sea views from its sun-drenched terrace, casual but on-the-ball service and superb eats. To-die-for calamari and the generous and well-selected wine by the glass make a long lunch here a must.

Isle of Wight Hotel (☎ 5952 2301; The Esplanade; mains A$8-18; lunch & dinner) Head upstairs to the bistro for the 'gourmet' take on chicken parmigiana – first-class views overshadow the shabby interior. The bar fires up on weekend nights, with three burly bouncers circling the 20-something crowds. See also Sleeping, opposite.

Getting There & Around

V/Line (☎ 13 61 96; www.vline.vic.gov.au) has at least one bus or train service daily between Melbourne and Cowes (A$17, 3½ hours).

Amaroo Park YHA (opposite) offers tour packages and a daily bus service between Melbourne and the hostel (you must be a guest of the hostel) for A$20 per person; bookings are essential.

Inter Island Ferries (☎ 9585 5730; www.interislandferries.com.au) runs between the Mornington Peninsula's Stony Point and Phillip Island (one way A$9), via French Island. There are at least two trips each day, year-round.

At least six trains a day run between Melbourne and Stony Point, via Frankston – where you'll need to change trains (Metcard zones 1, 2 and 3 A$7, one hour 40 minutes). For more information contact the **Met** (☎ 13 16 38; www.victrip.com.au).

There is no public transport on the island. You can hire bikes from Amaroo Park YHA for A$15 per day (nonguests welcome), which also runs tours to the main sights.

FRENCH ISLAND

☎ 03

Off the coast in Western Port, French Island is about 1½ hours' drive from Melbourne, but it feels a century away. In fact, residents have complained that visitors sometimes treat them like actors, as though French Island was a theme park along the lines of Sovereign Hill (p279). It does feel a bit like being on set, but an empty one – between takes. There are few houses, and the island's 68 permanent residents live mostly along the 144km of coast. There is no urban infrastructure: no rubbish collection or mail service, and no water-, electricity- or gas-supply services.

The semisealed road leading inland is trafficked intermittently by old cars that threaten to shed a rusted part as they shudder across the rain-corrugated unsealed roads. It's French Island's only main road, along which cows and disused chicory kilns punctuate vast, grassy pastures.

Visitors' cars are not allowed on the island. While not huge, French Island is too big to explore on foot. Cycling is more convenient and the right pace for koala spotting. Koalas are easily seen lounging in a branch, mostly around the cricket ground, but also in the state park that makes up two-thirds of the island. The island provides a safe natural habitat for koalas to flourish. (The first koala was brought to the island as a birthday present for a farmer's wife.)

The coastal landscape of the island changes rapidly. One of Victoria's two remaining mangrove forests grows here.

French Island Eco Tours (☎ 9770 1822; www.frenchislandecotours.com.au) conducts a variety of tours, including a half-day tour (A$60) focusing on the island's heritage and wildlife. This tour includes a two-course organic lunch.

French Island State Park Camping (☎ 5980 1294) is on the western shore, about 4km walk from the ferry. The lovely beachside spot has pit toilets and drinking water (you must treat the water). You aren't allowed to light fires, so bring a fuel stove. Tankerton General Store (about 6km away) sells limited supplies. Camping is free but bookings are essential.

McLeod Eco Farm (☎ 5678 0155; dm/d A$35/120) is a historic property (formerly the island's prison), with kitchen facilities, lounge, organic farm and beautiful gardens. It's 21km from the ferry, but pick-ups are included in the price. The dorm rooms sleep two; rooms are very basic, with shared bathroom.

Another good option is the **French Island B&B** (☎ 5980 1209; www.frenchislandbandb.com.au; s/d A$55/110), with a simple, but comfy cottage out the back. Breakfast is included. The general store is also located here.

Getting There & Around

See p275 for details of Inter Island Ferries services between Stony Point and French Island.

You can hire bikes (A$11 per day) from the kiosk at the jetty on summer weekends and public holidays, or from the **Tankerton General Store** (☎ 5980 1209) on weekdays.

WILSONS PROMONTORY NATIONAL PARK

The 'Prom' is the southernmost tip of Victoria. Surrounded on three sides by sea, it's one of the most popular national parks in Australia. There is a superb variety of natural attractions, including abundant wildlife and some wonderful beaches, and more than 130km of walking tracks.

The day visit fee of A$9.30 per car is included in the overnight charge if you're camping.

The only access road leads to **Tidal River** on the western coast, which has a Parks Victoria office and education centre, a petrol station, a general store, an open-air cinema (summer only), camp sites, cabins, lodges and facilities.

The **Parks Victoria office** (☎ 1800 350 552, 03-5680 9555; www.parkweb.vic.gov.au; Tidal River; 8am-5pm) takes reservations for accommodation, and issues permits for camping away from Tidal River. It also has details of walks, from 15-minute strolls to overnight and longer.

The northern area of the park is much less visited. Most walks in this 'Wilderness Zone' are overnight or longer and mainly for experienced bushwalkers. You'll need to carry drinking water in summer. Fires are banned except in designated fireplaces in Tidal River (between May and October).

Taking a tour is a good way of getting here if you don't have your own transport. **Bunyip Bushwalking Tours** (☎ 03-9531 0840; www.bunyiptours.com) has two-day bushwalking trips (adult/concession A$230/195), which include transport from Melbourne, camping equipment, entrance fees, permits and all meals. From Phillip Island, **Amaroo Park & Duck Truck Tours** (☎ 03-5952 2548) runs day trips to the Prom (A$70), visiting sights like Mt Oberon, Squeaky Beach, Tidal River and Picnic Bay. Lunch is included and there are YHA discounts (for more information, see Amaroo Park YHA, p274).

Sleeping

Foster Backpackers Hostel (☎ 03-5682 2614; 17 Pioneer St, Foster; dm/units A$20/60) There are no hostels in the park; this one is in nearby Foster. The V/Line bus stops outside and the owner runs a bus service to Tidal River and rents out camping gear.

There are **self-contained huts** (4/6 beds A$55/85), two-bedroom **cabins** (A$145) and **units** (A$105) located within the park, all booked through the **Parks Victoria office** (☎ 1800 350 552, 03-5680 9555; www.parkweb.vic.gov.au).

Tidal River has 450 camp sites (bookings essential in holiday periods). During the high season, sites cost A$20 for up to three people and one car, plus A$4.20 per extra person and A$6 per extra car. At other times, rates are slightly cheaper. There are another 11 bush camping areas around the Prom, 10 with pit toilets and most with water. Overnight bushwalkers need camping permits (A$5), which should be booked ahead through the Parks Victoria office.

Getting There & Away

There's no direct public transport between Melbourne and the Prom. **V/Line** (☎ 13 61 96) has daily coaches from Melbourne to Foster (A$26, 3½ hours), about 60km north of Tidal River. **Foster Backpackers Hostel** (☎ 03-5682 2614) runs a daily bus service to and from the Prom (A$15 each way), departing early from Foster.

LAKES DISTRICT

Gippsland's Lakes District is the largest inland waterway system in Australia. There are three main lakes that interconnect: Lake King, Lake Victoria and Lake Wellington. The 'lakes' are actually shallow lagoons, separated from the ocean by a narrow strip of sand dunes known as Ninety Mile Beach.

GETTING THERE & AWAY

V/Line (☎ 13 61 96) trains and coaches leave Southern Cross station in Melbourne for Bairnsdale at least nine times daily (A$60, four hours). It also runs from Melbourne to Lakes Entrance (A$70, 4½ hours) four times daily. Daily V/Line coaches run along the Princes Hwy from Bairnsdale into New South Wales (NSW).

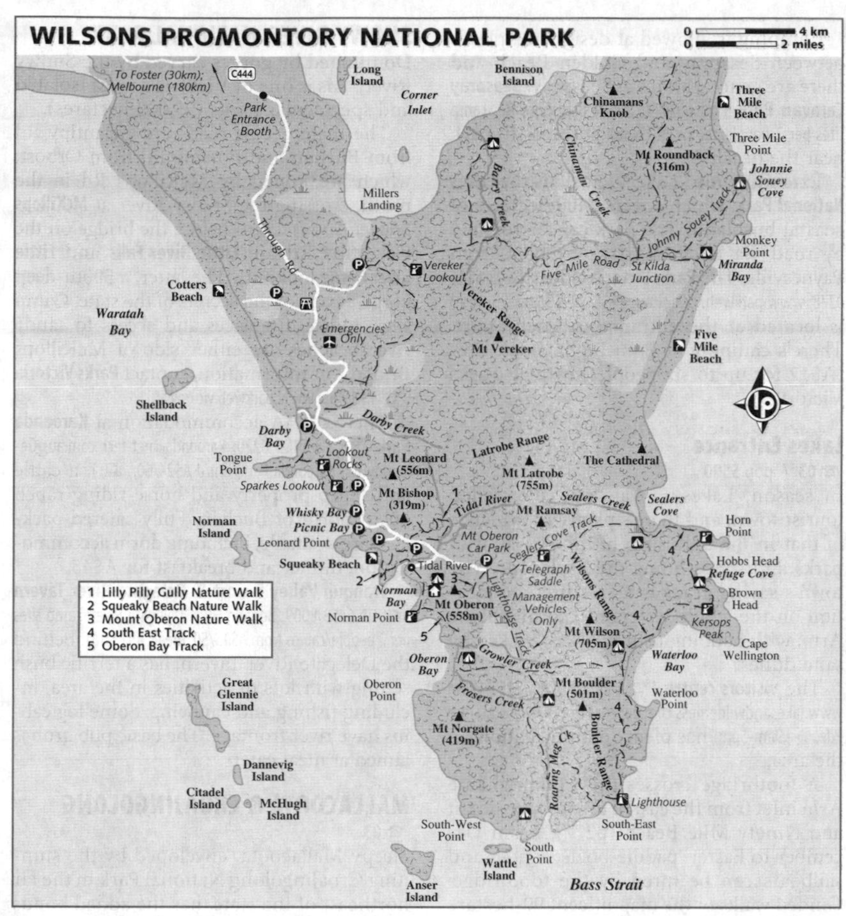

Bairnsdale

☎ 03 / pop 10,670

Bustling Bairnsdale is the major town of this district; from here you can also access the Alpine region (p288). The **visitors centre** (☎ 1800 637 060, 5152 3444; 240 Main St; 9am-5pm) can book accommodation.

The **Krowathunkoolong Keeping Place** (☎ 5152 1891; 37-53 Dalmahoy St; admission A$4; 9am-5pm Mon-Fri) is a cultural centre with displays and information on the local Aboriginal people.

For budget accommodation options, there's the **Commercial Hotel** (☎ 5152 3031; 124 Main St; dm/s/d A$15/20/40), which is good value, despite being a little threadbare around the edges. Dorm rooms sleep up to four.

Mitchell Gardens Holiday Park (☎ 5152 4654; mitchell.gardens@net-tech.com.au; 2 Main St; camp sites per 2 people A$15, cabins A$70-110) is east of the centre and by the Mitchell River. The facilities at this holiday park are well kept and clean. The cabins have river views.

Ninety Mile Beach

Stretching from Seaspray to Lakes Entrance, dunes, swamplands and lagoons back this pristine and seamless sandy beach. There's a sizable kangaroo and emu population, so drive slowly, especially at dusk and in the night. The beach is great for surf fishing and walking, but be advised it can be dangerous for swimming, except where it's patrolled at Seaspray.

Camping is allowed at designated places between Seaspray and Golden Beach and there are general stores at Seaspray. **Seaspray Caravan Park** (☎ 03-5146 4364; Foreshore Rd; camp sites per 2 people/cabins A$17/48) is the only park near the beach.

Extending into Lake Victoria is the **Lakes National Park**, which covers 2400 hectares of coastal bushland. The park can be reached by road via Loch Sport or by boat from Paynesville. The **Parks Victoria office** (☎ 03-5146 0278; www.parkweb.vic.gov.au; 8.30-9.30am & 3-4pm) is located at the entrance to Loch Sport. There's camping at Emu Bight. Book sites (A$12 for up to six people) through Parks Victoria.

Lakes Entrance

☎ 03 / pop 5500

In season, Lakes Entrance is a crowded tourist town, and there's plenty of evidence of that in the ugly strip of motels, caravan parks and shops lining the Esplanade. The town's saving grace is its picturesque location on the gentle waters of Cunninghame Arm, with bobbing fishing boats, backed by sand dunes.

The **visitors centre** (☎ 1800 637 060, 5155 1966; www.lakesandwilderness.com.au; cnr Princes Hwy & Marine Pde; 9am-5pm) has plenty of information on the area.

A footbridge crosses the Cunninghame Arm inlet from the east of town to the ocean and Ninety Mile Beach (p277). From December to Easter, paddle-boats, canoes and sailboats can be hired by the footbridge. Guided walks of the magnificent 90-hectare Gippsland forest are offered by the **Nature Sanctuary** (☎ 5156 5863; Toorloo Arm; A$20); night are walks are available.

If you're planning to stay overnight here, **Riviera Backpackers** (☎ 5155 2444; www.yha.com.au; 669-671 The Esplanade; dm/d A$18/38;) is a good, clean option, It has a large kitchen, and there's a pool table. Guests receive discounts at nominated restaurants and on some tours.

The wide open spaces at clean and shady **Eastern Beach Caravan Park** (☎ 5155 1581; Eastern Beach; camp/caravan sites from A$15/17) are in stark contrast to those on the inner-town circuit. The friendly owners will help out wherever possible, and the facilities are reasonable. There's excellent fishing at the nearby beach.

SNOWY RIVER NATIONAL PARK

Dominated by gorges carved by the Snowy River, this is one of Victoria's most isolated and spectacular parks (95,000 hectares).

The main access roads are Gelantipy Rd from Buchan and Bonang Rd from Orbost, which are joined by McKillops Rd in the north, crossing the Snowy River at **McKillops Bridge**. About 25km before the bridge on the Gelantipy Rd are **Little River Falls** and **Little River Gorge** lookouts. The latter, a 500m-deep gorge, is one of the secrets of the state. Camp sites, toilets, fireplaces and access to sandy river beaches are either side of McKillops Bridge. For information, contact **Parks Victoria** (☎ 13 19 63; www.parkweb.vic.gov.au).

There's YHA accommodation at **Karoonda Park** (☎ 03-5155 0220; karoonda@net-tech.com.au; Gelantipy Rd, Karoonda Park; dm/d A$24/60;), a cattle and sheep property and horse-riding ranch 40km north of Buchan. Fully catered packages are available, including dorm accommodation, dinner and breakfast for A$45.

Tranquil Valley Resort & Delegate River Tavern (☎ 03-6458 8009; Bonang Hwy, Delegate River; camp sites per 2 people/cabins from A$15/50, meals A$13-15), behind the Delegate River Tavern, has a terrific bush setting with lots of activities in the area, including fishing and canoeing. Some log cabins have river frontage. The basic pub grub is aimed at meat eaters.

MALLACOOTA & CROAJINGOLONG

☎ 03

Sleepy Mallacoota, enveloped by the stunning Croajingolong National Park in the far northeast of the state, has the added bonus of nearby ocean beaches. There are ample opportunities for bushwalking, surfing and swimming. But it's no secret, and can become crowded at Christmas and Easter.

The **Parks Victoria information centre** (☎ 5158 0219; www.parkweb.vic.gov.au; 9.30am-noon & 1-3.30pm Mon-Fri) is opposite the main wharf. The informal **visitors centre** (www.mallacoota.com; 9am-5pm), in the green shed on the wharf, has sufficient maps and information on conditions at Croajingolong. It can also issue the necessary permits for camping overnight.

Prices for accommodation vary significantly with the seasons and you'll need to book ahead for Christmas or Easter.

Mallacoota Hotel Motel & Mallacoota Lodge YHA (☎ 5158 0455; inncoota@vicnet.net.au; 51-55 Maurice Ave; lodge dm/d A$20/40, motel s/d A$50/60;) is

MELBOURNE & VICTORIA

nothing fancy, but offers good value for this pack-'em-in tourist town. The large motel rooms overlook an excellent pool and lawn; rates vary seasonally. The YHA has good accommodation with a shared kitchen; book through the hotel-motel.

Mallacoota Foreshore Camp Park (☎ 5158 0300; Camping Reserve; camp/caravan sites per 2 people A$21/35) has sites which extend right along the foreshore and have sublime views of the lake, with its resident population of black swans and pelicans.

Croajingolong National Park

Stunning **Croajingolong** (87,500 hectares) is one of Australia's finest national parks. It stretches for about 100km from Bemm River to the NSW border and includes unspoilt beaches, inlets and forests. The 200m sand dunes at Thurra are the highest on the mainland. Mallacoota Inlet is the largest and most accessible area. The plentiful wildlife in the park includes huge goannas. The main camping areas are Wingan Inlet, Shipwreck Creek, Thurra River, Peachtree Creek and Mueller Inlet. You may need to bring water, so check first with Parks Victoria. You'll also need to book during the main holiday seasons; camping fees are up to A$17 a site.

Getting There & Away

Princes Hwy is the main access road to this region. Mallacoota is 23km off the highway.

INLAND

Victoria's flat farming land begins to crumple up a little bit around the historic gold-mining centres of Ballarat and Bendigo, and is in stark contrast to the always-spectacular mountains of the Alpine National Park. So buckle up ski boots or lace up hiking boots to appreciate this beautiful area year-round.

Activities

Pan for gold at Ballarat's Sovereign Hill – but don't plan on giving up your day job. Bushwalk around the lush Grampians, whose ancient rocks are loved for their indigenous paintings, as well as for rock climbing and abseiling. There's also caving, horse riding and canoeing. In winter, ski or snowboard in the glorious Alpine National Park, which offers bushwalking at other times.

BALLARAT

☎ 03 / pop 73,000

Ballarat is a historic gold-mining town best known for its simulated town, Sovereign Hill – where 300 actors, 40 horses and 60 buildings keep the 'township' stuck firmly in the 1860s.

The area was originally known to its indigenous custodians, the Watha Warrung people, as 'Ballaarat' (resting place). Things became decidedly busy when European pastoralists discovered gold at nearby Buninyong in 1851. Thousands of diggers flooded the area, working alluvial goldfields and sinking deep shaft mines, which tapped into incredibly rich quartz reefs. Work continued until the end of WWI, by which time Ballarat had grown into major provincial hub, with grand Victorian architecture lining its broad streets. Lydiard St is one of Australia's finest streetscapes. Impressive buildings include Her Majesty's Theatre, the art gallery and Craig's Royal Hotel; the visitors centre distributes a brochure on these sights.

The **visitors centre** (☎ 1800 446 633, 5320 5672; www.ballarat.com; 39 Sturt St; 9am-5pm) books accommodation and sells the Ballarat 'Eureka Pass' (A$36 per adult), which allows two days unlimited entry to Sovereign Hill, the Gold Museum and Eureka Stockade Centre; this pass is also available from the venues. The **Gold Shop** (☎ 5333 4242; 8a Lydiard St North), in the old Mining Exchange building, sells miners' rights and detailed maps, and rents out metal detectors to hopefuls.

Sights

Ballarat has a few sights worth finding. The main attraction, **Sovereign Hill** (☎ 5331 1944; www.sovereignhill.com.au; Bradshaw St; admission A$29; 9am-5pm) is an entertaining living history museum, with costumed characters going about daily 1860s life. You can pan for gold and may find a speck or two. There are also two underground tours of re-created mines, plus a gold pour, which transforms A$50,000 of liquid gold into a 3kg bullion bar.

The nightly sound-and-light show **Blood on the Southern Cross** (☎ 5333 5777; admission A$35) is a simulation of the Eureka Stockade battle – the 1854 uprising of miners against corrupt colonial rulers heralded as the beginnings of Australian democracy. Starting times depend on the sunset; bookings are essential.

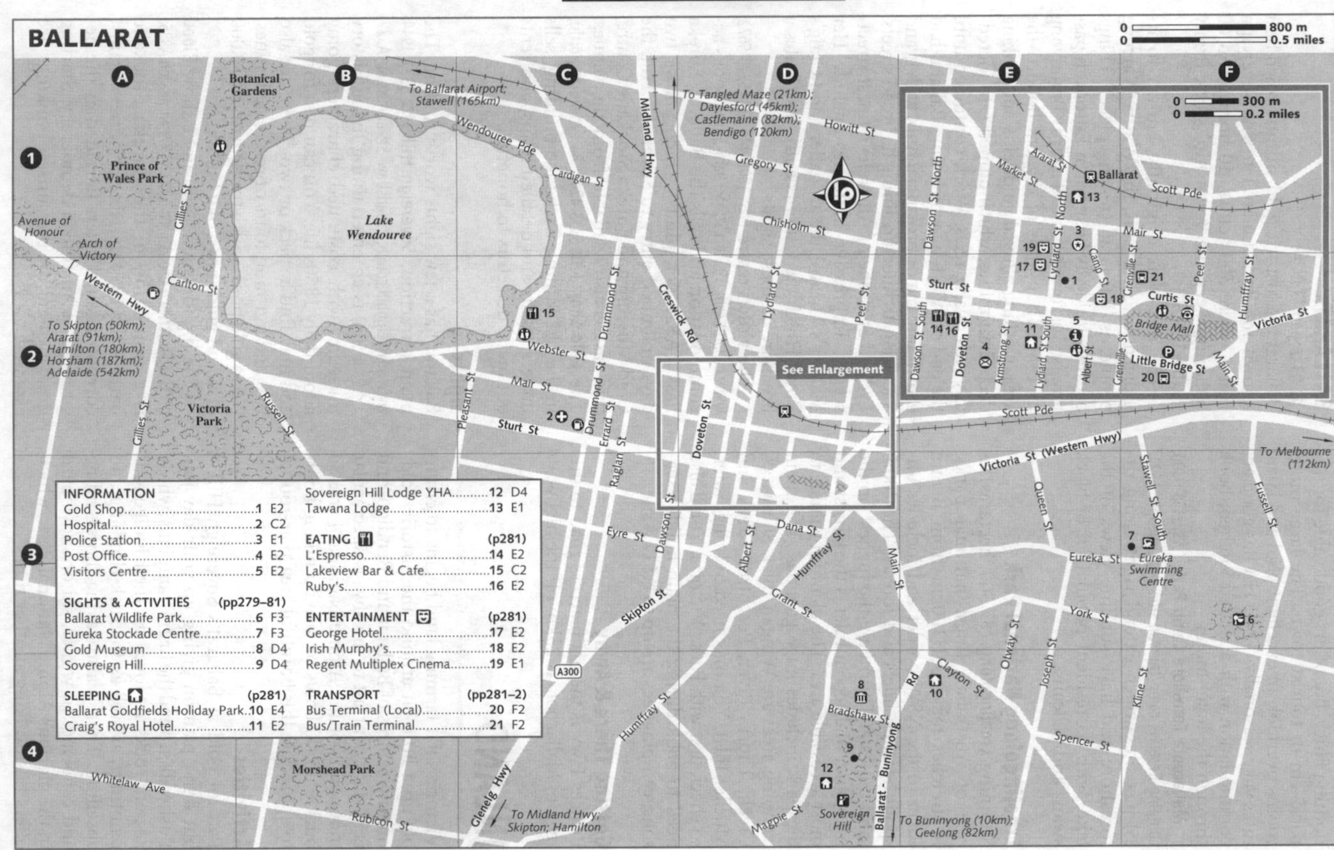
BALLARAT
0 800 m
0 0.5 miles
0 300 m
0 0.2 miles
See Enlargement
INFORMATION
Gold Shop....1 E2
Hospital....2 C2
Police Station....3 E1
Post Office....4 E2
Visitors Centre....5 E2
SIGHTS & ACTIVITIES (pp279–81)
Ballarat Wildlife Park....6 F3
Eureka Stockade Centre....7 F3
Gold Museum....8 D4
Sovereign Hill....9 D4
SLEEPING (p281)
Ballarat Goldfields Holiday Park..10 E4
Craig's Royal Hotel....11 E2
Sovereign Hill Lodge YHA....12 D4
Tawana Lodge....13 E1
EATING (p281)
L'Espresso....14 E2
Lakeview Bar & Cafe....15 C2
Ruby's....16 E2
ENTERTAINMENT (p281)
George Hotel....17 E2
Irish Murphy's....18 E2
Regent Multiplex Cinema....19 E1
TRANSPORT (pp281–2)
Bus Terminal (Local)....20 F2
Bus/Train Terminal....21 F2
To Skipton (50km); Ararat (91km); Hamilton (180km); Horsham (187km); Adelaide (542km)
To Ballarat Airport; Stawell (165km)
To Tangled Maze (21km); Daylesford (45km); Castlemaine (82km); Bendigo (120km)
To Melbourne (112km)
To Buninyong (10km); Geelong (82km)
To Midland Hwy; Skipton; Hamilton
Lake Wendouree
Botanical Gardens
Prince of Wales Park
Victoria Park
Morshead Park
Avenue of Honour
Arch of Victory
Eureka Swimming Centre
Sovereign Hill
Bridge Mall
Western Hwy
Midland Hwy
Victoria St (Western Hwy)
Glenelg Hwy
Ballarat - Buninyong Rd
A300

Over the road from Sovereign Hill, the **Gold Museum** (☎ 5337 1107; Bradshaw St; admission included in Sovereign Hill ticket, separate admission A$7.30; 9.30am-5.20pm) displays gold and memorabilia, as well as an audiovisual presentation that tells the story of the Watha Warrung.

Standing on the site of the Eureka Stockade rebellion, the **Eureka Stockade Centre** (☎ 5333 1854; cnr Eureka & Rodier Sts; admission A$9; 9am-5pm) has multimedia galleries simulating the battle.

If you've had enough gold for one day, head for **Lake Wendouree**. This large artificial lake was used for the 1956 Olympics' rowing events. Wendouree Pde, which circles the lake, is where jaw-dropping houses mix it with charming old timber boatsheds along the lake's shores.

Ballarat's immaculate 40-hectare **botanical gardens** are beside Lake Wendouree. If you have the stomach for it, you can come face to face with the likes of Paul Keating and John Howard in the gardens' Prime Ministers' Avenue, with its collection of bronze busts.

The **Ballarat Wildlife Park** (☎ 5333 5933; cnr Fussell & York Sts; admission A$15.50; 9am-5.30pm) has native animals, reptiles and a few exotics. Guided tours are at 11am and there are several daily shows.

Who can resist a maze? The **Tangled Maze** (☎ 5345 2847; Midland Hwy; admission A$7; 10am-5.30pm), 21km north of town, covers over an acre with plenty of twists and turns. There's also a mini golf course, tearoom and picnic areas.

Sleeping

Ballarat's 100-year-old Begonia Festival (in early March) attracts thousands of visitors, so accommodation can be hard to find at this time (book in advance).

Sovereign Hill Lodge YHA (☎ 5333 3409; www.yha.com.au; Magpie St; dm/s/d A$21/30/60) You've struck gold here, with super facilities including a bar, barbecue and large communal lounge. Single and double rooms with bathrooms are available. Book well in advance to avoid disappointment.

Craig's Royal Hotel (☎ 5331 1377; www.craigsroyal.com; 10 Lydiard St South; d A$60, with bathroom A$95-115) This grand Victorian building is one of the best old pubs in the state. It took its 'Royal' moniker after the Prince of Wales and Duke of Windsor visited.

Tawana Lodge (☎ 5331 3461; 128 Lydiard St North; s/d A$33/44) Basic hotels rooms with shared facilities are a fair deal here. Have a look up the stairwell at the murals of reclining chaste young ladies.

Ballarat Goldfields Holiday Park (☎ 5332 7888; 108 Clayton St; camp sites per 2 people A$20-23, cabins A$60-70;) This is the closest caravan park to Sovereign Hill and one of the best-equipped in these parts. There's a pool, games room and tennis courts.

Eating

L'Espresso (☎ 5333 1789; 417 Sturt St; dishes A$10-24; lunch daily, dinner Fri & Sat) Sink into a comfy chocolate-coloured banquette between the wall of jazz and blues records and the opposing wall of artistically displayed produce. Mainstay breakfasts, such as porridge with honey and dried fruit, have a classy finish. Lunch is traditional Italian, with unfussy pasta, focaccia and meat dishes.

Ruby's (☎ 5333 3386; 423 Sturt St; dishes A$8-20; breakfast Sat & Sun, lunch Tue-Sun, dinner Sat) Cosy Ruby's is a lovely place to linger; you'll need longer than usual to be able to peruse the extensive menu. Café standards, such as risotto, curry and laksa, are given a sophisticated spin, and there are plenty of meat-free options.

Lakeview Bar & Café (☎ 5331 4592; 22 Wendouree Pde; dishes A$7.50-23; breakfast, lunch & dinner) Hip young things buzz around this bistro-style restaurant by the lake, especially on live-music nights.

Entertainment

George Hotel (☎ 5333 4866; 27 Lydiard St North) The historic George is one of the better venues for bands, from 9.30pm to 4am on Friday and Saturday nights.

Irish Murphy's (☎ 5331 4091; 36 Sturt St) This Guinness theme pub has bands from Thursday to Sunday night.

Regent Multiplex Cinema (☎ 5331 1556; 49 Lydiard St North) This is a super, central cinema showing all the latest big-screen favourites.

Getting There & Around

V/Line (☎ 13 61 96) trains run frequently between Melbourne and Ballarat (A$17, 1½ hours).

V/Line also has daily bus services from Ballarat to Warrnambool (A$20, three hours) and Bendigo (A$21, two hours), and two services per day to Mildura (A$60, seven hours).

McCafferty's/Greyhound (☎ 13 14 99, 13 20 30, 9670 7500; www.mccaffertys.com.au) and **Firefly** (☎ 1300 730 740; www.fireflyexpress.com.au) buses stop at the train station on the Melbourne–Adelaide run.

The local bus line, **Davis Bus Service** (☎ 5331 7777; www.kefford.com.au) covers most of the town; timetables are available at the visitors centre.

BENDIGO

☎ 03 / pop 68,700

The gracious sandstone edifices of Bendigo hark back to the heady goldrush days. When gold was discovered at Ravenswood in 1851 thousands of diggers, many of them Chinese, converged on the fantastically rich Bendigo Diggings. Named after a famous bare-knuckle boxer, William 'Abednigo' Thompson, Bendigo is a distinguished regional centre that supports a number of boutique industries. The **Easter Fair** attracts thousands of visitors with its carnival atmosphere and Chinese-dragon procession.

The **visitors centre** (☎ 1800 813 153, 5444 4445; www.bendigotourism.com; 51-57 Pall Mall; 9am-5pm) in the historic post office is also an interpretative centre. The staff book accommodation and activities.

The 500m-deep **Central Deborah Gold Mine** (☎ 5443 8322; www.central-deborah.com; 76 Violet St; guided tour A$17, self-guided tour A$8; 9am-5pm) gave up about 1000kg of gold during its 15 years as a working mine from 1939 to 1954.

One of Victoria's largest regional galleries, the **Bendigo Art Gallery** (☎ 5443 4991; 42 View St; admission by donation; 10am-5pm) has outstanding collections of Australian and 19th-century European art, plus regular visiting overseas exhibitions.

Bendigo Pottery (☎ 5448 4404; Midland Hwy; admission free; 9am-5pm), the oldest pottery works in Australia (1858), is at Epsom, 6km north of Bendigo. There's a café, sales gallery and historic kilns, and you can watch potters at work, or have a pottery lesson for A$12. **Living Wings & Things** (☎ 5448 3051; admission A$7; 9am-5pm) is on the same site. It has lizards, pythons, butterflies, walk-through parrot enclosures, wallabies and dingoes.

Sleeping

Nomads Ironbark Bushcabins (☎ 5448 3344; www.bwc.com.au/ironbark; Watson St; dm/d A$20/55) Nomads is a horse-riding camp out in the bush, with free pick-up from Bendigo train station. A two-day package of two nights' accommodation with food and enough riding to make it difficult to walk costs A$95. Shorter trail rides are also available.

Bendigo YHA (☎ 5443 7680; www.yha.com.au; 33 Creek St South; dm A$21;) This homey little hostel is in a weatherboard cottage and has all the usual facilities, for a bargain-bucket price.

Central City Caravan Park (☎ 5443 6937; 362 High St, Golden Sq; dm A$15, camp/caravan sites per 2 people A$18/37, cabins A$65) One of about 10 caravan parks in and around Bendigo, this one includes a basic hostel section in prefab cabins (four bunks each), with separate cooking and kitchen facilities. Central City is about 2km south of the centre – you can get to it by bus from Hargreaves St.

Getting There & Around

At least four **V/Line** (☎ 13 61 96) trains run between Bendigo and Melbourne daily (A$25, two hours). Buses from Bendigo, departing outside the train station, include daily services to Ballarat (A$21, two hours) and Mildura (A$60, six hours), and twice-daily services to Echuca (A$7.30, 1½ hours).

Walkers Buslines (☎ 5443 9333) and **Christian's Buslines** (☎ 5447 2222) service the area. Timetables are available at the visitors centre.

ECHUCA

☎ 03 / pop 10,950

Echuca, a local Aboriginal term meaning 'the meeting of the waters', is where the Goulburn and Campaspe Rivers join the Murray River. Ex-convict Harry Hopwood, who established punt and ferry crossings over the Murray and Campaspe Rivers, founded the town in 1853. He built the Bridge Hotel in 1858 and watched his town grow into the busiest inland port in Australia, when at its peak over 100 paddle-steamers plied the Murray River. The wharf was once over a kilometre long and lined with shops and hotels.

The **visitors centre** (☎ 1800 804 446, 5480 7555; www.echucamoama.com; 2 Heygarth St; 9am-5pm) can book accommodation and sells V/Line tickets.

Sights & Activities

At the wharf, the old-fashioned **Port of Echuca** (☎ 5482 4248; www.portofechuca.org.au; 52 Murray

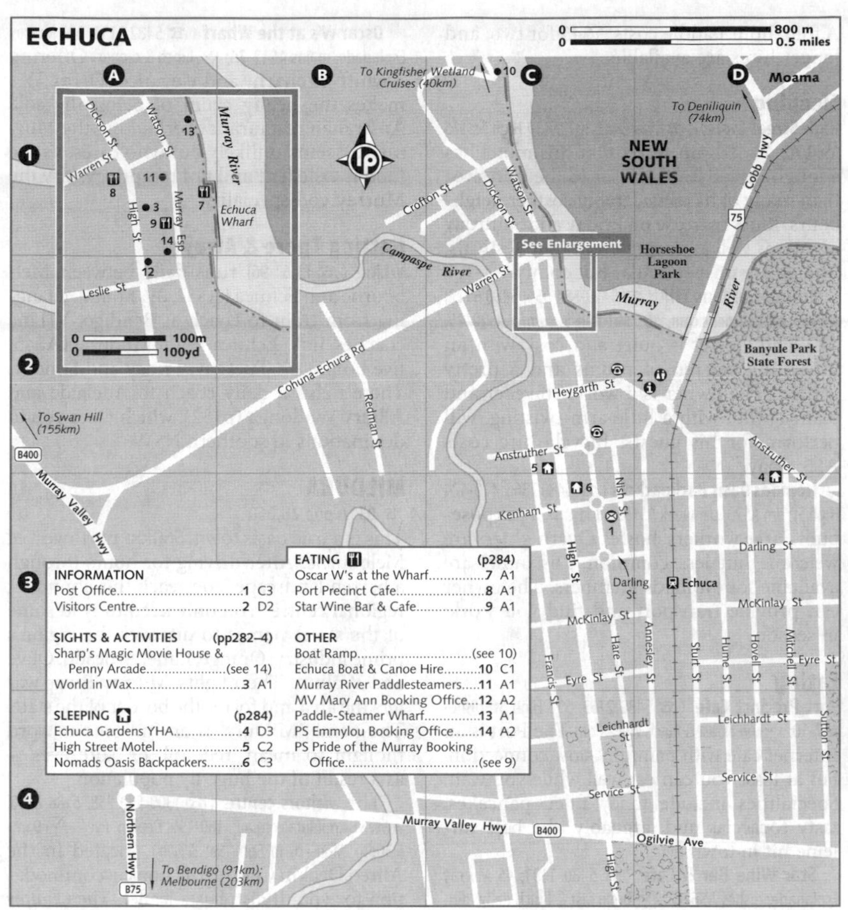

Esplanade; admission A$11; 9am-5pm) has a quasi-Disneyland appeal. A ticket combining the port's attractions with a paddle-steamer cruise costs A$23 per adult. You can escape from the **Star Hotel** (45 Murray Esplanade), built in 1867, through an underground tunnel built to help drinkers avoid the police during the years when the pub was a 'sly grog shop'. The **Sharp's Magic Movie House & Penny Arcade** (☎ 5482 2361; Murray Esplanade; admission A$13; 9am-5pm) has a collection of penny-arcade machines and shows old movies; try the home-made fudge here as well.

World in Wax (☎ 5482 3630; 630 High St; adult A$8.80; 9am-5.30pm) eerily immortalises a 'cast' of 60 famous people ranging from the British royal family to Paul Hogan.

A **paddle-steamer cruise** along the Murray is a real treat. **Murray River Paddlesteamers** (☎ 5480 2237; www.emmylou.com.au; 57 Murray Esplanade; 9am-5pm) sells tickets for the **PS Emmylou** (90-min cruise A$17) with overnight cruises available, and the **PS Pride of the Murray** (cruise per hr A$13). **PS Adelaide** (☎ 5482 4248; 1hr adult A$17.50) is the oldest wooden-hulled paddle-steamer still operating anywhere in the world; it occasionally has cruises. There's also **MV Mary Ann** (☎ 5480 2200; 624 High St), a cruising restaurant rather than a paddle-steamer.

Echuca Boat & Canoe Hire (☎ 5480 6208; www.echucaboatcanoehire.com) hires out motor boats, kayaks and canoes from the Victoria Park boat ramp, about 700m north of the wharf.

A four-hour paddle costs A$45 for two, and longer hires are available.

Sleeping

High Street Motel (☎/fax 5482 1013; 439 High St; s/d A$60/70; ❄) It's no secret that this motel has a lot going for it: it's closer to the port area than many of its considerably costlier neighbours. Rates increase on Friday and Saturday nights, as well as during events and festivals. Rooms are unspectacular but comfy.

Echuca Gardens YHA (☎0419-881 054, 5480 6522; www.echucagardens.com; 103 Mitchell St; dm/d A$20/45; 💻) This hostel is quiet and cosy with an intriguing warren of rooms and a pretty garden. The owner is a world traveller and pianist who, with a little arm-twisting, will perform for his guests. Bicycle hire costs A$5 a day.

Nomads Oasis Backpackers (☎5480 7866; 410-424 High St; dm A$23, per week A$135) This is a purpose-built, large workers' hostel. Overnighters are welcome but less common. Discounts are available for Nomads members. The owner can provide transport and find you work, in season.

Eating

Port Precinct Café (☎5480 2163; 591 High St; dishes A$7-10; 🕐 breakfast & lunch Wed-Mon) The Port is an Internet café with painfully slow connection, but at least you can eat well while you wait. Specialities include fancy filled pancakes, tasty focaccias and, arguably, the best caffeine hit in town.

Star Wine Bar & Café (☎5480 1181; 45 Murray Esplanade; dishes A$6-12; 🕐 breakfast & lunch daily, dinner Fri & Sat) Part of the Star Hotel, this café sells snacks and light meals during the day and dinner on Friday and Saturday. The bar has a nice moody atmosphere with interesting artwork, and there's a leafy patio at the back. The food is typically cross-cultural with just enough Eastern influence to spice things up.

> **FRUIT FLY**
>
> An exclusion zone surrounding the Murray River protects the fruit and vegetable crops from fruit fly by prohibiting the carrying of fresh fruit into the zone. There are warning signs and disposal bins on the roads leading into the zone.

Oscar W's at the Wharf (☎5482 5133; 101 Murray Esplanade; mains A$12-26; 🕐 lunch & dinner) Offering a whiff of charm and elegance, Oscar W's makes the heady claim of being the sole Australian restaurant overlooking the Murray. It seems unlikely but who cares, as the food is excellent and not too pricey. Try the Murray cod speciality.

Getting There & Away

V/Line (☎13 61 96) runs daily between Melbourne and Echuca (A$32, 3½ hours), changing from train to coach at Bendigo. V/Line coaches link Echuca with Mildura (A$45, five hours) on Tuesday, Friday and Sunday. There's also a daily coach to Adelaide and Albury Wodonga (p132), which takes you to destinations in southern NSW.

MILDURA

☎03 / pop 28,060

This is a true oasis town, 560km northwest of Melbourne. After driving for hours through a barren landscape, you reach this abundant regional centre. You only need to read some of the street names to discover the region's prime industry: Orange, Lime, Avocado, Olive and Walnut. The mighty Murray River waters the area and forms the border of the state. The name 'Mildura' is an indigenous word thought to mean 'red soil' or 'sore eyes' – as a result of the huge fly population.

The **visitors centre** (☎1300 550 858, 5188 8380; www.visitmildura.com.au; 180-190 Deakin Ave; 🕐 9am-5.30pm Mon-Fri, to 5pm Sat & Sun), located in the Alfred Deakin Centre, will book accommodation for you. It also has a leaflet, *The Chaffey Trail*, which guides you around local sights. Also in the Alfred Deakin Centre is a café and aquatic centre. The library next door to the centre provides Internet access.

Contact the employment agency **Madec** (☎5021 3359/2203, 5022 1797; cnr 10th St & Deakin Ave) for fruit-picking work. The main harvest season runs from about January to March and some casual work is available year-round. The visitors centre has a useful leaflet on fruit-picking work.

The **Mildura Arts Centre & Rio Vista** (☎5018 8322; 199 Cureton Ave; admission A$4; 🕐 10am-5pm) combines an art gallery, theatre and museum in the former home of WB Chaffey, who planned the town.

A number of wineries in the area are open daily for tastings:

Lindeman's Karadoc (☎ 5051 3285; Karadoc; ⌚ 10am-4.30pm) A huge complex 20km south of Mildura off the Calder Hwy. The café is open 10am to 3pm Monday to Friday.
Mildara Blass (☎ 5025 2303; Merbein; ⌚ 9am-5pm Mon-Fri, 10am-4pm Sat & Sun) On the Murray River, 9km west of Mildura.
Trentham Estate (☎ 5024 8888) A small winery across the border in NSW, 12km from Mildura; the restaurant is open for lunch Tuesday to Sunday.

Tours

Harry Nanya Tours (☎ 1800 630 864, 5027 2076) is the best known of several Aboriginal tour operations, offering a wide range of cultural tours. Day tours run to Mungo National Park (p455) for A$75. The park is part of the Willandra Lakes system – containing the longest continual record of Aboriginal life in Australia, dating back some 46,000 years.

Running a tour similar to that offered by Harry Nanya, **Jumbunna Walkabout Tours & Charter** (☎ 0412-581 699; www.jumbunnawalkabout.com.au) includes barbecue lunch on Monday, Friday and Sunday (A$85). Tours depart from the visitors centre at 7.30am in summer and 8.30am in winter.

PADDLE-STEAMER CRUISES

Cruises depart from the Mildura Wharf at the end of Deakin Ave.

PS Melbourne (☎ 5023 2200) is the only original boat here still driven by steam. Two-hour cruises (A$20) depart daily at 10.50am and 1.50pm. The **PV Rothbury** (☎ 5023 2200) has two cruises on Thursday only. A winery cruise (A$46 including lunch) departs at 10.30am, and an evening dinner cruise (A$45) departs at 7pm.

Sleeping & Eating

Mildura Park Motel (☎ 5023 0479; fax 5022 1651; 250 Eighth St; s/d A$50/55; ❄) The no-frills Mildura Park is located in a quiet residential area 1km or so west of Deakin Ave. All rooms have bathrooms, and fancier rooms are available, with kitchenettes (s/d A$69/76).

Riverboat Bungalow (☎ 0418-147 363, 5021 5315; 27 Chaffey Ave; dm A$20, per week A$120; 💻) Most people stay a week at the homely Bungalow, although overnighters are welcome, too. There's also a second smaller property round the corner at 206 Eighth St, with the added perk of a small pool.

Riverbeach Camping Ground (☎ 5023 6879; apex@ruralnet.net.au; Cureton Ave; camp/caravan sites per 2 people A$20/30, cabins A$55-95) Blissfully located right on the sandy riverbanks, Riverbeach has spick-and-span cabins and plenty of trees for shady sites. The fully licenced café-bar is a plus.

Mildura Grand Hotel (☎ 5023 0511; Seventh St) has a number of dining options. You could try authentic thin-crust pizza at **Pizza Café** ($14-17; lunch & dinner), get an iron fix with a steak at the **Spanish Grill** ($20-25; lunch & dinner) or totally splurge at **Stefano's** (banquet A$85; dinner Mon-Sat).

Getting There & Away

AIR

Mildura's airport is 10km west of town off the Sturt Hwy (A20). Low-end fares to Melbourne start at about A$120.
Qantas (☎ 13 13 13; www.qantas.com.au)
Rex (☎ 13 17 13; www.regionalexpress.com.au)

BUS

V/Line (☎ 13 61 96) has four services per day between Melbourne and Mildura (A$65, eight hours) via Bendigo. V/Line also connects Mildura with Ballarat (A$60, seven hours) twice daily, and has a service connecting towns along the Murray River, including Echuca (A$45, five hours) on Tuesday, Friday and Sunday.

Long-distance coaches operate from near the train station on Seventh Ave.

THE GRAMPIANS

The Grampians are a major Victorian attraction with a rich diversity of plant and animal wildlife, rock formations, Aboriginal rock art, bushwalking, climbing and plenty of other activities. The Grampians lie west of Ararat and stretch some 90km from Dunkeld in the south, almost to Horsham in the north. **Halls Gap**, the most central town in the Grampians, has a supermarket, restaurants and cafés, and a range of accommodation.

The **Grampians & Halls Gap Visitors Centre** (☎ 1800 065 599, 03-5356 4616; www.visitgrampians.com.au; Grampians Rd, Halls Gap; ⌚ 9am-5pm) will book accommodation and look after your backpack while you explore the area.

Housed in a striking building shaped like a cockatoo, the **Brambuk Cultural Centre** (☎ 03-5356 4452; brambuk@netconnect.com.au; Grampians Rd, Halls Gap; ⌚ 9am-5pm) is run by five Koorie communities. There are great displays, a bush tucker café (offering Internet access)

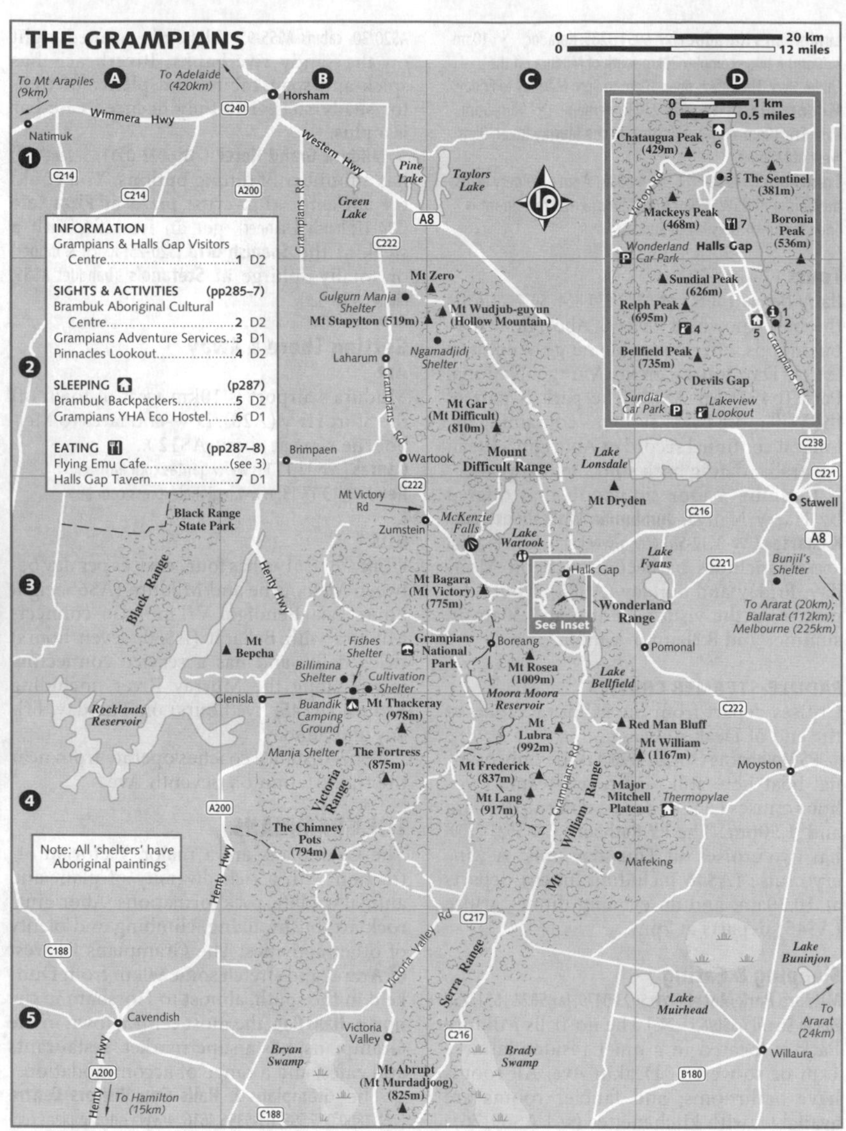

and, during holiday periods, Aboriginal music and dance. The **Gariwerd Dreaming Theatre** (admission A$4.40) at the cultural centre has a multimedia narration of traditional stories. Tours of rock-art sites depart from the centre most days at 10am. Tours cost A$15 (four-person minimum) and need to be booked 24 hours in advance.

The cultural centre also houses the **Parks Victoria office** (☎ 03-5356 4381; www.parkweb.vic.gov.au), providing advice on walks and camping in the area.

Much of the **rock art** in the Grampians is not publicised or accessible. In the northern Grampians near Mt Stapylton, the main sites are **Gulgurn Manja Shelter** and **Ngamadjidj**

Shelter. In the southwestern Grampians, near the Buandik camping ground, the main sites are **Billimina Shelter** and **Manja Shelter**.

Close to Halls Gap, the **Wonderland Range** has some spectacular and accessible scenery. There are scenic drives and walks – from an easy half-hour stroll to Venus Baths, to a five-hour walk to the **Pinnacles Lookout**. Walking tracks start from Halls Gap, and the Wonderland and Sundial car parks.

There are two tracks from the Zumstein picnic area, northwest of Halls Gap, to the spectacular **McKenzie Falls**. The first track, taking two to three hours, follows the McKenzie River upstream via another set of falls. The second is a cop-out five- to 10-minute walk for those in a hurry – or just lazy!

Activities

Rock climbing and abseiling are popular activities in the park; a half-day introductory course costs around A$60.

The **Grampians Mountain Adventure Company** (☎ 0427-747 047; grampiansadventure.com.au) is led by accredited instructors, for those who fancy a taste of the vertical world.

Grampians Adventure Services (GAS; ☎ 03-5356 4556; www.visitgrampians.com.au/gas) offers rock climbing, abseiling, canoeing, bike tours, bushwalking and caving.

Hangin' Out (☎ 03-5356 4535; www.hanginout.com.au) is another multiactivity adventure company offering abseiling, bushwalking and single- or multipitch climbing.

Activities may be booked by phone, via each company's website or from the Grampians Central Booking Office in the Halls Gap Newsagency.

BUSHWALKING

There are more than 150km of tracks in the Grampians, ranging from half-hour strolls to overnight treks through difficult terrain. The rangers at the Parks Victoria office can provide maps and advice on choosing a walk.

Be sure to take a map and wear appropriate footwear; take a hat and sunscreen in summer and carry water. Before you set off, always let someone (preferably the rangers) know where you're going.

HORSE RIDING

Grampians Horse Riding Centre (☎ 03-5383 9255) gives you the opportunity to explore the forests and valleys by horseback. Rides cost from A$45 for 90 minutes.

Sleeping

Grampians YHA Eco Hostel (☎ 03-5356 4544; www.yha.com.au; Grampians Rd; dm/s/d A$25/55/65; 💻) This 60-bed YHA is a real original. As the name suggests, there are several ecofriendly features, such as solar electricity and water conservation, plus a veggie patch and a chicken run for fresh free-range eggs. Rooms are five-star hostel style and dorm rooms have either two or four beds.

Brambuk Backpackers (☎ 03-5356 4250; Grampians Rd; dm/r A$22/55; 💻) Brambuk is a light and airy hostel with a mellow friendly feel and mountain views. There's a large sitting room with outside terrace.

Tim's Place (☎ 03-5356 4288; www.timsplace.net; Grampians Rd; dm/s/d A$23/40/55; 💻) This long-established place is showing the signs of age, but gets good reviews from travellers. Several tour companies drop off here and there's free use of mountain bikes.

Halls Gap Lakeside Caravan Park (☎ 03-5356 4281; www.hallsgaplakeside.com.au; Tymna Dr; sites A$18-24, basic cabins A$55-65) The park is one of several in the area and new facilities include some luxury cabins (from A$105) and a glassed-in dining area. This is a good spot for bird-watching. The park also looks onto grassland where kangaroos habitually congregate at dusk.

Parks Victoria (☎ 13 19 63; www.parkweb.vic.gov.au) has 13 camp sites with toilets and fireplaces, and most have at least limited drinking water. Permits (A$11) cover one car and up to six people. You can self-register or pay at Brambuk Cultural Centre. Bush camping is permitted everywhere except in the Wonderland Range area, around Lake Wartook, and in marked parts of the Serra and Victoria Ranges and some other sites. Check at the centre for any other regulations that may be in force at the time.

Eating

The Halls Gap **general store** (🕓 8am-8pm) has a café, takeaway and supermarket.

Flying Emu Café (☎ 03-5356 4400; Shop 5, Stony Creek Stores, Grampians Rd; dishes A$6-10; 🕓 lunch) The Emu serves a good range of gourmet snacks including the all-time favourite *eggs à la emu* with smoked salmon and hollandaise sauce.

TOTAL FIRE BAN

High temperatures combined with strong winds provide conditions of extreme fire danger throughout Victoria. To prevent bushfires in summer, stringent laws are put into place. On days of Total Fire Ban, no campfires of any type are permitted.

It is the individual's responsibility to know when fire restrictions have been declared. To help, Parks Victoria has erected signs in camping areas, towns display warning flags, and there are frequent radio messages and warnings in local newspapers.

Halls Gap Tavern (☎ 03-5356 4416; Grampians Rd; mains A$4-14; lunch & dinner) The best value in this modern colonial-style setting is a daily changing three-course meal for A$10. Alternatively, order from the menu with plenty of pasta choices. The desserts are pretty yummy as well.

Black Panther Café & Bar (☎ 03-5356 4511; 6 Stoney Creek Stores; mains A$7.50-13; breakfast, lunch & dinner) The menu here boasts an all-day bumper breakfast plus pizza, pasta, lunch specials, vegetarian lentils and the like. You can take away, or have meals delivered for a small charge within a reasonable distance.

Getting There & Away

V/Line (☎ 13 61 96) has a coach service that does the daily run from Melbourne to Halls Gap (A$46, four hours).

ALPINE NATIONAL PARK & SKI RESORTS

The Alpine National Park (646,000 hectares) links the high-country areas of Victoria, New South Wales and the Australian Capital Territory (ACT).

There's an increasing number of summer activities in the region, but in winter it's everything to do with snow and the incumbent après-ski partying.

The official website (www.skivic.com) has loads of information on the various resorts.

Most ski resorts are in or near the park but otherwise the area is largely wilderness. Some of the many access roads are closed in the snow season. See www.vicsnowreport.com.au for an up-to-date report on snow and road conditions. To save a few dollars, consider staying off the mountain in neighbouring towns and commuting to the snowfields each day.

There are several camping areas, and bush camping is allowed in most of the park. The region has many walking tracks, including the Australian Alps Walking Track, which wends 655km from Walhalla to Canberra.

The following snowfields offer cross-country skiing but lack accommodation:

Lake Mountain (☎ 03-5963 3288) Ski region, 120km northeast of Melbourne via Marysville, with 37km of beginners, intermediate and advanced cross-country trails.

Mt Bogong Some tough downhill skiing routes around the summit of Mt Bogong.

Mt St Gwinear (☎ 03-5165 3204) Cross-country trails on this mountain (171km from Melbourne via Moe) connect with Mt Baw Baw.

Mt Stirling (☎ 03-5777 0815) An excellent cross-country area a few kilometres northeast of Mt Buller Alpine Village, with over 60km of mostly advanced trails and a ski school.

Mt Baw Baw

☎ 03 / elevation 1564m

Mt Baw Baw Alpine Village (1480m) has stunning views of much of Gippsland and is a mere three-hour drive from Melbourne via the Princes Hwy (M1) and the C426.

The **Mt Baw Baw Resort office** (☎ 5165 1136; www.mountbawbaw.com.au) provides an information service.

Baw Baw is a good place for novice skiers and is more relaxed than the big resorts. The ski-able downhill area is 25 hectares and the runs are 25% beginners, 64% intermediate and 11% advanced, with a vertical drop of 115m. It's also a base for cross-country trails, one of which connects to the Mt St Gwinear trails.

Snow-season entry fees for the day car park cost A$26 per car. The lifts only operate if there is snow and daily passes cost A$65 (A$370 for five days).

Mt Baw Baw Ski Hire (☎ 1800 629 578, 5165 1120; www.bawbawskihire.com.au) books accommodation. In the snow season, ski-club (lodge) accommodation is available from A$30 per person mid-week and A$40 on Saturday and Sunday (minimum two nights).

Kelly's Lodge (☎ 5165 1129; lodge@kellyslodge.com.au; summer/snow-season beds A$50/70), apart from being a cosy and friendly place, is the only accommodation open year-round. You can cook in the shared kitchen or have meals in the restaurant.

Mt Buller

☎ 03 / elevation 1805m

Mt Buller is Victoria's largest and liveliest ski resort, 47km east of Mansfield and 237km (three hours) northeast of Melbourne.

The **Mt Buller Resort Management Board** (☎ 5777 6077; www.mtbuller.com.au; 8.30am-5pm snow season, 10am-4pm other times) shares premises with the post office. During peak ski season there's an information booth at the Clock Tower. There are several places where you can rent ski and snowboard gear, including **Buller Sports Horse Hill** (☎ 5777 6244), handily located at the bottom of the Horse Hill Chair Lift.

The ski-able downhill area is 180 hectares and runs are divided into 25% beginner, 45% intermediate and 30% advanced, with a vertical drop of 400m. Cross-country trails link Mt Buller with Mt Stirling.

Snow-season entry fees for the day car park are A$20 per car. Lift tickets for a full day cost from A$75 and include the use of up to 26 lifts and 400 hectares of varying terrain. Lift-and-lesson packages start at A$110.

SLEEPING & EATING

There are over 7000 beds on the mountain. Rates vary according to season and the number of beds per room. **Mt Buller Central Reservations** (☎ 1800 039 049) books accommodation in lodges from around A$75 per person.

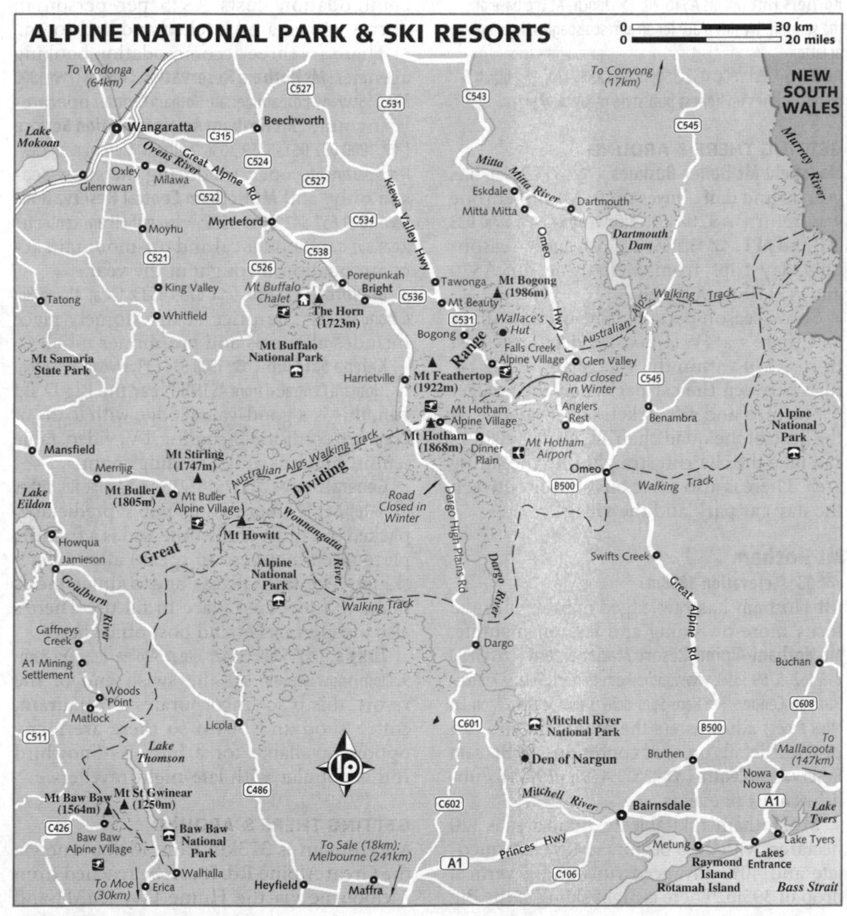

Avalanche Alpine Lodge (☎ 9873 5151; www.avalanchealpinelodge.com.au; Delatite Lane; summer/snow season d for 2 nights A$170/190, apt for 2 nights A$970/1090) Appropriate for all seasons, this alpine lodge, with an open fire and a pool table, offers a choice of rooms and apartments. Prices increase on weekends.

Mt Buller YHA Lodge (☎ 5777 6181; The Avenue; dm mid-week/weekend A$55/100) Only open during the ski season, so it pays to book well in advance. It's in a great location – you can ski right to the front door. Budget-priced packages available include accommodation, ski/snowboard hire, a lift ticket and transport from Melbourne.

Slick Mt Buller has a big-city range of places to eat. Try:

Kofflers Hut (mains A$16-20; lunch) At the base of the summit, try this place for an alfresco spaghetti bolognese or latte.

Arlberg (☎ 1800 032 380; mains A$12-20; lunch & dinner) Dishes up honest pub-style meals and pizza.

GETTING THERE & AROUND

Mansfield-Mt Buller Buslines (☎ 5775 2606) has year-round daily buses up to Mt Buller (one way/return A$20/35). **Snowcaper** (☎ 1800 033 023) and **APT** (☎ 1300 655 965) run snow-season-only day trips from Melbourne for A$70 and A$110 respectively.

Snow-season parking is below the village and there's a 4WD taxi service; fares cost from A$14 within the village and A$22 return between the car parks and the village.

Ski hire and lift tickets are available at the base of the quad chairlift, so day visitors can take the chairlift straight into the skiing area. There is also a free bus shuttle between the day car park and the village.

Mt Hotham

☎ 03 / elevation 1868m

Mt Hotham has raw-edged appeal, with the focus more on skiing and less on nightlife. **Mt Hotham Alpine Resort Management** (☎ 1800 246 462, 5759 3550; www.mthotham.com.au; Village Administration Centre; 8am-5pm daily snow season, Mon-Fri other times) administers the mountain and can provide details on road conditions. **Mt Hotham Reservation Centre** (☎ 1800 354 555, 5759 4444) publishes a list of events.

Mt Hotham's ski-able downhill area is 320 hectares, with 20% beginner, 40% intermediate and 40% advanced runs and a vertical drop of 395m. There is night skiing at the Big D and over 35km of sheltered, scenic ski trails between Mt Hotham and Dinner Plain.

Adventuresome off-piste skiing is in steep and narrow valleys; ski touring on the Bogong High Plains over to Falls Creek is excellent. This is also the starting point for trips across Razorback to beautiful Mt Feathertop. On the eastern side, below the village, trails run as far as Dinner Plain.

The snow-season entry fee is A$26 per car. Lift tickets cost A$85 per day (A$400 per week).

SLEEPING & EATING

Snow-season accommodation is abundant but availability varies considerably during the rest of the year. Typically, summer accommodation costs A$25 per person in dorms with shared kitchen and bathroom.

There are three accommodation booking agencies: **Mt Hotham Reservation Centre** (☎ 1800 354 555; www.hotham.net.au; Hotham Central) operates year-round; **Mt Hotham Accommodation Service** (☎ 1800 032 061, 5759 3636; hotham@netc.net.au; Lawlers Apartments) operates during the snow season only; and **Mt Hotham Central Reservations** (☎ 1800 657 547, 5759 3522; www.mthotham-centralres.com.au) can book local and off-mountain accommodation throughout the year.

Gravbrot Ski Club (☎ 5759 3533; Great Alpine Rd; d from A$110) The price at this homely place includes all meals and pre-dinner nibbles.

Kalyna Ski Club (☎ 1800 633 611; www.kalyna.com.au; Hotham Central; d from A$150) Near the Big D ski run, this is a good-value lodge with loads of creature comforts including TV, video, table tennis, billiards and a reading room.

General Store (☎ 5759 3523; Great Alpine Rd; dishes A$11-16) Mt Hotham's only pub is predictably packed out most of the time and is a friendly place to chill out (so to speak) after a day's skiing. The tasty pizzas and counter meals make it a low-cost place to fill up. There's also a supermarket and post office here.

Zirky's (☎ 5759 3542; Great Alpine Rd; 8am-9.30pm snow season) At the swish end of the resort, this place incorporates a restaurant, coffee shop and bistro so there are many options available for a bite. Its Snowbird Inn is popular with late-night revellers.

GETTING THERE & AROUND

Mt Hotham is 373km from Melbourne via the Great Alpine Rd. It can be reached from Melbourne via the Hume Fwy (M31) and

Harrietville (4½ hours) or via the Princes Hwy and Omeo (5½ hours).

During the snow season, **Trekset** (☎ 1300 655 546, 9370 9055; www.mthothambus.com.au) runs a daily bus service between Melbourne and Mt Hotham (A$125 return) stopping at Wangaratta, Myrtleford, Bright and Harrietville.

Mt Hotham's airport also services Dinner Plain. **QantasLink** (☎ 13 13 13) flies daily in the snow season from Melbourne (return from A$120, one hour).

The village sprawls along a ridge, with free shuttle minibuses frequently running back and forth from 7am to 3am. Another shuttle service operates to Dinner Plain.

Mt Buffalo National Park

Mt Buffalo (1500m) is a handsome ski resort, although it's not known for reliable snow. It's in an area (31,000 hectares) that was declared a national park in 1898. The main access road leads off the Great Alpine Rd at Porepunkah to just below the summit of the Horn (1723m). Apart from Mt Buffalo itself, the park is noted for its scenery of granite outcrops, streams and waterfalls, and an abundance of birdlife and walks.

There are two skiing areas: Cresta Valley and Dingo Dell. Cresta has five lifts, and the graded downhill runs cover 27 hectares with 45% beginner, 40% intermediate and 15% advanced runs, and a vertical drop of 157m. Cresta Valley is the starting point for many of the cross-country trails while Dingo Dell is perfect for beginner skiers.

The Bright **visitors centre** (☎ 1800 033 079, 03-5758 3490; www.parkweb.vic.gov.au; bottom of Gully chair lift; 9am-6pm in snow season, 9am-5pm other times) covers this region. Dingo Dell has a day visitor shelter with a kiosk.

The entry fee during the snow season is A$12.90 per car (A$9 at other times). Lift tickets cost A$39 per day.

Mt Buffalo is paradise for experienced hang-gliders, and the walls of the Gorge provide really challenging rock climbs. **Lake Catani** is good for swimming and canoeing. **Adventure Guides Australia** (☎ 03-5728 1804; www.adventureguidesaustralia.com.au) has rock climbing, caving, ski touring and other summertime activities from around A$80 per half-day.

SLEEPING & EATING

Mt Buffalo Wilderness Lodge (☎ 1800 037 038, 03-5755 1988; Mt Buffalo; d mid-week/weekend A$140/220) The lodge has motel-style units or four-bed bunk rooms with shared bathrooms, plus a games room, indoor climbing wall, restaurant and ski hire. Breakfast and dinner are included in the rates.

Mt Buffalo Chalet (☎ 1800 037 038, 03-5755 1500; www.mtbuffalochalet.com.au; Mt Buffalo; d summer/snow season A$150/270) The chalet is a huge guesthouse built in 1909 and retains a warm old-fashioned feel with simple bedrooms, large lounges and a games room with open fires. The chalet is open year-round, and there's a three-night minimum stay. Its **café** (buffet lunches A$29-39; dinner from A$20) is open to non-guests. Dinners are à la carte.

Camping is allowed at Rocky Creek. Pick up the permit from the Parks Victoria ranger at the **Mt Buffalo entrance station** (☎ 03-5756 2328).

GETTING THERE & AROUND

There is no public transport to the plateau, although a **V/Line** (☎ 13 61 96) coach can drop you at Porepunkah, near the base of the mountain. A taxi to or from Bright costs about A$55 (40 minutes). Transport from Wangaratta train station can be arranged for chalet and lodge guests.

Falls Creek

☎ 03 / elevation 1780m

Falls Creek is the most fashion-conscious of the resorts and combines great skiing with equally great après-ski entertainment. It's a 4½-hour drive from Melbourne and gets packed with city folk on weekends during the snow season. There are some great **walking tracks** that start here, including the walk to **Wallace's Hut** (said to be the oldest cattlemen's hut in the alpine region).

The **visitors centre** (☎ 1800 033 079, 5758 3490; www.fallscreek.com.au; bottom of Gully chairlift; 9am-6pm in snow season, 9am-5pm in summer) is the place to go for information about the whole region, including Mt Buffalo. The snow-season entry fee is A$24 per car. Full-day lift tickets cost A$85 (A$400 for five days). Skiing at Fall's Creek is spread over two main areas: the Village Bowl and Sun Valley. There are 19 lifts, and the ski-able downhill area covers 451 hectares, with 17% beginner, 60% intermediate and 23% advanced runs and a vertical drop of 267m. On Wednesday and Saturday there is night skiing in the Village Bowl.

Some of Australia's best cross-country skiing can be found here. A trail leads around Rocky Valley Pondage to some old cattlemen's huts, and the more adventurous can tour to the summits of Nelse, Cope and Spion Kopje. Australia's major cross-country skiing event, the Kangaroo Hoppet, is held on the last Saturday in August. It's part of the Worldhoppet series of long-distance races.

SLEEPING & EATING

Accommodation may be booked via several agencies including **Falls Creek Central Reservations** (☎ 1800 033 079, 5758 3733; www.skifallscreek.com.au; Bogong High Plains Rd), **Mountain Multiservice** (☎ 1800 465 566, 5758 3499; www.mountainmultiservice.com.au; Schuss St) and **Go Snow Go Falls Creek** (☎ 1800 253 545, 9873 5474; fallscreek.albury.net.au/~gosnow).

Alpha Ski Lodge (☎ 5758 3488; www.alphaskilodge.com.au; 5 Parallel St; d summer A$65, d snow season midweek/weekend A$110/240) This is a great choice for larger groups. There's a huge kitchen with eight cooking stations, plus sauna and large lounge/TV area with panoramic views. The four-bed bunk rooms cost slightly less.

Viking Alpine Lodge (☎ 5758 3247; www.vikinglodge.com.au; 13 Parallel St; d summer/snow season A$70/200) Viking has good views and a good location, with full facilities including handy ski hire, a shop and even a ski-tuning service for the pros. You can hire mountain bikes here in summer.

Summit Ridge (☎ 5758 3800; sumridge@fallscreek.albury.net.au; Schuss St; d A$110) This place manages to be rustic and classy within a perfectly feng-shui cradle of mountains. Rooms are nothing to write home about but are comfy enough, and a bumper breakfast is included in the price. This place organises loads of special events, including wine tasting on weekends.

There are many dining options in Falls Creek. For traditional English-style stodge and hearty ales head to **Cock 'n' Bull** (☎ 5758 3210; mains A$16-21; lunch & dinner). Or get retro with cheese or chocolate fondue at **JB's Bar & Restaurant** (☎ 5758 3278; mains A$14-20; lunch & dinner).

GETTING THERE & AROUND

The only way to get to Falls Creek from Melbourne is with **Pyle's Coaches** (☎ 5754 4024; www.pyles.com.au), which runs daily snow-season services from Melbourne (Southern Cross station) to Falls Creek (A$125). There are reductions for children and students. Advance bookings are essential.

On the mountain, the **Over-Snow Taxi service** (☎ 5758 3285; A$25 return) operates between the car parks and lodges from 8am to midnight (to 2am Saturday morning).

Tasmania

CONTENTS

HIGHLIGHTS

- **Seafood stalls** Pig out on delish fish and other yummy seafood at one of these stalls on Hobart's floating waterfront (p302)
- **Overland Track** Suck in the refreshing, eucalyptus-scented air on a ramble through this track in the rugged Cradle Mountain-Lake St Clair National Park (p321)
- **Wineglass Bay** Sun yourself at this dreamy spot on the postcard-perfect Freycinet Peninsula (p310)
- **Port Arthur** Imagine what convict life must have been at the hauntingly beautiful ruins here (p307)
- **Bay of Fires** Get high on the (free) million-dollar views of this mystical bay (p317)
- **Salamanca Market** Shop like a mad thing at Hobart's spirited marketplace (p300)
- **Fresh Produce** Fill your belly – without emptying your moneybelt – on Tasmania's bottomless 'picnic basket' of fabulous fresh food

- **Cheer for:** Glenorchy Magpies in the STFL (Aussie rules)
- **Eat:** at a floating fish punt in Hobart (p302)
- **Drink:** a 10oz (285mL) of Cascade (in the south) or Boags (in the north)
- **Listen to:** Monique Brumby's *Thylacine*, Australian Crawl's *Errol*
- **Party at:** Hobart's Salamanca Pl and harbourside pubs (p304)
- **Swim at:** Freycinet's Wineglass Bay (p310) or Kingston Beach (p305) near Hobart (brrrr … next stop, Antarctica!)
- **Avoid:** logging trucks and narrow roads, dissing the crown princess of Denmark
- **Locals' nickname:** Hillbillies, Taswegians

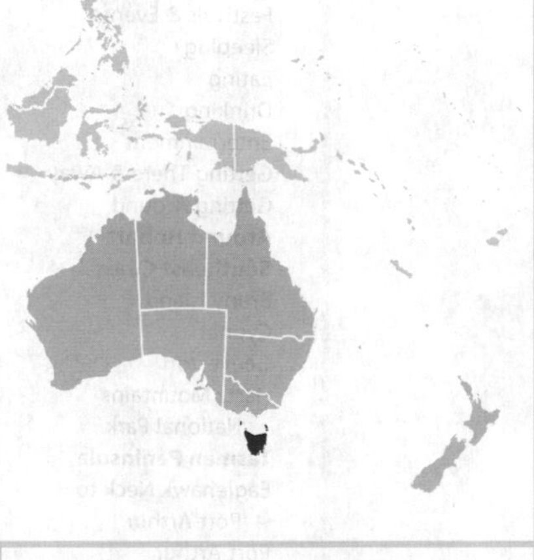

- TELEPHONE CODE: 03
- WEBSITE: www.discovertasmania.com.au

Affectionately dubbed 'Tassie' by Australians, the island-state of Tasmania is home to some of the country's most mind-bending coastal and inland wilderness regions. Almost one quarter of this breathtakingly beautiful island is comprised of wildlife-filled national parks, many awarded the status of World Heritage Area.

Tasmania was known to European settlers as Van Diemen's Land until 1856 when its name was changed to Tasmania. It's estimated that there were between 5000 and 10,000 Aborigines in Tasmania when Europeans arrived and despite being brutally subjugated (almost to the point of annihilation), Tasmanian Aborigines have survived changes in government policy and settler attitudes to proudly maintain their cultural identity.

Compact in comparison with the mainland states, Tasmania is a splendid place to kick back and cruise the back roads at leisure, gawking at sublime scenery en route – from the majestic beauty of mighty Cradle Mountain to the tantalising gin-clear waters of east coast beaches.

Apart from its treasure trove of outdoor attractions, Tasmania also has some phenomenal cafés, restaurants and pubs – perfect places to swap stories with locals and fellow travellers while tucking into luscious local produce and quaffing fruity home-grown wine.

Tasmania is home to some of the friendliest folk you'll ever meet and few travellers leave here without a bundle of fond memories and an address book filled with new friends. So don't let the rough waters of Bass Strait deter you – make your way to magical little Tassie and your efforts will be richly rewarded.

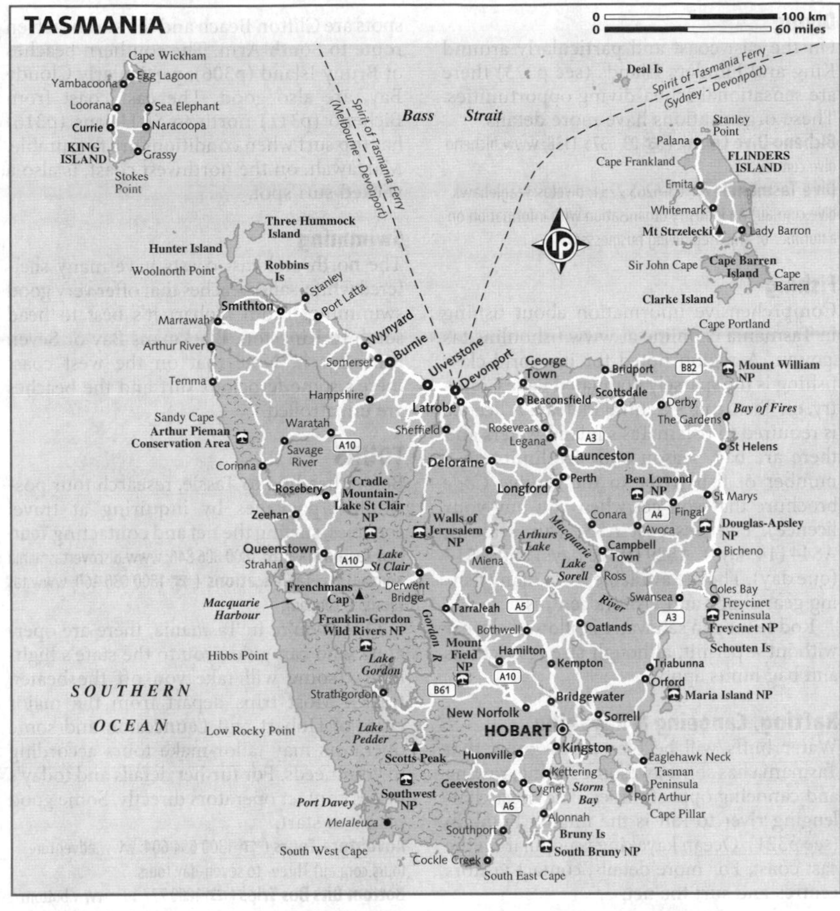

ACTIVITIES

Tasmania is an outdoor lover's paradise, with everything from surfing to abseiling. Plenty of information is available at Tasmania's visitors centres as well as on the Internet. One good website is that of **Tourism Tasmania** (www.discovertasmania.com); click on 'things to do & see'. Fellow travellers are another excellent source of what's hot and what's not.

Bushwalking

The best-known of many superb bushwalks in Tasmania is the **Overland Track** (p321) in the Cradle Mountain-Lake St Clair National Park. The Lonely Planet guide *Walking in Australia* has a section devoted to some of the prime (longer) walks to be done in Tasmania.

On long walks it's important to remember that in any season a fine day can quickly turn ugly, so warm clothing, waterproof gear, a tent and a compass are essential. Tasmap produces an excellent series of maps available at visitors centres, **Service Tasmania** (☎ 1300 135 513; 134 Macquarie St, Hobart), the **Tasmanian Map Centre** (☎ 03-6231 9043; 100 Elizabeth St, Hobart), outdoor-equipment shops, The Wilderness Society shops and newsagencies throughout the state.

There are several shops selling camping gear around the state, and a few youth hostels hire out equipment and/or take guided bushwalking tours.

Diving

On the east coast and particularly around King and Flinders Islands (see p323) there are sensational scuba-diving opportunities. These organisations have more details:

Bicheno Dive Centre (☎ 03-6375 1138; www.bichenodive.com.au)

Dive Tasmania (☎ 03-6265 2251; divetas@eaglehawkdive.com.au) An industry organisation with information on a number of affiliated diving businesses.

Fishing

Comprehensive information about fishing in Tasmania is online at www.fishonline.tas.gov.au. A region noted for its world-class fishing is the sparsely populated Lake Country, on Tasmania's Central Plateau. A licence is required to fish in Tas's inland waters and there are bag, season and size limits on a number of fish (refer to the *Fishing Code* brochure that you get when you buy your licence). Licences cost A$56 (full season), A$44 (14 days), A$29 (three days) and A$17 (one day). They're available from many fishing gear shops and visitors centres.

Rod fishing in salt water is allowed all year without a permit, although size restrictions and bag limits apply.

Rafting, Canoeing & Kayaking

Water buffs will be pleased to know that Tasmania has some awesome rafting, rowing and canoeing opportunities. The most challenging river to raft is the mighty Franklin (see p321). Ocean kayaking is popular on the east coast. For more details, contact visitors centres and surf the net.

Rock Climbing & Abseiling

If you relish defying gravity, Tasmania has some amazing cliffs that are ideal for climbing, particularly along the east coast, where the weather is usually best. If you wish to climb or abseil with an experienced instructor, try one of these outfits:

Aardvark Adventures (☎ 0408-127 714; www.aardvarkadventures.com.au)

Freycinet & Strahan Adventures (☎ 03-6257 0500; www.adventurestasmania.com)

Tasmanian Expeditions (☎ 03-6334 3477; www.tas-ex.com)

Surfing

Catch a wave on one of Tasmania's numerous surf beaches. Close to Hobart, the best spots are Clifton Beach and the surf beach en route to South Arm. The southern beaches of Bruny Island (p306), particularly Cloudy Bay, are also good. The east coast from Bicheno (p311) north to St Helens (p316) has top surf when conditions are favourable. Marrawah, on the northwest coast, is also a wicked surf spot.

Swimming

The north and east coasts have many sheltered white-sand beaches that offer very good swimming. From Hobart it's best to head south to Kingston, Blackmans Bay or Seven Mile Beach. Note that on the west coast there's some ferocious surf and the beaches are unpatrolled.

TOURS

Before heading to Tassie, research tour possibilities/packages by inquiring at travel agencies, surfing the net and contacting **Tourism Tasmania** (☎ 1800 806 846; www.discovertasmania.com.au) or **Tas Vacations** (☎ 1800 030 160; www.tasvacations.com.au).

Once you're in Tasmania, there are operators who can guide you to the state's highlights (some will take you off the beaten track). Most trips depart from the major cities of Hobart and Launceston and some operators may tailor-make tours according to your needs. For further details and today's prices contact operators directly. Some good places to start:

Adventure Tours (☎ 1300 654 604; www.adventuretours.com.au) Three- to seven-day tours.

Bottom Bits Bus Trips (☎ 1800 777 103; www.bottombitsbus.com.au) Backpacker-friendly day trips from A$90.

Craclair (☎ 03-6424 7833; www.craclair.com.au) Guided walks (day walks and longer) in wilderness areas.

Island Cycle Tours (☎ 1300 880 334; www.islandcycletours.com) Guided cycling trips starting at A$55.

Tasmanian Expeditions (☎ 03-6334 3477; www.tas-ex.com) A variety of activity-based tours ranging from half a day to 13 days and with a choice of bushwalking, river rafting, cycling and canoeing tours.

Tigerline Travel (☎ 1300 653 633; www.tigerline.com.au) Coach tours (day trips and short breaks) to major attractions in and around Hobart and Launceston.

Tiger Trails (☎ 03-6234 3931; www.tigertrails.green.net.au) Ecotours – one-day and multiday – to pristine wilderness areas, ranging in difficulty from easy to challenging.

Under Down Under Tours (☎ 1800 064 726; www.underdownunder.com.au) Has nature-based, backpacker-friendly trips from two to seven days.

HOBART

☎ 03 / pop 128,048

Straddling the mouth of the Derwent River and backed by towering Mt Wellington, Hobart combines modern city verve with a rich colonial heritage and a serene natural beauty. The attractive Georgian buildings, the buzzing harbour and a friendly, easy-going vibe make Hobart one of Australia's most welcoming state capitals. It's a top spot in which to chill out for a few days, snack on seafood so fresh it's almost still wiggling, and hook up (and possibly make onward travel plans) with other backpackers.

The deep-water harbour of the Derwent River estuary has been important in Hobart's development; many merchants made their fortunes from the whaling trade, shipbuilding and the export of products such as merino wool and corn. Today, Hobart is Australia's second-oldest city and its southernmost capital.

ORIENTATION

The airport is 16km east of the centre. The **Airporter shuttle bus** (☎ 0419-382 240) operates a service between the city (via various hostels and hotels) and the airport for A$9.20, one way. If you wish to be picked up for an airport drop then you must let them know a day ahead, before 8pm. A taxi between the airport and city centre costs A$30 to A$35.

Being fairly small and simply laid out, Hobart is a breeze to navigate. The streets in the city centre, many of which are one way, are arranged in a grid around the Elizabeth St mall. The Tasmanian Travel & Information Centre and the main post office are on Elizabeth St, and the main shopping area extends west from the mall on Elizabeth St.

Salamanca Pl, a row of Georgian warehouses, is along the southern waterfront, and just south of this is Battery Point, Hobart's well-preserved early colonial district. If you follow the river south from Battery Point you'll come to Sandy Bay.

The northern side of the city centre is bounded by the recreation area known as the Domain (short for Queen's Domain), which includes the Botanical Gardens and the Derwent River. From here the Tasman Bridge crosses the river to the eastern suburbs and the airport.

Maps

The best maps of Hobart are the *Hobart Street Directory* (A$18) and the Hobart maps in the *Tasmanian Towns Street Atlas* (A$28). You can usually purchase these and other good maps at large newsagents and bookshops.

Other sources for maps in Hobart:

Royal Automobile Club of Tasmania (RACT; ☎ 6232 6300, 13 27 22; www.ract.com.au; cnr Murray & Patrick Sts)

Service Tasmania (☎ 1300 135 513; www.service.tas.gov.au; 134 Macquarie St)

Tasmanian Map Centre (☎ 6231 9043; www.map-centre.com.au; 100 Elizabeth St)

Disabled travellers can get a copy of the useful *Hobart CBD Mobility Map* at the Tasmanian Travel & Information Centre; it's a guide to the relevant facilities.

INFORMATION

Bookshops

Déjà Vu Books (☎ 6223 4766; 77 Salamanca Pl) Sells (and may buy) good second-hand books.

Fullers Bookshop (☎ 6224 2488; 140 Collins St) Well-stocked, with a popular café upstairs.

Hobart Bookshop (☎ 6223 1803; 22 Salamanca Sq) New and second-hand books. May buy second-hand books.

Tasmanian Map Centre (☎ 6231 9043; 100 Elizabeth St) Specialises in maps and guidebooks.

Emergency

Ambulance & Fire (☎ 000)

Police station (☎ 000, 6230 2111; 37-43 Liverpool St)

Internet Access

Most of Hobart's hostels have Internet access for their guests. In town, Internet centres charge around A$5 to A$8 per hour.

Mouse on Mars (☎ 6224 0513; 27 Salamanca Pl; 🕙 10am-10pm)

Pelican Loft (☎ 6234 2225; 35a Elizabeth St; 🕙 8am-7pm Mon-Fri, 10.30am-5pm Sat)

Service Tasmania (☎ 1300 135 513; 134 Macquarie St; 🕙 8.15am-5.30pm Mon-Fri)

State Library (☎ 6233 7529; 91 Murray St; sessions free for Australians; 🕙 9.30am-6pm Mon & Tue, to 9pm Wed-Fri, to 2.30pm Sat)

Medical Services

Chemist on Collins (☎ 6235 0257; 93 Collins St)

City Doctors Travel Clinic (☎ 6231 3003; 93 Collins St) Enter through the pharmacy.

Royal Hobart Hospital (☎ 6222 8308; 48 Liverpool St) Use the Argyle St entry for the emergency department, which is open 24 hours.

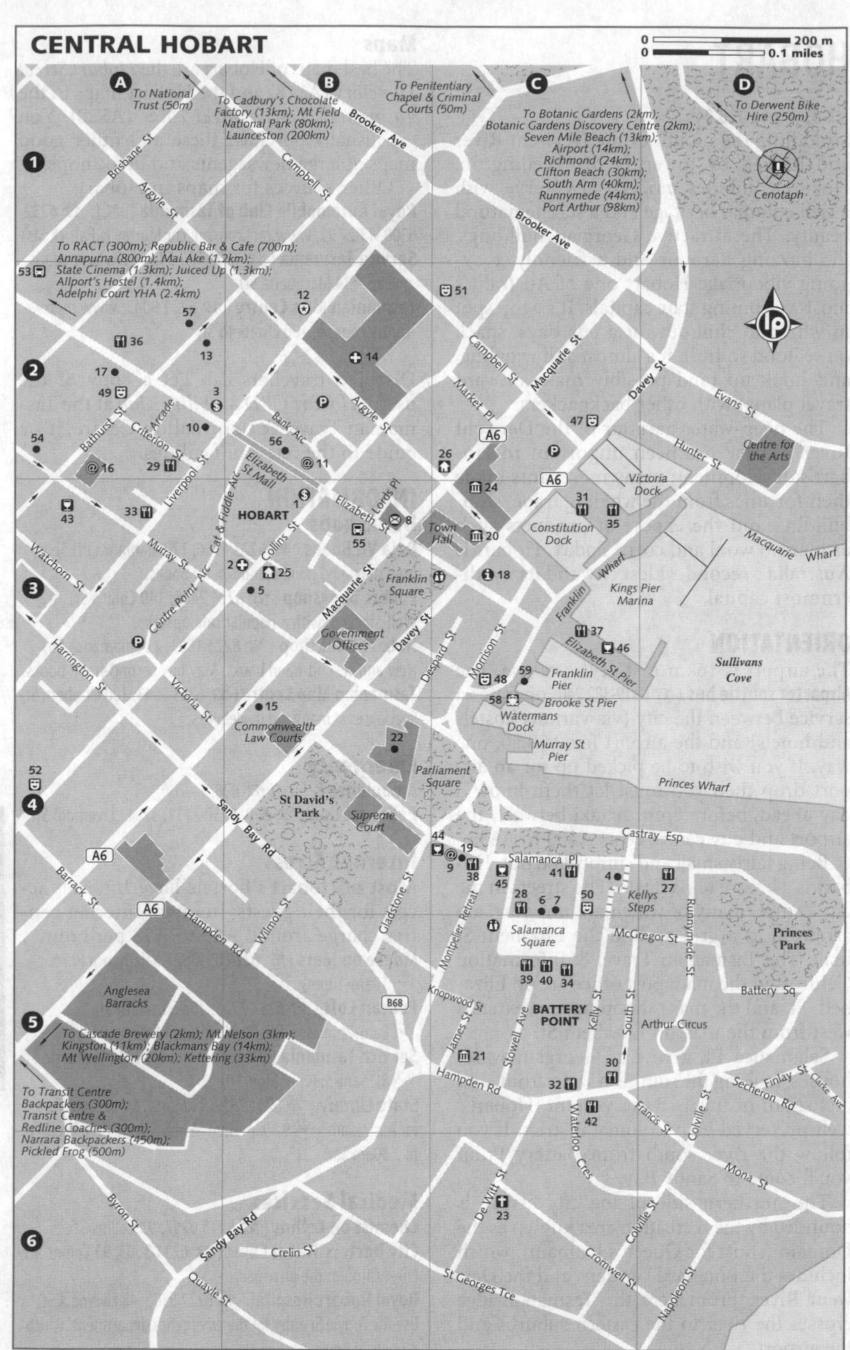
CENTRAL HOBART
0 200 m
0 0.1 miles
To National Trust (50m)
To Cadbury's Chocolate Factory (13km); Mt Field National Park (80km); Launceston (200km)
To Penitentiary Chapel & Criminal Courts (50m)
To Botanic Gardens (2km); Botanic Gardens Discovery Centre (2km); Seven Mile Beach (13km); Airport (14km); Richmond (24km); Clifton Beach (30km); South Arm (40km); Runnymede (44km); Port Arthur (98km)
To Derwent Bike Hire (250m)
Cenotaph
To RACT (300m); Republic Bar & Cafe (700m); Annapurna (800m); Mai Ake (1.2km); State Cinema (1.3km); Juiced Up (1.3km); Allport's Hostel (1.4km); Adelphi Court YHA (2.4km)
To Cascade Brewery (2km); Mt Nelson (3km); Kingston (11km); Blackmans Bay (14km); Mt Wellington (20km); Kettering (33km)
To Transit Centre Backpackers (300m); Transit Centre & Redline Coaches (300m); Narrara Backpackers (450m); Pickled Frog (500m)
HOBART
BATTERY POINT
Sullivans Cove
Centre for the Arts
Victoria Dock
Constitution Dock
Kings Pier Marina
Franklin Pier
Brooke St Pier
Watermans Dock
Murray St Pier
Princes Wharf
Elizabeth St Pier
Macquarie Wharf
Franklin Wharf
Town Hall
Franklin Square
Government Offices
Commonwealth Law Courts
Parliament Square
St David's Park
Supreme Court
Anglesea Barracks
Salamanca Square
Kellys Steps
Princes Park
Battery Sq
Arthur Circus
Brooker Ave
Brisbane St
Argyle St
Campbell St
Macquarie St
Davey St
Evans St
Hunter St
Market Pl
Bathurst St
Arcade
Criterion St
Liverpool St
Elizabeth St Mall
Bank Arc
Lords Pl
Elizabeth St
Collins St
Cat & Fiddle Arc
Murray St
Centre Point Arc
Watchorn St
Harrington St
Victoria St
Despard St
Morrison St
Sandy Bay Rd
Barrack St
Hampden Rd
Wilmot St
Gladstone St
Montpelier Retreat
Salamanca Pl
Castray Esp
McGregor St
Runnymede St
Knopwood St
James St
Stowell Ave
Kelly St
South St
Finlay St
Clarke Ave
Secheron Rd
Francis St
Colville St
Waterloo Cres
Mona St
De Witt St
Cromwell St
Napoleon St
St Georges Tce
Byron St
Crelin St
Quayle St
A6
B68
TASMANIA

INFORMATION
ANZ Bank & ATM....................1 B3
Chemist on Collins....................2 B3
City Doctors Travel Clinic....................(see 2)
Commonwealth Bank & ATM....................3 A2
Déjà Vu Books....................4 C4
Fullers Bookshop....................5 B3
Hobart Bookshop....................6 C4
Kathmandu....................7 C4
Main Post Office....................8 B3
Metro Office....................(see 8)
Mouse on Mars....................9 C4
Paddy Pallin....................10 A2
Pelican Loft....................11 B2
Police Station....................12 B2
Recycled Recreation....................13 A2
Royal Hobart Hospital....................14 B2
Service Tasmania....................15 B4
State Library....................16 A2
Tasmanian Map Centre....................17 A2
Tasmanian Travel & Information Centre....................18 C3
The Wilderness Society Shop....................19 C4

SIGHTS & ACTIVITIES (pp299–300)
Carnegie Gallery....................(see 20)
Maritime Museum of Tasmania....................20 C3
Narryna Heritage Museum....................21 C5
Parliament House....................22 B4
St George's Anglican Church....................23 C6
Tasmanian Museum and Art Gallery....................24 C3

SLEEPING (pp301–2)
Central City Backpackers....................25 B3
Montgomery's Private Hotel & YHA Backpackers....................26 C2

EATING (pp302–3)
Ball & Chain Grill....................27 D4
Bar Celona....................28 C4
Criterion St Cafe....................29 A2
Da Angelo Ristorante....................30 C5
Fish Frenzy....................(see 37)
Floating Seafood Stalls....................31 C3
Jackman & McRoss....................32 C5
Kafe Kara....................33 A3
Machine Laundry Café....................34 C5
Mures....................35 C3
Nourish....................36 A2
Orizuru Sushi Bar....................(see 35)
Pashas....................37 C3
Retro Café....................38 C4
Salamanca Bakehouse....................39 C5
Say Cheese....................40 C5
Vietnamese Kitchen....................41 C4
Z's....................42 C5

DRINKING (p304)
Cow....................43 A3
Irish Murphy's....................44 C4
Knopwood's Retreat....................45 C4
T-42°....................46 C3

ENTERTAINMENT (p304)
Federation Concert Hall....................47 C2
Isobar....................48 C3
New Sydney Hotel....................49 A2
Salamanca Arts Centre Courtyard....................50 C4
Syrup....................(see 45)
Theatre Royal....................51 C2
Village Cinema....................52 A4

TRANSPORT (pp304–5)
Hobart Bus Terminal....................53 A2
Lo-Cost Auto Rent....................54 A2
Metro City Bus Station....................55 B3
Qantas....................56 B2
Selective Car Rentals....................57 A2
TassieLink....................(see 53)
Wanderer Ferry....................58 C4

OTHER
Booking Offices for Boat Cruise Companies....................59 C3

Money

There are 24-hour ATMs scattered throughout Hobart (you can find several at Salamanca Place). Two major bank branches with ATMs:

ANZ Bank (☎ 13 13 14; 40 Elizabeth St)
Commonwealth Bank (☎ 13 22 21; 81 Elizabeth St)

Outdoor Equipment

Kathmandu (☎ 6224 3027; 16 Salamanca Sq)
Paddy Pallin (☎ 6231 0777; 119 Elizabeth St)
Recycled Recreation (☎ 6234 3575; 54 Bathurst St) Sells second-hand outdoor gear at the Climbing Edge indoor rock-climbing centre.

Post

Main post office (☎ 13 13 18; cnr Elizabeth & Macquarie Sts; 🕒 8.30am-5.30pm Mon-Fri)

Tourist Information

Tasmanian Travel & Information Centre (☎ 6230 8233; tasbookings@tasvisinfo.com.au; cnr Davey & Elizabeth Sts; 🕒 8.30am-5.30pm Mon-Fri, 9am-5pm Sat, Sun & public holidays) Staffed by helpful souls, this office has zillions of glossy brochures (including some informative booklets and maps) and a selection of souvenirs, and also offers a booking service for the entire state (a booking fee is charged for accommodation and car hire).

SIGHTS

Salamanca Place

The row of beautiful sandstone warehouses on the harbour front at Salamanca Pl is a prime example of Australian colonial architecture. Dating back to the whaling days of the 1830s, these warehouses were the hub of Hobart Town's trade and commerce. Today, they have been tastefully developed to house galleries, restaurants, cafés, nightspots and shops selling everything from kitsch knick-knacks to dainty antiques. It's the perfect place to cool your heels (and engage in people-watching) over a hot cuppa.

Battery Point

Behind Princes Wharf is the historic core of Hobart, the old port area known as Battery Point. Its name comes from the gun battery that stood on the promontory by the guardhouse (1818). During colonial times this area was a colourful maritime village.

Don't miss **Arthur Circus** – a circle of quaint cottages built around a village green – or **St George's Anglican Church**. To help with your exploration of the area, get the *Battery Point and Sullivan's Cove Trail of Discovery* pamphlet (A$2) from the Tasmanian Travel & Information Centre.

Narryna Heritage Museum (☎ 6234 2791; 103 Hampden Rd; adult/student A$6/5; 🕒 10.30am-5pm Tue-Fri, 2-5pm Sat, Sun & public holidays, closed Jul) is a Georgian sandstone mansion that was built in 1836. It's set in beautiful grounds and contains a treasure-trove of domestic colonial artefacts.

Historic Sites

Hobart has some of the best-preserved old buildings in Australia.

Close to the city centre is St David's Park, with **gravestones** dating from the earliest days

TASMANIA

SENSATIONAL SALAMANCA MARKET

Every Saturday morning the colourful, buzzing **Salamanca Market** (8.30am-3pm) is held outdoors along Salamanca Pl, and browsing through the hundreds of stalls is a joy. There's a mishmash of items for sale, including some high-quality locally produced items (great gifts for family and friends back home) at reasonable prices. Tasty eats are available from market stalls or nearby cafés, and there's engaging entertainment provided by buskers and other street performers. Don't miss it!

of the colony, while opposite is **Parliament House**, built in 1835. Hobart's prestigious **Theatre Royal** (6233 2299; 29 Campbell St) is the oldest theatre in Australia, established in 1837.

The fascinating **Penitentiary Chapel & Criminal Courts** (6231 0911; cnr Brisbane & Campbell Sts; adult/student A$8/6) can be explored via the excellent National Trust–run tours at 10am, 11.30am, 1pm and 2.30pm. Get ready for goosebumps on the **ghost tours** (0417-361 392; adult/student A$8.80/7.70; 8pm) that are also held here nightly; bookings essential.

Runnymede (6278 1269; 61 Bay Rd, New Town; adult/student A$7.70/5.50; 10am-4.30pm Mon-Fri, noon-4.30pm Sat & Sun), in the northern part of the city, is a gracious 1830s residence.

Museums

The **Tasmanian Museum & Art Gallery** (6211 4177; 40 Macquarie St; admission free; 10am-5pm) incorporates Hobart's oldest existing building, the Commissariat Store (1808). The museum section features an Aboriginal display and relics from the state's colonial heritage, while the gallery has a collection of Tasmanian colonial art. Free guided tours take place at 2.30pm from Wednesday to Sunday.

The **Maritime Museum of Tasmania** (6234 1427; 16 Argyle St; adult/student A$6/5; 9am-5pm) has an interesting salt-encrusted collection of photos, paintings, models and relics highlighting Tasmania's shipping past. Upstairs from the museum is the **Carnegie Gallery** (admission free; 9am-5pm), exhibiting Tasmanian art and photography.

Cadbury Chocolate Factory

Chocolate has in all likelihood sustained you through the most trying on-the-road ordeals, so to stock up, visit the **Cadbury chocolate factory** (1800 627 367; Cadbury Rd, Claremont; tours adult/student A$13/9, bookings essential). The factory has guided tours on weekdays (except public holidays) from 9am to 1.30pm. Participants enjoy sweet samples along the way, and can purchase discounted products at the completion of the tour. The factory is about 15km north of the city centre.

Cascade Brewery

Australia's oldest brewery **Cascade** (6221 8300; Cascade Rd; tours adult/student A$14/10; 9am-4pm Mon-Fri, bookings essential) was established on the southwestern edge of the city centre in 1832. It's still in use today, brewing beverages for nationwide consumption. Tours run at 9.30am, 10am, 1pm and 1.30pm (more if there's demand), and include free samples.

Natural Attractions

Just by the Tasman Bridge is the beguiling **Botanical Gardens** (www.rtbg.tas.gov.au; admission free but donations welcome; 8am-6.30pm Oct-Mar, to 5.30pm Apr & Sep, to 5pm May-Aug). The gardens were established in 1818 and today boast the largest collection of mature conifers in the southern hemisphere. After wandering through the gardens, you can explore their world in more detail at the interactive **Botanical Discovery Centre** (6236 3075; Queens Domain; admission free; 9am-4.30pm mid-May–late Aug, 9am-5pm late Aug–mid-May).

Hobart is dominated by 1270m-high **Mt Wellington**, which has sweeping views and walking tracks – the *Mt Wellington Walks* map (A$4; available at the Tasmanian Travel & Information Centre) has details. To get here, you can drive up winding roads, take a guided tour or hop on local bus No 48 or 49 from the Macquarie St side of Franklin Sq – the bus will take you to Fern Tree at the base of the mountain and from there it's a stunning walk to the top (five to six hours return, via the Springs and the Organ Pipes). **Mt Wellington Shuttle Bus Service** (0417-341 804; return A$25) departs from central Hobart thrice daily; city pick-ups can be arranged. See Cycling (opposite), for information on bicycle trips down the mountain.

There are also wonderful views from **Mt Nelson**, a good alternative when Mt Wellington is wrapped in cloud.

ACTIVITIES

Cycling

If you fancy a ride beside the Derwent, you can hire a bicycle from **Derwent Bike Hire** (☎ 6234 2143; Regatta Grounds; ⏰ daily 20 Dec-14 Feb, weekends only Sep-May) for A$7/20 per hour/day (touring bikes are also available from A$100 per week). It can be found by the cenotaph in the Regatta Grounds.

A useful navigational tool is the *Hobart Bike Map* (A$4), available from the Tasmanian Travel & Information Centre and containing details of the city's cycle paths and road cycling routes.

You can also participate in an organised ride from the top of Mt Wellington for A$55 (takes around three hours), including transport to the summit, bikes and safety equipment. One local operator offering tours is **Island Cycle Tours** (☎ 1300 880 334; www.islandcycletours.com).

TOURS

Tigerline Coaches (☎ 1300 653 633; www.tigerline.com.au) Tigerline takes full- and half-day bus tours in and around Hobart. Typical half-day tours include the Cadbury chocolate factory (adult/student A$44/38), and Mt Wellington and city sights (adult/student A$45/39).

Gregory Omnibuses (☎ 6224 6169) Offers double-decker sightseeing trips, including a trip that visits the Cascade brewery (A$29) and the Cadbury chocolate factory (A$46).

City Sights Under Lights (☎ 0418-576 489; www.showyoutasmania.com.au) has several tours including a night-time coach excursion around Hobart (A$35).

Cruises

Several boat-cruise companies operate from the Franklin Pier, Brooke St Pier and Watermans Dock area, offering a variety of affordable harbour cruises.

Captain Fell's Historic Ferries (☎ 6223 5893) Offers good-value lunch (A$18/26 for a small/large meal) and dinner (A$30) cruises, plus has sightseeing packages that include ferry and double-decker bus trips.

Cruise Company (☎ 6234 9294) Has a popular 4½-hour 'Cadbury Cruise', which leaves from Brooke St Pier at 10am Monday to Friday (adult/student A$45/40 including lunch); the boat chugs to the Cadbury chocolate factory, where you disembark and tour the premises before returning to the city.

Guided Walks

Hobart Historic Tours (☎ 6278 3338) Conducts an informative two-hour Hobart Historic Walk (adult/student A$19/17, 10am September to May, on request June to August) and also the lively two-hour Hobart Historic Pub Tour (adult/student A$19/17, 5pm Sunday to Thursday). All bookings and inquiries can be made at the Tasmanian Travel & Information Centre, which is also the departure point for the tours.

National Trust (☎ 6223 7570) Has a 2½-hour Battery Point Heritage Walk (A$15 including morning tea, 9.30am Sat), which heads off once a week from the wishing well at Franklin Sq.

FESTIVALS & EVENTS

February

Australian Wooden Boat Festival (www.awoodboatfest.com) Held every two years (odd-numbered years) to coincide with the regatta (see following), this festival features vessels from around Australia and celebrates Tasmania's boat-building heritage.

Royal Hobart Regatta A major annual aquatic carnival, with boat races and other activities.

March & April

Ten Days on the Island (www.tendaysontheisland.org) Tasmania's major cultural festival – this biennial event (odd-numbered years) is a state-wide celebration of local and international 'island culture'.

October

Royal Hobart Show A large agricultural festival showcasing the state's primary industries, held annually in late October.

December & January

Hobart Summer Festival (www.hobartcity.com.au/hsf) Hobart's premier festival, held from late December to mid-January. The docks are at their most festive for 10 days or so around the finish of the annual Sydney to Hobart Yacht Race and New Year. Highlights include the 'Taste of Tasmania' – a week-long food and wine extravaganza.

SLEEPING

Hobart has some terrific hostels, many found in the Central Business District (CBD) or at nearby North Hobart.

Most hostels have a 'key hire' fee of around A$5, which is refunded upon checkout, and some places have a small charge for linen/towel hire. Hostels may offer cheaper rates during winter and discounts if you stay at least one week.

In the following list, private rooms have a shared bathroom unless otherwise stated.

Allport's Hostel (☎ 6231 5464; www.tassie.net.au/~allports; 432 Elizabeth St, North Hobart; dm/s/d/tr A$20/50/60/70; Ⓟ 💻) Close to the excellent North Hobart restaurant strip, this well-kept hostel in an atmospheric old mansion has plenty of character, two well-equipped kitchens, a laundry and pleasant living areas. The rooms are tidy and spacious, the bathrooms are clean, the beds are comfortable and the vibe is relaxed. Bicycles and bushwalking/camping gear can be hired here. Allport's friendly owner, Jan, has lots of good advice and her cat, Gorgeous, appreciates a tummy rub or three.

Pickled Frog (☎ 6234 7977; www.thepickledfrog.com; 281 Liverpool St; dm A$19-22, s A$27-30, d A$44-48; P 💻) This big, red, ramshackle hostel, with its convivial ambience, attracts a constant stream of young backpackers. Apart from a café-bar and lounge, there's a large communal kitchen, tour information and bicycles for hire. The private rooms are a tad small but otherwise OK.

Central City Backpackers (☎ 6224 2404; www.centralbackpackers.com.au; 138 Collins St; dm A$18-22, s/d A$36/48; 💻) In the heart of the CBD, this rambling, popular hostel has plenty of communal space, reasonably good (if somewhat small) rooms and amiable staff. Sheet/towel/doona (continental quilt) hire is A$1/1/2 and bicycles can be rented for A$20 per day.

Narrara Backpackers (☎ 6231 3191; nigelruddock@hotmail.com; 88 Goulburn St; dm/s/tw/tr A$19/40/48/63; 💻) This central, well-maintained hostel has the appealing atmosphere of a group house. The communal areas are smaller than those of many other hostels, but the place is certainly comfortable and the owner has lots of regional knowledge.

Montgomery's Private Hotel & YHA Backpackers (☎ 6231 2660; www.montgomerys.com.au; 9 Argyle St; dm A$25, s & d A$65, s & d with bathroom A$89; 💻) This central, modern hotel includes decent hostel rooms but cramped communal facilities. The rooms with private bathroom are better value than those with shared bathroom. Next door there's a pub with good booze and meals (some rooms can cop noise from the pub at night so choose carefully). Montgomery's lacks the personal touch found in other hostels.

Adelphi Court YHA (☎ 6228 4829; adelphi@yhatas.org.au; 17 Stoke St, New Town; dm/d A$24/60, d with bathroom & breakfast A$69; P) Hobart's other YHA hostel is the more laid-back Adelphi, offering rooms in a spruced-up 1950s-style block built around a courtyard. It's 2.5km from the city but reasonably close to the North Hobart restaurant strip. Make sure there are no school groups checked in during your intended stay, as the otherwise peaceful setting is then transformed into a noisy school playground.

Transit Centre Backpackers (☎ 6231 2400; www.salamanca.com.au/backpackers; 199 Collins St; dm/s/d A$19/25/45) This nondescript hostel is upstairs at the Redline bus station – a convenient place to stay if you're catching a bus at a silly hour. The dormitories are tightly packed and the rooms lack oomph, but the place has a mellow atmosphere and is run by lovely people.

EATING

Hobart's CBD has some good spots for brunch and lunch, but evening options are better closer to the water, in historic precincts or in North Hobart. Salamanca Place has some charming cafés and restaurants, especially brunch-time during the Saturday market. For the most diverse selection of eateries (patronised predominantly by locals), head to Elizabeth St in North Hobart, a cosmopolitan strip of pubs, cafés and restaurants. This is the place to come if you want to escape the touristy Salamanca and waterfront eateries.

City Centre

Criterion St Cafe (☎ 6234 5858; 10 Criterion St; lunch A$6-13; 🕒 breakfast & lunch Mon-Sat) This popular city-centre eatery dishes up quality café fare including crisp salads, flavoursome pastas and divine cakes.

Kafe Kara (☎ 6231 2332; 119 Liverpool St; lunch A$8.50-18; 🕒 breakfast & lunch Mon-Sat) Also popular, Kafe Kara offers a tempting array of light bites and more filling meals. A satiating serve of risotto is A$15, salads are around A$9.50 and hearty soups start at A$8.50.

Nourish (☎ 6234 5674; 129 Elizabeth St; meals under A$11; 🕒 10am-4pm Mon-Wed, to 8pm Thu & Fri, 11am-3pm Sat) Marketing itself as a mainly vegetarian restaurant, Nourish features curries, salads, stir-fries, risottos and more. All dishes are gluten-free and largely dairy-free, too.

Waterfront

Constitution Dock has a string of floating takeaway seafood stalls (you can't miss them) that are marvellous for a cheap dockside feed; a bag of calamari and chips is around A$6.

Fish Frenzy (☎ 6231 2134; Elizabeth St Pier; meals A$8-14; 🕒 lunch & dinner) Spicy calamari salad (A$11) and fish burgers (A$10) are just two options from a simple but appealing and affordable menu of fresh seafood.

Pashas (☎ 6231 9822; Elizabeth St Pier; meals A$6-20; breakfast & lunch Tue-Sun) Next door to Fish Frenzy, Pashas is another moneybelt-friendly and unpretentious eatery. Try their 'signature dips', a selection of yummy home-made dips (including chilli and eggplant, and feta and walnut) that come with all-you-can-eat Turkish bread; the small platter (A$7.50) is enough for two. The Tasmanian scallop pie (A$9) is another hot seller.

Mures (☎ 6231 2121; Victoria Dock; meals A$6-29; lunch & dinner) This Hobart institution has a Lower and Upper Deck. On the Lower Deck you'll find a fishmonger and an inexpensive food bistro; try the marinade fish (A$9.50). Be prepared to fork out A$19 to A$29 for a meal at the fancier Upper Deck. Also part of the Mures complex is the **Orizuru Sushi Bar** (☎ 6231 1790; sushi A$2-3 each, mains A$13-18; lunch & dinner Mon-Sat), which gets the thumbs up for its sushi creations and other Japanese fare. A bowl of miso soup is A$2.50.

Salamanca

Salamanca Bakehouse (☎ 6224 6300; 5-6 Salamanca Sq; 24hr) The place to come for some late night, post-party sustenance. Choose from the usual bakery assortment of savoury and sweet goodies, from crusty loaves to creamy cakes. Although its curried chicken pie (A$4.50) won a gourmet pie award in 2003, spice junkies will find it bland.

Retro Café (☎ 6223 3073; 31 Salamanca Pl; meals A$8-13; breakfast & lunch) This hip café has long been loved for its well-brewed coffee and wholesome meals. For breakfast (on request if not on the menu) try the highly palatable pan-fried mushrooms on rye toast (A$10).

Machine Laundry Café (☎ 6224 9922; 12 Salamanca Sq; meals A$8-13; breakfast & lunch) With its groovy on-site laundry, this is the ideal place to slurp on an apricot smoothie (A$4.50) or eat eggs while catching up on some long overdue washing.

Vietnamese Kitchen (☎ 6223 2188; 61 Salamanca Pl; meals A$7.50-10; lunch & dinner) If you're sick of subsisting on meals of the do-it-yourself few-minute noodle variety, make a beeline for the godsend little VK, which will fill your belly without depleting your funds. A delicious veg laksa is A$7.50.

Say Cheese (☎ 6224 2888; 7 Salamanca Sq; meals A$10-17; breakfast & lunch) Serves fine platters of cheese (of course), seafood, antipasto and more. Its Julius Caesar salad (A$14) is a winner.

Bar Celona (☎ 6224 7557; 23 Salamanca Sq; meals A$10-15; breakfast & lunch) This stylish café-wine bar has a varied menu with everything from delicate Tasmanian smoked salmon (A$10.50) to chunky nachos (A$9.90).

Ball & Chain Grill (☎ 6223 2655; 87 Salamanca Pl; mains A$17-26; lunch & dinner Mon-Fri, dinner Sat & Sun) If you're missing meat, this place cooks big fat steaks on an authentic charcoal grill. Or perhaps the wallaby sausages (A$9.70 per small serve) are more your thing? An all-you-can-eat salad is included with orders – if you're strapped for cash, choose a small serve (a Porterhouse steak is A$11) and fill any tummy gaps with the smorgasbord salads, which include those of the filling noodle and bean variety.

Battery Point

Jackman & McRoss (☎ 6223 3186; 57-59 Hampden Rd; snacks A$0.70-8; 7.30am-5pm) A bakery-café deservedly popular for its wonderful array of fresh pies, tarts, baguettes and pastries. Sourdough rolls are A$0.70 each; buttermilk-and-raisin loaves are A$2.80. Recommended treats include the baked ricotta and mushroom tart (A$4), and the rhubarb and hazelnut torte (A$4.50 per heavenly slice).

Da Angelo Ristorante (☎ 6223 7011; 47 Hampden Rd; mains A$12-19; dinner) Da Angelo specialises in authentic Italian cuisine, sporting an assortment of home-made pasta, veal and chicken dishes. An entrée serve of gnocchi (A$8) is surprisingly filling.

Z's (☎ 6224 7124; 60 Hampden Rd; meals A$12-26, tapas plates A$9-15; lunch & dinner Wed-Fri, breakfast, lunch & dinner Sat, breakfast & lunch Sun) Z's is an upbeat, trendy café-wine bar with two menus – the à la carte menu has standard café-bistro fare, but the tapas list is much more interesting: graze on Moroccan lamb, fried *haloumi* (salty Greek cheese) and mini *frittatas* (pastryless quiche; all A$10 each).

North Hobart

Elizabeth St in North Hobart has a sterling reputation for good-value cuisine that reflects a range of nationalities.

Annapurna (☎ 6236 9500; 305 Elizabeth St; mains A$12-18; lunch & dinner Mon-Fri, dinner Sat & Sun) Offers a mouthwatering variety of Indian fare – lunch is especially recommended, with a plate of curry costing just A$5.50. À la carte possibilities include tandoori mushrooms (A$12), *saag* lamb (curried lamb with spinach; A$13) and even masala *dosa* (large lentil-flour crepe stuffed with spiced potatoes; A$12).

Mai Ake (☎ 6231 5557; 322 Elizabeth St; meals A$12-16; dinner) Gets positive reports for its tasty Thai food, which includes traditional favourites such as red curry (A$13).

DRINKING

Juiced Up (☎ 6231 1570; 367 Elizabeth St; meals A$5-9, juices A$3.50-5.50; breakfast & lunch Mon-Sat) A brilliant place for a vitamin top-up, with a focus on freshly squeezed juices. If you're feeling woozy after a big night out, the 'Hangover' (carrot; apple; watermelon; and orange and beetroot) will bring you back to the land of the living. There's a limited but commendable selection of wholesome meals.

Hobart has a medley of upbeat watering holes – some old favourites:

Knopwood's Retreat (☎ 6223 5808; 39 Salamanca Pl) A perennial Hobart favourite, usually hidden behind a solid mass of sozzled Friday-night drinkers loitering on the pavement section.

Irish Murphy's (☎ 6223 1119; 21 Salamanca Pl)

Republic Bar & Cafe (☎ 6234 6954; 299 Elizabeth St, North Hobart) One of Hobart's most atmospheric pubs, with fabulous food (generous serves ranging from A$9 to A$18), live music, a beer garden and a loyal following. The perfect place to down a beer before or after seeing a blockbuster at the nearby State Cinema (see Entertainment on below).

If you're seeking more stylish wining and reclining, these options should tickle your fancy:

Bar Celona (☎ 6224 7557; 23 Salamanca Sq) For a full review, see p303.

T-42° (☎ 6224 7742; Elizabeth St Pier)

Cow (☎ 6231 1200; 112 Murray St)

See also some drinking options with live music on right.

ENTERTAINMENT

Cinemas & Theatres

State Cinema (☎ 6234 6318; www.statecinema.com.au; 375 Elizabeth St, North Hobart) Established in 1913, this splendid little cinema is a rare gem, with unbeatable old-world charm and a stress-banishing ambience. You can even sip on a glass of wine while surrendering yourself to the big screen.

Village Cinema (☎ 6234 7288; 181 Collins St) This large, modern inner-city complex shows mainstream releases.

Federation Concert Hall (☎ 6235 3633, 1800 001 190; 1 Davey St) This modern concert hall is home to the Tasmanian Symphony Orchestra (www.tso.com.au); tickets start at A$41/22 per adult/student.

Theatre Royal (☎ 6233 2299; www.theatreroyal.com.au; 29 Campbell St) Australia's oldest theatre stages a range of music, ballet, theatre and opera performances by local and touring companies. Tickets usually range from A$20 to A$65.

Live Music

The *Mercury* newspaper lists most of Hobart's entertainment options in its Thursday insert called 'Pulse'. Also worth a browse is the online gig guide at www.nakeddwarf.com.au.

Good live music is usually held every Friday from 5.30pm to 7.30pm at the Salamanca Arts Centre courtyard (off Salamanca Sq).

There's regular live music at many pubs.

Irish Murphy's (☎ 6223 1119; 21 Salamanca Pl) Local bands play from Wednesday to Saturday, with a session on Sunday afternoons.

Syrup (☎ 6223 2491; upstairs, 39 Salamanca Pl) A popular place for late-night drinks and has a mixture of live music and DJs. It's open Wednesday to Saturday nights.

Isobar (☎ 6231 6600; 11 Franklin Wharf) Has a decent bar downstairs and a club upstairs.

Republic Bar & Cafe (☎ 6234 6954; 299 Elizabeth St, North Hobart) and the **New Sydney Hotel** (☎ 6234 4516; 87 Bathurst St) have an eclectic range of live music most nights of the week.

GETTING THERE & AWAY

Air

There are no direct flights between Tasmania and overseas destinations. At the time of writing, low-end airfares started at: Sydney A$110; Melbourne A$80.

Jetstar (☎ 13 15 38; www.jetstar.com.au)

Qantas (☎ 13 13 13; www.qantas.com.au; 77 Elizabeth St Mall, Hobart)

Regional Express (Rex; ☎ 13 17 13; www.regionalexpress.com.au)

Virgin Blue (☎ 13 67 89; www.virginblue.com.au)

Bus

Main bus companies with travel to/from Hobart include **Redline Coaches** (☎ 1300 360 000;

www.tasredline.com.au), which operates from the Transit Centre at 199 Collins St, as well as **TassieLink** (☎ 1300 300 520; www.tassielink.com.au, 64 Brisbane St), operating from the new Hobart Bus Terminal.

TassieLink has a seven-/10-/14-/21-day Explorer Pass that must be used within 10/15/20/30 days and costs A$160/190/220/260. The pass is valid on all scheduled services for unlimited kilometres and can be bought from mainland Tasmanian travel centres, Youth Hostels Association (YHA) and STA offices, most travel agents, or directly from TassieLink.

If you intend to buy an Explorer Pass, ask for timetables in advance or check TassieLink's website and plan your itinerary carefully before making your purchase. This is the only way to ensure that you'll be able to get where you want to go within the life of the pass.

Car & Motorcycle

There are many car-rental firms in Hobart; most have representation at the airport. The large multinationals (eg Avis, Budget, Hertz, Thrifty) have desks inside the terminal; smaller local companies have representation in the airport's car park area. Local budget firms include the following:

Lo-Cost Auto Rent (☎ 1800 647 060; www.locostautorent.com; 105 Murray St)

Selective Car Rentals (☎ 6234 3311; www.selectivecarrentals.com.au; 47 Bathurst St)

GETTING AROUND

For information about getting to/from the airport, see p297.

Bicycle

See Cycling on p301 for details of bicycle rental.

Boat

The **Wanderer** (☎ 6223 1914; return A$15) ferry, operated by Derwent River Cruises, visits various sites including the Botanical Gardens and Battery Point. It has a service departing Brooke St Pier (1.30pm and 3pm Monday to Friday; noon, 1.30pm and 3pm Saturday; 10.30am, noon, 1.30pm and 3pm Sunday).

Bus

Metro (☎ 13 22 01; www.metrotas.com.au) operates the local bus network; there's an information desk inside the main post office on the corner of Elizabeth and Macquarie Sts. Most buses leave from this area of Elizabeth St, or from around the edges of nearby Franklin Sq. If you're planning to bus around Hobart it's worth buying Metro's timetable (A$1). For A$3.90 you can buy a daily pass that can be used after 9am Monday to Friday, and all day Saturday, Sunday and public holidays.

CRUISE WITH CARE

Whizzing around in your own set of wheels is a fantastic way of exploring Tasmania, but one-lane bridges on country roads, and piled-high log-trucks that speed around sharp corners, demand constant caution. In cold weather be wary of 'black ice', an invisible layer of ice over the bitumen, especially on the shaded side of mountain passes. Furthermore, always keep your eyes peeled for wildlife and, if possible, avoid driving between dusk and dawn, as this is when marsupials are most active.

Taxi

Try **City Cabs** (☎ 13 10 08) or **Taxi Combined Services** (☎ 13 22 27). As well as regular taxis, **Maxi Taxi** (☎ 6234 3573) has vehicles catering to disabled people.

AROUND HOBART

Hobart is near some interesting historic and scenic sites such as **Richmond**, 24km northeast of the capital. With more than 50 buildings dating from the 19th century, it's Tasmania's premier historic town. For further details see www.richmondvillage.com.

Mt Field National Park, 80km northwest of Hobart, has dramatic mountain scenery, abundant wildlife and babbling waterfalls. For more information, contact the park's **Mt Field National Park visitors centre** (☎ 03-6288 1149; Lake Dobson Rd; 8.30am-5pm Dec-Apr, 9am-4pm Apr-Dec).

Eleven kilometres south of Hobart is the town of **Kingston**, which has the Kingston Beach – a popular swimming and sailing spot. Nearby is the smaller, more secluded Boronia Beach and its deep rock pool and further south is Blackmans Bay, which has a blowhole.

Getting There & Around

The **Richmond Tourist Bus** (☎ 0408-341 804; return A$25) runs a twice-daily service from Hobart that gives you three hours to explore Richmond before returning.

TassieLink (☎ 1300 300 520; www.tassielink.com.au) has a bus service from Hobart to the east coast that passes through Richmond (A$5.20, 40 minutes) on weekdays (except on school holidays). It also has regular services from Hobart to Mt Field National Park from November to April (A$25, 1¾ hours).

Day trips to places near Hobart are also offered by **Tigerline Coaches** (☎ 1300 653 633; www.tigerline.com.au).

SOUTHEAST COAST

South of Hobart are some pretty timber- and fruit-growing areas (providing opportunities for seasonal work – see p474 for information on working in Australia), as well as beautiful Bruny Island and the Hartz Mountains National Park. Information about the region can be found online at www.huontrail.org.au and at www.farsouth.com.au.

Getting There & Around

Hobart Coaches (☎ 13 22 01; www.hobartcoaches.com.au) runs several buses on weekdays from Hobart to Kettering (A$7). One bus runs each weekday from Hobart to Cygnet (A$8.70).

TassieLink (☎ 1300 300 520; www.tassielink.com.au) has regular services from Hobart through to Kingston (A$3.50, 30 minutes) and Geeveston (A$12, 1½ hours).

BRUNY ISLAND

☎ 03 / pop 520

Bruny Island is almost two islands, joined by an isthmus where mutton birds and other waterfowl breed. The island has superb coastal scenery, swimming and surf beaches, good fishing, and picturesque walking tracks within the spectacular **South Bruny National Park**. For more information about the island see www.brunyisland.net.

The small port of Kettering, on a sheltered bay 34km south of Hobart, is the terminal for the Bruny Island car ferry. The **Kettering visitors centre** (☎ 6267 4494; kettering@tasvisinfo.com.au; 81 Ferry Rd; ⏰ 9am-5pm), by the ferry terminal, has information about accommodation and services on the island.

Getting There & Around

There are frequent daily **ferry services** (☎ 6272 3277) from Kettering. There's no charge for foot passengers; a car costs A$21 return (A$26 on public holidays and public holiday weekends). Motorcycles cost A$11 (A$15 on public holidays and public holiday weekends) and bicycles are A$3. At least two buses operated by **Hobart Coaches** (☎ 13 22 01; www.hobartcoaches.com.au) connect passengers from Hobart with the ferry at Kettering daily for A$7.10.

The ferry terminal on Bruny Island is a long way from anywhere and travellers will need their own transport to get around the island.

CYGNET

☎ 03 / pop 800

The environs of Cygnet are known for their bountiful orchards – fruit grown here includes apples, stone fruits and berries – and the area attracts a stream of backpackers in search of fruit-picking work from November to May. The region also offers fine fishing, bushwalking and good beaches with safe swimming conditions.

Huon Valley Backpackers (☎ 6295 1551; www.balfeshill.alltasmanian.com; 4 Sandhill Rd, Cradoc; camp sites per person A$15, dm A$20, tw & d A$45) Off the Channel Hwy 4.5km north of town, this hostel has good facilities and is especially busy from November to May (advance bookings recommended), when the friendly host helps backpackers find fruit-picking work.

GEEVESTON

☎ 03 / pop 827

Geeveston is the gateway to the Hartz Mountains National Park and the popular Tahune Forest AirWalk. The **Forest & Heritage Centre** (☎ 6297 1836; geeveston@tasvisinfo.com.au; Church St; admission A$2; ⏰ 9am-5pm) incorporates the visitors centre, and has comprehensive displays on all aspects of forestry and a gallery where local craftspeople have taken to wood with artistic fervour. It costs A$11 to enter the forest room and gallery, and to do the AirWalk, which is out of town.

The **Tahune Forest AirWalk & visitors centre** (☎ 6297 0068; ⏰ 9am-5pm), 29km from Geeveston, is a 620m-long elevated stroll between 25m and 45m above the ground. The walk takes you though the canopy of the forest where you can enjoy panoramic views.

HARTZ MOUNTAINS NATIONAL PARK

This national park, 84km from Hobart, is renowned for its rugged mountains, glacial lakes, gorges, alpine moorlands and dense rainforest. The area is subject to rapid changes in weather, so even on a one-day walk you should take waterproof gear and warm clothing. There are some amazing views from the **Waratah Lookout** (24km from Geeveston), including the jagged peaks of the Snowy Range and the Devils Backbone. Good walks include tracks to **Arve Falls** (20 minutes return), **Lake Osborne** (40 minutes return) and the more-challenging **Hartz Pass** (3½ hours return).

TASMAN PENINSULA

The Tasman Peninsula is renowned for the convict ruins at Port Arthur and for its striking 300m-high cliffs, dazzling beaches and bays, and bushwalking opportunities, much of which constitutes the Tasman National Park. Information on the region is available at www.portarthur-region.com.au.

Getting There & Around

TassieLink (☎ 1300 300 520; www.tassielink.com.au) connects Hobart and the Tasman Peninsula, but the timetable's geared more to students than to travellers. There's a weekday bus service between Hobart and Port Arthur (A$20, 2¼ hours) during school terms, and one service three days a week in school holidays. Buses stop at all the main towns on the peninsula.

Those without their own transport might prefer to join a coach tour out of Hobart run by **Tigerline Coaches** (☎ 1300 653 633; www.tigerline.com.au); full-day tours cost A$77, which includes a hotel pick-up and drop-off and the entry fee to the Port Arthur site.

EAGLEHAWK NECK TO PORT ARTHUR

Near Eaglehawk Neck are the incredible coastal formations of the **Tessellated Pavement**, the **Blowhole**, **Devils Kitchen**, **Tasmans Arch** and **Waterfall Bay**. South of Port Arthur is **Remarkable Cave**.

There are some enchanting walks in the **Tasman National Park** (per person A$3.50, vehicle with max 8 passengers A$10), including Waterfall Bay (one to 1½ hours return), Cape Raoul (1½ hours to the lookout, five hours return to the cape) and Cape Hauy (five hours return).

You can visit the remains of the **penal outstations** at Eaglehawk Neck, Koonya, Premaydena and Saltwater River, and the restored ruins at the **Coal Mines Historic Site**.

The **Tasmanian Devil Park** (☎ 03-6250 3230; Arthur Hwy, Taranna; admission A$20; 9am-6pm) is a wildlife rescue centre with plenty of native birds and animals, besides devils. There are scheduled animal feedings (devil feedings are at 10am, 11am, 1.30pm and 5pm), plus shows featuring birds of prey (11.15am and 3.30pm).

Sleeping

Eaglehawk Neck Backpackers (☎ 03-6250 3248; 94 Old Jetty Rd, Eaglehawk Neck; camp sites per person A$7, dm A$18) Down Old Jetty Rd you'll find this earthy, tranquil hostel. On offer is a very small area for tents, as well as nicely kept rooms – you need to bring your own sheets and doona although pillows are provided – and bicycle rental for guests. Advance bookings are recommended.

Fortescue Bay Campground (☎ 03-6250 2433; Tasman National Park; camp sites A$11, max six people per site) This remote and captivating area has good facilities (including a small kiosk selling basic supplies) and is 12km off the highway on an unsealed road. National park entry fees apply in addition to camping fees; book ahead for the busy summer holiday period.

Eating

Officers' Mess (☎ 03-6250 3635; 443 Pirates Bay Dr, Eaglehawk Neck; meals A$5-12; 8am-6pm) Whips up light lunches and takeaways, and has a well-supplied store. A curried scallop pie with chips and salad is A$9.50.

Eaglehawk Cafe (☎ 03-6250 3331; Arthur Hwy, Eaglehawk Neck; lunch under A$12; breakfast & lunch Thu-Tue) With its laid-back ambience and a menu of tempting dishes emphasising local produce, the Eaglehawk is a good choice. For a hearty morning fill you can't beat the Pirates' Bay breakfast (A$15).

Mussel Boys (☎ 03-6250 3088; 597 Arthur Hwy, Taranna; meals A$11-18; lunch only Wed, lunch & dinner Thu-Sun) Offers delights from the deep such as crumbed scallops/prawns/calamari for A$1/1/0.50 (each), and prawn-and-scallop kebabs (A$7).

PORT ARTHUR

☎ 03 / pop 170

In 1830 Governor Arthur chose the Tasman Peninsula as the place to confine prisoners who had committed further crimes in the colony. He called the peninsula a 'natural penitentiary' because it was connected to the mainland by a strip of land less than 100m wide, called Eaglehawk Neck. To deter escape, ferocious guard dogs were chained in a line across the isthmus and a rumour circulated that the waters on either side were shark-infested. Between 1830 and 1877 about 12,500 convicts served their sentences at Port Arthur.

The historic township of Port Arthur became the centre of a network of penal stations on the peninsula but was much more than just a prison town. It also had fine buildings and thriving industries built on convict labour, including shipbuilding, coal mining, shoemaking and brick and nail production.

Australia's first railway 'ran' the 7km between Norfolk Bay and Long Bay: convicts pushed the carriages along the tracks. A semaphore telegraph system allowed instant communication between Port Arthur, the penal outstations and Hobart. Convict farms provided fresh vegetables; a boys' prison was built at Point Puer to reform and educate juvenile convicts; and a church (today one of the most readily recognised tourist sights in Tasmania) was erected.

Tragedy struck Port Arthur in late April 1996 when a gunman opened fire on visitors and staff, killing 35 people and wounding several others. The gunman was finally captured after he burned down a local guesthouse, and he was subsequently imprisoned. There is now a poignant memorial garden at the site. Please refrain from asking Port Arthur staff questions about the tragedy.

The **Port Arthur Historic Site** (☎ 1800 659 101; www.portarthur.org.au; adult/student A$24/19; ⌚ grounds & ruins 8.30am-dusk) is among Tasmania's premier tourist attractions, containing over 30 historic buildings and ruins. The **visitors centre** (☎ 6251 2371; ⌚ 8.30am to around 9pm) is in the entrance building and includes an information counter, eateries and a gift shop. Downstairs is an interesting interpretation gallery, where you can follow the convicts' journey from England to Tasmania.

At the Convict Study Centre, you can find out whether you have convict ancestry by accessing a computer database of convicts who came here.

For disabled visitors, some areas of the site require assisted access, and a courtesy buggy can be arranged – inquire at the visitors centre.

Forty-minute guided tours of the site are included in the entry fee. The tours are worthwhile and leave regularly (at least one per hour) from outside the visitors centre. The admission ticket – which includes a small booklet containing details of the site as well as a handy map – is valid for two consecutive days. The ticket also entitles you to a short harbour cruise of about 20 minutes that circumnavigates but does not stop at the **Isle of the Dead**. Should you wish to visit this island on a highly recommended one-hour guided tour to see the remaining headstones and hear some of the stories, it costs an additional A$10. Note that the cruises and Isle of the Dead tours don't operate in August.

There's also a **Point Puer Boys Prison Tour** on the mainland, which is a guided walk (A$10; not operational in August). Some 3000 boys, ranging in age from nine to 18, passed through this prison between 1834 and 1849.

Another extremely popular tour at the site is the spooky, 90-minute, lantern-lit **ghost tour** (A$15.50); bookings essential. The tour leaves from the visitors centre at dusk and takes in a number of historic buildings, with guides telling of some spine-chilling occurrences. There is a minimum of two tours per night.

Tasmanian Seaplanes (☎ 6227 8808; www.tas-seaplane.com) is based at the site and offers scenic seaplane flights starting at A$65 for 20 minutes.

Sleeping & Eating

Roseview Youth Hostel (☎ 6250 2311; roseview@southcom.com.au; Champ St; dm/d A$19/45) With a great location at the edge of the Port Arthur site, this YHA hostel has slightly crowded dorms but is otherwise very nice. To get here, continue 500m past the Port Arthur turn-off and turn left at the sign for the hostel into Safety Cove Rd.

Port Arthur Caravan & Cabin Park (☎ 6250 2340; www.portarthurcaravan-cabinpark.com.au; Garden Point; camp/caravan sites A$16/18, dm A$15, cabins May-Aug A$75-85, Sep-Apr A$85-95) This well-equipped park is about 1km before Port Arthur and not far from a sheltered beach.

At the historic site there are a few eating options, including the Museum Coffee Shop in the old Asylum, and Port Café in the visitors centre, which serve standard café fare; a salad roll is A$4.80.

Felons (☎ 6251 2310; mains A$15-25; ⏲ dinner) Also in the visitors centre, this is a more upmarket choice with menu offerings such as cajun fish of the day (A$23) and lemon ginger cheesecake (A$8). Advance bookings are recommended.

Phudies (☎ 6250 2227; Tasman Hwy; meals under A$15; ⏲ breakfast & lunch Wed-Mon, lunch Sat) Back on the highway, almost opposite the turn-off to the historic site, this place serves a selection of light meals including pies, sandwiches, quiches and the occasional curry.

Convict Kitchen Bistro (☎ 6250 2101; Comfort Inn Port Arthur, 29 Safety Cove Rd; meals A$13-16; ⏲ breakfast, lunch & dinner) Conveniently located near the historic site, this motel-restaurant welcomes nonguests and is a particularly handy option for people staying at the nearby Roseview Youth Hostel. Roast of the day is A$16.

EAST COAST

Tasmania's east coast is known for its long sandy beaches, good fishing and mild, sunny climate. The region's best-known scenic features are the national parks of Maria Island and Freycinet. The jaw-dropping scenery around Coles Bay shouldn't be missed, and Bicheno and Swansea make for relaxing seaside stays.

Getting There & Around

Redline Coaches (☎ 1300 360 000; www.tasredline.com.au) runs a weekday service between Launceston and Bicheno (A$28, 2¾ hours) via Swansea (A$23.30, two hours).

TassieLink (☎ 1300 300 520; www.tassielink.com.au) has a service from Hobart to Swansea (A$22, 2½ hours) as well as a service from Hobart to Bicheno (A$26, three hours) and St Helens (A$38, 3¾ hours). Call for current schedules. TassieLink also links Launceston and Bicheno (A$25, 2½ hours).

For the Freycinet Peninsula, **Bicheno Coach Service** (☎ 03-6257 0293) has at least five services a week from Bicheno to Coles Bay (A$10, 30 minutes), with return trips on the same day.

MARIA ISLAND NATIONAL PARK

This secluded island has eye-popping scenery (and bird-watching), including fossil-studded sandstone and limestone cliffs, pleasant beaches, forests and fern gullies. The marine life around the island is also diverse and plentiful. For more details check out www.key.org.au/mariaisland.

There's a **visitors centre** (☎ 6257 4772; triabunna@tasvisinfo.com.au; cnr Charles St & Esplanade, Triabunna; ⏲ 10am-4pm) on the waterfront at Triabunna (departure point for the Maria Island ferry), which can provide details about the island.

The Maria Island **ferry** (☎ 0427-100 104) leaves from the town jetty at Triabunna and runs at least once daily (telephone ahead to confirm timings as they're subject to change). The return fare is A$25 per adult; bicycles are carried for A$2.

SWANSEA

☎ 03 / pop 529

On the shores of Great Oyster Bay, with super views across to Freycinet Peninsula, Swansea is a delightful place for camping, boating, fishing and surfing.

Settled in the 1820s, Swansea has a number of historic buildings, including the original 1860 **council chambers** (Noyes St) and the 1838 **Morris' General Store** (☎ 6257 78101; 13 Franklin St), which is still trading. The community centre dates from the 1860s and houses the **Glamorgan War Memorial Museum** (☎ 6257 8215; 22 Franklin St; admission A$3; ⏲ 9am-5pm Mon-Sat, to 4pm Tue), which has various exhibits including old B&W photos, sewing machines and even some Fijian spears. It also houses an exquisite 120-year-old billiard table, with games available from 5pm to 7pm Wednesday to Monday (A$2 per person per game, advance bookings essential).

At the **Swansea Bark Mill & East Coast Museum** (☎ 6257 8382; 96 Tasman Hwy; admission A$5.50; ⏲ 9am-5pm summer, 10am-4pm winter), a restored mill displays working models of equipment used in the processing of black-wattle bark, a basic ingredient used in the tanning of heavy leathers. The adjoining museum features displays of Swansea's early history.

Sleeping & Eating

Swan Inn (☎ 6257 8899; 1 Franklin St; d with bathroom A$60) Brilliant budget beachfront rooms are available here, in front of the old pub. Set right on the beach and with million-dollar sea views, the rooms are a bit cramped but are clean and comfortable. Advance bookings (request the best sea-facing room) are recommended. The pub here does meals that are good value (lunch from A$10 to A$19; dinner from A$14 to A$23).

Swansea Holiday Park (☎ 6257 8177; www.swansea-holiday.com.au; Shaw St; unpowered/powered camp sites A$16/18, cabins A$40-85) This neat park has a beachfront location signposted off the main road just north of town. On offer are camp sites right on the beach, and fully self-contained cabins.

Left Bank (☎ 6257 8896; cnr Franklin & Maria Sts; meals A$6-14; 🕑 breakfast & lunch Wed-Mon Aug-Apr, breakfast & lunch Thu-Mon May-Jul) Behind the bright red door is one of the east coast's best stops for great coffee and winning café fare in an easy-going atmosphere. Tasty breakfast choices include buttered toast with pesto and slow-roasted tomatoes (A$6), and smoked salmon in cheesy scrambled eggs (A$12). A luscious slice of lemon tart is A$7.

Pier Cafe (☎ 6257 8266; 14 Franklin St; meals A$5-8; 🕑 breakfast, lunch & dinner) This small, no-frills takeaway has cheap eats such as seafood boxes (A$7.50), burgers (around A$5) and chips with gravy (A$3).

Kate's Berry Farm (☎ 6257 8428; Addison St; 🕑 8.30am-6pm summer, to 5pm in winter) About 3km south of Swansea, this friendly farm has breathtaking views, a store selling home-made produce such as fruity jams (A$4.50 to A$7.80) and absolutely divine ice cream (from A$2 – the small serves are huge). There are also Devonshire teas (A$7.50 per person) and cakes.

COLES BAY & FREYCINET NATIONAL PARK

☎ 03 / pop 120

The small township of Coles Bay is dominated by the awesome 300m-high pink granite outcrops called the **Hazards**. The town is the gateway to many gorgeous beaches, se-cluded coves, rocky cliffs and excellent bushwalks in the **Freycinet National Park**. The park, incorporating Freycinet Peninsula, beautiful Schouten Island and the Friendly Beaches (on the east coast, north of Coles Bay), is noted for its coastal wildflowers, and for its wildlife, which includes black cockatoos, yellow wattlebirds, honeyeaters and Bennett's wallabies.

Information

Park information and organised tour information is available from the helpful **visitors centre** (☎ 6256 7000; freycinet@parks.tas.gov.au; 🕑 8am-5pm May-Sep, to 6pm Oct-Apr) at the park's entrance. See www.freycinetcolesbay.com for a useful online guide to the area.

Coles Bay Trading (☎ 6257 0109; 1 Garnet Ave; 🕑 7am-7pm summer, 8am-6pm winter) is the general store and post office. It has an ATM, and sells groceries and petrol.

Activities

This area is a walker's paradise, with walks such as a 27km circuit of the peninsula and many shorter tracks. The best known of these is the beautiful **Wineglass Bay**. The walk to the beach itself takes 2½ to three hours return, or you can just head to the Wineglass Bay Lookout for breathtaking views of white sand and crystal-clear water (about 1½ hours).

Shorter, less-strenuous walks include the 500m-long lighthouse boardwalk at **Cape Tourville**, which affords great coastal panoramas (including a glimpse of Wineglass Bay).

On any long walk remember to sign in (and sign out) at the registration booth in the car park. An entry fee is charged for all of Tasmania's national parks; a pass is needed whether or not there is a collection booth. Passes are available at park entrances, from many tour operators, on the Spirit of Tasmania ferries, at some local stores and from **Service Tasmania** (☎ 1300 135 513; 134 Macquarie St, Hobart). A 24-hour pass to any number of parks costs A$10 per car or A$3.50 per person. The best value for most travellers is the two-month pass, which costs A$33 per vehicle or A$14 per person for bushwalkers, cyclists and motorcyclists.

Freycinet & Strahan Adventures (☎ 6257 0500; www.adventurestasmania.com; cnr Coles Bay Esplanade & Freycinet Dr) offers a range of activities from rock climbing and abseiling (from A$85 per person) to mountain-biking (from A$50).

Coles Bay Trading (☎ 6257 0109; 1 Garnet Ave; 🕑 7am-7pm summer, 8am-6pm winter) has bicycle hire (A$11/17 for a full/half-day), and in summer and during Easter, inquire at the **visitors centre** (☎ 6256 7000; freycinet@parks.tas.gov.au; 🕑 8am-5pm May-Sep, to 6pm Oct-Apr) about free, ranger-led activities (eg walks, talks and slide shows).

Sleeping & Eating

The scenery at the free camp sites of Wineglass Bay (one to 1½ hours' walk from the car park), Hazards Beach (two to three hours) and Cooks Beach (about 4½ hours) is well

TASMANIA

worth the walk. There's little reliable drinking water at any of these sites or elsewhere on the peninsula, so carry your own. Campfires are not permitted inside the park.

Richardsons Beach at the national park entrance is the main **camping ground** (☎ 6256 7000; camp/caravan sites per person A$5.50/6.60). Facilities here include powered sites, toilets and water. Only cold-water showers are available. Camping at Richardsons Beach is extremely popular in summer, and sites for the period from mid-December to mid-February are determined by a ballot drawn on 1 October (applications must be made before 30 September). During this peak period there is limited tent space available in the designated backpacker camping area (no vehicle access, no bookings taken; camping A$5.50 per person), but this fills quickly. Outside of the ballot period, advanced bookings are highly recommended.

Iluka Holiday Centre (☎ 6257 0115; www.ilukaholidaycentre.com.au; Coles Bay Esplanade; camp sites unpowered/powered per 2 people A$20/25, on-site caravans per 2 people A$65, cabins & units per 2 people A$80-130) This large well-maintained park has good amenities, plus a shop, pub and bakery next door. It's wise to book ahead. Also here is **Iluka Backpackers** (☎ 6257 0115; dm/d A$23/59), a YHA hostel that's light-on for character but is clean and popular (so book ahead).

Freycinet Rentals (☎ 6257 0320; 5 Garnet Ave, Coles Bay) Manages a number of properties in and around Coles Bay – these are primarily self-contained holiday houses that can sleep up to six people. Prices range from A$120 to A$170 for two, with additional guests costing A$15 to A$25; prices are lower in the low season (winter). Rates include linen, and the majority of properties have a full kitchen, barbecue, laundry, TV and video.

Freycinet Café & Bakery (☎ 6257 0272; Coles Bay Esplanade; pizzas A$10-22; 🕓 breakfast & lunch) Offers all-day breakfast, sandwiches, cakes, freshly baked pies, and after 4pm, pizzas. Toasted foccacias are A$8.

Iluka Tavern (☎ 6257 0115; Coles Bay Esplanade; meals A$10-16; 🕓 lunch & dinner) A little lacking in personality, but worth a visit for its good pub-style meals, such as quiche with salad (A$10.50).

Getting There & Around

Bicheno Coach Service (☎ 6257 0293; biccoa@vision.net.au) runs buses from Coles Bay to Bicheno, meeting east-coast TassieLink and Redline services at the Coles Bay turn-off. There are up to four services on weekdays, one on Saturday and two on Sunday. Some services only run if bookings exist and it's wise to book at least the night before. The bus will pick you up from your accommodation if requested. In Coles Bay, buses depart from the general store and run via Iluka Holiday Centre. The fare between Bicheno and Coles Bay is A$10/16 one way/return; from the turn-off to Coles Bay the fare is A$7/13.

It's more than 5km from Coles Bay to the national park's walking-tracks car park, and, if booked, the buses will drop off or pick up passengers at the car park. There is also a morning shuttle bus service between Coles Bay and the walking-tracks car park on weekdays (Saturday and Sunday only if booked); the cost is A$4/7 one way/return.

BICHENO

☎ 03 / pop 711

In the early 1800s, whalers and sealers used Bicheno's narrow harbour (called the Gulch) to shelter their boats. These days, fishing is still one of the town's major occupations. Bicheno has beautiful beaches and is the ideal spot to let your hair down, meditate and contemplate where your life is going.

Information

The **Bicheno Information Service** (☎ 6375 1500; 46 Foster St; 🕓 9.30am-4.30pm summer, 11am-3pm winter) is staffed by volunteers who happily disseminate free brochures and advice.

Sights & Activities

An interesting 3km **foreshore walk**, from Redbill Point to the blowhole, continues south around the beach to Courland Bay. You can also walk up to **Whalers Lookout** for good views.

There's a **fairy penguin rookery** at the northern end of Redbill Beach. To see the penguins, join a one-hour **tour** (☎ 6375 1333; A$16) that leaves nightly at dusk from East Coast Surf on the main road. You can also book **glass-bottom boat tours** (☎ 6375 1294; A$15) here. There's a good dive operator in Bicheno – **Bicheno Dive Centre** (☎ 6375 1138; www.bichenodive.com.au; 2 Scuba Ct) – where a dive costs A$105 (A$32 if you have your own diving gear).

For something a little different, **Le Frog** (☎ 6375 1777) offers passenger rides on a three-wheeled trike (a cross between a motorcycle and convertible car) in and around town. Rides are with a gregarious French driver – hence the name. Prices start at A$12 for a 10- to 15-minute jaunt around Bicheno.

Other tours are also available.

Seven kilometres north of town is the 32-hectare **East Coast Natureworld** (☎ 6375 1311; www.natureworld.com.au; Tasman Hwy; admission A$13; ⌚ 9am-5pm), which boasts a walk-through aviary, lots of native animals and a scenic lookout.

A few kilometres south of the animal park is the turn-off to the picturesque **Douglas-Apsley National Park** (☎ 6257 0107). There's rough road access to Apsley Gorge in the park's south, where there's a waterhole with very good swimming.

Sleeping & Eating

Bicheno Backpackers (☎ /fax 6375 1651; bichenobackpackers@bigpond.com; 11 Morrison St; dm A$18) With its well-designed bunks (each with lockers), this laid-back and clean hostel is a super choice.

Bicheno East Coast Holiday Park (☎ 6375 1999; bichenoecholidaypark@bigpond.com; 4 Champ St; camp/caravan sites A$16/18, cabins A$65-85) This well-maintained park has a central location and all the requisite amenities. If it's booked out, try **Bicheno Caravan Park** (☎ /fax 6375 1280; 52 Burgess St; camp sites per person A$15).

Freycinet Café & Bakery (☎ 6375 1972; 55 Burgess St; ⌚ breakfast & lunch) As good as its namesake in Coles Bay, this place has mouthwatering pies and other freshly baked treats. Try the lip-smacking chicken and Camembert pie (A$3.90) and chocolate berry cake (A$3.50 per slice).

Cod Rock Café (☎ 6375 1340; 45 Foster St; meals A$6-16; ⌚ lunch & dinner) Rock up to the Cod Rock Café for cheap, tasty seafood such as fish burgers (A$6.50) and calamari with chips (A$7.80).

Getting There & Around

Bicheno Coach Service (☎ 6257 0293; biccoa@vision.net.au) runs buses to Coles Bay (A$10/16 one way/return) from the Freycinet Café & Bakery (55 Burgess St). There are up to four services every day from Monday to Friday, one on Saturday and two on Sunday. It is advisable to book at least the night before.

NORTHEAST

LAUNCESTON

☎ 03 / pop 68,443

Although Launceston lags behind Hobart in the cosmopolitan stakes, its appeal to tourists has grown in recent times, with the opening of new eateries and museums. If you're planning a trip here in mid-February try to coincide your visit with the summer **Festivale** (www.festivale.com.au), a three-day event celebrating food, wine and the arts, staged in City Park.

Founded in 1805, Launceston is Australia's third-oldest city and the commercial centre of northern Tasmania. It was the third attempt by the British to establish a permanent settlement on the Tamar River and was originally called Patersonia, after its founder. In 1907 the city was renamed in honour of Governor King, who was born in Launceston, England.

Orientation

Launceston airport is about 15km south of the city centre. **Tasmanian Shuttle Bus Services** (☎ 0500 512 009) runs a door-to-door airport service for A$10 (book a day in advance). A taxi to the city centre costs about A$28.

The compact city centre is arranged in a grid pattern around the Brisbane St mall, between Charles and St John Sts. Two blocks north, in Cameron St, there's another public area in the centre of Civic Sq, home to two churches, the town hall, library and police.

For road maps and motoring information, including a map of Launceston (A$2.50), go to the **Royal Automobile Club of Tasmania** (RACT; ☎ 6335 5633; cnr George & York Sts).

Information

EMERGENCY

Police station (☎ 000; Cimitiere St)

INTERNET ACCESS

Cyber King (☎ 6334 2802; 113 George St; per hr A$8; ⌚ 8.30am-7pm Mon-Sat)

OUTDOOR EQUIPMENT

For bushwalking maps and camping gear (sales or rental), try the following:

Allgoods (☎ 6331 3644; cnr York & St John Sts)
Paddy Pallin (☎ 6331 4240; 110 George St)

TASMANIA

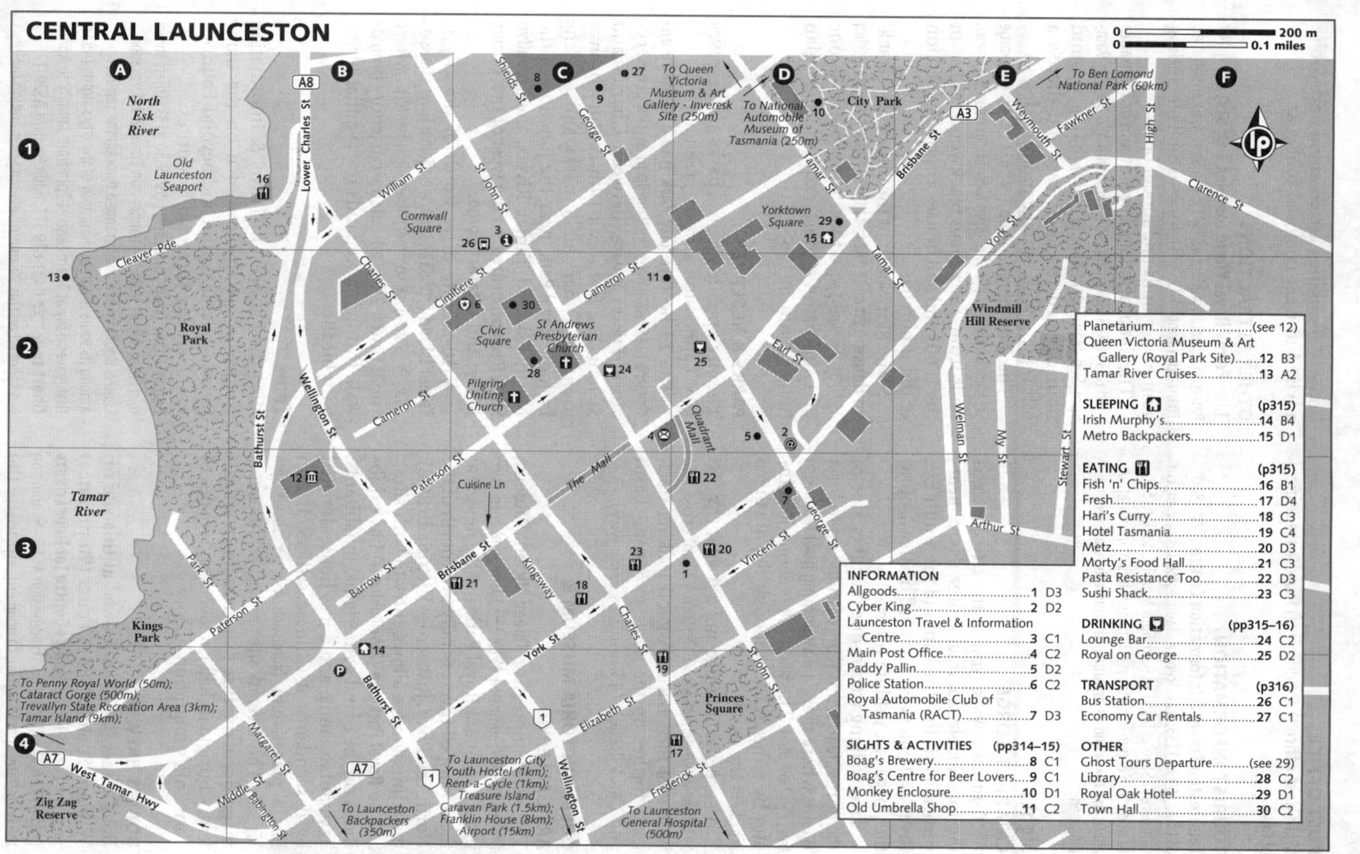
CENTRAL LAUNCESTON
0 200 m
0 0.1 miles
Planetarium (see 12)
Queen Victoria Museum & Art Gallery (Royal Park Site) 12 B3
Tamar River Cruises 13 A2
SLEEPING (p315)
Irish Murphy's 14 B4
Metro Backpackers 15 D1
EATING (p315)
Fish 'n' Chips 16 B1
Fresh 17 D4
Hari's Curry 18 C3
Hotel Tasmania 19 C4
Metz 20 D3
Morty's Food Hall 21 C3
Pasta Resistance Too 22 D3
Sushi Shack 23 C3
DRINKING (pp315–16)
Lounge Bar 24 C2
Royal on George 25 D2
TRANSPORT (p316)
Bus Station 26 C1
Economy Car Rentals 27 C1
OTHER
Ghost Tours Departure (see 29)
Library 28 C2
Royal Oak Hotel 29 D1
Town Hall 30 C2
INFORMATION
Allgoods 1 D3
Cyber King 2 D2
Launceston Travel & Information Centre 3 C1
Main Post Office 4 C2
Paddy Pallin 5 D2
Police Station 6 C2
Royal Automobile Club of Tasmania (RACT) 7 D3
SIGHTS & ACTIVITIES (pp314–15)
Boag's Brewery 8 C1
Boag's Centre for Beer Lovers 9 C1
Monkey Enclosure 10 D1
Old Umbrella Shop 11 C2
North Esk River
Old Launceston Seaport
Tamar River
Royal Park
Kings Park
Zig Zag Reserve
Cornwall Square
Civic Square
City Park
Yorktown Square
Windmill Hill Reserve
Princes Square
Quadrant Mall
The Mall
St Andrews Presbyterian Church
Pilgrim Uniting Church
To Queen Victoria Museum & Art Gallery - Inveresk Site (250m)
To National Automobile Museum of Tasmania (250m)
To Ben Lomond National Park (60km)
To Penny Royal World (50m); Cataract Gorge (500m); Trevallyn State Recreation Area (3km); Tamar Island (9km);
To Launceston Backpackers (350m)
To Launceston City Youth Hostel (1km); Rent-a-Cycle (1km); Treasure Island Caravan Park (1.5km); Franklin House (8km); Airport (15km)
To Launceston General Hospital (500m)
Lower Charles St
Cleaver Pde
Bathurst St
Wellington St
Paterson St
Park St
Margaret St
Middle St
Babington St
West Tamar Hwy
Barrow St
Brisbane St
Cuisine Ln
Kingsway
York St
Charles St
Cameron St
Cimitiere St
William St
St John St
Shields St
George St
Elizabeth St
Frederick St
Vincent St
Earl St
Tamar St
Weymouth St
Fawkner St
High St
Clarence St
Welman St
My St
Stewart St
Arthur St
A8
A3
A7
1

TASMANIA

POST OFFICE

Main post office (107 Brisbane St) Found in the centre of town.

TOURIST INFORMATION

Launceston Travel & Information Centre (☎ 1800 651 827, 6336 3133; travelcentre@launceston.tas.gov.au; cnr Cimitiere & St John Sts; 🕑 9am-5pm Mon-Fri, to 3pm Sat, to noon Sun & public holidays) Dispenses lots of information about the town and its environs, although the staff seem a bit jaded.

Sights

CATARACT GORGE

A 10-minute walk west of the city centre is the formidable Cataract Gorge. Here, near-vertical cliffs line the banks of the South Esk River as it enters the Tamar. The area around the gorge is a wildlife reserve.

Two walking tracks, one on either side of the gorge, lead from Kings Bridge up to First Basin, where there's a **swimming pool** (admission free; 🕑 Nov-Mar). The walk takes about 30 minutes by either track, although the northern track is the easier.

A suspension bridge and a **chairlift** (☎ 6331 5915; one way/return A$7/8.50; 🕑 9am-4.30pm) cross the waters of First Basin. A good walking track leads further up the gorge to Second Basin and Duck Reach (45 minutes each way).

QUEEN VICTORIA MUSEUM & ART GALLERY

The very impressive **Queen Victoria Museum** (☎ 6323 3777; admission A$10; 🕑 10am-5pm) has two branches, one at Royal Park and the newest at the revamped Inveresk railyards (north of the North Esk River, just across Victoria Bridge); the admission fee allows entry to both sites.

The **Royal Park site** (2 Wellington St) has exhibitions on the island's Aboriginal inhabitants, Tasmanian fauna, and a joss house donated by descendants of Chinese settlers. It also has a **planetarium** (admission A$5; 🕑 shows 3pm Tue-Sat). The **Inveresk site** (Invermay Rd) houses a magnificent mixture that includes an art gallery, Aboriginal shell necklaces and stories of Tasmania's migration history.

BOAG'S BREWERY

Boag's beer has been brewed at this site on William St since 1881. Tours (90 minutes) are operated from **Boag's Centre for Beer Lovers** (☎ 6332 6300; 39 William St; admission A$16; 🕑 tours on the hour 9am-1pm Mon-Thu, to noon Fri), opposite the brewery. Bookings are essential and you're advised to wear enclosed footwear.

OTHER ATTRACTIONS

The **Penny Royal World complex** (☎ 6331 3377; 147 Paterson St; adult/student A$15/12; 🕑 9am-4.30pm summer, 10am-4pm winter) has historic exhibits including gunpowder mills and model boats.

The **National Automobile Museum of Tasmania** (☎ 6334 8888; 86 Cimitiere St; admission A$8.50; 🕑 9am-5pm Sep-May, 10am-4pm May-Sep) has a ground floor devoted to classic cars and there's a loft replete with vintage motorcycles.

The **Old Umbrella Shop** (☎ 6331 9248; 60 George St; admission free; 🕑 9am-5pm Mon-Fri, to noon Sat) was built from Tasmanian blackwood timber in the 1860s and still houses a curious selection of old umbrellas.

Some 8km south of the city centre, **Franklin House** (☎ 6344 7824; 413-419 Hobart Rd; admission A$7.70; 🕑 9am-5pm Oct-Mar, to 4pm Apr-Sep) is one of Launceston's most exquisite Georgian homes, built in 1838.

PARKS & RESERVES

The city's public squares, parks and reserves give Launceston a fresh, green appeal.

The 13-hectare **City Park** has a **monkey enclosure** (admission free; 🕑 9am-4pm) and a conservatory. **Princes Square**, between Charles and St John Sts, features a 19th-century bronze fountain. Other public parks and gardens include: **Royal Park**, near the junction of the North Esk and Tamar Rivers; the **Trevallyn State Recreation Area**, to the west of the Tamar River; and **Cataract Gorge**.

A 10-minute drive north of the city is **Tamar Island** (☎ 6327 3964; West Tamar Hwy; admission A$2; 🕑 9am-dusk summer, 10am-4pm winter), where you'll find a 2km wheelchair-friendly boardwalk through a wetlands reserve that teems with birdlife.

Tours

Visit the Launceston Travel & Information Centre to get the lowdown on the many tours available within and beyond Launceston. Here are some old favourites:

Coach Tram Tour Company (☎ 6336 3133) Offers three tours that depart from the Launceston Travel & Information Centre. Bookings are also arranged through the centre. Among its tours is a three-hour tour of the city's sights (A$32) that leaves daily at 10am (also at 2pm from January to April).

Ghost tour (☎ 0421-819 373; adult/student A$20/17) Get spooked on this 90-minute evening tour around the city's back alleys. Tours depart from the front of the Royal Oak Hotel (14 Brisbane St) at dusk and bookings are essential.

Historic walk (☎ 6331 3679; adult/student A$15/11; ⏲ tours 9.45am Mon-Fri) This one-hour guided tour takes you around the city centre.

Tamar River Cruises (☎ 6334 9900; www.tamar-river-cruises.com.au) Based at Home Point in Royal Park, this company offers various cruises including a 50-minute tour of the Cataract Gorge (A$14).

Sleeping

Launceston has some pleasing budget offerings. Private rooms are with shared bathroom unless otherwise stated.

Metro Backpackers (☎ 6334 4505; www.backpackersmetro.com.au; 16 Brisbane St; dm/d A$23/55; P 💻) This is a first-rate YHA hostel with a swish interior and central location. It has lots of tour information, and excellent facilities including an outdoor rooftop terrace and barbecue, laundry and bikes for rent. Highly recommended.

Launceston Backpackers (☎ 6334 2327; www.launcestonbackpackers.com.au; 103 Canning St; dm/s/d A$17/38/40; 💻) Another fine budget choice is this large hostel, in a renovated Federation building. Facilities include spacious communal areas and a laundry. There's also plenty of travel information.

Launceston City Youth Hostel (☎ 6344 9779; tasequiphire@email.com; 36 Thistle St; dm/s/f A$15/22/40) Located nearly 2km from the city centre, this rambling hostel is another sound choice – unless you're averse to the strict single-sex dorm policy. The hostel also rents out bicycles (see p316) and bushwalking gear.

Irish Murphy's (☎ 6331 4440; www.irishmurphys.com.au; 211 Brisbane St; dm/d A$17/35) This atmospheric pub has decent, informal budget accommodation and plenty of hobnobbing opportunities in the bar and restaurant downstairs. Good for live music, see right.

Treasure Island Caravan Park (☎ 6344 2600; treasureislandlaunceston@netspace.net.au; 94 Glen Dhu St; camp/caravan sites A$19/20, on-site caravans A$46, cabins A$70-80) About 2.5km south of the city, this park has good facilities but is in a somewhat noisy location beside the highway.

Eating

For a quick, cheap nibble head for **Morty's Food Hall** (cnr Brisbane & Wellington Sts; ⏲ 10am-9.30pm), which has something to satisfy most taste buds, from Caesar salad (A$9.50) to Asian noodles (A$8 to A$15).

Fresh (☎ 6331 4299; 178 Charles St; meals A$6-13; ⏲ breakfast & lunch) This retro-style vegetarian café, opposite Princes Sq, serves tasty light meals and terrific coffee. The pizza topped with mushrooms, feta, and onion marmalade (A$11) is yummy.

Sushi Shack (☎ 6331 4455; 134 York St; sushi A$3.50-18; ⏲ lunch & dinner Mon-Sat) Recommended for fresh sushi to eat in or take away, as well as classic Japanese mains such as tempura, *yakisoba* (fried noodles) and teriyaki. Starve all day before pigging out on all-you-can-eat sushi (A$18) every Wednesday and Thursday night.

Metz (☎ 6331 7277; 119 St John St; meals A$7-24; ⏲ breakfast, lunch & dinner) The Metz is a classic all-day café-bar that attracts a mixed crowd of locals who enjoy the casual setting and modern fare – from traditional breakfasts through to wood-fired pizzas.

Pasta Resistance Too (☎ 6334 3081; 23 Quadrant Mall; meals A$5-6; ⏲ lunch Mon-Sat) This tiny lunch spot has a marvellous medley of freshly made pasta and sauces at piddling prices, which is why it's often packed. The chicken pesto gets a big tick.

Hotel Tasmania (☎ 6331 7355; 191 Charles St; meals A$6-15; ⏲ lunch & dinner) The restaurant here is nothing fancy but the meals are incredibly good value. Roast of the day is A$6, and with burgers or lasagne for A$8, shoestring travellers can feast without fiscal fear. For a review of the bar here, see below.

Fish 'n' Chips (☎ 6331 1999; 30 Seaport Blvd; meals A$10-15; ⏲ lunch & dinner) Offers simple, affordable fish and chips (from around A$6), seafood salads and antipasto platters.

Hari's Curry (☎ 6331 6466; 150 York St; mains A$10-15; ⏲ lunch & dinner Mon-Fri, dinner Sat & Sun) Cooks an admirable selection of the usual Indian suspects. The spices may pack a punch, but the prices certainly won't.

Drinking & Entertainment

There is a sprinkling of inviting pubs in Launceston, many with regular live music.

Irish Murphy's (☎ 6331 4440; 211 Brisbane St) This themed pub is an excellent venue with live music six days a week (usually Wednesday to Monday). See also left.

Lounge Bar (☎ 6334 6622; 63 St John St) Has a cool loungey interior and hosts regular live music (usually Thursday to Saturday).

Hotel Tasmania (☎ 6331 7355; 191 Charles St) The bar here isn't bad for a game of pool over a drop of amber fluid. A mix of bands and DJs entertain the locals from Wednesday to Saturday nights – it can sometimes get pretty rowdy after midnight. See also p315.

Royal on George (☎ 6331 2526; 90 George St) The Royal is a great refurbished pub dating from 1852, which has live bands on Friday and Saturday nights.

Getting There & Away

AIR

Flights to Melbourne start at about A$100.

Jetstar (☎ 13 15 38; www.jetstar.com.au)
Qantas (☎ 13 13 13; www.qantas.com.au)
Virgin Blue (☎ 13 67 89; www.virginblue.com.au)

BUS

The main bus companies operating out of Launceston are **Redline Coaches** (☎ 1300 360 000; www.tasredline.com.au) and **TassieLink** (☎ 1300 300 520; www.tassielink.com.au), and the depot for their services is on Cornwall Square (on the corner of St John and Cimitiere Sts).

Redline runs buses to various destinations including Bicheno (A$25, 2½ hours), Devonport (A$19, 1½ hours), Hobart (A$26.20, 2½ hours), St Helens (A$26, 2¾ hours) and Swansea (A$23.30, two hours).

TassieLink has a regular city express service linking Launceston with Devonport (A$17, 1¼ hours), tying in with the ferry schedules, and Hobart (A$24, 2½ hours). It services the north and west from Launceston, including Sheffield (A$23, two hours), Cradle Mountain (A$55, three hours) and Strahan (A$75, 8¾ hours). TassieLink also runs a twice-weekly service between Launceston and Bicheno (A$25, 2½ hours) – the service is increased to four times weekly in summer.

CAR & MOTORCYCLE

All of the major car-rental firms (ie Budget, Hertz, Europcar, Avis) have desks at the airport, and most also have an office in town. Local budget operators include **Economy Car Rentals** (☎ 6334 3299; 27 William St); call for current rates.

Getting Around

For information about getting to/from the airport see p312.

BICYCLE

Rent-A-Cycle (☎ 6344 9779; 36 Thistle St), at the Launceston City Youth Hostel (p315), has a range of touring/mountain bikes from A$12/18 per day.

BUS

The local bus service is run by **Metro** (☎ 13 22 01; www.metrotas.com.au). The main departure points are on the two blocks of St John St between Paterson and York Sts. For A$3.90 you can buy a daily pass that can be used after 9am Monday to Friday and all day Saturday, Sunday and on public holidays. Most routes, however, don't operate in the evenings and Sunday services are limited.

AROUND LAUNCESTON

The 165-sq-km **Ben Lomond National Park**, 50km southeast of Launceston, is best known for its skiing facilities (the ski season is usually from early July to late September) but is picturesque at any time of the year.

Wine buffs should visit Rosevears, a pretty riverside settlement with some noteworthy wineries: **Strathlynn** (☎ 03-6330 2388; www.pbv.com.au; 95 Rosevears Dr; tastings A$3; ⏲ 10am-5pm); **St Matthias** (☎ 03-6330 1700; www.moorilla.com.au; 113 Rosevears Dr; tastings free; ⏲ 10am-5pm) and **Rosevears Estate** (☎ 03-6330 1800; www.rosevearsestate.com.au; Waldhorn Dr; tastings A$2; ⏲ 10am-5pm).

Getting There & Around

Redline Coaches (☎ 1300 360 000; www.tasredline.com.au) runs two to three buses daily on weekdays along the eastern side of the Tamar River between Launceston and George Town (A$10, 45 minutes).

NORTHEAST COAST

The northeast has some of Tasmania's most secluded, magnificent beaches, yet it sees comparatively few travellers. If you're in this area, the Bay of Fires is a must-see.

St Helens

☎ 03 / pop 1800

St Helens, sprawled around Georges Bay, is an old whaling town first settled in 1830. Its interesting and varied past is recorded in the **History Room** (☎ 6376 1744; 61 Cecilia St; admission A$2; ⏲ 9am-5pm Mon-Fri, to noon Sat, 10am-2pm Sun, closed Sun during winter), which shares its space and phone lines with the town's visitors centre.

Although the town's beaches are not crash hot for swimming, there are superb scenic beaches at **Binalong Bay** (12km from St Helens), **Sloop Rock** (14km), **Stieglitz** (7km) and St

TASMANIA

Helens and Humbug Points. Out on St Helens Point are the spectacular **Peron Dunes**.

About 20km west of St Helens you'll encounter the turn-off to tiny **Pyengana**, worth a detour for the scenic 90m-high **St Columba Falls**. The return walk from the car park to the base of the falls takes 20 minutes.

SLEEPING & EATING

Kellraine Units (☎/fax 6376 1169; 72 Tully St; d/tr A$55/75) The best-value accommodation in St Helens is this unassuming collection of large, self-contained units. They're next to the highway about 800m northwest of the centre, and each roomy unit has laundry, video, living and dining areas, and a full kitchen.

St Helens Youth Hostel (☎ 6376 1661; 5 Cameron St; dm/d A$21/45) This simple hostel, in a converted house, is in a quiet spot and only a block from the town centre. The rooms are nothing flash but the price is kind on the wallet. Bicycle hire is A$10 per day.

St Helens Caravan Park (☎ 6376 1290; Penelope St; camp sites A$14-17, powered caravan sites A$18-22, on-site caravans A$35-45, cabins A$55-90) This park has a pleasant bushland setting to the south of town, and has good amenities.

Wok Stop (☎ 6376 2665; 57a Cecilia St; meals A$4-15; 🕗 8am-8pm) Drop into this little eatery for your tomato or spinach dhal, butter chicken, beef vindaloo or one of the other piquant curries on offer. Or you could unwind over a pot of refreshing lemon balm and mint tea (A$2.50).

Milk Bar Cafe (☎ 6376 2700; 57b Cecilia St; meals A$6-13; 🕗 breakfast & lunch, closed Sun in winter) Next door to the Wok Stop, this cosy place serves tasty café fare with flair.

GETTING THERE & AROUND

Redline Coaches (☎ 1300 360 000; www.tasredline.com.au) runs buses from Launceston to Conara Junction near Campbell Town, then through Fingal and St Marys (A$20, two hours) to St Helens (A$26, 2¾ hours).

TassieLink (☎ 1300 300 520; www.tassielink.com.au) has several weekly services between Hobart and St Helens via the east coast (A$38, four hours).

Bay of Fires

From St Helens a minor road heads northeast to meet the coast at the start of the stunning Bay of Fires and continues up as far as The Gardens.

Early explorers named the bay after seeing Aboriginal fires along the shore. It's a series of sweeping beaches, rocky headlands, heath lands and lagoons, all part of a coastal reserve. The ocean beaches provide some good surfing and the lagoons some safe swimming; it's not advisable to swim in the ocean, due to the many rips.

NORTH

Rolling hills and farmlands extend from the Tamar Valley north of Launceston and west to the Great Western Tiers. The best way to explore this area is to abandon the highways and follow the quiet minor roads through small towns.

Getting There & Around

Redline Coaches (☎ 1300 360 000; www.tasredline.com.au) has several services daily from Launceston to Devonport (A$19, 1½ hours). Some of these services call at the ferry terminal in Devonport.

TassieLink (☎ 1300 300 520; www.tassielink.com.au) runs a daily express service designed to work in with the Bass Strait ferry schedules; it provides an early-morning service from Devonport to Launceston (A$17, 1¼ hours) and Hobart (A$41, about four hours), and an afternoon service in the opposite direction to meet evening boat departures.

DEVONPORT

☎ 03 / pop 21,575

Nestled behind the lighthouse-topped Mersey Bluff, Devonport is the terminal for the *Spirit of Tasmania* vehicular ferries that run between Victoria and Tasmania and New South Wales and Tasmania. Devonport's visitors are usually arriving or departing rather than staying, as the town has few attractions.

The airport is 5km east of town. An **airport shuttle** (☎ 6424 6333) operates on weekdays and the fare is A$10. A taxi costs about A$17.

Information

Devonport visitors centre (☎ 6424 8176; ttic@dcc.tas.gov.au; 92 Formby Rd; 🕗 7.30am-5pm or 9pm) is across the river from the ferry terminal. It's open to meet all ferry arrivals; the 9pm closure applies when there are day crossings of the ferry, which arrive at 7pm.

For more information about Devonport and Tasmania, particularly in regards to bushwalking and tours, head for the central **Backpacker's Barn** (☎ 6424 3628; 10-12 Edward St; 9am-5.30pm Mon-Fri, to noon Sat). It has a great bushwalking shop and useful traveller services, including outdoor equipment hire, storage lockers (A$1 per night) and shower use (A$2).

Internet access is available at the **online access centre** (☎ 6424 9413; 21 Oldaker St; per 30min A$3.30; 9.30am-5.30pm Mon-Sat).

Sights & Activities

The **Tasmanian Aboriginal Culture Centre** (☎ 6424 8250; Bluff Rd; admission A$3.80; 9am-5pm), also known as 'Tiagarra' (the Tasmanian Aboriginal word for 'keep'), was established to preserve the art and culture of the Tasmanian Aborigines.

The **Devonport Maritime Museum** (☎ 6424 7100; 6 Gloucester Ave; admission A$3; 10am-4.30pm Tue-Sun Oct-Mar, to 4pm Mar-Oct) has a scintillating display of maritime paraphernalia. The **Devonport Regional Gallery** (☎ 6424 8296; 45-47 Stewart St; admission free; 10am-5pm Mon-Sat, noon-5pm Sun) houses predominantly 20th-century Tasmanian paintings, ceramics and glasswork.

Sleeping & Eating

Accommodation here can fill up in a flash, especially from late December to February – so advance bookings are wise.

Inner City Backpackers (☎ 6424 1898; mollymalones@vantagegroup.com.au; 34 Best St; dm A$15, d with/without bathroom A$50/35) As the most central backpacker lodgings in Devonport, situated above Molly Malones Irish pub, the rooms here are lacklustre but comfortable enough. Facilities include a communal kitchen, lounge and laundry.

Tasman House Backpackers (☎ 6423 2335; www.tasmanhouse.com; 114 Tasman St; dm/s/d A$13/30/39;) This unpretentious hostel has basic budget rooms and good facilities. It's a 15-minute walk from town and can be accessed from both Tasman and Steele Sts.

MacWright House (☎ 6424 5696; 115 Middle Rd; dm/s A$14/19) This down-to-earth YHA hostel, 3km southwest of town, has basic accommodation in a clean and humble old house. From the town centre, it's a 40-minute walk or a five-minute bus ride (No 40).

Abel Tasman Caravan Park (☎ 6427 8794; 6 Wright St; camp/caravan sites A$17/22, on-site caravans A$45, cabins A$95) Boasting a good beachfront view at the northern tip of East Devonport, this park's location (500m to the ferry terminal) makes it especially popular.

Molly Malones (☎ 6424 1898; 34 Best St; meals A$8-21; lunch & dinner) Friendly, cavernous MMs has good-value pub standards (roast of the day for A$10, Irish stew for A$12). There's often live music, usually towards the end of the week.

Cheap eats are available at the bakeries that line Rooke St, and the street's northern end has a few reasonably priced stand-outs such as the **Indian Affair** (☎ 6423 5141; 153 Rooke St; mains A$16-18; dinner), offering, as the name suggests, Indian cuisine. The serves are filling so don't let hunger pangs cajole you into over-ordering.

Getting There & Away

AIR

Fares to Melbourne start at about A$100.

Qantas (☎ 13 13 13; www.qantas.com.au)

Rex (☎ 13 17 13; www.regionalexpress.com.au)

BOAT

Three high-speed **Spirit of Tasmania ferries** (☎ 13 20 10; www.spiritoftasmania.com.au) cruise nightly between Melbourne and Devonport, and three times a week between Sydney and Devonport. The vessels more closely resemble a floating hotel than a ferry, with restaurants, bars etc. The public areas of the ship and a handful of on-board cabins have been designed to cater for wheelchairs.

The **ferry terminal** (☎ 13 20 10) is on the Esplanade in East Devonport.

Melbourne–Devonport

At 9pm nightly year-round, one ferry departs from Port Melbourne's Station Pier and the other departs from Devonport's Esplanade, with both arriving at their destinations across Bass Strait at around 7am the next day. Additional daytime sailings are scheduled during the peak summer period, and weekends from December to April. These daytime sailings depart at 9am, arriving at 7pm.

Fares depend on whether you're travelling in the peak (early December to late January), shoulder (late January to late May, and September to early December) or off-peak (late May to late August) season. One-way adult fares to Melbourne cost A$140/112/105 peak/shoulder/off-peak for airline-style seats on a night crossing or A$212/193/184 for the cheapest berth (in a four-bed cabin). A bed in a twin-berth cabin costs A$257/217/207. Passage on a day crossing costs A$145/115 in the peak/shoulder season (no day crossings in the off-peak season). There are discounts of 25% on cabin berths for students. Linen is supplied in the cabins, and each cabin has a bathroom.

On both ferry routes the cost for accompanied vehicles depends on the size of the vehicle and the season. The fare for a standard car (5m or less in length) or a campervan is A$55 in peak season, free for the rest of the year.

Sydney–Devonport

One-way adult fares to/from Sydney cost A$304/255/230 in the peak/shoulder/off-peak season for the cheapest berth (in hostel-style accommodation). A bed in a three- or four-bunk cabin costs A$475 to A$492 in the peak season, A$400 to A$415 in the shoulder season and A$360 to A$372 in the off-peak season. Twin and double cabins are also available. Dinner and brunch are included in the price of the fares.

The Devonport–Sydney ferry departs Devonport at on 3pm Monday, Thursday and Saturday, and arrives in Sydney at 11.30am the following day. In the opposite direction, the ferry leaves Sydney at 3pm on Tuesday, Friday and Sunday, arriving in Devonport at 11.30am the following day. In June, July and August it departs Sydney on Friday and Sunday and departs Devonport on Thursday and Saturday.

BUS

Redline Coaches (☎ 1300 360 000; www.tasredline.com.au; 9 Edward St) has its terminal opposite Backpacker's Barn (10-12 Edward St). Buses also stop at the ferry terminal when the ferry is in town. Redline runs at least three services daily from Hobart to Launceston, then on to Devonport, and return. The fare from Launceston to Devonport is A$19 and the trip takes 1½ hours.

TassieLink (☎ 1300 300 520; www.tassielink.com.au) also covers various destinations. The arrival and departure point for TassieLink coaches is directly outside the visitors centre and the *Spirit of Tasmania* terminal (92 Formby Rd).

Maxwells (☎ 6492 1431) runs buses on demand to Cradle Mountain, Lake St Clair, the Walls of Jerusalem, Frenchmans Cap and other hiking destinations. You can arrange the pick-up/drop-off point when making a booking.

Getting Around

For information about getting to/from the airport see p317.

Local buses, operated by **Merseylink** (☎ 1300 367 590; www.merseylink.com.au), run from Monday to Saturday – you can get a timetable at the Devonport visitors centre.

AROUND DEVONPORT

Quaint **Sheffield**, 30km south of Devonport, promotes itself as the 'town of murals' due to the fact that around 32 murals depicting the history of the area have been painted in and around the town, since 1986. The scenery around Sheffield is another of its features, with lofty **Mt Roland** (1231m) dominating the landscape. More details can be obtained from the **Sheffield Information Centre** (☎ 6491 1036; sheffield@tasvisinfo.com.au; Pioneer Crescent; 🕑 9am-5pm).

About 86km from Devonport is the **Walls of Jerusalem National Park**, comprising a series of glacial valleys and lakes on top of the Central Plateau. The park is popular with experienced bushwalkers seeking an isolated and spectacular hiking challenge.

TassieLink has a service linking Launceston and Sheffield (A$19, two hours).

WEST

Grand mountains, grassy plains, ancient rivers, tranquil lakes, dense rainforests and a treacherous coast are all features of this beautiful region, some of which is now a World Heritage Area. Before the arrival of Europeans, the west was home to many of the island's Aboriginal people, and plenty of archaeological evidence of these original inhabitants – some of it more than 20,000 years old – has been found.

See www.westcoasttourism.com.au for more information on the region.

Getting There & Around

TassieLink (☎ 1300 300 520; www.tassielink.com.au) runs buses to various destinations including from Hobart to Lake St Clair (A$38, three to 3½ hours), and Strahan (A$57, six to nine hours, times vary depending on Queenstown stopover). There are return services along this route on the same days. TassieLink also has services from Launceston to Cradle Mountain (A$55, three hours) and Strahan (A$75, 8¾ hours), also with return services on the same days. Similarly priced is **Redline Coaches** (☎ 1300 360 000; www.tasredline.com.au), which has a daily service between Cradle Mountain and Devonport, with connecting services from Launceston on weekdays only.

STRAHAN

☎ 03 / pop 758

Strahan is the only sizable town on the rugged west coast. Its harbourside main street is undeniably attractive, but in a somewhat artificial way. The town's real appeal lies in the natural and historical attractions around it rather than in the town itself.

Information

Strahan visitors centre (☎ 6471 7622; strahan@tasvisinfo.com.au; Esplanade; 9am-6pm Sep-May, 2-5pm Jun-Aug) Offers Internet access (A$3 per 30 minutes) and comprehensive regional information.

Sights & Activities

The walk to **Hogarth Falls** starts east of the town centre at Peoples Park; allow one hour, return. Other natural attractions include the impressive 33km-long **Ocean Beach**, 6km from town. In October the beach becomes a **mutton bird rookery** when the birds return from their winter migration. About 14km along the road from Strahan to Zeehan are the brilliant **Henty Dunes**, a series of 30m-high sand dunes.

GORDON RIVER CRUISES

Both of the following companies offer popular river cruises that include a rainforest walk at Heritage Landing, views of, or passage through, Hells Gates (the narrow entrance to Macquarie Harbour) and a land tour of Sarah Island, a former penal settlement.

World Heritage Cruises (☎ 6471 7174; Esplanade) runs six-hour cruises (A$65) departing at 9am, and also at 2pm in the summer. There are half-day cruises offered from October to April (departing 9am, returning 1.30pm). This shorter tour costs A$60; it doesn't stop at Sarah Island.

Gordon River Cruises (☎ 6471 4300; Esplanade) has 5½-hour cruises (A$65) that depart at 8.30am, and also at 2.30pm in summer.

JET-BOAT RIDE

Wild Rivers Jet (☎ 6471 7174; www.wildriversjet.com.au; Esplanade) runs exhilarating 50-minute jet-boat rides up the rainforest-lined gorges of the King River for A$50.

SCENIC FLIGHTS

Wilderness Air (☎ 6471 7280; wildair@tassie.net.au; Esplanade) offers excellent 80-minute seaplane flights (A$150) that fly up the Gordon River to Sir John Falls. The plane lands at the falls so that you can enjoy a rainforest walk. The planes depart regularly from Strahan harbour and fly back via the Franklin River valley and Frenchmans Cap.

Seair Adventure Charters (☎ 6471 7718; Esplanade) has 60-minute helicopter flights for A$150 (landing in the Teepookana Forest), and 45-/65-minute flights for A$140/175.

Sleeping & Eating

There is a dearth of budget accommodation in Strahan; advance reservations are a good idea in the busy summer season.

Strahan Backpackers (☎ 6471 7255; 43 Harvey St; dm/s/d A$20/24/50) This in-demand hostel, in a lovely bush setting, is a 10-minute walk from the centre. It has ordinary but well-kept rooms.

Strahan Caravan & Tourist Park (☎ 6471 7239; cnr Andrew & Innes Sts; camp site per person A$10, on-site van A$50, cabin A$90) A well-maintained beach-front park that's only a short distance from the heart of the village and offers good-value accommodation and facilities.

West Coast Yacht Charters (☎ 6471 7422; Esplanade; bunks A$40, d A$80) An interesting option is to stay on a sailing boat moored at the wharf. Linen and a light breakfast are included in the price, but be prepared to check in at around 7.30pm and disembark before 9am. The yacht is not moored every night (overnight cruises on the Gordon River are available), so you'll need to book ahead.

Banjo's Bakehouse (☎ 6471 7794; Esplanade; breakfast A$10-17, pizzas from A$10; 6am-8.30pm) This popular central bakery serves satiating breakfasts, as well as snacks such as sandwiches and hot pies. Pizzas are a possibility after 6pm.

Fish Café (☎ 6471 4386; Esplanade; meals A$4.50-7; breakfast, lunch & dinner) This bustling, casual takeaway café offers a variety of quick meals, with a focus on seafood. Good options include the crumbed flounder (A$4.50) and battered Tasmanian scallops (A$1.80 each).

Hamer's Hotel (☎ 6471 7191; Esplanade; meals A$13-25; 🕑 lunch & dinner) Serves commendable vegetarian options as well as something for carnivores, such as wallaby sirloin. Its public bar is a good spot to down a couple of beers.

Getting Around

Strahan Taxis (☎ 0417-516 071) has services to surrounding attractions like Henty Dunes (A$25 per taxi, maximum four people). **Risby Cove** (☎ 6471 7572) rents out bicycles (A$15 per hour or A$10/20 per half/full day).

FRANKLIN-GORDON WILD RIVERS NATIONAL PARK

This World Heritage–listed park includes the catchment areas of the Franklin and Olga Rivers and part of the Gordon River, as well as the glorious bushwalking and climbing region known as **Frenchmans Cap**. It has a number of unique plant species and a major Aboriginal archaeological site at **Kutikina Cave**.

Much of the park is impenetrable rainforest, but the Lyell Hwy traverses its northern end and there are a few short walks starting from the road. These include hikes to **Donaghys Hill** (40 minutes return), from where you can see the Franklin River and the mesmerising white-quartzite dome of Frenchmans Cap, and a stroll to **Nelson Falls** (20 minutes return).

Rafting the Franklin

The Franklin is a wild river and rafting it can be sensational but hazardous. Rafting the length of the river, starting at Collingwood River and ending at Sir John Falls, takes between eight and 14 days (shorter trips on certain sections of the river are also possible). For tours and packages contact the **Lake St Clair visitors centre** (☎ 03-6289 1172; Lyell Hwy, via Derwent Bridge; 🕑 8am-7pm summer, to 5pm winter), which also has the latest information on permits and regulations. Also useful are the Franklin rafting notes on the website for **Parks & Wildlife** (PWS; www.parks.tas.gov.au). Once you're in the website, click on Outdoor Recreation, then Boating, Kayaking & Rafting.

CRADLE MOUNTAIN-LAKE ST CLAIR NATIONAL PARK

Tasmania's best-known national park is the superb 1262-sq-km World Heritage Area of Cradle Mountain-Lake St Clair. Its dramatic mountain peaks, deep gorges, sublime lakes and wild moorlands extend from the Great Western Tiers in the north to Derwent Bridge on the Lyell Hwy in the south. It's one of the areas affected most by glacial activity in Australia and includes Mt Ossa (1617m), Tasmania's highest peak, and Lake St Clair, Australia's deepest natural freshwater lake.

There are plenty of day walks in both the Cradle Valley and Cynthia Bay (Lake St Clair) regions, but it's the spectacular 80.5km walk between the two that has turned this park into a bushwalkers' magnet. The Overland Track is one of the finest bushwalks in the country and can be walked in either direction, but most people walk from north to south.

Sights & Activities

CRADLE VALLEY

At the northern park boundary is the **Cradle Mountain visitors centre** (☎ 03-6492 1110; Cradle Mountain Rd; 🕑 8am-5pm), staffed by helpful rangers who can advise on weather conditions, walking gear and bush safety. Ask here about the many free activities (eg walks, talks and slide shows) held during summer.

For visitors in wheelchairs, behind the centre is an easy 500m circular **boardwalk** through the adjacent rainforest.

Whatever time of the year you visit, be prepared for cold, wet weather in the Cradle Valley area. On average it rains here seven days out of 10, is cloudy eight days in 10, has all-day sunshine only one day in 10 and snows on 54 days each year!

LAKE ST CLAIR

Occupying a wing of the large building at the southern end of the walking track is the **Lake St Clair visitors centre** (☎ 03-6289 1172; via Derwent Bridge; 🕑 8am-7pm summer, to 5pm winter), with good advice and displays on the park. Register here to walk the Overland Track in the northerly direction. At the adjacent, separately run **Lakeside St Clair Wilderness Holidays** (☎ 03-6289 1137; www.view.com.au/lakeside), you can organise a cruise (starting at A$25 for a 1½-hour trip) on the lake or hire canoes (A$15 per hour) and dinghies (A$50/90 per half/full day).

OVERLAND TRACK

For prospective walkers, the visitors centre at Cradle Mountain has an Overland Track information kit, including map and track notes, for A$20 (plus postage and handling if you want it sent to you).

The best time to walk the Overland Track is during summer, when flowering plants are most prolific, although spring and autumn also have their attractions. You can walk the track in winter, but only if you're experienced.

Walkers sometimes start the track at Dove Lake, but the recommended route begins at Ronny Creek, about 5km from the visitors centre.

The track is well marked along its entire length and, at an easy pace, takes around five or six days to walk. There are many secondary paths leading up to mountains such as Mt Ossa or other natural features, so the length of time you actually take is really only limited by the amount of supplies you can carry. There are unattended huts (first-in-first-served basis) along the track that you can use for overnight accommodation, but in summer they fill quickly so make sure you carry a tent. Campfires are banned so you must carry a fuel stove.

The most hazardous part of the walk is the exposed high plateau between Waldheim and Pelion Creek, near Mt Pelion West. The southwest wind that blows across here can be surprisingly strong and bitterly cold.

If you're walking from Cradle Valley to Cynthia Bay, you have the option of radioing from Narcissus Hut on the northern end of Lake St Clair for a **ferry** (☎ 03-6289 1137, per person A$20) to come to pick you up, saving a five- to six-hour walk.

More-detailed descriptions of the walk are given in Lonely Planet's *Tasmania* and *Walking in Australia* guides. A number of outfits offer guided walks of the Overland Track – inquire at visitors centres and travel agents, or scan the Internet.

Sleeping & Eating

CRADLE VALLEY

Waldheim Cabins (☎ 03-6492 1110; cradle@parks.tas.gov.au; Waldheim; s & d A$70) These basic four- to eight-bunk huts are some 5km into the national park. Each contain gas stoves, cooking utensils and wood or gas heaters, fridge and 24-hour power, but no bedding. Bathroom facilities are shared. Check-in or book at the Cradle Mountain visitors centre.

Cradle Mountain Tourist Park (☎ 03-6492 1395; www.cosycabins.com/cradle; Cradle Mountain Rd; camp sites unpowered/powered per 2 people A$25/30, dm A$25) Situated 2.5km from the national park entrance, this bushland complex is the only place in the area offering budget accommodation and is therefore in demand – book ahead.

Cradle Mountain Wilderness Cafe (☎ 03-6492 1018; Cradle Mountain Rd; lunch A$5-11, dinner A$14-17; 🕑 lunch & dinner) Part of the Wilderness Village apartment complex but on the opposite side of the road from the accommodation, this café serves cheap meals and has an extensive takeaway section.

CYNTHIA BAY & DERWENT BRIDGE

Derwent Bridge Wilderness Hotel (☎ 03-6289 1144; Derwent Bridge; dm A$25, d with/without bathroom A$105/85) Although the accommodation is nothing to write home about, it's comfortable and clean, and a welcoming lounge bar (open for lunch and dinner) is on site.

Lakeside St Clair Wilderness Holidays (☎ 03-6289 1137; www.view.com.au/lakeside; Cynthia Bay; camp/caravan sites A$12/15, dm A$25) This place has its office at Cynthia Bay by the visitors centre. It has a lake-side camping ground not far away, plus basic two- to four-bunk dorm rooms. Pricey cabins are also available. The restaurant has good breakfast, lunch and dinner options, plus a range of takeaways.

Getting There & Away

TassieLink (☎ 1300 300 520; www.tassielink.com.au) has bus services from Launceston to Cradle Mountain (via Devonport) and from Hobart to Lake St Clair every day from November to late April. There are three services weekly between Cradle Valley and Lake St Clair; less frequent outside of these months. TassieLink also offers packages (bookings essential) dropping you off at one end of the Overland Track and picking up at the other.

Maxwells (☎ 03-6492 1431) runs services on demand from Devonport to Cradle Mountain (A$40); Launceston to Cradle Mountain (A$60); Hobart, Devonport or Launceston to Lake St Clair (A$70); and Cradle Valley to Lake St Clair (A$85).

Getting Around

In Cradle Valley, **Maxwells** (☎ 03-6492 1431) runs a shuttle bus between the tourist park, the visitors centre and Dove Lake (A$9 one way, bookings essential). This company also runs a taxi bus on demand between Cynthia Bay and Derwent Bridge (A$7 one way).

A **ferry service** (☎ 03-6289 1137) does trips between Cynthia Bay and Narcissus Hut, at the northern end of Lake St Clair, for A$20/25 (one way/return). It departs numerous times daily; expect to pay more if there are fewer than four people on board. Bookings are essential; if using this service at the end of your walk, you must radio the ferry operator on arrival at Narcissus Hut.

SOUTHWEST

SOUTHWEST NATIONAL PARK

There are few places left in the world as isolated and untouched as Tasmania's southwest wilderness, home to the state's largest national park. The best-known walk in the park is the **South Coast Track**, between Port Davey and Cockle Creek, near Southeast Cape. This walk takes about 10 days and should only be tackled by experienced hikers who are well prepared for the often vicious weather conditions. Light planes are used to airlift bushwalkers into the southwest. Details are available in Lonely Planet's *Walking in Australia*. A range of escorted wilderness adventures is possible in the area, involving flying, hiking, rafting, canoeing, mountaineering and camping. As a starting point, contact the **Mt Field PWS** (☎ 03-6288 1149). Mt Field is also the place to pick up your national parks' pass.

Getting There & Around

A popular way to tackle the South Coast Track is to fly into remote Melaleuca and walk out. **Tasair** (☎ 1800 062 900; www.tasair.com.au) and **Par Avion** (☎ 03-6248 5390; www.paravion.com.au) offer air services to bushwalkers, flying between Hobart and Melaleuca for around A$150 one way. The airlines also offer scenic flight day trips, which can include landings and bushwalks.

From November to April, **TassieLink** (☎ 1300 300 520; www.tassielink.com.au) runs two to three buses a week between Hobart and Scotts Peak (A$60, four hours) via Mt Field, and between Hobart and the eastern end of the South Coast Track at Cockle Creek (A$53, 3½ hours).

LAKE PEDDER & STRATHGORDON

☎ 03 / pop 70

At the northern edge of the southwest wilderness lies Lake Pedder, once a stunningly beautiful natural lake considered the ecological jewel of the region. In 1972, however, it was flooded to become part of the Gordon River power development.

Strathgordon is the base to visit Lakes Pedder and Gordon. It's become fairly popular for bushwalking, climbing, fishing and watersports. A **visitors centre** (☎ 6280 1134; Gordon River Rd; ⌚ 10am-5pm Nov-Mar, 11am-3pm Apr-Oct) at the 140m-high **Gordon Dam**, 12km west of the township, provides information about the area, including accommodation.

BASS STRAIT ISLANDS

Tasmania has two groups of islands, the Hunter and Furneaux Groups, at the western and eastern entrances to Bass Strait, respectively. These islands are rich in wildlife and natural beauty and will appeal to those wishing to get well off the beaten track. On the western side of Bass Strait in the Hunter Group, **King Island** has beautiful beaches and quiet lagoons. The main township is Currie on the west coast, and other notable settlements are Naracoopa on the east coast and Grassy in the southeast.

Pretrip information can be obtained from **King Island Tourism** (☎ 1800 645 014; www.kingisland.org.au). King Island is particularly renowned for its dairy produce, especially its award-winning cheeses: **King Island Dairy** (☎ 03-6462 1348; www.kidairy.com.au; North Rd, Loorana), 7.5km north of Currie, has tastings and sales.

Flinders Island is the largest of the 52 islands in the Furneaux Group. The island's main industries are farming, fishing and seasonal mutton-birding. Pretrip information can be sought from the **Flinders Island Area Marketing & Development Office** (☎ 1800 994 477; www.flindersislandonline.com.au; ⌚ 8.30am-5pm Mon-Fri). For further information also see www.focusonflinders.com.au. Bushwalking is popular and many visitors climb **Mt Strzelecki**. The walk starts about 12km south of Whitemark and the return trip takes three to five hours. There are beautiful **beaches** around the island as well as several **shipwrecks** (some clearly visible from shore).

Probably the best way to visit King or Flinders Islands is to buy a fly-drive package that includes accommodation. Contact **Tourism Tasmania** (☎ 1800 806 846; www.discovertasmania.com.au) or **Tasmanian travel centres** (www.tastravel.com.au; Sydney ☎ 1300 655 145, 60 Carrington St; Melbourne ☎ 1300 655 145, 259 Collins St) for details.

Darwin & Around

CONTENTS

HIGHLIGHTS

- **Kakadu National Park** Encounter ancient rock art at Ubirr and Nourlangie (p340)
- **Nitmiluk National Park** Paddle along breathtaking Katherine Gorge (p348)
- **Croc-jumping tour** Witness dinosaur-like crocodiles leap for their lunch on the Adelaide River (p337)
- **Museum & Art Gallery of the Northern Territory** Visit the Cyclone Tracy exhibit at this excellent gallery in Darwin (p328)
- **Buley Rockhole** Enjoy some 'hydro'-therapy in the crystal-clear waters of Litchfield National Park's oasis (p339)
- **Mindil Beach Night Market** Feast on world fare while watching the sun drop into the ocean (p334)
- **Fishing expeditions** Hook a silvery barramundi on a cruise off Darwin's coast (p331)
- **Deckchair Cinema** Catch a 'flick' at Darwin's fabulous open-air cinema (p335)
- **Darwin Harbour** Take a catamaran cruise at sunset, with champagne in hand (p331)

- **Cheer for:** the Tigers or the All Stars at the Tiwi Islands Football League grand final (held the last Sunday in March)
- **Eat:** a barramundi that you've caught yourself
- **Drink:** a 'green can', or a Darwin stubby
- **Watch:** *Crocodile Dundee* (filmed near Katherine), *We of the Never Never*
- **Party at:** Starving backpacker' nights at pubs near Mitchell St (p334)
- **Swim at:** Mindil for the night market, or Casuarina for the nudies (p330)
- **Avoid:** swimming with saltwater crocodiles
- **Locals' nickname:** Top Enders

TELEPHONE CODE: 08	WEBSITE: www.nt.holidays.com.au

Australia's Top End is surprising and enticing. It's here that you can spot a croc, soak up the perennial heat and hit roads less travelled, revelling in a land endowed with waterfalls, lush growth, and creeks that meld into giant flood plains. If you're after urban action, Darwin – the capital of the Northern Territory (NT) – has one of the liveliest backpacker scenes in the country.

At Darwin's doorstep lies an unrivalled natural playground. South of the city is Litchfield National Park: jump from waterfall to gorge to swimming hole and bask in the park's monsoonal rainforests. To Darwin's east lies Australia's largest mainland park – World Heritage–listed Kakadu National Park. If you're an adventure seeker–cum–nature junkie, a visit here is a must. Bountiful billabongs, an abundance of plant and animal life, wondrous waterfalls and some of the best rock art on the planet can be found here. Kakadu and its remote neighbour, Arnhem Land, retain a strong and fascinating Aboriginal heritage. Aboriginal culture is also active on the Tiwi Islands of Bathurst and Melville, to Darwin's north. Towards the Red Centre (for Alice Springs and Uluru, see p419), paddling a canoe along the spectacular Nitmiluk (Katherine Gorge) National Park is one of the best ways to enjoy the Katherine region.

ACTIVITIES

Cycle around Darwin or go scuba diving in Darwin Harbour to get up-close and personal with soft corals and tropical fish. Hike through diverse habitats at Kakadu National Park or head to Nitmiluk and hire a canoe. And at the end of an arduous day's activity, revitalise in cool plunge pools, waterfalls and thermal pools scattered throughout the Top End. Ah, life is tough at the top.

DARWIN

☎ 08 / pop 71,350

Sticky, friendly and eclectic, Darwin is Australia's most northern city. It possesses a distinctly Australian demeanour – informal and a bit rough around the edges – yet its proximity to Asia can make it feel as though it is indeed Indonesia's far south.

Multiculturalism is alive and well here and best observed at one of the colourful markets held in the dry season (April to September). In the wet season (roughly November to March) the skies light up with electrical storms, dark clouds roll in and the humidity hits its peak.

With the infrastructure of a small city but the feel of a big country town, Darwin is on the verge of cosmopolitan. Rodeo die-hards coexist with market-dwelling bohemians, divers and young up-and-comers. Tourists savour barramundi at chic Cullen Bay, while you'll find locals engaging in the popular activity of 'pigging' (hunting feral pigs) on Darwin's outskirts.

The boom kicked off by Kakadu's exposure in the classic Aussie film *Crocodile Dundee* did a lot for Darwin's transformation from something on an outpost to the colourful place it is today.

At its doorstep a natural playground (Kakadu, Litchfield, and Nitmiluk National Parks) awaits. But the sun-drenched lure of Darwin is seductive enough for drifters who harbour dreams of reinvention, and for the steady stream of party-goers who visit Darwin's shores.

HISTORY

In 1839 HMS *Beagle* commander John Lort Stokes came across the area now known as Darwin, and called it Port Darwin after his former shipmate (the then unknown evolutionist, Charles Darwin). However, the first European settlement on the site was known as Palmerston, with a later unofficial name of Port Darwin. In 1911 it received the official title of 'Darwin'.

It took a long time to decide on Darwin as the site for the region's centre. Even after the city was established its growth was slow and troubled. The city was officially founded in 1869. In 1872 the erection of the Overland Telegraph Line linked Darwin – indeed, Australia – to the rest of the world.

Darwin was bombed to its core by Japanese fighter planes on 19 February 1942, which was the impetus for the swift construction of the Stuart Hwy that connects Darwin to the southern states.

Natural forces struck on Christmas Eve of 1974 when ferocious Cyclone Tracy left a path of devastation never witnessed before in Australia (see the boxed text on p329). Today, the city's good-looking Esplanade, modern buildings and streets that run off into mangroves hide the havoc caused on that fatal day.

ORIENTATION

Darwin's centre is a fairly compact area at the end of a peninsula. The Alice Springs–bound Stuart Hwy enters the city to become Daly St. The main shopping area, around the Smith St Mall, is about 500m southeast of Daly St. Mitchell St, a prominent backpacker thoroughfare, runs alongside Smith St.

Darwin's airport is 12km north of the city centre. The **airport shuttle bus** (☎ 1800 358 945, 8991 5066) will pick you up or drop you off almost anywhere in the city centre for A$8/14 one way/return. Several hostels in town reimburse guests for the one-way fare (keep your receipt). Taxi fares between the airport and city centre are around A$16 to A$20.

INFORMATION

Emergency

After-hours Medical Service (☎ 8922 8888)
Ambulance (☎ 000)
Fire (☎ 000)
Marine Stinger Emergency Line (☎ 1800 079 909)
Police (☎ 000; cnr Mitchell & Knuckey Sts)

Internet Access

Most Internet cafés charge about A$5 to A$6 per hour for access.
Global Gossip (☎ 8942 3044; 44 Mitchell St)

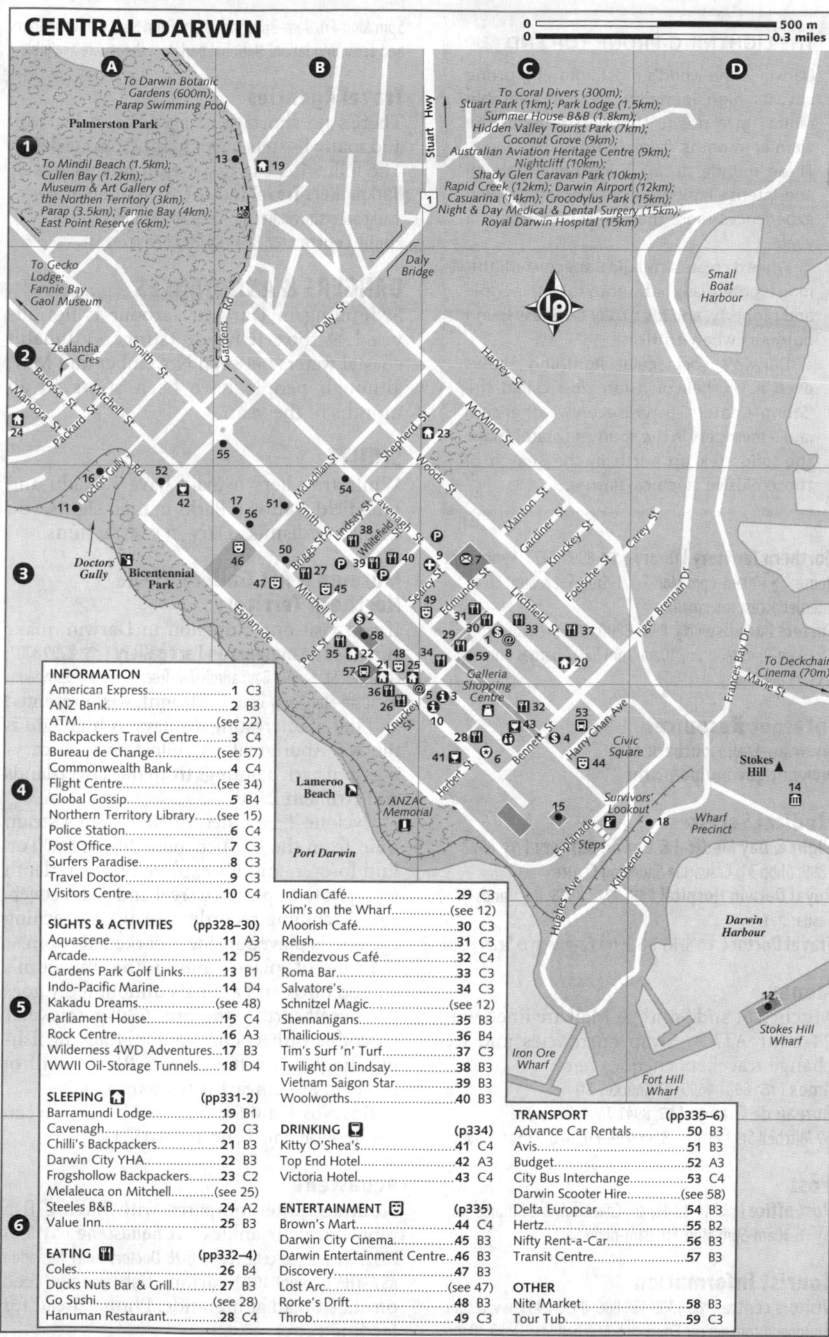
CENTRAL DARWIN
0 500 m
0 0.3 miles
A
B
C
D
1
2
3
4
5
6
To Darwin Botanic Gardens (600m); Parap Swimming Pool
Palmerston Park
To Mindil Beach (1.5km); Cullen Bay (1.2km); Museum & Art Gallery of the Northern Territory (3km); Parap (3.5km); Fannie Bay (4km); East Point Reserve (6km);
To Coral Divers (300m); Stuart Park (1km); Park Lodge (1.5km); Summer House B&B (1.8km); Hidden Valley Tourist Park (7km); Coconut Grove (9km); Australian Aviation Heritage Centre (9km); Nightcliff (10km); Shady Glen Caravan Park (10km); Rapid Creek (12km); Darwin Airport (12km); Casuarina (14km); Crocodylus Park (15km); Night & Day Medical & Dental Surgery (15km); Royal Darwin Hospital (15km)
Stuart Hwy
To Gecko Lodge; Fannie Bay Gaol Museum
Daly Bridge
Small Boat Harbour
Daly St
Gardens Rd
Zealandia Cres
Smith St
Barossa St
Manoora St
Mitchell St
Packard St
Harvey St
McMinn St
Shepherd St
Woods St
McLachlan St
Doctors Gully Rd
Smith St
Cavenagh St
Lindsay St
Whitefield St
Briggs St
Manton St
Gardiner St
Knuckey St
Carey St
Doctors Gully
Bicentennial Park
Mitchell St
Searcy St
Edmunds St
Litchfield St
Foelsche St
Tiger Brennan Dr
Esplanade
Peel St
Frances Bay Dr
To Deckchair Cinema (70m)
Mavie St
Galleria Shopping Centre
Knuckey St
Harry Chan Ave
Civic Square
Bennett St
Herbert St
Stokes Hill
Lameroo Beach
ANZAC Memorial
Survivors' Lookout
Wharf Precinct
Esplanade Steps
Port Darwin
Kitchener Dr
Hughes Ave
Darwin Harbour
Stokes Hill Wharf
Iron Ore Wharf
Fort Hill Wharf

INFORMATION
American Express....1 C3
ANZ Bank....2 B3
ATM....(see 22)
Backpackers Travel Centre....3 C4
Bureau de Change....(see 57)
Commonwealth Bank....4 C4
Flight Centre....(see 34)
Global Gossip....5 B4
Northern Territory Library....(see 15)
Police Station....6 C4
Post Office....7 C3
Surfers Paradise....8 C3
Travel Doctor....9 C3
Visitors Centre....10 C4

SIGHTS & ACTIVITIES (pp328–30)
Aquascene....11 A3
Arcade....12 D5
Gardens Park Golf Links....13 B1
Indo-Pacific Marine....14 D4
Kakadu Dreams....(see 48)
Parliament House....15 C4
Rock Centre....16 A3
Wilderness 4WD Adventures....17 B3
WWII Oil-Storage Tunnels....18 D4

SLEEPING (pp331-2)
Barramundi Lodge....19 B1
Cavenagh....20 C3
Chilli's Backpackers....21 B3
Darwin City YHA....22 B3
Frogshollow Backpackers....23 C2
Melaleuca on Mitchell....(see 25)
Steeles B&B....24 A2
Value Inn....25 B3

EATING (pp332–4)
Coles....26 B4
Ducks Nuts Bar & Grill....27 B3
Go Sushi....(see 28)
Hanuman Restaurant....28 C4
Indian Café....29 C3
Kim's on the Wharf....(see 12)
Moorish Café....30 C3
Relish....31 C3
Rendezvous Café....32 C4
Roma Bar....33 C3
Salvatore's....34 C3
Schnitzel Magic....(see 12)
Shennanigans....35 B3
Thailicious....36 B4
Tim's Surf 'n' Turf....37 C3
Twilight on Lindsay....38 B3
Vietnam Saigon Star....39 B3
Woolworths....40 B3

DRINKING (p334)
Kitty O'Shea's....41 C4
Top End Hotel....42 A3
Victoria Hotel....43 C4

ENTERTAINMENT (p335)
Brown's Mart....44 C4
Darwin City Cinema....45 B3
Darwin Entertainment Centre....46 B3
Discovery....47 B3
Lost Arc....(see 47)
Rorke's Drift....48 B3
Throb....49 C3

TRANSPORT (pp335–6)
Advance Car Rentals....50 B3
Avis....51 B3
Budget....52 A3
City Bus Interchange....53 C4
Darwin Scooter Hire....(see 58)
Delta Europcar....54 B3
Hertz....55 B2
Nifty Rent-a-Car....56 B3
Transit Centre....57 B3

OTHER
Nite Market....58 B3
Tour Tub....59 C3

THE LIGHTNING-PRONE TOP END

Darwin is the world's most lightning-prone city. Its high humidity and considerable rainfall give rise to thunderstorms in the warmer months from October to March. These thunderstorms bring heavy rainfall and intense lightning. On average, Darwin experiences more than 80 thunder days a year.

While it creates a magical spectacle, lightning is potentially hazardous to both people and property, and it's a risky business being outdoors when it strikes.

Darwin's spectacular lightning shows even have their own fan club called the 'Storm Chasers' (www.severeweather.com.au) – members in the southern states make the long trek up north in the search of those elusive electrical flashes.

Northern Territory Library (☎ 8999 7177; Parliament House; ⌚ 10am-6pm Mon-Fri, 1-5pm Sat & Sun) Free Internet access (no email).
Surfers Paradise (☎ 8941 3800; 21 Cavenagh St; ⌚ 9am-9pm Mon-Fri, 10am-3pm Sat) Charges only A$3.95 per hour.

Internet Resources

www.australiasoutback.com
www.nt.gov.au/ipe/pwcnt

Medical Services

Night & Day Medical & Dental Surgery (☎ 8927 1899; Shop 31, Casuarina Shopping Centre)
Royal Darwin Hospital (☎ 8922 8888; Rocklands Dr, Casuarina)
Travel Doctor (☎ 8981 7492; cnr Cavenagh & Searcy Sts)

Money

Mitchell St and Smith St Mall are lined with 24-hour ATMs. Swap currencies and exchange travellers cheques here:
Amex (☎ 8981 4699; 27 Knuckey St)
Bureau de Change (☎ 8941 7401; Shop 27, 69 Mitchell St; ⌚ 8am-8pm Mon-Fri, to 6pm Sat & Sun)

Post

Post office (☎ 13 13 18; cnr Cavenagh & Edmunds Sts; ⌚ 8.30am-5pm Mon-Fri, 9am-noon Sat)

Tourist Information

Visitors centre (☎ 1300 138 886, 8936 2499; www.tourismtopend.com.au; cnr Knuckey & Mitchell Sts; ⌚ 8.30am-5pm Mon-Fri, 9am-3pm Sat, 10am-3pm Sun) Can book tours and accommodation. National park fact sheets are available.

Travel Agencies

There's no shortage of agencies in Darwin, and many hostels have their own tour desks. The following can assist with further travel:
Backpackers Travel Centre (☎ 1800 020 007; www.backpackerstravel.net.au; Shop 3b, 14 Knuckey St)
Flight Centre (☎ 8941 6878; 21 Knuckey St)

DANGERS & ANNOYANCES

Swimming in Darwin Harbour is not advised as box jellyfish (stingers) inhabit coastal waters between November and May, although people have been stung in all months of the year.

SIGHTS

While travellers usually have Kakadu and Litchfield National Parks in their sights, you shouldn't dismiss Darwin's attractions.

Museum & Art Gallery of the Northern Territory

If you visit one attraction in Darwin, make sure it's the **museum and art gallery** (☎ 8999 8201; Conacher St, Fannie Bay; admission free; ⌚ 9am-5pm Mon-Fri, 10am-5pm Sat & Sun). It's bright, well presented and full of interesting displays. A highlight is the NT Aboriginal art collection with carvings and bark paintings from the Tiwi Islands and Arnhem Land.

Cyclone Tracy (described as 'like a steam train from the sky') changed life in the Top End forever, and it's explored here in depth with photographs, newsreel and radio coverage. A chilling recording of the screeching cyclone is played inside a darkened room.

Pride of place among the museum's stuffed birds and animals undoubtedly goes to 'Sweetheart' – the 5m, 780kg saltwater crocodile with a penchant for attacking fishing dinghies on the Finniss River south of Darwin. Sweetheart is truly impressive.

Bus Nos 4 and 6 travel close by, or you can get here on the Tour Tub (p331).

Aquascene

Nothing quite compares with having fish nibble at your ankles. At **Aquascene** (☎ 8981 7837; www.aquascene.com.au; 28 Doctors Gully Rd; adult A$7, YHA discount 10%) various fish species feed on stale bread at high tide. Phone ahead for feeding times.

East Point Reserve

If you're keen to see some wallabies, then East Point Reserve, north of Fannie Bay, is the place to go in the late afternoon. There's year-round swimming at saltwater Lake Alexander, plus walking and cycling paths.

On the northern side of the point is a series of **wartime gun emplacements** and the sobering **Military Museum** (☎ 8981 9702; www.epmm.com.au; East Point Reserve; adult A$10; 🕐 9.30am-5pm), devoted to Darwin's WWII activities.

Fannie Bay Gaol Museum

Comprised of rudimentary cells, this **museum** (☎ 8999 8201; cnr East Point Rd & Ross Smith Ave; admission free; 🕐 10am-4.30pm) housed Darwin's prisoners from 1883 to 1979. The gallows, constructed for a hanging in 1952, are the most compelling aspect.

Darwin Botanic Gardens

Picnic or simply while away the hours at the sprawling **botanic gardens** (☎ 8981 1958; Gardens Rd; admission free; 🕐 7am-7pm) – an easy bicycle ride from the city centre.

Parliament House

Dubbed 'the wedding cake', the white edifice of **Parliament House** (☎ 8946 1425; 90min tours free; 🕐 9am-6pm Mon-Fri, tours 9am & 11am Sat) dominates the southeastern end of Mitchell St. The building also houses the Northern Territory Library. Tour bookings are essential.

Wharf Precinct

The old **Stokes Hill Wharf**, below the cliffs at the southeastern end of the city centre, is worth exploring.

At the end of the jetty an old warehouse, known as the **Arcade**, houses a food centre that's great for an alfresco lunch or a cool drink on a balmy evening.

Back on the mainland, the precinct also encompasses the **oil-storage tunnels** (☎ 8985 6333; adult A$4.50; 🕐 9am-5pm May-Sep, 10am-2pm Tue-Fri Oct-Apr), which were built during WWII.

Indo-Pacific Marine

A great prelude to any snorkelling trip in the area is the **marine aquarium** (☎ 8981 1294; Stokes Hill Wharf; adult/student A$18/15; 🕐 10am-5pm Apr-Oct, 9am-1pm Mon-Sat & 10am-5pm Sun Nov-Mar). The aquarium is the long-term work of its passionate guide, John. It recreates Darwin's marine environment beautifully (no feeding, no filters). Study box jellyfish, intriguing stonefish and other sea creatures up close.

Crocodylus Park

To maximise the hefty entry cost, time your visit to this **crocodile park** (☎ 8922 4500; www.wmi.com.au/crocpark; 815 McMillans Rd, Berrimah; adult A$25, YHA & VIP discount 15%; 🕐 9am-5pm) to coincide with one of the 45-minute tours. There's also a mini zoo, and a museum covering all things croc-related. You can even see the remains of the last meal of Darwin personality, 'Sweetheart'. Tours are at 10am, noon and 2pm. Bus No 5 from Darwin (weekdays only) gets you to within a five-minute walk of the park.

Australian Aviation Heritage Centre

About 10km from the city centre is Darwin's **aviation museum** (☎ 8947 2145; 557 Stuart Hwy, Winnellie; YHA or VIP cardholder A$11, adult/student A$9/7.50; 🕐 9am-5pm). It was built to house an enormous American B-52 bomber used in the

A CYCLONE CALLED TRACY

Cyclone – a violent tropical storm (or) hurricane (Collins English Dictionary, 3rd Australian edition)

The eye of Cyclone Tracy was first detected on 22 December 1974, over 200km north of Darwin. Two days later it changed its predicted course and headed straight for Darwin, hitting the city in the early hours of 25 December. The airport anemometer failed at 3.05am after recording a gust of 217km/h. During the next few hours, as the rest of the country roused for the festivities of Christmas Day, estimates suggest that the cyclone's peak wind speeds were as high as 280km/h, mangling cars and sending lampposts to the ground.

The aftermath: 49 people died on land and another 16 were missing at sea; almost 90% of Darwin's 11,200 houses were destroyed; the estimated damage bill was tipped at over A$500 million.

A similar cyclone flattened Darwin (originally called Palmerston) in 1897. Since Cyclone Tracy, several other comparatively weak cyclones have passed over Darwin – the city now sits in a state of readiness for these violent acts of nature.

Vietnam War. Lots of space is dedicated to Darwin during the war years. Tours are held at 10am and 2pm, and bus Nos 5 (weekdays only) and 8 run along the Stuart Hwy.

ACTIVITIES

Cycling

The main bicycle track runs from the northern end of Cavenagh St to Fannie Bay, Coconut Grove, Nightcliff and Casuarina. At Fannie Bay a side track heads out to East Point Reserve.

For more information on bicycle hire see Bicycle & Scooter on p336.

Diving

Darwin Harbour offers some excellent year-round wreck diving. Try these operators:

Cullen Bay Dive (☎ 8981 3049; www.divedarwin.com; 66 Marina Blvd, Cullen Bay) Two dives with tanks A$100.

Coral Divers (☎ 8981 2686; 42 Stuart Hwy, Stuart Park) Single boat dives with tanks for A$55; Open Water Certification courses for A$450.

Golf

Near the Botanical Gardens, the lush greens of **Gardens Park Golf Links** (☎ 8981 6365; www.gardensparkgolf.com.au; Gardens Rd; 9-holes adult/student A$13/8, 18-holes adult/student A$18/13; 🕓 6.30am-7pm) are enough to inspire golfers of most standards. There's minigolf and a driving range on which to strut your stuff. Inquire about backpacker deals.

Rock Climbing

There are a lot of impressive rocks to climb in the NT, so if you want some training, head to the **Rock Centre** (☎ 8941 0747; rockcentre@octa4.net.au; Doctors Gully Rd; adult climb with/without gear A$22/16; 🕓 Tue-Thu 9am-9pm, Fri-Mon 9am-6pm), near Aquascene.

Swimming

Popular beaches outside the stinger season include **Mindil**, **Vestey's** on Fannie Bay and **Casuarina** further north, which doubles as a nude beach.

The main public **swimming pool** (☎ 8981 2662; Ross Smith Ave; adult/student A$3/1.40; 🕓 6am-7.30pm Mon, Tue, Thu & Fri, to 6pm Wed, 8am-6pm Sat, 10am-6pm Sun), at Parap, has a partly shaded 50m pool and diving boards. Take bus No 6 or 10 from the city centre.

TOURS

The visitors centre and most places to stay have a plethora of tour information on Darwin and the Top End.

Aboriginal Cultural Tours

A few tours specialising in Aboriginal culture depart from Darwin. Tours to remote communities that involve a chartered flight are quite expensive.

Tiwi Tours (☎ 1800 183 630, 8924 1115; www.aussieadventure.com.au) will fly you northwest to Bathurst Island to experience some Tiwi culture

---

FANCY WORKING HERE?

Who could blame you for wanting to hang around Darwin and pick up some work? With the right working permits, it's possible. The daily *Northern Territory News* has job listings.

The hospitality industry hits its peak from April to October. Hospitality-oriented **Forward Recruitment** (☎ 08-8981 3228) can give you some leads.

It's mango season in the Top End from October to November, and farmers are always on the lookout for extra hands. Approximately 50km outside of Darwin, **Noonamah Tavern** (☎ 08-8988 1054) has budget cabins that are a 15-minute drive from most mango farms. Go to www.jobsearch.gov.au/harvesttrail for more details about seasonal employment opportunities.

Territory schools often seek casual teaching staff. For more information check out www.teaching.nt.gov.au.

There's often casual nursing work available in Aboriginal communities as well as in Darwin, Gove and Katherine, and further south. Nurses can register with the **NT Nurses Board** (☎ 08-8999 4157).

For other casual work opportunities contact **Drake** (☎ 08-8924 3333), **Grunt** (☎ 08-8947 4475) or **Intergrated** (☎ 08-8941 6522).

Willing Workers on Organic Farms Australia has over 50 hosts in the Territory – register at wwoof.com.au or check out the various environmental projects of Conservation Volunteers (www.conservationvolunteers.com.au).

For more details visit www.theterritory.com.au and www.australiasoutback.com.

(p336) on a one-/two-day all-inclusive tour for A$310/570. Prices include the charter flight, permits, meals and, on the two-day tour, accommodation.

City Sights

The **Tour Tub** (☎ 8985 6322), an open-sided minibus, does a circuit of the city, calling at the major places of interest. You can hop on or off anywhere along its route. In the city centre it leaves from Knuckey St. There's a set fare (A$25 per adult) for the day; buses operate hourly from 9am to 4pm.

Cruises & Charters

City of Darwin (☎ 0417-855 829; www.darwincruises.com; cruises adult/student A$50/35) For a taste of how the other half lives, enjoy a sunset cruise on Darwin Harbour. *Very* relaxing. Bring your own (BYO) drinks. Meet at Cullen Bay marina at 4.45pm.

Equinox Fishing Charters (☎ 1800 199 000, 8942 2199; www.equinoxcharters.citysearch.com.au; Cullen Bay; tours from A$110; 9am-5pm Mon-Fri, 9am-noon Sat) If you dream of hooking a big one then a trip out on Darwin's waters might be just the answer.

Tours Further Afield

As with the hostel scene, tour operators are always matching each other to get bums on seats, especially during the Wet. Most operators offer discounts.

Adventure Tours Australia (☎ 1300 654 604, 8309 2277; www.adventuretours.com.au) Action-packed one- to 10-day tours throughout the Territory.

Billy Can Tours (☎ 1800 813 484; www.billycan.com.au) Upmarket tours of Kakadu, Litchfield, Arnhem Land and Katherine. Camping or budget accommodation. German and French language tours, too.

Darwin Day Tours (☎ 1800 811 633, 8924 1124) The full-day Wildlife Spectacular Tour (A$135 per adult) takes in the Territory Wildlife Park, Darwin Crocodile Farm, the Jumping Croc cruise and nearby Fogg Dam. There are also day trips to Litchfield National Park (from A$86), Kakadu (from A$144) and Katherine (from A$149).

Desert Venturer (☎ 1300 858 099; www.desertventurer.com) Four-day road trips between Darwin and Cairns (and vice versa) for A$390 per adult plus A$75 meal kitty.

Kakadu Dreams (☎ 1800 813 266; www.kakadudream.com.au; 50 Mitchell St) 'No oldies allowed' camping safaris. Litchfield trip from A$80. Two- to three-day Kakadu expeditions departing daily (from A$290 to A$410 in the high season and A$270 to A$380 in the low season).

Kakadu 4WD Safaris (☎ 1300 551 112; www.kakadu4wdsafaris.com) These owner-operated trips get rave reviews. Three-day Kakadu trips from A$410.

Wilderness 4WD Adventures (☎ 1300 666 100, 8941 2161; www.wildernessadventures.com.au; 88 Mitchell St) Competitively priced three- to five-day Kakadu trips from A$405. Emphasis on fun. 'Top End Blitz' trip to Kakadu, Katherine and Litchfield from A$595.

Xplore (☎ 1300 136 133, 8941 4311; Shop 15, Mitchell St) 'Get wet (and dirty)' on three-day all-inclusive Kakadu trips, from A$415.

FESTIVALS & EVENTS

Down Under International Film Festival See big name features and local shorts; held in May.

Darwin Fringe Festival A fusion of dance, poetry and music; held in July/August.

Beer Can Regatta Territorian eccentricity is at its best at this festival. It features races of boats made entirely from beer cans, off Mindil Beach; held in July/August.

Darwin Rodeo Yeehah! The whips crack as international teams compete in numerous cowboy events; held in August.

Festival of Darwin An arts and culture festival over 17 days; held in August.

National Aboriginal & Torres Strait Islander Art Awards The premier national Aboriginal art event, at the Museum & Art Gallery of the Northern Territory; held in August.

SLEEPING

Hostels

Some hostels are tucked-away bohemian places while others enjoy prime positions and streamlined service. Hostels generally charge around A$20 a bed in the Dry, but in the Wet price wars ensure a better deal for travellers.

Melaleuca on Mitchell (☎ 1300 723 437, 8941 7800; www.melaleucaonmitchell.com.au; 52 Mitchell St; dm/d A$25/65 Wet, dm/d A$30/80 Dry) The newest kid on the block, this 452-bed 'backpacker resort' opened in 2004 and has a kitchen, bar, spa, good communal areas and laundry facilities.

Darwin City YHA (☎ 8981 3995; darwinyha@yhant.org.au; 69 Mitchell St; dm from A$17, d with/without bathroom A$65/55, nonmembers extra A$3.50) Looking for a clean and central pad? This friendly place is the best choice – it's run like a well-oiled machine (having 24-hour reception is handy). There's an orderly kitchen plus a TV room.

Cavenagh (☎ 8941 6383; www.thecavenagh.com; 12 Cavenagh St; dm/d from A$16/55) A happening choice with a trendy bar attached (p334). Your best bet is a room towards the back. Space is limited in the dorms but they all have bathrooms. Reasonably helpful staff.

Frogshollow Backpackers (☎ 1800 068 686, 8941 2600; www.frogs-hollow.com.au; 27 Lindsay St; dm/d from A$17/55;) This two-storey hostel is a bit like a frog's nook with a relaxed feel and attentive staff. The dorms are clean enough but can get crowded. There's a decent kitchen and two shaded spas.

Gecko Lodge (☎ 1800 811 250, 8981 5569; www.geckolodge.com.au;146 Mitchell St; dm/d from A$16/45;) Run by Dutchman and former backpacker, Marcel, this is a friendly hostel recommended by readers. It's a bit rundown but little extras like free pancakes and muesli at breakfast, and nightly lifts to town make up for it. The front balcony rooms are the best.

Chilli's Backpackers (☎ 1800 351 313, 8941 9722; www.chillis.com.au; 69a Mitchell St; dm from A$18, d & tw from A$50;) This three-storey hostel is quite loud and attracts a mostly young crowd in cool threads who are up for a party. The four- and eight-bed dorms have a basin but the latter feel cramped. Some doubles include bathrooms (right next door to the bed). Soak away in the rooftop spa. Air-con is available between 7.30pm and 8.30am.

Park Lodge (☎ 8981 5692; 42 Coronation Dr, Stuart Park; s/d from A$45/50;) Tucked away from the action in Stuart Park, this is friendly, clean and quiet with a mix of older and refurbished rooms. Budget rooms have a fridge and share bathrooms. There's a well-equipped kitchen, TV and sitting room, and laundry.

Wilderness Lodge (☎ 1800 068 886, 8981 8363; www.wildlodge.com.au; 88 Mitchell St; dm/d A$18/50;) A central – albeit simple – and friendly lodge. Bright doubles are on the small side. There are plenty of places to sit and read, or to get through that postcard backlog, and there's bike hire here.

Hotels

Barramundi Lodge (☎ 8941 6466; www.barramundilodge.com.au; 4 Gardens Rd, The Gardens; s/d Oct-Apr A$30/50, May-Sep A$50/75;) This quiet lodge gets good reports from our readers. Spotless rooms have a TV and kitchenette. Bathrooms are communal. There's a laundry, common area, banana lounges by the inviting pool, and a barbecue.

Value Inn (☎ 8981 4733; www.valueinn.com.au; 50 Mitchell St; d Nov-May A$60, Jun-Aug A$90;) A bit of a rabbit warren but it *is* in the centre of Mitchell St. Every room sleeps three people and has a TV, mini bathroom and bar fridge. The ground floor is dedicated to smokers.

SPLURGE!

Steeles B&B (☎ 8941 3636, 0411-442 373; 4 Zealandia Cres, Larrakeyah; d from A$50;) Couples or singles travelling during the Wet and looking for a quiet place to stay might be in luck if either one of the two well-accessorised rooms at Steeles' Spanish Mision-style B&B are available.

Camping & Caravan Parks

Hidden Valley Tourist Park (☎ 8947 1422; www.hvtp.com.au; 25 Hidden Valley Rd, Berrimah; camp sites unpowered/powered per 2 people A$23/25, bunkhouse rooms s/d A$33/45, budget cabins from A$70;) Ideal if you have your own vehicle. The air-con bunkhouse rooms are a steal. Self-contained cabins are super-clean and camp sites are neatly divided by gardens.

Shady Glen Caravan Park (☎ 8984 3330; www.shadyglen.com.au; cnr Farrel Cres & Stuart Hwy, Stuart Park; camp sites unpowered/powered per 2 people A$22/25, s/d A$30/35, cabins without bathroom from A$60;) About 10km from central Darwin, this leafy spot has all the facilities you'd expect, and friendly staff. The tidy cabins are better than the bed-in-a-box donga-style budget rooms near the highway (a donga is a small, transportable building widely used in the outback).

EATING

City Centre

SELF-CATERING

There's a **Woolworths** (☎ 8941 6111) supermarket between Smith and Cavenagh Sts (near Peel St) and a 24hr **Coles** (☎ 8941 8055; 55-59 Mitchell St) right opposite Value Inn in Mitchell St. The **Brumby's** bakery chain has outlets at both complexes.

CAFÉS

Moorish Café (☎ 8981 0010; 37 Knuckey St; mains A$19-30; breakfast, lunch & dinner) Eat well at this Moroccan-meets-Spanish café, complete with comfy corner lounges and candles. The char-grilled vegetable stack (A$19) is heavenly, and check out the flavoursome tapas (A$5.50 to A$7.50). Don't go past the Turkish delight ice cream ensemble (A$10.50). Divine dining!

Relish (☎ 8941 1900; cnr Air Raid Arcade & Cavenagh St; mains A$5-6.50; breakfast & lunch Mon-Sat)

> **SPLURGE!**
>
> **Pee Wee's at the Point** (☎ 8981 6868; Alec Fong Lim Dr, East Point Reserve; mains A$20-45; dinner) Simple concept, nicely done, with a fabulous view and great pan-Asian food. Relish some of the best food Darwin has to offer: Thai-style snapper (A$35), or Shanghai prawns with chilli and garlic sauce (A$45), perhaps? Mmm. Limited vegetarian options. Bookings essential.

Cosy and welcoming. Linger over a mango melt (A$5) at lunch time. *Chai* (spiced tea; A$3.30) served with something sinfully sweet is perfect for an afternoon sojourn. Takeaways are available.

Roma Café (☎ 8981 6729; 30 Cavenagh St; mains A$5-11; breakfast & lunch) A "hippy stuck in the '70s", says one local. This place is a Darwin institution. Much-loved morning heart starters include the banana pancakes (A$7) and the tad more adventurous Indian brekkie (A$9) of dhal, roti and yoghurt.

Ducks Nuts Bar & Grill (☎ 8942 2122; 76 Mitchell St; mains A$12-24; breakfast, lunch & dinner) A trendy eatery-cum-bar. The slick, emporium-style Bar Espresso coffee shop in the Ducks Nuts complex delivers so-so service but good brekkies.

Salvatore's (☎ 8941 4679; cnr Knuckey & Smith Sts; mains A$6.50-18; breakfast, lunch & dinner) A middle-of-the-road option serving all-day brekkie (from 7am) and aromatic espresso. Ideal for late-night munchies.

Indian Café (☎ 8941 0752; Shop1, 15 Knuckey St; mains A$7; lunch & dinner Mon-Sat) A couple of our readers have recommended this authentic-looking café for its mango lassis and good-value curry combos.

RESTAURANTS

Go Sushi (☎ 8941 1008; Shop 5, 28 Mitchell St; sushi trains per piece A$3-5.50; lunch & dinner Mon-Sat) Sit by the oh-so-cool sushi train and you'll be faced with the daunting task of deciding what to have. The tempura flake, chilli and vegetable rolls are scrummy.

Thailicious (☎ 8981 1122; Shop 18, 69 Mitchell St; mains A$7.70-21; lunch Mon-Fri & dinner daily Dry & lunch Tue-Fri, dinner Tue-Sun Wet) This family-run eatery does modern Thai and other Asian delights well, not to mention some pretty mean cocktail concoctions. Try Pattaya paradise (A$19) – noodles wrapped in a pancake omelette – or a reliable green curry. Get here early to score a triangle bolster seat.

Hanuman Restaurant (☎ 8941 3500; 28 Mitchell St; mains A$9.50-27; lunch & dinner) Hanuman's imposing looks are deceiving – it's competitively priced, with snappy service and delicious Thai cuisine and tandoori dishes. The spicy pumpkin *jalfrezi* (A$14) is particularly tasty. Swap your thongs and shorts for some smart-casual gear.

Vietnam Saigon Star (☎ 8981 1420; Harry Chan Arcade, Shop 9, 60 Smith St; mains A$8.50-17; lunch & dinner Mon-Sat) Need a Vietnamese fix? This simple BYO place will satisfy your taste buds for spring rolls (A$7) and *pho* (A$8.50).

Twilight on Lindsay (☎ 8981 8631; 2 Lindsay St; mains A$17-28; lunch & dinner) Best at night when the fairy lights are glowing, Twilight's Asian-meets-colonial style is ambient. Servings are a touch on the delicate side. Lunch-time tapas is an affordable A$2.50 per serve – try grilled sardines, *frittata* (pastryless quiche) or perhaps salt-and-pepper squid. Yum!

Rendezvous Cafe (☎ 8981 9231; Shop 6, Star Village Arcade, 32 Smith St Mall; mains A$3.80-12; breakfast & lunch Mon-Sat, dinner Thu-Sat) In a quiet arcade off Smith St Mall, this BYO Thai-Malaysian place gets repeated raps for its laksa, and the home-made iced tea is also pretty good. Breakfast is served from 10.30am.

Tim's Surf 'n' Turf (☎ 8981 1024; 10 Litchfield St; mains A$8-28; lunch Mon-Fri & dinner daily) Prides itself on its fun vibe and 1kg steaks. Fill up on scotch fillet with prawns (A$22), and chicken schnitzel (A$15). Revel in Tim's magic tricks and greet resident crocodile, 'Schnitzel Von Crumb'.

PUBS

Shenannigans (☎ 8981 2100; 69 Mitchell St; mains A$14-25; 10.30am-2am) Tuck into beef in Guinness (A$15) or traditional bangers and mash (A$14).

Rorke's Drift (☎ 8941 7171; 46 Mitchell St; mains A$7.50-25; breakfast, lunch & dinner) The English-style brekkie is said to work wonders on a hangover (breakfast is served from 10am) – a hangover you may well have procured from drinking here the night before (p334).

Wharf Precinct

Cheap eats rule at the end of Stokes Hill Wharf, where half of Darwin descends on weekend nights.

Kim's on the Wharf (☎ 8981 6009; Shop 4, Starboard Café, Stokes Hill Wharf; ⌚ lunch & dinner) Locals *loooove* the barra (barramundi), prawn, calamari and salad combo (A$9.90).

Schnitzel Magic (☎ 8981 6009; Shop 14, Port Arcade, Stokes Hill Wharf; ⌚ lunch & dinner) Another Darwin institution serving local delights – namely freshly crumbed camel, croc, buffalo or roo.

Cullen Bay & Fannie Bay

Million-dollar views coupled with cheap-as-chips takeaway and relaxed dining make this a popular precinct.

Sawasdee Thai Nonya Seafood Restaurant (☎ 8941 3335; Shop 1, 52 Marina Blvd, Cullen Bay; mains A$15-22; ⌚ lunch Dry, dinner Dry & Wet) Darwin's climate is made for indulging in Thai food. Feast on the usual line-up.

Buzz Café (☎ 8941 1141; 48 Marina Blvd, Cullen Bay; mains A$14-30; ⌚ brunch Sat & Sun, lunch & dinner daily) There's certainly a buzz about this café's nouveau cuisine. There's a big deck for sun adoration and a spiffy bar made of lava pieces. Lots of bites to share, or lash out with the pan-fried barramundi on potato mash (A$30) – all to oneself.

Bay Seafood Café (☎ 8981 8789; 57 Marina Blvd, Cullen Bay; barramundi & chips A$8.50; ⌚ lunch & dinner) Nothing beats fish and chips by the water and this place is lauded as having the best in town. Try the Morton Bay Bug burger (A$9.90), chilli and garlic prawns (from A$16.90) or the tasty barra, chips & prawns option (from A$11.50).

MARKET MADNESS

It's a quintessential Top End experience to head to Asiatic **Mindil Beach Night Market** (Mindil Beach; ⌚ 5-10pm Thu May-Oct & 5-9pm Sun mid-May–early Oct), off Gilruth Ave. Take your choice – there's mouthwatering Thai, Sri Lankan, Brazilian, Greek, Portuguese and more, all at around A$4 to A$6 per serve. Top off your oodles of noodles with luscious crepes before cruising past arts and crafts stalls bulging with hand-crafted jewellery, art and New Age tie-dyed clothes.

Similar stalls can be found at **Parap Village Market** (⌚ 8am-2pm Sat), **Nightcliff Market** (⌚ 8am-2pm Sun), **Palmerston Market** (⌚ 5-10pm Fri Dry only) and **Rapid Creek Market** (⌚ 5-9pm Fri, 8am-2pm Sun).

Seafood on Cullen (☎ 8981 4666; Shop 8, 51 Marina Blvd; buffet A$28; ⌚ dinner) If the salt air has induced major seafood cravings, then head for a big feed at this no-frills place, which has a seafood buffet (plus steak and dessert).

Cornucopia Café (☎ 8981 1002; Conacher St, Fannie Bay; mains A$7-18; ⌚ breakfast & lunch) A pleasant spot to digest culture after a visit to the attached Museum & Art Gallery of the Northern Territory. The antipasto platter (A$18) is packed with Mediterranean treats.

DRINKING

Most of the popular pubs are on Mitchell St, within a short walk or long stumble of each other.

Cavenagh (☎ 8941 6383; www.thecavenagh.com; 12 Cavenagh St) Quench summer thirsts at this hip 'n' happening bar, part of the Cavenagh hotel (p331). Outdoor fans disperse refreshing mist in the heat.

Ducks Nuts Bar & Grill (☎ 8942 2122; www.ducksnuts.com.au; 76 Mitchell St) Vodka aficionados will enjoy the swanky bar, or you can savour Sunday sessions (2pm to 6pm) of blues and jazz. Part of the Ducks Nuts (p333) complex.

Shenannigans (☎ 8981 2100; 69 Mitchell St; ⌚ 10.30am-2am) You may well be in the Top End but you could be forgiven for thinking you're somewhere in Dublin here. Travellers can be spotted at this bustling watering hole during the day and through the night. You can also grab a bite here (p333).

Top End Hotel (☎ 8981 6511; cnr Mitchell & Daly Sts) Big and brassy. This is a hotbed of entertainment and drinking action from the tropical gardens of Lizards Outdoor Bar, with its big-screen sports broadcasts and weekend bands, to the funkier Retro Club (Tuesday to Saturday).

Victoria Hotel (The Vic; ☎ 8981 4011; 27 Smith St Mall) A lively backpacker haunt. Vie for a spot on the balcony overlooking the mall. Live bands play from Tuesday to Friday and there are often different kinds of wild party themes.

Rorke's Drift (☎ 8941 7171; 46 Mitchell St) Deliberate over 14 types of beer on tap, and people-watch from the shady outdoor beer garden. Inside is reminiscent of a typical English pub (only with the air-con cranking away). You can also grab a bite here (p333).

Kitty O'Shea's (☎ 8941 7947; Mitchell St; ⌚ 10am-4am) Another Irish pub! This one has Guinness, Kilkenny, Harp lager and Bulmer's cider on tap.

Darwin Sailing Club (☎ 8981 1700; Atkins Dr, Fannie Bay) This is where you'll find the locals hanging out – for live music on a Saturday night (dry season only), or on a Sunday arvo for a few sundowners. Travellers can get temporary membership (free) on the spot.

CLUBBING

Keep an eye out for bills posted on notice boards and telegraph poles that advertise dance and full-moon parties.

Discovery & Lost Arc (☎ 8942 3300; 89 Mitchell St; 🕑 from 9.30pm) Darwin's pretty young things head here for a boogie to commercial dance anthems. Next door, the open-fronted Lost Arc is a kissy-kissy nook.

Throb (☎ 8942 3435; 64 Mitchell St; admission A$10; 🕑 from 10pm Thu-Sun) Playing progressive house this is Darwin's premier gay- and lesbian-friendly club. It throbs with drag shows on Friday and Saturday nights, showcasing performances by Darwin's much-loved Aboriginal performer and community worker, Crystal Love, plus other glamours.

ENTERTAINMENT

For up-to-date event information go to www.darwinarts.com.au.

Cinemas

Deckchair Cinema (☎ 8981 0700; www.deckchaircinema.com; Kitchener Dr, Wharf Precinct; adult/concession A$12/10; box office 🕑 from 6.30pm Apr-Oct) Recline in an old-fashioned deckchair and watch an arty flick under the stars. Bring mosquito repellent and a cushion for extra comfort. The snack bar sells alcohol (no BYO).

Darwin Film Society (☎ 8981 0700; Conacher St, Fannie Bay; adult/concession A$12/10) Art-house films screen during 'Flix in the Wet' at the Museum & Art Gallery Theatrette.

Darwin City Cinema (☎ 981 5999; 76 Mitchell St; adult/student A$14/10.50) This is the city's large cinema complex, screening the latest release blockbuster films. Head down on Tropical Tuesday for A$9 entry (all day).

Theatre

Darwin Entertainment Centre (box office ☎ 8980 3333; www.darwinentertainment.com.au; 93 Mitchell St; 🕑 10am-5.30pm Mon-Fri & 1hr prior to shows) This large complex houses the Playhouse and Studio Theatres, and stages cabaret, touring concerts and amateur plays. Online ticketing available.

The hipper **Brown's Mart** (☎ 8981 5522; www.brownsmart.com.au; cnr Harry Chan Ave & Smith St) presents off-beat theatre performances in one of Darwin's oldest buildings. An arty crowd congregates here for Bamboo Lounge on selected Friday nights: an eclectic and always bohemian line-up of performances and acts.

Live Music

Rorke's Drift (☎ 8941 7171; 46 Mitchell St) 'Always a good night out', says one local rager. Rorke's has a jam-packed line-up: karaoke on Wednesday, cover bands on Tuesday and Saturday nights, Sunday blues sessions and cheap drinks for girls on Thursday.

If you can't do without live music, head to Ducks Nuts Bar & Grill, Top End Hotel, and Victoria Hotel (all opposite), and Darwin Sailing Club (left).

GETTING THERE & AWAY

Air

International and interstate flights operate out of Darwin. At the time of writing, low-end one-way fares (with Jetstar, Qantas and Virgin Blue) started at: Sydney A$210, Brisbane A$180, Cairns A$250, Melbourne A$190, Adelaide A$240, Perth A$270, Alice Springs A$210.

Airnorth (☎ 8920 4001; www.airnorth.com.au)
Qantas (☎ 13 13 13; www.qantas.com.au)
Virgin Blue (☎ 13 67 89; www.virginblue.com.au)

Airnorth connects Darwin with Broome, Groote Eylandt, Gove, Kununurra and Dili (East Timor).

Other, smaller routes are flown by local operators; ask your travel agent.

Bus

Interstate buses pull in behind the Transit Centre.

McCafferty's/Greyhound (☎ 13 20 30; www.mccaffertys.com.au) has daily services to and from Darwin. From Darwin, destinations include Kununurra (A$160, 10 hours), Broome (A$300, 24 hours), Katherine (A$65, four hours), Alice Springs (A$240, 20 hours) and Townsville (A$390, 35 hours).

Train

In early 2004 the **Ghan** (☎ 13 21 47; www.gsr.com.au) officially started its long run from Adelaide to Darwin, linking south and north in

CAR RENTAL TIPS

- Find out the day's best deal at the visitors centre in Mitchell St.
- You may save money by booking in advance.
- Make sure you get enough mileage – the Top End is a big place.
- It may be worthwhile hiring a campervan for touring when you consider that this option includes cooking facilities and accommodation.

the middle of this wide brown land. The one-way economy seat/twin-berth sleeper trip from Adelaide to Darwin costs A$440/1390 (concessions are available). The train departs Adelaide at 5.15pm on Sunday, and the trip takes 47 hours.

Car & Motorcycle

HIRE

Darwin has numerous budget car-rental operators, as well as all the major national and international companies:

Advance Car Rentals (☎ 1800 002 227, 8981 2999; 86 Mitchell St)
Avis (☎ 136 333, 8981 9922; 89 Smith St)
Budget (☎ 8981 9800; cnr Daly St & Doctors Gully Rd)
Delta Europcar (☎ 1800 811 541; 77 Cavenagh St)
Hertz (☎ 1300 132 105, 8941 0944; cnr Smith & Daly Sts)
Nifty Rent-a-Car (☎ 8941 7090; 86 Mitchell St)

GETTING AROUND

Pick up a free Darwin map at the visitors centre to help you navigate your way around.

Bicycle & Scooter

Most of the backpacker hostels hire out bicycles; the usual charge is A$6/17 per hour/day.

Darwin Scooter Hire (☎ 0418-892 885; Nite Market, Mitchell St) rents out scooters for A$40/20 per day/two hours; two-seater scooters are also available. You'll need to show your drivers licence.

Bus

The transit centre, where Darwin's long-haul buses come and go, is in the centre of town behind Darwin City YHA on Mitchell St.

Darwinbus (☎ 8924 7666; www.nt.gov.au/ipe/dtw/public/bustimes; Harry Chan Ave) runs a comprehensive service from the small depot near the corner of Smith St and Harry Chan Ave.

Fares are on a zone system: one-/six-zone single trips cost A$1.40/2.80, or you can buy unlimited all-zone daily/weekly passes for A$5/25. Bus No 4 (to Fannie Bay, Nightcliff, Rapid Creek and Casuarina) and No 6 (Fannie Bay, Parap and Stuart Park) are useful for getting to Mindil Beach, the Museum & Art Gallery of the Northern Territory, Fannie Bay Gaol Museum and East Point. Bus Nos 5 and 8 travel along the Stuart Hwy past the airport to Berrimah. Bus Nos 5 and 6 don't run on weekends.

Pedicab

Prestige Pedicabs (☎ 0415-528 390, 0439-337 561; fares from A$5; ⌚ from 1pm) will chauffeur you around in an Asian-style cyclo. Half-hour tours are available from A$25.

Taxi

As well as the regular taxi service, Darwin's handy 24-hour **Arafura Shuttle** (☎ 8981 3300) has taxi-bus services that will take you anywhere in the central area for a flat A$3, and elsewhere (such as Fannie Bay and East Point) for a fixed fee.

AROUND DARWIN

Take a deep breath, inhale the fresh air and be inspired by the great outdoors around Darwin. This area boasts excellent bushwalking and has some great get-away-from-it-all camping options.

TIWI ISLANDS

The Tiwi Islands – Bathurst and Melville – are about 80km north of Darwin across Beagle Gulf and are home to the Tiwi Aboriginal people. Most Tiwi Islanders live on Bathurst Island's Nguin settlement and follow a non-traditional lifestyle. On Melville Island the settlements are Pularumpi and Milikapiti.

The Tiwi's island location have kept them fairly isolated and their culture has retained several unique features. Perhaps the best known are the *pukumani* burial poles, carved and painted with symbolic and mythological figures (used by Tiwi Islanders to mark grave sites). More recently the Tiwi have started producing highly acclaimed art for sale (www.tiwiart.com).

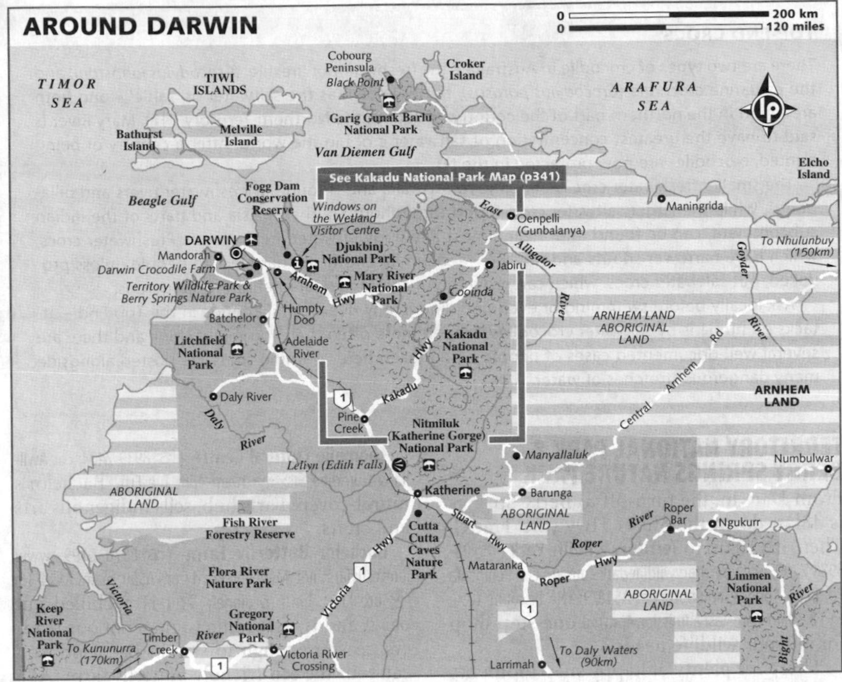

You need a permit to visit the islands and the easiest option is to take a tour. **Tiwi Tours** (☎ 1800 183 630, 8924 1115; www.aussieadventure.com.au) is the main operator (see Aboriginal Cultural Tours, p330).

DARWIN CROCODILE FARM

Just a little south of the Arnhem Hwy turn-off is this **crocodile farm** (☎ 08-8988 1450; www.crocfarm.com.au; Stuart Hwy; adult/concession A$10/8; ⌚ 9am-4pm) You'll get within kissing distance of 'Snowy', 'Maurice' and 'Bert', the latter being a 5.2m beast best known for his cameo in *Crocodile Dundee*.

Some of the croc-filled lagoons and enclosures are on the smelly side. Tours run daily at 2pm, with an extra tour at noon on Sunday.

ARNHEM HIGHWAY

The Arnhem Hwy branches off towards Kakadu 33km southeast of Darwin. At the intersection is the blink-and-you'll-miss-it **Didgeridoo Hut & Art Gallery** (☎ 08-8988 4457; www.didgeridoohut.com.au), where you can watch indigenous artists at work.

About 50km east of Darwin is the fantastically named town of Humpty Doo (not much here, though) and 15km further is the turn-off to **Fogg Dam Conservation Reserve**, which is frequented by a plethora of water birds. There are three short nature walks (2.2km to 3.6km) here. **Window on the Wetlands Visitors Centre** (☎ 08-8988 8188; wow.pwcnt@nt.gov.au; admission free; ⌚ 7.30am-7pm) sits atop Beatrice Hill, by the Arnhem Hwy 3km past the Fogg Dam turn-off. It's a good place to stretch your legs and take in expansive views over the Adelaide River flood plains.

If you're desperate to see crocodiles, then consider one of the 'jumping croc' cruises that leave from the Adelaide River Crossing. Huge saltwater crocodiles rise out of the water for bits of meat held on the end of poles (apparently in the name of 'exercise'). It's a bit of a circus but an amazing sight. Most backpacker tours en route to Kakadu generally stop here. Down Fogg Dam Rd off the Arnhem Hwy, **Hunter Safaris** (☎ 1800 670 640, 8983 3224; www.huntersafaris.com.au; adult A$25) has one-hour jumping croc tours at 9am, 11am, 1pm and 3pm all year.

TOP-END CROCS

There are two types of crocodile in Australia – the freshwater or 'freshie' *(Crocodylus johnstoni)* and the estuarine crocodile *(Crocodylus porosus)*, better known as the saltwater or 'saltie' – and both are found in the northern part of the country, including the Northern Territory (NT). Mary River is said to have the greatest concentration of saltwater crocs in the world. After a century of being hunted, crocodiles are now protected in the NT.

The smaller freshwater croc is endemic to Australia and is found in freshwater rivers and billabongs, while the larger saltwater croc, found throughout Southeast Asia and parts of the Indian subcontinent, can be found in or near almost any body of water, fresh or salt. Freshwater crocs, which have narrower snouts and rarely exceed 3m in length, are harmless to people unless provoked, but saltwater crocs, which can grow to 7m and longer, are definitely dangerous.

Ask locally before swimming or even paddling in any rivers or billabongs in the Top End – attacks on humans by saltwater crocodiles happen more often than you might think and there are several well-documented cases of people being taken here. Warning signs are posted alongside many dangerous stretches of water.

TERRITORY NATIONAL PARK & BERRY SPRINGS NATURE PARK

From Darwin, the turn-off to Berry Springs is 48km down the Stuart Hwy (the Track). Then, it's 10km to **Territory Wildlife Park** (☎ 08-8988 7200; www.territorywildlifepark.com.au; Cox Peninsula Rd, Berry Springs; adult/student A$18/9; YHA discount 10%; 🕑 8.30am-6pm, last admission 4pm), a one-stop shop for all your wildlife needs!

There are plenty of happy snap moments to be had with lounging kangaroos. The aquarium, replicating the entire Top End river system, is a captivating 3D-impression of life underwater: watch leisurely turtles and fresh water crocs enjoy a swim, before going eye-to-eye with a massive saltwater croc. Don't miss the birds of prey show at 10am and 3pm.

It's easy to spend the greater part of a day here. There's a buffet-style **cafeteria** (mains A$6-10; 🕑 8.30am-4.30pm; ⊠) serving home-made goodies.

BATCHELOR

☎ 08 / pop 730

This tiny town enjoys close proximity (18km) to a favoured Darwinite weekend haunt, the luscious Litchfield National Park.

For park-related inquiries, a ranger at the **parks office** (☎ 8976 0282; cnr Pinaroo & Nurdina Sts; 🕑 8am-5pm Mon-Fri) may be around to assist.

The well-stocked **Batchelor General Store & post office** (☎ 8976 0045; 🕑 7am-6pm Mon-Sat, 8am-5pm Sun) is where you can grab takeaway from 8am to 1pm Sunday, 7am to 4pm Monday and Tuesday, 7am to 8pm from Wednesday to Friday and 8am to 8pm Saturday.

Coomalie Cultural Centre (☎ 8939 7404; cnr Awillia & Nurndina Sts; 🕑 10am-4pm Tue-Fri), Bachelor's mural-covered arts hub, sells indigenous arts and crafts.

Bachelor Butterfly Farm (☎ 8976 0199; www.butterflyfarm.net; Meneling Rd; d from A$50, mains A$14-16; 🕑 breakfast, lunch & dinner; ⊠) is a chilled-out oasis, and is, according to many of our readers, reason enough to stay in Bachelor. You can tour the eco-friendly butterfly farm (A$6 per adult) before having a relaxed bite to eat on the veranda, complete with Nepalese prayer flags and dream-catchers. There's always an eclectic crowd of Willing Workers on Organic Farmers in residence. Yoga-loving owner, Chris, has set up a shared-house arrangement with three separate bedrooms, each with TV. Rates and room arrangements (beds from A$20) are negotiable in the Wet.

The quaint **Banyan Tree Caravan Park** (☎ 8976 0330; www.banyan-tree.info; Litchfield Park Rd; camp sites unpowered/powered per 2 people A$15/19, budget d A$40; ⊠) is close to Litchfield. The camp kitchen contains a barbecue, stove and fridge.

Batchelor Resort (☎ 8976 0123; www.batchelor-resort.com; Litchfield Park Rd; camp site unpowered/powered per two people A$10/26; ⊠) is closer to town than the Banyan Tree Caravan Park. You can feed parrots here as the sun goes down. There's also minigolf (A$5).

LITCHFIELD NATIONAL PARK

While Kakadu gets all the hype, chances are you'll be pleasantly surprised by the lesser-known **Litchfield National Park** (www.nt.gov.au/ipe/pwcnt), 115km south of Darwin. With its many pools, falls and rivers, expect to spend most of your day wet. It gets crowded on weekends so try to visit midweek.

There are two routes to the park from the Stuart Hwy that join up and loop through the park. The southern access road via Batchelor is sealed all the way, while the Cox Peninsula Rd access into the park is only partially sealed.

About 17km after entering the park from Batchelor, there's a field of **magnetic termite mounds**. It's essential to have a picture taken in front of one of these 6m masterpieces… made out of termite faeces and saliva!

Near the termite mounds, **Buley Rockhole** (2km) and **Florence Falls** (5km) are highlights. You'll reach stunning Florence Falls via Shady Creek walk (1.8km return), one of the park's best walks through monsoon forest. Be aware of the depths and strong currents when swimming here or you might end up down Florence Creek! There's a 3.2km track linking the falls to the gorgeous series of plunge pools that make up Buley Rockhole.

Breathe in the serenity at **Tolmer Falls**. Rare bats inhabit these caves so swimming is a no-go for the sake of these creatures. A walking track (1.5km loop) offers beautiful views of the area.

It's a further 7km along the main road to the turn-off for the park's centrepiece – **Wangi Falls** (pronounced *wong*-guy), 1.5km up a side road. Get sprayed by the misty waterfalls before preparing for a dip in the swimming hole (dry season only). There's a short walk circumnavigating the falls (40 minutes return).

Pick up a copy of Map NT's *Litchfield National Park* (Edition 5) if you're considering any of the longer walks. These walks include the 39km **Circuit Tabletop track** (one to two nights, dry season only). You'll need to register with the **Parks & Wildlife Commission of the Northern Territory** (☎ 1300 650 730; www.nt.gov.au/ipe/pwcnt; returnable deposit of A$50).

See the Darwin Tours Further Afield section on p331 for information on tours to Litchfield National Park.

Roll out the swag or pitch a tent at Litchfield's **camp sites** (per adult A$6.60): Wangi Falls, Buley Rockhole, Florence Falls and Tjaynera (Sandy Creek) Falls. All sites have toilets and fireplaces. Fees are usually collected by the ranger. There is no fee for camping at Surprise Creek. See Batchelor (opposite) for information on caravan parks just outside the park.

The kiosk, next to the camping grounds at Wangi Falls, serves fast food and refreshments until late in the afternoon. Nearby **Monsoon Café** (☎ 08-8978 2077; Litchfield Park Rd, 9am-late;), 4km north of Wangi Falls, is good for the budget and has home-made cakes and brewed coffee.

SPLURGE!

Jungle Drum Bungalows (☎ 8976 0555; 10 Meneling Rd; d bungalows Wet/Dry from A$75/100; restaurant breakfast & dinner;) Surrounded by lush foliage, Jungle Drum is a stylish choice. At night the pavilion restaurant is lit up with Balinese-style lamps, creating an intimate feel. It serves home-style meals like steak drizzled with pepper sauce (A$18) and chicken kebabs (A$15). Bungalows 5 and 6 have the best positions near the saltwater pool. Each bungalow has a fridge and TV.

ADELAIDE RIVER

☎ 08 / pop 230

This minor settlement, 111km south of Darwin on the Stuart Hwy, was established in 1870 to service the construction of the Overland Telegraph Line. Adelaide River now serves the daily procession of tour buses and passing tourists with fuel and snacks.

The immaculate **cemetery** is worth a visit, with its sea of white crosses honouring those who died in the 1942–43 Japanese air raids.

Pop into the town's pub, the **Adelaide River Inn** (☎ 8976 7047; fax 8976 7181; Memorial Tce; camp sites unpowered/powered per 2 people A$10/15, d A$60, mains A$8.50-19;), behind the roadhouse, to see 'Charlie' – the water buffalo who shot to fame in *Crocodile Dundee*. He's now stuffed atop the pub's bar. Oh, and the barra and chips here is supposed to be among the best in the Top End.

PINE CREEK

☎ 08 / pop 470

Nothing much happens in this slow-paced settlement and its future is actually hanging in the balance since the closure of the local mine in late 2003. It's worth a fleeting visit, at least. The Kakadu Hwy branches off the Stuart Hwy at Pine Creek, connecting it to Cooinda and Jabiru.

Pine Creek Museum (Railway Pde; adult A$2.20; 11am-5pm Mon-Fri & 11am-1pm Sat Dry, 1-5pm Mon-Fri Wet) has served many functions during its time – private residence, hospital and communications outpost – but now you can visit it to learn about Pine Creek's mining days.

Sleeping & Eating

Pine Creek Diggers Rest Motel (☎ 8976 1442; 32 Main Tce; s/d/q cabins A$80/90/100;) The pick of the town's accommodation, this place has uber-clean self-contained cabins. Friendly owner, Pat, doubles as the town's voluntary visitor information officer and she'll happily tell you about things to see and do around town.

Lazy Lizard Tourist Park (☎ 8976 1224; camp sites unpowered/powered per 2 people A$13/16, mains A$7-23; lunch & dinner;) Camp sites are a bit exposed but there is a landscaped pool. Step back in time at the park's colonial-style tavern. Wondering what the metal triangle out the front is for? Lasso practice, of course!

Mayse's Café (☎ 8976 1241; Moule St; mains A$4-12) There's breakfast (A$3.50 to A$12) all day. Come lunch, enjoy a mango smoothie (A$4.50) or chomp on a big chicken burger (A$7.50) as a suave, life-sized James Dean looks on.

KAKADU & ARNHEM LAND

Anyone who is serious about outdoor activities will want to visit legendary Kakadu National Park. Its amazing array of differing environments beckon naturalists, birdwatchers and serious bushwalkers. Arnhem Land is even more untouched, and largely inaccessible to tourists. The select group of tour operators working here incorporate cultural activities such a rock-art exploration into their itineraries.

KAKADU NATIONAL PARK

Delight the senses at Kakadu National Park with its sunsets, plunge pools, grassland walks, river cruises and rock-art. Kakadu is one of Australia's greatest natural assets, spanning 20,000 sq km – a haven of extraordinary flora and fauna and oversized landscapes, a place where the lives of animals, paintings and people are intricately woven. Kakadu's Unesco World Heritage status recognises its dual significance: natural and cultural. It *is* the Top End, complete with crocodiles, mozzies (mosquitoes) and pit toilets.

The name Kakadu is derived from Gagudju, a local Aboriginal word referring to a clan and language group. The park is managed jointly by its traditional Aboriginal owners and the Australian government's Director of National Parks. The recognition of traditional ownership has ensured the land is managed as it would have been thousands of years ago, including the use of age-old burning practices. Active Aboriginal settlements are scattered throughout the park.

Kakadu stretches more than 200km south from the coast and for 100km from east to west, with the main entrance 153km east of Darwin, along a bitumen road. Enclosed by the park, but not part of it, are a few tracts of land designated for other purposes – principally uranium mining.

The East Alligator River runs as a trajectory between Kakadu National Park and Arnhem Land Aboriginal Reserve, the vast stretch of largely uninhabited sacred land positioned to Kakadu's east occupying an area about the size of Victoria. The only settlements of any size here are Gove, on the peninsula at the northeastern corner, and Oenpilli (Gunbalanya), just across the East Alligator River from Ubirr in Kakadu National Park. To Arnhem Land's north is the isolated Cobourg Peninsula, most of which is preserved as Gurig National Park.

Travelling independently through Kakadu means you can soak up the park's atmosphere at your own leisure. However, going on an organised tour means you'll get the benefit of a guide. Give yourself at least three days in the park (this will provide you with a 'snapshot'), but a week here is even better.

CLIMATE

The average maximum temperature in Kakadu is 34°C year-round. The transition from the droughtlike conditions of the Dry (April to September) to the Wet (October to March) transforms Kakadu's landscape. Kakadu's average rainfall of 1400mm occurs during the Wet. The season determines what you can do within the park: seeing Kakadu at the tail end of the Wet or the early Dry is to see it at its best.

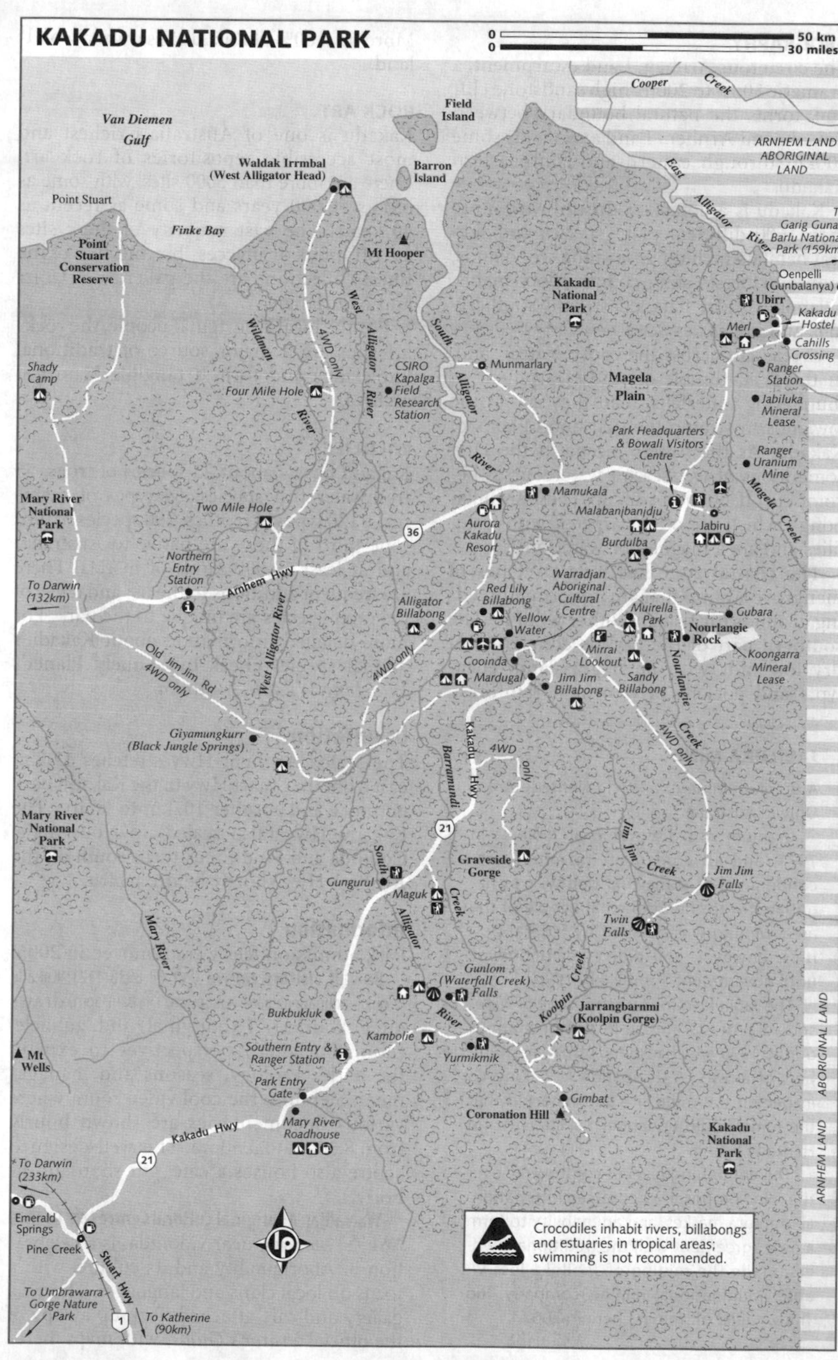
KAKADU NATIONAL PARK
0 50 km
0 30 miles
Van Diemen Gulf
Field Island
Barron Island
Waldak Irrmbal (West Alligator Head)
Point Stuart
Finke Bay
Point Stuart Conservation Reserve
Mt Hooper
Cooper Creek
ARNHEM LAND ABORIGINAL LAND
East Alligator River
To Garig Gunak Barlu National Park (159km)
Oenpelli (Gunbalanya)
Ubirr
Kakadu Hostel
Merl
Cahills Crossing
Ranger Station
Jabiluka Mineral Lease
Kakadu National Park
Magela Plain
Munmarlary
Shady Camp
Four Mile Hole
CSIRO Kapalga Field Research Station
Wildman River
West Alligator River
South Alligator River
4WD only
Park Headquarters & Bowali Visitors Centre
Ranger Uranium Mine
Magela Creek
Mamukala
Malabanjbanjdju
Jabiru
Burdulba
Mary River National Park
Two Mile Hole
Aurora Kakadu Resort
36
Northern Entry Station
Arnhem Hwy
To Darwin (132km)
Red Lily Billabong
Warradjan Aboriginal Cultural Centre
Alligator Billabong
Yellow Water
Muirella Park
Gubara
Nourlangie Rock
Koongarra Mineral Lease
Cooinda
Mirrai Lookout
Mardugal
Jim Jim Billabong
Sandy Billabong
Nourlangie Creek
Old Jim Jim Rd 4WD only
Giyamungkurr (Black Jungle Springs)
Kakadu Hwy
Barramundi
4WD only
Jim Jim Creek
Mary River National Park
21
Graveside Gorge
South
Gungurul
Maguk
Creek
Alligator
Jim Jim Falls
Twin Falls
Mary River
Gunlom (Waterfall Creek) Falls
Koolpin Creek
Jarrangbarnmi (Koolpin Gorge)
Bukbukluk
River
Kambolie
Yurmikmik
Southern Entry & Ranger Station
Mt Wells
Park Entry Gate
Mary River Roadhouse
Gimbat
Coronation Hill
Kakadu Hwy
21
Kakadu National Park
ARNHEM LAND
ABORIGINAL LAND
To Darwin (233km)
Emerald Springs
Pine Creek
Stuart Hwy
To Umbrawarra Gorge Nature Park
1
To Katherine (90km)
Crocodiles inhabit rivers, billabongs and estuaries in tropical areas; swimming is not recommended.

GEOGRAPHY

The circuitous Arnhem Land escarpment, a dramatic 30m- to 200m-high sandstone cliff line, forms the natural boundary between Kakadu and Arnhem Land and winds some 500km through eastern and southeastern Kakadu.

Kakadu is a botanist's dream, with more than 1600 different plant species and several habitats including: savanna woodlands, monsoon forests, stone country, flood plains, billabongs, tidal flats, coast, and southerly hills and ridges.

Creeks cut across the rocky plateau and, in the Wet, tumble off the escarpment as thundering waterfalls, then flow across the lowlands to swamp the vast flood plains of Kakadu. As the waters recede in the Dry, some loops of wet-season watercourses become cut off, but don't dry up. These are billabongs, which are often carpeted with water lilies and are a magnet for water birds.

The coastal zone has long stretches of mangrove swamp that are important breeding grounds for fish and other wildlife. The southern part of the park is comprised of dry lowlands with open grassland, eucalypts and pockets of monsoon rainforest. More than 80% of Kakadu is savanna woodland.

JABILUKA MINE

A uranium mine in a World Heritage Area? Only in Australia.

Uranium was discovered at Jabiluka in 1971, and an agreement to mine (later condemned as somewhat dodgy) was negotiated with the Aboriginal people of the area. Mining was delayed by federal politics, however, and didn't get underway until government approval in 1996.

The Jabiluka mine was the scene of widespread protests and sit-in demonstrations during 1998, which resulted in massive numbers of arrests. A delegation from Unesco inspected the mine site and reported that the mine would endanger Kakadu's World Heritage listing.

The continuing level of controversy over the mine proposal, a depressed international uranium market, and an inability to form a new agreement with the traditional owners, made the mining of Jabiluka less viable. Multinational mining company, Rio Tinto, called off mining here in 2002.

ROCK ART

Kakadu is one of Australia's richest and most accessible repositories of rock art. There are more than 5000 sites, with some as old as 50,000 years and some as recent as 40 years. The vast majority of these sites are off limits or inaccessible, but two of the finest collections are the galleries at Ubirr and Nourlangie.

For the local Aboriginal people, the rock-art sites are a major source of traditional knowledge and form a tangible historical archive.

WILDLIFE

Kakadu boasts about 25 species of frogs, 55 freshwater fish species, 64 types of mammals, 120 types of reptiles, 290 species of bird (one-third of those are native to Australia) and at least 10,000 kinds of insects. There are frequent additions to the list and a few of the rarer species are unique to the park. For more-detailed information about Kakadu's animal species check out Lonely Planet's *Watching Wildlife Australia.*

Orientation

The sealed Arnhem Hwy stretches 120km east from the Stuart Hwy to the Kakadu park entrance and another 107km to Jabiru. The Kakadu Hwy (also sealed) to Nourlangie, Cooinda and Pine Creek turns south off the Arnhem Hwy shortly before Jabiru.

Information

Park admission fees were removed in 2005.

Bowali visitors centre (☎ 08-8938 1121; Kakadu Hwy; kakadunationalpark@ea.gov.au; 8am-5pm) draws on 'gukburlerri' (Aboriginal) and 'guhbele' (non-Aboriginal) perspectives to explain the park's ecology, seasons and management. Step into the cool video room where various documentaries are shown hourly from 8.30am to 3.30pm. This well-designed centre also houses a café, gift shop and library.

Warradjan Aboriginal Cultural Centre (☎ 08-8979 0051; 9am-5pm), near Cooinda, is a celebration of Aboriginality and its culture, with a focus on local clans and languages. There's a gallery and café attached. Pick up a copy of the official *Visitor's Guide*, with maps, here.

Fuel is available at Aurora Kakadu Resort, Border Store (Ubirr), Jabiru, Cooinda and Mary River Roadhouse (just outside the park). Jabiru also has a supermarket, post office and Westpac bank. The **Northern Land Council office** (☎ 08-8979 2410) in Jabiru issues permits (A$14) on the spot for the highly recommended trip to the Injalak Arts & Crafts Centre in Oenpelli (Gunbalanya), a 30-minute trip into Arnhem Land across the East Alligator River.

Free ranger talks are conducted throughout Kakadu during the Dry. The official Kakadu website (www.deh.gov.au/parks/kakadu) is jam-packed with information about the park.

Sights

UBIRR

Located in the East Alligator region, Ubirr is an outlying outcrop of the Arnhem escarpment. It's famous for its spectacular Aboriginal **rock-art site** (🕒 8am-sunset Apr-Nov, 2pm-sunset Dec-Mar), and for some of the best panoramic views in Kakadu, at **Narab Lookout**. Ubirr lies 39km north of the Arnhem Hwy.

Guluyambi Cruises (☎ 1800 089 113; 1¾-hr tours per adult A$40) runs comprehensive Aborigine-guided cruises on the East Alligator River. The cruises rival the well-known Yellow Waters options at Cooinda. The tours depart from the upstream boat ramp at 9am, 11am, 1pm and 3pm from May to November. In the wet season alternative cruises operate on the Magela wetlands; ring to inquire.

JABIRU

The township of Jabiru, 250km east of Darwin, is Kakadu's major service centre, with a bank, newsagent, medical centre, supermarket, bakery, service station and Olympic-sized pool (adult swim A$2.70). About 6km northeast is Jabiru airport and the Ranger uranium mine.

NOURLANGIE

As you approach Nourlangie Rock, the sheer vertical enormity of the escarpment is overwhelming. This is Kakadu's most famous site renowned for its Aboriginal rock-art galleries associated with Namarrgon (Lightning Man).

You reach Nourlangie at the end of a 12km sealed road that turns east off Kakadu Hwy 21km south of Arnhem Hwy. The road is open from 8am to sunset daily.

A 1.5km circular walk takes you first to the **Anbangbang rock shelter**, where Aboriginal people lived during the Wet. Look for circular markings on rocks in the shelter, which reveal where Aboriginal people ground seeds for food and ochre to make paint. A series of open-air galleries leads to **Gunwarddehwardde Lookout**, from where you can see the start of the Arnhem Land escarpment – the land of Lightning Dreaming.

The 12km **Barrk walk** takes you over the top of Nourlangie Rock and is an excellent walk in the Wet season.

Other nearby sights of interest back towards the highway include the gorgeous **Anbangbang billabong** (seen in *Crocodile Dundee*), **Nawurlandja lookout**, **Nanguluwurr** rock gallery and **Gubara** (Baroalba Springs), an area of shaded pools in monsoonal forest at the end of a 3km walking track.

JIM JIM FALLS & TWIN FALLS

These two spectacular waterfalls are along a 4WD dry-season track that turns south off the Kakadu Hwy between the Nourlangie and Cooinda turn-offs. It's about 57km along this road to Jim Jim Falls past towering sandstone walls (the last 1km on foot), and a further 10km to Twin Falls. The grandeur of these deep gorges will leave you breathless, and both are best seen in the early Dry when some water still flows over the falls. The only way to see them in the Wet is from the air (see Scenic Flights, p344).

In early 2004 the traditional owners and the Kakadu Board of Management decided that swimming at the base of Twin Falls – an extremely popular activity – should stop due to cultural reasons and safety concerns (the number of estuarine crocodiles moving into the Twin Falls Gorge each wet season had increased). Consequently, access to Twin Falls is by boat shuttle service, and a walking track on boulders, sand and a 400m boardwalk. Swimming is only allowed at the top of the escarpment. Visits to Twin Falls are for two hours only.

YELLOW WATER & COOINDA

The turn-off to the Cooinda accommodation complex and the superb Yellow Water wetlands is 47km down the Kakadu Hwy from its junction with the Arnhem Hwy.

The **boat trip** (☎ 1800 500 401, 8979 0111; tour .res@gagadjulodgecooinda.com.au) on Yellow Water Billabong is one of the more sedate highlights of a visit to Kakadu but you'll witness the amazing birdlife and even the odd giant croc. The dawn trip is the best. Two-hour cruises cost A$45 per adult and depart at 6.45am, 9am and 4.30pm. Shorter (1½-hour) cruises leave at 11.30am, 1.15pm and 2.45pm and cost A$40. During the Wet, 1½-hour cruises at the same cost depart at 8.30am, 11.45am, 1.30pm and 3.30pm. Book your cruise the day before at Cooinda Lodge, especially for the early departure.

COOINDA TO PINE CREEK

Just south of the Yellow Water and Cooinda turn-off, the Kakadu Hwy heads southwest out of the park on the Stuart Hwy to Pine Creek, 160km away. On the way there is a turn-off to the superb escarpment waterfall and clear plunge pool at **Gunlom** (Waterfall Creek) – another *Crocodile Dundee* location. It's 37km from the turn-off, along a good dirt road.

Activities

BUSHWALKING

Kakadu has rewarding but tough bushwalking country. Many people will be satisfied with the marked tracks, which range from 1km to 12km in length. For the more adventurous there are infinite possibilities, especially in the drier southern and eastern sections of the park. Follow the lore of bushwalking – prepare well, tell people where you're going and don't walk alone. And keep up the fluids! You'll need a permit from the **Bowali visitors centre** (☎ 08-8938 1121; Kakadu Hwy; kakadunationalpark@ea.gov.au; ⏲ 8am-5pm) to camp outside established camp sites. For overnight bushwalks, you must have a walking companion and apply for a permit at the same centre, providing a topographical map reference outlining your route.

Parks Australia's *Kakadu by Foot* (A$3.30) is a helpful guide to the marked walking tracks in Kakadu (available at the Bowali visitors centre).

Tours

All meals are generally included in the tour price, and some operators offer discounts to VIP, Youth Hostels Association (YHA) and Nomads members. For more information on Kakadu tours contact the **Jabiru Travel Centre** (☎ 08-8979 2548).

Adventure Tours Australia (☎ 1300 654 604, 08-8309 2277; www.adventuretours.com.au) See Kakadu's seasonal best on a range safari trip (two/three days from A$320/450).

Kakadu Animal Tracks (☎ 08-8979 0145; www .animaltracks.com.au; adult A$95) Gets rave reviews from our readers. Search for wildlife, gather bush tucker and have a sunset campfire cook-up. These seven-hour tours depart from Cooinda at 1pm (May to October).

Kakadu Gorge & Waterfall Tours (☎ 08-8979 0111, 08-8979 0145) Trips to Jim Jim Falls and Twin Falls.

Lord's Kakadu & Arnhem Land Safaris (☎ 08-8948 2200; www.lords-safaris.com) All-inclusive trips into Arnhem Land (to Gunbalanya) for A$180.

Magela Cultural & Heritage Tours (☎ 08-8979 2114; magela@austarnet.com.au; adult incl lunch & permit A$185) Highly regarded small-group 4WD day tours from Jabiru, including the 'Arnhemlander' tour.

Wilderness 4WD Adventures (☎ 1300 666 100, 08-8981 8363; www.wildernessadventures.com.au) Four-wheel drive camping tours into Kakadu (three/five days A$450/670). Emphasis on fun.

Xplore Backpacker Wilderness Tours (☎ 1300 136 133) Go 4WD touring, backpacker style (three/five days A$420/690).

SCENIC FLIGHTS

The view of Kakadu from the air is spectacular. Try these operators:

Kakadu Air (☎ 1800 089 113; kakair@kakair.com.au) Half-/one-hour fixed-wing flights for A$90/150.

North Australian Helicopters (☎ 1800 898 977; www .northaustralianhelicopters.com.au) Half-hour helicopter tours of the escarpment and Minkinj Valley for around A$170, or you can go sky-high on a flight over Jim Jim Falls and Twin Falls for around A$420.

Sleeping & Eating

Prices for accommodation in Kakadu can vary tremendously depending on the season or where you decide to stay – camping under the starry skies is a fantastic option (see the boxed text on opposite).

SOUTH ALLIGATOR

Aurora Kakadu Resort (☎ 1800 818 845, 08-8979 0166; kakadu@aurora-resorts.com.au; Arnhem Hwy; camp sites per person A$7.50, bar mains A$6.50-25, restaurant mains A$15-27; ❄ 🏊) This resort is set in sprawling gardens that are made for camping. It also has a tennis court and barbecue area, and comfy hotel rooms are available. Same-sex shared budget rooms are available for A$20 per adult, or A$80 per room. Rooms have a bar

CAMPING UNDER THE STARS IN KAKADU

Kakadu is the ideal place for camping in the dry season. Although you can pitch a tent on the manicured lawns of the Aurora Kakadu Resort (opposite), Kakadu Lodge (below) or Gagadju Lodge (below), the best way to appreciate nature here is to set up camp at one of the 18 designated areas. Most of these sites are free, but there five larger camping areas that have showers, flush toilets and running water and cost A$5.40 per adult per night. To camp away from a designated site, you need a permit from the **Bowali visitors centre** (☎ 08-8938 1121; Kakadu Hwy; kakadunationalpark@ea.gov.au; 🕑 8am-5pm).

The five main national park camping areas are: Merl, near the Border Store at Ubirr; Muirella Park, a few kilometres south of the Nourlangie turn-off and then 6km off the Kakadu Hwy; Mardugal, just off the Kakadu Hwy 1.5km south of the Cooinda turn-off; Garnamarr near Jim Jim Falls; and Gunlom, in the southern part of the park. Only the Mardugal site is open during the Wet.

There are 14 free camping areas throughout the park. The most basic (with no toilets or facilities) are: Two Mile Hole, Four Mile Hole, Red Lily Billabong, Bucket Billabong and Alligator Billabong. The other free camping areas have pit toilets but no showers or running water. Malabanjbanjdju and Burdulba are camping sites near Jabiru. You can also go bush at Waldak Irrmbal (West Alligator Head), Sandy Billabong (near Nourlangie Rock), Jim Jim Billabong (near Yellow Water) and Giyamungkurr (Black Jungle Springs; permit required) on the Old Jim Jim Rd. At the southern end of the park are Maguk, Kambolie and Jarrangbarnmi (Koolpin Gorge). For more information check with the Bowali visitors centre.

and a fridge, and linen is provided. Splurge at the restaurant or eat on the cheap at the bar.

UBIRR

Kakadu Hostel (☎ 08-8979 2232; dm A$25, d & tw A$65; ❄ 🅿) Kakadu's only true backpacker hostel. This simple place has rooms with two to 14 beds, a communal kitchen and a lounge room.

The **Border Store** (☎ 08-8979 2474) has supplies and fuel and its café serves lunch.

JABIRU

Kakadu Lodge with Caravan Park (☎ 1800 811 154, 08-8979 2422; www.aurora-resorts.com.au; Jabiru Dr; camp sites unpowered/powered per 2 people A$20/25, dm A$31, mains A$10-22; 🕑 breakfast, lunch & dinner; ❄ 💻 🅿) This excellent resort has shady grassed sites, and the comfortable cabins share facilities. There are coin-operated barbecues, a camp kitchen (no utensils) and laundry facilities. Book ahead for dorm beds.

Lakeview Park Bush Bungalows (☎ 08-8979 3144; www.lakeviewkakadu.com.au; 27 Lakeview Dr; bush bungalows Wet/Dry A$70/85) The safari-style fan-cooled rooms here sleep up to four people. The facilities are shared and guests have the use of a fridge, barbecues and a laundry.

COOINDA

Gagadju Lodge Cooinda (☎ 1800 500 401, 08-8979 0145; reservations@gagadjulodgecooinda.com.au; Kakadu Hwy; camp sites unpowered/powered per 2 people A$15/28, dm A$31; ❄ 🅿) A busy camping ground with dongas. Fuel, basic supplies, insect repellent (you'll need it!) and film are sold at the shop.

Barra Bistro (mains A$12.50-23; 🕑 lunch & dinner) Dishes out largish but ordinary buffet meals, and fast food nosh is sold near the bar.

Getting There & Around

Ideally, take your own vehicle. In the Dry you can easily get to most sites in a conventional vehicle, excluding Jim Jim Falls, which is also off limits to many 4WD hire vehicles (check your policy).

It's possible to explore Kakadu and its surrounds by getting around with a bus pass to Jabiru, Ubirr and/or Cooinda and combining this with a trip to Jim Jim Falls and/or Twin Falls, the Yellow Waters cruise and/or an Aboriginal cultural tour.

Camping gear can be hired inexpensively (and with free delivery) in Darwin from **Gone Bush** (☎ 0413-757 000; gonebush@octa4.net.au).

McCafferty's/Greyhound (☎ 13 20 30) has a daily return service between Darwin and Cooinda via Jabiru. Tickets cost A$55/105 one way/return.

Plenty of tours (p331) depart from Darwin for Kakadu – some combining Kakadu with Mary River, Litchfield National Park, Katherine and Arnhem Land.

ARNHEM LAND

Mysterious and remote, Arnhem Land Aboriginal Reserve is a continuation of Kakadu east to the Gulf of Carpentaria. It's a vast, sparsely inhabited area owned solely by Aboriginal people. Clans living throughout Arnhem Land fish, hunt animals and gather seasonal plants. Pristine scenery and numerous rock-art sites are major attractions but Arnhem Land is virtually closed to independent travellers, apart from Oenpelli (Gunbalanya), just across the East Alligator River in Kakadu, the remote Garig Gunak Barlu (formerly Gurig) National Park (on the Cobourg Peninsula at the northwest corner) and Gove or Nhulunbuy (the peninsula at the northeast corner). For more information visit East Arnhem Land Tourism Association website: www.ealta.org.

Tours

Birds Bees Trees & Things (☎ 08-8987 1814; www.birdsbeestreesandthings.com.au) Go spearfishing, harvest yam or learn about indigenous art. Tours depart from Nhulunbuy (from A$100 per adult).

Arnhem Land Tours (☎ 1800 089 113) Daily departures from Jabiru and Cooinda (A$185 per adult).

Nomad Charters (☎ 8987 8085; www.nomadcharters.com.au) Half-day fishing safaris from A$180 per person.

See also Magela Cultural & Heritage Tours (p344) and Lord's Kakadu & Arnhem Land Safaris (p344).

KATHERINE REGION

Make a beeline for Nitmiluk National Park and paddle a canoe through awe-inspiring Katherine Gorge between towering rock walls. This is one of the NT's real treats.

KATHERINE

☎ 08 / pop 6720

Katherine itself is a 'one-street' kind of town, but it's real attraction is the ravishing Nitmiluk National Park, 30km away.

There's an edginess about Katherine. You'll most likely find that it makes a striking contrast to the images of Aboriginal ecotourism promoted by glossy tourist brochures. However, it's certainly a great place to buy a didgeridoo.

Terrible floods ripped through Katherine on Australia Day in 1998. Apparently the flood waters could have filled an empty Sydney Harbour in just nine hours. A crocodile was even spotted cruising down the submerged aisles at Woolworths!

Orientation & Information

The Stuart Hwy makes its way through town, becoming Katherine's main street, Katherine Tce. Giles St, the road to Nitmiluk National Park, branches off to the northeast in the middle of town. Katherine's airport is 8km south of town.

Katherine Visitor Information Centre (☎ 1800 653 142, 8972 2650; www.krta.com.au; cnr Stuart Hwy & Lindsay St; 🕓 8.30am-5pm Mon-Fri, 9am-2pm Sat & Sun Apr-Nov) is packed with information. The town's **transit centre** is opposite on Katherine Tce. The major banks, with ATMs, line Katherine Tce.

Katherine hospital (☎ 8973 9211; Giles St) is about 2.5km north of the town, and the **police station** (☎ 8972 0111; Stuart Hwy) is southeast of town.

Sights & Activities

Katherine Low Level Nature Park, by Katherine River 5km from town, beckons swimmers in the Dry. A bike/walking path links the nature park with town and passes Katherine's bubbling **thermal pools**, which have wheelchair access.

Katherine Museum (☎ 8972 3945; katherinemuseum@bigpond.com; Gorge Rd; adult A$3.50; 🕓 10am-4pm Mon-Fri & to 1pm Sat Mar-Oct, 10am-1pm Mon-Sat Nov-Feb, 2-5pm Sun year-round) is on the way to Nitmiluk National Park. It gives a fascinating insight into the region's past, from its famous cattle empires to its wartime bombing in 1942. The Gypsy Moth biplane flown by Dr Clyde Fenton, the pioneering flying doctor, is housed here.

Take an excursion to the world's largest classroom (strictly during tour times) at the **School of the Air** (☎ 1800 653 142, 8972 1833; www.schools.nt.edu.au/ksa; Giles St; adult A$5; 🕓 tours 9am, 10am & 11am Mon-Fri, mid-Mar–Nov only, closed school holidays). This is an opportunity to see how kids in the remote outback are taught. Listen in on a live lesson on the guided tour (45 minutes).

Tours

Gecko Canoeing (☎ 1800 634 319, 8972 2224; www.geckocanoeing.com.au) Extended canoe trips along the Katherine River. All-inclusive one-/three-day trips cost A$155/595. A 10-day 'Escarpment & River Escape' combines hiking along the awesome Jatbula Trail (p348) in Nitmiluk National Park with canoeing (A$1980).

North Australian Helicopters (☎ 1800 089 103, 8972 1253; www.northaustralianhelicopters.com.au) Fly over Nitmiluk from A$60 per person.

Travel North (☎ 1800 089 103, 8971 9999; www.travelnorth.com.au; Transit Centre, Katherine Tce) Tour options galore in the Katherine area, including a Crocodile Night Adventure (A$44 per adult).

Sleeping

Discounts are available at most hostels to YHA/VIP members, and the hostels generally offer free transfers from the transit centre.

Kookaburra Lodge Backpackers (☎ 1800 808 211, 8971 0257; www.kookaburrabackpackers.com.au; cnr Lindsay & Third Sts; dm/tw A$20/55;) Nothing much to look at, but the friendly owners (and 'Scully' the resident terrier) are very welcoming. There are dorm 'units' with kitchens and a free pancake brekkie each morning, plus table tennis and a tour booking service. Bike hire is available (half-/full day A$10/15).

Victoria Lodge (☎ 1800 808 875, 8972 3464; 21 Victoria Hwy; dm/d A$18/55;) This distinctive red-brick hostel has vaguely modern rooms with muted hues. It's cheap and cheerful, with a kitchen and bathroom for each shared 'unit'.

Katherine River Lodge (☎ 1800 800 188; www.katherineriverlodge.net; Giles St; 50 Giles St; budget tw A$40, standard d A$70;) There are a couple of decent budget rooms here, with bathroom, fridge and TV. They're ideal for backpackers – you're basically getting the same deal as the motel rooms but much cheaper!

Palm Court Backpackers (☎ 1800 626 722, 8972 2722; www.travelnorth.com.au; cnr Third & Giles St; dm/tw A$18/50;) The motel-style rooms here are popular but pretty basic. There's a shared kitchen and barbecue area, and all dorms have bathrooms. Double rooms also have fridges.

Coco's Accommodation, Music & Art (☎ 8971 2889; coco@21firstst.com; 21 First St; camp sites per 2 people A$9, dm A$16;) A popular stop on the cycling circuit. A hippy crowd stays at this ramshackle place, and there's a great didgeridoo and art showroom attached.

Knotts Crossing Resort (☎ 1800 222 511, 8972 2511; www.knottscrossing.com.au; cnr Giles & Cameron Sts; camp sites unpowered/powered per 2 people A$20/25, cabins from A$75, village room A$90;) Tropical gardens, efficient service and excellent facilities. Self-contained cabins are bright and have detached bathrooms – the cabins are similar to (but cheaper than) the village rooms.

Shady Lane Tourist Park (☎ 8971 0491; www.shadylanetouristpark.com.au; 1828 Gorge Rd; camp sites unpowered/powered per 2 people A$20/23, cabins A$50-90;) Palm-fringed grounds towards Nitmiluk National Park, with exceptionally clean facilities. The budget rooms offer privacy and the free-standing cabins are a step up in quality.

SPLURGE!

Jan's B&B (☎ 8971 1005; jcomleybbaccom@yahoo.com.au; 13 Pearce St; shared guesthouse s/d A$33/85, B&B s/d A$110/160;) The nondescript street doesn't sell this B&B particularly well but inside the gates you'll find rather decadent accommodation that's well-suited to those seeking a homey atmosphere with all the mod-cons. Plush rooms share bathroom facilities and guests are welcome to use the pool table, piano, lounge area, spa and kitchen.

Eating

Katherine is by no means 'foodie central' but there are a few good-value choices to keep you ticking over.

If you're self-catering, **Woolworth's** (Katherine Tce; 7am-10pm) is the cheapest place for supplies for hundreds of kilometres around. It has a liquor shop and a bakery.

Stockman's Camp Tucker Night (☎ 0427-112 806; Katherine Museum grounds, Gorge Rd; dinner Tue & Thu) Try this for something different – for A$35 per person you can sample camp-oven delights like kangaroo stew and damper. Dinner is served at 6pm.

Katie's Bistro (☎ 8972 2511; Knotts Crossing Resort, cnr Giles & Cameron Sts; mains A$16-25; dinner) Part alfresco, part à la carte, you'll get obliging service and carefully presented meals from chilli prawns (A$25) to Parisian-style croc (entrée/main A$14/24) at this bustling bistro. A big tick goes to the couscous patties served with Greek salad (A$17). There is a 'tropical' barbecue on Sunday, and a buffet dinner (A$20 per person) on Monday.

Diggers Den (☎ 8971 0422; Victoria Hwy; mains A$14-A$25; lunch & dinner) All-you-can-eat pizza, pasta and salad (A$9.90) at this low-key hang-out on Thursday. There's also a pasta and schooner backpacker special for

A$7 on presentation of a voucher from your hostel.

Starvin' (☎ 8972 3633; 32 Katherine Tce; mains A$13-18; 🕑 from 3.30pm Mon-Sat) Vegetarians are well catered for at this café dedicated to all things Italian. Try a pizza topped with king prawns (A$15).

Kumbidgee Lodge Tea Rooms (☎ 8971 0699; Giles St; mains A$6-18; 🕑 breakfast, lunch & dinner) Favoured by locals on Sunday afternoon, this run-down but likable spot can be found along the gorge road. The ample 'bush brekkie' (A$12) will give you enough fuel to canoe Nitmiluk (Katherine Gorge).

Entertainment

Get into some live music at **Diggers Den** (☎ 8971 0422; Victoria Hwy) every Friday night at 8pm, and on Sunday afternoon.

Catch the latest blockbuster at **Katherine Cinema 3** (☎ 8971 2522; www.katherinecinemas.com.au; 20 First St; adult/student A$13/9.70), preferably on Wednesday when all tickets are A$9.20.

Getting There & Away

All buses stop at Katherine's transit centre. Typical fares from Katherine include Alice Springs (A$190, 15 hours), Darwin (A$65, four hours) and Kununurra (A$100, four hours).

The **Ghan** (☎ 13 21 47; www.gsr.com.au) train goes from Adelaide to Darwin (one-way economy seat/twin-berth sleeper A$440/1390) but stops in Katherine en route. It's possible to do a gorge cruise before pushing on: the train stops in Katherine for four hours enabling passengers to do a two hour cruise. Train staff take bookings; prebookings are not available. Cruises are paid for on arrival and include transfers.

NITMILUK FAST FACTS

- Title of the land was handed back to the Jawoyn people in 1989. A 99-year lease guarantees them traditional rights over the area.
- Katherine River is home to around 45 fish species and 168 species of birds.
- Part of Australia's first colour feature film, Charles Chauvel's *Jedda*, which was also the first film to cast Aboriginal actors in leading roles, was filmed at Nitmiluk.
- The gorge was formed 20 to 25 million years ago.

AROUND KATHERINE

Nitmiluk (Katherine Gorge) National Park

Straddled between the Territory's monsoonal tropics and arid zone, stunning Nitmiluk is 13 gorges – or one continuous cleft spanning 15km depending on who you ask – carved out by the Katherine River. The gorge walls aren't high but they are rugged and colourful. During the Dry the gorge waters are calm, but from November to March they can become a raging torrent, so swimming and canoeing are restricted.

INFORMATION

The **Nitmiluk Centre** (☎ 08-8972 1253; 🕑 7am-7pm Dry, 7am-4pm Wet), at the gorge, is an imaginative and interactive information centre. There's also a desk for the **Parks & Wildlife Commission of the Northern Territory** (☎ 08-8972 1886), which has information sheets on the marked walking tracks. As a safety precaution, you must register here between 7am and 1pm for overnight walks (refundable deposit of A$50 required), and for extended canoeing trips and camping (A$3.30 per person per night).

SLEEPING & EATING

Nitmiluk Caravan Park (☎ 08-8972 3150; camp sites unpowered/powered per 2 people A$18/22) Right next to the gorge entrance, this often-crowded caravan park has plenty of grass and shade, as well as showers, toilets, barbecues and a laundry. Wallabies and goannas are frequent visitors at dusk. You can book and pay at the visitors centre.

Fast food–oriented **Nitmiluk Café** (Nitmiluk Centre; mains A$7.50-10.50; 🕑 breakfast & lunch) has indoor-outdoor seating, and there's a gift shop where you can pick up film.

ACTIVITIES

Bushwalking

There are fantastic marked bushwalking tracks in the park. The one-way **Jatbula Trail** (subject to closure October to May) is a sensational 66km, five-day hike over the Arnhem Land escarpment from Nitmiluk National Park to Leliyn (Edith Falls). There isn't any transport at the end of the track, so pre-arrange your pick-up. Map NT's semidetailed topographic *Nitmiluk National Park Map* (A$6.60), available at the Parks & Wildlife Commission desk within the visitor information centre, is invaluable on extended walks in the park.

Canoeing

Self-guided paddling along the gorge is extremely popular with backpackers. In the Dry you may have to drag your canoe over rocks to get from one gorge to the next. Don't expect to paddle to the 13th gorge in a day, either.

Nitmiluk Tours (☎ 1800 089 103, 08-8972 1253; www.travelnorth.com.au) hires out single/double canoes from the boat ramp for a half-day (A$33/50) or full day (A$45/70). Three-day guided canoeing trips are also available (A$500, departing Tuesday). The boat ramp is by the main car park, about 500m beyond the Nitmiluk Centre.

See also Tours on p346.

TOURS

Nitmiluk Tours (☎ 1800 089 103, 08-8972 1253; www.travelnorth.com.au) has a two-hour gorge cruise from the boat ramp to the second gorge and a rock-art gallery. It leaves at 9am, 11am, 1pm and 3pm daily and costs A$40 per adult. Half- and full-day trips are also available. It's best to go on one of the cooler morning trips.

GETTING THERE & AWAY

It's 30km by sealed road from Katherine to the Nitmiluk Centre and gorge. **Travel North** (☎ 1800 089 103, 08-8972 1044) shuttles run from Katherine's transit centre to the gorge at 8am, 12.15pm and 4.15pm and make the return trip at 9am, 1pm and 5pm (subject to demand). One-way/return fare is A$14/21.

Leliyn (Edith Falls)

Also in Nitmiluk National Park, but reached via a turn-off from the Stuart Hwy about 43km north of Katherine and 20km down a sealed road, these pretty **falls** cascade through three pools to the pandanus-lined Sweetwater Pool. The ranger-staffed **Leliyn Camp Ground** (☎ 08-8975 4869; camp site per person A$8) at the main pool has grassed camp sites, toilets and hot showers. The kiosk sells snacks.

Manyallaluk Aboriginal Community

This **community** (☎ 08-8975 4727; www.manyallaluk.com; camp sites per 2 people A$17.60; Apr-Nov only) is about 80km east of Katherine (35km is unsealed road) and offers highly regarded **cultural tours** (full-day tours per adult with/without transfers from Katherine A$143/110); in association with Odyssey Tours. Take the opportunity to see how this friendly community, consisting of three indigenous groups, have lived for centuries. The community isn't accessible to tourists in the wet season.

Adelaide & Around

CONTENTS

HIGHLIGHTS

- **Kangaroo Island** Explore the rugged coastlines, and see the abundant wildlife and sealife in this natural environment (p371)
- **Barossa Valley** Pose as a wine connoisseur (p363)
- **Cuisine** Feast on Adelaide's top quality yet inexpensive cuisine (p358)
- **Festivals** Get cultured at one of Adelaide's abundant arts festivals (p357)
- **Fleurieu Peninsula** Watch for dolphins on the beaches of the peninsula (p370)
- **McLaren Vale** Cycle to cellar doors with a cheese box along the old railway line (p369)
- **Flinders Ranges** Take an awe-inspiring walk (p375)

- **Cheer for:** Port Power in the AFL (Aussie rules); refer to them as 'Port Adelaide' for added cred
- **Eat:** a pie floater
- **Drink:** a schooner (285mL) of Coopers
- **Listen to:** Superjesus' *Jet Age* or The Angels' Am I Ever Gonna See Your Face Again
- **Watch:** *Storm Boy* (boy meets pelican…)
- **Party at:** the east end of Rundle St, or the west end of Hindley St, in Adelaide (p360)
- **Swim at:** Henley beach (p356), near the city, pubs and cafés
- **Avoid:** drinking the tap water, king brown snakes
- **Locals' nickname:** Crow Eaters

- TELEPHONE CODE: 08
- WEBSITE: www.southaustralia.com

While South Australia (SA) is the driest state of Australia, it's also the most understated. Colonised by free settlers, the progressive state initiated the relaxing of many social and censorship laws and encouraged free expression (and the creation of Australia's first nudist beach). Culture and hedonism pervade the psyche with world-class festivals, celebrated wines and epicurean delights, which perhaps add to the general friendliness and lack of pretension. You too can head home with a high-brow education after sampling the wines at cellar doors in famed regions such as the Barossa Valley and McLaren Vale.

High on the ecotourism register, its wilderness areas are varied and accessible – from the ancient and majestic Flinders Ranges, to the wild coasts of Kangaroo Island, with its bountiful native flora and fauna. On the city's doorstep, the Adelaide Hills offer bushwalking and interaction with wildlife, including a bit of koala cuddling, amid atmospheric villages.

You'll often see dolphins on the stunning swimming and surfing beaches of the Fleurieu Peninsula, and even the occasional whale on its migratory path past Victor Harbor between June and October. If you've got time to cruise, take in the less-beaten path along the wild and rugged Southeast Coast.

For information on the opal mining outpost of Coober Pedy, in SA's arid north, see p455.

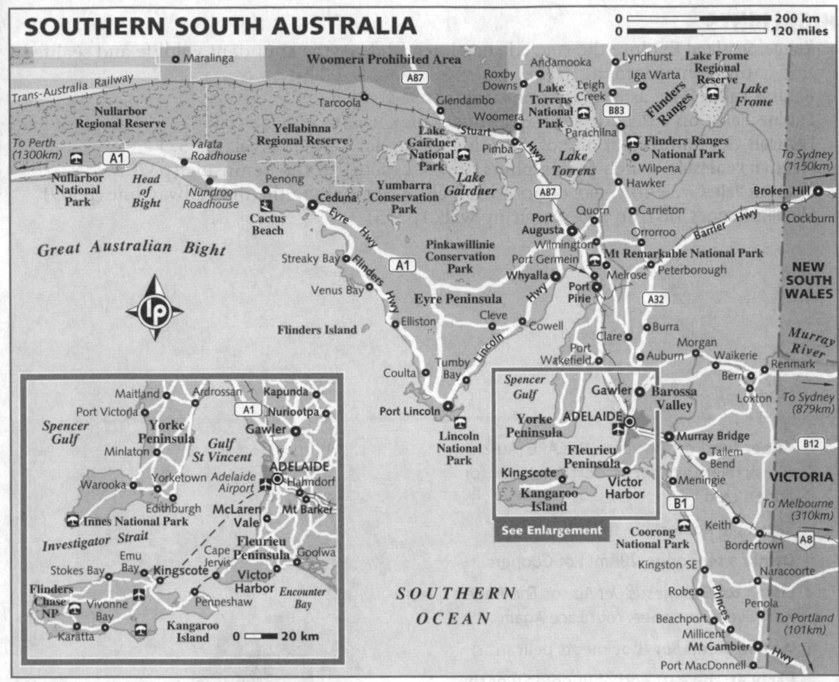

ADELAIDE

☎ 08 / pop 1,045,854

Cosmopolitan Adelaide is bordered by the enchanting hills of the Mt Lofty Ranges and the long, sandy beaches of Gulf St Vincent.

Early European colonists built with stone, pride and plenty of style a capital with a European feel encircled by green parklands. Successive settlers have provided a vibrant hedonistic spirit with varied cuisines, magnificent wines and numerous galas that celebrate a thriving arts community.

A good quality of life is affordable – even on a backpacker's budget – so indulge in the healthy live music and arts scene, and work on your tan on the stunning beaches.

ORIENTATION

Adelaide's compact city centre is laid out on an orderly grid bordered by North, East, South and West Tces. King William St is the main thoroughfare dissecting the city and most cross streets change their name here. Victoria Sq, the city's geographical centre, has bus stops and the Glenelg tram terminus. Franklin St, which runs off the square, contains Adelaide's central bus station.

Rundle St, lined with cafés, restaurants, bookshops, retro clothing shops and independent cinemas, is the social centre for all ages. Heading west the street becomes Rundle Mall, the main shopping strip. Across King William St, Rundle Mall turns into Hindley St, with its mix of bars, dance clubs and strip joints.

Elegant North Tce hosts a string of magnificent public buildings, including the art gallery, museum, state library and the University of Adelaide. Continue north and you're in the lush North Parklands, with the Festival Centre and the casino located in the historic train station; King William Rd then crosses into North Adelaide at the Torrens River, which has walking and cycling paths.

INFORMATION

Bookshops

Adelaide Booksellers (☎ 8410 0216; www.adelaidebooksellers.com.au; 1st fl, shop 6a, Rundle St Mall) Quality second-hand books.

Blue Beat (☎ 8410 7679; 109 Hindley St) Forget reading and seek out new sounds from the excellent and eclectic CD range.
Borders Books, Music & Café (☎ 8223 3333; 97 Rundle Mall) A vast collection of books and CDs.
Imprints Booksellers (☎ 8231 4454; 107 Hindley St) The booklover's bookshop.
Map Shop (☎ 8231 2033; cnr Peel & Hindley Sts) Good map selection.
Mary Martin's Bookshop (☎ 8359 3525; 249 Rundle St) An Adelaide institution.

Emergency
Ambulance (☎ 000, 13 29 62)
Fire (☎ 000, 8204 3600)
Lifeline (☎ 13 11 14, 8202 5820) 24-hour counselling.
Police (☎ 000, 8303 0525; 26 Hindley St)
RAA Emergency Roadside Assistance (☎ 13 11 11, 8202 4600)
Rape & Sexual Assault Service (☎ 8226 8777/87; 55 King William Rd, North Adelaide)

Internet Access
Most hostels offer Internet access, though prices vary. Other providers:
Kappy's Bettanet Internet Café (☎ 8294 8977; 55 Jetty Rd, Glenelg; per 15/60 min A$2/5; 🕑 7.30am-10.30pm) Fast connections attached to a great café.
State Library of SA (bookings ☎ 8207 7242; cnr North Tce & Kintore Ave; access free; 🕑 9.30am-8pm Mon-Wed & Fri, 9.30am-6pm Thu, noon-5pm Sat & Sun) Book ahead.
Zone Internet Café (☎ 8223 1947; 238 Rundle St; per min A$0.10; 🕑 9.30am-11pm)

Medical Services
Emergency Dental Service (☎ 8272 8111; 🕑 Sat, Sun & after hours) Provides dentist contact details.
Royal Adelaide Hospital (☎ 8222 4000; North Tce)
Simpsons Pharmacy (☎ 8231 6333; cnr West Tce & Waymouth St; 🕑 8am-midnight Mon-Fri, 9am-noon Sat & Sun)
Traveller's Medical & Vaccination Centre (☎ 8212 7522; 29 Gilbert Pl; 🕑 9am-5pm Mon-Fri, to 7pm Wed, 9am-12.30pm Sat)

Money
Banks and ATMs are prevalent throughout the city centre, particularly on and around Rundle Mall.

To change foreign currencies try **American Express** (Amex; ☎ 1300 139 060; Shop 32, Rundle Mall; 🕑 9am-5pm Mon-Fri, 9am-noon Sat) or **Thomas Cook** (☎ 8231 6977; Shop 4, Rundle Mall; 🕑 9am-5pm Mon-Fri, 10am-4pm Sat), or head to the airport or casino out of hours.

GETTING INTO TOWN

Adelaide airport is 7km west of the city centre.

Skylink (☎ 8332 0528; www.skylinkadelaide.com; one way A$7.50; bookings 🕑 7am-10pm) runs hourly shuttles between 5.30am and 9.30pm. If you're catching a flight on one of the smaller regional airlines, inform the driver. The shuttle also picks up passengers from the interstate train terminal (see p362).

A taxi charges around A$17 between the airport and city centre.

Post
Main post office (☎ 13 13 18; 141 King William St; 🕑 8am-5.30pm Mon-Fri, 9am-12.30pm Sat) Handles poste restante; have mail addressed to you c/o Poste Restante, Adelaide 5001.

Tourist Information
Disability Information & Resource Centre (DIRC; ☎ 8223 7522/79; www.dircsa.org.au; 195 Gilles St; 🕑 9am-5pm Mon-Fri) Provides information on accommodation, venues, tourist destinations and travel agencies for people with disabilities.
Information kiosk (King William St; 🕑 10am-5pm Mon-Thu, 10am-8pm Fri, 10am-3pm Sat, 11am-4pm Sun) This kiosk at the end of Rundle Mall provides Adelaide-specific information and free walking tours at 9.30am Monday to Friday.
South Australian Tourism Commission Visitors Centre (SATC; ☎ 1300 655 276, 8303 2033; www.southaustralia.com; 18 King William St; 🕑 8.30am-5pm Mon-Fri, 9am-2pm Sat & Sun) Abundantly stocked with leaflets and publications on Adelaide and SA. There's also a booking service and BASS ticket-selling outlet.
Visitors centre (☎ 8294 5833; Glenelg foreshore; 🕑 9am-5pm Mon-Fri, 10am-3pm Sat & Sun) Behind the Town Hall.

SIGHTS
The superbly curated **Art Gallery of South Australia** (☎ 8207 7000; www.artgallery.sa.gov.au; North Tce; admission free; 🕑 10am-5pm) represents all the big names in Australian art through the eras. It also has an impressive international art collection (including Rodin) and hosts temporary exhibitions. You could easily return here over a couple of days but if you've got limited time, perhaps start with the Australian galleries, featuring extensive Southern Australian landscapes. Guided tours (free)

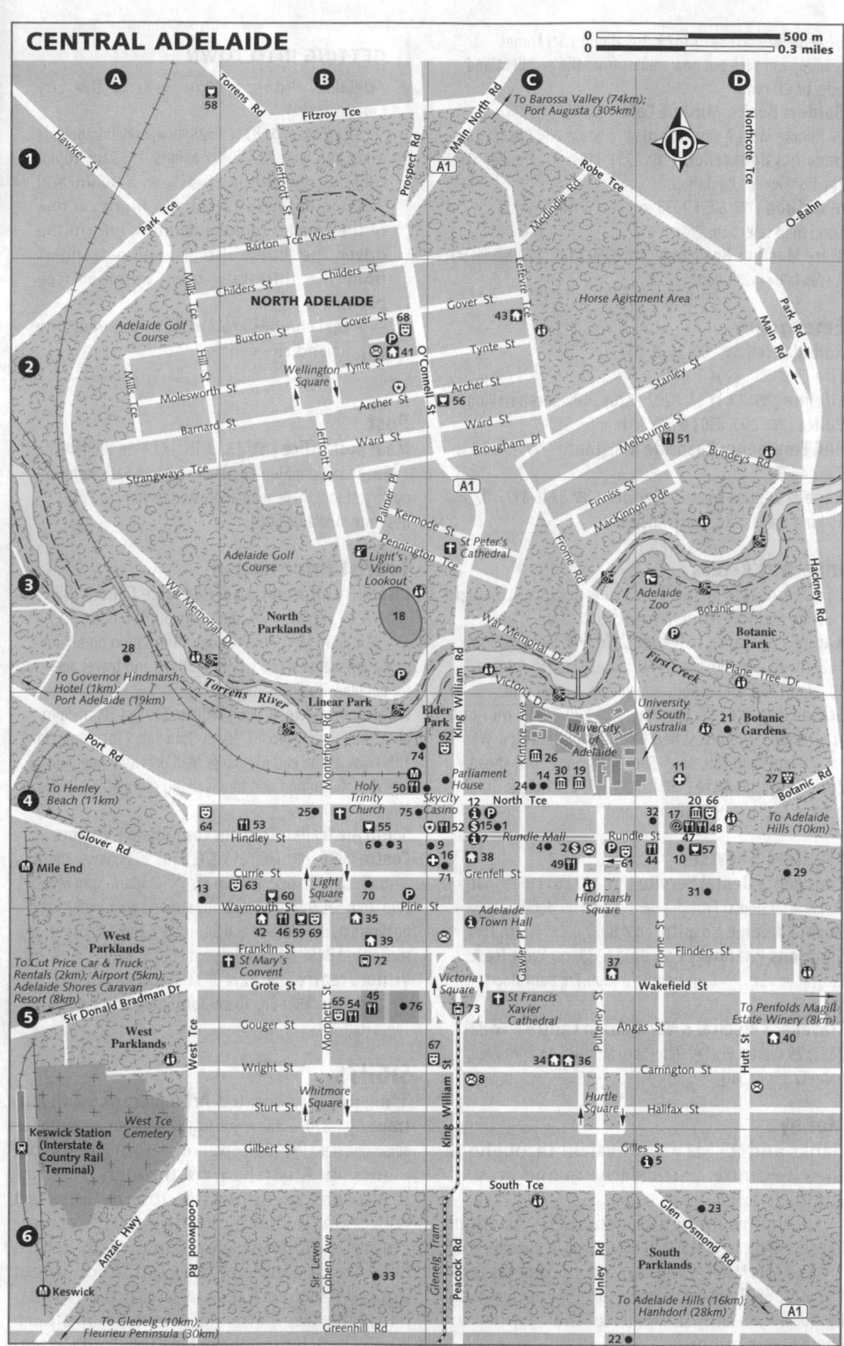
CENTRAL ADELAIDE
0 500 m
0 0.3 miles
To Barossa Valley (74km); Port Augusta (305km)
NORTH ADELAIDE
Horse Agistment Area
Adelaide Golf Course
Wellington Square
Light's Vision Lookout
St Peter's Cathedral
Adelaide Golf Course
North Parklands
Adelaide Zoo
Botanic Park
To Governor Hindmarsh Hotel (1km); Port Adelaide (19km)
Torrens River
Linear Park
Elder Park
University of Adelaide
University of South Australia
Botanic Gardens
To Henley Beach (11km)
Parliament House
Holy Trinity Church
Skycity Casino
Rundle Mall
To Adelaide Hills (10km)
Mile End
Light Square
Hindmarsh Square
Adelaide Town Hall
West Parklands
To Cut Price Car & Truck Rentals (2km); Airport (5km); Adelaide Shores Caravan Resort (8km)
St Mary's Convent
Victoria Square
St Francis Xavier Cathedral
To Penfolds Magill Estate Winery (8km)
West Parklands
Whitmore Square
Hurtle Square
Keswick Station (Interstate & Country Rail Terminal)
West Tce Cemetery
South Parklands
Keswick
To Adelaide Hills (16km); Hanhdorf (28km)
To Glenelg (10km); Fleurieu Peninsula (30km)
Glenelg Tram

INFORMATION
Adelaide Booksellers 1 C4
American Express 2 C4
BASS (see 12)
Blue Beat 3 B4
Borders Books, Music & Café 4 C4
Disability Information & Resource Centre 5 D6
Imprints Booksellers 6 B4
Information Kiosk 7 C4
Main Post Office 8 C5
Map Shop 9 C4
Mary Martin's Bookshop 10 D4
Royal Adelaide Hospital 11 D4
SATC Visitors Centre 12 C4
Simpsons Pharmacy 13 A4
State Library of SA 14 C4
Thomas Cook 15 C4
Traveller's Medical & Vaccination Centre 16 C4
Zone Internet Café 17 D4

SIGHTS & ACTIVITIES (pp353–6)
Adelaide Oval 18 B3
Art Gallery of South Australia 19 C4
Ayers Historic House 20 D4
Botanic Gardens 21 D4
Bradman Collection (see 24)
Haigh's Chocolates Visitors Centre 22 C6
Himeji Gardens 23 D6
Institute Building 24 C4
Jam Factory Contemporary Craft & Design 25 B4
Migration Museum 26 C4
National Wine Centre of Australia 27 D4
Old Adelaide Gaol 28 A3
Rymill Park 29 D4
South Australian Museum 30 C4
Tandanya 31 D4
Urban Cow Studio 32 D4
Veale Gardens 33 B6

SLEEPING (pp357–8)
Adelaide Backpackers Inn 34 C5
Adelaide Central YHA 35 B5
Adelaide Travellers Inn 36 C5
Backpack Oz 37 C5
Blue Galah Backpackers Hostel 38 C4
Cannon St Backpackers 39 B5
East Park Lodge 40 D5
Fire Station 41 B2
My Place 42 B5
Princes Lodge Motel 43 C2

EATING (pp358–60)
Austral Hotel 44 D4
Botanic Café (see 66)
Chinatown 45 B5
Coles Supermarket (see 76)
Cumberland Arms 46 B5
Exeter Hotel 47 D4
Falafel House 48 D4
Jasmin Indian Restaurant 49 C4
Ky Chow (see 45)
Lucia's Pizza & Spaghetti Bar (see 76)
Pie Cart 50 B4
Sprouts (see 49)
Store 51 D2
T Bar (see 76)
Thai in a Wok (see 49)
Vego and Lovin' It (see 17)
Wok-in-a-Box 52 C4
Worldsend Hotel 53 B4
Ying Chow Chinese Restaurant 54 B5
Zuma Caffé (see 76)

DRINKING (p360)
Apothecary 1878 55 B4
Archer Hotel 56 C2
Belgian Beer Café 57 D4
Bombay Bicycle Club 58 A1
Garage Bar 59 B5
Grace Emily Hotel 60 B4

ENTERTAINMENT (pp360–1)
Academy Cinema City 61 C4
Adelaide Festival Centre 62 C4
Edinburgh Castle Hotel 63 B4
Heaven Nightclub Complex 64 A4
Mars Bar 65 B5
Nova & Palace East End Cinemas (see 10)
PJ O'Brien's 66 D4
Queen's Arms Hotel 67 C5
Royal Oak Hotel 68 B2
Savvy 69 B5

TRANSPORT (pp361–2)
Access Rent-a-Car 70 B4
Adelaide Metro Information Centre 71 C4
Central Bus Station 72 B5
Glenelg Tram Terminus 73 C5
Hawk-Rent-A-Car (see 72)
Linear Park Mountain Bike Hire 74 B4
Qantas 75 B4

OTHER
Central Market 76 B5

run at 11am and 2pm weekdays, 11am and 3pm weekends. Peruse the great bookshop and revitalise at the café.

You can browse around the studios, art spaces and glass-blowing rooms at **Jam Factory Contemporary Craft & Design** (☎ 8410 0727; 19 Morphett St), which displays local artists' innovative and colourful work, and **Urban Cow Studio** (☎ 8232 6126; 11 Frome St).

Directed by Tim Flannery, Australia's answer to David Suzuki, the enthralling exhibits of the **South Australian Museum** (☎ 8207 7368; www.samuseum.sa.gov.au; North Tce; admission free; 10am-5pm) include Australia's natural history, whales and Antarctic explorer Sir Douglas Mawson (with expedition footage). The absorbing Aboriginal Cultures Gallery displays artefacts and explores Aboriginal Dreaming stories.

The fascinating **Migration Museum** (☎ 8207 7580; www.history.sa.gov.au; 82 Kintore Ave; admission by donation; 10am-5pm Mon-Fri, 1-5pm Sat & Sun) tells the stories of migrants who made SA their home. There's information on more than 100 nationalities in their database, along with poignant personal tales.

Visit **Tandanya** (☎ 8224 3200; 253 Grenfell St; adult A$4; 10am-5pm), an indigenous cultural institute, to learn about the local Kaurna people. It offers a free didgeridoo show (noon Monday to Friday) and Torres Strait Islander dance (noon Saturday and Sunday), and contains galleries, a café, and art and crafts.

Built in 1878 and decommissioned in 1988, the **Old Adelaide Gaol** (☎ 8231 4062; Gaol Rd, Thebarton; adult/student A$7/5.50; 11am-4pm Mon-Fri, 11am-3.30pm Sun) displays a range of home-made escape devices. Commentary tapes are provided for self-guided tours, or take a guided tour on Sunday. Spooky ghost tours are by appointment only.

If you're craving chocolate, you need settle only for the best at the iconic **Haigh's Chocolates Visitor Centre** (☎ 8372 7077; www.haighschocolates.com.au; 154 Greenhill Rd, Parkside; admission free). Dedicated to fine chocolate production, Haigh's takes you through the life-cycle of chocolate on tours of the factory (1pm and 2pm Monday to Saturday, 20 minutes); samples are included, bookings are essential.

Cricket fans can pour over the personal items of cricketing legend Sir Donald Bradman at the **Bradman Collection** (☎ 8207 7271; Institute Bldg, cnr North Tce & Kintore Ave; admission free; 9.30am-6pm Mon-Thu, to 8pm Fri, noon-5pm Sat & Sun). Tours (A$6.50) run at 11.30am and 12.30pm weekdays. Continue the theme north of the Torrens River at the **Adelaide Oval** (☎ 8300 3800; www.cricketsa.com.au; King William Rd, North Adelaide), where a statue of 'the Don' graces this most picturesque of Test cricket grounds. Adelaide Oval/Museum Tours (adult/student A$10/5, two hours) depart at 10am Monday to Friday and 2pm Sunday from the south gate on War Memorial Dr.

Shark victim turned shark advocate Rodney Fox promotes understanding of the much-maligned creature and its position in the delicate ocean ecosystem at **Rodney Fox Shark Experience** (☎ 8376 3373; www.rodneyfox.com.au; Glenelg Town Hall, Moseley Sq, Glenelg; adult A$6.50; 10am-5pm). It offers a fascinating insight into the 'smoke and mirrors' of the filming of *Jaws*.

North Adelaide is a pretty suburb with old bluestone cottages, pubs, alfresco restaurants and a fair bit of old money. It's separated from the city by the Torrens River and the **North Parklands**, part of a green belt surrounding Adelaide which also includes the **Botanic Gardens**, where you can take free guided walks (see Activities right). **Rymill Park**, in the East Parklands, has a boating lake and possums in the trees (they emerge at night); the South Parklands contain the **Veale Gardens**, with streams and flowerbeds, and the Japanese **Himeji Gardens**; and there are a number of sports grounds to the west.

Ayers Historic House (☎ 8223 1234; 288 North Tce; admission A$8; 10am-4pm Tue-Fri, 1-4pm Sat & Sun), built in 1845, was the elegant residence of Sir Henry Ayers, seven times SA's premier, and now features period furnishings and costume displays.

Adelaide Beaches

Adelaide's sandy **beaches** are excellent for swimming, sunbaking, bodyboarding and taking in the sunset, and often feature a few dolphins.

Glenelg, or 'the Bay', is a relaxed seaside suburb where locals mingle happily with tourists to stroll the promenade. Weekend crowds devour mountains of ice cream and a bustling alfresco café strip leads to a great swimming beach. Take a vintage tram from Victoria Sq in the city centre for the sunset views. **Beach Hire** (☎ 8294 1477; Sep-Apr), near the visitor centre, hires out deck chairs, umbrellas, wave skis and bodyboards on sunny days.

The proclamation of SA was read in 1836 at **Old Gum Tree** on MacFarlane St, and Governor Hindmarsh and the first colonists landed on the beach nearby. In 1836 the original free European settlers travelled from England on **HMS Buffalo**; a full-size replica sits on the Patawalonga, north of Moseley Sq. The **Bay Discovery Centre** (☎ 8179 9504; Moseley Sq, Glenelg; admission free; 10am-5pm) depicts life and hardships experienced by the first European settlement and addresses the plight of the local Kaurna Aboriginal people, who lost both their land and voice.

Henley Beach, also on the sea, is much smaller and quieter than Glenelg, but has the best pub on the coast: the **Ramsgate Hotel** (☎ 8356 5411; 328 Seaview Rd, Henley Beach). Take bus Nos 130 to 137 from Grenfell and Curry Sts.

ACTIVITIES

The peaceful **Botanic Gardens** (North Tce) has free guided walks departing from the information kiosk at 10.30am on Monday, Tuesday, Friday and Sunday (90 minutes). The kiosk also stocks free track guides: *Historical Walking Trails* tells the story of Adelaide's many fine buildings, while others cover **public art** and the wonderful riverside **Linear Park** – a 40km walking/cycling path that follows the Torrens River from the Adelaide foothills right through to the sea.

Pick up excellent **cycling** maps (free) from **Transport SA** (TSA; ☎ 8343 2225; www.transport.sa.gov.au/personal_transport/bike_direct/index.asp) vehicle-licensing centres or bike shops.

Head out on a catamaran with **Temptation Sailing** (☎ 0412-811 838; www.dolphinboat.com.au; Holdfast Shores Marina, Glenelg) to swim with dolphins (A$98, 3½ hours) or spot dolphins (A$48, 3½ hours).

Perched on the city's doorstep, the historic **Penfolds Magill Estate Winery** (☎ 8301 5569; 78 Penfolds Rd, Magill; 10.30am-4.30pm Mon-Fri, 11am-5pm Sat & Sun) is home to perhaps Australia's best known wine. Enjoy a **wine tasting** at the cellar door, indulge at the gourmet restaurant sporting great city views, or partake in the 'Great Grange Tour'. You can also take a self-guided tour with tastings of Australian wines (A$8.50) at the **National Wine Centre of Australia** (☎ 8222 9222; www.wineaustralia.com.au; cnr Botanic & Hackney Rds; 10am-6pm).

Contact **Adelaide Dive Centre** (☎ 8231 6144; www.adskin.com.au) or **Glenelg Scuba Diving Centre** (☎ 8294 7744; www.glenelgscuba.com.au; Patawalonga

Frontage, North Glenelg) for impressive southern oceans diving at sites such as the wreck of the HMAS *Hobart* (see p370).

TOURS

A huge variety of tours cover Adelaide, the Adelaide Hills, Fleurieu Peninsula and Barossa Valley. Most hostels will recommend backpacker-friendly wine tours, but check the number of wineries to be visited and ensure that you won't spend the day at tourist shops. Day trips to the southern Flinders Ranges and Kangaroo Island are very rushed and not recommended. See the regional SA sections for details of tours and operators.

Tauondi Aboriginal Cultural Tours (☎ 8341 2777; tours A$10-15) offer 45-minute Aboriginal guided tours covering plants and their uses in the Botanic Gardens (Wednesday to Friday and Sunday), Dreaming stories in Cleland Wildlife Park (see p367), and the Aboriginal Cultures Gallery in the South Australian Museum. Bookings are essential.

Adelaide's Top Food & Wine Tours (☎ 8231 4144; www.food-fun-wine.com.au) uncovers SA's gastronomic soul with dawn tours of the buzzing Central Market, on which stallholders introduce their varied produce. See the website for changing tour details.

Prime Mini Tours (☎ 8293 4900; www.primeminitours.com; tours A$50; ⏲ Tue-Thu) runs City & Brewery Tours (minimum six people; 5½ hours) combining the Rodney Fox Shark Experience, Haigh's Chocolates and the South Australian Brewing Company.

FESTIVALS & EVENTS

Adelaide is Australia's festival epicentre with a continuous stream of fantastic international and local events. The calibre of local and international performers attracts audiences from around the world, particularly for the Glenelg Jazz Festival and the Adelaide Festival of Arts. At the Adelaide Fringe Festival, Aussie stand-up comedians are joined by their European and American counterparts and other headline acts from the Edinburgh Fringe Festival.

March

Adelaide Festival of Arts Culture vultures absorb international and Australian dance, drama, opera and theatre performances on even-numbered years.

Adelaide Fringe A biennial independent arts festival, second only to the Edinburgh Fringe.

Clipsall 500 Rev heads rejoice as Adelaide's streets become a four-day Holden vs Ford racing track.

Womadelaide One of the world's best live music events with more than 400 musicians and performers from around the globe.

August

Royal Adelaide Show

South Australian Living Artists Innovative exhibitions and displays across the city.

October

Glenelg Jazz Festival First-class New Orleans & Australian jazz bands.

Feast A three-week lesbian and gay cultural festival with a carnival, theatre performances, talks and dances.

November

Horse Trials An Olympic-level event held in the city-centre parklands.

Christmas Pageant An Adelaide institution for more than 70 years – floats, bands and marching troupes take over the city streets for the day.

December

Bay Sports Festivals A large sports fest held in Glenelg, including beach volleyball, an aquathon, a surf carnival, hockey and gridiron.

Proclamation Day The day SA was put on the world map – 28 December.

SLEEPING

Hostels

A couple of city pubs have rooms, but hostels offer the best value. Choosing one may just depend on whether you prefer free apple pie or cheesecake for supper. Most hostels have dedicated TV rooms with a selection of movies, and well-stocked guest kitchens. They generally offer a free service to/from the airport, and bus and train stations, and have their own travel agencies or will book tours and car hire.

Adelaide Central YHA (☎ 8414 3010; www.yha.com.au; 135 Waymouth St; dm/d from A$20/57, non-YHA members extra A$5; ⏲ 24hr; P ✲ 💻) It may not be party central, but you will get plenty of sleep in the spacious and comfortable rooms (with luggage lockers), and it's surrounded by great bars and nightspots. Gleaming facilities, excellent communal areas with a pool table, TV rooms, free nightly movies and good security are the go. Daily bike hire is A$10.

My Place (☎ 8221 5299; 257 Waymouth St; www.adelaidehostel.com.au; dm A$20, d with TV A$54; P 💻)

The wonderfully welcoming atmosphere will soon have you calling this relatively small and quiet hostel 'home'. It's just a stumble away from pubs and Light Sq nightspots and has a cosy TV room, sauna and plant-rimmed terrace to laze on. Affable, multilingual staff will get you out on the town with evening adventures to local pubs – particularly good for solo travellers. Rates include a bumper breakfast and daily bus to Glenelg, or you can hire a bike (A$10 per day).

Backpack Oz (☎ 8223 3551; www.backpackoz.com.au; cnr Wakefield & Pulteney Sts; dm/s/d A$22/55/60;) Alternately friendly and brusque, this gleaming family-run hostel has spacious dorms and a guesthouse over the road (great for couples). Guests can still get a coldie and shoot some pool at the converted bar of this former hotel. There's a comfortable communal area, free breakfast and free dinner on Wednesday. Full linen is provided.

Blue Galah Backpackers Hostel (☎ 8231 9295; www.bluegalah.com.au; 1st fl, 62 King William St; dm/tw from A$22/64;) Slap bang in the city centre, this friendly hostel has a grand old balcony with a pool table and barbecue, a bar and a comfy lounge area. Rooms are clean if a little cramped and some lack windows. There's good security and toast for breakfast.

Adelaide Backpackers Inn (☎ 8223 6635; 118 Carrington St; dm/s/tw/d A$20/44/50/55;) A relaxed and ultraclean place with roomier dorms than most and an annex across the road. Free breakfast, rice, spices, tea, supper and laundry powder draws them in.

Glenelg Beach Resort (☎ 8376 0007; www.glenelgbeachhostel.com.au; 7 Moseley St, Glenelg; dm A$25, d/f from A$60/70;) With a fabulous beachside location, this charming terrace dating from 1879 is Adelaide's budget golden child. Fan-cooled rooms sport period details and are bunk-free. There's an open fireplace and large plasma TV screen in the lounge, a pool room with jukebox, nightly entertainment in the bar, and a courtyard garden. Rates include linen, breakfast and airport pick-ups.

Other backpacker hostels:

Adelaide Travellers Inn (☎ 8224 0753; 112 Carrington St; dm/tw A$20/50;) Not for the picky 'packer, its qualities lie in the impressive manga collection, casual employment office and bilingual Japanese-speaking staff.

Cannon St Backpackers (☎ 1800 069 731, 8410 1218; www.cannonst.com.au; 110 Franklin St; dm/tw A$20/55;) If you're looking for the frat house–style party place, check right in – the bar's open. Others bemoan the lack of sleep and tattiness.

Motels

Princes Lodge Motel (☎ 8267 5566; princeslodge@senet.com.au; 73 Lefevre Tce, North Adelaide; s with bathroom A$46, d with/without bathroom A$82/65;) In a grand old house overlooking parkland and the hills, this friendly but tired lodging is close to chichi North Adelaide's restaurants and within walking distance of the city. Rates include continental breakfast.

Camping

Adelaide Shores Caravan Park (☎ 8356 7654; www.adelaideshores.com; 1 Military Rd, West Beach; camp sites per 2 people A$25, caravans/cabins from A$50/65;) Nestled behind dunes on a lovely beach with a walking/cycling track extending to Glenelg (3.4km) in one direction and Henley Beach (3.5km) in the other, this is a great spot to be in summer. Lush sites, glistening amenities and passing dolphins.

> **SPLURGE!**
>
> **North Adelaide Heritage Group** (☎ 8272 1355; www.adelaideheritage.com) manages a range of beautifully refurbished cottages around Adelaide. The c1866 bluestone **Fire Station** (80 Tynte St, North Adelaide; d from A$140;) was operational during Victorian times – line up to book the Fire Engine Suite, outfitted with a genuine red and shiny fire engine.

EATING

To borrow and corrupt a phrase, 'Just because you're backpacking doesn't mean you have to eat bad food and drink bad coffee.' Dining out in Adelaide sits high on the social register – aided by inexpensive prices and high standards.

Foodies flock to Gouger St, where you can sample from every continent and get some of the gutsiest Chinese food around. Choose from the market's delights, café quickies, and restaurant dining from Argentine to Vietnamese and everywhere in between. In **Chinatown** (by the Central Market), many Asian eateries serve cheap lunches and *yum-cha* brunches (all you can eat for around A$10).

Pull up a people-watching pew at the lively Italian and Thai alfresco cafés and restaurants in Rundle Street or Jetty Rd in Glenelg, or relax at the quiet cluster of good restaurants on Hindmarsh Sq.

Pub bar meals and noodle shops offer good tastes at great prices.

Self-Catering

Central Market Precinct (btwn Grote & Gouger Sts; 7am-5.30pm Tue & Thu, 7am-9pm Fri, 7am-3pm Sat) You can find just about everything at the Central Market's 250-odd shops – abundant and fresh vegetables, breads, cheeses, seafood and gourmet produce – you name it. Good luck making it out without succumbing to the temptation to eat here. Bargain hunters should head down on Tuesday afternoon or after lunch on Saturday. There's also a **Coles Supermarket** (Central Market Arcade, cnr King William & Gouger Sts) here.

Cafés

T Bar (8410 5522; 44 Gouger St; breakfast A$2.50-7.50, lunch A$6-7.50; breakfast & lunch) Take a side-step out of the market and indulge at this 140-variety tea emporium, also serving great coffee, cakes, and tasty meals.

Zuma Caffé (8231 4410; 56 Gouger St; meals A$2.20-8; breakfast & lunch Tue, Thu & Sat, breakfast, lunch & dinner Fri) On the edge of the market, Italian-style Zuma's big breakfast fry-up (A$7.70) will keep you humming through the day. Voluptuous muffins (A$2.20) and lunch dishes are also a good bet.

Store (8361 6999; 157 Melbourne St, North Adelaide; breakfast A$5-12, lunch A$8.50-15.50; breakfast, lunch & dinner) Gourmet gremlins champ at the bit to pile into this northside haunt for breakfast, lunch and dinner, and anything in between.

Pubs

Worldsend Hotel (8231 9137; 208 Hindley St; bar meals A$7-11, dining room A$16-19) Enjoy great-value bar meals with a good casual vibe and mixed crowd. Upmarket meals are available in a separate dining room.

Exeter Hotel (8223 2623; 246 Rundle St; snacks A$1.20-5.50, meals A$10-17) Like a country pub in the middle of the city, but with more inspired meals ranging from venison vindaloo and roo fillets to chicken laksa and tofu burgers.

The **Austral Hotel** (8223 4660; 205 Rundle St) serves excellent food and the **Cumberland Arms** (8231 3577; 205 Waymouth St) is a popular spot with cheap meals.

Quick Eats

Pie cart (Adelaide train station; pies A$2.50; 6pm-midnight Mon-Fri, 4pm-4am Sat, 4-11pm Sun) Detour past this Adelaide icon for late night munchies on your stumble home.

Falafel House (258 Rundle St; dishes A$5-7.50; lunch & dinner) Chow down on felafels or *yiros* (kebabs) bursting with fresh salad until at least 2am.

Vego and Lovin' it (8223 7411; 1st fl, 240 Rundle St; burgers A$8.20, wraps from A$4.40; lunch Mon-Fri) Get a weekly vitamin dose disguised in a scrumptious veggie burger or wrap at this artsy, hippy sharehouselike kitchen.

Noodle shops dotted around the city and Glenelg are great places to get filling, cheap and tasty meat and vegetarian meals fast:

Thai in a Wok (8224 0969; 37 Hindmarsh Sq; mains A$7.50-13.50; lunch Mon-Fri, dinner Wed-Sat) A small restaurant serving Thai favourites with plenty of lemongrass.

Wok-in-a-Box (8231 0121; cnr King William & Hindley Sts; meals A$7-8)

Glenelg Spices (8376 1388; 111 Jetty Rd, Glenelg; meals A$10-17) Delightful spicy aromas waft from this very popular Malaysian/Thai restaurant.

Restaurants

Lucia's Pizza & Spaghetti Bar (8231 2303; 2 Western Mall, Central Market; meals A$6-7.50; breakfast & lunch Mon-Thu & Sat, breakfast, lunch & dinner Fri) This little piece of Italy is an Adelaide institution renowned for some of the finest coffee in town. Breakfast and cheap tucker are served during market hours, and all sauces are home-made – try Friday's lasagne special or the home-made pizzas.

Sprouts (8232 6977; 39 Hindmarsh Sq; meals A$11-17) Vegetarians and vegans – you're in good company here. Famous herbivores are prominently named at the entry to this small, stylish dining room which serves dishes such as Cajun spiced tofu and mushroom crepe wraps.

Ying Chow Chinese Restaurant (8211 7998; 114 Gouger St; mains A$7.50-14; dinner daily, lunch Friday) Behind the utilitarian decor hides a culinary gem. It's not your typical Chinese restaurant – rather than ubiquitous Cantonese, the cuisine is styled from the Guangzhou region and the flavours are delightful. Try Eshan chicken or aniseed tea duck (A$12). It gets packed nightly, but it's worth the wait – or you can grab a takeaway. For lunch, head to its action-packed sister restaurant **Ky Chow** (8221 5411; 82 Gouger St; mains A$7-13;

SPLURGE!

Jasmin Indian Restaurant (☎ 8223 7837; 31 Hindmarsh Sq; mains A$19.50; 🕒 lunch Tue-Fri, dinner Tue-Sat) Mrs Singh's mouth-watering North Indian cuisine garners a full house and keeps Jasmin among Australia's top 100 restaurants. If you like it hot, try the vindaloo.

🕒 lunch Mon-Fri, dinner daily) which serves dishes such as duck with sundried Chinese bayberries (A$9).

Botanic Café (☎ 8224 0925; 4 East Tce; mains A$17-25) Order from a seasonal menu styled from the best regional produce in this swish, contemporary hot spot opposite the Botanical Gardens. On Friday and Saturday nights it turns into a buzzing tapas bar.

DRINKING

To get a true Adelaide experience, head for the bar and order a schooner (half pint) or pint of Coopers, the local brew, or a glass of SA's impressive wine. Most pubs feature a 'happy hour' with reduced price drinks at some stage in the evening. In Hindley St, grunge and sleaze collides with student energy, and groovy bars sit amid adult bookshops and strip joints.

Grace Emily Hotel (☎ 8231 5500; 232 Waymouth St) Backpackers congregate for the free bands and barbecue on Monday nights. There's live music most nights, featuring some great up-and-coming Australian performers. If you're up for a bit of wildlife spotting, look out for the tiny native bats that feed on insects under the street lights near the beer garden.

Worldsend Hotel (☎ 8231 9137; 208 Hindley St) A mixed crowd gathers here to soak up the casual vibe. Popular with Uni students.

Exeter (☎ 8223 2623; 246 Rundle St) Enter the front bar at this inner city pub and you can imagine yourself re-emerging into a country town. Pull up a stool or claim a wooden table in the atrium-like beer garden and settle in for the evening. Music (playing most nights) ranges from acoustic to electronica.

Garage Bar (☎ 8212 9577; 163 Waymouth St, Light Sq) Kick back at this groovy, converted-garage bar with darts, pool and foosball. Thursday is bingo night.

Archer Hotel (☎ 8361 9300; 47 O'Connell St, North Adelaide) A trendy spot for food or a drink, with rooms such as the library and music room, and a great beer garden.

Other cool spots to see and be seen include the following:

Apothecary 1878 (☎ 8212 9099; 118 Hindley St) Get a dose from the old dispensary–turned–wine bar.

Belgian Beer Café (☎ 8359 2233; 27-29 Ebenezer Pl, off Rundle St) A European-style drinking hall with 26 imported Belgian superbrews and lots of noisy chatter.

Bombay Bicycle Club (☎ 8269 4455; 29 Torrens Rd, Ovingham) Relish the Rudyard Kipling–inspired décor and become a member of the 100-beer club.

CLUBBING

Put on your dancing shoes and bust some funky moves at these inner city clubs:

Garage Bar (☎ 8212 9577; 163 Waymouth St, Light Sq) A good vibe. On weekends it takes off with the resident DJ.

Savvy (☎ 8221 6030; 149 Waymouth St, Light Sq) Very popular. Features DJs and guests.

Heaven Nightclub complex (☎ 8216 5216; www.heaven.com.au; 7 West Tce; 🕒 8pm-6am) Nectar for clubbers – different bars play different music including retro, rhythm and blues, house and dance.

Mars Bar (☎ 8231 9639; 120 Gouger St; 🕒 10.30pm-late Wed-Sat) A popular dance club.

Gay & Lesbian Venues

For details on the local scene, pick up a copy of **Blaze** (www.blazemedia.com.au), available around the city; reviews, community news and popular gay and lesbian venues are listed on its website.

Good places to start:

Edinburgh Castle Hotel (☎ 8410 1211; 233 Currie St) With a dance floor, bistro and beer garden.

Mars Bar (☎ 8231 9639; 120 Gouger St; 🕒 10.30pm-late Wed-Sat) A popular and lively gay and lesbian dance club with drag shows on weekends.

Queen's Arms Hotel (☎ 8211 8000; 88 Wright St) Nightly entertainment.

ENTERTAINMENT

For arts connoisseurs, Adelaide has a phenomenal cultural life that compares favourably with much larger cities. To get your finger on the pulse, grab a copy of free street press papers *Rip it Up* or *db* – available at record shops, hotels, cafés and nightspots – which have listings and reviews of bands and DJs playing around town. The **Advertiser** (www.theadvertiser.com.au) newspaper lists events, cinema programmes and gallery details on

Thursday and Saturday. The free monthly **Adelaide Review** (www.adelaidereview.com) features theatre and gallery listings.

Bookings for the big events can be made through **BASS** (☎ 13 12 46; www.bass.sa.com.au; Visitors Centre, 18 King William St) and the riverside **Adelaide Festival Centre** (☎ 8216 8600; King William Rd), which hosts touring and local plays, festival events, concerts and musicals.

Cinemas

Cinemas slash ticket prices to A$9 on Tuesday. **Nova & Palace East End Cinemas** (☎ 8232 3434; 251 & 274 Rundle St, Adelaide; adult/concession A$13.50/9.50) feature new-release independent, art-house and foreign-language films, while **Academy Cinema City** (☎ 8223 5000; Hindmarsh Sq; tickets A$14) screens new-release mainstream films. In summer, pack a picnic and mosquito repellent, and spread out on the lawn to watch old and new classics under the stars at the **Moonlight Cinema** (☎ 1900 933 899; www.moonlight.com.au; Botanic Gardens; adult/concession A$14/10; mid-Dec–mid-Feb).

Live Music

Governor Hindmarsh Hotel (the Gov; ☎ 8340 0744; www.thegov.com.au; 59 Port Rd, Hindmarsh) Live music fans should check out the line-up at the Gov when heading into town. It received the Australian 'Live music venue of the year award' and features some legendary local and international acts. The atmospheric bars attract a mixed crowd of all ages (and flavours) – while the odd Irish fiddle band sits around in the bar, a back venue hosts folk, jazz, blues, salsa, reggae and dance music.

Royal Oak Hotel (☎ 8267 2488; 123 O'Connell St, North Adelaide) A great pub with a lively crowd and a variety of music.

Other pubs offering good live music:

Grace Emily Hotel (☎ 8231 5500; 232 Waymouth St) Cosy.

Austral Hotel (☎ 8223 4660; 205 Rundle St) Friday and Saturday nights.

Exeter Hotel (☎ 8223 2623; 246 Rundle St) See under Drinking (opposite).

PJ O'Brien's (☎ 8232 5111; 14 East Tce)

Sport

Sport is a huge part of the city's daily life. Adelaide hosts a number of world-class international events that take over the city streets and turn into big parties, including tennis matches, car-racing and one-day and test cricket matches.

The Australian Football League (AFL) rules the city, with two local competitive teams: the Adelaide Crows and 2004 premiership winners Port Adelaide. The Redbacks are the state's cricket team and basketball has the Adelaide 36ers.

GETTING THERE & AWAY

Air

Low-end one-way fares (Qantas and Virgin Blue) at the time of writing started at: Sydney A$120, Brisbane A$160, Melbourne A$80, Perth A$190 and Alice Springs A$150. Emu, Great Western and Regional Express Airlines (Rex) fly within SA.

Emu Airways (☎ 8234 3711; www.emuair.citysearch.com.au) Kangaroo Island.

Great Western Airlines (☎ 8355 9299; www.gwairlines.com.au) Flies between Adelaide and Kangaroo Island/Port Lincoln.

O'Connor Airlines (☎ 13 13 13, 8723 0666; www.oconnor-airlines.com.au) Flies between Adelaide, Melbourne, Mildura, Mt Gambier and Whyalla.

Qantas (☎ 13 13 13; www.qantas.com.au; 144 North Tce)

Regional Express (Rex; ☎ 13 17 13; www.regionalexpress.com.au) Flies between Adelaide and Kingscote on Kangaroo Island (A$120), and Coober Pedy (A$170).

Virgin Blue (☎ 13 67 89; www.virginblue.com.au)

Bus

Adelaide's **central bus station** (101-111 Franklin St) contains terminals and ticket offices for all major interstate and statewide services, and left-luggage lockers. For bus timetables see the **State Guide** (www.bussa.com.au). Discounts are available for backpacker associations/international student ID card holders.

McCafferty's/Greyhound (☎ 13 14 99; www.mccaffertys.com.au; 6am-8.30pm) has services between Adelaide and these cities: Melbourne (A$65, 11 hours), Sydney (A$140, 25 hours), Alice Springs (A$210, 21 hours) and Perth (A$284, 35¼ hours).

V/Line (☎ 13 61 96, 8231 7620; www.vlinepassenger.com.au; 7.30am-5pm Mon-Fri) runs daily bus and train services to Melbourne (A$62, 11½ hours), and Sydney (A$155, 21 hours).

Firefly Express (☎ 1300 730 740; www.fireflyexpress.com.au; 7am-8.30pm) departs at 7.30am and 8.30pm for Melbourne (A$50, 11 hours) and Sydney (A$100, 24 hours).

Premier Stateliner (☎ 8415 5555; www.premierstateliner.com.au; 7am-9pm) services destinations from Adelaide including Ceduna (A$91, 12 hours), McLaren Vale (A$7, one hour), Mt Gambier (A$53, 6½ hours), Nuriootpa in the Barossa Valley (A$7.40), Victor Harbor (A$16, two hours) and Wilpena Pound (A$70, seven hours).

Backpacker-style bus tours offer a great way to get from 'A to B' and see the sights on the way. Outback tours generally include the Flinders Ranges, Coober Pedy and Uluru (Ayers Rock). Operators include the following:

Groovy Grape (☎ 1800 661 177, 8371 4000; www.groovygrape.com.au) Three-day Melbourne–Adelaide (A$285), seven-day Adelaide–Alice Springs (A$750).

Heading Bush (☎ 1800 639 933; www.headingbush.com.au) A 10-day Adelaide–Alice Springs 4WD outback expedition (also including the Simpson Desert and West MacDonnell Ranges) with a maximum of 10 people (with/without YHA or VIP card A$1195/1400).

Wayward Bus (☎ 1800 882 823; www.waywardbus.com.au) 3½-day Melbourne–Adelaide via the coast (A$295), eight-day Adelaide–Alice Springs (A$790).

Car

If you want to hitch a ride (sharing petrol costs) or buy a second-hand car, check out the hostel notice boards. Expect to pay around A$45 per day for car hire with the cheaper companies:

Access Rent-a-Car (☎ 1800 812 580, 8359 3200; 60 Frome St)

Cut Price Car-&-Truck-Rentals (☎ 8443 7788; cnr Sir Donald Bradman Dr & South Rd, Mile End South)

Hawk-Rent-A-Car (☎ 1800 004 295, 8371 2824; 101 Franklin St)

Wicked Campers (☎ 1800 246 869; 07-3257 2170; www.wickedcampers.com.au) Fitted-out caravans from A$48/60 per day for eight/one week rental.

Train

The interstate train terminal is at Railway Tce, Keswick, just southwest of the city centre. **Skylink** (☎ 8332 0528; www.skylinkadelaide.com; bookings 7am-10pm) will pick up pre-booked passengers from the station (A$4) on its airport–city runs (see Getting into Town on p353).

Great Southern Railway (☎ 13 21 47, 8213 4444; www.trainways.com.au; 7.30am-8pm Mon-Fri, 8am-6pm Sat, 9am-5pm Sun) operates all train services in and out of SA. Backpackers are eligible for huge discounts (around 50%) and cheap six-month passes (A$450) if they have specific ID.

The following trains depart from Adelaide regularly:

Ghan To Alice Springs (economy seat/twin-berth sleeper A$215/680, 19 hours); to Darwin (economy seat/twin-berth sleeper A$440/1390, 47 hours).

Indian Pacific To Perth (economy seat/twin-berth sleeper A$310/960, 39 hours); to Sydney (economy seat/twin-berth sleeper A$223/450, 25 hours).

Overland To Melbourne (economy seat/twin-berth sleeper A$60/150, 11 hours).

GETTING AROUND

Bicycle

Hire bikes from hostels, **Linear Park Mountain Bike Hire** (☎ 8223 6271; Elder Park; bikes & in-line skates per day/week A$20/80; 9am-5pm), just below the Festival Centre, and **Glenelg Cycles** (☎ 8294 4741; 754 Anzac Hwy, Glenelg; bikes per day A$18; 9am-5pm Mon-Fri, 9am-4pm Sat & Sun).

Public Transport

The **Adelaide Metro Information Centre** (☎ 8210 1000; www.adelaidemetro.com.au; cnr King William & Currie Sts; 8am-6pm Mon-Sat, 10.30am-5.30pm Sun) provides timetables and sells tickets for the integrated metropolitan buses, trains and Glenelg tram. Tickets can also be purchased on board, or at staffed train stations. There are day-trip tickets (A$6.20) and two-hour peak (A$3.30) and off-peak (A$2) tickets. The peak travel time is before 9am and after 3pm. The Bee Line and City Loop buses are free.

Bee Line (No 99B) runs in a loop from the Glenelg tram terminus at Victoria Sq, up King William St and around the corner past the train station to the City West campus of the University of South Australia.

City Loop (No 99C) runs around the margins of the CBD from the train station, passing the Central Market en route. It generally runs every 15 minutes.

Wandering Star Service (☎ 8303 0844; www.adelaidemetro.com.autickets; A$6; 12.30-5am Fri & Sat) will pick you up from designated spots/nightclubs and deliver you to your front door within most city suburbs. Pick up a brochure from the Adelaide Metro Information Centre or visitors centre.

Classic old trams rattle between Moseley Sq (Glenelg) and Victoria Sq (city) approximately every 15 minutes from 6am to 11.50pm daily.

The **suburban train station** (North Tce) terminal is by the casino.

Taxi

There are licensed taxi ranks all over town, or call **Adelaide Independent Taxis** (☎ 13 22 11, wheelchair users 1300 360 940) or **Suburban Taxis** (☎ 13 10 08).

AROUND ADELAIDE

North of Adelaide is the wine and gourmet region of the Barossa Valley, while east of the city is Adelaide Hills; both rich in German heritage. Regions south of Adelaide include the Fleurieu Peninsula, offering fabulous beaches and epicurean haunts.

Activities

Head to Adelaide's nearby hills to walk through native bush, and get up close to plenty of wildlife at Cleland Wildlife Park. Not even a teetotaller could pass up a chance to taste wines at cellar doors in the Barossa and McLaren Vale. Get your hands on a bike and cycle your way through these world-famous regions. Hire a board and carve up the waves on the Fleurieu Peninsula. In season, head off on a whale-spotting adventure.

BAROSSA VALLEY

☎ 08

The Barossa Valley, 75km northeast of Adelaide, is Australia's best-known wine district. Its gnarled old vineyards have been producing wines for around 160 years and now make up a quarter of the Australian vintage and some immensely quaffable red wines.

The rolling landscape is dotted with modest Lutheran churches and old cottages that date back to the original settlement of 1842. Fleeing religious persecution in Prussia and Silesia, these first settlers weren't actually wine makers, but came clutching vines that are the origin of today's full and silky red wines. Prior to WWI, place names in the Barossa probably sounded even more Germanic, but during the war many names were patriotically anglicised.

One cannot live on bread and cheese alone. While in the region, taste (and fill your backpack with) the local produce such as dill cucumbers, pickled onions, olive oils, relishes, jams and chutneys. You can pick up regional produce at the **Barossa Farmer's Market** (Vitners Sheds, Angaston; 🕑 7-11.30am Sat).

WHISPERING WALL

About 7km southwest of Lyndoch, en route from Adelaide (via Gawler), is the famous **Whispering Wall**, a concrete dam wall with amazing acoustics. Normal conversations held at one end can be heard clearly at the other end, 150m away – so sing your lungs out!

INFORMATION

Internet access is available at **Barossa Council Libraries** (🕑 9am-5pm Mon-Fri, 9am-noon Sat; access free; Tanunda 83 Murray St; Nuriootpa 10 Murray St).

There are ATMs in the main street in Nuriootpa and Tanunda.

The **visitors centre** (☎ 8563 0600; www.barossa-region.org; 66 Murray St, Tanunda; 🕑 9am-5pm Mon-Fri, 10am-4pm Sat & Sun) stocks a plethora of information on local sights, B&B accommodation, wineries and contacts for vineyard work. All you want to know about the history of the Barossa, viticulture in the region, and wines in general is covered at the attached **Wine Centre** (admission A$2.50).

TOURS

If you've got the time, make your own way up to the Barossa, as many of the wineries are within walking/cycling distance and you'll get a lot more variety and choice.

Some organised tours:

Barossa Valley Tours (☎ 8563 2233, 0417-852 453; www.barossavalleytour.com; full-day tours A$39, with lunch A$47) A local operator that will whisk you around the major sites in the area, including a selection of wineries, and a stop for a two-course lunch (optional).

Groovy Grape Getaways (☎ 1800 66 11 77; www.groovygrape.com.au; tours A$65) Fun backpacker tours from Adelaide including the Whispering Wall, Big Rocking Horse, a few wineries and a barbecue lunch.

Prime Mini Tours (☎ 1300 667 650; www.primeminitours.com; tours A$65) One of the best tours from Adelaide; includes lunch.

FESTIVALS & EVENTS

Big events in the Barossa are the week-long **Barossa Vintage Festival** (www.barossa-region.org/vintagefestival) which runs from Easter Monday in odd-numbered years, and August's hugely popular **Barossa Jazz Weekend** (www.barossa-region.org).

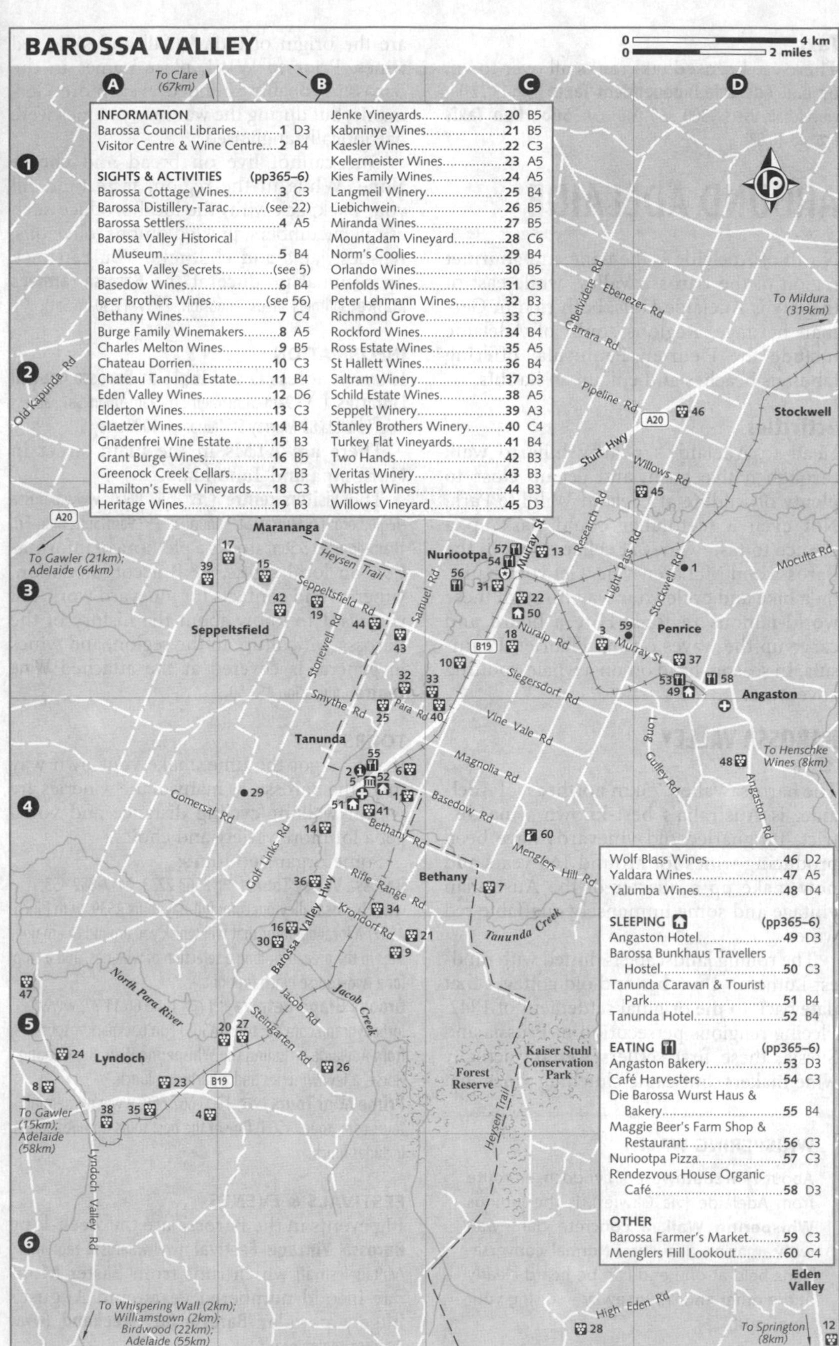
BAROSSA VALLEY
0 4 km
0 2 miles
A
B
C
D
1
2
3
4
5
6
To Clare (67km)
INFORMATION
Barossa Council Libraries............1 D3
Visitor Centre & Wine Centre....2 B4
SIGHTS & ACTIVITIES (pp365–6)
Barossa Cottage Wines.............3 C3
Barossa Distillery-Tarac..........(see 22)
Barossa Settlers........................4 A5
Barossa Valley Historical Museum.....................5 B4
Barossa Valley Secrets.............(see 5)
Basedow Wines..........................6 B4
Beer Brothers Wines...............(see 56)
Bethany Wines...........................7 C4
Burge Family Winemakers.........8 A5
Charles Melton Wines...............9 B5
Chateau Dorrien.......................10 C3
Chateau Tanunda Estate..........11 B4
Eden Valley Wines...................12 D6
Elderton Wines.........................13 C3
Glaetzer Wines.........................14 B4
Gnadenfrei Wine Estate...........15 B3
Grant Burge Wines..................16 B5
Greenock Creek Cellars...........17 B3
Hamilton's Ewell Vineyards......18 C3
Heritage Wines........................19 B3
Jenke Vineyards.......................20 B5
Kabminye Wines......................21 B5
Kaesler Wines..........................22 C3
Kellermeister Wines.................23 A5
Kies Family Wines...................24 A5
Langmeil Winery.....................25 B4
Liebichwein.............................26 B5
Miranda Wines........................27 B5
Mountadam Vineyard..............28 C6
Norm's Coolies........................29 B4
Orlando Wines.........................30 B5
Penfolds Wines........................31 C3
Peter Lehmann Wines..............32 B3
Richmond Grove......................33 C3
Rockford Wines.......................34 B4
Ross Estate Wines....................35 A5
St Hallett Wines......................36 B4
Saltram Winery.......................37 D3
Schild Estate Wines.................38 A5
Seppelt Winery........................39 A3
Stanley Brothers Winery..........40 C4
Turkey Flat Vineyards..............41 B4
Two Hands..............................42 B3
Veritas Winery.........................43 B3
Whistler Wines........................44 B3
Willows Vineyard.....................45 D3
Wolf Blass Wines....................46 D2
Yaldara Wines.........................47 A5
Yalumba Wines.......................48 D4
SLEEPING (pp365–6)
Angaston Hotel........................49 D3
Barossa Bunkhaus Travellers Hostel.....................................50 C3
Tanunda Caravan & Tourist Park..51 B4
Tanunda Hotel.........................52 B4
EATING (pp365–6)
Angaston Bakery.....................53 D3
Café Harvesters.......................54 C3
Die Barossa Wurst Haus & Bakery....................................55 B4
Maggie Beer's Farm Shop & Restaurant..............................56 C3
Nuriootpa Pizza.......................57 C3
Rendezvous House Organic Café..58 D3
OTHER
Barossa Farmer's Market.........59 C3
Menglers Hill Lookout.............60 C4
Old Kapunda Rd
Belvidere Rd
Ebenezer Rd
Carrara Rd
Pipeline Rd
To Mildura (319km)
A20
Sturt Hwy
Willows Rd
Stockwell
Research Rd
Light Pass Rd
Stockwell Rd
Moculta Rd
To Gawler (21km); Adelaide (64km)
Marananga
Heysen Trail
Nuriootpa
Murray St
Samuel Rd
Seppeltsfield Rd
Seppeltsfield
Stonewell Rd
Nuraip Rd
Penrice
B19
Siegersdorf Rd
Angaston
Smythe Rd
Para Rd
Vine Vale Rd
Long Gulley Rd
Tanunda
Magnolia Rd
To Henschke Wines (8km)
Angaston Rd
Gomersal Rd
Basedow Rd
Bethany Rd
Golf Links Rd
Menglers Hill Rd
Bethany
Rifle Range Rd
Krondorf Rd
Barossa Valley Hwy
Tanunda Creek
North Para River
Jacob Rd
Jacob Creek
Steingarten Rd
Lyndoch
Kaiser Stuhl Conservation Park
Forest Reserve
To Gawler (15km); Adelaide (58km)
Lyndoch Valley Rd
Eden Valley
High Eden Rd
To Whispering Wall (2km); Williamstown (2km); Birdwood (22km); Adelaide (55km)
To Springton (8km)

GETTING THERE & AROUND

There are several routes to the Barossa Valley from Adelaide, with the most direct being via Main North Rd through Elizabeth and Gawler.

More picturesque routes go through the Torrens Gorge, then via either Williamstown or Birdwood. If you're coming from the east and want to tour the wineries before hitting Adelaide, take the scenic route via Springton and Eden Valley to Angaston.

Barossa Valley Coaches (☎ 8564 3022) has twice daily (once on Sunday) return services from Adelaide to Tanunda (A$13, 1½ hours), Nuriootpa (A$14, two hours) and Angaston (A$15, two hours).

Premier Stateliner (☎ 8415 5555; www.premierstateliner.com.au) services Nuriootpa from Adelaide (A$7.40) three times daily.

Cycling is a good way to get around the Barossa, particularly along the Para Rd Trail which wends its way past wineries. Hire bikes from the **Bunkhaus Travellers Hostel** (☎ 8562 2260; Barossa Valley Way, Nuriootpa; bikes from A$8), **Tanunda Caravan & Tourist Park** (☎ 8563 2784; Tanunda; bikes ½/full-day A$15/20) or **Barossa Secrets** (☎ 8563 0665; 91 Murray St, Tanunda; 🕑 10am-4.30pm; bikes daily/overnight A$16.50/25).

Barossa Valley Taxis (☎ 8563 3600) has a 24-hour service.

Tanunda

pop 3865

It's worth taking a wander around Tanunda, the most Germanic of the towns in the centre of the valley, which has some early cottages around **Goat Sq** on John St and some fine old Lutheran churches. The **Barossa Valley Historical Museum** (☎ 8563 0507; 47 Murray St; admission A$4; 🕑 11am-5pm Mon-Sat, 1-5pm Sun) has exhibits on the valley's early settlement. A few galleries and antique shops line the main street, while **Barossa Secrets** (☎ 8563 0665; 91 Murray St; 🕑 10am-4.30pm) sells local produce, and fascinating things made out of lavender and old oak wine barrels.

At **Norm's Coolies** (☎ 8563 2198; Barossa Valley Way, off Gomersal Rd; adult A$8; shows 2pm Mon, Wed & Sat), at Breezy Gully Farm about 3km from Tanunda, you can watch trained sheepdogs going through their paces.

Turn off the main road southeast of Tanunda and take the scenic drive through the sleepy historic hamlet of Bethany, the first German settlement in the valley, and via **Menglers Hill Lookout** for a superb view over the valley before reaching Angaston and Nuriootpa. The route runs through beautiful, rural country featuring large gums. From Nuriootpa, take the palm-fringed road to Seppeltsfield and Marananga, before heading back to Tanunda.

Tanunda Hotel (☎ 8563 2030; 51 Murray St; s/d A$50/60; mains A$13-18), a family-run hotel in the centre of town, has comfortable rooms and a broad menu.

Tanunda Caravan & Tourist Park (☎ 8563 2784; www.tanundacaravantouristpark.com.au; Barossa Valley Way; camp sites unpowered/powered per 2 people A$17/22, caravans from A$38, cabins from A$58; 💻) is just a short walk from the town and pub. This park has good facilities, a camp kitchen and laundry, and hires out bikes (half/full day A$15/20) to explore nearby wineries.

Die Barossa Wurst Haus & Bakery (☎ 8563 3598; 86a Murray St, Tanunda; breakfast A$3.50-9, meals A$8-12.50; 🕑 breakfast & lunch) is a deli-cum-bakery and the home of mettwurst and cheeses, where pies, value-packed all-day breakfasts, German cakes and apple strudel are gobbled up in record time. Delve into the region's heritage with a Bavarian Feast roll (A$12.50) with wurst, sauerkraut, potato salad and mustard.

There's a supermarket, bakery, and take-away food shops in the centre of town.

Nuriootpa

pop 3865

At the northern end of the valley, the small town of Nuriootpa is surrounded by vineyards. You can follow the Para Rd Trail cycling and walking path along the river to a number of cellar doors.

A relaxed and friendly vine-fringed hostel, the **Barossa Bunkhaus Travellers Hostel** (☎ 8562 2260; Barossa Valley Way; dm/d A$17/50; 🅿) is a kilometre south of town. It has a well-appointed kitchen, barbecues, a summer-only pool and wood fires, and makes a great base for winery exploration by foot or bike (from A$8).

At 'jack-of-all-cuisines' **Nuriootpa Pizza** (☎ 8562 1896; 51 Murray St; small pizzas A$8.50-11.50; 🕑 dinner Mon-Wed, lunch & dinner Thu-Sun), munch on thick or thin-style pizzas, pasta, fish and chips, *yiros*, burgers and more. Can't decide? Cover a few options with the 'chicken and chips' pizza.

Locals and visitors alike savour the Mediterranean cuisine at **Café Harvesters** (☎ 8562 1348; 29D Murray St; mains A$17-22; 🕑 lunch Wed-Sat,

THE GOOD DROP

South Australia is well-marked on the world wine map for its excellent wines from the regions of, among others, the Clare Valley, McLaren Vale, Coonawarra and the Barossa Valley. Here's the deal when heading to the cellar door for tastings: swirl, sniff, sip, and swill before swallowing or spitting out. Listed here are some exciting boutique wineries, together with world-renowned names regularly quaffed at home, which make up the 50-odd wineries with cellar door tastings in the Barossa Valley (see the Barossa Valley map, p364, for more).

Bethany Wines (☎ 8563 2086; www.bethany.com.au; Bethany Rd, Tanunda; 10am-5pm Mon-Sat, 1-5pm Sun) Offering a stunning hill-side vista, this friendly family winery makes a killer white port and classic dry reds.

Henschke Wines (☎ 8564 8223; www.henschke.com.au; Henschke Rd, Kyneton; 9am-4.30pm Mon-Fri 9am-noon Sat) In nearby Eden Valley, 14km from Angaston, the home of 'Hill of Grace' produces exceptional wines.

Kabminye Wines (☎ 8563 0889; www.kabminye.com; Krondorf Rd, Tanunda; 11am-5pm Wed-Sun) Check out the straw-bale building at this family-owned winery, which incorporates a cellar door, gallery and Krondorf Rd Café, specialising in Barossan heritage food.

Langmeil Winery (☎ 8563 2595; www.langmeilwinery.com.au; cnr Para & Langmeil Rds, Tanunda; 10.30am-4.30pm) Some legendary wines in a beautiful setting. Pre-arrange a winery tour and explore its history and vineyards.

Penfolds Wines (☎ 8568 9290; www.penfolds.com; Tununda Rd, Nuriootpa; 10am-5pm Mon-Fri, from 11am Sat & Sun) You know the name. The 'Barossa Ultimate Tasting Experience' (A$100 per person) allows you to pass some Grange Hermitage across your lips; book ahead.

Peter Lehmann Wines (☎ 8563 2500; Para Rd, Tanunda; 9.30am-5pm Mon-Fri, 10.30am-4.30pm Sat & Sun) Partner your tastings with a food platter or buy a classic Barossa red and enjoy it with a picnic by the Para River. A parkland walk links to Richmond Grove.

Rockford Wines (☎ 8563 2720; Krondorf Rd, Tanunda; 11am-5pm Mon-Sat) The converted stone building makes this small winery's cellar door a picturesque winner. It's widely noted for its black shiraz. Fabulous chutneys, jams and mustards are often available for tasting also.

Two Hands (☎ 8562 4566; www.twohandswines.com; Neldner Rd, Marananga; 11am-5pm Wed-Fri, 10am-5pm Sat & Sun) People swoon in delight over these wonderful wines – complete with eccentric names and labels – produced at this boutique winery. Try the moscata, the 'Garden series'… and all the others – they're fabulous, and wine reviewer Robert M Parker thinks so too.

dinner Thu-Sat). Styled with regional produce and served up in rustic charm, lunchtime focaccias (A$9 to A$10) hit the spot, or sink an espresso and piece of home-made cake to get you back on the winery track. Dinner bookings are essential.

Maggie Beer's Farm Shop & Restaurant (☎ 8562 4477; www.maggiebeer.com.au; Pheasant Farm Rd; lunch A$25) Maggie dishes up seasonal specialties from the celebrity-gourmet's kitchen – she's famous for her pheasant dishes. Book ahead for a table overlooking the water, or cruise in for great coffee and taste Maggie's gourmet produce and Beer Brothers' wines.

Angaston

pop 1933

On the eastern side of the valley, the quiet town of Angaston has a couple of galleries and studios along its main street.

Angaston Hotel (the Corner Pub; ☎ 8564 2428; 59 Murray St; B&B per person A$35; mains A$9-16) has traditional hotel rooms that are clean and as comfortable as grandma's house. Pub grub features steak and grills, and schnitzel any way you like it.

Rendezvous House Organic Café (☎ 8564 3533; 22 Murray St; breakfast A$6-15, lunch A$7-17) will enrapture your tastebuds with flavoursome organic food amid casually stylish arty chic. Yum! Carnivores, vegans and vegetarians are welcome and well catered for.

Grab a cheap-and-cheerful egg and bacon roll (A$3) or baguette (A$3.60) at **Angaston Bakery** (63 Murray St).

ADELAIDE HILLS

☎ 08

Even in the driest summer months the Adelaide Hills, a 30-minute drive from the city, offer crisper air, lush woodland shade and the delicious scent of eucalyptus from stands of gum trees. Numerous conservation and wildlife parks contain walking tracks, stunning views and the chance to view and interact with native fauna.

Travelling along picturesque narrow roads you'll pass carts of fresh produce for sale, stone cottages, olive groves and vineyards. Locals wear grins from ear to ear, happy with the good life.

INFORMATION

Adelaide Hills Visitor Information Centre (Mt Lofty Summit ☎ 8370 1054; www.visitadelaidehills.com.au; 9am-5pm; Hahndorf ☎ 1800 353 323; 41 Main St; 9am-5pm Mon-Fri, 10am-4pm Sat & Sun) has oodles of information and can assist with B&B accommodation; the Hahndorf centre has Internet access (A$2 per 15 minutes).

SIGHTS & ACTIVITIES

Just a 12km ride or drive from the city (or take bus No 105 from Currie St to stop 26, then walk the extra 1km), you can follow walking tracks that wend through the woodlands, rugged gorges and waterfalls of **Morialta Conservation Park**.

Make like Dr Dolittle and walk with the animals at **Cleland Wildlife Park** (☎ 8339 2444; www.environment.sa.gov.au/parks/cleland; Summit Rd, Cleland; adult/student A$12/9; 9.30am-5pm). You can get up close and interact with many species of Australian fauna, feed kangaroos and emus, and even have your photo taken with a koala (A$12, 2pm to 4pm). The hissing Tasmanian devils are particularly fascinating to watch when active at feeding time, while the koalas and wombats are generally catching some zzzs. You could easily spend a good few hours here. Dusk **wildlife** and **Aboriginal tours** (adult A$20), which bring Dreaming stories to life, run with minimum numbers only, so call ahead. Public transport is limited; take bus No 163F from Grenfell St at 9.52am, 10.52am or 12.52pm and get off at Crafers for a connecting No 823 service to the wildlife park.

From the Cleland Wildlife Park, walk through the bush (2km) or drive up to **Mt Lofty Summit** (727m), which has beautiful views over Adelaide and the Gulf St Vincent. From here continue south for 1.5km to the stunning **Mt Lofty Botanical Gardens** (☎ 8370 8370; 8.30am-4pm Mon-Fri, 10am-6pm Sat & Sun). There are gates on both Mawson Dr and Lampert Rd, and parking costs A$2.20.

The first exported Australian wine was a case of Adelaide Hills' hock, sent to Queen Victoria in 1845. There are now around a dozen cellar doors in the area including **Petaluma's Bridgewater Mill Winery & Restaurant** (☎ 8339 3422; bridgewatermill@petaluma.com.au; cellar door 10am-5pm), set in a beautifully restored 200-year-old flour mill, complete with an award-winning restaurant overlooking Cox's Creek and 'The Old Rumbler' waterwheel. See Hanhdorf (p368) for other wineries.

TOURS

Bikeabout (☎ 0413 525 733; www.bikeabout.com.au) offer downhill cycling tours (A$45) from Mt Lofty summit to Hahndorf.

SLEEPING

Mount Lofty Railway Station (☎ 8339 7400; www.mlrs.com.au; 2 Sturt Valley Rd, Stirling; d B&B with/without bathroom A$85/65) Trainspotters rejoice. *The Ghan* and *The Overland* whoosh through this converted heritage-listed train station in otherwise quiet and lush Stirling. There are simple rooms in clean, self-contained accommodation.

Fuzzies Farm (☎ 8390 1111; fuzzyt@ozemail.com.au; Norton Summit; cabins per week around A$90) In a great setting at the edge of Morialta Conservation Reserve 15km east of Adelaide, this friendly organic farm has self-contained bushland cabins and a café. Weekly rates for helpers include meals. Bookings are essential.

Burnslea Log Cabin (☎ 8388 5803; burnslealc@yahoo.com; Leslie Creek Rd, Mylor; d A$85) A great self-contained log cabin with complimentary breakfast provisions and alpaca petting.

In Belair, **Nunyara Holiday Units** (☎ 8278 1673; 5 Burnell Dve, Belair; d A$70, extra person A$7.50; P) offer excellent value self-contained units with million-dollar views of the city and coast.

At the edge of Belair National Park, is **Belair Caravan Park** (☎ 8278 3540; Upper St Rd; camp sites unpowered/powered per 2 people A$16/19, cabins A$50-65). The rustic and basic cottages in national parks along the Heysen Trail at Mt Lofty, Norton Summit and Mylor offer a fantastic opportunity to get out into nature. Make bookings at the **Adelaide Central YHA** (☎ 8414 3000; www.yha.com.au; 135 Waymouth St, Adelaide; cottages from A$50), where you'll need to collect keys, and bring your own sleeping sheets.

EATING

Organic Market & Café (☎ 8339 7131; 5 Druids Ave, Stirling; meals A$3.50-12) Hill-types flock to this vibrant and lively café off Mt Barker Rd. It's perhaps the busiest spot in Stirling – and rightly so, the food's delicious and everything's made with love. Gorge on plump savoury or sweet muffins and great coffee, and leave feeling virtuous and healthy. The Portuguese custard tarts are wicked.

Stirling Pub (☎ 8339 2345; 52 Mt Barker Rd; bar meals A$10) Grab a meal at the bar and soak up the atmosphere.

Aldgate Café (☎ 8339 2530; 6 Strathalbyn Rd, Aldgate; pizza A$6.50-10, pasta A$10, meat dishes A$12.50; lunch & dinner) Solid and tasty meals are served up opposite the pub, with featured A$8 specials from Monday to Wednesday.

Jimmies (☎ 8339 1534; 6 Main St, Crafers; mains A$10.50-18; breakfast & lunch Sat & Sun, dinner nightly) A lively evening spot loved for its wood-fired oven pizzas. Live jazz on Thursday night.

The pretty towns of Aldgate and Stirling are blessed with great pubs, groovy cafés, bakeries and supermarkets.

GETTING THERE & AROUND

It's worth hiring a car to encompass early morning views and breakfast at Mt Lofty Summit and a guided wildlife walk at sunset. Take a good map. A good tour of the Hills loops north from Adelaide, leaving the city via North Tce, Botanic Rd and Payneham Rd, and continuing on to Lower North East Rd. This scenic route takes you to Birdwood, from where you can continue north to the Barossa Valley, or travel south to loop around Hahndorf and Mt Lofty before returning to Adelaide via the South Eastern Fwy.

Regular buses from Adelaide's central bus station (A$3.30) stop at Crafers, Stirling and Aldgate, though there are few No 823 buses from Crafers to Mt Lofty Summit and Cleland Wildlife Park. Bus Nos 840 and 164F depart hourly from Adelaide's central bus station for Hahndorf (A$3.30, 70 minutes).

There are also **taxis** (☎ 8389 5566) in the area.

Adelaide to Birdwood

Heading out of Adelaide along the Lower North East Rd, the celebrated **Chain of Ponds Winery** (☎ 8389 1415; www.chainofponds.com.au; Main Adelaide Rd, Gumeracha; cellar door 10.30am-4.30pm) is about 35km from the city centre. A few kilometres further on, the very stationary **Big Rocking Horse** (☎ 8389 1085; The Toy Factory, Main Adelaide Rd; 9am-5pm) is another fascinating example of giant Aussie kitsch, though this time constructed of corrugated iron rather than deteriorating fibreglass. In the historic Birdwood Mill about 6km further on, the **National Motor Museum** (☎ 8568 5006; www.history.sa.gov.au; Shannon St, Birdwood; adult A$9; 9am-5pm) has an impressive collection of immaculate vintage and classic cars and motorcycles.

Hahndorf

pop 1842

You could be forgiven for thinking you've arrived slap-bang in the centre of a German theme park at Hahndorf, the oldest surviving German settlement in Australia, located 28km southeast of Adelaide. European trees flirt with gums and cascades of colourful flowers flow from half wine-barrels along the main street, which contains plenty of antique, vintage and knick-knack shops, and is surrounded by quality wineries. Settled in 1839 by Lutherans who left Prussia to escape religious persecution, the town took its name from the ship's captain, Hahn; *dorf* is German for village.

The 1857 **Hahndorf Academy** (☎ 8388 7250; 68 Main St; 10am-5pm Mon-Sat, noon-5pm Sun) houses an art gallery with rotating exhibitions and several original sketches by Sir Hans Heysen, the famed landscape artist and resident of Hahndorf. The academy houses the **German Immigration Museum**, which is worth the gold coin donation. It illustrates the early life of German settlement in the Adelaide Hills and has an extensive collection of bizarre carved pipes (depicting a ballerina, a woman's shrivelled head and a talon).

You'll see more than 300 of Sir Hans' original works on a tour through his studio and house, the **Cedars** (☎ 8388 7277; Heysen Rd; tours A$8), about 2km northwest of Hahndorf. Tours run at 11am, 1pm and 3pm every day except Saturday.

Pick your own strawberries between November and May from the famous **Beerenberg Strawberry Farm** (☎ 8388 7272; Mount Barker Rd; 9am-5pm), also renowned for its plethora of jams, chutneys and sauces.

You can reach some quality wineries in the Hahndorf area from Balhannah Rd, off Main St in the centre of town:

Shaw & Smith (☎ 8398 0500; Lot 4 Jones Rd, Balhannah; 10am-4pm Sat & Sun)

Nepenthe Wines (☎ 8388 4439; Jones Rd, Balhannah; 10am-4pm)

Hahndorf Hill Winery (☎ 8388 7512; Lot 10 Pains Rd, Hahndorf; 10am-5pm)

SLEEPING & EATING

Hahndorf Resort (☎ 1800 350 143; www.hahndorfresort.com.au; 145 Main St, Hahndorf; camp sites unpowered/powered per 2 people A$15/17, cabins A$49; P) In keeping with the local theme, Bavarian-style chalets encircle this sprawling, verdant resort. It has ample facilities, tennis courts, a swimming pool and fauna park, and **Hans Heysen Restaurant** (mains from A$10). Located 1.5km from town, bus Nos 840 and 164F stop at the gate. Half-/full-day bike hire is A$7.50/15.

Wurst, sauerkraut, pretzels, strudel and German beer abound in Hahndorf.

Hahndorf Inn (☎ 8388 1000; 35a Main St; breakfast A$4.50-15, mains A$10-22) Fancy a meal of cheese Krasky, Vienna sausage, sauerkraut and apple strudel? There's a friendly buzz in this cosy, rustic place – perhaps it's the lack of pokies chinking and chiming in the background. Gather around a wine barrel with a stein of German beer (on tap).

German Arms Hotel (☎ 8388 7013; 50 Main St; mains A$7.50-16) Lively and packed on weekends, the pub's bratwurst and pies are popular as are the economical 'old favourites'.

FLEURIEU PENINSULA

☎ 08

Stunning beaches stretch along the Fleurieu (*floo*-ree-o) Peninsula coastline south of Adelaide. Boutique wineries – dotted like liquid gems throughout the adjacent rolling hills of the lower Mt Lofty Ranges – create a vivid and contrasting landscape.

The smuggling businesses of early settlers on the Peninsula was replaced by whaling in 1837 from Encounter Bay. Nowadays, protected baby whales and their doting mothers can be watched off the southern beaches. The region's website is www.fleurieupeninsula.com.au.

TOURS

Prime Mini Tours (☎ 1300 667 650; www.primeminitours.com; tours A$48) visits Hahndorf, Victor Harbor and McLaren Vale, while **Enjoy Adelaide** (☎ 8332 1401; www.enjoyadelaide.com.au; tours A$60) combines wine- and almond-tasting with penguin viewing at Victor Harbor.

GETTING THERE & AROUND

Premier Stateliner (☎ 8415 5555) runs up to four buses daily from Adelaide's central bus station to McLaren Vale (A$6.70, one hour), Willunga (A$7.10, 70 minutes), Victor Harbor (A$15.60, two hours), Port Elliot (A$15.60, two hours) and Goolwa (A$15.60, two hours).

McLaren Vale Wine Region

A patchwork of vineyards and almond groves covers the scenic rolling hills around the McLaren Vale region, approximately 35km south of Adelaide, which supports more than 50 wineries. The area is particularly well suited to red wines. Wineries with great cellar door tastings include, among others: **Wirra Wirra** (☎ 8323 8596; www.wirrawirra.com; McMurtie Rd, McLaren Vale), home of the sensational 'wood henge'; **Fox Creek Wines** (☎ 8556 2403; www.foxcreekwines.com; Malpas Rd, McLaren Vale), which produces one of the region's top bottles of shiraz, the Last Chance Reserve Shiraz; **Coriole Vineyards** (☎ 8323 8305; www.coriole.com; Chaffeys Rd, McLaren Vale), with delightful gardens, cheeses and olives; and **Chapel Hill** (☎ 8323 8429; Chapel Hill Rd, McLaren Vale), which has beautiful views. For vineyard work in the area, contact **Boston Recruitment** (☎ 8323 9935).

For a fantastic day of wine tasting with matched cheeses, hire a bike (three hours A$21, per day A$30) and buy a cheese box (three cheeses, crackers, olives and raisins for A$10 per person) from Blessed Cheese (see below), then hit the old railway line walking/cycling track from McLaren Vale to **Willunga**, a lovely town 6km to the south.

The **McLaren Vale & Fleurieu visitors centre** (☎ 8323 9944; www.mclarenvale.info or www.fleurieupeninsula.com.au; Main Rd, McLaren Vale; 9am-5pm, Mon-Fri 10am-5pm Sat & Sun), at the northern end of McLaren Vale, can assist with accommodation and shares space with **Stump Hill Café & Wine Bar** (☎ 8323 8999), which offers tastings from local wineries with no cellar door. The **art galleries** along the main street of McLaren Vale are also worth a look.

Providing the only budget accommodation in McLaren Vale, and information on winery labour, **McLaren Vale Lakeside Caravan Park** (☎ 8323 9255; www.mclarenvale.net; Field St, McLaren Vale; camp sites per 2 people/caravans with bathroom A$18/50) is in a pretty rural setting close to town.

Most of the town's eateries are spread along Main Rd. Superb coffee and tasty meals comprised of local and regional SA gourmet produce are served at **Market 190** (☎ 8323 8558; 190 Main Rd; meals A$6-14), and **Blessed Cheese** (☎ 8323 7958; www.blessedcheese.com.au; 150 Main St). Duck into **Brian's Olive Shop**, nearby, for plump olives and local produce.

Gulf St Vincent Beaches

There are superb swimming beaches along the Gulf St Vincent coastline, extending from **Christies Beach**, popular with experienced surfers, onto the partially nudist and gay hang-out (at the southern end) of **Maslin Beach**, **Port Willunga**, home of acclaimed cliff-top restaurant **The Star of Greece** (☎ 8557 7420; The Esplanade; mains A$20-30; lunch), and **Sellicks Beach**, home of the **Victory** (☎ 8556 3083; Main South Rd; mains A$12-22) pub, with fine views, good food and an impressive cellar. Beyond here the coastline becomes rockier. There are good beaches at **Carrickalinga** and **Normanville**. Dolphins can usually be spotted at most beaches along the coastline, although of course there's no guarantee.

Scuttled off Yankalilla Bay in 2002, the destroyer HMAS *Hobart* now entertains scuba divers as a **wreck dive**, obtain permits from the **Dolphin Dive** (☎ 8558 2733; www.diveexhmashobart.com; 52 Main St, Normanville), which also organises dives. See also p356 for dive operators.

Along the south coast near Cape Jervis (and the Kangaroo Island ferry terminal) is the **Deep Creek Conservation Park**, with bush camping areas and walking tracks, including the Heysen Trail. This 1200km series of tracks which wind along rugged coastline, through ridgetops of the Mt Lofty and Flinders Ranges, and finish in Parachilna Gorge north of Wilpena Pound.

Encounter Bay

The stunning coastline between Victor Harbor and Goolwa has some beautiful swimming beaches and great surf. It's very popular in summer and between June and October you might be lucky enough to see a southern right whale on its migratory path.

The **visitors centres** (The Causeway ☎ 8552 5738; www.tourismvictorharbor.com.au; Goolwa Wharf ☎ 8555 3488; www.visitalexandrina.com;) can help you book accommodation.

Hire a bike to cycle the **Encounter Bikeway Trail** (23km) between Victor Harbor and Goolwa; maps are available from visitors centres. You can hire bikes (A$10/20 per hour/day) from **Victor Harbor Cycles & Skates** (☎ 8552 1417; 73 Victoria St) or **Goolwa Caravan Park** (☎ 8555 2737; www.goolwacaravanpark.com.au; Noble Ave, Goolwa). On Sunday, the steam **Cockle Train** (☎ 8552 2782; one way/return A$16/23) travels between Goolwa and Victor Harbor via Port Elliot.

VICTOR HARBOR

This one-time sealing and whaling centre turned popular holiday town is 83km south of Adelaide. You can ride on a double-decker tram pulled by Clydesdale draught horses (one way/return A$4/6) across the short causeway connecting the mainland with tiny **Granite Island**, which has a penguin rookery. Watch the penguins waddle home on a one-hour dusk penguin tour; book at **Granite Island Gift Shop** (☎ 8552 7555; tour A$10). Maintain the aquatic theme at the **South Australian Whale Centre** (☎ 8552 5644; www.sawhalecentre.com; 2 Railway Tce; adult/student A$6/4.50; 11am-4.30pm), or watch sharks being fed through underwater windows at the **Below Decks Shark Aquarium** (adult A$15; 11am-5pm), which opens depending on visibility.

The heritage-listed **Anchorage** (☎ 8552 5970; anchoragevh@ozemail.com.au; cnr Coral St & Flinders Pde; s/d from A$40/70;) has comfortable and clean rooms (book ahead) or try **Victor Harbor Beachfront Caravan Park** (☎ 8552 1111; 114 Victoria St; camp sites per 2 people/cabins A$22/65).

You can get a decent feed and watch the miniature trains run around the top of the room at **Grosvenor Junction Hotel** (☎ 8552 1011; 40 Ocean St; bar specials A$5, meals A$10-12).

Join the regulars for pub grub at the **Royal Family Hotel** (☎ 8554 2219; rfhotel@chariot.net.au; 32 North Tce, Port Elliott; mains A$9-16;) or join the queue at the excellent **Port Elliot Bakery** across the road.

PORT ELLIOTT

On the picturesque **Horseshoe Bay**, laid-back Port Elliot has a beautiful swimming beach and a cliff-top walk perfect for seasonal whale-watching.

Nearby surf beaches include **Boomer Beach** on the western edge of town and **Middleton Beach**, the best surf beach in the area, to the east. Rent surfing gear at **Southern Surf Shop** (☎ 8554 2376; 36 North Tce, Port Elliot), or **Big Surf Australia** (☎ 8554 2399; Main Rd, Middleton), or learn with **Surf Academy** (☎ 8552 2541); 90-minute lessons including all equipment cost A$30.

Port Elliott has the best range of budget accommodation along this stretch. Fans of shabby-chic will love cosy **Arnella by the Sea** (☎ 8554 3611; narnu@bigpond.com; 28 North Tce, Port Elliott; dm/d A$25/60) which has some of the nicest budget doubles around.

In an unbeatable position behind sand dunes on Horseshoe Bay, **Port Elliot Tourist**

Park (☎ 8554 2134; www.portelliotcaravanpark.com.au; Middleton Rd, Port Elliott; camp sites per 2 people/cabins from A$21/60) has all the Big-4 facilities.

Beachside **Flying Fish** (1 The Foreshore, Port Elliott; takeaway A$9-14.50) serves great Coopers-battered flathead (a fish) and chips.

GOOLWA

At the point where Australia's largest river, the Murray, enters the ocean, Goolwa is a restful and unassuming place, with the best surf beach on the southern coast and great sunsets. **Hindmarsh Island Bridge**, with its unusual land- and sea-based animal murals, links the mainland to Hindmarsh Island. You can hire **bodyboards** from Goolwa beach kiosk in summer (A$10).

Goolwa Caravan Park (☎ 8555 2737; www.goolwacaravanpark.com.au; Noble Ave; camp sites per 2 people A$16, cabins from A$60), 3.5km from town, is close to the river.

KANGAROO ISLAND & THE SOUTHEAST COAST

South of Adelaide is the wildlife wonderland of Kangaroo Island, and the rugged Southeast Coast which joins SA to Victoria.

Activities

On Kangaroo Island, the only thing limiting you is your imagination. The most attractive aspect of a visit is the chance to view wildlife in its own habitat – though you'll have to walk to see it, or you could roar around on a nocturnal quad bike tour. Hiking here is superb, as is the surfing, snorkelling, sandboarding on inland dunes, and diving to see hard and soft corals and the elusive dragons.

Watersports continue to dominate along the Southeast Coast, with plenty of great surfing, swimming and fishing spots. Hike tracks through the dunes or take a bush tucker or Aboriginal medicine tour in the Coorong, and explore pock-marked Mt Gambier.

KANGAROO ISLAND

☎ 08

Kangaroo Island (KI), 13km off SA's coast, is a wildlife wonderland of birds, animals and ocean-based creatures. Its wild and rugged coastline shelters beaches edged with turquoise seas, while the interior contains forest and bush. Its small population mainly inhabits the eastern towns.

Kangaroo Island's isolation from European diseases and (introduced) feral species greatly protected the island's native flora and fauna. The care of the natural ecosystem continues, with 30% of land now maintained as either conservation or national parks.

Many island place names are in French – the first thorough survey of its coast was carried out in 1802 and 1803 by the French explorer Nicholas Baudin. His English counterpart, Matthew Flinders, named the island after his crew enjoyed a feast of kangaroo meat here.

Car hire is inexpensive and distances are not vast (you can drive the length of the island in two hours), so head for the southern coast and western end of the island. While here, try the local produce, including Clifford's Honey, Kangaroo Island Cheese, local wines and Emu Ridge Eucalyptus oil.

INFORMATION

Kingscote **library** (☎ 8553 2015; Dauncey St, Kingscote) has Internet access.

There are banks in Kingscote; in Penneshaw, **Grimshaw's Corner Store & Cafe** (cnr Third St & North Tce) has an ATM and the **post office** (Nat Thomas St; 🕑 9am-5pm Mon-Fri, 9-11am Sat) acts as a bank agency.

The **visitors centre** (☎ 8553 1185; www.tourkangarooisland.com.au; 🕑 9am-5pm Mon-Fri, 10am-4pm Sat & Sun), just outside Penneshaw on the road to Kingscote, is stocked with information on all the island's offerings, books accommodation and sells park entry tickets and Island Parks Passes (adult/student A$42/30), which are also sold at **National Parks & Wildlife South Australia** (NPWSA; ☎ 8559 7235; Flinders Chase National Park; 🕑 9am-5pm) outlets.

ACTIVITIES

KI Outdoor Action (☎ 8559 4296; South Coast Rd, Vivonne Bay) hires out sea and river kayaks/surfboards (A$25/35) and runs quad bike tours (A$50).

Rewards for scuba divers include fur seals and the elusive leafy seadragon; for details, contact **Kangaroo Island Diving Safaris** (☎ /fax 8559 3225; www.kidivingsafaris.com) and **Adventureland Diving** (☎ 1800 686 620, 8553 1284; advhost@bigpond.com).

TOURS

Most backpacker trips from Adelaide include ferry fares, accommodation and meals.

Campwild Adventures (☎ 8132 1333; www.campwild.com.au) Two- and three-day tours (from A$295) include sandboarding and bushwalking.

Kangaroo Island Sealink (☎ 13 13 01, 8202 8688; www.sealink.com.au; 440 King William St, Adelaide) The one-day tour (A$180) from Adelaide is only for those extremely short on time.

Wayward Bus (☎ 1300 653 510; www.waywardbus.com.au) Two-day tours (A$310) cover all the major sights; stays can be extended.

SLEEPING & EATING

Penguin Walk YHA Hostel (☎ 8553 1233; www.ki-ferryconnections.com; 33 Middle Tce, Penneshaw; dm/d A$23/76; ☒) Near the ferry terminal, this place has spacious modern rooms with bathrooms and fridges. Shared kitchen facilities are limited.

Kangaroo Island Central Backpackers Hostel (☎ 8553 2787; ki_backpackers@hotmail.com; 19 Murray St, Kingscote; dm/d A$20/50) A small and friendly hostel.

Flinders Chase Farm (☎ 8559 7223; chillers@kin.net.au; West End Hwy; dm/cabins A$15/50) This place has a casual charm with cosy 'shacks', dorms in wooden buildings and tropical bathrooms. There's a good outdoor kitchen and campfire area, and roaming kangaroos.

Kangaroo Island Wilderness Resort (☎ 8559 7275; bliss@austdreaming.com.au; South Coast Rd; dm A$40; mains A$10-20; ☐) This resort has a bar, a good restaurant and a takeaway shop.

There are private cabins around the coast starting at around A$85 for two people; off-season rates are negotiable. Inquire at the visitors centre in Penneshaw, or try the cabins at **Emu Bay Holiday Homes** (☎/fax 8553 5241; www.emubayholidays.com.au; Emu Bay).

The **NPWSA** (☎ 8559 7235; kiparksaccom@saugov.sa.gov.au; cottages from A$75) has some beautiful refurbished heritage accommodation; best to book lighthouse keepers' cottages at Cape Willoughby, Cape Borda and Cape du Couedic in advance.

Small and basic camping grounds are found around the island, including at Emu Bay, Stokes Bay, Vivonne Bay and Western River Cove. The **visitors centre** (☎ 8553 1185; www.tourkangarooisland.com.au; Penneshaw; ⏲ 9am-5pm Mon-Fri, 10am-4pm Sat & Sun) issues camping permits for bush sites at Chapman River, Brown Beach and American River. Within Flinders Chase National Park, there's camping at **Rocky River** (camp sites per 2 people A$19), Snake Lagoon, West Bay or **Harveys Return** (camp sites per 2 people A$6.50). Or try **Western Kangaroo Island Caravan Park** (☎ 8559 7201; beckwith@kin.on.net; South Coast Rd; camp sites per 2 people/cabins A$15/80; ☒) near Flinders Chase National Park.

There are restaurants and quick bite options in Penneshaw and Kingscote, and general stores with petrol pumps and hot food at American River, Parndana and Vivonne Bay. There's a café in the visitors centre at Flinders Chase National Park and a kiosk at Stokes Bay. Kangaroo Island Wilderness Resort has a bar, restaurant and petrol pump.

GETTING THERE & AWAY

Flights between Adelaide and Kingscote cost about A$129.

Emu Airways (☎ 8234 3711; www.emuair.citysearch.com.au)

Great Western Airlines (☎ 8355 9299; www.gwairlines.com.au)

Regional Express (Rex; ☎ 13 17 13; www.regionalexpress.com.au)

If you don't have your own vehicle, catch the bus to Cape Jervis and ferry across to the island, then hire a car booked for collection at the ferry terminus at Penneshaw.

Kangaroo Island Sealink (☎ 13 13 01) operates three vehicular ferries between Cape Jervis and Penneshaw daily (one way fares for passengers/bicycles/cars A$32/5.50/70).

Sealink's bus service (☎ 13 13 01) connects with ferry departures at Port Jervis. Buses run from Adelaide's central bus station (adult/student A$18/15, two hours) and Goolwa and Victor Harbor (A$12, 40 minutes). Bookings are essential.

GETTING AROUND

A **shuttle bus** (☎ 8553 2390; A$12) connects the airport and Kingscote (14km), while the **Sealink Shuttle** (☎ 13 13 01) connects Kingscote (A$11) with the morning and evening ferries. Bookings are essential.

The island's main roads are sealed; some gravel roads can give you a wild ride if it's been a while since grading. Drive particularly carefully from dusk to dawn and watch out for roos. Not all Adelaide car-rental companies will rent cars for Kangaroo Island trips; with ferry prices it's cheaper to hire on the island – but book ahead.

Car hire agencies:

Budget (☎ 8553 3133; www.budget.com.au; Kingscote airport)

Hertz (☎ 1800 088 296, 8553 2390; Kingscote airport)

Wheels over Kangaroo Island (☎ 1800 750 850, 8553 3030; Kingscote airport)

Dudley Peninsula

Looking across Backstairs Passage to the Fleurieu Peninsula, **Penneshaw** is a quiet town with a white sandy beach at **Hog Bay**. Ferries from Cape Jervis arrive here.

Book fairy penguins tours at **Penneshaw Penguin Centre** (☎ 8553 1103; tours adult/child A$8/6.50) on the foreshore near the ferry terminal. You'll see more penguins here than at Kingscote. Tours depart at 7.30pm and 8.30pm (an hour later during daylight saving, in which clocks are put forward an hour).

The **Cape Willoughby Lightstation** (☎ 8553 1191; Willoughby Rd; tours adult/student A$10.50/7.50) first operated in 1852 and is now used as a weather station. Tours run from 10am to around 3.15pm daily.

North Coast

Kingscote, 60km from and 117km from Flinders Chase National Park, is the main town on the island. Rangers take the daily **Discovering Penguins Walk** (adult/student A$12/9.50) at 7.30pm and 8.30pm (9pm and 9.40pm during daylight saving); arrive 30 minutes early at the Penguin Burrow at the Ozone Hotel.

The **Kangaroo Island Marine Centre** (☎ 8553 3112; Kingscote Wharf; tours A$10) includes a saltwater aquarium (A$3). Tours run at 7.30pm and 8.30pm (also 1pm and 5pm in school holidays). The **tidal pool** about 500m south off the jetty is the best place to swim in town. However, most locals head out to the lovely **Emu Bay**, 18km away, with its beautiful long sweep of sand. There are several fine, sheltered beaches along the north coast, including **Stokes Bay** (hidden away through a limestone tunnel), **Snelling Beach** and **Western River Cove**.

Flinders Chase National Park

Occupying the western end of the island, Flinders Chase is one of SA's most significant national parks. There is plenty of mallee scrub, but also beautiful tall forests with amazing birdlife, koalas, echidnas, possums and platypuses (if you're lucky enough to see them). Resist the urge to feed the brazen kangaroos.

NPWSA visitors centre (☎ 8559 7235; 🕑 9am-5pm) has interesting displays, a souvenir shop and café, and handles cabin bookings (see opposite).

On the northwestern corner of the island is the **Cape Borda lightstation** (☎ 8559 3257; Playford Hwy), built in 1858, which has 45-minute guided tours (A$10.50/7.50) from 11am to 3pm daily (10am to 4pm in summer). At nearby **Harvey's Return** are great views, a small, poignant cemetery on the cliff top and a bush camping area.

Just south of Cape Borda is the **Ravine des Casoars**, named by Baudin after the dwarf emus he saw there (*casoars* means 'cassowaries'), which became extinct soon after European settlement. There's a beautiful walking track (6.5km return) here.

In the southeastern corner of the national park, **Cape du Couedic** is wild and remote with towering cliffs. A picturesque lighthouse built in 1906 tops the cape; you can follow the path from the car park down to **Admirals Arch** – a large natural archway formed by pounding seas. New Zealand fur seals are usually seen here, including cows nursing their pups.

At Kirkpatrick Point, 2km east of Cape du Couedic, the **Remarkable Rocks** are a cluster of large, weather-sculpted granite boulders on a huge dome swooping to the sea. It's a surreal sight.

South Coast

The south coast is rough and wave swept compared with the north. At **Seal Bay Conservation Park** (☎ 8559 4207; Seal Bay Rd; 🕑 9am-4.15pm, to 7pm summer), 60km southwest of Kingscote, you can wander past a large colony of Australian sea lions lolling about on the beach. Tours (adult/student A$12.50/9.50) run every 45 minutes.

Near Seal Bay and close to South Coast Rd is **Little Sahara**, a series of enormous white-sand dunes. The long and beautiful **Vivonne Bay** has a camp site, excellent fishing and surfing, but bathers should take great care: the undertows are fierce so stick close to the jetty or the river mouth. There's a general store on the main South Coast Rd.

Horseshoe-shaped **Hanson Bay** is connected to **Kelly Hill Conservation Park** (☎ 8559 7231; South Coast Rd; 🕑 10am-3.30pm, to 4.30pm summer) via a great bush track that passes by lagoons (18km return, 8 hours); there are cave tours (adult/student A$10.50/7.50) and adventure-caving tours (adult/student A$26/16) of the dry limestone caves.

SOUTHEAST COAST

☎ 08

Dukes Hwy provides the most direct route between Adelaide and Melbourne (729km) via Bordertown, but the coastal Princes Hwy route, which runs adjacent to the Coorong, is definitely the more scenic. Along the rugged, wind and salt parched Southeast coast (Limestone Coast) you'll find tranquil harbours with fishing and holiday towns and some great swimming and surfing beaches. From Robe to Mt Gambier, the road passes through a sea of plantation forests, interspersed with the odd patch of cleared farmland or stand of gum trees.

You can gorge on saltwater fare along the Southeast Coast; October to April is crayfish (rock lobster) season. For regional information, see www.thelimestonecoast.com.

GETTING THERE & AWAY

Premier Stateliner (☎ 8415 5555) runs a daily coastal bus service between Adelaide and Mt Gambier (A$52.50, 6½ hours) via the Coorong including Meningie (A$25.50, two hours), Kingston SE (A$41, four hours), Robe (A$46, 4½ hours) and Beachport (A$48.50, five hours). A daily inland route travels to Bordertown (A$39, four hours).

V/Line (☎ 1800 817 037) runs a combined bus and train service daily between Mt Gambier and Melbourne (A$60, 6½ hours).

Wayward Bus (☎ 1300 653 510; www.waywardbus.com.au) has a 'classic coast' tour (A$295, 3½ days) between Melbourne and Adelaide which is a fabulous way see the SA coast and Great Ocean Rd, in Victoria.

Coorong National Park

The dunes, lagoons, freshwater soaks and ephemeral lakes of the Coorong form a wetland of international importance and support vast numbers of waterbirds. From the mouth of the Murray it stretches 145km southeast and is rarely more than 4km in width. The Ngarrindjeri Aboriginal people are still closely connected to this area; the name Coorong is derived from the Ngarrindjeri word 'Karangk' (long neck). Travelling through at sunset is serenely beautiful.

The easiest access point to the ocean is a 3km drive from the Princes Hwy at **42 Mile Crossing**, 19km south of Salt Creek. From here, it's a 1.3km 4WD or walk to a great view of the Southern Ocean. You can take the dirt Old Coorong Rd as an alternative to the Princes Hwy when roads are dry. Permits for bush **camp sites** (per car A$6.50) are available from the roadhouse at Salt Creek and the **NPWSA office** (☎ 8575 1200; 34 Main St, Meningie; 🕑 9am-5pm Mon-Fri), which also has general park and track information.

Meningie, on Lake Albert, is a popular windsurfing spot and the main town in the centre of the Coorong. Ngarrindjeri-owned **Coorong Wilderness Lodge** (☎ 8575 6001; off the Princes Hwy, Point Hack), about 25km south of Meningie, offers a bush food and medicine walk and bush-tucker (book ahead). **Camp Coorong** (☎ 8575 1557; nlpa@lm.net.au; Princes Hwy; camp sites per 2 people/dm/cabins A$10/22/55; ♿), 10km south of Meningie, has simple modern cabins and dorms and good kitchen facilities. Book in advance, ask about linen hire, and bring your own food.

Kingston SE is the proud hometown of 'Larry the giant Lobster'. Satisfy your 'cray'-vings (sorry!) at **Lacepede Lobster** (🕑 9am-6pm), a swimmingly-fresh take-away by the jetty. Between here and Robe, gently undulating farmland is interspersed with plantation pine forests and the occasional vineyard around Mt Benson, near Cape Jaffa.

Robe

This relaxed and charming fishing port gets inundated with sun, sand and surf seekers in summer. It's blessed with quaint limestone cottages, a protected sandy swimming beach near the town centre, and **Long Beach** (2km from town off the Kingston SE road), a good windsurfing and surfing spot. The beachfront walking track has interpretative signs, while other marked tracks meander through the coastal dunes at **Little Dip Conservation Park**, extending 13km south of town.

The **visitors centre** (☎ 8768 2465; www.robe.sa.gov.au; Mundy Tce; 🕑 9am-5pm Mon-Fri, 10am-4pm Sat & Sun) has free Internet access and an interesting photo display on Robe's heritage. **Wilsons at Robe** (☎ 8768 2459; 5 Victoria St) sells local and Australian coast–inspired art and craft.

There's stiff competition for Robe's seemingly abundant accommodation in summer. An ivy-covered façade hides beachside **Caledonian Inn** (☎ 8768 2029; caled@seol.net.au; Victoria St; s/d A$45/60) and its atmospheric Scottish bar. Of Robe's three caravan parks, **Sea-Vu Caravan Park** (☎ 8768 2273; 1 Squire Dr; camp sites unpowered/powered per 2 people A$19.50/22, cabins from A$72), quietly set on the beachfront, is closest to town and has good amenities.

Tasty gourmet lunches and decadent cakes are baked on site at the soulful **Wild Mulberry Café** (☎ 8768 5276; 46 Victoria St; breakfast & lunch A$7-16.50), which also serves all-day cooked breakfast and Robe-roasted Mahalia coffee. Dine alfresco on the foreshore with freshly hooked and cooked takeaway from **Robe Seafood & Takeaway** (Victoria St).

Beachport

Tranquil Beachport's milky turquoise waters and beautiful location make it a great chill-out spot. There's a decent **surf beach**, or you can float like never before on the hyper-saline **Pool of Siloam**.

There's a **visitors centre** (☎ 8735 8029; Millicent Rd; 9am-5pm Mon-Fri, 11am-2pm Sat & Sun), a couple of caravan parks and **Bompa's** (☎ 8735 8333; 3 Railway Tce; dm/d A$25/45), which has accommodation, a cosy bar and a café.

The giant sand dunes of **Canunda National Park** lie 22km south of town and feature 4WD tracks, Boandik Aboriginal middens (traces of old camp sites), and cliff-top walks. You can **camp** (per vehicle A$7) near Southend.

Mt Gambier

Mt Gambier (486km from Adelaide, 471km from Melbourne), appears like a lush oasis built on the slopes of its extinct volcano. The crater – **Blue Lake** – is a stunning sight in an almost implausible shade of sapphire during summer. The **visitors centre** (☎ 8724 9750, 1800 087 187; Jubilee Hwy East; 9am-5pm) provides details on the region.

If you're planning to stay in town, **Blue Lake Holiday Park** (☎ 8725 9856; www.bluelakeholidaypark.com.au; Bay Rd; camp sites unpowered/powered per 2 people A$20/24, cabins from A$65) is close to the Blue Lake, or become a jail bird for the night at the **Old Jail** (☎ 8723 0032; turnkey@seol.net.au; Langlois Dr; dm/tw A$22/56).

FLINDERS RANGES

The glowing red and purple folds of the majestic Flinders Ranges are a spectacular sight. Beloved of artists and bushwalkers alike, this ancient colossus rises from the northern end of the Spencer Gulf and runs 400km north into the arid outback. In the far north, the ranges are hemmed in by sand ridges and barren salt lakes.

As in many other dry regions of Australia, the vegetation here is surprisingly diverse and colourful, and the country is carpeted with wildflowers in the early spring. Winter and early spring (June to September) are the best times to visit.

Bushwalking is a major attraction of the area, but this is wild, rugged country and walkers should be adequately equipped with drinking water, maps and sun protection. Solo walks are not recommended; let someone know where you're headed and when you expect to return from your walk. The park has a number of marked bushwalking tracks, listed in a free NPWSA leaflet. The Heysen Trail ends in Parachilna Gorge, near Blinman, having come up through the Ranges.

Information

Westprint and Hema print good maps of the area.

Quorn visitors centre (☎ 08-8648 6419; 3 Seventh St, Quorn; 9am-5pm) Next to the council chambers.

Wilpena Pound visitors centre (☎ 08-8648 0048; admin@wilpenapound.com.au; 8am-6pm) Near the pound entrance.

Activities

Put on your walking shoes and get active on your own steam, exploring this ancient landscape. Go climb a rock at Warren Gorge, or gain extra insight into this land on one of the excellent cultural tours run from Iga Warta.

Tours

Wayward Bus (☎ 1800 882 823; www.waywardbus.com.au) has an excellent tour incorporating Flinders Ranges and Coober Pedy (A$550), which includes the option of one week at Iga Warta. See p362 for details on overland tours visiting the Flinders Ranges.

You can also pick up tours departing from Port Augusta, Quorn, Hawker, Wilpena Pound, Iga Warta and Arkaroola; see local visitors centres and backpacker hostels for details.

Other tours:

Ozzie's Bush Track Tours (☎ 08-8648 6567; www.aboutozzietours.com; 22 Pool St, Quorn) Bush walks (A$12), tours (one/three/five days A$140/480/890 inclusive), and a popular half-day tour to nearby Dutchman Stern Conservation Park (A$78) are on offer. Minimum numbers apply.

Wallaby Tracks Adventure Tours (☎ 08-8648 6655; www.users.bigpond.com/headbush/wadtours.html) Recommended and good-value tours (A$99 to A$399) depart from Quorn and Port Augusta, and there are transfers to/from Adelaide.

Getting There & Around

Premier Stateliner (☎ 08-8415 5555) departs from Adelaide on Wednesday and Friday to Wilpena Pound (A$70, seven hours), Quorn (A$49.50, five hours) and Hawker (A$65, six hours). Return trips are on Thursday, Friday and Sunday.

You can call ahead for recorded information on **road conditions** (☎ 1300 361 033) in the Flinders Ranges and the outback. An interesting loop from Wilpena Pound continues north through the Flinders Ranges National Park past Oraparinna Homestead, then west through Brachina Gorge to the main Leigh Creek road.

The 20km self-guided **Brachina Gorge Geological Trail** features an outstanding sequence of sedimentary rock – pick up a leaflet from the Wilpena Pound visitors centre. Following this, either turn back to Hawker or head north to Parachilna and take the scenic road east through Parachilna Gorge and Blinman, before heading south back to Wilpena through the national park.

QUORN

☎ 08

About 330km north of Adelaide and 40km northeast of Port Augusta, Quorn is the picturesque gateway to the Flinders.

Andu Lodge (☎ 8648 6655; www.users.bigpond.com/headbush; 12 First St; dm/s/d A$20/30/50; 💻) is a lovely YHA hostel in an old hospital with excellent facilities and a peaceful atmosphere. It also runs Wallaby Tracks Adventure Tours (above).

HAWKER

☎ 08

The **Moralana Scenic Route** loops from Hawker, taking in the magnificent scenery along the Elder and Wilpena Pound ranges. It's 24km to the Moralana turn-off, then 28km along an unsealed road that joins up with the sealed Hawker to Leigh Creek road. From here it's 46km back to Hawker.

The **Flinders Ranges Caravan Park** (☎ 8648 4266; jsitters@flinderscpk.com.au; 1 Leigh Creek Rd; camp sites per 2 people/caravans/cabins A$21/45/55; ❄) is about 1km from town, and is spacious, friendly and has a good kitchen. Four-wheel-drive tours are available.

WILPENA POUND

☎ 08

The large natural basin of **Wilpena Pound** (park entry A$6.50) is the park's main attraction. The external wall soars 500m, while inside the basin slopes away from the encircling ridge top. Access is via the narrow gap through which Wilpena Creek exits the pound. There is plenty of wildlife in the park. **Sacred Canyon**, 20km east of the visitors centre on a rough road, has many petroglyphs (rock carvings). To the north are striking scenic attractions, such as **Bunyeroo Gorge** and the **Aroona Valley**. There are several bush-camping areas.

Most of the walks start from the visitors centre, which is near the main camp site. From **St Marys Peak** and **Tanderra Saddle**, you can enjoy the white glimmer of **Lake Torrens** off to the west, the beautiful Aroona Valley to the north, and the pound spread out below your feet. A popular three-hour walk is **Ohlssen Bagg**, which will take you to the top of the mountain that sits on the rim above the Wilpena Pound Resort and offers tremendous views. **Arkaroo Rock**, which is about 10km south of Wilpena off the Hawker road, has well-preserved Aboriginal paintings and also offers good views in spring. It's a 3km walk from the car park to the rock shelter. **Wangara Hill** lookout is a 7km return walk and **Cooinda** is the bush-camping area within the pound.

Wilpena Pound Resort (☎ 8648 0004; www.wilpenapound.com.au; Wilpena Rd; camp sites per 2 people A$16, dm/d A$25/100; ❄ 🏊) is just outside the pound and has motel-style units; there's a bar/bistro but no kitchen.

Off the Hawker road, about 20km south of Wilpena and close to the pound's outer edge is **Rawnsley Park** (☎ 8648 0030; www.rawnsleypark.com.au; Wilpena Rd; camp sites per 2 people/caravans A$17/48, cabins from A$68; ❄ 💻). There's a restaurant and several good bushwalks start from here, or you can take horse rides (one hour, A$45), 4WD tours, or hire mountain bikes (A$10/50 per hour/day).

You can **bush camp** (per car incl entry A$11) within the national park; pay fees at the visitors centre, which is well-stocked with groceries.

BLINMAN TO PARACHILNA

The quaint hamlet of Blinman is on the circular route around the Flinders Ranges National Park. Dramatic **Chambers Gorge**, 64km to the northeast of Blinman towards Arkaroola (a wilderness sanctuary in the northern Ranges), features a striking gallery of Aboriginal rock carvings. From Mt Chambers you can see Lake Frome to the east and Wilpena Pound to the south.

An inspiring scenic drive links Blinman with Parachilna, home of the renowned Prairie Hotel, to the west via **Parachilna Gorge** and some lovely camping spots.

The **Prairie Hotel** (☎ 08-8648 4844; www.prairiehotel.com.au; Hawker–Leigh Creek Rd; camp sites per 2 people/dm A$10/35; dishes A$10-24;) is famous for its 'Flinders feral food': camel, roo and emu.

In Parachilna Gorge, the dusty **Angorichina Tourist Village & Store** (☎ 08-8648 4842; www.angorichinavillage.com.au; Parachilna Gorge Rd; camp sites per 2 people A$16, cabins from A$58;) camping ground is surrounded by magnificent steep hills. The shared cabins are short on facilities. Bike hire costs a staggering A$50 per day.

IGA WARTA

☎ 08

About 60km from Leigh Creek, on the Arkaroola Rd, **Iga Warta** (☎ 8648 3737; www.igawarta.com; Arkaroola Rd, via Copley; camp sites per person A$18), run by members of the local Adnyamathanha Aboriginal community, offers a fantastic range of cultural tours focusing on the surrounding country and Aboriginal history. You can hire tents and swags for A$18.

Perth & Around

CONTENTS

HIGHLIGHTS

- **Perth** Savour the city life, but really it's just a big, friendly country town (p380)
- **Fremantle** Live the good life with Freo's never-ending choice of hip cafés, pubs and bars (p391)
- **Rottnest Island** Lie back on the beaches (p396)
- **Bunbury** Interact with dolphins, and eat your way down Victoria St (p399)
- **Margaret River** Learn to surf, and sample some of the finest wine in the country (p404)
- **Underground caves** Explore the caves that dot the coast from Cape Naturaliste to Cape Leeuwin (p404)
- **Pemberton** Discover amazing karri forests around this picturesque spot (p408)
- **Cape Leeuwin** Watch the waves crash into the coast at Australia's most southwesterly point (p407)
- **Tree Top Walk** Gaze down at the forest floor from 40m above the ground (p411)
- **Scuba diving** Enjoy some of the best underwater views in the country at historic Albany (p413)

- **Cheer for:** the Perth Orioles in the Commonwealth Trophy (netball)
- **Eat:** fish'n'chips at Cicerello's (p395) in Fremantle
- **Drink:** a middy (285mL) of Emu Bitter
- **Listen to:** John Butler Trio's *Sunrise Over Sea* or Eskimo Joe's *A Song is a City*
- **Party at:** Sundays at Northbridge (p388) or any day in Fremantle (p396)
- **Swim at:** Perth's Scarborough Beach for the surf, and Cottesloe for the beachside pub (p383)
- **Avoid:** great white sharks, and telling the locals that the eastern states are more fun
- **Locals' nickname:** Sand Gropers

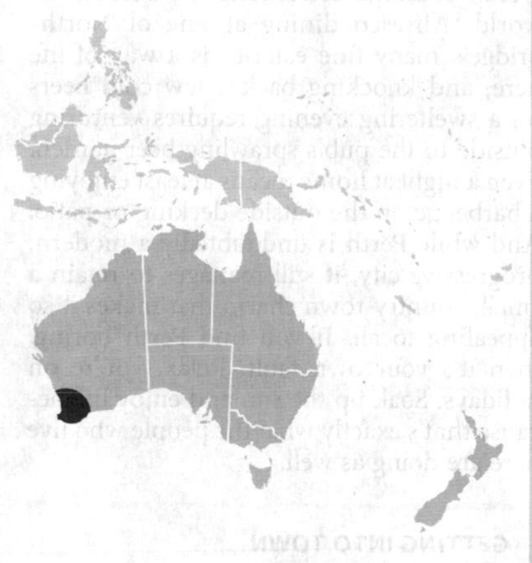

- TELEPHONE CODE: 08
- WEBSITE: www.westernaustralia.com/en

We could spend this whole introduction waxing lyrical about southwestern Australia's superb beaches, great climate, fine wines, thrilling water sports, dramatic coastal scenery, abundant wildlife, towering karri forests and extensive underground cave systems. Really, we could. But chances are if you're reading this, you'll already know about these picture-perfect highlights that make this incredible corner of the state so alluring.

What we can tell you is that the southwest and southern pockets of Western Australia (WA) hold countless little surprises around every corner. Where else can you find a giant sand-dune system rising abruptly from the forest floor with the ocean nowhere in sight? Who would have thought that one of the most popular backpacker hostels in the state would have no Internet, no TV and actually encourage you to leave the place in search of nature? How many people would know that the 950km-plus Bibbulmun Track, an eight-week slog for most, has been jogged by one amazing individual in 2½ weeks? And did you know that the most popular bird in the state, the West Coast Eagle, doesn't have feathers but has a penchant for chasing an oval-shaped ball around?

Free of crowds and the sometimes crass development that seems to plague the eastern states, WA's southwest is a hidden gem begging to be uncovered. For travels up the west coast to outback WA, see p445.

PERTH

☎ 08 / pop 1,380,000

The first thing you notice about Perth is that it's so damn clean. The footpaths are almost totally devoid of rubbish, the parks and gardens are pristine and even the skyscrapers seem to gleam differently from other cities.

It's obvious that the people love living here, and with good reason. With an awesome climate, Perth is an outdoors city. You'll find people cycling or jogging along the meandering banks of the Swan River or Kings Park at any time of the day and the white-sand beaches that hug the Indian Ocean coastline are among the best in the world. Alfresco dining at one of Northbridge's many fine eateries is a way of life here, and knocking back a few cold beers on a sweltering evening requires venturing outside to the pub's sprawling beer garden. Even a night at home means at least enjoying a barbecue on the outside decking or patio. And while Perth is undoubtedly a modern, progressive city, it still manages to retain a small, country-town charm that makes it so appealing to all. If you find Perth boring, then it's your own fault. Relax, you're on holidays. Soak up the sun and enjoy life because that's exactly what the people who live here are doing as well.

GETTING INTO TOWN

Perth's international and domestic airport terminals are about 13km and 10km east of the city centre respectively. The **Airport-City Shuttle Bus** (☎ 9479 4131) costs A$11/13 from the domestic/international terminals to the city centre and will drop off at hostels and hotels. This service gets pretty busy so if you're travelling from Perth to the airport, try to book at least a day in advance. If you need to travel between the domestic and international terminals to catch an onward flight, the shuttle can do this for a whopping A$7. A taxi will set you back around A$25/30 to and from the domestic/international terminals.

Transperth bus No 37 travels to the domestic airport from the City Busport (A$3) every 30 minutes from 6.15am to 11.20pm, returning to the city from 5.30am to 11pm.

Don't Miss: Watching the sun sink slowly into the Indian Ocean at Cottesloe Beach, joining in the fun at one of Perth's legendary Sunday sessions, painting the town red at Northbridge's many bars, pubs and clubs, working up a sweat at gorgeous Kings Park.

ORIENTATION

The train station and Wellington St Bus Station sit conveniently on the northern fringe of the city centre on Wellington St.

Despite having less than 1.5 million people, Perth is very spread out, although the city centre is quite compact. The two main streets in the central business district (CBD) are Hay St and Murray St, both running east–west. Northbridge, where many backpackers prefer to base themselves, is northeast of the city centre, and within easy walking distance. Trendy inner-city suburbs like Subiaco (west) and Leederville (northwest) are close to the city centre while the Swan River pretty much forms the CBD's southern barrier.

INFORMATION

Bookshops

All Foreign Languages Bookshop (☎ 9321 9275; 101 William St) Travel guides, foreign-language books, dictionaries and phrasebooks.

Arcane Bookshop (☎ 9328 5073; 212 William St, Northbridge) Gay and lesbian literature.

Elizabeth's Secondhand Bookshop Barrack St (☎ 9225 6094; 80 Barrack St) Hay St (☎ 9481 8848; 820 Hay St) Excellent selection of paperbacks.

Emergency

Ambulance (☎ 000)

Fire (☎ 000)

Police (☎ 000)

RACWA Roadside Assistance (☎ 13 11 11; 228 Adelaide Tce)

Internet Access

Internet access costs pretty much the same wherever you go in WA. You'll fork out around A$2 to A$3 for the first 15 minutes and generally, around A$6 per hour.

All backpacker hostels have Internet facilities, but if you find yourself cruising around town and need access fast, then the following will do the trick:

Backpackers Travel Centre (☎ 9228 1877; www.backpackerstravel.net.au; 246 William St)

Internet Cafe (☎ 9225 7555; 126-128 Barrack St)

Traveller's Club (☎ 9226 0660; 499 Wellington St)

Medical Services

Central City Medical Centre (☎ 9221 4747; 420 Wellington St; 8am-6pm) Next to the train station.
Lifecare – Dentist (☎ 9221 2777; Wellington St; 8am-8pm) Opposite the Central City Medical Centre.
Royal Perth Hospital (☎ 9224 2244; Victoria Sq)
Travel Medicine Centre (☎ 9321 7888; 5 Mill St)

Money

All major banks have plenty of branches scattered around the city. In fact it's hard not to run into one at regular intervals. The imposing BankWest skyscraper is easily identifiable because it's the tallest building in the city. You'll also find the following:
American Express (Amex; ☎ 1300 132 639; 109 St George's Tce)
Thomas Cook (☎ 9321 7811; 760 Hay St)

Post

Main post office (☎ 9326 5211; Forrest Pl; 8am-5.30pm Mon-Fri, 9am-12.30pm Sat)

Tourist Information

i-City Information Kiosk (Murray St Mall; 10am-4pm Mon-Thu & Sat, 10am-8pm Fri, noon-4pm Sun) With helpful volunteers, this kiosk is an excellent alternative to the visitors centre.
Western Australian visitors centre (☎ 1300 361 351; www.westernaustralia.net; Forrest Pl, cnr Wellington St; 8.30am-6pm Mon-Thu, 8.30am-7pm Fri, 8.30am-12.30pm Sat) Heaps of info on anywhere in the state. Also has a speedy Internet terminal.

SIGHTS

Perth's major sights are easy to get to. The museum and art gallery are based in the southern outskirts of Northbridge while most of the other attractions are in the city centre or near the Swan River. Even the aquarium is not that difficult to find by public transport. The modern city centre is mostly devoid of old architecture, but the area around Government House and the Supreme Court Gardens is worth a stroll to escape the traffic fumes.

Perth Cultural Centre

This sprawling complex houses enough stuff to keep even the most reluctant of museum and art gallery goers interested for at least half a day, and the best thing is it will cost you next to nothing.

Spread over two floors, the **Western Australian Museum** (☎ 9427 2700; www.museum.wa.gov.au; James St Mall, Northbridge; admission A$2; 9.30am-5pm) will give you an insight into the state's geological history including a superb meteorite display. There's a large collection of stuffed animals (including a massive bison), which is actually far more interesting than it sounds. Check out the dinosaur skeletons, including a fearsome T-Rex. Wander around and admire Aboriginal art and pay a visit to Megamouth, an enormous species of shark, wallowing in his own preservative bath.

The showcase of the excellent **Art Gallery of Western Australia** (☎ 9492 6600; www.artgallery.wa.gov.au; 47 James St, Northbridge; admission free; 10am-5pm) is undoubtedly the incredible array of indigenous art. Evocative images depicting the Dreamtime and traditional bark paintings are not to be missed. The gallery also contains European, Australian and Asia-Pacific art.

Perth Institute of Contemporary Arts (PICA; ☎ 9227 6144; www.pica.org.au; 51 James St, Northbridge; admission free; 11am-7pm Tue-Sun) is a nonprofit organisation that promotes contemporary Australian art. It features a changing programme of temporary exhibitions.

Aquarium of Western Australia

Don't be fooled by the name because this is not just another ho-hum water tank stuffed with fish. The emphasis is on WA marine life and it's definitely worth the effort of dragging yourself away from the beach and getting out here, at Hillarys, approximately 15km northwest of the city. This outstanding **aquarium** (AQWA; ☎ 9447 7500; www.aqwa.com.au; Hillarys Boat Harbour, 91 Southside Dr, Hillarys; admission A$22; 10am-5pm) takes you on a 98m underwater walk with around 2500 examples of 200 marine species as your tour guides (well, sort of). If you're feeling courageous, you can snorkel or dive with the sharks in the giant aquarium (A$90, plus A$30/15 diving/snorkelling equipment hire) at 1pm and 3pm daily. Take the Joondalup train to Warwick Interchange and then transfer to bus No 423 to get to the aquarium.

Kings Park

Spectacular Kings Park is where the good people of Perth go to briefly escape city life. This 4-sq-km park of natural bushland sits on the southwestern fringe of the city centre. Take the **tree-top walk** (admission free; 9am-5pm) through the southwestern corner of the park and admire the awesome views or indulge in

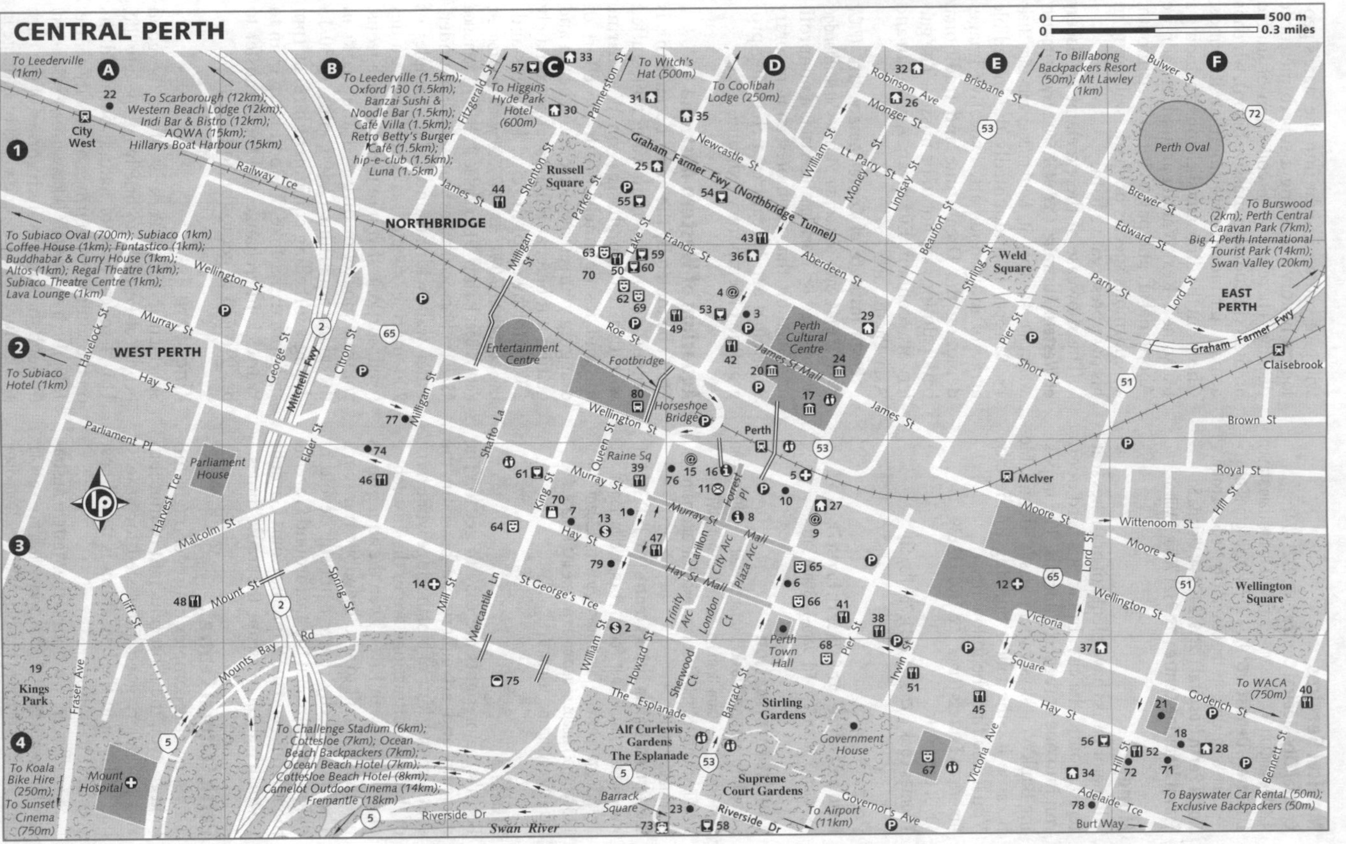
CENTRAL PERTH
0 500 m
0 0.3 miles
To Leederville (1km)
To Scarborough (12km); Western Beach Lodge (12km); Indi Bar & Bistro (12km); AQWA (15km); Hillarys Boat Harbour (15km)
City West
To Leederville (1.5km); Oxford 130 (1.5km); Banzai Sushi & Noodle Bar (1.5km); Café Villa (1.5km); Retro Betty's Burger Café (1.5km); hip-e-club (1.5km); Luna (1.5km)
To Higgins Hyde Park Hotel (600m)
To Witch's Hat (500m)
To Coolibah Lodge (250m)
To Billabong Backpackers Resort (50m); Mt Lawley (1km)
Perth Oval
To Burswood (2km); Perth Central Caravan Park (7km); Big 4 Perth International Tourist Park (14km); Swan Valley (20km)
EAST PERTH
NORTHBRIDGE
Russell Square
Weld Square
To Subiaco Oval (700m); Subiaco (1km) Coffee House (1km); Funtastico (1km); Buddhabar & Curry House (1km); Altos (1km); Regal Theatre (1km); Subiaco Theatre Centre (1km); Lava Lounge (1km)
WEST PERTH
To Subiaco Hotel (1km)
Graham Farmer Fwy (Northbridge Tunnel)
Graham Farmer Fwy
Mitchell Fwy
Railway Tce
Entertainment Centre
Perth Cultural Centre
Footbridge
Horseshoe Bridge
Perth
McIver
Claisebrook
Parliament House
Raine Sq
Forrest Pl
James St Mall
Murray St Mall
Hay St Mall
Carillon Arc
City Arc
Plaza Arc
Trinity Arc
London Ct
Sherwood Ct
Perth Town Hall
Wellington Square
Victoria Square
Stirling Gardens
Government House
Supreme Court Gardens
Alf Curlewis Gardens
The Esplanade
Barrack Square
Kings Park
Mount Hospital
Swan River
To Challenge Stadium (6km); Cottesloe (7km); Ocean Beach Backpackers (7km); Ocean Beach Hotel (7km); Cottesloe Beach Hotel (8km); Camelot Outdoor Cinema (14km); Fremantle (18km)
To Koala Bike Hire (250m); To Sunset Cinema (750m)
To Airport (11km)
To WACA (750m)
To Bayswater Car Rental (50m); Exclusive Backpackers (50m)
Burt Way
Wellington St
Murray St
Hay St
St George's Tce
Adelaide Tce
Riverside Dr
Mounts Bay Rd
Governor's Ave

INFORMATION
All Foreign Languages Bookshop........1 C3
American Express........2 C3
Arcane Bookshop........3 D2
Backpackers Travel Centre........4 D2
Central City Medical Centre........5 D3
Elizabeth's Secondhand Bookshop........6 D3
Elizabeth's Secondhand Bookshop........7 C3
i-City Information Kiosk........8 D3
Internet Cafe........9 D3
Lifecare – Dentist........10 D3
Main Post Office........11 D3
RACWA........(see 34)
Royal Perth Hospital........12 E3
Thomas Cook........13 C3
Travel Medicine Centre........14 B3
Traveller's Club........15 D3
Western Australian Visitors Centre........16 D3

SIGHTS & ACTIVITIES (pp381–3)
Art Gallery of Western Australia........17 D2
Cycle Centre........18 F4
Kings Park........19 A4
Perth Institute of Contemporary Arts........20 D2
Perth Mint........21 F4
Scitech Discovery Centre........22 A1
Swan Bells........23 D4
Western Australian Museum........24 D2

SLEEPING (pp384–6)
Backpackers International........25 C1
Governor Robinsons........26 E1
Grand Central Backpackers........27 D3
Hay St Backpackers........28 F4
Old Swan Barracks........29 D2
One World Backpackers........30 C1
Ozi Inn........31 C1
Shiralee Backpackers........32 E1
Spinner's Backpackers........33 C1
Townsend Lodge........34 E4
Underground Backpackers........35 D1
YHA Britannia International........36 D2
YMCA-Jewell House........37 E4

EATING (pp386–8)
Bernadi's Cafe........38 D3
Bobby Dazzler's Ale House & Eatery........39 C3
Cafe Asia........40 F4
City Bakery & Lunch Bar........41 D3
Govinda's Hare Krishna Restaurant........42 D2
Little India........43 D1
Lotus Vegetarian........44 C1
Magic Apple Wholefood Kitchen........45 E4
Matsuri........46 B3
Metro Food Hall........47 C3
Mount St Foodstore........48 A3
Old Shanghai Markets Food Hall........49 D2
Toledo Cafe........50 C2
Topiary Bar & Restaurant........51 E4
Wasabi........52 F4

DRINKING (pp388–9)
Brass Monkey........53 D2
Deen........54 D1
Elephant & Wheelbarrow........55 C1
Grosvenor Hotel........56 E4
La Bog........57 C1
Lucky Shag........58 D4
Mustang Bar........59 C2
Novaks Inn........60 C2
Universal Bar........(see 53)
Westende Belgian Beer Cafe........61 C3

ENTERTAINMENT (pp389–90)
Base........62 C2
Cinema Paradiso........63 C2
His Majesty's Theatre........64 C3
Hoyts Cine Centre........65 D3
Hoyts Cinema City........66 D3
Pallas Hotel........(see 59)
Perth Concert Hall........67 E4
Playhouse Theatre........68 D4
Rise........69 C2

SHOPPING (p390)
Creative Native........70 C3
Didges We Doo........(see 4)

TRANSPORT (pp390–1)
Ace Rent-a-Car........71 F4
Avis........72 F4
Barrack St Jetty........73 C4
Budget........74 B3
City Busport........75 C4
Easyrider Backpacker Tours........76 D3
Hertz........77 B2
Perth Rent-a-Car........78 E4
Qantas........79 C3
Wellington St Bus Station........80 C2

OTHER
Captain Cook Cruises........(see 73)

the free guided walks of the park and **botanic garden** offered by the **visitors centre** (☎ 9480 3569; 9.30am-4pm) at 10am and 2pm daily. Alternatively, you can wander around the well-marked walking tracks yourself.

Perth Mint

Opened in 1899, the **Perth Mint** (☎ 1800 098 817; www.perthmint.com.au; 310 Hay St; admission A$7; 9am-4pm Mon-Fri, 9am-1pm Sat & Sun) is an outstanding example of Victorian colonial architecture. Here you can join a guided tour and watch gold being poured every hour from 10am to 3pm Monday to Friday and 10am to noon Saturday and Sunday. Check out the Golden Beauty, a whopping 11.5kg gold nugget that would end all of your cash-flow problems forever.

Scitech Discovery Centre

Well worth a visit is the excellent **Scitech Discovery Centre** (☎ 9481 6295; www.scitech.org.au; 1st fl, City West Centre, cnr Sutherland St & Railway Pde, West Perth; admission A$12; 10am-5pm), a planetarium, science exhibition and puppet show (yes, puppet show!) all rolled into one. Here, you'll find changing hands-on exhibits (we enjoyed testing our balance on the space motion sickness display) that will enthral any science buff. The admission price drops to A$9 if you visit after 3pm.

Swan Bells

Containing the bells of St Martin's-in-the-Fields, given to WA by the British government in 1988 to commemorate Australia's bicentenary, the **Swan Bells** (☎ 9218 8183; www.swanbells.com.au; Barrack Sq, Riverside Dr; admission A$6; 10am-5pm) are not that interesting despite all the fuss that's made in the tourist brochures. There are excellent views from the top of the tower though, and if you visit on the first Tuesday of the month, you won't have to pay a cent.

ACTIVITIES

Perth's Mediterranean climate lends itself perfectly to enjoying the great outdoors. The beaches are world class and the water is warm enough to make swimming a blissful experience almost year-round. Walking, jogging, cycling and rollerblading are popular activities, especially along the banks of the meandering Swan River.

Beaches

Perthites boast that their beaches are equal, if not better, than anything Sydney or Queensland can serve up. They're not joking. **Cottesloe** and **Scarborough** are the most popular and plonking yourself on the sand at either to watch the sun set majestically into the Indian Ocean is something you just have to do at least once. The swimming at Cottesloe in particular is excellent and downing a beer or two at the **Ocean Beach Hotel** (OBH; p388) or the **Cottesloe Beach Hotel** (p388) after a hard day's sunbathing is a fine reward. Scarborough has some good waves if you want to dust the cobwebs off your surfboard. Other beaches include **Port** near Fremantle; safe and quiet **City Beach**; **Floreat**; and **Trigg**. Surf-free beaches on the Swan River include **Crawley**, **Peppermint Grove** and **Como**.

Cycling, Jogging & Walking

On a warm, sunny afternoon it seems like everyone in Perth gets busy doing their thing on the path that runs along the banks of the **Swan River**. If you're especially energetic, it winds all the way to Fremantle. Cyclists, joggers and walkers all share the path and it can get pretty crowded – stay to the left or suffer the consequences! **Cycle Centre** (☎ 9325 1176; 282 Hay St; ⏰ 9am-5.30pm Mon-Fri, 9am-1pm Sat, 1-4pm Sun) rents bikes for A$20 per day, while **Koala Bike Hire** (☎ 9321 3061; Fraser Ave) costs A$16 per day.

Kings Park (p381) is a haven for walkers and joggers who prefer the relaxing bush setting and the sounds of birds chirping happily away.

Whale-Watching

Humpback whales pass by Perth on their annual migration from September to December. Several companies can take you out to see these majestic creatures including **Mills Charters** (☎ 9246 5334; www.millscharters.com.au; 3hr tours A$45), which leaves from Hillary's Boat Harbour. Catch the Warwick train and then hop on bus No 423 to get there. Other operators:

Boat Torque (☎ 9421 5888) Leaves from Barrack St Jetty.

Oceanic Cruises (☎ 9335 2666; www.oceaniccruises.com.au) In Fremantle.

Scuba Diving & Snorkelling

Most diving is done from Rottnest Island, but the Marmion Marine Park, just north of Scarborough, is also a prime spot.

Sorrento Quay Dive Shop (☎ 9448 6343; www.sorrentoquaydive.com.au; Northside Dr, Hillarys Boat Harbour) does dives here from Thursday to Sunday at 6.30am, 9am and 11am for A$30, and there's also snorkelling on Saturday and Sunday at 1.45pm.

TOURS

If you haven't got time to sample the wines down at Margaret River, then the Swan Valley is the next best thing. Conveniently located east of Perth, the Swan Valley is the second best-known wine producing area in WA.

Out & About Tours (☎ 9377 3376; www.outandabouttours.com.au) does a full-day tour visiting five wineries from Tuesday to Sunday at 9.30am for A$75, including a hefty lunch. **Swan Valley Tours** (☎ 9299 6249; www.svtours.com.au) offers a similar deal.

For something a little different **Captain Cook Cruises** (☎ 9325 3341; www.captaincookcruises.com.au) does winery tours by boat down the Swan River (A$100), leaving from Barrack St Jetty. It also does half-day scenic tours of the Swan River (A$32).

Oceanic Cruises (☎ 9325 1191; www.oceaniccruises.com.au) runs one of the more interesting tours – a cruise to Carnac Island (A$80), an A-class nature reserve off the coast of Perth. There you can snorkel, see sea lions and marine birds, and go on a guided walk with a marine biologist.

Itchyfeet Adventure Tours (☎ 1800 198 189; www.itchyfeettours.com) operates a day tour to Penguin Island (A$85), just off the coast of Rockingham, south of Perth.

FESTIVALS & EVENTS

A fun time to be in Perth is for several weeks around January and February when the **Perth International Arts Festival** (www.perthfestival.com.au) and the **WA Fringe Festival** (www.adventureworld.net.au) take centre stage on the city's entertainment scene. They feature a plethora of entertainment from music, dancing, drama and film.

Royal Perth Show (www.perthroyalshow.com.au), held in September, is like a cross between an amusement park and a big animal exhibition. Take the Fremantle train and hop off at the Showgrounds station.

Perth Pride (www.pridewa.asn.au) takes place in October, as does the annual Pride March. **Artrage** (www.artrage.com.au) is a biennial contemporary arts festival with an always-interesting programme.

SLEEPING

Perth is overrun with backpacker hostels. You won't be without a cheap place to sleep here. This is both good and bad news for the budget traveller. Competition between owners is fierce, which keeps prices down. That's the good news. It also means that with so many places, many of them struggle to make even a small profit, so standards vary from incredibly bad to amazingly good. Most travellers choose to stay in Northbridge where the party action is.

City Centre

Exclusive Backpackers (☎ 9221 9991; www.exclusivebackpackers.com; 158 Adelaide Tce; dm/s/d A$17/35/50, d with bathroom A$58;) You'll receive a warm welcome at this quaint little backpackers on the eastern edge of the city centre. The place is spotless and there's a friendly, cruisey vibe in the downstairs lounge area. The single rooms with TV must be the best value in town.

Hay St Backpackers (☎ 9221 9880; haystbackpackers@hotmail.com; 266-268 Hay St; dm/s A$20/35, d with/without shower A$60/50;) For a laid-back atmosphere, it's hard to beat this sprawling hostel on the fringe of the CBD. The free Red Central Area Transit (CAT) bus stops just across the road to whisk you into town in a matter of minutes.

Grand Central Backpackers (☎ 9421 1123; grandcentralbp@hotmail.com; 379 Wellington St; dm/s A$18/36, d with bathroom A$50;) You won't complain about dust and dirt at this cavernous old hostel, close to the train station. The place is spotless, including the bathrooms, and the water pressure pumping out of the showers makes this place worth every cent.

YMCA-Jewell House (☎ 9325 8488; www.ymcajewellhouse.com; 180 Goderich St; dm/s/d A$20/36/50, s/d with TV & fridge A$40/55;) Cleaner than grandma's spring-cleaning spree, we challenge you to find a speck of dirt anywhere here – although atmosphere and fun are just as absent.

Townsend Lodge (☎ 9325 4143; 240 Adelaide Tce; www.townsend.wa.edu.au; s A$35;) Claustrophobics beware! It's a little cramped here and there are single rooms only, but it's central, cheerful and clean and the rate drops to A$28 if you stay more than one night.

Northbridge

One World Backpackers (☎ 9228 8206; www.oneworldbackpackers.com.au; 162 Aberdeen St; dm A$18-25; s/d A$50/55, s/d with bathroom A$60/65;) This absolute gem of a hostel welcomes travellers with a happy smile, big, clean rooms and a refreshing attitude. It's eco-friendly and caters for disabled travellers. Brilliant!

Coolibah Lodge (☎ 9328 9958; www.coolibahlodge.com.au; 194 Brisbane St; dm/s A$19/37, d A$55-60;) Wander through the Coolibah and the tranquillity of the place really hits you. Rooms are clean, there's a huge kitchen, and the relaxed courtyard is good for a breather or a party, depending on the mood of its guests.

Underground Backpackers (☎ 9228 3755; underground@iinet.au; 268 Newcastle St; dm A$20-24;) A big, cavernous place with plenty to keep you occupied whether it's a dip in the pool, a sip in the bar or vegging out in front of the free movies in the massive lounge area.

Witch's Hat (☎ 9228 4229; www.witchs-hat.com; 148 Palmerston St; dm/tw/d A$21/55/65;) The grand lady of all backpackers, this beautiful old house boasts a superb courtyard, a relaxed ambience and freshly painted rooms. Being just far enough away from Northbridge's hustle and bustle, peace and quiet is virtually assured here.

Spinner's Backpackers (☎ 9328 9468; www.spinnersbackpackers.com.au; 342 Newcastle St; dm/tw A$17/50;) Spinner himself is the host with the most and genuinely cares about his guests. There's a good vibe going on here and the dorms are roomy, making this place a brilliant option. Check out the radical artwork on the walls, an attraction in itself.

Billabong Backpackers Resort (☎ 9328 7720; www.backpackersresort.com.au; 381 Beaufort St; dm A$18-20, d A$55;) This popular backpackers has bathrooms in all dorms, and you can work out in the gym or grab a bite to eat at the café. Once you've done all that, you can sit back and relax on the balcony that opens up from all the rooms.

Shiralee Backpackers Hostel (☎ 9227 7448; www.shiralee.com.au; 107 Brisbane St; dm/d A$17/50;) Travellers can't stop raving about this funky hostel set in a beautiful Federation home in a quiet area of Northbridge. Guests have access to a modern, well-equipped kitchen and spacious TV lounge.

Governor Robinsons (the Guv; ☎ 9328 3200; www.govrobinsons.com.au; 7 Robinson Ave; dm A$20, tw & d A$55, d with bathroom A$65;) Intimate and relaxed, the Guv has immaculate bathrooms and a cool outside courtyard.

Ozi Inn (☎ 9328 1222; www.oziinnbackpackers.com.au; 282 Newcastle St; dm A$17, d & tw A$50;) A friendly welcome awaits at the Ozi, which has had a fresh coat of paint and offers clean, comfy dorms.

SPLURGE!

Seashells (☎ 9341 6644; www.seashells.com.au; 178 The Esplanade, Scarborough; d & tw A$200; P ✱ 💻 🏊) You can't beat the seaside location at these self-contained apartments that exude a touch of class. If you can tear yourself away from the balcony and the awesome views, you can pop downstairs for a work-out in the gym or sweat in the sauna.

Old Swan Barracks (☎ 9428 0000; www.oldswan barracks.com; 6 Francis St; dm A$18-20, s/d/tr A$45/50/60; 💻) In an old army barracks building, this sprawling hostel has 120 beds, and plans to add more. The fan-cooled rooms are adequate, there's a huge lounge area and cheap meals at the café next door.

Backpackers International (☎ 9227 9977; 110 Aberdeen St; dm/tw A$15/45, d with bathroom & air-con A$60; 💻) Big fan-cooled dorms dominate this funky hostel upstairs from a well-stocked bottle shop (gotta love that!). The windows open right up to catch the afternoon sea breeze. There's a more upmarket hostel right next door, operated by the same people.

Britannia International (☎ 9427 5155; 253 William St; britannia@yhawa.com.au; dm/s/d A$22/35/60; 💻) This old building (c 1901) is a little jaded these days, but that hasn't stopped its popularity. The high ceilings keep the heat at bay and the fan-cooled dorms are spacious. The Brit should have a new baby sister at 300 Wellington St by the time you read this.

Cottesloe & Scarborough

Ocean Beach Backpackers (☎ 9384 5111; www.obh .com.au; cnr Marine Pde & Eric St, Cottesloe; dm/s/d A$21/ 60/65; P 💻) Just a short stagger from the beach, travellers rave about the dorms with ocean views, the bathrooms and the location cannot be beaten.

Western Beach Lodge (☎ 9245 1624; 6 Westborough St, Scarborough; dm/d A$17/45; P 💻) In a quiet suburban street, this intimate place is just a quick stroll from the beach.

East of the City

Perth Central Caravan Park (☎ 9277 1704; 34 Central Ave, Ascot; camp sites per 2 people A$18) This park boasts an excellent location just 8km from the city centre with a pleasant riverside setting.

Big 4 Perth International Tourist Park (☎ 9453 6677; www.perthinternational.com.au; 186 Hale Rd, Forestfield; camp sites per 2 people A$25, tw A$60; 🏊) More a luxury holiday village than a caravan park, this awesome place is 15km east of the city and has backpacker rooms (stay seven nights and pay for six) as well as camp sites.

EATING

City Centre

A hard day's lying on the beach or a big night out requires a big feed. The city centre caters for every craving imaginable, although it does get quite deserted on weekends.

City Bakery & Lunch Bar (cnr Hay & Pier Sts; pies A$2.50, Asian dishes A$4.50-6.50; 🕒 breakfast & lunch) Don't expect much fanfare at this busy city bakery and café. Do expect filling, tasty, inexpensive tucker real fast.

Magic Apple Wholefood Kitchen (☎ 9325 8775; 447 Hay St; sandwiches & rolls from A$4; 🕒 lunch Mon-Fri; ✱) It may not look pretty from the outside, but they do the best salad rolls and sandwiches in town.

Mount St Foodstore (☎ 9485 1411; 42 Mount St; meals A$10-20; 🕒 breakfast & lunch; ✱) The breakfasts here are amazing and the emphasis is on gourmet produce, which is good news if you're sick of burgers and chips.

Topiary Bar & Restaurant (☎ 9326 7000; cnr Hay & Irwin Sts; meals A$8-14; 🕒 breakfast, lunch & dinner Mon-Fri; ✱) Big burgers, sumptuous fish and chips and tasty salads all washed down with an ice-cold beer.

Bernadi's Cafe (☎ 9221 9999; 528 Hay St; meals A$6-13; 🕒 breakfast & lunch; ✱) Bernadi's draws a steady stream of hungry patrons all too willing to sample a giant burger, focaccia or schnitzel.

Bobby Dazzler's Ale House & Eatery (☎ 9481 0728; 300 Murray St; meals A$11-16; 🕒 lunch & dinner; ✱) Bobby Dazzler's is always full with hungry locals and visitors eagerly chowing down on *nasi goreng* (spicy fried rice), beef-and-Guinness pie or good old spag bol. Wash it all down with a pint of the house-brewed Nail Ale.

Wasabi (☎ 9225 6868; 323 Hay St; meals A$8; 🕒 lunch & dinner Mon-Fri; ✱) Good, inexpensive Japanese food in a no-frills environment. The teriyaki fish is particularly inviting.

Cafe Asia (☎ 9325 1822; 72 Bennett St; meals A$8-16; 🕒 lunch Tue-Sun, dinner daily; ✱) Specialising in seafood, but catering for vegetarians as well, Cafe Asia will deliver between 6pm and 9pm anywhere in Perth city and East Perth. Try the Thai chilli chicken rice or the tasty stewed tofu with minced pork (it's damn spicy!).

Matsuri (☎ 9322 7737; QV1 Bldg, 250 St George's Tce; mains A$13-18; lunch & dinner;) Reliable Japanese fare that gets pretty popular with the after-work crowd wanting a quick bite on the run.

Down an escalator from the Hay St Mall is the **Metro Food Hall** (cnr Hay & William Sts) with surprisingly good meals for around A$6.

Northbridge

Northbridge is the home of all things food and drink. There are scores of eateries on James St, west of its intersection with Lake St. Walk along, have a look and take your pick. However, nearly every street in central Northbridge will have at least a few options to satisfy even the loudest of rumbling tummies.

Toledo Cafe (☎ 9227 9222; 35 Lake St; meals A$10; lunch & dinner Tue-Sun) Holy Toledo, you can't beat the all-you-can-eat pizza for A$10 from Sunday to Thursday between 6pm and 8pm – this place is a genuine backpacker favourite.

Govinda's Hare Krishna Restaurant (☎ 9227 1684; 200 William St; meals A$2-6; lunch & dinner) Not many people know about this low-key eatery that offers A$2 curries from 5pm to 6pm Monday to Friday and a sumptuous A$6 veg buffet at lunch time. Amazing value!

Little India (☎ 9328 8485; 275 William St; meals A$14; lunch & dinner;) If you're craving a good curry, Little India offers sizeable portions for the ravenously hungry.

Old Shanghai Markets Food Hall (James St; meals A$7-10; lunch & dinner) This heaving collection of Asian eateries all under the one roof offers a megachoice of Chinese, Indian, Japanese, Malaysian and Thai dishes to suit the budget conscious. The only trouble is deciding what country your taste buds should visit.

Lotus Vegetarian (☎ 9228 2882; 1/220 James St; meals A$7-15; lunch & dinner Tue-Sun;) Choose from more than 25 international dishes from this vegan-friendly eatery in a quiet location.

Subiaco

Stylish 'Subi' is every local's favourite hang-out on weekends. The place throbs with day trippers who plonk themselves down for brunch and coffee and a serious session of people watching.

Lava Lounge (☎ 9382 2889; 1 Rokeby Rd; meals A$7.50-16; breakfast, lunch & dinner;) Big eaters need look no further than Lava's big breakfasts (try the Eggs on Fire), massive sandwiches or filling pastas.

Coffee House (☎ 9381 4300; cnr Rokeby Rd & Churchill Ave; meals A$5-12; breakfast & lunch) Subi is not really the place to grab a quick bite, but if you're the unconventional type then this simple place has tasty sandwiches and rolls and more-substantial fare like lasagne or crumbed sausages.

Funtastico (☎ 9381 2688; 12 Rokeby Rd; meals A$12-19; breakfast, lunch & dinner;) Check out the giant wood-fired pizzas while the beef and chestnut pie and various lunch specials are sure to please.

Buddhabar & Curry House (☎ 9382 2941; 88 Rokeby Rd; meals A$10-18; lunch Thu-Sat, dinner Tue-Sun;) Tucked away just off the main drag, this intimate little Indian restaurant has an extensive á la carte menu plus a A$15 banquet every Sunday night and A$10 curries on Tuesdays.

Leederville

Not as pretentious as Subiaco, Oxford St in Leederville is low key, but still pleasant enough to warrant a short train trip from the city.

Oxford 130 (130 Oxford St; light meals A$5-10; breakfast & lunch) Busier than busy, this little café-bakery sometimes has queues of hungry people stretching out the front door. Check out the sandwiches, cakes, huge biscuits (bigger than the palm of your hand), excellent coffee and yummy wheat-free chocolate cake.

Banzai Sushi & Noodle Bar (☎ 9227 7990; 741 Newcastle St; meals A$10-16; lunch & dinner) Vegetarians will be well looked after at this modern

SPLURGE!

Altos (☎ 9382 3292; 424 Hay St, Subiaco; meals A$23-30; lunch Mon-Fri, dinner Mon-Sat;) Italian food at its supreme best. Altos serves up some of the best risottos you are ever likely to taste, with an emphasis on fresh seafood as well as an extensive wine list. Try the squid ink risotto and you will not be disappointed. Depending on the mood of the staff, the service can range from attentive to nonplussed.

Japanese eatery opposite the Leederville Hotel. Carnivores won't feel left out either.

Café Villa (☎ 9242 1554; cnr Oxford & Newcastle Sts; meals A$12-18; breakfast, lunch & dinner;) When you claim to have the best breakfasts in town, you'd better be able to back it up. We won't get into any arguments, but can report that they're damn good and the legendary sandwiches served with huge chips will keep you going until late at night.

Retro Betty's Burger Café (☎ 9444 0499; 127 Oxford St; meals A$8-15; breakfast, lunch & dinner) Popular with youngsters, this American-style diner offers big pancakes, burgers and milkshakes.

Cottesloe

Cottesloe's two cool pubs are the perfect places to grab a meal before or after hitting the white sands of beautiful Cottesloe Beach:

Ocean Beach Hotel (☎ 9384 2555; 1 Eric St; meals A$8-18; lunch & dinner;) See right.

Cottesloe Beach Hotel (☎ 9383 1100; 104 Marine Pde; meals A$8-18; lunch & dinner;) See right.

DRINKING

Perth's Sunday sessions are legendary. It seems everyone heads to their favourite local on a sunny Sunday arvo to down a few ales and catch up with friends. Northbridge thrives any day or night of the week as does Cottesloe, while the city centre is usually deserted on weekends when office workers head to their homes in the suburbs.

Brass Monkey (☎ 9227 9596; 209 William St, Northbridge) Trendy locals and thirsty travellers love this sprawling pub for its boutique brews and big beer garden. It seems everyone in Perth is here on a Friday night downing after-work ales and cocktails.

Deen (Aberdeen Hotel; ☎ 9227 9361; 84 Aberdeen St, Northbridge) If you're a backpacker and you're in Perth on a Monday night, your trip is incomplete without hitting the Deen. It's just gotta be done. It's also popular on other nights for live music, DJs and pool tables.

Mustang Bar (☎ 9328 2350; 46 Lake St, Northbridge) This American-style sports bar is hugely popular with travellers sinking beers while watching ESPN and Star Sports on the big screen. It sometimes has live music, and many of the backpacker hostels offer deals that get you cheap or free entry and discounted drinks at this place.

Ocean Beach Hotel (☎ 9384 2555; 1 Eric St, Cottesloe) After sunning yourself on the beach, the OBH is the place to go to watch the sun slide into the Indian Ocean. Many a local or traveller has ducked in here for a quick drink and stayed for hours.

Cottesloe Beach Hotel (☎ 9383 1100; 104 Marine Pde, Cottesloe) With a cool, big balcony overlooking the beach, you could easily spend an afternoon here and not realise the time.

Subiaco Hotel (☎ 9381 3069; cnr Rokeby Rd & Hay St, Subiaco) This imposing big building looks a bit like an old castle. We dare you to walk past the Subi without popping inside for a drink. We tried and failed.

Westende Belgian Beer Cafe (☎ 9321 4094; cnr King & Murray Sts, Perth) Beer connoisseurs will love this trendy bar on the west side of the city with its plethora of draught and bottled amber nectar.

Grosvenor Hotel (☎ 9325 3799; 339 Hay St) This low-key pub shows sport on a big screen in the main bar; the superb beer garden is a great spot to relax on a warm day.

Novaks Inn (☎ 9328 7974; 147 James St) Big and brash, Novaks happy hour (9.30pm to 10.30pm) draws in scores of thirsty party-goers ready to hit Base (opposite) nightclub next door.

Other places to drink the night away:

Elephant & Wheelbarrow (☎ 9448 4433; 53 Lake St, Northbridge) Homesick Brits will love this huge pub with a good range of beers on tap.

BUT I JUST WANT A BEER...

Ordering a beer at a bar seems simple enough doesn't it? You ask the bartender for a beer, he/she hands it over, you hand over your money and you sip away without a care in the world. Not so. Depending on what state you're in (that's geographically speaking!) the humble beer answers to more than one name in this huge country. For example, in NSW you'll be drinking schooners (425mL), in Victoria you'll swig on a pot (285mL) and in Tassie you'll need to ask for a 10 ounce (285mL) to be understood. It's no different here in WA. Simply ask the bartender for a middy (285mL). Of course British backpackers would not be caught dead drinking from a vessel so small. So do as they do and ask for a pint (568mL). Cheers!

La Bog (☎ 9228 0900; 361 Newcastle St, Northbridge; 🕑 8pm-late) Be early to secure a prime spot at this good old-fashioned Irish pub.
Universal Bar (☎ 9227 6771; 221 William St, Northbridge; 🕑 5pm-late) Popular any night of the week, with live music.
Lucky Shag (☎ 9221 6011; Barrack St Jetty, Perth) Cool name, great views of the Swan River and perfect if you've just staggered off the ferry from Rottnest Island.

CLUBBING

Perth's club scene doesn't heave like Melbourne's or Sydney's, but that's not to say it's dead either. Most places don't really get rocking until 11pm and most stay open until around 4am.

hip-e-club (☎ 9227 8899; cnr Oxford & Newcastle Sts, Leederville; 🕑 Tue-Sun) Travellers love the Tuesday backpackers' night at this trendy club that's still going strong when others have come and gone.

Rise (☎ 9328 7447; 139 James St, Northbridge) The real deal when it comes to clubbing, Rise is especially packed on weekends.

Base (☎ 9226 0322; cnr Lake & James Sts, Northbridge; 🕑 9pm-late Wed-Sun) More a lounge bar than a club, Base is incredibly popular on Friday and Saturday nights.

Pallas Hotel (☎ 9382 3235; 44 Lake St, Northbridge) You'll have to queue on weekends, but many say the wait is worth the effort.

ENTERTAINMENT

To escape Perth's beer and beach culture (you sure now?), you need to delve deep. Still, there's plenty to keep you interested if you're into theatre, the movies or watching big men kick an oval ball made out of pigskin around. *Xpress* magazine's website, www.xpressmag.com.au, has details of happenings in Perth, while the *Heatseeker* website also has lots of info: www.heatseeker.com.au.

Theatre

Check the *West Australian* newspaper for its theatre programs. Popular theatres:
His Majesty's Theatre (☎ 9265 0900; 825 Hay St)
Regal Theatre (☎ 9484 1133; 474 Hay St, Subiaco)
Subiaco Theatre Centre (☎ 9382 3385; 180 Hamersley Rd, Subiaco)
Playhouse Theatre (☎ 9231 2377; 3 Pier St)

Dance and classical music performances are often held at the **Perth Concert Hall** (☎ 9484 1133; 55 St Georges Tce), home to the Western Australian Symphony Orchestra.

Cinemas

Art-house films screen at the following:
Cinema Paradiso (☎ 9227 1771; Galleria complex, 164 James St, Northbridge)
Luna (☎ 9444 4056; www.lunapalace.com.au; 155 Oxford St, Leederville)
Astor (☎ 9370 1777; 659 Beaufort St, Mt Lawley)

You can also watch films outdoors in summer at **Sunset Cinema** (☎ 9385 5400; Kings Park) and **Camelot Outdoor Cinema** (☎ 9385 4793; Memorial Hall, Lochee St, Mosman Park). Ticket prices range from A$8 to A$15.

All of the Hollywood favourites are shown at **Hoyts Cinema City** (☎ 9325 2377; Hay St) opposite the town hall and **Hoyts Cine Centre** (☎ 9325 4992; 139 Murray St). Budget night is Tuesday (A$9).

Sport

From March to September you won't be able to escape Australian Rules Football (AFL, or lovingly referred to by Aussies as 'the footy') and it seems nearly every conversation is centred on how Perth's two teams – the West Coast Eagles and Fremantle Dockers – are going. Both sides play at **Subiaco Oval** (☎ 9381 2187) on alternate weekends and tickets (A$16) are available at the gate, unless the two big Victorian clubs (Essendon and Collingwood) are visiting when games are likely to be sold out well in advance.

In summer, the **West Australian Cricket Association** (WACA; ☎ 9265 7222; Nelson Cres, East Perth) ground hosts international limited-overs and Test cricket matches.

Perth Glory, the city's successful soccer team, will play its part in the newly formed nationwide A League, part of Soccer Australia's push to retain the country's talented players rather than lose them to the lucrative overseas market. The team is very popular and plays at Perth Oval.

The Perth Wildcats compete in the National Basketball League and the Perth Orioles compete in the Commonwealth Trophy (netball).

Live Music

Perth has some terrific live-music venues:
Universal Bar (☎ 9227 6771; 221 William St, Northbridge) Pulls in a fun lovin' crowd nightly (see left).

Higgins Hyde Park Hotel (☎ 9328 6166; cnr Bulwer & Fitzgerald Sts, North Perth) Jazz on Monday and Tuesday, country rock on Wednesday, and other bands on weekends.

Mustang Bar (☎ 9328 2350; 46 Lake St, Northbridge) Often has live music (see p388).

Indi Bar & Bistro (☎ 9341 1122; 27 Hastings St, Scarborough) Never fails to disappoint.

Check out Thursday's edition of the *West Australian* for a comprehensive round-up of live music venues.

PERTH & AROUND

SHOPPING

There are several places around town selling genuine indigenous art and didgeridoos.

Indigenart (☎ 9388 2899; 115 Hay St, Subiaco) This place displays certified authentic Aboriginal art on canvas, paper and bark as well as artefacts and crafts. There's another branch at **Fremantle** (Map p394; ☎ 9335 2911; 82 High St).

Creative Native (☎ 9322 3398; 32 King St, Perth) You can purchase works from internationally renowned artists at this superb gallery. Don't forget to ask for a private didgeridoo lesson. Creative Native also has a branch in **Fremantle** (Map p394; ☎ 9335 6995; 65 High St).

Didges We Doo (☎ 9228 1896; 223 William St, Northbridge) Potential didgeridoo buyers need look no further. This workshop has hundreds of termite-hollowed didgeridoos.

GETTING THERE & AWAY

Air

Low-end one-way fares (Qantas and Virgin Blue) at the time of writing: Sydney A$200, Brisbane A$280, Melbourne A$200, Adelaide A$200, Darwin A$270, Alice Springs A$270, Broome A$210. Skywest flies within WA.

Qantas (☎ 13 1313; www.qantas.com.au; 55 William St)

Skywest (☎ 1300 660 088; www.skywest.com.au) Has flights from Perth to several towns and cities in regional WA including Albany.

Virgin Blue (☎ 13 67 89; www.virginblue.com.au)

Bus

McCafferty's/Greyhound (☎ 13 20 30; www.greyhound.com.au) operates from the Wellington St Bus Station to just about everywhere in WA. See the Getting There & Away sections under individual regions throughout this chapter for more information. **Easyrider Backpacker Tours** (☎ 9226 0307; www.easyridertours.com.au; 144 William St) offers an excellent hop-on, hop-off bus service down to the southwest and Great Southern regions (p399).

Car & Motorcycle

Car rental is becoming increasingly popular among budget travellers who want to see as much of this huge state as they can. There are several budget car-rental firms in Perth as well as the major players. If you're renting a car, make absolutely certain you read the fine print otherwise you may end up with a nasty shock when you return the vehicle and find that the free unlimited kilometres that was promised only applied within a 100km radius from Perth!

Some reputable dealers that could save you a few bucks:

Ace Rent-a-Car (☎ 9221 1333; www.acerent.com.au; 311 Hay St)

Bayswater Car Rental (☎ 9325 1000; www.bayswatercarrental.com.au; 160 Adelaide Tce)

Perth Rent-a-Car (☎ 9225 5855; www.perthrentacar.com.au; 229 Adelaide Tce)

Of course, if you want the security of the big companies then they are all here:

Avis (☎ 13 63 33; www.avis.com; 46 Hill St)

Budget (☎ 13 27 27; www.budget.com; 960 Hay St)

Hertz (☎ 13 30 39; www.hertz.com; 39 Milligan St)

Ferry

Ferries to Rottnest Island depart from the Barrack St Jetty, just south of the city centre. See p397 for more details.

Train

The only service down the southern coast from Perth is the *Australind* train to Bunbury operated by **Transwa** (☎ 1300 662 205; www.transwa.wa.gov.au). See p399 for fares and schedules.

GETTING AROUND

Perth's transport system makes getting around town a breeze. The free CAT buses will get you to anywhere in the city centre and Northbridge (see opposite), while the public bus and train system, run by Transperth, are affordable and reliable. For information on getting to and from the airport, see p380.

The city's excellent bus and rail system means you'll probably only need a car for travel further afield; for information on car hire, see above.

Bus & Train

Transperth (☎ 13 62 13; www.transperth.wa.gov.au) operates the city's public buses, trains and ferries, and has information offices in the

Plaza Arcade (off the Hay St Mall), Perth train station, the City Busport (on Mounts Bay Rd) and at Wellington St bus station. These offices are open from 7.30am to 5.30pm Monday to Friday, but the Plaza Arcade office also opens from 8am to 5pm on Saturday, and the City Busport office from noon to 4pm on Sunday.

The free city-transit zone involves Transperth buses and trains within the area bounded by Northbridge (Newcastle St) in the north, the river in the south, Kings Park in the west and the Causeway.

On regular Transperth buses and trains, a short ride of one zone costs A$2, two zones A$3 and three zones A$3.80. Zone 1 includes the city centre and the inner suburbs (including Subiaco and Claremont), and Zone 2 extends all the way to Fremantle, Sorrento and Midland.

The CAT buses that whiz you around the city centre, South Perth and Northbridge are reliable, comfortable and, best of all, free. There are three different routes and each bus stop has computer read-outs that tell you how far away the next service is.

The Red CAT operates east–west from the WACA in East Perth to Outram St (next to Kings Park) and back; it runs every five minutes from 6.50am to 6.20pm Monday to Friday, and every 35 minutes from 10am on the weekend.

The Blue CAT operates north–south from Barrack St Jetty to Northbridge; services run every seven minutes from 6.50am to 6.20pm Monday to Friday, and every 15 minutes from 10am on the weekend. Special Friday (6.50am to 6.20pm, every seven minutes; 6.20pm to 1am, every seven minutes), Saturday (8.30am to 1am, every 15 minutes) and Sunday (10am to 6.15pm, every 15 minutes) services operate later hours (every 15 minutes), which come in handy if you're staying in the city centre and partying in Northbridge.

The Yellow CAT runs pretty much east–west on Wellington St and then does a short loop north and then northwest around East Perth (6.50am to 6.20pm Monday to Friday, 10am to 6.15pm Saturday and Sunday; every 15 minutes).

Transperth also operates the Fastrak suburban train lines to Armadale, Fremantle, Midland and the northern suburb of Currambine from around 5.20am to midnight Monday to Friday, with reduced services on Saturday and Sunday. During the day, some of the Joondalup trains continue to Armadale and some Fremantle trains run through to Midland. Under the plans for a new railway system linking Perth with Mandurah and Rockingham by 2007, there will be new stations on Canning and Leach Hwys.

All trains leave from Perth station on Wellington St. Your rail ticket can also be used on Transperth buses and ferries within the ticket's area of validity. You can travel without paying in the free transit zone between Claisebrook and City West train stations.

Taxi

If you need to call a cab, there are two main companies:

Black & White (☎ 9333 3333)
Swan Taxis (☎ 13 13 30)

AROUND PERTH

Perth's environs have more to keep you occupied than the city itself. Rottnest Island is a must see, and travellers have been known to bypass Perth altogether for the cruisy vibe found in Fremantle.

Activities

You can be as active or as lazy as you like. Fremantle is the perfect place to sit and watch the world go by, while Rottnest Island offers amazing **swimming** and **cycling** and world-class **scuba diving**.

FREMANTLE

☎ 08 / pop 25,000

Nowadays Fremantle has been all but swallowed by Perth's urban sprawl, but if you know what's good for you, you won't tell a Freo local that their town is part of the city. They'll staunchly defend their own turf, are proud of their town's individuality and will rightly point out that Fremantle retains a unique character and charm not found anywhere else in the state. This beautiful port city is busy every day, but especially on weekends when Perthites visit to sip coffee and people-watch along the bustling cappuccino strip, or partake of a liquid of a different variety at the many boutique pubs.

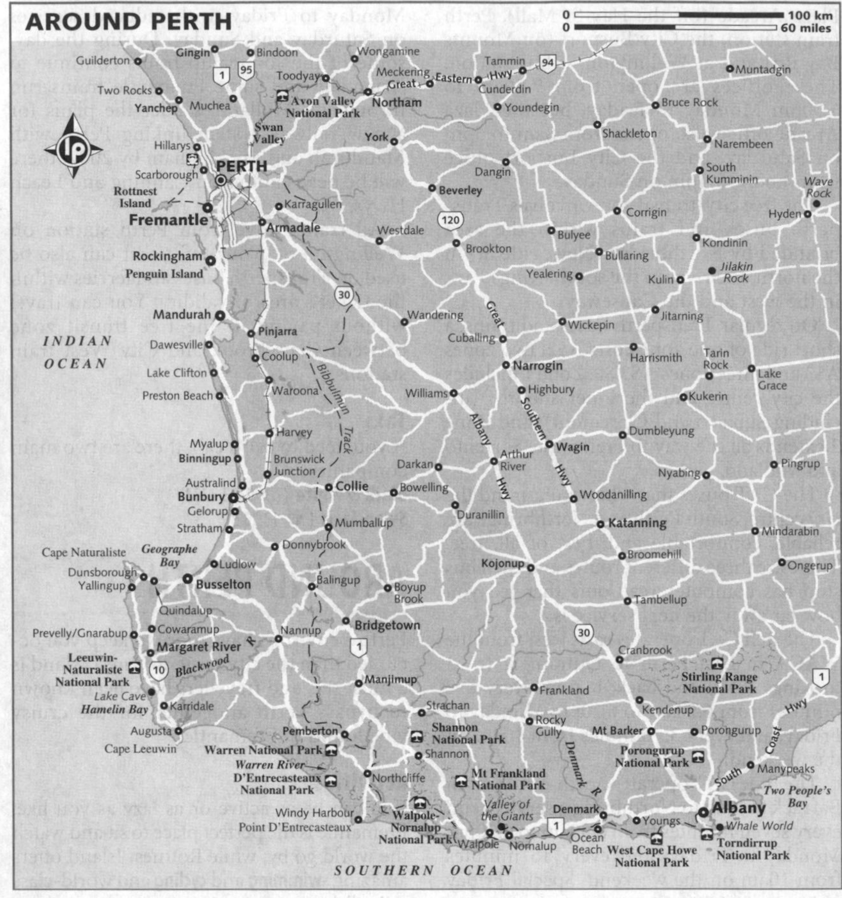

The weekend markets, seafood restaurants along the waterfront and the interesting museums are also good reasons to spend at least a few days in Freo.

Orientation

If you're heading straight to Fremantle from Perth airport, the **Fremantle Airport Shuttle** (☎ 9335 1614) will whisk you there for A$20, and the cost drops to A$13/10 per person for two/three people.

From the train station, it's an easy walk down Market St into the town centre.

Fremantle is situated at the mouth of the mighty Swan River, 18km southwest of Perth's city centre. The train station sits in between Victoria Quay Rd and Phillimore St with the Rottnest ferry terminal a short stroll southwest. South Tce, also known as the cappuccino strip, is the main eating and drinking artery and most of the places selling fish and chips, and seafood restaurants are lined up along Mews Rd.

Information

Chart & Map Shop (☎ 9335 8665; 14 Collie St) Stocks an impressive array of maps.
Fremantle Hospital (☎ 9431 3333; Alma St)
Fremantle Post Office (☎ 13 13 18; 13 Market St)
Travel Lounge (☎ 9335 8776; www.thetravellounge.com.au; 16 Market St; 🕒 7am-11pm) Internet access and an abundance of travel information.
Visitors centre (☎ 9431 7878; Town Hall, Kings Sq; 🕒 9am-5pm Mon-Fri, 10am-3pm Sat, noon-3pm Sun)

Sights

MUSEUMS

In an impressive building on the waterfront, the **Western Australian Maritime Museum** (☎ 9431 8444; www.mm.wa.gov.au; Victoria Quay; admission A$10; ⏲ 9.30am-5pm) is packed with permanent and temporary exhibitions focussing on WA's maritime links with the Indian Ocean. Must-sees include *Australia II*, the controversial winged-keeled yacht that won the America's Cup in 1983; half-hourly tours of the **Ovens Submarine** (admission A$8; ⏲ 10.30am-4.30pm), situated at the western end of Victoria Quay via a set of 9m-high stairs; recovered material from the Dutch wrecks *Zuytdorp*, *Zeewijk*, *Vergulde Draeck* and the *Batavia*; and the fascinating fishing exhibition, which explains old Aboriginal fishing techniques to present-day technology.

While on the nautical theme, don't forget to check out the **Shipwrecks Museum** (☎ 9431 8444; Cliff St; admission free; ⏲ 9.30am-5pm), in a restored convict-built commissariat building. It features displays of ships that met their fate along WA's treacherous coastline, including the hull of the Dutch ship *Batavia*, Australia's second-oldest known shipwreck, which came to grief in 1629.

Revheads will love the **Fremantle Motor Museum** (☎ 9336 5222; www.fremantlemotormuseum.net; B Shed, Victoria Quay; admission A$10; ⏲ 9.30am-5pm) located in a classic 1920s heritage building. Here you'll find historic racing cars including Allan Jones' Formula One–winning Williams, and Bob Morris' Bathurst Torana A9X. There are also cars that were once owned by the rich and famous, Vietnam War jeeps and one of the oldest Land Rovers in the world.

Housed in the convict-built **Arts Centre** (☎ 9432 9555; www.fac.org.au; cnr Ord & Finnerty Sts; admission free; ⏲ 10am-5pm), the **Fremantle History Museum** (☎ 9430 7966) recounts the port city's Aboriginal history and the town's European settlement. The arts centre is worth a look for its contemporary arts and crafts, and sometimes stages courtyard music concerts.

FREMANTLE PRISON

Guided tours of the **Fremantle Prison** (☎ 9336 9200; www.fremantleprison.com.au; 1 The Terrace; admission A$15; ⏲ 10am-5pm) offer an excellent introduction to Australia's gruesome convict history. Built in the 1850s, it was used as a maximum-security prison until 1991. Climb the gun tower for an aerial view of the complex and check out the main cell block, which housed up to 1000 men in tiny quarters (1.2m by 2.1m). Tours are held every 30 minutes, but particularly recommended are the 1½-hour candlelight tours (A$18), which leave every 15 minutes from 7pm on Wednesday and Friday.

MARKETS

Originally built as a market hall in 1897, the bustling **Fremantle Markets** (☎ 9335 2515; www.fremantlemarkets.com.au; cnr South Tce & Henderson St; ⏲ 9am-9pm Fri, 9am-5pm Sat, 10am-5pm Sun) exude sights, smells and a fun atmosphere. Visitors can stroll around in search of knick-knacks, jewellery, clothes, fruit and veg, gourmet spices and more.

For a more low-key shopping experience, check out the **E-Shed Markets** (E Shed, Victoria Quay; ⏲ 9am-6pm Fri-Sun), while waiting for your ferry to Rottnest Island.

ARCHITECTURE

The oldest public building in WA is the **Round House** (10 Arthur Head; admission A$2; ⏲ 10am-3.30pm), a solid stone structure originally built as a prison in 1831. The stately **Samson House** (61 Ellen St; admission A$3; ⏲ 1-5pm Sun) was constructed in the late 1880s for a notable Fremantle family that lived there for two generations.

Activities

If all that eating and drinking wears thin after a while, there's good scuba diving, snorkelling and fishing to be enjoyed off the coast. **All Water Adventures** (☎ 9433 6966; Shop 1, E Shed, Victoria Quay) offers diving courses, snorkelling, parasailing and deep-sea fishing.

For an adventure of a different kind, **Leeuwin Ocean Adventures** (☎ 9430 4105; www.leeuwin.com; B Berth, Victoria Quay) offers day sails (A$100) aboard the tall ship *Leeuwin* as well as half-day (A$70) and twilight (A$55) cruises.

Festivals & Events

The 10-day **Festival of Fremantle** in November is the city's biggest annual event, featuring street parades, concerts, exhibitions and free performances. Freo's January **Sardine Festival** is fun for foodies, with gourmet yabbies, crocodile, seafood and sardines on offer. There's also the **Busker's Festival** in April, and the **Blessing of the Fleet** in October. Check out www.fremantlefestivals.com/main/html for more information.

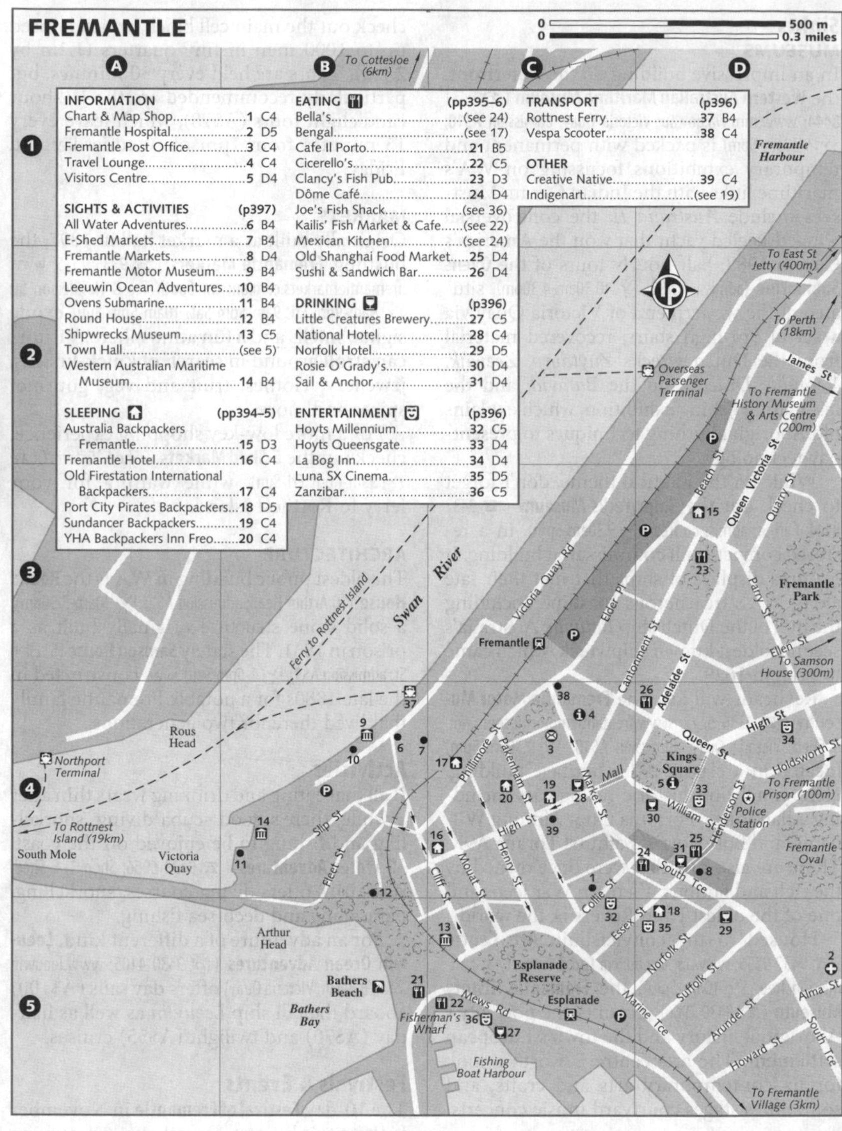

Sleeping

Freo caters well for the budget traveller.

Sundancer Backpackers (☎ 9336 6080; www.sundancerbackpackers.com; 80 High St; dm/s/d A$16/40/50, d with bathroom A$65; P 💻) The free car parking and the big outdoor spa make this place well worth the effort. The dorms are a little on the small side, but are compensated by the large, clean kitchens and fun atmosphere.

Port City Pirates Backpackers (☎ 9335 6635; www.innoz.com.au; 11 Essex St; dm A$18, s & d A$50; 💻) Relaxed and comfortable, and tucked away on a side street not far from the action, this place has an excellent courtyard, and the high ceilings keep the heat at bay. There's free airport pick-up and drop-off if you stay a few nights.

Old Firestation International Backpackers (☎ 9430 5454; 18 Phillimore St; dm/s/d A$17/22/45; P 💻) Women travellers will feel very safe here with constant, but unobtrusive, video surveillance. Management will help with finding work, there's free computer games and big clean kitchens.

Australia Backpackers Fremantle (☎ 9433 2055; 4 Beach St; dm/s/d A$17/30/45; P 💻) Formerly the Cheviot, this sprawling hostel spread over two floors boasts good-value double rooms with fridge, and a cool courtyard and massive lounge area. You can't beat the 24-hour food stop across the road.

YHA Backpackers Inn Freo (☎ 9431 7065; bpinn_freo@hotmail.com; 11 Pakenham St; dm/s/d A$18/35/50; 💻) There's a low-key vibe at this big old hostel, which boasts a roomy lounge area, OK dorms and squeaky clean kitchen.

Fremantle Village (☎ 9430 4866; 1 Cockburn Rd; camp sites unpowered/powered per 2 people A$22/24) Only 3km from the city centre, this is Fremantle's only caravan park and has grassy tent sides, free barbecues and a good campers kitchen.

SPLURGE!

Fremantle Hotel (☎ 9430 4300; cnr Cliff & High Sts; s/d A$60/85, s/d with bathroom A$85/95) Without doubt the best value-for-money place in town, the Fremantle Hotel exudes charm and grace without going over the top. You could do so much worse for this price. All rooms have TV, fridge and phone, and are spotlessly clean.

Eating

To come to Fremantle and not indulge yourself at one of the many fine cafés or restaurants would be outright cruelty to your tastebuds. If the cappuccino strip along South Tce doesn't grab you, then at the very least try some freshly cooked fish and chips along Fishing Boat Harbour.

SOUTH TERRACE & AROUND

Sitting down anywhere along the trendy, buzzing cappuccino strip on South Tce and taking in nourishment is all part of the Fremantle experience.

Dôme Café (☎ 9336 3040; 13 South Tce; meals A$10-20; 🕑 breakfast, lunch & dinner) Always busy with hungry patrons wanting a quick bite or caffeine pick-me-up. Sit outside and be part of the busy South Tce scene, if you can grab a seat.

Mexican Kitchen (☎ 9335 1394; 19 South Tce; meals A$12-20; 🕑 lunch & dinner) You can't beat the half-price nachos (A$10) between 6pm and 7pm every Tuesday, and the A$12 chicken and steak fajitas on Wednesday nights are as popular as ever.

Bella's (☎ 9336 1599; 33 South Tce; meals A$11-19; 🕑 lunch & dinner) Plonk yourself down at Bella's and prepare for a feast of pastas, gourmet salads and big burgers.

Old Shanghai Food Market (4 Henderson St; meals A$5-14; 🕑 lunch & dinner) Even those with the most discerning of palates will be satisfied at this little food hall that serves up Asian tucker to the masses.

Clancy's Fish Pub (☎ 9335 1351; 51 Cantonment St; meals A$11-20; 🕑 lunch & dinner) Backpackers love the fish and chips and jug of beer deal (A$40) that satisfies four people.

Bengal (☎ 9335 2400; meals A$3.50-8; 🕑 lunch & dinner) Conveniently located at the Old Firestation International Backpackers (left), Bengal has been dishing up cheap, filling Indian food for years.

Sushi & Sandwich Bar (☎ 9336 6685; Shop 3b, 2 Queen St; meals A$5.50; 🕑 lunch) This unpretentious Japanese hole-in-the-wall eatery is perfect for those wanting a healthy option on the run.

FISHING BOAT HARBOUR

Wandering along the picturesque waterfront with the smell of freshly cooked fish and chips wafting past your nostrils doesn't have to be a form of torture – just give yourself over to temptation.

Joe's Fish Shack (☎ 9336 7161; 42 Mews Rd; meals A$8-11; 🕑 lunch & dinner) Overlooking the port, this low-key eatery serves generous helpings of fish and chips.

Cicerello's (☎ 9335 1911; 44 Mews Rd; meals A$8-12; 🕑 lunch & dinner) It's difficult not to feel hungry once you stroll through the doors of this big barnlike place that serves fresh seafood, although the tanks filled with live fish and crustaceans are not there for consumption (we think).

Kailis' Fish Market & Cafe (☎ 9335 7755; 46 Mews Rd; meals A$7.50-12; 🕑 breakfast, lunch & dinner) One of the few places along Mews Rd that caters to nonseafood lovers. The café offers the normal fare from pies and chicken rolls to coffee and cake and, yes, there's the obligatory fish and chips.

Cafe Il Porto (☎ 9335 6726; 47 Mews Rd; meals A$14-20; ⏲ breakfast Sun, lunch & dinner daily) You can't come to Freo and not try the local delicacy, chilli mussels, at this popular restaurant.

Drinking

Few things can be better than sampling a brew in one of Freo's many boutique pubs or bars.

Little Creatures Brewery (☎ 9430 5555; 40 Mews Rd; ⏲ 10am-midnight) This award-winning microbrewery's popularity has skyrocketed as the Australian beer drinker's palate shifts ever so slowly from the tasteless mass-produced filth that is served up by some of the nation's big breweries. The pale ale and mid-strength, amber coloured Rogers' beer is served straight from the vats of this brilliant, busy brewery that also does excellent food and boasts an extensive wine list.

Sail & Anchor (☎ 9335 8433; 64 South Tce) Rub shoulders with locals and day trippers at this hugely popular pub with a vast array of naturally brewed beers and a good selection of quality wines.

Norfolk Hotel (☎ 9335 5405; 47 South Tce) The sprawling beer garden at this relaxed pub is the place to be on a warm, sunny afternoon.

National Hotel (☎ 9335 1786; cnr Market & High Sts) In the heart of town, the Nash goes off, especially when the Dockers are winning, and there's live music Thursday to Sunday.

Rosie O'Grady's (☎ 9335 1645; 23 William St) Huge Irish pub opposite the town hall.

Clubbing & Entertainment

Zanzibar (☎ 9433 3999; 42 Mews Rd; ⏲ 6pm-late Thu, noon-late Fri-Sun) This ageless nightclub-bar still pulls in the crowds thanks to its ear-blowing sound system and smooth talkin' DJs.

La Bog Inn (☎ 9336 7751; 189 High St; ⏲ 6pm-late Tue-Thu, 6pm-6am Fri & Sat, 8pm-midnight Sun) Thursday is backpackers night at La Bog with A$8 jugs and A$4 bourbons.

Luna SX Cinema (☎ 9430 5999; Essex St) Screens the latest art-house and independents. For Hollywood action, try **Hoyts Millennium** (Collie St) or **Hoyts Queensgate** (6 William St). Tickets cost between A$9 and A$14.

Getting There & Away

Fremantle sits at the end of the (surprise, surprise) Fremantle train line from Perth. The 35-minute journey costs A$3 and departs every 15 minutes.

Bus Nos 105, 106 and 111 from the City Busport in Perth go along St George's Tce to Fremantle via Canning Hwy. Bus Nos 103 and 104 depart from St George's Tce and head to Fremantle station via the north side of the river.

A more-pleasant, although costly and time-consuming, option is the ferry that leaves from Perth's Barrack St Jetty. **Oceanic Cruises** (☎ 9325 1191) operates four trips per day leaving Perth at 8.45am, 10am, noon and 2pm and departing from Fremantle at 11am, 1pm, 3.15pm and 5pm (one way/return A$14/22).

Ferries to Rottnest leave from the Rottnest Ferries Terminal at Victoria Quay. For more information see opposite.

Getting Around

The free CAT bus (7.30am to 6pm Monday to Friday, 10am to 6pm Saturday and Sunday; every 10 minutes) does a loop around the town starting from the train station, travelling around the northern stretches of the city centre, making its way to Market St and then South Tce, snaking its way to Marine Tce, up Cliff St and back to the train station.

Vespa Scooter (☎ 9336 3003; 10 Elder Pl) rents scooters for buzzing around town (A$30/45/60 for 1½/three/five hours or A$70 per day).

ROTTNEST ISLAND

☎ 08

Vehicular transport on Rottnest Island is almost nonexistent, making this little piece of paradise, 19km off the coast of Fremantle, a cyclist's dream. Only 11km long and around 4.5km wide, Dutch explorer Willem de Vlamingh named the island Rotte-nest (rat's nest) in 1696 after the large rats he saw there. It turned out these creatures were not rats at all, but small marsupials called quokkas. 'Rotto' has some of the best white-sand beaches on the west coast and offers superb swimming. The island was a brutal prison for Aborigines in the early 20th century, but these days it offers respite to Perth families who flock here en masse for their summer holidays.

Information

At the end of the jetty where the ferries dock, you'll find the helpful **accommodation office**

(☎ 9432 9111; www.rottnest.wa.gov.au; Thomson Bay) while the nearby **visitors centre** (☎ 9372 9752; 8.30am-4.45pm) offers useful information about the island. The main settlement, Thomson Bay, has a post office and an ATM.

Sights & Activities

You shouldn't miss the **Oliver Hill Gun Emplacement**, west of Thomson Bay. Installed in 1937 to protect the mainland port and its ships from attack in WWII, the guns are linked by a railway line (train ride and tour A$16). Trains leave Thomson Bay at 10.30am, 11.30am, 12.30pm, 1.30pm and 2.30pm daily. Alternatively the **visitors centre** (☎ 9372 9752) offers one-hour tours for A$4.50 (phone for times). Either cycle (20 minutes) or walk (45 minutes) there yourself.

Rottnest Voluntary Guides (☎ 9372 9757) holds some excellent free historical tours, including an Aboriginal historical walk (11am Wednesday and Saturday) and a quokka tour (1pm daily).

The small **museum** (☎ 9372 9753; Kitson St; admission A$2.50; 11am-4pm) has exhibits about the island's brutal prison history, wildlife and shipwrecks.

Vlamingh's Lookout on Lookout Hill offers superb vistas. Built in 1870, the **Lomas Cottage** (Thomson Bay; 10.30am-12.30pm) was the home of freed convict John Lomas, while the nearby **Quod** (British slang for prison) was constructed in 1864.

Of course, the main reason why so many people flock here in summer is for the **beaches**. The best way to see them is to hire a bike (see p398) and cycle around the island, taking a breather and a swim at the Basin, Longreach and Geordie Bays. Strickland, Salmon and Stark Bays offer good waves for surfers.

The temperate waters surrounding Rottnest Island support an extensive reef system and an abundance of marine life. The *Underwater Explorer II* does 45-minute reef and shipwreck tours daily from September to May (A$20) and snorkelling tours (1½ hours, November to April) for A$22. For tour times and bookings contact the **visitors centre** (☎ 9372 9752). **Malibu Dive** (☎ 9292 5111; Thomson Bay) does scuba diving off the coast for A$50/70 without/with equipment.

If getting active on top of the water is more your style, then **Time-Out** (☎ 0413-181 322; Geordie Bay) hires mini glass–bottom boats (per half-hour A$18).

Sleeping

Sleeping wise, the news is not great for budget travellers. Apart from the YHA and camping ground, accommodation options are geared towards families on mid-range budgets.

Kingstown Barracks Youth Hostel (☎ 9372 9780; kingstown@rottnest.wa.gov.au; dm/d A$19/45;) It is vital to book ahead (often more than weeks in advance in summer) if you want to stay at this 54-bed former army barracks. Check in at the accommodation office at the main jetty before you make the 1.2km walk, bike or bus trip to Kingstown. Facilities include an excellent kitchen and a large lounge area. Non-YHA members pay slightly more.

Cabins, Bungalows & Villas (☎ 9432 9111; reservations@rottnest.wa.gov.au; 1st/2nd night 4-bed bungalows A$80/40, 6-bed bungalows A$95/40) If you've got a few mates and the YHA is full and camping doesn't appeal, these self-contained bungalows are your next best bet.

Allison camping ground (☎ 9432 9111; Thomson Bay; camp sites per 2 people A$16) This dusty old camping ground, also known as Tentland, at least provides good shade from the scorching summer sun.

Eating & Drinking

Rottnest Bakery (☎ 9292 5023; Thomson Bay Mall; light meals A$3-8; breakfast & lunch) Grab a pie on the run and you may even be tempted to go back for the delicious cakes and pastries.

Rottnest Tearooms (☎ 9292 5171; Thomson Bay; meals A$10-26; breakfast, lunch & dinner) If the views don't rope you in, then the sandwiches, rolls and big burgers will.

Dôme Café (☎ 9292 5026; Thomson Bay; meals A$10-25) A branch of the popular Dôme chain, this pleasant eatery offers caffeine addicts their daily morning hit and some half-decent food too.

Rottnest Hotel (☎ 9292 5011; Bedford Ave) It's inevitable that at some stage you'll end up in the enormous beer garden of this sprawling old pub (also known as the Quokka Arms).

Getting There & Away

Return fares on most of the ferries are A$45 from Fremantle and A$60 from Perth's Barrack St Jetty. The trip takes about 30 minutes from Freo and 1½ hours from Perth.

Boat Torque (☎ 9335 6406; www.rottnestexpress.com.au) Seven ferries daily from Fremantle (adult return A$48) and three from Perth (adult return A$63).

Oceanic Cruises (☎ 9325 1191, 9430 5127; www.oceaniccruises.com.au) Four services from Perth (adult return A$60), five from Fremantle's B Shed and one from its East St jetty (adult return A$45).
Hillarys Fast Ferries (☎ 9246 1039; www.hillarysfastferries.com.au) Three boats daily from Hillarys Boat Harbour (adult return A$63) north of Perth, from September to June.

Getting Around

Get off your backside and hire a bike – everybody else does. **Rottnest Bike Hire** (☎ 9292 5105; Thomson Bay; per hr/day A$7/15; 8.30am-5pm) will have you on your way, but remember to return your bike by 4.30pm.

The free shuttle bus travels between the main bus stop in Thomson Bay, to Geordie Bay, Fay's and Longreach Bays before returning to Thomson Bay and then out to the airport and Kingstown Barracks YHA from 7.45am to 9.20pm. The separate Bayseeker Service drops you off at the island's best bays (A$7).

SWAN VALLEY

☎ 08

Beautifully situated around the Swan River is the **Swan Valley** wine region, WA's oldest. Although overshadowed by Margaret River, this region, only 18km northeast of the city centre, is WA's second most well-known wine-producing area. It makes a pleasant day trip from Perth, particularly if you haven't got time to explore down south.

Margaret River Chocolate Company (☎ 9250 1588; 5123 West Swan Rd; 10am-5pm), with its good-quality chocolates, jams and preserves, is mobbed by families on weekends. **Swan Valley Cheese Company** (☎ 9296 0600; 640 Great Northern Hwy, Herne Hill; 10am-5pm Tue-Sun) is also popular.

Feral Brewing Co (☎ 9296 4657; www.feralbrewing.com; 152 Haddrill Rd, Baskerville; 11am-6pm Wed, 11am-late Thu-Sun) is an award-winning brewery, not what its name suggests. All the beers are handcrafted on site.

There are two art galleries specialising in WA art, which are worth a look: **Lamont's Gallery** (☎ 9296 4485; 85 Bisdee Rd, Millendon), and the **Gomboc Gallery** (☎ 9274 3996; 50 James Rd, Middle Swan) which has an excellent sculpture garden.

The following list of Swan Valley wineries is by no means exhaustive, but here are some of our favourites.
Brigadoon Estate Wines (☎ 9296 2476; 65 Cathedral Ave, Brigadoon) Family-owned, with some fabulous boutique wines.
Houghton Wines (☎ 9274 9540; Dale Rd, Middle Swan) Giant among the Swan Valley wineries, WA's largest winemaker is famous for its white burgundy.
Ledaswan Winery (☎ 9296 0216; 179 Memorial Ave, Baskerville) The award-winning shiraz is reason enough to visit.
Paul Conti Wines (☎ 9309 1634; 529 Wanneroo Rd, Woodvale) Produces a good pinot noir, something Margaret River doesn't do.

For more information on Swan Valley winery tours from Perth, see p384.

THE SOUTHWEST

As you leave the 'big city' of Perth behind, you begin to anticipate what riches southwest WA has in store. Beautiful long stretches of wild ocean beaches, relaxed seaside towns, fine wines, big waves, thrilling water sports and rugged caves are some of the surprises waiting ahead.

Most travellers head straight for wonderful Bunbury, bypassing the ho-hum slightly overdeveloped coastal cities of Rockingham and Mandurah.

Activities

The southwest offers plenty to get you off your backside. You can explore the region's many superb limestone caves, and the **surfing** here is world class, particularly at Yallingup and Prevelly. The **scuba diving** around Busselton and Dunsborough is excellent while many a traveller has indulged in a bit of elbow bending at Margaret River's fantastic wineries.

Tours

If you haven't got your own wheels and don't have enough time to hike it by public transport, there are some excellent organised tours from Perth to the southwest coast.

Redback Safaris (☎ 08-9371 3695; www.redbacksafaris.com.au) has a three-day tour that covers Pemberton and the nearby karri forests, and Margaret River, although the main focus of this tour is Albany and Denmark. The tour (A$350) departs Monday and Friday from September to April.

Planet Perth (☎ 08-9225 6622; www.planettours.com.au) offers a similar deal, but over four days (YHA and VIP members/full price A$430/480) and you get a little extra time in

Margaret River. It also goes all the way down to Augusta. It departs every Thursday.

Easyrider Backpacker Tours (☎ 08-9226 0307; www.easyridertours.com.au; 144 William St) offers a tourlike atmosphere, with the flexibility of choosing your own itinerary. It offers fully guided tours, but doubles as a hop-on, hop-off bus service: you get to decide how long you spend at each place, and catch the bus when it passes through to continue your journey. It's a fun, relaxed way to travel and a good way to meet people. Options include a Southern Curl tour (YHA and VIP members/full price A$200/210), valid for three months, that departs two to five times a week from Perth and stops at Bunbury, Dunsborough, Margaret River, Augusta, Nannup, Pemberton, Walpole, Denmark and Albany.

Western Travel Bug (☎ 08-9204 4600; www.travelbug.com.au) has a four-day tour (YHA and VIP members/full price A$530/550) to Albany, Margaret River and the southwest, leaving Perth Tuesday and Thursday.

Active Safaris (☎ 08-9450 7776; www.activesafaris.com.au) has two-day southwest tours (A$260) departing Perth every Wednesday and Saturday.

Tall Timber Treks (☎ 08-9761 7076; www.talltimbertreks.com.au) offers tailored tours. Half-day kayak trips, including barbecue, costs A$45.

Getting There & Away

Transwa (☎ 1300 662 205) buses go daily from Perth to Bunbury (A$22, three hours), Busselton (A$26, 4¼ hours), Dunsborough (A$26, 4½ hours), Yallingup (A$29, 4¾ hours), Margaret River (A$30, 5½ hours) and Augusta (A$36, six hours).

South West Coachlines (☎ 08-9324 2333) also services the region daily from Perth to Bunbury (A$21), Busselton (A$25), Dunsborough (A$27), Margaret River (A$28) and Augusta (A$34).

Transwa's *Australind* train travels twice daily in both directions between Perth and Bunbury (A$22, 2½ hours). It leaves Perth at 9.30am and 5.55pm, and departs Bunbury at 6am and 2.45pm.

BUNBURY

☎ 08 / pop 28,000

Don't believe anyone when they say the best thing about Bunbury is the highway out of town. These same people have probably only ever seen the industrial bypass road on the outskirts of town on their way from Perth to Margaret River. Bunbury offers superb beaches, a dolphin experience that rivals Monkey Mia, a café, bar and restaurant scene not found outside Perth and a wonderful temperate climate. Hell, it even has its own skyscraper (well, sort of), the Bunbury Tower. Bunbury has heaps going for it and if you take the time to explore the place properly, you'll see a side that many West Australians simply couldn't be bothered looking for.

Orientation

The train station is about 3km south of the city centre and is a fair old hike with a loaded backpack. Fortunately **Bunbury City Transit** (☎ 9791 1955) will whisk you between the town's visitor information centre and the train station for free.

The bus station is at the visitors information centre on Carmody Pl, in the middle of town.

The city centre is reasonably compact and no doubt you'll be spending a bit of time wandering up and down Victoria St, where most of the cafés and restaurants are.

Information

Bunbury City Realty (☎ 9791 2200; 79 Victoria St) Plenty of computer terminals for speedy Internet access.

Bunbury Visitor Information Centre (☎ 9721 7922; Carmody Pl; 🕑 9am-5pm Mon-Fri, 9.30am-4.30pm Sat, 10am-2pm Sun) Good source of info with helpful staff, and plenty of brochures, as well as an Internet café next door.

Main Post Office (153-55 Victoria St)

Sights & Activities

If you really want to see dolphins and haven't got the time or money to get all the way up to Monkey Mia, then Bunbury offers a similar, albeit less-reliable experience. While you're pretty much guaranteed to see the dolphins at Monkey Mia (see p447), Bunbury is a bit hit and miss; the success rate is reasonably good in summer, much less so in winter.

Head out along Koombana Drive to the **Dolphin Discovery Centre** (☎ 9791 3088; www.dolphindiscovery.com.au; Koombana Beach; admission A$4; 🕑 8am-5pm Sep-May, 9am-3pm Jun-Aug) where wild bottlenose dolphins regularly visit the shallow waters during the day, though mornings are usually your best bet. You're allowed to wade in waist deep while the dolphins swim around you, but in no way are you allowed

PERTH & AROUND

to touch them (for your safety as much as theirs – some are known to bite when touched!). The centre also has an interpretive centre and minitheatre showing short films. Worth doing are the 1½-hour **Dolphin Eco Cruises** (YHA members/nonmembers A$30/33) that leave from the Discovery Centre at 11am and 2pm. From November to April you can swim with the dolphins, under the watchful eye of a marine biologist, via three-hour boat tours (A$115): 8am and 11am from December to March, and noon in November and April. If you don't fancy swimming and just want to tag along on the boat, it will set you back A$65.

Bunbury offers excellent scuba diving around the *Lena* wreck, scuttled in December 2003, 5km offshore. **Bunbury Dive Charters** (☎ 9721 6070; Bunbury Service Jetty, Boat Harbour) will take you there at 7am and 10am (per single/double dive A$70/110). Also, **Coastal Water Dive** (☎ 9721 7786; www.coastalwaterdive.com.au; 87 Albert Rd) does dives around the 55m-long *Lena* (per single/double dive A$70/105).

Dekked Out (☎ 9796 1000; dekkedout@iprimus.com.au) offers sea-kayaking (A$50) around the Leschenault Peninsula and estuary, Collie River and Koombana Bay at 8.30am from the Eaton Boat Ramp. It also does kayak tours to the Cape Region (A$90) and Hamelin Bay (A$35).

Bunbury's brilliant **surf beaches** include Lighthouse Beach and Surf Club Beach, both along Ocean Drive. Koombana Bay is protected from the surf, thanks to its sheltered harbour.

If golf is your game, **Bunbury Golf Club** (☎ 9725 1231; www.bunburygolfclub.com.au; Lot 1, Lucy Victoria Ave, Clifton Park), just north of the town of Australind, is one of the top 10 courses in the state. Green fees are A$12/23 for nine/18 holes and club hire is A$15/20.

Art lovers can wander around the **Bunbury Regional Art Galleries** (☎ 9721 8616; 64 Wittenoom St; admission free; 🕑 10am-4pm) housed in a pink building that was once a convent.

Built in 1880 by the King family, the **King Cottage Museum** (☎ 9721 7546; 77 Forrest Ave; admission A$2; 🕑 2-4pm) has rooms that are furnished with items from 1880 to 1920, and features changing exhibits and outdoor displays.

Climb the **Marlston Hill Lookout** (admission free) up the steps off Victoria St for sweeping views over town, the Indian Ocean and the harbour.

Sleeping

Bunbury's two backpacker hostels are conveniently located close to the beach and the city centre.

Wander Inn (☎ 9721 3242; www.bunburybackpackers.com.au; 16 Clifton St; dm A$16-20, s/d A$36/50; 💻) With a huge outside area at the back, good, clean rooms and a wonderfully laid-back vibe, this superb hostel is deservedly popular. Don't forget the free coffee and cake at 6.30pm every evening, and the regular barbecues (A$8). Non-VIP members pay a little extra.

Dolphin Retreat YHA (☎ 9792 4690; 14 Wellington St; dm/s A$18/28, d & tw A$50; 💻) Only six-weeks old at the time of research, and undergoing extensive renovations, this YHA hostel offers free pool and table tennis, big dorms sleeping a maximum of four and a good kitchen. The back shed should be completely covered by murals by the time you read this. Non-YHA members pay A$2 more.

Bunbury has several decent caravan parks for those wanting to pitch a tent:

Koombana Bay Holiday Resort (☎ 9791 3900; www.kbhr.com.au; Koombana Dr; camp sites unpowered/powered per 2 people A$20/25; 🏊) Opposite the Dolphin Discovery Centre, this big park has a good campers kitchen and is conveniently located about 600m from the town centre. The self-contained cabins (A$60) are excellent value.

Waterloo Village Caravan Park (☎ 9725 4434; Lot 9, South Western Hwy, Waterloo; camp sites unpowered/powered per 2 people A$18/20) Just 10 minutes from the city.

Glade Caravan Park (☎ 9721 3800; www.glade.com.au; cnr Timperley Rd & Bussell Hwy; camp sites unpowered/powered per 2 people A$15/22, cabins without/with bathroom A$50/70; 🏊) Excellent undercover barbecue area, and the resort-style pool is especially inviting.

Eating

While it may not quite grab your attention like Fremantle's, Bunbury's version of the cappuccino strip, on Victoria St, is a pleasant surprise.

Just One Thai (☎ 9721 1205; 109a Victoria St; meals A$8.50-17; 🕑 lunch & dinner) Talk about popular! It seems all of Bunbury comes here at least once a week for consistently good Thai food including some mouth-watering vegetarian options. Whether dining in or grabbing take away, expect to wait.

Walkabout Cafe (☎ 9791 6922; 66 Victoria St; meals A$11-15; 🕑 lunch & dinner; 🎲) The burgers here are filling, and the seafood and salads are decent, too. For a splurge, try the barramundi

(A$22) and feel no guilt whatsoever afterwards.

Henrys (☎ 9721 6000; 97 Victoria St; meals A$7.50-16; breakfast, lunch & dinner) Henrys is always teeming with famished locals wanting a piece of the all-day breakfasts or fresh seafood. If caffeine is your go, then they don't make it better anywhere in town.

Wah Sing (☎ 9791 8799; 68 Victoria St; meals A$9.50-16; lunch Sun-Fri, dinner daily;) This busy Chinese restaurant is not fancy, but it's always busy and gets the job the done.

Drooley's Pizza Lounge (☎ 9721 3417; 70 Victoria St; pizzas A$7.50-15; dinner) You'll find very good pizzas here, including the Heart Smart Pizza – a low fat, no-cheese, vegetarian pizza with more than 13 ingredients.

Raang Mahal (☎ 9792 1555; 27 Victoria St; meals A$15; lunch Tue-Fri, dinner daily;) Intimate and nicely furnished, this polished Indian restaurant at the top end of town has an A$8 veg curry-and-rice lunch special, and 15% off all take-away orders.

Do It Yourself Lunch Bar (☎ 9791 1868; 42 Victoria St; sandwiches & rolls A$5.50; lunch;) For those who want to know exactly what goes in their lunch-time sandwich, this do-it-yourself place allows you to build your own.

Drinking

Bunbury has a young, vibrant population, which makes ducking out for a sip an enjoyable affair.

Rose Hotel (☎ 9721 4533; cnr Victoria & Wellington Sts) Sophisticated pub with a good range of beers on tap.

Fitzgerald's (☎ 9791 2295; 22 Victoria St) This big Irish pub-bar has a massive dance floor and a beer garden with a relaxed feel.

Trafalgar's (☎ 9721 2600; 36 Victoria St) Good for a low-key drink while gazing at live sports on the big screen.

Jane's Jungle Juice (☎ 9791 8808; 52 Victoria St; juices A$5) For a natural pick-me-up try the staggering array of juices, smoothies and wheatgrass shots available here, and perhaps some vegetarian tucker thrown in for good measure.

Clubbing & Entertainment

Grand Cinemas (☎ 9791 4418; cnr Victoria & Clifton Sts) Settle back and watch a movie from one of the six big screens.

Prince of Wales (☎ 9721 2016; 41 Stephen St) The best pub in town for live music, this big, rambling place is incredibly popular on weekends.

Exit (☎ 9791 6522; Victoria St; 6pm-late Fri & Sat) In a little alleyway off the main street, Exit claims to be as good as any club in Melbourne, Sydney or Perth. It can accommodate up to 1000 partygoers so we'll let you decide for yourself.

Barbados Lounge Bar (☎ 9791 6555; 15 Bonnefoi Blvd, Marlston Waterfront; 7am-midnight Mon-Sat, 7am-10pm Sun) Bunbury's Marlston Waterfront is thriving after an extensive redevelopment and Barbados is a sprawling club that also doubles as a bar and restaurant. You'll find a wide range of beers on tap, comfy sofas and a big dance floor.

Getting Around

Bunbury City Transit (☎ 9791 1955; Bicentennial Sq, Carmody Pl) covers the region around the city as far north as Australind and south to Gelorup. You can get a bus from the visitor information centre to the train station for free.

BUSSELTON

☎ 08 / pop 11,000

This low-key, picturesque seaside town virtually triples in size during summer when West Aussie holidaymakers are drawn to its sheltered beaches and relaxed atmosphere. Busselton is a town on the go with real estate prices soaring as investors take advantage of the area's popularity surge. Long-term travellers are drawn here for grape-picking work.

Information

Busselton Tourist Bureau (☎ 9752 1288; 38 Peel Tce; 8.30am-5pm Mon-Fri, 9am-4pm Sat, 10am-3pm Sun) Busy visitors centre that operates on reduced hours in winter.

Novatech Computers (☎ 9754 2838; Shop 10, Busselton Blvd) Check your email here.

Sights & Activities

One of the most popular tourist attractions in the state – in fact, some unofficial sources say *the* busiest – is undoubtedly **Busselton Jetty** (☎ 9754 3689; jetty/train/observatory A$2.50/5/13; 7.30am-6pm). It's hard to argue when you turn up to view the underwater observatory at the end of the jetty, only to be told it has been booked out for the day (phone ahead a day in advance to be sure of getting in). This is the town's pride and joy. It's the longest wooden jetty in the southern hemisphere, stretching almost 2km into the clear blue waters of the Indian Ocean. The underwater observatory is as close as you're going to get to scuba diving without having to struggle into a wetsuit. Once you're past the admission kiosk, stroll down to the observatory (give the 20-minute, and costly, miniature-train ride a big miss) where you'll see colourful reef fish and coral. On windy days, the walk out there can be an adventure in itself.

You can dive the nearby *Swan* wreck (double dive without/with gear A$130/160) and the coral reefs with **Dive Shed** (☎ 7754 1615; www.diveshed.com.au; 21a Queen St).

Daredevils can skydive with **Southern Skydivers** (☎ 0439-979 897; Busselton Regional Airport), with barely a 10-minute briefing before you're ready to jump out of that plane.

For more water action go for a spin, weather permitting, with **Busselton Jet Ski Hire** (☎ 0428-382 382; 15min A$45), located on the waterfront. **Boats 'n Bikes** (☎ 0439-979 360; Busselton Jetty) rents boats, kayaks and bikes.

Sleeping

Busselton markets itself unashamedly towards families, but is a popular stop for backpackers as well. There are scores of caravan parks if the hostel or motor inn doesn't appeal.

Busselton Backpackers (☎ 9754 2763; www.bsnbpk.com; 14 Peel Tce; dm/d A$23/45; 🖳) You'll feel like you're a guest in someone's house at this cosy little retreat tucked away in a side street, just a short stroll from the town centre. It's immaculately clean and has a huge backyard big enough for a game of mini cricket.

Paradise Motor Inn (☎ 9752 1200; paradisemotorinn@bigpond.com; 6 Pries Ave; dm/d A$20/50; 🏊) This budget motel has a few dorm rooms stashed quietly away. The comfy beds come with a freshly folded towel, but there are no cooking facilities.

There are half a dozen or so caravan parks in and around town. Check at the tourist bureau for a full list. A couple worth checking out:

Amblin Caravan & Camping Park (☎ 9755 4079; www.amblin-caravanpark.com.au; Lot 5 Bussell Hwy; camp sites per 2 people A$24) In a beachfront location 6km south of town, this park has grassy, shady sites.

Kookaburra Caravan Park (☎ 9752 1516; 66 Marine Tce; camp sites per 2 people A$26) Just a two-minute stroll to town, this place only takes weekly bookings from Christmas until the end of January, but you can stay for as little or as long as you like the rest of the year.

Eating & Drinking

Busselton offers a decent selection of eating options, although those with exotic palates might be somewhat disappointed.

Timeless Cafe (☎ 9752 3900; 105 Queen St; meals A$7-15; 🕑 breakfast, lunch & dinner Wed-Mon, breakfast & lunch Tue) As well as standard opening hours, this unpretentious eatery stays open until 2am Wednesday to Monday, offering burgers, rolls, and old favourites like chicken parma and steaks. A little birdy told us that by the time you read this, there may be budget accommodation upstairs.

Old Chapel Cafe (☎ 9752 4155; Shop 5, Blvd Shopping Centre; meals A$4-8; 🕑 breakfast & lunch) Locals say you can't go past the A$8 breakfasts at the old St Joseph's Church, while others will politely swear by the sandwiches, coffee and cakes.

Cafe Tara (☎ 9752 3399; 62 Kent St; meals A$3-9.50; 🕑 breakfast & lunch) Hiding away in a cosy little corner of Kent St, Cafe Tara serves up good Mexican dishes as well as big club sandwiches.

Kent St Bakery (☎ 9754 2918; Kent St; cakes & slices A$2; 🕑 breakfast & lunch) This unassuming little bakery will give sweet tooths their daily sugar fix.

Vasse Bar Cafe (☎ 9754 8560; 44 Queen St; pastas A$11, pizzas A$14; 🕑 breakfast, lunch & dinner) Choose one of the many draught beers and sit outside on the undercover footpath. There's good grub here too.

Albies Bar & Bistro (☎ 9752 1166; cnr Queen & Albert Sts; mains A$10-20) With a pleasant beer garden out the back, Albies is a fine place to end the day with a well-earned bevvy.

DUNSBOROUGH

☎ 08 / pop 2500

Dunsborough has taken off in a big way with Perth retirees looking to escape the city and buy into an affordable market (although real estate prices are beginning to skyrocket). Development is starting to take hold, particularly along the picturesque beachfront, but Dunsborough still manages to retain a quintessential coastal town feel (for how long, though, we don't know). What does all this mean? Well, for a start, Dunsborough is not some large retirement village. There's enough going on to justify spending a few days here. With some superb shallow beaches, a bustling town centre and a backpacker hostel with a location to die for, Dunsborough is on the move.

Information

Dunsborough Yallingup Information Centre (☎ 9755 3299; Dunsborough Park Shopping Centre, Seymour Blvd; 9am-5pm Mon-Fri, 9am-4pm Sat & Sun) Staff here will go that extra bit to help.

Juice & Bytes (☎ 9756 8358; Shop 16, Dunsborough Park Shopping Centre) Grab a freshly squeezed juice while surfing the Internet.

Sights & Activities

Dunsborough's position on Geographe Bay makes it ideal for scuba diving. **Cape Dive** (☎ 9756 8778; www.capedive.com; Shop 3, 222 Naturaliste Tce) and **Bay Dive & Adventures** (☎ 9756 8577; baydive@westnet.com.au; 26 Dunn Bay Rd) ferries groups out to the *Swan* wreck, 2.5km offshore (single/double dive A$50/105).

If you are talking beaches then **Meelup**, **Eagle Bay** and **Bunker Bay** are your best bets; if you want thrills on top of the water, **Cape Kayaks** (☎ 9755 2728) has four-hour kayak tours departing from the boat ramp. **SeaEco Yacht Cruises** (☎ 9755 2039) has 2½-hour cruises on Geographe Bay (per person A$40), four-hour cruises (A$60) and twilight trips (A$40).

Naturaliste Charters (☎ 9755 2276) does whale-watching tours (A$45) from June to September leaving at 10am from the boat ramp on Geographe Bay Rd.

If you have your own transport, drive or ride out to the tip of Cape Naturaliste to take a guided tour of the **Cape Naturaliste Lighthouse** (☎ 9755 3955; admission A$7; 9.30am-4.30pm), otherwise it's a 13km slog on foot from town. There are some excellent walking tracks near the lighthouse.

Travellers rave about the **Quindalup Fauna Park** (☎ 9755 3933; cnr Caves & Quindalup Siding Rds; admission A$10; 9.30am-5pm) where you can wander through an aviary (and be used as a perch by resting birds), see kangaroos, wombats, quokkas and gaze at the aquarium.

Sleeping

For a small town, Dunsborough looks after the budget traveller with three backpackers.

Dunsborough Beach House YHA (☎ 9755 3107; 201-205 Geographe Bay Rd, Quindalup; dm/s A$20/30, d & tw A$50;) If this backpacker hostel were to be described in real-estate agent speak, then the word 'location' would be used repeatedly as a selling point. Situated right on the beach with superb views across the bay and access to the most awesome sunrises (if you're early enough), this hostel is popular with the party crowd. Pig out on the barbecue (A$8.50) every Tuesday and Thursday night. Bring earplugs if you want a good night's sleep though – the floorboards in the upstairs dorms and hallways creak worse than granddad's old wooden rocking chair.

Dunsborough Inn (☎ 9756 7277; www.dunsboroughinn.com; 50 Dunn Bay Rd; dm/s A$22/25;) This motel-style lodge in the heart of town has backpacker accommodation, with a clean, modern kitchen and good facilities – although the whole place is a little sterile as far as atmosphere goes.

Dunsborough Lodge (☎ 9756 8866; 13 Dunn Bay Rd; dm A$20, d with/without bathroom A$75/60;) Absolutely spotless and modern, with a breezy balcony. The future of this place was uncertain at the time of writing; it was up for sale but, as the owner insisted, only for the right price – and that could take a few years. The room with four bunks, a double bed and TV (A$95) spells excellent value.

Yallingup is your best bet for camping (p404).

Eating & Drinking

Evviva (☎ 9755 3811; Shop 1/233 Naturaliste Tce; day menu A$8-10, dinner mains A$10-30; breakfast & lunch daily, dinner Mon & Tue, Fri & Sat) The all-day breakfasts at this cosy little café will keep you going until dinner time. Night-time diners can eat alfresco, wrapping themselves in genuine Tunisian rugs that the owner brought back from her travels in North Africa.

Cafe Mozza's (☎ 9756 7104; Shop 4, Dunsborough Village; meals A$6-11; breakfast, lunch & dinner) A steady stream of locals is a fine testimony that this café is getting it right. Try the value breakfast of an egg-and-cheese muffin, a hash brown and tea or coffee (A$11).

Shakes Diner (☎ 9755 3599; Shop 9, 34 Dunn Bay Rd; meals A$8-15; breakfast & lunch) With old LPs (that's records, not our guidebooks) posted on the walls, Shakes dishes up big breakfasts and the best burgers in town.

Three Bears Bar (☎ 9755 3657; cnr Caves Rd & Naturaliste Tce) With a good range of beers on tap, this is the place to be for live music on Friday and Saturday nights.

YALLINGUP

☎ 08

Surfers will want to check out the waves at Yallingup; but while it's a pleasant place to spend a day, there's not much to warrant staying the night as most of the attractions near here can be visited using Dunsborough as base.

Sights & Activities

When the surf is up, the beach at Yallingup is the place to be. If you can't surf, **Yallingup Surf School** (☎ 9755 2755) will get you riding those waves in no time.

Serious beer lovers will want to sample the produce at **Wicked Ale Brewery** (☎ 9755 2848; www.wickedalebrewery.com.au; Hemsley Rd; 🕑 10am-5pm Sun-Thu, 10am-6pm Fri & Sat), roughly halfway between Dunsborough and Yallingup. Try the flavoured beers: Bad Frog Citrus, chocolate, passionfruit and Mama's (alcoholic) ginger beer. Trust us, it tastes better than it sounds.

About 6km south of Yallingup, **Wardan Aboriginal Centre** (☎ 9756 6566; www.wardan.com.au; Injidup Springs Rd; admission A$10; 🕑 10am-4pm Wed-Mon) does guided bush walks by the Wardani people, traditional owners of most of the land in this region for 55,000 years.

About 12km south of Yallingup on the way to Margaret River, you should set aside some time to visit the **Bootleg Brewery** (☎ 9755 6300; www.bootlegbrewery.com.au; Pusey Rd, Wilyabrup; 🕑 free tastings 10am-noon Mon-Fri), which produces some truly outstanding brews including the delicious Wils Pils and Settlers Creek Pale Ale. Apart from the free tastings, you can buy 170mL glasses for A$2.50. People drive from Margaret River regularly for the renowned food (mains A$12 to A$20); bookings are essential.

Sleeping & Eating

Caves Caravan Park (☎ 9755 2196; park@caveshouse.com.au; Yallingup Beach Rd; camp sites unpowered/powered per 2 people A$25/30) Quiet and shady and a 50m stumble from the pub, this pleasant caravan park's rates drop considerably during the low season.

Yallingup Beach Holiday Park (☎ 9755 2164; www.yallingupbeach.com.au; Valley Rd; camp sites per 2 people A$25) Close to the surf beach, this large park has access to a safe swimming lagoon.

Surfside Kiosk (☎ 9755 2545; Lot 105 Valley Rd; meals A$4.50-8; 🕑 breakfast & lunch) Serious surfing requires serious nourishment and this little kiosk is packed with starving locals and day-trippers feasting on fish and chips, burgers and sandwiches. Take a number and be prepared to wait.

Caves House Hotel (☎ 9755 2131; Caves Rd; meals A$9-25; 🕑 breakfast, lunch & dinner) The breakfast pancakes are a touch different from the usual pub fare, but this is a pub after all and the stock standards are here if that's what you really want.

MARGARET RIVER

☎ 08 / pop 6000

You don't have to be a surfer or a wine buff to enjoy Margaret River, but it certainly helps. The town and its surrounding area continues to flourish as a major tourist destination, especially in summer and at Easter

CAVING IN TO TEMPTATION

While surf beaches and wine are the major attractions between Cape Naturaliste and Cape Leeuwin, there can be no denying the popularity of the region's spectacular underground limestone caves.

CaveWorks visitors centre (☎ 9757 7411; Caves Rd), about 25km north of Margaret River at Lake Cave, sells tickets, runs guided tours, and has excellent information about all the caves. Single-cave tickets cost A$16, and three-cave passes, which can be used over several days, include entry to Lake, Jewel and Mammoth Caves for A$38.

You can enter some caves yourself – such as **Mammoth** (🕑 9am-4pm) and **Calgardup** (🕑 9am-4.15pm), both about 2km north of the visitors centre – but at most you have to take a compulsory tour.

Enter **Lake Cave** (🕑 9.30am-3.30pm) on a guided tour with CaveWorks, while its tours of **Jewel Cave** (🕑 9.30am-3.30pm), 8km north of Augusta, leave on the half-hour. **Moondyne Cave**, near Jewel Cave was closed to the public at the time of writing.

Entry to the mystical **Ngilgi Cave** (☎ 9755 2152; ☎ 9.30am-4pm), 1km from Yallingup on the way to Dunsborough, is on the half-hour; tours (A$15) are semiguided with guides available to answer questions.

when it seems everyone in WA is here. Margaret River somehow finds a way to drift between being busy and sleepy, which appeals to almost everyone.

Information

Medical Centre (☎ 9757 2733; Bussell Hwy; 🕐 8am-6pm)

Post office (53 Townview Tce)

River Video (☎ 9757 2097; Shop 5, 103 Bussell Hwy) Plenty of computer terminals for Internet access.

Visitors centre (☎ 9757 2911; 100 Bussell Hwy; 🕐 9am-5pm) Excellent source of info including wine displays and accommodation bookings.

Sights & Activities

Travelling to Margaret River and not trying the wines would be like going to Ireland and not sampling a Guinness. There are a bewildering number of tours that whisk you to a handful of the region's wineries and throw in a gourmet lunch. A full-day tour costs around A$70 to A$80 and includes pick-up from your accommodation.

Wine for Dudes (☎ 9758 8699; www.winefordudes.com) A fun way to spend the day; this award-winning operator has excellent commentary and a real personal touch.

Bushtucker Tours (☎ 9757 1084; www.bushtuckertours.com) Very popular with the party crowd.

Cheers (☎ 9757 2270) Cheese and biscuits on board this bus tour.

South West Adventure Tours (SWAT; ☎ 9758 7654; www.swatmr.com.au) The half-day wine trail from 2pm to 6pm covers four wineries and includes a vineyard platter.

Margaret River Tours (☎ 0419-917 166; www.margaretrivertours.com) Also does surfing and sightseeing tours.

Chocoholics should head straight for **Margaret River Chocolate Company** (☎ 9755 6555; www.chocolatefactory.com.au; cnr Harman's Mill & Harman's Sth Rds, Metricup; 🕐 10am-5pm), where all of the chocolate is imported from Belgium and moulded here.

First-time visitors may not be aware that Margaret River is actually 12km inland and not right on the beach.

Surfers Point is the place to head for all things surf, and is where four-time WA state surfing champion Josh Palmateer from the **Surf Academy** (☎ 9757 3850; joshpal@westnet.com.au) will teach you to ride those waves (boards and wetsuits provided) for A$40 per person in a group of three.

Seafari Charters (☎ 9757 1050; seafari@highway1.com.au) offers scuba diving (full day charters A$160), fishing (A$150) and whale-watching charters.

Adventure In (☎ 9757 2104; Bussell Hwy) just up from the visitors centre will keep thrill seekers happy with abseiling (full day A$160), climbing, canoeing (half/full day A$90/160) and caving (half day A$90).

Housing the largest collection of birds of prey in Australia, **Eagles Heritage Raptor Wildlife Centre** (☎ 9757 2966; www.eaglesheritage.com.au; Boodjidup Rd; admission A$9; 🕐 10am-5pm) virtually opposite Xanadu winery has a flying display at 11am and 1.30pm.

If you have your own transport and can bribe someone into being the designated driver then there's no reason why you can't visit some of the region's wineries by yourself. There are far too many good vineyards to list them all here, but we did some serious investigating (all in the name of research, you understand) and came up with the following:

Alexandra Bridge (☎ 9758 5988; www.alexandrabridgewines.com.au; Brockman Hwy, Karridale) Robust reds and cool whites.

Cullen (☎ 9755 5277; www.cullenwines.com.au; Caves Rd, Cowaramup) Taste the 2002 Ellen Bussell Red and you probably won't leave without a bottle tucked under your arm.

Evans & Tate (☎ 9755 6244; www.evansandtate.com.au; cnr Caves & Metricup Rds, Wilyabrup) Award-winning winery; staggering variety.

Leeuwin Estate (☎ 9759 0000; www.leeuwinestate.com.au; Stevens Rd, Margaret River) The Art Series chardonnay is widely considered Australia's best white wine.

Vasse Felix (☎ 9755 5242; www.vassefelix.com.au; cnr Caves & Harmans Rds, Cowaramup) One of Australia's favourite wineries.

Voyager Estate (☎ 9757 6354; www.voyagerestate.com.au; Stevens Rd, Margaret River) Huge old estate with some of the finest drops in the country.

Sleeping

Book well ahead during Christmas and especially Easter (when the Salomon Masters surfing championships are held).

Surfpoint Resort (☎ 9757 1777; www.surfpoint.com.au; Riedle Dr, Gnarabup; dm/d/tr A$24/75/85; 💻) About 12km from Margaret River on the beach in the Prevelly/Gnarabup area, this brilliant, modern place is right up there with the best of them. Built in 1996 and winner of the Best Backpackers in WA award in 2003, it has a huge, clean kitchen. The well-manicured lawns and abundant greenery make it a peaceful place to crash.

Margaret River Lodge (☎ 9757 9532; www.mrlodge.com.au; 220 Railway Tce; dm/s/d A$19/40/55; 🖳 🅿) This YHA hostel about 1.5km from town attracts the younger party-going crowd and has plenty of showers, a groovy TV room and brilliant swimming pool. The doubles with bathroom and TV are great value. Non-YHA members pay a little extra.

Inne Town Backpackers (☎ 9757 3698; www.margaretriverbackpacker.com; 93 Bussell Hwy; dm A$20-22, d/tr A$55/75; 🖳) The kitchen was being renovated when we passed through and will give this place the spruce up it needs. Conveniently located in the heart of town, this backpackers has 42 beds, an outside pool table and a happy vibe.

Riverview Cabins & Camping (☎ 9757 2270; www.riverviewcabin.com; 8-10 Willmott Ave; camp sites per 2 people A$20, cabins A$55) Only about 1km from town, this caravan park has a campers kitchen, good nearby walking tracks and a friendly resident kookaburra named Wally, who sometimes visits guests.

Big Valley (☎ 9757 5020; Wallis Rd, off Rose Brook Rd; camp sites unpowered/powered per 2 people A$7/8) Catering especially for campers with tents, Big Valley is 9km southeast of Margaret River and has hot water, fridges, a campers kitchen, barbecues and camp fires. It's closed from May to October.

Eating & Drinking

Whether it's a bite in one of the excellent cafés or a gourmet splurge at a winery, you won't go hungry in Margaret River.

Ashtons Bakery (☎ 9757 2539; Shop 4, Settlers Arcade, 116 Bussell Hwy; light meals A$5; 🕒 breakfast & lunch) This little hole-in-the-wall bakery keeps 'em coming back for the big filled rolls, pies and beef burgers.

Goodfellas Cafe (☎ 9757 3184; 97 Bussell Hwy; meals A$12-20; 🕒 lunch & dinner) Opposite the visitors centre, Goodfellas has been dishing out pasta, steak, calamari and tasty woodfired pizzas for yonks.

Chill-E-Cafe (☎ 9758 7222; 111 Bussell Hwy; meals A$10-14; 🕒 breakfast & lunch) Surf the Net while chowing down on a grilled fish burger or a BLT.

Sea Gardens Café (☎ 9757 2374; Lot 99, Mitchell Dr, Prevelly Park; meals A$8-19; 🕒 breakfast, lunch & dinner) Famished surfers and beachgoers love the hearty pizzas, pastas, burgers and salads at this place on the beach.

Aloha Sushi & Juice Bar (☎ 9757 9300; BankWest Bldg, Shop 2b, 142 Bussell Hwy; meals A$9.50-12; 🕒 lunch) Health-conscious types enjoy the low-cal Japanese food and vitamin-packed juices (small/large A$5/7). We loved the bento beef, although there could have been more of it.

Settlers Tavern (☎ 9757 2398; 114 Bussell Hwy) With live music Wednesday to Saturday, Settlers is the place to wind down after a hard day.

Wino's (☎ 9758 7155; 85 Bussell Hwy) With a wide selection of local wines and premium bottled beers, Wino's fits the bill for a quiet drink.

Margarets Beach Resort (☎ 9757 1227; 1 Resort Pl, Gnarabup) A short stumble from Surfpoint Resort (p405), the Thursday and Friday sundowner drinks and live music one Friday per month are popular. Travellers give the take-away pizzas the big thumbs up.

Getting Around

Margaret River Scooter Hire (☎ 9757 3698; Bussell Hwy) just down from the visitor centre hires scooters (per hour/four hours/full day A$10/30/45).

AUGUSTA

☎ 08 / pop 2000

Where the Indian and Southern Oceans collide, Augusta's sleepiness is part of its charm. Locals love the unhurried atmosphere of their little town and are ready to fight the inevitable mass development when it finally arrives from the north.

Information

Augusta visitors centre (☎ 9758 0166; cnr Blackwood Ave & Ellis St; 🕒 9am-5pm) At the time of research they were planning to move a bit further up Blackwood Ave.

Leeuwin Movie World (☎ 9758 1444; Lot 91, Shop 2, Blackwood Ave) Grab a coffee from the coin-operated machine and surf the Net.

Sights & Activities

Naturaliste Charters (☎ 9755 2276; www.whales-australia.com) does whale-watching tours (A$45) from June to September.

Hop aboard the **Sea Dragon** (☎ 9758 4003; cdragon@west.net.com.au) or **Miss Flinders** (☎ 9758 1944) for cruises of the scenic Blackwood River (A$20). Both skippers are women, and possess a vast knowledge of the area. The boats leave from the Ellis St jetty.

Southwest Fishing Adventures (☎ 9758 1950) does fishing tours on the Blackwood River.

The small, but interesting **Augusta Historical Museum** (☎ 9758 1948; 47 Blackwood Ave; admission A$2; ⏲ 10am-noon & 2-4pm Sep-Apr, 10am-noon May-Aug) focuses on local history, including a must-see display of the 1986 whale rescue that catapulted Augusta into the international spotlight.

If you have your own wheels, or feel like an 8km walk, the **Cape Leeuwin Lighthouse** (☎ 9758 1944; admission A$7; ⏲ 8.45am-5pm) should not be missed. You can take a guided tour of this 39m-high structure, or you can wander around the lighthouse and surrounding area for free. Indeed, standing on the edge of Cape Leeuwin with the waves of the Indian and Southern Oceans crashing into the cliffs, makes you feel very, very small.

Sleeping

Baywatch Manor Resort (☎ 9758 1290; enquiries@baywatchmanor.com.au; 88 Blackwood Ave; dm/d A$20/50; 💻) Best YHA in Oz six years running and it's not slowing down. This place exudes personal charm and grace. All beds, even the dorms, have a neatly folded towel and bar of soap. It's not a party place, but then again neither is Augusta.

Leeuwin House (☎ 9758 1290; Blackwood Ave; dm A$18-22, s A$22-26, d A$50-55, tr A$60-70) Operated by the Augusta Hotel-Motel across the road (go there to check-in) this place is clean and perfectly acceptable, but there's no full-time caretaker and it lacks atmosphere.

Clovelly Holiday Units (☎ 9758 1577; 78 Blackwood Ave; d/tr A$60/80) Worth considering for a little more luxury at a little more cost.

Check at the visitors centre for a list of caravan parks around Augusta (there are four of them), although we did like **Flinders Bay Park** (☎ 9758 1380; flindersbaypark@westnet.com.au; Albany Tce; camp sites unpowered/powered per 2 people A$20/23), which has full beachfront access.

Eating & Drinking

Augusta Bakery & Café (☎ 9758 1664; 121 Blackwood Ave; light meals A$3-10, pizzas A$12; ⏲ breakfast & lunch daily, dinner Fri) The Friday night pizzas are going strong (nightly in January) and the breakfasts, pies and light meals are as good.

Cosy Corner Cafe (☎ 9758 1408; 100 Blackwood Ave; meals A$7-18; ⏲ breakfast, lunch & dinner) Gotta love the huge, filled rolls and views over the river. This place has everything a fussy eater could want: focaccias, burgers, hot meals, takeaways.

Squirrels (☎ 9758 1858; 63 Blackwood Ave; meals A$7-9; ⏲ breakfast & lunch) With a big reputation, Squirrels has been dishing out massive burgers, fresh fish and chips and steaming hot coffee for years.

Augusta Hotel-Motel (☎ 9758 1944; Blackwood Ave) Have a drink with the locals in the main bar or grab a bite in the bistro (A$10 to A$20) with magnificent views.

SOUTHERN FORESTS

As you leave the coast and head inland, you begin to anticipate the forests and towering karri trees that wait ahead. This is real bush country and the forests here are a logger's dream. The government has scaled down logging in recent years, which has allowed the forests to prosper. Unfortunately, the same cannot be said about some of the towns, which are struggling as the population leaves in droves to search for work.

Activities

The forests in this part of the world make for some of the best **walking** tracks in the country. Northcliffe Forest Park has several short tracks that won't test your fitness level too much. For (much) more of a challenge, there's the Bibbulmun Track which runs straight through to Albany.

Getting There & Away

Transwa (☎ 1300 662 205) has six buses per week from Perth to Pemberton; some go via Bunbury and Bridgetown (A$32, 4½ hours) and some take the longer cape route via Margaret River and Augusta (A$37, eight hours). The Pemberton–Albany bus (3½ hours) goes via Northcliffe. **South West Coachlines** (☎ 08-9324 2333) travels to Nannup (A$29).

NANNUP

☎ 08 / pop 520

With the timber industry being scaled down, Nannup has done a superb job reinventing itself as a tourist destination. It bills itself as an outdoors town, with bushwalking, canoeing and relaxation the prime activities. The town really fires up during the **Tulip Festival** on the second Saturday in August and the **Music Festival** on the long weekend in March.

Information

Nannup visitors centre (☎ 9756 1211; 4 Brockman St; ⌚ 9am-5pm) In the old police station; you can also wander through the jail and prisoner exercise yard.

Telecentre (☎ 9756 3022; Lot 31, Warren Rd) Access the Internet (per hr A$6) here.

Sights & Activities

One of the main reasons travellers come to Nannup is for **canoeing** on the mighty Blackwood River.

About 25km from Nannup towards Augusta (leave the Brockman Hwy and turn into Poison Swamp Rd 8km after Stewart Rd) is **Blackwood River Canoeing** (☎ 9756 1209; blackwoodrivercanoeing@wn.com.au; Poison Swamp Rd). It offers both quick paddles and full-day downriver adventures from A$20 to A$35.

Blackwood Forest Canoeing (☎ 9756 1252; River Rd), about 12km from Nannup (after 7km travelling south, turn into River Rd and then it's 5km to the river), offers canoeing trips starting at A$25/35 for a half/full day.

Halfway between Busselton and Nannup is the **Mythic Maze** (☎ 9756 2121; St John's Brook, Vasse Hwy; admission A$4; ⌚ 10am-4pm) with a maze and sculpture garden that's actually more fun than it sounds. The **Blythe Gardens** (Brockman St; admission A$2) in Nannup is a relaxing spot.

Sleeping

Black Cockatoo (☎ 9756 1035; 27 Grange Rd; dm/s/d A$20/30/45) It's not unknown for travellers to come to Nannup specifically to stay at the Black Cockatoo, such is its reputation. Guests are encouraged to get out and explore nature at this peaceful retreat, which is why you'll find no TV or Internet here. You can sleep in the tepee, a caravan painted in Aboriginal art, and to do your stuff there's the traditional Aussie outside dunny.

Nannup Hotel Motel (☎ 9756 1164; 12 Warren Rd; dm/s/d A$22/35/60) As well as dorm rooms for backpackers and basic singles and doubles, this pub has motel-style units (A$85).

The visitors centre operates these two caravan parks under the same banner: **Nannup Caravan Parks** (☎ 9756 1211) Brockman St (camp sites unpowered/powered per 2 people A$18/19); Balingup Rd (camp sites unpowered/powered per 2 people A$13/18).

Eating & Drinking

Blackwood Cafe (☎ 9756 1120; 24 Warren Rd; meals A$4-11; ⌚ breakfast, lunch & dinner) We loved the inexpensive breakfasts (A$6 to A$10), so we came back at lunch time for the big salad rolls.

Hamish's Café (☎ 9756 1287; 1 Warren Rd; meals A$14-20; ⌚ lunch Wed-Sun, dinner Fri & Sat) Hamish's does the job if you're searching for the usual fare: pasta, steak or fish.

Good Food Shop (☎ 9756 1351; 15 Warren Rd; meals A$7-13; ⌚ breakfast & lunch) Comfort food in the form of burgers, toasted sandwiches, lasagne, nachos and hot soup can be found at this busy little place on the main drag.

Nannup Hotel Motel (☎ 9756 1164; 12 Warren Rd) It's the only pub in town, so if you want a drink of the alcoholic variety, this is your one-stop shop.

PEMBERTON

☎ 08 / pop 800

With Warren and Gloucester National Parks as next door neighbours, Pemberton's enviable location is a constant source of pride for the people who live here. The scenery is stunning and 'Pemby', as it's commonly referred to, is the sort of place where you plan to spend an afternoon and end up staying for days.

Information

CALM office (☎ 9776 1207; Kennedy St) Sells national park passes.

Pemberton visitors centre (☎ 9776 1133; Brockman St; ⌚ 9am-6pm)

Telecentre (☎ 9776 1745; 29 Brockman St) Check email here.

Sights & Activities

About 3km out of town (head down Ellis St), climbing the **Gloucester Tree** requires a big, deep breath and a carefree attitude, but the dizzy 60m scramble has deterred many a soul. It's free if you walk there, but if you have your own car, national park fees apply (A$9 per car). Tree climbers can also try the Dave Evans Bicentennial Tree in the glorious **Warren National Park**.

To appreciate the surrounding karri forests and the awesome Yeagarup sand dunes, you will need to take a 4WD tour.

Pemberton Discovery Tours (☎ 9776 0484) does tours (A$60) at 9am and 2pm daily and will take you to places you just cannot go by yourself. **Pemberton Hiking & Canoeing** (☎ 9776 1559; pemhike@wn.com.au) does four-hour walks, two- to five-day hikes through the ancient karri forests and canoeing. If abseiling or rock climbing is more your go, **Strungout Adventures** (☎ 0427-084 015) will get your heart rate up in no time (full-day abseiling tours A$140).

If you still haven't had your fill of vino from Margaret River then Pemberton's thriving wine industry is worth checking out. **Gloucester Ridge** (☎ 9776; Burma Rd) is the best known, but there are others worthy of a taste test (or two!):

Donnelly River (☎ 9776 2052; Vasse Hwy)
Hidden River Estate (☎ 9776 2052; Mullineaux Rd)
Phillips Estate (☎ 9776 0381; Channybearup Rd)

The brilliant artificial beach at **Big Brook Dam**, 6km from town in the middle of the forest, is packed with locals on warm summer days. If you're feeling energetic you can jog or walk the scenic 3.9km circumference.

The **pioneer museum** (admission A$2) is worth a quick look, while the excellent **Karri Forest Discovery Centre** (admission A$2) tells the story of the karri forest and its inhabitants. Both are housed in the visitors centre, although you must pass through the pioneer museum to get to the discovery centre.

While its appeal lies mainly with families and oldies, there's no denying the popularity of the **Pemberton Tramway Co** (☎ 9776 1322; www.pemtram.com.au; Pemberton Train Station) trains that chug their way through the karri and marri forests to Warren Bridge (A$18, 1¾ hours, 10.45am and 2pm), Eastbrook (A$23, 1¾ hours, 10.30am and 2.15pm) and Lyall (A$28, three hours, 10.30am Sunday only). If you haven't got your own transport, this is probably the best way to see the forests up close.

Sleeping

Pemby doesn't look after the budget traveller very well, but there are a few options to be found that won't blow your bank balance to smithereens.

Pemberton Backpackers & Budget Cottages (☎ 9776 1105; pembertonbackpackers@wn.com.au; 7 Brockman St; dm/s/d A$17/31/50, self-contained cottage A$70; 💻) This busy YHA has a virtual monopoly on the local budget accommodation scene, but doesn't let that lower its standards. The place exudes friendliness and its position in the middle of town is a bonus.

Pemberton Forest Stay (☎ 9776 1153; www.pembertonforeststay.com; Stirling Rd; cottages A$65) Set in a former timber-workers village 9km from town, there are six self-contained cottages here, sleeping from four to 20 people.

Pemberton Caravan Park (☎ 9776 1300; Club Rd; camp sites per 2 people A$22) Behind the backpackers hostel, this caravan park has laundry facilities and budget cabins (without/with bathroom A$70/90).

Eating

Coffee Connection (☎ 9776 1159; Dickinson St; meals A$10-13; 🕑 breakfast & lunch) This place is about 500m from town (follow the sign on Brockman St); you won't get a better cup of coffee in Pemby, and the lunches and humungous scones will keep the hunger at bay.

Pemberton Millhouse Café (☎ 9776 1122; 14 Brockman St; meals A$6-12; 🕑 breakfast & lunch) Opposite the backpackers, this quaint little tearoom-style place has a loyal following with big lunches, coffee, cakes and seven flavours of ice cream.

Jan's Diner (☎ 9776 0011; Brockman St; mains A$5-12; 🕑 breakfast & lunch) The façade paints a false picture – Jan's is actually quite large inside. Once you've had breakfast here, you won't need to fill up for the rest of the day. We loved the enormous rolls.

SHANNON NATIONAL PARK

Some of the region's most magnificent karri country can be found in this 535-sq-km national park, 53km south of Manjimup. The 48km **Great Forest Trees Drive** leads you through the old-growth forest with the bonus of onboard commentary if you tune your radio in to 100 FM when you see the signs. The full-colour *Great Forest Trees Drive* (A$15) is a detailed map and drive guidebook that's available from CALM. As you would expect from a region renowned for its pristine forests, Shannon National Park offers some excellent bushwalking opportunities.

There is a fine **camping ground** (camp sites per 2 people A$13) on the spot where the original timber-milling village used to be. The ground also has huts equipped with potbellied stoves (A$13) – all fees are on a self-registration basis.

NORTHCLIFFE

☎ 08 / pop 240

Northcliffe has been hit as hard as any town in the region thanks to a dramatic reduction in logging. But rather than sit back and wallow in self pity, this tiny town has used its misfortune as a spur to delve into other activities, namely tourism. With a network of superb walking tracks that don't require you to be a world-class athlete, you could easily spend a day exploring the surrounding forests and bushland. There's still a long way to go for Northcliffe, and many shopfronts are still unoccupied, but this feisty little town is starting to win the battle.

Information

Northcliffe visitors centre (☎ 9776 6066; Wheatley Coast Rd; 9.30am-4pm Mon-Fri, 10am-2pm Sat & Sun)

Telecentre (☎ 9776 7330; 28 Mill Rd) Internet access is available here but, given it's located about 14km from town, you may need to wait until you get to Walpole.

Sights & Activities

The annual **Karri Cup** mountain-bike championships attracts mountain bikers from all over the state.

Most people come to Northcliffe for the abundant **walking** tracks close to town in **Northcliffe Forest Park**. The 400m Twin Karri Loop just out of town, off Forest Park Drive, is a good place to start. Once you've done that it's time to tackle the 3.5km Marri Meander route nearby. A path next to the visitors centre leads to the Bardi Creek Trail, a 700m walk to the Gardner River Trail that drifts for a further 1km.

The **Pioneer Museum** (admission A$2) next to the visitors centre gives a good insight into what life was like for the early settlers of the region in 1924. Check out the old washing machine and never again curse about having to wash your dirty clothes.

Windy Harbour, 26km south of Northcliffe, has a sheltered beach on a stretch of wild coastline and the cliffs of the fine **Point D'Entrecasteaux** are accessible from here. The road here has been improved and allows easy access for 2WD vehicles. About halfway between Northcliffe and Windy Harbour, the 187m-high lookout at **Mt Chudalup** offers superb views.

Sleeping & Eating

One of the things that makes Northcliffe appealing is that accommodation is dirt cheap. There is an abundance of inexpensive farmstays and B&Bs in the area. Ask at the visitors centre for a full list.

Northcliffe Hotel (☎ 9776 7089; Wheatley Coast Rd; s/d/tw A$35/55/65) Bibb Track walkers and backpackers get a A$5 discount at this friendly local pub.

Round Tu-It Holiday Park (☎ 9776 7276; Muirillup Rd; dm A$15, camp sites per 2 people A$20, caravans A$45, B&B s/d A$45/65) About 2km from town with a campers kitchen, this park has a number of accommodation options.

Northcliffe Caravan Park (☎ 9776 7295; Zamia St; camp sites unpowered/powered per 2 people A$6/9) This basic caravan park is right in the centre of town.

Hollowbutt Cafe (☎ 9776 6050; Zamia St; meals A$3.50-7; breakfast & lunch daily, dinner Fri) We didn't ask (and didn't want to know) how this place got its name, but the coffee, home-made pies, sausage rolls and sandwiches make it the most popular place in town.

GREAT SOUTHERN

With nothing separating it from the Antarctic, the Great Southern coastline is spectacularly wild and rugged. When the weather is good there are some fine beaches for lazing about, the national parks are stunning and the friendly little towns that dot the coast will leave a lasting impression.

Activities

Bushwalking near Walpole and Denmark is a favourite activity while the **scuba diving** off Albany's coast is reputed to be among the best in the world.

Tours

All the tour companies servicing the southwest cover the Great Southern area as well. For tour information, see the Southwest tours, p398.

Getting There & Away

Skywest (☎ 1300 660 088, 08-9334 2288; www.skywest.com.au) has daily flights from Perth to Albany (A$210).

Transwa (☎ 1300 662 205) offers a daily train/bus service from Perth to Albany (via Bunbury) that uses a combination of the *Australind* and road coach (A$55). It passes through Walpole (A$50) and Denmark (A$50), and takes about 8½ hours. Another daily bus service from Perth to Albany (A$45, six hours) travels inland via Williams and stops in Mt Barker (A$37, 5½ hours).

GARY MUIR: LOCAL LEGEND

Debate rages on how long the **Bibbulmun Track** actually is. Some say it's 972km, others reckon it's 962km, and you'll speak to people who swear it's closer to 950km. Who cares? It's a bloody long way. The track, designed specifically for hikers, starts from the outskirts of Perth and continues through the southwest of the state until it ends in Albany. It takes most fit (and slightly crazy) people about eight weeks to complete the gruelling task although many just do a small portion of the track at a time. But in September 2002, local Walpole legend Gary Muir jogged the Bibb Track in an amazing 17½ days. Using the aid of special walking sticks that allowed him to glide across the ground, Muir did the deed to raise money for his beloved Nuyts Wilderness Area, near Walpole. He averaged around 60km per day (and one day travelled a whopping 90km).

While 17½ days is quite staggering, it could have been less. Muir spent a whole day flat on his back due to injury (his knees still give trouble) and had to wait around for half a day, just short of the finishing line, specifically for the media to arrive. (Because the media contingent – and nobody else for that matter – didn't expect Muir to complete the journey so quickly, they were unprepared for his arrival in Albany and kept him waiting while the journos flew in from the capital.) You will hear of Gary Muir's trek the whole way down the southwest and southern coasts, but Walpole is where his heart is. His energy is boundless and the enthusiasm he has for Walpole's wilderness areas and his eagerness to share it with travellers makes for a fascinating conversation.

WALPOLE

☎ 08 / pop 450

Walpole (wall-poll) is the perfect base to explore the surrounding coastline, forests and wilderness areas. Walpole itself doesn't do a lot to keep travellers within its town limits, but when you've got Mother Nature living on your doorstep, it doesn't really matter.

Information

CALM office (☎ 9840 1027; South Coast Hwy)
Telecentre (☎ 9840 1395; Vista St) Has email facilities.
Walpole Tourist Bureau (☎ 9840 1111; South Coast Hwy; 9am-5pm Mon-Fri, 9am-4pm Sat & Sun)

Sights & Activities

To get a real feel for the surrounding inlets, islands and forests, you can't beat the energetic Gary Muir's commentary aboard his **WOW Wilderness Eco Cruises** (☎ 9840 1036, 9480 1036). His boat, which leaves from the town jetty at 10am, will take you into the heart of Walpole-Nornalup National Park with a short walk down to a secluded beach for A$30. For more on Gary's exploits, see above.

The best **beaches** are at Rest Point (west) and Coal Mine (east) while **Conspicuous Cliffs** offers stunning views and good surfing.

As you travel down the **Valley of the Giants**, take note of the magnificent Tolkienesque trees overhead. Worth a quick stop along the way is the 24m-tall **Giant Tingle Tree**, with a girth that makes it the largest of any known living eucalypt on earth.

Most people come here for the forest experience with an aerial twist, the **Tree Top Walk** (☎ 9840 8263; off South Coast Hwy; admission A$6; 9am-4.15pm), 18km east of Walpole. This 600m-long steel ramp rising up to 40m above the forest floor gives a perspective from high up in the canopy of the giant tingle trees. It sways a bit, so vertigo sufferers might feel safer with both feet on the ground, among the huge red tingle trees along the **Ancient Empire Walk** below.

Sleeping

Walpole Lodge (☎ 9840 1244; info@walpolelodge.com.au; cnr Pier St & Park Ave; dm/s/d A$20/40/55, d with bathroom A$65; 💻) With a friendly, cosy feel, staying here is like sharing a big house. There's a huge backyard and a pot-bellied stove to warm you up in winter.

Tingle All Over Budget Accommodation YHA (☎ 9840 1041; cnr Nockolds & Inlet Sts; dm/s A$20/36, d & tw A$50; 💻) There are no bunk beds here, which many say is a good thing. The place is absolutely spotless, quiet and has a giant chess set in the backyard.

Coalmine Beach Caravan Park (☎ 9840 1026; coalmine@agn.net.au; Knoll Dr; camp sites unpowered/powered per 2 people A$20/22) About 3km east off South Coast Hwy, this pleasant park occupies a prime spot on Nornalup Inlet.

Eating

Top Deck Cafe (☎ 9840 1344; 25 Nockolds St; meals A$5.50-13; breakfast & lunch daily, dinner Jan) If the gourmet pies, burgers and seafood don't rope you in, the sticky date pudding will.

Wooz & Suz Cafe (☎ 9840 1214; Lot 13 Nockolds St; meals A$7-14; breakfast, lunch & dinner) Home-style cooking at its finest with all the standard grub from focaccias and burgers to steaks.

Eagle Rock Cafe (☎ 9840 1322; 20 Nockolds St; meals A$5.50-12; breakfast, lunch & dinner) We dare you to have a go at the big bushman's breakfast, but if you're not up to the challenge, there's plenty of calamari, fresh sandwiches and milkshakes to satisfy.

DENMARK

☎ 08 / pop 2000

Wedged snugly between the ocean and the hills, picturesque Denmark's appeal is obvious. The stunning natural beauty surrounding the town has made it a haven for city types seeking a fresh start and a slice of the good life. There's a close community feel here with an emphasis on alternative living.

Information

Denmark visitors centre (☎ 9848 2055; www.denmarkvisitorcentre.com.au; 60 Strickland St; 9am-5pm)

Spot News (☎ 9848 1362; 39 Strickland St) A newsagency on the main street with several quick Internet terminals.

Sights & Activities

There are some superb **walking** tracks in and around Denmark. The Wilson Inlet Trail starts from the bridge in the town centre, runs down the Denmark River and out onto Wilson Inlet for 6km. The Mokare Trail follows a 4km circuit around the river. Madfish Bay, Greens Pool and Ocean Beach are the best **beaches**. Because Denmark is protected by Wilson Inlet, there's no surf right in town. For that you have to venture 9km south to Ocean Beach. **South Coast Surfing** (☎ 9848 2057) has two-hour lessons from 9am daily.

Little River Discovery Tours (☎ 9848 2604) does 4WD tours around West Cape National Park and trips out to the Valley of the Giants and Tree Top Walk. **Wild About Wilderness Tours** (☎ 9848 3502; www.westnet.com.au/windrose) does excellent walking tours as well as beach hopping, twilight and two-day tours. **Denmark River Cruises** (☎ 0428-374 464) does a one-hour river cruise that also ventures out to Wilson Inlet, departing from Berridge Park on Hollings Rd. A better option though is the twilight tour that leaves at 6pm and you can bring your own booze.

Denmark's flourishing wineries produce some excellent cool-climate reds. These places make some fine drops:

Kent River (☎ 9840 8136)
Old Somerset Hill (☎ 9840 9388)
Springviews (☎ 9853 2088)
Tingle Wood (☎ 9840 9218)
West Cape Howe (☎ 9848 2959)

Sleeping

Denmark Budget Accommodation (☎ 9848 1700; cnr South Coast Hwy & Strickland St; dm A$19, d A$60-65; 💻) Only a few days old at the time of research and in a prime location in the centre of town, this backpacker hostel offers bathrooms in all dorms and breezy balconies. If you can scrounge together a group of four, the family room with TV, bathroom and fridge is awesome value (A$80).

Blue Wren Travellers' Rest YHA (☎ 9848 3300; http://bluewren.batcave.net/; 17 Price St; dm/d A$19/55, s & tw A$50; 💻) Intimate and relaxed, the Blue Wren is a little worn around the edges, but Flint, the friendly dog, will welcome you with open paws and the fresh, free rain water from an outside tank tastes better than anything you'll buy in a bottle. Noisy neighbours early in the morning make the en-suite double impossible for sleeping-in.

Rivermouth Caravan Park (☎ 9848 1262; 1 Inlet Dr; camp sites per 2 people A$18) Just 1km south of town, this well-grassed park has a good campers kitchen.

Riverbend Caravan Park (☎ 9848 1107; East River Rd; camp sites unpowered/powered per 2 people A$18/20) This small, but surprisingly spacious, park is 2km north of Denmark.

Eating & Drinking

Denmark Bakery (☎ 9848 2143; Shop 9, 27 Strickland St; pies & pasties A$3-3.50; breakfast & lunch) The vegie pie here won the 2003 Great Aussie Pie Competition. You can't argue with that, nor can you ignore the constant queue of locals popping in for a snack or lunch on the go.

McSweeney's Gourmet Café (☎ 9848 2362; 5b Strickland St; meals A$7-11; breakfast & lunch) Big brekkies, strong coffee, gourmet rolls and yummy desserts make McSweeney's one of the most popular cafés in town.

Lushus (☎ 9848 1299; 18 Hollings Rd; meals A$4-15; breakfast & lunch) Fine food, great prices, cool setting.

Food Haven (☎ 9848 1636; cnr South Coast Hwy & Hollings Rd; meals A$5-14; breakfast, lunch & dinner)

If you can't find what you're looking for at this café–fast food joint, then you're not really looking are you?

Spot Café (☎ 9848 2899; 39 Strickland St; meals A$5-14; ⌚ breakfast & lunch) Vegetarians are looked after at this intimate little café tucked away off the main street. The tandoori chicken and salad rolls are worth seeking out and when you ask for strong coffee here, that's exactly what you get.

Heng Wah Chinese Restaurant (☎ 9848 3033; cnr North & High Sts; meals A$8-14; ⌚ lunch Tue-Fri, dinner Sat-Mon) It's small and it doesn't look like much from the roadside, but the lunchbox specials here are truly massive.

Denmark Hotel (☎ 9848 2206; cnr Hollings Rd & Walker St; mains A$12-22) Some locals say the meals in the main bar are the most reliable in town. We just liked the front courtyard beer garden overlooking the river.

ALBANY

☎ 08 / pop 29,900

If you've travelled down the southwest and southern coasts, Albany (that's *al*-buh-nee, not *awl*-buh-nee) seems like a mega metropolis compared to the tiny towns you've been through. For this reason, travellers who are a little sick of one-pub, one-street towns, look forward to Albany. With its rolling hills (not completely unlike Hobart in appearance), fantastic beaches and world-class diving, Albany is the oldest European settlement in WA and is one of the highlights of the southern coast.

Information

Albany Hospital (☎ 9892 2222; cnr Warden Ave & Hardie Rd)
Albany visitors centre (☎ 9841 1088; Old Train Station, Proudlove Pde; ⌚ 9am-5pm)
CALM office (☎ 9842 4500; 120 Albany Hwy)
Eco Tourist Centre (☎ 9842 6886; cnr Stirling Tce & York St) Check email here.
Main post office (4/218 York St)

Sights & Activities

King George Sound offers some of the best **scuba diving** in the country around the spectacular reefs, the HMAS *Perth* wreck and a whale chaser boat that was sunk in 1982. **AlbanyDive.com** (☎ 9842 6886; www.albanydive.com; cnr York St & Stirling Tce) and **Albany Scuba Diving Academy** (☎ 9842 3101; www.albanyscuba.com.au) are reputable organisations. Dive costs for both are around A$160 for a double dive if you hire equipment, and around A$85 if you have your own gear.

If getting wet doesn't appeal, you can explore the reef by boat with **Albany Reef Explorer** (☎ 0418-950 361; www.albanyreefexplorer.net.au), which leaves from Whale World three times daily.

Whale World (☎ 9844 4021; www.whaleworld.org; Frenchman Bay Rd; admission A$15; ⌚ 9am-5pm), 21km south of Albany at the former Cheynes Beach Whaling Station at Frenchman Bay, is a huge whale exhibition–type museum thingy. The name says it all really. Here you can see whale skeletons, a shark exhibit that shows the relationship between whale hunting and sharks, a 3D whale movie and learn about the gruesome history of whale hunting.

Albany is prime **whale-watching** territory. From July to October southern right whales continue their migration through the waters of King George Sound. The humpback whale season is from June to November. **Silver Star Cruises** (☎ 9842 9876; silverstar@albanyis.com.au) and **Southern Ocean Charters** (☎ 0409-107 180) will take you out to see these majestic creatures (A$45). Boats depart from the town jetty, just south of the city centre.

Middleton Beach, about 4km east of town, is the place to go for sand and sea while **Emu Point**, 4km by road northeast of Middleton, has excellent swimming. You can walk or jog the scenic 5km path from Middleton Beach to Emu Point. Panoramic vistas can be enjoyed from **Mt Clarence** and **Mt Melville**, which overlook the town.

For a better understanding of Australia's defence history, head to **Princess Royal Fortress Military Museum** (☎ 9841 9333; Forts Rd; admission A$4; ⌚ 9am-5pm). About 12km from town, the **Albany Wind Farm** has 12 65m-high wind turbines that generate enough electricity for 17,000 homes. Each blade is 35m long.

There are some beautiful national parks around Albany.

West Cape Howe National Park, 30km west, is a favourite with naturalists, bushwalkers, rock climbers and anglers.

South of Albany, off Frenchman Bay Rd, is **Torndirrup National Park**, with a stunning if treacherous stretch of coastline. Southern right whales can be seen from the cliffs during season.

Don't take lightly the warning signs at the park's natural attractions, the **Gap**, the

Natural Bridge and the **Blowholes**; tragic accidents still occur thanks to carelessness and strong wind gusts. Other popular spots in the park are **Jimmy Newhill's Harbour** and **Salmon Holes** (popular with surfers, although these coves are quite dangerous).

East of Albany is **Two People's Bay**, a nature reserve with a fine swimming beach, scenic coastline and a small colony of noisy scrub birds, a species once thought extinct.

Sleeping

Albany Backpackers (☎ 9842 5255; www.albanybackpackers.com.au; cnr Stirling Tce & Spencer St; dm A$20-22, s A$36, d & tw A$50; 💻) Bright and happening, this popular backpackers is virtually covered with some of the coolest murals you're likely to see (even the rooms have them). Make no plans at 6.30pm every evening, other than the free coffee and cake upstairs.

Albany Bayview Backpackers YHA (☎ 9842 3388; 49 Duke St; dm A$19, d & tw A$50; 💻) Finally getting the facelift it needs, the YHA-affiliated Bayview is a low-key hostel on the fringe of the city centre that sleeps 42 people. The 'bunker' TV room with free videos is a fine place to relax and all guests get 10 minutes of free Internet use on arrival.

Albany's Cruize-Inn (☎ 9842 9599; www.cruizeinn.com; 122 Middleton Rd; s/tw/d A$35/55/60) Wedged between city and beach, this friendly, personal guesthouse is a perfect option if you want peace and quiet and a little more luxury for a bargain price.

Discovery Inn (☎ 9842 5535; www.discoveryinn.com.au; 9 Middleton Rd; dm/s/A$25/40, d & tw A$65; 💻) Superbly located just a healthy drop punt from Middleton Beach, this friendly guesthouse welcomes backpackers, and you can't knock back the free substantial breakfast.

London Backpackers (☎ 9841 6599; www.londonbackpackers.com.au; 160 Stirling Tce; dm A$20, s with/without bathroom A$40/30; d with/without bathroom A$55/50; 💻) With more name changes than Prince, the London's plumbing needed serious work when we visited (the taps in the sinks in some of the rooms were constantly trickling). Still, the dorms were roomy and the pub downstairs is a good place for a drink or two.

Premier Hotel (☎ 9841 1544; cnr York St & Grey St East; s with/without bathroom A$35/25, d with/without bathroom A$65/55) Clean and perfectly acceptable, the rooms here are perhaps the biggest surprise in town. The bar downstairs isn't particularly welcoming, especially for lone women travellers.

The visitors centre has a complete list of the many caravan parks around Albany. Some recommended ones:

Albany Holiday Park (☎ 9841 7800; www.albanyholiday.com.au; 550 Albany Hwy; camp sites unpowered/powered per 2 people A$18/21, on-site vans A$39) About 4km from town this park has a campers kitchen, general store and liquor shop.

Middleton Beach Holiday Park (☎ 9841 3593; www.holidayalbany.com; Middleton Rd; camp sites unpowered/powered per 2 people A$29/30) It ain't cheap, but the location right on Middleton Beach is superb. There's a good campers kitchen and TV room.

Eating

Shamrock Cafe (☎ 9841 4201; 184 York St; meals A$6.50-18; 🕑 breakfast & lunch) Vegetarians will be excited by the big full-veg breakfast (A$9) while the burgers, bangers and mash, chicken parma and the obligatory Guinness pie (it is the Shamrock, after all) will keep meat-eaters happy.

Dylans On the Terrace (☎ 9841 8720; 82-84 Stirling Tce; meals A$5-15; 🕑 breakfast, lunch & dinner) Dine alfresco at this incredibly busy café-restaurant. It will fix you up with all the pancakes, burgers, kebabs and rolls you'll need to keep you going all day.

Earl of Spencer (☎ 9841 1322; cnr Earl & Spencer Sts; meals A$12-28; 🕑 lunch & dinner) Simply a wonderful place to spend an hour, an afternoon or an evening. With 15 beers on tap, this mellow English-style pub is as good as it gets in Albany. You get a certificate if you can finish the famous pie and pint (A$15). We tried and succeeded!

Harvest Moon Café (☎ 9841 8833; 86 Stirling Tce; meals A$6.50-17; 🕑 lunch daily, dinner Thu) Health fanatics and vegetarians will be in their element at this gem of a place overlooking the waterfront. The home-cooked food here is brilliant and the Thursday night curries are magic.

Cosi's Cafe (☎ 9841 7899; cnr York St & Peel Pl; meals A$6-12; 🕑 breakfast & lunch) With a steady stream of customers grabbing takeaways or lazing about at the outdoor tables, Cosi's does all the standard fare in style.

Naked Bean (☎ 9841 1815; 14 Peel Pl; meals A$8-10; 🕑 breakfast & lunch Mon-Sat) The Naked Bean's light meals and great coffee will kick start your day in style.

Bangkok Rose (☎ 9842 2366; 112 York St; meals A$12-19; 🕑 lunch Thu & Fri, dinner Tue-Sun) Good, wholesome Thai food a stone's throw from the waterfront. You can bring your own grog.

Drinking

Earl of Spencer (☎ 9841 1322; cnr Earl & Spencer Sts) For variety and class, the Earl (see opposite) is the place for a beverage any time of day or night.

White Star Hotel (☎ 9841 1733; 72 Stirling Tce) This rowdy pub hums on Thursday nights with live music and a younger clientele.

Legends Bar (☎ 9842 1711; cnr Adelaide Cres & Flinders Pde, Middleton Beach) Located at the historic Esplanade Hotel, Legends buzzes with live sports on the big screen, a busy pool table and an energetic crowd.

Entertainment

If you feel like catching a movie, **Albany 3 Cinemas** (☎ 9842 2210; Albany Hwy) shows the latest flicks. **Heaven Dance Club** (☎ 9841 7688; 148a Stirling Tce; ⌚ Thu-Sat) stays open long after the pubs have shut.

Getting Around

Love's (☎ 9841 1211) runs bus services along the Albany Hwy from Peel Place to the main roundabout, and to Middleton Beach, Emu Point and Bayonet Head. A short trip around town costs A$2.

If you need a cab then **Albany Taxis** (☎ 9844 4444) will come to your aid.

MT BARKER

☎ **08 / pop 1650**

You can use sleepy Mt Barker as a base for exploring the nearby Porongurup and Stirling Ranges. The town itself is pleasant enough but not mind-blowingly interesting. The fertile soil around Mt Barker supports a growing wine industry.

Information

Mount Barker Tourist Bureau (☎ 9851 1163; Unit 6, Lot 622, Albany Hwy; ⌚ 9am-5pm Mon-Fri, 9am-3pm Sat, 10am-3pm Sun)

UPS Computers (☎ 9851 2880; 61 Lowood Rd) Log onto the Internet here.

Sights & Activities

The outstanding **Old Police Station Museum** (☎ 9851 1735; Albany Hwy; admission A$5; ⌚ 10am-4pm) deserves a few hours to do it justice. Take the guided tour around the complex, which houses an old lock-up, a school room made with recycled aluminium parts and a pioneer room that pays tribute to the families that settled the area in 1839.

The picturesque **St Werburgh's Chapel** (☎ 9857 6041; St Werburgh's Rd), built in 1873, is worth a quick look. Five kilometres out of town, the **Mt Barker Lookout** offers panoramic views of the surrounding area.

The Mt Barker region has some fine wineries that produce cool-climate varieties like pinot noir and grenache that don't thrive in warmer areas like Margaret River. If you fancy a tipple these places are worth seeking out:

Gilberts (☎ 9851 4028; Albany Hwy, Kendenup)
Goundrey (☎ 9851 1777; Muir Hwy, Mt Barker)
Plantagenet (☎ 9851 2063; Albany Hwy, Mt Barker)
Springviews (☎ 9853 2088; Woodlands Rd, Porongurup)

Sleeping

Chill Out Backpackers (☎ 9851 2798; 79 Hassell St; s A$25, d & tw A$45) The great thing about this place is you get B&B facilities (without the brekky) at backpackers prices. This private home can accommodate eight guests on its five-acre property. It's clean and friendly and the balcony is a great spot to sit and relax.

Mt Barker Caravan Park & Cabins (☎ 9851 1691; Albany Hwy; s A$18, camp sites unpowered/powered per 2 people A$16/18; cabins A$55) Near the Old Police Station Museum, this is one of the few caravan parks in WA that has budget single rooms. The cabins are a steal and can sleep six people.

Eating

Jondels Diner (☎ 9851 2888; 43b Lowood Rd; meals A$4.50-10; ⌚ breakfast & lunch) With tasty omelettes, steak sandwiches, seafood baskets and sandwiches, Jondels is not fancy, but will satisfy a sizeable hunger.

Mt Barker Hotel (The Top Pub; ☎ 9851 1477; 39 Lowood Rd) For a counter meal (A$10 to A$20) and a beer, the Top Pub is a local favourite.

PORONGURUP & STIRLING RANGES

☎ **08**

The region north of Albany is one of spectacular natural beauty with two rugged, mountainous national parks to explore. National park fees (A$9) apply to vehicles entering both parks. For further information, contact Albany's **CALM office** (☎ 9842 4500; 120 Albany Hwy) or the rangers at **Porongurup National**

Park (☎ 9853 1095) and **Stirling Range National Park** (☎ 9827 9230).

Porongurup National Park

With towering karri trees, 1100-million-year-old granite outcrops and excellent bush tracks, the panoramic **Porongurup National Park** is a popular stomping ground for bushwalkers and naturalists. Tracks include Castle Rock (two hours), and the challenging Marmabup Rock walk (three hours) via Devil's Slide (two hours). There's a 6km **scenic drive** along the park's northern edge that starts at the ranger's residence.

SLEEPING & EATING

Porongurup Villa Inn (☎ 9853 1110; homebake@omninet.net.au; Porongurup Rd; dm/d A$20/60) At the time of research, the popular Porongurup Shop & Tearooms was in the process of renovating its budget accommodation (hence the separate name). By the time you read this you'll be able to rest your head in the dorms at the inn, or couples can enjoy the self-contained mud-brick cottage.

Porongurup Range Tourist Park (☎/fax 9853 1057; Porongurup Rd; camp sites unpowered/powered per 2 people A$16/18, caravans A$35-40, cabins A$60;) With one of the best campers kitchens in the region, a tennis court and a barbecue area, this caravan park is popular so book ahead.

Maleeya's Thai Cafe (☎ 9853 1123; 1376 Porongurup Rd; mains A$13-21; lunch & dinner) You may need to book in advance to eat at this wildly popular Thai restaurant.

Stirling Range National Park

Rising abruptly from the surrounding flat and sandy plains, the 96km-long **Stirling Range** is famous for its spectacular colour changes through blues, reds and purples, and its amazing **wildflowers** from late August to early December.

Most day-trippers try to squeeze in at least one half-day walk to **Toolbrunup Peak** (both for the views and to burn off a few calories), **Bluff Knoll** (at 1073m, the highest peak in the range) or **Toll Peak** (prolific wildflowers).

SLEEPING & EATING

Stirling Range Retreat (☎ 9827 9229; www.stirlingrange.com.au; Chester Pass Rd; camp sites per 2 people A$18, dm/s/d/tr A$19/45/45/60) Superbly situated, this peaceful retreat encourages its visitors to get out and experience nature, which is why there's no TV.

Bluff Knoll Cafe (☎ 9827 9293; Chester Pass Rd; meals A$5-15; breakfast, lunch & dinner) Set opposite the Stirling Range Retreat, this convenient little place offers good, standard café fare.

Outback Australia

CONTENTS

HIGHLIGHTS

- **Uluru** Gaze at Uluru's luminous flanks as they reflect the setting sun (p429)
- **Kings Canyon** Discover secluded pools within this outrageously picturesque canyon in Watarrka National Park (p427)
- **Devonian Reef national parks** Explore the archaeological wonders of the Kimberley's Geikie Gorge, Tunnel Creek and, most captivating, Windjana Gorge (p440)
- **Cape Leveque** Swim in crystal-clear waters at this soul-restoring spot on the tip of the striking Dampier Peninsula (p445)
- **Living Desert Reserve** Watch the sun rise over the sculptures outside Broken Hill (p453)
- **Jandra** Plough down the Darling River in this paddleboat and spot kangaroos grazing on the semiarid plains around Bourke (p452)
- **Monkey Mia** Share the shallow waters of Shark Bay with wild dolphins (p447)
- **Coober Pedy** Go underground and fossick for your fortune (p455)

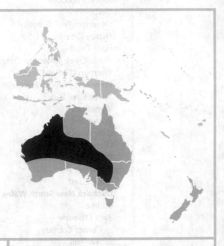

- **Eat:** bush tucker in Alice: emu, crocodile, kangaroo and camel (p424)
- **Drink:** plenty of water!
- **Listen to:** redneck country radio stations
- **Watch**: *Mad Max* or *The Adventures of Priscilla, Queen of the Desert*
- **Party at:** Alice Springs (p424) or Broome (p439)
- **Swim:** with whale sharks and manta rays at Ningaloo Reef (p449) or at Broome's Cable Beach (p436)
- **Avoid:** taipan snakes, running out of petrol
- **Locals' nickname:** Dust Eaters

- TELEPHONE CODES: 08, 02
- WEBSITE: www.alicesprings.nt.gov.au

Tropical islands, glorious beaches, modern metropolises and quirky wildlife may bring travellers to Australia's shores, but for many visitors it is the remote regions that give a trip down under its unique flavour. Some of Australia's most extraordinary sights can be found here, from the iconic Uluru, gorgeous Shark Bay and the monsoonal desolation of the remote Kimberley to the blasted landscape of Coober Pedy. And the outback also evokes the twin pillars of Australia's history – the ancient cultures and beliefs of Aboriginal nations contrasting with the pioneer spirit of white colonists in towns such as Bourke, Broken Hill and Alice Springs.

For many travellers the mind-boggling scale of Australia's back country is a highlight (consider that a Perth-Darwin-Alice Springs-Adelaide trip will take you along more than 7000km of roads), and almost everyone is taken aback by the sheer variety and abundance of landscapes and vegetation – the continent's remote reaches are anything but lifeless deserts. Add some stunning natural features, the renowned hospitality of country Australia and the chance to gain insights into some of the world's oldest cultures and you have an experience that will stay with you forever.

This vast region has one thing in common: the best time to visit is between June and September, avoiding the blistering summer heat in the Red Centre and the stifling humidity and torrential rains of the Wet in the tropical north.

THE RED CENTRE

For the red-hot experience of a lifetime, head for the very centre of Australia.

Awe-inspiring Uluru is the undisputed champion of the Red Centre's attractions, but there are many more treasures within this harsh and remote region. These include the spectacular cliffs and hidden water holes of Kings Canyon, to the eerie domes of Kata Tjuta and the ancient waterways of the MacDonnell Ranges.

And don't be too quick to leave the desert town of Alice Springs – this thriving centre has an attractive mix of contemporary culture and outback larrikinism, leavened by the timeless art and culture of regional Aboriginal peoples.

Activities

Activities in the Red Centre are limited a little by distance and environment, but there are some great ways to see the sights: by camel or motorbike at ground level, or in a helicopter, balloon or light plane from above. The fitter folk (or masochists) can shoulder a backpack for some bushwalking – the Larapinta Trail in the West MacDonnells will test the most committed walkers.

ALICE SPRINGS

☎ 08 / pop 25,000

In its brief 125-year history, the Alice (as it is usually known) has gone from a simple station on the Overland Telegraph Line to a modern regional centre and mustering point for the endless stream of travellers heading to 'the Rock'.

While for many visitors the Alice is a place to replenish supplies after a number of days on the road, it has plenty to recommend itself and is worth a visit of at least a couple of days.

Orientation

The centre of Alice Springs is a compact and uniform grid just five streets wide, bounded by the (usually dry) Todd River on one side and the Stuart Hwy on the other, with the Todd St pedestrian mall running north–south in between.

You will find most hostels east and south of the town centre, while there is a cluster of good caravan parks even further south.

The Alice Springs airport is 15km south of the town; it's about A$30 by taxi. An **airport shuttle** (☎ 8953 0310; Gregory Tce) meets flights and picks up/drops off at city accommodation (one way/return A$11/18).

Information

BOOKSHOPS

Big Kangaroo Books (☎ 8953 2137; Todd Mall) Specialises in Australian titles, including good art and natural-history titles.

Boomerang Book Exchange (☎ 8952 5843; Reg Harris Lane, off Todd Mall) Cheap paperbacks.

EMERGENCY & MEDICAL SERVICES

Alice Springs Hospital (☎ 8951 7777; Gap Rd)
Ambulance (☎ 000)
Fire (☎ 000)
Lifeline Crisis Line (☎ 1800 019 116)
Police station (☎ 000; cnr Parsons & Bath Sts)

INTERNET ACCESS

There are heaps of local choices, all with fast ADSL connections.

Green Frog Internet (☎ 8952 1141; Shop 10, 76 Todd St)

Outback Email (☎ 8955 5288; Outback Travel Shop, 2a Gregory Tce)

MONEY

Major banks and ATMs can be found in and around Todd Mall in the town centre.

POST

Post office (31-33 Hartley St; 🕒 8.15am-5pm Mon-Fri, 9am-noon Sat)

MPARNTWE

The Alice Springs area is known as Mparntwe to its traditional residents, the Arrernte Aboriginal people. The heart of the area is the junction of the Charles (Anthelke Ulpeye) and Todd (Lhere Mparntwe) Rivers, just north of Anzac Hill.

All the topographical features of the town were formed by the creative ancestral beings – the Yeperenye, Ntyarlke and Utnerrengatye caterpillars – as they crawled across the landscape from Emily Gap (Anthwerrke), in the MacDonnell Ranges southeast of town. Alice Springs' sizable Aboriginal community retains strong spiritual links to the area.

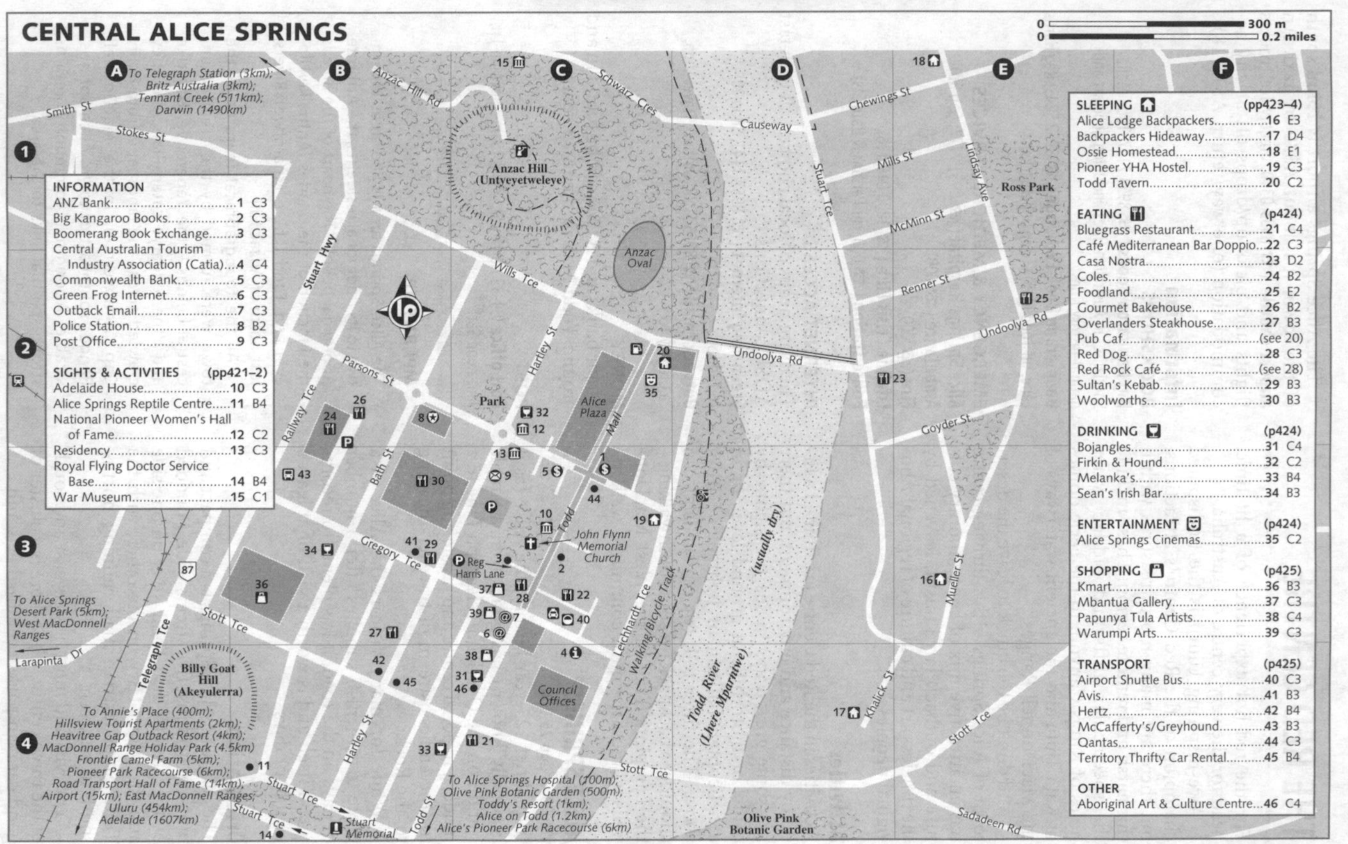
CENTRAL ALICE SPRINGS
0 300 m
0 0.2 miles
INFORMATION
ANZ Bank 1 C3
Big Kangaroo Books 2 C3
Boomerang Book Exchange 3 C3
Central Australian Tourism Industry Association (Catia) 4 C4
Commonwealth Bank 5 C3
Green Frog Internet 6 C3
Outback Email 7 C3
Police Station 8 B2
Post Office 9 C3
SIGHTS & ACTIVITIES (pp421–2)
Adelaide House 10 C3
Alice Springs Reptile Centre 11 B4
National Pioneer Women's Hall of Fame 12 C2
Residency 13 C3
Royal Flying Doctor Service Base 14 B4
War Museum 15 C1
SLEEPING (pp423–4)
Alice Lodge Backpackers 16 E3
Backpackers Hideaway 17 D4
Ossie Homestead 18 E1
Pioneer YHA Hostel 19 C3
Todd Tavern 20 C2
EATING (p424)
Bluegrass Restaurant 21 C4
Café Mediterranean Bar Doppio 22 C3
Casa Nostra 23 D2
Coles 24 B2
Foodland 25 E2
Gourmet Bakehouse 26 B2
Overlanders Steakhouse 27 B3
Pub Caf (see 20)
Red Dog 28 C3
Red Rock Café (see 28)
Sultan's Kebab 29 B3
Woolworths 30 B3
DRINKING (p424)
Bojangles 31 C4
Firkin & Hound 32 C2
Melanka's 33 B4
Sean's Irish Bar 34 B3
ENTERTAINMENT (p424)
Alice Springs Cinemas 35 C2
SHOPPING (p425)
Kmart 36 B3
Mbantua Gallery 37 C3
Papunya Tula Artists 38 C4
Warumpi Arts 39 C3
TRANSPORT (p425)
Airport Shuttle Bus 40 C3
Avis 41 B3
Hertz 42 B4
McCafferty's/Greyhound 43 B3
Qantas 44 C3
Territory Thrifty Car Rental 45 B4
OTHER
Aboriginal Art & Culture Centre 46 C4
To Telegraph Station (3km); Britz Australia (3km); Tennant Creek (511km); Darwin (1490km)
Smith St
Stokes St
Anzac Hill Rd
Schwarz Cres
Anzac Hill (Untyeyetweleye)
Anzac Oval
Causeway
Stuart Tce
Chewings St
Mills St
Lindsay Ave
Ross Park
McMinn St
Renner St
Undoolya Rd
Goyder St
Mueller St
Khalick St
Stott Tce
Sadadeen Rd
Stuart Hwy
Wills Tce
Parsons St
Hartley St
Railway Tce
Park
Alice Plaza
Mall
Bath St
Todd
John Flynn Memorial Church
Gregory Tce
Reg Harris Lane
Leichhardt Tce
Walking/Bicycle Track
(usually dry)
Todd River (Lhere Mparntwe)
Council Offices
Olive Pink Botanic Garden
Telegraph Tce
Billy Goat Hill (Akeyulerra)
To Alice Springs Desert Park (5km); West MacDonnell Ranges
Larapinta Dr
To Annie's Place (400m); Hillsview Tourist Apartments (2km); Heavitree Gap Outback Resort (4km); MacDonnell Range Holiday Park (4.5km) Frontier Camel Farm (5km); Pioneer Park Racecourse (6km); Road Transport Hall of Fame (14km); Airport (15km); East MacDonnell Ranges; Uluru (454km); Adelaide (1607km)
Stuart Memorial
Todd St
To Alice Springs Hospital (700m); Olive Pink Botanic Garden (500m); Toddy's Resort (1km); Alice on Todd (1.2km) Alice's Pioneer Park Racecourse (6km)

LET'S GET THIS PARTY STARTED

While it's always wise to do some basic research before you head off, this is especially true in remote Australia, where so much time can be spent just getting from place to place. Some good introductory websites:

Australia's Outback (www.australiasoutback.com)
Territory Discoveries (www.territorydiscoveries.com.au)
Visit Outback NSW (www.visitoutbacknsw.com.au)
Shark Bay – World Heritage Area (www.sharkbay.asn.au)
Coober Pedy (www.opalcapitaloftheworld.com.au)

And although independent transport offers you the most flexibility in exploring this vast region, there are plenty of private tours and regular bus services to get you from town to town. If you have your own wheels, just remember that you'll be travelling along some pretty remote routes – take enough food and drinking water to last your party at least a couple of days, just in case you find yourself squinting into the blazing sun as you stand next to a motionless vehicle.

TOURIST INFORMATION

Central Australian Tourism Industry Association (Catia; ☎ 1800 645 199, 8952 5800; www.centralaustraliantourism.com; 60 Gregory Tce; ⌚ 8.30am-5.30pm Mon-Fri, 9am-4pm Sat & Sun) Pick up brochures and the free *Central Australia Visitors Guide* and *Welcome to Central Australia* booklets.

Dangers & Annoyances

Avoid walking alone at night in the town centre or on poorly lit backstreets. Get a taxi back to your accommodation if you're out late.

Sights

While there's a smattering of minor attractions in the town centre, the best places (especially the Desert Park and cultural precinct) are a little further out. If you're fit and game, a bike is a great way to get about; otherwise the Alice Wanderer (see p425) is your best option.

ALICE SPRINGS DESERT PARK

The town's number-one attraction is the superb **Alice Springs Desert Park** (☎ 8951 8788; www.alicespringsdesertpark.com.au; Larapinta Dr; adult/concession A$18/9; ⌚ 7.30am-6pm), spectacularly situated at the base of the MacDonnell Ranges, 5km west of town. Divided into sand, woodland and riverine ecosystems, the region's unique plant and animal life is presented through a series of walk-in aviaries and an outstanding nocturnal house, where you can see rare critters such as bilbies, mala hare-wallabies and phascogales, plus snakes, lizards and bats. Ranger talks are held at various exhibits throughout the day. Allow at least three hours to get the most out of your visit.

It's an easy 5km cycle out to the park but if you don't have your own wheels, **Desert Park Transfers** (☎ 8952 4667; adult/concession A$30/20) operates return trips with the park entrance fee included in the price.

ALICE SPRINGS CULTURAL PRECINCT

A compact area west of the town centre, the **Alice Springs Cultural Precinct** (☎ 8951 1120; www.nt.gov.au/dam; Larapinta Dr; adult/concession A$8/5; ⌚ 10am-5pm) combines several historical and cultural attractions in one ticket.

The **Araluen Arts Centre** (☎ 8952 5022) features the Albert Namatjira Gallery, with paintings by Namatjira as well as his mentor Rex Battarbee and other artists from the Hermannsburg school. It also has galleries that showcase art from the central desert region, and travelling exhibitions.

Close by, the **Museum of Central Australia** (☎ 8951 5532) has superb exhibits on natural history, including local megafauna fossils and meteorites, and Aboriginal culture. Check out the world's biggest bird, the intimidating *Dromornis stirtoni*, an ancient relative of the modern goose.

The small circular building just to the south houses the wreck of the **Kookaburra**, a tiny plane that crashed in the Tanami Desert in 1929, while the nearby **Aviation Museum** has exhibits on pioneer aviation in the Territory. Lastly, there's the **Alice Springs cemetery**, containing the graves of local luminaries like Harold Lasseter (who perished in 1931 trying to re-find a rich gold reef he had supposedly found earlier, west of Uluru) and Albert Namatjira.

ROYAL FLYING DOCTOR SERVICE BASE

The **RFDS base** (☎ 8952 1033; www.flyingdoctor.net/central/alice.htm; 8-10 Stuart Tce; adult A$6; 🕑 9am-4pm Mon-Sat, 1-4pm Sun) operates an aero-medical service to isolated communities. The visitor centre here has 45-minute tours every half-hour, taking you through the radio communications centre and museum (with its scary, ancient medical gear). There's also a reasonable café.

ALICE SPRINGS REPTILE CENTRE

While it's not a patch on the Desert Park, the **reptile centre** (☎ 8952 8900; www.reptilecentre.com.au; 9 Stuart Tce; adult A$8; 🕑 9am-5pm) allows you get up close and personal with some of the world's most venomous snakes, along with thorny devils, pythons and a saltwater croc.

FRONTIER CAMEL FARM

About 5km south of town is **Frontier Camel Farm** (☎ 8953 0444; www.cameltours.com.au; Ross Hwy; short ride adult A$10; 🕑 9am-5pm), where you can ride one of these strange 'ships of the desert'. An interesting museum pays tribute to the Afghan cameleers who opened up the desert here to white folks.

OTHER ATTRACTIONS

You can do an easy town walk taking in most of the heritage buildings. Starting in Todd Mall, you'll find **Adelaide House** (☎ 8952 1856; adult A$3; 🕑 10am-4pm Mon-Fri, 10am-noon Sat), built in the early 1920s and now preserved as a memorial museum to John Flynn, who founded the flying doctor service.

The **Residency** (cnr Hartley & Parsons Sts; admission free; 🕑 9am-5pm Mon-Fri, 10am-4pm Sat & Sun), dating from 1927, was originally the home of the first governor of central Australia and has been refurbished to reflect the period.

Across the road is the Old Courthouse, which now houses the **National Pioneer Women's Hall of Fame** (☎ 8952 9006; www.pioneerwomen.com.au; 27 Hartley St; adult A$2.20; 🕑 10am-5pm Feb–mid-Dec), a thought-provoking tribute to pioneering women from all over Australia.

Just across the Todd River from the town centre, the **Olive Pink Botanic Garden** (☎ 8952 2154; www.opbg.com.au; Tuncks Rd; admission free; 🕑 10am-6pm) has a fine collection of arid-zone flora, plus marked trails, a visitors centre and a café.

Just north of the town centre is **Anzac Hill**, where you get fine views of the MacDonnell Ranges – it's especially popular at sunset.

A little further north, off the Stuart Hwy, is the old **Telegraph Station** (☎ 8952 3993; telegraphstation@octa4.net.au; Heritage Dr; adult A$6.50; 🕑 8am-5pm), which dates from the 1870s. The station, which includes restored homestead buildings and a blacksmith shop. It's also home to the original Alice Springs (known as 'Thereyurre' to the Arrernte Aboriginal people), a semipermanent water hole in the Todd River. The station is an easy 3.5km walk or ride to the station from town – just follow the path on the western side of the riverbed.

At the MacDonnell siding, about 14km south of Alice Springs along the Stuart Hwy, the **Road Transport Hall of Fame** (☎ 8952 7161; Norris Bell Ave; adult A$6; 🕑 9am-5pm) is a motor-vehicle buff's delight with superbly restored vehicles, original road trains and vintage cars.

Several easy **bushwalks** radiate from the Olive Pink Botanic Garden and the Telegraph Station, which is the first stage of the rugged Larapinta Trail. **Central Australian Bushwalkers** (☎ 8953 1956; http://home.austarnet.com.au/longwalk) is a local group that organises a wide variety of walks in the area.

You could also take flight in a **balloon** (from A$210). See the visitors centre for details.

Tours

The tourist office has details on all sorts of tours from Alice Springs. See p429 for details of tours to Uluru and Kings Canyon.

Popular tours and operators include the following:

Aboriginal Art & Culture Centre (☎ 8952 3408; 86 Todd St) Has half-day Aboriginal desert-discovery tours (A$85) covering bush tucker, flora and fauna, and art and culture.

Alice Wanderer (☎ 1800 722 111; www.alicewanderer.com.au) Offers one-day tours to the West MacDonnell Ranges (A$120).

Centre Highlights (☎ 8953 2843) Has small-group tours to the West MacDonnell Ranges (A$95, including lunch), plus day tours to Palm Valley and Hermannsburg (A$105).

Emu Run (☎ 8953 7057; www.emurun.com.au) Offers full-day trips to the East and West MacDonnell Ranges (each A$100, including lunch).

Festivals & Events

Most of the local community gets involved in the Alice's many colourful activities.

OUTBACK AUSTRALIA

Alice Springs Cup (www.alicespringsturfclub.org.au) Main annual carnival held at Alice's Pioneer Park Racecourse each May.
Finke Desert Race (www.finkedesertrace.com.au) A three-day, rev-head event held on the Queen's Birthday weekend in June.
Alice Springs Beanie Festival (www.beaniefest.org) An arts and crafts festival held during June and July that brings together Aboriginal communities from around central Australia.
Camel Cup (www.camelcup.com.au) A series of camel races held in mid-July.
Alice Springs Rodeo Bow-legged stockmen abound during this August event.
Henley-on-Todd Regatta (www.henleyontodd.com.au) Draws the biggest crowds of all in late September, with 'boat' races on the dry Todd River. The boats are all bottomless, with the well-lubricated crews simply running down the course.

Sleeping

Alice has an abundance of reasonable accommodation options, with plenty of good hostels and caravan parks.

HOSTELS

Discounts (usually A$1) apply at most hostels for Youth Hostels Association (YHA)/VIP/Nomads members. All hostels are air-conditioned and provide a light breakfast as well as bus and train pick-ups and drop-offs. Most also rent bikes (half-/full day from A$6/12).

Annie's Place (☎ 1800 359 089, 8952 1545; www.anniesplace.com.au; 4 Traeger Ave; dm A$17, d A$55; P ✿ 💻 🏊) A converted motel, Annie's boasts the best hostel doubles in town, plus clean six-bed dorms. There's a great pool, a well-equipped kitchen and tasty meals at its café-bar (dinner A$5). All rooms have a bathroom and fridge, and it's just a short walk to town.

Toddy's Resort (☎ 1800 806 240, 8952 1322; www.toddys.com.au; 41 Gap Rd; dm A$17-18, budget tw & d A$50, motel d A$60; ✿ 💻 🏊) A little further south from Annie's, Toddy's has a relaxed friendliness despite its size. Brightly coloured with a good range of accommodation options, it has a decent-sized pool with open-air bar, clean facilities, spacious common areas and all-you-can-eat evening meals (A$8.50).

Alice Lodge Backpackers (☎ 1800 351 925, 8953 1975; www.bpf.com.au; 4 Mueller St; dm A$16-19, s/d A$40/50; ✿ 🏊) A friendly place on a quiet backstreet east of the Todd River, the Lodge has a well-grassed central courtyard with a small pool, a narrow but functional kitchen and a tour office. Try for the four-bed dorm.

Ossie Homestead (☎ 1800 628 211, 8952 2308; 18 Warburton St; dm A$16-18, d A$45; P ✿ 💻 🏊) Out of the way and a bit starchy, but quiet with good facilities, keypad security, spotless rooms, a pool table and central courtyard with barbecue. The owners also run good regional tours (see www.ossies.com.au).

Also recommended:
Backpackers Hideaway (☎ 8952 8686; www.bpf.com.au; 6 Khalick St; dm A$16-20, d A$45; P ✿) A very welcoming and relaxed place in a slightly ramshackle old house with a spa out the back.
Pioneer YHA Hostel (☎ 8952 8855; www.yha.com.au; cnr Parsons St & Leichhardt Tce; dm A$19-25, d/tw A$70/80; ✿ 💻 🏊) The most central of the hostels. It's a bit cramped but facilities are generally good.

HOTELS

Todd Tavern (☎ 8952 1255; www.toddtavern.com.au; 1 Todd Mall; budget/standard d A$50/60; ✿) Rooms at the Todd are good-sized, clean and have keyless entry, but the bar downstairs can get noisy. Budget rooms share facilities. The Todd also has excellent-value meals (see Pub Caf, p424) and a bottle shop (liquor shop).

SELF-CONTAINED ACCOMMODATION

Here are some more-luxurious apartment choices for self-catering small groups.

Alice on Todd (☎ 8953 8033; www.aliceontodd.com; cnr Strehlow St & South Tce; 2-/3-bedroom apt from A$150/190; P ✿ 🏊) Peering over the banks of the Todd, these self-contained apartments can take up to six people (extra adult A$20), and there's a nice pool, barbecue area and games room.

Hillsview Tourist Apartments (☎ 0407-602 379; www.hillsviewapartments.com; 16 Bradshaw Dr; standard/deluxe apt d A$105/125; ✿) Across the train line, each of these slightly daggy but well-equipped, two-bedroom apartments (sleeps six, extra adult A$16.50) has a private courtyard and views of the MacDonnell Ranges.

CAMPING & CARAVAN PARKS

Most camping grounds are on the outskirts of Alice, with the main cluster south of town off the Ross Hwy. High-season rates are quoted here.

Heavitree Gap Outback Resort (☎ 1800 896 119, 8950 4444; www.aurora-resorts.com.au; Palm Circuit; camp/caravan sites per 2 people A$18/20, dm A$25, motel d A$85-110; P ✿ 💻 🏊) The pick of the parks,

Heavitree's population of black-footed rock wallabies draws in the punters, along with immaculate camp sites, clean dorms and motel rooms. The motel rooms come with bathroom and fridge (both motel and dorms have free movies). Meals are available at the pub and there's a supermarket on-site.

MacDonnell Range Holiday Park (☎ 1800 808 373, 8952 6111; www.macrange.com.au; Palm Pl; camp/caravan sites per 2 people A$20/24, budget d A$55, cabin d with/without bathroom A$115/80, villa d A$125-140; P) Not far from Heavitree, this holiday park has excellent facilities including a shop, TV and games room, and camp kitchen. If you're in a group, cabins and villas sleep six (extra adult A$14) and have decent kitchens.

Eating

SELF-CATERING

If you're stocking up for a trip into the wilds, there are several good supermarkets located around the centre of the city: **Coles** (☎ 8952 5166; Bath St; ☎ 24hr), **Woolworths** (40 Hartley St; ☎ 7am-midnight) and **Foodland** (Lindsay Ave; ☎ 7.30am-9pm) are open daily. The enormous **Gourmet Bakehouse** (☎ 8953 0041; Coles Complex, Bath St; ☎ 7am-5.30pm Mon-Fri, to 2pm Sat) has pastries, cakes and sourdough bread.

CAFÉS, PUBS & RESTAURANTS

Alice has a good range of cheap eateries, but prices rise sharply for better-quality nosh.

Café Mediterranean Bar Doppio (☎ 8952 6525; Fan Arcade; mains A$6-11; breakfast, lunch & dinner) Alice's standout budget eatery. Doppio is an agreeable place that serves up huge and wholesome brekkies, focaccias and curries, plus fresh juices, smoothies and a great cup of coffee. Vegetarians will probably find themselves haunting this place: try the excellent polenta with tomato and basil.

Pub Caf (☎ 8952 1255; Todd Tavern, 1 Todd Mall; mains A$6-16; breakfast, lunch & dinner) A popular spot for bistro pub grub, with the best-value steaks in town, plus a generous veggie and salad bar, and well-priced wine list. Theme nights include Monday's movie-and-meal deal (A$16.50) and great Sunday-evening roasts (A$7).

Sultan's Kebab (☎ 8953 3322; cnr Hartley St & Gregory Tce; kebabs A$6-9, mains A$17; lunch & dinner) Delicious, fresh and authentic Turkish food is on offer at this local haunt (plus belly dancers on Friday and Saturday nights). You can eat in or take away.

Casa Nostra (☎ 8952 6749; cnr Undoolya Rd & Stuart Tce; meals A$10-16; dinner Tue-Sun) Across the river from the town centre, Casa Nostra is a longstanding, family-run pizza and pasta place that offers pretty good value. BYO (bring your own) wine for a cheap night out.

Bluegrass Restaurant (☎ 8955 5188; cnr Stott Tce & Todd St; mains A$15-23; lunch & dinner Wed-Mon) The place to come for a special occasion, this intimate space has a lovely garden setting and a thoughtful seasonal menu of Australian-Mediterranean fusion cuisine.

Overlanders Steakhouse (☎ 8952 2159; 72 Hartley St; mains A$24-28; ☎ dinner) Pretty gimmicky and pricey, but the place to come to chow down on Oz fauna like emu, crocodile, kangaroo and camel.

Red Dog (Todd Mall; ☎ breakfast & lunch) and **Red Rock Café** (Todd Mall; ☎ breakfast & lunch), almost side by side in the pedestrian mall, serve early breakfasts, pastries, burgers and coffee.

Drinking

Bojangle's (☎ 8952 2873; 80 Todd St) Wild West meets Aussie outback at this place, where shells from the complimentary peanuts carpet the floor by the end of the night. Some hard drinking goes on here to the strains of live music most nights.

Melanka Backpackers (☎ 8952 4744; 94 Todd St) This cavernous hostel bar attracts a younger crowd, and it absolutely goes off some nights. There's live music, dancing, jelly wrestling, shots, theme nights – the whole shebang. It's not for the faint-hearted.

Firkin & Hound (☎ 8953 3033; 21 Hartley St) A far quieter affair, this English-themed pub serves, curiously, mostly Irish and European beers. There are big-screen sports and bands from Wednesday to Sunday (in season).

Sean's Irish Bar (☎ 8952 1858; 51 Bath St) This open-air bar pulls a fine Guinness and has karaoke on Thursday, live music Friday to Sunday and a jam session at 4pm on Sunday. The attached restaurant serves passable Indian food.

Entertainment

Alice Springs Cinemas (☎ 8952 4999; Todd Mall) Latest-release movies screen between 10am and 9pm. Some hostels offer two-for-one movie ticket deals.

If it's live music you're after, head to Bojangle's (above), Melanka (above) or Sean's Irish Bar (above).

OUTBACK AUSTRALIA

Shopping

As a regional centre, Alice sells pretty well everything you'll need. Start with **Kmart** (☎ 8952 8188; Bath St) for general goods and see the tourist office for advice on specialist items. Alice is also the centre for Aboriginal arts and crafts from all over central Australia. You can buy direct from the artists at **Papunya Tula Artists** (☎ 8952 4731; www.papunyatula.com.au; 78 Todd St), **Warumpi Arts** (☎ 8952 9066; 105 Gregory Tce), and **Mbantua Gallery** (☎ 8952 5571; 71 Gregory Tce). The **craft market** (Todd Mall; 9am-1pm) lines the mall with knick-knack stalls each Sunday.

Getting There & Away

AIR

Low-end flights to/from Alice Springs at the time of writing started at Sydney A$190, Brisbane A$260, Melbourne A$240, Adelaide A$150, Darwin A$210 and Perth A$270. Qantas also flies from Alice to Yulara (at Uluru) from A$110.

Qantas (☎ 13 13 13; www.qantas.com.au; cnr Todd Mall & Parsons St)
Virgin Blue (☎ 13 67 89; www.virginblue.com.au)

BUS

McCafferty's/Greyhound (☎ 13 20 30, 8952 7888; www.mccaffertys.com.au; cnr Gregory & Railway Tces) has daily services from Alice Springs to Adelaide (A$210, 21 hours), Uluru (A$75, 5½ hours), Cairns (A$375, 33 hours), Darwin (A$240, 20 hours) and Katherine (A$190, 15 hours).

Backpacker-type buses cover the distance while savouring the sights along the way. **Desert Venturer** (☎ 1800 079 119; www.desertventurer.com.au) makes three-day runs (A$330, food kitty A$55) between Cairns and the Alice twice weekly. **Groovy Grape Getaway Australia** (☎ 1800 661 177; www.groovygrape.com.au) has a two-day Alice to Adelaide run, via Coober Pedy (A$150) twice weekly, and longer camping trips from Adelaide to Alice Springs.

CAR & MOTORCYCLE

Alice Springs is a long way from anywhere but the roads are sealed to the north and south. When travelling, carry drinking water and emergency food at all times – even the Stuart Hwy can become impassable due to flooding, which could leave you stranded.

Rentals don't come cheap as most firms offer only 100km free a day (which won't get you anywhere), but at the time of writing you could get unlimited-kilometre rentals by booking through **Territory Discoveries** (☎ 13 43 83; www.territorydiscoveries.com.au). Rental companies include the following:

Avis (☎ 8953 5533; Shop 5, 52 Hartley St)
Britz (☎ 8952 8814; cnr Stuart Hwy & Power St)
Hertz (☎ 8952 2644; 76 Hartley St)
Territory Thrifty Car Rental (☎ 1800 891 125; cnr Stott Tce & Hartley St)

TRAIN

A great way to reach Alice Springs is aboard the *Ghan*, which departs from Adelaide at 5.15pm on Sunday and Friday and from Darwin at 4pm on Tuesday. Simple seat fares are competitive (one way from Adelaide/Darwin A$215/240), but prices rise steeply for sleepers. Tickets can be booked through **Trainways** (☎ 13 21 47; www.gsr.com.au).

Getting Around

Alice's flat terrain is perfect for cycling, and makes it a breeze to visit the Telegraph Station, Cultural Precinct, Desert Park or Simpsons Gap. Most hostels rent bikes for around A$6/12 per half-/full day. Alternatively, **Alice Wanderer** (☎ 1800 722 111; www.alicewanderer.com.au) has a hop-on, hop-off bus (A$35) that services 16 town attractions seven times a day.

Alice Springs' public bus service, **Asbus** (☎ 8950 0500; short trip A$2.20) can take you to the Cultural Precinct (Route No 1) or the southern hostels and caravan parks (Route No 4). See the tourist office for timetables.

Taxis (☎ 13 10 08) congregate near the corner of Todd St and Gregory Tce.

AROUND ALICE SPRINGS

East, west and south of Alice Springs are some fine attractions, including the gorges, water holes and walking tracks of the East and West MacDonnell Ranges, fabulous Finke Gorge and the spectacular cliffs of Kings Canyon.

There are tours to all of the places mentioned below, plus limited bus services, but having your own transport will give you far more flexibility and allow you to cover a lot more ground.

East MacDonnell Ranges

The East MacDonnell Ranges stretch for 100km east of Alice Springs, and get far fewer visitors than the West MacDonnell Ranges. The sealed Ross Hwy, south of town, leads to most of the highlights, but from the 100km mark it becomes a dirt road, which usually requires a 4WD. There are currently no facilities in the East MacDonnell Ranges, so take all provisions with you.

Emily Gap (Anthwerrke), 16km out of town, is the first stop on the way to the East MacDonnells, and features rock art and a fairly deep water hole in the narrow gorge. **Jessie Gap**, 8km further, is an equally scenic and usually much quieter place. There is a walk (18km one way, two hours, unmarked) between the two gaps. Both of these sites have toilets.

Fifty-one kilometres from Alice Springs is **Corroboree Rock**, one of many strangely shaped outcrops scattered over the valley floor. Another 15km from here brings you to the turn-off to **Trephina Gorge Nature Park**, where that are some excellent walks, deep swimming holes, abundant wildlife and low-key camping areas. The main attractions here are the gorge itself, **Trephina Bluff** and **John Hayes Rockhole**.

Just after a **roadside shrine** (complete with glistening motorcycle), the road forks and it's all dirt from here. The southern fork takes you to **N'Dhala Gorge**, which features around 5900 ancient Aboriginal rock carvings, although they're not easy to spot. The eastern fork takes you to the old gold-mining ghost town of **Arltunga**, which was worked from 1887 until 1912.

The last stop is **Ruby Gap Nature Park**, 154km from Alice, a little-visited and remote park that rewards its visitors with wild and beautiful scenery. Camping is allowed anywhere along the river; you'll need to bring your own drinking water and firewood. It is essential to get a map from the website of the **Parks & Wildlife Commission** (www.nt.gov.au/ipe/pwcnt) and to register with the **Voluntary Walker Registration Scheme** (☎ 1300 650 730). You can register by filling out a form at particular trailheads, but it's easiest to register by phone.

West MacDonnell Ranges

Spectacular gorges and fine walks punctuate the West MacDonnells, and the sealed roads make them very popular with day-trippers. Heading west from the Alice, Namatjira Dr turns northwest off Larapinta Dr 6km beyond Standley Chasm and is sealed all the way to Glen Helen, 132km from town. From the dirt road beyond, there is a turn-off south through Tylers Pass to Tnorala (Gosse Bluff), which meets up with the Mereenie Loop Rd. Larapinta Dr (see opposite) continues southwest from Standley Chasm to Hermannsburg (sealed), then the Mereenie Loop Rd (a dirt road) loops all the way to Kings Canyon. See p422 for details of tours out of Alice.

SIGHTS & ACTIVITIES

Bushwalking

The ranges provide ample opportunity for walking, with many excellent tracks in the parks and reserves. Before attempting an overnight walk, register with the **Voluntary Walker Registration Scheme** (☎ 1300 650 730).

The **Larapinta Trail** is a demanding, 12-stage, 220km track along the backbone of the West MacDonnells, stretching from the Telegraph Station on the outskirts of Alice Springs to Mt Sonder, beyond Glen Helen Gorge. The whole track takes around two weeks, although it's easy to tackle individual sections (one to two days each). While there's drinking water at some stops, it's wise to be completely self-sufficient. Detailed track notes and maps are available from the website of the **Parks & Wildlife Commission** (www.nt.gov.au/ipe/pwcnt) and from the visitors centre in Alice Springs.

Simpsons Gap

Westbound from Alice Springs on Larapinta Dr you pass **John Flynn's Grave** on the way to the turn-off to **Simpsons Gap** (🕒 8am-5pm). The Gap is 22km from town, and the area is a popular picnic spot and has some good walks. However the star attraction is the small population of endangered **black-footed rock wallabies** on either side of the gap.

Standley Chasm (Angkerle)

The most spectacular gap around the Alice, **Standley Chasm** (☎ 08-8956 7440; adult A$6; 🕒 8am-5pm) is incredibly narrow – the near-vertical walls almost meet above you. Refreshments are sold at the kiosk and there are picnic facilities and toilets. It's 51km east of Alice Springs.

NAMATJIRA DRIVE

Not far beyond Standley Chasm, Namatjira Dr heads northwest off Larapinta Dr. West along Namatjira Dr is another series of gorges and gaps in the range. **Ellery Creek Big Hole** is 93km from Alice Springs and has a

OUTBACK AUSTRALIA

large permanent water hole – a great place for a swim on a hot day, but the water can be freezing. **Serpentine Gorge**, a narrow gorge with a water hole at the entrance (no swimming), is 13km further on.

The **Ochre Pits**, just off the road 11km west of Serpentine, are a source of paints for Aboriginal people. Next is the large, rugged **Ormiston Gorge**, arguably the most impressive gorge in the West MacDonnells and well worth a couple of hours. There's an inviting water hole and the gorge curls around to the enclosed valley of Ormiston Pound. There are some good short walking tracks around here, plus a **visitors centre** (☎ 08-8956 7799) and a good camping area.

Only about 2km further is the turn-off to the scenic **Glen Helen Gorge**, where the ancient Finke River (the world's oldest) cuts through the MacDonnells.

The idyllic view of Glen Helen Gorge's massive walls lit up at night is reason enough to venture out to **Glen Helen Resort** (☎ 1800 896 110; www.glenhelen.com.au; Namatjira Dr; camp/caravan sites per person A$11/13, budget rooms A$85, motel d A$150;), a historic homestead. The ambient bar and restaurant features live music five nights a week (March to December). The exposed camping area is grassy, and budget rooms share facilities.

There are national park **camping areas** (camping per person A$3.30-6.60) at Ellery Creek Big Hole, Serpentine Gorge, Ormiston Gorge and Redbank Gorge, with Ormiston the best of them. Camping fees are payable to the honesty box.

Larapinta Drive

The spectacular James Ranges form an east-west band south of the West MacDonnell Ranges. While not as well known as the MacDonnells, the ranges contain some of the Centre's best attractions: Hermannsburg, Palm Valley and Kings Canyon.

Heading south from Standley Chasm, Larapinta Dr heads to Hermannsburg, passing the **Wallace Rockhole** turn-off and the **Namatjira Monument** on the way. The latter commemorates Hermannsburg's most famous son, Aboriginal watercolourist Albert Namatjira. Only 8km beyond the Namatjira Monument you reach the Hermannsburg Aboriginal settlement, 125km from Alice Springs. Although the town is restricted Aboriginal land, permits are not required to visit the historic precinct, store and art gallery, where you can see the distinctive ceramic works by the Hermannsburg Potters group.

From Hermannsburg a 4WD track follows the Finke River south to the **Finke Gorge National Park**, 12km away. Famous for the rare central Australian cabbage palm *(Livistona mariae)*, **Palm Valley** is the park's most popular attraction (see also Tours, p422). The main gorge features high red cliffs, majestic river red gums, plenty of sand and stately palms. The shady camping area has a serene setting, plus hot showers and flushing toilets.

Mereenie Loop Road

From Hermannsburg you can continue west along the Mereenie Loop Rd to **Kings Canyon**. This dirt road is suitable for robust conventional vehicles, although motorcycles and bicycles are not allowed. To travel this road you need a permit as it passes through Aboriginal land. The one-day permits are issued on the spot (A$2.20) at the visitors centre in Alice Springs, and from Glen Helen Homestead, Kings Canyon Resort service station and Hermannsburg service station.

Watarrka (Kings Canyon) National Park

This superb national park includes one of the most spectacular sights in central Australia – the sheer, 100m-high walls and secluded water holes of **Kings Canyon**. The short **Kings Creek Walk** follows the rocky creek bed to a raised platform with amphitheatre-like views of the towering canyon's rim. Better is the **Kings Canyon Walk** (6km loop, four hours), where walkers are rewarded with awesome views. After a steep climb, the walk skirts the canyon's rim, which overlooks sheer cliff faces. It then enters the **Garden of Eden** with its tranquil pools and prehistoric cycads, and passes through a maze of giant eroded domes. Watch your step – the cliffs are unfenced and the wind can be strong. Carry plenty of water and a hat.

The **Giles Track** (22km one way, overnight) is a marked track that follows the ridge between the gorge and Kathleen Springs. You can register for the walk with the **Volunteer Walker Registration Scheme** (☎ 1300 650 730).

TOURS

Free, one-hour **guided ranger walks** (3pm Tue & Thu Jul-Oct) operate from the Canyon car park. Helicopter flights (from A$60) are available from **Kings Canyon Resort** (☎ 08-8956 7873) and **Kings Creek Station** (☎ 08-8956 7474). For information on tours combining Kings Canyon and Uluru see opposite.

SLEEPING & EATING

Kings Canyon Resort (☎ 1800 089 622, 08-8956 7442; www.voyages.com.au; Luritja Rd; camp/caravan sites per 2 people A$28/32, dm A$45, lodge r A$170, d A$100, motel d A$330-420;) You'll pay top dollar for the well-maintained facilities at this resort, 6km west of the canyon. The grassy camping ground has plenty of shade, a laundry and barbecues. Four-bed dorm and lodge rooms share kitchen and bathroom facilities. There's a bar, café, restaurant, shop and fuel. The resort's **Outback BBQ & Grill** (mains A$16-27; dinner) has pizza, grills and some nonmeat options to live Australiana music, while **Carmichael's Restaurant** (breakfast A$16-22, buffet A$45; breakfast & lunch) serves swish breakfasts and an evening seafood buffet.

Kings Creek Station (☎ 08-8956 7474; www.kingscreekstation.com.au; Luritja Rd; camp sites per person A$12, power per site A$3.10, s/d cabins incl breakfast A$70/104;) Around 35km south of the canyon, this friendly spot has pristine camp sites, a small pool, a shop with fuel and limited supplies, and a good kitchen-barbecue area. The rather corny evening entertainment (adult A$20) is of the whip-cracking, billy tea and damper variety, but it's harmless enough.

GETTING THERE & AWAY

You can reach Kings Canyon, 230km southwest of Alice Springs, via the unsealed Mereenie Loop Rd (see p427), although most people head north from the Lasseter Hwy on their way to or from Uluru. If you're travelling via the Stuart Hwy, the gravel Ernest Giles Rd is a tempting short cut that wipes 150km off the sealed route, but it's often impassable after heavy rain and is not recommended for conventional vehicles.

Stuart Highway

The main road south of Alice has a few minor attractions on the way to the Uluru turn-off. Around 75km south of town is the turn-off to **Rainbow Valley Conservation Reserve**, a beautiful series of sandstone bluffs and cliffs in shades ranging from cream to red. It's 22km from the turn-off along a 4WD track.

You can jump out of your car and onto a camel at **Stuarts Well**, a roadhouse 90km south of Alice Springs, or head west for 11km along the Ernest Giles Rd to check out the **Henbury Meteorite Craters**. Another 70km south is **Erldunda**, a roadhouse on the turn-off to the Lasseter Hwy and Uluru.

Lasseter Highway

The Lasseter Hwy connects the Stuart Hwy with Uluru–Kata Tjuta National Park, 244km to the west. There are a couple of roadhouses along the way, plus a lookout for **Mt Conner** (350m), the large mesa (table-top mountain) that some eager souls mistake for Uluru.

If you have your own wheels, **Curtin Springs Station** (☎ 08-8956 2906; www.curtinsprings.com; Lasseter Hwy; camp sites free, s/d A$35/45, showers A$1), 85km east of Yulara (Ayers Rock Resort), is a fair alternative to the busy and somewhat pricey resort. There's a bar and restaurant, plus the obligatory camel rides.

ULURU–KATA TJUTA NATIONAL PARK

This entire area is of deep cultural significance to the owners, the Pitjantjatjara and Yankunytjatjara Aboriginal peoples (who refer to themselves as Anangu). The area once known to white Australians – and tourists – as Ayers Rock has always been known to Aborigines as Uluru, and the Olgas as Kata Tjuta. These names are now the preferred official names of these sites, although die-hards and bloody-minded continue to use the English names. The national park is leased to Environment Australia (the federal government's national parks body), which administers it in conjunction with the traditional owners.

It's easy to spend several days in the Uluru–Kata Tjuta area; there are plenty of walks and other activities, and the Rock never seems to look the same no matter how many times you see it. Most group tours are very rushed, but it's best experienced at your own pace, if you have the time.

Information

Uluru–Kata Tjuta National Park Cultural Centre (☎ 08-8956 3138; 7am-5.30pm Apr-Oct, to 6pm Nov-Mar) is 1km before the Rock on the road from Yulara. You can easily spend an hour or three here before visiting Uluru itself. The two inspiring buildings represent the ancestral figures of Kuniya and Liru and contained within them are two main display areas – the Tjukurpa display features Anangu art and *tjukurpa* (Aboriginal law, religion and custom), while the Nintiringkupai display focuses on the history and management of the national park. The centre also houses a gallery, souvenir shop and café.

PARK ENTRY

The park itself is open daily from half an hour before sunrise to sunset. Three-day entry permits to the national park, available at the park entry station, are a hefty A$25 per adult.

Tours

A huge variety of tours is available, taking in everything from guided walks and motorcycle tours to all-inclusive tours from Alice Springs (but avoid those that bundle you there and back in a day – you'll spend far too much time looking out the bus window and a distressingly short period at the sites). All local tours can be booked at the **Tour & Information Centre** (☎ 8957 7324; resort shopping centre; 🕓 7.30am-8.30pm) at Yulara. The Uluru Express (p432) also provides transport from Yulara to Uluru and Kata Tjuta.

Owned and operated by the Mutitjulu community, **Anangu Tours** (☎ 08-8956 2123; www.anangutours.com.au; tours adult from A$52) offers a range of tours led by Aboriginal guides. The tours include aspects of Anangu culture and law, and demonstrations of bush skills and spear-throwing. Self-drive options are also available.

Discovery Ecotours (☎ 1800 803 174; www.discoveryecotours.com.au; tours from A$110) offers tours around the base of Uluru, and Kata Tjuta walks, while **AAT-Kings** (☎ 1800 334 009; www.aatkings.com; tours adult from A$80), a major operator, runs a range of daily coach tours.

Other operators:

Ayers Rock Helicopters (☎ 08-8956 2077; flights from A$85)

Ayers Rock Scenic Flights (☎ 08-8956 2345; flights from A$130)

Uluru Motorcycles (☎ 08-8956 2019; tours from A$150)

FROM ALICE SPRINGS

All-inclusive camping trips to Uluru by private operators start at A$280/400 for two/three days, which includes Kings Canyon. If you're rushed for time there are two- or even one-day tours. Prices can vary with the season and demand, and sometimes there may be cheaper 'stand-by' fares available.

Popular companies:

Adventure Tours Australia (☎ 08-8981 4255; www.adventuretours.com.au)

Mulga's Adventures (☎ 08-8952 1545; www.mulgas.com.au)

Sahara Outback Tours (☎ 08-8953 0881; www.saharatours.com.au)

AAT-Kings (☎ 1800 334 009; www.aatkings.com) and **McCafferty's/Greyhound** (☎ 13 14 99; www.mccaffertys.com.au) offer three-day tours of Uluru and Kings Canyon from A$280. If your time is limited, **Day Tours** (☎ 08-8953 4664; adult A$150) will race you to Uluru and back, including lunch and sunset viewing, but it's a very long day.

Uluru (Ayers Rock)

Nothing in Australia is as readily identifiable as Uluru (Ayers Rock), the world's biggest monolith. Australia's favourite postcard image is 3.6km long and rises a towering 348m from the surrounding sandy scrubland. If your first sight of the Rock is during the afternoon it appears as an ochre-brown colour. But as the sun sets, it illuminates the Rock in burnishing orange, then a series of deeper and darker reds before it fades into charcoal. A performance in reverse, with marginally fewer spectators, is given at dawn at this World Heritage site.

WALKS

There are several good walking tracks around Uluru; pick up the *Insight into Uluru*

> **CLIMBING ULURU**
>
> For decades, this demanding climb, which takes about two hours return, has been the highlight of a trip to the Centre. For the Anangu, however, the path up the side of the Rock is part of the route taken by Mala men on their arrival at Uluru, and as such has great spiritual significance. As custodians of these lands, the Anangu are also distressed by the injuries and deaths that occur on the Rock. For these reasons, the Anangu don't climb and they ask that you don't either. If you compare climbing the Rock to, say, clambering over the altar in Notre Dame Cathedral or striding through a mosque during prayer, it's not hard to understand the Anangu perspective – it's a question of respect.

brochure (A$1) from the cultural centre to get the most out of your experience.

The **Base Walk** (10km, three to four hours) takes you right around the circumference of the Rock, and allows you to escape the madding crowds. The **Mala Walk** (2km, one hour) is an interpretative walk explaining the *tjukurpa* of the Mala (hare-wallaby people). The **Mutitjulu Walk** (1km, 30 minutes) takes you to a permanent water hole, and tells of the clash between two ancestral snakes, Kuniya and Liru.

Kata Tjuta (the Olgas)

A bizarre collection of huge rounded rocks, Kata Tjuta (the Olgas) stands about 30km to the west of Uluru. Less famous than Uluru, the monoliths are still impressive and many people find them more captivating. Kata Tjuta (meaning 'many heads') is of great *tjukurpa* significance: climbing on the domed rocks is definitely not on.

The main walking track here is the **Valley of the Winds**, a 7.4km loop track (two to four hours) that winds through the gorges giving surreal views of the domes. The short (2km return) signposted track into the pretty **Olga Gorge** (Tatintjawiya) is especially beautiful in the afternoon when sunlight floods the gorge.

There's a picnic and sunset-viewing area with toilet facilities just off the access road a few kilometres west of the base of Kata Tjuta. Like Uluru, the Olgas are at their glorious, blood-red best at sunset.

Yulara (Ayers Rock Resort)

☎ 08

Lying just outside the national park, 21km from Uluru and 53km from Kata Tjuta, Yulara (pop 2530, including Mutitjulu) is the service village for the area. The complex is a well-equipped – though expensive – base for exploring the area.

ORIENTATION & INFORMATION

Yulara is built around a vaguely circular drive, with all hotels and facilities strung along its outer edge. *The Resort Guide* is a useful sheet available at the visitors centre and hotel desks.

The Connellan airport is about 5km north of Yulara. A free shuttle bus to Yulara meets all flights and will drop you at your accommodation.

The **visitors centre** (☎ 8957 7377; 🕑 8.30am-8pm) contains good displays on the geography, wildlife and history of the region.

Accommodation other than the camping ground can be booked through **central reservations** (☎ 1300 139 889; www.voyages.com.au).

Most tour operators (see p429) and car-hire firms have desks at the **Tour & Information Centre** (☎ 8957 7324; 🕑 7.30am-8.30pm) at the shopping centre. The centre includes a supermarket, photo shop and eateries, and a **post office** (☎ 8956 2288; 🕑 9.30am-6pm Mon-Fri, 10am-2pm Sat & Sun), which is the bank agency for the Commonwealth and Westpac banks. **ANZ** (☎ 8956 2070) has an ATM here.

There are coin-operated Internet machines in the Tour & Information Centre and Outback Pioneer Hotel & Lodge.

SIGHTS & ACTIVITIES

Each evening you can take in the **Night Sky Show** (☎ 1800 803 174; adult A$32), an informative look into Anangu and Greek astrological legends, with views of the startlingly clear outback night sky through telescopes and binoculars; bookings are required.

If you're hanging out to meet some local beasties, check out **Predators of the Red Centre** (☎ 8956 2563; adult A$22; 🕑 noon), in the Inmapiti Amphitheatre next to Sails in the Desert.

Frontier Camel Tours (☎ 8956 2444; arock@cameltours.com.au; tours from A$90) can take you on a saunter through the dunes.

SLEEPING

Given the excessive prices charged for most food and accommodation at Yulara, it's nice to discover that you can actually visit the Rock without breaking the bank. You'll cook your own meals or eat lots of takeaway, and you'll either rub shoulders with the masses in the camping ground or sleep in a high-volume dorm, but it can be done. Couples looking for a reasonably priced double, however, are out of luck. With the exception of camp sites (which are unlimited), you'll need to book your accommodation in advance, especially during school holidays.

Ayers Rock Resort Camp Ground (☎ 8956 2055; camp.ground@ayersrockresort.com.au; camp/caravan sites per 2 people A$26/31, cabins A$150; P) Grassy and well maintained, the camping ground gets insanely busy in the high season. There's a small pool, clean amenity blocks and a very basic camp kitchen (sink, fridge and two

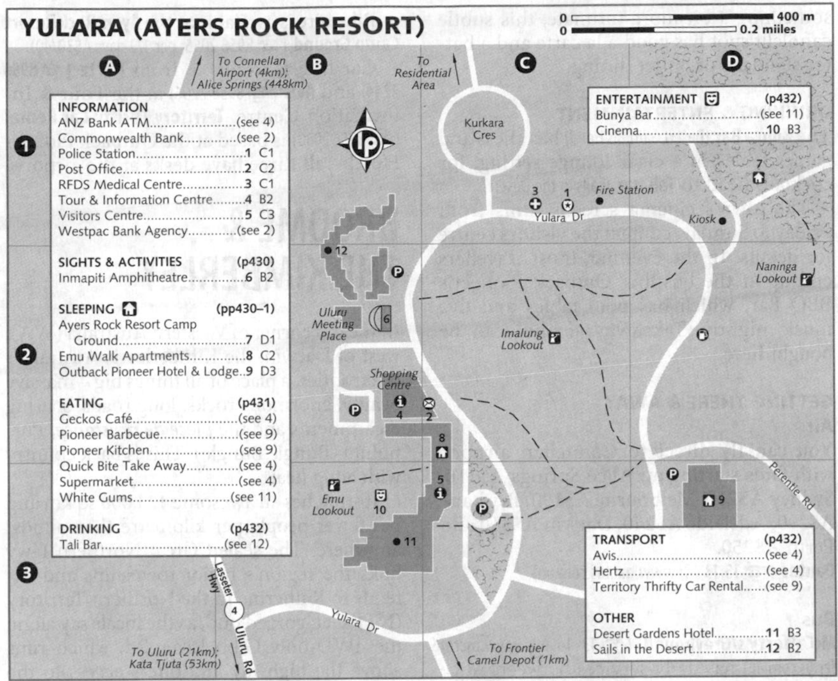

barbecues) that's in high demand. Everyone wakes before dawn to the sounds of people crashing about in preparation for a trip to the Rock, so try instead for one of the self-contained cabins. They sleep up to six people, and are relatively good value, but get booked out weeks or months in advance.

Outback Pioneer Hotel & Lodge (☎ 8957 7605; dm A$33-41, budget d with/without bathroom A$190/170, standard d from A$330; P ✿ 💻) The Pioneer has cramped but OK four- and 20-bed dorms, and plain double rooms. There's an excellent, well-equipped kitchen (open 24 hours), plus laundry, TV room and Internet machines, and you can use the hotel pool – a pretty good deal, all up.

From here prices head into the stratosphere, although the spacious, self-contained **Emu Walk Apartments** (2-bedroom apt A$450, extra adult A$36; ✿) sleep six and might be attractive to small groups seeking a little more luxury.

EATING

The well-stocked **supermarket** (resort shopping centre; 🕒 8.30am-9pm) has a salad bar and delicatessen, and sells fresh fruit and vegetables and meat, and camping supplies. The range and competitive prices make self-catering an attractive option.

Pioneer Kitchen (Outback Pioneer Hotel & Lodge; burgers A$8; 🕒 lunch & dinner) A hole-in-the-wall that offers a range of good burgers and wraps, plus hot chips, which can be washed down with a beer from the nearby bar.

Quick Bite Take Away (resort shopping centre; 🕒 breakfast, lunch & dinner) has the usual fast-food suspects, like burgers (A$6.50) and barbecued chicken (half/whole A$5/8.50).

Geckos Café (☎ 8956 2562; resort shopping centre; pizza A$19-26, pasta & mains A$21-29; 🕒 lunch & dinner) Serves pretty good pizza and OK pasta, if you don't choke on the prices. The attached ice-cream parlour also serves thickshakes.

Pioneer Barbecue (Outback Pioneer Hotel & Lodge; barbecue A$17-25, salad bar only A$16; 🕒 dinner) Self-sizzle modest portions of sausages, steak, fish or crocodile, aided and abetted by an unremarkable salad bar. Meals are accompanied by live Australiana music and the banter of lively crowds.

White Gums (Desert Gardens Hotel; ☎ 8956 2100; mains A$10-19, dinner buffet A$50; 🕒 dinner) For something a bit more intimate, this subtle candlelit spot has good à la carte and a better standard of buffet dining.

DRINKING & ENTERTAINMENT

The **Bunya Bar** (Desert Gardens Hotel) has chess and games tables in a cigar lounge setting; for cocktails head to **Tali Bar** (Sails in the Desert).

The town's cinema screens films from Friday to Sunday; contact the visitors centre for details. In the evening, most travellers end up at the bustling Outback Pioneer's BBQ Bar, which has pool tables and live music nightly. Takeaway alcohol can be bought here.

GETTING THERE & AWAY

Air

You can fly direct to Connellan airport, with fares starting at: Alice Springs A$110, Sydney A$210, Melbourne A$190, Brisbane A$290, Adelaide A$240, Darwin A$310 and Perth A$250.

Qantas (☎ 13 13 13; www.qantas.com.au)

Bus

McCafferty's/Greyhound (☎ 13 14 99; www.mccafferty s.com.au) has daily services between Alice Springs and Uluru (A$75, 5½ hours). Services between Adelaide and Uluru (A$210) connect with the bus from Alice Springs at Erldunda.

Car & Motorcycle

The road from the Alice to Yulara (441km) is sealed and there are food and petrol stops at Stuart Wells, Erldunda and Curtin Springs. The whole journey takes about four to five hours. If you don't have your own vehicle, renting a car in Alice Springs can be expensive, unless you can get an unlimited kilometre deal (see Car & Motorcycle, p425).

GETTING AROUND

The resort itself sprawls a bit, but it's not too large to get around on foot. A free shuttle bus runs between all accommodation points, the shopping centre and Frontier Camel Depot (every 15 minutes, 10.30am to 6pm and 6.30pm to 12.30am daily).

Uluru Express (☎ 8956 2152) provides return transport from the resort to Uluru for A$30 per adult. Morning shuttles to Kata Tjuta cost A$45; afternoon shuttles include a stop at Uluru for sunset and cost A$50.

Bike hire is available at the **Ayers Rock Resort Camp Ground** (☎ 8956 2055; per 1/2 days A$30/40).

Car hire is available from **Hertz** (☎ 8956 2244) and **Avis** (☎ 8956 2266) at the Tour & Information Centre. **Territory Thrifty Car Rental** (☎ 8956 2030) is based at the Outback Pioneer Hotel – all three have desks at the airport.

BROOME & THE KIMBERLEY

In the top corner of Western Australia (WA), west of Darwin, the Kimberley is Australia's last frontier, a place of all things big – massive beauty, enormous rocks, long roads, soaring escarpments and the *pièce de résistance*, Purnululu (Bungle Bungle). This is back country with a big heart.

It stretches an awesome 423,000 sq km and has fewer people per kilometre than almost anywhere. The sealed Great Northern Hwy links the region's major townships and extends to Katherine in the Northern Territory (NT). Get 'gorged out', as the locals say along the 4WD-only Gibb River Rd, which runs above the highway and offers access to the spectacular Mitchell Plateau.

During the Wet (November to April), you'll be greeted with waterfalls galore, mosquitoes, lashings of spear grass and almost-nightly lightning shows. It's party time for the wildlife! In the Dry (May to October), the weather is more tolerable and the Kimberley's radiant palette gleams.

For more information pick up a copy of the *Kimberley Holiday Planner* from the Broome visitor centre, call the **Western Australia Visitor Centre** (☎ 1300 361 351) or visit the websites www.westernaustralia.com, www.kimberleytourism.com or www.ata.org.au.

Northwest Regional Airlines (☎ 1300 136 629) and **Skippers Aviation** (☎ 08-9478 3989) has daily flights throughout the region.

Activities

This part of Australia offers a rare glimpse into an ancient landscape. Get off the beaten track bushwalking, enjoy horse riding, or 4WD touring high-country style. For those seeking pure adrenaline, head inland for some mountain-range rock climbing or try abseiling down ravines. More experienced adventure-seekers may like to conquer some of the world's most extensive cave systems or kayak through timeworn gorges.

Tours

There are numerous tour operators in the Kimberley:

Adventure Tours (☎ 1300 654 604, 08-8309 2277; www.adventuretours.com.au; 8-day 4WD Darwin-Broome A$1350) These Broome to Darwin (or vice versa) trips are strenuous but fun.

East Kimberley Tours (☎ 1800 682 213, 08-9168 2213; www.eastkimberleytours.com.au) Overnight Bungle Bungle trips. Explorations of the Mitchell Plateau.

Easyrider Backpacker Tours (☎ 1800 247 848, 08-9226 0307; www.easyridertours.com.au; 4-day trip adult/concession A$509/499) The 'Kimberley Krossing' trip will whiz you across the outback.

Kimberley Adventure Tours (☎ 1800 083 368, 08-9191 2655; www.kimberleyadventures.com.au; Kimberley tour from A$1295) Darwin to Broome (or vice versa) along the Gibb River Rd, seeing the Bungle Bungles and Lake Argyle. Only nine passengers on any trip.

Kimberley Wild Outback Tours (☎ 08-9193 7778; www.kimberleywild.com.au; 8-day tour from A$1695) 'Do' the Kimberley on an eight-day 'Explorer tour'.

Kimberley Wilderness Adventures (☎ 1800 675 222; www.kimberleywilderness.com.au; 6–13-day tours adult from A$1575) Travel the rugged terrain with this award-winning company and stay at safari camps adjacent to major Kimberley icons.

Remote Outback Cycle Tours (☎ 08-9279 6969; www.cycletours.com.au; tours adult from A$549; 🕑 May-Nov) Combine mountain biking with 4WD on an 11-day Darwin to Broome 'Gibb River Rd Cycling Experience' (A$1695). Bikes and gear supplied.

Wilderness 4WD Adventures (☎ 1300 666 100; www.wildernessadventures.com.au; Kimberley Challenge adult from A$1350) Go for adventure! See the Bungles, and the Gibb River Rd's plethora of gorges.

Willis's Walkabouts (☎ 08-8985 2134; www.bushwalkingholidays.com.au; per day from A$138) Bushwalking in the Kimberley. Discounts for advance bookings.

The **West Australian Indigenous Tour Operators Committee** (Waitoc; www.waitoc.com) lists contact information for local Aboriginal tour operators.

BROOME

☎ 08 / 14,000

Atmospheric Broome looms large in the nation's imagination as a far-flung paradise where fortunes are made. The Kimberley's semiarid landscape envelopes this laconic town, but it's the azure Indian Ocean that has really put Broome on the map as the centre of the Australian pearling industry.

Tucked in a tiny cavity of Western Australia's northwest, Broome enjoys an enviable average temperature of 31°C. Its population balloons in the dry season (May to October), but in the Wet (November to April) Broome puts on its green cloak and lightning dissects the sky. You'll soon be seduced by 'Broome-time': its languid heat, unbuttoned living and blinding light take your senses into an altered state.

A frontier town with a bloody past, fast-growing Broome is now a comfortable conduit for crosscultural pollination: there's a strong sense of Aboriginality balanced with a Chinese legacy and New Age–meets–new money vibe.

Orientation

Broome is positioned on the eastern coast of the Dampier Peninsula, on Roebuck Bay. The Great Northern Hwy (Broome Hwy) curls into Roebuck Bay from the north to become Hamersley St, which hits Town Beach. Adjacent is palm-lined Carnarvon St, the centre of Broome's Asiatic commercial and historical hub – Chinatown. Dampier Tce is parallel to Carnarvon St and is lined with shops. Frederick St extends northwest and meets Broome's premier attraction, Cable Beach.

The airport on Macpherson St is less than a kilometre west of Chinatown.

Information

EMERGENCY & MEDICAL SERVICES

Broome Dental Clinic (☎ 9192 1624; 6 Barker St)

Hospital (☎ 9192 9222; Robinson St; 🕑 24hr)

Police station (☎ 9194 0200; Hamersley St)

INTERNET ACCESS

Get wired at the following Internet cafés from A$6 per hour:

Broome Telecentre (☎ 9193 7153; 40 Dampier Tce; 🕑 9am-5pm Mon-Fri, to 1pm Sat)

Internet Outpost (☎ 9193 6534; 16 Carnarvon St; 🕑 9am-4.30pm)

Library (☎ 9191 3477; library@broome.wa.gov.au; cnr Haas & Hamersley Sts; 🕑 10am-5pm Mon, Wed & Fri, to 7pm Tue & Thu, 9am-noon Sat) Free Internet access (subject to availability).

MONEY

There are ATMs in Carnarvon and Short Sts.

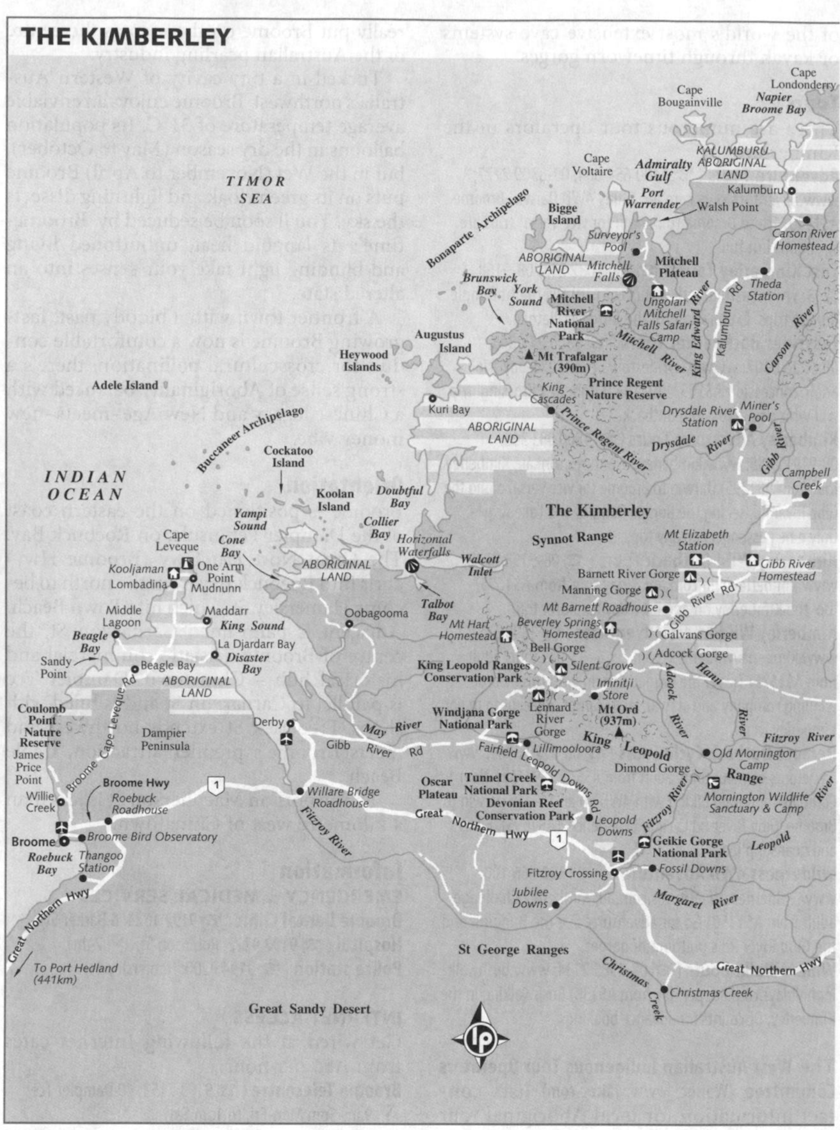

POST

Post office (☎ 9192 1380; 28 Carnarvon St; 🕓 9am-5pm Mon-Fri)

TOURIST INFORMATION

Broome visitors centre (☎ 9192 2222; www.broomevisitorcentre.com.au; cnr Great Northern Hwy & Bagot St; 🕓 8am-5pm Mon-Fri, 9am-4pm Sat & Sun dry season, 8am-5pm Mon-Fri, 9am-1pm Sat & Sun Wet) A worthwhile pit-stop. Grab a copy of the *Broome Visitor Centre Holiday Guide*.

TRAVEL AGENCIES

There are always last-minute backpacker specials being offered at the hostels and the Courthouse market (Saturday, dry season).

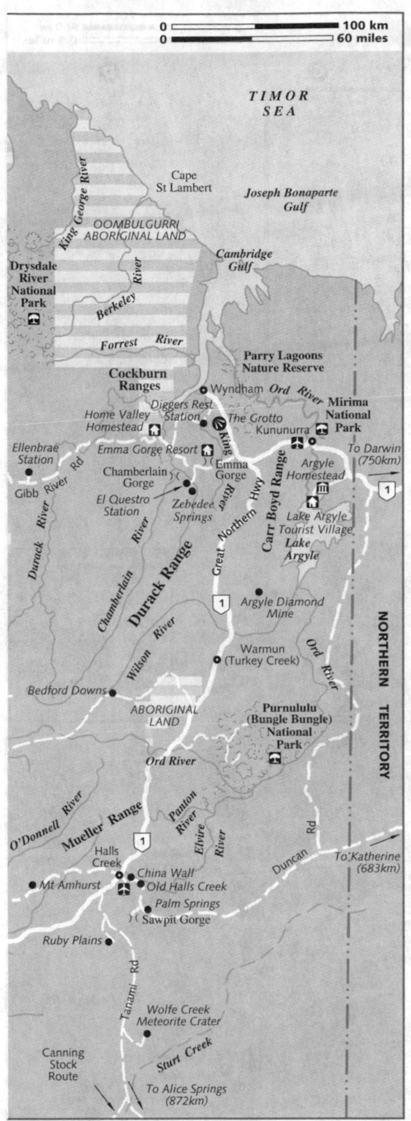

Harvey World Travel (☎ 9193 5599; broome@harveyworld.com.au; Paspaley Plaza, Carnarvon St) For onward and upward travel.

Dangers & Annoyances

Poisonous stingers frequent Broome's prime swimming stretch, Cable Beach (November to March), and Roebuck Bay.

Sights

Lined with former pearling sheds and pavement cafés, **Chinatown** is Broome's heart and soul. Explore it with a copy of *Broome Heritage Trail* (from the visitors centre; A$3).

Sun Pictures (see p439) is the world's oldest open-air cinema (1916) with classic deck chairs, charm galore and even the odd light aircraft flying overhead.

Watch a sunset worthy of hanging on your wall at iconic **Cable Beach**; learn about native plants along the marked tracks of **Miniyirr Park**; head to **Gantheaume Point** where low tide reveals 120-million-year-old dinosaur tracks, or take a dip in **Anastasia's Pool** right next door.

An **evening market** (☎ 9192 2222; from 5pm) at **Town Beach** coincides with the somewhat overrated **Staircase to the Moon** (March to October) phenomenon. The illusion of a staircase is created when the rising full moon reflects on mud flats at low tide. The **Flying Boat Wrecks** – remains of Japanese Zero fighter planes – can be seen 1km from Town Beach at low tides (March to October).

Broome Historical Society Museum (☎ 9192 2075; Saville St; adult/student A$5/3; 🕓 10am-1pm Mon-Fri Nov-May, 10am-4pm Mon-Fri, to 1pm Sat & Sun Jun-Oct) gives a real sense of bygone Broome. View the journal of English explorer William Dampier (1651–1715), who voyaged past present-day Broome in 1699.

Learn about the heady pearling days at **Pearl Luggers** (☎ 9192 2059; pearlluggers@bigpond.com; 31 Dampier Tce; admission free, tours adult/concession A$20/18; 🕓 tours 11am & 2pm Mon-Fri, 11am Sat & Sun). Delve into indigenous water practices at **Manbana Aquaculture Hatchery & Discovery Centre** (☎ 9192 3844; www.manbana.com; adult/concession A$15/12; Murakami Rd; 🕓 tours 9am, 11am, 1pm & 3pm Mon-Fri, 11am & 1pm Sat & Sun) near the port, southeast of the town centre.

In need of a makeover, **Broome Crocodile Park** (☎ 9192 1489; Cable Beach Rd; adult/concession A$18.50/15; 🕓 10am-5pm Mon-Fri, 2-5pm Sat & Sun Apr-Nov, 3.30-5.15pm Dec-Mar) is chock-a-block with crocs. The admission fees are hefty but include a tour, so time your visit to coincide with a tour (3pm from April to November and 3.45pm December to March).

Activities

No visit to Broome is complete without being a beach-bum on the white sands of **Cable Beach** – all 22km of it. At the bottom

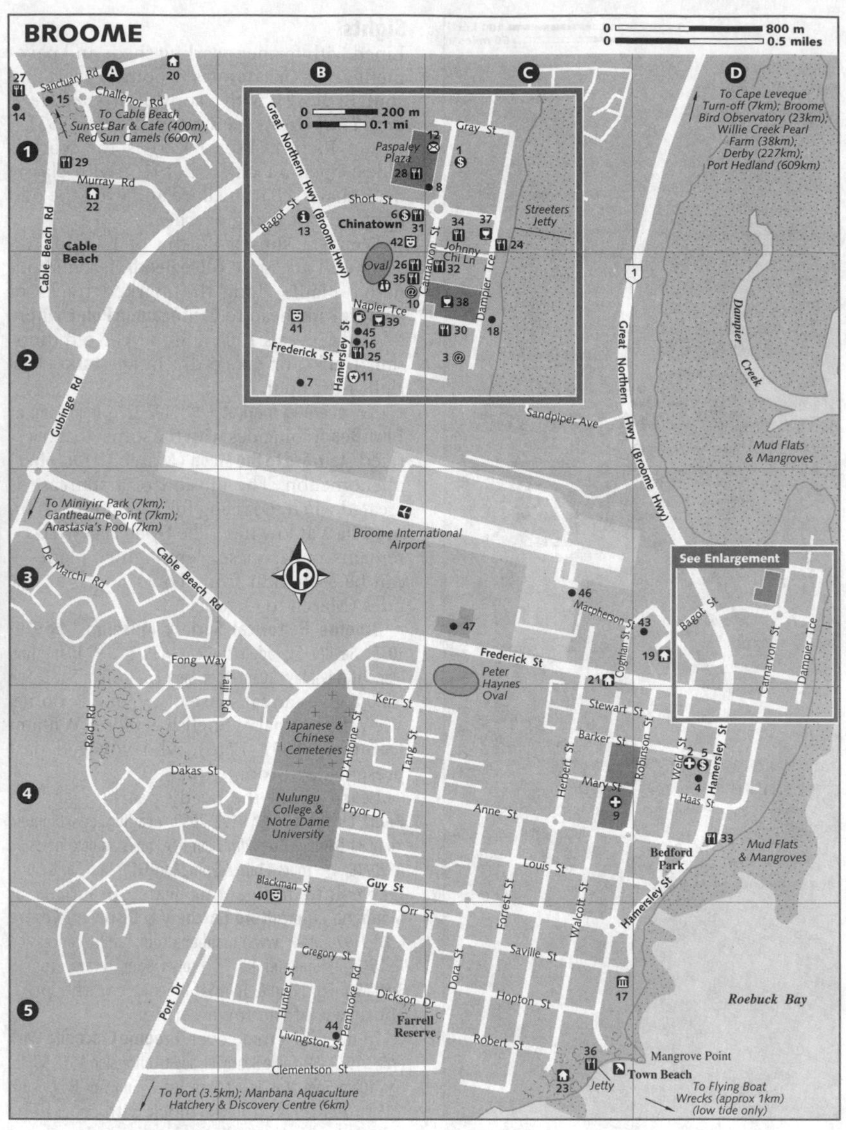

of Broome Surf Lifesaving Club, you'll find **Beach Hut** (bodyboards per hr/day A$3/9, surfboards & wave skis per hr/day A$10/30), which hires umbrellas and deck chairs from A$3 and a range of boards.

Red Sun Camels (☎ 1800 184 488, 9193 7423; www.redsuncamels.com.au; tours adult sunset 1hr A$40, morning 40min A$30) offers sunset camel tours on Cable Beach. Watching the sun melt into the Indian Ocean on humpback is an essential Broome experience.

Broome is made for cycling. Get yourself two wheels at **Broome Cycles** (☎ 9192 1871; 2 Hamersley St; per 1/7 days A$18/70; 8.30am-5pm Mon-Fri, to 2pm Sat, 10am-2pm Sun). It also has an outlet near Cable Beach.

INFORMATION
- ANZ Bank....1 C1
- Broome Dental Clinic....2 D4
- Broome Telecentre....3 C2
- Civic Centre....4 D4
- Commonwealth Bank ATM....5 D4
- Commonwealth Bank ATM....6 B1
- Courthouse Markets....7 B2
- Harvey World Travel....8 C1
- Hospital....9 C4
- Internet Outpost....10 B2
- Library....(see 4)
- Police Station....11 B2
- Post Office....12 C1
- Visitors Centre....13 B1

SIGHTS & ACTIVITIES (pp435–6)
- Beach Hut....14 A1
- Broome Crocodile Park....15 A1
- Broome Cycles....16 B2
- Broome Historical Society Museum....17 C5
- Pearl Luggers....18 C2

SLEEPING (pp437–8)
- Broome's Last Resort....19 D3
- Cable Beach Backpackers....20 A1
- Kimberley Klub....21 C3
- Palm Grove Holiday Resort....22 A1
- Roebuck Bay Caravan Park....23 C5

EATING (p438)
- 2 Rice....24 C1
- Aarli Bar....25 B2
- Action Supermarket....(see 47)
- Bloom's Café & Licensed Restaurant....26 B2
- Cable Beach Sandbar & Grill....27 A1
- Coles....28 B1
- Diver's Tavern....29 A1
- Frangipanis Café Restaurant....30 C2
- Henry's Café....31 B1
- Ice Creamery....32 C2
- Matso's Café & Brewery....33 D4
- Shady Lane Café....34 C1
- Son Ming Chinese Restaurant....35 B2
- Sri Curry House....(see 8)
- Town Beach Café....36 C5

DRINKING (p439)
- Nippon Inn....37 C1
- Roebuck Bay Hotel....38 C2
- Tokyo Joe's....39 B2

ENTERTAINMENT (p439)
- Gimme Gimme Club....40 B4
- Sun Cinemas....41 B2
- Sun Pictures....42 B1

TRANSPORT (p439)
- Avis....43 D3
- Britz....44 B5
- Broome Broome....45 B2
- Budget....46 C3

OTHER
- Boulevard Shopping Centre....47 C3

Tours

Learn about indigenous culture and coast care on the excellent 90km **Lurujarri Songcycle Heritage Dreaming Trail** (☎ 9192 3337; http://trails.heritage.wa.gov.au; adult/concession incl food, luggage transport & guide A$1200/650), which traverses some spectacular country around Broome while travelling with the Goolarabooloo Aboriginal people over nine days.

Also recommended:

Astro Tours (☎ 9193 5362; www.astrotours.net; 2hr shows adult A$56; Apr-Dec) A close encounter with Broome's diamond-studded night sky.

Broome Aviation (☎ 9192 1369; www.broomeaviation.com; adult from A$150) Soar sky-high for unforgettable views.

LizArt Broome Tours (☎ 9192 6948; www.lizartbroome.com; adult A$50; tours 8.30am & 12.30pm Mon, Tue, Thu & Fri) Meet Broome's arty set on this half-day tour.

Outback Ballooning (☎ 1800 809 790; www.outbackballooning.com.au; flights adult A$240; Jun-Sep) Get a bird's-eye view over the bay and desert with the 45- to 60-minute Broome Balloon Flight.

Western Blue Sea Kayak (☎ 1300 665 888, 0419 895 367; www.westernblue.com.au; 3hr tour adult/concession A$65/58; Apr-Oct) Hit the waves with turtles and dolphins.

Festivals & Events

The people of Broome love a party.

Broome Art & Music Foundation Ten days of home-grown and imported talent, held during April.

Shinju Matsuri (Festival of the Pearl) A long-running 10-day celebration of Broome's pearling identity featuring a street parade and fireworks finale in August.

Stompen Ground A cultural festival in September or October featuring indigenous bands from around the country and traditional foods.

Worn Art Presents over 150 artworks exploring the human form from late September to early October.

Sleeping

Most of the budget accommodation is clustered around Chinatown, although there are a few options at Cable Beach. Prices escalate in the Dry when demand peaks; book ahead.

HOSTELS

Kimberley Klub (☎ 1800 004 345, 9192 3233; www.kimberleyklub.com; 62 Frederick St; dm A$19, d & tw A$45;) A miniresort set up with a poolside bar, big communal kitchen and roomy dorms make this the pick of the hostels. It's clean and secure with a breezy atmosphere. A five-minute walk to Chinatown.

Cable Beach Backpackers (☎ 1800 655 011, 9193 5511; www.cablebeachbackpackers.com; 12 Sanctuary Rd; dm A$19-22, s/d A$45/62;) This hostel is well positioned near its namesake, making it the choice for lounge lizards wanting to work on their tans. Smallish bright doubles. Free shuttle service.

Broome's Last Resort (☎ 1800 801 918, 9193 5000; www.yha.com.au; 2 Bagot St; dm A$18-26, s, d & tw A$70, surcharge for YHA nonmembers A$3.50;) This old-style place suits those in the mood to party. Spartan rooms with coin-operated aircon (A$1 for four hours). Bathrooms are in need of an overhaul.

CAMPING

Roebuck Bay Caravan Park (☎ 9192 1366; roebuckbaycp@broome.wn.com.au; 91 Walcott St; camp/caravan sites per 2 people A$20/24, on-site caravan d A$60) Sites at this large park fronting pretty Roebuck Bay are some of the best real estate in town.

The park's adjacent mango camping ground (camp sites A$10; April to September only) offers a shady and cheap alternative.

Palm Grove Holiday Resort (☎ 1800 803 336, 9192 3336; www.palmgrove.com.au; cnr Cable Beach Rd & Murray Rd; camp/caravan sites per 2 people A$27/31, s & d studio A$110, d cabins from A$165;) Palm Grove has a prime position near Cable Beach and boasts immaculate grounds. The self-contained studios and cabins are extremely clean. The nearby corner store has groceries and snacks.

Eating

Broome isn't renowned for its cheap eats, but if you're craving succulent seafood then you've come to the right place.

CENTRAL BROOME

Self-Catering

For supplies, head to **Coles** (☎ 9193 5928; Paspaley Plaza, Carnarvon St; 6am-midnight) or **Action Supermarket** (☎ 9192 3383; Broome Boulevard Shopping Centre, Frederick St; 8am-8pm).

Cafés

Matso's Café & Brewery (☎ 9193 5811; matzos@tpg.com.au; 60 Hamersley St; mains A$13-28; breakfast, lunch & dinner) This café oozes charm. There's a well-rounded breakfast menu (go for the pearlers' brekkie) and hearty lunch-time options.

Bloom's Café & Licensed Restaurant (☎ 9193 6366; 31 Carnarvon St; mains A$12-22, tapas A$4.50-8; breakfast, lunch & dinner) Dining on the fan-cooled veranda is a very pleasant way to watch the world go by. Cruisey service, vegetarian options and tasty tapas.

Aarli Bar (☎ 9192 5529; cnr Hamersley & Frederick Sts; seafood mains to share from A$31; breakfast, lunch & dinner) Foodies will favour this trendy new kid on the block, tucked away in a thick of frangipani. Char-grilled figs with spicy ricotta and honey (A$10.50) figures on the yummy brekkie line-up. *Baba ghanoush* or maybe a rustic pizza (A$12 to A$14.50) for lunch, perhaps?

Town Beach Café (☎ 9193 5585; Robinson St; mains A$16.50-18.50; breakfast, lunch & dinner) Thumbs up for relaxed waterside dining. Pancakes are the order of the day in the morning while whopping burgers hit the mark at lunch time.

Henry's Café (☎ 9192 3222; cnr Carnarvon & Short Sts; mains A$13.80-27; breakfast, lunch & dinner) A wide choice of eats are available at this can't-go-wrong corner café.

2 Rice (☎ 9192 1395; 26 Dampier Tce; mains A$4-12; 10am-3pm Mon-Fri Wet, 8am-5pm Mon-Fri Dry, 9am-1pm Sat year-round) It's sushi (A$6.50) heaven at lunch time and locals love the Balinese chicken curry (A$12). They flock to this trendy little spot on Saturday morning for freshly baked bread, muffins and calzone.

Shady Lane Café (☎ 9192 2060; Johnny Chi Lane; mains A$6.50-15; breakfast & lunch, closed Sun Wet) For eggs any way you like 'em, or maybe a jungle juice (A$4.50), this café is a fine choice. Plumped-up Lebanese wraps (A$7), salads and toasted sandwiches will tempt.

Quick Bites

Sri Curry House (☎ 9192 2688; Paspaley Plaza, Carnarvon St; mains A$12.50-17.50; lunch & dinner Mon-Sat) Housed in a no-frills shop front this is one of the few places in these parts serving nosh from the Indian subcontinent.

Ice Creamery (☎ 9193 5400; Shop 3, 34 Carnarvon St; 9am-5pm) An old-fashioned ice-cream bar serving a wicked mango flavour. Eat it quick before it melts!

Restaurants

Frangipanis Café Restaurant (☎ 9193 6766; 5 Napier Tce; mains A$15.50-37.50; lunch & dinner, closed Sun in the Wet) Although a touch on the expensive side, Frangipanis dishes out reliable pastas and more-adventurous dishes. Come-hither desserts.

Son Ming Chinese Restaurant (☎ 9192 2192; Carnarvon St; mains A$13.50-23; lunch & dinner) When in Chinatown it's almost obligatory to have a chow down and this BYO place fits the bill.

CABLE BEACH

Cafés

Cable Beach Sandbar & Grill (☎ 9193 5090; Cable Beach Rd; mains A$14-22; breakfast & dinner) Position, position, position. Perfectly placed overlooking the beach and an all-round fave with locals and sandy tourists alike. The Greek salad (A$9) is satisfying. The novel beep-and-collect-your-meal system is kitsch but works.

Cable Beach Sunset Bar (☎ 1800 199 099, 9192 0400; www.cablebeachclub.com; mains A$18-30; dinner) Part of the exclusive Cable Beach Club Resort, you're paying for to-die-for views here. Pizzas (A$16 to A$18) are ideal for sharing over a couple of drinks.

Divers Tavern (☎ 9193 6066; cnr Murray & Cable Beach Rds; mains A$9.50-22.90; lunch & dinner) Huge counter meals; a T-bone steak (A$22.90) here will give you your weekly B12 fix! Vegetarians have a few options, too.

Drinking

Broome's drinking scene is fairly relaxed, and sophisticated down at the Cable Beach end of town.

Matso's Café & Brewery (☎ 9193 5811; 60 Hamersley St; 3-9pm) For a bit of local fermentation action, head here. There's a fine selection of local ales (A$3.70 to A$6), including Ginger Beer and Chilli Lager.

Roebuck Bay Hotel (☎ 9192 1221; 45 Dampier Tce; 10am-midnight Sun-Wed, to 1am Thu, to 2am Fri & Sat) The 'Roey' is a classic Aussie pub – a touch raucous but likeable nonetheless. Bad karaoke guaranteed on Monday night.

Tokyo Joe's (☎ 9193 7222; 52 Napier Tce) This is a favourite backpacker haunt belting out dance-worthy tunes.

Nippon Inn (☎ 9192 1941; Dampier Tce; 9pm-4am Mon-Wed, Fri & Sat) Specialises in dry-season partying until the wee hours.

Cable Beach Sunset Bar & Café (☎ 1800 199 099, 9192 0400; wine by the glass A$6.50-9.50, cocktails A$13; 4pm-late) Has an enviable beachside position for sundowners like the aptly named 'Postcards from Broome' and 'Kimberley Kool.'

Entertainment

LIVE MUSIC

Goolarri Media Enterprises' **Gimme Gimme Club** (☎ 9192 1325; www.gme.com.au; 7 Blackman St) showcases the sounds of the Kimberley in a series of concerts from July to September.

Head to Matso's Café & Brewery (see above) for live music on Sunday.

CINEMA

Watch the latest films under the stars at **Sun Pictures** (☎ 9192 1077; ross@sunpictures.com.au; Carnarvon St; adult/concession A$13.50/11.50) to really experience 'Broome-time.' **Sun Cinemas** (☎ 9192 3199; 3 Weld St; adult/concession A$13.50/11.50) shows films in less character-filled surrounds.

Getting There & Away

Visitors sure come a long way from anywhere to get to Broome's shores.

AIR

At the time of writing, the cheapest fares to/from Broome (on Qantas and Virgin Blue) were Sydney A$360, Brisbane A$410, Melbourne A$220, Adelaide A$310 and Perth A$210. Skywest flies from Broome to Perth and Darwin (very reasonable at A$200); North West Regional and Airnorth operate within WA and the NT.

Airnorth (☎ 1800 627 474; www.airnorth.com.au) Throughout WA, the NT and East Timor.

North West Regional Airlines (☎ 1300 136 629; www.northwestregional.com.au) Broome to Halls Creek and Fitzroy Crossing.

Qantas (☎ 13 13 13; www.qantas.com.au)

Skywest Airlines (☎ 1300 660 088, www.skywest.com.au) Perth–Broome and Broome–Darwin.

Virgin Blue (☎ 13 67 89; www.virginblue.com.au)

BUS

McCafferty's/Greyhound (☎ 13 20 30; www.mccaffertys.com.au) operates a daily Perth to Darwin service, which stops at the Broome visitors centre. From Broome, fares include Perth (A$310, 35 hours), Darwin (A$300, 24 hours), Port Hedland (A$77, eight hours), Derby (A$55, three hours) and Kununurra (A$180, 14 hours).

Getting Around

CAR & MOTORCYCLE

If you want to venture beyond Chinatown and Cable Beach, you really need your own four wheels. Most of the car-hire operators have airport offices.

Avis (☎ 9193 5980; Coghlan St)

Britz (☎ 9192 2647; www.britz.com; 10 Livingstone St)

Broome Broome (☎ 1800 676 725, 9192 2210; www.broomebroome.com.au; 7/6 Hamersley Street)

Budget (☎ 1300 305 888, 9193 5355; www.budget.com.au; Broome International Airport, Macpherson St)

BUS

The **Broome Bus** (☎ 9193 6585; adult one way A$2.70; 7.10am-6.15pm Mon-Sat, 10.23am-6.15pm Sun) links Chinatown with Cable Beach every hour. The **Nightrider bus** (☎ 9192 8987; adult one way/return A$3.50/6; 6.30pm-3am April-Dec daily, 6.30pm-12.20am Thu-Sat Jan-Mar) runs every 30 minutes and stops just about everywhere.

TAXI

Broome Taxis (☎ 9192 1133; 24hr)

Roebuck Taxis (☎ 1800 880 330; 24hr).

AROUND BROOME

Broome Bird Observatory (☎ 9193 5600; http://home.it.net.au/~austecol/observatories/broome.htm; Crab Creek Rd; admission adult A$5, unpowered/powered camp

OUTBACK AUSTRALIA

sites per person A$11/13.50, s/d A$30/52, bunk r A$38), 24km east of Broome (15km unsealed road), has over 310 species of migratory birds coming and going. Tours of the observatory cost A$48 (A$72 with a Broome pick-up).

Willie Creek Pearl Farm (☎ 9193 6000; www.williecreekpearls.com.au; self-drive adult A$28, tours adult A$59; tours 9.15am, 10.30am, 11.45am, 1pm & 2.15pm Dry, 9.15am & 2.15pm Wet), 38km from Broome, is the only pearl farm in the Kimberley that's open to the public.

DERBY

☎ 08 / pop 5000

The oldest town (gazetted 1883) in the Kimberley, 220km northeast of Broome, Derby isn't much more than a supply stop. It is the western entrance to the Gibb River Rd and the jumping-off point to the isolated islands of the magnificent Buccaneer Archipelago (also known as Thousand Islands). The archipelago, accessible by a short flight (adult from A$170) or cruise, boasts the amazing Horizontal Waterfalls – one of the Kimberley's more unusual sights.

Information

Derby hospital (☎ 9193 3333)

Derby visitor centre (☎ 1800 621 426, 9191 1426; www.derbytourism.com.au; 2 Clarendon St; 8.30am-4.30pm Mon-Fri year-round, 9am-1pm Sat & Sun Apr-Sep, 9am-4pm Sat & Sun Jun-Aug, 9am-noon Sat Oct-Mar;)

Sights

The 1500-year-old **Boab Prison Tree**, 7km south of town, is Derby's most famous attraction and a symbol of indigenous belief and practice. Prisoners (mostly Aborigines) were locked up here by 'blackbirders' en route to labour camps or the grim **Old Derby Gaol** (Loch St).

Wharfinger's House Museum (☎ 9191 1426; cnr Loch & Elder Sts; by appointment) was the 1920s abode of the harbour master and now houses a museum and gallery (get the key from the visitors centre). Derby's lofty **wharf** is a good fishing spot and the best place to see the town's colossal tidal flow.

Tours

Derby Sea Plane (☎ 9192 6208; day tours adult from A$279) Fly-and-cruise tours to the Horizontal Waterfalls.

Windjana Tours (☎ 9193 1550; tours adult from A$99) Explore stunning Windjana Gorge and Tunnel Creek.

Sleeping & Eating

West Kimberley Lodge (☎ 9191 1031; Lot 50, Sutherland St; powered camp sites per 2 people A$24, s/d A$45/65;) A tidy guesthouse and camping ground near Woolworths supermarket.

Derby Boab Inn (☎ 9191 1044; boabinn@bigpond.com; Loch St; dm A$25, s/d A$50/40;) Has a range of basic budget rooms and a restaurant.

Spinifex Hotel (☎ 9191 1233; Clarendon St; spinifexhotel@westnet.com.au; dm A$20, budget s/d A$50/55, motel s/d A$60/75;) Rooms at the 'Spinny' are not among the Kimberley's best, but this central pub has Derby's only backpacker beds, and is the place to go for drinking, pool and the occasional band.

The BYO **Wharf Restaurant** (☎ 9191 1195; mains A$10-24), right on the jetty, is famed for its seafood. **Oasis Restaurant** (☎ 9193 1044; Loch St; mains A$11-22) does a roast and seafood buffet (A$22) on Sunday.

Getting There & Away

Daily **McCafferty's/Greyhound** (☎ 13 20 30) buses to Darwin and Perth stop at the visitors centre.

DEVONIAN REEF GORGES

In the Devonian period 350 million years ago the West Kimberley was the site of an enormous inland sea with its own 'great barrier reef'. Now you can witness the reef's remnants in three national parks. **Windjana Gorge** and **Tunnel Creek National Parks** are accessed via Fairfield Leopold Downs Rd (which links the Gibb River Rd and the Great Northern Hwy), while **Geikie Gorge National Park** is northeast of the town of Fitzroy Crossing.

There's a 3.5km walk through the tree-lined Windjana Gorge – look out for primeval life forms fossilised within the gorge walls.

The walk through the tunnel in the Napier Range (as the reef is known here) at Tunnel Creek, is not to be missed but a torch and walking boots are essential.

Bell Gorge's cool waters beckon time out from the Kimberley's rugged terrain but be wary of leeches here. About 220km east of Derby there's a turn-off that leads to **Silent Grove**, where camping is permitted along the banks of Bell Creek.

Geikie Gorge is truly awe-inspiring. **Darngku Heritage Cruises** (☎ 9191 5552; 2½hr cruise adult A$44, 5½hr walk incl lunch adult A$105; mid-Apr–Nov) operates tours of Geikie Gorge, with tickets

OUTBACK AUSTRALIA

THE GIBB RIVER ROAD

The 665km, mostly unsealed, **Gibb River Rd** – a cattle route between Derby and Kununurra/Wyndham – cuts straight through the Kimberley and is only accessible in the Dry. The equally rough **Kalumburu Rd** heads 267km further north to Kalumburu. For more information, grab a copy of the comprehensive *Gibb River & Kalumburu Roads Travellers Guide* (A$3), available at Broome or Derby visitor centres, with handy tips on accommodation, preparing your vehicle and being self-sufficient.

Gibb River Road Bus Services (☎ 08-9169 1880; www.gibbriverbus.com.au; adult one way/return A$240/360; ⏲ Tue-Sun, May-Sep only) operates one of the most remote bus trips around, covering the 705km route from Kununurra to Derby, and vice versa, along the dusty Gibb River Rd in five-star comfort. Stop off at any of the sights along the way (tickets are valid for three months). The bus leaves either Kununurra or Derby at 6am and arrives at the end destination around 5.30pm.

Western Section

The 5km-long **Lennard River Gorge** is ideal for a cooling swim. Nearby **Bell Gorge** is one of the Kimberley's standouts.

Central Section

Dimond Gorge is one of the Kimberley's largest and most spectacular gorges. **Mt Barnett Roadhouse** is a pit-stop to get supplies and, all importantly, to refuel. North of here, **Manning Gorge** has a lovely waterfall. **Mt Elizabeth Station** (☎ 08-9191 4644) has homestead accommodation, camping facilities and a store. About 12km south, **Barnett River Gorge** is another rustic spot to camp.

Eastern Section

Some stations in these parts with camping include authentic **Home Valley Station** (☎ 08-9161 4322; www.homevalley.com.au) and **Diggers Rest Station** (☎ 08-9161 1029), both of which organise horse trekking through the Kimberley – yee-hah!

El Questro (☎ 08-9169 1777; www.elquestro.com.au; camping per person A$12.50, Emma Gorge standard d A$135, Station Township bungalows A$220; ⏲ Apr-Oct) is a *million*-acre private wildlife park 100km west of Kununurra, with showstoppers such as Zebedee Springs, Chamberlain and Emma Gorges. Seven-day park permits cost A$12.50 per adult; transfers from Kununurra to El Questro cost from A$50; and all-inclusive day tours from Kununurra are A$165 per adult.

Mornington Wildlife Sanctuary & Camp (☎ 1800 631 946, 08-9226 0340; www.australianwildlife.org; unpowered camp sites per 2 people A$30) is an ideal base from which to explore over 3000 sq km of the central Kimberley. Camping is upmarket, complete with flushing toilets and showers. Self-guided canoeing trips are available (A$55 per canoe). Self-cook barbecues are from A$16 per person. From Derby, you'll find this haven 240km up the Gibb River Rd and a further 95km inland from the Mt House turn-off.

Kalumburu Rd

Drysdale River Station (☎ 08-9161 4326; www.drysdaleriver.com.au; camp sites per person A$7.50, d A$99; ⏲ 8am-noon & 1-5pm Apr-Nov) and **Kalumburu community** (☎ 08-9161 4333; camp sites unpowered/powered per 2 people A$10/15, dongas per person A$60, tw A$80 ⏲ 7am-4pm Mon-Fri; A$25 vehicle permit required on arrival) offer homestead accommodation, camping and fuel.

Gibb River Road to Mitchell Plateau

The biologically rich **Mitchell Plateau** (Ngauwudu) is an area of significant Aboriginal heritage to the Wunambal people. At the **Mitchell Falls** (Punamii-unpuu) gorges a four-tiered waterfall has been carved into the sandstone. It's an adventurous destination but one that involves considerable forward planning due to its isolation.

available from Fitzroy Crossing Tourist Bureau. The Department of Conservation and Land Management (CALM) also offers tours that depart at 8am and 3pm (tickets available at the gorge).

FITZROY CROSSING

☎ 08 / pop 1500

A sleepy settlement 392km east of Broome by the flood-prone Fitzroy River, Fitzroy Crossing is a convenient access point for Geikie (20km) and Windjana (145km) Gorges and is home to several Aboriginal communities.

Fitzroy Crossing Tourist Bureau (☎ 9191 5355; fxinfo@sdwk.wa.gov.au; Flynn Dr; 8am-5pm Apr-Sep, 9am-5pm Mon-Fri & 9am-1pm Sat Oct-Mar) has lots of information and can make bookings for Geikie Gorge tours. The town also has a **hospital** (☎ 9191 5001).

Fitzroy River Lodge Motel Hotel & Caravan Park (☎ 9191 5141; Great Northern Hwy; camp/caravan sites per 2 people A$21/24, safari tent d A$130;) is a steady if somewhat overpriced option. **Crossing Inn** (☎ 9191 5080; crossinginn@bigpond.com.au; Skuthorpe Rd; camp sites per 2 people from A$15;), more or less a tin shed, is a popular local watering hole. Newer motel rooms (doubles A$95) are attached and have great verandas overlooking the river; there's also a bistro. **Tarunda Caravan Park** (☎ 9191 5330; Forrest Rd; camp/caravan sites per 2 people A$20/23, d A$110) has affordable camping and pricier self-contained units.

Self-caterers can stock up at **Tarunda Supermarket** (☎ 9191 5004; Forrest Rd).

McCafferty's/Greyhound (☎ 13 20 30) has daily buses to Perth and Darwin that stop at the tourist bureau and Fitzroy River Lodge.

HALLS CREEK

☎ 08 / 1590

A cluster of roadhouses 288km west of Fitzroy Crossing, Halls Creek was established in 1955 and isn't altogether exciting. Sixteen kilometres south of present-day Halls Creek you'll find **Old Halls Creek**, the site of WA's own gold rush that was sparked in 1855.

Six kilometres from town off Duncan Rd, the Kimberley's own **China Wall** is an impressive natural phenomenon of 6m sub-vertical quartz extending for 16km. When the weather is right, you can walk the length of it. If you're looking for a top bush-camping spot, try picturesque **Sawpit Gorge** (52km southeast of Halls Creek).

Information

Halls Creek hospital (☎ 9168 6003)

Halls Creek information centre (☎ 9168 6262; visitors@hcshire.wa.gov.au; cnr Halls St & Great Northern Hwy; 8.30am-4.30pm May-Sep) In the middle of town.

Halls Creek Telecentre (☎ 9168 5230; Community Resource Centre, cnr Great Northern Hwy & Roberta Ave; per hr A$5) Internet access.

Tours

The following operators take tours to the Bungle Bungles (opposite) and Wolfe Creek (below).

Bungle Bungle Scenic Flights (☎ 1300 136 629; 80min Wolfe Creek Crater flight A$180, 90min Bungles flight A$200)

Oasis Air (☎ 1800 501 462; 80min Bungles flight from A$169, 80min Wolfe Creek Crater flight from A$145)

Sleeping & Eating

Comfort Inn Kimberley Hotel Motel (☎ 1800 355 228, 9168 6101; dm A$18, budget d A$89) The town's only pub that has a backpacker room.

Best Western Halls Creek Motel (☎ 9168 6001; hallscreekmotel@westnet.com.au; 194 Great Northern Hwy; dongas A$30-50, motel s/d A$88/112;) Budget accommodation with dongas (small transportable buildings) offering shared bathrooms, while the motel rooms have private bathrooms. Russian Jack's restaurant serves dinner daily (mains A$14 to A$27).

Old Halls Creek Lodge (☎ 9168 8999; camp/caravan sites per 2 people A$17/20, budget r A$50) Has camping in a bushy setting.

Halls Creek Caravan Park (☎ 1800 355 228, 9168 6169; lanus@bigpond.com.au; Roberta Ave; camp/caravan sites per 2 people A$18/21, on-site vans A$44, d & tw cabins A$55;) The park is nothing much to look at, but it's central.

JK's Café (☎ 9168 6444; cnr Halls St & Great Northern Hwy; mains around A$7.50; breakfast & lunch) is attached to the information centre. With something for everyone, you'll find hearty café fare and cakes here. Breakfasts cost from A$9.50.

Getting There & Away

McCafferty's/Greyhound (☎ 13 20 30) buses running to Perth and Darwin stop at the Poinciana Roadhouse.

WOLFE CREEK METEORITE CRATER

To get to Wolfe Creek, head 19km south from Halls Creek to Tanami Rd (the turn-off to Alice Springs). About 146km down this stretch you'll find **Wolfe Creek Meteorite Crater** (accessible May to November) – the second largest of its kind in the world.

Known for thousands of years as 'Kandimalal' by the Jaru and Walmajarri Aboriginal peoples, this place is intrinsically linked with the rainbow snake. Scientific study suggests the crater is the result of a meteorite thumping into earth 300,000 years ago. Climb 50m deep into the crater (watch your step) and admire its 850m diameter expanse.

WARMUN (TURKEY CREEK)

This town is home to a sizable Aboriginal community and is officially a dry area (no alcohol permitted). The **roadhouse** (☎ 9168 7882; camp sites per person A$6, dm A$20) has no-frills accommodation and fuel.

Leading Aboriginal painters including Rover Thomas and Queenie McKenzie have painted around these parts. The **Warmun Art Gallery** (☎ 9168 7496; www.warmunart.com; 9am-4pm Mon-Fri, phone ahead) is a top spot to view artworks and potentially catch indigenous artists at work.

Daily **McCafferty's/Greyhound** (☎ 13 20 30) buses to Darwin and Perth stop at Turkey Creek.

PURNULULU (BUNGLE BUNGLE) NATIONAL PARK

The 3000-sq-km Purnululu National Park contains the extraordinary Bungle Bungle Range, with its famous striped rock towers, and attracts huge numbers of visitors during the Dry. These 360-million-year-old formations possess a similar majesty to Uluru (Ayers Rock). Amazingly, they were only 'discovered' during the 1980s (although the Kidja people were pretty familiar with them) and the park was created in 1987. The Bungle Bungles were added to the World Heritage list in 2003. The name *purnululu* means 'sandstone' in the local Kidja dialect and Bungle Bungle is thought to be a misspelling of 'bundle bundle', a common grass.

The art of the Kidja people is sprinkled throughout the park. Add the park's hidden gorges, vast chasms, newly discovered plants, nailtail wallabies and 130 bird species to the mix and you have one of the world's great landscapes.

It takes a bit of legwork to get to the park's main attractions. The best time to explore the southern end of the park, including **Piccaninny Gorge**, is in the morning. The northern end of the massif is at its best in the afternoon – choose from **Echidna Chasm** (2km return walk, easy) or **Mini Palms** (5km return walk, easy to moderate). The overnight Piccaninny Gorge walking track (30km return, moderate to difficult) will appeal to hard-core bushwalkers. Register at the park's visitor centre for the latter walk.

The park is only open April to December (weather permitting). If you're driving, the turn-off from the highway is 53km south of Warmun. It's then 52km along a rough 4WD-only Spring Creek track (it can take up to three hours to travel this leg!) to the Three Ways junction and the **visitor centre** (☎ 9168 7300; admission per vehicle A$9; 8am-1pm & 2-4pm). From here it's 20 minutes north to **Kurrajong Camp** near Echidna Chasm and 45 minutes south to the more picturesque **Walardi Camp**; both have fresh water and toilets, and camp sites cost A$9 per person.

Tours

Several operators also include Purnululu in multiday Kimberley tours – see p433 for details or check out these operators:

Alligator Airways (☎ 1800 632 533; www.alligatorairways.com.au; 2hr flight from A$200) Soar over the Bungle Bungles and Lake Argyle in a plane.

Slingair Heliwork WA (☎ 1800 095 500, 9168 7337; www.slingair.com.au; 45min scenic flight adult A$220; 7am-4.30pm) Helicopter flights for an instant buzz; from Turkey Creek roadhouse over the Bungles.

WYNDHAM

☎ 08 / pop 1000

Fringed by the muddy banks of the Cambridge Gulf, Wyndham is accessible by car only. This is real crocodile country – say 'g'day' to the 20m rock-solid crocodile at the town's entrance. Call into **Kimberley Motors** (☎ 9161 1281; www.eastkimberley.com; Great Northern Hwy; 6am-6pm) for tourist information.

On a clear day, it's worthwhile heading to the top of Mt Bastion to the **Five Rivers Lookout**. Here you'll get a 360-degree view over the Cambridge Gulf which is the confluence of the King, Pentecost, Durack, Forrest and Ord Rivers.

The **Grotto**, 35km southeast of Wyndham township, has an impressive waterfall during the Wet.

About 9km along a dirt track, 20km south of Wyndham, you'll find **Parry Creek Farm** (☎ 9161 1139; camp/caravan sites per 2 people A$20/30, motel d/tw with shared bathroom A$75;) where you can stay in the midst of a wetlands mecca. There's a campers' kitchen and restaurant-bar (April to November). Be warned, the mozzies are ferocious here in the Wet!

The Greyhound/McCafferty's bus service doesn't go to Wyndham. Travellers must get off at the Great Northern Hwy/Victoria Hwy intersection or Kununurra and pre-arrange transport (car or taxi) to Wyndham.

KUNUNURRA

08 / pop 6000

Kununurra's name, meaning 'meeting of big waters', is particularly apt – the town was established in 1960 to service the Ord River Irrigation Scheme. A growing town with prosperous crops (heavenly mangos in November) and close proximity to the regional delights of the Gibb River Rd, Purnululu National Park and Lake Argyle, Kununurra has a decisively more upbeat feel than its Kimberley counterparts.

Information

CALM (9168 4200; Lot 249, Ivanhoe Rd; 9am-5pm Mon-Fri)
Kununurra hospital (9168 1522)
Kununurra Telecentre (9169 1868; Banksia St; per hr A$8; 9.30am-5pm Mon-Fri)
Kununurra tourist bureau (91681177; www.eastkimberley.com; Coolibah Dr; 8am-5pm, shorter hours in the Wet)

Sights & Activities

Mirima National Park (entry per car A$9) is an idyllic park 2km northeast of Kununurra; you can easily while away a couple of hours exploring the gorges and soaking up the views. There are two walks through the sandstone cliffs, which were once part of the ocean floor: the **Derdbe-gerring banan lookout trail** (800m return walk, moderate) and the **Demboong banan gap trail** (500m return walk, easy). Camping isn't permitted here. There are toilets but you must bring your own water.

There's a host of natural attractions around Kununurra, including **Ivanhoe Crossing**, **Valentine's Springs**, **Middle Springs**, **Black Rock Pools**, **Lily Creek Lagoon** and **Kelly's Knob**. Lake Kununurra, also called **Diversion Dam**, is popular for picnics and boating: try your luck fishing in the Lower Dam.

Worth a stop, **Waringarri Arts** (9168 2212; www.waringarriarts.com.au; off Speargrass Rd; 8am-4pm Mon-Fri Dry, 8am-noon Mon-Fri Wet) has a broad range of affordable pieces by Aboriginal artists from northeast Kimberley.

Tours

Argyle Expeditions (9168 7040; www.argyleexpeditions.com.au; adult from A$45) Lake Argyle's highlights including a barramundi feeding frenzy.
Big Waters Kimberley Canoe Safaris (1800 641 998, 9169 1998; www.adventure.kimberley.net.au) Gear up for a three-day, self-guided canoe safari from Lake Argyle to Kununurra along the Ord River. Park your canoe at designated bush camps along the way.
Kimberley Canoeing (1300 663 369; self-guided tours per person from A$155, one day guided tour A$125) Explore the Ord River at your leisure (equipment supplied). Rock-climbing (from A$60), caving (from A$110) and abseiling (from A$50) are also covered by this active outfit.
Lake Argyle Tours & Cruises (9168 7361; www.lakeargyle.com; tours from A$38) The name says it all.

Sleeping

Kununurra Backpackers (1800 641 998, 9169 1998; www.adventure.kimberley.net.au; 24 Nutwood Cres; dm/d A$20/50;) Does budget well. There's everything you need here to relax or get organised for your next adventure, plus a big kitchen for an equally big cook-up.

Kimberley Croc Backpackers (9168 2702; www.yha.com.au; 257 Konkerberry Dr; dm/tw/d A$18/27/54, surcharge for YHA nonmembers A$3.50;) Well set up for short- and long-term travellers. Kununurra and Kimberley Croc Backpackers both offer adventure tours throughout the Kimberley.

Ivanhoe Village Caravan Park (9169 1995; big4kununurra@westnet.com.au; cnr Coolibah Dr & Ivanhoe Rd; camp/caravan sites per 2 people A$12-24/25, d cabins from A$65;) One of the region's best budget choices with grassy camp sites and spick-and-span cabins.

Eating

Apart from one good café-restaurant, choices here are restricted to motel eateries, pub counter meals and a few takeaway places, but the quality is generally OK.

Stars in the Kimberley (9168 1122; 4 Papuana St; mains A$20-30; lunch & dinner;) Readers have recommended this somewhat pricey restaurant for its 'delicious and imaginative food' and decent coffee.

Valentine's Pizzeria (9169 1167; Cottontree Ave; pizza A$8-18; 5pm-late) The pizza here is yummy enough, or you can go for Mexican eats.

OUTBACK AUSTRALIA

LAKE ARGYLE FAST FACTS

- Lake Argyle is a 1000-sq-km body of water.
- Approximately 25,000 freshwater crocodiles inhabit Lake Argyle.
- Barramundi are all born male and at age six they transform into females to breed.
- You can only view 2% of Lake Argyle from any vantage point on land.
- Lake Argyle barramundi was consumed by Hollywood types at the 2003 Oscars.

Getting There & Around

McCafferty's/Greyhound (☎ 13 20 30) has daily buses to Darwin and Perth that stop at the visitors centre.

LAKE ARGYLE

A marvel of engineering, Lake Argyle was built from 1969 to 1971 – and it only took the biggest non-nuclear explosion in Australia to make it happen! Lake Argyle is officially the largest body of fresh water on the continent, holding 12 to 18 times more than Sydney Harbour (depending on who you ask). It's 70km from Kununurra (sealed road).

The best way to experience Lake Argyle is on a boat. It's relaxing to be out on the water surrounded by verdant mountains after being in the Kimberley's rugged interior on an extended road trip – bring your swimming gear.

DAMPIER PENINSULA

Sea-sculpted red rocks meet sparkling waters in the stunning Dampier Peninsula, which extends 200km north of Broome along the 4WD-only Cape Leveque Rd to epic **Cape Leveque**. Here you can dive into the blue abyss that is the Indian Ocean. Middle Lagoon offers brilliant swimming, snorkelling and fishing, while further north Kooljaman boasts incredible sunsets. Check water conditions with locals first.

If you want to learn about indigenous culture or you're simply after a footprint-free beach, it's *the* region to discover. The *Dampier Peninsula Travellers Guide* (A$2) highlights all the options – pick up a copy at the Broome visitors centre.

At the tip of the peninsula, **Kooljaman at Cape Leveque** (☎ 9192 4970; www.kooljaman.com.au; PMB 8, Cape Leveque; camp sites per person A$14, beach shelter d A$50, unit d A$90, safari tent d A$190, bookings essential) makes the arduous trip worthwhile. Go for the basic huts right on the beach and imagine yourself as a castaway. There's a small shop and **Dinka's Restaurant** (mains A$15-27; lunch & dinner Apr-Oct).

Tours

Renowned as a true oasis and favoured by the occasional movie star seeking escape, this part of WA deserves a couple of days at least. See it in style with one of these operators:

Kimberley Wild Outback Tours (☎ 9193 7778; www.kimberleywild.com.au; 1-/3-day Cape Leveque tours adult from A$209/597; Apr-Nov) Uncovering Cape Leveque and around.

Over the Top Adventure Tours (☎ 9192 5211; Dampier 1-/2-day tours adult A$205/310) Tours to Cape Leveque. 'Well worth the expense,' says a reader.

UP THE WEST COAST

As you make your way from Perth up the west coast, be prepared for outback Australia with a twist. With endless stretches of empty beach, the warm waters of the Indian Ocean and a seemingly year-round summer, you can be easily tricked into thinking, 'This isn't the outback!'. Then, as you make your way further north along the dusty main highway, the land changes into a warm, earthy, red tone and each roadhouse seems further away than the last. It's then that you realise how far you've come and how far you still have to go.

Activities

You can get as physical or as lazy as you want here. If you can convince yourself that laying in the warm sun on a beautiful beach is an activity, then go for it. Otherwise the area offers good diving and swimming possibilities or, if you feel like being active on top of the water, there are numerous boat trips to be enjoyed.

SHARK BAY AREA

Shark Bay's status as a World Heritage site makes it one of the more remarkable places on earth. Situated in the middle of

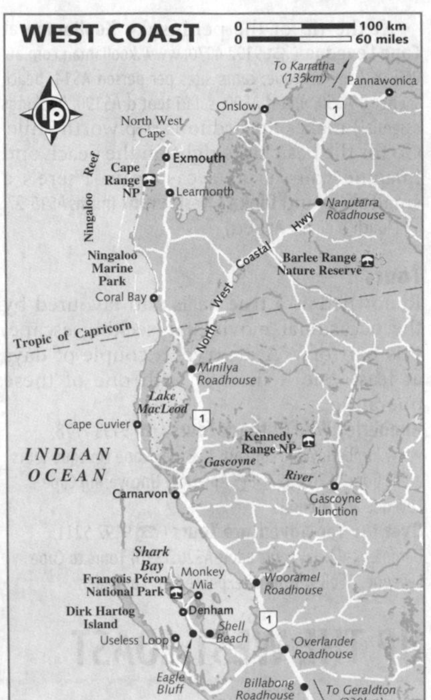

some of the most stunning natural beauty in the state, this sunny, peaceful haven is still very remote. To get here, particularly as you make your way north up the Brand Hwy from Perth, you pass through some inhospitable terrain that reminds you just how harsh this part of the world can be. Then, long stretches of white-sand beach and crystal-clear water appear out of the blue, looking like the cover of some tourist brochure. It's amazing how many people come here for a short visit and end up staying for good.

For a better look at the natural beauty of the area, check out www.sharkbay.asn.au/world_heritage_area.html.

TOURS

Most travellers visit the Denham–Monkey Mia area via one of the many organised budget tours that leave from Perth, or with the convenient hop-on, hop-off buses that operate up and down the coast. **Easyrider** (☎ 08-9446 1800; www.easyridertours.com.au) is by far the most popular hop-on, hop-off option with full commentary along the way. It also offers fully guided tours up to Monkey Mia with its Exmouth Exposure four-day excursion (A$320, meals not included).

Most organised budget tours are of around 3½ to four days' duration, cost pretty much the same (around A$470), offer accommodation in hostels and working farm stations, and include meals. Some popular tour companies that travel to Monkey Mia from Perth:

Active Safaris (☎ 08-9450 7776; www.activesafaris.com.au)
Aussie Scenic Tours (☎ 0417-975 906; www.aussiescenictours.com.au)
Australian Adventure Travel (☎ 08-9226 0660; www.travellersclub.com.au)
Planet Perth Tours (☎ 08-9225 6622; www.planettours.com.au)
Redback Safaris (☎ 08-9371 3695; www.redbacksafaris.com.au)

Denham

☎ 08 / pop 1140

Denham's proximity to Monkey Mia (opposite) – minus the resort-style atmosphere and full-on crowds – makes it a more appealing place to base yourself than 'Dolphin City'. There are more eating and drinking options here and a range of activities to keep you busy once you've seen the dolphins. **Shark Bay Information & Booking Office** (☎ 1300 135 887; 29 Knight Tce) is a better source of information than **Shark Bay Tourist Bureau** (☎ 9948 1253; 71 Knight Tce) further up the main street. Check your email at the **Telecentre** (Knight Tce; per hr A$6; Tue-Fri).

SIGHTS & ACTIVITIES

Shark Bay didn't get its name for nothing. Yes, there are sharks here and swimming is at your own peril. About 6km from town, **Ocean Park** (☎ 9948 1765; Denham Hamelin Rd; admission A$7) is like a small marine park, but at the time of research was building a huge aquarium that should be worth checking out.

Eagle Bluff, 24km from town on the Denham Hamelin Rd, has a superb vantage point from where you can clearly see sharks swimming in the bay. **Shell Beach**, 45km from town on the Denham Hamelin Rd, has tiny shells instead of sand, up to 10m deep in some parts (footwear is a sensible idea as these shells can dig into your feet).

Perhaps the best-kept secret is the **hot springs tub** (admission free), at Péron Homestead, which is about 6km from the town towards Monkey Mia.

OUTBACK AUSTRALIA

TOURS

See Shark Bay and Dirk Hartog Island from the air on a plane tour with **Shark Bay Air Charter** (☎ 1300 135 887; 29 Knight Tce; tours A$50). **Shark Bay Majestic Tours** (☎ 9948 1627; www.ozpal.com/majestic) does excellent full-day tours of François Péron National Park (A$125), the stromatolites (a colony of prehistoric microbes; A$125), the hot springs tub (A$35) and a half-day tour to Shell Beach (A$65). **Shark Bay Coaches & Tours** (☎ 9948 1081) offers interesting day tours (A$55) of the area, including Eagle Bluff, the stromatolites, Shell Beach and Ocean Park on Tuesday, Friday and Sunday. A tour with a twist is the popular hands-on experience that takes you out to the working pearl farm off the coast, where you get to see how the famous black pearls of the area are made. These full-day tours cost just A$5 and fill up fast. Book at **Bay Lodge** (☎ 9948 1278).

SLEEPING & EATING

Bay Lodge (☎ 9948 1278; baylodge@wn.com.au; 113 Knight Tce; dm/d A$20/50;) You may not want to explore Shark Bay once you check in at this superb YHA hostel, only paces from the beach. The hammocks near the pool are a perfect excuse to laze away the day and the dorms are more like roomy units, with their own TV area. The lodge runs a daily bus to and from Monkey Mia and the self-contained doubles are an absolute bargain.

Blue Dolphin Caravan Park & Holiday Village (☎ 9948 1385; www.ozpal.com/bluedolphin; Lot 5 Hamelin Rd; camp sites unpowered/powered per 2 people A$16/20) Close to town, this caravan park has a good campers kitchen, a supermarket next door and on-site vans for A$50.

Self-caterers can stock up at **Foodland** (☎ 9948 1351; 1 Knight Tce) or **Tradewinds Supermarket** (☎ 9948 1147; cnr Knight Tce & Denham Hamelin Rd).

Jetty Café (☎ 9948 1047; 51 Knight Tce; meals A$7-16; breakfast, lunch & dinner;) With a huge range of home-cooked meals, this large café has massive filled rolls and whips up a fine seafood basket.

Bay Café (☎ 9948 1308; 69 Knight Tce; meals A$7.50-20; breakfast, lunch & dinner;) Choose from the foot-long hot dogs, big breakfasts or nachos. However, if you've almost used up your calorie allowance for the day, the low-fat ice cream will please.

GETTING THERE & AWAY

Shark Bay Coaches & Tours (☎ 9948 1081) offers a shuttle bus (A$30, 1½ hours, departs at 5.30am) that does the 128km trip from Denham to the Overlander Roadhouse on Monday, Wednesday, Thursday and Saturday (it will pick you up). It times its run to connect with the two **McCafferty's/Greyhound** (☎ 13 20 30) coaches that continue their journeys from the roadhouse south to Perth and north to Broome.

There's a public bus running daily between Denham (from the Caltex station in the town centre) and Monkey Mia for A$10.

François Péron National Park

About 4km from Denham on the Monkey Mia Rd is the turn-off to the wild **François Péron National Park** (car/bus passenger/pedestrian A$9/4/free), renowned for its pristine beaches, dramatic cliffs, salt lakes and rare marsupial species. The 52,000-hectare park was a sheep station from the 1880s until it was bought by the government and turned into a national park in 1990. There's a visitors centre at the old Péron Homestead, 6km from the main road. **Camp sites** (per person A$8) with limited facilities are at Big Lagoon, Gregories, Bottle Bay, Cape Péron and Herald Bight.

Monkey Mia

It's important to keep things in perspective when you get to **Monkey Mia Dolphin Resort** (☎ 08-9948 1320; www.monkeymia.com.au; admission A$6), 27km from Denham. Many a traveller has ventured here expecting their socks to be blown off by a life-changing interaction with one of Mother Nature's most beautiful creatures – the bottlenose dolphin – and have left feeling short-changed. At the same time, countless people have begrudgingly trudged their way out here to please their more-enthusiastic travelling companions and have not wanted to leave.

It's likely your experience of interacting with the dolphins will lie somewhere in between, and it *is* worth doing, especially when any of the females bring their calves along. These wild mammals venture into the shallow waters virtually every day (early morning is the best time to see them) to get a small feed of fish from the knowledgeable volunteers who run the show. Only a handful of female dolphins (some males were getting too aggressive) are given just a fraction of their daily food requirements here. The amount is limited to two feeds of 0.6kg and one of 0.7kg per dolphin per day so that they don't become reliant on hand-outs and can keep teaching their young to hunt.

At times you wonder whether it's the dolphins that are checking *you* out rather than the other way around. They're shy at first, but pluck up the courage to come right into the shallows and swim around your feet. It's important not to touch the dolphins, for your safety as much as theirs. They have been known to bite and to lash out with their tails in annoyance. No sunscreen on your legs, either – it irritates their eyes. Leave your expectations behind and your trip will definitely be worth it.

The **Dolphin Information Centre** (☎ 08-9948 1320; 🕑 7.30am-4pm), near the beach viewing area, shows a 45-minute video and hosts talks by wildlife researchers.

TOURS

The dolphin thing alone doesn't take up a lot of time (probably an hour or so), but you can easily spend a full day here, including lazing about on the superb beach. **Shotover** (☎ 08-9948 1481; www.monkeymiawildsights.com.au) offers hour-long, marine-wildlife cruises on a catamaran (A$35) that leave from the jetty next to the dolphin interaction zone. You may spot dolphins, dugongs, loggerhead and green turtles, sea snakes, sharks (including a 4.5m tiger shark), stingrays and whales. Two-hour tours (A$55) are also available. Not to be outdone, **Aristocat II** (☎ 08-9948 1446; www.monkey-mia.net) offers similar cruises as Shotover, for the same prices.

SLEEPING & EATING

Monkey Mia is not a town, but a resort complex that masquerades as a small village. Accommodation for all budgets is plentiful, but food is expensive and the on-site minimart is not well stocked. You'd be wise to bring in food from Denham (there are two supermarkets on Knight Tce, see p447). You won't be able to buy takeaway alcohol anywhere in the resort so, if you're camping and want to enjoy a drink while sitting outside your tent in the sun, bring alcohol with you. The following places share the resort's phone number of ☎ 9948 1320.

Monkey Mia Dolphin Lodge & Backpackers (4-/7-bed dm A$18.50/21.50; 💻) A sprawling, modern hostel a short stagger from the beach with an impressive state-of-the-art kitchen. The popular attached Monkey Bar has a brilliant beer garden with a TV screen and sells the resort's cheapest booze (A$3.50 beers and A$3 glasses of wine).

The resort's **camping ground** (camp sites per 2 people per day/week A$18/55) will satisfy those with their own tents and has a serviceable campers' kitchen while the double units (A$65 with shared bathroom) provide a bit more comfort.

Monkey Bar (meals A$3.50-15) The backpacker hostel's bar has cheap takeaway food and also light bar snacks including pizzas, barbecued chickens, hot chips, burgers and sandwiches.

Peron Café (meals A$8-18; 🕑 breakfast, lunch & dinner) Attached to the more expensive Bough Shed Restaurant, this pleasant café serves light meals and takeaway tucker.

GETTING THERE & AWAY

For details on getting to and from Monkey Mia from Denham and from Denham to the Overlander Roadhouse and further afield, see p447.

CORAL COAST

The Coral Coast extends from Coral Bay to Onslow and takes in the magnificent Ningaloo Marine Park, arguably WA's greatest and most precious natural attraction. The awesome Ningaloo Reef rivals the Great Barrier Reef in beauty and biodiversity, is far more accessible and doesn't get anything like the tourist numbers of its east-coast counterpart.

Coral Bay

☎ 08 / pop 120

At the southern end of Ningaloo Marine Park, Coral Bay is a tiny community nestled at the edge of a picturesque bay. Coral Bay consists of one street – Robinson St – from where you can easily amble to the beach and reef just off-shore. The town is a good base for outer-reef activities as well, with plenty of tour operators and booking offices. The bay is enclosed by a protective reef that provides good snorkelling within 50m of the shore.

INFORMATION

Coral Bay's two small shopping centres have supermarkets with Eftpos facilities. Internet access is available at **Fins Cafe** (☎ 9942 5900) and **Ningaloo Club** (☎ 9948 5100; www.coralbaywa.com.au/ningalooclub) for A$6 per hour.

TOURS

For dive trips and whale shark, manta ray and whale-watching tours see Ningaloo Marine Park on right. The five booking offices in Coral Bay are within 100m of each other on Robinson St.

ATV Eco Tours (☎ 9942 5873) A range of self-drive, quad-bike tours around the bay, including snorkelling (A$70) and sunset (A$60) tours.

Coral Bay Adventures (☎ 9942 5955; www.users.bigpond.com/coralbay) Scenic flights over Ningaloo Reef (from A$50 for 30 minutes).

Coral Breeze (☎ 9948 5190) A small catamaran that cruises the reef for a half-/full day (A$65/85); includes lunch.

Coral Coast Tours (☎ 9948 5190) Full-day tour to Exmouth via 4WD coastal track, including Turquoise Bay in Cape Range National Park (A$150).

Glass Bottom Boats (☎ 9942 5885) and **Sub-Sea Explorer** (☎ 9942 5955) Spy on coral communities (A$25, one hour); the latter can also combine snorkelling (A$35, two hours).

SLEEPING & EATING

Ningaloo Club (☎ 9948 5100; dm A$18-25, d A$60-85;) This modern hostel has a well-equipped kitchen and the pool-side bar area has a TV lounge and pool table. There are lockers in the dorms (four or 10 beds) and you can pay extra for air-con.

Peoples Park Caravan Village (☎ 9942 5933; camp sites unpowered/powered per 2 people A$24/28;) A small, attractive park with lush lawns; it's also close to the beach and has a good café.

Self-caterers should stock up in Carnarvon or Exmouth.

Shades Restaurant (☎ 9942 5863; Ningaloo Reef Resort; takeaways A$7-12, dinner mains A$17-28; lunch & dinner) Shades offers takeaway food during the day and bistro meals for dinner (bookings essential).

Ningaloo Reef Cafe (☎ 9942 5882; Bayview Holiday Village, Robinson St; pizzas A$10-20; dinner) bakes tasty pizzas, while **Fins Cafe** (☎ 9942 5900; 4 Robinson St; meals A$18-28; breakfast, lunch & dinner;) opens early for good-value breakfasts, followed by café-style lunches, and offers an upmarket seafood menu as the finale (BYO alcohol).

GETTING THERE & AWAY

See p451 for transport information.

Ningaloo Marine Park

Stunning Ningaloo Reef stretches more than 250km along North West Cape Peninsula and is protected by the boundaries of Ningaloo Marine Park. The reef is amazingly accessible, lying only 100m offshore from some parts of the peninsula, and is home to a staggering variety of marine life. More than 220 species of hard coral have been recorded here. It's this coral that attracts the park's biggest drawcard, the *Rhiniodon typus*, otherwise known as the whale shark. These gentle giants arrive like clockwork each year to feed on plankton and small fish. Ningaloo is the only place in the world where these creatures reliably appear every year. They are the largest fish in the world, and can weigh up to 21 tonnes, although most are between 13 and 15 tonnes. They can also reach up to 18m in length.

For more information on the park, contact **CALM** (☎ 08-9949 1676; 22 Nimitz St) in Exmouth, which has the excellent pamphlet *Parks of the Coral Coast*.

TOURS

Swimming with a whale shark is what most people are here for. Full-day whale shark tours cost around A$350 and operate out of both Exmouth (up to eight boats) and Coral Bay (two boats). There's not much between them – Exmouth operators have shorter travel times and also adhere to a 'no sighting policy' (ie you can go on the next available trip if a whale shark isn't spotted), but Coral Bay operators have a higher encounter rate and you don't have to battle seven other boats and scores of people to reach a shark. All use spotter planes, and the price generally includes snorkelling gear, wetsuit, food and park fees. Outside the whale shark season, half-day manta ray tours cost around A$120 and include snorkelling gear, wetsuit and snacks. You need to be a capable swimmer to get the most out of either experience.

Most operators also offer dive trips (A$80 to A$140) and courses (around A$380 for PADI Open Water Certificates), although conservation laws prevent you from diving with the whale sharks. Snorkelling equipment is available for around A$10/15 per half-/full day.

Coral Bay Adventures (☎ 9942 5955; Coral Bay)

Exmouth Diving Centre (☎ 9949 1201; www.exmouthdiving.com.au; Exmouth)

OUTBACK AUSTRALIA

Ningaloo Blue (☎ 9949 1119; www.ningalooblue.com.au; Exmouth)
Ningaloo Reef Dive (☎ 9942 5824; www.ningalooreefdive.com; Coral Bay)
Three Islands Marine (☎ 9949 1994; www.whalesharkdive.com; Exmouth)

Cape Range National Park

The arid inland gorges of Cape Range National Park (admission per vehicle A$9) gradually soften and give way to white sand, which leads to the crystal waters, coral and sea life of Ningaloo Reef. It's a stunning place to spend a few days. The Milyering **visitors centre** (☎ 08-9949 2808; ⏰ 10am-4pm) has useful maps and publications.

ACTIVITIES

Good snorkelling spots include **Lakeside**, **Oyster Stacks** and **Turquoise Bay**. You can walk into Mandu Mandu Gorge (3km return) via an access road 20km south of the visitors centre, as well as to Yardie Creek (1.5km return) in the park's far south. Those with 4WDs can continue south to Coral Bay via the coast (check at the visitors centre that Yardie Creek is passable). **Yardie Creek Tours** (☎ 08-9949 2659) has one-hour boat rides up this short, sheer gorge for A$25. They run daily during school holidays and by appointment at other times.

SLEEPING

There are many compact **camping grounds** (camp sites per 2 people A$10) along the coast within the park. Facilities and shade are usually minimal or nonexistent, but most have pit toilets; good options include Neds Camp, Mesa Camp, Lakeside and Osprey Bay. Sites are limited and allocated on arrival; check the situation with **CALM** (☎ 08-9949 1676; 22 Nimitz St, Exmouth).

GETTING THERE & AWAY

For those without transport, the **Ningaloo Reef Bus** (☎ 1800 999 941) is the best way to get to and from the park. It leaves Exmouth Shopping Centre at 8.50am (daily April to October; Monday, Tuesday, Friday and Saturday only November to March), returning from Ningaloo Reef Retreat at 2pm. En route it stops at Vlamingh Head Lighthouse (A$6), Tantabiddi (A$10), Milyering (A$20), Turquoise Bay (A$20) and Mandu Mandu Gorge (A$30, including lunch at the Reef Retreat).

Exmouth

☎ 08 / pop 2500

Exmouth was established in 1967 to support the nearby US naval communications base. Although the army has shipped out, Exmouth has a prosaic hangover, evident in its utilitarian layout and buildings. Today, it caters to an increasing number of people eager to experience the reef, offering plenty of good tours and accommodation.

ORIENTATION & INFORMATION

Most of Exmouth's eateries are concentrated in the centre of town near the Exmouth Shopping Centre. Accommodation options are no more than a 1km walk south from the town centre down Murat Rd.

The airport is 37km south of Exmouth and the **Airport Shuttle Bus** (☎ 9949 1101; A$17) meets all flights, and shuttles into town.

Blue's Internet Café (☎ 9949 1119; cnr Kennedy & Thew Sts; ⏰ 9am-7pm) Fast Internet access.
CALM (☎ 9949 1676; 22 Nimitz St; ⏰ 8am-5pm Mon-Fri) Can supply maps and guides to the national park.
Visitors centre (☎ 9949 1176; www.exmouth-australia.com; Murat Rd; ⏰ 8.30am-5pm) Has information on tours and takes bookings.

TOURS

Apart from Ningaloo Marine Park cruises and dives (see p449), tours from Exmouth include gulf and gorge safaris and some other water-based options; the visitors centre has full details:

Capricorn Kayak Tours (☎ 9438 1911; www.capricornkayak.com.au) A range of coastal and camping tours between late March and November, including a sunset barbecue (A$55) and full-day (A$130) options.
Learn to Surf (☎ 0438-125 423) Will have you standing in two hours (A$35).
Neil McLeod's Ningaloo Safari Tours (☎ 9949 1550; www.ningaloosafari.com) Well-regarded, half-/full-day (A$65/145) trips through Ningaloo Reef, Cape Range National Park and Vlamingh Head.
Ningaloo Coral Explorer (☎ 9949 2424, 0417-971 998) Two-hour coral-viewing and snorkelling tour at 2pm daily from Bundegi Beach (A$40).
Southern Cross Safaris (☎ 9574 4692; www.scsafaris.com.au)

SLEEPING

Pete's Exmouth Backpackers (☎ 9949 1101; www.exmouthvillage.com; cnr Truscott Cres & Murat Rd; dm/s/d A$21/30/52;) Based at Exmouth Cape Tourist Village, travellers rave about this

YHA hostel that offers a free beach bus, inexpensive tours and free mountain bikes. YHA nonmembers pay a little extra.

Excape Backpackers (☎ 9949 1200; www.potshotresort.com; Murat Rd; dm A$20-22, tw A$60;) Part of the sprawling Potshot Hotel Resort, this complex is like a small town; there are several levels of accommodation, two restaurants, four bars, two pools, a bottle shop and a free shuttle service to the McCafferty's/Greyhound bus stop.

Ningaloo Club (☎ 9949 1805; ningaloo.exmouth@westnet.com.au; 50 Market St; dm/d A$24/48;) Formerly Marina Beach Retreat and now affiliated with Ningaloo Club in Coral Bay, the spacious fan-cooled permanent tents here are surprisingly comfortable. Just 2km south of town, with direct access to the beach, there are stellar facilities at this laid-back place, and free bike use.

Ningaloo Caravan & Holiday Resort (☎ 9949 2377; www.exmouthresort.com; Murat Rd; camp sites unpowered/powered per 2 people A$21/26;) The best of the caravan parks, this shady resort has modern facilities including a campers' kitchen. Attached is **Winston's Backpackers** (dm/d A$20/60;), with reasonable four-bed dorms and use of the park's facilities.

EATING

Continental Café (☎ 9949 4111; Exmouth Shopping Centre; meals A$4-12; breakfast & lunch) This buzzing little café serves gourmet pies, custom-made sandwiches, muffins and espresso.

Sea Urchin (☎ 9949 1249; 73 Maidstone Cres; meals A$17-22) You can bring your own booze, sit outside and feast on à la carte laksa, seafood and pasta, as well as decent fish and chips (A$8.50).

BJ's Takeaway & Pizza (☎ 9949 1244; Exmouth Shopping Centre; pizzas A$14-19; dinner Tue-Sun) BJ's has all the traditional toppings, as well as a few gourmet combinations to get you through until breakfast time.

GETTING THERE & AWAY

Air

There are daily **Skywest** (☎ 1300 660 088) flights to Karratha and Carnarvon, with links to Denham and Perth.

Bus

All buses stop at Exmouth's visitors centre. **McCafferty's/Greyhound** (☎ 13 20 30) operates three services a week from Perth (A$175, 18 hours), via the Overlander Roadhouse (for Denham; A$115, 10 hours) and Coral Bay (A$165, 15½ hours). Alternatively, you can hop off the daily McCafferty's/Greyhound Perth–Darwin bus at the Giralia turn-off ($145 one way, 17 hours) and pick up the Exmouth shuttle which comes to meet the bus (A$22, one hour). From Exmouth there are three weekly services to Coral Bay (A$65, 1¾ hours). Going north from Exmouth, you have to change buses at the Giralia turn-off. **Integrity Coach Lines** (☎ 1800 226 339) has four weekly services to Perth and two to Broome, also with connecting shuttles.

OUTBACK NEW SOUTH WALES

Head into the far west of New South Wales (NSW) and you'll hit the state's very own red chunk of the outback, complete with endless horizons and vast blue skies. It's contradictory country, with rugged Broken Hill producing mineral wealth but also artistic masterpieces. Far-flung Bourke was once a trade centre linked to the world by paddle steamer, which you can still ride if the Darling River's cooperating. Then there's sweltering Tibooburra (consistently blowing the mercury with the state's highest temperatures) and the ancient remains in Lake Mungo National Park.

Activities

Getting out into the great outdoors is made difficult by the extremes of climate and landscape out here. There's plenty of **walking** to be had in Mungo and Kinchega National Parks, but remember to register before walks and take plenty of water and sunscreen. For a shorter walk, the Living Desert Reserve just outside of Broken Hill will give you stunning views of the surrounding area especially at sunset.

BOURKE

☎ 02 / pop 2600

Roughly 800km northwest of Sydney, Bourke has been a frontier town since it was settled. At the edge of the outback, the expression 'back o' Bourke' is a measurement of extreme distance for Australians. On the Darling River, it was once a major river port, but today it's a sleepy town. Bourke's bored youth occasionally cause trouble at night, but it's usually only vandalism.

The **visitors centre** (☎ 6872 1222; tourinfo@lisp.com.au; Anson St; 9am-5pm daily Easter-Oct, 9am-5pm Mon-Sat Nov-Easter) is a mine of information. Half-day **Mateship Country Tours** (A$22) start here, taking a very personal tour of the town, river and citrus farms. The **National Parks & Wildlife Service office** (NPWS; ☎ 6872 2744; 51 Oxley St; 8.30am-4.30pm Mon-Fri) can help you explore the surrounding area.

Leaving from Kidman's Camp, the paddle-boat **Jandra** (☎ 6872 1321; adult/concession A$13/10; cruises 9am, 11am & 3pm) takes you on a historic tour down the Darling including Bourke's river-port history. If you keep your eyes peeled you'll be able to spot kangaroos lolling on the dry plains around town. The new **Back O'Bourke Exhibition Centre** (☎ 6872 1321; www.backobourke.com.au; Kidman Way, North Bourke; adult/concession A$3.50/2.50), a museum showing interactive films complete with outback sights, sounds and smells, was almost complete at the time of writing.

Sleeping & Eating

Gidgee Guesthouse YHA (☎ 6870 1017; www.yha.com.au; cnr Oxley & Sturt St; dm A$22-25, s A$32, d & tw A$55-60, surcharge for YHA nonmembers A$3.50;) This fully renovated bank is easily the best budget option in town. Friendly owners arrange camel treks.

Port O'Bourke (☎ 6872 2544; 32 Mitchell St; s/d A$38/59, d with bathroom A$85;) Recently renovated, this is new, basic pub-style accommodation. The **bar** (mains A$7-13; lunch & dinner Mon-Sat) serves burgers, steaks and hearty outback grub.

Morrall's Bakery (☎ 6872 2086; 37 Mitchell St; pies A$3, pizzas A$8) This tiny shop front makes award-winning pastries, becoming Tiffanie's pizzeria Friday to Sunday nights.

Getting There & Away

Air Link (☎ 13 17 13; www.airlinkairlines.com.au) flies from Bourke weekdays to Dubbo (A$150). **CountryLink** (☎ 13 22 32) buses run to Dubbo (A$60, 4½ hours) four times a week, connecting with trains to Sydney (A$66).

BACK O'BOURKE – CORNER COUNTRY

The state's far western corner is a semi-desert of heat, red dust and flies. Along the Queensland border, the **Dog Fence** restrains the northern dingoes and is regularly patrolled by boundary riders.

Tiny **Tibooburra**, NSW's hottest spot with a sweltering *average* temperature of 28 degrees, is in the far northwestern corner and has several attractive 19th-century stone buildings. **Sturt National Park** starts right on the northern edge of town with a handy **NPWS office** (☎ 08-8091 3308; Briscoe St; 8.30am-4.30pm Mon-Fri).

BROKEN HILL

☎ 08 / pop 19,800

Lost in the far west, Broken Hill is an oasis in semiarid wilderness. Mining put the 'Silver City' on the map, but a huge population of artists keeps it on the tourist trail. Artists are drawn to the area's raw beauty and intense, reliable light. Walking around town, you'll spot numerous wall murals, sculptures and art galleries.

Orientation & Information

The city is laid out in an easily navigable grid with Argent St the main drag. The airport is about 5km south of town and with no shuttle bus, so a cab will cost you around A$15.

City Perk Internet Cafe (☎ 8088 1443; 305 Argent St; per 20min A$3; 8.30am-5pm).

NPWS office (☎ 8080 3200; 183 Argent St; 8.30am-4.30pm Mon-Fri) A visit here is a must if you're heading further into the outback.

Visitors centre (☎ 8087 6077; www.murrayoutback.org.au; cnr Blende & Bromide Sts; 8.30am-5pm) Dispenses useful information including gallery guides, and books buses

Sights

Sightseeing around town is made difficult by heat and the distance between each sight. Start early in the morning and avoid the middle of the day if you are on foot.

MINES

There's an excellent underground tour at **Delprat's Mine** (☎ 8088 1604; Federation Hill; 2hr tours

ZONED OUT

Broken Hill is so remote that it barely knows what state it's in. Technically, it's part of New South Wales (NSW), but both the phone code (08) and time zone – Adelaide (central) time, which is half an hour behind Sydney (eastern) time – are South Australian.

OUTBACK AUSTRALIA

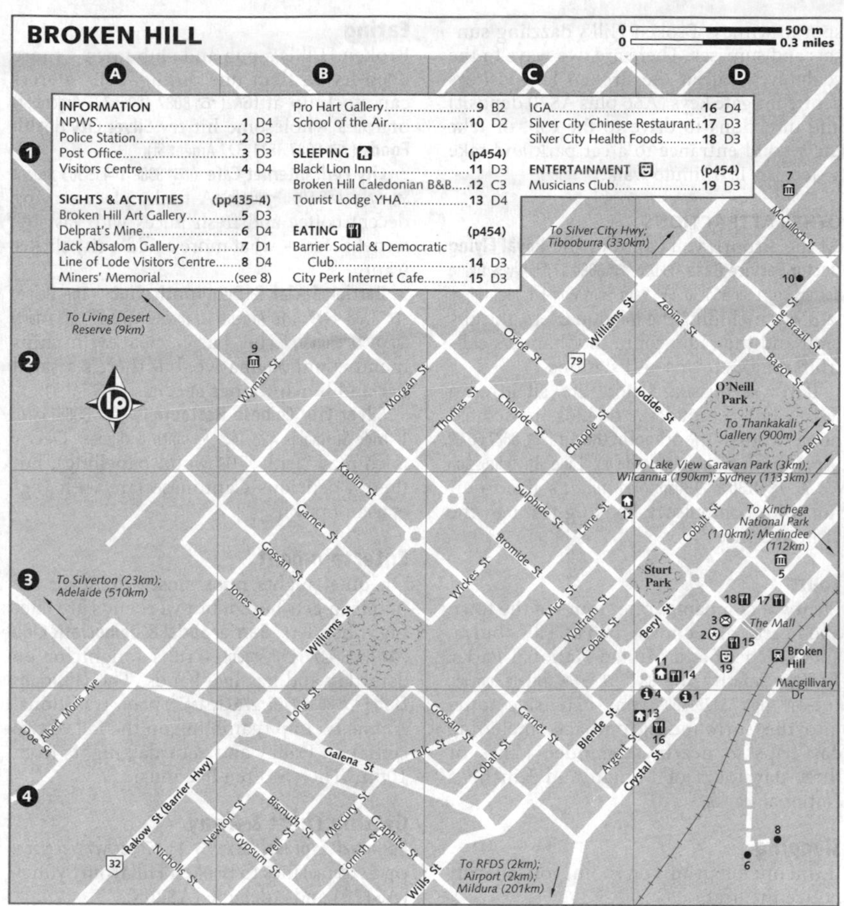

adult/concession A$38/34; tours 10.30am Mon-Fri, 2pm Sat), where you descend 130m in miner's gear. It's a detailed look at mining from the grease of the winder house to the grit of the mines.

Crowning a huge hill of mine waste, the **Line of Lode Visitors Centre** (☎ 8088 6000; Federation Hill; memorial adult/concession A$2.50/2; 9am-10pm) is the town's most obvious landmark. The rusting ship-like **memorial** to Broken Hill's deceased miners is a worthy tribute, and the sunrise and sunset views are impressive.

ART GALLERIES

Broken Hill's red earth and harsh light inspired the works at **Broken Hill Regional Art Gallery** (☎ 8088 5491; www.artgallery.brokenhill.nsw.gov.au; Sully's Bldg, 404-408 Argent St; admission by donation; 10am-5pm Mon-Fri, 1-5pm Sat & Sun), including the famous *Silver Tree* sculpture. **Pro Hart Gallery** (☎ 8087 2441; www.prohart.com.au; 108 Wyman St; adult A$4; 9am-5pm Mon-Fri, 1.30-5pm Sat) crams in a huge collection including Picassos, Dalis and Pro's gaudy Rolls Royce. **Jack Absalom Gallery** (☎ 8087 5881; 638 Chapple St; 10am-5pm) showcases realist landscapes by Absalom, an artist/author who periodically pops in for a chat. **Thankakali** (☎ 8087 6111; cnr Beryl & Buck Sts; 9am-4pm Mon-Fri, 10am-3pm Sat & Sun) is an extensive gallery of Aboriginal works.

The most impressive gallery is located outdoors – the **Living Desert Reserve**, including an international sculpture project on a hill top 9km from town. There are wide views over the plains making it the perfect spot to witness Broken Hill's dazzling sunsets and sunrises. There are two ways to the sculptures: call at the Broken Hill visitors centre for gate keys (A$6 plus A$20 deposit) and directions to drive to the top, or take the second entrance to a car park and take a steepish 15-minute walk.

OTHER ATTRACTIONS

At the airport, you can tour the **Royal Flying Doctor Service Base** (RFDS; ☎ 8080 1777; www.flyingdoctors.org; tour A$5.50; 9am-5pm Mon-Fri, 11am-4pm Sat & Sun), including the headquarters, the aircraft and the radio room that handles calls from remote towns and stations.

If you're missing school life, sit in on a lesson being broadcast to kids in isolated homesteads at the **School of the Air** (☎ 8087 6077; www.schoolair-p.schools.nsw.edu.au; Lane St; admission A$3.50; 8.30am-9.30am Mon-Fri). It's live-to-air fun, with compulsory booking through the visitors centre.

Tours

Plenty of companies offer tours of the town and nearby attractions, such as Tibooburra, and Kinchega and Mungo National Parks. **Tri State Safaris** (☎ 8088 2389; www.tristate.com.au; 1-/3-day trips A$129/690) runs extensive tours into the surrounding outback, including day trips to nearby Menindee Lakes or three-day tours of Mungo and Kinchega National Parks.

Sleeping

If you opt for an air-con room, you'll hardly notice the heat.

Tourist Lodge YHA (☎ 8088 2086; mcrae@pcpro.net.au; 100 Argent St; dm/s/d A$19/29/46;) This popular YHA hostel has a small pool, and dorms are often doubles or twins.

Broken Hill Caledonian B&B (☎ 8087 1945; www.caledonianbnb.com.au; 140 Chloride St; s/d A$55/66) Featuring excellent homey rooms and friendly staff, this old-fashioned charmer is a well-converted hotel.

Black Lion Inn (☎ 8087 4801; 34 Bromide St; s/d A$24/31) This friendly pub has good-value rooms in an adjoining building, so you'll sleep through the bar-room banter.

Lake View Caravan Park (☎ 8088 2250; 1 Mann St; unpowered/powered sites per 2 people A$20/18, on-site vans/cabins A$35/46;) Three kilometres northeast of town, this park enjoys a prime location on the edge of the bush.

Eating

Broken Hill is a pub and club town – more deep-frying than fine dining. Self-caterers can stock up at **IGA** (☎ 8087 4806; 135 Argent St) or for a wholesome hit try **Silver City Health Foods** (☎ 8087 3811; 322 Argent St).

City Perk Internet Cafe (☎ 8088 1443; 305 Argent St; mains A$8.50; lunch) A funky place serving decent coffee and fresh juices with fast Internet access – what more could a city slicker want?

Barrier Social & Democratic Club (The Demo; ☎ 8088 4477; 218 Argent St; mains A$8; breakfast, lunch & dinner) The basic meat-with-chips menu is unimaginative, but there's a salad bar and lunch/dinner specials (A$7/13).

Silver City Chinese Restaurant (☎ 8088 5860; 1 Oxide St; mains A$8-15; lunch & dinner) Décor is chintzy (with '70s wood panelling), but there's delicious Cantonese fare with vegetarian options.

Entertainment

On quiet nights pubs close whenever the publican gets bored, but weekends are late-night benders. **Barrier Social & Democratic Club** (☎ 8088 4477; 218 Argent St) runs a nightclub on Saturday and has live bands. The **Musicians Club** (☎ 8088 1777; 276 Crystal St) plays traditional Aussie two-up (gambling on the fall of two coins) on Friday and Saturday nights from 10pm. There's often live music.

Getting There & Away

Regional Express (Rex; ☎ 13 17 13; www.regionalexpress.com.au) flies to Broken Hill from Sydney (A$120) and Adelaide (A$265).

McCafferty's/Greyhound (☎ 13 20 30) runs daily to Adelaide (A$58) and Sydney (A$89). Most buses depart from the visitors centre.

The *Indian Pacific* (☎ 13 21 47; www.trainways.com.au) passes through Broken Hill twice a week, bound for Sydney (A$165, 16 hours), Perth (A$375, three days) and for Adelaide (A$64, seven hours). The direct **CountryLink** (☎ 8087 1400; 8am-5pm Mon-Fri) service leaves for Sydney on Tuesday (A$117, 14 hours).

AROUND BROKEN HILL

Silverton is an old silver-mining town found along a bumpy road 25km northwest of Broken Hill. This interesting ghost town has served as the desolate setting for films including *Mad Max II* and *A Town Like Alice*. Old buildings remain, including the **Silverton**

Hotel (☎ 8088 5313; ⌚ 9am-9pm), home to movie memorabilia and the owner's Mad Max car. Don't leave without taking the infamous 'Test', a taste of larrikinism. On the road from Broken Hill, **camel tours** (☎ 8088 5316; Silverton Rd, half-/1hr rides A$15/25, 2hr sunset rides A$50) through the desertscape are unforgettable.

One hundred and eleven kilometres southeast of Broken Hill, **Kinchega National Park** has spectacular lakes to explore. The visitors centre is at the old Kinchega woolshed (16km from the park entrance) and there are well-marked roads throughout the park.

MUNGO NATIONAL PARK

The World Heritage–listed Mungo is a dry lake and the site of Australia's oldest archaeological finds: human skeletons dating back 46,000 years. The other attraction is the **Walls of China** – a 25km semicircle ('lunette') of sand dunes created by the unceasing westerly wind (which exposes ancient remains).

Pay your day-use (A$6 per car) and camping fees (A$3 per person) at the often-unstaffed **visitors centre**, by the old Mungo woolshed. It has a self-guided drive brochure here.

There's camping at Main Camp (2km from the visitors centre) and Belah Camp (east of the dunes). Hostel-style beds are available at the **Shearers' Quarters** (dm A$17), near the visitors centre.

The easiest way to Mungo is to take a tour from Broken Hill (see Tours on opposite) or Mildura (see Tours on p285).

COOBER PEDY

☎ 08 / pop 2624

You may think you've reached the end of the world when you head eight hours north of Adelaide and arrive in Coober Pedy – the opal capital of Australia, if not the world. The name Coober Pedy is from an Aboriginal language, said to mean 'white man's hole in the ground'. About half the population lives in dugouts (underground rooms) to shelter from the extreme climate: daytime summer temperatures can soar to over 50°C and the winter nights are freezing. Apart from the dugouts, there are over 250,000 mine shafts in the area, so keep your eyes open!

Opal was discovered here by a teenage boy in 1915, and it since has lured people from all over the world to live here. You'll soon hear outrageous stories of fortunes made and lost, shady deals, vendettas, intrigues and crazy old-timers. Every few years someone makes a million-dollar find, but some miners spend decades hard at work and make very little for their efforts.

Information

Underground Books (☎ 8672 5558; Post Office Hill Rd; ⌚ 8.30am-5pm Mon-Fri, 10am-4pm Sat) sells the Desert Parks Pass (yearly pass per vehicle A$90), which is required to visit most of the outback's conservation areas.

The **visitors centre** (☎ 1800 637 076; www.opalcapitaloftheworld.com.au; District Council offices, Hutchison St; ⌚ 8.30am-5pm Mon-Fri) is diagonally opposite the Ampol Roadhouse and bus station.

Bottled water is an expensive commodity here; you can refill water bottles at the coin-operated **24-hour water dispenser** (30L for A$0.20) by the Oasis Caravan Park.

Sights & Activities

Keen fossickers can have a 'noodle' for opals in the mullock (waste dumps); the safest area is the **Jeweller's Shop opal field** in the northeast corner of town.

There are plenty of wild and eccentric sights in Coober Pedy. There's an underground **Serbian Orthodox Church** and a unique bare-earth **golf course**, which reveals how bizarre this place is. The prominent **Big Winch Lookout** (Italian Club Rd; ⌚ 9am-5pm Mon-Sat) provides views over the town.

Many of the early **dugout homes** were simply worked-out mines; these days they're usually cut specifically as residences and sell for A$70,000 to A$80,000. **Faye's Underground Display Home** (☎ 8672 5029; Jewellers Shop Rd; admission A$4.50; ⌚ 9am-5pm Mon-Sat) was hand-dug by three women in the 1960s, while **Diggers Dream** (☎ 8672 5442; Nayler Pl; admission A$3; ⌚ 11.30am-5pm) has a more contemporary décor.

Opal is still embedded in the rock at the early mine and underground home at **Old Timers Mine & Museum** (☎ 8672 5555; Crowders Gully Rd; adult/student A$10/9; ⌚ 9am-6pm).

Umoona Opal Mine & Museum (☎ 8672 5288; Hutchison St; ⌚ 8am-7pm), in the centre of town, offers tours (A$10), which include information on local Aboriginal beliefs. It also has an

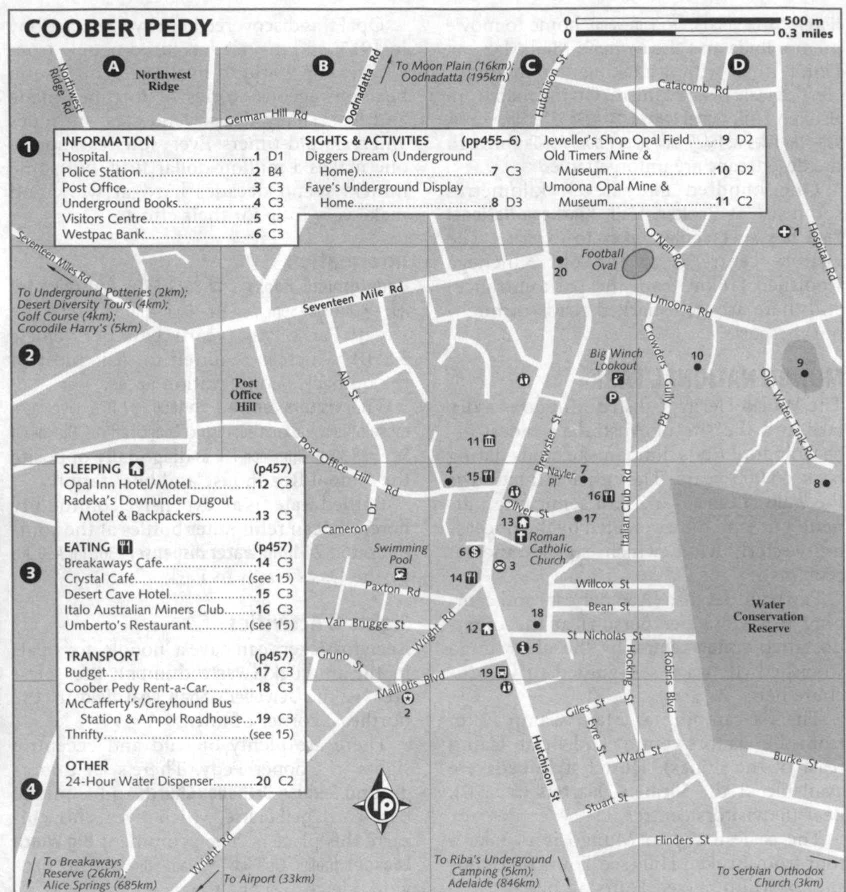

excellent 18-minute documentary on opals and opal mining. About 2km northwest of town, you can watch the potters at work at **Underground Potteries** (☎ 8672 5226; Rowe St; 🕑 8.30am-6pm). About 3km further on is **Crocodile Harry's** (☎ 8672 5872; Seventeen Mile Rd; admission A$2; 🕑 9am-6pm), an amazing, decorated dugout home. It is the work of many artists who have stayed with Harry over the years, and it also featured in *Mad Max III* and *Stark*. Some readers found it sleazy, others sad.

The lunar landscape of **Moon Plain**, 15km northeast of Coober Pedy, is a wonderful sight, as is the **Breakaways Reserve** (entry permit A$4), about 35km north off the Stuart Hwy. This stark but colourful area of mesa hills and scarps contains a white-and-yellow formation known as the **Castle**, which featured in the films *Mad Max III* and *The Adventures of Priscilla, Queen of the Desert*. Pick up an entry permit from the visitors centre or Underground Books.

If you're interested in purchasing opals, shop around and be wary of discounts over 30%. An international guarantee provides some measure of security, as does dealing with members of the Coober Pedy Retail Business and Tourism Association.

Tours

Various tours between Adelaide and Alice Springs explore Flinders Ranges, Oodnadatta Track, Coober Pedy, Uluru and Kings Canyon:

Adventure Tours Australia (☎ 1300 654 604, 8309 2299; www.adventuretours.com.au)
Groovy Grape Getaways Australia (☎ 1800 661 177; www.groovygrape.com.au)
Wayward Bus Touring Company (☎ 1800 882 823, 8410 8833; www.waywardbus.com.au)

Local day tours:
Desert Diversity Tours (☎ 1800 069 911, 8672 5226; www.desertdiversity.com;) One-day ecotours to the Painted Desert (A$145) and Lake Eyre (A$155); book through Underground Books.
Martin's Star Gazing (☎ 8672 5223; tours A$22) Explores the heavens from the Moon Plain (night only).
Radeka's Downunder Dugout Motel & Backpackers (☎ 8672 5223; tours A$40) Popular with backpackers; includes opal mine, underground home, Serbian church, fossicking for opals, Breakaways and Harry's.
Stuart Range Tours (☎ 8672 5179) The morning town tour (A$30) covers the history, lifestyle and fields of Coober Pedy; the afternoon tour (A$40) also includes the Breakaways.

If you really want to get the expanse into perspective and visit small, remote outback communities, travel with the **mail truck** (tours A$125; Mon & Thu) along 600km of dirt roads on its round trip (12 hours) from Coober Pedy to Oodnadatta and William Creek. Book ahead.

Sleeping

Radeka's Downunder Dugout Motel & Backpackers (☎ 8672 5223; www.radekadownunder.com.au; Oliver St; underground dm A$22, d & tw A$55;) This backpacker mecca has bunks in open alcoves, and pleasant private rooms. It has a good kitchen, laundry, restaurant and bar. There are free airport and bus station transfers if you book in advance.

Opal Inn Hotel/Motel (☎ 8672 5054; www.opalinn.com.au; Hutchison St; pub s/d A$48/55, motel s/d/tr A$62/69/76; meals A$13-18; dinner;) Central to the action, the pub and motel rooms here are basic but clean. The saloon bar serves counter meals and has pool tables and cable TV. There are A$8 specials on Thursday and Friday.

Riba's Underground Camping (☎ /fax 8672 5614; ribascamping@hotmail.com; William Creek Rd; above-ground/underground camp sites per person A$6/9) This unique and friendly place on the William Creek road, 5km from town, has cool underground facilities, a TV lounge and free showers. The one-hour evening mine tour (A$14) includes the night's camping fee.

Eating & Drinking

There are plenty of cafés and takeaways on the main street, and larger hotels and motels have cafés and restaurants (see Sleeping, left).

Italo Australian Miners Club (Italian Club; ☎ 8672 5101; Italian Club Rd; mains with salad bar A$10; dinner Wed-Sun) The local institution for steak and schnitzels on Thursday and Friday nights, and a good place for a beer at other times.

Breakaways Cafe (☎ 8672 3177; Hutchison St; meals A$4-8.50; 7am-8pm) A friendly and popular café serving value-packed cooked breakfasts, burgers and specials such as schnitzel with salad (A$7.50).

Desert Cave Hotel (☎ 8672 5688; www.desertcave.com.au; Hutchison St) Has the upmarket **Umberto's Restaurant** (mains A$18-26; dinner), and **Crystal Café** (breakfast A$3.50-11, lunch A$6-12; breakfast & lunch), where you can start the day with a maple syrup pancake stack (A$8.50) and good coffee. The Sunday lunch buffet (A$14.50) is a local favourite.

Getting There & Around

Coober Pedy is just off the Stuart Hwy 846km north of Adelaide in South Australia and 688km south of Alice Springs, in the Northern Territory.

Regional Express (Rex; ☎ 13 17 13; www.regionalexpress.com.au) flies to/from Adelaide (A$170). Most motels and hostels will pick up at the airport if you ring ahead.

McCafferty's/Greyhound (☎ 13 14 99) bus services are every day from Adelaide (A$125, 10½ hours) and Alice Springs (A$125, eight hours).

Bear in mind that there are no refuelling stops between Glendambo and Coober Pedy (259km). You can rent 4WDs to explore Lake Eyre from these places:
Budget (☎ 8672 5333; cpdbudget@ozemail.com.au; Oliver St) One-way rentals available.
Coober Pedy Rent-a-Car (☎ 8672 3003; Mud Hut Motel, St Nicholas St)
Thrifty (☎ 8672 5688; reserve@desertcave.com.au; Desert Cave Hotel)

Australia Directory

CONTENTS

ACCOMMODATION

Budget accommodation in Australia is plentiful and usually of a high standard. Whether you stay within the communal ruckus of entrepreneurial hostels, on the creaking upper storeys of age-weathered pubs or in the bush-enclosed camping sites of national park, there'll be no shortage of satisfying snoozing during your trip.

The accommodation listings in the Australian chapters of this guidebook are devoted almost entirely to budget establishments – we also provide a couple of big-city 'splurge' options, for those times when you feel like spoiling yourself with a bit of space and/or luxury. Listings are ordered so they start with the most recommended places, with our authors' preferences based on a mixture of atmosphere, cleanliness, facilities, location and totally unreliable subjectivity. Places that primarily offer tent and campervan sites (eg camping grounds and holiday parks) appear at the end of accommodation sections.

We treat any place charging up to A$40 per single or A$80 per double as true budget accommodation. That said, in the more expensive areas like metropolitan Sydney and Melbourne, 'budget' can mean paying up to A$50 per single and A$100 per double.

Accommodation prices given throughout this book are for dorms or rooms with shared bathroom unless stated otherwise (ie 'with bathroom').

During summer (December to February) and at other peak times, particularly school and public holidays, prices are usually at their highest, whereas outside these times useful discounts and lower hotel walk-in rates can be found. One exception is the Top End, where the wet season (summer) is the low season and prices can drop substantially. The weekend escape is a notion that figures prominently in the Australian psyche, meaning accommodation from Friday night through Sunday can be in greater demand (and pricier) in major holiday areas. High-season prices are quoted in this guidebook unless otherwise indicated.

B&Bs

Bed and breakfasts (or guesthouses) are a growing niche industry, with new places opening all the time in everything from restored miners' cottages and converted barns to rambling old houses and simple bedrooms in a family home. B&Bs are rarely budget-oriented and tend to be upmarket, particularly in areas that cater to those wanting to swap city living for a pampered weekend in the country.

Local tourist offices can usually provide a list of places. For online information, try the **Bed & Breakfast Site** (www.babs.com.au) or **Inn Australia** (www.innaustralia.com.au).

Camping & Caravan Parks

The cheapest accommodation lies outdoors, where the nightly cost of camping for two people is usually somewhere between A$15 and A$25, or slightly more for a powered site. Whether you're packing a tent, driving a campervan or towing a caravan (house trailer in North American–speak), camping in the bush is a highlight of travelling in Australia. In places like the outback and northern Australia you often won't even need a tent, and nights spent around a campfire under the stars are unforgettable. Stays at designated sites in national parks normally cost between A$4 and A$9 per person. When it comes to urban camping, remember that most city camping grounds are kilometres away from the town centre.

Most caravan parks are good value; the vast majority are equipped with hot showers, flushing toilets and laundry facilities, and occasionally a pool. Many have old on-site caravans for rent, but these are largely being replaced by on-site cabins. Cabin sizes and facilities vary, but expect to pay A$50 to A$90 for two people in a cabin with a kitchenette. If you intend doing a lot of caravanning or camping, consider joining one of the major chains such as **Big 4** (www.big4.com.au), which offers discounts at member parks.

Hostels

Hostels are a highly social but low-cost fixture of the Australian accommodation scene. Note that not all dorms are same-sex rooms – double-check this if you're after a single-sex dorm. The website www.allbackpackers.com.au lists hostels around the country.

HOSTEL ORGANISATIONS

There are over 130 hostel franchisees of **VIP Backpacker Resorts** (☎ 07-3395 6111; www.backpackers.com.au; 3/41 Steele Pl, Morningside, Qld 4170) in Australia and many more overseas. For A$39 you'll receive a 12-month membership, entitling you to a A$1 discount on accommodation and a 5% to 15% discount on other products such as air and bus transport, tours and activities. You can join online, at VIP hostels or at larger agencies dealing in backpacker travel.

Nomads Backpackers (☎ 02-9264 5533; www.nomadsworld.com; 6th fl, 204 Clarence St, Sydney, NSW 2000) has several dozen franchisees in Australia alone. Membership (A$34 for 12 months) entitles you to numerous discounts. Join at participating hostels, backpacker travel agencies, online, or via the Nomads head office.

INDEPENDENT HOSTELS

Australia has numerous independent hostels, with the fierce competition for the backpacker dollar prompting plenty of enticements such as free breakfasts, courtesy buses and discount meal vouchers. In the cities, some places are run-down hotels trying to fill empty rooms; the unrenovated ones are often gloomy and depressing. Others are converted motels where each four-to-six-bed unit has a fridge, TV and bathroom, but communal areas and cooking facilities may be lacking. There are also purpose-built hostels, often with the best facilities but sometimes too big and impersonal – avoid 'we love to party' places if you're in an introspective mood. The best places tend to be the smaller, more intimate hostels where the owner is also the manager.

Independent backpacker establishments typically charge A$19 to A$27 for a dorm bed and A$40 to A$60 for a twin or double room (usually without bathroom), often with a small discount if you're a member of YHA, VIP and sometimes Nomads (see left).

Some places will only admit overseas backpackers; they're mainly urban hostels that have had problems with locals sleeping over and bothering the backpackers. Hostels that discourage or ban Aussies say it's only a rowdy minority that makes trouble, and will often just ask for identification in order to deter potential troublemakers, but it certainly can feel annoying and discriminatory for genuine people trying to travel in their own country. Also watch out for those hostels catering expressly to working backpackers, where wages and facilities can be minimal but rent can be high.

PRACTICALITIES

Electricity

- Use a three-pin adaptor (different to British three-pin adaptors) to plug into the electricity supply (230V AC, 50Hz)

Videos

- Videos you watch will be based on the PAL system

Weights & Measures

- Use the metric system for weights and measures

YHA HOSTELS

Australia has over 140 hostels associated with the **Youth Hostels Association** (YHA; ☎ 02-9261 1111; www.yha.com.au; 422 Kent St, Sydney, NSW 2000). YHA is part of the **International Youth Hostel Federation** (IYHF; www.hihostels.com), also known as Hostelling International (HI), so if you're already a member of that organisation in your own country, your membership entitles you to YHA rates in the relevant Australian hostels. Nightly charges are between A$10 and A$30 for members; most hostels also take non-YHA members for an extra A$3.50. Visitors to Australia should purchase a HI card preferably in their country of residence, but you can also buy one at major local YHA hostels at a cost of A$35 for 12 months. Australian residents can become full YHA members for A$55/85/115 for one/two/three years; join online, at a state office or any youth hostel.

YHA hostels provide basic accommodation, usually in small dormitories (bunk rooms), although many provide twin rooms and even doubles. They have 24-hour access, cooking facilities, a communal area with a TV, laundry facilities and, in larger hostels, travel offices. There's often a maximum-stay period (usually five to seven days). Bed linen is provided (sleeping bags are not welcomed due to hygiene concerns) in all hostels except those in wilderness areas, where you'll need your own sleeping sheet.

The annual *YHA Accommodation & Discounts Guide* booklet details all Australian hostels and any membership discount entitlements (transport, activities etc).

Hotels & Motels

Hotels in cities or well-touristed places are generally of the business or luxury variety where you get a comfortable room with all the mod cons in a multistorey block. These places tend to have a pool, restaurant/café, room service and various other facilities. Where we recommend such hotels we quote 'rack rates' (official advertised rates), though significant discounts can be offered when business is quiet.

Motels (or motor inns) are characterised by comfortable mid-range rooms. Prices vary and there's rarely a cheaper rate for singles, so motels are better for couples or groups of three. Most motels are modern, low-rise and have similar facilities (tea- and coffee-making, fridge, TV, air-con and bathroom) but the price will indicate the standard. You'll pay at least A$50 for a room.

Pubs

For the budget traveller, hotels in Australia are the ones that serve beer – commonly known as pubs (from the term 'public house'). In country towns, pubs are invariably found in the town centre. Many pubs were built during boom times, so they're often among the largest and most extravagant buildings in town. In tourist areas some pubs have been restored as heritage buildings, but generally the rooms remain small and old-fashioned, with a long amble down the hall to the bathroom. You can sometimes rent a single room at a country pub for not much more than a hostel dorm bed, and you'll be in the social heart of the town. But if you're a light sleeper, avoid booking a room right above the bar and check whether a band is playing downstairs that night (especially on Friday and Saturday nights).

Standard pubs have singles/doubles with shared facilities starting from around A$30/50, more if you want a private bathroom. Few have a separate reception area – make inquiries in the bar.

Rental Accommodation

The ubiquitous holiday flat resembles a motel unit but has a kitchen or cooking facilities. It can come with two or more bedrooms and is often rented on a weekly basis – higher prices are often reserved for shorter stays. For a two-bedroom flat, you'll pay from A$60 to A$95 per night.

If you're interested in a shared flat or house for a long-term stay, check the classified advertisements sections of the daily newspapers; Wednesday and Saturday are usually the best days. Noticeboards in universities, hostels, bookshops and cafés are also worth browsing.

Other Accommodation

Many farms offer a bed for a night. At some you sit back and watch other people raise a sweat, while others get you involved in day-to-day activities. At a couple of remote outback stations you can stay in homestead rooms or shearers' quarters and try activities such as horse riding. Check out the options on offer on the website of **Australian Farmhost Holidays** (www.australiafarmhost.com); state tourist offices can also tell you what's available.

It's sometimes possible to stay in the hostels and halls of residence normally occupied by university students, though you'll need to time your stay to coincide with the longer uni holiday periods.

ACTIVITIES

Although Australia provides plenty of excuses to kick back and do little more than work on a tan, it also encourages travellers to throw themselves into the thick of the outdoor action. Innumerable activities are possible here, many on the cliffs, wilderness trails and mountains of dry land, and many more on the offshore swells, reefs and islands. These activities often give you a chance to see parts of the country that you wouldn't encounter if you just hung around your hostel or the nearest pub.

The following is a summary of what's possible; for specifics, read the individual activities entries in each state and territory chapter.

Bushwalking

You can follow fantastic trails through national parks around the country. Notable walks include the **Overland Track** (p321) in Tasmania; the **Thorsborne Trail** (p203) across Hinchinbrook Island in Queensland; the **Larapinta Trail** (p426) in the Centre; and **Mt Kosciuszko** (p129) in NSW.

Lonely Planet's *Walking in Australia* provides detailed information on local bushwalking.

Cycling

Avid cyclists have access to lots of great cycling routes and touring country for day, weekend or longer trips. Most large cities have a recreational bike-path system and an abundance of bike-hire places. The rates charged by most outfits for renting road or mountain bikes (not including the discounted fees offered by budget-accommodation places to their guests) are anywhere between A$8 and A$12 per hour, A$18 to A$40 per day. Security deposits can range from A$50 to A$200, depending on the rental period.

If you're considering getting around Australia by bike, see p477.

Diving & Snorkelling

There's excellent scuba diving (as well as many dive schools) along the **Great Barrier Reef** (p184). The **Professional Association of Diving Instructors** (PADI; www.padi.com) offers Open Water Certificate courses that typically cost A$300 to A$650 for three to five days, depending on how much time you actually spend on the reef. You'll need to procure a medical certificate (about A$50) for all certified PADI courses.

In Western Australia the **Ningaloo Reef** (p449) is every bit as interesting as the east-coast reefs, but without the tourist numbers, and numerous tours are available at **Coral Bay** (p448) and **Exmouth** (p450). In the southern waters around Melbourne, Adelaide, Perth, Tasmania and NSW you can dive around shipwrecks and with seals and dolphins; courses are also generally cheaper in the south, too. And of course it's cheap to hire a mask, snorkel and fins.

Extreme Sports

The elastic entertainment of **bungy jumping** is big on the Gold Coast (see Breakfast Again Anyone? on p156) and in Cairns (see p209).

Fantastic sites for **abseiling** and **rock climbing** include the Blue Mountains (p87) in New South Wales, Mt Buffalo in Victoria's high country (p291) and the spectacular Hazards at Coles Bay (p310) on Tasmania's east coast. Local professionals can set you up with equipment and training. For online info, visit **Climbing Australia** (www.climbing.com.au) or **Wild Publications** (www.rock.com.au).

Tandem **paragliding** flights are available anywhere there are good take-off and landing points and thermal winds; try Rainbow Beach (Queensland) and Bright (Victoria). **Sky-diving** and **parachuting** are also widely practised, especially in Byron Bay, the Gold Coast and Townsville.

Horse & Camel Riding

Exploring the bush by horseback is a distinctly Australian activity, even without an Akubra to flap in the wind as you ride. In Victoria, go horse riding in the **high country** (p278) and follow the spectacular routes of the Snowy Mountains cattle people. In northern Queensland, ride horses through rainforests and along sand dunes, and swim with them in the sea. There are also sundry riding opportunities in Australia's north and west.

Camel riding is an offbeat alternative, especially in central Australia and outback South Australia where there are camel farms. Originally brought in from the Middle East to be used as transport in Australia's harsh desert environment, camels now run wild all over the interior. A sunset camel ride on Cable Beach is *de rigueur* in **Broome** (p435), while you can also ride these desert-savvy animals just south of **Alice Springs** (p422).

Skiing & Snowboarding

Australia has a small but enthusiastic snow-sports industry, with snowfields straddling the NSW–Victoria border. The season is relatively short, however, running from about mid-June to early September, and snowfalls can be unpredictable. The top places to ski are **Thredbo** (p131) and **Perisher** (p131) in NSW's Snowy Mountains, and **Falls Creek** (p291) and **Mt Hotham** (p290) in Victoria. Equipment can be hired at the snowfields.

The website for **Skiing Australia** (www.skiingaustralia.org.au) has links to major resorts.

Surfing

World-class waves can be ridden all around the country, from Queensland's **Gold Coast** (p157), the great beaches in **Sydney** (p60) and Victoria's reowned **Bells Beach** (p265) to SA's **Fleurieu Peninsula** (p370) and **Margaret River** (p405) in WA.

For surf-cams and photos: **Coastalwatch.com** (www.coastalwatch.com).

Water Sports

Australia's coast isn't just for surfing and diving. Most major resorts rent windsurfing gear and there are outfits on the east coast offering **parasailing** (behind a speedboat) and **jetboating**: parasailing is good at Port Douglas in Queensland and at WA's Fremantle, while jetboating is popular on the Huon River in Tasmania. The places offering the most activities are those with the most visitors, such as **Airlie Beach** (p189), **Cairns** (p208) and the **Gold Coast** (p157) in Queensland.

Sailing is a popular activity around the islands of the **Great Barrier Reef** (p193) and all along the east coast, where you can take lessons or just pitch in and help crew a yacht.

Great **white-water rafting** trips are possible on the **Nymboida River** (p102) in northern NSW, the **Tully River** (p203) in north Queensland and the mighty **Franklin River** (p321) in Tasmania. **Canoeing** and **kayaking** can be enjoyed on rivers at locales like **Katherine Gorge** (p349) in the Northern Territory and **Blackwood River** (p408) in southern WA.

Whale- & Dolphin-Watching

Migrating southern right and humpback whales pass close to Australia's southern coast on their way between the Antarctic and warmer waters, and whale-watching cruises allow you to get close to these magnificent creatures. The best spots are the mid-north coast of NSW, **Warrnambool** (p270) in Victoria, and **Albany** (p413) on the southwest cape of WA. Whale-watching seasons are roughly May to October on the west coast and in southwestern Victoria, and September to November on the east coast.

Dolphins can be seen year-round along the east coast, at places such as **Jervis Bay** (p113) and **Byron Bay** (p106), both in NSW, and off WA at places like **Bunbury** (p399) and **Monkey Mia** (p447).

BOOKS

Lonely Planet publishes numerous state/territory and regional guides to Australia, including *East Coast Australia*, *Queensland & the Great Barrier Reef*, *Tasmania*, *Aboriginal Australia & the Torres Strait Islands* and *Northern Territory*.

Considering Australia's huge size, it's surprising that relatively little travel literature has appeared on this continental subject. That said, some thought-provoking and just plain entertaining books have been written about this country.

Robyn Davidson's *Tracks* (1980) details her wilfully lunatic trek across 2700km of the outback equipped only with humour, determination and a handful of wild camels. Bruce Chatwin's *The Songlines* (1987) has the famously self-indulgent but outwardly perceptive author writing about (and sometimes embodying) the cultural collision between central Australian Aborigines and 'modern' society.

Affable Tim Bowden drives his beloved 4WD ('Penelope') across the Kimberley, Pilbara and Nullarbor, and writes in a knowledgeable and occasionally twee style on his ensuing meditations in *Penelope: Bungles to Broome* (2002). A different kind of road trip is described in Tony Horwitz's entertaining *One for the Road* (1999), a high-speed account of life on and along the highway during a round-Oz hitchhiking trip.

For comfortably predictable reading, pick up Bill Bryson's *Down Under* (2001), in which the mass-market humorist takes his usual well-rehearsed potshots at a large target. The book is sold in the USA under the title *In a Sunburned Country*.

BUSINESS HOURS

Business hours vary a little from state to state but most shops and businesses open at 9am and close at 5.30pm Monday to Friday, with Saturday hours usually from 9am to either noon or 5pm. Sunday trading is becoming increasingly common but it is currently limited to the major cities and, to a lesser extent, regional Victoria. There are usually one or two late shopping nights each week, normally Thursday and/or Friday, when doors stay open until 9pm. Most supermarkets are open until at least 7pm and are sometimes open 24 hours; milk bars (general stores) and convenience stores are also often open late.

Banks normally operate from 9.30am to 4pm Monday to Thursday and until 5pm on Friday. Some large city branches are open from 8am to 6pm on weekdays, and a few are also open from 8am to 9pm on Friday. Post offices are open from 9am to 5pm Monday to Friday, but you can also buy stamps on Saturday morning at post office agencies (operated from newsagencies) and from Australia Post shops in all the major cities.

Restaurants are typically open from noon to 3pm for lunch, and they open between 6pm and 7pm for dinner. They normally stay open until at least 9pm but tend to serve food until later in the evening on Friday and Saturday; the main restaurant strips in large cities keep longer hours all week. Cafés tend to be all-day affairs that either close around 5pm or continue their business into the night. Pubs usually serve food from noon to 2pm and from 6pm to 8pm. Pubs and bars often open for drinking at lunchtime and continue well into the evening, particularly from Thursday to Saturday.

Nearly all attractions across Australia are closed on Christmas Day.

CLIMATE

Australia's size means there's a lot of climatic variation, but without severe extremes. The southern third of the country has cold (though generally not freezing) winters (June

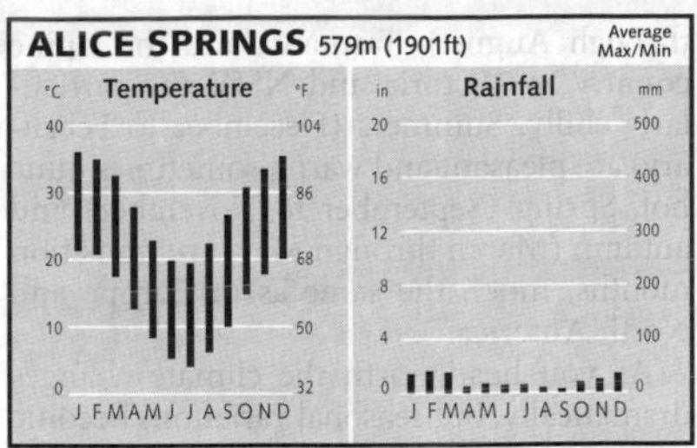

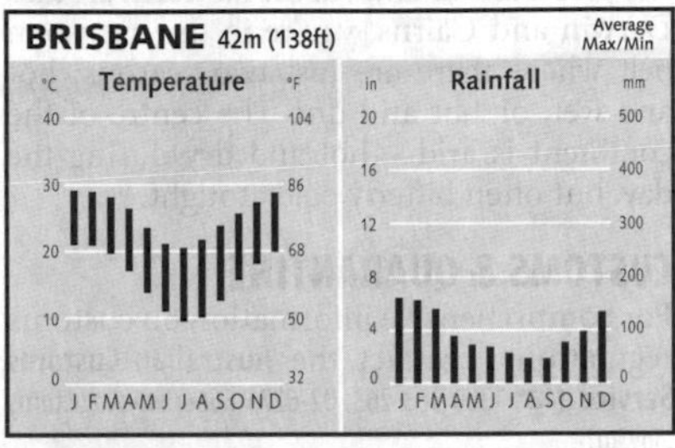

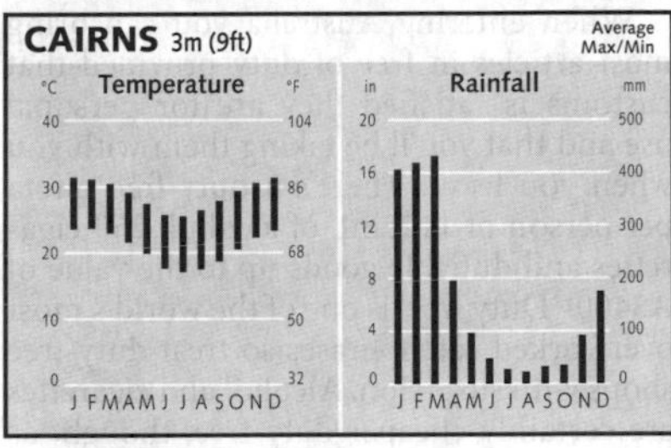

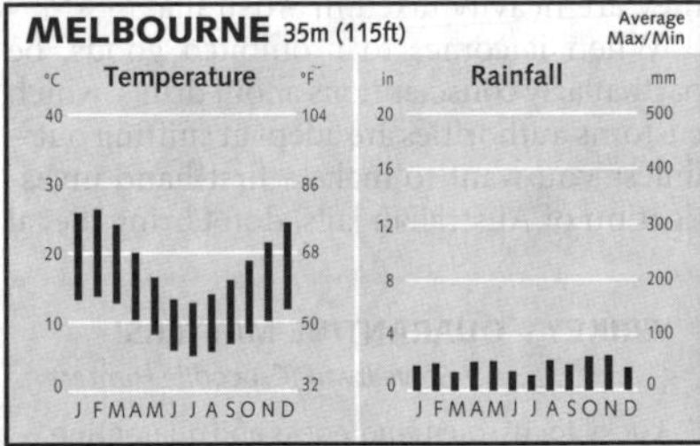

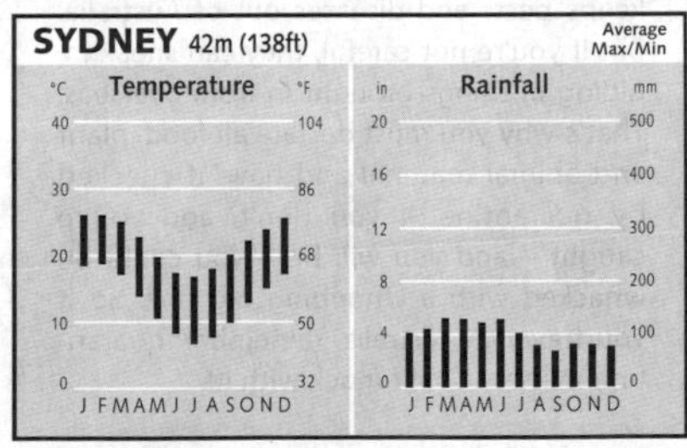

through August). Tasmania and the alpine country in Victoria and NSW get particularly chilly. Summers (December to February) are pleasant and warm, sometimes quite hot. Spring (September to November) and autumn (March through May) are transition months, much the same as in Europe and North America.

As you head north the climate changes dramatically, but seasonal variations become less pronounced until, in the far north around Darwin and Cairns, you're in the monsoon belt where there are just two seasons: hot and wet, or hot and dry. The centre of the continent is arid – hot and dry during the day, but often bitterly cold at night.

CUSTOMS & QUARANTINE

For comprehensive information on customs regulations, contact the **Australian Customs Service** (☎ 1300 363 263, 02-6275 6666; www.customs.gov.au).

When entering Australia you can bring most articles in free of duty provided that customs is satisfied they are for personal use and that you'll be taking them with you when you leave. There's a duty-free quota per person of 1125mL of alcohol, 250 cigarettes and dutiable goods up to the value of A$400. 'Duty free' is one of the world's most overworked catchphrases so treat duty-free shops with suspicion. Alcohol and cigarettes are certainly cheaper duty free, though, as they are heavily taxed in Australia.

When it comes to prohibited goods, be particularly conscientious about drugs, which customs authorities are adept at sniffing out – unless you want to make a first-hand investigation of Australian jails, don't bring illegal drugs in with you. Note that all medicines must be declared.

Also be forthright about all food, plant material and animal products. You will be asked to declare on arrival all goods of animal or plant origin (wooden spoons, straw hats, the lot) and show them to a quarantine officer. The authorities are naturally keen to protect Australia's unique environment and important agricultural industries by preventing weeds, pests or diseases getting in – Australia has so far managed to escape many of the pests and diseases prevalent elsewhere in the world. Food is also prohibited, particularly meat, cheese, fruit, vegetables and flowers, plus there are restrictions on taking fruit and vegetables between states. And if you lug in a souvenir, such as a bongo with animal hide for a skin, or a wooden article that shows signs of insect damage, it won't get through. Some items may require treatment to make them safe before they are allowed in.

Other restricted goods include weapons, products made from protected wildlife species (eg animal skins, coral, ivory) and live animals.

Remember that Australia takes quarantine very seriously. All luggage is screened or X-rayed – if you fail to declare quarantine items on arrival and are caught, you risk an on-the-spot fine of up to A$220, or prosecution which may result in fines over A$60,000, as well as up to 10 years imprisonment. For more information on quarantine regulations contact the **Australian Quarantine and Inspection Service** (AQIS; ☎ 1800 020 504, 02-6272 3933; www.aqis.gov.au).

CRIKEY – QUARANTINE MATTERS!

Steve Irwin (Crocodile Hunter)

Lucky for us, our remoteness and quarantine keeps pests and diseases out of Australia. But if you're not careful, they can sneak in, hiding in things brought in from overseas. That's why you must declare all food, plant and animal material and have it checked by quarantine. If you don't, and you're caught – and you will be – you could be whacked with a whopping big fine. So if you travel to Australia, remember: quarantine matters. Don't muck with it!

DANGERS & ANNOYANCES

Animal Hazards

Judging by Australia's remarkable profusion of dangerous creatures, Mother Nature must have been really pissed off when she concocted the local wildlife. The country has poisonous snakes and spiders, its share of shark and crocodile attacks and, to top it off, it's home to the world's deadliest creature, the box jellyfish (see following). Travellers don't need to be in a constant state of alarm, however – you're unlikely to see many of these creatures in the wild, much less be attacked by one.

Hospitals have antivenin on hand for all common snake and spider bites (dial ☎ 000 for an ambulance), but it helps to know what it was that bit you.

BOX JELLYFISH

There have been numerous fatal encounters between swimmers and these large jellyfish on the coast north of Bundaberg in Queensland, and along the coast of the NT. Also known as the sea wasp or 'stinger', their venomous tentacles can grow up to 3m long. You can be stung during any month, but the worst time is from November to the end of April, when you should stay out of the ocean unless you're wearing protective clothing such as a 'stinger suit', available from swimwear and sporting shops in the stinger zone. The box jellyfish also has a tiny, lethal relative called an Irukandji.

For information on treating box jellyfish stings, see p808.

CROCODILES

In the tropics, saltwater crocodiles ('salties') are a real danger. As well as living around the coast they are found in estuaries, creeks and rivers, sometimes a long way inland. Observe safety signs or ask locals whether an inviting waterhole or river is croc-free before plunging in – these precautions have been fatally ignored in the past.

INSECTS

For four to six months of the year you'll have to cope with those two banes of the Australian outdoors: the fly and the mosquito ('mozzie'). Flies aren't too bad in the cities but they get out of hand in the outback. In central Australia the flies emerge with the warmer spring weather (late August), particularly if there has been good winter rain, and last until the next frosts kill them off. Flies also tend to be bad in coastal areas. The humble fly net, which fits on a hat, is very effective (though utterly unfashionable). Widely available repellents such as Aerogard and Rid may also deter the little bastards, but don't count on it.

Mozzies are a problem in summer, especially near wetlands in tropical areas, and some species are carriers of viral infections. Try to keep your arms and legs covered as soon as the sun goes down and make liberal use of insect repellent.

For details of what ticks can get up to, see p808.

SNAKES

There are many venomous snakes in the Australian bush, the most common being the brown and tiger snakes, but few are aggressive – unless you're interfering with one, or have the misfortune to stand on one, it's extremely unlikely you'll be bitten. The golden rule if you see a snake is to do a Beatles and *let it be*.

For information on treating snake bites, see p809.

SPIDERS

The deadly funnel-web spider is found in NSW (including Sydney) and its bite is treated in the same way as a snake bite – with antivenin. Another eight-legged critter to stay away from is the black one with a distinctive red stripe on its body, called the redback spider for obvious reasons; for bites, apply ice and seek medical attention. The whitetail is a long, thin black spider with, you guessed it, a white tail, and has a fierce bite that can lead to local inflammation and ulceration. The disturbingly large huntsman spider, which often enters homes, is harmless, though seeing one for the first time can affect your blood pressure.

Bushfires & Blizzards

Bushfires are, unfortunately, a regular occurrence in Australia. In hot, dry and windy weather, be extremely careful with any naked flame – cigarette butts thrown out of car windows have started many a fire. On a total fire ban day it's forbidden even to use a camping stove in the open; the penalties are severe.

When a total fire ban is in place, bushwalkers should delay their trip until the weather improves. If you're out in the bush and you see smoke, even a long way away, take it seriously – bushfires move quickly and change direction with the wind. Go to the nearest open space, downhill if possible. A forested ridge, on the other hand, is the most dangerous place to be.

More bushwalkers actually die of cold than in bushfires. Even in summer, temperatures can drop below freezing at night in the mountain areas and the weather can change rapidly. Blizzards in the mountains of Tasmania, Victoria and NSW can occur at any time of the year, even January. Exposure in even moderately cool temperatures can sometimes result in hypothermia – for more information see p809.

Crime

Australia is a relatively safe place to visit but you should still take reasonable precautions. Make sure that you don't leave hotel rooms or cars unlocked, and don't leave your valuables unattended or visible through a car window. Sydney, the Gold Coast, Cairns and Byron Bay all get a dishonourable mention when it comes to theft, so keep a careful eye on your belongings.

Many pubs in Sydney and other major cities carry posted warnings about drugged drinks, after several reported cases of women accepting a drink from a stranger only to later fall unconscious and be sexually assaulted. Women are advised to refuse drinks offered by strangers in bars. If you're really worried, drink bottled alcohol rather than from a glass.

On the Road

Australian drivers are generally a courteous bunch, but risks are posed by speedsters and drink drivers. Potential dangers on the open road include animals, such as kangaroos, which can leap out in front of your vehicle (mainly at dusk); fatigue, caused by travelling long distances without the necessary breaks (stop for a rest or switch drivers every two hours); and excessive speed. Driving on dirt roads is also tricky if you're not used to them. For more information on such potential dangers see Road Conditions and Road Hazards, p484.

Swimming

Popular beaches are patrolled by surf lifesavers and patrolled areas are marked off by red-and-yellow flags. Even so, surf beaches can be dangerous places to swim. Undertows (or 'rips') are the main problem. If you find yourself being carried out by a rip, the important thing to do is just keep afloat; don't panic or try to swim against the rip, which will exhaust you. In most cases the current stops within a couple of hundred metres of the shore and you can then swim parallel to the shore for a short way to get out of the rip and make your way back to land.

A number of people are also paralysed every year by diving into waves in shallow water and hitting a sand bar; check the depth of the water before you leap.

DISABLED TRAVELLERS

Disability awareness in Australia is pretty high and getting higher. Many of Australia's key attractions provide access for those with limited mobility and a number of sites have also begun addressing the needs of visitors with visual or aural impairments; contact attractions in advance to confirm the facilities. Tour operators with accessible vehicles operate from most capital cities. Major airports and rail services have wheelchair access and other facilities for disabled travellers, while most taxi companies in major cities and towns have modified vehicles that take wheelchairs. Accommodation facilities are improving, but there are still far too many older (particularly 'historic') establishments where the required renovations haven't been done.

The best source of reliable, Australia-wide information is the **National Information Communication and Awareness Network** (Nican; ☎/TTY 02-6285 3713, TTY 1800 806 769; www.nican.com.au; 4/2 Phipps Cl, Deakin, ACT 2600). The website of the **Australian Tourist Commission** (www.australia.com) has downloadable information for people with disabilities – look under the 'Plan Your Trip' link, then 'Specific Travel Needs'. Another excellent resource is the **Disability Information & Resource Centre** (DIRC; ☎ 08-8236 0555, TTY 08-8223 7579; www.dircsa.org.au; 195 Gilles St, Adelaide, SA 5000). The publication *Easy Access Australia* (www.easyaccessaustralia.com.au) is available from various bookstores and provides details on easily accessible transport, accommodation and attraction options. Visit the **National Public Toilet Map** (www.toiletmap.gov.au) for details of toilets with disability access.

The **Carers Concession Card** (☎ 13 13 13, TTY 1800 652 660; www.qantas.com.au), accepted only by Qantas, entitles a disabled person and the carer travelling with them to a 50% discount on full economy fares; contact Nican for eligibility and an application form.

DRIVING LICENCE

You can generally use your home country's driving licence in Australia, as long as it's in English (if it's not, a certified translation must be carried) and shows your photograph for identification. Confusingly, some states prefer that you have an International Driving Permit (IDP), which must be supported by your home licence. It's easy enough to get an IDP – just go to your home country's automobile association and they issue it on the spot. The permits are valid for 12 months.

EMBASSIES & CONSULATES

See also p474 for information on getting a visa.

Embassies & Consulates in Australia

Addresses of major offices include the following. Look in the *Yellow Pages* (www.yellowpages.com.au) phone directories of the capital cities for a more complete listing. For the locations of these and other consulates, see the individual city maps.

Canada (www.dfait-maeci.gc.ca/australia) Canberra (Map p116; ☎ 02-6270 4000; Commonwealth Ave, Canberra, ACT 2600); Sydney (Map pp48-50; ☎ 02-9364 3000; 5th fl, 111 Harrington St, Sydney, NSW 2000)

France Canberra (Map p116; ☎ 02-6216 0100; www.ambafrance-au.org; 6 Perth Ave, Yarralumla, ACT 2600); Sydney (Map pp48-50; ☎ 02-9261 5779; www.consulfrance-sydney.org; 26th fl, St Martins Tower, 31 Market St, Sydney, NSW 2000)

Germany (www.germanembassy.org.au) Canberra (Map p116; ☎ 02-6270 1911; 119 Empire Circuit, Yarralumla, ACT 2600); Sydney (Map pp44-5; ☎ 02-9328 7733; 13 Trelawney St, Woollahra, NSW 2025); Melbourne (☎ 03-9864 6888; 480 Punt Rd, South Yarra, Vic 3141)

Ireland Canberra (Map p116; ☎ 02-6273 3022; irishemb@cyberone.com.au; 20 Arkana St, Yarralumla, ACT 2600); Sydney (Map pp48-50; ☎ 02-9231 6999; 30th fl, 400 George St, Sydney, NSW 2000)

Netherlands (www.netherlands.org.au) Canberra (Map p116; ☎ 02-6220 9400; 120 Empire Circuit, Yarralumla, ACT 2600); Sydney (Map pp44-5; ☎ 02-9387 6644; 23rd fl, Plaza Tower II, 500 Oxford St, Bondi Junction, NSW 2022)

New Zealand (www.nzembassy.com/australia) Canberra (Map p116; ☎ 02-6270 4211; Commonwealth Ave, Canberra, ACT 2600); Sydney (Map pp48-50; ☎ 02-8256 2000; 10th fl, 55 Hunter St, Sydney, NSW 2000)

UK (www.uk.emb.gov.au) Canberra (Map p116; ☎ 02-6270 6666; Commonwealth Ave, Yarralumla, ACT 2600); Sydney (Map pp48-50; ☎ 02-9247 7521; 16th fl, 1 Macquarie Pl, Sydney, NSW 2000); Melbourne (☎ 03-9652 1600; 17th fl, 90 Collins St, Melbourne, Vic 3000)

USA (canberra.usembassy.gov) Canberra (Map p116; ☎ 02-6214 5600; 21 Moonah Pl, Yarralumla, ACT 2600); Sydney (Map pp48-50; ☎ 02-9373 9200; 59th fl, 19-29 Martin Pl, Sydney, NSW 2000); Melbourne (☎ 03-9526 5900; 553 St Kilda Rd, Melbourne, Vic 3004)

It's important to realise what your own embassy – the embassy of the country of which you are a citizen – can and can't do to help you if you get into trouble. Generally speaking, it won't be much help in emergencies if the trouble you're in is even remotely your own fault. Don't forget that while in Australia, you are bound by Australian laws.

In genuine emergencies you might get some assistance, but only if other channels have been exhausted. For example, if you need to get home urgently, a free ticket is exceedingly unlikely – the embassy would expect you to have insurance. If you have all your money and documents stolen, it might assist with getting a new passport, but a loan for onward travel is out of the question.

Australian Embassies & Consulates Abroad

The website of the **Department of Foreign Affairs & Trade** (www.dfat.gov.au) provides a full listing of all Australian diplomatic missions overseas. They include:

Canada Ottawa (☎ 613-236 0841; www.ahc-ottawa.org; Suite 710, 50 O'Connor St, Ottawa, Ontario K1P 6L2) Also in Vancouver and Toronto.

France Paris (☎ 01-40 59 33 00; www.austgov.fr; 4 Rue Jean Rey, 75724 Cedex 15, Paris)

Germany Berlin (☎ 030-880 0880; www.australian-embassy.de; Wallstrasse 76-79, Berlin 10179) Also in Frankfurt.

Ireland Dublin (☎ 01-664 5300; www.australianembassy.ie; 2nd fl, Fitzwilton House, Wilton Terrace, Dublin 2)

Netherlands The Hague (☎ 070-310 82 00; www.australian-embassy.nl; Carnegielaan 4, The Hague 2517 KH)

New Zealand Wellington (☎ 04-473 6411; www.australia.org.nz; 72-78 Hobson St, Thorndon, Wellington); Auckland (☎ 09-303 2429; 7th fl, Price Waterhouse Coopers Bldg, 186-194 Quay St, Auckland)

UK London (☎ 020-7379 4334; www.australia.org.uk; Australia House, The Strand, London WC2B 4LA) Also in Edinburgh and Manchester.

USA Washington DC (☎ 202-797 3000; www.austemb.org; 1601 Massachusetts Ave NW, Washington DC 20036-2273) Also in Los Angeles, New York and other major cities.

FESTIVALS & EVENTS

Details of significant local festivals and events are provided in the state and territory chapters of this book. The following events, however, are celebrated throughout a particular region, state or even around the country.

January

Big Day Out (www.bigdayout.com) Huge open-air, big-name rock concert that spends a day each in Sydney, Melbourne, Adelaide, Perth and the Gold Coast.

February

Tropfest (www.tropfest.com) Selected entries to this short-film festival are aired simultaneously at locations in Sydney, Melbourne, Canberra, Brisbane, Hobart and Perth on the last Sunday in February.

March & April (around Easter)

Targa Tasmania (www.targa.org.au) Six-day rally for exotic cars that runs around the entire state, appropriating 2000km of road as it goes.

Ten Days on the Island (www.tendaysontheisland.org) Major biennial Tasmanian cultural festival. Held in odd-numbered years in venues around the state.

May

Sorry Day (www.journeyofhealing.com) On 26 May each year, the anniversary of the tabling in 1997 of the *Bringing Them Home* report, concerned Australians acknowledge the continuing pain and suffering of indigenous people affected by Australia's one-time child-removal practices and policies. Events are held in most cities countrywide.

July

Naidoc Week (www.atsic.gov.au) Communities across Australia celebrate the National Aboriginal and Islander Day of Celebration (inaugurated in 1957).

December & January

Sydney to Hobart Yacht Race (http://rolexsydneyhobart.com) Sydney Harbour is a fantastic sight as hundreds of boats farewell the competitors in the gruelling Sydney to Hobart Yacht Race.

GAY & LESBIAN TRAVELLERS

Australia is a popular destination for gay and lesbian travellers, with the so-called 'pink tourism' appeal of Sydney highlighted by the city's annual, world-famous and spectacular Sydney Gay and Lesbian Mardi Gras.

Certain areas are the focus of the gay and lesbian communities, among them **Cairns** and **Noosa** in Queensland; **Oxford St** and **King's Cross** in Sydney; the **Blue Mountains**, **Hunter Valley** and south coast in NSW; the Melbourne suburbs of **Prahran**, **St Kilda** and **Collingwood**; and the low-key WA capital **Perth**.

Major gay and lesbian events include the aforementioned **Sydney Gay and Lesbian Mardi Gras** (www.mardigras.org.au) in February and March, Melbourne's **Midsumma Festival** (www.midsumma.org.au) from mid-January to mid-February, and Adelaide's **Feast** (www.feast.org.au) in November.

See also Gay & Lesbian Sydney (p62), Out in Queer Melbourne (p246) and Gay & Lesbian Brisbane (p146).

In general Australians are open-minded about homosexuality, but the further into the country you get, the more likely you are to run into overt homophobia. Having said that, you will find active gay communities in places such as Alice Springs and Darwin. Even Tasmania, once a bastion of sexual conservatism, now actively encourages gay and lesbian tourism. Homosexual acts are legal in all states but the age of consent between males varies – in the Australian Capital Territory, Victoria, NSW and WA it's 16, in SA and Tasmania it's 17, and in the NT and Queensland it's 18.

Publications & Contacts

All major cities have gay newspapers, available from gay and lesbian venues. National gay lifestyle magazines include *DNA*, *Lesbians on the Loose* and the bi-monthly *Blue*. There's also the WA-focused *Women Out West*. Perth has the free monthly *Shout* and Adelaide has the fortnightly *Blaze*.

The website of **Gay and Lesbian Tourism Australia** (GALTA; www.galta.com.au) has general information, though you need to become a member to receive the full benefits. Other helpful websites include **Gay Australia** (www.gayaustralia.com.au) and the Sydney-based **Pinkboard** (www.pinkboard.com.au). Gay telephone counselling services (you'll find them in most capital cities) are another useful resource.

HOLIDAYS

Public Holidays

The following is a list of the main national public holidays. There are also various state, territory and local (ie town/city) holidays – check with tourist offices for exact dates.

New Year's Day 1 January
Australia Day 26 January
Easter (Good Friday to Easter Monday inclusive) March/April
Anzac Day 25 April
Queen's Birthday (except WA) Second Monday in June
Queen's Birthday (WA) Last Monday in September
Christmas Day 25 December
Boxing Day 26 December

School Holidays

The Christmas holiday season, from mid-December to late January, is part of the summer school holidays – it's the time you are most likely to find transport and accommodation booked out, and long, restless queues at tourist attractions. There are three shorter school-holiday periods during the year, but they vary by a week or two from state to state. They fall roughly from early to mid-April, late June to mid-July, and late September to early October.

INSURANCE

Don't underestimate the importance of a good travel-insurance policy that covers theft, loss and medical problems – nothing is guaranteed to ruin your overseas adventure quicker than an accident or having essential belongings stolen. Some policies specifically exclude 'dangerous activities' such as scuba diving, parasailing, bungy jumping, motorcycling, skiing and even bushwalking. If you plan on doing any of these things, make sure the policy you choose fully covers you for your activity of choice.

You may prefer a policy that pays doctors or hospitals direct rather than making you pay on the spot and claim later. If you have to claim later make sure you keep all documentation. Check that the policy covers ambulances and emergency medical evacuations by air.

For information on insurance matters relating to cars that are bought or rented, see p482.

INTERNET ACCESS

Email and Internet addicts will find it fairly easy to get connected throughout Australia. The local 'cybercafés' aren't as futuristic as their name implies, and connection speeds and prices can vary significantly, but they all offer straightforward Internet access. Most public libraries also have free online access, but generally there are a limited number of terminals and these are provided for research needs, not for travellers to check their emails. You may have to join the library to use the service – head for a cybercafé first. Access costs range from A$3 an hour in cut-throat King's Cross in Sydney to A$10 an hour in more remote locations. The average is about A$6 an hour, usually with a minimum of 10 minutes access. Most youth hostels and backpacker places can hook you up, as can many hotels and caravan parks. In remote areas of WA, SA and NSW, telecentres provide Internet access, while Tasmania has set up access centres in numerous local libraries and schools.

Free web-based email services include **ekit** (www.lonelyplanet.ekit.com), **Yahoo** (www.yahoo.com), **MSN Hotmail** (www.hotmail.com) and **Excite** (www.excite.com).

INTERNET RESOURCES

Australian Government (www.gov.au) Gateway to all federal, state, territory and local government sites.

Australian Newspapers Online (www.nla.gov.au/npapers) National Library–maintained listing of Australian newspaper websites.

Australian Tourist Commission (www.australia.com) Official, federal government–run tourism site with nationwide info for travellers.

Guide to Australia (www.csu.edu.au/australia) Links to sundry domestic sites focusing on attractions, culture, the environment, transport etc.

Lonely Planet (www.lonelyplanet.com) Get started with summaries on Australia, links to Australia-related sites and travellers trading information and tall stories on the Thorn Tree.

TNT (www.tntmagazine.com/au) Website for an independent traveller-focussed magazine, with employment, accommodation and vehicle-for-sale classifieds.

LEGAL MATTERS

First offenders caught with small amounts of illegal drugs are likely to receive a fine rather than go to jail, but the recording of a conviction against you may affect your visa status. Speaking of which, if you stay in Australia beyond the life of your visa, you will officially be an 'overstayer' and could face detention and expulsion, and then be prevented from returning to Australia for up to three years.

Police have the power to stop your car and ask to see your licence (you're required to carry it), check your vehicle for roadworthiness, and also to insist that you take a breath test for alcohol – drink driving-offences are taken very seriously here.

If you are arrested, it's your right to telephone a friend, relative or lawyer before any formal questioning begins. Legal Aid is available only in serious cases and only to the truly needy – for links to Legal Aid offices see **National Legal Aid** (www.nla.aust.net.au). However, many solicitors do not charge for an initial consultation.

COMING OF AGE

- You can drive when you're 17, and generally must be 21 to hire a car (see p481).
- The legal age for voting is 18.
- The homosexual age of consent varies from state to state (see p468); for heterosexuals it's 16 in all states and territories except SA and Tasmania, where it's 17.
- The legal drinking age is 18.

MAPS

Lonely Planet publishes handy fold-out city maps of *Sydney*, *Melbourne* and *Brisbane & Gold Coast*, as well as the highly detailed *Australia Road Atlas*. Local tourist offices usually supply free maps, though the quality varies.

If you plan on bushwalking or taking part in other outdoor activities for which large-scale maps are an essential item, browse the topographic sheets published by **Geoscience Australia** (☎ 1800 800 173, 02-6249 9111; www.ga.gov.au; cnr Jerrabomberra Ave & Hindmarsh Dr, Symonston, ACT 2609). The more popular sheets are usually available over the counter at map shops or places selling specialist bushwalking gear and outdoor equipment.

MEDIA

As far as the newspapers go, you can leaf through the daily *Sydney Morning Herald*, Melbourne's *Age* or the national *Australian* broadsheet. Tabloid titillation can be found in the *Daily Telegraph* (Sydney), *Herald Sun* (Melbourne) and *Courier Mail* (Brisbane) papers.

The advertising-free, government-funded national TV and radio network is the Australian Broadcasting Corporation (ABC). Triple J is the ABC's youth FM radio station, which plays a lot of local and international non-mainstream music. **ABC Online** (www.abc.net.au) lists programming and frequencies.

Besides ABC TV, there are three commercial TV stations – the Seven, Nine and Ten networks – and SBS, which is a government-sponsored multicultural station. Many of the pubs and clubs have big-screen TVs showing sports beamed in via satellite Pay TV stations.

MONEY

ATMs & Eftpos

Many Australian banks have 24-hour automated teller machines (ATMs) attached to them. But don't expect to find ATMs *everywhere* (you certainly shouldn't count on finding them off the beaten track or in very small towns). Most ATMs accept cards issued by other banks, and are linked to international networks.

Eftpos (Electronic Funds Transfer at Point Of Sale) is a convenient, widespread service that lets you use your bank card (credit or debit) to pay direct for services or purchases, and often withdraw cash as well. Eftpos is available practically everywhere these days, even in outback roadhouses where it's a long way between banks. As with an ATM, you need to know your Personal Identification Number (PIN) to use it.

Bank Accounts

If you're planning to stay in Australia a while (on a working-holiday visa for instance) it makes sense to open a local bank account. This is easy for overseas visitors provided it's done within six weeks of arrival. You simply present your passport and provide the bank with a postal address and they'll open the account and send you an ATM card.

After six weeks it's much more complicated. A points system operates and you need a minimum of 100 points before you can earn the privilege of letting the bank take your money. Passports or birth certificates are worth 70 points; an international driving licence with photo earns you 40 points; and minor IDs, such as credit cards, get you 25 points. You must have at least one ID with a photograph. Once the account is open, you should be able to have money transferred across from your home account (for a fee, of course).

If you don't have an Australian Tax File Number (TFN), interest earned from your funds will be taxed at a rate of up to 47%. See p475 for tax-related information.

Credit & Debit Cards

Perhaps the best way to carry most of your money is in the form of a plastic card. Credit cards such as Visa and MasterCard are widely accepted by many hostels, restaurants and tour companies, and are essential (in lieu of a large deposit) if you want to hire a car.

They can also be used to get cash advances at banks and from many ATMs, depending on the card, but be aware that these incur immediate interest. Charge cards such as Diners Club and American Express (Amex) are not as widely accepted.

The obvious danger with credit cards is maxing out your limit. A safer option is a debit card with which you can draw money directly from your home bank account using ATMs, banks or Eftpos machines around the country. Any card connected to the international banking network – Cirrus, Maestro, Plus and Eurocard – should work, provided you know your PIN. Fees for using your card at a foreign bank or ATM vary depending on your home bank; ask before you leave.

The most flexible option is to carry both a credit and a debit card.

Currency

Australia's currency is the Australian dollar; made up of 100 cents. There are 5c, 10c, 20c, 50c, $1 and $2 coins, and $5, $10, $20, $50 and $100 notes. Although the smallest coin in circulation is 5c, prices are often still marked in single cents and then rounded to the nearest 5c when you come to pay.

Unless otherwise stated, all prices given in the Australian chapters of this book (including the Australia Directory and Australia Transport chapters) are in Australian dollars (A$). For an idea of the money required to travel Down Under, see p18.

Exchanging Money

Changing your foreign currency or travellers cheques is usually no problem at banks throughout Australia or at licensed moneychangers such as Thomas Cook or Amex in the major cities.

This table shows currency rates at the time this book went to press. For the latest exchange rates see www.oanda.com/convert/classic.

Country	Unit	A$
Canada	C$1	1.10
euro zone	€1	1.75
Indonesia	10,000Rp	1.58
Japan	¥100	1.29
New Zealand	NZ$1	0.9
UK	£1	2.55
USA	US$1	1.42

Tipping

It's customary but by no means obligatory to tip in restaurants and cafés if the service warrants it – a gratuity of between 5% to 10% of the bill is the norm.

Travellers Cheques

The ubiquity and convenience of internationally linked credit- and debit-card facilities across Australia means that travellers cheques are not heavily relied upon.

Amex, Thomas Cook and other well-known international brands of travellers cheques are easily exchanged. Transactions at their bureaux are commission-free if you use their cheques, while local banks charge hefty fees (often in excess of A$7 per transaction) for the same service. You need to present your passport for identification when cashing travellers cheques.

POST

All post offices will hold mail for visitors. You need to provide some form of identification (such as a passport) to collect mail. You can also have mail sent to you at city Amex offices if you have an Amex card or travellers cheques.

See p463 for post-office opening times.

Letters

It costs A$0.50 to send a standard letter or postcard within the country. **Australia Post** (www.auspost.com.au) has divided international destinations into two regions: Asia-Pacific and Rest of the World; airmail letters up to 50g cost A$1.10 and A$1.65, respectively. The cost of sending a postcard (up to 20g) anywhere is A$1 and an aerogram to any country is A$0.85.

Parcels

There are five international parcel zones. Sea mail is only available to the USA and Canada (Zone 4) and to Europe and South Africa (Zone 5); it's cheap but can take forever. A 1/1.5/2kg parcel costs A$15/21/27 to both zones. Each 500g over 2kg costs A$3 extra with a maximum of 20kg. Economy airmail rates are A$18/26/34 to Zone 4 and A$20/29/38 to Zone 5. To all other destinations, including New Zealand (Zone NZ), only airmail is available. A 1/1.5/2kg parcel sent by 'economy air' to New Zealand costs A$12/17/22, while parcels to any of the Asia-Pacific nations (Zones 1, 2 and 3) will cost A$15/21/27.

STUDYING

Australia has a sizeable population of international students who temporarily settle in the country to undertake English-language courses or degrees at tertiary institutions. During semester breaks or even after their courses are completed, many of these students take the opportunity to swap academic texts for backpacks and head off to explore the Australian landscape.

If you're considering further studies in Australia, visit the federal government's **Study in Australia** (www.studyinaustralia.gov.au) website for information on all facets of advanced education, as well as tips on living and travelling here. Once you've enrolled, you'll find that most institutions have international student advisers who can supply info on how to make the most of your travel breaks and may even be able to put you in touch with other foreign students who are willing to share their recent experiences on the road. Some tour and travel companies specifically cater to international students and will advertise their services on campus.

TELEPHONE

The two main telecommunication companies are the mostly government-owned **Telstra** (www.telstra.com.au) and the fully private **Optus** (www.optus.com.au). Both are also major players in the mobile (cell) market, along with **Vodafone** (www.vodafone.com.au) – other mobile operators include **AAPT** (www.aapt.com.au) and **Orange** (www.orange.net.au).

Domestic Calls

Local calls from private phones cost A$0.18 to A$0.30 while local calls from public phones cost A$0.40; both involve unlimited talk time. Calls to mobile phones attract higher rates and are timed. Blue phones or gold phones that you sometimes find in pubs or other businesses usually cost a minimum of A$0.50 for a local call.

For long-distance calls, Australia uses four STD (Subscriber Trunk Dialling) area codes. STD calls can be made from virtually any public phone and are cheaper during off-peak hours, generally between 7pm and 7am. Long-distance calls (ie to more than about 50km away) within these areas are charged at long-distance rates, even though they have the same area code. The main area codes are:

State/Territory	Area code
ACT	☎ 02
NSW	☎ 02
NT	☎ 08
Queensland	☎ 07
SA	☎ 08
Tasmania	☎ 03
Victoria	☎ 03
WA	☎ 08

Area-code boundaries don't always coincide with state borders – NSW, for example, uses each of the four neighbouring codes. See the individual town entries for details.

Numbers starting with ☎ 190 are usually recorded information services, charged at anything from A$0.35 to A$5 or more per minute (more from mobiles and payphones). To make a reverse-charge (collect) call from any public or private phone, dial ☎ 1800 REVERSE (738 3773), or ☎ 12 550.

Toll-free numbers (prefix ☎ 1800) can be called free of charge from almost anywhere in the country – they may not be accessible from certain areas or from mobile phones. Calls to numbers beginning with ☎ 13 or ☎ 1300 are charged at the rate of a local call – the numbers can usually be dialled Australia-wide, but may be applicable only to a specific state or STD district. Telephone numbers beginning with ☎ 1800, ☎ 13 or ☎ 1300 cannot be dialled from outside Australia.

International Calls

Most payphones allow ISD (International Subscriber Dialling) calls, the cost and international dialling code of which will vary depending on which provider you're using. It's worth shopping around for special deals.

The **Country Direct service** (☎ 1800 801 800) connects callers in Australia with operators in nearly 60 countries to make reverse-charge (collect) or credit-card calls.

When calling overseas you need to dial the international access code from Australia (☎ 0011 or ☎ 0018), the country code and the area code (without the initial 0). So for a London number you'd dial ☎ 0011-44-171, then the number. Also, certain operators have you dial a special code to access their service.

Country	International country code
France	☎ 33
Germany	☎ 49
Ireland	☎ 353
Netherlands	☎ 31
New Zealand	☎ 64
UK	☎ 44
USA & Canada	☎ 1

If dialling Australia from overseas, the country code is ☎ 61 and you need to drop the 0 (zero) in the state/territory area codes.

Mobile Phones

Local numbers with the prefixes ☎ 04xx or ☎ 04xxx belong to mobile phones. Australia's two mobile networks (digital GSM and digital CDMA) service more than 90% of the population but leave vast tracts of the country uncovered. The east coast, southeast and southwest get good reception, but elsewhere (apart from major towns) it's haphazard or nonexistent.

Australia's digital network is compatible with GSM 900 and 1800 (used in Europe). It's easy and cheap enough to get connected short-term as the main service providers all have prepaid mobile systems. Buy a starter kit, which may include a phone or, if you have your own phone, a SIM card (around A$15) and a prepaid charge card. The calls tend to be more expensive than with standard contracts, but there are no connection fees or line-rental charges and you can buy the recharge cards at convenience stores and newsagents. Don't forget to shop around.

Phonecards

A variety of phonecards can be bought at newsagents, hostels and post offices for a fixed dollar value (usually A$10, A$20 etc) and can be used with any public or private phone by dialling a toll-free access number and then the PIN number on the card. Some public phones also accept credit cards.

The **ekit** (www.lonelyplanet.ekit.com) global communication service provides low-cost international calls – for local calls you're usually better off with a local phonecard. ekit also offers free messaging services and email, plus travel information and an online travel vault where you can securely store details of all important documents. You can join online, where you'll find local-access numbers for the 24-hour customer-service centre. Once you've joined, always check the ekit website for the latest access numbers for each country. Current dial-in numbers for Australia are Sydney ☎ 02-8208 3000, Melbourne ☎ 03-9909 0888, Brisbane ☎ 07-3102 8880 and elsewhere ☎ 1800 114 478 (toll free).

TIME

Australia is divided into three time zones: the Western Standard Time zone (GMT/UTC plus eight hours) covers WA; Central Standard Time (plus 9½ hours) covers the NT and SA; and Eastern Standard Time (plus 10 hours) covers Tasmania, Victoria, NSW, the ACT and Queensland. There are minor exceptions – for instance, Broken Hill (NSW) is on Central time.

'Daylight saving' (for which clocks are put forward an hour) operates in most states during the warmer months (October to March). However, things can get pretty confusing, with WA, the NT and Queensland staying on standard time, while in Tasmania daylight saving starts a month earlier than in SA, Victoria, the ACT and NSW.

For international timing, see the map of world time zones (p811).

TOURIST INFORMATION

Tourist information is provided in Australia by various regional and local offices, details of which are given in the relevant city and town sections throughout this book.

The **Australian Tourist Commission** (ATC; ☎ 1300 361 650, 02-9360 1111; www.australia.com; 4th fl, 80 William St, Woolloomooloo, NSW 2011) is the government body charged with improving foreign tourist relations and has a website with information in nine languages (including French and German).

Countries with ATC offices include:

Germany (☎ 069-2740 0622; Neue Mainzer Strasse 22, Frankfurt D 60311)

New Zealand (☎ 09-915 2826; 3rd fl, 125 The Strand, Parnell, Auckland)

UK (☎ 020-8780 2229; Gemini House, 10-18 Putney Hill, London SW15 6AA)

USA (☎ 310-229 4870; Suite 1920, 2049 Century Park East, Los Angeles, CA 90067)

VISAS

All visitors to Australia need a visa – only New Zealand nationals are exempt, and even they receive a 'special category' visa on arrival. Application forms for the several types of visa are available from Australian diplomatic missions overseas, travel agents or the website of the **Department of Immigration & Multicultural & Indigenous Affairs** (☎ 13 18 81; www.immi.gov.au).

Passport holders of some 33 countries, including the USA, Canada, Japan, the UK and most other Western European countries, can get an Electronic Travel Authority (ETA). The ETA replaces the usual passport stamp and is available through travel agents or overseas airlines; travel agents can charge up to US$15 for this service. You can also apply for the ETA online (www.eta.immi.gov.au), which attracts a nonrefundable service charge of A$20.

If you're from a country not covered by the ETA, or you want to stay longer than three months, you'll need to apply for a tourist visa. Standard visas cost A$65 and allow one entry (in some cases multiple entries) and stays of up to three months, and are valid for use within 12 months of issue. A long-stay tourist visa (also A$65) can allow a visit of up to a year.

Visitors are allowed a maximum stay of 12 months, including extensions. Visa extensions are made through the Department of Immigration & Multicultural & Indigenous Affairs and it's best to apply at least two or three weeks before your visa expires. The application fee is A$165 and is nonrefundable.

Single visitors between 18 and 30 years of age from 16 countries, including Canada, France, Germany, Ireland, Japan, the Netherlands and the UK are eligible for a Working Holiday (WH) visa, which allows you to visit for up to 12 months and gain casual employment. The emphasis is on casual (not full-time) employment, so you are only able to work for any one employer for a maximum of three months. Apply for this visa online (www.immi.gov.au/e_visa/visit.htm) or at Australian diplomatic missions abroad – you can't change from a tourist visa to a WH visa once you're in Australia. Applications (A$165) can be made up to a year in advance and are conditional on having a return air ticket or enough money for a return or onward fare. For employment possibilities, see below, and visit the **Lonely Planet** (www.lonelyplanet.com) website for up-to-date visa information.

VOLUNTEERING

Several organisations can arrange fulfilling volunteer work in Australia.

Australian Volunteers International (AVI; ☎ 08-8941 9743; www.ozvol.org.au; Darwin) places skilled volunteers into Aboriginal communities in northern and central Australia. Most of the placements are paid contracts for a minimum of a year and you'll need a work visa. There are also occasional short-term placements and unskilled jobs.

The nonprofit **Conservation Volunteers Australia** (☎ 1800 032 501, 03-5333 1483; www.conservationvolunteers.com.au; 13-15 Lydiard St Nth, Ballarat, Vic 3350) organises practical conservation projects such as tree planting, walking-track construction and wildlife surveys that enable you to see some interesting parts of the country.

Most projects are either for a weekend or a week and all food, transport and accommodation is supplied in return for a small cost-covering contribution (A$30 per day). Many travellers join a Conservation Experience package of four/six weeks (A$815/1200). Both packages comprise several different projects; additional weeks can be added for A$200 per each seven-day block.

The concept behind the well-established **Willing Workers on Organic Farms** (WWOOF; ☎ 03-5155 0218; www.wwoof.com.au; Mt Murrindal Co-op, W Tree, Vic 3885) is that you do several hours of work each day on a farm in return for bed and board. Almost all places have a minimum stay of two nights. The farms are supposed to be organic (including permaculture and biodynamic growing), but some places aren't even farms – you might help out at a pottery or do the books at a seed wholesaler. To join, send A$50/60 for singles/couples to Wwoof, or join online. Wwoof will send you a membership number and a booklet listing participating enterprises.

WORKING

New Zealanders can work in Australia without having to apply for a special visa or permit, but other short-term visitors can only work in Australia if they have a Working Holiday visa (WH). Major tourist centres like Alice Springs, resort towns along the Queensland coast and the ski fields of Victoria and NSW are all good prospects for casual work during peak seasons.

Seasonal fruit-picking (harvesting) relies on casual labour and there is something to be picked, pruned or farmed somewhere in Australia all year round. It's hard work that involves early- morning starts, and you're usually paid by how much you pick (per bin, bucket or whatever) – expect to earn A$50 to A$60 a day to start with, more when you get quicker at it. Some work, such as pruning or sorting, is paid by the hour at around A$12. **Harvest Hotline** (☎ 1300 720 126) can connect you with the relevant fruit-picking regions.

Other options for casual employment include factory work, labouring, bar work, waiting on tables, nanny work and working as a station hand (jackaroo/jillaroo). People with computer, secretarial, nursing and teaching skills can find work temping in the major cities by registering with a relevant agency. Be prepared to hunt around for worthwhile opportunities, and make your own wellbeing the priority if you're subjected to unsatisfactory conditions.

Resources

Australian Job Search (www.jobsearch.gov.au) is a Commonwealth government agency with plenty of jobs on offer, including a 'Harvest Trail' for backpackers to follow around the country. **My Career** (www.mycareer.com.au) is one of the country's busiest employment websites.

Backpacker accommodation, magazines and newspapers are good resources for local work opportunities. **Workabout Australia** (www.workaboutaustralia.com.au), a book by Barry Brebner, details seasonal work opportunities.

Tax & Superannuation

If you have a WH visa, you should apply for a TFN (Tax File Number). Without it, tax will be deducted from any wages you receive at the maximum rate (around 47%). Apply for a TFN online via the **ATO** (www.ato.gov.au); it takes about four weeks to issue.

Even with a TFN, nonresidents (including WH visa holders) pay a higher rate of tax than Australian residents, especially those on a low income. There's no tax-free threshold, so you pay tax on every dollar you earn, starting at 29% on an annual income of up to A$21,600 (A$415 per week).

If tax is deducted as you earn, it's unlikely you'll be entitled to a tax refund when you leave Australia. However, if you have had tax deducted at 47% because you didn't submit a TFN, you will be entitled to a partial refund of tax paid. To get the refund you must lodge a tax return with the **Australian Taxation Office** (ATO; ☎ 13 28 61; www.ato.gov.au).

To lodge a tax return, you need a TFN and also a Group Certificate (an official summary of your earnings and tax payments) provided by your employer – give them written advice at least 14 days in advance that you want the certificate on your last day at work, otherwise you may have to wait until the end of the financial year (30 June).

As part of the government's compulsory superannuation scheme, if you're earning more than A$450 per calendar month your employer must make contributions on your behalf to a retirement or superannuation (super) fund. These contributions are at the rate of 9% of your wage, and the money must remain in the fund until you reach 'preservation age', currently 60 years. Find out the latest from the ATO and the relevant super fund.

Australia Transport

CONTENTS

Some of the world's more diminutive nations can be traversed on the ground in a matter of hours. The exploration of a country the size of Australia obviously takes a teensy bit more effort, both in getting here in the first place and in deciding on some cost-effective yet reliable means of transportation to get you around.

Most travellers arriving in Australia will find themselves dragging their backpacks off carousels at international terminals in Sydney and Melbourne. For detailed information on international flights arriving in and departing from the country, including flights across the Tasman Sea to New Zealand, ticket options and a full list of Australia's international airports, see the Australia & New Zealand Transport chapter (p799).

GETTING AROUND

AIR

Time pressures combined with the vastness of the Australian continent may lead you to consider taking to the skies at some point in your trip. Nicotine fiends should note that all domestic flights are nonsmoking.

Airlines in Australia

Qantas is the country's chief domestic airline, represented at the budget end of the national air-travel market by its subsidiary Jetstar. Another highly competitive carrier that flies all over Australia is Virgin Blue.

Australia also has numerous smaller operators flying regional routes. In many places, such as remote outback destinations or islands, these are the only viable transport option. Many of these airlines operate as subsidiaries or commercial partners of Qantas.

Regional airlines include the following:

Airnorth (☎ 08-8920 4001; www.airnorth.com.au) Flies across northern Australia, taking in destinations such as Darwin, Alice Springs, Katherine and Broome; also flies across the Timor Sea to Dili (East Timor) and Kupang (West Timor).

Alliance Airlines (☎ 1300 130 092; www.allianceairlines.com.au) Touches down in Townsville, Cairns, Brisbane, Norfolk Island and Sydney.

Australian Airlines (☎ 1300 799 798; www.australianairlines.com.au) This Qantas subsidiary flies between Cairns and the Gold Coast; Sydney and Melbourne.

Jetstar (☎ 13 15 38; www.jetstar.com.au) A budget-oriented Qantas subsidiary flying to Brisbane, Sydney and Melbourne, and other east-coast destinations such as the Gold Coast and Cairns, as well as Hobart and Launceston in Tasmania.

Macair (☎ 13 13 13; www.macair.com.au) Commercially partnered with Qantas, this Townsville-based airline flies throughout western and northern Queensland (Qld).

O'Connor (☎ 13 13 13, 08-8723 0666; www.oconnor-airlines.com.au) Another Qantas partner, flying between Melbourne, Adelaide, Mildura, Mount Gambier and Whyalla.

Qantas (☎ 13 13 13; www.qantas.com.au) Qantas is the chief domestic airline.

QantasLink (☎ 13 13 13; www.qantas.com.au) Flying across Australia under this Qantas subsidiary brand is a collective of regional airlines that includes Eastern Australia Airlines and Sunstate Airlines.

Regional Express (Rex; ☎ 13 17 13; www.regionalexpress.com.au) Flies to Sydney, Melbourne, Adelaide, Canberra, Devonport and around 25 other destinations in New South Wales (NSW), Victoria, South Australia (SA) and Tasmania.

Skywest (☎ 1300 66 00 88; www.skywest.com.au) Flies from Perth to many western towns, including Albany, Esperance, Exmouth, Karratha, Port Hedland, Carnarvon, Kalgoorlie and Broome, plus Darwin up north.

Virgin Blue (☎ 13 67 89; www.virginblue.com.au) Highly competitive, Virgin Blue flies all over Australia; Virgin fares are cheaper if booked online (A$10 less per one-way ticket).

DEPARTURE TAX

You must pay a A$38 departure tax when leaving Australia. This tax is included in the price of airline tickets.

> **CHECK THOSE FARES, MATE**
> The information in this chapter is particularly vulnerable to change. Check airline websites for current fares and routes. Prices quoted throughout this book are low-end starting fares at the time of research.

Air Passes

With discounting being the norm these days, air passes are generally not great value. Qantas' **Boomerang Pass** (☎ 13 13 13) can only be purchased overseas and involves buying coupons for either short-haul flights (up to 1200km, eg Hobart to Melbourne) from A$175 one way, or multizone sectors (including NZ and the Pacific) from A$330. You must purchase a minimum of two coupons before you arrive in Australia, and once here you can buy more.

Regional Express (Rex) has a **Rex Backpacker** (☎ 13 17 13) scheme, where international travellers clutching either a VIP, YHA, ISIC or IYTC card (Australian residents aren't eligible) pay for unlimited travel (one month/two months A$500/900) on the airline – note that where flights are heavily booked, seats will not always be guaranteed.

BICYCLE

It's not that uncommon for intrepid cyclists to pedal their way around much (and in some cases all) of Australia. There are literally thousands of kilometres of good country roads where you can wear out your chain wheels. Also, 'mountainous' is not an adjective that applies to this country – instead, there's lots of flat countryside and gently rolling hills.

Bicycle helmets are compulsory in all states and territories, as are white front lights and red rear lights for riding at night.

If you are bringing in your own bike, check with your airline for costs and the degree of dismantling and packing required. Within Australia, bus companies require that you dismantle your bike, and some don't guarantee that it will travel with you on the same bus. On trains, supervise the loading, if possible tie your bike upright, and check for possible restrictions: most intercity trains will only carry two to three boxed bikes per service.

Eastern Australia was settled on the principle of not having more than a day's horse ride between pubs, so it's possible to plan even ultra long routes and still get a shower at the end of each day. Most riders carry camping equipment but, on the east coast at least, it's feasible to travel from town to town staying in hostels, hotels or caravan parks.

You can get by with standard road maps but, as you'll probably want to avoid both the highways and the low-grade unsealed roads, the government series is best. The 1:250,000 scale is the most suitable, though you'll need a lot of maps if you're going a long way. The next scale up, 1:1,000,000, is adequate and is widely available in speciality map shops.

Carry plenty of water to avoid becoming dehydrated. Cycling in the summer heat can be made more endurable by wearing a helmet with a peak (or a cap under your helmet), using plenty of sunscreen, not cycling in the middle of the day, and drinking lots of water (not soft drinks). It can get very cold in the mountains, so pack appropriate clothing. In the south, beware the blistering hot northerlies that can make a north-bound cyclist's life hell in summer. The southeast trade winds begin to blow in April, when you can have (theoretically at least) tail winds all the way to Darwin.

Travel in the Outback needs to be properly planned, with the availability of drinking water the main concern – those isolated water sources (bores, tanks, creeks and the like) shown on your map may be dry or the water may be undrinkable, so you can't depend entirely on them. Also make sure you've got the necessary spare parts and bike-repair knowledge. Check with locals if you're heading into remote areas, and let someone know where you're headed before setting off.

Information

The **Bicycle Federation of Australia** (☎ 02-6249 6761; www.bfa.asn.au) is the national cycling body. Each state and territory has a touring organisation that can also help with cycling information and put you in touch with touring clubs.

Bicycle New South Wales (☎ 02-9281 4099; www.bicyclensw.org.au)
Bicycle Queensland (☎ 07-3844 1144; www.bq.org.au)
Bicycle SA (☎ 08-8232 2644; www.bikesa.asn.au)
Bicycle Tasmania (www.biketas.org.au)
Bicycle Transportation Alliance (☎ 08-9420 7210; www.multiline.com.au/~bta/) In Western Australia (WA).

Bicycle Victoria (☎ 03-8636 8888; www.bv.com.au)
Northern Territory Cycling Association (☎ 08-8932 2869; www.nt.cycling.org.au)
Pedal Power ACT (☎ 02-6248 7995; www.pedalpower.org.au)

See Lonely Planet's *Cycling Australia* for other useful contacts and popular routes. Also check out www.bicycles.net.au.

Purchase

If you arrive in Australia without a set of wheels and want to buy a new road cycle or mountain bike that won't leave a trail of worn-out or busted metal parts once it leaves the city limits, your starting point (and we mean your absolute bottom-level starting point) is A$400 to A$500. To set yourself up with a new bike, plus all the requisite on-the-road equipment such as panniers, helmet etc, your starting point becomes A$1500 to A$2000. Second-hand bikes are worth checking out in the cities, as are the post-Christmas sales and midyear stocktakes, when newish cycles can be heavily discounted.

Your best bet for reselling your bike is via the **Trading Post** (www.tradingpost.com.au), which is distributed in newspaper form in urban centres around Australia, and which also has a busy online trading site.

BOAT

There's a hell of a lot of water around Australia but unless you're fortunate enough to hook up with a yacht, it's not a feasible way of getting around. The only regular domestic passenger services of note are run by **TT-Line** (☎ 1800 634 906; www.spiritoftasmania.com.au), which dispatches three high-speed, vehicle-carrying ferries – *Spirit of Tasmania I, II* & *III* – between both Sydney and Melbourne and Devonport. See p318 for more details.

BUS

Australia's extensive bus network is a relatively cheap and reliable way to get around, though it can be a tedious form of transport at times and requires planning if you intend to do more than straightforward city-to-city trips. Most buses are equipped with air-conditioning, toilets and videos, and all are smoke-free zones. The smallest towns eschew formal bus terminals for a single drop-off/pick-up point, usually outside a post office, newsagent or shop.

It may look like there are two national bus networks, **McCafferty's** (☎ 13 14 99; www.mccaffertys.com.au) and **Greyhound Pioneer** (☎ 13 20 30; www.greyhound.com.au), but McCafferty's took over Greyhound a few years ago, making the tickets, terminals and passes of both companies interchangeable. Despite this, both brand names continue to be used, which is why we refer to 'McCafferty's/Greyhound' throughout this guidebook. Fares purchased online are roughly 5% cheaper than over-the-counter tickets.

Small regional operators running key routes or covering a lot of ground include the following:

Firefly Express (☎ 1300 730 740, 03-8318 0318; www.fireflyexpress.com.au) Runs between Sydney, Melbourne and Adelaide.
Integrity Coach Lines (☎ 1800 226 339, 08-9226 1339) Heads north from Perth up to Exmouth and Port Hedland.
Premier Motor Service (☎ 13 34 10; www.premierms.com.au) Runs along the east coast between Cairns and Melbourne.
Premier Stateliner (☎ 08-8415 5555; www.premierstateliner.com.au) Services towns around SA.
Redline Coaches (☎ 1300 360 000; www.tasredline.com.au) Services Tasmania's northern and eastern coasts.
TassieLink (☎ 1300 300 520, 03-6271 7320; www.tassielink.com.au) Criss-crosses Tasmania, with extra summer links to bushwalking locales.
Transwa (☎ 1300 662 205; www.transwa.wa.gov.au) Hauls itself around the southern half of WA.
V/Line (☎ 13 61 96; www.vline.vic.gov.au) Runs to most major towns and cities in Victoria.

Backpacker Buses

While the companies offering transport options for budget travellers in various parts of Australia are pretty much organised-tour operators, they do also get you from A to B (sometimes with hop-on, hop-off services) and so can be a cost-effective alternative to the big bus companies. The buses are usually smaller, you'll meet lots of other travellers, and the drivers sometimes double as tour guides; conversely, some travellers find the tour-group mentality and inherent limitations don't suit them. Discounts are usually given to card-carrying students and members of hostel organisations (see p459).

Adventure Tours Australia (☎ 1300 654 604, 08-8309 2277; www.adventuretours.com.au) does budget tours in all states except for Victoria and NSW. It also runs a hop-on, hop-off minibus service around Tasmania, taking in key tourist destinations and some out-of-the-way places like Arthur River – the Hop On Hop Off Pass (A$325) allows two months' travel in an anticlockwise direction around the state, starting from either Devonport, Launceston or Hobart.

Autopia Tours (☎ 1800 000 507, 03-9419 8878; www.autopiatours.com.au) runs three-day trips along the Great Ocean Rd from Melbourne to Adelaide via the Grampians for A$170, not including accommodation or meals (both can be arranged). The four-day Melbourne to Sydney tour goes via the Snowy Mountains, Canberra and the Blue Mountains (A$185).

Easyrider Backpacker Tours (☎ 08-9446 1800; www.easyridertours.com.au) is a true hop-on, hop-off bus, but you can also do trips as tours. It covers the west coast from Albany to Broome, with trips out of Perth. The Southern Curl goes Perth–Margaret River–Albany–Perth (A$210) in three days; Perth to Exmouth costs A$310, while Exmouth to Broome costs A$290.

Groovy Grape (☎ 1800 661 177, 08-8371 4000; www.groovygrape.com.au), a SA-based operator formerly dedicated to Barossa Valley tours, now also offers a seven-day Adelaide–Alice camping trip for an all-inclusive A$750, a two-day Boomerang return (with a night in Coober Pedy) for A$160, and a three-day Great Ocean Rd trip between Adelaide and Melbourne for A$285.

Nullarbor Traveller (☎ 08-8390 3297; www.the-traveller.com.au) is a small company that runs relaxed minibus trips across the Nullarbor – there's a nine-day Adelaide–Perth trip (A$990) via the southern forests, while the seven-day return journey (A$770) goes straight through Kalgoorlie. Prices include accommodation (camping and hostels), entry fees and most meals.

Oz Experience (☎ 1300 300 028, 02-9213 1766; www.ozexperience.com) is a hop-on hop-off tour service. The country's biggest backpacker bus network, Oz concentrates on east coast Australia and the Centre. Travel is in the one direction (in either direction but you can't backtrack) and passes are valid for 12 months. A Sydney–Cairns pass (21-day minimum with standard price including bushwalking, kayaking and cycling) is A$595. Melbourne–Canberra–Sydney (five-day minimum including sand-boarding, cycling and bushwalking) is A$295. The price includes transport, activities equipment and fees. Accommodation and food aren't included in the fare.

Most trips with the reputable **Wayward Bus** (☎ 1300 653 510, 08-8410 8833; www.waywardbus.com.au) allow you to get on or off where you like. The eight-day Face the Outback run travels from Adelaide to Alice Springs via Wilpena Pound, the Oodnadatta Track, Coober Pedy and Uluru (A$790 including meals, camping and hostel charges; national park entry fees cost an extra A$25). Classic Coast is a 3½-day trip along the Great Ocean Rd between Adelaide and Melbourne (A$300).

Wild-Life Tours (☎ 03-9534 8868; www.wildlifetours.com.au) offers various trips ex-Melbourne, including Adelaide and Sydney runs. Melbourne to Adelaide can be done in two, three or four days (costs range from A$150 to A$210).

Bus Passes

The following McCafferty's and Greyhound passes can be used on either bus service. There's a 10% discount for members of YHA, VIP, Nomads and other approved organisations.

AUSSIE EXPLORER PASS

This popular pass gives you from one to 12 months to cover a set route – there are 25 in all and the validity period depends on distance. You haven't got the go-anywhere flexibility of the Kilometre Pass (you can't backtrack), but if you can find a route that suits you it generally works out cheaper.

The Aussie Highlights pass allows you to loop around the eastern half of Australia from Sydney, taking in Melbourne, Adelaide, Coober Pedy, Alice Springs, Darwin, Cairns, Townsville, the Whitsundays, Brisbane and Surfers Paradise for A$1470, including tours of Uluru-Kata Tjuta and Kakadu National Parks. Or there are also one-way passes, such as the Aussie Reef & Rock, which goes from Sydney to Alice Springs (and Uluru) via Cairns and Darwin (and Kakadu) for A$1130; the Top End Explorer, which takes in Cairns to Darwin (and Kakadu) for A$470; and the Western Explorer from Perth to Darwin (A$620).

AUSSIE KILOMETRE PASS

The Aussie Kilometre is the simplest pass and gives you a specified amount of travel, starting at 2000km (A$330) and going up in increments of 1000km to a maximum of 20,000km (around A$2400). The pass is valid for 12 months and you can travel where, and in what direction, you like, and stop as many times as you like. For example, a 2000km pass will get you from Cairns to Brisbane, 4000km (A$560) from Cairns to Melbourne, and 12,000km (A$1500) will cover a loop from Sydney to Melbourne, Adelaide, central Australia, Darwin, Cairns and back to Sydney. On the west coast you will need 3000km to get from Perth to Broome and 5000km from Perth to Darwin.

Telephone at least a day ahead to reserve a seat if you're using this pass and bear in mind that side-trips or tours off the main route (eg to Kakadu, Uluru or Shark Bay) may be calculated at double the actual kilometre distance.

Classes

There are no separate classes on buses, and the vehicles of the different companies all look pretty similar and are equipped with air-con, toilets and videos. Smoking is not permitted on Australian buses.

Costs

Following are average one-way bus fares on some well-travelled Australian routes.

Route	Adult/Concession (A$)
Adelaide–Darwin	445/400
Adelaide–Melbourne	60/55
Adelaide–Perth	290/260
Brisbane–Cairns	200/180
Canberra–Melbourne	70/65
Canberra–Sydney	35/30
Sydney–Melbourne	75/70
Sydney–Brisbane	100/90

Reservations

During summer, school holidays and public holidays, you should book well ahead on the more popular bus routes, including intercity and east-coast services. At other times of the year you should have few problems getting on to your preferred service. But if your long-term travel plans rely on catching a particular bus, book at least a day or two ahead just to be safe.

If using a McCafferty's/Greyhound pass, you should make a reservation at least a day in advance.

CAR & MOTORCYCLE

Australia is a vast and mostly sparsely populated country where public transport is often neither comprehensive nor convenient, and sometimes nonexistent. Anyone whose experience of Australia is limited to travelling the east coast might hotly dispute this, but on the whole it's true. Many travellers find that the best way to see the place is to buy a cheap car, and it's certainly the only way to get to those interesting out-of-the-way places without taking a tour.

Motorcycles are another popular way of getting around. The climate is good for bikes for much of the year, and the many small tracks from the road into the bush lead to perfect spots to spend the night. A fuel range of 350km on a bike will cover fuel stops up the Centre and on Hwy 1 around the continent. The long, open roads are really made for large-capacity machines above 750cc, which Australians prefer once they outgrow their 250cc learner restrictions.

For information on driving licences, see p466.

Automobile Associations

The national **Australian Automobile Association** (www.aaa.asn.au) is the umbrella organisation for the various state associations and maintains links with similar bodies throughout the world. Day-to-day operations are handled by the state bodies, which provide emergency breakdown services, literature, excellent touring maps and detailed guides to accommodation and camping grounds.

The state organisations have reciprocal arrangements with other states in Australia and with some similar organisations overseas. So if you're a member of the NRMA in NSW, for example, you can use the RACV's facilities in Victoria. Similarly, if you're a member of the AAA in the USA, you can use any of the Australian state organisations' facilities. Bring proof of membership with you.

Association details for each state are:

Automobile Association of the Northern Territory (AANT; ☎ 08-8981 3837; www.aant.com.au)

National Roads & Motorists Association (NRMA; ☎ 13 11 22; www.nrma.com.au) In NSW and the Australian Capital Territory (ACT).

Royal Automobile Association of South Australia (RAA; ☎ 08-8202 4600; www.raa.net)

Royal Automobile Club of Queensland (RACQ; ☎ 13 19 05; www.racq.com.au)

Royal Automobile Club of Tasmania (RACT; ☎ 13 27 22; www.ract.com.au)
Royal Automobile Club of Victoria (RACV; ☎ 13 19 55; www.racv.com.au)
Royal Automobile Club of Western Australia (RACWA; ☎ 13 17 03; www.rac.com.au)

Fuel & Spare Parts

Fuel (super, diesel and unleaded) is available from service stations sporting the well-known international brand names. Gas (LPG) is not always stocked at more remote roadhouses; if you're on gas it's safer to have dual-fuel capacity. Prices vary from place to place and from price war to price war – conflicts such as the one in Iraq are also a major influence on prices – but basically fuel is heavily taxed and continues to hike up, much to the shock and disgust of local motorists. Unleaded petrol (used in most new cars) now regularly hovers around A$1 per litre even in the cities. Once out into the country, prices soar – in outback Northern Territory (NT) and Qld they can go as high as A$1.50 per litre. Distances between fill-ups can be long in the outback but there are only a handful of tracks where you'll require a long-range fuel tank. On main roads there'll be a small town or roadhouse roughly every 150km to 200km.

The further you get from the cities, the better it is to be in a Holden or a Ford – if you're in an older vehicle that's likely to require a replacement part, life is much simpler if it's a make for which spare parts are more readily available. Volkswagen Kombi vans may be the quintessential backpackers' wheels, but they're notoriously bad for breaking down and difficult to find parts for, and so are a poor choice for remote Australia.

Hire

For cheaper alternatives to the car-hire prices charged by big-name international firms, try one of the many local outfits. Remember, though, that if you want to travel a significant distance you will want unlimited kilometres, and that cheap car hire can often come with serious restrictions.

You must be at least 21 years old to hire from most firms – if you're under 25 you may have to pay a surcharge (from A$15 to A$28 per day). It's cheaper if you rent for a week or more and there are often low-season and weekend discounts. Credit cards are the usual payment method.

In the larger east-coast cities, major companies typically charge from about A$55 to A$60 per day for a small car (Holden Barina, Ford Festiva, Hyundai Excel). They all have offices or agents in most cities and towns. Some companies include:

Avis (☎ 13 63 33; www.avis.com.au)
Budget (☎ 1300 362 848; www.budget.com.au)
Delta Europcar (☎ 1800 030 118; www.deltaeuropcar.com.au)
Hertz (☎ 13 30 39; www.hertz.com.au)
Thrifty (☎ 13 61 39; www.thrifty.com.au)

You can usually get a small car with limited kilometres from a smaller local company from around A$45 a day. **Apex** (☎ 1800 804 392, 07-3265 9250; www.apexrentacar.com.au) is a good-value company. It has offices in mainland capital cities, Alice Springs and Cairns.

For a less orthodox form of car rental, that is an organised car-pooling scheme where travellers prepared to pay for lifts and drivers looking for cash-paying passengers are brought together, check out **Ezi-Ride** (☎ 07-5559 5938; www.ezi-ride.com).

You can also check out the possibilities for long-distance lifts on the virtual notice board, www.needaride.com.au.

Although you can bring vehicles from the mainland to Tasmania, renting may be cheaper and more convenient, particularly on short trips. **Tasmanian Travelways** (www.travelways.com.au), a free bimonthly newspaper available from visitors centres in Tasmania, lists many of the rental options, including campervan rental companies. Car and motorcycle hire options in Tasmania include:

Economy Car Rentals (☎ 03-6334 3299)
Lo-Cost Auto Rent (☎ 1800 647 060; www.locostautorent.com)
Tasmanian Motorcycle Hire (☎ 03-6391 9139; www.tasmotorcyclehire.com.au)

CAMPERVAN HIRE

Britz Rentals (☎ 1800 331 454, 03-8379 8890; www.britz.com) hires out fully equipped 2WD and 4WD campervans, which are commonplace on northern Australian roads. The high-season costs start from around A$100 (two-berth) or A$170 (four-berth) per day for a minimum hire of five days (with unlimited kilometres), but the price climbs from there; to reduce the insurance excess from A$5000 to a few hundred dollars costs an extra A$35 per day for a 2WD and A$50 per day for a 4WD. Britz has offices in all the mainland capitals except Canberra, as well as in Alice Springs, Broome and Cairns, so one-way rentals are also possible.

Many other places rent campervans, especially in Tasmania and the Top End where they're very popular. Check out **Backpacker Campervans** (☎ 1800 670 232, 03-8379 8893; www.backpackercampervans.com) and the loud colour schemes of **Wicked Campers** (☎ 1800 246 869, 07-3257 2170; www.wickedcampers.com.au).

Insurance

In Australia, third-party personal injury insurance is always included in the registration cost of the vehicle. This ensures that every registered vehicle carries at least minimum insurance. You would be wise to extend that minimum to at least third-party property insurance as well – minor collisions with other vehicles can be amazingly expensive.

When it comes to hire cars, know exactly what your liability is in the event of an accident. Rather than risk paying out thousands of dollars if you do have an accident, you can take out your own comprehensive insurance on the car, or (the usual option) pay an additional daily amount to the rental company for an 'insurance excess reduction' policy. This brings the amount of excess you must pay in the event of an accident down from between A$2000 and A$5000 to just a few hundred dollars.

Be aware that if you're travelling on dirt roads you will not usually be covered by insurance unless you have a 4WD – in other words, if you have an accident you'll be liable for all the costs involved. Also, most companies' insurance won't cover the cost of damage to glass (including the windscreen) or tyres. Always read the small print.

Outback Travel

You can drive all the way around Australia on Hwy 1 and through the Centre from Adelaide to Darwin without leaving sealed roads. However, if you really want to see outback Australia, there are plenty of routes that bring new meaning into the phrase 'off the beaten track'.

While you may not need 4WD or fancy expedition equipment to tackle most of these roads, you do need to be carefully prepared for the loneliness and lack of facilities. Vehicles should be in good condition and have reasonable ground clearance. Always carry a tow rope so that some passing good Samaritan can pull your broken-down car to the next garage.

When travelling to very remote areas, such as the central deserts, it's advisable to have a 4WD, and carry a high-frequency (HF) radio transceiver equipped to pick up the relevant Royal Flying Doctor Service bases. A satellite phone and Global Positioning System (GPS) finder can also be handy. Of course, all this equipment comes at a cost, but travellers have perished in the Australian desert after breaking down.

Always carry plenty of water. In warm weather allow 5L per person per day and an extra amount for the radiator, carried in several containers.

It is wise not to attempt the tougher routes during the hottest part of the year (October to April inclusive) – aside from the risk of heat exhaustion, simple mishaps can very easily lead to tragedy at this time. Conversely, there's no point going anywhere on dirt roads in the outback if there has been recent flooding. Get local advice before heading off into the middle of nowhere. For more information regarding Australia's climate see p463.

If you do run into trouble in the back of beyond, don't wander off – stay with your car. It's easier to spot a car than a human being from the air, and you wouldn't be able to carry a heavy load of water very far anyway. South Australian police suggest that you carry two spare tyres (for added safety) and, if stranded, try to set fire to one of them (let the air out first) – the pall of smoke will be seen for miles.

Of course, before you set out, let family, friends or your car-hire company know where you're going and when you intend to be back. For the full story on safe outback travel, including exhaustive firsthand detail of prime tracks like the Birdsville Track and the Great Central Rd, get hold of Lonely Planet's *Outback Australia*. See also The Gibb River Road boxed text, p441.

Purchase

You should be able to pick up a 1982 to 1984 XE Ford Falcon station wagon (a very popular model with backpackers) in good condition from A$1500 to A$2500. The XF Falcon

(1985 to 1986) is also popular and costs around A$3000 to A$3500. Japanese cars of a similar size and age are more expensive, but old Mitsubishi Sigmas and Nissan Bluebirds are usually cheap and reliable. If there are only two of you, a panel van with a mattress in the back is a good option – it's cheaper than a campervan and more comfortable to sleep in than a station wagon.

You can buy a vehicle from a car dealer, but it will work out much cheaper if you buy one via car markets, automobile auctions or privately through newspapers or traveller notice-boards. Buying through a car dealer does have the advantage of some sort of guarantee, but this is not much use if you're buying a car in Sydney for a trip to Perth.

Sydney, Perth and Darwin are particularly good places to buy cars from backpackers who have finished their trip. These vehicles will have done plenty of kilometres but they often come complete with camping gear, Eskies, water containers, tools, road maps and old Lonely Planet guides.

When it comes to buying or selling a car, every state has its own regulations, particularly in regard to registration (rego). In Victoria, for example, a car has to have a compulsory safety check (Certificate of Roadworthiness) before it can be registered in the new owner's name. In NSW and the NT, safety checks are compulsory every year when you come to renew the registration. Stamp duty has to be paid when you buy a car and, as this is based on the purchase price, it's not unknown for buyer and seller to agree privately to understate the price.

For information on the rego requirements and fees applicable in all states and territories, visit the online resource www.onlinedmv.com/australia_department_of_transport.htm, where you'll find links to the websites of all the relevant government transport authorities.

Note that it's much easier to sell a car in the same state that it's registered in, otherwise you (or the buyer) must re-register it in the new state, and that's a hassle. Vehicles with interstate plates are particularly hard to get rid of in WA.

If you do not have your own motorcycle but do have a little bit of spare time up your sleeve, getting mobile on two wheels in Australia is quite feasible. The beginning of winter (June) is a good time to start looking. Australian newspapers and the local bike-related press have classified advertisement sections; A$3500 should get you something that will take you around the country, provided you know a bit about bikes. The main drawback is that you'll have to try to sell it afterwards.

Good starting points for those considering the purchase of a motorcycle are the monthly *Motorcycle Trader* magazine and the **BikePoint website** (http://bikepoint.ninemsn.com.au). The odds of tracking down a reliable and affordable bike are greater in the bigger cities, particularly Sydney, Brisbane and Melbourne.

The registration procedures for motorcycles in each state and territory are usually the same as those that apply to cars, but the fee is significantly less (it's often calculated on weight).

BUY-BACK DEALS

A way of getting around the hassles of buying and selling a vehicle privately is to enter into a buy-back arrangement with a dealer. Be aware that dealers may find ways of knocking down the price when you return the vehicle (even if the price was agreed to in writing), often by pointing out expensive repairs allegedly required to gain the dreaded roadworthy certificate needed to transfer the registration.

A company that specialises in buy-back arrangements on cars and campervans is **Travellers Auto Barn** (☎ 02-9360 1500; www.travellers-autobarn.com.au), which has offices in Sydney, Melbourne, Brisbane and Cairns, and offers a range of vehicles. The buy-back arrangement is guaranteed in writing before you depart and the basic deal is 50% of the purchase price if you have the vehicle for eight weeks, 40% for up to six months, or 30% for up to 12 months. You can probably get better value if you purchase and/or sell on your own, but the convenience of a guaranteed buyback is handy. If you're driving long distances, we strongly urge you to get an independent mechanical check before you buy.

Another option, for cars and motorcycles, is **Car Connection** (☎ 03-5473 4469; www.carconnection.com.au). Rather than requiring you to outlay the full amount and then sell it back, you post a bond that is actually less than the value of the vehicle (a credit-card imprint is fine) and only pay a fixed 'user fee' for any period up to six months. A Ford Falcon station wagon or Yamaha XT600 trail bike will set you back A$2150 for any period up to six months; a diesel Toyota Landcruiser, suitable for serious outback exploration, costs around A$5000; a campervan costs A$6000. Information and bookings are also handled by the company's Germany-based agent, **Travel Action GmbH** (☎ 0276-47824).

Road Conditions

Australia has few multilane highways, although there are stretches of divided road (four or six lanes) in some particularly busy areas, including the Princes Hwy from Murray Bridge to Adelaide, most of the Pacific Hwy from Sydney to Brisbane, and the Hume and Calder Hwys in Victoria. Elsewhere the major roads are sealed two-laners.

You don't have to get far off the beaten track to find dirt roads. In fact, anybody who sets out to see the country in reasonable detail should expect some dirt-road travelling. And if you seriously want to explore remote Australia, you'd better plan on having a 4WD and a winch. A few basic spare parts, such as fan belts and radiator hoses, are worth carrying if you're travelling in places where traffic is light and garages are few and far between.

Motorcyclists should beware of dehydration in the dry, hot air – carry at least 5L of water on remote roads in central Australia and drink plenty of it, even if you don't feel thirsty. If riding in Tasmania (a top motorcycling destination) or southern and eastern Victoria, you should be prepared for rotten weather in winter and rain at any time of year. It's worth carrying some spares and tools even if you don't know how to use them, because someone else often does. Carry a workshop manual for your bike and spare elastic (octopus) straps for securing your gear.

Road Hazards

The 'road-kill' that you unfortunately see a lot of in the outback and alongside roads in many other parts of the country (Tasmania being a prime example) is mostly the result of cars and trucks hitting animals during the night. Many Australians avoid travelling altogether once the sun drops because of the risks posed by animals on the roads.

Kangaroos are common hazards on country roads, as are cows and sheep in the unfenced outback – hitting an animal of this size can make a real mess of your car. Kangaroos are most active around dawn and dusk. They often travel in groups, so if you see one hopping across the road in front of you, slow right down, as its friends may be just behind it.

If you're travelling at night and a large animal appears in front of you, hit the brakes, dip your lights (so you don't continue to dazzle and confuse it) and only swerve if it's safe to do so – numerous travellers have been killed in accidents caused by swerving to miss animals.

A not-so-obvious hazard is driver fatigue. Driving long distances (particularly in hot weather) can be so tiring that you might fall asleep at the wheel – it's not uncommon and the consequences can be unthinkable. So on a long haul, stop and rest every two hours or so – do some exercise, change drivers or have a coffee.

Road Rules

Driving in Australia holds few real surprises, other than the odd animal caught in your headlights. Australians drive on the left-hand side of the road and all cars are right-hand drive. An important road rule is 'give way to the right' – if an intersection is unmarked (unusual), you must give way to vehicles entering the intersection from your right.

The general speed limit in built-up areas was 60km/h but in recent years this has been reduced to 50km/h on residential streets in most states – keep an eye out for signs. Near schools, the limit is 40km/h in the morning and afternoon.

On the open highway it's usually 100km/h or 110km/h – in the NT there's no speed limit outside built-up areas, except along the Lasseter Hwy to Uluru where the limit is 110km/h. The police have speed radar guns and cameras and are fond of using them in strategically concealed locations.

Oncoming drivers who flash their lights at you may be giving you a friendly warning of a speed camera ahead – or they may be telling you that your headlights are not on. Whatever, it's polite to wave back if someone does this. Try not to get caught doing it yourself, since it's illegal.

All new cars in Australia have seat belts both in the back and the front, and it is the law to wear yours – you are likely to get a fine if you don't. Small children must be belted into an approved safety seat, and most car rental agencies should be able to set you up with one for free or for a small charge.

Drink-driving is a real problem, especially in country areas. Serious attempts to reduce the resulting road toll are ongoing and random breath-tests are not uncommon in built-up areas. If you're caught with a blood-alcohol level of more than 0.05% be prepared for a hefty fine and the loss of your licence. In Victoria you must be *under* 0.05%.

PARKING

One of the big problems with driving around big cities like Sydney and Melbourne (or popular tourist towns such as Byron Bay) is finding somewhere to park. Even if you do find a spot there's likely to be a time restriction, meter (or ticket machine) or both. It's one of the great rorts in Australia that by overstaying your welcome (even by five minutes) in a space that may cost only a few dollars to park in, local councils are prepared to fine you anywhere from A$50 to A$120. Also note that if you park in a 'clearway' your car will be towed away or clamped – look for signs.

In the cities there are large multistorey car parks where you can park all day for between A$10 and A$25.

Many towns in NSW have a peculiar form of reverse-angle parking, a recipe for disaster if ever there was one. If in doubt, park your car in the same direction and at the same angle as other cars.

HITCHING

Travellers who decide to hitch should understand that they are taking a small but potentially serious risk. People who do choose to hitch will be safer if they travel in pairs and let someone know where they are planning to go.

In Australia, the hitching signal can either be a thumbs up or a downward-pointed finger.

TRAIN

Rail travel in Australia is something you do because you really want to – not because it's cheaper or more convenient, and certainly not because it's fast. That said, trains are more comfortable than buses, and on some of Australia's long-distance train journeys the romance of the rails is alive and kicking.

Rail services within each state are run by that state's rail body, either government or private.

The three major interstate services in Australia are operated by **Great Southern Railways** (☎ 13 21 47, 08-8213 4592; www.gsr.com.au), namely the *Indian Pacific* between Sydney and Perth; *The Overland* between Melbourne and Adelaide; and *The Ghan* between Adelaide and Darwin via Alice Springs.

Costs

Some standard one-way train fares include:

Adelaide–Darwin Adult/concession in a travel seat A$440/220, from A$1390/840 in a cabin.
Adelaide–Melbourne Adult/concession in a travel seat A$60/45, from A$150/90 in a cabin.
Adelaide–Perth Adult/concession in a travel seat A$310/160, from A$960/580 in a cabin.
Brisbane–Cairns A$190 per adult (economy seat).
Canberra–Melbourne A$95 per adult (economy seat); involves a bus ride from Canberra to Cootamundra, then a train to Melbourne.
Canberra–Sydney A$50 per adult (economy seat).
Sydney–Melbourne A$115 per adult (economy seat).
Sydney–Brisbane A$115 per adult (economy seat).
Sydney–Perth Adult/concession in a travel seat A$520/260, from A$1250/810 in a cabin.

Reservations

As the railway-booking system is computerised, any station (other than those on metropolitan lines) can make a booking for any journey throughout the country. For reservations telephone ☎ 13 22 32; this will connect you to the nearest main-line station.

Discounted tickets work on a first-come/first-served quota basis, so it can help to book in advance.

Train Passes

The **Great Southern Railways Pass** (☎ 13 22 32; www.trainways.com.au), which is only available to passport-equipped non-Australian residents, allows unlimited travel on the rail network for a period of six months. The pass costs A$590 per adult and A$450 per student or card-carrying backpacker (relatively inexpensive considering the amount of ground you could cover over the life of the pass), but note that you'll be travelling in a 'Daynighter' reclining seat and not a cabin. You need to prebook all seats at least 24 hours in advance.

CountryLink (☎ 13 22 32; www.countrylink.info) is a rail and coach operation that visits destinations in NSW, the ACT, Qld and Victoria, and offers two types of pass to foreign nationals with valid passports. The **East Coast Discovery Pass** (☎ 13 22 32) allows one-way economy travel between Melbourne and Cairns (in either direction) with unlimited stopovers, and is valid for six months – the full trip costs A$390, while Brisbane to Cairns is A$230 and Sydney to Cairns is A$310. The **Backtracker Rail Pass** (☎ 13 22 32; www.backpackerrailpass.info) allows travel on the entire CountryLink network and comes in four versions: a 14-day/one-/three-/six-month pass costing A$220/250/270/380 respectively.

New Zealand

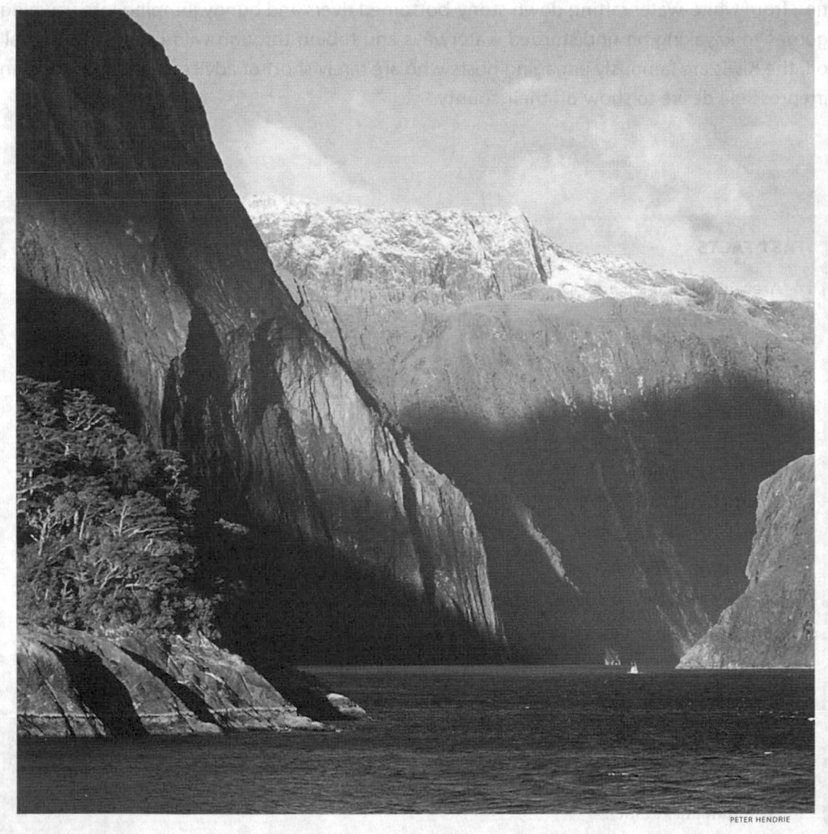

PETER HENDRIE

New Zealand

The two enigmatic main islands of New Zealand are not identical twins – rather, each has a unique physical character that can independently stop awestruck travellers in their tracks. The North Island has a volcanic nature and has blown its stack a few memorable times in the past, though lately it's been content with subterranean smouldering while backpackers enthusiastically walk around crater lakes, dip themselves in thermal pools and crane their necks up the tumble-down slopes of soaring cones. The South Island, meanwhile, has forsaken volcanoes for the snow-capped grandeur of the Southern Alps and the magnificent flooded basins of Fiordland National Park, which between them offer travellers unparalleled tramps, cool skiing slopes, cruises on utterly remote sounds and some of the freshest air you'll ever breathe.

In case you haven't got the picture, NZ is one of the most scenic and profoundly beautiful places anyone could hope to explore. It also offers a thrilling abundance of outdoor activities, from white-water rafting down stony-bottomed rivers and bungy jumping into yawning gorges to kayaking on undisturbed waterways and tubing through wild caves. To top it all off, the Kiwis are famously engaging hosts who are rarely short of advice, friendliness and an irrepressible desire to show off their county.

FAST FACTS

- **Area** 268,680 sq km
- **ATMs** In all tourist areas and many small towns
- **Budget** NZ$50-70 per day
- **Capital** Wellington
- **Costs** Dorm bed NZ$18-25; bottled beer NZ$3-5; takeaway snack NZ$2-3
- **Electricity** 230V AC, 50Hz
- **Money** US$1 = NZ$0.61
- **Population** 3,950,000
- **Seasons** High Nov-Apr; low Jun-Sep
- **Telephone** Country code ☎ 64
- **Time** GMT/UTC + 12hrs

NORTH ISLAND p506

SOUTH ISLAND p643

TRAVEL HINT

Outdoor activities can suck your finances dry. Prioritise activities you're really keen on and forgo the rest (until next time).

Snapshot New Zealand

CURRENT EVENTS

A contentious and divisive issue in 2003/04 was about the ownership of, and access to, New Zealand's foreshores and seabeds. In mid-2003 a court decision paved the way for the Maori to claim customary title over the *whenua* (land). New Zealand's Labour government, led by Prime Minister Helen Clark responded by stating that land ownership should reside with the Crown, re-igniting a land rights debate that's as old as the 1840 Treaty of Waitangi. In early 2004 more than 15,000 protestors marched on parliament chanting a clear message: don't confiscate our land. (Despite wind and rain gusts of over 120km per hour, the protest was one of the biggest since the 1981 Springbok tour.)

During the 1950s and 1960s, apartheid policies had an impact on All Blacks selection and Maori players were excluded from some South African tours. In 1981, amid massive protests, the South African Springbok rugby team toured NZ, dividing the nation. Protestors disrupted telecommunications, invaded sports grounds and, in Auckland, dropped flour bombs onto the pitch from a plane. The All Blacks didn't tour South Africa again until apartheid ended.

Maoris see the decision to grant the Crown ownership of the foreshores and seabeds as a weakening of their traditional rights.

With a national election planned for 2005, the seabeds and foreshores issue could change the face of NZ politics. A new political party, the Maori Party, appeared on the scene in mid-2004, led by ex-Labour MP Tariana Turia. The National Party, the opposition, has been campaigning on a platform of 'tough on crime', and restricting race-based funding and policies. The right-wing New Zealand First Party (one of the country's minor political parties) is campaigning on the deeply xenophobic social equation that immigration equals an increase in violent crime and economic hardship.

Rugby is always a hot topic in NZ. Late 2003 saw the first reverential invocation of All Blacks' names like Spencer, Mealamu and McCaw in the early stages of the prized World Cup, followed by a pride-thumping semifinal loss to less-fancied Australia, and then gutter-press attacks on a team that had apparently let the nation down. Sadly, 2004 saw more of the same, with the phrase 'flat back line' muttered over many a beer.

In the arts, is *Lord of the Rings* really only a trilogy? New Zealand has been dining out on the *Rings'* massive international success for years, culminating in *Return of the King* winning Best Everything – 11 awards in total – at the 2004 Academy Awards. Even if you don't encounter one of the thousands of people who worked on the films, you'll inevitably hear someone shamelessly announcing the most tenuous connection: 'My best friend's husband's hairdresser played an orc, you know'. Kiwis claim the movies as their own, and the tourism industry is milking the concept of NZ as legendary realm. Hopefully Peter Jackson can continue to ride the wave with his remake of *King Kong*.

Forget hobbits, wizards and that gold trinket. The real star of Peter Jackson's epic film trilogy *Lord of the Rings* is the breathtaking NZ landscape. If nothing else, the movie makes a fine trip planner.

Arguably due to the mass advertising of its Middle Earth landscape in the *Rings* flicks, and also to a widespread international perception of NZ as a haven far removed (geographically and historically) from global mayhem, the country received a record 2.1 million visitors in 2003, up 3% on the previous year. A common talking point in NZ is the prospective boost to its relatively stable economy if its profile remains 'pure'.

The 'NZ Dream' of the quarter-acre section is taking a battering as the urban sprawl advances. Auckland is expanding rapidly, fuelled by a 'drift north' and immigration, and there's concern about public transport keeping up with the influx. There's also a trend of people moving to the coastlines. In Nelson, for example, property values have skyrocketed and orchards have been ploughed under to make way for more housing. In the process, the *bach* (pronounced batch) – a rough beach house, passed down through generations – is disappearing. Many New Zealanders feel this is a great loss, especially when the land is sold to foreign buyers.

HISTORY

New Zealand's history is short. And fast. In less than a thousand years the islands produced two new peoples: the Polynesian Maori and European New Zealanders (generally referred to by their Maori name, 'pakeha').

First Settlers

Landscapes in Conflict: A field guide to the New Zealand Wars, by Nigel Prickett – a traveller's guide to important battle sites, Maori *pa* fortifications and pakeha history, with striking photographic images.

It's certain that NZ's first settlers were the Polynesian forebears of today's Maori people. Much of the migration took place between 1000 and 1200, and within the first hundred years they spread from the tip of the North Island to the bottom of the South, choosing warm coastal areas that offered fertile growing conditions, sources of workable stone from which to carve knives and adzes, and abundant big game. The population flourished, feasting on high-protein flightless birds, such as moa, and plants brought from Polynesia, such as kumara (definitely try some salty kumara chips!).

By about 1400 big-game supply was in rapid decline. Except in the far south, fur seal breeding colonies were hunted out and moa were nearly extinct. Rumours of spotting moa persist, so if you see one, photograph it – you've just made the greatest zoological discovery of the last 100 years.

DID YOU KNOW?

The largest moa weighed up to 240kg!

Maori economics turned to small game – forest birds and rats – and from hunting to gardening and fishing. To make a good living required detailed local knowledge, and complex communal organisation, hence the rise of Maori tribes. Competition for resources increased, as did conflict, and this led to the building of increasingly sophisticated fortifications, known as *pa*. You'll still see vestiges of many *pa* earthworks around the country – on the hilltops of Auckland for example.

Enter Europe

New Zealand became an official British colony in 1840, but the first authenticated contact between Maoris and the outside world took place in 1642, at Golden Bay. Two Dutch ships sailed from the Dutch East Indies (Indonesia), to search for the 'Great South Land'. Commander Abel Tasman was instructed to pretend to any natives 'that you are by no means eager for precious metals, so as to leave them ignorant of the value of the same'. When Tasman's ships anchored, local Maoris approached in their canoe, making the traditional challenge: friend or foe? Misunderstanding this, the Dutch challenged back by blowing trumpets. When a boat was lowered to take a party between the two ships, it was attacked and four crewmen were killed. Tasman sailed away and no other Europeans returned for 127 years. But the Dutch had left a name: Nieuw Zeeland.

TIMELINE

1642: First European contact by Abel Tasman

AD 1000 — 1640 — 1760

AD 1000–1200: Polynesians, ancestors of the modern Maori, settle NZ by ocean-going canoe

1769: Captain James Cook and De Surville 'rediscover' NZ

Contact between Maoris and Europeans was renewed in 1769 when explorers arrived under James Cook and Jean De Surville. Cook visited again between 1773 and 1777, and there were further French expeditions. Unofficial visits, by whaling ships in the north and sealing gangs in the south, began in the 1790s. The first mission station was founded in 1814, in the Bay of Islands.

New England whaling ships favoured the Bay of Islands for 'rest and recreation' (sex and alcohol), and 271 ships called there between 1833 and 1839. Their favourite haunt? Kororareka, now Russell, known to the missionaries as 'the hellhole of the Pacific'.

One or two dozen bloody clashes dot the history of Maori-European contact before 1840 but, given the number of visits, interracial conflict was modest. Europeans needed Maori protection, food, and labour, and the Maori traded for European articles, especially muskets (depicted in the film, *The Piano*).

Most warfare was between Maori and Maori: the terrible intertribal Musket Wars of 1818–36. Because Northland had the earliest contact with Europe, its Ngapuhi tribe acquired muskets first. Under their great general Hongi Hika, Ngapuhi then raided south, winning bloody victories against tribes without muskets. Once these other tribes acquired muskets, they fought off the Ngapuhi and, in turn, raided further south. The domino effect continued to the far south of the South Island.

As well as muskets, Europeans brought such things as pigs, potatoes and diseases. It's estimated that the Maori population was around 100,000 in 1769. The Musket Wars killed perhaps 20,000, and new diseases also wreaked havoc. By 1840 the Maori population numbered about 70,000.

The Maori bent under the weight of European contact, but they certainly didn't break.

Treaty of Waitangi

By 1840 Maori tribes were describing local Europeans as 'their pakeha', and valued the profit and prestige they brought. They wanted more, and concluded that accepting nominal British authority was the way to get it. At the same time, the British government was overcoming its reluctance to undertake potentially expensive intervention in NZ. It believed that the Maori couldn't handle the increasing scale of unofficial European contact. The two peoples struck a deal, symbolised by the treaty first signed at Waitangi on 6 February 1840. The Treaty of Waitangi is NZ's founding document with a standing similar to that of the US Constitution. The original problem was a discrepancy between British and Maori translations: the English version promised Maoris full equality as British subjects in return for complete rights of government. The Maori version also promised that Maoris would retain their chieftainship, which implied local rights of government. The problem wasn't great at first, because the Maori version applied outside the small European settlements.

Waitangi National Reserve (p542), where the treaty was first signed in 1840, is now a tourist attraction. Every 6 February Waitangi hosts treaty commemorations, and protests. Online, check out www.waitangi-tribunal.govt.nz and www.treatyofwaitangi.govt.nz.

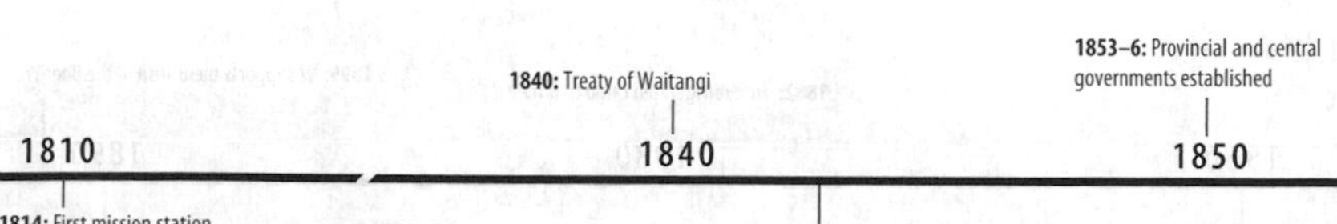
1853–6: Provincial and central governments established
1840: Treaty of Waitangi
1810
1840
1850
1814: First mission station founded in Bay of Islands
1845: Hone Heke fights the Norhtland war

Making Pakeha

In 1840, there were only about 2000 Europeans in NZ, and Kororareka (Russell) was the capital and biggest settlement. By 1850 the settlements of Auckland, Wellington, New Plymouth, Nelson, Christchurch and Dunedin were formed, with 22,000 settlers between them. About half of these had come under the auspices of the New Zealand Company, brainchild of Edward Gibbon Wakefield. With limited success, Wakefield tried to short-circuit the barbarous frontier phase of settlement with 'instant civilisation'. From the 1850s his settlers, who included a high proportion of upper-middle-class gentlefolk, were swamped by waves of immigrants until the 1880s. These people were part of the great British and Irish diaspora that also populated Australia and much of North America. But the NZ mix was distinctive. New Zealand's lowland Scot settlers were prominent and the Irish, even the Catholics, tended to come from the north of Ireland. The English tended to come from the counties close to London and small groups of Germans, Scandinavians and Chinese immigrated when the pakeha population reached half a million. As settlements grew, conflict brewed.

Maori Resistance

Utu (1983), which means 'revenge', is a historically based film set in the 1860s and directed by Geoff Murphy. It's a fascinating, though amateurish, primer about the NZ Land Wars fought between the Maori and Europeans.

Maori resistance was one of the most formidable ever mounted against European expansion. The first clash took place in 1843 at Wairau Valley (see p645) when a posse of settlers attempted to enforce British control but encountered the reality of Maori control. Twenty-two settlers were killed, including Wakefield's brother, along with about six Maoris. In 1845, more serious fighting broke out in the Bay of Islands when the young Ngapuhi chief Hone Heke cut down the British flag at Russell, then sacked the town. Heke baffled the British, using a modern variant of the traditional *pa* fortification – vestiges can still be seen at Ruapekapeka. The fighting of the 1840s confirmed that the North Island consisted of a European fringe around an independent Maori heartland.

Fighting broke out again in 1860 and wars burned sporadically until 1872 over much of the North Island; five separate major conflicts made up what are now collectively known as the New Zealand Wars (also referred to as the Land Wars or Maori Wars. A Maori nationalist organisation, the Maori King Movement, was the backbone of resistance. In later years some remarkable prophet-generals, notably Titokowaru and Te Kooti (p619), took over. In the Waikato War of 1863–64 up to 5000 Maoris resisted an invasion mounted by imperial, colonial and 'friendly' Maori troops numbering 20,000. This conflict involved armoured steamships, ultramodern heavy artillery, telegraph and 10 British regiments. The Maori won several battles but European numbers and resources proved too powerful. Maori political independence finally ended when police invaded its last sanctuary, the Urewera Mountains, in 1916. Today, the Lake Waikaremoana Track in Te Urewera

1860

1860–72: Land Wars (Waikato, Taranaki and the East Coast)

1882: First refrigerated cargo to Britain

1880

1890

1893: NZ gives women the vote

1899: NZ supports the British in the Boer War

National Park is one of the most popular and beautiful walks on the North Island.

Welfare & Warfare

From the 1850s to 1880s the pakeha economy boomed on the back of wool exports, gold rushes and massive overseas borrowing for development. The crash came in the 1880s, when NZ experienced its Long Depression.

With a reputation as 'the world's social laboratory', NZ was the first country to give women the vote in 1893, and introduced old age pensions in 1898.

In 1935 the First Labour Government took office, led by Michael Joseph Savage, easily NZ's favourite Australian. This government created NZ's pioneering version of the welfare state.

For a peaceful country, NZ has spent much of its history at war, both at home and overseas. It backed Britain in the Boer War (1899–1902); and in WWI (1914–18) about 100,000 NZ men served overseas and close to 60,000 became casualties. Kiwi soldiers earned a reputation for skill and bravery – most notably at the famous battle of Gallipoli. You'll see a memorial lined with names at any square or park in most NZ towns. New Zealand did its share of fighting during WWII (1939–1945) as well: roughly 100,000 New Zealanders fought in Europe and the Middle East. In 1999 NZ sent its largest number of military personnel since the Korean war – around 1400 – on a peacekeeping mission to East Timor.

Season of the Jew by Maurice Shadbolt – the first in a series of novels about the NZ Wars, this covers the second Taranaki war (1865–69) and the exploits of the remarkable one-eyed general Titikowaru who, for a short while, brought imperial NZ to its knees.

Better Britons?

British visitors have long found NZ hauntingly familiar. This is not simply a matter of the British and Irish origin of most pakeha. It also stems from the tightening of NZ links with Britain from 1882, when refrigerated cargoes of food were first shipped to London. By the 1930s, a hundred giant ships carried frozen meat, cheese, and butter, as well as wool, on regular voyages. The NZ economy adapted to feeding London, and cultural links were also enhanced. New Zealand children studied British history and literature, not their own. New Zealand's leading scientists and writers, such as Ernest Rutherford and Katherine Mansfield, gravitated naturally to Britain.

This tight relationship has been described as 'recolonial', but it's a mistake to see NZ as an exploited colony. Average living standards in NZ were normally better than in Britain, as were the welfare and lower-level education systems. Especially in war and sport, New Zealanders sometimes saw themselves as the Better Britons of the south.

In recolonial NZ it was illegal for farmers to allow their cattle to mate in fields fronting public roads until the 1950s. Sunday newspapers were illegal until 1969, and full Sunday trading was not allowed until 1989. Licensed restaurants hardly existed in 1960, nor did supermarkets or TV. Notoriously, from 1917 to 1967, pubs were obliged to shut at 6pm.

DID YOU KNOW?

Kate Sheppard spearheaded NZ's suffragist movement. After years of constant lobbying, her third petition in 1893 was signed by 32,000 women (about one-third of the adult female population at the time) and it was the largest petition ever presented to parliament.

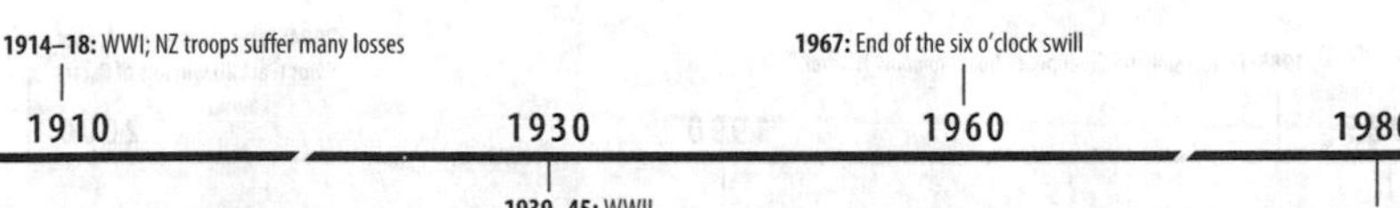

1914–18: WWI; NZ troops suffer many losses
1967: End of the six o'clock swill
1910
1930
1960
1980
1939–45: WWII
1981: Springbok rugby tour rips NZ society apart

Coming In, Coming Out

The recolonial system managed to survive until 1973, when Mother England ran off and joined the Franco-German commune now known as the EU. Other forces of change also occurred around this time: NZ developed alternative markets to Britain, women penetrated the workforce and political sphere, gays came out of the closet, university-educated youth became more assertive, and environmental protests and political movements burgeoned. Tourism rapidly expanded and visitors to NZ, which numbered 36,000 in 1960, now number more than two million per year.

The country's more recent Big Shift is associated with the politics of 1984, when the elected Labour government adopted an antinuclear foreign policy and a more market-driven economic policy. Social restrictions were removed almost as fast as economic ones – the pubs still closed at six, but am, not pm. In 1985 French spies sank the antinuclear protest ship *Rainbow Warrior* in Auckland Harbour (see p539). The lukewarm American condemnation of the French act rallied New Zealanders' support for the antinuclear policy, which became associated with national independence. New Zealand investors engaged in a frenzy of speculation, and suffered even more than the rest of the world from the economic crash of 1987.

Economic recovery began in the late 1990s. In 1999 Labour won a general election and Helen Clark became NZ's first elected woman prime minister; Labour was re-elected in 2002.

The early 21st century is an interesting time for NZ. New Zealanders of the 1960s would hardly recognise Auckland's main streets, and Wellington's nightlife is a riot of colour and late-night partying. Like NZ food and wine, film and literature are flowering, and the new ethnic mix is creating a potent energy in popular music. There are constants, however – the pub, sports ground, bush, beach, and *bach*. New Zealand's powerful history, rich with ancient legends and *Maoritanga* (Maori culture), continues to unfold.

THE CULTURE

The National Psyche

The Ministry for Culture & Heritage's history resource: www.nzhistory.net.nz.

What riles a New Zealander?

Being mistaken for an Australian, losing the rugby, social injustice, social justice, genetically engineered food, nuclear testing, land rights.

What is the single-most important aspect of NZ culture?

The Land. Marketed to the rest of the world as 100% Pure NZ, it's the spiritual essence of the country, as is the belief that people belong to the land, rather than the land belonging to people.

What is Kiwiana?

Kiwiana is symbols and icons that represent national identity, such as the fearsome *haka* performed by the All Blacks, gumboots, Buzzy Bee toys, the national soft drink – L&P (Lemon & Paeora), and Paua (abalone) shell.

1985: French sink the Greenpeace boat, *Rainbow Warrior*

2004: Peter Jackson and *Lord of the Rings* (Part III) win lots of Oscars

1985 — 1990 — 2000

1984: NZ becomes nuclear free

1999: NZ's first female prime minister is elected

Kiwiana encapsulates the national myth that with a bit of 'Kiwi ingenuity' and some 'number-eight wire' – the gauge used for making fences – New Zealanders can solve anything.

What are New Zealanders proud of?
New Zealand; Maori culture; 'Kiwi' sense of humour; internationally renowned filmmakers, directors, musicians, designers and inventors; international sporting prowess; being nuclear free; fresh seafood, gourmet cheese and fine wine; strong work ethic; not selling out to superpowers; flightless birds.

Dictionary of NZ Biography: www.dnzb.govt.nz.

What do New Zealanders worship?
The rugby, All Blacks, a *hangi*, sheep, the All Blacks beating Australia in rugby, beer.

Why does the friendly rivalry exist between New Zealand and Australia?
Kiwis believe they invented pavlova and that Russell Crowe comes from NZ; Aussies believe they invented pavlova and that Russell Crowe comes from Australia.

Lifestyle

New Zealanders are passionate travellers and you're bound to run into a Kiwi in any country. With young New Zealanders, the 'big OE' (overseas experience) is considered a rite of passage, but the primary destination has changed: Australia, rather than Britain.

Walking and gardening are listed as prime leisure activities, along with swimming and fishing – over a quarter of the population throws a line in.

People are marrying later or not marrying at all and de facto relationships are most common for under-25s. Roughly 20,000 couples get married each year, but about 10,000 get divorced.

NZ is 21st on the OECD's 30-country ladder, which means that New Zealanders are about one-third less affluent than Canadians and Irish, and as wealthy as the average Spaniard.

A recent government survey debunked NZ as a 'cultural backwater', finding that the nation's most popular cultural activity is reading. During 2003, more than a million people attended a live-music performance, 750,000 watched some theatre and over 500,000 visited a *marae* (Maori meeting house). Wellingtonians' long-standing claim as the country's most culturally active hub was also borne out (sorry, Aucklanders!).

LANGUAGE

Maori and English are both official languages of NZ, and many European New Zealanders know a smattering of Maori. Maori is taught at most schools and all government material is bilingual. Maori is still spoken casually in the Far North, East Cape and Te Urewera regions as well as on *marae* and in official capacities.

Common Maori Greetings

Kia ora – Hello/Good luck/Good health.
Haere mai! – Welcome!
Tena koe – Hello (to one person).
Tena koutou – Hello (to three or more people).
Hei konei ra – See you later.

People

New Zealand's population is 3.95 million humans (and 39.2 million sheep). The racial mix is 74.5% NZ European, 9.7% Maori, 4.6% Pacific Islander, and 7.4% Asian and others. Over 70% of the population lives in cities and almost one in three people live in Auckland.

Auckland is home to more Pacific Islanders than the Pacific Island nations themselves and has also been the prime destination for ethnic Chinese since immigration rules were relaxed in 1987. Thousands of Asian students reside in Auckland's central city.

In 1936 Maoris were 17% urban and 83% rural; in 1986, these proportions had reversed. High birth rates see about 15% of New Zealanders identifying as Maori, a proportion likely to grow.

MAORI CULTURE

Below Ranginui (Sky Father) and Papatuanuku (Earth Mother) were various gods of land, forest and sea, joined by deified ancestors over time. In legend, demi-god Maui fished up the North Island; the South Island was known as Te Waka o Maui (The Canoe of Maui), the one in which he was sitting when he caught the fish.

Modern Maoris refer to themselves in terms of their *iwi* (tribe), often named after an ancestor. Traditionally of great relevance was the *hapu* (subtribe) and the village structure based around *whanau* (extended family groups).

Essential to beliefs and society were *tapu* (complex rules of sacredness) and *mana* (personal spiritual power or prestige). *Tapu* applied to forbidden objects; *mana*, or personal spiritual power, was possessed by chiefs, flowing from them to their tribe. *Mana* could be lost and gained.

Battle increased a tribe's *mana* and the Maori had a highly developed warrior society. *Pakanga* (war) had its own worship, sacrifices, rituals, dances and art forms. Tribes engaged in numerous battles over territory, for *utu* (revenge). Cooking and eating an enemy destroyed that enemy's *tapu*.

On the *whenua* (land), geographical features such as *maunga* (mountains) and *awa* (rivers) delineated tribal boundaries. Today each tribe has one or more sacred *maunga*. Tribal *whakapapa* (oral genealogies) always refer to the names of mountains.

The proper reverence for *tipuna* (ancestors) was important to the Maori. In the absence of a written language, long *whakapapa*, going back hundreds of years, were committed to memory. Maoris saw themselves as part of the collective knowledge and experience of their ancestors.

The Marae

Strictly, the *marae* is the open area in front of the *whare whakairo* (carved meeting house), but today it describes the entire complex of buildings. Visiting a *marae* will help towards understanding *Maoritanga* (Maori culture). It's a sacred place to be treated with great respect.

A welcoming ritual called *te powhiri* occurs when visitors come onto the *marae*. After appropriate ancestors have been praised, the visitor's *tapu* is deemed lifted and hosts and visitors are permitted *hongi* (pressing of noses). In some places the *hongi*, a sharing of life breath, is a single press, in others it's press, release, press. It's never a rubbing together of noses. (Neither is it a kiss on the nose, as was delivered by one confused Australian prime minister!)

Marae protocol varies but shoes must be removed before entering. If you receive hospitality, it's customary to offer a *koha* (donation).

Marae Visits

Rotorua (p593) in the Bay of Plenty has the most *marae* set up for tours, performances or visits. Other options around the country:

Nga Hau e Whai (p678) In Christchurch.

Te Papa (p628) In Wellington's Te Papa museum; not an operating *marae* in the traditional sense.

Te Poho-o-Rawiri (p621) In Gisborne.

Waitangi National Reserve (p542) In Northland; not an operating *marae* but fascinating to visit.

New Zealand's small but active gay and lesbian communities predominantly cluster around the cities, particularly Auckland and Wellington.

Media

Most cities have daily newspapers – Auckland's *New Zealand Herald* has the biggest national circulation. For entertainment check out the readily available music, and gay and lesbian street-press publications (see p519 and p633).

Pavement magazine is 'the contemporary culture magazine for modern youth'. Other mags worth a flick-through are Auckland's *Metro*, a glossy guide to the city; and Wellington's authoritative music mag *A Low Hum*. For those who love food-porn, salivate over a copy of *Cuisine*.

New Zealand Herald Online: www.nzherald.co.nz

Listen to student radio network, bNet, broadcast from Auckland (95bFM) and other major cities for local gig-guides, new music and alternative programming. Tune into Radio Sport for the true sounds of NZ summer: cricket commentary, and National Radio for news and features. Auckland and Queenstown have the dance station George FM.

There's a nationwide network of *iwi* (tribal) stations, such as Waikato's Radio Tainui and Auckland's Mai FM. Niu FM is the national Pacific Island station.

Arts

New Zealanders have a high profile in many of the arts. Common themes and inspirations stem from the Land Wars, independence from the 'other country', Maori and English identity, immigration and mythology.

LITERATURE

New Zealand has an active literary scene. Katherine Mansfield (p629) began a NZ tradition in short fiction, carried on by accomplished novelist, Janet Frame (1924–2004). James Baxter (1926–72) is one of NZ's best-known poets, and Maurice Shadbolt is a renowned historian. Elizabeth Knox is a well-known modern novelist.

NZ literary links: www.piperpat.co.nz/nz/society/writing.html.

Although the Maori lack a tradition of written culture, there is some dynamic Maori and Pacific contemporary fiction such as Witi Ihimaera's *Whale Rider* and the controversial *Once Were Warriors*, by Alan Duff. *The Bone People* by Kerri Hulme attracted much recognition after winning the 1988 Booker Prize. Displacement and colonial life is explored by Peter Walker's biography *The Fox Boy*. Samoan author Albert Wendt wrote the brilliant *Leaves of the Banyan Tree*.

TOP READS

- *The Bone People* (Kerri Hulme) A poetic, depressing, heart-warming and violent story about a father, son and their friend Kerewin.
- *Electric* (Chad Taylor) Tight and sparse writing that gives a seamy, drugged view of Auckland during severe power outages.
- *Dogside Story* (Patricia Grace) Heart-warming and powerful story of contemporary issues facing an East Coast Maori community.
- *The Trespass* (Barbara Ewing) A young woman escapes the 1849 London cholera epidemic by migrating to Wellington.
- *In a Fishbone Church* (Catherine Chidgey) Named the country's best novelist under 40, Chidgey's book focuses on one family and transcends time.

TOP FLICKS

- *The Whale Rider* (Niki Caro) Maori mythology and social hierarchy told through the eyes of a 12-year-old girl.
- *The Piano* (Jane Campion) A tale of erotic longing between Maori and pakeha.
- *Stickmen* (Hamish Rothwell) Fun, easy-pleaser about a fiercely competitive pool competition run at the local pub.
- *Scarfies* (Robert Sarkies) Comic thriller about a group of Dunedin students.
- *Topless Women Talk About Their Lives* (Harry Sinclair) twenty-somethings discuss their lives, featuring Danielle Cormak from *Xena*.

CINEMA & TV

New Zealand's mystical, magical landscapes – black-sand beaches and snow-capped, mist-shrouded peaks – and its relatively low exchange rate makes it an enormously popular country for film shoots. Peter Jackson's *Rings* trilogy is the most recent success story, but Oscar-winning director Jane Campion brought NZ's landscapes to the world stage with *The Piano* and the disturbing biographical account of Janet Frame in *An Angel at My Table*. New Zealand actor Sam Neill describes the country's 'uniquely strange and dark film industry' as producing bleak, haunted work. Lee Tamahori's *Once Were Warriors* paints a violent picture of Maori life, balanced by Niki Caro's mythical *Whale Rider*.

The world-leading Weta postproduction facility in Wellington proves NZ's dedication to filmmaking, as does its Mediaplex, and the number of film festivals held annually (p782).

Free-to-air TV is dominated by the two publicly-owned Television New Zealand (TVNZ) channels (TV One and TV2), versus the Canadian-owned TV3 and its sibling music channel C4. Maori TV, going live in 2004, has started well. Regional TV struggles to be entertaining.

MUSIC

There's been music in NZ since first human occupation. Local music comprises around 20% of commercial stations' playlists, instead of 2%, as it was in the early '90s. Perennial local heroes are brothers Tim and Neil Finn of Split Enz and Crowded House.

Local music news, free and paid downloads (including videos) and more: www.amplifier.co.nz.

Contemporary Maori music has never been stronger or more varied and singer-songwriter Bic Runga is a leading artist. Te Vaka's tribal beats draw from their Polynesian roots. New Zealand's hip-hop scene is burgeoning, and Scribe simultaneously topped the national album and singles charts and sold triple platinum. Rapper Mareko is backed by Auckland enterprise Dawn Raid.

Flying Nun was the record label at the centre of a creative boom in the 1980s (and is still a source of cult fascination for indie music buffs).

Auckland is home to the garage-rock scene, providing a springboard for D4 and the Datsuns, and spawning respected drum-and-bass crews Concord Dawn and Bulletproof.

In Wellington, no-one grooves harder than Fat Freddy's Drop, who merge jazzy flights of improvisation with a dub heartbeat. In Dunedin – where the vibe is scruffy, arty and independent – pick up second-hand records at Records Records (p739). Christchurch is home of downbeat masters Salmonella Dub. Taranaki-born MC Tali is a hot drum-and-bass talent – check her out.

VISUAL ARTS

Kiwis have infiltrated the art world in all its forms.

Karen Walker, Trelise Cooper, Zambesi and World are internationally recognised fashion labels.

At Bronx Zoo stands a totem carved by Polynesian artist Shane Eagleton; Luke Jacomb is attracting attention in Seattle as a 'pioneering glassmaker'; Nina Sherson is a leading UK floral designer; and Maori *moko* (tattoo) featured in a 2002 exhibition at Britain's Maritime Museum. And of course, there's baby-photographer Anne Geddes. Len Lye's boundary-exploding work can be seen at Govett-Brewster Art Gallery (p583).

Leading contemporary Maori artists include Shane Cotton and Peter Robinson, and multimedia artist Lisa Reihana received acclaim for her 2002 exhibition *Digital Marae*. Charles Frederick Goldie (1870–1947) painted a series of highly realistic Maori portraits, now acknowledged and valued by Maoris as ancestral representations.

Dunedin-born David Low (1891–1963) was a highly influential cartoonist whose notorious work was banned during Nazi Germany.

Bone fish-hook pendants, carved in traditional and modernised styles are common NZ souvenirs – a badge of honour for most expat Kiwis – worn on a piece of leather around the neck. Paua shell is carved into beautiful ornaments and jewellery and makes an impressively tacky ashtray!

Sport

Though golf is the most *popular* sport, NZ's obsession is rugby union, a game interwoven with the country's history and culture. The All Blacks rugby team has almost mythical status and when they lose the semifinal of the Rugby World Cup (as they've done no fewer than three times!) there is national mourning – NZ's economy has actually been known to dip. Rugby crowds at Auckland's Eden Park (p527) are as restrained as their teams are cavalier, but things get noisier as you head south: fans at Canterbury's Jade Stadium (p687) are reputed to be the most one-eyed in the land.

Links to everything: www.sports.co.nz.

Auckland is home of the NZ Warriors rugby league team, which plays in the Australian NRL, and a Warriors home game at Ericsson Stadium (p527) is a noisy spectacle.

Netball is the leading winter sport for women (although more than 10,000 women play rugby), and the Silver Ferns perpetually challenge Australia for world supremacy. The Invercargill-based Southern Sting (p762) attract a fanatical local following.

Cricket is the sport of summer. See international matches at Wellington's Basin Reserve.

HAKA

Haka is Maori for any form of dance but it's come to be associated with the war chant that precedes battle. The most famous *haka* comes from Te Rauparaha (1768–1849), a chief of the Ngati Toa tribe. Made famous by the All Blacks, it's a powerful national symbol of pride and identity.

Te Rauparaha's Haka

Ka mate, ka mate (It is death, it is death)
Ka ora, ka ora (It is life, it is life)
Tenei te tangata puhuruhuru (Behold the hairy man)
Nana nei i tiki mai i whakawhiti te ra (Who caused the sun to shine)
Upane, aupane (Abreast, keep abreast)
Upane, ka aupane (The rank, hold fast)
Whiti te ra (Into the sunshine)

ENVIRONMENT Vaughan Yarwood

The Land

New Zealand is a young country – its present shape is less than 10,000 years old. Having broken away from the supercontinent of Gondwanaland (which included Africa, Australia, Antarctica and South America) in a stately geological dance some 130 million years ago, it endured eons of uplift and erosion, buckling and tearing, and the slow fall and rise of the sea as ice ages came and went. Straddling the boundary of two great colliding slabs of the earth's crust – the Pacific plate and the Indian/Australian plate – to this day NZ remains the plaything of nature's most powerful forces.

Vaughan is a historian and travel writer who is widely published in NZ and internationally. His most recent book is *The History Makers: Adventures in New Zealand Biography* and he is currently researching a book on Antarctic exploration.

The result is one of the most varied and spectacular series of landscapes in the world, ranging from snow-dusted mountains and drowned glacial valleys to rainforests, dunelands and an otherworldly volcanic plateau. It is a diversity of landforms you would expect to find across an entire continent rather than a small archipelago of islands in the South Pacific.

Evidence of NZ's tumultuous past is everywhere. The mountainous spine of the South Island – the 650km-long ranges of the Southern Alps – is one product of the clash of the two plates; the result of a process of rapid lifting that, if anything, is accelerating. Despite the country's highest peak, Mt Cook, losing 10m from its summit overnight in a 1991 landslide, the Southern Alps are on an express elevator that, without erosion and landslides, would see them reach 10 times their present height within just a few million years.

On the North Island, the most impressive changes have been wrought by volcanoes. Auckland, the country's biggest city, is built on an isthmus peppered by distinctive scoria cones, on many of which you can still see the earthworks of *pa* (fortified villages) built by early Maoris. The city's biggest and most recent volcano, 600-year-old Rangitoto Island, is just a short ferry ride from the downtown wharves. Some 300km further south, the classically shaped cone of snow capped Mt Taranaki/Egmont overlooks tranquil dairy pastures.

But the real volcanic heartland in NZ runs through the centre of the North Island, from the restless bulk of Mt Ruapehu in Tongariro National Park northeast through the Rotorua lake district out to the country's most active volcano, White Island, in the Bay of Plenty. Called the Taupo Volcanic Zone, this 250km-long rift valley – part of a great chain of volcanoes known as the Pacific Ring of Fire – has been the seat of massive eruptions that have left their mark on the country both physically and culturally.

New Zealand *is* Middle Earth. It has every geological formation and geographical landscape you can imagine…and some you can't.

ELIJAH WOOD (FRODO BAGGINS)

Most spectacular were the eruptions from the volcano which created Lake Taupo. Considered the world's most productive volcano in terms of the amount of material ejected, Taupo last erupted 1800 years ago in a display which was the most violent anywhere on the planet within the past 5000 years (see p570).

You can experience the aftermath of volcanic destruction on a smaller scale at Te Wairoa (the Buried Village; p603) near Rotorua on the shores of Lake Tarawera. Here, partly excavated and open to the public, lie the remains of a 19th-century Maori village overwhelmed when nearby Mt Tarawera erupted without warning.

The famous Pink and White Terraces (one of several claimants to the popular title 'eighth wonder of the world') were destroyed overnight by the same upheaval. For more information, see p602.

But when Nature sweeps the board clean with one hand she often rebuilds with the other: Waimangu Valley, born of all that geothermal violence, is the place to go to experience the hot earth up close and personal amid geysers, silica pans, bubbling mud pools and the world's biggest hot spring. Or you can wander around Rotorua's Whakarewarewa Thermal Village (p592) where descendants of the Maori displaced by the eruption live in the middle of steaming vents and prepare food for visitors in boiling pools.

A second by-product of movement along the tectonic plate boundary is seismic activity – earthquakes. Not for nothing has NZ been called 'the Shaky Isles'. Though most quakes do little more than rattle the glassware, one was indirectly responsible for creating an internationally celebrated tourist attraction…

Landforms: the shaping of New Zealand, by L Molloy and R Smith; takes digital modelling to its aesthetic limits to show nature at work. A delectable series of topographical 'snapshots' with explanatory text tells the story of how NZ became the way it is.

In 1931 an earthquake measuring 7.9 on the Richter scale levelled the Hawkes Bay city of Napier causing huge damage and loss of life. Napier was rebuilt almost entirely in the then-fashionable Art Deco architectural style, and walking its streets today you can relive its brash exuberance in what has become a mecca for lovers of Art Deco (p610).

Travellers to the South Island can also see some evidence of volcanism; if the remains of the old volcanoes of Banks Peninsula were not there to repel the sea, the vast Canterbury Plains, built from alpine sediment washed down the rivers from the Alps, would have eroded away long ago.

But in the south it is the Southern Alps themselves that dominate, dictating settlement patterns, throwing down engineering challenges and offering outstanding recreational opportunities. The island's mountainous backbone also helps shape the weather, as it stands in the path of the prevailing westerly winds which roll in, moisture-laden, from the Tasman Sea. As a result bush-clad lower slopes of the western Southern Alps are among the wettest places on earth, with an annual precipitation of some 15,000mm. Having lost its moisture, the wind then blows dry across the eastern plains towards the Pacific coast.

The North Island has a more even rainfall and is spared the temperature extremes of the South – which can plunge when a wind blows in from Antarctica. The important thing to remember, especially if you are tramping at high altitude, is that NZ has a maritime climate. This

RESPONSIBLE TRAVEL

Toitu te whenua – Care for the land. Help protect the environment by following these guidelines:

- Treat NZ's forests and native wildlife with respect. Damaging or taking plants is illegal in most parts of the country.
- Remove rubbish. Litter is unsightly and can encourage vermin and disease. Rather than burying or burning, carry out what you carry in.
- In areas without toilet facilities bury toilet waste in a shallow hole away from tracks, huts, camp sites and waterways.
- Keep streams and lakes pure by cleaning away from water sources. Drain waste water into the soil to filter out soaps and detergent. If you suspect contamination, boil water for three minutes, filter or chemically treat it before use.
- Where possible use portable fuel stoves. Keep open fires small, use only dead wood and make sure the fire is out by dousing it with water and checking the ashes before leaving.
- Keep to tracks where possible. Get permission before crossing private land and move carefully around livestock.

ENVIRONMENTAL ISSUES IN AOTEAROA NEW ZEALAND *Nandor Tanczos*

Aotearoa New Zealand is famous for having won some significant environmental battles. Since the 1980s we have seen the NZ Forest Accord (developed to protect native forest) and the end of all native logging on public land. Our national parks and reserves now cover around a third of our land area, and the first few marine reserves have been established. We are also famous for our strong antinuclear stance.

To describe ourselves as 'clean and green', however, is 100% pure fantasy. A drive in the country soon reveals that much of our land is more akin to a green desert.

The importation of European sheep and cattle grazing systems to Aotearoa New Zealand has left many hillsides with marginal productivity; they are bare of trees and prone to erosion. In many areas grazing threatens our waterways, with stock causing damage to stream and lake margins and runoff leading to nutrient overload of waterways. Regional councils and farming groups are starting to fence and plant stream banks to protect water quality but their efforts may be outstripped by the growth in dairy farming.

Despite increasing international and local demand for organic food, most farming in Aotearoa New Zealand relies on high levels of chemical inputs in the form of fertilisers, pesticides and herbicides. In addition, the Labour government, backed by most other political parties, has voted to end the ban on the release of genetically engineered (GE) organisms into the environment, in the face of overwhelming public opposition. However, we are still GE free and many of us are determined to keep it that way.

Our record on waste is regrettable. The Parliamentary Commissioner for the Environment recently stated that the average New Zealander generates 900kg of waste a year, which is more than the average American. Recycling facilities barely exist in some areas, although many local councils have been working with communities to combine waste reduction, job creation and reuse of reclaimed materials. Even so, some items, such as batteries, remain almost impossible to recycle, and the packaging industry has largely been left to 'self-regulate', with predicable consequences.

Energy consumption in Aotearoa New Zealand has grown three times more than population over the last 20 years. We are one of the most inefficient users of energy in the developed world and a staggering two-thirds of our energy comes from nonrenewable resources (although most other countries use an even higher proportion of nonrenewable resources!).

Add to that the ongoing battle being fought in many communities over the disposal of sewage and toxic waste, a conflict often spearheaded by *tangata whenua* (Maori), and the 'clean and green' label begins to look seriously compromised.

We do have a number of things in our favour. Our biggest saving grace is our small population, so the cumulative effect is reduced. Also, there are many national park and reserve areas set aside to protect native ecosystems making Aotearoa New Zealand a place well worth visiting. This is a beautiful land with enormous geographical and ecological diversity. Our forests are unique and magnificent, and the bird species that evolved in response to an almost total lack of mammalian life are spectacular, although now reduced in numbers.

The responsibility of New Zealanders is to make change, not just at a personal level, but at an institutional and infrastructural level, for ecological sustainability. The responsibility of visitors to Aotearoa New Zealand is to respect our unique biodiversity, and to query and question. Every time you ask where the recycling centre is; every time you express surprise at the levels of energy use, car use and water use; every time you demand organic food at a café or restaurant; you affect the person you talk to.

Aotearoa New Zealand has the potential to be a world leader in ecological wisdom. We have a strong tradition to draw from – the careful relationship the Maori developed with the natural world over the course of many, many generations. We live at the edge of the Pacific, on the Rim of Fire, a remnant of the ancient forests of Gondwanaland. We welcome conscious travellers.

Nandor is a Member of Parliament (NZ Greens), a high-profile campaigner on genetic engineering and a keen user of public transport means the weather can change with lightning speed, catching out the unprepared.

Wildlife

New Zealand may be relatively young, geologically speaking, but its plants and animals go back a long way. The tuatara, for instance, an ancient reptile unique to these islands, is a Gondwanaland survivor closely related to the dinosaurs, while many of the distinctive flightless birds (ratites) have distant African and South American cousins.

Due to its long isolation, the country is a veritable warehouse of unique and varied plants, most of which are found nowhere else. And with separation of the landmass occurring before mammals appeared on the scene, birds and insects have evolved in spectacular ways to fill the gaps.

The now extinct flightless moa, the largest of which grew to 3.5m tall and weighed over 200kg, browsed open grasslands much as cattle do today (skeletons can be seen at Auckland Museum, p511), while the smaller kiwi still ekes out a nocturnal living rummaging among forest leaf litter for insects and worms much as small mammals do elsewhere.

One of the country's most ferocious looking insects, the mouse-sized giant weta, meanwhile, has taken on a scavenging role elsewhere filled by rodents.

As one of the last places on earth to be colonised by humans, NZ was for millennia a safe laboratory for such risky evolutionary strategies, but with the arrival first of the Maori and soon after of Europeans, things went downhill fast.

Many creatures, including moa and the huia, an exquisite songbird, were driven to extinction and the vast forests were cleared for their timber and to make way for agriculture. Destruction of habitat and the introduction of exotic animals and plants have taken a terrible environmental toll and New Zealanders are now fighting a rearguard battle to save what remains.

DID YOU KNOW?

Found only in NZ, tuatara have a redundant third eye and are covered with scales. Unlike other reptiles (and surprisingly for something that has been around for 200 million years), the male has no penis. Living wild now only on offshore islands, you can see them in captivity in the Southland Museum & Art Gallery in Invercargill (p760).

BIRDS & ANIMALS

The first Polynesian settlers found little in the way of land mammals – just two species of bat – but forests, plains and coasts alive with birds. Largely lacking the bright plumage found elsewhere, NZ's birds – like its endemic plants – have an understated beauty which does not shout for attention.

Among the most musical is the bellbird, common in both native and exotic forests everywhere except Northland, though like many birds more likely to be heard than seen. Its call is a series of liquid bell notes, most often sounded at dawn or dusk.

The tui, another nectar eater and the country's most beautiful songbird, is a great mimic, with an inventive repertoire that includes clicks, grunts and chuckles. Notable for the white throat feathers which stand out against its dark plumage, the tui often feeds on flax flowers in suburban gardens but is most at home in densely tangled forest ('bush' to New Zealanders).

Fantails are commonly encountered on forest tracks, swooping and jinking to catch insects stirred up by passing trampers, while pukeko, elegant swamp-hens with blue plumage and bright red beaks, are readily seen along wetland margins and even on the sides of roads nearby – be warned, they have little road sense.

If you spend any time on the South Island high country, you are likely to come up against the fearless and inquisitive kea – an uncharacteristically

B Heather and H Robertson's *Field Guide to the Birds of New Zealand* is the most comprehensive guide for bird-watchers and a model of helpfulness for anyone even casually interested in the country's remarkable birdlife.

KIWI SPOTTING

The kiwi is a threatened species, and with the additional difficulty of them being nocturnal, it's only on Stewart Island that you easily see one in the wild. However, they can be observed in many artificially dark 'kiwi houses':

Kiwi & Birdlife Park (p719) Queenstown.
National Aquarium of New Zealand (p611) Napier.
Wellington Zoo (p630)
Willowbank Wildlife Reserve (p680) Christchurch.

drab green parrot with bright red underwings. Kea are common in the car parks of the Fox and Franz Josef Glaciers where they hang out for food scraps or tear rubber from car windscreens.

Then there is the takahe, a rare flightless bird thought extinct until a small colony was discovered in 1948, and the equally flightless kiwi, the country's national emblem and of course the nickname for New Zealanders themselves.

DID YOU KNOW?

The egg of the flightless kiwi can weigh as much as a quarter of the female bird and, not having an egg tooth, the chick uses its feet to break out of the shell. With whiskers, tiny hidden wings, a low metabolic rate, no tail feathers, hairlike plumage and a keen sense of smell, the ground-dwelling kiwi is rather more like a mammal than a bird.

The kiwi has a round body covered in coarse feathers, strong legs and a long, distinctive bill with nostrils at the tip for sniffing out food. It is not easy to find them in the wild, but they can be seen in simulated environments at excellent nocturnal houses.

To get a feel for what the bush used to be like, take a trip to Tiritiri Matangi Island (p536), not far from Auckland. This regenerating island is an open sanctuary and one of the country's most successful exercises in community-assisted conservation.

Encountering marine mammals is one of the great delights of a visit to NZ, now that well-regulated ecotourism has replaced the commercial whaling and sealing that drove many NZ species to the brink of extinction in the early 19th century. Sperm whales can be seen off the coast of Kaikoura and licensed companies offer swimming with wild dolphins in the Bay of Islands and elsewhere; forget aquarium shows – sea encounters are the real thing.

TREES

No visitor to NZ (particularly Australians!) will go for long without hearing about the damage done to the bush by that bad-mannered Australian import, the brush-tailed possum. The long list of mammal pests introduced accidentally or for a variety of misguided reasons includes deer, rabbits, stoats, pigs and goats. But the most destructive by far is the possum, 70 million of which now chew through millions of tonnes of foliage a year despite the best efforts of the Department of Conservation (DOC) to control them.

Herbert Guthrie-Smith's *Tutira* is a book like no other. Subtitled 'the story of a New Zealand sheep station', it is really much more: a teeming mix of geology, geography, botany, animal husbandry and natural history leavened with dry Scottish humour… an undisputed classic.

Among favoured possum food are NZ's most colourful trees: the kowhai, a small-leaved tree growing to 11m, that in spring has drooping clusters of bright yellow flowers (NZ's national flower); the pohutukawa, a beautiful coastal tree of the northern North Island which bursts into vivid red flower in December, earning the nickname 'Christmas tree'; and a similar crimson-flowered tree, the rata. Species of rata are found on both islands; the northern rata starts life as a climber on a host tree (that it eventually chokes).

The few remaining pockets of mature centuries-old kauri are stately emblems of former days. Their vast hammered trunks and towering, epiphyte-festooned limbs, which dwarf every other tree in the forest, are reminders of why they were sought after in colonial days for spars and building timber. The best place to see the remaining giants is Northland's Waipoua Kauri Forest (p552), home to three-quarters of the country's surviving kauri.

Now, the pressure has been taken off kauri and other timber trees including the distinctive rimu, or red pine, and the long-lived totara (favoured for Maori war canoes), by one of the country's most successful imports – *pinus radiata*. Pine was found to thrive in NZ, growing to maturity in just 35 years, and plantation forests are now widespread through the central North Island – the Southern Hemisphere's biggest, Kaingaroa Forest, lies southeast of Rotorua.

You won't get far into the bush without coming across one of its most prominent features – tree ferns. New Zealand is a land of ferns (with more than 80 species) and most easily recognised are the mamuka (black tree fern), which grows to 20m and can be seen in damp gullies throughout the country; and the 10m high ponga (silver tree fern) with its distinctive white underside. The silver fern is equally at home as part of corporate logos and on the clothing of many of the country's top sportspeople.

DID YOU KNOW?

Tane-mahuta (p552), the biggest surviving kauri tree – 51m high and with a girth of 13m – is only a quarter of the size of the largest known, a kauri that grew on the Coromandel Peninsula, said to have had a girth of over 26m.

National Parks

A third of the country – more than five million hectares – is protected in environmentally important parks and reserves which embrace almost every conceivable landscape: from mangrove-fringed inlets in the north to the snow-topped volcanoes of the Central Plateau, and from the forested fastness of the Ureweras in the east to the Southern Alps' majestic mountains, glaciers and fiords. The 14 national parks, three maritime parks and two marine reserves, along with numerous forest parks, offer huge scope for wilderness experiences, ranging from climbing, snow skiing and mountain biking to tramping, kayaking and trout fishing.

The Department of Conservation website has useful information on the country's national parks, tracks and walkways. It also lists backcountry huts and camp sites: www.doc.govt.nz.

Three places are World Heritage areas: NZ's Subantarctic Islands, Tongariro National Park (p576) and Te Wahipounamu (p748), an amalgam of several national parks in southwest NZ which boast the world's finest surviving Gondwanaland plants and animals in their natural habitats.

Access to the country's wild places is relatively straightforward, though huts on walking tracks require passes and may need to be booked in advance. In practical terms, there is little difference for travellers between a national park and a forest park, though dogs are not allowed in national parks without a permit. Camping is possible in all parks, but may be restricted to dedicated camping grounds – check first. Permits are required for hunting (game birds) and licences needed for inland fishing (trout, salmon). Both can be bought online at www.fishandgame.org.nz.

TOP FIVE NATIONAL PARKS

- **Aoraki/Mt Cook** (p702) Alpine landscape; home to the wonderfully naughty kea and NZ's highest mountain. Alpine track, glacier flights, climbing.
- **Fiordland** Vast untouched fiords, waterfalls, sandflies, pristine lakes. Outstanding walks include the Milford (p755) and Keplar (p750) tracks.
- **Te Urewera** (p617) Rugged forested hills; steeped in Maori history. Lake Waikaremoana walking track.
- **Tongariro** (p576) Active volcanic wilderness; the world's fourth-oldest national park. Ski fields, rock climbing, Tongariro Northern Circuit.
- **Whanganui** (p589) Primeval river valleys; rich Maori and settler history. Canoe journeys, *marae* stays.

North Island

CONTENTS

HIGHLIGHTS

- **Tongariro National Park** Visit smoking Mt Ruapehu and walk the Tongariro Crossing (p576)
- **Bay of Islands** Jet-boat, sail and kayak around these beautiful islands (p537)
- **Rotorua** Experience geothermal magnificence and splendid Maori culture (p590)
- **Auckland** Drink your way downtown (p525)
- **Waitomo** Abseil into incredible glow-worm-studded caves and go tubing along underground rivers (p559)
- **Mt Taranaki/Egmont** Check out the massive cone of this volcano (p587)
- **Te Urewera National Park** Tramp the Lake Waikaremoana Track (p617)
- **Wellington's Bohemian cafes** Discuss Kafka over strong black espressos (p636)

- **Cheer for:** Bay of Plenty Steamers in the NPC (rugby union)
- **Eat:** paua fritters from Auckland's White Lady (p523)
- **Drink:** a handle (425mL) of Steinlager
- **Listen to:** The Black Seeds' *Keep on Pushing* or Betchadupa's *The Alphabetchadupa*
- **Watch:** *Whale Rider* or *Lord of the Rings*
- **Party at:** Central Auckland (p525) or Courtenay Pl in Wellington (p638)
- **Swim:** in a geothermal pool that you dig yourself at Hot Water Beach (p567)
- **Avoid:** complaining about the weather
- **Locals' nickname:** JAFA (Aucklander)

- TELEPHONE CODES: 09, 07, 06, 04
- WEBSITE: www.purenz.com

The backpack was invented for places like New Zealand's North Island, a rugged, adventurous, yet easily explorable place where volcanic mountains, craters and lakes give way to lush, rambling forests, which in turn yield to stunning surf beaches and gulf-moored islands. Travellers have to cross oceans to get here but are soon rewarded by finding themselves scrambling up the sides of active volcanoes, snorkelling alongside dolphins, descending into the maws of alien underground caverns and learning to ride atop some fine South Pacific rollers. Other popular activities on this island, which has a warmer climate and a rougher, lava-hewn persona than its southern sibling, include pressing noses with a friendly Maori, trying unsuccessfully to hug the trunk of a massive kauri tree, base jumping from high up an inner-city building, and hanging about in pubs and bars while marvelling at how many other backpackers followed you here.

All you need to do to get inspired about travelling to the North Island is to chant the sometimes fearsome names of this island's prime attractions – Tongariro, Taranaki, Waitomo, Rotorua, Taupo. Even the gentrified names given to the beautiful collection of turquoise coves known as the Bay of Islands and to the entertainment-infatuated city of Auckland paint enigmatic pictures that will come to vivid life once you land on northern Kiwi soil.

AUCKLAND

☎ 09 / pop 1.2 million

Situated on a narrow strip of land between two scenic harbours, Auckland is surrounded by more sandy beaches and islands than arguably any other city in the world. It's a self-proclaimed 'City of Sails' and NZ's 'pretend capital' with an energetic outdoor culture both on the harbours and on dry land, where plenty of sports are played and watched. The city is also splashed with green parks that include the terraced volcanic hills where Maori people once lived in *pa* (fortified villages).

Auckland is challenging Queenstown as the country's adventure capital, as it has installed enough daredevil leaps, climbs and rides to satisfy any thrill-seeker. Those looking for indoor entertainment will find a downtown brimming with late-night clubbing, a great live-music scene, theatres, concert halls and comedy venues.

For many Polynesians living on isolated and undeveloped South Pacific islands, Auckland's streets have a modern allure and many islanders now live in the southern and western suburbs. Recent Asian immigrants attracted by the city's clean, green image and relatively stress-free lifestyle have also helped give the city an international cosmopolitan style.

Don't Miss: a base jump off Sky Tower, checking out islander culture at the Auckland Museum, chilling out at Kelly Tarlton's Antarctic Encounter & Underwater World, clubbing on K Rd, upmarket drinking at Viaduct Harbour, swimming with a dolphin, and having a laugh at the Classic Comedy Club.

HISTORY

Maori habitation in the Auckland area dates back at least 800 years, with initial settlements drifting from the coastal regions of the Hauraki Gulf islands to the fertile Auckland isthmus. From the 17th century, tribes from outside the region challenged the local Ngati Whatua tribe for this desirable place. The locals in response built *pa* on Auckland's numerous volcanic cones. But when the first Europeans arrived in the area in the 1830s they reported a land largely devoid of inhabitants. The Auckland isthmus (Tamaki Makaurau, literally 'Tamaki Desired by Many') had largely been forsaken, either ravaged by war or the threat of it.

After the 1840 signing of the Treaty of Waitangi (p491), Captain William Hobson, NZ's first governor, moved the capital to Auckland because of its fine harbour (Waitemata, or 'Sparkling Waters'), fertile soil and central location. Hobson named the settlement after his commanding officer, George Eden (Lord Auckland). However, it lost capital status to Wellington after just 25 years.

Since the beginning of the 20th century, Auckland has been NZ's fastest-growing city and its main commercial centre.

ORIENTATION

The city's commercial heart is Queen St, which runs from Britomart Station near the waterfront up to Karangahape Rd (K Rd). On the way it passes Aotea Sq, and comes within a few blocks of the landmark Sky Tower.

With its ethnic restaurants, funky bars and nightclubs, K Rd is a lively, Bohemian alternative to the more reserved downtown. Parnell Rd, just east of the centre, is a street of renovated wooden villas converted into restaurants and boutiques, and continues to the fashion outlets in Newmarket. Just west of the centre is Ponsonby Rd, its many restaurants, bars and cafés abuzz with the chatter of diners, the hiss of cappuccino machines and the ringing of mobile phones.

Further out, Mt Eden and Mission Bay are residential suburbs with restaurants, bars and cafés. Devonport, easily reached by ferry across the harbour, is a quaint waterside suburb on the southern tip of the residential North Shore, equipped with beaches and art galleries. The nearby suburb of Takapuna also has its share of restaurants, bars and cafés. For bush walks, surf beaches and wineries, head west to the Waitakere Ranges.

INFORMATION

Bookshops

Auckland Map Centre (Map pp514-15; ☎ 309 7725; 209 Queen St) Pick up city and country maps here.

Borders (Map pp514-15; ☎ 309 3377; Skycity Metro Mall, 291 Queen St; 🕓 10am-10pm Sun-Thu, 10am-midnight Fri & Sat) For books, music and DVDs.

Hard to Find But Worth the Effort Second-hand Bookshop (☎ 446 0300; 81A Victoria Rd, Devonport; 🕓 9.30am-5.30pm)

Whitcoull's (Map pp514-15; ☎ 356 5400; 210 Queen St; 🕓 8am-6pm Mon-Thu, 8am-9pm Fri, 9am-6pm Sat,

GETTING INTO TOWN

Auckland Airport (Map pp510-11; ☎ 256 8899; www.auckland-airport.co.nz) is 21km south of the city centre. A free shuttle service operates every 20 minutes between the international and domestic terminals and there's also a signposted footpath between them (about a 1km walk).

The **AirBus** (☎ 0508 247 287, 375 4702; adult one way/return NZ$15/22, backpacker NZ$11/18) runs every 20 or 30 minutes (from 6.20am to 10pm) between the international and domestic terminals and the city, stopping outside major hostels and hotels; buy a ticket from the driver. The trip takes about 50 minutes one way (longer during rush hour).

Door-to-door **shuttle minibuses** (first person NZ$20, each subsequent person NZ$5) also run to and from the airport. It pays to get a group together and for you all to get off at the same place. The price increases if you want to go to an outlying suburb. Each shuttle is supposed to stay a maximum of 15 minutes so you may be able to negotiate a lower price if one is about to leave. The main operator is **Super Shuttle** (☎ 306 3960).

A taxi to the airport from the city costs around NZ$40.

The **Sky City Coach Terminal** (Map pp514-15; 102 Hobson St), where long-distance buses arrive, is in the heart of Auckland's downtown. Trains shunt into and out of **Britomart Station** (Map pp514-15; Quay St), 1km east of the centre. The free City Circuit bus does an inner-city loop that includes this station every 10 minutes from 8am to 8pm; for earlier or later connections into town, hop on the **Link bus** (tickets NZ$1.20). For further details see p529.

10am-6pm Sun) Another large bookshop with good NZ, travel and fiction sections.

Women's Bookshop (☎ 376 4399; 105 Ponsonby Rd, Ponsonby; 10am-6pm) A community resource as well as a bookshop.

Emergency

AIDS Hotline (☎ 0800 802 437)

Ambulance, Fire Service & Police (☎ 111)

Auckland Central Police Station (Map pp514-15; ☎ 302 6400; cnr Vincent & Cook Sts)

Auckland Victim Support (☎ 302 6653)

Internet Access

Expect to pay from NZ$2 to NZ$4 per hour at Auckland's numerous Internet cafés; several are open 24 hours.

Internet Resources

Auckland Regional Council (www.arc.govt.nz) Info on Auckland's parks and transport.

DineOut (www.dineout.co.nz) Customers' comments on local restaurants.

Tourism Auckland (www.aucklandnz.com) Lots of tourist information.

Laundry

Clean Green Laundromat (Map pp514-15; ☎ 358 4370; 18B Fort St; 8am-6.30pm Mon-Fri, 8am-5pm Sat)

Left Luggage

Most hostels offer storage and there are some left-luggage lockers on the lower level of Britomart Station (small lockers NZ$0.50 per hour or NZ$10 for 24 hours, big lockers NZ$1 per hour or NZ$15 for 24 hours).

Media

Auckland A-Z Visitors Guide Has maps and events.

Jason's Auckland What's On This free publication comes out monthly.

New Zealand Herald (www.nzherald.co.nz/nznews) Auckland's widely circulated newspaper also has a website.

Medical Services

Ascot Accident & Medical Clinic (Map pp510-11; ☎ 520 9555; 90 Greenlane East, Remuera; consultations from NZ$55; 24hr)

Auckland City Hospital (Map pp514-15; ☎ 379 7440; Park Rd, Grafton; consultations NZ$120; 24hr) The main accident and emergency hospital; be warned you could face a wait of up to three hours.

Quay Med (☎ 919 2555; 68 Beach Rd, Parnell; consultations adult NZ$50-55, student NZ$30-35; 8am-8pm Mon-Fri, 10am-2pm Sat & Sun) Provides a wide range of medical services without the long queues of Auckland City Hospital. There is a pharmacy (9am-6pm Mon-Fri) and a dentist (8am-8pm Mon-Fri).

Travel Care Medical Centre (Map pp514-15; ☎ 373 4621; 125 Queen St; consultations NZ$54; 9am-5.30pm Mon-Fri, 10am-5pm Sat, noon-4pm Sun) Specialises in health care for travellers.

Money

There are plenty of moneychangers, banks and ATMs on Queen St. The exchange rates

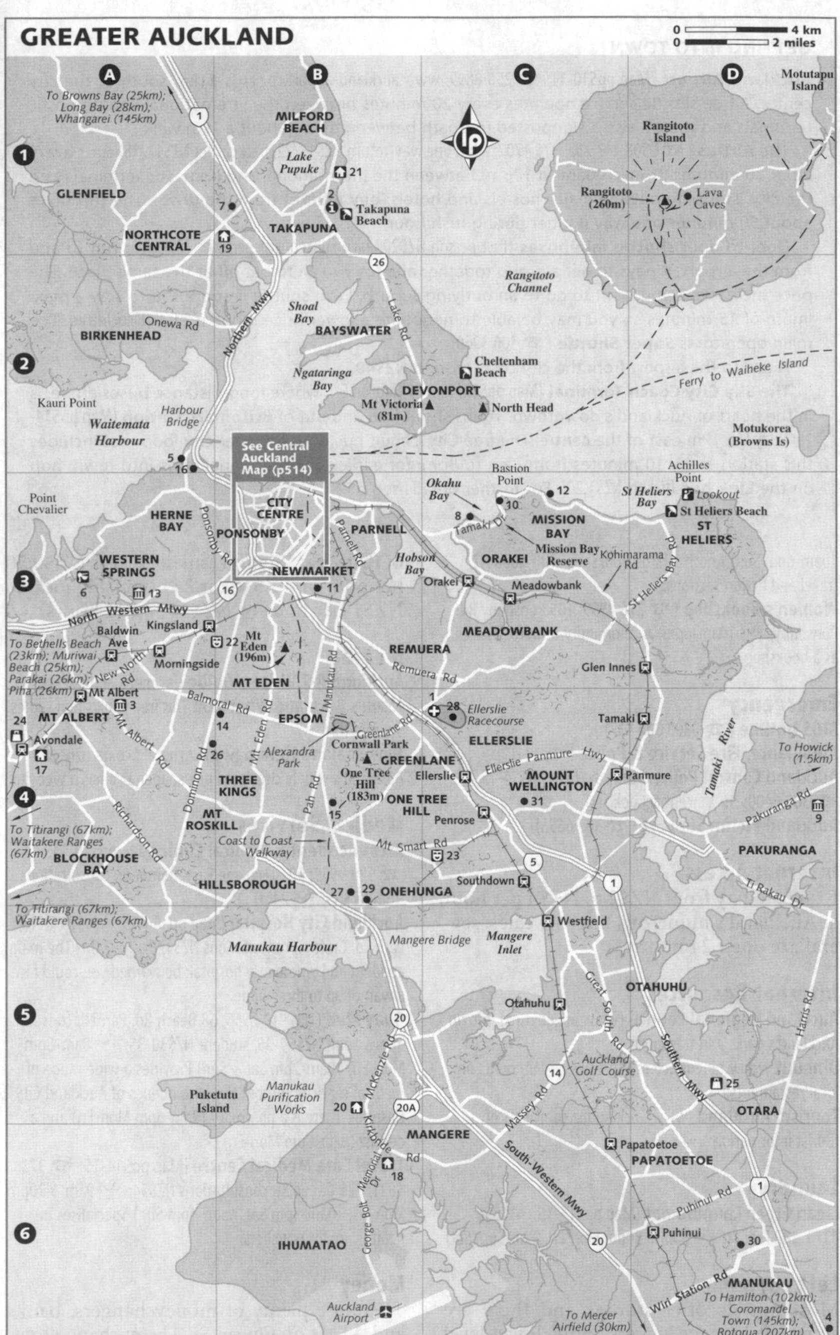
GREATER AUCKLAND
0 4 km
0 2 miles
To Browns Bay (25km); Long Bay (28km); Whangarei (145km)
MILFORD BEACH
Lake Pupuke
GLENFIELD
NORTHCOTE CENTRAL
TAKAPUNA
Takapuna Beach
Motutapu Island
Rangitoto Island
Rangitoto (260m)
Lava Caves
Rangitoto Channel
Shoal Bay
BAYSWATER
Lake Rd
Northern Mwy
Onewa Rd
BIRKENHEAD
Ngataringa Bay
Cheltenham Beach
DEVONPORT
Mt Victoria (81m)
North Head
Ferry to Waiheke Island
Kauri Point
Harbour Bridge
Waitemata Harbour
Motukorea (Browns Is)
See Central Auckland Map (p514)
Bastion Point
Okahu Bay
Achilles Point
St Heliers Bay
Lookout
St Heliers Beach
Point Chevalier
HERNE BAY
CITY CENTRE
PONSONBY
PARNELL
Parnell Rd
Ponsonby Rd
Tamaki Dr
MISSION BAY
ST HELIERS
WESTERN SPRINGS
NEWMARKET
Hobson Bay
ORAKEI
Mission Bay Reserve
Kohimarama Rd
St Heliers Bay Rd
Orakei
Meadowbank
North Western Mtwy
Kingsland
Baldwin Ave
MEADOWBANK
To Bethells Beach (23km); Muriwai Beach (25km); Parakai (26km); Piha (26km)
Morningside
New North Rd
Mt Eden (196m)
REMUERA
Remuera Rd
Glen Innes
MT EDEN
Mt Albert
Balmoral Rd
Manukau Rd
Ellerslie Racecourse
Tamaki
MT ALBERT
EPSOM
Mt Eden Rd
Mt Albert Rd
Avondale
Greenlane Rd
Cornwall Park
ELLERSLIE
Tamaki River
To Howick (1.5km)
Alexandra Park
GREENLANE
Ellerslie Panmure Hwy
Dominion Rd
THREE KINGS
One Tree Hill (183m)
Ellerslie
MOUNT WELLINGTON
Panmure
Pah Rd
ONE TREE HILL
Pakuranga Rd
Richardson Rd
To Titirangi (67km); Waitakere Ranges (67km)
MT ROSKILL
Penrose
PAKURANGA
Coast to Coast Walkway
Mt Smart Rd
BLOCKHOUSE BAY
HILLSBOROUGH
Southdown
ONEHUNGA
Ti Rakau Dr
To Titirangi (67km); Waitakere Ranges (67km)
Westfield
Mangere Bridge
Mangere Inlet
Manukau Harbour
OTAHUHU
Otahuhu
Great South Rd
Harris Rd
Southern Mwy
Auckland Golf Course
McKenzie Rd
Puketutu Island
Manukau Purification Works
Massey Rd
OTARA
MANGERE
Kirkbride Rd
South-Western Mwy
Papatoetoe
PAPATOETOE
George Bolt Memorial Dr
Puhinui Rd
Puhinui
IHUMATAO
MANUKAU
Wiri Station Rd
Auckland Airport
To Mercer Airfield (30km)
To Hamilton (102km); Coromandel Town (145km); Rotorua (207km)

INFORMATION		KELLY TARLTON'S...		ENTERTAINMENT	
INFORMATION		Kelly Tarlton's Antarctic Encounter & Underwater World	10 C3	**ENTERTAINMENT**	(p527)
Ascot Accident & Medical Clinic	1 C4	Lionzone Brewery	11 B3	Eden Park	22 B3
Takapuna Visitors Centre	2 B1	Mission Bay Watersports	12 C3	Ericsson Stadium	23 C4
SIGHTS & ACTIVITIES	(pp511–18)	Motat	13 A3	**SHOPPING**	(p528)
Alberton House	3 A4	Rocknasium	14 B4	Avondale Market	24 A4
Auckland Botanical Gardens	4 D6	Stardome Observatory	15 B4	Otara Markets	25 D5
Auckland Harbour Bridge Bungy Jump	(see 16)	Westhaven Marina	16 A2	**TRANSPORT**	(p529)
Auckland Harbour Bridge Climb	5 A2	**SLEEPING**	(pp519–22)	Auckland Rentals & Buy-Back	26 A4
Auckland Zoo	6 A3	Avondale Motor Park	17 A4	Car Warehouse	27 B4
Dive Centre	7 B1	Jet Inn	18 B6	Ellerslie Racecourse Car Fair	28 C4
Fergs Kayaks	8 C3	North Shore Motels & Holiday Park	19 B1	Hammer Car Auctions	29 B4
Gulfwind Sailing Academy	(see 16)	Skyway Lodge	20 B5	Manukau Car Fair	30 D6
Howick Historical Village	9 D4	Takapuna Beach Holiday Park	21 B1	Turner's Car Auctions	31 C4

offered at private moneychangers are usually similar but it pays to shop around.

ASB Bank (Map pp514-15; Westfield Downtown Shopping Centre; 9am-4.30pm Mon-Fri, 9am-4pm Sat & Sun) Try ASB for weekend banking.

Post

Wellesley St post office (Map pp514-15; 7.30am-5pm Mon-Fri) Near Aotea Square. This is the place to pick up post-restante mail (ID is required).

Tourist Information

Auckland visitors centre (Map pp514-15; ☎ 979 2333; www.aucklandnz.com; cnr Victoria St West & Federal St; 8am-8pm Sun-Wed, 8am-10pm Thu-Sat) In the Sky Tower Atrium.

Automobile Association (AA; Map pp514-15; ☎ 377 4660; 99 Albert St; 9am-5pm Mon-Fri, 9am-3pm Sat) Has maps and accommodation directories.

Department of Conservation Information Centre (DOC; Map pp514-15; ☎ 379 6476; www.doc.govt.nz; Ferry Bldg, 99 Quay St; 10am-5.30pm Mon-Fri, 10am-3pm Sat)

Domestic Airport visitors centre (Map pp510-11; ☎ 256 8480; 7am-5pm) In the Air New Zealand section of the domestic airport, just a short walk from the international airport.

North Shore visitors centre (☎ 446 0677; 3 Victoria Rd, Devonport; 8.30am-5pm) For info on attractions around Devonport.

NZ visitors centre (Map pp514-15; ☎ 979 2333; nzvc@aucklandnz.com; cnr Quay & Hobson Sts; 9am-5pm) Info on the whole country.

Takapuna visitors centre (Map pp510-11; ☎ 486 8670; www.tourismnorthshore.org.nz; 49 Hurstmere Rd, Takapuna; 8.30am-5pm Mon-Fri, 10am-3pm Sat & Sun) Covers the less touristy North Shore.

Visitors Information Centre (Map pp510-11; ☎ 275 6467; International Airport) Open from arrival of first to last flight. It's on your left as you walk onto the concourse; you can make free calls to Auckland accommodation providers.

SIGHTS

Central Auckland is the easy-to-navigate repository for many of the city's prime sights, including the heights of Sky Tower, sundry high-quality museums and galleries, the yacht-crowded waterfront and the green reaches of Auckland Domain. East of downtown in Parnell are numerous historic buildings.

Sky Tower

The imposing **Sky Tower** (Map pp514-15; ☎ 363 6422; www.skycityauckland.co.nz; cnr Victoria St West & Federal St; adult/concession NZ$15/10; 8.30am-11pm Sun-Thu, 8.30am-midnight Fri & Sat) is part of the **Sky City complex** (24hr), a casino with restaurants, cafés, bars and a hotel. At 328m it's the tallest structure in the southern hemisphere; a lift takes you up to the observation decks in 40 seconds. It costs NZ$3 extra to catch the skyway lift to the 'ultimate' viewing level. Late afternoon is a good time to go up, and the Sky Lounge sells beer and coffee to slurp as the sun sets. For details of the Sky Jump and Vertigo Climb, see under Activities (p516).

Auckland Museum

The country's oldest **museum** (Te Papa Whakahiku; ☎ 309 0443; www.akmuseum.org.nz; Parnell; admission by donation; 10am-5pm) sits atop a sweeping expanse of lawn that forms part of the Auckland Domain (Map pp514–15). It has a comprehensive display on Pacific Island and Maori culture on the ground floor, including a 25m-long war canoe. The first floor is dedicated to the natural world and has a first-class activities centre for children. The 2nd floor focuses on New Zealanders at war, from 19th-century battles to the peace-keeping assignments of today, and includes a re-creation of 19th-century Auckland shops.

For many, the highlight is the performance of Maori song and dance by **Manaia** (☎ 306 704; adult/concession NZ$15/12). The informal shows at 11am, noon and 1.30pm are a good introduction to Maori culture.

Kelly Tarlton's Antarctic Encounter & Underwater World

This unique **aquarium** (Map pp510-11; ☎ 0800 805 050, 528 0603; www.kellytarltons.co.nz; 23 Tamaki Dr; adult/concession NZ$26/20; 9am-8pm Dec-Feb, 9am-6pm Mar-Nov) is housed in old storm-water holding tanks. A transparent acrylic tunnel runs along the centre of the aquarium, through which you travel on a conveyor belt, with the fish (including sharks and stingrays) swimming around you. You can step off at any time to take a closer look.

The big attraction, however, is the Antarctic Encounter, which includes a walk through a replica of Scott's 1911 Antarctic hut and a ride aboard a heated snow cat through a frozen environment where a colony of King and Gentoo penguins lives at subzero temperatures. Displays include an Antarctic scientific base of the future and exhibits on the history of Antarctica.

To get here take bus Nos 74 to 76 from outside Britomart Station, or the Explorer Bus (p518). It's 6km from downtown on the road to Mission Bay.

Lionzone Brewery

Lion Breweries (Map pp510-11; ☎ 358 8366; www.lionzone.co.nz; 380 Khyber Pass Rd, Newmarket; adult/concession NZ$15/12) has turned its plain old brewery tours into an interactive 'beer experience'. Two-hour tours are held daily except Sunday at 9.30am, 12.15pm and 3pm, and include a history of brewing, an audiovisual presentation, a virtual tour of the brewing process and, of course, some quality time spent sampling Steinlager and Lion Red beers in a replica brewhouse.

Minus 5° Bar

Minus 5° Bar (Map pp514-15; Princes Wharf; 2-10pm) is an extraordinary bar where everything from the seats to your glass is made of ice. Put on special clothing (including gloves and shoes), pay NZ$20 and sip a vodka-based drink or a juice from an edible ice glass. You can only stay inside the shimmering ice world for 30 minutes. Lenin Bar (p526) next door offers a good view inside.

Auckland Zoo

Auckland Zoo (Map pp510-11; ☎ 360 3819; www.aucklandzoo.co.nz; Motions Rd, Western Springs; adult/concession NZ$13/10; 9.30am-5.30pm) isn't huge, but has spacious, natural compounds. The primate exhibit is well done and the African animals enclosure, 'Pridelands', is excellent, as is the meerkat domain which can be explored through tunnels. A nocturnal house has native birds such as kiwis, but they are hard to see. Newish additions to the zoo include a penguin enclosure and the sea lions, which you can watch through an underwater viewing window. Last admission is at 4.15pm.

To get there take the Explorer Bus (p518), or bus Nos 042 to 045 from outside Britomart Station. Electric **trams** (return fare NZ$2) run every 20 minutes to Motat (opposite).

National Maritime Museum

This **museum** (Map pp514-15; ☎ 0800 725 897, 373 0800; www.nzmaritime.org.nz; cnr Quay & Hobson Sts; adult/concession NZ$12/6; 9am-6pm summer, 9am-5pm winter) is the place to learn about NZ's seafaring history. It's a well-designed, extensive display of dozens of boats, from Maori canoes and immigrant ships to jet-boats, and includes the history of the America's Cup.

An old steamboat, SS *Puke*, is moored outside the museum and runs free 20-minute trips around the harbour on either Saturday or Sunday between 11am and 3pm. The **Ted Ashby** (adult/concession NZ$15/7, boat & museum NZ$19/12), a flat-bottomed scow, operates one-hour cruises from the museum at noon and 2pm on Tuesday, Thursday, Saturday and Sunday.

Auckland Art Gallery

The **Auckland Art Gallery** (Map pp514-15; ☎ 379 1349; www.aucklandartgallery.govt.nz; admission free, special exhibitions adult/concession NZ$7/5, Mon free; 10am-5pm) is housed in two neighbouring buildings and the entry fee covers both galleries. The **Main Gallery** (cnr Wellesley St East & Kitchener St), built in French chateau style, has an extensive permanent collection of NZ art, including Charles Goldie's stark Maori portraits of a vanished age. The gallery café has a deck overlooking Albert Park. The **New Gallery** (Map pp514-15; cnr Wellesley & Lorne Sts) concentrates on contemporary art. Ten private art galleries can be found in the streets around these two public galleries.

Stardome Observatory

Stardome Observatory (Map pp510-11; ☎ 624 1246; off Manukau Rd; www.stardome.org.nz; adult/concession NZ$12/10) is in the One Tree Hill Domain. As well as viewing the sky inside the planetarium, on clear nights it's possible to gaze at the night sky and stars through the courtyard telescopes. The night sky can also be viewed through a large 50cm telescope (NZ$8). The planetarium's hour-long Stardome Show is not dependent on Auckland's fickle weather and is usually held Wednesday to Saturday evenings (phone the observatory or check the website for scheduled times).

Motat (Museum of Transport & Technology)

This 19-hectare **museum** (Map pp510-11; ☎ 846 0199; www.motat.org.nz; Great North Rd; admission NZ$10; 🕑 10am-5pm) is at Western Springs, near the zoo, and comprises two parts. Motat I has exhibits on transport, communications and energy, including vintage cars, a display about pioneer aviator Richard Pearse and the hands-on Science Centre. Motat II features rare and historic aircraft, plus railway and military hardware; exhibits include a V1 flying bomb and a Lancaster bomber from WWII, but pride of place goes to the huge Solent flying boat that ran a Pacific islands loop in the days of luxury flying. Electric **trams** (return fare NZ$2) run every 20 minutes from Motat I to Motat II and the zoo.

To get there, take the Explorer Bus (p518), or bus Nos 042 to 045 from outside Britomart Station.

Historic Buildings

The NZ Historic Places Trust owns three 19th-century properties with period furnishings that give an insight into the lifestyle of wealthy pioneer families in Auckland. **Alberton House** (Map pp510-11; ☎ 846 7367; 100 Mt Albert Rd, Mt Albert; admission NZ$7.50; 🕑 10.30am-noon & 1-4.30pm Wed-Sun) is a true colonial-style mansion. **Highwic House** (☎ 524 5729; 40 Gillies Ave, Newmarket; admission NZ$7.50; 🕑 10.30am-noon & 1-4.30pm Wed-Sun) is a wooden Gothic building; entry is via Mortimer Pass. **Ewelme Cottage** (☎ 379 0202; 14 Ayr St, Parnell; admission NZ$3; 🕑 10.30am-noon & 1-4.30pm Fri-Sun) was built for a clergyman in the 1860s.

Near Ewelme Cottage is the restored **Kinder House** (☎ 379 4008; 2 Ayr St, Parnell; admission NZ$2; 🕑 11am-3pm Tue-Sun), built of stone in 1857 and displaying the art and memorabilia of the Rev Dr John Kinder, who died in 1903.

St Mary's Church (Parnell Rd, Parnell; 🕑 10am-4pm Mon-Sat, 11am-4pm Sun) is a perfect example of a wooden Gothic church (1886). It's next door to **Holy Trinity Cathedral**, worth seeing for its stained-glass windows.

Howick Historical Village (Map pp510-11; ☎ 576 9506; Bells Rd, Pakuranga; adult/student NZ$10/8; 🕑 10am-4pm) is an interesting collection of 30 restored 19th-century buildings, including a thatched sod cottage, forge, school, toy museum and chapel.

Parks & Gardens

Albert Park (Map pp514–15) is a good central spot in which to relax or have a picnic surrounded by flower beds and historical monuments, such as an 1899 statue of Queen Victoria.

Covering about 80 hectares, the **Auckland Domain** (Map pp514–15) is a large public park that contains Auckland Museum, sports fields and the **Wintergarden** (Map pp514-15; ☎ 379 2020; admission free; 🕑 9am-4.30pm), with its fernery, tropical house, cool house and café.

On Gladstone Rd in Parnell are the **Parnell Rose Gardens**, which are in bloom from November to March.

The 65-hectare **Auckland Botanical Gardens** (Map pp510-11; ☎ 267 1457; Hill Rd; admission free; 🕑 8am-dusk) has a café and visitors centre, as well as rose, herb, cacti, native plant and edible gardens. Take bus Nos 471 or 472; it's 53 minutes from Britomart Station to the bus stop in South Mall, Manurewa, then a 20-minute walk along Hill Rd.

Mt Eden & One Tree Hill — Map pp510–11

Auckland is punctuated by some 48 volcanoes, many of which provide parkland retreats and great views. The view from Mt Eden (Maungawhau) is superb. At 196m, it's the highest volcanic cone in the area. You can see the entire Auckland district – all the bays and land between Manukau Harbour and Hauraki Gulf – and look 50m down into the volcano's crater. Drive to the top or take bus Nos 274 to 277 from Britomart Station to Mt Eden and then walk.

The 183m-high Maungakiekie ('Mountain of the Kiekie Tree'), or **One Tree Hill**, is a distinctive bald hill, topped by a huge obelisk. It was the largest and most populous of the Maori *pa*, and the terracing and dugout storage pits are still visible.

Tamaki Drive — Map pp510–11

This scenic coastal road, lined with pohutukawa trees which turn red at Christmas time,

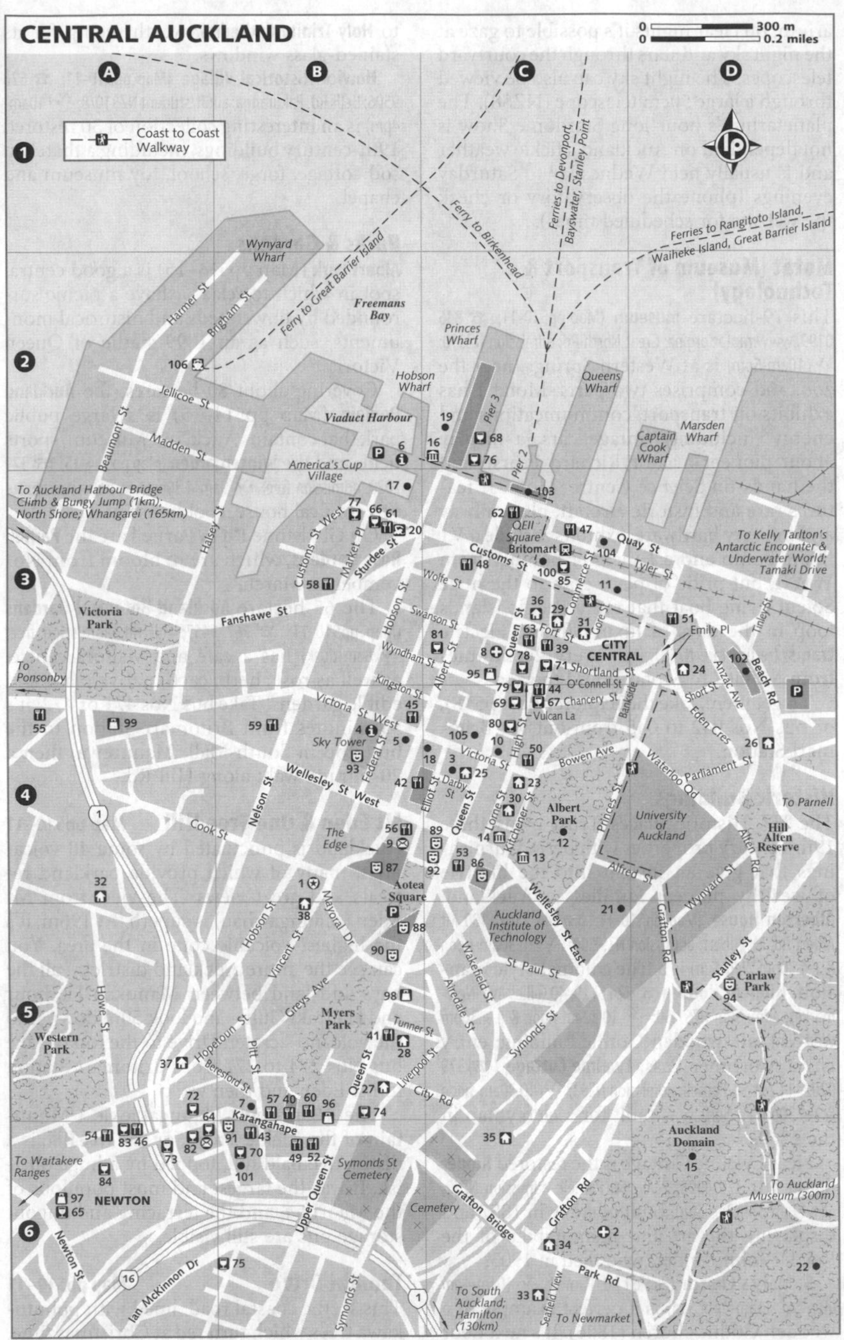

CENTRAL AUCKLAND
300 m
0.2 miles
Coast to Coast Walkway
Wynyard Wharf
Freemans Bay
Ferry to Great Barrier Island
Ferry to Birkenhead
Ferries to Devonport, Bayswater, Stanley Point
Ferries to Rangitoto Island, Waiheke Island, Great Barrier Island
Princes Wharf
Hobson Wharf
Viaduct Harbour
Queens Wharf
Captain Cook Wharf
Marsden Wharf
America's Cup Village
QEII Square
Britomart
To Auckland Harbour Bridge Climb & Bungy Jump (1km); North Shore; Whangarei (165km)
To Kelly Tarlton's Antarctic Encounter & Underwater World; Tamaki Drive
Victoria Park
To Ponsonby
CITY CENTRAL
Sky Tower
The Edge
Aotea Square
Albert Park
University of Auckland
Hill Alten Reserve
To Parnell
Auckland Institute of Technology
Myers Park
Carlaw Park
Western Park
NEWTON
To Waitakere Ranges
Symonds St Cemetery
Cemetery
Auckland Domain
To Auckland Museum (300m)
To South Auckland; Hamilton (130km)
To Newmarket

INFORMATION

- ASB Bank (see 62)
- Auckland Central Police Station 1 B4
- Auckland City Hospital 2 C6
- Auckland Map Centre 3 C4
- Auckland Visitors Centre 4 B4
- Automobile Association (AA) 5 B4
- Borders (see 92)
- Clean Green Laundromat (see 29)
- DOC Information Centre (see 103)
- NZ Visitors Centre 6 B2
- Pride Centre 7 B5
- Starship Children's Hospital (see 2)
- Ticketek (see 87)
- Travel Care Medical Centre 8 C3
- Wellesley St Post Office 9 B4
- Whitcoull's 10 C4

SIGHTS & ACTIVITIES (pp511–18)

- Adventure Cycles 11 C3
- Albert Park 12 C4
- Auckland Art Gallery (Main) 13 C4
- Auckland Art Gallery (New) 14 C4
- Auckland Domain 15 D6
- Dolphin Explorer (see 19)
- Fullers Cruises (see 103)
- Ground Rush (see 85)
- Minus 5° Bar (see 76)
- National Maritime Museum 16 C2
- Ocean Rafting 17 B3
- Pride of Auckland (see 16)
- Sky Jump (see 93)
- Sky Screamer 18 C4
- Soren Larsen 19 C2
- Tepid Baths 20 B3
- University Recreation Centre 21 C5
- Vertigo Climb (see 93)
- Wintergarden 22 D6

SLEEPING (pp519–21)

- Albert Park Backpackers 23 C4
- Aspen House 24 D3
- Auckland Central Backpackers 25 C4
- Auckland City Hotel 26 D4
- Auckland City YHA 27 B5
- Auckland International YHA 28 B5
- base Backpackers 29 C3
- Central City Backpackers 30 C4
- Fat Camel Hostel 31 C3
- Freeman's B&B 32 A4
- Grafton Hall of Residence 33 C6
- Huia Residence 34 C6
- International House 35 C6
- Queen St Backpackers 36 C3
- Sky City Hotel (see 93)
- Verandahs 37 A5
- YWCA 38 B5

EATING (pp522–5)

- A1 Sushi 39 C3
- Alleluya 40 B5
- Asian Restaurants 41 B5
- Atrium on Elliot 42 B4
- Brazil 43 B6
- Café Melba 44 C4
- Café Midnight Express 45 B4
- Caluzzi 46 A6
- Daikoku Ramen 47 C3
- Food Alley 48 C3
- Food for Life 49 B6
- Foodoo 50 C4
- Good Fortune 51 D3
- Guranga's 52 B6
- Kangnam Station Korean Restaurant (see 90)
- Kiwi Music Bar & Café 53 C4
- Little Turkish Café (see 57)
- Monkey House 54 A6
- New World Supermarket 55 A4
- Orbit (see 93)
- Pie Mania 56 B4
- Rasoi 57 B5
- Raw Power (see 78)
- Seamart Deli & Café 58 B3
- Toto 59 B4
- Verona 60 B5
- Wangthai 61 B3
- Westfield Downtown Shopping Centre 62 C3
- White Lady 63 C3

DRINKING (pp525–6)

- Cruising Rock Bar 64 A6
- Dogs Bollix 65 A6
- Europa 66 B3
- Flesh Bar & Nightclub 67 C4
- Float 68 C2
- Fu Bar 69 C4
- Galatos 70 B6
- Globe Bar (see 25)
- Honey 71 C3
- Ibiza 72 A5
- Kamo 73 A6
- Khuja Lounge 74 B5
- Kings Arms Tavern 75 B6
- Lenin Bar 76 C2
- Mojo 77 B3
- Occidental Belgian Beer Café 78 C3
- Papa Jack's Voodoo Lounge 79 C4
- Rakinos 80 C4
- Shakespeare Tavern 81 C3
- Staircase 82 A6
- Thirsty Dog 83 A6
- Urge 84 A6
- Vertigo Bar 85 C3

ENTERTAINMENT (pp526–7)

- Academy Cinema 86 C4
- Aotea Centre 87 B4
- Auckland Town Hall 88 B5
- Civic 89 C4
- Classic Comedy Club 90 B5
- NZ Film Archives 91 B6
- O'Carrolls (see 78)
- Sky City Casinos (see 93)
- Sky City Theatre (see 93)
- Sky City Village Multiplex 92 C4
- Sky City 93 B4
- Stanley St Tennis Courts 94 D5

SHOPPING (pp527–8)

- Aotea Square Market (see 87)
- Kathmandu 95 C3
- Modus Operandi (see 80)
- Paper Bag Princess 96 B5
- R&R Sport 97 A6
- Real Groovy Records 98 B5
- Victoria Park Market 99 A4

TRANSPORT (pp528–30)

- Air New Zealand 100 C3
- Backpackers Car Market 101 B6
- Car Rental Companies 102 D3
- Ferry Building 103 C3
- Fullers (see 103)
- Magic Travellers Network 104 C3
- Qantas 105 C4
- Sky City Coach Terminal (see 93)
- Subritzky Ferry Terminal 106 A2

crosses Hobson Bay to **Orakei**, where you can hire kayaks and inline skates. It continues past Kelly Tarlton's Antarctic Encounter & Underwater World to **Bastion Point**, which was occupied by members of the Ngati Whatua tribe in a 1978 land protest. The garden **memorial** to an early prime minister, Michael Joseph Savage, has a good viewpoint.

Tamaki Drive continues to **Mission Bay**, which has a popular beach with water-sports gear for hire (see p517), pavement restaurants, bars and a cinema multiplex. Further on, **St Heliers Bay** is smaller and more relaxed. Further east along Cliff Rd, the **Achilles Point lookout** has dramatic views of the city, harbour and Hauraki Gulf.

You can hire a bicycle and cycle along this route, or else take a bus (Nos 745 to 746).

Devonport

Devonport (Map pp510-11; www.devonport.co.nz), on the tip of North Shore peninsula and easily reached by ferry from downtown, retains a 19th-century feel with many well-preserved Victorian and Edwardian buildings. It also has two volcanic cones, Mt Victoria and North Head, both former Maori *pa* with good views and old fortifications. Get info on local attractions at the **North Shore visitors centre** (☎ 446 0677; 3 Victoria Rd; ⌚ 8.30am-5pm).

There are lots of small, tourist-trampled art and craft galleries, bookshops and cafés. There are also some good beaches, including the lovely **Cheltenham Beach**, and a great view of Auckland's skyline from the foreshore, especially in the evening. Sample a fine range of eateries and bars here, mostly crowded along Victoria Rd.

Buses to Devonport run regularly from outside Britomart Station, but you have to pass through Takapuna and traffic can be slow. Quicker and far more enjoyable is the 12-minute **ferry** ride from the Auckland Ferry Building, departing every 30 minutes from 6.15am to 11pm Monday to Thursday, until 1am Friday and Saturday, and from 7.30am to 10pm on Sunday and public holidays. The last ferries back from Devonport are at 11.30pm Monday to Thursday, 1.15am Friday and Saturday, and 10.30pm Sunday. The fare is NZ$5.20 for a one-way ticket and NZ$9 for an open return. You can hire a **bicycle** (per 4hr NZ$15) outside the Auckland ferry ticket office and cycle around Devonport.

Fullers operates ferries to Waiheke and Rangitoto Islands that call in at Devonport; see under Hauraki Gulf Islands (p533 and p530).

ACTIVITIES

Auckland has become more and more adventurous in recent years and there's no shortage of challenging activities in and around this harbour-hemmed city, everything from sliding through watery canyons and skydiving to climbing or jumping off the harbour bridge, throwing yourself off the Sky Tower and swimming alongside some gregarious flippered mammals.

Look around for backpacker reductions or special offers before booking anything.

Spiderman Activities

Auckland Harbour Bridge Bungy Jump (Map pp510-11; ☎ 0800 462 8649, 361 2000; www.ajhackett.co.nz; Westhaven Marina) offers a 40m leap off the bridge and a quick dip in the harbour for NZ$125; discounts may be available. A video is NZ$39, photos are NZ$12 and a T-shirt is NZ$25.

Sky Jump (Map pp514-15; ☎ 0800 759 586, 368 1835; www.skyjump.co.nz; Sky Tower, cnr Victoria St West & Federal St; adult/concession NZ$195/145; ⏰ 10am-5.30pm) is a 192m, 16-second, 75kph base wire jump from the observation deck of the Sky Tower. It's more like a parachute jump than a bungy jump. Beware, it can be addictive – one guy has already jumped 87 times. Photos cost NZ$25 and a second jump is NZ$75.

Sky Screamer (Map pp514-15; ☎ 578 0818; cnr Albert St & Victoria St West; 1st/2nd rides NZ$35/15; ⏰ 10.30am-10pm Sun-Thu, 10.30-2am Fri & Sat) involves being strapped into a seat and hurled 70m up in the air. A video costs NZ$20.

Ground Rush (Map pp514-15; ☎ 0800 7275 867; www.groundrush.co.nz; Customs St; NZ$80) offers rappelling (forward abseiling) down the Mercure Hotel. The price includes two walks down the building and a 20m freefall if you want to try it, and takes around one hour.

Auckland Harbour Bridge Climb (Map pp510-11; ☎ 0800 462 5462, 377 6543; www.ajhackett.co.nz; Westhaven Reserve, Curran St; NZ$110) is a 2½-hour guided climb involving walking to one of the support pylons, into which you descend, then climbing the arch itself up to the summit and back down the other side. You wear a climbing suit with a harness attached to a static line. Bookings are essential.

Vertigo Climb (Map pp514-15; ☎ 0800 4837 8446, 368 1917; www.4vertigo.com; NZ$145) involves climbing inside the Sky Tower mast up to the crows nest, 80m above the observation deck. These climbs take two hours and run at 10am, noon, 2pm and 4pm; a photo costs NZ$17.

Canyoning

Awol Canyoning (☎ 0800 462 965, 834 0501; www.awoladventures.co.nz; NZ$135) takes you abseiling down waterfalls, sliding down rocks and jumping into pools in the Waitakere Ranges. The pick up from Auckland, lunch and snacks are included in the price. The whole trip takes from 10am to 5pm but the actual canyoning takes two to three hours.

Cliffhanger Adventures (☎ 827 0720; www.cliffhanger.co.nz; half-/full-day trips from NZ$95/125) also runs abseiling and rock-climbing trips around Auckland. Trips further afield cost NZ$300 (NZ$340 overnight). Sea-kayaking and other adventures are also possible.

Dolphin Swimming

Dolphin Explorer (Map pp514-15; ☎ 357 6032; www.dolphinexplorer.com; NZ$100; ⏰ 10.30am-4pm) has daily dolphin swimming trips departing from Pier 3. Common or bottlenose dolphins, orcas and Brydes whales can all be seen. Swimming with dolphins is strictly controlled (for example, you can only swim with common dolphins and no swimming is allowed if there are baby dolphins sleeping or feeding). Wetsuits, masks, snorkels and fins are provided. If you don't see any dolphins or whales you can take another trip free. Whales are sighted on over 60% of the trips and dolphins on 95% of trips.

Water Sports

Fergs Kayaks (Map pp510-11; ☎ 0800 333 999, 529 2230; www.fergskayaks.co.nz; 12 Tamaki Dr, Okahu Bay; ⏰ 8am-6pm Mon-Fri, 9am-6pm Sat & Sun) sells and hires out kayaks (NZ$9 to NZ$15 per hour, NZ$30 to NZ$40 per day) and in-line skates (NZ$15/30 per hour/day). Day and night guided kayak trips are available to Devonport (NZ$65, 4½ hours, 8km) or Rangitoto Island (NZ$75, six hours, 13km). They're open extended hours from December to March.

Mission Bay Watersports (Map pp510-11; ☎ 521 7245; Mission Bay Beach; 🕒 10am-evening Dec-Mar) has sailboard hire (NZ$25 per hour) and tuition (NZ$35 per hour), kayak hire (NZ$10 per hour) and wakeboarding (NZ$30 for 15 minutes). Wetsuits are free.

For good **surf** less than 50km from the city, try **Piha**, **Muriwai** or **Bethells Beach** (Te Henga) on the west coast, where the water is often very rough. Most of the surfing beaches have surf clubs and lifeguards. **Aloha Surf School** (☎ 489 2846; 1½-2hr lessons/practice NZ$80/25, pick up NZ$30) is a long-running surf school with experienced and safety-conscious instructors, conducting lessons at Piha and elsewhere.

NZ Surf Tours (☎ 832 9622; www.newzealandsurftours.com; day tours from NZ$100) runs weekend surfing courses (October to June) that include transport, all equipment and three hours of lessons per day. A five-day course (NZ$700) includes food and accommodation.

Dive Centre (Map pp510-11; ☎ 444 7698; www.divecentre.co.nz; 128 Wairau Rd, Takapuna) has a large dive shop, runs PADI courses, and does dive trips to Little Barrier Island (NZ$155 for two dives), Mokohinau Island and the Hen and Chickens Islands (NZ$170 for two dives).

Skydiving

Skydive Parakai (☎ 0800 425 867, 420 7327; www.nzskydive.com; Parakai Airfield, Greens Rd) does tandem skydives from 8000ft (NZ$185) and 16,000ft (NZ$400). Four to five hours of training and a solo jump from 12,000ft is NZ$390. A video and photos is NZ$150. Parakai is a half-hour drive northwest of Auckland.

Skydive Auckland (☎ 0800 865 867; www.skydiveauckland.com) offers a tandem skydive from 12,000ft (including a 50-second freefall) for NZ$250, or training followed by a solo jump for NZ$350. A video costs NZ$125; a video plus photos costs NZ$150. It all takes place at Mercer airfield, 55km south of Auckland.

Cycling

Adventure Cycles (Map pp514-15; ☎ 309 5566; 36 Customs St E; 🕒 7am-7pm) hires out road and mountain bikes (NZ$18 to NZ$35 per day). Cycle along Tamaki Dr to Mission Bay (p513), or put the bike on a ferry and cycle around Devonport (p515).

Swimming

Auckland is noted for its fine and varied beaches dotted around the harbours and coastline. Popular east-coast beaches along Tamaki Dr (p513) include **Mission Bay** and **St Heliers Bay**. Popular North Shore beaches include **Cheltenham** (Map pp510–11) and **Takapuna** (Map pp510–11), and further north, **Browns Bay** and **Long Bay**.

The **Tepid Baths** (Map pp514-15; ☎ 379 4754; 100 Customs St; admission NZ$4.50; 🕒 6am-9pm Mon-Fri, 7am-7pm Sat & Sun) has two undercover pools, a sauna, spa bath and steam rooms. A workout in the gym is an extra NZ$10.50, and yoga/pilates is NZ$15.

The **Olympic Swimming Pool** (☎ 522 4414; 77 Broadway, Newmarket; adult/student NZ$5/4; 🕒 5.45am-10pm Mon-Fri, 7am-8pm Sat & Sun) has a spa, steam room and sauna, as well as a large indoor pool. A work-out in the fitness centre costs NZ$12.

Parnell Saltwater Pools (☎ 373 3561; Judges Bay Rd, Parnell; admission NZ$5; 🕒 6am-8pm Mon-Fri, 8am-8pm Sat & Sun Dec-Apr) is popular in summer for its outdoor saltwater pools and sunbathing areas.

Harbour & Other Cruises

Fullers Cruises (Map pp514-15; ☎ 367 9111; www.fullers.co.nz; Quay St) has lots of cruises, operating almost all the ferries that run from the ferry building. Fullers runs 1½-hour harbour cruises (NZ$30, includes free return ticket to Devonport) at 10.30am and 1.30pm, visiting a long list of sights. Ferries go to many of the nearby islands in the gulf. Rangitoto and Waiheke are easy to reach and make good day trips from Auckland.

Ocean Rafting (Map pp514-15; ☎ 0800 801 193, 577 3194; www.oceanrafting.co.nz), based in Viaduct Basin, has a fast inflatable boat that whips you round the harbour or further out into the gulf. A 45-minute trip costs NZ$45, while a one-hour trip out to Rangitoto Island costs NZ$70 and a trip round Waiheke Island costs NZ$130. Bookings are essential for the Waiheke trip.

Sailing

This is the 'City of Sails' and nothing gets you closer to the heart and soul of Auckland than sailing on the harbour.

Pride of Auckland (Map pp514-15; ☎ 377 0459; www.prideofauckland.com; 45/90min cruises NZ$45/$55), based next to the Maritime Museum, offers sailing trips around the harbour. There's also a 1½-hour cruise with lunch (NZ$70) and a 2½-hour dinner cruise (NZ$90).

Based at Princes Wharf during the summer, the tall ship **Soren Larsen** (Map pp514-15; ☎ 411 8755; www.sorenlarsen.co.nz; day trips adult/concession NZ$95/80) offers hands-on day sailing. It also does four-day trips to the Bay of Islands (NZ$200 per night). In winter you can join them cruising around tropical South Pacific islands.

Gulfwind Sailing Academy (Map pp510-11; ☎ 521 1564, 027-480 2462; www.gulfwind.co.nz; Westhaven Marina) can provide day sailing cruises (NZ$395 for four people) as well as personalised tuition and flexible small-group sailing courses for beginners or experienced sailors. Courses run all year; a three-day competent crew certificate costs NZ$600.

Other Activities

Rocknasium (Map pp510-11; ☎ 630 5522; rocknasium@clear.net.nz; 610 Dominion Rd; admission NZ$20) is a funky indoor climbing centre with a café. The price covers all-day instruction and free basic accommodation upstairs in a 14-bed dorm or one of two doubles, with access to a kitchen and lounge.

At the **University Recreation Centre** (Map pp514-15; ☎ 373 7999; 17 Symonds St; admission NZ$11; ⌚ 6am-9.30pm Mon-Thu, 9am-5.30pm Sat & Sun) you can play squash, badminton or basketball, or work out in the gym.

TOURS

You can spend a day touring Auckland's major attractions via the hop-on, hop-off **Explorer Bus** (☎ 0800 439 756; www.explorerbus.co.nz; day pass NZ$30). It departs daily from the ferry building every half-hour from 9am to 4pm from October to April and every hour from 10.30am to 4.30pm from May to September. The bus runs to Kelly Tarlton's, Mission Bay, Parnell, Auckland Museum, Sky Tower, Victoria Park Market and back to the ferry building. At Auckland Museum you can pick up the **Satellite Link** (⌚ Oct-Apr) to Lionzone Brewery, Mt Eden, Westfield St Lukes Shopping Mall, Auckland Zoo, Motat and Eden Park. The Explorer Bus day pass price includes the Satellite Link. If you're at the airport or in South Auckland, the service offers a free pick up to take you to the Explorer Bus (bookings required).

Auckland has plenty of tour operators. Three-hour bus tours will typically take you around the city centre, over the harbour bridge and out along Tamaki Dr, including stops at Mt Eden, Auckland Museum and Parnell, for about NZ$50.

Scenic Pacific Tours (Map pp514-15; ☎ 0800 698 687, 307 7880; 172 Quay St) and **Great Sights** (Map pp514-15; ☎ 0800 744 487, 375 4700; www.greatsights.co.nz; 180 Quay St) are major operators doing city tours, as well as tours to the Bay of Islands, Waitomo and Rotorua. Free pick up and drop off at your hotel is usually included with city tours.

ABC Tours (☎ 0800 222 868; half-/full-day tours NZ$65/95) Has an afternoon tour covering Devonport, the Henderson wine region, the Waitakere Ranges and Manukau Harbour. The full-day tour draws a good picture of the Auckland region.

Auckland Adventures (☎ 379 4545; www.aucklandadventures.co.nz; afternoon/day tours NZ$65/100) Runs good-value tours. The afternoon tour (12.45pm to 5pm) includes the Muriwai gannet colony, an orchard, wineries and Mt Eden, while the day tours (9am to 5pm) also include either a 1½-hour hike or a one-hour downhill mountain-bike ride.

Bush & Beach (☎ 575 1458; www.bushandbeach.co.nz) Has a tour to the Waitakere Ranges that includes hiking and a visit to Karekare Beach for NZ$75. If you include a city tour the cost is NZ$120.

FESTIVALS & EVENTS

The **Auckland visitors centre** (Map pp514-15; ☎ 979 2333; www.aucklandnz.com; cnr Victoria St West & Federal St; ⌚ 8am-8pm Sun-Wed, 8am-10pm Thu-Sat) keeps a list of the many annual events held in Auckland, or visit **Tourism Auckland's events page** (www.eventsauckland.com).

January

ASB Open Tennis Championships (Women) See the latest fashions as some leading players warm up for the Aussie Open.

Heineken Open Tennis Championships (Men) See some famous tennis names in action as the new season gets underway in Stanley St.

Auckland Anniversary Day Regatta The City of Sails lives up to its name.

Big Day Out (www.bigdayout.com; Ericsson Stadium) Auckland's largest multiband concert.

February

Devonport Wine & Food Festival (www.devonportwinefestival.co.nz) Sip and sup with the smart set at this two-day festival.

HERO Festival (www.gaynz.com/hero/default.asp) The gay parade has had financial problems but will no doubt continue.

GAY & LESBIAN AUCKLAND

The **Pride Centre** (Map pp514-15; ☎ 302 0590; www.pride.org.nz; 281 K Rd; 10am-5pm Mon-Fri, 10am-3pm Sat) is the main contact point for the gay and lesbian community.

Express is a fortnightly magazine with masses of info on the Auckland gay scene. *Up* is a monthly magazine, while the *New Zealand Gay Guide* (www.gogaynewzealand.com) is a pocket-sized booklet with listings. Log on to www.gaynz.com for news and venue listings.

Auckland hosts a HERO festival every February with two weeks of events including the Big Gay Out, the HERO parade and a Heroic Gardens weekend when 20 gay gardens go on view to the public to raise money for AIDS sufferers.

Kamo (Map pp514-15; ☎ 377 2313; 382 K Rd; mains NZ$15-20; 10.30am-10.30pm Tue-Sun) is a low-key restaurant and bar.

Urge (Map pp514-15; ☎ 307 2155; 490 K Rd; 9pm-late Thu-Sat) is a gay men's bar and club with a friendly owner, a DJ on Friday and Saturday nights and occasional theme nights.

Flesh Bar & Nightclub (Map pp514-15; ☎ 336 1616; 15 O'Connell St; 6pm-late) is a dimly lit downtown lounge bar with free snacks and karaoke on Wednesday. The **nightclub** (11pm-late Fri & Sat) is downstairs. It usually has no cover charge and features regular drag shows by the resplendent Ms Ribena.

For more gay- and lesbian-specific information, see the New Zealand Directory chapter (p782).

Aotearoa Maori Performing Arts Festival A rare chance to see Maori culture in action.
Asian Lantern Festival Three days of Asian food and culture in Albert Park to welcome the lunar New Year.
Mission Bay Jazz & Blues Street Fest (www.jazzandbluesstreetfest.com) New Orleans comes to the bay as jazz and blues bands line both sides of the street as the sun sets.

March/April

Waiheke Jazz Festival (www.waihekejazz.co.nz) The wine island is booked up months ahead for this annual music fest.
Pasifika Festival (www.aucklandcity.govt.nz/whatson/events/pasifika) Western Springs Park hosts this giant Polynesian party with music, dancing and food.
Royal NZ Easter Show (www.royaleastershow.co.nz) Fun with an agricultural flavour.

October

Lindauer Coastal Classic (www.coastalclassic.co.nz) Fleet yacht race from NZ's pretend capital (Auckland) to its first capital (Russell).
Wine Waitakere Wet your whistle at the westie wineries.

November

Ellerslie Flower Show (www.ellersliefIowershow.co.nz) Five days of flowers, music and food lure crowds of visitors to Auckland Botanical Gardens.

December

Auckland Cup Pick the winner at the biggest horse race of the year.
Christmas in the Park (www.aucklandcity.govt.nz/whatson/events/cocacola) This party is so big it has to be held in the Auckland Domain.
First Night (31 December) A free and alcohol-free music party in Aotea Sq.

SLEEPING

Auckland has plenty of hostels in the city centre and inner suburbs, but you'll still need to book ahead in summer, especially if you want a private room. The city centre has the largest hostels in town, mostly on or just off Queen St – bookended by the nightlife of K Rd in the south and Viaduct Basin in the north – but they tend to be crowded and some need upgrading. For quieter but still sociable environments, try the hostels in the inner-city suburbs of Parnell, Mt Eden or Ponsonby, the latter with its own sizeable collection of bars and clubs along Ponsonby Rd.

Other budget sleeping options in Auckland include university student accommodation, plain pub and cheap hotel lodgings, and outer suburb holiday parks.

City Centre — Map pp514–15

HOSTELS

base Backpackers (☎ 0800 227 369, 300 9999; www.basebackpackers.com; 16-22 Fort St; dm NZ$22-24, d & tw NZ$65-85; 💻) This large, ultra-smart backpackers sets high standards with a café (all meals under NZ$10), a busy bar and nightclub, a quiet library room, a travel agency and a roof deck with a sauna and hot pool (payment required). Dorms have eight to 12 beds, and the immaculate rooms have bathrooms, TVs, linen, heaters and hairdryers. One floor is reserved for women. Everything is well designed with bright colours, big windows and even big mirrors. The TVs in the washrooms are a bit much but the toilet seat wipes are a nice touch. This downtown haven has bubbly, well-trained staff and tries exceptionally hard to please its customers.

Auckland Central Backpackers (☎ 358 4877; www.acb.co.nz; cnr Queen & Darby Sts; dm NZ$22-24, d & tw NZ$65-85; 💻) This 500-bed backpackers is so popular that it buzzes day and night like a beehive, so stay away if you don't like crowds. The dorms have four beds or four double bunks. Full linen is supplied except in bunk dorms. Rooms with bathroom, and family rooms, have their own TV. Some rooms have no windows but all rooms have air-con/heating and a small fridge. Facilities include a large Internet area and a job-search agency, and downstairs is the Globe Bar which parties late every night.

Auckland City YHA (☎ 309 2802; www.yha.org.nz; cnr City Rd & Liverpool St; dm/s NZ$25/45, d & tw NZ$65; 💻) On a quiet street just off the southern end of Queen St, this ever-popular, purpose-built, high-rise hostel is clean and well run, with artworks on the walls and linen supplied. Dorms have three to six beds, YHA members pay NZ$4 less. Tommy's Bistro (meals NZ$7 to NZ$12) is on the ground floor along with a tour desk. Upstairs is a sun deck.

Auckland International YHA (☎ 302 8200; www.yha.org.nz; 5 Turner St; dm NZ$27, d & tw NZ$70-85; Ⓟ 💻) This bright, modern and clean accommodation is the nearby City YHA's twin but has rooms with private bathroom which are only available to members. It's child- and disabled-friendly, linen is supplied, and dorm rooms have individual lights and four or eight beds. YHA members pay NZ$4 less except for the rooms with private bathroom. The dining room is nicer than the windowless TV room and some rooms only have small high windows. There's a travel desk and a board for job vacancies.

YWCA (☎ 377 8763; www.akywca.org.nz; 103 Vincent St; s NZ$40, d & tw NZ$60; Ⓟ 💻) This place is much better than most YWCAs and both men and women can stay here, although there are some female-only zones. The refurbished rooms have cheerful décor, linen, a fridge, heating and a desk. Staff are helpful and the fast Internet access is free. It's often booked out by long-term residents, even during quiet periods, so it's best to ring ahead.

Queen St Backpackers (☎ 373 3471; www.qsb.co.nz; 4 Fort St; dm/s NZ$24/45, d & tw NZ$60; 💻) A large lounge area with a bar and pool table makes this a sociable hotel-turned-backpackers. It's gradually being upgraded, starting with the showers and carpets. Most rooms have a sink and a table and chairs, and dorms vary from four to eight beds.

Verandahs (☎ 360 4180; www.verandahs.co.nz; 6 Hopetoun St; dm NZ$22-28, s NZ$40, d & tw NZ$65; 💻) The well-named Verandahs is in an appealing, turn-of-the-century, balcony-encircled villa on a fairly busy road but backs on to the lovely expanse of Western Park, Auckland's oldest park. It was just getting a lick of white

SPLURGE!

Bavaria B&B (☎ 638 9641; www.bavariabandbhotel.co.nz; 83 Valley Rd, Mt Eden; s NZ$80-95, d NZ$110-135; Ⓟ) This long-running B&B is in a spacious villa wreathed in native timber. It offers near-luxurious rooms with bathrooms decorated in pastel shades and a convivial TV-lounge, dining room and deck where guests can mingle.

Jet Inn (Map pp510-11; ☎ 0800 538 466, 275 4100; www.jetinn.co.nz; 63 Westney Rd; r NZ$110-170; Ⓟ 💻 🏊) This superior accommodation has a stylish restaurant and bar, an attractive pool area and memorable décor comprising hundreds of authentic African carvings. Rates are negotiable, especially from Friday to Sunday, and each room has a safe. The airport is only 4km away.

Sky City Hotel (Map pp514-15; ☎ 0800 759 2489, 363 6000; www.skycity.co.nz; cnr Victoria St West & Federal St; d & tw NZ$190-340; Ⓟ 💻 🏊) Rooms in this popular luxury hotel have large windows, TV, Internet, a bath and a shower, and there's also a pool, business centre, gym and sauna. But the big attraction is its brilliant location in Auckland's entertainment hub, with a buzzing atrium foyer, surrounded by Sky Tower, restaurants, bars and a 24-hour casino. It's as close to Las Vegas as Auckland gets.

paint and other final renovations when we visited. Singles are on the small side.

Other recommended city-centre hostels:

Albert Park Backpackers (☎ 309 0336; www.albertpark.co.nz; 27 Victoria St East; dm NZ$21-23, s NZ$45, d & tw NZ$55; 💻)

Central City Backpackers (☎ 358 5685; www.backpacker.net.nz; 26 Lorne St; dm NZ$22-25, d & tw NZ$60; 💻)

Fat Camel Hostel (☎ 0800 220 198, 307 0181; www.fatcamel.co.nz; 38 Fort St; dm NZ$20-23, s & d NZ$50-60; 💻)

HOTELS & B&BS

Auckland City Hotel (☎ 303 2463; www.aucklandcityhotel.co.nz; 131 Beach Rd; backpacker dm/d NZ$25/50, hotel s/d NZ$70/80; 💻) Stay here if you want cheap but clean rooms in a central location. Hotel rooms have a TV, a fridge, a table and chairs, and a bathroom. In the loft is a tiny backpacker section with a kitchen, TVs in the rooms and shared facilities. The Mascot Café downstairs does a full breakfast for NZ$5.50.

Aspen House (☎ 379 6633; www.aspenhouse.co.nz; 62 Emily Pl; s from NZ$55, d & tw NZ$75-110; Ⓟ 💻) A budget hotel with 27 uninspiring rooms without bathrooms, but the price includes breakfast. The other plus points are the lounge and the outdoor and laundry areas where guests can relax and discuss the day's events. Next door in the 'Lodge' are 30 newish rooms with private bathroom.

Freeman's B&B (☎ 0800 437 336, 376 5046; www.freemansbandb.co.nz; 65 Wellington St; s NZ$65, d & tw NZ$85; 💻) Internet access, tea and coffee, and a substantial continental breakfast are included in the price at this refurbished accommodation with new beds and hardworking owners. All B&B rooms have shared facilities. Freeman's and its shady garden are in a quiet street away from the downtown hubbub.

UNIVERSITY ACCOMMODATION

Huia Residence (☎ 377 1345; 110 Grafton Rd; s NZ$40, d & tw NZ$50, apt NZ$85; Ⓟ 💻) Available year-round to travellers, this student-style high-rise accommodation is a good deal, with central heating, fridges, linen and some furniture in the rooms. Each floor has a kitchen. The self-contained, spacious apartments with kitchens and TVs are a good deal too.

Grafton Hall of Residence (☎ 373 3994; graftonhall@auckland.ac.nz; 40 Seafield View Rd; s/tw incl breakfast NZ$37/65; 💻 Ⓟ) Free laundry, Internet and tennis makes for a tempting offer at this spacious student accommodation in a quiet street. It's open to travellers from mid-November to mid-February.

International House (☎ 379 7192; 27 Whitaker Pl; s incl breakfast & dinner NZ$30) A great deal is offered to solo travellers from mid-November to mid-February in these typical student rooms with linen, desks, chairs and cupboards. There's a games room and a lounge with TV, video and DVD.

Parnell

City Garden Lodge (☎ 302 0880; city.garden@compuweb.co.nz; 25 St Georges Bay Rd; dm NZ$20-22, s NZ$45, tw NZ$45-50, d NZ$55; Ⓟ 💻) Housed in an elegant two-storey palace built for the Queen of Tonga, this TV-less and well-run backpackers with a courtyard and BBQ area is filled with character and decorative flair. The cheaper dorm has eight beds; the others have three or four beds.

Auckland International Backpackers (☎ 358 4584; international.bp@xtra.co.nz; 2 Churton St; camp sites per person NZ$10, dm NZ$22, d & tw NZ$50; 💻) Eat in the sunroom, the pleasant dining room or out in the small garden at this large, rambling, but comfortable and friendly backpackers that used to be a YHA hostel. There are single-sex dorms.

Lantana Lodge (☎ 373 4546; 60 St Georges Bay Rd; dm/s NZ$22/50, d & tw NZ$55; 💻) Pleasant Lantana is located at the peaceful end of the St Georges Bay Rd cul-de-sac. It's fairly cosy due to a maximum capacity of 20 guests. A lot of work has been put into the surrounding garden, though the rooms are plain.

Aloe Tree Lodge (☎ 358 0665; aloetree@backpackers-nz.co.nz; 17 St Georges Bay Rd; camp sites per person NZ$10, dm/s/tw/d NZ$22/45/50/55; Ⓟ 💻) The exuberant colour scheme at this hostel can make your eyes water and the facilities are fairly basic, but the staff are very friendly, there's free Internet and a jungly garden, and the place has a laid-back, roughshod appeal. The sign out front may say 'Leadbetter Lodge', but don't fret, you're still in the right place.

Railway Campus (☎ 367 7100; railcamp@auckland.ac.nz; 26 Te Taou Cres; studio/2-/3-bed apt from NZ$80/115/145) Auckland's spacious 1930s railway station has retained many period features and offers accommodation with private bathrooms to travellers all year, with plenty of vacancies between mid-November and mid-February; winter prices for some rooms can be up to NZ$50 higher. An odd mixture of grand architecture and budget student-style rooms, it's packed with facilities such as a large industrial kitchen, gym, games room, library and a large-screen TV. You can play a game of giant chess in the impressive atrium concourse.

Mt Eden

Bamber House (☎ 623 4267; www.hostelbackpacker.com; 22 View Rd; dm NZ$20-23, s NZ$45, d & tw NZ$55; P 💻 🏊) One of Auckland's best backpackers, with young, personable staff. It consists of two smart, clean and colourful houses with a large garden, a pool and a trampoline. One house is colonial style while the other is modern. Tennis courts are across the road. Dorms vary from three to eight beds, but singles are in outbuildings.

Oaklands Lodge (☎ 0800 220 725, 638 6545; www.oaklands.co.nz; 5A Oaklands Rd; dm/s/d NZ$23/45/55; 💻) More smart and bright accommodation with a small garden and friendly staff can be found here. Its neighbours include the lively cosmopolitan scene of Mt Eden village and the slopes of Mt Eden itself. The lodge is managed by the same people who run Bamber House.

Pentlands Backpackers (☎ 638 7031; www.pentlands.co.nz; 22 Pentland Ave; dm NZ$20-23, s NZ$45, d & tw NZ$55; P 💻) Pentlands is yet another accommodating urban outpost of the Bamber empire. It's a colourful and comfortable place with small dorms, a large lounge, a log fire, a garden deck and a tennis court.

Ponsonby

Uenuku Lodge (☎ 378 8990; 217 Ponsonby Rd; dm NZ$22-24, d & tw NZ$50-55; P 💻) A high-quality, gay-friendly backpackers, with two storeys raised up above eatery-crowded Ponsonby Rd. It has an outdoor area, a touch of style and good views from most private rooms, while the rear upper deck looks out towards the dart-shaped outline of the Sky Tower. Non-dorm rooms have sinks and bedside lamps, and all linen is supplied.

Brown Kiwi (☎ 378 0191; www.brownkiwi.co.nz; 7 Prosford St; dm NZ$22-24, d & tw NZ$55; P 💻) Another smart, gay-friendly backpackers with an exterior dripping with shingles. The dorms have either four or eight beds, and the triples are out the back in the small garden courtyard. It's located on a small side street only a few minutes' walk from Ponsonby Rd.

Ponsonby Backpackers (☎ 0800 476 676, 360 1311; www.ponsonby-backpackers.co.nz; 2 Franklin Rd; camp sites per person NZ$15, dm/s from NZ$22/35, d & tw NZ$55; P 💻) This slightly dishevelled, colonial-style backpackers has all the requisite facilities, a garden, and a good location only a 15-minute walk from the centre. The biggest dorm has only six beds, but the singles are rather boxy. There's usually a guest BBQ on Monday night.

Airport

Skyway Lodge (Map pp510-11; ☎ 275 4443; www.skywaylodge.co.nz; 30 Kirkbride Rd, Mangere; dm NZ$24, s NZ$45-60, d & tw NZ$55-65; 🏊) This is the best budget option near the airport, with a friendly and helpful owner, and a large communal lounge and kitchen. Dorms have four beds and a ride to/from the airport is free.

Other Areas

Map pp510–11

Apart from the parks listed below, you can also camp at several hostels, including Auckland International Backpackers (p521) and Ponsonby Backpackers (above).

North Shore Motels & Holiday Park (☎ 418 2578; info@nsmotels.co.nz; 52 Northcote Rd, Takapuna; camp sites per person NZ$16, dm NZ$33, s from NZ$55, d NZ$60-140; 💻 🏊) An indoor pool and spa are available at this large holiday park near Takapuna on North Shore, 4km north of the Harbour Bridge. It's the best such park in Auckland.

Takapuna Beach Holiday Park (☎ 489 7909; www.kiwiholidayparks.co.nz; 22 The Promenade, Takapuna; camp/campervan sites per person NZ$11/15, s & d NZ$55-90) Another holiday park option in Takapuna, located right on the beach and equipped with its own shop, BBQs and other camper mod cons. The foreshore locale is attractive, but the park's facilities could be improved.

Avondale Motor Park (☎ 0800 100 542, 828 7228; www.aucklandmotorpark.co.nz; 46 Bollard Ave, Avondale; camp/campervan sites per person NZ$10/12, s & d NZ$45-65) Avondale has an attractively leafy and rural setting, filled with all manner of accommodation from tent sites to self-contained tourist flats with private bathrooms, and embellished by a kid's playground. However, the kitchen and TV-lounge are poor.

EATING

Due to its size and ethnic diversity, Auckland has NZ's best range of dining options. For good-value fast food, you can't beat the city's numerous Asian eateries (many clustered around the corner of Queen and Tunner Sts, Map pp514–15) and cheap takeaway kebab places, while Lorne St, High St and traffic-free Vulcan Lane are lined with cafés of all shapes, sizes and philosophies. K Rd is best known for its late-night clubs but cafés and inexpensive ethnic restaurants are mixed in with the fashion boutiques, tattooists and adult shops. Ponsonby Rd is by far the trendiest café strip, with Parnell, Mt Eden Village and Newmarket presenting other options. The upmarket Princes Wharf and Viaduct waterfront area is awash with restaurants, most of which have outdoor areas.

City Centre

Map pp514–15

SELF-CATERING

New World supermarket (☎ 307 8400; 2 College Hill Rd; 🕑 7am-midnight) This is the most central supermarket for all your food and alcohol needs. The Link bus (p529) stops nearby.

Star Mart (most 🕑 24hr) convenience stores are dotted around the downtown area.

CAFÉS

Raw Power (☎ 303 3624; 1st fl, 10 Vulcan Lane; meals NZ$10; 🕑 breakfast & lunch Mon-Fri, brunch Sat) This small, no-frills vegetarian café is worth seeking out and is popular with young women. Fresh fruit juices are NZ$5, while food such as a tofu burger and felafel in pitta bread with salad is carefully prepared and tasty.

Café Melba (☎ 377 0091; 33 Vulcan Lane; meals NZ$11-15; 🕑 breakfast & lunch) For breakfast try the eggs or salmon Benedict, bagels, croissants or the porridge and plums in this small but lively café with indoor and outdoor seating.

Foodoo (☎ 373 2340; 62 High St; meals NZ$10-13; 🕑 breakfast & lunch Mon-Sat) Lots of deli food and more substantial items make a tempting display at this everything-is-home-cooked café and gourmet takeaway.

Seamart Deli & Café (☎ 302 8980; cnr Fanshawe St & Market Pl; 🕑 breakfast & lunch) This is a great place for fresh fish and seafood, with a wide choice of sashimi, sushi and deli items to eat in or takeaway.

Kiwi Music Bar & Café (☎ 309 7717; 332 Queen St; regular/large pizzas NZ$12/16; 🕑 lunch & dinner Mon-Fri, dinner Sat & Sun) This laid-back pizzeria and bar in Queen St only plays NZ music, so it's your chance to discover Scribe, Zed and Betchadupa...

QUICK EATS

Food Alley (☎ 373 4917; 9 Albert St; meals NZ$7-9; 🕑 lunch & dinner) For authentic Asian fare, you can't beat this large, no-frills food court where nearly every meal is under NZ$9. Come here for *bibimbap* (veg, meat and rice topped with a fried egg), *roti* (flat, flaky bread), laksa, *okonomiyake*, Thai desserts and all your other Asian favourites.

Pie Mania (☎ 377 1984; 36 Wellesley St; pies NZ$2.50-4.50; 🕑 breakfast & lunch Mon-Fri) Lovers of the humble pie can eat in or take out 30 varieties here, including fruit versions, plus weekly specials like herb chicken, cranberry and camembert pie.

Kangnam Station Korean Restaurant (☎ 309 1588; 329 Queen St; meals NZ$8-20; 🕑 lunch & dinner Mon-Sat, dinner Sun) Lots of meals are under NZ$10 at this authentic Korean restaurant with a jovial host. It doesn't close until 2am.

Good Fortune (☎ 302 0928; 16 Emily Pl; 🕑 lunch & dinner Mon-Fri, dinner Sat & Sun) Twenty-four lunch choices for NZ$5.50 and dinner specials from NZ$5.50 to NZ$9 make this budget Chinese restaurant popular with Asian students, many of whom say it tastes just like the cooking at home.

Daikoku Ramen (☎ 309 2200; Tyler St; noodles NZ$8-14; 🕑 lunch & dinner) This small, funky Japanese fast-food joint doesn't waste money on décor but is the place for cheap and fast noodles.

White Lady (Shortland St; burgers NZ$8-13; 🕑 breakfast, lunch & dinner) This long white bus has been in business here serving fast food to late-night revellers here since 1950. It's open 24 hours from Friday to Sunday.

For a food-court feed, head for the international fast food at **Westfield Downtown Shopping Centre** (QE Sq) or **Atrium on Elliot** (Elliot St).

RESTAURANTS

A1 Sushi (☎ 377 8008; 18 Shortland St; meals NZ$7-30; 🕑 lunch & dinner Mon-Sat) All sorts of fresh-made Japanese lunch items come round on the mini conveyor belt and you can eat as much as you like for NZ$13. Don't miss out! Dinner is *sukiyaki* and *shabu shabu*.

Wangthai (☎ 358 4131; 96 Customs St; mains NZ$17-24; 🕑 lunch & dinner Mon-Fri, dinner Sat & Sun) This reasonably priced Thai place near the Viaduct Basin has cool and smart surroundings.

Café Midnight Express (☎ 303 0312; 59 Victoria St West; mains NZ$8-16; 🕑 lunch & dinner) This authentic ethnic restaurant has Middle Eastern food, music and décor.

SPLURGE!

Orbit (Map pp514-15; ☎ 363 6000; mains NZ$28-31; lunch & dinner) This is the place to go for a special meal as the restaurant is 52 storeys up, revolves once an hour and has stunning views of the Auckland region. The food is not as good as the view, so avoid vegetarian dishes and stick to basic mains and a stylish dessert (NZ$13). The service is leisurely so you can stay a couple of hours and revolve twice. There's a minimum charge of NZ$25 per head; free entry to the observation deck (normally NZ$15) is included.

Toto (Map pp514-15; ☎ 302 2665; 53 Nelson St; mains NZ$24-30; lunch & dinner Mon-Fri, dinner Sat & Sun) Italian and NZ wines accompany fine modern Italian cuisine with professional opera singers on Saturday and Thursday (NZ$10 cover charge). Lunch is unique 'Yum Ciao' – lots of small items.

Caluzzi (Map pp514-15; ☎ 357 0778; 461 K Rd; dinner & show NZ$45; dinner Tue-Sat) A unique restaurant and bar with 'garden shed' décor where three drag queen waitresses put on a cabaret show as they serve you. Booking is essential and the thin-skinned should stay well away.

Parnell

QUICK EATS

Al & Pete's (☎ 377 5439; 496 Parnell Rd; burgers NZ$4-9, meals NZ$15; lunch & dinner) Legendary gourmet burgers (such as chicken and camembert or scotch fillet), as well as fish and chips, sandwiches and other meals are available here.

Kebab Kid (☎ 373 4290; 363 Parnell Rd; dishes NZ$8; lunch & dinner) This is the place for cheap shwarmas, pitta breads and kebabs.

RESTAURANTS

Java Room (☎ 366 1606; 317 Parnell Rd; mains NZ$16-21; dinner Mon-Sat) This charming restaurant serves up a mixture of Indonesian, Malaysian, Thai and Indian food at reasonable prices. The chilli prawns and orange duck curry are popular.

Thai Friends (☎ 373 5247; 311 Parnell Rd; mains NZ$16-20; lunch & dinner Tue-Sat, dinner Sun & Mon) Sit on floor cushions in this cosy and reasonably priced BYO Thai restaurant.

La Porchetta (☎ 309 0807; 167 Parnell Rd; mains NZ$10-20; lunch & dinner Wed-Fri, dinner Sat-Tue) Join the crowds and tuck into bargain pizzas and pastas in this bright BYO diner and takeaway.

Oh Calcutta (☎ 377 9090; 151 Parnell Rd; mains NZ$17-19; lunch & dinner) One of Auckland's best Indian restaurants, with tandoori meals, lamb *rogan josh*, Goa fish curry and NZ$15 vegetarian meals, but (unlike the original stage show of the same name) no nudity.

K Rd — Map pp514–15

CAFÉS

Brazil (☎ 302 2677; 256 K Rd; meals NZ$8-14; breakfast, lunch & dinner) Unusual music ('electro-industrial soundscapes') and décor are the main attractions at this dark, tunnel-like café with a DJ on Saturday afternoon.

Alleluya (☎ 377 8424; St Kevin's Arcade; meals NZ$8-14; breakfast, lunch & dinner Tue-Sat, breakfast & lunch Sun & Mon) Super-thick pizza slices, Thai chicken pies, tuna bakes and homemade baked beans are included in the lengthy and eclectic menu at this relaxed licensed café with a view.

Monkey House (☎ 358 1884; 501 K Rd; breakfasts NZ$3-14, lunches NZ$9-15; breakfast, lunch & dinner) K Rd's smartest and roomiest café-bar, with outside area, European beers on tap, some organic food, and Cuban dancing on Friday night. Closes at 7pm Monday to Thursday.

QUICK EATS

Little Turkish Café (☎ 302 0353; 217 K Rd; meals NZ$5-9; lunch & dinner) Authentic Middle Eastern kebabs, salads and desserts are available here until late at night. Smoke a *shisha* (pipe) for NZ$8.

Food for Life (☎ 300 7585; 268 K Rd; meals NZ$5; lunch & dinner Mon-Fri, lunch Sat) This Hare Krishna vegetarian restaurant serves a bargain seven-item combination meal that may include lasagne, pizza and semolina pudding, as well as the usual Indian items.

Guranga's (☎ 303 1560; 214 K Rd; meals NZ$5; lunch Mon-Sat) A smaller, rival Hare Krishna restaurant with Indian combination meals. Large juices cost only NZ$3, and seating on floor cushions is available upstairs.

RESTAURANTS

Verona (☎ 307 0508; 169 K Rd; mains NZ$14-24; lunch & dinner Mon-Sat, dinner Sun) The best restaurant on K Rd offers mainly organic food but is also a bar and sells deli snacks. It's usually busy and service can be haphazard.

Rasoi (☎ 377 7780; 211 K Rd; meals NZ$5-15; 🕒 lunch & dinner Mon-Sat) Good cheap vegetarian *thali* (rice and assorted curries on one platter) and South Indian food can be found here together with *lassi* and Indian sweets such as *barfi* and *laddoo*.

Ponsonby

CAFÉS

Atomic Café (☎ 376 4954; 121 Ponsonby Rd; meals NZ$7-15; 🕒 breakfast, lunch & dinner) Popular and long-established, this café with a covered garden area offers delights such as Atomic porridge (NZ$6.50) and leafy greens with roast vegetables and fetta (NZ$11).

Fusion (☎ 378 4573; 32 Jervois Rd; breakfasts NZ$5-14, lunches NZ$10-14; 🕒 breakfast & lunch) A licensed café complete with a garden and children's sandpit out the back, Fusion offers a menu that lives up to its name and delivers *miso* soup, *lassi*, Turkish delight and even curried banana salad.

Logos (☎ 376 2433; 265 Ponsonby Rd; mains NZ$8-16; 🕒 breakfast, lunch & dinner) This café-bar has mainly vegetarian food, including vegan muffins, and plays New Age music.

QUICK EATS

Ponsonby Pies (☎ 361 3685; 288 Ponsonby Rd; 🕒 breakfast & lunch) More than 20 varieties of these famous-in-NZ pies are on sale for around NZ$3 each, including fruit ones which cost NZ$1 extra with ice cream. Usually closes around 6pm.

Otto Woo (☎ 360 1989; 47 Ponsonby Rd; meals NZ$6-13; 🕒 lunch & dinner Mon-Fri, dinner Sat & Sun) Eat in or take away at this clean, bright, Asian-style eatery that serves its original fusion food in a neat white cardboard box.

Burger Fuel (☎ 378 6466; 114 Ponsonby Rd; burgers NZ$6-10; 🕒 lunch & dinner) This is the place for gourmet burgers – try the 'Bastard' for size.

RESTAURANTS

One Red Dog (☎ 360 106; 151 Ponsonby Rd; medium pizzas NZ$18; 🕒 lunch & dinner) As well as serving popular pizzas, this place has microbrewery beers and bare-brick décor.

Other Areas

NEWMARKET

Poppadom (☎ 529 1897; 471 Khyber Pass Rd; lunches from NZ$5.50, dinner mains NZ$10-18; 🕒 lunch & dinner Mon-Fri, dinner Sat & Sun) This reliable and modestly priced BYO Indian tandoori eatery is in an area of cheap ethnic restaurants. A vegetarian banquet is NZ$20 per person (minimum two).

Kenzie (☎ 522 2647; 17A Remuera Rd; meals NZ$11-16; 🕒 breakfast & lunch) Light meals, good coffee and backpacker-sized cake slices are available at this roadside café.

MT EDEN

De Post Belgian Beer Café (☎ 630 9330; 466 Mt Eden Rd; mains NZ$12-17; 🕒 breakfast, lunch & dinner) A two-storey Belgian pub with good food; another branch is at the Occidental Belgian Beer Café (below) in the city.

Tea Time Café (☎ 623 2319; 442 Mt Eden Rd; 🕒 breakfast & lunch) There are 130 teas to drink or buy here, as well as snacks and good coffee.

DRINKING

Auckland's nightlife tends to be quiet during the week, but wakes up late on Friday and Saturday when most pubs and bars are open till 1am or later. There are lots of busy watering holes in the downtown district, including the extroverted Viaduct Harbour area, while along Ponsonby Rd the line between café, restaurant and bar gets blurred (or rather, blurry). For Live Music options see p527.

City Centre Map pp514–15

Globe Bar (☎ 357 3980; cnr Queen & Darby Sts) This is a solid backpacker favourite with NZ$4.50 beers and wines, happy hour until 8pm, Miss Backpacker competitions, karaoke, theme parties, and a DJ most nights at 10pm, usually playing funked-up house music.

Occidental Belgian Beer Café (☎ 300 6226; 6-8 Vulcan Lane) Belgian beer is on tap and Belgian food is on the menu at this smart and popular bar. Accompany a monastic brew with some mussels in a blue-cheese topping.

Shakespeare Tavern (☎ 373 5396; 61 Albert St; mains NZ$12-19) This English-style pub has 10 of its own brews, including Pucks, which packs a punch with an alcohol content of 11%. There's an upstairs balcony.

Thirsty Dog (☎ 377 9190; 469 K Rd; closed Sun) This pub has Newcastle Brown, Tetleys (the beer, not the tea), Irish and Australian beers.

Vertigo Bar (☎ 302 9424; 13th fl, Mercure Hotel, 8 Customs St) Buy a beer here (NZ$5) and you can sit back and enjoy the harbour and city views from up on the 13th floor.

Honey (☎ 369 5639; 5 O'Connell St) This pricey champagne bar with sofas sells unique Kiwi drinks like South, a NZ-made gin, and 42 Below, a NZ-made vodka, which can be infused with feijoa or even manuka honey. Bubbly stuff costs from NZ$10 a glass.

Viaduct Harbour & Princes Wharf

Lenin Bar (Map pp514-15; ☎ 377 0040; Princes Wharf) This is a strange bar with a Russian theme, lots of vodkas and DJs from Thursday to Saturday. Next door is the even stranger Minus 5° Bar (p512).

Parnell

Parnell is more a place for dining than drinking, but there are a couple of options.

Bog (☎ 377 1510; 196 Parnell Rd) Also serves hearty food and has live music on Thursday, Friday and Sunday.

Exchange Hotel (☎ 377 4968; 99 Parnell Rd) Has DJs and pool competitions.

Ponsonby

Opus (☎ 376 6373; 43 Ponsonby Rd) This large, smart brasserie-bar specialises in NZ wines and serves up jugs of beer, including five microbrewery brews.

Sponge (☎ 360 0098; 198 Ponsonby Rd) This is a trendy bar with a nightclub upstairs (see Chicane; right).

CLUBBING

K and Ponsonby Rds are the main places to find late-night clubs, but there are a few establishments lurking around Vulcan Lane and Viaduct Basin. A number of clubs have a NZ$5 to NZ$20 cover charge depending on the night and the event; most clubs are closed Monday and several only open on Friday and Saturday nights.

See the Gay & Lesbian Auckland boxed text (p519) for gay and lesbian venues.

Fu Bar (Map pp514-15; ☎ 309 3079; 166 Queen St) This long-running basement dance club has live bands and DJs playing house, techno, drum'n'bass and hip-hop. It also has some pool tables.

Papa Jack's Voodoo Lounge (Map pp514-15; ☎ 358 4847; 9 Vulcan Lane) This is the home of hard rock, with skulls, ripped seats, a pool table, a live band on Wednesday and a DJ on Friday and Saturday.

Khuja Lounge (Map pp514-15; ☎ 377 3711; 536 Queen St) Above the Westpac building, this laid-back venue offers DJs and live jazz, soul and hip-hop bands.

Staircase (Map pp514-15; ☎ 374 4278; 340 K Rd) This large venue is into hard house.

Ibiza (Map pp514-15; ☎ 302 3354; 253 K Rd; 🕑 24hr Fri & Sat) This is a nonstop house and trance venue.

Cruising Rock Bar (Map pp514-15; 262 K Rd; 🕑 10pm-late Fri & Sat) This spacious black cellar with couches and a pool table has a DJ who plays rock, hard rock and rock'n'roll.

Safari Lounge (☎ 378 7707; 116 Ponsonby Rd, Ponsonby) This dimly lit den is outfitted with bar football and pool tables and has a DJ on Wednesday, Friday and Saturday nights from 9pm.

Chicane (☎ 360 0098; 198 Ponsonby Rd, Ponsonby; 🕑 10pm-late Fri & Sat) Upstairs from Sponge bar (left), this nightclub has a DJ, curtained booths and purple furniture.

Float (Map pp514-15; ☎ 307 1344; Shed 19, Princes Wharf) This venue has a black box area with a DJ on Friday and Saturday nights.

Mojo (Map pp514-15; ☎ 374 4255; Customs St) and neighbouring **Europa** (Map pp514-15; ☎ 358 5060; cnr Customs St West & Market Pl, Viaduct Basin) are both good venues for a night of R&B hip-hop (Polynesian style) on Friday or Saturday night. They enforce a strict dress code.

ENTERTAINMENT

The *NZ Herald* has 'The Guide' section from Monday to Friday with gig listings and entertainment features, and a larger 'Time Out' section on Saturday. *Backpacker Xpress* (free every Thursday) also tells you what's on at many of Auckland's pubs and bars. The **Fix** (www.thefix.co.nz), free every Thursday, also has live-music listings.

Tickets for major events can be bought from **Ticketek** (Map pp514-15; ☎ 307 5000; www.ticketek.co.nz) which has outlets at the Aotea Centre and Sky City Atrium.

Theatre & Music

Aotea Sq and the buildings that surround it comprise Auckland's main performance arts complex. The Town Hall, Civic and Aotea Centre venues (see individual listings following) are collectively known as **The Edge** (☎ 309 2677; www.the-edge.co.nz; Queen St).

Auckland Town Hall (Map pp514-15; ☎ 309 2677; 50 Mayoral Dr) This venue hosts concert performances and is home to the NZ Symphony Orchestra and **Auckland Philharmonia** (☎ 0800 744 542; www.aucklandphil.co.nz).

Aotea Centre (Map pp514-15; ☎ 307 5060; 50 Mayoral Dr) Auckland's main venue for theatre, dance, ballet and opera. The excellent and challenging Auckland Theatre Company puts on a regular programme here.

Civic (Map pp514-15; ☎ 309 2677; cnr Queen St & Wellesley St West) This grand restored theatre with a lavish Eastern-fantasy interior is used by major touring productions to stage opera, musicals and live theatre.

Classic Comedy Club (Map pp514-15; ☎ 373 4321; www.comedy.co.nz; 321 Queen St; tickets NZ$8-15) This is Auckland's top venue for comedy. Shows run from Wednesday to Saturday from around 8pm, with late shows on Friday and Saturday. Telephone or check the website for the schedule.

Sky City (Map pp514-15; ☎ 0800 759 2489; cnr Victoria & Hobson Sts) This is Auckland's biggest single entertainment venue. As well as restaurants, bars, the observation deck and a 700-seat theatre, it has two 24-hour casinos: the huge Sky City Casino (level 2) and the smaller Alto Casino (level 3).

Cinema

Sky City Village Multiplex (Map pp514-15; ☎ 979 2400; www.villageskycity.co.nz; 291 Queen St) This 13-screen multiplex is part of Sky City Metro, a modernistic mall. Tickets are cheaper on weekdays before 5pm and all day Tuesday.

Academy Cinema (Map pp514-15; ☎ 373 2761; www.academy-cinema.co.nz; 64 Lorne St; tickets NZ$10-13) Located in the basement of the central library, this cinema shows independent foreign and art-house films. A glass of champagne with the film is NZ$7. The **Rialto Cinemas** (☎ 529 2218; www.rialto.co.nz; 167 Broadway, Newmarket) screens similar film genres.

NZ Film Archives (Map pp514-15; ☎ 379 1688; www.filmarchive.org.nz; 300 K Rd; 🕑 11am-5pm Mon-Fri, 11am-4pm Sat) Wonderful resource of over 1000 Kiwi feature films and documentaries, dating from 1905, which you can watch for free on a TV screen.

Sport

Eden Park (Map pp510-11; ☎ 815 5551; www.edenpark.co.nz; Reimers Ave, Kingsland) Eden Park is the stadium for top rugby (winter) and cricket (summer) matches. The All Blacks, the Black Caps and the Auckland Blues all play here. To get there, take the train from Britomart to Kingsland Station.

Ericsson Stadium (Map pp510-11; ☎ 571 1699; www.ericssonstadium.co.nz; Beasley Ave, Penrose) Hosts soccer, rugby league (NZ Warriors) and the occasional big-name concert or music festival.

Live Music

O'Carrolls (Map pp514-15; ☎ 300 7117; 10 Vulcan Lane) This Irish pub has live acoustic acts on Wednesday, Thursday and Saturday.

Rakinos (Map pp514-15; ☎ 358 3535; 35 High St) This upstairs retro café, bar and music venue has NZ$12 cocktails, live music and DJs. Come for the music rather than the offhand staff.

Dogs Bollix (Map pp514-15; ☎ 376 4600; cnr K & Newton Rds) This Irish pub becomes a live-music venue at 9pm from Tuesday to Sunday; Monday is quiz night.

Kings Arms Tavern (Map pp514-15; ☎ 373 3240; 59 France St) This is one of Auckland's leading small venues for live rock bands, which play most nights.

Galatos (Map pp514-15; ☎ 303 1928; 17 Galatos St) There are three venues in one here, with DJs, top local live bands and hip-hop and drum'n'bass in the basement.

Java Jive (☎ 376 5870; www.javajive.co.nz; Pompallier Tce, Ponsonby) Offers reasonably priced bar meals and live Kiwi rock, blues and jazz outfits.

Alhambra (☎ 376 2430; 283 Ponsonby Rd, Ponsonby) Hosts live jazz and blues from Wednesday to Sunday night.

SHOPPING

NZ and international fashion designers manage to keep boutiques around Auckland well stocked. Aficionados of the couturier world should head to High St and Chancery Lane in the city as well as Newmarket and Ponsonby Rd, with K Rd (Map pp514–15) also worth a look. For a taste of what's in store, check out the following two stores.

Modus Operandi (Map pp514-15; ☎ 309 4008; 51 High St) This hip, Kiwi-designer-focused place makes imaginative use of mirrors and life-like mannequins.

Paper Bag Princess (Map pp514-15; ☎ 307 3591; 145 K Rd) Bargain second-hand designer outfits.

For sports goods, try **R&R Sport** (Map pp514-15; ☎ 309 6444; cnr K Rd & Ponsonby Rd), a huge store with camping, hiking, cycling, skiing, surfing and other outdoor-activities stuff.

MARKETS

Auckland has several markets that are worth browsing for their eclectic wares and discounted bargains.

Victoria Park Market (Map pp514-15; ☎ 309 6911; 210 Victoria St West; 9am-6pm) sells mostly clothes, shoes, accessories and souvenirs, but also has massages (NZ$10 for 10 minutes) and a spacious pub.

For ethnic food stalls, arts and crafts, and live music on Saturday (noon to 3pm) visit **Aotea Square Market** (Map pp514-15; Aotea Sq; 10am-6pm Fri & Sat), while more diverse goodies are sold at the **Avondale Market** (Map pp510-11; ☎ 818 4931; Avondale Racecourse, Ash St; 8am-noon Sun).

The **Otara Markets** (Map pp510-11; ☎ 274 0830; Newbury St; 6am-noon Sat) are held in the car park between Manukau Polytech and Otara town centre and have a real Polynesian atmosphere, with South Pacific food, music and fashions; take bus No 487 or 497 from outside Britomart Station.

Music lovers should visit the megastore **Real Groovy Records** (Map pp514-15; ☎ 302 3940; 438 Queen St).

Kathmandu (Map pp514-15; 151 Queen St) is a good place for outdoor gear.

GETTING THERE & AWAY

Air

Auckland Airport (Map pp510-11; ☎ 0800 247 767, 256 8899; www.auckland-airport.co.nz), 21km southwest of the city centre, is the major aerial gateway to NZ. It has an international terminal and a domestic terminal, each with a visitors information centre (p511) and left-luggage facilities; the international terminal also has a free phone for accommodation bookings. For information on international flights, see p799.

Auckland is also a hub for domestic flights; key destinations regularly serviced include Rotorua (from NZ$90), Wellington (from NZ$90), Christchurch (from NZ$95) and Queenstown (from NZ$150).

Domestic airlines operating to/from Auckland include:

Air New Zealand (Map pp514-15; ☎ 0800 737 000, 357 3000; www.airnz.co.nz; cnr Customs & Queen Sts)
Great Barrier Airlines (☎ 0800 900 600, 275 9120; www.greatbarrierairlines.co.nz)
Mountain Air (☎ 0800 222 123, 09-256 7025; www.mountainair.co.nz)
Origin Pacific (☎ 0800 302 302; www.originpacific.co.nz)
Qantas (Map pp514-15; ☎ 0800 808 767; 357 8900; www.qantas.co.nz; 191 Queen St)

Bus

The main long-distance bus company is **InterCity Coachlines** (☎ 913 6100; www.intercitycoach.co.nz), which in tandem with its subsidiary, **Newmans Coach Lines** (☎ 913 6200; www.newmanscoach.co.nz), operates services to/from key NZ towns and cities. InterCity and Newmans prices are usually interchangeable, but Newmans sometimes charges a higher fare than InterCity for an identical route. These operators are based at the **Sky City Coach Terminal** (Map pp514-15; ☎ 916 6222; 102 Hobson St).

Northliner Express (☎ 307 5873; www.northliner.co.nz) serves Northland, with buses heading to the north from Auckland to Whangarei (NZ$35), the Bay of Islands (NZ$45) and Kaitaia (NZ$70). Buses leave from 172 Quay St. **Guthreys Express** (☎ 0800 759 999, 309 0905; www.guthreys.co.nz) operates services southwards to Hamilton (NZ$20), Rotorua (NZ$40) and Waitomo (NZ$40). Buses depart from 168 Quay St, which is opposite the ferry building, in downtown Auckland.

Backpacker bus operators with their main offices in Auckland include **Kiwi Experience** (☎ 366 9830; www.kiwiexperience.com; 195 Parnell Rd, Parnell) and **Magic Travellers Network** (Map pp514-15; ☎ 358 5600; www.magicbus.co.nz; 136 Quay St), which both offer a door-to-door service with pick ups and drop offs at any city hostel. For more information on such outfits and the territory they cover, see p792.

Car & Campervan

HIRE

A swag of **car-rental companies** (Map pp514-15) can be found conveniently grouped together along Beach Rd, opposite the old train station. All the big international firms are represented at the airport.

All of the following car-rental companies except Avis rent out campervans as well as cars:

Ace (☎ 0800 502 277, 303 3112; www.acerentals.co.nz)
Alternative Rental Cars (☎ 373 3822; www.hireacar.co.nz)
Avis (☎ 0800 655 111, 526 2847; www.avis.com)
Backpacker Campervans (☎ 0800 422 267, 275 0200; www.backpackercampervans.com)

Britz NZ (☎ 0800 831 900, 275 1834; www.britz.com)
Budget (☎ 0800 652 227, 375 2270; www.budget.co.nz)
Hertz (☎ 0800 654 321, 367 6350; www.hertz.co.nz)
Hertz Campervans (☎ 0800 525 5000, 256 9698)
Maui (☎ 0800 651 080, 255 0620; www.maui.co.nz)

PURCHASE

For stays of two months or more, consider buying a cheap car via car markets, fairs, auctions or ads at hostels. Before handing over your money, check that the car is mechanically sound, has not been stolen, and does not have money owing on it; see p796 for more information.

The **Backpackers Car Market** (Map pp514-15; ☎ 377 7761; 190 Hobson St; ⌚ 9.30am-5pm) can give you the A to Z of buying and selling cars in NZ. A full mechanical check with a one-month guarantee is NZ$110 and third-party insurance can be arranged (around NZ$190 for three months with an NZ$800 excess). To display a car there to sell costs NZ$55 for three days.

Auckland has several car fairs, where people bring their own cars to sell; arrive between 8.30am and 9.30am for the best choice. Mechanical inspection services, credit agencies and Auto Check details are on hand at the fairs at **Ellerslie Racecourse** (Map pp510-11; ☎ 529 2233; www.carfair.co.nz; Greenlane East Rd, Ellerslie ⌚ 9am-noon Sun), where it costs NZ$30 to display a vehicle, and **Manukau** (Map pp510-11; ☎ 358 5000; Manukau City Centre Car Park; ⌚ 9am-1pm Sun), where you can display your vehicle for NZ$20.

Alternatively, try finding a vehicle at one of Auckland's car auctions. **Turner's Car Auctions** (Map pp510-11; ☎ 525 1920; www.turners.co.nz; cnr Leonard & Penrose Rds, Penrose) has auctions daily except Monday; a mechanical inspection will cost NZ$95 and a NZ$250 'Protection Plan' avoids any ownership or money-owing hassles. **Hammer Car Auctions** (Map pp510-11; ☎ 636 4900; cnr Neilson & Alfred Sts, Onehunga) also has auctions daily except Sunday.

Buy-back deals, whereby the dealer agrees to buy back your car for an agreed price (usually 50% of what you pay), aren't such a great deal but they do offer a safety net if you have trouble reselling the car. See p797 for further information. Dealers working on this system include **Auckland Rentals & Buy-Backs** (☎ 629 5455; 746 Dominion Rd) and **Car Warehouse** (Map pp510-11; ☎ 0800 888 850, 636 9903; 34 Alfred St, Onehunga).

Train

Trains arrive at and depart from **Britomart Station** (Map pp514-15; ☎ 0800 872 467; www.tranzscenic.co.nz; Quay St; booking office ⌚ 8am-8.30pm).

Only one train belonging to **Tranz Scenic** (☎ 0800 872 467; www.tranzscenic.co.nz) operates out of Auckland, going to Wellington via Hamilton and Palmerston North. The *Overlander* runs daily, leaving Auckland/Wellington each morning and arriving in the other city that night (two trains going in opposite directions). Check the website for departure/arrival times as they change during the year. The standard adult fare is NZ$145, but a seat in an older-style 'backpacker carriage' costs only NZ$75. A variety of discount and concession fares are available for purchase within NZ, usually available during off-peak periods only.

GETTING AROUND

A Discovery Pass (NZ$12) allows a day's travel on most bus, train and ferry services. For details of how to get into town from the airport and train station, see the boxed text (p509).

Bus

The Auckland city bus service is primarily run by **Stagecoach** (☎ 366 6400; www.rideline.co.nz). There's no downtown bus station; most buses leave from bus stops scattered around Britomart Station (Map pp514–15). Single-ride inner-city fares are NZ$0.50 (pay the driver); if you're travelling further afield, fares range from NZ$1.20 to NZ$7.90. A one-day pass (which includes downtown to North Shore ferries) costs only NZ$8, while a three-day pass costs NZ$19.

The **Link bus** (tickets NZ$1.20) leaves every 10 to 15 minutes from 6am to 11.30pm Monday to Friday and from 7am to 11.30pm Saturday and Sunday. It's a handy service travelling a loop that includes Queen St, Sky City, Victoria Park Market, Ponsonby Rd, K Rd, Newmarket, Parnell and Britomart Station.

The **City Circuit bus** (free) leaves every 10 minutes from 8am to 8pm and negotiates the inner city from Britomart Station up Queen St, past Albert Park to Auckland University, across to Sky Tower and back to Britomart.

The **Niterider** (☎ 366 6400; fare NZ$4-6) runs from the **Civic** (Map pp514-15; cnr Queen St & Wellesley

St West) along 10 routes between 1am and 3am on Friday and Saturday nights.

Ferry

Fullers (Map pp514-15; ☎ 367 9111; www.fullers.co.nz; ticket NZ$8.40-14) operates passenger ferries between the city and Devonport, Stanley Bay, Birkenhead and Bayswater on the North Shore, the gulf islands and Half Moon Bay near Howick.

Taxi

The biggest operator is **Auckland Co-Op Taxis** (☎ 300 3000).

Train

Tranz Metro (☎ 366 6400; www.rideline.co.nz; fares NZ$1.10-5, bikes NZ$1) runs three routes from Britomart Station; one line runs west to Waitakere, while the other two run south to Pukekohe. Services are at least hourly and run from around 6am to 8pm from Monday to Saturday. All train carriages have wheelchair ramps.

HAURAKI GULF ISLANDS

There are 47 islands off Auckland in the DOC-administered Hauraki Gulf Maritime Park; some of them are good-sized, easily visited islands, while others are no more than rocks jutting out of the sea. The isles that receive the most visitors include wine-soaked Waiheke, volcanic Rangitoto and rugged Great Barrier.

Get advance info on the highlights of the gulf at the Auckland **DOC Information Centre** (see p511).

Activities

The islands of Hauraki Gulf offer a multitude of hiking and mountain biking possibilities above sea level, and swimming, surfing, kayaking and sailboarding down in the ebb and flow of the ocean.

RANGITOTO & MOTUTAPU ISLANDS

☎ 09 / pop 105

A mere 10km northeast of downtown Auckland is Rangitoto (260m, Map pp514–15), which literally means 'Blood Red Sky' and is the largest and youngest of the area's volcanic cones. It erupted from the sea 600 years ago, an event almost certainly witnessed by Maori people living on nearby **Motutapu Island** (www.motutapu.org.nz), to which Rangitoto is now joined by a causeway.

Rangitoto is a good place for a picnic and for **walks**, which are detailed on an information board at the wharf. The hike from the wharf to the island's summit takes about an hour; you can then do a loop walk around the crater's rim, including a side trek (30 minutes return) to some **lava caves**. The island's black volcanic rock can get hot in summer, so bring good shoes and plenty of water.

In contrast to Rangitoto, Motutapu is mainly covered in sheep- and cow-grazed grassland. Traces of some 500 years of continuous human habitation are etched into the island's landscape.

The **Outdoor Education Camp** (☎ 445 4486; www.motutapucamp.com; per person/cottage NZ$15/150) has three-bedroom, self-contained cottages sleeping up to 12 people. Prices are reduced in winter and include free pick up from the Rangitoto ferry. Kayaking, sailing, abseiling and other activities are available.

There's a basic **DOC camping ground** (☎ 372 7348; Home Bay, Motutapu; camp sites per person NZ$5) three-hours' walk from Rangitoto wharf. A water tap and flush toilet are provided, but bring cooking equipment as open fires are forbidden.

Getting There & Around

Fullers (☎ 367 9111; www.fullers.co.nz; return fare NZ$20) has boats leaving at 9.15am and 2.15pm daily from Auckland's Ferry Building for the 20-minute trip to Rangitoto.

Fullers also does one-day tours to Rangitoto: on the **Volcanic Explorer** (tickets NZ$50) you ride in a canopied trailer, towed by a 4WD tractor, to a 900m boardwalk leading to the summit; the cost includes the return ferry trip. Some of these services go via Devonport.

WAIHEKE ISLAND

☎ 09 / pop 8500

Waiheke is the most visited of the gulf islands and, at 93 sq km, is one of the largest. Waiheke enjoys a slow pace of life and a fine climate; its many picturesque bays and safe beaches make it a great place to relax, and vineyards and olive groves are scattered across it. The island also attracts artistic types who exhibit their work in local galleries and craft shops.

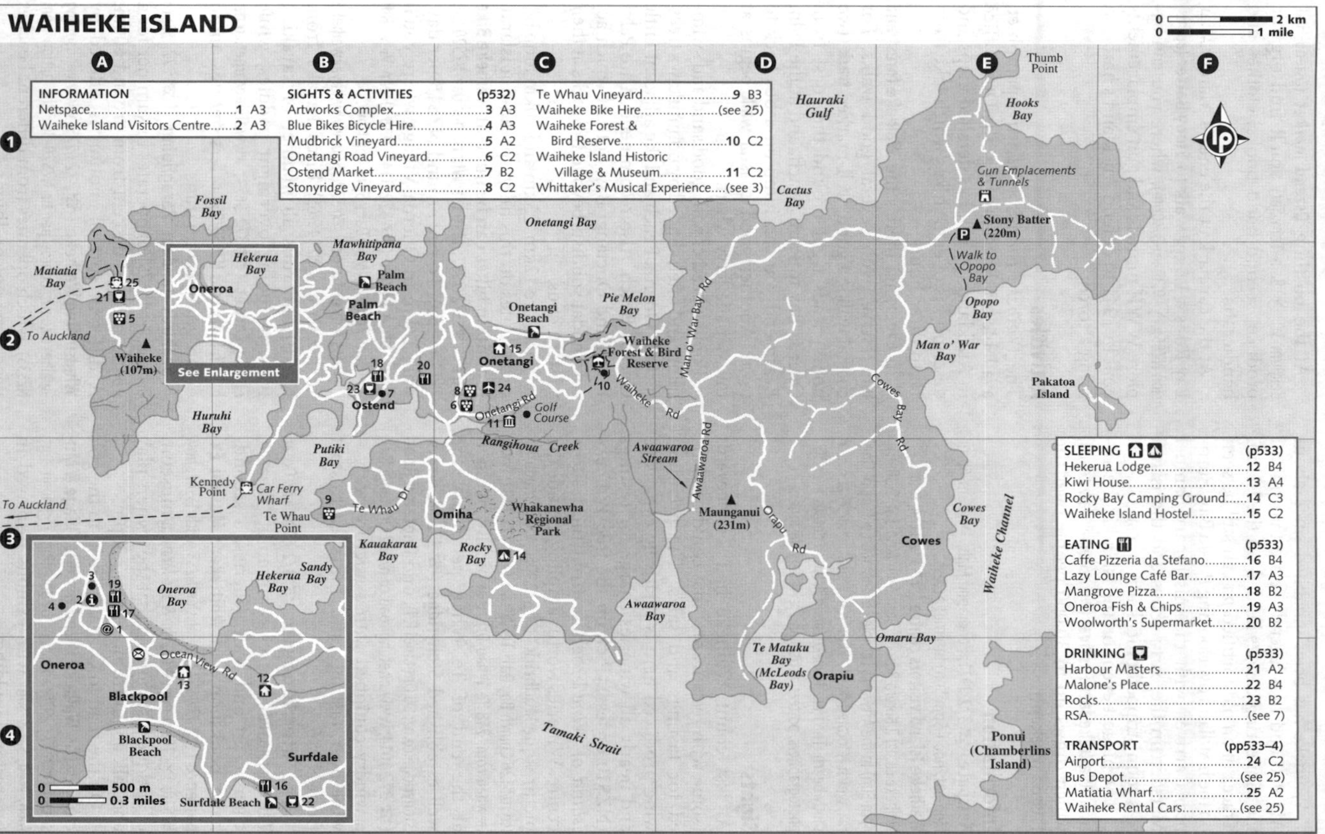
WAIHEKE ISLAND
0 2 km
0 1 mile
INFORMATION
Netspace.....1 A3
Waiheke Island Visitors Centre.....2 A3
SIGHTS & ACTIVITIES (p532)
Artworks Complex.....3 A3
Blue Bikes Bicycle Hire.....4 A3
Mudbrick Vineyard.....5 A2
Onetangi Road Vineyard.....6 C2
Ostend Market.....7 B2
Stonyridge Vineyard.....8 C2
Te Whau Vineyard.....9 B3
Waiheke Bike Hire.....(see 25)
Waiheke Forest & Bird Reserve.....10 C2
Waiheke Island Historic Village & Museum.....11 C2
Whittaker's Musical Experience.....(see 3)
Hauraki Gulf
Thumb Point
Hooks Bay
Gun Emplacements & Tunnels
Stony Batter (220m)
Walk to Opopo Bay
Opopo Bay
Man o' War Bay
Cactus Bay
Onetangi Bay
Fossil Bay
Matiatia Bay
To Auckland
Waiheke (107m)
Hekerua Bay
Oneroa
See Enlargement
Mawhitipana Bay
Palm Beach
Onetangi Beach
Onetangi
Pie Melon Bay
Waiheke Forest & Bird Reserve
Man o' War Bay Rd
Waiheke Rd
Cowes Bay Rd
Pakatoa Island
Ostend
Onetangi Rd
Golf Course
Huruhi Bay
Putiki Bay
Rangihoua Creek
Awaawaroa Stream
Awaawaroa Rd
Kennedy Point
Car Ferry Wharf
Te Whau Point
Te Whau Dr
Omiha
Whakanewha Regional Park
Maunganui (231m)
Orapu Rd
Cowes Bay
Waiheke Channel
Cowes
Kauakarau Bay
Rocky Bay
Awaawaroa Bay
Te Matuku Bay (McLeods Bay)
Orapiu
Omaru Bay
Tamaki Strait
Ponui (Chamberlins Island)
Oneroa Bay
Sandy Bay
Ocean View Rd
Blackpool
Blackpool Beach
Surfdale
Surfdale Beach
0 500 m
0 0.3 miles
SLEEPING (p533)
Hekerua Lodge.....12 B4
Kiwi House.....13 A4
Rocky Bay Camping Ground.....14 C3
Waiheke Island Hostel.....15 C2
EATING (p533)
Caffe Pizzeria da Stefano.....16 B4
Lazy Lounge Café Bar.....17 A3
Mangrove Pizza.....18 B2
Oneroa Fish & Chips.....19 A3
Woolworth's Supermarket.....20 B2
DRINKING (p533)
Harbour Masters.....21 A2
Malone's Place.....22 B4
Rocks.....23 B2
RSA.....(see 7)
TRANSPORT (pp533–4)
Airport.....24 C2
Bus Depot.....(see 25)
Matiatia Wharf.....25 A2
Waiheke Rental Cars.....(see 25)

Waiheke has been inhabited since about AD 950 and oral legends relate that one of the pioneering canoes landed on the island. Traces of an old fortified *pa* can still be seen on the headland overlooking Putiki Bay. Europeans arrived with the missionary Samuel Marsden in the early 1800s and the island was soon stripped of its kauri forest.

The biggest event on the island is the annual **Waiheke Jazz Festival** (www.waihekejazz.co.nz), which draws up to 30,000 people over the Easter weekend.

Information

Netspace (☎ 372 9921; Pendragon Mall; 🕑 9am-6pm Mon-Sat, noon-5pm Sun) Internet access.

Waiheke Island visitors centre (☎ 372 1234; info@waiheke.co.nz; 2 Korora Rd; 🕑 9am-5pm Mon-Sat, 9.30am-4pm Sun) In the Artworks complex in the main village of Oneroa, which is located nearly 2km from Matiatia wharf above a sandy beach. The free *Waiheke Island Art Map* details over 30 photographers, potters, artists and jewellery designers.

Sights

At last count Waiheke had 24 **vineyards** (some with restaurants) that could be visited for tastings and sales. The premium wine produced here is relatively expensive and nearly all wineries charge for tastings (NZ$10 or less). Pick up the free *Waiheke Island of Wine* brochure from the visitors centre. Wineries worth sampling include the picturesque **Mudbrick** (☎ 372 9050; www.mudbrick.co.nz; 126 Church Bay Rd); **Te Whau** (☎ 372 7191; www.tewhau.com; 218 Te Whau Dr), scenically perched at the end of Te Whau peninsula; the well-established **Stonyridge** (☎ 372 8822; www.stonyridge.co.nz; 80 Onetangi Rd); and **Onetangi Road** (☎ 372 1014; www.onetangiroad.co.nz; 82 Onetangi Rd), a winery equipped with a microbrewery – wine/beer tastings and tours each start from NZ$6.

The **Artworks complex** (☎ 372 6900; cnr Ocean View & Kororoa Rds) houses a community theatre, cinema, art and craft galleries, a second-hand bookshop and **Whittaker's Musical Experience** (☎ 372 5573; admission NZ$3, with 1½hr show NZ$10; 🕑 10am-4pm Wed, Thu & Sat-Mon), a museum of antique instruments that the owners play and talk about from 1pm to 2.30pm.

On the road to Onetangi, next to the golf club, is the **Waiheke Island Historic Village & Museum** (☎ 372 2970; admission by donation; 🕑 noon-4pm Mon, Wed, Sat & Sun) with exhibits displayed in five restored buildings.

At the bustling **Ostend market** (Ostend Hall, Belgium St; 🕑 8am-1pm Sat) you'll find organic produce, second-hand books, clothes and handicrafts.

At the car park at the end of Man o' War Bay Rd is a 1.5km walk to **Stony Batter** (admission NZ$5; 🕑 9.30am-3.30pm), where you can explore WWII tunnels and gun emplacements built in 1941 to defend Auckland's harbour; bring a torch.

Activities

The *Waiheke Islands Walkways* pamphlet, available on the island or at the DOC office in Auckland (p511), has detailed maps and descriptions of eight hikes which take from 1½ to three hours.

In Onetangi there's the **Waiheke forest and bird reserve**, with several good walks. For coastal walks, a good, well-marked **track** (two hours) leads right around the coast from Oneroa Bay to Palm Beach, and at the Palm Beach end you can jump on a bus back to town. Another good coastal **walk** begins at the Matiatia ferry wharf.

Popular **beaches** with good sand and swimming, and often shaded by pohutukawa trees, include Oneroa Beach and the adjacent Little Oneroa Beach. Also recommended are Palm Beach and Onetangi Bay, both of which accommodate nudists beyond the rocks at their western ends.

There are 12km, 25km and 70km loop bicycle routes on this hilly, spread-out island. Mountain bikes can be hired at **Waiheke Bike Hire** (☎ 372 7937; Matiatia Wharf; per day NZ$20-30; 🕑 9am-5pm). To pay around NZ$15 per day, walk 1½km to Oneroa Village where you'll find **Blue Bikes** (☎ 372 3143; 113 Ocean View Rd; 🕑 9am-7pm Dec-Mar, 9am-5pm Apr-Nov).

Ross Adventures (☎ 372 5550; www.kayakwaiheke.co.nz; 2/4hr trips NZ$45/65) hires kayaks from NZ$10 and runs all manner of kayaking trips, including overnight paddles, while **Flying Carpet** (☎ 372 5621; www.flyingcarpet.co.nz; half-/full-day trips NZ$50/95) offers outings on an ocean-going catamaran.

Seabirds Tandem Paragliding (☎ 372 5556; Onetangi Beach; NZ$160) operates in summer for a gentle rise and descent from around 600m. A different sort of motion is offered by **Windsurfing Waiheke** (☎ 372 6275; www.windsurfing-waiheke.co.nz; boards per hr NZ$20-30, 2hr tuition from NZ$35), which operates from different beaches depending on conditions.

Waiheke Air Services (☎ 372 5000; trips NZ$25-65) offers scenic flights for a gannet's view of the island.

Sleeping

Waiheke has a ready supply of backpackers' hostels and other types of accommodation. Prices at most places jump from mid-December to the end of January, and also at Easter (when you'd be lucky to get a bed anywhere).

Hekerua Lodge (☎ 372 8990; www.hekerualodge.co.nz; 11 Hekerua Rd; camp sites per person NZ$15, dm NZ$21-25, s NZ$35, d NZ$50-65;) Nestled in native bush, this small backpacker haven has a deck, garden, outdoor pool and hot spa pool. The atmosphere is relaxed and friendly; TV/videos can only be watched after 6pm. It's a 15-minute walk to Oneroa but buses stop nearby.

Waiheke Island Hostel (☎ 372 8971; www.waiheke.cjb.net; 419 Seaview Rd, Onetangi Bay; dm/s NZ$24/36, d NZ$50-70;) This clean and colourful YHA associate (NZ$4 less for members) has a large garden and helpful staff, and overlooks Onetangi Beach. The dorms have only two bunk beds. Linen is provided, mountain bikes can be hired (NZ$20 per day) and other activities can be booked.

Kiwi House (☎ 372 9123; kiwihouse@clear.net.nz; 23 Kiwi St; s NZ$45, d & tw from NZ$80) This friendly guesthouse offers a filling continental breakfast, pleasant decks and a shared kitchen, all at reasonable prices.

At remote Rocky Bay, at the far end of Gordons Rd in the Whakanewha Regional Park, is a council-run **camping ground** (☎ 303 1530; camp site per person NZ$5). Telephone to make a reservation and for the combination number to unlock the gate. Only drinking water and long-drop toilets are provided.

Eating & Drinking

The main place for cafés, bars and restaurants is Oneroa's main street, but other eating and drinking venues are scattered throughout Matiatia, Surfdale, Palm Beach, Ostend and Onetangi.

Oneroa Fish & Chips (☎ 372 8752; 29 Waikare Rd, Oneroa; lunch & dinner) Hidden away between the police station and a café is this superior fishy takeaway. It also does burgers (NZ$5 to NZ$10).

Lazy Lounge Café Bar (☎ 372 5732; 139 Ocean View Rd, Oneroa; meals NZ$8-22; breakfast, lunch & dinner) This funky laid-back place above the Rockit Gallery has varied indoor/outdoor areas (some of which have a 1960s feel, with scruffy sofas), a pool table, music, art on the walls, sea views and a great range of food from deli items to pizzas.

Caffe Pizzeria da Stefano (☎ 372 5309; 18 Hamilton Rd, Surfdale; meals NZ$15-25; dinner Tue-Sun) This is a locally recommended, BYO indoor/outdoor place serving Italian pizza, pasta and even *gelati*.

RSA (☎ 372 9250; Belgium St, Ostend; mains NZ$8-18; lunch & dinner) Located in the centre of Ostend, this place has little character but cheap food and beer. Also reasonably priced is **Mangrove Pizza** (☎ 372 8789; 14 Belgium St; dinner), where you can get pizzas (large NZ$18) or burgers (NZ$5 to NZ$8).

Self-caterers should head to **Woolworth's supermarket** (102 Ostend Rd, Ostend).

Harbour Masters (☎ 372 2950; Matiatia Bay; dinner mains NZ$15-22) This modern pub near the ferry has a beach-volleyball court, a garden and deck area, weekly live entertainment and a DJ on Friday and Saturday.

Malone's Place (☎ 372 8011; 6 Miami Ave, Surfdale; mains NZ$12-25) This Irish pub has a garden area, hearty bistro meals and live music on Friday, Saturday and Sunday.

Rocks (☎ 372 3722; 11 Belgium St, Ostend; meals NZ$14-16) This modern pub has a nice outdoor area, Waiheke oysters on the menu (six for NZ$14), a pool table and karaoke on Thursday.

Getting There & Away

Waiheke Air Services (☎ 0800 372 5000, 372 5000) has flights between Waiheke and Auckland (one way for one person NZ$110, NZ$80 per person for two or more people), Great Barrier Island (NZ$90) and Whitianga (one way for one person NZ$160, NZ$90 per person for two or more people).

Fullers (☎ 367 9111; www.fullers.co.nz; return fare NZ$25) runs ferries approximately hourly every day between downtown Auckland and Matiatia Wharf. The trip takes 35 minutes and a few ferries go via Devonport (one-way fare adult/child NZ$5.20/2.20).

Subritzky Line (☎ 534 5663; www.subritzky.co.nz; return fare NZ$25, car/motorcycle return NZ$110/31) takes cars and passengers on its route from Half Moon Bay in Auckland's east to Kennedy Point on Waiheke. The ferry runs at least every two hours from early morning to early evening daily; the trip takes 45 minutes. Bookings are essential.

Getting Around

Fullers (☎ 366 6400) operates four bus routes on the island that all connect with the arriving and departing ferries. All buses go from Matiatia Wharf to Oneroa, then depending on the route you can get to Little Oneroa, Palm Beach, Ostend and Rocky Bay; or Blackpool, Surfdale, Ostend and Onetangi. Matiatia to Oneroa costs NZ$1.10, MatiaitiaWharf to Palm Beach costs NZ$2.70 and an all-day bus pass is NZ$10.

Waiheke Rental Cars (☎ 372 8635; Matiatia Wharf) rents out cars from NZ$50 per day (plus NZ$0.50 per kilometre and an insurance excess, or deposit, of NZ$750). They also rent 50cc scooters (NZ$40 per day, NZ$500 excess) and motorcycles (NZ$65 per day, NZ$750 excess), neither of which attract a per-kilometre charge.

Taxi services include **Waiheke Taxis** (☎ 372 8038) and **Dial-a-Cab** (☎ 372 9666).

GREAT BARRIER ISLAND

☎ 09 / pop 1200

Scenic, rugged Great Barrier Island (Aotea), 88km from the mainland, is the largest island in the gulf. It's a hardy place, lacking an electricity grid (there are only private generators) or a bank, but this is compensated for with unspoilt beaches, hot springs, old kauri dams, a forest sanctuary, a network of tramping tracks and numerous activity options. Named by James Cook, Great Barrier Island was initially a whaling, mining and logging centre, but is now publicly owned and managed by DOC.

Tryphena is the main settlement, 3km from the ferry wharf at Shoal Bay.

> **PIGEON-GRAMS**
>
> Great Barrier's first pigeon-gram service took flight in 1897, a year after an enterprising Auckland newspaper reporter used a pigeon to file a report from the island. From small beginnings, the service expanded to include a good part of the Hauraki Gulf. Shopping lists, election results, mine claims and important pieces of news winged their way across land and sea tied to the legs of the canny birds. The arrival of the telegraph in 1908 grounded the service. Pigeon-gram stamps are now prized collector's items.

Information

DOC office (☎ 429 0044; 🕑 8am-4.30pm Mon-Fri) At Port Fitzroy, the main harbour on the west coast.

Great Barrier Island visitors centre (☎ 429 0033; www.greatbarrier.co.nz; 🕑 9am-4pm Mon-Fri, 9am-1pm Sat & Sun) The information centre is opposite the airfield at Claris, a small settlement 16km north of Tryphena, which also has a general store, bottle shop and laundrette.

Activities

SWIMMING & SURFING

The west-coast beaches, such as the sheltered sands of **Tryphena Bay**, are safe, but care needs to be taken on the surf-pounded (and surfing-conducive) eastern beaches. **Medlands Beach**, with its wide sweep of white sand, is one of the island's best and is easily accessible from Tryphena. Remote **Whangapoua** in the north-east requires more effort to get to, while **Kaitoke**, **Awana Bay** and **Harataonga** on the east coast are also worth a visit. **Okiwi Bar** has an excellent right-hand break, while Awana has both left- and right-hand breaks.

WALKING

The island's many worthwhile walks are not always well signposted, although they are being upgraded. This means you should be properly equipped with water and food, and prepared for bad weather. The best tramping trails are in the Great Barrier Forest north of Whangaparapara. The DOC's fold-out *Great Barrier Island* hiking brochure (NZ$2 donation) details 23 hikes.

Windy Canyon is only a 15-minute walk from the main Port Fitzroy–Harataonga (Aotea) road and has spectacular rock outcrops and island views. From here, an excellent trail continues for another 1½ hours through scrubby forest to **Hirakimata** (Mt Hobson; 621m), the highest point on the island. Another very popular walk is the **Kaitoke Hot Springs Track** (45 minutes), accessible from Whangaparapara Rd.

For details of a useful trampers bus service, see under Getting Around (p536).

MOUNTAIN BIKING

A good ride is from Tryphena to Whangaparapara: cycle about an hour to Medlands

Beach where you can stop for a swim, then cycle another hour to the hot springs, from where it's another half-hour to accommodation in Whangaparapara. Spend another day cycling through the forest up to Port Fitzroy, stopping on the way for a hike up to the kauri dams on a good, well-marked 4WD track. **Paradise Cycles** (☎ 429 0303; Claris) and **GBI Adventure Rentals** (☎ 429 0062; Mulberry Grove, Tryphena & Claris) both hire out mountain bikes.

OTHER ACTIVITIES

Aotea Sea Kayak (☎ 429 0664; aoteakayak@hotmail.com) runs sunset (NZ$35), night (NZ$50), snorkelling (NZ$55) and overnight (NZ$85) guided paddles. You can even paddle right round the island, but it takes 10 days. Night paddlers experience phosphorescence on the water's surface.

Hooked on Barrier (☎ 09-429 0417; Claris) hires out diving, snorkelling, fishing, surfing and kayaking gear.

Great Barrier Island Horse Treks (☎ 429 0274; Medlands; 1hr/2hr/half-day rides NZ$35/75/95) offers beach riding and swimming with horses (the horses do the swimming).

Sleeping

Stray Possum Lodge (☎ 0800 767 786, 429 0109; www.straypossum.co.nz; camp sites per person NZ$12, dm NZ$20, d & tw NZ$60, chalet NZ$125) Nestled in the bush south of Tryphena is this popular place with its own bar and a restaurant serving pizza and other takeaways. The chalets are self-contained and sleep up to six.

Crossroads (☎ 429 0889; xroads@ihug.co.nz; 1 Blind Bay Rd, Claris; dm/s/tw NZ$25/35/60; 💻) This comfortable backpackers is in the middle of the island, 2km from the airfield. Mountain bikes can be hired, and golf clubs can be borrowed to play on the nearby nine-hole golf course (NZ$10 to play all day).

Medlands Beach Backpackers & Villas (☎ 429 0320; www.medlandsbeach.com; 9 Mason Rd; dm NZ$22, d NZ$50-70) Basic accommodation is provided at the cheaper rates, but it's a five-minute walk to a beautiful beach and water-sports equipment is usually available.

Orama (☎ 429 0063; www.orama.org.nz; Karaka Bay; camp sites per person NZ$10, dm/cabins NZ$18/35; 🚐) Surrounded by hectares of bush, this Christian community just north of Port Fitzroy has plenty of diverse accommodation. There's a small store and you can hire kayaks, rowing dinghies and fishing and snorkelling gear.

DOC camping grounds (☎ 429 0044; camp sites per person NZ$7) The DOC has sites at Harataonga Bay, Medlands, Akapoua Bay, Whangapoua, The Green (Whangaparapara) and Awana Bay. All have basic facilities, including water (cold showers) and chemical toilets; BYO gas cooking stove. Bookings are essential in December and January. Camping is not allowed outside the camping grounds without a permit.

DOC Kaiaraara Hut (accommodation per person NZ$10, camp sites per person NZ$5) This hut sleeps up to 30 and is in the Great Barrier Forest, a 45-minute walk from Port Fitzroy wharf. Facilities include cold water, chemical toilets and a kitchen with a wood stove; bring your own sleeping bag and cooking equipment. It operates on a first-come, first-served basis, but is almost never full. You can also camp outside.

Eating & Drinking

Tipi & Bob's Restaurant (☎ 429 0550; Puriri Bay Rd, Tryphena; mains NZ$24-29; 🕒 breakfast, lunch & dinner) This popular haunt has an inviting deck overlooking the harbour, and fresh fish, seafood and steaks on the menu. There's a bistro menu in the bar (meals NZ$6 to NZ$20), including high-quality fish and chips.

Cruisy Café (☎ 429 0997; Blackwell Dr, Tryphena) This café sells bread, cakes, doughnuts and lunch items.

Claris Store 2000 (☎ 429 0852) This store is near the airport and is well stocked with groceries, bread, organic meat, pizzas and pies.

Currach Irish Pub (☎ 429 0211; Blackwell Dr, Tryphena; mains NZ$10-20) This lively pub has a changing menu of seafood, steak and Asian-style meals, and is the island's social centre. Thursday is the big music night when anyone can get up and perform, but there's also live music on the weekend in summer.

Getting There & Away

AIR

Great Barrier Airlines (☎ 0800 900 600, 275 9120; www.greatbarrierairlines.co.nz; one way/return NZ$90/180) flies three times daily to Great Barrier Island from Auckland Airport and twice daily from Dairy Flat aerodrome, on Portman Rd on the way to Orewa (North of Auckland). Flights take 35 minutes. Great Barrier Airlines also fly in from Whangarei, in Northland, or from Whitianga (p565) on the Coromandel Peninsula.

POOR KNIGHTS ISLANDS – AN ABSOLUTE DIVE

On your way north to the Bay of Islands from Auckland and Hauraki Gulf, divert northeast from Whangarei for 26km to reach **Tutukaka Marina**, where a multitude of yachts, dive boats and game-fishing boats are moored together. This is the main year-round base for trips to the Poor Knights Islands, 24km offshore and rated as one of the world's top 10 diving spots.

The Poor Knights Islands Marine Reserve was established in 1981. The islands are bathed in a subtropical current from the Coral Sea, so varieties of tropical and subtropical fish not seen in other coastal waters are observed here. The waters are clear, with no sediment or pollution problems. The 40m to 60m underwater cliffs drop steeply to the sandy bottom, and are a labyrinth of archways, caves, tunnels and fissures that attract a wide variety of sponges and colourful underwater vegetation. Manta rays are common.

The two main volcanic islands, Tawhiti Rahi and Aorangi, were once home to members of the Ngati Wai tribe but, since a raiding-party massacre in the early 1800s, the islands have been *tapu* (forbidden). Even today no-one is allowed to set foot on the islands, in order to protect their pristine environment. Not only do tuatara (prehistoric reptiles) and Butler's shearwater birds breed there, but there are unique species of flora, such as the Poor Knights red lily.

A major operator at Tutukaka Marina is **Dive! Tutukaka** (☎ 0800 288 882, 09-434 3867; www.diving.co.nz; day trip NZ$175), with a standard day trip that includes two dives, plus time for snorkelling and kayaking. Wannabe divers will find plenty of experienced instructors on hand; a five-day PADI open-water course costs NZ$595 (medical certificate required). Dive trips for first-timers or experts can also be organised from Whangarei.

Shuttle buses leave Whangarei for Tutukaka at 7.10am and 3pm, and depart Tutukaka at 8.15am and 4.30pm. In summer a shuttle also runs from Whangarei to Paihia (Bay of Islands) at 5.30pm and leaves Paihia for Whangarei at 7.30pm.

Mountain Air (Great Barrier Express; ☎ 0800 222 123, 256 7025; www.mountainair.co.nz; one way/return NZ$105/175) flies three or four times a day from Auckland Airport, and four times a week from Whangarei (both trips cost the same).

You can fly to Great Barrier Island one way with either carrier and take a Subritzky ferry the other way for NZ$125.

FERRY

Subritzky (☎ 373 4036; www.subritzky.co.nz; adult/student one way NZ$55/40, return NZ$85/70) sails daily through December and January, but not on Tuesday and Saturday the rest of the year. The boats also take cars (NZ$500 return December and January, NZ$300 return February to November) and run from Wynyard Wharf in Auckland to Tryphena.

Fullers (☎ 367 9111; www.fullers.co.nz; one way/return NZ$60/120) runs services from the Auckland Ferry Building to Tryphena from mid-December to the end of January, usually at the weekend; the trip takes two hours.

Getting Around

Great Barrier Buses (☎ 429 0474) runs five buses a day from Stray Possum Lodge (p535) to Claris via Tryphena and Medlands Beach, with two services continuing on to the hot pools and White Cliffs. It also offers an excellent trampers transport service, which can drop you off at any of the main trail heads and pick you up at the other end. A one-day pass that includes trampers transport or scheduled services is NZ$30; a three-day pass costs NZ$49.

Aotea Bus (☎ 429 0055) has airport and wharf transfers (NZ$12 from Claris to Tryphena) and a bus service from Tryphena to Port Fitzroy (NZ$15) which runs daily December to February, and from Monday to Friday the rest of the year.

GBI Rent-A-Car (☎ 429 0062; gbi.rentacar@xtra.co.nz; Mulberry Grove Bay, Tryphena & Claris) hires out a wide range of hardy vehicles, including mini mokes starting at NZ$50, as well as adventure gear.

Many of the accommodation places will pick up from the airport or wharf if notified in advance.

TIRITIRI MATANGI ISLAND

☎ 09

This magical 210-hectare, predator-free **island** (www.tiritirimatangi.co.nz) is home to lots of endangered **native birds**, including the very rare and colourful takahe. Other birds that can be seen here are the bell bird (NZ's nightingale), the stitch bird, the rare saddleback, the whitehead, kakariki, kokako, little spotted kiwi, brown teal, New Zealand robin, fernbird and penguins.

The island's original forests were decimated by early farmers, but since 1984 hundreds of volunteers have planted 250,000 native trees and the forest cover has regenerated. An 1865 **lighthouse** stands on the eastern end of the island. A **guided walk** on the island is a good deal at NZ$5.

The **bunkhouse** (☎ 479 4490; dm NZ$15) has a kitchen, hot showers and flush toilets.

Fullers (☎ 367 9111; www.fullers.co.nz; ticket NZ$45) usually has ferries heading to the island from Auckland on Thursday, Saturday and Sunday, running more often between December and March. The ferries leave Central Auckland at 9am and arrive back in the city at 4.45pm; you can also get to the island from Gulf Harbour on the Whangaparaoa Peninsula, north of Auckland.

MOTUIHE ISLAND

☎ 09

Enjoy the remoteness, regenerating bush, **walking tracks** and sandy **beaches** of this 176-hectare island for a couple of nights at a bargain price. Formerly a prison camp during WWI, it now has only four permanent residents. There's a self-contained **farmhouse** (☎ 534 5419; 1-4 people NZ$60) that's rented out to one group at a time (BYO linen, towels and food) and an ultra-basic **camping ground** (camp site per person NZ$5).

Fullers (☎ 367 9111; www.fullers.co.nz; return NZ$20) runs a ferry to Motuihe from Auckland at 7pm on Friday and another back to Auckland around 5.15pm on Sunday.

GOAT ISLAND BEACH

☎ 09

This is one of NZ's special places, out near Cape Rodney to the north of Auckland. The country's first **marine reserve** (547 hectares) was established here in 1978 and subsequently its waters have become a giant aquarium. Walk to the right over the rocks and you can usually see snapper (the big fish with blue dots and fins), blue maomao and stripy parore swimming around. Alternatively, **snorkel** or **scuba dive** from the black-sand beach, or **dive** off Goat Island itself to encounter colourful sponges, forests of brown seaweed, stingrays and, if you're very lucky, orca whales and bottle-nosed dolphins.

The glass-bottomed boat **Habitat Explorer** (☎ 422 6334; www.glassbottomboat.co.nz; cruises NZ$20) offers a great 45-minute trip around Goat Island, viewing the underwater life as you go. Trips run from the beach year-round, except when the sea is too rough.

Snorkelling, diving gear and wetsuits can be hired at **Seafriends** (☎ 422 6212; www.seafriends.org.nz; 7 Goat Island Rd; 🕒 10am-5pm), 1km before Goat Island Beach. Also on the premises is a saltwater aquarium, marine education centre and café.

BAY OF ISLANDS

☎ 09

In the heart of the Northland region and famed for its stunning coastal scenery is the Bay of Islands, one of NZ's major attractions. The bay is punctuated by dozens of coves and when the sun is shining its clear waters range in hue from turquoise to deep blue. Although a hugely popular tourist and sailing destination, the 150 or so islands have thankfully escaped development; townships are all on the mainland.

As the site of NZ's first permanent English settlement, the Bay of Islands also has enormous historical significance. It was here that the Treaty of Waitangi (p491) was drawn up and first signed by 46 Maori chiefs in 1840; the treaty remains the linchpin of race relations in modern-day NZ.

The small town of Paihia is the area's activity hub, while only a short passenger-ferry ride away are the fine old buildings of Russell, which has all the charm and character that Paihia lacks. To the northwest is Kerikeri, famous for its orchards and outdoor Mediterranean-style cafés.

Activities

The Bay of Islands has a mind-boggling, highly competitive array of activities, with most subject to backpacker discounts. Hostels can book all tours and can generally arrange cheap deals. Most of the following activities depart from Paihia, but pick ups from Kerikeri can be arranged and most of the cruises call in at Russell.

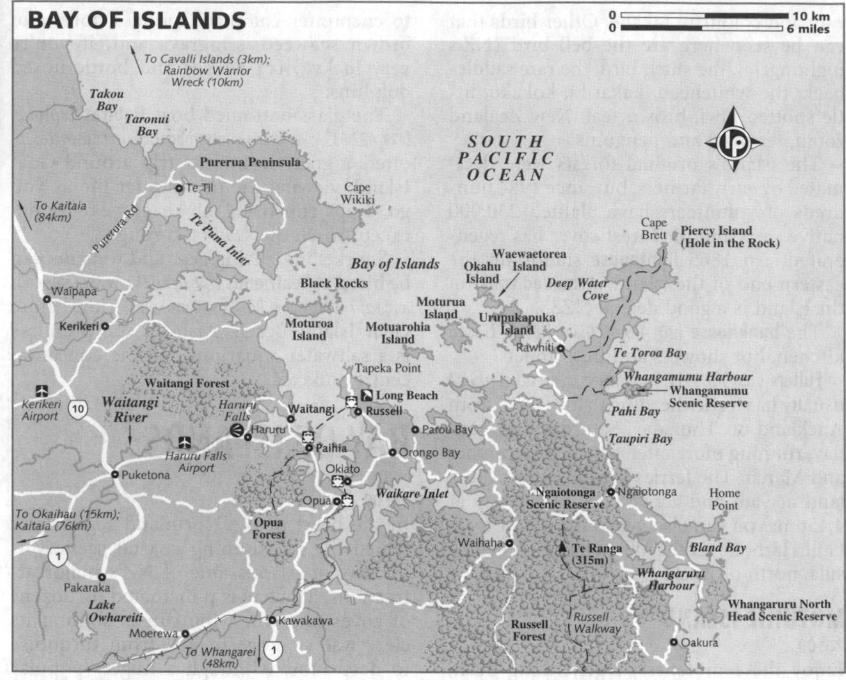

CRUISING, JET-BOATING & SAILING

You can't leave the Bay of Islands without taking some sort of cruise and there are plenty of operators keen to get you on board. The two biggest operators are **Fullers** (☎ 402 7422; www.fullers-bay-of-islands.co.nz; Maritime Building, Paihia) and **Kings Tours & Cruises** (☎ 0800 222 979, 402 8288; www.kings-tours.co.nz; Maritime Building, Paihia).

Fullers has the four-hour **Hole in the Rock** (NZ$62) tour off Cape Brett. Boats pass through the hole if conditions are right. There's also a stopover on Urupukapuka Island, where Westerns writer Zane Grey went big-game fishing and where a tourist submarine called the **Nautilus** (admission NZ$12) is submerged.

Fullers' **'Cream Trip'** (tickets NZ$85) is a day trip which started back in 1920 when one Captain Lane picked up dairy products from the many farms around the bay. As more roads were built and the small dairy farms closed, it became a mail delivery service. It's now part of the 'Supercruise', which incorporates the Hole in the Rock tour and a one-hour stopover on Urupukapuka Island.

Kings has a **Day in the Bay** (tickets NZ$85) cruise, which is a combination of the 'Cream Trip' route and the Hole in the Rock with dolphin swimming.

Also very popular are the high-speed Hole in the Rock jet-boat trips, good fun and handy if you're short on time. Put on the waterproof gear provided and fasten your seatbelts! **Excitor** (☎ 402 7020; www.excitor.co.nz; tickets NZ$65) and **Mack Attack** (☎ 0800 622 528, 402 8180; www.mackattack.co.nz; tickets NZ$65) have regular 1½-hour trips.

A very pleasant way of exploring the bay is aboard a day sailing trip. In most cases you can either help crew the boat (no experience required), or just spend the afternoon sunbathing, swimming, snorkelling, kayaking and fishing. Operators generally charge similar rates – NZ$80 to NZ$120 for a full day's sailing, with lunch – and boats include the **R Tucker Thompson** (☎ 0800 882 537, 402 8430; www.tucker.co.nz; tickets NZ$95), which offers a barbecue lunch and a cruise on a classic schooner that has sailed around the world; **Carino** (☎ 402 8040; www.sailinganddolphin.co.nz; tickets NZ$70), which combines sailing and dolphin swimming; the **Phantom** (☎ 0800 224 421; tickets NZ$80), a speedy 15m ocean racer; and also the **Straycat** (☎ 402 6130; tickets NZ$75), which is a 16-passenger catamaran.

OVERNIGHT CRUISE

The **Rock** (☎ 0800 762 527; www.rocktheboat.co.nz; 24hr cruises NZ$140) is an unlikely looking form of overnight accommodation: a former vehicle ferry now set up for backpackers. This comfortable floating hostel has four-bed dorms, twins and double rooms (doubles cost an extra NZ$15 per person) and a bar. The cruise departs around 5pm from Paihia wharf and includes an excellent barbecue and seafood dinner with live music, then a full day spent cruising around and visiting islands, fishing, kayaking, snorkelling and swimming.

DOLPHIN SWIMMING

These trips operate all year and have a high success rate; operators generally offer a free trip if dolphins aren't sighted. The swims are subject to weather conditions, with restrictions if the dolphins have offspring. As well as encountering bottlenose and common dolphins, whales, orcas and penguins may also be seen. A portion of the fee charged by all operators goes towards marine research via DOC.

Dolphin Discoveries (☎ 402 8234; dolphin@igrin.co.nz; trips NZ$95), established 15 years ago, has 3½-hour trips with all equipment provided.

Dolphin Adventures (☎ 402 6985; www.awesomeadventures.co.nz; trips NZ$95) has similar trips, with an option to spend time on Urupukapuka Island.

SEA-KAYAKING

There are plenty of opportunities for kayaking around the bay, either on a guided tour or by renting a kayak and going it alone.

Coastal Kayakers (☎ 402 8105; www.coastalkayakers.co.nz; Te Karuwha Pde, Ti Bay, Waitangi) runs a half-day guided tour for NZ$50 per person (NZ$70 for a full day), and a two-day budget harbour wilderness tour for NZ$110. A minimum of two people is required. Kayaks can be rented for NZ$28/40 per half-/full day.

New Zealand Sea Kayak Adventures (☎ 402 8596; nzakayak@clear.net.nz; 2-/3-day trips NZ$175/250) runs kayaking and camping trips, and also has a day trip including lunch for NZ$125.

Island Kayaks (☎ 402 7111; 18 Kings Rd, Paihia; NZ$60) and **Bay Beach Hire** (☎ 402 6078, Marsden Rd, Paihia; NZ$50) have half-day guided trips.

SCUBA DIVING

The Bay of Islands offers some fine subtropical diving. Local operators all go out to the wreck of the *Rainbow Warrior* (see the boxed text, below) off the Cavalli Islands, about an hour from Paihia by boat.

Paihia Dive (☎ 0800 107 551, 402 7551; www.divenz.com; Williams Rd, Paihia) offers *Rainbow Warrior* dive trips (NZ$175 for two dives including gear) or you can do two adventure dives for the same price. Dive courses start at NZ$210.

Dive North (☎ 402 7079; divenorth@xtra.co.nz) also has trips to the *Rainbow Warrior* and other popular dive sites such as Deep Water Cove and Cape Brett.

SURFING

Auckland-based **NZ Surf Tours** (☎ 09-832 9622; www.newzealandsurftours.com; NZ$400) runs a three-day surfing course from Tuesday to Thursday at nearby surfing beaches, including meals, transport, surfboards, wetsuits and lessons.

OTHER ACTIVITIES

Boats can be chartered for **fishing** at the Maritime Building in Paihia or at Russell wharf.

Bay of Islands Skydive Centre (☎ 0800 427 593, 402 6744; Haruru Falls Airport) offers a tandem skydive for NZ$270. A video of the jump costs

THE RAINBOW WARRIOR

In 1985, the Greenpeace flagship *Rainbow Warrior* lay anchored in Auckland Harbour, preparing to sail to Moruroa near Tahiti to protest against French nuclear testing. But it never left Auckland because French saboteurs, in the employ of the French government, attached explosives to the side of the ship and sank her, killing a green campaigner, Fernando Pereira.

In the midst of international outrage, two of the saboteurs were captured, tried and found guilty. But in a farcical turn of events the agents were turned over to the French government, imprisoned on a French Pacific island as if they had won a trip to Club Med, and returned home within two years.

The skeletal remains of the *Rainbow Warrior* were taken to the waters of Northland's beautiful Cavalli Islands, where they can now be explored by divers.

NZ$125, and a video and photographs cost NZ$150.

Skywalk (☎ 021-415 556; Haruru Falls Airport; flights NZ$150) takes passengers up in a motorised hang-glider for half-hour flights. You can learn to fly the glider yourself for NZ$580.

Bay Beach Hire (☎ 402 6078; www.baybeachhire.co.nz; Marsden Rd, Paihia; 9am-5.30pm) hires out just about everything for a fun day: kayaks (half-day NZ$35), small sailing catamarans (NZ$125), mountain bikes (half-day NZ$15), boogie boards, fishing rods, wetsuits and snorkelling gear. Bay Beach Hire also runs **Flying Kiwi Parasail** (☎ 402 6078; www.parasail-nz.co.nz; trips NZ$75), which organises one-hour parasailing trips departing Paihia wharf hourly over summer.

The increasingly popular sport of kitesurfing, where you use a kite (more a mini parachute) to drag you across the waves on a surfboard, can be attempted via **Air Torn Kiteboarding** (☎ 402 6236). You can get full instruction for NZ$400.

Salt Air (☎ 402 8338; www.saltair.co.nz) has scenic flights ranging from a 30-minute tour of the Bay of Islands (NZ$95) to a five-hour flight-and-4WD tour of Cape Reinga and Ninety Mile Beach (NZ$330). You can also take helicopter flights out to the Hole in the Rock and Cape Brett (NZ$170).

Paihia Duck (☎ 402 8681; www.paihiaduck.co.nz; tours NZ$45) offers one-hour tours on an amphibious bus that leaves Paihia four times daily to head up to Waitangi, then across the water to Opua and back to Paihia.

Big Rock Springs Trail Rides (☎ 401 9923; half-/full-day ride NZ$55/80) is based in Okaihau, about 42km west of Paihia, but will pick up in Paihia. The full-day ride includes a river swim on horseback.

Cape Reinga Tours

It's cheaper and easier to do trips to Cape Reinga and Ninety Mile Beach from Kaitaia or Doubtless Bay if you're heading up that way (see p551). However, if you're short on time, it's possible to do a long day trip (10 to 12 hours) from the Bay of Islands. The various available bus tours are all pretty similar and usually include a visit to Puketi kauri forest, sandboarding on the dunes and other stopovers, but check out the itinerary and whether lunch is included.

4X4 Dune Rider (☎ 402 8681; www.dunerider.co.nz; trips NZ$90) Popular with backpackers as these small-group trips (20-seater buses) make plenty of stops for sandboarding and swimming.

Awesome Adventures (☎ 402 6985; www.awesomeadventures.co.nz; Maritime Bldg, Paihia; trips NZ$95) Orients its trips to backpackers, with sandboarding on the 85m-high dunes, swimming at Tapotupotu Bay and a visit to the kauri forest.

Fullers (☎ 402 7422; tours NZ$95, with BBQ lunch NZ$110) Has all-day trips departing from Paihia and Kerikeri.

Northern Exposure (☎ 0800 573 875, 402 8644; NZ$85) Offers similar stuff as Awesome Adventures, but doesn't allow children on its trips.

Getting There & Away

Air New Zealand (☎ 0800 737 000; www.airnz.co.nz) operates three to four flights daily from Auckland to Kerikeri (from NZ$85).

Buses serving Paihia arrive at and depart from the Maritime Building beside the wharf. **InterCity** (☎ 402 7857; www.intercitycoach.co.nz) and **Northliner** (☎ 402 7857; www.northliner.co.nz) run daily from Auckland to the Bay of Islands (from NZ$45, four hours) via Whangarei.

Getting Around

Ferries (fare NZ$5) connect Paihia with Russell, running regularly between around 7am and 7pm (to 10pm from October to June).

You can also get around the bay on a **water taxi** (☎ 403 8823).

PAIHIA & WAITANGI

☎ 09 / pop 7250

Paihia was first settled by Europeans as a mission station in 1823 with the arrival of Reverend Henry Williams. Paihia has a very pretty setting and is now a tourist town with countless activity and accommodation options. Adjoining Paihia to the north is Waitangi, site of the historic signing on 6 February 1840 of the treaty between the Maori people and the representatives of Queen Victoria's government. Various ceremonial events are held here every year on Waitangi Day (6 February), the anniversary of the Treaty of Waitangi's inception.

Information

Bay of Islands visitors centre (☎ 402 7345; visitorinfo@fndc.govt.nz; 8am-late summer, 8am-5pm winter) Near the wharf, next door to the Maritime Building.

Boots Off Travellers Centre (☎ 402 6632; Selwyn Rd; per hr NZ$9) Internet access.

Maritime Building (Marsden Rd; per hr NZ$6) There's Internet access here. Fullers, Kings, Awesome Adventures

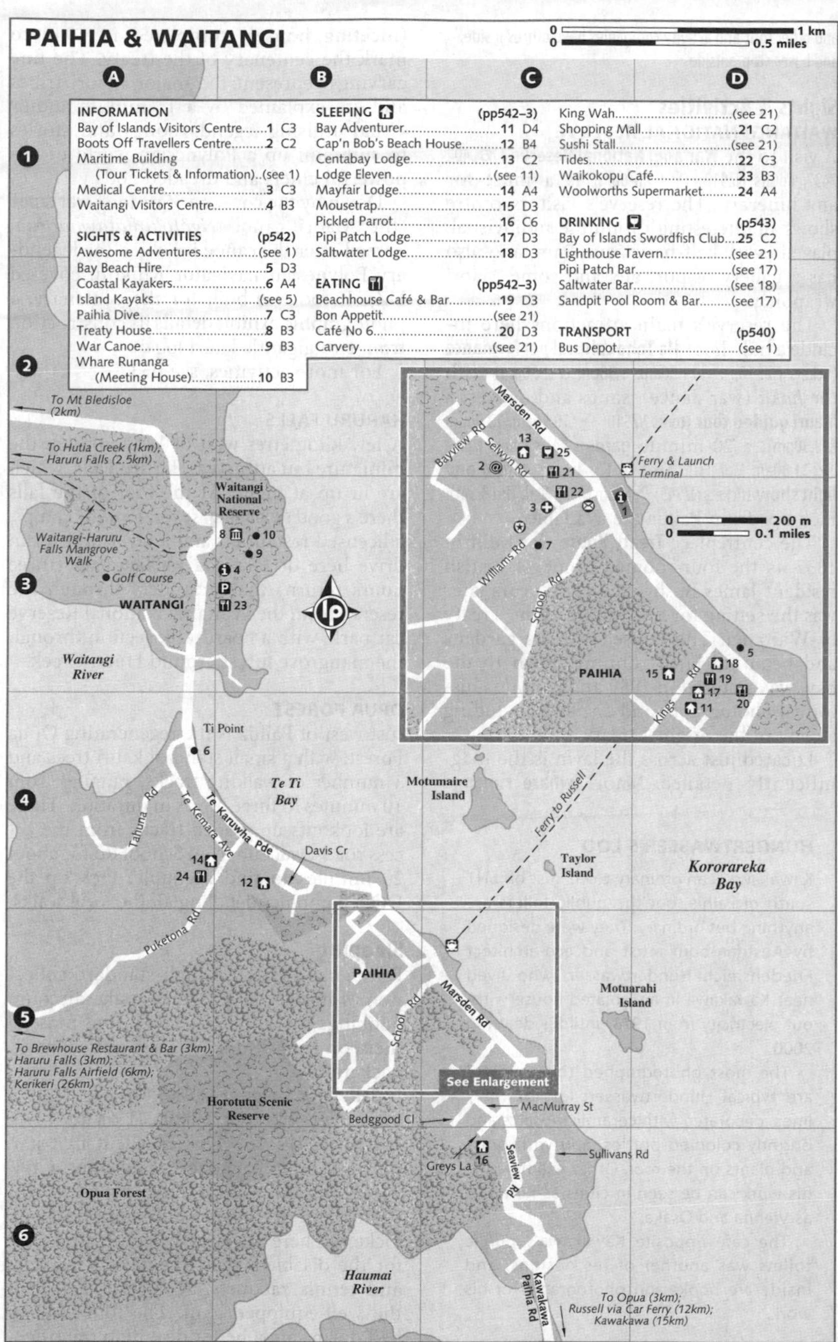
PAIHIA & WAITANGI
0 1 km
0 0.5 miles
A
B
C
D
INFORMATION
Bay of Islands Visitors Centre.......1 C3
Boots Off Travellers Centre.........2 C2
Maritime Building
(Tour Tickets & Information)..(see 1)
Medical Centre.............................3 C3
Waitangi Visitors Centre..............4 B3
SIGHTS & ACTIVITIES (p542)
Awesome Adventures.................(see 1)
Bay Beach Hire.............................5 D3
Coastal Kayakers..........................6 A4
Island Kayaks.............................(see 5)
Paihia Dive....................................7 C3
Treaty House.................................8 B3
War Canoe.....................................9 B3
Whare Runanga
(Meeting House)........................10 B3
SLEEPING (pp542–3)
Bay Adventurer.............................11 D4
Cap'n Bob's Beach House............12 B4
Centabay Lodge............................13 C2
Lodge Eleven..............................(see 11)
Mayfair Lodge...............................14 A4
Mousetrap.....................................15 D3
Pickled Parrot................................16 C6
Pipi Patch Lodge...........................17 D3
Saltwater Lodge............................18 D3
EATING (pp542–3)
Beachhouse Café & Bar................19 D3
Bon Appetit.................................(see 21)
Café No 6......................................20 D3
Carvery..(see 21)
King Wah.....................................(see 21)
Shopping Mall..............................21 C2
Sushi Stall....................................(see 21)
Tides...22 C3
Waikokopu Café............................23 B3
Woolworths Supermarket.............24 A4
DRINKING (p543)
Bay of Islands Swordfish Club....25 C2
Lighthouse Tavern......................(see 21)
Pipi Patch Bar.............................(see 17)
Saltwater Bar...............................(see 18)
Sandpit Pool Room & Bar.........(see 17)
TRANSPORT (p540)
Bus Depot.....................................(see 1)
1
2
3
4
5
6
To Mt Bledisloe (2km)
To Hutia Creek (1km); Haruru Falls (2.5km)
Waitangi National Reserve
Waitangi-Haruru Falls Mangrove Walk
Golf Course
WAITANGI
Waitangi River
Ti Point
Te Ti Bay
Motumaire Island
Tahuna Rd
Te Kemara Ave
Te Karuwha Pde
Davis Cr
Puketona Rd
Taylor Island
Kororareka Bay
Ferry to Russell
Motuarahi Island
PAIHIA
School Rd
Marsden Rd
See Enlargement
Horotutu Scenic Reserve
MacMurray St
Bedggood Cl
Sullivans Rd
Greys La
Seaview Rd
Opua Forest
Haumai River
Kawakawa Pahiia Rd
To Brewhouse Restaurant & Bar (3km); Haruru Falls (3km); Haruru Falls Airfield (6km); Kerikeri (26km)
To Opua (3km); Russell via Car Ferry (12km); Kawakawa (15km)
Marsden Rd
Bayview Rd
Selwyn Rd
Ferry & Launch Terminal
0 200 m
0 0.1 miles
Williams Rd
School Rd
PAIHIA
Kings Rd

and other tour and activity companies have offices inside, and buses stop outside.

Sights & Activities

WAITANGI NATIONAL RESERVE

A visit to the **Waitangi National Reserve** (☎ 402 7437; adults NZ$10; 🕑 9am-6pm) is a must for any itinerary. The reserve's visitors centre shows an interesting 15-minute audiovisual, played every half-hour from 9am, and also has a gallery of portraits and some Maori weaponry.

The reserve's main attractions here include a half-hour **He Toho cultural performance** (tickets NZ$10; 🕑 11.30am, 1.30pm & 2.30pm) with the *haka* (war dance), songs and dances; a **Maori guided tour** (tours NZ$10; 🕑 10.30am, 12.30pm & 2.30pm); a 20-minute **garden tour** (tours NZ$5; 🕑 11.30am Mon-Fri); and a 1½-hour **sound and light show** (tickets NZ$45; 🕑 8pm Mon, Wed, Thu & Sat). Pick ups from Paihia are available.

The centrepiece **Treaty House** was built in 1832 as the four-roomed home of British resident James Busby, and eight years later was the setting for the signing of the Treaty of Waitangi. The house, with its gardens and beautiful lawn running down to the bay, was restored in 1989 and contains historical photographs and displays, including a copy of the original treaty.

Located just across the lawn is the magnificently detailed Maori **whare runanga** (meeting house), completed in 1940 to mark the centenary of the treaty. The fine carvings represent the major Maori tribes and are explained by a 15-minute audiovisual utilising legends, songs and stories to summon up a Polynesian world of all-powerful chiefs and dreaded gods.

Down by the cove is a 35m-long **war canoe** (the Maori canoe *Ngatokimatawhaorua*, named after the canoe in which the legendary Polynesian navigator Kupe discovered NZ). It too was built for the centenary; a photographic exhibit details its construction from two gigantic kauri logs.

For more activities, see p537.

HUNDERTWASSER'S LOO

Kawakawa is an ordinary town, just off SH1 south of Paihia, but the public toilets are anything but ordinary. They were designed by Austrian-born artist and eco-architect Friedensreich Hundertwasser, who lived near Kawakawa in an isolated house without electricity from 1973 until his death in 2000.

The most photographed toilets in NZ are typical Hundertwasser: lots of wavy lines, decorated with ceramic mosaics and brightly coloured bottles, and with grass and plants on the roof. Other examples of his work can be seen in cities as far apart as Vienna and Osaka.

The café opposite Kawakawa's public toilets was another of his designs, and inside are books and photographs of his work.

HARURU FALLS

A few kilometres west of Waitangi are the miniature but attractive Haruru Falls, which are lit up at night. At the foot of the falls there's good **swimming**, several motor camps, a licensed restaurant and a tavern. You can drive here or take the **walking track** (three hours return) that meanders through the reserve from the Waitangi National Reserve car park, with a boardwalk section through the mangrove forest around Hutia Creek.

OPUA FOREST

Just west of Paihia is the regenerating Opua Forest, with a small stand of kauri trees and a number of walking tracks, ranging from 10 minutes to three hours in duration. There are lookouts up graded tracks from the access roads; walk up from School Rd for about 20 minutes to find a couple. Pick up the DOC pamphlet detailing all the local walks.

Sleeping

Paihia has a sizeable, high-standard collection of hostels, all of which make discount bookings for activities. You'll find most of them on Kings Rd, Paihia's so-called 'backpackers row'.

Saltwater Lodge (☎ 0800 002 266, 402 7075; www.saltwaterlodge.co.nz; 14 Kings Rd; dm NZ$21-23, d & tw NZ$100-115; 💻) This excellent five-star, purpose-built backpackers is only a few years old. All rooms have private bathrooms and are heated and equipped with lockers. There are large balconies and a lift for the disabled, plus free kayaks, bicycles and tennis racquets. A special feature is the well-equipped gym. The four- to six-bed dorms are a better deal than the pricey private rooms, but the latter are subject to discounts when things are quiet.

Cap'n Bob's Beach House (☎ 402 8668; capnbobs@xtra.co.nz; 44 Davis Cres; dm NZ$21, d NZ$50-70; 💻) This small but stylish backpackers makes for a spotless home away from home, with a hard-working owner, veranda views and a touch of luxury.

Bay Adventurer (☎ 402 5162; www.bayadventurer.co.nz; 28 Kings Rd; dm NZ$20, d NZ$55-85, studio NZ$75-95; 💻 ♿) Large, smart-to-luxurious establishment with a spa pool, free bikes and good, very clean facilities. Rooms have comfy mattresses with linen included. Note that this is not a party place, with prominent notices requesting that noise effectively stops after 11pm.

Centabay Lodge (☎ 402 7466; www.centabay.co.nz; 27 Selwyn Rd; dm NZ$20, d & tw NZ$50-65; 💻) This lodge is just behind the shops and the friendly owners maintain a high standard. The spa pool and kayaks are available for free, and the more expensive rooms with private bathroom are a good deal.

Mousetrap (☎ 402 8182; www.mousetrap.co.nz; 11 Kings Rd; dm NZ$19-22, d & tw NZ$45-55; 💻) There are plenty of small chill-out areas in this nautical-themed, wood-décor hostel, where a mixed bag of rooms have wardrobes and central heating.

Pickled Parrot (☎ 0508 727 768, 402 6222; theparrot@paradise.net.nz; Greys Lane; camp sites per person NZ$16, dm NZ$20-22, d & tw NZ$50; 💻) Breakfast, bikes and fishing rods are included in the price at this laid-back backpackers in a pleasant garden setting. The parrot nips.

Lodge Eleven (☎ 402 748; lodgeeleven@hotmail.com; cnr Kings Rd & MacMurray St; dm/d NZ$20/60; 💻) This YHA-associate hostel is in a converted motel. The rooms have private bathroom and come with bedding and heating, but the communal areas are not as good as the rooms.

Pipi Patch Lodge (☎ 402 7111; pipipatch@acb.co.nz; 18 Kings Rd; dm NZ$22, d & tw NZ$60-80; 💻 ♿) This backpackers lodge, popular with tour groups, has eight-bed dorms (all with bathroom, a sink and a fridge), a spa and the world's tiniest swimming pool. It's a party place with a bar.

Mayfair Lodge (☎ 402 7471; mayfair.lodge@xtra.co.nz; 7 Puketona Rd; camp sites per person NZ$12, dm/s/d NZ$22/40/50; 💻) This small, friendly backpackers is clean and colourful, though located a bit out of town.

Eating

Beachhouse Café & Bar (☎ 402 7345; 16 Kings Rd; meals NZ$6-15; 🕑 breakfast, lunch & dinner) This lively place has fresh juices for NZ$5.50, gourmet burgers for NZ$6 to NZ$10, all-day breakfasts and big beer glasses, plus a DJ (Friday), live music (Saturday) and a jam session (Sunday).

Café No 6 (☎ 402 6797; 6 Marsden Rd; mains NZ$11-20; 🕑 breakfast, lunch & dinner; 💻) An informal café that serves mainly Mediterranean food, including tapas and ciabatta bread, though occasionally Bavarian meatballs sneak onto the menu.

Waikokopu Café (☎ 402 6275; meals NZ$14-26; 🕑 9am-5pm, dinner summer) An excellent café near the visitors centre at the Waitangi National Reserve.

Tides (☎ 402 7557; Williams Rd; meals NZ$7-25; 🕑 breakfast, lunch & dinner summer) Provides light but tasty meals, with daily seafood specials. Opening times vary in winter.

The Shopping Mall is the place for cheap eats. **Bon Appetit** (☎ 402 7867; 🕑 lunch & dinner) offers lasagne (NZ$4.50), seafood soup (NZ$3) and a buffet selection (NZ$12 for a large plastic container). Next door is a **carvery** (🕑 lunch Mon-Sat, dinner Mon-Fri) which serves meat and salad rolls for NZ$6 and meals for NZ$12, and nearby is a **sushi stall** (NZ$7 a packet) and **King Wah's** (☎ 402 7566; 🕑 lunch & dinner) Chinese buffet dinner (NZ$24).

Self-caterers should head for the **Woolworths supermarket** (6 Puketona Rd; 🕑 7am-10pm).

Drinking

Saltwater Bar (☎ 402 7783; 14 Kings Rd) Serves popular pizzas and has shuffleboard and nightly karaoke, bar games and quizzes.

Pipi Patch Bar (☎ 402 7111; 18 Kings Rd) This bar has a DJ on Saturday, 'Wild Wednesdays', a moist-mouth competition (not what you think it is) and other backpacker fun and games.

Bay of Islands Swordfish Club (☎ 402 7723; Marsden Rd) There are great views and tall tales at this club bar that welcomes visitors.

Sandpit Pool Room & Bar (☎ 402 6063; 16 Kings Rd) Tables at this combination pool room and drinks dispenser cost NZ$10 per hour.

Lighthouse Tavern (☎ 402 8324) There's a DJ in summer and a dance area at this place above the Shopping Mall.

Brewhouse Restaurant & Bar (☎ 402 7195; Haruru Falls) This historical tavern, 4km from Paihia, brews its own draught beers. It's a convivial place with an open fire, a restaurant and a DJ or live music on summer weekends.

RUSSELL

☎ 09 / pop 1140

Historic, peaceful Russell is across the bay from the hustle of Paihia. It was originally a fortified, expansive Maori settlement known as Kororareka (Sweet Penguin). But in 1830 two Maori girls vied for the attention of a whaling captain and sparked the intertribal 'War of the Girls', which was only resolved when the area's *ariki* (high chief), Titore, decreed the two tribes be split on either side of a border at the base of the Tapeka Peninsula. A European settlement quickly sprang up in place of the abandoned Maori village.

In its early days Russell was a magnet for so-called rough elements like fleeing convicts, whalers, prostitutes and drunk sailors. Charles Darwin described it in 1835 as full of 'the refuse of society', but it was probably no worse than other ports. Today, cafés, gift shops and motels have replaced the grog shops and brothels.

Most Bay of Islands water-based tours pick up from Russell, making the township an alternative base to busy Paihia.

Information

DOC Pewhairangi Bay of Islands visitors centre (☎ 403 9003; www.doc.govt.nz; The Strand; 🕑 9am-5pm summer, 9am-4.30pm winter) This excellent centre has information on the sprawling reserve called Pewhairangi (opposite).

Innovation (☎ 403 8843; Trader's Mall) Internet access.

Russell Information & Booking Centre (☎ 403 8020; russell.information@xtra.co.nz; 🕑 7.30am-9pm summer, 8.30am-5pm winter) On the pier where the passenger ferry from Paihia docks.

Sights & Activities

Russell's waterfront is lined with stately colonial buildings and pohutukawa trees, and the town lays claim to some of NZ's oldest buildings, including **Christ Church** (1847), the country's oldest church, which is suitably scarred with musket and cannonball holes.

The small, modern **Russell Museum** (☎ 403 7701; 2 York St; admission NZ$5; 🕑 10am-4pm) has a fine 1:5 scale model of Captain Cook's *En-*

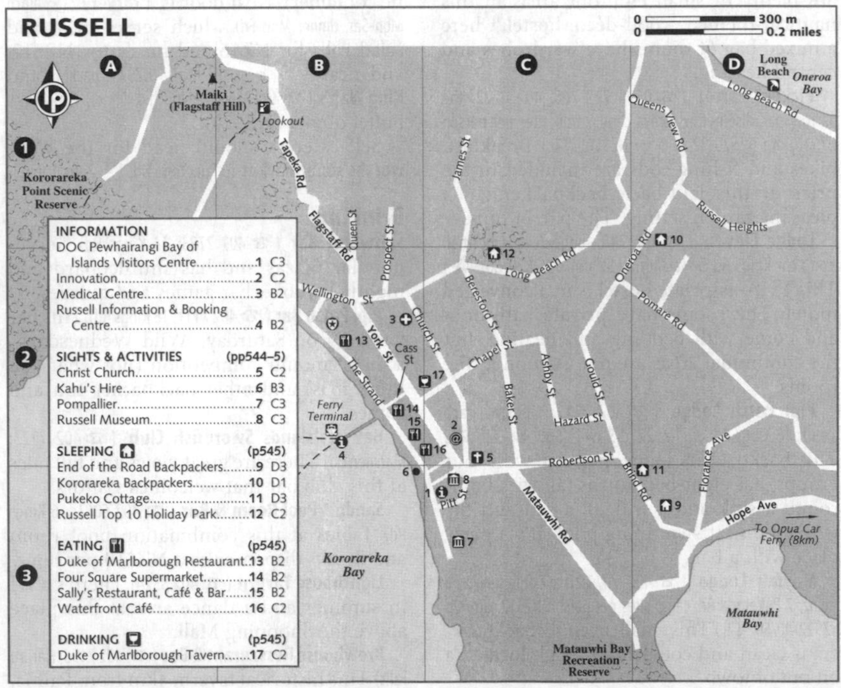

deavour (Cook visited the Bay of Islands in 1769) and an impressive 7kg crayfish, as well as Maori and pakeha relics and a 10-minute history video.

Pompallier (☎ 403 9015; adult/student NZ$7.50/3.50; 10am-5pm Dec-Feb & school holidays) was built in 1842 to house the Roman Catholic mission's printing press, which printed 40,000 books in Maori. During the 1870s it was converted into a private home but has since been restored to its original state. There are five tours daily from March to November.

Overlooking Russell is **Maiki** (Flagstaff Hill), where Ngapuhi leader Hone Heke chopped down the flagpole – a hated symbol of pakeha authority – four times in the mid-19th century. The view is worth the climb. By car take Tapeka Rd or, if on foot, take the track west of the boat ramp along the beach at low tide, or up Wellington St at high tide.

Russell Information & Booking Centre rents out **bicycles** for NZ$10/25 per hour/half-day, while in good weather **Kahu's Hire** (The Strand) rents out kayaks and dinghies (NZ$10 per hour).

About 1.5km east of Russell is **Long Beach** (Oneroa Bay Beach), which has an unusual adobe cottage. Turn left (facing the sea) to visit **Donkey Bay**, a small cove that is an unofficial nudist beach.

Sleeping

End of the Road Backpackers (☎ 403 7632; 24 Brind Rd; dm/d NZ$20/45) End of the Road is a small but comfortable backpackers with good views out over the marina. The sole dorm has just two beds.

Pukeko Cottage (☎ 403 8498; barrymp@xtra.co.nz; 14 Brind Rd; dm/d NZ$20/45;) This establishment is another small, homely hostel with an artistic owner.

Kororareka Backpackers (☎ 403 8494; korobp@xtra.co.nz; 22 Oneroa Rd; dm/d NZ$20/50;) Another comfortable, compact backpackers with a deck. The owners are knowledgeable on the subject of local Maori history.

Russell Top 10 Holiday Park (☎ 0800 148 671, 403 7826; russelltop10@xtra.co.nz; James St; camp/campervan sites per person from NZ$11/13, d NZ$45-105) This park has a small store, good facilities, an attractive setting and refurbished tourist flats.

Eating & Drinking

Duke of Marlborough Restaurant (☎ 403 7829; The Strand; mains NZ$12-25; lunch & dinner) The grand old Duke has period charm with a veranda, and the brief but interesting menu includes treats like smoked venison.

Cafés on the waterfront:

Sally's Restaurant, Café & Bar (☎ 403 7652; 25 The Strand; mains NZ$18-28; lunch & dinner)

Waterfront Café (☎ 403 7589; The Strand; breakfast & lunch, closed Mon winter)

You can stock up on groceries at **Four Square Supermarket** (The Strand).

Duke of Malborough Tavern (☎ 403 7851; York St) This sports bar has live music most Fridays, a bistro restaurant, draught Guinness and a table-tennis table.

Getting There & Around

From Paihia, the easiest way to reach Russell is with the regular **passenger ferry** (one way NZ$5). It runs from 7.20am to 7.30pm (until 10.30pm October to May), generally every 20 minutes. Buy your tickets on board.

A **car ferry** (vehicle & driver one way/return NZ$8/15, motorcycle & rider NZ$4/7, additional passenger NZ$1/2) runs roughly every 10 minutes between 6.50am and 10pm from Opua to Okiato Point. Buy tickets on board.

PEWHAIRANGI

☎ 09

This park consists of 40 separate areas which extend from Whangamumu Harbour in the south to Whangaroa in the north, where diverse hikes take in islands, *pa* sites and some spectacular scenery. The **DOC Pewhairangi Bay of Islands visitors centre** (☎ 403 9003; www.doc.govt.nz; The Strand, Russell; 9am-5pm summer, 9am-4.30pm winter) can provide information.

Rawhiti is the starting point for the **Cape Brett hike** (7½ hours), a hard 20km walk to the top of the peninsula, where overnight stays are possible in the **Cape Brett Hut** (☎ 403 9003; accommodation NZ$12); on top of the accommodation cost, there's also a NZ$30 trail fee.

You can camp at two bays on **Urupukapuka Island** (☎ 403 9003; camp site per person NZ$6), which has hikes of up to five hours and is accessible by water taxi or a **Fullers** (☎ 402 7422; www.fullers-bay-of-islands.co.nz) tour boat. Both Cable and Urupukapuka Bays have fresh water, cold showers and composting toilets, but you need your own food, stove and fuel. Also on the island is **Zane Grey's Restaurant & Bar** (☎ 403 7009; zanegrey@xtra.co.nz; Otehei Bay; camp sites per person NZ$12, dm NZ$20, d NZ$30-50; mains NZ$12-25), which provides accommodation.

KERIKERI

☎ 09 / pop 5000

Located at the northern end of the Bay of Islands, Kerikeri has a glut of historical and natural attractions, as well as a relaxed Mediterranean feel generated by the local citrus orchards and café culture.

'Kerikeri' means 'To Dig':– Maori people grew kumera (sweet potato) here before the pakeha arrived, and the area's fertile soils now produce kiwi fruit and oranges as well as vegetables. Picking and pruning go on virtually all year and attract workers at wage rates pegged at around NZ$9 per hour.

Information

DOC (☎ 407 8474; 34 Landing Rd) Hiking information.
Kerikeri Computers (☎ 407 7941; 88 Kerikeri Rd; per hr NZ$6) Internet access.
Visitors centre (☎ 407 9297; www.kerikeri.co.nz; Cobham Rd; 9am-5pm Mon-Fri, 10am-noon Sat) Part of a library complex that provides Internet access.

Sights & Activities

The **Stone Store** (☎ 407 9236; admission NZ$3.50; 10am-5pm Nov-Apr, 10am-4pm Mar-Oct), on the banks of Kerikeri River, was built between 1833 and 1836 and is NZ's oldest stone building. It's full of the type of goods that were bartered in the store, including muskets and blankets, as well as diaries and other relics of missionary endeavour. At one time a blanket was worth a pig, but a musket cost eight or 10 pigs (or blankets). The role of missionaries in arming northern Maori people with muskets remains a controversial topic.

Adjacent to the store is the even older **Mission House** (admission NZ$5; 10am-4pm), erected in 1822 by Reverend Butler. The country's oldest wooden building, it contains some original fittings and chattels. A ticket to visit both buildings is NZ$7.

Up the hill behind the Stone Store is a marked historical walk to **Kororipo Pa** (20 minutes return), the fortress of famous Ngapuhi chief Hongi Hika. Hika-led Ngapuhi raiding parties once set off from here to terrorise much of the North Island during the Musket Wars (p491). The walk emerges near **St James Anglican Church**, built in 1878.

Across the river from the Mission House is **Rewa's Village** (☎ 407 6454; admission NZ$3; 9am-5pm summer, 10am-4pm winter), a mock-up of a pre-European Maori village, with information boards on plants that were used at the time – by all accounts, food plants like fern roots did not taste good.

Also on this side of the river is a scenic reserve with several marked walking tracks, including the 4km **Kerikeri River Track** that leads to the 27m-high **Rainbow Falls**, passing **Wharepoke Falls** and the **Fairy Pools** (great for swimming and picnics) along the way. Alternatively, you can reach Rainbow Falls via a 10-minute walk from Waipapa Rd, and the Fairy Pools can be accessed from the dirt road beside the YHA hostel (below).

Pick up the free *Art & Craft Trail* brochure from the visitors centre to visit Kerikeri's many art, furniture, wool and pottery outlets, including an unusual **kaleidoscope shop** (☎ 407 4415; 256 Waipapa Rd).

On the road into Kerikeri from the south are orchards, fruit stalls and a cluster of shops, including the homemade edibles at **Shirley's Temple Gourmet Food** (☎ 403 7141), expensive but delicious handmade-on-the-premises chocolate at **Makana** (☎ 407 6800) and kauri products at **Kauri Workshop** (☎ 407 9196).

Aroha Island visitors centre (☎ 407 5243; www.aroha.net.nz; admission free; 9.30am-5.30pm Tue-Sun Sep-May) is on the tiny five-hectare **Aroha Island**, 12km northeast of Kerikeri, and is reached via a permanent causeway through the mangrove bushes. The centre has environmental displays, including information on the handful of adult North Island brown kiwi that live on the island along with lots of other birds such as fantails and tui. Kayaks can be rented here (NZ$20 for two hours).

On SH10, just south of Kerikeri Rd, are a couple of wineries that offer tastings. **Cottle Hill Winery** (☎ 407 5203) is a boutique place selling cheese and meat platters for lunch, while **Marsden Estate Winery** (☎ 407 9398; Wiroa Rd) offers a range of meals and platters (NZ$12 to NZ$20) on its decking.

Sleeping

Kerikeri YHA (☎ 407 9391; yhakeri@yha.org.nz; 144 Kerikeri Rd; camp sites per person NZ$18, dm/tw NZ$23/55, d NZ$55-80;) This hostel has some character and a tranquil setting with a large garden leading down to the river; you might see a kingfisher on the volleyball net.

Hone Heke Lodge (☎ 407 8170; honeheke@xtra.co.nz; 65 Hone Heke Rd; dm NZ$18, s NZ$35-45, d &

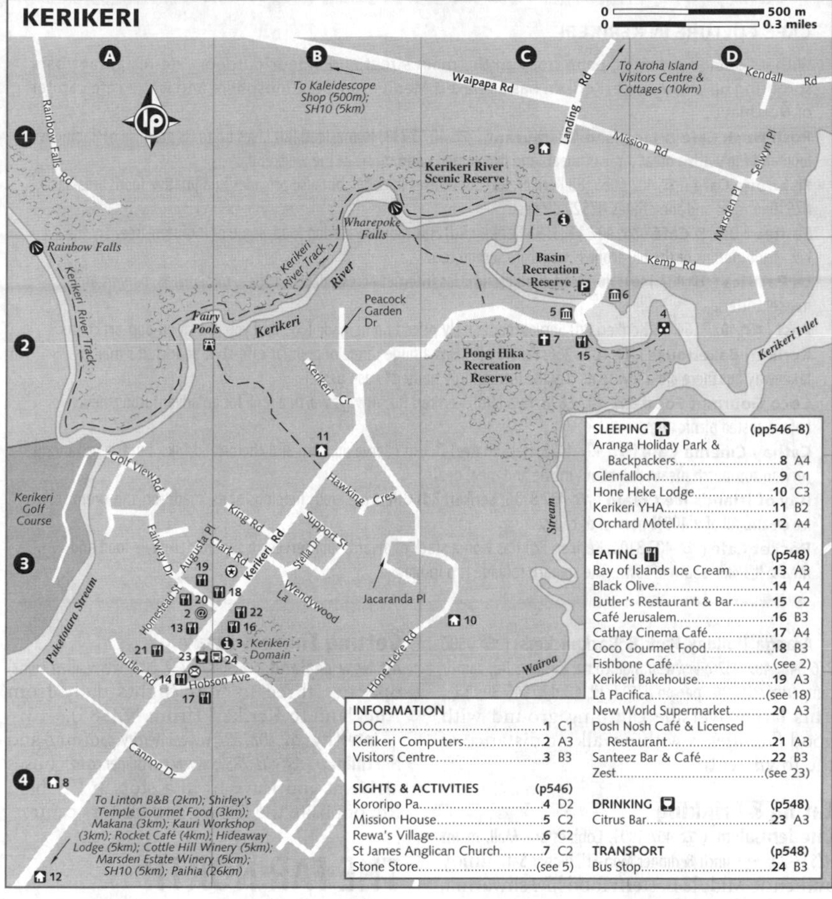

tw NZ$45-50;) Hone Heke has a line of single-storey units which caters mainly to those working in local orchards. Weekly rates range from NZ$85 to NZ$100 per person.

Hideaway Lodge (☎ 0800 562746, 407 9773; www.hideawaylodge.co.nz; 111 Wiroa Rd; camp sites per person NZ$10-13, dm per week NZ$85, d per week NZ$175-185;) Hideaway is a good place to stay if you're looking for work as they usually have jobs available year-round. The lodge is spacious, well equipped and usually busy and lively. It's 5km out of Kerikeri, west of the SH10 junction, but there are free rides to town twice a day.

Aroha Island Cottages (☎ 407 5243; www.aroha.net.nz; Aroha Island; camp sites per person NZ$9, cottage d NZ$80-95 & extra person NZ$12) The modern self-contained cottages on this small island sleep up to 10 people.

Glenfalloch (☎ 407 5471; glenfall@ihug.co.nz; 48 Landing Rd; s NZ$60, d NZ$80-95;) This relaxing homestay B&B with a beautiful garden and a tennis court is 500m north of the Stone Store. Rooms have bathroom or private facilities and the hosts enjoy their job.

Linton B&B (☎ 407 7654; 518 Kerikeri Rd; s/d NZ$40/60) Facilities are shared but there is a good cooked breakfast and a large garden.

Orchard Motel (☎ 407 8869; orchardmotel@xtra.co.nz; Kerikeri Rd; unit NZ$75-110;) Less than 1km south of the town centre among the orchards are these units with kitchens, a large outdoor pool and a spa.

CAFÉ CULTURE IN KERIKERI

With its orange orchards, palm trees on the main street and indoor/outdoor café-restaurant-bars sprouting up everywhere, Kerikeri has a relaxed Mediterranean atmosphere and is the café capital of Northland.

Posh Nosh Café & Licensed Restaurant (☎ 407 7213; Homestead Rd) Lives up to its promise of 'fabulous food and fun' with a great array of meals and live comedy and music at the weekend.

Fishbone Café (☎ 407 6065; 88 Kerikeri Rd) Specialises in coffee but also provides imaginative food: breakfasts, NZ$10 lunches and sometimes NZ$20 dinners.

Santeez Bar & Café (☎ 407 1185; 93 Kerikeri Rd) Has mouthwatering food, some of it gluten-free. Try the kiwi-fruit muffins or the big scones; mains are served too.

La Pacifica (☎ 407 1461; Hub Mall, Kerikeri Rd) Has Internet access, decent coffee, mini pizzas, *paninis* and mussel fritters.

Zest (☎ 407 7164; 73 Kerikeri Rd) Serves moderately priced homemade food and you can sit on pop-art chairs.

Kerikeri Bakehouse (☎ 407 7266; Fairway Dr) Has a huge range of popular café-style snacks. It's mainly takeaway but there are a few seats. Try the intriguingly named 'wasp nest'.

Coco Gourmet Food (☎ 407 8826; Hub Mall, Kerikeri Rd) Always worth a look for an adventurous, never-before-tasted picnic item.

Cathay Cinema Café (☎ 407 4428; Hobson Ave) Doesn't serve popcorn and chemical drinks, but is a restaurant serving top-notch meals. Ask about movie and meal deals.

Bay of Islands Ice Cream (☎ 407 8136; Kerikeri Rd) Offers generous helpings of its 'made-on-the-premises' ice cream. All of it 100% natural of course.

Rocket Café (☎ 407 3100; Kerikeri Rd) Has won a stack of awards and serves up superb deli-style food and meals. It's 4km south of town. The spinach roulade is popular.

Aranga Holiday Park & Backpackers (☎ 0800 276 648, 407 9326; www.aranga.co.nz; Kerikeri Rd; camp/campervan sites per person NZ$11/12, s & d NZ$45-80; 💻) This large riverside camping ground with good facilities is within walking distance of the town centre.

Eating & Drinking

Café Jerusalem (☎ 407 1001; Cobblestone Mall; mains NZ$13-20; 🕒 lunch & dinner Mon-Fri, dinner Sat) Enjoy authentic Middle Eastern food like shwarma, falafel and baklava that you can eat in or take away. A four-meat combo with yoghurt, rice, pitta bread and salad is NZ$20.

Black Olive (☎ 407 9693; Kerikeri Rd; meals NZ$12-25; 🕒 dinner Tue-Sun) Black Olive serves up popular pasta and pizza takeaways, or you can sit down and eat in the back.

Butler's Restaurant & Bar (☎ 407 8479; Stone Store Basin; mains NZ$8-25; 🕒 lunch & dinner Wed-Sun) There's beef, venison, lamb or fish for dinner on the veranda here overlooking the river.

The **New World Supermarket** (Fairway Dr) has everything self-caterers might need.

Citrus Bar (☎ 407 1050; Kerikeri Rd; meals NZ$10-24; 🕒 lunch & dinner) Citrus is a sports-music bar and the most popular nightspot in town, with live bands or a DJ on Friday night. The bistro menu includes pizza and nachos.

Getting There & Away

Air New Zealand (☎ 0800 737 000; www.airnz.co.nz) operates three to four flights daily from Auckland to Kerikeri (from NZ$85).

InterCity (☎ 402 7857; www.intercitycoach.co.nz) and **Northliner** (☎ 402 7857; www.northliner.co.nz) buses arrive at and leave from a stop in Cobham Rd, opposite the library and visitors centre.

THE FAR NORTH

Up beyond the Bay of Islands, Northland squeezes itself into a rugged, desolate tendril of earth called the Aupouri Peninsula, known to the Maori people as Te Hiku o te Ika a Maui (The Tail of Maui's Fish) from the creation legend that tells of how Maui hauled a great fish from the sea, which became the North Island. It's dominated by high dunes and flanked on its western side by the hard sand of Ninety Mile Beach – if it was metricated to Ninety Kilometre Beach, the name would be more accurate. At its northwestern extremity is the captivatingly isolated Cape Reinga.

The peninsula's gateway town, Kaitaia, is a good place to learn about and participate in Maori culture.

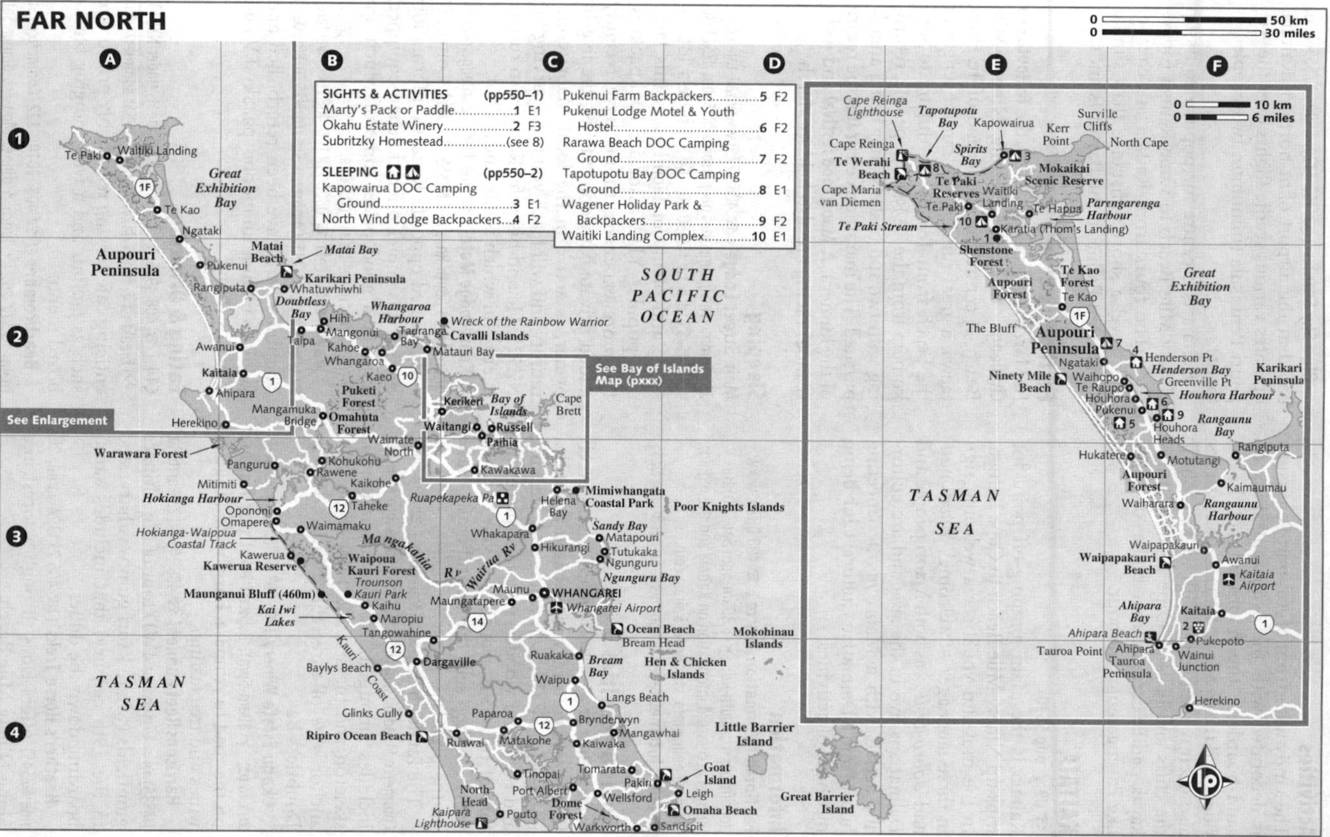
FAR NORTH
0 50 km
0 30 miles
A
B
C
D
E
F
1
2
3
4
SIGHTS & ACTIVITIES (pp550–1)
Marty's Pack or Paddle.................1 E1
Okahu Estate Winery...................2 F3
Subritzky Homestead.................(see 8)
SLEEPING (pp550–2)
Kapowairua DOC Camping Ground...................................3 E1
North Wind Lodge Backpackers...4 F2
Pukenui Farm Backpackers.............5 F2
Pukenui Lodge Motel & Youth Hostel...6 F2
Rarawa Beach DOC Camping Ground..7 F2
Tapotupotu Bay DOC Camping Ground..8 E1
Wagener Holiday Park & Backpackers..................................9 F2
Waitiki Landing Complex..............10 E1
See Enlargement
See Bay of Islands Map (pxxx)
SOUTH PACIFIC OCEAN
TASMAN SEA
Te Paki
Waitiki Landing
Great Exhibition Bay
Te Kao
Ngataki
Aupouri Peninsula
Pukenui
Matai Beach
Matai Bay
Karikari Peninsula
Rangiputa
Whatuwhiwhi
Doubtless Bay
Whangaroa Harbour
Wreck of the Rainbow Warrior
Hihi
Mangonui
Taipa
Tauranga Bay
Cavalli Islands
Awanui
Kahoe
Whangaroa
Matauri Bay
Kaeo
Kaitaia
Ahipara
Puketi Forest
Kerikeri
Bay of Islands
Cape Brett
Mangamuka Bridge
Omahuta Forest
Herekino
Waitangi
Russell
Paihia
Waimate North
Warawara Forest
Panguru
Kohukohu
Rawene
Kawakawa
Mitimiti
Kaikohe
Hokianga Harbour
Ruapekapeka Pa
Helena Bay
Mimiwhangata Coastal Park
Poor Knights Islands
Opononi
Omapere
Taheke
Whakapara
Sandy Bay
Matapouri
Hokianga-Waipoua Coastal Track
Waimamaku
Hikurangi
Tutukaka
Ngunguru
Kawerua
Kawerua Reserve
Waipoua Kauri Forest
Mangakahia Rv
Wairua Rv
Ngunguru Bay
Trounson Kauri Park
Maunu
WHANGAREI
Maunganui Bluff (460m)
Kaihu
Maungatapere
Whangarei Airport
Kai Iwi Lakes
Maropiu
Tangowahine
Ocean Beach
Bream Head
Mokohinau Islands
Kauri Coast
Ruakaka
Bream Bay
Hen & Chicken Islands
Baylys Beach
Dargaville
Waipu
Langs Beach
Glinks Gully
Paparoa
Brynderwyn
Mangawhai
Little Barrier Island
Ripiro Ocean Beach
Ruawai
Matakohe
Kaiwaka
Tinopai
Tomarata
Goat Island
Pakiri
Leigh
North Head
Port Albert
Wellsford
Great Barrier Island
Dome Forest
Omaha Beach
Kaipara Lighthouse
Pouto
Warkworth
Sandspit
0 10 km
0 6 miles
Cape Reinga Lighthouse
Tapotupotu Bay
Kapowairua
Kerr Point
Surville Cliffs
North Cape
Cape Reinga
Spirits Bay
Te Werahi Beach
Te Paki Reserves
Mokaikai Scenic Reserve
Cape Maria van Diemen
Waitiki Landing
Te Hapua
Parengarenga Harbour
Te Paki Stream
Karatia (Thom's Landing)
Shenstone Forest
Te Kao Forest
Aupouri Forest
The Bluff
Henderson Pt
Henderson Bay
Ninety Mile Beach
Waihopo
Te Raupo
Greenville Pt
Karikari Peninsula
Houhora Harbour
Houhora
Houhora Heads
Rangaunu Bay
Hukatere
Motutangi
Kaimaumau
Waiharara
Rangaunu Harbour
Waipapakauri
Waipapakauri Beach
Kaitaia Airport
Ahipara Bay
Ahipara Beach
Pukepoto
Tauroa Point
Ahipara
Tauroa Peninsula
Wainui Junction

Activities

The sandy waterfront of Aupouri Peninsula is decorated with the exuberant skids of sand-boarders, the hoofprints of horse riders and the treads of 4WD tours. Visitors also occupy themselves with walks around the cliffs and bays of Cape Reinga, and a kayak paddle across serene bodies of water like Parengarenga Harbour.

KAITAIA

☎ 09 / pop 5630

Kaitaia is the main jumping-off point for trips up Ninety Mile Beach to Cape Reinga. In the museum you'll see a welcome sign in three languages – 'welcome', '*haere mai*' and '*dobro dosli*' – as both Maori people and Dalmatians live in the area and are culturally active, with a Maori *marae* (meeting house) and a Dalmatian Cultural Club being the focus of activities.

Information

Far North Information Centre (☎ 408 0879; www.topofnz.co.nz; South Rd; 8.30am-5pm Sat-Thu) Has Internet access and information on Kaitaia and the region; for more online info, visit www.kaitaia.com.

Hacker's Internet café (84 Commerce St; per 30min NZ$5)

Sights & Activities

Te Wero Nui (☎ 408 4884; Commerce St) is an excellent Maori cultural centre based around a unique *whare* (house), where flax weaving and bone and woodcarving take place. Informal tuition is available or you can just watch. A shop sells the art and crafts made on the premises.

The **Far North Regional Museum** (☎ 408 1403; Commerce St; admission NZ$3.50; 10am-4pm Mon-Fri) includes among its exhibits a giant moa skeleton and the sizeable 1769 de Surville anchor, one of three the explorer lost in Doubtless Bay.

Okahu Estate Winery (☎ 408 0888; okahuestate@xtra.co.nz; 10am-5pm), 3.5km south of Kaitaia on the road to Ahipara, has a wide range of wines and free tastings.

Harrisons Reef Runner (☎ 408 1033; 123 North Rd; NZ$35) is a Unimog 4WD tour of the Ahipara gumfields (where kauri gum was harvested in the 19th century) that includes sand-boarding down the dunes.

Heather's Horse Treks (☎ 406 7133; Awanui; 2hr ride NZ$45) offers rides through a forest and along Ninety Mile Beach.

Blue Sky Scenics (☎ 406 7320; flights NZ$55-135), based at the airport 6km north of Kaitaia, operates various scenic flights over the Aupouri Peninsula (minimum two people per flight).

Kaitaia is a centre for popular tours up Ninety Mile Beach to Cape Reinga (opposite). The tours from Kaitaia are cheaper and travel a shorter distance than similar tours from Paihia in the Bay of Islands.

Festivals & Events

In March a special marathon, the **Te Houtawea Challenge**, takes place along Ninety Mile Beach. It centres on the legend of Te Houtaewa, a great runner who ran the length of the beach from Te Kao to Ahipara to steal kumera from the Te Rarawa people, returning with two full baskets after being angrily pursued. The marathon celebrates the return of the kumera. A **Maori food festival** and *waka* (canoe) racing are also held in March.

Sleeping

Main Street Lodge (☎ 408 1275; www.tall-tale.co.nz; 235 Commerce St; camp sites per person NZ$15, dm NZ$21-30, s NZ$45-55, d & tw NZ$50-60;) There's lots of space and plenty of facilities in this large and popular YHA-associate backpackers; the more expensive rooms have recently added private bathrooms. Peter, the live-in owner, is active in the local Maori community and will teach you bone carving for NZ$25. He and his wife, Kerry, also run Te Wero Nui which is sited next door.

Kauri Lodge Motel (☎ 408 1190; kaurilodgemotel@xtra.co.nz; 15 South Rd; s & d NZ$55-70;) Conveniently located opposite Kaitaia's information centre, this motel offers kitchen-equipped units at a good price, some of which are more spacious than others.

Wayfarer Motel (☎ 0800 118 100, 408 2600; wayfarermotel@xtra.co.nz; 231 Commerce St; s/d NZ$70/80;) The units here have been refurbished and facilities include an indoor spa, Sky TV and a games room.

Eating & Drinking

C14 (☎ 408 4935; 14 Commerce St; meals under NZ$13; breakfast & lunch daily, dinner Thu-Sat summer) An enticing café serving reasonably priced fare such as *paninis* and a wide-ranging blackboard menu.

Beachcomber (☎ 408 2010; 222 Commerce St; mains NZ$12-26; lunch & dinner Mon-Fri, dinner Sat)

A popular restaurant where the menu includes duck, ostrich, venison and salmon.

Sea Dragon (☎ 408 0555; 185 Commerce St; mains NZ$14; lunch & dinner) This inexpensive Chinese restaurant and takeaway has lunch specials (NZ$10) and a Sunday evening buffet (NZ$18 for 25 dishes).

The large **Pak N Save** (☎ 408 6222; West Lane) is the cheapest place for self-caterers. For a drink head to the **Kaitaia Hotel** (☎ 408 0360; 17 Commerce St), which has been quenching thirsts since 1839.

Getting There & Away

Air New Zealand (☎ 0800 737 000; www.airnz.co.nz) has daily flights between Kaitaia and Auckland (from NZ$75). The airport is 6km north of Kaitaia.

InterCity (☎ 408 0540; www.intercitycoach.co.nz) and **Northliner** (☎ 438 3206; www.northliner.co.nz) buses leave from **Kaitaia Travel** (Blencowe Street), and go daily (except Sunday) to Auckland (from NZ$65) via Paihia and Whangarei.

CAPE REINGA & NINETY MILE BEACH

☎ 09

Cape Reinga is 116km by road from Kaitaia at the northern tip of NZ, a trip shadowed for most of its length by the hard sands of Ninety Mile Beach. Standing at the windswept Cape Reinga lighthouse and looking out over the unbroken ocean is a contemplative experience. The lighthouse is still in use and directly below it is where the waters of the Tasman Sea and Pacific Ocean meet, creating waves up to 10m in stormy weather.

Sights & Activities

Still visible on the very tip of Cape Reinga is the 800-year-old **pohutukawa tree** whose roots hide the entrance to the mythical Maori underworld. This point is known in Maori legend as Te Rerenga Wairua, where the spirits of the dead depart the earth.

From Cape Reinga you can walk along Te Werahi Beach to **Cape Maria van Diemen** (five hours return), while a track from Cape Reinga car park leads past Sandy Bay and sundry cliffs to beautiful **Tapotupotu Bay** (four hours return). From Tapotupotu Bay you can then walk to **Kapowairua** (eight hours) at the eastern end of Spirits Bay, where there's a DOC camping ground (see p552).

Te Paki Reserves are public land with free access; just leave the gates as you found them and don't disturb the animals. There are about 7 sq km of giant sand dunes on either side of where Te Paki Stream meets the sea. A stop to take flying leaps off the dunes or toboggan down them is a highlight of locally operated tours.

Marty's Pack or Paddle (☎ 409 8445; www.packorpaddle.co.nz; half-/full-day trips NZ$80/125), at Karatia (Thom's Landing), offers combined fishing and sea-kayaking trips around the superb Parengarenga Harbour. Kayaks can be hired (NZ$55 per day), and sand-boarding and horse rides are also available. There's also backpacker accommodation here; two-/three-day all-inclusive trips cost NZ$175/340.

Bus tours (see Tours following) travel along **Ninety Mile Beach** on their way from Kaitaia or Paihia to Cape Reinga, or vice versa, depending on the tides. Private vehicles can also do the beach trip but all hire-car agreements prohibit driving on the beach. The usual access point for vehicles is **Waipapakauri**, just north of Kaitaia. The beach 'road' is only for those equipped with rugged vehicles – ordinary cars have hit soft sand and been swallowed by the tides, thus you may see the roof of an unfortunate vehicle poking through the sands. Check tide times before setting out, avoid travel 2½ hours either side of high tide, and watch out for 'quicksand' on Te Paki Stream (keep moving).

Tours

Bus tours go to Cape Reinga from Kaitaia, Mangonui (Doubtless Bay) and the Bay of Islands. It makes sense to take the tour from Kaitaia or Doubtless Bay since they are much closer to Cape Reinga and offer a cheaper deal.

Harrison's Cape Runner (☎ 0800 227 373, 408 1033; http://ahipara.co.nz/caperunner; 123 North Rd, Kaitaia; trips NZ$40) Schedules day trips that take in the main features of the cape, plus some sand tobogganing action. The various trips are pretty similar and include a picnic lunch.

Sand Safaris (☎ 0800 869 090, 408 1778; www.sandsafaris.co.nz; 221 Commerce St, Kaitaia; tours NZ$50) Runs buses seating around 30 people up to Cape Reinga, with a picnic lunch thrown in.

Sleeping & Eating

FAR FAR NORTH

Waitiki Landing Complex (☎ 409 7508; camp/campervan sites per person NZ$14/18, dm NZ$20, s & d NZ$55) This is the northernmost accommodation in NZ, 21km shy of Cape Reinga at Waitiki

Landing. There's a camp kitchen, laundrette and hot showers (NZ$1), as well as a liquor store, shop and a restaurant that does good pizzas (medium NZ$16) and ostrich burgers (NZ$5.50 takeaway or NZ$11 as a sit-down meal). Various trips can be arranged here, including to Cape Reinga (NZ$25 to NZ$45), to Te Paki for sand-boarding (NZ$30) and to the white silica sand across Parengarenga Harbour (NZ$10). Drop offs and pick ups for hiking trips are also possible, and sand-boards can be hired (NZ$10 for four hours, plus a NZ$50 bond).

North Wind Lodge Backpackers (☎ 409 8515; Otaipango Rd, Henderson Bay; dm/tw/d NZ$18/40/50; 💻) This unusual turreted house is an ocean-side retreat, 6km down an unsealed road on the peninsula's east side. It's spacious and modern, and near a great stretch of beach. Boogie boards and sand-boards are available to guests.

DOC camping grounds (camp sites per person NZ$5-6) in the Cape Reinga area include Kapowairua on Spirits Bay, with cold water and limited toilet facilities, and Tapotupotu Bay, with toilets and showers. Neither has electricity and you'll need to bring a cooker as fires aren't allowed; also bring insect repellent. DOC's **Rarawa Beach camping ground** (🕓 Sep-Apr), 3km north of Ngataki and 10km south of Te Kao, has water and toilet facilities only.

PUKENUI

There are several budget accommodation options in and around Pukenui, which is on Houhora Harbour about 45km north of Kaitaia.

Pukenui Lodge Motel & Youth Hostel (☎ 409 8837; pukenui@igrin.co.nz; dm NZ$18, d & tw NZ$45-100; 💻 🏊) This YHA-associate backpackers is in a historic 1891 house with pleasant rooms overlooking Houhora Harbour. Motel guests can also access a spa pool.

Pukenui Farm Backpackers (☎ 409 7863; Lamb Rd; camp sites per person NZ$8, dm/d NZ$13/34) Just 2km down the mostly unsealed Lamb Rd is this modern, comfortable cottage with a six-bed dorm, a twin, a double and a veranda from which you can see memorable sunsets. The owners will pick up from the Pukenui shops, and guests can collect their own vegetables and take part in farm activities.

Wagener Holiday Park & Backpackers (☎ 409 8564; www.northlandholiday.co.nz; Houhora Heads; camp/campervan sites per person NZ$10/12, dm, s & d per person NZ$18; 💻) Decent accommodation is on offer at this beautiful waterfront spot at Houhora Heads, 2km off the main road. There's a café, free museum and the 15-room **Subritzky Homestead** (☎ 406 7298; admission NZ$7.50), a 1862 homestead constructed of local swamp kauri. Kayaks, mountain bikes, surfboards and fishing gear can be hired.

TOWERING KAURI

Kauri forest once blanketed the Aupouri Peninsula, but nowadays the trees spread over the peninsula's western side are mostly pine planted for commercial timber. You can, however, still see a remnant of the North Island's once-extensive kauri groves at the superb **Waipoua Kauri Forest**, about 110km south of Kaitaia on the west coast. This sanctuary, proclaimed in 1952, contains some huge trees: a fully grown kauri can reach 60m and have a trunk 5m or more in diameter.

From the **visitors centre** (☎ 09-439 3011; SH12; 🕓 8.30am-5.30pm Mon-Fri, 9am-5pm Sat & Sun) on the Waipoua Kauri Forest's southern fringe, the highway winds north through jungly forest for 8km to the turn-off to the kauri walks, where several giant trees are easily reached. A 20-minute walk away from the car park is the massive **Te-matua-ngahere** (The Father of the Forest), believed to be 2000 years old and, with a trunk over 5m in diameter, to have the biggest girth of any kauri in NZ. Close by are the **Four Sisters**, a skyscraping quartet of trees, and a half-hour walk further on is the large **Yakas Tree**. Further north up the highway is the 51m-high **Tane-mahuta**, named for the Maori god of the forests and the country's largest kauri tree (it's taller than Te-matua-ngahere but doesn't have the same impressive girth).

Next to the Waipoua River just past the visitors centre is the **Waipoua DOC Forest Camp** (☎ 09-439 3011; camp sites per person NZ$7, cabins per person NZ$8-14), with spacious but spartan cabins; BYO bedding and book ahead in summer. The camp also has hot showers, flush toilets and a separate kitchen.

Buses operated by **InterCity** (☎ 09-408 0540; www.intercitycoach.co.nz) stop at Waipoua Kauri Forest.

WAIKATO & CENTRAL NORTH ISLAND

The Waikato region is the hub of rural NZ. It is filled with iconic pastoral landscapes of grazing cattle, sheep and thoroughbred horses. The region is named after the 420km-long Waikato River, the area's centrepiece and the source of the its fertility, which winds northwest from Lake Taupo past Hamilton to Port Waikato on the west coast. It's not surprising that Peter Jackson's Hobbiton was erected here on farmland near Matamata. Resort-ridden Lake Taupo is on the Central Plateau, where you'll also find the awesome Tongariro National Park, replete with snowcapped volcanic peaks.

Beneath the tame surface of the King Country region are the spectacular depths of Waitomo Caves, where you can float through dark limestone caves decorated by starry glow-worms. The watery theme continues at laid-back Raglan on the west coast, which has a world-famous surf break. Jutting northwards from the centre of the North Island is the rugged, densely forested Coromandel Peninsula, with some activity-laden coastal towns.

Activities

The central North Island is the perfect place to exhaust yourself by undertaking every

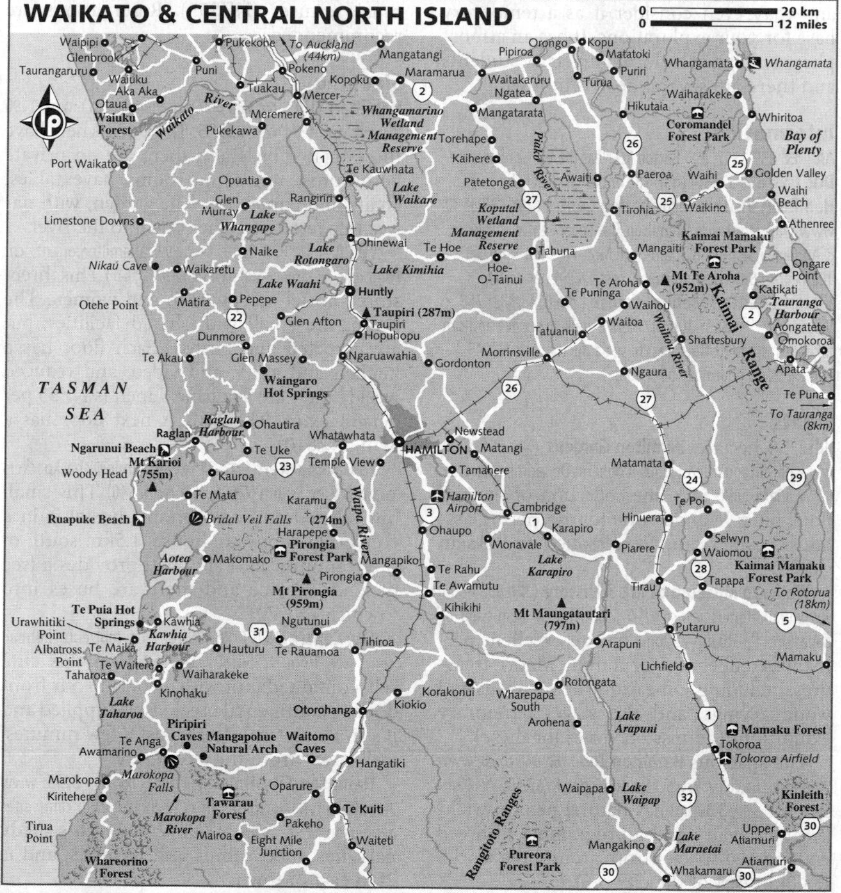

imaginable activity. Ride the awesome surf around Raglan, kayak around the limestone delights of Cathedral Cove, plumb the depths of Waitomo by going black-water rafting on inner tubes or abseiling straight down into a caving adventure, and tramp the brilliant Tongariro Crossing or the wilderness trails of Coromandel. For an encore, plunge into a thermal pool at Taupo, ski down Tongariro's volcanic slopes and build your own spa at Hot Water Beach.

HAMILTON

☎ 07 / pop 132,000

NZ's largest inland city, Hamilton is 129km south of Auckland and is the Waikato region's major centre. You'll doubtless pass through on your way around the region, and may even consider it as a temporary base for your explorations. It has an atmosphere enlivened by local university students and there are several hostels in town.

Information

AA (☎ 839 1397; 295 Barton St) Near the transport centre.

DOC (☎ 838 3363; 4th fl, 18 London St) Near the river.

Hamilton Visitors Information Centre (☎ 839 3580; www.waikatonz.com; Hamilton Transport Centre, cnr Brice & Anglesea Sts; 8.30am-5pm Mon-Fri, 9am-4pm Sat, 10am-4pm Sun) Has Internet access (NZ$4 per hour).

Victoria Central Medical Centre (☎ 834 0333; 750 Victoria St; 8am-10pm) Offers a walk-in service and can take x-rays and fix fractures; to see a doctor costs NZ$45 and there's a pharmacy next door.

Sights

The 50-hectare **Hamilton Gardens** (☎ 856 3200; www.hamiltongardens.co.nz; Cobham Dr; admission free; 7.30am-dusk) is a fine collection of themed floral plots. Wander around rose, herb, glasshouse, American, Renaissance and Asian gardens.

Waikato Museum of Art & History (☎ 838 6606; www.waikatomuseum.co.nz; 1 Grantham St; admission by donation; 10am-4.30pm) has an excellent permanent collection of Tainui Maori treasures, including some exquisite weavings and woodcarvings, and also stages temporary exhibitions (admission varies for these).

The spacious **Hamilton Zoo** (☎ 838 6720; www.hamiltonzoo.co.nz; Brymer Rd; admission NZ$7.50; 9am-5pm, last entry 3.30pm) has natural pens, a walk-through aviary and a programme to breed endangered species from around the world. It's 8km east of the city centre.

Activities

Extreme Edge (☎ 847 5858; www.sportsclimber.co.nz; 90 Greenwood St; 10am-10pm Tue-Sat, 10am-8.30pm Sun & Mon) offers a free introductory indoor climbing lesson and a full day of clambering for NZ$18. It also stages more expensive outdoor climbing courses.

Waterworld (☎ 849 4389; Garnett Ave; 6am-9pm Mon-Fri, 7am-9pm Sat, 9am-9pm Sun), located 4km north of the town centre, has indoor and outdoor pools, waterslides, a gym and spa. For NZ$10 you can do most things.

MV Waipa Delta (☎ 0800 472 3353; cruises Thu-Sun) is a replica of an 1876 Waikato paddle steamer and runs popular river cruises from Memorial Park. There are 1½-hour buffet lunch cruises (NZ$40), one-hour afternoon tea cruises (NZ$20) and evening buffet and music cruises (NZ$55). Reservations are recommended.

Sleeping

Hamilton YHA (☎ 838 0009; yhahamil@yha.org.nz; 1190 Victoria St; dm/s/d NZ$24/35/55;) Dorms here have three to five beds and there are no private bathrooms, but some rooms have tables, chairs and cupboards. The garden, with native tree ferns, stretches down to the river.

YWCA (☎ 838 2219; www.ywcahamilton.org.nz; cnr Pembroke & Clarence Sts; s/tw NZ$20/40;) This three-storey hostel accepts men and women. The rooms are small with shared facilities, but are carpeted and heated. Each floor has a kitchen and a TV and video, and reduced weekly rates are available. Linen is NZ$5 per person extra. The YMCA next door has a gym (NZ$10).

J's Backpackers (☎ 856 8934; admin@jsbackpackers.co.nz; 8 Grey St; dm NZ$18, d & tw NZ$40) This small but relaxed and comfortable hostel is in a converted suburban house, 1.5km south of the Hamilton East shops. It provides a free pick up service and there are buses into town (NZ$1.70).

City Centre B&B (☎ 838 1671; citycentrebb@hotmail.com; s/tw from NZ$50/80;) Stay in this cute self-contained unit with a pool at your front door. A continental breakfast is supplied and it's in a quiet cul-de-sac just a few minutes' walk away from the city centre.

Hamilton City Holiday Park (☎ 855 8255; www.hamiltoncityholidaypark.co.nz; 14 Ruakura Rd; camp sites per person NZ$12, s NZ$20-30, d NZ$30-60) This shady park has good cabins and facilities, and is 2km east of town.

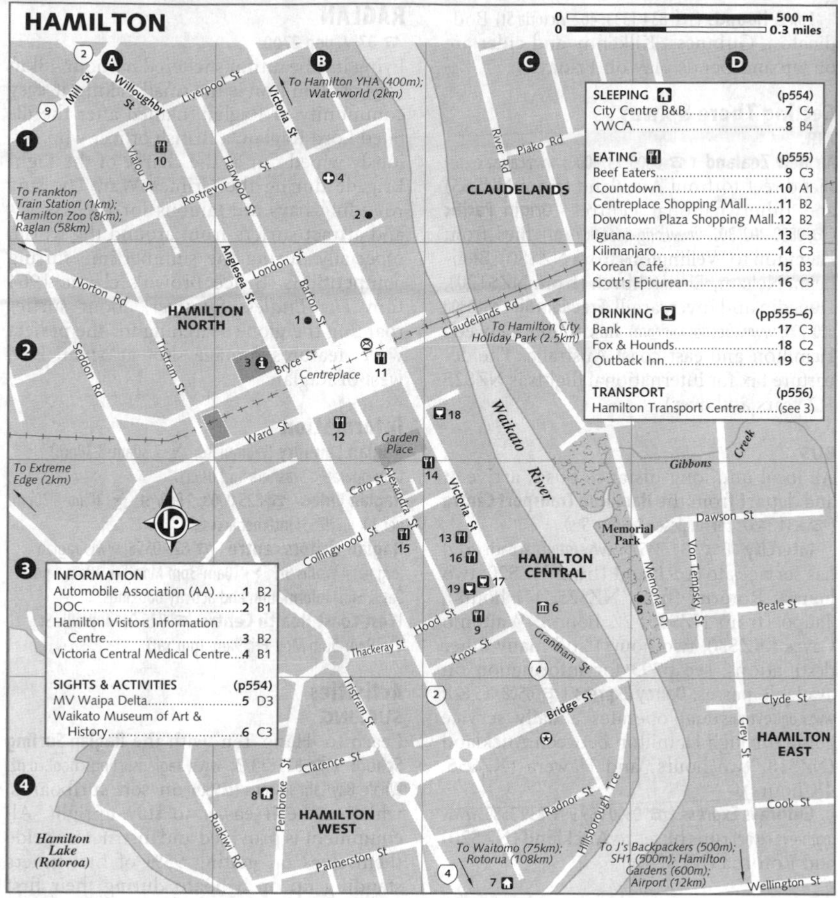

Eating & Drinking

Kilimanjaro (☎ 839 2988; 337 Victoria St; meals NZ$3.50-13; ⌚ breakfast & lunch) Delicious self-service, home-cooked food is available at this café in Garden Pl.

Scott's Epicurean (☎ 839 6680; 181 Victoria St; meals NZ$7-13; ⌚ breakfast & lunch) Sample interesting international food with an individual twist at this popular, reasonably priced café with an outdoor area. Try the *aglio olio* spaghetti.

Korean Café (☎ 838 9100; cnr Collingwood & Alexandra Sts; mains NZ$8-13; ⌚ lunch & dinner Mon-Sat) All the Korean favourites are here; try the *dolsot bibimbap* (a rice, meat, vegetable and chilli sauce hotpot).

Iguana (☎ 834 2280; 203 Victoria St; medium pizzas/mains NZ$17/25; ⌚ lunch & dinner) Iguana has a garden bar and serves up popular gourmet pizzas.

The Centreplace and Downtown Plaza malls have small international food courts, while **Beef Eaters** (☎ 839 5374; 5 Hood St; burgers NZ$5; ⌚ dinner Tue-Sun) is the place for late-night snacks (closes 4am).

You can pick up groceries at **Countdown** (☎ 834 1490, cnr Anglesea & Liverpools Sts; ⌚ 24hr).

Outback Inn (☎ 839 6354; 141 Victoria St) A large and popular student bar with TV screens, bar football, DJs and live music.

Bank (☎ 839 4740; cnr Victoria & Hood Sts) Venture inside this cream-coloured 1878 heritage building and you'll find eight beers on tap, good nachos and DJs on Friday and Saturday at 10pm.

Fox & Hounds (☎ 834 1333; 402 Victoria St) Boddington, Guinness, Kilkenny and cider are on tap and bands play on Friday.

Getting There & Away

AIR

Air New Zealand (☎ 0800 737 000; www.airnz.co.nz) flies direct to/from Auckland (from NZ$65) and other national centres. **Origin Pacific** (☎ 0800 302 302; www.originpacific.co.nz) flies from Hamilton to Wellington (from NZ$80), Blenheim, Nelson, Christchurch (from NZ$120), Dunedin and Invercargill. **Freedom Air** (☎ 0800 600 500; www.freedomair.com) has flights between Hamilton and east-coast Australia. The departure tax for international flights is NZ$25 (12 years and over).

BUS

All local and long-distance buses arrive at and depart from the **Hamilton Transport Centre** (☎ 834 3457; cnr Anglesea & Bryce Sts).

InterCity (☎ 834 3457; www.intercitycoach.co.nz) has services to Auckland (from NZ$20, two hours), Rotorua (from NZ$25, 1¾ hours), Taupo (from NZ$35, 2½ hours), Waitomo Caves (NZ$30, two hours) and many other destinations; see p793 for information on available passes. **Dalroy Express** (☎ 0508 465 622; www.dalroytours.co.nz) operates a daily service going through Hamilton between Auckland (NZ$18, two hours) and Hawera (NZ$55, 4¾ hours).

Guthreys Express (☎ 0800 759 999, 839 3580; www.guthreys.co.nz) runs buses to Auckland (NZ$20) and Rotorua (NZ$25).

TRAIN

Hamilton is on the main rail line between Auckland and Wellington; there is one train a day in each direction. Trains stop at the **Frankton Train Station** (☎ 846 8353; Queens Ave), 1km west of the city centre. Dinsdale buses run between the Hamilton transport centre and near the train station (NZ$2, every half-hour).

Getting Around

Hamilton Airport (☎ 843 3623; www.hamiltonairport.co.nz) is 12km south of the city. The **Super Shuttle** (☎ 843 7778; NZ$10) offers a door-to-door service. A taxi costs around NZ$35.

Hamilton's bus system, **Busline** (☎ 0800 4287 5463), operates Monday to Saturday from around 7am to 5.45pm (later on Friday).

RAGLAN

☎ 07 / pop 2700

Lying in a beautiful sheltered harbour 48km west of Hamilton is the small, taking-it-easy community of Raglan, named after the ill-fated Lord Raglan, a British officer who seriously wiped out at the charge of the Light Brigade during the Crimea War. The surrounding bays are famous for their waves and attract surfers from around the world, especially during the summertime surfing competitions. Bruce Brown's classic 1964 film *The Endless Summer*, about surfies roaming the globe searching for the perfect wave, features footage shot at Manu Bay, west of Raglan.

Information

Raglan Laundry (Wainui Rd; 🕑 7.30am-8.30pm) Coin-operated washers and driers.

Raglan Video (☎ 825 0008; 9 Bow St; 🕑 10am-8.30pm; per 30min NZ$5) Internet access.

Raglan visitors centre (☎ 825 0556; www.raglan.org.nz; 4 Wallis St; 🕑 10am-3pm Mon-Fri, 10am-5pm Sat & Sun) Information and activity bookings.

West Coast Health Centre ☎ 825 0114; Wallis St; 🕑 9am-5pm Mon-Fri, 9am-1pm Sat)

Activities

SURFING

Learn to 'Hang Ten' with the **Raglan Surfing School** (☎ 825 7873; www.raglansurfingschool.co.nz; Whale Bay; 3hr lessons NZ$80) on soft surfboards, which make it easier to stay upright. All equipment is provided and instructors pride themselves on getting 95% of first-timers standing up on a board during their first lesson. Those already experienced can rent surfboards (NZ$10 per hour), boogie boards (NZ$5 per hour) and wetsuits (NZ$5 per hour). The school operates from Ngarunui Beach, 7km west of Raglan, and lessons can be booked at the Raglan visitors centre.

Solscape (☎ 825 8268; 611 Wainui Rd, Manu Bay) offers surfing lessons provided by a female surfer. The company also rents out surfing equipment and kayaks, and offers scuba-diving trips to Gannet Island (NZ$80).

Skyrider (☎ 825 7453; lessons NZ$100) offers 1½-hour, one-on-one kitesurfing lessons at Rangipu Beach; book at the visitors centre.

SWIMMING

Te Kopua Recreational Reserve, over the footbridge by the camping ground, is a safe, calm

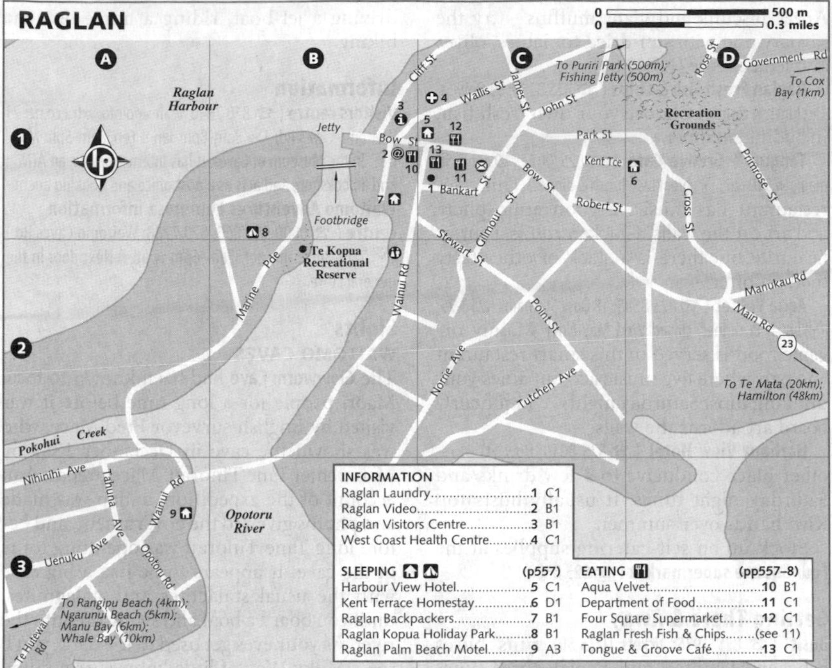

harbour beach that is popular with families despite the black sand. Other good beaches are at **Cox Bay**, reached by a walkway from Government Rd or from Bayview Rd, and **Puriri Park**, towards the end of Wallis St and a safe swimming spot around high tide.

OTHER ACTIVITIES

Kayaks can be hired by nonguests (two- to three-hour hire NZ$8) at Raglan Backpackers (see following section), while guests can use them free of charge. A 15-minute paddle brings you to the Rocks, with limestone pinnacles and sea caves.

Green Goose Cruises (☎ 825 8153; cruises NZ$17) runs trips around the harbour in summer, usually at noon and 5pm.

Sleeping

Raglan Backpackers (☎ 825 0515; info@raglanbackpackers.co.nz; 6 Nero St; dm NZ$18, d & tw NZ$40) On the water's edge with sea views from some rooms, this excellent purpose-built hostel is centred on a garden courtyard and has small but smart rooms and a helpful owner.

Kent Terrace Homestay (☎ 825 7858; rickraglan@hotmail.com; Kent Tce; d NZ$75) This centrally located, self-contained unit has two bedrooms and a kitchenette and opens onto decks. It's at the end of Kent Tce.

Harbour View Hotel (☎ 825 8010; Bow St; s/d NZ$50/70) The light and airy rooms in this two-storey, veranda-equipped heritage building are without bathrooms, but there is plenty of natural kauri wood décor. Restaurant meals (locals swear by the NZ$8.50 seafood chowder) and a bar within staggering distance downstairs add to its attraction.

Raglan Palm Beach Motel (☎ 825 8153; raglanmotel@paradise.net.nz; 50 Wainui Rd; d NZ$85-105) On the waterfront, this well-maintained motel offers canoes and kayaks free to guests.

Raglan Kopua Holiday Park (☎ 825 8283; raglanholidaypark@xtra.co.nz; Marine Pde; camp sites per person NZ$10, dm NZ$15, d NZ$45-80) This is a well-kept facility situated on a sheltered, inner-harbour beach across the inlet from town.

Eating & Drinking

Department of Food (☎ 825 7017; 35 Bow St; ⏲ lunch) This deli's goodies include *paninis*, hummus,

Anzac biscuits and giant muffins – try the savoury one with sun-dried tomatoes, olives and fetta cheese (NZ$3.50).

Raglan Fresh Fish & Chips (☎ 825 8119; 33 Bow St; lunch & dinner) Choose your own fresh fish, including snapper.

Tongue & Groove Café (☎ 825 0027; 19 Bow St; mains NZ$10-26; breakfast, lunch & dinner) This café-restaurant has music, a good atmosphere and art on the walls. Chicken *roti* is a surfer favourite but there is a stack of other tasty food on offer.

Aqua Velvet (☎ 825 8588; 18 Bow St; mains NZ$8-25; lunch & dinner, closed Wed May-Nov) Mainly organic food is served in this smart restaurant and bar, where live music accompanies your drinking most Saturday nights. Unique surfboard art adorns the walls.

Harbour View Hotel (☎ 825 8010; Bow St) Another place conducive to a few drinks and Saturday night tunes. It usually hosts top Kiwi bands over summer.

Stock up on self-catering supplies at the **Four Square supermarket** (☎ 825 8300).

Getting There & Away

Busit (☎ 825 1975; tickets NZ$5.50) runs buses between Hamilton and Raglan three times daily from Monday to Friday (there's no weekend service). **Beach Express** (☎ 0800 021 130) is a shuttle service running from Raglan to Hamilton (NZ$15) and to Auckland Airport or downtown Auckland (NZ$55, return NZ$85).

WAITOMO

☎ 07

The name of the Waitomo region, which comes from the Maori words *wai* (water) and *tomo* (hole or shaft), is highly appropriate: dotted throughout the countryside are numerous shafts dropping abruptly into underground cave systems and streams. There are over 300 mapped caves in the area and these limestone caverns and accompanying formations make up one of the North Island's premier attractions.

Tours through the Glowworm Cave (also known as Waitomo Cave) and the Aranui Cave have been feature attractions for decades. But in typical Kiwi fashion, the list of things to do has grown and become more daring. Now you can abseil, raft and tube through the caves, or try your hand at a number of above-ground activities such as driving a jet-boat, riding a horse or quad biking.

Information

Visitors centre (☎ 878 7640; waitomoinfo@xtra.co.nz; 21 Waitomo Caves Rd; 8am-8pm Jan & Feb, 8am-5pm Mar-Dec) In the Museum of Caves. It has Internet access, an ATM and a bookshop, and acts as a post office and booking agent.

Waitomo Adventures Luminosa information centre (☎ 0800 924 866, 878 7788; Waitomo Caves Rd; 7am-8pm summer, 7am-6pm winter) Next door in the general store.

Sights

WAITOMO CAVES

The **Glowworm Cave** had been known to local Maori people for a long time before it was visited by English surveyor Fred Mace, who was shown the cave in December 1887 by Maori chief Tane Tinorau. Mace prepared an account of the expedition, a map was made and photos given to the government, and before long Tane Tinorau was operating tours of the cave. It appears to be just a big cave with the usual stalactites and stalagmites, until you board a boat and swing off onto the river. As your eyes get used to the dark, you'll see a Milky Way of little lights surrounding you: these are the glow-worms. You can see them in other places around Waitomo and in other parts of NZ, but the ones in this cave are something special as the conditions for their growth are just about perfect, meaning there's a remarkable number of them. Try to avoid the big tour groups, most of which arrive 10.30am to 2.30pm and are bustled through the cave several groups at a time. Photography isn't allowed.

Three kilometres west of Glowworm Cave is **Aranui Cave**, a large cavern with no glow-worms but with thousands of tiny 'straw' stalactites hanging from the ceiling. Various scenes in the colourful formations are pointed out and photography is permitted. It's an hour's walk to the caves or the ticket office can arrange transport.

Tickets for tours of the aforementioned **Waitomo caves** (☎ 878 8227; www.waitomocaves.co.nz; either/both caves NZ$25/45) are sold at the entrance to the Glowworm Cave. The 45-minute tours of the Glowworm Cave leave daily on the half-hour from 9am to 5pm, with an extra tour at 5.30pm from November to Easter and more tours at the height of summer; there's also a 'museum-cave special' (NZ$26) that includes

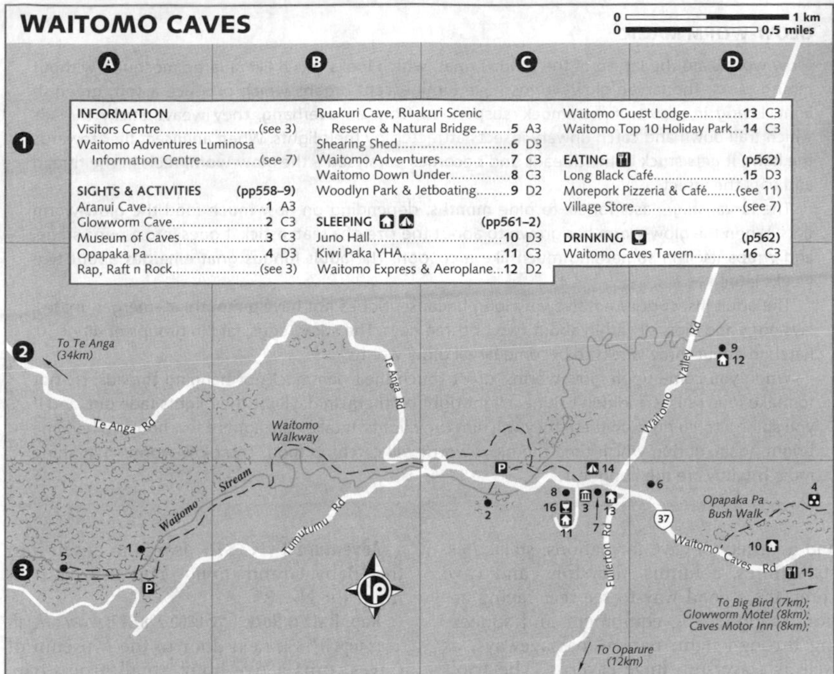

the Glowworm Cave tour and admission to the informative Museum of Caves. Aranui Cave tours also last 45 minutes and depart at 10am, 11am, 1pm, 2pm and 3pm.

MUSEUM OF CAVES

This **museum** (☎ 878 7640; admission NZ$5; 8am-8pm Jan & Feb, 8am-5pm Mar-Dec) has some excellent exhibits detailing how caves are formed and the flora and fauna that thrive in them. Displays include a cave model, fossils of extinct birds and animals that have been discovered in caves, and a cave crawl. There are also audiovisual presentations on caving, glow-worms and other Waitomo attractions.

Free entry is often included with various activities, or you can get a 'museum-cave special' (see previous section).

Activities

CAVING & ABSEILING

Waitomo Adventures (☎ 0800 924 866, 878 7788; www.waitomo.co.nz; Caveland Café) offers a range of cave adventures.

The amazing **Lost World** trip begins with 100m of abseiling, but you don't need prior abseiling or caving experience. The principal trip to Lost World is an all-inclusive, all-day affair (NZ$360) running from 10.30am to 5.30pm and including an underground lunch, followed afterwards by dinner. After the initial abseil, you'll spend about three hours negotiating your way through a 30m-high cave via a combination of walking, rock climbing, spider-walking, inching along narrow rock ledges, wading and also swimming through a subterranean river to get back out, passing glow-worms, stunning rock and cave formations, waterfalls and more.

Another option is a four-hour dry trip (NZ$230) that also starts with a 100m abseil (with a guide beside you on another rope) and then an hour's walk into the cave before exiting via another vertical cavern. These trips depart at 7.10am, 11.30am and 3pm, but times can vary.

The **Haggas Honking Holes** (NZ$165) is a four-hour caving trip that offers professional abseiling instruction followed by a caving trip with three abseils, rock-climbing, and travelling along a subterranean river with waterfalls. Along the way you see glow-worms

GLOW-WORM MAGIC

Glow-worms are the larvae of the fungus gnat, which looks much like a large mosquito without mouth parts. The larvae glow-worms have luminescent organs which produce a soft, greenish light. Living in a sort of 'hammock' suspended from an overhang, they weave sticky threads which trail down and catch unwary insects attracted by their lights. When an insect flies towards the light, it gets stuck in the threads and becomes paralysed – the glow-worm reels in the thread and eats the insect.

The larval stage lasts for six to nine months, depending on how much food the glow-worm gets. When the glow-worm has grown to about the size of a matchstick it goes into a pupa stage, and wraps itself in something much like a cocoon. The adult fungus gnat emerges about two weeks later.

The adult insect does not live very long because it does not have a mouth; it emerges, mates, lays eggs and dies, all within about two or three days. The sticky eggs, laid in groups of 40 or 50, hatch in about three weeks to become larval glow-worms.

When you come upon glow-worms, don't touch their hammocks or hanging threads, try not to make loud noises and don't shine a light right on them. In daylight their lights fade out, and if you shine a torch right on them they will dim their lights. It takes the lights a few hours to become bright again, during which time the glow-worm will catch no food. The glow-worms that shine most brightly are the hungriest.

and a variety of cave formations: stalactites, stalagmites, columns, flowstone and cave coral. It's a good way to see real caving action, using caving equipment and squeezing through tight, narrow passageways, as well as traversing huge caverns. The trip's name derives from a local farmer, 'Haggas', and characters in a Dr Seuss story, 'honking holers'. Trips depart at 10am and 3pm, but times can vary. The **Gruesome Twosome** option (NZ$370) combines this trip with the four-hour Lost World excursion.

Tumu Tumu Toobing (NZ$85) is a more physical, adventurous four-hour tubing trip, departing at 10am and 3pm. **Blackwater Fever** (NZ$230) combines this trip with Haggas Honking Holes.

St Benedict's Cavern (NZ$100) is an attractive cave with straw stalagmites, explorable via a three-hour trip with half that time spent underground abseiling and trying out a subterranean flying fox.

Waitomo Down Under (☎ 0800 456 9676, 878 6577; www.waitomocavesfloatthrough.co.nz), beside the Museum of Caves, operates 'float through' caving adventures for groups of up to 12 people. Prices include soup and toast.

In **Adventure I** (NZ$75) you go through Te Anaroa (Long Cave) in inner tubes, going over two waterfalls (one on a slide) and getting a good close-up view of glow-worms along the way. Roughly half the trip's three hours is spent underground.

Adventure II (NZ$75) is a 50m abseil into the 'Baby Grand' *tomo*. You can do it at night for NZ$85.

Rap, Raft n Rock (☎ 0800 228 372; www.caveraft.com; trips NZ$85), next door to the Museum of Caves, runs a five-hour, small group trip. It starts with abseil training followed by a 27m abseil into a natural cave, and then involves floating along a subterranean river on an inner tube. How fast you float will depend on the season and the recent rainfall level, but there are always plenty of glow-worms. After some caving you do a belayed rock climb up a stepped 20m pitch to the surface.

BLACK-WATER RAFTING

The **Legendary Black Water Rafting Company** (☎ 0800 228 464, 878 6219; www.blackwaterrafting.co.nz) runs three different adventures. The cost of each trip includes admission to the Museum of Caves.

Black Labyrinth (NZ$75) is a three-hour trip (one hour is spent underground) where you float on an inner tube down a subterranean river flowing through Ruakuri Cave. The excursion's high point is leaping off a small waterfall and then bobbing through a long, glow-worm-coated passage. The trip ends with hot showers, soup and bagels in a café. A wetsuit is provided to keep you warm, but raise your comfort level by eating or drinking something hot prior to the trip.

A trip of similar duration is **Spellbound** (NZ$37), a guided tour through parts of the Mangawhitiakau cave system at Oparure, 12km south of Waitomo. It includes a boat ride and is a good option if you don't want to get wet.

Black Abyss (NZ$145) is a more adventurous five-hour trip (with two to three hours underground) that includes a 30m abseil into Ruakuri Cave, more glow-worms, tubing and cave climbing. Hot showers and snacks are also provided.

WALKING

The Museum of Caves has free pamphlets on various walks in the area. The path from Aranui Cave to **Ruakuri Cave** is an excellent short walk. From the Glowworm Cave ticket office there's a walk to a grove of **California redwoods** (15 minutes). Also starting here is the **Waitomo Walkway** (three hours return), which heads through farmland and follows Waitomo Stream to the **Ruakuri Scenic Reserve**, where a half-hour return walk passes by the river, caves and a natural limestone bridge. At night, drive to the Ruakuri Reserve car park and walk across the bridge where glow-worms put on a magical display; bring a torch to find your way. The **Opapaka Pa Bush Walk** (one hour return) leads to a pre-European *pa* site on a hill and is lined with plaques describing traditional Maori medicines found in the forest, as well as forest lore.

OTHER ACTIVITIES

Woodlyn Park (☎ 878 6666; www.woodlynpark.co.nz; 1177 Waitomo Valley Rd; admission NZ$15; shows 1.30pm) has a rustic theatre where fair-dinkum Barry Woods puts on a helluva one-hour farm animal show combining history and humour. Snowy the sheep, Trev the black pig and Big Mac the steer are other stars, but the audience takes part too. The **jet-boating** (7 laps NZ$50; 9.30am-6.30pm Nov-Apr, 9.30am-5pm May-Oct) at the park is unique because instead of just being a passenger, you get the chance to drive a jet-boat around a figure-of-eight course.

At the **Shearing Shed** (☎ 878 8371; admission free; 9am-4pm) big, fluffy Angora rabbits are sheared rather than sheep, and top-quality angora fur products are sold.

Waitomo Caves Horse Treks (☎ 878 5065; 1/2hr rides NZ$40/50) offers various bush and farmland rides. All levels are catered for and long treks can be organised. The stables are a 15-minute drive west of Waitomo or they will pick up from Waitomo.

Big Red (☎ 878 7640; waitomoinfo@xtra.co.nz; 2hr trips NZ$75) offers self-drive, quad-bike trips through the countryside.

Track 'n' Paddle (☎ 957 0002; www.tracknpaddle.co.nz; tours NZ$100-300) runs mountain-biking, hiking and kayaking tours from Waitomo to Marakopa, on the coast due west of Waitomo, and to the sizeable Kawhia Harbour, to the northwest. Tours involve small groups (maximum eight people) and depart three times a week.

Caving company **Rap, Raft n Rock** (☎ 0800 228 372; www.caveraft.com) also has a two-hour high-ropes course (NZ$40), staged nine metres above the ground.

Sleeping

Kiwi Paka YHA (☎ 878 3395; www.kiwipaka-yha.co.nz; School Rd; dm NZ$22, d & tw NZ$50;) This excellent, jumbo-sized, alpine-style hostel has four-bed dorms and a popular restaurant (p562) that serves mainly pizzas. YHA Members and nonmembers pay the same rate.

Juno Hall (☎ 878 7649; junohall@junowaitomo.co.nz; 600 Waitomo Caves Rd; camp sites per person NZ$10, dm NZ$20, d & tw NZ$50-60;) This purpose-built, chalet-style hostel has lots of wood panelling, an outdoor pool and a tennis court, and can organise fishing, hunting and farmstays. It's clean, cosy and well run, and there are TVs in the rooms with bathroom.

Glowworm Motel (☎ 873 8882; Waitomo Caves Rd; s & d NZ$65-80;) These reasonably priced units, 8km before Waitomo, are equipped with kitchens.

Caves Motor Inn (☎ 873 8109; glow.worm@xtra.co.nz; SH3; backpacker lodge NZ$25, units s/d NZ$75/85) This motel on the main road by the Waitomo turn-off is better than it looks from the outside, and has a backpacker section, a bar and a restaurant (dinner only).

Waitomo Guest Lodge (☎ 878 7641; 7 Waitomo Caves Rd; s/d NZ$50/70) All rooms have private bathrooms in this well-located and comfortable B&B.

Big Bird (☎ 0800 733 244, 873 7459; www.waitomobigbird.co.nz; 17 Waitomo Caves Rd; s NZ$40, d NZ$65-80) The price includes continental breakfast; an ostrich bacon, ostrich egg and ostrich sausage breakfast is NZ$6 extra. With free tours of their ostrich farm and the glow-worms at Ruakuri Reserve, this is a guesthouse with extras and character at a good price.

Waitomo Express & Aeroplane (☎ 878 6666; billy@woodlynpark.co.nz; 1177 Waitomo Valley Rd; d NZ$90-100) You can stay in comfortable, motel-style units housed inside a 1950s railway carriage or in the front or tail of a Bristol fighter aeroplane that saw action in the Vietnam War. Everything in this place is unusual!

Waitomo Top 10 Holiday Park (☎ 878 7639; stay@waitomo park.co.nz; camp sites per person NZ$13, s & d NZ$40-75;) Opposite the museum is this modern and well-maintained park, with an outdoor pool and spa. Ask for a free torch for the Ruakuri Reserve glow-worm walk.

Eating & Drinking

Long Black Café (Waitomo Caves Rd; meals NZ$5-12; breakfast & lunch) This popular and spacious café is run by one of the caving companies. There's *paninis*, bagels, pasta and all-day breakfasts, as well as Internet access.

Morepork Pizzeria & Café (☎ 878 8395; School Rd; mains NZ$16-22; breakfast, lunch & dinner) Inside the upmarket Kiwi Paka YHA is this modern and popular restaurant, with an alpine look and a balcony. The pizzas are the main menu items (medium-sized versions cost NZ$18).

Waitomo Caves Tavern (☎ 878 8448; School Rd; mains NZ$12-15; lunch & dinner) This tavern has 11 beers on tap, good-value bistro meals and bands on Friday and Saturday nights. Relax here after a hard day of spelunking.

The village store beside the Museum of Caves is small but has an ice-cream parlour, a bar and Internet access.

Getting There & Away

InterCity (☎ 913 6100; www.intercitycoach.co.nz) runs a daily bus service to Waitomo from Auckland (NZ$50) and Rotorua (NZ$35).

Guthreys Express (☎ 0800 759 999; www.guthreys.co.nz) offers 'coach only' seats (NZ$40) on its Auckland–Waitomo tours.

Waitomo Wanderer (☎ 349 2509; www.waitomotours.co.nz) runs a useful daily loop from Rotorua to Waitomo via the rock-climbing hub of Wharepapa South. The bus leaves Rotorua at 7.45am, arrives at Waitomo at 10am, then departs Waitomo at 3.45pm, returning to Rotorua at 6pm. It costs NZ$30 one way.

MATAMATA

☎ 07 / pop 7800

Matamata, about 90km northeast of Waitomo, was once famous only for the local stud farms breeding thoroughbred horses. But then Peter Jackson decided to use nearby farmland to create Hobbiton for the filming of *Lord of the Rings*, and thousands of the film's fans have since undertaken a pilgrimage to the setting of the hobbit village. Enough remains of the set for your imagination to fill in the holes and the guides are full of stories about the making of the movies. Other attractions in the area include tandem skydiving at the nearby airport, a pioneer village and a hot-springs resort.

The **visitors centre** (☎ 888 7260; www.matamata-info.co.nz; 45 Broadway; 8.30am-5pm Mon-Fri, 9.30am-3pm Sat & Sun) books Hobbiton tours.

Sights & Activities

Visit Hobbiton with **Rings Scenic Tours** (☎ 888 6838; www.hobbitontours.com; tours NZ$50). Their two-hour tours proved to be so popular (13,000 went on them in one year) that they have been running three times a day, but the number may decrease.

The **Firth Tower** (☎ 888 8369; Tower Rd; admission NZ$5; 10am-4pm Wed-Sun) was built in 1882 by Auckland businessman Josiah Firth, who acquired 22,400 hectares from his friend Wiremu Tamihana, chief of the Ngati Haua, and then erected this tall concrete status symbol. The tower is filled with Maori and pioneer relics and around it are 10 other buildings, including a pioneer schoolroom, jail, cottage and a 14m-deep bricked well – hard work to dig and build. It's 3km from town.

Opal Hot Springs (☎ 0800 800 198, 888 8198; Okauia Springs Rd; pool/spa from NZ$4.50/5) is 2km down an access road off Tower Rd, north of Firth Tower and 6km from Matamata. Try Ramaroa Spa, a private outdoor hot spa, for a Garden of Eden experience. Near the complex is the 150m-high **Wairere Falls**.

Skydive Waikato (☎ 0508 759 3483, 029-759 3483; www.freefall.co.nz; SH27) runs tandem skydiving, usually on Wednesday and Saturday, from 10,000ft (NZ$220). The airfield is 8km north of Matamata.

Sleeping

Maple Lodge (☎ 888 8764; maplelodge@xtra.co.nz; 11 Mangawhero Rd; d NZ$70;) This motel is within walking distance of the town centre and has a spa pool.

Broadway (☎ 888 8482; www.broadwaymatamata.co.nz; 128 Broadway; d from NZ$80;) Located in the town centre, these recently refurbished motel units have Sky TV and share a spa pool.

Opal Hot Springs Holiday Park (☎ 0800 800 198, 888 8198; Okauia Springs Rd; camp/campervan sites per person NZ$11/12, s & d NZ$40-65) This park has basic facilities but is clean and offers free entry to the hot pools.

Eating & Drinking

Workman's Café & Bar (☎ 888 5498; 52 Broadway; mains to NZ$25; ⏲ breakfast, lunch & dinner Tue-Sun) The menu in this retro café-bar-restaurant changes every two weeks and has built itself a reputation that extends beyond Matamata.

Ronnie's Café (78 Broadway) Ronnie's has a huge self-service selection.

Lucky's (☎ 888 5630; 96 Broadway) This bar sometimes has live music.

Getting There & Away

InterCity (☎ 834 3457; www.intercitycoach.co.nz) buses pass through Matamata.

COROMANDEL PENINSULA

The mountainous, forested spine of the **Coromandel Peninsula** (www.thecoromandel.com) is threaded with hiking trails, while narrow roads wind along the attractive coastline. The historic gold-mining town of Thames retains a pioneer atmosphere. Whitianga and nearby Hahei are a mini-Bay of Islands, with plenty of activities in, on and below the water.

Thames

☎ 07 / pop 10,000

Thames, on the shallow Firth of Thames, is the western gateway to, and main service centre of, the Coromandel. Plenty of 19th-century wooden stores, pubs and houses have survived from the time when gold-mining and kauri logging made the town a thriving business centre, though nowadays Thames is a base for tramping or canyoning in the nearby Kauaeranga Valley (p565).

INFORMATION

Laundromat Internet (740 Pollen St) Internet access.

Thames visitors centre (☎ 868 7284; www.thames-info.co.nz; 206 Pollen St; ⏲ 8.30am-5pm Mon-Fri, 9am-4pm Sat & Sun) Has Internet access; closes later in summer.

SIGHTS & ACTIVITIES

The worthwhile **Gold Mine Experience** (☎ 868 8514; Pollen St; admission NZ$10; ⏲ 10am-4pm) includes a walk through a gold-mine tunnel, a stamping battery busily crushing rock and the option of panning for gold (NZ$2).

The **Butterfly & Orchid Garden** (☎ 868 8080; Victoria St; admission NZ$9; ⏲ 10am-4pm, closed mid-winter), at Dickson Holiday Park (p565), is an indoor tropical jungle full of hundreds of colourful butterflies.

Karaka Bird Hide is a great bird-watching hide overlooking the Firth of Thames that's easily reached by a boardwalk through the mangroves just off Brown Street. The best viewing time is two hours either side of the high tide.

The **local historical museum** (cnr Cochrane & Pollen Sts; admission NZ$2.50; ⏲ 1-4pm) has pioneer relics, rocks and old photographs of the town.

There's a **market** (⏲ 9am Sat) at the northern end of Pollen St (known as Grahamstown) with lots of organic produce and handicrafts.

Matatoki Farm Cheese (☎ 868 1284; SH26; ⏲ 10am-4pm Mon-Sat May-Oct) is a cheese factory and shop roughly 10km south of Thames, where you can taste and buy handmade cheeses.

Paki Paki Bike Shop (☎ 867 9026; Goldfields Mall; per day NZ$30) rents out fully equipped touring bikes.

SLEEPING

Gateway Backpackers (☎ 868 6339; 209 MacKay St; dm/d NZ$20/45; 💻) This well-located, relaxed backpackers takes up two neighbouring houses. It has light and airy rooms, plenty of facilities and a garden deck. Freebies for guests include bike and washing machine use, and tea and coffee.

Sunkist International Backpackers (☎ 868 8808; sunkist@xtra.co.nz; 506 Brown St; camp sites per person NZ$14, dm NZ$20, d & tw NZ$45; 💻) Four- to 10-bed dorms occupy this 1860s heritage building. The hostel has a garden, free bikes, lots of information and a shuttle-bus service to Kauaeranga Valley. Staff can be cranky.

Brian Boru Hotel & Motel (☎ 868 6523; brianboru@xtra.co.nz; 200 Richmond St; s/d NZ$25/60) This backpackers is above the pub, which the owner is renovating, and there's a more expensive motel on a separate block out the back. For a bizarre experience try the kauri room.

Awakite (Valley View) B&B (☎ 868 7213; 499 Kauaeranga Valley Rd; s/d NZ$50/80) About 7km up the valley, this guesthouse has clean bright

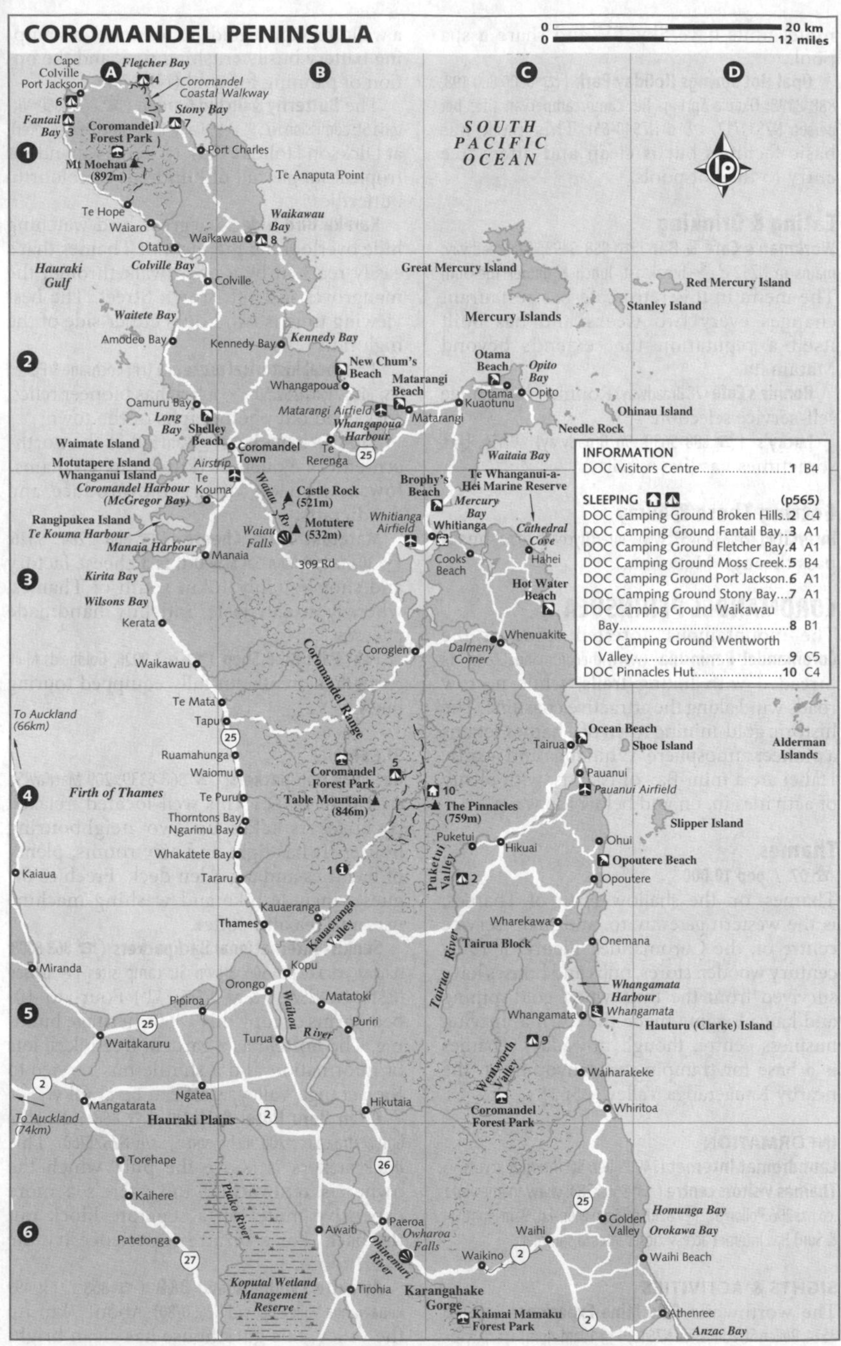
COROMANDEL PENINSULA
0 20 km
0 12 miles
SOUTH PACIFIC OCEAN
Hauraki Gulf
Firth of Thames
Cape Colville
Port Jackson
Fletcher Bay
Coromandel Coastal Walkway
Stony Bay
Fantail Bay
Coromandel Forest Park
Mt Moehau (892m)
Port Charles
Te Anaputa Point
Te Hope
Wairao
Waikawau Bay
Waikawau
Otatu
Colville Bay
Colville
Waitete Bay
Amodeo Bay
Kennedy Bay
New Chum's Beach
Whangapoua
Matarangi Beach
Matarangi
Matarangi Airfield
Whangapoua Harbour
Oamuru Bay
Long Bay
Shelley Beach
Waimate Island
Coromandel Town
Te Rerenga
Motutapere Island
Whanganui Island
Coromandel Harbour (McGregor Bay)
Airstrip
Te Kouma
Waiau Rv
Castle Rock (521m)
Motutere (532m)
Waiau Falls
Rangipukea Island
Te Kouma Harbour
Manaia Harbour
Manaia
309 Rd
Kirita Bay
Wilsons Bay
Kerata
Waikawau
Great Mercury Island
Red Mercury Island
Stanley Island
Mercury Islands
Otama Beach
Otama
Opito Bay
Opito
Kuaotunu
Ohinau Island
Needle Rock
Waitaia Bay
Te Whanganui-a-Hei Marine Reserve
Brophy's Beach
Mercury Bay
Whitianga Airfield
Whitianga
Cathedral Cove
Hahei
Cooks Beach
Hot Water Beach
Whenuakite
Coroglen
Dalmeny Corner
Coromandel Range
Te Mata
Tapu
To Auckland (66km)
Ruamahunga
Waiomu
Te Puru
Thorntons Bay
Ngarimu Bay
Whakatete Bay
Tararu
Kaiaua
Coromandel Forest Park
Table Mountain (846m)
The Pinnacles (759m)
Puketui
Puketui Valley
Hikuai
Ocean Beach
Tairua
Shoe Island
Alderman Islands
Pauanui
Pauanui Airfield
Slipper Island
Ohui
Opoutere Beach
Opoutere
Kauaeranga
Kauaeranga Valley
Thames
Wharekawa
Tairua Block
Onemana
Tairua River
Miranda
Kopu
Orongo
Waihou River
Matatoki
Puriri
Pipiroa
Turua
Waitakaruru
Whangamata Harbour
Whangamata
Hauturu (Clarke) Island
Wentworth Valley
Waiharakeke
Mangatarata
Ngatea
To Auckland (74km)
Hauraki Plains
Hikutaia
Coromandel Forest Park
Whiritoa
Torehape
Kaihere
Piako River
Patetonga
Awaiti
Paeroa
Owharoa Falls
Ohinemuri River
Waikino
Waihi
Golden Valley
Homunga Bay
Orokawa Bay
Waihi Beach
Koputal Wetland Management Reserve
Tirohia
Karangahake Gorge
Kaimai Mamaku Forest Park
Athenree
Anzac Bay
INFORMATION
DOC Visitors Centre....1 B4
SLEEPING (p565)
DOC Camping Ground Broken Hills..2 C4
DOC Camping Ground Fantail Bay..3 A1
DOC Camping Ground Fletcher Bay.4 A1
DOC Camping Ground Moss Creek..5 B4
DOC Camping Ground Port Jackson.6 A1
DOC Camping Ground Stony Bay...7 A1
DOC Camping Ground Waikawau Bay....8 B1
DOC Camping Ground Wentworth Valley....9 C5
DOC Pinnacles Hut....10 C4

rooms, a lounge, and friendly, enthusiastic hosts who grow their own organic fruit and vegetables.

Brookby Motel (☎ 868 6663; brookbymotel@xtra.co.nz; 102 Redwood Lane; s & d NZ$65-90) It's worth searching out this reasonably priced brookside gem where all the rooms have small decks and stylish furnishings.

Dickson Holiday Park (☎ 868 7308; www.dicksonpark.co.nz; Victoria St; camp/campervan sites per person NZ$11/12, dm NZ$18, d NZ$45-85; 💻 🅿) Situated in a quiet valley 4km north of Thames, this pleasant camping ground has a shop, free bikes and a three-hour bush hike up into the hills, which are riddled with gold mine tunnels.

EATING

Food for Thought (☎ 868 6065; 574 Pollen St; 🕑 breakfast & lunch Mon-Sat) This place has coffee and tea and lots of deli snacks for under NZ$5.

Sola Café (☎ 868 8781; 720b Pollen St; 🕑 breakfast & lunch daily, dinner Wed-Sat summer) This is a brilliant vegetarian café with vegan, dairy-free and gluten-free food.

Majestic Fish Shop (☎ 868 6204; 640 Pollen St; mains NZ$13-21) This popular fish-and-chips takeaway has a restaurant at the back.

Kaveeta's (☎ 868 7049; 518 Pollen St; mains NZ$10-12; 🕑 lunch & dinner) This distinctive, inexpensive restaurant serves up Indian food, pizzas (including Indian-style ones), a herby *lassi* and *kulfi* ice cream. It also has a tasty vegetarian selection.

Sealey Café & Bar (☎ 868 8641; 109 Sealey St; meals NZ$10-26; 🕑 breakfast, lunch & dinner) This all-day café-restaurant has a pleasant courtyard out the front and some unusual and tempting combinations and salads on its menu.

Goldmine (☎ 868 3180; 545 Pollen St; mains NZ$10-28; 🕑 lunch & dinner) This bar and grill has a surprisingly long and varied menu.

GETTING THERE & AWAY

InterCity (☎ 868 7284; www.intercitycoach.co.nz) buses run between Thames and various destinations, including Auckland (from NZ$30). See Intercity Passes p793 for more information.

Coromandel Forest Park

☎ 07

Over 30 walks and tramps criss-cross the Coromandel Forest Park, which covers a peninsular area stretching from the Maratoto Forest in the south right up to Cape Colville. The most popular hike leads to the dramatic **Pinnacles** (759m) in the **Kauaeranga Valley** behind Thames; there are old kauri dams in this valley, including the Tarawaere Waterfalls, Dancing Camp, Kauaeranga Main, Moss Creek and Waterfalls Creek dams. Other outstanding hikes include the walks around **Puketui Valley** and its historical gold-mine workings and the **Coromandel Coastal Walkway** (three hours) between Fletcher Bay and Stony Bay in the far north.

The **DOC visitors centre** (☎ 867 9080; Kauaeranga Valley Rd; 🕑 8am-4pm) has hiking information and displays on kauri logging. The centre is 14km off the main road; the hiking trails start a further 9km along a gravel road. Sunkist International Backpackers (p563) provides transport from Thames to the hiking trails.

The 80-bed **DOC Pinnacles hut** (☎ 867 9080; per person NZ$15) has gas cookers, heaters, toilets and cold showers, and must be prebooked. Very basic **DOC camping grounds** (camp sites per person NZ$7) are located at Fantail Bay, Port Jackson, Fletcher Bay, Stony Bay and Waikawau Bay in the north. There are also basic DOC camping grounds further south at Broken Hills and Wentworth Valley, and near the Pinnacles hut at Moss Creek. Over Christmas and New Year, bookings are required for **Waikawau Bay** (☎ 866 1106); all other camping sites work on a first-come, first-served basis.

Whitianga

☎ 07 / pop 3580

Whitianga is the main town on Mercury Bay and is a popular harbourside resort with plenty of marine activities such as scuba diving or kayaking around offshore islands and, on land, bone carving and horse riding.

BRING BACK THE KAURI

The Coromandel Peninsula once supported magnificent stands of the long-living kauri tree, but after continual logging between the 1870s and the 1930s, very few remain. For a NZ$10 donation you can help bring the kauri forests back to life, as a volunteer will plant a kauri seedling on your behalf. Pick up a leaflet at the **DOC visitors centre** (☎ 867 9080; Kauaeranga Valley Rd; 🕑 8am-4pm) or contact the **Kauri 2000 Trust** (☎ 07-866 0468; Box 174, Whitianga).

Nearby are two famous natural attractions: Cathedral Cove and Hot Water Beach.

The legendary Polynesian explorer and seafarer Kupe is said to have landed near here around AD 800, resulting in the area being called Te Whitianga a Kupe (Crossing Place of Kupe).

INFORMATION

Medical centre (☎ 866 5911; 87 Albert St; 🕑 8.30am-5pm Mon-Fri, 9-11am Sat & Sun summer) Has a 24-hour phone line.

Whitianga i-SITE visitors centre (☎ 866 5555; www.whitianga.co.nz; 66 Albert St; 🕑 9am-5pm Mon-Fri, 9am-4pm Sat & Sun) Has Internet access and hires out bicycles (NZ$25 per day).

SIGHTS & ACTIVITIES

The **museum** (☎ 866 0770; admission NZ$3; Esplanade; 🕑 10am-4pm summer, 11am-3pm Tue-Thu & Sun winter) has local history and nature displays, plus an interesting video about Maori and pakeha perceptions of Captain Cook.

Maurice Aukett of **Bay Carving** (☎ 866 4021; Esplanade; 🕑 9am-4pm), located beside the museum, will help you create your own high-quality Maori-style bone carving using a dentist drill and sandpaper. This two-hour exercise (NZ$35) is highly recommended. **Bone Studio** (☎ 866 2158; 16 Coghill St) offers more in-depth bone-carving tuition (NZ$80 per day).

The **Cave Cruzer** (☎ 0800 427 893, 866 2275; www.cavecruzer.co.nz; 1-3hr trips NZ$45-85) is a rigid-hull inflatable boat offering trips around the caves and islands that involve snorkelling, fishing and commentary.

The **Blue Boat** (☎ 866 4904; trips NZ$30) operates a two-hour trip to Cathedral Cove at 10am and 2pm, plus 5pm over summer; minimum four adults per trip.

Seafari Glass Bottom Boat (☎ 021-478 290; www.glassbottomboatwhitianga.co.nz; tours NZ$65) operates 2½-hour tours year-round allowing you to see what's under the water as well as the limestone coastal scenery. Three trips run per day over summer and snorkelling gear is available.

Seafari Windsurfing (☎ 866 0677; Brophy's Beach), based 4km north of Whitianga, hires out sailboards (NZ$20 to NZ$35 per hour) and kayaks (NZ$10 to NZ$20 per hour), and provides sailboarding lessons (NZ$40 for 1½ hours). Wetsuits cost NZ$5; lifejackets are included in the price.

For horse trekking, try the **Twin Oaks Riding Ranch** (☎ 866 5388; treks NZ$30), 9km north of Whitianga on the Kuaotunu Rd.

Highzone (☎ 866 2113; www.highzone.co.nz; 49 Kaimarama Rd; admission NZ$10-60) offers high adventure on a ropes course involving nine challenges staged 12m above ground level, including a leap onto a trapeze. It's 7km south of Whitianga, just off the main road.

SLEEPING

On The Beach Backpackers Lodge (☎ 866 5380; www.coromandelbackpackers.com; 46 Buffalo Beach Rd; dm/s NZ$22/45, d & tw NZ$55-75; 💻) Large, brightly painted and well-run, this YHA-associate hostel has lots of rooms and offers free kayaks, surfboards, spades (for digging a pool on Hot Water Beach) and bikes (NZ$20 per day).

Cat's Pyjamas (☎ 866 4663; www.cats-pyjamas.co.nz; 4 Monk St; camp sites per person NZ$12, dm NZ$12, d & tw NZ$45-50; 💻) A small and bright backpackers with friendly hosts who can arrange 30-minute scenic flights at a reasonable price.

Buffalo Peaks Lodge (☎ 866 2933; www.buffalopeaks.co.nz; 12 Albert St; dm/d NZ$22/50; 💻) This place has dorms of various sizes and is popular with backpacker tour groups. It has a spa pool and a free pool table.

Aladdin Holiday Park (☎ 866 5834; Bongard Rd; camp & campervan sites per person NZ$10-13, s & d NZ$45-110) Bush walks for all energy levels are available near this pleasant camping ground to the north of the town centre.

Mercury Bay Motor Camp (☎ 866 5579; 121 Albert St; camp/campervan sites per person from NZ$10/13, d NZ$40-120; 🏊) This camp is small and shady, with a spa, clean facilities and kayaks for hire (NZ$10 per day).

EATING & DRINKING

Café Nina (☎ 866 5440; 20 Victoria St; meals NZ$4.50-11; 🕑 breakfast & lunch) Barbecue breakfasts, an ever-changing lunch menu and afternoon tea are available at this popular café. Worth seeking out.

Coghill Café (10 Coghill St; meals NZ$8.50-14; 🕑 breakfast & lunch) This café opens early (7am) and provides home-made snacks, giant pies, date scones, smoothies and larger meals.

Snapper Jack's (☎ 866 5482; Albert St) This popular fast-food outlet serves up fish or chicken and chips, either for takeaway or sit-down munching.

Salt Bar & Restaurant (☎ 866 5818; 1 Blacksmith Lane; mains NZ$16-22; 🕑 lunch & dinner) Thai dishes are served inside or on the terrace overlooking the marina. The sports bar has live music and DJs on a regular basis.

Hairy's Bar & Grill (☎ 866 5249; 31 Albert St) Sports bar with table tennis, big screen TV, jukebox, pool table, live bands at weekends and, surprisingly, a swimming pool out back.

GETTING THERE & AWAY

Waiheke Air Services (☎ 0800 372 5000, 372 5000) and **Great Barrier Airlines** (☎ 0800 900 600, 275 9120; www.greatbarrierairlines.co.nz) connect Whitianga with Waiheke Island and Great Barrier Island respectively.

Go Kiwi (☎ 0800 446 549) has a daily shuttle bus from Whitianga to Thames (NZ$30, 1½ hours) and Opoutere, while **InterCity** (☎ 913 6100; www.intercitycoach.co.nz) passes through on its Coromandel Loop every day (see p793).

Hahei & Hot Water Beach

☎ 07

Hahei (www.hahei.co.nz), 38km by road from Whitianga via Coroglen, is a beautiful white-sand beach fronting islands scattered out over a bay. The islands and the dramatic limestone coastline are all part of the Te Whanganui a Hei Marine Reserve. Kayaking, snorkelling, diving and boat trips are all popular activities here. Just 9km south of Hahei is the famous Hot Water Beach.

SIGHTS & ACTIVITIES

About 1km north of Hahei is the car park marking the start of the walk to impressive **Cathedral Cove** (45 minutes), with its gigantic limestone arch. On the way, visit the rocky cove at **Gemstone Bay**, which has an excellent snorkelling trail, and the sandy cove at **Stingray Bay**. You can walk from Hahei Beach but it takes another 30 minutes.

At the southern end of Hahei Beach is a walk up to an old Maori *pa*, **Te Pare Point** (20 minutes). There are splendid coastal views, especially if you walk through the grass and look south.

Cathedral Cove Sea Kayaking (☎ 866 3877; www.seakayaktours.co.nz; 188 Hahei Beach Rd; half-day trips NZ$65) has guided kayaking trips around the fascinating Cathedral Cove area. The 'Remote' kayak trip heads the other way when conditions permit and is also highly recommended, yielding caves, blow holes, a long tunnel and great limestone scenery. Free pick up is available from Ferry Landing.

> **BEACH WARNING!**
>
> Hot Water Beach is plagued year-round by dangerous currents, also known as rips or undertows. It's one of the four most dangerous beaches in NZ in terms of drowning incidents. Swimming here is not safe.

Cathedral Cove Dive (☎ 866 3955; 3 Margaret Pl) has dives two or three times daily. Prices vary from NZ$40 (own gear) to NZ$80 (includes all gear). A 'Discover Scuba' half-day course is NZ$120, while PADI courses cost NZ$500 including all gear. Its shop in the shopping centre rents out scuba and snorkelling gear and boogie boards.

At **Hot Water Beach**, thermal waters brew just below the sand in front of a rocky outcrop. Join the crowd on the beach two hours each side of low tide, dig a hole in the sand with a spade, and then relax in your own natural spa pool. Spades can be hired (NZ$4) from **Tarte Café** (🕑 9am-7pm summer, 9am-5pm winter). Heed the warnings about the dangers of swimming here (see the Beach Warning boxed text, above).

SLEEPING

Tatahi Lodge (☎ 866 3992; tatahi_lodge@xtra.co.nz; Grange Rd; dm/d NZ$20/55) This is a spotless and smart choice next to the shops and cafés, with an alpine chalet design, brightly coloured furnishings, pine décor and views.

Hahei Beach Resort (☎ 866 3889; info@haheiholidays.co.nz; Harsant Ave; camp/campervan sites per person NZ$11/12, backpacker dm/d NZ$19/45, d cabin NZ$45-90) Large and perfectly located on the beachfront, the accommodation here is more modern than the facilities.

Fernbird (☎ 866 3080; fernbird@xtra.co.nz; 24 Harsant Ave; dm/d NZ$19/45; 💻) Fernbird has just two plain rooms, but the accommodation is homely, with a beautiful front garden.

EATING

Grange Road Café (☎ 866 3502; 7 Grange Rd; lunches NZ$5-10, dinners NZ$20-28; 🕑 breakfast, lunch & dinner summer) The kitchen here turns out excellent, original meals. It caters for everyone, including vegans, and has lots of NZ wines and beers as well as fresh juices. It has reduced hours in winter.

Luna Café (☎ 866 3016; 1 Grange Rd; mains NZ$14-26; 🕑 breakfast, lunch & dinner) This is another good restaurant-café that serves mainly Mediterranean-style food, including pizzas for NZ$20.

GETTING THERE & AROUND

The easiest way to get from Whitianga to Hahei (if you don't have a car) is by using the ferry crossing. The **passenger ferry** (adult/bicycle one way NZ$1/0.50) from Whitianga to Ferry Landing takes five minutes, and runs continuously from 7am to 10.30pm in summer, and from 7am to 6.30pm, 7.30pm to 8.30pm and 9.30pm to 10.30pm in winter.

Go Kiwi (☎ 0800 446 549) runs a bus several times daily from Ferry Landing to Cook's Beach (NZ$3), Hahei (NZ$7) and Hot Water Beach (NZ$10), with some services continuing to Dalmeny Corner on the highway for connections with buses to Auckland and Whitianga. A day pass costs NZ$20 and a NZ$35 explorer pass allows you to use the service as much as you like over a three-day period. You can pick up a timetable and make bookings at the Whitianga i-SITE visitors centre (p566).

TAUPO

☎ 07 / pop 21,040

The town of Taupo lies on the northeastern corner of Lake Taupo, NZ's largest lake (606 sq km), which was formed by one of the greatest volcanic explosions of all time (see the Big Bang boxed text, p570). This serene body of water is the source of NZ's longest river, the Waikato, and is also hailed as the world's trout-fishing capital. Taupo township makes it on to most backpackers' NZ hit lists because of its scenic views across the lake to the volcanic peaks of Tongariro National Park and its long list of attractions and activities, the latter ranging from fishing and boating to bungy jumping and skydiving.

The name 'Taupo' is possibly derived from the name Tapuaeharuru (Resounding Footsteps), bequeathed long ago by Maori chief Tamatea-arikinui, who noticed that the area's ground felt hollow and his footsteps seemed to reverberate. Another potential source of the name comes from the story of Tia, who discovered the lake and slept by it draped in his cloak – it became known as Taupo nui a Tia (The Great Cloak of Tia). Taupo, as it was later called, was first occupied by Europeans as a military outpost in the 1860s, with the government buying the land from the Maori people a decade later.

Information

AA (Map p569; ☎ 378 6000; 93 Tongariro St)

Backpack Lake Taupo (www.backpacklaketaupo.com) For details of budget accommodation, activities and other useful information, check out this website.

Cyberwash (Map p569; ☎ 0274-460 202; 10 Roberts St; per hr NZ$7-8) Offers a laundry service while you check your email.

Internet Outpost (Map p569; 11 Tuwharetoa St; per hr NZ$7-8)

Post office (Map p569; cnr Horomatangi & Ruapehu Sts) Exchanges money on Saturday morning.

Super Loo Near the visitors centre, this is a large shower and toilet complex, with showers for NZ$2 (for four minutes) and towels for NZ$1.

Taupo visitors centre (Map p569; ☎ 376 0027; www.laketauponz.com; Tongariro St; 8.30am-5pm) Handles bookings for all local accommodation, transport and activities, and also supplies DOC maps and information.

Sights

The **Lake Taupo Museum & Art Gallery** (Map p569; ☎ 378 4167; Story Pl; admission NZ$4; 10.30am-4.30pm) has many historical photos and mementos of the 'old days' around Lake Taupo. The centrepiece of the collection is a Maori meeting house, Te Aroha o Rongoheikume, adorned with traditional, elaborate carvings. Other exhibits include a moa skeleton, displays on the local forestry, boating and trout-fishing industries, and a mock-up of a 19th-century shop. There are also temporary art exhibitions.

Alongside the museum is the well-tended **Taupo Rose Garden** (Map p569; Story Pl; admission free), home to dozens of varieties of roses and with a shady pergola in the middle.

In the middle of the Waikato River, accessed by a footbridge, is **Cherry Island** (Map p569; ☎ 378 9427; admission NZ$8.50; 9am-5pm), a small trout and wildlife park with a café. The wildlife consists of a few goats, pigs, pheasants and ducks.

Acacia Bay, which has a pleasant, peaceful beach, is around 5km west of Taupo.

Activities

THERMAL POOLS

The AC Baths at the **Taupo Events Centre** (Map p575; ☎ 376 0340; www.taupovenues.co.nz; Spa Rd; admission NZ$6.50; 8am-9pm), 2km east of town, has a big, heated pool with a waterslide, an indoor

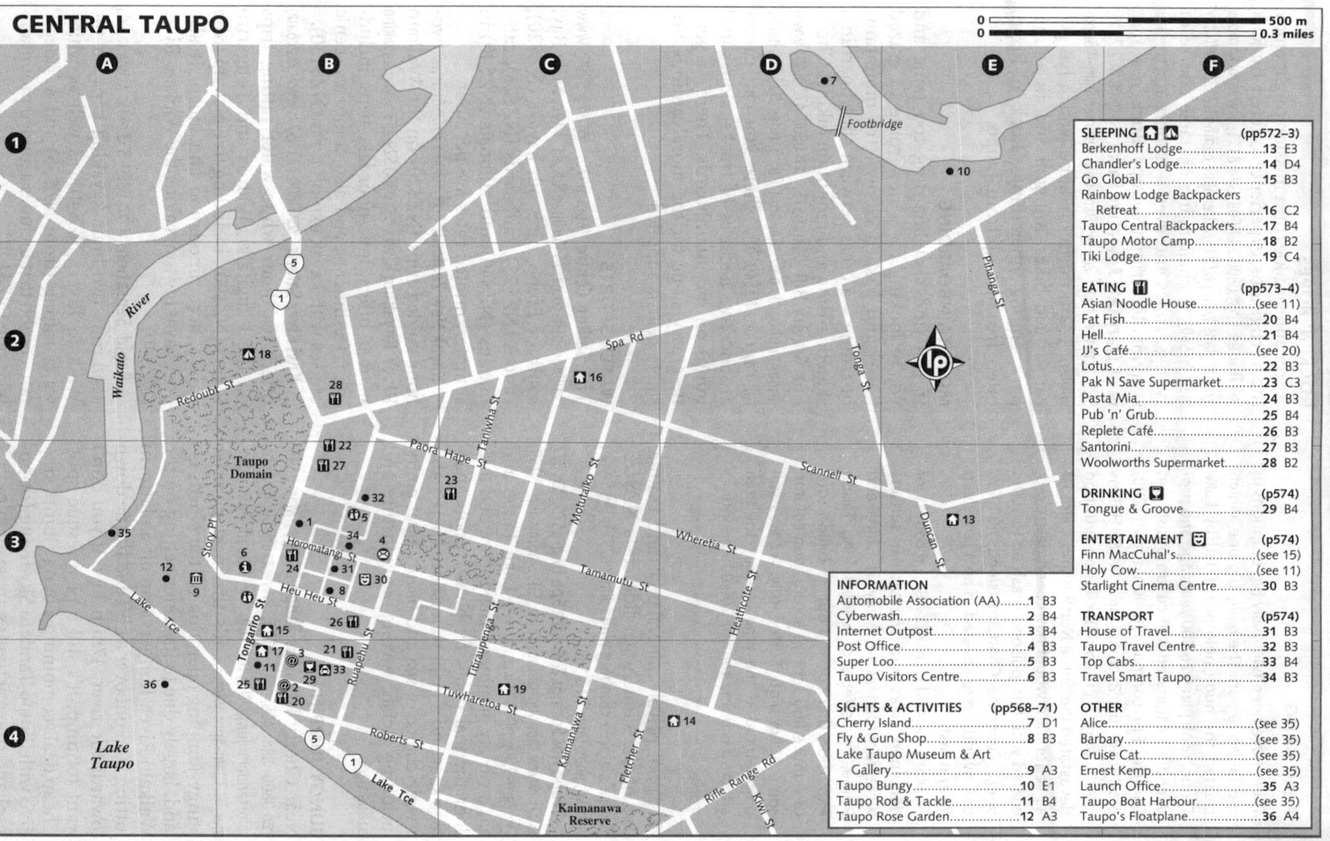
CENTRAL TAUPO
0 500 m
0 0.3 miles
SLEEPING (pp572–3)
Berkenhoff Lodge 13 E3
Chandler's Lodge 14 D4
Go Global 15 B3
Rainbow Lodge Backpackers Retreat 16 C2
Taupo Central Backpackers 17 B4
Taupo Motor Camp 18 B2
Tiki Lodge 19 C4
EATING (pp573–4)
Asian Noodle House (see 11)
Fat Fish 20 B4
Hell 21 B4
JJ's Café (see 20)
Lotus 22 B3
Pak N Save Supermarket 23 C3
Pasta Mia 24 B3
Pub 'n' Grub 25 B4
Replete Café 26 B3
Santorini 27 B3
Woolworths Supermarket 28 B2
DRINKING (p574)
Tongue & Groove 29 B4
ENTERTAINMENT (p574)
Finn MacCuhal's (see 15)
Holy Cow (see 11)
Starlight Cinema Centre 30 B3
TRANSPORT (p574)
House of Travel 31 B3
Taupo Travel Centre 32 B3
Top Cabs 33 B4
Travel Smart Taupo 34 B3
OTHER
Alice (see 35)
Barbary (see 35)
Cruise Cat (see 35)
Ernest Kemp (see 35)
Launch Office 35 A3
Taupo Boat Harbour (see 35)
Taupo's Floatplane 36 A4
INFORMATION
Automobile Association (AA) 1 B3
Cyberwash 2 B4
Internet Outpost 3 B4
Post Office 4 B3
Super Loo 5 B3
Taupo Visitors Centre 6 B3
SIGHTS & ACTIVITIES (pp568–71)
Cherry Island 7 D1
Fly & Gun Shop 8 B3
Lake Taupo Museum & Art Gallery 9 A3
Taupo Bungy 10 E1
Taupo Rod & Tackle 11 B4
Taupo Rose Garden 12 A3
Footbridge
Waikato River
Taupo Domain
Lake Taupo
Kaimanawa Reserve
Redoubt St
Spa Rd
Paora Hape St
Taniwha St
Motutaiko St
Tonga St
Pihanga St
Scannell St
Duncan St
Whereta St
Tamamutu St
Heathcote St
Horomatangi St
Heu Heu St
Tongariro St
Ruapehu St
Titiraupenga St
Tuwharetoa St
Kaimanawa St
Fletcher St
Roberts St
Lake Tce
Story Pl
Rifle Range Rd
Kiwi St

A BIG BANG

There have been two really big eruptions in the Taupo region. The *really* big one, which created the huge hole now filled by Lake Taupo, took place 26,500 years ago and produced an estimated 800 cu km of ash and pumice. For comparison, Krakatoa (1883) produced just 8 cu km and Mt St Helens (1980) only 3 cu km. The Taupo eruption devastated the entire North Island – almost all vegetation would have been destroyed, coated with hot, poisonous ash up to 100m deep. Even the Chatham Islands (800km downwind) were covered in an 11cm-deep layer of ash.

More recently, in AD 181, accounts of darkened skies and spectacular sunsets were recorded as far away as China and Rome, the effects of a week-long Taupo explosion that spewed out 33 billion tons of pumice and sent up an eruption column some 50km high. Fortunately, NZ was still uninhabited at the time – today the area affected is home to over 200,000 people.

kids' pool, private mineral pools and a sauna. Use of the sauna/waterslide costs NZ$4/3. There's also a **climbing wall** (climbs NZ$13; 5-9pm Mon-Fri, noon-9pm Sat & Sun).

Taupo Hot Springs & Health Spa (Map p575; ☎ 377 6502; www.taupohotsprings.com; SH5; admission NZ$9; 7am-9.30pm) is 1km from Lake Taupo and has a variety of mineral-rich indoor and outdoor thermal pools, freshwater pools, massage spas and a giant waterslide. There's also a wide choice of spa and beauty treatments, including facials, waxing, acupuncture and massages.

BUNGY JUMPING

Near Cherry Island is **Taupo Bungy** (Map p569; ☎ 0800 888 408, 377 1135; www.taupobungy.com; solo/tandem jump NZ$100/160; 8.30am-7pm summer, 8.30am-5pm winter). It's the most popular bungy-jumping operation on the North Island, largely due to its scenic setting on the Waikato River. Jumpers leap off a platform jutting 20m out over a cliff and hurtle down towards the river, 47m below. If you don't want to jump, it's still a picturesque spot. Cheap deals combining a bungy jump, skydive with Taupo Tandem Skydiving (opposite) and other activities are available.

ROCK 'N' ROPES

Adrenaline junkies on a mission might enjoy the vertiginous experience offered by **Rock 'n' Ropes** (☎ 0800 244 508, 374 8111; www.rocknropes.co.nz; giant swing NZ$15, adrenaline combo NZ$35, half-day blast NZ$60), a challenging obstacle course of swings, ropes and even a trapeze up in the swaying, teetering tree tops. Rock 'n' Ropes is at **Crazy Catz Adventure Park** (☎ 0800 462 7219; SH5; activities NZ$5-20; 9am-6pm summer, 9am-4.30pm winter), 13km north of Taupo, which has go-carts, quad bikes, minigolf and an animal park, among other things. Rock 'n' Ropes offers free pick up from Taupo.

MOUNTAINBOARDING

If you find skateboarding too tame and you're looking for a new route to grazed knees and bashed elbows, try mountainboarding – a cross between snowboarding, skateboarding and mountain biking. Check out **Gravity Hill** (Map p575; ☎ 0800 472 848; www.mountainboard.co.nz; Rakanui Rd; 5 rides NZ$29, half-/full-day rides NZ$40/70), where you can career around five hectares of tracks, slopes and jumps on mountainboards. There's a gentle grassy slope for the more cautious. All safety gear is supplied.

WATER SPORTS

The **Sailing Centre** (Map p575; ☎ 378 3299; www.sailingcentre.co.nz; 75 Kurupae Rd) at Two Mile Bay, south of Taupo, hires out kayaks (NZ$20), canoes (NZ$25), sailboards (NZ$25), catamarans (NZ$40) and sailboats (NZ$40) in summer; quoted rates are per hour.

Kayak New Zealand (☎ 0800 529 256) has two-hour guided trips (NZ$20) on the Waikato River. **Kayaking Kiwi** (☎ 0800 529 255; www.kayakingkiwi.co.nz) offers three-hour lake trips, including refreshments, and also combines scenic cruises with kayak explorations (NZ$130).

Kiwi River Safaris (☎ 0800 723 8577; www.krs.co.nz) offers two-hour white-water rafting trips on the Rangitaiki, Wairoa and Tongariro Rivers (NZ$90), including free pick up from Taupo, accommodation and lunch. It also does kayaking tours along the Waikato River (NZ$40).

Rapid Sensations (☎ 0800 353 435; www.rapids.co.nz) runs two-hour kayaking trips on the Waikato River (NZ$40), as well as white-water rafting (from NZ$55) and a 'ride 'n' raft' combo that includes a guided mountain-bike ride (NZ$140).

During summer there are lots of other activities on Lake Taupo, including swimming, water-skiing, sailboarding, paragliding and sailing. The visitors centre (see p568) has details; gear can be hired on the lakefront.

SKYDIVING

Skydiving at Taupo couples an adrenaline rush with a brilliant view over the lake and surrounding region. The **Great Lake Skydive Centre** (☎ 0800 373 335, 378 4662; www.freefly.co.nz; jumps incl ground video from NZ$195) and **Skydive Taupo** (☎ 0800 586 766; www.skydivetaupo.co.nz; jumps from NZ$180) do dives from 9000ft and 12,000ft, while **Taupo Tandem Skydiving** (☎ 0800 275 934; www.tts.net.nz; jumps NZ$170-300) do jumps from between 6000ft and 15,000ft. All three companies operate from Taupo Airport.

GLIDING

The **Taupo Gliding Club** (Map p575; ☎ 378 5627; Centennial Dr; from NZ$70) goes gliding on Saturday, Sunday and Wednesday afternoons (when the weather is suitable) at Centennial Park, about 5km up Spa Rd from the town centre.

FISHING

The Taupo region is world famous for its trout fly fishing, which is the only fishing you can do on all rivers flowing into the lake and within a 300m radius of the river mouths. Spin fishing (which involves the use of an artificial lure that spins as the fishing line is reeled in) is allowed on the Waikato River (flowing *out* of the lake) and on the Tokaanu tailrace, flowing into the lake from the Tokaanu Power Station. Several fly-fishing guides operate around Taupo, most notably in Turangi. The price of around NZ$250/450 per half-/full-day, everything included, is reasonable when you consider you are paying for years of local knowledge.

An alternative way to experience the thrill of catching your own dinner is to take a boat out on the lake. A number of fishing guides and charter boats operate in Taupo, including **Te Moana Charters** (☎ 378 4839) and **White Striker Charters** (☎ 378 2736), both charging from NZ$80 per hour. You can hire boats at the **launch office** (Map p569; ☎ 378 3444; 🕑 8.30am-5pm summer, 9am-2.30pm winter) for around NZ$30 per hour. If you take an organised trip, all equipment and licences will be supplied, and a minimum of two to three hours is normally required (or at least suggested). Both spin fishing and fly fishing are allowed on the lake.

Taupo Rod & Tackle (Map p569; ☎ 378 5337; 7 Tongariro St) and the **Fly & Gun Shop** (Map p569; ☎ 378 4449; www.huntingandfishing.co.nz; 34 Heu Heu St) have fishing tackle for hire.

Fishing licences are obligatory (there are huge fines for violations) and are available from the visitors centre (p568) or the launch office. Licences for fishing on Lake Taupo and the nearby rivers cost NZ$13/27/70 per day/week/year.

HORSE TREKKING

Taupo Horse Treks (Map p575; ☎ 378 0356; Karapiti Rd; 1/2hr rides NZ$30/50) has a good reputation for running forest treks.

CYCLING

Taupo is a cyclist-friendly place, with dedicated cycle lanes along Lake Tce and Heu Heu St, and plenty of cycle racks. Lake Taupo is the location of two of the biggest annual cycling events in NZ: the 160km **Lake Taupo Cycle Challenge** (www.cyclechallenge.org.nz), on the last Saturday in November, and the 12-hour Day-Night Thriller, held in October and regularly attracting over 3000 riders. The leaflet *Cycling Around Lake Taupo*, available from the visitors centre, has suggested routes.

Taupo Quad Adventures (☎ 377 6404; www.4x4quads.com; 1hr/full-day trips NZ$60/230) has fully guided off-road quad-bike trips. It's at the turn-off to Orakei Korako on SH1.

Both **Rainbow Lodge** (Map p569; ☎ 378 5754; 99 Titiraupenga St) and **Go Global** (Map p569; ☎ 377 0044; cnr Tongariro & Tuwharetoa Sts) rent bikes for around NZ$20 per day. **Rapid Sensations** (☎ 0800 353 435; www.rapids.co.nz) rents mountain bikes for NZ$45 per day and offers guided rides from NZ$55. **Cyberwash** (Map p569; ☎ 0274-460 202; 10 Roberts St) rents scooters from NZ$45 for two hours.

Bikes are forbidden on the track from Spa Park to Huka Falls due to track damage.

WALKING

An enjoyable, easy walk runs from Taupo to **Aratiatia** (Map p575; 3½ hours) along the Waikato River's east bank. The track follows the river to **Huka Falls** (Map p575), crossing a hot stream and riverside marshes en route, before continuing straight ahead on the 7km **Taupo Walkway** to Aratiatia. There are views of the river, Huka Falls and the power station across the river. From the town centre, head up Spa Rd, passing the Taupo Bungy site. To reach the start of the walk turn left at County Ave and continue through Spa Thermal Park to the end of the street. The path heads off to the left of the car park, up over a hill and down to the hot springs by the river. Alternatively, drive to the falls and park, cross the bridge and walk out to Aratiatia.

Another walk goes to the top of **Mt Tauhara** (Map p575; two hours), where there are magnificent views. Take the SH5 turn-off, 2km south of Taupo town centre, and about 6km along it turn left into Mountain Rd; the start of the track is signposted on the right-hand side.

A flat, easy **walkway** (Map p575) along public-access beaches heads from the Taupo lakefront to Five Mile Bay. Heading south from Taupo, there's a hot-water beach on the way to Two Mile Bay. At Two Mile Bay (4.2km south of Taupo) the walkway connects with the **Lions Walk to Five Mile Bay** (8km). Anywhere along here you can easily get back to SH1, the lakeside road.

There are plenty of other good walks and tramps in the area; the visitors centre has the relevant DOC pamphlets (NZ$1).

Tours

BUS TOURS

Kiwi Experience (☎ 09-366 9830; www.kiwiexperience.com) Operates the 'East As' backpacker bus trip from Taupo around the East Cape and back again, via Gisborne and Napier. The trip takes a minimum of four days and costs NZ$260, or NZ$250 as an 'add on' to a Kiwi Experience National Pass. Accommodation and food are extra.

Paradise Tours (☎ 378 9955; www.paradisetours.co.nz; tours NZ$40) Does three-hour tours to the Aratiatia Rapids, Craters of the Moon and Huka Falls; for information on these places, see the Wairakei Park section (p574). The company also offers tours to Tongariro National Park.

Taupo Tours (☎ 377 0774; www.taupotours.com; tours NZ$5) Runs 20-minute sightseeing tours of Taupo in a refurbished 1950s British double-decker bus. The bus stops behind the Super Loo and at the town end of the lakefront and runs every half-hour between 10am and 4pm from Boxing Day to Easter.

See also Getting Around, p574, for sights in and around Taupo.

AERIAL SIGHTSEEING

Air Charter Taupo (☎ 378 5467; www.airchartertaupo.co.nz; Taupo Airport; flights NZ$50-180) Does scenic flights ranging from 15-minute trips to one-hour jaunts across Lake Taupo, Tongariro, Wairakei Park and Mt Ruapehu.

Helistar Helicopters (Map p575; ☎ 0800 435 478; www.helistar.co.nz; Huka Falls Rd; flights NZ$75-950) This outfit, about 3km northeast of town, offers a variety of scenic helicopter flights, ranging from five minutes to two hours. Also available is the 'Hukastar Combo' (from NZ$170): a helicopter flight followed by a spin on the Huka Jet (p575).

Taupo's Floatplane (Map p569; ☎ 378 7500; www.tauposfloatplane.co.nz; flights NZ$60-430) Next to Taupo Boat Harbour, it does a variety of trips, including quick flights over the lake and longer ones over Mt Ruapehu and as far afield as Whakaari (White Island). If you're looking for a full day out, you could try the 'Taupo Trifecta Combo' (floatplane trip, followed by a jet-boat trip and a walk through Orakei Korako; NZ$260).

LAKE CRUISES & JET-BOATING

Four boats specialise in cruises on the lake. All the boats offer similar trips, including visiting a modern Maori rock carving beside the lake. The carving is on private land and can only be reached by boat; trips take between 1½ and 2½ hours. All boats leave from the wharves at **Taupo Boat Harbour** (Map p569; off Redoubt St). Bookings can be made at the visitors centre or the **launch office** (Map p569; ☎ 378 3444; 🕒 8.30am-5pm summer, 9am-2.30pm winter).

Alice (Map p569; trips NZ$15; 🕒 11am, 12.30pm & 2pm Sat & Sun) A steamboat plying Lake Taupo's waters.

Barbary (Map p569; cruises NZ$30; 🕒 10am & 2pm, plus 5pm summer) Built in 1926, the *Barbary* is a 15m ocean-going racing yacht once briefly possessed by actor Errol Flynn. 'Barbary Bill', the skipper, is much loved by tourists and locals and his trip is probably the most popular.

Cruise Cat (Map p569; trips NZ$28; 🕒 11.30am Mon-Sat, 10.30am Sun) For something with a little more zip, try the Cruise Cat, which is a large, modern launch. On Sunday there's brunch (NZ$45).

Ernest Kemp (Map p569; trips NZ$28; 🕒 10.30am & 2pm) Built to resemble a 1920s steamboat. There are written commentaries in various languages for the trips.

Sleeping

Tiki Lodge (Map p569; ☎ 377 4545; www.tikilodge.co.nz; 104 Tuwharetoa St; dm/d from NZ$26/30; 💻) This newish lodge is a friendly hostel with Maori décor and spotless rooms. It has comfortable, well-equipped communal areas, including a huge kitchen, TV and reading lounges, and a wide balcony with a BBQ and views of the lake.

Berkenhoff Lodge (Map p569; ☎ 378 4909; bhoff@reap.org.nz; 75 Scannell St; dm/d NZ$20/50; 💻 🍴) This is a big, rambling old place in a quiet spot away from the town centre, but handy for Taupo Bungy and the AC Baths. It has good-sized rooms, all with private bathrooms, and there's a spa pool, games room, TV-lounge and kitchen, plus a barbecue and bar.

Rainbow Lodge Backpackers Retreat (Map p569; ☎ 378 5754; rainbowlodge@clear.net.nz; 99 Titiraupenga St; dm/d from NZ$18/45) Rainbow Lodge is a very popular place, with clean, spacious rooms, and it books up quickly. It has a large communal area, a sauna and a games area, and can arrange lots of activities and tours. Mountain bikes, fishing tackle and camping gear are available for hire.

Orange House (☎ 376 8105; orangehouse@ihug.co.nz; rooms per week NZ$80) Orange House is a small, private house with a pleasant garden, in a central (but secret!) location, designed to be a private, quiet, long-stay alternative to hostel accommodation (minimum stay one week). Phone ahead or ask at Go Global for details.

Chandler's Lodge (Map p569; ☎ 378 4927; chandlertaupo@xtra.co.nz; 135 Heu Heu St; s/d incl breakfast NZ$55/80; 💻) Could this lodge be any cosier? This is a small, friendly and intimate place, just a short walk from the town centre, with four self-contained motel units and two rooms with shared facilities. Other meals can be provided at an extra cost.

Go Global (Map p569; ☎ 0800 464 562, 377 0044; www.go-global.co.nz; cnr Tongariro & Tuwharetoa Sts; dm/s/d from NZ$21/35/50) Go Global is an ageing, knocked-about backpackers that has undergone some renovation in recent times. It's a big, sociable place, with rooms above Finn MacCuhal's pub and TVs in most rooms, so it's not the quietest place to stay. Check out the circular pool table.

Taupo Central Backpackers (Map p569; ☎ 378 3206; 7 Tuwharetoa St; dm/d NZ$23/55) This is another big old party-central backpackers that's now looking frayed around the edges, and it's all a little jaded and impersonal. There's a rooftop bar that gets lively at weekends, and all rooms have an attached bathroom.

De Bretts Thermal Resort (Map p575; ☎ 378 8559; www.debrettsresort.co.nz; SH5; camp sites per person from NZ$24, s/d from NZ$28/50; 💻) De Bretts is a five-star-rated holiday park next to Taupo Hot Springs. It's set in well-tended, park-like grounds and has a good choice of accommodation options, including sheltered sites, backpacker dorms and motel-style units.

Taupo Motor Camp (Map p569; ☎ 377 3080; www.taupomotorcamp.co.nz; 15 Redoubt St; camp sites per person from NZ$24, s/d from NZ$40/45) This is Taupo's most central camping ground, occupying a pleasant and spacious spot beside the Waikato River. It has stationary caravans, with or without showers (costing between NZ$45 and NZ$75) and a TV-lounge.

Eating & Drinking

Hell (Map p569; ☎ 0800 864 355, 377 8181; 30 Tuwharetoa St; pizzas NZ$6-14; 🕑 dinner) Hell is an excellent takeaway pizza joint, with a variety of diabolically innovative toppings such as 'Mordor', with venison pepperoni, and 'Underworld', with smoked mussels. It also has a good range of pastas and salads. Delivery is available.

JJ's Café (Map p569; ☎ 377 1545; 8 Roberts St; mains NZ$6.50-25; 🕑 breakfast, lunch & dinner) JJ's has a cheap, daytime menu, including all-day breakfasts, bagels and pasta. It has indoor and outdoor seating, and it's a popular backpacker hang-out.

Fat Fish (Map p569; ☎ 377 0086; 10 Roberts St; mains NZ$17-26; 🕑 breakfast, lunch & dinner) Fat Fish offers, as you might expect, varied fishy dishes as well as lamb, chicken, pizzas and *paninis*. It also serves good breakfasts and has outdoor seating.

Pub 'n' Grub (Map p569; ☎ 378 0555; Lake Tce; mains NZ$9.50-20; 🕑 breakfast & lunch) This is a friendly pub serving up traditional pub-grub standards like fish and chips, and bacon and eggs, plus a few surprises, such as oysters. It's also a good place for a beer or two.

Pasta Mia (Map p569; ☎ 377 2930; 26 Horomatangi St; mains from NZ$8; 🕑 breakfast, lunch & dinner) Relaxed Pasta Mia serves lots of pasta dishes, as well as sandwiches and cakes. It's a popular place for sitting back with a coffee.

Replete Café (Map p569; ☎ 377 3011; www.replete.co.nz; 45 Heu Heu St; mains from NZ$3.50; 🕑 breakfast & lunch) This perpetually busy café, with its menu of pies, *paninis*, burritos and sandwiches, is an excellent place for breakfast or brunch, and there's a well-stocked culinary shop attached.

Santorini (Map p569; ☎ 377 2205; 133 Tongariro St; mains NZ$16-25; 🕑 dinner Mon-Sat) Seat yourself at Santorini's first-floor balcony and enjoy Greek and Italian cuisine such as moussaka, linguini and chicken souvlaki.

Lotus (Map p569; ☎ 376 9497; 137 Tongariro St; mains NZ$10-20; 🕑 lunch & dinner Wed-Fri, dinner Sat-Mon)

Lotus is a gaudily decorated restaurant next door to Santorini. It serves up good-quality Thai food such as stir-fries and curries and it also does takeaways.

Asian Noodle House (Map p569; ☎ 377 6449; 9 Tongariro St; mains NZ$7-15; lunch & dinner) A large selection of vegetarian dishes, friendly service and generous portions makes this place a good takeaway or eat-in option.

Tongue & Groove (Map p569; ☎ 378 3900; 11 Tuwharetoa St) The Tongue & Groove is a smart upstairs bar and brasserie. There's a balcony, pool table and occasional live bands.

For self-caterers, **Pak N Save** (Map p569; ☎ 376 0999; Ruapehu St) and **Woolworths** (Map p569; ☎ 378 7040; Spa Rd) are both open late daily.

Entertainment

Holy Cow (Map p569; ☎ 378 7533; 11 Tongariro St) Located upstairs, the Holy Cow absolutely heaves after 11pm with much dancing and partying, mostly on table tops. People generally gravitate to this place once other places close.

Finn MacCuhal's (Map p569; ☎ 378 6165; Tuwharetoa St) This lively, dimly lit Irish pub packs in the punters, with DJs on weekends and a large outdoor patio, though it's pretty quiet during the day.

For movies, there's the **Starlight Cinema Centre** (Map p569; ☎ 378 7515; Starlight Arcade, off Horomatangi St).

Getting There & Away

AIR

Air New Zealand (☎ 0800 737 000, 378 5428; www.airnz.co.nz) flies direct to Auckland (from NZ$75) and Wellington (from NZ$85) each day, with onward connections. In Taupo, ticketing is handled through travel agencies, including **House of Travel** (Map p569; ☎ 378 2700; 37 Horomatangi St) and **Travel Smart Taupo** (Map p569; ☎ 378 9028; 28 Horomatangi St).

BUS

InterCity (☎ 378 9032; www.intercitycoach.co.nz) and **Alpine Scenic Tours** (☎ 386 8918) arrive at and depart from the **Taupo Travel Centre** (Map p569; ☎ 378 9032; 16 Gascoigne St). The travel centre also sells tickets for trains and the *Interislander* ferry (p641).

InterCity has several daily buses to Turangi (NZ$18, 45 minutes), Auckland (NZ$53, 4½ hours), Hamilton (NZ$33, 2¾ hours), Rotorua (NZ$23, one hour), Tauranga (NZ$45, 2¾ hours), Napier (NZ$36, two hours) and Wellington (NZ$70, 5¾ hours). In addition, the **Purpil People Mover Shuttle** (☎ 0800 787 745; www.purpilpeoplemover.co.nz) runs to Napier on weekdays (one way/return NZ$25/35), picking up and dropping off at your accommodation.

Shuttle services operate year-round between Taupo, Tongariro National Park and the Whakapapa Ski Area. Transport to the Tongariro Crossing costs NZ$30. During winter, shuttles travel daily and may include package deals for lift tickets and ski hire. Bookings can be made at the visitors centre (see p568) or at any hostel. **Tongariro Expeditions** (☎ 377 0435; www.tongariroexpeditions.com) has services departing Taupo at 5.40am and 6.20am (6am only June to October), returning at 3.30pm and 4.30pm. Note, though, that transport can be delayed or cancelled due to changeable weather conditions.

Getting Around

Taupo's Hot Bus (☎ 377 1967) does an hourly circuit of all the major attractions in and around Taupo. It leaves from the visitors centre on the hour from 10am to 6pm (each stop NZ$4, day pass NZ$10).

For a taxi, try **Taupo Taxis** (☎ 378 5100) or **Top Cabs** (Map p569; ☎ 378 9250), which has a taxi rank on Tuwharetoa St.

AROUND TAUPO

☎ 07

Wairakei Park

If you cross the river at Tongariro St and head north from town on SH1, you'll arrive at the Wairakei Park area, also known as the Huka Falls Tourist Loop.

On Tongariro St, take the first right turn after you cross the river and you'll be on Huka Falls Rd, which passes along the river. When returning to Taupo, turn left back to the highway and you'll pass other interesting spots on your way back.

There's no public transport but tours go to a few places along here; otherwise walk or hire a mountain bike for the day.

HUKA FALLS

Along Huka Falls Rd are the spectacular Huka Falls (Map p575), known as Hukanui in Maori, meaning 'Great Body of Spray'. A footbridge crosses the Waikato River above the falls – a great torrent of water, more like

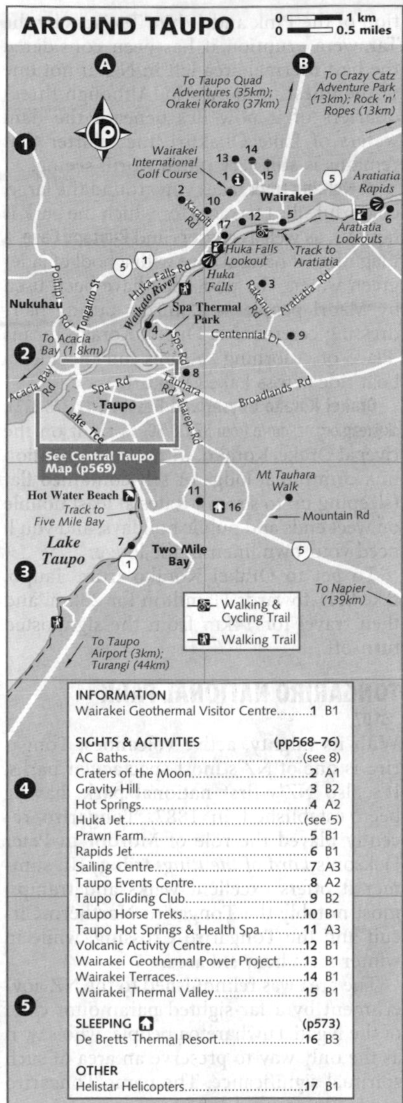

a giant rapid that plunges through a narrow cleft in the rock. The water here is clear and turquoise, particularly on a sunny day.

VOLCANIC ACTIVITY CENTRE

Budding vulcanologists will love this **activity centre & bookshop** (Map p575; ☎ 374 8375; www.volcanoes.co.nz; Huka Falls Loop Rd; admission NZ$6; 9am-5pm Mon-Fri, 10am-4pm Sat & Sun). The observatory monitors volcanic activity in the volatile Taupo Volcanic Zone, and the visitors centre has excellent displays on NZ's geothermal and volcanic activity. Exhibits include a large relief map with push-button highlighters to show the volcanic regions, and old documentaries about the eruptions of Ngauruhoe and Ruapehu in 1945 – the largest NZ eruptions last century. There's also a little booth you can sit in to experience what an earthquake feels like: press a button to shudder and shake in your seat.

HUKA JET & PRAWN FARM

The **Huka Jet** (Map p575; ☎ 0800 485 2538, 374 8572; www.hukajet.com; trips NZ$75) does a 30-minute jet-boat trip down the Waikato River to the Aratiatia Dam and up to Huka Falls. Trips run all day (price includes transport from Taupo).

Next door is the world's only geothermal-heated freshwater **prawn farm** (Map p575; ☎ 374 8474; www.prawnpark.com; admission NZ$6). There are tours on the hour between 11am and 4pm; tours are more frequent in summer. There's also **Killer Prawn Golf** (balls NZ$1 each, NZ$10 for 20).

ARATIATIA RAPIDS

Two kilometres off SH5 are the **Aratiatia Rapids** (Map p575), a spectacular part of the Waikato River until the government, in its wisdom, plonked down a powerhouse and dam, shutting off the water. To keep visitors happy it opens the control gates at various times: 10am, noon, 2pm and 4pm from 1 October to 31 March, and 10am, noon and 2pm from April to September. You can see the water flow through from three good vantage points (entry is free).

The **Rapids Jet** (Map p575; ☎ 0800 727 437, 378 5828; trips NZ$55) shoots up and down the lower part of the Aratiatia Rapids. It's a sensational 45-minute ride, with the jet-boats departing from the end of the access road to the Aratiatia lookouts. Go down Rapids Rd; look for the signpost to the National Equestrian Centre.

WAIRAKEI THERMAL VALLEY

This **thermal valley** (Map p575) gets its name from the water having once been used as a mirror, similar to Orakei Korako (p576). It is the remains of what was once known as

Geyser Valley, which before the geothermal power project started in 1958 was one of the most active thermal areas in the world, with 22 geysers and 240 mud pools and springs. It's now the site of **Wairakei Terraces** (Map p575; ☎ 378 0913; www.wairakeiterraces.co.nz; admission NZ$18; ⌚ tours 9am-5pm Oct-Mar, 9am-4.30pm Apr-Sep), a man-made landscape of silica terraces, pools and geysers, which attempts to recreate, in some small part, the appearance of the fabled Pink and White Terraces (see the Mt Tarawera Eruption boxed text; p602). There's also a **Maori Cultural Experience** (admission NZ$75; ⌚ 6.30pm), including a concert and *hangi* (traditional Maori earth-oven food). Other attractions on the site include an animal park, carriage rides, a 'Maori village' and a restaurant.

WAIRAKEI GEOTHERMAL POWER PROJECT

NZ was the second country in the world to produce power from natural steam. If you dive into all of that steam you'll find yourself at the **Wairakei Geothermal Power Project** (Map p575), which generates about 190MW, providing about 5% of NZ's electricity. The **visitors centre** (Map p575; ☎ 378 0913; admission NZ$2; ⌚ 9am-5pm summer, 9am-4.30pm winter) has information on the bore field and powerhouse, including an audiovisual.

CRATERS OF THE MOON

An interesting and unexploited thermal area is **Craters of the Moon** (Map p575; admission free, donations appreciated; ⌚ dawn-dusk), run by DOC and therefore less touristy than other commercially exploited thermal areas. Don't miss the lookout just before the car park – it's the best place for photos.

This thermal area sprang up in the 1950s. The power station lowered underground water levels, reducing the pressure of the heated water and causing more vigorous boiling and steam. New mud pools and steam vents appeared, and you can wander through them on a walkway.

Craters of the Moon is signposted on SH1, about 5km north of Taupo.

Orakei Korako

Between Taupo and Rotorua is the thermal area **Orakei Korako** (☎ 378 3131; www.orakeikorako.co.nz; admission NZ$21; ⌚ 8am-5pm). It receives fewer visitors than similar sites because of its remote location, but since the destruction of the Pink and White Terraces by the Tarawera eruption it has been considered the best thermal area left in NZ, if not one of the finest in the world. Although three-quarters of it now lies beneath the dam waters of Lake Ohakuri, the quarter that remains is still very much worth seeing.

A **walking track** takes you around the large, colourful silica terraces for which the park is famous, as well as geysers and **Ruatapu Cave**, a magnificent natural cave with a pool of jade-green water. The pool may have been used by Maori people as a mirror during hairdressing ceremonies: Orakei Korako means 'Place of Adorning'. Admission includes a boat ride across Lake Ohakuri.

Orakei Korako Geyserland Resort (☎ 378 3131; ok@reap.org.nz; dm/d from NZ$20/80) is right on the river at Orakei Korako, with accommodation in a communal lodge or self-contained flat (sleeping up to seven). Rates at least double on weekends and public holidays, and you'll need your own linen in the lodge.

To get to Orakei Korako from Taupo, take SH1 towards Hamilton for 23km, and then travel for 14km from the signposted turn-off.

TONGARIRO NATIONAL PARK

☎ 07

With its mighty, active volcanoes, Tongariro is one of NZ's most spectacular parks. It's also NZ's first national park, having been established in 1887. Tongariro recently played the role of Mordor in Peter Jackson's *Lord of the Rings* trilogy. In summer it offers excellent walks and tramps, most notably the Tongariro Northern Circuit and the Tongariro Crossing, while in winter it's a busy ski area.

The area was relinquished to the NZ government by a far-sighted paramount chief of the Ngati Tuwharetoa people, who saw it as the only way to preserve an area of such spiritual significance. The name Tongariro originally covered the three mountains of the park (Tongariro, Ngauruhoe and Ruapehu) and comes from *tonga* (south wind) and *riro* (carried away). The story goes that the famous *tohunga* (priest) Ngatoro-i-rangi was stuck on the summit and had almost perished from the cold. He called to his sisters in Hawaiki for fire, saying he was being 'carried away by the south wind'. As the sisters approached they stopped at

Whakaari (White Island), Tarawera, Rotorua and Taupo, igniting the fires that still smoulder in those places.

Information

The **visitors centre** (☎ 892 3729; 🕑 8am-6pm Dec-Apr, 8am-5pm May-Nov) is in Whakapapa (pronounced 'fa-ka-pa-pa') Village, on the park's northwestern side. It has lots of information on the park, including walks, huts and current skiing, track and weather conditions. The many displays on Tongariro's geological and human history make the centre an interesting place to visit. The detailed *Tongariro National Park* map (NZ$15) is worth buying before you go tramping, and you can pick up a number of DOC brochures on local walks.

DOC centres serving the park are in **Ohakune** (Ohakune Field Centre; ☎ 06-385 0010; www.ohakune.info; Ohakune Mountain Rd; 🕑 8am-3pm, 8am-5pm public hols), to the southwest, and **Turangi** (☎ 386 8607; near junction SH1 & Ohuanga Rd), to the north.

If you're visiting Tongariro National Park, remember that much of it experiences alpine conditions, which means that weather can change faster than you can say, 'Where did all those clouds come from?' See the boxed text (p580) for safety tips before setting out on your adventure.

There are no ATM facilities in either Whakapapa Village or National Park township, so stock up on cash at larger townships nearby such as Turangi.

Sights

MT RUAPEHU

The multipeaked summit of Mt Ruapehu (2797m) is the highest of the park's volcanoes, and the most active. The upper slopes were showered with hot mud and water in the volcanic activity of 1969 and 1975, and in December 1988 the volcano threw out some hot rocks. These were just tame precursors to the spectacular eruptions of September 1995, when Ruapehu sprayed volcanic rock and emitted massive clouds of ash and steam. From June to September the following year the mountain rumbled, groaned and sent ash clouds high into the sky. The 1996 ski season was pretty much a write-off, and local businesses really felt the pinch. The locals in Ohakune set up deck chairs at the end of their main street, sipped wine and observed the mountain's antics.

These eruptions were not the worst of the century, however. Between 1945 and 1947 the level of Crater Lake rose dramatically when eruptions blocked the overflow. On Christmas Eve 1953 the overflow burst and the flood led to one of NZ's worst natural disasters. The volcanic mudflow (known as a lahar) swept away a railway bridge at Tangiwai (between Ohakune and Waiouru) moments before a crowded express train arrived and 153 people lost their lives in the resulting collision.

The 1995–96 eruption once again blocked the overflow of Ruapehu's Crater Lake and caused it to start filling once more. Scientists predict that if the lake continues to fill at its current rate, another lahar will occur sometime in the not-too-distant future. DOC has set up alarm systems at Crater Lake's edge to monitor its build-up so that locals and emergency teams have plenty of warning should it decide to burst its banks.

MT TONGARIRO

Another old but still active volcano is Mt Tongariro (1967m). Red Crater last erupted in 1926. It has a number of coloured lakes dotting its uneven summit, as well as hot springs gushing out of its side at Ketetahi. The Tongariro Crossing (p579) is a magnificent walk passing beside the lakes, right through several craters and down into lush native forest.

MT NGAURUHOE

Much younger than the other volcanoes in the park is Mt Ngauruhoe (2287m); it's estimated to have formed in the last 2500 years and the slopes to its summit are still perfectly symmetrical. In contrast to Ruapehu and Tongariro, which have multiple vents, Ngauruhoe is a conical, single-vent volcano. It can be climbed in summer, but in winter (under snow) it is definitely only for experienced mountaineers. It's a steep but rewarding climb.

Both Ngauruhoe and Ruapehu were used in the *Lord of the Rings* films, but as you can see, it was Ngauruhoe that most resembled Mordor's Mt Doom.

Activities

TONGARIRO NORTHERN CIRCUIT

Classed as one of NZ's Great Walks (p777), the Northern Circuit, which starts and

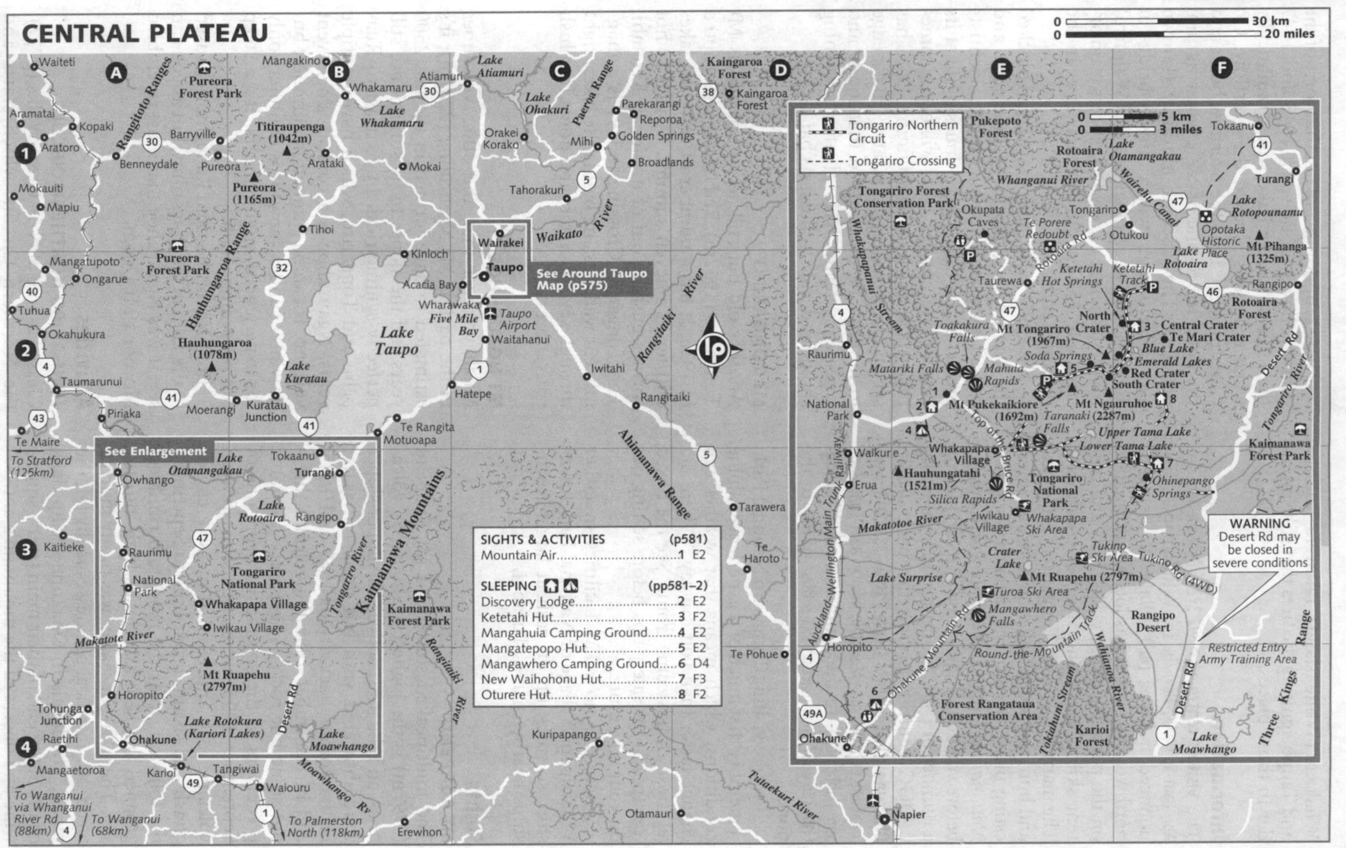
CENTRAL PLATEAU
0 30 km
0 20 miles
SIGHTS & ACTIVITIES (p581)
Mountain Air....1 E2
SLEEPING (pp581–2)
Discovery Lodge....2 E2
Ketetahi Hut....3 F2
Mangahuia Camping Ground....4 E2
Mangatepopo Hut....5 E2
Mangawhero Camping Ground....6 D4
New Waihohonu Hut....7 F3
Oturere Hut....8 F2
See Around Taupo Map (p575)
See Enlargement
Tongariro Northern Circuit
Tongariro Crossing
0 5 km
0 3 miles
WARNING
Desert Rd may be closed in severe conditions
Lake Taupo
Taupo
Wairakei
Kaimanawa Mountains
Ahimanawa Range
Hauhungaroa Range
Rangitoto Ranges
Pureora Forest Park
Kaingaroa Forest
Tongariro National Park
Tongariro Forest Conservation Park
Kaimanawa Forest Park
Forest Rangataua Conservation Area
Rangipo Desert
Restricted Entry Army Training Area
Three Kings Range
Mt Ruapehu (2797m)
Mt Tongariro (1967m)
Mt Ngauruhoe (2287m)
Mt Pukekaikiore (1692m)
Hauhungatahi (1521m)
Mt Pihanga (1325m)
Titiraupenga (1042m)
Pureora (1165m)
Hauhungaroa (1078m)
Whakapapa Village
Iwikau Village
National Park
Ohakune
Turangi
Tokaanu
To Stratford (125km)
To Wanganui via Whanganui River Rd (88km)
To Wanganui (68km)
To Palmerston North (118km)

finishes at Whakapapa Village (you can begin at Mangatepopo car park), normally takes three to four days to complete. The walk takes in Ngauruhoe, Tongariro and much of the famous one-day Tongariro Crossing.

Highlights of the circuit include tramping through several volcanic craters, including the **South Crater**, **Central Crater** and **Red Crater**; some brilliantly colourful volcanic lakes, including the **Emerald Lakes**, **Blue Lake** and the **Upper** and **Lower Tama Lakes**; the cold **Soda Springs** and **Ohinepango Springs**; and various other volcanic formations such as cones, lava flows and glacial valleys.

There are several possibilities for side trips that can take you from a few hours to overnight to complete. The most popular side trip from the main track is to **Ngauruhoe summit** (three hours), but it is also possible to climb from **Red Crater to Tongariro** (two hours) or walk from **New Waihohonu Hut to Ohinepango Springs** (30 minutes).

The safest, most popular time to walk the track is from December to March. The track is served by four huts: Mangatepopo, Ketetahi, Oturere and New Waihohonu. These have mattresses, gas heating (cookers in summer), toilets and water. Camping is allowed near all of the huts.

During the full summer season (from late October to early June), a Great Walks pass is required and must be bought in advance, whether you stay in the huts or camp beside them. All park visitors centres sell **Great Walks huts passes** (per person per night prebooked NZ$14, bought from hut warden NZ$18) and **camping passes** (per person NZ$10/12).

Outside (not during) the summer season, you can use ordinary **back-country hut tickets** (hut per night/camping per person NZ$10/5), and annual passes; for more info on tickets, see p774. However, the track is transformed into a tough alpine trek in winter, when it's covered in snow.

TONGARIRO CROSSING

Regarded as the finest one-day walk in NZ, the Tongariro Crossing covers many of the most spectacular features of the Tongariro Northern Circuit between Mangatepopo and Ketetahi Huts. On a clear day the views are magnificent. The track passes through vegetation zones ranging from alpine scrub and tussock, to places at higher altitudes where there is no vegetation at all, to the lush podocarp forest as you descend from Ketetahi Hut towards the end of the track. This is what many trampers do as day two of the Northern Circuit, with the extra walk along the Ketetahi track. Because of its popularity, shuttles are available to both ends of the track.

There are a couple of steep spots along the way, but most of the track is not terribly difficult. It's billed as a six- to seven-hour walk, but expect it to take longer if you're not in top condition. Some prefer to do it as a two-day walk, especially if side trips are included.

Worthwhile side trips include ascents of Mt Ngauruhoe and Mt Tongariro. Mt Ngauruhoe can be ascended most easily from the Mangatepopo Saddle, reached near the beginning of the track after the first steep climb. The summit of Tongariro is reached by a poled route from Red Crater.

The Mangatepopo Hut, reached via Mangatepopo Rd, is near the start of the track, and the Ketetahi Hut is a couple of hours before the end; to stay at or camp beside either hut in summer you must have a Great Walks pass, purchased in advance and valid from the end of October until the Queen's Birthday weekend. The Ketetahi Hut is the most popular in the park. It has bunks to sleep 24 people, but regularly has 50 to 60 people trying to stay there on Saturday night and at the busiest times of year (summer and school holidays). As bunks are claimed on a first-come, first-served basis, it's not a bad idea to bring camping gear, just in case. Campers can use all of the hut facilities, which can make the kitchen crowded, especially during peak times.

CRATER LAKE WALKS

When Ruapehu is volcanically active, the area within 1.5km of Crater Lake is off limits; check with DOC park offices for the latest information.

The walk to Crater Lake (seven hours return: four hours up, three hours down) in the crater of Ruapehu begins at Iwikau Village, at the end of Top of the Bruce Rd above Whakapapa Village. It's definitely not an easy stroll and the track isn't marked. Even in summer there may be ice and snow to get through; in winter, forget it unless you are an experienced mountaineer.

TRACK SAFETY

The weather on the mountains is capricious – it can change from brilliant sunshine to snow, hail or wind within a few minutes. Be sure to check with a DOC office for current track and weather conditions before setting out. Bring a raincoat and warm woollen clothing. Take local advice seriously: they know the mountains best and it's their time, money and effort that's going to be expended getting you back safe and sound.

Accidents occur on tracks when people misjudge loose rocks or go sliding down the volcanic slopes, so watch your step! On Ngauruhoe, watch out for loose scoria, and be careful not to dislodge rocks onto people coming up behind you.

Essential equipment for walking in the park:

- waterproof raincoat and overtrousers
- warm clothing
- tramping boots
- food and drink
- first-aid kit
- sunscreen and sunglasses
- sun hat and warm hat

In winter, alpine or mountaineering experience is essential if you are walking many tracks, especially climbing peaks. If you don't know how to use ice axes, crampons and avalanche gear, do not attempt the summits.

Be sure to check with the Whakapapa visitors centre for current weather conditions before you set off. Boots, sunglasses and windproof clothing are always essential, while ice axes and crampons may be needed on some parts of the track.

From December to April you can use the **chairlift** (adult NZ$17; 9am-4pm) at the Whakapapa Ski Area to get you up the mountain, cutting about three hours off the walk. **Guided walks** (892 3738; incl lift pass adult NZ$65) to Crater Lake leave daily at 9.30am from the chairlift.

You can reach Crater Lake from the Ohakune side, but the track is steeper and ice axes and crampons are always necessary (to ascend a steep glacier). From this side, allow five hours to go up and three hours to go down.

OTHER WALKS

Keen trampers can do the entire **Round-the-Mountain Track** (four to six days), which circumnavigates Ruapehu. It's one of the least-tramped tracks in the park, and the terrain varies from beech forest to desert. Be sure to get a good map (such as Parkmaps No 273-04) before attempting to walk this track.

From Whakapapa Village

A number of fine walks begin at or near the Whakapapa visitors centre and from the road leading up to the centre. Several other good walks take off from the road leading from Ohakune to the Turoa Ski Area. DOC's *Whakapapa Walks* (NZ$1) has details of many such walks, including the following:

Ridge Track A 30-minute return walk, which climbs through beech forest to alpine shrub for views of Ruapehu and Ngauruhoe.

Silica Rapids A 7km loop track to the Silica Rapids (2½ hours), named for the silica mineral deposits formed here by the rapids on Waikare Stream. The track passes interesting alpine features.

Tama Lakes A 17km track to the Tama Lakes (five to six hours return). These lakes, on the Tama Saddle between Ruapehu and Ngauruhoe, are great for a refreshing swim. The upper lake affords fine views of Ngauruhoe and Tongariro (beware of winds on the saddle).

Taranaki Falls A 6km loop track to the 20m-high Taranaki Falls (two hours) on Wairere Stream.

Whakapapa Nature Walk A 15-minute loop track suitable for wheelchairs, beginning about 200m above the visitors centre and passing through beech forest and gardens typical of the park's vegetation zones.

North of Whakapapa Village

Still more tracks take off from SH47, on the national park's northern side, including the following:

Lake Rotoaira On the shores of Lake Rotoaira are excavations of a pre-European Maori village site, the Opotaka Historic Place.

Mahuia Rapids About 2km north of the turn-off leading to Whakapapa, SH47 crosses the Whakapapanui Stream just below the rapids, which makes a nice destination for a walk.

Matariki Falls A 20-minute return track to the falls takes off from SH47 about 200m from the Mahuia Rapids car park.

SKIING & SNOWBOARDING

The two main ski areas are **Turoa** and **Whakapapa** (☎ 892 3738; www.whakapapa.co.nz; daily lift pass NZ$70); Whakapapa (1630m) lies above Whakapapa Village, while Turoa is to the south. The **Tukino Ski Area** (☎ 06-387 6294; www.tukino.co.nz; daily lift pass NZ$30), on the eastern side of Ruapehu, is only accessible by a 4WD road.

The only accommodation at the ski fields is in private lodges, so most skiers stay at Whakapapa Village, National Park township or Ohakune. One pass is valid for both Whakapapa and Turoa.

OTHER ACTIVITIES

Mountain Air (☎ 0800 922 812; www.mountainair.co.nz; SH47; flights from NZ$70) conducts memorable flights over the volcanoes.

Plateau Outdoor Adventure Guides (☎ 892 2740) is based at Raurimu, 6km north of National Park township. It offers a wide variety of activities around Tongariro and the Whanganui River, including canoeing, kayaking, whitewater rafting and tramping.

Sleeping

Whakapapa Village has a limited supply of accommodation. The towns of National Park, Ohakune and Turangi are all near the park and offer a greater range of overnight options.

Skotel Alpine Resort (☎ 0800 756 835, 892 3719; www.skotel.co.nz; dm NZ$20, d from NZ$110; 💻) This is a cosy, woody hotel with a homely and relaxing ambience. There's a choice of accommodation including self-contained chalets, sleeping up to seven people, while facilities include a sauna, spa pool, gym, ski shop, games room and a licensed restaurant and bar. Bedding for dorm rooms costs NZ$5 extra.

Whakapapa Holiday Park (☎ 892 3897; whakapapaholpark@xtra.co.nz; camp sites per person NZ$22, dm/d NZ$18/55) This well-maintained, popular park is opposite the visitors centre, 6km from the Whakapapa Ski Area. It's in a pretty spot and offers a wide range of accommodation options, including a 32-bed backpackers lodge.

The park has two basic **DOC camping grounds** (camp sites per person NZ$5): **Mangahuia** (SH47) is between National Park and the SH48 turn-off to Whakapapa, while **Mangawhero** (Ohakune Mountain Rd) is near Ohakune. Both grounds are basic, with cold water and pit toilets. Payment is via an honesty box.

Eating & Drinking

Tussock (SH48, Whakapapa Village; mains NZ$11-17; 🕑 lunch & dinner) Serves up above-average pizzas, plus burgers and other tavern-style fare. The bar area and big-screen TV get a workout when major sports events are on. There's also occasional live entertainment in winter, when an open fire helps to warm things up.

Whakapapa Camp Store (SH48, Whakapapa Village) Sells a range of takeaway snacks and food for self-catering.

Getting There & Away

The main gateway to Tongariro is National Park township; see that section (p582) for details of bus and train transport to the area.

Alpine Scenic Tours (☎ 386 8918; www.alpinescenictours.co.nz; tickets NZ$30) has a shuttle departing Taupo (6.30am) for Whakapapa Village (arriving 8.25am) via Turangi (7.30am), Ketetahi car park (at the end of the Tongariro Crossing) and Mangatepopo car park (for the Tongariro Crossing). Various shuttles run between Turangi, Whakapapa Village and National Park township during the day, and they go up to the ski area at Top of the Bruce Rd by request. Book in advance to guarantee a spot, as seats are limited, and there are no phones at the trail heads.

Tongariro Track Transport (☎ 892 3716; tickets NZ$20) specialises in the Tongariro Crossing and has buses departing Whakapapa and National Park.

NATIONAL PARK

☎ **07 / pop 460**

The small settlement of **National Park** (www.nationalpark.co.nz) is 15km west of Whakapapa Village and serves as one of the gateways to Tongariro. It caters to the ski-season crowds with plenty of accommodation, but has little else apart from great views of Ruapehu. In summer, it's a good base for the walks and attractions of the park.

Activities

Howard's Lodge, Pukenui Lodge and Ski Haus (all listed under Sleeping, below) hire out gear for the Tongariro Crossing and other treks. The spa pools at Ski Haus and Pukenui Lodge can be hired by nonguests.

Howard's Lodge takes guided **mountain-bike tours** (2hr trips from NZ$20). It also provides transport and bike hire for the 21km downhill **Fishers Track**, as well as the **42nd Traverse**, an excellent 46km mountain-bike trail through Tongariro Forest that is classed among the best one-day rides in NZ.

Adrift Guided Outdoor Adventures (☎ 0800 462 374; www.adriftnz.co.nz) runs canoe adventures (one-/six-day trips NZ$230/800) and guided treks (from NZ$135). **Tongariro River Rafting** (☎ 0800 101 024; www.tongariro-riverrafting.com) offers white-water rafting on the Tongariro River, as well as kayaking and mountain-biking excursions.

For those rainy days there's an 8m-high indoor **climbing wall** (☎ 892 2870; www.npbp.co.nz; Finlay St; admission NZ$12, with own gear NZ$9; 9am-9pm) at National Park Backpackers (see following), with 55 different climbs.

Sleeping

Ski Haus (☎ 892 2854; www.skihaus.co.nz; Carroll St; camp sites per person NZ$18, dm/d from NZ$18/55; 💻) Ski Haus is a cosy wood-cabin affair that's been operating for a quarter of a century. It features an alpine-style lounge with a welcoming log fire at its heart. It has a spa pool and billiards table for chilly evenings and there is a bar, kitchen and a restaurant offering breakfast and dinner. Dorm rooms and doubles are simple but comfortable and there's also a three-bedroom cottage (from NZ$90) if you're after a bit more privacy.

Howard's Lodge (☎ 892 2827; www.howardslodge.co.nz; 11-13 Carroll St; dm/d from NZ$19/55; 💻) Howard's Lodge is an excellent place, and has a spa pool, comfortable lounge and spotless, well-equipped kitchens. There's a range of rooms to choose from, and meals are available at an extra cost. Ski, snowboard, tramping gear and mountain-bike hire are available.

National Park Backpackers (☎ 892 2870; www.npbp.co.nz; Finlay St; camp sites per person NZ$24, dm/d from NZ$18/50; 💻) This popular and welcoming backpackers has basic but neat rooms, most with bathroom facilities. The big attraction is the climbing wall (discounted use for guests), and there's also a barbecue, hot tub and indoor badminton court.

Discovery Lodge (☎ 0800 122 122; www.discovery.net.nz; SH47; camp sites from per person NZ$16, dm from NZ$30; 💻) Located between National Park and Whakapapa, this place has a spa pool, restaurant, bar and comfy lounge with a pool table and big-screen TV. The pricier backpacker cabins (NZ$65) have a bathroom and bedding. There's room for campervans.

Adventure Lodge & Motel (☎ 892 2991; www.adventurenationalpark.co.nz; Carroll St; dm/d from NZ$20/80; 💻) Adventure Lodge is a friendly, laid-back, modern place with good package deals on offer. It has excellent facilities, including spa pools, volleyball, *boules* and a barbecue, and meals are available. Bring your own bedding for the dorm rooms or hire it for NZ$7.

Pukenui Lodge (☎ 0800 785 368; www.tongariro.cc; Millar St; dm/d from NZ$22/95; 💻) The picturesque Pukenui has a variety of rooms, including a smart self-contained three-bedroom chalet (from NZ$100). Prices rise on weekends, when dinner is included. There is a spa, kitchen and restaurant, and the lodge sells lift passes and can organise Tongariro track transport and activities.

Eating

All the places to stay in National Park provide either meals or kitchens (or both) for their guests.

Basekamp (☎ 892 2872; Carroll St; burgers around NZ$6; lunch & dinner) Basekamp offers a menu of 19 different hearty 'gourmet' burgers, as well as pizzas.

Schnapps (☎ 892 2788; Findlay St; mains around NZ$15; dinner) Schnapps is a congenial place for a drink or a meal. There are excellent pizzas, burgers, steaks and more, and in winter there are often bands on Saturday night.

Getting There & Away

BUS

The buses of **InterCity** (☎ 09-913 6100; www.intercitycoach.co.nz) arrive at and depart from outside Ski Haus on Carroll St daily except Saturday; buy tickets at Ski Haus and Howard's Lodge. Journeys north to Auckland (NZ$60) via Hamilton (NZ$35) or south to Wellington (NZ$80) via Palmerston North (NZ$50) take between five and six hours.

Alpine Scenic Tours (☎ 386 8918) has twice-daily shuttles that make a return trip between Turangi and National Park (NZ$25), with stops at Whakapapa Village, Whakapapa Ski Area (by request), the Mangatepopo and Ketetahi car parks (Tongariro Crossing), and on from Turangi to Taupo. Arrange any track transport beforehand, as there are no phones at the trail heads.

Tongariro Track Transport (☎ 892 3716) operates a daily shuttle from National Park to the Mangatepopo car park, stopping at Whakapapa Village on the way (return NZ$20).

Howard's Lodge also runs a shuttle (NZ$18 return) for the Tongariro Crossing; bookings essential.

TRAIN

Tranz Scenic (☎ 0800 872 467, 04-495 0775; www.tranzscenic.co.nz) operates the *Overlander* trains on a route between Auckland and Wellington, stopping at National Park along the way. Train tickets (National Park to Auckland from NZ$35, to Wellington from NZ$35) are available from Ski Haus and Howard's Lodge, not from the train station.

TARANAKI

The **Taranaki** (www.taranakinz.org) region juts into the Tasman Sea on the west coast of the North Island, about halfway between Auckland and Wellington. The region is named after the Mt Taranaki volcano, also called Mt Egmont, the huge cone of which dominates the landscape. It's the 'most climbed' mountain in NZ and was the stand-in for Mt Fuji in Tom Cruise's *The Last Samurai*, filmed here in 2003; see the boxed text (p585). The 'big smoke' for the area is New Plymouth.

The names Taranaki and Egmont are both widely used in the region; Taranaki is the Maori name for the volcano and Egmont is the name James Cook gave it in 1770, after the Earl of Egmont. Egmont National Park retains its name but Taranaki and Egmont are *both* official names for the volcano.

Activities

Tramping in Egmont National Park and climbing up or skiing down the park's centrepiece volcano, Mt Taranaki/Egmont, are popular things to do in this area, though heed the mountain's dangerous reputation (see Tramping & Climbing, p588). The Taranaki region is also renowned for its world-class surfing and sailboarding beaches along SH45, appropriately dubbed the 'Surf Highway'.

NEW PLYMOUTH

☎ 06 / pop 49,100

A coastal city surrounded by fertile agricultural and dairy lands, New Plymouth is a friendly community and a superb base for visiting Egmont National Park. Apart from excellent beach and parkland walkways, there are some established leafy parks and the spectacular backdrop of Mt Taranaki/Egmont.

Information

For information about the region pick up the *Taranaki* guide from the visitors centre, or visit www.windwand.co.nz.

DOC office (☎ 758 0433; www.doc.govt.nz; 220 Devon St West; 8am-4.30pm Mon-Fri) Info on Egmont National Park.

Interplay Internet Café (☎ 758 1918; Top Town Complex; per 30min/1hr NZ$3/5)

New Plymouth visitors centre (☎ 759 6060; www.newplymouthnz.com; 1 Ariki St; 9am-6pm Mon, Tue, Thu & Fri, 9am-9pm Wed, 9am-5pm Sat & Sun) Offers Internet access.

Phoenix Urgent Doctors (☎ 759 4295; 95 Vivian St; 8am-10pm) For medical help.

Sights

GOVETT-BREWSTER ART GALLERY

The **Govett-Brewster Art Gallery** (☎ 759 6060; www.govettbrewster.com; cnr Queen & King Sts; admission free; 10.30am-5pm) is a fantastic contemporary art gallery that is renowned throughout NZ. It has a reputation for adventurous, often international shows where artists look at life from unique and bizarre perspectives. Even if art's not your thang, a visit to the Govett-Brewster is totally worthwhile. Fans of abstract animation should seek out the films of Len Lye, pioneer animator of the 1930s, whose works are held here and shown from time to time.

PUKE ARIKI & MAORI CRAFTS

Puke Ariki (☎ 759 6060; www.pukeariki.com; 1 Ariki St; admission free; 9am-6pm Mon-Fri, 9am-5pm Sat & Sun), meaning 'Hill of Chiefs' and named after a New Plymouth Maori *pa*, is a stunning complex housing the visitors centre and a **museum** (admission free) with an extensive collection of Maori artefacts, wildlife and colonial exhibits.

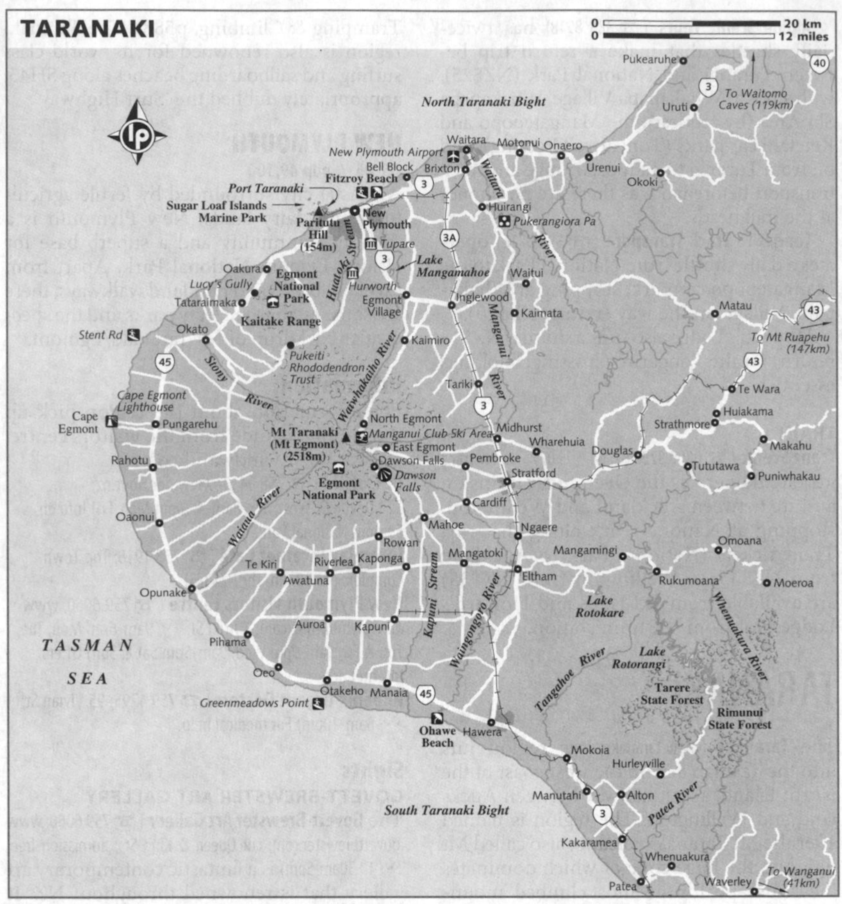

Also here is the **Richmond Cottage & Heritage Garden** (admission NZ$1). Unlike most early cottages, which were made of timber, sturdy Richmond Cottage was built of stone in 1853. The interior is still under development, but the gardens are a mixture of old-world and rare NZ natives.

Bone and woodcarvings from local students are on display at the **Rangimarie Maori Arts & Crafts Centre** (☎ 751 2880; www.windwand.co.nz; 80 Centennial Dr; admission free; 9am-4pm Mon-Fri), 3km west of town at the foot of Paritutu Hill.

HISTORIC PLACES

The free *Heritage Walkway* leaflet, obtainable from the visitors centre, outlines an interesting self-guided tour of around 30 historic sites.

St Mary's Church (Vivian St), built 1846, is the oldest stone church in NZ. Its graveyard has headstones of early settlers and of soldiers who died during the Taranaki Land Wars (1860–61 and 1865–69), when local Maori warriors fought settlers and the colonial government for the fertile land around Waitara. Impressed by their bravery, the British also buried several Maori chiefs here.

At the eastern end of the city is the **Fitzroy Pole** (Devon St), erected by the Maori community in 1844 to mark the point beyond which Governor Fitzroy had originally forbidden settlers to acquire land (later revoked). The carving on the bottom of the pole depicts a sorrowful pakeha topped by a cheerfully triumphant Maori.

PARITUTU

Above the power station is Paritutu, a steep hill with a magnificent view from the top. The name means 'Rising Precipice' and it's worth the tiring but quick scramble to the summit. You look out over the city and the rocky Sugar Loaf Islands looming just offshore.

PARKS

Pukekura Park (☎ 759 6060; www.newplymouthnz.com) is a 10-minute walk south of the city centre and has 49 hectares of gardens, bushwalks, streams, waterfalls and ponds. There are also **display houses** (admission free; 🕑 8am-4pm) with orchids and other exotic plants, and **rowboats** (per 30min NZ$5) can be hired on the lake at weekends and on summer evenings.

Adjoining Pukekura is the lovely **Brooklands Park** and, between them, the Bowl of Brooklands, an outdoor sound-shell in a bush and lake setting. Brooklands Park was once the land around an important early settler's home; the fireplace and chimney are all that remain of the house after the Maori burnt it down. Highlights include a 2000-year-old puriri tree, a rhododendron dell with over 300 varieties, a great children's **zoo** (admission free; 🕑 8.30am-5pm), which has a walk-through monkey enclosure, and the **Gables** (admission free; 🕑 1-4pm Sat & Sun), one of the oldest hospitals in NZ, now converted into an art gallery and medical museum.

SAMURAI TOURS

Fans of the Tom Cruise flick *The Last Samurai* should hightail it to Uruti, 50km northeast of New Plymouth, where a Japanese village set was erected in a valley situated on a 800-hectare cattle-and-sheep farm. The original set (which took six months to build) was dismantled after Cruise and co wrapped up a seven-week shoot early in 2003, but the farm's owners have re-created several of the structures, including a Japanese hut and a water wheel, and embellished them with photos and props. You can take 1½-hour tours of the **Samurai Village** (☎ 06-752 6806; www.samuraivillagetours.com; adults NZ$35; tours 🕑 Mon, Wed, Fri & Sun), accompanied by a commentary on the making of the film; bookings are essential. A splendid backdrop is provided by Mt Taranaki/Egmont to the south, which acted as a stand-in for Japan's Mt Fuji.

InterCity (☎ 06-759 9039; www.intercitycoach.co.nz) buses run from New Plymouth to Uruti, or talk to the tour operators about arranging transport from New Plymouth.

SUGAR LOAF ISLANDS MARINE PARK

This marine park, established in 1986, includes the rocky islets offshore from the power station, Back Beach on the west side of Paritutu and the waters up to about 1km offshore. The islands are eroded volcanic remnants and are an isolated refuge for sea birds, **NZ fur seals** and marine life; the greatest number of seals appears from June to October but some are there year-round.

Boat trips to these islands are popular in summer. **Happy Chaddy's Charters** (☎ 758 9133; www.windwand.co.nz/chaddiescharters; adult NZ$20) has boats departing from Lee Breakwater, tide and weather permitting.

Activities

SURFING & SAILBOARDING

Besides being beautiful, the Taranaki coastline is a world-class surfing and sailboarding area. **Fitzroy** and **East End Beaches** are both at the eastern end of New Plymouth. There's also decent surf at **Back Beach**, by Paritutu at the western end of the city, and at **Oakura**, about 15km west of New Plymouth. There are no buses to Oakura but hitching is easy. Fine surf beaches extend all along SH45.

Vertigo (☎ 752 8283; vertigosurf@xtra.co.nz; 605 Surf Hwy 45, Oakura) hires out surfboards and sailboards and offers instruction. **Tangaroa Adventures** (☎ 021-701 904; tangaroa.adventures@xtra.co.nz; 25 Collins St, Hawera) and **Taranaki Coastal Surf Charters** (☎ 025-592 306) both provide guided surf tours of the area, while the inexperienced can get some experience with **Tandem Surfing** (☎ 752 7734; www.hang20.com; 27 Maise Tce, Oakura) – they guarantee you'll stand up. **Carbon Art** (☎ 0508 946 376; carbonart@xtra.co.nz; Ngamotu Beach) specialises in sailboard hire and lessons.

WALKING

The visitors centre has useful leaflets detailing walks around New Plymouth, including coastal, reserve and park walks, in addition to the **Heritage Walkway** (opposite). The 7km

Coastal Walkway, from Lake Rotomanu to Port Taranaki, is a personal favourite. **Te Henui Walkway**, from the coast at East End Reserve to the city's southern boundary, is one of the most interesting and varied walks. **Huatoki Valley Walkway**, following Huatoki Stream, makes an attractive walk to the city centre.

CYCLING

Cycle Inn Bike Hire (☎ 758 7418; 133 Devon St; bikes per day NZ$20-30) rents bicycles.

Tours

Several operators offer scenic flights over the snowcapped summit of Mt Taranaki/Egmont, including **New Plymouth Aero Club** (☎ 755 0500; www.airnewplymouth.co.nz; flights from NZ$65).

Sleeping

Sunflower Lodge (☎ 759 0050; www.sunflowerlodge.co.nz; 25 Ariki St; dm NZ$20-22, s NZ$40, tw & d NZ$50-60; 💻) Has great single and double rooms with your own TV, cupboard, lounge chair (and footrest!). A fantastic balcony overlooks the ocean and there's a homey lounge room and a big clean kitchen. Sunflower Lodge has friendly owners and is great value.

Shoestring Budget Backpackers (☎ 758 0404; shoestringb@xtra.co.nz; 48 Lemon St; dm/s NZ$19/27, tw & d NZ$40-50) Shoestring backpackers is friendly and central but the real drawcard is the beautiful heritage building, built in 1910 (they think), its interior made with rimu timber. Rooms are upstairs (away from the communal areas), there's a small kitchen and separate dining area, small sauna and mega-relaxing sunroom with superb ocean views.

Cottage Mews (☎ 758 0403; shoestringb@xtra.co.nz; 48 Lemon St; s/d NZ$65/75) This place is next door to Shoestring Budget Backpackers (where you check in) and has good-value, well-kept studios and one-bedroom units.

Egmont Lodge YHA (☎ 753 5720; www.taranaki-bakpak.co.nz; 12 Clawton St; camp sites per person NZ$22, dm/s NZ$20/30, d & tw NZ$50) A tranquil hostel in park-like grounds with a stream running through it – you can even feed the eels. There are 10-bed mixed dorms, a small kitchen and a communal living area that opens onto a veranda surrounded by tree ferns. It's 15 minutes from town on a pleasant streamside walkway or phone for a free pick up from the bus station. The famous 'Mt Egmont' cake, made nightly, is a sight to behold.

Central Motel (☎ 758 6444; central.new.plymouth@xtra.co.nz; 86 Elliot St; s/d NZ$65/75) Up the hill on Elliot St, Central Motel is indeed central and has tidy studio units with a small kitchen and optional Sky TV. Excellent value.

Burton's State Hotel (☎ 758 5373; statehotel@burtons.org.nz; cnr Devon St East & Gover St; s NZ$55, d & tw NZ$70) Above Burton's Restaurant & Bar, this is excellent pub accommodation at reasonable rates. Rooms have a bathroom and TV.

Belt Road Holiday Park (☎ 0800 804 204, 758 0228; www.beltroad.co.nz; 2 Belt Rd; camp sites per person NZ$20, s & d NZ$30-75) This pohutukawa-sheltered holiday park is on a bluff overlooking the port, 1.5km west of the town centre. Cabin prices depend on facilities.

New Plymouth Top 10 Holiday Park (☎ 758 2566; www.nptop10.co.nz; 29 Princes St; camp sites per person NZ$20, d NZ$40-100) This park is in Fitzroy, 3.5km east of the centre. It has a shady camping area.

Eating & Drinking

Simply Read Café & Bookshop (☎ 757 8667; cnr Dawson & Hine Sts; meals NZ$6-12; 🕑 breakfast, lunch & dinner) With beautiful water views, Simply Read is a cheerful, popular café with a small bookshop. Its blackboard menu changes regularly and home-style meals include mushroom strudel, chicken lasagne and vegetable filos, plus a tempting selection of cakes and muffins.

Daily News Café (☎ 759 6060; 1 Ariki St; meals NZ$5-10; 🕑 lunch) Where current affairs cost a cup of coffee. In the south wing of the Puke Ariki complex, you can select from a range of daily newspapers or listen to the radio through headphones while drinking espresso and eating fresh focaccias and *panini*.

Ozone Coffee Factory (☎ 779 9020; 121 Devon St East; meals NZ$6.50-13; 🕑 lunch) A terrific café for a strong, heart-starting brew of aromatic Ozone coffee (these guys supply many of the cafés around New Plymouth). Lunchtime sandwiches and hot food are equally delicious.

Ultra Lounge (☎ 758 8444; 75 Devon St East; lunch NZ$5-14, dinner NZ$17-30; 🕑 lunch & dinner) Ultra Lounge falls into many categories and does each one equally well – funky café with full-bodied coffee and sticks of loose-leaf tea, a superb restaurant, and mellow cocktail lounge bar. Food here is truly excellent. For brunch the bacon and egg butty with wholegrain mustard hollandaise can't be beaten.

Baja (☎ 757 8217; 17 Devon St; mains NZ$9.30-20) A great range of Mexican food with a delightful lack of sombreros. Feast on Tex-Mex *quesadillas*, enchiladas and *fajitas* with chicken, beef or veg fillings. There's a big screen for sport and Baja is also fun for a drink or two.

El Condor (☎ 757 5436; 170 Devon St East; meals NZ$11-24; dinner Tue-Sat) El Condor, near the corner of Gover St, is a pizza and pasta place with a difference – it's Argentinean. Feast on home-made cannelloni and double-layered pizza.

Portofino (☎ 757 8686; 14 Gill St; mains NZ$15-19; dinner) This Italian restaurant has a huge selection of pasta dishes and steaming wood-fired pizzas with thick and tasty toppings. Takeaways are available and it's fully licensed.

Mill Bar & Restaurant (☎ 758 1935; 2 Courtenay St; meals NZ$11-25; lunch & dinner) The Mill specialises in Stonegrill – a piping hot stone (supposedly heated to 400°C) is used to cook your meat selection at your table. This way you get to cook your steak just the way like it. The large bar is a popular place for a night out, and often has live bands at weekends.

Sandwich Extreme (☎ 759 6999; 52 Devon St East; dishes NZ$5.50-7.50; lunch) This little eatery makes fresh, filling sandwiches, toasties and baked potatoes to eat in or take away.

Grabba kebab (☎ 757 8158; 211a Devon St East; kebabs NZ$7-9) Tasty kebabs are served at this ever-reliable takeaway.

In the Centre City shopping centre there's a food hall with Chinese and Italian food, seafood, wholefood, sandwich and dessert counters.

Pak N Save (☎ 758 1594; Gill St) is a supermarket selling cheap groceries. Another useful supermarket is **Woolworths** (☎ 759 7481; btwn Leach & Courtenay Sts). **Down to Earth** (☎ 7585 9677; cnr Devon St West & Morley St) is an organic wholefood shop selling dry goods, dairy, honey etc.

Peggy Gordon's Celtic Bar (☎ 758 8561; cnr Devon St West & Egmont St) is a relaxed Irish bar with live music at the weekends. Go here at night.

Entertainment

Ultra Lounge (☎ 758 8444; 75 Devon St East) Ultra Lounge has DJs spinning ambient house and mellow hip-hop on Friday nights.

Crowded House (☎ 759 4921; www.crowdedhouse.co.nz; Devon St East) Another very popular night-spot, welcoming people of all ages into its literally crowded interior.

Bowl of Brooklands (☎ 759 6080; www.bowl.co.nz; Brooklands Park) A large outdoor theatre. Check with the visitors centre for current concert schedules and prices.

Getting There & Away

AIR

Air New Zealand Link (☎ 0800 737 000, 737 3300; www.airnz.co.nz; 12-14 Devon St East) has daily direct flights to/from Auckland (from NZ$75) and Wellington (from NZ$80), with onward connections to Christchurch and Nelson. **Origin Pacific** (☎ 0800 302 302, 03-547 2020; www.originpacific.co.nz) also has direct flights to Wellington (from NZ$80) and Auckland (from NZ$70) with onward connections.

BUS

InterCity (☎ 759 9039; www.intercitycoach.co.nz; behind Centre City shopping centre) runs buses to/from Hamilton (NZ$33, four hours, one daily), Auckland (NZ$55, six hours, one daily), Wanganui (NZ$16, three hours), Palmerston North (NZ$45, four hours) and Wellington (NZ$60, four hours). Book tickets at **Travel Centre** (☎ 759 9039; 2nd fl, Centre City, 120 Devon St).

Dalroy Express (☎ 0508 465 622; www.dalroytours.co.nz; 7 Erica Pl) operates a daily service between Auckland (NZ$65, four hours) and Hawera (NZ$13, four hours) via New Plymouth and Hamilton (NZ$45, two hours).

White Star (City to City) (☎ 06-758 3338; 25 Liardet St) has two daily buses during weekdays and one at weekends to/from Wanganui (NZ$22, 2½ hours), Palmerston North (NZ$30, 3¾ hours) and Wellington (NZ$45, 6¼ hours).

See p590 for details of shuttle services from New Plymouth to Mt Taranaki/Egmont.

Getting Around

New Plymouth Airport (☎ 755 2250) is 11km east of the centre. **Withers** (☎ 0800 751 177, 751 1777; www.withers.co.nz; adult NZ$12) operates a door-to-door shuttle to/from the airport; you can book online.

Okato Bus Lines (☎ 758 2799; okatobus@xtra.co.nz; Stanley St) serves the city and its surrounding suburbs from Monday to Saturday; timetables sell for NZ$0.50. The main bus stop is outside the Centre City shopping centre.

MT TARANAKI/EGMONT

☎ 06

The massive cone of 2518m-high Taranaki, a dormant volcano that looks remarkably like

Japan's Mt Fuji or the Philippines' Mayon, dominates the Taranaki region.

Geologically, Mt Taranaki is the youngest of a series of three large volcanoes on one fault line, the others being Kaitake and Pouakai. Mt Taranaki/Egmont last erupted 350 years ago and is considered dormant rather than extinct. The top 1400m is covered in lava flows, a few of them descending to 800m above sea level. An interesting feature is the small subsidiary cone on the flank of the main cone, 2km south of the main crater, called Fantham's Peak (1962m).

Mt Taranaki is supremely sacred to the Maori community, both as a burial site for chiefs and as a hide-out in times of danger. According to legend, Taranaki was once a part of the Tongariro group of volcanoes. He was forced to leave rather hurriedly when Tongariro caught him with the beautiful Pihanga, the volcano near Lake Taupo who was Tongariro's lover. Taranaki gouged a wide scar in the earth (the Whanganui River) as he fled south in anger, pain and shame, moving west to his current position where he hides his face behind a cloud of tears.

There's a saying in Taranaki that if you can see the mountain it's going to rain and if you can't see the mountain it's already raining! The mountain is one of the wettest spots in NZ, with about 7000mm of rain recorded annually at North Egmont (compared with about 1500mm in New Plymouth) as it catches the moisture-laden winds coming in from the Tasman Sea and pushes them up to freezing heights. Still, it doesn't *always* rain there and the volcano is a spectacular sight on a clear day.

The surrounding Egmont National Park was created in 1900 and is NZ's second-oldest park.

Information

If you plan to tramp in Egmont National Park, it's essential you first get up-to-date information about track and weather conditions from the **North Egmont visitors centre** (☎ 756 0990; www.doc.govt.nz; North Egmont; 🕑 8am-4pm Oct-Apr, 9am-4pm May-Sep). Another good source of this info is the New Plymouth DOC office (p583).

Other information sources:

Dawson Falls visitors centre (☎ 025-430 248; www.doc.govt.nz; RD 29; 🕑 8am-4.30pm Wed-Sun, daily summer school holidays) Located around the other side of the mountain.

Stratford DOC (☎ 765 5144; www.doc.govt.nz; Pembroke Rd; 🕑 8am-4pm) Visited by coming up the mountain from Stratford.

Stratford visitors centre (☎ 765 6708; www.stratfordnz.co.nz; cnr Miranda & Prospero Sts, Stratford; 🕑 8.30am-5pm Mon-Fri, 9.30am-noon Sat)

Activities

TRAMPING & CLIMBING

Due to its accessibility, Mt Taranaki/Egmont ranks as the 'most climbed' mountain in NZ. But be warned that although the mountain looks like an easy climb, it has actually claimed 63 lives. The principal hazard is the erratic weather, which can change from warm and sunny to raging gales and white-out conditions unexpectedly quickly and within a distance of 100m; snow can fall at any time of year on the mountain, even in summer. There are also precipitous bluffs and steep icy slopes. Don't be put off, but don't be deceived. It's *crucial* to get advice before departing and to fill out the intentions book at a DOC office or visitors centre. If you intend to walk or climb for any distance or height, be sure to have the appropriate map. Pick up the brochure *Taranaki: The Mountain* from DOC offices or visitors centres for more safety tips.

In summer the mountain can be climbed in one day. There are numerous excellent tramping possibilities, including hikes to the summit or right round the mountain. Shorter tracks ranging from easy to difficult, and which require anything from 30 minutes to several hours, start from the three roads heading up the mountain. Pick up a copy of the DOC brochure *Short Walks in Egmont National Park*. Some of the higher alpine tracks are suffering erosion and DOC is encouraging people to use the lower tracks, which are well maintained and can still provide good views. An existing northern circuit is in the process of being upgraded, check with the North Egmont visitors centre.

Other walks include the **York Loop Track**, which follows part of a disused railway line (DOC produce a leaflet on the walk); York Rd provides access to the walk.

The 55km **round-the-mountain track** (three to five days) is accessible from all three mountain roads. You can start or finish this track at any park entrance and there are a number of huts on the mountain. Buy hut tickets (see Sleeping, below) and DOC's handy *Around the Mountain Circuit* brochure at visitors centres or DOC offices.

There is one main **summit route** (six to eight hours return), a pole route that starts at North Egmont visitors centre. This route is on the northern side of the mountain and loses its snow and ice earliest in the year – it's advisable not to make the climb in snow and ice conditions if you're inexperienced. Another route to the summit, beginning at Dawson Falls visitors centre, requires more technical skill and keeps its ice longer; it's best attempted with an experienced guide.

You can hike without a guide from February to March when snowfalls are at their lowest, but if you are an inexperienced climber, want other people to climb or tramp with, or want to try your hands at rock climbing, DOC can put you in contact with tramping clubs and guides in the area. It generally costs around NZ$300 per day to hire a guide. Some reliable operators:

MacAlpine Guides (☎ 025-417 042, 765 6234; www.macalpineguides.com; 30 Ceilia St, Stratford)

Mountain Guides (☎ 025-474 042, 758 8261; www.mountainguides.co.nz)

Top Guides (☎ 0800 448 433, 021-838 513; www.topguides.co.nz)

SKIING

In winter the mountain is popular with skiers. At the top of Pembroke Rd is Stratford Plateau, from where it's a 1.5km walk to the small **Manganui club ski area** (☎ 759 1119; http://snow.co.nz/manganui; daily lift pass from NZ$37). Skiing equipment can be hired at **Mountain House Motor Lodge** (☎ 765 6100; www.mountainhouse.co.nz; Pembroke Rd, Stratford). Stratford visitors centre has useful daily weather and snow reports, and there's also a **snow phone service** (☎ 765 7669).

Sleeping

There are many DOC-administered tramping huts scattered about the mountain, accessible only by walking trails. Most cost NZ$10 per night (for two tickets, purchased from DOC offices), but two cost NZ$5 (Syme and Kahui Huts). Huts have bunks and mattresses, but you provide all cooking, eating and sleeping gear. No bookings are necessary as it's all on a first-come, first-served basis, but you must purchase tickets before starting the walks. Camping is permitted in the park, though it's not encouraged as DOC prefers you to use the huts.

For DOC places (the first two places in the following list) bookings are essential and you must carry out *all* your rubbish. You must also bring your own sleeping bag, food and cooking utensils.

Konini Lodge (☎ 025-430 248; Dawson Falls; adult NZ$20) This lodge is situated beside the Dawson Falls visitors centre and offers bunkhouse accommodation.

Camphouse (☎ 756 0990; North Egmont; adult NZ$20) The Camphouse also has bunkhouse accommodation and is located beside North Egmont visitors centre.

Eco Inn (☎ 752 2765; www.homepages.paradise.net.nz/ecoinn; 671 Kent Rd; camp sites per person NZ$20, s NZ$24, d & tw NZ$45) Located about 6.5km south of Tatam, this small, ultra-ecofriendly place is made from recycled timber, while a mixture of solar, wind and water power provides hot water and electricity. A hot tub is available for use. Eco Inn is 3km from the border to Egmont National Park and it provides transport to the mountain (for a price).

Missing Leg (☎ 752 2570; missingleg@xtra.co.nz; 1082 Junction Rd, Egmont Village; dm/d NZ$16/37) Missing Leg backpackers is a casual communal place where you can come in and brew yourself a cuppa. There's dorm beds only, a loft section, a log fire and a potbellied stove. It's in Egmont Village and there's a swimming hole here.

WHANGANUI JOURNEY

The centrepiece of the mellow, rural Wanganui region, which lies in the southwest of the North Island, is **Whanganui National Park**. The park is based around the beautiful Whanganui River, a lazy curl of water that is NZ's longest navigable river and one of the country's most popular canoeing destinations. In fact, this wilderness area attracts so many ardent fans that someone in the Department of Conservation made the rather mysterious decision to denote the 145km stretch of river from Taumarunui south to Pipiriki one of NZ's Great Walks (p777), calling it the 'Whanganui Journey'. This canoeist's wet dream takes roughly five days to complete.

Getting There & Away

Public buses don't go to Egmont National Park. However, a couple of shuttle buses (one way NZ$25 to NZ$30, return NZ$35 to NZ$40) travel to/from New Plymouth and the mountain, including **Mt Taranaki Shuttle** (☎ 758 9696), **Withers** (☎ 751 1777; www.withers.co.nz) and **Cruise NZ Tours** (☎ 758 3222; kirstall@xtra.co.nz).

Central Cabs (☎ 765 8395) provides a taxi service from Stratford.

ROTORUA & BAY OF PLENTY

Rotorua is far and away the most popular and, inevitably, the most commercialised tourist destination on the North Island. Nicknamed 'Sulphur City', it has the most energetic thermal activity in the country, with bubbling mud pools, gurgling hot springs, gushing geysers and evil eggy smells hovering around. Rotorua also has a large Maori population and this is a good place to experience a traditional *hangi* and Maori concert.

Rotorua is less than 60km inland from the Bay of Plenty, a scenic and prosperous area blessed with a warm, sunny climate and some stunning sandy beaches. Tauranga is the bay's main town, the centre of NZ's kiwifruit trade and only a short ferry trip from the swimmer- and surfer-crowded beaches of Mt Maunganui. To the east off Whakatane lies the moonscape island of Whakaari (White Island), NZ's most active volcano and a breathtaking place to visit.

You can travel from here along the coast of the remote East Cape to Gisborne; see the boxed text on p623 for details.

Activities

White-water rafting and sledging, as well as jet-boating and thermal-pool and mud bathing are prime activities in and around sulphuric Rotorua. And don't forget the unparalleled mountain biking in Whakarewarewa State Forest Park or the downhill tumble of Kiwi-invented zorbing.

The superb Bay of Plenty beaches near Tauranga are a big draw for holidaying swimmers and surfers, while quieter stretches of pristine sand run eastwards. A wide range of water sports are on hand, including diving off the active Whakaari volcano, and this is also a great place to go swimming with dolphins or whale-watching.

ROTORUA

☎ 07 / pop 76,000

Rotorua is a major stop on the international backpacker route, a thriving city consistently buoyed by a huge influx of tourists. Needless to say, it can get extremely busy, especially during the summer months. It's scenically located 297m above sea level on the shores of Lake Rotorua, which teems with trout, and is surrounded by other serene lakes and thermal areas.

Don't Miss: visiting Wai-O-Tapu Thermal Wonderland and Te Whakarewarewa, checking out the excavated Buried Village, taking in a concert and *hangi* at Tamaki Maori Village, having a mud bath at Wai Ora Spa and riding a zorb downhill at Agrodome Adventure Park.

History

The Rotorua district was first settled in the 14th century when the canoe *Te Arawa*, captained by Tamatekapua, arrived from Hawaiki at Maketu in the central Bay of Plenty. The settlers took the tribal name Te Arawa to commemorate the vessel that had safely brought them so far. Much of the inland forest was explored by Tamatekapua's grandson, Ihenga, who also named many geographical features of the area. The name Rotorua means 'The Second Lake' (*roto* means 'lake' and *rua* 'two'), as it was the second lake Ihenga discovered.

In the next few hundred years, various subtribes split into more subtribes and territorial conflicts broke out. In 1823 the Arawa lands were invaded by Northland's Ngapuhi chief, Hongi Hika, in the so-called Musket Wars. Both the Arawa and the Northlanders suffered heavy losses and the Ngapuhi eventually withdrew. During the Waikato Land War (1863–67) the Arawa tribe threw in their lot with the government against their traditional enemies in the Waikato, gaining the backing of its troops. This also prevented East Coast reinforcements getting through to support the Maori King Movement (an initiative by those Maoris unwilling to sell or lose their land to Europeans to band together under their current king to resist pakeha incursions).

GETTING INTO TOWN

All major intercity buses stop at **Tourism Rotorua** (Map pp592-3; ☎ 348 0366; 1167 Fenton St), in the centre of town.

The airport (Map p601) is located about 10km out of town, on the eastern side of the lake. **Super Shuttle** (☎ 349 3444) offers a door-to-door service to/from the airport (NZ$12 for the first person, NZ$3 for each additional passenger). A taxi to the airport from the city centre costs about NZ$18.

With peace returning in the early 1870s, European settlement around Rotorua took off, as did the early tourism industry when word of the area's scenery and supposed health-giving waters got around. The main attraction was the fabulous Pink and White Terraces, formed by the sinter deposits of silica from volcanic activity. Touted at the time as the eighth natural wonder of the world, they were destroyed in the 1886 Mt Tarawera eruption; see the boxed text (p602).

Orientation

The main shopping and restaurant-café strip is Tutanekai St, the central part of which is a parking area and pedestrian mall. Running parallel, Fenton St starts near the Government Gardens near the lake and runs all the way to the Whakarewarewa ('Whaka') thermal area 3km away. It's lined with motels for much of its length.

Information

At Tourism Rotorua you can pick up the weekly magazine *Thermal Air*, a useful, free tourist publication, as well as the free annual *Rotorua Visitors Guide*, which is a more basic affair, and the *Gateway to Geyserland* (NZ$1), a good map of the city and surrounding area.

American Express agent (Galaxy United Travel; Map pp592-3; ☎ 347 9444; cnr Amohau & Tutanekai Sts)

Arthritis Centre (☎ 348 5121; 1115 Haupapa St) Can arrange a wheelchair for disabled travellers; call them between 10am and 3pm Monday to Friday.

Cyber World (Map pp592-3; 1174 Haupapa St; per hr NZ$5-6) Internet access.

Cybershed (Map pp592-3; ☎ 349 4965; 1176 Pukuatua St; per hr NZ$5-6) Internet access.

Laundry (Map pp592-3; 1209 Fenton St) Opposite the police station.

Planet 4 Cyber Café (Map pp592-3; Rotorua Central Mall, off Amohau St; per hr NZ$5-6) Internet access.

Police (Map pp592-3; ☎ 348 0099; Fenton St) The phone line is staffed 24 hours.

Rotorua Hospital (Map pp592-3; 24hr phone access ☎ 348 1199; Pukeroa St).

Rotorua Taxis (☎ 348 1111) Runs a taxi with a wheelchair hoist.

Thomas Cook (Map pp592-3; ☎ 348 0640; cnr Fenton & Hinemoa Sts) There's a foreign exchange desk here, and plenty of banks will change foreign currencies.

Tourism Rotorua (Map pp592-3; ☎ 0800 768 678; www.rotoruanz.co.nz; 1167 Fenton St; 🕑 8am-6pm Oct-Apr, 8am-5.30pm May-Sep) Makes bookings for activities and accommodation around Rotorua (and elsewhere in NZ), and comprises a travel agency and DOC office. There's also a money changing bureau (8am to 5.30pm) and other services for travellers, including showers, luggage storage and public telephones (buy your phonecard from the money changing bureau).

Victim support line (☎ 349 9471)

Sights

Excepting lakeside attractions such as Ohinemutu Maori village and the Museum of Art & History, not to mention Lake Rotorua itself, most of Rotorua's main sights are arrayed to the southeast of the town: from the geysers of Te Whakarewarewa that lie only a few kilometres from the centre, to the 'Buried Village' of Te Wairoa and the thermal wonderland of Wai-O-Tapu further afield.

TE WHAKAREWAREWA

Te Whakarewarewa (Map p601) is Rotorua's largest and best-known thermal reserve, and a major Maori cultural area. It's pronounced 'fa-ka-re-wa-re-wa' – most simply call it 'Whaka'. However, even Whakarewarewa is a shortening of its full name, Te Whakarewarewatanga o te Ope Taua a Wahiao, which means 'The Gathering Together of the War Party of Wahiao'.

There are historical links between the tribe that now owns and runs Whakarewarewa and the Tarawera eruption. Some small tribes were all but wiped out by that eruption (see p602), but one small group re-established themselves on land donated by another tribe at Whakarewarewa.

Entry to Whaka's geyser area is through the **NZ Maori Arts & Crafts Institute** (Map p601; ☎ 348 9047; www.nzmaori.co.nz; Hemo Rd; admission NZ$20; 🕑 8am-6pm summer, 8.15am-5.15pm winter). Its most spectacular geyser is **Pohutu** (Maori for

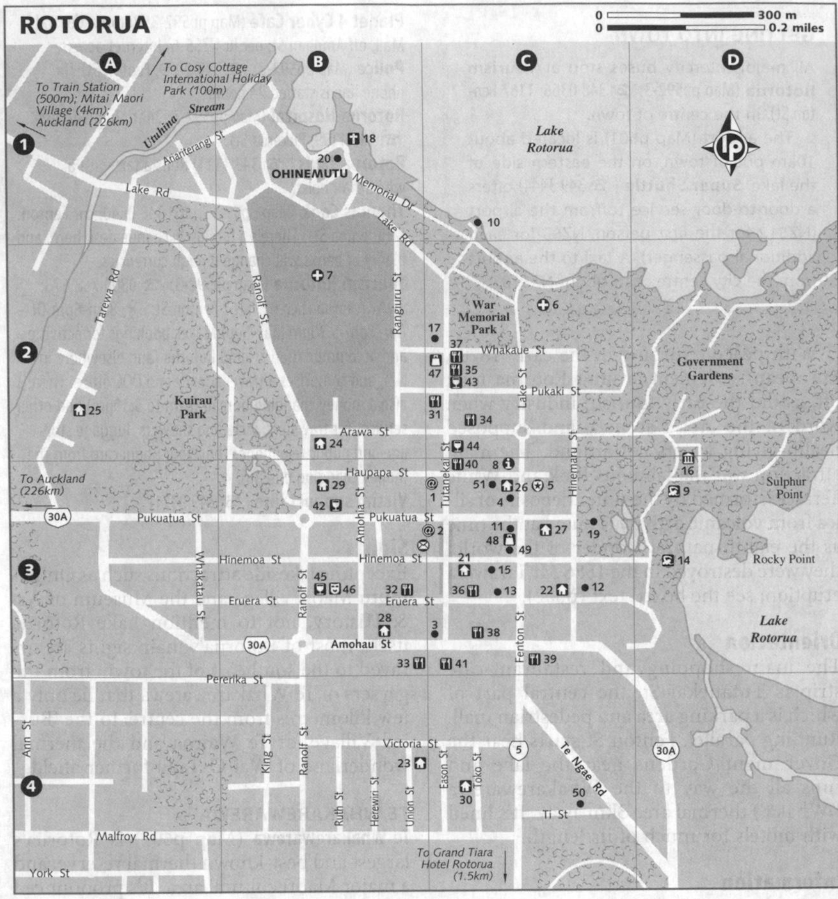

'Big Splash' or 'Explosion'), which usually spurts hot water about 20m (sometimes over 30m) into the air between 10 and 20 times a day. The average eruption lasts about five to 10 minutes, though the longest is reputed to have lasted for 15 hours – a world record. You get a warning because the **Prince of Wales' Feathers** geyser always starts off shortly before Pohutu. The institute also has working craftspeople, an art gallery, a replica Maori village, kiwi house, a Maori concert held daily at 12.15pm and access to the thermal area.

Whakarewarewa Thermal Village (Map p601; ☎ 349 3463; www.whakarewarewa.com; Tryon St; admission NZ$20; 8.30am-5pm) is on the eastern side of Whaka. There are concerts in the meeting house at 11.15am and 2pm, and guided tours through the village (with its souvenir shops and café) and the thermal area every hour between 9am and 4pm daily; the admission fee covers all concerts and tours. There's plenty of thermal activity in the village but no access to the geysers.

Whaka is 3km south of the city centre, straight down Fenton St. City buses drop you near Tryon St.

KUIRAU PARK

West of the centre off Ranolf St is **Kuirau Park** (Map pp592–3), an area of volcanic activity that you can wander around free of charge. Its most recent eruption in late 2003 covered much of the park (including the trees) in mud, and drew crowds of

INFORMATION
Cyber World....................1 C3
Cybershed....................2 C3
DOC....................(see 8)
Galaxy United Travel & American Express Agent....................3 C3
Laundry....................4 C3
Money Changing Bureau....................(see 8)
Planet 4 Cyber Café....................(see 41)
Police Station....................5 C3
Queen Elizabeth Hospital....................6 C2
Rotorua Hospital....................7 B2
Thomas Cook....................(see 49)
Tourism Rotorua....................8 C3

SIGHTS & ACTIVITIES (pp591–7)
Blue Baths....................9 D3
Indoor Climbing Wall....................(see 21)
Lakeland Queen Paddle Steamer....................10 C1
Map & Track Shop....................11 C3
Millennium....................12 C3
O'Keefe's....................13 C3
Planet Bike....................(see 21)
Polynesian Spa....................14 D3
Rotorua Cycle Centre....................15 C3
Rotorua Lakes Cruises....................(see 10)
Rotorua Museum of Art & History....................16 D3
Royal Lakeside Novotel Hotel....................17 C2
St Faith's Anglican Church....................18 B1
Tamaki Maori Village....................19 C3
Tamatekapua Meeting House....................20 B1

SLEEPING (pp597–8)
base Backpackers....................21 C3
Crash Palace....................22 C3
Funky Green Voyager....................23 B4
Hot Rock....................24 B2
Kiwi Paka YHA....................25 A2
Planet Nomad Backpackers....................26 C3
Rotorua Central Backpackers....................27 C3
Spa Lodge Backpackers....................28 B3
Treks Backpackers....................29 B3
Tresco B&B....................30 C4

EATING (pp598–9)
Café Ephesus....................31 C2
Capers Epicurean....................32 B3
Cocos....................(see 34)
Countdown Supermarket....................33 B3
Fat Dog....................34 C2
Herb's....................35 C2
Indian Star....................(see 43)
Katsubi....................36 C3
Lady Jane's Ice Cream Parlour....................37 C2
Mr India....................38 C3
Pak N Save Supermarket....................39 C3
Pig & Whistle....................40 C3
Rotorua Central Mall....................41 C3

DRINKING (p599)
Bar Barella....................42 B3
Echo....................(see 21)
Fuze....................43 C2
Hennessy's Irish Bar....................44 C2
Lava Bar....................(see 24)
O'Malley's....................45 B3

ENTERTAINMENT (p599)
Hoyts Movieland 5....................46 B3

SHOPPING (pp599–600)
Best of Maori Tourism....................(see 26)
Madhouse Design....................47 C2
Souvenir Centre....................48 C3

TRANSPORT (p600)
Air New Zealand....................49 C3
Bus Depot....................(see 8)
Rent-a-Dent....................50 C4

OTHER
Carey's Sightseeing Tours....................51 C3

spectators hoping for more displays. It has a crater lake, pools of boiling mud, plenty of steam and small mineral baths.

MAORI CONCERTS & HANGI

Although Maori culture in Rotorua has been heavily commercialised, it's still well worth experiencing. The two big activities are concerts and *hangi*; often the two are combined.

The concerts are put on by locals. Chances are that by the evening's end, you'll have been dragged up on stage, experienced a Maori *hongi* (nose-to-nose contact) and have joined hands for a group sing along. Other features of a Maori concert are *poi* dances (a women's dance where balls of woven flax are twirled) and action songs.

Whakarewarewa Thermal Village puts on daily concerts and also offers the three-hour **Mai Ora concert & hangi** (adult NZ$70; 6.15pm summer, 5.15pm winter).

For a combined concert and *hangi*, one of the best options is **Tamaki Maori Village** (Map p601; ☎ 346 2823; www.maoriculture.co.nz; adult NZ$85; tours 5pm, 6pm & 7pm summer, 5pm & 7pm winter), which does an excellent Twilight Cultural Tour to a *marae* and village complex 15km south of Rotorua. It provides transport and on the way explains the traditional protocol involved in visiting a *marae*. Their **city-centre location** (Map pp592-3; 1220 Hinemaru St) also offers the daytime Tamaki Heritage Experience (adult NZ$26), an interesting 45-minute guided tour and drama performance.

One of the newer venues is **Mitai Maori Village** (☎ 343 9132; www.mitai.co.nz; 196 Fairy Springs Rd; concert & hangi adult NZ$75; 6.30-9.45pm), which also offers guided bush walks. You can pass up the *hangi* and just take in a concert (NZ$25), but to do this you'll need to organise your own transport.

Many of the big hotels in Rotorua offer Maori concerts and *hangi*, charging around NZ$50 for adults (roughly half that for concerts alone). Some of the main venues include: **Millennium** (Map pp592-3; ☎ 347 1234; cnr Eruera & Hinemaru Sts), **Kingsgate Hotel** (☎ 348 0199; Fenton St), **Royal Lakeside Novotel Hotel** (Map pp592-3; ☎ 346 3888; Tutanekai St) and **Grand Tiara Hotel Rotorua** (☎ 349 5200; Fenton St). Exact times and prices are liable to change, so check with the hotels or Tourism Rotorua before booking.

LAKE ROTORUA

Lake Rotorua, the largest of 16 lakes in the Rotorua district, was formed by an eruption and subsequent subsidence of the area.

Two cruises depart from the Rotorua lakefront jetty, at the northern end of Tutanekai St. The **Lakeland Queen paddle steamer** (Map pp592-3; ☎ 0800 862 784; www.lakelandqueen.co.nz) does one-hour breakfast (NZ$28), luncheon (NZ$30), afternoon tea (NZ$20) and dinner cruises (NZ$55), while **Rotorua Lakes Cruises** (Map pp592-3; ☎ 347 9852; cruises NZ$30) does a one-hour circuit of Mokoia Island.

If you prefer to explore under your own steam, **Hamill Adventures** (☎ 348 4186) rents out

HINEMOA & TUTANEKAI

The true story of Hinemoa and Tutanekai is one of NZ's best-known lovers' tales. Descendants of the pair still live in the Rotorua area today.

Hinemoa was a young woman of a subtribe that lived on the western shore of Lake Rotorua. Tutanekai was a young man of the subtribe that lived on Mokoia Island, on the lake. The two subtribes sometimes visited one another; that was how Hinemoa and Tutanekai met. But though both were of high birth and deeply in love, Tutanekai was illegitimate and so Hinemoa's family were against the two marrying.

At night, island-bound Tutanekai would play his flute and sometimes the wind would carry his melody across the water to Hinemoa, who could hear his declaration of love for her. Her people tied their canoes up at night so she could not go to him. But one night, Hinemoa was so overcome by the music that she undressed and swam the long distance from the shore to the island.

Arriving naked on Mokoia, Hinemoa sought refuge in a hot pool to figure out what to do next. Eventually a man came to fetch water from a cold spring beside the hot pool. In a deep man's voice, Hinemoa called out, 'Who is it?' The man replied that he was the slave of Tutanekai, come to fetch water. Hinemoa reached out of the darkness, seized the slave's calabash gourd and broke it. She did this each time the slave tried to collect water, until finally Tutanekai himself came to confront the interloper, only to discover it was Hinemoa.

Tutanekai stole Hinemoa into his hut. The two lovers emerged the next morning, and when Hinemoa's efforts to reach Tutanekai were revealed, their union was celebrated.

This story is memorialised in NZ's most cherished traditional song, *Pokarekare ana*, adapted from a poem by Paraire Henare Tomoana (1868–1946) of the Ngati Kahungunu tribe. Almost anyone from NZ can sing this song for you. Often you will hear only the first verse and the chorus sung, but there are several verses. If you want to sing along, the first verse and chorus go like this:

Pokarekare ana nga wai o Rotorua.
Troubled are the waters of Rotorua.
Whiti atu koe, e hine, marino ana e.
If you cross them, maiden, they will be calm.

E hine e, hoki mai ra,
Come back to me, maiden,
Ka mate ahau i te aroha e.
I will die for love of you.

pontoon boats (NZ$75 per hour) and pedal boats (from NZ$10 per 20 minutes).

OHINEMUTU

Ohinemutu is a lakeside Maori village. Its name means 'Place of the Young Woman who was Killed' and was bestowed by Ihenga in memory of his daughter.

The historic Maori **St Faith's Anglican Church** (Map pp592-3; 8am-5pm) by the lakefront has a beautiful interior decorated with Maori carvings, *tukutuku* (woven panels), painted scrollwork and stained-glass windows. An image of Christ wearing a Maori cloak is etched on a window so that he appears to be walking on the waters of Lake Rotorua.

Opposite the church is the impressive 1887 **Tamatekapua Meeting House** (Map pp592–3). Named for the captain of the *Arawa* canoe, this is an important meeting house for all Arawa people.

There's also a small Maori craft shop on the site.

ROTORUA MUSEUM OF ART & HISTORY

This impressive **museum** (Map pp592-3; ☎ 349 4350; www.rotoruamuseum.co.nz; Government Gardens; admission NZ$10; 9.30am-6pm Oct-Mar, 9.30am-5pm Apr-Sep), better known as the Bath House, is in a grand Tudor-style edifice in the Government Gardens and originally opened as an elegant spa retreat in 1908. Displays in the former shower rooms give a fascinating insight into eccentric therapies once practised here, including 'electric baths' and the Bergonie Chair, into which patients suffering from constipation were strapped and then 'vibrated rapidly'. Venture into the basement (hard-hats provided) to see the complex piping system and audiovisual presentations.

The museum has an interesting exhibition of the *taonga* (treasures) of the local Arawa people, including elaborate woodcarvings and jade. Other exhibitions relate stories of the WWII 28th Maori Battalion, with a 25-minute film, and the disastrous 1886 Mt Tarawera eruption. The survivors' stories have been preserved, as has the strange tale of the ominous, ghostly war canoe that apparently appeared before a boatload of astonished tourists hours before the eruption. A gripping 20-minute film on the history of Rotorua, including the eruption (accompanied by shuddering seats), runs every 20 minutes in a small theatre off reception.

The museum admission fee also gives you access to the Blue Baths, though a swim in the Baths' pool costs extra.

In the surrounding **Government Gardens** are typical English touches such as croquet lawns, bowling greens and rose beds, as well as steaming thermal pools. If you fancy a game of **bowls** (☎ 025-245 4433; 30/60min NZ$15/20; 🕒 4.30-6.30pm Mon-Wed, 9am-6.30pm Thu-Sun), reservations are essential. Also in the grounds are the **Blue Baths** (Map pp592-3; admission NZ$10; 🕒 10am-5pm), a refurbished 1930s swimming-pool complex housing a small museum recalling the building's heyday. If it all makes you feel like taking a dip yourself, there's a modern heated pool here too (adult NZ$8).

Activities

Soaking in a thermal pool is the chief activity in and around Rotorua, but there are other possibilities requiring a little more physical exertion, including riding a mountain bike along the trails of Whakarewarewa State Forest Park, white-water rafting and sledging on nearby rivers, kayaking on scenic lakes and tramping through forests.

THERMAL POOLS

The popular **Polynesian Spa** (Map pp592-3; ☎ 348 1328; www.polynesianspa.co.nz; off Hinemoa St; main pools NZ$14, private pools per 30min NZ$14, spa therapies from NZ$65; 🕒 6.30am-11pm, last tickets 10.15pm, spa therapies 9am-9pm) is in the Government Gardens. A bathhouse was opened at these springs in 1886 and people have been swearing by the health-giving properties of the waters ever since. The modern complex has several pools at the lake's edge that range in temperature from 36°C to 43°C, and a main pool at 38°C. Aix massage (a hydrotherapy treatment) and a variety of mud spa treatments are available. Towels and swimsuits can also be hired. It's advisable to put all valuables in a safe-deposit box at the ticket office.

There are two natural open-air pools with medicinal mineral waters (hotter than 39°C) at **Waikite Valley Thermal Pools** (Map p601; ☎ 333 1861; public pools NZ$6, private pools per 40min NZ$10; 🕒 10am-10pm). To get there, go 30km south on SH5 (the highway to Taupo) to a signposted turn-off opposite the Wai-O-Tapu turn-off; the pools are another 6km down this road.

Those wishing to swim in hot water can visit **Kerosene Creek** (Map p601), out on SH5. Turn left on the unsealed old Waiotapu Rd and follow it for 2km. This is one of the few places where travellers can bathe in natural thermal pools for free.

WHITE-WATER RAFTING

Of the rafting trips on offer, those taking place on the grade V Kaituna River, off SH33 about 16km northeast of Rotorua, are the most popular. Time spent on the river is about 45 minutes and you go over the 7m Okere Falls, then over another 3m drop and about 14 rapids. The cost is around NZ$80.

All of Rotorua's rafting companies tackle the Kaituna. **Raftabout** (☎ 0800 723 822; www.raftabout.co.nz), **River Rats** (☎ 0800 333 900; www.riverrats.co.nz) and **Whitewater Excitement Co** (☎ 349 2858; www.raftnz.co.nz) also visit the Rangitaiki River (grade III to IV; day trips NZ$95) and the fast-flowing Wairoa River (grade IV to V; from NZ$80). **Kaituna Cascades** (☎ 0800 524 8862; www.kaitunacascades.co.nz) also does the Motu River (grade III to IV).

WHITE-WATER SLEDGING

Kaitiaki Adventures (☎ 0800 338 736, 357 2236; www.raft-it.com) does white-water sledging on the Kaituna River (NZ$115). You zoom along on a sledge specially designed for manoeuvrability on the river. Also on offer are white-water rafting trips on the Kaituna (NZ$75) and Wairoa (NZ$80) Rivers and a sledge/raft combo on the Kaituna (NZ$170).

KAYAKING

Adventure Kayaking (☎ 348 9451; www.adventurekayaking.co.nz) has half-day kayaking trips on

Lake Rotorua and Lake Rotoiti (NZ$55); full-day trips on Lake Tarawera (NZ$75) and Lake Rotoiti (NZ$80); a twilight lake paddle with a soak in a hot pool (NZ$65); and two- and three-day trips starting at NZ$160. They also rent kayaks from NZ$40 per day.

Kaituna Kayaks (☎ 0800 465 292; www.kaitunakayaks.com; NZ$130) runs half-day guided kayaking trips on the Kaituna River.

MOUNTAIN BIKING

The **Whakarewarewa State Forest Park** (below) has 10 of the best mountain-bike trails in the country. **Planet Bike** (Map pp592-3; ☎ 348 9971; Hinemoa St) hires bikes and gear (one-hour/full-day hire NZ$15/50), does drop offs and pick ups, and also organises guided rides (NZ$60 to NZ$100).

Other bicycle-hire places include **Lady Jane's Ice Cream Parlour** (Map pp592-3; ☎ 347 9340; cnr Tutanekai & Whakaue Sts) and **Rotorua Cycle Centre** (Map pp592-3; ☎ 348 6588; 1120 Hinemoa St). 'City bikes' cost around NZ$25 per day.

WALKING

The **Map & Track Shop** (Map pp592-3; ☎ 349 1845; 1225 Fenton St) has pamphlets and excellent maps outlining the area's many fine walks. A handy booklet is DOC's *Your Pace, Our Place* (free).

On the southeastern edge of town, **Whakarewarewa State Forest Park** (Map p601) was planted early in the 20th century as an experiment to find the most suitable species to replace NZ's rapidly dwindling, slow-growing native trees. The **Fletcher Challenge Visitor Information Centre** (Map p601; ☎ 346 2082; 🕒 8.30am-6pm Mon-Fri, 10am-4pm Sat & Sun), located in the park, has a woodcraft shop and displays on the history of the forest, plus info on local walks. Walks range in duration from half an hour to four hours, and include some great routes to the **Blue** and **Green Lakes**. Several walks start at the visitors centre, including the walk through **Redwood Grove** (30 minutes), a grove of large Californian redwood trees.

The 22.5km **Western Okataina Walkway** (Map p601, seven hours) heads through native bush from Lake Okareka to Ruato, on the shores of Lake Rotoiti. There's public transport past the Ruato end only.

The 10.5km **Eastern Okataina Walkway** (Map p601, three hours) goes along the eastern shoreline of Lake Okataina to Lake Tarawera. The 6km **Northern Tarawera Track** (two hours) connects to the Eastern Okataina Walkway and makes it possible to do a two-day walk from either Lake Okataina or Ruato to Lake Tarawera, with an overnight stop at a **DOC camping ground** (Map p601; camp sites per person NZ$6). From here you can walk another two hours to the Tarawera Falls, where there's another DOC camping ground.

Note that as **Mt Tarawera** (Map p601) is a protected area and a sacred site for the local Ngati Ragitihi tribe, access is restricted and it is not possible to go tramping independently. The only access is via organised 4WD or helicopter trips (see opposite).

The 7m-high **Okere Falls** (Map p601) are about 16km northeast of Rotorua on SH33; the walk to them is through native podocarp forest and takes about 30 minutes.

Just north of Wai-O-Tapu on SH5, a short but fairly strenuous trail leads to Maunga kakatamea Lookout on the top of **Rainbow Mountain** (Map p601, 1½ hours), with its small crater lakes and fine views.

OTHER ACTIVITIES

For a bit of indoor exercise, try the **indoor climbing wall** (Map pp592-3; ☎ 350 1400; thewall1140@hotmail.com; 1140 Hinemoa St; adult with/without gear NZ$14/10, student NZ$6/10; 🕒 noon-late Mon-Fri, 10am-late Sat, 10am-8pm Sun) at base Backpackers. They also organise full-day outdoor climbing trips (NZ$100).

Go tandem skydiving with **NZOne** (☎ 345 7569; www.nzone.biz; Rotorua Airport; jumps NZ$250-400). The initial flight includes some amazing views over the region's lakes and volcanoes, and the dives go from 9000ft, 12,000ft and 15,000ft.

Operators doing horse treks include **Farmhouse** (Map p601; ☎ 332 3771), northeast of Lake Rotorua, and **Peka** (Map p601; ☎ 346 1755), south of Rotorua. It costs about NZ$30 for the first hour, less for consecutive hours.

Mountain Action (Map p601; ☎ 0800 682 284, 348 8400; www.mountainaction.co.nz; 525 Ngongotaha Rd) organises 4WD tours through farms and bush (NZ$60 to NZ$150), horse treks (half-hour/half-day NZ$20/210), paintball (NZ$40), and rides in an eight-wheel, all-terrain amphibious vehicle called an Argo (from NZ$10).

Off Road NZ (☎ 332 5748; www.offroadnz.co.nz; 193 Amoore Rd), 20km north of Rotorua, is the place to go for self-drive bush tours. Prices start at NZ$80 for the 4WD bush safari, and you can also try your hand at driving 'monster trucks' (from NZ$35) and sprint cars (from NZ$30). Other activities include clay-pigeon shooting (NZ$18 for five shots) and archery (NZ$15 for 10 arrows).

You can wander down to the Rotorua lakefront and **fish** if you have a licence. You can get a fishing licence directly from the **Map & Track Shop** (Map pp592-3; ☎ 349 1845; 1225 Fenton St; licences per day/week/season NZ$17/34/90) and hire fishing gear at **O'Keefe's** (Map pp592-3; ☎ 346 0178; 1113 Eruera St). Guided fishing trips cost about NZ$80 per hour per person (minimum two people); ask at Tourism Rotorua or at the lakefront for fishing operators.

Tours

BUS & 4WD TOURS

Carey's Sightseeing Tours (Map pp592-3; ☎ 347 1197; 1108 Haupapa St) The largest outfit in Rotorua. Trips include a half-day tour of the Wai-O-Tapu and Waimangu thermal areas (NZ$85). The full-day 'world-famous' Waimangu Round Trip focuses on the 1886 Mt Tarawera eruption and incorporates a visit to the Waimangu Volcanic Valley, a cruise on Lake Rotomahana past the site of the Pink and White Terraces, a cruise on Lake Tarawera, a visit to the Buried Village, and a dip in the Polynesian Spa (NZ$190).

Mt Tarawera New Zealand Ltd (☎ 349 3714; www.mt-tarawera.co.nz) Organises guided half-day 4WD tours to the top of Mt Tarawera (NZ$110) as well as helicopter landings on the summit (NZ$300) and a Volcanic Eco Tour combining the 4WD trip with visits to Wai-O-Tapu and Waimangu (NZ$195).

Tarawera Legacy (☎ 349 3463; trips NZ$65) Runs day trips visiting the Rotorua Museum of Art & History, the Buried Village and Whakarewarewa Thermal Village, picking up from hotels.

AERIAL SIGHTSEEING

Flights over the city and lake start at around NZ$70, with Tarawera flights costing around NZ$150. You can also fly further afield to Whakaari (White Island) and down to Mts Ruapehu and Ngauruhoe in Tongariro National Park.

Helipro (☎ 357 2512; www.helipro.co.nz) Based at Rainbow Farm and the NZ Maori Arts & Crafts Institute. Does a variety of trips including city flights (NZ$55) and Mt Tarawera buzzes (NZ$300).

Redcat (☎ 0800 733 228; flights from NZ$95) Uses a 1950s Grumman Ag Cat biplane for trips ranging from 12-minute 'city scenic' flights (NZ$95) to the 45-minute 'sulphur spectacular' over Wai-O-Tapu and other thermal areas (NZ$280). Leather jackets, silk scarves and goggles are provided for that dashing Biggles look.

Volcanic Air Safaris (☎ 0800 800 848, 348 9984; www.volcanicair.co.nz) Offers float-plane and helicopter flights (from NZ$60), including a combined Mt Tarawera helicopter flight and guided tour of Hell's Gate (NZ$300).

Volcanic Wunderflites (☎ 0800 777 359; flights from NZ$70) Particularly popular for flights over the awesome chasm of Mt Tarawera.

Sleeping

HOSTELS

Kiwi Paka YHA (Map pp592-3; ☎ 347 0931; stay@kiwipaka-yha.co.nz; 60 Tarewa Rd; camp sites per person from NZ$18, dm/s/d from NZ$22/35/50; 💻 ♿) This well-maintained YHA hostel is just over 1km from the city centre (it runs a transfer service for travellers). It's a quiet place that attracts a slightly older backpacker clientele. Facilities include a thermal pool, a pleasant café (the Twisted Pippie) and a bar.

base Backpackers (Map pp592-3; ☎ 350 2040; www.basebackpackers.com; 1140 Hinemoa St; dm/d from NZ$18/50; 💻) This is a branch of the scrupulously clean, upmarket 'base' backpackers chain, with good-sized rooms and great communal areas. There's a female-only floor, personal lockers in each room, and mountain bikes for hire. There's also a bar called Echo (p599) and a climbing wall.

Planet Nomad Backpackers (Map pp592-3; ☎ 346 2831; www.planetnomad.co.nz; 1193 Fenton St; dm/s/d from NZ$18/35/45; 💻) This clean and airy place is on a busy road near Tourism Rotorua and the bus station. It lacks individual character but the rooms are of a decent size and there's a large lounge and modern kitchen, as well as barbecue facilities. Discounts on activities around NZ are on offer.

Funky Green Voyager (Map pp592-3; ☎ 346 1754; 4 Union St; dm/d from NZ$18/45) This is one of the smallest and nicest of Rotorua's backpackers. Located in a tranquil residential neighbourhood, close to the centre, the hostel is comfortable and casual with a spacious backyard and a pleasant sunny conservatory.

Rotorua Central Backpackers (Map pp592-3; ☎ 349 3285; rotorua.central.bp@clear.net.nz; 1076 Pukuatua St; dm/s/d NZ$20/26/45; 💻) Convivial, well-managed hostel in a quiet side-street location just off Fenton Rd. The cheerful atmosphere is heightened by biggish double rooms, comfortable beds (not bunks) throughout and good facilities that include a spa.

Crash Palace (Map pp592-3; ☎ 348 8842; www.crashpalace.co.nz; 1271 Hinemaru St; dm/d from NZ$19/45; 💻) This sociable two-storey hostel is a pleasant, homely place in a fairly quiet location, but still very close to central Rotorua. It has a small but well-stocked kitchen, a relaxing garden area, spa pool and a lounge with pool table.

Hot Rock (Map pp592-3; ☎ 348 8636; hotrock@acb.co.nz; 1286 Arawa St; dm/s/d from NZ$20/50/60;) Hot Rock is a big, brash hostel with decent rooms and well-kept communal areas. It's a firm favourite with the party-hearty, bussed-in-backpacker crowd and not exactly the place to come for quiet reflection. There are three hot pools (indoor and outdoor) and the lively Lava Bar (opposite).

Spa Lodge Backpackers (Map pp592-3; ☎ 348 3486; www.spalodge.co.nz; 1221 Amohau St; dm/s/d from NZ$18/28/40) This hostel comprises a pair of worn-out houses in the centre of town, filled with a hotchpotch of furnishings and decoration. But it's cheap, friendly, and, judging by the many travellers' notes scrawled in the hallway, gets a lot of traffic. There are smoking and nonsmoking lounges and a free thermal spa. They only accept payment in cash.

Treks Backpackers (Map pp592-3; ☎ 349 4088; www.treks.co.nz; 1278 Haupapa St; dm from NZ$23, d & tw from NZ$55) Big, brand-new backpacker complex sited across from Kuirau Park (p592) that was in the final stages of construction at the time of research and will be worth checking out. Dorms here will have only four beds, and doubles and twins with/without bathroom will be available.

SPLURGE!

Waiteti Lakeside Lodge (Map p601; ☎ 357 2311; www.waitetilodge.co.nz; 2 Arnold St, Ngongotaha; s & d from NZ$145) The luxurious Waiteti lodge enjoys an enviable location in private grounds on the lake, at the mouth of the Waiteti trout stream. There are just five spacious, wood-cabin-style rooms and the hosts can arrange fly-fishing trips and other activities.

Kotare Lodge (Map p601; ☎ 332 2679; www.kotarelodge.co.nz; 1000j Hamurana Rd; s/d NZ$100/150) Kotare is a secluded, peaceful single-storey lodge set in well-manicured gardens overlooking Lake Rotorua. The elegantly appointed rooms have great views and there are some nice extra touches including abundant fresh flowers and home baking.

B&BS

Tresco B&B (Map pp592-3; ☎ 0800 873 726, 348 9611; www.trescorotorua.co.nz; 3 Toko St; s/d from NZ$50/90) This is a small, friendly B&B set up in a cosy white-timber house built almost a century ago and renovated over the past couple of years. Choose between simple doubles with bathrooms and singles with or without private facilities. There's free pick up from the airport or bus stop.

CAMPING

Blue Lake Top 10 Holiday Park (Map p601; ☎ 0800 808 292, 362 8120; www.bluelaketop10.co.nz; 723 Tarawera Rd; camp/campervan sites per person from NZ$22/26, s/d from NZ$40/45;) This holiday park is 10km from town, set amid native bush near the soporific shores of Blue Lake. Kayaks, canoes, fishing boats and bicycles are available for hire.

Friendly Waiteti Trout Stream Holiday Park (Map p601; ☎ 357 5255; www.waiteti.com; 14 Okona Cres; camp sites per person from NZ$20, dm/d from NZ$12/35) This is a secluded camping ground set in lovely mature gardens on the bank of the Waiteti stream, 6km north of town. As the name implies, it's a friendly place popular with family groups and anglers. There's a good range of accommodation, plus spa, playground, TV-room and fishing facilities, and it's handily placed for out-of-town attractions such as the Agrodome and Rainbow Springs Nature Park.

Cosy Cottage International Holiday Park (☎ 0800 222 424, 348 3793; www.cosycottage.co.nz; 67 Whittaker Rd; camp sites per person from NZ$24, d from NZ$45;) Beside the Utuhina stream, this peaceful, family-friendly park has thermally heated camp sites, a hot-water beach, natural steam *hangi* cooker, hot mineral pools and an adventure playground. Canoes, bicycles and fishing tackle can be rented.

Eating

Fat Dog (Map pp592-3; ☎ 347 7586; 1161 Arawa St; mains NZ$8-20; breakfast, lunch & dinner) A big, warm, soothing place, with twee poetry scrawled on the backs of chairs and a huge menu of fresh, lovingly made breakfasts, burgers, salads and *paninis*. Perfect for a relaxing, filling late-morning meal.

Café Ephesus (Map pp592-3; ☎ 349 1735; 1107 Tutanekai St; mains NZ$16-20; lunch daily, dinner Tue-Sun) This is a small Turkish place offering a good range of traditional meat and fish dishes, plus pizzas and lighter meals.

Cocos (Map pp592-3; ☎ 348 4220; 1151 Arawa St; mains NZ$10-18; ⌚ breakfast, lunch & dinner Thu-Sun, lunch & dinner Mon-Wed) Cocos is a great-value place specialising in fresh 'hot plate' meat and vegie dishes, with set lunch and dinner menus, including an 'all you can eat Mongolian-style BBQ'.

Pig & Whistle (Map pp592-3; ☎ 347 3025; cnr Haupapa & Tutanekai Sts; mains NZ$12-23; ⌚ lunch & dinner) This busy restaurant-bar in a former police station has fish and chips, smoked-chicken pizza, burgers and sandwiches on the menu. It also runs its own microbrewery.

Katsubi (Map pp592-3; ☎ 349 3494; 1123 Eruera St; mains NZ$12-45; ⌚ breakfast, lunch & dinner) Drop in here to sample authentic Japanese and Korean specialities, from sushi and sashimi to *golbaengi muchim* (seasoned moon snail with noodles).

Indian Star (Map pp592-3; ☎ 343 6222; 1118 Tutanekai St; mains NZ$11-20; ⌚ lunch & dinner) A broad range of meat and veggie curries and tandoori dishes are on the menu at this popular Indian eatery, and there's also a takeaway service.

Mr India (Map pp592-3; ☎ 349 4940; 1161 Amohau St; mains NZ$15-20; ⌚ lunch & dinner) Mr India is moderately priced and has all the authentic subcontinental favourites, as well as a good selection of vegetarian dishes.

Sweet-toothed visitors will love the extensive selection of ice creams at **Lady Jane's Ice Cream Parlour** (Map pp592-3; ☎ 347 9340; 1092 Tutanekai St). For a range of hot quick eats, including baked goods, Asian food and burgers, try the food court at **Rotorua Central Mall** (Map pp592-3; Amohau St; ⌚ 8am-5.30pm Mon-Thu, 9am-7pm Fri, 9am-5pm Sat, 10am-4pm Sun).

Self-caterers can ransack the local **Pak N Save** (Map pp592-3; ☎ 347 8440; cnr Fenton & Amohau Sts) and **Countdown** (Map pp592-3; ☎ 350 3277; Central Mall, Amohau St) supermarkets.

Drinking

Lava Bar (Map pp592-3; ☎ 348 8616; 1286 Arawa St) At this boisterous bar in the Hot Rock backpackers (see opposite), you can mix with an international and local crowd, play pool and listen to good music.

Echo (Map pp592-3; ☎ 350 3291; 1140 Hinemoa St) Within base Backpackers (p597), Echo is another bustling hostel bar attracting a mix of locals and travellers.

Pig & Whistle (Map pp592-3; ☎ 347 3025; cnr Haupapa & Tutanekai Sts) A popular, renovated pub with a range of meals (left) and its own microbrewed beers: Snout dark ale and Swine lager.

Fuze (Map pp592-3; ☎ 349 6306; cnr Pukaki & Tutanekai Sts; ⌚ 3pm-late Tue-Sat) A chilled-out bar attracting a more mature crowd. It has a nice ambience, good cocktails and snack food.

Inevitably, Rotorua has its share of 'Irish' theme pubs, most notably **O'Malley's** (Map pp592-3; ☎ 347 6410; 1287 Eruera St) and the dimly lit **Hennessy's Irish Bar** (Map pp592-3; ☎ 343 7902; 1206 Tutanekai St) which has a seemingly unceasing jolly-Irish-pub-song soundtrack.

SPLURGE!

Capers Epicurean (Map pp592-3; ☎ 348 8818; 1181 Eruera St; mains NZ$15-27; ⌚ breakfast, lunch & dinner) This stylish, gourmet place serves up tasty and intriguing concoctions such as venison with blue cheese and chervil tagliatelle, smoked lamb and baked bluenose. There's also a big breakfast menu, takeaway deli counter and upmarket condiments and kitchenware for sale.

Herb's (Map pp592-3; ☎ 348 3985; 1096 Tutanekai St; mains NZ$25-33; ⌚ dinner) Herb's is a large, refined steakhouse with a formal air and lots of roasted and grilled meats on the menu, including lamb rump, sirloin fillet and ostrich, plus the odd curry.

Entertainment

Live-music venues in the area include Pig & Whistle (left), which usually has live bands on Friday and Saturday nights, and Fuze (above), which occasionally sees performers on stage.

Bar Barella (Map pp592-3; ☎ 347 6776; 1263 Pukeuatua St) Good for some drum'n'bass on the weekends.

For movies, go to **Hoyts Movieland 5** (Map pp592-3; ☎ 349 0061; 1281 Eruera St; adult/student NZ$12.50/10), where all tickets are discounted to NZ$8 on Tuesday.

Shopping

Rotorua has many tourist-oriented shops selling traditional woodcarvings, greenstone, thermal-mud products and much more. Fenton St is a good place to start buying up souvenirs.

Best of Maori Tourism (Map pp592-3; ☎ 347 4226; 1189 Fenton St) Has a large assortment of Maori craftwork for sale, including woodcarvings, greenstone jewellery and clothing.

Souvenir Centre (Map pp592-3; ☎ 348 9515; 1231 Fenton St) Sports a comprehensive stock of Kiwiana to satisfy all your wooden *tiki* and tacky T-shirt needs. Paua-shell jewellery, woolly jumpers and thermal-mud cosmetics can also be had here.

Madhouse Design (Map pp592-3; ☎ 347 6066; 1093 Tutanekai St) Very interesting contemporary gallery shop showcasing paintings, sculptures, glass and other works by local artists.

Getting There & Away

AIR

Air New Zealand (Map pp592-3; ☎ 0800 737 000, 343 1100, airport counter ☎ 345 6175; www.airnz.co.nz; cnr Fenton & Hinemoa Sts; 🕑 8.30am-5pm Mon-Fri) offers daily direct flights to Auckland (from NZ$90), Christchurch (from NZ$120), Nelson (from NZ$115), Queenstown (from NZ$165) and Wellington (from NZ$90).

Qantas (☎ 0800 808 767; www.qantas.co.nz) flies between Rotorua and Christchurch (from NZ$105) and Queenstown (from NZ$155).

BUS

All major bus companies stop at **Tourism Rotorua** (☎ 348 0366), which handles bookings (see Information, p591).

InterCity (☎ 348 0366; www.intercitycoach.co.nz) has daily buses to/from Auckland (NZ$45, four hours), Wellington (NZ$80, eight hours), Tauranga (NZ$21, 1½ hours), Palmerston North (NZ$60, 5½ hours) and Hamilton (NZ$20, 1½ hours). On the east-coast routes, InterCity goes daily to Gisborne (NZ$50, 4½ hours) via Opotiki (NZ$25, 2¼ hours) and Whakatane (NZ$25, 1½ hours), and to Napier (NZ$55, three hours) via Taupo (NZ$21, one hour). See p793 for information on passes.

Guthreys Express (☎ 0800 759 999, 343 1730; www.guthreys.co.nz) runs daily buses to Auckland (NZ$40, four hours) and Hamilton (NZ$25, two hours).

Getting Around

BUS

There are a multitude of shuttle services to attractions around Rotorua; check with Tourism Rotorua centre for details. One such operator is **Ritchies Coachlines** (☎ 345 5694); one stage costs NZ$1.60 and an all-day pass is NZ$7. Ritchies also runs suburban buses to Whakarewarewa (route 3) and Rainbow Springs (route 2; Ngongotaha), departing/arriving Rotorua on Pukuatua St.

Waitomo Wanderer (☎ 0800 924 866; trips NZ$30) does return trips to Waitomo (p562).

CAR

Rotorua has a host of highly competitive car rental companies. **Rent-a-Dent** (Map pp592-3; ☎ 349 3993; 14 Ti St) and **Link Low Cost Rentals** (☎ 349 1629; 1222 Fenton St) are two economical companies.

HITCHING

Hitching to Rotorua is generally easy, except on SH38 from Waikaremoana – past Murupara the road is unsealed and traffic is very light. The problem hitching out of Rotorua is often the sheer number of backpackers leaving town; you may have to join the queue and wait.

AROUND ROTORUA Map p601

☎ 07

Hell's Gate

Known as Tikitere to the Maori people, **Hell's Gate** (☎ 345 3151; www.hellsgate.co.nz; Te Ngae; admission NZ$16; 🕑 9am-8.30pm) lies 16km northeast of Rotorua on the road to Whakatane (SH30). George Bernard Shaw visited Tikitere in 1934 and said of it, 'I wish I had never seen the place, it reminds me too vividly of the fate theologians have promised me', and proceeded to give the place its English name. The reserve covers 10 hectares, with a 2.5km walking track to the various attractions, including the largest hot thermal waterfall in the southern hemisphere. Long regarded by Maori people as a place of healing, the site also houses the **Wai Ora Spa & Wellness Centre** (mud bath & spa NZ$50; 1hr massage NZ$100), where you can relax with a variety of mud and spa treatments.

Waimangu Volcanic Valley

This **thermal area** (☎ 366 6137; www.waimangu.com; valley walk NZ$25, boat trip NZ$25, walk & boat NZ$50; 🕑 8.30am-5pm Feb-Dec, to 6pm Jan) was created during the eruption of Mt Tarawera in 1886 (see the boxed text, p602), making it brand spanking new in geological terms. The easy, peaceful downhill path through the valley passes many interesting thermal and volcanic features, including the Inferno Crater Lake, where overflowing water can reach 80°C, and

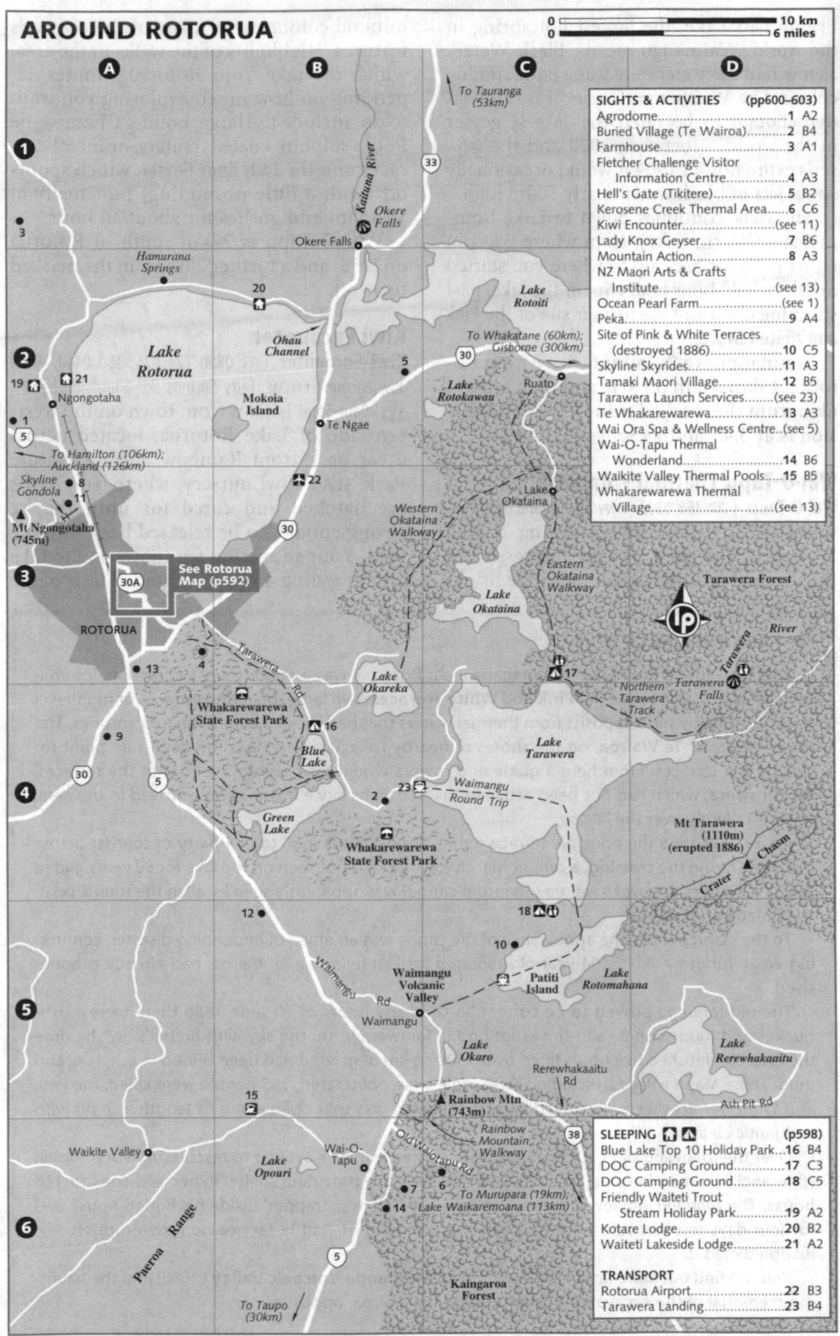
AROUND ROTORUA
0 10 km
0 6 miles
A
B
C
D
1
2
3
4
5
6
SIGHTS & ACTIVITIES (pp600–603)
Agrodome....1 A2
Buried Village (Te Wairoa)....2 B4
Farmhouse....3 A1
Fletcher Challenge Visitor Information Centre....4 A3
Hell's Gate (Tikitere)....5 B2
Kerosene Creek Thermal Area....6 C6
Kiwi Encounter....(see 11)
Lady Knox Geyser....7 B6
Mountain Action....8 A3
NZ Maori Arts & Crafts Institute....(see 13)
Ocean Pearl Farm....(see 1)
Peka....9 A4
Site of Pink & White Terraces (destroyed 1886)....10 C5
Skyline Skyrides....11 A3
Tamaki Maori Village....12 B5
Tarawera Launch Services....(see 23)
Te Whakarewarewa....13 A3
Wai Ora Spa & Wellness Centre....(see 5)
Wai-O-Tapu Thermal Wonderland....14 B6
Waikite Valley Thermal Pools....15 B5
Whakarewarewa Thermal Village....(see 13)
SLEEPING (p598)
Blue Lake Top 10 Holiday Park....16 B4
DOC Camping Ground....17 C3
DOC Camping Ground....18 C5
Friendly Waiteti Trout Stream Holiday Park....19 A2
Kotare Lodge....20 B2
Waiteti Lakeside Lodge....21 A2
TRANSPORT
Rotorua Airport....22 B3
Tarawera Landing....23 B4
To Tauranga (53km)
Kaituna River
Okere Falls
Okere Falls
33
Hamurana Springs
Lake Rotoiti
Ohau Channel
Lake Rotorua
Mokoia Island
To Whakatane (60km); Gisborne (300km)
30
Ruato
Lake Rotokawau
Ngongotaha
Te Ngae
To Hamilton (106km); Auckland (126km)
5
Skyline Gondola
Mt Ngongotaha (745m)
Western Okataina Walkway
Lake Okataina
Eastern Okataina Walkway
See Rotorua Map (p592)
30A
ROTORUA
Tarawera Rd
Tarawera Forest
Tarawera River
Lake Okareka
Whakarewarewa State Forest Park
Blue Lake
Northern Tarawera Track
Tarawera Falls
Lake Tarawera
Waimangu Round Trip
Green Lake
Whakarewarewa State Forest Park
Mt Tarawera (1110m) (erupted 1886)
Crater Chasm
Waimangu Rd
Waimangu Volcanic Valley
Waimangu
Patiti Island
Lake Rotomahana
Lake Okaro
Lake Rerewhakaaitu
Rerewhakaaitu Rd
Ash Pit Rd
Rainbow Mtn (743m)
Rainbow Mountain Walkway
Old Waiotapu Rd
38
Waikite Valley
Wai-O-Tapu
Lake Opouri
To Murupara (19km); Lake Waikaremoana (113km)
Paeroa Range
Kaingaroa Forest
To Taupo (30km)

Frying Pan Lake, the largest hot spring in the world. Waimangu means 'Black Water', as much of the water here was a dark, muddy colour. The Waimangu Geyser was once active enough to be rated the 'largest geyser in the world' – between 1900 and the geyser's extinction in 1904 it would occasionally spout jets of black water nearly 500m high.

The walk continues down to Lake Rotomahana (Warm Lake), from where you can either get a lift back up to where you started or take a half-hour boat trip on the lake, past steaming cliffs and the former site of the **Pink and White Terraces**.

Waimangu is a 20-minute drive from Rotorua, 19km south on SH5 and then around 6km from the marked turn-off. Last admission is at 3.45pm (4.45pm in January).

Wai-O-Tapu Thermal Wonderland

Wai-O-Tapu (☎ 366 6333; www.geyserland.co.nz; admission NZ$19; 🕑 8.30am-5pm), meaning 'Sacred Waters', is the most visually impressive of the thermal areas to visit, due to the bright mineral colouring of many of the reserve's features. Highlights of the walks in the area, which can take from 30 to 90 minutes depending on how much exploring you want to do, include the large, boiling Champagne Pool, sulphur-coated craters, mineral terraces and the **Lady Knox Geyser**, which spouts off (with a little prompting) punctually at 10.15am and gushes for about an hour.

Wai-O-Tapu is 27km south of Rotorua on SH5, and a further 2km from the marked turn-off.

Kiwi Encounter

Kiwi Encounter (☎ 0800 724 626, 350 0440; www.kiwiencounter.co.nz; Fairy Springs Rd; admission NZ$21; 🕑 10am-5pm) is 6km from town on the western side of Lake Rotorua, located across a car park from Rainbow Springs Nature Park. It's a kiwi nursery, where baby kiwis are hatched and cared for until they're strong enough to be released back into the wild. Your admission fee allows you to take an interesting 45-minute guided tour of the

MT TARAWERA ERUPTION

In the mid-19th century Lake Rotomahana, near Rotorua, was a major tourist attraction. International visitors came to see the **Pink and White Terraces**: two large, beautiful terraces of multilevel pools, formed by silica deposits from thermal waters that had trickled over them for centuries. The Maori village of **Te Wairoa**, on the shores of nearby Lake Tarawera, was the departure point for visiting the terraces. From here a guide and rowers would take visitors by boat to the terraces. **Mt Tarawera**, which had not been active in the 500 years since Maori people arrived in the area, towered silently over the lakes.

On 31 May 1886 the principal terrace guide, Sophia Hinerangi, took a party of tourists across the lake. During the crossing, a ceremonial canoe of a kind not seen on the lake for 50 years glided across its waters. The *waka wairua* (phantom canoe) was apparently seen by all in the tourist boat, both Maori and pakeha.

To the Maori people, the appearance of the canoe was an omen of impending disaster, confirming what Tuhoto Ariki, a 104-year-old *tohunga* (priest) living in Te Wairoa, had already prophesised.

The old *tohunga* proved to be correct. In the early hours of 10 June 1886 there were earthquakes and loud sounds, and the erupting Mt Tarawera lit up the sky with fireballs. By the time the eruption finished five hours later, over 1500 sq km of ground had been buried in ash, lava and mud. Three Maori villages, including Te Wairoa, were obliterated, 153 people were killed, the Pink and White Terraces were destroyed and Mt Tarawera was split open along its length as if hit with a gigantic cleaver.

Over the following days, excavations were carried out at Te Wairoa to rescue survivors. Sophia Hinerangi became a heroine, having saved many lives by providing shelter in her well-constructed house. The *tohunga*, however, was not so fortunate. He was trapped inside his buried house and for four days rescuers refused to dig him out, claiming he had in fact caused the eruption, not just predicted it.

You can find out more about the eruption at **Waimangu Volcanic Valley** (p600) and the haunting memorial of the excavated **Buried Village** (Te Wairoa; opposite).

facility and helps ensure the continuation of this important conservation effort. Tours usually depart hourly, though the number of tours held daily depends on demand.

Skyline Skyrides

Skyline Skyrides (☎ 347 0027; www.skylineskyrides.co.nz; Fairy Springs Rd; gondola NZ$17, luge NZ$6, gondola & 5 luge rides NZ$33; 🕑 from 9am) is just south of Kiwi Encounter. Take a gondola ride up Mt Ngongotaha (745m) for a panoramic view of the lake area, then fly back down the mountain on one of three concrete tracks on a luge (a sort of toboggan on wheels), coming back up again on a chairlift. There's also a café and restaurant on the mountaintop, plus a flight simulator, mountain bikes, 'sky swing' and other attractions to spend money on. Several walking tracks weave around the mountain.

Agrodome

If seeing millions of sheep in rural NZ wasn't enough, visit **Agrodome** (☎ 357 1050; www.agrodome.co.nz; Western Rd; show NZ$18, tour NZ$20, show & tour NZ$35), 7km north of Rotorua on SH1. This is where 19 breeds of sheep are on show amid sheep-shearing demonstrations, sheepdog displays, a chocolate factory and a woollen mill, as well as **Ocean Pearl Farm** (admission NZ$10), where you're guided through a facility producing paua pearls.

AGRODOME ADVENTURE PARK

As the name suggests, the Adventure Park is a little more adventurous than watching sheep being shorn.

Like bungy jumping, **zorbing** (dry or wet NZ$40, from three-quarters of the way up NZ$35) is another unusual Kiwi innovation. The rules are simple: climb into an inflated double plastic sphere (the two spheres are held together with shock cords), strap in and roll downhill for about 150m. You'll rotate within the sphere, and eventually the sphere will come to a stop. If that's not enough for you, skip the tying in and ask for a couple of buckets of cold water to be tossed inside the sphere – you literally slip downhill.

Other system-shocking experiences include a 43m-high **bungy** (NZ$80); a rather large swing called the **swoop** (NZ$45), which reaches speeds of up to 130km/h; the **agrojet** (NZ$35), which whips you around a 1km manmade jet-boat course before you can even catch your breath; and **free fall xtreme** (NZ$65), a free-fall skydive simulator that floats you 5m in the air on a powerful column of wind.

Buried Village (Te Wairoa)

The **Buried Village** (Te Wairoa; ☎ 362 8287; www.buriedvillage.co.nz; admission NZ$18; 🕑 8.30am-5.30pm Nov-Mar, 9am-4.30pm Apr-Oct) is reached by a 15km scenic drive from Rotorua along Tarawera Rd, which passes the Blue and Green Lakes. There's a museum just beyond the ticket counter that has many artefacts and background info on the events before and after Tarawera's 1886 eruption. There's also a small theatre where you can watch a dramatised film about the eruption, seen through the eyes of a young English tourist who died in the village hotel, and learn the story of Tuhoto Ariki who, according to some, was to blame for the destruction (see the Mt Tarawera Eruption boxed text; opposite). The site of his *whare* has been excavated and the dwelling reconstructed. Other buildings buried by volcanic debris and since excavated include the Rotomahana Hotel, the blacksmith's and a number of houses, where sealed wine bottles, smashed crockery and other grim scenes of daily domesticity cut short can be seen.

There's also a peaceful bush walk through the valley to Te Wairoa Falls, which drops 80m over a series of rocky outcrops. The last part of the track to the falls is steep and slippery.

Lake Tarawera

About 2km past the Buried Village is Tarawera Landing, on the shore of Lake Tarawera. Tarawera means 'Burnt Spear', named by a visiting hunter who left his bird spears in a hut and on returning the following season found both the spears and hut had been burnt.

Tarawera Launch Services (☎ 362 8595; cruises NZ$29) has a cruise at 11am crossing over Lake Tarawera towards Lake Rotomahana. It stays on the other side for about 45 minutes, long enough for people to walk across to Lake Rotomahana, then returns to the landing. The trip takes 2½ hours. A shorter one-hour cruise (NZ$18) on Lake Tarawera leaves at 1.30pm, 2.30pm and 3.30pm (the latter two trips operate in summer).

Boats from Tarawera Landing can also provide transport to Mt Tarawera and to **Hot Water Beach** on Te Rata Bay. The beach has hot thermal waters and a very basic **camping ground** run by DOC.

TAURANGA

☎ 07 / pop 58,500

Tauranga is the principal city of the Bay of Plenty and one of NZ's largest export ports, shipping out the produce of the rich surrounding region. As the centre of NZ's principal kiwi-fruit region, work is available when the fruit is being picked (May and June), but you may be able to find some orchard or agricultural work at almost any time; check with local hostels for work contacts.

Tauranga has great restaurants and an attractive waterfront, which includes two huge marinas. Swimming with dolphins, diving, surfing, sailing and other water-borne activities are all at hand. Just across the harbour are the fabulous beaches and headland scenery of Mt Maunganui (p607).

Information

AA (☎ 578 2222; cnr Devonport Rd & First Ave)

DOC office (☎ 578 7677; 253 Chadwick Rd West, Greerton) About a 10-minute drive from the centre of Tauranga down Cameron Rd.

Public library (95 Willow St) Offers Internet access, and there are plenty of Internet cafés scattered around town.

Tauranga visitors centre (☎ 578 8103; www.tauranga.govt.nz; 95 Willow St; 7am-5.30pm Mon-Fri, 8am-4pm Sat & Sun)

Sights

The **Elms Mission Station House** (☎ 577 9772; Mission St; admission NZ$5; 2-4pm Sun & public holidays) was founded in 1835. The present house was built in 1847 by a pioneer missionary and is furnished in period style. Another well-preserved colonial home with original furnishings is **Brain-Watkins House** (☎ 577 7672; 233 Cameron Rd; admission NZ$2; 2-4pm Sun), built in 1881 from native kauri wood.

Te Awanui is a fine replica Maori canoe on display in an open-sided building at the top end of The Strand. Continue uphill beyond the canoe to **Monmouth Redoubt** (Monmouth St), a fortified site during the Maori Wars. Further along is **Robbins Park** (Cliff St), with a rose garden and hothouse.

Activities

DOLPHIN SWIMMING

The **Tauranga Dolphin Company** (☎ 0800 836 574), **Dolphin Seafaris** (☎ 0800 326 8747; www.nzdolphin.com; 90 Maunganui Rd, Mt Maunganui) and **Butler's Swim with Dolphins** (☎ 0508 288 537; www.swimwithdolphins.co.nz) run dolphin-swimming trips. Even if you don't meet the dolphins, you'll enjoy a good-value day cruise and get to snorkel on the reefs. Trips cost around NZ$100 per adult.

WHITE-WATER RAFTING

White-water rafting is popular on the Wairoa River, which has some of the best falls and rafting in NZ. This is definitely a rafting trip designed for thrill-seekers, ranging from grade II cascades to grade V rapids, with a highlight being a plunge over a 4m waterfall! The water level here is controlled by a dam, so it can only be rafted on 26 days of the year; advance bookings are essential. **Wet 'n' Wild Rafting** (☎ 0800 462 7238; www.wetnwildrafting.co.nz; 2 White St, Rotorua) offers 1½-hour trips down the Wairoa River (NZ$85) and also rafts the Waituna River (NZ$75). **River Rats** (☎ 0800 333 900; www.riverrats.co.nz) operates similar trips on the Wairoa River (NZ$90) and Kaituna River (NZ$80).

DIVING

Tauranga Underwater Centre (☎ 571 5286; www.diveunderwater.com; 50 Cross Rd) operates a number of snorkelling, scuba and PADI diving courses, including open-water courses (NZ$450) and speciality courses (from NZ$130).

WALKING

Many local walks are outlined in the free pamphlet *Walkways of Tauranga*, including paths visiting the fascinating **Waikareao Estuary**. For walks further afield pick up a copy of *Short Walks of the Western Bay of Plenty* (NZ$1). Both are available from visitors centres.

The backdrop to the western part of the Bay of Plenty is the rugged, 70km-long **Kaimai Mamaku Forest Park**, which has some adventurous tramps; for information see the DOC pamphlet *Kaimai Mamaku Forest Park Day Walks* (NZ$1).

Some 15km to the southwest of Tauranga is **McLaren Falls** (admission free; McLaren Falls Rd; 8am-7.30pm summer, 8am-5.30pm winter), a 170-hectare park in the Wairoa River valley, just off SH29, which is filled with walking tracks, barbecue sites, exotic trees and rich birdlife.

Sleeping

Tauranga Central Backpackers (☎ 571 6222; www.tgabackpack.co.nz; 64 Willow St; dm/s/d NZ$20/40/50; 💻) This bright, well-run place is bang in the centre of town, with a large TV-lounge, pool table, modern kitchen and friendly staff. They can also help with finding work and rent out bikes (NZ$10 per day).

Apple Tree Cottage (☎ 576 7404; mark.gail@clear.net.nz; 47 Maxwell St, Pillans Pt, Otumoetai; camp sites per person NZ$10, dm/d NZ$20/40) This is a friendly, family-run backpackers in a quiet residential area close to the harbour. There's a basic wooden cottage and simple bunkrooms set in an attractive garden.

Bell Lodge Motel & Backpackers (☎ 578 6344; www.bell-lodge.co.nz; 39 Bell St; camp sites per person NZ$12, dm/s/d NZ$19/60/70; 💻) Bell Lodge, 4km west of town, is a spruce, purpose-built hostel, pleasantly situated on three hectares of land. This is a well-equipped place, with a big kitchen, barbecue and a lounge.

Just the Ducks Nuts (☎ 576 1366; www.justtheducksnuts.co.nz; 6 Vale St; camp sites per person NZ$14, dm/d NZ$20/45) This six-bedroom house is in a peaceful residential area, with a good view of the harbour. It has a laid-back atmosphere, good communal areas, a library and comfy rooms. They will drop off and pick up.

Tauranga YHA (☎ 578 5064; yhataur@yha.org.nz; 171 Elizabeth St; camp sites per person NZ$11, dm/d NZ$18/50; 💻) This YHA is a cosy, well-equipped hostel, conveniently close to the city centre. There's a large garden, spotless bunkrooms and lockers for your gear.

Silver Birch Thermal Holiday Park (☎ 578 4603; silverbirch@xtra.co.nz; 101 Turret Rd; camp sites per person from NZ$11, d from NZ$35) Silver Birch is on the Waimapu Estuary, just south of town. It's a relaxing, family-friendly place with good facilities, including thermal pools and a shop. Kayaks can be hired.

There are three basic modern **hostels** (NZ$15) and **camp sites** (per person NZ$4) at McLaren Falls (opposite); contact **Tauranga District Council** (☎ 577 7000; www.tauranga.govt.nz) for bookings.

Eating & Drinking

Crown & Badger (☎ 571 3038; cnr The Strand & Wharf St; mains NZ$8.50-15; 🕑 breakfast, lunch & dinner) This friendly British-style pub serves up Anglo-inspired concoctions like Nelson's nachos (NZ$8.50), Park Lane pork (NZ$15) and Northampton ham and eggs (NZ$14). It's also a nice place for a quiet drink.

Bravo (☎ 578 4700; Red Sq; mains NZ$10.50-16; 🕑 breakfast, lunch & dinner) This trendy, well-regarded restaurant and bar is a pleasant spot for inexpensive light meals, bagels, pizzas and drinks, with outdoor seating on the pedestrianised street.

Café Hasan Baba (☎ 571 1480; 107 Grey St; mains NZ$10-25; 🕑 lunch & dinner) Hasan Baba serves good-value Middle Eastern cuisine, including couscous, salads and lamb, in an atmospheric setting.

Krazy Jacks (☎ 587 4111; 47 The Strand; mains NZ$7.50-20; 🕑 lunch & dinner) Krazy Jacks is a popular bar and restaurant serving up steaks, surf 'n' turf and the like, as well as salads and pasta. Has occasional live jazz and rock gigs.

Takara (☎ 579 4177; 18 Hamilton St; mains NZ$12-19; 🕑 lunch & dinner Tue-Sun) Takara offers a good selection of Japanese sushi and *tempura* dishes. Set menus start at NZ$18, and there's free green tea.

New Delhi Café (☎ 578 5533; 20 Wharf St; mains NZ$14-20; 🕑 lunch & dinner) New Delhi has a good choice of spicy and not-so-spicy Indian dishes, such as beef vindaloo, chicken korma and vegetable biryani. They do takeaways.

Stars & Stripes Diner (☎ 577 1319; West Plaza, 75 Devonport Rd; burgers from NZ$5.80, mains from NZ$14; 🕑 breakfast Tue-Sat, lunch daily, dinner Tue-Sun) This cheap American-style fast-food joint has lots of burgers, chilli dogs and sandwiches, plus steaks, burritos and breakfasts.

Fresh Fish Market (☎ 578 1789; 1 Dive Cres; meals from NZ$5; 🕑 lunch & dinner) Down on the waterfront, this place serves excellent fish and chips and is a local legend.

Grumpy Mole (☎ 571 1222; 41 The Strand; 🕑 Tue-Sat) Big and very woody Wild West theme bar, adorned with cattle skulls and buffalo heads, and sporting some pool tables.

Bahama Hut (☎ 571 0839; Wharf St) One of the more popular joints in town. It has resident DJs, a dance floor and a surfing theme.

Getting There & Away

AIR

Air New Zealand (☎ 0800 737 000, 577 7300; www.airnz.co.nz; cnr Devonport Rd & Elizabeth St) has daily direct flights to Auckland (from NZ$75), Nelson (from NZ$140) and Wellington (from NZ$100).

BUS

InterCity (☎ 578 8103; www.intercitycoach.co.nz) arrives at and departs from Tauranga visitors

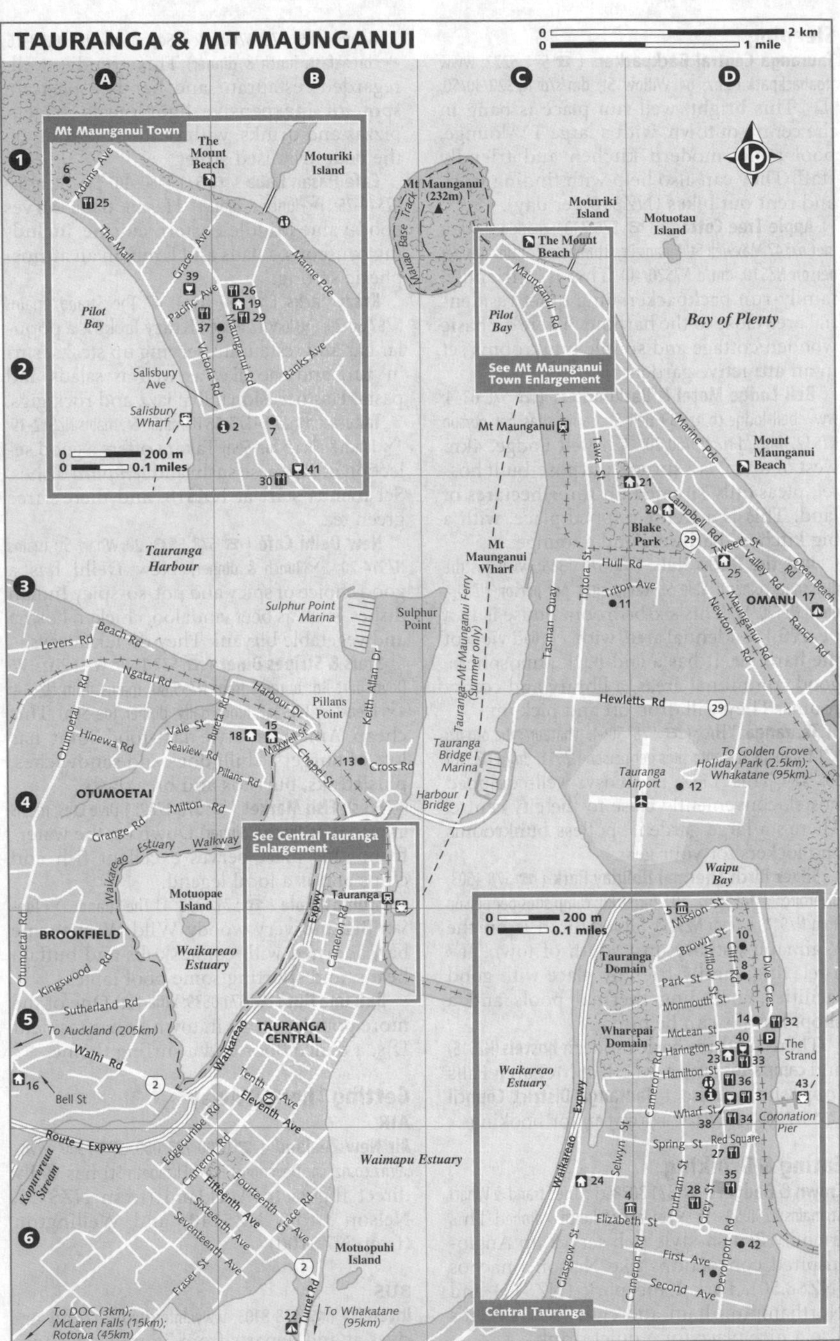
TAURANGA & MT MAUNGANUI
Mt Maunganui Town
See Mt Maunganui Town Enlargement
See Central Tauranga Enlargement
Central Tauranga
Bay of Plenty
Tauranga Harbour
Mt Maunganui (232m)
Pilot Bay
Moturiki Island
Motuotau Island
Sulphur Point
Tauranga Airport
Waikareao Estuary
Waimapu Estuary
Motuopae Island
Motuopuhi Island
OTUMOETAI
BROOKFIELD
OMANU
TAURANGA CENTRAL
To Auckland (205km)
To Golden Grove Holiday Park (2.5km); Whakatane (95km)
To DOC (3km); McLaren Falls (15km); Rotorua (45km)
To Whakatane (95km)
Tauranga–Mt Maunganui Ferry (Summer only)

INFORMATION
Automobile Association (AA)....1 D6
Mt Maunganui Visitors Centre....2 B2
Public Library....(see 3)
Tauranga Visitors Centre....3 D5

SIGHTS & ACTIVITIES (pp604, 607)
Brain-Watkins House....4 C6
Elms Mission Station House....5 D5
Hot Saltwater Pools....6 A1
Island Air Charter....(see 12)
Island Style Surf Shop....7 B2
Monmouth Redoubt....8 D5
Mount Surf Shop....9 B2
Robbins Park....10 D5
Rock House....11 C3
Tandem Skydiving....(see 12)
Tauranga Glider Club....12 D4
Tauranga Underwater Centre....13 B4
Te Awanui....14 D5

SLEEPING (pp605, 608)
Apple Tree Cottage....15 B4
Bell Lodge Motel & Backpackers....16 A5
Cosy Corner Motor Camp....17 D3
Just the Ducks Nuts....18 B4
Mount Backpackers....19 B2
Mount Maunganui B&B....20 D3
Pacific Coast Lodge & Backpackers....21 D3
Silver Birch Thermal Holiday Park....22 B6
Tauranga Central Backpackers....23 D5
Tauranga YHA....24 C6

EATING (pp605, 609)
Beaches Café....25 A1
Bombay Brasserie....26 B2
Bravo....27 D6
Café Hasan Baba....28 D6
Café Istanbul....29 B2
Clippers Restaurant & Bar....30 B3
Crown & Badger....31 D5
Fresh Fish Market....32 D5
Krazy Jack's....33 D5
New Delhi Café....34 D5
Stars & Stripes Diner....35 D6
Takara....36 D5
Thai-Phoon....37 A2

DRINKING (pp605, 609)
Aclantis....(see 30)
Bahama Hut....38 D5
Barmuda....39 A2
Grumpy Mole....40 D5
Mount Mellick....41 B2

TRANSPORT (pp605–6)
Air New Zealand....42 D6
Bus Depot....(see 2)
Ferry Service....43 D5
Tauranga Bus Terminal....(see 3)

centre, which books tickets. From Tauranga buses head to Auckland (NZ$35, 4½ hours), Hamilton (NZ$24, two hours), Thames (NZ$18, 1½ hours), Rotorua (NZ$21, 1½ hours), Taupo (NZ$45, 2½ hours) and Wellington (NZ$90, nine hours).

Bay Coaster (☎ 0800 422 9287) runs a daily service to Whakatane (NZ$12, 1½ hours) via Te Puke.

Supa Travel (☎ 571 0583) and **Tauranga Airport Shuttles** (☎ 574 6177) are local companies operating buses on demand to Auckland Airport (NZ$85).

Most buses continue to Mt Maunganui after stopping in Tauranga. Bay Hopper buses run from Wharf St to Mt Maunganui.

FERRY

The **ferry service** (☎ 578 5381; ticket NZ$6; 8.15am-4.15pm) to Mt Maunganui takes about 30 minutes and operates from Boxing Day (26 December) to Waitangi Day (6 February).

Getting Around

Tauranga's airport is located at Mt Maunganui. A taxi from Tauranga's centre to the airport costs around NZ$11; options include **Citicabs** (☎ 577 0999), **Tauranga Taxis** (☎ 578 6086) and **Coastline** (☎ 571 8333).

Tauranga's local bus service runs from Monday to Saturday to most locations in the area, including Papamoa and Te Puke.

MT MAUNGANUI

☎ 07 / pop 16,800

The town of Mt Maunganui (Large Mountain) stands at the foot of the 232m-high hill of the same name (also called 'the Mount', or Maumo). New Zealand's 'Surf City' is just across the inlet from Tauranga, and its fine beaches make it a popular holiday resort for Kiwis. The Mount attracts large numbers of surfers, and a planned artificial reef to be constructed 250m offshore should make it a world-class surfing spot; check out the **Mount Reef Project** (www.mountreef.co.nz) website for progress reports.

All the info you need is at the **Mt Maunganui visitors centre** (☎ 575 5099; Salisbury Ave; 9am-5pm Mon-Fri, 9am-4pm Sat & Sun Oct-Easter).

Activities

The **Mount Beach** between Moturiki and Maunganui is good for surfing and swimming. If you're keen to ride a wave, the **Mount Surf Shop** (☎ 575 9133; 96 Maunganui Rd) rents out wetsuits (NZ$15 per day), surfboards (NZ$30 per day) and boogie boards (NZ$20 per day). **Island Style Surf Shop** (☎ 575 3030; www.nzsurfschools.co.nz; 227 Maunganui Rd) organises one-hour lessons from NZ$60, including hire of all necessary gear.

At the foot of the Mount are some **hot saltwater pools** (☎ 575 0868; Adams Ave; admission NZ$2.50; 6am-10pm Mon-Sat, 8am-10pm Sun & hols).

The **Rock House** (☎ 572 4920; www.therockhouse.co.nz; 9 Triton Ave; per day NZ$12; 4-8pm Mon, noon-8pm Tue-Fri, 10am-6pm Sat & Sun) has an indoor climbing wall.

Tauranga's airport is located at Mt Maunganui and is the base for a number of air clubs and scenic flight providers. The **Tauranga Glider Club** (☎ 575 6768; flights per hr from NZ$30) flies every weekend, weather permitting, while **Tandem Skydiving** (☎ 576 7990; freefall@xtra.co.nz; jumps from NZ$190) does 8000ft jumps. **Island Air Charter** (☎ 575 5795; www.islandair.co.nz) does one-hour scenic flights over Whakaari (White Island; from NZ$120), the Rotorua thermal area (from NZ$120) and 15-minute flits above the Tauranga/Mount Maunganui area (NZ$40).

Walking trails go around Mt Maunganui; the route to the top, where there are magnificent views, should take about an hour and gets steeper towards the summit. You can also climb around the rocks on **Moturiki Island**, which is actually joined to the peninsula; check out the *Walkways of Tauranga* brochure. Moturiki Island and the base of the Mount also make up the **Crimson Trail**, which offers spectacular views of pohutukawa trees in full bloom between November and January; leaflets are available at the visitors centre, or you can log on to the **Project Crimson** (www.projectcrimson.org.nz) website.

Sleeping

Accommodation prices at Mt Maunganui tend to be slightly higher than in Tauranga.

Pacific Coast Lodge & Backpackers (☎ 0800 666 622; www.pacificcoastlodge.co.nz; 432 Maunganui Rd; dm/d from NZ$20/50; 💻) This spotless, purpose-built hostel has great facilities and comfy, wood-panelled bunk rooms, though the dividing walls could be thicker. It's decorated throughout with colourful murals, and the friendly staff are happy to book activities for you.

Mount Backpackers (☎ 575 0860; www.mountbackpacker.co.nz; 87 Maunganui Rd; dm/d from NZ$18/50; 💻) Mount Backpackers is located in the heart of the town centre, only a few minutes' walk from the beach. Boogie boards and bikes can be hired and special deals are offered on a range of local activities, including surf lessons.

Mount Maunganui B&B (☎ 575 4013; www.mountbednbreakfast.co.nz; 463 Maunganui Rd; s/d incl breakfast from NZ$45/75) The five rooms at this homely place are a bit small, but they're cheap and well cared for. There's also a guest billiard lounge.

Golden Grove Holiday Park (☎ 575 5821; 73 Girven Rd; camp sites per person from NZ$12, d from NZ$40) Golden Grove is a big, family-friendly camp with spruce, modern accommodation close to the Mount's sandy beaches. Note that it can be popular with school groups.

Cosy Corner Motor Camp (☎ 575 5899; www.cosycorner.co.nz; 40 Ocean Beach Rd; camp sites per person

WHAKAARI (WHITE ISLAND)

Whakaari, or White Island, is NZ's most active volcano, a small, 324-hectare island lying 50km off the coast from **Whakatane** (www.whakatane.com), a service town to the east of Tauranga. Whakaari was formed by three separate volcanic cones, all of different ages. Erosion has worn away most of the surface of the two older cones and the youngest, which rose up between the two older ones, now occupies most of the island's centre. Hot water and steam continually escape from vents over most of the crater floor and temperatures of 600°C to 800°C have been recorded.

Before the arrival of Europeans, Maori people caught sea birds on the island for food. In 1769 Captain Cook named it White Island, inspired by the dense clouds of white steam hanging above it. The island's most recent active period was between 1976 and 1981, when two new craters were formed and 100,000 cu m of rock was ejected.

A visit to Whakaari is an unforgettable, if disconcerting, experience, but the constant rumblings and plumes of steam don't (necessarily) mean that it's about to blow up. The island is privately owned and the only way you can visit is with a helicopter or boat tour. There's no jetty so boats have to land on the beach, which means that visits are not possible in rough seas.

Most trips to Whakaari include a one- or two-hour tour on foot around the island. All trips (except for fixed-wing aerial sightseeing) incur a NZ$20 landing fee, which is normally included in the quoted price. There are numerous tour outfits, most of which operate from Whakatane (for details of the daily Bay Coaster service between Tauranga and Whakatane, see p605) and include the following:

Dive White (☎ 0800 348 394; www.divewhite.co.nz; from NZ$120) Diving and snorkelling trips to Whakaari (White Island).

Pee Jay (☎ 0800 733 529; www.whiteisland.co.nz; NZ$130) Six-hour tours, with two hours on the island plus extra time for whale- and dolphin-watching if you're lucky. Lunch is included in the price.

Scott Air (☎ 0800 535 363; www.scottair.co.nz; from NZ$135) Aerial sightseeing tours over the island.

White Island Adventure Tours (☎ 0800 733 529; NZ$100) Offers a 4½- to six-hour boat trip, including lunch and a bit of dolphin-watching en route. You spend about two hours on the island.

NZ$12, d NZ$50;) Close to the beach in a quiet suburban area, this is another good-quality, family camping ground with a sociable atmosphere. There's a good range of facilities on offer, including a barbecue and a games room.

Eating & Drinking

Beaches Café (574 8075; cnr Adams Ave & Marine Pde; mains around NZ$8-10; breakfast, lunch & dinner) This pleasant spot at the base of the Mount serves light meals, sandwiches and the like, and is a popular place to hang out with a coffee.

Thai-Phoon (572 3545; 14a Pacific Ave; mains NZ$13-17; dinner) Authentic Thai specialities such as red and green curries, stir-fries and sweet-and-sour dishes are the order of the day here.

Bombay Brasserie (575 2539; 75-77 Maunganui Rd; mains around NZ$18; dinner) This place offers all the popular Indian dishes and has a good wine list. There's also a takeaway menu available.

Clippers Restaurant & Bar (575 3135; cnr Rata St & Maunganui Rd; mains NZ$14-20; breakfast, lunch & dinner) This modern, nautically themed restaurant does great daily roasts, as well as seafood and steak. There's also a bar and a giant chess set for patrons on the outside decking.

Café Istanbul (574 1574; 91 Maunganui Rd; mains NZ$16-25; lunch Sat & Sun, dinner daily) Busy Café Istanbul serves up traditional Turkish dishes, plus salads, pasta and roasts.

Mount Mellick (574 0047; 317 Maunganui Rd) An Irish pub that hosts live bands on Friday night and varied entertainment on other nights. It also offers standard pub grub all day long.

Barmuda (575 8363; 19c Pacific Ave) Laid-back locals' bar above Bardelli's restaurant, with pool tables, video jukebox, pokies and Sky sports.

Aclantis (575 3135; 290 Maunganui Rd) Another popular place, with regular live music, three bars and a dance floor.

Getting There & Away

A bridge spans the harbour between Mt Maunganui and Tauranga, or you can drive up from the southeast via Te Maunga on SH2. See under Tauranga (p605) for bus details. Most continue on from Tauranga to Mt Maunganui visitors centre.

EAST COAST

The East Coast region of the North Island harbours some of NZ's most varied, most dramatic and least travelled landscapes, from the rich wine country around beautiful Hawkes Bay to the primeval forests crowding Lake Waikaremoana, and northwards to the remote, rugged terrain and scattered Maori communities of East Cape.

Gisborne, NZ's most easterly city, is a relaxed, sunny destination internationally renowned for its surf and beaches, while further south is the seaside resort of Napier, with an amazing collection of Art Deco architecture.

Activities

The waterfronts around Gisborne and Napier provide some excellent surfing and swimming, while inland, the superb shoreline of Lake Waikaremoana is encircled by one of NZ's Great Walks. The East Cape has more wilderness than you can tramp through and some splendidly isolated rivers to raft down.

NAPIER

06 / pop 55,000

Napier occupies a fine coastal plot at the southern end of sweeping Hawkes Bay and, like most places in the bay area, enjoys its fair share of sunshine all year. Napier also makes a good base for exploring many of the region's top wineries, which are a short distance from the city limits. The city's biggest drawcard, however, is its architecture. It could challenge Miami for the title of 'Art Deco Capital of the World', with numerous examples of the style around the city centre.

The area was originally occupied by Maori people, who found food plentiful in the bay and the hinterland (you can see the Otatara Pa, with its barricades now rebuilt, on Gloucester St beyond the Eastern Institute of Technology). A trading base was established in 1839 and the town was officially planned in 1854, subsequently being named after the British general and colonial administrator, Charles Napier. But the biggest transformation began in 1931, when Napier was virtually destroyed by an earthquake measuring 7.9 on the Richter scale. In Napier and nearby Hastings 258 people died, and Napier suddenly found itself 40 sq km larger when the

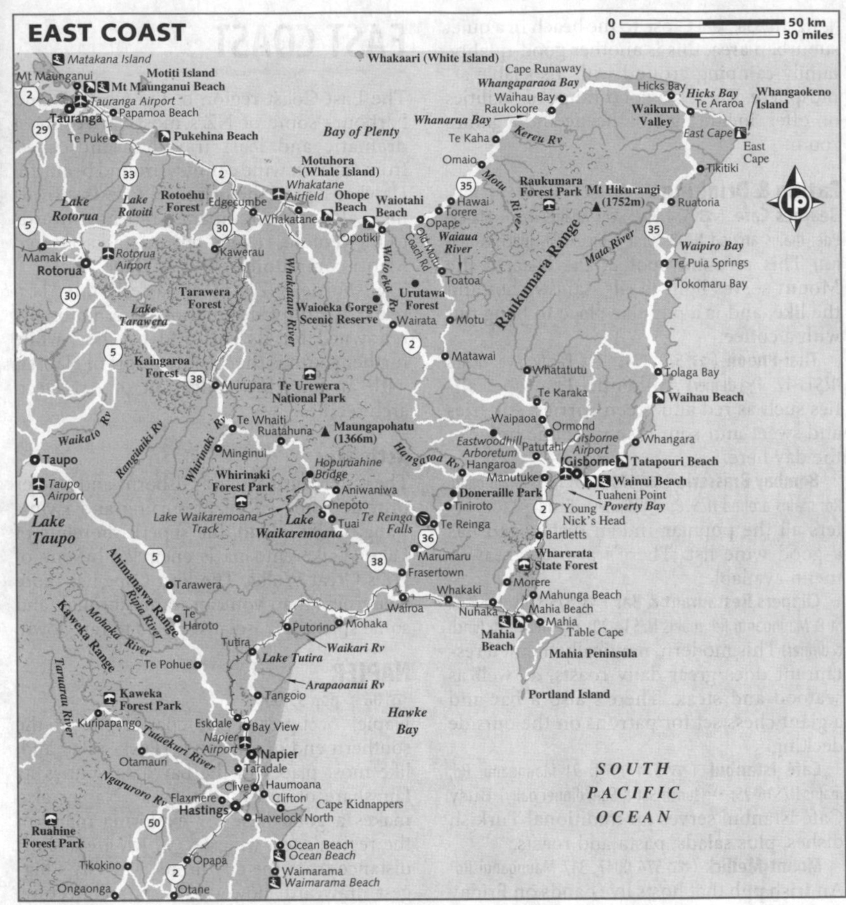

quake heaved the sea bed above sea level – in some places the land level rose by over 2m. The rebuilding program that followed produced a memorable Art Deco city.

Orientation

At the northern end of town looms Bluff Hill, a natural boundary between the centre and the Ahuriri and port areas. The prime commercial streets are Hastings and Emerson Sts. Emerson St is a pedestrian thoroughfare with many Art Deco features.

Information

AA (☎ 834 2590; 87 Dickens St)

And Computers Internet Café (Ocean Boulevard Mall, off Dickens St)

DOC office (☎ 834 3111; 59 Marine Pde) In the Old Courthouse. It has information on the sundry natural attractions around the city.

Visitors centre (☎ 834 1911; www.isitehawkesbaynz.com; 100 Marine Pde; 🕑 8.30am-5pm, closes later summer) A well-informed centre.

Sights

ART DECO ARCHITECTURE

The earthquake and accompanying fire of 1931 caused the destruction of most of Napier's older brick buildings. The city's two frantic years of reconstruction from 1931 to 1933 took place during the peak years of the Art Deco architectural style, resulting in a unique assemblage which has won international acclaim.

The Napier Art Deco Trust promotes and protects the city's architectural heritage. Its excellent, one-hour **guided Art Deco walks** (walks NZ$8; 10am) leave from the visitors centre, while its two-hour walks depart from the **Deco Centre** (835 0022; www.artdeconapier.com; 163 Tennyson St; tours NZ$12; 9am-5pm, tours 2pm summer & 2pm Wed, Sat & Sun winter). The walks are preceded by a half-hour introductory talk and short video.

Walks brochures (NZ$4) are available at the visitors centre, the Deco Centre and Hawkes Bay Museum. There's also an *Art Deco Scenic Drive* map (NZ$4) to the Art Deco– and Spanish Mission–style architecture around Napier and Hastings. The *Marewa Meander* (NZ$2) leads you through a suburb transformed after the quake.

Guided tours in a 1934 Buick can be arranged through **Deco Affair Tours** (025-241 5279; tours NZ$15-75); tours last from 20 minutes to 2½ hours. **Fairway Tours** (0800 428 687; www.fairwaytours.co.nz; tours NZ$15) run one-hour 'city highlights' tours, leaving from the visitors centre.

In the third week of February, Napier holds an **Art Deco weekend**, when there are dinners, balls, bands and much fancy dress. You might also encounter Bertie, Napier's Art Deco ambassador, who likes to promenade around town in period togs.

See the boxed text (below) for a summary of Art Deco architecture in Napier.

MARINE PARADE

Lined with Norfolk pines, **sunken gardens** and some fine old wooden buildings that survived the quake, Marine Pde has retained its air of an old-fashioned English seaside resort. It comes complete with pebble beach, but a strong riptide makes swimming far too hazardous. The statue of **Pania of the Reef**, a tragi-romantic figure from local Maori folklore, is at the parade's northern end.

Marineland (834 4027; admission NZ$9; Marine Pde; 10am-4.30pm) has performing seals and dolphins, with shows at 10.30am and 2pm (plus at 4pm in summer). You can also swim with dolphins (NZ$40, wetsuit hire NZ$10). A tour of Marineland (NZ$15) includes touching and feeding dolphins, while a tour of the penguin recovery workshop (NZ$15) will have you help feed and care for penguins. Bookings are essential.

The **National Aquarium of New Zealand** (834 1404; www.nationalaquarium.co.nz; Marine Pde; admission NZ$12; 9am-5pm Easter-Dec, to 9pm Jan, to 7pm Feb-Easter) has saltwater crocodiles, piranha, turtles and several land-dwelling animals, including kiwis and the unique tuatara (indigenous lizards). It also has sharks, and you can swim

DECOED OUT

Art Deco is the name given to a decorative style that made headlines in 1925 at the International Exposition of Modern Decorative and Industrial Arts in Paris. Zigzags, lightning flashes, geometric shapes and rising suns all characterise this distinctive style. Ancient cultures, such as those of Egyptians and Mayans, were also drawn upon for inspiration. Soft pastel colours are another Art Deco giveaway and have been employed by Napier's restorers, though many of the city's buildings were originally monochrome plaster.

Emerson St has some excellent examples of Art Deco, though many of the shopfronts have been modernised and you'll have to look up to the second storeys to see the fine Art Deco detail. Good examples on Emerson St are the **Provincial Hotel**, **Kidson's Building**, the **Esprit buildings**, the **Criterion Hotel & Criterion Art Deco Backpackers** and the **ASB Bank**, with its wonderfully restored interior. On Dalton St, the **Hotel Central** is a superb example of the style. Around the corner, look for the extravagant Moorish- and Spanish Mission–style building which used to be the **Gaiety de Luxe Cinema** (Dickens St). On the corner of Dickens and Dalton Sts is the former **State Cinema** (now a shopping complex).

Tennyson St has some fine preserved buildings. The restored **Municipal Theatre** stands out with its neon light fittings and wall decorations. The **Daily Telegraph building** is one of the finest examples of Art Deco in Napier and the **Deco Centre**, facing Clive Sq, is also impressive despite some modifications. At the intersection of Tennyson and Hastings Sts are more fine buildings, particularly the block of Hastings St from Tennyson to Browning Sts. Check out the **Soundshell** (Marine Pde) and the paving of the plaza. From here you can admire the Art Deco clock tower (neon-lit at night) of the **A&B building** and also the **Masonic Hotel**.

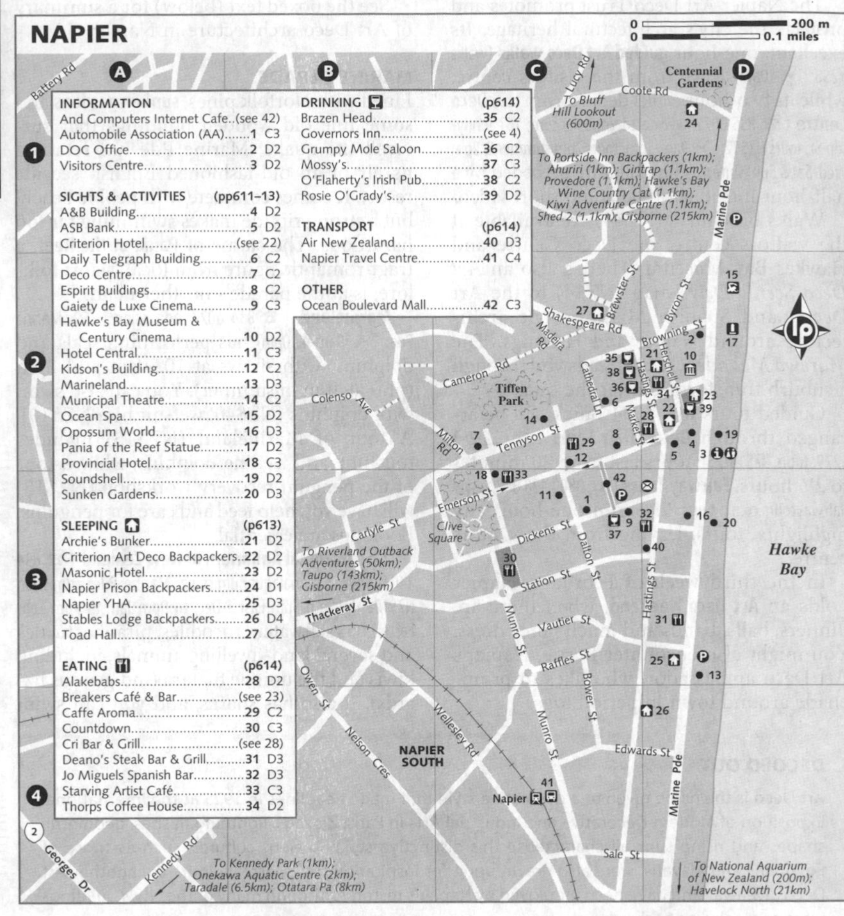

with them if you're a qualified diver (NZ$40, plus NZ$30 for gear). Hand feedings take place at 10am and 2pm, and there's a 'behind the scenes' tour at 9am and 1pm (NZ$20).

To find out more about the most vilified creature in NZ, head to **Opossum World** (☎ 835 7697; www.opossumworld.co.nz; 157 Marine Pde; 9am-5pm). There's a display on the pesky varmint and a shop with all manner of possum-pelt products, from socks to sweaters.

HAWKES BAY MUSEUM

Also on Marine Pde is a well-presented **art gallery & museum** (☎ 835 7781; www.hawkesbaymuseum.co.nz; 65 Marine Pde; admission NZ$7.50; 9am-6pm Oct-Apr, 9am-5pm May-Sep). There are exhibitions on Maori art and culture, including artefacts from the East Coast's Ngati Kahungunu tribe, and displays on the early colonial settlers. There are also interactive displays on dinosaurs and the story of amateur palaeontologist Jean Wiffen, who discovered evidence of several prehistoric species in NZ after professional sceptics had claimed there were none to be found. The fascinating section on earthquakes includes a 35-minute audiovisual in which Napier quake survivors tell their stories. Other rooms host temporary art exhibitions.

Also on site is the **Century Cinema** (☎ 835 9248; www.centurycinema.co.nz; tickets NZ$10), with a regular programme of art-house movies.

BLUFF HILL LOOKOUT

There's an excellent view over all of Hawkes Bay from atop the sheer cliff-face of **Bluff Hill** (sunrise-sunset), 102m above the Port of Napier, though the route to the top is rather circuitous.

Activities

Although the beach along Marine Pde is considered too dangerous for swimming, there's great **swimming** and **surfing** on the beach up past the port.

The **Onekawa Aquatic Centre** (834 4150; Maadi Rd; admission NZ$2.50, unlimited waterslide rides NZ$4; 6am-9pm) has waterslides and various other attractions.

Ocean Spa (835 8553; 42 Marine Pde; admission NZ$6; 6am-10pm Mon-Sat, 8am-10pm Sun) is an excellent waterfront swimming pool complex, with spas (NZ$8) and the option to indulge in a half-hour massage (NZ$35).

There's a climbing wall at the **Kiwi Adventure Centre** (834 3500; 58 West Quay, Ahuriri; climb plus harness NZ$15; 11am-9pm Tue-Fri, 10am-6pm Sat & Sun), which also organises canyoning, caving and kayaking trips.

Riverland Outback Adventures (834 9756), 50km north of Napier on SH5, organises various activities, including horse trekking (NZ$25 to NZ$50), one- and two-day white-water rafting trips (NZ$25 to NZ$230), and a horse trek and canoeing combo (NZ$75). There's also accommodation here, including tent sites (around NZ$9) and self-contained lodge units (around NZ$20/50 per single/double), as well as a spa, sauna and swimming pool.

Riverside Jet (874 3841) runs trips on the scenic Ngaruroro River (from NZ$25).

The **Hawkes Bay Wine Country Cat** (0800 946 322; www.hbwinecountrycat.com) runs daily lunch (NZ$50) and dinner-dance cruises (NZ$50) from West Quay out into the bay, departing 11am and 6.30pm respectively.

Sleeping

Archie's Bunker (833 7990; www.archiesbunker.co.nz; 14 Herschell St; dm/s/d from NZ$20/25/50;) This modern, well-cared-for hostel is centrally located, with clean, spacious rooms and good communal areas, including TV-lounges and a pool table. The friendly owners help organise work and rent out bikes.

Napier Prison Backpackers (835 9933; www.napierprison.com; 55 Coote Rd; dm/d NZ$20/50;) For atmosphere, try this Victorian prison (which was decommissioned in 1993). It has plenty, from the creaking cell doors to the liberal scribbling of gang graffiti. You can even sleep on the former prisoners' bunks. Guided one-hour tours cost NZ$10 (free for inmates).

Stables Lodge Backpackers (835 6242; www.stableslodge.co.nz; 370 Hastings St; dm/d from NZ$13/50;) Stables Lodge is a charming, spotless old house with horse-themed décor and a quiet, relaxed atmosphere. There's a peaceful inner courtyard, hammocks in the garden and a couple of friendly dogs.

Portside Inn Backpackers (833 7292; www.portsideinn.co.nz; 52 Bridge St; camp & campervan sites per person from NZ$10, dm from NZ$17;) On the other side of Bluff Hill at Ahuriri is this sociable modern hostel. There's a huge lounge bar, space for campervans and a small garden. Its main selling point is its proximity to the bars and restaurants at Ahuriri.

Napier YHA (835 7039; yhanapr@yha.org.nz; 277 Marine Pde; dm/s/d from NZ$18/24/50) This large wooden house enjoys a good location opposite the beach, though street-facing rooms can be noisy. It's an older building with a lot of character and there's a sunny courtyard out back.

Toad Hall (835 5555; www.toadhall.co.nz; cnr Shakespeare Rd & Brewster St; dm/s/d from NZ$18/20/40) Toad Hall is one of the few survivors of the 1931 earthquake. It's now a basic hostel with simple, clean rooms, none with more than two beds. There's a bar downstairs and a great rooftop terrace.

Criterion Art Deco Backpackers (835 2059; www.criterionartdeco.co.nz; 48 Emerson St; dm/s/d from NZ$20/24/45;) This place is upstairs in the former Criterion Hotel, one of Napier's best examples of Spanish Mission architecture. There's a large lounge with a balcony, though some rooms are small and stuffy, and it can get noisy.

Masonic Hotel (835 8689; www.masonic.co.nz; cnr Marine Pde & Tennyson St; s/d NZ$75/85) The fine old Art Deco Masonic Hotel couldn't be more conveniently sited, right in the heart of town and part of the huge Masonic Establishment complex, which includes a pub and a couple of good restaurants. All rooms have bathrooms, and there's a restaurant and bar with a dance floor.

Kennedy Park (0800 457 275; www.kennedypark.co.nz; Storkey St; camp sites per person from NZ$12, d from NZ$38;) This park is in Marewa, 2.5km from the centre, and has a range of simple but cosy and clean accommodation, including motel-style units. There's a restaurant on site.

Eating

Jo Miguels Spanish Bar (☎ 835 8477; 193 Hastings St; mains from NZ$7.50; ⏰ lunch Wed-Sun, dinner daily) Jo Miguels is a thoroughly Spanish place, complete with guitars and matador posters on the walls. It serves good tapas dishes and pizzas, and there's also a little geranium- and vine-filled courtyard.

Shed 2 (☎ 835 2202; West Quay; mains NZ$15-25; ⏰ lunch Tue-Sun, dinner daily) This open and very popular restaurant-bar overlooks the marina and concentrates on seafood and meat dishes, but also has pizzas.

Provedore (☎ 834 0189; West Quay; mains NZ$10-26; ⏰ lunch & dinner Tue-Sun) Provedore is a trendy restaurant by day and a popular bar by night. There's an eclectic menu and a long wine list.

Gintrap (☎ 835 0199; www.gintrap.com; West Quay; mains NZ$16-28; ⏰ lunch & dinner) This large place has excellent views of the marina, and is good for bar snacks and more substantial meals such as pasta, fish and grills.

Breakers Café & Bar (☎ 835 8689; cnr Marine Pde & Tennyson St; mains from NZ$6; ⏰ breakfast, lunch & dinner) This is a relaxed place with outdoor seating, offering good-value, all-day breakfasts, salads, steaks and seafood.

Deano's Steak Bar & Grill (☎ 835 4944; 255 Marine Pde; mains from NZ$12; ⏰ lunch & dinner) Deano's has a good range of steaks at reasonable prices and special NZ$14 meal deals on Monday and Wednesday nights, which include a drink.

Caffe Aroma (☎ 835 3922; 20 Dalton St; bagels from NZ$4; ⏰ breakfast & lunch) If you're into espresso coffee, bagels and Vespas, this is definitely your place. They also do cooked breakfasts from NZ$7.

Starving Artist Café (☎ 835 1646; 260 Emerson St; mains from NZ$5; ⏰ breakfast & lunch) This place does good-value breakfasts, salads and pasta, and is adorned with colourful works by local artists, most of it for sale.

Alakebabs (☎ 834 1170; 4 Market St; kebabs NZ$3-10.50; ⏰ lunch & dinner) Excellent-value takeaway place for tasty doner kebabs and filled pitta breads. There's also outdoor seating.

Thorps Coffee House (☎ 835 6699; 40 Hastings St; mains from NZ$5; ⏰ breakfast & lunch Mon-Sat) Thorps is a good spot for light snacks, *panini*, muffins and pastries.

Self-caterers can stock up at **Countdown** (☎ 834 1401, cnr Munro & Dickens St) supermarket.

Drinking

Governors Inn (☎ 835 0088; cnr Emerson St & Marine Pde) Governors Inn is a sedate pub with pool tables in its back bar.

O'Flaherty's Irish Pub (☎ 834 1235; Hastings St) O'Flaherty's is a rough-edged Irish pub with mismatched furniture and stripped floorboards. They have live bands Thursday to Saturday night.

Rosie O'Grady's (☎ 835 8689; Hastings St) Rosie's is a dimly lit 'Irish' pub which has occasional live music. It's part of the Masonic Establishment.

Brazen Head (☎ 834 3587; 21 Hastings St) Yet another 'Irish' pub, this one a much smarter place with a good-value lunch and dinner menu and occasional live music.

Cri Bar & Grill (☎ 835 7162; Market St) This is a lively local bar with pool tables and cheap food, popular with backpackers.

Grumpy Mole Saloon (☎ 835 5545; cnr Hastings & Tennyson Sts) This Wild West wood-cabin-style chain pub regularly pulls in the crowds with cheap drink offers and loud music.

Mossy's (☎ 835 6696; 88a Dickens St) Mossy's is a regular café by day and has live bands on Friday and Saturday night.

Getting There & Away

AIR

Air New Zealand (☎ 0800 737 000, 833 5400; www.airnz.co.nz; cnr Hastings & Station Sts) offers daily direct flights to Auckland (from NZ$90), Christchurch (from NZ$120) and Wellington (from NZ$80). **Origin Pacific** (☎ 0800 302 302; www.originpacific.co.nz) flies from Napier to Auckland (from NZ$85).

BUS

InterCity (☎ 834 2720; www.intercitycoach.co.nz) buses operate from **Napier Travel Centre** (☎ 834 2720; Munro St; ⏰ 8.30am-5pm Mon-Fri, 8-11.30am & 12.30-1.30pm Sat & Sun). InterCity has services running to destinations of Auckland (NZ$80, seven hours), Hamilton (NZ$60, five hours), Rotorua (NZ$55, three hours), Taupo (NZ$36, two hours), Tauranga (NZ$80, five hours), Gisborne (NZ$35, four hours), Palmerston North (NZ$38, 2¾ hours) and Wellington (NZ$60, 4¼ hours).

THERE'S WORK IF YOU WANT IT

Many overseas travellers come to this region to work so they can extend their trip to other parts of the country.

The NZ fruit industry is big business, bringing in about NZ$1.4 billion in export earnings each year. There's plenty of work available in this sector year-round, though the busiest time of year is between November and May; the peak of activity in Hawkes Bay is February and March. Payment is either worked out on a contract basis, where you can expect to earn from NZ$10 to NZ$15 per hour, or by the number of bins you fill with fruit (roughly NZ$10 to NZ$12 per bin). The working week is normally six days. Dairy-farm work pays around NZ$9 to NZ$12 per hour, but you will usually need to have prior experience in this area. Check if accommodation is provided by the employer, and if you're expected to have your own transport.

Foreign nationals (except Australians) will need a work visa; check with the **New Zealand Immigration Service** (www.immigration.govt.nz) for details, including working holiday schemes (18 to 30 year olds only).

Hostels will generally help find orchard contracting work if you are staying with them.

For online information on employers check out the **Hawkes Bay Fruitgrowers Association** (www.hbfruitgrowers.co.nz), the **New Zealand Fruitgrowers Federation** (www.fruitgrowers.org.nz), **Seasonal Work NZ** (www.seasonalwork.co.nz) and **Agworkers** (www.agworkers.co.nz). If you're interested in doing voluntary work on organic farms, log onto **Wwoof New Zealand** (www.wwoof.co.nz).

Bay Express (☎ 0800 422 997) runs daily to Wellington (NZ$35, five hours).

The **Purpil People Mover Shuttle** (☎ 0800 787 745) runs between Napier and Taupo on weekdays (one way/day return NZ$25/35), picking up and dropping off at your accommodation.

HITCHING

If you're heading north catch a bus and get off at Westshore, or try thumbing closer in. If you're heading south stick to SH2. The alternative inland route (SH50) is much harder going, with less traffic.

Getting Around

Napier Airport is about 2km north of town. The airport **shuttle bus** (☎ 844 7333) charges NZ$10 for the trip between the airport and Napier's city centre, while **Napier Taxi Service** (☎ 835 7777) charges about NZ$13.

Nimbus (☎ 877 8133) operates Napier's suburban bus services, including regular buses between Napier and Hastings via Taradale (NZ$5.20, one hour). All local buses depart from the corner of Dickens and Dalton Sts.

AROUND HAWKES BAY

☎ 06

Wineries, Food, Arts & Crafts

The Hawkes Bay area is one of NZ's premier wine-producing regions. It's very much the country's chardonnay capital, but cabernet sauvignon and merlot grapes from the area are also highly regarded and many other varieties are produced here. Local wine makers produce the handy *Guide to the Wineries* (which lists the ever-increasing number of wineries open to visitors) and an excellent free map.

Vineyards offering tastings include **Sileni Estate** (☎ 879 8768; 2016 Maraekakaho Rd, Hastings), **Sacred Hill Winery** (☎ 844 0138; 1033 Dartmoor Rd, Puketapu, Napier), **Crab Farm Winery** (☎ 836 6678; 511 Main Rd, Bay View), **Brookfields** (☎ 834 4615; Brookfields Rd, Meeanee), **Mission Estate Winery** (☎ 845 9350; 198 Church Rd, Taradale), the oldest in the country, **Esk Valley Estate Winery** (☎ 836 6411; Main Rd, Bay View), **Vidal Estate** (☎ 876 8105; 913 St Aubyn St East, Hastings), **Ngatarawa Wines** (☎ 879 7603; 305 Ngatarawa Rd, Hastings), **Alpha Domus** (☎ 879 6752; 1829 Maraekakaho Rd, Hastings) and **Trinity Hill Winery** (☎ 879 7778; 2396 SH50, Hastings).

Church Road Winery (☎ 844 2053; 150 Church Rd, Taradale) also has tastings and offers an informative tour of its facilities, which include a small **wine museum** (admission NZ$7.50). There's an excellent jazz concert every February, plus Sunday jazz over summer.

Havelock North has a concentration of wineries, especially out on Te Mata Rd. **Te Mata Estate Winery** (☎ 877 4399; Te Mata Rd, Havelock North), **Akarangi Wines** (☎ 877 8228; River Rd, Havelock North), **Lombardi Wines** (☎ 877 9018; Black Barn Rd, Havelock North) and **Craggy Range Winery**

(☎ 873 7126; 253 Waimarama Rd) are all worth a visit. A number of wineries are open for lunch and offer excellent dining.

Every year around the beginning of February, **Harvest Hawkes Bay** (☎ 0800 442 946; www.harvesthawkesbay.co.nz) puts on a big show to celebrate wine and food. The weekend event of tastings and concerts involves upwards of 25 wineries.

A fine way of visiting the wineries is by bicycle, since most of the wineries are within easy cycling distance and it's all flat land. **Bike D'Vine** (☎ 833 6697; www.bikedevine.com), **Bike About Tours** (☎ 843 9991; www.bikeabouttours.co.nz) and **On Yer Bike** (☎ 879 8735) arrange self-pedalling bike tours of the vineyards (day tour around NZ$40), and will pick you, or your purchases, up if you get tired.

Motorised tour operators include **Grape Escape** (☎ 0800 100 489), **Bay Tours** (☎ 843 6953), **Vince's Vineyard Tours** (☎ 836 6705), **Vicky's Wine Tours** (☎ 843 9991) and **Hawkes Bay Tours** (☎ 0800 868 742). Tours generally last four hours, take in four or five wineries, and cost from NZ$40 per person; day tours cost around NZ$85. All tour operators pick up in Napier, Hastings or Havelock North.

Food is now an integral part of vineyard tours, with food markets an extremely popular feature. Two markets of particular note are the **HB Food Group Farmers Market** (☎ 877 1001; Hawkes Bay Showgrounds, Kenilworth Rd, Hastings; 🕑 8.30am-12.30pm Sun) and the **Village Growers Market** (☎ 877 7985; The Sun Dial, Lombardi Estate, Black Barn Rd, Havelock North; 🕑 9am-noon Sat Nov-Mar), which specialises in organic produce. The map-accompanied brochure *Hawkes Bay Food Trail* lists produce growers in the area.

Some local craftspeople open their studios to the public. For info on these, get the *Hawkes Bay Arts Trail* leaflet from a visitors centre.

Cape Kidnappers Gannet Colony

From late September to late April, the Cape Kidnappers gannet colony comes to life. Elsewhere these large birds usually make their nests on remote and inaccessible islands, but here (and also at Muriwai near Auckland) they nest on the mainland, unfazed by human spectators. Cape Kidnappers, so-named because it's where local Maoris tried to kidnap a Tahitian servant boy from Cook's expedition, is administered by DOC, which produces a handy leaflet and booklets on the colony (NZ$1).

The gannets usually begin turning up in late July after the last heavy storm of the month, which apparently casts driftwood and other handy nest-building materials high up the beach where it's easy for the birds to collect. In October and November eggs are laid and take about six weeks to hatch. By March the gannets start to migrate and by April only the odd straggler will be left. The best time to see the birds is between early November and late February.

To see the colony, you can do a 10km **walk** (five hours return) along the beach from Clifton, just along from Te Awanga. You must leave no earlier than three hours after high tide and start back no later than 1½ hours after low tide. It's a long walk with no refreshment stops, so go prepared! All trips are dependent on the tides, schedules for which are available from the Napier visitors

THE LONGEST PLACE NAME IN THE WORLD

Hold your breath and then say this name as fast as you can:

Taumatawhakatangihangakoauauotamateaturipukakapikimaungahoronukupokaiwhenuakitanatahu.

The name is a shortened form of 'The Brow of a Hill Where Tamatea, the Man with the Big Knees, Who Slid, Climbed, and Swallowed Mountains, Known as Land Eater, Played his Flute to his Lover'. Tamatea Pokaiwhenua (Land Eater) was a chief so famous for his long travels across the North Island that it was said he ate up the land as he walked. There are many other place names in the region also attributed to this ancient explorer, an inspiration to the modern traveller.

To get to the long-winded hill, travel about 65km south of Napier to Waipukurau (usually simply called 'Wai-puk'). From here, head towards Porangahau on the coast. Follow this road for 40km to the Mangaorapa junction and then follow the 'Historic Sign' indicators. The much-photographed AA road sign is a few kilometres up the hill (on private property) from Mangaorapa station.

centre. No regular buses go to Te Awanga or Clifton from Napier, but **Kiwi Shuttle** (☎ 027-459 3669; tickets NZ$20) goes on demand. There is a rest hut at the colony.

TOURS

Cape Kidnappers Guided Walks (☎ 875 0837; half-/full-day walks NZ$45/90) Offers walks over Summerlee Station, a 2000-hectare sheep-and-cattle run about 2km from Te Awanga.

Gannet Beach Adventures (☎ 0800 426 6387; www.gannets.com; trips NZ$28) Offers rides on a tractor-pulled trailer along the beach, departing the Clifton Beach car park. It's a 20-minute walk from where they drop you off to the main saddle colony. The guided return trip takes about four hours.

Gannet Safaris (☎ 0800 427 232; www.gannetsafaris.com; admission NZ$45) Has a 4WD overland trip that takes you right to the gannet colonies across farmland. It departs from Summerlee Station near Te Awanga.

Beaches

Two popular surf beaches south of Cape Kidnappers are **Ocean Beach** and **Waimarama Beach**. To get to them, take Te Mata Rd out of Havelock North and continue east past Te Mata Peak.

TE UREWERA NATIONAL PARK

☎ 06

Te Urewera is home of the Tuhoe people, one of NZ's most traditional tribes. The army of Te Kooti (see the boxed text, p619) found refuge here during its battles against the government. Te Kooti's successor, Rua Kenana, led a thriving community at Maungapohatu, beneath the sacred mountain of the same name, from 1905 until his politically inspired arrest in 1916. Maungapohatu never recovered after that and only a small settlement remains. Slightly larger is nearby **Ruatahuna**, where the extraordinary Mataatua Marae celebrates Te Kooti's exploits.

Te Urewera National Park is one of the country's most attractive parks and protects part of the largest untouched native forest area in the North Island. It's a marvellous area of lush forests, lakes and rivers, with plenty of birds, trout, deer and other wildlife. The main focus of the park is the superbly scenic Lake Waikaremoana (Sea of Rippling Waters). Most visitors come to walk the Lake Waikaremoana Track, one of NZ's Great Walks (p777), but many other walks are on offer.

Information

The **Aniwaniwa visitors centre** (☎ 837 3803; urewerainfo@doc.govt.nz; 9am-5pm), beside the lake, has interesting displays on the park's natural history and supplies info on walking tracks and accommodation. Hut and camping passes for the Lake Waikaremoana Track can also be bought at DOC offices and visitors centres in Gisborne, Wairoa, Whakatane and Napier.

For online information about the area, check out **Lake Waikaremoana** (www.lake.co.nz).

Activities

Te Urewera Adventures (☎ 366 3969), based out of Ruatahuna, offers one- to three-day horse treks (NZ$120 to NZ$600) in the thick of Te Urewera National Park.

LAKE WAIKAREMOANA TRACK

This three- to four-day tramp is one of the North Island's most popular walks. The 46km track has spectacular views from Panekiri Bluff, but all along the walk – through fern groves, beech and podocarp forest – there are vast panoramas and beautiful views of the lake. The walk is rated as easy and the only difficult section is the climb to Panekiri Bluff. Because of its popularity it's very busy from mid-December to the end of January and at Easter.

The walk can be done year-round, but the cold and rain in winter deter most people and make conditions much more challenging. Because of the altitude, temperatures can drop quickly, even in summer. Walkers should take portable stoves and fuel as there are no cooking facilities in the huts. It's not recommended that you park your car at either end of the track – there have been break-ins.

Five huts and five camping grounds are spaced along the track. It's essential to book through DOC; if you intend doing the walk over the Christmas or New Year period, book as far ahead as possible.

The track can be done either clockwise from Onepoto in the south or anticlockwise from Hopuruahine Bridge in the north. Starting from Onepoto, all the climbing is done in the first few hours. Water on this section of the track is limited so fill your water bottles before heading off. For those with a car, it is safest to leave it at Waikaremoana and then take a boat to the trail heads.

OTHER WALKS

The **Whakatane River Round Trip** (three to five days) starts at Ruatahuna on SH38, 45km from Aniwaniwa visitors centre towards Rotorua. The five-hut track follows Whakatane River then loops back via Waikare River, Motumuka Stream and Whakatane Valley. You can walk north down Whakatane River and out of the national park at Ruatoki, from where you'll probably have to hitch.

The **Manuoha–Waikareiti Track** (three days) is only for experienced trampers. It begins near Hopuruahine and heads up to Manuoha Hut (1392m), the highest point in the park. It then follows a ridge down to pretty Lake Waikareiti via Sandy Bay Hut, before ending at Aniwaniwa.

Popular short/day walks include the **Old Maori Trail** (four hours return), starting at Rosie Bay and following a traditional Maori route to Lake Kaitawa; the **Lake Waikareiti Track** (two hours return) through beech and rimu forest; and the **Ruapani Circuit** (six hours), which takes in wetlands. The DOC booklet *Lake Waikaremoana Walks* (NZ$2.50) lists many good short walks.

Sleeping

There are various camps and cabins along SH38, including a camp, cabins and motel 67km inland from the Wairoa turn-off.

Lake Whakamarino Lodge (☎ 837 3876; www.lakelodge.co.nz; s/d NZ$60/70) This lodge is at Tuai and overlooks peaceful Lake Whakamarino. It offers a high standard of accommodation, as well as lunch (NZ$19) and dinner (NZ$25).

Waikaremoana Motor Camp (☎ 837 3826; misty@lake.co.nz; camp sites per person from NZ$10, dm/s from NZ$20/40) This camping ground is in a wonderful spot on the shore of Lake Waikaremoana, near the visitors centre. It has well-designed wooden chalets, 'fisherman's cabins' sleeping up to five people and camp sites with panoramic views. There's an on-site shop and good fishing facilities.

Big Bush Holiday Park (☎ 0800 525 392, 837 3777; www.lakewaikaremoana.co.nz; camp sites per person from NZ$10, dm/d from NZ$20/65; 💻) Another attractively sited camping ground, located between Lake Waikaremoana and Tuai, with neat cabins and backpacker rooms. It has its own small lake and a licensed restaurant.

There are over 50 DOC back-country huts along the walkways throughout the national park. The five **Lake Waikaremoana Track huts** (per night NZ$14) are rated and priced as Great Walks huts (see p777) and must be prebooked at any time of year; ditto the five DOC **camping grounds** (camp sites per person NZ$10) that also lie along the track.

Getting There & Around

Approximately 105km of road between Wairoa and Rotorua remains unsealed; it's a winding and time-consuming drive. Traffic is light, making it slow for hitching. **Big Bush Holiday Park** (☎ 837 3777) runs a shuttle from Wairoa through to Rotorua (NZ$30) on Monday, Wednesday and Friday, and from Wairoa to the lake daily (NZ$25).

A **shuttle or boat service** (☎ 837 3729) operates on demand from Waikaremoana Motor Camp to either Onepoto or Hopuruahine Stream (NZ$15).

GISBORNE

☎ 06 / pop 32,700

Situated on the small, half-moon sweep of Poverty Bay is Gisborne, NZ's most easterly city and one of the closest in the world to the International Date Line. The Maori name for the area, Tairawhiti, means 'the coast upon which the sun shines across the water' – Gisborne is the first city in the world to see the dawn of each new day. The fertile plains around Gisborne support intensive farming of subtropical fruits, market-garden produce and vineyards. Within easy reach of the city are a number of great surf beaches, making Gisborne something of a surfers' hotspot.

The Gisborne region has been settled for over 1000 years. Two skippers of ancestral migratory *waka* – Paoa of the *Horo-uta* and Kiwa of the *Takitimu* – made an intermarriage pact which led to the founding of Turanganui a Kiwa (now Gisborne) soon after their arrival from Hawaiki. The newly introduced kumera flourished in the fertile soil and the Maori settlement spread to the hinterland.

Even though Gisborne was the site of Cook's first landing in NZ in 1769, European settlement of the region only began in 1831. When the Treaty of Waitangi was signed in 1840 many chiefs from the East Coast refused to acknowledge it (let alone sign it), and by the early 1860s numerous battles between government and Maori forces had broken out. But by 1866 the government

TE KOOTI

The enigmatic Te Kooti was born into the Rongowhakaata tribe in Poverty Bay in the 1830s. As a young man, he was accused of assisting the Hauhau in Gisborne during a siege by government troops and in 1865, along with a number of others, was packed off to exile in the Chatham Islands. Here he experienced the visions that were to eventually lead to the establishment of the Ringatu Church.

In 1867 Te Kooti led an escape from the Chathams; more than 200 men, women and children sailed away on a captured supply ship, the *Rifleman*. They landed at Poverty Bay where, during a ceremony of thanks for their safe return, Te Kooti urged his followers to raise their right hands to pay homage to God rather than kneel in submission. This is believed to be the first time the 'raised hand', from which Ringatu takes its name, was used.

The escapees intended to make their way peaceably into the interior, but resident Poverty Bay magistrate Reginald Biggs demanded they give up their arms. They refused and a series of skirmishes followed, during which government troops suffered a series of humiliating defeats.

Te Kooti attacked Matawhero, killing Biggs and, later, several chiefs, including the father of his first wife. He became both hated and feared, and some of his prisoners decided it would be prudent to become supporters.

Te Kooti became for a while the bogeyman of the entire East Coast, moving his forces in and out of the Urewera range, and attacking both Poverty Bay and Bay of Plenty townships. Finally in 1872, as government forces closed in from three directions, he retreated into the King Country, at that time a vast area entirely under the reign of the Maori king, where government troops dared not venture.

Once under the protection of the king, in Te Kuiti, Te Kooti swore he'd fight no more. He devoted the rest of his life to making peace with his former enemies and formulated the rituals of the Ringatu Church. His reputation as a prophet and healer spread, and he made a series of predictions about a successor (Rua Kenana claimed this mantle in 1905).

After his pardon Te Kooti lived in the Bay of Plenty near Opotiki, and he spent much time visiting other Ringatu centres in the region. He never returned to Poverty Bay and eventually died at Ohiwa Harbour in 1893. His body was removed by his followers from its original burial place and to this day no-one knows for sure exactly where he was finally laid to rest.

Go to Te Kuiti, 19km south of Waitomo, to visit the magnificently carved **Te Tokanganui-o-noho Marae** that Te Kooti helped build for those who looked after him; the *marae* overlooks the southern end of Rora St. The intrepid might also visit the Urewera base of Te Kooti and his successor, Rua Kenana, at Ruatahuna (p617).

had crushed opposition and transported many survivors, including the charismatic Te Kooti (see the boxed text, above), to the remote Chatham Islands, paving the way for an influx of European farmers. However, much of the pasture is today leased from the Maori community.

Information

AA (☎ 868 1424; 363 Gladstone Rd)

DOC office (☎ 869 0460; 63 Carnarvon St; 🕒 8am-4.30pm Mon-Fri) Seek information from the visitors centre before approaching this office.

Gisborne visitors centre (☎ 0800 447 267, 868 6139; www.gisbornenz.com; 209 Grey St; 🕒 7.30am-5.30pm Mon-Fri, 9am-5pm Sat & Sun) Beside the unmissable Canadian totem pole. It has Internet access and stocks the handy free booklet *Gisborne & the Eastland Region* and has info on seasonal fruit picking; also see the There's Work If You Want It boxed text (p615).

Treb-Net (Treble Court, Peel St) Internet access.

Verve (☎ 868 9095; 121 Gladstone Rd) Internet access.

Sights

TAIRAWHITI MUSEUM

This excellent regional **museum** (☎ 867 3832; 18 Stout St; admission by donation; 🕒 10am-4pm Mon-Fri, 1.30-4pm Sat & Sun) has displays on East Coast Maori and colonial history, as well as natural history. The gallery has changing art exhibitions. Outside is a sled house, stable and Wyllie Cottage (1872), the oldest house still standing in Gisborne, with reconstructed Victorian interiors.

Also part of the complex is the **Te Moana Maritime Museum**, behind the main museum.

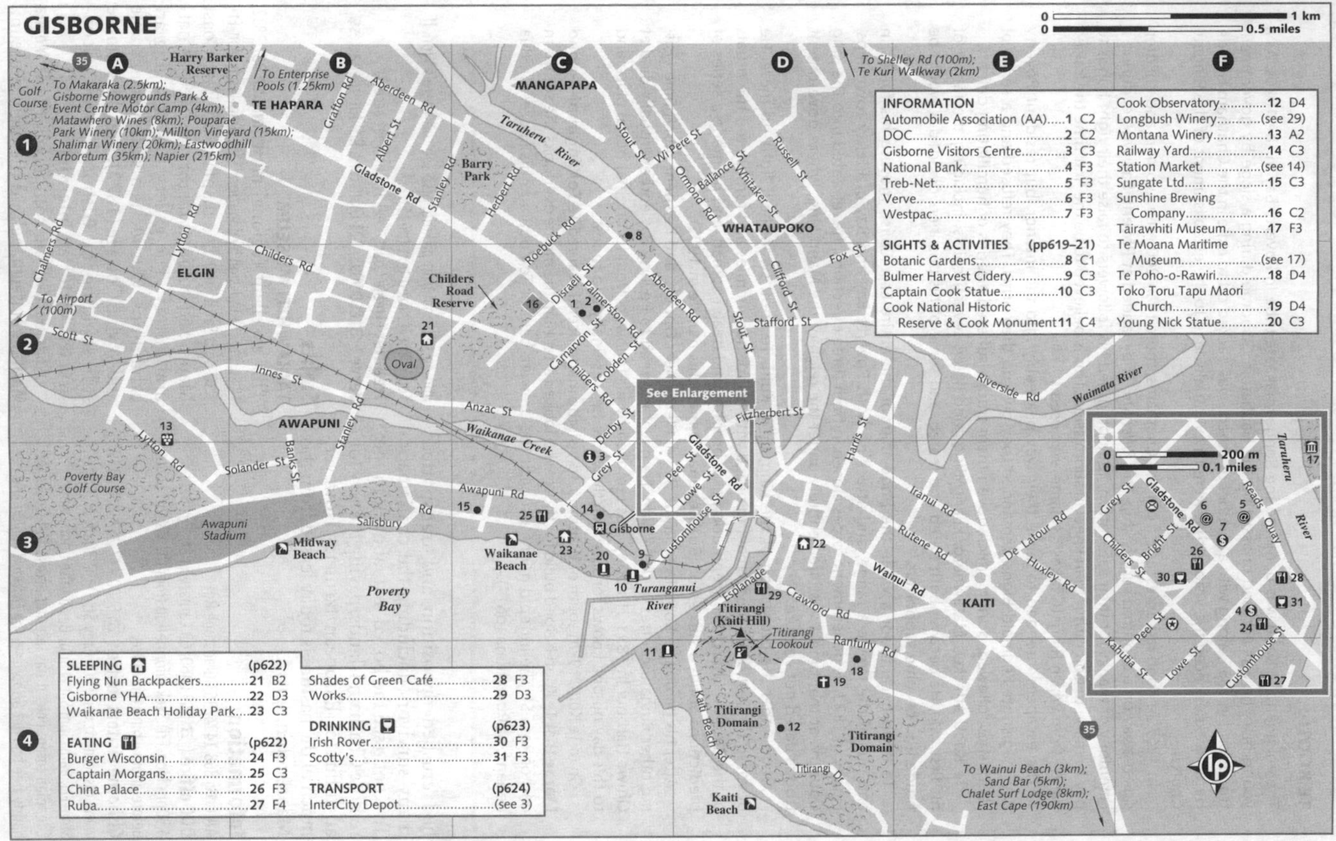
GISBORNE
0 1 km
0 0.5 miles
INFORMATION
Automobile Association (AA).....1 C2
DOC.....2 C2
Gisborne Visitors Centre.....3 C3
National Bank.....4 F3
Treb-Net.....5 F3
Verve.....6 F3
Westpac.....7 F3
SIGHTS & ACTIVITIES (pp619–21)
Botanic Gardens.....8 C1
Bulmer Harvest Cidery.....9 C3
Captain Cook Statue.....10 C3
Cook National Historic Reserve & Cook Monument.....11 C4
Cook Observatory.....12 D4
Longbush Winery.....(see 29)
Montana Winery.....13 A2
Railway Yard.....14 C3
Station Market.....(see 14)
Sungate Ltd.....15 C3
Sunshine Brewing Company.....16 C2
Tairawhiti Museum.....17 F3
Te Moana Maritime Museum.....(see 17)
Te Poho-o-Rawiri.....18 D4
Toko Toru Tapu Maori Church.....19 D4
Young Nick Statue.....20 C3
SLEEPING (p622)
Flying Nun Backpackers.....21 B2
Gisborne YHA.....22 D3
Waikanae Beach Holiday Park.....23 C3
EATING (p622)
Burger Wisconsin.....24 F3
Captain Morgans.....25 C3
China Palace.....26 F3
Ruba.....27 F4
Shades of Green Café.....28 F3
Works.....29 D3
DRINKING (p623)
Irish Rover.....30 F3
Scotty's.....31 F3
TRANSPORT (p624)
InterCity Depot.....(see 3)
To Makaraka (2.5km); Gisborne Showgrounds Park & Event Centre Motor Camp (4km); Matawhero Wines (8km); Pouparae Park Winery (10km); Millton Vineyard (15km); Shalimar Winery (20km); Eastwoodhill Arboretum (35km); Napier (215km)
To Enterprise Pools (1.25km)
To Shelley Rd (100m); Te Kuri Walkway (2km)
To Airport (100m)
To Wainui Beach (3km); Sand Bar (5km); Chalet Surf Lodge (8km); East Cape (190km)
Harry Barker Reserve
Golf Course
TE HAPARA
MANGAPAPA
WHATAUPOKO
ELGIN
AWAPUNI
KAITI
Barry Park
Childers Road Reserve
Oval
Poverty Bay Golf Course
Awapuni Stadium
Midway Beach
Waikanae Beach
Poverty Bay
Taruheru River
Waimata River
Turanganui River
Waikanae Creek
Titirangi (Kaiti Hill)
Titirangi Lookout
Titirangi Domain
Kaiti Beach
Gisborne
See Enlargement
0 200 m
0 0.1 miles

One wild night in 1912, the 12,000-ton *Star of Canada* was blown ashore on the reef at Gisborne. The ship's bridge and captain's cabin were salvaged and eventually installed in what became the town's best-known home, since restored and made into a museum. There are displays on Maori canoes, early whaling and shipping, and Cook's visit to Poverty Bay, and an awesome collection of vintage surfboards.

MONUMENTS

There's a statue of '**Young Nick**' (Nicholas Young), Cook's cabin boy, in a little park on the river mouth. A press-ganged member of Cook's crew, he was the first to sight NZ. Across the bay are the white cliffs that Cook named Young Nick's Head. Also in this park is a statue of **Captain Cook**, standing atop a globe etched with the routes of his voyages.

Across the river at the foot of Kaiti Hill is a **monument** to Cook, near the spot where he first set foot on NZ (on 9 October 1769 in 'ship time' according to Cook's journal, but really the 8th). It's in the Cook National Historic Reserve.

TE POHO-O-RAWIRI

Also at the foot of Titirangi is Te Poho-o-Rawiri Maori meeting house, one of the largest in NZ. It has a richly decorated interior and its stage is framed by *maihi* (ornamental carved gable boards). The human figure kneeling on its right knee with its right hand held upwards is the *tekoteko* (carved figure) representing the ancestor who challenges those who enter the *marae*. The meeting house is always open, except when a function is in progress; seek permission before entering (☎ 868 5364). A little Maori church, **Toko Toru Tapu**, stands on the side of Titirangi, not far from the meeting house.

The free leaflet *Tairawhiti Heritage Trails: Gisborne District* provides good information on historic sites in this Maori ancestral land.

OTHER SIGHTS

Titirangi (Kaiti Hill) has fine views of the area. There's a walking track up from the Cook monument, starting near Waikahua Cottage, which was once a refuge during the Hauhau unrest. Near the top is yet another monument to Cook, but it's a fine one. At the 135m summit is the **Cook Observatory**. The **Gisborne Astronomical Society** (☎ 867 7901; admission NZ$2) meets here at 8.30pm on Tuesday in summer, 7.30pm in winter; all are welcome.

Down on **Kaiti Beach**, low tide attracts a wealth of bird life, including stilts, oystercatchers and other pelagic visitors.

The huge **Eastwoodhill Arboretum** (☎ 863 9003; www.eastwoodhill.org.nz; 2392 Wharekopae Rd, Ngatapa; admission NZ$8; 🕒 9am-5pm), 35km west of town, has NZ's largest collection of northern hemisphere temperate trees, shrubs and climbers. To get there follow the Ngatapa-Rere Rd; there's a 45-minute walk marked through the trees and budget accommodation in the park (dorm bed NZ$25). The **Botanic Gardens** are in town beside the Taruheru River.

Also of interest is the **Station Market** (Grey St; 🕒 10am-4pm Tue-Sat), consisting of a string of small shops and a homely café on the long-disused railway station platform. The **Gisborne City Vintage Railway** (☎ 867 5083; 2hr trip NZ$35) runs steam-train excursions on the track to Wairoa three to four times a year; the engine is kept in the adjoining **Railway Yard** (☎ 867 0385; admission by donation; 🕒 9am-1pm Sat).

Gisborne is a major wine-producing area noted for its white varietals; more than a third of NZ's chardonnay grapes are grown here. Wineries to visit include **Matawhero Wines** (☎ 868 8366; 185 Riverpoint Rd), **Millton Vineyard** (☎ 862 8680; 119 Papatu Rd, Manutuke), **Pouparae Park** (☎ 867 7931; 385 Bushmere Rd) and **Shalimar** (☎ 863 7776; Ngatapa Rd), and the **Longbush** (☎ 863 0627; The Esplanade) and **Montana** (☎ 868 2757; Lytton Rd) vineyards in town. The visitors centre has details on opening hours and tours.

There is also a natural beer brewery, the **Sunshine Brewing Company** (☎ 867 7777; 109 Disraeli St), and **Bulmer Harvest Cidery** (☎ 868 8300; Customhouse St); both have tastings and cellar-door sales.

Activities

SWIMMING & SURFING

You can swim at **Waikanae Beach** in the city, while **Midway Beach** has a surf club and a swimming complex with a big waterslide and children's playground. **Wainui Beach** also has a surf club where you can safely swim between the flags. **Enterprise Pools** (☎ 867 9249; Nelson Rd; admission NZ$2.50; 🕒 6am-3pm Mon & Fri, 6.30am-8pm Tue-Thu, 2-5pm Sat & Sun) is an indoor complex open to the public.

Surfing is hugely popular in Gisborne, with many surf beaches close to the city.

Waikanae Beach is good for learners, while more experienced surfers can choose from the **Pipe**, south of town, or **Sponge Bay Island**, just to the north. The bays of **Wainui** and **Makrori**, on SH35 heading towards East Cape, also have plenty of breaks.

Sungate Ltd (☎ 868 1673; 55 Salisbury Rd) hires out an array of water-sports equipment, including surfboards (NZ$10 per hour) and boogie boards (NZ$5 per hour). **Surfing with Frank** (☎ 867 0823) offers private lessons for NZ$40 and group lessons for NZ$30; wetsuits and boards are provided.

OTHER ACTIVITIES

The adventurous can get in submersible metal cages for close-ups of mako sharks ('waterborne pussycats') with **Surfit Charters** (☎ 867 2970; www.surfit.co.nz; 48 Awapuni Rd; adult from NZ$165). Tamer snorkelling on the reefs around Gisborne can also be arranged.

Gisborne Quad Adventures (☎ 868 4394; www.gisbornequadadventures.co.nz; 176 Valley Rd; adult per hr from NZ$60) runs quad-bike safaris through local farmland and bush.

The 5.6km **Te Kuri Walkway** (three hours) starts 4km north of town at the end of Shelley Rd and leads through farmland and some forest to a commanding viewpoint. The walk is closed from August to October for lambing.

Waimoana Horse Trekking (☎ 868 8218; Wainui Beach; 1hr treks NZ$30) takes you up over hilly farmland and down onto sandy Wainui Beach.

Tours

Whale Rider Tours (☎ 868 5878; tereiputald@xtra.co.nz; tours NZ$50) offers guided tours of the locations used in the award-winning *Whale Rider* film. Bookings can be made at the Gisborne visitors centre.

Sleeping

Chalet Surf Lodge (☎ 868 9612; www.chaletsurf.co.nz; 62 Moana Rd, Wainui Beach; dm/d NZ$20/50; 💻) This mellow place is in a great spot opposite Wainui Beach, around 8km from town, and is popular with surfers. There's a big, open communal area and a range of rooms available. Surf lessons start at NZ$35 and there's free bike and boogie-board use.

Flying Nun Backpackers (☎ 868 0461; 147 Roebuck Rd; dm/s/d from NZ$17/27/45) This historic former convent was where famous NZ opera diva Dame Kiri Te Kanawa had her early singing lessons. They're big on security and there are spacious rooms and a big, open garden.

Gisborne YHA (☎ 867 3269; yha.gis@clear.net.nz; 32 Harris St; dm/d from NZ$17/40; 💻) Situated 1.5km from the city centre across the river, this hostel is in a substantial old home full of character, with spacious grounds. It's a sociable place but big enough, and far enough away from the city, to be a quiet retreat too.

Waikanae Beach Holiday Park (☎ 867 5634; Grey St; camp sites per person from NZ$10, d from NZ$30) This family-friendly camp has an enviable location on glorious Waikanae Beach, with 'ranch house'-style cabins and motel units. Surfboards and bikes are available for hire and there's a tennis court next door.

Gisborne Showgrounds Park & Event Centre Motor Camp (☎ 867 5299; www.gisborneshow.co.nz; 20 Main Rd; camp sites per person from NZ$10, d from NZ$30) This huge park, 4km from the city centre at Makaraka, is a shady, restful place with newish cabins and good on-site facilities.

Eating

Ruba (☎ 868 6516; 14 Childers Rd; mains NZ$12-23; 🕑 breakfast & lunch Mon-Sat, dinner Thu-Sat) Ruba is a stylish licensed restaurant and coffee bar with an eclectic menu of salads, pasta, fish and lamb. It's a pleasant stop for a drink, too, and sells packaged coffee and mugs.

Shades of Green Café (☎ 868 1450; cnr Lowe St & Reads Quay; mains from NZ$12; 🕑 breakfast & lunch Mon-Sat, dinner Thu-Sat) This laid-back café with its 'ethnic' décor serves salads, pasta and organic veggie options. It's also a good place for tea and muffins.

Burger Wisconsin (☎ 867 6442; 26 Gladstone Rd; burgers NZ$6.50-9.50; 🕑 lunch & dinner) It's hard to beat the variety of burgers at this takeaway chain. Pumpkin, tofu, satay and blue cheese are just some of the flavours on offer, and there's a small seating area.

Captain Morgans (☎ 867 7821; 285 Grey St; burgers NZ$4-7; 🕑 breakfast, lunch & dinner) This popular eatery is close to Waikanae Beach. The burgers are particularly good and particularly large.

China Palace (☎ 867 4911; 55 Peel St; mains NZ$10-19; 🕑 lunch & dinner) China Palace offers a good-value smorgasbord on Friday, Saturday and Sunday evenings, and, alas, karaoke on weekdays.

Works (☎ 863 1285; Esplanade; mains NZ$10-26; 🕑 lunch & dinner) Housed in part of Gisborne's original freezing works, this is an excellent winery-restaurant serving imaginative meat, fish and vegetarian dishes. It also has a predictably extensive wine list, if you just want to sit back and sample the local produce.

Drinking

Irish Rover (☎ 867 1112; 66 Peel St) This Irish theme pub is packed at the weekend, and there's occasional live music. Watch out for the 'no hats, no undesirable tattoos' sign on the door.

Scotty's (☎ 867 8173; 35 Gladstone Rd) Scotty's is a popular local hang-out and gets lively on the weekend. The large garden bar fills up on hot summer afternoons and there's the occasional live band.

EAST CAPE

North of Gisborne is the isolated, little-visited East Cape, with a wild bushy interior divided by the Raukumara Range, and a cove-riddled coastline shadowed for 330km by the magnificently scenic SH35. On a sunny day the water is an inviting turquoise, while at other times a layer of clouds hangs on the craggy mountains rising straight up from the beaches and everything turns a misty green. Dozens of fresh, clear streams flow through remote gorges to meet the sea, and during summer the coastline turns crimson with the blooming of the pohutukawa trees that line the seashore. The region is inhabited by friendly, predominantly Maori communities living a slow-paced life. Locals are passionate about rugby and especially their rugby team, Ngati Porou East Coast – don't pass up the chance to see a match.

Highlights of a trip east from Opotiki along the cape's northern coast include the beaches at **Torere** and **Hawai**, both steeply shelved and covered with driftwood; the superb carvings at the Tukaki meeting house at **Te Kaha**; beautiful **Whanarua Bay**; and **Raukokore Anglican Church**, standing like a picture postcard on a lone promontory. **Hicks Bay** is a magnificent place, complemented by nearby Horseshoe Bay, while **Te Araroa** has in its school grounds one of NZ's largest pohutukawa, **Te Waha o Rerekohu**, reputed to be over 600 years old. East of Te Araroa is **East Cape Lighthouse**, the most easterly tip of mainland NZ.

South of Te Araroa is the important Maori town of **Ruatoria**, centre of the Ngati Porou tribe, with 1752m-high **Mt Hikurangi** as an impressive backdrop; **Tokomaru Bay**, a crumbling, picturesque town with a splendid beach and activity options for surfers, trampers and swimmers; and **Tolaga Bay**, with another fine beach (3km south of town) and the **Cooks Cove Walkway** (2½ hours return). South of Tolaga Bay is the small settlement **Whangara**, the setting for Witi Ihimaera's wonderful novel *The Whale Rider*, which was also filmed here; tours of locations used in the film are conducted from Gisborne (opposite).

The cape's interior is one of NZ's last frontiers, as wild as parts of south Westland. To go white-water rafting on the **Waioeka** and **Motu Rivers**; contact **Wet 'n' Wild Rafting** (☎ 0800 462 7238; www.wetnwildrafting.co.nz). See DOC offices in Opotiki and Gisborne for details of the area's wild **walks** and rare wildlife like the whio (blue duck) and Hochstetter's frog *(Leiopelma hochstetteri)*.

The **Maori Tourism Network** (☎ 06-864 4694) produces a leaflet on activities and accommodation around the cape, available in various visitors centres. The **Opotiki visitors centre** (☎ 07-315 8484; www.eastlandnz.com; cnr St John & Elliott Sts, Opotiki; 🕑 8am-5pm) distributes the *Opotiki & East Cape* booklet and shares its building with **DOC** (☎ 07-315 1001). Note that the telephone area code from Opotiki east to Hicks Bay is ☎ 07, while from Te Araroa onwards past the cape and south to Gisborne the code is ☎ 06.

Travel around East Cape is often slow and sometimes nonexistent, especially on weekends, but several operators link Hicks Bay near the tip of the cape with Opotiki (on the Bay of Plenty) and Gisborne, including **Matakaoa Coast Line Couriers** (☎ 0800 628 252), **East Land Couriers** (☎ 07-315 6350), **Polly's Passenger Courier** (☎ 06-864 4728) and **Cook's Courier** (☎ 06-864 4711); book all shuttle services, which will either pick you up from where you're staying or arrange a place to meet. Another transport option is to join **Kiwi Experience's** (☎ 09-366 9830; www.kiwiexperience.com) 'East As' backpacker bus, which does a circuit from Taupo (NZ$260), taking a minimum of four days. **Kiwi Trails** (☎ 07-343 7922; www.kiwitrails.co.nz) does round-cape trips on demand (NZ$280), operating out of Rotorua. Hitching can be challenging at times due to the general lack of traffic heading around the cape, but your hostel or motel will usually be able to find you a ride.

Sand Bar (☎ 868 6828; Oneroa Rd) The Sand Bar is a friendly, convivial place out at Wainui. The best nights are Thursday to Saturday; a shuttle runs from the bar to Gisborne's centre at midnight.

Getting There & Away

AIR

Air New Zealand (☎ 0800 737 000, 868 2700; www.airnz.co.nz; 37 Bright St) has daily direct flights to Auckland (from NZ$85) and Wellington (from NZ$100), with onward connections to places like Rotorua and Hamilton.

BUS

The **InterCity** (☎ 868 6139; www.intercitycoach.co.nz) depot is at the visitors centre. InterCity has one bus daily (leaves at 9am) to Napier (NZ$35, four hours) via Wairoa (NZ$20, 1½ hours) and also runs a service (leaves 8am) between Gisborne and Auckland (NZ$70, nine hours) via Opotiki (NZ$25, two hours), Whakatane (NZ$35, three hours) and Rotorua (NZ$50, 4½ hours).

HITCHING

Hitching is OK from the south of the city, and not too bad through Waioeka Gorge to Opotiki – it's still best to leave early. To hitch a ride out, head along Gladstone Rd to Makaraka, 6km west, for Wairoa and Napier, or the turn-off to Opotiki and Rotorua.

Getting Around

Taxi Buses (☎ 867 2222) runs the town's bus service, which only operates on weekdays. Taxis include **Gisborne Taxis** (☎ 867 2222) and **Eastland Taxis** (☎ 868 1133). **Link Taxis** (☎ 868 8385) runs between Gisborne's centre and the airport (around NZ$12), which is located about 2km west of town.

WELLINGTON

☎ **04 / pop 205,500**

A thriving café and entertainment scene, steep hills and spectacular views of a rugged coastline, challenging walks, a sheltered and water-sports-conducive harbour, and a serious dedication to the arts make Wellington an enormously enjoyable city, with much to keep you occupied and satisfied within its funky and energetic confines. As NZ's capital city, Wellington is also home to the country's parliament and its national treasures, the latter on prominent display in several fine museums and galleries.

Wellington is perched on the southeastern tip of the North Island, squaring off to a tangle of islands in Marlborough Sounds across Cook Strait. Its location makes the city a major travel crossroads between the North and South Islands. As every visitor soon finds out, this off-strait locale is also the reason why the city has inherited the well-deserved nickname 'Windy Welly'.

Wellington's most recent claim to fame was as host for the world premiere of *The Return of the King* (2003), the final instalment of director Peter Jackson's epic cinematic trilogy, *The Lord of the Rings*.

Don't Miss: browsing the treasures of Te Papa (the 'Museum of New Zealand'), riding the cable car up to the Botanic Garden's great views, kayaking and surfing out on the water, drinking in a slick bar on Courtenay Pl or Cuba St, then having a strong wake-up espresso in a Bohemian café the next morning.

HISTORY

Maori legend has it that the explorer Kupe was the first person to discover Wellington harbour. The original Maori name for the area was Te Whanga Nui a Tara, Tara being the son of a Maori chief named Whatonga who had settled on the Hawkes Bay coast. Whatonga sent Tara and his half-brother to explore the southern part of the North Island. When they returned over a year later, their reports were so favourable that Whatonga's followers moved there, founding the Ngati Tara tribe.

The first European settlers arrived in the NZ Company's ship *Aurora* on 22 January 1840, not long after Colonel William Wakefield arrived to buy land from the Maori people. The idea was to build two cities: one would be a commercial centre by the harbour (Port Nicholson) and the other, further north, would be the agricultural hub. However, the Maori community denied they had sold the land at Port Nicholson, or Poneke, as they called it. As it was founded on hasty and illegal buying by the NZ Company, land-rights struggles followed and were to plague the country for years, still affecting it today.

GETTING INTO TOWN

Wellington Airport (☎ 385 5100; www.wellington-airport.co.nz; closed 2-4am) is 7km southeast of the city centre. **Super Shuttle** (☎ 0800 748 885, 387 8787; www.supershuttle.co.nz; tickets NZ$15-20) provides a door-to-door minibus service between the city and the airport at any hour.

The **Stagecoach Flyer** (☎ 387 8700; www.stagecoach.co.nz; airport-city NZ$5) is a local bus running between the airport, Wellington city and the Hutt Valley. Buses run from the city to the airport from 5.45am to 7.45pm weekdays and 6.15am to 8.15pm weekends; from the airport, buses run 6.20am to 8.20pm weekdays and 6.50am to 8.50pm weekends.

A taxi between the city centre and the airport costs NZ$15 to NZ$20.

Wellington Train Station (Map pp626-7; ☎ 498 2058; off Waterloo Quay; 7.15am-5.30pm Mon-Fri, 7.15am-12.15pm Sat & Sun) is less than 1.5km north of the city centre; long-distance buses arrive at and depart from here. To get into the centre of Wellington, head for the bus stop (Map pp626–7) outside the station and catch one of the many city-bound services; a good option is the distinctive yellow **City Circular bus** (fare NZ$2) that loops the main inner-city sites regularly each day.

Three ferry operators plough across Cook Strait (see Getting There & Away, p641): Interislander services arrive and depart from the Interislander terminal (Map pp626–7) in the north of town, while Lynx and Bluebridge/Strait Shipping services are based at Waterloo Quay (Map pp626–7), not far from the train station. A free ferry shuttle-bus service operates between the ferries and the train station (where long-distance buses also depart), departing from the train station 35 minutes before each sailing. A shuttle meets all arriving ferries.

In the 1850s Wellington was a thriving settlement of around 5000 people. In 1855 an earthquake razed part of Hutt Rd and the area from Te Aro flat to the Basin Reserve, which initiated the first major land reclamation. In 1865 the seat of government was moved from Auckland to Wellington, a political status that the city has since embellished with numerous cultural institutions.

ORIENTATION

The city congregates on one side of the harbour, which was formed by the flooding of a huge valley, but it's so cramped for space that many workers live in the two narrow valleys leading north between the steep, rugged hills; one is the Hutt Valley and the other follows SH1 through Tawa and Porirua.

Lambton Quay, the main business street, wriggles along almost parallel to the seafront (which it once was). The heart of the city stretches from the train station, at the northern end of Lambton Quay, to Cambridge and Kent Tces. Thorndon, immediately north of the centre, is the historic area and embassy district.

The waterfront along Jervois Quay, Cable St and Oriental Pde is an increasingly revitalised area – Oriental Pde is Wellington's premier seafront boulevard. Cuba Mall, Courtenay Pl, Manners St, Willis St and Queens Wharf, as well as Lambton Quay, are where the action is, be it for eating, drinking or shopping.

INFORMATION

Bookshops

Arty Bees (Map pp630-1; ☎ 385 1819; 17 Courtenay Pl; www.artybees.co.nz) Massive second-hand bookshop specialising in science fiction, fantasy and detective novels.

Bellamy's (Map pp630-1; ☎ 384 7770; 105 Cuba St) Second-hand bookshop, with a wide selection of *Maoritanga* (Maori culture) and NZ books.

Dymocks (Map pp626-7; ☎ 472 2080; 366 Lambton Quay)

Map Shop (Map pp630-1; ☎ 385 1462; www.mapshop.co.nz; 193 Vivian St; 8.30am-5.30pm Mon-Fri, 10am-1pm Sat) Carries a great range of NZ city and regional maps, plus topographic maps for trampers.

Unity Books (Map pp630-1; ☎ 499 4245; 57 Willis St) Local institution with an excellent fiction section, including NZ literature.

Whitcoull's (Map pp630-1; ☎ 384 2065; 91 Cuba Mall)

Emergency

For police, fire and ambulance emergencies call ☎ 111.

Internet Access

Internet facilities are plentiful with fast connections; most places charge a minimum of NZ$1 per 15 minutes. Most backpackers also have Internet facilities. Central places with numerous terminals include:

GREATER WELLINGTON

0 — 400 m
0 — 0.2 miles

INFORMATION

Accident and Urgent Medical Centre........1 C8
After-Hours Pharmacy........(see 1)
American Express........(see 56)
Australian High Commission........2 C2
Automobile Association (AA)........3 B5
Canadian High Commission........4 B3
DOC Visitors Centre........5 B4
Dymocks........6 B5
German Embassy........7 C2
Israeli Embassy........8 B4
Main Post Office........9 C4
Netherlands Embassy........10 B4
Thomas Cook........(see 6)
UK High Commission........11 B3
US Embassy........12 B2

SIGHTS & ACTIVITIES (pp628–32)

Academy Galleries........13 B5
Beehive........14 B4
Botanic Gardens........15 A4
Cable Car Museum........(see 63)
Carter Observatory........16 A5
Colonial Cottage Museum........17 A8
Fergs Rock 'n' Kayaks........18 C5
Freyberg Swimming Pool & Fitness Centre........19 D6
Government Buildings........(see 5)
H2OSports........20 D6
Katherine Mansfield's Mansfield's Birthplace........21 C2
Lady Norwood Rose Garden........22 A4
Mt Victoria Lookout........23 E7
Museum of Wellington City & Sea........24 B5
National Archives........25 C3
National Cricket Museum........26 C8
National Library Gallery........27 B3
National Tattoo Museum........28 B7
Old St Paul's Cathedral........29 C3
Parliament House........30 B3
Parliamentary Library........31 B3
Premier House........32 A3

To Otari-Wilton's Bush (1.8km)

To Omega Rental Cars (500m); Ace Rental Cars (950m)

To SH1 & SH2; Hutt Park Holiday Village (13km); Lower Hutt (18km); Plimmerton (23km); Moana Lodge (25km); Upper Hutt (28km); Harcourt Holiday Park (35km); Kapiti Coast (71km); The Wairarapa (98km)

To Makara Peak Mountain Bike Park (4km)

Wellington-Picton Ferry (Interislander Services)

Wellington-Picton Ferry (Lynx Catamaran Services)

Ferry to Days Bay & Matiu-Somes Island

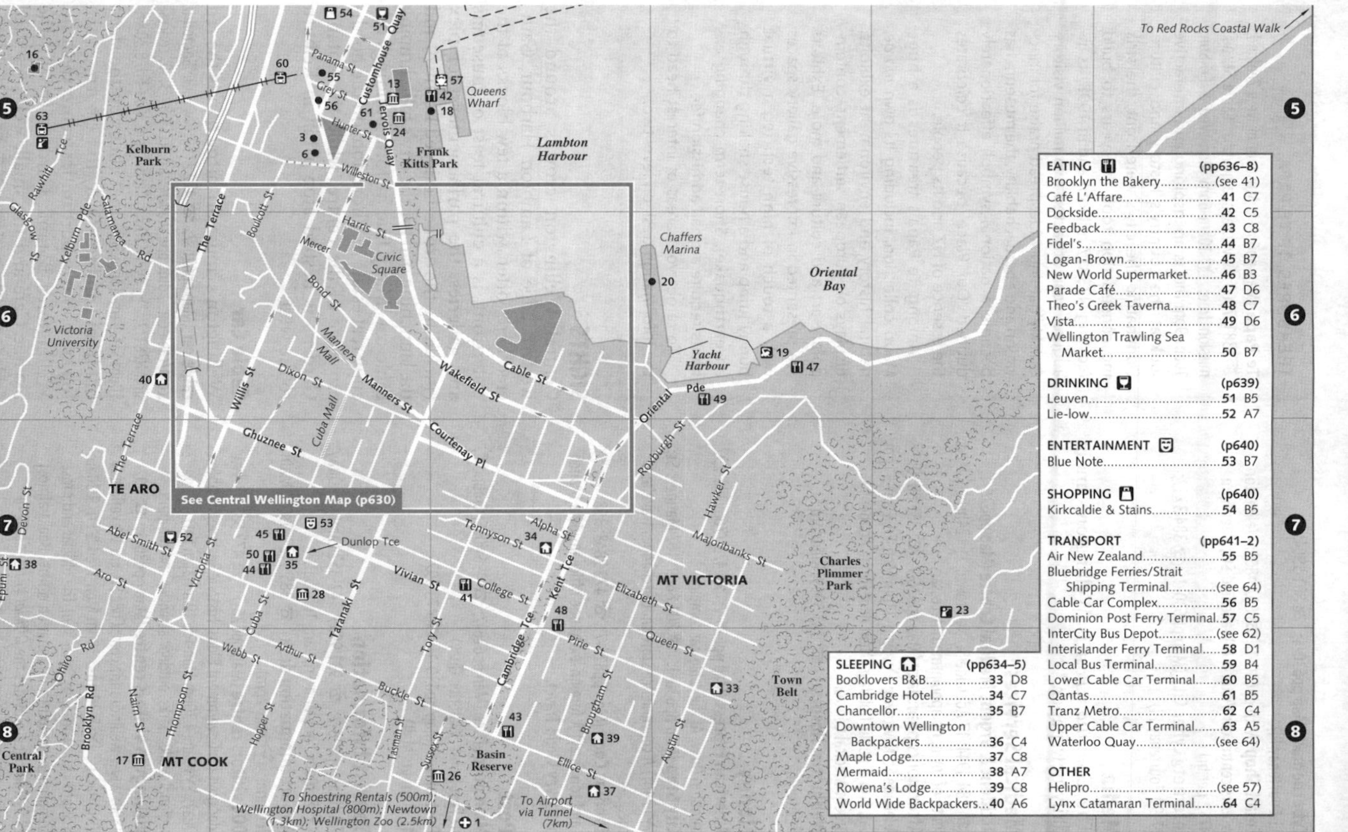
EATING (pp636–8)
Brooklyn the Bakery...............(see 41)
Café L'Affare..........................41 C7
Dockside................................42 C5
Feedback................................43 C8
Fidel's....................................44 B7
Logan-Brown..........................45 B7
New World Supermarket.........46 B3
Parade Café...........................47 D6
Theo's Greek Taverna.............48 C7
Vista.......................................49 D6
Wellington Trawling Sea Market.....50 B7
DRINKING (p639)
Leuven....................................51 B5
Lie-low....................................52 A7
ENTERTAINMENT (p640)
Blue Note................................53 B7
SHOPPING (p640)
Kirkcaldie & Stains..................54 B5
TRANSPORT (pp641–2)
Air New Zealand......................55 B5
Bluebridge Ferries/Strait Shipping Terminal.............(see 64)
Cable Car Complex.................56 B5
Dominion Post Ferry Terminal.57 C5
InterCity Bus Depot................(see 62)
Interislander Ferry Terminal.....58 D1
Local Bus Terminal..................59 B4
Lower Cable Car Terminal.......60 B5
Qantas....................................61 B5
Tranz Metro............................62 C4
Upper Cable Car Terminal.......63 A5
Waterloo Quay.......................(see 64)
OTHER
Helipro...................................(see 57)
Lynx Catamaran Terminal.......64 C4
SLEEPING (pp634–5)
Booklovers B&B.................33 D8
Cambridge Hotel................34 C7
Chancellor..........................35 B7
Downtown Wellington Backpackers..................36 C4
Maple Lodge.......................37 C8
Mermaid.............................38 A7
Rowena's Lodge.................39 C8
World Wide Backpackers...40 A6
To Red Rocks Coastal Walk
Lambton Harbour
Queens Wharf
Frank Kitts Park
Chaffers Marina
Oriental Bay
Yacht Harbour
Oriental Pde
Civic Square
Kelburn Park
Victoria University
See Central Wellington Map (p630)
TE ARO
MT VICTORIA
MT COOK
Charles Plimmer Park
Town Belt
Basin Reserve
Central Park
Panama St
Grey St
Hunter St
Customhouse Quay
Jervois Quay
Willeston St
Harris St
Mercer
Bond St
Manners Mall
Manners St
Wakefield St
Cable St
Courtenay Pl
Dixon St
Cuba Mall
Ghuznee St
Willis St
Boulcott St
The Terrace
Salamanca Rd
Kelburn Pde
Rawhiti Tce
Glasgow St
Devon St
Epuni St
Abel Smith St
Aro St
Victoria St
Dunlop Tce
Vivian St
Tennyson St
Alpha St
Kent Tce
Cambridge Tce
College St
Taranaki St
Cuba St
Arthur St
Webb St
Tory St
Pirie St
Elizabeth St
Majoribanks St
Hawker St
Roxburgh St
Queen St
Brougham St
Austin St
Buckle St
Tasman St
Sussex St
Hopper St
Thompson St
Nairn St
Brooklyn Rd
Ohiro Rd
Ellice St
To Shoestring Rentals (500m); Wellington Hospital (800m); Newtown (1.3km); Wellington Zoo (2.5km)
To Airport via Tunnel (7km)

Cybernomad (Map pp630-1; ☎ 801 5964; 43 Courtenay Pl)
Email Shop (Map pp630-1; ☎ 802 4860; Wellington visitors centre, cnr Victoria & Wakefield Sts; after 6pm NZ$2 per hr)
Internet@Cyber City (Map pp630-1; ☎ 384 3717; 97-99 Courtenay Pl)

Media

The *Dominion Post* is Wellington's main daily newspaper.

Medical Services

Accident & Urgent Medical Centre (Map pp626-7; ☎ 384 4944; 17 Adelaide St, Newtown; 24hr) Located south of town; no appointment necessary.
After-hours pharmacy (Map pp626-7; ☎ 385 8810; Adelaide St, Newtown; 5pm-11pm Mon-Fri, 8am-11pm Sat, Sun & public holidays) Next door to the Accident & Urgent Medical Centre.
Wellington Hospital (☎ 385 5999; Riddiford St, Newtown)

Money

American Express (Map pp626-7; ☎ 473 7766; 280-292 Lambton Quay) At the cable-car complex.
City Stop (Map pp630-1; ☎ 801 8669; 107 Manners St; 24hr) A convenience store that exchanges travellers cheques.
Thomas Cook (Map pp626-7; ☎ 472 2848; 358 Lambton Quay) A foreign-exchange office inside a branch of Harvey World Travel.

Post

Main post office (Map pp626-7; ☎ 496 4065; Ground fl, NZ Post House, Waterloo Quay)
Post office (Map pp630-1; ☎ 473 5922; 43 Manners Mall)

Tourist Information

AA (Map pp626-7; ☎ 931 9999; 342-352 Lambton Quay; 8.30am-5pm Mon-Fri, 9am-1pm Sat)
Airport information desk (☎ 385 5123; 1st fl, Main Terminal; 7am-7pm)
DOC visitors centre (Map pp626-7; ☎ 472 5821; www.doc.govt.nz; Government Bldgs, Historic Reserve, Lambton Quay; 9am-4.30pm Mon-Fri, 10am-3pm Sat) Info on regional walks, parks, outdoor activities and camping.
Wellington visitors centre (Map pp630-1; ☎ 802 4860; www.wellingtonnz.com; Civic Sq, cnr Wakefield & Victoria Sts; 8.30am-5.30pm Mon-Wed & Fri, 9.30am-5.30pm Thu, 9am-5pm Sat & Sun) The official and most comprehensive tourist information centre. Books almost everything and provides the *Official Visitor Guide to Wellington*, plus other useful brochures.

TREASURES OF TE PAPA

Te Papa (Map pp630-1; Museum of New Zealand; ☎ 381 7000; www.tepapa.govt.nz; Cable St; admission free; 10am-6pm Mon-Wed & Fri-Sun, 10am-9pm Thu) is an inspiring and interactive look at the country's history and culture. Dominating the city's waterfront, the striking construction took five years to build (costing NZ$317 million) and in 1998, its inaugural year, attracted two million visitors. Quickly gaining widespread praise for innovation and approachability, the museum has become a national symbol, affectionately dubbed 'Our Place' because it celebrates the essence of NZ and its people.

Among Te Papa's treasures is a huge Maori collection, including its own *marae*, natural history and environment exhibits, displays on European settlement, contemporary art and culture and more. Exhibits are presented in impressive gallery spaces with a touch of high tech (eg a virtual bungy jump and a house shaking through an earthquake). Short-term changing exhibits require a small admission fee.

To target your areas of interest head to the information desk on level two.

SIGHTS

Central Wellington crowds around the western edge of Lambton Harbour. Gathered here, often within a few blocks of the waterfront, is a cultural feast of museums and galleries, the parliamentary complex (including the drone-besieged Beehive) and the launching pad for the city's hill-climbing cable car. Many fine historic buildings occupy real estate in Thorndon, on the northern edge of the centre, while the Botanic Gardens is nestled atop a hill in Kelburn to the west.

Cable Car

Wellington's 'must-do' attraction is the red **cable car** (Map pp626-7; ☎ 472 2199; www.wellingtonnz.com/cablecar; adult one way/return NZ$1.80/3.60, concession NZ$1/2; every 10min 7am-10pm Mon-Fri, 8.30am-10pm Sat, 9am-10pm Sun) that chugs up the steep hill from Lambton Quay to Kelburn. At the top are photo opportunities galore, fresh air, Wellington's Botanic Gardens (p630), the Skyline Café and the small, well-presented **Cable Car Museum** (Map pp626-7; ☎ 475 3578; admission free; ⏲ 9am-5pm), which tells the cable car's tale since it began in 1902.

Stroll back down to central Wellington either through the Botanic Gardens or by a series of steps which interconnect with roads (a 30- to 40-minute walk).

Museums

MUSEUM OF WELLINGTON CITY & SEA

The three-storey **Museum of Wellington City & Sea** (Map pp626-7; ☎ 472 8904; www.museumofwellington.co.nz; Queens Wharf; admission free; ⏲ 10am-5pm) offers an imaginative interactive experience of Wellington's rich maritime history and social heritage since Maori settlement. There's an impressive lighthouse lens, and ancient Maori legends are dramatically told using tiny hologram actors and excellent special effects. There's also a moving documentary about the *Wahine*, a Wellington–Christchurch car ferry that in 1968 was blown by fierce winds onto Barrett's Reef just outside the harbour entrance, eventually sinking with the loss of 51 lives.

MEDIAPLEX & FILM ARCHIVE

Highlighting Wellington's square-eyed dedication to film and television is **Mediaplex** (Map pp630-1; ☎ 384 7647; www.filmarchive.org.nz; 84 Taranaki St; admission free; ⏲ noon-5pm Sun-Thu, noon-8pm Fri & Sat), a new, innovative complex combining film, archive, a library, cinema and research centre all under one architecturally designed roof. It has an extensive collection of over 90,000 NZ film, television and video titles, dating from 1895 and stretching right up to current-day sitcoms.

OTHER MUSEUMS

The **National Tattoo Museum** (Map pp626-7; ☎ 385 6444; www.mokomuseum.org.nz; 42 Abel Smith St; adult/concession NZ$5/4; ⏲ noon-5.30pm Tue-Sat) has thousands of examples of tattoo art on show, including Maori *moko* (facial tattoos), traditional and contemporary tools, and a tattoo studio in case the urge strikes. For dedicated ink-lovers only.

Cricket aficionados will be bowled over by the historical memorabilia at the **National Cricket Museum** (Map pp626-7; ☎ 385 6602; Basin Reserve; admission NZ$3; ⏲ 10.30am-3.30pm Nov-Mar, 10.30am-3.30pm Sat & Sun Apr-Oct). There's an extensive range of videos, displays on cricket's arrival in the colonies and the first international test in 1894, as well as the original Addington bat.

The **Colonial Cottage Museum** (Map pp626-7; ☎ 384 9122; www.colonialcottagemuseum.co.nz; 68 Nairn St; admission NZ$5; ⏲ noon-4pm late Dec to Apr, noon-4pm Wed-Sun May to late Dec) is central Wellington's oldest building, built in 1858 by carpenter William Wallis and lived in by his family until 1977. The museum relates the story of family life in colonial Wellington.

Galleries

For a comprehensive list of Wellington's public, independent and dealer galleries, pick up a copy of the *Arts Map* brochure from the visitors centre.

KATHERINE MANSFIELD

Katherine Mansfield is NZ's most distinguished author, famous for her short stories and often compared to Chekhov and Maupassant.

Born Kathleen Mansfield Beauchamp in 1888, she left Wellington at 19 for Europe, where she spent the rest of her short adult life. She mixed with Europe's most famous writers, such as DH Lawrence, TS Eliot and Virginia Woolf, and married the literary critic and author John Middleton Murry in 1918. In 1923, aged 34, she died of tuberculosis at Fontainebleau in France. It was not until 1945 that her five books of short stories (*In a German Pension, Bliss, The Garden Party, The Dove's Nest* and *Something Childish*) were combined into a single volume, *Collected Stories of Katherine Mansfield*.

Katherine Mansfield's birthplace (Map pp626-7; ☎ 473 7268; http://www.bookcouncil.org.nz/tourism/destinations/kmbirthplace.html; 25 Tinakori Rd; admission NZ$5.50; ⏲ 10am-4pm) is a lovingly restored house with a restful heritage garden. Mansfield spent five years of her childhood here, and the house is mentioned in her stories *The Aloe* (which in its final form became *Prelude*) and *A Birthday* (a fictionalised account of her own birth). The excellent video *A Portrait of Katherine Mansfield* screens here and the 'Sense of Living' exhibition displays period photographs alongside excerpts from her writing. The No 14 Wilton bus stops nearby on Park St.

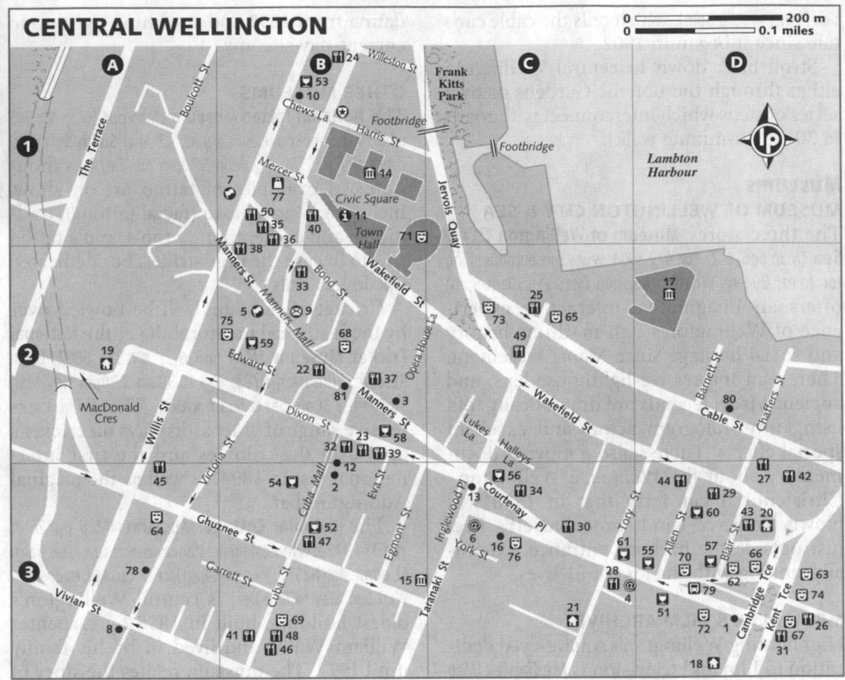

City Gallery Wellington (Map pp630-1; ☎ 801 3952; www.city-gallery.org.nz; Civic Sq, 101 Wakefield St; NZ exhibits admission by donation; 🕑 10am-5pm) has regularly changing contemporary exhibitions of art, architecture and design. New Zealand artists feature but it's also where you'll find major international shows, a recent example of which was a photographic exhibition by film maker Wim Wenders. There's often a fee for international exhibits.

Part of the New Zealand Academy of Fine Arts, **Academy Galleries** (Map pp626-7; ☎ 499 8807; nzafa@xtra.co.nz; 1 Queens Wharf; admission free; 🕑 10am-5pm) is a contemporary space for international fine arts. When the gallery isn't exhibiting the work of academy graduates, it's available for hire and may have paintings from Iran and Peru, embroidery, ceramics and quilts.

Historic Buildings

Completed in 1866, **Old St Paul's Cathedral** (Map pp626-7; ☎ 473 6722; 34 Mulgrave St; admission by donation; 🕑 10am-5pm) looks quaint from the outside, but the striking interior is a good example of early English Gothic timber design. It features magnificent stained-glass windows and houses displays on Wellington's early history.

At the northern end of Lambton Quay stands the 1876 **Government Buildings** (Map pp626–7), among the world's largest all-wooden buildings. With its block corners and slab wooden planking, you have to look twice to realise that it's not made of stone. The building has been restored and houses a university law department and various offices, including the DOC visitors centre.

Dating from 1843, **Premier House** (Map pp626-7; Tinakori Rd) is the official prime ministerial residence. An early Labour prime minister, Michael Joseph Savage, spurned such luxury, however, and the house was used for a variety of purposes between 1935 and 1990 until it was restored.

Other Sights

BOTANIC GARDENS & ZOO

The tranquil, 26-hectare **Botanic Gardens** (Map pp626-7; ☎ 499 1400; 🕑 dawn-dusk) are easily visited in conjunction with a cable-car ride (p628). Besides native bush, you can wander the **Lady Norwood Rose Garden** (Map pp626–7).

INFORMATION
Arty Bees....1 D3
Bellamy's....2 B3
City Stop....3 B2
Cybernomad....4 C3
Email Shop....(see 11)
French Embassy....5 B2
Internet@Cyber City....6 C3
Japanese Embassy....7 B1
Map Shop....8 A3
Post Office....9 B2
Unity Books....10 B1
Wellington Visitors Centre....11 B1
Whitcoull's....12 B3

SIGHTS & ACTIVITIES (pp628–33)
Bungy Rocket....13 C3
City Gallery Wellington....14 B1
Mediaplex & Film Archive....15 B3
Penny Farthing Cycles....16 C3
Te Papa....17 D2

SLEEPING (pp634–5)
base Backpackers....18 D3
Rosemere Backpackers....19 A2
Wellington City YHA....20 D3
Wildlife House....21 C3

EATING (pp636–8)
Abrakebabra....22 B2
Angkor....23 B2
BNZ Centre....24 B1
Brewery Bar & Restaurant....25 C2
Café Bastille....26 D3
Chaffers Park Market....27 D3
Chow....28 C3
Commonsense Organics....29 D3
Courtenay Central....30 C3
Deluxe Café....31 D3
Dixon St Deli....32 B2
Ed's Juicebar....33 B2
Espressoholic....34 C3
Fisherman's Plate Seafood....35 B1
Hell....36 B1
James Smith Corner....37 B2
Kopi....38 B2
La Casa della Pasta....39 B2
Lido....40 B1
Midnight Espresso....41 B3
New World Supermarket....42 D3
One Red Dog....43 D3
Pandora Panetteria....44 D3
Sunday Market....45 A3
Sushi takeaways....46 B3
Tulsi....47 B3
Vegetarian Café....48 B3
Wellington Market....49 C2
Wholly Bagels....50 B1

DRINKING (pp638–9)
Grand....51 D3
JJ Murphy & Co....52 B3
Malthouse....53 B1
Matterhorn....54 B3
Mercury Lounge....55 D3
Molly Malone's....56 C3
Ponderosa....57 D3
Sovereign....58 B2
Tupelo....59 B2
Vespa Lounge....60 D3
Wellington Sports Café....61 C3

ENTERTAINMENT (pp639–40)
Amba....62 D3
BATS Theatre....63 D3
Bodega....64 A3
Circa Theatre....65 C2
Downstage Theatre....66 D3
Embassy Theatre....67 D3
Hoyts Regent on Manners....68 B2
Indigo....69 B3
Kitty O'Shea's....70 D3
Michael Fowler Centre....71 B1
Paramount....72 D3
Pound Nite Club....(see 58)
Reading Cinemas....(see 30)
Rialto....73 C2
Sandwiches....74 D3
Studio Nine....75 B2
Westpac Trust St James Theatre....76 C3

SHOPPING (p640)
Mainly Tramping....77 B1

TRANSPORT (p641)
Apex Car Rental....78 A3
Bus Stop....79 D3
Cable St Car Fair....80 D2

OTHER
Wellington - The Dark Side Tours....81 B2

There's also a teahouse, visitors centre and the NZ headquarters of World Wide Fund for Nature. The gardens are also accessible from Glenmore St. In the gardens is **Carter Observatory** (Map pp626-7; ☎ 472 8167; www.carterobs.ac.nz; 40 Salamanca Rd; planetarium adult/concession NZ$10/8; 10am-5pm Sun-Tue, 10am-late Wed-Sat), where there are astronomy displays and you can view the night sky through the telescope (weather permitting).

The main entrance to **Otari-Wilton's Bush** (☎ 475 3245) is north of the city at the junction of Wilton Rd and Gloucester St; catch the No 14 Wilton bus. Devoted to the cultivation and preservation of indigenous NZ plants, it has a number of walks through densely forested areas and flax clearings, plus picnic areas and an information centre.

The well-maintained **Wellington Zoo** (☎ 381 6750; www.zoo.wcc.govt.nz; 200 Daniell St; admission NZ$10; 9.30am-5pm) has a wide variety of native and non-native wildlife and is committed to conservation and research. There are outdoor lion and chimpanzee parks, and a nocturnal kiwi house which also houses tuatara and giant weta (indigenous insects). The zoo is 4km south of the city; catch Stagecoach bus Nos 10 and 23.

MT VICTORIA LOOKOUT

The best view of the city, harbour and surrounding region is from the lookout on top of **Mt Victoria** (Map pp626–7; 196m), east of the city centre. Take bus No 20 (Monday to Friday) to the top or make the taxing walk. To drive, take Oriental Pde along the waterfront and then Carlton Gore St.

BEEHIVE & PARLIAMENT

Three buildings on Bowen St form NZ's parliamentary complex.

Office workers swarm around the distinctive, modernist Beehive (Map pp626–7), which is exactly what it looks like. It was designed by architect Sir Basil Spence and controversy surrounded its construction between 1969 and 1980. It's the architectural symbol of the country.

Next door is Parliament House (Map pp626–7), completed in 1922, and beside this is the neo-Gothic Parliamentary Library (Map pp626–7) building, dating from 1899. There's a **visitors centre** (☎ 471 9503; www.ps.parliament.govt.nz; 10am-4pm Mon-Fri, 10am-3pm Sat, noon-3pm Sun) in the ground-floor foyer of Parliament House, from where free guided tours of the building depart hourly.

NATIONAL LIBRARY & ARCHIVES

Opposite the Beehive is the **National Library** (Map pp626-7; ☎ 474 3000; www.natlib.govt.nz; cnr Molesworth & Aitken Sts; admission free; 9am-5pm Mon-Fri, 9am-1pm Sat), NZ's most comprehensive book collection. Housed here is the

Alexander Turnbull Library, an early colonial collection with many historical books, maps, newspapers and photographs, and the **National Library Gallery** (Map pp626-7; admission free; 9am-5pm Mon-Fri, 9am-4.30pm Sat, 1-4.30pm Sun) with its changing exhibits.

One block away, the **National Archives** (Map pp626-7; ☎ 499 5595; www.archives.govt.nz; 10 Mulgrave St; admission free; 9am-5pm Mon-Fri, 9am-1pm Sat) displays several significant national treasures, including the original Treaty of Waitangi (p491).

ACTIVITIES

With all its wind and surrounding water, Wellington is a great place for sailboarding: choose from sheltered inlets, rough harbours and wave-beaten coastal areas. The various bays around the harbour are also quite receptive to kayaks, while the coastline out beyond the harbour mouth yields some excellent surf breaks and a good seaside walk. Trans-harbour ferry trips, bay beach swims and mountain biking over local hills are other active options.

Ferry to Days Bay & Matiu-Somes Island

Trips across the harbour to **Days Bay** can be made on the **Dominion Post Ferry** (Map pp626-7; ☎ 499 1282; www.eastbywest.co.nz; Shed 5, Queens Wharf; adult one way NZ$7.50), departing Queens Wharf around nine times daily weekdays and five times daily at weekends. It's a 30-minute trip to Days Bay, where there are beaches, a fine park and a boatshed with canoes and rowing boats for hire. There are also a couple of houses that Katherine Mansfield's family kept for summer homes; her story *At the Bay* recalls summer holidays here. A 10-minute walk from Days Bay brings you to the upmarket settlement of **Eastbourne**, which has good cafés and picnic spots.

At least three Days Bay ferries per day also call in at **Matiu-Somes Island** (adult return NZ$17), a former prisoner-of-war camp and quarantine station. Now a DOC-managed reserve, it has walking trails and beaches.

Mountain Biking

Makara Peak Mountain Bike Park (www.makarapeak.org.nz) is a 200-hectare, council-run park in the hills of Karori, west of the city centre. The main entrance is on South Karori Rd (accessible by bus Nos 12 and 17). The park has numerous tracks ranging from easy to very difficult. **Mud Cycles** (☎ 476 4961; www.mudcycles.co.nz; 1 Allington Rd, Karori; bike hire half-/full day NZ$25/40) offers free inner-city pick up and drop off (or can drop bikes to your accommodation) and track information. They also do guided tours from NZ$55 per half-day.

There are other good opportunities for mountain biking around town; the visitors centre or any of Wellington's bike stores can give you specific information and maps. **Penny Farthing Cycles** (Map pp630-1; ☎ 385 2279; penny.farthing.wgtn@xtra.co.nz; 89 Courtenay Pl) rents out bikes.

Walking

The easy **Red Rocks Coastal Walk** (2½ hours) follows the volcanic coast to the south of the city from Owhiro Bay to Red Rocks and Sinclair Head, where there's a seal colony. Take bus No 1 or 4 to Island Bay, then No 29 to Owhiro Bay Pde (or walk 2.5km along the Esplanade). From the start of Owhiro Bay Pde it's 1km to the quarry gate where the coastal walk starts.

Other Activities

H2OSports (Map pp626-7; ☎ 224 2223; www.h2osports.co.nz; 251 Marine Pde, Seatoun; 1hr beginners lesson NZ$40, kit rental NZ$30; 9am-sunset) has sailboarding lessons for beginners; the price includes all equipment.

At the long-running **Fergs Rock 'n' Kayaks** (Map pp626-7; ☎ 499 8898; www.fergskayaks.co.nz; Shed 6, Queens Wharf; in-line skates/kayaks per 2hr NZ$10/18, rock climbing per adult/student NZ$12/9; 10am-8pm Mon-Fri, 9am-8pm Sat & Sun) you can challenge your calf muscles with indoor rock-climbing, cruise the waterfront on a pair of in-line skates and see the sights from a kayak. Fergs also offers a range of introductory courses and guided kayaking trips on the bay.

Gnarly surfing breaks are found near the airport at **Lyall Bay** (where Viggo Mortensen and Billy Boyd, AKA Aragorn and Pippin respectively, took time off from their quest for the ring to learn how to surf) and southeast of Wellington at **Palliser Bay**. The visitors centre can help you with fishing and diving charters.

Freyberg Swimming Pool & Fitness Centre (Map pp626-7; ☎ 384 3107; www.wellington.govt.nz/services/swimpools; 139 Oriental Pde; admission NZ$3.50; 6am-9pm) has a heated indoor pool, a spa and a sauna.

For something more dramatic, try a reverse **bungy rocket** (Map pp630-1; ☎ 382 8438; cnr Taranaki St & Courtenay Pl; 1st/2nd ride NZ$35/15), where you sit in a capsule-like device that's flung into the air at high speed.

TOURS

Helipro (Map pp626-7; ☎ 472 1550; www.helipro.co.nz; Shed 1, Queens Wharf; 10/20/30min flights NZ$75/135/250) Does scenic helicopter flights along various routes.

Rover Ring Tour (☎ 021-426 211; www.wellingtonrover.co.nz; tours NZ$150; 🕑 8.30am-4.30pm) A fantastic, day-long *Lord of the Rings* tour with an enthusiastic guide who manages to bring the scene locations (minus the sets and props) to life; lunch at the Chocolate Fish café, where the film's stars downed many meals, is included. There's a maximum of six people per tour, and a minimum requirement of two people.

Seal Coast Safari (☎ 0800 732 527; safari with/without barbecue NZ$70/60; 🕑 departs 10.30am & 1.30pm, barbecue safari 5pm Nov-Mar) Runs 2½-hour 4WD excursions that guarantee seal sightings. Tours depart from Wellington visitors centre.

Walk Wellington (☎ 384 9590, 802 4860; www.wellingtonnz.com/walkwellington; tour NZ$20; 🕑 10am Wed & Fri-Sun & 5.30pm Mon-Fri Nov-Mar, 10am Sat & Sun Apr-Oct) Leads informative 90-minute walking tours that focus on the city or waterfront, and depart from the visitors centre.

Wally Hammond's City Tours (☎ 472 0869, after hours 528 2248; www.wellingtonsightseeingtours.co.nz; adult city tour NZ$40, Kapiti NZ$65, Wairarapa NZ$130; 🕑 city tours depart 10am & 2pm, Kapiti 9am & 1.30pm, Wairarapa 9am) Offers several tours in and around Wellington, including a 2½-hour city highlights tour; a four-hour tour of the fine beaches and forests on the Kapiti coast (so-named because it lies opposite the bird and marine sanctuary of Kapiti Island, 5km offshore); and a full-day visit to the Wairarapa region, which includes Martinborough's wineries, Palliser Bay and some *Lord of the Rings* sites. They pick up and drop off at your accommodation.

Wellington – the Dark Side (Map pp630-1; ☎ 0800 215 411; will@top.net.nz; departs cnr Manners & Cuba Malls; adult/backpacker NZ$24/20; 🕑 10am-noon & 1-3pm Mon-Fri, 10am-noon Sat & Sun Nov-Mar) A two-hour guided walk full of 'murder, mayhem and nefarious activity' that has received positive reports.

Wellington Rover (☎ 021-426 211; www.wellingtonrover.co.nz; adult day pass NZ$35; 🕑 8.30am, 11am, 2pm & 4.30pm Mon-Sat) A popular tour that gives you the option of a hop-on, hop-off minibus and covers places that are tricky to reach without a car.

GAY & LESBIAN WELLINGTON

Wellington's gay scene is tiny, but friendly and inclusive. Sovereign and Pound nite club are the main long-running entertainment venues but there are heaps of other bars and cafés around the inner-city area that are also gay-friendly, especially around Courtenay Pl, Lambton Quay and Cuba St.

At the visitors centre, you can pick up a copy of the pocket-sized quarterly *New Zealand Gay Guide* brochure, which gives details of cruise clubs, saunas, bars, restaurants and accommodation in Wellington.

Media such as the fortnightly **express** (www.gayexpress.co.nz; NZ$2.50) and the monthly **UP Newspaper** (NZ$3.50) profile the latest gay-scene happenings. The publications are free from selected venues or you can buy them from newsagents.

Around March is the **Annual Gay & Lesbian Fair** (www.gayfair.wellington.net.nz), which has a host of stalls and entertainment and culminates in a rip snorting dance party.

For information, or just to talk, phone the **Wellington Gay Switchboard** (☎ 473 7878; gayswitchboard@yahoo.com; 🕑 7.30-10pm) or **Lesbian Line** (☎ 499 5567; wgtnlesbianline@hotmail.com; 🕑 7.30-10pm Tue, Thu & Sat).

Excellent online resources include **Gay NZ** (www.gaynz.com), which has comprehensive national coverage of all things queer, **Gay Line Wellington** (www.gayline.gen.nz) and **Lesbian Wellington** (www.wellington.lesbian.net.nz).

Unity Books (p625) stocks a wide variety of gay and lesbian titles.

Sovereign (Map pp630-1; ☎ 384 5054; www.pound.co.nz; 1st fl, Oaks Complex, Dixon St; 🕑 4.30pm-late Tue-Sun) is a cosy, relaxed retro bar with a mixed gay and lesbian clientele; just look for the door with 'The straight route is often boring' painted above it. Thursday night from 8pm is karaoke night at Sovereign, but for disco and drag head to the adjacent **Pound nite club** (Map pp630-1; 🕑 11pm-late Fri & Sat), which sparks up at around 1am.

For more gay- and lesbian-specific information, see p782.

FESTIVALS & EVENTS

Wellingtonians love to celebrate. Check at the visitors centre or online on the **Wellington** (www.wellingtonnz.com) site for a comprehensive listing of festivals. Tickets to most events can be booked through Ticketek (p639).

January/February

Summer City Festival (☎ 801 3500; www.feelinggreat.co.nz) A two-month celebration of summer that begins on New Year's Eve and includes many free outdoor events.

February/March

New Zealand Festival (☎ 473 0149; www.nzfestival.telecom.co.nz) Beginning late February, this biennial event (held in even-numbered years) involves a month of culture, including theatre, dance, music and opera performances, with many top international artists involved.

Fringe NZ (☎ 495 8015; www.fringe.org.nz) A month-long festival of visual arts, music, dance and theatre. Its home is BATS Theatre (p640).

May

International Laugh Festival (☎ 09-309 9241; www.laugh.co.nz) Held early May, with national and international comedians performing in venues around town.

July

International Film Festival (☎ 385 0162; www.enzedff.co.nz) A three-week event showcasing the best of NZ and international cinema.

September

Montana World of Wearable Art Show (www.worldofwearableart.com) Exported from Nelson, this show challenges local and international artists to create fashionable art. For the background to this event, see the boxed text (p664).

October

International Jazz Festival (☎ 385 9602; www.jazzfestival.co.nz) A popular fortnight of jazz concerts, workshops, jazz crawls and street performances.

November

Toast Martinborough Wine, Food & Music Festival (☎ 06-306 9183; www.toastmartinborough.co.nz) Held on the third Sunday in November, this wine-tasting extravaganza sees tiny Martinborough, east of Wellington, swelling by around 11,000 people.

SLEEPING

Typically, accommodation in Wellington is more expensive than in regional areas, but the overall standard is generally high and there are a heap of great places to stay right in, or within easy walking distance of, the city centre.

Budget accommodation is mainly in the form of multistorey hostels or smaller guest-house-style hostels in Victorian houses. The cheaper places to stay are scattered throughout the city, but there's a grouping around Courtenay Pl and close by (a five- to 10-minute walk) along Brougham St in Mt Victoria, a quiet residential area at the eastern edge of the city. From the train station, catch bus No 2 to Brougham St; Nos 1 and 4 will take you to Basin Reserve, near the southern end of Brougham St.

Camping grounds are scarce in Wellington. Rowena's Lodge (opposite) can accommodate a few tents. Otherwise head northeast of town to Hutt Valley, easily reached by train or bus from Wellington (see under Getting Around; p642).

Hostels

Wellington City YHA (Map pp630-1; ☎ 801 7280; yhawgtn@yha.org.nz; cnr Cambridge Tce & Wakefield St; dm NZ$25-29, d & tw NZ$60-90) These guys know how to run a hostel. Staff are friendly, efficient and knowledgeable, and can book anything you need with minimum fuss. The main communal area is excellent: a kitchen that Jamie Oliver would call 'lovely jubbly', big dining area, pool table and a TV/video room. Rooms are clean and well maintained.

Wildlife House (Map pp630-1; ☎ 0508 005 858, 381 3899; www.wildlifehouse.co.nz; 58 Tory St; dm NZ$24-26, s & d NZ$60-70; 💻) You can't miss this large zebra-striped building. Rooms are spacious, many with a desk and couch. Communal areas are funkily designed with wood and corrugated iron and include reading, TV and video rooms, a gym and a modern kitchen. It could, however, be cleaner.

World Wide Backpackers (Map pp626-7; ☎ 0508 888 555, 802 5590; www.worldwidenz.co.nz; 291 The Terrace; dm NZ$25, d & tw NZ$50-60; 💻) Set in an old homely house, this friendly and well-regarded backpackers is small, clean and offers winning free extras like local calls, breakfast and wine in the evening, not to mention warmly decorated rooms with beds that have a high snooze rating. It's down-to-earth and chilled.

base Backpackers (Map pp630-1; ☎ 0800 227 369, 801 5666; www.basebackpackers.com; 21-23 Cambridge Tce; dm/d from NZ$20/75; 💻) Very comfortable multistorey hostel packed with pristine rooms (many with access to windswept balconies), facilities and lots of spaces to just hang out, including a café and a raucous basement bar that makes noise all week long. The doubles all have private bathrooms.

Rosemere Backpackers (Map pp630-1; ☎ 384 3041; www.backpackerswellington.co.nz; 6 MacDonald Cres; dm/s/tw/d NZ$22/38/50/55; 💻) Rosemere has received some serious refurbishment in recent times. It's a short walk uphill from the centre and has a fun, relaxed atmosphere. The attractive extras on offer include free city pick up, soup in winter and a barbeque in summer.

Downtown Wellington Backpackers (Map pp626-7; ☎ 473 8482; www.downtownbackpackers.co.nz; 1 Bunny St; dm/s NZ$23/45, tw NZ$50-60, d NZ$55-75) Located opposite the railway station, Downtown is huge and busy. It's one of the largest Art Deco buildings in NZ and a young Queen Elizabeth II stayed here in 1953. It has a big-city feel with slightly dingy rooms, but amenities are sound: a restaurant serving cheap food; a large bar with billiard table; a huge kitchen and lounge; and pubs next door.

Maple Lodge (Map pp626-7; ☎ 385 3771; 52 Ellice St; dm/s/tw/d NZ$21/35/45/50; Ⓟ) Cosy and welcoming Maple Lodge offers clean accommodation in small bunk-equipped dorms (which have the best views) and wee doubles, all with sinks except the twin. There's no TV; instead there's ambient chill-out music, board games and conversation. It's a popular option for solo travellers.

Rowena's Lodge (Map pp626-7; ☎ 0800 801 414, 385 7872; www.wellingtonbackpackers.co.nz; 115 Brougham St; camp sites per person NZ$13, dm/s/d NZ$20/28/50; Ⓟ) It's the views that have it at Rowena's. A women's hostel during WWII, this is a rambling, friendly place with an outdoor barbecue area and is the only accommodation in town to offer camping. There are free shuttle services to ferries, buses and trains.

Moana Lodge (☎ 233 2010; www.moanalodge.co.nz; 49 Moana Rd, Plimmerton; dm NZ$22-24, tw NZ$50-60, d NZ$50-60) If you'd prefer to stay out of the city, try this exceptional backpackers on the beach in Plimmerton, 25km north of town off SH1. It's well run and friendly, and the caring owners are more than happy to share their local expertise and pick you up from the train station (suburban trains between Wellington and the Kapiti Coast stop in Plimmerton). There's free use of kayaks and bikes.

SPLURGE!

Mermaid (Map pp626-7; ☎ 384 4511; www.mermaid.co.nz; 1 Epuni St; s NZ$75-NZ$125, d NZ$85-135, tw NZ$110-140) Situated in the cool Aro Valley neighbourhood, a mere short black away from Cuba St, is the Mermaid, a small women-only guesthouse in a wonderfully restored villa. Each room is individually themed with colourful artistic flair. White robes and fluffy towels make Mermaid a luxurious experience and there's a guest kitchen, lounge and deck area.

Chancellor (Map pp626-7; ☎ 385 2153; www.grandhotelsinternational.com; 213 Cuba St; r NZ$190; Ⓟ 💻) Formerly Trekkers Lodge, this place has been renovated within an inch of its life and now sports modern, boutique, motel-style rooms with comfortable beds, TVs, phones and private bathrooms. Right on Cuba St, the Chancellor is a great choice. Cheaper rates are usually available.

Booklovers B&B (Map pp626-7; ☎ 384 2714; www.bbnb.co.nz; 123 Pirie St; s NZ$90-120, d NZ$100-160) Booklovers is an elegant old home run by award-winning NZ author Jane Tolerton. There are four inviting rooms with sweeping views, TVs and CD players, and the home is (of course) filled with books. Breakfast is superb – berry compote and homemade granola. From the front gate bus No 2 runs to Courtenay Pl and the railway station.

Hotels

Cambridge Hotel (Map pp626-7; ☎ 385 8829; www.cambridgehotel.co.nz; 28 Cambridge Tce; dm NZ$23-25, s NZ$55, d & tw with bathroom NZ$90-95) This restored heritage hotel provides quality pub accommodation. Its central position, well-equipped kitchen, Sky TV and cheap weekly rates make it popular for long stays. Guests can purchase barbecue fare (steaks NZ$10, burger ingredients NZ$6) and cook downstairs on the pub grill.

Camping

Hutt Park Holiday Village (☎ 0800 488 872, 568 5913; www.huttpark.co.nz; 95 Hutt Park Rd, Seaview, Lower Hutt; camp & campervan sites per person NZ$26, s & d NZ$39-85; Ⓟ 💻) This busy park is 13km north of Wellington. Its excellent facilities include three communal kitchens, Sky TV, a trampoline and a spa, but its industrial and inconvenient location detracts. It's a 15-minute drive from the ferry, a five-minute walk from the bus stop (take the Eastbourne bus) or a 20-minute walk from Woburn Train Station.

Harcourt Holiday Park (☎ 526 7400; www.harcourtholidaypark.co.nz, 45 Akatarawa Rd, Upper Hutt; camp/campervan sites per person NZ$18/20, s & d NZ$35-80) This well-designed, well-maintained park is 35km northeast of Wellington, just off SH2. It's set in native bush with a river nearby. Facilities aren't as plentiful as at Hutt Park, but the location is prettier.

EATING

Wellington serves up old-school arty establishments cooking vegetarian comfort food (lasagnes, veggie burgers, burritos etc), pubs serving quality counter meals, and relaxed restaurants and takeaways selling mainly Malaysian, Indian and Chinese staples. In keeping with the expectations of its flourishing literati, Wellington also boasts more cafés (per capita) than New York City.

Cuba St is one of the best food strips. Courtenay Pl, traditionally Chinatown, also has plenty of cafés and restaurants, as does the Manners Mall–Willis St area. Not surprisingly, most of the seafood restaurants can be found on the city's waterfront.

Self-Catering

Dixon St Deli (Map pp630-1; ☎ 384 2436; 45 Dixon St; meals NZ$4.50-16; ⌚ lunch) For something gourmet try Dixon St deli, a foodstore and café selling its own range of produce.

Commonsense Organics (Map pp630-1; ☎ 384 3314; 260 Wakefield St) has a range of organic produce.

There's also **New World supermarket** (city centre Map pp630-1; ☎ 384 8054; 279 Wakefield St; ⌚ 7am-midnight; Thorndon Map pp626-7; ☎ 499 9041; Molesworth St; ⌚ 8am-10pm).

Cafés

Lido (Map pp630-1; ☎ 499 6666; cnr Victoria & Wakefield Sts; mains NZ$13-22; ⌚ lunch & dinner) Popular corner café with curved windows and a sunny aspect. In its unpretentious atmosphere you can dine on the likes of Mediterranean and Indochinese platters, pastas, Italian-style pork and mozzarella balls and plum crumble (mmm). Service is friendly and professional.

Espressoholic (Map pp630-1; ☎ 384 7790; 128 Courtenay Pl; breakfast NZ$4-16, lunch & dinner NZ$12-18; ⌚ breakfast, lunch & dinner) Serious supporters of coffee addiction, this grungy café, with chipped black tables and colourful graffiti-art, serves strong brews of Italian coffee. There's a broad veggie selection such as corn fritters and ricotta ravioli. Espressoholic plays cool music, has a courtyard and closes late (midnight weekdays, 3am on Saturday and Sunday).

Midnight Espresso (Map pp630-1; ☎ 384 7014; 178 Cuba St; meals NZ$7-14; ⌚ breakfast, lunch & dinner) Dine on primarily vegetarian and vegan food among the hessian-sack art and metal sculptures at this cool, high-ceilinged café. This long-running local stalwart serves food until around 2am and is an institution for paper reading, coffee drinking and philosophising.

Fidel's (Map pp626-7; ☎ 801 6868; 234 Cuba St; meals NZ$5-20; ⌚ breakfast, lunch & dinner) Fidel's is an institution for caffeine-craving, left-wing subversives, watched over by images of Castro. Terrific eggs (Benedict, Florentine, with salmon, mushrooms, hash browns – you name it) are miraculously pumped from the itsy-bitsy kitchen. Pierced, tattooed staff are studiously vague, but friendly.

Vegetarian Café (Map pp630-1; ☎ 384 2713; 179 Cuba St; meals NZ$6-12; ⌚ lunch) A gem for non-carnivores, this cheap, cheerful and inviting place has great veggie and vegan options. Try the Tex-Mex burrito or sate your hunger with a well-priced bowl of chilli or steamed vegetables.

Deluxe Café (Map pp630-1; ☎ 801 5455; 10 Kent Tce; meals from NZ$8; ⌚ lunch) At lunch time this cosy, well-loved café is packed with funky

IN THE MARKET

The **Porirua** or **Poly Market** (☎ 236 7066; Cobham Court; ⌚ 6-9am Sat) is both a source of fantabulous foodstuffs, from fresh vegetables to seafood, and a unique experience in Maori and Polynesian culture. If you're serious about the quality of your food supplies, get here very early as the best edibles are sold well before the 9am closing time. But if healthy eating isn't your primary concern, turn up any time and buy yourself yummy Pacific Island fast-food like pork buns and satay literally drenched in fat. If you miss the next Poly Market, try the Sunday morning **produce market** (Map pp630-1; cnr Ghuznee & Willis Sts), or the Sunday morning **Chaffers Park Market** (Map pp630-1) selling fruit and vegies, eggs, flowers and lots more.

Gen-Xers, businesspeople and chilled locals. Right next to the Embassy theatre, Deluxe serves rich, full-bodied Havana espresso, loose-leaf herbal teas, dense chocolate brownies, filos, lasagne, healthy rolls and sandwiches, and sushi.

Café L'Affare (Map pp626-7; ☎ 385 9748; 27 College St; meals NZ$6-16; 🕑 breakfast & lunch Mon-Sat) Doing everything right, L'Affare is a massive, atmospheric café with fast service, high communal tables, couches, a disco ball and industrial stage lights. A prominent coffee roaster and supplier, the café smells of freshly ground Colombian beans. Sensational toasted baps are a bargain.

Brooklyn the Bakery (Map pp626-7; ☎ 802 4111; 29 College St; meals NZ$9-13; 🕑 breakfast & lunch) The sister store of Dixon St Deli (opposite), Brooklyn has the same stylish chocolate-brown interior and makes bread, bagels and coffee.

Ed's juicebar (Map pp630-1; ☎ 4473 1769; Bond St; meals NZ$5-10; 🕑 lunch) Tiny Ed's has a substantial selection of pure juices and smoothies such as the Floo Fighter and the Liver Lover. Soups change daily and for lunch there are hot meals, fresh salads and sandwiches. Produce is locally sourced, organic and GE-free.

Two very popular cafés by the water are **Parade Café** (Map pp626-7; ☎ 939 3935; 148 Oriental Pde; meals NZ$8-15; 🕑 lunch & dinner) and **Vista** (Map pp626-7; ☎ 385 7724; 106 Oriental Pde; meals NZ$10-15; 🕑 lunch & dinner), both offering mixed menus, great brunch choices, reasonable prices and outdoor seating.

Quick Eats

Pandoro Panetteria (Map pp630-1; ☎ 385 4478; 2 Allen St; meals NZ$1.50-7; 🕑 breakfast & lunch) An Italian bakery with smooth, flavoursome coffee, savoury and sweet muffins, stuffed breads, pastry scrolls, cakes, tarts and brownies.

Wholly Bagels (Map pp630-1; cnr Willis & Bond Sts; bagels NZ$1.60-8; 🕑 lunch) Sells authentic boiled bagels, sold 'naked' or with a selection of flavoured cream cheeses, and filled with the likes of tuna salad or pastrami.

Feedback (Map pp626-7; ☎ 385 9000; 87 Kent Tce; meals NZ$5-10; 🕑 dinner) 'One step beyond' burgers that satisfy the most deep-seated burger cravings. Buns are filled with traditional or gourmet fillings that include steak, lamb, beef and chicken, and veggie options like Mexican chilli bean and chick pea. Terrific.

Hell (Map pp630-1; ☎ 0800 864 355; 14 Bond St; meals NZ$12-14; 🕑 dinner) Demon gourmet pizzas are themed after all things evil. Try the seven deadly sins range or the vegetarian 'purgatory'. Attached is **Syn bar**, which is fun for drinks.

Sushi takeaways (Map pp630-1; ☎ 385 0290; 189 Cuba St; meals NZ$5-10; 🕑 lunch) Has super fresh Japanese treats that are cheap and tasty.

Abrakebabra (Map pp630-1; ☎ 473 3009; 90 Manners St; meals NZ$6-12; 🕑 lunch & dinner) Serves chicken and lamb kebabs and burgers on thick fluffy bread with a variety of dips, and the all-important baklava finisher. If you love a kebab, this is the place.

Wellington Trawling Sea Market (Map pp626-7; ☎ 384 8461; 220 Cuba St; meals NZ$5-13; 🕑 lunch & dinner) Sells caught-that-morning fish, wonderful fish dinners with chips and salad, and fat burgers.

Fisherman's Plate Seafood (Map pp630-1; ☎ 473 8375; 12 Bond St; meals NZ$8-14; 🕑 dinner) Eat straight off the butchers' paper at this classic fish 'n' chipper with its tiny 'dining' area – orange plastic swivel chairs, fake pine-wood panelling and a jaunty fish mural. The battered scallops and hand-cut chips are delicious.

Wellington Market (Map pp630-1; Wakefield St; meals NZ$3-12; 🕑 10am-5.30pm Fri-Sun) Has excellent Asian choices, including Indian and even Nepalese food. A speciality here is Maori cuisine; you can buy food prepared in a *hangi*.

Food courts include **Courtenay Central** (Map pp630-1; Courtenay Pl; meals NZ$3.50-9; 🕑 lunch & dinner), **BNZ Centre** (Map pp630-1; Willis St; meals NZ$4-10; 🕑 lunch) and **James Smith Corner** (Map pp630-1; ☎ 801 8813; 55 Cuba St; meals NZ$2-9; 🕑 lunch).

Restaurants

Kopi (Map pp630-1; ☎ 499 5570; 103 Willis St; meals NZ$9-16; 🕑 lunch & dinner) Malaysian for 'coffee', Kopi is consistently voted the city's best Malaysian eatery – the crowds here attest to its popularity. Choose from *roti* (flat, flaky bread dipped in a creamy coconut curry), curries such as goat korma, and *nasi kandar* (coconut rice). For dessert, try feijoa ice cream.

Angkor (Map pp630-1; ☎ 384 9423; 43 Dixon St; mains NZ$15-25; 🕑 lunch & dinner Mon-Fri, dinner Sat) Highly rated Cambodian restaurant where you can sample such delights as *amok trei* (spicy steamed fish) and *yao-horn* (a charcoal broiler steam boat created for sharing).

Tulsi (Map pp630-1; ☎ 802 4144; 135 Cuba St; mains NZ$16-22; 🕑 lunch & dinner) A spacious, bright and contemporary Indian place with a central circular bar, Tulsi has excellent lunch deals (cheap curries, naan and rice). Overall the food is outstanding.

Chow (Map pp630-1; ☎ 382 8585; 45 Tory St; meals NZ$11-19; lunch & dinner) This super stylish eatery-bar serves fresh Asian cuisines amid '70s décor – pots of spiky mother-in-law's tongue, cream-coloured retro chairs and orange low-hanging lamps. Try a fragrant broth of marinated whitefish, Japanese barbeque pork and fresh fried tofu in a spicy tomato and tamarind gravy. 'Motel' is the fabulous lounge bar.

La Casa della Pasta (Map pp630-1; ☎ 385 9057; 37 Dixon St; NZ$12-20; lunch Mon-Fri, dinner daily) Reasonably priced, home-style Italian food is what this no-fuss place does well. Authentic pasta dishes include comforting staples like lasagne, ravioli, tortellini and gnocchi.

Theo's Greek Taverna (Map pp626-7; ☎ 801 8806; 13 Pirie St; mains NZ$17-25; lunch & dinner) A whitewashed Mediterranean-style building with an outdoor courtyard and live music and dancing (Thursday, Friday and Saturday) to complement the authentic cuisine. The *mezze* platters are a great way to sample a variety of tasty appetisers.

SPLURGE!

Dockside (Map pp626-7; ☎ 499 9900; Queens Wharf; mains NZ$22-32; lunch & dinner) An upmarket, nautically themed restaurant with superb waterside frontage and quality seafood with an emphasis on local produce. Feast on Nelson scallops or smoked groper and sweet paprika fishcakes.

Café Bastille (Map pp630-1; ☎ 382 9559; 16 Majoribanks St; mains NZ$22-24; dinner) A modern French restaurant that also favours local produce, along with an expansive wine list and knowledgeable staff. Try Lake Pukaki salmon with warm potato salad and watercress and finish with orange-caramel crepes. If you don't love the French, you will after this meal.

Logan-Brown (Map pp626-7; ☎ 801 5114; 192 Cuba St; mains NZ$26-40; lunch & dinner Mon-Fri, dinner Sat & Sun) A fine-dining experience in a former 1920s bank chamber that's worth the splurge. Service is excellent, neither fussy nor obtrusive, and the simple, elegant food is delicious. The weekday lunch and pre-theatre set menus are top value and the wine list extensive.

One Red Dog (Map pp630-1; ☎ 384 9777; 9 Blair St; meals NZ$16-26; dinner) A bustling, upmarket brewery-pub, popular for late-night weekend drinks, with a wide selection of beers. On offer are excellent gourmet pizzas, pastas, calzones and salads. Families take the early dinner sitting and young 20-somethings create a fun, upbeat atmosphere.

Brewery Bar & Restaurant (Map pp630-1; ☎ 381 2282; www.thebrewerybar.co.nz; cnr Taranaki & Cable Sts; mains NZ$11-27; lunch & dinner) In a prime waterfront position in a renovated warehouse, the Wellington Brewing Company takes beer seriously. Stuff brewed on site includes Sassy Red and Wicked Blonde. Families, tourists and businessfolk come for big serves of beer-battered fish 'n' chips, sirloin and linguini.

DRINKING

Courtenay Pl is the boisterous drinking centre of Wellington, with its fair share of Irish and microbrewery pubs. Blair and Allen Sts, running off Courtenay Pl, are also fertile hunting grounds for booze, but here you'll find it's moody, upmarket lounge bars that are the norm. Cuba St also does a roaring trade in quickly emptied glasses, as does Edward St which is best visited after midnight.

JJ Murphy & Co (Map pp630-1; ☎ 384 9090; 119-23 Cuba St) Popular bar in Cuba Mall with outdoor tables. It's a great spot to watch sporting events. Inside it's all dark-wood booths and big barrels, with plenty of pool tables.

Malthouse (Map pp630-1; ☎ 499 4355; 47 Willis St) A shrine for lovers of naturally brewed beer, from local ales through to fine international drops like Tuborg and Kronenbourg. Extremely popular with corporate types, but don't hold that against it. There's a couple of big balconies and some pool tables.

Matterhorn (Map pp630-1; ☎ 384 3359; 106 Cuba St) Set in a smart, architecturally designed space with low lighting and polished concrete floors, Matterhorn is way cool. Three bars dispense quality drinks to 20-somethings and its leather-bound menu reveals salty tapas.

Mercury Lounge (Map pp630-1; ☎ 384 6737; 1/46 Courtenay Pl) Well-attended by young professionals, this slick upstairs lounge bar has faux-suede lounges and premium beers.

Molly Malone's (Map pp630-1; ☎ 384 2896; cnr Courtenay Pl & Taranaki St) This is a rousing, very popular pub. Upstairs is the Dubliner, a combination Irish restaurant and whisky bar with a scary 100 whiskeys to choose from!

Ponderosa (Map pp630-1; ☎ 384 1064; 28 Blair St) An intimate, cowboy-themed cocktail bar with tree-stump tables and a tiny mezzanine to crowd onto.

Wellington Sports Café (Map pp630-1; ☎ 801 5115, cnr Courtenay Pl & Tory St) With its big-screen TVs and cheap meals, this is the perfect spot to watch the big games. See also Entertainment, right.

Leuven (Map pp626-7; ☎ 499 2939; 135 Featherston St) This 'beer café' (their description) is more upmarket than your everyday pub and a great place to sample hearty Belgian cuisine, such as mussels and *frites* (fries), washed down by one or more beers from their huge selection.

Tupelo (Map pp630-1; ☎ 384 1152; 6 Edward St; ⏲ Tue-Sat) We all love a back-alley bar. Intimate Tupelo is warm, red and lit by chandeliers, and has above-average service.

Lie-low (Map pp626-7; ☎ 385 0647; 186 Willis St; ⏲ 8pm-6am Thu-Sat) A groovy late-night opener that is kitsch, Bohemian and plays a great range of music in the electroclash genre. The well-mixed cocktails are a treat. Lie-low is lots of fun.

Vespa Lounge (Map pp630-1; ☎ 385 2438; 21 Allen St) A smooth bar with low-hanging red lamps casting a moody glow, red velvet drapes, slate-grey walls, a pool table and a shiny polished wood bar. Keeps the drinks coming until 6am.

Grand (Map pp630-1; ☎ 801 7800; 69 Courtenay Pl) An upmarket ground-floor bar that's all chocolate-brown, exposed brick, black ottoman-style lounges and gilt mirrors. Pool tables occupy level three and a casino level four.

CLUBBING

There are a couple of good, dedicated nightclubs in Wellington, though invitations to DJs are also extended by many pubs and bars throughout the week. Sample the city's clubbing scene on main entertainment drags like Courtenay Pl, Cuba St and Edward St, where it all starts to go rambunctiously wrong in the early hours of the morning. There's usually little to no clubbing action on Sunday and Monday nights.

Studio Nine (Map pp630-1; ☎ 384 9976; 9 Edward St) A cool dance club hosting international DJs and with a fab lounge area. This is the place to head for all-night doof – make sure you bring plenty of stamina.

Sandwiches (Map pp630-1; ☎ 385 7698; www.sandwiches.co.nz; 8 Kent St; ⏲ Tue-Sat) Funk it up at cool-man-cool Sandwiches, a bar and nightclub with live performances – comedy, jazz, electronica – from Wednesday to Saturday. Platters such as 'Mafia madness', gourmet pizzas and club sandwiches are available.

Some bar-club hybrids:

Matterhorn (Map pp630-1; ☎ 384 3359; 106 Cuba St) DJs spin ambient funk here at weekends.

Mercury Lounge (Map pp630-1; ☎ 384 6737; 1/46 Courtenay Pl) DJs spin happy house on weekends.

Ponderosa (Map pp630-1; ☎ 384 1064; 28 Blair St) Funk, house, hip-hop and retro are the sounds of choice from Thursday to Saturday.

Tupelo (Map pp630-1; ☎ 384 1152; 6 Edward St) Where DJs play hip-hop, jazz and housey soul Wednesday through Friday.

Vespa Lounge (Map pp630-1; ☎ 385 2438; 21 Allen St) Smooth tunes in a funky house vein.

Wellington Sports Café (Map pp630-1; ☎ 801 5115, cnr Courtenay Pl & Tory St) There's often a DJ when there are no big sporting contests to televise. See also Drinking, left.

ENTERTAINMENT

Wellington has a vibrant performing arts scene, with numerous well-established and highly respected professional and amateur theatre companies. Meanwhile, jazz, rock, soul and grunge get regular airings in the city's live music venues; the cover charge varies, though most pub gigs are free.

Purchase tickets for shows and concerts from **Ticketek** (☎ 384 3840; www.ticketek.co.nz) outlets at the Queen Wharf Events Centre, Westpac St James Theatre or the Michael Fowler Centre. For gig listings, pick up a copy of the free brochure *The Package*, available at venues, cafés and record stores around town.

Show times for movies around town are listed in local newspapers or on the **Wellington Film Guide** (www.film.wellington.net.nz) website. Adult tickets cost around NZ$12; most cinemas have a cheap day early in the week.

Theatre & Music

Circa Theatre (Map pp630-1; ☎ 801 7992; www.circa.co.nz; 1 Taranaki St; adult/stand-by ticket NZ$30/16; ⏲ box office 10am-4pm Mon-Fri, performances Tue-Sun) Circa has been running for over 25 years. Its main auditorium seats 250 people and its studio seats 100. Cheap tickets are available for preview shows (the night before opening night) and stand-by tickets are obtainable one hour before a show.

Downstage Theatre (Map pp630-1; ☎ 801 6946; www.downstage.co.nz; cnr Courtenay Pl & Cambridge Tce; tickets NZ$35-40) NZ's longest-running professional theatre company, now over 40 years of age. Its 250-seat auditorium also hosts contemporary dance.

BATS Theatre (Map pp630-1; ☎ 802 4175; www.bats.co.nz; 1 Kent Tce; adult/concession around NZ$15/12) Alternative, avant-garde theatre and home of Fringe NZ (p634). Reduced-price, same-day theatre tickets are available at the visitors centre, subject to availability (tickets go on sale from noon).

Westpac Trust St James Theatre (Map pp630-1; ☎ 802 4060; www.stjames.co.nz; 77 Courtenay Pl) A grand old heritage building often used for opera, ballet, major musical shows and major musicians (eg Jack Johnson). It provides a permanent home for the **Royal New Zealand Ballet** (www.nzballet.org.nz).

Michael Fowler Centre (Map pp630-1; ☎ 801 4231; www.wellingtonconventioncentre.com; Wakefield St) A massive centre, part of the Civic Sq complex, with 19 venues. It has great acoustics and hosts performances from popular bands to the New Zealand Symphony Orchestra.

Cinemas

Embassy Theatre (Map pp630-1; ☎ 384 7657; www.theembassytheatretrust.org.nz; 10 Kent Tce) Boasting the largest screen in the southern hemisphere, this grand dame underwent major restoration in November 2003 before hosting the world premiere of the final hobbit flick, *Return of the King*. It usually screens mainstream films.

Hoyts Regent on Manners (Map pp630-1; ☎ 472 5182; http://hoytsnz.ninemsn.com.au/cinema/1MML.asp; 73 Manners St) Screens all the latest Hollywood schlockbusters.

Paramount (Map pp630-1; ☎ 384 4080; www.paramount.co.nz; 25 Courtenay Pl) Shows mainly art-house movies; NZ$6 tickets Monday.

Reading Cinemas (Map pp630-1; ☎ 801 4600; www.readingcinemas.co.nz; Courtenay Central, Courtenay Pl) Screens mainstream, new-release films.

Rialto (Map pp630-1; ☎ 385 1864; www.rialto.co.nz; cnr Jervois Quay & Cable St) Screens independent productions.

Live Music

Bodega (Map pp630-1; ☎ 384 8212; 101 Ghuznee St) Welly's longest-running live-music venue, cool Bodega has music every night from around 10pm. Expect to hear dirty rock, Latin, soul, DJs and reggae-mon. There are over 17 beers on tap and the vibe here is rockin'.

Indigo (Map pp630-1; ☎ 801 6797; 171 Cuba St; 🕑 closed Mon) A hard-core live-music haunt with local DJs spinning experimental techno, comedy nights on Tuesday, and music that prompts parents to say, 'What's this racket?'. It's grungy, with dreadlocked punters smoking Lucky Strikes.

Amba (Map pp630-1; ☎ 801 5212; 21 Blair St) A fancy lounge bar and popular live-music venue that specialises in jazz but also incorporates swing, funk and dub. On Monday nights there's free mussels at the bar.

Blue Note (Map pp626-7; ☎ 801 5007; 191 Cuba St) Punters from all walks of life – gay, straight, transgender – come to the slightly seedy Blue Note to sing; Wednesday, Sunday and Monday are dedicated karaoke nights. There are also open-mike nights and jam sessions.

Some pub venues:

JJ Murphy & Co Irish-themed place with live music Wednesday to Sunday night. See Drinking, p638.

Kitty O'Shea's (Map pp630-1; ☎ 384 7392; 28 Courtenay Pl) Live music every night: catch an open jam session early in the week, some unplugged traditional Irish noises midweek and some amped-up pub rock at weekends.

Molly Malone's Live music nightly. See Drinking, p638.

SHOPPING

Two publications that keep the city's fashionistas in the loop are *Wellington's Shopping Guide*, published twice a year, and *Fashion Map*, the guide to NZ and international designers and boutique clothes shops. For second-hand records and books, plus retro clothing, stroll along Cuba St. Shops selling outdoor equipment are on Mercer St.

Kirkcaldie & Stains (Map pp626-7; ☎ 472 5899; 165-177 Lambton Quay) NZ's answer to Bloomingdale's or Harrods, Kirkcaldie & Stains is an up-market department store that's been running since 1863.

Mainly Tramping (Map pp630-1; ☎ 473 5353; 39 Mercer St) The place for all your specialist outdoor needs, be they concerned with tramping, kayaking or mountain climbing.

GETTING THERE & AWAY

Air

Wellington Airport (☎ 385 5100; www.wellington-airport.co.nz; 🕑 closed 2-4am) is 7km southeast of the city centre. There's an **information desk** (☎ 385 5123; 1st fl, Main Terminal; 🕑 7am-7pm), a bureau de change, ATMs, storage lockers, car-rental desks, cafés and shops. Those in transit or with early flights are not permitted to stay overnight inside the airport. Departure tax on international flights is NZ$25 per adult.

Air New Zealand (Map pp626-7; ☎ 0800 737 000; www.airnz.co.nz; cnr Lambton Quay & Grey St) offers regular, direct domestic flights to/from Wellington and most major centres, including Auckland (from NZ$90), Christchurch (from NZ$65), Dunedin (from NZ$100), Rotorua (from NZ$90) and Westport (from NZ$90).

Origin Pacific (☎ 0800 302 302; www.originpacific.co.nz) flies into Nelson (from NZ$70, daily), where there's a connection to Christchurch. **Qantas** (Map pp626-7; ☎ 0800 808 767; www.qantas.co.nz; 2 Hunter St) has direct flights from Wellington to Auckland (from NZ$85) and Christchurch (from NZ$65). **Soundsair** (☎ 0800 505 005, 03-520 3080; www.soundsair.co.nz) runs a service between Wellington and Picton (NZ$80).

Holders of backpacker and student cards are eligible for discounts.

Bus

InterCity (☎ 472 5111; www.intercitycoach.co.nz) and **Newmans** (☎ 499 3261; www.newmanscoach.co.nz) coaches depart from Platform 9 at **Wellington Train Station** (Map pp626-7; off Waterloo Quay).

White Star (City to City) (☎ 478 4734) has one to two buses daily from Bunny St, near Downtown Wellington Backpackers. Buses run along the North Island's west coast to Palmerston North (NZ$20, 2¼ hours), Wanganui (NZ$27, 3½ hours) and New Plymouth (NZ$45, six hours). Connect at Palmerston North for services to Napier and Gisborne.

Car

Wellington has a number of hire-car operators that will negotiate cheap deals, especially for longer-term rental (a couple of weeks or more), but overall rates aren't as competitive as in Auckland. Advertised rates range from around NZ$45 to NZ$110 per day; cars are usually about two or three years old and in excellent condition.

Recommended companies:

Ace Rental Cars (☎ 0800 525 500, 471 1178; 150 Hutt Rd)

Apex Car Rentals (Map pp630-1; ☎ 0800 300 110, 385 2163; www.apexrentals.co.nz; 186 Victoria St)

Omega Rental Cars (☎ 0800 667 722, 472 8465; www.omegarentals.com; 92-96 Hutt Rd)

Shoestring Rentals (☎ 0800 746 378, 389 2983; www.carhire.co.nz/shoestring; 138 Adelaide Rd)

For details of some of the bigger, international car-hire firms operating in the country, see p794.

If you plan on travelling on both the North and South Islands, it's a much cheaper option to return your hire car to either Picton or Wellington and pick up another after crossing the strait. This is common practice and car-hire companies make it a painless exercise.

There are often cheap deals on car relocation from Wellington to Auckland (most renters travel in the opposite direction); a few companies offer very cheap rental on this route – the catch being that you may only have 24 or 48 hours to make the journey.

For those looking to buy or sell a car, the **Cable St Car Fair** (☎ 499 3322; Cable St; 9am-noon Sat) is in the car park near Te Papa. **Turners Auctions** (☎ 0800 282 8466, 587 1400; www.turners.co.nz; 120 Hutt Park Rd, Lower Hutt) buys and sells used cars by auction. Also check noticeboards at backpackers for ridiculously cheap deals.

Ferry

There are three ferry options for crossing Cook Strait from Wellington to Picton in the South Island. These large boats have lounges, cafés, bars and an information desk (some Interislander ferries even have a movie theatre). Note that sailing times are subject to change.

Bluebridge Ferries/Strait Shipping (Map pp626-7; ☎ 0800 844 844, 473 1479; www.strait.co.nz; adult NZ$40) Crossing takes three hours, 20 minutes. Departs Wellington 3am (excluding Monday) and 1pm. Returns from Picton 8am (excluding Monday) and 7pm. Car or campervan costs an extra NZ$150, motorcycle NZ$45, and bicycle or surfboard NZ$10.

Interislander (Map pp626-7; ☎ 0800 802 802, 498 3302; www.interislandline.co.nz; adult NZ$60) Crossing takes three hours. There are roughly nine sailings per day but regular daily services depart Wellington 1.30am (excluding Monday), 9.30am, 2pm and 5.30pm; and return from Picton 5.30am (excluding Monday), 10am, 1.30pm, 6pm and 9.30pm. Car or campervan costs an extra NZ$220, motorcycle NZ$60, bicycle or surfboard NZ$10. Discount fares often available for advance bookings.

Lynx (Map pp626-7; ☎ 0800 802 802, 498 3302; www.interislandline.co.nz; adult NZ$60) Crossing takes 2¼ hours. Departs Wellington 8am and 3.30pm; returns from Picton 11.30am and 7pm. A faster option for the same price on a high-speed catamaran. Car or campervan costs an extra NZ$220, motorcycle NZ$60, bicycle or surfboard NZ$10.

You can book ferries at your accommodation, by phone, online, at travel agents and directly at individual offices. A free ferry shuttle-bus service is provided on both sides of the strait. For details of Wellington services, see the Getting into Town boxed text (p625). On the Picton side, a free shuttle runs between the ferry and the Picton–Christchurch *Tranz Coastal* train. Car-hire companies also pick up and drop off at the ferry terminal; if you arrive outside business hours, arrangements can be made to collect your hire vehicle from the terminal car park.

Hitching

It's not easy to hitch out of Wellington – the highways heading out of the city, SH1 and SH2, are motorways for a long distance and hitching is illegal on motorways. The best option is to catch a bus or train to one of the towns on the Kapiti Coast or to Masterton and hitch from there.

Train

Wellington Train Station (off Waterloo Quay) has a **travel centre** (☎ 498 2058; 🕑 7.15am-5.30pm Mon-Fri, 7.15am-12.15pm Sat & Sun) that books and sells tickets for trains, buses, ferries, tours and more. Luggage lockers are also available.

One long-distance train operated by **Tranz Scenic** (☎ 0800 872 467, 495 0775; www.tranzscenic.co.nz) runs between Wellington and Auckland. The *Overlander* runs daily, leaving Wellington/Auckland each morning and arriving in the other city that night (two trains going in opposite directions). Check the website for times as they change during the year. The standard adult fare is NZ$145, but a seat in an older 'backpacker carriage' is only NZ$75. Various concessions are available, usually only for off-peak services.

GETTING AROUND

For comprehensive timetable and fare information, check online at the **Wellington Regional Council** (www.wrc.govt.nz/timetables) website. Call **Ridewell** (☎ 801 7000; ridewell@gw.govt.nz) for timetable and ticketing info for all bus and train services.

For details of how to get into town from the airport and train station, see the Getting into Town boxed text (p625).

Bus

Wellington has an efficient local bus system. **Stagecoach** (☎ 387 8700; www.stagecoach.co.nz; 45 Onepu Rd, Kilbirnie) has frequent services from 7am to 11.30pm on most routes. Most depart from beside the train station (Map pp626–7) and from the major **bus stop** (Map pp630-1; cnr Courtenay Pl & Cambridge Tce). Useful colour-coded bus route maps and timetables are available at the visitors centre.

Bus fares are determined by zones: there are eight zones; the cheapest fare is NZ$1.50 for rides in zone one, NZ$2 for two zones and up in 50 cent increments to NZ$5. A Single Daytripper Pass is NZ$8 and allows unlimited bus travel for one day (excluding the airport bus, After Midnight buses and services to Hutt Valley). An all-day StarPass (NZ$9) allows unlimited rides on all routes.

The City Circular is the name given to the distinctive bright-yellow buses that take in Wellington's prime inner-city sights. These buses loop the city every 15 minutes between 10am and 4.45pm daily; the fare is NZ$2.

The **After Midnight Bus Service** (☎ 801 7000) has buses departing the central entertainment district (Courtenay Pl, Cuba St) at 1am, 2am and 3am Saturday and Sunday and heading off on a number of routes to the outer suburbs. The flat fare is NZ$3.50.

To get to the Hutt Valley from Courtenay Pl, take the **Stagecoach Flyer** (☎ 387 8700; www.stagecoach.co.nz) to Upper Hutt ($8.50, one hour) or Eastbourne-bound bus No 81 or 83 to Lower Hutt ($5, 45 minutes).

Taxi

The city's taxi companies include **Wellington Combined Taxis** (☎ 384 4444) and **Wellington Ace** (☎ 388 8100).

Train

Tranz Metro (Map pp630-1; ☎ 801 7000; www.tranzmetro.co.nz) operates four suburban train routes. Trains run frequently from 6am to midnight, departing from Wellington Train Station. These routes are: Johnsonville, via Ngaio and Khandallah; Paraparaumu, via Porirua and Paekakariki; Melling, via Petone; and Upper Hutt, going on to Masterton. Timetables are available from the train station, visitors centre, or online.

South Island

CONTENTS

HIGHLIGHTS

- **Queenstown** Let your adrenaline go crazy (p719)
- **Milford Track** Pit your feet against a 'Great Walk' like this one (p755)
- **Milford Sound** Kayak the coves here (p756)
- **Kaikoura** Frolic with seals and dolphins (p658)
- **Christchurch** Toast your travels in the cruisey bars (p685)
- **Franz Josef & Fox Glaciers** Take in these frozen splendours (p711)
- **Stewart Island** Enjoy the walks and sheer isolation (p763)
- **Abel Tasman National Park** Experience the lush wilderness of this park (p670)

- **Cheer for:** Otago Highlanders in the Super12 (rugby union)
- **Eat:** crayfish (lobster) in Kaikoura (p661)
- **Drink:** a handle (425mL) of Speight's
- **Listen to:** Bic Runga's *Drive*, Scribe's *The Crusader*
- **Watch:** *Heavenly Creatures* (murderous Christchurch schoolgirls), *Scarfies* (murderous Dunedin uni students) or *Perfect Strangers* (murder on the West Coast)
- **Party at:** Queenstown (p728) or Dunedin (p743)
- **Swim at:** Abel Tasman National Park (p670)
- **Avoid:** sandflies (p754 and p781)
- **Locals' nickname:** Mainlanders

- TELEPHONE CODE: 03
- WEBSITE: www.purenz.com

Like its northern companion across Cook Strait, the South Island of New Zealand is blessed with awesome geographical assets that attract backpackers like bare skin attracts Kiwi sandflies. The terrain down south is not an imitation of the volcanic north, however, but is a unique landscape with its own scenic extremes – from the frozen heights of the Southern Alps that run down the island's spine and the grand fiords that flood the uninhabited southwest to the sheep-grazed greenery of inland pastures, dazzling lakes that were dug out by mountains of ice, and the spectacular island clutter of Marlborough Sounds. Travellers allow themselves to go completely wild here by bungy jumping into canyons, jet-boating up rocky gorges, tramping into the hearts of remote national parks, picking their way over glaciers and letting dolphins and seals teach them how to swim.

The island's pristine air is a revelation, as any backpacker who's kayaked on Milford Sound, wandered into Stewart Island's undergrowth or caught their breath in the shadow of Mt Cook can tell you. The cities and towns often have their own distinctive, refreshing appeal, which you can sample in the crowded clubs of mountain-backed Queenstown and the riverside bars of Christchurch.

MARLBOROUGH & NELSON

Crossing Cook Strait from Wellington to Picton is an exciting prospect, a bit like entering a new country. (Wellington is actually a tad south of Picton, so you move east to west.) Compared with the North Island, the South Island is less populated, slower paced, geographically different and the Maori presence is less apparent.

There is plenty to occupy the traveller in the Marlborough region, in particular the myriad beautiful inlets and bays of Marlborough Sounds, the incredibly popular, coast-hugging Queen Charlotte Track and the famous wineries around Blenheim. To the south is the ocean-front town of Kaikoura, a mecca for marine wildlife enthusiasts – Kaikoura technically lies in the Canterbury region and is often accessed from Christchurch, but we've included it here due to its proximity to Blenheim and Picton, and the ease of travelling between these towns.

West of Picton is the Nelson region, which has some of NZ's best tramping and kayaking possibilities in and around the verdant, neighbouring national parks of Abel Tasman and Kahurangi. Also here is the engagingly artistic town of Nelson.

The first European to visit the Marlborough district was Abel Tasman, but it wasn't until a whaling station was set up in 1827 that the area received its first permanent European settlement. In June 1840, Major Bunbury arrived on HMS *Herald* on the hunt for Maori signatures to the Treaty of Waitangi (p491). Soon after, Nelson settlers came into conflict with Maori tribes over ownership of part of the Wairau Plain, which led to an infamous massacre; see the boxed text on below. In March 1847, Wairau was finally bought and added to the Nelson territory. Settlers petitioned for independence and the colonial government established the region of Marlborough.

Activities

The northern end of the South Island is a tramper's dream, with high-profile walks like the Queen Charlotte and Abel Tasman Coastal Tracks. If you want to put your arms to use rather than your feet, paddle a sea-kayak around the region's sheltered mainland bays and the serene island coves of Marlborough Sounds. You can also go rock-climbing on limestone crags, loiter in numerous palate-pleasing wineries and make eye contact with whales, several species of dolphin and other sea critters offshore.

PICTON

☎ 03 / pop 3600

Picton, a small, pretty port built around an enclosed harbour at the head of Queen Charlotte Sound, is not just the marine gateway to the South Island but is also the best base from which to explore the Marlborough Sounds and tackle the Queen Charlotte

WAIRAU MASSACRE

One of the most infamous early conflicts between settlers in the Nelson region and Maori tribes occurred in 1843. The opportunistic New Zealand Company tried to settle part of the Wairau Plain after buying the alleged rights from the widow of a trader, John Blenkinsopp. He claimed he bought the land from the Maori for a 16lb cannon, and had obtained a dubious deed signed by local chiefs.

The Maori denied all knowledge of the Wairau sale and two chiefs of the Ngati Toa tribe, Te Rauparaha and Te Rangihaeata, arrived from Kapiti to resist survey operations. The pakeha sent out a hurriedly co-opted armed party led by Arthur Wakefield, brother of the then governor of NZ, to arrest them. The party was met peacefully by the Ngati Toa at Tuamarina, but the pakeha precipitated a brief skirmish, during which Te Rangihaeata's wife was shot. The pakeha (white New Zealanders) were forced to surrender and Rangihaeata, mad with rage, demanded vengeance. Twenty two of the party, including Wakefield, were killed; the rest escaped through the scrub and over the hills. The event came to be known as the Wairau Massacre.

Tuamarina, the site of the massacre, is 19km south of Picton. In the cemetery near the road is a pakeha monument designed by Arthur Wakefield's youngest brother, Felix Wakefield.

SOUTH ISLAND

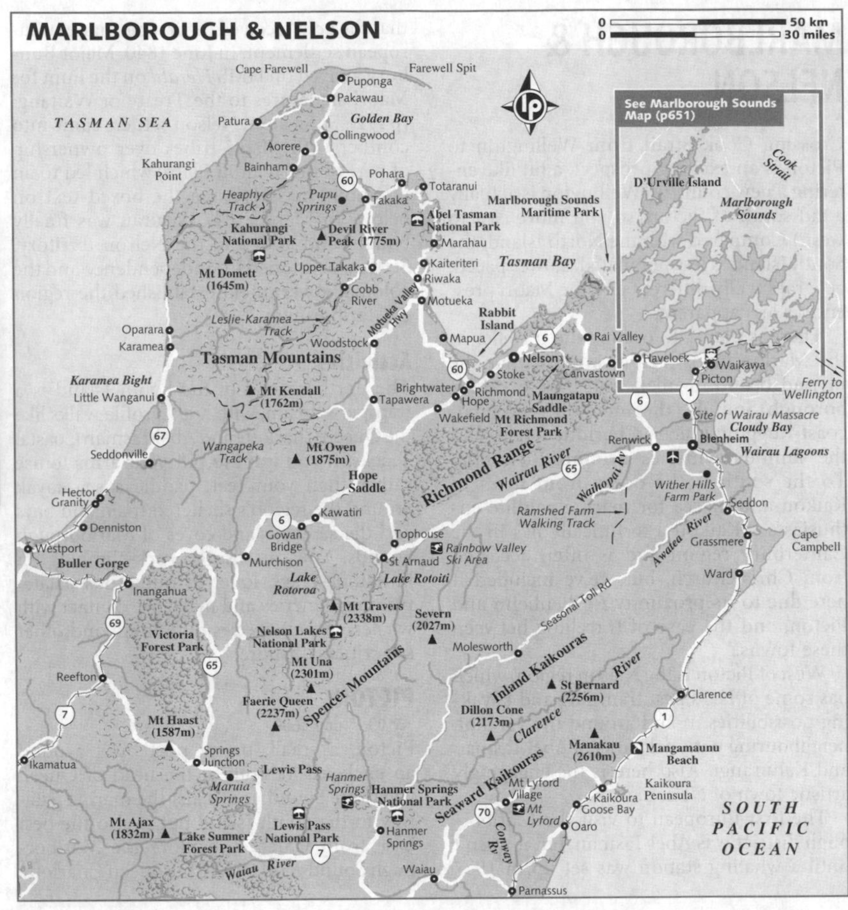

Track. Picton is a hive of activity when a ferry docks and during the peak of summer, but is slow and sleepy at other times.

Information

Automobile Association (AA; ☎ 573 6784; www.aaamarlinmotel.com; 33 Devon St)

Creek Pottery & Gift Shop (☎ 573 6313; 26 High St; per 15min NZ$4) Internet access.

Picton Medical Centre (☎ 573 6092; 71 High St)

Picton visitors centre (☎ 520 3133; www.destinationmarlborough.com; Foreshore; 🕑 8.30am-5pm) Maps and info on walking in the Marlborough Sounds area; the Department of Conservation (DOC) counter here is staffed during summer.

United Video (☎ 573 7466; 63 High St; per 15min NZ$3) Internet access. In the Marlin Motel.

Sights & Activities

The **Edwin Fox Maritime Centre** (☎ 573 6868; edwinfoxsoc@xtra.co.nz; Dunbar Wharf; adult NZ$5; 🕑 8.45am-5pm) has a few maritime exhibits and provides access to the battered but still-floating hull of the old East Indiaman *Edwin Fox*, purportedly the ninth-oldest ship in the world. Built of teak in Bengal, the 48m-long, 760-ton vessel was launched in 1853. During its long and varied career it carried convicts to Perth (Australia), troops to the Crimean War and immigrants to NZ. It's gradually being restored.

Next door is the **Aquarium of the Marlborough Sounds** (☎ 573 6030; Dunbar Wharf; adult NZ$8; 🕑 9am-5pm), a hit with kids and with a playground opposite.

The visitors centre has a map showing several walks, including the easy 1km **Bob's Bay Path** along the eastern side of Picton Harbour to Bob's Bay. The **Snout Walkway** (three hours) carries on along the ridge from the Bob's Bay Path and has great views the length of Queen Charlotte Sound. The **Tirohanga Walkway** (45 minutes) begins on Newgate St and offers panoramic views of Picton and the Sounds.

Diving opportunities around the Sounds include the wreck of the *Mikhail Lermontov*, a Russian cruise ship that sank in Port Gore in 1986. It's said to be the world's biggest diveable cruise shipwreck. **Diver's World** (☎ 573 7323; www.pictondiversworld.co.nz; London Quay; dives NZ$90-190) organises dive trips to the *Mikhail Lermontov* (bookings essential) and to Karaka Point and Double Bay, as well as night dives, equipment hire (two-dive minimum) and courses.

Buzzy Bikes & Boats (☎ 573 7853; todd.fam@xtra.co.nz; London Quay; bikes/kayaks per day NZ$40/50) hires mountain bikes and kayaks. It also runs a water taxi to/from Picton to Marlborough Sounds.

Marlborough Sounds Adventure Company (☎ 573 6078; www.marlboroughsounds.co.nz; Waterfront; bikes per day NZ$40) hires mountain bikes recommended for riding the Queen Charlotte Track.

See p756 for details of sea-kayaking excursions into the Sounds.

Tours

There are heaps of tours to choose from in Picton, mostly cruise-and-walk combinations around Queen Charlotte Sound.

Dolphin Watch Marlborough (☎ 573 8040; www.dolphinwatchmarlborough.co.nz; ecotours NZ$35-70, bird-watcher tours NZ$85) does ecotours around Queen Charlotte Sound and Motuara Island bird sanctuary. You can spot dolphins, sea birds or fur seals, and there's a bird-watcher special on Tuesday, Thursday and Sunday.

Southern Wilderness (☎ 0800 266 266, 578 4531; www.southernwilderness.com; railway station, 3 Auckland St; half-/full-day trips from NZ$90/130) is an enthusiastic company doing great tours of the Marlborough region, including winery tours (pick up/drop off in Picton), white-water rafting trips on the Gowan and Buller Rivers, and three-day rafting trips on the Clarence River.

Two-hour and four-hour cruise/walk options are offered by **Beachcomber Fun Cruises** (☎ 0800 624 526, 573 6175; www.beachcombercruises.co.nz; Waterfront; Magic/Pelorus mail run NZ$65/95, cruises NZ$45-55; 🕐 Pelorus mail run Tue, Thu & Fri, Magic Mail Run Mon-Sat). It also runs full-day mail boat cruises on Queen Charlotte and Pelorus Sounds, which are genuine NZ Post rural delivery services.

Endeavour Express (☎ 573 5456; www.boatrides.co.nz; Waterfront; NZ$45-55) is a backpacker-friendly company that offers a range of cruises and cruise/walks, as does **Cougar Line** (☎ 0800 504 090, 573 7925; www.cougarlinecruises.co.nz; Waterfront; NZ$55-65).

Waka Whenua Tours (☎ 573 7877; www.picton.co.nz/for/wakawhenuatours; NZ$40-60; 🕐 10.30am, noon & 1.30pm) visits Marlborough vineyards with a descendant of the Tangata Whenua tribe Te Atiawa. Scenic, historic, cultural and back country–themed tours are also available.

Sleeping

Sequoia Lodge Backpackers (☎ 0800 222 257, 573 8399; www.sequoialodge.co.nz; 3a Nelson Sq; dm NZ$20-22, d & tw NZ$60) Named after one of the enormous trees out the front, this is a big, comfortable and well-run place. It has a giant outdoor chess set, fresh bread nightly and percolated coffee morning and evening.

Villa (☎ 573 6598; www.thevilla.co.nz; 34 Auckland St; dm NZ$22-23, d & tw NZ$55-60; 💻) A deservedly popular hostel with a beautiful rose-covered cottage with cosy rooms and communal areas, well-equipped kitchens, friendly owners and even friendlier dogs. Free perks include bike hire, tea and coffee, breakfast, hot spa pool and broadband Internet (two terminals).

Bayview Backpackers (☎ 573 7668; www.truenz.co.nz/bayviewbackpackers; 318 Waikawa Rd; dm NZ$17, s NZ$30-36, d & tw NZ$40-45) Situated on Waikawa Bay, 4km from central Picton, with bay views and pleasant porch areas. The friendly owners offer free pick up and drop off in town. Water sports equipment and bicycles are also free.

Juggler's Rest (☎ 573 5570; jugglers-rest@xtra.co.nz; 8 Canterbury St; dm/d NZ$20/45; 🚭) If you're a juggler or even marginally interested in learning, this is the place to be – it's run by professional jugglers and lessons are offered free. Juggler's is a small hostel that's surrounded by bush.

Atlantis (☎ 573 8876; www.atlantishostel.co.nz; cnr Auckland St & London Quay; dm NZ$17-19, tw NZ$20-21, d NZ$21-24; 🚭) Rooms are cheap but the dorms are massive (some have 30 beds). Facilities

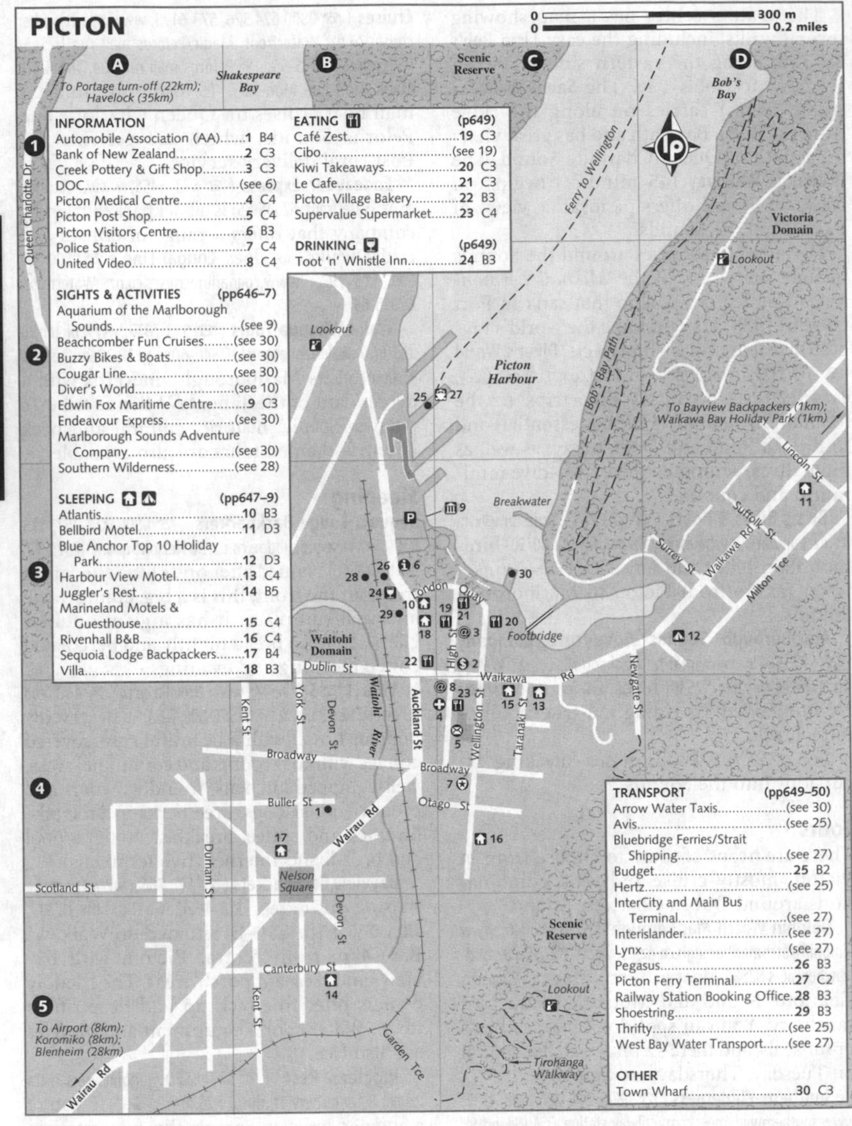

include a small indoor heated pool, pool table, Sky TV and more than 300 DVDs to keep your eyes square.

Bellbird Motel (☎ 573 6912; 96 Waikawa Rd; d NZ$60-70) Slightly out of town, '70s-style Bellbird has six spacious self-contained units that are old-school and feel more like houses than units. Great value.

Marineland Motels & Guesthouse (☎ 573 6429; www.marinelandaccom.co.nz; 26-28 Waikawa Rd; s NZ$50-65, d with bathroom NZ$65-90, self-contained units NZ$75-95;) Marineland has old-fashioned B&B guesthouse rooms in a beautiful character home with a guest lounge and dining room. Continental breakfast is included in the rates; cooked breakfast is supplied on request. The modern motel rooms are fully self-contained and have Sky TV.

Rivenhall B&B (☎ 573 7692; rivenhall.picton@xtra.co.nz; 118 Wellington St; s/d NZ$55/80) Perched high on the hill overlooking Picton and the Marlborough Sounds, Rivenhall is a lovely homestay option with friendly hosts. Breakfast of your choice is provided and for an additional NZ$25 Nan will cook you dinner.

Harbour View Motel (☎ 0800 101 133, 573 6259; 30 Waikawa Rd; s & d NZ$65-80) Harbour View has an elevated position that offers watery views of Picton's endearing harbour. Units are fully self-contained and a reasonably priced option.

Blue Anchor Top 10 Holiday Park (☎ 573 7212; www.blueanchor.co.nz; 70-78 Waikawa Rd; camp sites unpowered/powered per 2 people NZ$20/22, s & d NZ$35-80; 💻 ♿) About 1km from the town centre, Blue Anchor is a well-kept, modern park with a range of facilities, including spa and swimming pools, and a recreation room stuffed with games.

Waikawa Bay Holiday Park (☎ 0800 924 529, 573 7434; www.waikawa.kiwiholidayparks.com; 302 Waikawa Rd; camp sites per 2 people NZ$18, s & d NZ$30-75) About 4km from Picton, this park is a pleasant spot to stay and has a good range of accommodation, grassy sites and a courtesy van.

Eating & Drinking

Café Zest (☎ 573 6616; 31 High St; meals NZ$6-15; 🕒 breakfast & lunch) A cheery spot with blue walls and a classic black-and-white tiled floor. Food is served with a modern twist – breakfast toast may come with chunky plum jam and pesto as the condiments of choice.

Le Cafe (☎ 573 5588; 33 High St; mains NZ$12-15; 🕒 breakfast & lunch; 💻) Right on the waterfront and with a slightly Bohemian character, Le Cafe is a great place for a lingering breakfast or lunch – it also has one computer with Internet access. It's a cruisey place for a coffee and a read of the paper.

Cibo (☎ 573 7171; 33 High St; meals NZ$6-14; 🕒 breakfast & lunch) This licensed and bring-your-own (BYO) café offers something different, with treats like Spanish tapas for lunch and thick pancake stacks for breakfast at weekends.

Picton Village Bakery (☎ 573 7082; 46 Auckland St; meals NZ$4-6) Dutch owners bake a range of European treats, including 'dark long-baked rye bread' – good for tramping (as it doesn't break up). Pies here are scrumptious, as are the focaccias and ciabatta sandwiches. Gluten-free bread is available on request.

Toot 'n' Whistle Inn (☎ 573 6086; 7 Auckland St; meals NZ$9.50-15; 🕒 lunch & dinner) A classic local right by the ferry terminal. Head here for big portions of pub grub (with plenty of chips) that should be washed down with big portions of lager.

If you're hankering for fish and chips, try **Kiwi Takeaways** (☎ 573 5537; 14 Wellington St; meals NZ$4-9; 🕒 dinner).

Self-caterers head to **Supervalue supermarket** (☎ 573 6463; Mariners Mall, 71 High St).

Getting There & Away

AIR

A courtesy shuttle bus to/from the airstrip at Koromiko, 8km south of Picton, is included in the price of flights.

Soundsair (☎ 0800 505 005, 520 3080; www.soundsair.co.nz) runs a service between Picton and Wellington (from NZ$80, 25 minutes, eight daily). There are discounts for card-carrying backpackers and students.

BUS

There are numerous buses travelling south to Christchurch and plenty heading west to Nelson. Buses serving Picton operate from the ferry terminal or the visitors centre.

InterCity (☎ 573 7025; www.intercitycoach.co.nz; Picton ferry terminal, Auckland St) runs services to/from Christchurch (NZ$50, five hours, two daily) via Kaikoura (NZ$27, 2¼ hours), with connections to Dunedin and Invercargill. Services also run to/from Nelson (NZ$29, two hours, three daily), with connections to Motueka (NZ$30, one daily), Greymouth and the glaciers, and to/from Blenheim (NZ$10, 25 minutes, five daily). At least one bus daily on each of these routes connects with a Wellington ferry service.

Buses running between Picton and Nelson stop at Havelock. There are no buses on the 35km back road between Picton and Havelock (Queen Charlotte Dr), but this is a scenic route if you're driving or cycling.

A profusion of smaller shuttle buses heads south to Christchurch, usually offering a door-to-door service to central accommodation places. Companies include the following:

Atomic Shuttles (☎ 0800 248 885, 573 7477; www.atomictravel.co.nz)

K Bus (☎ 525 9434; www.kahurangi.co.nz)

Magic Travellers Network (☎ 548 3290; www.magicbus.co.nz)
South Island Connections (☎ 0508 742 669, 366 6633; www.southislandconnections.co.nz)
Southern Link Shuttles (☎ 573 7477; www.yellow.co.nz/site/southernlink)

FERRY

Ferries depart from and arrive at the **Picton ferry terminal** (Auckland St), where there are Bluebridge Ferries/Strait Shipping and Interislander/Lynx booking desks. The terminal has conveniences such as a laundrette, public showers, phones and Internet access.

There are three options for crossing Cook Strait by boat (note that timetables are subject to change):

Bluebridge Ferries/Strait Shipping (☎ 0800 844 844, 04-473 1479; www.strait.co.nz; adult NZ$40) Crossing takes three hours 20 minutes. Departs Picton 8am (excluding Monday) and 7pm. Returns from Wellington 3am (excluding Monday) and 1pm. Car or campervan costs an extra NZ$150, motorcycle NZ$45 and bicycle or surfboard NZ$10.

Interislander (☎ 0800 802 802, 04-498 3302; www.interislandline.co.nz; adult NZ$60) Crossing takes three hours. There are roughly nine sailings a day with services departing Picton 5.30am (excluding Monday), 10am, 1.30pm, 6pm and 9.30pm, and returning from Wellington 1.30am (excluding Monday), 9.30am, 2pm and 5.30pm. Car or campervan costs an extra NZ$220, motorcycle NZ$60 and bicycle or surfboard NZ$10. Discount fares often apply to advance bookings.

Lynx (☎ 0800 802 802, 04-498 3302; www.interislandline.co.nz; adult NZ$60) A faster option for the same price on a catamaran. Crossing takes 2¼ hours. Departs Picton 11.30am and 7pm, and returns from Wellington 8am and 3.30pm. Car or campervan costs an extra NZ$220, motorcycle NZ$60 and bicycle or surfboard NZ$10.

TRAIN

Tranz Scenic (☎ 0800 872 467; www.tranzscenic.co.nz; 🕑 7am-7pm) runs the scenic *TranzCoastal* service between Picton and Christchurch (NZ$85, 5½ hours, one daily) via Blenheim (30 minutes) and Kaikoura (2½ hours). The service connects with the *Interislander* ferry. It departs Picton at 1.40pm; from Christchurch it departs at 7.30am. A free shuttle service links the train station and ferry terminal on both sides of the strait.

Getting Around

Renting a car in Picton usually costs between NZ$45 and NZ$110 per day; most agencies also allow drop offs in Christchurch. If you're planning to drive in the North Island it's cheaper to return your car to Picton and pick up another car in Wellington after crossing the strait.

Picton's car-hire companies:

Avis (☎ 573 6363; www.avis.com; Picton ferry terminal, Auckland St)
Budget (☎ 573 6081; www.budget.com; Picton ferry terminal, Auckland St)
Hertz (☎ 520 3044; www.hertz.com; Picton ferry terminal & 12 York St, Picton)
Pegasus (☎ 573 7733; www.rentalcars.co.nz; 1 Auckland St) Cheaper than the major operators.
Thrifty (☎ 573 7387; www.thrifty.com; Picton ferry terminal, Auckland St)

MARLBOROUGH SOUNDS

☎ 03

The Marlborough Sounds feature many delightful bays, islands, coves and waterways, which were formed by the sea flooding its deep valleys after the ice ages. Parts of the Sounds are now included in the Marlborough Sounds Maritime Park, which is actually many small reserves separated by private land, mostly pastoral leases. As an example of how convoluted the Sounds are, Pelorus Sound is 42km long but has 379km of shoreline.

The Queen Charlotte Track is the main attraction for trampers, but there are other walks such as the Nydia Track (two days), which stretches between Kaiuma Bay and Duncan Bay; the track is accessed from the town of Havelock, 35km west of Picton.

Activities

QUEEN CHARLOTTE TRACK

The Queen Charlotte Track has wonderful coastal scenery, beautiful coves and some pristine camping spots. The coastal forest is lush, and from the ridges you can look down on either side to Queen Charlotte and Kenepuru Sounds. The track is 71km long and connects historic Ship Cove with Anakiwa. The terrain it passes through is not national park but is a mixture of privately owned land and DOC reserves – access depends on the cooperation of local landowners, so it's important to respect their property by staying in designated camping grounds and carrying out all your rubbish.

Queen Charlotte is a well-defined track and is suitable for people of all ages of aver-

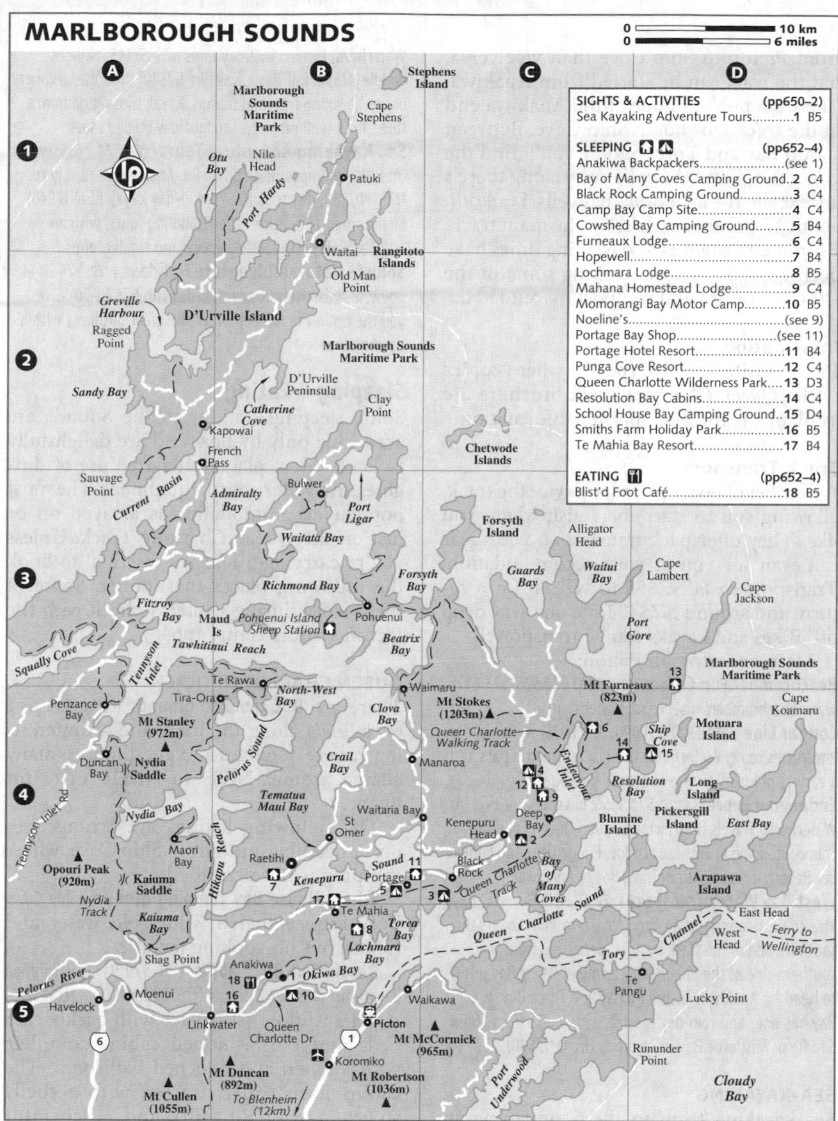

age fitness. You can do the tramp in sections using local boat transport, or walk the whole three- to four-day journey. Sleeping options are only half a day's walk apart. Though there aren't the hordes who walk the Abel Tasman Track, there's still some solid traffic on this path.

Mountain biking is also an option and it's possible to ride the track in two or three days. Note that the section between Ship Cove and Punga Cove is closed to cyclists between 1 December and 28 February. At this time you can still get dropped off by boat at Punga Cove and ride to Anakiwa. As with the Abel Tasman Track, you can do part of the trip by sea-kayak.

Ship Cove is the usual starting point, mainly because it's easier to arrange a boat from Picton to Ship Cove than vice versa, but the walk can be started from Anakiwa. There's a public phone at the Anakiwa end of the track, but not at Ship Cove. Between Camp Bay and Torea Saddle you'll find the going toughest. About halfway along there's an excellent viewpoint, Eatwells Lookout, about 15 minutes walk from the main track. Estimated distances and walking times have been recently revised, making some of the DOC literature and signposting outdated.

Information

Picton visitors centre (p646), where copies of the *Queen Charlotte Track* brochure are available, is the best spot for information.

Track Transport

A number of boat operators service the track, allowing you to start and finish where you like. They offer pack transfers so your gear can wait for you at your accommodation. Transport costs NZ$55 to NZ$60 for a return, and around NZ$40 for a one-way drop off. Bikes and kayaks can be transported.

Main operators in Picton:

Beachcomber Fun Cruises (☎ 0800 624 526, 573 6175; www.beachcombercruises.co.nz; Waterfront)

Cougar Line (☎ 0800 504 090, 573 7925; www.cougarlinecruises.co.nz; Waterfront) Offers a return-trip pass and a variety of luxury 'cruise and walk' packages.

Endeavour Express (☎ 573 5456; www.boatrides.co.nz; Waterfront) Travels from Picton to outer Queen Charlotte Sound, stopping at Furneaux Lodge, Punga Cove and Endeavour Resort; it picks up from Torea Bay or Anakiwa.

West Bay Water Transport (☎ 573 5597; west_bay@xtra.co.nz; floating jetty, Picton ferry terminal) Covers the southern end of the track by boat, departing from the southern side of the Picton ferry terminal (West Bay jetty) to head for Anakiwa, Lochmara Bay and Torea Bay. West Bay has one- and two-day specials with walks from Torea Saddle or Mistletoe Bay to Anakiwa (from NZ$40).

SEA-KAYAKING

Sea-kayaking trips on the Sounds operate from Picton, Anakiwa and Havelock – many water taxis operate out of Havelock and nature cruises can be organised to Maud Island.

Havelock Sea Kayaking Company (☎ 574 2114; havelockseakayak@ihug.co.nz; trips NZ$80-150, kayak hire NZ$35) Full-day sea-kayaking trips on the Marlborough Sounds, including a deluxe overnight version.

Marlborough Sounds Adventure Company (☎ 0800 283 283, 573 6078; www.marlboroughsounds.co.nz; Waterfront, Picton; 1-/2-day tours NZ$85/145, twilight paddle NZ$50, full-day kayak hire NZ$40) Organises a variety of sea-kayaking trips and tramps. Kayak trips range from a three-hour twilight paddle to four-day guided tours.

Sea Kayaking Adventure Tours (☎ 574 2765; www.nzseakayaking.com; Anakiwa Rd, Anakiwa; 1-/2-day tours NZ$180/280, day trips NZ$75, full-day kayak hire NZ$40) Environmental, nature-based paddling tours, with an emphasis on personalised service and small groups.

Sounds Natural Adventure Holidays (☎ 574 2144; www.soundsnatural.co.nz; full-day trip NZ$70-90) Gives you the option to fully embrace the great outdoors with a naturist tour.

Sleeping & Eating

Some sleeping options in the Sounds are accessible only by boat and are delightfully isolated. Most places offer free use of dinghies and water sports equipment. The most popular accommodation is arrayed on or just off the Queen Charlotte Track. Unless you're carrying a tent it's essential to book the following places in summer. Some of them close during winter – check with the Picton visitors centre (p646).

QUEEN CHARLOTTE TRACK

There are **DOC camping grounds** (camp sites per 2 people NZ$10) along the track and an interesting variety of lodges and guesthouses; many charge around NZ$5 to NZ$10 extra for linen.

The following listings are arranged in order heading south from Ship Cove, where camping is not permitted.

School House Bay camping ground (Ship Cove) Beautifully situated, with cold water and toilets, but no cooking facilities.

Resolution Bay Cabins (☎ 579 9411; Resolution Bay; camp sites per 2 people NZ$20, dm/d from NZ$25/75) A delightfully rustic place with backpacker beds and old-fashioned cabins complete with kitchen and attached bathroom. The cabins have real character, with potbelly stoves, ageing furniture and a generator providing the electricity. It's incredibly peaceful.

Furneaux Lodge (☎ 579 8259; www.furneaux.co.nz; dm NZ$30-35, d NZ$135-185) A century-old place set amid lovely gardens, and is a godsend for thirsty trampers – it has a genuine pub, one of the only pubs in NZ accessible only by boat or foot. The backpacker section is in an old stone cottage with a big open fire, and there are also comfortable studios and one-bedroom chalets. Meals are available in the bar and restaurant.

Camp Bay camp site (Camp Bay) On the western side of Endeavour Inlet.

Punga Cove Resort (☎ 0800 809 697, 579 8561; www.pungacove.co.nz; Endeavour Inlet; dm NZ$35, d NZ$160-350;) Backpackers will find a separate area overlooking the bay amid this resort's huge upmarket range of self-contained, studio, family and luxury A-frame chalets. The resort also has a pool, spa, shop, bar and an excellent restaurant.

Mahana Homestead Lodge (☎ 579 8373; www.mahanahomestead.com; Endeavour Inlet; dm NZ$25, d & tw NZ$55) Mahana gets a huge rap from those who've stayed in this purpose-built lodge. Every room has sea views. There's only a natural water supply here so use water wisely, and bring your own linen if possible. Mahana's chocolate cake is renowned throughout the Sounds.

Noeline's (☎ 579 8375; tw NZ$45) Noeline's, five minutes up the hill from Mahana, is a friendly, relaxed homestay with a handful of beds, cooking facilities and great views.

Bay of Many Coves camping ground (Bay of Many Coves) On the saddle above the track.

Black Rock camping ground (Kumutoto Bay) Further along the track from Black Rock camping ground.

Portage Hotel Resort (☎ 573 4309; www.portage.co.nz; Kenepuru Sound; dm NZ$25, d NZ$160-265) This resort is a stalwart on Kenepuru Sound. It's flash, with an à la carte restaurant, casual café and bar. The backpacker section is great, with lounge and cooking facilities. Even if you're not staying, drop in for a beer. The hotel has sailboats, sailboards, fishing, a spa, gym and tennis courts.

Portage Bay Shop (☎ 573 4445; www.portagecharters.co.nz; Kenepuru Sound; s/d NZ$30/60) Offers backpacker accommodation and hires yachts, dinghies, kayaks and bikes, and sells fuel.

Cowshed Bay camping ground (Portage) Located just east around the bay from the Portage Hotel Resort, it can easily be reached by road from Picton or Havelock, or by boat to Torea Bay, where there's a shuttle service.

Lochmara Lodge (☎ 573 4554; www.lochmaralodge.co.nz; Lochmara Bay; dm NZ$25-28, d NZ$60-120; Oct-May) A superb retreat on Lochmara Bay, reached by a side track south of the Queen Charlotte Track, or by boat from Picton. Facilities include an outdoor hot spa, hammocks, barbecues and a volleyball court. It has a homely backpackers lodge with four- and eight-bed dorms set in lush surroundings.

Te Mahia Bay Resort (☎ 573 4089; www.temahia.co.nz; Kenepuru Sound; dm NZ$30, d NZ$105-140) This resort is north of the track, just off the main road, on a beautiful bay facing Kenepuru Sound. It has dorm beds and very roomy self-contained units looking out over the water. There's a store, plus kayaks for hire.

Anakiwa Backpackers (☎ 574 1338; anakiwa@ihug.co.nz; 401 Anakiwa Rd; dm NZ$19, d & tw NZ$50) This small place is right at the southern end of the track. There are only six beds in the self-contained section, and there's home-made bread.

Blist'd Foot Café (Anakiwa) After days of walking, this is the place to rest your feet at the end of the track and debrief with fellow trampers. It's near the pick-up point for water transport back to Picton.

OTHER SOUNDS ACCOMMODATION

Queen Charlotte Wilderness Park (☎ 579 9025; www.truenz.co.nz/wilderness; Cape Jackson; 2 nights & 3 days NZ$260) North of Ship Cove and extending right up to Cape Jackson, this park is a private farming lease that allows you to continue exploring north of the Queen Charlotte Track. The package includes accommodation, dinner and transfers from Picton. As well as opportunities for tramping on a virtually deserted track, there's also boating, kayaking and horse riding.

Hopewell (☎ 573 4341; www.hopewell.co.nz; Kenepuru Sound; d & tw NZ$40) A comfortable, highly rated backpackers in a remote part of Kenepuru Sound. It's surrounded by native bush and opens onto the sea. There's also an outdoor spa. Access by road is possible but the bumpy drive makes the water taxi from Portage the best option.

Momorangi Bay Motor Camp (☎ 573 7865; momorangi.camp@xtra.co.nz; Queen Charlotte Dr; camp sites per 2 people NZ$23-30, cabins NZ$30) Momorangi Bay, 15km from Picton on the road to Havelock, is one of several motor camps along Queen Charlotte Dr. There are around 30 camp sites with water frontage.

Smiths Farm Holiday Park (☎ 574 2806; www.smithsfarm.co.nz; Queen Charlotte Dr, Linkwater; camp sites unpowered/powered per 2 people NZ$18/20, s & d NZ$40-90) A cut above your average holiday park, with lush camping areas and relatively new cabins (shared facilities or self-contained). It's just before the turn-off to Portage and is part of a working beef farm.

There are almost 30 **DOC camping grounds** (camp sites per 2 people NZ$10) throughout the Sounds, with water and toilet facilities but not much else; none have cooking facilities.

Getting There & Around

The best way to get around the Sounds is still by boat, although the road system has been extended. No scheduled buses service the Sounds but much of it is accessible by car. Most of the road is sealed to the head of Kenepuru Sound, but beyond that it's nothing but narrow, forever-winding gravel roads. To drive to Punga Cove from Picton takes at least two hours – the trip is 45 minutes by boat.

Scheduled boats service most of the accommodation on the Queen Charlotte Track and are the cheapest way to get around. Another option is to contact **Arrow Water Taxis** (☎ 573 8229, 027-444 4689; www.arrowwatertaxis.co.nz; Town Wharf, Picton), a well-known operator servicing Queen Charlotte Sound, which takes passengers on demand.

BLENHEIM

☎ 03 / pop 25,900

Blenheim is 29km south of Picton on the Wairau Plain, a landscape contrast to the Sounds. The flatness of the town, located at the junction of the Taylor and Opawa Rivers, was a problem in the early days as Blenheim grew up around a swamp – now the reclaimed Seymour Sq with its attractive lawns and gardens.

Blenheim is a classic NZ country town and is one of the best places to access NZ's biggest wine-growing district. During the second weekend of February, Blenheim hosts the **BMW Wine Marlborough Festival** (☎ 577 9299, 04-384 8630; www.bmw-winemarlborough-festival.co.nz) at Montana Brancott winery.

Information

AA (☎ 578 3399; www.nzaa.co.nz; 23 Maxwell Rd)

Blenheim Library (☎ 578 2784; library@marlborough.govt.nz; cnr Arthur & Seymour Sts; per 15min/hr NZ$2/6) Internet access.

Marlborough Visitors Information Centre (☎ 577 8080; www.destinationmarlborough.com; railway station, Sinclair St; 🕒 8.30am-5pm Mon-Fri, 9am-4pm Sat & Sun) Friendly and efficient; in the refurbished railway station building.

Sights & Activities

The main sights are around Blenheim at the lush vineyards with their gourmet restaurants; see the boxed text on p656.

Near Seymour Sq are relics of Blenheim's violent early history. The tiny **Blenkinsopp's cannon** (Seymour St) is outside the council offices. Originally from the whaling ship *Caroline*, captained by John Blenkinsopp, it's reputedly the cannon for which Te Rauparaha was persuaded to sign over the Wairau Plain; for more on Blenkinsopp and the bloody aftermath of this alleged land deal, see the boxed text on p645.

Opposite Seymour Sq, the **Millennium Art Gallery** (☎ 579 2001; Seymour St; admission by gold-coin donation; 🕒 10am-5.30pm) is a contemporary art gallery with changing exhibitions by local, national and international artists.

Spokesman (☎ 0800 422 453; spokes@xtra.co.nz; 61 Queen St; half-/full-day bike hire NZ$35/60) hires bikes and mobility scooters.

Sleeping

Koanui Backpackers (☎ 578 7487; www.koanui.co.nz; 33 Main St; dm NZ$20, s NZ$45, d & tw NZ$50-60) A bright, friendly place with cosy rooms and a big, modern kitchen. It's toasty in winter with the log fire burning and electric blankets on the bed, and there's a TV lounge with free videos. Koanui is popular with fruit pickers. Discounted single rooms are available in the low season.

Grapevine (☎ 578 6062; rob.diana@xtra.co.nz; 29 Park Tce; dm NZ$17, d NZ$36-40) In an old maternity home, the Grapevine is a homely place with cotlike dorm beds. The big attraction is the Opawa River running right past the back door – you can borrow canoes for free.

Raymar Motor Inn (☎ 0800 361 362, 578 5104; 164 High St; d NZ$70-75) Very reasonably priced motel that's centrally located. Studio rooms have comfortable beds, TVs and telephones.

Blenheim Bridge Top 10 Holiday Park (☎ 0800 268 666, 578 3667; www.blenheimtop10.co.nz; 78 Grove Rd; camp sites unpowered/powered per 2 people NZ$22/24, d NZ$40-80) North of the town centre, this holiday park has camp sites by the river plus a range of cabins and units.

Spring Creek Holiday Park (☎ 570 5893; www.holidayparks.co.nz/spring; Rapaura Rd; camp sites unpowered/powered per 2 people NZ$21/22; d NZ$30-180) Spring Creek is 6km out of Blenheim towards Picton, in a peaceful location about 500m off SH1 near a good fishing creek. It

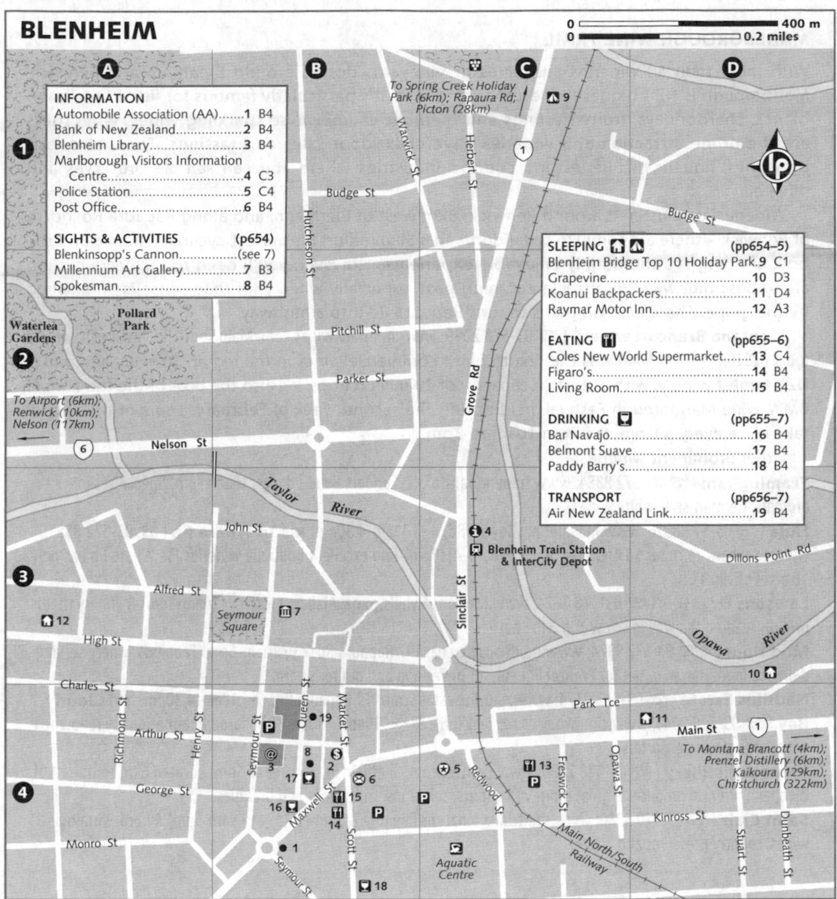

has a mixture of cabins, self-contained units and motel rooms, covering all budgets.

Eating & Drinking

Living Room (☎ 579 4777; cnr Scott St & Maxwell Rd; meals NZ$7-20; lunch & dinner Mon-Thu) The popular Living Room is a chic café–wine bar decorated in warm copper and brown tones with artistic style. It's great for a cosy drink on the couches or for a quality breakfast of poached eggs and tomatoes.

Figaro's (☎ 577 7277; 8 Scott St; meals NZ$10-14; breakfast & lunch) Superb coffee is served at this stylish cream-and-brown café, perfect for a lingering breakfast; alternatively, just take away one of the fat muffins stuffed with fruit.

Paddy Barry's (☎ 578 7470; 51 Scott St; meals NZ$10-14; lunch & dinner) For pub food and occasional live entertainment there's this big, vaguely-Irish pub, which serves filling meals and has a fun atmosphere and an outdoor deck.

Belmont Suave (☎ 577 8238; 67 Queen St) A cool, funky, split-level bar that goes off at night, with people spilling out onto the pavement. A feature wall with forest wallpaper, orange-and-green swivel chairs, and mirrors complement the retro feel. Disk Jockeys play at weekends and it's the place to boogie.

Bar Navajo (☎ 577 7555; 70 Queen St; mains NZ$14-30; 8.30-3am) A busy, Native American–themed bar with a colourful totem (authenticity yet to be verified), booths, pool tables and a

MARLBOROUGH WINE TRAIL

With more than 50 wineries and acres of vineyards dotted around Blenheim and Renwick, Marlborough is NZ's biggest wine-producing area. It's particularly famous for floral sauvignon blancs, chardonnays, fruity rieslings and *méthode champenoise* sparkling wines. Wine tours are the prime attraction and wineries have cellar-door sales and tastings. Tours also visit breweries, liqueur distilleries and cottage industries where you can sample preserves and olive oil.

Wineries are clustered around Renwick, 8km west of Blenheim, and along Rapaura Rd, north of Renwick – there are some 25 cellar doors in a 5km radius. It's perfect cycling distance and the bulk of riding is a thoroughly enjoyable experience. However, you'll need to take care cycling along busy highways with trucks zooming past, especially when your road sense is diminished by the grape. There are also plans to turn Rapaura Rd into a highway.

Montana Brancott winery (☎ 03-578 2099; www.montanawines.com; Main South Rd, Blenheim; winery tours NZ$10; ⌚ 9am-5pm) was the first to plant commercial vines in the region 30 years ago and is NZ's largest winery, with a storage capacity of 20 million litres. It's also the host of the the annual BMW Wine Marlborough Festival, held during the second week of February. Tours of the winery take place every 30 minutes from 10am to 3pm.

Other prominent wineries:

Framingham (☎ 03-572 8884; www.framingham.co.nz; Conders Bend Rd; ⌚ 10am-5pm) Specialises in aromatic German-style white wines.

Huia (☎ 03-572 8326; www.huia.net.nz; Boyces Rd; ⌚ 11am-4.30pm) and **Te Whare Ra** (☎ 03-572 8581; www.te-whare-ra.co.nz; 56 Anglesea St; ⌚ 10am-4.30pm) Two excellent boutique wineries (Te Whare Ra has only 18 acres of vines).

Lawsons Dry Hills (☎ 03-578 7674; www.lawsonsdryhills.co.nz; Alabama Rd; ⌚ 10am-5pm) A winery that is proudly leading the way in screw-top wine bottles.

Mud House (☎ 03-572 9374; www.mudhouse.co.nz; 197 Rapaura Rd; ⌚ 10am-5pm) Fabulous winery serving delicious food. Has an outlet for Prenzel liqueur, an olive shop and quilter's barn.

Nautilus Estate (☎ 03-572 9374; www.nautilusestate.com; 12 Rapaura Rd; ⌚ 10am-4.30pm) and **Cloudy Bay** (☎ 03-520 9040; www.cloudybay.co.nz; Jackson Rd; ⌚ 10am-4.30pm) Two large, internationally renowned wineries (both big exporters).

Prenzel Distillery (☎ 03-578 2800; www.prenzel.com; Sheffield St; ⌚ 10am-5pm) Located 6km southeast of Blenheim, Prenzel produces a great range of liqueurs, schnapps, fruit wines and brandies.

Saint Clair (☎ 03-570 5280; www.saintclair.co.nz; cnr Rapaura & Selmes Rd; ⌚ 9am-5pm) Award-winning wines, country preserves and a café.

rather beaten-up mannequin that has suffered the ravages of time. The varied menu has items such as venison sandwiches, salmon and fettuccini. At weekends DJs play from 10.30pm.

For self-catering head to **Coles New World** (☎ 520 9030; Freswick St).

Getting There & Away

AIR

Blenheim airport is about 6km west of town on Middle Renwick Rd. **Air New Zealand Link** (☎ 0800 737 000, 578 4059; www.airnz.co.nz; 29 Queen St) has direct flights to/from Wellington (from NZ$80, 25 minutes, 10 daily), with connections to other centres.

Soundsair (☎ 0800 505 005, 520 3080; www.soundsair.co.nz) flies from Wellington to Korimoko (from NZ$80, 25 minutes, eight daily), about 20km north of Blenheim. The airport shuttle bus only goes to Picton; see below for details of bus transport between Picton and Blenheim.

BUS

Deluxe Travel Lines (☎ 578 5467; blenheim.depot@ritchies.co.nz; 45 Main St) has regular services between Blenheim and Picton (NZ$8, 20 minutes, two to four daily).

The **InterCity** (☎ 577 2890; www.intercitycoach.co.nz) Nelson–Christchurch bus stops at Blenheim en route; Blenheim to Picton costs NZ$10 and takes 25 minutes (five buses daily). There's also a host of shuttle buses that stop at Blenheim on the Nelson–Christchurch route; see p649.

Villa Maria Estate (☎ 03-255 0660; www.villamaria.co.nz; cnr New Renwick & Paynters Rds; ⏰ 10am-5pm) A big, highly regarded winemaker that consistently reels in major awards.

Tours

Wine Tours by Bike (☎ 03-572 9951; www.winetoursbybike.co.nz; 106 Jeffries Rd, Rapaura; half-/full-day bike hire NZ$35/50) runs a pick-up and drop-off service between Blenheim and Jeffries Rd. Its hire bikes come equipped with a winery map, pannier and mobile phone so you can call to be picked up if you get too tipsy.

There are several wine tours (by minibus) available from Blenheim and a couple from Picton. Pick up from your accommodation is easily arranged.

Deluxe Travel Lines (☎ 0800 500 511, 03-578 5467; www.deluxetravel.co.nz; tours NZ$50) A bigger operator with a six-hour excursion that includes the Montana tour; departures can be arranged from Picton.

Highlight Tours (☎ 03-577 9046; www.marlborough.co.nz/highlight; half-day tours NZ$50) Offers personalised small-group tours.

Marlborough Wine Tours (☎ 03-578 9515, 025-248 1231; www.marlboroughwinetours.co.nz; tours NZ$50-70) Has a range of tours.

Marlborough Wine Trails (☎ 03-578 1494, 025-264 4704; www.yellow.co.nz/site/barryswinetours; half-/full-day tours NZ$50/85) Offers personalised tours; Barry is an effusive guide.

Food

Of course, with wine there should ideally be food and a gourmet lunch at one of the vineyards. Most vineyards have attached cafés or restaurants, many of them with stunning views, serving fresh local produce. Splurge on perfectly matured cheeses, broths and consommés, plump scallops, herb-encrusted this and Manuka-smoked that; you may need to brush up on your gourmet speak beforehand!

The following eateries serve delicious meals (see also Mud House, above):

Gibbs at Cairnbrae (☎ 03-572 8048; www.cairnbrae.co.nz; 258 Jacksons Rd; meals NZ$15-25; ⏰ lunch & dinner)

La Veranda Vineyard Café (☎ 03-572 9177; www.marlboroughwinevalley.co.nz/39.html; Domaine Georges Michel, Vintage Lane; meals NZ$24-28; ⏰ lunch & dinner)

Twelve Trees (☎ 03-572 9054; www.allanscott.com/restaurant.asp; Allan Scott winery, Jacksons Rd; meals NZ$14-22; ⏰ lunch) Has an innovative blackboard menu.

Wairau River Wines (☎ 03-572 9800; www.wairauriverwines.com; Rapaura Rd; meals NZ$15-21; ⏰ lunch)

Whitehaven (☎ 03-577 6634; www.whitehaven.co.nz/café.htm; 1 Dodson St; mains NZ$26-30; ⏰ lunch)

TRAIN

Tranz Scenic (☎ 0800 872 467; www.tranzscenic.co.nz; ⏰ 7am-7pm) runs the scenic *TranzCoastal* service between Picton and Christchurch, stopping at Blenheim; between Blenheim and Picton (30 minutes, one daily) costs NZ$10 to NZ$20, while to/from Christchurch (five hours, one daily) costs NZ$35 to NZ$75.

KAIKOURA

☎ 03 / pop 3850

Kaikoura is a stunning town with a superb setting on a bay backed by the steeply rising foothills of the Seaward Kaikouras, which are magnificently snowcapped in winter. Many travellers make their way here from Christchurch, which lies 183km to the south. In Maori legend, the tiny Kaikoura Peninsula (Taumanu o te Waka o Maui) was where the demigod Maui sat when he fished the North Island up from the depths of the sea.

The first European to settle in Kaikoura was Robert Fyffe, who established a whaling station in 1842. Kaikoura was a whaling centre from 1843 until 1922, after which sheep farming and agriculture continued flourished. Excavations near Fyffe House (p658) revealed the largest moa egg ever found (240mm long, 178mm in diameter) and showed that the area was a moa-hunter settlement about 800 to 1000 years ago – at least 14 Maori *pa* (fortified village) sites have also been identified.

Nature Watch Charters began whale-watching trips in 1987 and the tours' fame escalated, putting Kaikoura on the tourist

SOUTH ISLAND

map. Thousands of international visitors come to see the local wildlife and during the busy summer months it pays to book whale-watching and dolphin-swimming tours at least a few days ahead.

The 'Big Five' most likely to be seen are the sperm whale, Hectors dolphin (the smallest and rarest of dolphins), dusky dolphin (found only in the southern hemisphere), NZ fur seal and bottlenose dolphin. Other animals frequently seen include orcas (killer whales), common dolphins, pilot whales and blue penguins. Sea birds include shearwaters, fulmars, petrels and royal and wandering albatross. Seals are easily seen on the rocks at the seal colony.

There's no guarantee of seeing any specific animal on any one tour, but something of interest will be sighted. Sperm whales are most likely to be seen from October to August and orcas from December to March. Most other fauna is seen year-round.

Marine animals are abundant at Kaikoura because of the currents and continental shelf formation. From land, the shelf slopes gradually to a depth of about 90m, then plunges to more than 800m. Warm and cold currents converge here, and when the southerly current hits the continental shelf it creates an upwelling current, bringing nutrients up from the ocean floor and into the light zone. The waters are often red with great clouds of krill, the sperm whale's favourite food, attracting larger fish and squid.

Information

Ambulance (☎ 319 5199; Beach Rd)
Hospital (☎ 319 7760; Deal St)
Internet Outpost (☎ 319 7970; 19 West End; per hr NZ$5.50)
Kaikoura visitors centre (☎ 319 5641; www.kaikoura.co.nz; West End; 🕒 9am-5.30pm Mon-Fri, 9am-4.30pm Sat & Sun summer, 9am-5pm Mon-Fri, 9am-4pm Sat & Sun winter) By the car park (on the beachside). Staff are very helpful and can make tour bookings. There's a DOC representative here during summer.

Sights

George Fyffe, cousin of NZ's first European settler, Robert Fyffe, came to Kaikoura from Scotland in 1854 and built **Fyffe House** (☎ 319 5835; fyffe.bill@xtra.co.nz; 62 Avoca St; adult NZ$5; 🕒 10am-4pm) in around 1860. The house is the only architectural survivor from the town's whaling days.

Kaikoura Museum (☎ 319 7440; kk.museum@xtra.co.nz; 14 Ludstone Rd; adult NZ$3; 🕒 12.30-4.30pm Mon-Fri, 2-4pm Sat & Sun) includes the old town jail (1910), historical photographs, Maori and colonial artefacts, and an exhibit on the region's whaling era.

In 1828, the Kaikoura beachfront, now the site of the **Garden of Memories**, was the scene of a tremendous battle. Here a Ngati Toa war party, led by chief Te Rauparaha, bore down on Kaikoura, killing or capturing several hundred of the Ngai Tahu tribe.

Up on the hill at the eastern end of town is a water tower with a **lookout**; you can see both sides of the peninsula and along the coast. Take the walking track up to the tower from Torquay St or drive up Scarborough Tce.

Activities

DOLPHIN & SEAL SWIMMING

Busy Dolphin Encounter (☎ 0800 733 365, 319 6777; www.dolphin.co.nz; 58 West End; observation/swim NZ$55/115; 🕒 trips 8.30am & 12.30pm, extra trip 5.30am summer) Gives you the chance to swim with huge pods of dusky dolphins. It provides wetsuits, masks and snorkels for the three-hour 'dolphin encounter'. Book in advance as participants rave about this popular trip.
Seal Swim Kaikoura (☎ 319 6182; www.sealswimkaikoura.co.nz; 202 the Esplanade; tours NZ$50; 🕒 Nov-Apr) does two-hour guided snorkelling tours that expose you to NZ fur seals.

WALKING

There are two **walkways** that start from the seal colony, one along the seashore and one above it along the cliff top; a loop takes 2½ hours. If you go on the seashore track, check out the tides with the visitors centre beforehand (it's best to go within two hours of low tide). Both walks afford excellent views of fur seal and red-billed seagull colonies. A track from **South Bay** (45 minutes) leads over farmland and back to town.

Mt Fyffe Walking Track centres on Mt Fyffe (1602m), which dominates the narrow Kaikoura Plain and the town. Information about history, vegetation, birds and the walking tracks is detailed in the *Mt Fyffe and the Seaward Kaikoura Range* brochure.

Kaikoura Coast Track (☎ 319 2715; www.kaikouratrack.co.nz; tours NZ$130) is a three-day tramp through private farmland and along the Amuri coast, 50km south of Kaikoura. The 43km tramp has spectacular coastal views and accommodation is in comfortable farm

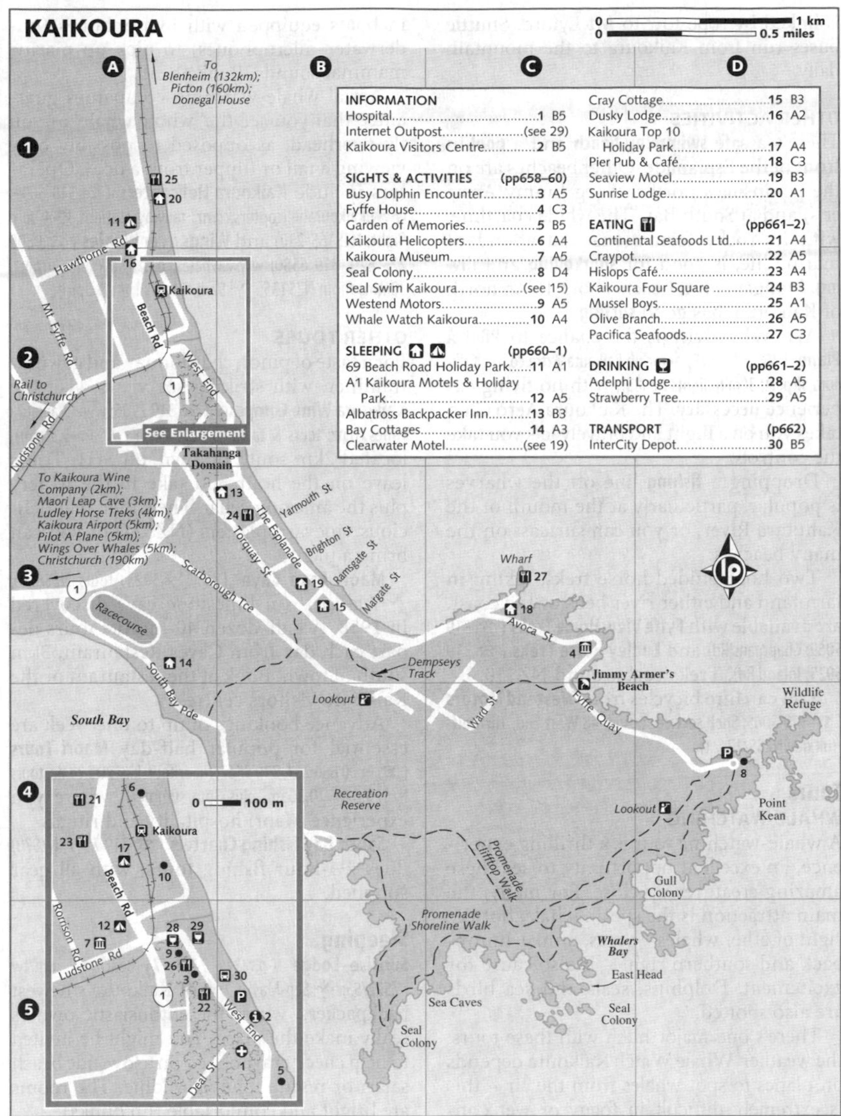

cottages. The cost includes three nights' accommodation and pack transport; bring your own sleeping bag and food. A two-day mountain-bike option is NZ$70.

SKIING & SNOWBOARDING

In winter, skiers and snowboarders head to **Mt Lyford** (Amuri; ☎ 315 6178, snowphone 366 1220; www.mtlyford.co.nz; daily lift passes NZ$45), which is about 60km from Kaikoura and 4km from Mt Lyford Village, where accommodation is available. The Lake Stella field has skiing at all levels, basin and off-piste cross-country skiing, 15km of groomed trails for ski touring, and a natural pipe for snowboarding, while nearby Terako Basin has advanced skiing and is linked by rope tow to Mt Lyford. Shuttle buses run from Kaikoura to the mountain daily.

OTHER ACTIVITIES

There's a safe **swimming beach** and a **pool** in front of the Esplanade. Other beaches are on the peninsula's northeast (eg Jimmy Armer's) and at South Bay. The whole coastline, with its rocky formations and abundant marine life, is good for **snorkelling** and **diving**. Mangamaunu Beach, about 15km north of Kaikoura, has good **surfing**.

A novel activity is the chance to **Pilot A Plane** (☎ 319 6579; aeroclub.kaikoura@xtra.co.nz; Kaikoura airport; 30min flights NZ$85), with no flying experience necessary. The Kaikoura Aero Club takes you on a flight and bravely lets you take the controls.

Dropping a **fishing** line off the wharves is popular, particularly at the mouth of the Kahutara River, or you can surfcast on the many beaches.

Two-hour guided horse treks, taking in farmland and either river beds or the coast, are available with **Fyffe View Horse Treks** (☎ 319 5069; Chapmans Rd) and **Ludley Horse Treks** (☎ 319 5925; Inland Rd). Treks cost around NZ$50.

You can hire bicycles from **Westend Motors** (☎ 319 5065; Shell service station, 48 West End; 1hr/half-/full day NZ$5/12/21).

Tours

WHALE-WATCHING

A whale-watching tour is a thrilling experience, an excellent opportunity to see these amazing creatures up close. For many, the main attraction is the sperm whale, but the sight of other whales – orcas, minke, humpback and southern right – is also cause for excitement. Dolphins, seals and sea birds are also spotted.

There's one major hitch with these tours: the weather. Whale Watch Kaikoura depends on planes to spot whales from the air – this is extremely difficult in foggy or wet conditions, when the Whale Watch office then cancels line after line of disappointed customers. If this trip is a *must* for you, allow a few days.

Whale Watch Kaikoura (☎ 0800 655 121, 319 6767; www.whalewatch.co.nz; Whaleway Station, Whaleway Rd; NZ$110; 🕑 3-16 trips daily) is based at the old train station, from where 3½-hour tours set out to sea in search of whales and other wildlife in boats equipped with hydrophones (underwater microphones) to pick up marine mammal sounds. Book ahead.

Aerial whale-watching companies guarantee that you see the 'whole whale' as you fly overhead, as opposed to possibly only viewing a tail or flipper from a boat. Operators include **Kaikoura Helicopters** (☎ 319 6609; www.kaikourahelicopters.co.nz; railway station; 30-40min flights NZ$165-230) and **Wings over Whales** (☎ 0800 226 629, 319 6580; www.whales.co.nz; Kaikoura Airport; 30mins flight NZ$135; 🕑 9am, 11am, 1pm & 3pm).

OTHER TOURS

For a taste of pinot, chardonnay and gewürztraminer, with striking sea views, visit the **Kaikoura Wine Company** (☎ 319 7966; www.kaikourawines.co.nz; tours & tastings NZ$8.50; 🕑 10am-5.30pm), located 2km south of town, off SH1. Tours leave on the hour and take in the winery plus the amazing cellar. The winery has delicious vineyard platters (NZ$24) or you can bring a picnic.

Maori Leap Cave (☎ 319 5023; tours NZ$8.50; 🕑 7am-7pm) is a limestone cave discovered in 1958. A half-dozen 40-minute tours depart each day from Caves Restaurant, 3km south of town. Book at the restaurant or the Kaikoura visitors centre.

Advance bookings of up to one week are essential for popular half-day **Maori Tours** (☎ 0800 866 267, 319 5567; maoritourskk@xtra.co.nz; tours NZ$75; 🕑 10.30am, plus 3pm summer), where you experience Maori hospitality and rituals.

South Bay Fishing Charters (☎ 319 7517; NZ$70) does 2½-hour fishing tours, with all gear supplied.

Sleeping

Sunrise Lodge (☎ 319 7444; 74 Beach Rd; dm/tw NZ$22/55; 🕑 Sep-May) One of Kaikoura's newest backpackers, where the enthusiastic owners really make the place. You might be invited to help check craypots, go on a low-tide beach safari or rescue injured wildlife. The rooms are bright and comfortable (no bunks).

Cray Cottage (☎ 319 5152; 190 the Esplanade; dm NZ$20-22, tw NZ$50; 🕑 Aug-May) A small, friendly and tranquil place with a self-contained hostel behind the owners' house. It's about 1km east of the town centre and free pick up/drop off is available.

Albatross Backpacker Inn (☎ 319 6090; www.albatross-kaikoura.co.nz; 1 Torquay St; dm NZ$20-22, s NZ$40, d & tw NZ$55) High-quality backpackers with a lovely large TV/living area, plus decks, verandas and even an aviary. Some of the dorms have 'Turkish-theme' bunks – semi-enclosed beds with a unique design.

Dusky Lodge (☎ 319 5959; duskyjack@hotmail.com; 67 Beach Rd; dm NZ$21, d & tw NZ$55) A busy hostel, with all the facilities to cope. There's a brilliant outdoor deck and spa with mountain views, and a good-sized kitchen and lounge.

Pier Pub & Café (☎ 319 5037; pierhotel@xtra.co.nz; 1 Avoca St; s/d NZ$40/55) A classic establishment, way down the southern end of the beach. Apart from being a friendly spot for a drink, there's cheap accommodation – many rooms have views of the water and Kaikoura Ranges, and there's a big old balcony.

Seaview Motel & Clearwater Motel (☎ 0800 456 000, 319 6149; 164 & 168 the Esplanade; d from NZ$75) Two motels next to each other, both run by the same enthusiastic owner, who has a pin board to mark your country of origin. The self-contained units are clean and nifty, many with sea views. This is a popular choice with Asian travellers.

Bay Cottages (☎ 319 5506; baycottages@xtra.co.nz; 29 South Bay Pde; cottages NZ$60) Excellent-value tourist flats (with kitchenette and bathroom) capable of sleeping four to six. They're on South Bay, a few kilometres south of town, and are close to swimming beaches. The friendly owner may take you out crayfishing and often puts on a coffee-and-cray brunch.

69 Beach Road Holiday Park (☎ 319 6275; www.holidayparks.co.nz/69beach; 69 Beach Rd; camp sites unpowered/powered per 2 people NZ$21/22; s & d NZ$30-180) This creek-side park is an excellent place right by a bakery. It has friendly, helpful owners and clean facilities, including a well-equipped communal kitchen.

Kaikoura Top 10 Holiday Park (☎ 319 5362; www.kaikouratop10.co.nz; 34 Beach Rd; camp sites unpowered/powered per 2 people NZ$24/26, d NZ$45-100; ♿) Tucked behind a large hedge is this well-maintained camping ground. The excellent facilities include a range of quality cabins.

A1 Kaikoura Motels & Holiday Park (☎ 319 5999; www.kiwiholidayparks.com; 11 Beach Rd; camp sites per 2 people NZ$20, d NZ$45-100; ♿) On SH1, about 200m from the town centre, is this peaceful camping ground with a number of comfortable cabins and units. The small, green camping area backs onto a creek. There's a trampoline to keep the kids bouncing.

Eating & Drinking

If you're not into seafood you might struggle for choice in Kaikoura but if you love crustaceans and all things fishy you'll be in gastronomic heaven.

Hislops Café (☎ 319 6971; 33 Beach Rd; meals NZ$6-15; 🕒 breakfast, lunch & dinner) This smart café has a reputation for fresh organic food. Start the morning with fruit salad, toasted muesli, omelettes or French toast and feel healthy and smug all day. There's also a daytime blackboard menu (salads, pasta, open sandwiches) and evening dining.

Craypot (☎ 319 6027; 70 West End; snacks NZ$7-18, mains NZ$20-30; 🕒 lunch & dinner) This mellow, large, long-running restaurant and bar serves lots of fresh and tender seafood. Try the mussel chowder or stop messing about and head directly for the cray.

Continental Seafoods Ltd (☎ 319 5509; 47 Beach Rd; meals NZ$4-12) Just north of town is the place for a grease hit – fish and chips, battered shellfish and fat, salty chips.

Olive Branch (☎ 319 6992; 54 West End; meals NZ$7-20) The most reasonably priced cray in town. It's also classy and elegant and has a

PICK YOUR POISSON

As well as all the marine life you can encounter in Kaikoura, in town you certainly can't avoid one sea creature: the crayfish. The town's name reflects its abundance in these waters – in Maori 'kai' means food and 'koura' means crayfish. In season, crayfish is always featured in Kaikoura restaurants and local takeaways. Unfortunately, it's pricey – you'll pay the export price, which at the time of research was hovering around NZ$70 per kilogram. If you're not too keen on the idea of paying around NZ$50 for a restaurant meal of half a cray (NZ$90 to NZ$100 for a whole), you can purchase fresh, nongarnished crays at **Pacifica Seafoods** (☎ 319 5817; wharf; 🕒 9am-5pm Mon-Fri), or from **Nin's Bin**, a rustic beachside caravan 20km towards Picton.

You could also take a **fishing tour** (opposite) and crack into some cray that way. Alternatively, you might strike it lucky and find a local who'll kindly take you out crayfishing and allow you to share in the catch. This is an economical way to taste the local produce, not to mention fun.

lovely balcony. The menu features venison pizza, vegetarian cannelloni, Marlborough mussels and vegetarian nachos.

Mussel Boys (☎ 319 7160; www.musselboys.co.nz; 80 Beach Rd; meals NZ$20-30; ⏰ lunch & dinner) Part of a small regional chain, this is a bright, cheery and kid-friendly restaurant. It's a little out of town but worth the trip, especially if you're into bivalves – you can get them as flats (grilled on the half-shell) or steamers (whole shell). Tempting sauces include roast tomato and chilli, green curry and coconut milk.

Strawberry Tree (☎ 319 6451; 21 West End) An atmospheric pub with couches, pool table and live music twice a month – jamming sessions encouraged. Snack food is available and there's sometimes free crayfish in summer! Be sure to check out the journalistic photos taken by the owner. All the furniture and décor has been taken from demolished historic buildings.

Adelphi Lodge (☎ 319 6555; West End) Opposite Strawberry Tree, Adelphi is popular with punters and pool sharks as there are four pool tables.

Donegal House (☎ 319 5083; www.donegalhouse.co.nz; Mt Fyffe Rd) The Donegal is an unexpected 'little Irish pub in the country' and a real gem. Guinness and Kilkenny are available and there's regular live music, plus a huge outdoor area.

For self-catering head to **Kaikoura Four Square** (☎ 319 5332; 31-33 West End).

Getting There & Away

BUS

There are **InterCity** (☎ 04-472 5111; www.intercitycoach.co.nz) services operating between Kaikoura and Nelson (NZ$50, five hours, two daily), Picton (NZ$27, 1½ hours, two daily) and Christchurch (NZ$25, 2½ hours, two daily). Buses arrive and depart from the town car park; tickets and information are available at the visitors centre.

Other shuttle services to/from Kaikoura:

Atomic Shuttles (☎ 0800 248 885, 322 8883; www.atomictravel.co.nz)
East Coast Express (☎ 0508 830 900)
Hanmer Connection (☎ 0800 377 378, 315 7575)
K Bus (☎ 525 9434; www.kahurangi.co.nz)
South Island Connections (☎ 0508 742 669, 366 6633; www.southislandconnections.co.nz)
Southern Link (☎ 358 8355; www.yellow.co.nz/site/southernlink)

TRAIN

Tranz Scenic (☎ 0800 872 467, 04-495 0775; www.tranzscenic.co.nz; ⏰ 7am-7pm) runs the *TranzCoastal* service between Picton and Christchurch, which stops at Kaikoura; between Kaikoura and either Picton (2½ hours, one daily) or Christchurch (three hours, one daily) costs NZ$20 to NZ$45. The northbound service departs Kaikoura at 10.25am, and the southbound at 4.05pm.

Getting Around

You can hail down or telephone for a **taxi** (☎ 319 6214).

NELSON

☎ 03 / pop 52,300

Nelson is an inspiringly active place, noted for its wineries, breweries and energetic arts and crafts community, and is a fine starting point for explorations of the South Island's wonderful northwestern coastal region.

Among the first Maori to arrive in Nelson were the Ngati Tumatakokiri tribe, who by 1550 occupied most of the province. The Tumatakokiri reigned supreme in Tasman Bay until the 18th century, when the Ngati-apa from Wanganui and the Ngai Tahu – the largest tribe on the South Island – combined for a devastating attack. The Ngati-apa's victory was short-lived, as between 1828 and 1830 they were practically annihilated by armed tribes from Taranaki and Wellington who sailed into the bay in the largest fleet of canoes ever assembled in NZ.

The region's first pakeha settlers sailed in response to advertisements by the NZ Company, set up by Edward Gibbon Wakefield in an attempt to systematically colonise the country. His grandiose scheme was to transplant a complete slice of English life from all social classes. But 'too few gentlemen with too little money' accepted the initial challenge and the new colony almost foundered in its infancy.

The colony was plunged into gloom in 1843 with the deaths of 22 of Nelson's most able citizens during an infamous massacre (see the boxed text on p645). A year later the NZ Company was declared bankrupt and the settlement had to endure near-famine conditions. Only the later arrival of hard-working German immigrants saved the region from economic ruin.

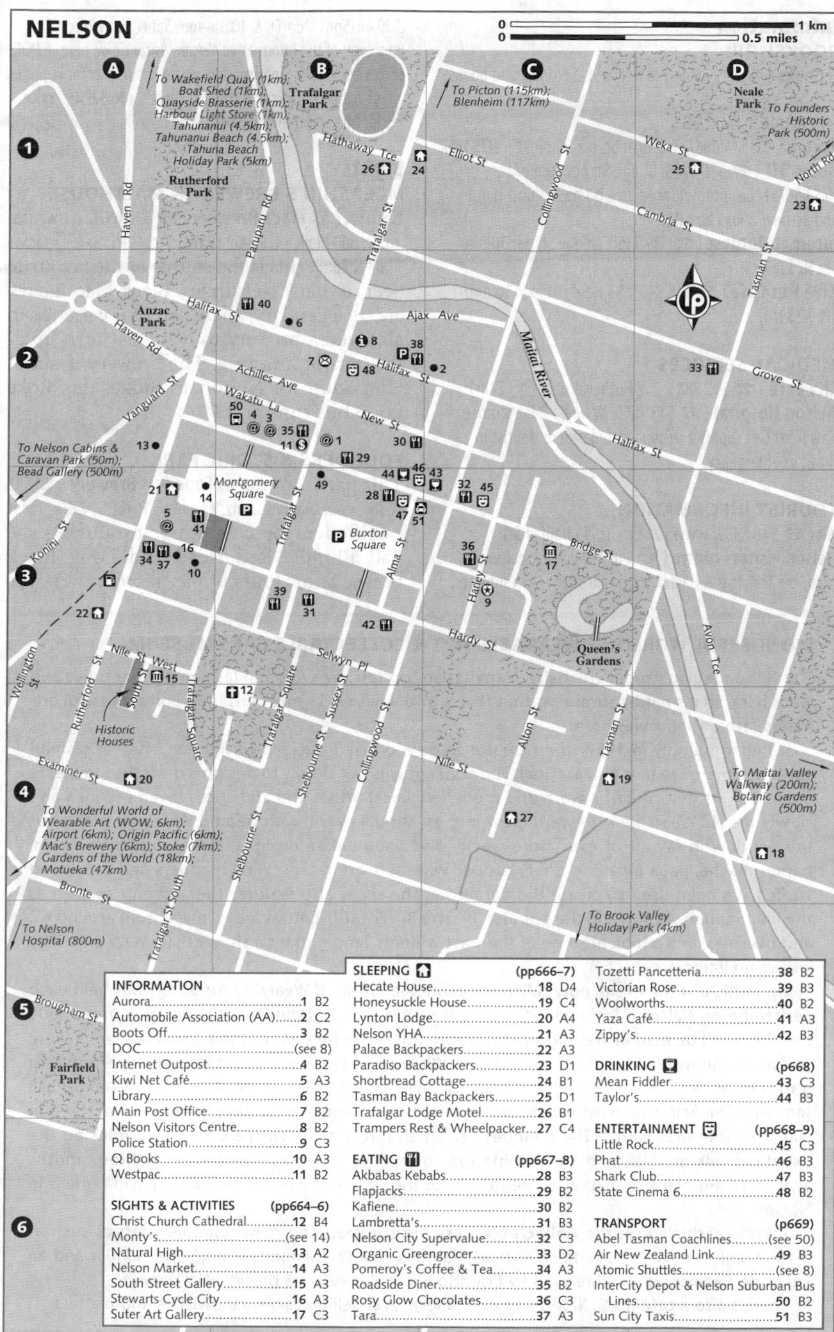
NELSON
0 1 km
0 0.5 miles
A
B
C
D
1
2
3
4
5
6
To Wakefield Quay (1km); Boat Shed (1km); Quayside Brasserie (1km); Harbour Light Store (1km); Tahunanui (4.5km); Tahunanui Beach (4.5km); Tahuna Beach Holiday Park (5km)
Trafalgar Park
To Picton (115km); Blenheim (117km)
Neale Park
To Founders Historic Park (500m)
Rutherford Park
Anzac Park
Hathaway Tce
Elliot St
Weka St
North Rd
Cambria St
Collingwood St
Trafalgar St
Paruparu Rd
Haven Rd
Halifax St
Ajax Ave
Achilles Ave
Wakatu La
New St
Vanguard St
Maitai River
Grove St
Tasman St
To Nelson Cabins & Caravan Park (50m); Bead Gallery (500m)
Montgomery Square
Buxton Square
Alma St
Bridge St
Harley St
Konini St
Hardy St
Selwyn Pl
Queen's Gardens
Avon Tce
Nile St West
Wellington St
Rutherford St
South St
Trafalgar Square
Sussex St
Shelbourne St
Collingwood St
Alton St
Tasman St
Nile St
Historic Houses
Examiner St
To Maitai Valley Walkway (200m); Botanic Gardens (500m)
To Wonderful World of Wearable Art (WOW; 6km); Airport (6km); Origin Pacific (6km); Mac's Brewery (6km); Stoke (7km); Gardens of the World (18km); Motueka (47km)
Bronte St
Trafalgar St South
To Brook Valley Holiday Park (4km)
To Nelson Hospital (800m)
Brougham St
Fairfield Park
SOUTH ISLAND

INFORMATION
Aurora 1 B2
Automobile Association (AA) 2 C2
Boots Off 3 B2
DOC (see 8)
Internet Outpost 4 B2
Kiwi Net Café 5 A3
Library 6 B2
Main Post Office 7 B2
Nelson Visitors Centre 8 B2
Police Station 9 C3
Q Books 10 A3
Westpac 11 B2

SIGHTS & ACTIVITIES (pp664–6)
Christ Church Cathedral 12 B4
Monty's (see 14)
Natural High 13 A2
Nelson Market 14 A3
South Street Gallery 15 A3
Stewarts Cycle City 16 A3
Suter Art Gallery 17 C3

SLEEPING (pp666–7)
Hecate House 18 D4
Honeysuckle House 19 C4
Lynton Lodge 20 A4
Nelson YHA 21 A3
Palace Backpackers 22 A3
Paradiso Backpackers 23 D1
Shortbread Cottage 24 B1
Tasman Bay Backpackers 25 D1
Trafalgar Lodge Motel 26 B1
Trampers Rest & Wheelpacker 27 C4

EATING (pp667–8)
Akbabas Kebabs 28 B3
Flapjacks 29 B2
Kafiene 30 B2
Lambretta's 31 B3
Nelson City Supervalue 32 C3
Organic Greengrocer 33 D2
Pomeroy's Coffee & Tea 34 A3
Roadside Diner 35 B2
Rosy Glow Chocolates 36 C3
Tara 37 A3
Tozetti Pancetteria 38 B2
Victorian Rose 39 B3
Woolworths 40 B2
Yaza Café 41 A3
Zippy's 42 B3

DRINKING (p668)
Mean Fiddler 43 C3
Taylor's 44 B3

ENTERTAINMENT (pp668–9)
Little Rock 45 C3
Phat 46 B3
Shark Club 47 B3
State Cinema 6 48 B2

TRANSPORT (p669)
Abel Tasman Coachlines (see 50)
Air New Zealand Link 49 B3
Atomic Shuttles (see 8)
InterCity Depot & Nelson Suburban Bus Lines 50 B2
Sun City Taxis 51 B3

Information

BOOKSHOPS

Q Books (☎ 545 7555; 130 Hardy St) Second-hand books.

INTERNET ACCESS

Aurora (☎ 546 6867; Trafalgar St; per 30min/1hr NZ$4/6)
Boots Off (☎ 546 8789; Bridge St; per 30min/1hr NZ$3.50/5) Has Internet facilities. Also has second-hand and as-new books for sale.
Internet Outpost (☎ 539 1150; Bridge St; per 30min/1hr NZ$3.60/5)
Kiwi Net Café (☎ 548 8404; 93 Hardy St; per 30min/1hr NZ$3/4)

MEDICAL SERVICES

City Care (☎ 546 8881; 202 Rutherford St; 24hr)
Nelson Hospital (☎ 546 1800; Waimea Rd, entrance Kawai St) Can supply a doctor, ambulance or dentist in times of emergency.

TOURIST INFORMATION

AA (☎ 548 8339; www.nzaa.co.nz; 45 Halifax St)
Nelson visitors centre (☎ 548 2304; www.nelsonnz.com; cnr Trafalgar & Halifax Sts; 8.30am-6pm summer, 8.30am-5pm Mon-Fri & 10am-4pm Sat & Sun winter) Pick up a copy of the informative *Nelson Visitor Guide* here. A DOC officer attends the information centre in summer for inquiries about national parks and tramps. There's a NZ$2.50 service fee for bus and tour bookings.

Sights

MCCASHIN'S BREWERY & MALTHOUSE

Known as **Mac's Brewery** (☎ 547 0526; www.macs.co.nz; 660 Main Rd, Stoke; tastings/tours NZ$3/7; tours 11am & 2pm), this is the source of the favourite beer of many Nelsonites. Black Mac, a dark ale, is legendary; there are five varieties in all. Take a brewery tour or just turn up at the bar for a tasting. The brewery is about 6km south of Nelson in Stoke; the Stoke Loop bus runs past it.

FOUNDERS HISTORIC PARK

This park is home to **Founders Brewery** (☎ 548 4638; www.biobrew.co.nz; Founders Park), NZ's first certified organic brewery, producing the Tall Blonde, Red Head and Long Black brews. Short tours of the microbrewery are

WONDERFUL WORLD OF WEARABLE ART & COLLECTABLE CARS MUSEUM

The Nelson region exudes creativity. Many artists, potters, weavers and fashion designers live and work here, so it's hardly surprising that this is also where NZ's most inspiring and successful art-meets-fashion show was born.

It began humbly in 1987 when creator Suzie Moncrieff decided to hold an off-beat fashion show in a marquee tent in Wakefield. The concept was not simply to design a dress, but to create a piece of art that could be worn and modelled. Local artists and audiences loved the idea and slowly the NZ Wearable Art Award grew into an annual event, with traditional fabrics going out the window in favour of ever-more wacky and imaginative designs. Everything from wood, papier mâché, paua (abalone) shell, copper wire, soft-drink cans, wine bladders and even food stuffs have been used to create the garments. The show also features themed entries such as the illumination section and the popular 'Bizarre Bra Award'. Entries are received from around NZ and overseas, and a look at some of the past winners (and entrants) shows that WOW creativity knows no limits.

Up until 2004 the event, now called the Montana World of Wearable Art Show, was held each September in Nelson's Trafalgar Sq, where it would attract around 10,000 people – from 2005 the show will be held in Wellington, probably still in September, but the date and venue were still to be confirmed at the time of research. While you're in Nelson, check out the eye-popping **gallery** (☎ 548 9299; www.worldofwearableart.com; 95 Quarantine Rd; adult NZ$15; 9am-6.30pm summer, 10am-5pm winter), which showcases the bizarre but spellbinding 'garments' featured in the Wearable Art awards. The galleries are small but hi-tech, with a carousel mimicking the usual catwalk models, and an illumination room. The artworks change every three months and there are plans to display more in the future. Unlike the show, the gallery will remain in Nelson.

Equally enthralling is the **Collectable Cars** display, featuring mint-condition classics such as a 1959 pink Cadillac, a 1908 Renault made famous as a Parisienne taxi, an E-type Jaguar and an Eldorado Cadillac convertible used by Eisenhower in the 1953 US presidential parade.

There's also a **café** (meals NZ$6-14) in the gallery foyer selling cakes, sandwiches and platters.

available. Founders Park is near the waterfront, 1km from the city centre, easily spotted by the large windmill.

Next door to the brewery are the beautiful **Miyazu Japanese Gardens.**

NELSON MARKET

This is an excellent local **market** (☎ 546 6454; Montgomery Sq; 🕑 8am-1pm Sat), with produce and food stalls, and arts and crafts utilising wood, oils, possum-fur products and glass. Sunday sees a flea market, **Monty's** (🕑 9am-1pm), at the same place.

GALLERIES

Suter Art Gallery (☎ 548 4699; www.thesuter.org.nz; 208 Bridge St; adult NZ$3; 🕑 10.30am-4.30pm) adjoins Queen's Gardens and has a few interesting lithographs and paintings. It's the city's main repository of high art, with changing exhibitions, musical and theatrical performances, films, a craft shop and café.

South St Gallery (☎ 548 8117; www.nelsonpottery.co.nz; 10 Nile St West; admission free; 🕑 9am-5pm Mon-Fri, 10am-4pm Sat & Sun) is noted for its extensive collection of pottery.

HISTORIC BUILDINGS

The traditional symbol of Nelson is its Art Deco **Christ Church Cathedral** (☎ 548 1008; Trafalgar Sq; 🕑 8am-7pm), at the top of Trafalgar St. Work began in 1925 but was delayed and arguments raged in the 1950s over whether the building should be completed according to its original design. Finally completed in 1965 to a modified design, it was consecrated in 1972, 47 years after the foundation stone was laid.

Close to the cathedral is **South St**, home to a row of restored workers' cottages dating from 1863 to 1867, and said to be the oldest preserved street in NZ.

The beautiful **Isel Park gardens** are worth a visit, and in the grounds is the historic **Isel House** (☎ 547 1347; isel@ihug.co.nz; 16 Hilliard St, Stoke; admission by donation; 🕑 11am-4pm).

GARDENS

The **Botanic Gardens** has a lookout at Botanical Hill, with a spire proclaiming it NZ's exact geographical centre.

Gardens of the World (☎ 542 3736; www.gardensoftheworld.co.nz; 95 Clover Rd East, Hope; adult NZ$5; 🕑 10am-dusk) features beautifully landscaped gardens from Asia, America, Europe and Australia.

Activities

Many of the available activities take place some way out of the city, but the following operators will pick up and drop off in Nelson.

Go paragliding with **Adventure Paragliding and Kiteboarding** (☎ 546 6863; www.skyout.co.nz; 6 Bridge St; 🕑 9.30am-5.30pm Mon-Fri, 9.30am-12.30pm Sat) or **Nelson Paragliding** (☎ 544 1182; www.nelsonparagliding.co.nz; 108 Queen St). Both charge NZ$155 for a tandem flight and NZ$190 for a full-day introductory course.

You can also tandem skydive with **Skydive Abel Tasman** (☎ 0800 422 899, 528 4091; www.skydive.co.nz; 16 College St, Motueka airstrip; jumps 9000/12,000ft NZ$210/260). The cost includes transport to Motueka airstrip, 10 minutes' instruction and a certificate.

Another aerial possibility is hang-gliding with **Nelson Hang Gliding Adventures** (☎ 548 9151; gmeadows@clear.net.nz; 20min flights NZ$140) at Takaka Hill and Richmond Ranges.

If you want to nip from town to the beach, or do some serious off-road touring on the local mountain biking tracks, hire a bike from **Natural High** (☎ 546 6936; www.naturalhigh.co.nz; 52 Rutherford St; bike hire per day NZ$25-80), which has a large specialist cycle range. **Stewarts Cycle City** (☎ 548 1666; www.stewartscyclecity.com; 114 Hardy St; half-/full day NZ$20/40) also hires bikes and does repairs; it offers cheap deals to overseas travellers.

Rock climbing on the sheer limestone cliffs of the Golden Bay and Takaka area has long been popular with local outdoor enthusiasts. **Vertical Limits** (☎ 545 7511; www.verticallimits.co.nz; 34 Vanguard St; full day NZ$130; 🕑 10am-9pm Mon-Fri, 10am-6pm Sat & Sun) offers various rock-climbing trips, no experience necessary. **Nelson Bays Adventure** (☎ 0800 379 842, 526 7842; Moutere Hwy, Lower Moutere; day trips NZ$120) offers rock climbing, caving and tramping.

Another popular activity is the skywire and quad-bike tours with **Happy Valley Adventures** (☎ 0800 157 300, 545 0304; www.happyvalleyadventures.co.nz; 194 Cable Bay Rd; skywire NZ$65, quad-bike driver NZ$65-125, passenger NZ$20-30), which is a 10-minute drive northwest along SH6.

Stonehurst Farm Horse Treks (☎ 0800 487 357, 542 4121; www.stonehurstfarm.co.nz; Rd 1, Richmond; 2hr/half-day rides NZ$35/85) offers one-hour farm rides, two-hour sundowner treks and, for experienced riders, the chance to take part in a cattle muster.

Nelson Bonecarver (☎ 546 4275; 87 Green St, Tahunanui; day courses NZ$55) offers instruction and materials so you can design and carve your own pendant out of bone. You can also create your own bead necklace at the **Bead Gallery** (☎ 546 7807; www.beads.co.nz; 18 Parere St; 9am-5pm Mon-Sat, 10am-4pm Sun). **Creative Tourism NZ** (☎ 548 0250; www.creativetourism.co.nz) are thoroughly recommended for other short courses on culture, arts and cuisine in and around Nelson.

There are many opportunities for sailing in Tasman Bay. To help out on a yacht, the best option is the Wednesday night race run by **Catamaran Sailing Charters** (☎ 547 6666; www.sailingcharters.co.nz; 46 Martin St; Wed night races NZ$40, day trips from NZ$85). You get two hours to help crew a boat around the harbour in racing conditions.

Of the area's many walks, the **riverside footpath** makes a pleasant stroll through the city, and the **Maitai Valley Walkway** is particularly restful and beautiful.

Tours

For details of some exceptional tramping and sea-kayaking tours, see p671.

Bay Tours (☎ 0800 229 868, 544 4494; www.baytoursnelson.co.nz; 48 Brougham St; half-/full-day wine tours NZ$60/135, craft NZ$50/75, scenic NZ$50-135) One of several operators doing winery tours in the Richmond and Upper Moutere area, as well as 'craft & scenic tours'.

JJ's Scenic Tours (☎ 0800 568 568; www.jjs.co.nz; 10 Musgrave Cres, Tahunanui; half-day tours NZ$55) Visits four vineyards and a brewery on its main half-day tour.

Tasman Helicopters (☎ 528 8075; www.tasmanhelicopters.co.nz; from NZ$110) A host of chopper tours, including *Lord of the Rings* locations, D'Urville Island sea fishing, wine tours and flights over Farewell Spit and Kahurangi and Abel Tasman National Parks.

Festivals & Events

Arts Festival (☎ 546 0212; www.nelsonfestivals.co.nz; Sep) Events such as a masked carnivale parade, cabaret, literary readings, theatre and music performances.

Nelson Jazz Festival (☎ 546 9269; www.nelsonjazz.co.nz/3Festival.htm; late Dec) Jazz cats from all round NZ gather for this musical extravaganza.

Sleeping

Paradiso Backpackers (☎ 546 6703; www.backpackernelson.co.nz; 42 Weka St; camp sites per 2 people from NZ$12, dm NZ$20-22, d & tw NZ$55;) Club Med for the financially challenged, this is a sprawling place. There's plenty of pool-side action, watched over by the glassed-in main kitchen, plus a high-rotation hammock, volleyball court and sauna. Rooms are nothing special. Dorms are four- and eight-bed with mezzanines, and there are heated A-frame tents. Free veggie soup in winter and the NZ$8 barbecue in summer are big hits.

Tasman Bay Backpackers (☎ 548 7950; www.tasmanbaybackpackers.co.nz; 10 Weka St; dm NZ$22, d & tw NZ$55) This popular option is light and airy, with great views, communal living areas and a well-used hammock and swing chair. Colourful rooms have four to six beds, with individual reading lights and shared facilities. The kitchen is well organised and the friendly young owners bake bread in winter. Tasman is a cool place.

Shortbread Cottage (☎ 546 6681; 33 Trafalgar St; dm/d NZ$22/55) A small, homely, 13-bed hostel. Cosy rooms are freshly painted and beds have new mattresses; only two bedrooms have bathrooms. There's a small kitchen and a great outdoor garden area. Home-made shortbread is served at 6pm.

Trampers Rest & Wheelpacker (☎ 545 7477; 31 Alton St; dm/d NZ$20/50) Just a few beds, but Trampers is hard to beat for a homely environment. The enthusiastic owner, a keen tramper and cyclist, provides information as well as free use of bikes. There's a small kitchen, book exchange, piano and lots of CDs.

Nelson YHA (☎ 545 9988; yhanels@yha.org.nz; 59 Rutherford St; dm NZ$20, d & tw NZ$50-70) This spotless, central place is purpose-built with facilities such as a soundproof, vaultlike TV room and a well-organised modern kitchen opening onto an outdoor terrace.

Hecate House (☎ 546 6890; www.brazen.co.nz/hecate; 181 Nile St; dm/s/d NZ$20/45/50) Chilled, female energy radiates from Hecate House, a women-only hostel in a lovely historic house. There's a cosy TV room, small kitchen and laundry facilities, and the cedar hot tub, in the organic garden, is a therapeutic way to iron out those tramping kinks.

Honeysuckle House (☎ 548 7576; 125 Tasman St; s NZ$35, d & tw NZ$55) A friendly, family-run, 11-bed backpackers in a quiet part of town. A lovely, homely environment, complete with a garden, and twin and double rooms equipped with TVs.

Palace Backpackers (☎ 548 4691; www.thepalace.co.nz; 114 Rutherford St; dm NZ$20, d & tw NZ$50) The Palace is in an early-20th-century villa set above the street with views from the balconies. It doesn't look like much from the street but this is perhaps the nicest of the big backpackers. It has plenty of character, no bunks and lots of little common areas.

Lynton Lodge (☎ 548 7112; www.nzmotels.co.nz/lynton/index.html; 25 Examiner St; self-contained apartments NZ$90) Located high on a hill, with wonderful views of Nelson and the cathedral lit up at night, Lynton Lodge has excellent older-style self-contained apartments. It looks and feels more like a guesthouse than a motel, with relaxed common areas.

Trafalgar Lodge Motel (☎ 0800 000 051, 548 3980; www.trafalgarlodge.co.nz; 46 Trafalgar St; B&B NZ$55, studios NZ$85-95) Centrally located, Trafalgar has options for all budgets. There's cheaper B&B-style rooms in the guesthouse and studios with phone and Sky TV in the motel section. The B&B rooms have a sink, electric blankets, a couch and an area to make hot beverages; price includes breakfast.

Nelson Cabins & Caravan Park (☎ 548 1445; www.holidayparks.co.nz/nelson; 230 Vanguard St; s & d NZ$50-60) Clean, friendly and the most central park in Nelson. There are no camp sites; the basic cabins are a mixture of twins, bunk beds and tourist flats.

Tahuna Beach Holiday Park (☎ 548 5159; www.tahunabeachholidaypark.co.nz; 70 Beach Rd; camp sites per 2 people NZ$22, s & d NZ$30-90) A huge park accommodating thousands – like a mini village with its own supermarket, on-site dairy, minigolf and *pétanque*. It's near the beach, 5km from the city, with an enormous range of accommodation.

Brook Valley Holiday Park (☎ 548 0399; 584a Brook St; camp sites per 2 people NZ$20, s & d NZ$23-40) This place is at the end of Tasman St in the upper Brook Valley, in a superb forest setting by a stream. It's the same distance from the centre as Tahuna, but smaller and more personal.

Eating

The wealth of local produce, particularly seafood, makes eating out in Nelson an exciting prospect. Deep-sea fish such as orange roughy and hoki, scallops from the bays, and mussels and oysters are available, complemented by microbrewed beers and well-rounded NZ wines. Food is often organic and there are loads of vegetarian options.

SELF-CATERING

Organic Greengrocer (☎ 548 3650; www.organicgreengrocer.co.nz; cnr Tasman & Grove Sts; pies NZ$3; 🕑 lunch) Stocking all things wheat-, dairy- and gluten-free, this organic food store has a range of fresh produce, dry goods and vegetarian pies and cakes that are baked on the premises. You can also join up for Willing Workers on Organic Farms (Wwoof) memberships here (see p788).

Supermarkets include **Woolworths** (☎ 546 6466; cnr Paruparu Rd & Halifax St) and the **Nelson City Supervalue** (☎ 548 0191; 69 Collingwood St; 🕑 8am-9pm), which claims to stock more than 480 organic products.

CAFÉS

Kafiene (☎ 545 6911; 22 New St; meals NZ$8.50-12; 🕑 breakfast & lunch Mon-Sat, dinner Sat) Kid-friendly Kafiene is a chilled place, set in a pebble-covered courtyard dotted with well-loved couches, decorative mirror mosaics, a dedicated children's play area with toys and heavy-duty sandpit, and established greenery. Feast on bagels, veggie burgers, nachos, thumpin' breakfasts and delicate butterfly cupcakes. Also has a range of loose-leaf herbal teas.

Rosy Glow Chocolates (☎ 548 3383; 20 Harley St; per chocolate NZ$3-3.50, boxed selections NZ$18-36; 🕑 9am-5pm Mon-Fri, 10am-1pm Sat) A sibling of the original Rosy Glow shop in Collingwood, on Golden Bay, this is a must for any chocoholic. Sells home-made logs of rich, creamy chocolate such as conquistador (hazelnut praline in dark chocolate) and ginger bar (caramel and chopped ginger).

Flapjacks (☎ 548 0270; 75 Bridge St; burgers NZ$6-10, mains NZ$17-23; 🕑 breakfast, lunch & dinner) Nelson's version of the American diner, with pine tables, booths and an outdoor eating area. The burgers are big and extremely popular. There's a range of pancakes and toasted sandwiches. Closes early Monday.

Zippy's (☎ 546 6348; 276 Hardy St; meals NZ$4.50-7; 🕑 lunch Mon-Sat) At this biorhythmically aligned vegetarian lunch spot, the décor is a crazy combo of purple, teal and red, and service is zippy yet earnest. Food includes risotto cakes, fabulous frittata and the 'locally famous' chocolate afghans. Drinks include ice-cream shakes, *chai* and heart-startingly rich, full-flavoured coffee.

Yaza Café (☎ 548 2849; Montgomery Sq; meals NZ$4-11; 🕑 breakfast & lunch Wed-Sun, dinner Thu-Sat) At the site of the weekend markets, Yaza is a cosy, kid-friendly café with all-day breakfasts. The food is free-range and organic, and patchouli lingers in the air – it's 'your lounge in town'. Also has live music Friday and Saturday; see right.

QUICK EATS

Akbabas Kebabs (☎ 548 8825; 130 Bridge St; meals NZ$6.50-10.50; lunch & dinner) Tiny Turkish kebab house. Dine at low tables surrounded by rugs and carpets in the small corner lounge. Perfect for a quick bite.

Tozetti Pancetteria (☎ 546 8484; 41 Halifax St; NZ$3.50-5.50; breakfast Mon-Sat, lunch Mon-Fri) You'll smell fresh bread baking before you see Tozetti, a tiny bakery serving beautiful breads, sandwiches and sweet treats, plus strong Pomeroy's coffee.

Roadside Diner (Trafalgar St; meals NZ$6-12; 6pm-3.30am Fri & Sat) A big white pie cart near Bridge St that has been serving food since 1933. Claims the 'biggest burgers in NZ'.

Pomeroy's Coffee & Tea (☎ 548 7524; www.pomeroys.co.nz; 80 Hardy St; 9am-6pm) A coffee and tea supplier that will have coffee connoisseurs beaming. Sells the best beans and fresh loose-leaf tea imported from overseas.

RESTAURANTS

Victorian Rose (☎ 548 7631; 281 Trafalgar St; mains NZ$13-18; lunch & dinner) This place is a pastiche of English/Irish pub styles in airy high-ceilinged premises. Substantial counter meals include mussels and cockles steamed in Mac's beer and served with fresh buttered bread, lamb and chicken roast, seafood mornay and fish or chicken curry. Backpacker specials are available.

Tara (☎ 548 0881; 104 Hardy St; mains NZ$8.50-15; lunch Tue-Sat, dinner Mon-Sat) A well-priced restaurant serving sushi, *udon* noodles and miso soup.

Boat Shed (☎ 546 9783; 351 Wakefield Quay; mains NZ$16-27; breakfast, lunch & dinner) An ambient seafood restaurant sitting on stilts over the sea. The food here is undeniably delicious. There's an interesting menu, including a range of 'breakfast cocktails' – perfect for continuing your hangover.

Lambretta's (☎ 545 8555; 204 Hardy St; mains NZ$22-28; lunch & dinner Mon-Sat) Named after the Italian scooter, this predominantly pizza and pasta restaurant is reasonably priced and has a busy, casual atmosphere. There are no run-of-the-mill toppings here – all are interesting gourmet combinations. It's a big place with Grecian columns.

For excellent seafood by the sea and a touch of the Côte d'Azur in sunny Nelson, head to the **Quayside Brasserie** (☎ 548 3319; 309 Wakefield Quay; meals NZ$16-30; lunch & dinner) or the casual **Harbour Light Store** (☎ 546 6685; 341 Wakefield Quay; meals NZ$8-24; lunch & dinner).

Drinking

Most of Nelson's late-night pubs and bars are clustered around Bridge St, where the action starts to build around 10pm.

Victorian Rose (☎ 548 7631; 281 Trafalgar St) Backpackers (and locals) often start with a meal and a few drinks at the popular Victorian Rose, where Guinness is served with care and there's a large selection of beers; happy hour stretches from 4pm to 7pm Friday. Bands also play here (jazz on Tuesday, blues on Thursday).

Mean Fiddler (☎ 546 8516; 145 Bridge St) A real bar. This pub is traditionally Irish (it's owned by a Dubliner) but isn't obnoxiously so with leprechauns and shamrocks everywhere. It has the biggest range of whiskies in Nelson (some up to NZ$1000) and a range of imported beers. There's also an outdoor courtyard. Also hosts live, free music daily.

Taylor's (☎ 548 0508; 131 Bridge St) Full of glitzy lights and blinking pokie machines. A party place popular with backpackers – there are NZ$10 drink-and-food deals.

Entertainment

Suter Art Gallery (☎ 548 4699; www.thesuter.org.nz; 208 Bridge St) Hosts theatre, music and dance performances.

Phat (☎ 548 3311; 137 Bridge St; admission NZ$5-25; 10pm-late Wed-Sat) DJs at this righteous club spin techno, dub, drum and bass, breaks and hip-hop, often courtesy of big-name international acts. There's a cover charge every night, which those who worship the beats happily pay.

Little Rock (☎ 546 8800; 165 Bridge St) Popular bar and café decorated in Flintstone-era décor; turns into a dance club after about 11pm.

Yaza Café (☎ 548 2849; Montgomery Sq; admission NZ$3; Fri & Sat night) Yaza is a café that doubles as a live-music venue, its musical tastes ranging from folk, acoustic, blues and roots to punk, pop and reggae.

State Cinema 6 (☎ 548 3885; www.statecinema6.co.nz; 91 Trafalgar St) Has six big screens and is the place to see mainstream, new-release flicks.

MORE WINING

The Nelson region has a flourishing wine-making industry and although it doesn't rival the Marlborough region in size, there are enough wineries to keep you busy (around 20 at last count). Many vineyards on the Nelson Wine Trail can be visited by doing a loop from Nelson through Richmond to Motueka, following the SH60 coast road in one direction and the inland Moutere River road in the other. Wineries are open for tastings and sales, and several have cafés and restaurants. For information about wine tours, see p666.

Grape Escape (☎ 03-544 4054; www.grapeescape.co.nz; McShane Rd; 10am-4.30pm) is a complex housing two wineries – Richmond Plains (certified organic wine) and Te Mania – as well as a café-bar and an art and craft gallery. It's on the wine tour itineraries.

Other wineries worth a visit:

Denton Winery (☎ 03-540 3555; alex@dentonwinery.co.nz; Awa Awa Rd; 11am-5pm)
Moutere Hills Winery (☎ 03-543 2288; www.mouterehills.co.nz; Sunrise Valley; 11am-6pm 24 Oct-Easter)
Neudorf Vineyards (☎ 03-543 2643; www.neudorf.co.nz; Neudorf Rd; 10am-5pm Mon-Sat Sep-May, daily 27 Dec-31 Jan)
Ruby Bay Winery (☎ 03-540 2825; rubybay@xtra.co.nz; Korepo Rd; 10am-5pm Dec-Easter, Sat & Sun only Oct & Nov)
Seifrieds (☎ 03-544 1555; www.seifried.co.nz; Redwood Rd; 10am-5pm) One of the region's biggest wineries, with a decent restaurant.

Shark Club (☎ 546 6630; 132-136 Bridge St; noon-late) If you're hankering for a game of stick with some of the fiercest white pointers around, head to this pool hall. There's a pool comp every Wednesday and Thursday (entry NZ$2), a jukebox for inspiration and cheap bar snacks (nachos, wedges etc) for fuel.

Getting There & Away

AIR

Air New Zealand Link (☎ 0800 737 000; www.airnz.co.nz; cnr Trafalgar & Bridge Sts; 9am-5pm Mon-Wed & Fri, 9.30am-5pm Thu, 9.30am-12.30pm Sat) has direct flights to/from Wellington (from NZ$95, 35 minutes, 10 daily), Auckland (from NZ$140, 1¼ hours, eight daily) and Christchurch (from NZ$100, 50 minutes, seven daily), with connections to other cities.

Origin Pacific (☎ 0800 302 302, 547 2020; www.originpacific.co.nz; Trent Dr), which is based in Nelson, has direct connections to several major centres, including Auckland (NZ$100 to NZ$225, 1¼ hours, two daily), Christchurch (from NZ$75, 50 minutes, two to five daily) and Wellington (from NZ$75, 35 minutes, six to 10 daily). There's a service to Hamilton (from NZ$100, 2¼ hours, three to four daily) via Wellington.

BUS

Abel Tasman Coachlines (☎ 548 0285; www.abeltasmantravel.co.nz; 27 Bridge St) runs services to Motueka (NZ$9, one hour, two to three daily), Takaka (NZ$22, 2¼ hours, two daily) and Kaiteriteri (NZ$14, 1¼ hours, one daily).

Atomic Shuttles (☎ 0800 248 885, 322 8833; www.atomictravel.co.nz; cnr Trafalgar & Halifax Sts) runs to Picton (NZ$15, two to 2½ hours, one to two daily) and Greymouth (NZ$40, 7¾ hours, one daily), with connections to Fox Glacier.

InterCity (☎ 548 1538; www.intercitycoach.co.nz; 27 Bridge St) runs daily to Picton (NZ$29, two hours, three daily), Christchurch (NZ$70, 8½ hours, one daily) and Greymouth (NZ$70, six hours, one daily) via Murchison and Westport, with connections to Franz Josef and Fox Glaciers.

K Bus (☎ 525 9434; www.kahurangi.co.nz) provides transport to regional walking tracks, shuttling to/from Picton (NZ$20, two hours, two to three daily), Collingwood (NZ$34, three hours, one to two daily) and the beginning of the Heaphy Track (NZ$45, four hours, one daily).

Getting Around

TO/FROM THE AIRPORT

Super Shuttle (☎ 0800 748 885, 547 5782; www.supershuttle.co.nz; NZ$10) offers 24-hour door-to-door services to and from the airport, which is 6km southwest of town. A taxi to the airport costs about NZ$15.

BUS

Nelson Suburban Bus Lines (☎ 548 3290; www.nelsoncoaches.co.nz; 27 Bridge St) operates local services from its terminal on Bridge St. Buses run out to Richmond via Tahunanui and Stoke until about 5pm or 6pm Monday to Friday, and until 2pm or 3pm Saturday. These connect with two loop services in Stoke, which will get you to Isel Park and Mac's Brewery.

The **Bus** (☎ 547 5912; single trip NZ$4) is a central bus service running every hour or so on four routes, all starting from the bus depot.

TAXI

Sun City Taxis (☎ 0800 422 666, 548 2666; 140 Bridge St) has a convenient rank on Bridge St. Also try **Nelson City Taxis** (☎ 0800 108 855, 548 8223).

ABEL TASMAN NATIONAL PARK

The coastal Abel Tasman National Park is an accessible and popular tramping area. The park is at the northern end of a range of marble and limestone hills extending from the vast Kahurangi National Park (p672) and the interior is honeycombed with caves and potholes. There are various tracks in the park, including an inland path, although the coastal track is the most popular.

Activities

ABEL TASMAN COASTAL TRACK

This 51km, three- to five-day track is one of the most beautiful in the country, passing through pleasant native bush that overlooks beaches of golden sand, which are lapped by gleaming blue-green water. The numerous bays, small and large, are like a travel dream come to life. The tramp is classified as one of NZ's Great Walks (p777). Once little known outside the immediate area, this track has well and truly been 'discovered' and in summer hundreds of people may be on it at any one time – far more than can be accommodated in the huts, so bring your tent.

From Bark Bay to Awaroa Head, there is an area classified as the **Tonga Island Marine Reserve**, which is home to a seal colony and visiting dolphins. Tonga Island itself is a small island out from Onetahuti Beach.

Information

The **Abel Tasman Coastal Track booking desk** (☎ 03-528 0005) is at the **Motueka visitors centre** (☎ 03-528 6543; www.abeltasmangreenrush.co.nz; 20 Wallace St, Motueka; ⌚ 8am-5pm, until 7pm summer) – Motueka is 35km northwest of Nelson. It's here that you can book Great Walks hut and camping passes. You can also obtain passes from the Takaka office of **DOC** (☎ 03-525 8026; www.doc.govt.co.nz; 62 Commercial St, Takaka; ⌚ 8am-4pm Mon-Fri) and at the Nelson visitors centre (p664). Try to plan your trip a couple of days beforehand – staff at Motueka visitors centre are experts and can offer suggestions to tailor the track to your needs and organise transport at each end.

Walking the Track

Many visitors combine tramping and kayaking on the track; see the boxed text on opposite.

Several sections of the main track are tidal, with long deviations required during high tides. There is no alternative walking route around Awaroa estuary. Check local newspapers, subtracting 20 minutes from the Nelson tidal times. Tide tables and advice are also available at DOC and the Motueka visitors centre.

Take additional food so you can stay longer should you have the inclination. Bays around all the huts are beautiful but you should definitely bring generous amounts of sandfly repellent. At the tiny, picturesque beach of Te Pukatea near Anchorage Hut there are no sandflies.

Many walkers finish at Totaranui, the final stop for boat services and a pick-up point for buses, but it is possible to keep walking around the headland to Whariwharangi Hut (two hours) and then on to Wainui (1½ hours), where buses service the car park.

Tours

Abel Tasman Seal Swim (☎ 0800 252 925; www.sealswim.com; swim/watch NZ$120/60; ⌚ 8.45am & 1pm) Trips to a seal colony, departing from Marahau. You can also be dropped off in the park and walk back after the swim.

Abel Tasman Wilson's Experiences (☎ 0800 223 582, 03-528 7801; www.abeltasmannz.com; 3hr/half-day cruises NZ$45/60, kayak & walk NZ$85-110, cruise & walk NZ$50-85) Cruises, walks and kayak (and combinations of) tours. The launch services from Kaiteriteri can also be used as trampers' transport.

Kaiteriteri Kayaks (☎ 0800 252 925, 03-527 8383; www.seakayak.co.nz; Kaiteriteri Beach; seal swim NZ$100-120, seal watch NZ$40-60)

Sleeping & Eating

At the southern edge of the park, Marahau is the main jumping-off point for the Abel Tasman National Park. From the northern end of the park, the nearest towns with ac-

PADDLING THE ABEL TASMAN

The Abel Tasman Coastal Track has long been famous among trampers, but its main attractions – the scenic beaches, coves and bays – make it an equally alluring spot for sea-kayaking.

Many travellers choose to kayak around at least part of the park, cruising the relatively safe, sheltered waters and calling in at those impossibly pretty beaches. You can easily combine kayaking, tramping and camping here. It's not necessarily a matter of hiring a kayak and looking after yourself (although it is possible to do that) – a string of professional outfits can get you out on the water, and the possibilities for guided or freedom trips are vast. You can kayak from half a day to three days, camping or staying in huts. You can kayak one day, camp overnight and walk back, or walk further into the park and catch a water taxi back. Trips can be fully catered or you can arrange to stay in huts or other accommodation. A popular choice if your time is tight is a guided kayak trip to Anchorage Bay, where you stay overnight, walk unguided to Onetahuti Beach and catch a water taxi back – it costs around NZ$130 plus camping or hut fees. Most companies offer a three-day trip where you get dropped at the northern end of the park and paddle back (or vice versa) for around NZ$400 with food included. What you decide to do may depend on your own time (and financial) constraints – pick up the brochures, look at the options and talk to other travellers.

Instruction is given to first-timers and double kayaks are used by all outfits unless you can demonstrate that you're competent enough to control and keep upright in a single kayak. If you're on your own you'll be matched with someone else in the group.

Freedom rentals (kayak and equipment hire) are around NZ$100 per person for two days; most companies require a minimum two-day hire and do not allow solo hires.

The peak season is from November to Easter but you can paddle year-round. December to February is by far the busiest time, so it's worth timing your visit earlier or later. Winter is a good time as you will see more birdlife and the weather is surprisingly calm and mild.

Most of the sea-kayaking operators have plenty of experience and all offer similar trips at similar prices. Marahau is the closest base but trips are also run out of Motueka, Kaiteriteri and even Nelson.

Abel Tasman Kayaks (☎ 0800 732 529, 03-527 8022; www.abeltasmankayaks.co.nz; Marahau Beach; 2-day kayak & walk NZ$130, 3-day guided tours, incl meals NZ$400)

Kaiteriteri Kayaks (☎ 0800 252 925, 03-527 8383; www.seakayak.co.nz; Kaiteriteri Beach; half-day & sunset paddles NZ$65, full-day guided trips NZ$95-170, overnight guided tours NZ$160-310, overnight freedom NZ$100-180)

Kiwi Kayaks (☎ 0800 695 494; www.kiwikayaks.co.nz; Main Rd, Riwaka; full-day kayak & walk NZ$75, full-day guided tours NZ$95-130, 2-day NZ$145-300, 3-day NZ$300-390)

Ocean River Sea Kayaking (☎ 0800 732 529, 03-527 8266; www.seakayaking.co.nz; Main Rd, Marahau; 1-day trip NZ$115-170, 2-day NZ$330-600)

Sea Kayak Company (☎ 0508 252 925, 03-528 7251; www.seakayaknz.co.nz; 506 High St, Motueka; 1-day tour NZ$100, 2-day NZ$200-250, 3-day NZ$400)

Southern Exposure (☎ 0800 695 292, 03-527 8424; www.southern-exposure.co.nz; Moss Rd, Marahau; 1-day trip NZ$95-125, 2-day noncatered/catered NZ$250/310, 3-day NZ$300/390)

commodation are Pohara and Takaka, plus there's **Totaranui Campground** (☎ 03-525 8083; camp sites unpowered/powered per 2 people NZ$20/24), accessible by road in the north of the park; only sites for tents and campervans are available here.

Within the park itself there are four huts – Anchorage (24 bunks), Bark Bay (28 bunks), Awaroa (22 bunks) and Whariwharangi (19 bunks) – as well as 21 designated camp sites. None of the huts have cooking facilities, so you should carry your own stove. Some of the camp sites have fireplaces but, again, you should carry cooking equipment. If you don't have a prebooked **Great Walks huts pass** (per night NZ$14 Oct-Apr, NZ$10 May-Sep) for a particular night in the main season (1 October to 30 April), you will be refused entry to a hut; in winter you don't need to book but you still need to purchase a pass. Individuals keen on sleeping outside will need a **camping pass** (per night NZ$7). As with hut tickets, camp passes should be purchased before you start walking the track. From Christmas Day to late January, huts and camp sites are usually full.

Aquapackers (☎ 0800 430 744; www.aquapackers.co.nz; Anchorage Bay; dm NZ$55) Moored in Anchorage Bay, the MV *Parore* is a great option for backpackers, especially those who like a lager. The former patrol boat is decked out with accommodation for 14 passengers and the cost includes a big dinner, breakfast and a packed lunch for you to take on the day's walk.

MV Etosha (☎ 0800 386 742; Anchorage Bay; d NZ$75) Also in Anchorage Bay, the MV *Etosha* has been upgraded and has three double cabins.

The best way to get to the boats is by water taxi (see below).

Getting There & Away

Motueka is your best base for accessing the Abel Tasman Coastal Track. Transport options to/from the track are extremely flexible – you can kayak, take a helicopter, a bus or water taxi.

Abel Tasman Coachlines (☎ 03-548 0285; www.abeltasmantravel.co.nz) operates buses between Nelson and Motueka (NZ$9, one hour, two to three daily). From Motueka there are services to/from Marahau (NZ$8, 40 minutes, two to three daily), Totaranui (NZ$22, 2¼ hours, two to three daily), Takaka (NZ$15, one hour, two to three daily) and the Wainui car park at the northern end of the track (NZ$26, 1¾ hours, two to three daily).

K Bus (☎ 03-525 9434; www.kahurangi.co.nz) runs buses from Picton and Nelson to Motueka (NZ$9, one hour, four daily). Services run between Motueka and Takaka (NZ$22, two hours, three daily), Marahau (NZ$8, 40 minutes, two daily), Totaranui (NZ$22, 2¼ hours, one daily) and the Wainui car park (NZ$26, 1¾ hours, one daily).

Getting Around

The beauty of Abel Tasman is that it's easy to get to and from any point on the track by water taxi. Prices from Marahau and Kaiteriteri include Anchorage or Torrent Bay (NZ$22), Bark Bay (NZ$25), Tonga (NZ$27), Awaroa (NZ$30) and Totaranui (NZ$32).

Operators include:

Abel Tasman Sea Shuttle (☎ 0800 732 748, 03-528 9759; www.abeltasmanseashuttles.co.nz; 415 High St, Motueka)

Abel Tasman Water Taxis (☎ 0800 423 397, 03-528 7497; www.abeltasman4u.co.nz; Kaiteriteri)

Aqua Taxi (☎ 0800 278 282, 03-527 8083; www.aquataxis.co.nz; Marahau)

Marahau Water Taxis (☎ 0800 808 018, 03-527 8176; www.abeltasmanmarahaucamp.co.nz; Marahau Beach Camp, Franklin St, Marahau)

KAHURANGI NATIONAL PARK

This is the second largest of NZ's national parks and undoubtedly one of the greatest. Its 500,000 hectares comprise an ecological wonderland – more than 100 bird species, 50% of all NZ's plant species, 80% of its alpine plant species and a karst landscape with the largest known cave system in the southern hemisphere. Kahurangi means 'treasured possession'.

Information

The best spot to pick up detailed information, park maps and Great Walks huts and camping passes for the Heaphy Track is from **Takaka DOC** (☎ 03-525 8026; www.doc.govt.co.nz; 62 Commercial St, Takaka; 🕐 8am-4pm Mon-Fri). Alternatively, pay a visit to either the Nelson (p664) or Motueka (p670) visitors centres.

Activities

HEAPHY TRACK

The Heaphy Track is classified as one of NZ's Great Walks (p777). This 82km, four- to six-day tramp doesn't have the spectacular scenery of the Routeburn or Milford Tracks, but it certainly has its own distinctive beauty. The track lies almost entirely within Kahurangi National Park.

Highlights include the view from the summit of Mt Perry (two-hour return walk from Perry Saddle Hut), and the coast, especially around Heaphy Hut where it's worth spending a day or two resting up. It's possible to cross the Heaphy River at its mouth at low tide.

There are seven huts, for which you need a **Great Walks huts pass** (per night NZ$14 Oct-Apr, NZ$10 May-Sep). The huts are set up for around 20 or more people, and beds are on a first-come-first-served basis. All have gas stoves, except Heaphy and Gouland Downs Huts, which need wood.

Camp sites, which require a **camping pass** (per night NZ$7), are available at Gouland Downs, Aorere Shelter and Brown Hut, as well as on the coastal part of the track – Heaphy Hut, Katipo Shelter and Scotts Beach. At the time of writing it was likely that you needed to prebook huts and camp sites before setting off on the tramp.

Walking the Track

Most people travel southwest from Collingwood to Karamea. From Brown Hut the track passes through beech forest to Perry Saddle. The country opens up to the swampy Gouland Downs, then closes in with sparse bush all the way to MacKay Hut. The bush becomes denser towards Heaphy Hut, with the beautiful nikau palm growing at lower levels.

The final section is along the coast through heavy bush and partly along the beach. Unfortunately, the sandflies can be unbearable along this, the most beautiful part. The climate here is surprisingly mild, but do not swim in the sea as the undertows and currents are vicious. The lagoon at Heaphy Hut is good for swimming, and fishing is possible in the Heaphy River.

The Heaphy has kilometre markers; the zero marker is at the southern end of the track at the Kohaihai River near Karamea.

WANGAPEKA & LESLIE-KARAMEA TRACKS

After walking the Heaphy from north to south, you can return to the Nelson/Golden Bay region via the more scenic, though harder, Wangapeka Track, which starts just south of Karamea. Although not as well known as the Heaphy, the Wangapeka is thought by many to be a more enjoyable tramp. It starts 25km south of Karamea at the end of Wangapeka Rd, runs 52km east to the Rolling River near Tapawera and takes about five days. There is a chain of **huts** (per night NZ$7-14) along the track.

The 91km Leslie-Karamea Track is a medium-to-hard tramp of five to seven days. It connects the Cobb Valley near Takaka with Wangapeka Rd, south of Karamea, on the West Coast (thus including part of the Wangapeka Track on the final two days).

Getting There & Away

Abel Tasman Coachlines (☎ 03-528 8850, 03-548 0285) has a service between Nelson and the Heaphy Track (NZ$45, 3¾ hours, one daily), going via Takaka and Collingwood; in winter it runs on demand and is expensive.

K Bus (☎ 03-525 9434; www.kahurangi.co.nz) provides transport between Nelson and the beginning of the Heaphy Track (NZ$45, 3¾ hours, one daily). There's a phone at the trailhead to call buses.

Wadsworths Motors (☎ 03-522 4248; Main Rd, Tapawera) services the Wangapeka and Leslie-Karamea Tracks.

Karamea Express (☎ 03-782 6757; www.lastresort.co.nz) runs from Karamea to Kohaihai at the southern end of the Heaphy Track (NZ$8), departing Karamea at 1.45pm and returning 2.10pm from mid-October to Easter, plus 12.30pm (returning 1pm) from December to February. At other times it runs on demand and for a higher price; ring for a quote. Karamea Express runs on demand to the Wangapeka Track (the ends of the Heaphy and Wangapeka Tracks have phones to arrange transport). It also travels south to the main town of Westport (NZ$20, 1½ hours), departing 7.50am weekdays from May to October, plus Saturday from November to April. Another Westport-bound option is **Cunningham's Coaches** (☎ 03-789 7177), which departs Karamea at 6.15pm Monday to Friday (NZ$15). From Westport, there are numerous options for heading east or further down the West Coast.

Hitchhiking to either the Karamea or Collingwood end of the Heaphy Track is difficult.

CHRISTCHURCH

☎ 03 / pop 331,400

Christchurch, the South Island's biggest city and the urban centre of the Canterbury region, is often described as the most English of NZ's cities, a description bolstered by the punts gliding down the picturesque Avon River, a grand Anglican cathedral rising above the city's central square, and the trams rattling past streets with oh-so-British names. Even the tranquil suburbia to the west, with its manicured gardens dotted with geraniums, chrysanthemums and crisply cut lawns with nary a blade of grass out of place, do little to challenge this.

But for all its self-consciously inherited charm, Christchurch should not be dismissed as simply a facsimile of somewhere else. It's a city with puritan roots but an energetic enthusiasm for the trappings of modern life, as exemplified by a multitude of great cafés, restaurants and bars, and the Kiwi art that has pride of place in the city's newish gallery.

There are also wildlife reserves teeming with native animals.

Don't Miss: taking a gondola ride up to some mountain-top walking, hitting a club in Lichfield St or a cocktail list on Oxford Tce, braving a storm at the International Antarctic Centre, filling your stomach at one of the many good, cheap Asian restaurants, and indulging in booze and bands at Dux de Lux.

HISTORY

Though it still has the Gothic architecture and wooden villas bequeathed by its founders, Christchurch has strayed from the original urban vision of its founders. In 1850 the settlement of Christchurch was an ordered Church of England enterprise, and the fertile farming land was deliberately placed in the hands of the gentry. Christchurch was meant to be a South Pacific model of class-structured England, not just another scruffy colonial outpost. Churches were built rather than pubs, and wool made the elite of Christchurch wealthy. In 1862 it was incorporated as a very English city, but its character slowly changed as other migrants arrived, new industries followed and the city formed its own aesthetic and cultural notions.

ORIENTATION

Cathedral Sq marks the centre of town and is itself marked by the spire of Christchurch Cathedral. The western half of the inner city is dominated by the Botanic Gardens.

Christchurch is compact and easy to walk around, although it's slightly complicated by the river twisting through the centre and constantly crossing your path.

Colombo St runs north–south past Cathedral Sq and is one of the main shopping strips. Oxford Tce is the prime dining boulevard, while the pedestrianised New Regent St is worth a look for its pastel-painted Spanish mission–style architecture, complete with stunted fire escapes.

Map World (☎ 374 5399; cnr Manchester & Gloucester Sts) carries a wide range of NZ city and regional maps, guidebooks and topographic maps for trampers. The local office of **AA** (☎ 379 1280; www.aa.co.nz; 210 Hereford St) has a good range of touring and town maps.

INFORMATION

Bookshops

Arts Centre Bookshop (☎ 365 5277; Arts Centre) Great range of NZ titles.

Scorpio Books (☎ 379 2882; 79 Hereford St) Lots of travel, history and Maori culture, plus international periodicals.

Smith's Bookshop (☎ 379 7976; 133 Manchester St) Excellent second-hand bookshop with unruly book-squashed shelves over three floors.

Whitcoulls (☎ 379 4580; 111 Cashel St) Veritable hangar of all-ages books.

Emergency

Police, Ambulance & Fire (☎ 111)

Safecare (☎ 364 8791; 🕑 24hr) Help for victims of rape/sexual assault.

Internet Access

The going hourly rate in Christchurch's cybercafés is often as low as NZ$3. Most hostels also have Internet terminals or kiosks. Some local options:

Cyber Café Christchurch (☎ 365 5183; 166 Gloucester St; 🕑 10am-10pm Mon-Fri, 10am-9pm Sat)

GETTING INTO TOWN

Christchurch Airport (☎ 358 5029; www.christchurch-airport.co.nz) is at the northwestern end of Memorial Ave, 7km from the city centre. **Super Shuttle** (☎ 0800 748 885, 357 9950) is one of several airport shuttles operating 24 hours and charging NZ$12 to NZ$18, depending on the pick-up/drop-off point. The airport is also serviced by public bus, namely the **City Flyer** (☎ 366 8855; adult NZ$5), which runs from Cathedral Sq between 6am and 11pm weekdays and from 7.30am to 10.30pm weekends; it departs every 20 to 30 minutes up to 5pm or 6pm, then every hour. A taxi to/from the airport costs between NZ$25 and NZ$30.

The buses of the main NZ coach line, InterCity, arrive at and depart from Worcester St, right in the city centre, between Christchurch Cathedral and Manchester St. **Christchurch Railway Station** (☎ 0800 872 467, 341 2588; Troup Dr, Addington), located about 2.5km southwest of Cathedral Sq, just beyond South Hagley Park, is serviced by a free shuttle that picks up from various accommodation places; ring the visitors centre to request pick up.

E-caf (☎ 365 6480; Arts Centre; 8am-11pm)
Netopia (☎ 365 2612; 728 Colombo St; 11am-11pm Sun-Thu, 11am-late Fri & Sat)
Vadal Internet Fone Shop (☎ 377 2381; 57 Cathedral Sq; 8am-late)

Internet Resources

www.christchurchnz.net Exhaustive website for Christchurch and the Canterbury region.
www.christchurch.org.nz Council-run site with the latest tourism developments.
www.localeye.info Local news and visitor info.

Medical Services

Bealey Ave Medical Centre (☎ 365 7777; cnr Bealey Ave & Colombo St; 24hr)
Christchurch Hospital (☎ 364 0640, emergency dept 364 0270; Riccarton Ave)

Money

Hereford St is home to several major banks. For moneychanging, you'll find **Thomas Cook** (☎ 366 2087; cnr Colombo & Armagh Sts) inside a branch of Harvey World Travel.

Post

Post office (☎ 377 5411; 3 Cathedral Sq; 8am-6pm Mon-Fri, 10am-4pm Sat)

Tourist Information

Christchurch & Canterbury visitors centre (☎ 379 9629; www.christchurchnz.net; Cathedral Sq; 8.30am-5pm Mon-Fri, 8.30am-4.30pm Sat & Sun) Loads of information. Books transport, activities and accommodation. Also here is the Southern Encounter Aquarium & Kiwi House.
DOC (☎ 379 9758; 133 Victoria St) Information on South Island national parks and walkways.
Travel & Information Centre (☎ 353 7040; travel&info@cial.co.nz) At both terminals of the airport; can book transport and accommodation.

SIGHTS

Most of Christchurch's worthwhile sights are packed into the city centre, including the cathedral-dominated central square, the history-enriched Arts Centre, the nearby modernistic art gallery and the calming Avon River, which gently snakes its way around the Botanic Gardens. But other highlights are scattered to the far corners of the city, with the cool International Antarctic Centre out near the airport, the gondola down south towards Lyttelton, and the country's largest *marae* (meeting house) out east.

Cathedral Square

Cathedral Sq, named after the building that dominates it, is where locals and tourists continually criss-cross each other's paths, giving the city's flat centrepiece a lively bustle. In the centre of the square is the 18m-high **Metal Chalice** sculpture, created by Neil Dawson to acknowledge the new millennium. A human landmark is provided by local eccentric the **Wizard**, who dresses like a Harry Potter film extra and harangues crowds with his soapbox philosophy.

The striking, Gothic **Christchurch Cathedral** (☎ 366 0046; www.christchurchcathedral.co.nz; admission free; 8.30am-7pm Mon-Fri, 9am-6pm Sat & Sun) was consecrated in 1881 and has an impressive rose window, wood-ribbed ceiling and tilework emblazoned with the distinctive Fylfot Cross. You can also climb halfway up the 63m-high **spire** (adult NZ$4). The administrators are keen to charge for whatever they can (eg a camera or video permit costs NZ$2.50), but the proceeds help maintain this wonderful building.

Southern Encounter Aquarium & Kiwi House (☎ 359 0581; www.southernencounter.co.nz; Cathedral Sq; adult/student NZ$11/9; 9am-4.30pm), accessed through the visitors centre, has disturbingly large eels, sea horses, red-eared slider turtles and other marine life, and also has a touch tank. Don't expect much from the kiwi enclosure; these endangered birds don't like light and are hypersensitive to sound.

International Antarctic Centre

This **centre** (☎ 353 7798; www.iceberg.co.nz; 38 Orchard Rd; adult/concession NZ$20/18, audio guide NZ$5; 9am-8pm Oct-Apr, 9am-5.30pm May-Sep) is part of a huge complex built for the administration of the NZ, US and Italian Antarctic programmes. Learn all about the icy continent through historical, geological and zoological exhibits, including videos of life at Scott Base, an aquarium of creatures gathered under the ice in McMurdo Sound, and an 'Antarctic Storm' chamber where you get a first-hand taste of -18°C wind chill (check at reception for 'storm' forecasts). The 15-minute **Hägglund Ride** (NZ$12, admission & ride NZ$30) involves a zip around the centre's backblocks in an all-terrain vehicle. Visiting the centre is expensive, but worthwhile if you make the most of the Antarctic education on offer. You can reach it on the airport bus, or it's a short walk from the airport.

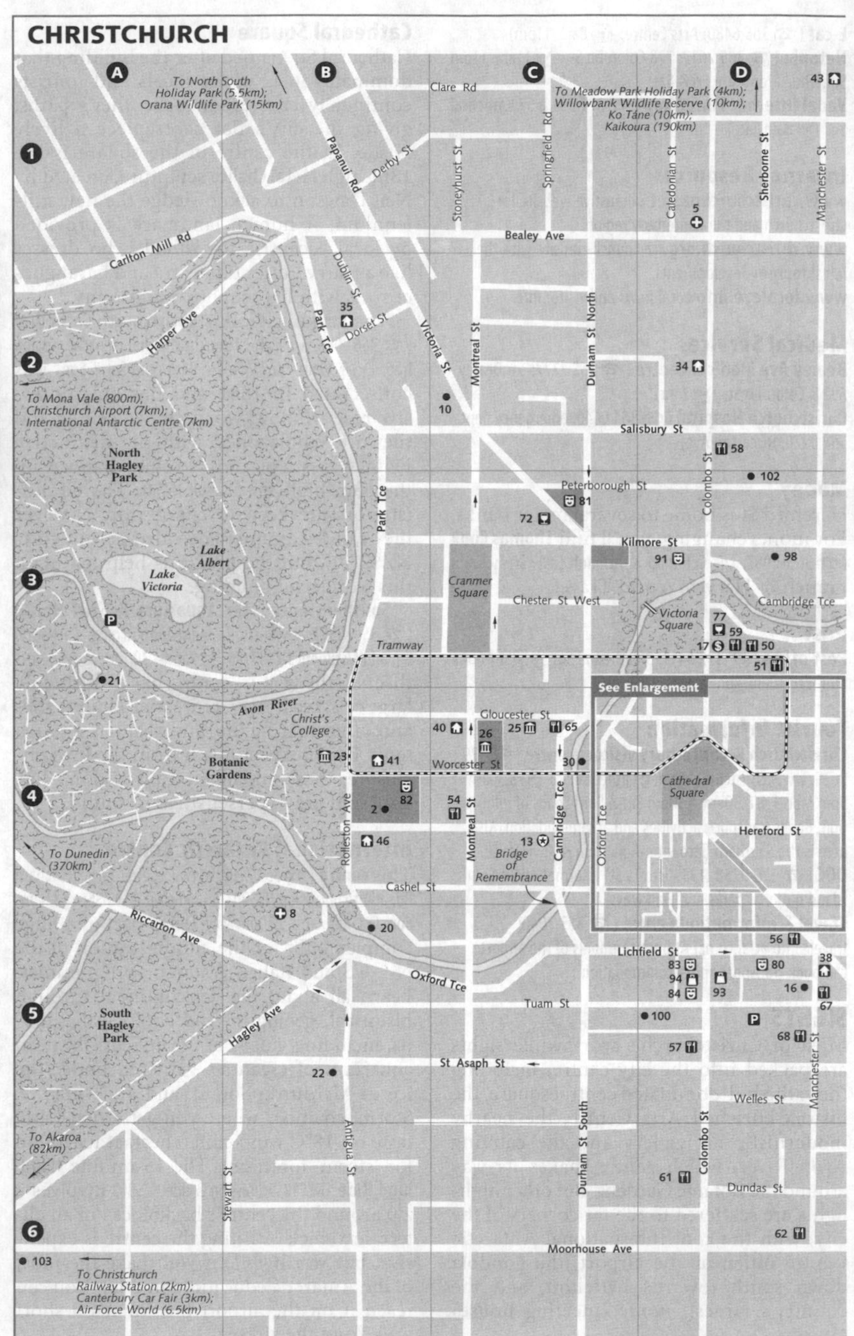
CHRISTCHURCH
To North South Holiday Park (5.5km); Orana Wildlife Park (15km)
To Meadow Park Holiday Park (4km); Willowbank Wildlife Reserve (10km); Ko Tāne (10km); Kaikoura (190km)
To Mona Vale (800m); Christchurch Airport (7km); International Antarctic Centre (7km)
To Dunedin (370km)
To Akaroa (82km)
To Christchurch Railway Station (2km); Canterbury Car Fair (3km); Air Force World (6.5km)
North Hagley Park
South Hagley Park
Lake Victoria
Lake Albert
Avon River
Christ's College
Botanic Gardens
Cranmer Square
Victoria Square
Cathedral Square
Bridge of Remembrance
See Enlargement
Tramway
Clare Rd
Papanui Rd
Derby St
Stoneyhurst St
Springfield Rd
Caledonian St
Sherborne St
Manchester St
Carlton Mill Rd
Bealey Ave
Harper Ave
Dublin St
Dorset St
Park Tce
Victoria St
Montreal St
Durham St North
Salisbury St
Colombo St
Peterborough St
Kilmore St
Chester St West
Cambridge Tce
Gloucester St
Worcester St
Rolleston Ave
Cambridge Tce
Oxford Tce
Hereford St
Cashel St
Riccarton Ave
Oxford Tce
Hagley Ave
Lichfield St
Tuam St
St Asaph St
Welles St
Antigua St
Stewart St
Durham St South
Dundas St
Moorhouse Ave

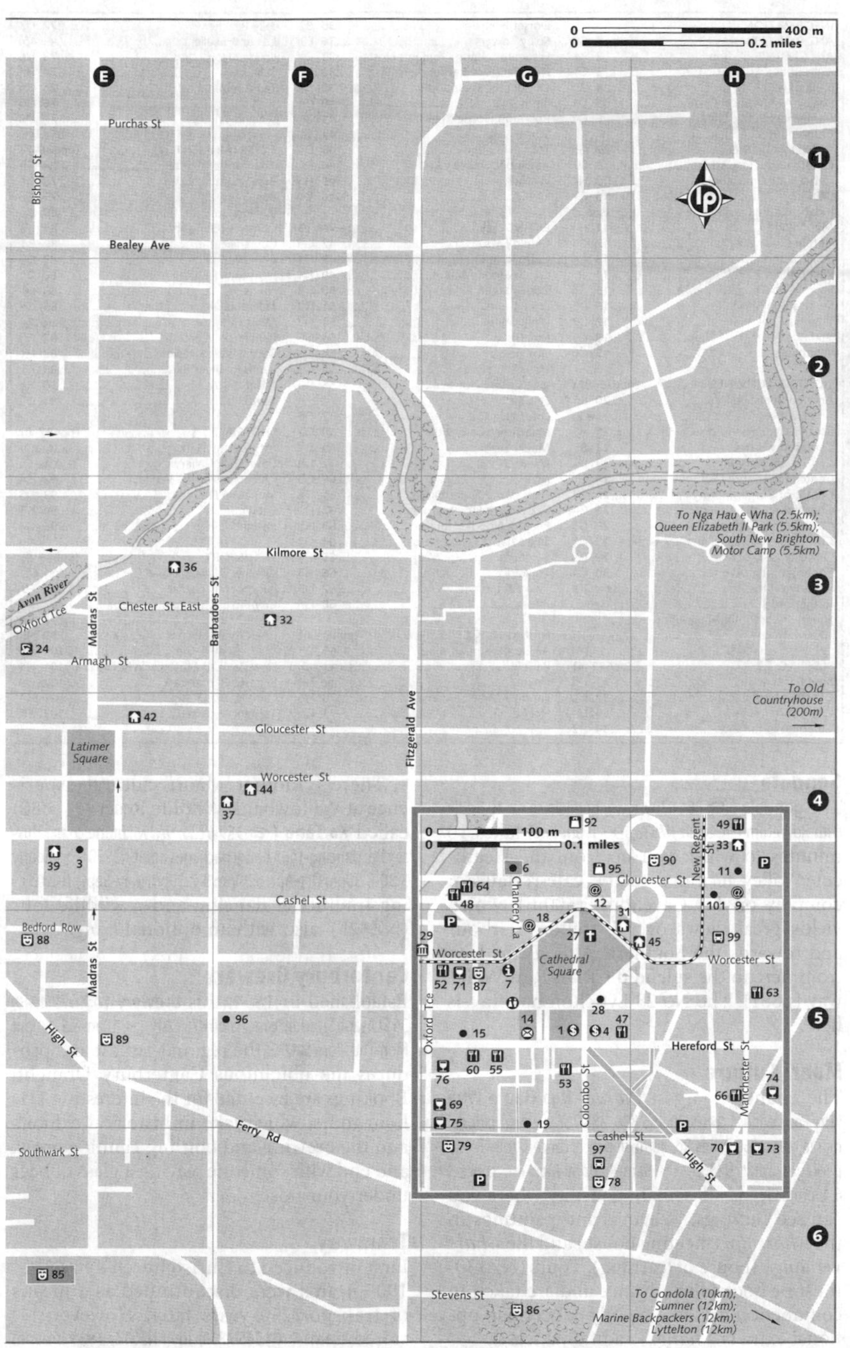

0 400 m
0 0.2 miles
E
F
G
H
1
2
3
4
5
6
Purchas St
Bishop St
Bealey Ave
Kilmore St
Avon River
Oxford Tce
Madras St
Chester St East
Barbadoes St
Armagh St
Gloucester St
Latimer Square
Worcester St
Fitzgerald Ave
Cashel St
Bedford Row
High St
Ferry Rd
Southwark St
Stevens St
To Nga Hau e Wha (2.5km); Queen Elizabeth II Park (5.5km); South New Brighton Motor Camp (5.5km)
To Old Countryhouse (200m)
To Gondola (10km); Sumner (12km); Marine Backpackers (12km); Lyttelton (12km)
0 100 m
0 0.1 miles
Chancery La
Gloucester St
New Regent St
Worcester St
Cathedral Square
Oxford Tce
Hereford St
Manchester St
Colombo St
Cashel St
High St

SOUTH ISLAND

INFORMATION
ANZ Bank (ATM) **1** G5
Arts Centre Bookshop **2** B4
Automobile Association (AA) **3** E4
Bank of NZ (ATM) **4** G5
Bealey Ave Medical Centre **5** D1
Canterbury Public Library **6** G4
Christchurch & Canterbury Visitors Centre **7** G5
Christchurch Hospital **8** B5
Cyber Café Christchurch **9** H4
DOC **10** C2
E-caf (see 2)
Map World **11** H4
Netopia **12** G4
Police Station **13** C4
Post Office **14** G5
Scorpio Books **15** G5
Smith's Bookshop **16** D5
Thomas Cook **17** D3
Vadal Internet Fone Shop **18** G5
Whitcoulls **19** G5

SIGHTS & ACTIVITIES (pp675–82)
Antigua Boatsheds **20** B5
Arts Centre (see 2)
Botanic Gardens Visitors Centre & Café **21** A3
Canterbury Brewery **22** B5
Canterbury Museum **23** B4
Centennial Leisure Centre **24** E3
Centre of Contemporary Art **25** C4
Christchurch Art Gallery **26** C4
Christchurch Cathedral **27** G5
Christchurch Personal Guiding Service **28** G5
Our City O-Tautahi **29** G5
Punting on the Avon **30** C4
Punting on the Park (see 20)
Rutherford's Den (see 2)
Southern Encounter Aquarium & Kiwi House (see 7)

SLEEPING (pp682–4)
base Backpackers **31** G5
Chester Street Backpackers **32** F3
City Central YHA **33** H4
Colombo in the City **34** D2
Dorset House **35** B2
Foley Towers **36** E3
Frauenreisehaus Women's Hostel **37** F4
New Excelsior Backpackers **38** D5
Occidental Backpackers **39** E4
Orari B&B **40** C4
Rolleston House YHA **41** B4
Stonehurst **42** E4
Tranquil Lodge **43** D1
Vagabond Backpackers **44** F4
Warners **45** H5
YMCA **46** B4

EATING (pp684–5)
Café d'Fafo **47** G5
Caffe Roma **48** G4
City Seafood Market **49** H4
Copenhagen Bakery & Café **50** D3
Daily Grind **51** D3
Daily Grind **52** G5
Dimitris **53** G5
Dux de Lux **54** C4
Ebisu **55** G5
Java Coffee House **56** D5
Le Café (see 2)
Lotus Heart **57** D5
Mainstreet Café & Bar **58** D2
Matsu Sushi **59** D3
Mum's (see 12)
Mythai **60** G5
New World Supermarket **61** D6
Pak N Save Supermarket **62** D6
Penang Noodle House **63** H5
Sala Sala **64** G4
Santorini **65** C4
Topkapi **66** H5
Two Fat Indians **67** D5
Zydeco **68** D5

DRINKING (pp685–6)
All Bar One **69** G5
Bailie's (see 45)
Coyote (see 76)
Grumpy Mole Saloon **70** H6
Holy Grail **71** G5
Jolly Poacher **72** C3
Le Bar Bruxelle (see 45)
Loaded Hog **73** H6
Sullivans **74** H5
Tap Room **75** G5
Viaduct **76** G5
Vic and Whale **77** D3

ENTERTAINMENT (pp686–7)
Arts Centre Cinemas (see 2)
Base **78** G6
Bog **79** G6
Carbon **80** D5
Christchurch Casino **81** C3
Court Theatre **82** B4
eye spy **83** D5
Heaven **84** D5
Hoyts **85** E6
Jade Stadium **86** G6
Ministry/Smile (see 80)
Regent on Worcester **87** G5
Sammy's Jazz Review **88** E5
Southern Blues Bar **89** E5
Theatre Royal **90** H4
Town Hall **91** D3

SHOPPING (pp687–8)
Arts Centre Market (see 2)
Cave Rock Gallery (see 2)
Champions of the World **92** G4
Mountain Designs **93** D5
Snowgum **94** D5
Swanndri Shop **95** G4

TRANSPORT (pp688–9)
Air New Zealand Travel Centre (see 61)
Backpackers Bazaar **96** F5
City Bus Exchange **97** G6
First Choice **98** D3
InterCity Bus Depot **99** H5
Mac's Rent-A-Car **100** D5
New Zealand Motorcycle Rentals **101** H4
Pegasus Rental Cars **102** D3
Qantas (see 50)
Turners Auctions **103** A6

Gondola

The **gondola** (☎ 384 0700; www.gondola.co.nz; 10 Bridle Path Rd; return fare adult NZ$18; ⏲ 10am-late) takes 10 minutes to whisk you up from the Heathcote Valley terminal to the café-restaurant complex on Mt Cavendish (500m), which yields great views over Lyttelton Harbour and towards the Southern Alps. Paths lead from here to the splendid Crater Rim Walkway (p681). The No 28 Lyttelton bus travels here.

Maori Culture

The country's largest *marae*, **Nga Hau e Wha** (The Four Winds; ☎ 0800 456 898, 388 7685; www.nationalmarae.co.nz; 250 Pages Rd; admission free, concert-tour-hangi packages adult NZ$65; ⏲ 9am-4.30pm Mon-Fri, concert 6.45pm daily), is a fascinating facility where you can see carvings, weavings and paintings in the *whare nui* (meeting house) and the *whare wananga* (house of learning). Tours (NZ$30) must be booked in advance and are taken in conjunction with the nightly concert; an optional extra is a *hangi* (traditional feast).

There's another Maori cultural experience at Willowbank Wildlife Reserve (p680) called **Ko Tāne** (☎ 359 6226; www.kotane.co.nz; Hussey Rd; dancing-tour-hangi packages adult NZ$70; ⏲ hourly 5.30-8.30pm Oct-Apr, 6.30pm & 7.30pm May-Sep), featuring traditional dancing and a wildlife tour (NZ$25), also with an optional *hangi*.

Canterbury Brewery

Established in 1854, this **brewery** (☎ 379 4940; 36 St Asaph St; adult/concession NZ$12/8; ⏲ 10am & 12.30pm Mon-Thu, 1pm Sat) is the region's largest and produces the ubiquitous Canterbury Draught. Bookings are essential for the interesting 1½-hour tours, which take in historical exhibits and the brewing and bottling/canning areas, and end with someone waving a glass of beer under your nose.

Tramway

First introduced to Christchurch's streets in 1905, trams were discontinued as a means of transport 50 years later. However, restored **trams** (☎ 366 7830; adult NZ$13; ⏲ 9am-9pm

Nov-Mar, 9am-6pm Apr-Oct) now operate a 2.5km inner-city loop that takes in prime local features and shopping areas; tickets are valid for two consecutive days and can be bought from the driver.

Canterbury Museum

This absorbing **museum** (☎ 366 5000; www.cantmus.govt.nz; Rolleston Ave; admission free; 9am-5pm) has amassed a wonderful collection of natural and man-made items of significance to NZ. Highlights include the Maori gallery, with some stunning *pounamu* (jade) pieces; the coracle in the 'Antarctic Hall' used by a group of people shipwrecked on Disappointment Island in 1907; and the child-oriented **Discovery** (admission NZ$2), with interactive displays and living exhibits such as some docile tarantulas. The 4th-floor café has good views of botanic greenery.

Christchurch Art Gallery

Set in an eye-catching metal-and-glass collage, the city's relatively new **art gallery** (Te Puna o Waiwhetu; ☎ 941 7300; www.christchurchartgallery.org.nz; cnr Worcester & Montreal Sts; admission free, audio guide NZ$2.50; 10am-5pm Thu-Tue, 10am-9pm Wed) has an engrossing permanent collection divided into pre-20th century, 20th-century and contemporary galleries, plus temporary exhibitions featuring modern NZ artists such as Margaret Hudson-Ware, Margaret Elliott and Peter Siddell. Thematic guided tours are regularly held (ask at the information desk) and there's also a spacious café–wine bar.

Other Museums & Galleries

The **Centre of Contemporary Art** (CoCA; ☎ 366 7261; www.coca.org.nz; 66 Gloucester St; admission by donation; 10am-5pm Mon-Fri, noon-4pm Sat & Sun) is a big white canvas of a place with major renovations on the drawing board. It showcases the work of creative modern-day NZ photographers, painters and sculptors (including recent fine arts graduates), as well as multi-hued exhibitions of international works.

Nearly 30 classic aircraft and exhaustive detail of NZ's military aviation history are warehoused at **Air Force World** (☎ 343 9532; www.airforcemuseum.co.nz; 45 Harvard Ave, Sockburn; adult/student NZ$15/9; 10am-5pm, tours 11am, 1pm & 3pm). After exploring the underbelly of a Vampire, Skyhawk or the rather less scary-sounding Beaver, take the one-hour tour (included in admission price) of the hangars and restoration workshops. Bus Nos 5, 51 and 81 take you there.

Our City O-Tautahi (☎ 941 7460; www.ccc.govt.nz/ourcity; cnr Oxford Tce & Worcester St; admission free; 10am-4pm Mon-Fri) is a free, Christchurch-focused exhibition in the old Municipal Chambers, revealing interesting facets of the city's history. There are diplomatic gifts such as a gold scimitar from the Amir of Bahrain, an old ejector seat salvaged from an air race between London and Christchurch in 1953, and drier displays on current and future developments.

Arts Centre

The former Canterbury College (later Canterbury University) site, with its enclave of wonderful Gothic Revival buildings, has been transformed into the excellent **Arts Centre** (☎ 363 2836; www.artscentre.org.nz; 2 Worcester St; admission free; visitors centre 9.30am-5pm), where arts and craft outlets share the premises with theatres, cafés and restaurants. The visitors centre, located in the clock tower on Worcester St, provides details of free guided tours of the complex. From here, you can also access the

THE ATOMIC MAN

Staring out from the NZ$100 bill is the face of Ernest Rutherford, the first person to split the atom. He achieved this feat in 1917 at Manchester University. Prior to this, he picked up a Nobel Prize for Chemistry in 1908 and later discovered that atoms were not thin, easily penetrated objects, but in fact had a small, heavy nucleus – after firing alpha particles at a thin strip of foil and observing the end result, he exclaimed that 'It was as if you fired a 15-inch shell at a sheet of tissue paper and it came back to hit you'. (He also once said that 'All science is either physics or stamp collecting', which perhaps explains his limited fan base in the wider scientific community.)

Before these discoveries, though, he was a student at Canterbury College in Christchurch, where his future career was inspired by the teachings of Professor Alexander Bickerton. Have a look at an evocative old lecture theatre, with its graffiti-carved desks, and one of Rutherford's early work spaces in the Rutherford's Den exhibit in the Arts Centre (above).

interesting **Rutherford's Den** (www.rutherfordsden.org.nz; admission gold coin donation; 10am-5pm); see the boxed text on p679.

Banks of the Avon

The city's **Botanic Gardens** (941 7590; www.ccc.govt.nz/parks/botanicgardens; Armagh St; admission free; 7am to 1hr before sunset, visitors centre 10am-4pm Sep-Apr & 11am-3pm May-Aug) comprise 30 riverside hectares planted with 10,000-plus specimens of indigenous and introduced plants. There are lots of greenhouses and thematic gardens to explore, lawns to sprawl on, and a café at the visitors centre.

Mona Vale (348 9660; 63 Fendalton Rd; admission free; 9.30am-4pm daily Oct-Apr, 10am-3.30pm Wed-Sun May-Sep) is a charming Elizabethan-style homestead sitting on 5.5 riverside hectares of landscaped gardens, ponds and fountains. Have some food in the café inside the homestead, wander the gorgeous grounds or take a 30-minute Avon River **punt** (NZ$16; operates 10am-5pm Jun-Apr). Bus No 9 gets you there.

Wildlife Reserves

Orana Wildlife Park (359 7109; www.oranawildlifepark.co.nz; McLeans Island Rd; adult/concession NZ$14/12; 10am-5pm) has an excellent walk-through native-bird aviary, a nocturnal kiwi house and a reptile exhibit featuring the wrinkly tuatara (a type of lizard). But most of the extensive grounds are devoted to Africana, including lions, rhinoceros, giraffes, zebras, oryx and cheetahs. Animal feeding times are scheduled daily and there's a 'farmyard' area where children can pet the more domesticated animals.

Willowbank Wildlife Reserve (359 6226; www.willowbank.co.nz; Hussey Rd; adult/concession NZ$16/14; 10am-10pm) is another good faunal reserve, with a focus on native NZ animals and hands-on enclosures that contain alpacas, wallabies and deer. Tours are held several times a day and also at night for spotting nocturnal critters. Maori performances also take place here (see p678).

Lyttelton

Southeast of Christchurch are the prominent Port Hills, which slope down to the city's port, Lyttelton Harbour. Christchurch's first European settlers landed here in 1850 to embark on their tramp over the hills, and this is where you'll find the historic port of Lyttelton, only 12km from Christchurch and popular with day-trippers because of its scenic setting, attractive old buildings and some good café-bars. **Lyttelton visitors centre** (328 9093; lyttinfo@ihug.co.nz; 20 Oxford St; 9am-5pm) has numerous information leaflets on the town and surrounding area.

Lyttelton Museum (328 8972; Gladstone Quay; admission by donation; 2-4pm Tue, Thu, Sat & Sun) has interesting maritime exhibits such as wreck-recovered artefacts and ship models (there's a 6ft version of the *Queen Mary*), plus historical paraphernalia such as a 19th-century pipe organ and an Antarctic gallery (both Scott and Shackleton used the port as a base).

The neo-Gothic **Timeball Station** (328 7311; 2 Reserve Tce; adult NZ$5; 10am-5pm), built in 1876, was where (for 58 years) a huge timeball was hoisted on a mast and then dropped at exactly 1pm, Greenwich Mean Time, allowing ships in the harbour to set their clocks and thereby accurately calculate longitude. Note that it requires a short, steep climb, and that the wind can really rip across the tower's top.

Black Cat (0800 436 574, 328 9078; www.blackcat.co.nz; 17 Norwich Quay; NZ$45) operates two-hour 'Christchurch Wildlife Cruises' on Lyttelton Harbour, where you may (but may not) see rare Hectors dolphins, blue penguins and various sea birds.

Head down the laneway off London St, walk behind the supermarket and clamber up the stairway to enter the decidedly uplifting **Wunderbar** (328 8818; 19 London St; 1pm-late), where you can have a drink on the balcony while looking out over the docks, nurture a glass in a red-velvet booth or have an eventful time in the fabulously eccentric, upholstered back room, which hosts everything from discos to trannie shows and live music.

Bus No 28 runs regularly from Christchurch to Lyttelton. You can drive straight to Lyttelton via a road tunnel, an impressive piece of engineering with gleaming tiles reminiscent of a huge, elongated public toilet.

ACTIVITIES

The most popular activities around Christchurch are rather gentler than the high-powered pursuits of places such as Wanaka and Queenstown. Punting down the Avon River is a good example, as are the inner-city walks, the tracks further south at Lyttelton Harbour, and the swimming off New Brighton and Sumner beaches. But up-tempo activities such as water-skiing, skydiving and jet-boating the Waimakariri River can be had too.

Walking

The visitors centre (p675) has info on Christchurch walks. Within the city are the **Riverside Walk** and various historical strolls, while out past Sumner is the excellent clifftop walk to **Taylors Mistake** (2½ hours).

For great views of the city, take the walkway from the **Sign of the Takahe** on Dyers Pass Rd. The various 'Sign of the…' places in this area were originally roadhouses built during the Depression as rest stops. Now they vary from the impressive tearooms at the Sign of the Takahe to a simple shelter at the Sign of the Bellbird and are referred to primarily as landmarks. This walk leads up to the **Sign of the Kiwi** through Victoria Park and then along Summit Rd to Scotts Reserve, with several lookout points along the way.

You can walk to Lyttelton on the **Bridle Path** (1½ hours), which starts at Heathcote Valley (take bus No 28). The **Godley Head Walkway** (two hours return) begins at Taylors Mistake, crossing and recrossing Summit Rd, with beautiful views on a clear day.

The **Crater Rim Walkway** (nine hours) around Lyttelton Harbour goes 20km from Evans Pass to the Ahuriri Scenic Reserve.

From the gondola terminal on Mt Cavendish, walk to **Cavendish Bluff Lookout** (30 minutes return) or the **Pioneer Women's Memorial** (one hour return).

Swimming & Surfing

Queen Elizabeth II Park (☎ 941 6849; www.qeiipark.org.nz; Travis Rd, Burwood; pool adult NZ$5; 🕑 6am-9pm Mon-Fri, 7am-8pm Sat & Sun) is a huge sports complex with indoor pools (including a 40m wave pool), waterslides, a gym and squash courts; take bus No 43. Closer to town is the **Centennial Leisure Centre** (☎ 941 6853; www.centennial.org.nz; 181 Armagh St; pool adult NZ$5; 🕑 6am-9pm Mon-Thu, 7am-7pm Fri-Sun), which has a heated indoor pool.

The closest **beaches** to the city are Waimairi, North, New Brighton and South Brighton; bus Nos 5, 49 and 60 head there. Sumner, to the city's southeast, is also popular (take bus No 30 or 31), while there are some good surfing breaks further east at Taylors Mistake.

Cycling

City Cycle Hire (☎ 0800 343 848, 339 4020; www.cyclehire-tours.co.nz; bikes half-/full day from NZ$20/30) will deliver bikes to where you're staying. It also runs half- and full-day **tours** (NZ$75-135) to Port Hills and Akaroa.

You can pedal downhill from the gondola terminal with the **Mountain Bike Adventure Company** (☎ 0800 424 534; NZ$45). Price includes the gondola ride up the mountain; booking is essential.

Boating

The historic green-and-white **Antigua Boatsheds** (☎ 366 5885; www.boatsheds.co.nz; 2 Cambridge Tce) rents out canoes (per hour NZ$7), rowboats (per 30 minutes NZ$12) and paddle boats (per 30 minutes NZ$14) for Avon River exploration. The boatsheds are also the starting point for **Punting in the Park** (☎ 366 0337; NZ$13; 🕑 10am-dusk), where someone else does all the elbow work during a 30-minute trip in a flat-bottomed boat.

A similar experience is offered by **Punting on the Avon** (☎ 379 9629; 20min trip NZ$18; 🕑 10am-dusk Mon-Fri, by arrangement Sat & Sun) from the landing stage at the Worcester St bridge.

Other Activities

Several **skiing** and **snowboarding** areas lie within a two-hour drive of Christchurch, near Kaikoura (p659), Arthur's Pass (p696) and Methven (p698).

Other active options in and around Christchurch include **jet-boating** (from NZ$55) on the Waimakariri River, **tandem skydiving** (NZ$250), **tandem paragliding** (NZ$120), **ballooning** (NZ$220), **rafting** (NZ$145) on the Rangitata River and **horse trekking** (from NZ$35); ask at the visitors centre.

TOURS

Numerous companies conduct tours of the city and will also trundle you out to nearby towns (Lyttelton, Akaroa) and sites further afield (Arthur's Pass, Hanmer Springs, the wineries of the Waipara).

The nonprofit **Christchurch Personal Guiding Service** (☎ 379 9629; NZ$8; 🕑 10am & 1pm Oct-Apr, 1pm May-Sep) does informative, two-hour city walks. Get tickets from the visitors centre; during summer, tickets are also available from a red-and-black kiosk on the south-eastern side of Cathedral Sq.

Christchurch Bike Tours (☎ 366 0337; www.chchbiketours.co.nz; NZ$28; 🕑 2pm Nov-Apr) pedal around the city on informative two-hour tours.

Christchurch Sightseeing Tours (☎ 0508 669 660, 366 9660; www.christchurchtours.co.nz; from NZ$30) offers comprehensive 3½-hour city tours year-round, a three-hour circuit of private gardens in the city during spring and summer, and twice-weekly tours of heritage homes from September to May.

For a host of touring options in and around Christchurch, try **Canterbury Leisure Tours** (☎ 0800 484 485, 384 0999; www.leisuretours.co.nz; from NZ$40). You can do everything from three-hour city tours to full-day Akaroa, Mt Cook, Arthur's Pass and Kaikoura outings (the day tours are fine if you're short on time, but otherwise try to spend longer in each of these fine places).

Canterbury Vin de Pays (☎ 357 8262; www.vindepays.co.nz; from NZ$65) combines sightseeing with regional wine and cheese tasting, including a nicely flavoured reconnaissance of Waipara Valley wineries.

FESTIVALS & EVENTS

The **World Buskers Festival** (www.worldbuskersfestival.com) entertains the city streets from mid- to late January, concentrated around Cathedral Sq and the Arts Centre. Mid-February sees the **Flowers and Romance Festival** (www.festivalofflowers.co.nz) – the city provides gardens in full bloom, the romance is up to you. **Showtime Canterbury** (www.showtimecanterbury.co.nz) dominates the first half of November with major horse races such as the New Zealand Cup, fashion shows, fireworks and the centrepiece **A&P Show** (Agricultural & Pastoral Show; www.theshow.co.nz).

SLEEPING

Christchurch has a growing population of hostels, most of them within a 10-minute shuffle of Cathedral Sq.

Several budget stalwarts are found around Latimer Sq, a few blocks east of Cathedral Sq, with some smaller, homelier options further east from there. There are also several well-established budget places close to the foliage of the Botanic Gardens. Camping grounds are located at least several kilometres from the city centre.

Stonehurst (☎ 0508 786 633, 379 4620; www.stonehurst.com; 241 Gloucester St; dm NZ$22, s from NZ$55, d NZ$60-85; P 💻 🏊) Well-managed all-budgets complex opposite Latimer Sq where you can rent everything from a dorm bunk to a three-bedroom apartment (see the boxed text on opposite) and then celebrate your arrival with a dip in the heated swimming pool or a drink at the bar. Decide in advance what you're after (eg don't get a pool-side bunk room if you want peace and quiet) and book ahead at peak times.

Foley Towers (☎ 366 9720; foley.towers@backpack.co.nz; 208 Kilmore St; dm/d from NZ$19/50; P 💻) Friendly Foley Towers provides lots of well-maintained rooms encircling quiet inner courtyards, and a warm welcome in dorms warmed by under-floor heating. Great to stay in if you need a break from places specialising in mass off-the-bus arrivals.

Frauenreisehaus Women's Hostel (☎ 366 2585; jesse-sandra@quicksilver.net.nz; 272 Barbadoes St; dm/s/tw NZ$23/35/50; 💻) The refreshing, welcoming Frauenreisehaus is a women-only hostel that offers free bikes, a well-equipped kitchen and the opportunity to plunder fresh herbs and spices from the garden. It's essential you reconfirm your booking before arrival.

Vagabond Backpackers (☎ 379 9677; vagabondbackpackers@hotmail.com; 232 Worcester St; dm NZ$19-22, s/d NZ$32/50; P 💻) Small, homely place with an appealing garden that accentuates Vagabond's peaceful, unruffled air. Its pinkish façade is only a short walk from Cathedral Sq.

Old Countryhouse (☎ 381 5504; http://homepages.ihug.co.nz/~oldhouse; 437 Gloucester St; dm NZ$21-28, d NZ$50-65; P 💻) Popular for its cosiness and taking-it-easy ambience, the Countryhouse has split itself into two separate, very clean villas. It's a bit further out than other hostels, but is still only 1km east of Latimer Sq; if you don't feel like walking, bus No 30 stops opposite.

Chester Street Backpackers (☎ 377 1897; chesterst@free.net.nz; 148 Chester St East; dm/d from NZ$20/50; 💻) It has a suburban location but definitely not a suburban feel. Rather, this small and welcoming backpackers has an enticingly cosy atmosphere, and the barbecue set up in the boot of an old Anglia Deluxe is a nice touch.

Occidental Backpackers (☎ 379 9284; www.occidental.co.nz; 208 Hereford St; dm NZ$18-22, s/tw/d NZ$35/45/50; P 💻) The Occidental rarely gets rave reviews from backpackers, as not everyone finds the tatty lounge and the sometimes violent colour scheme endearing. But you could do worse than one of the balcony-equipped front-facing rooms, and we found staff irrepressibly friendly. They supply a free breakfast and cheap bar food (meals NZ$4 to NZ$12).

City Central YHA (☎ 379 9535; yha.christchurchcity@yha.org.nz; 273 Manchester St; dm/d from NZ$26/55; P 💻) Comfortable bunks and beds, huge, spotless lounges and kitchens (of which there are two), a pool table and helpful staff are some of the characteristics of this well-equipped, central hostel.

Warners (☎ 377 0550; www.warnerscentral.co.nz; 50 Cathedral Sq; dm NZ$20-25, s NZ$45-55, d NZ$50-60; P 💻) The hostel section of the square-facing Warners Hotel has been spruced up in recent years and has a pleasant feel, though the TV room and kitchen have aged facilities. The building's western arm has been transformed into a luxury hotel.

base Backpackers (☎ 0800 942 225, 982 2225; www.basebackpackers.com; 56 Cathedral Sq; dm NZ$22-25, s NZ$35-45, d & tw NZ$50-75; P 💻) As central as Warners, fronting Cathedral Sq. It's a well-kept place with good kitchen and laundry facilities, reliable Internet access and the sociable Saints & Sinners bar.

New Excelsior Backpackers (☎ 0800 666 237, 366 7570; www.newexcelsior.co.nz; cnr Manchester & High Sts; dm NZ$22-25, s NZ$35-40, d NZ$55; 💻) This revamped pub (which has a history as a hotel dating back to the 1860s) is a decent, central and well-equipped backpackers with its own café-bar and a great outdoor deck.

Dorset House (☎ 366 8268; www.dorsethouse.co.nz; 1 Dorset St; dm/s/d from NZ$23/45/55; P 💻) Lovely, 130-year-old weatherboard home with a nice atmosphere, a large, regal lounge, a pool table and single beds instead of bunks. It's a short stroll from expansive parklands.

Rolleston House YHA (☎ 366 6564; yha.rollestonhouse@yha.org.nz; 5 Worcester St; dm/tw NZ$22/50; P 💻) Pleasant Rolleston House is in an excellent position beside the tramline and can count both the Arts Centre and the Botanic Gardens as neighbours. It's a good choice for those who don't have the energy or the inclination for a party-till-you-drop hostel.

YMCA (☎ 0508 962 224, 365 0502; www.ymcachch.org.nz; 12 Hereford St; dm NZ$18, s NZ$45-70, d NZ$55-90; P 💻) Functional accommodation that focuses on facilities and cleanliness rather than style or character, with a choice of private or shared bathroom. You can get cheap breakfasts and dinners (NZ$6 to NZ$12) in the dining room and also hire time in the adjoining gym or on the climbing wall.

Tranquil Lodge (☎ 366 6500; 440 Manchester St; dm/s/d NZ$22/45/55; 💻) Sizeable place in a peaceful north-of-the-centre location. The linoleum floor doesn't give it much character and the kitchen is poky, but this is balanced out by comfortable beds (no bunks), a spacious lounge, pool table and wheelchair access throughout.

Marine Backpackers (☎ 326 6609; www.themarine.co.nz; 26 Nayland St; dm/s NZ$18/25, d NZ$45-55; P 💻) Only a short walk from the beachfront at Sumner, this old pub was being fitted out with more rooms when we visited. The plain rooms are embellished by a sun-soaked veranda, back garden, downstairs bar (with meals) and a busy local café scene. Bus Nos 30 and 31 run between Sumner and the city centre.

Meadow Park Holiday Park (☎ 0800 396 323, 352 9176; www.meadowpark.co.nz; 39 Meadow St; camp sites unpowered/powered per 2 people NZ$28/30, d NZ$45-85; P) Good place to pitch a tent or park a campervan. It's also well equipped for leisure activities, with an indoor pool, spa

SOUTH ISLAND

SPLURGE!

Stonehurst (☎ 0508 786 633, 379 4620; www.stonehurst.com; 241 Gloucester St; motel d NZ$95-165, apartments from per week NZ$500; P 💻) The place to go for some good deals on a variety of motel rooms (from studios to two-bedroom units) and self-contained tourist flats. The accommodation is central, comfortable and modern, staff are exceedingly helpful and reception is manned around the clock.

Colombo in the City (☎ 0800 265 662, 366 8775; www.motelcolombo.co.nz; 863 Colombo St; d NZ$95-150; P) It may sound like a Peter Falk telemovie, but it's actually a bunch of roomy ultramodern units only a few blocks north of Oxford Tce; handy if you feel like sampling some late-night culture and sleeping it off in comfort. Wheelchairs are accommodated.

Orari B&B (☎ 365 6569; www.orari.net.nz; 42 Gloucester St; s/d from NZ$135/150; P) A fine late-19th-century home that's been stylishly updated with light-filled rooms, inviting guest areas and a front garden that's lovely in full bloom. Art connoisseurs note: it's located across the road from Christchurch Art Gallery.

and a big playground for the kids to unleash their energies. Accommodation with a roof ranges from old 'standard' cabins to plain motel units.

North South Holiday Park (☎ 0800 567 765, 359 5993; www.northsouth.co.nz; 530 Sawyers Arms Rd; camp sites unpowered/powered per 2 people NZ$19/21, d NZ$37-60; P) If you don't want to travel far after picking up your campervan at the airport, consider driving here. The many facilities include a pool, sauna, tennis courts and playground. If you don't have your own transport, airport transfers can be arranged.

South New Brighton Motor Camp (☎ 388 9844; www.holidayparks.co.nz/southnewbrighton; 59 Halsey St; camp sites unpowered/powered per 2 people NZ$18/20, d NZ$35-60; P) The cabins are nothing special, but the sheltered grounds and the location (a short walk from South Brighton Beach) are why people come here.

EATING

Christchurch offers a great variety of cuisines and eateries, and the quality is generally high. Cafés range from minimalist caffeine specialists to upmarket European-style places and less-polished, more-Bohemian joints. Restaurants dish up a hearty mixture of Asian and European food.

The largest concentration of cafés and restaurants is found along 'the Strip', the eastern side of Oxford Tce between Hereford and Cashel Sts. The common characteristics here are good vantage points, outdoor tables and meat-heavy international dishes.

Self-Catering

Self-caterers should head to the large **Pak N Save supermarket** (☎ 377 1000; 297 Moorhouse Ave) or the **New World supermarket** (☎ 377 6778; South City Centre, Colombo St).

Cafés

Mainstreet Café & Bar (☎ 365 0421; 840 Colombo St; meals NZ$5-13; breakfast & lunch) Bright, airy, upstairs/downstairs affair serving vegan and vegetarian food with panache. A good place to get a breakfast with the works or a teriyaki tofu wrap after a late night. Mainstreet also has an eclectic live-music programme (see p687).

Café d'Fafo (☎ 366 6083; 137 Hereford St; meals NZ$8-14; breakfast & lunch) Claims to cater to the coffee connoisseur and backs it up by delivering large, tasty, pumped-up, double-shot lattes. The extensive breakfast menu includes a vegetarian eggs Benedict with pesto hollandaise.

Java Coffee House (☎ 366 0195; cnr High & Lichfield Sts; mains NZ$9-13; breakfast & lunch) Funky, bright-paint-splattered place with groovin' music, hungover staff and leaflets for upcoming dance events. It's a good place for a late-morning serve of eggs on pancakes, and you can get your latte or *chai* in a cup or bowl.

Le Café (☎ 366 7722; Clock Tower, Arts Centre; meals NZ$11-17; breakfast, lunch & dinner) Only a restaurant set in an arts centre would choose a name of such simple pretentiousness. That said, the nice fresh food is decidedly mainstream – pizza, pasta, focaccias, fish and chips, chicken Caesar salad – and the surroundings pleasantly historic.

Caffe Roma (☎ 379 3879; 176 Oxford Tce; mains NZ$10-18; breakfast & lunch) This imitation European café has a refined continental persona, making it a relatively quiet, semiformal place for breakfast. Savour a plateful of lamb kidneys or rosemary brioche.

Quick Eats

A variety of food stalls set themselves up daily in Cathedral Sq, or you can accost one of the many food vans selling everything from Lebanese to Thai at the Arts Centre market (see p688).

Daily Grind (☎ 377 4959; cnr New Regent & Armagh Sts; meals from NZ$5; lunch & dinner) Provides express delivery of coffee, juices (including a 'flu chaser') and smoothies, plus tasty solids such as focaccias, *panini*, bagels and salads. There's also a second **Daily Grind** (☎ 377 6288; cnr Worcester St & Oxford Tce).

Lotus Heart (☎ 379 0324; 595 Colombo St; mains NZ$7-13; breakfast Mon-Fri, lunch daily, dinner Fri only) Meditative, meat-free eatery, where Buddhist chanting or ethereal melodies may accompany your delicious Cajun veg stew, mushroom stroganoff or African beans. Also has organic coffee and great smoothies.

City Seafood Market (☎ 377 3377; 277 Manchester St; lunch Mon-Fri) The place to go to browse a variety of fresh, ice-packed seafood or to pick up some consistently cheap fish and chips (NZ$3).

Matsu Sushi (☎ 365 3822; 105 Armagh St; meals NZ$5-9; lunch Mon-Fri) This atmospheric little Japanese eatery doles out a sushi lunch box for NZ$5, plus noodle soups and other dishes for less than NZ$10.

Penang Noodle House (☎ 377 2638; 172 Manchester St; meals NZ$6.50-14; ⌚ lunch & dinner Mon-Sat) Don't be put off by the tattered menu out front and the browbeaten interior. This place serves good-value Malaysian food, including veg choices and the uncommon option of ostrich with satay sauce.

Copenhagen Bakery & Café (☎ 379 3935; Price Waterhouse Coopers Centre, 119 Armagh St; ⌚ breakfast & lunch) If the medals strung proudly above the display counter are anything to go by, you can snaffle some much-awarded tarts, quiches, cakes and breads here. Don't pass up the apple pie.

For reliable souvlaki, try **Dimitris** (☎ 377 7110; 709 Colombo St).

Restaurants

Topkapi (☎ 379 4447; 185 Manchester St; mains NZ$9.50-18; ⌚ lunch & dinner Mon-Sat) Grab yourself a cushioned, low-slung bench in the tapestry-draped interior and enjoy some great Turkish food, including a wide range of meat or veg kebabs. The takeaway counter does brisk business.

Dux de Lux (☎ 366 6919; cnr Hereford & Montreal Sts; mains NZ$15-22; ⌚ lunch & dinner) This vivacious place is a deserved crowd favourite for its hearty vegetarian and seafood menu, with veggie-packed curries, Mediterranean pizza and mushroom filo served up alongside Akaroa salmon and salt-and-pepper squid. It also scores highly for its outdoor courtyards, house-brewed beer and generally festive vibe. Most nights of the week there's also live music to aid your digestion (see p687).

Mythai (☎ 365 1295; 84 Hereford St; mains NZ$15-18; ⌚ lunch & dinner Mon-Sat) The cuisine of playfully exotic Mythai includes some flavoursome seafood, noodle and rice meals, with several veg choices. A memorable dish is the *pha sarm lot* (fish of the day in garlic and hot chilli sauce).

Ebisu (☎ 374 9375; 96 Hereford St; mains NZ$10-18; ⌚ lunch Fri, dinner nightly) This *izakaya* (Japanese-style pub) is outfitted with long bars and tables, and murals on the walls. It serves sashimi and other traditional fare, plus grilled dishes that are ideal for a group feast.

Two Fat Indians (☎ 371 7273; 112-114 Manchester St; mains NZ$13-20; ⌚ lunch & dinner) Attracting young backpackers and mixed-age locals alike, this polished twin-room eatery lives by the tagline, 'The art of pint and curry'. The extensive menu pleases both carnivores and vegetarians, and includes *palak kofta* (spinach dumplings) and a reliable chicken *tikka masala*. A minimum order of NZ$15 per person often applies.

Mum's (☎ 365 2211; cnr Colombo & Gloucester Sts; mains NZ$10-18; ⌚ lunch & dinner) Get a double hit of Asian flavours (Japanese and Korean) at this maternal restaurant. Korean meals include octopus and *sundae gugbab* (pork soup), while sushi and noodles round out the Japanese tastes, including a half-dozen vegetarian options.

> **SPLURGE!**
>
> **Santorini** (☎ 379 6975; cnr Gloucester St & Cambridge Tce; mains around NZ$25; ⌚ dinner Tue-Sat) A double-storey, wood-soaked place with an atmosphere that often imitates the outside mural of an impromptu Greek party. It serves up great moussaka, *brizola* (marinated rib-eye steak) and a range of *mezedakia* (appetisers), sometimes accompanied by live (and loud) bouzouki music.
>
> **Zydeco** (☎ 365 4556; 113 Manchester St; mains NZ$20-28; ⌚ dinner nightly) Blackened lamb, wild venison ragout and a hearty gumbo are just some of the Creole/Cajun dishes you can sample in this laid-back eatery. They couldn't resist some kitsch deep-South embellishments, like the 'gator stapled to one wall.
>
> **Sala Sala** (☎ 366 6755; 184 Oxford Tce; mains NZ$16-30; ⌚ lunch Mon-Fri, dinner nightly) This spacious, orderly restaurant serves all the usual Japanese standards, from tempura to sashimi and sushi platters (the latter for around NZ$20). The service is soothingly mild-mannered.

DRINKING

The chameleonic nature of the city's eating and drinking scene sees numerous restaurants and cafés packing away their menus later in the evening and distributing beer, wine and cocktail lists. Predictably, fashionable Oxford Tce is a prime area for after-dark bar hopping, but there are plenty of other places around the city centre to drink at, from crusty old pubs to taverns with thick knots of people around their pool tables.

Holy Grail (☎ 365 9816; 88 Worcester St) Set in a converted Art Deco theatre, the Holy Grail is a multilevel complex that includes a 10m-high screen with its own set of padded bleachers, pool tables, balcony bars and a minimalist dance floor. Caters mainly to sports lovers but there are also free DJs most nights.

Sullivans (☎ 379 7790; 150 Manchester St) Unsurprisingly, lots of Guinness and Kilkenny are downed here amid the usual Irish-pub décor. But, surprisingly, the bar doesn't usually open until 4pm and has been known to close on Sunday.

Loaded Hog (☎ 366 6674; cnr Manchester & Cashel Sts) Nonrustic place with brewery equipment strewn along the walls (in testimony to its naturally brewed beers) and a fondness for major sports events.

Grumpy Mole Saloon (☎ 371 9301; cnr Manchester & Cashel Sts) Unapologetically hewn from all manner of Wild West kitsch.

Jolly Poacher (☎ 379 5635; 31 Victoria St; 🕑 noon-dawn) Keeps dangerously long hours, so what starts off as a casual lunch could become a gruelling liquid marathon. The comfortable booths can get packed out by groups, particularly when a sporting contest is in the offing.

Vic & Whale (☎ 366 6355; 772 Colombo St) Large one-room saloon equipped with pool tables and oversized TVs. All the drinking action takes place around the big central bar and spilt drinks are not uncommon when things get busy.

Bailie's and the Belgian beer–themed Le Bar Bruxelle are both inside **Warners Hotel** (☎ 366 5159; 50 Cathedral Sq), with access to a good beer garden.

There are numerous establishments on Oxford Tce that swap their knives and forks for tumblers, wine glasses and beer goggles once meal time is over. They include **All Bar One** (☎ 377 9898; 130 Oxford Tce), which has a subdued interior and a manic outdoor area once the cocktail hour kicks in; **Coyote** (☎ 366 6055; 126 Oxford Tce), ostensibly a Tex-Mex eatery but with well-established bar credentials with younger night owls; **Viaduct** (☎ 366 6055; 126 Oxford Tce), popular for its food and its bar service; and the **Tap Room** (☎ 365 0547; 124 Oxford Tce), where the long-lunch and after-work crowds like to hang out.

CLUBBING

Nightclubs are mostly on Lichfield St, between Colombo and Manchester Sts, with their doors usually creaking open from 10pm Wednesday through Saturday. When you've exhausted the authentic clubbing options, head to Oxford Tce where numerous restaurants transform into late-night watering holes with DJs and impromptu dance floors. Nightclub admission normally ranges from free to NZ$10, though big-name DJ events can cost upwards of NZ$20.

Carbon (downstairs, 76 Lichfield St) Prominent, cocktail-shaking underground club that regularly hauls in DJs from around NZ and the UK, resulting in some huge house, jazz, hip-hop, dub and broken-beat gigs.

Base (☎ 377 7149; 1st fl, 674 Colombo St) Specialises in drum and bass, hard house and trance, with some nights seeing up to a half-dozen DJs sharing the turntables. Occasionally, this multilevel club lowers its colours with something tacky, like a 'Night in Ibiza' party.

eye spy (☎ 379 6634; 56 Lichfield St) One of the better bar-club hybrids on the Lichfield St clubbing strip, infused with a chilled-out orange glow and with some cute little seats out the back and funky DJ sounds from around 11pm. A good place for early-evening cocktail slurping.

Other clubs to try:

Heaven (☎ 377 9879; 633 Colombo St; 🕑 11pm-late Fri & Sat) Techno is the aural weapon of choice here.

Ministry/Smile (☎ 379 2910; 90 Lichfield St) Two venues in one big space, with all-star DJs often in attendance.

ENTERTAINMENT

Christchurch is the hub of the South Island's performing arts scene, with several excellent theatres; a major concert ticketing company is **Ticketek** (☎ 377 8899; www.ticketek.co.nz).

Live music in pubs, bars and cafés is mostly free. For info on live gigs (and clubbing events), get the free weekly flier the **Package** (www.thepackage.co.nz) and the free fortnightly leaflet **JAGG** (www.jagg.co.nz), available from Java Coffee House (p684) and other nightlife-conscious cafés, shops and venues. Also check out entertainment listings in the *Press* newspaper.

Theatre, Dance & Music

Town Hall (☎ 377 8899; www.ticketek.co.nz; 86 Kilmore St; adult/student from NZ$20/10; 🕑 box office 9am-5.30pm Mon-Fri, 10am-5pm Sat, later when events are on) The riverside town hall is one of the main venues for local performing arts, where you can hear a chamber or symphony orchestra, choirs and bands, or catch some theatre and the odd visiting hypnotist.

Theatre Royal (☎ 0800 205 050, 377 0100; 145 Gloucester St; NZ$25-85) Another stalwart of the local scene, where the Royal New Zealand Ballet might stage *Peter Pan* before being upstaged by the Canterbury Opera doing *La Traviata*.

Court Theatre (☎ 0800 333 100, 963 0870; www.courttheatre.org.nz; 20 Worcester St; adult/student from NZ$30/20; box office 9am-8pm Mon-Fri, 10am-8pm Sat) Located within the Arts Centre, the Court Theatre hosts year-round performances of everything from Samuel Beckett to *My Fair Lady*. The resident Court Jesters troupe stages its long-running improvised comedy show, *Scared Scriptless*, every Friday night at 11pm.

Cinemas

Average movie ticket prices are NZ$13/11/7.50 per adult/concession/child, with cheaper matinee sessions.

Hoyts (☎ 377 9945, session times 366 6367; www.hoyts.co.nz; 392 Moorhouse Ave) *American Pie* and *Matrix* sequels will probably keep appearing here for years to come.

Regent on Worcester (☎ 366 0140; 94 Worcester St) A classic, old cinema favouring middle-of-the-road films; not quite art house, but not blockbusters either.

Arts Centre Cinemas (☎ 366 0167; Arts Centre) Comprises two venues (the Academy and Cloisters) and, appropriately enough, they show art-house films.

Sport

Jade Stadium (☎ 379 1765, tickets 377 8899; 30 Stevens St) This stadium has been known to host cricket internationals, but it's best known as Canterbury's rugby heartland, where you can see the Crusaders in action in the Super 12 competition.

Live Music

Dux de Lux (☎ 366 6919; cnr Hereford & Montreal Sts) Invites ska, reggae, rock, pop and dub artistes to cater to demanding crowds at least several nights a week. It's also one of the city's busiest watering holes, particularly on a sunny day when the outdoor areas are a mass of raised glasses.

Mainstreet Café & Bar (☎ 365 0421; 840 Colombo St; admission free) Acoustic gigs and laid-back electronica can be heard in this casual café-bar space, as well as regular open mic nights (usually Tuesday).

Vic & Whale (☎ 366 6355; 772 Colombo St; admission free) The wood-panelled walls of this saloon resound with the noise of bands and DJs on Saturday night, sometimes Friday night too.

Southern Blues Bar (☎ 365 1654; 198 Madras St; admission free) This lively blues bar has nightly gigs (starting around 10.30pm) and a dance floor for aficionados of good blues music. It pulls a mixed, loquacious crowd of musicians, office workers and the terminally fashionable.

Sammy's Jazz Review (☎ 377 8618; www.sammys.co.nz; 14 Bedford Row; admission free) This great brick-walled, wood-floored jazz den is patronised nightly by notable local singers such as Gennine Bailey, and also accommodates the odd funk outfit. When the weather allows, retreat to the outdoor courtyard for some alfresco listening. There may be an admission charge for big-name acts.

Other places where you can catch live sounds:

Bailie's (☎ 366 5159; Warners Hotel, 50 Cathedral Sq) Free end-of-week gigs.

Sullivans (☎ 379 7790; 150 Manchester St) Free bands and regular Irish dancing.

Bog (☎ 379 7141; 82 Cashel St) Pub programme of DJs, live music and quiz nights.

Casino

Christchurch Casino (☎ 365 9999; www.christchurchcasino.co.nz; 30 Victoria St) The country's oldest casino is actually just over a decade old, but has quickly come to grips with the rewards of round-the-clock gambling.

SHOPPING

Colombo St, High St and Cashel St (including its pedestrianised mall) are all crammed with money-hungry places, particularly the fashion and accessories stores where the creative output of NZ designers is on display.

Swanndri Shop (☎ 379 8674; 123 Gloucester St) Fans of the 'Swannie', NZ's ubiquitous woollen checked shirt, will find what they're looking for here. Swanndri has also branched out into upmarket 'streetwise' garments, which presumably means your clothes can find their way home by themselves if necessary.

Champions of the World (☎ 377 4100; 767 Colombo St) All Blacks merchandise outlet with a rather immodest choice of name that has haunted it since the most recent World Cup. Snap up the NZ rugby union team's official jerseys, socks, ties, shorts, scarves…

The Arts Centre has dozens of craft shops and art galleries selling pottery, jewellery, woollen goods, Maori carvings, handmade toys and more; in some cases you can see the craftspeople at work. One of the best shops is **Cave Rock Gallery** (☎ 365 1634), with an excellent range of ceramics, glassware, fabrics (including kaleidoscopic blouses) and jewellery carved from jade and paua (abalone) shells. Every weekend the Arts Centre also has a lively craft and produce **market** (🕓 10am-4pm Sat & Sun), with buskers regularly in attendance.

For camping gear, tramping boots and other outdoors equipment, trek over to **Snowgum** (☎ 365 4336; 637 Colombo St) or **Mountain Designs** (☎ 377 8522; 654 Colombo St).

GETTING THERE & AWAY

Air

Christchurch Airport (☎ 358 5029; www.christchurch-airport.co.nz), 7km northwest of the city centre, is the main international gateway to the South Island; for info on the city's direct connections with several overseas destinations, including key Australian cities, see p799. The airport has excellent facilities, including a bureau de change, ATMs, baggage storage, car-rental desks, cafés and shops. It also has a **travel and information centre** (☎ 353 7040; travel&info@cial.co.nz) in both the domestic terminal (open 7.30am to 8pm) and the international terminal (open for all international flight arrivals). Passengers on international flights are charged a departure tax of NZ$25.

In conjunction with small affiliated airlines under the collective banner Air New Zealand Link, **Air New Zealand** (☎ 0800 737 000; www.airnz.co.nz) offers numerous direct domestic flights, with connections to other centres. There are direct flights to/from Auckland (from NZ$90), Blenheim (from NZ$85), Dunedin (from NZ$75), Hamilton (from NZ$120), Hokitika (from NZ$65), Invercargill (from NZ$85), Nelson (from NZ$75), Queenstown (from NZ$75), Wanaka (from NZ$80) and Wellington (from NZ$65). The airline has a large inner-city **travel centre** (☎ 363 0600; 549 Colombo St).

Qantas (☎ 0800 808 767, 379 6504; www.qantas.co.nz; Price Waterhouse Coopers Centre, 119 Armagh St) offers direct flights to Auckland (from NZ$90), Dunedin (from NZ$95), Invercargill (from NZ$150), Nelson (from NZ$125), Queenstown (from NZ$75), Rotorua (from NZ$105) and Wellington (from NZ$65).

Origin Pacific (☎ 0800 302 302, 547 2020; www.originpacific.co.nz) has direct flights to Dunedin (from NZ$75), Invercargill (from NZ$85), Nelson (from NZ$75) and Wellington (from NZ$65), with connections to other places.

Bus

InterCity (☎ 379 9020; www.intercitycoach.co.nz) buses depart from Worcester St, between the cathedral and Manchester St. Northbound buses go to Kaikoura (NZ$32, three hours), Blenheim (NZ$60, five hours) and Picton (NZ$65, 5½ hours), with connections to Nelson (NZ$70, eight hours). Buses also go west direct to Queenstown (NZ$60, 7½ hours), or to Queenstown (NZ$135, 10 hours) via Mt Cook (NZ$75, 5½ hours). There are also direct services to Wanaka (NZ$95, seven hours). Heading south, buses run along the coast via the towns along SH1 to Dunedin (NZ$55, six hours), with connections to Invercargill (NZ$75, 9¾ hours) and Te Anau (NZ$75, 10½ hours).

Coast to Coast (☎ 0800 800 847; www.coast2coast.co.nz) and **Alpine Coaches** (☎ 0800 274 888; www.alpinecoaches.co.nz) run from Christchurch to Greymouth and Hokitika (both NZ$35) via Arthur's Pass (NZ$25).

Myriad shuttle buses run to destinations such as Akaroa, Dunedin, Hanmer Springs, Picton, Queenstown, Wanaka, Hokitika and points in between, most of them can be booked at the visitors centre; see the sections on the respective towns for details.

For information about backpacker buses rumbling through Christchurch, see p792.

Car, Campervan & Motorcycle

HIRE

Major car and campervan rental companies all have offices in Christchurch, as do numerous smaller local companies; see the lengthy list in the *Yellow Pages*. Operators with national networks often want cars to be returned from Christchurch to Auckland because most renters travel in the opposite direction, so special rates may apply. For reliable national rental companies, see p794.

Smaller-scale rental companies:

First Choice (☎ 0800 736 822, 365 9261; www.firstchoice.co.nz; 132 Kilmore St)

Mac's Rent-A-Car (☎ 0800 154 155, 377 9660; www.macsrentals.co.nz; 156 Tuam St)

New Zealand Motorcycle Rentals (☎ 377 0663; www.nzbike.com; 166 Gloucester St) Also does guided tours.
Pegasus Rental Cars (☎ 0800 803 580, 365 1100; www.rentalcars.co.nz; 127 Peterborough St)

BUYING A CAR

If you want to buy or sell a car, check out **Backpackers Bazaar** (☎ 379 3700; www.backpackercars.co.nz; cnr Tuam & Barbadoes Sts). The **Canterbury Car Fair** (☎ 338 5525; Addington Raceway, Wrights Rd entrance; 9am-noon Sun) has a sellers fee of NZ$20. **Turners Auctions** (☎ 366 1807; www.turners.co.nz; 32 Moorhouse Ave) buys and sells used cars by auction; vehicles priced under NZ$6000 usually go under the hammer (metaphorically) at 6pm on Tuesday and Thursday.

Train

Christchurch Railway Station (☎ 0800 872 467, 341 2588; Troup Dr, Addington; ticket office 7am-4.30pm) is where you can catch the *TranzCoastal* train service, which runs daily each way between Christchurch and Picton via Kaikoura and Blenheim, departing Christchurch at 7.30am and arriving in Picton at 12.50pm; fares to Picton start around NZ$40 per person. The *TranzAlpine* runs daily between Christchurch and Greymouth via Arthur's Pass (see the boxed text on p709); there are various fares, with the cheapest one-way tickets starting around NZ$70. For more information about both these services and the various fares available, contact **Tranz Scenic** (☎ 0800 872 467; www.tranzscenic.co.nz).

GETTING AROUND

For details of how to get into town from the airport and train station, see the boxed text on p674.

Bus

The Christchurch **bus network** (Metro; ☎ info line 366 8855; www.metroinfo.org.nz; info line 6.30am-10.30pm Mon-Sat, 9am-9pm Sun), operated by a private business/government consortium, is inexpensive and efficient. Most buses run from the **City Bus Exchange** (Colombo St), with its pedestrian entrance opposite Ballantynes department store. The exchange has an information desk; or, get timetables from the visitors centre. A cash fare to anywhere in the city proper is NZ$2. Metrocards allow two-hour/full-day travel for NZ$1.50/3, but the catch is that the cards must be loaded up with a minimum of NZ$10 first.

For information about the following two services, contact **Red Bus** (☎ 0800 733 287; www.redbus.co.nz). The Shuttle is a free inner-city service (it goes as far north as Kilmore St, and south to Moorhouse Ave) with about 20 pick-up points; it runs every 10 to 15 minutes from 8am to 10.30pm Monday to Thursday, to midnight Friday, from 9.30am to midnight Saturday, and 10am to 8pm Sunday. The After Midnight Express (NZ$4) operates on four suburban routes, most of them departing Oxford Tce; it departs hourly between midnight and 4am Friday and Saturday.

The **Best Attractions Shuttle** (24hr pass NZ$15) is operated by **Canterbury Leisure Tours** (☎ 0800 484 485, 384 0999) and links major attractions such as the International Antarctic Centre, the gondola and Willowbank Wildlife Reserve. It departs Cathedral Sq every 1½ to two hours from 9am to 7pm late December to late April, and 10am to 5.10pm the rest of the year.

Car, Campervan & Motorcycle

For drivers, Christchurch's network of one-way streets can create a little confusion, particularly for those of us whose sense of direction deserts them once they leave their own driveway – equip yourself with a decent map. If you want to avoid the metered parking or car parks of the inner-city streets, check out the all-day parking areas a half-dozen blocks out of the centre (eg east of Latimer Sq).

Taxi

Christchurch's main taxi companies:
Blue Star (☎ 379 9799)
First Direct (☎ 377 5555)
Gold Band (☎ 379 5795)

CANTERBURY

The Canterbury region has a physical presence that slowly builds from the volcanically uplifted hills of Banks Peninsula and the expansive, well-farmed flat lands of Canterbury Plain to the mountaineer-calling pinnacles of the Southern Alps. It's the stuff of classic NZ holiday snaps and still-life videos: emerald, sheep-strewn pastures backed by jagged, snow-tipped mountains.

Beyond the urban attractions of Christchurch are numerous environmental treats,

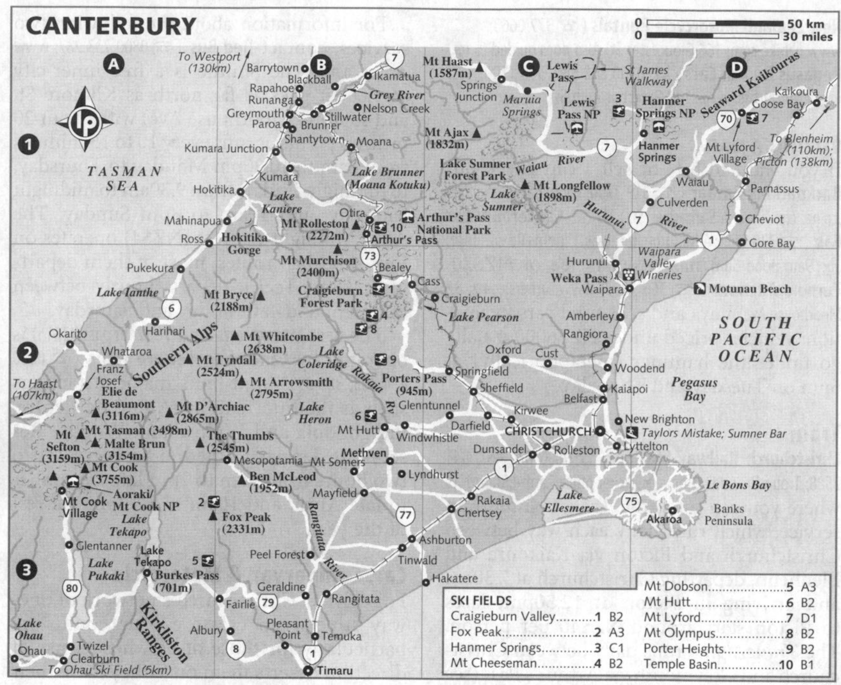

such as the dolphin-cruised harbour just off the Francophile town of Akaroa, the sulphur pools and jet-boat-happy canyons at Hanmer Springs, the forested terraces lining Arthur's Pass, and the vivid hues of Lake Tekapo. One of NZ's most inspiring sights is of the highest peak in Aoraki/Mt Cook National Park on a bright day, with the névés and seracs of nearby Tasman Glacier providing impressive scenic support.

Activities

Tramp across the hills of Banks Peninsula or the heights of Arthur's Pass National Park, walk under the massive icy overhang of Aoraki/Mt Cook, swim with dolphins in Akaroa Harbour, bungy jump or jet-boat in Thrillseekers Canyon and snowboard the wild slopes of Craigieburn and Mt Hutt; these are just some of the possibilities to exhaust yourself with around Canterbury.

BANKS PENINSULA

Banks Peninsula and its appealing hills were formed by two giant volcanic eruptions. Small harbours such as Le Bons, Pigeon and Little Akaroa Bays radiate out from the peninsula's centre, giving it a cogwheel shape. The historic town of Akaroa is a highlight.

James Cook sighted the peninsula in 1770 and thought it was an island, promptly naming it after naturalist Sir Joseph Banks. The Ngai Tahu tribe, who occupied the peninsula at the time, were attacked at the Onawe *pa* by the Ngati Toa chief Te Rauparaha in 1831, dramatically reducing their population.

In 1838 whaling captain Jean Langlois negotiated the purchase of Banks Peninsula from the local Maori and returned to France to form a trading company. With French-government backing, 63 settlers headed for the peninsula in 1840. But only days before they arrived, panicked British officials sent their own warship to raise the flag at Akaroa, claiming British sovereignty under the Treaty of Waitangi. Had the settlers arrived two years earlier, the South Island may well have become a French colony.

The French did settle at Akaroa, but in 1849 their land claim was sold to the New Zealand Company and the following year a large group of British settlers arrived. The heavily forested land was cleared and soon dairy farming (later supplanted by sheep farming) became the peninsula's main industry.

SLEEPING

Onuku Farm Hostel (☎ 03-304 7066; Onuku Rd; dm NZ$14-22, d NZ$45; ⏲ Sep-Apr) Wonderful backpackers on a 340-hectare sheep farm near Onuku, 5km south of Akaroa. The owners organise swimming-with-dolphins tours (NZ$80) and kayaking trips (NZ$25) for guests, and will also lob a free fishing line your way. They pick up from Akaroa.

Le Bons Bay Backpackers (☎ 03-304 8582; Le Bons Bay Rd; dm/d NZ$20/50; ⏲ Oct-May) Six kilometres before Le Bons Bay is this excellent restored farmhouse, wedged in a glorious valley. Besides bucolic splendour, you can also enjoy gourmet dinners (NZ$12, including veg options) and two-hour wildlife-spotting bay tours (NZ$22). The owners will pick up from Akaroa. Book ahead as beds are in demand.

Le Bons Bay Holiday Park (☎ 03-304 8533; lebonsholiday@xtra.co.nz; Le Bons Bay Rd; camp sites per 2 people NZ$22, d NZ$50) Speaking of things bucolic, occupy a stream-side camp site or one of the trim little cabins at this secluded holiday park.

Okains Bay Camping Ground (☎ 03-304 8789; 1162 Okains Bay Rd; camp sites per 2 people from NZ$12) Nice, pine tree–peppered place. Permits to unfold and erect your sheets of canvas are available from the house at the camping ground's entrance.

Ten kilometres before Akaroa at Duvauchelle is the basic **Duvauchelle Reserve Board Motor Camp** (☎ 03-304 5777; Seafield Rd; camp sites per 2 people NZ$20, s & d NZ$30), with pleasant foreshore sites and ultra-simple cabins backed by green hills. The friendly **Hotel des Pecheurs** (☎ 03-304 5803; Duvauchelle; dm NZ$15, d NZ$75-85) has plain motel rooms, simple backpacker accommodation across the road (add NZ$5 for linen) and good-value meals.

Akaroa

☎ 03 / pop 650

Akaroa is a Maori word for 'Long Harbour' and is the site of the country's first French settlement; in fact, descendants of the original French settlers still reside here.

Located 82km from Christchurch, this is a charming town on a scenic harbour that strives to re-create the feel of a French provincial village, down to the names of its streets (rues Lavaud, Balguerie, Jolie) and houses (Langlois-Eteveneaux).

INFORMATION

There's heaps of information stockpiled at **Akaroa visitors centre** (☎ 304 8600; www.akaroa.com; 80 Rue Lavaud; ⏲ 9am-5pm). There's an ATM-equipped Bank of New Zealand branch opposite the visitors centre and Internet access at **Bon-E-Mail** (☎ 304 7447; 41 Rue Lavaud; per 20min NZ$2; ⏲ 9am-8pm).

SIGHTS & ACTIVITIES

The interesting **Akaroa Museum** (☎ 304 1013; cnr Rues Lavaud & Balguerie; adult/student NZ$4/3.50; ⏲ 10.30am-4.30pm Oct-Apr, 10.30am-4pm May-Sep) is spread over several historic buildings, including the old courthouse, the tiny Custom House by Daly's Wharf, and one of NZ's oldest houses, Langlois-Eteveneaux. It has modest displays on the peninsula's once-significant Maori population, a courtroom diorama and Akaroa community relics and archives (check out the weird timeline entwining major global events with NZ history).

The **Maori & Colonial Museum** (☎ 304 8611; Okains Bay; adult NZ$5; ⏲ 10am-5pm) started life as a private collection of indigenous and pioneer artefacts but went public 25 years ago. Located northeast of Akaroa, it features a reproduction Maori *whare runanga* (meeting house), a sacred 15th-century god stick and a war canoe.

The *Akaroa Historic Area Walk* booklet (NZ$5) details an excellent **walking tour**, starting at the 1876 **Waeckerle Cottage** and finishing at the old Taylor's Emporium premises near the wharf, along the way taking in all the wonderful old wooden buildings and churches that give the town its character.

To really break into stride, tackle the **Banks Peninsula Track** (☎ 304 7612; www.bankstrack.co.nz; NZ$180). It's a 35km, four-day walk across private farmland and then around the dramatic coastline of Banks Peninsula; cost includes transport from Akaroa and hut accommodation. There's also a more leisurely two-day option (NZ$120).

Dolphins Up Close (www.swimmingwithdolphins.co.nz; Main Wharf; cruise & swim NZ$95, cruise only NZ$45) attempts to get you swimming alongside harbour-cruising dolphins, assuming the animals are around and feeling sociable. **Dolphin**

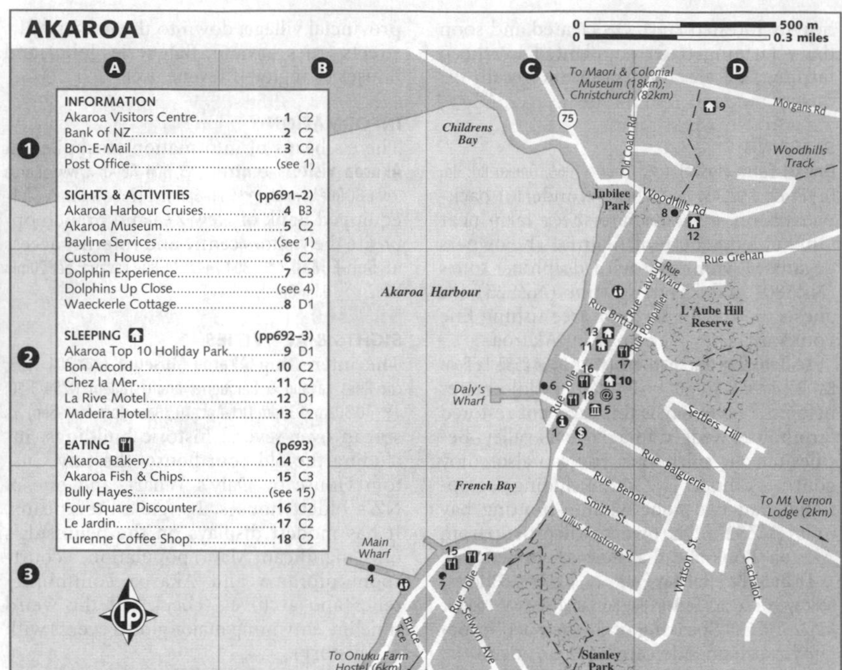

Experience (☎ 0508 365 744, 304 7726; www.dolphinsakaroa.co.nz; 61 Beach Rd; cruise & swim NZ$80, cruise only NZ$35) also has popular dolphin-swimming trips.

TOURS

To go in search of Hectors dolphins and blue penguins, take a two-hour harbour cruise with **Akaroa Harbour Cruises** (☎ 0800 436 574, 304 7641; www.canterburycat.co.nz; Main Wharf; NZ$39; 1.30pm, plus 11am Nov-Mar).

Bayline Services (☎ 304 7207; 108 Rue Jolie; NZ$20; 8.20am Mon-Sat) operates the Eastern Bays Scenic Mail Run, a 140km, five-hour delivery service to remote parts of the peninsula, and visitors can come along to visit the isolated communities and bays. It departs from the visitors centre; bookings are essential. It also does a 2½-hour tour of the inner bays (NZ$20; departs 2pm with a minimum of four people).

SLEEPING

Bon Accord (☎ 304 7782; www.bon-accord.co.nz; 57 Rue Lavaud; dm/d NZ$22/50;) Friendly backpackers in a compact 150-year-old house, complete with a garden in which to empty your mind and summer barbecues to occupy your stomach.

Chez la Mer (☎ 304 7024; chez_la_mer@clear.net.nz; 50 Rue Lavaud; dm NZ$20, s/d from NZ$35/50) Similarly historic and garden-equipped, and offering free mountain bike use.

Mt Vernon Lodge (☎ 304 7180; Rue Balguerie; camp sites per 2 people NZ$30, dm/d from NZ$18/50;) Laid-back Mt Vernon is a YHA-associated lodge 2km from town (free pick up is offered), set in the middle of extensive rural grounds where you can choose between dorms and self-contained cabins. Nature walks and horse treks are two of the possible distractions.

Madeira Hotel (☎ 304 7009; 48 Rue Lavaud; s/d NZ$20/40) An excellent accommodation deal is provided by this big, atmospheric hotel, with dirt-cheap prices for clean, well-kept rooms.

La Rive Motel (☎ 0800 247 651, 304 7651; larive@paradise.net.nz; 1 Rue Lavaud; d from NZ$75) Another good deal, this old-style motel has big, light-filled rooms and good facilities, well priced considering each unit is self-contained.

Akaroa Top 10 Holiday Park (☎ 304 7471; akaroa.holidaypark@xtra.co.nz; 96 Morgans Rd; camp sites per 2 people NZ$24, d NZ$40-70) On a hillside above town but connected by a pathway to Woodhills Rd, this pleasant park has good harbour views and options for every budget, including low-cost cabins.

EATING

Le Jardin (☎ 304 7447; 41 Rue Lavaud; meals NZ$6-15; ⏲ lunch & dinner Wed-Sun) Set in a converted old house cradled by delightful gardens, Le Jardin has good light meals such as chicken laksa and ricotta, and rice and spinach cakes to munch at a table out the front or in the stylish interior.

Madeira Hotel (☎ 304 7009; 48 Rue Lavaud; mains NZ$13-17; ⏲ lunch & dinner) Good NZ pub fare such as pork bangers in brown-onion sauce is served in the Madeira's red-boothed dining room. There's a pleasant beer garden and live bands often play on summer weekends.

Bully Hayes (☎ 304 7533; 57 Beach Rd; mains NZ$10-17; ⏲ breakfast, lunch & dinner) Brasserie-style waterfront café-bar with a small outdoor terrace and a menu consisting of pesto chicken, char-grilled beef salad, green-lipped mussels and breakfast pancakes.

Turenne Coffee Shop (☎ 304 7005; 74 Rue Lavaud; meals NZ$4-8; ⏲ breakfast & lunch; 💻) Inventive tearoom fare such as *gado gado* flan, and pumpkin and mushroom pie.

French Farm Winery (☎ 304 5784; French Farm Valley Rd; mains NZ$14-22; ⏲ lunch) Through the lavender-wreathed entrance of the winery's main house, set amid beautiful grounds on the western side of Akaroa Harbour, is a good restaurant. A cheese board for two costs NZ$22, and in summer pizzas are served alfresco. Try one of the winery's white wines or its orange-steeped liqueur.

Barrys Bay Cheese (☎ 304 5809; Barrys Bay; ⏲ 9.30am-5.30pm) Pick up fine cheddar, havarti, gouda and flavoured cheeses. Near to French Farm Winery.

For pastries, sandwiches and cakes, try the **Akaroa Bakery** (☎ 304 7663; 51 Beach Rd; ⏲ breakfast & lunch), while **Akaroa Fish & Chips** (☎ 304 7464; 59 Beach Rd) serves up marine takeaway.

Self-caterers should head for the **Four Square Discounter** (Rue Lavaud; ⏲ 9am-6pm Mon-Sat).

GETTING THERE & AWAY

The **Akaroa Shuttle** (☎ 0800 500 929; www.akaroashuttle.co.nz) departs from outside the Christchurch visitors centre at 8.30am and 2pm daily from November to April, and 8.30am Saturday to Thursday (plus 4.30pm on Friday) from May to October (bookings essential in winter), returning from Akaroa two to three times daily; return fare NZ$20. **French Connection** (☎ 0800 800 575) leaves Christchurch visitors centre at 8.45am, returning from Akaroa at 2.30pm daily (plus 3.45pm April to August, and 4.15pm September to March). Fares are NZ$15, or NZ$20 return; bicycles cost NZ$5 extra and must be pre-booked.

HANMER SPRINGS

☎ 03 / pop 750

Hanmer Springs, the main thermal resort on the South Island, is 10km off SH7, also called the Lewis Pass Hwy – this highway branches off SH1 to the north of Christchurch and after the Hanmer Springs turn-off, it wiggles its way west along a beautiful route to the 907m-high Lewis Pass, then Maruia Springs, Springs Junction and eventually the West Coast.

Apart from its body-crowded hot pools, Hanmer Springs is extremely popular for high-energy outdoor activities that include jet-boating, rafting, bungy jumping and skiing. Visitors swell the population year-round, as Hanmer is a favourite weekend destination for Christchurch-based folk.

Information

Bank of New Zealand ATM (Hurunui visitors centre; ⏲ 9am-9pm)

Hanmer Springs Adventure Centre (☎ 315 7233; 20 Conical Hill Rd; fishing rods per day NZ$25, scooters per hr NZ$28; ⏲ 9am-5pm) Supplies info on (and handles bookings for) various activities, and rents a wide range of sports equipment, including skiing and snowboarding gear.

Hanmer Springs Medical Centre (☎ 315 7503; 20 Amuri Ave)

Hurunui visitors centre (☎ 0800 442 663, 315 7128; www.hurunui.com; Amuri Ave; ⏲ 10am-5pm) Books accommodation, transport and local activities.

Activities

SOAKING & SWIMMING

Visitors have been soaking in the waters of **Hanmer Springs Thermal Reserve** (☎ 315 7511; www.hotfun.co.nz; cnr Jacks Pass Rd & Amuri Ave; adult NZ$10; ⏲ 10am-9pm) for more than 100 years. Local legend has it that the thermal springs are a piece of the fires of Tamatea that dropped from the sky after an eruption of Mt Ngauruhoe on the North Island –

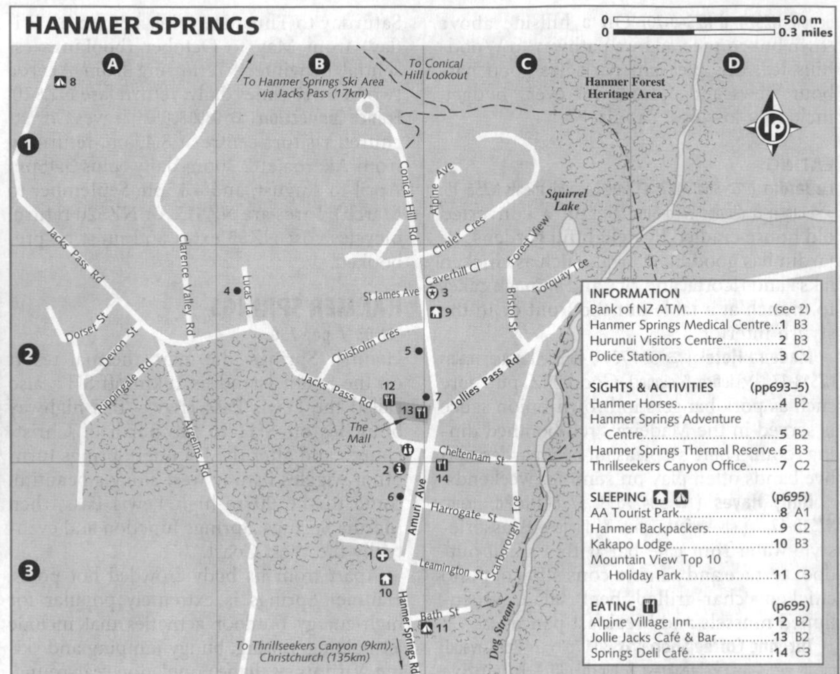

Maori call the springs Waitapu (sacred waters).

The hot spring water mixes with freshwater to produce pools of varying temperatures. In addition to the mineral pools, there are landscaped rock pools, sulphur pools, a freshwater 25m lap pool, private sauna/steam suites (NZ$17 per half-hour), massage facilities, a restaurant (see Garden House Café, opposite) and a family activity area that includes a waterslide (NZ$5).

THRILL SEEKING

In case the name isn't a big enough hint, **Thrillseekers Canyon** (☎ 315 7046; www.thrillseeker.co.nz; bungy jump NZ$115, jet-boating from NZ$70, rafting NZ$85) is the adrenaline centre of Hanmer Springs. You can hurl yourself off a 35m-high ferry bridge with a bungy cord, jet-boat through the Waiau Gorge or go white-water rafting (grade two to three) down the Waiau River. Book at the Thrillseekers Canyon centre, next to the bridge where the Hanmer Springs turn-off meets SH7. There's also an **information/booking office** (☎ 315 7346; the Mall) in town.

SKIING & SNOWBOARDING

The **Hanmer Springs Ski Area** (☎ 341 806; www.snow.co.nz/hanmersprings/index.htm; daily lift passes NZ$35) is based on Mt St Patrick, 17km from Hanmer Springs, and has mostly intermediate and advanced runs. Another snowy option is **Mt Lyford** (p659), about 60km from Hanmer Springs. The **Hanmer Springs Adventure Centre** (☎ 315 7233; 20 Conical Hill Rd) operates shuttle buses to the Hanmer Springs Ski Area (NZ$20) and Mt Lyford (NZ$30).

OTHER ACTIVITIES

The pamphlet titled *Hanmer Forest Recreation* (NZ$1) outlines pleasant short walks near town, mostly through picturesque forest. The easy **Woodland Walk** starts from Jollies Pass Rd, 1km from town, and goes through Douglas fir, poplar and redwood stands. It joins the **Majuba Walk**, which leads to **Conical Hill Lookout** and then back to Conical Hill Rd, about 1½ hours all up. The visitors centre has details of longer tramps, including in Lake Sumner Forest Park.

Hanmer Horses (☎ 0800 873 546, 315 7444; www.hanmerhorses.co.nz; Lucas Lane; 1hr rides NZ$40) will go riding over hill, dale, tussock and mountain, should they be required to. They'll even lead littlies on a 20-minute pony ride (NZ$10).

BackTrax (☎ 0800 422 258, 315 7684; www.backtrax.co.nz; 2½hr trip NZ$130) organises quad-bike trips up into the hills and along (and across) the Hanmer River; minimum age for participants is 16. The region is also popular for mountain biking – the **Hanmer Springs Adventure Centre** (☎ 315 7233; 20 Conical Hill Rd; bike hire per hr/half-day/full day NZ$15/25/35; 🕑 9am-5pm) offers trail maps, advice and bike rental, and also does an organised ride (NZ$75) over Jacks and Jollies Passes.

Sleeping

Hanmer Backpackers (☎ 315 7196; hanmerbackpackers@hotmail.com; 41 Conical Hill Rd; dm/d NZ$20/50; 💻) The township's original backpackers has had some good work done to its small dimensions in recent times and now sports a bigger kitchen and a mezzanine lounge. It's inviting and comfortable, and has a barbecue area to hang about in during summer and a log fire to huddle next to in winter.

Kakapo Lodge (☎ 315 7472; stay-kakapo@xtra.co.nz; 14 Amuri Ave; dm NZ$20-24, d NZ$55-75; 💻) The YHA-affiliated Kakapo Lodge has a simple, uncluttered aesthetic enhanced by a roomy kitchen and lounge, under-floor heating to banish winter chills, and an outdoor deck. Besides rooms in the main lodge, there are also several motel-style units.

Mountain View Top 10 Holiday Park (☎ 0800 904 545, 315 7113; www.holidayparks.co.nz/mtnview; Bath St; camp sites unpowered/powered per 2 people NZ$20/24, d NZ$40-80) This fresh-aired, amenity-ridden and fairly busy park is located only a few minutes' walk from the thermal reserve. You'll need your own linen and towel for all accommodation except some self-contained units.

AA Tourist Park (☎ 315 7112; aatouristpark@xtra.co.nz; 200 Jacks Pass Rd; camp sites unpowered/powered per 2 people NZ$18/24, d NZ$26-65) This large, well-run park is 3km from town and has cheap, no-frills caravans, plus some budget cabins with the power unplugged. The camp and campervan sites are sizeable.

Eating & Drinking

Springs Deli Café (☎ 315 7430; 47Amuri Ave; meals NZ$9-15; 🕑 breakfast & lunch) Cruisey main-street café with great breakfast selections and a variety of quiches, focaccias and sweet nibbles for lunch. One of Hanmer Springs' better-value cafés, and usually crowded for this reason.

Garden House Café (☎ 315 7115; Amuri Ave; mains NZ$10-14; 🕑 lunch & dinner) This café in the thermal reserve has an outside deck on which you can dry out your wrinkly skin and fill your stomach with burgers, omelettes, salads and pastas; it also has a kids' menu.

Alpine Village Inn (☎ 315 7005; 10 Jacks Pass Rd; mains NZ$12-20; 🕑 lunch & dinner) Timber-clad place better known as the local boozer but doing a sideline in reasonably priced bistro meals such as giant T-bone steaks and chicken cordon bleu.

Jollie Jacks Café & Bar (☎ 315 7388, 12a Conical Hill Rd; mains NZ$13-25; 🕑 lunch & dinner) A decent spot for an extended meal. It has a pleasant, high-ceilinged interior and a scattering of outdoor tables. The daytime fare is along the lines of pizza, Asian beef salad and corn and crab fritters.

Getting There & Away

The **Hanmer Connection** (☎ 0800 377 378) runs from Hanmer Springs to Christchurch (NZ$25) and Kaikoura (NZ$30).

ARTHUR'S PASS

☎ 03

About a two-hour road trip west from Christchurch on SH73 is the glorious mountainscape of **Arthur's Pass National Park**. The island crossing from Christchurch to Greymouth, over Arthur's Pass, is a scenic route covered by buses and the *TranzAlpine* train (see the boxed text on p709).

Nowhere else in NZ do you get a better picture of the climb from sea to mountains. From Christchurch, almost at sea level, the road heads over the flat Canterbury Plains, then winds up into the skiing areas of Craigieburn before following the Waimakariri and Bealey Rivers to Arthur's Pass, passing handsome lakes such as Pearson and Grasmere along the way.

The settlement of Arthur's Pass is 4km from the pass of the same name and is the highest town in NZ. The 924m pass was on the route used by the Maori to reach Westland but its European discovery was made by Arthur Dobson in 1864, when the Westland gold rush created enormous pressure to find a crossing over the Southern Alps from Christchurch. A coach road was completed within a year of Dobson's discovery, but the coal and timber trade later demanded a railway, duly completed in 1923.

The town is a handy base for walks, climbs, views and winter skiing in Arthur's Pass National Park and nearby Craigieburn Forest Park.

Information

Arthur's Pass visitors centre (☎ 318 9211; SH73; 8.30am-5pm), run by DOC, has information on all park walks, including route guides for the longer, hut-lined tramps. It doesn't make onward bookings or reservations, but can help with local accommodation and transport info. The centre also screens a 17-minute video (per adult NZ$1) on the history of Arthur's Pass and has excellent displays – check out the 1888 Cobb & Co coach in a back room. About 150m from the visitors centre is the local **chapel** – make time for a visit and enjoy a lovely surprise inside.

Trampers can hire detailed topo maps (NZ$1 per day, with NZ$20 refundable deposit) from the visitors centre. Staff also offer invaluable advice on the park's often savagely changeable weather conditions. Check conditions here and fill out an intentions card before going on any walk; be sure to sign out after returning, otherwise it'll send a search party to find you!

For online info, visit www.softrock.co.nz/apis. There's Internet access at the **Sanctuary** (SH73; per hr NZ$5), a gift shop with a couple of terminals stowed away in a small annex.

Activities

WALKING

Day-long walks in the Arthur's Pass National Park offer fantastic 360-degree views of snow-capped peaks, many of them over 2000m; the highest is Mt Murchison (2400m). There are huts on the tramping tracks and several areas suitable for camping. The leaflet *Walks in Arthur's Pass National Park* (NZ$1) details walks to scenic places such as **Temple Basin** (three hours return), **Mt Bealey**, **Mt Aicken** and **Avalanche Peak** (all six to eight hours return).

Longer tramps with superb alpine backdrops include the two-day-long **Goat Pass Track** and the difficult **Harman Pass** and **Harpers Pass Tracks**. Such tracks require previous tramping experience as flooding can make the rivers dangerous to cross and the weather is extremely changeable; seek advice from DOC first.

Craigieburn Forest Park, 42km south of Arthur's Pass, has a significant system of walking tracks, with longer tramps possible in the valleys west of the Craigieburn Range – see the DOC pamphlet *Craigieburn Forest Park: Day Walks* (NZ$1).

SKIING & SNOWBOARDING

There are five ski areas in the Arthur's Pass and nearby Craigieburn regions.

Temple Basin (☎ 377 7788; www.templebasin.co.nz; daily lift passes NZ$38) is a club area just 4km from Arthur's Pass township, with half its terrain taken up by advanced runs. It's a 50-minute uphill walk from the car park to the ski-area lodges. There's floodlit skiing at night and good back-country runs for snowboarders.

Craigieburn Valley (☎ 365 2514, snowphone 366 7766; www.craigieburn.co.nz; daily lift passes NZ$45), centred on Hamilton Peak in Craigieburn Forest Park, is a ski area 40km from Arthur's Pass. It's one of NZ's most challenging club areas, with intermediate and advanced runs and a shredder's 'soggy dream'. It's a pleasant 10-minute walk through beech forest from the car park to the ski area.

Another good club area in the Craigieburn Range is **Mt Cheeseman** (☎ 379 5315; www.mtcheeseman.com; daily lift passes NZ$45). The ski area, based on Mt Cockayne, is in a wide, sheltered basin.

Also in Craigieburn and hard to find, but worth the search, is **Mt Olympus** (☎ 318 5840; www.mtolympus.co.nz; daily lift passes NZ$35). This club area has four tows that lead to intermediate and advanced runs. Snowboarding is allowed, there are good cross-country areas and ski-touring trails to other areas. Transport by 4WD is advisable from the bottom hut.

To the south of the Craigieburn Range, about 65km from Arthur's Pass township and 96km from Christchurch, is the commercial ski area of **Porter Heights** (☎ 318 4002; www.porterheights.co.nz; daily lift passes NZ$50). Its 720m-long 'Big Mama' is the steepest run in NZ and there's a half-pipe for snowboarders, plus good cross-country areas and ski touring out along the ridge.

Sleeping & Eating

Arthur's Pass Alpine YHA (☎ 318 9230; yha.arthurspass@yha.org.nz; SH73, Arthur's Pass; camp sites per 2 people NZ$20, dm/d from NZ$20/50) Friendly, well-maintained hostel, with a near-permanent log fire blazing away due to the Southern Alps' chill. Offers lots of advice on regional walks and there's plenty of room to stow gear and bikes.

Mountain House Backpackers (☎ 318 9258; www.trampers.co.nz; SH73, Arthur's Pass; camp sites per 2 people NZ$24, dm/d NZ$21/55) This lodge gets the thumbs up from many travellers for its cosy feel, good facilities and predisposition towards local walks and tramps.

Alpine Motel (☎ 318 9233; alpine.motels@xtra.co.nz; SH73, Arthur's Pass; d NZ$70-95) Tucked away in the southern part of town is this small complex of comfortable motel units. Car storage is available if you're going to disappear into the wilderness for a while.

Bealey Hotel (☎ 318 9277; www.bealeyhotel.co.nz; SH73, Bealey; dm NZ$20, d NZ$85-95) This hotel is 12km east of Arthur's Pass at Bealey, a tiny settlement famous for a hoax staged by the local publican in 1993 that led New Zealanders to believe that a live moa had been sighted in the area. There is the budget Moa Lodge (with 10 double rooms), self-contained motel units and a restaurant and bar.

Flock Hill Lodge (☎ 318 8196; www.flockhill.co.nz; SH73; dm/d NZ$18/120) High-country sheep station 44km east of Arthur's Pass, adjacent to the Craigieburn Forest Park. Backpackers after a rustic experience can stay in old shearers' quarters, while others can opt for two-bedroom motel units or large cottages with kitchenettes; one room is fully equipped for disabled travellers. When you're not renting mountain bikes or fishing gear, feed your face in the restaurant or bar.

Smylie's Accommodation (☎ 318 4740; Main Rd, Springfield; s NZ$20-45, d NZ$65) A YHA-associated hostel around 30km southeast of Craigieburn, run by a family whose surname is fortunately not Simpson. There's a strong Japanese influence here, most evident in the food, the popular Japanese bath, *kotatsu* (foot warmer) and some futon-equipped rooms. In winter, ski equipment, meals and ski-field transport are provided.

You can camp within Arthur's Pass township at the basic **public shelter** (NZ$5), where there's stream water, a sink, tables and toilets. Camping is free at Klondyke Corner, 8km south of Arthur's Pass, and Kelly Shelter, 17km northwest; both have toilets and the water must be boiled before drinking.

Arthur's Pass Store & Tearooms (☎ 318 9235; SH73, Arthur's Pass; ⏰ 7.30am-7pm) Sells sandwiches, pies, other hot snacks, basic groceries and expensive petrol; at the time of research it was expanding its premises.

Oscar's Haus Alpine Café (☎ 318 9234; SH73, Arthur's Pass; mains from NZ$10; ⏰ lunch & dinner) A licensed café serving good-value meals (open until late in summer).

Chalet Restaurant (☎ 318 9236; SH73, Arthur's Pass; mains NZ$13-30; ⏰ lunch & dinner) Downstairs in the Chalet accommodation complex, this restaurant is where you can eat the likes of chicken or veg hotpot and lamb shanks in the bistro or à la carte restaurant. For an upmarket eatery, the food and service aren't always reliable.

Getting There & Around

Arthur's Pass is on the main run for buses between Christchurch (NZ$25) and Greymouth (NZ$20); **Atomic Shuttles** (☎ 322 8883; www.atomictravel.co.nz), **Alpine Coaches** (☎ 0800 274 888; www.alpinecoaches.co.nz) and **Coast to Coast** (☎ 0800 800 847; www.coast2coast.co.nz) all stop here.

The *TranzAlpine* train, operated by **Tranz Scenic** (☎ 0800 872 467; www.tranzscenic.co.nz), runs between Christchurch and Greymouth via Arthur's Pass. It leaves Arthur's Pass for Greymouth (from NZ$37) at 10.45am and for Christchurch (from NZ$50) at 4pm. Bus and train tickets are sold at the **Arthur's Pass Store & Tearooms** (☎ 318 9235; SH73, Arthur's Pass).

The road over the pass was once winding and very steep – the most tortuous of all the South Island passes – but a new, spectacular viaduct has removed many of the treacherous hairpin bends. It's slowly being extended to eliminate areas prone to rock fall.

Mountain House Taxi (☎ 318 9258), based at Mountain House Backpackers (left), offers a transport service to the walking tracks and Temple Basin ski field.

METHVEN

☎ 03 / pop 1070

Methven, about 115km west of Christchurch, hibernates for most of the year but gets a massive wake-up call in winter when it fills with skiers heading to/from Mt Hutt and other ski areas. That said, there are some nonwinter distractions here, including forest walks and jet-boat rides.

Information

E-mail Shop (☎ 302 8982; Forest Dr) Internet access.

Medical centre (☎ 302 8105; Main St) Opposite the visitors centre.

Methven visitors centre (☎ 302 8955; www.methven.net.nz; Main St; 🕒 7.30am-8pm daily winter, 9am-5pm Mon-Fri & 10am-4.30pm Sat & Sun summer) Books accommodation, skiing packages, transport and activities (also see the website www.nz-holiday.co.nz/methven) Internet access available.

Activities

SKIING & SNOWBOARDING

Nearby **Mt Hutt** (☎ 308 5074, snowphone 0900 997 66; www.nzski.com/mthutt; daily lift passes adult/student NZ$75/55) is one of NZ's best ski areas, and one of the highest ski fields in the southern hemisphere. Mt Hutt has beginner, intermediate and advanced slopes, with a quad and a triple chairlift, three T-bars, various other lifts and heli-skiing from the car park to slopes further afield. The wide open faces are good for those learning to snowboard. There's usually a full five months of skiing here (June to October), which is perhaps the longest ski season of any resort in NZ.

The place to go in Methven for ski rental and advice is **Big Al's Snow Sports** (☎ 302 8003; www.bigals.co.nz; cnr Main St & Forest Dr), which also rents out mountain bikes and fishing gear.

Black Diamond Safaris (☎ 302 9696; www.blackdiamondsafaris.co.nz) can take you to the area's uncrowded club ski fields by 4WD. Prices start at NZ$50 for 4WD transport only; NZ$125 gets you transport, a lift pass and lunch.

OTHER ACTIVITIES

Mt Hutt Bungy (☎ 302 9969; NZ$100) is an exhilarating bungy jump from a cantilevered platform at Kea Rock. It markets itself misleadingly as 'NZ's highest bungy', true in terms of the altitude but not the actual bungy height (43m; Queenstown has much higher jumps). It usually operates only over winter.

The **Mt Hutt Forest**, predominantly mountain beech, is 14km west of Methven. Adjoining it are the **Awa Awa Rata Reserve** and the **Pudding Hill Scenic Reserve**. There are two access roads: Pudding Hill Rd leads to foot access for Pudding Hill Stream, and McLennan's Bush Rd leads to both reserves. There are many walking tracks here, including the water-crossing **Pudding Hill Stream Route** (2½ hours) and the **Awa Awa Rata Reserve Loop Track** (1½ hours).

There's a good, easy walk across farmland and through the impressive **Rakaia River Gorge** (three to four hours return), beginning at the car park just south of the bridge on SH77. **Rakaia Gorge Alpine Jet** (☎ 318 6574; www.rivertours.co.nz; NZ$70) and **Rakaia Gorge Scenic Jet** (☎ 318 6515; NZ$60) both do 40-minute jet-boat trips through the gorge.

Sleeping

Due to the influx of skiers over winter, many places have drying rooms and ski storage. Some places are closed in summer. The following are open year-round, with their lowest prices applicable only outside the ski season.

Mt Hutt Bunkhouse (☎ 302 8894; mthuttbunks@xtra.co.nz; 8 Lampard St; dm/d from NZ$17/34; 💻) Offers simple accommodation just off Methven's main street. There are all the requisite winter facilities, such as ski tuning, boot drying, gear storage and room heating, and a barbecue for when the snow thaws.

Skiwi House (☎ 302 8772; www.skiwihouse.co.nz; 30 Chapman St; dm/d from NZ$17/40) Good facilities and a backpacker-popular atmosphere.

Redwood Lodges (☎ 302 8964; www.methvennz.com; 5 Wayne Pl; s NZ$20-25, d NZ$50) Has been transformed from a one-time vicarage into two well-appointed travellers' lodges, with a communal kitchen area and brightly decorated rooms. Choose between bunk rooms, quads, doubles and twins (some rooms with bathroom).

Alpernhorn Chalet (☎ 302 8779; nzbcoutfitters@xtra.co.nz; 44 Allen St; per person from NZ$25) Small and inviting budget chalet, with a wonderful conservatory housing an indoor garden and spa pool, and other nice alpine touches such as rimu-carved kitchen benches. Rooms come in double or twin variations and all have shared facilities.

Snow Denn Lodge (☎ 302 8999; info@methvenaccommodation.co.nz; cnr McMillan & Bank Sts; dm/d NZ$25/65) This centrally located, YHA-associated lodge is a modern, purpose-built house with lots of room to lounge in and some appealing dining/living areas, a large kitchen and a spa pool. Prices are a bit higher than your average hostel.

Bed Post (☎ 302 8508; www.mthuttbeds.com/bedpost.htm; 177 Main St; dm NZ$18-22, d NZ$70-95) Has room in its lodge for 20 budget-conscious souls, who can make the most of full kitchen and laundry facilities. Others can opt for the one- to three-bedroom motel units; larger units can sleep up to eight.

Ryton Station (☎ 0800 926 868, 318 5818; www.ryton.co.nz; camp sites per 2 people NZ$5, dm NZ$25, d NZ$120-135) Beautifully isolated, 14,800-hectare sheep station, located 50km northwest of Methven on the northern shore of Lake Coleridge. The high-country accommodation here ranges from a wilderness camping ground and 16-bed budget lodge (bedding and meals available from the homestead) to DB&B lake-view chalets. There are also great activities here, including fishing, tramping, horse riding and mountain biking.

Methven Camping Ground (☎ 302 8005; Barkers Rd; camp sites unpowered/powered per 2 people NZ$19/20, d NZ$30-50) Small park keeping to itself, close to the centre of town. It's in a scenic location and the facilities (including a TV room) and cabins are serviceable.

Eating & Drinking

Most of Methven's eateries do a roaring trade in winter, but are often open only three to five nights a week in summer; some close down for the entire sunny season.

Canterbury Hotel (☎ 302 8045; cnr Main St & Forest Dr; mains NZ$10-20; 🕑 lunch & dinner) One of Methven's two pubs, known for obvious reasons as the Brown Pub. This is where locals tend to hang out, either conversing at the bar or eating one of the many solid pub grills, including sausages, schnitzel and 'brontosaurus steak' (500g of rump steak).

Blue Pub (☎ 302 8046; Barkers Rd) The other pub option, a favourite among the visiting ski crowd for discussing the day's exploits on the mountain. Its **Base Café** (mains from NZ$15; 🕑 lunch & dinner) goes for slightly more upmarket fare than its counterpart pub across Main St.

Steel-Worx (☎ 302 9900; 36 Forest Dr; meals from NZ$10) Opens over winter but usually stays shut over summer. Has standard main meals complemented by cheaper bar snacks such as burgers and pizza.

Lisah's (☎ 302 8070; Main St; mains NZ$15-21; 🕑 dinner Wed-Sat) Mellow, red-walled Lisah's is a top local choice, where you can satisfy your stomach with lemongrass chicken or carpet bag steak (stuffed with oysters). It's also an intimate wine bar and cocktail lounge.

For good pizzas and kebabs, pay a visit to **Uncle Dominic's** (☎ 302 8237; the Square; pizzas NZ$11-21; ⏲ lunch Sat & Sun, dinner daily), while **Café 131** (☎ 302 9131; Main St; meals NZ$9-14; ⏲ lunch winter) has reasonably priced salads, roast vegetable filo and BLTs.

Getting There & Around

Methven Travel (☎ 302 8106) picks up from Christchurch city and airport and delivers you to your accommodation (NZ$27); other companies also offer this service during the ski season.

InterCity (☎ 379 9020; www.intercitycoach.co.nz) has daily buses between Methven and Christchurch (NZ$21).

Many shuttles run from Methven to Mt Hutt ski field in winter for around NZ$20 to NZ$25; inquiries and pick ups are dealt with at the visitors centre.

LAKE TEKAPO

☎ 03 / pop 295

This small town at the southern end of its namesake lake has unobstructed views across turquoise water, with hills and snow-capped mountains as a backdrop – for an explanation of why this and other nearby lakes have such striking coats of blue, see the boxed text on left. Tekapo derives its name from the Maori words *taka* (sleeping mat) and *po* (night), though it's not clear if this refers to indigenous sleeping habits or a Maori encounter with early explorers.

The expansive high ground on which the lake is located is known as Mackenzie Country after the larger-than-life James 'Jock' McKenzie, who is said to have run stolen flocks of sheep around 1843 in this then-uninhabited region (nobody's sure why the region and the chap himself have different spellings).

Lake Tekapo is a popular first stop on tours of the Southern Alps, with Mt Cook and Queenstown buses chugging up to the cluster of main-road tourist shops to create some short-lived retail chaos.

BLUE CRUSH

The blazing turquoise colour of Lake Tekapo is due to 'rock flour' (sediment) in the water. This so-called flour was created when the lake's basin was gouged out by a stony-bottomed glacier moving across the land's surface, with the rock-on-rock action grinding out fine particles that ended up being suspended in the glacial melt water. This sediment gives the water a milky quality and refracts the sunlight, hence the brilliant colour.

Lake Tekapo's unreal colouring is a characteristic shared by other regional bodies of water such as Lake Pukaki, 45km southwest of Lake Tekapo and 2km northeast of the turn-off to Mt Cook. On this lake's southern shore is the **Lake Pukaki visitors centre** (☎ 03-435 3280; lake.pukaki@xtra.co.nz; SH8; ⏲ 9.30am-5pm Mon-Sat, 10am-5pm Sun), fronted by a sterling lookout that, on a clear day, gives a picture-perfect view of Mt Cook and its surrounding peaks, with the ultrablue lake in the foreground.

Information

Kiwi Treasures (☎ 680 6686; SH8; ⏲ 7.30am-8pm summer, limited hours winter) Serves as both a souvenir shop and a visitors centre; for Web-based info visit www.laketekapountouched.co.nz.

Tekapo Helicopters (per 20min NZ$2) Internet access.

Sights & Activities

The diminutive, picturesque **Church of the Good Shepherd** beside the lake was built of stone and oak in 1935. Further along is a **statue** of a collie dog, a tribute to the sheep-dogs that helped develop the Mackenzie Country.

Popular walks include the track to the summit of **Mt John** (three hours) from just beyond the motor camp. From there, continue on to **Alexandrina** and **McGregor Lakes**, making it an all-day tramp. Other walks are detailed in the brochure *Lake Tekapo Walkway* (NZ$1).

Lake Tekapo Adventures & Cruises (☎ 0800 528 624, 680 6629; www.laketekapo.co.nz; cruises from NZ$38) organises activities in the vicinity of Godley Glacier, ranging from 4WD safaris and mountain-bike runs to fishing and lake cruises. **Mackenzie Alpine Trekking Company** (☎ 0800 628 269, 680 6760; www.laketekapo.cc/matc; 1hr rides NZ$45, full-day rides NZ$220) organises high-country horse rides.

In winter, Lake Tekapo provides transport and ski hire for downhill skiing at **Mt Dobson** (☎ 685 8039; www.dobson.co.nz; daily lift passes NZ$50), a commercial ski area northeast of town that caters for learners and has NZ's largest intermediate area. You can also ski at **Fox Peak**

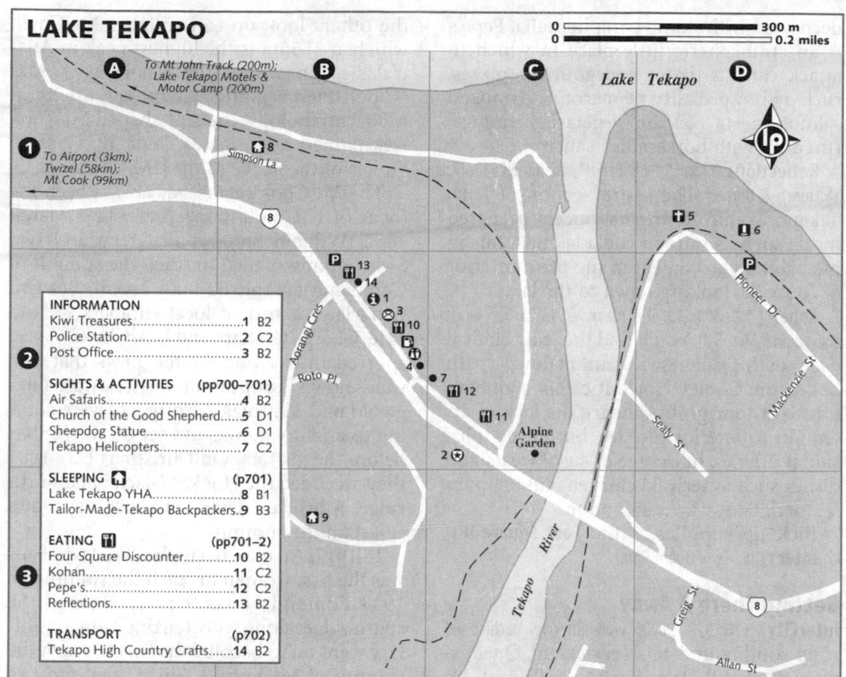

(☎ 688 0044; www.foxpeak.co.nz; daily lift passes NZ$40), a club ski area in the Two Thumb Range, and at **Ohau** (☎ 438 9885; www.ohau.co.nz; daily lift passes NZ$50), 105km south of Lake Tekapo and with the country's longest T-bar and excellent terrain for snowboarding, cross-country skiing and ski touring.

Lake Tekapo also has an open-air **ice-skating rink** (Jun-Sep).

Tours

Air Safaris (☎ 0800 806 880, 680 6880; www.airsafaris.co.nz; SH8; NZ$240) does 50-minute flights over Mt Cook and its glaciers, taking you up the Tasman Glacier, over the upper part of the Fox and Franz Josef Glaciers, and by Mts Cook, Tasman and Elie de Beaumont.

Tekapo Helicopters (☎ 0800 359 835, 680 6229; www.tekapohelicopters.co.nz; SH8) has 25-minute (NZ$180) and 45-minute (NZ$320) flights that include ice-field landings and grand viewings of Mt Cook and the glaciers.

Sleeping

Lake Tekapo YHA (☎ 680 6857; yha.laketekapo@yha.org.nz; 3 Simpson Lane; camp sites per 2 people NZ$20, dm/d from NZ$21/50) Friendly, well-equipped little place, its living room adorned with open fireplaces and outstanding views across the lake to the mountains – and there's no TV to dominate the atmosphere. There are limited camp sites here, so book ahead if you want one.

Tailor-Made-Tekapo Backpackers (☎ 680 6700; www.tailor-made-backpackers.co.nz; 9-11 Aorangi Cres; dm/d from NZ$19/45;) This hostel favours beds rather than bunks and is spread over a pair of well-tended houses on a peaceful side street, well away from the main-road bus traffic. An effort has been made to brighten up the interior and there's a barbecue-equipped garden. Couch potatoes note, there's no TV here.

Lake Tekapo Motels & Motor Camp (☎ 0800 853 853, 680 6825; www.laketekapo-accommodation.co.nz; camp sites per 2 people NZ$24, d NZ$45-120) Has an exceptionally pretty and peaceful lake-side locale, plus everything from budget cabins to motel units. Bedding hire for the cabins costs NZ$10.

Eating

Pepe's (☎ 680 6677; SH8; meals from NZ$12; lunch & dinner) Filled with large booths and its walls decorated with skiing paraphernalia, Pepe's is an atmospheric little place in which to attack various pastas and gourmet pizzas, such as its speciality pepperoni, a 'smoked salmon siesta', or the 'vegetarian vintage' (fired up with horseradish sauce).

Reflections (☎ 680 6808; SH8; mains NZ$15-27; ⏰ lunch & dinner) The bistro section of Lake Tekapo Scenic Resort has nicely prepared meals such as salmon roulade and venison pie, which you can eat in the plain interior or outside, looking down to the lake.

Kohan (☎ 680 6688; SH8; mains NZ$13-25; ⏰ lunch daily, dinner Mon-Sat) You'll find the truly clinical décor of this Japanese restaurant down a path beside the Godley Hotel. It caters mainly to transient tour groups, hence the lack of attention to interior niceties, but on the plus side it offers a full range of sushi treats and dishes such as teriyaki chicken and tempura seafood; takeaway is an option.

Pick up supplies at the **Four Square Discounter** (SH8; ⏰ 7.30am-9pm).

Getting There & Away

InterCity (☎ 379 9020; www.intercitycoach.co.nz) runs southbound bus services to Queenstown (NZ$40), Wanaka (NZ$50) and Mt Cook (NZ$25), and eastbound services to Christchurch (NZ$40). **Southern Link Shuttles** (☎ 358 8355; www.yellow.co.nz/site/southernlink), **Atomic Shuttles** (☎ 322 8883; www.atomictravel.co.nz) and the **Cook Connection** (☎ 0800 266 526, 027-458 3211; www.cookconnect.co.nz) include Lake Tekapo on their routes; ticket prices range from NZ$20 to NZ$45 for most destinations.

Between them, **Kiwi Treasures** (☎ 680 6686; SH8) and **Tekapo High Country Crafts** (☎ 680 6656; SH8) handle bookings for visiting buses.

AORAKI/MT COOK NATIONAL PARK

☎ 03

The spectacular 700-sq-km Aoraki/Mt Cook National Park is part of the Southwest New Zealand (Te Wahipounamu) World Heritage Area (see the boxed text on p748), which extends from Westland/Tai Poutini National Park's Cook River down to the chilly toes of Fiordland National Park. Fenced in by the Southern Alps and the Two Thumb, Liebig and Ben Ohau Ranges, more than one-third of the national park has a blanket of permanent snow and glacial ice.

Of the 27 NZ mountains over 3050m high, 22 are in this park. The peak that all the others look up to is mighty Mt Cook, which at 3755m is the highest peak in Australasia. Known to the Maori as Aoraki (Cloud Piercer), after an ancestral deity in Maori mythology, the tent-shaped Mt Cook was named after James Cook by Captain Stokes of the survey ship HMS *Acheron*.

The Mt Cook region has always been the focus of NZ mountaineering. On 2 March 1882, William Spotswood Green and two Swiss alpinists failed to reach the summit of Cook after an epic 62-hour ascent. But two years later a trio of local climbers – Tom Fyfe, George Graham and Jack Clarke – were spurred into action by the news that two well-known European alpinists, Edward Fitzgerald and Matthias Zurbriggen, were coming to attempt Cook, and set off to climb it before the visitors. On Christmas Day 1884 they ascended the Hooker Glacier and north ridge, a brilliant climb in those days, and stood on the summit.

In 1913, Australian climber Freda du Faur was the first woman to reach the summit. In 1948 Edmund Hillary's party climbed the south ridge; along with Tenzing Norgay, Hillary went on to become the first to reach the summit of Mt Everest. Since then, most of the daunting face routes have been climbed. Among the region's many great peaks are Sefton, the beguiling Tasman, Silberhorn, Elie de Beaumont, Malte Brun, Aiguilles Rouges, Nazomi, La Perouse, Hicks, De la Beche, Douglas and the Minarets. Many can be ascended from Westland/Tai Poutini National Park, and there's a system of climbers' huts on both sides of the divide.

In the early hours of 14 December 1991, a substantial piece of Mt Cook's east face (around 14 million cubic metres) fell away in a massive landslide. Debris spewed out over the surrounding glaciers for 7.3km, cleaving a path down the Grand Plateau and Hochstetter Icefall and reaching as far as the Tasman Glacier.

Mt Cook is a wonderful sight – assuming there's no cloud in the way. Most visitors arrive on tour buses, jump out at the Hermitage hotel for photos, and then zoom off back down SH80. Those who choose not to take this awesome peak and its glorious surrounding landscape for granted stick around and try some of the excellent short walks. While on the tracks, look out for the thar, a goat-like creature and excellent climber; the chamois, smaller and of lighter build than the thar but an agile climber; and red deer. In summer, you'll see the large mountain buttercup, often called the Mt Cook lily, as well as mountain daisies, gentians and edelweiss.

Like the Fox and Franz Josef Glaciers on the other side of the divide, the Mt Cook glaciers move fast. The Alpine Memorial, located near the old Hermitage site on the Hooker Valley Walk and which commemorates one of the mountain's first climbing disasters, illustrates the glaciers' speed. Three climbers were killed by an avalanche in 1914. Only one of the bodies was recovered at the time but 12 years later a second body melted out of the bottom of the Hochstetter Icefall, 2000m below where the party was buried.

Information

Aoraki/Mt Cook visitors centre (☎ 435 1186; mtcookvc@doc.govt.nz; Bowen Dr; 🕑 8.30am-6pm Oct-Apr, 8.30am-5pm May-Sep), run by DOC, advises on weather conditions, guided tours and tramping routes, and screens a 20-minute audiovisual (NZ$3) on the history and mountaineering of the Mt Cook region. Online information is available at www.mount-cook.com.

Post is handled by the souvenir shop in the Hermitage hotel (right), which is open from 7am until 10pm in summer. The hotel's coffee shop sells some groceries, as does the Mt Cook YHA (p704), but you'd fare better by stocking up on supplies before you head up SH80. Mt Cook has no banking facilities.

At the **Alpine Guides Shop** (☎ 435 1834; Bowen Dr), you can rent day packs, sleeping bags, ice axes and crampons.

Sights

TASMAN GLACIER

High up, the Tasman Glacier is a predictably spectacular sweep of ice, but further down it's downright ugly. Glaciers in NZ (and elsewhere in the world) have generally been retreating over the past century, although they are now advancing. Normally, as a glacier retreats it melts back up the mountain, but the Tasman is unusual because its last few kilometres are almost horizontal. So in recent decades it has melted from the top down, exposing a jumble of stones, rocks and boulders. In other words, in its 'ablation zone' (where it melts) the Tasman is covered in a more or less solid mass of debris, which slows down its melting rate and makes it unsightly.

Despite this considerable melt, the ice by the site of the old Ball Hut is still estimated to be more than 600m thick. In its last major advance (17,000 years ago), the glacier crept south far enough to carve out Lake Pukaki (see the boxed text on p700). A later advance did not reach out to the valley sides, so the old Ball Hut Rd runs between the outer valley walls and the lateral moraines of this later advance.

HERMITAGE

This is arguably the most famous hotel in NZ, principally for its location and the fantastic views of Mt Cook. Originally constructed in 1884, when the trip up from Christchurch took several days, the first hotel was destroyed in a flash flood in 1913; you can see the foundations in Hooker Valley, 2km from the current Hermitage. Rebuilt, the hotel survived until 1957, when it was completely burnt out; the present Hermitage was built on the same site.

Even if you're not staying at the Hermitage, you can still have a drink in the bar and look out the huge windows at the indomitable face of Mt Cook.

Activities

The visitors centre, the Hermitage, the YHA and Glentanner Park (see p704 for details of the last three) provide information and make bookings for a multitude of activities in the area, though be aware that most are weather-dependent.

WALKING

Easy walks from the Hermitage area are outlined in the brochure *Walks in Aoraki/Mt Cook National Park* (NZ$1), available from the visitors centre. Always be prepared for sudden weather changes.

The track to **Kea Point** (two hours return) is lined with native plant life and kea, and ends at a platform with excellent views of Mt Cook, the Hooker Valley and the ice faces of Mt Sefton and the Footstool. The walk to **Sealy Tarns** (three to four hours return) branches off the Kea Point Track and continues up the ridge to the gas-equipped, 28-bunk **Mueller Hut** (dm NZ$22).

It's a four-hour return walk up the **Hooker Valley** and across a couple of swing bridges to

Stocking Stream and the terminus of Hooker Glacier. After the second swing bridge, Mt Cook totally dominates the valley.

Tasman Valley walks are popular for their views of Tasman Glacier. Walks start at the end of the unsealed Tasman Valley Rd, 8km from the village. The **Tasman Glacier View track** (40 minutes return) leads to a viewpoint on the moraine wall, passing the Blue Lakes (more green than blue these days) on the way. Views of Mt Cook and the surrounding area are spectacular, but the view of the glacier is limited mostly to the icy grey sludge of the terminal lake and Tasman River. To approach the snub of the glacier, take the route to **Ball Shelter** (three to four hours) from the car park; you can stay here at **Ball Shelter Hut** (dm NZ$5).

If you intend staying at any of the park's huts, register your intentions at the visitors centre and pay the hut fee; besides the aforementioned two, most huts cost NZ$20 per night.

Longer tramps are only recommended for those with mountaineering experience, as conditions at higher altitudes are severe, the tracks dangerous and many people have died here; the majority of walkers shouldn't even consider tackling these tracks.

From November to March, **Alpine Guides Trekking** (☎ 435 1809; www.ultimatehikes.co.nz; full-day tramp NZ$95) offers a day-long, 8km tramp from the Hermitage through the Hooker Valley to the terminal lake of Hooker Glacier; half-day walks can also be organised.

MOUNTAINEERING

For the experienced, there's unlimited scope here for climbing. But regardless of your aptitude, take every precaution: more than 200 people have died in climbing accidents in the park. These are recorded in the bleak 'In Memoriam' book in the visitors centre, which begins with the first death on Mt Cook in 1907. Several tragedies in December 2003 showed just how terribly capricious the mountains can be – a total of eight climbers died on Mt Tasman and Mt Cook, three of them experienced mountain guides who were well known in Mt Cook village.

The highly changeable weather is an important factor around here. Check with the park rangers before attempting any climb, and heed their advice. You must fill in a climbers' intentions card before starting on any climb, so rangers can check on you if you're overdue coming out. Make sure you sign out again when you return.

Alpine Guides (☎ 435 1834; www.alpineguides.co.nz; Bowen Dr) has guided climbs in summer, and in winter does tailored ski-touring trips and ski-mountaineering and alpine snowboarding courses.

OTHER ACTIVITIES

The highly rated **Glacier Explorers** (☎ 435 1077; www.glacierexplorers.com; NZ$85) heads out on the terminal lake of the Tasman Glacier. It starts with a 30-minute walk to the shore of Lake Tasman, where you board a small motorised inflatable and get up close and personal with the ice for an hour. The three-hour trips conducted by **Southern Alps Guiding** (☎ 435 1890; www.mtcook.com; NZ$75) enable you to kayak across glacial bays, circumnavigating the odd iceberg as you paddle.

Another way of checking out the area is with **Glentanner Horse Trekking** (☎ 435 1855; 1hr/2hr rides NZ$50/70), which does summer-only guided horse treks on a high-country sheep station.

Tours

From October until April, **Alan's 4WD Tours** (☎ 435 0441; www.mountcooktours.co.nz; NZ$85) runs 2½-hour 4WD trips from the Hermitage up to Husky Flat, from where it's a 15-minute walk to a glacier viewpoint; there's plenty of interesting commentary and alpine flora to gaze at along the way.

Mount Cook Ski Planes (☎ 0800 800 702, 435 1026; www.mtcookskiplanes.com) buzzes over this magnificent iced-in terrain during 40-minute (NZ$280) and 55-minute (NZ$370) flights, both with glacier landings. Flights without a landing are much cheaper, such as the 25-minute 'Mini Tasman' trip (NZ$190).

Sleeping

Mt Cook YHA (☎ 435 1820; yha.mtcook@yha.org.nz; cnr Bowen & Kitchener Dr; dm/d from NZ$24/65) This excellent hostel is equipped with a free sauna, drying room, a decent video collection, warming log fires and (for those who haven't expended all their energy on local tracks) an in-house bouldering wall. Book at least a few days in advance in the summer.

Unwin Hut (☎ 435 1100, 435 1840; SH80; dm NZ$25) This lodge is about 3.5km before the village and belongs to the NZ Alpine Club (NZAC).

Members get preference but beds are usually available for climbing groupies. There are basic bunks and a big common room with a fireplace, kitchen and excellent views up the Tasman Glacier to the Minarets and Elie de Beaumont.

White Horse Hill Camping Area (☎ 435 1186; Hooker Valley; camp sites per 2 people NZ$5) This basic DOC-run camping ground is at the old Hermitage site, 2km from Aoraki/Mt Cook village and the starting point for the Hooker Valley Track. There's running water and toilets but no electricity, showers or cooking facilities. Book at the visitors centre. There's also a handy public shelter in the village, with running water, toilets and coin-operated showers.

Glentanner Park Centre (☎ 0800 453 682, 435 1855; www.glentanner.co.nz; SH80; camp sites unpowered/powered per 2 people NZ$20/22, dm NZ$20, d NZ$50-80) Located on the north shore of Lake Pukaki, this is the nearest commercial camping ground to the national park and has great views of Mt Cook, 25km to the north. It's well set up with various cabins, a dormitory (open October to April only), a restaurant (right) and a booking service for horse treks and scenic flights.

You can also stay at several trampers' huts in the national park – for details, see p703.

Eating & Drinking

Hermitage (☎ 435 1809; Terrace Rd) The only budget option in the hotel is a mezzanine-level coffee shop that dispenses daytime snacks. Nonetheless, duck into the top-notch à la carte Panorama Room to see the outrageously good view: Sefton is to your left, Cook is in the centre and the Ben Ohau Ranges, dark brown and forbidding, are to your right. Adjacent to the Panorama Room is the Snowline Lounge Bar, with well-upholstered lounges in which to down a warming liquid. The smaller, less-formal Chamois Bar is upstairs in Glencoe Lodge, 500m from the main hotel, near the YHA, where it entertains with a pool table and big-screen TV; beer-drinking food such as nachos, burgers and steak sandwiches are also served here.

Old Mountaineers Café Bar & Restaurant (☎ 435 1890; Bowen Dr; mains NZ$15-25; ⏰ lunch & dinner; 💻) Sitting next to the visitors centre, this relatively new, attractive café-bar has a cosy interior, outdoor seating and views straight up the mountain. In a village that's been dominated by the high-priced Hermitage for over a century, this place is a breath of fresh, independent air.

Glentanner Restaurant (☎ 435 1855; SH80; meals NZ$11-17; ⏰ breakfast & lunch) The caféteria-style eatery at Glentanner Park throws together basic cooked and continental breakfasts, and lunch-time burgers, BLTs and *panini*. Dinners (usually served only over summer) are just as simple: think vegetarian quiche and steak sandwiches.

Getting There & Away

InterCity (☎ 435 1809; www.intercitycoach.co.nz) heads to Mt Cook from Christchurch (NZ$75), Queenstown (NZ$65) and Wanaka (NZ$55); buses stop at the YHA and the Hermitage, both of which handle bookings. **High Country Shuttles** (☎ 0800 435 050, 435 0506) runs between Mt Cook and Twizel (one way/return NZ$15/25), and you can usually connect there with **Southern Link Shuttles** (☎ 358 8355; www.yellow.co.nz/site/southernlink) and **Atomic Shuttles** (☎ 322 8883; www.atomictravel.co.nz) to travel on to Queenstown, Wanaka or Christchurch. **Cook Connection** (☎ 0800 266 526, 027-458 3211; www.cookconnect.co.nz) shuttles to Timaru and Oamaru (both NZ$45).

The InterCity subsidiary **Newmans Coach Lines** (☎ 379 9020; www.newmanscoach.co.nz) offers the 'Mt Cook Wanderer', a Christchurch–Mt Cook–Queenstown sightseeing trip costing NZ$130 from Christchurch and NZ$115 from Queenstown.

If you're driving, it's best to fill up at Lake Tekapo or Twizel. There is petrol at Mt Cook, but it's expensive and involves summoning an attendant from the Hermitage.

THE WEST COAST

The West Coast region (also known as Westland) is a rugged, salt-sprayed stretch of wild rocky beaches and bush-clad hills sweeping up to towering, icy peaks. Often the narrow coastal strip is nothing but *pakihi* (dried-up swamp) or farmland, but the contrast between the energetic wash of the ocean on one side and the hilly heights on the other is striking. Easy access to solitude is also one of the West Coast's major characteristics.

The biggest attractions of this region are the huge, icy dimensions of Franz Josef and

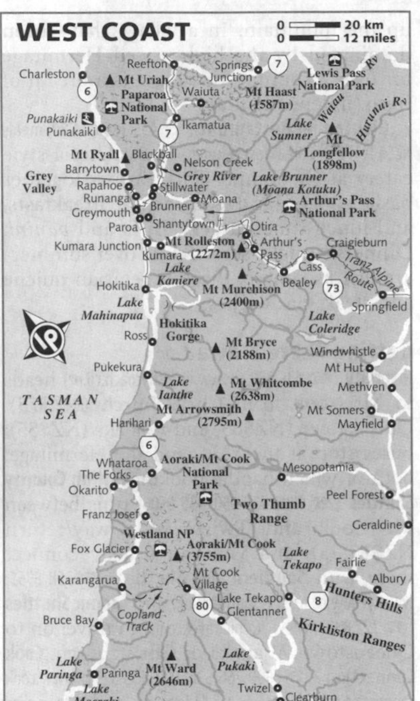

Fox Glaciers, framed by the dominating peaks of Mts Cook and Tasman. But there are other features that provide some scenic competition, such as the wonderful geological layering at Punakaiki Rocks. The West Coast is also a major source of *pounamu* (greenstone, or jade) and Hokitika is the best place in NZ to see it being crafted.

Activities

There are some breathtaking walks to take along the stunning West Coast, including the track around iconic Lake Matheson, the overgrown tracks in isolated Paparoa National Park and the tramps up and over the formidable icy reaches of Fox and Franz Josef Glaciers. Water activities include kayaking on the Pororari River or on Lake Mapourika, while a popular indoor pursuit is the personalised carving of a piece of jade in Hokitika.

HOKITIKA

☎ 03 / pop 4000

Hokitika ('Hoki' for short) was settled during the 1860s gold rush and became a busy port. This is NZ's major centre for the working of greenstone, which is what attracts the bulk of its visitors. But there's more to do around here than looking at stone being mass produced into bookends in the form of *tiki* (or *hei tiki*, a stylised human figure) and *taniwha* (fear-inducing water spirit). Hoki is also rich in history and nearby is a wealth of native forests, lakes and rivers. Although quieter than the larger hub of Greymouth (see the boxed text on p709), 40km to the north, it makes for a more interesting overnight stop.

Information

Aim West Sports (☎ 755 8481; 20 Weld St; per 20min NZ$2; 🕐 9am-8pm Mon-Fri, 9am-5pm Sat & Sun) Internet access.

DOC (☎ 755 8301; 10 Sewell St)

Westland visitors centre (☎ 755 6166; hkkvin@xtra.co.nz; cnr Hamilton & Tancred Sts; 🕐 8.30am-6pm Nov-Mar, 8am-5pm Apr-Oct) In the historic Carnegie Building, which was originally established as a library.

Sights

One of Hoki's premier attractions is its profusion of arts and crafts outlets; see Shopping on p708.

New Zealand Eco Centre (☎ 755 5251; 60 Tancred St; adult NZ$12; 🕐 9am-5pm) is predominantly an aquarium set up with tanks devoted to marine life such as sharks, snake-necked turtles, crayfish and square-jawed piranhas. The star attractions, however, have to be the enormous long-finned eels flopped over wooden platforms and draped over rocks in the central enclosure; feedings occur at 10am, noon and 3pm daily. There's also a dimly lit kiwi enclosure and some wrinkly tuataras.

A short signposted walk from the highway leads you to a dead-end **glow-worm dell** (admission free; 🕐 24hr). Visit after dark to see the lit-up worms suspended on their sticky threads – the multitude of glow-worms here makes for a magical sight.

The **West Coast Historical Museum** (☎ 755 6898; Carnegie Bldg, cnr Hamilton & Tancred Sts; adult NZ$5; 🕐 9.30am-5pm) contains an interesting history parade of old photos, a Maori artefact-filled cabinet, settlers' relics such as a Scottish ceremonial powder horn, an opium pipe bowl and a working Meccano-set replica of the Grey River Gold Dredge.

Activities

Try some jade carving with **Just Jade Experience** (☎ 755 7612; www.jadecountry.co.nz; 197 Revell St;

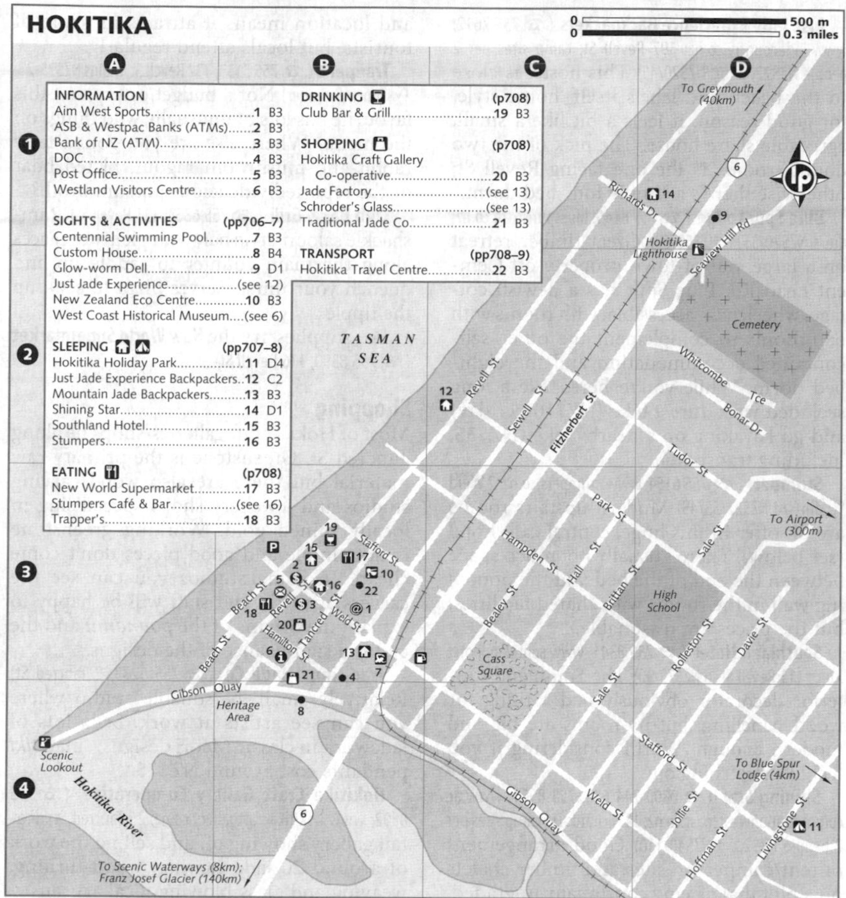

workshop NZ$80-150), at the backpackers of the same name (see p708). The all-day activity begins with designing your own piece or choosing a traditional design, and includes instruction on cutting, working and polishing the greenstone. Workshop prices vary depending on the design's complexity.

Pick up a copy of the *Hokitika Heritage Walk* leaflet (NZ$1) from the visitors centre and explore the waterfront along **Gibson Quay** – it's not hard to imagine the river and wharf choked with sailing ships of yesteryear. At the Sewell St end, the **Custom House** is sometimes open to the public as a craft centre.

Scenic Waterways (☎ 755 7239; www.paddleboatcruises.com; NZ$25) offers 1½-hour paddleboat cruises on Mahinapua Creek. For even more leisurely water sports, visit the heated **Centennial Swimming Pool** (☎ 755 8119; 53 Weld St; adult/student NZ$3/2).

Festivals

In mid-March, Hokitika hosts the increasingly popular **Wildfoods Festival** (Cass Sq), a major bush food event attracting up to 20,000 curious gourmands.

Sleeping

Mountain Jade Backpackers (☎ 0800 838 301, 755 8007; mtjade@minidat.co.nz; 41 Weld St; dm NZ$20, d from NZ$50) Spacious, open-plan backpackers centrally located above a jade shop. It has neat dorms and doubles, and self-contained units. Wheelchair access is provided.

Just Jade Experience Backpackers (☎ 755 7612; www.jadecountry.co.nz; 197 Revell St; camp sites per 2 people NZ$22, dm/d NZ$20/45) This hostel is close to the beach and labels itself 'home-style' for good reason: it feels a bit like a small, agreeable share house. The pick of the two double rooms is the one facing Revell St; otherwise there's a simple four-bed dorm.

Blue Spur Lodge (☎ 755 8445; bluespur@xtra.co.nz; dm/s NZ$20/35, d NZ$50-60) Great timber retreat on a large, out-of-town property off Cement Lead Rd. Blue Spur has a newish cottage, wheelchair-accessible, with rooms with bathrooms to complement the other self-contained accommodation and the eight-bed dorm. While you're here, take a long secluded walk, hire a bike (NZ$10 per day) and go kayaking on a nearby lake (NZ$35, including transport).

Stumpers (☎ 755 6154; www.stumpers.co.nz; 2 Weld St; dm/s/d NZ$22/35/45) Modern upstairs rooms are on offer in this huge, central café-hotel (see below). There's usually not much space between the end of the bed and the opposing wall in the rooms with shared facilities, but the prices are reasonable.

Southland Hotel (☎ 755 8344; www.southlandhotel.com; 111 Revell St; d NZ$75-90) The Southland's interior decorator obviously had a thing for wood panelling, but its rooms are big and modern enough. Worth considering if you feel like stretching out.

Shining Star (☎ 0800 744 646, 755 8921; www.accommodationwestcoast.co.nz; 11 Richards Dr; camp sites per 2 people NZ$20, d NZ$40-110) Good arrangement of tent/campervan sites and timber chalets on a plot that's being continually upgraded. The priciest accommodation faces the beach but all the cabins are well maintained and there's plenty of adjacent pastureland in which to let your mind roam.

Hokitika Holiday Park (☎ 0800 465 436, 755 8172; www.hokitika.com/holidaypark; 242 Stafford St; camp sites unpowered/powered per 2 people NZ$18/20, d NZ$30-80) There's a wide range of accommodation here, including a wheelchair-accessible two-bedroom abode. The colourful playground could distract the kids for a little while.

Eating & Drinking

Stumpers Café & Bar (☎ 755 6154; 2 Weld St; mains NZ$12-25; 🕒 breakfast, lunch & dinner) Simply prepared, filling meals such as beer-battered blue-eye cod and pork *parmigiana* are the mainstays here. The café's conspicuous size and location means it attracts its share of tourists, but locals attend regularly.

Trapper's (☎ 755 5133; 137 Revell St; mains NZ$25-28; 🕒 lunch & dinner) Not a budget eatery, but this favourite has lots of unusually wild things on the menu. Where else are you gonna taste rabbit-and-mushroom ragout, plated boar or the reportedly delicious possum broth?

Club Bar & Grill (☎ 755 6868; 131 Revell St) Ramshackle saloon-style bar, with plenty of places along the main counter to saddle up and quench your thirst. Serves pizza to soak up the tipple.

For supplies, try the **New World Supermarket** (☎ 755 8390; 116 Revell St).

Shopping

Most of Hoki's craft galleries/shops lie along Tancred St. Greenstone is the primary raw material but there are also wood-carving studios and jewellery shops specialising in locally mined gold. Working greenstone is not simple and good pieces don't come cheap. In some studios you can see the carvers at work, and staff will be happy to explain the origins of the *pounamu* and the cultural significance of the designs.

Traditional Jade Co (☎ 755 5233; 2 Tancred St) Relatively small, personable studio where you can see artists at work. Sells lots of jadework in classic Maori designs; small *tiki* pendants cost around NZ$75.

Hokitika Craft Gallery Co-operative (☎ 755 8802; www.hokitikacraftgallery.co.nz; 25 Tancred St) Retail gallery showing off and selling the work of around 20 jade-carving, wood-turning, weaving and glass-blowing local artisans.

Jade Factory (☎ 755 8007; 41 Weld St) Part of the Mountain Jade complex, this outlet has a big range of well-presented jade sculpture. You probably won't be interested in snapping up a golf putter with a jade head for NZ$200 and stuffing it in your backpack, but the intricacy of some pieces makes it worth a look.

Schroder's Glass (☎ 755 8484; 41 Weld St) Has a workshop where you can come to grips with terms such as 'glory holes' and 'marvering', and a gallery where you can browse some of Schroder's original, craftily twisted and colourful creations, from huge platters to diminutive glasses.

Getting There & Away

Hokitika Travel Centre (☎ 755 8557; 60 Tancred St) books flights and is where most buses stop.

THE TRANZALPINE

One of the world's great rail journeys is the *TranzAlpine*'s traverse of the Southern Alps between Christchurch and Greymouth – it begins near the Pacific Ocean and ends by the Tasman Sea.

Not so long ago, this popular rail journey, now made in the comfort of specially designed carriages, was undertaken in a ramshackle railcar. In times of bad weather and road closure, it was often the only means that West Coasters had to get to the eastern side of the divide.

The *TranzAlpine* crossing offers a bewildering variety of scenery. It leaves Christchurch at 8.15am, then speeds across the flat, alluvial Canterbury Plains to the foothills of the Southern Alps. In the foothills it enters a labyrinth of gorges and hills known as the Staircase; the climb here is made possible by a system of three large viaducts and most of the tunnels that will be encountered along the line.

The train emerges into the broad Waimakariri and Bealey Valleys and (on a good day) the surrounding vista is stupendous. The river valley is fringed with dense beech forest, which eventually gives way to the snowcapped peaks of Arthur's Pass National Park (p695).

At the small alpine village of Arthur's Pass, the train enters the longest of the tunnels, the 'Otira' (8.5km), and heads under the mountains to the West Coast.

There are several more gems on the western side – the valleys of the Otira, Taramakau and Grey Rivers, patches of podocarp forest and the pleasant surprise of trout-filled Lake Brunner (Moana Kotuku), fringed with cabbage trees.

The train arrives in Greymouth around 12.45pm and departs for Christchurch an hour later, arriving at 6.05pm.

Few travellers who make this rail journey will have regrets, except when the weather is bad. Chances are if it's raining on one coast, it'll be fine on the other.

Being at the other end of the coast-to-coast route from Christchurch (by road or rail), Greymouth gets decent tourist traffic. Here you can visit **Monteith's Brewing Co** (☎ 03-768 4149; www.monteiths.co.nz; cnr Turumaha & Herbert Sts; admission NZ$10; 🕑 tours 10am, 11.30am & 2pm Mon-Fri, 11.30am & 2pm Sat & Sun), the original West Coast brewery, with a beer list that includes the delicious Monteith's Black. Get info on local activities such as white-water rafting at **Greymouth visitors centre** (☎ 0800 473 966, 03-768 5101; cnr Herbert & Mackay Sts; 🕑 9am-7pm daily Oct-Apr, 9am-5pm Mon-Fri & 10am-4pm Sat & Sun May-Sep). **Greymouth Travel Centre** (☎ 0800 767 080, 03-768 7080; railway station, 164 Mackay St; 🕑 9am-5pm Mon-Fri, 10am-3pm Sat & Sun) is the bus depot and books all forms of transport; it has luggage-storage facilities.

The *TranzAlpine* rail service is operated by **Tranz Scenic** (☎ 0800 872 467; www.tranzscenic.co.nz; 🕑 7am-7pm).

AIR

Air New Zealand Link (☎ 0800 737 000, 09-357 3000; www.airnz.co.nz) has regular direct flights from Hokitika to Christchurch (from NZ$80), with connections to other centres. The airport is about 2.5km east of the visitors centre.

BUS

From Hokitika there are daily **InterCity** (☎ 755 8557; www.intercitycoach.co.nz) services to Greymouth (NZ$22, one hour), Nelson (NZ$75, seven hours) and Fox Glacier (NZ$45, 3½ hours). **Atomic Shuttles** (☎ 322 8883; www.atomictravel.co.nz) has services (bookings essential) to Fox Glacier (NZ$30), Greymouth (NZ$10) and one to Queenstown (NZ$70, 10 hours). **Coast to Coast** (☎ 0800 800 847; www.coast2coast.co.nz) and **Alpine Coaches** (☎ 0800 274 888; www.alpinecoaches.co.nz) run to Christchurch (NZ$35) via Arthur's Pass.

PUNAKAIKI & PAPAROA NATIONAL PARK

☎ 03

Almost midway between Greymouth and the northern West Coast town of **Westport** (www.westport.org.nz) is the small settlement of Punakaiki, which has some of the region's finest scenery and is on the doorstep of the beautifully rough, 30,000-hectare Paparoa National Park.

Information

The **Paparoa National Park visitors centre** (☎ 731 1895; punakaikivc@doc.govt.nz; SH6; 🕑 9am-6pm Oct-Apr, 9am-4.30pm May-Sep) has interesting displays on the park and supplies info on activities, accommodation and track conditions.

Sights

Punakaiki is best known for the wondrous **Pancake Rocks** and their accompanying **blowholes**. Through a layering and weathering process known as stylobedding, the limestone rocks at Dolomite Point have formed into what look like stacks of thin pancakes. When a good tide is running (check at the visitors centre for times), the water surges into caverns below the rocks and squirts out from impressive geyserlike blowholes. A 15-minute walk loops from the highway around the rocks and blowholes.

Paparoa National Park has many other natural attractions besides its gritty pancakes. The region is blessed with sea cliffs, fine mountains (the Paparoa Range), rivers, diverse flora and a Westland black petrel colony, the world's only nesting area of this rare sea bird.

Activities

Interesting tramps in the national park include the 27km **Inland Pack Track** (two to three days), established by miners in 1867 to circumvent the more rugged coastal walk, and are detailed in the DOC *Paparoa National Park* pamphlet (NZ$1). The **Croesus Track** (one to two days) is covered by another DOC leaflet (NZ$0.50) and is an 18km tramp over the Paparoa Range from the former coal mining centre of Blackball to Barrytown (16km south of Punakaiki), passing through historic gold-mining areas. If you're planning on walking, register your intentions at the park's visitors centre. Many of the inland walks are subject to river flooding, so check conditions before setting out.

Punakaiki Canoes (☎ 731 1870; www.riverkayaking.co.nz; SH6; canoe hire per 2hr/day NZ$30/50) hires out canoes and kayaks near the Pororari River bridge. **Punakaiki Horse Treks** (☎ 731 1839; www.pancake-rocks.co.nz; 2½hr ride NZ$80) arranges four-legged excursions in the national park.

Locally based **Green Kiwi Tours** (☎ 0800 474 733; www.greenkiwitours.co.nz; tours per hr from NZ$60, caving from NZ$40) does information-laden tours throughout the region, including to the Westland black petrel breeding colony, as well as caving, bouldering and heli-hiking trips.

Sleeping & Eating

Punakaiki Beach Hostel (☎ 731 1852; www.punakaikibeachhostel.co.nz; Webb St; dm/s/d from NZ$23/39/55; 💻) Snug beach-bumming hostel sporting a large veranda and an outdoor spa, only a short trudge from Pancake Rocks and some bushy tracks. It also rents out rooms in the **Seaside House** (Owen St).

Punakaiki Beach Camp (☎ 731 1894; beachcamp@xtra.co.nz; SH6; camp sites unpowered/powered per 2 people NZ$20/22, d NZ$30-40) An appealingly landscaped plot of land beside the water, drenched with ocean smells and studded with budget cabins.

Wild Coast Café (☎ 731 1873; SH6; mains NZ$9-16; 🕑 breakfast & lunch) Beside the visitors centre, this tourist-swamped café, fittingly serves a pancake stack with fruit, cream and maple syrup. It also cooks veg lasagne and various other light meals.

WHITEBAIT

Whitebait are small, translucent, elongated fish – the imago (immature) stage of the river smelt. They swarm up West Coast rivers in dense schools and are caught in set seine-net traps or large, round scoop nets. Many an argument has been had along a riverbank or near a river mouth about the best rock to position yourself on to catch the biggest haul.

The fishing season has been limited in recent times to allow the declining whitebait stocks to regroup. The breeding season is usually from September to mid-November but varies from year to year. Cooked in batter, these small fish are delicious and highly prized by locals.

One of the West Coast's culinary doyennes provided this recipe for whitebait patties:

Take a pint of whitebait (about 500ml – yes, the fish are measured as a liquid rather than a solid, as they used to be piled into pint-size glass milk bottles for sale) and pour into a bowl. For the batter take one egg, three tablespoons of flour, a pinch of salt and a little milk to make a smooth paste. Mix this and then pour over the whitebait. Cook in smoking-hot fat until golden brown and serve immediately with mint sauce and hot potato chips. Pickled onions are a fine accompaniment.

Punakaiki Tavern (☎ 731 1188; SH6; mains NZ$14-23; ⌚ lunch & dinner) Help yourself to a glass or two of something cold in the beer garden or in front of the fireplace when the drizzle settles in. Big, hearty mains vie with cheaper bar snacks for your attention. If you're lucky, you may even find whitebait fritters or burgers on the menu (see the boxed text on opposite).

Getting There & Away

Services between Westport and Greymouth, operated by both **InterCity** (☎ 789 7819; www.intercitycoach.co.nz) and **Atomic Shuttles** (☎ 322 8883; www.atomictravel.co.nz), stop at Punakaiki daily, allowing enough time to see the Pancake Rocks.

FRANZ JOSEF & FOX GLACIERS

Franz Josef and Fox are the two most famous glaciers within the frosty, mountainous splendour of **Westland/Tai Poutini National Park**, and rank among the major attractions in a country full of natural wonders. Nowhere else at this latitude have glaciers advanced so close to the sea. Unlike the Tasman Glacier on the other side of the dividing range, these two are just what you expect glaciers to be – mighty cascades of ice, tumbling down a valley towards the sea.

The glaciers' stunning development is partly due to the West Coast being subject to prevailing rain-drenched westerlies, which fall as snow high up in the névés – the snow crystals fuse to form clear ice at a depth of about 20m. Also, ice-accumulation zones on the glaciers are very large, meaning there's a lot of ice to push down the valley. Finally, the glaciers are very steep, so the ice can travel a long way before it finally melts.

The rate of descent is staggering: wreckage of a plane that crashed on Franz Josef in 1943, 3.5km from the terminal face, made it down to the bottom 6½ years later – a speed of 1.5m a day. At times the Franz Josef can move at up to 5m a day, over 10 times as fast as glaciers in the Swiss Alps, but it usually advances about 1m per day.

The heavy tourist traffic is catered for in the twin towns of Franz Josef (referred to by locals simply as 'Franz') and Fox Glacier, 23km apart. These small, modern tourist villages provide accommodation and facilities at higher-than-average prices. Franz is the busier of the two, with more nightlife and accommodation options, but Fox has more of an Alpine-village charm.

Franz Josef Glacier

☎ 03

Early Maori knew this area as Ka Roimata o Hine Hukatere (Tears of the Avalanche Girl). Maori legend has it that a girl lost her lover after he fell while climbing the local peaks, and that her flood of tears eventually froze into a glacier.

Franz Josef Glacier was first explored in 1865 by Austrian Julius Haast, who named it after the Austrian emperor. In 1985, after a long period of apparent retreat, the glacier started advancing again and progressed nearly 2km until 1996, when the retreat started again.

The glacier is 5km from Franz, with its terminal only a 20-minute walk from a car park. Keep your fingers crossed for a fine day so that you'll have great views of the ice and the snowcapped peaks behind. The glaciers are roped off to stop people getting close to where there is a risk of ice fall; if you want to venture further you should take a guided walk.

INFORMATION

Alpine Adventure Centre (☎ 0800 800 793, 752 0793; SH6) A major activity booking agent and screens the 20-minute *Flowing West* movie (NZ$10) on a giant screen (great visuals, shame about the Jerry Bruckheimer soundtrack).
Franz Josef DOC visitors centre (☎ 752 0796; www.glaciercountry.co.nz; SH6; ⌚ 8.30am-6pm) Has an excellent interpretive display and information on walks in the area.
Medical centre (☎ 753 4172; SH6) Attended by a doctor based in nearby Whataroa.
Scott Base Tourist Information Centre (☎ 752 0288; SH6; per 20min NZ$2) Internet access.

ACTIVITIES

Independent Walks

There are several good glacier viewpoints close to the road leading from the glacier car park, including **Sentinel Rock** (10 minutes) and the **Ka Roimata o Hine Hukatere Walk** (40 minutes), which leads towards the terminal face.

Other walks require a little worthwhile footslogging. The **Douglas Walk** (one hour return), off Glacier Access Rd, passes by the terminal moraine from the 1750 advance and Peter's Pool, a small kettle lake. **Roberts**

SOUTH ISLAND

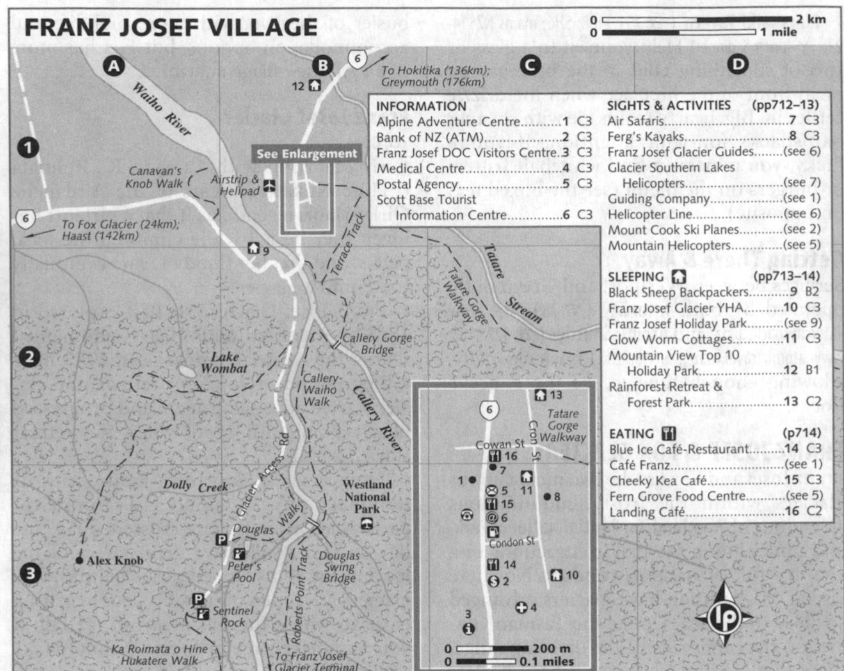

Point (five hours return) overlooks and is quite close to the terminal face and involves a longer walk over more rugged terrain.

The **Terrace Track** (one hour return) starts on the old Callery Track, a former gold-mining area, and leads up onto a terrace behind the village with pleasant views of the Waiho River. From the Tatare Gorge walkway off Cowan St, you can join the rough **Callery-Waiho Walk** (four hours return), which joins up with the Roberts Point track at Douglas Swing Bridge.

Guided Walks & Heli-hikes

The best way to experience the glaciers is to walk on them. Small-group walks with experienced guides, and with boots, jackets and other equipment supplied, are offered by the **Guiding Company** (☎ 0800 800 102, 752 00467; www.nzguides.com; Alpine Adventure Centre) and the well-established **Franz Josef Glacier Guides** (☎ 0800 484 337, 752 0763; www.franzjosefglacier.com; Scott Base Tourist Information Centre). With both outfits, half-/full-day walks cost NZ$65/110 – the full-day trip is much better value, with around six hours on the ice, as opposed to about two hours with the half-day trip. Full-day ice-climbing trips (NZ$200) are another option.

Heli-hikes not only give you an aerial view of the glacier but allow you to get much further up where there's a better chance of exploring those incredible blue-ice caves, seracs and pristine ice formations – don't pass up the opportunity to do one if at all possible. A heli-hike with about two hours on the glacier costs NZ$260.

Glacier Valley Eco Tours (☎ 752 0699; www.glaciervalley.co.nz; NZ$30) does guided walks up the river valley to the terminal.

Other Activities

For a lower-altitude experience, try one of the three-hour guided kayaking trips on Lake Mapourika (10km north of Franz) offered by **Ferg's Kayaks** (☎ 0800 423 262, 752 0230; www.glacierkayaks.com; 20 Cron St; NZ$55). Trips include mountain views and a detour down a serene channel.

Bikes can be hired from various accommodation places in Franz. The average price is around NZ$10/20 per half-/full-day hire.

GLACIER-SPEAK

It's a little-known fact that glaciers always advance and never really retreat. However, sometimes the ice melts faster than it advances, which is when the end face of the glacier moves backwards up the mountain and the glacier appears to be retreating.

The last ice age (15,000 to 20,000 years ago) saw the Franz Josef and Fox Glaciers reach right to the sea. Then warmer weather came and they may have retreated even further than their current position. In the 14th century a new mini–ice age started and for centuries the glaciers advanced, reaching their greatest extent around 1750; the terminal moraines from this time can be clearly seen. But in the 250-odd years since then, the glaciers have steadily retreated and their terminals are now several kilometres further back.

If you want to impress/bore new friends with glacial knowledge while you're all comparing exploits on the West Coast's magnificent glaciers, refer to the following:

ablation zone – where the glacier melts
accumulation zone – where the snow collects
bergschrund – large crevasse in the ice near the headwall or starting point of the glacier
blue ice – as the accumulation zone, or névé, snow is compressed by subsequent snowfalls, it becomes firn and then blue ice
crevasse – cracks in the glacial ice as it crosses obstacles and moves down the mountain
dead ice – as a glacier retreats, isolated chunks of ice may be left behind
firn – partly compressed snow on the way to becoming glacial ice
glacial flour – the river of melted ice that flows off glaciers is a milky colour from the suspension of finely ground rocks
icefall – when a glacier descends so steeply that the upper ice breaks up in a jumble of ice blocks
kettle lake – lake formed by the melt of an area of dead ice
moraine – walls of debris formed at the glacier's sides (lateral moraine) or end (terminal moraine)
névé – snowfield area where firn is formed
seracs – ice pinnacles formed, like crevasses, by the glacier passing over obstacles
terminal – the final ice face at the end of the glacier

SOUTH ISLAND

TOURS

As Julie Andrews once pointed out, the hills are alive with the sound of… buzzing helicopters and planes doing runs over the glaciers and Mt Cook. The flights are a superb experience, particularly the helicopters, which can fly right in and bank close to the glacier face, and many flights include a snow landing. A 10-minute flight without a snow landing costs between NZ$100 and NZ$145, while a 20-minute flight to the head of Franz Josef Glacier or Fox Glacier costs between NZ$150 and NZ$180. Flights past both glaciers and to Mt Cook cost around NZ$310. Prices quoted are for adults; kids under 15 will pay between 50% and 70% of the adult price.

Some recommended local operators:

Air Safaris (☎ 0800 723 274, 680 6880; www.airsafaris.co.nz)
Fox & Franz Josef Heliservices (☎ 0800 800 793, 752 0793; www.scenic-flights.co.nz)
Glacier Southern Lakes Helicopters (☎ 0800 800 732, 752 0755; www.heli-flights.co.nz)
Helicopter Line (☎ 0800 807 767, 752 0767; www.helicopter.co.nz)
Mountain Helicopters (☎ 0800 369 423, 752 0046; www.mountainhelicopters.co.nz)
Mount Cook Ski Planes (☎ 0800 800 702, 752 0714; www.mtcookskiplanes.com)

SLEEPING

Franz Josef Glacier YHA (☎ 752 0754; yha.franzjosef@yha.org.nz; 2-4 Cron St; camp sites per 2 people NZ$20, dm NZ$24-26, s NZ$40, d NZ$55-75; 💻) High-standard, recently renovated place with more than 100 beds, not including the compact camp sites in a small interior courtyard. The hostel has barrier-free rooms and the needs of disabled travellers have been taken into account throughout the building.

Rainforest Retreat & Forest Park (☎ 0800 873 346, 752 0220; www.forestpark.co.nz; Cron St; camp sites per 2 people NZ$24, d NZ$60-125) This exceptional place has camp sites plotted within rainforest and excellent facilities (including sauna and spa). There are tidy cottages with bathrooms, stand-alone elevated 'tree houses' and 'tree lodges' – the difference between the tree houses and lodges is that the latter have central heating and kitchen facilities.

Glow Worm Cottages (☎ 0800 151 027, 752 0172; www.glowwormcottages.co.nz; 27 Cron St; dm/s from NZ$22/50, d NZ$50-90) The service can be dismissive but the rooms and facilities are pretty impressive and you can hire bikes (half-day NZ$10). There are three- to five-bed dorms, motel units and numerous distractions such as a spa, video library and pool table.

Franz Josef Holiday Park (☎ 752 0766; www.franzjosef.co.nz; SH6; camp sites per 2 people from NZ$16, dm/d NZ$21/70; 💻) This park is just south of town and home to Black Sheep Backpackers, which opts for facilities and cleanliness over aesthetics (there's enough of that in the surrounding countryside). The backpackers is often filled up by tour buses, so try to book ahead at peak times. The park and the hostel seem pleasant enough, but they do get mixed reviews from travellers.

Mountain View Top 10 Holiday Park (☎ 0800 467 897, 752 0735; www.mountainview.co.nz; SH6; camp sites per 2 people NZ$26, d NZ$45-125; 💻) Spread over a big highway-side plot and fitted out with barbecues and a spa pool. Cabin-wise, it has everything from standard BYO-linen models to one- and two-bedroom units with bathrooms, sleeping up to seven people.

EATING & DRINKING

Cheeky Kea Café (☎ 752 0139; SH6; dinner NZ$15-22; 🕑 breakfast, lunch & dinner) This no-frills, caféteria-style place will suit budget consumers. The food includes lots of roasts, venison sausages and the like, with a vegetarian lasagne and several salads thrown in for vegetarians.

Café Franz (☎ 752 0793; Alpine Adventure Centre, SH6; meals NZ$9-15; 🕑 breakfast & lunch) Tucked away in a corner, this small café serves filling light meals such as bangers and mash, *panini*, roast vegetable salad and nachos. It's usually filled with tourists exhausted from considering all the activity options around town.

Landing Café (☎ 752 0229; SH6; mains NZ$10-27; 🕑 lunch & dinner) Casual, tile-floored place with a big, modern interior and tables flung across a front deck. Has a good selection of alcohol, regularly changing soups, pastas and risotto, and other dishes such as venison casserole and marinated feta salad.

Blue Ice Café-Restaurant (☎ 752 0707; SH6; mains NZ$15-28; 🕑 dinner, lunch at peak times) Stylish eatery dressed up with white linen tablecloths, but beyond the extensive wine list and well-presented meals it's still down-to-earth enough to cook up several styles of pizza. The upstairs bar has a pool table and is licensed to mix cocktails until late – it stays open if there's a decent (invariably young) crowd.

Self-caterers can shop at the well-stocked **Fern Grove Food Centre** (☎ 752 0731; SH6).

GETTING THERE & AROUND

Buses operated by **InterCity** (☎ 752 0242; www.intercitycoach.co.nz) shuttle between the two glacier towns, with daily buses south to Fox Glacier (NZ$20, 40 minutes) and Queenstown (NZ$95, eight hours), and north to Nelson (NZ$85, 10 hours). You can also get to Franz Josef from Christchurch (via Arthur's Pass) in a day. In the high season (summer) these buses can be heavily booked, so plan and book well ahead or be prepared to wait until there's space.

Atomic Shuttles (☎ 322 8883; www.atomictravel.co.nz) has daily services to Queenstown (NZ$50, 7½ hours) and Greymouth (NZ$30, 3½ hours). A ticket to Fox costs NZ$10.

Glacier Valley Eco Tours (☎ 752 0699; www.glaciervalley.co.nz) runs shuttles to the glacier (return NZ$10).

Fox Glacier

☎ 03

This glacier was named in 1872 in the wake of a visit by Sir William Fox, the country's prime minister at the time. Even if you've already visited Franz Josef Glacier, 25km up the road, it's worth stopping at Fox to see this particular mass of mountain-descending ice. At the very least, you should take the beautiful walk around Lake Matheson. The same activities offered at Franz Josef – glacier walks, flights and so on – are available from Fox township.

The petrol station here is the last fuel stop until you reach Haast, 120km further south.

INFORMATION

Alpine Guides (☎ 0800 111 600, 751 0825; www.foxguides.co.nz; SH6; 🕑 7.30am-9pm Oct-Apr, reduced hours winter) Books most activities and bus services. It's also the local postal agency and money exchange.

Fox Glacier DOC visitors centre (☎ 751 0807; SH6; 🕑 9am-12.30pm & 1-4.30pm) Has a small display

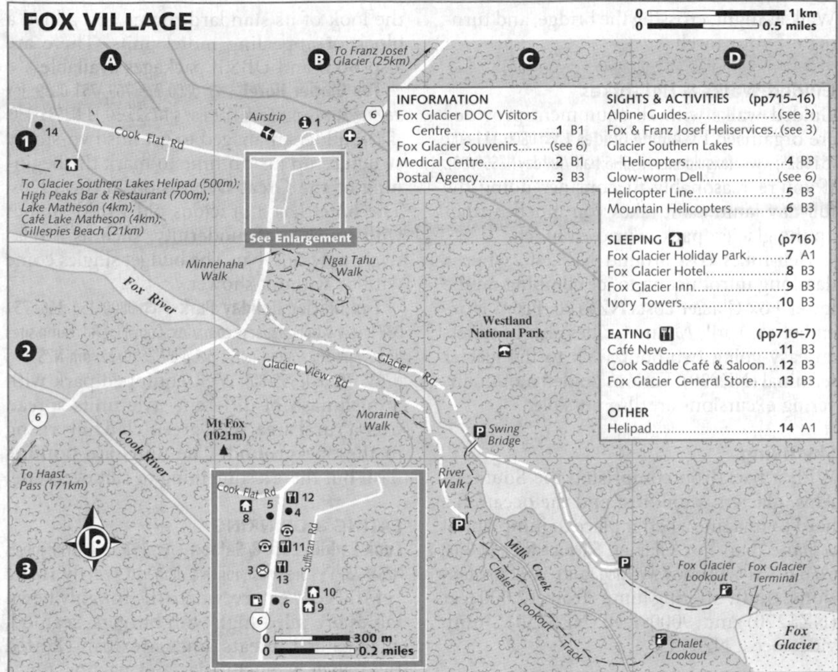

on the glacier environment and leaflets on short walks around the ice.

Fox Glacier Souvenirs (☎ 751 0765; SH6; per 12min NZ$2) The fastest Internet connection in town.

Medical centre (☎ 753 4172; SH6) Consultations provided by a doctor based in nearby Whataroa.

ACTIVITIES

Independent Walks

About 6km along Cook Flat Rd is the turn-off to **Lake Matheson** and one of the most famous panoramas in NZ. It's an hour's walk around the lake and at the far end (assuming it's a fine day) are unforgettable postcard views of Mt Tasman and Mt Cook reflected in the water. The best time to catch the view is dawn, when the lake is at its calmest, but late afternoon, when the setting sun illuminates the mountains, is also a great time.

Other than from the air, the best view of Fox Glacier and the neighbouring mountains is from further west on Cook Flat Rd – follow this unsealed road for its full 21km to the remote black sand and stunning rimu forest of **Gillespies Beach**. Another excellent viewpoint is **Mt Fox** (1021m; six hours return), off the highway 3km south of town, but this rugged tramp is recommended only for equipped trampers.

Other good walks around the glacier include the **moraine walk** over a major 18th-century advance, the short **Minnehaha Walk** or the **River Walk**. The **Chalet Lookout Track** (1½ hours return) leads to a lookout over the terminal.

It's 1.5km from Fox to the glacier turn-off, and the ice is another 5km from the main road. From the car park you can follow the marked track to the glacier, but as with Franz Josef it's roped off before you get to the terminal.

Leading from the building containing Mountain Helicopters and Fox Glacier Souvenirs is a short path to a **glow-worm dell** (NZ$4; 🕑 for 1hr from nightfall). But unlike in Hokitika, which has a freely accessible glow-worm dell (p706), some Fox entrepreneur has decided to overcharge for this brief walk (across private property) and limit the access times. We've been told it may also be possible to see glow-worms by taking the Minnehaha

Walk at night, crossing the bridge, and turning off your torch.

Guided Walks & Heli-hikes

Guided walks with all equipment provided are organised by **Alpine Guides** (☎ 0800 111 600, 751 0825; www.foxguides.co.nz; SH6; half-/full day NZ$50/80). If you're reasonably fit consider doing the full-day jaunt, as it takes you much further up the glacier; pack your own lunch.

Heli-hikes cost around NZ$240, while a day-long introduction to ice climbing on the lower Fox Glacier costs NZ$190. From November to April, Alpine Guides also conducts an easy-going two-hour walk to the glacier terminal (NZ$30). Various guided mountaineering excursions are also possible.

Skydiving

With a backdrop comprising the Southern Alps, glaciers, rainforest and the ocean, it's hard to imagine a better place to jump out of a plane than Fox Glacier. **Skydive NZ** (☎ 0800 697 593, 751 0080; www.skydiving.co.nz) is a professional outfit offering jumps from 12,000 feet (NZ$270) and 9000 feet (NZ$230). Jump videos cost NZ$145.

TOURS

The cost of aerial sightseeing at Fox is pretty much the same as at Franz Josef. Dependable operators include:

Fox & Franz Josef Heliservices (☎ 0800 800 793, 751 0866; www.scenic-flights.co.nz)

Glacier Southern Lakes Helicopters (☎ 0800 800 732, 751 0803; www.heli-flights.co.nz; SH6)

Helicopter Line (☎ 0800 807 767, 751 0767; www.helicopter.co.nz; SH6)

Mountain Helicopters (☎ 0800 369 423, 751 0045; www.mountainhelicopters.co.nz; SH6)

Mount Cook Ski Planes (☎ 0800 800 702, 752 0714; www.mtcookskiplanes.com)

SLEEPING

Ivory Towers (☎ 751 0838; www.ivorytowerslodge.co.nz; Sullivan Rd; dm/s NZ$20/38, d & tw NZ$50-90; 💻) As a backpackers should be: tidy, laid-back, draped in greenery and with good facilities, plus most of the small dorms have single beds (rather than bunks) with duvets supplied. There's also a spa, videos and a book exchange.

Fox Glacier Inn (☎ 0508 369 466, 751 0022; www.foxglacierinn.co.nz; 39 Sullivan Rd; dm/s NZ$20/50, d NZ$50-85) In the last few years this inn has refreshed the look of its standard rooms and added a block of appealing motel units. There are also B&B and DB&B packages available.

Fox Glacier Hotel (☎ 0800 273 769, 751 0839; fox.resort@xtra.co.nz; Cook Flat Rd; s NZ$25-30, d NZ$85-130; 💻) Builders managed to get this two-storey structure up just in time to mark the beginning of the Great Depression in the 1920s. The hotel has a gracious old-world air but with touches of modernity, such as a relatively new café-bar. The budget singles come with or without shower.

Fox Glacier Holiday Park (☎ 0800 154 366, 751 0821; www.holidayparks.co.nz/fox; Cook Flat Rd; camp sites unpowered/powered per 2 people NZ$20/22, dm NZ$18, s NZ$35-70, d NZ$55-80) Well-equipped park with a mishmash of different-style units spread over a rural area, with green-clad hills rising in the background. The units are nothing flash but there's something to suit everyone.

EATING & DRINKING

Cook Saddle Café & Saloon (☎ 751 0700; SH6; meals NZ$8-25; 🕑 breakfast, lunch & dinner) Overtly rustic yet still cosy eatery, where the roughly hewn tables are piled high with burgers, seafood, char-grilled meats and Mexican-slanted food such as enchiladas and nachos. Once the food is downed, there's plenty of beer and wine to follow.

Café Neve (☎ 751 0110; SH6; mains NZ$14-30; 🕑 lunch & dinner) Good food and outdoor seating are the staples here. The lunch menu mixes Asian noodles (veg or chicken), lamb hotpot, pizzas and breakfast bagels, while dinner dishes include chicken supreme and venison loin.

Fox Glacier Hotel (☎ 751 0839; Cook Flat Rd; mains NZ$14-18; 🕑 dinner) For pub-style meals, check out this hotel's past-era dining room, which serves venison casserole and good old roast of the day.

High Peaks Bar & Restaurant (☎ 751 0131; Cook Flat Rd; mains NZ$12-30; 🕑 dinner) Fresh-looking complex with a back-corner restaurant and a front-of-house bar-café with a pool table. The café has cheaper meals such as bangers and mash, and T-bone steak, while the restaurant serves pan-fried scallops and rack of lamb.

Café Lake Matheson (☎ 751 0878; Lake Matheson Rd; mains NZ$14-18, sunset barbecue NZ$25; 🕑 breakfast, lunch & dinner) Hybrid café and shop at the edge of the Lake Matheson car park, where it pleases the tourist hordes with calamari salad, Thai red curry chicken and seafood laksa. Also has a sunset barbecue nightly (6pm to 9pm, rain or shine).

Fox Glacier General Store (☎ 751 0829; SH6; ⏰ 8am-8pm) A reasonable selection of vittles, plus beer and wine takeaways.

GETTING THERE & AROUND

Most buses stop outside the Alpine Guides building.

The services offered by **InterCity** (☎ 751 0701; www.intercitycoach.co.nz) overlap – southbound services from Greymouth go to Fox Glacier, while northbound ones from Queenstown continue on to Franz Josef (NZ$20, 40 minutes). Both northbound and southbound services from Fox village depart around 8.45am daily. Services run to/from Nelson (NZ$90, 11 hours) and Queenstown (NZ$90, seven hours).

Atomic Shuttles (☎ 322 8883; www.atomictravel.co.nz) also runs between Queenstown and Greymouth daily, stopping at Fox Glacier. Fares include Queenstown (NZ$50), Greymouth (NZ$40) and Franz Josef (NZ$10). There's an additional northbound service to Punakaiki (NZ$40).

Fox Glacier Shuttle/Tours (☎ 0800 369 287) will drive you to Lake Matheson or Fox Glacier (NZ$10 return).

QUEENSTOWN REGION

Queenstown is NZ's self-styled outdoor-adventure capital, but when the adrenaline ebbs and the partygoers have called it a night (or morning), stunning Lake Wakatipu and the surrounding mountains materialise as the truly intoxicating attractions. The aptly named Remarkables and the Eyre Mountains form a breathtaking backdrop to this super-active town – superlatives can't do justice to the sight of the snowcapped peaks at sunrise or in the afterglow of dusk.

At the northern head of Lake Wakatipu is the small town of Glenorchy, a springboard to the Routeburn Track and some other fine tramps (see the boxed text on p731), while to the northeast of Queenstown is the satellite outdoor-activity hub of Wanaka.

Don't Miss: jumping into thin air at the end of a rubber cord, white-water rafting or sledging down either (or both) the Kawarau or Clutha Rivers, riding the Skyline Gondola up and the luge back down, walking the Routeburn or Rob Roy Valley Tracks, jet-boating the Dart River and celebrating your endeavours with a well-earned drink in a Queenstown watering hole.

Activities

High-excitement activities abound in and around Queenstown. White-water rafting, sledging, canyoning and jet-boating are all great ways to get wet, while bungy jumping and skydiving are exciting ways to fly. Earth-bound pursuits include skiing, rock-climbing and mountain biking. For advice on how to start making up your mind about which activities to tackle, see the boxed text on p723.

QUEENSTOWN

☎ 03 / pop 7500

Queenstown, on the northern shore of serpentine Lake Wakatipu, is the epitome of the big-budget resort town, awash with organised tour groups and plenty of hustling for the tourist dollar. There's great skiing in winter and plenty of substitute summer pastimes. Most outdoor activities are centred on the lake and the many nearby rivers. The town is also well equipped for indoor pursuits such as beer drinking, pool playing and café snacking.

This is not an irredeemably brash place – in fact, some of the cafés, bars and other places to hang out are remarkably laid-back – but with its innumerable activities, great facilities and magnificent scenery, Queenstown is understandably a huge destination for travellers. So be forewarned that its streets are often paved with humanity – if you're averse to major crowds or have long-held illusions about the sacredness of your personal space, you probably won't like it.

The region was deserted when the first pakeha arrived in the mid-1850s, although there is evidence of previous Maori settlement. Sheep farmers came first, but in 1862 two shearers discovered gold on the banks of the Shotover River, precipitating a deluge of prospectors. A year later Queenstown was a mining town with streets and permanent buildings. Then the gold petered out and by 1900 the population had dropped from several thousand to a mere 190. The

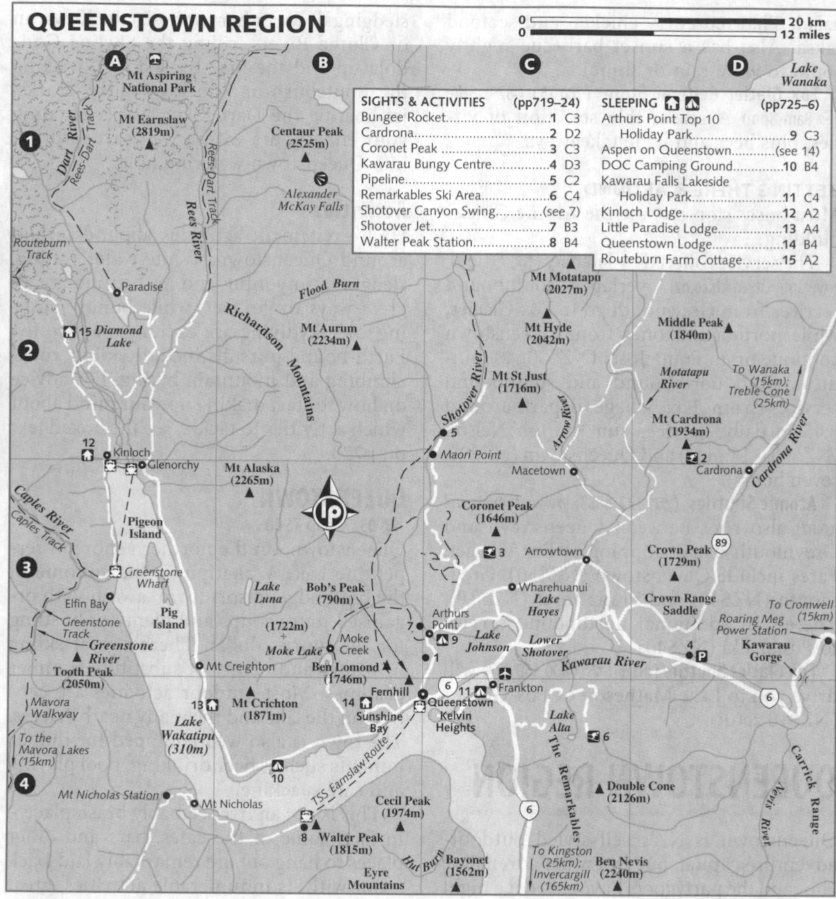

lake was the principal means of transport and at the height of the mining boom there were four paddle steamers and 30 other craft plying the waters.

Orientation & Information

This compact town is scattered over steep hills that slope up from the lake. The main streets are the pedestrian-only Mall and Shotover St, with its activity-booking offices.

EMERGENCY

Police, ambulance or fire (☎ 111)

INTERNET ACCESS

Most hostels in Queenstown have Internet access and, as well, there are several cybercafés charging around NZ$0.10 per minute:

Budget Communications (Map pp720-1; ☎ 441 1562; 2nd fl, O'Connells Shopping Centre, cnr Camp & Beach Sts; 9am-11pm) Not the quickest connection but has NZ$3 per hour early-morning and late-night deals.

Ecafé (Map pp720-1; ☎ 442 9888; 50 Shotover St; 9am-11pm) Super-quick connection.

Internet Laundry (Map pp720-1; 1 Shotover St; 8am-10pm) Rates as low as NZ$4 per hour, but only four terminals.

Internet Outpost (Map pp720-1; ☎ 441 3018; 27 Shotover St; 10am-11pm)

MEDICAL SERVICES

Queenstown Medical Centre (Map pp720-1; ☎ 441 0500; 9 Isle St)

POST

Post office (Map pp720-1; ☎ 442 7670; Camp St; 🕑 8.30am-6pm Mon-Fri, 9am-4pm Sat) Has poste restante.

TOURIST INFORMATION

Destination Queenstown (Map pp720-1; ☎ 0800 478 336, 441 1800; www.queenstown-nz.co.nz; 44 Stanley St; 🕑 8.30am-5.30pm Mon-Fri) Doesn't make bookings but is very informative.

DOC visitors centre (Map pp720-1; ☎ 442 7935; queens townvc@doc.govt.nz; 37 Shotover St; 🕑 9am-5pm May-Nov, 9am-6pm Dec-Apr) Has details of the area's natural attractions.

Info & Track Centre (Map pp720-1; ☎ 442 9708; www.infotrack.co.nz; 37 Shotover St; 🕑 7am-9pm) Next door to DOC and handles tramper transport to the Routeburn, Greenstone, Caples, Kepler, Milford and Rees-Dart trailheads.

Kiwi Discovery (Map pp720-1; ☎ 0800 505 504, 442 7340; www.kiwidiscovery.com; 37 Camp St; 🕑 7am-8.30pm peak times) Also organises summer-time track transport and winter-time ski transport and hire.

Queenstown visitors centre (Map pp720-1; ☎ 0800 668 888, 442 4100; info@qvc.co.nz; Clocktower Centre, cnr Shotover & Camp Sts; 🕑 7am-7pm Dec-Apr, 7am-6pm May-Nov) The biggest booking agent in town.

Real Journeys (Map pp720-1; ☎ 0800 656 503, 442 7500; www.realjourneys.co.nz; Steamer Wharf, Beach St; 🕑 7.30am-8.30pm) A subsidiary of the prominent South Island travel firm Fiordland Travel and books a huge range of lake trips and tours.

Station (Map pp720-1; ☎ 442 5252; www.thestation.co.nz; cnr Camp & Shotover Sts; 🕑 8am-7.30pm) A prime activity-booking office, housing AJ Hackett Bungy and various other operators.

Sights

The **Skyline Gondola** (Map pp720-1; ☎ 441 0101; www.skyline.co.nz; Brecon St; return fare adult NZ$17; 🕑 9am-6.30pm) is a cable-car ride to the summit of a hill where there are excellent views and various cash-hungry features, namely a restaurant, the 30-minute hi-tech film **Kiwi Magic** (adult NZ$9) and a luge (p724). You can, however, walk the summit **loop track** (30 minutes) for free.

The **Maori Concert & Hangi** (Map pp720-1; ☎ 442 8878; qtownmaori@paradise.co.nz; 1 Memorial St; adult NZ$50; 🕑 dining & concert 7-9.30pm), involving a show and a *hangi*-style feast, is something of a rarity on the South Island, but this Queenstown version does its best to cater to throngs of tourists. Bookings essential.

Kiwi & Birdlife Park (Map pp720-1; ☎ 442 8059; www.kiwibird.co.nz; Brecon St; adult NZ$16; 🕑 9am-5pm) is a large, peaceful bird sanctuary with two kiwi houses, a nursery where endangered birds are raised and a free-range duck pond. The birdlife also includes the rare black stilt, kea, moreporks and parakeets.

Underwater World (Map pp720-1; ☎ 442 8538; Jetty; adult NZ$5; 🕑 8.30am-dusk) is a submerged observation gallery that's overpriced and may still have streaky windows, though the agile little scaup or 'diving' ducks do make quite a sight. Perhaps save your money for the Milford Deep underwater observatory (p755).

Minus 5° Bar (Map pp720-1; ☎ 442 6050; Steamer Wharf; adult NZ$25; 🕑 from 3pm) is a frosty mirror image of the similarly named bar in Auckland (p512). Just about everything inside is made of ice. The admission fee allows you to get suited up in protective clothing and enjoy a cocktail in the bar; subsequent drinks cost NZ$12 each. Visits are limited to 30 minutes and a maximum of three cocktails.

SOUTH ISLAND

Activities

BUNGY JUMPING

Queenstown is famous for its bungy jumping and the activity's local master of ceremonies is **AJ Hackett Bungy** (Map pp720-1; ☎ 442 4007; www.ajhackett.com; Station, cnr Camp & Shotover Sts). Prices for the following options include transport out of town and gondola rides where relevant.

The historic 1880 **Kawarau Bridge** (NZ$130), 23km from Queenstown on SH6, became the world's first commercial bungy site in 1988 and offers a 43m-high leap. The NZ$8 million **Kawarau Bungy Centre** (Map p718; ☎ 442 1177; adult NZ$5; 🕑 8am-8pm) opened here at the beginning of 2004 and includes the multimedia Bungy Dome theatre, a bungy museum, café and bar.

At the top of the gondola, 400m above Queenstown, is the **Ledge Bungy** (Map pp720-1; NZ$130), the most scenic of the latex-rubber-cord options and one you can do at night.

If these aren't high enough, then do the 102m-high **Pipeline** (Map p718; NZ$160), a rather dramatic jump from a single-span suspension bridge across Skippers Canyon (a 45-minute trip from town), on the site of an 1864 gold-sluicing water pipeline. Higher still is the **Nevis Highwire** (Map p718; NZ$195) – see the boxed text on p722. If you're a true masochist, you can do AJ Hackett's **'Thrillogy'** (NZ$290), combining the Kawarau, Ledge and Nevis jumps.

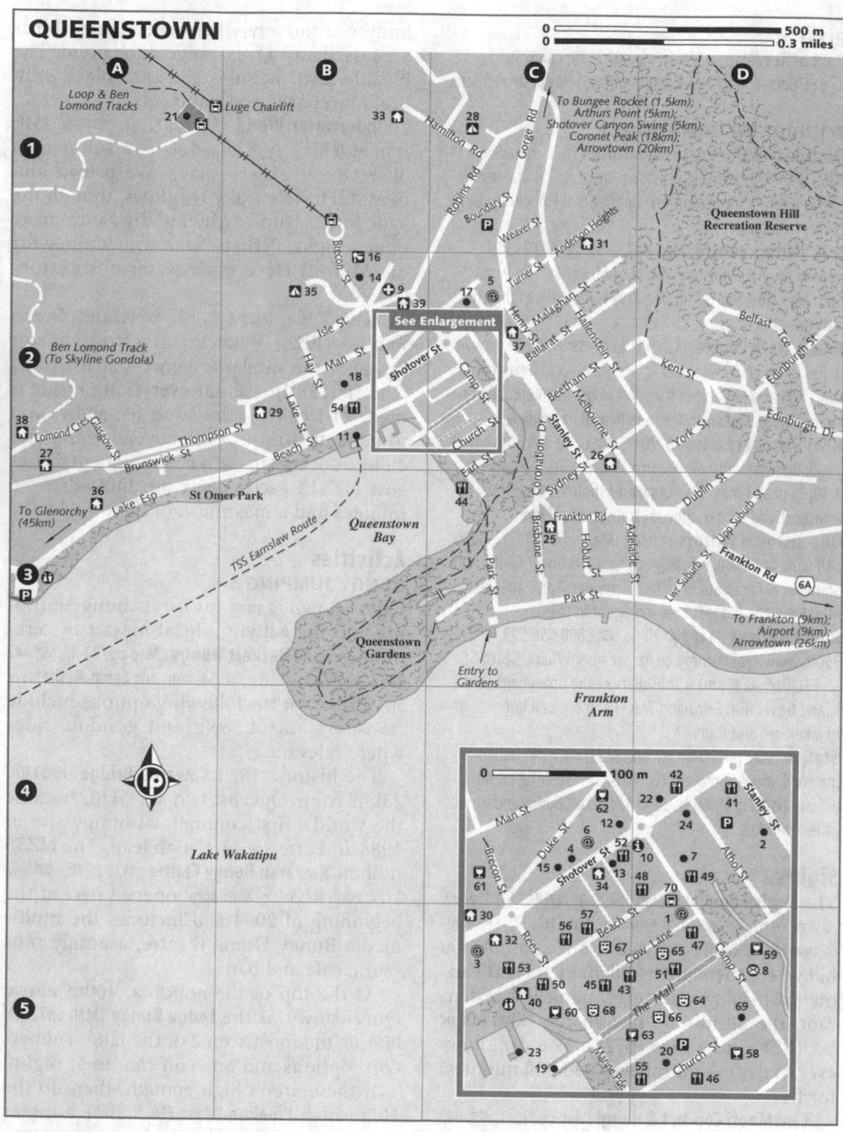

The highest of the local bungy plummets, however, takes place between 150m and 180m above Lake Wakatipu courtesy of **Parabungy** (Map pp720-1; ☎ 442 8507; www.parabungy.co.nz; Jetty; NZ$230), which uses a speedboat to tow you up in the air with a parasail and then has you take a long-distance plunge towards the lake.

Bungy Variations

The **Shotover Canyon Swing** (☎ 0800 279 464, 442 6990; www.canyonswing.co.nz; NZ$110) is touted as the world's highest rope swing (109m), where you jump from a cliff-mounted platform in a full body harness and take a wild swing across the canyon at 150km/h. On a similar theme, at Hackett's Ledge bungy

INFORMATION
Budget Communications 1 D5
Destination Queenstown 2 D4
DOC Visitors Centre (see 4)
Ecafé 3 C5
Info & Track Centre 4 C4
Internet Laundry 5 C2
Internet Outpost 6 C4
Kiwi Discovery 7 D4
Post Office 8 D5
Queenstown Medical Centre 9 B2
Queenstown Visitors Centre 10 D4
Real Journeys 11 B2
Station 12 C4

SIGHTS & ACTIVITIES (pp719–24)
Adventure Biking (see 62)
AJ Hackett Bungy (see 12)
Alpine Sports 13 C4
Caddyshack City 14 B2
Challenge Rafting (see 10)
Extreme Green Rafting (see 7)
Gravity Action 15 C4
Kawarau Jet (see 19)
Kiwi & Birdlife Park 16 B2
Kiwi Magic (see 21)
Ledge Bungy (see 21)
Ledge Sky Swing (see 21)
Luge (see 21)
Maori Concert & Hangi 17 C2
Minus 5° Bar (see 11)
NZONE (see 15)
Off Road Adventures 18 B2
Parabungy 19 C5
Paraflights NZ (see 19)
Queenstown Bike Hire 20 D5
Queenstown Rafting (see 15)
Skyline Gondola 21 A1
Small Planet Sports Co 22 D4
Tandem Paragliding (see 21)
TSS Earnslaw (see 11)
Twin Rivers Jet 23 C5
Underwater World (see 19)
Vertigo 24 D4

SLEEPING (pp725–6)
Black Sheep Lodge 25 C3
Bungi Backpackers 26 C2
Butterfli Lodge 27 A2
Creeksyde Top 10 Holiday Park 28 C1
Deco Backpackers 29 B2
Discovery Lodge 30 C5
Hippo Lodge 31 C1
McFees 32 C5
Pinewood Lodge 33 B1
Queenstown Accommodation Centre 34 C4
Queenstown Lakeview Holiday Park 35 B2
Queenstown YHA 36 A3
Resort Lodge 37 C2
Scallywags Travellers Guesthouse 38 A2
Southern Laughter 39 B2
Thomas's Hotel 40 C5

EATING (pp726–8)
Alpine Supermarket 41 D4
Bakery 42 D4
Bunker 43 C5
Coronation Bathhouse Café & Restaurant 44 C3
Cow 45 C5
Dux de Lux 46 D5
Fergburger 47 D5
Fishbone Bar & Grill 48 D4
Freiya's 49 D4
Habebes 50 C5
Kappa Sushi Café 51 D5
Ken's Noodles (see 49)
Leonardo's 52 C4
Minami Jujisei 53 C5
Naff Caff 54 B2
Night 'n Day (see 50)
O'Connell's Food Hall (see 1)
Planet 1 55 D5
Turkish Kebabs 56 C5
Vudu Café 57 C5

DRINKING (p728)
Loaded Hog (see 11)
Monty's 58 D5
Pig & Whistle 59 D5
Pog Mahones 60 C5
Rattlesnake Room 61 C4
Red Rock Bar & Grill 62 C4
Shooters (see 61)
Winnie Bagoes 63 D5

ENTERTAINMENT (p729)
Chico's 64 D5
Debajo 65 D5
Embassy Cinemas 66 D5
Sky Alpine Casino 67 C5
Subculture (see 58)
Surreal 68 C5
Tardis Bar (see 43)
Wharf Casino (see 11)
World Bar (see 6)

TRANSPORT (pp729–30)
Air New Zealand 69 D5
Bus Stop (Shopper Bus, Arrow Express) 70 D4
InterCity Booking Office (see 10)

site is the **Ledge Sky Swing** (Map pp720-1; NZ$85), where you go into free fall in a harness before soaring through the air on a huge arc.

Another option is the **Bungee Rocket** (Map p718; ☎ 442 9894; Gorge Rd; NZ$65), which one local said was 'for couch potatoes yearning for an adrenaline rush' – you're strapped into a seat in a cagelike device that's flung into the air at high speed, then bounces around at the end of bungy cords.

JET-BOATING

The Shotover and Kawarau are the preferred rivers to hurtle along near Queenstown, but the Dart River (p730) is less travelled, lengthier and more scenic. Trips either depart from Queenstown or go via minibus to the river in question before boarding the jet-boat.

Shotover Jet (Map p718; ☎ 0800 746 868, 442 8570; www.shotoverjet.co.nz; NZ$90) does half-hour trips through the rocky Shotover Canyons, with an emphasis on 360-degree spins; the thrill factor of these trips is loudly trumpeted but in reality they're very safe.

Twin Rivers Jet (Map pp720-1; ☎ 442 3257; www.twinriversjet.co.nz; NZ$75) and **Kawarau Jet** (Map pp720-1; ☎ 442 6142; www.kjet.co.nz; Jetty; NZ$75) both do one-hour trips on the Kawarau and Lower Shotover Rivers.

WHITE-WATER RAFTING

The Shotover and Kawarau Rivers are equally good for rafting. For rafting purposes, rivers are graded from I (easy) to VI (unraftable). The Shotover canyon varies from III to V+, depending on the time of year, and includes shooting the darkness of the 170m-long Oxenbridge Tunnel, carved out by miners to divert the river. The Kawarau River is IV and is fine for first-time rafters. Trips typically take four to five hours, but half of this time is spent getting there and back by minibus.

Rafting companies include **Queenstown Rafting** (Map pp720-1; ☎ 0800 723 8464, 442 9792; www.rafting.co.nz; 35 Shotover St), **Extreme Green Rafting** (Map pp720-1; ☎ 442 8517; www.nzraft.com; 39 Camp St) and **Challenge Rafting** (Map pp720-1; ☎ 0800 423 836, 442 7318; www.raft.co.nz; Queenstown visitors centre, cnr Camp & Shotover Sts); prices for all three operators start around NZ$140 for half-day trips.

RIVER SURFING & WHITE-WATER SLEDGING

Serious Fun (☎ 0800 737 468, 442 5262; www.riversurfing.co.nz; NZ$130) leads exhilarating trips over the warmer months down sections of the Kawarau River, surfing river waves, running rapids and riding whirlpools using modified boogie boards. **Mad Dog River Boarding** (☎ 442 7797; www.riverboarding.co.nz; NZ$130) does likewise.

NERVOUS ON NEVIS

No safety-standard reassurances can remove the trepidation prior to leaping from the gondola jump pod of the 134m-high Nevis Highwire bungy. The world's first gondola jump is an engineering marvel, with 30 international patents on its many innovations. It spans a remote gorge on the Nevis River and the gondola is suspended by 380m-long cables.

Several aspects of the construction have been deliberately designed to maximise exposure and titillate the fear factor. This fear increases when, bedecked in a safety harness, you take the airy cable car out to the pod, and literally thunders when you peer through the glass-bottomed floor to watch the reactions of the first jumpers.

Your turn comes. You're briefed while sitting in a chair and adjustments are made to the bungy cords based on your weight. The chair is turned and you shuffle towards the abyss.

Countdown, then six-plus seconds of free fall with the river bed far beneath hurtling towards you – what an incredible ground-rush! Relief as the bungy extends and you're catapulted to the top of the first bounce. At the top of the second bounce you release a rip cord and swing over into a sitting position. Now you can enjoy the bouncing and admire the view. A short bump, the clever recovery system swings into action, and you are winched back to the safety of the pod.

A relieved jumper quipped: 'This is great, you don't have to walk up from the river.'

Frogz Have More Fun (☎ 0800 338 737, 443 9130; www.frogz.co.nz; NZ$100-120) gets you to steer buoyant, highly manoeuvrable sleds through rapids on the Clutha and Hawea Rivers (both good for beginners) and the Kawarau River (more challenging).

CANYONING

XII-Mile Delta Canyoning (☎ 0800 222 696; www.xiimile.co.nz; NZ$135) has half-day trips in the 12-Mile Delta Canyons that expose you to all canyoning fundamentals: waterslides, rock jumps, swimming through narrow channels, abseiling and a few surprises. Canyoning in the remote Routeburn Valley is possible with **Routeburn Canyoning** (☎ 0800 222 696; NZ$250); price includes transport from Queenstown.

FLYING & SKYDIVING

Tandem Paragliding (Map pp720-1; ☎ 0800 759 688, 441 8581; www.paraglide.net.nz; NZ$185) takes off from the top of the gondola for dreamy aerial cruises, though the trips last only 10 minutes. **Flight Park Tandems** (☎ 0800 467 325; www.tandemparagliding.com; NZ$170) does similar flights from Coronet Peak.

Lazy paraflights up to 200m above the lake can be done with **Paraflights NZ** (Map pp720-1; ☎ 442 8507; www.parasail.co.nz; solo/tandem NZ$75/65). For those who prefer a delta wing there's **Skytrek Hang Gliding** (☎ 442 6311; NZ$165) and **Antigravity** (☎ 0800 426 445, 441 8898; www.antigravity.co.nz; NZ$185).

Fly by Wire (☎ 0800 359 299, 442 2116; www.flybywire.co.nz; NZ$155) is a unique experience that allows you to control a high-speed tethered plane at speeds of up to 170km/h for a six-minute flight.

NZONE (Map pp720-1; ☎ 0800 376 796, 442 5867; www.nzone.biz; 35 Shotover St; 9000/12,000ft jumps NZ$250/300) lets you tandem free fall to terminal velocity (up to 200km/h) before your parachute opens and you're nursed safely to ground.

SKIING & SNOWBOARDING

The region's oldest ski field is **Coronet Peak** (Map p718; ☎ 442 4620; daily lift passes adult/student NZ$80/60), 18km from Queenstown. The season here is reliable because of a multimillion-dollar snow-making system, and the treeless slopes and good snow provide excellent skiing – the chairlifts run to altitudes of 1585m and 1620m. The consistent gradient and the many undulations also make this a snowboarder's paradise.

The visually impressive **Remarkables ski area** (Map p718; ☎ 442 4615; daily lift passes adult/student NZ$75/55) is 23km from Queenstown. It has beginner, intermediate and advanced runs, with chairlifts and beginners' tows. Look out for the sweeping run called Homeward Bound.

There are plenty of shuttles from Queenstown to both Coronet Peak and the Remarkables during the ski season; for details, see p729.

MOUNTAIN BIKING

Adventure Biking (House of Safari; Map pp720-1; ☎ 441 0065; 48 Camp St; from NZ$80) organises uphill/

downhill riding action from Moke Lake along Moke Creek Gorge, taking in river crossings along the way.

If you're not fit enough for any strenuous uphill pedalling, choose an operator who'll take you and your bike to a suitable high point. **Gravity Action** (☎ 441 1021; www.gravityaction.com; 37 Shotover St; from NZ$100) does a trip into Skippers Canyon, while **Vertigo** (Map pp720-1; ☎ 0800 837 8446, 442 8378; www.heli-adventures.co.nz; 14 Shotover St; from NZ$110) does guided downhill trips.

Queenstown Bike Hire (Map pp720-1; ☎ 442 6039; Marine Pde; bikes per day from NZ$20, kayaks per 2hr NZ$18) has a wide variety of bikes (and some kayaks) and suggestions on where to cycle. **Small Planet Sports Co** (Map pp720-1; ☎ 442 6393; 17 Shotover St; bikes per half-/full day NZ$25/35) also hires mountain bikes.

WALKING

Stroll along the waterfront through town and into the peaceful **Queenstown Gardens** (Map pp720–1) on the peninsula. One of the shortest local climbs is the two- to three-hour return trip up/down 900m-high **Queenstown Hill**; access is from Belfast Tce.

For a more spectacular view, take the six- to eight-hour return climb of 1746m-high **Ben Lomond** (Map p718). It's a difficult tramp requiring high-level fitness and shouldn't be underestimated; consult DOC on this and the region's many other walks.

Alpine Sports (Map pp720-1; ☎ 442 7099; 28 Shotover St) hires packs, sleeping bags and boots for NZ$6 per day; tents cost NZ$10 per day. **Kiwi Discovery** (Map pp720-1; ☎ 442 7340; 37 Camp St) and **Info & Track Centre** (Map pp720-1; ☎ 442 9708; 37 Shotover St) also rent equipment. **Small Planet Sports Co** (Map pp720-1; ☎ 442 6393, 17 Shotover St) sells new and used outdoor equipment for tramping, skiing and biking.

Encounter Guided Day Walks (☎ 442 8200; www.ultimatehikes.co.nz; NZ$130; ⏲ Oct-Apr) offers a day of tramping on the Routeburn Track.

OTHER ACTIVITIES

There are plenty of wild tracks heading to otherwise inaccessible historical areas amid the region's canyons and hills. **Off Road Adventures** (Map pp720-1; ☎ 442 7858; www.offroad.co.nz; 61a Shotover St; half-day tours from NZ$220) offers guided biking (motorcycles or quads) through this challenging backcountry terrain.

Via Ferrata (☎ 409 0696; dave@viaferrata.co.nz; 3hr climbs NZ$110) guides inexperienced climbers via rock-embedded rungs and wire ropes up stony faces and ledges above Queenstown.

ACTIVITIES AU-GO-GO

There really is a bewildering array of activities in Queenstown, suitable for either the reluctant challenge seeker or the true adrenaline junkie. Sifting through all the options and choosing your preferred modes of fun can be a daunting task, but there are some things you can do to make your decisions easier. A handy activity overview is offered by **iTAG** (Independent Traveller's Adventure Guide; www.itag.co.nz) in one of its free booklets, widely available in Queenstown and elsewhere in NZ. If possible, get online and check the websites mentioned in this section to get the latest information on what tour operators are offering. Another good website is www.queenstownadventure.com.

Unless you have weeks up your sleeve, you probably won't be able to squeeze in every appealing activity. So work out a rough budget and list your top priorities. You might choose to stay in the cheapest possible accommodation to free up more cash for more activities.

Once in Queenstown you can either book directly with activity companies, at your accommodation (most backpackers have a booking service) or at one of the town's many booking agencies, located mainly on Camp and Shotover Sts. Choose the most convenient, as prices won't vary from place to place. Also bear in mind that countless activity combinations (combos) are arranged between major operators – one example is the 'Ultimate Trio' (NZ$450), which comprises a jet-boat ride, white-water rafting trip and tandem skydive from 9000 feet.

Also note that in Queenstown (and throughout NZ), participation in all adventure activities involves a degree of risk – they wouldn't be half as much fun if the adrenaline wasn't pumping. Most operators do everything in their power to ensure that participants are safe and have a great time, but accidents do happen and Lonely Planet receives many emails and letters from travellers with sad tales of broken bones and the like. So if you plan to dive headfirst into the aforementioned activities, get the appropriate travel insurance to cover any potential mishap.

The **Luge** (Map pp720-1; ☎ 441 0101; www.skyline.co.nz; Brecon St; NZ$6) involves taking to one of two 800m-long tracks at the top of the gondola in a three-wheel cart.

Minigolf enthusiasts will enjoy the intricacy of the model-decorated 'course' at **Caddyshack City** (Map pp720-1; ☎ 442 6642; 25 Brecon St; NZ$15; ⏰ 10am-5.30pm), but prices are steep.

You can also do horse riding, diving and more, including just collapsing in an exhausted heap. See the visitors centre or any of the major booking agencies for details.

Tours

SKIPPERS CANYON

Popular Skippers Canyon trips take the very scenic, winding (some would say hair-raising) 4WD-only road from Arthurs Point towards Coronet Peak and then above the Shotover River, passing sights leftover from the area's gold-mining days. **Nomad Safaris** (☎ 442 6699; www.outback.org.nz; NZ$110) heads out this way on four-hour tours.

Skippers Canyon Heritage Tours (☎ 442 5949; qtown.heritage.tours@clear.net.nz; NZ$95) does four-hour tours brimming with gold-mining facts. It's owned by a descendant of the area's early settlers.

LAKE CRUISES

The stately, steel-hulled **TSS Earnslaw** is the most famous of Lake Wakatipu's many cruise boats. Built over a century ago and licensed to carry more than 800 passengers, it churns across the lake at 13 knots, burns a tonne of coal an hour and was once the lake's major means of transport. It's been used for lake cruises since 1969. In case you're wondering, 'TSS' stands for 'Twin Screw Steamer'. Book trips through **Real Journeys** (Map pp720-1; ☎ 0800 656 503, 442 7500; www.realjourneys.co.nz; Steamer Wharf, Beach St).

Cruise options include the standard 1½-hour navigation of the lake (NZ$36) and 3½-hour excursions to the high-country **Walter Peak Station** (Map p718; NZ$55), which include sheep-shearing demonstrations and sheep-dog performances.

AERIAL SIGHTSEEING

No possibility is ignored in Queenstown – if you can't boat up it, down it or across it, or walk around it, then you can fly over it. **Over The Top Helicopters** (☎ 442 2233; www.flynz.co.nz; from NZ$135), **Queenstown Air** (☎ 442 2244; www.queenstownair.co.nz; from NZ$130), **Air Fiordland** (☎ 0800 103 404, 442 3404; www.airfiordland.com; 1hr flights NZ$290) and **Milford Sound Scenic Flights** (☎ 0800 207 206, 442 3065; www.milfordflights.co.nz; from NZ$280) are all local operators.

For a little more excitement, take a 15-minute aerobatic flight in a Pitts Special biplane with **Actionflite** (☎ 442 9708; www.actionflite.co.nz; NZ$240).

MILFORD & DOUBTFUL SOUNDS

Day trips via Te Anau to Milford Sound take 12 to 13 hours and cost around NZ$190, including a two-hour cruise on the sound; bus-cruise-flight options are also available.

Operators include **Real Journeys** (Map pp720-1; ☎ 0800 656 503, 442 7500; www.realjourneys.co.nz; Steamer Wharf, Beach St), **Great Sights** (☎ 0800 744 487; www.greatsights.co.nz), **Kiwi Discovery** (Map pp720-1; ☎ 442 7340; www.kiwidiscovery.com; 37 Camp St) and **InterCity** (☎ 442 8238; www.intercitycoach.co.nz). The **BBQ Bus** (☎ 442 1045; www.milford.net.nz) takes groups of no more than 20 people and throws in a barbecue lunch.

To save on tour travel time and cost, consider visiting Milford from Te Anau (p750).

In a similar vein, tours of Doubtful Sound cost around NZ$270 from Queenstown, but are around NZ$70 cheaper if taken from Manapouri (p758).

WINERY TOURS

Taking a guided tour of the region's fine wineries means being able to enjoy a drink or three without having to drive yourself. **Queenstown Wine Trail** (☎ 442 3799; www.queenstownwinetrail.co.nz; from NZ$80) offers a personalised, informative, five-hour tour with tastings at four wineries, while **It's Wine Time** (☎ 0508 946 384; www.winetime.co.nz; from NZ$75) is also recommend for its tours of central Otago vineyards.

KINGSTON FLYER

At Kingston, 45km from Queenstown, on the southern tip of Lake Wakatipu, is the **Kingston Flyer** (☎ 0800 435 937, 248 8848; www.kingstonflyer.co.nz; one-way/return fare NZ$25/30; ⏰ Oct-May), a heritage steam train plying a 14km stretch of track between Kingston and Fairlight – the original Flyer ran between Kingston and Gore from 1878 to the mid-1950s. Transport to/from Queenstown by bus, catamaran or helicopter can be arranged.

Sleeping

Accommodation prices tend to rocket during the peak summer and ski seasons; book well in advance at these times. You'll pay extra for rooms with guaranteed lake views.

A good resource for bedroom-seeking groups is the **Queenstown Accommodation Centre** (Map pp720-1; ☎ 442 7518; www.qac.co.nz; 30 Shotover St), which has a range of holiday homes and apartments (sleeping four to twelve people) on its books. Prices range from NZ$250 to NZ$1000 per week and there's a minimum stay of three days (one week at peak times such as Christmas).

HOSTELS

Queenstown YHA (Map pp720-1; ☎ 442 8413; yha.queenstown@yha.org.nz; 88-90 Lake Esplanade; dm from NZ$24, s/d NZ$50/65; 💻) Big, rambling, chalet-style place, though without much character inside. If you're going to take one of the smallish doubles, try for one of the two rooms with lake views; no such views accompany any single rooms. Staff in this ever-busy place are exceedingly helpful.

Hippo Lodge (Map pp720-1; ☎ 442 5785; www.hippolodge.co.nz; 4 Anderson Heights; camp site per person NZ$14, dm/s/d from NZ$24/35/65; 💻) Relaxed, good-quality, multilevel lodge subjected recently to appealing renovations. It doesn't offer town pick ups, which means you face a steep, backpack-burdened climb, but it's worth it. Optimistic wildlife lovers note: 'Hippo' is the name of the owner's dog.

McFees (Map pp720-1; ☎ 442 7400; www.megalo.co.nz/mcfees; 48a Shotover St; dm NZ$22, d NZ$70-80) An old-style place with some unusual design features (one room we saw had a nicely carpeted wall), extremely amenable front-desk staff and good facilities (particularly the kitchen), and is excellent value considering the location. There are two room rates: for rooms with a lake view, and without; some of the latter come with their own courtyard.

Butterfli Lodge (Map pp720-1; ☎ 442 6367; www.butterfli.co.nz; 62 Thompson St; dm/d NZ$23/60) Butterfli has positioned itself on a hill so that it has great lake views from an outside deck and an above-it-all feel, though the interior is fairly plain. The cheapest beds are in a four-bed room.

Pinewood Lodge (Map pp720-1; ☎ 0800 7463 9663, 442 8273; www.pinewood.co.nz; 48 Hamilton Rd; dm NZ$22, d from NZ$50; 💻) Scattered enclave of budget to family lodges, each with its own lounge. There's free pick up from town, a spa and a small shop at reception, plus a 24-hour TV and pool room.

Black Sheep Lodge (Map pp720-1; ☎ 442 7289; www.blacksheepbackpackers.co.nz; 13 Frankton Rd; dm/d NZ$23/55; 💻) This former motel is now a good-standard backpackers with the air of a large bunkhouse, particularly in the rooms adjacent to the front entry. It's attractively casual and has central heating, a fire-stoked lounge and a spa.

Deco Backpackers (Map pp720-1; ☎ 442 7384; www.decobackpackers.co.nz; 52 Man St; dm/d NZ$20/50) Two semidetached, ex-residential Art Deco places joined forces to create this distinctive backpackers. The rooms are nothing special, but the hill-side aspect lends it some good views and there's freshly percolated coffee to wake up to in the morning.

Bungi Backpackers (Map pp720-1; ☎ 0800 728 286, 442 8725; www.bungibackpackers.co.nz; 15 Sydney St; dm/d NZ$19/50; 💻) This exuberant hostel has overdosed on colour and has so much paraphernalia plastered to the walls you can't actually see what's holding the roof up. One of several hostels offering a 'smoking room' to fume-starved travellers.

Southern Laughter (Map pp720-1; ☎ 0800 5284 4837, 441 8828; www.southernlaughter.co.nz; 4 Isle St; dm/s from NZ$21/50, d NZ$55-65; 💻) The balconies, hammocks and clinging foliage in parts of this place give it almost a tropical-retreat feel. The smallish share rooms range from four-bed dorms to eight-bed 'units', and there's a pool table, spa and videos. You'll need an affinity with pink to stay here.

Scallywags Travellers Guesthouse (Map pp720-1; ☎ 442 7083; 27 Lomond Cres; dm/d NZ$24/60) Small, view-blessed backpackers up a steep hill, with a jumble of odds and ends inside that give it a lived-in atmosphere rather than a sense of transience. Offers free pick up from town.

Resort Lodge (Map pp720-1; ☎ 442 4970; www.resortlodge.co.nz; 6 Henry St; dm/d NZ$22/55; 💻) Small hostel squeezed onto a diminutive plot of land on a central side street. It does have some outdoor decks to pose on, splashes of colour brighten the rooms and you can make free local calls from in-room phones, but it's really the location that makes it worthwhile.

HOTELS

Thomas's Hotel (Map pp720-1; ☎ 442 7180; www.thomashotel.co.nz; 50 Beach St; dm NZ$24-30, d NZ$75-120) The central, lake-side location is a real winner and the rooms (all with bathrooms) are spacious. Rooms on the building's back corner come with large windows along two walls and thus have grand views over the harbour, mere metres away. The hotel's eponymous mascot is a sleepy, much-petted cat.

Discovery Lodge (Map pp720-1; ☎ 441 1185; www.dlq.co.nz; 47-49 Shotover St; dm/s NZ$26/70, d NZ$70-130; 💻) The recently built Discovery Lodge offers budget eight-bed modern dorms, but goes decidedly upmarket with its other rooms – all rooms with bathroom boast a TV and a CD/DVD player, and many rooms afford good views of the surrounding mountains. On the ground floor is a party-minded club-bar and a café.

Queenstown Lodge (Map p718; ☎ 0800 756 343, 442 7107; www.queenstownbackpackers.co.nz; Sainsbury Rd, Fernhill; dm/d from NZ$29/80; 💻) Located on the hill behind the Heritage Hotel land grab, this was originally built as a Contiki lodge but has since transformed into a large accommodation complex with some agreeable shared rooms and an on-site bar/eatery called **Peppers** (mains around NZ$15). Its shuttle heads into town hourly from 8am to 11pm.

SPLURGE!

Little Paradise Lodge (Map p718; ☎ 442 6196; www.littleparadise.co.nz; Glenorchy–Queenstown Rd; s NZ$45, d NZ$100-120) Handmade, environmentally dedicated house 28km from Queenstown. The owner has hewn the bed headboards, various carvings and adornments around the idiosyncratic house, created a duck pond and a wade-in pool, and established beautiful gardens. Fantastic location opposite the lake.

Coronet Alpine Hotel (☎ 0800 877 999, 442 7850; www.coronetalpinehotel.co.nz; 161 Arthurs Point; d from NZ$130; 💻 🅿) Large hotel in spacious grounds north of town at Arthurs Point. It's the closest hotel to Coronet Peak and offers great facilities for skiers, plus summer extras such as a swimming pool. Has a van shuttling to/from Queenstown.

Aspen on Queenstown (Map p718; ☎ 0800 427 688, 442 7688; www.queenstownhotel.com; 139 Fernhill Rd, Fernhill; d NZ$130-300; 🅿) This Colorado wannabe has a range of suites and one- and two-bedroom apartments, with suitably plush fittings and a choice of courtyard or lake views. The indoor heated pool and pool table–equipped bar may eat into your leisure time.

CAMPING & CAMPERVAN PARKS

Queenstown Lakeview Holiday Park (Map pp720-1; ☎ 0800 482 7352, 442 7252; www.holidaypark.net.nz; Brecon St; camp sites per 2 people NZ$24, d NZ$65-95) Only a short stroll from the gondola, this park has exposed camp sites, very good facilities and an arc of tall flats keeping sentinel-like watch over the lake. You have to admire the restrained immodesty of its advertising slogan: 'Arguably New Zealand's No 1 Holiday Park'.

Creeksyde Top 10 Holiday Park (Map pp720-1; ☎ 0800 786 222, 442 9447; www.camp.co.nz; 54 Robins Rd; camp sites per 2 people NZ$27, d NZ$45-135) Creeksyde's pine needle–covered grounds contain everything from plain lodge rooms to tourist flats; most sites and rooms are booked out for the Christmas/New Year season by the start of December. The reception area is impaled on a 10-tonne boiler tube salvaged from an old woollen mill.

Kawarau Falls Lakeside Holiday Park (Map p718; ☎ 0800 226 774, 442 3510; www.campsite.co.nz; SH6; camp sites unpowered/powered per 2 people NZ$24/26, dm NZ$19, d NZ$50-90; 💻) Foreshore camp sites and a six-bedroom lodge (three rooms have balconies and views of the lake) are two overnight options here. There's also a three-bedroom house that sleeps 10 (from NZ$120). Great water-side location.

Arthurs Point Top 10 Holiday Park (☎ 0800 462 267, 442 9311; www.top10arthurspt.co.nz; Gorge Rd; camp sites per 2 people NZ$24, d NZ$40-90) This park is located about 5km from town towards Arrowtown, where it's right outside the well-trafficked bustle of Queenstown and is scenically hemmed in by some chunky hills.

DOC camping ground (Map p718; 12-Mile Creek Reserve; camp sites per person NZ$5) Fifteen kilometres from Queenstown towards Glenorchy.

Eating

Vudu Café (Map pp720-1; ☎ 442 5357; 23 Beach St; breakfast NZ$9-12, lunch NZ$13-15; 🕑 breakfast, lunch & dinner) Head to this always-crowded café for an early-morning cholesterol fix via the brekkie *quesadillas* (with pesto, cheese, avocado and sour cream). This cool but by no means pretentious place also does great creative light lunches and dinners, such as potato and dill pikelets, a chicken-and-cashew noodle bowl and venison bangers and mash.

Naff Caff (Map pp720-1; ☎ 442 8211; 1/66 Shotover St; meals NZ$3-12; 🕑 breakfast & lunch) Small, welcoming place with bagels, muffins, *pain au chocolat* (chocolate croissant), home-made muesli, great coffee and various teas (which can be purchased in 100g bunches). Not so naff after all.

Leonardo's (Map pp720-1; ☎ 442 8542; 22 Shotover St; meals NZ$8-14; 🕑 breakfast & lunch) The main attractions in Leonardo's mellow interior are the organic, freshly roasted coffee and sweet tastes such as chunks of tiramisu, ginger crunch and baked cheesecake.

Ken's Noodles (Map pp720-1; ☎ 442 8628; 37 Camp St; meals NZ$4-12; 🕑 lunch daily, dinner Mon-Sat) *Udon* and *ramen* noodle meals such as *miso-ramen* (noodles in miso soup) and six-piece sushi packs (NZ$4) are efficiently dished out in Ken's sparse, no-fuss interior.

Kappa Sushi Café (Map pp720-1; ☎ 441 1423; Level 1, 36a the Mall; mains NZ$10-25; 🕑 lunch) This place is a well-established upstairs café with a small weather-proof balcony where you can tuck into sushi, sashimi, tempura, noodles – all the Japanese standards.

Fergburger (Map pp720-1; ☎ 441 1232; Cow Lane; burgers NZ$8-15; 🕑 noon-5am) High-quality gourmet burger counter hidden down Cow Lane, with bun-enclosed offerings ranging from the classic 'Fergburger' to the 'Sweet Bambi' (with cervena) and the whopping 'Big Al'.

O'Connell's Food Hall (Map pp720-1; ☎ 442 7760; cnr Camp & Beach Sts; 🕑 8am-8pm) A basement food court with budget nosh, including Turkish, fish and chips, Thai, Japanese and burgers.

Bakery (Map pp720-1; ☎ 442 8698; 15 Shotover St; 🕑 breakfast & lunch) Standard bakery treats, with some tables on an upstairs terrace.

Habebes (Map pp720-1; ☎ 442 9861; Wakatipu Arcade; meals NZ$5-11; 🕑 lunch) A fresh assortment of quiches, delicious pita rolls and impressive pies (lentil, chicken), with plenty of veg options.

Turkish Kebabs (Map pp720-1; ☎ 441 3180; 31 Beach St; meals NZ$8-15; 🕑 breakfast, lunch & dinner) Felafels, kebabs, shish kebabs and mixed grills are on the menu.

Planet 1 (Map pp720-1; cnr Church St & Marine Pde; 🕑 lunch) Cheap Japanese takeaway at this van on the waterfront.

Winnie Bagoes (Winnie's; Map pp720-1; ☎ 442 8635; 1st fl, 7 the Mall; meals NZ$15-28) Eat in a booth or on the outside balcony; meals include gourmet pizzas, Mexican, seafood and Thai-flavoured fare.

Dux de Lux (Map pp720-1; ☎ 442 9688; 14 Church St; mains NZ$10-25; 🕑 lunch & dinner) A sister branch of Christchurch's ultrapopular Dux de Lux vegetarian/seafood restaurant-cum-brewery (see p685) has been set up in Queenstown, though on a much smaller scale than the original. You can get cheapish snacks in the bar section, which is set up in the stony interior of the former McNeill's Cottage Brewery, or dine on delicious mains in the stylish dining hall next door.

Freiya's (Map pp720-1; ☎ 442 7979; 33 Camp St; mains NZ$12-18; 🕑 lunch & dinner) Well-prepared dine-in (and takeaway) Indian. Start with the usual array of samosas and pakoras, followed by a good *rogan josh* or *dal makhani* (lentils) simmered among ginger, onions and garlic. There are a half-dozen veg selections.

Cow (Map pp720-1; ☎ 442 8588; Cow Lane; mains NZ$15-26; 🕑 lunch & dinner) The dark, cosy, stone-walled interior of the Cow takes a little getting used to, particularly if you've just entered

SPLURGE!

Gantley's (☎ 442 8999; Arthurs Point Rd; mains NZ$29-40; 🕑 dinner) Fine contemporary NZ dining in an 1863 stone-and-timber building at Arthurs Point, with a highly regarded wine list and plenty of candlelight at dinner-time. Reservations essential. It runs a courtesy bus to/from town.

Bunker (Map pp720-1; ☎ 441 8030; Cow Lane; mains NZ$40; 🕑 dinner) Set in a former ski-tuning den, the Bunker is a low-lit restaurant with terrific food, an equally terrific selection of Australian and NZ wines and a couple of framed James Bond photos on the wall. There's only a handful of tables so book ahead. Mains have included horopito-rubbed roast venison, twice-cooked duck leg and seared rare tuna. After dinner it becomes a cosy, upmarket bar in which to have a dry martini, shaken, not stirred.

Coronation Bathhouse Café & Restaurant (Map pp720-1; ☎ 442 5625; Marine Pde; lunch NZ$15-21, dinner NZ$27-38; 🕑 lunch & dinner) Treat yourself to brunch, lunch or dinner in this restored historic bathhouse (built 1911) in lake-side gardens. Dinner mains include ragout of rabbit, roasted spatchcock and terrine of wild venison.

from bright sunlight. It's popular with locals for its tasty range of pizzas and pastas, but has been more hit-and-miss with travellers. The laneway it's on was where cows were brought in to be milked from nearby paddocks during the 1860s gold rush.

Fishbone Bar & Grill (Map pp720-1; ☎ 442 6768; 7 Beach St; mains NZ$15-30; ⏰ lunch & dinner) A bright spray of colour in a town full of sombre stylishness. Mains include calamari in chilli-plum sauce, wine-steamed mussels and char-grilled cod. Ocean-going calypso sometimes accompanies meals.

Minami Jujisei (Map pp720-1; ☎ 442 9854; 45 Beach St; mains NZ$15-30; ⏰ lunch Mon-Sat, dinner daily) Accomplished Japanese restaurant with various dishes cooked *nabe mono* (hotpot-style) and lots of seafood to choose from. A delicious choice is the venison *tatati;* 'tatati' means to briefly sear then put into ice and serve.

The 24-hour **Night 'n Day** (Map pp720-1; ☎ 442 8289; 24 Rees St) convenience store has lots of goodies, including pies, sandwiches, wine and beer. For fully-fledged self-catering, head to the **Alpine Supermarket** (Map pp720-1; ☎ 442 8961; cnr Stanley & Shotover Sts; ⏰ 8am-9pm Mon-Fri, 9am-9pm Sat & Sun).

Drinking

Winnie Bagoes (Winnie's; Map pp720-1; ☎ 442 8635; 1st fl, 7 the Mall) Deservedly popular place for a beer due to its laid-back ambience and retractable roof. Lounge in front of the log fire on cold afternoons, play pool or eat in a booth or on the outside balcony.

Dux de Lux (Map pp720-1; ☎ 442 9688; 14 Church St) When you're not stuffing your face with good food or listening to live music at Dux de Lux, just sit back and let the liquid-fuelled cheer of the crowd and the aftertaste of a microbrewed beer wash over you. See also review under Eating, p727.

Monty's (Map pp720-1; ☎ 441 1081; Church St) The front bar here is so rustic you half expect to see a bunch of fur trappers having a fist fight over a card game. The West Coast brew Monteith's is its preferred beer-verage.

Pog Mahones (Map pp720-1; ☎ 442 5382; 14 Rees St) Wood-saturated Irish pub right by the lake, where it gets a multitude of view-seeking drinkers. Has a cosy upstairs bar with a teensy first-come-first-seated balcony.

Pig & Whistle (Map pp720-1; ☎ 442 9055; 19 Camp St) Escape the boisterous crowds elsewhere by heading to this sedate pub with a quieter crowd, low-key music and a large beer garden out front.

Loaded Hog (Map pp720-1; ☎ 441 2969; Steamer Wharf, Beach St) Cavernous bar, a bit less rustic than its English-tavern name suggests, although it has enough farming paraphernalia nailed to the ceiling and floors to start up several agricultural ventures. Also has outside tables and a long list of NZ wines.

Red Rock Bar & Grill (Map pp720-1; ☎ 442 6850; 48 Camp St) From the same mould as many other places around town: alcove-riddled interior, pockmarked floors, some outside seating, light daytime meals and little to make a lasting impression except when a sizeable drinking crowd gathers.

Rattlesnake Room (Map pp720-1; ☎ 442 9995; 14 Brecon St) One of NZ's many saloon-style places attempting to invoke some rough-and-ready spirit by looking like the set of a cowboy film. This one is even more distinctive for its Santa Fe adobe design, the enormous six-shooter hanging from the ceiling and decorative long-horn skulls. In keeping with the anachronistic interior, it was blasting ancient David Bowie when last we visited.

Shooters (Map pp720-1; ☎ 442 4144; 10 Brecon St) A big generic sports bar, next door to the Rattlesnake Room.

Clubbing

There's plenty of free DJ-hosted entertainment around town, though some nightclubs (eg Subculture, Debajo) charge NZ$3 to NZ$5 admission after midnight Thursday to Saturday – a few dollars more for out-of-town DJs.

Subculture (Map pp720-1; ☎ 442 7685; downstairs, 12-14 Church St) Friendly, underground Subculture has some skilful DJs toying with the turntable to make satisfying drum and bass, hip-hop, dub and reggae noises.

Debajo (Map pp720-1; ☎ 442 6099; Cow Lane) Smallish downstairs affair with a tentative Latin décor (a couple of toreador posters) but a solid reputation for house beats and decent cocktails.

Tardis Bar (Map pp720-1; ☎ 441 8397; Skyline Arcade) Seems an ill-fitting name, as it's no bigger on the inside than it looks on the outside. It is, however, a good dance bar with regular DJs and a foot-worn floor.

World Bar (Map pp720-1; ☎ 442 6757; 27 Shotover St) This place was recently refitted to accommodate demanding crowds of DJ-listening, boozing backpackers. There are low benches to slump on after too many drinks and low lighting to make sure no-one notices.

Several Queenstown restaurants and bars quick-change into late-night clubs:

Chico's (Map pp720-1; ☎ 442 8439; 1st fl, the Mall) A grill above the Old Man Rock café-bar that turns into a classic-hits disco.

Rattlesnake Room (Map pp720-1; ☎ 442 9995; 14 Brecon St) On Friday and Saturday nights DJs usually mosey in.

Surreal (Map pp720-1; ☎ 441 8492; 7 Rees St) Has a mixture of drum and bass, hip-hop, trance, garage and soul, plus great food and vivacious staff.

Entertainment

The free weekly flyer the *Source* details many of the entertaining goings-on around Queenstown.

Embassy Cinemas (Map pp720-1; ☎ 442 9994; www.embassymovies.co.nz; 11 the Mall; adult/student NZ$13/9) Hosts a programme of new-release movies. Pre-5pm sessions are cheaper.

The low-rolling **Sky Alpine Casino** (Map pp720-1; ☎ 441 0400; Beach St; ⏲ noon-4am) has several bars and gaming areas, with the main tables squeezed into one large room. Another place where you can put your money at stake is the **Wharf Casino** (Map pp720-1; ☎ 441 1495; Steamer Wharf, Beach St; ⏲ 11am-3am).

Numerous bars stage live-music gigs, usually for free, including **Pog Mahones** (see Drinking, opposite), which has occasional live (and loud) Irish music and solo musicians, and **Winnie Bagoes** (see Drinking, opposite), which has acoustic shows (and DJs) during summer and winter.

Getting There & Away

AIR

Direct daily flights are offered by **Air New Zealand** (Map pp720-1; ☎ 0800 737 000, 441 1900; www.airnz.co.nz; 8 Church St) between Queenstown and both Auckland (from NZ$150) and Christchurch (from NZ$75), with connections to other major centres. **Qantas** (☎ 0800 808 767, 379 6504; www.qantas.co.nz) also has direct flights to Christchurch (from NZ$75), with connections to Auckland and Rotorua.

BUS

The booking office for **InterCity** (Map pp720-1; ☎ 442 8238; www.intercitycoach.co.nz; Queenstown visitors centre, cnr Camp & Shotover Sts) has details of daily bus services, including to Christchurch (from NZ$60), Te Anau (NZ$35), Milford Sound (NZ$70), Dunedin (NZ$55) and Invercargill (NZ$38), plus a daily West Coast service to the glaciers (NZ$95) via Wanaka (NZ$26) and Haast Pass.

'Alternative' bus tours such as the West Coast Express, Kiwi Experience, Magic Bus and the Flying Kiwi also go up the West Coast to Nelson; see p792 for details.

The **Bottom Bus** (www.bottombus.co.nz) does a loop service around the south of the South Island; for more info, see p769. Book tickets at the **Info & Track Centre** (Map pp720-1; ☎ 442 9708; 37 Shotover St).

Myriad shuttle buses can also be booked at the visitors centre. Shuttles go to Wanaka (NZ$15 to NZ$25), Dunedin (NZ$25 to NZ$30), Te Anau (NZ$25 to NZ$35) and Christchurch (NZ$45 to NZ$50). Operators include Wanaka Connexions, offering regular services to Wanaka; Atomic Shuttles, which goes to Christchurch, Dunedin and Invercargill; Southern Link Shuttles, with services to Dunedin, Christchurch and Wanaka; Catch-a-Bus, which goes to Dunedin; and Topline Tours, heading to Te Anau.

TRAMPER & SKIER TRANSPORT

Both the **Info & Track Centre** (Map pp720-1; ☎ 442 9708; 37 Shotover St) and **Kiwi Discovery** (Map pp720-1; ☎ 0800 505 504, 442 7340; 37 Camp St) can arrange transport to notable walking tracks. **Backpacker Express** (☎ 442 9939; www.glenorchyinfocentre.co.nz; 2 Oban St, Glenorchy) runs to/from the Routeburn, Greenstone, Caples and Rees-Dart Tracks, all via Glenorchy. The morning bus picks up at various accommodation points around Queenstown. Prices: NZ$15 between Queenstown and Glenorchy, and NZ$15 between Glenorchy and any of the tracks.

Bus services between Queenstown and Milford Sound via Te Anau can be used for track transport. See p754 for information on the tramper-servicing company Tracknet.

Kiwi Discovery (Map pp720-1; ☎ 0800 505 504, 442 7340; 37 Camp St) operates ski-season shuttles to Coronet Peak and the Remarkables (NZ$25). It also has services to Cardrona and Treble Cone (NZ$35) – for details of these two ski areas, see p735.

Getting Around

TO/FROM THE AIRPORT

Queenstown Airport (☎ 442 3505; www.queenstownairport.co.nz; Frankton) is located 8km from town. **Super Shuttle** (☎ 0800 748 8853, 442 3639) picks up and drops off in Queenstown (from NZ$8). The **Shopper Bus** (☎ 442 6647) runs to the airport (NZ$3.50) hourly from 8.15am to 5.15pm. **Alpine Taxis** (☎ 442 6666) or **Queenstown Taxis** (☎ 442 7788) charge around NZ$20 for the trip between airport and town.

BUS

The **Shopper Bus** (☎ 442 6647) has services to Fernhill and Frankton accommodation spots (NZ$2.50).

GLENORCHY

☎ 03 / pop 215

The tiny, beautifully situated hamlet of Glenorchy lies at the head of Lake Wakatipu, 47km or a scenic 40-minute drive from Queenstown. Regrettably, most people rush through here to knock off the Routeburn Track and bypass other great tramping opportunities in the Rees and Dart River Valleys.

Information

DOC visitors centre (☎ 442 9937; glenorchyvc@doc.govt.nz; cnr Mull & Oban Sts; 🕓 8.30am-4pm) Has info on the latest walking-track conditions and hut tickets. Get camping gear and supplies in Queenstown or Te Anau.

Activities

JET-BOATING & KAYAKING

Dart River Safaris (☎ 0800 327 853, 442 9992; www.dartriver.co.nz; Mull St; NZ$160) journeys by jet-boat into the heart of the glorious Dart River wilderness, where you can savour the grandeur of Mt Earnslaw and the bush-clad mountain walls that sandwich the river before taking a 4WD trip down a back road to Paradise. The return trip from Glenorchy takes three hours. Transfers from Queenstown cost an extra NZ$20 and add three hours to the trip. Shuttles leave Queenstown at 8am and noon daily.

Dart River Safaris also offers trips starting with a 1¼-hour jet-boat ride up the Dart and then a river descent in an inflatable three-seater canoe called a 'funyak' (www.funyaks.co.nz). From Glenorchy the whole ride takes 6½ hours and costs NZ$240; for transfers from Queenstown add NZ$20.

Dart Wilderness Adventures (☎ 0800 109 139, 442 9939; www.glenorchyinfocentre.co.nz; NZ$160) also jet-boats along the Dart River between Glenorchy and Sandy Bluff; it's a three-hour, 80km return trip. Shuttles from Queenstown (NZ$20) depart at 9.30am and 1.30pm daily.

WALKS & DRIVES

The DOC leaflet *Glenorchy Walkway* (free) details an easy water-side walk around the outskirts of town, with several picnic areas to stop at along the way.

Those with wheels should do some walking in the superb valleys north of Glenorchy. **Paradise**, in case you've been seeking it, lies 15km northwest of town, just before the start of the Rees-Dart Track. Paradise is just a paddock but the gravel road there runs through beautiful farmland surrounded by majestic mountains (there are several small creek crossings). Alternatively, you can explore the Rees Valley or take the road to Routeburn, which goes via the Dart River Bridge. Near the start of the Routeburn Track in Mt Aspiring National Park is a day hut and the short **Double Barrel** and **Lake Sylvan Walks**.

OTHER ACTIVITIES

Catering to all levels of horse-riding experience is **Dart Stables** (☎ 0800 474 3464, 442 5688; www.dartstables.com; Coll St), with options that include a two-hour ride at the head of Lake Wakatipu (NZ$85; NZ$105 from Queenstown), a full-day hoof (NZ$160) or an overnight trek with a sleep-over in Paradise (NZ$380). **High Country Horses** (☎ 442 9915; www.high-country-horses.co.nz) offers one- and two-hour guided rides for beginners (NZ$40 and NZ$60 respectively), full-day rides (NZ$110) and various overnight trips.

Glenorchy has an 18-hole **golf course** (cnr Oban & Mull Sts; green fees NZ$5); for club hire, inquire at Glenorchy Hotel (below) or Glen-Roydon Lodge (p732).

Sleeping & Eating

Glenorchy Hotel (☎ 0800 453 667, 442 9902; relax@glenorchynz.com; Mull St; dm NZ$18, d from NZ$70) Very comfortable shared-facility and rooms with bathroom are available in this pub. Out the back is the simple Backpackers Retreat. The pub also has a **café-restaurant** (mains NZ$15-30; 🕓 breakfast, lunch & dinner) which serves broccoli-and–blue cheese penne and the 'Lord of the Locals' (a dish comprising grilled meats such as chicken, beef and venison).

Kinloch Lodge (Map p718; ☎ 442 4900; www.kinlochlodge.co.nz; Kinloch Rd; dm NZ$24, d NZ$55-160) Across Lake Wakatipu from Glenorchy is

LAKE WAKATIPU REGION TRAMPS

The mountainous region at the northern head of Lake Wakatipu has some of the greatest scenery in NZ, which you can view while tramping along the famous Routeburn and lesser-known Greenstone, Caples, and Rees-Dart Tracks. Glenorchy is a convenient base for all these tramps.

Department of Conservation staff will advise on maps and track conditions, and sell Great Walks passes. For more detailed information on all these tracks, see Lonely Planet's *Tramping in New Zealand*. Also check out the DOC brochure *Lake Wakatipu Walks and Trails* (NZ$1) for shorter tracks in the area.

Routeburn Track

The three- to four-day Routeburn Track is one of the country's Great Walks (p777) and is also one of NZ's most popular rainforest/subalpine tracks because of the great variety of landscapes it passes through. Unfortunately, it has become the surrogate for those who have missed out on the Milford Track and pressures on the track have necessitated the introduction of a booking system, similar to Milford's.

Advance bookings are required throughout the main season (late October to April), either through DOC offices in Te Anau, Queenstown or Glenorchy, or by emailing greatwalksbooking@doc.govt.nz. The **Great Walks huts pass** (per night NZ$35) allows you to stay at Routeburn Flats, Routeburn Falls, Lake Mackenzie and Howden Huts – variously priced 'family' passes are also available. A **camping pass** (per night NZ$15) allows you to pitch a tent only at Routeburn Flats and Lake Mackenzie. Outside the main season, huts passes are still required (NZ$10 per night), while camping is free. Note that the Routeburn Track is often closed by snow in winter and stretches of the track are very exposed and dangerous in bad weather; always check conditions with DOC before setting out.

There are car parks at the Divide and Glenorchy ends of the Routeburn; they're unattended, so don't leave valuables in your car. **Glenorchy Holiday Park** (☎ 03-442 7171; 2 Oban St, Glenorchy) stores gear for free if you use its transport, otherwise it charges NZ$3 per day.

The Routeburn Track can be started from either end. Many people travelling from the Glenorchy end try to reach the Divide in time to catch the bus to Milford and connect with a cruise on the sound. Highlights of the track include the views from Harris Saddle and the top of nearby Conical Hill – you can see waves breaking on the beach at Martins Bay. These are almost as good as the view from Key Summit, which offers a panorama of the Hollyford, Eglinton and Greenstone Valleys.

Greenstone & Caples Tracks

The Routeburn can be combined with the Greenstone and Caples Tracks for a return trip back to the Glenorchy area. Access at the Greenstone and Caples end is at Greenstone Wharf. The road from Kinloch to Greenstone Wharf is unsealed and rough; **Backpacker Express** (☎ 03-442 9939) usually runs a boat across the lake from Glenorchy. These two tracks form a loop; the huts en route are Mid Caples, Upper Caples, McKellar and Mid Greenstone (all NZ$10 per night).

From McKellar Hut you can walk two to 2½ hours to Howden Hut on the Routeburn Track (you'll need to book this hut from late October to April). Other options from McKellar Hut include turning off for the Divide before reaching Howden Hut.

Rees-Dart Track

This difficult four- to five-day circular route goes by way of the Dart Valley, Rees Saddle and Rees Valley, with the possibility of a side trip to the Dart Glacier if you're suitably equipped. Access by vehicle is possible as far as Muddy Creek on the Rees side, from where it's two hours to Twenty Five Mile Hut.

You can park at Muddy Creek; transport is also available to and from the tracks. Most people go up the Rees first and then back down the Dart. The three DOC huts (Shelter Rock, Dart and Daleys Flat) cost NZ$10 per night.

this excellent retreat, a great place to unwind or prepare for a tramp (track transfers can be organised). Stay in the main house's 'Heritage' rooms (top choices are the two front-facing rooms) and have a three-course meal in the fine restaurant for an all-inclusive NZ$220 for two people. There's also a bar and hot tub. Kinloch is a 26km drive from Glenorchy or you can organise a three-minute boat ride (NZ$5).

Routeburn Farm Cottage (Map p718; ☎ 442 9901; elfinbay@queenstown.co.nz; Routeburn Rd; d NZ$85) The rural grounds of Routeburn Farm are on the road to the Routeburn Track – they're 6km before the start of the tramp and 21km from Glenorchy. Here you'll find a comfortable, three-bedroom, self-contained cottage surrounded by walking opportunities. The owners also conduct one-on-one horse rides (NZ$90).

Glenorchy Holiday Park (☎ 442 7171; 2 Oban St; camp sites unpowered/powered per 2 people NZ$18/20, dm NZ$16, d NZ$32-80) A spread-out park that's well set up for trampers and is fronted by a jet-boat and track shuttle booking office and a small shop with limited supplies. It has rustic bunks and cabins and a self-contained villa.

Glenorchy Café (☎ 442 9958; Mull St; meals NZ$8-15; 🕘 breakfast & lunch, dinner in summer) Eating here is like eating in someone's warm living room, a feeling accentuated by the artful domestic décor, complete with carpet and the well-aged sounds of some old vinyl 45s.

Glen-Roydon Lodge (☎ 442 9968; www.glenroydon.com; Argyle St) This lodge has a front-of-house **café** (lunch NZ$8-15; 🕘 lunch) and an expansive, more expensive **restaurant** (dinner NZ$20-25; 🕘 dinner) serving ample portions of blue cod.

Stock up on groceries in Queenstown.

Getting There & Away

The sealed Glenorchy-Queenstown Rd is wonderfully scenic, but its constant hills are a killer for cyclists. In summer, trampers buses such as **Backpacker Express** (☎ 442 9939; www.glenorchyinfocentre.co.nz; 2 Oban St), based at the Glenorchy Holiday Park, travel this road daily and also drive from Glenorchy to the start of the Routeburn, Rees-Dart, Greenstone and Caples Tracks (all NZ$15); the Routeburn Track service can be caught from Queenstown (NZ$30), with first departures around 8am. Prices quoted are for prebooked trips; there'll be an extra NZ$5 levy if you just turn up and hop on.

WANAKA

☎ 03 / pop 3500

Wanaka is a popular summer and winter resort town, known for its New Year revelries. But the splendour of the surrounding mountains and lakes, plus the long list of adrenaline-inducing outdoor activities, make it a favoured tourist destination year-round. This sporty yet laid-back town offers a sharp contrast to the hype of Queenstown, though many locals fear that all the development taking place here will ultimately change that.

Wanaka is located just over 100km from Queenstown, at the southern end of Lake Wanaka, and is the gateway to the Treble Cone, Cardrona, and Waiorau ski areas (see p735).

The town is also a gateway to **Mt Aspiring National Park**, a mountainous area in north-western Otago and southern Westland that was earmarked as a national park in 1964 and named after its highest peak, Mt Aspiring (3027m). The park, which has wide valleys, secluded flats, more than 100 glaciers and sheer mountains, now blankets more than 3500 sq km of the Southern Alps, from the Haast River in the north to its border with Fiordland National Park in the south.

Information

Lake Wanaka visitors centre (☎ 443 1233; www.lakewanaka.co.nz; 🕘 8.30am-6pm) is in a conspicuous log cabin off Ardmore St, on the waterfront.

The **DOC Wanaka visitors centre** (☎ 443 7660; Ardmore St; 🕘 8am-4.45pm Mon-Fri year-round, 9.30am-3.45pm Sat May-Oct, 8am-4.45pm Sat & Sun Nov-Apr) is the place to inquire about walks and tramps, including those in Mt Aspiring National Park.

Cybercafés include **Budget Communications** (☎ 443 4440; 38 Helwick St; per 10min NZ$1; 🕘 10am-10pm) and **Wanakaweb** (☎ 443 7429; 1st fl, 3 Helwick St; per 10min NZ$1; 🕘 9am-late).

Sights

PUZZLING WORLD

The **Puzzling World** (☎ 443 7489; www.puzzlingworld.com; adult NZ$9; 🕘 8am-5.30pm) complex harbours the three-dimensional 'Great Maze', where you must navigate 1.5km of passages to the towers at each corner and then back to the exit; it's more difficult than you think. The 'Puzzling World' section has lots of illusional treats to keep you amused and engrossed, including a series of holographic photographs,

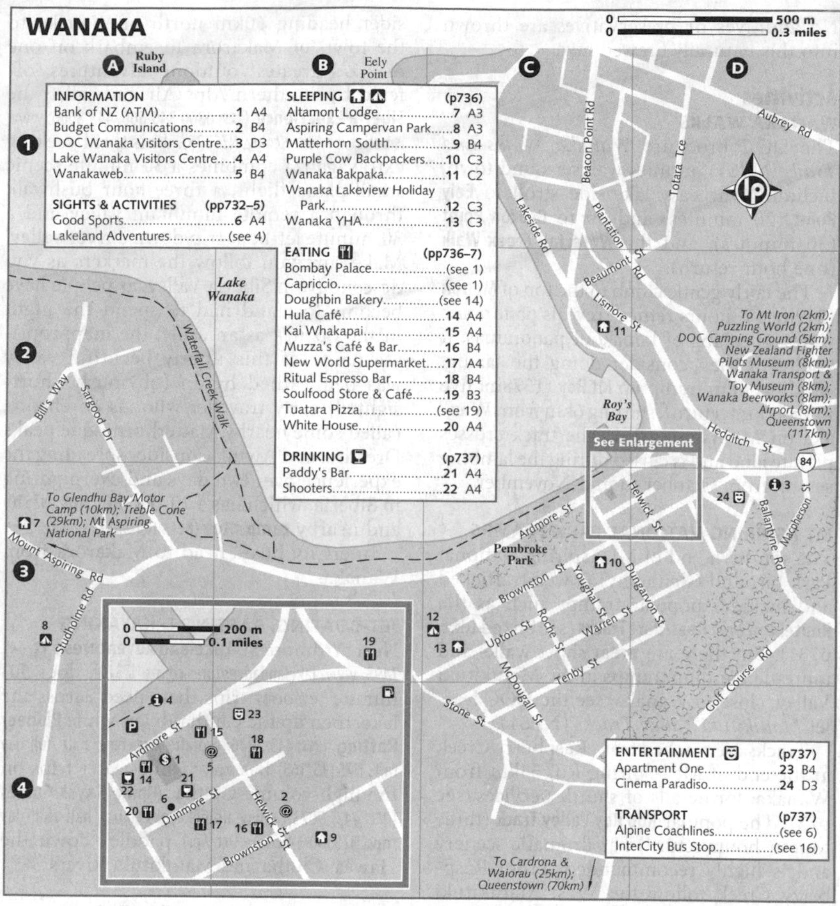

the unsettling Hall of Following Faces and a balance-testing tilted room. The complex is on the road to Cromwell, 2km from Wanaka, and is reasonably priced considering the engaging exhibits. To choose between Puzzling World or the maze, rather than doing both, costs NZ$6.

MUSEUMS

New Zealand Fighter Pilots Museum (☎ 0800 927 247, 443 7010; www.nzfpm.co.nz; Wanaka Airport; adult NZ$8; 🕑 9am-4pm Feb-Dec, 9am-6pm Jan), located 8km out of town, is dedicated to NZ combat pilots, their wartime experiences and the aircraft they flew. Besides the well-preserved collection of Hawker Hurricanes, de Havilland Vampires and the odd-sounding Chipmunk, there's also a desktop aerial combat game to try out.

Wanaka Transport & Toy Museum (☎ 443 8765; SH6; adult NZ$6; 🕑 8.30am-5pm) is the result of one man's obsessive collecting over 40 years, and will make spouses who complain about unruly tool sheds think differently. The transport section has a movie-starring Cadillac, antique motorcycles and aircraft – just how the MIG jet fighter was acquired is anyone's guess. The toy section provides nostalgic moments for just about everyone.

At **Wanaka Beerworks** (☎ 443 1865; SH6; 🕑 9.30am-6pm, tours 2pm) you can taste this small brewery's three carefully brewed products – a malt lager, a dark ale and the tasty bitter 'Brewski' – for a total cost of around NZ$5.

No additives or preservatives are thrown into this naturally brewed mix.

Activities

WANAKA WALKS

The DOC brochure *Wanaka Walks and Trails* (NZ$1) outlines walks around town, including the easy lake-side stroll to **Eely Point** (20 minutes) and on to **Beacon Point** (30 minutes), and the **Waterfall Creek Walk** (one hour return).

The fairly gentle climb to the top of **Mt Iron** (549m; 1½ hours return) reveals panoramic views. Speaking of knockout panoramas, if you're fit then consider doing the taxing, winding, 8km tramp up **Mt Roy** (1578m; five to six hours return), starting 6km from Wanaka on Mt Aspiring Rd. The track crosses private land and is closed during the lambing season from October to mid-November.

MT ASPIRING NATIONAL PARK TRAMPS

The southern end of Mt Aspiring National Park (around Glenorchy) is well trafficked and includes popular tramps such as the **Routeburn** and **Rees-Dart Tracks** (see boxed text, p731). But there are great short walks and more-demanding tramps in the Matukituki Valley, close to Wanaka; see the DOC leaflet *Matukituki Valley Tracks* (NZ$1).

Tracks are reached from Raspberry Creek at the end of Mt Aspiring Rd, 54km from Wanaka; for details of shuttle services, see p737. The popular **Rob Roy Valley Track** (three to four hours return) has dramatic scenery and is highly recommended. From Raspberry Creek follow the West Matukituki Valley path and turn off to head up the Rob Roy Stream to a point below the Rob Roy Glacier. The **West Matukituki Valley** track goes on to Aspiring Hut (four to five hours return), a scenic walk over mostly grassy flats. For overnight or multiday tramps, continue up the valley to **Liverpool Hut** for great views of Mt Aspiring, or over the very scenic but difficult **Cascade Saddle** to link up with the Rees-Dart Track north of Glenorchy.

The longer tramps are subject to snow and can be treacherous in adverse weather. Register your intentions with (and seek advice from) DOC in Wanaka before heading off.

SIBERIA EXPERIENCE

If you feel inspired by the magnificent terrain of Mt Aspiring National Park, consider heading 60km north of Wanaka to the town of Makarora to embark on one of NZ's greatest outdoor adventures, offered by Southern Alps Air and called the **Siberia Experience** (☎ 0800 345 666, 443 8666; www.siberiaexperience.co.nz; NZ$225). This thrill-seeking extravaganza combines a 30-minute scenic small-plane flight, a three-hour bushwalk through a remote mountain valley and a 30-minute jet-boat trip down a river valley. Make sure you follow the markers as you descend from Siberia Valley, as people have become lost and had to spend the night in the open – as an aside, the inappropriate name of this utterly beautiful valley was bequeathed by an (obviously short-sighted) early traveller who, as an encore, called some nearby Matterhornesque peaks Dreadful and Awful. Consider spreading the experience over two days and overnighting in Siberia, which has a 20-bed **DOC hut** (NZ$10) and nearby **camp sites** (per site NZ$5).

InterCity buses head to Makarora from Wanaka.

JET-BOATING, RAFTING & KAYAKING

Near Ardmore St, **Lakeland Adventures** (☎ 443 7495; www.lakelandadventures.co.nz; NZ$70), does 50-minute jet-boat trips that speed across the lake, then up the Clutha River, while **Pioneer Rafting** (☎ 443 1246; ecoraft@xtra.co.nz; half-/full-day rafts NZ$115/165) has easy white-water trips on the high-volume Clutha. **Alpine Kayak Guides** (☎ 443 9023; www.alpinekayaks.co.nz; half-/full-day trips NZ$100/145; 🕑 Oct-Apr) paddles down the Hawea, Clutha and Matukituki Rivers.

CANYONING & RIVER SLEDGING

Adventurous souls will love canyoning, a summer-only activity staged by **Deep Canyon** (☎ 443 7922; www.deepcanyon.co.nz; trips from NZ$195; 🕑 Nov-Apr) and involving climbing, swimming and waterfall-abseiling through confined, steep and wild gorges. Transport to the canyon, lunch, instruction and equipment are included. **Frogz Have More Fun** (☎ 0800 338 737, 443 9130; www.frogz.co.nz; NZ$100-120) offers white-water sledging on boogie board–style rafts. The cheaper trips are on the gentler Clutha and Hawea Rivers; the more expensive are on the challenging Kawarau.

SKYDIVING & PARAGLIDING

Tandem Skydive Wanaka (☎ 443 7207; www.skydivenz.com; 9000/12,000ft NZ$250/300) does jumps at

9000 feet and 12,000 feet; the latter takes 45 seconds and will have the atmosphere whistling past your ears at 200km/h.

Wanaka Paragliding School (☎ 443 9193; www.wanakaparagliding.co.nz) will take you on tandem flights at 800m (NZ$160) and 1500m (NZ$200); the higher glide is at Matukituki Bowl.

SKIING & SNOWBOARDING

The highest of the southern lake ski areas is **Treble Cone** (☎ 443 7443; www.treblecone.co.nz; daily lift passes adult/student NZ$75/55), which is in a spectacular location 29km west of Wanaka and has steep slopes that are best for intermediate to advanced skiers. It also has a natural half-pipe for snowboarding.

Around 25km south of Wanaka is **Cardrona** (☎ 443 7341, snowphone 0900 476 69; www.cardrona.com; daily lift passes NZ$70), which has high-capacity chairlifts, beginners' tows and a radical half-pipe for snowboarders. Cardrona has acquired a reputation for the services it offers to disabled skiers, and it was the first resort on the South Island to have an on-field crèche. In summer it attracts mountain bikers.

New Zealand's only commercial Nordic ski area is **Waiorau** (☎ 443 7542; www.snowfarmnz.com; daily passes NZ$30), 26km south of Wanaka in the Pisa Range, high above Lake Wanaka. Here there are 25km of groomed trails and thousands of hectares of open rolling country for the ski tourer. Huts with facilities are dotted along the top of the Pisa Range.

For details of transport to/from these ski areas, see p737.

OTHER ACTIVITIES

Lakes Wanaka and Hawea (16km away) have excellent trout fishing and numerous guides are based in Wanaka. **Lakeland Adventures** (☎ 443 7495; www.lakelandadventures.co.nz), off Ardmore St, can hire you a motorised runabout for NZ$40 per hour and a rod for NZ$20 per day; a 24-hour licence costs NZ$17 (NZ$34 per week). Lakeland Adventures also offers **Wild Wanaka**, a combo experience that can include jet-boat, helicopter, rally car and quad-bike rides; the all-inclusive experience costs NZ$450 or you can reduce the price by customising the itinerary. It also hires out kayaks (from NZ$10 per hour) and bikes (from NZ$25/35 per half-/full day).

Wanaka Rock Climbing & Abseil Adventures (☎ 443 6411; www.wanakarock.co.nz) has an introductory rock-climbing course (one day NZ$165), a half-day introduction to abseiling (NZ$95) and bouldering and multipitch climbs for the experienced.

Produced by the DOC, *Mountain-biking around Wanaka* (NZ$0.50), describes **mountain bike rides** ranging from 2km (the steep Mt Iron track) to 20km (West Matukituki Valley). For high-altitude guided mountain biking, contact **Alpine & Heli Mountain Biking** (☎ 443 8943; www.mountainbiking.co.nz; NZ$130-300), which does heli-biking trips at Treble Cone and Mt Pisa, as well as 4WD tours of the Pisa Range.

Lake Wanaka Horse Trekking (☎ 443 7777) leads two-hour rides on a forested track to Mt Iron (NZ$55), and two-hour open-country ride for more experienced riders (NZ$60).

Criffel Peak Safaris (☎ 0800 102 122, 443 1711; www.criffelpeaksafaris.com; 2/4hr trips NZ$110/250) has quad-bike excursions that explore the Criffel Range. The four-hour trip also includes a barbecue and a visit to 19th-century gold diggings.

Good Sports (☎ 443 7966; www.good-sports.co.nz; Dunmore St) hires out a vast array of sports equipment, including bikes, camping and tramping accessories, fishing rods and water-sports gear.

Tours

Lakeland Adventures (☎ 443 7495; www.lakelandadventures.co.nz) has one-hour lake cruises (NZ$50) and a three-hour trip with a guided walk on Mou Waho (NZ$90).

The following companies are all based at Wanaka Airport.

Aspiring Air (☎ 0800 100 943, 443 7943; www.nz-flights.com) has a range of scenic flights, including a 50-minute flight over Mt Aspiring (NZ$155) and a Milford Sound flyover and landing (NZ$300). **Wanaka Flightseeing** (☎ 0800 105 105, 443 8787; www.flightseeing.co.nz; from NZ$175) offers a similarly wide range of flights, several with a discount of around NZ$35 for early-morning departures. Chopper outfits include **Wanaka Helicopters** (☎ 443 1085; www.heliflights.co.nz), whose flights include a 20-minute flutter around Wanaka (NZ$145), and **Aspiring Helicopters** (☎ 443 1454; www.aspiringhelicopters.co.nz), with similar journeys and prices.

Festivals

Every second Easter (even-numbered years) Wanaka hosts the incredibly popular **Warbirds**

Over Wanaka (☎ 0800 496 920, 443 8619; www.warbirdsoverwanaka.com; Wanaka Airport; three-day admission NZ$110, first day only NZ$30, each of last two days NZ$50), a huge international air show that can attract more than 100,000 people to the town.

Sleeping

Purple Cow Backpackers (☎ 443 1880; www.purplecow.co.nz; 94 Brownston St; dm from NZ$19, d & tw NZ$55-70) Very popular, roomy and comfortable hostel with a definite ski-lodge feel, thanks partly to its chalet-style frontage, and with the great views that seem standard for most Wanaka hostels. Facilities include a separate video lounge, outdoor decks and rental of bikes and kayaks. Front desk staff are efficient.

Wanaka Bakpaka (☎ 443 7837; wanakabakpaka@xtra.co.nz; 117 Lakeside Rd; dm/d NZ$21/45) Opposite the jetty on the northern side of Roy's Bay, with great views of the lake and mountains from its lounging areas. The cosiest double is the room facing the lake, to the left of the main entrance. Eschews large backpacker bus groups (and TVs) for a constant flow of travel-happy individuals.

Matterhorn South (☎ 443 1119; www.matterhornsouth.co.nz; 56 Brownston St; dm NZ$25, s & d NZ$80; 💻) Judging by its name, this place is keen on the snowcapped mountain persona, an impression bolstered by its stark white paint job. Large dorms with bathroom, and a pleasant deck and barbecue area make this a nice place to stay.

Wanaka YHA (☎ 443 7405; yha.wanaka@yha.org.nz; 181 Upton St; camp sites per 2 people NZ$20, dm/d NZ$24/60; 💻) Appealing, slightly rough-around-the-edges YHA, far less boisterous and traveller-jammed than many other hostels around town. Has good storage facilities, and advice on the local activity options.

Altamont Lodge (☎ 443 8864; altamontlodge@xtra.co.nz; 121 Mt Aspiring Rd; s/d NZ$35/55) Excellent, friendly budget place on a tree-lined main road, with tennis court, spa pool and video lounge. At peak times (such as winter, when skiers make the most if its drying room and ski storage) it can be booked out by selfishly large groups, so book ahead. There's a one-off linen charge of NZ$5.

Aspiring Campervan Park (☎ 0800 229 843, 443 6603; www.campervanpark.co.nz; Studholme Rd; campervan sites per 2 people NZ$31) Adjacent to the Bay View Motel is this modern, well-equipped campervan park. Guests have access to a spa and sauna, and there's a fine barbecue area.

Wanaka Lakeview Holiday Park (☎ 443 7883; 212 Brownston St; camp sites per 2 people NZ$20, d NZ$35-65) No prizes for guessing Lakeview's chief characteristic. This sprawling park is Wanaka's most central outdoor accommodation centre and has a range of cabins (with and without bathroom).

Glendhu Bay Motor Camp (☎ 443 7243; glendhucamp@xtra.co.nz; Mt Aspiring Rd; camp sites per 2 people NZ$19, d NZ$30-36) Located 10km out of town, where its spacious grounds also have a lovely lake-side aspect. The cheapest doubles are in a 16-bed lodge.

There's a **DOC camping ground** (Albert Town reserve; camp sites per person NZ$5) adjacent to SH6, 5km northeast of Wanaka.

Eating

Ritual Espresso Bar (☎ 443 6662; 18 Helwick St; meals NZ$10-16; ⏰ lunch) Popular dispenser of decent coffee and very good filos, focaccias, quiches and other light fare.

Kai Whakapai (☎ 443 7795; cnr Helwick & Ardmore Sts; meals NZ$10-28; ⏰ lunch & dinner) Cooking with flair, from roast couscous and feta to some good salads (including a great chilli beef version), pancake and egg brekkies, focaccias and pastas. This perennially popular place always seems to have a sizeable crowd packed within or hanging around outside.

Soulfood Store & Café (☎ 443 7885; 74 Ardmore St; mains NZ$8-13; ⏰ breakfast & lunch) The fairly cheap pancakes, padang-style noodle and rice meals, soups, salads and smoothies here are all very wholesome – naturally for a place that also doubles as an organic food store. They're also delicious, particularly the breakfast omelettes.

Hula Café (☎ 443 9220; Pembroke Mall; meals NZ$9-15; ⏰ breakfast & lunch) Cool café tucked in behind the bakery, doing fine coffee and light food such as toasted bagels. Just to be eclectic, it also serves up 'porker' schnitzels.

Doughbin Bakery (☎ 443 7290; Ardmore St; ⏰ breakfast & lunch) Cheap baked goods on the lake front.

Capriccio (☎ 443 8579; 1st fl, 123 Ardmore St; mains NZ$14-30; ⏰ dinner) Well-established restaurant gazes out over the lake as it dishes out spaghetti and meatballs, pumpkin and basil *pan soti* and seafood meals such as tuna steak and green-lip mussels.

Tuatara Pizza (☎ 443 8186; 72 Ardmore St; pizzas NZ$15-25; ⏰ lunch & dinner) Some of the more interesting gourmet combinations in this fresh-food pizzeria are chicken and cranberry, cajun chicken with chilli, and tofu with teriyaki sauce – reassuringly, tuatara is not one of the official toppings.

Bombay Palace (☎ 443 6086; Level 1, Pembroke Mall; mains NZ$15-20; ⏰ dinner) Serves large, satisfying portions of all the usual Indian suspects, including a half-dozen vegetarian options. Let staff know when booking if you're a coeliac sufferer or have other food-related allergies and they'll do their best to accommodate you.

Muzza's Café & Bar (☎ 443 7296; 57 Helwick St; mains NZ$10-25; ⏰ lunch & dinner) With a name like that, this couldn't be anything but a laid-back, unassuming place with a family-friendly atmosphere and standard pub/tavern meals.

White House (☎ 443 9595; cnr Dunmore & Dungarvon Sts; mains NZ$15-25; ⏰ lunch & dinner) No political connections, rather a literal one – this place belongs by all rights on a Cycladian island and has a breezy, feel-good interior. Be tempted by numerous veg dishes, such as baked polenta and aubergine, as well as tiger prawns and mutton tagine (lean-meat casserole).

For self-catering, Wanaka has a **New World supermarket** (☎ 443 7168; Dunmore St; ⏰ 8am-8pm).

Drinking

Paddy's Bar (☎ 443 7645; 21 Dunmore St) This is where Wanaka's youthfully loud carousers go for a drink. It has few real Irish touches other than a preponderance of green paint and dual happy hours (5pm to 6pm and 9pm to 10pm).

Shooters (☎ 443 4345; 145 Ardmore St) Not the spot for a *Melrose Place* flashback, but rather an alcohol-flushed, barn-sized tavern catering to a ready-to-drink crowd. There are usually DJs spinning something (free) from 10pm on Friday and Saturday.

Entertainment

Apartment One (☎ 443 4911; Level 1, 99 Ardmore St; admission 11pm-3am NZ$3, other times free; ⏰ 6pm-4am Tue-Sun) Up a stairway round the back of Relishes restaurant you'll find some relaxed people slurping cocktails or shuffling to house, deep house, and drum and bass dance nights.

Cinema Paradiso (☎ 443 1505; www.paradiso.net.nz; 1 Ardmore St; tickets NZ$12) The former town hall has been turned into a wonderful, character-filled cinema decked out with old lounge chairs and sofas. Doors open one hour before film screenings. Dinner can be preordered and is served during intermission.

Getting There & Away

AIR

Flights between Wanaka and Christchurch (from NZ$80) are offered by **Air New Zealand** (☎ 0800 737 000; www.airnz.co.nz).

Aspiring Air (☎ 0800 100 943, 443 7943; www.nz-flights.com) has up to three flights daily between Queenstown and Wanaka (NZ$120, 20 minutes).

BUS

The bus stop for **InterCity** (☎ 443 7885; www.intercitycoach.co.nz; Helwick St) is outside Muzza's Café & Bar. Wanaka receives daily buses from Queenstown (NZ$26), which motor on to Franz Josef (NZ$70) via Haast Pass. From here, buses also go via Mt Cook (NZ$55) to Christchurch (NZ$130), and a daily bus to Cromwell (NZ$10) connects with the Queenstown-Dunedin route.

The town is well serviced by door-to-door shuttles, nearly all of which can be booked at **Lake Wanaka visitors centre** (☎ 443 1233), off Ardmore St. Southern Link Shuttles goes to Queenstown (NZ$15) and Christchurch (NZ$35), while Wanaka Connexions drives regularly to Queenstown (NZ$25) and Atomic Shuttles goes to Queenstown (NZ$15), Dunedin (NZ$30), Invercargill (NZ$35) and Greymouth (NZ$70).

Getting Around

Alpine Coachlines (☎ 443 7966; www.good-sports.co.nz; Dunmore St), operating out of Good Sports, has regular transport to Raspberry Creek in Mt Aspiring National Park (NZ$25), and to the ski fields of Cardrona, Waiorau and Treble Cone (return NZ$22). **Mount Aspiring Express** (☎ 443 8422; www.adventure.net.nz) has daily services to Raspberry Creek (one way/return NZ$25/45) from October to May.

DUNEDIN & THE OTAGO PENINSULA

The attractive, increasingly urbane city of Dunedin is wedged at the southwestern end of fiordlike Otago Harbour. This tidal harbour's southern shoreline is defined by the fauna-rich mass of Otago Peninsula, and between them these two features host a wealth of ecotourism activities. One of the most engaging things about this region is the highly enjoyable contrast between arts-loving city and animal-loving peninsula.

Activities

Wildlife watching is the main event in the Dunedin region, with sea lions and fur seals spottable in Otago Harbour, an albatross colony at Taiaroa Head, and enigmatic yellow-eyed and blue penguins leaving webbed footprints on the beaches of Otago Peninsula. When you get tired of just watching, try swimming and surfing off St Clair Beach, horse riding over local hills and sea-kayaking across the harbour's sheltered waters.

DUNEDIN

☎ 03 / pop 110,800

Dunedin is the South Island's second city (after Christchurch) and home of NZ's first university. The city has a statue of Robert Burns guarding its centre, echoing its foundation by Scottish settlers – 'Dunedin' is Celtic for 'Edinburgh'.

The area's early Maori history was particularly bloody, involving a three-way feud between peninsular tribes. *Utu* (revenge) followed attack as the feud between the Ngai Tahu and Ngati Mamoe tribes escalated in the early 19th century. Coastal sealing and whaling then brought ravaging diseases, and by 1848 the once considerable population of Otakau Pa had decreased to just over 100.

The first permanent European settlers arrived at Port Chalmers in March 1848, six years after a plan for a Presbyterian settlement on the South Island's east coast was mooted. Gold was soon discovered in Otago and the province quickly became the colony's richest, most influential entity, with the grand Victorian city of Dunedin as its centrepiece. But after its heady start, Dunedin declined economically and much of its population drifted away. Contemporary life in the city is more stabilised, with well-tended suburbs surrounding a socially busy centre.

Though central Dunedin now has modern intrusions, much of the fetching Victorian architecture survives: solid public buildings dot the city and wooden villas are scattered across the hilly suburbs. The city is cultured, graceful and lively for its size, with its 20,000-plus tertiary students helping drive the local arts, entertainment, café and pub scenes.

Information

Internet access costs between NZ$3 and NZ$5 per hour and is available at several hostels and cafés.

AA (☎ 477 5945; 450 Moray Pl)

DOC (☎ 477 0677; 1st fl, 77 Stuart St) Has info on regional walking tracks.

Dunedin Hospital (☎ 474 0999; 201 Great King St)

Dunedin visitors centre (☎ 474 3300; www.cityofdunedin.com; 48 the Octagon; 🕓 8.30am-5.30pm Mon-Fri, 9am-5.30pm Sat & Sun) In the magnificently restored municipal chambers.

Friendly Cyberlounge (☎ 477 8433; 1st fl, 434 George St) Internet access above Khmer Satay Noodle House, with high-performance, high-speed machines (and low rates).

General Post Office (☎ 477 3517; 243 Princes St) Handles post-restante.

Internet Depot (☎ 470 1730; 18 George St; 🕓 9am-11pm Mon-Thu, 9am-midnight Fri & Sat, 10am-11pm Sun) Big and clean, with lots of terminals.

Police, ambulance or fire (☎ 111)

University Book Shop (☎ 477 6976; 378 Great King St; 🕓 8.30am-5.30pm Mon-Fri, 9.30am-3pm Sat, 11am-3pm Sun) Dunedin's finest paper emporium. Upstairs is a great range of discounted books.

Urgent Doctors & Accident Centre (☎ 479 2900; 95 Hanover St) Has a pharmacy that's open outside normal business hours.

Sights

CADBURY WORLD

One-hour tours of Dunedin's **chocolate factory** (☎ 0800 223 287, 467 7967; www.cadburyworld.co.nz; 280 Cumberland St; adult/student NZ$14/12; 🕓 tours every 30min 9am-3.30pm) will expose you to a Willy Wonka–style foyer and details of the choc making that's been conducted in this factory since the 1930s. It handles 85% of NZ chocolate production.

SPEIGHT'S BREWERY

To see the production of a different kind of confection, take a 1½-hour tour of this **brewery** (☎ 477 7697; www.speights.co.nz; 200 Rattray St; adult/concession NZ$15/12; 🕓 tours 10am, 11.45am & 2pm daily, plus 4.30pm Sat & Sun), at the end of which you can try each of the six beers brewed here.

BALDWIN ST & OTHER RECORDS

Baldwin St, north of the city centre, is listed in *Guinness World Records* as the world's steepest street, with a gradient of 1 in 1.266.

The Dunedin City Explorer bus (see p741) will get you there. The annual 'Gutbuster' race (February) sees the winner run up and back in around two minutes.

Speaking of records, if you'd like an education in NZ indie music, dive into the piles of predominantly second-hand vinyl and CDs at **Records Records** (☎ 474 0789; www.recordsrecords.co.nz; 213 Stuart St), an iconic Dunedin music store that's been in business in the same building for more than 30 years.

OTAGO MUSEUM

Give yourself a few hours in this wonderful **museum** (☎ 474 7474; www.otagomuseum.govt.nz; 419 Great King St; admission by donation; 10am-5pm). In the Tangata Whenua Gallery is a Maori war canoe, grand meeting-house carvings and a Kiribati warrior carrying a shark-tooth sword. Exhibits in the 'Nature Galleries' include a large wasp's nest and a rather terrifying specimen of the Japanese spider crab, the world's largest. The nature theme continues in the excellent hands-on science of **Discovery World** (adult/child/family NZ$6/3/14), with live animals such as tarantulas and frogs.

DUNEDIN PUBLIC ART GALLERY

Dunedin's **art gallery** (☎ 474 3240; www.dunedin.art.museum; 30 the Octagon; permanent exhibition free; 10am-5pm) is an excellent fine-arts exhibition space with an appropriately airy, sky-lit foyer. The permanent exhibition showcases NZ art of the past 150 years – such as a corrugated-steel piece from Ralph Hotere and a room dedicated to Frances Hodgkins – plus the odd Monet, Turner and a prominent Goldie. Temporary exhibitions (admission charged) have included 'The Pre-Raphaelite Dream', a 19th-century collection borrowed from London's Tate Gallery.

OTHER MUSEUMS & GALLERIES

Even if you're not into old steam locomotives such as the 1872-built 'Josephine', it's worth visiting the **Otago Settlers Museum** (☎ 477 4000; 31 Queens Gardens; adult/concession NZ$4/3; 10am-5pm) just to see the fantastic old Art Deco bus-depot foyer that's now the museum's southern wing. There are also some great pioneer exhibits, including the eerie Smith Gallery, its walls crammed with the stolid faces of 19th-century immigrants.

New Zealand Sports Hall of Fame (☎ 477 7775; www.nzhalloffame.co.nz; Dunedin railway station, Anzac Ave; adult/student NZ$5/3; 10am-4pm) is for die-hard sports buffs who want to read cricketer Richard Hadlee's motivational mottos and then learn which wrestler patented the 'octopus clamp' (Lofty Blomfield) and who won gold in the long jump at the Helsinki Olympics (Yvette Williams).

TAIERI GORGE RAILWAY

Some visitors rate this **railway** (☎ 477 4449; www.taieri.co.nz; Dunedin railway station, Anzac Ave; NZ$60; 2.30pm Oct-Mar, 12.30pm Apr-Sep, extra 9.30am summer services) one of the world's great train journeys, similar to Colorado's Silverton-Durango line. While winding through the rocky gorge, the train crosses a dozen viaducts, one of them 50m above the creek bed. The four-hour excursion involves a 58km trip to Pukerangi and back again; some trains continue a further 19km to Middlemarch (NZ$65).

Most people take the train as a day trip, but you can travel one way and continue by bus to Queenstown (NZ$110). Before boarding the train, take some time to inspect Dunedin station's striking Edwardian façade and Royal Doulton mosaic-tile floor.

OTHER SIGHTS

Designed by a London architect and completed in 1906, grandiose **Olveston** (☎ 477 3320; www.visit-dunedin.co.nz/olveston.html; 42 Royal Tce; adult NZ$14; guided tours 9.30am-4pm) looks as it did when lived in by the ostentatious Theomin family in the early 1900s. Though the building itself is not overwhelmingly impressive, the lavish furnishings and artworks are. To see it, you must book a place on a one-hour guided tour.

Dating from 1868, the 28-hectare **Dunedin Botanic Gardens** (☎ 477 4000; cnr Great King St & Opoho Rd; admission free; gardens dawn-dusk, visitors centre 9.30am-4.30pm) has cultivated clusters of azaleas, camellias, roses and native plants, plus a four-hectare rhododendron dell and an aviary with 50 species of bird.

For a man-made contrast, visit the **University of Otago** (☎ 479 1100; www.otago.ac.nz), founded with 81 students in 1869 and with an interesting mishmash of old and new architecture.

Activities

SWIMMING & SURFING

St Clair and St Kilda are popular swimming beaches, the former equipped with the heated,

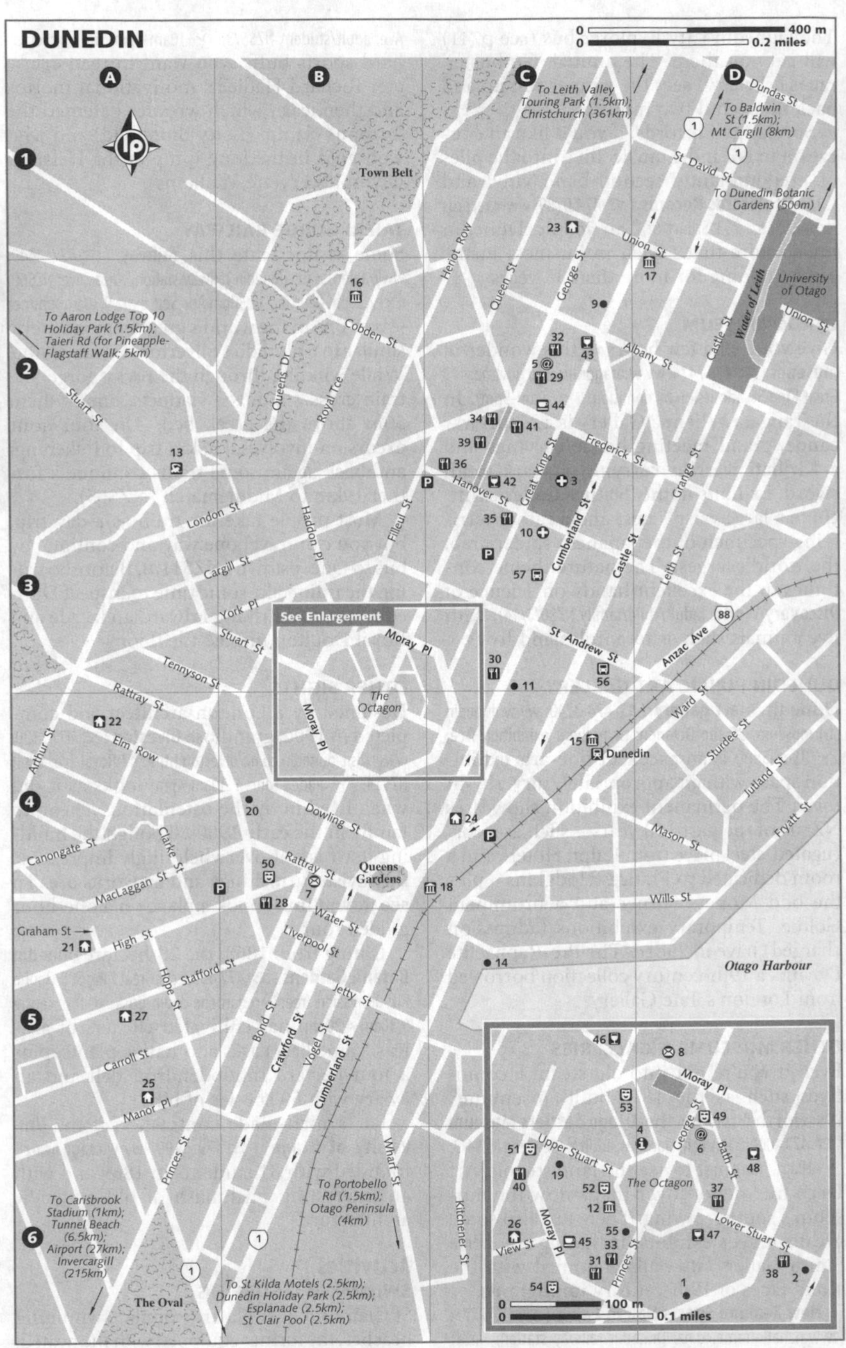
DUNEDIN
0 400 m
0 0.2 miles
Town Belt
To Leith Valley Touring Park (1.5km); Christchurch (361km)
To Baldwin St (1.5km); Mt Cargill (8km)
To Dunedin Botanic Gardens (500m)
University of Otago
Water of Leith
To Aaron Lodge Top 10 Holiday Park (1.5km); Taieri Rd (for Pineapple-Flagstaff Walk; 5km)
See Enlargement
The Octagon
Queens Gardens
Dunedin
Otago Harbour
To Carisbrook Stadium (1km); Tunnel Beach (6.5km); Airport (27km); Invercargill (215km)
The Oval
To St Kilda Motels (2.5km); Dunedin Holiday Park (2.5km); Esplanade (2.5km); St Clair Pool (2.5km)
To Portobello Rd (1.5km); Otago Peninsula (4km)
0 100 m
0 0.1 miles

INFORMATION
Automobile Association (AA) 1 D6
DOC 2 D6
Dunedin Hospital 3 C3
Dunedin Visitors Centre 4 D6
Friendly Cyberlounge 5 C2
Internet Depot 6 D6
Main Post Office 7 B4
Post Office 8 D5
University Book Shop 9 C2
Urgent Doctors & Accident Centre 10 C3

SIGHTS & ACTIVITIES (pp738–42)
Cadbury World 11 C3
Cycle Surgery (see 2)
Dunedin Public Art Gallery 12 C6
Moana Pool 13 A2
Monarch Wildlife Cruises & Tours 14 C5
New Zealand Sports Hall of Fame 15 C4
Olveston 16 B2
Otago Museum 17 D2
Otago Settlers Museum 18 C4
Records Records 19 C6
Speight's Brewery 20 B4
Taieri Gorge Railway (see 15)

SLEEPING (p742)
Chalet Backpackers 21 A5
Elm Lodge Backpackers 22 A4
Kiwis Nest 23 C1
Leviathan Heritage Hotel 24 C4
Manor House Backpackers 25 A5
Next Stop Dunedin Backpackers 26 C6
Stafford Gables YHA 27 A5

EATING (p743)
Arc Café 28 B4
Azi Jaan 29 C2
Countdown Supermarket 30 C3
Etrusco at the Savoy 31 C6
Governors Café 32 C2
Jizo Japanese Café & Bar 33 C6
London Lounge 34 C2
Mission 35 C3
New Satay Noodle House 36 C2
Percolator 37 D6
Potpourri 38 D6
Reef 39 C2
Tangenté 40 C6
Thai Over 41 C2

DRINKING (pp743–4)
Abalone 42 C3
Albert Arms (see 34)
Captain Cook 43 C2
Di Lusso (see 47)
Fix 44 C2
Mazagran Espresso Bar 45 C6
Poolhouse 46 C5
Pop Bar 47 D6
Woolshed 48 D6

ENTERTAINMENT (p744)
Bath St 49 D5
Dunedin Casino 50 B4
Fortune Theatre 51 C6
Hoyts 52 C6
Metro 53 C5
Rialto Cinemas 54 C6

TRANSPORT (p745)
Air New Zealand 55 C6
InterCity 56 C3
Suburban Bus Stop 57 C3

saltwater **St Clair Pool** (☎ 455 6352; Esplanade, St Clair Beach; adult NZ$4.50; late Oct-late Mar). Based at St Clair Pool is **Southern Coast Surf Clinic** (☎ 455 6007; www.surfcoachnz.com), which teaches surfing to beginners, organises trips for the experienced and rents out surfboards, boogie boards and wetsuits – the western end of St Clair Beach also happens to have swell surfing. Alternatively, swim at **Moana Pool** (☎ 471 9780; 60 Littlebourne Rd; adult swim NZ$4.50, swim & waterslide NZ$8.50).

WALKING

There's a short walkway across farmland to **Tunnel Beach**, southwest of central Dunedin. Catch a Corstorphine bus from the Octagon to Stenhope Cres and walk 1.5km along Blackhead Rd to Tunnel Beach Rd, then 400m to the start of the walkway (45 minutes return; closed August to October due to lambing). The hand-hewn stone tunnel was built by John Cargill to enable secluded, beachside family picnics. The impressive sandstone cliffs contain small fossils.

Catch a Normanby bus to the start of Norwood St, then walk two hours uphill (1½ hours down) to the **Mt Cargill-Bethunes Gully Walkway**. The highlight is the view from Mt Cargill (also accessible by car). In Maori legend, the three peaks of Cargill (named after a leader of early Otago colonists) represent the petrified head and feet of a princess of an early Otakau tribe. From Mt Cargill, a track continues to the 10-million-year-old, lava-formed **Organ Pipes** and, after another 30 minutes, to Mt Cargill Rd on the other side of the mountain.

Northwest of Dunedin, the 5km-long **Pineapple-Flagstaff Walk** (two hours) has great views of the harbour, coastline and inland ranges; look for the signpost at Flagstaff-Whare Flat Rd, off Taieri Rd.

The **Otago Tramping & Mountaineering Club** (www.otmc.co.nz) organises full-day and weekend tramping trips and meets every Thursday evening at 3 Young St, St Kilda; nonmembers most welcome.

OTHER ACTIVITIES

Cycle Surgery (☎ 477 7473; 67 Stuart St; bike hire per day NZ$25) rents out bikes and is a good source of mountain biking info. For details of rides in and around Dunedin, pick up the free brochure *Fat Tyre Trails* from the visitors centre.

Local horse trekkers include **Hare Hill** (☎ 0800 437 837, 472 8496; www.horseriding-dunedin.co.nz; half-/full day from NZ$50/95), based north of Dunedin and offering beach and hill-trail rides.

Tours

Dunedin City Explorer (☎ 0800 322 240; day ticket NZ$15; buses depart the Octagon 9.45am, 11.30am, 1pm, 2.30pm & 4pm) is a hop-on, hop-off bus service that loops around the city's main sights, including Baldwin St, Otago Museum, Olveston and the Botanical Gardens.

Hair Raiser (☎ 477 2258; NZ$15; 6pm Wed & Fri) is a factual evening tour of the city's darker side, which departs outside the visitors centre.

Newton Tours (☎ 477 5577; www.transportplace.co.nz; NZ$15) does one-hour double-decker tours of

Dunedin five times daily, taking in historic homes, the university and the railway station. Newton also runs numerous other double-decker routes and peninsula wildlife tours.

Monarch Wildlife Cruises & Tours (☎ 477 4276; www.wildlife.co.nz; wharf, cnr Wharf & Fryatt Sts) ships out daily on the MV *Monarch* for tours of the harbour and peninsula. The half-day peninsula cruise (from NZ$70) passes fur seal, shag and gull colonies, as well as the albatross colony at Taiaroa Head. You can also join the cruise for an hour's sail at Wellers Rock on the peninsula (NZ$30).

For more wildlife-centric tours, see p747.

Sleeping

Stafford Gables YHA (☎ 474 1919; yha.dunedin@yha.org.nz; 71 Stafford St; dm/d from NZ$23/55; 💻) Set in a late-19th-century former private hotel, this is a large-roomed, relatively peaceful hostel with a rooftop garden and balconies attached to some rooms. Staff happily give the lowdown on Dunedin activities.

Chalet Backpackers (☎ 479 2075; kirsti@paradise.net.nz; 296 High St; dm/d NZ$20/50) Small, homely brick building that adds to its character with a games room (with pool table), an expansive kitchen, a piano and rumours of a resident ghost. Has opted for comfy single beds rather than bunks in all dorms.

Elm Lodge Backpackers (☎ 0800 356 563, 474 1872; www.elmwildlifetours.co.nz; 74 Elm Row; dm/d from NZ$18/40; 💻) Good place to stay if you feel like looking down on Dunedin and the harbour from a nearby hill top, and if you appreciate cosiness and quick access to a sheltered garden. It's a short walk up from the Octagon, or it'll pick up. It also does wildlife tours (p747).

Kiwis Nest (☎ 471 9540; kiwisnest@ihug.co.nz; 597 George St; dm/s NZ$20/40, d NZ$50-80) It's quite an accomplishment for such a rambling place to retain a cosy, personal feel, but Kiwis Nest somehow manages this trick. If privacy is a priority, try for the self-contained unit with its own small piece of outdoor decking. Doubles come with or without bathroom (bathroom NZ$10 extra).

Manor House Backpackers (☎ 0800 477 0484, 477 0484; www.manorhousebackpackers.co.nz; 28 Manor Pl; dm/d NZ$20/50) Another of Dunedin's trademark warm, well-aged hostels, set in twin historic homes overlooking some parkland. The dorms are smallish but tidy affairs and staff are pretty relaxed.

Next Stop Dunedin Backpackers (☎ 0800 463 987, 477 0447; www.nextstop.co.nz; 2 View St; dm/d NZ$18/45; 💻) This mural-daubed hostel clings to the side of a steep street, with most of its rooms arranged around a nice fire-warmed central space. The doubles are small but upper-level rooms are brightened by skylights (only one dorm has this feature). There's also a small rooftop terrace.

Leviathan Heritage Hotel (☎ 0800 773 773, 477 3160; leviathan@xtra.co.nz; 27 Queens Gardens; d NZ$70-135) This landmark building is in pretty good nick despite its years of toil, and its well-appointed rooms are very popular with visitors. There's an on-site bar and café to encourage you not to leave the premises. Cooked/continental breakfast is an extra NZ$14/10.

St Kilda Motels (☎ 455 1151; stkildamotels@xtra.co.nz; cnr Queens Dr & Victoria Rd; s/d from NZ$55/65) Cheap suburban option, appealingly close to St Kilda Beach but at a busy intersection. Due to its price and location, its two one-bedroom units and several two-bedroom units can book out well in advance at peak times.

Leith Valley Touring Park (☎ 467 9936; lvtpdun@southnet.co.nz; 103 Malvern St; camp sites per 2 people NZ$22, d NZ$32-65) Lovely little park snuggled up against a cliff face north of town; take Duke St, at the top end of George St. Some camp sites are beside a small creek and the park has a very cosy timber lounge-dining-kitchen area. Continental breakfasts cost an extra NZ$5.

Dunedin Holiday Park (☎ 0800 945 455, 455 4690; www.dunedinholidaypark.co.nz; 41 Victoria Rd; camp sites unpowered/powered per 2 people NZ$20/22, d NZ$30-65) This sizeable park is several hundred metres east along Victoria Rd from St Kilda Motels (see above), over a hill from St Kilda Beach. It has around 100 camp sites and can get pretty crowded at peak times. The cheapest accommodation with bathroom is in a lodge room.

Aaron Lodge Top 10 Holiday Park (☎ 0800 879 227, 476 4725; www.aaronlodgetop10.co.nz; 162 Kaikorai Valley Rd; camp sites unpowered/powered per 2 people NZ$24/26, d NZ$40-80; 💻 ♿) Well-tended holiday plot about 2.5km northwest of the city, with good bus access (take a Bradford or Brockville bus from the Octagon). It has great gardens climbing the hill behind reception, where secluded camp sites are secreted. Kids are well catered for, with everything from play equipment to a pool and an under five's playroom.

Eating

Governors Café (☎ 477 6871; 438 George St; meals NZ$8-15; lunch & dinner) Cool, happening café decorated with student notices and serving all-day breakfasts for late risers, plus an array of milkshakes and light meals such as pizzas and nachos.

Tangenté (☎ 477 0232; 111 Moray Pl; meals NZ$10-25; lunch daily, dinner Fri & Sat) Overdoes the 'casual funk' and 'designer cuisine' angles, but this taste-conscious bakery-café nonetheless serves a delicious range of brunch fare and various seafood, meat and pasta dishes. It also does organic breads and serves coffee in towering ceramic goblets.

Percolator (☎ 477 5462; 142 Stuart St; meals NZ$7-14; breakfast, lunch & dinner) Hip little place with a relaxed young crowd and ironically grandiose touches such as an opulent paint job. Egg-heavy brunches are the big deal here and there's lots of arts-related material to browse.

Arc Café (☎ 474 1135; www.arc.org.nz; 135 High St; meals NZ$7-15; lunch daily, dinner Mon-Sat;) The highly entertaining Arc Café is famous for the variety of its on-stage performances (see p744) but is just as well known for the tasty vegetarian and vegan food it dishes out to hungry patrons.

London Lounge (☎ 477 8035; 387 George St; mains NZ$9-15; lunch & dinner) Upstairs in the Albert Arms tavern is this student-attended local, which serves gourmet pub fodder such as MacDuff sausages and Rob Roy roast of the day, all at heavily deflated prices.

Jizo Japanese Café & Bar (☎ 479 2692; 56 Princes St; meals NZ$6-15; lunch & dinner Mon-Sat) Good-value Japanese eatery with a black-coated interior and a small mezzanine level. Try the squid teriyaki or any of the excellent *udon* noodle dishes.

New Satay Noodle House (☎ 479 2235; 16 Hanover St; meals NZ$6-9; lunch & dinner) Dirt-cheap, no-frills place serving a wide variety of Chinese and Thai dishes, plus some kormas and vindaloos. Judging by the consistently full tables, the food is popular.

Azi Jaan (☎ 477 0505; 424 George St; lunch & dinner) Turkish takeaway selling tasty *shwarmas*, shish kebabs and burgers. On either side of it is a strip of cheap noodle, curry and pizza places.

Potpourri (☎ 477 9983; 97 Stuart St; meals NZ$6-9; breakfast & lunch) Wolf down organic pizzas, burritos, pies and quiches in this wholefoods café while something groovy like James Brown plays in the background.

Etrusco at the Savoy (☎ 477 3737; 1st fl, 8a Moray Pl; mains NZ$12-18; dinner) Reasonably priced Italian (pizza, pasta, antipasto) is served in a lovely pillar-supported room within the grand old Savoy building. Small circles of stained glass in the windows add colour to the wood-heavy atmosphere. Crowds dress semiformal to partake of the elegance.

Mission (☎ 477 1637; 65 Hanover St; mains NZ$13-25; lunch & dinner) Extraordinary venue – an old church that became a club and was then turned into an immaculate conception of a restaurant-bar. The menu includes pizza, calzone and various pastas (including roast veg and pesto), plus *hoy sin* pork and pumpkin-cheese fritters.

Thai Over (☎ 477 7815; 388 George St; mains NZ$17; dinner) Good central Thai restaurant with familiar dishes such as pad thai, but also serving newcomers such as lamb shank curry (the 'spaghetti drunken' Thai/Italian fusion, however, leaves us baffled).

Esplanade (☎ 456 2544; Esplanade; mains NZ$15-25; brunch & dinner) Inside the old Hydro Hotel that overlooks St Clair Beach, where ocean-front views are accompanied by jazzy background music to get you in the mood to munch a hearty brunch. Of the mains choices, spaghetti chicken livers is one of the more unusual offerings.

Reef (☎ 471 7185; 333 George St; mains NZ$19-24; lunch & dinner) Wade into Reef's deep-blue interior and try the 'express' lunches (NZ$10, served within 15 minutes): prawns, calamari rings and seafood chowder. Alternatively, fork out a bit more for the excellent chilli crab or pig out on a seafood platter with a friend (around NZ$60).

For 24-hour supplies, try **Countdown supermarket** (☎ 477 7283; 309 Cumberland St).

Drinking

Mazagran Espresso Bar (☎ 477 9959; 36 Moray Pl; 8am-6pm Mon-Fri, 10am-2pm Sat & Sun) International coffee-bean emporium, roughly the size of a large espresso machine and usually with a queue of addicts reading the *Socialist Review* and *Real Groove*.

Fix (☎ 479 2660; 15 Frederick St; early morning Mon-Thu, later in the morning Fri-Sun) Another good espresso place, where you're welcome to BYO food to accompany its coffee – the courtyard is always crammed with uni folk.

Pop Bar (☎ 474 0842; 14 the Octagon) Booth-sized downstairs bar-club that gets going late, with vinyl benches and plenty of bar stools to warm up while you're waiting for the music to start.

Di Lusso (☎ 477 3776; 12 the Octagon) A loungey hideaway dressed to impress at night and fond of its vodka and its aquarium.

Captain Cook (☎ 474 1935; 354 Great King St) The 'Cook' is a classic hang-out for procrastinating students during term, supplying them with a beer garden, a big-screen TV, cheap food and plenty of freshly filled glasses.

Albert Arms (Royal Albert Mine Host Bar; ☎ 477 2952; 387 George St) Another popular pub, the refurbished, Flatiron-shaped Albert Arms attracts low-key locals and the odd student grouping.

Woolshed (☎ 477 3246; 318 Moray Pl) Country-comfort drinking spot full of alcohol-soaked good cheer, rural wall-hung paraphernalia and several pool tables. Can get quite raucous when the crowd starts to build.

Poolhouse (☎ 477 6121; 12 Filleul St; pool per hr NZ$6-9) Not one of your run-of-the-mill seedy pool halls, but a clean, well-run, relatively quiet place where you can knock balls around on seven-foot and nine-foot tables, sipping a skill-lowering ale between pots. A new backpackers was being installed upstairs when last we visited, which may change the ambience somewhat.

Abalone (☎ 477 6877; cnr George & Hanover Sts) Shiny 1st-floor restaurant-bar that stays open until late for cocktails and other refined boozing against a background of chic muzak once the dinner crowds have been packed away. There are lots of chairs to sink into and a long elegant bar to slump over.

Entertainment

The *Otago Daily Times* newspaper lists what's on around the city. So does the free weekly pamphlet **f*INK** (www.fink.net.nz), available at cafés and bars around town. A number of nightspots close on Sunday and Monday.

Fortune Theatre (☎ 477 8323; www.fortunetheatre.co.nz; 231 Stuart St; tickets NZ$25; box office 9am-5pm Mon-Fri, also 4.30-8.30pm Sat & 1.30-4pm Sun when shows are on) Local company that's been treading the floorboards in a graceful old church for more than 25 years. Tickets are NZ$2 more expensive when booked online.

Dunedin Casino (☎ 0800 477 4545; www.dunedincasino.co.nz; 118 High St) Part of the Southern Cross Hotel, Dunedin's casino has engulfed the former Grand Hotel building's ostentatiously refurbished architecture, from the gilded grand staircase right up to the glass dome.

Hoyts (☎ 477 3250, info line 477 7019; 33 the Octagon; adult/student NZ$13/11) Commercial movie releases.

Rialto Cinemas (☎ 474 2200; www.rialto.co.nz; 11 Moray Pl; adult/student NZ$13/11) Shows a mixture of mainstream and independent releases in a halcyon-era cinema.

Metro (☎ 474 3350; www.metrocinema.co.nz; town hall, Moray Pl; tickets before/after 5pm NZ$8.50/10) Prefers art-house titles.

Carisbrook Stadium (☎ 455 1191; Burns St; tickets NZ$15-30) This is the so-called 'home of NZ rugby', also known less congenially as the 'House of Pain'. Attending a rugby game here (the season runs February to October) is a great way to expose yourself to the Kiwi passion for this sport. Terrace tickets to low-key games are usually available at the ground. Alternatively, **Bottom Bus** (☎ 434 7370; www.bottombus.co.nz) runs rugby trips combining meals, drinks, face painting and transport (with/without bus pass NZ$175/230). Transport can also be arranged from Queenstown (from NZ$200).

Arc Café (☎ 474 1135; www.arc.org.nz; 135 High St; admission free-NZ$10;) The pick of the local live-music venues is the ultradiverse Arc Café. Within the space of a week, you can catch acoustic gigs, funk, jazz, stand-up comedy, DJs and drumming circles while surrounded by a young, laid-back crowd.

Bath St (☎ 477 6750; 1 Bath St; admission free-NZ$8) Like all respectable late-night clubs, the perennial Bath St is accessed through a small unsignposted doorway and down a bare corridor. It's not that big, but the dance floor is bigger than most other clubs around town and hosts popular hip-hop and house gigs.

Some bars and restaurants that are keen on musical inspiration (most events are free):

Abalone (☎ 477 6877; cnr George & Hanover Sts) Makes clubbing sounds from 10pm Friday and Saturday.

Pop Bar (☎ 474 0842; 14 the Octagon) Usually has DJs playing Thursday to Saturday, progressing from soul to house as the days pass.

Mission (☎ 477 1637; 65 Hanover St; from 11pm Fri & Sat) Play pool under the stained glass, drink beer sitting on an old pew or just hang about staring at the organ pipes until the postdinner DJs take over.

Woolshed (☎ 477 3246; 318 Moray Pl) Hosts rustic live music (such as bush bands) from midweek onwards.

Getting There & Away

AIR

Direct, budget-priced flights between Dunedin and eastern Australia destinations are offered by **Freedom Air** (☎ 0800 600 500, 09-523 8686; www.freedomair.co.nz).

Air New Zealand (☎ 0800 737 000, 479 6594; www.airnz.co.nz; cnr Princes St & the Octagon) has direct flights to/from Auckland (from NZ$165), Christchurch (from NZ$75) and Wellington (from NZ$100). **Qantas** (☎ 0800 808 767, 379 6504; www.qantas.co.nz) also offers direct flights to Christchurch (from NZ$95). **Origin Pacific** (☎ 0800 302 302, 547 2020; www.originpacific.co.nz) flies direct to Christchurch (from NZ$75).

BUS

InterCity (☎ 474 9600; www.intercitycoach.co.nz; 205 St Andrew St) has direct services to Christchurch (NZ$60), Queenstown (NZ$55) and Te Anau (NZ$45).

A number of door-to-door shuttles service Dunedin, arriving and departing at **Dunedin railway station** (Anzac Ave); you can make inquiries and bookings at the station's **travel desk** (☎ 477 4449; 8.30am-5pm Mon-Fri, 9am-5pm Sat & Sun). Atomic Shuttles runs to/from Christchurch (NZ$30), Invercargill (NZ$25) and Queenstown or Wanaka (NZ$30). Knight Rider operates a night-time service on the Christchurch–Dunedin–Invercargill route (NZ$35 each segment). Catch-A-Bus operates daily between Dunedin and Te Anau (NZ$45) and also has services to Christchurch (NZ$45), Queenstown (NZ$30) and Wanaka (NZ$38). Wanaka Connexions runs from Dunedin to Wanaka and then Queenstown (both NZ$35).

From Dunedin, **Bottom Bus** (☎ 434 7370; www.bottombus.co.nz) and **Catlins Coaster** (☎ 0800 304 333, 021-682 461; www.catlinscoaster.co.nz) both do the scenic route through the Catlins; for details see p769.

TRAIN

The magnificent **Dunedin railway station** (Anzac Ave) is visited by the Taieri Gorge Railway (p739).

Getting Around

Dunedin Airport (☎ 486 2879; www.dnairport.co.nz) is located 27km southwest of the city. **Kiwi Shuttles** (☎ 473 7017; www.kiwishuttles.co.nz) handles airport transfers (around NZ$15). **Dunedin Taxis** (☎ 477 7777) and **City Taxis** (☎ 477 1771) also operate door-to-door shuttles; a standard taxi ride between the city and airport costs around NZ$50 to NZ$60.

City buses (www.orc.govt.nz/bustt/bus.asp) leave from stops on the Octagon, while buses to districts around Dunedin leave from Cumberland St. Buses run regularly during the week, but routes either combine on Saturday and Sunday to form limited services or they simply stop. The visitors centre has timetables; the average trip costs less than NZ$2.

For details of the hop-on, hop-off Dunedin City Explorer, see p741.

OTAGO PENINSULA

☎ 03

Otago Peninsula has a reputation as the most accessible wildlife area on the South Island – albatross, yellow-eyed penguins, blue penguins, fur seals and sea lions all thrive here – and also harbours a score of historical sites, walkways and natural formations. For an overview, pick up the *Otago Peninsula* brochure and map from Dunedin's visitors centre and check out www.otago-peninsula.co.nz.

Sights

ALBATROSS COLONY

Taiaroa Head, at the peninsula's eastern end, has the world's only mainland royal albatross colony. The birds arrive at the nesting site in September, court and mate in October, lay eggs in November, then incubate the eggs until January, when the chicks hatch. Between March and September parents leave their chicks while collecting food, returning only for feeding. By September the fledged chicks leave.

The **Royal Albatross Centre** (☎ 478 0499; www.albatross.org.nz; Taiaroa Head; 9am-7pm summer, shorter hours winter) has excellent displays on the albatross and other peninsular wildlife, plus a pretty good **café** (mains NZ$11-17). The only public access to the colony is from the centre, with tours offered every 30 minutes (bookings essential). The one-hour 'Royal Albatross' tour (NZ$25) includes a 30-minute video-accompanied talk at the centre, then heads up the hill to a glassed-in viewing area overlooking the nesting sites. In calm weather it's unlikely you'll see an albatross flying but chances are better later in the day when the wind picks up; ask if the birds are around before you pay. The centre is open

SOUTH ISLAND

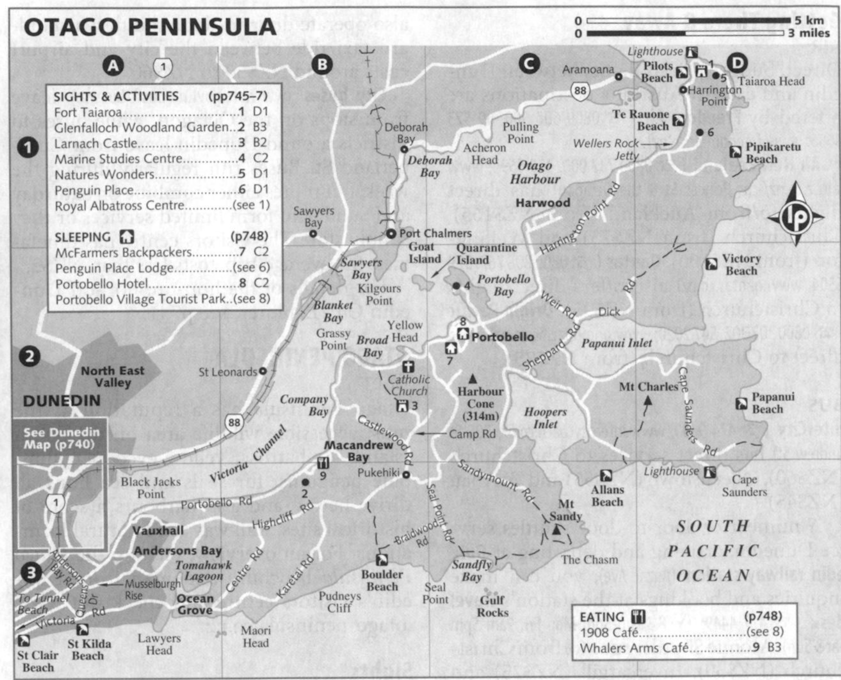

year-round but the main viewing area is closed to the public during the breeding season (mid-September to late November). At this time you can still attend the 'Albatross Insight' introductory talk and video confined to the centre (NZ$8).

Also here are the tunnels of historic 1886 **Fort Taiaroa**, featuring a 150mm Armstrong Disappearing Gun. The gun was installed during the late 19th century to counter the improbable threat of attack from Tsarist Russia, and was so named because it could be withdrawn into its bunker after firing. Fort Taiaroa tours (NZ$12) depart from the albatross centre; there's also a 1½-hour 'Unique Taiaroa' tour (NZ$30) combining visits to the albatross colony and fort.

PENGUINS

The yellow-eyed penguin (hoiho in Maori), one of the rarest penguin species, faces an ongoing loss of habitat, especially the low-lying coastal vegetation in which they nest. Sadly, many farmers in Southland and Otago allow cattle to trample the remaining patches of vegetation favoured by these animals.

On the peninsula, a private conservation reserve called **Penguin Place** (☎ 478 0286; www.penguin-place.co.nz; Harrington Pt Rd; tours NZ$30; ⏲ tours every 30min) has been set-up by the owners of Penguin Place Lodge, who have replanted the breeding habitat, built nesting sites, cared for sick and injured birds and trapped predators. From the lodge, you can do tours of the reserve, comprising a talk on penguin conservation and close-up viewing from a system of trenches and hides; these trips are very popular, so book ahead. There's also accommodation here; see p748.

Several tour operators (see opposite) go to other yellow-eyed penguin beaches via land owned by farmers who charge for the privilege. Yellow-eyed penguins also nest at other public beaches, including Sandfly Bay, which has a DOC hide; follow all signs, don't approach the penguins, and view them only from the hide. Unfortunately, the penguins have been badly disturbed at some beaches by first-class idiots wielding flash photography and car headlights, to the point where (according to some concerned locals) the animals are moving further down the coast.

SEA LIONS

The New Zealand (or Hooker) sea lion can usually only be seen on a tour (see right) to a 'secret' beach where the first pup was born on the NZ mainland after a breeding absence of 700 years. They are also often present at Allans and Victory Beaches. The sea lions, visitors from Campbell Island and the Auckland Islands, are predominantly bachelor males.

LARNACH CASTLE

This **castle** (☎ 476 1616; www.larnachcastle.co.nz; Camp Rd; castle & grounds NZ$15, grounds only NZ$8; 9am-5pm) is a monumental extravagance, a mashing of architectural styles and fantasies on the highest point of the peninsula, funded (to the tune of £25,000, or about NZ$25 million by today's standards) by one William Larnach in 1871 to impress his French nobility–descended wife. Larnach, a merchant and politician, committed suicide in a Parliament House committee room in 1898, one of the many scandals presented inside the castle for tourist titillation.

Larnach Castle can be reached from Dunedin by guided tour or by taking the Portobello bus to Company Bay and walking 4km uphill. If you buy access to the gardens only, you can still visit the café in the castle's ballroom.

OTHER SIGHTS

Glenfalloch Woodland Garden (☎ 476 1775; 430 Portobello Rd; admission by donation; 9.30am-dusk) is a gorgeous florescent landscape covering 12 hectares, with walking tracks leading through a profusion of rhododendrons, azaleas, magnolias and fuchsias. The café–wine bar here is open over summer. The Portobello bus stops out the front.

The University of Otago–run **Marine Studies Centre** (☎ 479 5826; www.otago.ac.nz/marinestudies; Hatchery Rd; NZ$8; noon-4.30pm) showcases the work of the adjacent marine lab. The main attraction is a one-room aquarium displaying octopus, crayfish and sea horses, plus a rock pool–style touch tank. There are guided tours of the facility (NZ$16, 10.30am daily).

Activities

WALKING

The peninsula has numerous scenic farmland and beach walks, accessible with your own transport and detailed in the free brochure *Otago Peninsula Tracks*.

From the car park at the end of Seal Point Rd, trudge down huge sand dunes to the beautiful beach at **Sandfly Bay** (40 minutes). From the end of Sandymount Rd, there's a walk to the impressive cliff scenery of the **Chasm** and **Lovers Leap** (40 minutes return), plus a one-hour side track to Sandfly Bay.

OTHER ACTIVITIES

E-Tours (☎ 476 1960; www.inmark.co.nz/e-tours; NZ$95) does full-day cycling trips along rural tracks and beaches, which include admission to either the albatross or penguin centres, or a cruise. The price also includes pick up from Dunedin.

Wild Earth Adventures (☎ 473 6535; www.wildearth.co.nz; from NZ$80) takes sea-kayaking trips in the area, spending about two hours on the water. It also picks up from Dunedin. More sea-kayaking options, including trips out to Quarantine Island, are offered by **Just Kayaking** (☎ 0800 867 325; info@justkayaking.co.nz; from NZ$80).

Those keen on sinking to new depths in the harbour should contact **Dive Otago** (☎ 466 4370; www.diveotago.co.nz; day dives from NZ$135), which also heads further afield to plunge into places such as Milford Sound.

Tours

Natures Wonders (☎ 0800 246 446; www.natureswondersnaturally.com; Taiaroa Head; NZ$30; 9am-7pm summer, shorter hours winter) does 45-minute return trips in an eight-wheel-drive amphibious vehicle through property at Taiaroa Head, taking in great coastal scenery and wildlife. It's based not far from the albatross centre.

Newton Tours (☎ 477 5577; www.transportplace.co.nz) heads from Dunedin to Larnach Castle along Highcliff Rd (NZ$32, including castle entry), and visits various wildlife locations on and around Taiaroa Head (from NZ$50).

Otago Explorer (☎ 0800 322 240, 474 3300; from NZ$35; 9am & 3pm) is the only peninsula operator to offer guided tours inside Larnach Castle, with the guide giving a good spin on the Larnach family history.

Elm Wildlife Tours (☎ 0800 356 563, 474 1872; www.elmwildlifetours.co.nz; standard tours NZ$65), based out of Elm Lodge Backpackers (p742) in Dunedin, conducts small-group wildlife-spotting tours of up to six hours' duration, with pick up and drop off included in the cost. **Back to Nature Tours** (☎ 0800 477 0484, 477

0484; www.backtonaturetours.co.nz; from NZ$50), based out of Manor House Backpackers (p742), does a similar trip, departing Dunedin in the afternoon.

Sleeping & Eating

McFarmers Backpackers (☎ 478 0389; mcfarmersbackpackers@hotmail.com; 774 Portobello Rd; dm/d NZ$20/45) Friendly, highly rated hill-top farmstay that combines a harbour-side position with a rural nature. Backpackers are well catered for. It's located 1km from Portobello village; the local bus usually stops out the front.

Portobello Hotel (☎ 478 0759; 2 Harrington Pt Rd; s/d NZ$35/70) Portabello's old pub has a pair of decent rooms, one with bathroom. There are plans to embellish the hotel with some outdoor decking and a bistro in the future; in the meantime, you'll find plenty of locals yabbering away in the front bar.

Penguin Place Lodge (☎ 478 0286; Harrington Pt Rd; dm NZ$20) Simple but well-maintained lodge accommodation with shared facilities on private farmland. Linen is NZ$5 extra but harbour and pasture views are free of charge.

Portobello Village Tourist Park (☎ 478 0359; portobellotp@xtra.co.nz; 27 Hereweka St; camp sites unpowered/powered NZ$20/24, d NZ$30-65) Pretty little park in Portobello township, with a fine removed-from-it-all feel, bike hire, basic bunkrooms and fully equipped tourist flats. It's a short walk from the bright lights of Portobello's town centre.

Whalers Arms Café (☎ 476 1357; 494 Portobello Rd; mains from NZ$10; lunch & dinner) A something-for-everyone café and bar, with a watery vista at Macandrew Bay and a good range of light and heavy meals, as well as a variety of wine to choose from.

1908 Café (☎ 478 0801; 7 Harrington Pt Rd; mains NZ$10-25; breakfast, lunch & dinner) The best dining choice on the peninsula, in Portobello and with a mod-NZ à la carte menu and gourmet blackboard specials. Those with dietary requirements will be accommodated wherever possible.

Getting There & Around

There are a half-dozen bus services each weekday between Dunedin and Portobello (NZ$4), several of which continue on to Harrington Pt, though weekend services are limited. Once you get to the peninsula, however, you'll find it's tough to get around without your own transport.

Note that the petrol station in Portobello keeps unpredictable hours, so it's best to fill up in Dunedin before driving out.

SOUTHLAND & STEWART ISLAND

The Southland region of the South Island is a glorious collage of undisturbed mountain-rimmed fiords, sleepy beachside towns, enigmatic coastal forests and rough-edged ocean bays. Fiordland National Park stakes its claim across most of the southwest. This spectacular park, part of the Southwest New Zealand (Te Wahipounamu) World Heritage Area (see the boxed text on below), is a raw wilderness area of mist-wreathed peaks separated by numerous deeply recessed sounds – its immensity can only really be appreciated from the air or from a boat or kayak on the water.

Milford Sound hogs most of the tourist attention in these parts, not just for its high cliffs and deep-water calm but also for the magnificent wilderness-surrounded road that carries people here from the lake-side town of Te Anau. Doubtful Sound is another naturally splendid outpost, where cruise boats plough around Bauza Island to get a

TE WAHIPOUNAMU

In the southwest corner of the South Island, four huge national parks have joined forces to create the Southwest New Zealand World Heritage Area. Known in Maori as Te Wahipounamu (the Place of Greenstone), the region measures 2.6 million hectares and is recognised as much for its cultural importance as for its extraordinary landscape, unique vegetation and wildlife. A World Heritage Area is a global concept that identifies natural and cultural sites of international significance, places so special that protecting them is a priority to people of all countries.

Te Wahipounamu comprises the following national parks:

Aoraki/Mt Cook National Park (p702)
Fiordland National Park
Mt Aspiring National Park (p734)
Westland/Tai Poutini National Park (p711)

glimpse of the Tasman Sea. You've probably also heard of the Milford Track, definitely not your average walk in the (national) park. The Catlins, a region of serene forested hills and coastal dunes due east of Invercargill, is well worth an extended exploration.

Offshore is marvellous Stewart Island, more than three quarters of which is national park land. It's a favourite destination of trampers, bird-watchers and those seeking a rejuvenating mixture of natural beauty and isolation.

Activities

The most famous activity you can do in NZ's deep south is walking the sublime Milford

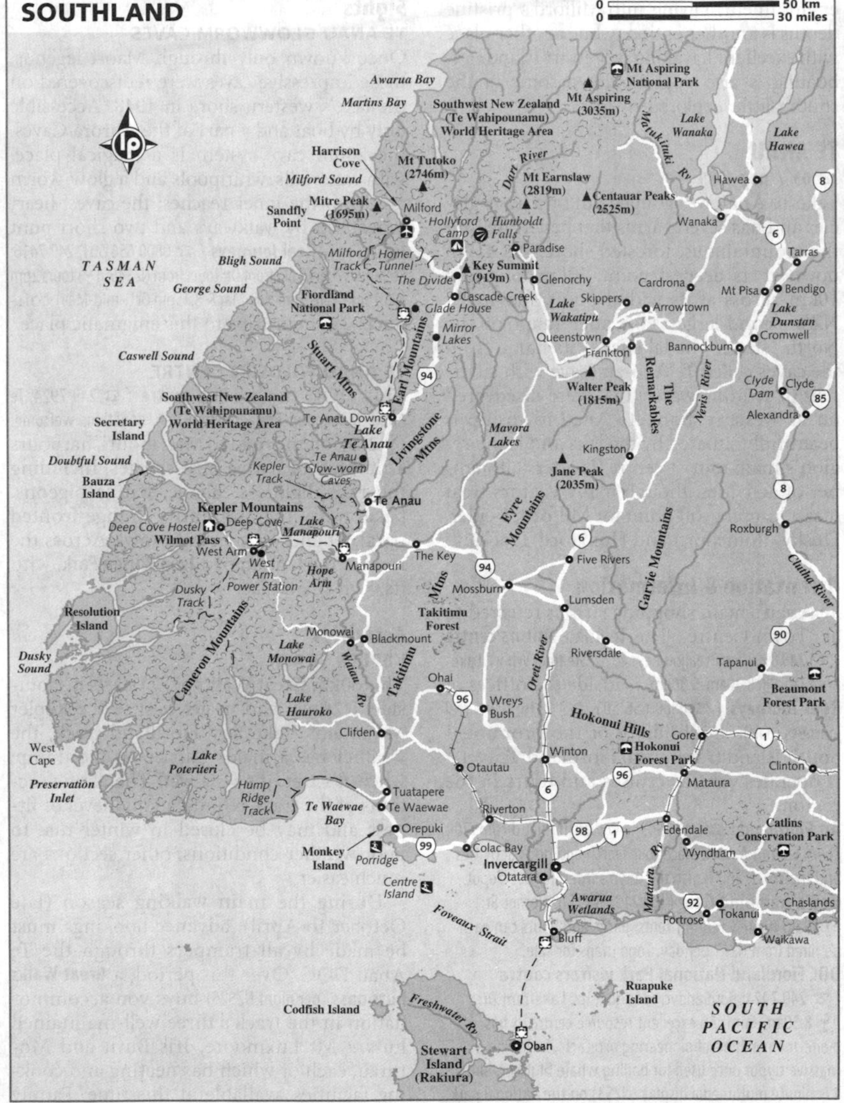

Track – and if that doesn't leave you too footsore, you might consider some encore tramping along such other notable pathways as the Kepler, Dusky or Rakiura Tracks. Milford Sound and its remote neighbour Doubtful Sound are highly accommodating to cruise boats, but sea-kayaking on the surface of these magnificent sounds is the best way to appreciate the stature of the surrounding environment. Diving into Milford's pristine depths is another option, while another place with excellent kayaking is Stewart Island. Jetboating is also popular down some of the south's little-explored rivers.

TE ANAU

☎ 03 / pop 1785

Lake Te Anau was gouged out by a huge glacier and has several arms that penetrate into the mountainous, forested shore. It's 417m down at its deepest point, 53km long and 10km across at its widest point, making it NZ's second-largest lake, after Taupo on the North Island. The lake takes its name from the caves called Te Ana-au (cave with a current of swirling water) that were discovered on its western shore. Te Anau township is beautifully situated by the lake and is the region's main tourist centre. It offers all manner of activities, though many visitors treat it as a jumping-off point for Milford, Kepler, Dusky, Routeburn and Hollyford Tracks.

Orientation & Information

Te Anau's main shopping strip is referred to as 'Town Centre'. The **Te Anau visitors centre** (☎ 249 8900; vin@realjourneys.co.nz; Steamer Wharf, Lakefront Dr; 🕑 8.30am-5.30pm) is inside the offices of **Real Journeys** (☎ 0800 656 501, 249 7416; www.realjourneys.co.nz), a subsidiary of the prominent South Island travel firm, Fiordland Travel – it operates various cruises and tours in the region.

Air Fiordland (☎ 249 7505; www.airfiordland.com; 70 Town Centre) A good place to research and book activities and transport, and is also the town's InterCity bus depot.

Bev's Tramping Gear (☎ 249 7389; 16 Homer St; 🕑 9am-noon & 6-8pm) Tents, packs and boots can each be hired from NZ$7 per day. Topo maps for sale.

DOC Fiordland National Park visitors centre (☎ 249 7924; fiordlandvc@doc.govt.nz; Lakefront Dr; 🕑 8.30am-6pm) An excellent resource centre. It has a one-room exhibit of pioneering artefacts, including a massive trypot once used for boiling whale blubber, and a 17-minute multimedia display (NZ$3) on the national park.

E-Stop (50 Town Centre; 🕑 9am-8.30pm) Internet access available via a dozen coin-operated terminals.

Great Walks counter (☎ 249 8514; greatwalksbooking@doc.govt.nz) Those planning to tramp the Milford, Routeburn or Kepler Tracks can book here, inside the DOC visitors centre.

Medical centre (☎ 249 7007; Luxmore Dr)

Post shop (☎ 249 7348; 102 Town Centre) Inside the newsagency.

Sights

TE ANAU GLOWWORM CAVES

Once known only through Maori legends, these impressive caves were rediscovered on the lake's western shore in 1948. Accessible only by boat and a part of the Aurora Caves, the 200m cave system is a magical place, with waterfalls, whirlpools and a glow-worm grotto in the inner reaches; the caves' heart is reached by walkways and two short punt journeys. **Real Journeys** (☎ 0800 656 501, 249 7416; Steamer Wharf, Lakefront Dr; tours from NZ$45; 🕑 tours 2pm & 6.15pm, plus 5pm Nov-Mar & 8.15pm Oct–mid-May) conducts 2½-hour trips to this enigmatic place.

TE ANAU WILDLIFE CENTRE

This DOC-run **wildlife centre** (☎ 249 7924; Te Anau–Manapouri Rd; admission free, donations welcome; 🕑 24hr), on the road to Manapouri, harbours a number of native bird species, including the rare flightless takahe, native pigeons, kaka, weka, the diminutive orange-fronted parakeet and various waterfowl. Across the road is the landscaped **Ivon Wilson Park**, with its own small lake.

Activities

KEPLER TRACK

This 60km Great Walk (p777) starts just outside Te Anau and heads west to the Kepler Mountains. Like any Fiordland track, the weather has a major impact on the tramp; when it's wet, it's *very* wet. The alpine sections of the track require a good level of fitness and may be closed in winter due to poor weather conditions; other sections are much easier.

During the main walking season (late October to April), advance bookings must be made by all trampers through the Te Anau DOC. Over this period, a **Great Walks huts pass** (per night NZ$25) buys you accommodation in the track's three well-maintained huts – Mt Luxmoore, Iris Burn and Moturau, each of which has heating and cooking facilities available at this time. Family

discounts and a three-night package are also available. A **camping pass** (per night NZ$12) permits you to camp only at the designated sites at Brod Bay and adjacent to Iris Burn Hut. Outside the main season, hut passes still need to be prepurchased (NZ$10 per night) but no heating or cooking is on offer. Off-season camping is free.

The walk can be done over four days and features a variety of vegetation and both lake-side and riverside terrain, then a climb out of beech forest up to the tree line and panoramic views. The alpine stretch between Luxmoore and Iris Burn Huts goes along a high ridge, well above the bush and offers fantastic views when it's clear. Other sections cross U-shaped, glacier-carved valleys. It's recommended that the track be done in the Luxmoore–Iris Burn–Moturau direction.

See p754 for details of services to Rainbow Reach and Brod Bay.

KAYAKING & JET-BOATING

Guided kayaking trips on the enthralling waterways of the World Heritage Area are run by **Fiordland Wilderness Experiences** (☎ 0800 200 434, 249 7700; www.fiordlandseakayak.co.nz; 66 Quintin Dr). Day paddles on Milford Sound (including transport to/from Te Anau) cost NZ$115, or NZ$95 if you meet the guides at Milford. Two-day trips on Doubtful Sound cost NZ$300 (three- to five-day Doubtful tours are also available). Independent kayak rental costs around NZ$50 per day.

Luxmore Jet (☎ 0800 253 826, 249 6951; www.luxmorejet.co.nz; Te Anau Tce; NZ$75) sets off on a one-hour ride from Queens Reach on the Upper Waiau River; its bus will pick up at your door.

OTHER ACTIVITIES

Trips 'n' Tramps (☎ 249 7081; www.milfordtourswalks.co.nz) offers small-group guided tramps, including an 11km Milford Track day walk (NZ$125) and a 2½-hour Milford Sound cruise followed by a three-hour walk on the Routeburn Track up to Key Summit (NZ$145).

High Ride Four Wheeler Adventures (☎ 249 8591; www.highride.co.nz; NZ$120) does three-hour backcountry trips on quad bikes, with great views over the lakes.

The visitors centre provides information on the abundance of guided **trout fishing** (fly, trolling or spinning). River/stream fishing takes place roughly October through May, while lake fishing occurs year-round.

For more easily accessible water sports, try the chlorine-scented **Fiordland Community Pool** (Howden St; adult NZ$3; 3.30-5pm & 7-8.30pm Mon-Fri, 2-5pm & 7-8.30pm Sat & Sun). Roughly from December to March, **Lakeland Boat Hire** (☎ 249 8364; Te Anau Tce) rents out rowing boats, pedal boats and canoes from a lake-side caravan.

Te Anau Bike Hire (☎ 0800 483 2628, 249 7211; 7 Mokonui St; bike hire per hr/day from NZ$10/25) hires mountain bikes and quadricycles.

Tours

CRUISES

As well as Te Anau Glowworm Caves trips (p750), **Real Journeys** (☎ 0800 656 501, 249 7416; Steamer Wharf, Lakefront Dr) runs boat transfers from November to March from Te Anau Downs to Glade Wharf, the Milford Track's starting point. You can do the trip one way (NZ$45 or NZ$55, the cheaper price applying to earlier departures) if you're walking the track, or the return cruise (NZ$75). **Sinbad Cruises** (☎ 249 7106; www.sinbadcruises.co.nz) offers yacht charters and scenic cruises on a 36ft gaff ketch yacht, *Manuska*. You can cruise on Lake Te Anau (from NZ$50) and sail to Glade Wharf for the Milford Track (NZ$70) or to Brod Bay for the Kepler Track (NZ$20).

AERIAL SIGHTSEEING

Wings & Water Te Anau (Waterwings Airways; ☎ 249 7405; wingsandwater@teanau.co.nz; Te Anau Tce) has floatplane flights right off Te Anau Tce. It does a 10-minute zip around the local area (NZ$65), a 20-minute Kepler Track flyover (NZ$125), a 40-minute Doubtful Sound flight (NZ$225) and one-hour flights over Milford Sound (NZ$320). There's also a 1¼-hour 'Fiordland Fantastic' trip over the remote Dusky and Doubtful Sounds (NZ$380).

Air Fiordland (☎ 249 7505; www.airfiordland.co.nz; 70 Town Centre) offers scenic flights on fixed-wing aircraft, including a 70-minute Milford Sound flight (NZ$275) and a 40-minute flight to Doubtful Sound (NZ$180). It also does 4½-hour Milford Sound flight-and-cruise packages (NZ$310).

Southern Lakes Helicopters (☎ 0508 249 7167, 249 7167; www.southernlakeshelicopters.co.nz; Lakefront Dr) has a 'triple buzz' heli-hike-cruise package (NZ$140) and also does one-hour hovers over Doubtful Sound (NZ$240).

Sleeping

Te Anau Lakefront Backpackers (☎ 249 7713; info@teanaubackpackers.co.nz; 48-50 Lakefront Dr; dm from NZ$23, d & tw from NZ$55;) The ad hoc collection of buildings that make up this backpackers comes with attentive staff, a spa pool, a barbecue area and a good waterfront location, though the atmosphere is a little lacklustre. Beware the charmless doubles in a pair of buildings across Quintin Dr, particularly the 'Southern Lakes' annex.

Te Anau YHA (☎ 249 7847; yhatanau@yha.org.nz; 29 Mokonui St; dm NZ$24-26, s/d NZ$36/55;) Bright, clean, modern hostel with excellent facilities and a laid-back vibe – you can be physically laid-back on the sun deck. It's well set up for trampers and will store gear.

Steamers Beach Lodge (☎ 0800 483 2628, 249 7457; www.teanauholidaypark.co.nz/steamers_beach_lodge.htm; 1 Te Anau-Manapouri Rd; dm NZ$21-23, d NZ$55;) Roughly steamboat-shaped lodge with comfortable rooms (BYO or hired bedding) and roomy communal areas, including a newish kitchen, dining room and lounge. Extras include car and gear storage, plus track transport.

Barnyard Backpackers (☎ 249 8006; rainbowdowns@xtra.co.nz; Rainbow Downs, 80 Mt York Rd; dm from NZ$20, s/d NZ$45/50) This tranquil backpackers, on a deer farm 9km from Te Anau, offers great trans-valley views and horse rides (NZ$25 per hour). The main building is very cosy, with a wood heater and a mezzanine level with pool table.

Edgewater XL Motel (☎ 0800 433 439, 249 7258; edgewater.xl.motels@xtra.co.nz; 52 Lakefront Dr; s/d NZ$80/90) Doesn't have the most appealing street-frontage, but it's excellent value considering you get a well-equipped, one-bedroom unit a mere backpack's throw from the water.

Te Anau Great Lakes Holiday Park (☎ 0800 249 555, 249 8538; www.teanaugreatlakes.co.nz; cnr Luxmore Dr & Milford Rd; camp sites per 2 people NZ$24, dm NZ$19, d NZ$50-100; 💻) Expansive park fronted by an appealing low-slung building with well-serviced rooms and facilities. It also has a range of cabins and makes a good base.

Te Anau Lakeview Holiday Park (☎ 0800 483 2628, 249 7457; www.teanauholidaypark.co.nz; 1 Te Anau-Manapouri Rd; camp sites unpowered/powered per 2 people NZ$22/25, s from NZ$30, d NZ$50-100; 💻) Another large, well-equipped park, this one opposite the lake. Besides a hostel bed (see Steamers Beach Lodge, opposite), you can get budget singles in the West Arm Lodge (they're tiny but you can't complain about the price or their condition) and roomy camp sites, some yielding great water views.

Te Anau Mountain View Top 10 Holiday Park (☎ 0800 249 746, 249 7462; www.teanautop10.co.nz; Te Anau Tce; camp sites NZ$27, d NZ$50-125; 💻) Well-managed park with pristine units, gas barbecue, kid's playground, picnic tables, guest lounge and spa, plus lots of info on activities. Linen and bedding for the cabins cost an extra NZ$7.

Strung out along the SH94 to Milford are more than a dozen basic **DOC camping grounds** (per person NZ$5). They all operate on an honesty system.

Eating & Drinking

La Toscana (☎ 249 7756; Town Centre; mains NZ$10-20; 🕑 dinner) Italian eatery doing brisk business with various rich pastas (including several veg versions) and a sizeable list of pizzas. Has lots of booths lining the walls. Very popular towards the end of the week.

Ranch Café, Bar & Grill (☎ 249 8801; Town Centre) Pioneer-style establishment with a popular happy hour (8pm to 9pm) and an upstairs bar with pool tables. Also has appalling musical tastes, unless you happen to think *Me and You and a Dog Named Boo* is a great song. It does, however, do a decent NZ$12 Sunday roast and good-value schnitzels.

Olive Tree Café (☎ 249 8496; 52 Town Centre; lunch NZ$8-18, dinner NZ$23-30; 🕑 breakfast, lunch & dinner) At the end of a tiny arcade, the licensed Olive Tree has great food and a courtyard for coffee in the sun. Lunch menus have included Kashmiri lamb curry and baked ricotta, while dinner has seen mushroom ravioli and 'roti of ocean blue nose'.

Ming Garden Chinese Restaurant (☎ 249 7770; Loop Rd; mains NZ$14-20; 🕑 dinner) Convivial place with a long list of Chinese standards and several set meals (from NZ$45 for two people).

Redcliffe Café & Bar (☎ 249 7431; 12 Mokonui St; mains NZ$16-30; 🕑 dinner) Cottage restaurant with a semiformal air and meaty dinners such as green Thai fish curry and chicken breast stuffed with mushrooms and *bocconcini*. Also has fine desserts such as chocolate and passionfruit *brûlée*, and a nice garden bar.

Fiordland Bakery (☎ 249 8899; Town Centre; 🕑 breakfast & lunch) A ready supply of fresh-baked cakes, biscuits and pies.

Supervalue Supermarket (☎ 249 9600; 1 the Lane; 🕑 8am-8pm Mon-Fri, 8.30am-7pm Sat, 10am-7pm Sun) For do-it-yourself meals.

Moose (☎ 249 7100; Lakefront Dr) Has the standard NZ small-town tavern trifecta: pokies, pool and TAB. It's a cavernous place that usually has some kind of sport blaring loudly from its big-screen TV.

Getting There & Away

InterCity (☎ 249 7559; www.intercitycoach.co.nz) has daily bus services between Queenstown and Te Anau (NZ$35) and on to Milford (NZ$35), plus daily runs to Invercargill (NZ$40) and to Dunedin (NZ$45), continuing on to Christchurch (NZ$75).

Topline Tours (☎ 249 8059; www.toplinetours.co.nz) operates a daily shuttle between Te Anau and Queenstown (NZ$35), departing Te Anau at 10am and Queenstown at 2pm. **TrackNet** (☎ 0800 483 2628, 249 7777; www.tracknet.net) also operates on this route (NZ$35), and runs between Te Anau and Milford Sound (NZ$38).

Running between Te Anau and Invercargill (NZ$40) is **Scenic Shuttle** (☎ 0800 277 483, 249 7654; reservations@scenicshuttle.com), which departs Te Anau at 8.15am daily and Invercargill at 1pm (May to October) or 2pm (November to April) daily. Travelling the 4½ hours to Dunedin (NZ$45) is **Catch-A-Bus** (☎ 249 8900), leaving Te Anau at 1pm and Dunedin at 8.15am; bookings essential.

Fill up with petrol in Te Anau if you're driving to Milford Sound. Chains should be carried in winter and can be hired from most service stations.

NATURE STRIKES BACK

Once you leave Te Anau, you encounter two of the menaces of Fiordland: rain and sandflies. Rain in this area is very heavy – Milford gets more than 6m annually. Sandflies, for those who haven't (yet) met them, are nasty little biting insects. They're actually blackflies, but were christened 'sandflies' by Captain Cook after he encountered them in Dusky Sound – the local Maori name for them is Te Namu. They're smaller than mosquitoes, with a similar bite, and you'll see clouds of them at Milford.

Don't be put off sightseeing during a downpour; the masses of water hurtling down the sheer walls of Milford Sound are an incredible sight and the rain tends to keep the sandflies away. For walking and tramping it's a different story, as the rain means flooded rivers and poor visibility.

TRAMPERS TRANSPORT

A shuttle operated by **TrackNet** (☎ 0800 483 2628, 249 7777; www.tracknet.net) runs daily from October to April to the Routeburn, Kepler, Hollyford and Milford Tracks (call to inquire about winter services). The shuttle to Milford passes the Divide at the start/end of the Routeburn and Greenstone Tracks. For the Kepler Track, TrackNet operates a shuttle between Te Anau and the control gates (NZ$5) and then Rainbow Reach (NZ$8).

Kiwi Discovery (☎ 249 7505), which can be booked through Air Fiordland, shuttles between Queenstown and Milford via Te Anau; from Te Anau to Milford and back costs NZ$120.

The **Kepler Water Taxi** (☎ 249 8364) runs regularly to Brod Bay (NZ$20, return NZ$35) from the jetty adjacent to the Lakeland Boat Hire caravan. **Sinbad Cruises** (☎ 249 7106) also operates a service to Brod Bay (NZ$20).

Wings & Water Te Anau (Waterwings Airways; ☎ 249 7405) provides transport to Supper Cove (NZ$225) for Dusky Sound trampers.

MILFORD SOUND

☎ 03 / pop 170

Milford Sound is the most visited of all the Southland fiords and is one of NZ's biggest tourist attractions. The calm 22km-long fiord is dominated by the sheer weather-scuffed cliffs and peaks that surround it, in particular the stunning 1695m-high Mitre Peak. Visitors should prepare themselves for an absence of blue sky, as Milford is synonymous with rain. But although fine weather means crystal-clear exposure to Milford's beauty, a deluge also creates an unforgettable vista, thanks to the water cascading spectacularly down the rock faces. Occasionally Milford experiences an earthquake-triggered landslide, with a relatively recent one bulldozing its way down a 700m-high cliff.

Milford Sound receives tens of thousands of visitors each year. Around 14,000 arrive annually via the Milford Track, which ends at the sound, but most hitch a ride on the buses that pull into the cruise wharf; at peak times, the visitors centre here resembles a busy international air terminal.

Sights

TE ANAU TO MILFORD ROAD

The grand views start well before you arrive at Milford Sound, as the 119km road from Te Anau to Milford (SH94) is one of the most scenic roads you could hope for. After veering north from Te Anau through the undulating farmland that sits atop the lateral moraine of the glacier that gouged out Lake Te Anau, the road enters a patch of mountain beech forest and heads towards the entrance of Fiordland National Park and the Eglinton Valley. There's a wheelchair-accessible walk at **Mirror Lakes** (five minutes), 58km from Te Anau; you need clear weather to enjoy the lakes.

At the 77km mark is the area now referred to as O Tapara, but known more commonly as **Cascade Creek**. O Tapara is the original name of nearby Lake Gunn (largest of the Eglinton Valley lakes) and refers to a Ngai Tahu ancestor, Tapara; the lake was a stopover for parties heading to Anita Bay in search of greenstone.

The vegetation alters significantly as you approach the **Divide**, which is the lowest east–west pass in the Southern Alps. The size of the bush is reduced and ribbonwood and fuchsia are prominent. A 1½-hour walk from here along the Routeburn Track brings you to **Key Summit**, where there are numerous tarns and patches of alpine bog.

From the Divide, the road falls into the beech forest of the **Hollyford Valley**, where there's a side road leading to the start of the Hollyford Track (p756); at the end of this unsealed road is a walk to the high **Humboldt Falls** (30 minutes return).

The road to Milford, meanwhile, continues up to the east portal of the **Homer Tunnel**, 101km from Te Anau and preceded by a spectacular, high-walled, ice-carved amphitheatre. The tunnel is named after Harry Homer, who discovered the Homer Saddle in 1889. Work on the tunnel didn't begin until 1935, providing work for the otherwise unemployed during the Depression, and wasn't finished until 1953. Rough-hewn, the tunnel has a steep east-to-west gradient but emerges after 1207m into the spectacular **Cleddau Canyon** on its Milford side.

About 10km before Milford is the wheelchair-accessible **Chasm Walk** (20 minutes return). The Cleddau River plunges through eroded boulders in a narrow chasm, the 22m-deep Upper Fall. About 16m lower it cascades under a natural rock bridge to another waterfall. Views of **Mt Tutoko** (2746m), Fiordland's highest peak, are glimpsed above the beech forest just before you arrive in Milford.

MILFORD DEEP UNDERWATER OBSERVATORY

Unique environmental circumstances have allowed Milford Sound to become home to some rarely glimpsed marine life. Heavy rainfall creates a permanent tannin-stained freshwater layer above the warmer sea water. This layer filters out much of the sunlight and, coupled with the sound's calm, protected waters, replicates deep-ocean conditions. The result is that deep-water species such as black coral (which is actually white while still alive) thrive here not far below the surface. A similar situation exists at Doubtful Sound (p758).

Milford Deep underwater observatory (☎ 249 9442; www.milforddeep.co.nz) dangles from a system of interlinked pontoons attached to Milford's rock face. Here, in a circular chamber 10.5m underwater and accompanied by an informative commentary, you can check out the resident corals, tube anemones, large horse mussels, bottom-dwelling sea perch and other diverse creatures. The 30-minute observatory visits are highly recommended, even though the often-large size of accompanying tour groups may dilute the experience. You can stop here with various cruise operators (NZ$20) or catch the **observatory shuttle** (☎ 0800 326 969; NZ$45) from Milford wharf.

Activities

MILFORD TRACK

The famous Milford Track is a four-day, 53.5km tramp that is one of NZ's Great Walks (p777) and is often described as one of the finest in the world; many visitors make a special effort to do it. The number of walkers is limited each year. Accommodation is only in huts (camping isn't allowed) and you must follow a set itinerary. Some walkers resent these restrictions, but the benefits far outweigh the inconvenience: keeping numbers down protects the environment and, though it's a hassle to book, you're guaranteed the track won't be overcrowded.

In the off-season it's still possible to walk the track, but there's limited track transport, the huts aren't staffed and some of the bridges are removed. In the height of winter, snow and avalanches make it unwise.

Expect lots of rain, in the wake of which water will cascade *everywhere* and small streams will become raging torrents within minutes. Remember to bring wet-weather gear and to pack belongings in an extra plastic bag or two.

Bookings

For bookings, contact the Great Walks counter (p750) in Te Anau. The track can only be done in one direction: Lake Te Anau to Milford. Your DOC permit allows you to enter the track on one particular day and no other. The track must be booked from November to April, and it pays to book as far ahead as possible (bookings commence on 1 July for the following season). A **Great Walks pass** (NZ$105) allows you three nights in the huts.

The Great Walks counter in Te Anau can also book transport: bus from Te Anau to Te Anau Downs (NZ$15), ferry to Glade Wharf (NZ$45 to NZ$55), launch from Sandfly Point (the track's end) to the Milford Sound cruise terminal (NZ$26) and bus back to Te Anau (NZ$38). The total transport cost is from NZ$120.

Walking the Track

The track starts at Glade House, at the northern end of Lake Te Anau and accessed by boat from Te Anau Downs or Te Anau. It follows the fairly flat Clinton Valley up to Mintaro Hut, passing through rainforest. From Mintaro the track runs over the scenic Mackinnon Pass, down to Quintin Hut and through the rainforest in the Arthur Valley to Milford Sound. You can leave your pack at Quintin Hut while you make the return walk to Sutherland Falls, NZ's highest. If the pass appears clear when you arrive at Mintaro Hut, make the effort to climb it, as it may not be clear the next day. The highlights of Milford are the beautiful views from **Mackinnon Pass**, the 630m-high **Sutherland Falls**, the rainforest and the crystal-clear streams. An intricate and highly unnatural staircase has been built beside the rapids on the descent from Mackinnon Pass.

Groups taking part in expensive guided walks down the track stop at their own huts – Glade House, Pompolona and Quintin.

Transport to Glade Wharf

Buses operated by **TrackNet** (☎ 0800 483 2628, 249 7777; www.tracknet.net) drive from Te Anau to Te Anau Downs (NZ$15). **Real Journeys** (☎ 0800 656 501, 249 7416; www.realjourneys.co.nz) runs boat transfers from November to March from Te Anau Downs to Glade Wharf (the track's starting point); the 10.30am service costs NZ$45 and the 2pm service costs NZ$55. Alternatively, **Sinbad Cruises** (☎ 249 7106; www.sinbadcruises.co.nz) sails from Te Anau to Glade Wharf (NZ$70).

Transport from Sandfly Point

There are ferries leaving Sandfly Point (at the track's end) at 2.30pm and 3.15pm for the Milford Sound cruise wharf (NZ$26).

Fiordland Wilderness Experiences (☎ 0800 200 434, 249 7700; www.fiordlandseakayak.co.nz; 66 Quintin Dr, Te Anau) has guided kayaking from Sandfly Point to Milford (NZ$65).

HOLLYFORD TRACK

This well-known track, accessed via a road that branches off SH94 on Te Anau side of the Homer Tunnel, travels along the broad Hollyford Valley through rainforest to the Tasman Sea at Martins Bay. Because of its length (four to five days one way), it should not be undertaken lightly. Check with DOC in Te Anau for detailed information and the latest track and weather conditions.

Eight kilometres along Hollyford Rd from SH94 is the wilderness-hidden **Hollyford Camp** (camp sites per 2 people NZ$10, s/d NZ$17/28), also known as Gunns Camp. Cabins here are ultrarustic: you need your own linen (not available for hire), and cooking and heating is via a coal/wood-fired stove, with fuel provided. A generator supplies limited electricity each night. There's also a small shop and a **museum** (adult NZ$1) with pioneering memorabilia and historical flotsam such as some pumice from the 1883 eruption of Krakatoa that washed up in Martins Bay.

There are six **DOC huts** (per person NZ$5) along the track – Hidden Falls, Lake Alabaster, McKerrow Island, Demon Trail, Hokuri and Martins Bay.

TrackNet (☎ 0800 483 2628, 249 7777; www.tracknet.net) has a regular shuttle from Te Anau to the Hollyford Rd turn-off (NZ$25), then to the start of the track (NZ$38).

You can also charter **Air Fiordland** (☎ 249 7505; www.airfiordland.com) to fly between Milford and Martins Bay (NZ$420) or between Te Anau and Martins Bay (NZ$830). The charge is per load; four people can be transported.

SEA-KAYAKING

One of the most memorable perspectives you can have of Milford Sound is from water level in the sound's awesome natural amphitheatre. **Rosco's Milford Sound Sea Kayaks** (☎ 0800 476 726, 249 8500; www.kayakmilford.co.nz) has a trip that takes in Bowen Falls, Stirling Falls and Harrison Cove beneath the bulk of Pembroke Glacier – NZ$130/100 with/without return transport to Te Anau. Trips are good value and doable by those of average fitness. There's also an afternoon trip involving a short paddle to Sandfly Point and a walk on Milford Track (NZ$60).

Fiordland Wilderness Experiences (☎ 0800 200 434, 249 7700; www.fiordlandseakayak.co.nz) offers similar guided trips on the sound; see p751.

DIVING

Tawaki Dive (☎ 249 9006; www.tawakidive.co.nz; with/without own gear NZ$185/240) explores the depths of the sound. Day trips from Te Anau include two dives. The cost is NZ$40 less if you take your own transport to Milford.

Tours

MILFORD SOUND CRUISES

Cruises on Milford Sound are hugely popular; it's a good idea to book a few days ahead. On all trips you can expect to see Bowen Falls, Mitre Peak, Anita Bay and Stirling Falls, with the added possibility of glimpsing wildlife such as the hoiho or yellow-eyed penguin (one of the world's rarest). All cruises leave from the huge wharf visitors centre, a five-minute walk from the café and car park on an elevated walkway through a patch of Fiordland bush; the boardwalk goes beyond the visitors centre to Bowen Falls (30 minutes return).

Real Journeys (☎ 0800 656 501, 249 7416; www.realjourneys.co.nz) operates 1½-hour scenic cruises (NZ$50); opportunistically, it charges NZ$60 for the 1pm cruise simply because it's more popular. It also stages 2½-hour nature cruises (NZ$60; 12.30pm and 1.30pm sailings NZ$65) with a nature guide on board for commentary and to answer questions. During its months of operation (September to May), the small MV *Friendship* is a good choice because its capacity is only 45 people; the 10am cruise costs NZ$50 and the 12.45pm trip costs NZ$60. The larger boats can supply preordered picnic lunches (NZ$14) or a buffet spread (from NZ$26).

Mitre Peak Cruises (☎ 249 8110; www.mitrepeak.com) has small boats with a maximum capacity of 60. Its 1¾-hour cruises cost NZ$50, while 2¼-hour trips venturing out to the Tasman Sea cost NZ$55 (noon sailing NZ$60). The 4.30pm summer cruise is an excellent choice as many of the larger boats are heading back at this time.

Red Boat Cruises (☎ 0800 264 536, 441 1137; www.redboats.co.nz) recently added a prominent new catamaran to its fleet, the *Pride of Milford*. Sailings lasting 1¾ hours cost NZ$45 (the noon cruise lasts only 1½ hours but you pay NZ$50). Cruises lasting 2¼ hours and taking in the observatory cost NZ$65. Picnic and buffet lunches are available here too.

Between them, these operators have well over a dozen cruises between 9am and 3pm daily over summer; try to go on the day's first or last cruise (or on an overnight cruise) to avoid the middle-of-the-day crowds and extra cost.

Overnight Cruises

Three boats operated by **Real Journeys** (☎ 0800 656 501, 249 7416; www.realjourneys.co.nz) undertake overnight cruises, letting you appreciate the fiord when all other traffic has ceased. Kayaking, shore visits, swimming and wildlife viewing are possibilities as the boats sail the full length of the sound.

The budget-oriented *Milford Wanderer*, modelled on an old trading scow, carries 60 passengers overnight from November to April, leaving around 4.30pm or 4.45pm and returning the next morning at 9.15am or 9.30am. Accommodation in tiny four-bunk cabins (with shared bathrooms) costs NZ$195 if departing Milford, NZ$260 from Te Anau and NZ$320 from Queenstown; linen and meals are provided. The *Wanderer* is YHA affiliated, so a 10% member discount applies.

The *Milford Mariner* also sleeps 60 but has more upmarket twin-share cabins with bathroom. Between November and April, it departs Milford at either 4.30pm or 5pm and returns the following day at 9.15am. The cost is NZ$310 from Milford, NZ$375 from Te Anau and NZ$440 from Queenstown.

The MV *Friendship* departs between November and March at either 4.45pm or 5pm, returning 9.30am the next day. The multi-share bunk rooms cost NZ$195 from Milford, NZ$260 from Te Anau and NZ$320 from Queenstown.

Cheaper overnight cruises take place in May, September and October, when the weather is least dependable.

AERIAL SIGHTSEEING

Numerous scenic flights are also offered in Milford. **Milford Sound Flightseeing** (☎ 0800 656 503, 249 7416; www.realjourneys.co.nz) flies over the sound for periods ranging from 10 minutes (from NZ$70) to 40 minutes (from NZ$280), with prices dropping the more passengers there are.

Sleeping & Eating

Independent walkers seeking a bit of luxury after completing the Milford Track will be disappointed. The Mitre Peak Lodge caters only to those doing guided Milford Track walks.

Milford Sound Lodge (☎ 249 8071; milford.sound.lodge@xtra.co.nz; SH94; camp sites unpowered/powered per 2 people NZ$24/28, dm/d NZ$22/55; 💻) Milford's main accommodation is beside the Cleddau River, 1km from the Mitre Peak Cafe, and is a friendly, well-run place to stay. There's a small shop selling supplies and a **café** (mains NZ$16-22; 🕓 7-8.30pm) plying pizza, apricot chicken and various 'vegetation' meals.

Also see left for details of floating accommodation options.

Milford Café (☎ 249 7931; SH94; 🕓 lunch) is on the edge of the car park and sells a basic menu of sandwiches, pies and packaged snacks; there's also a tour booking counter here. Next door is **Milford Tavern** (☎ 249 7427; SH94; mains NZ$12-23; 🕓 lunch & dinner), with limited snacks, beer and a smattering of local workers, but not much else.

Getting There & Away

You can reach Milford Sound by flight, bus, tramping or driving. The most spectacular involves flying from Queenstown or Te Anau (see p724 and p752). A good combination trip is to visit Milford by bus and return by air, or vice versa.

The 119km road trip is also spectacular, with the added excitement of ploughing through the lightless, water-dripping Homer Tunnel; for a description, see p755. **InterCity** (☎ 249 7559; www.intercitycoach.co.nz) runs daily bus services from Queenstown (NZ$70) and Te Anau (NZ$35), but most passengers come on day trips that include a cruise. Trampers' buses also operate from Te Anau (p754) and Queenstown (p729) and will pick up at Milford Sound Lodge. All buses pass the Divide and the start/end of the Routeburn, Greenstone and Caples Tracks.

Many visitors make the return trip from Queenstown in one long 12- to 13-hour day. Te Anau is a better starting point as it's only five hours return by bus. **Real Journeys** (☎ 0800 656 501, 249 7416; www.realjourneys.co.nz) has a coach-cruise-coach excursion that leaves Te Anau at 8am and returns at 4.30pm, costing NZ$110 for the scenic cruise and NZ$125 for the nature cruise. **InterCity** (☎ 249 7559; www.intercitycoach.co.nz) has basically the same excursion for a similar price, except the cruise is with Red Boat. **Trips 'n' Tramps** (☎ 249 7081; www.milfordtourswalks.co.nz) also has a coach-and-cruise option out of Te Anau (NZ$125). The **BBQ Bus** (☎ 442 1045; www.milford.net.nz) offers small, personalised trips from Queenstown (NZ$170); price includes a barbecue lunch (veg option by request).

By car, the drive from Te Anau should take about 2½ hours, not allowing for stops. Fill up with petrol in Te Anau.

MANAPOURI

☎ **03 / pop 210**

Situated beside Lake Manapouri, 19km south of Te Anau, Manapouri is a popular base for Fiordland cruises, walking expeditions and other trips, with the emphasis on excursions to the naturally fantastic environs of Doubtful Sound. The lake is the second deepest in NZ, after nearby Lake Hauroko, and is in a spectacular setting, surrounded by mountains with native bush rambling over their lower reaches. Near town is the picturesque Frasers Beach.

Information

The **Real Journeys visitors centre** (☎ 0800 656 502, 249 6602; www.realjourneys.co.nz; Pearl Harbour; 🕓 7.30am-8pm Oct-Apr, 8.30am-6pm May-Sep) organises most West Arm Power Station and Doubtful Sound trips.

Sights

DOUBTFUL SOUND

Cliff-hemmed Milford Sound may be more spectacular, but Doubtful Sound is larger, gets much less tourist traffic and is an equally magnificent wilderness area of rugged peaks, dense forest and thundering post-rain waterfalls. Some of the cliffs are marked with huge chalky swathes, where tree avalanches or rock slides triggered by earthquakes have passed, while at the sea-roughed mouth of the sound is seal-inhabited Nee Island.

Until relatively recently, only the most intrepid tramper or sailor entered Doubtful Sound's inner reaches. Even Captain Cook, who named it, did not enter – observing it from off the coast in 1770, he was 'doubtful' whether the winds in the sound would be sufficient to blow the ship back out to sea, and sailed on. In 1793 the Spanish sailed in, naming Malsapina Reach after one of the expedition's leaders and Bauza Island after another.

Doubtful Sound became more accessible when the road over Wilmot Pass opened in 1959 to facilitate construction of the West Arm Power Station, intended to provide electricity for the aluminium smelter near Bluff. A tunnel was dug through the mountain from Lake Manapouri to Doubtful Sound and the massive flow of water from lake to sound now drives the power station's turbines. The project did not go entirely smoothly, however, and early plans to raise the level of Lake Manapouri met with fierce environmental resistance (see the boxed text on opposite). This is one of the reasons that hydroelectricity generation and tourism are uneasy bedfellows in the region.

Fortunately, Doubtful Sound remains exquisitely peaceful. Bottlenose and dusky dolphins and fur seals can be glimpsed in its waters, and Fiordland crested penguins nest in October and November. As in Milford Sound, black coral and other deep-sea life exist at unusually shallow levels in Doubtful because sunlight is filtered out by a permanent layer of fresh water above the sea water. On top of the water pumped in from Lake Manapouri, the sound receives around 6m of rain annually.

Activities

Adventure Kayak & Cruise (☎ 0800 324 966, 249 6626; www.fiordlandadventure.co.nz), beside the garage in Manapouri, rents kayaks (from NZ$45 per person per day, minimum two people) for paddles on Lake Manapouri. It also does Doubtful Sound day trips that combine a cruise with kayaking (NZ$170).

With a kayak you can cross the Waiau River for some fine walks, which are detailed in the DOC brochure *Manapouri Tracks* (NZ$1). A walk along the **Circle Track** (three hours return) can be extended to **Hope Arm** (five to six hours return). Although Te Anau is the usual access point for the **Kepler Track** (p750), this track touches the northern end of Lake Manapouri and part of it can be done as a day tramp from Manapouri; access is via the swing bridge at Rainbow Reach, 10km north of town. From Pearl Harbour there's also a walk along the river to **Frasers Beach** (1½ hours return), where you'll find an undisturbed plot of sand on which to sit and gaze across the beautiful lake.

Manapouri is also a staging point for the remote **Dusky Track**, a tramp that takes eight days if you travel between Lakes Manapouri and Hauroko, walking the track from Loch Maree Hut to Supper Cove on Dusky Sound as a side trip along the way. This is a challenging wilderness walk, suitable only for well-equipped, experienced trampers. Contact DOC and see Lonely Planet's *Tramping in New Zealand* for more details.

Tours

Real Journeys (☎ 0800 656 502, 249 6602; www.realjourneys.co.nz; Pearl Harbour) has a 'Wilderness Cruise', beginning with a 30-minute ride across Lake Manapouri, followed by a bus ride that ventures 2km underground (by road) to the West Arm Power Station. After a tour of the power station, the bus travels over Wilmot Pass to Doubtful Sound, which you explore on a three-hour cruise. The eight-hour trip costs NZ$200 from Manapouri, NZ$210 from Te Anau and NZ$270 from Queenstown; picnic lunches can be pre-ordered (NZ$20). It's possible to restrict your trip to the Lake Manapouri cruise and the power-station tour and not visit Doubtful Sound but, seriously, why would you?

From November to April, Real Journeys also has a Doubtful Sound overnight cruise, departing Manapouri at 12.30pm and returning at noon the next day. The *Fiordland Navigator* sleeps 70 and offers twin-share cabins with bathroom (NZ$450 from Manapouri, NZ$460 from Te Anau, NZ$520 from Queenstown) or quad-share bunkrooms (NZ$290 from Manapouri, NZ$300 from Te Anau, NZ$360 from Queenstown); 10% discounts are available for YHA members. Fares include meals and kayaking.

Fiordland Explorer Charters (☎ 0800 434 673, 249 6616; explorercharters@xtra.co.nz; Pearl Harbour) does trips with a maximum of 12 people on Doubtful Sound. A 7½-hour trip costs NZ$160 and pick up from Te Anau can be arranged. This environmentally committed operation also sells berths to independent travellers on far-travelling scientific research vessels to help offset the costs of such expeditions.

SAVING MANAPOURI

The original proposal to build the West Arm Power Station included a plan to raise the level of Lake Manapouri by 30m so it would join with Lake Te Anau. The possibility that this pristine lake and the ecological beauty around it would be swamped by a hydroelectricity scheme led, in 1969, to the initiation of what's been called NZ's first major environmental campaign. A year later, a staggering 265,000 signatures had been added to the Save Manapouri Petition (the longest such document in the country's history) and by 1972 NZ had elected a new national government based in no small part on the support of the party in question for the lake's protection.

Sleeping & Eating

Freestone Backpackers (☎ 249 6893; freestone@xtra.co.nz; Hillside-Manapouri Rd; dm NZ$20, d NZ$50-55) An excellent place to stay, with several four-bunk cabins arrayed along a serene, view-blessed hill 3km east of town. The personable owner has equipped each cabin with a wood-fired stove for cooking/heating.

Deep Cove Hostel (☎ 216 1340, 249 6602; dm/tw NZ$22/50) This remote hostel is right on Doubtful Sound, where it's predominantly used by school groups, but independent travellers can stay here from mid-December to mid-February. Arrangements must be made well in advance.

Manapouri Lakeview Motor Inn (☎ 249 6652; manapouri@clear.net.nz; 68 Cathedral Dr; dm from NZ$21, d NZ$75; 💻) This friendly motor inn's three-bed budget rooms (no bunks) look a bit tatty but are a great deal, as they all come with bathroom and lake view.

Manapouri Glade Motel & Motor Park (☎ 249 6623; Murrell Ave; camp sites per 2 people NZ$24, dm NZ$20, d NZ$55-75) Peacefully located by the lake, this small park was undergoing redevelopment when we last visited, including the establishment of a backpackers called Possum Lodge, so prices may have risen. Sandflies are well represented here, so bring something to deter them.

Manapouri Lake View Chalets & Motor Park (☎ 249 6624; www.holidayparks.co.nz/manapouri; SH95; camp sites per 2 people NZ$20, s from NZ$20, d NZ$35-100) Quirky motor park decorated with a collection of old Morris Minors and a range of distinctive cabins. Stand-alone budget shacks have a bed, table, chairs and strip heater; we got one to ourselves for NZ$20 (plus NZ$5 for linen).

Cathedral Café (☎ 249 6619; Waiau St; meals NZ$5-20; 🕘 breakfast, lunch & dinner) Attached to Hay's Store, this café serves everything from veg soup to chops and schnitzel. Ask for a coffee and you'll get it in a cup the size of a mini-salad bowl. Last orders are taken at 6.30pm.

Beehive Café (☎ 249 6652; 68 Cathedral Dr; mains NZ$12-29; 🕘 lunch & dinner) This extension of the public bar at the motor inn has ostrich medallions, venison hotpot and seafood lasagne among its heartier mains, plus lighter (and cheaper) bar snacks.

Getting There & Away

Scenic Shuttle (☎ 0800 277 483, 249 7654; reservations@scenicshuttle.com) drives between Manapouri and both Te Anau (NZ$15) and Invercargill (NZ$35). Alternatively, ask **Real Journeys** (☎ 0800 656 502, 249 6602; Pearl Harbour) if there are spare seats on its coaches to Te Anau.

INVERCARGILL

☎ 03 / pop 49,300

New Zealand's southernmost city has a fairly low skyline that gives it the impression of being bigger than it actually is. Scattered throughout the orderly street grid of this farm-servicing community are some attractive old buildings and a worthwhile museum and art gallery, but there's little else to hold the interest of transients keen on hightailing it to nearby natural attractions such as Stewart Island, the Catlins and Lake Manapouri.

On our last visit, we found that a number of hotels, bars and restaurants had closed their doors, though it wasn't clear whether this was due to lack of clientele or in preparation for rebirthing as brand-new concerns.

Information

Internet access costs between NZ$4 and NZ$5 per hour and is available at **Comzone.net** (☎ 214 0007; 45 Dee St; 🕘 9.30am-10pm), **Global Byte Café** (☎ 214 4724; 150 Dee St; 🕘 7.30am-5pm Mon-Fri, 9am-4pm Sat & Sun), the **library** (☎ 218 7025; 50 Dee St; 🕘 9am-8pm Mon-Fri, 10am-1pm Sat, 1-4pm Sun) and the visitors centre.

AA (☎ 218 9033; 47 Gala St)

DOC (☎ 214 4589; www.doc.govt.nz; 7th fl, State Insurance Bldg, 33 Don St)

Invercargill visitors centre (☎ 214 6243; www.invercargill.org.nz; Victoria Ave, Queens Park; 🕘 8am-7pm Oct-Apr, 8am-5pm May-Sep) In the same building as the Southland Museum & Art Gallery.

Post office (☎ 214 7700; Don St)

Sights

SOUTHLAND MUSEUM & ART GALLERY

This **museum and gallery** (☎ 218 9753; www.southlandmuseum.com; Victoria Ave, Queens Park; admission gold-coin donation; 🕘 9am-5pm Mon-Fri, 10am-5pm Sat & Sun) has permanent exhibits featuring Maori tools and ornamentation (as well as with a long, old canoe), scenes of Victoriana, and the Roaring '40s Subantarctic Islands exhibit, which has the skeleton of a rather awesome spider crab (plus a primitive animatronic seal). Art exhibits have included the intriguing photos, paintings and multimedia creations of contemporary Ngai Tahu artists.

A prime attraction here is the tuatara enclosure, which you can also peer into through a glass window on the north side of the building. One of the resident lizards is Henry, more than 100 years old and apparently still going strong.

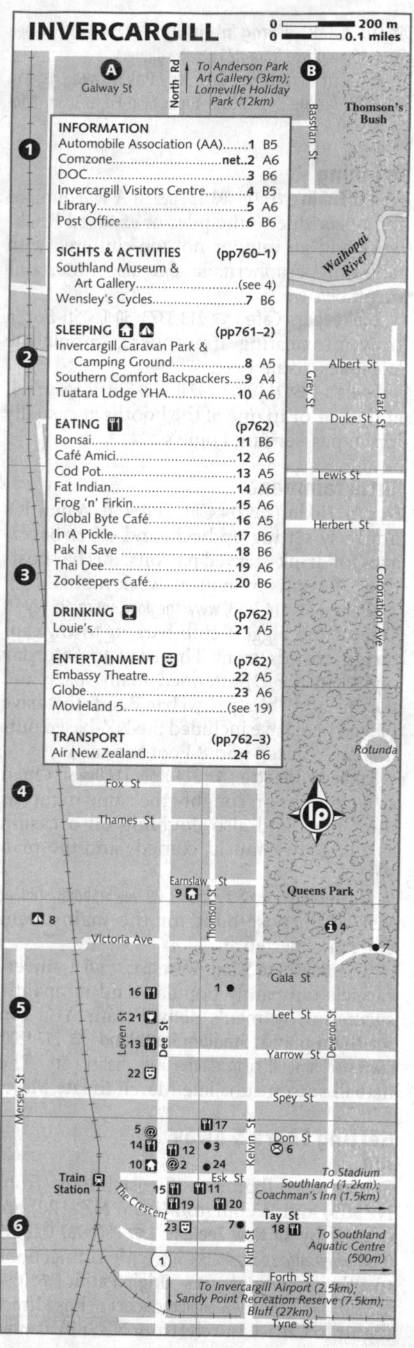

ANDERSON PARK ART GALLERY

Anderson Park (☎ 215 7432; andersonparkgallery@xtra.co.nz; McIvor Rd; admission by donation; 10.30am-5pm) is an attractive Georgian house built in 1925 and surrounded by 24 hectares of beautiful formal gardens, part of it taken up by a playground. It contains a growing collection of NZ art hanging above splendid antique furniture in some gracious old rooms.

Activities

The **Southland Aquatic Centre** (Splash Palace; ☎ 217 3838; Elles Rd; adult/student NZ$3.80/2.80) has a 50m main pool, a kid's pool, waterslide and steam room.

Wensley's Cycles (☎ 218 6206; cnr Tay & Nith Sts; per day NZ$20) hires bikes.

There are short walks 7km from town at **Sandy Point Recreation Reserve**, which has a mixture of totara scrub forest, fern gullies, coastal views and birdlife.

Sleeping

Southern Comfort Backpackers (☎ 218 3838; 30 Thomson St; dm/s/d NZ$21/45/50) Set in a vintage old villa with a calming colour scheme and a nice little garden, this is a consistently excellent hostel. Stay in one of the pleasant dorms or in the 'Playhouse', a little shed out back that costs NZ$21/34 single/double. It only accepts cash payment.

Tuatara Lodge YHA (☎ 214 0954; tuataralodge@xtra.co.nz; 30-32 Dee St; dm/d from NZ$20/50;) Makes a big deal about being the world's southernmost YHA, though we didn't meet anyone who'd come here solely for that reason. It has a spacious, modern interior, very good facilities, a range of rooms (including 'executive suites' with stereos, towels etc), efficient staff, and attracts a fair number of backpackers.

Coachman's Inn (☎ 217 6046; www.coachmans.co.nz; 705 Tay St; campervan sites per 2 people NZ$15, s from NZ$15, d NZ$25-95) Good-value motor lodge, with a double-storey block of budget 'cabins'. Also has a restaurant offering a NZ$13 roast.

Invercargill Caravan Park & Camping Ground (☎ 218 8787; 20 Victoria Ave; camp sites unpowered/powered per 2 people NZ$15/17, d NZ$28-36) Has an unusual location on the edge of Invercargill's showgrounds. Lacks a true camping ambience, but if it's really pouring you can pitch a tent indoors on a sawdust-covered dirt floor. Guests also get free bike use.

Lorneville Holiday Park (☎ 235 8031; www.holidayparks.co.nz/lorneville; SH98; camp sites per 2 people NZ$20, d NZ$36-70) Good-quality camping ground on its own large farmed plot. From town, head north along SH6 for 8km, then turn right on SH98 and travel a further 3.5km.

Eating

Zookeepers Café (☎ 218 3373; 50 Tay St; meals NZ$7-15; breakfast, lunch & dinner) Brightly coloured café with an enthusiastically applied zoological theme, hence the cheetah pedalling away on a bicycle suspended from the ceiling. Serves hearty breakfasts and various pastas and focaccias, and is a hang-out for young locals in tune with local arts.

In A Pickle (☎ 218 7340; 16 Don St; meals NZ$4-12; breakfast Mon-Fri, lunch Mon-Sat) The place to go for a late breakfast, and one of Invercargill's busiest lunch spots through the week. Has a big list of breakfast treats and lots of *panini*, quiches and cakes, plus good coffee and lots of teas to round it all out. Golden walls give it a healthy glow.

Café Amici (☎ 214 1914; 73 Dee St; meals NZ$5-13; breakfast & lunch) This café is always full of mixed-age crowds simultaneously deep in conversation and stuffing their faces with sun-dried tomato and olive chicken strudel.

Global Byte Café (☎ 214 4724; 150 Dee St; meals NZ$5-14; breakfast & lunch) Arc-shaped, table-crowded modern space that does big breakfasts. Usually crowded at weekday lunch times.

Fat Indian (☎ 218 9933; mains NZ$14-18; lunch & dinner) Laneway Indian–food dispenser, off Dee St, laying on some good vindaloo, korma and balti curries. You can get a 'tandoori sampler' (mixed tandoori platter) for NZ$15, and there are several veg options.

Bonsai (☎ 218 1292; 35 Esk St; mains NZ$7-14; lunch & dinner Mon-Sat) Idiosyncratic restaurant with a splash of Japanese decoration but the feel of a Western café. Start with the chicken and *udon* noodles, then attack some teriyaki salmon or ginger beef steak.

Thai Dee (☎ 214 5112; 9 Dee St; mains NZ$10-16; lunch Mon-Fri, dinner daily) Saffron-coloured Thai Dee serves up well-spiced Thai salads and soups, plus plenty of noodle and curry dishes. Try the yummy coconut cream-, ginger- and peanut-flavoured Musuaman curry (either with meat or veg).

If you need a break from café culture, try the fish and chips or burgers at the **Cod Pot** (☎ 218 2354; 136 Dee St; dine-in meals NZ$5-15; lunch & dinner) or the gourmet pizza place at the back of **Frog 'n' Firkin** (☎ 214 4001; 31 Dee St; medium pizzas from NZ$12; dinner).

For supermarket fare, try **Pak N Save** (☎ 214 4864; 95 Tay St; 8.30am-10pm Mon-Fri, 8.30am-8pm Sat & Sun).

Drinking

Frog 'n' Firkin (☎ 214 4001; 31 Dee St) A warm place for a beer due to the piles of exposed brickwork and an interior not too cluttered with tables or paraphernalia. See also Entertainment, below.

Zookeepers Café (☎ 218 3373; 50 Tay St) For a truly intoxicating atmosphere, sample the laid-back scene here.

Louie's (☎ 214 2913; 142 Dee St) Settle yourself at the bar or in one of the booths at casually hip, tapas-serving Louie's .

Entertainment

Frog 'n' Firkin (☎ 214 4001; 31 Dee St) When it's not busy setting up beers and other beverages for drink-starved patrons, this bar hosts free DJ events on end-of-week nights.

Globe (☎ 214 3938; www.theglobe.net.nz; 25 Tay St) One of the biggest club-bars in town, capturing crowds from Thursday to Saturday nights in the DJ-attended main space and the upstairs Thirsty Kiwi bar. Bands that have played here have included the NZ-based outfits Panichicken and 8 Foot Sativa.

Embassy Theatre (☎ 214 0050; 112 Dee St) Open as a club-bar on roughly the same nights as the Globe, and also doubling on occasion as a large live-music, comedy and thespian venue.

Movieland 5 (☎ 211 1555; 29 Dee St; adult/student NZ$12/9) Purpose-built for the mainstream cinema experience.

The **Southern Sting** (www.sting.co.nz) is Invercargill's rampantly popular (and rampantly successful) women's netball team. You can see them play at **Stadium Southland** (☎ 217 1200; www.stadiumsouth.co.nz; Surrey Park, Isabella St). The netball season runs late March to late May.

Getting There & Away

AIR

Direct daily flights to Christchurch (from NZ$85) and Wellington (from NZ$120) are offered by **Air New Zealand** (☎ 0800 737 000, 215 0000; www.airnz.co.nz; 46 Esk St), with connections to other major centres. **Origin Pacific** (☎ 0800 302 302, 547 2020; www.originpacific.co.nz) has direct flights to Christchurch (from NZ$85). **Qantas**

(☎ 0800 808 767, 379 6504; www.qantas.co.nz) also flies direct to Christchurch (from NZ$150).

Stewart Island Flights (☎ 218 9129; www.stewartislandflights.com) flies to Oban (NZ$80, return NZ$145) three times daily.

BUS

Based at the train station on Leven St, **InterCity** (☎ 214 6243; www.intercitycoach.co.nz) buses run daily from Invercargill to Te Anau (NZ$40) and to Dunedin (NZ$45) and then Christchurch (NZ$90). **Hazlett Tours** (☎ 216 0717) does the leg to Queenstown (NZ$38) for InterCity daily.

Scenic Shuttle (☎ 0800 277 483, 249 7654; reservations@scenicshuttle.com) runs daily between Invercargill and Te Anau (NZ$40). **Catch-A-Bus** (☎ 249 8900) and **Atomic Shuttles** (☎ 214 6243; www.atomictravel.co.nz) run buses between Invercargill and Dunedin (both from NZ$25), and **Knight Rider** (☎ 342 8055) operates a night-time service on the Christchurch–Dunedin–Invercargill route.

Campbelltown Passenger Services (☎ 212 7404; cps.bluff@southnet.co.nz) has door-to-door services between Invercargill and Bluff (NZ$10 to NZ$15), connecting with the Stewart Island ferry.

Catlins Coaster and Bottom Bus services pass through Invercargill; see p769.

Getting Around

Invercargill Airport (☎ 218 6920; 106 Airport Ave) is 2km west of central Invercargill. **Spitfire Shuttle** (☎ 214 1851) charges from NZ$8 for trips between the airport and town, depending on which part of Invercargill you need to be dropped in or picked up from. By taxi the trip costs between NZ$10 and NZ$15; try **Blue Star Taxis** (☎ 218 6079) or **Taxi Co** (☎ 214 4478).

Southland Express runs a free bus service around the town centre (Dee, Tay, Esk, Kelvin and Gala Sts), departing every 15 minutes from 10am to 4.30pm weekdays, and 10am to 2.30pm Saturday. Otherwise, regular **city buses** (☎ 218 2320) run to the suburbs (single trip NZ$1.50, day pass NZ$3.50; 7am to 6pm weekdays, 9am to 3pm Saturday); these buses are free from 9am to 2.30pm weekdays and from 9am to 3pm Saturday.

STEWART ISLAND

☎ 03 / pop 420

New Zealand's third-largest island, due south of Invercargill across Foveaux Strait, Stewart Island is an increasingly popular wilderness destination. Maori call it Rakiura (Glowing Skies), perhaps referring to the aurora australis often seen in the southern sky, or the island's spectacular blood-red sunrises and sunsets. In March 2002, 85% of Stewart Island was designated Rakiura National Park. It's often thought of as being isolated and battered by harsh southern winds – actually it's not so inhospitable, but it certainly is unspoilt.

The minuscule population of hardy, independent islanders is congregated in Oban, the only sizeable township, situated on Halfmoon Bay. Half an hour's walk away is a sanctuary of forest, beaches and hills. There are also good swimming beaches here, some easily accessible off Kamahi Rd in Oban; that said, the water is invariably chilly.

According to Maori myth, NZ was hauled up from the ocean by Maui, who said, 'Let us go out of sight of land, far out in the open sea, and when we have quite lost sight of land, then let the anchor be dropped'. The North Island was the fish that Maui caught; the South Island his canoe and Rakiura was the anchor – 'Te Punga o te Waka o Maui'.

There is evidence that parts of Rakiura were occupied by moa hunters as early as the 13th century. The titi (mutton birds) on adjacent islands were an important seasonal food source for the southern Maori and their annual harvest continues. Today's southern Maori population is predominantly Ngai Tahu, with its lineage traceable to Ngati Mamoe and Waitaho.

The first European visitor was Captain Cook, who sailed around the eastern, southern and western coasts in 1770 but still couldn't figure out if it was an island or a peninsula. Deciding it was attached to the South Island, he called it South Cape. In 1809, the sealing vessel *Pegasus,* under the command of Captain Chase, circumnavigated Rakiura and proved it to be an island. It was named after William Stewart, first officer of the *Pegasus,* who charted the southern coast of the island in detail.

In June 1864, Stewart and the adjacent islets were bought from the Maori for £6000. Early industries consisted of sealing, timber milling, fish curing and shipbuilding. The discovery of gold and tin towards the end of the 19th century led to an increase in settlers but the 'rush' didn't last long. Today the island's

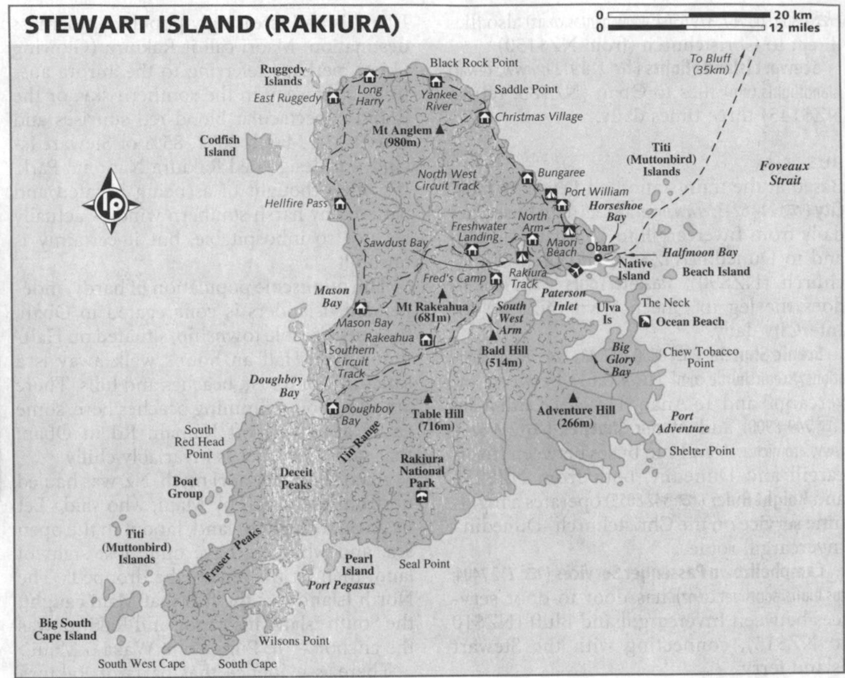

economy depends on tourism and fishing – crayfish, paua, salmon, mussels and cod.

Orientation

Stewart Island is roughly 65km long and 40km across at its widest point. It has less than 20km of roads and a rocky coastline incised by numerous inlets, the largest of which is Paterson Inlet. The highest point on the island is Mt Anglem (980m). The principal settlement is Oban on the shores of Halfmoon Bay – it's named after a place in Scotland and means 'many coves' in Gaelic. There are around 360 homes on the island, many of them holiday homes.

Information

There are no banks on Stewart Island. Credit card payment is accepted for many services, but it's wise to bring a supply of cash to last the duration of your stay.

The island is a local (not long-distance) phone call from Invercargill. You can get access to the Internet at a coin-operated computer inside the South Sea Hotel (p768), or at Justcafé (p768).

For online information, visit www.stewartisland.co.nz.

DOC Stewart Island visitors centre (☎ 219 0009; stewartislandfc@doc.govt.nz; Main Rd; 🕑 8.30am-7pm Mon-Fri & 9am-7pm Sat & Sun summer, 8.30am-5pm Mon-Fri & 10am-noon Sat & Sun winter) A few minutes' walk from the wharf and provides detailed information on flora, fauna and walks. It sells hut passes and has detailed pamphlets on local tramps; it also has folders with pictures and details of local accommodation.

Oban Tours & Taxis (☎ 219 1456; Main Rd) Books activities, organises sightseeing tours and rents scooters, cars, fishing rods and dive gear.

Postal agency (☎ 219 1090; Stewart Island Flights, Elgin Tce; 🕑 7.30am-5.45pm Mon-Fri, 8.30am-1pm Sat)

Stewart Island Adventure Centre (☎ 219 1134; main wharf) Booking agency for local activities, the Bluff ferry and water taxis.

Sights

FLORA & FAUNA

Unlike NZ's North and South Islands, there is no beech forest on Stewart Island. The predominant lowland vegetation is hardwood but there are also lots of tree ferns, a variety of ground ferns and several different kinds of orchid. Along the coast the vegetation consists of mutton bird scrub, grass tree, tree daisies, supplejack and leatherwood – there are warnings not to go tramping off the beaten track, as the bush is impenetrable in most places. Also around the shores are clusters of bull kelp, common kelp, fine red weeds, delicate green thallus and bladders of all shapes and sizes.

Budding ornithologists will have many field days here, examining locally bred sea birds and abundant bush birds such as tui, parakeets, kaka, bellbirds, fernbirds, robins, dotterels and kiwis. The weka can sometimes be spotted, as well as Fiordland crested, yellow-eyed and blue penguins.

Two species of deer, the red and the Virginia (whitetail), were introduced to the island in the early 20th century. Also introduced were brushtail possums, which are numerous in the northern half of the island and highly destructive to the native bush. Stewart Island has lots of NZ fur seals too.

ULVA ISLAND

The paradisal Ulva Island in Paterson Inlet covers only 250 hectares, but packs a lot of natural splendour. An early naturalist, Charles Traill, was honorary postmaster here. He would hoist a flag to signal to other islands (including Stewart) that the mail had arrived and hopefuls would stream in from everywhere. His postal service fell out of favour in 1921, however, and was replaced by one at Oban. A year later, Ulva Island was declared a bird sanctuary.

Bird-watchers go all woozy here. As soon as you get off the launch the air is alive with the song of tui and bellbirds, and you'll see kaka, weka, kakariki and NZ pigeon (kereru); some birds come so close that you don't need a telephoto lens to snap them. The abundance of birdlife here is due mainly to the absence of predators.

Good walking tracks have been developed in the island's northwest and are detailed in DOC leaflets, including walks to **Flagstaff Point Lookout** (20 minutes return) and **Boulder Beach** (1½ hours return). The forest has a mossy floor and many paths intersect beautiful stands of rimu, miro, totara and rata.

You can get to Ulva by water taxi for a return fare of between NZ$20 and NZ$25; see Getting Around (p769).

OTHER SIGHTS

Rakiura Museum (Ayr St; adult NZ$2; ⌚ 10am-noon Mon-Sat, noon-2pm Sun) shares its building with the Southland District Council office and is worth a look if you're interested in the island's history. It has info on whaling, sealing, tin mining, timber milling and fishing, and a particularly interesting section on Maori heritage.

Empress Pearl Visitors Centre (☎ 219 1123; 45 Elgin Tce; adult NZ$8.50; ⌚ 10am-5pm) has a makeshift, work-in-progress aquarium comprising numerous small tanks (without explanatory labels) set up in one large room, though you do get unusually close looks at starfish, urchins, sea horses and sea slugs, plus more unusual fish such as the spotted stargazer and southern pigfish. You can buy paua and pearl jewellery here and there are plans for an ocean-viewing restaurant.

At Harrold Bay, about 3km southwest of town, is a **stone house** built by Lewis Acker around 1835. It's one of the oldest stone buildings in NZ.

Despite Stewart Island's isolation, world events do reach this far, as revealed by the modest **world wars memorial** on the waterfront, dedicated to the 11 islanders who died over both campaigns.

Activities

WALKING

Stewart Island is trampers' heaven, but although some walks take only a few hours, a day trip to the island is hardly worthwhile. Plan on spending at least a few days here so you can really enjoy the beaches and rare bird and plant life. Gear can be stored at the DOC visitors centre in small/large lockers for NZ$2.50/5 per day.

There's a good network of tracks and huts on the northern part of the island, but the southern part is undeveloped and has desolate, isolated areas. You're advised not to go off on your own, particularly from the established walks, unless you've discussed your itinerary with someone beforehand.

Each hut has foam-rubber mattresses, wood stoves, running water and toilet facilities but you need to take food, sleeping bags, eating and cooking utensils and first-aid equipment with you. A tent and portable gas stove can be very useful over the summer holidays and at Easter, when the huts tend to fill up.

The 29km, three-day **Rakiura Track** is one of NZ's Great Walks (p777), a well-defined, easy circuit starting and ending at Oban. Partly because of its undemanding and scenic nature, this extensively boardwalked track gets very crowded in summer. Besides the shelter of huts at Port William and North Arm (both with room for 30 trampers), there are camp sites at Sawdust Bay, Maori Beach and Port William. Overnight trampers need to buy either a date-stamped **Great Walks huts pass** (per night NZ$10) or **camping pass** (per night NZ$6); there's a limit of two consecutive nights in any one hut. For more info, see the DOC pamphlet *Rakiura Track* (NZ$1).

In the island's north is the **Northwest Circuit Track**, a 125km track that takes between 10 and 12 days to complete. This tramp is only suitable for well-equipped, very experienced trampers, as is the 56km **Southern Circuit Track** that branches off it. A **Northwest Circuit Pass** (NZ$38) gives you a night in each of that track's huts. Alternatively, you can use **backcountry hut tickets** (per night NZ$5) or an **annual hut pass** (NZ$65), but you'll still have to buy a Great Walks huts pass for use at Port William and North Arm. See the DOC brochure *North West & Southern Circuit Tracks* (NZ$1) for full details.

Both the Rakiura and Northwest Circuit Tracks are detailed in Lonely Planet's *Tramping in New Zealand*.

The various short walks in the vicinity of Halfmoon Bay are outlined in the DOC pamphlet *Stewart Island Day Walks* (NZ$1). The walk to **Observation Rock** (30 minutes return) results in good views over Paterson Inlet. Continue past the old stone house at Harrold Bay to **Acker's Point Lighthouse** (three hours return), where there are good views of Foveaux Strait; blue penguins and a colony of shearwaters (mutton birds) can be seen near the rocks here.

OTHER ACTIVITIES

Paterson Inlet consists of 100 sq km of sheltered, kayak-friendly waterways, with 20 islands, DOC huts and two navigable rivers. A popular trip is the paddle to Freshwater Landing (7km upriver from the inlet) followed by a three- to four-hour walk to Mason Bay to see kiwis in the wild. **Rakiura Kayaks** (☎ 219 1368) rents kayaks from NZ$40 per day and also does guided trips around the inlet (half-/full-day trips NZ$45/70).

Ruggedy Range Wilderness Experience (☎ 219 1066; www.ruggedyrange.com) is an excellent eco-tourism operator offering guided walks and nature tours. Excursions include a half-day trip to Ulva Island (NZ$65).

Oban Tours & Taxis (☎ 219 1456; Main Rd) hires snorkel/scuba gear (NZ$40/80 per day; add NZ$18 for scuba tank hire and fill).

The island's **community centre** (☎ 219 1477; 10 Ayr St) houses a gym, coin-operated sauna, squash courts and a library (seldom open), all of which are open to visitors.

Tours

KIWI SPOTTING

The search for *Apteryx australis lawryi* is a highly rewarding eco-activity. The Stewart Island kiwi is a distinct subspecies of the brown kiwi, and has a larger beak and legs than its northern cousin. These kiwis are common over much of Stewart Island, particularly around beaches where they forage for sand-hoppers under washed-up kelp. Unusually, Stewart Island's kiwis are active both in the day and night; the birds are forced to forage for longer to attain breeding condition. Many trampers on the Northwest Circuit Track spot them, especially at Mason Bay.

Bravo Adventure Cruises (☎ 219 1144; philldismith@xtra.co.nz; tours NZ$90) runs night-time tours to spot these flightless marvels. Tour-group numbers are limited for the protection of the kiwis; a maximum of 15 people travel on the MV *Volantis*. Tour demand outstrips supply and trips only run on alternate nights, so make sure you book *well* ahead to avoid disappointment.

CRUISES & MINIBUS TOURS

Bravo Adventure Cruises (☎ 219 1144; philldismith@xtra.co.nz) is one of many charter outfits available for sightseeing (and fishing trips) – as long as you have a decent-sized group (six or more people), you can organise half-day trips from NZ$60 per person. A similar operator is **Thorfinn Charters** (☎ 219 1210; www.thorfinn.co.nz), which has an 11m launch that does half- to full-day wildlife-viewing cruises (mutton birds, seals, penguins), also from around NZ$60 per person.

Talisker Charters (☎ 219 1151; www.taliskercharter.co.nz) has a 17m steel sailing ketch available for half-day cruises around Paterson Inlet (NZ$55 per person), day trips to Port Adventure (NZ$100) and live-aboard charters

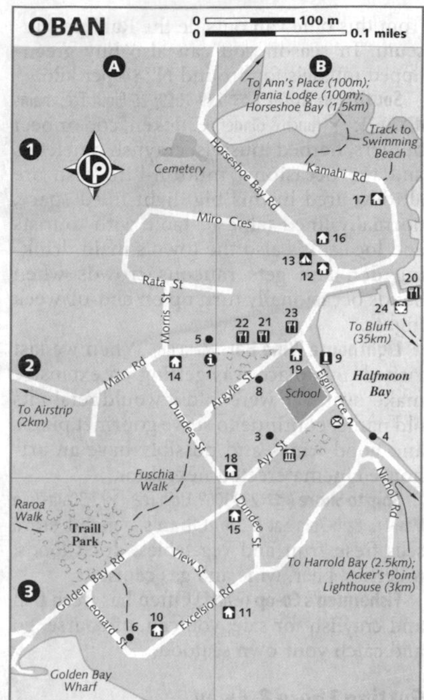

INFORMATION
DOC Stewart Island Visitors Centre 1 A2
Postal Agency 2 B2

SIGHTS & ACTIVITIES (pp764–7)
Community Centre 3 B2
Empress Pearl Visitors Centre 4 B2
Oban Tours & Taxis 5 A2
Observation Rock 6 A3
Rakiura Museum 7 B2
Seabuzzz Tours 8 B2
Stewart Island Adventure Centre .... (see 20)
World Wars Memorial 9 B2

SLEEPING (pp767–8)
Bayview Apartment 10 A3
Bellbird Cottage 11 B3
Dave's Place 12 B2
Ferndale Campsites 13 B2
Joy's Place 14 A2
Michael's House Hostel 15 B3
Pilgrim Cottage 16 B1
Room With a View 17 B1
Shearwater Inn/Stewart Island Backpackers 18 B2
South Sea Hotel 19 B2

EATING (p768)
Boardwalk Café & Bar 20 B2
Fishermen's Co-op .... (see 24)
Justcafé 21 B2
Kai Kart .... (see 7)
Lighthouse Wine Bar 22 B2
Ship to Shore 23 B2

TRANSPORT (pp768–9)
Foveaux Express 24 B2
Stewart Island Flights .... (see 2)

along the Fiordland coast (from NZ$90 per night).

Seabuzzz Tours (☎ 219 1282; www.seabuzz.co.nz; 5 Argyle St) runs one-hour glass-bottomed boat trips (NZ$25) and two-hour tours of the mussel and salmon farms at Big Glory Bay (NZ$50).

Oban Tours & Taxis (☎ 219 1456; Main Rd) zips around Halfmoon Bay, Horseshoe Bay and various other places on 1½-hour minibus tours (NZ$20).

Sleeping

HOSTELS, CAMPING & HOMESTAYS

Several homes in and around Oban offer hostel-style accommodation at low rates. Usually no advance booking is possible and for most you'll need your own sleeping bag and food. Some of the accommodation is available only over summer.

There is ongoing concern on the NZ backpacker circuit about the safety of female travellers; check with the visitors centre before booking your accommodation and if you don't feel comfortable in the place you're staying, move on.

Shearwater Inn/Stewart Island Backpackers (☎ 219 1114; www.stewart-island.co.nz/shearwater; cnr Dundee & Ayr Sts; camp sites per 2 people NZ$16, dm NZ$20, s NZ$26-36, d NZ$45-60; 💻) Neat and clean rooms, attractive camp sites and a well-equipped kitchen are some of the features of this prominent establishment. A splash of colour brightens many of the rooms, and there's a big, sociable collection of lounge chairs in the main communal hanging-out space.

Ferndale Campsites (☎ 219 1176; Miro Cres; camp sites per person NZ$8) Ferndale has plenty of room on a well-maintained swathe of lawn near the waterfront. The ablution block has a cooking shelter (cookers can also be hired), washing machine (NZ$2) and coin-operated showers (NZ$2). The shower and laundry facilities are open to the general public.

Commendable backpacker-accommodating homes include:

Ann's Place (☎ 219 1065; dm NZ$14) Across Mill Creek from the township and offering tramping-style accommodation in a family house off Mapau Rd.

Dave's Place (☎ 219 1427; Elgin Tce; dm NZ$20)

Joy's Place (☎ 219 1376; Main Rd; dm NZ$20) Has bunk-room beds and a restraining order on drinking and smoking.

Michael's House Hostel (☎ 219 1425; Golden Bay Rd; dm NZ$20) Basic accommodation.

HOTELS & MOTELS

South Sea Hotel (☎ 219 1059; www.stewart-island.co.nz; 26 Elgin Tce; s NZ$40-80, d NZ$80-120; 💻) Ostensibly a gregarious waterfront place with decent rooms, an upstairs balcony and separate detached motel units out the back. If offered an upstairs room on a Friday or Saturday, check whether any bands are playing downstairs that night; if they are, you may end up experiencing serious sleep deprivation.

Room With A View (☎ 214 9040; topship@xtra.co.nz; Kamahi Rd; d NZ$75) More ocean scenery is on offer in this self-contained motel-style unit, on a site tucked away around a headland from Oban's wharf (only a few minutes' walk from town, though) and opposite a path leading down to a swimming beach.

HOLIDAY HOMES & FLATS

If you're part of a group, consider hiring one of the island's many self-contained flats or holiday homes. These can represent great value if there are enough of you to share the cost – such places usually charge between NZ$10 and NZ$20 for each extra adult beyond the first two people. Good self-contained options include:

Bayview Apartment (☎ 219 1465; Excelsior Rd; d NZ$120) Near the sunset-conducive Observation Rock viewpoint and usually available only over summer.

Bellbird Cottage (☎ 219 1330; Excelsior Rd; d NZ$95) Three-bedroom place surrounded by bush and birdlife.

Pania Lodge (☎ 215 7733; halstead@xtra.co.nz; d NZ$125) Ten people can fit into this cosy house on a bushy four-hectare plot off Horseshoe Bay Rd near Butterfield Beach.

Pilgrim Cottage (☎ 219 1144; Horseshoe Bay Rd; d NZ$95) Attractive weatherboard cottage accessible down a short bush track.

Eating & Drinking

Boardwalk Café & Bar (☎ 219 1470; wharf; lunch NZ$7-14, dinner NZ$15-27; 🕑 lunch & dinner) Amenable café upstairs in the ferry wharf terminal, with all-round water views and a menu of whitebait fritters, mutton-bird fillets and pan-fried cod. There's also a pool table and many spots to just lounge with a drink in hand.

Justcafé (☎ 219 1567; Main Rd; meals NZ$5-10; 🕑 lunch; 💻) Warm little place with plenty of benches. Provides muffins, quiche, soup, toasted sandwiches and caffeine fixes.

Kai Kart (☎ 219 1225; Ayr St; meals NZ$6-15; 🕑 lunch & dinner) Bacon and eggs, chook burgers, mussel melts and seafood patties are all served from this blue van outside the Rakiura Museum. In season you can also buy green-lipped mussels for around NZ$4 per kilo.

South Sea Hotel (☎ 219 1059; 26 Elgin Tce; mains NZ$10-25; 🕑 lunch & dinner) Chicken, cod or beef burgers, herbed mussels, crayfish omelettes and the occasional mutton-bird dish are all devoured in this big, light-filled space, normally lined table-to-table with tourists and locals. It's also the town's main drinking den and gets raucous crowds when bands occasionally turn up on end-of-week nights.

Lighthouse Wine Bar (Main Rd) When we last visited, this place was getting an extensive make-over. We were told it would retain its old name, continue to serve gourmet pizzas and good wines and possibly have an art-house cinema erected next door.

Ship to Shore (☎ 219 1069; Elgin Tce; 🕑 7.30am-7pm Mon-Fri, 8am-7pm Sat & Sun) Oban's general store sells fresh fruit and vegetables, dried foods, toiletries, beer, wine and gas canisters.

Fishermen's Co-op (wharf) Often has fresh fish and crayfish for sale; you can, of course, go and catch your own seafood.

Getting There & Away

AIR

Stewart Island Flights (☎ 218 9129; www.stewartislandflights.com; Elgin Tce) handles flights between the island and Invercargill (NZ$80, 20 minutes; return NZ$145). There are sometimes discount stand-by fares; phone ahead to check this. Flights depart three times daily year-round. The bus trip from the island's Ryan's Creek airstrip to Oban is included in the air fare.

FERRY

The passenger-only **Foveaux Express** (☎ 212 7660; www.foveauxexpress.co.nz) runs between Bluff and Oban (NZ$45, return NZ$84), departing Bluff at 9.30am and 5pm September to April, and 9.30am and 4.30pm May to August. Definitely book a few days ahead in summer; YHA members are eligible for a 10% fare discount. The strait crossing takes one hour and is often subject to rough, stormy conditions.

Campbelltown Passenger Services (☎ 212 7404; cps.bluff@southnet.co.nz) runs a door-to-door shuttle service (NZ$10 to NZ$15), picking up from anywhere in Invercargill and connecting with the ferry to Stewart Island.

Getting Around

Oban Tours & Taxis (☎ 219 1456; Main Rd) rents cars for NZ$55/75 per half-/full day (petrol and mileage included) and hires motor scooters for NZ$25/45/50 per hour/half-day/day. Handily for trampers, it also does pick ups and drop offs to remote parts of the island, as do a number of charter boats, including **Seaview Water Taxi** (☎ 219 1014), **Stewart Island Water Taxi & Eco Guiding** (☎ 219 1394) and **Seabuzzz Tours** (☎ 219 1282). Several operators are based at Golden Bay Wharf, about a 10-minute walk from the township.

All the aforementioned charter outfits offer a water-taxi service to Ulva Island; return fares cost between NZ$20 and NZ$25.

THE CATLINS

☎ 03

The coastal route between Invercargill and the sleepy town of Balclutha passes through the enigmatic Catlins, a region of beautifully isolated forests and wildlife-filled bays stretching from Waipapa Point in Southland to Nugget Point in South Otago. The distance is similar to that of the inland route, which sticks to SH1, but vehicles travel much more slowly as 22km of road is unsealed; slow progress is being made on sealing this stretch of road, with the work expected to be completed in 2005.

Unless you've got your own transport or choose to hitch, the only way you can reliably get around this untrammelled region is with an organised bus trip, several of which cater specifically to backpackers; see right.

The Catlins was once inhabited by moa hunters, and evidence of their camp sites and middens has been found at Papatowai. Between 1600 and 1800 the Maori population thinned out because of the decline of the moa and the lack of kumara cultivation – the Maori also feared a wild, legendary, yeti-like creature called a *maeroero* (wild man of the forest), who they believed lived in the area. Later, whalers occupied sites along the shore, including Waikawa Harbour, Tautuku Peninsula and Port Molyneaux. Timber millers then moved into the dense stands of beech forest in the 1860s (at the height of the logging craze there were about 30 mills in the area), followed by a wave of settling pastoralists.

There are still reserves of podocarp forests in the Catlins, containing trees such as kahikatea, totara, rimu and miro. Behind the sand dunes of Tahakopa and Tautuku Bays are swathes of native forest extending several kilometres inland. The vegetation zones are best seen at Tautuku: sand-dune plants (marram, lupin, flax) are found near the beach; behind these are low trees such as rata, kamahi and five-finger; in the peaty sands behind the dunes is young podocarp forest; and there's mature forest with emergent rimu and miro and a main canopy of kamahi beyond. A good example of young forest is found near Lake Wilkie, where growth has occurred on the sediments that have gradually filled in the lagoon.

The local fauna includes large populations of New Zealand fur seals and Hooker sea lions, while elephant seals breed at Nugget Point. The variety of birdlife is an ornithologist's delight, with many sea, estuary and forest birds, plus the endangered yellow-eyed penguin, the kaka, blue ducks and the rare mohua (yellowhead).

INFORMATION

For information, contact or visit the main **Catlins visitors centre** (☎ 415 8371; info@catlins-nz.com; 20 Ryley St, Owaka; 9am-5pm Mon-Fri) or the smaller **Waikawa visitors centre** (☎ 246 8444; dolphinmagic@xtra.co.nz; Main Rd, Waikawa; 9am-5pm), and check the websites www.catlins.org.nz and www.catlins-nz.com. Some info is also available in Balclutha at the **Clutha visitors centre** (☎ 418 0388; balvin@nzhost.co.nz; 4 Clyde St; 8.30am-5pm Mon-Fri, 9.30am-3pm Sat & Sun).

The DOC pamphlet *The Catlins – Walking & Tramping Opportu bnities* (NZ$2.50) is useful, though the number of tracks has been halved in recent years due to a lack of track maintenance. A good general guide to the Catlins environment, written by local wildlife ranger K Widdowson, is *Stay A While In The Catlins* (NZ$2), available at Nugget Lodge (p772) and local info centres.

The Catlins has no banks, few petrol stations and limited options for eating out or grocery shopping. So if you plan to spend some time here, make the most of the facilities at Invercargill, Dunedin or Balclutha first.

TOURS

Bottom Bus (☎ Dunedin 434 7370, Queenstown 442 9708; www.bottombus.co.nz) motors along a regular loop that visits Queenstown, Dunedin, Te

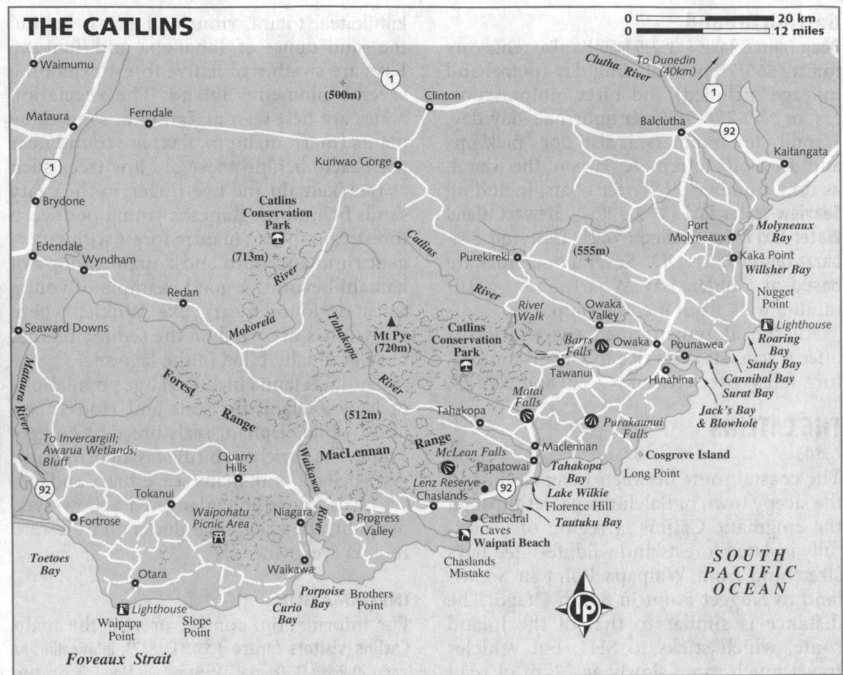

Anau and Milford Sound via the Catlins and Invercargill. It stops at all main points of interest and you can always hop off and catch the next bus through. One of the packages available, the Southlander pass (NZ$300), allows you to start and finish anywhere and includes a Milford Sound cruise.

Catlins Coaster (☎ 0800 304 333, 021-682 461; www.catlinscoaster.co.nz), run by the same folks as Bottom Bus, offers a day tour through the Catlins from Dunedin or Invercargill (from NZ$120); add an extra NZ$130 to include flights to Stewart Island.

Papatowai-based **Catlins Wildlife Trackers** (☎ 0800 228 5467, 415 8613; www.catlins-ecotours.co.nz) does guided walks and specialist ecotours of the region. Food, accommodation and transport to/from Balclutha (if required) is included in its two-night (NZ$290) or four-night tour (NZ$580). It also manages the **Top Track**, a two-day, 26km self-guided tramp (NZ$35 per person) through beaches and a private forest, with accommodation in a converted trolleybus or backpackers.

Catlins Natural Wonders (☎ 0800 353 941; www.catlinsnatural.co.nz) also offers first-rate guided trips. Day trips cost NZ$130/85 out of Dunedin/Balclutha, or there's an overnight trip (NZ$200/150, plus accommodation).

Invercargill to Papatowai

The road southeast from Invercargill passes the 14,000-hectare **Awarua Wetlands**, which supports various wading bird species, before arriving at Fortrose and the turn-off to **Waipapa Point**. New Zealand's second-worst maritime disaster occurred here in 1881, when the SS *Tararua* struck the Otara Reef, 1km offshore. Of the 151 passengers and crew, only 20 survived; 65 victims are buried in the nearby graveyard. A lighthouse was erected on the point three years after the tragedy.

Further east is **Slope Point**, the South Island's most southerly point. A walk across private land (20 minutes) leads to a small beacon atop a spectacular spur of rock; the track is closed September and October for lambing.

For four hours either side of low tide at **Curio Bay**, one of the world's most extensive fossil forests (160 million years old) is revealed. The petrified stumps, fallen log fossils and plant species identified here prove NZ's one-time connection to the ancient supercontinent Gondwana.

In nearby **Porpoise Bay** you used to see Hectors dolphins surfing the beach breaks, but we were told the dolphins have not been spotted for some time. If they come back and you try to swim with them, don't touch or otherwise harass them, as they only come close to shore over summer to rear their young. Yellow-eyed penguins, fur seals and sea lions also live here.

Inside the old Waikawa church is **Dolphin Magic** (☎ 246 8444; dolphinmagic@xtra.co.nz; Main Rd), which normally does dolphin-watching trips but these are obviously dependent on whether the dolphins reappear. However, they still visit places such as Brothers Point, where there are fur seals and numerous sea birds. The company also acts as an information centre and store.

The **Cathedral Caves** (admission per tramper or cyclist NZ$2, per car NZ$5) on Waipati Beach, so-named for their resemblance to an English cathedral, are accessible for two hours either side of low tide (tide tables are posted at the highway turn-off or at visitors centres). From the highway it's 2km to the car park, then a 15-minute walk to the beach and a further 25 minutes to the caves. The turn-off to pretty **McLean Falls** is just before the caves car park; the falls are 3.5km up a dirt road, followed by a 40-minute return walk.

Lenz Reserve has a bird lodge and the remains of the old Tautuku sawmill just a short walk from the road. At **Tautuku Bay** there's a 15-minute walk to the beach, a stunning sandy sweep punctuated by drifts of seaweed, and another walk to **Lake Wilkie** and its unique plant life. Past Tautuku is a great lookout at **Florence Hill**.

Further east at the mouth of the Tahakopa River is **Papatowai**, a base for forays into the nearby forests.

SLEEPING & EATING

Slope Point Backpackers (☎ 246 8420; justherb@xtra.co.nz; Slope Point Rd; camp sites per 2 people NZ$16, dm/d NZ$15/35) Cottage backpackers on a 140-hectare sheep and cattle station, with ordinary dorms and a lounge well lit by daytime rays. Take the turn-off at Tokanui signposted 'Haldane' for the 13km drive to Slope Point.

Nadir Outpost (☎ 246 8544; www.geocities.com/nadir_outpost; 174 Slope Point Rd; camp sites per 2 people NZ$16, dm NZ$15, B&B per person NZ$50) Next door to Slope Point Backpackers, this place has some dark little dorms (though one has a window) but nice garden surrounds. Also sells basic supplies and snacks such as microwaved sausage rolls and mini pizzas.

Curio Bay Camping Ground (☎ 246 8897; 601 Curio Bay Rd; camp sites unpowered/powered per 2 people NZ$10/15) Pleasant sites staked out right on the beach, and a small on-site store.

Curio Bay Accommodation (☎ 246 8797; 501 Curio Bay Rd; dm NZ$20, d NZ$50-70) Modern cottage with two doubles (one with bathroom), some bunks and water views.

Papatowai Scenic Highway Motels & Store (☎ 415 8147; b.bevin@paradise.net.nz; Main Rd, Papatowai; d NZ$80) Mouthful of a name, but has well-appointed motel units lying behind a well-stocked grocery, fuel and takeaway shop (which sports the world's trickiest public phone). Behind the motels is the simple **Papatowai Motor Camp** (☎ 415 8500; pest@es.co.nz; camp sites per 2 people NZ$14, dm/d NZ$12/30), with doubles in basic cabins.

Hilltop (☎ 415 8028; hilltop@ihug.co.nz; 77 Tahakopa Valley Rd, Papatowai; dm NZ$20, d NZ$55-60) An exceptional backpackers reached along the road just before the bridge near Papatowai, offering fantastic views and two beautifully furnished farmhouses. Mountain bikes and canoes are available for those who prefer activity to just sitting still and drinking in the peace and quiet.

Papatowai to Owaka

From Papatowai, follow the highway north to **Matai Falls** on the Maclennan River, then head southeast on the signposted road to the more scenic, tiered **Purakaunui Falls**, accessible along a short bush-parting walk. In the **Catlins Conservation Park** you can do the **River Walk** (five hours) through silver beech forest. In the middle of paddocks on the southern side of the Catlins River's mouth is the 55m-deep **Jack's Blowhole** (closed Sep & Oct for lambing), 200m from the sea but connected to it by a subterranean cavern. On the river mouth's northern side is the **Pounawea Nature Walk** (45 minutes return), which loops through kahikatea, ferns, kamahi, rimu, totara and southern rata.

SLEEPING & EATING

Five minutes beyond Purakaunui Falls is the peaceful **Falls Backpackers** (☎ 415 8724; sparx@es.co.nz; Purakaunui Falls Rd; dm/d NZ$20/50), where

SOUTH ISLAND

you can bed down in one of two doubles, a twin or a two-bed dorm (all bedding supplied) in a lovely old farmhouse. There's a **DOC camping ground** (camp sites NZ$4; Purakaunui Bay) down on the water.

There's another **DOC camping ground** (camp sites NZ$4; Tawanui) at one end of the River Walk in the Catlins Conservation Park.

Owaka

pop 395

Owaka is the Catlins' main town. The **Catlins visitors centre** (☎ 415 8371; info@catlins-nz.com; 9am-5pm Mon-Fri) and **DOC** (☎ 419 1000) are both at 20 Ryley St; the visitors centre lists accommodation, including the area's many farmstays.

SLEEPING & EATING

Blowhole Backpackers (☎ 415 8998; catlinsbb@xtra.co.nz; 24 Main Rd; dm/d NZ$20/45) Attractive reddish-brown cottage warmed by a fire and with a sunny veranda to exploit come summer.

Surat Bay Lodge (☎ 415 8099; www.suratbay.co.nz; Surat Bay Rd, Newhaven; dm/d NZ$21/50;) Very inviting hostel in a great beachside spot at Newhaven, 5km east of Owaka. On the adjacent Catlins estuary is a resident sea lion colony, and there's a variety of tours and mountain bike hire (half-/full day NZ$15/25) to make use of.

Catlins Gateway Motels (☎ 0800 320 242, 415 8592; cnr Main Rd & Royal Tce; s/d NZ$70/80) Conveniently located on Owaka's main road, this motel has conjoined, self-contained units that are well maintained.

Keswick Park Camping Ground (☎ 419 1110; pounawea@ihug.co.nz; Park Lane; camp sites unpowered/powered per 2 people NZ$16/20, dm NZ$15, d NZ$24-60) This camping ground is in a lovely setting at nearby Pounawea, with ramshackle cabins and functional old-style tourist flats. Follow the signs to Surat Bay down Royal Tce but veer right instead of crossing the river.

Lumberjack Bar & Café (☎ 415 8747; 3 Saunders St; mains from NZ$12; dinner) An inviting spot with a good-looking timber bar (made from a 6m-long piece of macrocarpa), open fire and comfy lounge, plus some reputable lunch and dinner selections.

Owaka to Nugget Pt

Cannibal Bay, east of Owaka, is a Hooker sea lion breeding ground. The bay got its name from a surveyor who discovered human bones in a midden and assumed a cannibalistic feast. There's a **walk** (30 minutes) between here and Surat Bay.

Further around the coast, on a not-to-be-missed side-track from the Kaka Point road, is **Nugget Point**. The wave-thumped rocky outcrops off the lighthouse-topped promontory, a 15-minute walk from the car park, lead off into the ocean's vast deep blue – the rocks were so-named because of their rough, varied shapes, which suggested overgrown gold nuggets. Fur seals, sea lions and elephant seals occasionally bask together on the rocks; it's the only place on the NZ mainland where these species coexist. There's also a wealth of birdlife, with yellow-eyed and blue penguins, gannets, shags and sooty shearwaters all breeding here. On your way to the 1869-built lighthouse, you'll pass **Roaring Bay**, which has a well-placed hide that may allow observation of yellow-eyed penguins coming ashore (usually two hours before sunset).

SLEEPING & EATING

Nugget Lodge (☎ 412 8783; www.nuggetlodge.co.nz; Nugget Rd; d NZ$95) Two units in a great setting, 3.5km before the Nugget Pt lighthouse. The upstairs pad has the best view and breakfast is provided for an extra NZ$15 per person. One of the owners is also the local wildlife ranger and can provide a wealth of local naturalist information.

Kaka Point Camping Ground (☎ 412 8818; 39 Tarata St; camp sites per 2 people NZ$20, d NZ$30) Has a sheltered grove of sites and basic cabins located near the beach, on a hill behind the main road; the caretaker's residence is at 21 Esplanade.

Fernlea Backpackers (☎ 412 8834; Moana St; s/d NZ$15/30) Compact, hill-top backpackers, perfect for those who like the sound of crashing surf carried to them on the breeze; head up the steps from Moana St.

Nugget View & Kaka Point Motels (☎ 0800 525 278, 412 8602; www.catlins.co.nz; 11 Rata St; d NZ$65-170) An impressive collection of ocean-viewing units only a few minutes' walk from the sand. Operating from here is **Nugget Point Ecotours** (1hr tours NZ$50).

Point (☎ 412 8800; 58 Esplanade, Kaka Pt; mains NZ$11-28; lunch & dinner) Beachfront eatery with a standard upmarket tavern menu and a driftwood bar attached.

New Zealand Directory

CONTENTS

ACCOMMODATION

Across New Zealand, budget travellers can tuck themselves in at night in hostels that range in character from the refreshingly relaxed to the tirelessly extroverted, in beautifully situated tent and campervan sites, and in guesthouses that creak with history.

You'll find lots of budget-accommodation reviews throughout the NZ chapters of this guidebook, ordered so they start with the places we recommend the most in terms of their ambience, cleanliness, facilities and other factors. In sections on the biggest cities, we also provide a couple of 'splurge' options so you can swap typical shoestring places for a little space and/or luxury once in a while. Camping grounds and holiday parks are listed at the end of accommodation sections.

We generally designate a place as budget accommodation if it charges up to NZ$65 per single or NZ$80 per double. We occasionally list places that charge a little more if they are good value considering their location, facilities etc.

If you're travelling during peak tourist seasons, you'll usually need to book a bed well in advance. The periods when accommodation is most in demand (and at its priciest) include the summer holidays from Christmas to the end of January, Easter, and winter in snowy resort towns like Queenstown and Wanaka. At other times of the year, you'll find that hotels charge cheaper rates during the week than over the weekend – many hotels also offer walk-in rates that are significantly lower than their advertised rates. We quote high-season prices in this guidebook unless otherwise indicated.

B&Bs & Guesthouses

Bed and breakfast (B&B) accommodation is set up in everything from suburban bungalows and weatherboard beach cottages to stately manors that have been owned by generations of one family. Dinner is sometimes also available, hence places with DB&B (dinner, bed and breakfast) packages. It's an unwritten law that NZ B&B brochures must depict a dog of some description, often a vacant-eyed golden retriever.

Guesthouses are usually spartan, cheap, 'private' (unlicensed) hotels, mostly low-key places patronised by people who eschew the impersonal atmosphere of many motels. However, some are quite fancy and offer self-contained rooms.

Typically you pay between NZ$80 and NZ$150 per double, though there are more than a few places where you can pay upwards of NZ$300 for a room.

Camping & Campervan Parks

Campers and campervan drivers alike are thrown together in 'holiday parks' (sometimes still called motor camps) that provide unpowered and powered sites, as well as cheap bunkrooms, a range of cabins, and

PRACTICALITIES

Electricity

- Use a three-pin plug (different to British three-pin plugs) to plug into the electricity supply (230V AC, 50Hz)

Videos

- Videos you watch will be based on the PAL system

Weights & Measures

- New Zealand uses the metric system

self-contained units that are often called tourist flats. They also have well-equipped communal kitchens and dining areas, and often games and TV rooms too. In cities, such parks are usually located away from the centre, but in smaller townships they can be central or near lakes, beaches, rivers or forests.

The nightly cost of holiday-park camping is usually between NZ$10 and NZ$12 per person, with powered sites being slightly more expensive. Sheltered accommodation normally ranges from NZ$30 to NZ$80 per double.

BACKCOUNTRY HUTS & CAMPING GROUNDS

If you'll gladly swap facilities for wilder, less developed locations such as national parks, head for one of the numerous camping grounds and huts managed by the **Department of Conservation** (DOC; www.doc.govt.nz). The DOC has a huge network of backcountry huts (over 1000) in NZ's national, maritime and forest parks. There are 'serviced huts' (with mattress-equipped bunks or sleeping platforms, water, heating, toilets and sometimes cooking facilities), 'standard huts' (no cooking equipment or heating) and 'basic huts' or bivvies. Hut fees range from free to NZ$25 per night, paid with tickets purchased in advance at DOC offices or park visitors centres. When you arrive at a hut, date the tickets and put them in the box provided.

The DOC also manages 200 camping grounds that are accessible by vehicles. The most basic of these ('informal' sites) are free, while 'standard' and 'serviced' grounds cost between NZ$3 and NZ$12 per person per night.

Farmstays

Farmstays enable you to learn about the significant agricultural side of NZ life, with travellers encouraged to 'have a go' at typical activities on dairy, sheep, high-country, cattle or mixed-farming spreads, as well as orchards. Costs vary widely, with B&B generally starting around NZ$70, sometimes less. Some farms have separate cottages where you fix your own food, while others have low-cost, shared, backpacker-style accommodation. **Rural Holidays NZ** (☎ 03-355 6218; www.ruralhols.co.nz) lists farmstays throughout the country on its website.

Hostels

NZ is practically overflowing with backpacker hostels, from small, homestay-style affairs with a handful of beds to refurbished hotels with scuffed façades and the towering modern structures you'll find blocking the skyline in the big cities. The prices given for hostel beds throughout this guidebook are the nonmembership rates.

HOSTEL ORGANISATIONS

The biggest NZ hostel group (and growing all the time) is **Budget Backpacker Hostels** (BBH; ☎ 03-379 3014; www.bbh.co.nz), which has around 325 hostels on its books, including homestays and farmstays. Membership costs NZ$40 (the membership card doubles as a phonecard with NZ$20 worth of calls) and entitles you to stay at any of the member hostels at a cost no greater than the rates advertised in the annual (free) *BBH Backpacker Accommodation* booklet. Nonmembers pay an extra fee of between NZ$1 and NZ$4, though not all hostel owners charge the difference. The membership card can be bought at any member hostel, or you can have it sent overseas for NZ$45 (including postage; see the website for details). BBH rates each hostel according to traveller feedback, using a percentage figure which in theory tells you how good (or at least how popular) each hostel is. While the system is generally pretty accurate, our experience is that some highly rated hostels are not that great, and some poorly rated places are not that bad.

VIP Backpacker Resorts (☎ 09-816 8903; www.vip.co.nz) represents over 80 hostels, particularly in the cities and major tourist spots. An advantage with VIP is that it's international, with a huge network of hostels in Australia,

Southern Africa, Europe, America and Fiji. For NZ$39 you'll receive a 12-month membership, entitling you to a NZ$1 discount on accommodation. You can join online, at VIP hostels or at larger agencies dealing in backpacker travel.

Nomads Backpackers (www.nomadsworld.com) also has franchisees in NZ. Membership costs A$34 for 12 months and, as with VIP, results in NZ$1 off the cost of nightly accommodation. You can join at participating hostels, backpacker travel agencies or online.

All of the aforementioned membership cards also entitle the user to sundry discounts on transport, tours, activities and dining.

INDEPENDENT HOSTELS

NZ is an incubator for independent hostels, hatching them across both islands at an impressive rate. With so many places vying for the overnight attention of backpackers and other travellers, it's no surprise that these businesses try hard to differentiate themselves from their competitors – some promote themselves purely on their low-key ambience, lazy gardens, personable owner/managers and avoidance of noisy backpacker bus groups, while others will bury you in extras like free breakfasts, free videos, spa pools, use of bikes and kayaks, shuttle buses, theme nights and tour bookings. If possible, check out your chosen place to stay before committing to a night there, to make sure the atmosphere and facilities correspond at least roughly to your expectations. Note that a number of hostels designate themselves 'unsuitable for children'.

Independent backpacker establishments typically charge NZ$19 to NZ$25 for a dorm bed, NZ$38 to NZ$45 for a single and NZ$45 to NZ$65 for a twin or double room (usually without bathroom), with a small discount if you're a member of BBH, VIP or Nomads (see opposite). Some have space for tents.

If you're a Kiwi travelling in your own country, be warned that some hostels only admit overseas travellers; typically they're inner-city places that cite problems they've had with locals bothering the guests. If you encounter such discrimination, insist you're a genuine traveller, or try another hostel.

YHA HOSTELS

NZ has over 60 **Youth Hostels Association** (YHA; ☎ 0800 278 299, 03-379 9970; www.stayyha.com) hostels, which accommodate individuals, families and groups. The YHA is part of the **International Youth Hostel Federation** (IYHF, www.hihostels.com), also known as Hostelling International or HI, so if you're already a member of that organisation in your own country, your membership entitles you to use NZ hostels. Nightly charges are between NZ$18 and NZ$35 per person for members; hostels also take non-YHA members for around an extra NZ$3 per night. Visitors to NZ should preferably purchase a HI card in their country of residence, but you can also buy one at major local YHA hostels at a cost of NZ$40 for 12 months; see the HI website for further details. New Zealand residents can become full YHA members for NZ$40/60 for one/two years; join online, at any youth hostel, or at most visitors centres.

YHA hostels provide basic accommodation in small dormitories (bunk rooms, usually with four to six beds) and most also have a limited supply of single, twin, double and en suite rooms. They have 24-hour access, cooking facilities, a communal area with a TV, laundry facilities and, in larger hostels, travel offices. There's often a maximum-stay period (usually five to seven days). Bed linen is provided in all hostels; sleeping bags are not welcomed as a general hygiene precaution.

The annual *YHA New Zealand Hostel & Discount Guide* booklet details all Kiwi hostels and the discounts (transport, activities etc) members are entitled to.

Pubs, Hotels & Motels

The least expensive form of hotel accommodation is the humble pub, which gets its name from the term 'public house'. These are older-style establishments which purvey beer and assorted social moments, but do a sideline in relatively cheap upstairs beds. Some old pubs are full of character and local characters, while some are grotty, ramshackle places that are best avoided, especially by solo women travellers. If you're considering renting a room above a pub's bar towards the end of the week, always check whether live music is scheduled for that night, or you could find yourself listening to the muted thump of a sound system until the early hours. In the cheapest pubs, singles/doubles might cost as little as NZ$25/40 (with a shared bathroom that's inevitably a long trek down the hall), though NZ$40/55 is more common.

Further up the hotel scale are the anonymous, well-equipped modern edifices you'll find pretty much everywhere that tourists visit. These face stiff competition from NZ's glut of nondescript low-rise motels, most of which have similar facilities (tea and coffee making, fridge, TV, air-con, private bathroom) – the price will indicate the standard. We quote 'rack rates' (official advertised rates) for such places throughout this book, but regular discounts and special deals are commonplace.

Rental Accommodation

The basic Kiwi holiday home is called a 'bach', short for 'bachelor' as they were often used by single men as hunting and fishing retreats; in Canterbury and Otago they're known as 'cribs'. These are simple self-contained cottages that can be rented in rural and coastal areas, often in a soothingly private location. They can be good for longer stays in a region, although many are only available for one or two nights at a time. Prices are typically NZ$70 to NZ$130, which isn't bad for a whole house or self-contained bungalow.

ACTIVITIES

Few activities are off-limits in NZ, a fact exemplified by the startling variety of ways in which Kiwis and visitors move over or through land, air and water. The following is just a summary of what's possible; for specifics, read the individual activities entries in the North Island and South Island chapters.

Bungy Jumping

Bungy jumping was made famous by Kiwi AJ Hackett's dive from the Eiffel Tower in 1986. Nowadays, people regularly hurtle earthwards from high places in NZ, with nothing between them and kingdom come but a gigantic rubber cord strapped to their limbs. For exhibitionist backpackers, the days of bungy jumping nude for free are well and truly over, though you might still get a discount.

Queenstown (p719) is virtually surrounded by bungy cords and bungy variations such as the bungy rocket, parabungy and Shotover Canyon Swing. Another South Island bungy jump awaits you outside **Hanmer Springs** (p694). Jumping is also done on the North Island at **Taupo** (p570) and in **Auckland** (p516) from the Harbour Bridge and the Sky Tower.

Caving

Caving opportunities abound in the honeycombed karst regions of the islands. One of the most spectacular caving experiences is the 100m abseil into the Lost World *tomo* (cave entrance) near **Waitomo** (p559). Underground organisations include the **Wellington Caving Group** (http://caving.wellington.net.nz) and the **Auckland Speleo Group** (www.asg.org.nz).

Cycling & Mountain Biking

Most towns offer bike hire, either at backpacker hostels or specialist bike shops, but quality mountain bikes can usually only be hired in major towns or adventure-sports hubs. The **Queen Charlotte Track** (p650) is one of the few tramping tracks you can bike down, but part of it is closed to bikes in summer.

The rates charged by most outfits for renting road or mountain bikes, not including the discounted fees or freebies offered to guests by some accommodation places, are anywhere from NZ$10 to NZ$20 per hour and NZ$20 to NZ$35 per day.

The **New Zealand Mountain Bike Web** (www.mountainbike.co.nz) has a good website, or contact **Mountain Bike NZ Inc** (MTBNZ; ☎ 04-473 8386; www.mountainbike.co.nz/nzmba).

If you're considering getting around NZ by bike, see p791.

Diving

The **Poor Knights Islands** (p536), off the east coast of the North Island, is reputed to have the best diving in NZ. **Marlborough Sounds** (p647) also has some interesting dives, including the *Mikhail Lermontov*, the largest diveable cruise ship wreck in the world.

Fiordland in the South Island is highly unusual in that the region's extremely heavy rainfall and mountain run-off leaves a layer of often peaty brown freshwater sitting on top of some of the saltwater fiords, notably **Milford Sound** (p756). The freshwater filters out light and discourages the growth of seaweed, so divers get to experience amazingly clear pseudo-deepwater conditions not far below the surface.

For more about NZ's explorable depths, pick up a copy of Lonely Planet's *Diving*

& Snorkeling New Zealand, contact the **NZ Underwater Association** (☎ 09-623 3252) in Auckland, or visit **Dive New Zealand** (www.divenewzealand.com).

Horse Riding

Unlike some parts of the world where horse riding beginners get led by the nose around a paddock, in NZ you really can get out into the countryside on farm, forest and beach rides. On the South Island, all-day horseback rides are a fine way to see the country around **Kaikoura** (p660), **Nelson** (p665) and **Dunedin** (p741). On the North Island, **Taupo** (p571) has options for wilderness horse trekking, as does the **Coromandel Peninsula** (p566).

Jet-boating

Jet-boats make short work of shallow and white water because there are no propellers to damage, there's better clearance under the boat and the jet can be reversed instantly for quick braking. The instant response of the jet enables these craft to execute passenger-drenching 360° spins almost within the length of the boat.

On the South Island, it's well worth taking the jet-boat rides down the Shotover and Kawarau Rivers near **Queenstown** (p721) and the Dart River near **Glenorchy** (p730), while the same can be said for the jet-boating trips on the **Bay of Islands** (p538).

Kayaking

Many backpacker hostels situated close to water will have kayaks for hire or for free, and loads of commercial guided trips are on offer. Highly rated sea-kayaking areas in NZ's north include **Waiheke Island** (p532), the **Bay of Islands** (p539) and **Coromandel Peninsula** (p567), and, in the south, **Marlborough Sounds** (p652), **Milford Sound** (p756) and along the coast of **Abel Tasman National Park** (p671).

Rafting

There are almost as many white-water rafting possibilities as there are rivers in NZ, and there's no shortage of companies to take you on an exhilarating ride down some magnificently wild watercourses. Popular raft carriers on the South Island include the **Shotover and Kawarau Rivers** (p721), while the **Rangitata River** (p681) is considered one of the country's best. In the North Island, try rafting the **Tongariro** (p570), the **Rangitaiki**, or the **Kaituna Cascades** (both p595), the highlight of which is the 7m-high Okere Falls.

A variation of white-water rafting is river sledging, a form of aquatic manoeuvring involving a polystyrene sled or a modified boogie board, flippers, a wetsuit and a helmet. Try it on rivers around **Wanaka** (p734) and **Rotorua** (p595). You can also go cave rafting, which is called 'tumu tumu toobing' and 'black-water rafting' at **Waitomo** (p560), though it's technically not rafting as it involves donning a wetsuit, a lighted hardhat and a black inner tube and floating along underground rivers.

Skiing & Snowboarding

NZ is one of the most popular southern-hemisphere destinations for snow bunnies. Lifts cost from NZ$30 to NZ$75 a day. Ski-equipment rental starts at around NZ$30 a day, while daily snowboard-and-boots hire starts at around NZ$35. The ski season is generally from June to October, although it varies from one ski area to another and can go as late as November. The websites **Snow** (www.snow.co.nz) and **nzski** (www.nzski.com) provide ski reports, employment updates and webcams.

The North Island is dominated by volcanic cone skiing; active **Mt Ruapehu** (p581) and dormant **Mt Taranaki** (p589) are the premier ski areas. New Zealand's best-known (and top-rated) skiing, however, is in the South Island, most of it revolving around **Queenstown** (p722), **Wanaka** (p735) and **Arthur's Pass** (p696).

Tramping

Tramping (that's Kiwi-speak for bushwalking, hiking or trekking) is a fine way to see NZ's natural beauty. There is an excellent network of huts and thousands of kilometres of tracks, many well marked but some only a line on a map. Before plodding along any track, get up-to-date information from offices of the **Department of Conservation** (DOC; www.doc.govt.nz). Another good resource is Lonely Planet's *Tramping in New Zealand*. The best walking weather is from January to March, though most tracks can be walked enjoyably any time from about October to April.

GREAT WALKS

The fittingly named Great Walks are the most popular tracks and can get very crowded,

SURFING IN NEW ZEALAND *Josh Kronfeld*

As a surfer I feel particularly guilty letting the reader in on a local secret – NZ has a sensational mix of quality waves perfect for both beginners and experienced surfers. As long as you're willing to travel off the beaten track, you can score some great, uncrowded waves. The islands of NZ are hit with swells from all points of the compass throughout the year. So, with a little weather knowledge and a little effort, numerous options present themselves. Point breaks, reefs, rocky shelves and hollow sandy beach breaks can all be found – take your pick!

Surfing has become increasingly popular in NZ and today surf schools are up and running at most premier surf beaches. It's worth doing a bit of pretravel research: **Surfing New Zealand** (www.surfing.co.nz) recommends a number of schools on its website. If you're on a surf holiday, consider buying a copy of either *New Zealand Surfing Guide* by Mike Bhana or Wayne Warrick's *Surf Riding in New Zealand*.

The Surfing New Zealand website includes information on many great surf spots, but most NZ beaches hold good rideable breaks. Some of the ones I particularly enjoy:

- Bay of Plenty: Mt Maunganui (p607), Matakana Island
- Canterbury: Taylors Mistake (p681), Sumner Bar
- Coromandel: Whangamata
- Marlborough & Nelson: Kaikoura Peninsula, Mangamaunu (p660), Meatworks
- North Island East Coast: Hicks Bay (p623), Gisborne city beaches (p621), Mahia Peninsula
- North Island West Coast: Punakaiki, Tauranga Bay (p604)
- Otago: Dunedin (p738) is a good base for surfing on the South Island, with access to a number of superb breaks such as St Clair Beach (p739)
- Southland: Porridge, Centre Island
- Taranaki: Fitzroy Beach, Stent Road and Greenmeadows Point all lie along the 'Surf Highway' (p583)
- Waikato: Raglan (p556), NZ's most famous surf break and usually the first stop for overseas surfies
- Wellington: City beaches such as Lyall Bay(p632), Castlepoint and Tora

NZ water temperatures and climate vary greatly from north to south. For comfort while surfing, wear a wetsuit. In the summer on the North Island you can get away with a spring suit and boardies; on the South Island, use a 2–3mm steamer. In winter on the North Island use a 2–3mm steamer, and on the South Island a 3–5mm with all the extras.

Josh is a keen surfer hailing originally from the Hawke's Bay region. While representing the All Blacks (1995–2000) he successfully juggled surfing, pop music and an international rugby career.

especially over summer. All nine Great Walks are fully detailed in Lonely Planet's *Tramping in New Zealand*, and are also described in DOC-produced pamphlets.

To tramp them you'll need to buy a Great Walks hut or camping pass, sold at DOC offices and visitors centres in the vicinity of each walk – on some walks, ordinary backcountry hut tickets and passes (see p774) can be used to procure a bunk or camp site in the track's low (nonsummer) season. Hut prices vary from NZ$10 to NZ$35 per night depending on the track and the season; camping fees range from NZ$6 to NZ$15 per night. You can only camp at designated camping grounds; there's no camping on the Milford Track.

Abel Tasman Coastal Track (p670)
Heaphy Track (p672)
Kepler Track (p750)
Lake Waikaremoana Track (p617)
Milford Track (p755)
Rakiura Track (p766)
Routeburn Track (p731)
Tongariro Northern Circuit (p577)
Whanganui Journey (p589)

Whale-Watching & Dolphin Swimming

Kaikoura (p658) is the NZ nexus of marine mammal-watching, though this activity is very dependent on weather conditions. The sperm whale, the largest toothed whale, is seen from October to August, while most of the other mammals are seen year-round.

Kaikoura is also an outstanding place to swim with dolphins; pods of up to 500 playful dusky dolphins can be seen on any given day. Dolphin swimming can also be done off the North Island near **Paihia** (p539) and **Tauranga** (p604), and off **Akaroa** (p691) on the South Island's Banks Peninsula.

Zorbing

At the eccentric end of the activity scale is zorbing, a Kiwi-invented pastime which involves rolling downhill in a transparent plastic ball – sit it out if you're prone to motion sickness, otherwise try it at **Rotorua** (p603).

BOOKS

Lonely Planet publishes a comprehensive *New Zealand* guidebook.

There's a noticeable dearth of dedicated travel literature on NZ, but the country's ability to inspire its explorers is obvious in published accounts of local wanderings.

Greenstone Trails (1994) by Barry Brailsford retraces with descriptive zeal the arduous journeys undertaken by the Maori into the wild tangle of the Southern Alps in search of the highly prized *pounamu* (greenstone).

Chris Duff's *Southern Exposure* (2003) details a 2700km sea-kayak circumnavigation of the South Island. It's written in a style reserved for self-obsessed sportspeople who regard their own exploits as spiritual revelations, but has some interesting descriptions of NZ's coastline.

If you like the way Paul Theroux cheers himself up by denigrating everything around him, leaf through the ultra-brief NZ entry in *The Happy Isles of Oceania* (1993), where Theroux flees to the Routeburn Track after Christchurch apparently makes him contemplate suicide.

BUSINESS HOURS

Most shops and businesses open their doors at 9am and close at 5.30pm weekdays and either 12.30pm or 5pm on Saturday. Late-night shopping usually occurs on Thursday and/or Friday, when hours are extended until 9pm. Supermarkets usually open from 9am until at least 7pm, often until 9pm or later in big towns and cities. Dairies (corner stores) and superettes (small supermarkets) close later than most other shops.

Banks are normally open from 9.30am to 4.30pm Monday to Friday. Post offices are open 9am to 5pm Monday to Friday, with main branches also open 9.30am to 1pm Saturday; postal outlets situated in other businesses like newsagencies may be open longer than the hours quoted here.

Restaurants are typically open from noon to 3pm and 6pm until at least 9pm, but tend to serve food until 11pm or later on Friday and Saturday night. Cafés can open as early as 7.30am and close around 5pm, though café-bar hybrids tend to their patrons until well into the night. Pubs usually serve food from noon to 2pm and from 6pm to 8pm. Pubs and bars often start pouring drinks at noon and stay open until late, particularly from Thursday to Saturday.

Don't count on any attractions being open on Christmas Day.

CLIMATE

NZ's location within the Roaring Forties means it gets freshened (and sometimes blasted) by relatively warm, damp winds blowing in from the Tasman Sea.

In the South Island, the Southern Alps act as a barrier for these moisture-laden easterlies, creating a wet climate on the west side of the mountains (over 7500mm annually) and a dry climate on the east side (about 330mm). After losing their moisture, the dry winds continue east, gathering heat and speed as they blow downhill and across the Canterbury Plains towards the Pacific coast.

In the North Island, the western sides of the high volcanoes get a lot more rain than the eastern sides but the rain shadow isn't

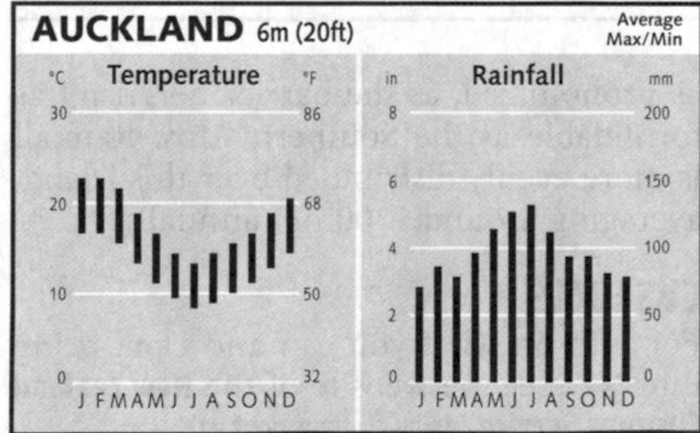

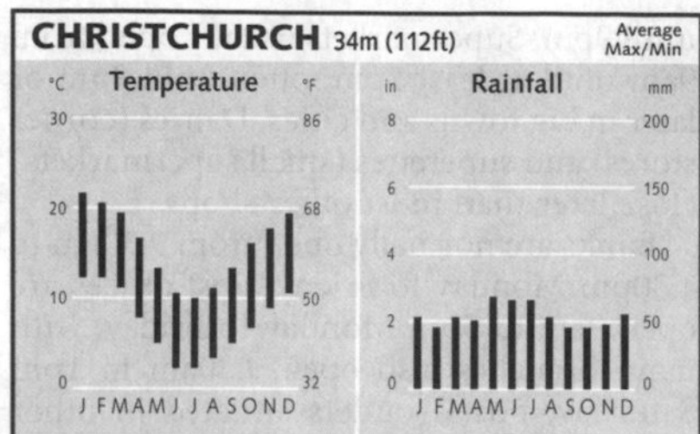

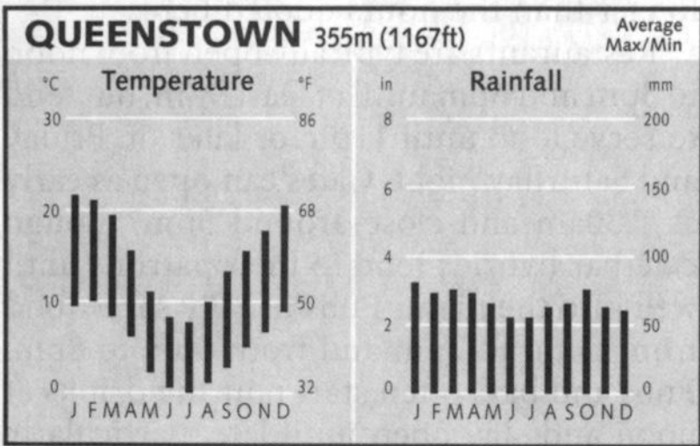

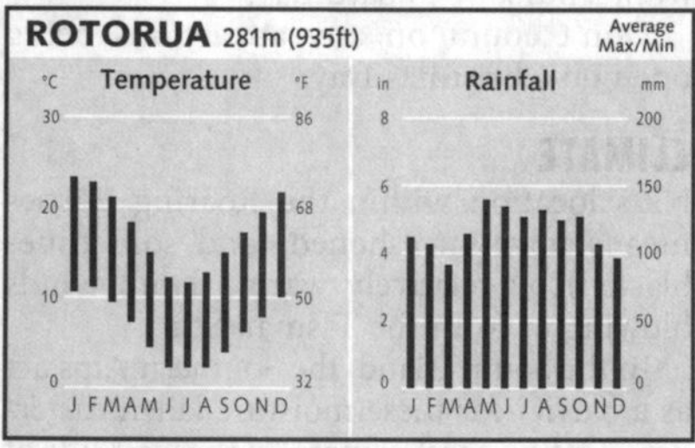

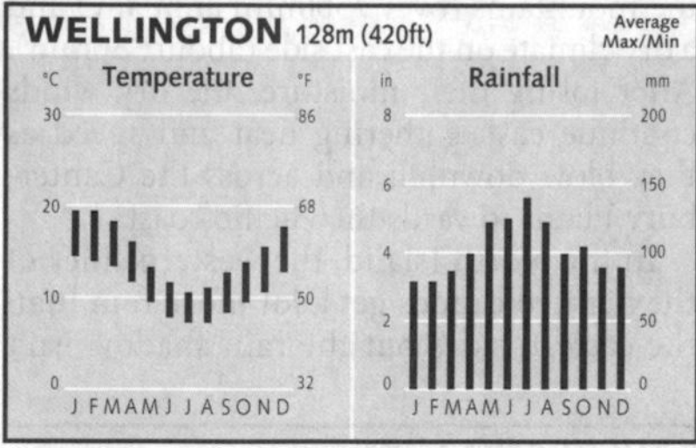

as pronounced, as the barrier here isn't as formidable as the Southern Alps. Rainfall is more evenly distributed over this island, averaging around 1300mm annually.

CUSTOMS

For info on what you can and can't bring into NZ, see the website of the **New Zealand Customs Service** (www.customs.govt.nz).

When entering NZ you can bring most articles in free of duty provided that customs is satisfied they are for personal use and that you'll be taking them with you when you leave. There's also a duty-free quota per person of 1125mL of spirits or liqueur, 4.5L of wine or beer, 200 cigarettes (or 250g of tobacco) and dutiable goods up to the value of NZ$700.

Customs are understandably fussy about drugs – declare all medicines and leave any bongs, hookahs and roach clips at home. Biosecurity is another customs buzzword, with authorities keen to keep out any diseases that may harm the country's significant agricultural industry. Tramping gear such as boots and tents will be checked and may need to be cleaned before being allowed in. You must declare any plant or animal products (including anything made of wood), and food of any kind. You'll also come in for extra scrutiny if you've arrived via Africa, Southeast Asia or South America.

DANGERS & ANNOYANCES

Though often reported in salacious detail by headline-hungry newspapers, violent crime is not common in NZ. Auckland is considered the 'crime capital' of the country, but it's very safe by international city standards.

Theft, primarily from cars, is a major problem. Avoid leaving any valuables in a vehicle no matter where it's parked; the worst places to tempt fate are tourist parking areas and the car parks at the start of walks. If the crown jewels simply must be left behind, pack them out of sight in the boot (trunk).

NZ has thankfully been spared from the proliferation of venomous creatures found in neighbouring Australia (poisonous spiders, snakes, jellyfish, Collingwood football-team supporters etc), but don't underestimate the risks posed by NZ's unpredictable, ever-changing maritime climate in high-altitude areas; for information on the dangers of hypothermia, see p809. Rips or undertows haunt some beaches and are capable of dragging swimmers right out to sea – take notice of any local warnings when swimming, surfing or diving, and see p466 for more information.

The islands' roads are often made hazardous by speeding locals, wide-cornering campervans and traffic-ignorant sheep. Try

SANDFLIES *Sir Ian McKellen*

As an unpaid but enthusiastic proselytiser on behalf of all things Kiwi, including the New Zealand tourist industry, I hesitate to mention the well-kept secret of sandflies. I first met them en masse at the glorious Milford Sound, where visitors (after the most beautiful drive in the world) are met, at least during the summer, by crowds of the little buggers. There are patent unctions that cope, and tobacco repels them too, but I would hope that travellers find them an insignificant pest compared with the glory of their habitat. Oddly, when actually filming scenes for *The Lord of the Rings*, I don't recall being bothered by sandflies at all. Honestly. Had there been, we would have set the Orcs on them.

Sir Ian is a UK-based actor who spent several years in NZ filming and has become something of an unofficial ambassador for NZ tourism.

to stay alert on the road despite the distractingly beautiful scenery.

In the annoyances category, it's hard to top a sandfly visitation (see above). Equip yourself with insect repellent in coastal areas unless you're keen to imitate a whirling dervish when these little fiends start biting.

DISABLED TRAVELLERS

A significant number of hostels and other Kiwi accommodation options are equipped with wheelchair-accessible rooms as well as disability-friendly bathrooms; true barrier-free rooms, however, are few and far between. Many tourist attractions provide wheelchair access, with wheelchairs often available with advance notice.

Tour operators with accessible vehicles operate from most major centres. Key cities are also serviced by kneeling buses (the steps on these buses can be lowered until they're flush with the ground), and taxi companies have wheelchair-accessible vans. Large car-hire firms such as Avis and Hertz provide cars with hand controls at no extra charge; advance notice is required.

The website of **Enable New Zealand** (www.enable.co.nz) has links (in the 'Kiwi Explorer' section) to organisations catering to people with disabilities, although its focus is not on travellers. A good contact point is the **Disability Information Service** (☎ 03-366 6189; dis@disinfo.co.nz; 314 Worcester St, Christchurch).

Disabled travellers who enjoy tramping should buy *Accessible Walks* by Anna Jameson and Andrew Jameson, which offers first-hand descriptions of over 100 South Island walks.

Riding for the Disabled (☎ 07-849 4727; Foreman Rd, Hamilton) is another useful organisation.

DRIVING LICENCE

International visitors to NZ can use their home country's driving licence; if your licence isn't in English, it's a good idea to carry a certified translation with you. Alternatively, use an International Driving Permit (IDP), which is valid for 12 months and usually issued on the spot by your home country's automobile association.

EMBASSIES & CONSULATES

Embassies & Consulates in New Zealand

Addresses of major diplomatic representations include the following. Look in local *Yellow Pages* (www.yellowpages.co.nz) phone directories (particularly in Wellington) for a more complete listing.

Australia (Map pp626-7; ☎ 04-473 6411; www.australia.org.nz; 72-78 Hobson St, Thorndon, Wellington)
Canada (Map pp626-7; ☎ 04-473 9577; www.dfait-maeci.gc.ca/newzealand; 3rd fl 61 Molesworth St, Wellington)
France (Map pp630-1; ☎ 04-384 2555; www.ambafrance-nz.org; 12th fl 34-42 Manners St, Wellington)
Germany (Map pp630-1; ☎ 04-473 6063; www.wellington.diplo.de; 90-92 Hobson St, Thorndon, Wellington)
Ireland (☎ 09-977 2252; consul@ireland.co.nz; 6th fl, 18 Shortland St, Auckland)
Netherlands (Map pp626-7; ☎ 04-471 6390; www.netherlandsembassy.co.nz; 10th fl, Investment Centre, cnr Featherston & Ballance Sts, Wellington)
UK (Map pp626-7; ☎ 04-924 2888; www.britain.org.nz/thebhc.html; 44 Hill St, Thorndon, Wellington)
USA (Map pp626-7; ☎ 04-462 6000; http://wellington.usembassy.gov; 29 Fitzherbert Tce, Thorndon, Wellington)

It's important to realise what your own embassy – the embassy of the country of which you are a citizen – can and can't do to help you if you get into trouble. Generally speaking, it won't be much help in emergencies if the trouble you're in is even remotely your own fault. Don't forget that while in NZ, you are bound by NZ laws.

In genuine emergencies you might get some assistance, but only if other channels have been exhausted. For example, if you need to get home urgently, a free ticket is exceedingly unlikely – the embassy would expect you to have insurance. If you have all your money and documents stolen, it might assist with getting a new passport, but a loan for onward travel is out of the question.

New Zealand Embassies & Consulates Abroad

The **Ministry of Foreign Affairs & Trade** (www.nzembassy.com) has a site listing all NZ diplomatic missions. The website provides contact details of representatives both in the country and abroad. Representative abroad include the following:

Australia Canberra (☎ 02-6270 4211; nzhccba@austarmetro.com.au; Commonwealth Ave, Canberra, ACT 2600); Sydney (☎ 02-8256 2000; nzcgsydney@bigpond.com; 10th fl, 55 Hunter St, Sydney, NSW 2000) Also in Melbourne.

Canada Ottawa (☎ 613-238 5991; info@nzhcottawa.org; Suite 727, 99 Bank St, Ottawa, Ontario K1P 6G3) Also in Vancouver and Toronto.

France Paris (☎ 01-45 01 43 43; nzembassy.paris@wanadoo.fr; 7ter, rue Léonard de Vinci, 75116 Paris)

Germany Berlin (☎ 030-206 210; nzembassy.berlin@t-online.de; Friedrichstrasse 60, 10117, Berlin) Also in Hamburg.

Ireland Dublin (☎ 01-660 4233; nzconsul@indigo.ie; 37 Leeson Park, Dublin 6) Also in Belfast.

Netherlands The Hague (☎ 070-346 93 24; nzemb@xs4all.nl; Carnegielaan 10, 2517 KH, The Hague)

UK London (☎ 020-7930 8422; email@newzealandhc.org.uk; New Zealand House, 80 Haymarket, London SW1Y 4TQ)

USA Washington DC (☎ 202-328 4800; nz@nzemb.org; 37 Observatory Circle NW, Washington DC 20008); Los Angeles (☎ 310-207 1605; www.nzcgla.com; Suite 1150, 12400 Wilshire Blvd, Los Angeles, CA 90025) Also in New York.

FESTIVALS & EVENTS

Details of major festivals and events that take place in a single city or town are provided throughout the destination chapters of this book. The following events, however, are pursued across several cities, throughout a particular region or even around the country.

February

Harvest Hawke's Bay (www.harvesthawkesbay.co.nz) Indulgent wine and food celebration, with participating wineries scattered around Napier and Hastings.

NZ Masters Games (www.nzmastersgames.com) The country's biggest multisport event, held in Dunedin (even-numbered years) and Wanganui (odd-numbered years).

Waitangi Day Commemorates the signing of the Treaty of Waitangi on 6 February 1840 with various events around NZ.

May

New Zealand International Comedy Festival (www.comedyfestival.co.nz) Three-week laugh-fest in venues across Auckland and Wellington.

July

New Zealand International Film Festival (www.enzedff.co.nz) After separate film festivals in Wellington, Auckland, Dunedin and Christchurch, a selection of flicks spends the next three months touring major provincial towns.

November & December

Coromandel Pohutukawa Festival (www.pohutukawafest.com) Biennial event dedicated to the conservation of the crimson pohutukawa tree, and featuring numerous concerts and sports events.

GAY & LESBIAN TRAVELLERS

The gay and lesbian tourism industry in NZ is fairly low-key, but homosexual communities are prominent in Auckland and Wellington (see the boxed texts on p519 and p633).

The **NZ Gay & Lesbian Tourism Association** (☎ 0800 123 429, 09-917 9184; www.nzglta.org.nz) in Auckland promotes local gay and lesbian tourism, while **Travel Gay New Zealand** (www.gaytravel.net.nz) is a gay information and reservation service. Other useful gay websites include **Gay NZ** (www.gaynz.com), **Gay Line Wellington** (www.gayline.gen.nz) and **Gay New Zealand** (www.gaynz.net.nz). The free *New Zealand Gay Guide* is a booklet available in key cities.

Gay festivals include the huge **HERO festival** (www.gaynz.com/hero), held every February in Auckland, and the **Gay & Lesbian Fair** (www.gayfair.wellington.net.nz) in Wellington in March. Queenstown stages the annual midwinter **Gay Ski Week** (www.gayskiweeknewzealand.com).

HOLIDAYS

Public Holidays

The following is a list of NZ's main public holidays. There are also various provincial anniversary day holidays, hangovers from the old days when each province was separately administered – check with tourist offices for exact dates.

New Year 1 & 2 January
Waitangi Day 6 February

Easter March/April
Anzac Day 25 April
Queen's Birthday 1st Monday in June
Labour Day 4th Monday in October
Christmas Day 25 December
Boxing Day 26 December

School Holidays

The Christmas holiday season, from mid-December to late January, is part of the summer school vacation – it's the time you are most likely to find transport and accommodation booked out, and long, restless queues at tourist attractions. There are three shorter school-holiday periods during the year, falling roughly from mid- to late April, early to mid-July, and mid-September to early October.

INSURANCE

Don't underestimate the importance of a good travel-insurance policy that covers theft, loss and medical problems. You may prefer a policy that pays doctors or hospitals direct rather than making you pay on the spot and claim later. If you have to claim later make sure you keep all documentation. Check that the policy covers ambulances and emergency medical evacuations by air.

Some policies specifically exclude designated 'dangerous activities' such as bungy jumping, scuba diving, white-water rafting, skiing and even bushwalking. If you plan on doing any of these things (a distinct possibility in NZ), make absolutely sure that the policy you choose fully covers you for your activities of choice.

It's worth mentioning that under NZ law, you cannot sue for personal injury (other than exemplary damages). Rather, the country's **Accident Compensation Corporation** (ACC; www.acc.co.nz) administers an accident compensation scheme that provides accident insurance for NZ residents and temporary visitors to the country, regardless of who is at fault. While some people cry foul, others point to the hugely expensive litigation 'industries' in other countries and raise a silent cheer. This scheme does not, however, cancel out the necessity for your own comprehensive travel insurance policy, as it doesn't cover you for such things such as loss of income or treatment in your home country, as well as other possible eventualities like illness. Also see the Health chapter (p806). For information on insurance matters relating to cars that are bought or rented, see p795.

INTERNET ACCESS

Getting connected in NZ is relatively simple in all but the most remote locales. So-called 'cybercafés' are usually brimming with terminals, high-speed connections and a bit of independent character in main tourist centres, but facilities are more unpredictable in small, out-of-the-way towns. Most hostels can also hook you up, sometimes for free. Many public libraries have Internet access too, but generally there are a limited number of terminals and these are provided for research needs, not for travellers to check their emails – so head for a cybercafé first.

The cost of access ranges from NZ$2 to NZ$10 per hour, with the lowest rates found in cities where competition generates dirt-cheap prices. There's often a minimum period of access, usually around 10 minutes.

Free Web-based email services include **ekit** (www.lonelyplanet.ekit.com), **Yahoo** (www.yahoo.com), **MSN Hotmail** (www.hotmail.com) and **Excite** (www.excite.com).

INTERNET RESOURCES

Destination New Zealand (www.destinationnz.co.nz) Has an excellent listing of informative websites.
Lonely Planet (www.lonelyplanet.com) Get started with summaries on NZ and travellers trading info on the Thorn Tree.
NZ Government (www.govt.nz) Everything you ever wanted to know about NZ bureaucracy, including services and regulations.
Pure New Zealand (www.purenz.com) NZ's official tourism site has comprehensive info for travellers.
Te Puna Web Directory (http://webdirectory.natlib.govt.nz) Exhaustive directory of domestic websites maintained by the National Library of NZ.

LEGAL MATTERS

Marijuana (aka 'New Zealand green', 'electric puha' or 'dac') is widely indulged in but illegal, and anyone caught carrying this or other illicit drugs faces stiff penalties. Even if the amount of drugs is small and the fine not too onerous, a conviction will still be recorded against your name and this may affect your visa status.

Always carry your licence or IDP when you drive; see p781. Drink-driving is a very serious offence; the legal blood alcohol limit is 80mg per 100mL of blood (0.08%).

COMING OF AGE

For the record:

- The legal age for voting in NZ is 18.
- You can drive when you're 15, but you can't rent a car until you're 21.
- The legal age of consent (for heterosexuals and homosexuals) is 16.
- The legal drinking age is 18.

If you are arrested, it's your right to consult a lawyer before any formal questioning begins.

MAPS

Free maps are provided by local tourist offices and are mostly of a quality good enough to help you navigate your way around town.

The best topographical maps for bushwalking are those produced by **Land Information New Zealand** (LINZ; www.linz.govt.nz), usually available from LINZ outlets in major centres and at DOC offices.

MEDIA

For daily news, check out Auckland's *New Zealand Herald*, Wellington's *Dominion Post* or Christchurch's *Press* newspapers.

Tune in to National Radio for current affairs and Concert FM for classical and jazz – see **Radio New Zealand** (www.radionz.co.nz) for frequencies – or one of the many regional or local commercial stations crowding the airwaves. There are also four national commercial TV stations and the subscriber television service Sky TV; the latter is favoured by bars equipped with big-screen TVs.

MONEY

ATMs & Eftpos

The country's major banks have 24-hour automated teller machines (ATMs) attached to various branches, which accept cards from other banks and provide access to overseas accounts. You won't find ATMs everywhere, but they're widespread across both islands.

Eftpos (Electronic Funds Transfer at Point Of Sale) is a convenient service that allows you to use your bank card (credit or debit) to pay for services or purchases direct, and often withdraw cash as well. It's available practically everywhere these days and you need to know your Personal Identification Number (PIN) to use it.

Bank Accounts

We've heard mixed reports on how easy it is for nonresidents to open a NZ bank account. Some sources say it's as simple as flashing a few pieces of identification, providing a temporary postal address (or your permanent address) and then waiting a few days while your request is processed. Other sources say that many banks won't allow visitors to open an account with them unless they're planning to stay in NZ for at least six months, or unless the application is accompanied by some proof of employment. The websites of local banks are also rather vague on the services offered to short-term visitors. Be prepared to shop around to get the best banking deal.

Credit & Debit Cards

Arguably the best way to carry your money is within the electronic imprint of a plastic card. Credit cards such as Visa and MasterCard are widely accepted for everything from a hostel bed or a restaurant meal to a bungy jump or a bus ticket, and such cards are pretty much essential (in lieu of a large deposit) if you want to hire a car. They can also be used to get cash advances over the counter at banks and from ATMs, depending on the card, though such transactions incur immediate interest. Charge cards such as Diners Club and American Express (Amex) are not as widely accepted.

Apart from losing them, the obvious danger with credit cards is that you'll go home to a steaming pile of debt and interest charges. A safer option is a debit card with which you can draw money directly from your home bank account using ATMs, banks or Eftpos machines. Any card connected to the international banking network (Cirrus, Maestro, Plus and Eurocard) should work, provided you know your PIN.

The most flexible option is to carry both a credit and a debit card.

Currency

The currency is the NZ dollar (NZ$), made up of 100 cents – there are 5c, 10c, 20c and 50c, $1 and $2 coins, and $5, $10, $20, $50 and $100 notes.

Unless otherwise stated, all prices given in the NZ chapters of this book (including the NZ Directory and NZ Transport chapters) are in NZ dollars. For an idea of the money required to travel around the islands, see p18.

Exchanging Money

Changing foreign currency or travellers cheques is usually no problem at banks throughout NZ or at licensed moneychangers such as Thomas Cook or Amex in the major cities.

The NZ dollar is a relatively strong currency, though in recent times it has lost a little ground to the high-flying Australian dollar.

This table shows currency rates at the time this book went to press. For the latest exchange rates see www.oanda.com/convert/classic.

Country	Unit	NZ$
Australia	A$1	1.06
Canada	C$1	1.17
euro zone	€1	1.85
Indonesia	10,000Rp	1.64
Japan	¥100	1.36
UK	£1	2.70
USA	US$1	1.50

Tipping

Tipping is by no means entrenched in NZ but is becoming more widespread, and is appreciated (if not anticipated) in eateries in main tourist areas. Tip if you feel the service was good – 5% to 10% of the bill is the norm.

Travellers Cheques

The ubiquity of internationally linked credit- and debit-card facilities in NZ tend to make travellers cheques seem rather clumsy. Nonetheless, Amex, Thomas Cook and other well-known international brands of travellers cheques are easily exchanged. Transactions at their bureaux are commission-free if you use their cheques, while per-transaction fees vary from bank to bank. You need to present your passport for identification when cashing travellers cheques.

POST

NZ post offices are often called 'post shops', as many are set up in modern shop-style premises. You can have mail addressed to you care of 'Poste Restante, Main Post Shop' in any town. Mail is usually held for 30 days and you need some form of identification (such as a passport) to collect it. You can also have mail sent to you at city Amex offices if you have an Amex card or travellers cheques.

See p779 for post-office hours.

Letters

Reliable services are offered by **New Zealand Post** (www.nzpost.co.nz). Within NZ, standard post costs NZ$0.45 for medium-sized letters and postcards.

International destinations are divided into five zones: Australia (zone A), South Pacific (B), East Asia and North America (C), UK and Europe (D) and 'Rest of World' (E). Airmail postcards (up to 10g) cost NZ$1.50 to anywhere in the world. Airmail letters (up to 200g) cost NZ$1.50 to zones A and B, and NZ$2 to zones C, D and E. Approximate delivery times are three to six days for zone A, three to 10 days for zone B, four to 10 days for zones C and D, and five to 10 days for zone E.

Parcels

International parcel zones are the same as for letters; pricing depends on weight and whether you send the parcel 'economy' (three to five weeks), 'air' (one to two weeks) or 'express' (within several days). You can send a parcel weighing 1/2/5kg by 'economy' to Australia for NZ$11/19/35, to North America and East Asia for NZ$23/42/83, and to the UK and the rest of Europe for NZ$25/47/92. To send such parcels by 'air' is roughly 20% more expensive, and by 'express' at least 50% more.

STUDYING

Significant numbers of international students enrol in courses throughout NZ every year and spend their holidays getting to know every corner of the North and South Islands. If you're interested in studying in NZ, whether you plan to undertake a university degree or attend an English-language course, visit the **New Zealand Immigration Service** (www.immigration.govt.nz/Migrant/Stream/Study) website, where you'll find detailed information on study opportunities (including links to various educational institutions), the local cost of living and the country's attractions, as well as testimonials from various foreign students who've already acquainted themselves with daily Kiwi life.

Most higher-education establishments have international student advisers on staff who can help you establish yourself in NZ and can offer advice on general lifestyle matters, including domestic travel. Some tour and travel companies specifically cater to international students and will advertise their services on campus.

TELEPHONE

Telecom New Zealand (www.telecom.co.nz) is the country's key domestic player and also has a stake in the local mobile (cell) market. The other mobile network option is **Vodafone** (www.vodafone.co.nz).

Domestic Calls

Local calls from private phones are free, while local calls from payphones cost NZ$0.50; both involve unlimited talk time. Calls to mobile phones attract higher rates and are timed.

For long-distance calls, NZ uses five regional area codes. National calls can be made from any payphone. The main area codes:

Region	Area code
Auckland	☎ 09
Bay of Plenty	☎ 07
Central Plateau	☎ 07
Coromandel Peninsula	☎ 07
East Coast	☎ 06
Hawke's Bay	☎ 06
King Country	☎ 07
Manawatu	☎ 06
Northland	☎ 09
South Island	☎ 03
Taranaki	☎ 06
Waikato	☎ 07
Wanganui	☎ 06
Wellington Region	☎ 04

If you're making a local call (ie to someone else in the same city or town), you don't need to dial the area code. But if you're dialling within a region (even if it's to a nearby town) you do have to dial the area code, regardless of the fact that the place you're calling has the same code as the place you're dialling from.

Numbers starting with ☎ 0900 are usually recorded information services, charging upwards of NZ$1 per minute (more from mobiles); these numbers cannot be dialled from payphones.

Toll-free numbers in NZ have the prefix ☎ 0800 or ☎ 0508 and can be called free of charge from anywhere in the country, though they may not be accessible from certain areas or from mobile phones. Telephone numbers beginning with ☎ 0900, ☎ 0800 or ☎ 0508 cannot be dialled from outside NZ.

International Calls

Payphones allow international calls, the cost and dialling code of which will vary depending on the service provider. Hunt around for the specials and the lowest rates.

The toll-free Country Direct service connects callers in NZ with overseas operators to make reverse-charge (collect) or credit-card calls. Details, including Country Direct access numbers, are listed in the front of telephone directories or are available from the NZ international operator. The access number varies, depending on the number of phone companies in the country you call, but is usually ☎ 000-9 (followed by the country code).

To make international calls from NZ, dial the international access code (☎ 00), the country code and the area code (without the initial 0). So for a London number you'd dial ☎ 00-44-171, then the number. Certain operators will have you dial a special code to access their service.

Country	International country code
Australia	☎ 61
Canada	☎ 1
France	☎ 33
Germany	☎ 49
Ireland	☎ 353
Netherlands	☎ 31
UK	☎ 44
USA	☎ 1

If dialling NZ from overseas, the country code is ☎ 64 and you need to drop the 0 (zero) in the area codes.

Mobile Phones

Local mobile (cell) phone numbers have the prefix ☎ 021, ☎ 025 or ☎ 027. Mobile-phone coverage is good in cities and towns and most parts of the North Island, but can be patchy away from urban centres on the South Island.

If you want to bring your own phone and go on a prepaid service using a local SIM card, any Vodafone shop will set you up with a SIM card and phone number (about NZ$35, including up to NZ$15 worth of calls); prepaid charge cards can be purchased at newsagents and shops practically anywhere. Telecom also has a prepaid system, but you must buy one of its phones to get on the network (there are no SIM cards).

Phonecards

A wide range of phonecards can be bought at hostels, newsagents and post offices for a fixed dollar value (usually NZ$5, NZ$10, NZ$20 and NZ$50) and can be used with any public or private phone by dialling a toll-free access number and then the PIN number on the card. Shop around, as call rates vary from company to company.

The **ekit** (www.lonelyplanet.ekit.com) global communication service provides low-cost international calls – for local calls you're usually better off with a local phonecard. Ekit also offers free messaging services and email, plus travel information and an online travel vault where you can securely store details of all important documents. You can join online, where you'll find local-access numbers for the 24-hour customer-service centre. Once you've joined, always check the ekit website for the latest access numbers for each country. Current dial-in numbers (toll-free), accessible anywhere in NZ, are ☎ 0800 445 108 or ☎ 0800 446 843.

TIME

NZ is 12 hours ahead of GMT/UTC and two hours ahead of Australian Eastern Standard Time. In summer NZ observes daylight-saving time, where clocks are put forward by one hour on the first Sunday in October; clocks are wound back on the first Sunday of the following March.

For international timing, see the map of world time zones (p811).

TOURIST INFORMATION

Almost every Kiwi city or town (whether it has any worthwhile attractions or not) seems to have a visitor information centre. The bigger centres stand united within the i-SITE Network (www.i-site.org) and double as booking agents for activities, transport and accommodation. Details of local tourism offices are given throughout this guidebook.

The **Tourism New Zealand** (☎ 04-917 5400; www.purenz.com; 16th fl, 80 The Terrace, Wellington) website is a good place to start your pre-trip research and has information in four languages (including German and Japanese). Overseas offices of this organisation include:

Australia (☎ 02-8220 9000; Suite 3, 24th fl, 1 Alfred St, Sydney, NSW 2000)

UK (☎ 020-7930 1662; New Zealand House, Haymarket, London SW1Y 4TQ)

USA (☎ 310-395 7480; Suite 300, 501 Santa Monica Blvd, Santa Monica, CA 90401)

VISAS

Visa application forms are available from NZ diplomatic missions overseas, travel agents or the website of the **New Zealand Immigration Service** (NZIS; ☎ 0508-558 855, 09-914 4100; www.immigration.govt.nz). The NZIS also has over a dozen offices overseas; see the website for details.

Citizens of Australia do not need a visa or permit to visit or work in NZ and can stay indefinitely (if they don't have any criminal convictions). UK citizens don't need a visa either and can stay in the country for up to six months. Citizens of another 48 countries that have visa-waiver agreements with NZ do not require a visa for stays of up to three months, provided they can show an onward ticket, sufficient funds (usually NZ$1000 per month) and a passport valid for three months beyond the date of their planned departure – nations in this group include Canada, France, Germany, Ireland, Japan, the Netherlands and the USA.

All other foreign nationals will need the standard NZ visitor visa, valid for three months and costing around NZ$85 if processed in Australia or certain South Pacific countries like Samoa and Fiji, and NZ$120 if processed elsewhere in the world.

Visitors' visas can be extended for stays of up to nine months within one 18-month period (some travellers may be granted a further extension of three months, depending on the circumstances). Apply for extensions at any NZIS office.

Travellers interested in short-term employment to supplement their travel funds should check out the NZ Working Holiday Scheme (WHS). Under this scheme, people aged 18 to 30 years from 17 countries (including Canada, France, Germany, Ireland, the Netherlands, Sweden and the UK) can apply for a 12-month visa. It's only issued to those seeking a genuine working holiday, not for permanent work, so you can't work for one employer for more than three months. Most eligible nationals must apply in (or from) their own country and present an onward ticket, a passport valid for at least three months from the date they will depart NZ, and evidence of a minimum NZ$4200 in accessible funds. However, citizens of Canada, Malaysia, the Netherlands and Singapore who are equipped with a standard NZ visitor visa can apply once they're in NZ. The application fee is NZ$120 (refunded if your application is unsuccessful). Rules differ slightly for different nationalities, so check out the requirements on the NZIS website. Only a limited number of these visas are issued annually, so apply early. See right for NZ employment opportunities and for info on Bunac, through which US citizens (who aren't eligible for a WHS) and nationals of other countries can apply for a work permit.

VOLUNTEERING

An economical way of travelling around NZ which involves doing some voluntary work is to join **Willing Workers on Organic Farms** (Wwoof; ☎ 03-544 9890; www.wwoof.co.nz; PO Box 1172, Nelson). Membership of this well-established international organisation provides you with a book of some 800 organic farms, permaculture farms, market gardens and other environmentally sound cottage industries throughout the country where, in exchange for daily work, you'll receive food, accommodation and hands-on experience in organic farming. You must contact the farm owner or manager beforehand to arrange your stay; don't turn up at a farm without warning.

Membership costs NZ$40/50 per single/double (a 'double' meaning two people travelling together) if you join within NZ; to have your book sent overseas costs an additional NZ$5. It doesn't hurt to be part of a Working Holiday Scheme when you join.

Farm Helpers in NZ (FHINZ; www.fhinz.co.nz) produces a booklet (NZ$25) that lists around 190 farms throughout NZ providing lodging in exchange for four to six hours work per day.

WORKING

If (and only if) you've been approved for a Working Holiday Scheme (see p787), you can begin to check out the possibilities for temporary employment in fields such as agriculture, hospitality, ski resorts and office work.

Seasonal fruit picking, thinning, pruning and harvesting is readily available. Apples, kiwi fruit and other produce are picked in summer and early autumn. Pay rates are low (you can usually expect to earn between NZ$10 and NZ$15 each hour) and the work is hard, so the demand for workers is usually high. You're usually paid by how much you pick (per bin, bucket or kilo). The main picking season is from December to May, though there's some form of agricultural work in the country year-round. Places where you may find picking work include the Bay of Islands (Kerikeri and Paihia), rural Auckland, Tauranga, Gisborne and Napier in the North Island; and Nelson, Marlborough (around Blenheim) and Central Otago in the South Island. Approach prospective employers directly where you can, or stay at hostels or holiday parks in the picking areas that specialise in helping travellers to find work.

The winter work available at ski resorts, or in the towns that service them, includes bar tending, waiting tables, cleaning, working on ski tows and, if you're properly qualified, ski or snowboard instructing. Have a look at the website for each resort for announcements of prospective work.

Registering with an agency in Auckland is your best bet for inner-city office work in areas such as IT, banking and finance, and telemarketing.

Be aware that finding something suitable will not always be easy, regardless of how straightforward it may look from afar on work-touting websites. Be prepared to look around for worthwhile opportunities, and don't put up with unsatisfactory conditions such as exploitative pay.

Resources

Seasonal Work NZ (www.seasonalwork.co.nz) has a database of thousands of casual jobs. It gives the contact details of employers looking for workers, rates of pay and nearby accommodation.

Another worthwhile resource, specialising in temporary positions in the heartland of the South Island, is the website of **Mid Canterbury Employment** (www.mces.co.nz).

The website of the **New Zealand Fruitgrowers Federation** (☎ 04-472 6559; www.fruitgrowers.org.nz) has lots of info on fruit-picking possibilities, including contact details for people charged with coordinating seasonal employment opportunities in various regions.

New Zealand Job Search (☎ 09-357 3996; www.nzjobs.go.to) is a handy employment service run out of Auckland Central Backpackers.

Hostels and backpacker publications, not to mention word of mouth, are also good sources of information on local work possibilities.

AgriVenture (☎ 07-823 5700; www.agriventure.com; PO Box 134, 55 Victoria St, Cambridge 2352) organises farming and horticultural exchanges for people aged 18 to 30 years from Australia, North America, Europe and Japan, for stays of between four and 15 months. Visas, jobs (regarded as 'traineeships') and accommodation with a host family are arranged in advance and you don't necessarily need an agricultural background to apply.

Citizens of the USA, who are unable to take part in the Working Holiday Scheme, should check out **Bunac** (www.bunac.com). Its 'Work New Zealand' program is similar to the WHS in that American citizens aged 18 to 30 can apply for a 12-month visa that allows them to work and travel. It costs US$475 to apply for the program, which includes arrival orientation, help with finding jobs and some accommodation (the first two nights are included). Application forms can be ordered online. The NZ scheme is very popular and books out well in advance, so get your application in early. Nationals of numerous other countries can also take part in this program.

Tax

For the vast majority of travellers, any money earned while working in NZ will have income tax deducted from it by their employer, a process called Pay As You Earn (PAYE). Standard NZ income tax rates start at 19.5% for annual salaries up to NZ$38,000 (NZ$730 per week). A NZ accident compensation scheme premium will also be deducted from your pay packet.

A minority of travellers may face a different tax scenario if their country has a Double Tax Agreement (DTA) with NZ, and may be entitled to a tax refund when they leave NZ. Interest earned in bank accounts may also be subject to nonresident withholding tax deductions. For information on all these scenarios, contact the **Inland Revenue Non-Resident Centre** (☎ 03-467 7020; nonres@ird.govt.nz; Private Bag 1932, Dunedin NZ).

Tourists undertaking paid work in NZ are required to get an IRD number for tax purposes. Apply on the website of **Inland Revenue** (www.ird.govt.nz/library/publications/irdnumber.html). The issuing of an IRD number normally takes eight to 10 working days.

New Zealand Transport

CONTENTS

It's relatively easy to transport yourself around New Zealand's pair of main islands after you've endured your long-haul international flight or popped over to say hello from nearby Australia.

International backpackers feeling crumpled from a lengthy stint in economy class will usually disembark in Auckland, while travellers jetting in from Australia could end up in an airport terminal in Wellington, Auckland, Christchurch, Dunedin or several smaller places. For detailed information on international flights arriving in and departing from NZ, including flights connecting the country with Australia and ticket options, see the Australia & New Zealand Transport chapter (p799).

GETTING AROUND

AIR

New Zealand has a widespread network of intra- and interisland flights. All domestic flights are nonsmoking.

Airlines in New Zealand

The country's major domestic carrier, Air New Zealand, flies between the country's major (and many minor) destinations. It does this with the help of several smaller airlines – including Eagle Air and Air Nelson – that are partly owned by or share a partnership with Air New Zealand and are collectively represented under the banner Air New Zealand Link. You can book these flights through Air New Zealand.

The next biggest carrier is regional airline Origin Pacific, which has services to most sizeable cities and towns lying between Auckland and Invercargill. Australia-based Qantas also maintains routes between main urban areas, mostly using the planes of other airlines.

Several small-scale outfits provide essential transport services to small outlying islands such as Great Barrier Island in Hauraki Gulf and Stewart Island.

New Zealand regional airlines:

Air New Zealand (☎ 0800 737 000, 09-357 3000; www.airnz.co.nz) Offers direct flights between main destinations in conjunction with a couple of small affiliated airlines under the banner Air New Zealand Link.

Great Barrier Airlines (☎ 0800 900 600, 09-275 9120; www.greatbarrierairlines.co.nz) Connects Great Barrier Island with Auckland, Whangarei and the Coromandel Peninsula; also flies direct between Auckland and the Coromandel.

Mountain Air (☎ 0800 222 123, 09-256 7025; www.mountainair.co.nz) Flies regularly between Auckland, Whangarei and Great Barrier Island.

Origin Pacific (☎ 0800 302 302, 03-547 2020; www.originpacific.co.nz) Flies to 10 locations across both islands. The Wing It pass, for YHA members only ($295, five standby flights), is great value.

Qantas (☎ 0800 808 767, 09-357 8900; www.qantas.co.nz) Joins the dots between Auckland, Wellington, Rotorua, Christchurch and Queenstown.

Soundsair (☎ 0800 505 005, 03-520 3080; www.soundsair.co.nz) Hops across Cook Strait between Wellington and

> **CHECK THOSE FARES, AY?**
>
> The information in this chapter is particularly vulnerable to change. The best place to check out current fares is on the airline websites.

> **DEPARTURE TAX**
>
> On leaving NZ, you will be charged a departure tax of NZ$25. This tax is not included in the price of airline tickets, but must be paid separately at the airport before you board your flight.

Picton up to 16 times per day; also flies between Wellington and Kaikoura.

Stewart Island Flights (☎ 03-218 9129; www.stewartislandflights.com) Flies between Invercargill and Stewart Island.

BICYCLE

Pannier-lugging cycle tourists are numerous in NZ, particularly over summer. The country is so popular with cyclists because it's clean, green, relatively uncrowded and has lots of cheap accommodation (including camping options) and easily accessible fresh water. The roads are also good and the climate generally not too hot or too cold, except on the rain-loving west coasts (particularly on the South Island). The abundant hills make for hard going at times, but there are plenty of flats and lows to accompany the highs. Bikes and cycling gear (to rent or buy) are readily available in the main centres, as are bicycle repair services.

Needless to say, the choice of itineraries is limited only by your imagination. Cycling along the extensive coastline is an obvious highlight, but the inland routes have their share of devotees. One increasingly popular expedition is to follow an upgraded path along an old railway line into the former gold-mining heartland of Otago on the South Island – detailed information on the **Otago Central Rail Trail** (www.otagocentralrailtrail.co.nz) is available on the website.

By law you must wear an approved safety helmet (or risk a fine) and it's also good to have reflective gear for cycling at night or on dull days. Cyclists who use public transport will find that major bus lines and trains only take bicycles on a 'space available' basis (meaning bikes may not be allowed on) and charge up to NZ$10. Some of the shuttle or backpackers buses, on the other hand, make sure they always have storage space for bikes, which they carry for a reasonable surcharge.

If importing your own bike or transporting it by plane within NZ, check with the relevant airline for costs and the degree of dismantling and packing required.

Carry plenty of water to avoid the possibility of dehydration. Cycling in summer heat can be made more endurable by wearing a helmet with a peak (or a cap under your helmet) and plenty of sunscreen, not cycling in the middle of the day, and drinking lots of water (not soft drinks). It can get very cold in the mountains, so pack appropriate clothing. On the South Island, the hot katabatic or föhn wind that sweeps across the Canterbury Plains during summer can cause a lot of discomfort.

Information

The national bicycle-promotion body is **Cycling New Zealand** (www.cyclingnz.org.nz). Lonely Planet's *Cycling New Zealand* is a comprehensive guide to two-wheel tours of the country, with detailed maps, route descriptions and elevation profiles. The *Pedallers' Paradise* booklets by Nigel Rushton cover the North and South Islands. *Classic New Zealand Mountain Bike Rides* by the Kennett brothers, Paul, Simon and Jonathan, suggests a wide variety of short and long rides all over NZ.

Purchase

Bicycles can be readily bought in NZ's larger cities, but prices for newer models are high. For a decent hybrid bike or rigid mountain bike you'll pay anywhere from NZ$700 to NZ$1500, though you can get a cheap one for around NZ$400 to NZ$500 – however, then you still need to get panniers, a helmet and other essential touring gear, and the cost quickly climbs. Arguably you're better off buying a used bike, but finding something that's in good enough shape for a long road trip is not always easy. Other options include the post-Christmas sales and mid-year stocktakes when newish cycles can be heavily discounted.

BOAT

New Zealand may be an island nation but there's hardly any long- or medium-distance water transport around the country. Obvious exceptions include the boat services between Auckland and various islands in Hauraki Gulf (see p536), the interisland ferries that chug across Cook Strait between the North and South Islands – see details under Wellington (p641) and Picton (p650) – and the passenger ferry that negotiates the width of Foveaux Strait between Bluff and the town of Oban on Stewart Island (p768).

BUS

Bus travel in NZ is relatively easy and well organised, with services transporting you to the far reaches of both islands (including the start/end of various walking tracks), but depending on your itinerary it can be expensive, tedious and time consuming. The bus 'terminals' in smaller places usually comprise a parking spot outside a prominent local business.

The dominant bus company is **InterCity Coachlines** (www.intercitycoach.co.nz; Auckland ☎ 09-913 6100; Christchurch ☎ 03-379 9020), which can drive you to just about anywhere on the North and South Islands, from Invercargill and Milford Sound in the south to Paihia and Kaitaia in the north. InterCity is closely associated with **Newmans Coach Lines** (☎ 09-913 6200, 03-374 6149; www.newmanscoach.co.nz), which emphasises the luxury aspect of its limited scheduled services and conducts various sightseeing excursions and day tours.

Smaller regional operators running key routes or covering a lot of ground on the North Island:

Alpine Scenic Tours (☎ 07-386 8397; www.alpinescenictours.co.nz) Has services between Turangi and National Park, with useful stops for trampers in Tongariro National Park and extension services up to Taupo.

Go Kiwi Shuttles (☎ 0800 446 549, 07-866 0336; www.go-kiwi.co.nz) Links places such as Auckland, Rotorua and Hamilton with various towns across the Coromandel Peninsula.

Guthreys Express (☎ 0800 759 999, 09-309 0905; www.guthreys.co.nz) Daily services between Auckland, Hamilton and Rotorua.

Northliner (☎ 09-307 5873; www.northliner.co.nz) Runs from Auckland up to Paihia (Bay of Islands) and Kaitaia.

Waitomo Wanderer (☎ 07-349 2509; www.waitomotours.co.nz) Does a daily loop from Rotorua to Waitomo.

White Star (City to City) (☎ 06-758 3338) Shuttles to/from Wanganui to Wellington and New Plymouth.

South Island bus companies:

Abel Tasman Coachlines (☎ 03-548 0285; www.abeltasmantravel.co.nz) Runs services between Nelson and the neighbouring national parks of Kahurangi and Abel Tasman.

Alpine Coaches (☎ 0800 274 888; www.alpinecoaches.co.nz) Heads across the island from Christchurch to Hokitika and Greymouth via Arthur's Pass.

Atomic Shuttles (☎ 03-322 8883; www.atomictravel.co.nz) Has daily services throughout the South Island, including to Christchurch, Dunedin, Invercargill, Picton, Nelson, Greymouth, Queenstown and Wanaka.

Coast to Coast (☎ 0800 800 847; www.coast2coast.co.nz) Motors from Christchurch to Hokitika and Greymouth via Arthur's Pass.

Hanmer Connection (☎ 0800 377 378, 03-315 7575) Has daily services from Hanmer Springs to Christchurch and Kaikoura.

K Bus (☎ 03-525 9434; www.kahurangi.co.nz) Roams across the top of the South Island from both Blenheim and Picton.

Knight Rider (☎ 03-342 8055) Runs from Christchurch to Invercargill via Dunedin.

Lazerline (☎ 0800 220 001, 03-388 7652) Heads from Christchurch to Nelson via Lewis Pass daily.

Scenic Shuttle (☎ 0800 277 483, 03-249 7654; reservations@scenicshuttle.com) Runs between Te Anau and Invercargill via Manapouri.

Southern Link Coaches (☎ 03-358 8355; www.southernlinkcoaches.co.nz) Runs from Christchurch to Queenstown, Wanaka and Nelson.

South Island Connections (☎ 0508-742 669, 03-366 6633; www.southislandconnections.co.nz) Operates daily shuttles between Dunedin, Christchurch and Picton.

Cook Connection (☎ 0800 266 526, 0274-583 211; www.cookconnect.co.nz) Runs between Mt Cook and both Timaru and Oamaru on the east coast several times a week.

Topline Tours (☎ 03-249 8059; www.toplinetours.co.nz) Connects Te Anau and Queenstown.

Wanaka Connexions (☎ 03-443 9122; www.wanakaconnexions.co.nz) Links Wanaka, Queenstown, Christchurch and Dunedin.

Backpacker Buses

The handful of bus companies in NZ that focus their transport services on budget travellers are basically organised tours, but they can be a cost-effective travel alternative to the big bus companies. The buses are usually smaller, you'll meet lots of other travellers, and the drivers sometimes double as tour guides; conversely, some travellers find the tour-group mentality (which sometimes includes being stuck in 'life is a party' mode) and inherent limitations don't suit them. Discounts are usually given to card-carrying students and members of hostel organisations (see p774).

We get lots of feedback about such companies, a real mixed bag of rave reviews and lengthy criticisms. It's a good idea to compare outfits and the deals they offer when you arrive in NZ, particularly by talking to the other travellers you'll see piling out of such buses at hostels.

Affiliated with the Kiwi Experience (see opposite), **Bottom Bus** (www.bottombus.co.nz; Dunedin ☎ 03-434 7370; Queenstown ☎ 03-442 9708) is a hop-on, hop-off service that runs a deep-south loop taking in Queenstown, Dunedin, Te Anau and Milford Sound via the Catlins, Invercargill and the Southern Scenic Route. The options include Dunedin to Te Anau

(NZ$260 including Milford Sound), Dunedin to Queenstown (NZ$410 including Milford and Stewart Island) and the In a Stew route (NZ$500 including visits to Milford, Stewart Island and either the Otago Peninsula or Te Anau Caves).

The **Flying Kiwi** (☎ 0800 693 296, 03-547 0171; www.flyingkiwi.com) is very much a tour rather than a bus service. With an emphasis on outdoor activities, its 'rolling travellers' home' includes hot showers and a kitchen and carries mountain bikes, a Canadian canoe, a windsurfer, fishing gear and more. Accommodation is in the form of camping – you can bring you own tent or hire one. There's an additional fund for food and the group takes turns at cooking. South Island excursions include eight-day West Coast tours (NZ$450) and 10-day explorations of the island's south and east (NZ$690), plus a 16-day loop (NZ$930). North Island options include a comprehensive nine-day jaunt (NZ$510) and the two-day Northern Express (NZ$110). The 27-day, trans-NZ Ultimate Explorer costs from NZ$1300.

The biggest operation of the hop-on, hop-off backpacker/tour buses, **Kiwi Experience** (☎ 09-366 9830; www.kiwiexperience.com) has pea-green buses that operate a comprehensive service around the North and South Islands. There are numerous routes and most passes are valid for one year. Trips include Northern Roundup (NZ$370, nine-day minimum), Southern Roundup (NZ$435, 11-day minimum) and the Full Monty trip (from NZ$1540, minimum 31/38 days in summer/winter). Useful small loops where other services are limited include the Awesome & Top Bit route (NZ$175) around Northland, the Bottom trip (NZ$330; run by Bottom Bus) through the Catlins, East As (NZ$300) and Milford Overland (NZ$155).

Magic Travellers Network (☎ 09-358 5600; www.magicbus.co.nz) runs Magic Bus, another hop-on, hop-off bus operating an extensive network on the North and South Islands, with 16 main trips from a minimum of four days. Trips range from the basic Top of the North (from NZ$210) or Top of the South (from NZ$290) to the countrywide Spirit of NZ (from NZ$1110, minimum 23 days).

Bus Passes

InterCity offers numerous bus passes, either covering the whole country or concentrating on North or South Island travel. If you're planning to cover a lot of ground, the passes can work out cheaper than paying as you go, but they lock you into using InterCity buses (rather than, say, the convenient shuttle buses that cover much of the country).

Northliner offers backpackers discount passes for travel around the top end of the North Island.

INTERCITY PASSES

The appropriately named **Flexi-Pass** (www.flexipass.co.nz) is valid for one year and allows you to travel pretty much anywhere (and in any direction) on the InterCity/Newman's network. You can get on and off wherever you like and can change bookings up to two hours before departure without getting penalised. The pass is purchased in five-hour blocks of travel time, from a minimum of 15 hours (NZ$150) up to a maximum of 60 hours (NZ$540) – the average cost of each block is cheaper the more hours you buy. You can top up the pass if you need more time.

InterCity (www.intercitycoach.co.nz; Auckland ☎ 09-913 6100; Christchurch ☎ 03-379 9020) offers a range of other passes involving a fixed itinerary of travel on each island and across the country, most with a maximum life of three months. North Island passes include: Coromandel Loop (NZ$55), allowing travel from Thames to Whitianga and Tairua, then back to Thames; Coromandel Trail (NZ$90), starting from Auckland and heading to Rotorua via the Coromandel Peninsula; and Forests, Islands and Geysers (NZ$350), combining a circuit of the North Island with flights to Great Barrier Island and Whitianga.

South Island passes include: West Coast Passport (NZ$150 ex-Picton), allowing travel from Picton to Queenstown via the West Coast; Milford Bound Adventure (NZ$180), going from Christchurch to Milford via Queenstown and Mt Cook; and South Island Extreme (NZ$470), allowing a loop from Picton to Picton or Christchurch to Christchurch.

Dual-island passes include: NZ Pathfinder (NZ$540), taking you from Auckland to Christchurch or vice versa, including trips along the South Island's West Coast and to Milford Sound; NZ Trail Blazer (NZ$560), describing a loop that starts/finishes at Auckland; and the self-explanatory Total New Zealand Experience (NZ$680).

There may be a reservation charge of NZ$3 per sector, depending on the agent. This fee will not apply if you book by telephoning InterCity direct.

For details of a pass combining travel on InterCity coaches, Tranz Scenic trains and interisland ferries, see under Train Passes (p798) later in this chapter.

NORTHLINER

Northliner (☎ 09-307 5873; www.northliner.co.nz) offers card-carrying backpackers (YHA, VIP, BBH and Nomads, see p774) various passes enabling unlimited travel on different routes. The Bay of Islands (NZ$55), Loop (NZ$85) and Northland Freedom (NZ$115) passes are all valid for one month from date of purchase, while the Top Half (NZ$80) pass is valid for two months.

Classes

There are no separate classes on buses. Smoking isn't permitted on these vehicles.

Costs

Following are average one-way bus fares on some well-travelled NZ routes.

Route	Adult/Concession (NZ$)
Auckland-Pahia	45/36
Auckland-Rotorua	45/36
Auckland-Wellington	90/75
Christchurch-Dunedin	55/45
Christchurch-Greymouth	35/28
Christchurch-Picton	60/50
Christchurch-Queenstown	60/50
Picton-Greymouth	70/55
Queenstown-Dunedin	30/24
Queenstown-Greymouth	80/65
Wellington-Rotorua	80/65

The majority of bus companies offer discounts of between 15% and 30% to card-carrying backpackers and students.

Reservations

During summer, school holidays and public holidays (see p782), you should book well ahead on the more popular routes. At other times you should have few problems getting on to your preferred service. But if your long-term travel plans rely on catching a particular bus, book at least a day or two ahead just to be safe.

Bus fares vary widely according to how far ahead they're booked and their availability, and the best prices are generally obtained a few weeks in advance.

CAR & MOTORCYCLE

Without doubt, the best way to explore NZ in depth is to have your own transport, as it allows you to create your own flexible itinerary. Good-value, short-term car- and campervan-hire rates can be tracked down, but budget travellers intent on a lengthy trip should consider buying their own set of wheels.

For information on driving licences see p781. For details on taking a vehicle across the strait between the North and South Islands, see the Wellington (p641) and Picton (p650) sections.

Automobile Association

New Zealand's **Automobile Association** (AA; ☎ 0800 500 444; www.aa.co.nz) provides emergency breakdown services and excellent touring maps. It also maintains links with similar bodies throughout the world, so if you're a member of an affiliated organisation in your home country, bring proof of membership with you.

Fuel

Fuel (super, diesel and unleaded) is available from service stations sporting the well-known international brand names. Gas (LPG) is not always stocked by rural suppliers; if you're on gas it's safer to have dual fuel capacity. Prices vary from place to place, but basically petrol (gasoline) isn't pumped cheaply in NZ, with per-litre costs averaging around NZ$1.05. Some of the more remote destinations will charge a smallish fortune to fill your tank and you're better off getting fuel before you reach them – places that fall into this category include Milford Sound (fill up at Te Anau) and Mt Cook (fill up at Lake Tekapo or Twizel).

Hire

Competition between car-rental companies in NZ is pretty fierce, so rates tend to be variable and lots of special deals come and go; car rental is most competitive in Auckland, Christchurch, Wellington and Picton. The main thing to remember when assessing your options is distance: if you want to travel far, you need unlimited kilometres. You must be at least 21 years old to hire a vehicle.

Sizeable companies which all have offices or agents in most major cities and towns include the following:

Avis (☎ 09-275 7239; www.avis.com)
Budget (☎ 0800 652 227; www.budget.co.nz)
Hertz (☎ 0800 654 321; www.hertz.co.nz)
Thrifty (☎ 09-256 1405; www.thrifty.com)

There are also numerous local firms, which we detail throughout the NZ chapters of this guide. These are almost always cheaper than the big operators (sometimes as much as half the going rate) but the cheapest car hire often comes with serious restrictions. Some less-expensive operators have national networks, including the highly recommended ones below:

Omega Rental Cars (☎ 0800 525 210; www.omegarentalcars.com)
Pegasus (☎ 0800 803 580; www.rentalcars.co.nz)

The big firms sometimes offer one-way rentals (eg pick up a car in Auckland and leave it in Christchurch) but there are a variety of restrictions and sometimes a substantial drop-off fee may apply if you're not returning the car to the city of hire. However, on rental of a month or more this should be waived between Auckland and Wellington or Christchurch. On the other hand, an operator in Christchurch may need to get a vehicle back to Auckland and will offer a great one-way deal.

Some car-hire firms will not allow you to take their vehicles on the ferries that cross Cook Strait. Instead, you drop your car off at either the Wellington or Picton terminal and pick up another car once you've crossed the strait.

Daily rates typically start around NZ$45 to $NZ50 per day for a compact, late-model, Japanese car (including GST, unlimited kilometres and insurance). Local firms sometimes advertise cars for as low as NZ$25 per day. It's obviously cheaper if you rent for a week or more and there are often low-season and weekend discounts. Credit cards are the usual payment method.

New Zealand has great terrain for motorcycle touring, despite the changeable weather in parts of the islands. Most of the country's motorcycle-hire shops are in Auckland and Christchurch, where you can hire anything from a little 50cc moped (nifty-fifty) for zipping around town to a big 750cc touring motorcycle and beyond. **New Zealand Motorcycle Rentals** (www.nzbike.com; Auckland ☎ 09-377 2005; Christchurch ☎ 03-377 0663) rents out low-grunt motorcycles like the Yamaha XT225 from NZ$80 per day (as low as NZ$60 per day for rentals of three weeks or more).

CAMPERVAN HIRE

Campervans (also known as mobile homes, motor homes or RVs) are enormously popular for slow-paced NZ tours, so popular that in well-trafficked parts of the South Island during peak tourist season you can feel socially inadequate if you're driving anything else.

You can hire campervans from an assortment of companies for an assortment of prices, depending on the time of year and how big you want your home-on-wheels to be. **Maui** (☎ 0800 651 080, 09-275 3013; www.maui.co.nz) and **Britz** (☎ 0800 831 900, 09-275 9090; www.britz.co.nz) are two of the biggest operators. Some cheaper operators:

Auto Rentals (☎ 0800 736 893, 03-371 7343; www.autorentals.co.nz)
Backpacker Campervans (☎ 0800 422 267, 09-275 0200; www.backpackercampervans.com)
Kea Campers (☎ 09-441 7833; www.kea.co.nz)

A small van suitable for two people typically has a well-equipped minikitchen and fold-out dining table; the latter transforms into a double bed when mealtime is over. Four- to six-berth campervans are the size of light trucks (and similarly sluggish) and besides the extra space usually contain a toilet and shower.

During summer, rates offered by the main rental firms for two-/four-/six-berth vans are usually around NZ$200/280/310 per day, dropping to as low as NZ$60/85/105 in winter; the lowest rates are offered for rentals of three weeks or more. The summer rates of smaller operators start at around NZ$170 per day for kitted-out minivans (from NZ$50 per day in winter).

Insurance

When it comes to renting a vehicle, know exactly what your liability is in the event of an accident. Rather than risk paying out a large amount of cash if you do have an accident (minor accidents are common in NZ), you can take out your own comprehensive insurance policy, or (the usual option) pay an additional daily amount to the rental company for an 'insurance excess reduction' policy. This brings down the amount of excess you must pay in the event of an accident from around NZ$1500 or NZ$2000 to around NZ$150 or NZ$200. Smaller operators offering cheap rates often have a compulsory insurance excess, taken as a credit-card bond, of around NZ$900.

Most insurance agreements won't cover the cost of damage to glass (including the windscreen) or tyres, and insurance coverage is often invalidated on beaches and certain rough (4WD) unsealed roads, so always read the small print.

Purchase

For a longer stay and/or for groups, buying a car and then selling it at the end of your travels can be one of the cheapest and best ways to see NZ. You can often pick up a car as cheap as (or cheaper than) a one- or two-month rental, and you should be able to get back most of your money when you sell it. The danger, of course, is that you'll buy a lemon and it will break down every five minutes.

Auckland is the best place for travellers to buy a car, followed by Christchurch. An easy option for a cheap car is to scour the notice boards of backpacker hangouts, where other travellers sell their cars before moving on – you can often pick up an old car for only a few hundred dollars. Some backpackers specials are so cheap it may be worth taking the risk that they will finally die on you. Besides, these vehicles often come complete with water containers, tools, road maps and even camping gear.

Car markets and car auctions are also worth investigating. There are three weekly car markets/fairs in Auckland, the Canterbury Car Fair in Christchurch and a smaller market in central Wellington. At auctions you can pick up cheap cars from around NZ$1000 to NZ$4500, but you don't have the luxury of a test drive – **Turners Auctions** (☎ 0800 282 8466, 04-587 1400; www.turners.co.nz) is the country's largest such outfit with 11 locations. For details of all the aforementioned places, see the relevant sections for Auckland (p529), Wellington (p641) and Christchurch (p689).

Make sure any car you buy has a Warrant of Fitness (WoF) and that the registration lasts for a reasonable period. A WoF certificate, proving that the car is roadworthy, is valid for six months but must be less than 28 days old when you buy a car. To transfer registration, both you and the seller fill out a form and lodge it within seven days of the car purchase. It is the buyer's responsibility to organise a change of ownership card and to take care of the fee for this (around NZ$10). Vehicles usually get registered only once, but you then have to pay a licensing fee to use the car on the road. You can obtain a licence valid for either three months (NZ$55), six months (NZ$105) or 12 months (NZ$200). Third-party insurance, covering the cost of repairs to another vehicle in an accident that is your fault, is also a wise investment.

Car inspections are highly recommended as they'll protect you against any dodgy WoFs (many such scams have been reported) and may well save you a lot of money in repair bills later. Various car inspection services will check any car you intend to buy for less than NZ$100. They stand by at car fairs and auctions for on-the-spot inspections, or will come to you. The **Automobile Association** (AA; ☎ 0800 500 444; www.aa.co.nz) also offers a mobile inspection service – it's slightly cheaper if you bring the car to an AA-approved mechanic. AA checks are thorough, but most garages will look over the car for less money.

Another wise precaution before you buy a car is to confirm the ownership of the vehicle, and find out if there are any outstanding debts on it, by registering with the online **Personal Properties Securities** (www.ppsr.govt.nz) and conducting a search; searches cost NZ$3 and are done using the Vehicle Identification Number (VIN; found on a plate near the engine block), licence plate or chassis number.

Buying a motorcycle in NZ is a realistic option. The beginning of winter (June) is a good time to start looking. Regional newspapers and the local bike press have classified advertisement sections. The main drawback of buying a bike is obviously that you'll have to try to sell it afterwards.

Good places to start your search for a two-wheeler are the monthly *NZ Motorcycle*

Trader magazine and the **BikePoint New Zealand website** (www.bikepoint.co.nz). Once you factor in the on-the-road costs, you'll be lucky to purchase a decent second-hand road bike (as opposed to a trail bike) through a motorcycle dealer for less than around NZ$3200. You'll have a greater chance of success in bigger cities like Auckland and Wellington. The WoF requirements and registration procedures for motorcycles are the same as for cars, but the cost of the on-road licence is higher: to license a motorcycle for three/six/12 months costs around NZ$70/130/250.

BUY-BACK DEALS

One way of getting around the hassles of buying and selling a vehicle privately is to enter into a buy-back arrangement with a car or motorcycle dealer. However, dealers may find ways of knocking down the price when you return the vehicle (even if it was agreed to in writing), often by pointing out expensive repairs that allegedly will be required to gain the WoF certificate needed to transfer the registration. The buy-back amount varies, but may be 50% less than the purchase price. In a strictly financial sense, hiring or buying and selling the vehicle yourself (if you have the time) is usually much better value.

Road Hazards

The full spectrum of drivers and driving habits is represented on NZ roads, from the no-fuss motorist who doesn't mind pulling over to let you past, to back-roads tailgaters who believe they know a particular stretch of bitumen so well that they can go as fast as they like – this despite narrow, twisting roads. Traffic is usually pretty light, but it's easy to get stuck behind a slow-moving truck or campervan on uphill climbs, so bring plenty of patience with you for your time on the road. There are also lots of gravel or dirt roads to explore, which require a very different driving approach than sealed roads.

Road Rules

Kiwis drive on the left-hand side of the road and all cars are right-hand drive. A 'give way to the right' rule applies and is interpreted to a rather strange extreme here – if you're turning left and an oncoming vehicle is turning right into the same street, you have to give way to it.

The speed limit on the open road is generally 100km/h; in built-up areas the limit is usually 50km/h. An 'LSZ' sign stands for 'Limited Speed Zone', which means that the speed limit is 50km/h (although the speed limit in that zone is normally 100km/h) when conditions are unsafe due to bad weather, limited visibility, pedestrians, cyclists or animals on the road, or excessive traffic. Speed cameras and radars are used extensively. At single-lane bridges (of which there are a surprisingly large number), a smaller red arrow pointing in your direction of travel means that *you* give way, so slow down as you approach and pull a little to the side if you see a car approaching the bridge from the other end.

All new cars in NZ have seat belts back and front and it's the law to wear one – you're risking a fine if you don't. Small children must be belted into an approved safety seat, and most car rental agencies should be able to set you up with one for free or a small charge.

Get hold of a copy of the *New Zealand Road Code*, a wise investment that will tell you all you need to know about life on the road. Versions applicable to both cars and motorcycles are available at AA offices and bookshops, or check the online rundown of road rules on the website of the **Land Transport Safety Authority** (www.ltsa.govt.nz/roadcode/index.html).

HITCHING

In NZ hitching is common. The hitching signal can either be a thumbs up or a downward-pointed finger. See also p642.

TRAIN

In NZ you travel by train for the journey, not just in order to get somewhere (with the exception of the single commuter service detailed below). The company **Tranz Scenic** (☎ 0800 872 467, 04-495 0775; www.tranzscenic.co.nz) operates several visually stunning routes, namely the *Overlander*, the *TranzCoastal* between Christchurch and Picton, and the *TranzAlpine* which rattles over the Southern Alps between Christchurch and Greymouth. It also operates the weekday *Capital Connection* commuter service between Palmerston North and Wellington.

Costs

An variety of discounts and concessions apply to tickets within NZ, usually only in off-peak periods. These include discounts of between 30% and 50% off standard fares for tickets booked well in advance and for a seat in a 'backpacker carriage' (which has smaller viewing windows than other carriages).

Price ranges for some one-way train fares:

Route	Fare (NZ$)
Auckland-Hamilton	20-40
Auckland-Wellington	70-140
Christchurch-Greymouth	60-105
Picton-Kaikoura	20-45
Picton-Christchurch	35-80

Reservations

Reservations can be made by contacting Tranz Scenic and at most train stations, travel agents and visitors centres, where you can also pick up booklets detailing timetables.

Train Passes

The Tranz Scenic **Best of New Zealand Pass** (☎ 0800 692 378; www.bestpass.co.nz), offered in conjunction with several coach and ferry operators, enables you to undertake a variety of land and sea trips throughout NZ. If you plan your itinerary well enough, you could save as much as 30% on the cost of booking each bus, train or ferry leg independently.

With validity for six months, the Best of New Zealand Pass works on a points system, with each leg of your trip 'costing' you a certain number of points. You can buy 600 points for NZ$500, 800 points for NZ$650 and 1000 points for NZ$790; you can also top-up points when you need them (100 extra points costs around NZ$90). A 1000-point trip could include Auckland to Wellington by train and coach, the *Interislander* ferry, and a fair whack of the South Island by train (including the *TranzAlpine*) and coach.

Australia & New Zealand Transport

CONTENTS

They don't call Australia the land 'down under' for nothing. It's a long way from just about everywhere, and getting there usually means a long-haul flight. That 'over the horizon' feeling doesn't stop once you're there either – the distances between key cities (much less opposing coastlines) can be vast, requiring a minimum of an hour or two of air time but up to several days of highway cruising or dirt-road jostling to traverse. For information on how to get around this big place, see the Australia Transport chapter (p476).

New Zealand has its own peaceably isolated South Pacific location, which is one of its primary drawcards, but it also means that unless you fly over from Australia you also have to contend with many hours in the air to get there. Travelling around the country is a much less taxing endeavour – see the New Zealand Transport chapter for details of the options (p790).

GETTING THERE & AWAY

ENTERING THE COUNTRIES

Disembarkation in both Australia and NZ is generally a straightforward affair, with only the usual customs declarations (for Australia's requirements, see p464; for NZ's, see p780) and the fight to be first to the luggage carousel to endure. However, recent global instability has resulted in conspicuously increased security in airports, both in domestic and international terminals, and you may find that customs procedures are now more time-consuming. One relatively new Kiwi procedure has the Orwellian title 'Advance Passenger Screening', a system whereby the documents that used to be checked after you touched down in NZ (passport, visa etc) are now checked via computer before you board the flight that will transport you there – Australia has been using a similar system for more than five years. Make sure all your documentation is in order so that your check-in is as smooth as possible.

Passport

There are no restrictions when it comes to citizens of foreign countries entering either NZ or Australia. If you have a visa, you should be fine – for information on Australian visas see p474, and for the lowdown on NZ visas see p787.

AIR

There are lots of competing airlines and a wide variety of air fares to choose from if you're flying to NZ or Australia from Asia, Europe or North America, but you'll still pay a lot for a flight. Jetting across the Tasman Sea between the two countries is fortunately a much cheaper proposition.

Because of Australia's size and diverse climate, any time of year can prove busy for inbound tourists. If you plan to fly at a particularly popular time of year (Christmas is notoriously difficult for Sydney and Melbourne) or on a particularly popular route (such as Hong Kong, Bangkok or Singapore to Sydney or Melbourne), make your arrangements well in advance of your trip.

Similarly, NZ's inordinate popularity and abundance of year-round activities, from tramping in summer to skiing and snowboarding in winter, means that passenger lists can overflow year-round. The advice given for Australia applies here too: plan your visit well ahead.

The high season for both Australia and NZ, when travel to either country is at its most expensive, is roughly over summer and

THINGS CHANGE

The information in this chapter is particularly vulnerable to change. Check directly with the airline or a travel agent to make sure you understand how a fare (and ticket you may buy) works and to be aware of the security requirements for international travel. Check airline websites for current fares and routes. Shop carefully. The details given in this chapter should be regarded as pointers and are not a substitute for your own careful, up-to-date research.

its shoulder months (November to March). Similarly, the low season is over winter and its shoulder months (May to September).

Airports

AUSTRALIA

Australia has a number of international gateways, with Sydney and Melbourne being the busiest:

Adelaide (code ADL; ☎ 08-8308 9211; www.aal.com.au)
Brisbane (code BNE; ☎ 07-3406 3190; www.brisbaneairport.com.au)
Cairns (code CNS; ☎ 07-4052 9703; www.cairnsport.com.au/airport)
Darwin (code DRW; ☎ 08-8920 1811; www.ntapl.com.au)
Melbourne (Tullamarine; code MEL; ☎ 03-9297 1600; www.melbourne-airport.com.au)
Perth (code PER; ☎ 08-9478 8888; www.perthairport.net.au)
Sydney (Kingsford Smith; code SYD; ☎ 02-9667 9111; www.sydneyairport.com.au)

NEW ZEALAND

Seven airports receive and farewell international flights, with Auckland handling most of the overseas traffic:

Auckland (code AKL; ☎ 0800 247 767, 09-256 8855; www.auckland-airport.co.nz)
Christchurch (code CHC; ☎ 03-358 5029; www.christchurch-airport.co.nz/airport)
Dunedin (code DUD; ☎ 03-486 2879; www.dnairport.co.nz)
Hamilton (code HLZ; ☎ 07-848 9027; www.hamiltonairport.co.nz)
Palmerston Nth (code PMR; ☎ 06-351 4415; www.pnairport.co.nz)
Queenstown (code ZQN; ☎ 03-442 3505; www.queenstownairport.co.nz)
Wellington (code WLG; ☎ 04-385 5100; www.wellington-airport.co.nz)

Airlines

Australia's overseas carrier is Qantas, which flies across Europe, North America, Asia and the Pacific. Australian Airlines, a subsidiary of Qantas, flies between the prime east-coast destination of Cairns (with connections to the Gold Coast) and Japan, Singapore, Hong Kong and Taiwan, as well as flying nonstop between Bali and both Sydney and Melbourne, and from Sydney to the Malaysian province of Sabah on Borneo. New Zealand's own overseas carrier is Air New Zealand, which touches down on runways across Europe, North America, eastern Asia and the Pacific. Both Qantas and Air New Zealand have very good safety records.

Airlines that connect Australia and NZ with international destinations (note all phone numbers mentioned here are for dialling from within Australia or NZ):

Air Canada (airline code AC; www.aircanada.ca; Australia ☎ 1300 655 787, 02-8248 5757; NZ ☎ 09-379 3371) Hub: Pearson International Airport in Toronto.
Air New Zealand (airline code NZ; Australia ☎ 13 24 76, 03-9613 4850; www.airnz.com.au; NZ ☎ 0800 737 000; www.airnz.co.nz) Hub: Auckland International Airport in NZ.
Air Paradise International (airline code AD; www.airparadise.com.au; Australia ☎ 03-9341 8000) Hub: Ngurah Rai in Denpasar, Bali, Indonesia.
Australian Airlines (airline code AO; www.australianairlines.com.au; Australia ☎ 1300 799 798) Hub: Kingsford Smith Airport in Sydney.
British Airways (airline code BA; www.ba.com; Australia ☎ 1300 767 177, 02-9258 3200; NZ ☎ 0800 274 847) Hub: Heathrow Airport in London.
Cathay Pacific (airline code CX; www.cathaypacific.com; Australia ☎ 13 17 47, 02-9667 3816; NZ ☎ 0508-800 454) Hub: Hong Kong International Airport.
Emirates (airline code EK; www.emirates.com; Australia ☎ 1300 303 777, 02-9290 9700; NZ ☎ 0508-364 728) Hub: Dubai International Airport in United Arab Emirates (UAE).
Freedom Air (airline code SJ; www.freedomair.com; Australia ☎ 1800 122 000; NZ ☎ 0800 600 500) Hub: Auckland International Airport in NZ.
Garuda Indonesia (airline code GA; www.garuda-indonesia.com; Australia ☎ 1300 365 330, 02-9334 9900; NZ ☎ 09-366 1862) Hub: Soekarno-Hatta International Airport in Jakarta.
Gulf Air (airline code GF; www.gulfairco.com; Australia ☎ 1300 366 337, 02-9244 2149) Hub: Abu Dhabi International Airport in Dubai, UAE.
Japan Airlines (airline code JL; www.jal.com; Australia ☎ 02-9272 1111; NZ ☎ 09-379 9906) Hub: Narita Airport in Tokyo.

KLM (airline code KL; www.klm.com; Australia ☎ 1300 303 747; NZ ☎ 09-309 1782) Hub: Schiphol Airport in Amsterdam.
Lufthansa (airline code LH; www.lufthansa.com; Australia ☎ 1300 655 727; NZ ☎ 09-303 1529) Hub: Frankfurt Airport in Germany.
Malaysia Airlines (airline code MH; www.malaysiaairlines.com; Australia ☎ 13 26 27, 02-9364 3500; NZ ☎ 0800 777 747) Hub: Kuala Lumpur International Airport in Malaysia.
Pacific Blue (airline code DJ; www.flypacificblue.com; Australia ☎ 13 16 45, 07-3295 3000; NZ ☎ 0800 670 000) Hub: Brisbane Airport in Australia.
Qantas (airline code QF; www.qantas.com.au; Australia ☎ 13 13 13; NZ ☎ 0800 808 767) Hub: Kingsford-Smith Airport in Sydney.
Royal Brunei Airlines (airline code BI; www.bruneiair.com; Australia ☎ 08-8941 0966; NZ ☎ 09-302 1524) Hub: Bandar Seri Begawan Airport in Brunei.
Singapore Airlines (airline code SQ; www.singaporeair.com; Australia ☎ 13 10 11, 02-9350 0100; NZ ☎ 09-303 2129) Hub: Changi International Airport in Singapore.
South African Airways (airline code SA; www.flysaa.com; Australia ☎ 1800 099 281, 08-9216 2200) Hub: Johannesburg International Airport in South Africa.
Thai Airways International (airline code TG; www.thaiairways.com; Australia ☎ 1300 651 960; NZ ☎ 09-377 3886) Hub: Bangkok International Airport in Thailand.
United Airlines (airline code UA; www.unitedairlines.com; Australia ☎ 13 17 77, 02-9292 4111; NZ ☎ 09-379 3800) Hub: Los Angeles International Airport in the USA.

Tickets

Generally there's nothing to be gained by buying a ticket direct from the airline. Discounted tickets are released to selected travel agents and specialist discount agencies, and these are usually the cheapest deals going. An exception is booking on the Internet, where reduced administrative costs (ie no customer service salaries) are often reflected in cheap fares.

Automated online ticket sales work well if you're doing a simple one-way or return trip on specified dates, but are no substitute for a travel agent with the lowdown on special deals, strategies for avoiding layovers and other useful advice.

Paying by credit card offers some protection if you unwittingly end up dealing with a rogue fly-by-night agency in your search for the cheapest fare, as most card issuers provide refunds if you can prove you didn't get what you paid for. Alternatively, buy a ticket from a bonded agent, such as one covered by the **Air Travel Organiser's Licence** (ATOL; www.atol.org.uk) scheme in the UK. If you have doubts about the service provider, at the very least call the airline and confirm that your booking has been made.

All the fares quoted in this chapter are regularly undercut by special deals and student-only fares. For that matter, they're also regularly blown way out of proportion by major carriers charging passengers a hefty premium on popular routes.

Online booking websites:

Airbrokers (www.airbrokers.com) This US company specialises in cheap tickets. To fly LA–Tokyo–Beijing–Shanghai–Hong Kong–Auckland–Christchurch–Sydney–LA will cost around US$2200.
Cheap Flights (www.cheapflights.com) Very informative site with specials, airline information and flight searches from the USA and other regions.
Cheapest Flights (www.cheapestflights.co.uk) Cheap worldwide flights from the UK; get in early for the bargains.
Expedia (www.expedia.msn.com) Microsoft's travel site; mainly US-related.
Flight Centre International (www.flightcentre.com) Respected operator handling direct flights, with sites for NZ, Australia, the UK, the USA, Canada and South Africa.
Flights.com (www.tiss.com) Truly international site for flight tickets; offers cheap fares and an easy-to-search database.
House of Travel (www.houseoftravel.co.nz) Cheapest airfares on any airline around NZ and from NZ to Australia and the South Pacific islands. Note you can only book for travel out of NZ.
Roundtheworldflights.com (www.roundtheworldflights.com) This excellent site allows you to build your own trips from the UK with up to six stops. A four-stop trip including Asia, Australia, NZ and the USA costs from UK£900.
STA (www.statravel.com) Prominent in world student travel but you don't have to be a student; the site is linked to worldwide STA sites.
Travel Online (www.travelonline.co.nz) Good place to check worldwide flights from NZ.
Travel.com (www.travel.com.au) Good Australian site; look up fares and flights out of and into the country.
Travelocity (www.travelocity.com) US site that allows you to search fares (in US dollars) to/from practically anywhere.

RTW TICKETS

If you're flying to NZ or Australia from the other side of the world, round-the-world (RTW) tickets can be real bargains. They are usually put together by the world's two biggest airline alliances, **Star Alliance** (www.staralliance.com) and **Oneworld** (www.oneworldalliance.com), and give you a limited period (usually a year) in which to circumnavigate the

DEPARTURE TAX

You must pay a A$38 departure tax when leaving Australia. This is included in the price of airline tickets.

On leaving NZ, you will be charged a departure tax of NZ$25. This tax is not included in the price of airline tickets, but must be paid separately at the airport before you board your flight.

globe. You can go anywhere the carrying airlines go, as long as you stay within the set mileage or number of stops and don't backtrack when flying between continents. Backtracking is generally permitted within a single continent, though with certain restrictions; see the relevant websites for details.

An alternative type of RTW ticket is one put together by a travel agent. These are usually more expensive than airline RTW fares but allow you to devise your own itinerary.

Round-the-world tickets start from about UK£850 from the UK or around US$1850 from the USA.

CIRCLE PACIFIC TICKETS

A Circle Pacific ticket is similar to a RTW ticket but covers a more limited region, using a combination of airlines to connect Australia, NZ, North America and Asia, with stopover options in the Pacific Islands. As with RTW tickets, there are restrictions and limits on how many stopovers you can make.

Asia

Most Asian countries offer fairly competitive air-fare deals, with Bangkok, Singapore and Hong Kong being the best places to shop around for discount tickets.

Hong Kong's travel market can be unpredictable, but excellent bargains are sometimes available. Some Asian agents:

Phoenix Services (☎ 2722 7378) Based in Hong Kong.

STA Travel (Bangkok ☎ 02-236 0262; www.statravel.co.th; Singapore ☎ 65-6737 7188; www.statravel.com.sg; Tokyo ☎ 03-5391-3205; www.statravel.co.jp)

TO/FROM AUSTRALIA

Flights between Hong Kong and Australia are notoriously heavily booked. Flights to/from Bangkok and Singapore are often part of the longer Europe–Australia route so they are also sometimes full. The moral of the story is to plan your preferred itinerary well in advance.

Typical one-way fares to Sydney are US$350 from Singapore, US$340 from Penang or Kuala Lumpur, and US$340 from Bangkok. From Tokyo, fares start at US$750 but are often much higher.

From east-coast Australia, return fares to Singapore and Kuala Lumpur range from A$850 to A$1600; to Bangkok from A$900 to A$1600; and to Hong Kong from A$950 to A$1700, depending on the airline and when you're travelling.

You can get cheap short-hop flights between Darwin and Indonesia, a route serviced by Garuda Indonesia and Qantas. Royal Brunei Airlines flies between Darwin and Bandar Seri Begawan, while Malaysia Airlines flies from Kuala Lumpur.

Air Paradise International operates regular flights between Denpasar in Bali and the state capitals of Sydney, Melbourne and Perth, with fares out of Australia from around A$900 (A$750 from Perth).

TO/FROM NEW ZEALAND

Common one-way fares to Auckland are US$600 from Singapore, US$700 from Penang or Kuala Lumpur, US$600 from Bangkok and Hong Kong, and US$750 from Tokyo.

Travelling in the other direction, one-way fares from Auckland to Singapore cost around NZ$1000, and around NZ$1200 to Kuala Lumpur, Bangkok, Hong Kong and Tokyo, depending on the airline.

Australia

Air New Zealand and Qantas operate a network of flights linking key NZ cities with most major Australian gateway cities, while quite a few other international airlines include NZ and Australia on their Asia-Pacific routes. Check out Air New Zealand's cheap Tasman Express fares.

Another trans-Tasman option is the no-frills budget airline Freedom Air, an Air New Zealand subsidiary that offers direct flights between destinations on Australia's east coast (Gold Coast, Brisbane, Sydney and Melbourne) and the NZ centres of Auckland, Christchurch, Dunedin, Wellington, Palmerston North and Hamilton – note that not all these cities are connected to each other by direct flights.

Also check Asian and US airlines, which often have reasonable fares, as does Emirates.

Pacific Blue, a subsidiary of budget airline Virgin Blue, flies between both Christchurch and Wellington and numerous Australian cities, including Perth, Hobart and Adelaide.

If you book early enough and do your homework, you can pay around A$200 for a one-way fare from either Sydney or Melbourne to either Auckland, Christchurch or Wellington, though you could be charged anything up to A$350; return fares cost between A$350 and A$700. You can fly into Auckland and out of Christchurch to save backtracking, but you probably won't get the cheapest fares with this itinerary.

From key NZ cities, you'll ordinarily pay between NZ$220 and NZ$270 for a one-way ticket to an Australian east-coast city, with a return flight costing between NZ$430 and NZ$570.

There's usually not a significant difference in price between seasons, as this is a popular route pretty much year-round. The intense trans-Tasman competition, however, inevitably results in some attractive discounting.

For reasonably priced fares, try one of the numerous Australian capital-city branches of **STA Travel** (☎ 1300 733 035; www.statravel.com.au). Another good option, also with dozens of offices around the country, is **Flight Centre** (☎ 13 16 00).

Canada

The routes flown from Canada are similar to those from mainland USA, with most Toronto and Vancouver flights stopping in one US city such as Los Angeles or Honolulu before heading on to NZ and Australia.

Canadian discount air ticket sellers are known as consolidators (although you won't see a sign on the door saying 'Consolidator') and their air fares tend to be about 10% higher than those sold in the USA. Travel pages of newspapers are probably the best place to look to find consolidators. Local backpacker magazines will also carry such ads, as will certain Canadian travel websites. **Travel Cuts** (☎ 866-246-9762; www.travelcuts.com) is Canada's national student travel agency and has offices in all major cities.

TO/FROM AUSTRALIA

One-way fares out of Vancouver to Sydney or Melbourne cost from C$1200/C$1500 in the low/high season. From Toronto, one-way fares go from around C$1300/C$1600.

In the low season, fares from Australia start at around A$2000 return from Sydney to Vancouver. In the high season, return fares start at around A$2200.

TO/FROM NEW ZEALAND

One-way fares out of Vancouver to Auckland cost from C$1200 via the US west coast. From Toronto, one-way fares cost from C$1300. One-way fares from NZ start around NZ$1500 to Toronto and NZ$1400 to Vancouver.

Continental Europe

From major destinations in Europe such as the hub of Frankfurt, most flights travel to Australia and NZ via one of the Asian capitals. A number of flights are also routed through London before flying via Singapore, Bangkok, Hong Kong or Kuala Lumpur.

A good agent in the Dutch travel industry is **Holland International** (☎ 0900-8858; www.hollandinternational.nl).

In Germany, a good option is the Berlin branch of **STA Travel** (☎ 030-2859 8264; www.statravel.de).

In France (more specifically, Paris), try **Usit Connect Voyages** (☎ 01 43 29 69 50; www.usitconnections.fr) or **OTU Voyages** (☎ 01 40 29 12 22; www.otu.fr) – both companies are student/youth specialists and have offices in many French cities. Other recommendations include **Voyageurs du Monde** (☎ 01 40 15 11 15; www.vdm.com/vdm) and **Nouvelles Frontières** (☎ 08 25 00 08 25; www.nouvelles-frontieres.fr/nf); the phone numbers given are for offices in Paris, but again both companies have branches elsewhere.

TO/FROM AUSTRALIA

One-way fares from Paris and Frankfurt in the low/high season cost from €900/€1200. Return fares from Amsterdam start around €1400.

Return air fares from Australia to key European hubs like Paris and Frankfurt usually cost between A$1700 and A$2500.

TO/FROM NEW ZEALAND

One-way fares from France and Germany cost from €1200; and from Amsterdam €1500 return.

To fly return to Europe from NZ costs from around NZ$1800 return.

New Zealand

Air New Zealand and Qantas operate a network of flights linking key cities such as Auckland, Wellington and Christchurch in NZ with most major Australian gateway cities; discounted fares are regularly available. Freedom Air is an Air New Zealand subsidiary that operates direct flights between the two countries and offers excellent rates year-round. Good deals are also available through Asian airlines such as Thai Airways International and US carriers such as United Airlines. A relative newcomer to the trans-Tasman route is Emirates, which is also offering some reasonable fares. The Virgin Blue subsidiary, Pacific Blue, has been granted some airspace between Australia and NZ, which has resulted in some very cheap fares as competition between all the aforementioned airlines heats up.

One-way fares from NZ to Sydney cost between NZ$220 and NZ$270, with return fares costing anything from NZ$430 to NZ$570. One-way/return fares going the other way can cost as little as A$200/A$350 if you shop around and book your ticket early enough. There's not a great deal of difference in price between seasons, as this is a popular route all year.

Popular local travel agencies include **Flight Centre** (☎ 0800 243 544; www.flightcentre.co.nz), which has a large central office in Auckland and many branches throughout the country, and **STA Travel** (☎ 0508 782 872; www.statravel.co.nz), which also has offices in various cities.

UK & Ireland

Depending on which airline you travel with from the UK, flights to Australia or NZ go via the Middle East and Asia, or via the USA. Flights via Asia are usually cheaper and more frequent, and you can often make stopovers in countries like India, Thailand and Singapore. Via the USA, stopover possibilities include New York, Los Angeles, Honolulu or a variety of Pacific Islands.

Some of the best deals around are with Emirates, Gulf Air, Malaysia Airlines, Japan Airlines and Thai Airways International. Unless there are special deals on offer, British Airways, Singapore Airlines and Qantas generally have higher fares but may offer a more direct route.

Discount air travel is big business in London. Advertisements for many travel agencies appear in the travel pages of the weekend broadsheet newspapers, in *Time Out*, the *Evening Standard* and also in the free magazine, *TNT*.

Popular agencies in the UK include the ubiquitous **STA Travel** (☎ 0870-160 0599; www.statravel.co.uk), **Trailfinders** (☎ 0207-628 7628; www.trailfinders.co.uk) and **Flight Centre** (☎ 0870-499 0040; www.flightcentre.co.uk).

TO/FROM AUSTRALIA

Typical direct fares from London to Sydney are UK£400/UK£600 one-way/return during the low season (March to May). At peak times such as mid-December, fares go up by as much as 30%. The rest of the year they're somewhere in-between.

From Australia you can expect to pay from A$1000/A$1700 one-way/return in the low season to London and other European capitals (with stops in Asia on the way), and upwards of A$1100/1800 during the high season.

TO/FROM NEW ZEALAND

Typical one-way fares from London to Auckland start around UK£450; note that in June, July and mid-December, fares can go up by as much as 30%. From NZ you can expect to pay around NZ$1250 for one-way fares to London.

USA

Most flights between the North American mainland and NZ or Australia are to/from the US west coast, with the bulk routed through Los Angeles but some coming through San Francisco. If you're coming from some other part of the USA, your travel agent should be able to arrange a discounted 'add-on' fare to get you to the city of departure. There are also numerous airlines offering flights via Asia, with stopover possibilities including Tokyo, Kuala Lumpur, Bangkok, Hong Kong and Singapore; and via the Pacific with stopover possibilities like Nadi (Fiji), Rarotonga (Cook Islands) and Tahiti (French Polynesia).

As in Canada, discount travel agents in the USA are known as consolidators. San Francisco is the ticket consolidator capital of America, although some good deals can be found in Los Angeles, New York and other big cities. Look for ads from consolidators in travel pages of newspapers, local backpacker magazines and certain US travel websites.

STA Travel (☎ 800-781 4040; www.statravel.com) has offices all over the USA.

TO/FROM AUSTRALIA

Typically you can get a return ticket to Australia from the west coast from US$1100/US$1300 in the low/high season, or from the east coast starting at US$1400/US$1700.

Return fares from Australia to the US west coast cost around A$1850, and to New York from A$2100.

TO/FROM NEW ZEALAND

Typically you can get a return ticket to NZ from the US west coast for US$1300, or from the east coast from US$1600.

One-way fares from NZ to the US west coast cost from NZ$1200, and to New York from NZ$1700.

SEA

It's possible (though by no means easy or safe) to make your way between Australia and countries such as Papua New Guinea and Indonesia, and between NZ and Australia and some smaller Pacific Islands, by hitching rides or crewing on yachts – usually you have to at least contribute something towards food. Try asking around at harbours, marinas, and yacht and sailing clubs.

Good places to leave from on the Australian east coast include Coffs Harbour, Great Keppel Island, Airlie Beach and the Whitsundays, and Cairns – basically anywhere boats call in. Darwin could yield Indonesia-bound possibilities. A lot of boats move north to escape the winter, so April is a good time to look for a berth in the Sydney area.

Popular yachting harbours in NZ include the Bay of Islands and Whangarei (both in Northland), Auckland and Wellington. March and April are the best months to look for boats heading to Australia. From Fiji, October to November is a peak departure season as cyclones are on their way.

There are no passenger liners operating to/from Australia or NZ, and finding a berth on a cargo ship is difficult – that's if you actually want to spend months at sea aboard an enormous metal can.

Health

Dr David Millar

CONTENTS

Australia and NZ are remarkably healthy countries in which to travel. Tropical diseases such as malaria and yellow fever are unknown, while diseases of poor sanitation such as cholera and typhoid are unheard of. Thanks to their isolation and quarantine standards, animal diseases such as rabies and foot-and-mouth disease have yet to be recorded. Few travellers to these countries will experience anything worse than an upset stomach, sunburn or a bad hangover, and if you do fall ill the standard of hospitals and health care is high.

The absence of poisonous snakes or other dangerous animals in NZ makes it a very safe place to get off the beaten track and out into the beautiful countryside.

BEFORE YOU GO

Since most vaccines don't produce immunity until at least two weeks after given, visit a physician four to eight weeks before departure. Ask your doctor for an International Certificate of Vaccination (otherwise known as 'the yellow booklet'), which will list all the vaccinations you've received. This is mandatory for countries that require proof of yellow fever vaccination upon entry (sometimes required in Australia; see opposite), but it's a good idea to carry a record of all your vaccinations wherever you travel.

Bring medications in their original, clearly labelled, containers. A signed and dated letter from your physician describing your medical conditions and medications, including generic names, is also a good idea. If carrying syringes or needles, be sure to have a physician's letter documenting their medical necessity.

> David Millar is a travel-medicine specialist, diving doctor and lecturer in wilderness medicine who graduated in Hobart, Tasmania. He has worked in all states of Australia (except the Northern Territory) and as an expedition doctor with the Maritime Museum of Western Australia, accompanying a variety of expeditions around Australia, including the *Pandora* wreck in Far North Queensland and Rowley Shoals off the northwest coast. David is currently a Medical Director with The Travel Doctor in Auckland.

INSURANCE

If your health insurance doesn't cover you for medical expenses abroad, consider getting extra insurance – check subwwway on www.lonelyplanet.com for more details. Find out in advance if your insurance plan will make payments directly to providers or reimburse you later for overseas health expenditures. (Doctors expect payment at the time of consultation. Make sure you get an itemised receipt detailing the service and keep contact details for the health provider.)

RECOMMENDED VACCINATIONS

If you're really worried about health when travelling there are a few vaccinations you could consider: the World Health Organization recommends that all travellers should be covered for diphtheria, tetanus, measles, mumps, rubella, chickenpox and polio, as well as hepatitis B, regardless of the destination. A great time to ensure that all routine vaccination cover is complete is when you're making your travel plans.

ONLINE RESOURCES

There is a wealth of travel-health advice on the Internet. For further information, the **Lonely Planet website** (www.lonelyplanet.com) is a good place to start. The **World Health Organization** (www.who.int/ith/) publishes a superb book called *International Travel and Health*, which is revised annually and is available online at no cost. Another website of general interest

REQUIRED VACCINATIONS

New Zealand has no vaccination requirements for travellers.

Proof of yellow-fever vaccination is required only from those travellers entering Australia within six days of having stayed for one night or longer in a yellow fever–infected country. For a complete list of these countries visit the websites of the **World Health Organization** (www.who.int/wer/) or the **Centers for Disease Control and Prevention** (www.cdc.gov/travel/blusheet.htm).

is **MD Travel Health** (www.mdtravelhealth.com), which provides complete travel health recommendations for every country and is updated daily.

IN AUSTRALIA & NEW ZEALAND

AVAILABILITY & COST OF HEALTH CARE

Health insurance is essential for all travellers. While health care in both countries is of a high standard and is not overly expensive by international standards, considerable costs can build up and repatriation is extremely expensive. Make sure your existing health insurance will cover you – if not, organise extra insurance.

Both countries have excellent specialised public-health facilities for women and children in the major centres. No specific health concerns exist for women but greater care for children is recommended to avoid environmental hazards such as heat, sunburn, cold and marine hazards.

Health Care in Australia

Australia has an excellent health-care system. It's a mixture of privately run medical clinics and hospitals alongside a system of public hospitals funded by the Australian government. The Medicare system covers Australian residents for some health-care costs. Visitors from countries with which Australia has a reciprocal health-care agreement are eligible for benefits specified under the Medicare programme. Agreements are currently in place with NZ, the UK, the Netherlands, Sweden, Finland, Italy, Malta and Ireland – check the details before departing from these countries. In general the agreements provide for any episode of ill health that requires prompt medical attention. For further details visit www.hic.gov.au/yourhealth/services_for_travellers/vtta.htm.

Health Care in New Zealand

New Zealand does not have a government-funded system of public hospitals. All travellers are, however, covered for medical care resulting from accidents that occur while in NZ (eg motor-vehicle accidents, adventure-activity accidents) by the Accident Compensation Corporation (ACC). Costs incurred for treatment of a medical illness that occurs while in NZ will only be covered by travel insurance. For more details see www.moh.govt.nz.

Pharmaceutical Supplies

Over-the-counter medications are widely available in both countries through private chemists. These include pain killers, antihistamines for allergies and skin-care products.

Some medications that are available over the counter in other countries are only available by a prescription obtained from a general practitioner. These include the oral contraceptive pill, most medications for asthma and all antibiotics. If you take medication on a regular basis, bring an adequate supply and ensure you have details of the generic name as brand names differ between countries. The majority of medications in use outside of the region are available.

Self-Care

In either country, particularly in Australia's remote locations, it is possible there'll be a significant delay in emergency services reaching you in the event of serious accident or illness. Do not underestimate the vast distances between Australia's outback towns; an increased level of self-reliance and preparation in the outback is essential.

If you're heading into the wild, consider taking a wilderness first-aid course, such as those that are offered at the **Wilderness Medicine Institute** (www.nols.edu/wmi/index.shtml); take a comprehensive first-aid kit that is appropriate for the activities planned; and ensure that you have adequate means of communication.

Both countries have extensive mobile-phone coverage but you'll need additional radio communications if you're heading into the Australian outback or Tasmanian wilderness. Australia's **Royal Flying Doctor Service** (www.rfds.org.au) provides an important backup for remote communities.

INFECTIOUS DISEASES

Giardiasis

The giardia parasite is widespread in waterways throughout NZ and Australia. Drinking untreated water from streams and lakes is not recommended. Using water filters and boiling or treating water with chlorine tablets or iodine are effective ways of preventing the disease. Symptoms consist of intermittent bad-smelling diarrhoea, abdominal bloating and wind. Effective treatment is available (tinidazole or metronidazole).

Hepatitis C

This disease is still a growing problem among intravenous drug users. Blood-transfusion services fully screen all blood before use.

HIV

Levels of HIV are similar to other Western countries. Clean needles and syringes are widely available.

Meningococcal Disease

This occurs worldwide and is a risk with prolonged dorm-style accommodation. A vaccine exists for some types of the disease (meningococcal A, C, Y and W).

Sexually Transmitted Diseases

STDs (including gonorrhoea, chlamydia and herpes) occur at rates similar to most Western countries. The most common symptoms are pain on passing urine and a discharge. Infection can be present without symptoms, so seek medical screening after any unprotected sex with a new partner. Sexual-health clinics are run by major hospitals.

Tick Typhus

Tick typhus cases have been reported throughout Australia, but are predominantly found in Queensland and New South Wales. A week or so after being bitten a dark area forms around the bite, followed by a rash and possible fever, headache and inflamed lymph nodes. The disease is treatable with antibiotics (doxycycline), so see a doctor if you suspect you have been bitten.

ENVIRONMENTAL HAZARDS

Animal Bites & Stings

CROCODILES

The risk of crocodile attack in tropical northern Australia is real, but predictable and preventable. Before swimming anywhere in northern Australia (sea, river or waterhole), talk to the locals first. For more information on crocs, see p338 and p465.

INSECT-BORNE ILLNESS

Various insects can be a source of irritation and, in Australia, may be the source of specific rare diseases (dengue fever, Ross River fever).

Protection from mosquitoes, sandflies, ticks and leeches can be achieved by a combination of the following strategies:

- Wear loose-fitting, long-sleeve clothing.
- Apply 30% DEET on all exposed skin, and repeat application every three to four hours.
- Impregnate clothing with permethrin (an insecticide that kills insects but is completely safe for humans).

In NZ, mosquitoes and sandflies are more of a nuisance than an actual hazard (see p781).

MARINE ANIMALS

Australia has a few marine nasties you should watch for. Spikes, such as those found on sea urchins, stonefish, scorpion fish, catfish and stingrays, can cause severe local pain. If this occurs, immediately immerse the affected area in hot water (as high a temperature as can be tolerated). Keep topping up with hot water until the pain subsides and medical care can be reached. The stonefish is found only in tropical Australia, from northwestern Australia around the coast to northern Queensland. Antivenin is available.

Stings from jellyfish such as box jellyfish and Irukandji also occur in Australia's tropical waters, particularly during the wet season (November to April). The box jelly-fish has an incredibly potent sting and has been known to cause fatalities. Warning signs are present at affected beaches and stinger nets are in place at more popular beaches. Never dive into the water unless you have checked that it's safe with the local beach lifesavers. 'Stinger suits' (full-body Lycra swimsuits) prevent stinging, as do wetsuits. If you are stung, first aid consists of washing the skin with vinegar to prevent further discharge of remaining stinging cells, followed by rapid transfer to a hospital; antivenin is widely available.

The chances of being bitten by a shark are minimal, and the risk is no greater than in other countries with extensive coastlines. Check with surf lifesaving groups or talk to the locals before swimming.

NZ is free of marine stingers and biters, though if you stand on a kina (sea urchin) it will hurt a bit.

SNAKES

Australian snakes have a fearful reputation that is justified in terms of the potency of their venom, but unjustified in terms of the actual risk to travellers and locals. Snakes are usually quite timid in nature and in most instances will move away if disturbed. They only have small fangs, making it easy to prevent bites to the lower limbs (where 80% of bites occur) by wearing protective clothing (such as gaiters) around the ankles when bushwalking. The bite marks are very small and may even go unnoticed.

In all confirmed or suspected bites, preventing the spread of toxic venom can be achieved by applying pressure to the wound and immobilising the area with a splint or sling before seeking medical attention. Firmly wrap an elastic bandage (you can improvise with a T-shirt) around the entire limb, but not so tight as to cut off the circulation. Along with immobilisation, this is a life-saving first-aid measure.

There are no snakes in NZ. None.

SPIDERS

Australia has a number of poisonous spiders, but only one is really dangerous: the Sydney funnel-web spider (found only in and around Sydney) causes severe local pain, as well as vomiting, abdominal pain and sweating. Antivenin exists, so apply pressure to the wound and immobilise the area before transferring to a hospital.

Red-back spiders are found throughout Australia. Bites cause increasing pain at the site followed by profuse sweating and generalised symptoms (including muscular weakness, sweating at the site of the bite and nausea). First aid includes application of ice or cold packs to the bite, then transfer to hospital.

Some spider bites may cause sores or ulcers that are very slow and difficult to heal. Clean the wound thoroughly and seek medical assistance.

NZ has only two poisonous spiders: the native katipo, which is not very poisonous and uncommon to the point of being endangered, and the introduced (thanks, Australia) white-tailed spider, which is also uncommon.

Heat Illness

Very hot weather is experienced all year in northern Australia and during the summer months for most of the country. When arriving from a temperate or cold climate (eg chilly NZ), remember that it takes two weeks for acclimatisation to occur. Before the body is acclimatised an excessive amount of salt is lost in perspiration, so increasing the salt in your diet is essential.

Heat exhaustion occurs when fluid intake does not keep up with fluid loss. Symptoms include dizziness, fainting, fatigue, nausea or vomiting. On observation the skin is usually pale, cool and clammy. Treatment consists of rest in a cool, shady place and fluid replacement with water or diluted sports drinks.

Heatstroke is a severe form of heat illness that occurs after fluid depletion or extreme heat challenge from heavy exercise. This is a true medical emergency, with heating of the brain leading to disorientation, hallucinations and seizures. Prevention is by maintaining an adequate fluid intake to ensure the continued passage of clear and copious urine, especially during physical exertion.

Hypothermia

This is a significant risk in NZ, especially during the winter months, or year-round in the mountains of the North Island and all of the South Island. Mountain ranges and/or strong winds produce a high chill factor that can result in hypothermia even in moderately cool temperatures. Early signs include the inability to perform fine movements (such as doing up buttons), shivering and a bad case of the 'umbles' (fumbles, mumbles, grumbles, stumbles). The key elements of treatment are changing the environment to one where heat loss is minimised, changing out of any wet clothing, adding dry clothes with wind- and waterproof layers, adding insulation and providing fuel (water and carbohydrates) to allow shivering to build the internal temperature. In severe hypothermia, shivering actually stops; this is a medical emergency requiring rapid evacuation in addition to taking all the measures detailed above.

Surf Beaches & Drowning

New Zealand and Australia both have exceptional surf beaches. The power of the surf can fluctuate as a result of the varying slope of the seabed at many beaches. Check with local surf lifesaving organisations before entering the surf and be aware of your own limitations and expertise. For more information, see p466.

Ultraviolet Light Exposure

Australia and NZ have some of the highest rates of skin cancer in the world, so you should monitor UV exposure closely. UV exposure is greatest between 10am and 4pm, so avoid exposing your skin to the sun during these times. Always use 30+ sunscreen, making sure you apply it 30 minutes before exposure and that you reapply regularly to minimise sun damage.

Water

Tap water is universally safe to drink in both countries. Increasing numbers of streams, rivers and lakes, however, are being contaminated by bugs that cause diarrhoea, making water purification when bushwalking (tramping) essential. The simplest way of purifying water is to boil it thoroughly. You should also consider purchasing a water filter, chlorine tablets or iodine.

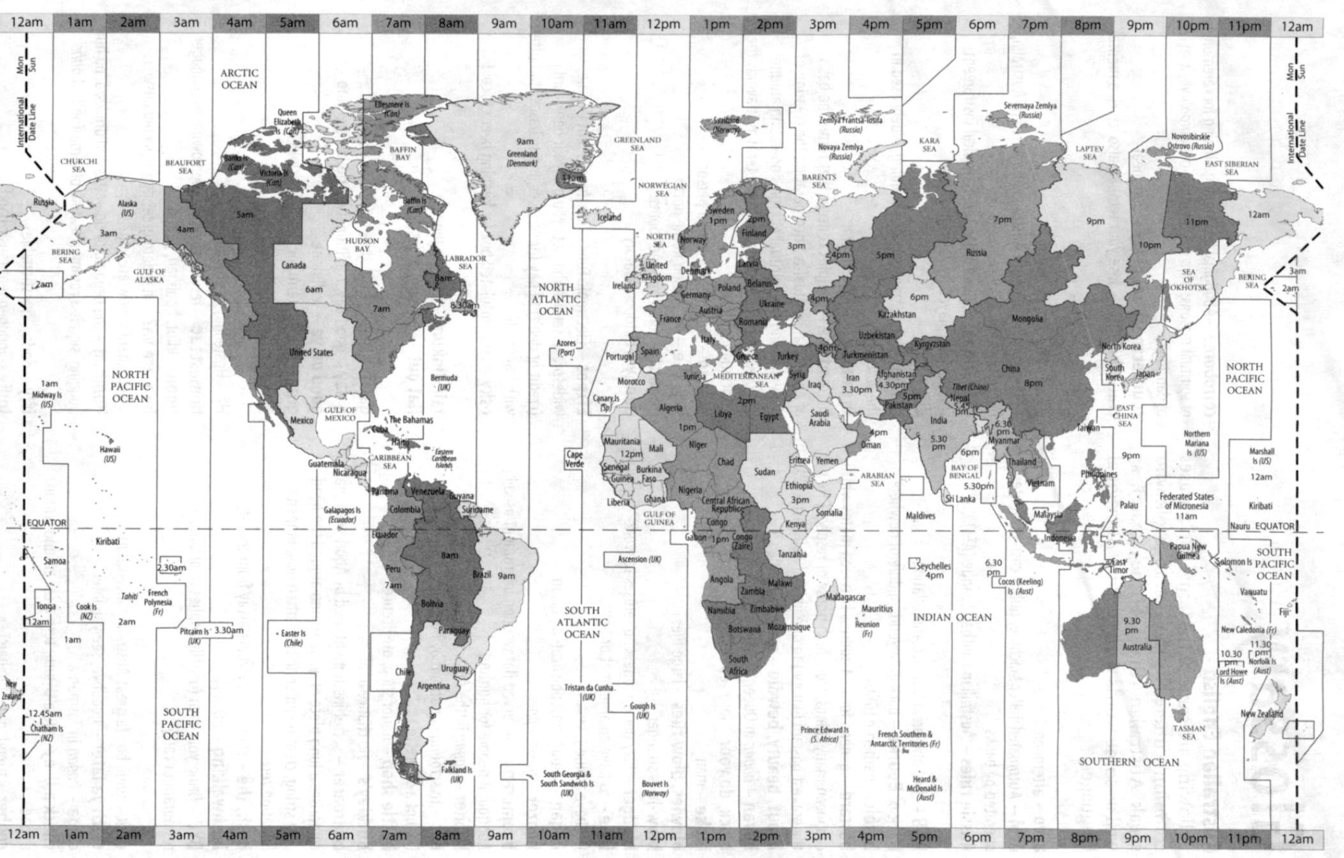
12am
1am
2am
3am
4am
5am
6am
7am
8am
9am
10am
11am
12pm
1pm
2pm
3pm
4pm
5pm
6pm
7pm
8pm
9pm
10pm
11pm
12am
International Date Line
Mon
Sun
ARCTIC OCEAN
NORTH PACIFIC OCEAN
NORTH ATLANTIC OCEAN
SOUTH ATLANTIC OCEAN
INDIAN OCEAN
SOUTH PACIFIC OCEAN
SOUTHERN OCEAN
EQUATOR
CHUKCHI SEA
BEAUFORT SEA
BERING SEA
GULF OF ALASKA
HUDSON BAY
BAFFIN BAY
LABRADOR SEA
GREENLAND SEA
NORWEGIAN SEA
NORTH SEA
BARENTS SEA
KARA SEA
LAPTEV SEA
EAST SIBERIAN SEA
SEA OF OKHOTSK
GULF OF MEXICO
CARIBBEAN SEA
MEDITERRANEAN SEA
ARABIAN SEA
BAY OF BENGAL
EAST CHINA SEA
GULF OF GUINEA
TASMAN SEA
Russia
Alaska (US)
Canada
United States
Mexico
Greenland (Denmark)
Iceland
Norway
Sweden
Finland
United Kingdom
Ireland
France
Germany
Poland
Spain
Portugal
Italy
Turkey
Egypt
Libya
Algeria
Morocco
Sudan
Iran 3.30pm
India 5.30 pm
China
Mongolia
Kazakhstan
Japan
Australia
New Zealand
Brazil
Argentina
Chile
Peru
Bolivia
Hawaii (US)
Midway Is (US)
Fiji
Madagascar
Sri Lanka
Indonesia
Philippines

Glossary

Australian English

Following are some of the terms and phrases commonly uttered by those strange folk who speak Australian (that's 'Strine', mate), as well as some words derived from Aboriginal languages.

arvo – afternoon
ATM – Automated Teller Machine; public cash dispenser operated by banks
Aussie rules – Australian Football League (AFL)

B&B – 'bed and breakfast' accommodation
back o' Bourke – back of beyond, middle of nowhere
barbie – barbecue (BBQ)
bastard – general form of address between mates which can mean many things, from high praise or respect ('He's the bravest bastard I know') to dire insult ('You bastard!')
beaut, beauty, bewdie – great, fantastic
bevan – *bogan* in Queensland
block, do your – lose your temper
bloke – man
blowies, blow flies – large flies
blow-in – stranger
bludger – lazy person, one who refuses to work
blue – to have an argument or fight (ie 'have a blue')
bogan – young, unsophisticated person
bonzer – great, *ripper*
boomerang – a curved flat wooden instrument used by Aboriginal people for hunting
booner – *bogan* in the Australian Capital Territory
bot – to scrounge or obtain by begging or borrowing (ie 'bot a cigarette')
bottle shop – liquor shop, off-licence
Buckley's – no chance at all
bullroarer – secret instrument used by Aborigines that comprises a long piece of wood swung around the head on a string, creating an eerie roar; often used in men's initiation ceremonies
bush, the – country, anywhere away from the city
bushwalking – hiking
BYO – bring your own (usually applies to alcohol at a restaurant or café)

cask – wine box (a great Australian invention)
catch ya later – goodbye, see you later
chiga – *bogan* in Tasmania
chuck a U-ey – do a U-turn, turn a car around within a road
cobber – friend, *mate* (archaic)
corroboree – Aboriginal festival or gathering for ceremonial or spiritual reasons; from the Dharug word *garaabara*, a style of dancing
counter meal, countery – *pub* meal
crack the shits – lose your temper, also 'crack a mental'

daks – trousers
dead set – true, dinkum
deli – *milk bar* in South Australia and Western Australia, but, elsewhere, a delicatessen
didgeridoo – cylindrical wooden musical instrument traditionally played by Aboriginal men
dill – idiot
donga – small, transportable building widely used in the *outback*
Dreaming – see *Dreamtime*
Dreamtime – complex concept that forms the basis of Aboriginal spirituality, incorporating the creation of the world and the spiritual energies operating around us; '*Dreaming*' is often the preferred term as it avoids the association with time
drongo – worthless or stupid person
Dry, the – dry season in the north
dugouts – underground rooms
dunny – outdoor lavatory

Eftpos – Electronic Funds Transfer at Point Of Sale; widespread service that lets you use your bank card (credit or debit) to pay for services or purchases, and often withdraw cash
esky – large insulated box for keeping beer etc cold

fair dinkum – honest, genuine
flat out – very busy or fast

galah – noisy parrot, thus noisy idiot
g'day – good day; traditional Australian greeting
good on ya – well done
grog – general term for alcoholic drinks
grouse – very good

HI – Hostelling International
homestead – residence of a station owner or manager
hoon – idiot, hooligan, yahoo
how are ya? – standard greeting (expected answer: 'Good, thanks, how are you?')
humbug – the begging of cigarettes and drinks; a 'no humbugging' sign is a common feature of some Top End *pubs*

iffy – dodgy, questionable
indie – independent music bands

jocks – men's underpants
jumped-up – full of self-importance, arrogant

Kiwi – New Zealander
knackered – broken, tired
Koori – Aboriginal person (mostly south of the Murray River)

larrikin – hooligan, mischievous youth

mate – general term of familiarity, whether you know the person or not
milk bar – small shop selling milk and other basic provisions
mobile phone – cell phone
mozzies – mosquitoes

never-never – remote country in the *outback*
no worries – no problems, that's OK

ocker – an uncultivated or boorish Australian; a knocker or derider
outback – remote part of the *bush, back o' Bourke*

pie floater – meat pie served in green-pea soup, a South Australian favourite
piss – beer
pissed – drunk
pissed off – annoyed
piss weak – no good, gutless
plonk – cheap wine
pokies – poker machines
Pom – English person
pot – large beer glass (Victoria); beer gut; to sink a billiard ball
pub – bar, often doubling as a cheap hotel; from 'public house'

rapt – delighted, enraptured
ratbag – friendly term of abuse
ratshit (RS) – lousy
reckon! – you bet! absolutely!
ripper – good (also 'little ripper')
root – have sexual intercourse
rooted – tired, broken

saltie – saltwater crocodile (the dangerous one)
sanger – sandwich
schooner – large beer glass (New South Wales, South Australia)
shanks's pony – to travel on foot
sheila – woman
she'll be right – no problems, no worries
shonky – unreliable
shout – buy a round of drinks ('Your shout!')
sick – (pronounced 'seek') good; great (as in 'fully sick, mate')
slab – two dozen *stubbies* or *tinnies*
station – large farm
story – the tale from the *Dreaming* that taps into the concepts of legend, myth, tradition and the law, and is meant to carry much more weight than the average historical account (given the importance of oral traditions in Aboriginal and Torres Strait Islander cultures)
stubby – 375ml bottle of beer

take the piss – deliberately telling someone a mistruth, often as social sport
tea – evening meal
thingo – thing, whatchamacallit, doovelacki, thingamajig
thongs – flip-flops, an ocker's idea of formal footwear
tinny – 375ml can of beer; also a small, aluminium fishing dinghy (Northern Territory)
too right! – absolutely!
Top End – northern part of the Northern Territory
tucker – food
two-pot screamer – person unable to hold their alcohol
two-up – traditional heads/tails coin gambling game

unsealed road – dirt road
ute – short for utility; a pick-up truck

walkabout – lengthy walk away from it all
Wet, the – rainy season in the north
whinge – complain, moan
whoop-whoop – *outback*, miles from anywhere
woomera – stick used by Aboriginal people for throwing spears

YHA – Youth Hostels Association
yobbo – uncouth, aggressive person
yonks – ages, a long time
youse – plural of you, pronounced 'yooze', only used by the grammatically challenged

New Zealand English

Here's a selective list of 'Kiwi English' and Maori terms and phrases that you'll probably come across in your New Zealand travels.

AA – New Zealand Automobile Association, which provides road information and roadside assistance
afghan – popular homemade chocolate biscuit
All Blacks – NZ's revered national rugby union team (the name comes from 'All Backs', which the press called the NZ rugby team on an early visit to England)
Aotearoa – *Maori* name for NZ, most often translated as 'Land of the Long White Cloud'
ATM – Automatic Teller Machine; public cash dispenser operated by banks

B&B – 'bed and breakfast' accommodation
bach – a holiday home, usually a wooden cottage (pronounced 'batch'); see *crib*
black-water rafting – rafting or tubing underground in a cave or *tomo*
boozer – a public bar
box of birds – an expression meaning 'on top of the world', usually uttered in response to 'How are you?'
bro' – literally 'brother'; usually meaning mate, as in 'just off to see the bros'
bush – heavily forested areas
BYO – bring your own (usually applies to alcohol at a restaurant or café)

campervan – caravan
Captain Cooker – a large feral pig, introduced by Captain Cook and now roaming wild over most of NZ's rugged bush land
chillie bin – cooler; large insulated box for keeping food and drink cold
choice – fantastic; great
ciggies – cigarettes
crib – the name for a *bach* in Otago and Southland
cuzzie or cuz' – cousin; relative or just mate; see *bro'*

dairy – a small corner store which sells milk, bread, newspapers, ice cream and pretty much everything else
Dalmatian – a term applied to the predominantly Yugoslav gum diggers who fossicked for kauri gum (used as furniture polish) in the gum fields of Northland
DB&B – 'dinner, bed and breakfast' accommodation
DOC – Department of Conservation (or *Te Papa Atawhai*); government department which administers national parks and thus all tracks and huts
dropkick – a certain method of kicking a rugby ball; a personal insult

EFTPOS – Electronic Funds Transfer At Point Of Sale; widespread service that lets you use your bank card (credit or debit) to pay for services or purchases, and often withdraw cash

farmstay – accommodation on a *Kiwi* farm where you're encouraged to join in the typical day-to-day activities
football – rugby, either union or league

Godzone – New Zealand (from Richard Seddon who referred to NZ as 'God's own country')
good as gold, good as – very good; no problem
greenstone – jade; *pounamu*

haka – any dance, but usually refers to the traditional challenge; war dance
hakari – feast
handle – a beer glass with a handle
hangi – oven made by digging a hole and steaming food in baskets over embers in the hole; a feast of traditional *Maori* food
hapu – subtribe or smaller tribal grouping
hard case – an unusual or strong-willed character
hei tiki – carved, stylised human figure worn around the neck, often a carved representation of an ancestor; also called a *tiki*
hoa – friend; usually pronounced 'e hoa'
homestay – accommodation in a family house where you're treated (temporarily, thank God) as one of the family
hongi – *Maori* greeting; the pressing of noses and sharing of life breath

'Is it what!' – strong affirmation or agreement; 'Yes isn't it!'

jandals – sandals; flip-flops; usually rubber footwear
jersey – a jumper, usually woollen; the shirt worn by rugby players
judder bars – bumps in the road to make you drive slowly; speed humps

kai – food; almost any word with kai in it has some food connection
ka pai – good, excellent
kia ora – the *Maori* word for hello
Kiwi – New Zealander
kiwi – the flightless, nocturnal brown bird with a long beak which is the national symbol; the NZ dollar; a member of the national rugby league team; an adjective to mean anything of or relating to NZ
kiwi bear – the introduced Australian brush-tailed possum
kiwi fruit – a small, succulent fruit with fuzzy brown skin and juicy green flesh; also known as Chinese gooseberry
koha – a donation
kumera – sweet potato

league – rugby league football
LOTR – *Lord of the Rings*
lounge bar – a more-upmarket bar than a public bar; called a 'ladies bar' in some countries

Maori – the indigenous people of NZ
Maoritanga – *Maori* culture
marae – literally refers to the sacred ground in front of the *Maori* meeting house, more commonly used to refer to the entire complex of buildings
metal/metalled road – gravel road (unsealed)
moko – tattoo; usually refers to facial tattoos

nifty-fifty – 50cc motorcycle
NZ – the universal appellation for New Zealand; pronounced 'enzed'

pa – fortified *Maori* village, usually on a hill top
pakeha – *Maori* for a white or European person; once derogatory, and still considered so by some, this term is now widely used for white New Zealanders
paua – abalone; tough shellfish pounded, minced, then made into patties (fritters), which are available in almost every NZ fish and chip shop
pillocking – 'surfing' across mud flats on a rubbish-bin lid
pounamu – the *Maori* name for *greenstone*
powhiri – a traditional *Maori* welcome onto the *marae*

quad bikes – four-wheel farm bikes

Rheiny – affectionate term for Rheineck beer
rigger – a refillable half-gallon plastic bottle for holding draught beer
riptide – a dangerously strong current running away from the shore at a beach
Roaring Forties – the ocean between 40° and 50° south, known for very strong winds

scrap – a fight
sick – (pronounced 'suck') good; great (as in 'fully sick, bro')
silver fern – the symbol worn by the *All Blacks* and other national sportsfolk on their jerseys, representative of the underside of a ponga leaf; the national netball team are the Silver Ferns
Steinie – affectionate term for Steinlager beer
superette – grocery store or small supermarket open outside normal business hours

tapu – sacred; forbidden; taboo
tarseal – sealed road; bitumen
tiki – short for *hei tiki*
tomo – hole; entrance to a cave
tramp – bushwalk, trek, hike; a more serious undertaking than an ordinary walk, requiring some experience and equipment
tuatara – a prehistoric reptile dating back to the age of the dinosaurs (perhaps 260 million years)

Waikikamukau – mythical NZ town; somewhere in the *wopwops*
Waitangi – short way of referring to the Treaty of Waitangi
waka – canoe
whare – house
whare runanga – meeting house
whenua – land
whitebait – a small, elongated, translucent fish which is scooped up in nets and eaten whole (head, eyes and all!) or made into patties
wopwops – remote; 'out in the wopwops' is out in the middle of nowhere

Behind the Scenes

THIS BOOK

This is the first edition of *Australia & New Zealand on a shoestring* – we're very excited! The entire Australian region was researched anew for this shoestring by a troupe of authors armed with backpacks, notebooks, laptops...and an 80-page author brief. In New Zealand Paul Smitz researched the South Island solo, as well as northern hotspots such as Auckland, Rotorua and Wellington. He was assisted in the North Island research by Martin Robinson, Richard Watkins and Nina Rousseau.

Paul also coordinated the authors' efforts; see The Authors chapter for which author wrote which chapters.

THANKS FROM THE AUTHORS

Paul Smitz Many thanks to all the people who contributed to my work on this book despite the social and moral consequences. They include all the New Zealanders I harangued mercilessly over several trips to the islands, all the Australians who helped me out at home, all the travellers who were regrettably exposed to my Inspector Clouseau eavesdropping skills and interview techniques, and the other authors and Lonely Planet bods whose efforts on this book will undoubtedly make me look good by association (too bad for them it doesn't work the other way around). Speaking of Mars, special thanks to Tim Burton for the alien expletives, and to the enigmatic woman who is secretly waiting for the Ziggy Stardust haircut to come back into fashion.

Sandra Bao Sydney is full of gracious and very helpful folks whose contributions greatly aided my research on this book. I met them everywhere I went, and their friendliness made this Lonely Planet gig one of my best ever. But I'd like to thank one person especially for his help and companionship – my friend Dilip Varma. A quick nod also to Victoria and Andrew Grimes, Melissa Lysaght and Tricia Wilden for the warmth and opinions they offered this weary traveller. See you all next time around!

Pete Cruttenden This trip into Australia's heart was a largely solo affair, but special thanks go to Rebecca Cole for sharing the journey, and to Errol Hunt and the good folk of Lonely Planet for their continuing support.

George Dunford Nikki (for patience, proofing and pandering), all those who gave me a bed, couch, cars or barstool especially (in order of appearance) Michael and Glynis (have you guys checked your car for dints?); Gina and Gazim (and now Honest Abe); Mike, Mel and SGT (welcome aboard, young fella); the Ads and Sara; mum (who would have made a great travelling companion for Bill B) and dad (made the ultimate sacrifice of his Land Rover). With a nod to Smitzy del Mar for coordinating the whole shebang and The Crutter for pulling the Outback chapter together. Let's not forget all on the inside at Lonely Planet (especially Errol Hunt, for signing me up and updating those briefs), Princess Coriander (of the Mapping Realms), Tom Hall–US, the hard-working folks of Talk2US, all the DPU crew (maximum respect to tha Jay-Bu for the travelling tunes, KT F for keeping it real, Rosie for her savvy agentry and Zebediah for the constant good humour) and all the folks along the way who gave tips or tricks for NSW (with special mention to Peta Lee at Newcastle visitors centre). Big shout-outs to the Rou for supreme mentoring and daily phonecalls on the road.

Simone Egger Thank you to Verity Campbell for her stellar text, and to Errol Hunt and Paul Smitz. Thanks also to the travellers who wrote in with advice and opinions. Special thanks to Ruth Davis, Simon King, Warren Egger, John Cope-Williams, Jonathan Leahy and Jessica Klingender.

Susannah Farfor Utmost thanks to navigator Ian Malcolm – surf buddy, hiker, feaster and shiraz quaffer extraordinaire. Huge thanks to the staff at the Caledonia Hotel in Robe who rang around to find us a place to stay when we arrived in the middle of the biggest agricultural swap meet in the state; Cape Willoughby's lighthouse keeper; Geoff and Hazel's well-needed oasis in the hills; Mark Potter for a low-down on gourmet haunts around McLaren Vale; and helpful, friendly and knowledgeable cellar door staff everywhere (particularly Two Hands, Langmeil and Wirra Wirra). Special thanks for the great local knowledge from Elizabeth Dankel, Annie McColl and family, Stephanie Vasileff, Jason and Louise James, Dan 'the dart champion' Webster, 'Scorch' and Ben Blake; and to all the fascinating and eccentric South Australians who went out of their way to answer oodles of questions which, no doubt, seemed very odd where details of the quest were not divulged. Cheers also to Paul Smitz, for his leniency, and Errol Hunt – the commissioner.

Justin Flynn To all the good people of WA, thanks for your hospitality, even after you found out that I was a Victorian. A huge *dank je vel* to Sascha for giving me the courage to go over the edge of that cliff at Kalbarri – the beer somehow tasted better that night didn't it? To Vasso in Perth, a sincere thank you for your help when I literally lost the shirt off my back. To John in Denham, your generosity was truly amazing, even though my head was cursing you the following day when I boarded that 5am bus! Big thanks to Errol at Lonely Planet for giving me the opportunity in the first place and to Paul who cobbled this monster together. Finally, special thanks to Wendy for not only minding the fort back home, but for giving me your blessing to follow my dreams.

Sarina Singh I'm very grateful to the many people in Tasmania who generously offered their time and insights during both research and write-up. Extra special thanks to Jan Dale for making me feel so at home and for cheerfully answering my perpetual questions. Many thanks also to John Kelly for kindly allowing me use of his office to write and for granting me access to the chocolate cupboard.

At Lonely Planet I'd like to say a big thank you to Paul Smitz for his stress-relieving tips and support and to Errol Hunt for making my job so delightfully straightforward from beginning to end.

Justine Vaisutis Special thanks to Alan for his unremitting support and to my sister Aidy for keeping me sane while on the road – a tall order even when I'm off it. For saving my technically inept behind, a big thank you goes to both Michaela and Nick in the London office.

While researching the Queensland chapter I was lucky enough to encounter plenty of friendly and helpful Queenslanders, particularly in tourist offices throughout the state. Their assistance was invaluable, as were the countless tips, laughs, pointers and entertaining conversations I enjoyed from the squillions of backpackers I met along the way.

Sarah Wintle Wholehearted thanks to my family and friends for their endless inspiration and support, especially my mum. Here's cheers to Errol Hunt for giving me the gig. Thanks also to the following Lonely Planet folk: Anna Bolger, Paul Smitz, George Dunford, David McClymont, Marika McAdam and Michelle Bennett. Thanks to Susannah Farfor for generous advice over nachos, and Kym 'travel agent to the stars' Smith, Robin Wintle, Jacqui Pringle and Tony Sedunary for proofreading services par excellence.

For a fair dinkum Broome perspective, thanks to Jade and Lanka. Thanks to Caroline and Stuart of Adventure Tours for cool headedness in the sweltering Kimberley heat and Dave Gross at CARE.

In the Top End, my gratitude extends to Andrea Wait and Paula Timson of the Northern Territory Tourist Commission; Georgianna Fien at Kakadu National Park; 'DJ' Steve at Wilderness 4WD Adventures; Geoff and Glenys Chambers for Darwin hospitality and Jamie at Tourism Top End in Darwin. Hats off to the efforts of all the helpful tourism staff.

Thanks also to the global nomads I've met on the open road, and the larger-than-life characters who made my job more interesting. Last but not least, I'd like to pay my respects to the indigenous elders of the Kimberley and the Top End, and acknowledge the traditional owners of those lands.

CREDITS

Australia & New Zealand on a shoestring was commissioned in Lonely Planet's Melbourne office by Errol Hunt, with assistance from Dazza O'Connell (managing editor) and Kate Cody (regional publishing manager), and from Corie Waddell (managing cartographer), Jack Gavran, and Bonnie Wintle (cartographers).

The new shoestring was coordinated inhouse by the überteam of Maryanne Netto (editing), Julie Sheridan (cartography) and Katherine Marsh (layout). The project was project managed inhouse by the unflappable Charles Rawlings-Way.

Maryanne was assisted by Joanne Newell, Monique Choy, Andrew Bain, Kate Evans, Yvonne Byron, Sasha Baskett, Charlotte Orr and Kate James. Thanks to Chris Love, Charlotte Harrison, Emma Koch, Kate McLeod, Laura Gibb, Lucy Monie, Nancy Ianni and Susannah Schwer for tying up loose ends. Big thank you also to Jennifer Garrett for conjuring up freelance help.

Julie was helped on the map front by Paul Bazalicki, Barbara Benson, Anneka Imkamp, Wayne Murphy, Jacqueline Nguyen and Chris Tsismetzis.

Katherine was assisted by David Kemp, Adam Bextream, Jenny Jones, Laura Jane, Wibowo Rusli, Yvonne Bischofberger, Jacqueline McLeod and Michael Ruff. Wendy Wright designed the cover.

Nicholas Stebbing and Rebecca Lalor from production services provided invaluable expertise and support, while Adriana Mammarella, Kate

McDonald and Sally Darmody did likewise on the layout front.

Thanks to numerous other Lonely Planet staff for massive input into the book in the planning and commissioning stages – especially Robert Reid and Virginia Maxwell. Also for help inhouse, thanks to Vivek Wagle, Gabrielle Green, Howard Ralley, Fiona Siseman, Jodie Farrelly, James Hardy, Pepi Bluck, Jennifer Mundy-Nordin, Sarah Finney, Amanda Jarvis, Paul Piaia, Gus Balbontin, Tom Hall, Anna Bolger, Helen Hewitt, Malcolm O'Brien, Carolyn Boicos, Adrian Persoglia, Cathy Lanigan, Owen Eszeki and Meg Worby. Thanks to Smitzy, and indeed all the other authors, for their patience, their passion and for just being really good people to work with.

Thanks also to the various clever souls whose research and writing informed the two Snapshots chapters: Eddie Butler-Bowdon (Australian history), Verity Campbell (Australian culture), Professor James Belich (NZ history) and Russell Brown (NZ culture).

ACKNOWLEDGEMENTS

Multitudinous thanks to the following for the use of their content:

John Stainton, Best Picture Show Company: Crikey – Quarantine Matters! boxed text (p464) by Steve Irwin.

Thanks also to Angela Sharpe at AQIS.

Thanks to Claire Dobbs for helping with the Sandflies boxed text (p781) by Sir Ian McKellen.

Index

D

INDEX

000 Map pages
000 Location of photographs

000 Map pages
000 Location of photographs

INDEX

000 Map pages
000 Location of photographs

INDEX

N

INDEX

000 Map pages
000 Location of photographs

000 Map pages
000 Location of photographs

INDEX

000 Map pages
000 Location of photographs

THE LONELY PLANET STORY

The story begins with a classic travel adventure: Tony and Maureen Wheeler's 1972 journey across Europe and Asia to Australia. There was no useful information about the overland trail then, so Tony and Maureen published the first Lonely Planet guidebook to meet a growing need.

From a kitchen table, Lonely Planet has grown to become the largest independent travel publisher in the world, with offices in Melbourne (Australia), Oakland (USA) and London (UK). Today Lonely Planet guidebooks cover the globe. There is an ever-growing list of books and information in a variety of media. Some things haven't changed. The main aim is still to make it possible for adventurous travellers to get out there – to explore and better understand the world.

At Lonely Planet we believe travellers can make a positive contribution to the countries they visit – if they respect their host communities and spend their money wisely. Every year 5% of company profit is donated to charities around the world.

SEND US YOUR FEEDBACK

We love to hear from travellers – your comments keep us on our toes and help make our books better. Our well-travelled team reads every word on what you loved or loathed about this book. Although we cannot reply individually to postal submissions, we always guarantee that your feedback goes straight to the appropriate authors, in time for the next edition. Each person who sends us information is thanked in the next edition – and the most useful submissions are rewarded with a free book.

To send us your updates – and find out about Lonely Planet events, newsletters and travel news – visit our award-winning website: **www.lonelyplanet.com/feedback**

Note: We may edit, reproduce and incorporate your comments in Lonely Planet products such as guidebooks, websites and digital products, so let us know if you don't want your comments reproduced or your name acknowledged. For a copy of our privacy policy, go to www.lonelyplanet.com/privacy

Published by Lonely Planet Publications Pty Ltd
ABN 36 005 607 983

Cover montage by Wendy Wright. Cover Photographs by Lonely Planet Images: John Hay, Chris Mellor, Patrick Horton, Krzysztof Dydynski, James Braund & Oliver Strewe; back cover: Daid Wall. Many of the images in this guide are available for licensing from Lonely Planet Images: www.lonelyplanetimages.com

Printed through Colorcraft Ltd, Hong Kong. Printed in China.

LONELY PLANET OFFICES

Australia
Head Office
Locked Bag 1, Footscray, Victoria 3011
☎ 03 8379 8000, fax 03 8379 8111
talk2us@lonelyplanet.com.au

USA
150 Linden St, Oakland, CA 94607
☎ 510 893 8555, toll free 800 275 8555
fax 510 893 8572, info@lonelyplanet.com

UK
72–82 Rosebery Ave,
Clerkenwell, London EC1R 4RW
☎ 020 7841 9000, fax 020 7841 9001
go@lonelyplanet.co.uk